D1621424

Whatever tiny bit of trivia Janne Stark doesn't know about Swedish metal isn't worth knowing. For years, he's researched and documented virtually every single band that ever existed and compiled his discoveries in an impressive encyclopedia in color that leaves all other attempts to shame. This is an effort of herculean size and a must-have for any metal head. It proves, once and for all, that Swedish metal rules.
Anders Tengner (Author and journalist)

I'm lucky Janne Stark speaks "Blekingska" (strange, rural Swedish idiom), otherwise he would easily have stolen my job, since he knows everything about Swedish hard rock and heavy metal.
Andreas Matz (Swedish radio personality)

No one would ever thump chest and avow that the Swedes invented heavy metal, but the classic, stirring, Euro, gothic... whatever you wanna call it — what Dio does — the Swedes perfected that back in the magical days of a little something a few of us call the New Wave Of Swedish Heavy Metal. Ah yes, the fictitious NWOSHM... well, maybe it wasn't so fictitious, but only tightly-knit and frankly a little Danish and Dutch as well (and there was Oz, from Finland). Whatever it was, come '84, '85, while the Americans were busy tarting up what they had learned from the New Wave Of British Heavy Metal and painting themselves hair metal, Swedish bands such as Axewitch, Torch, the magnificent Overdrive and, yes, Europe (In The Future To Come – quintessential polar molar-loosener), were mining the dark and chilly dungeon-mad medieval recesses of the form, basically from Maiden and Angel Witch down through Holocaust and Witchfinder General. The end result is a formidable style that was doomy, resolute, pure of metal intent, somehow classier than proposals from other countries, full up with mystique like Scorpions from the Uli era. History would prove that it was no fluke, with Sweden dominating the late '90s and 2000s with any number of high-flying acts strutting their command of genres from melodic thrash down to the world's best stoner rockers out-Sabbathing Sabbath. Oh yeah, and back to the original thought we opened with, it was indeed a Swedish band that had (arguably) kicked out the first NWOBHM album — or at least a record that was a candidate for one of the decade's heaviest albums and possibly the first of a new modern '80s metal — and that would have been Full Speed At High Level by the mighty Heavy Load, one of the root bands of Sweden's esteemed phalanx of heavy metal institutions. Really, it's so much quality from such a small country, which will become all too graphically clear as you stagedive into the moshpit of this book expertly compiled by Janne Stark, axe legend all over Dream Away, a song that is the locus of the greatest riff in this entire elegant encyclopaedia of thundering metal from the north.
Martin Popoff (Author, Senior editor and music journalist)

Truth be told, I haven't read any of these encyclopedias on Swedish Heavy Metal,..yet (and why I should I, for the last 30 years or so I've been busy living it)
So when Janne asked me to write the forewords for this new edition, not only was I honored, I also decided to close a deal with him: if I wrote a few introductory lines, I'd get a copy of his highly acclaimed book. Great! - there you go Janne, you're one helluva guy. I can't wait to get my hands on this unputdownable book. Thank you, stay metal!
Snowy Shaw (Therion, XXX, Notre Dame, Dream Evil etc)

When I started writing for hard rock fanzine The Hammer during the happy eighties, I knew very little about Swedish hard rock - and about writing, I should add. When I came in touch with the band Overdrive I had become better and was wise enough to realize I was dealing with a true guitar hero. Yes, there was room for those in the eighties. Several years later, when I have left most of that behind, Janne Stark is still here as a shining star on the hard rock heaven. Not only as a skilled musician, but also as producer, technician, talent seeker and expert. He has contributed markedly to Swedish hard rock keeping a strong hold both in Sweden and abroad. It shall also be noted that when I started at The Hammer, the style was still considered quite obscure. The band Europe and people like Janne Stark changed all that. Besides this, Janne manages to do what many others don't - to be both a guitar virtuoso and to review others. We, whose hearts beat for heavy rock, have Janne to thank for so much!
Annica Sundbaum-Melin (Journalist, author)

To fully embrace such a task as writing these books (now a third one) clearly borders on insanity, but that kind of insanity is something to be grateful for. Janne is one of those extremely motivated, heavily driven guys that the hardrock and metal community is known for. The determination comes from the power of music, where I have always found comfort, love and sheer lunacy!
Teddy Möller (Loch Vostok, F.K.Ü.)

Years of practicing the instrument, writing songs, rehearsals. Weeks on the road. Everything for the sake of rocking out on stage. This is not just an encyclopedia of Swedish rock music. It is also a dedication to everyone who have dedicated their life to Rock!
Max Flövik (Lillasyster)

I personally highly appreciate the work of Janne Stark taking his time to map the Swedish Rock scene in his encyclopedias. It gives You a great insight of past, present and who has played with who. You get to understand the Swedish foundation 'n rock heritage as well as keeping up with the new talented musicians that are coming out of Sweden. I learn new stuff every time a new encyclopedia is released! That, even though I am in this inner circle of musicians myself, I can only imagine how regular music lovers must enjoy these books. Janne Stark is not only The author and the burning spirit of these encyclopedias, he is very much contributing in his own right with his musical work in bands like Locomotive Breath etc, to this Swedish musical tree with brothers 'n sisters giving their time love 'n soul to something called Rock N Roll!!
Zinny Zan (Zan Clan, Easy Action etc.)

Growing up in Åkersberga, a small town north of Stockholm, my dreams were insanely big but who the Hell decided i was also worthy of having them all fulfilled?
Starting from our first band ATC and sitting here 30 years later having recorded or performed with everyone from Michael Jackson to Alice Cooper on more than 2300 albums, more than 50 gold and platinum awards, Grammy nominations, several number 1's on Billboard and so much more. Dreams do come true and i know that for countless of the 11.000 people listed in this book they all start out the same and for many they did come true! I can't thank Janne Stark enough for these amazing books and for reminding us all about the incredible Swedish rock legacy we are part of!!!
Tommy Denander (Guitarist, producer)

One of my first memories of Swedish hard rock was when me and my buddies in Trilogy went to Stockholm to check out the band Heavy Load, who were playing at Jarlateatern, sometime 1980-81. I had managed to nick half a bottle of whiskey from my old man, which we split on the train to the city, meaning we were pretty "strong" once we arrived. Of course, we had no money for the entrance fee, but a helluva lot of ideas on how to get in! We went up to the lady at the counter and said we were brothers of guitarist Ragne and that we were on the guest list. She said there was no guest list, but we insisted it was at the office. She told us to wait there while she went and got it. Of course, we said, and quickly ran in as soon as she disappeared. It wasn't much people there so we ran up to the stage and started headbang frantically when they started playing. I remember they blasted off a smoke bomb half a metre from where we were standing. It must've been powerful enough to make an impact on the Richter scale, and safe distance, what the hell is that?! I also remember we were extremely impressed by their backline and the mountain of Marshall amps, cabs and Styrbjörn's Ludwig kit with double bass drums, 40 tom toms and a million cymbals! Not to mention the band's stage outfits, leather trousers, fur vests, boots and I remember Styrbjörn playing in steel net armour... True Viking style!! At this time one of the world's most famous furniture designers, Eero Koivisto, played bass in the band. He became so excited he jumped off stage and started rocking with us. I got a notion and retuned his bass completely, but he didn't notice and just kept on rocking... Maybe it was a wise decision to go for a designer career instead. After the gig we were invited backstage by the band's manager/roadie, now renowned journalist Anders Tengner, to meet the band, which was huge! I remember we got their autographs, and Anders also wrote his. He had the writers itch already back then! Then we were on our way back home on the train to Märsta with ringing ears, burned eyebrows and a nascent hangover, but happy like children at Christmas after having sat in Santa's lap and been given the best present ever - Heavy Metal!!
Ian Haugland (Europe)

The constant question (especially when I did the documentary Så jävla metal) is how come there are so many metal bands in tiny Sweden? There are of course various answers to that, everything from the climate to easy access to rehearsal space etc. But why metal? Now it gets a bit more philosophical. Is there something in our nature? Melancholy? Anger? The Vikings... THIS we can speculate about until the cows come home. The main thing is that there's a lot of great music being made here, and that there are many gifted musicians and composers. Our responsibility is to make sure the possibilities are given to our children and future generations to continue this tradition. In your hand you're holding an encyclopedia of thousands of metal bands from Sweden, all the fantastic music they have created and all the inspiration they can provide. That's a great start!
Yasin Hillborg (Musician, producer of the documentary Så jävla Metal)

THE HEAVIEST
ENCYCLOPEDIA OF
SWEDISH HARD ROCK AND HEAVY METAL
EVER!

THE HEAVIEST
ENCYCLOPEDIA OF
SWEDISH
HARD ROCK AND
HEAVY METAL
EVER!

by

JANNE STARK

PREMIUM
PUBLISHING

STOCKHOLM

About the author

JANNE STARK, born 1963 in Karlshamn, Blekinge, Sweden. Freelance music journalist for Scandinavia's biggest guitar magazine, FUZZ and has previously written for various music magazines, such as Backstage, Metal Zone, Kool Kat News and Hard Roxx. Avid music collector. Has his own reviews blog (http://blogspot.com/starmusicreviews) and contributes to web zines www.metalcovenant.com and www.metalcentral.net when time allows it. Mechanical Engineer/Technical writer. Works as a project manager/technical writer at Avalon Information Systems AB. Janne is also a member of recording bands Overdrive, Constancia, Grand Design and Zoom Club, and has previously released recordings with bands like Locomotive Breath, BALLS, Zello, Planet Alliance, Paradize, Mountain Of Power, and has made numerous guest appearances on various recordings. Lives with his wife Ozzie and their three cats, Cosmo, Cleo and Kid. Has two daughters, Jennifer and Nathalie. Currently resides in Nyhamnsläge, Skåne.

PREMIUM PUBLISHING
Warfvinges väg 34
Box 30 184
SE-104 25 Stockholm
Sweden
Phone: +46 8 545 689 20
E-mail: info@premiumpublishing.com
www.premiumpublishing.com

The Heaviest Encyclopedia Of Swedish Hard Rock And Heavy Metal Ever!
by Janne Stark
ISBN: 978-91-89136-56-4

Executive producer: Wille Wendt
Design & Layout: Janne Stark

Printed in EU by Bulls Graphics, Halmstad, Sweden
Paper: MultiArt silk 115 gr
First edition: © MMXIII Premium Publishing – a div. of Internal AB
This edition contains an exclusive bonus CD - "Unreleased Gems" (SMCD 003) - see last pages for details.

CONTENT

The author's words 8
References 9
Designations.. 9
Peripheral bands 10
Compilation bands.. 12
Where are the bands from?.............................. 13
1-10 .... (1 Way Street - 454) 17
A .... (AB/CD - Azure) 21
B .... (BB Rock - By Night) 77
C .... (C.B Murdoc - Cut Out) 129
D..................... (D.I.Y - Dödfödd) 181
E .... (EF Band - Eye)........................ 249
F .... (F.K.Ü - Fuzzdevil)................... 293
G..................... (G.O.L.D - Gypsy Rose) 319
H..................... (H.E.A.L - Hädanfärd)................. 349
I...................... (Ice Age - IXXI) 385
J..................... (Jackwave - Justaquickstop) 415
K .... (Kaamos - Kyss) 425
L .... (Lack Of Faith - Lönndom) 441
M..................... (M.A.C - Mörrum's Own) 471
N .... (N.J.B - Nåstrond) 543
O..................... (Oberon - Ozium) 575
P .... (Pagan - Päst) 593
Q..................... (Qoph - Quorthon)..................... 625
R .... (R & R - Rävjunk) 631
S .... (S.K.U.R.K - System Shock) 661
T .... (T.A.R - Törsten Dricker) 763
U..................... (U.N.IT - Utumno) 809
V .... (Va-då? - Vörgus) 819
W .... (W.E.T - Wyvern) 837
X .... (X-Eryus - Xsavior) 857
Y .... (Yale Bate - Ypzilon) 859
Z .... (Zinny J Zan - Zpeedfreak) 862
Å, Ä, Ö .... (Mahnus Åhlin - Överslag) 870
Late additions .... (Angel King - Witherscape) 869
Name index 877
Photo credits... 908
Personal top lists 909
Bonus CD 913

The author's words

This is the final one! Yes, I know I said it after the first one and I did say it after the second one, but this time I mean it (yeah, right, just like you mean it the day after, swearing you'll never drink again…). Well, I may do it again, but not in this shape and form. This book is the mother of all, the grand opus, and the bible of my bibles. This time I have gathered all the bands from the first two books, updated and completed the information and discographies, plus added all new bands and all the ones I missed out earlier. Why would this be the last one then? Well, in the last couple of years releases have become much more difficult to categorise, in the sense that digital only albums are starting to grow and now even some label print on CD-R. So, that's why, this is the BIG one and this is the LAST one! I think...

How did I gather the information? Well, first of all, if possible, through the bands themselves, the members or the band's website, the record labels, collectors, magazine articles and I've also used a multitude of websites for information, especially on releases, labels, catalogue numbers and different pressings. These are listed on the reference page. I've also been in touch with several collectors and editors who have given me information, pics, scans, sounds etc., all to whom I'm deeply grateful!

At first my plan was to have the book out late 2010/early 2011, to make this an even "40 years of Swedish hard rock", from 1970-2010. This didn't happen, and now I've just tried to be as current as possible, hence the "Late additions" chapter. This time I have also weeded out some of the bands that snuck in, but weren't necessarily a clear case of hard rock/metal, some earlier labelled as "related". These bands have been listed in the "Peripheral bands" section. This also applies to bands that were on the verge of making it, but didn't. I wanted to include them anyway, as I've seen record dealers/traders state them as "mega rare, not even in The Book", while I sometimes excluded them since they were not heavy enough. Some bands in the book may still be "on the verge", and everyone may not agree they should be in there, but made it for some reason or another. Well, even the sun has its spots.

Website: **www.starkmusic.net**

8

Definitions

This book is by no means written as an unbiased, solely factual encyclop*ae*dia (it's actually an encyclop*e*dia). I am a music writer and reviewer, and I have taken the liberty of giving my personal points of view on the band's music and sound, like it or not. So, take the comments for what they are – one person's opinion, like any other review.

Also please note, the title of the book is "hard rock and heavy metal", meaning I 've included anything from the most commercial melodic hard rock/AOR to the blackest and heaviest of metal, also snuck in some hard-rocking funk, blues and fusion, that I felt landed on the right side of the fence. I also included a genre guide to give reference to how I have categorised the different styles.

My original plan was to include a detailed price guide, but with the variation of prices on different markets and the way the value of a record can switch from day to day, also depending on the quality, instead I decided to make a simple four-stage value guide. This will at least give an indication of the value. Some records are very rare, but since no one is interested in them, the value may still be low (until some member joins a well-known band or it becomes a hype...). I may also have missed some rarities, since you sometimes need to be a specified collector of the band to know.

Disclaimer (or... read this if you think I f****d up)

Regarding the band photos in this book, all have been received from the bands, labels or through the magazines I have written for as promotional photos. I have tried to be as complete and accurate as possible when it comes to photo credits (stated in the index), but in some cases the information has not been stated and I have not been able to find out who took the photo. If your photo is in here, un-credited, it's most unfortunate. I'd however be happy to add your information on the website, where other additional information will also be found.

I have tried to be as complete and accurate as possible when it comes to discographies, but sometimes information regarding pressings and artwork have varied, and at times which source to trust has been at the toss of a coin if it hasn't been found elsewhere. If you find information in the book that is incorrect (sometimes I have, for instance, found different spellings of names), e-mail me and I will put the correct info up on the site. The same applies to band information.

For further information or questions, e-mail me at: stark@starkmusic.net

Thanks

So many people have so helpful in so many ways. So my first huge thanks goes to all the bands, friends, collectors, fans, labels and musicians who have sent me records, scans, photos and information. You've made my life so much easier and unfortunately, this time, you are too many to mention (and I'd also HATE to unintentionally forget anyone). Still, my gratitude is no less. THANKS!!!!

The following people have been of invaluable help to me in various ways:
My lovely, patient and supportive wife Ozzie Adenborg!
My daughters Jennifer and Nathalie.
Our crazy cats Cleo, Kid and Cosmo.
All my family and friends!
Wilhelm Wendt, Roger Holegård, Liska Cersowsky and Camilla Dal @Premium Publishing!
Lennart "Phantom" Larsson for your invaluable help, knowledge, information and proof-reading.
Ola Gränshagen for your expertice and help on the pink and fluffy bands.
Mitsuhiro Nishida for your help and support!
Yasu Fuji for our Swedish Metal Conference!
PM Ström, Mikael Johansson & Rickard Nilsson for sharing your great photos.
Andy Gavin for checking my Enlg... Engisl... grammar.
The following persons also deserve a big thanks for their help and support:
Naoko Furuhashi, Per Winberg, Tord Karlsson, Christer Wedin, Johan Nylén, Mikitoshi Matsuo, Tomo Ando, Dan Ekman, Emil Öhman, Patrik Johansson, Stefan Renström@Thrash Palace, Patrik Leijen and Micke Persson@TPL Records, Swedmetal, Record Heaven, Burrn!!, Young Guitar and FUZZ Magazine.
My sponsors: Avalon Enterprise, True Temperament, VGS Guitars, Power Pedals and Nazenius Airbrush Art.
A HUGE special thanks to the bands, labels and musicians who helped me with material and information for the bonus CD!

Shoutouts to: Daniel Ekeroth, Peter Jandreus and Jörgen Holmstedt.

References

Websites

www.allmusic.com, amg.com, blabbermouth.net, cdbaby.com, cdon.com, discogs.com, ebay.com, facebook.com/(insert band name here), globaldomination.se, heavyharmonies.com, heavymetalrarities.com, melodicrock.com, metal-archives.com, musicmight.com, musik-sammler.de, musikon.se, myspace.com/(insert band name here), popsike.com, progg.se, recordheaven.net, reverbnation.com/(insert band name here), rocknytt.se, slba.se, stim.se, thecorroseum.com, tpl.se, tradera.com, wikipedia.com, strappadometalblog.blogspot.com

Magazines

Close Up, Burrn!!, Backstage, Slavestate, Classic Rock Magazine, Headbanger, Kick Ass Monthly, Metalized, FUZZ Magazine.

Genres

Genres I am referring to in the book and well-known bands of these genres.
AOR - The wimpy side of hard rock. (Journey, Survivor, Treat, Alien)
FM Rock - See *AOR*.
Westcoast (WC) - Very poppy AOR. Not included in the book.
Pomp - AOR with a proggy twist. (Boston, Trillion, Styx, Starcastle)
Melodic Hard Rock - The heavier side of AOR. (Hardline, Axe, Europe)
Sleaze - Bluesy, sleazy hard rock. (Aerosmith, Cinderella, Crazy Lixx)
Glam - Pop metal/hard rock with mascara. (Poison, Easy Action)
Hair Metal - Derogatory term of the entire eighties melodic hard rock scene.
Hard Rock/Heavy Rock - (Deep Purple, Led Zeppelin, Mountain, Neon Rose)
Seventies Hard Rock - See *Hard Rock/Heavy Rock*
Stoner - Fusion of doom, hard rock, psychedelic rock. (Kyuss, Half Man)
Sludge - Fusion of doom, southern rock, punk. (Eyehategod, St:Erik)
Drone - Veeery slow sludge/stoner. (Earth, Sunn O))), Neurosis, Suma)
Doom - Slow, doomy, heavy rock. (Cathedral, Trouble, Candlemass)
NWoBHM - New Wave of British Heavy Metal. (Saxon, Maiden, Trespass)
Heavy Metal - (Accept, Wild Dogs, Hammerfall, Dream Evil, Axewitch)
NWoSHM - New Wave of Swedish Heavy Metal. (Enforcer, Steelwing)
Neoclassical Metal - Classically influenced metal. (Impellitteri, Yngwie)
Power Metal - German major scale metal. (Helloween, Stratovarius, Dragonland)
Speed Metal - High speed thrash (Agent Steel, Nuclear Assault, Slayer)
Thrash Metal - (Sodom, Death Angel, Testament, Overkill, F.K.Ü, Kazjurol)
Bay Area Thrash - Thrash in the vein of the classic four. (Anthrax, Metallica..)
Progressive Metal - Technical metal. (Dream Theater, Symphony X, Andromeda)
Progressive Rock - Technical hard rock. (Kansas, The Flower Kings, Anekdoten)
Symphonic Rock - (Yes, Marillion, Änglagård, Trettioåriga Kriget, Cross)
Opera Metal - Female fronted operatic metal. (Nightwish, Within Temptation)
Death Metal - (Death, Possessed, Carcass, Dismember, Death Breath)
Melodic Death Metal - (Children Of Bodom, Scar Symmetry, Soilwork)
Progressive Death Metal - Technical death metal. (Atheist, Cynic, CB Murdoc)
Symphonic Death Metal - Orchestrated death metal. (Cradle Of Filth)
Symphonic Black Metal - Orchestrated black metal. (Dimmu Borgir, Emperor)
Gothernburg Sound - Melodic death metal. (In Flames, Dark Tranquillity)
Black Metal - (Venom, Bathory, Dissection, Dark Funeral, Lord Belial)
Old School Death/Black - (Burzum, Mayhem, Sorhin, Watain, Arckanum)
Death & Roll - Death metal with groove. (Entombed, Helltrain, Furbowl)
Funk Metal - Mixing funk and metal. (Living Colour, Electric Boys)
Folk Metal - Mixing folk music and metal.(Finntroll, Turisas, Sorg, Fejd)
Viking Metal - Viking theme metal with a folky touch. (Mortiis, Thyrfing)
Metalcore - Mix of Hardcore and metal. (Killswitch Engage, LOK, Seventribe)
Hardcore - Verging on punk. Not included in the book.
Crust - Not included in the book.
Punk - Not included in the book.
Grindcore - Mix of Hardcore, Crust, Thrash and Death Metal. Some included.
Goregrind - Mix of Grindcore and Death Metal. (Repulsion, Repugnant)
Industrial Metal - (Ministry, Nine Inch Nails, Skold, late Shotgun Messiah)
Blues Rock - Heavy bluesy rock. (Joe Bonamassa, Bad Company, Sky High
Southern Rock - Country/blues/hard rock. (Blackfoot, Molly Hatchet,)
Shredders - Advanced, technical guitar playing. (Joe Satriani, Paul Gilbert)
Grunge Metal - Seattle stuff. (Alice In Chains, Soundgarden, Skintrade)
Alternative metal/Post grunge - (Hoobastank, Nickelback, Takida, Corroded)
Nu-metal - Fusion of grunge, rap, metal (Slipknot, Korn, Tribal Ink)
Rap Metal - Fusion of rap and metal. (RATM, Stuck Mojo, Clawfinger,)
Goth Metal - Dark metal with gothic themes. (Paradise Lost, Malaise)
Post Metal - Emo/Post-Rock fused with metal. (Isis, Neurosis, Cult Of Luna)

Designations

Biography

v = Vocals
g = Guitar
k = Keyboards
b = Bass
d = Drums
h = Harmonica
p = Percussion
f = Flute
acc = accordion (definitely a metal instrument!)
sax = saxophone
Others may be written out (violin, effects etc).
Göteborg = Gothenburg
Malmö= Malmoe

Discography

- -	No catalogue number/label stated on the record
( )	If the catalogue number is in brackets it means the number was only found on the disc (matrix number)
n/a	Information not available
□	Picture sleeve
■	Picture sleeve, depicted
○	No picture sleeve (also noted in the comments)
●	No picture sleeve (also noted in the comments), depicted
CD	Full length CD album
2CD	Double CD
3CD	Triple CD
Box	Box set
CDS	CD Single (1-2 tracks)
MCD	Maxi CD/CD EP (3 or more tracks)
tr	tracks
LP	Full length vinyl album
2LP	Double album
3LP	Triple album
PD	Picture Disc
d	Digi-pack
/d	Released as both regular CD and digi pack with the same catalogue number
p	Paper pocket sleeve
g	Gatefold sleeve
v	Vinyl replica CD cover
pg	Paper pocket gatefold sleeve (aka eco sleeve)
book	CD in digi book (hard paper book digi pack cover)
3”	3” CD single
7”	7” vinyl single
7” EP	7” Extended Play with more than two tracks
7” 3tr	7” Extended Play, tracks specified
10”	10” vinyl
12”	Maxi single, 12” single, 1-2 tracks.
MLP	12” Maxi EP/Mini LP. More than 2 tracks.
DVD	DVD
LD	Laser Disc
MC	Music Cassette
Flexi	Flexi disc (thin plastic record)
Promo	"Promotional copy" stamped or printed.

Price Guide

$= Value between 50-100 USD (330-660 SEK)
$$= Value between 100-300 USD (660-2000 SEK)
$$$= Value over 300 USD (over 2000 SEK)
All records with no symbol have a value of up to 50 USD (330 SEK).
The actual value then depends on condition, market etc. Price indication refers to a mint condition record.

Comments

Comments contain info on edition (if available), colour vinyl, additional things (poster, slipcase, patch etc) and tracks on everything except albums. Cover songs (original artist) versions (single edit, demo, live etc) have been noted where available.

Peripheral bands (honourable mentions)

This chapter contains bands that didn't make it into the book for various reasons. Mainly because they fell just outside of the musical borders of this book. However, to avoid any confusion that I may have missed these bands, I have listed them here, with a comment. Also, some bands may be within the musical borders, bit since I only feature bands who have released printed, pressed albums, and some bands have released commercial pro-printed CD-R albums, I have mentioned some here.

Bands that were left out because they didn't fit the formula of the book:

59 Times The Pain – Hardcore.
69-Hard – Punk/rockabilly.
9T9 – Too poppy. Featuring members of **Standby**, **Cross**, **Russell** and **Vampa**.
96 % – New wave/rock.
Abhinanda – More hardcore than metal.
Absolute Beginners – Pop/punk/new wave rock.
Achilleus – Definitely on the verge, but more psychedelic rock than hard rock.
Action – Too poppy.
AHA – Hard rocker Dick Bewarp on guitar, still - pop.
Akut – pop/new wave.
Alea Jacta Est – Great guitars, but not really hard rock.
Ambra – Symphonic rock.
Amott, Christopher – Soft mood music.
Anders – Folk/rock/psych.
Andersson, Stefan – Too poppy.
Angel – Pop.
Antblad, Chris – Too poppy/WC.
Anton Maiden – Iron Maiden covers sung to midi files.
Apati – Melancholic rock.
Arbogast - Punk.
Arcana – Classical music.
Arditi – Ambient/classic.
Arose – Pop/rock.
Arsedestroyer - Grindcore.
Asstronuts – Grunge with a garage touch.
Asylum - Pro printed CD-R.
Audio – Rock.
Aurora – Disco rock/rock.
Avenue (*Hur känns det imorgon*) – Melodic rock.
Aymeric – Pop.
BJH – Rock 'n roll.
Baby Jesus – Rock.
Badrock – On the verge, but mostly pop/disco/rock.
Baker Perkins – Soft pop/FM rock.
Bakrus – Pop/punk.
Baltik – Symphonic jazz rock.
Baron Bult – Rock/pop.
Bay Laurel – Goth rock.
Bazooka! – Garage rock.
Beautiful Grey – Known hard rockers, but way too pop.
Belltown – Alternative hardcore/rock.
Bhonus – Too pop.
Big Bang – Pop.
Big Deal – The single *Du du du kan ge mig kärlek* is close, but too pop.
Big Hoss And The Animals – Never released.
Big Money – Pop.
Birdflesh – Grindcore.
Blackmail – Punk.
Blind System - Punk.
Bloomingday's – Westcoast.
Blueset – More blues/rock than hard rock.
Blåljus – Pop.
Bo Wilson Band – Great band, but too blues to make it.
Boogietryck – Rock. Close at times, but no cigarr.
Borås Energi – Just plain odd.
Boxer – Despite metal musicians, this is melodic rock.
Boys, The – Pre-*Treat*, but still, pop.
Breach – Hardcore.

Brick – Hardcore/punk.
Brickhouse – Great band, but too bluesy.
Brilliant Mistake – Rock.
Broman, Tommy – Great guitarist, but too soft.
Bruce Banner – Hardcore.
Bubbles, The – Kee Marcello, but still, this is pop.
CB Band – More 60s rock than hard rock.
CP Borrmaskinen – Punk.
Caliber 44 – Pro printed CD-R.
Camera – Melodic rock.
Candy Heaven – pop/rock.
Capricone's – Distorted guitars, but way too pop.
Captain Murphy – Rock.
Careless – Synth-oriented light weight AOR.
Cavokey – Melodic rock/pop.
Charles – Punk.
Charlys Slavar – Punk/new wave/rock.
Checkpoint Charlie – Rock.
Cherokee (*Nightrider* – 7") – Pop.
Chico Bar – Pop/rock.
Chuck Norris Experiment – More rock than hard rock.
Circus – Rock.
Circuit – (Could not verify its existence).
Cindy – Pop.
City People – Soul/funk melodic rock.
Colt 45 – Too pop.
Cool Affair – Westcoast/pop.
Corin & Edman – Westcoast.
Cosmic Ballroom – Rock.
Counterblast – Hardcore/punk.
Criss 99 - Pop/rock/new wave.
Crossfade - Westcoast.
Crystal Caravan, The – Too 60s for comfort.
D'Accord – Kee Marcello, still: Westcoast/pop.
Daisy Glaze – Rock/funk/garage.
Dark Daily – Pop/WC/funk/AOR.
Dark Side Cowboys – Ambient goth rock.
Darxtar – Symphonic/psychedelic rock.
De Infernali – Featuring Jon Nödtveit, still this is electronic ambient music.
Dead Man – Folkish psychedelic acid rock.
Deadbeats, The – Garage rock.
Demented – Pro printed CD-R.
Desire – Goth rock.
Desperados – Westcoast/pop.
Dezire – Pop/rock.
Dia Psalma - Punk, albeit pretty hard-rocking.
Diamond Dogs – Rock/rhythm 'n' blues.
Dice – Symphonic rock.
Dirty Dixxx – Pro-printed CD-R.
Dirty Vikings, The – Garage rock.
Distorsion – Too punkish.
Djush Band – Melodic rock.
Do*In*It – Yes, it's Nalle Påhlsson solo, but pop.
Dolce Vita – Pop/rock.
Doll Squad – Punkish hard core.
Dom Där – Punk.
Doughnuts – Hardcore/punk.
Ducks Can Groove – Blues/fusion.
Dungen – Symphonic/folky rock.
E.T.K – Punk.

East Lane – Funky poppy melodic rock.
Easy Action (feat Pelle Almgren) – Glam rock.
Eftertryck Förbjudes – Progg rock. Heavy at times.
Ellen Jamesians, The – Punk.
Elope – Rock.
Elvärk – Rock.
Endless Day – Their demos were hard rock, but the single was pop.
Energy – Progressive jazz-rock.
Enterprize – Melodic rock.
Epizootic – Fusion/jazz rock.
Erika – Light weight FM rock that went pop/dance.
Erlandsson, Mikael – Pop.
Euphoria – Pop.
Evolution Cancer – Hardcore/Crust.
Ewa Bound - Pop.
F.R.E.E – Westcoast/melodic rock.
Factory – Had their AOR:ish moments, but rock/pop.
Fake Moss – Pop/rock.
Famne, Björn – One song, *Vampire* is awesome 70s heavy psych, but the rest is not hard rock.
Far East – On the verge, but too pop.
Fear & Loathing – Billy Idol style.
Fejd – Folk.
Fet Mule – Hardcore.
Filthy Christians – Grindcore.
Fingerprints – Pop/rock.
Fireside – Hardcore/grunge.
First Band From Outer Space – Psychedelica.
Five Grams Of Perfection – Neo-punk.
Flames (w Åke Noreén) – Close, but more westcoast.
Fläsket Brinner – Progressive rock.
Frontlash – Hardcore.
Frontalrock – Rock.
Fuzzter – Punk.
Fä – Electrified folk.
Gadget – Grindcore.
Garvin – Melodic rock.
Gary T'To Band – Melodic rock/pop.
Gastones – Rock.
Gavelin – Bluesy melodic rock.
General Surgery – Grindcore.
Gerfast, Jan – Blues.
Gerry And The Moonshiners – Boogie rock.
Glamour (pre-*Alien*) – Pop/rock.
Glenda – Pop/punk/rock.
Gläns över sjö och strand – Progg rock.
Good Clean Fun – Melodic rock.
Gotlands Teater – Pop/punk/rock.
Government
Grand Exit – Only digital releases.
Grovjobb – Folk rock.
Gun Smoke – More 60s rock.
Gösta Berlings Saga – Symphonic rock.
HF – Pop.
Harald Råg – Garagy rock.
Hellacopters, The – Definitely debatable, but they are more rock, garage and punk than hard rock.
Hellbounds – Rock.
Hide The Knives – Alternative rock, post-grunge.
High Plain Drifters - Powerpop/rock.

Highways Slugs – Rock.
Hoarse – Grunge/Alternative rock.
Hoffsten, Louise – Melodic rock/pop/blues.
Hoven Drover – More folk than hard rock.
Håkansson, Kenny – Folk rock.
ID – Melodic rock.
Icon X – Folk-pop.
Ictus – Rock/pop.
Imperial State Electric - Rock.
In Xtenso – Westcoast.
Indisciplined Lucy – Symphonic rock.
Infanticide (Gävle) – Crust/grindcore.
Injection – Pop/rock.
Intact – Pop.
Intermission – Rock/pop.
Introitus – Symphonic rock.
JAB (Johnny Arwidsson Band) – Pop/rock/new wave.
Jaconne – Pop/symphonic
Jarnack, Bo – Pop/prog.
Jet Set – Pop/rock.
KG 22 – Pop/rock.
Kaftanrock – Blues rock.
Kapoor – Grunge/indie-oriented psychedelic rock.
Karlstad Korv – Bluesy biker rock.
Katten – Melodic rock.
Kebnekajse – Folk rock.
Kee & The Kick (feat Kee Marcello) – Rock/pop.
Keep In Mind – Pop.
Kenneth & The Knutters – Biker rock.
Keplers Odd – Drone noise.
Kessy – Heavy pop/pop.
Kid Down – Post-punk.
Killers – Covers of *The Sweet* and *Alice Cooper*, but not hard rock.
King Here After – Indie rock.
Kiss & Run – Closer to pop than AOR.
Kultivator – Jazzy prog.
Kung Tung – On the verge, but too punk/progg rock.
Labyrint – More rock than hard rock.
Ladan – New wave rock.
Ladyland – Pop/rhythm & blues/rock.
Landberk – Symphonic.
Landlords – Hardcore.
Leif Norbergs Orkester – Hard rock songs in easy listening "dansband" versions.
Lidström, Peter – Instrumental guitar, classical music.
Lindh, Per – Prog.
Little Chris – Blues/pop/rock.
Live – Covers only, and mostly pop/rock.
Livin' Sacrifice – Closer to punk than hard rock.
Lizette & – Too poppy.
Los Concombres – Garagey, alternative rock with a touch of sleaze.
Lotus (feat Chico Lindvall) – Jazz rock.
Louders – Pop/rock.
Love Injection – Pop/rock with horrible vocals.
Lucyfire – Goth.
Lyftkraft – Jazz rock.
Madison (on Rage Of Achilles) - Hardcore.
Magic Broom, The – Psychedelic.
Magnum Bonum – The majority of the band's material is melodic rock/pop. Same genre as Snowstorm, Factory and several others.
Magnus Åhlin med 22 hästar utan öron – Too pop.
Mammon – Pop/rock.
Man At Arms – Hardcore.
Mantaray K-D – Hardcore/punk.
Marble Arch – Goth rock.
Martial Mosh – Hardcore.
Martyrdöd – Hardcore.
Märvel – Rock.

Mary Beats Jane – Hardcore.
Maryslim – Sleazy rock/punk.
Masque – Symphonic rock.
Masters Of Show – Soul/pop/rock.
Matterhorn – Rock.
Meadow (2005) – Hardcore.
Mean Thore – Booze rock.
Mecki Mark Men – Psychedelic rock.
Medicin Rain – Rock.
Meleeh – Hardcore.
Mendonca, Paul – Funk rock.
Mess – Goth.
Micro Midas – Punkish pop rock.
Midnight Sun (*Under My Gun*) – Light weight AOR.
Mighty Band – *Alice Cooper* cover, but not hard rock.
Mikeyla – Pop/rock.
Mindscape (*Bring You Down*) – Pop/rock .
Minx – Rock/punk/pop, close but no cigar.
Mizz Percy – Blues rock.
Moon Safari – Progressive pop/rock.
Moor, The – Symphonic.
Morte Macabre – Symphonic.
Motorjoke – Punk/hardcore.
Mr. Libido – Guitar hero Mattias Ia Eklundh, yes, but this is quirky electronic pop/rock.
My Brother The Wind - Psychedelica.
Mystery – Pop/westcoast.
Månsken – Rock.
Nasum – Hardcore.
Neon Leon – Not Swedish.
New Clear Daze – Symphonic.
New Grove project, The – Symphonic.
New Rose - Too punk/new wave.
New Wind, The – Too punkish.
Nilsson, Tommy – Pop/rock/WC.
Norrbottens Järn - Political rock/pop. Made one or two harder songs.
North Connection – Funk/disco rock.
Norum, Tone – Some of her stuff is AOR, but mostly melodic rock/pop.
Nuts, The – Pub-rock/punk.
O-Kult – Rock.
Occasion – Pop/rock.
Olsons Grova – Great acidy guitar, but more 60s psych.
Opus III – Rock.
Output – Symphonic rock/pop.
Overture – Symphonic rock.
Paatos – Symphonic.
Packet - On the verge, but more symphonic progg rock.
Pandora - Rock/symphonic.
Panta Rei – Progressive/psychedelic rock.
Peace Love & Pitbulls – Cyber techno rock.
Phrank – Industrial rock.
Physical Rocket – Sixies-oriented blues rock.
Pierce – *Nasty Idols'* singer goes melodic rock.
Pipeline (*6:e juni* – 7") – Punk/pop. Similar to *Noice*.
Porridgeface, The – Pro-printed CD-R.
Poseur Apart – Symphonic.
President Gas – Pub rock.
Primary Man – Melodic rock.
Prime Sth – Melodic rock.
Prime Time – Pop.
Proboscis – Funk/hardcore/hip hop/rock.
Pseudo Sun – Acid rock.
Public – Pop/rock.
Puissance – Electronic/classical mood music.
Puls 144 – Quite heavy guitars, but this is too pop.
Purusam – Hardcore.
Pyramid – Despite Chris Mentzer on vocals, this is Chicago blues.
Rabalder – Melodic pop/rock.
Rabatt – Rock.

Racoon – Pop.
Ragdolls – Horrorpunk.
Ragnarök – Symphonic.
Raised Fist – Hardcore.
Ralph Peeker Band – Melodic rock.
Razzia (*Släpp mej* – 7") – Like *Noice*-meet-*Snowstorm*. Rock/pop/new wave.
Refused – Hardcore.
Rentokiller – Hardcore.
Revenge Of Lorenzo – Strange rock…
Rififi – Funky proggy rock.
Rise, The – Feat *Leviticus/Jerusalem* members. Pop.
Rock Set – Bluesy rock.
Rocket – Glam rock/pop.
Rocket Roll – Rock.
Rockparty Brass Band – Mainstream rock.
Rockvindar – Rock.
Rogefeldt, Pugh – Too pop/rock to make it, even with some great moments.
Romance (*Segla i mörkret* – 7", Pang) – Too pop/disco to qualify.
Rose – Too pop.
Rough Diamond - Pro printed CD-R.
Royal Bastards - Punk/garage rock.
Rubbermen – Funk rock.
Rådimma – Blues rock.
S.P.Q.R – New wave/rock/pop.
Saga – Symphonic rock.
Sanctum – Industrial symphonic.
Sator – Despite some hard-rocking songs, a punk band.
Sayyadina – Punk/hardcore.
Schaffer, Janne – Great guitarist with some hard edged songs, still, too soft.
Scorched Earth – Hardcore.
Scorpion – Sixties rock.
Scratch (feat Brink, Gripe etc) – Punk-pop-funk.
Scurvy – Gore/grind.
Section 8 – Hardcore.
Selfmindead – Straight edge hardcore.
Senseless – Hardcore.
Seragon – May look metal, but it's pop/rock.
Sex På Scén/Soundation – Light-weight poppy melodic rock.
Sha-Boom – Rock/glam/pop.
Shades Of Orange – Sixties rock.
Shield – Straight edge.
Sidewalk – Too pop.
Silver – Syth pop with heavy guitars.
Simon Says – Symphonic.
Skyfall – Rock.
Skyron Orchestra – 70s psychedelica.
Slips – Melodic rock/pop.
Slug – Pro printed CD-R.
Smiling Dog – Glam rock.
Snowstorm/Snöstorm – Some AOR/hard rock tracks, but mainly rock/pop.
Solar Lodge, The – Punkish garage rock.
Solid Blue – Featuring Hasse Fröberg. Still, light-weight melodic rock.
Soul Patrol – Alternative/psychedelic rock.
Soulshake Express, The – 60s rock.
Speak Easy – Pop/rock.
Spyke – Industrial pop/rock.
State Cows – Westcoast.
Station – Pop/rock.
Stereolith – Emo-core/pop.
Stolt, Roine – *Kaipa/The Flower Kings* main man. Progressive pop.
Stone Antica – Great band with a heavy edge, but still too pop/rock.
Stonepark – Indie rock.
Stormvarning – Rock/new wave/pop.

Peripheral bands (contd.)

Streetfight Fighters – Garage rock.
Strix-Q – Pop/rock.
Sun, The – Hardcore.
Suppository – Punk/grind.
Swed LA – Melodic rock.
Super Eight Group – 60s-style garagey acid rock.
Sydkraft – Rock.
T. Coma Band – Rock.
TST (*All Through The Night* – 7") – Too punk.
Taikes – Grunge rock.
Teddybears STHLM – Hard core gone dance pop.
Tempest, Joey – Mellow rock.
Thunder Express (aka *Dundertåget*) – Rock.
Tid – Close to *Joy Division*.
Tiebreak - Rock.
Tak Tak - Pop/rock/WC/AOR.
Tommy Mac Frees – Despite Ragne Wahlquist's guitar this is too pop/rock.
Totalt Jävla Mörker – Love the name, but too grind.
Trainsistor – Funk rock.
Transport & Lennie Norman – One song sort of hard rock only, the rest not.
Ultimate Concern – Hardcore/punk.
User Of A Common Name – Pop.
Vaka – Synth ambient.
Violent Silence – Prog.
Vision – Pop/rock.
Vision Gallery – Pop/rock.
Von Lyx – Pop.
Vox – Pop/rock.
Walkinglight – Soft Toto style.
Wasa Express – Despite the odd hard rockier song this is more melodic rock. Great band, though!
Watergarden – Pop/rock.
Watertouch – Outstanding proggy rock, but too jazz/folk to make it in.
Westpoint – Westcoast.
White Stains – Ambient.
Wild Flowers – Rock.
Wildliw – Pop/rock.
Witnezz – Straight rock 'n roll.
Wonderland (feat Edmundsson, Vranjic) – Pop/rock.
Xport – Rock/pop.
Yellow Mellow – Funk rock.
Zeus – Psych.
Zorry – Rock/pop.
Ztation – Pop/rock.
Zthürehz Zthürehz – Symphonic rock.
Ågren, Jimmy – Blues.
Åke Octan – Rock.
Änglarna – Pop/rock.
Ättestupa – Krautrock/drone/ambient/folk.

Compilation bands (honourable mentions)

The following bands have not (yet?) made releases on their own, but still should be mentioned, since they are featured with one or several songs on various compilation albums. Some bands may however have the same name as bands in the book. For the bands in the book, compilation albums are mentioned in the band biography.

12 Gauge Dead

Absurdum, Accryl, Aceldama, Act, Ad Infinitum, After After, Aisle, Alcoholica, Ambush, Anders Ericson, Anders Karlsson, Anders Moberg, Annabell, Anthem, Appendix, Aquaholic, Aquarius, Arcana, Arcania, Archangel, Area, Area Turns Red, Arleep, Ars Moriende, Artifact, Asfarock, Ashtray, Astro Zombies, Atrocity, Attention, Axels Misär, Axid, Ayenna.

B.M.T, B4 Blues, Baby Blue, Bacchus, Back Tobac, Backslag, Backstage Queen, Bactrack, Bad Control, Bare Farmers, Believer, Below, Beneath, Beyond, Big Break, Billy Jonsson, Black Arrow, Black Sajme, Blackmail, Bleed, Bleeding Hearts, Blizzard, Blow Out, Blue Sky, Blue Town, Blue Turk, Bluetown, Blå Dunster, Bocca Bandet, Bonaroo, Bronx, Bäck Group

Caamora, Cairo, Capricorn, Captain Chill, Caress, Cargo, Carryon, Cat Calls, Cereborn, Chainsaw, Challenger, Chatman, Cheerness, Cherie, Chivaz, Cockburn, Coffinman, Conceled, Conny Wendel, Cool Runnings, Copycats, Cordial Attack, Corpse, Corruption, Cover Up, Cranial Dust, Crematorium, Crime, Crimson Tide, Cross-Nordenfelt, Cryptic Art

D-Dust, Damage Done, Damnations Pride, Dark Haagen, Dark Ice, Darkness, Daylight, Daze Of Twilight, Dead Dogs, Dead Line, Dead Meat, Deafaid, Delta, Desert Storm, Desire, Dick Bewarp, Die Mauer, Dirty Lies, Disgraced, Dogpound, Dolores Teacup, Dormitory, Double Deuce, Dusty Pilgrims, Dysdain

E-Type, Early To Bed, Easy Livin', Eden, Edicius, Eddy Malm Band, Electra, Electric Life, Endart, Enforce, Ensamble Nocturne, Enslavement, Enthralled, Eon, Epsilon, Eroticon IV, Euphoria, Eurotrash, Evil Knights, Exercise One, Exist, Exit, Exocet, Extas, Eyes

Face 2 Face, Fairy Tales, Farside Of Reality, Fearless, Fiction, First Century, Flaped Forge, Flashback, Flow, Foggy Trip, Force Ten, Forlorn, Fortress, Free Wheelin, Furious, Fusion

Gabbas, Gain, Gallow, Gathering Freak, Gehirm, Glam Slam, Gloat, Globe, Grand Design, Green Means Go, Greenscab, Grindstone, Groove Kings, Groove Kings, Guilty

Hangman Jury, Happy Baboons, Harlekin, Hatred, Headforce, Headquake, Heartline, Heaven, Hell On Earth, Hell Patrol, Hellacoaster, Hickory Heads, Highlight, Hindorf, Hog House, Hog's Breath, Holy Angel, Horned, Humpty, Hypocondria, Håkan Ericsson

Ian Haugland, Idiots Rule, In Grey, Invader, IQ Zero, Ironside, Isaiah, Isobel

Jane Crow, Janne Stark, Jolly Roger, Justified Violation

Kamax, Karavan, Karma Kain, Katalysator, Keffrots, Keitel, Killerhawk, Kings Club, Komotio, Kontra 82

Landslide, Laroche, Lars Johansson, Lars Åke Löwin, Legum Lang, Limelight, Link, Livingroom, Loud 'N Proud, Loudmess, Lupuz

Macbeth, Macrodex, Made Of Steel, Made Of Steel,

Magnus Rosling, Manic Sounds Panic, Marble Icon, Marionet, Marygold, Master Massive, Maurfahr, Megido, Melonia, Mentzer, Merlin, Messiah Marcolin, Metal Axe, Metal Dance, Micke Besvär Band, Midwinter, Mighty Light, Migty Light, Mindscape, Minstrels Of Marble, Monica Maze Band, Montezuma, Moonville, Mordancy, Morgue, Morpheus Descents, Mortality, Morticia, Mother Groove, Mother Mind, Mr : Hangpike And Adams Leafs, Mr Band, Mrs Hippie (Stockholm)

Nasty Music, Neck Rose, Nepharitus, Neptune, New Penthouse, Nightrain, No Fun, No Name, Northern Star, Novgore, Noztalgica, Nude Orchestra

Occrah, One Time Blues Band, One Touch, Orions Sword, Our Metal, Outland, Overkill

P, Painkillaz, Paradice, Paranoid, Party Zoo, Patrik Belgrave, PB.Mansion, Peo Hedin, Pet Umbrella, Peter Andersson, Pexilated, Phentalon, Piece Of Clay, Pilsner, Pipeline, Poseidon, Power Rain, Powerage, Prime Touch, Prometheus, Psycho Holiday, Puka, Purgatorium

Ra, Random Generator, Rat Race, Rawburt, Recycle, Release, Rickard Sporrong, Riffifi, Riffomania, Ritchie's Rainboots, Riverside, Roadkill, Robert Hansson Project, Rock Rivers, Rock's, Rockslag, Rockslide, Rocky Mountains, Roll On, Romeos Delight, Rubberhead, Rubycon

S.G.R, Saigon Rose, Sardonic Tears, Saturnine, SBF, Scarlet Garden, Scars, Scotch Whiskey, Scrooge, Season's End, Second Hand, Second Sight, Second Thought, Second Trip, Sentinel, Sex, Shed, Shylie, Shylock, Sickinside, Skin 'N' Bone, Skin The Goat, Skrock, Skull, Skybreaker, Slow Train, Snakebite Remedy, Snakeskin Cowboys, Snappy Cacky, Snöfall, Somersault, Sonic Boom, Sovereign, Spit The Fish, Squealer, State, Steamboat Connection, Steelemade, Stillwatch, Stormbringer, Stormcloud, Stormwarning, Strangers, Sub Luna, Subconscious, Submit, Subscream, Success, Sugarglider, Sunny Side Up, Suspiria, Svenssons Slavar, Swea

T For Trouble, T'quila, Taiwaz, Talking Terms, Tama, Target, Temper, Ten Feet Tall, Tengel, The Beer Hunters, The Boys Are Back, The Buttz, The Cosmos Band, The Duke, The Elysian Fields, The Flow, The Legacy, The Lizzard, The Moose, The Pilgrim Family, The Pleasure In Killing Small Animals, The Weird, Thin Lipsztick, Three Mile Smile, Thug, Thy Serpent, Thy Steamroller, TNT, Tonmord, Tony Barrera Band, Total Death, Trace, Tranquillity, Transylvania, Trazador, Trazy, Trigger Happy, Twice, Twilight, TZ

Under Cover, Underdog, Union, Unlord

Vain, Valiant, Valley, Velvet Chain, Viper, Virgin, Vlado Jozic, Void, Voltergest, Voodoo Gods

Walter Ego, Wasted Breed, WC, White Angel, White Falcons, White Knight, White Lightnin', Whrehouse Rockers, Windir, Witch, Wiz, World Full Of X, World Of Silence, Wraith, Wyre

Zahrim, Zanity, Zoom Club

Örjan Johansson, Ösregn

Where are the bands from?

So, all the bands in this book. Where are they from? The map on the next page also shows the Swedish counties (län) and some of the major musical cities in each county.

BLEKINGE

Asarum: Turbo, Paradize. **Karlshamn:** Blinded Colony, Constancia, Faith, Fjelltrone, The Graviators, Helvetes Port, Interaction, The Kaars, Kaptain Sun, Mercy, Nymf, Ocean (1), Overdrive, Parasite, Setback, Shubend, Skald, To Africa With Love, Vitality, Vulture Cavalry **Karlskrona:** Backyard Bullets, Deception, Disruption, Istapp, Locomotive Breath, Midvinter, Nidrike, Pax, Scratch (1), To Africa With Love, Tomas Bergsten's Fantasy, Unchained (2), Vanmakt. **Mörrum**: BALLS, The Kaars, Locomotive Breath, Mountain Of Power, Mörrum's Own, Paradize (1), Turbo. **Olofström**: Fourever, Omnispawn, Wanton. **Ronneby**: Buszer, Keystone, No Rules. **Sölvesborg**: Crier, Dust Bowl Jokies, Gabria, Horoscope (1), The Kaars, Mercy, On The Rocks.

DALARNA

Avesta: Altered Aeon, Brazen Riot, Chainwreck, Dedication, Demonical, Freeway, Frontiers, Interment, Isildur, Moondark, Scar Symmetry, Society Gang Rape, Subdive, Uncanny, Vanity Blvd, World Below. **Björbo**: Eternal. **Borlänge**: 1 Way Street, Anekdoten, Astral Doors, Bacon (Brothers), Boom Club, Buckshot O.D., Cryonic Temple, Death Organ, Demon Cleaner, Dozer, Dödföd, Fimbultyr, Genocrush Ferox, Greenleaf, Jammer, Junction, King Hobo, Kiss Of Thunder, Thomas Larsson, Mojobone, The Morning After Pound, Renaissance Of Fools, Six Feet Under, Sky Of Rage, Sorhin, Stonecake, Stonewall Noise Orchestra, Thalamus, Vantage, Volturyon, Yeah Bop Station. **Falun**: 21 Lucifers, Aquila, Bacon (Brothers), BALLS, Billion Dollar Babies, Chainwreck, Civil War, Deals Death, Diploma, In Mourning, In Solitude, The Law, Mozkovitch, Mustain, Nattas, Nerved, Oferd, Orphan Gypsy, Panzer Princess, Porklift, Prey, Renaissance Of Fools, Sabaton, (Clas Yngström &) Sky High, Sound Explosion, Svarti Loghi, Tungsten Axe, Volturyon. **Gagnef**: Eternal, Hydra (1), Third Stone, Zone Zero. **Hedemora**: Centinex, Young Force. **Leksand**: Voyager, Zone Zero. **Ludvika**: The Abyss, Epitaph (2), Hypocrisy, Sacred Night, Sahara (1), Spasmodic. **Malung**: Cavalince, Coastline. **Mora**: Arckanum, Craft, Omnizide, Sataros Grief, Sun Island, Tryckvåg, Twin Earth. **Morgårdshammar**: Mother Of God. **Nås**: Eternal. **Pärlby**: Pain. **Rättvik**: BALLS, Baltimoore, Rainfall, Six Feet Under. **Smedjebacken**: Colourdream. **Vansbro**: In Mourning, Keen Hue, Stefan Morén, United. **Älvdalen**: Jonny Cartong.

GOTLAND

Stenkyrka: Stonechurch. **Visby**: Grave (2), Stereo Generator, Trix

GÄVLEBORG

Alfta: Panic. **Arbrå**: Armauk. **Bergsjön**: De Tveksamma. **Bollnäs**: Averon, Babylon Bombs, Bloodbound, Enigmatic, Evercry, Fantasmagoria, Gormathon, Inmoria, Korp, Lefay, Morgana Lefay, Overload, Solitude (1), Street Talk, Trail Of Murder. **Edsbyn**: Evergrace, Incrave, Månljus, Narduz, Nirvana 2002. **Forsbacka**: Azotic Reign. **Gävle**: Steven Anderson, Beardfish, Brigada Illuminada, Broken Glass, Dieselkopf, Dominion, Ereb Altor, Facequake, Februari 93, Gungfly, Il Shy, Isole, Jezider, King Chrome, King Size, Los Bohemos, Marcus Brutus Band, Mason, Mindsplit, Nasty Groove, Prowoke, Reazon, Revenge, Rough Diamonds, Skydiverse, Slam, The Storyteller, Turning Point, Undivide, Wildborn, Windwalker, Withered Beauty, Zircus. **Hassela**: Teamwork. **Hofors**: Corrosive Carcass, Happy Cakes, Itchy Daze, Zeit. **Hudiksvall**: Fire & Ice, Mathias Holm, Iscarot, Madison, Regent, Rimfrost, Vildhjarta. **Ljusdal**: Angeline, Galleon, Hallonbomb, Hangover, Helium Head, Julie Laughs Nomore. **Sandviken**: Altered Aeon, Higher Ground, In Aeternum, Legia, Lipkin, Mutant, Outremer, Patronymicon, Rocka Rollas, Sorcery, Theory In Practice. **Storvik**: Diavox, Mandylion. **Söderala**: Authorize. **Söderhamn**: Book Of Hours, Divine Sin, Empire, Gasoline Queen, Lotus (1), Misfortune, Razorblade, Saigon, Solution, Solution .45, Splash, Two Eagles Request, Vital Sign, Wolverine. **Valbo**: Reazon. **Yxbo**: Helium Head.

HALLAND

Livsnekad. **Falkenberg**: Ablaze My Sorrow, The Ancient's Rebirth, Apostle, By Night, Damn Delicious, Entity, The Goddamned, Immemoreal, Innocent Rosie, Kalajs, Kaross, Moria, Oppression, Sign, Sonic Syndicate, The Unguided, Vains Of Jenna. **Halmstad**: Arch Enemy, Armageddon, Big Talk (2), Blind Dog, Craze, Evil Masquerade, Last Tribe, Lechery, Livsnekad, Lohengrin, Pagan Rites, Promille, Pussy Galore, Devil Lee Rot, Scenteria, Shining, Side By Side, Sonic Temple, Spiritual Beggars, Svart, Tristitia, Twelvestep, VII Gates, Who's Next. **Laholm**: Steelwings. **Onsala**: Crystal Age. **Torup**: X-Eryus, Savagers. **Ullared**: M.A.C. **Vallda**: Denial, Sacrilege. **Varberg**: Overlord, Anata, Cromlech, Double Diamond, Fatal Embrace, Frequency, Inhale, Jeremiah, Kamchatka, Lavett, Lezlie Paice, Livin' Parazite, Lothlorien, Parazite, Revengia, Sanity, Serenade For June, Silicone Valley, Spit It Out, Trendkill, Vildsvin. **Veddinge**: Eternal Lies, Eucharist. **Vinberg**: Autopsy Torment

JÄMTLAND

Backe: Gudars Skymning. **Bispgården**: Moonshine. **Brunflo**: Inzight. **Frösön**: Carrie, God Kills. **Hissmofors/Krokom**: Törsten Dricker. **Hoting**: Charity, Wizzard. **Lit**: April Sky. **Strömsund**: Gudars Skymning, Vivid. **Sveg**: Demons Of Dirt. **Östersund**: 220 Volt, A*Teem, Aeon (2), After Twelve, April Sky, Blackwood, Bulletsize, Central, Chastisement, Defaced Creation, Durthang, Equinox Ov The Gods, Eternal Desire, Extaz, Hin Haley, Magic, Mercenary Mustangs, Myrah, Ornias, Pride, Psycho Circus, Saltmine, Sanctification, Scamps, Skywalkers, Souldrainer, Suspekt, Transit, Uppgång 34.

JÖNKÖPING

Eksjö: Double Deuce, Dumper, Fair Child, Long John, Stefan Herde And His Broomdusters, Tumbleweed, Magnus Åhlin. **Frinnaryd**: Lenny Blade. **Habo**: Boderline (1). **Huskvarna**: Angelez, Headline (2), Hellfueled, Oriz. **Jönköping**: Admonish, Allan Beddo Band, Arrow, Big Thing, Big Train, Blind Alley, Colorblind, Cornerstone, Crut, Devian, Disciple, Domgård, East End, The Embodied, Exhale Swe, Fafner, Fortune (1), Grimmark, Headline (2), Heartcry, Hellspray, Hypothermia, Incinerator, Inevitable End, Johannes, Kyla, Lava Engine, Layout, The Legion, Lifelover, Macrocosmic Emotions, Mammuth, Metal Mercy, Miseration, Narnia, Nominon, Oblivion, Obscene, Pelle, Renegade (1), Retrace, Sanctifica, Shiva, Siebensünden, Sister, Sordid Death, Spice And The RJ Band, Stonefuze, Svartnar, System Breakdown, Tanaque, Trazer, Twilight Project, Two Franlin Grove, Wonderland (1), X-Hale, Yankee Heaven. **Nässjö**: Airborne, Attention (2), Backyard Babies, Crimson Moonlight, Dumper, El Camino, Emotion, Fear The Future, Grand Illusion, Kongh, Memoria, Pax Romana, Promotion, Prospect, Spearfish, Vermin, Wulcan. **Tranås**: Prisca, Sons Of Neverland, W.O. Band. **Vetlanda**: Dorian Grey, Green Sleeves, Seven Tears, Tumult, Aeon (1), Band Of Spice, Mushroom River Band, Solitude (2), Spice And The RJ Band.

KALMAR

Borgholm: Damnation Army. **Färjestaden**: Warcollapse. **Gamleby**: Bone Gnawer, Carve, Demiurg, Hemligt Uppdrag, Paganizer, Revolting, Ribspreader, Ypzilon. **Gunnebo**: Atrox. **Hultsfred**: Meadow. **Kalmar**: 2 Years After, Arena, Arfsynd, Aspected, Belladonna, Bluesbreath, Elimi, Hebron, Miss Behaviour, Press, Spawn Of Possession, Unlight Order, Visceral Bleeding, The Wagabond. **Luvehult**: Pantokrator. **Målilla**: Meadow. **Mönsterås**: Fatal Attraction, N.J.B, Plebb, Purple Haze, The Quill/Quil. **Nybro**: Elimi, Guns 'N' Horses, Snötårar. **Orrefors**: Spaps. **Oskarshamn**: Boom Shanker Group, Charizma. **Vimmerby**: Blacksmith, Victim. **Västervik**: Another Life, Atrox, Blodsrit, Blue Skies Bring Tears, Danger (1), Paganizer, Portal, Primitive Symphony, Raving Mad, Repulz, Sinners Burn, Tale, Thunder. **Överum**: Ypzilon.

KRONOBERG

Lagan: Priority. **Linneryd**: Entrails. **Ljungby**: By My Fear, Erottica, Screamer. **Strömsnäsbruk**: Loaded. **Tingsryd**: M-Train. **Väckelsång**: Epidemic. **Växjö**: Antichrist, Aphasia, Bullet, Carnage, Code, Danger (2), Dethronement, Devourment, Driver, Dynamite, Electra Top Raiders, Entrails, Epedemic, Erupted, Funeral, Furbowl, Hypnosia, Jesusexercise, Jet Trail, Jigsore Terror, The Killbilly 5'Ers, Lemon Bird, Mandrake Root, Mindcollapse, Muddy Road, Obscurity, Overdeth,The Scams, Silencer, Skogen, Sundell, Peter, Vidunder, Violent Work Of Art, Witchgrave, Wonderflow. **Älmhult**: My Dear Addiction, Universal Flytrap, Worship.

NORRBOTTEN

Arvidsjaur: Balthazar's Machine. **Boden**: Loud, Maninnya Blade, Satariel, Slowgate, Torch Bearer. **Glommersträsk**: Squetters. **Haparanda**: Chaossworn, Jan Granwick, Grave (1), Mörker, Raubtier. **Jokkmokk**: Diva (Deeva). **Kalix**: Thorbjörn Englund, Genie, Viperine, Winterlong. **Kiruna**: 8-Point Rosie, Coldspell, Comatose, R & R, Red Surface, Those Who Bring The Torture. **Luleå**: Battlelust, Cryonic, Dark Legions, The Duskfall, The Everdawn, Grace, Helltrain, Machinae Supremacy, The Moaning, Morthirim, Necromicon, Sobre Nocturn, Terra Tenebrosa, White Night. **Malmberget**: Septic Grave, Sunset Blade. **Malmköping**: Leukemia. **Piteå**: Cap Outrun, Chained, Cryonic, Infanticide, Laudamus, Maniac, Meduza, Nagazaki, Phoenix, Powertrip, Punishment, Savage Skülls. **Vuollerim**: Loudhell. **Älvsbyn**: Warning. **Övertorneå**: Helsefyr.

SKÅNE

Anderslöv: Bakteria, Johansson (Brothers). **Bjärred**: Moonstruck. **Bromölla**: Frank Thomsen, Wulfgar, Zap Yankeefy. **Fjälkinge**: TRP. **Furund**: Balthazar. **Helsingborg**: 9th Plague, 17/Seventeen, Agretator, Alyson Avenue, Bai Bang, Boogie Liquor Band, Bulletrain, Cloudscape, Darkane, The Darksend, Dawn Of Oblivion, The Defaced, Doctor Weird, Double Trouble, Fat Nelly, Fullforce, Gallery (Gaeleri), Gpd B.C., Hearse, Hearts Alive, Heavy Cargo, Hyste'riah G.B.C, Kayser, Mindfuel, Non-Human Level, Nonexist, Odyssey (1), Fredrik Pihl, Quix, Scandal Circus, Scratch (2), Second Heat, Shame (2), Soil-

work, Stefan Rosqvist Band, Terror 2000, Titan, Too Late, Unameus, Vanadis, Von Benzo. **Hjärup**: Broken Dagger, Deranged, Killaman, Murder Corporation. **Hässleholm**: Arrowz, Bergraven, Body Core, Dirty Passion, Evildoer, Keegan, Morpheena, Sacrifice, Sleazy Joe, Wham Glam Boys. **Höganäs**: Faithful Darkness, Quarterback Beat. **Hörby**: Merrygold. **Höör**: Anti-Christian Assault, Chaos Feeds Life, Magnus Karlsson's Freefall, Nae'blis, Skyfire, Yggdrasil. **Kirseberg**: Mothers Pride. **Klippan**: Daydream, King Koole, Panama Red. **Klågerup**: Geff. **Kristianstad**: Alcatraz, Aska, Blue Sky, Carnival Sun, Co Stone, Dimmz, Evildoer, Headline (1), Helvetes Port, In Black, Morpheena, Mortum, Necrovation, Neon, Peak, Physical Attraction, Portrait, Psyckadeli, The Rifles, Sanzia, Sgt. Carnage, Spin Air, Supreme Majesty, TRP, Unsolved, Verminious. **Landskrona**: The End, The Forsaken, The Gardnerz, Hyste'riah G.B.C, Mordgrim, Oxid, Proud, Spinnrock, Unreal. **Lund**: Art Metal, Bakteria, Blastrock, Bootleg, Crazy Lixx, Dibbukim, Havok, Hellbelly, Into The Void, KamaSutra, Milky, Miscellany, Pandemonium, Sgt. Sunshine, Shining Path, Sludge, Soniq Circus, Splattered Mermaids, Stonelake, Thee Expression, Tusen & En Natt, Veritate. **Löddeköpinge**: Torsten. **Malmö**: 8-Point Rosie, A.C.T, Aces High, After Life, Andromeda, Asoka, Backhander, Bad Habit, Bewarp, Billionaires Boys Club, Bonafide, The Brimstone Days, Burning Engines, The Carpet Knights, Chains, The Chair, Colorstone, Constancia, Cosmic Junk, Cross Bow, Crowpath, Cult Disciples, Cult Of The Fox, Dave Nerge's Bulldog, Deathboot, Deathening, Debase, Deville, Dogman, The Downtown Clowns, The Drugs, Embraced, Enshrined, Espinoza, Eurock, Faith Taboo, Fall Ov Seraphim, Flegma, Fleshcut, From Behind, GRK, Gin N' It, Great Ad, Jonas Hansson, Hellspell, Horizon (2), Ishtar, The Itch, Joke, Johas Hansson Band, Karmakanic, Last Tribe, Life Illusion, Lisa Gives Head, Little Yankees, Lovehandles, Machinegun Kelly, Majestic, Mansson, Massdistraction, Mega Slaughter, Merrygold, Midnight Sun, Misteltion, Murderplan, Nasty Idols, Nation Beyond, Nattsmyg, New Brand, Ningizzia, Nirvana 2002, Non Serviam, Nonexist, Nonworkinggeneration, Obscurity, Obscuro, Omnious, Opus Atlantica, Origin Blood, Original Sin, Payback, Pete Sandberg's Jade, Planet Alliance, Pleasure Avenue, The Point, Pretty Wild, Pyramido, Quadruple, Raise Cain, Reingold, Renegades, Reptilian, Ridge, Rockvaktmästarna, S.K.U.R.K, Sad Wings, Pete Sandberg, Sapphire Eyes, Sgt. Sunshine, Shining Path, Shubend, Silver Mountain, Silver Seraph, Skald, Kenneth Skoog, Snake Charmer, Space Odyssey (Richard Andersson's). Splattered Mermaids, Storm, Sub Second Rocket, Subway Rats, Suma, Supreme Majesty, Svarte Pan, Syron Vanes, Tenebre, Time Gallery, Time Requiem, Timeless Miracle, Truth, United Enemies, Eric de Van, Vandöd, Vanity Dies Hard, Virgin Sin, Void Moon, Whipping Princess, White, Wit, Wizzy Blaze, Wraptors, Zane. **Osby**: Enjoy The View. **Perstorp**: Alicate, Neofight. **Rydebäck**: Too Late. **Simrishamn**: Panndeads. **Skurup**: Richard Andersson, Space Odyssey (Richard Andersson's). **Staffanstorp**: John Huldt. **Svedala**: Bulldoggs, Hellmark. **Tomelilla**: New Bulsara. **Trelleborg**: Emerald, Mister Kite, Project L.E.E. **Trottatorp**: Zilch. **Vittsjö**: Melissa. **Ystad**: Carnalist. **Åhus**: Delve, Sven Hahne & Prästrock, Verminious. **Åstorp**: Midfuel. **Ängelholm**: Anyway, Daydream, Svartnad. **Örkelljunga**: Half Man, Mothercake, Skånska Mord.

STOCKHOLM

Botkyrka: Ian Olteanu Band. **Bro**: Stormrider. **Bromma**: Råg i ryggen. **Djursholm**: Incinia. **Ekerö**: Bloodstone. **Enskede**: Construcdead, Morpheus. **Farsta**: Morpheus. **Fisksätra**: Zeta **Handen**: Avalon (1)/Avalone. **Haninge**: A Mind Confused, Avalon (1)/Avalone, Kaamos, Skitarg. **Huddinge**: Dechas, Dry Dive, Nattfrost. **Hägersten**: Siena Root. **Johanneshov**: Necrophobic.

Järfälla: Flagellated Seraph, Infuneral. **Järna**: Septekh. **Kista**: Sorcerer. **Kungsängen**: Morbus Chron. **Lidingö**: Freddie Field, Stonehenge, Yale Bate. **Märsta**: Flame. **Mölnbo**: Prosperity. **Nacka**: Man From The Moon, Moberg-Talton, Unholy. **Norrtälje**: Dog Faced Gods, Månegarm, The Royal Ghost. **Nykvarn**: The Gypsies. **Nynäshamn**: Deep Diver, Imperious, Shotgun Bluez, Slodust, Svartsyn. **Rimbo**: Cleopatra, Opéra, Riksväg 77. **Rönninge**: Excretion, Serpent Obscene. **Saltsjö-Boo**: Machinery. **Skogås**: Slumber. **Sollentuna**: Chai Gang, Epitaph (1), Forkeyed, Gondoline, Grand Stand, Hungry Head Hunters, Tomterockers. **Solna**: Korea, Request. **Spånga**: Curse, Malign. **Stenhamra**: Cauterizer. **Stockholm**: 7Days, 7:e Himlen, 8th Sin, AB/CD, A Canorous Quintet, A Swarm Of The Sun, ATC, Abramis Brama, Abruptum, Abstrakt Algebra, Afflicted, Afterglow, Agony, Airlines, Alex's Pro, Alexander Lucas, Alfonzetti, Amaran, Amaxa, Amaze Me, Amkeni, Anaemia, Angel Kng, Angeline, Angrepp, Anima Morte, Annie For President, Ape, Coste Apetrea, Aphrodite, Astrophobos, Atlantic Tide, Atlantis, Attack, Attention (1), Audiovision, Avalon (1)/Avalone, Avenue, Backdraft, Backtalk, Badmouth, Bajen Death Cult, Ball, BALLS, Bam Bam Boys, Ban-Zai/Nio Liv, Bang & Out, Bathory, Bedlam, Beast, Åke Eriksson & Bedlam, Bedlam Erixon, Beyond Visions, Bibleblack, Bishop Garden, Black Cat Moan, Black Dog, Black Trip, Blackshine, Blacksmith, Blindside, Bloodbath, Bloodshed, Conny Bloom, Blowsight, Blue Matter, Blåeld, Bonafide, Tony Borg, Born Of Fire, Bosse, Brat Pack, Brighteye Brison, Brother Ape, C.B Murdoc, Candlemass, Candy Roxx, Cane, Canopy, Carbonized, Carnage, Casablanca, Casino Rangers, Castillion, Cellout, Cervello, Chainsaw, Chainwreck, Chaos Omen, Cheerleader, Cheers, Cheese, Cheri, Chiron, Clawfinger, Clockwise, Closer (1), Clown, The Codex, Coercion, Colossus, Come Sleep, Comecon, Confess, Confidence, Constancia, Cool For Cats, Core Of Nation, Corrosive Sweden, Count Raven, Covered Call, Cranium, Crash Dïet, Crash The System, Crematory, Creozoth, Cross, Crucified Barbara, Crucifyre, Cut 4, D.I.Y, Da President, Dagger, Dakks, Dalton, Damn Delicious, Damnation, Dark Funeral, Dark Illusion, Dark Legions, Dark Tranquillity, Darque, Dave Nerge's Bulldog, David Harleyson Powertrio, Deacon Street, The Dead, Death Breath, Deathwitch, Decadence, Deed, Defender, Defueld, Degradead, Dellamorte, Demon Seed, Demonical, Demenoid, Tommy Denander, Desultor, Devlin, Dexter Jones' Circus Orchestra, Diablo Swing Orchestra, Diabolical Masquerade, Diesel Down, Dimhymn, Dionda, The Dirty Old Men, Dirty Passion, Disdained, Dismember, Divinefire, Dominion Caligula, Dr. Living Dead, Drain (S.T.H), Dream Bank, Dynazty, Easy Action, Ebony Tears, Eclipse, Edge Of Sanity, Leif Edling, Eggs On Legs, Electric Boys, Elevener, Elsesphere, Elvira Madigan, Emmas Boogie Band, Enter The Hunt,

Entombed, Eventide, Evil Masquerade, Explode, Face Down, Face Of Evil, Faceshift, Fake, Fatal Smile (2), Feed, Fi5th Reason, Fingerspitzengefühl, Fire, Firecracker, Fistfunk, Flagellation, Flagship, Forest Of Shadows, Forkeyed, Fortuna, Fortune (2), Four Sticks, Fred's Fuel, Fuck Bitch, Fullmakt, Funeral Mist, G.O.L.D, Gallantry, Gas, Gemini Souls, Glorious Bankrobbers, Glory, Glory Bells (Band), God Among Insects, Godphobia, Golden Resurrection, Gone, Gordon Fights, Grand Magus, Grand Slam, Jan Granwick, Grave (2), Greasy Saddles, Great King Rat, Greed, Gregor Samsa, Griftegård, Ground Mower, Guardian Angels, Guidance Of Sin, Hardcore Circus, Harmäs Way, Hate Gallery, Haystack, Hearse, Heartbreak Radio, Heavy Load, Heresi, Hero, Hetsheads, Hexenhaus, Highbrow, Hiroshima, Hjärter Sex, Horizont, House Of Shakira, Houston, Human Clay, Human Rage, Humanimal, Hydra (2), Hydrogen, Hyperborean, Hypocrite, Hysterica, Impera, Impulsia, In Grey, In The Colonnades, Indian Red, Infernal (666), Ingo & Floyd, Insania (Stockholm), Insision, Insult, Iron Lamb,

Kiruna

Jämtlands län

Östersund

Dalarnas län

Luleå

Piteå

Sundsvall

Skellefteå

Norrbottens län

Hudiksvall

Falun

Bollnäs

Umeå

Västerbottens län

Värmlands län
Örebro län

Borlänge

Örnsköldsvik

Västernorrlands län

Västra Götalands län

Karlstad

Gävle

Gävleborgs län

Jönköpings län

Göteborg

Skövde

Örebro

Västerås

Västmanlands län

Hallands län

Uppsala län

Halmstad

Eskilstuna

Uppsala

Kronobergs län

Jönköping

Upplands Väsby

Helsingborg

Växjö

Stockholms län

Malmö

Norrköping

Stockholm

Skåne län

Linköping

Södermanlands län

Visby

Östergötlands län

Karlshamn

Kalmar län

Blekinge län Karlskrona Borgholm Gotlands län

It's Alive, IXXI, Jaguar, Benny Jansson, Jar, Jekyll & Hyde, Jennie Tebler's Out Of Oblivion, Marcus Jidell, Jonah Quizz, Jupiter Society, Iodine Jupiter, Katatonia, Kerberos, Kingsize, Knockout, The Krixhjälters, Krux, Kyss, Lack Of Faith, Jayce Landberg, Chris Laney, Last Autumns Dream, Last View, Life, Lifelover, Limitless, Line Up, Lingua, Lion's Share, Lipstixx 'N' Bullets, Liquid Scarlet, Liquidist, Lithium, Lizard Eye, Lobotomy, Loud, M.O.B, Maeday, Malign, Yngwie Malmsteen, Mamont, Man.Machine.Industry, Mandala, Mangrove, Maninnya Blade, Kee Marcello, Margoth And The Jabs, Mass Muder Agenda, Maze Of Time, Mefisto, Meldrum, Memento Mori, Mental Hippie Blood, Mentor's Wish, Mercury Fang, Middleage, Mind's Eye, Mindshift, Misanthropian, Misdemeanor, Misth, Moahni Moahna, Mogg, Moment Maniacs, Moosters, Morbid, Mordichrist, Mort, Mosexz, Movin' Globe, Mr. Death, The Murder Of My Sweet, Murder Squad, Mykorrhiza, Mårran, Mörk Gryning, Naked, Narnia, Nattas, Nebulosa, Necronaut, Necrophobic, Neon Rose, Nerved, Netherbird, New Keepers Of The Water Towers, Nex, Nightvision, Nihilist, Noctes, Nord, Göran Nordh, Pontus Norgren, Notorious, Novak (Andreas), November, Nubian Rose, Obnoxious Youth, Obrero, Ocean (2), October Tide, Odenwrath, Ofermod, Omnitron, Ondskapt, One Cent, One Hour Hell, Onyx, Opeth, Ophthalamia, Order Of Isaz, Ouijabeard, Daniel Palmqvist, Paperback Freud, Paradise (2), Parafine, German Pascual, Pest, Pinch, Plan Three, Polankton, Platitude, Point Of Existence, Pompei Nights, Ponamero Sundown, Pontus Snibb 3, The Poodles, Power, Pray For Locust, Pretty Wild, Prisoner, Psykotisk, Publikförakt AB, Pussy Galore, Qoph, Marc Quee, Queen Obscene, Quorthon, Raceway, Radioactive, Rain, Rainmaker, Rat Bat Blue, Rebelene, Reckless, Red Baron, Red Fun, Red Rocket, Redsun, Regurgitate, Reptile Smile, The Rest, Rev. 16:8, Revanch, Revelations, Revokation, Revolution Riot, Ride The Sky, The Riff, The Ring, Rise And Shine, Ritual, Roachpowder, Road II Ruin, Roadrats, Robeeo, Rolene, Roterock, Rough Rockers, Russell, Sabbtail, Sanctury In Blasphemy, Satan's Penguins, Satanarchy, Saturnalia Temple, Sayit, Scarpoint, Screamin' Mother, Scudiero, Sectu, Self Deception, Semlah, Sencelled, Septekh, Serpent, Seventh Wonder, Shadowgarden, Shadowland, Shadowseeds, Shalalee, Shock Tilt, Sideburn, Siebenbürgen, Siena Root, Silencer, Silent Call, Sins Of Omission, Sister, Sixcoveredkisssongs, Skellington, Skintrade, Thore (Goes Metal) Skogman, Skua, Slingblade, Slowlife, Slumber, Smokey Bandits, Snakes In Paradise, Solen Skiner, Solid Ground (1), Sonic Ritual, Sons Of Thunder, Source Of Ignition, Southfork, Southpaw, Spacebone, Spazmosity, Speedy Gonzales, Spektrum, Spin Gallery, Glen Spove, Stand By, State Of Mind, Steamboat Willies, Steamroller, Stench, Sterbhaus, Stonesilk, Stormwind, Straight Frank, Strike, Subcyde, Sundown, Superstition, Swedes, Swedish Metal Aid, Switchblade, T.A.R, Talisman, Talk Of The Town, Tears, Tears Of Anger, Tebler, Jennie, Tejp, Tempelrock, Ten 67, Terra Firma, Therion, This Ending, This Gift Is A Curse, Three Minute Madness, Thyrfing, Tiamat, Tippen Ruda, Titanic Truth (Conny Bloom's), Token, Tom Trick, Tommy Tysper & The Kida, Tore And The No Smokers, Total War, Toxic Rose, Trash, Treat, Treblinka, Trettioåriga Kriget, Tribal Ink, Tribulation (2), Trident, Trilogy, Triton Enigma, Truck, Twilight, Twins Crew, Two Rocks, Tyranex, Tyrant, The Ugly, Undecimber, Union Mac, Unleashed, Unpure, Uppåt Väggarna, Valley, Vampa, Vanguard (2), Vanhelgd, Vargton Project, Veni Domine, Via Tokyo, Vicious Art, Victory (2), Thomas Vikström, Vildsvin, Vindictiv, Vision, Vomitous, Vondur, Vredgad, Vörgus, W.E.T (2), War, The Weed, Wild Cat Sleazy, Wisdom Call, Withershin, Without Grief, Work Of Art, Wyvern, Xorigin, Xsavior, Yeah Bop Station, Zinny J Zan, Zan Clan, Zavorash, Zen, Zeudo, Zoic, Änglagård, Örby Mix, Överslag. **Sundbyberg**: Heave. **Södertälje**: Cartago, Desultory, Dispatched, Eternal Oath, Pike, Poor Boys, Stitch, Through Time Tomorrow, Wyvern, Zebulon. **Södertörn**: Big Business. **Tensta**: Rat Pack. **Tureberg**: Ellen B. **Tumba**: Amon Amarth, Eternal Oath. **Tyresö**: Bronto, Celestial Pain, John Norum, Profundi, Raise Hell, Rutthna. **Täby**: Absurd, Expulsion, Hungry Head Hunters, Wild Cat Sleazy, Skiller. **Upplands Väsby**: Anette Ax, Denied, Europe, Excruciate, Funeral Dirge, Grand Stand, H.E.A.T, Human Rage, Internal Decay, Hasse Karlberg, Mud & Blood, Nattsvart, Nemesis, John Norum, Pandemonic, Subtopia, Subztain, Therion, Universe. **Vallentuna**: Ape, Sheik Ahmeed Group. **Vällingby**: Screwball.Sthlm. **Årsta**: Excruciate, Unanimated. **Älvsjö**: Burn, Degreed.

SÖDERMANLAND

Eskilstuna: Avalon (1), Big Talk (1), The Black, Blood-Feud, Calm, Chronic Decay, Circle Of Chaos, Cirkus Crypt Of Kerberos, Crystal Pride, Days Of Anger, Eternal Darkness, Exanthema, Griffin, House Of Usher, King & Rozz, Lazy, Lynx, Madigan, Mistie, Pink Panther, Posh Filth, Rozz The Boss, Sapfhier, Scaar, Shakespear, Shere Khan, Torch, Tough Trade, Treasure, Tyrant, Tyrox, Wizz. **Flen**: Vanity Blvd. **Gnesta**: Dispatched. **Katrineholm**: Captor, Crow, Fatal Smile (2), Indomitus, Ninnuam, Spitfire, Tears, Triton Enigma. **Mellösa**: Blacklight **Nyköping**: Advice, The Case, Chive, Demon Seed, Dream Police, Galaxy Safari, Gorement, Helgedom, Last Laugh (1), Malison Rogue, Mamont, Mezzrow, Pipers Dawn, Silverdollar, Snakepit Rebels, Steel Arrows, Steelwing. **Oxelösund**: Hels, Souless. **Sparreholm**: Last Laugh (1). **Strängnäs**: A Virgin's Delight, Crystal Ocean, Deceiver, Entropy, Flesh, Harmony (1), Merciless, Powerbreeze, Satureye, Serpent Obscene, Thrown, Vinterland. **Trosa/Vagnhärad**: Adept. **Åker Styckebruk**: Demon Seed.

UPPSALA

Bålsta: Dionysus, Keehole, Kremlin-s Inn, Nation, Saint Deamon. **Enköping**: Cavus, The Curtain, Mother Misery, Sherlock Brothers. **Fjärdhundra**: Clench, Greyhate, RFP, Staiger, Surrender. **Gimo**: Valenze. **Heby**: Three Seasons. **Knivsta**: Pejling, Soils Of Fate **Knutby**: Team Custard. **Litslena**: Shaker. **Uppsala**: 454, Alonzo, Anguish, Anima Morte, Barrelhouse, Big Fish, Crawley, Crush On You, Damien, Defleshed, Degial, Deviant, Die Hard, Dimma, Dreamline, Enemy Is Us, F.K.Ü, Fatal Smile (1), The Flower Kings, Forcefeed, Freedom Bleeder, Fuzzdevil, Hagen, Hasse Fröberg & Musical Companion, HÅF-band, Immaculate, Imperial Domain, In Solitude, Inrage, Isildur, Kaipa, Lafayette, Lindberg, Zia (Cia), Loch Vostock, Lost Souls, Mac Blagick, Malaise, Manticore, JJ Marsh, Mayadome, Mellow Poetry, Midas Touch, Misery Loves Co., The Mist Of Avalon, Mother Superior, Noctum, Pain Of Salvation, Peter Martinsson Group, R.A.W, Rat Pack, Reveal, Rävjunk, Safemode, Sanctrum, Sarcasm, Searing I, Seethings, Sektor Skandal, Six Pack Sonic, Spacebone, Spellbound, Sportlov, S:t Erik, Stallion Four, Steve Eastside Band, Undergång, Veternus, Vomitous, Watain, Whimzy, Yersinia.

VÄRMLAND

Arvika: Corrupt, Devan, Enforcer, Gallows End, Lancer, Paganus, Pearly White, Sleeping Ape, Spectra, Stench, Thrashon, Tribulation (2). **Filipstad**: Bullseye, Caligula. **Forshaga**: Gehennah, Syrus, Turbocharged, Vomitory. **Hagfors**: Closer (2), Naughty Boys. **Karlstad**: Abacorn, Angel Heart, Convinced, Dawn Of Decay, Dogpound, The*End, Eucharist, Gallows End, Gehennah, The Generals, God Macabre, Godgory, Grave Flowers, Infernal Gates, Kisses From The Past, The Law, Loss, Lowrider, Macabre End, Mama Kin, Mental Crypt, Moaning Wind, Mordbrand, Ozium, Paganus, Quiz, Remuda Dust, Renegade Five, Satan's Penguins, Shee, Silent Scythe, Singer, Souldivider, Space Probe Taurus, Sparzanza, Texas Ego, Vargr, Wigelius, World Of Silence. **Kil**: Dave Rock, David Wilhelmsson. **Kristinehamn**: Armatur, Brimstone, Burst, Etos, Frenzy, Impale, Love Injection, Lucy, Memfis, Moonville, Motorcity Madhouse, Paradise (3), Sabbtail, Simson, Tyburn. **Säffle**: Doom: Vs, Draconian, Fairness, Scorched, Shadowgarden. **Torsby**: Morgan Mastling Band. **Vålberg**: Macabre End, Space Probe Taurus. **Årjäng**: Tribulation (2).

VÄSTERBOTTEN

Bjurholm: Heel. **Boliden**: Armagedda, LIK, Lönndom. **Burträsk:** Wynja, Scumkill. **Dorotea**: Rockvattnä. **Holmsund**: Dead Silent Slumber, Scumkill. **Norsjö**: Feral, Idiot. **Robertsfors**: Summoned Tide. **Skellefteå**: Black Bonzo, Blodskald, Boderline (2), Calm Chaos, Carpe Wade, Casket Casey, Dream, Dråpsnatt, Far North, Fission, Gin Lady, Hexagon, Jet, Leviathan, Lineout, Nightscape, Otyg, Rubbet, Sorgeldom, Stardog, TME, Terrortory, Tie 28, Vintersorg, Waterclime, Whirling. **Umeå**: 8-Point Rosie, Ancient Wisdom, Angst, Apostasy, April Divine, Arrows, Assailant, Auberon, B.C And The Envelopes, Bewitched, Bubonic Plague, Captain Crimson, Cult Of Luna, Cut Out, Daemonicus, Dexter Jones' Circus Orchestra, Embracing, Fredrik Thordendal's Special Defects, Furor, Gates Of Ishtar, Ghamorean, Gotham City, Guillotine, Hades, Hate Ammo, Havayoth, Hollow, Infra, Jimmy Nielsen & Band, Jonny's Bomb, Lethal, Lithany, Live Elephant, M.A.D, Ma Connection, Meshuggah, Midvinter, Mogg, Moloken, Mortuus, Mr. Tiger, Naglfar, Nasheim, Nocturnal Rites, Oberon, Persuader, Plastic Pride, Plector, Ramm, Redstorm, The Satellite Circle, Scheitan, Shredhead, Small Band, Spinning Black Circle, Steve Roper Band, Stoneload, Street Level, TBC, TNT, Terrortory, Three Minute Madness, Throne Of Ahaz, Torn Apart, Umeå Small Band, Woods Of Infinity, X-Union, Zonaria. **Vilhelmina**: Headache. **Vindeln**: ReinXeed, Swedish Hitz Goes Metal. **Åsele**: Another Hell.

VÄSTERNORRLAND

Härnösand: Cheyenne, Ornias, Solsting. **Kramfors**: Apostasy, Black Web, Divine Souls, Impiety. **Matfors**: Make Up. **Medelpad**: Vargavinter. **Sollefteå**: Firework, Scar, Sunflower, Wildmarken. **Sundsbruk**: Gilt, Moahni Moahna. **Sundsvall**: Abyssos, Angtoria, Apostasy, Behemoth, Big Price, Blackwinds, Bloodline, Blot Mine, Cherry Red, The Citadel, Coastline Ride, Conquest, Darklands, Diabolical, Diabolicum, Fenria, Horde Of Hel, Hyena, In Battle, Inferno, Ivory, Left Hand Solution, Lion's Share, Lovebone, Melek Taus, Mirage, Mortalicum, My Own Grave, Mystery, Neocori, Nidsang, Odhinn, Paradise (1), Pathos, Reflex, Renegade (2), Sargoth, Seremedy, Setherial, Slitage, Soreption, Sten, Syn:drom, Tyfus, Va-då, Yohio, Zpeedfreak. **Lillström**: Horde Of Hel. **Timrå**: Quicksand Dream/Epic Irae. **Ånge**: The Citadel, Corroded, Dr Booster, Takida. **Örnsköldsvik**: Nattas, Absorbing The Pain, April Divine, Blackrain, Boozeman's Simplex, Desert Rain, Destynation, Eternia, Justaquickstop, Killer Bee, Limit, Linehouse, Master Piece, Meadows End, Reflex, Romance, Sergeant.

VÄSTMANLAND

Arboga: Angelize, Carnal Grief, Lifeless Image, Roulette, Slick Stuff, Soulbreach, Walk Away, Within Reach. **Fagersta**: Apati, Black Rose, Gods Incorporated, Kazjurol, Lick The Dog, Sanctum Sanguis, Suffer, Svart. **Hallstahammar**: Mourning Sign, Thore (Skogman) Goes Metal, The Wild Bunch. **Kolsva**: Broke[N]Blue. **Kungsör**: El Gordo. **Köping**: Ambush, Kings N' Fools, Necroplasma, Rampant. **Sala**: Asperity, Carnal Forge, Demorian, Harvey Wallbanger, In Thy Dreams, Mother's Hope, Section Eight, Slip Into Silk, Steel Attack, Wombbath. **Skinnskatteberg**: Sticky Sweet. **Surahammar**: Backstreet, Tribulation (1).

Västerås: Abhoth, Academy, Acis, Andra Band, Apati, Axenstar, Beyond All Recognition, Blackworld, Bombs Of Hades, Bullhorn, Comandatory, Dead Awaken, Dunder, Dust, Entrench, Funeral Frost, GSO, Godhate, Grand Design, Haterush, Jotunheim, Mainline, Mascot Parade, Miscreant, Mornaland, Mother's Hope, Negro, Oxan, Psychotic Supper, Rockbox, Rosicrucian, Sanctum Sanguis, Sartinas, Scaar, Schizophrenic Circus, Seventribe, Skinfected, Slapdash, Soulgrinder, Source (1), Speednauts, Ten Foot Pole, Throneaeon, Twinball, Unchained (1), Utumno, Vanessa, Vicious, Vilefuck, White Line, Zeelion, Zello.

VÄSTRA GÖTALAND

Skuggan. **Alingsås**: Immemoreal, Arise, Born Electric, Crash, Evolution, Fatal Tabasco, Fraise, Frekvens, Inverted, New Breed, Prophanity, Putreaeon, Skymning. **Billdal**: At The Gates, Dark Tranquillity, Grotesque. **Borås**: Ablaze, As You Drown, Beseech, Big Times, The Bjorn, Bloodlit, Brainwave, Cemetary (1213), Conviction, Crystal Eyes, Damnatory, Darkwater, Diary, Dr Dream, Egonaut, Empire Saint, Enbound, Evocation, Fierce Conviction, Freternia, Ginger Trees, Harmony (2), Ironware, Lake Of Tears, Legbone, Lonely Hearts, Lost Horizon, Mac & Ploids, The Mary Major, Orient, S.L.R, Saint Deamon, Sanchez, Srodek, Stoneflow, Wild One, Zonata. **Dals Långed**: Liquid Phase, Mordant, Nifelheim. **Ed**: Shattered. **Falköping**: Electric Eastwood, Hell N' Diesel, Igneous Human, Majestic Vanguard, Sacramentum, Svartnatt, Valinors Tree. **Floda**: Reizon Band. **Fristad**: Rydell & Quick. **Frölunda**: Temperance, Sarcazm. **Färgelanda**: Shore, Wildness. **Göteborg**: Abandon, Adams Eve, Agape, Air Raid, Alien, All Ends, Christian Alsing, Amaranthe, Arise, Art Rebellion, At The Gates, Avatar, The Awesome Machine, BB Rock, B-Thong, Beneath The Frozen Soil, Benevolent, Bengalen, Big Easy, Big Wave, Billionaires Boys Club, Biscaya, The Black (Sweden), Black Ingvars, The Black Marbles, Blackmail, Blakk Totem, Blodulv, Blofly, Blue Balls, Blåkulla, Bonkyman, Boogieman, Boulevard, Brutaliator, Bult, Bussiga Klubben, Calilio, Cans, Capricorn, Cardinal Sin, Carizma Rain, Celestial Decay, Chillihounds, Chronic Torment, Coldtears, Comatose, Concrete Stuff, Cornel Band, Croc, Crossing Oceans, Crystal Age, Danger Avenue, Dawn Of Time, Deacon Street, Dead By April, Deadwood, Deals Death, Deathdestruction, Deathening, Deathstars, Decollation, Despite, Destiny, Develop, Devilicious, Diabolique, Diamond Dawn, Diesel, Dimension Zero, Disdain, Dissection, Distorted Wonderland, Dogface, Dom Dracul, Domgård, Don Patrol, Doom Dogs, Dracena, Dragonland, Dream Evil, Dreamland, Dyngrak, Dödaren, EF Band, Eaglestrike, Eldrimner, Eleven Pictures, Elevener, Elsy Band, Enemies Swe, Engel, Eternity Remains, Evercry, Evil's Eve, Evocation, Exhale Swe, Export, Eye, Flash, Foobar The Band, Forest, Freak Kitchen, Fretless, Frozen Eyes, Fruitcake, Full Metal Jacketz, Full Strike, Fullforce, The Funeral Orchestra, Gardenian, Geisha, Gemini Five, Generous Maria, Glanzig, Gloomy Sunday, Gosh!, Graveyard, The Great Deceiver, H.E.A.L, Hammerfall, Robert Hansson, Hardcore Superstar, The Haunted, Headplate, Heartbreak Radio, Heed, Helvetes Port, Highway, Hope, Horisont, Hostile Cell, Human Race, Hyperhug, Ice Age, Illwill, Immersed In Blood, In Flames, Inevitable End, Irrbloss, It Will Come, Jerusalem, The Jet Circus, Jim Jidhed, Karnarium, Katana, Kharma, Kill, Killaman, King Hobo, Kyrkstöt, Laethoria, Last Autumns Dream, Lava Engine, The Law, Leash, Liers In Wait, Likblek, Lillasyster, LOK, Loréne, Lost Horizon, Lotus (2), Lovers Under Cover, Luciferion, Lucky Stiff, Lugnoro, Långfinger, Madison, Madrigal, Majestic Dimension, Kee Marcello, Marionette, Marulk, The Mary Major, Massive Audio Nerve, Mega Slaughter, Memfis, Miasmal, Midnight Blue, M.ill.ion, Miosis, Mother Pearl, Motvind, Mrs. Hippie, Mustasch, Nadir, Nestor, Nifelheim, NME Within, No Hawaii, Norden Light, Nostradameus, Notre Dame (1), Nox Aurea, Nåstrond, Obitus, Obligatorisk Tortyr, On Parole, One Without, Opera Diabolicus, Osukaru, Outshine, Oxiplegatz, Pagan, Pagan Rites, Pagandom, Pain And Passion, Painfield, Panama, Passenger, Plain Zero, Power Unit, The Provenance, Quinzy, Quolio, Rallypack, RAM, Reclusion, Reece/Kronlund, Reenact, Relevant Few, The Resistance, Rickshaw, Rising Faith, Roach, Road Ratt, Ruined Soul, Runemagick, Sacramentum, Saffire, Sahara (2), Salute, Sanctuary In Blasphemy, Sten Sandberg, Sergej The Freak, Seventh One, Seventh Planet, Shaggy, Shame (1), Sharp Nine, Sinkadus, Skull Parade, Slow Train, Snakeskin Angels, Snakestorm, Solid, Somber, Sonic Walthers, Soulquake System, Soulreaper, Speedfreaks, Spiders, Stabwound, Status Two, Stillborn, Styggelse, Suicide Nation, Supergroupies, Supreme Majesty, Swedens Finest, Swedish Erotica, Swordmaster, Taetre, Tai Rose, Talent, Thunderhog, Time Code Alpha, Ton Of Bricks, Tonvikt, Tornado Babies, Transport League, Trash Amigos, Treasure Land, Treborian, Tribulation (2), Trident, Tube Screamer, Twin Age, The Ungrateful, Union Mac, United Fools, Urbandux, Vampire, Emma Varg, Vassago, Vatten, Vivaldi (Group), Von Rosen, The Waiting Rain, Waterline, Whipped Cream, White Silver, Witchery, Within Y, Wiz, Wonderland (2), Wonderland Dementation Dept., XXX, Zero Illusions, Zombiekrieg. **Hedekas**: Lord Belial. **Herrljunga**: Debbie Ray, Plan 9 (Nine), Source (2). **Hisings Backa**: Polluted Influence. **Hjo**: Robb And Friends, Björn Stigsson, Whiteness, XT. **Horred**: Memorium. **Hunnebostrand**: Decameron. **Hyppeln/Knippla**: Tatch. **Hällevadsholm**: Jeanne D'Arc. **Härryda**: Art Metal, Mattias la Eklundh. **Hönö**: Morbid Insulter, Akilles. **Höviksnäs**: Akilles. **Kinna**: Baddies. **Kungsbacka**: Mammal, Moonlight Agony, Nightshade, One Minute Left. **Kungälv**: The Cold Existence, Crazy Visions, Fagin, Tencider, Tension. **Lerum**: Carizma Rain, Maleficio, Sister Sin. **Lidköping**: Backwater, Bad Business, Degrade, Downstroke, Gallery, Holocaust, Nectaris, Orcivus, Rhapsody (Sweden), The Session, Taurus. **Limmared**: Hawk. **Lindome**: The Reehab. **Ljungskile**: Holocaustia, Sworn. **Lysekil**: Her Whisper, Mammoth Volume. **Majorna**: Major N.A. **Mariestad**: Galaxy, Implode, Infinity, Scatcats. **Mellerud**: Shore. **Mölndal**: Deletion, Frame, Thornium. **Mölnlycke**: Gypsy Rose. **Nödinge**: Vulcano. **Partille**: Iron Shit Snakes, Velvet Crash. **Pjugseryd**: Golden Dawn. **Romelanda**: Humble Bee. **Skara**: CC Rock, Cap Outrun, Mean Streak, T'Bell, Tracy Goes Crazy, Trouble, X-Ray. **Skövde**: Ammotrack, Axia, CC Rock, Detest, Enemies Swe, Exhale Swe, Extasy, Flintstens Med Stanley, The Gloria Story, House Of Heavy, Incapacity, Kaross, King Pin, Leviticus, Masquerade, Miseration, Niva, Nocturnal Alliance, Oxygen, Paradize (2), Peo, Quest Of Aidance, Shotgun Messiah, Skold, Solar Dawn, Solution .45, Syconaut, Torch Bearer, Tracy Goes Crazy, Trouble, Unmoored, Vomitous. **Smögen**: Excessum. **Sollebrunn**: Blue Orange. **Stenungsund**: Astrogname, Sadistic Grimness, Treasure Land. **Strömstad**: Aggregate, Aggressive Chill, Assault, Deathstars, Dissection, Reaktor 4. **Tanum**: Gypsy, Legions Of War. **Tanumshede**: Loud 'N' Nasty, Mindblaster. **Tibro**: Amity. **Tidaholm**: Railroad. **Tjörn**: Cipher System. **Trollhättan**: Angel Blake, Born Of Sin, The Crown (Of Thorns), Darkness, Electric Earth, Gooseflesh, Haze, Horoscope (2), House Of Heavy, I Am Hunger, Impious, Latex, Lord Belial, Miss Willis, NME Within, One Man Army And The Undead Quartet, Pathos, Rat Salad, Ravaged, Twilight Zone, Vassago, X-It. **Töreboda**: Eternal Autumn. **Uddevalla**: Axis Powers, Bestial Mockery, The Divine Baze Orchestra, Fuelhead, Grief Of Emerald, Hellennium, Ill-Natured, Karma, Matricide, Necrocurse, Sabotage, Sadistic Grimness, Seveth One, Stingray, Suicidal Winds, Ton Of Bricks, Trident, Vornth. **Ulricehamn**: Flood. **Vara**: Lucid Legend, Rhapsody (Sweden). **Vänersborg**: Death Tyrant, Earthquake, Remo, Rising, Skin Infection, White Cat. **Västra Frölunda**: In Flames. **Åmål**: Genesaret, Magnolia.

ÖREBRO

Askersund: Adventure, Anxious, Queensland. **Degerfors**: Damned Nation, Dead End Street, Easy-Street, Frozen Fire, Mörker, Silverfish, Succé, Thyreos. **Frövi**: Giant, Revival Band. **Hallsberg**: Nugatory. **Hällefors**: Fantasy. **Karlskoga**: Bonedog, Cicero, Dead End Space, Deep Zilents, THE Durango Riot, Edge, Eternal Fear, Goddefied, H2O, Heads Or Tales, Jet Airliner, Johnny Engström Band, Love Child, Misery, Pantheon, Plague Angel, Plutonium, Johan Randén, Seven Wishes, Shadows Past, Silverfish, Stallion, Stockholm Showdown, Story, Strangulation, Tyron, Wood. **Kopparberg**: Degreed. **Kumla**: Altar, Arsenite, Drama, Memory Garden, Suffer. **Laxå**: Victory (1), X-Perience. **Lindesberg**: Relentless, Vemoth, Maramon, My Endless Wishes. **Vretstorp**: Traction. **Åsbro**: Anxious. **Örebro**: 2 Ton Predator, All Hell, Asteroid, Azure, Bedroom Love, The Bereaved, Bloodbath, Blowback, Burning Saviours, Closer (2), Coldworker, Colt 45, Cowboy Prostitues, Cripple, Crossroad Jam, Crystal Blue, Darkcide, Dead End Space, Deadmarch, Dreamhunter, Fallen Angel, Firestone, Human Cometh, Infestdead, Iniuriua, Hyperborean, Johnny Engström Band, Karaboudjan, Kings Of Modern Swing, Lifeline, Molly's Gusher, Motherlode, Mörker, Necrony, Nightingale, Norrsken, Notre Dame (2), Odyssey (2), The Painted Man, Pan-Thy-Monium, The Project Hate MCMXCIX, Projekt UPA, Relentless, Rio, Route Nine, Slyside, Starterhead, Steel, Dan Swanö, This Haven, Tornado Soup, Torture Division, Total Terror, Troubled Horse, Truckfighters, Unicorn, Waving Corn, Whyte Ash, Witchcraft, Witherscape, Wolf, XT.

ÖSTERGÖTLAND

Boxholm: Jackwave. **Finspång**: Ashes, Attention (1), Blizzard, Darkified, Dawn Of Silence, Edge Of Sanity, Facebreaker, Mirador, Pan-Thy-Monium, Plague Warhead, Rock Squad, Route Nine, Tormented, Unicorn. **Kisa**: Air Condition. **Linghem**: Thornclad. **Linköping**: Axewitch, Corporation 187, Daisy Chain, Dawn, Demental, Denata, Eidomantum, Exciters, Freevil, Ghost (B.C), The Grand Trick, Hazy, Head Force, Iron Lamb, Isengard, Kliché, Los Sin Nombre, Maim, Maitreya, Maryscreek, Meadow In Silence, Mindless (Sinner), Morifade, Mother Ice Dog, Nephenzy (Chaos Order), Night, Nine, Nocturnal, Oblivious, Octinomos, Paralyce, Parnassus, Powerdise, Prime, Päst, Repugnant, Roswell, Sadatron, Satanic Slaughter, Saved By Insanity, Screams Over Northland, Seance, Silver Wings, Skinny Horse, Skogen Brinner, Sleazy Roze, The Social Scumbags, Solid Ground (2), Stright Up, Taketh, Taste, Triumphator, U.N.IT, Unlight Order, W.E.T (1). **Mjölby**: Ceremonial Execution, Choir Of Vengeance, Close Quarters, Falconer, Indungeon, King Of Asgard, Lucifer, Mithotyn, Niden Div. 187, Ocean Chief, Thy Primordial, Traumatic, Vanguard (1), Vanhelgd, Belsebub, Bring Your Own Knife, Drabness, Toxaemia. **Norrköping**: Abandoned Sphinx, Abyzimbel, Angst, Arconova, Battle Station, Bedrock Zity, Blackburns, Blazing Guns, Bokor, Brewmaster, Captain Freak's Freaky Funksters, Patric Carlsson, Cherokee, Dear Mutant, Death Wolf, Depzon, Devian, Devil's Whorehouse, Dizziness, Downbound Train, Empty Guns, For You (4U), Grand Vision, Happy Hour, Illfigure, Kansas City Rollers, Last Temptation, Lights Out, Marduk, Marshal Kane, Misericordia, Nefandus, Neondaze, Nifters, Northern Darkness, Ofermod, Optimystical, Overflash, Pole Position, Print, Rebels, Reptilian, Sarea, Sargatanas Reign, Saved By Insanity, Shineth, Skraeckoedlan, Spetälsk, Stormcrow, System Shock, Terrorama, Timescape, Vagh, Vilent Divine, Von Panzer, Warhammer, Year Of The Goat. **Skänninge**: Black Circle. **Söderköping**: Allegiance, Darkified. **Vadstena**: Close Quarters, Infernal Vengeance. **Vikbolandet**: Blues Bag. **Åtvidaberg**: Algaion, Maim, Vergelmer. **Ödeshög**: Vanguard (1).

1 WAY STREET
Mats Frimodigs: v, Håkan Frisk: g, Mats Uhrlander: k,
Göran Andersson: b, Kaj Podgorski: d

Borlänge - Excellent pompous AOR in the true late 80s *Europe* vein, but with a personal touch. The choruses should melt the heart of any AOR-fan. Very powerful sound, great arrangement and classy songs. Outstanding vocals by Mats Frimodigs, who later joined *Keen Hue*, and first class guitar twiddling from Håkan Frisk. A must for fans of melodic hard rock. Kaj was the man behind the Boom Town musical high school in Borlänge.

1988 ■ Can't Let Go/A Place In Your Heart..7" TMC ....TMCS 026

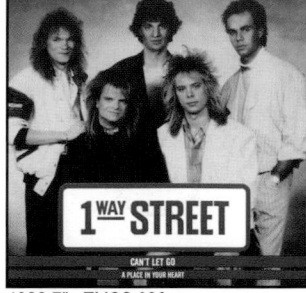
1988 7" - TMCS 026

2 TON PREDATOR
Mogge Lundin: v, Petter Samuel Freed: g, Tobbe Anger: b, Mattias Borg: d

Örebro - The foundation of *2 Ton Predator* was laid already back in 1993, when Tobbe and Mogge founded the band *Wedge*. They recorded some demos, but no label showed interest. When TBC finally approached the band Mogge, had to serve time. Once he was out, TBC went belly up. They now changed their name to *2 Ton Predator* and recorded a new demo in 1988, which caught the attention of Die Hard Records, who signed the band. Powerful metal somewhere between *Pantera* and *Down*. Produced by *Grope*'s Tue Madsen. Matte is also found in punksters *Genocide SS*, with whom he has recorded two albums. Anger later appeared in *All Hell*, Freed in *The Project Hate* and Borg in *Manifest* and *Whyte Ash*.
Website: www.myspace.com/2tonpredator

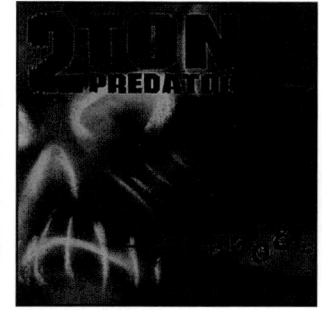
2001 CD - PCD 61

2000 □	IN THE SHALLOW WATERS...CD	Diehard	PCD 39/EFA10850
2001 ■	BOOGIE..CD	Diehard	PCD 61
2003 ■	DEMON DEALER ....CD	Diehard	PCD 63
2005 □	UNTITLED ....CD	private	- -

2003 CD - PCD 63

2 YEARS AFTER
David Sandström: v, Erik Johansson: g, Joel Nevrup: b, Daniel Öman: d

Kalmar - The band was formed in 2000, after the band *Aspected* had folded. However, they only lasted for a year. Joel and Öman are now found in rockers *The Whole Nine Yards*. *2 Years After* play messy and untight mid tempo hardcore/death metal, with horrible screaming vocals. The recording quality sounds like a pretty bad demo.

2001 ■ More Human, Less Alive/Damn The Day (split) ....7" EP Mäskdunc ....MDR 004
      Split with Skywalkers. Green or blue vinyl and a fabric-cover or paper cover.

2001 7" - MDR 004 (fabric cover)

7DAYS
Thomas Vikström: v, Markus Sigfridsson: g, Andreas Olsson: b, Daniel Flores: d

Stockholm - *7Days* started in 2004 when guitarist Sigfridsson had some songs that didn't fit his bands *Harmony* and *Darkwater*. He drafted his former *Harmony* colleague Olsson (*Narnia, Widsdom Call, Stormwind, Rob Rock*), who in his turn recommended drummer Flores (*Mind's Eye, Codex, The Murder Of My Sweet* etc). The band was picked up by Rivel Records, whose owner, Christian Liljegren (aka Rivel) recommended singer Thomas Vikström (*Talk Of The Town, Candlemass, Stormwind* etc). The band also used keyboard player Kaspar Dahlqvist (*Treasure Land, Dionysus* etc).
Website: www.sigfridsson.net/7days/

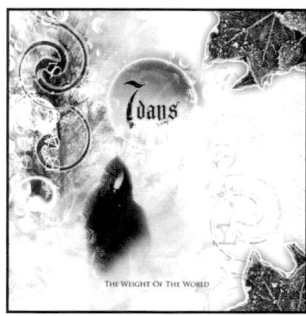
2006 CD - RRCD 028

2006 ■	THE WEIGHT OF THE WORLD ....CD	Rivel Records	RRCD 028
2010 ■	INTO FOREVER ....CD	Liljegren Records	LRCD 001

2010 CD - LRCD 001

7:E HIMLEN (aka SJUNDE HIMLEN)
Rosmarie "Rosa" Gröning: v, Anders Lago: g, Bert Östlund: k,
Tommy Gällhagen: b, Tomas Löfgren: d

Stockholm - Great melodic hard rock/AOR a bit like *Attack*, but not as poppy and with better vocals. Gällhagen was also a member of melodic rockers *Horizont*. Rosmarie has also recorded solo material in a pop vein and Östlund has written music for pop and country bands.

1982 □	Vilken natt för revolutionen/Dags att gå hem ....7"	Mill	MRS 1004
1983 ■	Se på mej (jag flyger)/Skönt att komma hem.....................................7"	Epic..	EPCA 3138

1983 7" - EPCA 3138

8-POINT ROSIE

Marcus Nygren: v, Alexander Timander: g/v, Adam Johansson: g/v,
Marcus Sjösund: b, Johannes Timander: d

Kiruna/Umeå/Malmö - *8-Point Rosie* was formed in 2009 by the members of former band *Ev-ermoore*. The band plays melodic, yet heavy metal, sounding a bit like *Morgana Lefay* meets *Nocturnal Rites*. Great vocals by Nygren (*Enbound, Stentorian*), mixed with some growls and gruffs from Timander and Johansson. A great sounding band indeed.

2010 CD - ESM 211

2010 ■ PRIMIGENIA...CD Escape..ESM 211

8TH SIN

Tony "It" Särkää: v, Michael Bohlin: g, Yxel "Y" Unutmas: g,
Johan Husgafvel: b, Zacharias "Zack" Ahlvik: d

Stockholm - *8th Sin* was founded by It and Bohlin in 1999 with the aim to mix metal, goth, synth and electro, which they do quite well, sounding a bit like a mix of *Rob Zombie*, *Deathstars* and *Pain*. Bohlin had earlier played in melodic hard rockers *Attention*, while It (Bohlin's brother-in-law) was formerly in *Abruptum, Ophthalamia, War, Vondur* etc. They drafted live bassist Johan Husgafvel (*Plague Divine*) and recorded the debut *Sinners Inc.,* from which the song *Dramaqueen* was featured in the roadmovie *Getaway In Stockholm 5*. In October 2005, the follow-up album was released, now with a full band which also featured guitarist Yxel "Y" Unutmas of *Fatal Smile*. Peter Tägtgren also made a guest appearance. The band, where drummer Thomas "TG" Lindgren had been replaced by Zacharias "Zack" Ahlvik, started recording the third album *Cosmogenesis*, but It decided to travel the world and Bohlin was touring with *Pain*, which delayed the release a few years.

2004 CD - BLOODCD 015

1005 CD - BLODCD 033

2004 ■ SINNERS INC...CD Black Lodge...............................BLODCD 015
2005 ■ ANGELSEED & DEMONMILK.................................CD Black Lodge...............................BLODCD 033
2012 □ COSMOGENESIS ....CD Soulseller Records.........................SSR 057

9TH PLAGUE

Tony Richter: v, Kristofer Örstadius: g, Johan Lindberg: b, Rafael Andersson: d

Helsingborg - Formed in 2000. The name refers to the Ten Plagues Of Egypt. The first demo *Spreading The Satanic Gospel* (2002) featured singer Tony Richter (ex-*The Darksend*), guitarists Johan Lindberg (ex-*Absus Ad Mortem*) and Stefan Stigert (ex-*The Darksend*), bassist Kristofer Örstadius and drummer Rafael Andersson (ex-*Absus Ad Mortem*). In 2003 the split cassette *Untied In Brutality* was released on Awaken Records and in 2004 the band released another demo entitled *Age Of Satanic Enlightenment*. At this time they were a quartet where Stigert was out of the band while Lindberg and Örstadius had switched instruments. Another demo, *Triumph Of Diaboilism*, saw the light of day in 2006 before they finally released the debut. The band split in 2008. The song *Demonic Conjuration* is found on *Voices Of Death Part IV: The Metal Crusade* (2000 Voices Of Death). The album was a solid slab of satanic death metal in the vein of *Morbid Angel*. Richter, who was also in *Gardens Of Obscurity*, is found in *Undecayed*.

2007 CD - BR 008

2007 ■ APOCATASTASIS REVERSED ....CD Butchered Records.........................BR 008

17 (aka SEVENTEEN)

Ulf "Chris Laney" Larsson: v, Jan "Jamie S:t Jan" Gripstedt: g,
Alex "Alec Farrara" Swerdh: b, Jack Daniel "J.D" Andersson: d

Helsingborg - After Ulf left the band *Unameus*, he formed the AOR/sleaze band *17*. The first single was produced by Thomas Vikström and Tommy Denander while the second by Thomas and Göran Elmquist. On the singles, the members were Ulf (v/g), Jonas "Jonni" Andersson (b), Niklas "Nick" Rollgard (g) and Patrik "Pat" Borgkvist (d). In 1993 Ulf left the others but kept the name. He recruited Alec and J.D from the band *Sabrosa* and Jamie from *U.L.C*. The three other ex-*17* members formed the band *Shooting Gallery*. After the MCD drummer J.D was sacked and they changed name to *Godsache*, they also changed style and recorded some demos. The first single doesn't really qualify into the higher league while *Rokket In My Pokket* (written by Thomas Vikström) and *17* are great. The MCD was produced by Göran Elmquist and Pontus Norgren (*Great King Rat, HammerFall* etc.) did some backing vocals. Ulf has later made quite a career as producer as well as musician, as solo artist as well as in *Zan Clan, Kyss, Randy Piper's Animal, Chris Laney, Chris Laney's Legion* etc., under the name Chris Laney.

1991 7" - S 002

1990 7" - S 001

1990 ■ Easy Come, Easy Go/Enough Is Enough ....7" private S-001
1991 ■ Rokket In My Pokket/When The Nite Cumz...........................7" private S-002
1994 ■ 17 ....MCD 5tr private ....SCD-001 A
    Tracks: Good Girl Gone Bad/2 Hot 2 Handle/Won't Waste My Time/Don't U Call It Luv/
    Mannerz Of A Monkey.

1994 MCD - SCD-001 A

21 LUCIFERS

**Erik Skoglund: v, Nicklas Lindh: g, Tobias Ols: g,
Per "Sodomizer" Eriksson: b, Olle Ferner: d**

Falun - A cold day early 2002 singer/guitarist Erik Skoglund (ex-*Five More Victims*), drummer Björn Åström (*Bludge*) and bassist Ola Berg (ex-*Without Grief*) started playing together as grindcore band *Gridlock*. They drafted second guitarist Nicklas Lindh (ex-*Without Grief*) and recorded a two-track demo. Since the name *Gridlock* was already taken, they changed it to *21 Lucifers*, after reading a headline in a newspaper. They recorded a second demo. Erik wanted to concentrate on vocals and second guitarist Tobias Ols (ex-*Without Grief*) was recruited. They recorded the demo *Retaliation*, after which Björn left the band. He was soon replaced by Olle Ferner. One week away from recording the next demo, bassist Berg left. Skoglund took over the bass and the recording was done. The basswork was soon taken over by Per "Sodomizer" Eriksson (*Bloodbath*) and the band was signed by Pulverised. *21 Lucifers* play fast and furious grind oriented death metal. Twenty songs in thirty-three minutes!
Website: www.21lucifers.com

2007 CD - ASH 025 CD

2007 ■	IN THE NAME OF…	CD	Pulverised	ASH 025 CD	

220 VOLT

**Joakim Lundholm: v, Peter Olander: g, Mats Karlsson: g,
Mikael "Mike" Larsson (now Krusenberg): b, Björn Höglund: d**

Östersund - Formed in 1979 by Mats Karlsson and Thomas Drevin. They found singer Christer Åsell (now Nääs), drummer Pelle Hansson and bassist Tommy Hällström. Hällström was replaced by Mikael Larsson (now Krusenberg) and in late 1981 Peter "Herman" Hermansson replaced drummer Hansson. In June 1982 they entered the studio to record their first seven track demo. The track *Woman In White* was later rerecorded for the debut album. In September the same year, the band again entered the studio to record another five tracks. Two of them were selected for the band's first single, released by local record dealer (and the band's first manager) Kjelle Björk, which has become a very sought after item. The B-side, *Sauron,* that was never rerecorded is a real seventies oriented riff-classic. Well worth looking for. The band was signed by CBS and the *Rainbow*-influenced début was released in 1983. Christer (later in *Empire* (where also Thomas Drevin was found), *Inzight* and *Magic)* was however rejected by the label during the recording of the debut and the band found singer Joakim Lundolm (*Mugabe*) to replace him. The debut was released May 30, 1983. Just before the release of *Power Games* Peter Olander replaced Thomas Drevin. They now toured extensively with bands like *Nazareth* and German metal band *Bullet*. By the Christmas of 1984 they recorded their best selling single *Heavy Christmas*, a non-LP track. Now the band had its first release in the US, a compilation of the first three albums, entitled *Electric Messengers*. They also opened up for the likes of *AC/DC*. Now things got really complicated when all except Olander had to do their military service. In the meantime Peter played with *Talisman* and John Norum. In March 1987 the boys were back in action and the single *Lorraine* went into the charts. *Eye To Eye* was produced by Max Norman (*Judas Priest, Ozzy* etc.) and the band went on a Swedish *Monsters Of Rock* tour together with *Electric Boys* and *Treat*. In 1990 Thomas formed *Daylight Dealer*, but nothing came out on record. After the release of the last 7" *Still In Love* differences with the record company and problems within the band put a halt to the career. The band split in 1992. Joakim quit singing and a while after Peter, Mats, Mike and Peter reformed with former *Blacksmith*/*Motherlode*-singer Per Englund under the name *Voltergeist*. They recorded an excellent demo. Mats also played with the melodic pop/rockers *Factory*. Mats, Peter and Thomas formed the band *Solar Moon*, but nothing came out of this. *220 Volt* had around 40 unreleased songs written and recorded. The track *Disappointed* is also found on the compilation-CD for the second encyclopedia and in 1997 some more of the unreleased recordings were unearthed on the compilation album *Lethal Illusion*. In 2002 *220 Volt* the first recording line-up reformed for a festival gig. It started as a re-union to celebrate the 20-years anniversary of the first single, but evolved into a full-blown re-union. New material was written, old material re-worked and the boys took it seriously, which was proved on the 2002 release, *Volume One*. The unreleased *Voltergeist* album was supposed to be released by Record Heaven in 2002, but it never happened. The band also released the live album *Made In Jämtland*. After this, drummer Peter Hermansson left the band and is now in *Zoom Club* and did a stint with *Grand Design*. In 2009 they did a new recording of *Heavy Christmas*, featuring original singer Joakim Lundholm and drummer Björn Höglund. In 2012 they re-united featuring new singer Anders Engberg (*Lion's Share*) and a new album is in the making. Johan Niemann (*Evergrey*) replaced bass-player Larsson (Krusenberg) early 2013. Mats is also in the band *Clover*. In 2013 Peter released his sigital solo EP, *Black Cloud*.
Website: www.220volt.se

Back in the days of muscles.

Reunited without any loss of power.

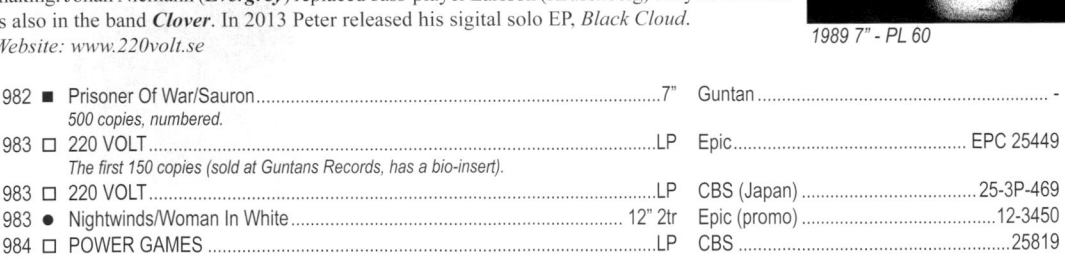

1989 7" - PL 60

1983 12" - 12-3450

1982 ■	Prisoner Of War/Sauron	7"	Guntan		-	$$
	500 copies, numbered.					
1983 □	220 VOLT	LP	Epic	EPC 25449		
	The first 150 copies (sold at Guntans Records, has a bio-insert).					
1983 □	220 VOLT	LP	CBS (Japan)	25-3P-469		
1983 ●	Nightwinds/Woman In White	12" 2tr	Epic (promo)	12-3450		
1984 □	POWER GAMES	LP	CBS	25819		

1984	☐	POWER GAMES	CD	CBS	CBS 258 19
		Bonus: Heavy Christmas			
1984	☐	Heavy Christmas/City Lights (re-mix)	7"	CBS	A 4967
1984	☐	Don't Go/Don't Go	12"	Epic (USA promo	EAS 2125
1984	☐	MIND OVER MUSCLE	LP	CBS (Japan)	28-3P-643
1985	☐	MIND OVER MUSCLE	LP	CBS	26254
1985	☐	MIND OVER MUSCLE	LP	CBS/Tonpress (Poland)	SX T 117
1985	☐	It's Nice To Be A King/Firefall (re-mix)	7"	CBS	A 6053
1985	☐	High Heels/Children Of The Plains	7"	CBS	A 6556
1985	☐	ELECTRIC MESSENGERS	LP	Epic (USA)	BFE 40099
1987	☐	Lorraine/Whiter Than White	7"	CBS	65000837
1987	☐	Heavy Christmas (re-mix)/Lorraine	7"	CBS	651254 7
1987	☐	Heavy Christmas (re-mix)/(original)/Lorraine	MLP 3tr	CBS	651254 6
1987	☐	Heavy Christmas (maxi-ver.)/Heavy Christmas (single)	12" 2tr	Epic (USA promo)	49-07500
1987	☐	Young And Wild/Dreams	7"	CBS	651048-7
		Dreams is previously unreleased.			
1987	☐	YOUNG AND WILD	LP	CBS	450 120 1
		This is a compilation with previously released tracks, only some are re-mixed.			
1987	☐	YOUNG AND WILD	CD	CBS	450 120 2
1988	■	EYE TO EYE	LP	CBS	460906-1
1988	☐	EYE TO EYE	CD	CBS	460906-2
1988	☐	Beat Of A Heart/Live It Up	7"	CBS	652 957 7
1988	☐	Beat Of A Heart/Beat Of A Heart	12" 1tr	Epic (USA promo)	EAS 1422
1988	☐	Love Is All You Need/On The Other Side	7"	CBS	653090 7
		The B-side is previously unreleased on vinyl.			
1989	■	EYE TO EYE	LP	Epic (USA)	FE 450 64
		Different artwork than on the European version.			
1989	☐	EYE TO EYE	CD	Epic (USA)	EK 450 64
		Bonus: On The Other Side			
1989	☐	EYE TO EYE	CD	Epic Sony (Japan)	25.8P-5089
		Bonus: On The Other Side			
1989	☐	EYE TO EYE	CD	Epic (Korea)	CPL-1048
1989	☐	Still In Love (re-mixed)/Criminal	7"	CBS	654694 7
1997	☐	LETHAL ILLUSION	CD	Empire	ERCD 1035
1997	☐	LETHAL ILLUSION	CD	Teichiku (Japan)	TECW-25520
		Bonus: Worlds Apart/Son In Law/Scene Of The Crime/What Have I Done			
1997	☐	220 VOLT	CD	Sony (Japan)	ESCA 7653
2002	☐	VOLUME 1	CD	private	VOLTCD 200201
2003	■	EYE TO EYE	CD	Power Play	PPRCD-1969001
		Bonus: Criminal/Still In Love (remix). Different artwork.			
2005	■	MADE IN JÄMTLAND	CD	Swedmetal	SM-01-CD
2009	☐	Heavy Christmas	MCD 4tr	MK Music	CD-03
		Tracks: Heavy Christmas/In The End/Firefall/Electric Messengers			

Unofficial releases:

1996	☐	Prisoner Of War/Sauron	7"	NWOSHM	001
199?	☐	220 VOLT	CD	-	-
1999	☐	220 VOLT	CD	Epic	ESCA 7653
		Greek counterfeit. ESCA 7653 on the matrix. Released around 2010.			
2001	☐	MIND OVER MUSCLE	CD	Metal Rendezvouz	MR 01013
		Bonus: High Heels/Dreams			
2001	☐	POWER GAMES	CD	Metal Rendezvouz	MR 01014
		Bonus: Heavy Christmas/Young And Wild/Lorraine			

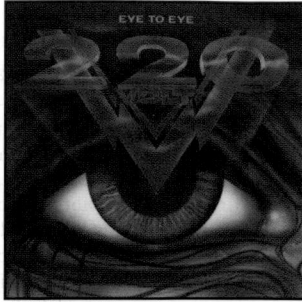
1988 LP - 460906-1

1989 LP - FE 450 64

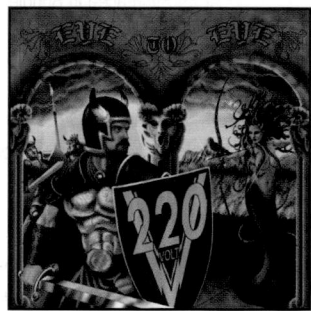

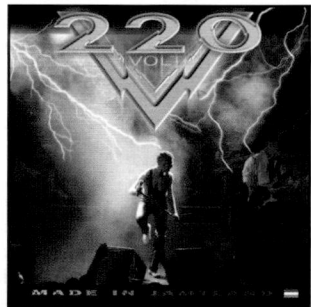
2003 CD - PPRCD-1969001

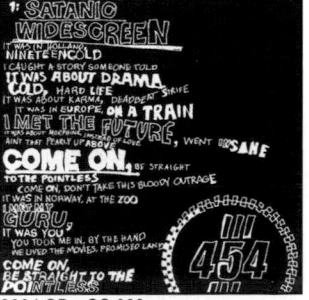
2005 CD - SM-01-CD

454

Anders E Rudström: v, Anders Stub: g. Tomas Gustavsson (now Rudström): g, Andreas Iverhed: b, Jakob Jennische: d

Uppsala - In the late nineties members of **Big Fish**, **Fuzzdevil** and **Mother Superior** got together to record a demo of loud, punkish, but heavy music, later labelled "stoner". Stub was supposed to sing, but it never happened, so they found Anders Rudström (**Ahimsa, Ded Zeb**). The first recording was made at the local radio studio. Stoner-oriented garagey heavy rock with influences of **Fu Manchu** and **Motörhead**. Jakob is also found in **Fuzzdevil, Spacebone** and **Six Pack Sonic**, plus he plays bass on the album *Pengar i sjön* by **Dimma**. Tomas (married to Anders Rudströms sister, hence the name change) and Andreas has previously played in **Big Fish**. After the CD Stub left the band and was replaced by Peter Rudström.

1999 2x7" - - -

1999	■	Free Ticket To The Ruble	2x7"g 8tr	Group Sounds	- -
		Tracks: Postmoon-Missils, Swampthing/Radio Murder/Hollywood 10/Over And Nowhere/ Eden Is Burning/Darby Cashed/The Bum And The Neon Bibles. Numbered.			
2000	☐	Maybe Legendary	MLP 7tr	Group Sounds	GS 004
		Tracks: Jonny Fackla/Welcome To Slavery/Brothers, Sisters, Bottles/Maybe Legendary/ Silverspoon Cages/Departure/Ghost Songs.			
2004	■	SATANIC WIDESCREEN	CD	Group Sounds	GS 009

2004 CD - GS 009

AB/CD

Mats "Brajan" Levén: v, Björn "Nalle/Nalcolm" Påhlsson: g, Bengt "Bengus" Ljungberger: g, Jim "Clim" Gustavsson: b, Nicco "Flint" Wallin: d

Stockholm - This is a true tongue-in-cheek band with Swedish top-notch musicians from bands like **Treat**, **Nord**, **Rickfors**, etc. paying homage to Australia's finest. They were actually one of Sweden's first true cover bands formed in 1983. In 1995 singer Mats Levén (**Abstrakt Algebra**, **Treat**, etc.) replaced Micke Hujanen, as he was tied up with other projects. (Unlike the originals the first singer has the ability to return). Björn has also made recordings with **Do*In*It** and **Easy Action**, while Bengt has recorded with the band **The Weed**, as well as a solo album in a far poppier vein. The lyrics are really something else. On *Cut The Crap*, **Yngwie** gets a slap in the face in the song *Rock 'N Rolex*, while **Michael Bolton** gets his in *Mikey's Butt*, not forgetting the **Scorpions** slaughter in *Elvis, Bugs And Oldies* - Killer!! If you're into **AC/DC**, you'll love them. The perfect placebo... and their songs are originals. The members have all been highly prolific. Påhlsson has recorded with **Therion, Mountain Of Power, Zan Clan, Treat, Randy Piper's Animal** etc, Nicco recorded an album with **Nord** and has made numerous studio sessions while Levén of course has been heard fronting **Yngwie Malmsteen, Southpaw, Therion, At Vance** etc. The exclusive track *Victory* was recorded for the tribute album of football team *Bajen, Bajen Forever* (2006) and *Wacko Jacko* was found on the bonus CD for the second encyclopedia. Hujanen has later backed up various artists such as **Ulf Lundell, Mats Ronander** etc and is also in power-trio **Zoom Club**. In 1993 Ljungberger recorded a CD with **BLJ Group**.

1986 MLP - FAMLP 001

1992 7" - PB 454 57

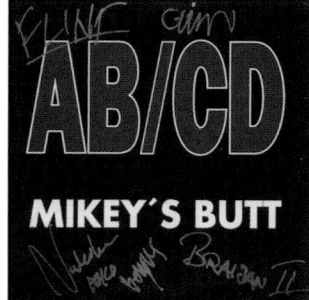
1995 CDS - 74321 28108 2

1986 ■	Victim Of Rock	MLP 6tr	Do-Re-Mi	FAMLP 001	
	Tracks: Victim Of Rock/The Rockin' Times/Time-Bomb/AB/CD/Poison In Your Veins/Blood-Money				
1992 □	THE ROCK AND ROLL DEVIL	CD	BMG	PD 75383	
1992 ■	The Rock 'N Roll Devil	7"	BMG	PB 454 57	
1995 ■	Mikey's Butt/Face-Lift Boogie	CDS 2tr	RCA	74321 28108 2	
1995 □	CUT THE CRAP	CD	RCA	74321 25309 2	

A.C.T

Herman Saming: v, Ola Andersson: g, Jerry Sahlin: k/v, Peter Asp: b, Thomas Lejon: d

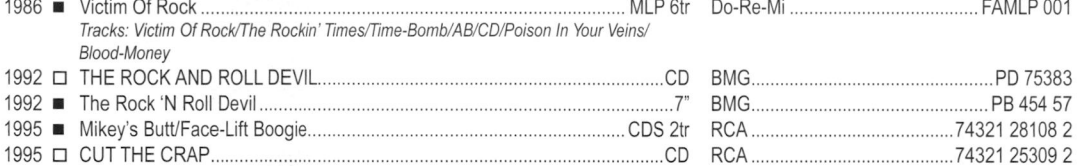
Young guys ACTing tough

Malmö - The band was formed under the moniker **Fairyland** in 1994. After a few member-changes they found the right line-up and in 1996 they found their new name and recorded their first demo. A second demo was recorded in 1998 and they were finally signed by MTM. High class pomp in the vein of early **Saga** and **City Boy** mixed with **It Bites** and a hint of **Dream Theater**. The songs are long and intriguing, going from lightweight poppy overtones to heavyweight guitar-riffs, all topped with a great sense of humor and incredibly catchy choruses. Right after the second album, drummer Tomas Erlandsson left the band and was replaced by Thomas Lejon. Herman was also a member of **Locomotive Breath** between 1995 and 2001 and Lejon is also found in **Andromeda** and he has formerly been a member of the band **Flow** that only made it onto a Dzynamite Records compilation, plus bands like **Nonexist** and **Embraced**. **A.C.T** started recording a new album in 2009, parts are already finished but child births put the band on hold. The new album was planned to be finished by November 2011, but is planned to be released late 2013. The 2002 release (*The Early Years*) is a seven track CD containing five demo tracks recorded before the debut, plus two live tracks taken from the compilation *Skånefinalen 1995 – Live*. In 2003 another CDR-promo was released on Acting Art. In 2013 former drummer Erlandsson and guitarist Andersson released the debut with the poppier band **Bella deBosco**. *Website: www.actworld.nu*

1999 CD - 0681-02

2003 CD - ATZ 02023

2003 CD - ATZ 02005

1999 □	TODAY'S REPORT	CD	Avalon Marquee (Japan)	MICCY 1140	
	Bonus: Granpa Phone Home				
1999 ■	TODAY'S REPORT	CD	MTM	0681-02	
2001 □	IMAGINARY FRIENDS	CD	Avalon Marquee (Japan)	MICP 10234	
	Bonus: New Age Polka (demo)				
2001 ■	IMAGINARY FRIENDS	CD	MTM	0681-31	
2002 □	(The Early Recordings)	MCD 7tr	Acting Art	--	$
	Tracks: Happy Days/Recall/Abandoned World/His Voice/The Chase/Dreamkeeping King (live)/Warsong (live)				
2003 ■	TODAY'S REPORT	CD	Atenzia	ATZ 02023	
	Bonus: Happy Days/Recall/Granpa Phone Home				
2003 ■	LAST EPIC	CD	Atenzia	ATZ 02005	
2003 □	LAST EPIC	CD	Avalon Marquee (Japan)	MICP-10349	

2003 CD - ATZ 02033

Year		Title	Format	Label	Catalogue
2004	☐	LAST EPIC	CD	Dope Entertainment (Korea)	DE-17005
2003	☐	IMAGINARY FRIENDS	CD	CD-Maximum (Russia)	CDM1103-1560
2003	■	IMAGINARY FRIENDS	CD	Atenzia	ATZ 02033

Bonus: Mouse In A Maze (Saga cover) + The making of

2006	■	SILENCE	CD	InsideOut	IOMCD 263
2006	☐	SILENCE	CD	Marquee Avalon (Japan)	MICP-10531

Bonus: Polish Reduce And Enlarge

2007	☐	TODAY'S REPORT	CD	InsideOut	IOMSECD 266
2007	☐	IMAGINARY FRIENDS	CD	InsideOut	SPV 79442 CD-E
2007	☐	LAST EPIC	CD	InsideOut	IOMSECD 268
2007	☐	LAST EPIC	CD	Soyus (Russia)	SPV79452

2006 CD - IOMCD 263

A CANOROUS QUINTET

Mårten Hansen: v, Linus Nirbrant: g, Leo Pignon: g, Jesper Löfgren: b, Fredrik Andersson: d

Stockholm - The band was formed in 1991 as a quartet, under the moniker *A Canorous Quartet*, which you might suspect. They split in 1993, but Fredrik and Mårten carried on changing the quartet to a quintet. Furious speed/death metal influenced by bands like *At The Gates* and *My Dying Bride*. Vocals of the type that kill vocal chords. Produced by Dan Swanö (*Edge Of Sanity, Nightingale, Bloodbath* etc.). Angela Ahola played synth on the first album. Leo is also found in *Niden Div. 187*. The band split after the 1998 album. Hansen guested on *October Tide*'s album *Grey Dawn* (1999) and sang in *Sins Of Omission* on *Flesh On Your Bones* (2010). Nirbrand and Andersson are also found in *Guidance Of Sin*. The LP *As Tears + The Time Of Autumn* contains the *As Tears* EP plus the *Time Of Autumn* demo. The 2012 single was recorded in 1994-95, originally meant to be featured on the debut album.

1995 MCD - CHAOSCD 02

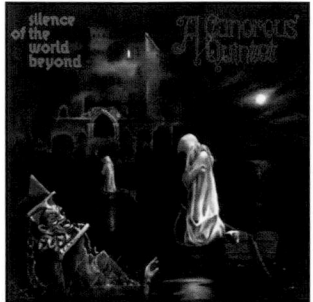

1996 CD - NFR 019

1995	■	As Tears	MCD 4tr	Chaos	CHAOSCD 02

Tracks: Through Endless Illusions/The Joy Of Sorrow/When Happiness Dies/Strangeland

1996	■	SILENCE OF THE WORLD BEYOND	CD	No Fashion	NFR 019
1998	■	THE ONLY PURE HATE	CD	No Fashion	NFR 028
2011	☐	AS TEARS + THE TIME OF AUTUMN	LPg	The Crypt	CRYPT 20 H

200 black, 300 magenta vinyl. poster.

2012	☐	Reflections Of The Mirror/The Offering	7"	Temple Of Darkness	TOD 032

500 copies..

1998 CD - NFR 028

A MIND CONFUSED

Johan Thörgren: v, Konstantin Papavassiliou: g, Rickard Wyöni: g, Nicklas Eriksson: b, Thomas Åberg: d

Haninge - The band existed between 1993 and 1998, when all except Johan formed *Kaamos*. The band made their first demo entitled *Demo 1 1995* in 1995 and the official *Poems Of A Darker Soul* in 1996 (Near Dark). Close in style to bands like *Dissection* and *Eucharist*. On the single, which was pretty cheap in sound and style, the line-up consisted of the above, minus Nicklas. Quite honestly the sound on the album is not that much better, but more like a mid-quality demo. Surprisingly enough it's recorded at Sunlight Studios by Fred Estby. Death metal with influences from thrash as well as *Iron Maiden*-type metal.

1996 7" - NDP 004

1996	■	Out Of A Chaos Spawn/Enchantress Of The Dark	7"	Near Dark	NDP 004

1000 numbered copies.

1998	■	ANARCHOS	CD	Near Dark	NDP 009
2002	☐	ANARCHOS	CD	Irond (Russia)	CD 02-176

1998 CD - NDP 009

A SWARM OF THE SUN

Jacob Berglund, Erik Nilsson

Stockholm - *A Swarm Of The Sun* is a two man project, on the debut with the addition of drummer Kalle Granström and bass player Anders Carlström (*Come Sleep, Lingua, Rövfitta*). Erik is also in the band *Aoria*, where he sings and plays guitar, and in *Kasual*. The band has some demos out, which are supposed to be available for purchase on the Version Studio website. Erik is also working on some film projects in different states of realization. Some loosely connected to *A Swarm of the Sun*, and some not. The band plays emo-oriented doom/stoner. The album also features Daniel Lindén (*Vaka, Dozer, Demon Cleaner, Greenleaf*) on drums and Anders Carlström on bass.

Website: www.aswarmofthesun.com/

2007	☐	The King Of Everything	MCD 6tr	Version Studio	VSCD 001

Tracks: Refuge/King Of Everything/A Mind But Not A Mouth/The Grip/An Animal In The Shape Of God/I Fear The

2010	■	ZENITH	CDd	Version Studio	VSCD 005

2010 CD - VSCD 005

ATC

Hans "Spider" Söder: v, Mats "Mappe" Björkman: g, Tommy Denander: g, Anders Gustafsson: b, Per Liljefors: d

Tommy Gun, age - young!

1984 LP- 818 416-1

Stockholm - The letters stand for Above The Clouds. The band made one album that didn't qualify into the higher leagues, although it has its nice moments. Quite standardish mid-80's hard rock in the early **Def Leppard**-vein. Worth noticing because of "Mappe" who later joined doomsters **Candlemass** and Tommy who has become a recognised guitarist and song-writer since. He later made recordings with **Cool For Cats**, **Cheese** (which also featured Liljefors), **Dag Finn, Prisoner, Talk Of The Town** etc. In 1995 he released two solo albums, *Skeleton* and *Less Is More*. In 1996 Tommy then released the first album with **Radioactive**, a project he recorded with members of **Toto** as back-up. On *Cut In Ice* he played a little over his limit though, however the dude was only 13 years old back then. Before the band split they recorded two tracks meant for a single (a video was also shot). They were produced by Michael B. Tretow (**ABBA**, a.o.), but never released. Tommy is now a highly prolific guitarist, producer and composer who has appeared on albums by artists like **Fee Waybill, Bruce Gaitch, Paul Stanley** etc. A live recording of ATC, made at Gröna Lund in 1985, is now circulating the web, both as audio and video. Mappe also recorded an album with **Zoic**.

1984 ■	CUT IN ICE	LP	Vertigo	818 416-1
2007 □	CUT IN ICE	CD	Shock Wave	n/a
	Budget re-issue, most likely a bootleg.			

A*TEEM

Rip Rhodes: v, Hank A*Teem: g, Carl "Speedergarben" Janfalk: g, Johan "Johny Tango" Törnqvist: g, Peter "Bad-Ass Bobby" Mellgren: b, Nils "Fastfills" Fjellström: d

Working men in jeans.

Östersund - Despite the tongue in cheek approach this is a killer heavy riff-oriented groovy hard rock/metal band in the vein of **The Cult** meets **Mustasch** with a singer quite reminiscent of Ralf Gyllenhammar. Mellgren is also in **Endless Torture**, while Fjellström has been found in various bands like **Aeon, Chastisement, In Battle, Odhinn, Sanctification, Souldrainer** and **Dark Funeral**. The band was formed in 1999, at first as a side project somewhat inspired by rock & roll, punk and **Entombed**. The initial line-up had Hank playing drums, but when they found Fastfills he switched to guitar. They also had L-G Putröv on vocals (nope, not the **Entombed** boy). Not sure who is who in the band, but the following people have appeared in the band in some form: Sebastian Nilsson (**Equinox Ov The Gods**), Per-Anders Enebro and Per Ove Eriksson. The band recorded a couple of demos that was finally released as the debut album. In the summer of 2002 L-G left. The members now started moving around geographically and things slowed down. In December 2007 the band started working on another five tracks, planned to be released in 2010, but nothing has been seen so far…

2002 □	KING IN JEANS	CD	New Noise Records	nnr013/BHR007
2002 ■	A*Men/A*Camp/A*Teem	7" 3tr	New Noise Records/Dimman	nnr017/Fog001
2005 □	Working Men	MCD 4tr	Dimman	Fog 005
	Tracks A*Teem – Working Men/A*Dam/A*Camp/A*Men			

2002 7" - nnr017/Fog001

A VIRGIN'S DELIGHT

Ola Johansson: v/g, Katja Andersson: k, Mats Johansson: b, Oscar Ekelund: d

Strängnäs - Good, solid melodic hard rock in the vein of **Dalton** or **Glory**. The tracks *Eden* and *Too Humble To Die* are featured on the *Tracks* (35:an, 1989) compilation.

1987 ■	The First Sight Of	7" 4tr	AVD Records	AVD 001
	Tracks: 2000 krig/By My Side/At First Sight/Eternal Life			

THE FIRST SIGHT OF Virgin's Delight

1987 7" - AVD 001

ABACORN

Michael "Miche" Johnson: v, Claes Engberg: g, Micke "Mike" Fröling: g, Frank Sundström: b, Johan Hidén: d

Karlstad - **Abacorn** was formed in the spring of 2002, when Claes' and Frank's prog metal band **Permanent Wave** was put on hold. Enter Mike, and after some more searching they found **Apple Brown Betty** drummer Johan. Claes finally convinced Frank, his old band mate, to join. In the spring of 2003, lead singer Miche (also ex-**Permanent Wave**) was drafted and **Abacorn** was finally complete. In November, the band entered RFM studios to record the songs *Bad Drug* and *Big Sleep* with producer Fredrik Hult, and in April 2004 they recorded four new songs. The demos finally became the band's self-financed debut CD, an outstanding ultra-powerful slab of metal with a modern touch. At times in the vein of **Sevendust**, but with a touch of **Pantera** in their prime. Great sounding stuff indeed! Heavy as Hell, yet melodic. In 2008 they released the demo *Ticking Bomb*. Guitarist Niclas Granath replaced Claes Engberg later the same year. In 2009 guitarist Micke Fröling left the band and was replaced by Mattias Frödén. Later the same year, the band recorded the EP *Message*, after which drummer Johan Hidén left the band

The band that doesn't compromise!

to join the band **Dunderman**. The song *Too Far* is found on the compilation *Big Balls Metal Compilation* (2010 Big Balls). In December 2010 the band announced they had decided to split.

2007 ■ IN A WORLD OF COMPRIMISE... WE DON'T..CD private BS6213

2007 CD - BS6213

ABANDON
Johan Carlzon: v, Ingvar Sandgren: g, Mehdi Vafaei: k,
David Fredriksson: b/v, Dani Cosimi: d
Göteborg - A doom band that seemed quite doomed. Singer Johan Carlzon (also in *Relevant Few*) died of a drug overdose in December 2008 while drummer Cosimi was serving a jail sentence and two of the other members were struck with cancer. David replaced Carl Linnaeus in 2000. Other former members include guitarist Johan Nilsson (*Relevant Few*) and drummer Magnus Häggman. Slow searing sludge doom with screeching vocals. Abandon split in 2005, but in 2011 they did a re-union show to honor singer Johan and the release of the 3LP. At this show the band was reinforced with singer/guitarist Ufuk Demir (*Relevant Few*).

2001 □ WHEN IT FALLS APART..CD Black Star Foundation ....BSF 08
2004 □ IN REALITY WE SUFFER ....CD Black Star Foundation ....BSF 16
       500 copies.
2005 □ IN REALITY WE SUFFER ....CD Codebreaker (UK)...........................CODEX002
       Different artwork.
2005 □ IN REALITY WE SUFFER ....CD Earache ....MOSH 303
2009 ■ THE DEAD END ....2CDd Black Star Foundation BSF034
2011 □ THE DEAD END ....3LP Black Star Foundation ....BSF 034
       275 copies.

2009 CDd - BSF 034

ABANDONED SPHINX
Henrik Lundgren: v/g, Ludvig Eklund: g, Klaus Gauffin: b, Anders Rösarne: d
Norrköping - Musically *Abandoned Sphinx* band delivers quite mainstream thrash in the vein of *Testament*, but the vocals are closer to the type you normally hear in death metal. The MCD is now a sought after item. Gauffin was later in *Violent Divine*.

1993 ■ Former Life..MCD 3tr Taltratten ....SphinxCd-s $
       Tracks: Intro: Former Life/String Of Innocence/Moments Of Advantage.

1993 MCD - SphinxCd-s

ABHOTH
Anders Ekman: v, Jörgen Kristensen: g, Anfinn Skulevold: g,
Dag Nesbö: b, Mats Blyckert: d
Västerås - Formed in 1989 as *MSA* (Morbid Salvation Army), playing grindcore. Singer Jörgen Bröms quit in 1990 to join *Afflicted*. They changed style and on the 7" *Abhoth* play death metal with tempo variations from ultra speed to slow doomy parts with some heavy riffs. Growling and warped vocals. Mats and Jörgen made some rehearsal recordings with the band *Suffer*, but nothing was ever released. After the 7", the band changed members and the new line-up featured guitarist/singer Jörgen, Mats, bassist Claes Ramberg and drummer Jens Klovegård. Mats and Jörgen are now found in *Dead Awaken*.

1993 ■ The Tide/Configuration...7" Corpse Grinder Records...................CGR 007
2012 □ THE TIDE...CD Dark Descent Records..................DDR072CD

1993 7" - CGR 007

ABLAZE
Pasi Humppi: v, Fredrik Jordanius: g, Oskar Lumbojev: d
Borås - It all started when Jordanius left *Rising Faith* to do his own thing in 2004. He approached former *Zonata* drummer Mikael "Cameron Force" Hörnqvist and the two started working. The band was soon completed with bass player Lukasz Strach and singer Pasi Humppi (*Freternia, Ironware, Crominic*). The band recorded their first three track demo *A* the same year. Jordanius is ex-*Fierce Conviction/Conviction* and *Rising Faith*. In 2005 the band parted ways with drummer Force, who was replaced by Lumbojev. On the album Strach was out of the band and session bassist Freddy Zielinsky (*Ironware*) was used. *Ablaze* produces well played traditional heavy metal with hints of bands like *Accept, Gamma Ray* and *Running Wild*. An album well worth checking out.

2007 ■ REAPERBAHN ....CD Stay Gold (Japan).........................ARTSG 023

2007 CD - ARTSG 023

ABLAZE MY SORROW
Kristian Lönnsjö: v, Magnus Carlsson: g, Dennie Linden: g,
Anders Brorsson: b, Alex Bengtsson: d
Falkenberg - Formed in 1993 by Magnus Carlsson and guitarist/singer Martin "Goatnecro" Qvist as *My Sorrow*. The band was soon completed by bass player Anders Brorsson and drummer

Fredrik Wenzel. The band recorded their first demo *For Bereavement We Cried* the year after. Wenzel left and was replaced by Alex Bengtsson. They recorded the demo track *The Song Of Dancing Sins* and in 1995 the demo *Demo-95*, which lead to a deal with No Fashion Records. Qvist wanted to concentrate on vocals and guitarist Roger Johansson was brought into the ranks. However, after the release of *If Emotion Still Burns,* Roger Johansson left and was shortly after replaced by Dennie. **Ablaze My Sorrow** play black metal influenced by the likes of **Entombed** and **Iron Maiden**. In 1997, shortly before the recording of *The Plague* singer Qvist left the band. He was replaced by Fredrik Arnesson. Right after the release Carlsson left the band and was replaced by Anders Lundin. The band now decided to take a break and a year later they all teamed up again, this time featuring both Carlsson and Qvist. The latter however left again and was later found in **Immemorial**. In 2002 they found a replacement in singer Kristian Lönnsjö (ex-**Deification**) and they recorded *Anger, Hate And Fury*.

Getting angry?

2002 CD - NFR 059

1996 ☐	IF EMOTION STILL BURNS	CD	No Fashion	NFR 015
1997 ☐	THE PLAGUE	CD	No Fashion	NFR 026
1997 ☐	THE PLAGUE	CD	Avalon Marquee (Japan)	MICY 10128
	Bonus: Rapist Of Life/Garden Of Sin			
2002 ■	ANGER, HATE AND FURY	CD	No Fashion	NFR 059
2002 ☐	ANGER, HATE AND FURY	CD	Irond (Russia)	CD 02-403

ABRAMIS BRAMA

Ulf Torkelsson: v, Per-Olof Andersson: g,
Dennis Berg: b, Fredrik "Trisse" Liefvendahl: d

Stockholm - Outstanding heavy, riff-oriented 70's hard rock, very similar to **November** in their heavier moments with an updated 70s sound. The band started out with lyrics only in Swedish, but the third release is for the English speaking listeners. In 1999 **Abramis Brama** unleashed their first 6-track demo *Ogräsblues*, which is a killer-CDR well worth looking for. The band does a Swedish version of *Mesmerization Eclipse* on the **Captain Beyond** tribute *Thousand Days Of Yesterdays* (1999 Record Heaven), entitled *Förtrollande Förmörkelse*. From the songs on the self-released 6-track promo: *Rökt, Smakar Söndag* and *Gravsten* are not found on the album. After the first album singer Christian Andersen was replaced by Ulf Torkelsson, who was ex-**Sunflower**. A cover of **November**'s *Men Mitt Hjärta Ska Vara Gjort Av Sten* can also be found on a demo-CDR and was later released on a split 7" with **Svarte Pan**. In 2003 they released their first, and only, album in English, *Nothing Changes*, which was rerecordings of old songs with English lyrics. After the recordings of *Rubicon* Fredrik Jansson was replaced by former **Grand Magus** drummer Liefvendahl. Jansson is now found in **Witchcraft, Atlantic Tide** and as bass player in **Count Raven**. On *Smakar söndag* (Tastes like Sunday) guestspots can be found from singer Moa Holmsten (**Meldrum**), keyboard player Rolf Leidestad and award winning saxophone player Jonas Kulhammar. In December 2012 Dennis left the band. He was replaced by Mats Rydström (**Backdraft, Pontus Snibb 3**) and a new album is planned to hit the streets in 2013. Ulf also joined **Atlantic Tide** in 2013.
Website: www.abramisbrama.com

Fishy, but hard-rocking!

1999 CD - RHCD 20

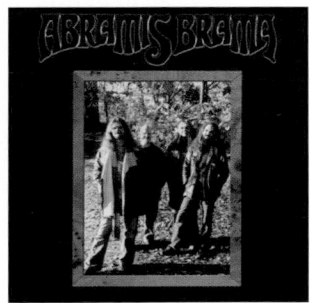
2002 CD - RHCD 67

2004 CDS - SRR MD1

1999 ■	DANSA TOKJÄVELNS VALS	CD	Record Heaven	RHCD 20
2001 ☐	NÄR TYSTNADEN LAGT SIG	CD	Record Heaven	RHCD 35
2002 ■	NOTHING CHANGES	CD	Record Heaven	RHCD 67
2003 ☐	Men mitt hjärta ska va gjort av sten (split)	7"	Ant Nest	ANR7" 001
	Split with Svarte Pan. Both bands doing covers of November.			
2003 ☐	NOTHING CHANGES	CDd	Sweden Rock	SRR 03
2003 ☐	NOTHING CHANGES	CD	Sweden Rock	SRR 012
2004 ■	Säljer din själ/Gravsten/Mamma talar	CDS 3tr	Sweden Rock	SRR MD1
2005 ☐	DANSA TOKJÄVELNS VALS	CD	Transubstans	TRANS 011
2005 ■	NÄR TYSTNADEN LAGT SIG	CD	Transubstans	TRANS 012
2006 ☐	RUBICON	2LP	Nasoni	NASONI 061
2006 ☐	RUBICON	2LP	Nasoni Records	NASONI 061 C
	Coloured vinyl.			
2007 ☐	LIVE	CD	Transubstans	TRANS 024
2009 ☐	SMAKAR SÖNDAG	CD	Transubstans	TRANS 046
2010 ☐	RUBICON	CD	Transubstans	TRANS 066

2005 CD - TRANS 012

ABRUPTUM

Tony "It" Särkää: v, Morgan "Evil" Håkansson: g/k

Stockholm - The band's first recording were two demos in 1990, entitled *Abruptum* and *The Satanist Tunes*. The titles of the two songs on the debut single are as impressive as the songs are strange. The first album contains two long (total over fifty minutes) experiments in death-growls, drum rhythms and meant-to-be frightening noises. *In Umbra...* is the same, only it's one sixtyminute track. When **Mayhem**-guitarist Euronymous died, his label Deathlike Silence folded and they were picked up by Hellspawn. Morgan is also found in **Marduk** and Tony was in **Ophthalamia**, a more traditional heavy satanic death/black metal band. Late 1995, he also released an album with his solo project **Vondur** (means evil in Icelandic), which is Nordic folk oriented music with evil Icelandic vocals. Tony was the founder of the Swedish satanic association *The Black Circle*. The title of the *Vi Sonus...* album means in English The Audial Essence Of Pure Black Evil, so now you know! *Evil Genius* is a compilation of the band's first two demos. Tony is now found in the more industrial band *8th Sin*.

1992 CD - ANTIMOSH 004

2001 MCD - BLOOD 006

1991 ☐ Evil	7"	Psycho-Slaughter	PS 003

Tracks: Hostes Orco Hostium Legiones Dis Manibus Pacis Ruptores Ultioni/Animum, Mentem Alcis, Iuventuem Largitionibus. Hostes Ad Dimicandum, Commotis Exita Sacris Thyias.

1992 ■ OBSCURITATEM ADVOCO AMPLECÉTREME	CD	Deathlike Silence	ANTIMOSH 004
1992 ☐ OBSCURITATEM ADVOCO AMPLECÉTREME	LP	Deathlike Silence	ANTIMOSH 004 LP
1994 ☐ IN UMBRA MALITIAE AMBULABO	CD	Deathlike Silence	ANTIMOSH 009
1994 ☐ IN UMBRA MALITIAE AMBULABO	LP	Deathlike Silence	ANTIMOSH 009 LP
1995 ☐ EVIL GENIUS	CD	Hellspawn	HELL 002

Contains the band's first two demo-tracks from Evil.

1996 ☐ VI SONUS VERIS NIGRAEMALITIAES	CD	Full Moon	FMP 007
2001 ☐ OBSCURITATEM ADVOCO AMPLECÉTREME	CD	Blooddawn	BLOOD 001
2001 ☐ IN UMBRA MALITIAE AMBULABO	CD	Blooddawn	BLOOD 002

New artwork.

2001 ■ De Profundis Mors Vas Cousumet/Dödsapparaten/Massdöd	MCD 3tr	Blooddawn	BLOOD 006
2001 ☐ De Profundis Mors Vas Cousumet/Dödsapparaten/Massdöd	10" 3tr	Blooddawn	BLOODLP 004
2001 ☐ IN ICTU OCULI	CD	Blooddawn	BLOOD 011
2001 ☐ IN ICTU OCULI	LP	Blooddawn	BLOODLP 011
2002 ☐ OBSCURITATEM ADVOCO AMPLECÉTREME	LP PD	Blooddawn	BLOODPLP 001

333 copies.

2004 ☐ CASUS LUCIFERI	CD	Bloddawn	BLOODCD 014
2004 ☐ CASUS LUCIFERI	LP	Bloddawn	BLOODLP 014
2004 ☐ CASUS LUCIFERI	LP PD	Bloddawn	BLOODPLP 014
2005 ☐ CASUS LUCIFERI	CD	CD-Maximum (Russia)	CDM 1104-2118
2007 ■ EVIL GENIUS	CD	Southern Lord (USA)	SUNNCD0000075
2007 ☐ EVIL GENIUS	LP	Southern Lord (USA)	SUNNLP0000075

1000 copies.

2007 ☐ EVIL GENIUS	CDd	Black Lodge	BLOD 027

New artwork..

2007 ☐ EVIL GENIUS	CD	Black Union	BUP01
2008 ☐ IN UMBRA MALITIAE AMBULABO	CD	Black Lodge	BLOD 002
2008 ☐ Maledictum/Maledictum	10"	Blooddawn	BLOOD 040

666 copies.

2011 ■ POTESTATES APOCALYPTIS	CDd	Blooddawn	BLOOD 048

1000 copies. Woven patch.

Unofficisal releases:

2007 ☐ OBSCURITATEM ADVOCO AMPLECÉTREME	7"	- -	- -

Track: Corpus Is As Transhere Abincere. Bootleg

2007 CD - SUNNCD0000075

2011 CDd - BLOOD 048

ABSORBING THE PAIN

Jonas Moström: v/g, Peo Hedin: g,
Anders "Sledge" Sandström: b, Magnus Grundström: d

Örnsköldsvik - *Absorbing The Pain* was formed in 2007 with its roots in bands like **Barophobia**, **Boozeman Simplex** and Danish band **Naked Rain**. Outstanding heavy riff oriented metal with hints of **Black Label Society**, but with cleaner vocals and more variation. Peo and Magnus have previously made records with melodic rockers **Killer Bee**. All three albums are solid pieces of lead, highly recommended!
Website: www.absorbingthepain.se

2010 CD - CD1001

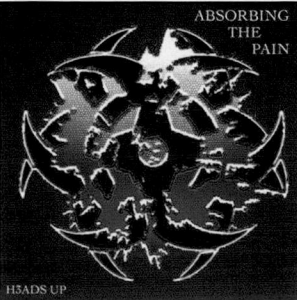

2011 CD - SAMCD11-01

2010 ■ ABSORBING THE PAIN	CD	Cold One	CD1001
2011 ■ SONGS OF HATE WITH LOVE	CD	Samsound/Rambo	SAMCD11-01
2012 ■ H3ADS UP	CD	Samsound/Rambo	SAMCD12-01

2012 CD - SAMCD12-01

ABSTRAKT ALGEBRA

**Mats Levén: v, Mikael "Mike Wead" Vikström: g, Simon Johansson: g,
Calle Westholm: k, Leif Edling: b, Jejo Perkovitch: d**

Stockholm - When *Candlemass* "took a break" in 1994, Leif compiled all of his unrecorded ideas, worked them out with drummer Jejo and called some more old friends to record the brilliant self-entitled album. Mike Wead was also a member of *Memento Mori* and has previously recorded with *Hexenhaus* and *Candlemass*, Jejo was in hardcore band *Brick* and dance units *Infinite Mass* and *Bearquartet*. Simon had his own band *Fi5th Reason*, while Mats (formerly *Treat, Capricorn, Swedish Erotica, Southpaw, Yngwie, AB/CD* etc) was in *Therion*. *Abstrakt Algebra* sound a bit like the missing link between *Black Sabbath* and *Savatage*, or as Leif describes it "A *Candlemass* of the 90s". The band split after the album, but they did record a second effort which was not released until the *Candlemass* re-issues in 2011. After this, Leif reformed *Candlemass*, which then included Jejo and Simon. Calle has release three albums with his progressive band *Jupiter Landing*, where Leif is guesting and he has recorded with soft symphonic band *Carptree*. Jejo is now found in *Mustasch*.

1996 CD - PRCD 024

1996 CD - MRRCD 024

1996	■	ABSTRAKT ALGEBRA	CD	Megarock	PRCD 024
		Promo with tray card only.			
1996	■	ABSTRAKT ALGEBRA	CD	Megarock	MRRCD 024
1996	□	ABSTRAKT ALGEBRA	CD	Zero (Japan)	XRCN-1227

ABSURD

Christopher Vowden: v/g, Mikael Bergström: g, Daniel Kangas: b, Marten Cederberg: d

Täby - *Absurd* released the demo *Storm Of Malevolence* in 1991, which was then followed by the EP the same year. Vowden has also been a member of *Expulsion, Abnormity, Stressfest* and *Mouthpeace*. Quite weird old-school death/grind/doom with warped spoken growl.

1991	■	Drained Of Body Chemicals	7" 3tr	Seraphic Decay	SCAM 018
		Tracks: Storm Of Malevolence/Drained Of Body Chemicals/See Through Me			

1991 7" 3tr - SCAM 018

ABUZIMBEL

**Jonas Franke-Blom: v/k, Magnus Bång: g, Niclas Brönner: k,
Mats Annemalm: b, Magnus Fritz: d**

Norrköping - *Abuzimbel* was formed when the guys were around fifteen and went to the same school in Norrköping. They rehearsed in the drummer's basement and after a show at the graduation show things started happening. They were influenced by bands like *Asia, Styx* and *Toto*, started writing their own material and entered the Rock SM two years in a row, where they ended up in the semi-finals. The single was recorded at their own expense by Ronny Roos of *Beatles* coverband *Liverpool* and printed in quite a big edition (more than 2 000 copies). After the single they recorded some demos that were even better than the single and when they finally entered the studio to record a second single a disagreement started that finally made the band split before its release. After the single they also had another singer, Max Malmgren, who is now fronting heavy rockers *Illfigure*. Franke-Blom later switched to cello and became a teacher and composer for movies and theatre; Fritz became a professional drummer and has played on numerous albums and shows, not in the heavier genres though. Niclas worked as a DJ, but has his own business today and Mats works as an optician. The name comes from Egypt and it is the name of the monument of the three famous pharao statues. The A-side is an up-tempo high-quality AOR in the vein of *Asia* with a heavy edge. The B-side is a semi-ballad goes up-tempo rocker, also quite close to *Asia*. Well worth looking for!

1986 7" - S&M 8603

1986	■	Beyond The Sun/Survive	7"	private	S&M 8603

ABYSS, THE

Mikael Hedlund: v/g, Lars Szöke: v/g, Peter Tägtgren: d/b/v

Ludvika - This is the same constellation that recorded a 1994-release under the name *Hypocrisy*, only the members have switched instruments. Peter plays guitar and Lars plays drums in *Hypocrisy*. In 1996 the band was reinforced by Mathias Kamijo (*Algaion, Vergelmer*), but he never appeared on record. The album contains uncompromising very fast and brutal black metal sung in Swedish and it's actually material not suitable for release under the *Hypocrisy* monicker. The first CD also features a cover of *Hellhammer*'s *Massacra*. Lars is guesting in the band *WAR*. Peter Tägtgen runs the studio with the same name as the band, where numerous classic death/black/thrash albums have been recorded under his command. He has also made several solo-releases under the name *Pain*.

1996 CD - NB 209 2

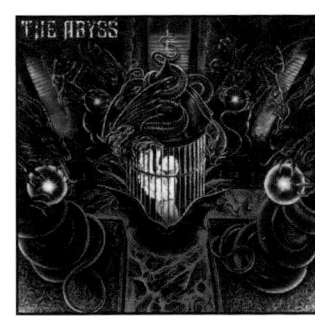
1995 CD - NB 126 2

2002 CDd - NB 653 2

1995	■	THE OTHER SIDE	CD	Nuclear Blast	NB 126 2
1995	□	THE OTHER SIDE	LP	Nuclear Blast	NB 126 1
1996	■	SUMMON THE BEAST	CD	Nuclear Blast	NB 209 2
2002	■	THE OTHER SIDE/SUMMON THE BEAST	CDd	Nuclear Blast	NB 653 2
2009	□	THE OTHER SIDE/SUMMON THE BEAST	CDd	Massacre	MASSCD 1292 DG

27

ABYSSOS

Christian "Lord" Rehn: v/g/k/b, Andreas Söderlund: d

Sundsvall - Formed by Christian Rehn, Daniel "Mad" Meidal and Andreas Söderlund in 1996. They recorded the first demo *Wherever The Witches Might Fly* later the same year. *Together We Summon The Dark* was also released as a cassette-album on Polish Mysic Productions. On the second release, bass-player Meidal was out and the band used session-singer Ah Fhinsta. The first album was in the vein of **Dissection**, while the follow-up was a bit more theatrical in its arrangements, more akin to **Dimmu Borgir**. On the second album they had also (like many other death metal bands) added more clean vocals, both male and female. The band is also featured on *The Unholy Bible* compilation (Cacophonous) as well as on *Independent Music For Independent People* (HOK 1999). In 1999 Söderlund also left the band. In 2002 the band began working on the third album entitled *Delomelanicon*, but it never surfaced. Rehn has also been found in **Evergrey**, **Sargoth** and **Angtoria**. Meidal and Söderlund are now found in **Insalubrious**.

1997 CD NIHIL 26 CD

1999 CD - NIHIL 34 CD

1997 ■	TOGETHER WE SUMMON THE DARK	CD	Cacophonous	NIHIL 26 CD
1999 ■	FHINSTHANIAN NIGHTBREED	CD	Cacophonous	NIHIL 34 CD

ACADEMY

Henrik Bladh: v/g, Michael Pyykkö: k, Stefan Hammarström: k, Patrik Sahlgren: d

Västerås - The A-side is a traditional hard rock ballad, while *Milk Energy* is pompous AOR in the heavier vein of **Toto**. High-quality stuff. The recording was sponsored by Arla Milk Company and others, to support the Childrens Cancer Foundation.

1989 ■	These Are The Dreams/Milk Energy	7"	Lynx	LRS 1008

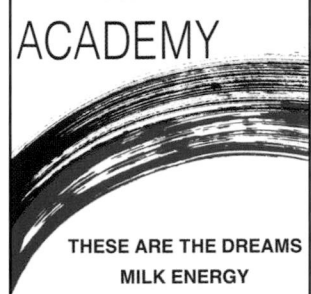
1989 7" - LRS 1008

ACES HIGH

Nikki Andersen: v, Joakim "Jake" Sandberg: g, Anders J:son: b,
David Brandt: k, Anders Johansson: d

Malmö - High-quality, guitar-driven melodic hard rock with a typically American, big and ballsy, AOR-sound. The singer is Danish but the remaining members hail from Malmö. Joakim, Anders and David were earlier in the band **Eyes** and their song *Rain Of Tears* can be found on the compilation *Rock Of Sweden*. David has also made several guest appearances on other albums for instance **Project L.E.E - Now Or Never**. Mats Björkman, who plays drums on the first album, is ex-**Quadruple**. After the first album, drummer Björkman was asked to leave and after some session-drummers the band finally engaged Anders Johansson (**Hammerfall, Silver Mountain, Johansson, Rising Force** etc). A limited edition of the first album also exists, with a misprint on the cover saying *Ten 'N*. A taster from the third album could be heard on the compilation *Rock The Nations II* (02 Z Records).

1994 CD - MRRCD 011

1998 CD - GMR 1098

1994 ■	TEN 'N OUT	CD	Megarock	MRRCD 011
1995 □	TEN 'N OUT	CD	JVC Victor (Japan)	VICP 5485
	Bonus: Take Me To Your Heart			
1998 ■	PULL NO PUNCHES	CD	GMR Music	GMR 1098
2002 □	FORGIVE & FORGET	CD	Z Records	ZR1997062
2004 ■	FORGIVE & FORGET	CD	Powerline	PLRCD 012
	Slipcase.			

2004 CD - PLRCD 012

ACIS

Johan Andersson: v, Peder Berglund: g, Peter Ledin: g,
Marco Malasagna: b, Jens Berglund: d

Västerås - A young melodic metal band with hints of **Saxon** and **Tygers Of Pan Tang**. Upper mid-league stuff. Peter Ledin was later lead singer of the band **Vanessa**. Some of the members later resurfaced in funk rock band **Trainsistor**.

1987 □	Lawbreaker/A Wanted Man	7"	Active Music	HEJ S-023	$

1987 7" - HEJ S-023

ADAMS EVE

Urban "Bam'C Slammer" Fermdal: v, Jörgen Fardvik: g,
Ronney Hedlund: b, Joacim Kjellgren: d

Göteborg - Riff-based melodic hard rock with a funky vibe, like a mix of **Van Halen** and **Extreme**. Great guitarwork! Jörgen and Joacim formed the band **Cristal** in 1987, with whom they recorded one demo. The band split in 1989 and the two went on to form **Adams Eve** the same year. They found bass-player Ronny and borrowed sleaze rockers **Big Bad Beat**'s singer Erik Dahl. When they decided to record a MCD they felt Erik wasn't the man for the job and they

called Urban, also ex-*Cristal*, now in a *Toto* cover band. Right after the MCD Ronney left the band and was replaced by Leif Strandqvist. Guitarist Nicklas Andersson (*Big Bad Beat, Export*) was added to the line-up. The band went from their happy *Extreme* funkishness to a darker and heavier vein, more influenced by *Skintrade* and *Mental Hippie Blood*. In 1994 Joacim quit and was replaced by Jörgen's brother Sören Fardvik (also in *Suicide Nation*). The band folded in late 1994, but they did record some more demos. Jörgen, Sören and Leif continued playing bluesy rock with singer Anneli Zachrisson under the name *Sister Jane*. The band later became *Gung*, who has recorded some highly promising demos. Fermdal is now handling the bass in melodic hard rockers *Elevener*.

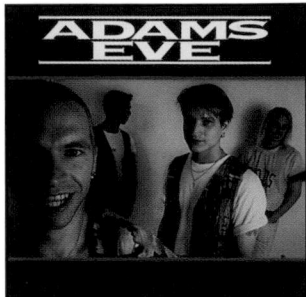

1993 ■ Adam's Eve ....MCD 4tr Local Hero ....LHM 0161 $
    Tracks: Bad Luck And Trouble/Break It Up/Woman/Get It Up

1993 MCD - LHM 0161

ADEPT

Robert Ljung: v, Jerry Repo: g, Gustav Lithammer: g,
Filip Brandelius: b, Gabriel Hellmark: d

Vagnhärad/Trosa - *Adept* was formed in 2004 and recorded their first demo, *Hopeless Illusions*, the same year. In 2005 the second demo, *When The Sun Gave Up The Sky*, was released. Metalcore with a touch of *In Flames*. Killer production by Fredrik Nordström and Henrik Udd, great musicians and great versatile vocals ranging from growl to clean. In 2011 guitarist Jakob Papinniemi was replaced by Gustav Lithammer.

2006 ■ The Rose Will Decay ....MCD 5tr Pretty Dirty Promotions 1
    Tracks: Introlude – The Collapse Of 2006/Let's Celebrate, Gorgeous! You Know Whose
    Party This Is/Incoherence; Blessed Upon A Phase/At Least Give Me My Dreams Back
    You Negligent Whore!/An Ode To Norah Barnes
2009 ■ ANOTHER YEAR OF DISASTER ....CD Pain & Action ....PANICCD 02
2011 □ DEATH DEALERS ....CDd Pain & Action ....PANIC 18
    Bonus: Playalong mp3-versions of: The Ivory Tower/This Could be Home
2011 □ DEATH DEALERS ....CD Pain & Action ....PANIC 32
2013 □ SILENCE THE WORLD ....CD Pain & Action ....PANIC 42

2006 MCD - 1

2009 CD - PANICCD 02

ADMONISH

Martin Norén: v, Emanuel Wärja: v/g, Emil Karlsson: g,
Jonas Karlsson: b, Robin Svedman: d

Jönköping - The band was formed in 1994 when Wärja and his friend Marcus started jamming. In 1995 the line-up started taking shape and they took the name *Admonish*. The members changed during the years and the activity varied. In 2002 things started happening and the line-up featured Emanuel, Martin and Robert. In 2003 guitarist Joel joined and they were re-inforced by former *Taketh* bassist Jonas. Joel left, but was finally replaced by former *Taketh* member (and Jonas' brother) Emil. The band now entered the studio to record the first MCD. The band play quite low rate death metal. On *Insnärjd* keyboards are played by Stormvit.
Website: www.admonish.org/

2005 MCD - AD 01

2005 ■ Den yttersta tiden ....MCD 3tr private ....AD 01
    Tracks: Epiphany/Den yttersta tiden/Var inte rädd
2007 ■ Insnärjd ....MCD 5tr Momentum Scandinavia MSD07
    Tracks: Tower Of Strength/A Glimpse/Istid/Journey Into Afterlife/Legacy. 850 copies with 8
    page 5 colour silver booklet.

2007 MCD - MSD07

ADVENTURE

Mats Ekstrand: v/g, Gert Karlsson: g, Kent Gustavsson: b, Peter Olsson: d

Askersund - Straight simple and very traditional mid 80s heavy metal. Mid-league stuff, well worth checking out if you're into bands like *Shakespeare*, *Arrowz* etc. The band's first singer was Matti Joutsen, but when they decided to relocate to Örebro, he and bass player Kent quit and joined the band *Queensland* with whom they recorded a single.

1985 ■ Destiny/Wonder Why ....7" Rolab Music..1101 $$

1993 MCD - LHM 0161

ADVICE

Dan Larsson: v/b, Tony Engström: v/k, Anders "Nippe" Fästader (aka Nilsson): g/k,
Stefan Larsson-Almén: g/k, Björn Ebbsjö: d

Nyköping - *Advice* was formed in 1982, influenced by bands like *Foreigner*, *Journey* and *Wrabbit* etc. They won the 1982 SN-Rocken competition, which resulted in studio time. Four tracks were recorded, of which two ended up on the single. The other two tracks; *Heartache* and *The Song Plays On*, were featured on the compilation *SN Rocken 82* (1983 SN).

Advice play commercial AOR with quite prominent keyboards but still some rough edged guitars. Musically it's really good, but the singer would need to work on his English. It's well worth looking for, for fans of 80s bands like *Harlequin*, *Hellfield* etc. The band split in 1983. Fästader (then Nilsson), moved to Stockholm and ended up in *Great King Rat* and has later on played with people like John Norum and Conny Bloom. Guitarist Stefan Larsson was in the initial line-up of *Treat*.

1983 ■ Eyes/Shadow Attack ....7" private ....A 66676 $

1983 7" - A 66676

AEON
Christian "Spice/Kryddan" Sjöstrand: b/v, Fredrik Finander: g, Urban "Ubbe" Lundin: d

Värnamo - When the single was recorded they were more of a heavy but thrashy band. After the single they started playing more traditional 70s influenced hard rock and recorded some demos with the following line-up: Christian (v/g), Fredrik (g), Karl Stork (b) and Ronnie Nielsen (d). Spice joined heavy 70's rockers *Spiritual Beggars* in 1993 and has also released albums with *Kayser*, *The Mushroom River Band* his own band *Spice And The RJ Band*, now known as *Band Of Spice*. Finander is also in *Kayser*. The 7" is well worth checking out.

1991 ■ Missing Ground/Under Silence ....7" private ....UNI 2578 $

1991 7" - UNI 2578

AEON
Tommy "Blackblood" Dahlström: v, Daniel Dlimi: g, Sebastian "Zeb" Nilsson: g
Marcus Edvardsson: b, Nils Fjellström: d

Östersund - Aeon was formed in 1999. All members except Daniel were previously in *Defaced Creation*. Soon after, guitarist Morgan Nordbekk entered the band. They recorded a six track demo, from which three tracks formed the *Promo 2000*, which was sent to several labels. They received interest from a few, but waited for a better deal, which came in August 2000, from Necropolis Records. Their demo recording was such a good production that the label and *Aeon* decided to release the full demo, with all the six tracks, as an MCD. It was realesed as *Dark Order* in May of 2001. On the recording all guitars were played by Zeb. Tommy, Zeb and Arttu are also found in *Diabolicum*. In about the same time, Morgan

Musicians of the dark order.

2001 MCD - DVR 009

Nordbekk decided to leave the band as he was moving to Stockholm. The band found a replacement in Daniel Dlimi (*Equinox Ov The Gods*, *Santification*, *Souldrainer*). *Aeon* continued to write material for their debut album, and did some gigs with this line-up. In 2002 drummer Arttu "Nathzion" Malkki decided to leave and he was replaced by Nils Fjellström (*In Battle*, *Chastisement*, *Souldrainer*, *Dark Funeral* etc). The band was finally signed by classic metal label Metal Blade and on the 2007 release bass player Johan Hjelm had been replaced by Max Carlberg (*Oltued*). *Aeon* play high-quality, blast-beat-filled furious death metal, but with great technique and quite a bit of variety. Great production and killer guitars. Before *Aeons Black*, bass player Max Carlberg was replaced by Marcus Edvardsson (*Souldrainer*, *Sanctification*, *In Battle* etc). In 2013 Nils was replaced by Erik Wiksten (*Fetus Stench*, *Blood Red Throne*) and Marcus by Tony Östman.
Website: www.aeon666.com

2010 CD - 3984-14901-2

2007 CD - 3984-14635-2

2001 ■ Dark Order ....MCD 6tr Deathvomit/Necropolis......................DVR 009
      Tracks: The Return Of Apolloun/Eternal Hate/With Blood They Pay/The Awakening/
      Bloodlust/Hell Unleashed
2005 ☐ BLEEDING THE FALSE...CD Unique Leader ....ULR 60026-2
2007 ■ RISE TO DOMINATE ....CD Metal Blade.............................3984-14635-2
2010 ■ PATH OF FIRE ....CD Metal Blade.............................3984-14901-2
2010 ☐ PATH OF FIRE ....CD Fono (Russia) FO834CD
2012 ☐ AEONS BLACK..CD Metal Blade.............................3984-15150-2
2012 ☐ AEONS BLACK..LP Metal Blade.............................3984-15150-1
      500 copies.

2012 CD - 3984-15150-2

AFFLICTED

Michael (Maciek) Van De Graaf: v, Jesper Thorsson: g,
Philip Von Segebaden: b, Yasin Hillborg: d

Stockholm - Formed late '88 under the name *Afflicted Convulsion* featuring the remains of the band *Defiance*. The albums were recorded in Sweden's premiere death metal studio - Sunlight and produced by Tomas Skogsberg. Fredrik Ling plays bass on the first two singles. On *Dawn Of Glory* they changed style from death to traditional heavy metal with influences from **Iron Maiden** and **Manowar**. They also changed singer from Jörgen Bröms to Michael (Maciek) Van De Graaf, who doesn't growl but sings. Bröms later joined **Abhoth** and later on, **Dissober**. Guitarist Joacim Carlsson, who was ex-**Dismember**, left after *Prodigal Sun* for the **Primus**-sounding **Proboscis** and later joined **Face Down**. In 1993 the band recorded the track *Seven Gates Of Hell* for the **Venom** tribute *Promoters Of The III World War*, on which Mikael Lindevall (**Proboscis**) filled Joacim's spot. In 1994 the track *Leper Messiah* was featured on the **Metallica**-tribute *Metal Militia* (Black Sun). The band can also be found on the 7" Nuclear Blast Sample *4 Way Split* (1992 Nuclear Blast) and on Relapse *Single Series Vol 5* (Relapse). Jesper is today working as manager at ADA Nordic Distribution., who actually distributed Nuclear Blast in Sweden. Yasin has produced the excellent movie *Så Jävla Metal* about the history of Swedish heavy metal.

1991 7" - THR 009

1992 7" - Single Series 019

2008 CDd - MASSCD1-190DG

1991 ■	Ingrained	7"	Thrash		THR 009
	Tracks: Viewing The Obscene/The Empty Word				
1992 ■	Astray/Spirit Spectrum	7"	Relapse	Singles Series 019	
1992 □	PRODIGAL SUN	LP	Nuclear Blast		NB 063-1
1992 □	PRODIGAL SUN	CD	Nuclear Blast		NB 063-2
1992 □	Rising To The Sun/Ivory Tower	CDS	Nuclear Blast		ST 45 NB 063
1992 □	Rising To The Sun/Ivory Tower	7"	Nuclear Blast		ST 45 NB 063
	1000 copies in yellow vinyl.				
1995 □	DAWN OF GLORY	CD	Massacre		MASSCD 055
2008 ■	PRODIGAL SUN	CDd	Metal Mind	MASSCD1-190DG	

AFRODITE

See Aphrodite.

AFTER LIFE

Bosse Andersson: v, Dick Bengtsson: g, Bengt Nilsson: b, Sonny Gröndahl: d

Malmö - Formed in 1969. The members were influenced by bands like **Steppenwolf** and **Deep Purple**. Some members originated from the local 60s band **Old Boots**. Side A is a quite light-weight track while side B is a cover of the **Purple**-song. Unfortunately the sound is quite weak, but they have a heavy attitude. A nice one to have in your 70s collection. They were much heavier live, which shows on some live recordings made by the local radio. The band broke up in 1971 due to two of the members doing their military service and it all fell apart. Bengt now lives in the USA. Dick has recorded with the **Malmö Big Band**, in a totally different musical direction.

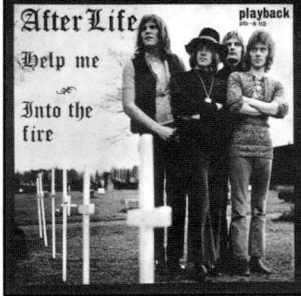

1971 7" - PB S112

1971 ■	Help Me/Into The Fire	7"	Playback	PB S112	$

AFTER TWELVE

Örjan Mårtensson: v/g, Bosse Karlsson: g, Tomas Björkbacka: k,
Håkan Mårtensson: b, Torbjörn Marcusson: d

Östersund - Pretty decent, quite typical eighties melodic hard rock/AOR. Worth checking out for fans of the typical eighties Epic Records AOR-bands like *4 Out Of 5 Doctors*, *Fortnox*, *Hellfield* etc.. Both tracks are up/mid tempo, so no ballad this time.

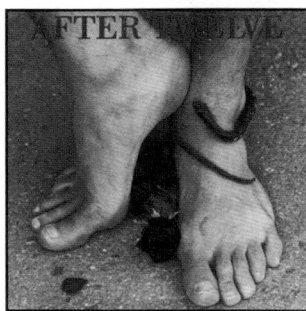

1988 7" - SSU 8801

1988 ■	All The Time/Moving On	7"	private	SSU 8801

AFTERGLOW

Germán Pascual: v, Fredrik Grünberger: g,
Johan Niemann: b, Daniel Flores: d

Stockholm - In my first encyclopedia I called this band "one of Sweden´s most promising un-signed bands of today". Since then they have had quite a nice career under the name **Mind's Eye**. *Afterglow* practically came out of nowhere and took me by storm. The band's private release contained high-quality prog-metal in the vein of **Dream Theater** (without keyboards) with astounding vocals and fantastic musicianship. Singer Germán was given the boot after the MCD was released, and they recorded several demos using various singers like Thomas Vikström (**Talk Of The Town**, **Candlemass**, **7Days** *etc*) and Robert Forse (**Heads Or Tails**). They ended up with singer Andreas Novak, changed their name to **Mind's Eye** and released the debut *Into The Unknown* in 1998, and several others followed (see **Mind's Eye**). In 2008 Lion Music released the **Mind's Eye** album *1994/The Afterglow*, which was a compilation of the *Afterglow* MCD plus three unreleased demo tracks and a video. Gérman returned to the scene in 2009 to

1995 MCD - AGCDS-9501

succeed Christian Liljegren in **Narnia** for one album before the band split. He is now sharing the vocal duties with Christian in the band **Divinefire**. Niemann has been in various bands like **Therion**, **The Murder Of My Sweet** and is now in **Evergrey**. Flores is also a prolific musician who has recorded with **The Murder Of My Sweet, Codex** and numerous other bands. In 2012 Gérman released his first solo album *A New Beginning*.

1995 ■ Afterglow..MCD 4tr   private ....AGCDS-9501 **$**
 *Tracks: Blind Justice/Cast Of Eternity/Ending A Story/Andromeda.*

AGAPE
Jalle Ahlström: v, Lars Carlsohn: g, Dan Tibell: k, Robert Wirensjö: k,
Ola Johansson: k, Jonas Axelsson: d
Göteborg - Side A is an OK melodic hard rocker with AOR-touch, while side B is a ballad. The singer is a very weak link. Dan Tibell was ex-**Jerusalem** and later joined **Heartcry**. Jalle was actually working as a "pub-priest" in Göteborg. He also recorded two solo-albums in a more straight west coast/rock vein under his own name. His vocal capacity has changed dramatically... to the better. The titles are *Breaking Ground* (89 Royal) and *That Lonely Road* (94 Stabel Hill).

1986 ■ Come On/Side By Side ....7"   Prim .... PRS 9006

1986 7" - PRS 9006

AGGREGATE
Joakim Wickgren: v/b, Morgan "Mogge" Rosörn: g, Johan Nylund: d
Strömstad - **Aggregate** was formed by former **Nugatory** members Wickgren and Rosörn together with Nylund, who all worked together at the time. In February 2008 the recorded their first CD. Later the same year second guitarist Emil Gustavsson was added to the line-up. **Aggregate** play death metal, at times with strong thrash influences, while in some songs they are almost a bit doomy.

2008 ■ FEEL THE PAIN...CD   Playwood (private).....................PlayCD008/5

2008 CD - PlayCD008/5

AGGRESSIVE CHILL
Mikael "Willy" Wilhelmsson: v/g, Krille Kellerman: g,
Robert Ottosson: b, Tommie Svanbo: d
Strömstad - **Aggressive Chill** was formed in 2003 by Wilhelmsson, Ottosson and drummer Tommie Svanbo. In 2006 Kellerman (**Mastema, Sarcastic, Diabolic, Whipping Post**) reinforced the band. *Destination 7734* was produced by reknowned producer Tobias Lindell (**Europe**). In 2009 drummer Svanbo was replaced by Tobias R Kellgren, who was later replaced by Jonas Kronberg. In 2011 Nidas Hammargren replaced Kronberg. **Aggressive Chill** play outstanding heavy, yet melodic metal with a modern touch, a bit similar to Swedish colleagues **Corroded**.

2008 CD - AC 2008

2008 ■	AGGRESSIVE CHILL	CD	Held	AC 2008
2009 ☐	Insomnia	CDSp 1tr	Held	ACCDS 309
2009 ☐	DESTINATION 7734	CDd	Held	AC CD 1-09
2013 ☐	BEFORE MY BREATH HOLDS ME DOWN	CD	Rambo	n/a

AGONY
Peter Lundström: v, Magnus Sjölin: g, Conny Wigström: g, Pelle Ström: g,
Nappe Benchemsi: b, Tommy Moberg: d
Stockholm - Formed as **Agoni** in 1984 playing punk/hard core, but they soon changed into a more thrash-oriented style. They recorded the demo *The Future Is Ours* and toured with punksters **Anti Cimex**. They now changed their name to **Agony** and in 1986 they recorded the demo *Execution Of Mankind* which lead to a deal with Music For Nations. Pelle Ström was sacked in 1987 and later joined **Krixhjälters/Omnitron** and after this, **Comecon**. Moberg has also been the singer of punk band **Mob 47** and was later in **Rubbermen**. Lundström sadly passed away in 2006.

1988 CD - CDFLAG 19

1988 ■	THE FIRST DEFIANCE	CD	Under One Flag	CDFLAG 19
1988 ☐	THE FIRST DEFIANCE	LP	Under One Flag	FLAG 19
1988 ☐	THE FIRST DEFIANCE	CD	Under One Flag (France)	100871
1988 ☐	THE FIRST DEFIANCE	CD	Combat (USA)	88561-8229
1988 ☐	THE FIRST DEFIANCE	LP	Combat (USA)	88561-8229-1

AGRETATOR
Pierre Richter: v/g, Christofer Malmström: g, Jörgen Löfberg: b, Peter Wildoer: d
Helsingborg - They started out under the name **Demise** and released two death metal demos. **Agretator** is a young and talented rough edged thrash band with more death-oriented vocals. They also have the tracks *Omnius Situation* and *Dull Reality* on the *Kompaktkraft* compilation (1994 Kompakt Kraft). The band split in 1998. Wildoer has been found in bands like **Silver**

1996 MCD - AR 002

Seraph, Darkane, Armageddon, Time Requiem etc. Richter in *Demise* and *God B.C*, Malmström in *Darkane* and *Non-Human Level*, and Löfberg has been in *Darkane* and *The Defaced*.

1994	□	DELUSIONS	CD	Crypta Records	8211-2
1996	■	DISTORTED LOGIC	MCD 5tr	Studiofabriken	AR 002

        Tracks: Chains Of Retribution/Distorted Logic/Water/Virtual Tragedy/Non-Human Level

AIR CONDITION

Kjell Gustavsson: v/d, Lars-Åke Nilsson: g,
Sven-Inge Nilsson: g, Lars Rulander: k, Jörgen Olsson: b

Kisa - Air Condition, despite the slightly daft name, plays pretty decent AOR/melodic hard rock, well-played and well-sung, but maybe not the hottest of songs.

1981	■	Street 69/Halfway Down	7"	Pang	PSI 012

1981 7" - PSI 012

AIR RAID

Michail Rinakakis: v, Andreas "Andy Stormchild" Johansson: g,
Johan "Johnny Nightshredder" Karlsson: g, Robin "Rob Thunderbolt" Utbult: b,
David "Dave Destructor" Hermansson: d

Göteborg - Air Raid, a new fresh upcoming bunch of metallurgists formed in 2009. Classic *Judas Priest* meets early *Metallica* over a drink at the NWoBHM bar. Hermansson is ex-*Solemn Dawn* and Michail was in *Event Horizon X*.

2012	□	Danger Ahead	MCD 7tr	Stormspell	SSR-DL80

        Tracks: When The Sky Turns Red/Annihilation/The Metal Cult/Midnight Burner/Free At Last/Traitor's Gate/Fight Street. 500 hand-numbered copies.

2012	■	NIGHT OF THE AXE	CD	Stormspell	SSR-DL97
2013	□	Danger Ahead	MLP 7tr	Underground Power	UP 004
2013	□	NIGHT OF THE AXE	LP	Underground Power	UP 005

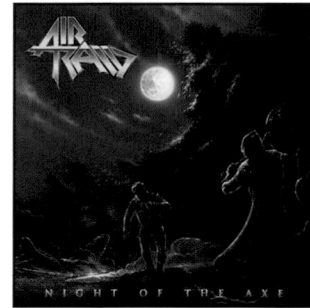

2013 CD - SSR-DL97

AIRBORNE

Mikael "Abbe" Sjöström: v, Christer "Chris" Andersson: g, Jocke Schön: g,
Tommy Johnsson: b, Stephen Axelsson: d

Nässjö - Formed in 1982, split in 1985. The single was recorded in the UK. Very UK sounding heavy metal in the vein of *Trespass*, which is why several collectors have mistaken it for a traditional UK NWoBHM release. Musically good and vocally average. Mikael moved to the US.

1983	■	In The United Kingdom	7" 3tr	Clubland	SJP 844

        Tracks: Burn In Hell/Lord Satan/Temple Of Metal

1983 7" - SJP 844

AIRLINES

Dan Pelleborn: v/b, Hans Larsson: g, Rolf Moberg: g,
Peter Westin: k, Bertil Stenström: d

Stockholm - This melodic AOR band was formed already in 1974, but during their nine year history they only released four singles. They all had overall poppy overtones, but some tracks are great. *Storstadskyla* (Big City Chill) is classy AOR in the vein of early *Balance*. The last single is probably the best one. Kjell Wallén handled the lead vocals on releases 2 and 3. He later joined *Universe*. Torbjörn Olsson plays keyboards on the first release. The band split in 1983.

1979	■	1979 (Lonely Child)/Eliza	7"	CBS	CBS 7892
1980	□	Charterresa/Tågluffa	7"	SOS	SOS 1034
1981	□	Emilia/Storstadskyla	7"	Rixi	TRIX 004
1982	□	Sista Valsen/Storstadskyla	7"	Rixi	TRIX 012

1979 7" - CBS 7892

AKILLES

Stefan: v, Thomas: g, Jarkko: g, Andreas Niemi: b, Janne: d

Höviksnäs - Formed in 1989 by former *Titan* bassist Andreas Niemi. The A-side is a metal ballad with a slight touch of old *Iron Maiden*, while the B-side is a mid-paced heavy rocker. A mid-quality recording, still worth checking out. In 2000 Andreas recorded a demo with a new line-up featuring Magnus Styrén on vocals, Peter Wold and Johnny Johansson on guitar. After the demo Wold and Johansson left the band. At one time the line-up featured Niemi, singer Robin Thuresson and drummer Michael Fuhrman, both also found in *Forbidden Dreams*. The last known line-up was quite different, featuring besides Niemi, singers Mia Lorentzon and Conny Thörnqvist, guitarists David Asp and Michael Fuhrman and drummer Robin Thuresson. In 2011 Niemi and Asp (also in *Candlemass* cover band *Ancient Dreams*) formed the band *Opera Diabolicus* who released their debut album *1614*.

1991	■	Passaway/Taste Of Blood	7"	Active Music	HEJ S-039	$

1991 7" - HEJ S-039

ALCATRAZ

Yvonne Andersson: v, Stefan Malmberg: g, Mats Mattsson: g,
Håkan Ekblad: b/v, Matz Winroth: d

Kristianstad - Decent ***Status Quo***-ish boogie rock with a slight southern feel. Yvonne has that typical country & western touch to her voice. They have the track *Love Can Be Too Dangerous* on the *Skånsk Rock I* (1982) compilation and another one on the Pang-compilation *Heavy Metal*.

1983 ■ Father Of My Son/Woman Charmer ....7" Pang ....PSI 068

1983 7" - PSI 068

ALEX'S PRO

Tony Qwarnström: v, Rolf Alex: v/d, Håkan Mjörnheim: g, Hans Engström: k,
Lars Hoflund: b, Tomas Opava: perc

Stockholm - This is a really strange band. Rolf Alex was one of Sweden's number one studio drummers, who played with people and bands like ***Glory, Wellander & Ronander, Tommy Broman, Forbes, Eva Dahlgren, ABBA, Scafell Pike*** etc. He has also produced bands like ***Great King Rat*** and ***Baltimoore***. *I'm Burnin'* is a great melodic hard rocker, while *Make It Easy* is pop. The first singled featured Danish singer Sös Fenger and Tamra Hope Rosanes. *Come Here To Me*, which was released under the name ***Alex's Pro Cussion***, is solid AOR. The LP *Alex's Pro Album* is just pop not worth looking for.

1984 7" - S-001

1984 ■ Make It Easy/I'm Burnin' ....7" Wale...S-001
1985 ■ Come Here To Me/Funny Invitations...7" RCA ....PB 60117
1985 ☐ Do It/Dancing On A Rainbow ....12" Wale...Wale Max 001

1985 7" - PB 60117

ALEXANDER LUCAS

Claes Alexander Von Post: g/v, Lucas Ekström: b, Benna Sörman: d

Stockholm - Formed in 1973 by Lucas and Clas Alexander. They simply put their first names together and came up with the band name (which also happens to be the Swedish name of Donald Duck's cousin Gladstone Gander). The band released only one single, a very high priced and sought after item today. The style was quite traditional solid, riff oriented 70's hard rock slightly reminiscent of ***November***. Lucas and Benna had previously played with the band ***Ljuso***, where popstar-to-be Magnus Uggla was also found. The band split in 1976. The only member who is still a professional musician is Benna, who later joined ***Strix-Q*** and Magnus Uggla. He later on recorded and played with ***Good Clean Fun***. Lucas was also in ***Strix-Q*** for a while. ***Alexander Lucas*** actually made a re-union gig in May 1995.

1973 ■ Speed/Svarta Skogen ....7" Efel..SEF 89 **$$**

1973 7" - SEF 89

ALFONZETTI

Matti Alfonzetti: v, Stefan Bergström: g, Mikael Höglund: b

Stockholm - Matti is formost known as the lead-singer of UK melodic rockers ***Jagged Edge*** and Swedish heavy-rockers ***Skintrade***. He has also sung with ***Talisman, Bad Society, Bam Bam Boys, Damned Nation, Road II Ruin*** etc. The first album featured Matti, guitarist Stefan Bergström (***Skintrade***), guitarist Göran Elmquist (***Bam Bam Boys, Dream Bank***), drummer Jamie Borger (***Talisman, Treat***) and bass player Nalle Påhlsson (***AB/CD, Therion, Vindictive, Kyss*** etc). The first album also features guest-spots from Mats Levén, Jonas Östman (***Malmsteen, Gotham City***) and Jocke Svanberg. Musically the first album is somewhere between Alfonzetti's soft AOR-side and his heavy edge things, while the second one is a bit heavier. Songs like *Ready, No Way Out* and *In The Groove* are actually old ***Skintrade***-songs, while *Out In The Cold* also can be found on the first ***Jagged Edge***-album. On the second album the line-up was slimmed down to a trio and the use of programmed drums (very well done, though) was predominant. The style was heavier and more modern. Both albums are great and well worth checking out! In 2011 Matti announced a new album was on the way. The album proved to be a great melodic platter, returning to the style of the debut. This time the line-up featured drummer/producer Daniel Flores (***Mind's Eye, The Murder Of My Sweet*** etc) and guests like Marcus Jidell (***The Ring, Evergrey***) and Emil Fredholm (***Plankton***). In 2011 Alfonzetti joined UK hard rockers ***Red White & Blues*** as singer/bassist and in 2012 ***Skintrade*** re-united. He is also fronting ***Impera***.

2000 CD - 0681-19

2002 CD - 0681-55

2000 ■ READY...CD MTM...0681-19
2002 ■ MACHINE ....CD MTM...0681-55
2011 ■ HERE COMES THE NIGHT...CD AOR Heaven...AORH00067
2011 ☐ HERE COMES THE NIGHT...CD Rubicon (Japan) RBNCD-1076

2011 CD - AORH00067

ALGAION

Mårten Björkman: v, Mathias Kamijo: g/b/k, Robert Eng: d

Åtvidaberg - High speed black metal with a furiously screaming singer. They however have some fine guitarwork and a really heavy sound. Recorded at Studio Abyss. Session musicians on the first album are Fredrik Söderlund: k/d, Elisabeth Magnusson and Mikael "Nattfurst" Österberg (**Sorhin, Necromancy**) on background vocals. Peter Tägtgren (**Hypocrisy, Pain**) assists on drums on *Vox Clemensis*. On *General Enemity* Tobbe Leffler (**Vergelmer, Nephenzy Chaos Order**) was session guitarist and Eric Krona session drummer. Mathias and Tobbe are also found in **Vergelmer**. The album also marks a drastic change of style to more doom/death oriented metal, on tracks like *Of Nature Red In Tooth And Claw* and *Mangod Hold The Sceptre* even similar to bands like **Vicious Rumours** or late **Judas Priest**, but with growl. Killer production. In 2001 the band recorded the MCD *The Herostratic Legacy* which was supposed to be released on Loud 'N Proud Records, but the label went bankrupt. After a long hiatus Mårten and Mathias returned, now with the addition of Robert Eng (**Satanic Slaughter, Corporation 187**). Björkman is also found in **Arditi**, while Kamijo has been part of **Pain, Morifade, TheAbyss, Vergelmer** and **Nephenzy Chaos Order**.

1996 MCD - WLR 009

2001 7" - MPEP08

1995	☐	OIMAI AI GEIOU	CD	Full Moon	FMP 003
1996	■	Vox Clementis	MCD 4tr	Wounded Love	WLR 009
		Tracks: Vox Clementis/Throughout Times/See What Is To Com/ Cupidus Imperii. The first pressing was misprinted.			
1997	☐	GENERAL ENEMITY	CD	Wounded Love	WLR 012
2002	■	On The Reach Of Zaphonia/And With Darkness I Pierce Him	7"	Miriquidi	MPEP08
		525 hand numbered copies			
2010	■	EXTHROS	CD	Pulverised	ASH 066

2010 CD - ASH 066

ALICATE

Jonas "Kim Miguel" Erixon: v/g, Glenn "Glen McKee" Ljungkvist: k, Fredrik "Fredric Alicia" Ekberg: b, Jesper Persson: d

Perstorp - *Alicate* was founded already back in 1985 by Erixon and Ekberg. Ljungkvist joined in 1989 before the first single (now a collector's item). Drums on the single were played by Jack White. The A-side of the single is a power ballad, while the B-side is a quite powerful melodic heavy rocker. The band took a long break between 1993 and 2006, when Erixon and Ekberg reformed the band. They found drummer Jesper Persson, also found in **Carnival Sun**. After a while Ljungkvist also returned to the ranks and the band started working on what became the album *World Of Hate*. The first release showed some great promise, and the members has been growing quite a lot since. The album is a great melodic hard rocker in the vein of 90s **Europe**. The 2013 release followed in the same tradition. Well worth checking out.

1989 7" - KIM 001

1989	■	The End/Too Shy To Take It	7"	private	KIM 001	$
2009	■	WORLD OF ANGER	CD	Forest Records	FRS002	
2013	☐	FREE FALLING	CD	Defox Records	- -	

2009 CD - FRS 002

ALIEN

Jim Jidhed: v, Tony Borg: g, Ulf "Ken" Sandin: b, Jimmy Wandroph: k, Toby Tarrach: d

Göteborg - In 1979 guitarist Tony Borg recorded a single with melodic hardrockers **Highway** and in 1981 another one, *Leaving You/Kisses In The Night* (Polar - POS 1290), with the band **Dolcevita**, a straight rocking band. When he later on formed **Alien** he was also working with female singer Lill-Babs in a totally different musical category. He had also been in **EF Band** and Icelandic pop/rockers **Vikivaki**. The first constellation of **Alien** featured singer Jim Jidhed, bassist Ken Sandin (later in **Swedish Erotica, Transport League, K2, TimeCode Alpha, DaVinci** and pop band **Strasse**), drummer Tobias Tarrach (also ex-**Highway**), keyboard player Jimmy Wandroph and Tony Borg. This constellation had a big hit with the old **Bee Gee's** cover *Only One Woman*. Jim surprisingly left the band as he wanted to slow down a bit, and was replaced by Pete Sandberg (ex-**Von Rosen, Madison, Sir Maxwell**). The US-remix was made by Duane Baron and John Purdell. On this release two new tracks with Pete on vocals were added and four old tracks were removed. On *Shiftin' Gear* the line-up featured Pete (v), Tony (g/b), Bert Andersson (k) and Imre Daun (d) (**Don Patrol, Snowstorm, The Black** etc). After the album Stefan Ridderstråle joined on drums, Richard on keyboards and ex-**Madison** man Conny Payne on bass. Pete left and Tomas Persson (later in **Red Fun**) joined for a tour. Pete later recorded with **Bewarp, Midnight Sun, Jade, Silver Seraph** and solo. In 1991 Rikard André (**J.R:s Glitter Band, Rossall & The Gang**) took over the drums. In 1992 Tony recorded an instrumental solo album using Conny, Richard and drummer Michael Wikman (later in **Planet Waves**). The record company persuaded Tony to record another **Alien**-album. The musicians on the new album were the ones from his solo album plus former **Shere Khan**-singer Daniel Zangger Borch. Daniel has also previously recorded a more pop/soul-influenced solo album under the monicker **Danny 'N Rocks**. He is also one of the singers on the **Flintsten Med Stanley**-project. The self-titled 1993-album *Alien* shows only a weak shadow of the early years, partly due to the albums horrible production. In 1995 **Alien** seemed to realise they needed a heavier edge and the 1995-album *Crash* has a more AOR:ish **Rainbow** influenced approach. It also showed

Alien in the headstrong days.

the talent of new drummer Staffan Scharin (*Talk Of The Town, Rossall & The Gang*). Daniel also made a guest appearance, singing the song *Love Is A Many-Splendored Thing* on jazz-guitarist Rune Gustavsson's album *Standards*. He also partcipated in the Swedish final of the Eurovision Song Contest in 1999. On the side, Borg had a cover band called **White Purple**, also featuring **Europe**'s Ian Haugland on drums. In 2002 Jim Jidhed proved he was ready to rock, as he released the strong AOR-oriented solo album *Full Circle*. In 2004 the world saw another re-union of **Alien**, this time featuring Jidhed, Borg, former **House Of Shakira**/**Grace** bass player Bernt Ek, drummer Jan Lundberg and keyboard player Mats Sandborg. The album is actually one of the better and more powerful **Alien** releases, also featuring a cover of Gary Moore's *Out In The Fields*… no, sorry its' the track *Fallen Eagle* that just has the entire begin-ning sounding like it. Borg has also participated in the project **Heartbreak Radio** and Conny Payne is now found in the band **Mindsplit**. In 2007 former singer Borch released his solo alhum *The One* (Voice Centre). In 2006 a downloadable live recording entitled *Live In Gothenburg 2004* was made available. Sandin is today found in **Kee Marcello's K2**. In the spring of 2009 the original line-up reunited for some shows. A new single, *Ready To Fly*, was recorded and released in October 2010 and the re-united band will release a new album late 2013.

Another step to success

1989 3" - VJD-10209

1987	☐	Headstrong/Headstrong(re-mix)	7"	Virgin	108 970
1987	☐	I'll Survive/I'll Survive (re-mix)	7"	Virgin	108 971
1988	☐	Only One Woman/Somewhere Out There	7"	Virgin	109 670
		Available with two different covers, glossy or matte.			
1988	○	Only One Woman/Tears Don't Put Out The Fire	12"	- - (Germany)	DM611781 178-88
		White label test pressing. No artwork.			
1988	☐	ALIEN	LP	Virgin	209 198
1988	☐	ALIEN	CD	Virgin	259 198
1988	☐	Tears Don't Put Out The Fire	CDS 1tr	Virgin (promo)	PRCD 2842
1988	☐	Tears Don't Put Out The Fire/Dreamer	7"	Virgin	111 564
1989	■	Tears Don't Put Out The Fire/Jaime Remember	3" CDS	Virgin (Japan)	VJD-10209
1989	☐	The Air That I Breathe/Now Love	7"	Virgin	112 005
1989	☐	The Air That I Breathe/Now Love	7"	Virgin (Australia)	VOZ 055 23586
		Different artwork.			
1989	☐	The Air That I Breathe	MLP 3tr	Virgin	612 005
		Tracks: The Air That I Breathe (Extended version)/Now Love/The Air That I Breathe			
1989	☐	ALIEN (US-remix)	LP	Virgin	209 775 1
		Same as the 88-release, but four track were removed and two new were added.			
1989	☐	ALIEN (US-remix)	CD	Virgin Records America (USA)	209 775 2
1989	☐	ALIEN (US-remix)	CD	Virgin Records America (USA)	7 90975-2
1989	☐	ALIEN (US-remix)	LP	Virgin (Canada)	VL 2543
1989	☐	ALIEN (US-remix)	CD	Virgin (Japan)	VJD-32214
1989	☐	Go Easy (US-remix)/Touch My Fire	7"	Virgin	111 819 7
1989	☐	Go Easy	MLP 3tr	Virgin	111 819 2
		Tracks: Go Easy (US-remix)/Touch My Fire/Tears Don't Put Out The Fire (US-remix)			
1989	☐	Go Easy	MCD 3tr	Virgin	611 819
1989	☐	Easy Livin'/How Long	7"	Virgin	112 370
1990	☐	Angel Eyes/Eagle	7"	Virgin	113 041
1990	☐	Angel Eyes(7" version)/"(12" version)/Eagle	CDS 3tr	Virgin	113 041
1990	☐	Angel Eyes(slow melodica version)/Angel Eyes/Eagle	MLP 3tr	Virgin	613 041
1990	☐	Turn On The Radio/Hot Summer Nights	7"	Virgin	113 139
1990	☐	SHIFTING GEAR	LP	Virgin	210 466
1990	☐	SHIFTING GEAR	CD	Virgin	260 466
1993	■	Number One	CDSp 1tr	Eagle	ECDS-10-63
1993	■	Take Me To Heaven/Strong Like A Warrior/A Little Ain't Enough	CDSp 3tr	Eagle (Promo)	ECDS-10-68
1993	☐	ALIEN	CD	Eagle	ECD 043
1993	●	Vit Jul	CDS 1tr	Eagle (Promo)	ECDS 1070 $
		Non-official recording for the record company as a Christmas card. Only a few copies were made for promotion. No artwork.			
1994	☐	ALIEN	CD	Zero (Japan)	XRCN-1105
1995	☐	ALIEN (US version)	CD	Virgin (Japan)	VJD-32214
1995	☐	CRASH	CD	Megarock	MRRCD 031
1995	☐	CRASH	CD	Zero (Japan)	XRCN-1239
		Bonus: Back On My Feet/Got This Great Thing Coming/With Every Little Beat Of My Heart/Message For Japan			
1997	■	BEST & RARE	2CD	Virgin	7243 8 42715 2 7/ALIENCD 1 $
1997	☐	Only One Woman/Tears Don't Put Out The Fire	CDS	Virgin	ALIPROCD 1
2001	☐	LIVE IN STOCKHOLM 1990	CD	Avalon Marquee (Japan)	MICP 10225
2005	☐	DARK EYES	CD	Frontiers	FRCD 261
2005	○	DARK EYES	CD	Irond (Russia)	CD 06-DD338
2005	○	DARK EYES	CD	Marquee (Japan)	MICP-10547
		Bonus tracks: Freedom			
2010	☐	Ready To Fly	CDSp 1tr	Manora Records	MRCDS011
2012	☐	ALIEN	CD	No Remorse Records	50999 953809 2 6
		1000 copies. EU version.			
2013	☐	ALIEN - 25TH ANNIVERSARY EDITION	2CD	EMI	50999 9930072 2
		Bonus: Feel My Love (Polar outtake)/Touch My Fire (Polar outtake)			

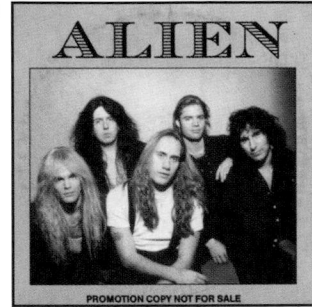

1993 CDS - ECDS-10-68

1993 CDS - ESCD-10-63

1993 CDS - ECDS 1070

1997 2CD - ALIENCD 1

ALL ENDS

Tinna Karlsdotter: v, Jonna Sailon: v, Fredrik Johansson: g,
Peter Mårdklint: g, Anders Janfalk: b, Joseph Skansås: d

Göteborg - A young, modern sounding band from Göteborg initiated by *In Flames* guitarists
Jesper Strömblad and Björn Gelotte in 2003. The original line-up also featured Björn's sister
Emma Gelotte on vocals, alongside Tinna and drummer Skansås. The band recorded a five track
demo at Studio Fredman. In 2005 Strömbland and Gelotte left in favour of bass player Michael
Håkansson (*Evergrey, Engel*) and guitarist Johansson (*Dimenzion Zero*). Later the same year
Mårdklint (*Embraced, Tenebre*) completed the line-up. In May 2007 the band made their debut
for Gun Records with the *Wasting Life* EP. They also rerecorded the initial demo tracks. In March
2009 Emma left the band and was replaced by Jonna Sailon. *Apologize* is a *One Republic* cover.
Quite kitchy and very catchy pop metal, like *Dead By April* meets *Evanescence*.
Website: www.allends.se

2007 MCD - GUN 283/8869708367 2

Year		Title	Format	Label	Cat. no.
2007	■	Wasting Life	MCD 5tr	Gun	GUN 283/88697 08367 2
		Tracks: Wasting Life/Alone/Am I Insane/Close My Eyes/The Day Has Come			
2007	□	ALL ENDS	CD	Gun	8869718876 2
2007	□	ALL ENDS	CD	BMG (Japan)	BVCP-21588
		Bonus: Alone/Am I Insane/Wasting Love (video)			
2007	■	Apologize/Walk Away	CDS	Gun	8869744177 2
2008	□	ALL ENDS	CD	Gun	886971887624
		New band artwork.			
2008	□	ALL ENDS	CD+DVDd	Gun	88697096502
		Bonus: Apologize/What Do You Want/What We Say/Treat Me Right. DVD with videos.			
2008	□	ALL ENDS	CD	BMG (Japan)	BVCP-21588
		Bonus: Alone/I Am Insane/Wasting Love (video)			
2008	□	ALL ENDS	CD+DVD	BMG (Japan)	BVCP-25172/3
		Bonus: Alone/Am I Insane + DVD. New band artwork.			
2008	□	Apologize/Apologize (video)	CDS	BMG	88697441772
2010	■	A ROAD TO DEPRESSION	CD	Nuclear Blast	NB 2638-2
2010	□	A ROAD TO DEPRESSION	CDd	Nuclear Blast	NB 2638-0
		Bonus: Blame/Make My Day			
2010	□	A ROAD TO DEPRESSION	CD	Sony Music (Japan)	SICP-2836
		Bonus: Blame/Make My Day			

2007 CDS - 8869744177 2

2010 - CD - NB 2638-2

ALL HELL

Andreas Åkerberg: v, Simon Follman: g, Tobias Anger: b, Jonas Lewén: d

Örebro - It all started in 2004 when bassist Anger (*2 Ton Predator*), singer Andreas Åkerberg
(*Breakout*) and Lewén (ex-*Within Reach*) started playing after some serious drinking. Follman (*Molly's Gusher*) was drafted. The band started rehearsing and writing, resulting in the
self-released debut. Åkerberg was later replaced by Einar Magnusson (*Ruin*). The band's style
is a bit like early *Entombed* meets *Nine*. Quite raw and punkish in its attitude, but still very
accomplished. Simon is also a guitar tech for Norwegian death metal band *Satyricon*. In 2008
the band released a free download album entitled *Knarkbrand* (drug fire). In 2010 Follman
left the band and was replaced by Tobias Johansson (now Sävenhed) (*Cowboy Prostitutes,
Flushed*). The band was planning a new album with the working title *Det sanna Sverige* (the
true Sweden), set for release in 2011, but is not to be found. In 2012 a new release was in the
works, with the working title *Folkbokförd*.

Year		Title	Format	Label	Cat. no.
2005	■	TRANSMITTER	CD	private	666-1

2005 CD - 666-1

ALLAN BEDDO BAND

Fabian Stanojevic: v, Tommy Hjälmberg: g, Jan Johansson: k,
Kent Pettersson: b, Mikael Andersson: d

Jönköping - Formed in 1985. The first single contains high-quality melodic hard rock with strong
influences of *Deep Purple* and *Uriah Heep*. Hammond organ is used, of course. It was recorded
with the above line-up. In 1991 the band was featured on the local compilation *LP-Projektet*
and two years later the MCD was recorded. Now the style had taken a change towards more
blues-oriented rock with the addition of horns. The line-up featured ex-*Metal Mercy* bass-player
Leif Andersson, Pierre Nilsson (g/v), Esse Nilsson (d) and Tommy. The name comes from a
local expression, Allan is when you show off and Beddo means cocky. The band resurfaced in
2010, now featuring Tommy, drummer/singer Hasse Frendin and bass player Peter Dahlstrand.

Year		Title	Format	Label	Cat. no.	
1988	■	Behind The Lines/Ride On	7"	Platina	PL 34	$
1993	□	Allan Beddo Band	MCD 5tr	private	- -	

1988 7" - PL 34

ALLEGIANCE

Roger "Bogge/B. War" Svensson: v/b, Pär Thornell: g/k, Fredrik Andersson: d

Söderköping - *Allegiance* was founded in 1989 and recorded a whole range of demos before being signed. They had titles such as *Sick World, Odin Äger Er Alle* (Odin owns you all) and *Höfdingadrapa* (Chief's murder). Fredrik and Roger are ex-*Marduk*. In the beginning the band also had Magnus "Devo" Andersson in the ranks as singer, then guitarist, but he left to join *Marduk*. Martin Gustafsson (*Darkified*) also had a stint with the band on vocals, but he was asked to leave as Bogge took over the vocal duties. The debut also saw Mikael Almgren (*The Sideburns*) on bass. The band's second album was produced by Peter Tägtgren (*Pain, Hypocrisy*). On the third album Almgren was out of the band. *Allegiance* started out as a death metal band but by time evolved into fast, furious and brutal black Viking metal with screeching vocals in Swedish. Roger is also found in *Devil's Whorehouse* and *Moment Manics*. Fredrik has also recorded with *A Canorous Quintet, This Ending, Triumphator, Moment Manics, Freevil* and *Amon Amarth*. The band was rejuvinted in 2009 and the trio has been reinforced with ex-*Vomitory* guitarist Ulf Dalegren. *Hymns Of Blood* is a compilation.

1996 CD - NFR 014

1997 CD - NFR 021

1996	■	HYMN TILL HANGAGUD	CD	No Fashion	NFR 014
1997	■	BLODÖRNSOFFER	CD	No Fashion	NFR 021
1998	■	VREDE	CD	No Fashion	NFR 031
2002	□	HYMNS OF BLOD	CD	Mercenary Music (USA)	CD 71123

ALONZO

Nippe Ungerh: v/g, Linus "Limpan" Sydstrand : b, Niklas "Nicke" Björnör: d

Uppsala - Man, it seems the new millennium has brought a huge retro-renaissance. In league with bands like *Siena Root, Blowback, Three Seasons* etc, *Alonzo*, formed in 2009 initially as an instrumental jam-band, bring their best 70s ammunition. Highly recommended!

| 2012 | ■ | VRÅNGVISOR | CD | Ozium Records | OZIUM003 |

1998 CD - NFR 031

ALSING, CHRISTIAN

Christian Alsing: g/b

Göteborg - Christian Alsing is a highly talented Swedish guitarist. Initially very influenced by Mattias Eklundh (*Freak Kitchen*), which showed on his 2001 demo CDR *Aggro*, but he soon developed his own style and tone. Instrumental guitar wizardry. On *Spasms For Two* the bass work was also handled by Simon Andersson (*Johan Randén, Pain Of Salvation, Urbandux*). Late 2012 Alsing joined brutal rockers *CB Murdoc*.

2012 CD - OZIUM003

| 2003 | □ | SPASMS FOR TWO | CD | - - (Italy) | - - |
| 2005 | ■ | THE LAST ROBOT | CD | private | CACD-004-2 |

ALTAR

Magnus Karlsson: v/b, Jimmy Lundmark: g, Fredrik Johansson: d

Kumla - *Altar* was formed under the name *Wortox* in 1988, and under that name they recorded the demo *The Unknown* in 1989. As *Altar* their only release is a split-CD together with Finnish band *Cartilage*. *Altar* play death metal with harmonies and listenable vocals. Dan Swanö also lends his guest vocals to the recording. Not to be confused with the Dutch band that released *Youth Against Christ*. After the CD the band released two demos in 1993-94 and then they split in 1995. The last demo also featured Mieszko Talarczyk (*Nasum*) on vocals and guitarist Johan Bülow of *Wolf, Fallen Angel* fame. *Dark Domains* is a compilations of *Ex Oblivione* and demos.

2005 CD - CACD-004-2

| 1992 | □ | EX OBLIVIONE (split) | LP | Drowned Products | DL 013 |

Split with Finnish band Cartilage. Tracks: Nothing Human/Lifeless Passion/Decapitated/
Daymare-A Message From The Grave/Ex Oblivione

| 1992 | □ | EX OBLIVIONE (split) | CD | Drowned Products | DC 013 |

Bonus: Severed On The Attic/No Flesh Shall Be Spared.

| 2012 | ■ | DARK DOMAINS | CD | Konqueror /Pulverised Records | ASH 089 CD |

ALTERED AEON

Kjell Andersson: v, Per Nilsson: g, Niklas Rehn: g,
Anders Hedlund: b, Henrik Ohlsson: d

Avesta/Sandviken - *Altered Aeon* was formed in 2001 by Henrik Ohlsson (*Mutant, Theory In Practice, Scar Symmetry, Diabolical*) and Kjell Andersson (*Azotic Reign*) under the name *Thrawn*. In 2002 guitarist Niklas Rehn was added to the band. They recorded the demo *Light Creates Shadows* the year after. On this recording the guitar solos were handled by Per Nilsson (*Scar Symmetry, World Below, Adversary*), who later joined full-time. Bass player Hedlund (*Theory In Practice*) completed the line-up. The recording was produced by Jonas Kjellgren (*Carnal Forge, Centinex*). The band was picked up by Greek label Black Lotus and during the recordings of the debut they changed their name to *Altered Aeon*. The album contains a

2012 CD - ASH 089 CD

cover of **King Diamond's** *Welcome Home*. In 2005 Nilsson left for personal reasons and he was replaced by Sami Mäki (**Theory In Practice, Undivine, Audioporn, Planet Rain**). In 2007 the band recorded a new demo entitled *Reborn As Gods*. **Altered Aeon** play great sounding, well-played thrash with touches of **Mercyful Fate** meets **Slayer**, but with cleaner vocals. Great stuff, indeed! In 2010 Andersson, Ohlsson and Hedlund formed thrash band **Clairvoyant Seed**.

2004 ■ DISPIRITISM ....CD   Black Lotus ....BLRCD 069
　　　　Slipcase.

2004 CD - BLRCD 069

ALYSON AVENUE
Arabella Vitanic: v, Tony Rohtla: g, Niclas Olsson: k,
Thomas Löyskä: g, Fredrik Eriksson: d

Helsingborg - Killer AOR, like a heavier and more guitar-oriented **Heart**. The band was formed in 1989, initially with a male singer. Anette Blyckert (now Olzon) was only supposed to add background vocals to a recording, but ended up fronting the band which was a really good choice as she's an outstanding singer. The line-up on the first two albums featured guitarist Thomas Löyskä, bass player Jarmo Piiroinen, drummer Roger Landin, keyboard player Nicklas Olsson and Anette. The band was featured on the local compilation *Total Frontkrock* (95 Rockfront) and also on *Melodic Rock Vol 4* (00 Point). Roger Landin and Niclas Olsson were also found in **Doctor Weird**. In 2007 Anette was recruited by Finnish melodic power metal band **Nightwish**. Both **Alyson Avenue** albums were re-issued in 2009, by popular demand and since they gained outrageous prices on Ebay. The debut was released as the original, while *Omega* was instrumentally re-recorded for the most part. Guest musicians on the rerecording include guitarist Janne Stark (**Overdrive** etc) on the track *I Still Believe*. In 2009 the band announced a comeback with new singer Arabella Vitanic. Some samples from the band's website revealed a heavier and rocking band showing great hopes for the future. The new album *Changes* features a new line-up containing original members Nicklas and Thomas together with Arabella, guitarist Tony Rohtla (**Bai Bang**) and drummer Fredrik Erikson. Niclas is also found in **Shiva**, **Second Heat** and has guested on albums with **Michael Bormann**. Changes also featured guest spots from former singer Anette, Fredrik Bergh (**Street Talk, Bloodbound**), Mike Andersson (Cloudscape, Fullforce), Michael Bormann, and Robert "Rob Marcello" Wendelstam (**Danger Danger, Chris Laney's Legion**). The album was produced by Chris Laney, and shows a fully revitalized band producing their best effort ever. Powerful, well-played melodic hard rock.

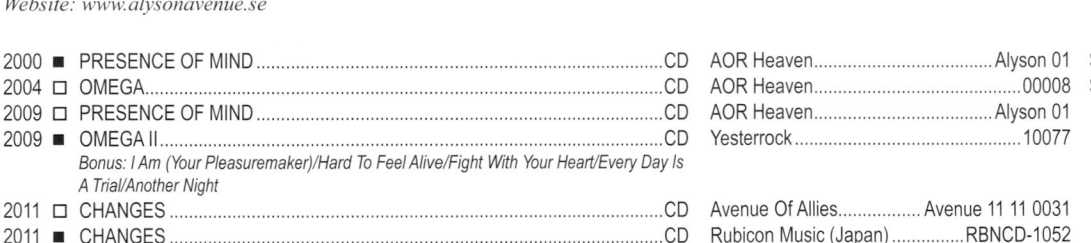

2000 CD - Alyson 01

Website: www.alysonavenue.se

2000 ■ PRESENCE OF MIND ....CD   AOR Heaven.....................................Alyson 01 $$
2004 □ OMEGA...CD   AOR Heaven...00008 $
2009 □ PRESENCE OF MIND ....CD   AOR Heaven.....................................Alyson 01
2009 ■ OMEGA II...CD   Yesterrock 10077
　　　　Bonus: I Am (Your Pleasuremaker)/Hard To Feel Alive/Fight With Your Heart/Every Day Is
　　　　A Trial/Another Night
2011 □ CHANGES ....CD   Avenue Of Allies................ Avenue 11 11 0031
2011 ■ CHANGES ....CD   Rubicon Music (Japan)..............RBNCD-1052
　　　　Bonus: Alone/What Comes Around

2009 CD - 10077

AMARAN
Johanna DePierre: v, Ronnie Backlund: g, Kari Kainulainen: g,
Mikael Andersson: b, Robin Bergh: d

Stockholm - In 2000 guitarists Kari Kainulainen (**Mourning Sign**) and Backlund started writing together and decided to form a band. Enter DePierre, Andersson and Bergh. In 2001 the band recorded the four track demo *Promo 2001*. *Pristine In Bondage* was recorded by Pelle Saether at Studio Underground. In 2003 Andersson left the band and was replaced by Ronnie Bergerståhl (**Centinex, Julie Laughs No More, World Below, Grave, Demonical**). Kainulainen left in November 2004 to concentrate on his band **Siliance**, but in April 2005 the band found a replacement in Gunnar Hammar. In May the same year Niklas Sandin (**Siebenbürgen, Katatonia, Shadows Past**) filled the empty bass spot, since Bergenståhl had also departed. In July 2005 the final blow came when Johanna decided to leave the band. After failing to find a suitable replacement, the band finally folded in December 2005. Bergh is also found in **Gorement, Piper's Dawn** and **October Tide**. **Amaran** play heavy rock almost bordering on melodic death, but with the clean vocals of Johanna they almost become closer to a mix between **Arch Enemy** and **Evanecence**. Outstanding stuff indeed.

2011 CD - Avenue 11 11 0031

2002 CD - POSH 038

2002 ■ A WORLD DEPRAVED..CD   Listenable ....POSH 038
2003 □ PRISTINE IN BONDAGE...CD   Avalon Marquee (Japan)..............MICP-10414
　　　　Bonus: As We Fly/Seven Long Years/Nocturnal
2004 ■ PRISTINE IN BONDAGE...CD   Listenable ....POSH 056
2004 □ PRISTINE IN BONDAGE...CD   Listenable ....POSH 056
　　　　Slipcase. Bonus: As We Fly
2004 □ PRISTINE IN BONDAGE...CD   CD-Maximum (Russia) .... CDM 1004-2029

2004 CD - POSH 056

AMARANTHE

Elize Ryd: v, Andy Sölveström: v, Jake E Lundberg: v, Olof Mörck: g/k,
Johan Andreassen: b, Mårten Löwe Sörensen: d

Göteborg/Denmark - Formed under the name *Avalanche* by former *Dragonland* and *Dream-land* members Olof and Jake. The band was initially supposed to use various singers, but the symbiosis between Elize and Jake worked so well they were both in. The band's first demo *Leaving Everything Behind* was published on Spotify in 2008. In 2009 the band changed name to *Amaranthe*. Great sounding, highly melodic power metal. The band mixes clean and growling male vocals with Elize's strong femme voice. Reminiscent of bands like *Within Temptation*. Andreassen is ex-*Engel*, Sölveström is ex-*Within Y, Evildoer, Cipher System*, while Danish bass player Sörensen has been a member of *The Arcane Order* and *Submission*.

2011 CD - SPI 391

2011 ■	AMARANTHE	CD	Spinefarm	SPI 391	
2011 ☐	AMARANTHE	CD	Universal (Japan)	UICO-1209	
	Bonus: Breaking Point/Splinter In My Soul				
2011 ☐	AMARANTHE	CD+DVD	Universal (Japan)	UICO-9060	
	Tour edition. Bonus: Breaking Point/Splinter In My Soul/Amaranthe (acoustic)/Leave Everything Behind (acoustic). DVD featuring videos, live and "the making of".				
2011 ☐	AMARANTHE - SPECIAL EDITION	CD+DVD	Spinefarm	SPI 391	
	Bonus: Breaking Point/Splinter In My Soul. Bonus DVD videos, live and "making of"				
2011 ■	Hunger	CDSp 1tr	Spinefarm	Spineranthe 1	
2013 ☐	THE NEXUS	CD	Spinefarm	0602537-25177	
2013 ☐	THE NEXUS	CDd	Spinefarm	0602537-27444	
	Bonus: Afterlife (acoustuc)/Leave Everything Behind (early version).				
2013 ☐	THE NEXUS	LP	Spinefarm	0602537-28413	

2011 CDS - Spinearanthe 1

AMAZE ME

Conny "Laz Basswood" Lind: v, Peter Broman: g/b/k

Stockholm - After having recorded a zillion good-quality demos Peter at last got his project on the road. Well, at least it made it on record. Peter is the brother of drummer Thomas Broman, previously with *Great King Rat, Elelctric Boys, John Norum* etc. Conny has previously worked with *State Of Mind, Vision, Raceway* and is now in *Mud & Blood*. *Amaze Me* is total AOR, with ultra melodic songs, nice arrangements and high musicianship. Very "American" sounding. Highly recommended for AOR-fans. A life-sign while waiting for the third album could be heard on *Rock The Nations II* (02 Z Records). The song was *Time*. *The Ultimate Collection* is a compilation, re-mastered by Chris Lyne (*Soul Doctor*). After the release of the compilation album in 2012, the duo finally re-joined forces and 2013 saw the release of the band's comeback album *Guilty As Sin*.

Amazing AOR duo

1996 CD - ALCB 3076

1996 ■	AMAZE ME	CD	Alfa/Brunette (Japan)	ALCB 3076	
1997 ■	DREAM ON	CD	Now & Then	NTHEN 35	
1997 ☐	DREAM ON	CD	Avalon Marquee (Japan)	MICY-1020	
1998 ☐	AMAZE ME	CD	Z Records	ZR1997008	
1998 ☐	WONDERLAND	CD	Z Records	ZR1997010	
1998 ☐	WONDERLAND	CD	Avalon Marquee (Japan)	MICY 1092	
	Bonus: You Say You Never Cry/Help Me Through The Night/Every Heartbeat/Next Train Back				
2012 ☐	ULTIMATE COLLECTION	CD	AOR Heaven Classix	Classix 0006	
	1000 copies.				
2013 ☐	GUILTY AS SIN	CD	AOR Heaven	00081	

1997 CD - NTHEN 35

AMBUSH

Ronny Starborg: v, Åke Cromnow: g, Ola Eriksson: g,
Mats "Finlay" Norström: b, Göran Levén: d

Köping - Formed in May 1982. Quite good hard rock with a folky touch. Like a mix of early *Heavy Load* and *Jethro Tull*. In the spring of 1984 the band was reinforced by keyboard-player Juha "Juba" Nurmenniemi, who was later found in *Darxtar, Achilleus* and *Pseudo Sun*. This line-up recorded the cassette-album *Don't Turn Your Back On Ambush* (1984 Aktiv Musik - HEJMC 004).They played their last gig on Christmas 1984, then with Lasse Andersson (son of *ABBA*'s manager Stickan Andersson) on drums. Lasse has later produced artists like *Tomas Ledin* and *Stefan Andersson*. The band made a short reunion in the spring of 1985, but was permanently dissolved in May 1985. Ronny and Åke later formed *Rampant*, that had 3 tracks on the compilation-cassette *Hårdrock* (Aktiv Musik - HEJMC 015), also featuring *Motherlode*. The bass duties in *Rampant* was actually handled by Juha Nurmenniemi.

1984 ■	4-track EP	7" 4tr	Aktive Musik	EP001	$	
	Tracks: Run Like Hell/Holy Ruler/Whole Man Again/Spirit Of A Fool.					

1984 7" - EP001

AMITY

Patrik Tibell: v/k, Junita Stomberg: v, Peo Pettersson: v

Tibro - Very slick AOR. Juanita was Peo's girlfriend at the time. The single was recorded for the Children's Cancer Foundation. Tibell was later in *T'Bell, Trace* and *CC Rock*, while Peo was in *Axia, Leviticus* and has since recorded several solo albums.

1984 ■ One Chance/I Can't Stay No More ....7" private ....AMI-001 $

One chance — I can't stay no more
1984 7" - AMI-001

AMKENI

Bosse Bäckström: v, Anders Jacobsson: g, Linus Bergström: k,
Peter Kadar: b, Pontus Hultgren: d

Stockholm - Even though the A-side starts out pretty weird it turns into a pretty decent melodic hard rocker. Vocally and lyrically the band however lacks a bit. The B-side is a totally horrible funk disco tune, not even close to being heavy (besides the guitar solo). Feels like the band didn't know which leg to stand on. For completists only.

1981 ■ You Are Right/Soul In My Mind ....7" private AK001

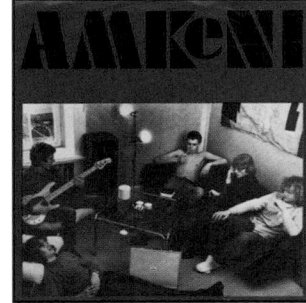
1981 7" - AK001

AMMOTRACK

Mikael de Bruin: v, Patrik Gardberg: g, Jonas Jeppsson: b, Anders Franssohn: d

Skövde - Formed already in 2004. After the debut, in 2009 Gardberg left the band for personal reasons, but he returned late 2010. He was temporarily replaced by Simon Roxx (*Easy Action*). In January 2011 the band started recording the follow-up. Outstanding heavy yet melodic metal with killer vocals and guitar playing. Highly recommended. Both albums were mixed by Tobias Lindell (*Europe, Mustasch* etc.). Gardberg is also in bands like *Solution .45* and *Torch Bearer*.
Website: www.ammotrack.org

2008 ■ AMMOTRACK...CD Gain ....GPCD 058
2011 □ COME DIE WITH US...CD Gain ....GPCD 084

2008 CD - GPCD 058

AMON AMARTH

Johan Hegg: v, Olavi Mikkonen: g, Johan Söderberg: g,
Ted Lundström: b, Fredrik Andersson: d

Tumba - The band was originally formed in 1991 under the name *Scum*. They recorded one demo. When teaming up with singer Hegg, they put the old band to rest and formed *Amon Amarth*, taking the name after the mountain of doom in *Lords Of The Ring* by J.R.R. Tolkien. In 1993 they recorded the demo *Thor Arise*. The second demo *The Arrival Of The Fimbul Winter* was recorded in 1994 and sold over 1 000 copies. Anders Hansson was initially part of the line-up, but left after the MCD was recorded. The first two albums were recorded by Peter Tägtgren, the debut at Sunlight and the second in The Abyss. *On One Sent...* drummer Martin Lopez, who got more involved in *Opeth*, had been replaced by Fredrik (ex-*A Canorous Quintet*) and Johan Söderberg was added to the line-up. They have also recorded the song *Eyes Of Horror* for a *Possessed*-tribute. *Amon Amarth* play high-quality technical death metal with a touch of thrash and a strong Viking theme. Brutal!
Website: www.amonamarth.com

Avengers from the golden hall

Once Sent From The Golden Hall
1998 CD - 3984-14133-2

1996 □ Sorrow Throughout The Nine Worlds...................................MCD/d 5tr Pulverised ....ASH 001
    Tracks: Sorrow Throughout the Nine Worlds/ The Arrival of the Fimbul Winter/ Burning Creation/ The Mighty Doors of the Speargod's Hall/ Under the Grayclouded Winter Sky
1998 ■ ONCE SENT FROM THE GOLDEN HALL ....CD Metal Blade.............................3984-14133-2
1998 □ ONCE SENT FROM THE GOLDEN HALL ....LP Metal Blade.............................3984-14133-1
1999 ■ THE AVENGER...CD Metal Blade.............................3984-14262-2
1999 □ THE AVENGER...CDd Metal Blade.............................3984-14262-2
1999 □ THE AVENGER...LP Metal Blade.............................3984-14262-1
1999 □ THE AVENGER...LP PD Metal Blade.........................3984-14262-1PD
2001 □ Sorrow Throughout The Nine Worlds...............................MLP PD 5tr Metal Supremacy.................................MS005
    500 copies.
2001 ■ THE CRUSHER...CD Metal Blade.............................3984-14360-2
    Bonus: Eyes Of Horror

1999 CD - 3984-14262-2

Year		Title	Format	Label	Catalogue
2001	☐	THE CRUSHER	2LP	Metal Blade	3984-14360-1

Bonus: Eyes Of Horror

2001	☐	THE CRUSHER	CD	Fono (Russia)	FO42CD
2002	■	VERSUS THE WORLD	CD	Metal Blade	3984-14410-2
2002	☐	VERSUS THE WORLD	2CD	Metal Blade	3984-14410-0

With bonus CD featuring: Sorrow Through The Nione Worlds (remastered)/The Arrival Of The Fimbul Winter (first unreleased demo)/Siegreicher March (German version of Victory March)

| 2002 | ☐ | VERSUS THE WORLD | 2LPg | Metal Blade | 3984-14410-1 |

Bonus: Burning Creation/Arrival Of Fimbul Winter/Without Fear/Risen From The Sea/Atrocious Humanity/Army Of Darkness/Thor Arise. All demo tracks.

| 2002 | ☐ | VERSUS THE WORLD | CD | Fono (Russia) | FO202CD |
| 2003 | ☐ | VERSUS THE WORLD | CD | Metal Blade (USA) | 3984-14410-2 |

Contains bonus CD featuring demos and Siegreicher Marsch.

2004	■	FATE OF NORNS	CD	Metal Blade	3984-14498-2
2004	☐	FATE OF NORNS	LP	Metal Blade	3984-14498-1
2004	☐	FATE OF NORNS	CD+DVD	Metal Blade	3984-14498-0
2004	☐	FATE OF NORNS	CD	Metal Blade Japan (Japan)	MBCY-1011
2004	☐	FATE OF NORNS	CD	Fono (Russia)	FO414CD
2005	☐	ONCE SENT FROM THE GOLDEN HALL	CD	Fono (Russia)	FO490CD
2005	☐	ONCE SENT FROM THE GOLDEN HALL	LP PD	Metal Blade	3984-14133-1PD
2005	☐	THE AVENGER	CD	Fono (Russia)	FO493CD
2006	☐	WITH ODEN ON OUR SIDE	2CD	Metal Blade	MB 14584-0

Bonus: Where Silent Gods Stand Guard (live)/Death In Fire (live)/With Oden On Our Side (demo)/Hermond's Ride To Hel-Lokes Treachery Part 1 (demo)/Once Sent From The Golden Hall (Sunlight demo)/Return Of The Gods (Sunlight demo)

| 2006 | ☐ | WITH ODEN ON OUR SIDE | CD | Metal Blade | MB 14584-2 |

Slipcase.

| 2006 | ☐ | WITH ODEN ON OUR SIDE | LPg | Metal Blade | MB 14584-1 |

Red vinyl.

| 2006 | ☐ | WITH ODEN ON OUR SIDE | CD | Metal Blade Japan (Japan) | MBCY-1075 |

Bonus: Where Silent Gods Stand Guard (live)/Death In Fire (live)/With Oden On Our Side (demo)/Hermond's Ride To Hel-Lokes Treachery Part 1 (demo)/Once Sent From The Golden Hall (Sunlight demo)/Return Of The Gods (Sunlight demo)

2006	☐	WITH ODEN ON OUR SIDE	CD	Fono (Russia)	FO624CD
2007	☐	WITH ODEN ON OUR SIDE	CD	Icarus (Argentina)	ICARUS 293
2007	☐	THE CRUSHER	LP PD	Metal Blade	3984-14360-1PD

500 hand numbered copies.

2008	☐	TWILIGHT OF THE THUNDER GOD	CD	Stomp	MB 024 CD
2008	☐	TWILIGHT OF THE THUNDER GOD	CD	Metal Blade	3984-14693-2
2008	☐	TWILIGHT OF THE THUNDER GOD	CDBox	Metal Blade	3984-14693-8 7

"Bobble Head" ltd ed box set.

| 2008 | ☐ | TWILIGHT OF THE THUNDER GOD | DCDd+DVD | Metal Blade | 3984-14693-0 |
| 2008 | ☐ | TWILIGHT OF THE THUNDER GOD | 2LPg | Metal Blade | 3984-14693-1 |

1500 copies with poster. D-side etched.

| 2008 | ☐ | TWILIGHT OF THE THUNDER GOD | LP PD | Metal Blade | 3984-14693-7 0 |

1000 hand numbered copies with poster.

| 2008 | ☐ | TWILIGHT OF THE THUNDER GOD | CD | Fono (Russia) | FO753CD |
| 2009 | ■ | ONCE SENT FROM THE GOLDEN HALL | 2CDd | Metal Blade | MB 14716 2 |

With bonus live CD.

| 2009 | ☐ | ONCE SENT FROM THE GOLDEN HALL | 2CDd | Metal Blade Japan (Japan) | MBCY-1108 |

With bonus live CD.

| 2009 | ☐ | THE AVENGER | 2CD | Metal Blade Japan (Japan) | MBCY-1111 |

With bonus live CD.

| 2009 | ☐ | TWILIGHT OF THE THUNDER GOD | CD | Metal Blade Japan (Japan) | MBCY-1101 |
| 2009 | ☐ | VERSUS THE WORLD | 2CD | Metal Blade Japan (Japan) | MBCY-1131 |

With bonus live CD (Bloodshed Over Bochum).

| 2009 | ■ | THE AVENGER | 2CDd | Metal Blade | 3984-14731-0 |

Re-issue with bonus: Thore Arise + extra CD with live recording of the entire album.

| 2009 | ☐ | THE CRUSHER | 2CD | Metal Blade Japan (Japan) | MBCY-1136 |

Re-issue with bonus: Eyes Of Horror + extra CD with live recording of the entire album

| 2009 | ☐ | VERSUS THE WORLD | LP PD | Metal Blade | 3984-41052-1PD |
| 2009 | ☐ | WITH ODEN ON OUR SIDE | LP | Back On Black (UK) | BOBV138LP |

Red vinyl. 1000 copies

| 2009 | ☐ | TWILIGHT OF THE THUNDER GOD | 2LP | Back On Black (UK) | BOBV036LP |

1000 copies blue vinyl. Also in white vinyl.

| 2009 | ☐ | TWILIGHT OF THE THUNDER GOD | 2LP | Back On Black (UK) | BOBV136LP |

Clear vinyl.

| 2009 | ☐ | ONCE SENT FROM THE GOLDEN HALL | 2LPg | Back On Black (UK) | BOBV135LP |

Clear vinyl. Bonus: Siegreicher March (Live)/Victorious March (live)

| 2009 | ☐ | THE AVENGER | 2LPg | Back On Black (UK) | BOBV133LP |

1000 copies. Transparent red vinyl.

| 2009 | ☐ | THE AVENGER | 2LPg | Metal Blade | MB 14731-1 |

1000 copies. Transparent red vinyl.

| 2009 | ☐ | FATE OF NORNS | LPg | Back On Black (UK) | BOBV134LP |

Grey vinyl. 1000 copies.

2001 CD - 3984-14360-2

2002 CD - 3984-14410-2

2004 CD - 3984-14498-2

2009 2CDd - MB 14716-2

2009 2CDd - 3984-14731-0

2009	■	THE CRUSHER	2CDd	Metal Blade	3984-14752-2

Bonus: Eyes Of Horror + live CD

2009	☐	VERSUS THE WORLD	2LPp	Back On Black (UK)	BOBV137LP
2009	☐	VERSUS THE WORLD – DELUXE EDITION	2CD	Metal Blade	3984-14791-0

Bonus live disc featuring: Death In Fire/For The Stabwounds In Our Backs/Where Silent Gods Stand Guard/Versus The World/Across The Rainbow Bridge/Down The Slopes Of Death/Thousand Years Of Oppression/Bloodshed/...And Soon The World Will Cease To Be

2010	☐	VERSUS THE WORLD	2LP	Back On Black (UK)	BOBV137LP
2010	☐	TWILIGHT OF THE THUNDER GOD	CD+DVD	Icarus (Argentina)	ICARUS 645
2010	☐	GREATEST HITS – HYMNS TO THE RISING SUN	CD	Metal Blade Japan (Japan)	MBCY-1130
2010	☐	ONCE SENT FROM THE GOLDEN HALL	2CD	Icarus (Argentina)	ICARUS 646
2010	☐	THE CRUSHER	CD	Icarus (Argentina)	ICARUS 647
2011	☐	SURTUR RISING	CD+DVD	Metal Blade	3984-99952-2
2011	☐	SURTUR RISING	CD+DVD	Icarus Music (Argentina)	ICARUS 771
2011	☐	SURTUR RISING	CDd	Metal Blade (USA)	3984-14972-2
2011	☐	SURTUR RISING	CDd book	Metal Blade (USA)	3984-14972-0
2011	☐	SURTUR RISING	LP PD	Metal Blade (USA)	3984-14972-1
2011	■	SURTUR RISING	CD	Metal Blade	3984-15006-2
2011	☐	SURTUR RISING	2LP	Metal Blade	3984-15006-1

Etched vinyl. Released in clear, orange, red, black and splatter vinyl.

2011	☐	SURTUR RISING	CD box	Metal Blade	3984-14986-2

Special edition in box featuring plastic figure

2011	☐	SURTUR RISING	CD	Howling Bull (Japan)	HWCY-1291

Bonus: War Machine (Kiss cover)

2011	☐	SURTUR RISING	CD	Fono (Russia)	FO851CD
2011	☐	ONCE SENT FROM THE GOLDEN HALL	2LPg	Back On Black (UK)	BOBV135LP

Orange vinyl. Bonus: Siegreicher March (Live)/Victorious March (live)

2013	☐	DECEIVER OF THE GODS	CD	Metal Blade	3984-15199-1
2013	☐	DECEIVER OF THE GODS	2CD	Metal Blade	3984-15208-1

2009 2CDd - 3984-14752-2

2011 CD - 3984-15006-2

AMSVARTNER

Marcus Johansson: v, Jonathan Holmgren: g, Daniel Nygaard: g, Albin Johansson: b, Alfred Johansson: d

Bygdeå - This was at the time one of the youngest death/black metal bands around. When they were formed in 1993, twin brothers Albin and Alfred were only 12 years old! In 1995 they released their first demo, simply entitled *Demo 1-95*. On the second demo, *Underneath The Thousand Years Gate*, older brother Marcus (also in *Disorge*) had also joined. The first EP was fairly impressive, but the second was highly praised. They play quite spacey death metal. Jonathan was also found in *Auberon* and *Invader*. The latter also included Alfred and Marcus. Nygaard left the band after two gigs and the recording of *Dreams,* to focus on being a sound engineer, he was later replaced by Kalle Lundin, who in his turn was later replaced by Mikko Savela. In 2002 the band recorded a new demo entitled *Theatrical Lunacy*.

1997 MCD - 3984-14246-2

1999 CD - BLACK 016 CD

1997	■	The Trollish Mirror	MCD 4tr	Metal Blade	3984-14246-2

Tracks: The Trollish Mirror/Underneath The Thousand Years Gate/Memories Of Faded Kingdoms/The Wilderness Of Wind

1999	☐	Amsvartner/Enthroned (split)	CD	Blackened	BLACK005CD

Split with Enthroned. Tracks from The Trollish Mirror

1999	☐	The Trollish Mirror	MCD 4tr	Blackened	B7 ER
1999	■	DREAMS	CD	Blackened	BLACK 016 CD

ANACHRONAEON

Patric Carlsson: v/g/b, Andreas Åkerlind: d

Västerås - It all started in *Eternally Devoured* who released two demos in 2000. Patric and Andreas continued as *Human Failure* and recorded the demo albums *Human Failure* (2002) and *Tales Of A Hollow Eternity* (2003). The track *Ages Ago* was featured on the *Metal Ostenation* (Enclave) compilation. They recorded a third demo in 2004, *As The Last Human Spot In Me Dies* and did one gig with bassist Kalle Ullbrandt. As there was a German punk band with the same name, they changed it to *Anachronaeon*, merging the words "anachronism" and "aeon". They were finally signed by Russian label Stygian Crypt who released the demo as the band's debut and also their subsequent release *The New Dawn*. The latter is a concept album dealing with findings of alien DNA in the USA. The band describes their music as progressive dark metal. It's actually quite hard to pinpoint the band's sound and style, and there sure is a lot of tempo and pace changes with switches between clean vocals and growl. At times it feels closer to dark progressive death metal, while at other times it's quite cheerful despite the subject. Quite varied stuff indeed. Unfortunately the production leaves a bit more to be desired, especially on the last album, where the vocals overpower the music and it has no power whatsoever.

2010 CD - SCP 053

2007 CD - SCP 036

2007	■	AS THE LAST HUMAN SPOT IN ME DIES	CD	Stygian Crypt	SCP 036
2007	☐	THE NEW DAWN	CD	Stygian Crypt	SCP 039
2010	■	THE FUTILE QUEST FOR IMMORTALITY	CD	Stygian Crypt	SCP 053
2012	■	THE ETHERAL THRONE	CD	Stygian Crypt	SCP 065

2013 CD - SCP 065

ANAEMIA

Kim Stranne: v, Krister Sundqvist: g, Martin Svensson: b, Tobias Ogenblad: d

Stockholm - The band was formed in 1994 when Kim and Tobias started playing in the local church. Through the Christian magazine *LTR* they found keyboard player Erik Hallåsen. The band was completed with Christer and Martin. Erik however left to devote his time to the technoproject **Pilot**. The band mixes influences of goth, doom, death and heavy rock. They can also be found on the *In The Shadow Of Death* (Endtime 00) compilation. After a long silence, a rerecording of the old demo song *Masquerade Of Sin* was released on the *Come Armageddon* compilation (2003), and the band was supposed to release a second album in 2004, but nothing has happened since. Geographical differences turned the band into a studio project but not much has happened in the later years. Kim also has a new pop band called **Kim Stranne & Kollektivet** with whom he has released the album *Slånbärssnår*, probably as far from **Anaemia** musically as you can come.

1999 CDd - ENDCD 02

TURN OR BURN !?!

1995 7" - 002

1995 ■	Turn Or Burn !?! (split)	7"	Turn Or Burn !?!	002
	Split with Immortal Souls. Track: Pseudo Freedom. 300 hand-numbered copies.			
1999 ■	THE SECOND INCARNATION	CDd	Endtime	ENDCD 02
	First 1000 copies as digi-pack			
1999 □	THE SECOND INCARNATION	CD	Endtime	ENDCD 02
1999 □	THE SECOND INCARNATION	CD	Gothenburg Noiseworks	GNW 07

ANATA

Fredrik Schälin: v/g, Andreas Allenmark: g, Henrik Drake: b, Conny Pettersson: d

Varberg - *Anata* was an Egyptian goddess of war who protected people from animal attacks. Pretty technical and brutal death metal in the vein of **Morbid Angel** or **Deicide**. The band was formed in 1993, then more in the thrash/death-vein. They recorded their first demo *Bury Forever The Garden Of Lie* in 1995 and their second *Vast Lands Of My Infernal Dominion* in 1997. Conny replaced drummer Robert Petersson in 2001. All four plus guitarist Björn Johansson also has a side-project called **Rotinject**. Fredrik guests on the debut by **Immemorial**. Allenmark, who left the band in 2008, is also found in **Cipher System** and **Exhale**, Schälin in **Immemoreal**, while Pettersson is found in **Trendkill, Beseech, Eternal Lies, Revengia** and **Justified**. The recordings of a new album was stated on the band's website, but nothing has happened since.
Website: www.anata.se/

Waiting for the departure?

1998 CDd - SOM 012

2001 CD - SOM 035

2006 CD - WICK22CD

1998 ■	THE INFERNAL DEPTHS OF HATRED	CDd	Seasons Of Mist	SOM 012
1999 □	WAR VOL. II (split)	CD	Seasons Of Mist	SOM 022
	Split with Bethzaida. Tracks: The Tranquillity Of My Lost Breath/Day Of Suffering/Let Me Become Your Fallen Messiah/With Me You Shall Fall			
2001 □	DREAMS OF DEATH AND DISMAY	CD	Relapse Records (USA)	RR 6480-2
2001 ■	DREAMS OF DEATH AND DISMAY	CD	Seasons Of Mist	SOM 035
2003 □	UNDER A STONE WITH NO INSCRIPTION	CD	Wicked World	WICK 15CD
2004 □	UNDER A STONE WITH NO INSCRIPTION	CD	Soyus (Russia)	WICK 15CD
2006 ■	THE CONDUCTOR'S DEPARTURE	CD	Wicked World	WICK22CD
2006 □	THE CONDUCTOR'S DEPARTURE	CD	Soyus (Russia)	WICK22CD

ANCIENT'S REBIRTH, THE

Dennis Widén: v/g, Henrik Bengtsson: g, Dan-Ola Persson: g, Martin Qvist: b, Thomas Hedlund: d

Falkenberg - Formed in 1992 under the name **Infernus Ritual.** They recorded their first rehearsal demo *Twisted Tales Of The Crucified* later the same year and *Culte De Diabolos* only a few months after. The first proper promo was *Of Wrath* in 1994 and then *Below The Nocturnal Skies* later that year. They were offered the deal with Dutch label Creations Of Necromancy Mysterii (CNM) and later signed a three album deal with Necropolis. Hedlund is also found in **Autopsy Torment, Cross Bow, Entity, Pagan Rites, Fall From Grace** and **Karnarium**, while Qvist is in **Ablaze My Sorrow, Immemoreal** and **Fall From Grace**. Death metal, inspired by the Norwegian style and bands like **Immortal** and Swedish fellows **Dissection**. Not the best sounding production, though.

1996 CD - CNM 001

1996 ■	DRAIN THE PORTAL IN BLOOD	CD	CNM	CNM 001
1998 □	Damnated Hell's Arrival	MCDd 4tr	Necropolis	NR 023
	Tracks: Damnated Hell's Arrival/Times To Come Are Frozen/ Flag Of Hate (Kreator cover)/ Armageddish Execution (The Feast Of The Ancient's Rebirth) Chapter I: The Gathering, Chapter II: The Sacrifice			
2006 □	DRAIN THE PORTAL IN BLOOD	LP	Perverted Taste	PT135

ANCIENT WISDOM

Marcus "Vargher" Norman: v/g/k/d

Umeå - **Ancient Wisdom** is the side-project of **Bewitched**/**Throne of Ahaz**-singer/guitarist Marcus. It was initiated in 1992 under the name **Ancient**, but he added the "wisdom" after the first demo *In The Eye Of The Serpent*. The second demo, *Through Rivers Of The Eternal Blackness,* was recorded the subsequent year. The debut album was recorded already in 1994, but due to technical reasons, released two years later. Very Viking-influenced black metal. *... And The Physical..* contains a cover of **Demon**'s *The Spell*. It was initially supposed to be a MCD and the first part was recorded already in 1998. He also recorded a cover of **Iron Maiden's** *Powerslave* for the compilation *A Call To The Irons* (1998 Dwell). The Line-up on the first album consisted of Marcus, guitarist Andreas Nilsson (**Midvinter, Naglfar**) keyboardist Jens Ryden (**Dead Silent Slumber/Naglfar, Thyrfing**) and bassist Fredrik "Beretorn" Jacobsson (**Throne Of Ahaz, Disorge**). From the second album on **Ancient Wisdom** became Marcus' solo project. Kristoffer Olivius (**Bewitched, Midvinter, Setherial, Naglfar**) lends some backing vocals on *The Calling*. Dark, melancholic and quite depressive black metal. Marcus has also recorded with **Naglfar** and **Havayoth**. He is still active in the latter plus **Bewitched**. Not to be confused with Americans Ancient VVisdom.

1996 CD - AV 015

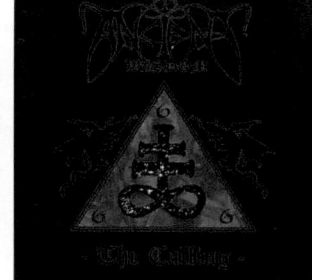

1997 CD - AV 020

1996	■	FOR SNOW COVERED THE NORTHLAND	CD	Avantgrade	AV 015
1997	■	THE CALLING	CD	Avantgarde	AV 020
2000	□	...AND THE PHSYICAL SHADE OF LIGHT BLED	CD	Avantgarde	AV 048
2003	□	...AND THE PHSYICAL SHADE OF LIGHT BLED	CD	Irond (Russia)	CD 03-421
		Bonus: The Spell (Demon cover)			
2004	□	COMETH DOOM, COMETH DEATH	CD	Avantgarde	AV 073
2004	■	COMETH DOOM, COMETH DEATH	CD	Irond (Russia)	CD 04-860

2004 CD - CD 04-860

ANDERSON, STEVEN

Steven Anderson: g, Bino Rindestig: k, Michael Nordmark: b, Mally Hoxell: d

Gävle - After having spent a year and a half at G.I.T and having studied gipsy music in Vienna for six months, Steven found himself a publishing company and recorded his debut-CD. It's a classy album filled with gipsy influenced Satriani style guitar music. A must for fans of **Steve Vai, Joe Satriani** etc. The debut was highly acclaimed in Japan. Steven also recorded a single with the band **Nasty Groove** and made his debut on the compilation album *Girls And Boys* (Andrew Mountain Records). The song featured was the soft instrumental track *The End Of Misery*. In the summer of 1998 Steven was touring with **Nordman**-singer Håkan Hemlin, doing mostly covers by bands like **Deep Purple**, **The Flesh Quartet** and **Nordman**. Steven later formed the band/project **Electric Religions** and has also made some demo-recordings with blues-band **Mrs. Hippie Blues**, where Bino is also found. In 2007 he released the CD *Invitation II Dig* with the oriental sounding rock band **Iubar**.

1994 MCD - SBA-P 004

1994 CD - MMON 9401

1994	■	Gipsy Power	MCD 3tr	Psychic Eye	SBA-P 004
		Tracks: Dance Of The Fortune Teller/The Child Within/Gipsy Fly. Promo with home-made cover in different colours			
1994	■	GIPSY POWER	CD	Moonage	MMON 9401
1994	□	GIPSY POWER	CD	Zero (Japan)	XRCN-1178
1996	□	MISSA MAGICA	CD	Zero (Japan)	XRCN-1281
1998	■	MISSA MAGICA	CD	Atrium	3984-22069-2. MOOG-002
		Slipcase			

1998 CD - 3984-22069-2.MOOG-002

ANDERSSON, RICHARD

Göran Edman: v, Magnus Nilsson: g, Richard Andersson: k,
Andy Rose: b, Jörg Andrews: d

Skurup - Richard Andersson is the keyboard player that once turned down working with Yngwie (well, maybe not so hard to understand considering his reputation). He has instead been pressing keys in bands like **Space Odyssey**, **Time Requiem**, **Silver Seraph**, **Evil Masquerade**, **Majestic** and non-Swedish acts **Iron Mask** and **Adagio**. On this album he has gathered a nice line-up (coincidently the same line-up that he continued to us on the subsequent **Time Requiem** album) and rerecorded tracks previously released by **Time Requiem**, **Majestic** and **Space Odyssey**, like a compilation with a new line-up. Göran is a well-established name in the scene having worked with **Yngwie Malmsteen, John Norum, Madison, Johansson, Xsavior, Vindictiv, Crash The System, Kharma, Karmakanic** etc. Magnus Nilsson has been heard in **Space Odyssey**, **Time Requiem** and **God B.C**. On his webpage Richard comments the album with the following words: "My favourite of all favourites, finally I can shape up some of the old songs that lack good production and some good musicians. Everything recorded under my closest supervision which I find extremely stimulating. I really love the new touch Göran Edman added to the old songs. Old good songs got what they deserved (a better treatment!!!)."
Website: www.anderssonmusic.com/

The master mind

2005 CD - 0009

2005	□	THE ULTIMATE ANDERSSON COLLECTION	CD	Toshiba-EMI	TOCP-67694
2005	■	THE ULTIMATE ANDERSSON COLLECTION	CD	Metal Heaven	0009

ANDROMEDA

**David Fremberg: v, Johan Reinholdz: g, Martin Hedin: k,
Fabian Gustavsson: b, Thomas Lejon: d**

Malmö - Andromeda was formed in 1999 when Johan submitted his demo *Welcome To Forever* to WAR Records, who signed him. When the debut *Extension Of The Wish* was recorded, in March 2000, the band had no singer and Lawrence Mackory (ex-*Darkane*, now *F.K.Ü*) stepped in as a session-singer to do the job. They found David Fremberg in August the same year, actually before the record was even released. David immediately rerecorded the vocals to the first album. The 2CD-version on NTS contains both Lawrence's and David's versions. Thomas is ex-*Tenebre* and is also found in *A.C.T* and *NonExist*. Bass on the debut was played by former *Horizon* man Gert Daun and the album was produced by Daniel Bergstrand (*Devin Townsend, Crawley* etc). WAR Records later changed their name to New Hawen and the album with Davids's vocals was released in 2004. On *II=I* the bass duties were handled by Reinholdz, but after this, Fabian Gustavsson became a solid part of a hereafter steady line-up. *Andromeda* play outstanding progressive metal in the vein of *Dream Theater* in their heavier moments, but with a more personal touch and with better vocals. Killer technical parts mixed with melodic vocals and really heavy riffing. On *II=I* they even stepped up a notch on the technical scale. In 2006 the band released their most melodic album, *Chimera*, while the follow-up, *The Immunity Zone,* probably is the band's darkest and most progressive release. David is also found in *Constancia* and has sung on albums by *Truth* and *Time Odyssey*. In 2007 the band released the live DVD *Playing off the Board. Chapters* is a double CD containing old songs, unreleased songs and rarities.
Website: www.andromedaonline.com/

Manifesting destiny

2001 2CD - 30171902

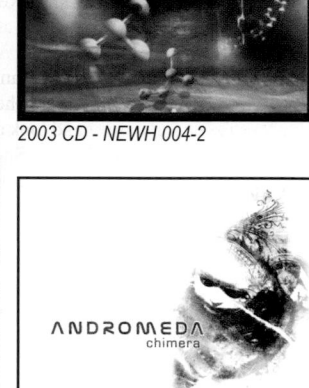
2003 CD - NEWH 004-2

2000	☐	EXTENSIONS OF THE WISH	CD	WAR	WAR 0015
2000	☐	EXTENSIONS OF THE WISH - FINAL EXTENSION	CD	New Hawen	NEWH003
2001	☐	EXTENSIONS OF THE WISH	CD	JVC (Korea)	JCKD 20052
		Bonus: Journey Of Polysphere Experience (demo version).			
2001	■	EXTENSIONS OF THE WISH - DEFINITIVE EXTENSION	2CD	Nothing To Say (France)	3071902
		Bonus: Journey Of Polysphere Experience/Eclipse, plus the WAR-version on one CD.			
2002	☐	II=I	CD	Pony Canyon Music (Korea)	PCKD-20129
2003	■	II=I	CD	New Hawen	NEWH 004-2
2003	☐	II=I	CD	Avalon Marquee (Japan)	MICP-10338
2003	☐	EXTENSIONS OF THE WISH	CD	Century Media	45003-2
		The Fremberg version.			
2004	☐	II=I	CD	Universal (China)	DSD-L1-012
2004	☐	EXTENSIONS OF THE WISH - FINAL EXTENSION	CD	New Hawen	NEWH 003
		Bonus: Journey Of Polysphere Experience/Eclipse			
2006	☐	CHIMERA	CD	Avalon Marquee (Japan)	MICP-10567
		Bonus: Chamelon Carnival (live)			
2006	■	CHIMERA	CD	Massacre	MAS PC518
2006	☐	CHIMERA	CD	Replica (France)	RPL 037
2006	☐	CHIMERA	CD	Avalon/Clairvoyant (Singapre)	CRS-10567
		Bonus: Chamelon Carnival (live).			
2006	☐	CHIMERA	CD	Clairvoyant (Korea)	CRS-10567
		Bonus: Chameleon Carnival			
2008	☐	THE IMMUNITY ZONE	CD	XIII Bis Records (France)	70022640703
2008	☐	THE IMMUNITY ZONE	CD	Avalon Marquee (Japan)	MICP-10767
2008	☐	THE IMMUNITY ZONE	CD	Nightmare (USA)	NMR-462
2009	■	THE IMMUNITY ZONE	CD	Silverwolf Productions	620062
2009	☐	PLAYING OFF THE BOARD	CD	Metal Mind	MASSCD1005
2009	☐	PLAYING OFF THE BOARD	CDd	Metal Mind)	MASSCDDG1005
		1000 copies.			
2011	■	MANIFEST TYRANNY	CD	Inner Wound	IW83015

2006 CD - MAS PC518

2009 CD - 620062

ANDRA BAND

**Urban "Ubbe" Carli: v/g, Rolf "Roffe" Gustafsson: g,
Johan "Joe" Danielsson: b, Urban "Ubbe" Gustafsson: d**

Västerås - I'm honestly not really sure how to categorise this. Very poppy melodic straight-ahead hard rock with typical Swedish political "progg" vocals, but with nice and biting twin guitars. Similar to *Dunder* or *Ocean* (Karlshamn). The band changed their name and released a more hard-rocking single in 1987, now under the moniker *Rockbox*. Carli is today playing in the duo *U&A* and in *Turnpike Road*, together with Rolf. For collectors only.

1984	■	Josefin/Leva mer	7"	CTR	CTR-684

2011 CD - NW83015

1984 7" - CTR-684

ANEKDOTEN

Nicklas Berg: g/k, Anna Sofi Dahlberg: cello/k/v,
Jan Erik Liljeström: b/v, Peter Nordin: d

Borlänge - This band has its musical roots in the 70s progressive era with bands like ***King Crimson***, the Italian 70s prog etc. They actually started out in 1990 as a ***King Crimson*** cover band featuring Nicklas, Jan-Erik and Peter, under the name ***King Edward***. In 1991, Anna Sofi joined the band and that marked the actual birth of ***Anekdoten***. Some demos were recorded and even though a few labels showed interest in the band, they release the debut on their own label Virta Levy. Two of the band's songs were featured on the local compilation *Eleven-On-A-One-To-Ten* (1993 Meantime) and the non-LP track *Cirkus* was featured on the compilation *This Is An Orange* (1995 Briskeby Records, BY-07). In 1994 ***Anekdoten*** embarked on a world tour which included an appearance at the US Progfest. Some tracks from this appearance are found on the compilation CD/DVD *Nearfest 1994*. In 1998 Nicklas and Peter teamed up with ***Landberk*** members Stefan Dimle and Reine Fiske to record an album with covers of theme songs from horror movies under the name ***Morte Macabre***. After the more contemporary sounding *From Within* the band took a break and when they were back with the album *Gravity*, Anna Sofi was not in the line-up. She however returned again. A Japan tour in 2005 resulted in the live-album *Waking The Dead – Live In Japan 2005* and in 2007 the band returned with the new studio album *A Time Of Day*, which went back to the style of *From Within*. ***Anekdoten*** play progressive rock in the vein of ***Änglagård*** and ***Landberk***, but with a heavier edge. *Vemod* is quite a heavy instalment, while they have later on produced some quite mellow stuff. The music features cello and Mellotron as well as distorted guitar and bass. Lars-Erik has also recorded a 7" with the more hard rock oriented ***Junction***. The second album was recorded with Tommy "Stommen" Andersson (***Stonecake***) at the helm. *Gravity* showed a different side of the band, with a more easy listening vibe to it. *Chapters* is a compilation also featuring unreleased tracks. Niklas also released his solo *Al Ultimo Fin De Semana* (with drummer Nordin) in a more sountrack style similar to ***Morte Macabre***.
Website: www.anekdoten.se/

Anekdoten - music from within!

1993	☐	VEMOD	CD	Virtalevy	VIRTA 001
1993	☐	VEMOD	LP	Colours	COSLP 017
1995	☐	VEMOD	CD	Arcàngelo (Japan)	ARC 1001
		Bonus: Sad Rain. The first 1.000 copies were released in a fold-out 10" LP-cover.			
1995	■	NUCLEUS	CD	Virta Levy	VIRTA 002
1995	☐	NUCLEUS	CD	Arcàngelo (Japan)	ARC 1002
1995	☐	NUCLEUS	CD	Musea (France)	FGBF 4165.AR
1996	☐	NUCLEUS	LP	Gates Of Dawn (USA)	GOD 003
1996	☐	VEMOD	LP PD	Record Heaven	RHPD 2
		300 copies.			
1997	☐	LIVE EP	MCD 4tr	Arcàngelo (Japan)	ARC 1035
		Tracks: Nucleus/The Flow/Away Of Life/Karenia.			
1997	☐	LIVE EP	MCDd 4tr	Arcàncelo (Japan)	ARC 1035
1997	☐	NUCLEUS	LP PD	Record Heaven	RHPD 9
		300 copies.			
1998	■	OFFICIAL BOOTLEG - LIVE IN JAPAN	2CDd	Arcàngelo (Japan)	ARC 1036/37
1999	☐	FROM WITHIN	CD	Virta Levy	VIRTA 003
1999	☐	FROM WITHIN	CD	Musea (France)	FGBG 4325.AR
1999	☐	VEMOD	CD	Rock Symphony (Brazil)	RSLN 012
2000	☐	FROM WITHIN	CD	Arcàngelo (Japan)	ARC 1049
2000	☐	FROM WITHIN	LP	Virta Levy	VIRTALP 003
2000	☐	FROM WITHIN	CD	Virta Levy	VIRTA 003
2000	☐	FROM WITHIN	CD	Musea (France)	FGBG 4325.AR
2003	☐	GRAVITY	CD	Arcàngelo (Japan)	ARC-1061
2003	☐	GRAVITY	CD	Virta Levy	VIRTA 004
2003	☐	GRAVITY	LP	Virta Levy	VIRTALP 004
2003	☐	GRAVITY	CD	Musea (France)	FGBG 4505.AR
2003	☐	GRAVITY	CD	Stickman (Germany)	Psychobabble 045
2003	☐	VEMOD	CD	Virta Levy	VIRTA 001
2004	☐	NUCLEUS	CD	Virta Levy	VIRTA 002
		Re-mastered re-issue with enhanced package. Bonus: Luna Surface.			
2005	☐	WAKING THE DEAD – LIVE IN JAPAN	2LPg	Virta Levy	VIRTADLP 001
2005	■	WAKING THE DEAD – LIVE IN JAPAN	CD	Arcàngelo (Japan)	ARC-1094
2007	☐	A TIME OF DAY	LP	Virta Levy	VIRTALP 005
2007	☐	A TIME OF DAY	CDd	Virta Levy	VIRTA 005
2007	☐	A TIME OF DAY	2CD	Arcangelo (Japan)	ARC-1121
		First 1000 copies with live bonus CD. Bonus: Firefly/Book Of Hours			
2009	☐	CHAPTERS	2CD	K-Scope	KSCOPE 115
2009	☐	CHAPTERS	2CD	Arcangelo (Japan)	ARC-1147/48
2011	☐	VEMOD	2LP	Virta Levy	VIRTALP 001
		Bonus: Sad Rain. 400 copies.			
2012	☐	A TIME OF DAY	CDd	Virta Levy	VIRTA 005
		Remastered re-issue.			
2012	☐	A TIME OF DAY	CD	Arcangelo (Japan)	ARC-1159

1995 CD - VIRTA 002

1998 2CDd - ARC 1036/37

2005 CD - ARC-1094

ANGEL BLAKE
Tobias Jansson: v, Marko Tervonen: g/b/d

Trollhättan - When *The Crown* was laid to rest (before the reunion), Tervonen decided to go solo. Guitarist Christian Älvestam (*Scar Symmetry*) was in the band's first live line-up, but left in 2008 and the vocals were handled by Tony Jelencovich (*Transport League, M.A.N*). A later live line-up also featured drummer Janne Saarenpää (*The Crown*), bassist Örjan Wressel and guitarist Anders Edlund (*Incapacity, Solar Dawn*). High-quality heavy Wagnerian, yet melodic metal.

2006	■	ANGEL BLAKE	CD	Metal Blade	3984-14566-2
2006	□	ANGEL BLAKE	CD	Metal Blade Japan (Japan)	MBCY-1081
2008	□	THE DESCENDED	CD	Dynamic Arts	DYN 029
2008	□	THE DESCENDED	CD	Spiritual Beast (Japan)	POCE-16041

Bonus videos: Retaliate (Live)/Defenseless

2006 CD - 3984-14566-2

ANGEL HEART
Daniel Mossberg: v, Jonas Wickström: g, Christer Olsson: k,
Patrik Johansson: b, Anders Forsberg: d

Karlstad - Formed in 1988, split late 1989. Quite low rate commercial 80's standard metal with quite horrible vocals. Jonas and Anders had previously recorded some demos with the band *Highway*. Patrik was later found in *Mindblizz*.

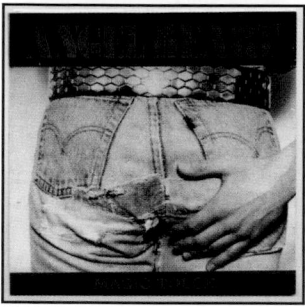

1989	■	Magic Touch/Crying Eyes	7"	private	MUFF 3001

1989 7" - MUFF 3001

ANGELEZ
Robert Molldius: v/g, Kenny Wendel: k, Björn Drott: b, Jan Snarberg: d

Huskvarna - Great melodic hard rock. *Need A Woman* is a killer! The band was formed around 1986-87. Wendel and Snarberg were later in melodic hard rockers *Yankee Heaven*, who were fronted by Jan's wife to be Anette Johansson (aka Nettie Q).

1990	■	Long Way From Home/Need A Woman	7"	Matchtown	MTR 1009	$

Long Way From Home

1990 7" - MTR 1009

ANGELINE
Jocke Nilsson: v/g, Janne Arkegren: g, Uffe Nilsson: b, Tobbe Jonsson: d

Ljusdal/Stockholm - The band was formed in 1987 in Ljusdal, and the name was taken from an old *Paul Sabu* song. They recorded their first demo entitled *The Legend* in 1988. The members on the Mini-LP were Jörgen "Sigge" Sigvardsson (v), Pär Åström (k), Janne, Jocke, Uffe and Tobbe. Sigge had some health issues while recording the album but pulled through and the record was released on his father's own label Wigwam. Just after its release, Pär left the band and went to the US. They started mixing in covers in their set, but also recorded a second MLP entitled *Masquerade*. Unfortunately it was never finished and the tapes were later erased. In 1991-92 they recorded some more demos with Mats Lindfors, but as it was now in the middle of the blooming grunge era, they received no label interest. They however gained some interest from Italy which spurred the band to make an 11-track live recording for promotional purposes. In September 1993 Janne also went to USA, Uffe had to do his military service and in the new year, 93/94, Sigge had to quit because of a heart condition. In April 1994 Janne was back from the US and *Angeline* found former *Ramm* singer Leif Grabbe from Umeå. The MCD was recorded and the band did about 40 gigs in Italy during June-July 1994. The new line-up was actually the strongest in the band's history and the style was now more traditional, melodic hard rock, slightly reminiscent of the 90's *Skid Row*, more than their earlier traditional AOR-sound. Check them out! February 13, 1995 Sigge sadly died in his sleep as a result of his cardial problems. In early 1995 Leif was sacked due to personal problems. In December the same year also Uffe left the band. *Angeline* now continued more or less as a cover band. In 1997 they released a live CD with covers only (very mixed styles, pop to hard rock), produced by Mats Lindfors. In 2001 they finally returned to writing original material. In 2004 some friends of Sigge made a short movie about his life. It was called *Sigge Stardust* and made a great impact at the Göteborg Film Festival in 2005. *Angeline* also has a track on the compilation-CDS *Ljudet Från Ljusdal* (Bombolaget). After some years of silence the band suddenly returned in 2007 when they performed at the *Sigge Bi-annual Family Day* event. In 2010 *Angeline* again gathered forces and made a comeback with the CD *Confessions*, now without singer Leif Grabbe and with Nilsson having taken over the vocals. A good choice, since he happens to be a killer singer. The comeback is a great bluesy AOR/melodic hard rocker well worth checking out. Grabbe later sang with *Shade Of Grey*. Late 2012 the band recorded the new four-track EP *Life*, which was initially only released as a digital release, but a printing is planned. The recording features a guest spot from Mikael Nord Andersson (*Nord, BALLS*) on mandolin.
Website: www.angelinetheband.se

Angelic melodic rockers.

1990 MLP - WLP 901   *1994 MCD - ANGCDS 1*

1990	■	Don't Settle For Second Best	MLP 6tr	Wigwam	WLP 901	$
1994	■	Rain.../Madness/Wanted Man	MCD 3tr	private	ANGCDS 1	
1997	□	LIVE	CDpg	private	17121012	
2004	□	GREATEST HITS	CD	private	Angecd 01	
2010	■	CONFESSIONS	CD	private	ACD 002	
2010	□	CONFESSIONS	CD	Avenue Of Allies	Avenue 10 09 0017	
2010	□	CONFESSIONS	CD	Bickee Music (Japan)	HMCX-1105	

Bonus: Nothing Changes/Remember America

| 2011 | □ | DISCON NEC TED | CD | Avenue Of Allies | Avenue 11 16 0036 | |

2010 CD - ACD 002

ANGELIZE

Petri Riipi: v, Peter Gustavsson: g/v, Ronnie Wicklander: g, Thomas Pettersson: k, Magnus Gustavsson: b, Magnus Hall: d

Arboga - Melodic hard rock/AOR with a typical 80s touch. Good stuff with strong melodies, good musicianship, good vocals and a great drummer. Both singles were first prizes from competitions, each one released in 500 copies. Gustavsson later became lead singer of AOR band *Broke[N]Blue*.

| 1988 | ■ | In It For Love/Ladies | 7" | CUF | CUF 009 |
| 1988 | □ | Strangers Paradise/Love Lies | 7" | SGV | SGV-S 811 |

1988 7" - CUF 009

ANGREPP

Adrian Lawson: v, Dawid Dahl: g, Karl Olsson: g, Andreas Fröberg: b, Fredrik Widigs: d

Stockholm - Angrepp (assault) made their debut with their 2006 demo *Prepare For Attack*. Adrian is also in *IXXI*, Fröberg in *Withershin* and Widigs in *The Ugly*. Thrash metal with a touch of black metal. Widigs has now been replaced by Jacob Hallegren (*Månegarm*)

| 2010 | ■ | WARFARE | CDd | Abyss Records | ABYSS 09 CD |

ANGST

Adimiron: g, Characith: g, Rudra "TRF" Fjäll: g/b, Stefan "Vrashtar" Kronqvist: d

Norrköping/Umeå - Characith, who had his previous solo project *Ondske*, formed the band with Adimiron in 2001. In 2003 the duo recorded the demo *Divine Wrath* (Death Propaganda). They also recorded an EP entitled *Lykania* in 2004, but this was never released. After the demos, Vrashtar was recruited. The album has a misprinted track listing with the incorrect order of the songs. TRF was drafted after the album was released. Daniel "DD Executioner" Johansson (*Sadistic Grimness, Kill, Diabolicum*) also played bass with the band for some time. Adimiron is also found in *Flagellant*, Characith (aka Ondske aka Rudra aka Naghor) in *Ondske*, *Nattstrype* and *Ofermod*. TRF (aka Naghor aka Sorgh) is also found in *Nattstrype*. Vrashtar in *Sargatanas Reign*. The band split in 2005 because of record label problems. *Angst* play old-school black metal in the vein of *Craft* and *Shining*.

2005 CD - BA 011

2010 CDd - ABYSS 09 CD

| 2005 | ■ | IN HOC SINGO VINCES | CD | Blakk Attack | BA 011 |
| 2005 | ■ | Hail Terror (split) | 7" | Eerie Art | EAR 006 |

Split with Diabolicum. Track: Evangelium Infernali

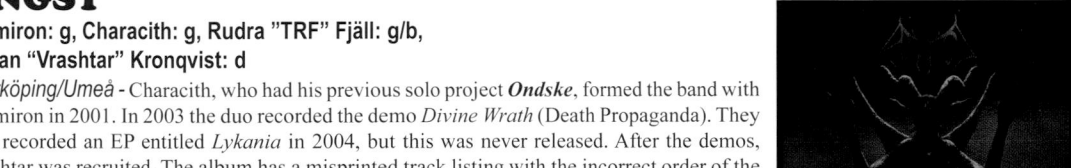

2005 7" - EAR 006

ANGTORIA

Sarah Jezebel Deva: v, Tommy Rehn: g/k, Christian "Chris" Rehn: g/k

Sundsvall/UK - The origin of the story can be traced back to 2001 when English singer Sarah Jezebel Deva (*Cradle Of Filth, Therion, Mortiis*) met Swedish keyboard player/guitarist Chris (*Abyssos, Evergrey*) on a mutual tour. They shared the same musical ambitions in working in an orchestrated project and soon became friends. In November 2002 they recorded a 5-track demo in Chris' brother Tommy's studio. Tommy had formerly recorded with the band *Moahni Moahna*. A promo was sent to various labels, but no deal was set. They now started talking about forming a band, more focused on metal. New songs were written and a new demo being recorded. Now Tommy, who was recording, was drafted and *Angtoria* was born. The demo was shopped around and the response was great, resulting in a deal with Listenable. In November 2005 they started recording the debut album *God Has A Plan For Us All*. Young drummer Anders Brobjer was used for the recording. There were guest appearances from people like Dave Pybus (*Cradle Of Filth*), Richard Andersson (*Time Requiem, Space Odyssey, Majestic*), Martin Häggström (*Moahni Moahna, Zool*). Dave was later drafted for the band and later on so was drummer John Henriksson. *Angtoria* plays high-quality melodic, heavy and orchestrated metal slightly similar to *Within Temptation*. Tommy is now found in *Corroded*.

2006 CD - POSH 085

| 2006 | ■ | GOD HAS A PLAN FOR US ALL | CD | Listenable | POSH 085 |
| 2006 | □ | GOD HAS A PLAN FOR US ALL | CD | Listenable | POSH 085 |

Bonus: A Child That Walks The Path Of A Man

ANIMA MORTE

Fredrik Klingwall: k/g, Daniel Cannerfelt: g, Stefan Granberg: g/b/k, Teddy Möller: d

Stockholm/Uppsala - *"Vintage Italian horror music from Sweden"*. This is how founder Fredrik describes *Anima Morte*. In 1999 Fredrik started working on a score for a friend's horror movie, *Gisslet från Swartöga*. It took only about 10 days to write and resulted in 40 minutes of classical music mixed with Italian-style horror movie music! A style which later would be the foundation of *Anima Morte*. The first EP consisted only of Fredrik and keyboardist Stefan Granberg, while on the album Fredrik utilised the forces of fellow *Loch Vostok* drummer Teddy Möller and guitarist Daniel Cannerfelt. Fredrik has also recorded with *Flagellation*, *Machinery*, *Desultor*, *Risining Shadows* as well as his solo material. Teddy has recorded with *Mellow Poetry*, *Mayadome* and *F.K.Ü.* The band also recorded a cover of Ennio Morricone's theme for the 1968 western movie *Il Grande Silencio*. The aforementioned musical description of founder Fredrik is quite accurate, but I would also add the words "heavy" and "progressive". It's at times a bit reminiscent of bands like *Landberk* and *Flower Kings* but with more power and a heavier mix with more distorted guitars. Very atmospheric though, and highly intriguing.

2007 MCD - LAST 008

2011 CDd - TRANS 067

2011 CDd - TRANS 080

2007	□	Viva Morte!...7" 4tr	Last Entertainment............................LAST 008
		Tracks: The Graveyard Plague/End f The Scourge/Are They Dead Yet?/Viva Morte!	
2007	●	Viva Morte!...MCD 4tr	Last Entertainment............................LAST 008
		Promo only.	
2007	□	Anima Morte/!Hooded Menace (split) ....7" PD	Dooementia ....DOOM 019
		500 copies. Track: Grasp Of The Beastwoman	
2007	□	FACE THE SEA OF DARKNESS..............................CD	Dead Beat Media ....DBM 01
2007	□	FACE THE SEA OF DARKNESS..............................LP	Horror Records ....HOR 026
2011	■	FACE THE SEA OF DARKNESS..............................CDd	Transubstans ....TRANS 067
		Bonus: A Ticket To Inferno	
2011	■	THE NIGHTMARE BECOMES REALITY ....CDd	Transubstans ....TRANS 080

ANNIE FOR PRESIDENT

Annie Kratz-Gutå: v, Jarmo Lindell: g/b/v

Stockholm - *Annie For President* started out in 1995 as a duo, featuring Annie (ex-*Rag Doll*) and Jarmo. When the album was recorded the two were the only members of the band, and among the guest musicians there are people like drummer Niclas Sigewall (*Electric Boys*), guitarist Ingemar Woody, bassist Daniel Bignert and keyboardist Erik Vårdstedt. The band even had a minor hit with a heavy rock version of *Elvis Presley's* song *Fever*. The duo however went separate ways and the band was put to rest. After eight years Annie re-started the band together with musicians from *Van Halen* cover band *Fan Heller* and recorded the track *The Night*. After this Annie started working with Peter Hermansson (*220 Volt, Talisman, Norum, Zoom Club*) who produced some new tracks, before he went to India and the band was again put to rest. Annie has also been backing singer for artists like Conny Bloom, E-Type etc. Today she is writing music and singing with *The Moose Brothers*, *Annie Is Joplin* and *Annie And The Extensions*. *Annie For President* play outstanding heavy funky hard rock in the vein of *Mother's Finest*.

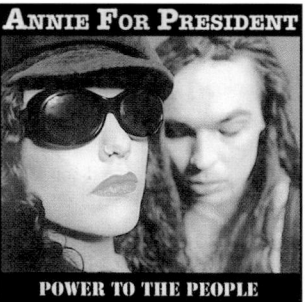

1996 CD - JAHA 02

1996	■	POWER TO THE PEOPLE ....CD	JAHA Records ....JAHA 02

ANOTHER HELL

Kristoffer Englund: v/g, Olof Gardeström: g, Jim Edström: b, Henrik Samuelsson: d

Åsele - The band was formed under the name *Aqua-Head* already in 1994, then consisting of Englund, Samuelsson, Markus Trysberg, Mattias Persson and Henrik Trysberg. The style was then a mix of thrash, sludge and groove metal. In 1997, they took a break and in 2004 Henrik and Kristoffer restarted the band, now with a more metal oriented attitude. Edström was drafted and when Gardeström later joined, the name was also changed. In 2010 *Another Hell* was established. The band plays melodic, yet brutal death metal in the vein of *Children Of Bodom* meets *Pantera*. The digital single *Capitol Hill* was released in 2011 and a full album is planned to be recorded in 2012.
Website: www.another hell.se

2010 MCD - - -

2010	■	Drowning In Dirt ....MCD 6tr	private .... - -
		Tracks: Capitol Hill/Redemption/Last Choking Breath/Face The Consequence/Watch It All Burn/Navigate To Nowhere	

ANOTHER LIFE

Andreas "Dea" Karlsson: v/k/d, Fredrik Pettersson: g, Dan Swanö: d/k

Västervik - *Another Life* is the brainchild of *Ribspreader/Sinners Burn* guitarist Andreas, formerly also in *Paganizer*. As the name may suggest this is a totally different bag of fruits, no death metal at all, but highly melodic, a bit melancholic and slightly progressive hard rock, quite similar to Dan Swanö's solo project *Nightingale*. Dan also plays keyboards on this album,

Andreas in Another Life

besides producing. Other musicians on the album are Joakim Diener (bass), Fredrik Petters-son (guitar), Peter Damin (drums) and Pär Fransson (lead guitars). Andreas recorded also two demos prior to the album, *Another Life* (2003) and *Melancholia* (2004). Great songs, great musicianship and great production. However, for the album to be fully enjoyable, Andreas should leave the vocal duties to someone more experienced. Swanö is in hundreds of bands such as **Bloodbath, Darkcide, Steel, Odyssey, Nightingale, Edge Of Sanity** etc etc. The bonus-CD features the demo tracks. Rogga Johansson has written lyrics for the album. A second album is said to be in the making.
Website: www.anotherlife.se

2008 CD - Vic 010

2008 ■ MEMORIES FROM NOTHING ....CD   Vic Records...Vic 010
2008 □ MEMORIES FROM NOTHING ....2CD   Vic Records...Vic 010
    Bonus: Empire/Tree Of Existence/Concealed By Fright/Reflections/Cotton Pines II/Life-time/Time/Standing Pale/Tree Of Existance – Unicorn Version.

ANTI-CHRISTIAN ASSAULT
Magnus Wohlfart: v/g/b, Christfucker: d/v

Höör - The band was formed in 2002. Wolhlfart is also found in **Nae'blis, Yggdrasil, Broken Dagger** and **Folkearth**. The recordings of the MCD started in 2004 but were not finished until two years later. A tape version was also released in 300 copies on Wulfrune Worxxx. The MCD has also been digitally released by Grand Master Music. Old school oriented fast black metal.

2006 MCD - Number one

2006 ■ Anti-Christian Assault...MCD 4tr   Daydream Nightmares Prod. ....Number one
    Tracks: Flames Of Hatred/Spread The Terror/Enter The Church Of Misery/Pray Before The Headsman. 500 copies.

ANTICHRIST
Anton Sunesson: v, Filip Runesson: g, Gabriel Forslund: g,
Gobbe Henningsson: b, Sven Nilsson: d

Växjö - Thrashers **Antichrist** was formed in 2007 and recorded the first demo, *Crushing Metal Tape* in 2008, followed by *Put To Death* two years later. The members had previously played with bands like **Witchgrave, Eviscerated, Disborn, The Rotten** and **Awaken Horror**. The album *Forgotten World* contains one song from each demo plus eight new songs. **Antichrist** play high-class raw, unpolished old-school thrash in the vein of **Kreator** and **Destruction** with authentic lo-fi demo style production. *Kill With Napalm* is an **Evil Blood** cover.

2011 CD - HRR 182 CD

2011 ■ FORBIDDEN WORLD ....CD   High Roller Records....................HRR 182 CD
2011 □ FORBIDDEN WORLD ....LP   High Roller Records..........................HRR 182
    First pressing: 1000 copies. Second pressing: 500 transparent red vinyl. 2012 pressing has different colour artwork. 250 copies white and 250 black vinyl.
2013 ■ Burned Beyond Recognition/Kill With Napalm...............................7"   Electric Assault Records ASLT-03
    1000 hand-numbered copies.

ANXIOUS
Åsa Andersson: v, Mirjam Andersson: v, Erik Wåke: g, Mattias Mattsson: g,
George Ellgren: k, Marcus Eriksson: b, Peter Larsson: d

Askersund/Åsbro - The band was formed in 1987 when a bunch of school mates just started playing around. At first they had a male singer, Fredrik Trossö, but later on they found Åsa. They participated in several band stands, but never won. They recorded some excellent demos, but finally recorded the single as a graduation project. The A-side is of course a cover of the song **The Animals** made famous. The band does their own arrange-ment, making it a bluesy ballad, which speeds up in the end and becomes a straight hard rocker. The B-side, on the other hand, is a great melodic hard rocker with heavy guitars, in the vein of **Toronto**. After the single Erik and George left the band as they wanted to play more heavy rock. Mattias, Peter and Marcus started playing in the dansband **Roffe Noveaux** together with Rolab studio owner Rolf Larsson. The three are now active as the cover band **Farbror Diesel**.

Anxious looking cool, calm and collected!

1991 7" - RM 1107

1991 ■ House of the Rising Sun/Somewhere in my Heart.........................7"   Rolab Music ....RM 1107   **$**
    500 copies

51

ANYWAY
Johan Freij: v, Pontus Nelderup: g, Anders Körmark: k,
Johan Häggman: b, Björn Roos: d
Ängelholm - Average-quality AOR, for collectors only. The band reunited in 2009.

1990 ■ The One I Need/Tina..7" private .... ANY 01

1990 7" - ANY 01

APATI
C9H13N: v, Fredrik "Obehag" Wolff (aka Torstenfelt): v,
Christian "Patient C" Larsson: g/b/d
Västerås/Fagersta - A depressive black metal band formed by Wolff in 2007. The name means apathy. C9H13N (the chemical name for Amphetamine) joined after the debut. Professor X (aka Avernus) (*Sanctum Sanguis* and *Promenia*) joined after the second album. The debut featured only Larsson and Wolff. Quite uninteresting, even though the second album is a tad better production-wise. Guitarist Fredrik "Obehag" Wolff (*Torstenfelt*) died of an overdose July 23, 2011. Christian "Patient C" Larsson is also in *Livsnekad, Svart, Shining, Promenia* and *Sanctum Sanguis*. Witty titel on the second album, which means "tomorrow canceled due to lack of interest".
Website: www.apatisk.se

2009 CD - THR 120

Year		Title	Format	Label	Cat. No.
2009	■	EUFORI	CD	Total Holocaust Records	THR 120
2010	□	EUFORI	2LPg	Art Of Propaganda/Obscure Abhorrence	- -
		Bonus: Alkohol (Lars Demian cover). Different artwork.. 100 white/red splatter + 400 black vinyl.			
2010	□	MORGONDAGEN INSTÄLLD I BRIST PÅ INTRESSE	CDd	Total Holocaust Records	THR 125
		500 copies			
2010	■	MORGONDAGEN INSTÄLLD I BRIST PÅ INTRESSE	CD	Total Holocaust Records	THR 125
		500 copies.			

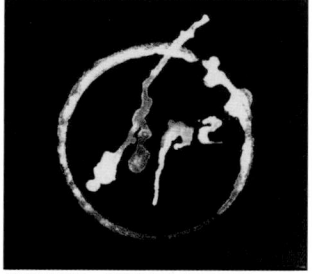

2010 CD - THR 125

APE
Daniel Riddersjö: v, Peter Söderlind: g, Oscar Simonson: b,
Peter "Pjorra" Johansson: fx, Peter "Bobby" Johansson: d
Vallentuna/Stockholm - *Ape* was formed out of the two bands *Disagree* and *Hurting Progress* that split in the late nineties. The members roots in the hardcore and metal scene shows in the interesting musical blend featured on the bands MCD. Outstanding brutal metal with a touch of hardcore, but still very melodic and quite technical. At times reminiscent of *Calm*, especially in *Cocktale*. The unreleased track *Echosong* is presented on the band's MySpace. Now split.
Website: www.myspace.com/apeclan

2003 ■ S/t..MCD 5tr s56 Recordings................... 5050466-9414-2-8
Tracks: Headrush/Barricades/Not Like You/Don't/Cocktale

2003 MCD - 5050466-9414-2-8

APETREA, COSTE
Coste Apetrea: g/b/k/v, Wilgot Hansson: d
Stockholm - Coste Apetrea, born in 1952, started his career back in 1972 in the jazz-rock oriented band *Samla Mammas Manna*. In 1976 he recorded the world music oriented self-titled album with the band *Ramlösa Kvällar*. After this he went to Finland to record with Jim Pembroke, where he also met Jukka Tollonen with whom he played for seven years. In 1977 he also recorded his first solo album *Nyspolat*. The album features drummer Åke Eriksson (*Bedlam, Wasa Express*) and Mats Glenngård (*Kebnekajse*). He also recorded an album with the band *De Gladas Kapell*. In 1983 he started a new career as producer/song writer. He recorded several albums with Finnish guitarist Jukka Tollonen, one being *Blue Rain* (Sonet). In 1986 he released the album *Stilla regn* which is a horrible attempt to break into the synth-pop market, sounding like *Paul Rein* or *Rick Astley* in style. What was he thinking? Avoid at all cost! In 1990 *Samla Mammas Manna* re-united and released the album *Kaka*. He also recorded the solo album *Airborne* and the subsequent year the album *Aqua, Music For Insomnia* was unearthed. In 1990 Coste formed the heavy blues rock unit *The Power Trio* together with drummer Peter Eyre and guitarist/bassist Max Åhman. In 1996 he recorded an acoustic album with the latter. It's however not until the album *Rites Of Passage* he actually qualifies into this book. This album is quite different from anything he had previously recorded. It's a really interesting mix of heavy rock with strong metal overtones, mixed with almost fusion-like guitar playing. The follow-up continued in the same footsteps, actually with an even more heavy rock orientation and less fusion, plus it saw Coste singing, too. Highly recommended for fans of great guitar playing! For all you Swedish readers, it was Coste who wrote the theme song for the children's TV show *Björnes magasin*.

Coste back in the days of afro.

2006 CD - LMC 167

2008 CD - LMC 250

Year		Title	Format	Label	Cat. No.
1977	□	NYSPOLAT	LP	MNW	MNW 81P
2006	■	RITES OF PASSAGE	CD	Lion Music	LMC 167
2008	■	SURPRISINGLY HEAVY	CD	Lion Music	LMC 250

APHASIA

**Hanna Rejdvik: v, Thomas Andersson: g, Emma Dahlqvist: k,
Håkan Fridell: b, Patrik Karlsson: d**

Växjö - **Aphasia** play pretty-good melodic hard rock, similar to **Shiva** or **Broke[N]Blue**. The band was formed in 2002 under the name **Image** consisting of Thomas, Håkan, singer Rosa Dahl and drummer Andreas Salomonsson. They were soon completed by keyboard player Emma Dahlqvist and late 2003 they recorded the single *A Late Night In November*. The band recorded *The Show Will Go On*, but when the album was ready the band parted ways with singer Rosa. Hanna joined and rerecorded the vocals in 2004. The band now also changed their name to **Aphasia**. Andreas Salomonsson played drums on the first release, but he left the band shortly after its release and was finally replaced by Patrik. After recording a three track demo they recorded the album *Shadow Of The Lonely*, which is actually a pro printed CD-R. A new album is said to be in the making.

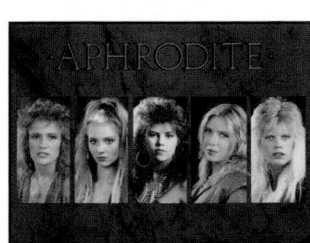

2005 CD - AACD001

2003 ☐	A Late Night In November	CDS 2tr	private	IMGCD001
	Tracks: Not Like Before/Together As One. As Image.			
2005 ■	THE SHOW WILL GO ON	CD	private	AACD001
	500 copies			

APHRODITE (aka AFRODITE)

**Malin Ekholm: v, Maria Landberg (now Tern): g,
Marianne Hall: b, Martina Axén: d**

Stockholm - After the punkish rock band **Living Sacrifice** (who released one album and two singles) split, Marianne joined forces with former **Revanch** guitarist Maria and they formed **Aphrodite**. *No Regrets* is a slab of good solid melodic hard rock/AOR. After the MLP, the band split, before reforming without second guitarist Flavia Canel, and changing their name to the Swedish **Afrodite** and the style was now more clear cut AOR, and good at that. The songs on the single were co-written with Dave Nerge (ex-**Highbrow, Dave Nerge's Bulldog** and **Dave & The Mistakes**). Landberg and Hall later recorded a 7" with the band **Shalale**. **Living Sacrifice** also temporarily reformed and made a live recording on November 4th 1995. Canel and Axén later formed **Rag Doll**, which later became **Drain (STH)**. Canel has also played bass in **Blowsight**, which she later managed. Tern resurfaced in **Hysterica**, and now plays in cover bands **Metalnun** and **Heartattack**.

1986 MLP - FAMLP 002

1989 7" - BOS 1043

1986 ■	No Regrets	MLP 5tr	Do-Re-Mi	FAMLP 002	$
	Tracks: No Regrets/Playing With Fire/Touch Me/Good And Evil/Bad Boys Boogie				
1989 ■	Cartoon Girl/All The Way	7"	Bozz	BOS 1043	
	Released under the name Afrodite.				

APOSTASY

Fredric Edin: v, Mathias Edin: g, Leif Högberg: k, Patrik Wall: b, Thomas Ohlsson: d

Kramfors/Umeå/Sundsvall - Formed in 2000 as **Marchosias** by brothers Fredric and Mattias Edin, drummer Håkan Björklund and guitarist Lars Engström. The band recorded their first demo in 2002 after which bass player Adreas Edin and keyboard player Dennis Bobzien were added to the line-up and Engström had quit. Henrik Johansson replaced the latter. The band recorded another demo and soon received interest from Black Mark Records. Andreas left and was replaced by Leif Högberg. They changed their name to **Apostasy** in 2003 and the debut album was produced by Pelle Saether and Lasse Lindén. After the album Björklund was sacked, Bobzien took over the drums and Daniel Lindgren (**Divine Souls/Setherial**) took over the bass duties. In 2004 it was Bobzien's turn to leave and he was replaced by Peter Sandin up until the recording of the second album, where Richard Holmgren performed the task, although not being a member. Daniel Lindgren now left and was replaced by Johan Edlund. On March 9, 2006 Henrik Johansson was stabbed to death by his girlfriend (who claims he ran into the knife himself). The band later recruited guitarist Ludvig Johansson (**Knife In Christ, Ghamorean**) and drummer David Ekevärn (**Knife In Christ, Putrevore, Shade Of Black**). Bass player Edlund was replaced by Patrik Wall. In 2009, after years of silence, the band presented a rough mix of the new track *Nuclear Messiah*. Later the same year their old label had received a request from Electronic Arts who wanted to use the track *Sulphus Injection* in the computer game *Brütal Legend*, which sure helped the band finance the new album. In 2010 Rambo Music signed **Apostasy**. In December the same year Ludvig was replaced by Peter Huss (**Shining, Cretoria**) and Ekevärn was replaced by Thomas Ohlsson (**The Project Hate MCMXCIC, Axenstar, Seven Wishes, Cellout**). **Apostasy** play quite melodic, almost heavy metal oriented black metal. Well played, killer production, great songs and semi-growling vocals. Similar to **Dimmu Borgir**. Website: *www.apostasysweden.se/*

2004 CD - BMCD 169

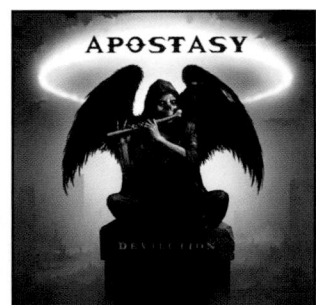

2005 CD - BMCD 178

2011 CD - AM CD 01

2004 ■	CELL 666	CD	Black Mark	BMCD 169
2005 ■	DEVILUTION	CD	Black Mark	BMCD 178
2011 ■	NUCLEAR MESSIAH	CD	Rambo Music	AM CD 01

APOSTLE

Patrik Andersson: v, Rickard Jakobson: g/b, Peter Callander: d

Falkenberg - Vegan death metal (Yes, first time I've heard of it, too). In 1998 the band released the four track cassette demo *...Till It Burns The Horizon*. Brutal old-school, blast-beat death metal.

1999 ■ DUSK FOR CONVENIENCE ....CD Abstract Communications...................ABS 002

1999 CD - ABS 002

APRIL DIVINE

Joakim Åström: v, Niklas Westberg: g, Peter Ulvén: b, Per Karlsson: d

Örnsköldsvik/Umeå - The band was formed in 1998 under the moniker *Starf*ck*. They recorded some demos and Swedish radio show *P3 Demo* played the band several times. In 2005 they signed up with a US management, making them change their name to *Bloody April*. In 2006 they were picked up by Swedish label Ninetone and now changed their name again to *April Divine*. The band made their debut in 2006 with the single *Almost Famous*, followed by the album *Chapter One*. In 2008 the band also recorded a cover of *Seal's Kiss From A Rose*, produced by Tobbe Lindell (*Europe, Mustasch, Aggressive Chill*). The second album was produced by Rick Beato (*Bullet For My Valentine, Shinedown, Dark New Day*) and *Sevendust* singer/guitarist Clint Lowery made a guest appearance on the album. *April Divine* could musically and quality-wise be placed alongside US bands like *Breaking Benjamin, Shinedown* or *Daughtry*. Heavy modern guitar riffs and clean melodic vocals. High class stuff.
Website: www.aprildivine.com

2007 CD - NRCD 101

2010 CD - SUPERCD 002

2006 □ Almost Famous	CDS	Ninetone	NRCDS 004
2007 ■ CHAPTER ONE	CD	Ninetone	NRCD 101
2010 ■ REDEMPTION	CD	Supernova	SUPERCD 002

APRIL SKY

Tom Åberg: v, Mike Åberg: g, Thomas Eriksson: b,
Robert Knutsson: k, Tomas Carlsson: d

Östersund/Lit - The A-side is a cover of the old Bette Middler classic, while the B-side is a powerful AOR-tune. Tom is a great singer. Robert is ex-*Wilderness* and Thomas Carlsson is ex-*Monaco Blues Band*.

1989 ■ The Rose/Come On ....7" private ....KUL 8908

1989 7" - KUL 8908

AQUILA

Patrik Carlsson: v/b, Johan Olsson: g, Hans Persson: g,
Pontus Larsson (now Lekaregård): k, Pelle Hindén: d

Falun - *Aquila* was formed in 1987. The A-side is a ballad, while the B-side shows more of an AOR-oriented side of the band. Quite good arrangements, with some nice guitar harmonies and above average vocals. The band lasted for 3-4 years. Some of the members formed the band *Deep Cee*, but only some demos came out of it. Pelle and Patrik are now found in the band *Fretless*. Pelle and Pontus are also found in *Eternal* and Johan plays in cover band *Raccoons & Moonshine*.

1988 ■ Dreams Of Africa/Love Is No Game...7" Active Music....................................HEJ S-029

1988 7" - HEJ S-029

ARCH ENEMY

Angela Gossow: v, Michael "Mike" Amott: g, Christopher "Chris" Amott: g,
Charles Petter "Sharlee D'Angelo" Andreasson: b, Daniel Erlandsson: d

Halmstad - *Arch Enemy* took their first steps when guitarist Michael "Mike" Amott left death metal band *Carcass* in 1996. He was also formerly a member of *Carnage* and is also found in *Spiritual Beggars*. Mike was soon joined by his younger brother Christopher (*Armageddon*), singer Johnny Liiva (*Carnage, Furbowl, Devourment*). Daniel Erlandsson (*Eucharist, The*End, In Flames*) was initially used as session drummer. What made *Arch Enemy* stick out a bit from other death metal bands at the time were the song structure and guitar solos, having a more 70s heavy rock touch. The band recorded the debut *Black Earth* in Studio Fredman (*Dimmu Borgir, Dream Evil* etc) and Wrong Again Records released it in 1996. Mike handled both his guitar duties as well as the bass playing on the album. The Japanese audience soon embraced the band and both brothers have been voted best guitarist several times in Japan's biggest hard rock magazine Burrn!! *Arch Enemy* was now picked up by Century Media, who released their second album *Stigmata*. The album also saw the addition of drummer Peter Wildoer and bass player Martin Begtsson. In 1999 the band was one of the four nominees in the Swedish Grammy Award "hard rock" category. Bengtsson was replaced by *Mercyful Fate/King Diamond/Witchery/Dismember* bassist Sharlee D'Angelo and Erlandsson again entered the band, now on a permanent basis. The band released the *Burning Bridges* album and on the

subsequent tour D'Angelo was temporarily replaced by Dick Lövgren (*Armegeddon, Meshuggah*) and later on by Roger Nilsson (*The Quill, Spiritual Beggars*). Liiva was sacked late 2000, as the band felt they were lacking a dynamic front man. His replacement was however not a man, but a woman, German music writer and singer Angela Gossow (she and Michael became a couple later on as well). Liiva instead formed the band *Nonexist*. Angela made her debut on the album *Wages Of Sin*, which marked a new era for the band. The guitars were more detuned than ever and the heaviness increased, topped with Angela's fearsome growls. *Anthems Of Rebellion* picked up where *Wages* left off. In July 2005, just after the recording of *Doomsday Machine*, Christopher decided to leave the band for personal reasons. He was, after a brief stint using Kostas "Gus G" Karamitroudis (*Dream Evil, Firewind, Ozzy Osbourne*), replaced by former *Talisman* guitarist Fredrik Åkesson. Fredrik however never made it on record with the band as Chris decided to return in March 2007. Fredrik went on to join *Opeth*. The band has toured extensively and the far east has always been a strong market for the band, which shows on the live album *Rise Of The Tyrant – Live In Japan*, where the live DVD *Tyrants Of The Rising Sun* was also recorded. *The Root Of All Evil* is an album of rerecordings of old songs before Angela's entry in the band. *Manifesto Of Arch Enemy* is a compilation. Chris has also made a great version of *Alcatrazz's Big Foot* for the Yngwie Malmsteen-tribute, *A Guitar Odyssey* (Black Sun). He also recorded a solo album of very soft and mellow music entitled *Follow Your Heart*, in 2010. The album *Dawn Of Khaos* was a special compilation given to the subscribers of Close-Up Magazine. It's a best of also featuring two new songs, two previously unreleased live tracks and a cover of *Kiss*' The Oath.

Website: www.archenemy.net

1996 CD - WAR 011 CD

1998 CD - 77212-2

1999 CD - 77276 2

2000 CD - TCFK 87217

1996 ■	BLACK EARTH	CD	Wrong Again	WAR 011 CD
1996 □	BLACK EARTH	LP PD	Wrong Again	WAR 011 PD
1996 □	BLACK EARTH	CD	Toys Factory (Japan)	TFCK-88792
	Bonus: Losing Faith/Ides Of March (Iron Maiden cover)			
1998 ■	STIGMATA	CD	Century Media	77212-2
1998 □	STIGMATA	CD	Century Media (USA)	7912-2
1998 □	STIGMATA	CD	Toy's Factory (Japan)	TCFK-87149
	Bonus: Diva Satanica/Hydra/Damnation's Way			
1999 ■	BURNING BRIDGES	CD	Century Media	77276 2
1999 □	BURNING BRIDGES	CD	Century Media (USA)	7976 2
1999 □	BURNING BRIDGES	CD	Toy's Factory (Japan)	TCFK 87184
	Bonus: Scream Of Anger (Europe-cover)/Fields Of Desolation (99 version)			
2000 □	BURNING LIVE	CD	Toy's Factory (Japan)	TCFK 87217
	Also a limited edition in paper box with poster.			
2000 □	BURNING LIVE	CD	Dream On (Korea)	PARK-9006
2001 □	BURNING BRIDGES	CD	Fono (Russia)	FO205CD
2001 ■	WAGES OF SIN	CD	Toy's Factory (Japan)	TFCK-87245
	Also available as limited edition in paper box and with mouse pad			
2001 □	WAGES OF SIN	CD	Dream On (Korea)	PARK-9004
2002 □	WAGES OF SIN	2CD	Century Media	77383-2
	Bonus: Starbreaker/Aces High/Scream Of Anger/Diva Satanica/Fields Of Desolation '99/ Damnation's Way/Hydra/The Immortal (video)			
2002 □	WAGES OF SIN	2CD	Century Media (USA)	8083-2
2002 ■	WAGES OF SIN	CD	Fono (Russia)	FO335CD
2002 □	WAGES OF SIN	LP	Century Media	77383-1
	Bonus: Lament Of A Mortal Soul			
2002 □	Burning Angel	MCD 3tr	Toy's Factory (Japan)	TFCK 87281
	Tracks: Burning Angel, Lament Of A Mortal Soul, Starbreaker, plus the video for Ravenous			
2002 □	BLACK EARTH	CD	Regain	RR 002-AS
	Bonus: Losing Faith/The Ides Of March (Iron Maiden cover)/Aces High (Iron Maiden cover)			
2002 □	BLACK EARTH	LP	Regain	RRASLP 2
	Vinyl version also featuring bonus-tracks.			
2002 □	BLACK EARTH	CD	Regain	REG-1001
	RRAS 2 plus bonus: Bury Me An Angel (video)			
2002 □	BLACK EARTH	CD	Regain (USA)	RGAR-1001
2002 □	BLACK EARTH	CDd	Regain	RR-101
	RRAS 2 plus bonus: Bury Me An Angel (video)			
2003 ■	ANTHEMS OF REBELLION	CD	Century Media	77483-2
2003 □	ANTHEMS OF REBELLION	CD	Century Media (USA)	8183-2
2003 □	ANTHEMS OF REBELLION	CD	Icarus (Argentina)	ICARUS 69
2003 □	ANTHEMS OF REBELLION	2CDd	Century Media	77483-8
2003 □	ANTHEMS OF REBELLION	2CDd+DVD	Toy's Factory (Japan)	TFCK-87322
	DVD with 3 live tracks + 5.1 mixes			
2003 □	ANTHEMS OF REBELLION	2CDd+DVD	Century Media	77483-8
2003 □	ANTHEMS OF REBELLION	2CDd+DVD	Century Media (USA)	8183-2
2003 □	ANTHEMS OF REBELLION	LP	Century Media	77483-1
2003 □	ANTHEMS OF REBELLION	CD	Fono (Russia)	FO318CD
2003 □	ANTHEMS OF REBELLION	2CD	Fono (Russia)	FO318CD
2003 □	ANTHEMS OF REBELLION	CD	Dream On (Korea)	PARK 9032
	Bonus: Special message for Korean fans.			

2002 CD - FO335CD

2003 CD - 77483-2

2003 ☐	BLACK EARTH ....CD	Dream On (Korea) .... PARK 9022	
	Bonus: Losing Faith/The Ides Of March (Iron Maiden cover)/Aces High (Iron Maiden)		
2004 ☐	STIGMATA ....CD	Dream On (Korea) .... PARK 9023	
2004 ☐	STIGMATA ....CD	Fono (Russia) FO334CD	
2004 ☐	DEAD EYES SEE NO FUTURE ....CD 6tr	Toy's Factory (Japan).................. TFCK-87358	
	Tracks: Dead Eyes See No Future/Burning Angel (live)/We Will Rise (live)/Symphony Of Destruction (Megadeth cover)/Kill With Power (Manowar cover)/Incarnated Solvent Abuse (Carcass cover)		
2004 ■	DEAD EYES SEE NO FUTURE ....CD 8tr	Century Media 77576-2	
	Tracks: Dead Eyes See No Future/Burning Angel (live)/We Will Rise (live)/Heart Of darkness (live)/Symphony Of Destruction (Megadeth cover)/Kill With Power (Manowar cover)/ Incarnated Solvent Abuse (Carcass cover)/ We Will Rise (video)		
2004 ☐	DEAD EYES SEE NO FUTURE ....CD 8tr	Century Media (USA)...........................8276-2	
2004 ☐	DEAD EYES SEE NO FUTURE ....CD 8tr	Fono (Russia) FO422CD	
2004 ☐	BURNING BRIDGES ....CD	Dream On (Korea) 2004-5	
	Bonus: Scream Of Anger (Europe cover)/Fields Of Desolation '99		
2005 ■	Doomsday Machine - Two-song Sampler .... CDS	Century Media (USA)...........................41270 6	
	Promo single. Tracks: Nemesis/I Am Legend-Out For Blood		
2005 ■	Arch Enemy/Nevermore (split) ....MCD	Century Media (USA)..............................8234 6	
	Promo single split with Nevermore.. Tracks: Nemesis/I Am Legend/Out For Blood		
2005 ☐	DOOMSDAY MACHINE ....CD	Century Media 77583-2	
2005 ☐	DOOMSDAY MACHINE ....CD	Century Media (USA)...........................8283-2	
2005 ☐	DOOMSDAY MACHINE ....CD	Fono (Russia) FO520CD	
2005 ☐	DOOMSDAY MACHINE ....CDd+DVD	Century Media 77583-8	
	DVD contains live video and live tracks		
2005 ☐	DOOMSDAY MACHINE ....LP	Century Media 77583-1	
2005 ☐	DOOMSDAY MACHINE ....CD	Toy's Factory (Japan).................. TFCK-87388	
	Bonus: Heart Of darkness (live)/Bridge Of Destiny (live). Also limited edition in paper box with postcards.		
2007 ☐	STIGMATA ....LP	Night Of The Vinyl Dead ....NIGHT 032	
2007 ☐	BURNING BRIDGES ....LP	Night Of The Vinyl Dead ....NIGHT 027	
2007 ☐	Revolution Begins ....MCD 4tr	Century Media 77721-3	
	Tracks: Revolution Begins/Blood On Your Hands/Walk In The Shadows (Queensryche cover)/I Am Legend-Out For Blood (live)		
2007 ☐	Revolution Begins ....MCD 4tr	Century Media (USA)...........................8421-2	
2007 ☐	RISE OF THE TYRANT ....CD	Century Media (USA)...........................8400-2	
2007 ■	RISE OF THE TYRANT ....CD	Century Media 77700-2	
2007 ☐	RISE OF THE TYRANT ....CD	Savage Messiah (Asia) MMMF-2231	
2007 ☐	RISE OF THE TYRANT ....CD	Mazzar (Russia) .... MYST CD270	
2007 ☐	RISE OF THE TYRANT ....CD	Dream On (Korea) ....n/a	
2007 ☐	RISE OF THE TYRANT ....CD+DVD	Toy's Factory (Japan) TFCK-87423	
	Bonus: The Oath (Kiss) + DVD live. Slipcase.		
2007 ☐	RISE OF THE TYRANT ....CD+DVD	Century Media 77700-0	
2007 ☐	RISE OF THE TYRANT ....LP+CD	Century Media 77700-1	
2008 ☐	TYRANTS OF THE RISING SUN – LIVE IN JAPAN 2CD	Century Media 997836-2	
2008 ■	TYRANTS OF THE RISING SUN – LIVE IN JAPAN 2LP	Century Media 997836-1	
	Different artwork.		
2009 ☐	BLACK EARTH ....LP	Back On Black .... BOBV 172LP	
2009 ☐	MANIFESTO OF ARCH ENEMY ....CD	Century Media 997890-0	
2009 ☐	THE ROOT OF ALL EVIL ....CD	Century Media 997946-0	
	Deluxe version with alternate artwork, patch and bonus tracks: Bury Me An Angel (live)/ The Immortal (live)/Bridge Of Destiny (live)		
2009 ☐	THE ROOT OF ALL EVIL................................LP	Century Media 997946-1	
2009 ☐	THE ROOT OF ALL EVIL................................CD	Yoshimoto R And C (Japan)........ YRCG-90019	
	Bonus: Bury Me An Angel (live)/The Immortal (live)/Bridge Of Destiny (live)/Wings Of Tomorrow (Europe cover)/Walk In The Shadows (Queensryche). Poster + slipcase		
2009 ☐	STIGMATA – DELUXE EDITION ....CD	Century Media (USA)...........................8624-2	
	Slipcase. Bonus: Hydra/Diva Satanica/Damnation's Way/Diva Satanica (live)/Beast Of Man (live)/Tears Of The Dead (live)/Bridge Of Destiny (live)		
2009 ☐	BURNING BRIDGES – DELUXE EDITION ....CD	Century Media (USA)...........................8623-2	
	Slipcase. Bonus: Fields Of Desolation '99/Star Breaker (Judas Priest)/Aces High (Iron maiden)/Scream Of Anger (Europe)/The Immortal (live)/Dead Inside (live)/Pilgrim (live)/ Silverwing (live)/Angelclaw (live)		
2009 ☐	THE ROOT OF ALL EVIL................................CD	Trooper (Japan) YRCG-90019	
2009 ☐	STIGMATA ....CD	Trooper (Japan) YRCG-90022	
2009 ☐	BURNING BRIDGES ....CD	Trooper (Japan) YRCG-90023	
2009 ☐	WAGES OF SIN ....CD	Trooper (Japan) YRCG-90024	
2009 ☐	ANTHEMS OF REBELLION ....CD	Trooper (Japan) YRCG-90025	
2009 ☐	STIGMATA ....CD	Rock Empire (Taiwan).................. MMMF-2314	
	Bonus: Hydra/Diva Satanica/Damnation's Way/Diva Satanica (live)/Beast Of Man (live)/ Bass Intro-Tears Of The Dead (live)/Bridge Of Destiny (live)		
2009 ☐	WAGES OF SIN 2CD	Rock Empire (Taiwan).................. MMMF-2305	
2009 ☐	DEAD EYES SEE NO FUTURE ....CD	Rock Empire (Taiwan).................. MMMF-2306	
	Bonus tracks: Heart of darkness (live)/We Will Rise (video)		
2009 ☐	BURNING BRIDGES ....CD	Rock Empire (Taiwan)..................... CEN7976.2	
2009 ☐	BLACK EARTH ....CD	Rock Empire (Taiwan)................. RGAR1001.2	

2004 CD - 77576-2

2005 CDS - 41270 6

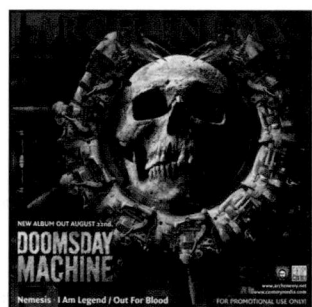

2005 MCD - 8234 6

2007 CD - 77700-2

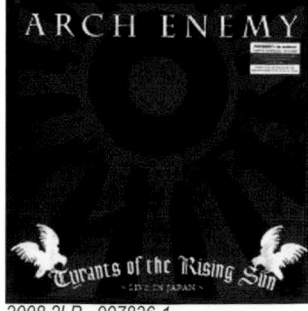

2008 2LP - 997836-1

2009	☐	DEAD EYES SEE NO FUTURE	CD	Trooper (Japan)	YRCG-90026
2011	■	DAWN OF CHAOS	CD	Century Media	998098-2P
2011	☐	KHAOS LEGIONS	CD	Trooper (Japan)	QATE-10001

Bonus: The Zoo (Scorpions cover)/Snowbound (acoustic)

2011	☐	KHAOS LEGION	CD	Trooper (Japan)	XNTE-10001

SHM-CD. Bonus: The Zoo (Scorpions cover)/Snowbound (acoustic)

2011	☐	KHAOS LEGIONS	CD	Century Media	9980632
2011	☐	KHAOS LEGIONS	2CDd	Century Media (USA)	8763-2

Bonus:Warning (Discharged cover)/Wings Of Tomorrow (Europe)/The Oath (Kiss)/The Book Of Heavy Metal (Dream Evil)

2011	☐	KHAOS LEGIONS	2CDd	Century Media (Eu+Australia)	9980630

King size media-book.

2011	☐	KHAOS LEGIONS	2LPg	Century Media	9980631

2200 black, 100 gold, 400 transparent+black marble and 300 red+black marble. -Bonus: Warning (Discharged cover)/Wings Of Tomorrow (Europe)/The Oath (Kiss)/The Book Of Heavy Metal (Dream Evil)

2011	☐	KHAOS LEGIONS	CD	Dope Entertainment (Korea)	2011-11
2011	☐	BLACK EARTH	2CD	Trooper (Japan)	XNTE-10007

SHM-CD. Bonus: The Ides Of March/Losing Faith + Live At W'ohol Osaka.

2011	☐	STIGMATA	CD	Trooper (Japan)	XNTE-10008

SHM-CD. Bonus: Aces High/Diva Satanica (live)/Beast Of Man (live)/Bass Intro-Tears Of The Dead (live)/Bridge Of Destiny (live)

2011	☐	BURNING BRIDGES	CD	Trooper (Japan)	XNTE-10009

SHM-CD. Bonus: Scream Of Anger/Fields Of Desolation '99/Starbreaker/The Immortal (live)/Dark Insanity (live)/Dead Inside (live)/Pilgrim (live)/Silverwing (live)/Transmigration Macabre (live)/Angelclaw (live)

2011	☐	WAGES OF SIN	CD	Trooper (Japan)	XNTE-10010

SHM-CD. Bonus: Lament Of A Mortal Soul/Shadows And Dust

2011	☐	ANTHEMS OF REBELLION	CD	Trooper (Japan)	XNTE-10011

SHM-CD. Bonus:Symphony Of Destruction/Kill With Power/Incarnated Solvent Abuse/Lament Of A Mortal Soul (live)/Behind The Smile (live)/Diva Satanica (live)f

2011	☐	DOOMSDAY MACHINE	CD	Trooper (Japan)	XNTE-10012

SHM-CD. Bonus: Heart Of Darkness (live)/Bridge Of Destiny (live)/Burning Angel (live)/ We Will Rise (live)/Heart Of Darkness (live)/Bridge Of Destiny (live)/I Am Legend-Out For Blood (live)

2011	☐	RISE OF THE TYRANT	CD	Trooper (Japan)	XNTE-10013

SHM-CD. Bonus: The Oath/The Book Of Heavy Metal/Dark Insanity (live)/I Will Live Again (live)/We Will Rise (live)

2011	■	THE ROOT OF ALL EVIL	CD	Trooper (Japan)	XNTE-10014

SHM-CD. Bonus: Wings Of Tomorrow/Walk ljn The Shadows/Warning/Bury Me An Angel (live)/The Immortal (live)/Bridge Of Destiny (live)

2011 CD - 998098-2P

2011 CD - 9980632

2011 CD - XNTE-10014

ARCKANUM
Johan "Shamaatae" Lahger: v/g/b/d

Mora - Extremely fast and evil Chaos-Gnostic old-school black metal with lyrics in medieval Swedish more or less screamed out. The band was formed in 1992, then also featuring Loke Svarteld (g) and Sataros (v) from **Sataros Grief**. On the first demo *Trulen*, it had become Shamaatae's solo-project. *Trulen* was supposed to be released on Carnal Records, but it didn't happen until 2006, now with 3 bonus tracks. The debut was produced by Peter Tägtgren, who also helps out with "monk vocals". The low sound level of the album *Kostogher* is meant to get people to turn up the volume so that the thunder of the track *Skoghens Minnen Vækks* blows their speakers. Nice way to treat your fans... The *11 Year Anniversary Album* contains previously unreleased material recorded between 1992-2003, most of it sounding like bad rehearsal recordings. Lahger has also been found in **Grotesque** and **Sorhin**. **Arckanum** play old-school-sounding black metal with desperate shouting vocals, quite badly recorded on the early releases. The **Arckanum** box set, released by Zyklon-B has been rejected by the band because the first press was mis-printed with pink logo and still sold despite the band's protests. The exclusive track *Aengin Oforhaerra* can be found on the Blut & Eisen compilation *Tormenting Legends II* (2006 Blut & Eisen). **Arckanum's** seventh album *Helvetismyrkr* features guitar solos from Set Teitan (**Dissection, Watain**) and is better sounding production-wise.

Lahger with an axe to grind

1995 CD - NR 008

1995	■	FRAN MARDER	CD	Necropolis	NR 008 $

First press 1000 copies, second press 1500 copies. Different cover between first and second press.

1997	■	KOSTOGHER	CD	Necropolis	NR 011
1998	☐	KAMPEN	2CD	Necropolis	NR 024
2001	■	Boka Vm Kaos	7" EP	Carnal	CR-000

Tracks: Vm Kaos Gatum Ok Kosmos, Bafomet. 500 copies.

2003	■	FRAN MARDER	LP	Blut & Eisen	- -
2003	■	FRAN MARDER	LP PD	Blut & Eisen	- -
2003	☐	Kosmos Wardhin Dræpas Om Sin (split)	7" EP	Carnal	CR-002/CR-003

Split with Contamino. 666 numbered copies.

2004	☐	THE 11 YEAR ANNIVERSARY ALBUM	LPg	Blut & Eisen	- -

1000 copies with poster.

1997 CD - NR 011

2004 ☐	THE 11 YEAR ANNIVERSARY ALBUM	LPgPD	Blut & Eisen	- -		

2004 ☐ THE 11 YEAR ANNIVERSARY ALBUM...LPgPD   Blut & Eisen .... - -
200 copies with poster.
2004 ☐ THE 11 YEAR ANNIVERSARY ALBUM...CD   Carnal CR-005
2004 ☐ KOSTOGHER ....2LPg   Blut & Eisen .... - -
2004 ☐ KOSTOGHER ....2LPg PD   Blut & Eisen .... - -
2004 ☐ KAMPEN ....2LP   Blut & Eisen .... - -
2004 ☐ KAMPEN ....2LP PD   Blut & Eisen .... - -
2005 ☐ KAOS SVARTA MAR ....MLP 5tr   Blut & Eisen .... - -
Tracks: Hæxhamar/Eldkniver/Ætergap/Frana (Anti-Cosmic Version)/ Spitælsker
2005 ☐ KAOS SVARTA MAR/SKINNING THE LAMBS (split) ....CD   Carnal CR-004
Split with Svartsyn. Tracks: Hæxhamar/Eldkniver/Ætergap/Frana/Spitælsker
2006 ☐ TRULEN ....2LP   Blut & Eisen .... - -
2006 ☐ TRULEN ....2LP PD   Blut & Eisen .... - -
2006 ■ TRULEN ....CD   Carnal CR-008
2007 ☐ FRAN MARDER ....CD   Full Moon productions (USA)............. FMP 046
2007 ☐ KAMPEN ....2CD   Full Moon Productions .... FMP 048
2008 ☐ ANTIKOSMOS ....CD   Debemur Morti Productions)............. DMP 037
2008 ☐ Antikosmos ....7"   Debemur Morti Productions)............. DMP 034
Red, black, yellow vinyl, 100 copies each. Tracks: Røkulfargnýr/Current Of Death
2008 ☐ ANTIKOSMOS ....LP   Debemur Morti Productions)............. DMP 037
Comes with 12-page booklet, A2 poster, 2 different versions of cover. Clear vinyl with black splatters or white vinyl with black splatters.
2008 ☐ ANTIKOSMOS ....CD   Moribund (USA) .... Dead 121 CD
2008 ☐ Arckanum/Sataros Grief (split) ....7"g   Blut & Eisen .... - -
Split with Sataros Grief. Track: Hadelik. 100 green, 600 black vinyl.
2008 ☐ Arckanum/Sataros Grief (split) ....7" PD   Blut & Eisen .... - -
300 copies.
2008 ☐ Grimalkinz Skaldi ....7"g   Carnal/Blut & Eisen.......................... CR-009
600 copies in black vinyl, 100 green/black splatter. Hand numbered
2008 ☐ Grimalkinz Skaldi ....7"g PD   Carnal/Blut & Eisen.......................... CR-009
300 copies.
2008 ☐ Hadelik (split) ....7"g   Carnal/Blut & Eisen.......................... --
Split with Sataros Grief.
2008 ☐ ARCKANUM ....5LP+10" box   Zyklon-B...ZBP **$$**
Box set containing 5 LPs,1 10", t-shirt, poster, sticker, pin and photo booklet.
2009 ☐ FRAN MARDER...CDd   Debemur Morti Productions ....DMP 054
2009 ☐ FRAN MARDER...LP PD   Hammer Of Hate (Finland) ....HOH 030
2009 ☐ FRAN MARDER...LP   World Wide War WWW-3
2009 ☐ KOSTOGHER ....CD   Full moon Productions ....FMP 047
2009 ☐ KOSTOGHER ....CD   Debemur Morti Productions ....DMP 0055
2009 ☐ KAMPEN ....CD   Debemur Morti Productions ....DMP 0056
2009 ☐ Þþþþþþþþþþþ...CD   Debemur Morti Productions ....DMP 049
2009 ☐ Þþþþþþþþþþþ...CD   Debemur Morti Productions ....DMP 049
500 copies in black, rest is normal silver CD.
2009 ☐ Þþþþþþþþþþþ ....LPg   Debemur Morti Productions ....DMP 049
White with red splatter vinyl.
2009 ■ Þþþþþþþþþþþ ....CD   Moribund Records (USA)...........DEAD 141 CD
2009 ☐ Þyrmir/Be Forwarned ....7"   Debemur Morti Productions ....DMP 0053
Black vinyl, plus limited edition in red.
2010 ☐ KOSTOGHER ....2LPg PD   Hammer Of Hate (Finland) ....HOH 031
2010 ☐ SVIGA LÆ...CD   Regain ....RR 179
Slipcase.
2010 ☐ ARCKANUM ....5LP+10" Box   Zyklon-B.......................................RR 179
500 copies, 100 first in splatter vinyl. The first batch was mis-prtinted with pink logo resulting in the band rejecting the label. Contains: 10 " Instrumental raw mixes, double Kampen,double Kostogher and Fran Marder) + t-shirt (Large) + poster + sticker + 1 pin + 1 photo booklet.
2011 ☐ HELVITISMYRKR ....LP   Seasons Of Mist ....SUA 019LP
2011 ☐ HELVITISMYRKR ....CD   Seasons Of Mist ....SUA 019
Bonus: Outro

Unofficial releases:
2008 ☐ FRAN MARDER...LP   World Wide War Prod ....-

2001 7" - CR-000

2003 LP PD - - -

2006 CD - CR-008

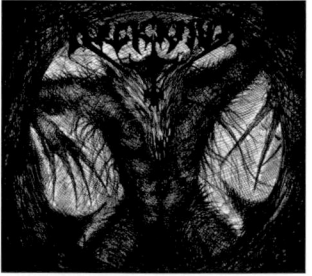
2009 CD - DEAD 141 CD

ARCONOVA

Andy Shore: v, Nicko DiMarino: g/k/b, Pontus Pfeiffer: b

Norrköping - Andy and Nicko formed the band in the spring of 2005. Highly accomplished melodic and slightly progressive metal. A bit thin production with poor-sounding programmed drums, but musically pretty good. After the album Pontus was replaced by bass player Marcel and guitarist Jimmy Wave was added to the line-up. Nicko also runs Deep Blue Studios.
Website: www.arconova.com/

2006 ■ LOST IN TIME...CD   Mimosound MIMO-012
1000 numbered copies.

2006 CD - MIMO-012

ARENA
Åke Thoresson: b/v, Henrik Swerkersson: g, Tony Jaensson: k, Dag Carlsson: d

Kalmar - The band was formed in 1984 and split in 1990. Pretty good hard rock/metal. Tony and Åke played in some other bands later on, but only demos came out of it. Not to be confused with the more pop-oriented band.

1987 ■ Breakin' Loose/Lost In Time..7" Platina...PL23 **$**

1987 7" - PL 23

ARFSYND
Perditor: g/v/b/d

Kalmar - Punkish death metal with desperately screeching vocals, close to **Shining** at times. Perditor is also found in **Orchivus, Grift** and **Haemophilia**.

2009 ■ ARFSYND..CD Daemon Worship Productions ....DWP 010
2013 □ HESYCHIA...CDd Daemon Worship Productions ....DWP 027

ARISE
**Patrik "Patsy" Johansson: v, Mattias "Sternberg" Svanborg: g,
L-G Jonasson: g, Kaj "Kai" Leissner: b, Daniel Bugno: d**

Alingsås/Göteborg - Formed by Johansson and Bungo in 1994 as a Bay Area thrash, and especially **Sepultura**, cover band. The two were completed by bass player Patrik Skoglöw. The name of course came from the **Sepultura**-song. The band went through various singers and made several demo recordings before putting a bit more effort into the recording, which resulted in the demo *Abducted Intelligence* in 2001, where Erik Ljungqvist (**Skymning**) handled the mike. The style evolved into a mix of death metal and thrash, often compared to **At The Gates.** The demo was recorded at Los Angered by Andy LaRocque and lead to a deal with Finnish Spinefarm Records. The line-up lasted for three albums, but for *The Reckoning* drastic changes were made. Ljungkvist and Skoglöw were out and Svanborg, Leissner and Jonasson were in. *The Reckoning* also features guest spots from people like Mikael Stanne (**Dark Tranquillity**), Jake Fredén (**Nostradameus**) and Jonas Kjellgren (**Carnal Forge, Scar Symmetry**). The band does a cover of *Communication Breakdown* on the **Led Zeppelin**-tribute *Dead Zeppelin* (Dwell Rec). The track *Cellbound* was featured on *The Metal Crusade* (01 VOD) and on *Witchcraft & Folklore Chapter One, The Last Of Cenruries* on AFM 79-99 (99 AFM). The band has split.

Skoglöw and Ljungqvist now play in the band **Mercury Monkeys**.

2003 CD - 067896-2

2009 CD - RR 144

2001	□	THE GODLY WORK OF ART...CD	Spinefarm	.....................................SPI 121 CD
2001	□	THE GODLY WORK OF ART...CDd	Spinefarm	.....................................SPI 121 DG
		Bonus: Motorbreath (Metallica cover)		
2003	■	KINGS OF THE CLONED GENERATION ....CD	Spinefarm	......................SPI 179 CD/067896-2
2005	□	THE BEAUTIFUL NEW WORLD ....CD	Spinefarm	......................................SPI 235 CD
2005	□	THE BEAUTIFUL NEW WORLD ....CD	Woodbell (Japan)	........................WBEX-25008
		Bonus: A Godly Work Of Art/Generations For Sale/Within/Haterush/Wounds/Abducted Intelligence/Motorbreath		
2009	■	THE RECKONING ....CD	Regain	....RR 144
2009	□	THE RECKONING ....CD	Regain (USA)	...........................REG-CD-1088

ARMAGEDDA
Stefan "Graav" Sandström: v/g, Andreas "A" Pettersson: g/b

Boliden - **Armagedda** was formed in 2000 by Andreas (also in **Leviathan, LIK, Lönndom**). He drafted singer/guitarist Graav and drummer Roger "Phycon" Markström (**Maleficium, Leviathan**). They started out under the moniker **Volkermord**. The actual German word for genocide is völkermord, but according to A it was not supposed to mean genocide and was just to be seen as a word. **Armagedda** is the name of the Israeli valley where the Armageddon is said to take place. In 2001 bass player Patrik "Mord" Högberg (also in **Demented**) completed the line-up and they were featured on the split-tape In Blackest Ruin (2001 Deathcult/Carnal). A and Graav were the band's primary members and others have also been acting as sessions musicians, such as drummer Tore "Necromorbus" Stjärna (**Watain**), Erik Danielsson (**Watain, Dissection**) and Fabian "Winterheart" Völker. *The Final War Approaching* featured, A, Graav and Phycon, while *Strength…* saw the addition of Mord. On *Only True Believers* drums were handled by Hor. Quite primitive black metal with spoken growls in the vein of **Burzum** and **Mayhem**. Quite uneventful mangling songs. After *Ond spiritism* the band decided to pack it in with the following statement: *"As you all may know, Armagedda will not bring you any future experiences. We decided after the release of Ond Spiritism that it was for the best to put this phenomenon of ours to the past, we felt that we had achieved everything we needed and seen in our dreams. To continue would have been a move in the wrong direction. Graav has chosen another path in life and is forever gone. But as certain as the end came hand in hand with Ond Spiritism a birth and beginning of something else grew in shape. However, that's another story and it will speak for itself somewhere else"*. The track *Domedagens triumf* can be found on the

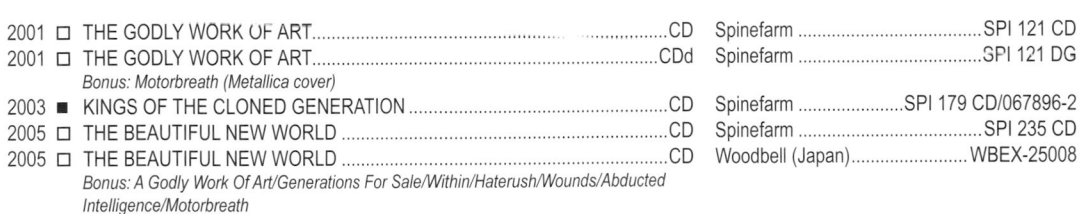

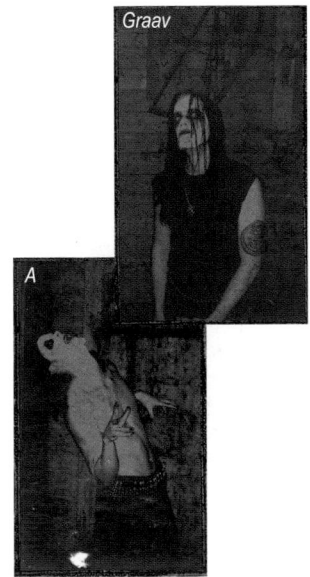
Graav

A

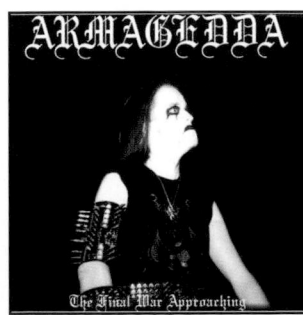
2001 LP - - -

2003 LP - FBP 022

Blut & Eisen compilation LP *Tormenting Legends* (2003). The track *Emperor From The Dark Eternal* is also found on the compilation 7" EP *Black Metal Endsieg III* (2002 Sombre). *Echoes Of Eternity* is a compilation of previously unreleased tracks, demos, EP tracks, live recordings and cover tracks. Due to an error, the first track is not *Armagedda*, but *Missfostret Tellus* by **Woods Of Infinity**. Pettersson is now handling vocals and guitar in the dark/avantgarde band **Whirling**. *Volkermord* is a collection of unreleased demos and rehearsal recordings. Most of the tracks are high speed, primitively recorded (in mono) old-school black metal. In 2010 the MCD *I Am* was released after the band's demise. It features recordings made in 2001-2002.

2008 CD - ARcd036

2001 ■	THE FINAL WAR APPROACHING	LP	Sombre	- -
	500 copies			
2001 □	THE FINAL WAR APPROACHING	CD	Breath Of Night/Mercilles	M.R.BON666CD
2001 □	Strength Through Torture	7"	Painiac Records	PAIN009
	Tracks: A World Full Of Lies/Dödens vind. 300 copies.			
2002 □	At The Edge Of Negative Existance (split)	7"g	Sombre	- -
	Split with Woods Of Infinity. Track: At The Edge Of Negative Existance. 666 copies.			
2002 □	Black Metal Endsieg III (split)	7"g	Sombre	- -
	Split with Secrets Of The Moon, Dark Storm, Bael. 666 copies. Track: Emperor From The Eternal Dark			
2003 ■	ONLY TRUE BELIEVERS	LP	From Beyond	FBP 022
	Bonus: Ghostwood (outro). 666 hand-numbered copies			
2003 □	ONLY TRUE BELIEVERS	LP PD	Agonia	Arplp002
	200 copies. Bonus: Night Of The Triumphator (Satyricon cover)/Ghostwood (outro)			
2003 □	ONLY TRUE BELIEVERS	CD	Agonia	ARCD006
	Bonus: Night Of The Triumphator			
2003 □	ONLY TRUE BELIEVERS	CD	Drakkar	DKCD 030
	Bonus: Night Of The Triumphator. 1000 copies.			
2004 □	ONLY TRUE BELIEVERS	CD	Agonia	ARCD006
	Second press. 1000 copies. Different back cover.			
2004 □	In Blackest Ruin	10" MLPg	Agonia	Armlp002
	Tracks: Intro (Fire Walk With Me)/Horde Of Demons/Whore Of God/Pain/Wrapped By Darkness/Satan My Master. Bonus: Only True Believers (rehearsal session 01)/Endless Fields Of Sorrow (rehearsal session 01). 500 copies			
2005 □	OND SPIRITISM	LPg	Agonia	ARlp010
	1000 copies, all smeared in blood.			
2005 □	OND SPIRITISM	LP PD	Agonia	ARplp012
	777 copies. Hand numbered. Poster.			
2005 □	OND SPIRITISM	CD	Agonia	ARcd015
2007 □	ECHOES OF ETERNITY	DLPg	Agonia	ARlp047
	500 copies.			
2007 □	ECHOES OF ETERNITY	CD	Agonia	Arcd047
2008 ■	THE FINAL WAR APPROACHING	CD	Agonia	ARcd036
	Re-mastered re-issue with new artwork.			
2010 □	THE FINAL WAR APPROACHING	LP	Inferna Profundus (Lithuania)	IPR018
	500 copies. First 50 with patch, first 200 with poster.			
2010 ■	I Am	MCDd 4tr	Nordvis	NVPTOS003
	Tracks: Den skrivna eskatologin/Den vanhelgade/I Am/Cold Eon			
2010 □	ONLY TRUE BELIEVERS	CDd	Agonia	Arcd006d
	Re-issue. Bonus: Ghostwood (outro)/Domedagens triumf/Night Of The Triumphator. Different artwork.			
2010 ■	VOLKERMORD – THE APPEARANCE	CD	Nordvis	NVP/TOS 001
2010 □	VOLKERMORD – THE APPEARANCE	CD	Blut & Eisen	Eisen 049
	226 marble vinyl + 266 white. hand numbered. Insert.			
2011 □	ONLY TRUE BELIEVERS	CD	Drakkar	DKCD 030
2011 □	ONLY TRUE BELIEVERS	LP	Drakkar	DKLP 011
2011 ■	I Am	MLP 4tr	Eisenwald Productions	Eisen 051
	100 copies in black vinyl, also available in red or white vinyl.			

2010 MCDd - NVPTOS 003

2010 CD - NVP/TOS 001

2011 MLP - Eisen 051

ARMAGEDDON

Christopher Amott: v/g, Tobias Gustafsson: b, Daniel Erlandsson: d

Halmstad - **Armageddon** has to be one of the most well-used band names of all times, starting in the UK in the 70s. Christopher is the younger brother of **Carcass/Spiritual Beggars**-guitarist Michael "Mike" Amott. Both he and Mike also played together in **Arch Enemy**. The line-up changed quite drastically between the albums. On the debut the band featured Christopher on guitar, singer Jonas Nyrén (**In Thy Dreams**), Martin Bengtsson (b) and Peter Wildoer (d) (**Darkane, Majestic, Arch Enemy** etc etc). On the second album the line-up had changed, with Dick Löwgren (**Last Tribe**) replacing Martin on bass, Daniel Erlandsson replacing Peter on drums and Rickard Bengtsson (**Last Tribe**) replacing Jonas on vocals. *Three* saw another change in the line-up, where Tobias Gustafsson (**The End, Croam, Revengia, Liers In Wait, Diabolique**) had replaced Löwgren on bass and singer Bengtsson was out with Amott himself now handling guitars and vocals. Chris also released the solo album *Follow Your Heart* in 2010, in a much softer vein. **Armageddon** are also featured on *Made In Tribute* (1997 Toy's Factory), where they do a cover of *Die With Your Boots On* and on *Mercyful Fate Tribute* (1997 Toy's Factory) where they do *Descecration Of Souls*.

1997 CD - TFCK-87103

2000 CD - TFCK-87234

Year		Title		Format	Label	Catalog
1997	☐	CROSSING THE RUBICON		CD	WAR	WAR 970304-1
1997	■	CROSSING THE RUBICON		CD	Toy's Factory (Japan)	TFCK-87103
2000	☐	EMBRACE THE MYSTERY		CD	Dream On (Korea)	PARK 9007
2000	■	EMBRACE THE MYSTERY		CD	Toy's Factory (Japan)	TFCK 87234

The first press also came with a slipcase.

2002	☐	THREE		CD	Toy's Factory (Japan)	TFCK-87286
2002	■	THREE		CD	Dream On (Korea)	PARK 9016
2003	☐	CROSSING THE RUBICON		CD	Toy's Factory (Japan)	TFCK-87286
2003	■	CROSSING THE RUBICON		CD	Dream On (Korea)	PARK 9027

Bonus: Die With Your Boots On (Iron Maiden cover)

| 2009 | ☐ | EMBRACE THE MYSTERY AND THREE | | 2CD | Century Media | 997966-2 |

Bonus: Worlds Apart (rehearsal)/The Broken Spel (rehearsal)/Die With Your Boots On/ Winter Skies (demo)/Sands Of Time (demo)/Descecration Of Souls (Mercyful Fate cover)

2002 CD - PARK 9016

ARMATUR
Johan Sterner: v, Peter Lindberg: g, Magnus Jakobsson: g, Håkan Hellgren: b, Leif Johansson: d

Kristinehamn - The A-side is straight rocking hard rock in the vein of *Ocean*, *Motvind*, *Dunder* or *Oxan*, while the B-side is heavy riff-oriented seventies hard rock. Mid-quality vocals with a punk-ish attitude. Three more songs were recorded but never released. Despite a strong local following, the band soon folded.

| 1980 | ■ | Rock 'N Roll/Mr X | 7" | Duvan | LJ 630920 |

500 copies.

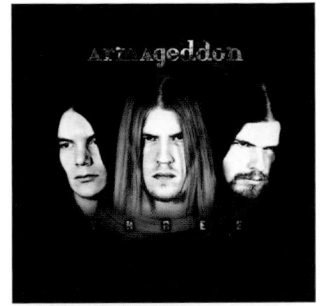

1980 7" - LJ 630920

ARMAUK
Jan Lindblom: v/g, Staffan: v/g, Per-Arne: b, Martin Stridh: d/g

Arbrå - Armauk means "enemy" in Orcish tongue. The first release was the 1998 demo *Where Life No Longer Is...*, printed in 100 copies. The CD also featured guest spots from keyboardists Johannes Thyr and Simon Jansson, and violinist Elin Hedlund. The CD was re-issued and remastered in 2004 as a self-released recording, however the band has no knowledge of its existance. Quite good, varied old-school-influenced death metal with progressive elements and desperate vocals. The band continued but with Martin and Staffan as the only remaining members.

| 1999 | ■ | RESURRECTED MEMORIES | CD | private | n/a |

1000 copies

1999 CD - n/a

ARROW
Mattias Höijer: v, Mats Ottosson: g, Mats Edström: g, Håkan Jardmo: b, Magnus Tallåker: d

Jönköping - Good melodic 80's hard rock/metal. This band is actually what later became the great AOR-band *Renegade*. On the first single Mattias handled both vocals and bass. Only three weeks before the MLP was recorded Håkan joined the band. Magnus switched his drums for a microphone and together with Håkan and Mats he formed *Renegade*. Mats has later recorded with his band *Shiva* and Tallåker has been found in *Hellspray* as lead singer on their first release. Both vinyls are well worth looking for. *Arrow* resurrected for a few shows in 2010. Håkan ran Zaragon Club in Jönköping for many years.

| 1988 | ■ | The Only Way/A Better Run | 7" | private | WSM 8401 | $$ |
| 1988 | ☐ | Diary Of A Soldier | MLP 4tr | private | ARF 001 | $ |

Tracks: Diary Of A Soldier/Straight To Your Heart/Tonight's The Night/Until The End Of Time.

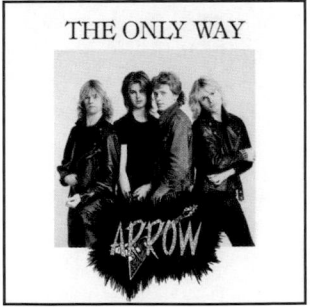

1988 7" - WSM 8401

ARROWS
Jonny Lindquist: v, Mikael Holmquist: g, Nicklas Lindquist: b, Patrik Andersson: d

Umeå - A quite amateurish metal band, showing the talent of a young Jonny Lindqvist, who later made several recordings with *Mogg*, *Jonny´s Bomb* and is now fronting metal band *Nocturnal Rites*. Although it's quite amateurish, it kind of feels like a diamond in the rough, so it's worth checking out.

| 1981 | ■ | Wounded In Love/I Want To Give You Rock `N` Roll | 7" | Studio 3L | S 3L-002 | $ |

ARROWZ
Per "Jeff Keegan" Lindstedt (aka Andersson): v/g, Ingvar Sylegård: b Hasse Gustavsson (now Gatu): d

Hässleholm - Another of the numerous Pang-singles. Although this is one of the better ones. Quite varied heavy metal in the vein of UK metal band *Trespass*, but not as classy. *Arrowz* also had the song *Backstreet Lady Sex Machine* on a New Renaissance Records compilation.

1981 7" - S 3L-002

61

The single is today a high priced item. The band drafted singer Zenny Hansson, now Zenny Gram (*Metal Muthaz, Spin Air*) and recorded three more demos. In 1984 Gustavsson relocated to Falun and the band folded. Zenny later joined *Faith*, *Destiny* and *Treasure Land*. Lindstedt took the stage name Jeff Keegan and formed the band *Keegan*.

1982 ■ Bird Of Steel/Help Me ....7" Pang ....PSI 051 $

1982 7" - PSI 051

ARSENITE
Tony Classon: v/g, Simon Hagberg: g, Martin Glaever: b, Richard Fredriksson: d

Kumla - Formed in 2009 and released their debut demo *High-Speed Thrashing Maniacs* in 2011. Tight, powerful and great melodic thrash similar to early *Megadeth* and *Metallica*, with a slight letdown in the "Swedish" vocals.

2012 ■ ASHES OF THE DECLINE ....CD Sliptrick Records SLP012.037

2012 CD - SLP012.037

ART METAL
Mattias "Ia" Eklundh: g, Jonas Hellborg: b, Jens Johansson: k, Salvaganesh: kanjeera, Anders Johansson: d

Härryda/Lund - Art Metal offers a highly interesting combination of sounds and styles. Anyone familiar with, and a fan of, guitar virtuoso Eklundh's other releases as solo artist or with *Freak Kitchen* will feel pretty much at home. Add the talent of bass virtuoso Hellborg (*Mahavishnu Orchestra, Alan Holdsworth, Ginger Baker, Shawn Lane*), keyboard virtuoso Jens Johansson (*Malmsteen, Johansson, Stratovarius*) and drummer Anders Johansson (*Malmsteen, Hammerfall, Johansson* etc). Anders, Jens and Jonas have also previously recorded together in various constellations such as *Shining Path*, *Jonas Hellborg Group* and the infamous filth metal band *Bakteria*. Mattias, Jonas and drummer Zoltan Czöcs have toured India several times as *Jonas Hellborg Group*. The style of this project, which is also shown by the presence of Indian artist Salvaganesh, who plays kanjeera, is however more drawn towards the Indian music culture and features a mix of heavy rock and Indian music in an intriguing mix. The band has also played several times in India. Eklundh by the way means "erect penis" in Hindi.

2007 ■ VYAKHYAN-KAR ....CDd Bardo ....Bardo 045

2007 CDd - Bardo 045

ART REBELLION
Erik Anell: v, Fredrik Lundstedt: g, Daniel Lundstedt: k, Mats Svensson: b, Hans Rasmusson: d

Göteborg - High-quality progressive hard rock influenced by the likes of *Dream Theater* and *Yes*. They are also featured on *The Lizzy Songs* (95 SMC) compilation, with the track *Angel Of Death*. SMC was also supposed to release the album *Descriptions* (SMC CD 2021-1) in 1996, which never happened, due to the label going bust.

1999 ■ EMBRACE THE FUTURE...CD Local Hero ....LHM 0568

As You Drown going down well

AS YOU DROWN
Henrik Blomqvist: v, Simon Exner: g, Mikael Åkerblom: g, Robert Karlsson: b, Martin Latvala: d

Borås - As You Drown was formed in 2003/2004 under the name *Etheral*, with an average age of only seventeen. The initial line-up featured singer/guitarist Mikael Åkerström, guitarist Simon Exner, drummer Martin Latvala and bassist Alexander Persson. Two demos were recorded between 2003-2005 and they supported bands like *Entombed*. In mid-2005 Mikael decided to step down from his vocal duties in order to focus on the guitar, and longtime friend Christopher Ranåsen was recruited as the new vocalist. During the same period Alexander left the band due to studies in Japan, and he was replaced by Robert Karlsson. They now recorded a new demo to send out to magazines, webzines and record labels, simply entitled *Demo 2007*. In early 2008 *Ethereal* was ready to record their debut album, and since the recording of the latest self-produced demo went beyond expectations, they came to the conclusion of building their own recording studio. They also announced the departure of vocalist Christopher due to commitment issues towards the band. In just four days over 20 auditions were mailed in, but the band already had their minds on ex-*Shadowbuilder* vocalist Henrik Blomqvist.

2009 CD - 3984-14735-2

With the line-up finally complete, the band decided it was time for a name change. And so *As You Drown* was born and ready to record its debut album which was mixed/mastered by Christian Silver (*The Crown, Sonic Syndicate, Impious*). *As You Drown* play death metal in the vein of *Behemoth* and *Cannibal Corpse* with an old-school touch.

2009 ■	REFLECTION	CD	Metal Blade	3984-14735-2	
2011 ■	RAT KING	CD	Metal Blade	3984-15050-2	

2011 CD - 3984-15050-2

ASHES

Jonas Magnusson: v/b, Andreas Sjöberg: g,
Robert "Mourning" Ivarsson: g, Mikael Wassholm: d

Finspång - Formed in 1996. *Ashes* produces black metal with a big dose of more traditional heavy metal. At times slightly reminiscent of *Ophthalamia*. Andreas is also found in *The Deadbeats* and *Plague Warhead*. Robert is also in *Ophthalamia, Facebreaker* and *Pan-Thy-Monium*, Jonas is also found in *Kill* and *Facebreaker*.

1997 □	DEATH HAS MADE IT'S CALL	CD	Necropolis	NR 015	
2001 ■	And The Angels Wept	MCD 6tr	Necropolis	NR 027	

Tracks: Betrayed/Son Of Mourning/Eternal Feelings/Nothing/And The Angels Wept/To The Bone

2001 MCD - NR 027

ASKA

Robban "Pisk" Wettersten: v/g/b/d

Kristianstad - *Aska* is the solo project of Robert Wettersten, started in 2003 when his previous band, *Demoriel*, split up. It was already back then all about making primitive sounding black metal, quite noise oriented and with simple monotonous songs. Some punk touches can also be found. A lot of the stuff was recorded direct into a digital portable recorder to avoid the material being polished and adjusted afterwards. Robert refers to *Aska* as anti-intellectual black metal, as opposed to the current wave of philosophical black metal bands. I will not disagree with this description. Very primitive old-school stuff.

2003 □	Förintelsehymner	MCD	Northern Sky Productions	--	

Tracks: Avsky/Blodshämnd/Livshat/En värld i förruttnelse/Utopisk tomhet

2005 □	THE PUREST COLD PRECISION (split)	CD	Eerie Art Productions	EAR 003	

Split with Blodulv. Tracks: Stank/Tortyr/Abort/C9H13N. 666 copies, first 100 with different artwork.

2006 □	Aska/Hypothermia (split)	7"	Unjoy	Unjoy 01	

Split with Hypothermia. Track:Abuse Myself (I Want To Die). 520 copies.

2007 ■	DÄR VANVETT GROR	CD	Total Holocaust Records	THR 108	

1000 copies.

2007 □	DÄR VANVETT GROR	LP	Unexploded	UER 014	

500 copies.

2007 CD - THR 108

ASOKA

Bo "Falsterbosse" Malmqvist: v, Tore Kjell: g, Kent "Tjobbe" Bengtsson: b,
Claes Ericsson: k, Alf "Daffy" Bengtsson: d

Malmö - A very interesting early 70's band in the progressive vein with some jazzy touches. They are quite reminiscent of *Trettioåriga Kriget*, but with a hint of early *Deep Purple*. The debut is filled with great Hammond organ/guitar interludes and interplays. The album is a very sought after item. The embryo of the band was formed in 1967 under the name *Taste Of Blues*. They recorded the album *Schizophrenia* in 1969. *Taste Of Blues* reformed into *Take Off* and with the addition of Tjobbe and Daffy they became *Asoka* in 1971. The band only lasted for one year. Claes and Robban later recorded two albums with jazz-rockers *Lotus*. In 2005 Mellotronen re-issued the album with some bonus material. This also lead to a band reunion. The re-united band featured original members Daffy, Tjobbe and Clas, with Patric Erixcon replaced by Falsterbosse and guitarist Robban Larsson replaced by Tore. A lot of songs were written by one of the members between 1979 and 1989, songs which fit well into the *Asoka* concept. These songs formed the basis of what became the *Asoka* return album *36 Years*, a great retro-oriented hard rocker with a strong touch of *Uriah Heep* and *Deep Purple*. The album *Asoka Plays Allan* is a slightly different album with *Asoka* paying tribute to the late Swedish actor Allan Edwall.

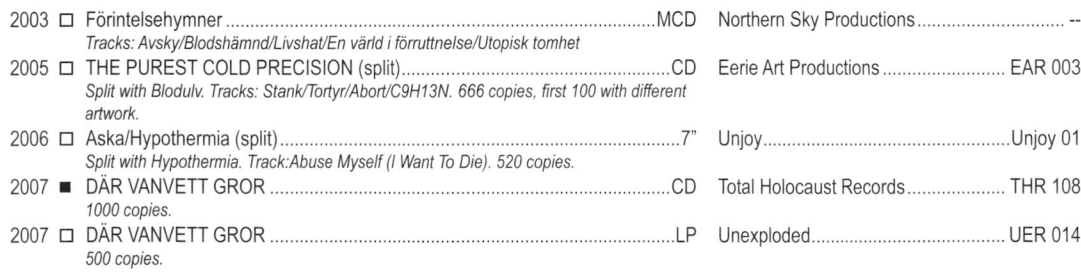
Asoka - 36 years ago?

1971 □	ASOKA	LP	Sonet	SLP-2527	$$
2005 □	ASOKA	CDd	Mellotronen	MELLOCD 019	

Bonus: The Seeker/At El Yago 9.3/Ohio

2007 ■	36 YEARS LATER	CDd	July Morning Records	JULY 001	
2009 □	ASOKA PLAYS ALLAN	CD	July Morning Records	JULY 002	

Unofficial release:

19?? □	ASOKA	LP	Ataxia (Italy)	7272	

This is a counterfeit, but the quality is very close to the original.

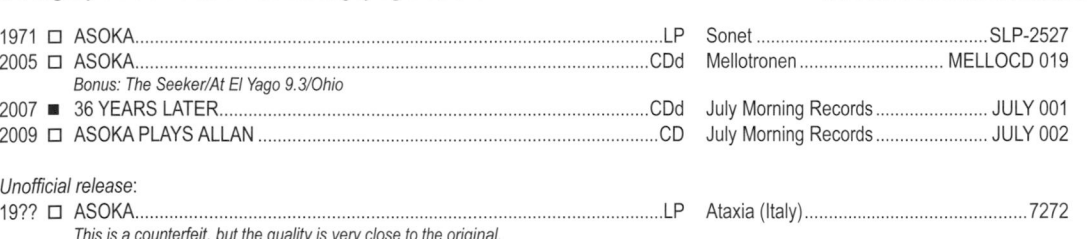

2007 CDd - JULY 001

ASPECTED

Johan "G" Sigurdsson: v, Erik Johansson: g, Joel Nevrup: b, Tony Heine: d

Kalmar - The band was formed around 1998. Quite quirky death metal with both growling and screaching vocals at the same time. Melodic passages mixed with quite technical and dissonant twists and turns. Actually a pretty intriguing musical mix. When Johan and Tony quit, the band split in 2000. Joel and Erik continued and changed name to *Two Years After*.

1998 ■ Aspected/Liquid Phase (split) ....7" EP   Take A Stand/No Appearance ....TAKE 006
Tracks: Fear/The Path Towards Nowhere/Worthless

1998 7" - TAKE 006

ASPERITY

Peter Kronberg: v/b, Johan Jahlonen: g, Petri Kuusisto: g/k, Stefan Westerberg: d

Sala - It all started when Stefan Westerberg (*Carnal Forge, In Thy Dreams, World Below*) and Petri Kuusisto (*Carnal Forge, In Thy Dreams, Soulskinner*) decided to leave *Steel Attack* to concentrate on their main band *Carnal Forge*. Stefan, who is originally a drummer, felt that he wanted to leave the job as the front man of *Steel Attack*. He however still wanted to do something different to *Carnal Forge*'s death/ thrash metal and still play the drums. Petri had the same type of feelings since he is originally a guitar player and not a keyboard player. After a year the two started talking about doing something together. The next day they met to work on some ideas. In the beginning the song writing was just for fun but as time went on, they felt this was something they really wanted to do. Months passed by and finally they had four songs ready to record. But they still had some problems to solve; first they had to find a good singer, bass player and another guitarist to complete the line up. They asked good friend Johan Jahlonen, who gladly accepted the offer since he had quit his former band and only played his own instrumental material. They still had to find a singer and bass player to complete the band. After a few weeks they found a two-in-one, Peter Kronberg (ex-*Section Eight*, solo). They recorded a demo and were soon signed by Arise Records. *Asperity* play outstanding melodic semi-progressive power metal with great musicianship, killer songs and a grade A singer in Peter. If you're into bands like early *Queensryche* or *Fifth Angel* don't miss this gem.

An aspiring bunch of lads

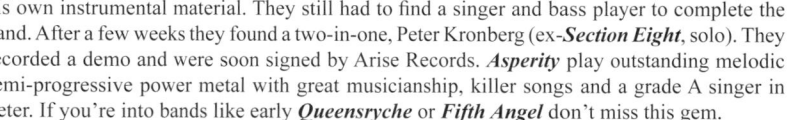
2004 CD - ARISE 053

2004 ☐ THE FINAL DEMAND ....CD   King Records (Japan) KICP-990
2004 ■ THE FINAL DEMAND ....CD   Arise..ARISE 053
2004 ☐ THE FINAL DEMAND ....CD   CD-Maximum (Russia) .... CDM 0404-1792

ASSAILANT

Peder Sundqvist: v, Oskar Norberg: g, Markus Sundbom: g,
Peder Sandström: k, Joakim Jonsson: b, Patrik Larsson: d

Umeå - *Assailant* was formed in 2004 when Oskar Norberg (younger brother of Nils of *Nocturnal Rites* and Emil of *Persuader/Savage Circus*) and Joakim Jonsson were the last men standing in their former band *Ecliptica*. They recruited singer Sundqvist, whose audition for the band meant writing lyrics and recording vocals for the song *Lies*, on the spot, in the studio. They also soon found Larsson, Sundbom (brother of Daniel in *Persuader*) and Sandström to complete the band. In 2005 they recorded the demo *Metal State* which lead to a deal with German label Dockyard 1 and early 2006 their debut was released. *Assailant* play slightly progressive melodic metal with a touch of melodic death, but with clean vocals. Strong song material and a great sound makes this a band well worth checking out. Sundqvist and Sundblom are ex-*Dead Street Journal*. Sundqvist has also been a member of *Lesra*. A third album is in the making. In 2009 Peder Sandström left the band and two years later they started recording new material and an excellent four track pre-production demo was recorded. 2012 will hopefully see a new album from the band.
Website: www.assailant.se

Wakey, wakey!!

2006 CD - DY 10019-2

2008 CD - DY 10055-5

2006 ■ NEMESIS WITHIN ....CD   Dockyard 1....................................DY 10019-2
2008 ■ WICKED DREAM ....CD   Dockyard 1....................................DY 10055-2
2008 ☐ WICKED DREAM ....CD   Soyus (Russia) ....DY 10055-2

ASSAULT

Martin Hellström: v, Johan Johnsson: g, Arthur Börjesson: g,
Hannes Rognås: b, Marcus Rosell: d

Strömstad - Started by Johan and Arthur in 2007, reinforced with Matin in 2009 and in 2010 they were a full band. Thrash with a touch of death metal, lots of blast beats and aggro vocals. Arthur is also in death metal band *When Hope Falls*.

2011 ■ CLOSER TO ETERNAL LIFE ....CD   Big Balls..BBR 1101

2011 CD - BBR 1101

ASTEROID

Robin Hirse: v/g/k, Johannes Nilsson: v/b, Elvis "47" Campbell: d

Örebro - **Asteroid** is one of Sweden's numerous stoner bands. However, they may be one of many, but they are actually quite diverse in their sound and style. **Asteroid** sounds quite influenced by early **Black Sabbath** and the guitar/Hammond interplay at times reminds me of German band **Night Sun**. The vocals are also slightly different, quite often with octave enhancement giving it a nice touch. They are also quite varied and dynamic in their songs which make the whole thing more interesting. On the second album the caretaker of the drumstool had been changed from Martin Ström to Elvis. Bass player Johannes is brother of Joakim Nilsson of **Graveyard**. Elvis is also found in **The Group Delisuion**.
Website: www.asteroid.se

2006 CD - FUZZCD 006

2006	■	ASTEROID	CD	Fuzzorama	FUZZCD 006
2007	■	ASTEROID + BLOWBACK (split)	CD	Fuzzorama	FUZZCD 005

Split with Blowback. Tracks: Sim-Sala-Bim/Anagram/Supernova/Hexagon/Walk Alone/The Big Trip Beyond

2010	☐	II	CD	Fuzzorama	FUZZCD 012

2007 CD - FUZZCD 005

ASTRAL DOORS

Nils Patrik Johansson: v, Joacim Nordlund: g/k/b, Jocke Roberg: k, Ulf Lagerström: b, Johan Lindstedt: d

Borlänge - It all started in the early 90s in the Rock House in Borlänge, a place where bands rehearse and musicians meet. Patrik was singing with the band **Staircase**, while Joachim was singing and playing guitar in progressive band **Erina**, a band were Jocke Roberg also resided. Patrik tried to draft drummer Johan Lindstedt, but he had just gotten a break with rap metal band **Buckshot O.D** and was not interested. It wasn't until 1998 things started happening when Johan and Patrik (then in **Purple** cover band **In Rock**) teamed up in the metal band **Barfly**, who recorded the outstanding demo CD-R *Slough* in 1998. The demo was engineered by Joachim Nordlund and soon Johan and Joachim decided to write some songs in the old **Purple** tradition. The band was born and the name taken from the song *Far Beyond The Astral Doors*. Now Martin Haglund (**Enslavement, Coffinman, Earflog, Pound**) was added to the line-up. Lokomotive Records signed the band and the debut *Of The Son And The Father* (entitled *Cloudbreaker* in Japan, because they didn't approve of the cover artwork) was recorded and mixed by Peter Tägtgren. The band has toured with acts like **Blind Guardian, Grave Digger** etc. Patrik is also found in **Lion's Share, Wuthering Heights** and **Space Odyssey**. **Astral Doors** sure have quite a few classic **Rainbow/Purple** overtones, especially since Patrik sounds like Ronnie James Dio's long lost brother, actually quite different from his days in **Barfly**. Before *Requiem Of Time* bass player Mika Itäranta (ex-**Pound**) was replaced by Ulf Lagerström. *Testament of Rock* is a compilation. The exclusive track *Fill Your Head With Rock* is found on the *Sweden Rock Festival 2008* compilation. The 2009 single *Hyllning till Leksand* is a celebration song for the local hockey team Leksand's 90th anniversary. *Jerusalem* was mixed by Daniel Bergstrand and Rickard Sporrong. In 2011 Metalville re-issued all the **Astral Doors** CDs as digi packs. In 2012 Patrik joined the former **Sabaton** members in the band **Civil War**.
Website: www.astraldoors.com

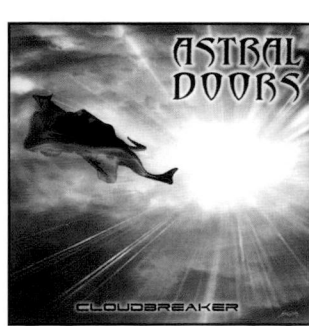

Stairway to Astral Doors.

2003	■	CLOUDBREAKER	CD	King Records (Japan)	KICP-974

Bonus: From Beyond The Astral Door/Moon Struck Woman

2003	☐	OF THE SON AND THE FATHER	CD	Locomotive Music	LM 137
2003	☐	OF THE SON AND THE FATHER	CD	Locomotive Music America (USA)	LM 137
2003	☐	OF THE SON AND THE FATHER	CD	Hellion (South America)	HEL 0405
2005	■	EVIL IS FOREVER	CD	Locomotive Music	LM 199
2005	☐	EVIL IS FOREVER	CD	Locomotive Music America	LM 199
2005	☐	EVIL IS FOREVER	CD	Hellion (South America)	HEL 0405
2005	☐	EVIL IS FOREVER	CD	King Records (Japan)	KICP-1051

Bonus: Another Day In Hell

2005	☐	Raiders Of The Ark	MCD 6tr	Locomotive Music	LM 221

Tracks: Raiders Of The Ark/Easy Rider/Far Beyond The Astral Doors/Another Day In Hell/ Moonstruck Woman/Time To Rock (video)

2005	☐	Raiders Of The Ark	MCD 6tr	Locomotive Music America (USA)	LM 221
2005	☐	Raiders Of The Ark	MCD 6tr	Hellion (South America)	n/a
2006	☐	ASTRALISM	CD	King Records (Japan)	KICP-1128

Bonus: The Astral Friar/Easy Rider

2006	☐	ASTRALISM	CD	Locomotive Music	LM 155
2006	☐	ASTRALISM	CDd	Locomotive Music	LM 290

Bonus: 21st Century Medieval

2006	☐	ASTRALISM	LP	Locomotive Music	LM 467
2007	☐	NEW REVELATION	CDd	Locomotive Music	LM 500
2007	☐	NEW REVELATION	CDd	Locomotive Music America (USA)	LM 500
2007	☐	NEW REVELATION	CD	Locomotive Music America (USA)	LM 527
2007	☐	NEW REVELATION	CD	King Records (Japan)	KICP-1269

Bonus: Lament Of The East/21st Century medieval

2003 CD - KICP-974

2005 CD - LM 199

2009 ☐	Hyllning till Leksand/Hyllning till Leksand (Karaoke version)	CDS	private	- -
2010 ☐	REQUIEM OF TIME	CD	Metalville	MTLV71566.2
2010 ☐	REQUIEM OF TIME	CDd	Metalville	MV003
2010 ☐	REQUIEM OF TIME	CD	Intergroove	MV00032
2010 ☐	REQUIEM OF TIME	CD	King Records (Japan)	KICP-1457
2010 ☐	TESTAMENT OF ROCK	CDd	Metalville	MV0092
2011 ☐	JERUSALEM	CDd	Metalville	MV0022
2011 ☐	JERUSALEM	CDd	Metalville	MV0022
2011 ☐	JERUSALEM *White vinyl.*	LP	Metalville	MV0022V1
2011 ☐	EVIL IS FOREVER	CDd	Metalville	MV0023
2011 ■	OF THE SON AND THE FATHER	CDd	Metalville	MV0028
2011 ☐	ASTRALISM	CDd	Metalville	MV0030

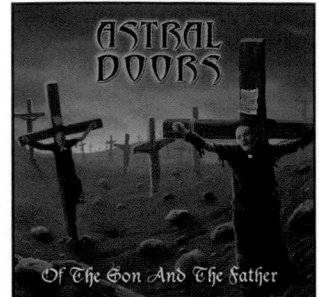
2011 CD - MV0028

ASTROPHOBOS

Mikael Broman: v/b, Martin Andersson: g, Jonas Ehlin: g

Stockholm - Melodic black metal in the vein of **Dissection** and **Necrophobic**. The band was formed in 2009, influenced by the Norwegian and Swedish death metal scene of the nineties. David Schelin-Andersen handled the drums on the album. The debut album *Remnants Of Forgotten Heroes* is due late 2013 on Abyss Records.
Website: www.astrophobos.com

2011 ■	Arcane Secrets	MCD 3tr	private	ASTRO 001
	Tracks: Divine Necromancy/Arcane Secrets/Crossing The Abyss. 500 copies.			

2006 CD - MIMO-012

ASTROQUEEN

Daniel Änghede: v/g, Daniel Tolegård: g, Mattias Wester: b, Johan Backman: d

Stenungsund - **Astroqueen** was formed in 1995-96 and they started out just jamming. It wasn't until 1997-98 they came up with the name and started getting some songs down and recorded their first demo. In 1999 they recorded the second demo *Themes From The Magic Ocean*. They were influenced by bands like **Kyuss** and **Black Sabbath**, but never saw themselves as a stoner band. Heavy stoner-oriented hard rock with a fat sound and a garagy touch. Pretty fuzzed out guitars at times, but still heavy and powerful. The track *Dragon Boozeiac* can also be found on *Molten Universe Volume One* (99 Molten Universe). The album was produced by Andy LaRocque.
Website: www.stonerrock.com/astroqueen

2001 CD - 76962-32382-2

1999 ☐	Rufus The Space Agent/Asteroid Blaster Part 1 *Red vinyl*	7"	Monster Zero	MZR 002
2001 ■	INTO SUBMISSION	CD	Pavement	76962-32382-2
2004 ■	ASTROQUEEN VS. BUFFALO (split)	CD	Dias De Garage	DIASCD 004
	Split with Buffalo. Tracks: Crashlander/Lava/The Untitled/The Shades Of John Doe/Chess Of Confusion/Fanstyg			

2004 CD - DIASCD 004

AT THE GATES

Tomas "Tompa" Lindberg: v, Martin Larsson: g, Anders Björler: g
Jonas Björler: b, Adrian Erlandsson: d

Göteborg/Billdal - This death metal band started out under the moniker **Grotesque** and released one album under that name. Alf, Tomas and Kristian went on to form **Liers In Wait**. Kristian left and the others formed **At The Gates** in the fall of 1990. On the debut the members were Tomas, Anders, Jonas, Adrian and guitarist Alf Svensson with the addition of violinist Jesper Jarold. On *With Fear...* Jesper was not in the band and just before the release, Alf (later in **Oxiplegatz**) left and was replaced by Martin. In 1995 they were signed by Earache. The hidden track on *With Fear...* is a cover of **Discharged's** *The Nightmare Continues*. Tomas also sings the song *Snotrocket* on Black Sun's **Metallica**-tribute *Metal Militia*. As Peaceville was bought by MFN, the old albums have been re-issued on that label. **At The Gates** play very heavy and guitar-dominated death metal with a sound quite reminiscent of **Slayer** and early **Entombed**. Lots of musical variations with the odd acoustic guitar and even keyboards. High musical quality and the compulsory growl/screeching vocals. Tompa is also found in **Skitsystem** and **The Great Deceiver**. In 1996 after having toured the US with **Napalm Death** and **Morbid Angel**, Anders decided to leave and the band consequently folded. Two new bands rose from the ashes. Tomas is now found in hardcore band **Hide** and has also played with **World Without End**. He is also involved with English band **Lock Up**. The Björler brothers and Erlandsson later formed **The Haunted**. **At The Gates** reformed in 2008 for some shows, which has since continued also resulting in some re-issues.
Website: www.atthegates.se

At The Gates at the gates

Year		Title	Format	Label	Catalog	
1991	■	Gardens Of Grief	MLP 4tr	Dolores Records	DOL005	

Tracks: Souls Of The Evil Departed/At The Gates/All Life Ends/City Of Screaming Statues

1992	☐	THE RED IN THE SKY IS OURS	LP	Deaf Records	DEAF 10	
1992	☐	THE RED IN THE SKY IS OURS	CD	Deaf Records	DEAF 10 CD	
1992	☐	THE RED IN THE SKY IS OURS	CD	Grind Core International	89810-2	
1993	☐	WITH FEAR I KISS THE BURNING DARKNESS	LP	Deaf Records	DEAF 14	
1993	■	WITH FEAR I KISS THE BURNING DARKNESS	CD	Deaf Records	DEAF 14CD	
1994	☐	TERMINAL SPIRIT DECEASE	LP	Peaceville	VILE 47	

Six tracks are studio recordings and three were recorded live at Magasinet, Göteborg.

1994	☐	TERMINAL SPIRIT DECEASE	CD	Peaceville	VILE 47 CD	
1994	☐	TERMINAL SPIRIT DECEASE	CD	Futurist (USA)	11061-2	
1995	☐	Gardens Of Grief	MCD 4tr	Black Sun Records	BS04	
1995	☐	Gardens Of Grief	7"	Peaceville	CC7	

Tracks: Souls Of The Evil Departed/All Life Ends. Ltd ed clear vinyl.

1995	■	SLAUGHTER OF THE SOUL	CD	Earache (promo)	MOSH 143CDPRO	
1995	☐	SLAUGHTER OF THE SOUL	CD	Earache	MOSH 143 CD	
1995	☐	SLAUGHTER OF THE SOUL	LP	Earache	MOSH 143 LP	$$

500 copies.

| 1995 | ☐ | SLAUGHTER OF THE SOUL | CD | Toy's Factory (Jap) | TFCK 88754 | |

Bonus: The Flames Of The End

| 1995 | ☐ | THE RED/WITH FEAR | 2CD | Peaceville | CDVILE 59 | |

A double CD for single price. Contains The Red Sky Is Ours and With Fear I Kiss The Burning Darkness.

| 1995 | ☐ | SLAUGHTER OF THE SOUL | CD | Earache | MOSH 143 CD | |
| 1996 | ☐ | CURSED TO TOUR (split) | CD | Earache | MOSH 14-3CD | |

Split with Napalm Death. Tracks: Slaughter Of The Soul/World Of Lies/Legion/The Dying. Free CD tour sampler.

| 1996 | ☐ | THE RED IN THE SKY IS OURS | CD | Pony Canyon (Japan) | PCCY-00966 | |

Bonus: All Life Ends (live)/Kingdom Gone (live)

| 2001 | ☐ | AT THE GATES/GROTESQUE (split) | CD | Century Media | 8040-2 | |

Split with Grotesque. Tracks: Souls Of The Evil Departed/At The Gates/All Life Ends/City Of Screaming Statues

| 2001 | ☐ | SUICIDAL FINAL ART | CDd | Earache | CDVILE 86 | |
| 2001 | ☐ | TERMINAL SPIRIT DECEASE | CD | Peaceville | CDVILEM 47 | |

Reissue with new package. Bonus: The Burning Darkness (live)/Kingdom Gone (live)

| 2001 | ☐ | TERMINAL SPIRIT DECEASE | CD | Soyus (Russia) | CDVILEM 47 | |
| 2001 | ☐ | THE RED IN THE SKY IS OURS | CD | Peaceville | CDVILEM 96 | |

Released both as normal jewel box and Super jewel box.

| 2001 | ☐ | THE RED IN THE SKY IS OURS | CD | Soyus (Russia) | CDVILEM 96 | |
| 2001 | ☐ | WITH FEAR I KISS THE BURNING DARKNESS | CDd | Peaceville | CDVILEM 97 | |

Bonus: Neverwhere (live)/Beyond Good And Evil (live)/The Architects. New artwork. Also released in jewel case.

| 2001 | ☐ | WITH FEAR I KISS THE BURNING DARKNESS | CD | Soyus (Russia) | CDVILEM 97 | |
| 2002 | ☐ | SUICIDAL FINAL ART | CD | Soyus (Russia) | CDVILE 86 | |

Bonus videos: Terminal Spirit Disease/The Burning Darkness

| 2002 | ☐ | SLAUGHTER OF THE SOUL | CD | Earache | MOSHCDX 143 | |

Reissue in new artwork. Bonus: Legion (Slaughterlord cover)/The Dying/Captor Of Sin (Slayer cover)/Unto The Others (demo)/Suicide Nation (demo)/Bister verklighet (No Security cover). Slipcase.

2002	☐	SLAUGHTER OF THE SOUL	CD/DVD dual	Earache	MOSH143CDD	
2002	☐	SLAUGHTER OF THE SOUL	CD	Soyus (Russia)	MOSH 143 CD	
2002	☐	SLAUGHTER OF THE SOUL	LP	Earache	MOSH 143	

Black or orange vinyl.

| 2003 | ☐ | THE RED IN THE SKY IS OURS | CDd | Peaceville | CDVILED 96 | |

Bonus: All Life Ends (live)/Kingdom Gone (live)/Ever-Opening Flower (demo). New artwork.

| 2003 | ☐ | WITH FEAR I KISS THE BURNING DARKNESS | CDd | Peaceville | CDVILED 97 | |

Bonus: Beyond Good And Evil (live)/The Architects (demo). New artwork.

| 2003 | ■ | TERMINAL SPIRIT DECEASE | CDd | Peaceville | CDVILED 47 | |

Bonus: The Burning Darkness (live)/Kingdom Gone (live). New artwork.

| 2004 | ☐ | Gardens Of Grief | MCD 4tr | Blackend | BLACK 087 CD | |
| 2006 | ☐ | SLAUGHTER OF THE SOUL | LP PD | Earache | MOSH 143 PD | $$ |

1500 copies. Bonus same as MOSHCDX 143.

| 2008 | ☐ | SLAUGHTER OF THE SOUL | CD+DVD | Earache | MOSH143CDV | |

Bonus DVD with "the making of", deleted scenes and videos. New artwork.

2008	☐	SLAUGHTER OF THE SOUL	CD+DVD	Earache USA)	MOSH1433	
2009	☐	Gardens Of Grief	MCD 4tr	Candlelight	CANDLE 267 CD	
2010	☐	THE RED IN THE SKY IS OURS	CD	Icarus (Argentina)	ICARUS 953	
2010	■	WITH FEAR I KISS THE BURNING DARKNESS	CD+DVD	Peaceville	CDVILEDD 259X	

Bonus: Neverwhere (live)/Beyond Good And Evil (live)/The Architects (demo) + DVD Live In Groningen. Super jewel case with new artwork.

| 2010 | ☐ | PURGATORY UNLEASHED – LIVE AT WACKEN | 2LP | Earache | MOSH 386 LP | |

Poster. 100 black/green, 200 yellow, 300 light blue, 1400 black.

| 2010 | ☐ | PURGATORY UNLEASHED – LIVE AT WACKEN | CD | Earache | MOSH 386 CDL | |

Contains patch and guitar pick.

| 2010 | ☐ | PURGATORY UNLEASHED: LIVE AT WACKEN | CD | Earache | MOSH 386 CDL | |

Woven patch + guitar pick.

1991 MLP - DOL 005

1993 CD - DEAF 14CD

1995 CD - MOSH 143CDPRO

2003 CDd - CDVILED 47

2010 CD+DVD - CDVILEDD 259X

2010 ☐	PURGATORY UNLEASHED: LIVE AT WACKEN 2LPg	Earache ....MOSH 386 LP
	100 green/black, 200 orange, 300 blue and 1400 in black vinyl.	
2011 ■	SLAUGHTER OF THE SOUL-PURGATORY UNLEASHED: LIVE..............2CD	Earache ....MOSH 386 CDT
	Slipcase with different artwork. Bonus: Legion (Slaughterlord cover)/Captor Of Sin (Slayer	
	cover)/Unto Others (demo)/Suicide Nation (demo)/Bister verklihet (No Security cover).	
2011 ☐	ULTIMATE COLLECTORS BOX...........................CD+2LPg+3DVD box	Earache ....MOSHPACK 143 BOX $$
	Purgatory Unleashed on CD, flame coloured vinyl and DVD. T-shirt, belt buckle, key ring,	
	poster, guitar pick, sew on patch, signed certificate. 300 copies.	
2011 ☐	Gardens Of Grief... MLP 4tr	Century Media 998072-1
	500 black, 100 transparent, 100 brown, 100 green, 100 gold/black marbled vinyl.	

2011 2CD - MOSH 386 CDT

Unofficial releases:

| 1996 ☐ | LIVE IN CLEVELAND OHIO 1996 ....LP | - - .... - - |
| | *Purple vinyl. Re-issued in 2001, 501 copies on dark red vinyl.* | |

ATLANTIC TIDE

Ulf Torkelsson: v, Fredrik "Eugene" Lindgren: g, Izmo Hedlund: b, Fredrik Jansson: d

Stockholm - Atlantic Tide was formed by former *Terra Firma/Unleashed/Loud Pipes* guitarist Fredrik in 2008. He brought in old friend, and former *Terra Firma* drummer Izmo, now on bass and *Hetsheads/Blackshine* guitarist Joakim Stabel. The band was christened by *Terra Firma/ Count Raven* singer Christian "Lord Chritus" Lindersson. *Atlantic Tide* feels musically like a natural continuation of *Terra Firma*, going back even more to the early 70s sound and style. Heavy, slightly psychedelic vintage hard rock. Great stuff! Fredrik programmed the drums on the first single, which was a little bit lacking in the vocal department. The last two singles saw a new line-up featuring Fredrik, Izmo, singer Ulf (*Abramis Brama*) and drummer Jansson (*Abramis Brama, Count Raven*). The band's logo was made by Erik Danielsson (*Watain*).

2009 7" - HHR 086

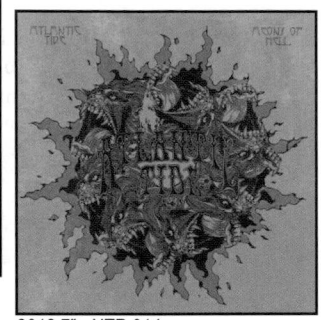

2013 7" - NTR 014

2009 ■	Bad Acid Queen/Eyestroids ....7"	High Roller ....HHR 086
	150 green + 350 black vinyl. Small poster.	
2013 ■	Aeons Of Hell/Way Of Living...7"	Night Tripper Records.......................NTR 014
	100 coloured vinyl including patch, 400 copies black vinyl.	
2013 ☐	Psychic Vampire/Massacre ....7"	Freedom Records ....n/a
	500 copies.	

ATLANTIS

Fredrik Glimbrand: g/v, Roger Averdahl: b, Patrik Sviberg: d

Stockholm - A really promising band that only produced one single. The style is melodic traditional hard rock with hints of Canadian seventies hard rockers *Teaze*. Well-produced and well played. Recommended. Roger is cousin of Patrik in *MOB*. Sviberg later turned up in *Raceway* and Glimbrand in *Mercury Fang* and now *Misth*.

| 1990 ■ | High On Music/Let's Go To My Place..7" | private ....F.I.S. 2112 |

1990 7" - F.I.S 2112

ATROX

Tobbe Johansson: v/g, Johan Larsson: g, Pelle Nilsson: g
Stephan Hermansson: b, Joakim "Isti" Loften: d

Västervik/Gunnebo - Formed in 1990. A thrash band with three guitarists very close to *Metallica* in the *Kill 'Em All*-era, both musically, soundwise and in the vocal department. Not bad at all. The band has since the release of the 7" recorded two demos, *Plague Of The Nature* (1993) and *Lack Of Respect* (1994) and changed line-up. The members were then: Stephan and Isti, singer Nicke Erikson plus guitarists Johan Gardestedt and Johan Dahlström. The sound also became heavier and more updated.

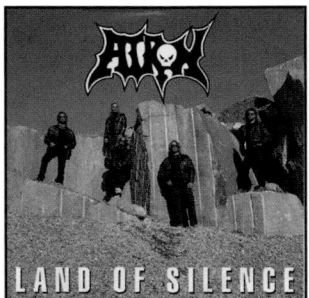

| 1992 ■ | Land Of Silence/The Oldest Wisdom..7" | PLC ....PLC 9201-02 |

1992 7" - PLC 9201-02

ATTACK

Anne-Mi "Rosa" Körberg: v, Björn Uhr: g, Claes "Fille" Lindström: b, Åke Eriksson: d

Stockholm - Attack, formed in 1980, plays very commercial hard rock sung in Swedish, actually quite similar to today's *Wig Wam* and *The Poodles*. The real strength of the band is Björn's phenomenal and brutally heavy guitars, and Åke's drumming, which is what saves the band. Not bad actually. Björn Uhr is ex-*Solid Ground/Tempelrock*. Original bass player Peter "P-J" Jägerhult recorded one album with *Trash* and was also in *Tempelrock*, while Åke Eriksson has beaten the skins with *Wasa Express, Bedlam* and several other acts. The band's hit *Ooa hela natten* is also available in an English version. Bassist Claes "Fille" Lindström replaced Peter "PJ" Jägerhult in 1982 and was later backing guitarist Benny Jansson. The title *Full Fart*... actually means Full speed... if you thought otherwise! After the band split Rosa and Björn made their own solo-singles on CBS, but both were uninteresting popsters. The band reformed in 1992 for a nostalgia tour and have also rerecorded some tracks for a compilation-CD on Dino Records.

1980 7" - SOS 1035

1980 LP - SOSLP-022

| 1980 ■ | Du får inte komma ikväll/Vill du ha, kom å ta ....7" | SOS ....SOS 1035 |

1980	■	VAMPYR ROCK	LP	SOS	SOSLP-022
1981	□	Kompaktmannen/Jag vill inte ner i källaren.	7"	CBS	1280
1981	□	Ooa hela natten/Kom fram	7"	CBS	1281
1981	□	RÄTT STUK	LP	CBS	85447
1982	■	Transnochando/Adelate	7"	Epic (Spain)	EPC A 1281

Spanish version of Ooa hela natten, but with Swedish lyrics.

1982	□	Tokyo/Tung Metall	7"	Epic	A 2163
1982	□	Ooin' In The Moonlight/Ooin.. (instrumental)	7"	Epic	A 2164
1982	□	Ooin' In The Moonlight/Ooin... (instrumental)	7"	Towerbell (UK)	TOW 23

Remixed by Tom Newman.

1982	□	Dag och natt/Grönt ljus	7"	Epic	A 2773
1982	□	FULL FART FRAMÅT	LP	Epic	EPC 25166
1982	□	Helt rätt/Dr Kildahr	7"	Epic	A 2975

1982 7" - EPC A 1281

ATTENTION

Björn Eriksson: v, Robert Mis: g, Peter Edwinzon: g, Martin Jensen: k, Philip Monell: b, Michael Bohlin: d

Finspång/Stockholm - Not to be confused with the Christian namesakes. The style is average-rate melodic 80s hard rock. The band was after the single decimated to two members, Philip and Michael (both on synth), and the style changed to more pop/ballad and instrumental music. They also recorded the albums *The Visual Symphony* ('93) and *Fairytales* ('95). Peter was later found in symphonic rockers *Unicorn* as well as in US-indie style band *Subway Mirror*. Michael has recorded two CDs with industrial goth/black metal band *8th Sin* and guests with *Vondur*.

| 1988 | ■ | Is This You/The Bird | 7" | Platina | PL33 |

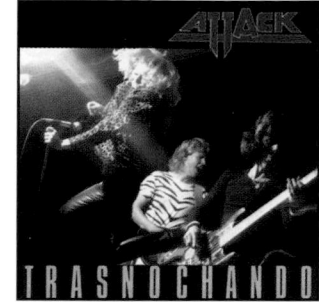

1988 7" - PL33

ATTENTION

Robert Johansson: v/d, Jon Peterson: g, Richard Eriksson: k, Fredrik Lundberg: b

Nässjö - A Christian band with a mixed musical direction. The debut has some tracks that are bluesy hard rock, some ballads and some straight hard rock. Good quality, though. On the album they have however softened and they do not qualify as hard rock. Keyboard-player Richard joined on *Please* and on *Mercystreet* drummer Tobias Fransson was out of the band and Robert handled that duty as well. Not to be confused with the band that released the single *Is This You*.

| 1997 | ■ | What Goes Up Must Come Down | MCD 5tr | Stefo Inter | KCJ 9409181-2 |

Tracks: Puzzle/Always Explain/I'm Alright/Jesus Is Groovy/Love Is A Person

| 1998 | □ | PLEASE | CD | Feedback | FBRCD 301 |
| 1999 | □ | MERCYSTREET | CD | Feedback | FBRCD 307 |

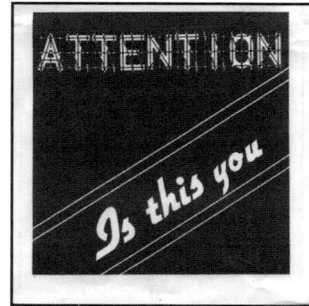

1997 MCD - KCJ 9409181-2

AUBERON

Fredrik Degerström: v, Andreas Johansson: g, Jonathan Holmgren: g, Morgan Lie: d

Umeå - The band was formed in 1988, as *Oberon*, playing thrash in the vein of *Metallica*. In 1993 they released their first demo *Follow The Blind* and two years later the second demo, *Insane* was unearthed, and lead to a deal with Black Mark. They changed their name to *Auberon* in 1997. Musically this band lies in the grey zone between power metal and death metal, like the missing link between *Hammerfall* and *Dissection*, with the vocals taken from the death metal genre and the melodic guitars from the power metal bag. The clean vocals are provided by Andreas Stoltz (*Hollow*), who is more or less a "hidden" member of the band. On the debut the line-up featured guitarists Johan Asplund and Johan Westerlund (*Mishrak*), who were both replaced before the second album. Their replacements were Jonathan Holmgren (*Amsvartner, Invader*) and Andreas Johansson (*Fatal Embrace, Sundown*). Bass player Pekka "Power" Kivi-aho (*Persuader, One Man Army*) never played on the album, and the bass-work was handled by Morgan and Fredrik. After the second album guitarists Christer Bergqvist (*Grief Of Emerald, Sadistic Grimness*) was also in the band. Fredrik has also been found in *Bewitched* and *Guillotine*. The title of the second album was misprinted and reads *Grossworld*. The band recorded the demo *Scum Of The Earth* in 2004. The last known line-up featured Fredrik, Jonathan and drummer Ibrahim Stråhlman (*Desultor*).

1998	■	THE TALE OF BLACK	CD	Black Mark	BMCD 103
2001	■	CROSSWORLD	CD	Black Mark	BMCD 145
2001	□	CROSSWORLD	CD	Irond (Russia)	01-52

1998 CD - BMCD 103

2001 CD - BMCD 145

AUDIOVISION

Christian Liljegren (aka Rivel): v, Torbjörn Weinesjö: g, Simeon Liljegren: b, Olov Andersson: k, Thomas Weinesjö: g

Stockholm - *Audiovision* is the side project intitiated by then *Narnia* singer Christian Liljegren (aka Rivel) and *Lion's Share/Road II Ruin* guitarist Lars "Chriss" Christmansson. The list of guests on the album is like a who-is-who of Swedish hard rock including singers Mats Leven, Thomas Vikström, Jeff Scott Soto, Hubertus Liljegren, guitarists Mattias Ia Eklundh, Carl

2005 CD - RRCD 019

69

Johan Grimmark, Janne Stark, Tommy Denander, keyboardists Mic Michaeli, Sampo Axelsson, Jörgen Schelander and Linus Kåse. The line-up on the first album ain't half bad either. Christian has been seen fronting bands like **Modest Attraction, Borderline, Flagship, Divinefire, Golden Resurrection** and **Wisdom Call**, bass-player Mikael Höglund has played with **Great King Rat, Tryckvåg, Thunder** (UK) and **Punchline**, while drummer Thomas Broman has played with **Great King Rat, Electric Boys, Road To Ruin, Glenn Hughes** and UK band **Send No Flowers**. Keyboards were handled by Andreas Lindahl. *The Calling* is an outstanding slab of guitar oriented powerful melodic metal with killer arrangements, strong songs and outstanding musical performances. The album also features the **Sweet** cover *Love Is Like Oxygen* which can also be found on the compilation *The Sweet According To Sweden* (Rivel), which also features Janne Stark, Mic Michaeli, Jeff Scott Soto and other guests. The follow-up saw a change of people, now with a more firm touring line-up featuring Christian, bassist and Christian's brother, Simeon Liljegren (**Modest Attraction, Borderline**), keyboard player Olov Andersson (**Grand Stand, Cross**), guitarist Torbjörn Weinesjö (**Veni Domine**), drummer Thomas Weinesjö (Veni Domine). *Focus* featured guest apperances from Erik Mårtensson (**Eclipse, W.E.T**) and Janne Stark (**Overdrive, Constancia** etc) and the album has a much more seventies oriented classic hard rock feel.

Focus, boys, focus!!

2010 CD - ULTCD 014

2005	■	THE CALLING	CD	Rivel	RRCD 019
2005	□	THE CALLING	CD	Avalon Marquee (Japan)	KICP-1048
		Bonus: Power From The Sky			
2010	■	FOCUS	CD	Ulterium Records	ULTCD 014
2010	□	FOCUS	CD	King Records (Japan)	KICP-1499
		Bonus: Are You Ready			

AUTHORIZE

**Thomas "Bizzon" Ek: v, Larsa Johansson: g/v,
Jörgen Paulsson: g, Putte Leander: b, Micke Swed: d**

Söderala (Söderhamn) - Formed in 1988 under the name **Morbid Fear**. **Authorize** play heavy thrash, on the verge of death metal. Thomas joined just before the album was recorded. Micke later joined **Under The Sun**. The band also has the track *Darkest Age* featured on the *Opinionate EP* (Opinionate 1990). The band split shortly after the album. The 2006 reissue features the tracks from the 1990 *Morbid Fear* demo as bonus.

1991	■	THE SOURCE OF DOMINION	CD	Putrefaction	PUT 007 $
2006	□	THE SOURCE OF DOMINION	CD	Arsenal Of Glory	ARSENAL 005
		Bonus: Intro/Broken Hypnosis/Darkest Age/Mindless Confusion/Thy Kingdom			
2010	□	THE SOURCE OF DOMINION	2CD	The Crypt	CRYPT 08
		Same bonus as above. Black or blue vinyl.			

1991 CD - PUT 007

AUTOPSY TORMENT

**Thomas "Devil Lee Roth" Karlsson: v, David "Slaughter" Stranderud: g,
Jimi "The Demon" Fagerstig: d, Thomas Hedlund: d**

Vinberg - The band was formed by Karlsson and guitarist Patrik "Onkel" Andersson in 1989-90 and recorded the demo *Splattered*. The duo was joined by Karl-Jan "Sexual Goatlicker/ Karl Vincent" Kristiansson and guitarist Daniel "Scyphe" Nilssen in 1991 and they recorded the *Darkest Rituals* demo using session bassist Henrik Paahle. In 1992 the band recorded two demos and two singles, that were never released. The band now split, or rather reformed into **Pagan Rites**. This band however only lasted for two years (before reforming later in 1995). Karlsson had joined **Tristitia** as singer, but left in 1998. In 1999 guitarist Scyphe and bass player Jimi "The Demon" Fagerstig reformed **Autopsy Torment**. With Thomas rejoining the duo they recorded the demo *Orgy With The Dead* in 2000. In 2001 they were reinforced with former **Ancient Rebirth**-drummer Thomas Hedlund. On *Graveyard Creatures* the line-up featured Karlsson on vocals, Hedlund on drums, David "Slaughter" Stranderud (**Portrait, Cross Bow**) on guitar and The Demon on bass. *7th Ritual…* is a collection of the band's first three demos. **Autopsy Torment** play old-school, simple death metal.

2002 7" - - -

2002 LP - MPLP 02

2002	■	Darkest Ritual	7" 4tr	Sombre Records	- -
		Tracks: Intro-Darkest Rituals/Rotting Flesh/Blasphemy Priest/Consumed Christ. 500 copies.			
2002	■	ORGY WITH THE DEAD	LP	Miriquidi/City Of The Dead	MPLP 02
		380 hand-numbered copies. Bonus: Gory To The Brave			
2003	■	TORMENTORIUM	CD	Painkiller	PKR 029
2003	□	TORMENTORIUM	LP	Painkiller	PKR 029
		500 copies, first 100 in red vinyl. Bonus track: Orgy With The Dead.			
2005	□	GRAVEYARD CREATURES	CD	Die Todesrune Records	DTM012
2005	□	GRAVEYARD CREATURES	LPg	Die Todesrune Records	DTM012
		Bonus: Splattered. 500 copies with insert			
2008	□	7TH RITUAL FOR THE DARKEST SOUL OF HELL	CD	Pulverised	ASH 044 CD

2003 CD - PKR 029

AVALON

Lena "Lana Dale" Dahlström: v, John Vesanen: g,
Sylvia "Sylvia Rice" Ristik: k, Michelle "Michel Rice" Ristik: b

Eskilstuna - A high-quality AOR band in the vein of late *Easy Action*, *Guardian Angels* and *Bam Bam Boys*. Highly recommended. Drums on the single were played by Håkan Hedlund (*Torch, Chrystal Pride*). The band split in 1987. Lena was later in the band *Tyrox*, but did not appear on their recordings. Not to be confused with Swedish dance band *Avalon*.

1986 ■ Dangerous Feelings/It's Hard..7" Backstage .... BSM 004-S

1986 7" - BSM 004-S

AVALON/AVALONE

Patric "Valentino" Fransson: v, Göran "G G Florence" Florén: g,
Tomas "Tom B" Walther: b

Stockholm/Handen/Haninge - This is another band on the verge of hard rock. *Avalon* was formed in 1985, initially as *Avalone*. On the first single, which was recorded in 1986, the band was a five-piece also featuring keyboardist Georgios "Georg Rozello" Charalambidis and drummer Fredrik "Fred Donelly" Lundfeldt. The A-side is good solid up-tempo AOR with the traditional B-side ballad. Musically it's really good, but the vocals are definitely a bit rough. In 1987 they won a band stand and signed a publishing deal with Tripple Music (which later became Lionheart Records) and recorded an album. *A View Of America* was released, but the album remains unreleased. On this single, Georgios was no longer in the band. The band left Little Big Apple and was picked up by Marianne Records sub label Eurozont, who released the third single, *Baby You're My Love*. The vocals had now become much better, but the music had on the other band become even more pop-oriented, even though there's some nice guitars, at least on the A-side. The same year, 1990, soccer club BK Söder asked Göran to write a pep song for the team, which resulted in *Nere på fältet* where the band was down to a trio. Around 1992 the band started breaking up and some of the members formed a band called *Midnight Sun* (not the recording band) on the side. Thomas and Patric did a lot of backing vocals on recordings (one being the horrible *Sommaren i city*), while Fredrik played with Erika. In the nineties Göran formed the pop band *Yummie* and arranged and produced all the songs for the TV show *Lilla melodifestivalen* in 2003 (a children's Eurovision Song Contest).

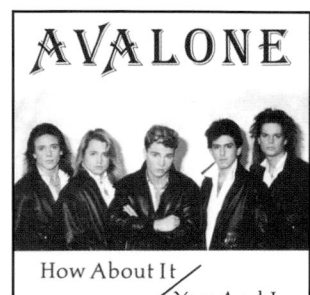

1987 7" - ASL 001

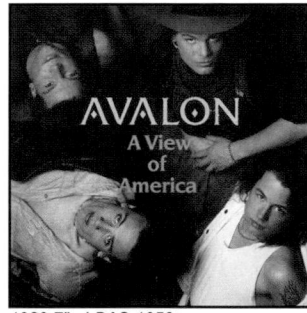

1989 7" - LBAS 1058

Year		Title	Format	Label	Cat. no.
1987	■	How About It/You And I	7"	private	ASL 001
		As Avalone.			
1989	■	A View Of America/Dansar I Dimmorna	7"	Little Big Apple	LBAS 1058
1989	□	A View Of America	MLP3tr	Little Big Apple	LBAM 1059
		Tracks: A View Of America (European Re-mix)/(7" version)/Dansar I Dimmorna.			
1989	□	A View Of America	MCD 3tr	Little Big Apple	LBACD-S 1060
1990	■	Baby You're My Love/Every Hour Every Day	7"	Eurozont	EZS 020
1990	□	Nere på fältet/Summer Night	7"	Eken Cup	EKEN 1

1990 7" - EZS 020

AVATAR

Johannes Eckerström: v, Jonas Jarlsby: g, Simon Andersson: g,
Henrik Sandelin: b, John Alfredsson: d

Göteborg - In 2001 John and singer Christian Rimmi started the band under the name *Lost Soul*, which also featured Jonas. The band however folded and the two started over as *Avatar*, now with Johannes on vocals. They started out playing covers by bands like *Cannibal Corpse*, *In Flames* and *Iron Maiden*. In 2003 Johannes quit the band, but he returned and Simon and Henrik were added to the line-up and they recorded the first demo *Personal Observations*. In 2004 the second, and far better, demo *4 Reasons To Die* (BSA 001) was recorded. In 2005 they decided to record an album on their own, but were picked up by Gain Records who released the debut album *Thoughts Of No Tomorrow* in 2006. The band toured with acts like *Impaled Nazarene, Evergrey, In Flames* and in 2007 the follow-up, *Schlacht* was released. 2009 saw the release of the third album. *Avatar* play quite technical yet melodic, at times on the verge of being almost too "major scale" for the genre, death metal in the vein of *Children of Bodom*. Lots of nice guitar harmonies, too. Late 2011 Simon was replaced by Tim Öhrström (*Eternity Remains, Shift*).

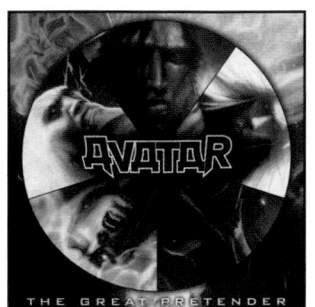

2009 CDS - GPCD 72

2009 CD - GPCD 71

Year		Title	Format	Label	Cat. no.
2006	□	THOUGHTS OF NO TOMORROW	CD	Gain	GPCD 28
2007	□	SCHLACHT	CD	Gain	GPCD 42
2009	■	The Great Pretender/Revolution Of Two	CDS	Gain	GPCD 72
2009	■	AVATAR	CD	Gain	GPCD 71
2010	□	AVATAR	CD	Stay Gold (Japan)	ARTSG-031
2010	□	AVATAR	CD	Columbia	n/a
2011	■	BLACK WALTZ	CD	Gain	GPCD 91
2011	□	Black Waltz	MCD 3tr	Gain	GPCD 92
		Tracks: Torn Apart/Black Waltz/One Touch			
2012	□	BLACK WALTZ	CD	eOne Music (USA)	EOM-CD-2411

2011 CD - GPCD 91

AVENUE

Björn Jansson: v, Benny Jansson: g, Jörgen Andersson: g,
Pierre Breidensjö: b, Roger Kindstrand: d

Stockholm - A very high class AOR-band with great musicians and great vocals. The A-side is
a power ballad in the vein of *Balance* or *Survivor* while the B-side is great melodic up-tempo
AOR-rocker similar to *Treat*. Well worth looking for. They recorded a full length album but the
record company went bankrupt before it was released. Björn and Benny (no *ABBA*-similarity pun
intended, I promise) later formed *Two Rocks*, with whom they recorded one album. They later
on formed the sadly unnoticed *Power United*. After that they formed *Mindcrime*, later known
as *Racketeer*, but nothing came out of it besides some great demos. Benny has also recorded
with *The Johansson Brothers*, *Snake Charmer* as well as some excellent solo albums. Björn
and Benny later formed *Tears Of Anger* with whom they released an album in 2004. Björn also
fronted German band *Ride The Sky*. Not to be confused with the Örebro-band who released
the far poppier single *Hur känns det imorgon/Förloraren*.

1985 7" - WEB 7-501

1985 ■ In My Life/Take Away ....7" WEB .... WEB 7-501

AVERON

Ola Persson: v/b, Micael Wikström: g, Per Rydberg: g, Stefan Halvarsson: d

Bollnäs - The *Averon*-story began in 1994. Per has previously recorded with the band *Enig-*
matic. *Averon* produces goth-oriented doom metal in the vein of *Candlemass* and *Solitude*
Aeternus. Quite simple and straightforward with average vocals and a pretty decent performance. Keyboard-player Anders Westling was also part of the line-up on the first album. After
the second album the band had some disputes with the label and has been more or less put on
hold until they finally split.
Website: http://listen.to/averon

1997 CD - USR 028

1997 ■ SERENITY ....CD Unisound..USR 028
1999 □ AN ECHO FROM BEYOND...CD Unisound..USR 032

AVSKY

TO: v/d, Anders "AE" Pers: g/b

(Dalarna) - *Avsky* (which means disgust in Swedish), formed in 2002, plays black metal with
a strong nod to the old school, but even some almost punkish elements, at times similar to
Darkthrone, but sometimes with the desperate vocal touch of *Shining*. The production is anything but old-school, instead it quite fat and pounding. No refined stuff, but plain and simple
song structures. The band released two demos in 2006; *Embrace Armageddon* and *No Cure*
For Mankind, before the debut was unearthed. The band's third album, *Scorn*, features guest
vocals from Mikael Nox Pettersson, and actually spawned the reunion of Nox and AE's old
band *Belzen*, now renamed *Omnizide*.

2007 CD - HPP 001 CD

2007 ■ MASS DESTRUCTION...CD Humanitys Plague Prod ....HPP 001 CD
2008 □ MALIGNANT ....CD Moribund..DEAD 108
2010 □ SCORN ....CD Moribund................................DEAD 146 CD

AWESOME MACHINE, THE

John Hermansen: v, Christian Smedström: g, Anders Wenander: b, Tobbe Bövik: d

Göteborg - The band was formed in 1996 by guitarist Christian and bass player Stefan Magnusson, both ex-*Tube Screamer*. The band's first demo was recorded in 1997. The 10" was
produced by Roberto Laghi (*B-Thong, Transport League, LOK*) and the album by Andy
LaRocque. After the 10" the band changed bass-player to from Stefan to Anders. Tobbe has
previously recorded some highly acclaimed demos with the band *Feel*. The band plays high-
quality stoner metal, in the vein of *Bozeman's Simplex*, *Lowrider* and *The Quill*. Christian
is also found on the postumely released *Mrs Hippie*-album, in *Chuck Norris Experiment*
and has previously recorded with *Full Metal Jacketz* while first singer Lasse Olausson was
ex-*Stoneflow*. John (*Mother Misery, Staiger, Greyhate*) replaced Lasse in 2004. Christian
left the band in 2006 to concentrate on his two other bands *Chuck Norris Experiment* and
On Parole (where Tobbe is also found). The band split in 2007. The song *Ompa Bomba*
can be found on *Burn The Streets Vol 1* (01 Daredevil) and *Fists Of Fury* on *Burned Down*
To Zero (01 Daredevil). The band has also been feaured on compilations like *The Mighty*
Desert Rock Avengers, Daredevil Magazine, Molten Universe Vol 1, Information Stoner
Highway, A Collection Of Great Dance Tunes Vol 2 and 3, Where The Bad Boys Rock, I Am
Vengeance and *Burn The Streets Vol 5*. Smedström is currently found in his footstompin'
crude blues project *Christan Smedström & The 2120's*.

Deus ex Awesome Machine

1998 ■	The Awesome Machine	10" 5tr	private		- -	$

Tracks: Mula/Fortune Teller/Burning Love/Sun Don't Shine On Me/Digging. 500 hand numbered copies.

1999 □	The Awesome Machine	MCD 7tr	Ellington Records	No. 6

Tracks: Mula/Fortune Teller/Burning Love/Sun Don't Shine On Me/Digging/God Damn Evil (demo)/Ompa Bompa (demo)

2000 □	Supernova/How Am I To Know/El Bajo	MCD 3tr	People Like You	- -
2000 □	IT'S UGLY OR NOTHING	LP	People Like You	PRISON 010-1

First press in golden marble yellow vinyl, second press in yellow vinyl.

2000 ■	IT'S UGLY OR NOTHING	CDd	People Like You	PRISON 010-2
2002 □	UNDER THE INFLUENCE	CD	People Like You	PRISON 047-2
2002 □	UNDER THE INFLUENCE	2CD	People Like You	PRISON 047-0

Second press, with green duplex cover, contains bonus CD with: Black Hearted Son (live)/God Damn Evil (live)/Emotion Water (live)/Supernova (live)//Under The Veil (Vincent Price remix)/Kick (Bite The Bullit remix)/Tomorrow (demo)/Emotion Water (demo)/Kick (video)/Still got no share pt 1 (video)

2002 □	UNDER THE INFLUENCE	2LP	People Like You	PRISON 047-1

First press of LP includes the first 10" as bonus tracks on side four. Second press, with green duplex cover, contains live tracks: Black Hearted Son/God Damn Evil/Emotion Water/Supernova

2002 □	The Awesome Machine vs. Duster 69 (split)	10" MLP	Daredevil	DD 019

Split with Duster 69. Tracks: Bleeder/Drowning In You/The Crailsheim Experience

2002 ■	Rickshaw/The Awesome Machine (split)	7" PD	Daredevil	DD 021

Split with Rickshaw. Tracks: Life In Hypercolour/Above All

2002 □	The Awesome Machine vs. Duster 69 (split)	CD	Fluid Groove (Australia)	FG001
2002 □	The Awesome Machine vs. Duster 69 (split)	CD	Bellaphon (Europe)	n/a
2003 □	THE SOUL OF A THOUSAND YEARS	CD	People Like You	PRISON 065-2
2003 □	THE SOUL OF A THOUSAND YEARS	LPg	People Like You	PRISON 065-1
2003 □	THE SOUL OF A THOUSAND YEARS	2CD	People Like You	PRISON 065-2

German only release with bonus single "Forgotten Words"

2002 □	Black Hearted Son/Under The Veil (Vincent Price Remix)	7"	World Records	World 003

500 copies. White vinyl.

2003 □	Forgotten Words/Burden Fall/Fragile Hearted Son+ (video)	MCD 3tr	People Like You	n/a
2005 □	Demon King/For The Weaker Ones	7"	Furthermocker	MOCK 3

Gimmick cover. 220 copies.

1998 10" - - -

2000 CDd - PRISON 010-2

2002 7" PD - DD 021

AX, ANETTE

Anette Ax (aka Richardsdotter): v

Upplands Väsby - Anette was born in the far north of Sweden, in Lappland. She made her AOR rocking debut single in 1987, followed by another one in Swedish, with two very cheesy pop songs that do not qualify into the book on their own. However, in 1989 she went to the US and recorded a single and an album with an all American line-up, featuring George Marinelli (g), Michael Thompson (g), Larry Wolf (k), Cliff Hugo (b) and John Molo (d). The album and single are way better, actually pretty good AOR with hints of Pat Benatar as well as Meatloaf. The single was actually released under the band name *Network*, but has a sticker saying Anette Ax on it. The subsequent singles are in the same style. Anette is also mother of Per Ax, drummer of *Excruciate*.

1987 7" - AA 1987

1987 ■	You're Not Worth It/Just One Minute	7"	private	AA 1987
1987 □	Jag vill inte förlora dig/Jag saknar dig	7"	private	AA 1987/2
1989 ■	It Is You/My Master	7"	Aim Records	AR 8901
1989 □	LOVE WAS THERE	LP	Aim Records	AR 8902
1989 □	Love Was There/Gimme Just Another Hour	7"	Aim Records	AR 8903
1990 □	Låt oss mötas/ Piece Of My Heart	7"	Aim Records	AR 9001
1996 □	Follow Your Heart/Du berör mig	CDS	Aiming Records	AIM 9601

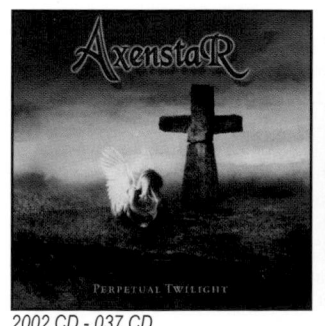

1989 7" - AR 8901

AXENSTAR

Magnus Winterwild (aka Eriksson): v/k, Joakim Jonsson: g,
Magnus Ek: b, Pontus Jansson: d

Västerås - *Axenstar* was formed as a cover band in 1998 by guitarist Peter Johansson and bass player Magnus Ek. The year after the line-up was completed by singer/keyboard player Magnus Eriksson (later Winterwild), guitarist and Magnus brother Thomas Eriksson and drummer Pontus Jansson. They entered Studio Underground with Pelle Saether in 2000 and recorded their first demo *The Beginning*. The subsequent year they followed it up with a demo simply entitled *Promo 2001* and they were soon signed by Spanish metal label Arise who released their debut, *Perpetual Twilight*, also produced by Saether, in 2002. After the second album, *Far From Heaven*, they went on their first European tour together with *Falconer*. As Magnus Ek could not make it, he was temporarily replaced by Joakim Jonsson (*Dust, Skyfire, Mornaland*). Right after the release of the band's third album *The Inquisition*, Peter and Thomas decided to leave the band. Their replacement was non other than the aforementioned Joakim Jonsson,

2002 CD - 037 CD

2003 CD - 049 CD

now on lead and rhythm guitar. The band now also changed label to Massacre Records and the album *The Final Requiem* was released in 2007. New changes happened soon after the release of the fourth album, when Pontus and Magnus Ek decided to leave the band. Drummer Thomas Ohlsson and bass player Henrik Sedell came and went within a year. In 2012 Magnus and Joakim recorded a new, as yet unreleased album and the current line-up now also features drummer Adam Lindberg (**Intrive**) and guitarist Jens Klovegård (**Liquid Suicide**). **Axenstar** play high-quality melodic power metal.
Website: www.axenstar.com

2005 CD - 069 CD

Year		Title		Label	Cat. No.
2002	■	PERPETUAL TWILIGHT	CD	Arise	037 CD
2002	□	PERPETUAL TWILIGHT	CD	King Records (Japan)	KICP-895
		Bonus: King Of Tragedy (demo)			
2002	□	PERPETUAL TWILIGHT	CD	Sail Productions (Korea)	SPCD-0021
		Bonus: King Of Tragedy (demo)			
2002	□	PERPETUAL TWILIGHT	CD	CD- Maximum (Russia)	CDM 1002-991
2002	□	PERPETUAL TWILIGHT	CDd	Scarecrow (Mexico)	SC02057
2003	■	FAR FROM HEAVEN	CD	Arise	049 CD
2003	□	FAR FROM HEAVEN	CD	King Records (Japan)	KICP-964
2003	□	FAR FROM HEAVEN	CDd	CD-Maximum	CDM 1103-1596
2005	■	THE INQUISITION	CD	Arise	069 CD
2005	□	THE INQUISITION	CD	CD-Maximum (Russia)	CDM 0405-2229
2005	□	THE INQUISITION	CD	King Records (Japan)	KICP-1075
		Bonus: Imaginary World			
2007	□	THE FINAL REQUIEM	CD	King Records (Japan)	KICP-1202
		Bonus: Storm			
2007	□	THE FINAL REQUIEM	CD	Massacre Records	MAS-CD 0528
2007	■	THE FINAL REQUIEM	CD	Locomotive Music (USA)	LM 437
2007	□	THE FINAL REQUIEM	CD	Mystic Empire (Russia)	MYSt CD 126
2011	□	AFTERMATH	CD	Ice Warrior	IWR-8
2011	□	AFTERMATH	CD	Rubicon Music (Japan)	RBNCD-1044

2007 CD - LM 437

AXEWITCH

Anders Wallentoft: v, Klas Wollberg: g, Magnus Jarl: g,
Magnus Hedin: b, Mats Johansson: d

Linköping - It all started back in 1979 when Magnus Jarl, Anders Wallentoft and bassist Tommy Brage formed *Hazy* and with drummer Rolf Holmström started playing mostly covers by *Rush*, *Judas Priest* and *UFO*. They called it quits in 1980. Anders kept the name *Hazy* and continued with a new line-up, while Magnus and Tommy formed *Iron Haze*, later *Black Stone*. Meanwhile Anders met guitarist Michael and drummer Mats and they joined *Hazy*, which soon folded. The three formed a new band with Tommy. Early 1981 they drafted Magnus, Anders took over lead vocalist duties and *Axewitch* was officially born. January 1982 they cut their first three-song demo. The band re-entered the studio in the summer of '82 to lay down tracks for their first MLP *Pray For Metal*. Late 1982 Web Records re-released *Pray For Metal* and another 1000 copies were pressed. In July 1983 *Axewitch* entered the legendary Decibel Studios in Stockholm (*Heavy Load, Yngwie Malmsteen*) to record their debut album *The Lord Of Flies* with *Torch* producer Olle Larsson. In the summer of 84 they returned to record their follow-up *Visions Of The Past*. In a smart move the band also released a 12" single called *Stand Up* which quickly mutated into an unexpected success story when entered the Swedish Rock single charts at a staggering number nine. Early 85 bass player Tommy Brage decided to part ways and was replaced by Magnus Hedin. Things seemed to be moving smoothly when all of a sudden another shift rocked the band's very foundation, prompting the Johansson brothers to pack their bags and leave in the summer. Mats would later re-appear in *Skinny Horse*. Despite this loss *Axewitch* commenced with the recording of their new LP, *Hooked On High Heels* later that summer. The band now consisted of Magnus, Anders and Magnus Hedin on bass, with Klas Wollberg adding guitars to some tracks. Per-Ove Johansson, sat in as a session drummer. New skins-man Abbe "Abbey" Enhörning arrived a little too late to leave his own mark on *Hooked On High Heels*. Although his picture can be seen on the back cover of the LP, he didn't play a single stroke on it. When *Hooked On High Heels* hit the streets it had an "artwork" that practically defied description. Take one look at the sleeve and you'll surely agree that this is one Hell of a top contender for any "Ugliest cover of the 80s" competition. It's hard not to imagine how shocked the band was when they first spotted the finished product in the stores. Late 1985/early 1986 the band toured a bit, but after a while Klas left Axewitch and was replaced by Ralf Petersson, a great guitarist and an old friend of Magnus and Anders. They kept on playing all over Sweden until late 1986. Abbey, their drummer left the band and Per-Ove Johansson rejoined the band, this time as their official drummer. Just a few weeks later Magnus Hedin (later in *Downbound Train*) went his own way, his place being taken by Dennis Printz. This line-up of *Axewitch* kept gigging and managed to record some demo material. After their third album *Axewitch* recorded three more demos, and also recorded several live shows with various line-ups whose common denominator remained the groups core of Magnus Jarl on guitar and Anders Wallentoft on vocals. Sadly none of these recordings saw the light of day - until 2005, that is. The band finally broke up in the summer of 1987. After *Axewitch*, Anders engaged in a few solo

Axewitch or Candlemass?

1982 MLP - AXE-MS-001   *1983 LP - FING LP 101*

projects. Magnus continued playing with the remains of the band, which they renamed *Sleazy Rose*. Magnus replaced guitarist Robban Persson in the band *Straight Up*. In Aug 1991 the original *Axewitch* line-up decided to play a ten year anniversary show. Klas Wollberg sadly died in 1996 after years of drug abuse. Ten years after Klas tragic death, *Axewitch* reunited for a 25 years anniversary gig in Linköping. Tommy was replaced by Lasse Fallman (*Straight Up*). A couple of gigs were made in 2007 and 2008. The band started writing songs for a new album. The new song *Fill Your Head With Rock* can be found on the compilation CD *Sweden Rock Festival 2008*. *Axewitch* also has the track *Nightmare* on the compilation *Linköpingsrock*. The band is still rocking at large.

1984 LP - FING LP 011

1982 ■	Pray For Metal	MLP 4tr	Axe	AXE-MS 001	$

Also pressed in 6 different colours (red, blue, green, orange, black and ?).Tracks: Born In A Hell/Heavy Revolution/In The End Of The World/Death Angel. 500 copies + 1000 black.

1983 ■	THE LORD OF FLIES	LP	Fingerprint	FING LP 101	
1983 ☐	THE LORD OF FLIES	LP	Megaton (Holland)	0005	
1983 ☐	THE LORD OF FLIES	LP	Discotto (Italy)	DM 0002	
1984 ■	Stand Up	MLP 3tr	Fingerprint	FINK M 404	

Tracks Stand Up/Time Traveller (non-LP)/Born In Hell (rerecorded)

1984 ■	VISIONS OF THE PAST	LP	Fingerprint	FING LP 011	
1984 ☐	VISIONS OF THE PAST	LP	Banzai (Can)	BRC 1922	
1985 ☐	VISIONS OF THE PAST	LP	Neat (UK)	NEAT 1025	
1985 ☐	VISIONS OF THE PAST	LP	Roadrunner (EU)	RR 9803	
1985 ☐	HOOKED ON HIGH HEELS	LP	Fingerprint	FING LP 012	
2005 ☐	PRAY FOR METAL	CD	Metal For Muthas	MFM 1016	

Bonus: Axewitch/Nightmare/Beyond The Realms of Death/We Salute This Town/Dance To The Music/Four Wheel Drive/It's A Lie(live)/City's On Fire(live) / Shadows Through The Night(live)/Back To Reality(live)/Four Centuries Ago(live)/Back In Trouble(live)/ Antisocial(live)

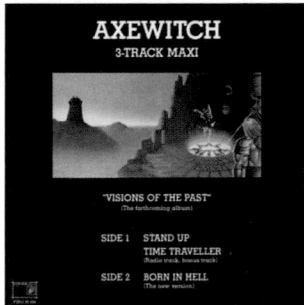

1984 MLP - FINK M 404

2005 ☐	THE LORD OF FLIES	CD	Metal For Muthas	MFM 1017	

Bonus: Rock This House Down (live)/Tracks Of Blood (live)/Love Can't Take It Away (live)/ Skull In The Mirror (live)/Queen Of Hearts (live)/Mary's Out Again (live)/World Of Illusions (live)/Get Out (live)/Deep Cuts The Knife (live)

2005 ☐	VISIONS OF THE PAST	CD	Metal For Muthas	MFM 1018	

Bonus: Evil Circle (demo)/Visions Of The Past (demo)/Give Them Hell (demo)/Tonight (demo)/Hot Lady (demo)/Heading For A Storm (demo)/Time To Live (demo)/Crazy And Wild (demo)/Nightmare (live)

2005 ■	HOOKED ON HIGH HEELS	CD	Metal For Muthas	MFM 1019	

Bonus: A Final Word/Get Out/Love Can't Take It Away/Runaway/Deep Cuts The Knife/ Young Girls In Love/Too Much Hollywood/Seven Angels

2005 CD - MFM 1019

AXIA

**Peo Pettersson: v, Robban Jacobsson: g, Morgan Blomquist: g,
Anders Biederbeck: k, Peter Andersson: b, Jonas Källsbäck: d**

Skövde - Formed in 1984. A very promising band that unfortunately never did lift off. The first two recordings are quite reminiscient of late *Rainbow*, while the 7" is more traditional melodic hard rock/AOR. On the first recording the line-up featured singer/guitarist Peo Pettersson, drummer Michael Alexandersen, bassist Niclas Ericson and guitarist Morgan Blomquist. Robban joined in 1986. This line-up lasted for the album only and the last 7" was recorded with the above members. In 1991 former *Swedish Erotica/Trazy Goes Crazy/Zanity*-singer Tony Niva (later in *Master Massive, Lion's Share* and *Oxygen*) replaced Håkan and the band recorded a full length demo-album in 1993. It was produced by Tomas Skogsberg, and drummer on the album was Ian Haugland. The band then changed their name to *Niva* and in 1994 the album *No Capitulation* was released in Japan. Peo joined *Leviticus* after the album and in 1995 he released his first solo-album. He also recorded a single with the band *Amity*, featuring his girlfriend at the time. Peo's solo-album *Look What I've Started* is in a far more commercial *Bryan Adams*-influenced style than his previous bands. Peo also sings three of the tracks on the *Flintsten Med Stanley*-CD and has a songwriting deal with Sweden Music Publishing. Although he now mostly writes pop/dance/country music, he does some cool solo stuff. *One Night* was pressed in around 200 copies but was never officially released. The line-up then consisted of singer Håkan Johansson, guitarists Robban and Morgan, bassist Peter and drummer Michael Pethrus. In 2000 the band made a re-union, remastered five tracks from the first LP and recorded five new excellent tracks which together became the CD-R *Axia 2000* (PopProdCD 1707). The last album was also made in the memory of Michael Pethreus and Jerry Karlsson, who were in the initial line-up of the band. The debut album was re-issued with the MLP as bonus by MTM in 2004. Bass player Peter Andersson has now recorded some albums with the band *Mean Streak*.

1985 MLP - MEP-1703

1988 LP - LP 1704

1985 ■	Charge It Up, Blast It Out	MLP 4tr	Pop Production	MEP-1703	$

Tracks: Increasing Action/Forced Into Darkness/ Never Ending Love,/The Savage Ramblers

1988 ■	AXIA	LP	Pop Production	LP 1704	
1989 ■	One Night/Raised	7"	NSL	NSL S 1001	$

200 copies. Not officially released.

2004 ☐	AXIA	CD	MTM Classix	0681-93	

The tracks from Charge It Up, Blast It Out as bonus.

1989 7" - NSL S 1001

AXIS POWERS

**Mathias "Matt The Desert Fox" Johansson: v, Peter "Pete Destroyer" Haglund: g,
Karl "Karl Kidd" Nilsson: g, Fredrik "Freddie Panzer" Andersson: b,
Christoffer "Mister" Larsson: d**

Uddevalla - The band was formed in 1997 by Mathias, Peter and Christoffer. Fredrik completed
the line-up two years after. They didn't record any demos before entering the studio in 1999 to
record the first self-financed single. After the release, the band recruited second guitarist Karl.
Christoffer has also recorded with punk band *Rallyholger*, while Mathias and Peter are found
in *Suicidal Winds*. *Axis Powers* burst out old-school Swedish death metal similar to *Grave*,
Carnage and early *Entombed*.

2000 7" - - -

2005 CD - IFPRCD 001

2000 ■	Evil Warriors...7" EP 4tr	private...................................... - -
	Tracks: Evil Warriors/Panzerblitz/Tanks Of War/I Wanna Be Your Dog (The Stooges cover)
2002 ☐	Born For War..MCD 5tr	Aftermath.......................................XV
	Tracks: Born For War/Scream For Jesus/Ashes/Trigger/Yellow Submarine (The Beatles cover)
2002 ☐	Born For War..7" 5tr	Aftermath.......................................XV
2005 ■	PURE SLAUGHTER...CD	Iron Fist.............................IFPRCD 001
2005 ■	Fresh Human Flesh (split)......................................7"	Deathstrike.............................DR 037
	Split with Ill Natured. Tracks: Fresh Human Flesh/Back To The Front
2009 ☐	MARCHING TOWARDS DESTRUCTION.................CD	Pulverised..............................ASH 061

2005 7" - DR 037

AZOTIC REIGN

**Kjell Andersson: v. Tord Eriksson: g, Patrik Gustavsson: g,
Andreas Vaple: b, Patrik Sjöberg: d**

Forsbacka - The band started under the moniker *Black Crusader* in 1989, influenced by bands
like *Slayer* and *Kreator*. They recorded their first self-titled demo in 1991, the second, *World of
Chaos* in 1993 and the third, *Dreamer*, in 1994. The MCD was produced by Daniel Bergstrand
(*Meshuggah, Strapping Young Lad, Crawley* etc). Heavy thrash/power metal with touches of
vintage *Metallica* and *Agony* but an up-dated and powerful sound. The band also recorded a
3-track demo in 2002, released on the final split album before splitting up. Vaple is also found
in *In Aeternum* and *King Chrome* while Kjell has recorded with *Altered Aeon*.

1998 MCD - TLSCD 4798

1998 ■	Beyond The Blood ....MCD 5tr	private.......................................TLSCD 4798
	Tracks: The Beginning (intro)/Sacrificed/Beyond The Blood/Heal My Soul/Reincarnation Denied
2000 ■	ABSTRACT MALEDICTIONS.....................................CD	Iron Glory...............................IG 1011
2003 ☐	SUDAMERICAN PORNO (split) ....CD	Blackened.......................................n/a
	Split with Jesus Martyr. Tracks: Childhood Memories/A Piece Of Soul/The Storm Is Coming

2000 CD - IG 1011

AZURE

Robert "Amorth Bredlave" Kanto: g/v, Mattias Holmgren: d/k/v, Peter Ulvén: b

Örebro - *Azure* started in 1995 as the brain child of Robert Kanto. On the first MCD the drums
were handled by Andreas "Velvet" Nilsson, lead guitar by Fredrik Pernros (now in *My Endless
Wishes*) and guest-vocals by Jonas Granvik. On the CD Mattias Holmgren from *Embracing* is
guesting on drums, keyboard and vocals, while the lead-guitars are handled by André Nylund
and Stefan Rådlund (*M.A.D*). Death metal in the vein of *Naglfar*. Robert also plays bass in
death metal band *Relentless*. In 2000 the band released the demo-CDR *Shadows In Midark*.
In 2004 Mattias called Robert and persuaded him to startrt writing and get on up to Umeå to
record. Said and done. They recorded four songs penned by Robert and sent the demo out to
some labels. The demo lead to a deal and with the help of *Embracing* members Mattias and
Peter they record the new album. Besides Robert, Mattias and Peter, the album featured guitar
solos from Nils Norberg (*Nocturnal Rites*), Ulph Johansson and Ronnie Björnström. The artwork
was made by Pär Johansson (*Satariel*).

Moonlight legends

1996 ■	A Vicious Age Lasting..MCD 3tr	Pentheselia......................MCD PHA 001
	Tracks: A Mountain Calls/Forlorn In The Dark/Arcthule Closes His Eyes. 500 copies.
1998 ☐	MOONLIGHT LEGEND...CD	Solistitium....................................SOL 024
2005 ☐	KING OF STARS – BEARER OF DARK.......................CD	Pulverised..............................ASH 016
2005 ☐	KING OF STARS – BEARER OF DARK......................CDd	Deathgasm (USA).....................DG 025

"A Vicious Age Lasting..."

1996 MCD - MCD PHA 001

BB ROCK

Robban Blennerhed: g/v, Claes Bergqvist: b/v, Benga Ragnewall: d

Göteborg - A powerful trio in the same vein as *ZZ Top* and Swedish fellows *Sky High*. In 1994 Robban released a solo album entitled *Seven* (Lake Side Records), but it's more of a fusion-rock platter. A shame the album still hasn't been reissued on CD.

1983 ■ MAKE IT MOVE ....LP Ewita ....LSPLP 207

1983 LP - LSPLP 207

B-THONG

Ralf "Lennart" Gyllenhammar: v, Stefan Thuresson: g,
Lars Häglund: b, Morgan Pettersson: d

Göteborg - The band was originally formed under the name *Concrete Stuff* with a more sleaze oriented approach and sound. They won a bandstand and first prize was the recording of two songs for a compilation entitled *Rockslaget 1992* as well as a single. They later changed style into a more hardcore *Pantera* meets *Skintrade* type of sound and found it best to change the name as well. The word "betong" means concrete in Swedish! Before the name-change they also changed drummer from Staffan Johansson to Morgan Pettersson (ex-*Boulevard, Midnight Blue*). Singer on the first two albums was Tony Jelencovich, who in December 1995 left to go full-time on his side project *Transport League* and today is also found in *Massive Audio Nerve* (aka *M.A.N*) and *DeathDestruction*. He has also recorded with *Iron Shit Snakes, Glanzig, Ton Of Bricks, Icon In Me* and had his metal side project *Commander*. *B-Thong*'s third album shows a more mature band, with a width from slow soft tracks to ultra heavy power. If Tony was a brutal screecher, Ralf sounds more like Ian Astbury from *The Cult*. Ralf was ex-*Grindstone* and is now found in *Mustasch*. The *Concrete Compilation* is as the name suggests a compilation, but also featuring 4 unreleased tracks: *Hatewheel, Seven Stitches, Itchy Fingers* and *My Kind Of Enemy*.

1994 CD - M 7007 2

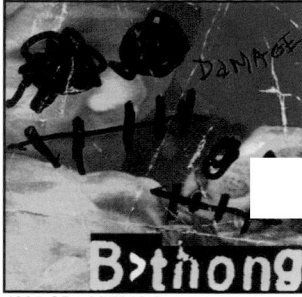

1995 CD - M 7013 2

1997 CD - M 7028 2

Year		Title		Label	Cat.no.
1994	■	SKINNED	CD	Mascot	M 7007 2
1995	□	SKINNED	CD	FEMS (Japan)	APCY-8177
1995	■	DAMAGED	CD	Mascot	M 7013 2
1997	■	FROM STRENGTH TO STRENGTH	CD	Mascot	M 7028 2
1997	□	FROM STRENGTH TO STRENGTH	CD	Dolphin (Japan)	BLCK-85977
2000	□	THE CONCRETE COMPILATION	CD	Mascot	M 7044 2
2004	□	FROM STRENGTH TO STRENGTH	CD	Irond (Russia)	CD 04-588/DD93

BABYLON BOMBS

Daniel "Dani" Persson: v/g, Jon Sundberg: g,
Rickard "Ricky" Harrysson: b, Svante "Swaint" Hedström: d

Bollnäs - The band was formed in 2001 and recorded the demo *Ten Things You Can't Live Without* the same year. The single *Louder* features a guest appearance from *Crucified Barbara* singer Mia Coldheart. After the debut, bass player Martin "Marty" Tronson was replaced by Ricky. When the bass player of *Sister Sin* walked out of the band mid-tour in 2009, Ricky stepped in and saved the day, but he was never a member of the band. *Babylon Bombs* play straight-ahead diesel infused hard rock in the vein of Swedish colleagues *Backyard Babies* or US bands like *Four Horsemen* and *Black Crowes*. Jon is also found in *Backdraft*. The bonus tracks on the Japanese version of *Doin' You Nasty* were taken from the 2003 promo.

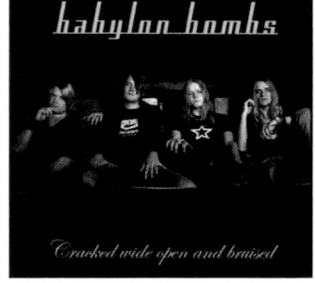

2005 CD - SMILCD 7102

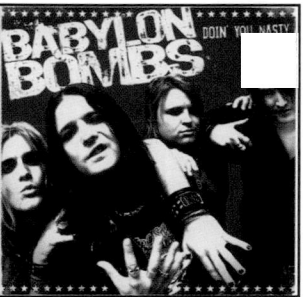

2006 CD - SMILCD 7106

2005	■	CRACKED WIDE OPEN AND BRUISED	CD	Smilodon	SMILCD 7102
2005	□	CRACKED WIDE OPEN AND BRUISED	CD	Victor (Japan)	VICP-63415
		Bonus: Round And Round/Suicide Street			
2006	■	DOIN' YOU NASTY	CD	Smilodon	SMILCD 7106
2007	□	DOIN' YOU NASTY	CD	Victor (Japan)	VICP-63672
		Bonus: Let's Roll/Delirious/Crucify			
2006	□	Louder/Suicide Street	CDS	Smilodon	SMILCDS 103
2006	■	Hometown Hero/Delirious	CDS	Smilodon	SMILCDS 105
2007	□	Jaded Heart/Kickin Bleedin Screamin	CDS	Smilodon	SMILCDS 108
2009	□	BABYLON'S BURNING	CD	Deaf & Dumb	BOAO 002
2009	□	Liberation	CDS	Deaf & Dumb	BOAO 003

2006 CDS - SMILCDS 105

BACKDRAFT

Jonas Åhlén: v, Robert "The Slob" Johansson: g, Jon Sundberg: g,
Mats Rydström: b, Niklas Matsson: d

Stockholm - *Backdraft* was formed in 1997 by Jonas (ex-*Soil, Anticipation*) and Robert (ex-*Mörkrets Furste*). They found drummer Fredrik "Trizze Trash" Liefvendahl (later in *Grand Magus*) and the name *Morningwood*. The line-up was completed with David and bass player Anders Sevebo (later in *Cellout*). In 1998 they recorded an excellent 3-track demo simply

entitled *Demo One 98*. They changed their name to *Backdraft*, drummer to Niklas (ex-*Killer Bee*), bass player to Mats and recorded another demo. In 2000 they finally recorded their first official EP, *The Goddamn Man*, which struck like a bomb. The debut album was another kick in the groin of dirty southern hard rock. The band had a long hiatus, during which Mats and Niklas played with US band *Raging Slab*. During this period the major part of *Backdraft* also formed a new band with *Raging Slab* front man Greg Strzempka under the moniker *Odin Grange*. A highly interesting combination that unfortunately has so far come up empty handed. When *Backdraft* returned in 2007 it was with another slab of outstanding heavy southern-sounding hard rock in the vein of *Pride & Glory* meets *Molly Hatchet* with a strong touch of *Badlands* and *Raging Slab*. In 2008 Nordlander decided to leave the band and was replaced by *Babylon Bombs* stringsman Jon Sundberg and a new album was being written. In April 2010 Matsson also joined *Bonafide*. *This Heaven Goes To Eleven* is slightly different in style, not as heavy and a bit more experimental.
Website: www.backdraft.se

2001 CD - LUNA 006 CD

2011 CD - GMRCD 9027

2000	☐	The Goddamn Man EP	MCD 4tr	Fandango	CD 03

Tracks: G'damn Man/Angels High/See U Burn/Hillbilly Blues

2001	■	HERE TO SAVE YOU ALL	CD	Lunasound	LUNA 006 CD
2007	☐	THE SECOND COMING	CDd	GMR	GMRCD 9008
2011	■	THIS HEAVEN GOES TO ELEVEN	CD	GMR	GMRCD 9027
2011	☐	THIS HEAVEN GOES TO ELEVEN	LPg+CD	GMR	GMRLP 9027

Bonus: Blue Sky (Allman Brothers band cover). 500 copies.

BACKHANDER
Mikael "Mike C" Svensson: v, Andreas Edlund: g,
Jonas Sjögren: b, Thomas Helgesson: d

Malmö - The band story goes back to 1998 when three of the members met up and started talking about forming a band. Other obligations however prevented them from starting up. In 2005 their paths crossed again and this time they realised their idea. Singer Mike is ex-*Corrosion*/*Road*, Jonas is ex-*Skyfire* and Andreas is also a member of *Skyfire* and *Chaos Feeds Life*. Helgesson is ex-*The Drugs*/*The Itch*/*Road*. *Backhander* play classic heavy rock with hints of the 70s as well as the 80s. In 2009 Mike and Thomas formed the band *Grand Rezerva*.

2006 MCDp - BAH 001

2006	■	Wanted Man/Your Way/Black Sinister	MCDp 3tr	Isma	BAH 001

BACKSTREET
Mikael Bojko: v/g, Ulf Andersson: g, Thomas Linde: k/h,
Mikael Saario: b, Mikael Englund: d

Surahammar - High-quality, traditional-sounding hard rock with a touch of *Deep Purple* and a strong Hammond-sound. Vocals of the upper-quality department. Recommended.

1992 MCD - BST 001

1992	■	Rollin' Down The Highway	MCD 4tr	private	BST 001

Tracks: Rollin' Down The Highway/Different Life/One Minute To Midnight/Stranger In My Kitchen.

BACKTALK
Lars "Hagis" Hagman: v/g, Assar Andersen: g,
Micke Brandtler: b, Tosse Wennerholm: d

Stockholm - Formed in 1977, split in 1983. This is no-nonsense straight hard rock with a lot of rock 'n roll in it, as well as some hints of *AC/DC*. Mid-class stuff.

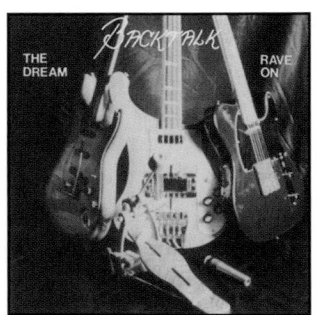
1982 7" - PSI 035

1982	■	The Dream/Rave On	7"	Pang	PSI 035

BACKWATER
Björn Wennerborg: v/g, Thomas Kihlberg: g,
Anders Thorstensson: b, Robert Andersson: d

Lidköping - *Backwater* was formed in 1997. Anders Thorstensson left the band in 2009 and was replaced by Viktor Ax. The band plays outstanding heavy rock/metal with a modern touch, at times similar to bands like *Shinedown*, *Alter Bridge* or Swedish colleagues *Cellout*. Great vocals, fat, detuned guitars and pounding drums. High-quality stuff! In 2012 the line-up saw Robert had been reaplaced by Mauritz Petersson.
Website: www.backwater.nu

2007 CDd - REV 666

2007	■	REVENGE	CDd	Bad Language	REV 666

BACKYARD BABIES

**Nicke Borg: g/v, Andreas Dregen (aka Svensson): g/v,
Johan Blomquist: b, Peder Carlsson: d**

Nässjö - This raunchy, sleazy hard rock band that was formed in 1987 in Nässjö became something of a Headbangers Ball fave-band. They started out as *Tyrant* and later changed it to *Dead Silent*. Their singer at the time, before Nicke joined in 1990, was Tobias Fischer. Shortly after the release of the debut, the album was out worldwide. Several of the single-tracks are non-album and even more are found on the *'95 Backstage Magazine* compilation-CD. Dregen was also found in *The Hellacopters*. By the time *Total 13* was released Dregen had again left *The Hellacopters*, with whom he had had huge success. The band supported *Kiss* on their 1999 Swedish dates, a band which had big impact on Dregen in his younger days. The debut was quite glammy and sleazy, while the follow-up was a bit more punkish. The band has become a kind of cult-band within its own lifetime, with an out and out rock 'n roll-drug-sex attitude. In 1999 the band also backed *Michael Monroe* on tour. *Making Enemies…* saw a return to a more hard rock oriented sound, while *Stockholm Syndrome* was more of a straight-ahead rock 'n roller. The band can also be found on numerous compilations, several featuring exclusive tracks, such as *Swedish Sins '97* (97 White Jazz), *Stranded In The Dollhouse* (97 Hurtin'), *Hell On Earth…Hail To Misfits* (97 Tribute), *Strangeland* (98), *Up In Flames* (99), *Gearfest* (00 Gearhead), *Again… This One's For JOHNNY* (01 Munster), *National Sånger* (02 National), *We Are Vengeance* (06 Century Media) and *Slam CD* (08 Slam Alternative Music Magazine). The track *Friends* features guest appearances recorded by people like *Danko Jones*, Nina Persson (*Cardigans*) and *Joey Ramone* (possibly the last recording before he died). In 2010 Andreas officially took the name Dregen (which was his nick name). In 2011 Nicke Borg entered the Swedish qualifying rounds of the Eurovision Song Contest with the song *Leaving Home*. He now has his solo project *Nicke Borg Homeland*.
Website: wwwbackyardbabies.com

Just Babies!

1994 CD - MRRCD 008

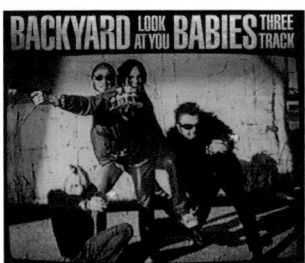
1994 MCDp - MRRCD S014

Year		Title	Format	Label	Cat. No.	
1991	☐	Something To Swallow	MLP 5tr	Opus 1 Productions	OPUS 3	$$

Tracks: Something To Swallow/Strange Kind Or Attitude/Juicy Lucy/Like A Child/Kickin' Up Dust

| 1994 | ■ | DIESEL AND POWER | CD | Megarock Records | MRRCD 008 | |

Sticker with the first pressing.

| 1994 | ■ | Electric Suzy/Shame/Lies/Taxi Driver (Hanoi Rocks cover) | MCDp 4tr | Megarock Records | MRRCD S014 | |
| 1995 | ☐ | Supershow | 7" | 5R Records | 5R0396 | |

Split with 69 Eyes. Track: Mommy's Little Monster (Social Distortion cover). Coloured vinyl

| 1997 | ☐ | Knockouts! | MCD 5tr | MVG | MVGCDS 47 | |

Tracks: UFO Romeo/Backstabber/Powderhead/Wireless Mind/Ghetto You

| 1997 | ☐ | Knockouts! | 10" 5tr | MVG | MVGV 47 | |
| 1997 | ■ | Look At You | MCD 3tr | MVG | MVGCDS 50 | |

Tracks: Look At You/Spotlight The Sun/Can't Find The Door (lost sunlight mixes)

| 1998 | ☐ | Total 05 | MCD 5tr | Coalition (UK) | SAM3204 | |

Tracks: Made Me Mama/UFO Romeo/Look At You/Bombed (Out Of My Head)/ Hey, I'm Sorry. Promo.

| 1998 | ☐ | Look At You | MCD 4tr | Coalition (UK) | COLA 046CD | |

Tracks: Look At You/Powderhead/Can't Find The Door/ Wireless Mind

1998	☐	Look At You/Powderhead	7"	Coalition (UK)	COLA 046	
1998	■	Look At You	MLP 4tr	Coalition (UK)	COLA 048	
1998	☐	TOTAL 13	CD	MVG	CDMVG 135	
1998	☐	TOTAL 13	LP	MVG	MVG 135	
1998	☐	Highlights CD1	MCD 3tr	Coalition (UK)	COLA058CD1	

Tracks: Highlights (studio)/Made Me Madman (live/Backstabber (live)

| 1998 | ☐ | Highlights CD2 | MCD 3tr | Coalition (UK) | COLA058CD2 | |

Tracks: Highlights (live)/Stars (live)/Fill Up This Bad Machine (live)

| 1998 | ☐ | Highlights (studio)/Look At You (studio) | 7"g | Coalition (UK) | COLA 058 | |
| 1998 | ☐ | Highlights CD | MCD 4tr | MVG | MVGCDS 53 | |

Tracks: Highlights (studio)/Rocker/Fill Up This Bad Machine (live)/Stars (live)

1998	☐	TOTAL 13	CD	MVG	MVG 135	
1998	☐	TOTAL 13	LP	MVG	MVG V135	
1998	☐	TOTAL 13	LP	Coalition/MVG (UK)	MVGV 135	

Bonus: Backstabber

| 1998 | ☐ | TOTAL 13 | CD | Coalition (UK) | 3984-22746-2 | |
| 1998 | ☐ | TOTAL 13 | CD | EastWest (Japan) | AMCE-2711 | |

Bonus: Powderhead/Wireless Mind/Can't Find The Door/ Rocker (featuring Michael Monroe)

| 1998 | ☐ | TOTAL 13 | LP | Scooch Pooch (USA)(Japan) | PO53 | |

Bonus: Babylon/Rocker

| 1998 | ☐ | (It Is) Still Allright To Smile/Babylon | 7" | Bad Afro | FRO 012 | |

3000 copies. Red, yellow or green vinyl.

| 1998 | ☐ | Bombed (Out Of My Mind)/Rocker | 7" PD | Coalition (UK) | COLA051 | |

2000 copies. Yellow vinyl. Autographed.

1998	☐	DIESEL & POWER	2LP	Megarock Records	MRRLP 036	
1998	☐	SAFETY PIN & LEOPARD SKIN	CD	MVG	3984-25361-2	
1998	☐	SAFETY PIN & LEOPARD SKIN	LP	MVG	MVGV 138	

1998 MLP - COLA 048

1998 ☐	SAFETY PIN & LEOPARD SKIN	CD	Coalition (UK)	3984-25361-2
1999 ☐	DIESEL & POWER	CD	EastWest (Japan)	ACME 7082
	Bonus: Lies			
1999 ☐	SAFETY PIN & LEOPARD SKIN	CD	EastWest (Japan)	ACME 2910
	With built in safety pin.			
1999 ☐	Babylon/Babylon (init fo' life remix)	12"	Pastor	BYBS1
	1000 copies. Poster.Single sided.			
1999 ☐	Babylon/Stars	7"	Coalition (UK)	COLA 073
	1000 copies. Red vinyl.			
2001 ☐	Brand New Hate/P.O.P/By The Phone	MCD 3tr	RCA (Australia)	74321 85560-2
2001 ☐	Brand New Hate/By The Phone	CDS 2tr	BMG/RCA	74321 85387 2
2001 ☐	Brand New Hate	CDS	BMG/RCA (promo)	BMGPROM 108
2001 ☐	Brand New Hate	MLP	BMG/RCA	74321 85560 1
2001 ☐	Brand New Hate	MCD	Supersonic/BMG	SUPERSONIC 073
	Tracks: Brand New Hate/The Kids Are Right/The Clash			
2001 ☐	MAKING ENEMIES IS GOOD	CD	BMG (Japan)	BVCP 21192
	Bonus: P.O.P, By The Phone/Fashion/The Clash			
2001 ☐	MAKING ENEMIES IS GOOD	LP	BMG/RCA	74321-85561 2
	A limited edition in white vinyl was also pressed.			
2001 ■	MAKING ENEMIES IS GOOD	CD	BMG/RCA	74321-85959-2
2001 ☐	MAKING ENEMIES IS GOOD	CDd	BMG/RCA	74321-86169-2
	Bonus: P.O.P			
2001 ☐	MAKING ENEMIES IS GOOD	CD	Supersonic	SUPERSONIC 074
2001 ☐	The Clash/Three Wise Monkeys/Fashion (Changes With You)	MCD 3tr	BMG/RCA	74321-88650-2
2001 ☐	The Clash/Three Wise Monkeys/Fashion (Changes With You)	MCD 3tr	BMG (Australia)	74321-88650-2
	Different artwork.			
2001 ☐	The Clash/Three Wise Monkeys	CDS 2tr	BMG/RCA	74321-88649-2
2001 ☐	INDEPENDENT DAYS	DCD	MVG	MVG 145
2003 ☐	Minus Celcius/Blackheart	CDS 2tr	BMG	82876-56878-2
2003 ☐	Minus Celcius/Blackheart/Please, Please, Please!	MCD 3tr	BMG	82876-56880-2
2003 ☐	FROM DEMOS TO DEMONS 1989-1992	CD	Powerline	PLRCD 007
2003 ☐	FROM DEMOS TO DEMONS 1989-1992	2CDd	Victor (Japan)	VICP-62146/-7
2003 ☐	STOCKHOLM SYNDROME	CD	BMG (Japan)	BVCP-21364
	Bonus: Big Bad Wolf/Shut The Fuck Up			
2003 ■	STOCKHOLM SYNDROME	CD	BMG/RCA	82876-57244-2
2003 ☐	STOCKHOLM SYNDROME	LP	BMG/RCA	82876-57244-1
2003 ☐	STOCKHOLM SYNDROME	CDd	BMG /RCA	82876-57587-2
	Bonus: Shut The Fuck Up			
2004 ☐	A Song For The Outcast/Devil-May-Care	CDS	BMG/RCA	82876-59405-2
2004 ☐	Friends/One Minute Silence For Joey/Pretty Ugly	MCD 3tr	BMG	82876 66322-1
2004 ☐	Remix For The Outcast	10" 3tr	Sound Pollution Single Club	SPS002
	Tracks: A Song For The Outcast/Devil-May-Care/Minus Celsius (Shieldstar & Play Remix)			
2004 ☐	LIVE LIVE IN PARIS	CD	Liquor & Poker (USA)	LP 6018-2
2005 ☐	TINNITUS	CDd	Liquor & Poker (USA)	LP 6009-2
	Comes with a Liquor & Poker bonus compilation.			
2005 ■	A Remix For The Outcast	10" 3tr	Sound Pollution	SPS002
	Tracks: A Song For The Outcast/Devil-May-Care/Minus Celsius (Shieldster And Player Remix)			
2005 ☐	LIVE LIVE IN PARIS	CD	RCA	82876-673902
2006 ■	TINNITUS + LIVE LIVE IN PARIS	2CD	Abacus	33001-2
2006 ☐	TINNITUS + LIVE LIVE IN PARIS	2CD	Icarus Music (Argentina)	ICARUS 195
2006 ☐	PEOPLE LIKE PEOPLE LIKE PEOPLE LIKE US	CD	Icarus Music (Argentina)	ICARUS 304
2006 ☐	PEOPLE LIKE PEOPLE LIKE PEOPLE LIKE US	CD	Abacus	0027
2006 ☐	PEOPLE LIKE PEOPLE LIKE PEOPLE LIKE US	CD	RCA	82876-82342-2
2006 ☐	PEOPLE LIKE PEOPLE LIKE PEOPLE LIKE US	LP	Century Media (UK)	77562-0
2006 ☐	PEOPLE LIKE PEOPLE LIKE PEOPLE LIKE US	CD	Century Media (UK)	77562-2
2006 ☐	PEOPLE LIKE PEOPLE LIKE PEOPLE LIKE US	CD	BMG (Jap)	BVCP-21477
2006 ☐	The Mess Age/Shattered Bonds	CDS	BMG/RCA	82876-82355-2
2006 ☐	Dysfunctional Professional	CDS 3tr	RCA	82876-86696-2
	Tracks: Dysfunctional Professional/Minor Major Problem/ Dysfunctional Professional (Rusiak Remix Swingfly)			
2006 ■	Fuck Off And Die/Zoe Is A Weirdo/Saved By The Bell	7" 3tr	Bootleg Booze	BOOZE 029
	1500 copies, 750 in transparent red vinyl w white splatter, 500 white vinyl w black splatter, 250 Boozers Club edition black vinyl.			
2006 ☐	DIESEL AND POWER	CD	Billion Dollar Babies	BYBBDB 001
	Bonus: Lies/Electric Suzy (video)			
2008 ☐	BACKYARD BABIES	CD	Billion Dollar Babies	BYBBDB 002
2008 ☐	BACKYARD BABIES	LP	Billion Dollar Babies	BYBBDBLP 002
2008 ☐	BACKYARD BABIES	CDd	Billion Dollar Babies	BYBBDBLI 002
	Extended booklet. Bonus: Fuck And Die (video)			
2008 ☐	BACKYARD BABIES	CD	Victor (Jap)	VICP-64386
	Bonus. Saved By The Bell (Piano Version)			
2008 ☐	Drool/F**k Off And Die	CDS	Spinefarm (UK) (promo)	SFCCDP09
2008 ☐	Drool/F**k Off And Die	7"	Spinefarm (UK)	1783070
	500 copies. Red vinyl.			

2001 CD - 74321-85959-2

2003 CD - 82876-57244-2

2005 10" 3tr - SPS 002

2006 2CD - 33001-2

2006 7" 3tr - BOOZE 029

2009 □	Degenerated/Star Wars Jr. (Supershit666) ....7"	Spinefarm (UK) 2701938			

2009 □ Degenerated/Star Wars Jr. (Supershit666) ....7"   Spinefarm (UK) 2701938
    500 copies. Blue vinyl.
2009 ■ THEM XX BOXSET (Photo book) ....Box set   Versity Rights ....BDBBOOK003 $$$
    4CD+DVD+Photo book. CDs featuring previously unreleased tracks: Fuck Off And Die (Hard Act To Follow Remix)(mix Johan Åberg)/The Mess Age (Greven & Gösen Remix)/ This Is How The World Ends. Bonus CD: Abandon (edit)/Degenerated (L'amour La Morgue edition). 300 copies
2010 □ THEM XX ....CD   Billion Dollar Babies ....BDB 003
2010 □ THEM XX ....CD   Victor (Japan) VICP-64805
    Bonus: Abandon (New Edit)
2010 □ 3 ORIGINAL ALBUM CLASSICS ....3CD   RCA 88697 55510 2
    Box set containing the albums Making Enemies Is Good, Stockholm Syndrome and Live Live In Paris
2011 □ DIESEL AND POWER ....LP   Billion Dollar Babies ....BDBVIN 001
    500 green + 500 black vinyl.

2009 Box set - BDBBOOK003

Unofficial Recordings:
1999 □ SPOTLIGHT THE BABIES ....CD   Bondage Music (Japan) ....BON 180
    Recorded in Tonhallen, Sundsvall (Swe) 990213 and Fujikyu Highland, Yananashi (Jap) 990809.
2001 □ BRAND NEW ENEMIES ....CD   8-Ball (Japan) CD02
    Recorded at Hultsfredsfestivalen June 14, 2001.

BACKYARD BULLETS
Leif Petersson: v, Joakim Karlsson: g, Christian Karlsson: b, André Andersson: d

Karlskrona - Formed in 1993. Singer Leif previously recorded an album with a band called **Tantrum**. **Backyard Bullets** split shortly after the MCD was released. Joakim and Christian later formed **Thrashyard Boys**, but nothing happened. *Who's Laughing Now* contains quite simple and uninteresting thrash with below average vocals. Joakim later spent some years in the US but returned to Sweden in the early 2000, where he's continued recording demos with various projects.

1995 ■ Who's Laughing Now ....MCD 5tr   private ....PPMCD 9501
    Tracks: Psycho Love/Rehabilitated/Try Help/Who's Laughing Now/ Dream On.

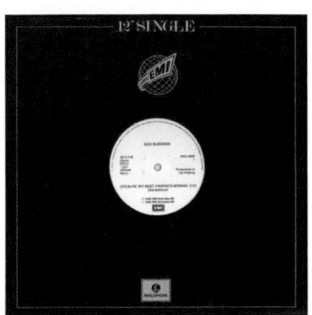
1995 MCD - PPMCD 9501

BACON (aka BACON BROTHERS)
Roberth Ekholm: v/g, Markus Aldén: b , Marcus Källström: d

Falun/Borlänge - Heavy blues-rock in the vein of **Sky High**, **ZZ Top** and **Blues Bag**. The band was formed in 1991 as **Bacon Brothers**, In 1997 original drummer and brother of bassist/singer Kimmo Ylitalo, Jari Ylitalo, left and was replaced by Mårten Ronsten. After the second release Mårten left to be replaced by Johan Sjöström. Per Wiberg (**Opeth, Mojobone, Spiritual Beggars** etc) guests on some of the releases. The band shortened their name to **Bacon** and on in 2009 the band had changed line-up, now featuring original member Roberth Ekholm and former **Stonecake** members Marcus Källström (d) and Markus Aldén (b). The album *Like It Black* is the band heaviest effort, a really hard-hitting melodic, stompin', hard rock blues album. The track *One Step Back* was penned by **ZZ Top**'s Billy Gibbons.

1996 □ Heavy Shit ....MCD 5tr   private ....- -
    Tracks: Backtrack/Feel So Good/The Feelgood Factor/Cut Off My Right Arm/Relocate Your Love
1997 □ TWO HEAVY ....CD   Agnas ....AMCD 003
2000 □ PIT STOP ....CD   Upp AB ....UPPCD 02
2009 ■ LIKE IT BLACK ....CD   Grammofonbolaget GRAM25

2009 CD - GRAM25

BAD BUSINESS
Stefan "The Flea" Larsson: v/g, Christer "Chris Crash" Hjort: g ,
Dan "TT Tonic" Högberg: b, Ola "Rich 'N Famous" Lugner: d

Lidköping - Stefan, Christer and Ola had previously recorded two albums and one single with the far more commercial band **Nectaris**. In 1984 they formed **Bad Boys**, which became **Bad Business**. This was a band that had quite a big potential and also recorded a very good demo after the album, but sadly dissappeared into obscurity. The style is quite close to **AC/DC** but with cleaner and brighter vocals. Good stuff, produced by Caj Högberg (**Proud**). The creativity-level when finding stage names are quite over the top. After the band split in 1987, the members have only played in occasional cover bands. Stefan played with **Voices And Noises**, together with Roger Ljunggren (**Twilight Project**) and Mikael Ellgren (**Gallery, Ambra**). The album is set to be digitally reissued by EMI in 2013.

1986 ● Stealin' My Best Friend's Woman/Rock This House ....12" 2tr   EMI ....PRO 4065
    No artwork.
1986 ■ THERE'S NO BUSINESS LIKE ....LP   EMI 136 226 1

1986 12" - PRO 4065

1986 LP - 136 226 1

BAD HABIT

Richard "Bax" Fehling: v, Hal (Johnsson) Marabel: g, Sven Cirnski: g, Patrik "Stevie Rose" Södergren: b, Jaime Salazar: d

Malmö - One of Sweden's premier AOR-bands. It all started out in the eighties under the name *Stratus* and the first demo-sign of *Bad Habit* was unearthed in 1987. The first MLP was initially recorded as a demo. After the first album it went all quiet and in 1990 the band felt beaten by the grunge and sleaze hypes, so they gave in. However, in 1994 things started moving once more and they reloaded the batteries with the release of *Revolution*. Keyboard player Doc Patric Schannong (Pat Shannon) was replaced by guitarist Cirnski. Salazar was at the time also playing with symphonic rocker *Roine Stolt* and occasionally with bass phenomenon Jonas Hellborg. On the MLP he was temporarily replaced by Janne Andersson. Hal (christened Hjalmar Johnsson) has produced the band *Project L.E.E.* and was also a member of *Bai Bang* in 1994, but quit to put his energy into *Bad Habit*. The MLP and first album contains ballsy top notch AOR in the vein of *Firehouse* etc. International sound, great vocals, classy musicianship and high-class arrangements. Highly recommended. *Revolution* was also classy AOR, but with pretty heavy edge at times, while on *Adult Orientation* the band had taken a slick westcoast turn. The band split after *Adult Orientation*, but in 2005 they reformed and returned to the world of AOR, still sticking to the poppier vein, although they do deliver a heavier package live. Hal (who took the family name Marabel) has also been one part of the pop duo *Arena Sweden*, together with Magnus Bäcklund. Doc moved to L.A, Bax is a pilot, working at Skyways. Sven recorded an outstanding heavy and bluesy solo CD under the name *Truth*, which was actually a continuation of his first solo album, which became Pete Sandberg's solo album *Push*. He has also contributed with guest solos on the two *Mountain Of Power* CDs, as well as on albums by *Blakk Totem* and *Raise Cain*. Salazar has appeared on numerous albums by bands like *Midnight Sun, Blakk Totem, Diabolique, Karmakanic, Last Tribe* and *The Flower Kings*. *Timeless* is a compilation featuring the two unreleased tracks *Turning Water Into Wine* and *Rock This Town*. On the 2011 album *Atmosphere* they actually turned up the distorted guitars a bit.

Bad habits die hard!

1987 7" - 651147 7

Never Find Another You

1988 7" - 651534 7

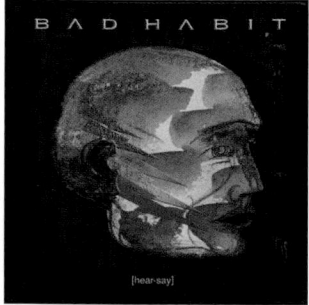

1989 7" - 112 076

2005 CD - FR CD 267

1987 ■	Need Somebody/Try Me	7"	CBS	651147 7
1988 ■	Never Find Another You/(long version)	7"	CBS	651534 7
1988 □	Young And Innocent	MLP 6tr	CBS	460402 1
	Tracks: Dreams Die Hard/Try Me/Never Find Another You/Need Somebody/Let It Go/ Young Young & Innocent			
1988 □	More Than A Feeling/Dancing	CDS	Virgin	661 820 2
1988 □	More Than A Feeling/Dancing	7"	Virgin	661 820 7
1989 □	AFTER HOURS	LP	Virgin	209 876 1
1989 □	AFTER HOURS	CD	Virgin	209 876 2
1989 ■	Rowena/Let It Go	7"	Virgin	112 076
1989 □	More Than I/Need Somebody	7"	Virgin	112 352
1995 □	REVOLUTION	CD	Megarock	MRRCD 033
1996 □	AFTER HOURS	CD	Zero (Japan)	XRCN-1271
	Bonus: Scandal Nights			
1996 □	REVOLUTION	CD	Zero (Japan)	XRCN-1260
1998 □	ADULT ORIENTATION	CD	MTM	199660
1998 □	ADULT ORIENTATION	CD	Pony Canyon (Japan)	PCCY 01313
2000 □	13 YEARS OF BAD HABIT	CD	Virgin	849129 2
2003 □	REVOLUTION / R.E.D.U.X	CD	GMR/Rock Treasures	RTCD004
	Bonus: I Live For You/Scandal Nights/Pray For The Children (by Arena Sweden)			
2005 ■	HEAR-SAY	CD	Frontiers	FR CD 267
2005 □	HEAR-SAY	CD	King Records (Japan)	KICP-1113
	Bonus track: Here I Am			
2005 □	ADULT ORIENTATION (RE-VISITED)	CD	King Records (Japan)	KICP-1114
	Bonus track: Anytime You Want It			
2005 ■	ABOVE AND BEYOND	CD	AOR Heaven	00037
2005 □	ABOVE AND BEYOND	CD	King Records (Japan)	KICP-1360
	Bonus track: Reaching Up			
2006 □	HEAR-SAY	CD	Irond (Russia)	CD 06-DD331
2009 □	ABOVE AND BEYOND	CD	Irond (Russia)	CD 09-DD700
2009 □	REVOLUTION (RE-VAMP)	CD	AOR Heaven/V.I.P Wonderclub	V500336
	Bonus: Need Somebody/In For The Count/Scandal Nights			
2010 □	TIMELESS	CD	AOR Heaven	AORH00046
2011 □	ATMOSPHERE	CD	AOR Heaven	00052
2011 □	ATMOSPHERE	CD	Irond (Russia)	CD 11-DD846
2011 □	ATMOSPHERE	CD	King Records (Japan)	KICP-1528
	Bonus: I'll Be True			

2005 CD - 00037

BADDIES

Christer Johnsson: v/g, Karl-Peter "Per" Resac: g,
Leif Training: b, Kenneth Johnsson: d

Kinna - *Don Juan* is pretty decent straight-ahead melodic hard rock with decent guitar work, unfortunately with uninteresting average Swedish vocals. *1984* is in the same vein but with an annoying disco beat. For collectors only. The single was produced by Swedish pop star *Nick Borgen*. Not to be confused with the UK band.

1984 ■	Don Juan/1984	7"	Pang	PSI 034

1982 7" - PSI 034

BADMOUTH

Tom Pearson: v, Randy Joy: g, Mike Hill: g, Chris LeMon: b,
Yngve "Vinnie Sharpe" Strömberg: d

Stockholm - Formed in 2007. The debut was quite average classic sleaze-tinged hard rock with decent vocals. The album was mixed by **Paul Sabu**, but lacks power. *Heavy Metal Parking Lot* was produced by **Chips Kisbye** (**Bonafide, Sator**) and is a way better effort. It feels like the band really stepped it up both regarding song material and playing. Really good sleazy hard rock. In 2011 drummer Rick Hard was replaced by Vinnie Sharpe. They also used drummer Robert Nilsson (**Killer Clan Of Fun**) on tour. In 2011 the band released the digital *EP, T – Part Three of H.A.T.E*, which was part of a project where four different bands cover songs by singer **Sofia Talvik** in different genres.

2008 CD - RXR007

2008 ■	BADMOUTH	CD	Romulus X	RXR007
2008 □	BADMOUTH	CD	Romulus X	RXR016
	Re-issue with new artwork (gagged lady)			
2011 ■	HEAVY METAL PARKING LOT	CD	Rambo/Danger Music & Media	DMMCD 001
2011 □	Blue Ribbon Days	MCDpg 3tr	Danger Music & Media	DMMCD 002
	Tracks: Blue Ribbon Days/Happy Go Lucky Guy/Rock Out. Came with Sweden Rock Magazine.			

2011 CD - DMMCD 001

BAI BANG

Diddi Kastenholt: v, Pelle "Eliaz" Eliasson: g, Joacim Sandin: b, Jonas Langebro: d

Sleazy rockers living their dream.

Helsingborg - Formed in 1980 under the name **Boogie Liquor Band**. A really good solid hard rock band that released one single. They changed their name to **Double Trouble** in 1983 and released four singles, of which some became great hits. The style then was poppy (hard) rock sung in Swedish. They recorded the first album under the name **Double Trouble** and the music was inspired by bands like **The Beatles, ELO** and **T-Rex**. Before the album was released they changed their name to **Bai Bang** because of too many bands with the same name. The members were Diddi, Clas, guitarist Eric Månsson (ex-**Vanadis,** now **Mansrock**), keyboardist Martyn Karlsson and drummer Mille Wendel. They wanted to move onto a harder rocking path and so they released a single with the **T Rex** cover *Hot Love*. On the second album *Cop To Con* they had changed style to more guitar oriented AOR. Most songs on the album were written by Mats Lindfors, Max Lorentz and Matti Alfonzetti (**Skintrade, Alfonzetti, Damned Nation, Red White & Blues**). It was however never released in Sweden. Bassist Mikael Persson joined after the first album was recorded and stayed for 18 months. In 1993 the band released the single *Little Child*. Now **Bad Habit** guitarists Hal Jonsson (now Marabel) was in the band and Martyn was out. After the single, Erik was replaced by **Nasty Idols/Espinoza/Majestic** bender Peter Espinoza, who left again in 1994, to put more effort into his band **Espinoza**. Hal also left to put more effort into the re-united **Bad Habit** and Jörgen Birch Jensen was recruited. Jörgen was also part of **Van Halen** cover band **Fan 'E De'**, also featuring members of **The Downtown Clowns**. The band recorded a new album originally entitled *Niceface*, which was long overdue and was released in Argentina late '95 under the title *Bai Bang* and later as *Ridin' High* in Europe. Most of the songs were written by Norwegian Ole Evinrude and are more or less loaded with clichés. It was produced by Berno Paulsson (**W.E.T, Nasty Idols, Spiritual Beggars** etc). In 1995 Joacim Sandin replaced Claes Wallin on bass and before *Attitude* guitarist Mikael Nilsson (**Sapphire Eyes, Nasty Idols, Alyson Avenue**) replaced Jörgen (later in **Silver Seraph**). **Bai Bang** is also featured on the compilation *Trilogy Of Stars* (92 Trilogy - TRCDC 9104). *Attitude* features a cover of **The Sweet's** *X-Ray Specs* (although **Sweet** aren't credited for it). Mikael was later replaced by guitarists Pelle Eliaz and Dave Aydin. The latter never appeared on any record. In 2009 Pelle also left the band, but returned again after a while. In 2012 the band however featured Kastenholt, Sandin, drummer Johan Bengtsson (also in **Pretty Wild**) and Jens Lundgren. Sleazy, glammy catchy hard rock. Sandin was replaced by Christoffer "Sikk Roxx" Svensson (**Famoüs Jameson**) early 2013.

1983 ■	Ung Kärlek/Goodbye Girl	7"	Rixi	TRIX 025
1984 □	Young Love/Junge Liebe	7"	Marie Marie	LC 9052
1985 □	Jag Kommer/Martini	7"	Start/Rixi	8408
1985 □	Tusen Och En Natt/Stopp Stopp Stopp	7	Sonet	T-10161
	The above were released under the name Double Trouble			

1983 7" - TRIX 025

Year		Title	Format	Label	Catalog
1987	□	Under Your Wings/To You	7"	Bozz	BOS 1001
1987	□	King For A Day/King For A Day (mini mix)	7"	Bozz	BOS 1004
1987	□	King For A Day/King For A Day (mini mix)	12"	Bozz	BOS 1004
1988	□	ENEMY LINES	LP	Bozz	BOLP 5001
1988	□	Behind Enemy Lines/(mini-mix)	7"	Bozz	BOS 1006
1989	□	Hot Love/To You	7"	Rush	RUSH 8809
1989	□	Next To You/Nobody Like You	7"	Beat Kingdom	BK5
1989	□	ENEMY LINES	CD	Vivo	imt 55007

Released in a box with four other bands. Hot love is featured as a bonus track.

1991	□	COP TO CON	CD	Trilogy (Canada)	TR-CD 9101
1991	□	COP TO CON	CD	Zero (Japan)	XRCN-1007
1992	□	Cop To Con/Love Is Strong	CDS 2tr	Zero (Japan)	XRCN-1027
1993	■	Little Child/F.O.F.D.	CDS 2tr	Ascendancy	ASCEN 1
1994	□	COP TO CON	CD	Jaguar	JA 11021-2

Yet another re-issue with a new artwork.

1994	□	Run To The End/Love Is Strong	7"	Jaguar	JA 1121
1995	□	BAI BANG	CD	Black Hole (Argentina)	MD 88018
1998	□	RIDIN' HIGH	CD	Rockfall	RRCD 501
1998	□	RIDIN' HIGH	CD	Avispa (Spain)	ACD 035
1999	□	RIDIN' HIGH	CD	Dream Circle (Germany)	DCD 9934
2000	□	ATTITUDE	CD	Riverside	RRCD 107
2000	□	ATTITUDE	CD	Avispa (Spain)	ACD 046
2002	□	Bai Bang	MCD 4tr	Riverside	RS 1006

Tracks: Rock 'N Roll City/Welcome To The Real World/X-Ray Specs (Sweet cover)/ Desperado

2005	□	BEST OF	CD	Swedmetal	SM-03-CD
2009	■	ARE YOU READY	CD	Metal Heaven	MVH00067
2009	□	ARE YOU READY	CD	Irond (Russia)	CD-09DD739
2011	□	LIVIN' MY DREAM	CD	AOR Heaven	AH 00060
2011	□	LIVIN' MY DREAM	CD	Rubicon Music (Japan)	RBNCD-1056

1993 CDS - ASCEN 1

2009 CD - MVH00067

BAJEN DEATH CULT

Tobias "Draugadrottir" Sidegård: v/g, Sebastian "Nidhögg" Ramstedt: g, Mats "Fox Skinner/Lodbror" Hedén: b, Anders "Mjölner" Bentell: d

Stockholm - The band was formed in the aftermath of the 1998 football season by members of the Swedish soccer fan club *Bajen Death Cult* for the team Hammarby IF. The band members are from several known Swedish bands. Lodbror has also been found in *Grand Magus* and Tobias in *Necrophobic*. Ramstedt is also in *Necrophobic* and *Morpheus*. These three are stated as composers of the released songs. However musicians like Fredrik Isaksson (*Grave*) and Johnny Hedlund (*Unleashed*) have also been part of the band at some point. Musically this is really classy, melodic powerful heavy metal in the good old *Accept*/*Priest* vein with nice guitar harmonies and clean vocals. Sidegård really proves he can sing great with a clean voice.

2004	■	Bajen-A-Voo-Doo	MCD 4tr	Tifo	BCD 001

Tracks: Vi som glöder/Nidvisa/El Corazon/Alla älskar en Bajare

| 2006 | ■ | NORDMÄN IFRÅN SÖDER | CD | private | BDC 002 |

2004 CD - BDC 001

BAKTERIA

Jeff Scott "Umberto Torres" Soto: v, Jens "Pedro Herrera" Johansson: k, Jonas "Jesus Ruiz" Hellborg: b, Anders "Manuel Gonzales" Johansson: d

Anderslöv/Lund/USA - The band bio says: "Originally founded in 1992, *Bakteria* was the first ones to come up with the concept of an all Mexican metal band!" Well, we know better don't we? *Bakteria* was mentioned already in the second encyclopedia. The band started out as a twisted experiment of four highly skilled musicians, Soto also found in *Rising Force, Eyes, Talisman, W.E.T* etc., Jens in *Rising Force, Silver Mountain* and now in *Stratovarius*, Anders in *Rising Force, Silver Mountain* and now in *Hammerfall*. Jonas is a highly gifted jazz bassist. He's also recorded a highly intriguing mertal fusion album with the band *Art Metal*, also featuring Anders and Jens plus guitar virtuoso Mattias Ia Eklundh. *Bakteria* was more of an experiment to see how far they could take the music and lyrics and still get signed, which they didn't succeed in back in 1993 when the album was actually recorded. Some of the songs were re-used (with other lyrics) for the *Shining Path* project. The music is hard driving, almost punk-oriented metal with no guitars, but heavily distorted keyboards. To give you an idea of the lyrical content let me just mention some song titles: *Shit On My Pubes, Castrate With A Rusty Scate, Shit In The Pussy*… well, you get the idea. The weird thing is, Anstalt Records reportedly released the CD in 2009, however noone seems to have ever seen it… does it exist? Well, it does, but only a few promo copies survived. According to Anders, 3000 copies were destroyed after the distributor had read the lyrics and gone through the roof. Even attorneys/ lawyers were called in. Four promo copies are said to have survived! A rarity!

The artwork meant to be.

2009 CD - NM 2503-2

| 2009 | ● | DEFECATE! SUFFOCATE! MUTILATE! MASTURBATE! | CD | Nuclear Blast/Anstalt Records | NM 2503-2 | $$ |

Only released as a promo in four copies. No artwork. The number was to be Patient 003

BALL

**Eero Raittinen: v, Nono Söderberg: g, Hillel Tokazier: k,
Kay Söderström: b/k, Henrik "Hempo" Hildén: d**

Stockholm - Straight 70s sounding hard rock with a strong bluesy touch. The B-side is not bad at all. Eero was previously with Finnish band *Tasavallan Presidentti*, Hillel was ex-*Help* and *Rotox*. Nono has made solo-recordings. Hempo and Kay were both previously in *Splash* and were later found in *Sarek* and *Trash*. Hempo has also played with *Baltimoore*, John Norum, Pugh Rogefeldt, *Dokken*, Glenn Hughes, *King Siguurd* and several other acts.

1986 ■ Leaving (For A New Band)/Ballgame ....7" Philips 6015 600

1986 7" - 6015600

BALLS

**Björn Lodin: v, Janne Stark: g, Mikael Nord Andersson: g,
Björn Lundkvist: b, Robert "Robban" Bäck: d**

Rättvik/Mörrum/Stockholm/Falun - BALLS was formed in 2007 when Björn Lodin contacted Janne to join forces after *Baltimoore* had folded. Janne was at the time writing songs together with Mikael Nord Andersson, who also joined. Björn and Janne started writing songs, as Mikael was at the time heavily involved with Swedish pop/rock singer Björn Skifs. Lundkvist (*Skyride*) and Bäck (*Eclipse, W.E.T, Billion Dollar Babies*) joined and the line-up was not only complete, but the members' last names actually made up the band name *BALLS* – Bäck, Andersson, Lodin, Lundkvist, Stark. The music is quite stripped down, traditional hard rock with hints of *AC/DC*. Unfortunately, due to different and strong opinions on various subjects, Björn left and the band folded just in time for the release. Janne and Mikael kept writing songs for what is to hopefully become Mikael's solo album, while Björn re-formed *Baltimoore* with Robert and Björn in the line-up. In 2009 Björn also joined Hungarian hard rockers *H.A.R.D.* The track *Chameleon* also appears on Versailles Records *AC/DC* tribute *Rock & Roll Train* (CD 2011), however cut down to 60 seconds without the band's consent. In 2009 Mikael and his colleague Martin produced the 2010 *Scorpions Sting In The Tail* and in 2011 started working on the two subsequent *Scorpions* releases. In 2012 Robban joined *Sabaton* and Björn released a pop/rock solo album in Swedish. Janne is still in *Overdrive*, *Grand Design*, *Constancia* and *Zoom Club*.

The shape of BALLS

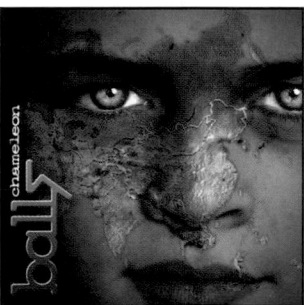

2008 CDd - BLP 2008-03

2008 ■ CHAMELEON ....CDd BLP ....BLP 2008-03

BALTHAZAR

**Peter Türsch: v, Jörgen Hansson: g, Stefan Rydberg: g,
Kent Persson: k, Mikael Johansson: b, Ronny Persson: d**

Furulund - Formed in 1979. Peter was ex-*Stonepepper* and *Mad Invasion*, the latter recorded a split-single with *High Level* which was never released due to the Studio going bust. The band split due to musical differences. Peter was offered the spot as lead singer in *Silver Mountain* but turned it down as the the music was a bit too "messy" (Peter was a huge *Journey* fan). He later wrote material for revues. Mid-weight and mid-class AOR. Quite similar to the stuff Epic Records used to release in the early 80's, such as *Hellfield*, *Fortnox*, *Air Raid* etc. Well worth looking for. Definitely time for a CD reissue.

1982 LP - YNF 508201

1983 7" - YNF 108310

1982 ■ HIDING IN THE CLOSET ....LP Holiday Music ....YNF 508201
1983 ■ Can't Cry Easy/Soldier Of Love ....7" Holiday Music ....YNF 108310

BALTHAZAR'S MACHINE

Börje Reinholdsson: v/d

Arvidsjaur - Quirky and highly interesting melodic hard rock mixing heavy riffs, odd twists and straight-ahead sing along choruses. Reminds me a bit of *Galactic Cowboys* at times. After the collapse of *X-Union* in 1997, Börje got involved with house project *Shrimp Cake*, but in 2000 he decided to go solo and called his project *Balthazar's Machine*. On the recordings he was helped out by rhythm guitarist Patrik Eklund and lead guitarist Ola Karlsson.

2004 CD - WW 0001

2004 ■ RECONSTRUCT ME ....CD Wobbling Wart ....WW 0001
2006 □ ROBOTICA ....CD Wobbling Wart .... WW 002

BALTIMOORE

Björn Lodin: v, **Emanuel Hedberg:** g, **Örjan Fernström:** k,
Björn Lundkvist: b, **Robban Bäck:** d

Rättvik - Björn Lodin started his recording career with a single in locals **Rainfall**, a compilation track with **Gathering Freak**, a demo with **Metal Studs** and then he fronted **Purple**-clones **Six Feet Under**. He was also one of the lead singers featured on the *Swedish Metal Aid* single. After this he went to Switzerland, but soon returned to Sweden. When returning he formed the band **Ready Steady** also featuring drummer Thomas Broman (**Tryckvåg, Great King Rat, Electric Boys, John Norum** etc), which never lifted off. In 1987 he formed **Baltimoore**. The band was initially a duo, featuring Björn and Ulf Wahlquist (**Secret Service**, now producer), who was actually featured on the early covers. However, it became Björn's solo-project. The first album also featured musicians such as guitarists Thomas Larsson (**Six Feet Under**, solo, **Glenn Hughes, Yeah Bop Station**) and Stefan Bergström (**Erika, Tone Norum** and later in **Skintrade** and **Alfonzetti**), drummer Rolf Alex (**Alex's Pro**) and keyboardist Mats Olausson (**Yngwie, Glory, Motvind** etc). The debut is a strong bluesy AOR-album while *Freak* is a deep soul blues thing. On the latter the guitars were handled by Stefan Bergström. On *Double Density* Björn joined forces with Hungarian-born guitarist Nikolo Kotzev (a resident of Åland/Finland, where Björn also lived for some years). When meeting Nikolo, he changed style and *Thought For Food* contains really good melodic hard rock. The band then featured Björn (v), Nikolo (g), Lars Pollack (k), Weine Johansson (b) and Ian Haugland (d). After *Thought For Food* the band split up and Nikolo concentrated on his band **Brazen Abbot**. Björn then sang on a couple of albums by **Lars-Erik Mattsson** and **Astral Groove**. In 2000 he decided to resurrect his old band. *Original Sin* is closer to his old solo-format, than his collaborations with Kotzev, musically as well. The line-up featured Joakim Larsson on bass, Lars Pollack on keyboards and Eiron Johansson on drums. The *Best Of* is more than an ordinary compilation. The album is all new rerecordings of old tracks; the way Björn intended them to be. The line-up now featured Björn (v), Thomas Larsson (g), Örjan Fernström (k), Weine (b) and Ian (d). It also featured guest keyboards from Per Wiberg (**Opeth, King Hobo, Mojobone**). *Ultimate Tribute* is a cover album where Björn pays tribute to bands like **Rainbow, Montrose, Nazareth, MSG, Deep Purple, Mountain** and **The Sweet**. Same line-up as the previous album minus Örjan. The 2005 effort *Fanatical* again featured a new line-up, this time featuring Björn, guitarists Stefan Bergström and Magnus "Mankan" Sedenberg (**Silver Seraph**), Weine and drummer Hempo Hildén (**Trash, John Norum, Glenn Hughes**). The same line-up lasted for another album, while on *X* Stefan was replaced by the returning Thomas Larsson. After a quite poorly promoted tour **Baltimoore** disbanded. Björn now contacted Janne Stark and together with Mikael Nord Andersson (who contributed with some backing vocals on the first **Baltimoore** LP) they formed the band **BALLS**. The bass was handled by Björn Lundkvist (**Skyride**) and drums by Robban Bäck (**Eclipse, W.E.T, Billion Dollar Babies**, now **Sabaton**). The line-up only released one CD, *Chameleon*, before disbanding. Björn again resurrected **Baltimoore** with yet another line-up featuring the aforementioned Björn and Robban, former colleague Örjan Fernström on keyboards and new guitarist Emanuel Hedberg. After releasing the album *Quick Fix*, which is more keyboard-oriented, less rocky but still quite bluesy, Björn fronted Hungarian hard rockers **H.A.R.D** and put **Baltimoore** on hold. In 2012 he was also recording pop-oriented solo material in Swedish, but later that year he revived **Baltimoore**, again featuring Hildén on drums, for a new album yet to be released.
Website: www.baltimoore.net

Young man with guitar

1988 7" - BOS 1003

1988 7" - BOS 1015

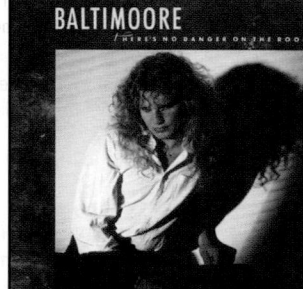

1989 LP - BOLP 5004

1990 7" - VS 1010

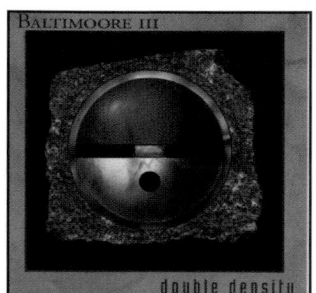

1992 CD - ONECD 041

2009 CDd - BLP 2009-01

1988	■	The Blues Is Just The Same/Too Many People	7"	Bozz	BOS 1003
1988	□	The Blues Is Just The Same	MLP 3tr	Bozz	BOST 1003
		Tracks The Blues Is Just The Same/The Blues..(extended version)/Too Many People			
1988	■	My Blue Moon/Happy Times	7"	Bozz	BOS 1015
1988	□	Ballerina(single vers.)/Ballerina(original vers.)	7"	Bozz	BOS 1022
1989	□	My Blue Moon/Happy Times	CDS	Bozz	BOSCD 1015
1989	□	THERE'S NO DANGER ON THE ROOF	CD	V.I.P	VCD 5004
1989	□	THERE'S NO DANGER ON THE ROOF	LP	Bozz	BOLP 5004
1989	□	Dance Dance/Hey Bulldog	7"	Bozz	BOS 1045
1990	□	Little Bye/In Love	7"	V.I.P	VS 1004
1990	□	FREAK	CD	V.I.P	VCD 5007
1990	□	FREAK	LP	V.I.P	VCD 5007
1990	■	Oh Darling/Fly So Gently	7"	V.I.P	VS 1010
1990	□	Memories Calling/Day To Come	7"	V.I.P	VS 1012
1992	□	My Kinda Girl	MCD 5tr	Alpha	PROMOCD 111
		Tracks My Kinda Girl/Till The End Of Day/My Blue Moon/Memories Calling/Little Bye			
1992	■	DOUBLE DENSITY	CD	Alpha	ONECD 041
1992	□	DOUBLE DENSITY	CD	Zero (Japan)	XRCN-1030
1992	□	My Kind Of Woman/Till The End Of Day	CDS 2tr	Alpha	ONECDS 111
1994	□	THOUGHT FOR FOOD	CD	Hawk	HAWKCD 2147
1994	□	THOUGHT FOR FOOD	CD	Zero (Japan)	XRCN-1114
1994	□	Alone/Full Speed Ahead	CDS 2tr	Hawk	HAWKPROM 019
2000	□	ORIGINAL SIN	CD	Lion Music	LMC 2006 2
2001	□	THE BEST OF	CD	Lion Music	LMC 2108 2
2003	□	ULTIMATE TRIBUTE	CD	Lion Music	LMC 2108 2

2005	□	FANATICAL	CD	Lion Music	LMC 149
2005	□	FANATICAL	CD	Irond (Russia)	CD 09-DD315
2006	□	KALEIDOSCOPE	CD	BLP	BLP 2006-01
2006	□	X	CDd	BLP	BLP 2006-02
2009	■	QUICK FIX	CDd	BLP	BLP 2009-01

BAM BAM BOYS

Matti Alfonzetti: v, Göran Elmquist: g, Gunnar Hallin: b, Fredrik Von Gerber: d

Stockholm - This band contains some highly acclaimed musicians. Matti has later been found in *Jagged Edge, Skintrade, Alfonzetti, Damned Nation* and now in UK hard rockers *Red White & Blues* and *Impera*, Gunnar was ex-*Neon Rose*, Freddie has played with tons of bands like *Easy Action, Voodoo X* and *Red Fun* while Göran has made several studio jobs and was also found in *Dream Bank*. The band was completed by keyboard-player Mats Olausson (*Yngwie, Glory, Motvind* etc) on tour. In 1989 *Bam Bam Boys* also recorded an album, which was not released due to the label going out of business. There was however a test-pressing made... in 4 copies. There was also a test-pressing made of a second single, *I Believe In Rock 'N Roll*, but never released as the label went bust. In 1999 the album was finally re-mastered and released. The band also made some reunion gigs.

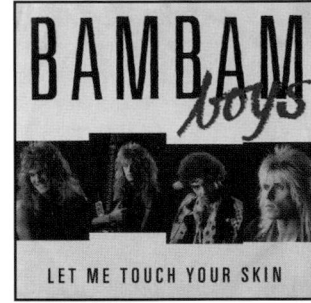

1988 7" - S 018

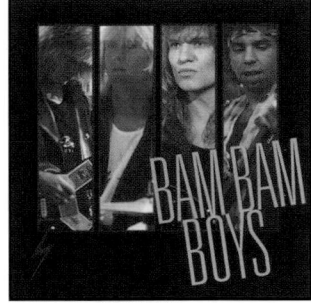

1999 CD - RRCD 104

1988	■	Let Me Touch Your Skin/White Lies	7"	KGR	S 018
1999	□	Let Me Touch Your Skin (Radio Edit)/(Album Version)	CDSp 2tr	Riverside	RS 1004
1999	■	BAM BAM BOYS	CD	Riverside	RRCD 104

BAN-ZAI (aka NIO LIV)

Magnus Brunzell: v, Ove Kilström: g, Johan Boding: k, Conny Goldschmidt: b, Jylle Sandberg: d

Stockholm - The band was originally called *Nio Liv* (Nine Lives), under which name they recorded a single (not to be confused with the Göteborg new wave band). Magnus was ex-*Candy Roxx*. Good AOR with strong, but very commercial melodies. A sound quite similar to *Alien*, but with vocals in Swedish. Not the same label as *Talisman, Masquerade* etc., but the one who also released a 7" with *Rising*. They recorded a full length album, but due to the record company going bust it was never released. Magnus, Conny and Ove were later in the *U2*-influenced band *Wasteland* (no recordings) and today Conny is found in hard rockers *M.O.B.* Johan has toured with *Sha-Boom* and several Swedish pop-artists.

1990 7" - EMPS-040

1989	□	Spillra Av En Man/En Galen Värld	7"	Empire	EMPS-010
		Released under the name Nio Liv.			
1990	■	13 Man/Maskerad	7"	Empire	EMPS-040

BAND OF SPICE

Christian "Spice" Sjöstrand: v/g, Anders Linusson: g, Johann: b, Robert "Bob Ruben" Hansson: d

Värnamo - The band was originally formed as *Spice And The RJ Band*, but changed their name when Anders Linusson (ex-*The Mushroom River Band*) joined the band and RJ (which stood for Ruben and Johan) wasn't correct anymore. Linusson is also a member of the Apladalen runners club (not a band, actually a runners club!). Spice is a former member of *Aeon, Kayser, Spiritual Beggars* and *The Mushroom River Band*. Bob was also in the first and last. *Band Of Spice* (as well as *Spice & The RJ Band*) play retro-oriented hard rock, with very pop-oriented melodies and a rock 'n roll attitude. The missing link between *The Mushroom River Band* and *The Hellacopters*?

2010 CD - WEED 11 CD

| 2010 | ■ | FEEL LIKE COMING HOME | CDd | We Deliver The Guts | WEED 11 CD |

BANG & OUT

Monica Larsson: v, Patric Köpman: g, Benny Björkh: b, Håkan Persson: d

Stockholm - Pretty high class melodic hard rock, slightly thin production, but it's compensated by the outstanding vocals of Monica. At times she sounds very much like *Lee Aaron*, and the music is also in the same melodic hard-rocking vein. Monica later fronted the sadly underrated and unsigned *Monica Maze Band*, also featuring Pontus Norgren (*Hammerfall, The Poodles, Great King Rat*). Well worth looking for if you're a fan of great melodic hard rock. Unfortunately Monica left the melodic rock vein and went into pop/folk music. Håkan was later found in *Skintrade*. In 2012 Monica returned to the scene with new solo material.

| 1989 | ■ | Riding On The Desert Wind/Wolves Cry | 7" | Platina | PL 61 |

1989 7" - PL 61

BARRELHOUSE

Hans Fröberg: v, Martin Högvall: g, Adam Johansson (Dahlberg): b, Björn Nilsson: d

Uppsala - The band was formed in 1979 and the 7" was recorded the same year. They actually only consisted of Martin and Björn. Adam owned the Tascam 4 track, on which the single was recorded. The band then played as a trio, featuring Martin, Björn and bass-player Janne Olander, later in **Solid Blue**. The split came in 1987, when Björn went to Texas. In 1993 he returned and the band reformed. The line-up then featured Martin, Björn, Hans (who was still in **Solid Blue**), Janne and keyboard-player Rickard Zander (yet another **Solid Blue** member). The band became more of a cover band, mostly doing **Led Zeppelin**-covers, such as *The Song Remains The Same, No Quarter* etc. No official recordings have yet emerged. The single is actually a great hard rocker in the true 70s vein, with serious riffing, good vocals and varied songs. Recommended. Adam changed his last name to Dahlberg and was found in fusion-band **Elexir**. Hans later joined **Spellbound, Solid Blue, The Flower Kings** and is alo in **Hasse & Fröberg & Musical Companion**.

1979 ☐ Far Away/Come On Down..7" Studio Högvall Records .... SHR 001

1979 7" - SHR 001

BATHORY

Thomas Ace "Quorthon" Forsberg: v/g

Stockholm - Sweden's first real death metal band with the charismatic Quorthon at the helm. He was born February 17, 1966 and died only 38 years old, of a heart failure June 7 (even though the Black Mark website stated June 3), 2004. He is buried at the Sandsborg cemetery in Gamla Enskede, south of Stockholm on July 13, 2004. He called himself Ace Shot in the beginning and actually took Ace as a middle name. Thomas' name was a well hidden secret, and many people tried to find it out. The Norwegian book *Lords Of Chaos* revealed his real name being **Pugh Rogefeldt**. Pop/rock star Pugh probably laughed his butt off. **Bathory** was formed in March 1983 by then seventeen year old Quorthon and three of his former Oi-punk buddies, bass player Fredrik "Fredrick Hanoi" Melander, singer Björn "The Animal" Kristensen and drummer Jonas "Vans McBurger" Åkerlund. The band was initially recognised for the two furious tracks *Sacrifice* and *The Return Of Darkness And Evil* on the compilation *Scandinavian Metal Attack* (1984) and was soon signed by Tyfon. This line-up only lasted until the debut was recorded. After this **Bathory** has been more of a project based around the persona of Quorthon. Bass player Koothar and

Bathory hunting for the primeval sound.

drummer Vvornth have actually been several different people such as bassist Rickard Bergman and drummer Stefan Larsson. On the **Bathory** website a quote by Thomas himself says: "There had always been some sort of a group situation up until shortly before *Twilight Of The Gods*. Though the people playing on most of those early albums would usually be friends of mine on a hired-guns level, friends with either no interest in a career whatsoever or possessing not enough of the qualities and enthusiasm one could usually ask of a full time band member". He was initially produced by his father Börje "Boss" Forsberg (owner of Black Mark Records). In some magazine features Quorthon denied Börje was his father claiming he was too young to be. However as records say Börje was born in 1944 (June 22), he was 22 when Quorthon was born, not 15, as stated in the interview. **Quorthon's** solo albums are quite far from the brutal death metal of **Bathory**, actually more in the vein of the latest **Bathory**-albums. The band started out sounding as primitive and raw as **Venom**. The first recordings were very primitively recorded in an old garage with a small amp, which shows... The goat on the cover of the debut album was supposed to be golden, but ended up yellow, which is probably one of the most fatal misprints in the history of death metal (besides the **Arckanum** box with pink print). **Bathory** however developed through the years and the album *Octagon* (the eighth album) contains pure heavy brain crushing metal with Quorthon's voice sounding cleaner than ever. *Destroyer Of Worlds* took this even a step further and added a doom-oriented and slightly symphonic touch to it all. All CD-reissues have been re-mastered. A cover of **Black Sabbath's** *War Pigs* can be found on *Black Mark Tribute Vol 2. Jubileum Vol. III* celebrated **Bathory**'s 15 years anniversary and contains 15 remastered tracks and 6 previously unreleased songs. Jonas Åkerlund is today a renowned video producer (**Metallica, U2, Madonna, Rammstein** etc). Thomas' sister Jennie Tebler now has a musical career of her own and also recorded a tribute single for her late brother. Quorthon's memory still hovers over the Swedish death/black metal scene and bands like **Watain** have performed tribute shows for **Bathory** and Quorthon.

1984 LP - BMLP 666-1

| 1984 | ■ | BATHORY | LP | Black Mark | BMLP 666-1 | $$$ |

The first pressing, approximately 800 copies with yellow goat.

| 1984 | □ | BATHORY | LP | Black Mark | BMLP 666-1 | $ |

White goat.

1985	□	BATHORY	LP	Banzai (Canada)	BRC 1934	
1985	□	THE RETURN... OF DARKNESS AND EVIL	LP	Black Mark	666-2	$
1985	□	THE RETURN... OF DARKNESS AND EVIL	LP	Combat (USA)	MX 8041	
1985	□	THE RETURN... OF DARKNESS AND EVIL	LP	Banzai (Can)	BRC 1955	
1986	■	UNDER THE SIGN OF THE BLACK MARK	LP	Under One Flag (UK)	FLAG 11	
1986	□	UNDER THE SIGN OF THE BLACK MARK	CD	Under One Flag (UK)	FLAG 11	
1986	□	UNDER THE SIGN OF THE BLACK MARK	LP	New Renaissance (USA)	NRR 033	
1986	□	UNDER THE SIGN OF THE BLACK MARK	CD	New Renaissance (USA)	NRR 033	
1986	□	UNDER THE SIGN OF THE BLACK MARK	LP	One Music Korea (Korea)	KPL 3055	

Different tracklisting and back cover artwork.

1986 CD - FLAG 11

1988	□	BLOOD FIRE DEATH	LP	Black Mark	BMLP 666-4	$
1988	□	BLOOD FIRE DEATH	LP	Under One Flag (UK)	FLAG 26	
1988	□	BLOOD FIRE DEATH	CD	Under One Flag (UK)	FLAG 26	
1988	□	BLOOD FIRE DEATH	LP PD	Under One Flag (UK)	FLAG 26 P	
1990	□	BLOOD FIRE DEATH	CD	Kraze/Maze America (USA)	MCD 1063	
1990	■	HAMMERHEART	LP	Black Mark	BMLP 666-5	
1990	■	HAMMERHEART	LP	Noise	N 0153	

Different artwork.

1990	□	HAMMERHEART	CD	Noise	N 0153	
1990	□	HAMMERHEART	LPg	Noise	N 0153	
1990	□	HAMMERHEART	LP	Seoul Records (Korea)	SIPR 038	
1990	□	BATHORY	CD	Black Mark	BMCD 666-1	
1991	□	TWILIGHT OF THE GODS	CD	Black Mark	BMCD 666-6	
1991	□	TWILIGHT OF THE GODS	LP	Black Mark	BMLP 666-6	
1991	□	TWILIGHT OF THE GODS	LP PD	Black Mark	BMPD 666-6	

Limited edition personally signed picture disc.

| 1991 | □ | TWILIGHT OF THE GODS | LP | One Music Korea (Korea) | KPL 3034 | |

Different artwork.

1990 LP - BMLP 666-5

1992	□	JUBILEUM VOLUME I	CD	Black Mark	BMCD666-7	
1993	□	HAMMERHEART	CD	Black Mark	BMCD 666-5	
1993	□	BLOOD FIRE DEATH	CD	Black Mark	BMCD 666-4	
1993	□	JUBILEUM VOLUME II	CD	Black Mark	BMCD666-8	
1994	□	REQUIEM	LP	Black Mark	BMLP666-10	
1994	□	REQUIEM	CD	Black Mark	BMCD666-10	
1994	□	BATHORY	LP	Hellion (Brazil)	HELL 014	
1995	□	OCTAGON	CD	Black Mark	BMCD666-11	
1995	□	HAMMERHEART	LPg	22 (Brazil)	22-05	
1996	■	Blood On Ice	MCDp 3tr	Black Mark (promo)	BMCDP-666-12	

Tracks: The Sword/The Lake/The Woodwoman

1996	□	BLOOD ON ICE	CD	Black Mark	BMCDP666-12	
1996	□	BLOOD ON ICE	LP	Black Mark	BMLP666-12	
1998	□	JUBILEUM VOL III	CD	Black Mark	BMCD666-16	
2001	□	KATALOG	CD	Black Mark	BMCD 666-17	

Compilation featuring ten tracks from the Bathory back-catalogue.

1990 LP - N 0153

2001	□	DESTROYER OF WORLDS	CD	Black Mark	BMCD 666-15	
2001	□	DESTROYER OF WORLDS	LP	Black Mark	BMLP 666-15	
2001	□	DESTROYER OF WORLDS	LP PD	Black Mark	BMPD 666-15	
2002	□	HAMMERHEART	CD	Irond (Russia)	CD 02-293	
2002	□	TWILIGHT OF THE GODS	CD	Irond (Russia)	CD 02-294	
2002	□	DESTROYER OF WORLDS	CD	Irond (Russia)	CD 02-295	
2002	□	NORDLAND I	CD	Black Mark	BMCD 666-18	
2002	□	NORDLAND I	CDd	Black Mark	BMDP 666-19	
2002	□	NORDLAND I & II	2LP	Black Mark	BMDP 666-21	
2002	□	NORDLAND II	CD	Black Mark	BMCD 666-20	
2002	□	NORDLAND II	CDd	Black Mark	BMDP 666-22	
2002	□	THE TRUE BLACK ESSENCE (HISTORY)	CD	-	RS 99	
2003	□	BATHORY	LP	Black Mark	BMLP 666-1	
2003	□	THE RETURN OF DARKNESS AND EVIL	LP	Black Mark	BMLP 666-2	
2003	□	UNDER THE SIGN OF THE BLACK MARK	LP	Black Mark	BMLP 666-3	
2003	□	BLOOD FIRE DEATH	LP	Black Mark	BMLP 666-4	
2003	□	HAMMERHEART	LP	Black Mark	BMLP 666-5	
2003	□	TWILIGHT OF THE GODS	LP	Black Mark	BMLP 666-6	
2003	□	JUBILEUM VOL. I	LP	Black Mark	BMLP 666-7	
2003	□	JUBILEUM VOL. II	LP	Black Mark	BMLP 666-8	
2003	□	JUBILEUM VOL. III	LP	Black Mark	BMLP 666-16	
2003	□	REQUIEM	LP	Black Mark	BMLP 666-10	
2003	□	OCTAGON	LP	Black Mark	BMLP 666-11	
2003	□	BLOOD ON ICE	LP	Black Mark	BMLP 666-12	
2003	□	NORDLAND I	CD	Irond (Russia)	CD 03-660	

1996 MCDp - BMCDP-666-12

89

Year		Title	Format	Label	Catalog
2003	□	NORDLAND II	CD	Irond (Russia)	CD 03-661
2003	□	BATHORY	CD	Irond (Russia)	CD 03-637
2003	■	OCTAGON	CD	Irond (Russia)	CD 03-679
2003	■	REQUIEM	CD	Irond (Russia)	CD 03-482
2003	□	THE RETURN	CD	Irond (Russia)	CD 03-638
2003	□	BLOOD FIRE DEATH	CD	Irond (Russia)	CD 03-432
2003	□	BLOOD ON ICE	CD	Irond (Russia)	CD 03-434
2003	□	NORDLAND II	CD	Black Mark	BMCD 666-20
2003	□	NORDLAND II	CDd	Black Mark	BMDP 666-20
2004	□	UNDER THE SIGN OF THE BLACK MARK	CD	Irond (Russia)	CD 04-715
2005	□	BATHORY	LP	Black Mark	BMLP 666-1

Re-mastered re-issue. Blood red vinyl.

| 2005 | □ | THE RETURN OF DARKNESS AND EVIL | LP | Black Mark | BMLP 666-2 |

Re-mastered re-issue. Blood red vinyl.

| 2005 | □ | UNDER THE SIGN OF THE BLACK MARK | LP | Black Mark | BMLP 666-3 |

Re-mastered re-issue. Blood red vinyl.

| 2005 | □ | BLOOD FIRE DEATH | LP | Black Mark | BMLP 666-4 |

Re-mastered re-issue. Blood red vinyl.

| 2005 | □ | HAMMERHEART | LP | Black Mark | BMLP 666-5 |

Re-mastered re-issue. Blood red vinyl.

| 2005 | □ | TWILIGHT OF THE GODS | LP | Black Mark | BMLP 666-6 |

Re-mastered re-issue. Blood red vinyl.

| 2005 | □ | NORDLAND I & II | 2LP | Black Mark | BMLP 666-12 |

Re-mastered re-issue. Blood red vinyl.

2006	□	IN MEMORY OF QUORTHON VOL I	CD	Black Mark	BMCD 666-23
2006	□	IN MEMORY OF QUORTHON VOL II	CD	Black Mark	BMCD 666-24
2006	□	IN MEMORY OF QUORTHON VOL III	CD	Black Mark	BMCD 666-25
2006	□	IN MEMORY OF QUORTHON	3CD+DVD Box	Black Mark	BMCD 666-27 $$
2007	□	BATHORY	LP PD	Black Mark	BMPD 666-1
2007	□	THE RETURN OF DARKNESS AND EVIL	LP PD	Black Mark	BMPD 666-2
2007	□	UNDER THE SINGN OF THE BLACK MARK	LP PD	Black Mark	BMPD 666-3
2007	□	BLOOD FIRE DEATH	LP PD	Black Mark	BMPD 666-4
2007	□	HAMMERHEART	LP PD	Black Mark	BMPD 666-5
2007	□	TWILIGHT OF THE GODS	LP PD	Black Mark	BMPD 666-6
2007	□	REQUIEM	LP PD	Black Mark	BMPD666-10
2007	□	OCTAGON	LP PD	Black Mark	BMPD666-11
2008	□	BLOOD ON ICE	LP PD	Black Mark	BMPD 666-12
2008	■	DESTROYER OF WORLDS	LP PD	Black Mark	BMPD 666-15
2008	■	NORDLAND I	LP PD	Black Mark	BMPD 666-18
2008	■	NORDLAND II	LP PD	Black Mark	BMPD 666-20
2010	□	BATHORY	LP	Black Mark	BMLP 666-1

Grey vinyl. Re-pressed in 500 copies gold vinyl in 2012 (also as BMLP 666-1)

| 2010 | □ | THE RETURN OF DARKNESS AND EVIL | LP | Black Mark | BMLP 666-2 |

Brown vinyl. Re-pressed in 500 copies gold vinyl in 2012 (also as BMLP 666-2)

| 2010 | □ | UNDER THE SINGN OF THE BLACK MARK | LP | Black Mark | BMLP 666-3 |

Blue vinyl. Re-pressed in 500 copies gold vinyl in 2012 (also as BMLP 666-3)

| 2010 | □ | BLOOD FIRE DEATH | LP | Black Mark | BMLP 666-4 |

White vinyl. Re-pressed in 500 copies gold vinyl in 2012 (also as BMLP 666-4)

| 2007 | □ | HAMMERHEART | 2LP | Black Mark | BMLP 666-5 |

Yellow. Re-pressed in 500 copies gold vinyl in 2012 (also as BMLP 666-5)

| 2010 | □ | TWILIGHT OF THE GODS | 2LP | Black Mark | BMLP 666-6 |

Light blue vinyl. Re-pressed in 500 copies gold vinyl in 2012 (also as BMLP 666-6)

Unofficial realeases:

| 1999 | □ | THE RETURN | LP | - | - |

Boot made from the Under One Flag-version in light-brown vinyl, probably made in South America.

| n/a | □ | Hail Sathanas | 7" | The Hordes | 666-666 |

Tracks: The Return Of Darkness And Evil/Sacrifice

2001	□	UNDER THE SIGN OF THE DARKNESS AND THE EVIL	CD	Bathory Hordes (Brazil)	-
2002	□	DIE IN FIRE	LP PD	Bathory Hordes (Brazil)	-
2005	□	BATHORY/VENOM (split)	LP	Black Mark	-

Split with Venom. 121 copies in white vinyl and 150 copies in yellow. Tracks: In Nomine Satanas/Die In Fire/Burning Leather/Satan My Master/The Return Of Darkness And Evil.

| 2009 | □ | TRUE BLACK ESSENCE | LP | - | - |

South American bootleg with demos and edits.

| n/a | □ | BATHORY/HELLHAMMER (split) | LP | - | - |

Bootleg split with Hellhammer. South America.

| n/a | □ | BLOODBACK | LP | - | - |

Tracks: Intro/In Conspiracy With Satan/Necromancy-Sacrifice/Raise The Dead (remastered demo 1984)/Sacrifice/The Return Of Darkness And Evil (edited version)/Valhalla/Satan My Master/In Nomine Of Satan/Resolution Greed/Witchcraft/Genocide (unreleased rehearsal)

2003 CD - CD 03-679

2003 CD - CD 03-679

2008 LP PD - BMPD 666-15

2008 LP PD - BMPD 666-18

2008 LP PD - BMPD 666-20

BATTLE STATION

Niklas "Nikki" Jonsson: v, Christian Fecht: g,
Robert Kenndal: b, Gustav "Gus" Liljenström: d

Norrköping - Formed in 1990 under the name *Nazty Habitz*, changed it to *Captain Freak's Freaky Funksters* (*CFFF*) and released a single. Bass player Robert Kenndal was replaced by Tomas and the band changed their name to *Battle Station*. The CFFF single was in the vein of *Electric Boys* and *Extreme*, while *Battle Station* owes more to the likes of *Ratt* and *Guns 'N Roses*. Powerful sleazy hard rock with some interesting riffs here and there. Typical sore-throat glam vocals á la Stephen Pearcy (*Ratt, Arcade*), a lot more powerful than on the *CFFF* 7". Great guitar-playing by Fecht. On the 7-track demo that preceded the CD they did a cover of *ABBA's Does Your Mutha Know*. In 1995 the band split and Gustaf and Christian formed the band *Millhouse*. Gustaf later recorded three albums with the band *Violent Divine*.

1994 MCD - TTCDS 01

1994	■	Battle Station	MCD 5tr	Taltratten	TTCDS 01

Tracks: Guillotine/Mental Confusion/Toys In The Attic (not the Aerosmith song)/Act Of Lies/Black Magic Woman.

BATTLELUST

Henrik "Baron De Samedi" Åberg: d/g/b/k, Lucichrist: g/b

Luleå - Black metal, unfortunately of the less interesting kind. Henrik is also found in *Necromicon, Hellmaster, Gates Of Ishtar, Incinerator* and *Satariel*. The band also has the track *The Acheron* on the compilation *A Tribute To Hell – Satanic Rites* (Full Moon Productions).

1997 CDd - HHR017

1997	■	OF BATTLE AND ANCIENT WARCRAFT	CDd	Hammerheart	HHR017

BEARDFISH

Rikard Sjöblom: v/g/k, David Zackrisson: g/k/v, Robert Hansen: b/v, Magnus Östgren: d

Gävle - Progressive band *Beardfish* was formed in 2001 by guitarist Zackrisson and Sjöblom, who had played together in school in the grunge band *Wooderson*. The debut also included keyboardplayer/guitarist Stefan Aronsson. Influenced by *Gentle Giant* and *Frank Zappa*, they may not qualify into the heavier league of progressive rock, but on some tracks there's some pretty fierce guitarplaying. They should appeal to fans of bands like *Anekdoten, Ritual, The Flower Kings* and *Cross*. Quite an outstanding progressive band with nice quirky musical twists, ranging from quite silly sounding simplicities to heavy guitar dominated parts, interesting arrangements and flawlessly executed. An intriguing band, indeed. They have also become one of *Dream Theater* drummer Mike Portnoy's favourite bands, resulting in the US prog metallers inviting *Beardfish* to open up for them on the North American leg of the 2009 *Progressive Nation* tour. Unfortunately they had to bail out of the tour as SPV filed for bankruptsy and no longer could support them financially. Rikard also has a side project called *Gungfly*, also in the vein of *Beardfish*, but mixing in other influences. *Mammoth* shows a slightly heavier side of the band.

2008 CD - IOMCD 294

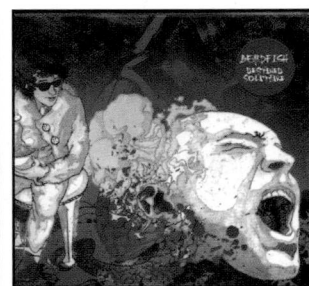
2009 CDd - IOMCD 314

2003	☐	FRÅN EN PLATS DU EJ KAN SE	CD	Jet-Set Music	JSM 002
2005	☐	THE SANE DAY	2CD	Beard & Breakfast	BEARD001/002
2007	☐	FRÅN EN PLATS DU EJ KAN SE	CD	Progress	PRCD 027
		Reissue with new artwork and bonus tracks: In Your Room/Spegeldans (live)			
2007	☐	THE SANE DAY	2CD	Progress	PRCD 028
2007	☐	SLEEPING IN TRAFFIC: PART ONE	CD	Inside Out	IOMCD 277
2007	☐	SLEEPING IN TRAFFIC: PART ONE	CDp	Belle Antique (Japan)	MAR-071262
2008	■	SLEEPING IN TRAFFIC: PART TWO	CD	Inside Out	IOMCD 294
2008	☐	SLEEPING IN TRAFFIC: PART TWO	CDp	Belle Antique (Japan)	MAR-081386
2009	■	DESTINED SOLITAIRE	CD/d	Inside Out	IOMCD 314
		First pressing released as digi-pack.			
2009	☐	DESTINED SOLITAIRE	CD	Inside Out	IOMCD 314
2009	☐	DESTINED SOLITAIRE	CD	Marquee Inc. (Japan)	MAR-91581
2011	■	MAMMOTH	CDd+DVD	Inside Out	50543-8
		Bonus DVD with a live show from Holland, plus "The making of…"			
2011	☐	MAMMOTH	CD	Century Media	50543-2
2011	☐	MAMMOTH	LP+CD	Century Media	50543-1
2011	☐	MAMMOTH	2CD	Marquee Inc. (Japan)	MAR-11826/7
2012	☐	THE VOID	CD	Inside Out	IOMCD 359
2012	■	THE VOID	CDd	Inside Out	IOMLTDCD 359
		Bonus: Ludvig & Sverker (Piano version)			

2011 CDd+DVD - 50543-8

2012 CDd - IOMLTDCD 359

BEDLAM

Bernt Ek: b/v, Thomas Jacobsson: g, Peter Carlsson: g/v, Åke Eriksson: d

Stockholm - The Kalix based band *Wildliw* recorded two melodic singles in 1983 and -84, but when the guys moved to Stockholm they recruited former *Wasa Express* drummer Åke Eriksson and *Bedlam* was born, a suitable name considering Åke's style of drumming and general flipouts. After the single *Tiger Feet* (*Mud*-cover) they changed singer to Micke Moberg (ex-*Zeta*),

with whom they recorded an excellent demo that was supposed to be the album *Sensurround*. He was however later replaced by Björn Lodin (*Baltimoore, Six Feet Under*), but shortly after, around 1989, the band broke up. Bernt joined *Wizz* in 1986 and after a year went on to AOR-rockers *The Station/House Of Shakira*. He later made some unreleased solo recordings as well as lending a helping hand to Tommy Denander, plus playing in hard rock cover band *Troop*. Before *Wildliw* he was in symphonic rock band *Grace*, with whom he recorded the album *Blind* in 1976. Tomas was later found in AOR band *Snakes In Paradise* and he has written songs for *Brett Walker* and Swedish pop singer *Carola*, while Peter made a successful career as pop/rock composer for radio and TV, but also for *Jim Jidhed* and *Nick Borgen*. *Bedlam* is straight-ahead hard rock in the same style as *Kiss*. The band made a, sadly, half-hearted attempt for a comeback in 2007. A couple of pretty nice sounding songs, one entitled *Hot Rocking*, were recorded but nothing more came out of it. Thomas is today in the band *Angel King* and Eriksson is in the resurrected *Wasa Express*.

1985 MLP - BEB LP 1

1985 7" - BED SI 2

1985	■	The Beauties And The Beast	MLP 6tr	Virgin		BED LP 1
1985	□	Take It To The Top/Take it To The Top (short)/Live It Up	MLP 3tr	Virgin		BED MA 1
1985	□	Take It To The Top/Live It Up	7"	Virgin		BED SI 1
1985	■	Tiger Feet/If You Want It Go And Get It	7"	Virgin		BED SI 2
1985	□	Tiger Feet (crazy mix)/Tiger Feet/Tiger Feet (extended version)	MLP 3tr	Virgin		BED MA 2

BEDLAM, ÅKE ERIKSSON &

Tony Ajayi: g, Olle Rönnbäck: b, Åke Eriksson: d/v

Stockholm - After Åke's previous band *Bedlam* split, he formed a new band but kept the name as a part of the new. Olle was previously in pop band *Vanessa* (not the hard rock act). The first single is a great piece of *Kiss*-type hard rock, with the B-side starting off with a long drumsolo. The second 7" was released under the name *Åke Eriksson Hot Shot 3*. The A-side is a 30s jazz-fling while the B-side is a real hard rocker with a drum solo ending it.

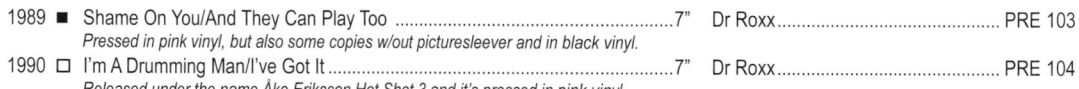
1989 7" - PRE 103

1989	■	Shame On You/And They Can Play Too	7"	Dr Roxx		PRE 103
		Pressed in pink vinyl, but also some copies w/out picturesleeve and in black vinyl.				
1990	□	I'm A Drumming Man/I've Got It	7"	Dr Roxx		PRE 104
		Released under the name Åke Eriksson Hot Shot 3 and it's pressed in pink vinyl				

BEDLAM ERIXON

Åke "Bedlam" Eriksson: d, Lasse "Dilldoo" Hajagos: v

Stockholm - This is weirdo-drummer Åke Eriksson's solo project. Åke started his professional drum career in the *Riksteatern* (The National Theater) in 1974, then joined jazz-rock group *Egba*, recorded four albums with *Wasa Express*, then toured with *Percussion All Stars* to continue with pop-metal band *Attack*. Then he recorded his solo singles, joined *Bedlam*, that later became *Åke Eriksson & Bedlam*. The second single is definitely for collectors only and is actually released under the moniker *Bedlam & Dilldoo*. *Helvetets Port* is a Swedish version of the *AC/DC* song *Highway To Hell*. Åke is now in the resurrected *Wasa Express*.

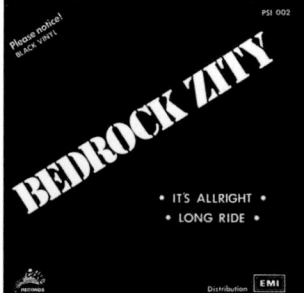
1982 7" - A 2976

1982	■	Let There Be Drums/Helvetets Port	7"	CBS		A 2976
1983	□	Läs högt ur din bankbok/Poltergeist	7"	CTR		CTR-383
		Released under the moniker Bedlam & Dildo.				

BEDROCK ZITY

Gunnar Hagman: v/g, Roger Hedin: g, Mikael Wiking: b, Jan Andersson: d

Norrköping - *It's Allright* is closer to a 50s rocker than hard rock, while *Long Ride* is straight low rate heavy metal with quite a thin sound. Label owner Lars E. Carlsson has co-written the songs.

1982	■	It's Allright/Long Ride	7"	Pang		PSI 002
		500 copies. Some without picture sleeve, but with band photo.				

1982 7" - PSI 002

BEDROOM LOVE

Stephen Nykvist: v, Roger Wahlsten: g, Andrew Axelsson: k ,
Danny Karlsson: b, Jesper "Jeppe" Lindbergh: d

Örebro - A short-lived band that released a high class soft AOR CD. Right after the release, Roger left the band to form *Wahlsten Band* together with his brother Peter, Stephen left for *Crystal Blue* and Andrew joined *Sly Side*. The CD is well worth investing in if you like well-played, high class AOR. Jesper recorded numerous demos and a CD with the band *The Painted Man*.

1993	■	Dreams Can Be Real	MCD 4tr	private		BEDCD 93001
		Tracks:You Are A Queen To Me/Give Love A Second Chance/Dreams Can Be Real/ Scared Without You				

1993 MCD - BEDCD 93001

BEHEMOTH

Stig "Sirre" Johansson: v, Gunnar "Fritz" Fritzell: g, Mikael Nilsson: b, Roger Wasell: d

Sundsvall - A great, powerful, heavy rock/metal band that only produced one single and some demos. Fritz sold all his belongings and moved to England to join *Angelwitch*. It however only ended up in a couple of jam sessions. Nilsson later joined *The Bereaved*. In 2009 the band reformed under the name *Deathwings* and some new songs can be found on the band's MySpace. Today's line-up features Sirre, Roger and new members Jörgen and Martin on guitars, plus bass player Leo. The single is a great FWoSHM gem in the vein of *Angelwitch*. Before the single the band also recorded a highly recommended demo. Not to be confused with the Polish death metal band (hence the name change to *Deathwings*).
Website: www.myspace.com/deathwingssweden

1982 7" - - -

1982 7" - CONT 1

1982	■	Deathwings/Vengeance	7"	private	- -	$
1982	■	Deathwings/Vengeance	7"	Bullet Euro Hit (France)	CONT 1	$
		Red cover.				

BELLADONNA

Kristian "Bobby Hott" Metsälä: v, H.B. Jewel: g, Andreas "Andy" Söderberg: g, Peter "Griffin" Eliasson: b, Rasmus "Raz Cadillac" Göransson: d

Kalmar - Straight ahead hard rock with a sleazy twist and a pretty good singer that, at times, is a bit reminiscent of *Bruce Dickinson*. Overall, not too impressive, though. The band recorded a bunch of demos, but soon broke up. Kristian (now called "Chriz Tyan") and Rasmus went on to form the band *Rasrisk* that plays powerful hard rock sung in Swedish. Rasmus is also in sleaze band *Spiders 'N Diamonds*.

| 2006 | ■ | Belladonna | MCD 4tr | private | BDR-1001 |
| | | *Tracks: Belladonna/Sweet Hell/Roadkill/Cloaser & Closer.* | | | |

2006 MCD - BDR-1001

BELSEBUB

Mika Savimäki: v/b/g, Peter "Blomman" Blomberg: g, Johny Fagerström: v/d

Motala - Formed in 1990. Recorded their first demo, *Lord Of Lucast* the same year and the second demo, *Disemboweled* the year after. I guess the name says it all. Furious death metal with a singer's voice from the depths of hell. The track *Cannibal Mind* was featured on the compilation *Rätt i örat* (91 Studiefrämjandet). The band then featured singer Stevo Bolgakoff (*Toxaemia*), guitarist Fredrik Åstrand and bassist Hans Gustavsson, besides Mika and Johny. Fagerström and Mika were also in *Lucifer*.

| 1992 | ■ | Elohim | 7" 3tr | Drowned | M-11620 |
| | | *Tracks: Chemical Warfare/Infected Organs/Masters To Reveal* | | | |

1992 7" - M-11620

BENEATH THE FROZEN SOIL

Linus Pilebrand: g, Robert Björk: b, Olof Holgersson: d

Göteborg - Doom band *Beneath The Frozen Soil* was formed in 2004, originally as a duo, consisting of Linus and Olof. The line-up is now completed by singer Gunnar Nilsson, while Robert has been replaced by Svante Enefalk. Linus is also found in *Gaia* and Olof in *Absebtia*. *Beneath The Frozen Soil* plays slow, searing doom with growling/screeching vocals.

2007	□	BENEATH THE FROZEN SOIL/NEGATIVE REACTION (split)	CD	Totalrust Music (USA)	TRUST 007
		Split with Negative Reaction. Tracks: The Wreathed Of This Afterbirth/The Time Is Now/ Signs Of That Grim Malady/So Still, So Overwhelmingly Silent. 1000 copies			
2010	■	BENEATH THE FROZEN SOIL/EVOKEN (split)	CD	I Hate	IHRCD 080
		Split with Evoken. Tracks: Ironlung/Monotone Black I/Monotone Black II			

2010 CD - IHRCD 080

BENGALEN

Bengt Ahlström: v/g, Stefan Storrank: b, Eje Gunnarsson: k, Mikael Nordström: d

Nykvarn - Christian melodic hard rock. Some tracks are more rock 'n roll, but with heavy guitars, a bit similar to *Motvind*. The first single featured drummer Mikael Holgersson and bassist Stefan Storrank, but when they had to do their military service bassist Thomas Skult and drummer Mikael "Mick" Nordström replaced them on the album. Nordström was later found in bands like *Modest Attraction* and *Spearfish*. The track *Åke Svensson* from the first single, was later rerecorded for the album. The last single saw Storrank replaced by Gunnarsson.

1980	□	Vi är kristna/Åke Svensson	7"	Trend Music	TRS 80-01
1981	■	BENGALEN	LP	Stanley & Andrew	5200002
1982	□	Löften/Läronlunk	7"	private	BEN 001

1981 LP - 5200002

BEREAVED, THE

Travis Neal: v, Henrik Tranemyr: g, Per Bergquist: g,
Tony Thorén: k, Mikael Nilsson: b, Tobhias Ljung: d

Örebro - In 1998 Mikael Nilsson (ex-*Behemoth*) and Henrik Tranemyr came to the conclusion they should start a metal band. They recruited guitarist Jonny Westerbäck and Tobhias Ljung. In 2000 they entered the studio to record a cover of *Welcome To Dying* for a *Blind Guardian* tribute album, now with Tobhias also handling the vocals. On the subsequent *Inverted Icons* demo (2002), Jonny took over the vocal task and the demo was recorded by Mathias Färm and the late Mieszko Talarczyk (*Nasum*). In 2003 they were signed by Black Lotus Records. The band had now also added the keyboard talents of Tony Thorén. The debut, which featured Jonny, Henrik, Tony, Mikael and Tobhias, was produced by Pelle Saether. In 2006 the band entered Studio Underground with Pelle as recording engineer and Dan Swanö mixing. When the album was recorded and ready Black Lotus had folded, but through the aid of Swanö the band was signed by Vic Records. In 2007 Jonny left the band. He was replaced by former *Closer* guitarist Per Bergquist and the vocal spot was filled by Denny Axelsson, who had made a stint with *Blinded Colony*. The latter however was not long after replaced by US singer Travis Neal, formerly of *Mother May I*, and who made his debut on *Daylight Deception*.

2009 CD - VIC012CD

2005 CD - BLR/CD070

2005 ■	DARKNENED SILHOUETTE	CD	Black Lotus Records	BLR/CD070
2009 ■	DAYLIGHT DECEPTION	CD	Vic Records	VIC012CD
2009 □	DAYLIGHT DECEPTION	CD	Spiritual Beast (Japan)	POCE-16060

BERGRAVEN

Pär "Bergraven" Gustafsson: v/g/b/d

Hässleholm - *Bergraven* is the brainchild of *Nex/Infernal Hellfire* man Pär Gustafsson. The band at times sounds like *Opeth* in their most melancholic moments. The music ranges from soft progressive rock to heavy doomy parts. Highly accomplished and intriguing music, great production, topped with spoken screeching growl. In 2003 Pär made his debut on the three track demo *Ty döden färdas snabbt. Till makabert väsen* was recorded at Necromorbus Studio. Session drums by Per "Perra" Karlsson (*Nominon, In Aeternum, Suffer, T.A.R, Nex, Altar*).

2004 CD - UER 003

2004 ■	FÖRDÄRV	CD	Un exploded	UER003
2007 □	DÖDSVISIONER	CD	Total Holocaust	THR100
2007 □	DÖDSVISIONER	CDd	Hydra Head (USA)	HH666-132
2009 ■	TILL MAKABERT VÄSEN	CD	Hydra Head (USA)	HH666-172

2009 CD - HH666-172

BESEECH

Erik Molarin: v, Lotta Höglin: v, Robert Spånglund: g, Mikael Back: k,
Klas Bohlin: g, Daniel Elofsson: b, Jonas Strömberg: d

Borås - Goth metal with influences of death and doom and a highly unusual instrumentation featuring cello, flute and violin. A bit reminiscent of *Type O Negative* and *Theatre Of Tragedy*. The band was formed in 1992 and recorded some demos, one being *A Lesser Kind Of Evil*. The first MCD, *Songs From A Bleeding Heart* was recorded in 1996 and produced by Christian Silver from *Sundown*. Unfortunately the label We Bite/Corrosion could not finance the release and it fell through. The album was finally picked up by Metal Blade. After the debut, Andreas Wiik was replaced by Daniel and Morgan Gredåker by Jonas. Singer Lotta Höglin was also added to the line-up and the earlier death/doom influences were toned down. The song *Edge Of Life* can be found on the compilation *Sometimes Death Is Better* (Shiver). The band also has three songs on the sound track for the B-movie *Alien Agenda 5 - Alien Conspiracy*. In 2001, before the latest album, singer Jörgen Sjöberg decided to leave the band and Erik replaced him. The band folded in 2006, and out of the ashes rose the more up-tempo band *The Mary Major* which features Lotta, Erik, Daniel and Jonas, plus Jörgen Ström.
Website: wwwbeseech.net

Beseech in their sunless days.

1998 ■	FROM A BLEEDING HEART	CD	Metal Blade	3984-14162-2
2000 □	BLACK EMOTIONS	CD	Pavement	32350
2002 □	SOULS HIGHWAY	CD	Napalm Records	NPR 104
2002 □	SOULS HIGHWAY	CDd	Napalm Records	NPR 104
	Bonus: Gimme Gimme Gimme (ABBA cover)			
2002 □	SOULS HIGHWAY	CD	Irond (Russia)	CD 02-221
	Bonus: Gimme Gimme Gimme (ABBA cover)			
2003 □	DRAMA	CD	Napalm Records	NPR 133
2004 □	DRAMA	CD	Irond (Russia)	CD 04-746
2004 □	BLACK EMOTIONS	CD	Irond (Russia)	CD 04-787
2005 □	SUNLESS DAYS	CD	Irond (Russia)	CD 05-1062
	Bonus: Manmade Dreams (re-make)/Lost (emotional version)			
2005 □	SUNLESS DAYS	CD	Napalm Records	NPR 170
2005 □	SUNLESS DAYS	CDd	Napalm Records	NPR 170
	Bonus: Manmade Dreams (re-make)/Lost (emotional version)			
2006 □	SUNLESS DAYS	CD	Icarus (Argentina)	ICARUS 181

1998 CD - 3984-14162-2

BESTIAL MOCKERY

Johan "Master Motorsåg" Sahlin: v, Michael "Doomfanger" Pettersson: g/b,
Ted "Bundy" Axelsson: g, Carl "Warslaughter" Wochatz: d

Uddevalla - Formed in 1995 by Master and Warslaughter. The band's first demo *Battle Promo* was recorded in 1996 as a duo why it contains no bass. For the 1997 demo *Christcrushing Hammerchainsaw* they found live bassist Anti-Fredrik. In 1998 they recorded *Chainsaw Demons Return*, in 1999 the split tape *Live Is Violence* and in 2000 *War: The Final Solution*. In 2000 Robert "Rob Devilpig" Hansson (*Rawhide*) replaced Fredrik. Doomfanger is also found in *Conspiracy* and Carl sings in *Kill*. Guitarist Ted "Bundy" Axelsson (*Mastema*) was added to the line-up in 2001. In 2004 the band was featured with the track *Chainsaw Demons Return* on the 7" compilation *Outbreak Of Evil* (Witching Metal). In 2008 the band also had four tracks on the four-way split/compilation *Deep Grave Dungeons* (Time Before Time). Carl is also found in *Zyclone System* and he is ex-*Sons Of Satan*. Sahlin was also in the latter. Fast and furious old-school death metal.

2002 7" - WREP 08

2002 CD - DOWN 008

2006 CD - RSR-0182

2007 CD - WHP 074D

2008 7" - HELLSEP 028

Year		Title	Format	Label	Cat. No.
1999	☐	LIVE FOR VIOLENCE (split)	CD	Impaler Of Trendies	n/a
		Split with Lust. Tracks: Distortion From The North/Chainsaw Enforcer/Shrapnel Fire/Possessed/Chainsaw Fucking/Chainsaw Demons			
2000	☐	Nuclear Goat	7"	private	-
		Split with Suicidal Winds. 300 hand numbered copies. Tracks: Nuclear Goat/Father In Heaven/Shrapnel Fire			
2001	☐	CHAINSAW EXECUTION	LP	Sombre	LP 012
		350 copies.			
2002	☐	CHRISTCRUSHING HAMMERCHAINSAW	CD	Metalblood	STRIKE 001
2002	☐	CHRISTCRUSHING HAMMERCHAINSAW	LP	Metalblood	STRIKE 001
		500 copies.			
2002	■	A Sign Of Satanic Victory	7" 4tr	Warlord (Italy)	WREP 08
		Tracks: Blackened Deat/ Fucking Dyke/Circumsising The Vagina/Bloodstained in Necronorth. 1000 copies.			
2002	■	EVOKE THE DESECRATOR	CD	Downfall	DOWN 008
2003	☐	EVOKE THE DESECRATOR	CD	Osmose	OPCD 154
2004	☐	Tribute to I-17 (split)	7"	Agonia Records	ARep005
		Split with Axis Powers. 666 hand numbered copies. Tracks: Prolapsing Orgy Of The Twisted Black//Chainsaw Metal/Lies Of Peace			
2005	☐	EVE OF THE BESTIAL MASSACRE (split)	LP	Deathstrike	DR 038
		Split with Unholy Massacre (Brazil). Tracks: Slay The God/I Will Puke On Christ/The Witches Song/Annihilist/Storm Of hate. 500 hand numbered copies.			
2005	☐	EVE OF THE BESTIAL MASSACRE (split)	CD	Agonia Records	ARcd 032
2006	■	GOSPEL OF THE INSANE	CD	Red Stream	RSR-0182
2006	☐	GOSPEL OF THE INSANE	CD	Osmose	OPCD 174
2006	☐	GOSPEL OF THE INSANE	LPg	Osmose	OPLP 174
		Bonus: Sledgehammer Sacrifice			
2006	☐	Sepulchral Wrath	10" 6tr MLP	Agonia Records	ARMLP 008
		666 numbered copies. Tracks: Sworn To Darkness/Devilworship			
2007	■	THE UNHOLY TRINITY	CD	Witchhammer	WHP 074D
		Compilation of the first three demos. 1000 hand numbered copies.			
2007	☐	BESTIAL SATANIC SACRIFICE (split)	CD	Division 666	HO12
		Split with Inquisitor (Holl). Tracks: Intro/Chainsaw Demons Return/Path Of Death/Bestial Satanic Sacrifice/Chainsaw Incarnated/Distortion From The North/Shrapnel Fire/Outro			
2007	☐	Poison Of The Underground (split)	7"	Turanian Honour	TURAN 006
		Split with Force Of Darkness (Chile).500 copies. Tracks: Chainsaw Kill/Pain Invocation			
2007	☐	Metal Of Death (split)	10" MLPg	Hells Headbangers	HELLSMLP 003
		Split with Destructor. First 200 copies in silver vinyl and with outer "razor wire" jacket. Tracks: Metal Fucking Death/Riding The Vortex/Master			
2007	☐	SLAYING THE LIFE	CD	Seasons Of Mist	SUA 001
2007	☐	SLAYING THE LIFE	LPg	Hells Headbangers	HELLSLP 023
2007	☐	SLAYING THE LIFE	LP PD	Hells Headbangers	HELLSPLP 017
2007	☐	CHAINSAW DESTRUCTION	CD	Terranis Productions	TP 011
		1000 copies. Compilation of live and unreleased tracks.			
2008	■	Hail Occult Masters	7"	Hells Headbangers	HELLSEP 028
		Split with Karnarium. Tracks: Bite The Bullet/Satan has Returned			
2009	☐	SEPULCHRAL WRATH	CD	Witchhammer	WHP 98D
2010	☐	CHRISTCRUSHING HAMMERCHAINSAW	CD	Hells Headbanders	HELLS 040

BEWARP

Pete Sandberg: v, Dick Bewarp: g, Dan J Ekfeldt: b, Richard Dahl: d

Malmö - Around 1985 Dick was the guitarist in the Swedish pop/rock band *AHA* (not to be confused with the Norwegian popsters) who recorded an album and a single for Tandan records. *Bewarp* however plays riff-oriented sleazy glam metal with glitter and stuff. The first album featured Anders "Theo" Theander (*Eurock*) on drums and Robert "Bobby" Vargkvist on vocals (previously with *Emerald* and *Sloppy Baboons*, later in *Espinoza*). Dick was also the promoter and driving force behind Sweden's solo guitar competition *Guitar Battle* and he has a song on

1991 7" - BW No 1

each of the *Guitar Heroes Of Sweden* CD's. *Upside Down* is, as you might suspect, a cover of the old disco tune. Pete is ex-*Alien, Madison* and later also in *Silver Seraph, Midnight Sun, Jade* as well as doing his solo-thing. *In Your Face* is highly recommended. In 1995 Dick pursued a successful career as video-producer, working with bands like *Bad Habit, Bai Bang; Keegan, Deranged* etc., but is now into TV-commercials. Theo runs Roastinghouse Productions.

1991 ■	Take Me To Heaven/Pleasure Of Fire	7"	B.O.R.G	BW No 1
1992 □	Upside Down/Funk It Up/Funk It Up	MCDp 3tr	B.O.R.G	BM921001
1992 □	FUNK'D RAPT'N TRASH'D	CD	Brunette (Japan)	ALCB-616
1994 □	FUNK'D RAPT'N TRASH'D	CD	SPM	MASS-502
1994 □	IN YOUR FACE	CD	Brunette (Japan)	ALCD-3009
1995 □	IN YOUR FACE	CD	Bellaphon	290.07.216

The European pressing is re-mastered with a much better sound.

1994 CD - MASS-502

BEWITCHED

Marcus "Vargher" Norman: g/v, A "Hellfire": g, Kristoffer "Wrathyr" Olivius: b

Umeå - Formed by former *Ancient Wisdom*-member Marcus and *Katatonia's* guitarist Anders "Blackheim" Nyström (also has a solo project called *Diabolical Masquerade*). In 1995 they recorded a four track demo entitled *Hellspell*. The 1996 MCD *Encyclopedia Of Evil* contains covers of **Venom, Mercyful Fate, Celtic Frost, Bathory** etc. The debut was speed-oriented death metal with clear eighties influences, while *Pentagram Prayer* contains pure 80s sounding metal with influences from **Iron Maiden, Judas Priest** and **Sodom**. *Hell Comes To Essen* is a live record that contains a quite different version of the classic *Born To Be Wild*. Marcus Norman joined *Naglfar* in 2000, where Olivius is also found. Some live-tracks can be found on the compilation *World Domination Live* (98 Osmose). Kristoffer is also found in **Setherial, Naglfar** and **Midvinter**. In 1997, after the recording of *Pentagram Prayer*, Blackheim left the band and was temporarily replaced by Fredrik "Spider" Degerström (**Auberon, Nocturnal Rites, Naglfar**). Before the recording of *At The Gates Of Hell*, drummer "Reaper" was replaced by Ulf "Stormlord" Andersson (**Nocturnal Rites**) and on the subsequent tour the band was reinforced by second guitarist A Hellfire. In 2006 Stormlord left and the drums on the last album were played by session drummer Marc Malice. Not to be confused with the band from Chile, who recorded the album *Somewhere Beyond The Mist*.

Bewitched and horny

1996 □	DIABOLICAL DESECRATION	CD	Osmose	OPCD 034
1996 □	DIABOLICAL DESECRATION	LP	Osmose	OPLP 034
1996 □	Encyclopedia Of Evil	MCD 7tr	Osmose	OPCD 041

Tracks: Prologue/Warhead (Venom cover)/Sacrifice (Bathory cover)/Evil (Mercyfull Fate cove)/Circle Of The Tyrants (Celtic Frost)/Come To The Sabbath (Black Widow)/Hellcult

1998 □	PENTAGRAM PRAYER	CD	Osmose	OPCD 057
1998 □	PENTAGRAM PRAYER	LP	Osmose	OPLP 057
1998 ■	HELL COMES TO ESSEN (live)	CD	Osmose	OPCD 57A
1998 □	HELL COMES TO ESSEN (live)	LP	Osmose	OPLP 57A
1998 □	HELL COMES TO ESSEN (live)	LP PD	Osmose	OPPIC 57A
1999 □	AT THE GATES OF HELL	CD	Osmose	OPCDL 076
1999 □	AT THE GATES OF HELL	LP	Osmose	OPLP 076
2002 □	RISE OF THE ANTICHRIST	CD	Osmose	OPCD 104
2002 □	RISE OF THE ANTICHRIST	LP	Osmose	OPLP 104

500 copies.

2004 □	Atrocities In A Minor	MLP 6tr	Regain	RRLP0311-042

The Devil's Children/Holy Whore/Cremations Of The Cross/Rise Of The Antichrist (live)/ Blade Of The Ripper (live)/Born Of Flames (live).

2004 □	Atrocities In A Minor	MCD	Regain	RRCD0311-042
2004 □	Atrocities In A Minor	MLP PD	Regain	RRPLP0311-042
2006 ■	SPIRITUAL WARFARE	CD	Regain	RR 050
2006 □	SPIRITUAL WARFARE	CD	Regain America (USA)	REG CD 1024

1998 CD - OPCD 057A

2006 CD - RR 050

BEYOND VISIONS

Rebecka Heijel: v, Alexander "Alex" Berg: g, Sauli Ranta: g, Håkan Nilsson: k, Morgan "Mogge" Andersson: b, Henrik "Nagge" Jansson: d

Stockholm - *Beyond Visions* was formed in 2007 and recorded their first demo *End Of The Beginning* the same year. Another demo was recorded the subsequent year and in 2010 they released a self-financed MCD. Well-written, well-produced and well-performed slightly symphonic power metal with a touch of **Within Temptation**. Great vocals from Rebecka. *Website: www.myspace.com/beyondvisions/*

2010 ■	V: Ex Animo	MCDd 4tr	private	- -

Tracks: My Immortal Tears/The Other Side Of Weakness/The Black Reign/Emperor Of The Sun

2010 MCDd - - -

BIBLEBLACK

**Kacper Rozanski: v, Mikael "Mike Wead" Wikström: g,
Simon Johansson: g, Jonaz Bylund: b, Tobhias Ljung: d**

Stockholm - **Bibleblack** is the brainchild of *Abstrakt Algebra/Mercyful Fate/King Diamond* guitarist Mike Wead. When King D had to make a halt because of back problems, Mike got his own thing going. He wrote a bunch of songs, drafted bassist Simon Johansson, with whom he had been playing in *Fifth Reason*, and programmed some drums, planning to sing the tracks himself. He found *Nattas* singer Kaspar and suddenly it all became quite serious. He now drafted *Hearse/The Bereaved* drummer Tobhias Ljung, Simon switched to guitar and they drafted Jonas Bülund on bass and recorded one crusher of an album. Outstanding teachnical progressive thrash with death-oriented, not over-growling, vocals. Try mixing *In Flames, Hexenhaus, Dream Theater* and a steamroller and you're in the neighbourhood of *Bibleblack*. The clean vocals on the album were provided by Kristian Andrén (*Memento Mori/Fifth Reason*) and Ronny Hemlin (*Steel Attack/Tad Morose/Lack Of Faith*). Simon has also been found in *Memory Garden* and *Steel Attack* and is also in *Wolf*. After the album Tobhias was replaced by *Circle Of Chaos*' Staffan Lundholm.
Website: www.bibleblack.se

2009	■	THE BLACK SWAN EPILOGUE	CDd	Vic Records	VIC 026 CD
2009	□	THE BLACK SWAN EPILOGUE	CD+DVD	Vic Records	VIC 026 CD
2009	□	THE BLACK SWAN EPILOGUE	CD	Spiritual Beast (Japan)	POCE-16056

2009 CD - VIC 026 CD

BIG BUSINE$$

Maria Isaacs: v, Magnus Hedlund: g, Niclas Nordlander: b, Stefan Cronebäck: d

Södertörn - This is definitely a borderline record. At times it's pure Westcoast oriented AOR with some nice distorted guitars, but remove the guitars and it's just pop. The B-side shows a bit more promise though, in the vein of *Toto* with a really nice guitar solo. Keyboard on the album played by Thomas Huttenlocher.

1989	■	Beat Of My Heart/Never Coming Back	7"	private	S-ROCK-01-89

1999 7" - S-ROCK-01-89

BIG EASY

**Stefan Haugsnes: v, Magnus Andersson (now Härsjö): g, Lars Lundin: k,
Dennis Österdahl: b, Michael Wallin: d**

Göteborg - Another of the numerous high-class melodic hard rock/AOR bands in Sweden. Like many others this one also hails from Göteborg. *Big Easy* was supposed to release their first full length album on Local Hero in 1996, but they changed the line-up a bit and changed their name to *Big Wave*, under which name they released the album (see *Big Wave* for further information). Their style also became a bit more blues infused. An early incarnation of the band featured singer Anders Möller (*Swedish Erotica, Black Ingvars*), bassist Conny Payne (*Madison, Mindsplit*) and keyboardist Calle Engelmarc (*Mercy, Turbo*).

1994	■	Big Easy	MCD 4tr	CePe	Big Sing 01

Tracks: Love Don't Come Easy/Red Blood/Will You Miss Me/Shine On.

1994 MCD - Bing Sing 01

BIG FISH

David Giese: v, Arvid Eriksson: g, Andreas Iverhed: b, Tomas Gustavsson: k/acc

Uppsala - In 1991 the band made their debut on the Tango Train split *Hydrology*. This is actually something really fresh and challenging. The music is an intriguing mix of Swedish folkmusic, folklore and heavy hard rock. Try mixing *Jethro Tull, Kebnekajse* and *Black Sabbath*. Could also be compared to a heavier *Va-Då*. The songs are performed on extremely heavy distorted riffing guitars, sampled drums, accordion, flutes and all types of scrap metal percussions. Highly recommended if you want to broaden your musical views. In 1994 the band switched from Strontium Records to Birdnest, who re-issued the first two releases. The last two albums are the heaviest.

1991	■	Hydrology/Blood 'N Fire (split)	MLP	Tango Train Productions	TTR 001

Split with New Form. Tracks: Into Three/Parasites/Cynical Days/Born To Be Naked

1992	□	VARGAVINTER	CD	Strontium	ASP 002
1992	□	Dans Mot Tiden	MCD 4tr	Strontium	ASP 003

Tracks: Dans mot tiden/Rörande själlösa vandrare/Hycklervisa/En flickas mörka rum

1994	■	VARGAVINTER	CD	Birdnest	BIRD 068 CD
1994	□	Dans Mot Tiden	MCD 4tr	Birdnest	BIRD 069 CD
1995	□	SÅNGER UR STEN	CD	Birdnest	BIRD 067 CD
1995	□	Nyårshambo/Vackra Vapen	CDS 2tr	Birdnest	BIRD 072 CD

Vackra Vapen is non-CD.

1996	□	ANDAR I HALSEN	CD	Birdnest	BIRD 094 CD

1991 MLP - TTR 001

1994 CD - BIRD 068 CD

BIG PRICE

**Markus Nordenberg: v, Mikael Hedström: g, Thomas Coox: k ,
Anders Nordström: k, Freddy Hedefalk: d**

Sundsvall - This is really good Westcoast-oriented AOR with nice guitar work. Should appeal to fans of *Toto, Alien* etc. The band was formed in 1990. Mikael is ex-*Paradise*. *Big Price* split in 1994 and turned into the cover band *Rock The House*.

1991 ■ We'll Be Together/Road To Your Heart...7" Garden Record P/CUF .....GAS 1005/CUF 015
    Available with gold or yellow dollar sign on cover.

1991 7" - GAS 1005/CUF 015

BIG TALK

Rasmus Uhlin: v/g, Christer Johansson: b, Robert Gustavsson: d

Eskilstuna - High-class melodic hard rock/AOR. Robert has previously recorded a 7" with the band *Tough Trade*. Rasmus now has a band called *Rasmus & The Reckless Band*, doing covers of *Bryan Adams*.

1993 ☐ Going Back ....MCD 3tr privat BTCD-01
    Tracks: Going Back/I Will Always Be Your Friend/Down The Road.

BIG TALK

Christer Schill: v, Jonas Christophs: g, Peter Bengtsson: k

Halmstad - High-quality AOR with great vocals and musical hints of *Saga* and *Toto*. The band tours under the name *Partykompaniet* (The Party Company) doing mostly covers, which is actually a pity. A must for pomp/AOR-fans.

1993 ■ TIME OF DREAMS ....CD private BTCJP-01

1993 CD - BTCJP-01

BIG THING

Jörgen Bolmstad: v, Mattias Rydell: g, P.O Häll: b, Tyrone Nilsson: d

Jönköping - *Big Thing* was a young band delivering guitar driven melodic hard rock that reminded a bit of *Dokken* meets *Victory*. Guitarist Mattias was very promising, while the vocals might sound a bit "Swedish".

1995 ■ FALLEN NATION ....CD SMC .... SMC CD 2019-1

1995 CD - SMC CD 2019-1

BIG TIMES

Pentti Von Fürstenrecht: k/v, Jimmy Årjes: k/v/b/g, Ingmar Eriksson: d/v

Borås - Quite good solid AOR. The band was quite a mystery as the cover contains no information on members. However it says the songs were taken from an album. The album was never released. Only 5-6 songs were finished when things started to fall apart. The songs are really good high-quality pomp and the album could have been really interesting. Jimmy also recorded a 7" with a pop/rock band called *Europe* (No, not **the** Europe) in the early 80s.

1991 ☐ Run the streets/Without you.....................................7" Roxx Music ....ROX 991

BIG TRAIN

Roger Frejd: v/g, Anders Karlsson: g, Thorbjörn Frejd: b, Johan Nyqvist: d

Jönköping - A-side is powerful rock/hard rock, B-side is bluesy hard rock. Roger and Thorbjörn also played in *Profile* who had the songs *Sheila* and *Red Water Blue Wine* on the *Vätterzound* compilation.

1990 ■ Dirty Town/Love Them An' Leave Them ....7" private ....RF 001

1990 7" - RF 001

BIG WAVE

**Stephan Haugsnes: v, Magnus Anderson: g,
Dennis Österdahl: b, Alexander Hedlund: d**

Göteborg - *Big Wave* started out under the name *Big Easy*, under which name they recorded a MCD. High-quality blues-based hard rock with a touch of vintage *Whitesnake*. The Japanese version is just the Massive pressing repacked and with a Japanese OBI. Dennis Österdahl was later part of *Human Race, Elsy Band* and *Rawburt*.

1997 ☐ BIG WAVE..CD Massive....................................MASS 507
1997 ■ BIG WAVE..CD Sound Treasure (Japan)................SRCD-009

1997 CD - SRCD-009

BILLION DOLLAR BABIES

Frank "Frankie Rich" Kooistra: v, **Patrik "Pat Kramer" Forsberg:** g,
Jon "Silver" Nilsson: g, **Niklas "Nic Lester" Hoven:** b, **Anton "Anthony Fox" Ryvang:** d

Falun - Sleaze of the heavier kind but a little touch of glam nevertheless. **Hardcore Superstar** and **Gemini Five** come to mind. The band was formed in 2005 and two years later released their self-financed EP and appeared in a TV-show which was the musical equivalent of the *Dragon's Den*. Drummer Robert "Robban XIII/Robby Rock" Bäck has also recorded albums with **BALLS, Baltimoore, W.E.T** and **Eclipse** and in October 2010 he left the band to pursue his other career. He was temporarily replaced live by Erik Berglund (*I Am So Me*). In March 2011 a permanent drummer was found in Anton "Anthony Edmund Fox" Ryvang (**Nanne Grönwall, Kalle Moraeus**). Robert joined **Sabaton** in 2012. *House Of Dreams* is a MCD trilogy released in 2012-13. Kooistra also recorded with the band **Mustain**.
Website: www.billiondollarbabies.nu

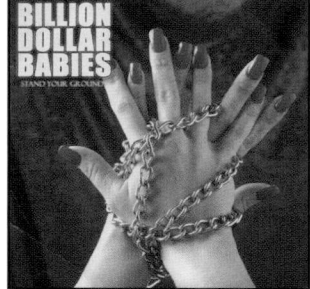
2007 MCDp - BCD001

2010 CD - ESM001

2007 ■	Stand Your Ground ....MCDp 4tr	BDB BCD001
	Tracks: Nineteen Ninty Four/Restless Minds/Stand Your Ground/We Don't Live Forever	
2010 ■	DIE FOR DIAMONDS ....CD	Esmeralda Music Group ESM001
2012 ■	House Of Dreams: Part 1.....................MCDd 3tr	Esmeralda Music Group .... ESM 003
	Tracks: In The Back Of My Limousine/A Millionaire's Dream/Crashing Down	

2012 MCDd - ESM 003

BILLIONAIRES BOYS CLUB

Mark Boals: v, **Jörg Fischer:** g, **Magnus Rosén:** b, **Anders Johansson:** d

Malmö/Göteborg/Germany/USA - OK, on the album they are only half-Swedish, but still worth mentioning, plus they were based in Sweden. The Swedish side consists of Anders Johansson (**Yngwie, Silver Mountain, Snake Charmer, Johansson Brothers, Hammerfall...**) and Magnus Rosén (**Von Rosen, Hammerfall, FullForce**). Mark has also been part of **Yngwie Malmsteen's Rising Force**. Anders and Jörg also toured together with Per Stadin and Pete Sandberg as a coverband under the moniker **Coverboys**. The bass tracks on the album were however recorded by Marcel Jacob and Per Stadin, which is quite evident. **Billionaires Boys Club** play top notch melodic hard rock very close to **Dokken** at their best. A hidden gem indeed.

1993 ■	SOMETHING WICKED COMES.....................CD	Blackbird BBCD-254
	Different artwork.	
1993 □	SOMETHING WICKED COMES.....................CD	Polydor (Germany) 517 761-2
1993 □	SOMETHING WICKED COMES.....................CD	Polydor K.K (Japan)..................... POCD-1321
	Bonus: Moshing In The Pit/Roadie Song	

1993 CD - BBCD-254

BISCAYA

Mads Clausen: v, **Pär Edwardsson:** g, **Martin Hedström:** g,
Magnus Strömberg: k, **Hans Johansson:** b, **Birger Löfman:** d

Göteborg - **Biscaya** was one of those bands who succeeded in writing intelligent hard rock without making it pass over the general listener's head. Great, slightly pomp-oriented melodic hard rock. On the 12", which is a gem, Martin was added to the line-up. Martin joined the band after the album, which actually was produced by PJ Jägerhult (**Trash, Attack**). Pär, Martin and Birger are session-musicians on the singles by **Hawk**. Magnus was previously in slick rockers **Public** and in 1995 he released a solo-album with piano music. It was actually a soundtrack to the Swedish TV-series *Svenska Hjärtan* (Swedish Hearts). Pär, Martin and Magnus brother Johan recorded a more pop-oriented album with **TNT**-producer Bjørn Nessjø. Pär became a well acclaimed producer/engineer who has worked with bands like **Million** and **Road Ratt**. Mads appeared on the TV-show *Sikta Mot Stjärnorna* (Aim for the stars) imitating singer **Björn Skifs** and is today found in the highly intriguing progressive band **Time Code Alpha**. Martin is playing with popster **Magnus Uggla**. In 2011 Löfman recorded an album with hard rockers **Fretless**.

1983 LP - PL 70034

1983 7" - BIS 1

1983 ■	BISCAYA.....................LP	RCA.....................PL 70034
1983 ●	Singing In Harmony/Summer Love ....7"	RCA (promo).........................BIS 1
1983 □	BISCAYA.....................LP	RCA (Japan) RLP-8260
1984 □	Summer Love/Fools ....7"	RCA (Japan promo) RPS-149
1984 ■	On 45 .... MLP 4tr	RCA.....................PG 70466
	Tracks: Hit It Hard/Space Bop/Swinging To A Melody/Greg's Song	
1985 □	Howl In The Sky/Rockin' Vehicles.....................7"	RCA (promo).....................RPS-163
1996 □	BISCAYA.....................CD	BMG (Japan) BVCP-7541
1996 □	BISCAYA.....................CD	RCA ....PK 70034
2008 □	BISCAYA.....................CDv	BMG (Japan) BVCM-37859
	Bonus: Hit It Hard/Space Bop/Swinging To A Melody/Greg's Song	

Unofficial recordings:

199? □	HOWL IN SWEDEN.....................CD	Bondage (Japan) ....BON 082
	31/3-84 Live in Göteborg. Japanese Bootleg.	
1996 □	BISCAYA.....................CD	Scandinavian Metal Attack.....................002
	Contains three tracks from the MLP as bonus.	

1984 MLP - PG 70466

BISHOP GARDEN
Fredrik Johansson: v, Stefan Olsson: g, Mattias Cederlund: k,
Mathias Wilhelmsson: b, Niclas Wilhelmsson: d
Stockholm - Outstanding slightly progressive hard rock with great melodies. In 1999 they released the six-track CD-R *Superpillow*, where the bass was played by Johan Bergkvist and keyboardist Cederlund (**Veni Domine**) was out. Here they had started exploring the outposts of bands like **King's X** and **Galactic Cowboys**. It was produced by Alex Losbäck. Stefan Olsson was later found in **Wisdom Call**.

1997 ■ GARDEN OF RELIEF ....CD T-bag...........................BGCD9701

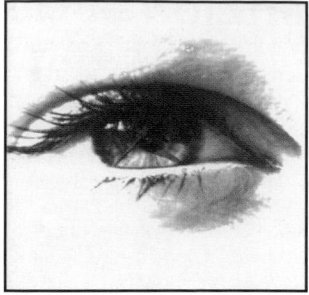

1997 CD - BGCD9701

BJORN, THE
Björn Johansson: v/g, Mikael Andersson: g, Jonathan Blomberg: b, Jonas Högberg: d
Borås - The band's musical motto is: "No rules, no excuses, no limitations". Musically **The Bjorn** are a bit reminiscent of **Metallica** with a touch of **Pantera**, but with many more musical inputs blending into the musical mix. Tight, heavy and powerful, but still quite melodic. In 2009 the band released the debut MCD through the singer's own label Strobesoul. The band also released the digital single *Hold On* in 2011.
Website: www.landofashes.com

2009 □ From The Land Of Ashes...MCD Strobesoul Productions................................ - -
    Tracks: Girlfriend America/Drown/Burn/Black Hole Frequency Shifter
2011 ■ 2011 ....CD Rambo Music................................STROB005

2011 CD - STROB 005

BLACK (SWEDEN), THE
Johan "Dr. A Force" Sahlén: v, Mats "Sir Richard Fireburn" Johansson: g,
Henrik "Johnny Flash" Thomsen: b, Imre "Steve Speed" Daun: d
Göteborg - This is more or less an **ABBA**-oriented version of **Black Ingvars** and not to be confused with the black metal band. The only difference is that instead of doing metal-versions of schlagers, pop-songs or dance-music, this band has concentrated on covering **ABBA**. Imagine a mix of *Smoke On The Water* and *Mamma Mia* or.., well you get the idea. After having heard **Black Ingvars** very thought through and well-arranged works, this does fall a bit short. Imre and Henrik are ex-**Snöstorm/Snowstorm** and **Don Patrol**. Johan is found in humor-popsters **Drängarna**. Mats has played with numerous well known artists such as Paul Young, **Asia** (on the Aqua-album), **Drama** (Norway) and also had a band together with John Sloman and Pino Palatino. Imre is also found in cover band **Partypatrullen** and has recorded with numerous other band like **Alien**, **Gypsy Rose**, **Kharma** and **Arose**. The CD has also been released under the name **The Black Sweden** with a different cover and also under the title *Rock Tribute To ABBA*. Mikael Erlandsson (**Crash**, solo, **Last Autumn's Dream**) provides backing vocals.

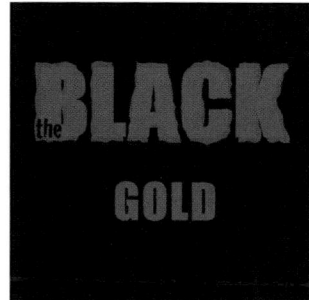

1999 CD - 74321 65191 2

2000 CD - 640441

1999 ■ GOLD..CD CIB/BMG................................74321 65191 2
1999 □ GOLD..CD Rock (Japan) ....RCCY 1063
    Some songs were re-arranged because of publishing problems.
1999 □ GOLD..CD EMI 7243 5 22 144 2
2000 □ GOLD..CD Great Vision/Universal (Russia)........159 208-2
2000 ■ ROCK TRIBUTE TO ABBA ....CD Bad Reputation 640441
    Different title, different artwork, same album.
2000 □ Gold Selection...MCD 4tr EMI ....CDP 000158
    Tracks: Ballroom Blitz(Dancing Queen)/Enter Sadman (Take A Chance On Me)/Smoke
    On The Water (Mamma Mia)/Heartbreaker (Knowing Me, Knowing You).
2000 ■ GOLD..CD EMI (Germany) 72435 22144 2
    Release under the name The Black Sweden.

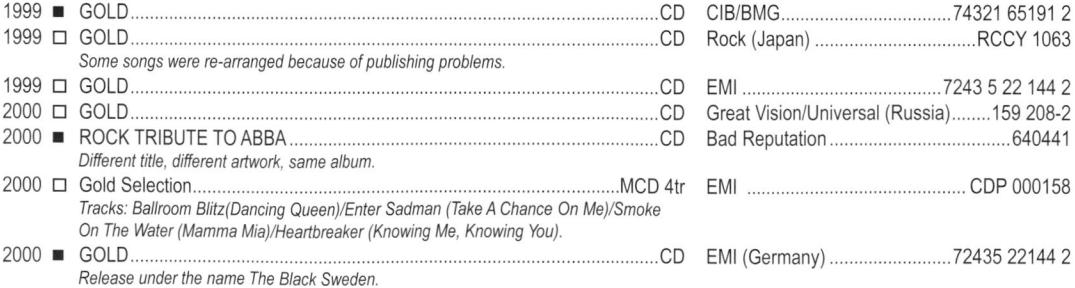

2000 CD - 72435 22144 2

BLACK, THE
Daniel Forn Bragman: v/g, Andreas Jonsson: b, Markus "Make/The Black" Pesonen: d
Eskilstuna - Swedish death metal band formed in 1991, which also featured **Dissection** main man, the late Jon Nödtveit back in 1992-93, under the alias Rietas. The band recorded the first cassette demo *Demo 1992* in 666 copies and then the *Black Blood* the same year. The latter has been re-issued on CD on *The Priest Of Satan*. Make is also found in **Eternal Darkness** and **Karjalan Sissit**, while Bragman and Jonsson has recorded with **Vinterland** and **Tyrant**. Nödtveit committed suicide in August 2006. The bass on the debut was handled by Marcus "Leviathan" Pedersen (**Crypt Of Kerberos, Infester**).

1996 □ Black Blood..MCD 7tr Necropolis Records ....NR 012
    Tracks: The Book Of Leviathan/Lady Lilith/The Spirit Of Solitude/Black Blood/Towards
    The Golden Dawn/The Goat Of Mendes/The Black Opal Eye

1994 CD - NR 003

1994 ■	THE PRIEST OF SATAN	CD	Necropolis Records	NR 003
2003 ☐	THE PRIEST OF SATAN	LP	Cryptia/Pakana	LCF IV/KULT 001
	300 copies. Heavy vinyl.			
2003 ☐	THE PRIEST OF SATAN	CD	Mutilation	MUT 034
	1000 copies. The tracks from the demo "Black Blood" as bonus.			
2003 ☐	THE PRIEST OF SATAN	LP	Miriquidi/City Of The Dead	MPLP 08
	666 copies.			
2008 ☐	ALONGSIDE DEATH	LPg	Hell's Cargo	- -
	666 copies with A2 poster.			
2008 ☐	THE PRIEST OF SATAN	CD	Miriquidi Productions	- -
2008 ☐	Black Blood	MCD 7tr	Miriquidi Productions	- -
	Different artwork.			
2009 ■	ALONGSIDE DEATH	CD	Pulverized	ASH 048 CD
	With OBI strip. First 2000 copies with free sticker.			

2009 CD - ASH 048 CD

BLACK & WHITE
Anders Wiberg (?)

Bonäs - The A-side is standard type melodic hard rock, while *This Is Love* is a ballad sung in the most horrible way. For collectors only.

1986 ■	Give Me Some Lovin'/This Is Love	7"	Active Music	HEJ S-016

1986 7" - HEJ S-016

BLACK BONZO
Magnus Lindgren (now Kärnebro): v, Joakim Karlsson: g, Nicklas Åhlund: k, Anthon Johansson: b, Mikael Israelsson: d

Skellefteå - *Black Bonzo* was formed in 2003 from the remains of psychedelic rockers *Soulshield*, which (after a short stint and a demo as *Kharma Cosmic*) split into the two bands *Moon Safari* and *Black Bonzo*. The bass on the first album was handled by Patrick Leanders-son. Singer Magnus Lindgren is also found in *Waterclime*. High class slightly progressive retro hard rock with a strong touch of vintage *Uriah Heep*. The debut album also goes under the title *Lady Of The Night*. Nicklas Åhlund has been replaced by Klas Holmgren. In 2012 the band died and was resurrected as *Gin Lady*, releasing their self-titled debut in My 2012. All albums are highly recommended for fans of classic seventies hard rock.
Website: www.blackbonzo.com

2004 CD - BCD 005

2007 CDp - GQCD 10072

2004 ■	BLACK BONZO	CD	B&B	BCD 005
2005 ☐	BLACK BONZO	CD	Argus/Avex (Japan)	GQCD 10003
	Bonus: Path/Siren			
2007 ☐	SOUND OF THE APOCALYPSE	CDd	B&B	BCD 017
2007 ☐	SOUND OF THE APOCALYPSE	LPg	Prima Vinyl	Blackb009
	1000 copies.			
2007 ☐	SOUND OF THE APOCALYPSE	CD	Argus/Avex (Japan)	GQCD 10058
	Bonus: Ten Feet Away/Losing Faith			
2007 ■	SOUND OF THE APOCALYPSE	CDp	Argus/Avex (Japan)	GQCD 10072
	Bonus: Ten Feet Away/Losing Faith			
2008 ☐	SOUND OF THE APOCALYPSE	CDd	Lazer's Edge (USA)	LE 1048
2009 ☐	BLACK BONZO	CDv	Argus/Avex (Japan)	GQCD 10071
	Bonus: Path/Siren			
2009 ☐	THE GUILLOTINE DRAMA	CD	B&B	BCD 029
2009 ■	THE GUILLOTINE DRAMA	CDv	Argus/Avex (Japan)	GQCD 10070
2009 ☐	THE GUILLOTINE DRAMA	3CDv box	Argus/Avex (Japan)	n/a
	3 CD box with all three releases as paper sleeve versions in a box.			

2009 CDp - GQCD 10070

BLACK CAT MOAN
Lars Axelsson: v, Jörgen Lantto: g, Hans Ludwig: g, Peter Melin: b, Bo Åström: d

Stockholm - Jörgen, Hans and Bo had previously recorded some demos with the great melodic hard rock band *Grinder*, later known as *Landslide*, who also had one song on the *Rockbox* compilation. Quite a good album, with well played and well sung melodic hard rock that just came and went. Too bad.

1991 ☐	BLACK CAT MOAN	LP	Microtrain	TUTLP 001
1991 ■	BLACK CAT MOAN	CD	Microtrain	TUTCD 001
1991 ☐	Heartbreak Jury/Out In The Cold	7"	Microtrain	LOK 002

1991 CD - TUTCD 001

BLACK CIRCLE
Strijd: v/g/b/d

Skänninge - Strijd is a one-man old-school black metal band in the vein of *Darkthrone* and *Judas Iscarot*. He recorded a bunch of demos both under the name *Strijd* and also *Svartr Strijd*.

2004	□	BEHOLD MY VISION AND WISDOM	CD	Perverted Taste	PT 110
2004	□	BEHOLD MY VISION AND WISDOM	LP	Anti-Xian Terror Records	AXTR666-001
2005	■	THE DISTANT WIND	CD	Total Holocaust	THR-72
		500 copies.			
2005	□	THE DISTANT WIND	LP	Turanian Honour	TURAN-002
		333 numbered copies. Different artwork.			
2008	□	A Living Hell (split)	7"	Turanian Honour Records	TURAN-005
		Split with US band Xasthur. 888 hand numbered copies and 244 in yellow viny + limited t-shirtl. Track: As Fire Scourged The Heavens			

2005 CD - THR-72

BLACK DOG
Henrik "Baffe" Olsson: v, Leo Dahlin: g , Kari Stehag: b, Thomas Andersson: d

Stockholm - Formed in 1993. Three songs, three styles. I find it hard to make up my mind, if this band is good or not, as the songs feel a bit too diverse. It has a grungy feel all over it though. After the MCD Kari left the band. He was temporarily replaced by André Skaug (*Clawfinger*). André's brother Morten was also in and out of the band in a few months time. In 1995 they recorded a new and far more interesting demo. It also showed a new line-up featuring Henrik, Leo, guitarist Morgan Zocek (*Sideburn*), bassist Fredrik Zackrisson and drummer Federico De Costa. Leo went to *Flying Green*. Federico left for progressive band *Qoph* and Baffe was later in *It's Alive*.

1994	■	Unleashed	MCD 3tr	Crown	CDS 1
		Tracks: Mentally Unsound/Take It In/Angel Of Soul.			

1994 MCD - CDS 1

BLACK INGVARS
Anders "Karl-Ingvar" Möller: v/g, Magnus "Lars-Ingvar" Tengby: g, Leif Larsson: v/b, Nisse "Niels-Ingvar" Nordin: d

Göteborg - The band was originally known as *The Few* and used to play covers and act as back-up for other artists, such as *Frankie Miller, Bonnie Tyler* and *Mick Ronson*. Just as a crazy whim they started making a heavy metal parody of Swedish dance music, mixing the names of the bands *Black Sabbath* and *Sven Ingvars* (Swedish dance/pop-band). They have stolen parts of songs by *AC/DC, Nazareth, Van Halen, Kiss* etc. and mixed these up with traditional Swedish dance/pop songs. It's quite funny, but as this type of dance music is so typically Swedish, it might sound a bit weird to non-Swedish listeners. As recording industry mogul, Bert Karlsson, couldn't sign this band he created the copies *Flinstens Med Stanley*, that was more of a hasty put together studio project containing musicians like Göran Edman, Thomas Vikström, Peo Pettersson etc. *Black Ingvars* however was far superior. The irony is that *Black Ingvars* was finally signed by Bert's label Mariann in 2000. The *Sjung och var glad*-albums contains children's songs such as *Bananas In Pajamas* etc. given the same treatment. Anders was also the lead singer of *Swedish Erotica*. In November 1995 the album had sold in the excess of 100 000 copies, in Sweden only (it probably wouldn't sell anywhere else for that matter...)! The label name SDM actually stands for Swedish Dance Metal. On *Heaven Metal* they made metal versions of Swedish hymns and Christian songs. Blasphemy? Well, some thought so... and the first version was even withdrawn and reworked. They even put a sticker on it saying it was "the legal version". After *Heaven Metal* bass player/singer Henrik "Pär-Ingvar" Ohlin was replaced by Leif (ex-*NME Within/Frozen Eyes*). On *Kids Super Hits* they do their renditions of popular radio-hits by *Britny Spears, Back Street Boys* etc. They also did a *Rammstein*-version of pop song *Schnappi*. After many years of absence they suddenly popped up again in 2009 at the dance-band bandstand on national TV called *Dansbandskampen*, playing their mix of dance band music and metal. They were voted out. The band also featured keyboard player Dan Helgesen.

Black and white Ingvars

1995	■	Mitt Eget Blue Hawaii/Leende Guldbruna Ögon	CDS 2tr	SDM	SDM 870
1995	□	EARCANDY SIX	CD	SDM	SDMCD 1805
1995	□	Tiotusen Röda Rosor/De Sista Ljuva Åren	CDS 2tr	SDM	SDM 871
1995	□	Sveriges Nationalsång	MCD 4tr	SDM	SDM 873
		A Metallica-nised version of the Swedish national hymn. Split CD with Top 40-singer Sven-Erik Magnusson.			
1995	□	Whole Lotta Engberg/Ljus Och Värme	CDS	SDM	SDM 874

1995 CDS - SDM 870

1995	☐	Black Christmas	MCD 3tr	SDM	SDM 875

Tracks: Ritsch Rap/Jag drömmer om en jul hemma/Sjömansjul på Hawaii

1995	☐	EARCANDY FIVE	CD	SDM	SDMCD 1808
1996	☐	Vem tänder stjärnorna/Karlstads kollage	CDSp 2tr	SDM	SDM 876
1997	☐	Idas Sommarvisa (Schwarzeneggeregger mix)/(together mix)	CDSp 2tr	SDM	SDM 501
1997	☐	SJUNG OCH VAR GLAD	CD	SDM	SDMCD 1809
1998	☐	Cherie/Dansa I Neon/La Det Swinge	MCDp 3tr	SMR	POOLS 027
1998	☐	SCHLAGERMETAL		SMR	POOLCD 007
1998	☐	Diggi-Loo Diggi Ley (Remixes)	MCDp 4tr	Pool Sounds	POOLS 037
1999	☐	HEAVEN METAL	CD	Pool Sounds	POOLCD 016

The first edition contained an intro speech by Runar Söögard, plus excerpts from a Prince-song.

1999	☐	Ovan Där	CDS	Pool Sounds	POOLS 039
1999	☐	Gospel medley/Varför skola människor strida	CDS	Pool Sounds	POOLS 052
2000	☐	THE VERY BEST OF DANSBANDSHÅRDROCK	CD	Mariann	MLPCD 3191
2000	■	KIDS SUPER HITS	CD	Mariann	MLPCD 3185
2000	☐	Baby One More Time/La Vida Loca/Popstar	MCDp 3tr	Mariann	MLPCDS 220
2000	☐	Funny Funny/Larger Than Life	CDS 2tr	Mariann	MLPCDS 231
2000	☐	EARCANDY FIVE	CD	Mariann	MLPCD 3229
2000	☐	EARCANDY SIX	CD	Mariann	MLPCD 3230
2001	☐	SJUNG OCH VAR GLAD 2	CD	Mariann	MLPCD 3307
2005	☐	Schnappi	CDS 1tr	Mariann	PROMOMLPCDS 445

2000 CD - MLPCD 3185

BLACK ROSE

Peter Thederan: v, Thomas Berg: g, Anders Haga: b, Peter Haga: d

Fagersta - Formed in 1990. Not to be confused with the UK band, *King Diamond* or *Cher*'s old bands with the same name. *Black Rose* is an upper mid-class melodic AOR/hard rock band. Quite reminiscent of *Europe* and *Glory*, but the first album is a step below their league. The track *Keep On*, recorded in 1995 showed a promising quality improvement, and appears on local compilation *Tid Är Musik*. They recorded several demos between 1995 and 2002, such as *Covers Up, Promo 99, A New Beginning - Promo 2000. Covers Up* features covers by *Van Halen, Talisman, Yngwie Malmsteen* and *Whitesnake*. On the second album guitarist Thomas Berg was replaced by Ola Carlsson and keyboard-player Håkan Karlström was replaced by Magnus Vesterlund. The style has also become a bit heavier, more akin to *Black Sabbath* in the *Seventh Sign*-era. In 2004 they returned with the album *Explode* and then there was silence. Haga was also found in *ShadowDivine*. The band however returned, featuring singer Peter Thederan, replacing Johan Spinord, guitarist Thomas Berg together with the Haga brohers. A demo with covers of *Malmsteen, Talisman, Hammerfall* etc was recorded in 2008. In 2012 the band returned with the new album, showing the band at their strongest so far. Great melodic hard rock/metal. Website: http://way.to/black_rose

1995 MCD - BR 007

1993	☐	FORTUNE FAVOURS THE BRAVE	CD	Büms	4 5123
1995	■	Winds Of Fire	MCD 4tr	private	BR 007

Tracks: Deceiver/Don't Wanna Lose You/On The Run/Winds Of Fire

2002	■	BLACK ROSE	CD	Shark/Crazy Life	SHARK 2016
2004	☐	EXPLODE	CD	Shark/Crazy Life	SHARK 2025
2012	■	TURN ON THE NIGHT	CD	Doolittle Group	DOOCD 006

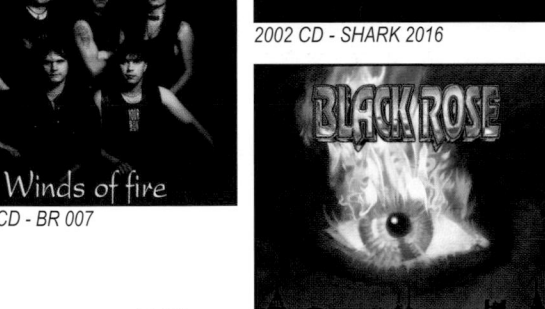

2002 CD - SHARK 2016

2012 CD - DOOCD 006

BLACK TRIP

Joseph Tholl: v, Peter Stjärnvind: g/b, Daniel Bergkvist: d

Stockholm - Now here's a really cool retro NWoBHM band that ticks all the boxes when it comes to authenticity. Stjärnvind, drummer in bands like *Krux, Entombed, Unanimated, Nifelheim, Murder Squad* and *Merciless*, here handles the strings, and he does it well. *Black Trip* sounds like the amalgamation and resurrection of bands like *Oxym, Triarchy, Diamond Head* and *Jameson Raid*. Bergkvis is ex-*Wolf* and Tholl is foremost guitarist in *Enforcer*. The band has also featured Erik Danielsson (*Watain*) on guitar and Erik "Tyrant" Gustavsson (*Nifelheim*) on bass. Great stuff indeed!

2012	■	Tvár Dábla	7"	Primitive Art	PAR 031

Tracks: Eyes Of The Night/The Sleeper. Sticker.

2012 7" - PAR 031

BLACK WEB

Urban Österberg: v/g, Andreas Melander: g, Lars Nilsson: b, Markus Ramström: d

Kramfors - *Black Web* was formed already back in 1992. Pretty good, slightly thrash-oriented metal with a touch of vintage *Metallica* mixed with some *Alice In Chains* overtones and at times some *Black Label Society* riffs thrown in for good measure. Well worth checking out. Urban, who also recorded an MCD with *Impiety* in 1996, sadly passed away in 2012.

2006	■	OLD HABITS DIE HARD	CD	private	BW 002

2006 CD - BW 002

BLACKBURNS

Johan Andersson: v/b, Fredrik Johansson: g, Johan Frisk: g, Fredrik Rehnqvist: d

Norrköping (?) **-** Mid class classic metal from a young band. Not bad, but not exactly exciting either. At times they sound a bit influenced by bands like *Dokken* and *Ratt*. Decent sound and decent performance with the vocals being the weak link.

1993 ■ Punishment Of Injustice ....MCD 4tr   Taltratten .... BLACKCD-S
     Tracks: Punishment Of Injustice/Annie/All I Got Is Rock 'N Roll/Sentence Of Death

1993 MCD - BLACKCD-S

BLACKLIGHT

Richard Karlsson: v, Jan Iso-Aho: g, Patric Hedberg: g, Kaj Ukura: b, Patrick Nygren: d

Mellösa - Local band that only recorded one MCD. The band was formed a couple of years before the release and have not been heard of since. Heavy death metal compared to *Dismember* during their *Massive Killing Capacity* period.

1997 □ Blacklight..MCD 4tr   private .... BLACK 001
     Tracks: Under The Moon/Cromwell Street/Black As Hell/Nightmare

BLACKMAIL

Jens Lundsbye: b/v, Robert Alsterlind: g/v, Danne Lundsbye: d

Göteborg - Young hungry hard rockers, with influences from *Freak Kitchen*, but then Mattias Ia Eklundh has produced three of the four tracks on the first MCD. They also have two tracks on the *Rockslaget 94* compilation. The band had been around for a long time and often boasted about being the most popular un-signed band on the web. They remained unsigned.

1996 MCDp - RARE 9601

1994 □ Schizophrenic ....MCDp 3tr   Ransom .... RARE CDEP 94001
     Tracks: Evil Enough/Feel Awrath/Stuck On You
1996 ■ A Female Impersonator.......................................MCDp 3tr   private .... RARE 9601
     Tracks: Female Impersonator/Demons Hide/World Of Misery

BLACKRAIN

Daniel Söderberg: v, Ronny Blylod: g, John Vigebo: b, Henrik "Honken" Söderqvist: d

Örnsköldsvik - The band initially started as Ronny's solo-project, where he played all instruments. He drafted singer Söderberg and in 2009 the two recorded the CD *One Week Notice* under the name *Justaquickstop*. Bass player Vigebo joined and finally drummer Söderqvist completed the line-up. After a few gigs with the new line-up and the adoption of a slightly heavier sound they decided to change the name to *Blackrain*. In the winter of 2010/11 the debut album was recorded. Great modern sounding melodic hard rock with great vocals and high class musicians. Söderberg and Vigebo have previously played with *Freelancer*, while Blylod has been found in bands like *Destynation, Engine No 9, Planet Storm* and *Eternia*.

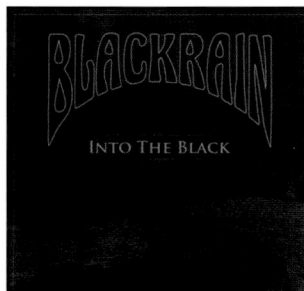

2011 CD - JAQSCD002

2011 ■ INTO THE BLACK...CD   JAQS Produktion JAQSCD002

BLACKSHINE

Anders "Atte" Strokirk: v/g, Albin Andersson: g
Fredrik Cardona (aka Holmberg): b, Martin Karlsson: d

Stockholm - The band was formed in August 1988 under the name *Hetsheads* and in 1995 released the album *We Hail The Possessed* (Repulse). *Our Pain...* was produced by Johnny Hagel (*Tiamat, Sundown, Sorcerer*). Strokirk was also found in *Necrophobc*. After *Our Pain Is Our Pleasure*, drummer Håkan Eriksson (ex-*Godblender, Inzight, Face Down*) replaced Anders Freimanis. Only three weeks before a tour with the latter, drummer Eriksson decided to jump ship. He was replaced by Stefan "Stipen" Carlsson (*Dia Psalma, Merciless, Harm's Way*). After the recording of the album, but before its release, Stipen left the band and was replaced by Chris Barkensjö (*Kaamos*). Dark and heavy but quite up-tempo, goth-oriented metal with melancholic parts and at times even with a touch of *Motörhead*. After five years of silence Strokirk returned with a new line-up and a heavier sound, seeing Joakim Stabel replaced by Andersson and Barkensjö by Karlsson (*Die Hard, Mykorrhiza, Bloodshed*). Great, heavy melodic death/thrash metal with Strokirk having a touch of Lemmy Kilminster in his voice.

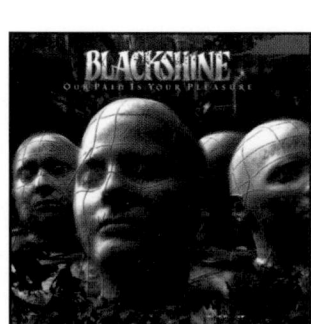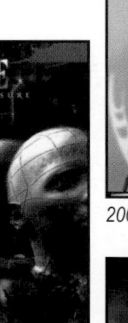

1997 CD - 74321501752

2002 CD - 085-72532

2006 CD - DY 100372

1997 ■ OUR PAIN IS YOUR PLEASURE	CD	G.U.N.	74321501752
2001 □ SOULLESS AND PROUD	CD	Nippon Crown (Jap)	CRCL 4796
2002 ■ SOULLESS AND PROUD	CD	Steamhammer/SPV	085-72532
2006 ■ LIFEBLOOD	CD	Dockyard 1	DY 100372
2006 □ LIFEBLOOD	CD	Soyuz Music (Russia)	DY 100372
2006 □ LIFEBLOOD	CD	Locomotive Music (USA)	LMUA 700151
2013 □ SOUL CONFUSION	CD	Trans-Am Productions	TAM001CD

BLACKSMITH

Per Englund: v, Robert "Bobby" Holmberg: g, Lars Johansson: k,
Claes "Fille" Lindström: b, David Wallin: d

Vimmerby/Stockholm - The band was formed in the early eighties and recorded the first two releases with the following line-up; Per Englund (v), Johan Nyström (g), Nicklas Andersson (k), Patrik Eklöf (b) and Mats Andersson (d). *Blacksmith* split and Per was later found in bands like *Voltergeist, Garbo, Motherlode* and *Mandrake Root*. In the 90s the band was partly reformed by guitarist Bobby Holmberg, but under the name *King's Crown*. When Per returned to the band, they also returned to using the *Blacksmith* moniker. The return album is killer hard rock with touches of *Ozzy, Malmsteen, Judas Priest* and *Led Zeppelin*, while the early releases are mid-league hard rock with a touch of *Deep Purple*. The drums, as well as production on the album were handled by Fredrik Thordendahl (*Meshuggah*). The kid on the cover is actually Bobby's son. Bobby was also in the band *MarysCreek*, while Fille is also in *Attack*.

1985 MLP - PR EP 002

Year		Title	Format	Label	Cat.No.
1985	■	GIPSY QUEEN	MLP 4tr	Party	PR EP 002
1986	□	Tomorrows Mystery/The King Has Lost His Crown	7"	Party	PRS 004
1999	□	ONCE UPON A STAR	CD	JVC Victor (Japan)	VICP 60851
		Bonus: Downhill Racer			
1999	■	ONCE UPON A STAR	CD	Sun Dance	SDR 0327

1999 CD - SDR 0327

BLACKWINDS

Magnus "Infaustus" Ödling: v, Per "Kraath" Hellqvist: v/g,
Anders "Zathanel" Löfgren: b, Håkan "Mysteriis" Sjödin: d

Sundsvall - The band was formed in 1998 by the three former *Setherial* members Per, Anders and Håkan. Anders is also found in *Midvinter, Blot Mine, Sorhin* and Håkan in *In Battle* and *Obscuratum*. Singer Magnus (*Diabolical, Setherial*) was added to the line-up on *Origin*, which is the first EP plus four new tracks. Not to be confused with the US dark ambient band of the same name. *Blackwinds* play standard formula fast, old-school style, black metal with Infaustus mostly shrieking style vocals.

Year		Title	Format	Label	Cat.No.
1999	□	The Black Wraiths Ascend	7" 3tr	Bloodstone	Blood 001
		300 copies, signed by the members. Tracks: The Black Wraiths Ascend/The Watchers/ Share My Doom			
2008	□	ORIGIN	CD	Nightmare Productiions	NP 017
		666 copies.			
2008	■	FLESH INFERNO	CD	Regain	RR 103
		Slipcase.			

2008 CD - RR 103

BLACKWORLD

Richard Holmgren: v/g/b/d, Peter Ledin: g, Johan Jalonen Penn: g

Västerås - *Blackworld* is the solo project of Richard Holmgren. He has used the lead guitar services of Peter Ledin (*Vanessa, Wolf, Grand Design, Soulskinner, Apostasy, Scaar*) and Johan Jalonen Penn. Richard is a multi-talented musician and a great singer. Musically the style is in the vein of later day *Ozzy Osbourne* mxed with *Black Label Society*. Highly recommended.

Year		Title	Format	Label	Cat.No.
2008	■	BLACKWORLD	CD	private	--

2008 CD - --

BLADE, LENNY

Lenny "Blade" Bladh: v/g/b

Frinnaryd/Thailand - A solo project from *Bullet/Incinerator/Pagan Rites/Hypnosia* bassist Lenny Blade, who also sings on this one. He says on the cover "I'm no singer" and so it is. However it's classic metal similar to bands like *Helvetets Port, Enforcer* etc. *Bullet* colleague Hampus Klang lays down some guitar solos, Jimmy "Hora/J. Voltage" Edström plays drums and *Pagan Rites* singer Thomas "Devil Lee Rot" Karlsson adds some vocals.

Year		Title	Format	Label	Cat.No.
2007	■	Taipei Nights	MCDd 5tr	Swed-Taiwan Records	STR 01
		Tracks: Shake Alley/Far East Hazard/Taipei Nights/Panzer Dragoon/Journey To Silius			

2007 MCDd - STR 01

BLAKK TOTEM

Peter "Pete Blakk" Jacobsson: v/g, Jens Lundahl: b, Jaime Salazar: d

Göteborg - *Blakk Totem* is the brain child of Pete Blakk. Pete has a long and exciting history, starting out with a single recording by local's *Trazer*, followed by a short stint in *EF Band*. He later formed the band *Geisha*, with whom he recorded one album. He left *Geisha* to join *King Diamond Band*, which at the time was more of a Swedish band with Andy LaRocqe, Mikkey Dee and Pete, leaving King as the only Dane. He recorded the albums *Them, Darkside,*

The Eye and *Conspiracy* with the King. After this he formed his own band *Totem*, that at one period featured singer Jakob "Jake Samuel" Samulesson (*Yale Bate, Jekyll & Hyde, The Ring, The Poodles*) on drums. On the 4tr MCD the name was changed to *Blakk Totem* as the other musicians are more or less hired. Sven Cirnski, who shared the lead guitar duties with Pete, is also found in **Raise Cain, Snake Charmer, Bad Habit, Truth**, bass-player Hal Patino in **King Diamond Band**, **=Y=** and Jaime is in **Midnight Sun, The Flower Kings** etc. On the MCD *Blakk Totem* played powerful hard rock with a touch of **Shotgun Messiah** (around *Second Coming*) and elements of sleaze as well as US power metal. Great dynamite loaded guitars, shit-heavy drum work from Jaime and an overall professional attitude. The musicians on the album can also be found on Pete Sandberg's album *Push*. On *The Secret Place* Cirnski was out. The music had also changed to a heavier degree of metal. The album also features guest spots from Hal Patino and Tony Jelencovic (**M.A.N, Transport League, B-Thong**). The band does a cover of *Callin' Dr Love* on the compilation *Kissin' Time – A Tribute To Kiss* (1996 Tribute Records) and a cover of *Battery* on the compilation *Metal Militia – A Tribute To Metallica II* (1996 Tribute). In 2012 Pete also recorded an album with **Disaster Peace** and Danish rocker **Maryann Cotton**.

1996 CD - CMCD 92006

2009 CD - CD 09-DD695

1995 ■	Blakk Totem	MCDgp 4tr	private/Warner Chappell	TOT CD 101
	Tracks: Blooddrained/Had Enough (Of You)/Bottomless Pit/Borderline Tribe			
1996 □	THE SECRET PLACE	CD	KOCH/CMC	CMCD 92006
2001 □	THE SECRET PLACE	CD	Black Sun	CD 0001
2009 □	THE SECRET PLACE	CD	Music Buy Mail	n/a
	Bonus: Sin After Sin (demo)/Calling Dr. Love (Kiss cover)/Battery (Metallica cover)			
2009 ■	THE SECRET PLACE	CD	Irond/Dark Division (Russia)	CD 09-DD695
	Bonus: Sin After Sin (demo)/Calling Dr. Love (Kiss cover)/Battery (Metallica cover)			

1995 MCDgp - TOT CD 101

BLASTROCK

Jonas Polling: v, Ola Wentrup: g, Harri Kolari: b, Peo Moogvall: d

Lund - The band was formed in 1996, or actually they changed their name from **Into The Void**, featuring Ola, bass player Joakim Bröms and drummer Per Olofsson and in 1995 the band had recorded the album *Facelift*. If **Into The Void** was influenced by **Monster Magnet** and **Soundgarden**, **Blastrock** owes more to **Motörhead** and general musical violence. In 2002 Bröms, who changed his career to war reporter, was replaced by ex-**Dipper** man Harri Kolari. At this time they also recruited singer Polling. Along the way drummer Per was also replaced by Peo. The band has also released a bunch of CD-R singles/Eps such as *Plunge, Now's The Time, Ruthless Fuck, That's Right Do It One More Time, Your Head Or Mine* and *Fire At Will*.

2002 □	Garage Metal	7" 4tr	Puberty Music Inc	PMP 005
	Tracks: One Man Army/Below The Belt/Age Or Beauty/Are You Ready			
2002 □	Like It Hard/A 1000 Scars/Special Forces	7" 3tr	Zorch	zs-19
2003 ■	BLASTROCK	CDd	Zorch	zs-25
2005 □	Hole In Your Head	MCD 5tr	Puberty Music Inc	PMP 006
	Tracks: Hole In Your Head/My Own Rules/My Fist Your Face/Losing My Mind/Time			

2003 CDd - zs-25

BLAZING GUNS

Magnus "Magnum" Lundström: v, Gabriel "Gabe Colt" Österlund: g,
Tommi "Tommy Trigger" Korkeamäki: g, Johnny Leadfinger: b, "Rikki Force": d

Norrköping - **W.A.S.P** style cowboy theme metal. The band recorded their first five-track demo *I'll Never (Give Up Leather)* in 2003. Magnus is also found in **Seven, Last Temptation** and **Hellbender**, Gabriel in **Seven** and **Von Panzer**, Tommi in **Hellbender** and Rikki in **Last Temptation**.

2005 □	1876	MCD	private	- -
	Tracks: Lawless/Forged In Steel/The Peacemaker/1876 (An Ode To The Brave).			
2005 ■	In The Sign Of Aces (split)	7"	Dream Evil	005
	Split with Not Fragile. Track: 1876 (An Ode To The Brave). 333 hand-numbered copies.			

2005 7" - 005

BLIND ALLEY

Hans Dimberg: v, Alec Bjöedal: v, Magnus Olsson: g/b/k,
Pierre Glans: g, Clas Magnusson: d

Jönköping - **Blind Alley** was formed out of the ashes of AOR band **Fortune** (the Jönköping band) by guitarist Magnus Olsson, formerly of **X-Hale**. The first album was only released through MP3.com. The first two albums featured Hans, Magnus and Pierre, while the third release saw an extended line-up also featuring former **Renegade** drummer Clas. The band is working on a new album and the vocals are now handled by **Hellspray** singer Anders Moberg. AOR of the highest order.

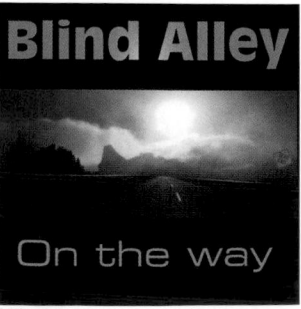

2001 ■	ON THE WAY	CD	MP3.COM	- -
2003 □	INFINITY ENDS	CD	AOR Heaven	00006
2007 □	DESTINATION DESTINY	CD	Perris	PER 1822

2001 CD - - -

BLIND DOG

Joakim Thell: g, Tobias Nilsson: v/b, Thomas Elnevik: d

Halmstad - **Blind Dog** have several great demos in their luggage. The track *Lose* was also featured on the compilation *Burn One Up* (Roadrunner), as well as on the label-version of the album. The band produces excellent heavy 70's influenced stonery hard rock. Recorded and mixed by Berno Paulsson (**The Quill, W.E.T, Spiritual Beggars** etc). On *Captain Dog Rides Again* Andreas Barringer is providing some Hammond organ. A last album, *Captain Dog Logs Out* was recorded but due to various reasons it was only released as a free download from the band's website in 2008. The band is sadly defunct.

1998	☐	10000 Reasons/Beyond My Reach	7"	Warpburner	WARP 002
		Yellow vinyl.			
1999	■	THE LAST ADVENTURES OF CAPTAIN DOG	CD	private	BLIND 1
1999	☐	THE LAST ADVENTURES OF CAPTAIN DOG	CD	Meteor City (USA)	MCY 015
2000	☐	THE LAST ADVENTURES OF CAPTAIN DOG	2LP	People Like You	PRISON 992-1
2000	■	THE LAST ADVENTURES OF CAPTAIN DOG	CDd	People Like You	PRISON 992-2
2003	☐	CAPTAIN DOG RIDES AGAIN	CD	Listenable Records	POSH 050

1999 CD - BLIND 1

2000 CDd - PRISON 992-2

BLINDED COLONY (aka BLINDED)

Johan Schüster: v, Johan Blomström: g, Tobias Olsson: g,
Roy Erlandsson: b, Staffan Franzén: d

Karlshamn - An angry young band, but with a lot of melodic feel to it, draws a lot of influences from the Gothenburg sound with hints of **In Flames** and **Dark Tranquillity**. The band was formed in 2000 as **Stigmata**. Vocals on the first album were handled by Niklas Svensson (**Carnival Sun, The Random Riots**), who is actually son of Kenta Svensson of **Overdrive**. He was replaced by Johan Schüster (**Skörda**). A 4 track promo CD-R was recorded in 2005, simply entitled *Promo 2005*. After *Bedtime Prayers* Schüster left the band for a career as songwriter in the US, where he's actually had number one hits with artists like **Pink** and **Britny Spears**, under the name Shellback. The band spent a long time looking for a vocal replacement after Denny Axelsson (**Maramon, Calm, Within Reach**) left before even having recorded with the band. *Divine* featured a guest solo from Janne Stark (**Overdrive, Constancia**). Bass player Roy Erlandsson was replaced by Martin Bergman. In 2010 the band had struggled long enough trying to find a new singer and two vocalists were drafted, Joel Andersson (clean vocals) and Johnny Blackout (growl). The band also shortened their name to **Blinded** and in December 2010 they released a new EP available from the band's website. Since then it has unfortunately been all quiet. *Website: www.blindedcolony.com*

2003 CDd - SC-067 2

2003	■	DIVINE	CDd	Scarlet	SC-067 2
2003	☐	DIVINE	CD	Toy's Factory (Japan)	TKCS-85073
		Bonus: Contagious Sin (demo)/Discrown The Holy (demo)			
2006	■	BEDTIME PRAYERS	CD	Pivotal	MORPH-13807

2006 CD - MORPH-13807

BLINDSIDE

Christian Lindskog: v, Simon Grenehed: g, Tomas Näslund: b, Marcus Dahlström: d

Stockholm - **Blindside** was formed in the suburbs of Stockholm. After a self-financed demo release in 1996, the band released their debut. A Christian band that sounds like a mix of **Korn** and **Deftones**. The band is far better known in the US than in their home country which started when Christian US fellows **P.O.D** started endorsing the band and even got them signed to Elektra. The band also toured with **Hoobastank**. Simon was surprisingly found in project band **Fuck Bitch**. *About A Burning Fire* featured guest spots from Jon Rekdahl (**Fuck Bitch**) and Billy Corgan (**The Smashing Pumpkins**) and was produced by Howard Benson (who also produced *Silence*). It even ended up on the Top 40 on the Billboard 200 chart. The latter also produced the album together with Chris Lord-Alge. Lindskog and Grenehed have also been working with side project **Lindforest** (a direct translation of Lindskog's last name). *Website: www.blindsideonline.com*

1997 CD - DGCD 01   *1999 CD - DGR 13*

1997	■	BLINDSIDE	CD	Day-Glo	DGCD 01
1997	☐	BLINDSIDE	CD	Solid State/Tooth And Nail	SS08/TND1096
1997	☐	Empty Box	MCD 5tr	Day-Glo	DGEP 02
		Tracks: Empty Box/Born/Replay/Teddybear/Daughter			
1999	■	A THOUGHT CRUSHED MY MIND	CD	Day-Glo	DGR 13
1999	☐	A THOUGHT CRUSHED MY MIND	CD	Solid State/Tooth And Nail	SS19/TND1132
2001	☐	Blindside	7"g 3tr	Structure	STRUCT 4
		Tracks: Walking Home/Sunrise/Knockin' On Another Door. 500 copies. Grey or clear vinyl.			
2002	■	SILENCE	CD	Elektra	7559-62765-2
2004	■	ABOUT A BURNING FIRE	CD	Elektra	7559-62918-2
2005	☐	THE GREAT DEPRESSION	CD	DRT Entertainment (USA)	RTE 00436 2
2005	☐	BLINDSIDE	CD	DRT Entertainment (USA)	RTE 00439 2
		Bonus: Liberty (demo)/Superman (demo)/Stolen (demo)/Forgiven (demo)			

2002 CD - 7559-62765-2

2005 ☐	A THOUGHT CRUSHED MY MIND...CD	DRT Entertainment (USA) ....RTE 00429 2

Bonus: Nothing But Skin/Knockin' On Another Door/Desert Flowers/All You Need/Sunrise/
(phatbeat 1303)

2007 ☐	The Black Rose EP...MCDd 8tr	Wasa Recording ....BSCD 001

Tracks: The Way You Dance/Slow Motion/Pretty Nights/The Color Of My Eyes/The Black
Rose/My Alibi (live)/Fell In Love With The Game (live)/When I Remember (live)

2007 ☐	The Black Rose EP.. MLP 8tr	Wasa Recording ....WASA 004
2011 ☐	WITH SHIVERING HEARTS WE WAIT.......................................CD	National.......................................NATCD 11-2

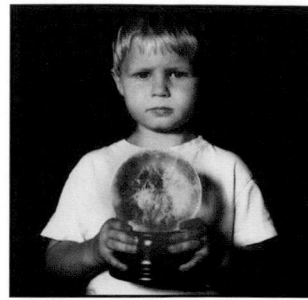

2004 CD - 7559-62918-2

BLIZZARD
Örjan Jonsson: v, Per Engström: g, Per Söderberg: g, Ulf Lundström: b, Kari Tapio: d

Finspång - Formed in 1984. A traditional sounding mid-80's melodic metal band. The MLP was produced by *Heavy Load* guitarist Ragne Wahlquist. In 1989 Engström, Söderberg and Tapio went on to form the band *Blackbird*, also featuring *Guitar Battle*-finalist Anders Karlsson. Besides recording some great demos they recorded two instrumental tracks found on the *Guitar Heroes Of Sweden* compilations, under Anders' name. Unfortunately the band split as Anders went to the US for golf and guitar training.

1987 ■	Fading Away .... MLP 4tr	private ....- -

Tracks: Illusions/Stronger Than The Wind/Lonely Nights/Fading Away.

1987 MLP - - -

BLODSKALD
Erik "Dr." Sundén": v, Halvar: g, Möller: g, Lage: d

Skellefteå - Quite horribly mixed, not even old-school, just bad sounding, black metal with puking vocals and untight drums. Sounds like it's been recorded at a rehearsal. Erik also sings in *Sorgeldom* and was previously in *Kaos Sacramentum*.

2009 ■	Vidundret...MCD 5tr	Death Dealers...................................DDA-005

Tracks: Fördärvets skog/Vidundret/Döden giver evig vila/Guds fördömda ätt/In The
Shadows Of The Horns (Darkthrone cover)

2009 MCD - DDA-005

BLODSRIT
Jimmie "Naahz/Nazgûl" Nyhlén: v/g, Stefan "Yxmarder" Johansson: g,
Emil "Brisheim" Koverot: b, Mattias Fiebig: d

Västervik - *Blodsrit* was formed already in the late 90s by singer Naahz. The first demo, *Dödens sändebud,* was recorded in 1999. In 2001 the band recorded the 4 track promo *Secrets Unveiled*. The style was decribed as raw black metal in the vein of *Darkthrone* or *Burzum*. The band has evolved quite a lot since the debut, but the style is more or less the same, quite varied black metal with shrieking vocals, at times more talking than singing. Quite raw and old-school style recording with drums sounding like they've been recorded with two distant mikes. Koverot (also found in *Portal*) was a thing in the media in 2008 when he was fired from his new job as a teacher due to his musical involvement not being at par with the head master's view of who the pupils should learn from. Fiebig is also in *Portal, Ribspreader* and *Paganizer*. Yxmarder is also a *Portal* man. The bass was handled by *Paganizer* member Patrik "Saphanoz" Halvarsson played on the *Occularis Inferium* album. Kristian "Kribbe" Halvarsson guested on vocals on *Supreme Misanthropy* and *Helveteshymner*. The latter was produced by the late Mieszko Talarczyk (*Nasum*) and contains a cover of *Candlemass*' Solitude. The 2008 version of *Supreme Misanthropy* is actually completely rerecorded and with new artwork.
Website: www.myspace.com/blodsritswe

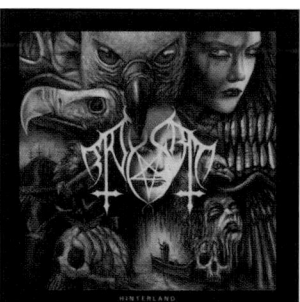

2007 CD - UER 018

2000 ☐	STORM OF IMMOLATION (split)..CD	Psychic Scream ....PSDL 9030-2

Split with Ritual Orchestra. Tracks: Shadowed Star Of Darkness/Godess Of Life Eternal/
Blinded By Fire/Master Of The Grim Domains/Torturing A Feeble Priest/Ablaze In The
Winter Night

2001 ☐	SUPREME MISANTHROPY...CD	Oaken Shield ....FPG 3
2002 ☐	...In Blood ....MCD 5tr	MP3.COM ....- -

Tracks: Torturing A Feeble Priest/Master Of The Grim Domains/Dödens sändebud/I spår
av Jesu blod/As Darkness Prevail

2003 ☐	OCCULARIS INFERIUM..CD	Oaken Shield ....FPG 18
2004 ☐	HELVETESHYMNER...CD	Oaken Shield ....FPG 25
2006 ☐	HELVETESHYMNER... LPg	Obscure Abhorence ....- -

500 copies, first 100 in splatter vinyl.

2006 ☐	THE WELL OF LIGHT HAS FINALLY DRIED.............................CD	Miniquiri Productions ....- -
2006 ☐	THE WELL OF LIGHT HAS FINALLY DRIED.............................LP	Miniquiri Productions ....- -

Artwork different from CD.

2007 ■	HINTERLAND ....CD	Unexploded Records ....UER 018
2007 ☐	HINTERLAND 2LPg	Unexploded Records ....UER 019

500 copies.

2008 CDd - UER 024

2008 CDd - UER 025

2008	☐	THE WELL OF LIGHT HAS FINALLY DRIED	LP	Unexploded Records	UER 023
		500 copies			
2008	■	SUPREME MISANTHROPY MMVIII	CDd	Unexploded Records	UER 024
2008	■	OCCULARIS INFERIUM/SECRETS UNVEILED	CDd	Unexploded Records	UER 025
		Bonus: Secrets Unveiled/Rulers Of The Desolate lands/Vid livets slut/Transilvanian Hunger (Darkthrone cover)			
2008	■	HELVETESHYMNER	CDd	Unexploded Records	UER 026
		Bonus: Choir Of Broken Bones/March Of The 22ⁿᵈ/Söndra			

2008 CDd - UER 026

BLODULV

Daniel "Nekro/Morn/Deadwood" Jansson: v, Grendel: g/b, Orcus:

Göteborg - The name was taken from the book *Röde Orm* by Frans G. Bengtsson. *Blodulv* (blood wolf in Swedish) is covered in mystery and darkness offering little info about its members besides Grendel being the main composer, Aeifur the lyricist and everything being written and recorded under the infuence of various drugs. The band was formed in 2002. Kriegwulff guests on vocals on the debut. The vocals have also been provided by Daniel "Nekro/Morn/ Deadwood" Jansson, who is also found in noise/drone band *Keplers Odd*, ambient noise band *Deadwood*, harsh noise crust punk band *Crest 218* (actually one of the worst sounding bands I've ever heard) and harsh noise electronica band *STUG 218* (sounds as bad as *Crest 218*, but more electronic). Other members that have been part of *Blodulv* are Nidhögg, Ulv and Stig Hailovic. *Blodulv* is black metal in the vein of *Darkthrone*. On all albums the drums are provided by a drum machine that goes under different names, such as Mr. Maachinaa, Dr. M. Electro and The One And Only Sir Electro. *Wehrkraft* is a compilation.

2005 CD - WW4

2005 CD - EAR 008

2004	☐	BLODULV	CD	Total Holocaust	THR 20
		1000 copies.			
2004	☐	BLODULV	LP	Eerie Art	EAR 001
		500 hand numbered copies.			
2004	☐	THE PUREST COLD PRECISION (split)	CD	Eerie Art	EAR 003
		Split with Aska. Tracks: Crusher Ov Covens/Amantia/Grimness/Dreadnought/Menacing Dark Relentless.			
2004	☐	II	CD	Total Holocaust	THR 36
2004	☐	II	LP	Forgotten Wisdom Productions	FWP 021
		500 copies.			
2004	☐	Pagan Panzer/Dead Star Rising	7"	Miriquidi/City Of The Dead	MPEP 10
		333 copies.			
2005	■	BLODULV	CD	Wolfrune Worxxx	WW 4
		New artwork.			
2005	☐	II	CD	Knightmare Recordings	KNIGHT 001
		New artwork.			
2005	■	III - Burial	CD	Eerie Art	EAR 008
		1000 copies.			
2005	☐	III - Burial	LPg	Knightmare Recordings	KNIGHT 002
2005	☐	Diatribe	MCD 4tr	Forgotten Wisdom Productions	FWP 028
		Tracks: Grim Disturbance/Divine Perversion/Famine Pulse/Poison Trait. 1000 copies.			
2009	■	WEHRKRAFT	CDd	Knightmare Recordings	KNIGHT 004
		666 copies.			

2009 CDd - KNIGHT 004

BLOFLY

Jesper Starander: v, Joacim Starander: g, Mattias Merking: g, Rasmus Grahm: b, Emil Asbjörnsen: d

Göteborg - Jesper and Joacim are ex-*Sharp Nine*. *Blofly* play aggressive contemporary metal with melodic vocals, but still angry enough, like a mix of *Pantera* and *Takida*. Website: www.myspace.com/blofly

2006 CDd - AI 101

| 2006 | ■ | PNEUMATIC DAMAGE OF THE GADGETS OF SUPERHEROES | CDd | All In records | AI 101 |

BLOOD-FEUD

Robert Hrusovar: v/k

Eskilstuna - This is a mix of thrash, speed and death metal made with sampling and computers. The "music" is actually very frightening and what could be described as the "soundtrack to World War 3". The voices on the record are in Serbocroatian and English. For people with steel reinforced nerves. Not to be confused with the Icelandic *Blood Feud* that released *Adjustment To The Sickest*.

| 1993 | ■ | GENOCIDE | CD | Voodoo | VOODOO 2 |

2009 CD - VIC012CD

BLOODBATH

**Mikael Åkerfeldt: v, Anders "Blackheim" Nyström: g, Per "Sodomizer" Eriksson: g,
Jonas Renkse: b, Martin "Axe" Axenrot: d**

Örebro/Stockholm - This started more or less as an old side-project that was resurrected in 1999, featuring Mikael Åkerfeldt, Anders "Blackheim" Nyström, Jonas Renkse and Dan Swanö. An all-star band indeed. On the first MCD and debut album Dan handled the drums, but on *Nightmare Made Flesh* he switched to guitar and bass, while Martin Axenrot (**Witchery, Nifelheim, Triumphator** etc) was drafted to take care of the drum stool. For this album only, Åkerfeldt also let his space open for **Pain/Hypocrisy** singer Peter Tägtgren. Simon Solomon guested on lead guitar. On *Unblessing The Purity* Swanö was replaced by Eriksson (*21 Lucifers*). *Bloodbath* produces great sounding technical old-school death metal in the vein of Dismember and Grave. The band also appears on a number of compilations such as *From Hell* (2002 This Dark Reign), *Harnessing Ruin* (2005 Olympic), *Fear Candy 59* (2008 Terrorizer Mag), *Dark Classics Vol 3* (2009 Peaceville) etc. In 2012 Åkerfeldt announced he was leaving the band. *Website: bloodbath.biz*

2000 MCD - 77255-3

2004 CD - 77555-2

2007 CD - CMBLOOD-2

Year		Title	Format	Label	Cat. No.
2000	■	Breeding Death	MCD 3tr	Century Media	77255-3
		Tracks: Breeding Death/Omnious Bloodvomit/Furnace Funeral			
2000	□	Breeding Death	MCD 3tr	Century Media America (USA)	7955-2
2002	□	RESURRECTION THROUGH CARNAGE	CD	Century Media	77455-2
2002	□	RESURRECTION THROUGH CARNAGE	CD	Century Media America (USA)	8155-2
2002	□	RESURRECTION THROUGH CARNAGE	LP	Century Media	77455-1
		Red vinyl. 500 copies.			
2002	□	RESURRECTION THROUGH CARNAGE	LP PD	Century Media	77455-1P
		500 copies. Comes in LP-cover with lyric sheet.			
2002	□	RESURRECTION THROUGH CARNAGE	CD	Fono (Russia)	FO 203 CD
2004	■	NIGHTMARE MADE FLESH	CD	Century Media	77555-2
2004	□	NIGHTMARE MADE FLESH	LP	Century Media	77555-1
		Red vinyl. Ltd ed 500 copies.			
2004	□	NIGHTMARE MADE FLESH	CD	Century Media America (USA)	8255-2
		Different artwork. Bonus: Breeding Death/Omnious Bloodvomit			
2004	□	NIGHTMARE MADE FLESH	CD	Fono (Russia)	FO 418 CD
2005	□	Breeding Death	MLP PD 5tr	Century Media	22001-1P
		Tracks: Breeding Death/Omnious Bloodvomit/Furnace Funeral/Breeding Death (demo)/ Omnious Bloodvomit (demo). 500 copies.			
2006	□	Breeding Death	MCD 5tr	Century Media	77618-2
		Different artwork. Bonus: Breeding Death (demo)/Omnious Bloodvomit (demo).			
2006	□	Breeding Death	MCD 5tr	Mystic Empire (Russia)	MYST CD 168
2007	■	RESURRECTION THROUGH CARNAGE/BREEDING DEATH	CD	Shock (Australia)	CMBLOOD-2
2008	□	RESURRECTION THROUGH CARNAGE	CD	Century Media	997827-2
2008	□	NIGHTMARE MADE FLESH	CD	Century Media	997838-2
2008	□	Unblessing The Purity	MCD 4tr	Peaceville	CDVILED 240
		Tracks: Blasting The Virginborn/Weak Aside/Sick Salvation/Mouth Of Empty Praise.			
2008	□	Unblessing The Purity	10" MLPg 4tr	Peaceville	VILELP 269
		1000 copies in blood red vinyl.			
2008	□	THE WACKEN CARNAGE	CD+DVD	Peaceville	CDVILEF 241X
2008	■	THE FATHOMLESS MASTERY	CDd	Peaceville	CDVILEF 242
2008	□	THE FATHOMLESS MASTERY	LP	Peaceville	VILELP 242
2008	□	THE FATHOMLESS MASTERY	CD	Soyus (Russia)	CDVILEF 242
2010	□	BREEDING DEATH	MLPg 6tr	Animate	ANR030
		Tracks: Breeding Death/Omnious Bloodvomit/Furnace Funeral/Etched Side. Bonus: Breeding Death (demo)/Omnious Bloodvomit (demo). 999 copies.			
2010	■	NIGHTMARE MADE FLESH	LP	Century Media	997838-1
		100 tellow, 200 blue and 200 marbled brownish vinyl. Different artwork.			
2010	□	Unblessing The Purity	10" MLP 4tr	Peaceville	VILELP 269
		Tracks: Blasting The Virginborn/Weak Aside/Sick Salvation/Mouth Of Empy Praise			
2010	□	Unblessing The Purity	MCD 4tr	Peaceville	VILED 240

CDVILEF 242

2010 LP - 997838-1

BLOODBOUND

**Patrik "Pata" Johansson: v, Tomas Olsson: g, Henrik Olsson: g,
Fredrik Bergh: k, Johan Sohlberg: b, Pelle Åkerlind: d**

Bollnäs - **Bloodbound** was formed in 2004 by **Street Talk** bassist/keyboardist Fredrik Bergh, **Street Talk** colleague Tomas Olsson and drummer Oskar Belin. They recruited **Tad Morose** singer Urban Breed and recorded the debut *Nosferatu*. The band did some shows, and during 2006 the band saw several members going in and out of the band such as guitarist Markus Albertsson (**7Sins, Tad Morose**), bass player Jörgen Andersson (**Baltimoore**) and Johan Sohlberg (**The Storyteller**). The drums were handled by Pelle Åkerlind (**Morgana Lefay**). The death metal style make-up did not appeal to singer Breed, who left the band to work on his solo career, and he was replaced by **Tad Morose** singer Kristian Andrén. The second album would however see the vocal talents of former **Jaded Heart/Bonfire** singer Michael Bormann and the band now had a more steady line-up also featuring Henrik Olsson (Tomas' brother) and Johan Sohlberg

Bloodbound in the name of METAL!

as steady members. The band also made some live shows with Bormann fronting the band. Bormann's busy schedule however collided with the plans of the band and Breed was asked to step in, and finally became a steady member of the line-up again for the band's third release *Tabula Rasa*. In 2010 Breed left the band again. After some searching they found *Dawn Of Silence* singer Patrik "Pata" Johansson and the album *Unholy Cross* was recorded. **Bloodbound** plays classic 80s influenced melodic metal in the vein of **Lost Horizon**.

2005	☐	NOSFERATU	CD	Avalon Marquee (Japan)	MICP-10562
2005	■	NOSFERATU	CD	Metal Heaven	00016
2007	☐	BOOK OF THE DEAD	CDd	Metal Heaven	00035
2009	☐	TABULA RASA	CD	Blistering Records	BR 022
2011	☐	UNHOLY CROSS	CD	AFM	AFMCD 351-2
2011	☐	UNHOLY CROSS	CD	Avalon Marquee (Japan)	MICP-10967
2012	☐	IN THE NAME OF METAL	CDd	AFM	AFMCD 422-9

2005 CD - 00016

BLOODLINE

Kristoffer "Wrathyr" Olivius: v, Fredric "Wredhe" Gråby: g/v, Björn "Sasrof" Holmberg: g, Nigris: b, Dödskommendanten: electronics/v

Sundsvall - Old-school sounding black metal with sadly, badly programmed drums and surprisingly melodic keyboards, by a bunch of well reputed musicians. Some songs are slightly drone-oriented, such as *Order Of The Parasite* or *The Great Becoming*, with desperate angst driven vocals, while others are high speed. It sounds surprisingly amateurish considering the skills of the musicians involved. A bit reminiscent of **Svartsyn** or, at times, **Shining**. Sasrof is also found in **Diabolicum, Setherial,** Wrede in **Ondskapt** and **Shining**, while Wrathyr is singing in **Setherial, Bewitched, Naglfar** and **Midvinter**. The 27 minute long dark ambient track *The Citadel Of Everlasting Tyranny* can be downloaded for free from Misantrof ANTIRecords website. Wredhe was added to the line-up before *Hate Procession*.

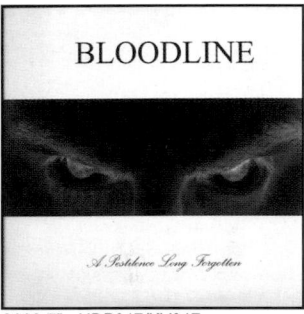

2002 7" - NDP017/KV017

2002	■	A Pestilence Long Forgotten/Was Einst War	7"	Neodawn/Ketzer Records	NDP017/KV017
		500 copies.			
2003	■	WEREWOLF TRAINING	CD	Selbstmord Services	CELLAR 011
2009	☐	HATE PROCESSION	CD	Blut & Eisen	- -
2009	☐	HATE PROCESSION	CDd	Blut & Eisen	- -
		Bonus: Aprés Moi, Le Deluge			
2009	☐	HATE PROCESSION	LPg	Blut & Eisen	- -
		Bonus: Aprés Moi, Le Deluge			
2009	☐	WEREWOLF TRAINING	LP	Blut & Eisen	- -

2003 CD - CELLAR 011

BLOODSHED

Erik Wall: v, Mats Nehl: g, Tommy "Talon" Åberg: g, Robin Verho: b, Martin Karlsson: d

Stockholm - Formed in 1996 by Joel and Mikael under the name **Scythe**. In 1997 they recorded their first demo *When The Night Betrays The Light* and two years after the second attempt *Laughter Of Destruction* was unearthed, now under the name **Bloodshed**. *Skullcrusher* featured Glenn Verho (v), Joel "Nefaustus" Geffen (g), Tommy "Talon" Åberg (g), Robin Verho (b), Mikael Vannequé (d). After *Inhabitants Of Dis* the band went through some major line-up changes. Joel, Mikael and Glenn left the band. They recruited singer Erik Wall, guitarist Johannes Pedro and drummer Marcus Jonsson (**Insision, Flagellation, Pandemonic**). Due to his commitments with **Insision**, Marcus left the band in 2005 and was replaced by **Mykorrhiza** drummer Martin Karlsson. Furthermore Johannes Pedro left and was replaced by Mats Nehl. In 2006 the band started rehearsing for the second album *Stale Cold Cell Recital*. In 2007 the album was available for free download, and the band also announced the return of guitarist Joel Geffen. After the album drummer Martin Karslsson also left and was replaced by Patrik "Pata" Frögéli (**Decadence**). **Bloodshed** play old-school death in the vein of **Marduk, Merciless** etc. In 2008 the ashes of **Bloodshed** reformed into **REV 16:8** and recorded their first CD on Temple Of Darkness in 2009. The line-up featured Joel, Tommy, Patrik and Paul "Themgoroth" Mäkitalo (**Dark Funeral**). Tommy is also found in **IXXI**. *Blade Eleventh* is a compilation of old demo tracks. The track *Kiss Of Cruelty* can be found on the *Better Undead Than Alive* compilation.

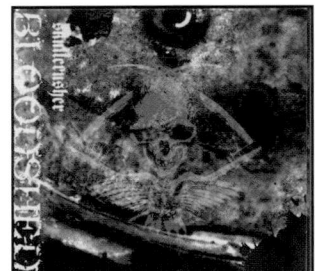

2001 MCDd - CODE 006

2003 CD - CODE 011

2001	■	Skullcrusher	MCDd 5tr	Code 666	CODE 006
		Tracks: Preparation-Aggression (intro)/Skullcrusher/Let The Bloodshed Begin/Laughter Of Destruction/The Ultimate Overthrow			
2002	☐	Skullcrusher	7" 5tr	Ledo Takas	LETA 005 EP
		666 hand numbered copies. White vinyl.			
2003	■	INHABITANTS OF DIS	CD	Code 666	CODE 011
2005	■	Blade Eleventh	MCD 7tr	Cursed Division	CURSE 001
		Tracks: Dead Men Walking/Shapeshifter Enemy/Intro/Living Palindrome/Kiss Of Cruelty/ Scythe – Blade Of Destruction(demo)/Act Of Retaliation (demo)			
2005	☐	Blade Eleventh	MCD 7tr	Horrifiend Records	n/a
		Tracks: Dead Men Walking/Shapeshifter Enemy/Intro/Living Palindrome/Kiss Of Cruelty/ Scythe – Blade Of Destruction(demo)/Act Of Retaliation (demo)			

2005 MCD - CURSE 001

BLOODSTONE

Damien Hess: v, Michael Samuelsson: g, Svante Friberg: b, Mats Wikberg: d

Ekerö - The band made two demos, *Branded At The Threshold Of The Damned* (1994) and *Hour Of The Gate* (1995). The demos became the CD, and later LP, *Hour Of The Gate*. Michael is also found in various demo bands such as *Cauterizer*, *Requiem* (featuring Messiah Marcolin) and *Goregoat 3007*, while Mats is found in *Face Of Evil* (as "Mad Witchburner"). Michael and Mats also recorded a demo with the project *Bifrost*. Death metal in the vein of *Morbid Angel*.

1996 ☐	HOUR OF THE GATE	CD	Burrn Records	BURNCD 003
2008 ■	HOUR OF THE GATE	LP	Blood Harvest	YOTZ #21
	Different artwork.			

2008 LP - YOTZ #21

BLOOM, CONNY

Conny "Bloom" Blomqvist: v/g/k/b/d

Stockholm - After the pretty low interest and thus sales of his previous project *Titanic Truth*, *Electric Boys* boy, Conny (according to Wikipedia: born Conquistador Juventus Junior Blomqvist November 20, 1964) went solo. The new style was sort of the missing link between his previous bands. Rough-edged and raunchy heavy rock actually closer to *MC5* than *Electric Boys*. Conny plays most of the instruments, but some occasional guest include bassist Ulf "Rockis" Ivarsson (*Sky High*), guitarist/keyboardist Anders Fästader (*Titanic Truth, Great King Rat, John Norum*), bassist Andy Christell (*Electric Boys*) and guitarist Andreas Dregen (aka Svensson) (*Backyard Babies, The Hellacopters*). The cover of *Love Scuplture's Sabre Dance* features *The Royal Disharmonic Orchestra* containing Dregen, drummer Gyp Casino (*Hanoi Rocks*) and Andy. In 2000 he joined UK-guitarist Ginger (*The Wildhearts*) in the band *Silver Ginger 5*, where Thomas Broman was also found. Conny also has a power-trio on the side and he has previously also recorded albums, singles and demos with bands like *Roadrat*, *Rolene* and *Neon Rose*. The live-CD *Been There, Done What? Live* features recordings of old *Electric Boys* stuff, as well as his solo songs and some covers. Conny was a part of *Hanoi Rocks* for their last album and tours before they split and he reformed *Electric Boys*. In 2009 he contributed with guest vocals and guitar for the *Rory Gallagher* cover *Bad Penny* on *Volume 2* by *Mountain of Power* and he also leant a helping hand on the debut by *Pontus Snibb 3* in 2011.
Website: www.connybloom.com

Conny was there, but did what?

1999 ☐	Last Mistake/Sabre Dance	CDSp 2tr	Telegram	3984-26272-9
1999 ☐	PSYCHONAUT	CD	Telegram	3984-26463-2
2003 ■	BEEN THERE, DONE WHAT? LIVE	CD	Feedback Boogie	FBRCD 019
2003 ☐	BEEN THERE, DONE WHAT? LIVE	CD	Victor (Japan)	VICP-63636

2003 CD - FBRCD 019

BLOT MINE

Jakob "Steril Vwrede" Andersson: v, Per-Erik "Thunaraz/Devothan" Karlsson: g,
Fredrik "Athel W" Eriksson: g, Daniel "Thron" Edström: b,
Anders "Zathanel" Löfgren: d

Sundsvall - The band was formed late 1995 by three *Setherial* members, Anders, Per-Erik and Daniel. The band released a 5-track demo in 1996 entitled *Kill For Inner Peace*. In 1997 Fredrik was added to the line-up. The album was recorded at Los Angered Studios. High speed black metal in the vein of *Emperor*, *Satyricon* and *Dark Funeral*.

1999 ■	PORPHYROGENESIS	CD	Near Dark	NDP 012
2004 ☐	ASH CLOUD	LP	W.T.C Productions	- -
	500 hand numbered copies.			
2005 ☐	ASH CLOUD	CD	Metal Fortress	MFE 009

1999 CD - NDP 012

BLOWBACK

Stefan Noren: v, Christian Kimber: b,
Sebastian Kimber: g, Henrik "Henke" Evertsson: d

Örebro - Swedish facial hair retro in the vein of colleagues *Witchcraft* with strong touches of *Black Sabbath* and *Trouble*. Well sung, well played and well worth checking out! *800 Miles* was recorded in Unisound by Dan Swanö.

2006 ☐	ASTEROID VS. BLOWBACK	CD	Fuzzorama Records	FUZZCD 005
	Split with Asteroid. Tracks: Holy Skies/Autumn Leaf/Fairies Dance/Cosmic Dust/Invisible Touch			
2008 ☐	MORNINGWOOD	CD	private	BL2008
2010 ■	800 MILES	CDd	Transubstans	TRANS 057

2010 CDd - TRANS 057

BLOWSIGHT

Niklas "Nic Red" Fagerström: v/g, Serban "Seb" Carapancea: g,
Marcus "Mao" Uggla: b, Fabien "Fabz" Perreau: d

Stockholm - Formed in 2003. Manga-influenced neo-punk oriented contemporary metal, like a mix of **Hoobastank** and **Avenged Sevenfold**. The first album version and CDS featured former **Drain (Sth)** guitarist Flavia Canel on bass Now the band's manager). The non-abum CDS track *Toxic* is a **Britny Spears** cover, actually written by Cathy Dennis and the three Swedes Henrik Jonback, Christian Karlsson and Pontus Winnberg. Bassist Marcus "Mao" Uggla, who replaced Mini, is also lead singer of **Mindshift**.

2007 CDd - --

2007	■	DESTINATION TERRORVILLE	CDd	private	- -
2007	□	I'll Be Around/Toxic (Britny Spears cover)	CDS	All Ears/Epic	8869708312 2
2009	□	DESTINATION TERRORVILLE	CD	Neo Bob	BM09C285
		Bonus: Bus Girl/Teenage Rockstar. Different artwork.			
2011	□	DYSTOPIA LANE	CD	Fastball Music	FB 10C483
2011	□	DYSTOPIA LANE	CD	Spiritual Beast (Japan)	IUCP-16100
2011	□	Shed Evil	MCD 5tr	Eclipse Records	ECLP 9028
		Tracks: Magic Eight Ball/The Girl & The Rifle/The Sun Behind The Rain/As Wicked As They Come/Live Die Surrender			
2012	□	LIFE & DEATH	CD	Fastball Music	FB 12C1194

BLUE BALLS

Björn "Nalle" Oscarsson: v/g, Patrick: b, Hasse Chapskate: d

Göteborg - The band was formed as **So What**, around 1988, but changed to **Blue Balls** because of the Norwegian pop band. The name came from a sexual experience Björn had at the age of 13, with a much older woman. Punkish, amateurish hard rock with juvenile lyrics, badly played and with horrible vocals. They even slaughter **Metallica's** *Motorbreath* beyond recognition. Patrik was only in the band for three gigs and bass on the album was played by Magnus Lind (**Treasure Land, Skull Parade**) and keyboards by Dan Helgesen. After the album, the band found a steady bass player in Tommi Ruuskanen. The style now became more punkish and due to drugs the band took a bit of a halt. After two year the band was supposed to reunite, but Tommie died in 1995, only 25 years old. Björn has directed and written movies and music videos.

1990 LP - UNI 2333

1990	■	THE NAKED TRUTH	LP	Roughie Records	UNI 2333

BLUE MATTER

Jesper Lindstedt: v, Jimmy Wahlsteen: g, Mathias "Matte" Gattefors: g,
Anders Sevebo: b, Olle Dahlstedt: d

Stockholm - A good band with a strong potential, at times similar to **Alice In Chains** but still on the hard-rocking side. Well worth checking out. Wahlsteen is today a much engaged session musician and a highly skilful guitarist in the pop genre with a great acoustic guitar album out, entitled *181ˢᵗ Songs* (Candyrat Records). Sevebo is found in modern heavy rockers **Cellout**.

1994 MCD - BMCD 9401

1994	■	Fact	MCD 4tr	private	BMCD 9401
		Tracks: Fact/To Your Sorrows/Share This Summer/Escape.			

BLUE ORANGE

E. Strömqvist, B. Lindgren, M. Ljungberg, Fredrik Källvik

Sollebrunn - On the first single the A-side is poor-man's funk metal á la **Electric Boys** *Lips 'N Hips*, while the B-side is basic hard rock with quite thin vocals. For collectors only.

1991 7" - FKS 9112

1991	■	No Fuckin' Covers	7"	private	FKS 9112
		Tracks: Such A Woman/Coming Home (2U).			

BLUE SKIES BRING TEARS

Niklas Ottosson: v/g, Christian Ahlsén: g, Andreas Ottosson: b, August Lengquist: d

Västervik - Formed as alternative rock trio **Threnody** in 1999, featuring August, Niklas and singer/bassist Josephine Kersten. In 2004 they took the name **Blue Skies Bring Tears** and also recorded their first demo. Five of those tracks are found on the debut album, even though two more demos were recorded. **Blue Skies Bring Tears** have quite a unique sound and their style is quite hard to describe. Doomy, dreamy and emotional with soft quite clean vocals similar to Ville Laihila (**Poisonblack**), yet heavy and ambient. **Opeth** meets **Poisonblack**. Really good and quite original. The album was released by the band in 2008 and then re-released by Supernova in 2011.
Website: www.blueskiesbringtears.com

2008 CD - SUPERCD 023

2008	□	ANOMALITY	CD	private	- -
		1000 copies.			
2008	■	ANOMALITY	CD	Supernova	SUPERCD 023

BLUE SKY
Wibbe: v/g, Maciek: g, Noffi: b, Mårten: d

Kristianstad - The single sounds more seventies than 1980. Quite heavy, but with quite clean guitar sound, a bit similar to **After Life**. Some good riffs in *Stranger In The City*.

1980 ■ Still In Love/Stranger In The City ....7" private ....HSP 2014

1980 7" - HSP 2014

BLUES BAG
Lennart Kåge: v/g, Hans Derestam: b, Sten Kåge: d

Vikbolandet - A great heavy blues band with some serious guitar twanging. Could be compared to early **ZZ Top**, but with their own personality. Lennart is a highly interesting guitarist. Vocals on the album are in Swedish. The band also recorded a cassette album with covers and an unreleased album produced by Robert Zima (**Trettioåriga Kriget**). Lennart and Sten are brothers of Claes Kåge in **Indian Red**. They were a hard touring band, more or less living on the road. Not long after the album, the band split. Lennart is now doing his own solo act, playing cover shows, after ski parties etc. Derestam is in **Mooster**.

1986 ■ Dirty Call/You Had Me Up ....7" private ....BBR 001
1991 ☐ BLÅ PÅSE...LP Pike...P 9111
1991 ☐ BLÅ PÅSE...CD Pike...P 9111

1986 7" - BBR 001

BLUESBREATH
Ronny Olsson: v/g, Christian Paulin: b, Peter Sundell: d

Kalmar - This is quite good mid-paced hard rock with nice 70's influences, at times similar to Australian band **Buffalo**. Good mid/low key vocals and fine bluesy guitar-work. Well worth looking for. **Bluesbreath** was not actually a band, but Ronny's project. He has also made several solo-recordings and some highly acclaimed demos with Åke Eriksson (**Bedlam, Attack, Wasa Express**). Christian is now in the fusion-oriented band **Mynta**. Ronny unfortunately died on midsummer's day in 1991, as a result of his severe diabetes.

1983 ■ I'm Tryin'/Bluesbreath ....7" S.O.S ....SOS 1152

1983 7" - SOS 1152

BLÅELD
Tommy Hammarsten: v/g, Lage Malmsten: v/b, Bengt Svensson: g, Harald Nygren: d

Stockholm - The first single is great seventies style hard rock a bit similar to a mix of **Wildmarken** and **Neon Rose** with a progressive touch on the B-side. The line-up features guitarist Hansi Cross and drummer Benny Hadders, later in **Von Lyx** and **Cross**, Tom Burton (k), Håkan Arnell (flute) and Danne Malm (percussion).

1979 ■ Hur står det till?/Regnuppehåll...7" G ....GMPS 7902
1985 ☐ Klockan 5/Frihetskänslans sång ....7" Knock Out Rock...........................KORPS 002

1979 7" - GMPS 7902

BLÅKULLA
Dennis Lindegren: v, Mats Öbergh: g, Bosse Ferm: k,
Hannes Råstam: b, Tomas Olsson: d

Göteborg - Formed in the fall of 1971 under the name **Kendal**. The original line-up featured bass player Steinar Andersson and and in the beginning they were influenced by early **Deep Purple**. In the spring of '74 they were offered to record a demo for free, at the recently opened Tal & Ton Studios. Shortly after the recording, Steinar left to join Icelandic band **Iceland** and the band almost split. They however received great interest from pop-label Anette Records and were reinforced by new bass player Hannes. The band had now changed into a symphonic rock band, heavily influenced by bands like **Yes**, **Focus** and **Genesis**. When Ferm decided to leave in December 1975 the band fell apart. Hannes and Tomas continued with folky **Text & Musik**. In 1978 Dennis made a popalbum under the moniker **Kaj Kristall,** that also featured Mats on guitar. Today Mats is working as a doctor and is mainly playing classical guitar, Bosse is/was head of a big Phillips-division in the USA and Tomas is a session-drummer. Hannes was a well known author and investigavtive reporter for the national Swedish television and sadly passed away January 12, 2012, from cancer. The vinyl is a very rare collector's item. The band plays heavy and complex, yet melodic symphonic rock with rough edged searing guitar-work and great vocals in Swedish. They could well be fit in somewhere between **Deep Purple** and early **Yes**. A true classic!

1975 ■ BLÅKULLA..LP Anette ....ALP 218
1997 ☐ BLÅKULLA..CD APM ....APM 9717 AT/SYMPHILIS 7
    Bonus: Mars/Linnéa/Idolen

1975 LP - ALP 218

BODY CORE

**Dan Hejman: v, Markus Wallén: g, Micke Jonsson: g,
Nicklas Wallén: b, Håkan Johansson: d**

Hässleholm - The band was formed in 1997 by Dan and Markus, at first using drum loops, soon hooking up with Håkan and starting out playing punk songs. Dan initially handled both vocals and bass, but soon left the latter over to Markus Nilsson. The demo *I Kill You In My Dreams* was recorded in 2000. After the demo, Nilsson was replaced by Nicklas Wallén, Markus' younger brother. They started leaning more towards black/death metal when second guitarist Daniel Larsson joined and the second demo *Parasite* was recorded in 2001. The demo was expanded and re-issued the subsequent year, now re-named *Welcome To Our Dying World*. Daniel was soon replaced by William Ekeberg (**Broken Dagger, Pandemonium**) and the demo *Idle Mind Amputation* was recorded in 2003. After the recording of the demo album *Blunt Force Trauma* in 2004 Ekekberg left for **Broken Dagger**. The band went through another guitarist, Jakob Löfdahl, before Micke Jonsson took over for the album *Decrepit Within*. The album was released by Cutting Edge, but due to a falling out between the band and the label it was supposed to be re-issued by Italian label Zero Effect. In 2009 Jonsson left and was replaced by former **Malum** stringsman Christian Vasselbring. Don't let the punk background fool you, **Body Core** play highly technical, intriguing and quirky death metal in the vein of Swedish colleagues **Calm**.

2007 CD - 320470 083789

2007 ■ DECREPIT WITHIN ....CD Cutting Edge 320470 083789

BOKOR

**Lars Carlberg: v, Thomas Eriksson (now Sabbathi): g, Jimmy Larsen: g,
Rickard Larsson: b, Daniel Ortega: d**

Norrköping - **Bokor** is quite a unique sounding Swedish band, sometimes very soulful and soft, a bit like later days **Opeth** in their softer moments, while in other moments it's quite progressive and heavy, almost adding a touch of **Tool** with singer Carlberg at times sounding like a mix of Eddy Vedder and Feargal Sharkey with a strong metal edge. Quite challenging but highly interesting music indeed. Well, played, well sung, well arranged and well produced. On the second album guitarist Fredrik "Lillis" Johansson and drummer Erik Wennerholm were exchanged for Jimmy and Daniel. Thomas is also found in **Griftegård, Dead Mutant** and **Year Of The Goat**.

2008 CD - SC 167-2

2007 □ ANOMIA 1 ....CD Scarlet...SC 130-2
2008 ■ VERMIN SOUL ....CD Scarlet...SC 167-2

BOLT

A Skare, E Skare

The A-side is decent keyboard-dominated AOR with limited vocals, while the B-side is a soft instrumental track. For collectors only.

1983 7" - PSI 096

1983 ● The Morning After/Interferenz ....7" Pang ....PSI 096

BOMBS OF HADES

**Jonas Stålhammar: v/g, P-O "Wolfie" Söderbäck: g,
Anders "Butch" Ekman: b, Magnus Forsberg: d**

Västerås - The band started out in 2002 playing crust punk, but soon switched to old-school death metal. Jonas is also found in **Macabre End, God Macabre, Utumno, Abhoth** and **Space Probe Taurus**. He also joined **The Crown** in 2009, before their comeback album *Doomsday King*. Magnus in **Tribulation, Dissober** and **Puffball**. Ekman is ex-**Abhoth** and Söderbäck is also ex-**Puffball**. Fast and furious punkish death metal, a bit like **Motörhead** goes death.

2011 7" - DR 026

2008 □ Carnivores... 7" 5tr Blood Harvest ....YOTZ #26
    Tracks: Necronomicus Kanth/Twisted Decay/Slaughter Of The Dead/Disrespect Their Bones/Coffin. 500 copies.
2011 ■ Into The Eternal Pit Of Fire .... 7" 4tr Detest Records ....DR 026
    Tracks: Prologue (The Ecstacy Of Blood)/Into The Eternal Pit Of Fire/The Day Man Lost/Confessor. 150 copies in white + 450 in black vinyl.
2011 ■ Bombs Of Hades/Unsurpress (split) .... 7"g 4tr Doomentia Records ....DOOM 056
    Split with Unsurpress. Tracks: Until Death (Hanged By The Neck)/Inside Teradome. 500 copies.
2011 □ Bombs Of Hades/Tormented (split)............................10" 4tr War Anthem Records...................WAR 041 EP
    Split with Tormented. Tracks: Ice Cold Grave/Clean Your Head (Loud Pipes cover). 300 copies.
2012 □ No Life (split)..10" 4tr Bifrost/Carnal Records.BRLP001/CRBRLP001
    Split with Mordbrand. Tracks: Burn/I'll Be Your Sister (Motörhead cover). 200 white/black splatter + 800 black vinyl.
2012 □ THE SERPENTS REDEMPTION ....CD Pulverised ....ASH 092 CD

2011 7"g - DOOM 056

BONAFIDE

Pontus Snibb: v/g, Mikael Fässberg: g, Martin Ekelund: b, Niklas Matsson: d

Malmö/Stockholm - In 2006 blues singer/drummer/guitarist Pontus Snibb stepped out of his comfortable blues cage to rock it out. Together with bass player Micke Nilsson, who also played with Pontus in his band *Snibb*, he started writing and demoing some songs in the good old *AC/DC* stomper rock genre. On the debut album Pontus, who also plays drums for US band *Jason & The Scorchers* and on the debut by *Brickhouse*, took care of the drums and vocals, but also drafted *Burning Engines/From Behind* guitarist Fässberg to share the rhythm guitars. The debut was highly acclaimed and the band played several high profile support shows. They found former *Wilmer X* sticksman Per-Åke "Sticky Bomb" Holmberg. In January 2009 the band locked themselves in the studio with producer and *Sator* singer/guitarist Chips Kiesbye and recorded the follow up *Something's Dripping*. Mia Coldheart (*Crucified Barbara*) is guesting on one track. The band is featured on the *Sweden Rock 2008* compilation with the exclusive track *Fill your Head With Rock*. In April 2010 Sticky left the band and was replaced by former *Backdraft/Raging Slab* drummer Niklas Matsson. In 2011 Pontus released the debut album of his side-project *Pontus Snibb 3*. In 2011 Micke Nilsson was replaced by Martin Ekelund.

Bonafide back in the Sticky days.

2007	□	BONAFIDE	CDd	Sweden Rock Records	SRR1
2009	□	BONAFIDE	CDd	Black Lodge	BLOD 063 CD
		Bonus: Miss Misery (Nazareth cover)/Hard Case To Break (live)/Night Time (live)			
2009	■	SOMETHING'S DRIPPING	CDd	Black Lodge	BLOD 065 CD
2009	□	Dirt Bound	CDS	Black Lodge	BLOD 066 CD
2010	□	Fill Your Head With Rock	MCD 6tr	Black Lodge	BLOD 076 CD
		Tracks: Fill Your Head With Rock/No Doubt About It/Kick Me Out/I Don't Need No Doctor (Ray Charles/Humble Pie cover)/I Can't Explain (The Who cover)/Nice Boys Don't Play Rock 'N Roll (Rose Tattoo cover) + Hard Livin' Man (video)/No Boubt About It (video)			
2012	□	ULTIMATE REBEL	CDd	Rootsy	ROOTSY 057
2013	□	BOMBO	CDd	Off Yer Rocka	OYR 006

2009 CD - BLOD 065 CD

BONE GNAWER

Kam Lee: v, Ronnie Björnström: g, Rogga Johansson: b, Morgan Lie: d

Gamleby/USA - A Swedish-American collaboration of an all-star kind. Rogga has been/is part of numerous bands like *Paganizer, Ribspreader, Edge Of Sanity, Demiurg, Sinners Burn* etc., Morgan in *Naglfar* and *Auberon*, Ronnie in *Embracing, Ribspreader* and American singer Kam is also found in *Death, Massacre* and *Mantas*. Heavy thrash oriented death metal with a fat and heavy production. Kam's vocals remind me of Jeff Scott Soto's semi-growling in *Bakteria*, and in combinations with the lyrics it's hard to take this seriously. The songs rock, though. After the recording of *Feast Of Flesh*, Rogga and Kam formed the new band *The Grotesquery*, an occult horror death metal band, also featuring Johan Berglund from *This Haven* and Brynjar Helgeton from Norwegian band *Liklukt*.

2009	□	FEAST OF FLESH	CDd	Pulverised	ASH 062 CD
2009	■	BONE GNAWER/BONESAW (split)	CD	Aphelion Productions	AP 052
		Split with Bonesaw. Tracks: Filthy Christian/Voices Within/Behind The Glass			
2010	□	FEAST OF FLESH	LP+7"	Metal Inquisition Records	MI 009
		99 copies + 7" EP Scissored. Tracks: Back To The Butchery/Leave Her To The Cleaver/ Scissored. Hand-numbered.			
2010	□	FEAST OF FLESH	LP	Metal Inquisition Records	MI 009
		201 copies.			

2009 CD - AP 052

BONEDOG

Micke Ladréhn: v/g, Peter Forss: b, Michael Andersson: d

Karlskoga - Formed in a sauna during the Christmas of 2009 when drummer Andersson was relaxing with some friends. One thing lead to another and on January 4, 2010, the trio was a reality. *Bonedog* is a power-trio carrying on the legacy of *Zeppelin, ZZ Top* and *Stevie Ray Vaughan*. Heavy, groovy, riff-oriented hard rock similar to Swedish fellows like *Sky High* and *Bacon*.

2011	■	BLAME THE CAT	CD	private	BONEDOG 01
2012	□	DESERT STORM	CD	private	BONEDOG 02

2011 CD - BONEDOG 01

BONKYMAN

Mats "Johnny Cherobiano" Lilienberg: v, Robert Hansson : g/b/d

Göteborg - This is just a one-off, half-crazy project from *Human Race/Rawburt*-guitarist Robert Hansson (in this case calling himself Rob Hanson, Pat Malone and Ron D-vous). He compiled and recorded a bunch of the material that didn't fit into the *Human Race*-concept, which was actually meant for a solo record, borrowed *Human Race* keyboard player Mats on vocals and released it through mp3.com. Melodic, guitar-based hard rock.

2000	■	THE ALCHEMIST	CD	mp3.com D.A.M	57639

2000 CD - 57639

BOOGIE LIQUOR BAND
Diddi Kasteholt: v, Eric Månsson: g, Jan Björk: g, Björn Mohlin: b, Mille Wendel: d

Helsingborg - **Boogie Liquor Band** has picked up one or two influences from **Thin Lizzy**, mixing it with the radio-oriented style **Magnum Bonum, Snowstorm** etc. Great guitar-work though. After the single the boys changed their name to **Double Trouble** and became hit-makers, and later on they became **Bai Bang**. Månsson was ex-**Vanadis** and is now in **Mansrock**.

1982 ■ Clownen/Plugga In (Alla Kontakter) ....7" private IA82TS

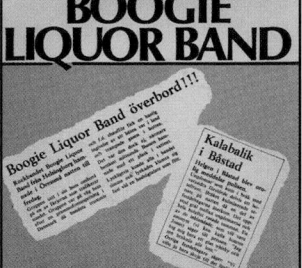
1982 7" - IA82TS

BOOGIEMAN
**Fredrik "Hellvis" Hansson: v, Johan "J.J. Scat" Johansson: g,
Nicklas "Nikki Oi" Jansson: b, Tobias "Shuffle" Olsson: d**

Göteborg - The band made their debut on the compilation *The Mighty Desert Rock Avengers* (People Like You) with the track *Red Sleeve*. Nikki is also found in the band **Woe,** while **Hellvis**, who made a stint in Hollywood, is also found in **The Hurricanez** and **VISE**. The latter recorded an album with **Kiss** guitarist Bob Kulick at the helm late 2009. **Boogieman** has a very 70s oriented fuzz-oriented sound lining up in the classic Swedish stoner colony together with bands like **Zebulon, The Awesome Machine, Mothercake** etc. Good stuff.

2002 □ Boogieman.........................MCDp 5tr private .... - -
    Tracks: Red Sleeve/14 Pictures/December/My Eyes/Infinity. Promo.
2003 ■ TRIPLE SIX BLUES.........................CD People Like You .... Prison 061-2
2003 □ TRIPLE SIX BLUES.........................LP People Like You .... Prison 061-1

2003 CD - Prison 061-2

BOOK OF HOURS
Anni Thulin: v, Adam Skogvard: g, Mattias Reinholdsson: b, Henrik Johansson: d/k

Söderhamn - After starting slowly around 1994, the band was finally formed in 1996, by Mattias and Henrik. Henrik drafted his former colleague singer Stefan Zell (both ex-**Arachnophobia, Pornographical Harmony**). Per Broddesson (ex-**Oberon**, not the recording band, now **Griftegård, Year Of The Goat**) and keyboard player Ulf Nygårds joined. Ulf however left before the first demo *Previously Unreleased* was recorded in 1997. It was followed by the four-track demo *We Find Your Lack Of Faith Disturbing* the year after. Zell actually left the band before the album, but agreed to help out on the recording. On the CDS the line-up was temporarily completed with former member Ulf on keyboards and singer Andreas Runesson. It contains two covers of **King Crimson** and **Van de Graaf Generator**. In 1999 Per left to join **Wolverine**. The latest release saw Anni Thulin on vocals and Adam Skogvard took Broddesson's place. Before Anni, the band featured singer Manne Ikonen (**Ghost Brigade**). In 2003 the band released the self-financed four-track CD-R *Transmissions*. Anni, Henrik and Mattias were also involved with electronic rock band **Ekrano**. Mattias and Henrik recorded a CD in 2005 with the highly odd **Iron Maiden** cover project **Food For Thought**. **Book Of Hours** play excellent, quirky, slightly avantgarde, heavy progressive rock in the vein of colleagues **Anekdoten**. Up until the band folded in 2004 Jonas Hansson played guitar. Jonas and Mattias today play in **Onda Radio** and Mattias runs his hard rock project **Astrakaan**.

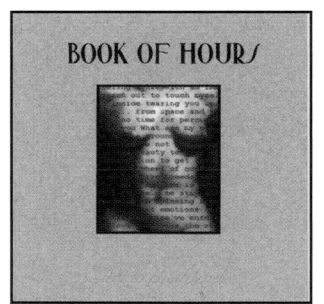
1999 CD - RHCD 16

2000 CDS - RHCDM11

1999 ■ ART TO THE BLIND ....CD Record Heaven........ RHCD 16
2000 ■ King Crimson & VDGG According To… .....CDSp 2tr Record Heaven........RHCDM11
2000 □ King Crimson & VDGG According To… .....CDSp 2tr Record Heaven........ RH promo 3

BOOM CLUB
Per Wiberg: v, Jan Bergman: g, Laban: b , Dan Andersson: d

Borlänge - This band is like a heavier version of **Stonecake** or a more hard-rocking version of **Primus** meets **Hendrix**. Jan was also part of popband **Apopocalypse** and Laban can also be heard in the band **Blue Crow Men**, that has two songs on the compilation *Eleven-On-A-One-To-Ten* (93 Meantime). Wiberg has since been found in numerous bands such as **Sky High, Spiritual Beggars, Death Organ, King Hobo, Mojobone, Opeth** etc.

1994 ■ BUY ONE OR BE ONE...........................CD Bolanche........ BOLCD 944
1994 □ Leather Distortion/Happy Holocaust .....CDS 2tr Bolanche........ BOLCDS 945

1994 CD - BOLCD 944

BOOM SHANKER GROUP
Mats Drehmer: v, John Viksten: g, Ulf Malm: g, Mikael Wester: b, Micael Hellström: d

Oskarshamn - The band was formed in 1985 with John and Mats being the foundation of the band. Dubious Danish label Büms heard a demo by the band and went to Oskarshamn to sign the band. Mats has later been found in **Dweebs** and **Drehmer**. Straighforward hard rock. Robert Triches (**The Quill**) also played bass in the band at one time.

1988 ■ BOOM SHANKER GROUP...........................LP Büms........67890

1988 LP - 67890

BOOTLEG

Mats Bergman: v, Christer: g, Svempa, Öjje, Jan Svedberg: d

Lund - *Dagdrömmar* is a really great straight-ahead early heavy metal, sounding a lot like UK colleagues like **Trespass, Buffalo** etc. *Tankar om dig* is unfortunately more of a less interesting straight boogie rocker. Well worth looking for anyway. Bergman was later in **The Scents** and the became a solo artist in a far poppier genre.

1982 7" - cWc024

1982 ■ Dagdrömmar/Tankar om dig ....7" CWC cWc024

BORDERLINE

Christian Liljegren: v, Stefan Selvander: g, Rickard Eriksson: k,
Simeon Liljegren: b, Per Johansson: d

Habo - Formed in 1989. This is really high-quality melodic hard rock, at times similar to the later **Leviticus** stuff. The band is Christian, which shows, especially on the second single. They later became **Modest Attraction**. On the first release the drums were handled by David Andersson. Christian has later appeared in bands like **Narnia, Audiovision, Divinefire, Flagship** etc. and today he is fronting **Golden Resurrection**. Simeon is found in the heavier **Pantokrator**.

1990 7" - LIN 001

1990 ■ Fri/Calling..7" private ....LIN 001
1991 ■ Can't Live Without Your Love/Let Me Rest In Your Arms ....7" private ....OPUS 01

BORDERLINE

Johan Paavola: v, Christer Lundgren: g, Urban Lundgren: k,
Anders Wikström: b, Per-Olof Andersson: d

Skellefteå - The band was formed in 1985 by Johan and Christer. The initial line-up also featured Anders, guitarist Fredrik Furberg and drummer Robert Larsson. Robert moved to Stockholm and Fredrik quit. The A-side is a up-tempo melodic hard rocker in the vein of early **Europe**. The B-side is a pretty decent ballad with some heavy guitars. Really good singer and good musicians.The band also had the previously unreleased track *Straight For The Heart* on the local compilation *R & R Skellefteå Musikförening* (1988 SMFLP 8801). On this compilation Johan also sings in the band **Ride The Sky**. Not long after, Olle moved to Södertälje and the band never found a suitable replacement and finally folded. Johan sang a while with soul band **HP-band**, but later joined Christer in hard rock cover band **Freetown**. They later became **Mr Quinn**.

1987 7" - WBS 0002

1987 ■ Keep On Waiting/Never Been Lonely ....7" Singapore Singles...........................WBS 0002

1991 7" - OPUS 01

BORG, TONY

Tony Borg: g, Conny Payne (aka Sundquist): b, Rickard André: k, Mikael Wikman: d

Göteborg/Stockholm - In 1979 guitarist Tony Borg recorded a single with melodic hardrockers **Highway** and in 1981 another one, *Leaving You/Kisses In The Night* (Polar - POS 1290), with the band **Dolcevita**, a straight rocking band. When he later on formed **Alien** he was also working with female singer Lill-Babs in a totally different musical category. He had also been in **EF Band** and Icelandic pop/rockers **Vikivaki**. In 1992 Tony was given the opportunity to do a solo album. This is not a show-off effort with flashy sweeps and arpeggios, but a melodic and at times almost pop/folky album. His backing band on this album later became the new **Alien**. Conny was ex-**Madison** and later in **Pete Sandberg's Jade**, now in **MindSplit**. **Alien** reformed in 2010 and a new album is to be expected late 2013.

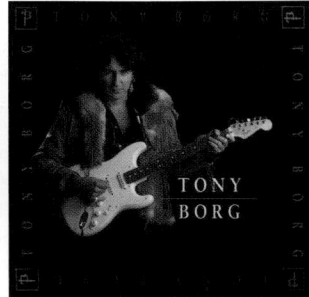

1992 CD - EMC 038

1992 ■ TONY BORG...CD Eagle...EMC 038
1992 ○ Song #32/Ode To Life ....CDS Eagle...ECDS 1060
1992 □ TONY BORG...CD Zero (Japan) XRCN-1121

BORN ELECTRIC

Jan Eliasson: v/g, Lars Eliasson: d, John Melander: b

Alingsås - The trio started playing together already back in the mid eighties, then as the cover band **After Beach**. In 1992 they formed the band **Crash**, featuring acclaimed AOR singer Mikael Erlandsson, and released one album. According to the band two disasters struck – the singer left and the tour bus… crashed. **After Beach** was resurrected in 1994. They released two live CDs and backed many famous Swedish pop singers. In 2002 they finally came to their senses and formed **Born Electric**, same line-up, but now playing high power 70s oriented hard rock. An outstanding ballsy hard rocker of an album. Powerful riffing, at times with a fat Hendrixy touch. Unfortunately the band's website hasn't been updated since 2004.

2004 CD EMCD 0403-2

2004 ■ BORN ELECTRIC..CD E.M.P ....EMCD 0403-2

BORN OF FIRE

**Piatos "Mr Dim" Dimitrios: v/g, Fredrik "Freddie Eugene" Lindgren: g,
Richard Cabeza: b, Peter Stjärnvind: d**

Stockholm - A thrash/death/metal all-star band. Freddie is also found in *Terra Firma, Loud Pipes, Unleashed* and *Harm's Way*, Richard in *Dismember, Unanimated, Dark Funeral, Murder Squad, Carbonized* and *General Surgery* and Peter is also found in *Entombed, Merciless, Unanimated, Face Down, Nifelheim, Krux, Murder Squad, Regurgitate* etc. Busy boys! Brutal technical thrash in the vein of *Slayer*, but with a strong touch of *Entombed*, especially the wall of guitars. The B-side is a high speed thrasher with lots of harmony guitars. Mr Dim, who sings in the vein of Phil Anselmo, is also found in the band *Harm's Way*. Highly recommended.

2001 ■ Chosen By The Gods/The Art Of Dying ....7"   Primitive Art..PAR 025
   Red vinyl. First 500 with postcard.

2001 7" - PAR 025

BORN OF SIN

**Jerry Backelin: v, Kristoffer Hjelm: g, Hjalmar Nielsen: g,
Robert Green: b, Henning Nielsen: d**

Trollhättan - Born Of Sin was formed in 2001. Two years after they recorded their first demo, entitled *The Beheader*, but because of line-up problems it was never made public. A new demo, *He Will Walk The Earth* was recorded the subsequent year. The band supported acts like *Lord Belial, Bestial Mockery, Transport League, Dismember* etc. In 2006 they were signed by Swedish label Unexploded Records and the first MCD was released. Due to personal problems bass player Axel Hjelm left the band and Robert Green switched from guitar to bass. The guitar spot was filled by Henning's brother Hjalmar, a fomer member of *Lord Belial* and also in *Enthralled*. Jerker is also found in *Nightspirit*, Kristoffer and Robert in *Conformatory*. *Born of Sin* play blast beat ridden death metal with a touch of thrash, a bit in the vein of *At The Gates* with raspy growl vocals. Quite nice production.

2006 MCD - UER 011

2006 ■ Let It Begin...MCD 5tr   Unexploded..UER 011
   Tracks: Walk With The Lord/Deceiver/She Must Be God's Whore/Hell Will Walk The Earth/Imperfect Breed Of Humanity
2009 ■ IMPERFECT BREED OF HUMANITY ....CD   Unexploded.. UER 017

2009 CD - UER 017

BOSSE

Per Hesselrud: v/g, Lars Martinsson: b, Olof "Hoss" Bergeus: d

Stockholm- This is something that is mostly interesting for the Swedish-speaking listeners. These guys are totally over the top with song-titles like *Sillunchen* (The Herring Lunch), *Per Får En Älg* (Per Gets A Moose), *Dä Ä Min Säl* (It Is My Seal) and *Kängurupelle* (Kangaroo Pelle) what do you expect? Of course the lyrics are in Swedish. However, the music is really heavy with some progressive touches here and there. They did previously record another CD under the name *Gaus*. The cover and title of the second release is a parody of *Yes'* album *99125* and *Judas Priest* live (Krylbo is a small Swedish town). In 1997 they released the CD-R *Live In What And Other Cities*, containing live recordings of their own stuff and covers by *Angelwitch, Larry Coryell* etc. In 2000 they recorded a demo-CD under the name *IFK Doom*, where they do hilarious covers of *Black Sabbath*-songs in Swedish, not forgetting a version of *Sex Pistols Anarchy In The UK* re-named *Anarki På OK*. In 2006 the band released another CD, only as pro printed CD-R however, entitled *F som i Flytrock, K som i Krossa* (Älgkräks Records). This time bass player Lars Martinsson had been replaced by Peter Söderström (*Ignition*). Hesselrud was formerly in melodic rockers *D.I.Y.* In 2005 Per, Peter and Olof became part of the *Eddy Malm Band*, lead by the former *Heavy Load* singer/guitarist.

1993 MCD - CD-02

1993 ■ Bosse ....MCD 6tr   Älgkräks CD-02
   Tracks: Sill lunchen/Pär får en älg/Tio mil hem/Dä ä min säl/Kängurupell/Bävern
1996 ■ 775 50 - UNLEASHED IN THE KRYLBO..CD   Wasa Vakt & Städ ....CD 03

-Unleashed in the Krylbo

1996 CD - CD 03

BOULEVARD

**Roy El Hoshy: v, Lennart Widegren: g, Dick Börtner: g,
Mikael Magnusson: b, Morgan Pettersson: d**

Göteborg - This band was just about to break, but something went wrong. The reason was actually that the record company president was busted for fraud. They deliver mid-class melody-oriented 80s hardrock/metal with average vocals, average songs, but quite interesting guitar work. The first single was released in December 1987, but re-released with a new cover the year after as the band thought the cover was too ugly to be acceptable. Roy, Lennart and Morgan recorded a more rock-oriented single with the project *Midnight Blue*. It was actually a parallel project on the same label. Dick and Lennart formed *Time Bomb Boys*, that later became *The Ungrateful*. Lennart moved to the USA after the band's debut and there joined the band *Elegantly Wasted*. Morgan was later found in *B-Thong* and *Glanzig*, while Mikael and Roy were found in the band *Gift*. Börtner, ex-*Steelemade*, joined *Innocent Rosie* and Mikael was also in *Easy Action*.

1987 7" - NJ111

1988 7" - NJ111

1987	□	WHAT'S UP?..	LP	Norman Ljudproduktion	LP 114
1987	■	On The Line/Still On The Way	7"	Norman Ljudproduktion	NJ 111
1988	■	On The Line/Still On The Way	7"	Norman Ljudproduktion	NJ 111

Re-released with new artwork.

| 1989 | ■ | WHAT'S UP?.. | CD | Satelit | SRCD 102350 |
| 2012 | □ | WHAT'S UP?.. | CD | Yesterrock | Y201225 |

Bonus: One The Line (demo)/Still On My Way (demo)/Running (demo)

1989 CD - SRCD 102350

BOZEMAN'S SIMPLEX

Patrik Fliesberg: v/g/k, Anders Harning: g, Mikael Olsson: b/k/g, Johan Abbing: d

Örnsköldsvik - The band was founded in 1992 with the intention of playing **Hendrix**-tunes. In 1994 they recorded the cassette album *Stoneheads And Other Freak Songs*. The band's 1996-demo *Spacewrapd* caught the attention of **Candlemass** man Leif Edling, who realeased the 10" *Hyperdrive* on his new Froghouse label. 70s sludgy-stoner-doom-hard rock, like a mix of **Black Sabbath** and **Hawkwind**. In 1999 Johan had to quit because of a bad shoulder, and he was replaced by Henrik Lundqvist. As the members spread out across Sweden in 2000 the band sadly disbanded the subsequent year. After the split Mikael started his own band **Khaki**, a solo project with a stoner touch, where he also uses the vocal aid of Fliesberg. The track *Blind* is also featured on the compilation *Musikhuset: So Far So Good* (1994 Musikhuset) and a cover of *Sin's A Good man's Brother* on the compilation *A Tribute To Grand Funk Rairoad – An American Band* (2000 Record Heaven). The band split around 2000, but made a reunion in 2004. *Website: www.musikhuset.org/~bozeman*

| 1998 | ■ | Hyperdrive... | 10" 4tr | Froghouse | FROG 003 |

Tracks: Come/Unknown Man/Head First/Into The Sun. Red vinyl

1998 10" - FROG 003

BRAINWAVE

Babis Argati: v/g, Gari Krajacic: g, Peter Stange: b, Krister Saarinen: d

Borås - Brutal power metal, similar to **Machine Head** meets **Pantera**. Great powerful riffing and brutal vocals. Babis is also found in **Damnatory**. The band also recorded several demos. The track *In The Eyes Of An Insect* is found on the compilation *Det hjälper inte att ropa på mamma* (97 Brosk) and *Outstretched* on *Unsigned Artists 1* (96 TBC)..

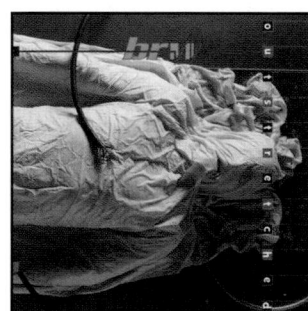

| 1997 | ■ | OUTSTRETCHED .... | CD | Sonus | AXCD 007 |

1997 CD - AXCD 007

BRAT PACK

Thomas Vikström: v, Kent Bill: g, Rickard André: k,
Torbjörn Westerhäll: b, Staffan Scharin: d

Stockholm - This is an odd and quite rare record. The members are pretty well known, especially singer Vikström, who has been found in bands like **Candlemass, Talk Of The Town, Stormwind** and **7Days** (to name a few). André is also in **Alien** where Scharin has also been found, besides being in **Talk Of The Town**. This project was an ode to the Oddevold hockey team and besides the hockey anthem *Bohus Bataljon -96* the band plays some live recorded covers by **Van Halen, Kiss** and **The Kinks**. They also do a great metal version of Amii Stewart's old disco hit **Knock On Wood**. By no means even close to a classic, but worth having for collector. The CD says it's five tracks, but tracks three and four are actually merged to one track.

| 1996 | ■ | Bohus Bataljon -96... | MCD 4tr | M.R.M Records | BPCD 960401 |

Tracks: Bohus Bataljon -96/You Really Got Me (The Kinks cover + Jump (Van Halen cover)/Knock On Wood (Amii Stewart cover)/I Was Made For Loving You (kiss cover)

1996 MCD - BPCD 960401

BRAZEN RIOT

Nicklas Franzén: v, Mikael Eriksson: g, Mattias Westlund: g,
Björn Lindborg: dj, Mikael Larsson: b, Emil Lantz: d

Avesta - The band was formed in 1997. Heavy and detuned hardcore-infused metal, similar to **LOK** meets **Rage Against The Machine**, or according to themselves "similar to **Spineshank**". Power to the max! In 2000 the band also recorded a 5-track demo CDR entitled *Higher Level* where none of the songs were found on the album. The album was recorded at Studio Underground and produced by Pelle Saether and Lasse Lindén. The band split in 2005. Emil is now found in **Chainwreck**.

| 2001 | ■ | FOLLOW THE MAINSTREAM... | CD | Dogbreath | DOGGY 005 |

2001 CD - DOGGY 005

BREWMASTER
Kristian "Bäckis" Bäckbrandt: v/b, Marcus "Makko" Bäckbrandt: g/v, Niclas "Klajja" Kleist: d

Norrköping - Ballsy brutal hard rock in the sign of… alcohol! *Black Label Society* meets *Motörhead*, not surprisingly. Niclas is also found in *Von Panzer* and Marcus in *Devil's Whorehouse*.

2004 ■ Whiskey God/Into You/Growin' Old (unplugged)..................................MCDp 3tr   private ....BREW 104

2004 MCD - BREW 104

BRIGADA ILLUMINADA
Anders Bohlin: v/g, Mats Brandt: g, Johan Sikberg: b, Andreas Skoglund: d

Gävle - The band was formed in 2004 by Bohlin and Brandt (*Caster, Openmindead*) as *Light Brigade*. After Skoglund (*Galder, Slingerbult*) joined in 2007, they also changed their name. Straight ahead retro hard rock with a psychedelic touch, in the vein of *Graveyard, Witchcraft* and *Siena Root*. The second album is in the making, set for release late 2013.

2011 ■ MONAD...CD   private ....ILL 001

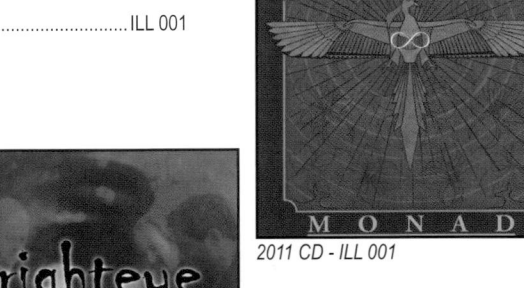
2011 CD - ILL 001

BRIGHTEYE BRISON
Linus Kåse: v/k, Johan Öijen: g, Per Hallman: k/v, Kristofer Eng: b, Erik Hammarström: d

Stockholm - The band was formed in 2000 by Linus, Kristofer and Linus' brother Daniel on drums. Johan joined six months later. The band recorded the four track demo *4:AM* in 2001, which lead to a deal with Rivel Records. The debut album was recorded between 2001 and 2002 and released in 2003. Sound engineer Per Hallman now joined the band, first as live sound engineer but later also on keyboards and vocals. The recordings of *Stories* started already in 2003, but took three years to finish. In the meantime a cover of *Mother Earth* was recorded for the tribute *The Sweet According To Sweden* (2004 Rivel). After shooting a video for the track *We Wanna Return* in 2006 Daniel decided to leave the band. His spot was filled by Erik Hammarström. His debut became the MCD *Believers & Deceivers*. The band has also recorded the exclusive track *Capaneus* for the compilation *Inferno* (Collossus). Linus has also recorded a CD with Rivel Records founder and *Narnia/Audiovision/DivineFire* singer Christian Rivel, under the name *Flagship*. *Brighteye Brison* produces well played, highly interesting progressive rock.

2003 CD - RRCD 002

2003 ■	BRIGHTEYE BRISON ....CD	Rivel.............................	RRCD 002
2006 □	STORIES ....CD	Progress	PRCD 019
2008 ■	Believers & Deceivers.....................................MCD 4tr	Progress	PRCD 031
	Tracks: Pointless Living/After The Storm/The Harvest/The Grand Event		
2011 □	THE MAGICIAN CHRONICLES – PART I ....CD	Progress	PRCD 047

2008 MCD - PRCD 031

BRIMSTONE
Jan-Erik Persson: v, Daniel Grahn: g/b

Kristinehamn - The band started under the name *Havoc* and recorded two demos under this name, before changing it to *Brimstone*. Up-tempo metal with a German touch. What differs the band from the likes of *Hammerfall* etc., is that the vocals are of the death metal-type. Drums programmed by Ola Larsson. Daniel (also found in *Memfis*) left the band in 2000 and was replaced by Tomas Ederer. The band is currently on hold.

1999 □	CARVING A CRIMSON CAREER.............................CD	TPL	TPL 005
1999 ■	CARVING A CRIMSON CAREER.............................CD	Nuclear Blast	NB 427-2
	Different artwork.		
2008 □	CARVING A CRIMSON CAREER.............................CDd	Metal Mind	MASS CD 1191 DG
	2000 numbered copies		

1999 CD - NB 427-2

BRIMSTONE DAYS, THE
Håkan Lanz: v/g, Hampus "Hampe" Hallgard: b, Johannes Malmqvist: d

Malmö - The band was formed after Håkan Lanz and Johannes Malmqvist came back from a trip to Australia. They started the blues duo *Blue Windmills*. They were soon completed by bassist Elias Dellow and the sound was more influenced by the seventies power trio format and bands like *Led Zeppelin, Free* and *Jimi Hendrix*. In 2009 they recorded their first demo EP, entitled *Flowers And Rainbows*. After this, bassist Dellow left the band and was replaced by Hampus Hallgard. *The Brimstone Days* play excellent retro hard rock with their aforementioned influenced showing clear and with a singer slightly reminiscent of Zakk Wylde.
Website: www.thebrimstonedays.com

2010 ■	THE BRIMSTONE DAYS.......................................CDgp	private	- -
2012 □	Brimstone Days/Bulldog Mack (split) ....7"	Transubstans Vinyl Club	TRANSV 704
	Split with Bulldog Mac. Track: I Need Soul		
2012 □	ON A MONDAY TOO EARLY TO TELL....................CDd	Transubstans	TRANS 099

2010 CDp - - -

BROKE[N]BLUE

Eva Aggesjö-Abrahamsson: v, Peter Gustansson: v,
Lars Abrahamsson: g/k, Ulf Vestlund: b/d

Kolsva - High class catchy AOR with mixed male/female vocals and pretty rough edged guitar work. Some songs, like *Enuff*, might as well have been written by Russ Ballard. The band recorded a highly acclaimed 7-track demo in 2000. Peter also recorded two singles with the band *Angelize* in the late eighties. Lars and Peter were also found in the cover band *Sixpack*.

| 2001 ■ NORTHERN LIGHT | CD | Maple Leaf | BROCD 01 |
| 2005 □ THE WAITING | CD | MTM | 0681-137 |

2001 CD - BROCD 01

BROKEN DAGGER

Niklas Olausson: v, Magnus Wohlfart: g, Urban Månsby: k,
William Ekeberg: b, Jeremy Child: d

Hjärup - **Broken Dagger** play progressive neoclassical power metal with a touch of speed metal. Well played, slightly thin production. The vocals are what makes me a bit dubious, as Niklas voice is quite… different, sounding a bit like a desperate Blackie Lawless. Magnus is also found in **Nae'blis, Yggdrasil, Wohlfart, Folkearth** etc. The latter also features Niklas, William and Jeremy. William is also found in **Pandemonium, Trymheim** and **Body Core**.

| 2007 ■ CHAIN OF COMMAND | CD | CMD | CMD001 |
| *Bonus: E.B.E.N* | | | |

2007 CD - CMD001

BROKEN GLASS

Ulrika Beijer: v, Anne Ekman: v, Victor Erdesjö: g, Fredrik Persson: g,
Johan Eckerblad: k, Jonas Sjödin: b, Johan Jämtberg: d

Gävle - Female fronted AOR in the vein of US bands **Tantrum** and **Sahara** with a touch of **Heart**. High quality stuff. The single is heavier than the album. The band was formed in 1988 and split in 1995. Jämtberg and Erdesjö had previously recorded two single with melodic rockers **II Shy**. Ulrika later moved to Stockholm and recorded the pop single *Heartbeat*. She was also part of the *Sound Of Music* musical. Jämtberg later formed cover-act **Midnight Express**, where Tobbe Damber (**Zircus, Skydiverse**) was also found. The band's heaviest song, *No Shadow*, can be found on the local compilation *Absolut Helges 1*, on which Jämtberg appears in none less than five bands and has written or co-written 13 of the 19 songs! They also recorded some demos with covers of **AC/DC** and **Aerosmith/Run DMC**.

1991 7" - VEZU-VIO 504

1991 ■ Arabian Nights/The Runner	7"	private	VEZU-VIO 504
500 copies.			
1993 ■ CRY BABY	CD	Büms	46123

1993 CD - 46123

BRONTO

Jonas Fritzon: v, Stefan Törnby: g, Patricio Carasco: b, Svante Nordström: d

Tyresö - Great riff-oriented hard rock with a touch of **Electric Boys** meets **Badlands** in some tracks, while others are almost a bit progressive. Really powerful and heavy sound. Great stuff!

| 1996 ■ Bronto | MCD 6tr | private | Bråska 251 |
| *Tracks: You Don't Wanna Stay/I Feel I Have To Laugh But No/She Lost Her Eye/No Life Allowed/Memories/Coffee* | | | |

1996 MCD - Bråska 251

BROTHER APE

Stefan Damicolas: v/g/k, Gunnar Maxén: b/k/v, Max Bergman: d

Stockholm - In 1979-80, Stefan had a band called **Abduhlas Profeter** playing classic hard rock influenced by bands like **Black Sabbath, Deep Purple** and **Led Zeppelin**. Max entered the scene and in 1981 also Gunnar. Four years later the band was reinforced by keyboard player Peter Dahlström, also on bass and vocals. The style now changed into symphonic rock inspired by bands like **Yes, Kansas, Genesis** and **Steve Hacket** and finally the name, **Brother Ape** was set into stone. In 2005, after the band's debut Peter left for personal reasons and the band kept going as a three-piece. The band plays symphonic, intricate, but at times quite groovy progressive rock which feels a bit like a melting pot of the aforementioned inspirational sources.

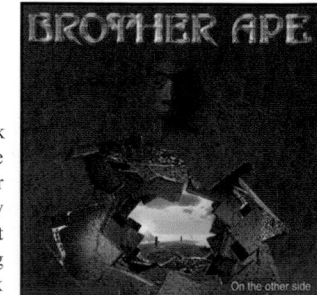
2005 CD - PRCD 014

2010 CD - PRCD 041

2005 ■ ON THE OTHER SIDE	CD	Progress Records	PRCD 014
2006 □ SHANGRI-LA	CD	Progress Records	PRCD 020
2008 □ III	CD	Progress Records	PRCD 032
2009 □ TURBULENCE	CD	Progress Records	PRCD 876
2010 ■ A RARE MOMENT OF INSIGHT	CD	Progress Records	PRCD 041

BRUTALIATOR
Stefan Karlsson: v, Jens Kjerrström: g, Fabian Helge: b, Johan Johannesson: d

Göteborg - The band formed in 1993 as *Profanity*, which was changed to *Brutaliator* in 2002. They also recorded an unreleased album in 2005 and a demo the previous year. *Brutaliator* split up in 2006. Karlsson is also found in *Soulreaper* and *Obligatorisk Tortyr*, where Kjerrström is also a member. The name is actually much heavier than the band. *Brutaliator* play outstanding thrash oriented metal with a touch of early *Metallica, Megadeth* and the Bay Area scene. Great vocals, great songs and well played. A sadly hidden gem.

2003 ■ BRUTALIATOR ....CD   private .... - -
　　　　CD in LP sleeve.

2003 CD - - -

BUBONIC PLAGUE
Stefan Eklund: v/g, Johan Sjögren: v/g/k, Johan Gustafsson: b, Kalle Gustafsson: d

Umeå - Incredibly varied, or rather, schizophrenic band. *Melting Concrete* is total hardcore, *A Man In Mexico* is like *Metallica* meets *Rage Against The Machine*, *Sociala* is punk-metal and *Technopad* is like *Ace Of Base* goes metal. Some vocals are in English and some in Swedish. Quite interesting though.

1994 ■ GOD DOESN'T PUNISH THE WICKED ....CD   private .... BUBCD 9409

1994 CD - BUBCD 9409

BUCKSHOT O.D.
Joachim Sjöström: v, Michael Nilsson: v/g, Tony Dicander: g,
Jonas Nyström: k/sampler, Christer Malmesjö: b, Johan "Joje" Lindstedt: d

Borlänge - Formed out of the rap-metal/hardcore band *Spit The Fish* in 1992, with Joachim replacing Jörgen Alriksson and adding Jonas. *Spit The Fish* recorded two tracks for the compilation *Eleven-On-A-One-To-Ten* ('93 Meantime). Joachim appeared on the same compilation, in the band *Riffomania*. He is also in the prog metal band *Death Organ*. *Buckshot O.D.* are in the same territory as *Clawfinger* but they have mixed more styles into their sound, a bit of *Snoop Doggy Dog*, a bit of *Red Hot Chili Peppers*, a bit of *Rage Against The Machine*. Production by Daniel Bergstand (*Crawley, Lost Souls* etc). The record company made a great job promoting the band. Over 2000 promo copies of the album were sent out. Destined to be big, but not much happened.

1995 MCD - FRONTPR 2

1995 ■ Sounfront Releases Spring 1995 (split) ....MCDp   Soundfront .... FRONTPR 2
　　　　Split with Lost Souls and Crawley. Tracks: Buss Dem Caps/War Zone Neighbourhood
1995 ■ OUTTA COARSE...CD   Soundfront .... FRONTCD 9

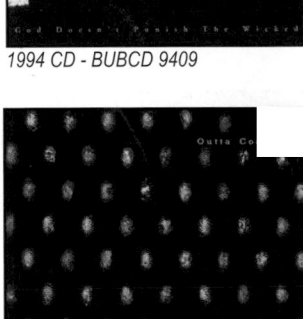
1995 CD - FRONTCD 9

BULLDOGGS
Johan Ericsson: v, Anders Pålsson: g, Rickard Ekvall: b, Daniel Lindberg: d

Svedala - *Bulldoggs* were formed in 2002 by four friends that had been playing in different bands since the 90s. The band has supported acts like *The Sweet, Nazareth* and *Hardcore Superstar*. Decent groovy heavy rock, slightly rough recorded and with slightly out of pitch harmony vocals at times. Lindberg has also played with *Embraced*.
Website: www.bulldoggs.com

2006 ■ NEVER MEANS MAYBE...CD   private .... BMNMM 0001

2006 CD - BMNMM 0001

BULLET
Dag "Hell" Hofer: v, Hampus Klang: g, Erik Almström: g,
Adam Hector: b, Gustaf Hjortsjö: d

Växjö - *Bullet* was formed in 2001 when Dag and Hampus decided it was time to put together a true heavy metal band looking at their heroes *Judas Priest, Accept* and *AC/DC*. In 2002 they recorded the demo *Heavy Metal Highway* which lead to a deal with Polish label Agonia. Soon things started happening and the band never seemed to turn down a gig. Finally they opened for *AC/DC* in August 2009. Adam Hector (one of the guys behind the Muskelrock festival) played bass on the first two releases, but was replaced by Lenny "Blade" Bladh on *Bite The Bullet*. After the album Adam was however back in the band again as Lenny moved to Thailand. Hampus is ex-*Birdflesh*. *Bullet* delivers all the clichés you can possibly imagine when thinking of the words "heavy metal" and "the 80s". Leather, denim and studs, sincere high-energy straight-ahead classic *AC/DC* influenced hard rock with an overloaded boost of energy. Dag's vocals sounds a bit like Bon Scott on an extra dose of adrenalin. In 2010 Lenny released the solo album *Taipei Nights*. On *Highway Pirates* the band is reinforced by *Saxon*'s Biff Byford, if only by a razor sharp whistling. Great on record, but a killer live act, and quite an active one at that! In December 2012 Almström left the band.
Website: www.bullet.nu

2006 CD - BLOD 029 CD

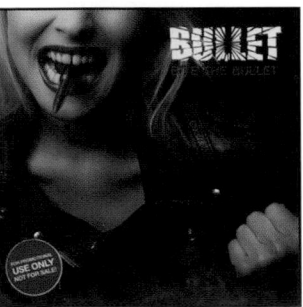
2008 CD - BLOD 046 CD

Highway pirates on the road to ruin.

2002 ☐ Heavy Metal Highway/Breaking Loose/Bang Your Head .... 7" 3tr	Swords & Sorcery .... STEEL 001	$$

225 copies.

2004 ◁ Speeding In The Night .... MCD 6tr   Agonia Records .... ARMCD 003
Tracks: Bang Your Head/No Turning Back/Leather Love/The Rebels Return/Breaking Bones/Heavy Metal Highway

2006 ☐ Heading For The Top .... CDS   Black Lodge BLODPRO029CDS
2006 ■ HEADING FOR THE TOP .... CD   Black Lodge .... BLOD 029 CD
2006 ☐ HEADING FOR THE TOP .... LPg   Black Lodge .... BLOD 029 LP
First edition including back patch.

2008 ☐ BITE THE BULLET .... CD   Black Lodge .... BLOD 046 CD
2008 ☐ BITE THE BULLET .... LPg   Black Lodge .... BLOD 046 LP
First edition including back patch. Also available in red vinyl.

2011 ☐ HIGHWAY PIRATES .... CD   Black Lodge .... BLOD 071 CD
2011 ☐ HIGHWAY PIRATES .... LP   Black Lodge .... BLOD 071 LP
2011 ☐ HIGHWAY PIRATES .... CD   Bickee Music (Japan) HMCX-1108
Bonus: Wild Wild Women

2011 ■ Bullet/Enforcer (split) .... 7"   Black Lodge .... BLOD 7004
Split with Enforcer. Track: Back On The Road

2012 ☐ Full Pull/Get On .... 7"   Nuclear Blast .... NB 2955-1
Pressed in 250 red, 250 white and 250 gold vinyl.

2012 ☐ FULL PULL .... CD   Nuclear Blast .... NB 2903-2
2012 ☐ FULL PULL .... CDd   Nuclear Blast .... NB 2903-0
250 copies + patch. Bonus: Get On

2012 ■ FULL PULL .... LPg   Nuclear Blast .... NB 2903-1
Bonus: Get On. 250 gold, red or black vinyl. Poster

2011 7" - BLOD 7004

2012 LP - NB 2903-1

BULLETRAIN

Robert "Robban" Lindell: v, Mattias "Matte" Persson: g,
Robin Bengtsson: g, Emil: b, Jonas Tillheden: d

Helsingborg - This young Helsingborg melodic sleaze unit recorded their first demo *1000 Miles Per Hour* in September 2006. Initially the bass player was Tim Svalö. A high-quality band that follow in the footsteps of the 80s bands together with current colleagues such as *Crazy Lixx, Crashdïet* and even more melodic bands like *Titan* and *H.E.A.T*.

2007 ☐ Johnny Gonebad .... MCD 4tr   private .... - -
Tracks: Johnny Gonebad/Joanna's Secret/Bad Blood (Outta Love)/Livin' A Dream. 500 copies

2010 ■ Turn It Up .... MCD 4tr   private .... - -
Tracks: My Way/Turn It Up/Fly Away (Don't Hide)/Even With My Eyes Closed

2010 MCD - - -

BULLETSIZE

Andreas "Diablo" Persson: v/g, Kjell Berg: g,
Christofer "Swanne" Swahn: b, Niklas "Nibbe" Gidlund: d

Östersund - The band was formed under the name *Metal Wings* in 2004, featuring former members of *Hellavator* and *Myra*. They recorded a couple of demos and in 2009 they added second guitarist Kjell Berg. *Bulletsize* play thrash-oriented death metal.
Website: www.bulletsize.se

2008 ☐	BULLETSIZE	CD	Taliesin Records	0001 7320470 107553
2013 ■	THE APOKALYPSE	CD	Sliptrick	SLP013.049

2013 CD - SLP013.049

BULLHORN

Lasse Holmgren: v, Jan Sandberg: g, Mats Andersson: g,
Kenneth Lamberg: b, Patrik Jonsson: d

Västerås - Previously known as *Ten Foot Pole*, under which name they recorded one album. The debut album contains a cover of *Four Horsemen's* *Rockin' Is My Business*. Jonas Hollsén handled drums on the first album, which was produced by Pelle Saether. *Suckerpunch* contains a cover of *Ozzy's* *Rock 'N Roll Rebel*. Standard classic hard rock with a touch of *AC/DC*, similar to *Bonafide* but with a bit more glam/sleaze-oriented vocals. Patrik was later in *Axenstar*.

1998 ☐	(LADISH)	CD	Crazy Life Music	a.b.s today 208
2001 ■	SUCKERPUNCH	CD	Shark	ALT SHARK 2101

2001 CD - ALT SHARK 2101

BULLSEYE

Johan Hallström: v, Bosse Norman: g, Jocke Ståhl: b, Jesper Magnusson: d

Filipstad - Hard rock with influences from *D.A.D* as well as *Volbeat*. Powerful and well played.
Website: www.bullseyeworld.com

2010 ■	Count On Me	MCDp 4tr	private	- -
	Tracks: Count On Me/YouSee/Back In The Time/Over The Top			

2010 MCDp - - -

BULT

Jonas Udd: v, Martin Andreasson: g, Sam Rönnberg: b, Cristian Sigurdsson: d

Göteborg - The band was initiated by Andreasson and Sigurdsson and took shape in 2010. Progressive death/thrash, a bit like *Mastodon* meets *Meshuggah*, well-played and really interesting. Bult means bolt in Swedish.
Website: www.bultband.com

2011 ■	Amidst The Throng	MCD 4tr	Hobo Records	HOBOCD 15
	Tracks: Overtly Powerless/Point Of No Return/The End/In The Image Of God			

2011 CDd - HOBOCD 15

BURN

Hans Bell: v, Ilpo "Paul Curry" Ylitalo: g, Patrik "Patrick Fox" Söderkvist: g,
Patrick Johansson: b, Ismo "Pete Curry" Ylitalo: d

Älvsjö (Stockholm) - The band's debut is more influenced by the NWoBHM and bands like *Iron Maiden*, while the second is a great, slightly *AC/DC* style, rocker with lots of good riffs and hooks. Just after the LP bassist Patrick replaced Hans "Alex Hill" Hernberg, singer Thomas "Tom Oakland" Eklund was replaced by Hans and instead of Patrik the guitar was handled by Tomas Ylivainio on the MLP. In 1991 Hans quit and the band split but they later partly reformed as *Squealer*, only releasing a demo.

1983 LP - SMSLP 1006

1983 ■	BURN	LP	Moonshine	SMSLP 1006
1988 ■	Still Going Wrong	MLP 4tr	Lonely Sailor	LSP-101
	Tracks: Brown Envelope Invasion/Lonely Sailor/Shotgun/Beerbelly.			

BURNING ENGINES

Kalle Johansson (now Nimhagen): v, Mikael Fässberg: g, Lotta Brolin: g,
Anders Mantler: b, Carl-Mikael "Hilton" Hildesjö: d

Malmö - *Burning Engines* was formed in 2001 by former *Embraced* singer Kalle who wanted to break free from the world of growling and go for a more groove oriented late 70s, early 80s vibe. The sound slowly turned a bit more stonerish and Dutch Daredevil Records signed the band. The band core of Kalle, Mikael and Hilton has been keeping the rock alive through the years and in 2005 they became the backing band of former *Iron Maiden* singer Paul DiAnno for his anniversary tour. Mikael, Martin and Hilton, together with three parts of *Locomotive*

1988 MLP - LSP-101

Breath formed the band *From Behind*, fronted by former *Samson/Mammoth* singer Nicky Moore. When the album finally was recorded only Mikael and Hilton were part of the constellation. Mikael is now found in *Bonafide*, Staffan Österlind, who replaced Lotta, has recorded with the band *Bloom* and is currently residing in the USA, playing with *Black Robot*. Martin has recorded with *Majestic* and pop band *Marygold*. Kalle is now fronting *Deathening*.

2002 ■ SERGEJ THE FREAK MEETS THE BURNING ENGINES (split) ....CD Daredevil..DD 017
   Tracks: Fly With Me/Garden Of Evil/Come On/Dreaming With The Eagle/Love Song

2002 CD - DD 017

BURNING SAVIOURS
Mikael Marjanen (now Monks): v/g, Jonas Hartikainen: g,
Fredrik Evertsson: b, Martin Wijkström: d

The third line-up going all Luciferian (or just drunk...)!

2005 CD - IHRCD 012

2007 CD - BRR 003

Örebro - *Burning Saviours* was formed in 2003 by guitarist Mikael Marjanen and drummer Martin Wijkström. The name came from a song on the album *Day Of Reckoning* by US band *Pentagram*. They teamed up with bass player Fredrik Evertsson and singer Andrei Amartinesei to record their first demo *Dayterrors* in 2004. Amartinesei added guitar to his vocal tasks for their second demo *The Crusade Of Evil*, recorded the same year. Later the same year they recorded yet a third demo, entitled *Into The Abyss*, which generated enough buzz to get the band on the roster of the German *Doom Shall Rise III* festival in 2005, and subsequently a deal with label I Hate Records. The self-titled debut was released in May 2005 and the follow-up a year later. Late 2006 Amartinesei parted ways with the band and was replaced by singer Frank Andersson and guitarist Henry Pyykkö. After the release of *Nymhs & Weavers* Andersson left the band which prompted Marjanen to switch from guitar to vocals. Second guitarist Andreas Eriksson was drafted. *Burning Saviours* play 70s hard rock at times quite reminiscent of bands like (early) *Granmax* and *Demian* with a strong touch of US doomsters *Pentagram*. Great stuff indeed! Marjanen, Pyykkö and Eriksson is now found in thrash/heavy metal band *Whyte Ash*, and have have release their debut on Transubstans Records. In 2011 the band returned with the 7" *Förbannelsen* (the damnation) and a new line-up where guitarist and Henry Pyykkö was replaced by Hartikainen and Marjanen had changed his name to Monks.

The second line-up more composed

2009 LP - SVR 002

2011 7" - NTR 004

2005 ■	BURNING SAVIOURS	CD	I Hate	IHRCD 012
2006 ☐	HUNDUS	CD	I Hate	IHRCD 021
2005 ○	The Giant/The Clown	7"	Rise Above	RISE 7 84
	100 copies in clear vinyl, 400 in black. No artwork.			
2007 ☐	NYMPHS & WEAVERS	CD	Transubstans	TRANS 033
2007 ■	NYMPHS & WEAVERS	LPg	Bloodrock Records	BRR 003
	500 copies.			
2008 ☐	BURNING SAVIOURS	CD	I Hate	IHRCD 059
	Reissue. New artwork.			
2009 ■	HUNDUS	LP	Svart Records	SVR 002
	500 copies. New artwork.			
2011 ■	Förbannelsen/Midnight	7"	Night Tripper	NTR 004
	400 black plus 100 hand numbered in red vinyl.			
2011 ☐	BURNING SAVIOURS	LP	Svart Records	SVR 020
	400 copies in clear vinyl. New artwork.			
2012 ■	The Offering/Spirit Of The Woods (Förbannelsen Part II)	7"	Night Tripper	NTR 006
	400 blackl plus 100 hand numbered in red vinyl plus patch.			
2012 ☐	The Nightmare/Doomus Maximus (Förbannelsen Part III)	7"	Night Tripper	NTR 008
	400 black and 100 red vinyl plus army cap.			
2012 ☐	I Am Lucifer/Hon dansar med döden (Förbannelsen Part IV)	7"	Night Tripper	NTR 009
	400 black and 100 red vinyl plus slipmat.			

2012 7" - NTR 006

BURST

Linus Jägerskog: v, Robert Reinholdz: g/v, Jonas Rydberg: g,
Jesper Liveröd: b, Patrik Hultin: d

Kristinehamn - Quite an interesting progressive metalcore band. **Burst** started out playing hardcore/crust punk under the name **Dislars** (as an homage to all the Dis-bands of this period) in 1993, formed by Liveröd (*Nasum*), Jägerskog and Hultin. The guitarists joined camp a bit later on. In 1994 they entered a bandstand, won, and the first prize was to record a CD. This became the band's debut on Zalt. The band mixes clean melodic vocals from Reinholdz with the screams of Jägerskog. As their playing skills improved they moved more towards a progressive edge, still sticking to their hardcore background. They changed their name to **Burst** and began working more seriously, recording demos and finally inking a deal with Melon Records. In 1999 they came to a real turning point and the musical path they are still on came to form. This showed on the album *Conquest: Writhe*, which the band states as their first in their own discography. The subsequent MCD was produced by Fredrik Reinedahl and Fredrik Nordström, giving the band a sound more suited to the music. It wasn't however until they were signed by Relapse and released *Prey On Life* they started gaining more success. The band toured with acts like **Dillinger Escape Plan** and **Mastodon**. Highly intriguing technical progressive metalcore. Hard to describe, but try mixing a bit of **In Flames** energy, a little bit of **Disharmonic Orchestra** whackyness, a little **Opeth** melancholy, a bit of **Mastedon** technicality and their own touch.

2001 CD - PRANK 044

2002 MCD - CSM#006

1995	☐	Burst	MCD 6tr	Zalt Records	ZALTREC 9501

Tracks: Illusion/I Fell/Passivity/Wide Awake/Attempt/Outro. 500 copies.

1996	☐	Shadowcaster	MCD 45tr	Melon/Birdnest	Melon961103

Tracks: Condemnation/Shadowcaster/Soulscarred/The Last Chapter

1998	☐	Lash Out/Burst (split)	7"	Impression	IR 701

Tracks: Forsaken, Not Forgotten/Corroded

1998	☐	TWO FACED	CD	Melon/Birdnest	Melon971003
2001	☐	CONQUEST: WRITHE	LP	Putrid Filth Conspiracy	PFC 014
2001	■	CONQUEST: WRITHE	CD	Prank	PRANK 044
2002	■	In Converting Ways	MCD 4tr	Chrome Saint Magnus	CSM#006

Tracks: Scavenger/Black But Shining/Paradise Regained/Ars Diavoli (The Devil In Me)

2003	☐	CONQUEST: WRITHE	2CD	Ritual (Japan)	HWCY-1147/48

Reissue with the tracks from "In Converting Ways" as bonus.

2003	☐	Burned By The Sun/Burst (split)	7"	Relapse Records	RR 051

Promo single given to mail order customers. 300 copies. Track: Sculpt The Lives

2003	☐	PREY ON LIFE	CD	Relapse Records	RR 6610-2
2003	☐	PREY ON LIFE	CD	Ritual (Japan)	HWCY-1155
2004	■	In Converting Ways	10" 4tr	Throne Records	CHAPTER 20

100 orange numbered + 200 orange + 700 black vinyl. New artwork.

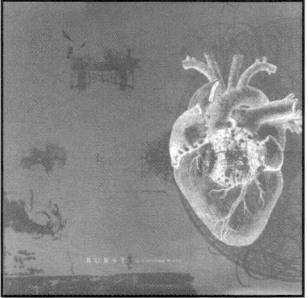

2004 10" - CHAPTER 20

2005	☐	Burst/The Ocean	7"	Garden Of Exile	GOELP 006

Track: Flight's End. Fold-out poster, 350 copies in clear vinyl, 350 copies blue transparent plus a limited number in other colours.

2005	■	ORIGO	CD	Replase Records	RR 6657-2
2005	☐	ORIGO	CD	Replase Records (Japan)	YSCY-1013

Bonus: video

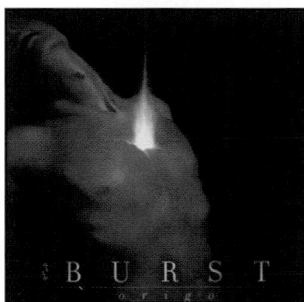

2005 CD - RR 6657-2

2006	☐	ORIGO	CD	Replase Records (USA)	RLS 766657
2006	☐	ORIGO + PREY ON LIFE	2LPg	Garden Of Exile	GOE 6

33 copies clear/white vinyl, 67 white/clear, 125 clear, 175 white.

2007	☐	ORIGO	CD	Irond (Russia)	CD 07-1291
2008	■	LAZARUS BIRD	CD	Replase Records	RR 6129-2
2008	☐	LAZARUS BIRD	CD	Replase Records (Japan)	YSCY-1122
2008	☐	LAZARUS BIRD	CD	Replase Records (USA)	RLS 766129
2008	☐	LAZARUS BIRD	2LPg	Garden Of Exile	GOE 21

69 copies in silver vinyl, 138 solid lime, 225 solid yellow, 375 black.

2008 CD - RR 6129-2

BUSSIGA KLUBBEN

Per Gustavsson: v, Anders Nyberg: g, Anders Billing: k,
Fredrik Ståhl: b, Jonas Ottander: d

Göteborg - It all started out as a pop-party-cover-band. The first single is a childrens song by Gullan Bornemark in a new wavish hard rock version. After the first album Billing joined. He felt the band could be heavier and re-arranged a lot of the band's poppy material and added the heavy edge. Heavy melodic hard rock, occasionally with a touch of **Deep Purple**. Brutal guitars and nice distorted Hammond. Great band! Vocals in Swedish. The name means "The Friendly Club" in Swedish. After *Grovmotorik* they went back to pop again. Billing quit and they hired a second guitarist, but the band split shortly after. Billing is now writing soundtracks and laying sound for TV and movies. He was also later in the band **15.01**, who recorded half an album for Slask Records, but took a long (still lasting) break.

1990 7" - hel 25-1

bussiga klubben
grovmotorik

1993 CD - hel cd-09

1990	■	Min Ponny/Jag Vill Ha En Egen Måne	7"	Helikopter	hel 25-1
1991	☐	PEACE, WAR & UNDERSTANDING	CD	Helikopter	HEL CD-02
1993	■	GROVMOTORIK	CD	Helikopter	hel cd-09

BUSZER

Daniel Barkman: v, Per Johansson: g, Andreas Andersson: g,
Johan Augustsson: b, Alexander Milsten: d

Ronneby - The first band to really put Ronneby on the metal map, besides Messiah Marcolin, of course. **Buszer** produced a 3-track demo CD-R entitled *Dark Pleasures* in 2001. On *Serenity* Daniel had replaced singer Sebastian Virtanen. Straight ahead classic heavy metal influenced by **Judas Priest** etc. Johansson was the man behind the NLP label.

2002 ■	Till The End	...MCD 4tr	NLP	NLP 0201
	Tracks: Till The End/War Anthem/The Devil In Miss Baines/Possessed			
2003 ■	SERENITY	...CD	NLP	NLP 0304

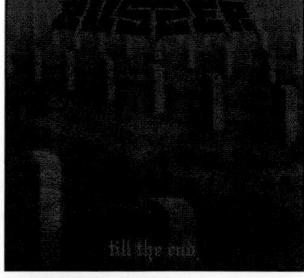

2002 MCD - NLP 0201

BY MY FEAR

David Gabrielsson: v, Niklas Andreasson: g, Torgny Johansson: g,
Pasi Salo: b, Morgan Hansson: d

Ljungby - In 1998 Torgny and David met, involved in music in different ways, but introduced through a common friend. They formed a band with the intention of sounding like a dark, angry, heavy **Iron Maiden**. They went thorugh various members before settling for the recording line-up. Not really sure if I buy into the **Iron Maiden** comparison, but they do add a bit of dual guitar flair into the melodic death metal brew. I'd compare them to a mix of **Dark Tranquillity** and **Avatar**.
Website: www.reverbnation.com/bymyfearofficial

2011 ■	CENTER	...CD	Supernova	SUPERCD 025

2003 CD - NLP 0304

BY NIGHT

Adrian Westin: v, Andre Gonzales: g, Henrik Persson: g,
Marcus Wesslen: b, Per Qvarnström: d

Falkenberg - The band was formed in 1999 and gradually developed their sound until their debut in 2004. Before this they were nominated "Sweden's Best Unsigned Band" in Close-Up magazine. The band produces a mix of thrash, metalcore with an almost industrial edge. Adrian, Andre and Marcus are also found in the band **Trendkill**, while the latter is also ex-**Eternal Lies**. In 2012 the band released their new album *Sympathy For Tomorrow*, only as a digital release.

2004 □	By Night/Sipher System (split)	...MCD 6tr	LifeForce	LFR 043-2
	Tracks: Lamentation/Unseen Oppression/Obsessed To Hate			
2005 ■	BURN THE FLAG	...CD	LifeForce	LFR 050-2
2006 □	A NEW SHAPE OF DESPERATION	...CD	LifeForce	LFR 063-2
2006 □	A NEW SHAPE OF DESPERATION	...LPg	LifeForce	LFR 063-1

2011 CD - SUPERCD 025

2005 CD - LFR 050-2

C.B MURDOC

Johan Ljung: v, Fredrik Boëthius: g, Henrik Hedberg: g, Johan Larsson: k,
Johan Hansen: b, Carl-Gustav "C-G" Bäckström: d

Stockholm - When *Mörk Gryning* folded in 2005 the members (except Goth and Kimera), with the addition of Johan Hansen, formed *C.B Murdoc*. Extremely well played metalcore-oriented technical death metal with a strong progressive touch. A band that delivers live, as well as on CD. Hedberg has also been in *Hypocrite*, while C-G is ex-*Meldrum*. The band's second album was recorded at Necromorbus Studio by Sverker Vidgren and mixed by Daniel Bergstrand (*Crawley, Devin Townsend* etc). *Meshuggah's* Fredrik Thordendahl does a guest solo. Bäckström, ex-*Wyvern, Hypocrite* and *Amaranth* is also found in *Sectu*. Technical blast beat heaven. Late 2012 Christian Alsing replaced Hedberg.

2009 CDd - BRK 001   *2012 CDd - SPI 413*

```
2009 ■ TWO IN ONE ..........................................................CDd  BRK Media.......................... BRK 001
2012 ■ THE GREEN ...........................................................CDd  Spinefarm ............................ SPI 413
```

CC ROCK

Patrik Tibell: v/k, Peter Lundin: g, Anssi Alatalo: g,
Roger Ljunggren: g/b, Marcus Nowak: d

Skara/Skövde - CC Rock was originally a continuation of the band *T'Bell* which featured Tibell (*Trace, Amity*) and Ljunggren (*Twilight Project*). Peter and Anssi, are main musicians according to the cover, however all the tracks were written by Tibell and Ljunggren, and Tibell also produced the CD. Other musicians that played on the album were singers Thomas Vikström, Mika Corpi, Peo Pettersson, guitarist Janne Strandh and drummer Marco Tapani. Musically it's very much in the vein of *T'Bell's* catchy AOR. Great production and high class song writing. After the CD the band has continued with a line-up featuring, besides Alatalo and Lundin, Mark E Gunnardo (v), Mikael Baden (b) and Magnus Thorn (d). Nowak was also in *Heads Or Tales*.

2007 MCDd - ZMCD 001

```
2007 ■ EP ............................................................MCDd 6tr  Zink Music..................... ZMCD 001
        Tracks: Wanna Feel Like The First Time/The Best I Can/Angel/Dreamer/My Special Lady/
        Dreamer (Radio Edit)
```

CALIGULA

Jörgen Zetterberg: v, Ola Paulsson: g, Tony Tomasson: b, Jesper Magnusson: d

Filipstad - Despite the death metal sounding name this band delivers great melodic sleaze in the vein of early *Mötley Crüe*, especially considering the Vince Neil sound-alike vocals. Well worth looking for. Jörgen and Jesper later formed sleaze/glam/AOR-band *Poseidon*, who are featured on *The Jukebox Collection* (1995 RFM) and *Gränslöst* (1995 RFM).

1991 7" - UNI 2577

```
1991 ■ So Fine/Must Get Out ........................................7"  private ...........................UNI 2577  $
```

CALILIO

Stefan Nilsson: v, Jonas Hörnqvist: g, Christian Joselfsson: k,
Magnus Lind: b, Magnus Hörnqvist: d

Göteborg - One of the numerous Platina-singles. They actually managed to find some really interesting acts and *Calilio* was one of them. The band plays melodic hard rock, not that far from early 80s *Europe*. The Hörnqvist brothers and Lind went on to form *Treasure Land*. Lind also played bass on the LP by *Blue Balls* and is today in *Skull Parade*. Jonas, who became quite the shredder, was a really talented kid already on this single. Well worth looking for.

1989 7" - PL 60

```
1989 ■ Lips/I Remember You........................................7"  Platina............................PL 60  $
```

CALM

Hans Forslund: v, Daniel Hermansson: v, Pierre Andersson: g,
Johan Magnusson: g, Tobias Lundh: b, Mathias Pettersson: d

Eskilstuna - Calm play highly intriguing, insanely experimental and technical metalcore that ranges from total hardcore mayhem to soft pop melodies, almost like a *System Of A Down* on turbo driven steroids. The band was formed already back in 1997. The debut featured singers Axel Jonsson, Daniel Bergwall and Per Åhlund (also sampling), guitarists Pierre Andersson and Richard Nyman, bass player Tobias Lundh and drummer Mathias Pettersson. On the second album, which was produced by Johan Blomström (*Overdrive, Kaptain Sun, Blinded Colony*), the line-up had changed to the above. Magnusson is ex-*Carnal Forge* and *Construcdead*.

2003 CDd - nu20031

2007 CD - CALM002CD

```
2003 ■ ARE WE SUPPOSED TO BE................................CDd  Nu Metal Recordz ............ nu20031
2007 ■ ARMY OF A FEW.............................................CD  private .........................CALM002CD
```

CALM CHAOS

Patric Wilén: v, Tobias "Toby" Backlin: g/v, Johnny Johansson: g,
Fredrik "FoaF" Forsfjäll: b, Daniel "Dannie" Wilén: b, Andreas "Nizze" Nilsson: d

Skellefteå - The first EP was only supposed to be a demo. *Calm Chaos* plays heavy, detuned rap-infused metal, a bit like a mix of *Limp Bizkit, Rage Against The Machine* and *Clawfinger*. The EP was more rap-oriented than the album, where melodic vocals started taking over slightly more. It's not surprising the band was invited to open up for *Clawfinger* in 2006. After the first leg of the tour Patric decided to leave and was replaced by Joakim Åström. The CD is also available in a Japanese version which is the same as the B&B but with an additional slipcase. Website: www.calmchaos.net

2003 ☐ All One ....MCD 5tr B&B Records .... BCD 001
Tracks: Alone/Justice/Fame/One Wish/Eternity
2005 ■ MELODY OF MOKUS..CD B&B Records .... BCD 007
2006 ☐ MELODY OF MOKUS..CD RB Records (Japan) .... BCD 007
Bonus: Stay Away/Justice. Slipcase
2007 ☐ MELODY OF MOKUS..CD India Records..................................53000072

2005 CD - BCD 007

CANDLEMASS

Mats Levén: v, Lars Johansson: g, Mats "Mappe" Björkman: g,
Leif Edling: b, Jan Lindh: d

Upplands Väsby/Stockholm - After *Nemesis* split in 1984, Leif formed *Candlemass*. The first demos, *Witchcraft* and *Second Demo 1984* were actually recorded under the name *Nemesis*, with bassist/singer Leif Edling, guitarists Klas Bergwall (*Arrow*) and Mats "Mappe" Björkman (ex-*ATC*) and drummer Matz Ekström. Two of the tracks were later found on the reissue of the *Nemesis*-MLP/MCD. In *Nemesis* and on the demos, Leif himself handled the vocals, which wasn't his strongest point, but on *Epicus...* he borrowed singer Johan Längquist (also found in *D-Project, Jonah Quizz* and now in *Impulsia*) and on *Nightfall* the huge singer with the huge voice, Eddie "Messiah" Marcolin, or Jan Alfredo Marcolin (ex-*Mercy, Rough Lizzards*) had taken over the mike. On the second album Klas Bergwall was replaced by ex-*Hexagon/Macbeth*-guitarist Lasse Johansson, and drummer Matz Ekström had been replaced by Jan Lindh. This is what became the classic *Candlemass* line-up. Additional guitars on *Nightfall* were played by Mikael "Mike Wead" Wikström (*Maninnya Blade, Hexenhaus, Memento Mori, Abstrakt Algebra* etc.). The band released the landmark Swedish doom albums *Ancient Dreams* (1988) and *Tales Of Creation* (1989), followed by a live album. After this internal friction resulted in Marcolin and the band parting company. On *Chapter 6* a replacement was found in former *Talk Of The Town* vocalist Thomas Vikström, who in 1993 made a very poppy solo-album. *Sigge Fürst* is *Candlemass* doing doom-versions of old Swedish cabaret songs in Swedish. Quite fun, but mostly for collectors. When *Candlemass* folded in 1993, Leif started his own project *Abstrakt Algebra* together with Mike Wead. Tomas was pursuing a diminished solo-career, doing session-jobs, made a demo with *Afterglow* and later ended up in *Stormwind*, with whom he recorded several albums. He was later moved on to bands like *Dark Illusion, 7Days* and *Covered Call*. Lasse formed the band *Zoic*, which also featured Mats and Jan. They released one album. In the late nineties he formed the band *Tarmac*, also featuring Michael (Storck) Uppman (*Rising Force, Paradise, Explode*), Tobbe Moen (*Red Fun*), Tom Forsell and former *Candlemass/Zoic*-colleague Jan Lindh. The band later became *Creozoth*, and who recorded one album. Eddie recorded two albums with *Memento Mori* before he left for doom rockers *Stillborn/Colossus* in 1994. Nothing however ever came out of that collaboration. The first five *Candlemass* albums contain first class doom-metal, clearly influenced by *Black Sabbath*. When Thomas joined, the tempos were a bit faster, but there was no reduction of the heaviness. The '98-release was initially meant to be a new *Abstrakt Algebra*-album, but as the band never lift off commercially, this was changed into *Candlemass*. Probably a correct move as it style wise is a true doom-album, pretty close to the doom-laden melodies of *Epicus Doomicus Metallicus*, but it also contains elements of 90s psychedelica more akin to *Abstrakt Algebra*. The line-up on this platter was Leif on bass, guitarist Mike Amott (*Spiritual Beggars, Arch Enemy, Carcass*), singer Björn Flodqvist (*Gone, Enter The Hunt*), drummer Jejo Perković (*Abstrakt Algebra, Mustasch*) and keyboardist Carl Westholm (*Abstrakt Algebra, Carptree, Jupiter Society*). Ian Haugland (*Europe*) also appears on a couple of tracks. In 1998 Leif started his own label Froghouse. The first release was the 10" EP *Wiz*. The songs were all recorded in 1997, with the *Dactylis* line-up, plus Patrik Instedt on guitar. On the subsequent album the guitars were handled by Mats Ståhl. *From The 13th Sun* is an outstanding performance in heavy doomy 70s *Sabbath*-orgy, first class! The 2001 re-mastered reissue of *Epicus...* contains a live-CD recorded in Birmingham 1988, with a *Black Sabbath*-medley. For all connoisseurs of dark metal, there is actually a demo floating around with the band *Witchcraft*, recorded in 1981 and with a young Leif Edling on vocals. Most of these tracks can however be found on the CD *Demos & Outtakes – The Black Heart Of Candlemass* released under Leif's name. In 2001 Leif

Epicus...

Doomicus...

Metallicus!!

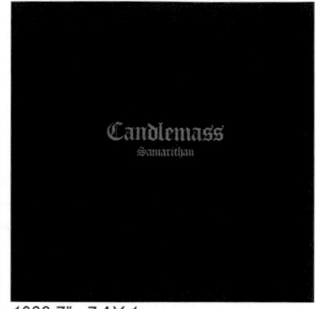

also formed the project **Krux** featuring members of **Entombed** and **Arch Enemy**, a band that has now released three albums. In 2001 the classic line-up featuring Marcolin, Johansson, Björkman, Edling and Ekström reformed. The old albums were re-issued with lots of bonus material. After a brief split in 2004, they re-united and recorded the self-titled album, for which they received a Swedish Grammy for "Best Hard Rock". The live DVD The *Curse Of Candlemass – Live In Stockholm 2003* was released. In 2007 the band celebrated a two year delayed 20th anniversary with a live show featuring some of the former members, including Johan Längquist. A DVD was filmed and released as *The 20 Year Anniversary Party*. In 2007 **Candlemass** and singer Marcolin parted ways. The vocal replacement came in the form of former **Solitude Aeternus** vocalist Robert Lowe, who made his debut on *King Of The Grey Islands*. *Ashes To Ashes* was recorded live in 2009 and **Candlemass** is without doubt Sweden's finest and foremost doom band, influential to, not only Swedish bands, but numerous international bands of the genre. *Doomology* is a really cool box set with tons of unreleased live material and demos ranging from 1992-2008, even a Eurovision Song Contest reject entitled *Vårt sista avsked* with Tomas Vikström on vocals. In 2010 the band recorded a cover of **Blue Öyster Cult's** *(Don't Fear) The Reaper* and **Dylan/Hendrix's** *All Along The Watchtower* on a limited edition 12". 100 copies were released by the band themselves on the 25th anniversary show on Doom Records, while 1000 copies were released by High Roller. When releasing *Psalms For The Dead*, the band announced this was the **Candlemass** swan song, the last album to be released. The band did not split up, but will just play live shows instead. We'll see, things have a way of changing over time. Shortly after Rob Lowe was sacked, he was replaced by Mats Levén.
Website: www.candlemass.net

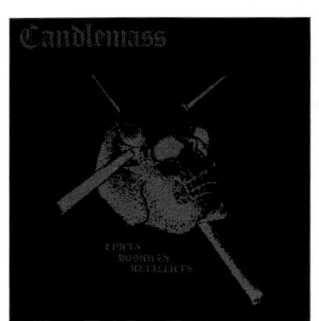

1986 LP - BD 013

Year		Title	Format	Label	Cat. No.	
1986	■	EPICUS DOOMICUS METALLICUS	LP	Black Dragon Records	BD 013	$
1986	□	EPICUS DOOMICUS METALLICUS	CD	Black Dragon Records	BDCD013	$
1986	□	EPICUS DOOMICUS METALLICUS	LP	Leviathan (USA)	LA 19882-1	$
1986	□	EPICUS DOOMICUS METALLICUS	CD	Leviathan(USA)	LD 19882-2	
1986	□	EPICUS DOOMICUS METALLICUS	LP PD	Black Dragon	-	
		1000 copies.				
1987	□	NIGHTFALL	LP	Active	LP 3	
1987	□	NIGHTFALL	CD	Active	ATV 3	
1987	□	NIGHTFALL	LP	Axis	AXIS LP 3	
1987	□	NIGHTFALL	LP PD	Megarock	CDP 004	
		500 copies.				
1998	□	NIGHTFALL	LP	Metal Blade (USA)	72241-1	
1998	□	NIGHTFALL	CD	Metal Blade	72241-2	
		Also released as long-box				
1988	□	At The Gallows End/Crystal Ball (1988 version)/Solitude (1988)	MLP 3tr	Metal Blade	72295-0	
1988	□	Samarithan/Solitude/Crystal Ball	MLP 3tr	Axis	12 AX 1	
1988	■	Samarithan/Solitude	7"	Axis	7 AX 1	$
		Also available in red vinyl.				
1988	□	ANCIENT DREAMS	LP	Active	LP 7	
1988	□	ANCIENT DREAMS	CD	Active	ATV 7	
1988	□	ANCIENT DREAMS	LP	Restless/Metal Blade	72241-2	
1988	□	ANCIENT DREAMS	LP	Metal Blade	73340-1	
1988	□	ANCIENT DREAMS	CD	Metal Blade	73340-2	
1989	■	TALES OF CREATION	LPg	Music For Nations	MFN 95	
1989	□	TALES OF CREATION	CD	Music For Nations	CDMFN 95	
		Bonus: Black Sabbath medley				
1989	■	TALES OF CREATION	LP PD	Music For Nations	MFN 95P	
1989	□	TALES OF CREATION	LP	New Electric Way (France)	104601	
1990	□	TALES OF CREATION	CD	Metal Blade	73417 2	
1990	□	TALES OF CREATION	CD	Pony Canyon (Japan)	PCCY-00053	
1990	□	TALES OF CREATION	CD	Paranoid Discos (Brazil)	UNROPRO 1991	
1990	□	LIVE	CD	Metal Blade	26444 2	
1990	□	LIVE	2LP	Music For Nations	MFN 109	
1990	□	LIVE	CD	Music For Nations	CDMFN 109	
1992	□	CHAPTER IV	LP	Music For Nations	MFN 128	$
1992	□	CHAPTER IV	CD	Music For Nations	CDMFN 128	
1993	■	Sigge Fürst	MCD 4tr	Megarock Records	MRRCDS003	$$
		Tracks: Bullfest/Samling vid pumpen/Bröllop på Hulda Johanssons pensionat/Tjo tjim och inget annat				
1994	□	LIVE	CD	Metal Blade	14061 2	
1994	□	AS IT IS, AS IT WAS	2CD	Music For Nations	CDMFN 166	
1996	□	EPICUS DOOMICUS METALLICUS	CD	Rising Sun	BDCD 013	
1998	□	DACTYLIS GLOMERATA	CD	Music For Nations	CDMFN 237	
1998	■	Wiz	10" 4tr	Froghouse	FROG 001	$
		Tracks: Wiz/Container/Bug Queen/Thirst. Red vinyl				
1999	□	FROM THE 13TH SUN	CD	Music For Nations	MFN 253	
2000	□	Nimis/Rock 'N Roll	7"	Trust No One	Trust No 14	
		1000 copies.				
2001	□	EPICUS DOOMICUS METALLICUS	2LP	Powerline	PLRLP 002	
		Contains a bonus live album.				
2001	□	EPICUS DOOMICUS METALLICUS	2CD	Powerline	PLRCD 002	

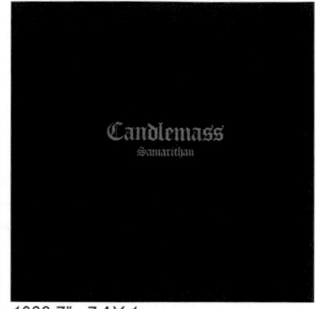

1988 7" - 7 AX 1

1989 LPg - MFN 95

1989 LP PD - MFN 95P

1993 MCD - MRRCDS003

1998 10" - FROG 001

2001 ☐	NIGHTFALL	2CD	Powerline	PLRCD 003

The bonus CD contains two demo-tracks, two live-tracks, two studio outtakes, an interview and a video of Bewitched.

2001 ☐	ANCIENT DREAMS	2CD	Powerline	PLRCD 004

The bonus CD contains four live-tracks, and interview and a video of Mirror Mirror.

2001 ☐	TALES OF CREATION	2CD	Powerline	PLRCD 005

The bonus CD contains five demo-tracks, and interview and a video of Dark Reflections.

2001 ☐	CHAPTER IV	CD+DVD	GMR	GMRCD 090

The bonus CD contains the "Bullfest" EP and a live DVD from Uddevalla 1993.

2002 ☐	EPICUS DOOMICUS METALLICUS	2CD	CD-Maximum (Russia)	CDM 0902-968/969
2002 ☐	NIGHTFALL	2CD	CD-Maximum (Russia)	CDM 0902-980/981
2002 ☐	ANCIENT DREAMS	2CD	CD-Maximum (Russia)	CDM 1002-987/987
2002 ☐	TALES OF CREATION	2CD	CD-Maximum (Russia)	CDM 1002-989/990
2003 ☐	DOOMED FOR LIVE - REUNION 2002	2CD	Powerline	PLRCD 009
2003 ☐	DOOMED FOR LIVE - REUNION 2002	2CD	CD-Maximum (Russia)	CDM 0403-1363/64
2003 ☐	DIAMONDS OF DOOM	2LP	Powerline	PLRLP 010

1000 copies. White marbled vinyl.

2003 ☐	DIAMONDS OF DOOM	2LP	Powerline	PLRLP 010	$$

2 copies in 1 blue + 1 black vinyl test pressing.

2004 ☐	ESSENTIAL DOOM	CD/d+DVD	Powerline	PLRCD 014

Best of plus new track "Witches" and a 5 track live DVD. First 3000 copies as digi pack.

2005 ☐	CANDLEMASS	CD	Nuclear Blast	NB 1448-2
2005 ☐	CANDLEMASS	LP	Nuclear Blast	NB 1448-1
2005 ☐	CANDLEMASS	CDd	Nuclear Blast	NB 1448-0

Bonus: Mars And Volcanos

2005 ☐	CANDLEMASS	CD	Irond (Russia)	CD 05-998
2005 ☐	CANDLEMASS	CD	NEMS (Argentina)	NEMS 358

Bonus: Mars And Volcanos

2005 ☐	Doom Songs – The Singles 1986-1989	4x7" box	Special Product Unit	SPUBOX 002	$$

Box with the below singles. 500 copies.

2005 ■	Solitude/Crystal Ball	7"	Vinyl maniacs	VMS 001
2005 ☐	At The Gallows End/Samarithan	7"	Vinyl Maniacs	VMS 002
2005 ■	Mirror Mirror/Bells Of Acheron	7"	Vinyl Maniacs	VMS 003
2005 ☐	Dark Reflections/Into The Unfathomed Tower	7"	Vinyl maniacs	VMS 004
2005 ☐	DOOMED FOR LIVE - REUNION 2002	2CD	Candlelight (USA)	CDL 0262 CD
2006 ☐	CANDLEMASS	2LPg	Black Lodge	BLOD 036 LP

Embossed cover. Bonus: Mars And Volcanos

2006 ☐	EPICUS DOOMICUS METALLICUS	2CD	Candlelight (USA)	CDL 0258 CD
2006 ☐	NIGHTFALL	2CD	Candlelight (USA)	CDL 0259 CD
2006 ☐	ANCIENT DREAMS	2CD	Candlelight (USA)	CDL 0260 CD
2006 ☐	TALES OF CREATION	2CD	Candlelight (USA)	CDL 0261 CD
2006 ☐	DACTYLIS GLOMERATA	2CD	GMR	GMRCD 2004

Bonus: Container/Thirst plus unreleased 9 track Abstrakt Algebra album. Slipcase..

2007 ☐	KING OF THE GREY ISLANDS	2LP	Nuclear Blast	NB 1818-1

Bonus: Solitude/At The Gallows End

2007 ☐	KING OF THE GREY ISLANDS	CDd	Nuclear Blast	NB 1818-0

Bonus: Solitude/At The Gallows End

2007 ■	KING OF THE GREY ISLANDS	CD	Nuclear Blast	NB 1818-2
2007 ☐	KING OF THE GREY ISLANDS	CD	Irond (Russia)	CD 07-1317
2007 ☐	KING OF THE GREY ISLANDS	CD	Icarus Music (Argentina)	ICARUS 361
2007 ☐	KING OF THE GREY ISLANDS	CD	Nuclear Blast America	NBA 11818B
2007 ☐	KING OF THE GREY ISLANDS – SPECIAL EDITION	CD box	Nuclear Blast	NB 1818-5

Steel box with the digi pack album + a 3" single with "Black Dwarf/Demonia 6. 500 copies.

2007 ☐	Black Dwarf (2007)/Demonia 6	7" PD	Nuclear Blast	NB 1988-7

500 copies.

2007 ■	FROM THE 13TH SUN	2LPg	Black Lodge/TNO	BLOD040LP/19

Bonus: Odessa Chamber/Socrates/John The Leper. New artwork. Lp 1 is red, Lp 2 transparent.vinyl.

2008 ☐	DACTYLIS GLOMERATA/ABSTRAKT ALGEBRA II	2CD	Peaceville	CDVILED217X

Bonus: Container/Thirst plus unreleased 9 track Abstrakt Algebra album.

2008 ☐	FROM THE 13TH SUN	CD	Peaceville	CDVILED 218

Bonus: Oil/Nimis/Rock 'N Roll

2008 ☐	LUCIFER RISING	CD	Nuclear Blast	2173-2
2008 ☐	LUCIFER RISING	CD	Irond (Russia)	CD 08-1530
2008 ☐	LUCIFER RISING	CD	Icarus Music (Argentina)	ICARUS 497
2008 ☐	LUCIFER RISING	CDd	Nuclear Blast	2173-0
2008 ☐	LUCIFER RISING	2LP	Nuclear Blast	2173-1
2008 ☐	LUCIFER RISING	CD	Nuclear Blast America	NBA 2173-2
2009 ■	If I Ever Die/Emperor Of The Void (Live)	7" PD	Nuclear Blast	NB 2372-9

500 copies.

2009 ☐	DEATH MAGIC DOOM	CD	Nuclear Blast	158071
2009 ☐	DEATH MAGIC DOOM	CD	Irond (Russia)	CD 09-1589
2009 ☐	DEATH MAGIC DOOM	CDd+DVD	Nuclear Blast	NB 2272-0

Bonus: Lucifer Rising. DVD featuring US Tour and Polar Studios

2009 ☐	DEATH MAGIC DOOM	LP+7"	Nuclear Blast	NB 2272-1

7" includes: Lucifer Rising (Album Outtake)/White God (NB 2272-1-2)

2005 7" - VMS 001

2005 7" - VMS 003

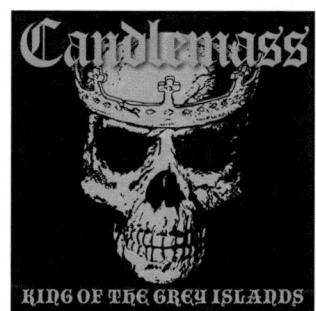

2007 CD - NB 1818-2

2007 2LPg - BLOOD040LP/19

2009 7" PD - NB 2372-9

2009 ■	DEATH MAGIC DOOM ....CD	Nuclear Blast America (USA)........ NBA 2272-2		
	Bonus: Lucifer Rising			
2009 ☐	DEATH MAGIC DOOM ....CDd+DVD	Nuclear Blast 158067		
2009 ☐	DEATH MAGIC DOOM ....LP+7"	Nuclear Blast 158153		
	7" includes: Lucifer Rising (Album Outtake)/White God			
2009 ☐	DEATH MAGIC DOOM ....CD	Avalon (Japan).............................MICP-10854		
	Bonus: Lucifer Rising/White God/Demons Gate (2009)/Emperor Of The Void (Live)/Black Dwarf (Live)			
2009 ☐	DEATH MAGIC DOOM ....CD	Icarus Music (Argentina)............. ICARUS 540		
2010 ☐	KING OF THE GREY ISLANDS.. 2LPg	Nuclear Blast ....NB 2591-1		
	Bonus: Solitude/At The Gallows End. 100 silver/grey vinyl. Also black vinyl.			
2010 ☐	Don't Fear The Reaper/All Along The Watchtower ....12"	Doom .... Doom 666	$	
	100 copies on blue vinyl. Only sold at anniversary gig.			
2010 ☐	Don't Fear The Reaper/All Along The Watchtower ....12"	High Roller ....HRR 155	$	
	100 black, 250 green, 250 red and 350 copies on blue vinyl.			
2010 ☐	NO SLEEP 'TIL ATHENS 2LPg	Nuclear Blast ....NB 2446-1		
	One blue and one white LP.			
2010 ■	ASHES TO ASHES ....CD+DVD	Nuclear Blast (USA)........................NB 2446-2		
2010 ☐	ASHES TO ASHES ....CD+DVD	Nuclear Blast ....NB 2562-2		
2010 ☐	ASHES TO ASHES 2LP	Nuclear Blast ....NB 2562-1		
	One blue and one yellow vinyl LP.			
2010 ☐	CANDLEMASS 2LP	Nuclear Blast ....NB 2590-1	$	
	100 copies in black/white flame vinyl + white or black vinyl. Bonus: Mars And Volcanos			
2010 ☐	EPICUS DOOMICUS METALLICUS.................................... LPg	Peaceville VILELP201		
	Red vinyl.			
2010 ☐	EPICUS DOOMICUS METALLICUS (+ Live in Birmingham) 2CD	Peaceville CDVILED201X		
2010 ☐	NIGHTFALL.. LPg	Peaceville VILELP202		
	Limited edition 180 g red vinyl.			
2010 ☐	DOOMOLOGY..5CD box	Nuclear Blast .... NB 2698-5		
	Box featuring: Live Jönköping 1987, Live Buckley Tivoli 1988, Demos 2003-2004, Demos King Of The Grey Islands, Demos 1992-2008. 1000 copies.			
2011 ☐	DOOMOLOGY...7LP box	High Roller ....HRR 166	$$	
	300 silver, 700 black, A1 poster, booklet.			
2012 ■	Dancing In The Temple Of The Mad Queen Bee/The Killing Of The Sun......12"	Napalm Records ....NPR 396		
	150 golden, 150 white and 500 on black vinyl.			
2012 ☐	PSALMS FOR THE DEAD...CD	Napalm Records ....NPR 427		
2012 ☐	PSALMS FOR THE DEAD..CD+DVD	Napalm Records ....NPR 427 LTD		
2012 ☐	PSALMS FOR THE DEAD..2LPg	Napalm Records ....NPR 427 LP	$	
	200 yellow + 250 green vinyl.			
2012 ☐	PSALMS FOR THE DEAD.......................................2LPg+7"	Napalm Records ....NPR 427 LP	$	
	Poster, post cards, booklet, bonus 7". 200 black, 300 gold/black, 300 gold marbled vinyl.			
2013 ☐	Candlemass vs. Entombed .... CDSg	Sweden Rock Magazine ..... (12-12/0446-4689)		
	Track: To Ride, Shoot Straight And Speak The Truth (Entombed cover).			

2009 CD - NBA 2272-2

2010 CD+DVD - NB 2446-2

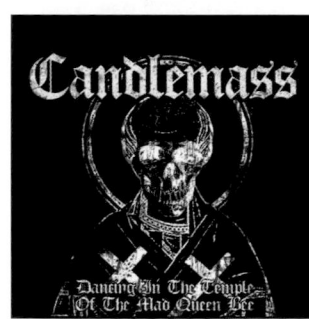

2012 12" - NPR 396

Unofficial recordings:

1989 ☐	CANDLEMASS 89 LIVE ....CD	- - .... - -		
	Live bootleg recorded in Greece 1989.			
1990 ■	DISCIPLES OF DOOM ....LP	Fan Club Records.............................. CLUB 5		
	Live bootleg recorded in Birmingham in 1988. 500 copies.			
1991 ☐	DARK ARE THE VEILS OF DETROIT ....LP	- - .... - -		
	Live bootleg recorded in Detroit in 1991.			
2002 ☐	DEMONS GATE...CD	Volve Recs..2002		
	Compilation of rare tracks. 550 copies.			
1995 ☐	SJUNGER SIGGE FÜRST...LP	Heavy Metal House 002 .... LP LE 001	$$	
	Contains 4 tracks from the Sigge Fürst MCD + Black Sabbath medley, Countess Bathory, Solitude '87, Crystal Ball '87, The End Of Pain. 200 copies.			
2002 ☐	LIVE REFLECTIONS ....CD	- - .... - -		
	Recorded in Stockholm and Sweden Rock 2002.			
2008 ☐	DACTYLIS GLOMERATA...LP	Music For Nations (Brazil) ....MFN 237		
	Black or blue vinyl.			
2008 ☐	Epicus Doomicus Hellenicus ....7"	- - (Greece) .... - -		
	Tracks: Solitude/Crystalk Ball. Live. Clear vinyl. 50 copies according to label.			
2010 ☐	DARK REFELCTIONS...LP	- - .... - -		
	100 numbered copies. Compilation.			

1990 LP - CLUB 5

CANDY KICKS ASS
Niklas Bentholm: v, Ronny Normi: g, Patric Wahlquist: g,
Örjan Andersson: b, Jonas Lundberg: d

Katrineholm/Stockholm - The band was formed in 1991 when Patric and Jonas left garage rockers *The Slammers. Candy Kicks Ass* play guitar-based garage attitude heavy rock with a touch of Seattle. The CDS was produced by Tomas Skogsberg. In 1995 the band moved from Katrineholm to Stockholm. After the MCD Daniel Andersson replaced Ronny. The band is also found on the compilation *Kakafoni* ('94 Kakafoni). A new demo-album was recorded in 1995.

1993 ■	Pain/Dirty Machine/Don't Get Me Wrong ....MCD 3tr	private .... ka 001		

1993 MCD - ka 001

CANDY ROXX

Magnus "Max Newman" Brunzell: v, Johan "Joan Strauss" Boding: g, Tord-Martin "Pat Raven" Pettersson: g, Ulf "Sebastian Gant" Waldekrantz: k, Mats "Randy Johansen" Johansson: b, Johan "Kid Tiffany" Malmgren: d

Stockholm - The band was formed in January 1983 under the name *Randy Coxx*, but had to change it to *Candy Roxx*. They recorded the first single four months later. Initially, they were more about image than actual music and with such stage-names... The songs on the first single were written by Kee Marcello and Peo Thyrén (at that time in *Easy Action*) just as an attempt to get the band a deal. The first singles are quite glam-poppy but they transformed into a sleazy glam-oriented hard rock band. On *Sex & Leather* Randy replaced Rex "Luger" Gisslén and Tord-Martin replaced Mats "Rio" Ingwall. The band recorded a full length album for UK label MFN (Music For Nations) after the MLP. They had then been asked to change into the same style as *Metallica*. However they overdid it and became too heavy for MFN (?!). Magnus later formed *Nio Liv*, that became *Ban-Zai*. Rex joined popsters *Shanghai*, recorded meek Euro-disco under his own name and later worked as producer (*Candlemass*). In 1995 *Candy Roxx* made a re-union gig with Magnus, Rex, Johan, Tord-Martin and ex-*Ban-Zai* man Conny Goldschmidt.

1983 7" - 818 026-7

1983 7" - 812 303-7

1983 ■	Signal/Som En Satellit	7"	Mercury	812 303-7
1983 ■	Tomorrow And Tonight/Churchyard Go Go	7"	Mercury	818 026-7
1984 ☐	Sex & Leather	MLP 6tr	Sword	SWORDMLP 006
	Tracks: Sex And Leather/Hey Hey Hey/Macho Man/I'm The Leader Of The Gang (Gary Glitter cover)/Over And Out			
1984 ■	Sex & Leather	MLP 6tr	Sword	SWO 12 006
	Second pressing with new artwork.			
1984 ☐	Sex & Leather/Macho Man	7"	Sword	SWO 7 006

SEX AND LEATHER
1984 MLP - SWO 12 006 (new artw.)

CANE

Anders Lindberg: v, Aris Restaino: g,
Reijo Suonuieri: b, Hans Lindström: d

Stockholm - The members themselves label their music "happy metal". Good solid melodic hard rock with powerful guitar work, high class vocals and an overall positive attitude. There's a slightly sleazy feel to some of the tracks. Good stuff.

1994 ○	It's Only In The Movies/I'll Do It For You	CDS 2tr	AHAR Production	CANECDS 01
1995 ■	With A Smile	MCD 5tr	AHAR Production	CANECDS 2
	Tracks: No, No, No, No/No Light On The Horizon/With A Smile/Eat Up Your Garbage/Two Mens Law			

1995 MCD - CANECDS 2

CANOPY

Fredrik Huldtgren: v, Jonatan Hedlin: g, Erik Björkman: g,
Daniel Ahlm: b, Peter Lindqvist: d

Stockholm - *Canopy* play quite melodic death metal in the vein of *Edge Of Sanity*. Great guitar work and great song, but quite uninteresting and low mixed growling vocals. Lindqvist is ex-*Decadence*. Dan Swanö makes a guest appearance on *During Day One*, while Kristian Niemann and John Råd Juvas guests on *Will & Perception*. The 2009 release *Will & Perception* features rerecordings of the tracks from the MCD plus three more tracks, one hailing back to *During Day One*. In 2010 the band released the new album *Menhir*, initially only as a digital release, but later as a digi-pack CD.

2004 ☐	During Day One	MCD	private	n/a
	Tracks: Common Walls/During Day One/Symbiotic/Shades Of Truth			
2005 ☐	Will & Perception	MCD 5tr	private	n/a
	Tracks: Decipher/Perception/For The Sickened Voice To Hear/Void/Will. The second pressing contains a bonus video of For The Sickened Voice To Hear.			
2006 ■	SERENE CATHARSIS	CD	Disconcert Music	DM 0989 2
2009 ☐	WILL & PERCEPTION	CD	Disconcert Music	DM 1433 2
2010 ☐	MENHIR	CDd	private	n/a

CANOPY
SERENE CATHARSIS
2006 CD - DM 0989 2

CANS

Joacim Cans: v, Metal Mike Chlasciak: g, Stefan Elmgren: g, Daniele Soravia: k
Mat Sinner: b, Mark Zonder: d

Göteborg - When *HammerFall* singer Joacim Cans decided to record a solo effort he didn't go as far as he did with the retro-rocking *Mrs. Hippe* album, but instead he went in a similar direction as his main band, melodic power metal, at time a bit more aggressive and at times adding keyboards to the brew. The musicians in the "band" are no noobes, Metal Mike has played with *Halford*, Soravia with *Moonlight Circus*, Mat Sinner with *Sinner* and *Primal Fear*, while Zonder is ex-*Warlord*, with whom Joacim recorded one album. The album also features guest appearances from Gus G (*Dream Evil, Ozzy, Firewind*), Danny Gill (*Speak No Evil*), Oscar Dronjac (*HammerFall*) and Mats Rendlert (*Infinity, Dreamland, Sandalinas*).

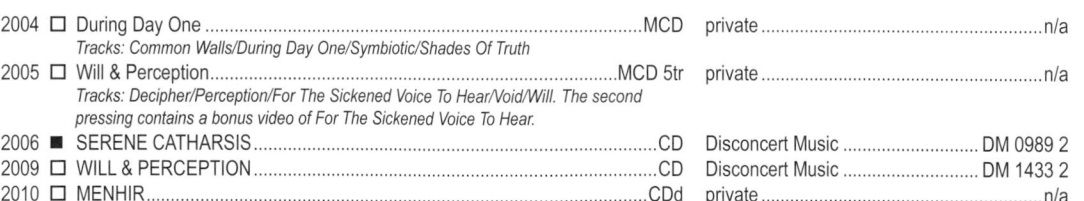

Cans imitating a carpenter?

2004 CD - N 0392 2

2004	☐ BEYOND THE GATES	CDd	Noise	N 0392 9
2004	■ BEYOND THE GATES	CD	Noise	N 0392 2

CAP OUTRUN
Andrée Theander: g, Erik Wiss: k

Skara/Piteå - *Cap Outrun* was formed in 2007 during the two members' education of Music And Sound Production in Skara/Skövde. The music is excellent well-played progressive rock/metal in the vein of **Galleon, Cross** meets **The Flower Kings**, but with a slightly heavier and more guitar driven edge. At times really heavy, at times quite jazzy with great guitar playing. Bass on the CD played by David Sivelind, drums by Mauritz Petersson (**Backwater**) and the vocal duties were shared among Thomas Kihlberg (**Backwater**), Martin Olsson, Jonas Källsbäck and Petter Boström. Wiss is also found in Lund-based pop/rockers **Fairfield**, with whom he has made several recordings. Because of geographical differences the band has been slow. Theander also has an AOR/Westcoast project called **Andrée Theander Expression**.

2008 MCDp - NB 805-1

2008	■ Influence Grind	MCDp	private	NB 805-1

Tracks: My Call/Spaces In Between/All I Need Is On My Kite/A Flash Of Deviation/Hand Of Time/Leaving The Grind

CAPRICORN
Mats Levén: v, Anders Ericson: g, Anders Skoog: k, Ulf Jansson: b, Jamie Borger: d

Göteborg - This was actually the debut for now highly acclaimed singer Mats Levén, later in **Swedish Erotica, Treat, Abstrakt Algebra, AB/CD, Therion, Candlemass** etc, as well as drummer Jamie Borger, who would later find fame in **Treat** and **Talisman**. You can certainly hear he was a diamond in the rough on this recording, even though Levén has come a long way since. Musically **Capricorn** delivers high-quality ballsy AOR with a strong American touch. Recommended. The band also recorded a 5-track demo well worth looking for.

1987 7" - W 45-01

1987	■ Sheyla/The Silent Cry (Tonight's The Night)	7"	private	W 45-01	$

CAPTAIN CRIMSON
Mikael Läth: d, Stefan Norén: v/g, Anders Tallfors: b, Andreas Eriksson: g

Umeå - Formed in November 2011. The name is most likely a combiantion of the bands **Captain Beyond** and **King Crimson**, which also the album title *Dancing Madly Backwards* points at (a **Captain Beyond** song title). The music is of course very retro-oriented early seventies hard rock, which should appeal to fans of new retro bands such as **Graveyard** and **Witchcraft**.

2012 CDd - TRANS 100

2012	■ DANCING MADLY BACKWARDS	CDd	Transubstans	TRANS 100
2013	☐ DANCING MADLY BACKWARDS	LP	White Dwarf	WHD 002

CAPTAIN FREAK'S FREAKY FUNKSTERS
Niklas Jonsson: v, Christian Fecht: g, Robert Kenndal: b, Gustav Liljenström: d

Norrköping - Formed in 1990 under the name *Nazty Habitz*. In 1991 they won the recording of a single in a bandstand. Just before the single was released they changed their name to **Captain Freak's Freaky Funksters**. **CFFF** are heavily influenced by **Electric Boys** and **Extreme**, with a fat and juicy guitar sound. A little weak in the vocal department, though. Great production by Stefan Pettersson and Daniel Gese (member of **Pole Position**). They later changed bass-player and in 1994 released a 5 track CD under the name **Battle Station**, but reformed as **Millhouse**.

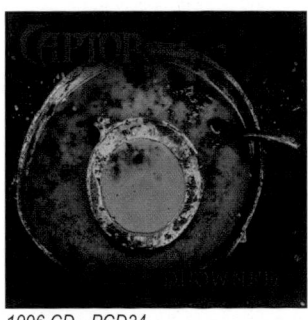
1991 7" - NASTY 01

1991	■ Cheap 'N Nasty/Suzie	7"	KFUM	NASTY 01

CAPTOR
Magnus Fasth: v, Fredrik Olofsson: g, Niklas Kullström: g,
Christoffer Andersson: b, Angelo Mikai: d

Katrineholm - Formed in 1989 and made their first demo in 1991. Well-played, tight death metal with a thrashy feel. Two songs can also be found on a local cassette *Christmas-compilation* and on the *Extreme Close-Up Vol 1* compilation CD. The first CD and the compilation tracks were recorded with Jacob Nordangård on bass and lead vocals. The track *My Head* was also featured on Border Music's '95 promo compilation *Svenskt*. On *Drowned* guitarist Jonnie Carlsson was repleaced by Nicklas. Also featured on *Die Hard 96 Catalogue Update* compilation (Die Hard 96).

1993	☐ LAY IT TO REST	CD	Euro Records	EURO 933-CD
1995	☐ Refuse To Die	MCD 5tr	Dolphin Productions	DMPCDS 07

Tracks: Refuse To Die/My Head/Insane/More Life/Circle Of Hate

1996	■ DROWNED	CD	Die Hard	PCD34
1997	☐ DROWNED	CD	Avalon Marquee (Japan)	MICY-1011

Bonus: Down

1997	☐ DOGFACE	CD	Die Hard	PCD 42

1996 CD - PCD34

CARBONIZED

Christofer Johnson: g/v, Lars Rosenberg: b, Piotr Wawrzeniuk: d

Stockholm - The band was founded by Lars in 1988 and the first demo *Au-To-Dafe* was recorded the year after. The line-up was the same as on the first 7"; drummer Markus Rüden, bassist Lars, singer Matti Kärki (later in **Therion, Carnage, Dismember**) and guitarists Stefan Ekström and Jonas Derouche. The debut 7" was well played technical death, with good production. Matti then left to join **Carnage** and off went Ekström and Rüden, too. They later turned up in **Morpheus**. Piotr took over the drums and Jonas took over the vocals. This line-up recorded the second demo *Recarbonized* in May 1990. When Christofer joined it became more of a studio project than a regular band. When they recorded *Disharmonization*, Piotr was also in **The Robots**, Christofer in **Therion** and Lars was in **Entombed**. The later recordings were more schizo death metal with disharmonic instrumental passages similar to **Heavy The World** or a more metallic and depressed **Primus**. *Screaming Machines* is even weirder with influences ranging from punk to psych to death. The album was recorded already in 1993. The band was put on hold and all three members later joined **Therion**. The records were born at Sunlight Studios. The track *The Monument* is also found on the 7" compilation *Chronology Of Death* (91 Blackout Zine).

1990 7" - THR 003

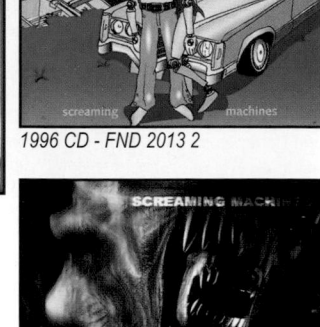

1996 CD - FND 2013 2

1990 ■	No Canonizations/Statues/Au-to-dafé	7" 3tr	Thrash Records	THR 003
	Available with black/white or blue cover.			
1990 ☐	FOR THE SECURITY	LP	Thrash Records	THR 011
1990 ☐	FOR THE SECURITY	CD	Thrash Records	THR 011 CD
1993 ☐	DISHARMONIZATION	CD	Foundations 2000	FDN 2006 2
1996 ■	SCREAMING MACHINES	CD	Foundations 2000	FND 2013 2
2003 ☐	DISHARMONIZATION	CD	Irond (Russia)	CD 03-699
2003 ☐	FOR THE SECURITY	CD	Irond (Russia)	CD 03-698
2003 ■	SCREAMING MACHINES	CD	Irond (Russia)	CD 03-703
2013 ☐	DEMO COLLECTION	CD	Flames Of Hell	FOH 00

2003 CD - CD 03-703

CARDINAL SIN

Magnus "Devo" Andersson: g, John Zweetsloot: g,
Alex Losbäck: b, Jocke Göthberg: v/d

Göteborg - **Cardinal Sin** was a thrash-oriented death metal formed by Zwetsloot in 1994. On the recording of the MCD, the band featured Zwetsloot, Göthberg and Andersson. "Devo" later joined **Marduk** and also had his solo project **Overflash**, John was ex-**Dissection, Nifelheim, The Haunted** and later in **Decameron** and Jocke was ex-**Grave, Marduk, In Flames, Miscreant** and **Darkified** later also in **Dimension Zero**.

1996 ■	Spiceful Intents	MCD 4tr	Wrong Again	WAR 010
	Tracks: Spiteful Intent/Probe With A Quest/The Cardinal Sin/Language Of Sorrow			

1996 MCD - WAR 010

CARIZMA RAIN

Arvin Yarollahi: v/g, Jonas Gembäck: g, Anders Kampe: k, Ellen Hjalmarsson: violin,
Jesper Arnö: b, Jesper Miller: d

Lerum/Göteborg - The band was formed in 1998, by, at the time, 16 year old boys Miller, Gembäck and Arnö. Later on Yarollahi and Kampe joined. They were inspired by bands like **Queen** and **Toto**, but also Latino music. The band added choir girls Caroline Stadelman and Angelica Dimakis live, but they left the band a year later. Two demos were recorded with this line-up. In 2000 they recorded the first demo CD-R *Clear Your Mind*, before Maja left the band. After this they recorded the second MCD, *Wide Awake*. The band folded in 2001, when singer Arvin moved to the UK for studies. The band changed its name to **50 Minutes Of Fame** and went through several singers, now playing covers. The band finally folded in 2006. *Carizma Rain* play melodic rock, ranging from quite poppy and funky AOR/Westcoast, to **It Bites** style melodic rock with folkish overtones. A great release for melodic rock fans.

2001 MCD - PROCK 2000

2001 ■	Wide Awake	MCD 4tr	private	PROCK 2000
	Tracks: Stay With Me/I Feel/Clear Your Mind/Free			

CARLSSON, PATRIK

Patrik Carlsson: g/b/d

Norrköping - Patrik was born in 1972, started out playing piano but soon wanted to be a guitar-equipped rocker instead. Influenced by **Steve Vai, Joe Satriani** and local hero **Pole Position/ Neondaze/Fair Of Freaks** guitarist Lars Boquist, he started recording his own stuff. His demo *Figstamper '02* lead to a deal with Lion Music. Patrik is an outstanding guitarist well worth checking out for fans of the Shrapnel catalogue of shredders. Great technique and great songs.

2004 ■	PHRASEOLOGY	CD	Lion Music	LMC 107
2006 ☐	MELODIC TRAVEL	CD	Lion Music	LMC 192

2004 CD - LMC 107

CARNAGE

Matti Kärki: v, Michael Amott: g, David Blomqvist: g, Johnny Dordevic: b, Fred Estby: d

Växjö/Stockholm - **Carnage** was formed in late 1988 by guitarist Michael Amott and Johan Axelsson (now Liiva) (ex-**Mortal Abuse**), initially as a grindcore band, but evolved into death metal, one of the first in Sweden. Michael had previously played with crust punk band **Disaccord**, whose song *Evil Lives Among Us* is found on the *Hardcore For The Masses* compilation (88 Uproar). He later joined English band **Carcass** with whom he recorded and toured. He later formed the awesome 70s influenced hard rock band **Spiritual Beggars**, and is also busy in **Arch Enemy**. The first demo *The Day Man Lost* (1989) was recorded with Michael, Johan, Johnny Dordevic (ex-**Mortal Abuse**) and drummer Jesper Larsson (ex-**Medicin Rain**) while the line-up on the second demo, *Infestation Of Evil* (1989) featured Estby on drums. The 7" also featured Michael, Fred, Johnny and Johan. The band only made three live performances. This is raw old-school death metal similar to **Dismember** and early **Entombed**. They were produced by Tomas Skogsberg (**Entombed** etc.). Dordevic was credited on the album, but the bass was actually played by Dordevic, Amott and Fred Estby. Axelsson/Liiva later joined **Jesusexercise**, **Furbowl** and **Arch Enemy** and recorded with his solo project **Nonexist**, while Johnny went to **Entombed** (as singer). David was also briefly in **Entombed**. Matti Kärki was also found in grindcore band **General Surgery**. Matti, David and Fred later reformed **Dismember** and Dordevic was found in **Hypnosia**.

1989 7" - DH 003

1990 CD - 88561-1105-2

2000 CD - MOSH 232 CD

1989 ■	Live Stockholm, Swe. 4.11.89	7" 4tr	Distorted Harmony (Mexico)	DH 003
	Tracks: Torn Apart/Crime Against Humanity/The Day Man Lost/Infestation Of Evil. 1000 copies.			
1990 ☐	DARK RECOLLECTIONS	LP	Necrosis	NECRO 003
1990 ☐	DARK RECOLLECTIONS/HALLUCINATING ANXIETY (split)	CD	Necrosis	NECRO 003/004 CD
	Split with Cadaver.			
1990 ■	DARK RECOLLECTIONS	CD	Relativity Records (USA)	88561-1105-2
2000 ■	DARK RECOLLECTIONS	CD	Earache	MOSH 232 CD
	Bonus: Crime Against Humanity/Aftermath/The Day Man Lost/Crime Against Humanity/ Aftermath/The Day Man Lost/Torn Apart/Infestation Of Evil			

CARNAL FORGE

Jens C Mortensen: v, Petri Kuusito: g, Jari Kuusisto: g,
Lars Lindén: b, Stefan Westerberg: d

Sala - The band was formed in 1997 by **In Thy Dreams** members Stefan (also in **Steel Attack**) and Jari. Guitarist Johan Magnusson, bass player Dennis Vestman and singer Jonas Kjellgren (**Centinex, Dellamorte, Scar Symmetry** etc.) made their way into the band and they soon recorded their first and only demo *Sweet Bride* in Studio Underground. They were soon picked up by Wrong Again Records and recorded the debut. Not much happened and soon Dennis left. He was replaced by Jari's brother Petri (**In Thy Dreams, Steel Attack**) and the band recorded the second album, *Firedemon*. Before the third album, Magnusson decided to leave. Petri switched to guitar and Lars Lindén (**Rosicrucian, Slapdash, Zeelion**), who had actually worked with the recordings of the band in Studio Undeground, took care of the bass duties. In 2004 the band recorded the live DVD *Destroy Live*. After this Kjellgren decided to leave the band and he was replaced by Jens C Mortensen. Extremely powerful old-school thrash, but with a touch of **Pantera**. *Please...Die* showed a bit more nuances than its predecessors. After *Testify For My Victims* some line-up changes happened. Mortensen was replaced by Peter Tuthill (**Construcdead, Backdraft, Dog Faced Gods**) and Jari was replaced by Dino Medanhodzic. In January 2010 the band also announced the departure of drummer Westerberg who would now join **Headstone** and the reunited **Steel Attack**. Chris Barkensjö (**Construdead, Grave**) replaced him, but he was also replaced, by Lawrence Dinamarca (**Loch Vostock**). Vestman later joined **Steel Attack** and is today in melodic rockers **Grand Design**.
Website: www.carnalforge.se

May the forge be with you!

2000 CD - 77312-2

2007 CD - CANDLE 178 CD

1998 ☐	WHO'S GONNA BURN	CD	WAR	WAR 0006
1999 ☐	WHO'S GONNA BURN	CD	Relapse Records	RR 6418
2000 ☐	FIREDEMON	CD	Century Media (USA)	8012-2
2000 ■	FIREDEMON	CD	Century Media	77312-2
2000 ☐	FIREDEMON	LP PD	Century Media	77312-1P
2001 ☐	PLEASE... DIE!	CD	Century Media (USA)	8098-2
2001 ☐	PLEASE... DIE!	CD	Century Media	77398-2
2003 ☐	THE MORE YOU SUFFER	CD	Century Media	74982-2
2003 ☐	THE MORE YOU SUFFER	CD	Century Media (USA)	8198-2
2003 ☐	THE MORE YOU SUFFER	CD	Soundholic (Japan)	TKCS-85056
	Bonus: Hits You Like A Hammer/Bullet Proof God Material			
2003 ☐	WHO'S GONNA BURN	CD	Regain Records	RR 0305-030
	Re-issue with new artwork.			
2004 ☐	AREN'T YOU DEAD YET?	CD	Century Media	75982-2
2004 ☐	AREN'T YOU DEAD YET?	CD	Soundholic (Japan)	TKCS-85097
	Bonus tracks: Ruler Of Your Blood/God's Enemy No 1			
2007 ■	TESTIFY FOR MY VICTIMS	CD	Candlelight	CANDLE 178 CD
2007 ☐	TESTIFY FOR MY VICTIMS	CD	Candlelight (USA)	CDL 346 CD

CARNAL GRIEF

Jonas Carlsson: v, André Alvinzi: g, Jonas Lindgren: g,
Johan Olsen: b, Henrik Brander: d

Arboga - This combo was formed in 1997 and released three demos before making their CD debut in 2004. André is also found in *Coldworker*. The track *Mythomania* is found on the *From The Underground* (1998 X-treme) compilation. Well played, well-produced melodic death metal with a metal edge and with lots of nice guitar harmony work.

2004 CD - TRHK 003

2004 ■	OUT OF CRIPPLED SEEDS	CD	Trinity Records (Hong Kong)	TRHK 003
2006 ☐	NINE SHADES OF PAIN	CD	GMR	GMRCD 9002

CARNALIST

Hampus Olsson: v, Niklas Lindeke: g, Jonas Nilsson: g, Sonny Mery: d

Ystad - *Carnalist* started out in 2005 under the name *H.I.V* formed by Mery and Lindeke. Metal and beer was what brought the two together. They changed their name to *Huj Babajaga* (means "cock-witch" in Polish…) and their style was thrash/death inspired by *Slayer* and *Behemoth*. Late 2006 Bruhn joined. They still had problems finding a suitable singer, but shortly after changing their name to *Carnalist* in 2007, they found singer Olsson and they finally could start playing live and soon recorded their first release, *The Art Of Extirpation*, which was released as a pro-printed CD-R. Quite technical and well played high-speed death metal.

2009 MCD - GORE 014

2009 ■	Genocide And The Supremacy Of Aggression	MCD 5tr	Goregeous Records	GORE 014

Tracks: Genocide And The Supremacy Of Aggression/Thus Spoke the Butcher's Knife/ Malicious Compulsion/Surgical Deviance/New Form of Life

CARNIVAL SUN

Niklas Svensson: v, Andreas Hall: g, Niclas "Ankan" Lundgren: b, Jesper Persson: d

Kristianstad - *Carnival Sun* was formed in 2004 by Hall and Persson (*Alicate*). They found singer Niklas Svensson (*Blinded Colony, The Random Riots*), who shared the same musical taste. Without having found a permanent bassist, they recorded their first demo *Beggars & Boozehounds* in 2006 and already then showed great promise with their fuel driven, raw, driving southern infused hard rock in, a bit like *Bonafide* meets *Rival Sons*. In April 2007 they found bass player Tobbe Skogh. He played on the debut album, but left before its release to devote his time to *The Itch*, and Lundgren was drafted. Niklas is the son of *Overdrive* drummer Kenta Svensson, who also makes a guest appearance on harmonica. Highly recommended. A new record is in the making, where the band does covers of *Overdrive* songs. Late 2012 Svensson left the band to devote his time to *The Random Riots*.
Website: www.carnivalsun.net

2011 LP - CSR 001

2011 ■	SUN OF A BITCH	LP+CD	private	CSR 001

LP with listening CD in paper pocket. 300 hand numbered copies.

2011 ☐	SUN OF A BITCH	CDp	private	CSR 001-1

CD in paper pocket., included with the LP.

CARPE WADE

Fredrik Enqvist: v/b, Jonathan Enmark: g, Mats Hammarström: g, Nils Angnarsson: d

Skellefteå - Formed in 1993. This started out as quite an interesting band that was picking and choosing riffs and chords from the good old 70s hard rock, *Hendrix* and *Pearl Jam* as well as the new power metal style. *Full Circle* is quite an outstanding rocker of an album with a great bluesy Strat-sound. *Elvis* is all *Elvis Presley* covers, except the tribute song *Elvis*. Through the years they however changed more and more towards power-pop/new wave and in 1998 they shortened their name to *Wade* (forced by their US label Interscope) and have released more records under that name in a less interesting vein.

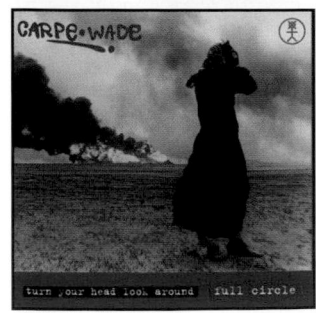

1994 CD - WeCD 070

1993 ☐	Porch Light	MCD	A Westside Fabrication	WeCD 067
1994 ■	FULL CIRCLE	CD	A Westside Fabrication	WeCD 070
1994 ☐	Snow	MCD	A Westside Fabrication	WeCD 077
1995 ☐	Spots	MCD	A Westside Fabrication	WeCD 092
1995 ☐	EVIDENCE	CD	A Westside Fabrication	WeCD 094
1996 ☐	Summer Party Romance	MCD 4tr	A Westside Fabrication	WeCD 125

Tracks: Summer Party Romance/Stop To Say Hello/Miss Universe/Insidiors Giver

1997 ☐	Never/Pavement	CDS 2tr	A Westside Fabrication	WeCD 136
1997 ☐	Superball	CDS	A Westside Fabrication	WeCD 140
1997 ☐	ODD MAN OUT	CD	A Westside Fabrication	WeCD 142
1997 ☐	Elvis	MCD 6tr	A Westside Fabrication	WeCD 147

Tracks: Elvis/Suspicious Minds/In The Ghetto/It's Now Or Never/Burning Love/Always On My Mind

CARPET KNIGHTS, THE
Magnus Nilsson: v/flute, Joakim Jönsson: g, Tobias Wulff: g,
Pär Hallgren: b, Pelle Engvall: d

Malmö - *The Carpet Knights* was formed in 1998 and recorded several demos before being picked up by Transubstans. Not sure how to label this band, but in the first track on *Lost And So Strange Is My Mind* **Jethro Tull** comes to mind. In other tracks they show a heavier side, a bit closer to Krautrockers **Epitaph** or **Granmax**, and even some acid riffing akin to **Sir Lord Baltimore**. Seventies influenced acidy proto-hard rock with a touch of psych. After the first album drummer Mattias Ankarbranth was replaced by **Svarte Pan** drummer Pelle and before the second release also bass player Nils Andersson was replaced by Hallgren (ex-**Sgt. Sunshine**). Jönsson, Wulff and Hallgren also play in the **Öresund Space Collective**. Jönsson is also in **Bland Bladen** together with former (not on record) *Carpet Knight* Andreas Gärtner.

2005 CD - TRANS 009   2009 CD - TRANS 049

2005 ■ LOST AND SO STRANGE IS MY MIND.......................................CD Transubstans ....TRANS 009
2009 ■ ACCORDING TO LIFE...CD Transubstans ....TRANS 049

CARRIE
Thord Jonsson: v, Bengt Thand: g, Lennart Thand: k,
Mats Pettersson: b, Roland Eriksson: d

Frösön - The band was formed in 1983, initially with Per Eriksson on vocals. Thord later replaced Per and the band released the self-financed single in 1000 copies. Bengt left and was replaced by Ulf Lagesten in 1987. Shortly after Lennart left. Thord, Mats and Roland are still around as a cover band with some original material. The name of the band is **Smalare Än Thord** (Thinner Than Thord). The A-side is a gem for fans of the 80s wave of melodic Swedish hard rock, in the vein of **Frontiers, Talk Of The Town** etc., while the B-side owes more to the likes of **Saga** and early **Toto**. Good performance, both vocally and musically, with a surprising slide-guitar solo on the B-side.

1985 7" - CAR 001

1985 ■ At Night (You're Stealing My Heart)/Lonely Man.............................7" private .... CAR 001

CARTAGO
Olle Ekstubbe: v, Peter Klintberg: g, Jesse Andersson: k/g,
Marku Larsson (Väkevä): b, Anders Viberg: d

Södertälje - The band was formed under the name **Högtryck,** initially playing jazz-rock. The first release was more poppy, in the vein of **Magnum Bonum**, while the second is first rate AOR with great vocals, quite similar to Daniel Borch (**Alien**). After the first single singer Thorbjörn Rapp was replaced by Olle and keyboardist/guitarist Jesse Andersson was added to the line-up. Classy production. The second single was partly recorded in Thunderload Studios (owned by the Wahlqvist brothers of **Heavy Load**). *Wait For The Dreams* is a great, driven melodic rocker with really heavy guitars. Highly recommended. The band split in 1995. In 2011 *Cartago* was resurrected, now featuring original members Peter, Marku and Anders, joined by **Reloaded** members Peter Alstermark (v) and Anders Plassgård (k).

1978 7" - BAS-S 007

1978 ■ Kontakt/Allt Det Du Gjort...7" Bastun.............................BAS-S 007
1990 ■ Hold On To Your Love/Wait For The Dreams..................................7" private CAR-001

1990 7" - CAR-001

CARVE
Rogga Johansson: v/g, Emil Koverot: g, C. Nyhlén: b, Mathias Fiebig: d

Gamleby - *Stillborn Revelations* was actually two separate recordings merged into one album. The only members featured on the entire album are Rogga (**Paganizer, Edge Of Sanity, Ribspreader, Deranged** etc) and Mathias (**Blodsrit, Portal, Paganizer**). Half the album features guitarist Andreas Carlsson and bass player Oskar Nilsson (**Paganizer, Unchained**), while the second half features Emil Koverot (**Portal, Blodsrit**) on lead guitar and J Diener on bass. According to Rogga the second album was actually also two separate recordings, but demos with drum machine recorded for the **Vomitory** drummer to check out. When the label wanted a new **Carve** album and couldn't offer any recording budget Rogga used the programmed drums for the recordings of the album. Brutal death metal in the vein of early **Entombed** with gut-wrenching artwork to top it off.

2002 CD - BHP 003

2002 ■ STILLBORN REVELATIONS ....CD Black Hole productions .... BHP 003
2004 ■ REVEL IN HUMAN FILTH...CD Black Hole productions .... BHP 010

2004 CD - BHP 010

CASABLANCA

Anders Ljung: v, Ryan Roxie: g, Erik Stenemo: g,
Mats Rubarth: b, Josephine Forsman: d

Stockholm - A new melodic hard rock act formed in 2008, featuring American gone Swedish guitarist Ryan Roxie (*Alice Cooper, Dad's Porno Mag, Roxie 77*). Ljung is ex-*Space Age Baby Jane*, Forsman in *Sahara Hotnights*, Stenemo is ex-*Melody Club*, while Rubath is a former soccer player in AIK. Style-wise it's not too far from *Roxie '77*'s *Cheap Trick* meets *Enuff Z'Nuff* with a touch of *Skid Row* style pop-tinged melodic classic seventies influenced hard rock. The band supported *Kiss* in Sweden in 2010. *Apocalyptic Youth* was produced by Chris Laney.

2011 CD - ROCKET 008

2010 ☐	Kings, Queens & Guillotines	MCD 6tr	Hagenburg	692.999 DR 853	$$

Tracks: Secret Angels Of Lust/Rich Girls/Celebrity Wasted/Love And Desperation/Beast Of Summer/Downtown

2011 ■	APOCALYPTIC YOUTH	CD	Rocket Songs	ROCKET 008	
2012 ☐	APOCALYPTIC YOUTH	CD	Rocket Songs	ROCKET 010	
2013 ☐	RIDING A BLACK SWAN	CD	Gain	n/a	

CASE, (THE)

Billy Nordström: v, Håkan Zetterkvist: g, Åke Andersson,
Peter Persson: b, Peter Sehlstedt

Nyköping - The first two singles were melodic hard rock, at times with a touch of *Magnum Bonum*. After the first singles the vocals were handled by Ubbe Rydeslätt (*Snakepit Rebels, Steel Arrows*), but he left before the third release. He had however co-written the single track. The last single is quite pompous AOR. Ubbe and Håkan were later in punksters *Blind System*. On the third single the "The" had been dropped. *Leader Of The Gang* is a cover of *Gary Glitter*.

1982 7" - ELO 1001

1982 ■	Ge Mig En Chans/Du Faller	7"	Election	ELO 1001
1982 ☐	Svara Hallå/Blå Kostym	7"	Election	ELO 1004
1988 ☐	Look At Me Now/Look At Me Now (instrumental)	7"	Hawk	HAWKS 1127
1989 ☐	Leader Of The Gang/Leader Of The Gang (Boys mix)	7"	Dixie	DIXIES 151

CASINO RANGERS

Mathias: v, Glenn: g, Nalle: g, Chris: b, Kicko: d

Stockholm - Quite energetic mid-range sleazy hard rock, at times similar to *Faster Pussycat* in *Nightmares*, while *Institution of Pain* is more rock 'n' roll glammy in its style.

1991 7" - CAS 006

1991 ■	Nightmares/Institution Of Pain	7"	Transfer Music Products	CAS 006

CASKET CASEY

Cia Hedmark: v, Mikael Lång: g, Mattias Marklund: g,
Patrik Pettersson: b, Stefan Strömberg: d

Skellefteå - The band was formed in 2001 by Pettersson and Marklund (*Vintersorg, Otyg*), but nothing happened until Cia Marklund (*Otyg, Vintersorg*) joined in 2003. Early 2004 drummer Strömberg joined. The band was named after a female necrophiliac (sounds like a paradox…). Even though the band is signed to a horror punk label, the music is way more elaborate. Good melancholic, melodic and slightly gothy, but not as dark hard rock. The band announced plans for a full length album in 2005, but nothing happened. Guitarist Lång is ex-*Soulreaper*.

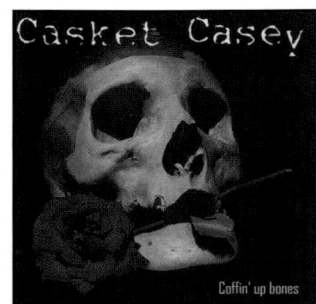

2005 ■	Coffin' Up Bones	MCD 4tr	Blood And Guts Records	BGRCD 005

Tracks: Back To Life/Cold Flesh And Blue/She's Been Bad/Still

CASTILLION

Ulf Sörman: g/v, Robert Örnesved: g, Magnus Stenberg: b, Johannes Berg: g

Stockholm - Formed in 2002 and recorded a video demo the same year, followed by *Demon Demon* in 2005. *Castillon* play high-quality progressive melodic metal similar to *Hollow*. Berg is also found in *Semlah*. The CD-R album *Triumph And Tragedy* was released in 2007.

2005 MCD - BGRCD 005

2013 ■	PIECES OF A SHATTERED ME	CD	private	(CASTILLION)

CAUTERIZER

Gunnar Berglindh: v, Jesper Bood: g, Michael Samuelsson: g,
Andreas Frisk: b, Iman Zolgharnian: d

Stehamra - This old-school death metal band was formed in 1990. In 1991 they released the cassette *The Summer Rehearsals -91* and the subsequent year they recorded the proper demo *Then The Snow Fell* which was officially released as a cassette EP by Wild Rags, and finally re-issued by Blood Harvest in 2008. After some line-up changes the band split in 1996. Samuelsson is also found in *Bloodstone, Bifrost, Goregoat, Utuk-Xul* and pop-electronica band

2013 CD - (CASTILLION)

Insolvent. Frisk runs punk label Kranium Records. *Grave*/*Coercion* member Pelle Ekegren was the band's first drummer.

2008 ■ Then The Snow Fell… .... 7" 4tr Blood Harvest .... YOTZ #16
     Tracks: Then The Snow Fell/Open Your Eyes/Never Give Birth/Chained To Reality

2008 7" - YOTZ #16

CAVALINCE
Olle Häggberg: v, Albert Cervin: g, Pähr Nilsson: g,
Alex Dahlqvist: k, Emil Wärmedal: b, Andreas Dahlqvist: d
Malung - The band was formed in 2002 by the Dahlqvist brothers, Cervin and Häggberg, influenced by bands like *Kamelot, Soilwork* and *Scar Symmetry* as well as *The Beatles* and *Frank Sinatra*. I would place them in the same category as *Scar Symmetry*, musically highly capable and great sounding melodic death metal with both clean and "angry" vocals in a well balanced mix. Emil and Pähr are ex-*Tempory*. The releases were recorded in The Abyss.

2006 □ On The Edge Of Madness ....MCD 5tr private CAVCD01
     Tracks: Within The World/A Moment Of Clarity/Memories/Left Alone/On The Egde Of Madness
2007 ■ EMBRYONIC ....CD private CAVCD02

2007 CD - CAVCD02

CAVUS
Tony Hermansen: v, Daniel Johansson: g, Peter Larsson: g,
Anders Johansson: b, Fredrik Söderström: d
Enköping - *Cavus* was formed in 2005. The band delivers high class riff-based heavy 70s oriented hard rock with a stoner touch, quite close to *The Quill* and *Thalamus*. Outstanding vocals and killer musicians. Not to be confused with the Finnish death metal band. Tony is also found in German stoner band *Grand Massive*, while Daniel is in the promising new stoner band *Dustifier* and Peter in *Manny Ribera*.

2006 ■ Cavus...MCD 5tr private 1824CD
     Tracks: Blow Your Mind/God I Will Be/Otherside/Pushed Around/Down There Again

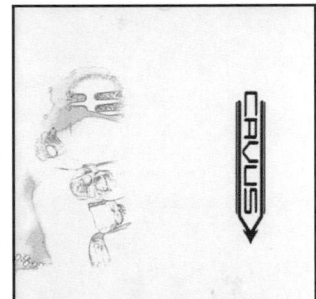

2006 MCD - 1824CD

CELESTIAL DECAY
Angelo Mayer: v, Robert Bjärmyr: g, Hobbe Housmand: g,
Håkan Olsson: k, Mattias Ryderman: b, Henrik Hedman: d
Göteborg - *Celestial Decay* was formed in 2008 by former *Last Kingdom* guitarist Housmand. He drafted his former colleague Hedman on drums, and the three *Breed* members Bjärmyr, Mayer and Olsson, plus bassist Ryderman. The band's conceptual debut album was mixed by renowned producer Beau Hill (*Europe, Ratt* etc). *Celestial Decay* play high-quality melodic power metal with a symphonic touch, quite similar to *Rhapsody In Fire* or *Angra*. The band's second album *Quantum X* is planned to be released late 2013. The line-up now features Housmand, guitarist Freddy Olofsson (*Last Kingdom*), bassist Anders Janfalk (*All Ends*), drummer Christian Wirtl (*Dragonforce, Soul Source*) and singer Andi Kravlajka (*Elsesphere, Silent Call*).

2010 CD - - -

2010 ■ CONTRADICTUM...CD private .... - -

CELESTIAL PAIN
Mikael "Mike Metalhead" Jansson; v/d, Johan "John Blackwar" Sandberg: g,
Victor "Vic Anders" Andersson: g, Benke "Benkr" Brogwall: b
Tyresö - Good old German-style thrash metal in the vein of *Kreator* and *Desaster* with quite desperate-sounding, high-pitched vocals. The band recorded two demos in 1994 and 1995. Jansson was earlier (and later) in *Unanimated*, while Sandberg and Andersson are ex-*Unpure*. The track *Celestial Pain* was also featured on the *Ultimate Swedish Vol. 1* (1996 Burn) compilation CD. The LP contains both demos. The band reformed and made some gigs in 2003.

2004 ■ AGGRESSION.. LPg Sway Records......................SR 02
     500 hand-numbered copies.

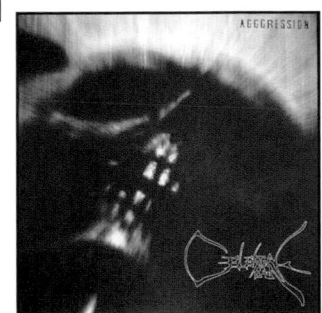

2004 LP - SR 02

CELLOUT
Percy Mejhagen: v/g, Robert Monegrim: g, Anders Sevebo: b, Thomas Ohlsson: d
Stockholm - It all started when bassist Mejhagen (ex-*Shopliftangels*) teamed up with guitarist Robert Monegrim. The two drafted bass player Sevebo and drummer Thomas Ohlsson. The band became *Cellout*. After the album, Thomas was replaced by Martin Karlsson, who in his turn left in 2012. In November 2011 guitarist Monegrim was replaced by Björn Kromm (*Keehole, Crometone*). *Cellout* play high-class modern melodic metal in the vein of bands like *Sevendust*, *Alter Bridge* and *Nickelback*, but also adding a heavier edge to it. A new album is in the making.

2010 ■ SUPERSTAR PROTOTYPE..CD Nuerra Records ....CELLO 35012

2010 CD - CELLO 35012

141

CEMETARY (1213)

Mathias Lodmalm: v/g, Anders Iwers: g, Tomas Josefsson: b, Markus Nordberg: d

Borås - Formed in 1989. Besides the slightly growling vocals the early recordings have a lot in common with bands like **Black Sabbath**. The debut was recorded at Sunlight Studios by Tomas Skogsberg and is in a more traditional death-vein. Christian Saarinen played guitar, Zrinko Culjak bass and Juha Sievers drums. On the second album the style changed towards a more gothic sound, and Anton Hedberg replaced Christian. Anders is also found in **Ceremonial Oath**. After *Last Confessions* Mathias Lodmalm split the band, joined forces with Kristian Wåhlin (**Liers In Wait, Diabolique**) and Johnny Hagel (ex-**Tiamat, Sorcerer**) to form the band **Sundown** (named after the **Cemetary** album). *Sweetest Tragedies* is a best of farewell album... before Lodmalm resurrected the band into **Cemetary 1213**, taken from the **Cemetary** song *1213 – Transgalactica*. It was to be a theme based trilogy, one sci-fi, one psychedelic and one horror. On the second, psychedelic, album *Phantasma* he however returned to the un-numbered original name. The world is still waiting for the third part entitled *Burial Theme*, which Lodmalm in interviews dating back to 2005, had started working on. However in 2006 he announced that the plans had been shelved due to him having enough of metal and the people in the business. The time between the last two albums he was also involved in various bands and styles such as **Lowrider** (not the stoner band), **Spektra, Domain ID** and electronic bands **The Distant Wake** and **Trauma Unit West**. The **Phantasma** LP was withdrawn shortly after its release.

1992 CD - BMCD 20

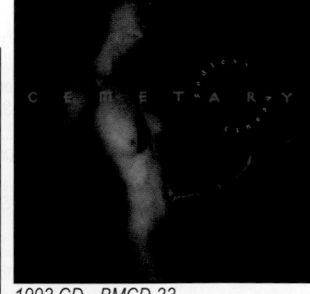

1993 CD - BMCD 33

1994 CD - BMCD 59

1992 □	AN EVIL SHADE OF GREY	LP	Black Mark	BMLP 20
1992 ■	AN EVIL SHADE OF GREY	CD	Black Mark	BMCD 20
1993 □	AN EVIL SHADE OF GREY	CD	King Records (South Korea)	KPL-3035
1993 ■	GODLESS BEAUTY	CD	Black Mark	BMCD 33
1994 ■	BLACK VANITY	CD	Black Mark	BMCD 59
1996 □	SUNDOWN	LP	Black Mark	BMLP 70
1996 □	SUNDOWN	CD	Black Mark	BMCD 70
1997 □	LAST CONFESSIONS	CD	Black Mark	BMCD111
1998 □	SWEETEST TRAGEDIES	CD	Black Mark	BMCD136
2000 ■	THE BEAST DIVINE	CDd	Century Media	77287-2
2003 □	SUNDOWN	CD	Irond (Russia)	CD 03-675
2003 □	AN EVIL SHADE OF GREY	CD	Irond (Russia)	CD 03-676
2003 □	BLACK VANITY	CD	Irond (Russia)	CD 03-678
2003 □	LAST CONFESSIONS	CD	Irond (Russia)	CD 03-672
2004 □	GODLESS BEAUTY	CD	Irond (Russia)	CD-04729
2005 □	PHANTASMA	CD	Black Mark	BMCD 170
2005 □	PHANTASMA	CDd	Black Mark	BMDP 170
2005 □	PHANTASMA	LP	Black Mark	BMLP 170
2013 □	The Funeral/Beyond The Grave	7"	To The Death	TTD 027

2000 CDd - 77287-2

CENTINEX

Johan Jansson: v, Jonas Kjellgren: g, Jonas Ahlberg: g, Martin Schulman: b, Ronnie Bergerståhl: d

Hedemora - Formed in 1990 and recorded their first demo *End Of Life* in 1991. In 1993 Wild Rags Records released *Under The Blackened Sky* on tape. In 1994 *Transcendent The Dark Chaos* was also released as a cassette through Evil Shit/Sphinx. The line-up on the first album featured singers Lasse Eriksson and Mattias Lamppu, guitarist Andreas Evaldsson, bassist Martin Schulman (**Interment**) and drummer Joakim Gustavsson. On *Malleus Maleficarum* Joakim had been replaced by Kaalima (which was actually not a person, but a drum machine) and Lasse was out. Since the 1996 CD, the band recorded two demos and they also appear on a German compilation-CD. The demo *Transcend The Dark Chaos* was supposed to be released as a MCD in 1996, through Wild Rags Records, but it never happened. Fred Estby from **Dismember** and **Carnage** makes a guest appearance on the track *Until Death Tear Us Apart*. On *Bloodhunt* Johan handled the vocals and on *Apocalyptic Armageddon* Kennet Englund (**Uncanny, Dellamorte, Interment**) took over the drum stool, while Jonas Kjellgren (**Scar Symmetry, World Below, Carnal Forge, Dellamorte**) replaced Andreas. In 1998 Novum Vox Mortiis released *Reborn Through Flames* as a cassette. In 2001 second guitarist Kenneth Wiklund left the band and he was replaced by Johan Ahlberg (**Subdive**) in 2002. After the recordings of *Decadence...* Englund left the band and was replaced by Bergerståhl (**Grave, Julie Laughs No More, World Below** etc). Jansson was also found in **Sportlov** under the moniker Ichtapp. **Centinex** mixes faster parts with slower **Paradise Lost** sounding parts, at times a bit reminiscent of **Hypocrisy** and **Dismember**. The band is featured on *Kreator Tribute Volume 1* (Full Moon). **Centinex** disbanded April 12, 2006. Jansson, Schulman and Bergerståhl continued under the name **Demonical**.

1992 ■	SUBCONSCIOUS LOBOTOMY	CD	Underground Records	U.G.R. 05
1992 □	SUBCONSCIOUS LOBOTOMY	LP	Underground Records	U.G.R. 05
	1000 copies.			
1995 □	Centinex/Inverted (split)	7" EP	VOD/Unholy Baphomet	VOD003/UBR 002
	Split with Inverted. 600 copies. Track:Sorrow Of The Burning Wasteland			
1996 □	MALLEUS MALEFICARUM	CD	Wild Rags Records	WRR 060
1997 □	REFLECTIONS	CD	Emanzipation/Die Hard	EMZ-2/RRS 954

1992 CD - U.G.R 05

Year		Title	Format	Label	Catalog
1998	☐	REBORN THROUGH FLAMES	CD	Repulse Records	RPS 032 CD
1998	■	Shadowland/Eternal Lies	7"	Oskorei Productions	OP 004

1000 copies, of which the first 500 were pressed in violet vinyl.

1998 7" - OP 004

| 1999 | ☐ | BLOODHUNT | MCD 6tr | Repulse Records | RPS 042 |

Tracks: Under The Pagan Glory/For Centuries Untold/Luciferian Moon/Bloodhunt/The Conquest Infernal/Like Darkened Storms

| 1999 | ■ | BLOODHUNT | 10" 7tr PD | Oskorei Productions | OP 008 |

Bonus: Mutilation (Death cover). 300 copies.

| 2000 | ☐ | Apocalyptic Armageddon | 7" 3tr | Deadly Art | DAP 095 |

Tracks: Apocalyptic Armageddon/Seeds Of Evil/Everlasting Bloodshed. 700 copies in grey splatter vinyl.

| 2000 | ☐ | HELLBRIGADE | CD | Repulse Records | RPS 046 |

First 3000 copies with special cardboard cover.

| 2000 | ☐ | HELLBRIGADE | CD | Soundholic (Japan) | TKCS 85003 |

Bonus: Apocalyptic Armageddon/Seeds Of Evil/Everlasting Bloodshed

| 2000 | ☐ | HELLBRIGADE | LP | Nocturnal Music | NMLP 030 |

500 copies.

| 2001 | ☐ | HELLBRIGADE | CD | World War III (USA) | CD 71158 |

Bonus: Apocalyptic Armageddon/Seeds Of Evil/Everlasting Bloodshed

2001	☐	HELLBRIGADE	CD	Picoroco (South Am)	PCOL 003-2
2001	☐	HELLBRIGADE	CD	Irond (Russia)	01-61
2002	☐	Hail Germania (split)	7" PD	Hells Headbangers	HELLS EP 001

Split with NunSlaughter.

1999 10" MLP PD - OP 008

2002	☐	DIABOLICAL DESOLATION	CD	Candelight	CANDLE 065
2002	☐	DIABOLICAL DESOLATION	CD	Candlelight (USA)	CANUS 015
2002	☐	DIABOLICAL DESOLATION	LP	Northern Sounds Records	NRS 008

1000 copies.

| 2003 | ☐ | Hail Germania (split) | 10" MLP PD | Painkiller Records | PKR-020 |

Split with NunSlaughter. Track: Enchanted Land (Sodom cover). 1000 copies.

| 2003 | ■ | Hail Germania (split) | 7" | Hells Headbangers | HELLS EP 001 |

Same as above. 800 black + 200 green vinyl.

| 2003 | ☐ | HELLBRIGADE | CD | Candlelight | CANDLE 084 |

Bonus: Apocalyptic Armageddon/Seeds Of Evil/Everlasting Bloodshed

| 2003 | ☐ | HELLBRIGADE | CD | Candlelight (USA) | CANUS 056 |
| 2003 | ☐ | MALLEUS MALEFICARUM | CD | Candlelight | CANDLE 085 |

Bonus: Only Slices Remain/Torn Within/Mutilation (Death cover)/Ripping Corpse (Kreator)

| 2003 | ☐ | MALLEUS MALEFICARUM | CD | Candlelight (USA) | CANUS 057 |
| 2003 | ☐ | BLOODHUNT/REBORN THROUGH FLAMES | CD | Candlelight | CANDLE 086 |

Bonus: Shadowland/Eternal Lies

2003 7" - HELLS EP 001

| 2003 | ☐ | BLOODHUNT/REBORN THROUGH FLAMES | CD | Candlelight (USA) | CANUS 058 |
| 2003 | ■ | Deathlike Recollections | 7" | Sword & Sorcery | STEEL 003 |

Tracks: Blood On My Skin/Shadows Are Astray. 500 copies.

2004	☐	DECADENCE: PROPHECIES OF COSMIC CHAOS	CD	Candlelight	CANDLE 089
2004	☐	DECADENCE: PROPHECIES OF COSMIC CHAOS	CD	Candlelight (USA)	CANUS 062
2004	☐	DECADENCE: PROPHECIES OF COSMIC CHAOS	LP	Hells Headbangers	HELLS LP 003

566 copies.

| 2004 | ☐ | DECADENCE: PROPHECIES OF COSMIC CHAOS | LP PD | Hells Headbangers | HELLS LP 003 |

100 copies.

| 2004 | ☐ | DECADENCE: PROPHECIES OF COSMIC CHAOS | CD | Soundholic (Japan) | TKCS-85100 |

Bonus: Towards Devastation (live)/Bloodhunt (live) + video.

| 2004 | ☐ | Live Devastation | 7" | Swedmetal | SM-01-7 |

Tracks: Towards Devastation/Bloodhunt. 500 copies.

2005	☐	WORLD DECLENSION	CDd	Regain Records	RR 081
2005	☐	WORLD DECLENSION	CD	Candlelight (USA)	CDL 0227
2011	☐	SUBCONSCIOUS LOBOTOMY	CD	Memento Mori	MEMENTO-III

New artwork. Bonus: Under The Blackened Sky and Transcend The Dark Chaos demos. 700 copies.

2003 7" - STEEL 003

| 2012 | ☐ | SUBCONSCIOUS LOBOTOMY | 2LP | The Crypt | CRYPT 26 |

New artwork. Bonus: Under The Blackened Sky, End Of Life and Transcend The Dark Chaos demos. 300 red/white splatter + 200 black vinyl copies.

| 2012 | ☐ | REFLECTIONS | LP PD | Night Of The Vinyl Dead | NIGHT 129 |

250 hand numbered copies.

| 2012 | ☐ | MALLEUS MALEFICARUM | LP PD | Night Of The Vinyl Dead | NIGHT 142 |

250 hand numbered copies.

| 2012 | ☐ | REBORN THROUGH FLAMES | LP PD | Night Of The Vinyl Dead | NIGHT 147 |

333 hand numbered copies.

| 2012 | ☐ | WORLD DECLENSION | LP PD | Night Of The Vinyl Dead | NIGHT 149 |
| 2013 | ☐ | Teutonische Invasion | 7" | Doomentia Records | DOOMEP 184 |

Tracks: Encahnted Land (Sodom)/Ripping Corpse (Kreator). 400 black + 100 splatter.

CENTRAL

Mikael Zakrisson: g/v, Conny Sparrman: g/v, Tomas Kålen: b/v/k, Sigge Kroon: d

Östersund - Really good melodic hard rock. *Om Du Kommer Igen* sounds quite similar to *Since You Been Gone*. The B-side is a rocking **Thin Lizzy**-influenced track. Kroon was later in **Magic**.

| 1982 | ■ | Om du kommer igen/Rik som ett troll | 7" | Pang | PSI 046 | $ |

1982 7" - PSI 046

CEREMONIAL EXECUTION

Robert "Gorebert" Kardell: v, Mattias "Flesh" Frisk: g,
Jimmy "Dolla" Johansson: g, Björn Ahlqvist: b, David Andersson: d

Mjölby - Formed in 2001 from the remains of **Blump**. Frisk and Johansson asked **Sinners Fate** singer David to join… on drums. Enter singer Robert and bassist Jonas Albrektsson (**Thy Primordial, Indungeon, Niden Div. 187** etc). On the 2003 demo Jonas had been replaced by Tommy "Zombie", who quit shortly after to be replaced by **Demons To Prefer** player Björn. The style had now evolved into a mix of Swedish and American death metal with some hardcore influences. They are in some rare moments very heavy, almost doom oriented, but mostly it's high speed quite technical and well played death metal. In 2004 the band recorded the album *Death Shall Set Us Free*, but due to problems with the label it was never released, until 2009, when Nuclear Winter Now released the album with some bonus material. Frisk and Johansson are also found in death metal band **Vanhelgd**, Kardell and Frisk have recorded several releases with experimental sludge band **The Jam Session** and Andersson is also found in stoner band **Ocean Chief**.

2006 7" - YOTZ #12

2009 CD - NWR 034

2004	☐	Ceremonial Execution/Borigor (split)	7" EP	Erode Records	ERODE 002

Split with Borigor. Tracks:Parasite/Abnormal Goring With A Broken Bottle. 1000 copies.

2006	■	Black God Rising	7" 3tr	Blood Harvest	YOTZ #12

Tracks: Life Denied/Black God Rising/Autopsy Of My Dying Bride. 500 copies.

2009	■	DEATH SHALL SET US FREE	CD	Nuclear Winter Records	NWR 034

Bonus: Wrapping In Goatskin/Chaosbringer/Fleshripper/Sessions Of Torment/Black Blood Rising/Autopsy Of My Dying Bride. 500 copies.

CEREMONIAL OATH

Anders Fridén: v, Anders Iwers: g, Mikael Andersson: g,
Thomas Johansson: b, Markus Nordberg: d

Billdal (Göteborg) - Formed in 1989 by Anders Iwers and Oscar Dronjak. Well played progressive death metal with lots of tempo changes. Nice guitar parts in the vein of old **Maiden**, but quite screeching vocals. Not the typical death-sound, but more traditional metal, especially on the last recording. Iwers and Nordberg were also found in **Cemetary**. Iwers was previously in **Tiamat**, between the albums *Astral Sleep* and *Clouds*. Mikael is ex-**Forsaken**. On the first 7" and CD the members were Iwers, Nordberg, guitarist/singer Dronjak, and bassist Jesper Strömblad. On *Carpet* they do a cover of **Iron Maiden's** *Hallowed Be Thy Name*. The album was recorded already in 1993 but not released until 1995. Jesper is now found in **In Flames** and Oscar in **Crystal Age** and **HammerFall**. Thomas "Tompa" Lindberg (**At The Gates**) and Anders Fridén (**Dark Tranquillity, In Flames**) sing on some tracks on the latest album. The non-CD tracks *New Sun* and *The Shadowed End* appears on the *W.A.R* compilation (Wrong Again Records) and the **Metallica**-cover *Disposable Heros* is featured on *Metal Militia* ('94 Black Sun).

1995 CD - BS 02

1992 7" - CGR 005

1992	■	The Lost Name Of God/For I Have Sinned/The Praise	7" 3tr	Corpse Grinder	CGR 005
1993	☐	THE BOOK OF TRUTH	CD	Modern Primitive	PRIM 3
1995	■	CARPET	CD	Black Sun	BS 02
2012	☐	THE BOOK OF TRUTH	2CD	Century Media	998269-2

Bonus: The Hour Between Darkness And Dawn/Remains Of Death/Force Of Habit/A Nocturnal Predator/Into The Abyss Of Hell/The Invocator/Necrosis/The Lost Name Of God/For I Have Sinned -The Praise

2012	■	THE BOOK OF TRUTH	2LP	Century Media	998269-1

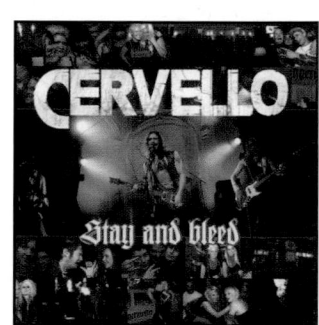
2012 2LP - 998269-1

CERVELLO

Michel Baioni: v/g, Martin Bohgard: g, Marcus Melander: b, Toni Baioni: d

Stockholm - On the band's first demo (*Drowning/Things/R.E.M*) from 2004, the band featured Michel, guitarist Magnus Lindbloom (**Lindbloom, Castle Royale, Jimmy Ågren Band**), bass player Emil Oscarsson and drummer Andreas Hellgren. When **Cervello** won the 2008 Radio Bandit *Best Unsigned* contest the line-up had drastically changed, featuring Michel, Martin, Marcus and Michel's brother Toni on drums. **Cervello** is one in the line of new heavy, yet melodic contemporary metal bands inspired by the likes of **Nickelback, Hinder** etc.

2009 CDS - 334 4242-1

2009	■	Stay And Bleed/C1	CDSp 2tr	Bonnier Music	334 4242-1

CHAI GANG

Jacqueline Anagrius: v, Mats Wennhag: g, Hans Ekman: g, Irene Tuomainen: k,
Peter Grimhall: b, Christer Lindgren: d

Stockholm (Sollentuna) - Really good, quite guitar driven melodic hard rock sung in Swedish, a bit in the vein of **Attack**, with Jacqueline sounding quite a lot like Rosa Körberg. Recorded in Studio Decibell by Robban Wellerfors. Mats recorded a single with punk rockers **Brontophobia** in 1979, while Irene later joined melodic rockers **Ladyland**.

1983	■	Guld som glimmar/Ta mig	7"	private	NR CG 001

1983 7" - NR CG 001

CHAINED

David Sandström: v/g, Daniel Persson: g, Jonas Stenlund: b, Stefan Nielsen: d

Piteå - **Chained** is a young Christian metal band, or a "radical worship band", as they have been called. Powerful and quite heavy steamroller metal a bit reminiscent of 90s **Metallica** with a touch of **Pantera** at times. In 2007 the band released a CD-R single *Shattered Minds/Like A Rattlesnake*. Stenlund is ex-**Laudamus**.
Website: www.chainedmetal.com

2010 ■ CHAINED...CD   private..CHCD001

2010 CD - CHCD001

CHAINS

Anthony Rascal: v, Gabby Force: g, Jason Stitch: g,
Matthias "Matt Haze": b, Martin "Rhyder" Erlandsson: d

Malmö - The band was formed in January 2003, but only drummer Stefan remains from the original trio. After a lot of name and member changes the recording line-up was completed in February 2008. The band, only having record a demo, supported **Kip Winger** in Denmark and won the *Nordic Challenge* in 2009. When they were finally on the brink of a break-through, the band split.

2008 ■ Fool For Your Love/Give It To Me ....CDSp 2tr   private......................................- -

2008 CDSp - - -

CHAINSAW

Pontus Arvidson: g/v, Christian Skärby: g, Tobias Backlund: b, Peter Lindqvist: d

Stockholm - **Chainsaw** was founded in 2003 by Pontus and Harry. Pontus was at the time without a band after the split-up of his old death metal band **Incendiary** and Harry (ex-**Pandemonic, Internal Decay**) was looking for a band on the side of his other band **Vörgus**. The style is pure old-school thrash metal, great sounding, too, and in the vein of classic **Anthrax**, early **Megadeth**, **Metallica** etc. Well worth checking out. After several try-outs and short term members, singer Jonas Åhlen (**Backdraft**) joined the band. This line-up recorded *Into The Pit* at Solna Soundlabs studios, produced by Mike Wead (**Mercyful Fate, King Diamond**). After the release, drummer Emil Holmgren joined the band. Late 2005, Jonas and Harry were replaced by vocalist Mario Ramos and bassist Tobias Backlund and in the beginning of 2006 lead guitarist Christian Skärby also reinforced the band. Emil Holmgren left the band in August 2006. In 2007 the band recorded a new demo, now using drummer Henrik Söderlund. **Chainsaw** has now found a permanent drummer in Peter Lindqvist and in October 2009 the band entered the studio with Mike Wead and Simon Johansson to record a full length album. The line-up on the album, finally released in 2012, saw another change in the line-up with Pontus handling the vocals.
Website: chainsawmetal.com

2005 CD - - -

2005 ■ Into The Pit...CD 6tr   private...--
  Tracks: Ancient Evil/Spawn Of Hatred/Twisting The Knife/Collective Entity/When There's
  No More Room In Hell/Lobotomy Of The Easter Bunny
2012 ■ FEED THE LIE...CDd   Emrinc..................................... E1002

2012 CDd - E 1002

CHAINWRECK

Sonny Jonasson: v, Mathias Henrysson: g, Björn Tauman: b, Emil Lantz: d

Falun/Stockholm/Avesta - In 2003 Henrysson, guitarist and singer of the band **Cudfish**, recorded some demos. **Malmsteen/Without Grief** drummer Patrik Johansson helped out with the drumming on the first two-track demo. Joined by Jonasson and former **Demon Cleaner** guitarist Kimmo Holappa they formed **Chainwreck**. **Cudfish/Without Grief** bass player Tauman joined ranks, but shortly after the drum stool had to be filled again due to Johansson's other engagements. Former **Cudfish**, now **Renaissance Of Fools** skinsman Magnus Karlsson stepped in, but had to leave and was replaced by **Dozer** drummer Olle Mårthans and this line-up recorded the demo *This Act Of Anger* late 2004. Early 2005 Holappa left to be replaced by Henrik Palm (**Sonic Ritual**). So, Jonasson, Henrysson, Palm, Taumans and Mårthans recorded the band's self-titled debut album, a heavy crusher of an album, mixing stoner, detuned grinding metal, melodic lines, clean vocals and almost death-ish growls into a pretty interesting craft metal ass-kicker. In January 2006 Mårthans left the band for studies in Stockholm and was replaced by Emil Lantz (**Brazen Riot, Bonedivers**). A few months later Palm took off and the band continued as a four-piece. The demo *Silence Equals Death* saw the light of day half a year later and the work with a second album started. The album was mixed by Jonas Kjellgren (**Scar Symmetry, Dellamorte** etc) and released in 2009. The second album, *A Season Of Hates Perfection*, has so far only been released digitally.
Website: www.chainwreck.com

2006 ■ CHAINWRECK ....CD   ADR .... ADR 102

2006 CD - ADR 102

CHAIR, THE

Chris Lee Smith: v, Janne Lindgren: g, Kenneth Braman: g,
Jonas "Jam" Strandberg: b, Peter "Stonebreaker": d

Malmö - Transubstans Records have a way of digging up great sounding retro-oriented bands, no difference here. *The Chair* bears some resemblance of vintage blues based, riff-oriented hard rockers like Aussie hard rockers *Buffalo* and *LeafHound* with acidy and very raw guitars. Great rough-edged bluesy vocals from American born singer Chris. The band was formed in the autumn of 2005. Chris, Janne and Kenneth had previously been playing together for a few years, after which Peter joined and in 2007 Peter replaced the previous unnamed bass player. In 2009 Jam left the band to become singer in *Suicide Messiah* (where Kenneth's son Christoffer plays drums).

2008 CD - TRANS 035

2008 ■ THE CHAIR...CD   Transubstans ....TRANS 035

CHAOS FEEDS LIFE

Martin Hanner: v/g, Andreas Edlund: b/g, Tobias Björk: d/v

Höör - *Chaos Feeds Life* was a side project of *Skyfire* members Hanner and Edlund (also in *Backhander*). The MCD was released on the short-lived Loud 'N ' Proud label. The band plays high speed thrash metal mixed with melodic power metal. The vocals are definitely thrashy on the verge of hardcore/death metal-ish. Like *Blind Guardian* meets *Children Of Bodom* meets *Avenged Sevenfold*, clearly ahead of their time.

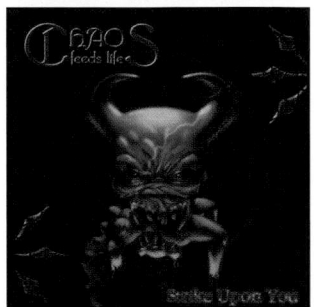

1999 MCD - LNP 015

1999 ■ ...Strike Upon You..MCD 6tr   Loud 'N' Proud ....LNP 015
       Tracks: Strike Upon You/Rise Above All Life/Suffer My Wrath/The Only True Blasphemy/
       Through The Lies/Into Despair

CHAOS OMEN

Tore Stjerna: v/g/b/d

Stockholm - *Chaos Omen* is the solo project of former *Watain* bassist Tore "Necromorbus" Stjerna, also the owner of Necromorbus studio. The single was released in 2004 and the subsequent year the track *Old Wounds* was recorded and put online for free download. The song was later featured on the *Let Clarity Succumb* MCD. In 2009 Tore started working on new material. Cold, fast, old-school-style black metal similar to bands like *Heresi*.

2006 MCD - NAIL 003

2004 ☐ Life Be Gone/Dwellers, Dwell No More..7"   Perverted Taste....................................PT 090
2006 ■ Let Clarity Succumb..MCD 4tr   Nails Of Christ....................................NAIL 003
       Tracks: Glare As I Reveal/To Admit And Allow/Let Clarity Succumb/Old Wounds

CHAOSSWORN

Anton Johansson: v/g, Janne Posti: g, Andreas Pelli: b, Niklas Pelli: d

Haparanda - The band was formed as *Cryptic Death* in 2004 and changed the name to *Chaossworn* in 2009. After the MCD drummer Niklas Pelli was replaced by Joni Salo. *Chaossworn* plays well-produced black metal-influenced by bands like *Dismember* and *Watain*.

2010 MCD - ABYSS 01-5 CD

2010 ■ Chalice Of Black Flames...MCD 3tr   Abyss Records........................ ABYSS 01-5 CD
       Tracks: Crowned & Winged/Bringer Of Storms/Chalice Of The Black Flames

CHARITY

Matti Norlin: v/g, Hans-Erik Jansson: g, Mikael Rönnberg: k,
Eskil Rönnberg: b, Michael Hallberg: d

Hoting - The band was formed in 1984 and released a 7" the year before, under the name *Wizzard*. *Charity* play traditional 80s melodic hard rock with a plus in the vocal department. They split just after the release of this single as some of the members were concentrating on the school work. Matti was at this point 14 years old. In 1995 he released a solo-CD with 20's/30's acoustic blues, entitled *Pre-War Blues*. He was also part of the musically multi-coloured duo *Matti & Haake* and is today in heavy blues rockers *Badge*. Rönnberg, who quit just before the release of the single, is now a concert pianist, while some of the others continued playing in cover-bands.

1987 7" - WBS 0006

1987 ■ In My Dreams/Two Of A Kind ....7"   Singapore Singles..........................WBS 0006 $

CHARIZMA

Bosse Nikolausson: b/v, Göran Nikolausson: g, Janne Nikolausson: d

Oskarshamn - This Christian AOR-band that consists of the three Nikolausson brothers was formed in 1981. Good melodic stuff with some weak spots in the vocal department. The first album has a more metal feel to it. *Join Hands* was only released in Estonia and *Rockin' The World Together* was only released in Russia. The band has toured in Germany, USA, Switzerland, Australia, England and also in Estonia four years in a row. On *To Be Continued…* the band turned into a more westcoast-ish/pop-unit closer to **Mr. Mister** and **Sting** than hard rock. The follow-up had a bit more edge, probably because it was produced by Mick Nordström (**Cornerstone, Spearfish, Modest Attraction**), but it still only qualifies into the arena-rock genre.

1985 LP - URR 8508

1985 ■	ROCK THE WORLD	LP	URR	URR 8508	
1986 ☐	Turn Me On/Try It (Feel The Love)	7"	URR	URR 8604	
1989 ☐	Join Hands	MLP 4tr	URR (Estonia)	URR 8910	
	Tracks: Join Hands/Where Do You Stand/Turn Me On/Take You High. Clear vinyl.				
1990 ■	ROCKIN' THE WORLD TOGETHER	LP	Melodiya (Russia)	C60 31041007	$
1993 ☐	THE ULTIMATE CALL	CD	93 Viva	CHMA9310	
1996 ☐	TO BE CONTINUED	CD	Asaph Music	6900004	
1999 ☐	Run To God (3 edits)	MCD 3tr	Megaphone	MS 13	
1999 ☐	THE BASICS OF LIFE	CD	Megaphone	MCD 14	
2000 ☐	ROCK THE WORLD	CD	Magdalene	MR 001	

1990 LP - C60 3104 1007

CHASTISEMENT

Johan Klitkou: v, Tommy Larsson: g, Marcus Edvardsson: g,
Nicklas Linnes: b, Nils Fjellström: d

Östersund - Death metal band **Chastisement** was formed in 1995 by guitarists Marcus Edvardsson and Fredrik Magnusson. Magnusson was later replaced by Larsson and they recorded their first demo in 1997. In 1999 they released the self-made seven-track debut, *But Lost We Are*, where the band themselves are unsure how many copies were made (between 50 and 200). The band also recorded a third album that was never released. Klitkou and Edvardsson are also found in **Souldrainer, Aeon, Endless Torture, Sanctification** and **In Battle** while Fjellström has played in bands like **Aeon, In Battle, Sanctification** and **Dark Funeral**. The band split in 2005. Highly interesting technical death metal in the vein of **Armegeddon**, with a touch of **Meshuggah** at times. Tight, well-played and well mixed. The band also released a live CD themselves.

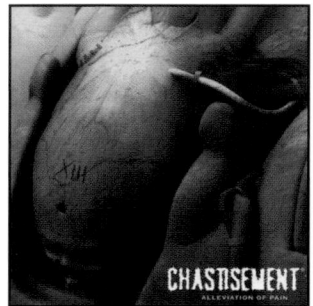
2002 CD - ILIAD 050

| 2002 ■ | ALLEVIATION OF PAIN | CD | Rage Of Achilles | ILIAD 050 | |

CHEERLEADER

Joel Ek: v/b, Joan Vieru: g, Niklas Ek: g, Andreas Westerlund: d

Stockholm - The name may suggest otherwise, but **Cheerleader** is a solid, sleazy, seventies influenced melodic hard rock trio, at times with some **Cheap Trick** overtones. The band was formed in 2009. Joan was ex-**Supragod**. The band was initially called **The Sh!t**, but changed it to **Cheerleader** and released their debut in 2011. Vieru's former band mate Rille Lindell also managed to get the band a UK tour slot together with the band he was in, **Warrior Soul**.

2011 CD - AS1101

| 2011 ■ | VEGAS OR BUST | CD | Angry Shark | AS1101 | |

CHEERS

Jorma Kujansuu: v/g, Jari Kujansuu: v/b, Mikael Eriksson: g,
Torbjörn Pettersson: k, Mikael Lundén: d

Stockholm - The A-side is in the same vein as a guitar dominated **Toto**, while the B-side is a bit more influenced by pop/funk. On the verge, but the A-side makes up for it.

1989 7" - ST 55-511

| 1989 ■ | Run Down/Lose Control | 7" | Studio 55 | ST 55-511 | $ |

CHEESE

Magnus Lange: v/k, Tommy Denander: g, Jonas Olsson: b, Per Liljefors: d

Stockholm - AOR in the same vein as late **Easy Action**. If it wasn't for the distorted guitar it would probably be labelled as pop. High-quality stuff anyway. Tommy was ex-**ATC** and later joined **Cool For Cats**. He has since done numerous session jobs as well as highly interesting solo-recordings and albums with **Radioctive, Talk Of The Town, Rainmaker** etc. The song *Hold On* can also be found on the compilation *The Recorder*.

1987 7" - KR 001

| 1987 ■ | Won't Come Easy/Hold On | 7" | private | KR 001 | $ |

147

CHERI

Joakim "Michael Ross" Lindquist: v, Anders "John Akefield" Åkerfeldt: g,
Mats "Sammy" Andersson: b, Anders "Jeff Lynn" Gärdelind: d

Stockholm - The band was formed in 1985. *Cheri* play very professional-sounding AOR, like a softer version of *Treat*. Well worth checking out. They started the recordings of an album, but the label went bust. Joakim was about to release his solo-album in 1996. He is however more influenced by the likes of *U2* and Swedish pop-singer *Thomas Ledin*.

1988 ■ She Looked The Other Way/Queen Of Heart ....7" Rio .... RIO 666

1988 7" - RIO 666

CHEROKEE

Peter Magnusson: v, Håkan Fried: g, Andreas Hansson: b, Jimmy Thörnfeldt: d

Norrköping - Formed in November 1992. Straight very 80s-influenced metal. Could easily have been recorded ten years earlier. Simple guitar work, chord patterns taken directly out of the beginners book of heavy metal and a singer who's sometimes a bit out of pitch. The MCD was the first prize in a competition. In the fall 1995 Jimmy was replaced by *Kansas City Rollers*-drummer Andreas Wahlberg. Håkan was also found in *Kansas City Rollers*.

1994 ■ Happy Family ....MCD 3tr Aktiv Musik.................................... RICD 001
       Tracks: Happy Family/Get Her In The Deep/Backseat Betty

1994 MCD - RICD 001

CHERRY RED

Thomas Lundgren: v, Magnus Nelin: g, Thomas Nesslin: k,
Hansi Fellbrink: b, Mats Nelin: d

Sundsvall - The whole thing started already back in 1985 when the guys formed under the name *Roulette*, under which name they released two singles and a posthumous CD (released in 2008 on AOR-FM Records). In 1990, influenced by their prospective label, they changed their name to *Cherry Red* and won a recording contract with CBS. They started recording their debut album, but after having recorded only three tracks the label changed it to a single (after having signed *Rat Bat Blue*) which was released on the CBS sub label Cupol. The band subsequently split, but continued playing together as a *Def Leppard* tribute band. High class AOR well worth checking out if you can find it. The single was never released with a printed sleeve.

1990 7" CS8

1990 ● Only The Strong/I Do ....7" Cupol CS8
       No picture sleeve.

CHEYENNE

Micke Olsson: v, Lasse Hedlund: g, Tomas Melin: k, Stefan Asplund: b, Micke Ståhl: d

Härnösand - Outstanding *Europe*-style melodic hard rock/metal with lots of dual guitars and keyboards. Classy vocals!

1989 ■ All You Got/Blinded By Love ....7" TAB TAB-ES-909

1989 7" - TAB-ES-909

CHILLIHOUNDS

Gabriel Aadland: v/g, Daniel Hessel: g, Carl Linnaeus: b, Stefan Johansson: d

Göteborg - According to the band's website: "We started this band because we were sick and tired of the music of today without heart and passion. Our philosophy hasn't changed since then, says singer Gabriel Aadland who formed the band in Gothenburg with lead guitarist Daniel Hessel". This was in 2003. Former *Aggressive* lead singer Stefan, who also played drums with punksters *Perkele*, joined the band. *Foobar The Band* bass player Robert Kulka joined, and they recorded two demos. Kulka left and former *Rickshaw* man Linnaeus (also toured with *Lucifyre*) joined. The demo *No Fashion, Just Rock 'N Roll* was recorded analogue in 2006. The band was finally signed by Italian indie label Nicotine and the debut saw the day the subsequent year. In 2009 Hessel left. *Chillihounds* play no-nonsense testosterone rock-out-with-the-cock-out hard rock with mixing touches of *AC/DC, Black Crowes, Mustasch* and vintage *Kiss*.

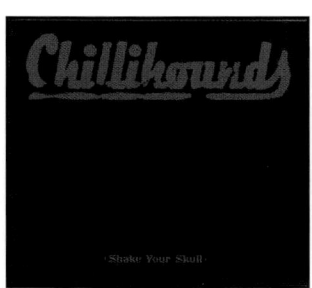

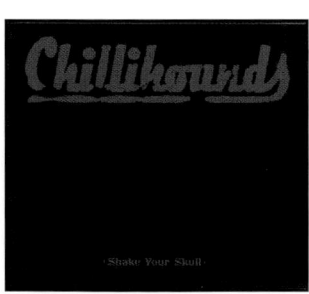

2010 CD - NIC 069

2011 CDd - TRANS 083

2007 ☐ THE ALBUM...CD Nicotine..............................NICO40
2010 ■ WELCOME TO THE SHOW ....CD Nicotine..............................NIC 069
2011 ■ SHAKE YOUR SKULL ....CDd Transubstans ....TRANS 083

CHIRON

Patrik Axelsson: v, Robin Tesch: g, Björn Åsander: k,
Klas Berg: b, Håkan Tingshagen: d

Stockholm - Great melodic hard rock in the vein of *Glory* and *Europe*. The first single being slightly heavier. Axelsson and Åsander later joined *Line-Up* and *Reckless*. The first single featured Chrille Eriksson (v), Patrik Axelsson (g), Jonny Lindberg (b) and Håkan on drums.

1986 7" - CH 001

1986 ■	Don't Lose Your Faith/Eyes Of Steel	7"	private	CH 001	$
1989 ☐	Endless/ Let You Go	7"	private	CHS 001	

CHIVE

Daniel Johansson: v, Fredrik Andersson: g,
Marcus Strandberg: b, Marcus Andersson: d

Nyköping - **Chive** was formed in the fall of 1997. Marcus and Marcus had previously recorded with punk band **Falling To Pieces** and Daniel with **Cascade**. They recorded a four-track demo in 1997 and in 1998 they released the self-financed 10". **Chive** produces high-quality stoner rock with phat riffing. New songs were written after the 10", but even though the band has not officially split things fizzled out. Marcus Andersson is found in **Disfear**, Daniel went back to **Cascade**. The track *Dragon* can also be found on *Burned Down To Zero* (01 Daredevil).

1998 10" - PWR 001

1998 ■	Chive	10" 6tr	Plant Woman	PWR 001

Tracks: Dragon/Evil Size/Evil Size 2(Someday)/Lifeless Eyes/Out Of Reach/Dressed In Black. 300 copies.

CHOIR OF VENGEANCE

Richard Martinsson: v/g, Lars Tängmark: g, Magnus Linhardt: b, Karsten Larsson: d

Mjölby - The band was formed by Karsten and Lars in 1987 and went through several line-up changes before recording the MCD. They also recorded two demos in 1997 and 2000. In 2000 the band slowly went to sleep. Lars (ex-**Dawn**) moved and Karsten (ex-**Dawn**, **Mithotyn**) devoted his time to **Falconer**. Richard is also ex-**Mithotyn** and **Dawn**. Furious death metal with warped and at times pitched down vocals, quite poorly recorded with quite fuzzed-out guitars and a thin drum sound. Musically it varies from high speed to traditional metal and almost punkish chord progressions.

1996 MCD - COV 001

1996 ■	Choir Of Vengeance	MCD 5tr	private	COV 001

Tracks: Frozen Valley/Warlock/Eternal/Premonition/Crown Of Flames

CHRONIC DECAY

Jocke Hammar: v/g, Roger Pettersson: g, Gunnar Norgren: b/v, Micke Karlsson: d

Eskilstuna - Started out under the name **Morbid Sin**. Varied death metal with a thrashy feel and traditional growling vocals. Micke Sjöstrand (also drummer in **Hypnosia**) who plays guitar on the first 7", passed away January 8, 2004 from skin cancer. The track *1st Of September* can be found on the *Projections Of A Stained Mind* (90 CBR) compilation and two tracks are featured on the compilation *Grindcore* (1993 Nuclear Blast).

1993 MCD - SFRCDS 9305

1990 ☐	Ecstasy In Pain/1:st Of September/Dark Before Dawn	7" 3tr	Studiefrämjandet	SFRS 613
1993 ■	Exanthema/Chronic Decay (split)	MCD	Studiefrämjandet	SFRCDS 9305

Split with Exanthema. Tracks: Return To Heaven/Silent Prayer/Visions Of A Madman.

2010 ☐	JUSTIFY YOUR EXISTANCE	LP	Me Saco Un Ojo	MSUO 05

500 copies.

2011 ☐	Exanthema/Chronic Decay (split)	MLP 5tr	Me Saco Un Ojo	MSUO 026

Vinyl reissue with new artwork.

CHRONIC TORMENT

Tommy "Tom Alcohol" Parkkonen: v/d, Pasi "Batong" Jaskara: g,
Simi "R Corps": g, Miika "Von Silli" Vains: b

Göteborg - **Chronic Torment** was formed in 1991 from the ashes of **Rotting Flesh**, **Hangover** and **H.B.D.**. The line-up featured drummer Tommy, guitarist Mirko "Hangover" Varis, singer Jouni "Joppe Jouppo" Parkkonen and guitarist Mikael "Mika 3,5" Vanhanen. They initially took the name **Sacretomia** and in 1992 released the demo *Altar Of Sin*. Due to lack of interest they split in 1995. Ten years later Tom and Miika started playing together again and this resulted in the *Doomed* album. **Reclusion** bassist Pasi joined in 2007 and before *Demons Of Chaos* Simi had entered. K. Ailo plays keyboards and has mixed *Doomed* and *Dream Of The Dead*. High-speed old-school-oriented death metal in the vein of **Napalm Death**.
Website: www.chronictorment.com

2007 CDp - DR 133

2006 ☐	DOOMED	CDp	private	DR 043

1000 copies.

2007 ■	DREAM OF THE DEAD	CDp	private	DR 133

1000 copies.

2008 ■	WIND OF INFECTION	CDp	private	- -

1000 copies.

2009 ■	DEMONS OF CHAOS	CDp	private	- -

1000 copies.

2008 CDd - - -

2009 CDp - - -

CICERO

Torbjörn Eriksson: v/k, Arto Pyykkö: g, Claes Aschan: g,
Mikael Nordh: b, Peter Lundin: d

Karlskoga - A hidden pomp/AOR gem! This album is a must for fans of early 80s AOR/pomp in the vein of *Styx*, *Morningstar*, *Trillion* etc. Very high-class stuff with great arrangements, raw guitars, well-played keyboards in the true early *Styx*-vein, nice melodies and lots of musical changes. Highly recommended. Production quite similar to *Morningstar* and the early 80s Canadian pompsters. 8 of the 9 songs sung in Swedish and one in English.

1982 ■ CICERO ....LP LiPhone...LiLP 3062 $

1982 LP - LiLP 3062

CIPHER SYSTEM

Karl Obbel: v, Johan Eskilsson: g, Magnus Öhlander: g,
Peter Engström: k, Henric Carlsson: b, Emil Frisk: d

Tjörn - The band was formed already in 1995 under the name *Eternal Grief*. The first line-up featured guitarists Johan Eskilsson and Andreas Allenmark, bass player Henric Carlsson (also in *The Unguided*) and drummer Pontus Andersson. After a desperate search for a vocalist, the band found Daniel Schöldström in 1997. They soon entered the studio to record the two-track demo *Path Of Delight*. In 1999 they entered Studio Fredman and recorded the three-track demo *Reaped By Chaos*, which was mixed by Anders Fridén of *In Flames*. However, dissatisfied with the production, the band let it collect dust on the shelf and soon after, Daniel and Andreas left the band. After being in limbo for a while the band again started moving early 2001, recruiting keyboard player Peter, who talked Daniel into returning (who ever said keyboard players were no good…). New songs were written and the band now took the name *Cipher System*. In 2002 they recorded the three-track demo *Eyecon* and recruited new guitarist Magnus Öhlander. In 2003 they once again entered the studio, this time Studio Fullmoon, where they recorded the three-track *Promo 2003*. This lead to a master deal with LifeForce and a first split-CD with Swedish colleagues *By Night*. In 2004 they once again entered Studio Fredman to record their first full length album. Allenmark can also be found in *Anata* and *Rotinjected*, while Carlsson is in *Nightrage*. After the first album the band did some gigs but slowly started fading away. Carlsson left the band to devote his time to *Nightrage*. At one time Jimmie Strimell (*Dead By April, Deathdestruction*) was the singer of the band and Carlsson and Eskilsson were actually in the initial line-up of *Dead By April*, in 2007, but left as they thought the label wanted the band to become too melodic. After a two year hiatus Eskilsson and Carlsson found it was time to blow some life into the beast again. They started writing songs and in 2008 *Cipher System* recorded another two-track demo and the line-up now featured singer Andreas Solveström, Johan Eskilsson, Andreas Allenmark, Peter Engström, Henric Carlsson and Emil Frisk. Before the second album singer Karl Obbel took over the vocal task. *Cipher System* hail from Tjörn, in the Göteborg area, so their sound is quite clearly influenced by their habitat. Melodic death metal, the Göteborg way, in the same vein as *Dark Tranquillity* and early *In Flames*.

2004 CD - LFR 048-2

2004 CD - LFR 043-2

2011 CD - NB 2773-2

2004 ■	CIPHER SYSTEM/BY NIGHT (split)......................CD	LifeForce.................................LFR 043-2
	Tracks: What If/Receive, Retrieve & Escalate/Sufferstream	
2004 ■	CENTRAL TUNNEL EIGHT ....CD	LifeForce.................................LFR 048-2
2011 ■	COMMUNICATE THE STORM ....CD	Nuclear Blast ....NB 2773-2
2011 □	COMMUNICATE THE STORM ....CD	Nippon Columbia (Japan)..........COCB-60029

CIRCLE OF CHAOS

Antonio Ravinio Da Silva: v, HG Hogström: g, Allan Lundholm: g,
Thomas Jonsson: b, Staffan Lundholm: d

Eskilstuna - Founded in the spring of 2008 by former *Abused* members Staffan and HG. Later the same year Da Silva (*Subcyde/Barbus*) reinforced the band, and the subsequent year Jonsson (ex-*Queensway*) joined. They started recording the album, and when it was almost finished second guitarist Allan (ex-*Convulsion*) completed the line-up. In 2011 Antonio left and was replaced by Julian Loaiza (*Rage Invest*). The CD-R *Twoheaded Serpent* was released in 2012.

2010 ■ BLACK OBLIVION ....CDp private .... - -

2010 CDp - - -

CIRKUS

Robin "Roux'd" Roux: v, Christopher "Snetan" Landstedt: g,
Rickard "Maston" Mattsson: b, Ric: d

Eskilstuna - Swedish glam with all the sounds, names, lyrics and moves according to the standard manual for 80s Sunset Strip glam. Produced by Chris Tsangarides (*Malmsteen, Tygers Of Pan Tang, Anvil*). The four-track CD-R *Let The Madness Begin* was released in 2005.

2008 ■ LET THE MADNESS BEGIN ....CD Cirkus Music .... CMR 008-001

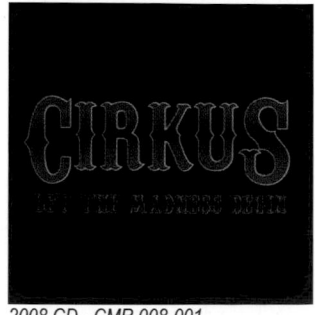
2008 CD - CMR 008-001

CITADEL, THE

Jonas Radehorn: v, Kenneth Johnsson: g, Janne Näsström: k,
Jörgen Andersson: b, Olov Groth: d

Sundsvall/Ånge - *The Citadel* was formed in 2002. They recorded their first demo in 2006 and released the first singel the same year. The single featured drummer Henka Johansson (*Clawfinger*) and Swedish pop singer Susie Päivärinta. *The Citadel* play a pretty unique mix of keyboard infused doom and almost symphonic melodic metal, with Radehorns outstanding vocals shining in the mix. Great songs and great sound. After the album bass player Jörgen Andersson replaced Rickard Persson and guitarist Janne Näsström replaced keyboard player Erik Sjögren. Johnsson is also found in *Torch, Tad Morose* and is preparing a solo release for 2013.

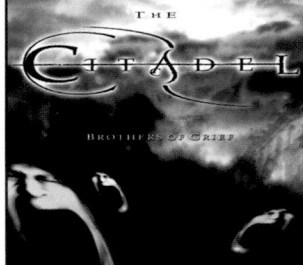

2006 ☐	The Creeper	CDS	Metal Fortress	MFE 016
2007 ■	BROTHERS OF GRIEF	CDd	GMR	GMRCD 9007
2011 ☐	A Passage Through Eternity	MCDd 5tr	GMR	GMRCD 9023
	Tracks: A Voice Within/Demon's Eye/Heaven/When The Storm Begins/7			

2007 CDd - GMRCD 9007

CIVIL WAR

Nils Patrik Johansson: v, Oskar Montelius: g, Rikard Sundén: g,
Daniel Mÿhr: k, Stefan Eriksson: b, Daniel Mullbäck: d

Falun - *Civil War* may be the the war remains of *Sabaton* (before the resurrection), but they actually sound quite different. Musically it's still war-oriented themes, pazer-infused stomping metal, but with Nils on vocals it takes another path. Not Nils' best work, but still good. Eriksson was ex-*Volturyon* and Nils Patrik is also in *Astral Doors, Lion's Share* etc.

2013 ☐	Civil War	MCDpg 5tr	Despotz	DZCD028
	Tracks: Rome Is Falling/Civil War/Forevermore/Custers Last Stand/Say It Right. 1900 copies.			
2013 ■	THE KILLER ANGELS	CDpg	Despotz	DZCD033
	Bonus: Children Of The Grave			
2013 ☐	THE KILLER ANGELS	2LPg+CD	Despotz	DZCD031
	Bonus: March Across The Belts. 1000 numbered copies.			

2013 CDd - DZCD033

CLAWFINGER

Zak Tell: v, Jocke Skoog: v/k/prog, Bård Torstensen: g,
André Skaug: b, Henka Johansson: d

Stockholm - Sweden's first real rap-metal band that made their debut on rappers *Just D*'s MCD *Klåfinger*, now a rarity. Formed by Jocke, Bård, Erlend and Zak, who worked together at the Rosenlund Hospital in 1990. The band's first single *Nigger* became a great hit in Sweden but caused quite a lot of problems for the band abroad, even though the lyrics were anti-racist. The 5-track *Warfair* includes some unreleased + live-material. The band made some successful tours as support for bands like *Anthrax* and *Alice In Chains*. The band is produced by "Sanken" (*Mental Hippie Blood, Peace Love & Pitbulls* etc). Session musicians used on several early recordings were bass player André Skaug and drummer Richard HuxFlux Nettermalm (*Plankton, Fistfunk, Paatos, Rammstein*). In 1995 they toured in South American on the Monsters Of Rock together with *Ozzy, Therapy?, Megadeth, Alice Cooper* and others. Around this time the drums were handled by Ottar Vigurst. For the recording of the self-titled 1997 album they used session drummer Henka (*The Citadel*), who soon became a firm member of the band. The non-album track *Better Than This* is also found on the compilation-CD delivered with my first book. *Two Sides* is a weird compilation featuring 2-3 different versions of songs like *Two Sides, Biggest & The Best* etc. Guitarist Erlend Ottem left in 2003. In 2008 Micke Dahlén replaced drummer Henka. In August 2012 the band announce they were calling it quits.
Website: www.clawfinger.net

Five white ni... no no no!

1993 MCD - 4509-93280-2

1993 ☐	Just D: Klåfinger	MCD 4tr	Telegram Records	TDEP 46
	Tracks: Vill ha allt (Faith No More)/Tbax tstan/BOS/Låt d goda rulla. Released as Just D featuring Clawfinger (or Klåfinger)			
1993 ☐	Nigger/Get It/Love	MCD 3tr	MVG	MVGCDS 7
1993 ☐	Nigger	MLP 4tr	WEA (Germany)	4509-93279-0
	Tracks: Nigger/Nigger (Me And The Reality Mix)/Nigger (D-Generator Mix)/Profit Preacher			
1993 ■	Nigger	MCD 4tr	WEA (Germany)	4509-93280-2
1993 ☐	Nigger	MCD 4tr	Warner Music (Australia)	4509-93280-2
1993 ○	Nigger/Nigger (BomKrash Re-mix)	12" 2tr	MVG (DJ-promo)	MVGPRMS 7
	No picture sleeve.			
1993 ☐	Clawfinger/The Wildhearts (split)	7"	EastWest (UK)	SAM 1262
	Promo-split. Track: Warfair			
1993 ☐	The Truth/The Truth (Cyber Glau Mix)	CDS 2tr	MVG	MVGCDS 15
1993 ☐	The Truth/Rosegrove	12" 2tr	MVG (promo)	CLAW 001
1993 ☐	The Truth/The Truth (Cyber Glau Mix)	12" 2tr	EastWest (UK) (promo)	SAM 1269
1993 ☐	The Truth/Get It/Love/Don't Get Me Wrong	MCD 4tr	Warner Music (Australia)	4509-93283-2
1993 ☐	The Truth/Get It/Love/Don't Get Me Wrong	MCD 4tr	WEA (Germany)	4509-93283-2
1993 ☐	The Truth/Get It/Love/Don't Get Me Wrong	MLP 4tr	EastWest	4509-94315-0

1994 MCD - MVGCDS 17

Year		Title	Format	Label	Catalogue

1993 ☐ The Truth/Don't Get Me Wrong (single sided)............................7" PD EastWest.............................YZ786P
1994 ■ Warfair ....MCD 5tr MVG ....MVGCDS 17
   Tracks: Warfair(Cybersank mix)/Profit Preacher/Stars & Stripes/The Truth(Live)/Warfair
1994 ☐ Warfair ....MCD 4tr WEA (Germany)......................4509-94989-2
   Tracks: Warfair(Cybersank mix)/Stars & Stripes/The Truth(Live)/Warfair
1994 ☐ Warfair (Cybersank mix)/Stars & Stripes (single sided) ....7" PD EastWest.............................YZ804P

1993 ■ DEAF DUMB BLIND ....CD MVG MVG112
1993 ☐ DEAF DUMB BLIND ....CD PolyGram (Norway) 514 952-2
1993 ☐ DEAF DUMB BLIND ....CD East West (Jap) AMCY-3093
1993 ☐ DEAF DUMB BLIND ....CD WEA (Germ) 4509-93321 2
1993 ☐ DEAF DUMB BLIND ....LP WEA (Germ) 4509-93321 1
1993 ☐ Rosegrove/Stars & Stripes..CDS MVG ....MVGCDS 9
1994 ☐ Warfair ....MCD 4tr WEA (Germany)......................4509-95629-2
   Tracks: Warfair(Cybersank mix)/The Truth(Cyber Gauman Mix)/Nigger (Zorbact mix)/
   Don't Get Me Wrong (Zorbact Techno Mix)

1993 CD - MVG112

1994 ☐ DEAF DUMB BLIND ....CD Metal Blade 3984-14073-2
1995 ☐ Pin Me Down...MCD 4tr MVG ....MVGCDS 28
   Tracks: Pin Me Down/Better Than This/Rosegrove (live)/Pin Me Down (Die Krupps
   re-mix)
1995 ☐ Pin Me Down...MCD 4tr WEA (Germany)......................4509-99933-0
1995 ☐ Pin Me Down...MCD 4tr EastWest (UK) YZ921CD1
1995 ○ Pin Me Down...MLP 3tr WMME (Germany)....................PRO 975
   Tracks: Pin Me Down/What Are You Afraid Of/Pin Me Down (Zorbact re-mix). Promo.
1995 ☐ Pin Me Down...MLP 3tr WEA (Germany)......................4509-99342-0
1995 ☐ Pin Me Down...MCD 3tr WEA (Germany)......................4509-99343-2
1995 ☐ Pin Me Down...MCD 3tr Vertigo (Norway) 856 669 2
1995 ☐ Pin Me Down...MCD 3tr MVG ....MVGCDS 27
1995 ☐ Pin Me Down/What Are You Afraid Of ....7" EastWest (UK) YZ921X
   Clear blue vinyl.

1995 MCD - MVGCDS 31

1995 ■ Do What I Say ....MCD 4tr MVG...MVGCDS 31
   Tracks: Do What I Say/Do What I Say (Hangar re-mix/ I Don't Want To/Pin Me Down (live)
1995 ☐ Do What I Say ....MCD 4tr MVG (Germany)......................0630-10978-2
1995 ■ Tomorrow ....MCD 4tr MVG...MVGCDS 34
   Tracks: Tomorrow (Sank mix)/Armageddon Down/Three Good Riffs/Tomorrow
1995 ☐ Tomorrow ....MCD 4tr MVG (Germany) EW012CD
   Tracks: Tomorrow (Sank mix)/Do What I Say (Hangar Remix)/I Don't Want To/Tomorrow
1995 ☐ USE YOUR BRAIN ....CD MVG ....MVG 121
1995 ☐ USE YOUR BRAIN ....CD Warner Music Sweden..............4509-99631 2
1995 ☐ USE YOUR BRAIN ....LP WEA Records (Germany) 4509-99340 1
1995 ☐ USE YOUR BRAIN ....CD WEA Music Gmbh (Germany) ...4509-99340 2
1995 ☐ USE YOUR BRAIN ....CD Vertigo (Norway) 526 882 2

1995 MCD - MVGCDS 34

1997 ☐ CLAWFINGER ....CD MVG ....MVG 134
1997 ☐ CLAWFINGER ....CD WEA...3984-20177-2
1997 ☐ CLAWFINGER ....CD The Music Cartel (USA)..............TMC018CD
1997 ☐ CLAWFINGER ....2CD Metal Blade 3984-22623 2
   Bonus CD containing: The Truth (Cyberglaumix)/Warfair (Cybersankremix)/Pin me down
   (Die Krupps Remix)/Do What I Say (Hanger Remix)/Tomowwor (Sank Remix)/Biggest &
   The Best (Pitchshifter Demix)/Two Sides (Witchman's Accelerator Mix.
1997 ☐ CLAWFINGER ....LP Liquacious (UK) ....SHOOSH 001
1997 ☐ The Biggest And The Best/Runner Boy ....7" Coalition (UK) ....COLA 031
   Blue vinyl.
1997 ☐ The Biggest And The Best ....MCD 4tr MVG ....MVGCDS 49
   Tracks: Biggest & The Best/Runner Boy/Biggest & The Best (Godhead Remix)/ Biggest &
   The Best (Pitchshifter Demix)
1997 ☐ The Biggest And The Best ....MCD 4tr Metal Blade 3984-20488 2
1997 ■ The Biggest And The Best ....MCD 4tr Coalition (UK) ....COLA 031CD
   Tracks: Biggest & The Best (Album Version)/Runner Boy/Biggest & The Best (Godhead
   Remix)/Hold Your Head Up

1997 MCD - COLA 031CD

1998 ☐ Two Sides ....MCD 4tr MVG ....MVGCDS 52
   Track: Two Sides/What Gives Us The Right/Two Sides (Witchman's Accelerator Mix)/Two
   Sides Of Every Vibe
1998 ☐ Two Sides/What Gives Us The Right (transparent vinyl) ....7" Coalition (UK) ....COLA 038
1998 ☐ Two Sides ....MCD 4tr Coalition (UK) ....COLA 038CD
   Track: Two Sides/What Gives Us The Right/Two Sides (Witchman's Accelerator Mix)/Two
   Sides Of Every Vibe
1998 ■ Two Sides (Witchman's Accelerator Mix) ....10" Coalition (UK) ....COLA 038TE
   One sided promo 10".
1998 ☐ Don't Wake Me Up ....MCD 4tr MVG...MVGCDS 54
   Tracks: Don't Wake Me Up (Radio Edit)/ Don't Wake Me Up (Yoga Remix)/Realitv/Don't
   Wake Me Up
2000 ○ ANOTHER TWO SIDES ....LP n/a (Japan).........................- -
   Promo only. No artwork, only leaflet.
2000 ☐ TWO SIDES ....CDd The Music Cartel (USA)................TMC 33CD
2001 ■ A WHOLE LOT OF NOTHING ....CDd Supersonic.............................74321 87033 2
2001 ☐ A WHOLE LOT OF NOTHING – LIMITED EDITION ....CDd Supersonic.............................74321 87034 2
   Bonus: Manic Depression (Hendrix cover)/Fake A Friend

1998 10" - COLA 038TE

2001 ☐	Out To Get Me	MCD 3tr	Supersonic	74321 87035 2

Tracks: Out To Get Me/Burn In Hell/Shine On You Crazy Diamond (Pink Floyd cover)

2001 ☐	Out To Get Me	MCD 5tr	Supersonic	SUPERSONIC 079

Tracks: Out To Get Me/Shine On You Crazy Diamond (Pink Floyd cover)/Megalomania/
The Ocean/I Love To Hate Myself

2001 ☐	A WHOLE LOT OF NOTHING	CD	BMG (Japan)	BVCP 21238

Bonus: Manic Depression (Hendrix coover)/Fake A Friend/The Ocean (Led Zeppelin
cover)/Shine On You Crazy Diamond (Pink Floyd cover)

2001 ☐	Nothing Going On	MCD 5tr	Supersonic	74321 88705 2

Tracks: Nothing Going On/Eat The Hand That Feeds Me/Braindead/Confrontation/Nigger

2001 ☐	Nothing Going On/Confrontation/Nigger (Live)	MCD 3tr	Supersonic	74321 88704 2
2001 ■	THE BIGGEST AND THE BEST OF	CD	MVG	MVG 144
2003 ☐	ZEROS & HEROES	CD	Supersonic	SUPERSONIC 132
2003 ☐	ZEROS & HEROES	CDd	Supersonic	SUPERSONIC 132

Bonus: Are You Talking To Me/Where Are You Now/Point Of No Return

2003 ☐	Recipe For Hate	MCD 5tr	Supersonic	SUPERSONIC 133

Tracks: Recipe For Hate/All My Greates Fears/Get It Off My Chest/Biggest & The Best
(Live)/Rosegrove (Live)

2005 ☐	DEAF DUMB BLIND	CD	MVG	MVG 149

Bonus: Get It/Profit Preacher/Stars & Stripes/Nigger (video)/Truth (video)/Warfair (video)

2005 ☐	Dirty Lies/The Faggot In You (Club/Radio Promo CD)	CDS	Nuclear Blast	NB 1578-2
2005 ■	HATE YOURSELF WITH STYLE	CD	Nuclear Blast	NB 1550-2
2005 ☐	HATE YOURSELF WITH STYLE	CDd+DVD	Nuclear Blast	NB 1550-5

Bonus DVD recorded live at Greenfield Festival.

2005 ☐	HATE YOURSELF WITH STYLE	CD	NEMS (Argentina)	NEMS 374
2005 ☐	HATE YOURSELF WITH STYLE	CD	Irond (Russia)	CD 05-1074
2005 ☐	HATE YOURSELF WITH STYLE	CD+DVD	Irond (Russia)	CD 05-1074DL
2006 ☐	Without A Case (Club/Radio Promo CD)	CDS	Nuclear Bast	NB 1657-2
2007 ☐	LIFE WILL KILL YOU	CD	Nuclear Blast	NB 1899-2
2007 ☐	LIFE WILL KILL YOU	CDd	Nuclear Blast	NB 1899-0

Bonus: Dying To Know/Picture Perfect Skies

2007 ☐	LIFE WILL KILL YOU	CD	Irond (Russia)	CD 07-1321

Bonus: Dying To Know/Picture Perfect Skies

2007 ☐	The Price We Pay/Life Will Kill You/Prisoners	MCD 3tr	Nuclear Blast	NB 1949-2

Club/Radio Promo CD

Unofficial recordings:

1994 ☐	RECORDED LIVE IN ROSKILDE JUNE 1994	CD	n/a	FFC 001
1994 ☐	LIVE DUMB UNRELEASED	CD	n/a	DRO 4850
1994 ☐	DON'T GET ME WRONG - LIVE 1994	CD	Clawfinger	CF 001
2001 ☐	B-SIDES AND RARITIES VOL 1	CD	Tradepoint	- -
2001 ☐	B-SIDES AND RARITIES VOL 2	CD	Tradepoint	- -

2001 CDd - 74321 87033 2

2001 CD - MVG 144

2005 CD - NB 1550-2

CLENCH

Nisse Bielfeld: v, Thomas Piehl: g, Thomas Hellquist: g, Örjan Baudin: b, Jens Wide: d

Fjärdhundra - **Clench** is a great hardcore/power metal band. They are quite close in style and sound to what **Pantera** produced on *Cowboys From Hell*. Quality musicians and raw vocals. Nisse is also found in **Surrender, RFP**. and **Sixcoveredkisssongs**.

1995 ■	GOATBREATH	CD	private	CLCD 1995

1995 CD - CLCD 1995

CLEOPATRA

Kristian Hermansson: v/g, Lars Hasselfeldt: g, Henrik Orgna: k,
Örjan Wahlström: b, Marcus Sjöblom: d/k

Rimbo - High class **Whitesnake**-influenced AOR with dominating guitars and top notch Coverdale-clone vocals. OK, there are some ballads and the odd funky rocker, but as a whole the first CD (actually a collection of demos in CD-format) is well worth checking out. This band showed great promise for the future. *I'm In Love* had the potential of becoming an AOR classic. The follow-up was a bit of a disappointment as the style was less edgy. The band split in 1999 when Kristian took part in a TV-show where the dance band **Friends** was put together. After some success the band split in 2002 and Kristian became the lead singer of **The Poodles**, whom he left after a year when he concentrated on writing music for other pop artists. In 2006 he started a new solo career and released the radio oriented melodic rock with an edge album *Learning To Fly*. He was also in metal band **Starmen** with an as-yet unreleased album under the belt. The band also has some killer tracks on compilations; *Read Between The Lines* and *How Many Times* are featured on *Made In Roslagen Vol. 1* (94 Norrtälje Rockförening) and *Comuer To De Ueo-Symphony No. 24* and *Overture La Papeleria Op. 27* on *Made In Roslagen CD 2* (96 M.I.R)

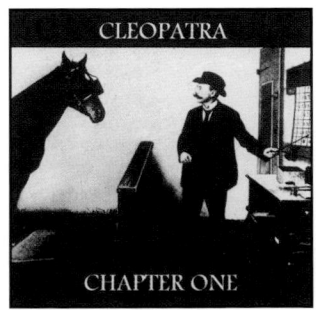
1995 CD - CLEO CD 001

1995 ■	CHAPTER ONE	CD	private	CLEO CD 001	$
1996 ■	RAIN	CD	private	CLEO CD 002	$

1996 CD - CLEO CD 002

CLOCKWISE
Benny Söderberg: v

Stockholm - Besides former *Fortune* singer Benny the debut consists of hired members: bassist John Levén (*Europe*), drummer Ian Haugland (*Europe, Trilogy*) and guitarist Jan Granvik (*Glory*). The style is very 80s-sounding melodic hard rock. On the second album the guitars were handled by Fredrik Åkesson (*Talisman, Southpaw, Krux, Opeth*) due to contractual problems for Granvik. The band has also recorded a third album which was never released.

1997 ■	NOSTALGIA	CD	Empire	ERCD 1034
1997 ☐	NOSTALGIA	CD	Pony Canyon	PCCY-01083
1998 ☐	NAÏVE	CD	Empire	W-CD 2041

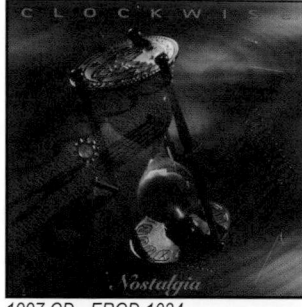

1997 CD - ERCD 1034

CLOSE QUARTERS
Viktor Granlund: v/g, Martin "KK" Karlsson: g, Martin Hederberg: b, David Svensson: d

Vadstena/Mjölby - Sounds like a mix of vintage *Kiss, Cheap Trick* and *The Hellacopters*. The album was recorded in Sunlight Studio by Tomas Skogsberg. The band was formed in 2006 by Granlund, Karlsson and Svensson and later they were joined by bass player Rasmus Ejneberg. The band recorded a couple of demos; *The Street Brawl EP* (2007), *Pleasure Under Pressure* (2008) and *Close Quarters* (2009) before Ejneberg was replaced by Hederberg. In 2010 they recorded the demo EP *Blackout* with Roberto Laghi at the helm. Late 2011 Viktor left the band to focus on his studies, and was replaced by Fredrik Josefsson.

2011 ☐	You Wanna Get Away/I Believe In Rock 'n' Roll	CDS	CQ Records/Rambo Music	- -
2011 ■	WE BELIEVE IN ROCK 'N ROLL	CD	CQ Records/Rambo Music	CQCD01

2011 CD - CQCD01

CLOSER
Joachim Dahlberg: v, Alx Reuterskiöld: g, Olle Cederborg: g,
Magnus Åsard: b, Jesper Örtegren: d

Stockholm - Formed in 2004. Not sure how to describe the band, but try mixing *Tool* in their melodic prime with a sober *Queens Of The Stone Age* and add a bit of intelligent melodies. It's a truly amazing recording, a must for any metal fan with an open mind In 2007 the band also made a second recording entitled The 39. Unfortunately it was only released digitally. The band was sadly put to rest in 2007. Alx has since made som more pop-oriented demos and mood music aimed for movies and laser shows, under the name *Carooze*. Not to be confused with death metal band *Closer*, on Pulverised.

2006 ■	Tokpela EP	MCD 4tr	private	CLRSREP-001

Tracks: Open Casket/Summon Their Cries/The Talker/Emergence. Slipcase

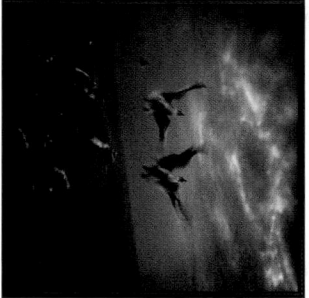

2006 MCD - CLRSREP-001

CLOSER
Andreas Melberg: v, Per Bergquist: g/v, Jonas Skoog: g,
Björn Ahlquist: b, Tobias Persson: d

Örebro/Hagfors - Formed in 2006 out of the ashes of the band *Withered*. Per is also found in *Smash Into Pieces*. During the recording of the album Skoog left the band, and Ahlquist was later replaced by Johannes. *Closer* play very technical and almost nu-metal-influenced melodic death metal, a great combination actually. Andreas does the growling and Per provides some clean vocals. Great-sounding band with well-written songs played well.

2006 ■	Darkness In Me	MCD 3tr	Pulverised	ASH020MCD

Tracks: Shelter From It/Darkness In Me/Nothing Is Everything

2008 ☐	A DARKER KIND OF SALVATION	CD	Pulverised	ASH047CD

2006 MCD - ASH020MCD

CLOUDSCAPE
Mikael "Mike" Andersson: v, Patrik Svärd: g, Stefan Rosqvist: g,
Håkan Nyander: b, Fredrik Joakimsson: d

The old era of Cloudscape

Helsingborg - In 2001 *Cloudscape* rose out of the ashes from the band *Doctor Weird*, that made a really good MCD in 1995 and an, as yet, unreleased album in 1999. Patrik Svärd, Björn Eliasson and Roger "Mini" Landin were part of *Doctor Weird*. They were completed with singer Mikael "Mike" Andersson and bass player Hans "Haynes" Persson. In 2002 *Cloudscape* recorded their first five track demo that finally lead to a deal with Roasting House Studios, who set the band up with Metal Heaven and Avalon Marquee. The self-titled debut saw the light of day in 2005. The band was compared to the likes of *Evergrey, Pagan's Mind* and *Queensryche*, well-played slightly progressive melodic metal. In 2006 the band returned to Roasting House Studios to record the second album with Pontus Lindmark (*Allen/Lande, Nostradameus, Planet Alliance*)

at the helm. The band now left Metal Heaven in the favour of Golden Core/Zyx Records who released the band's third album, also recorded by Lindmark at Roasting House. The album marks a more progressive side of the band. After *Global Drama* a couple of members decided to leave the band. Hans Persson has now been replaced by former *Sanzia/In Black/Supreme Majesy* stringsman Håkan Nyander and in February 2009 Landin decided to leave and the drums are now in the hands of *Jade/Damien/Cullooden* drummer Fredrik Joakimsson. Finally also guitarist/keyboardist Björn Eliasson decided to leave and was replaced by Daniel Pålsson. Andersson has also lent his voice to *Mountain of Power, Planet Alliance, Silent Memorial, Audiovision, Macel Coenen* and is also found in up-coming band *FullForce*. Svärd is also found in *Alyson Avenue* and *Second Heat*. The band entered the studio in 2011 to record the album *New Era*, this time using producer Micko Tweedberg (*Debase*). In November 2011 Pålsson left the band and was replaced by Stefan Rosqvist (*Dawn Of Oblivion, Stefan Rosqvist Band, FullForce*). Website: www.cloudscape.se

2006 CD - MH00020

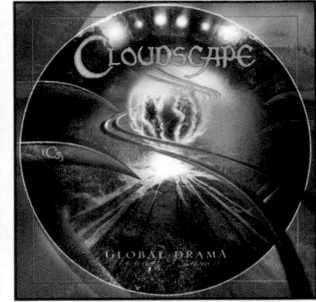
2008 CD - GCR 20036-2

2012 CD - RHRCD 687-2

2005	☐	CLOUDSCAPE	CD	Avalon Marquee (Japan)	MICP-10484
		Bonus: Inferno			
2005	☐	CLOUDSCAPE	CD	Metal Heaven	MH00004
2006	■	CRIMSON SKIES	CD	Metal Heaven	MH00020
2006	☐	CRIMSON SKIES	CD	Nightmare Records (USA)	NMR-262
		Bonus: You Belong			
2006	☐	CRIMSON SKIES	CD	Mystic Empire (Russia)	MYST CD 106
2008	☐	GLOBAL DRAMA	CD	Nightmare (USA)	NMR-442
2008	■	GLOBAL DRAMA	CD	Golden Core	GCR 20036-2
2012	■	NEW ERA	CD	Roasting House Records	RHRCD 687-2
2012	☐	NEW ERA	CD	Nightmare Records (USA)	NMR 563

CLOWN

Marianne Flynner: v, Staffan Astner: g, Lasse Hallberg: b, John Donelly: d

Stockholm - Great AOR in the mid-heavy league, with some biting guitar work. Great stuff, quite reminiscent of early *Pat Benatar*, with outstanding vocals. The actual band was initially only Marianne and Lasse. The latter sadly passed away a few years ago. The album also featured Björn Uhr on guitar (*Attack, Solid Ground*) and Leif Larsson on keyboards. Marianne pursued a solo-career in the 90s in a totally different musical direction, more towards acoustic westcoast pop. John, an Irishman that moved to Sweden, was previously playing with Gary Moore's *Skid Row*, and was later found in *Scaffel Pike*. Staffan is a highly acclaimed studio musician that has played with acts like *Eric Bibb* and in 2009 released a great fusion album with his own band *Bronk*. Unfortunately *Clown* never did lift off. After the album Staffan and John left. John was replaced by Sigge Frenzel (*Grand Slam*, Tone Norum), but the band soon folded. The album is set to be re-issued digitally, by EMI, in 2013. Both tracks on the single are non-LP.

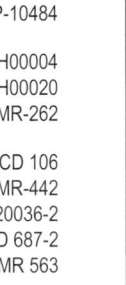
1981 7" - 7C 006-35854

1981 LP - 7C 062-35881

| 1981 | ■ | Night On The Town/Big Mouth | 7" | EMI | 7C 006-35854 |
| 1981 | ■ | CLOWN | LP | EMI | 7C 062-35881 |

CO STONE

Lars "Walle" Wallin: g/v, Lars Underdal: b, Lars "Kula" Andersson: d

Kristianstad - Great bluesy hard rock in the vein of *Sky High*/*BB Rock*. Well worth looking for!

1985 7" - HEP 2055

| 1985 | ■ | Co Stone | 7" 4tr | Hellrec | HEP 2055 $ |
| | | Tracks: Low Low Bad Bad/Pyramids/Beet-root Girl/All The Angels | | | |

COASTLINE

Helena Rosendahl: v, Thomas Hansson: g, Lars Melin: k,
Tomas Munters: b , Jan Hedlund: d

Malung - It all started in 2000 when Jan and Lars were playing in a cover band. One night at a gig Helena asked if she could sing a cover of *Anouk*. The boys loved her voice and asked if she would sing on their demo. Old friends Thomas and Tomas were asked to join and did so. In 2003 they released their debut album, recorded at former *Keen Hue* singer Stefan Morén's studio. The band plays high class AOR in the vein of *Heart*, *Pat Benetar* etc. Great vocals, killer guitar work, great songs. Truly a hidden gem! A second album was supposed to be released, but nothing has been heard so far. In 2004 the band recorded a three-track demo. The track *Maggie's Song* was also recorded for a local TV show and *We Are The Stars* for the local hockey team. The label has also disappeared. Hansson appeared in the TV show *Sikta mot stjärnorna* (Aim At The Stars) where he played the part of Angus Young.

2003 CD - VR-014

2003	■	COASTLINE	CD	Vinny Records	VR-014
2003	☐	COASTLINE	CD	Avalon Marquee (Japan)	MICP-10399
		Bonus: I'll Get Over You			

COASTLAND RIDE

Markus Nordenberg: v, Sven Larsson: g, Mikael Bohlin: k/g, Anders Rybank: k/g

Sundsvall - *Coastland Ride* was formed in 1997 by three friends that shared their love for melodic rock. The band plays quite poppy AOR in the vein of *Saga*, *I-Ten* and *Toto*. For the return album *On Top Of The World* super shredder Sven Larsson (*Street Talk, Lionville*, solo) was added to the line-up.

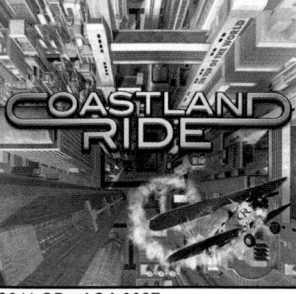

2003 ☐	COASTLAND RIDE	CD	AOR Heaven	00003
2011 ☐	COASTLAND RIDE	CD	Avenue Of Allies	AOA 0030
	Bonus: Jenny's Heart/The World IS Not Enough/Pitch Black Ride.			
2011 ■	ON TOP OF THE WORLD	CD	Avenue Of Allies	AOA 0037

2011 CD - AOA 0037

CODE

Sherwood Ball: v, Ola af Trampe: g, Anders Rydholm: b/g/k

Växjö/USA - This Swedish/American combo is something of an AOR-all-star band, featuring *Grand Illusion* members Anders, Ola and Per Svensson (the latter contributes with backing vocals on the album) and American AOR singer Sherwood (*Jay Graydon, Eddie Van Halen, Steve Morse* etc). It all started one day when Anders was listening to Sherwood singing an old *Jay Graydon* tune on the car radio wondering what he may be up to today. After an Internet search he found Sherwood's e-mail address and the collaboration started. Drums on the album were handled by Gregg Bissonette (*David Lee Roth, Joe Satriani, Toto* etc). *Code* play classic pompy AOR with great arrangements, killer vocals, nice keyboards and biting guitar-work, in the vein of *Survivor, Journey* or *Toto* (on *Turn Back*). Ola is currently workin on his melodic metal band *My Curse*, while Rydholm recorded an album with *FM* singer Steve Overland. Anders and Ola have also played with Japanese melodic metal singer *Demon Kogure*, whose album *Girls Rock* Anders produced. Anders, Ola and Per also plays on the album. Ola is also found in heavy rocking southern style band *The Killbilly 5'Ers*.
Website: www.codeband.net/

2007 CD - ESM 144

2007 ■	THE ENEMY WITHIN	CD	Escape	ESM 144
2007 ☐	THE ENEMY WITHIN	CD	Avalon/Marquee (Japan)	MICP-10632

CODEX, THE

Mark Boals: v, Magnus Karlsson: g/k, Linus Abrahamson: b, Daniel Flores: d

Stockholm/USA - A project featuring American singer Marc Boals (*Malmsteen, Ring Of Fire, Royal Hunt*) and Swedish musicians Flores (*The Murder Of My Sweet, Mind's Eye, ZooL, Tears Of Anger* etc), Karlsson (*Midnight Sun, Planet Alliance, Primal Fear* etc) and Abrahamsson (*Mister Kite, Nocturnal Alliance*). The album smells of Karlsson's song writing all over, so if you're into his other work with *Allen/Lande, Midnight Sun* etc, you'll know what to expect.

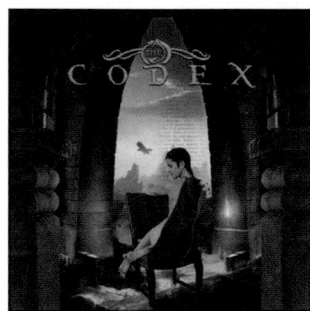

2007 CD - FR CD 353

2007 ■	THE CODEX	CD	Frontiers Records	FR CD 353
2007 ☐	THE CODEX	CD	Irond (Russia)	CD 07-DD558

COERCION

Kenneth Nyman: v, Rickard Thulin: g/b, Pelle Ekegren: d

Stockholm - The band was formed in 1992 by Kenneth, Rickard and bass player Pelle Liljenberg. They recorded their first demo, *Headway* in 1993 (here featuring drummer Gordon Johnston and guitarist Lasse Ortega), and another, *Human Failure*, in 1994, where Pelle and Lasse were out and Stefan Persson had joined on guitar, while the bass was handled by Thulin. On the debut album, *Forever Dead,* the line-up had again changed and now featured Nyman, Thulin, the returned Liljenberg, guitarist Stefan Söderberg and drummer Tor Frykhold. On the subsequent album and the last EP the band was back to the trio-format, now featuring Nyman, Thulin and drummer Pelle Ekegren (*Grave, Cauterizer*). The band officially split in 2005, but rumors of a re-union and a third album has been floating around. Old-school death metal. The tracks *Coughin' Blood* and *Blind Witness* were featured on the *Phased Out* (94 BlackBoone) compilation.

1999 CD - P.T 025

2003 MCD - AR 004

1997 ☐	FOREVER DEAD	CD	Perverted Taste	P.T 021
1999 ■	DELETE	CD	Perverted Taste	P.T 025
2003 ■	Lifework	MCD 5tr	Animate Records	AR 004
	Tracks: Man vs Logic/ Push And Hold/ Consumed/ Four Walls/ Passive Tool			

COLD EXISTENCE, THE

Jan Sallander: v/g, Jan Hellenberg: g, Patrik Syk: b, Joakim Antonsson: d

Kungälv - In the summer of 1998 Jan Sallander formed the band *Cold* together with an un-named bass player and drummer. In 1999 Jan Hellenberg joined and the subsequent year the old drummer and bass player left to be replaced by Patrik Syk (bass) and Björn Eriksson (drums). In 2003 they recorded their first official demo, *Beyond Comprehension* with Andy LaRoqcue at the helm. In 2004 Syk left to be replaced by Peter Laustsen (*Maleficio, Rimfrost, Nox Aurea*).

2005 MCD - KMP 008

A deal was inked with US label Khaosmaster Productions who released the demo as the band's first MCD. After the recording of *The Essence* Björn left and was replaced by Jimmie Olausson. Now it was Hellenberg's turn to throw in the towel due to lack of time. He was finally replaced by Wictor Lindström (*Garm*), but he was soon replaced by Robert Persson (*Nox Aurea*). In 2007 Olausson was replaced by *Vindicate* drummer Joakim Antonsson. The band recorded the album *Sombre Gates* in 2008 (produced by Pelle Saether), but due to problems with the label Open Grave it was delayed and finally taken over by Kolony Records. In 2009 Robert left the band and was replaced by Robin Lindström (*Vermillion Woods, Vanishing System*) and they were also reinforced by Thomas Backelin (*Lord Belial*), who was out again within a year. Sallander and Laustsen are ex-*Nox Aurea*, also in *When Nothing Remains*. **The Cold Existence** plays high-speed technical death metal in the vein of *Dissection, Nile* or *At The Gates*. They prove you can actually play old-school-influenced, but very varied and melodic death metal with nice guitar-work and lots of variations, even vocally, and have a great ballsy production at the same time. In 2012 Tobias Leffler took over the bass and the band signed a new deal with Non Serviam Records for a new album recorded in 2013. Antonsson is also out of the band.

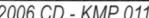

2006 CD - KMP 011   *2009 CD - KR 004*

2005	■	Beyond Comprehension	MCD 4tr	Khaosmaster Productions	KMP 008

Tracks: A Life Is Fading/Fallen To Ashes/Beyond Comprehension/Gates Of Silence

| 2006 | ■ | THE ESSENCE | CD | Khaosmaster Productions | KMP 011 |
| 2009 | ■ | SOMBRE GATES | CD | Kolony Records | KR 004 |

COLDSPELL

Niclas Swedentorp: v, Michael Larsson: g, Matti Eklund: k,
Anders Lindmark: b, Perra Johansson: d

Kiruna - **Coldspell** was formed in 2005 by guitarist and former *R.A.W* member Larsson. After recording some highly promising demos the band was finally signed by UK label Escape and the outstanding debut saw the light of day. Melodic, slightly retro-oriented hard rock with hints of early *TNT*, 1987 era *Whitesnake, Tesla, Tattoo Rodeo* etc. Well worth checking out! On the second album drummer Tobbe Broström had been replaced by Perra (*Crawley, Lost Souls*) and Tommi Partanen's bass spot had been filled by former *Dalton/R.A.W* man Anders Lindmark. *Europe*'s Ian Haugland also does some guest drumming on this album. All albums were recorded by Tommy Hansen (*TNT, Pretty Maids, Jorn* etc). On Frozen Paradise Chris Goldsmith (*Scarpoint*) had replaced bassist Anders Lindmark.
Website: www.coldspell.se

2009 CD - ESM 184

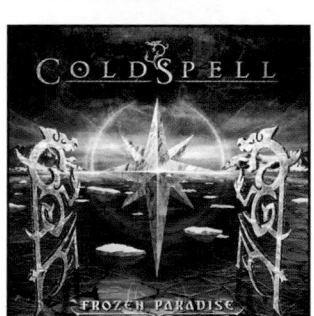

2011 CD - ESM 222

2009	■	INFINITE STARGAZE	CD	Escape Music	ESM 184
2009	□	INFINITE STARGAZE	CD	Bickee Music (Japan)	HMCX-1019
2011	■	OUT FROM THE COLD	CD	Escape Music	ESM 222
2013	■	FROZEN PARADISE	CD	Escape Music	ESM 258

2013 CD - ESM 258

COLDTEARS

Gustav Alander: v, David Johansson: g, Marcus Dahlström: b

Göteborg - It started in 2004 when David invited Gustav to sing on a track he had just written. This resulted in the foundation of **ColdTears**. In October 2005 Dahlström joined the band on bass, Adam Gelotte joined on drums and Ivar Anås on guitar. They recorded some demos, but in 2006 the latter two left the band. The trio featuring David, Gustav and Marcus recorded the MCD using programmed drums. **The Haunted**'s Peter Dolving guests on the track *No Ordinary Ghost*. In 2009 the band added two more members, Martin Färdigh on guitar and Rickard Johansson on drums. **ColdTears** planned to release their first full-length album, entitled *Silence Them All*, in 2011, it's recorded but still to be unearthed. These boys play high-class melodic death metal quite close to **The Haunted** and **Soilwork** in style. The album shows a bit more variation with some really heavy songs and more clean and effect ornamented vocals. Something to look forward to, indeed. David also wrote the music for the title track of **The Haunted**'s album *Unseen*.
Website: www.coldtears.se/

2008 MCDp - - -

2008	■	Warning	MCDp 4tr	private	- -

Tracks: No Ordinary Ghost/We Shine For All/Warning/Electric Kiss (Outro)

COLDWORKER

Joel Fornbrandt: v, Anders Bertilsson: g, Daniel Schröder: g,
Oskar Pålsson: b, Anders Jakobsson: d

Örebro - Formed in 2006. The debut featured singer André Alvinzi (*Carnal Grief*), who was fired in 2007, and replaced by *Phobos* singer Joel. *Rotting Paradise* was produced by Dan Swanö. Bertilsson and Schröder are also in thrash/death band *Ruin*, Pålsson in grindcore band *Relentless* and Jakobsson has recorded with bands like *Nasum, Route Nine* and *Necrony*. The track *Far Beyond Driven* is found on a three way split 7" EP released by Replase in 2007. The band contributes with the track *Crematorium* on the *Tribute To Repulsion* (LP 09 FDA Rekotz) compilation. High-energy, grind-infused death metal with elements of punk as well as techical metal.
Website: www.coldworker.com

2008 CD - RR 7019-2   *2006 CD - RR-6716-2*

2006 ■	THE CONTAMINATED VOID...CD	Relapse Records RR-6716-2	
2006 □	THE CONTAMINATED VOID...LP	Relapse Records RR-6716-1	
	100 clear vinyl, 300 grey, 600 white. Different cover.		
2006 □	THE CONTAMINATED VOID...CD	Relapse Japan (Japan)................. YSCY-1059	
	Bonus: Far Beyond Driven		
2008 ■	ROTTING PARADISE...CDd	Relapse Records RR-7019-2	
2008 □	ROTTING PARADISE...LP	Relapse Records RR-7019-1	
	100 clear, 300 red, 300 red with splatter, 300 yellow with red haze		
2008 □	ROTTING PARADISE...CD	Relapse Japan (Japan)................. YSCY-1102	
	Bonus: Rotting Paradise (Sepultura cover)		
2009 □	Coldworker/Deathbound (split) ....MCD 4tr	Power-It-Up............................... PIU101	
	Split with Finnish band Deathbound. Tracks: Identify With The Aggressor/Cold World Paranoia		
2012 ■	THE DOOMSAYER'S CALL...CD	Listenable Records ....POSH 162	

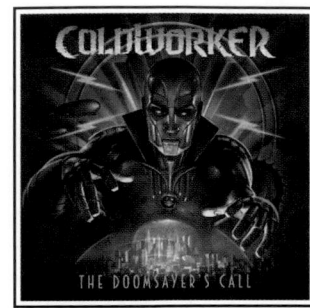

2012 CD - POSH 162

COLORBLIND
**Bengt "Boogie" Igefors: v, Fredrik Ljunge: g, Mattias Henriksson: g,
Ulrik Zander: b, Mikael Hilmersson: d**

Jönköping - The band contributed with the track *Letter To Mom* on the '93 compilation *Extreme Close-Up*, but under the name **Ten Feet Tall**. Before that they were called **Anona** and the song *Dark Life* was released on the *Loud 'N Proud* compilation (M&M). The song *Dark Life* was rearranged and rerecorded by **Colorblind** under the title *Darker*. Singer Boogie has previously recorded a 12" EP with the band **Metal Mercy**. **Colorblind** is a great powerful and heavy band. At times similar to bands like **Skintrade** and **Crawley**. Well worth checking out.

1995 ■	COLORBLIND..CD	Pyro Music Production .... PPC 001	

1995 CD - PPC 001

COLORSTONE
Johan Dahlström: v, Fredrik Bergengren: g, Johan Sandquist: b, Olle Nilsson: d

Malmö - **Colorstone** is somewhat of a Malmö who-is-who, featuring former **Time Gallery**/**Tricky Track** guitarist Bergengren, **Tricky Track** drummer Nilsson, **Silver Mountain** singer Dahlström and **Wasteland** bassist Sandquist. Together they form a great solid unit that really rocks the melodic rock foundation on their debut. If Hendrix would play AOR, he would probably sound something like this. At times quite similar to colleagues **Angeline**. A killer album!
Website: www.colorstone.se

2011 ■	INTO THE GARDEN ....CD+DVDd	CS Records SE26E11001	

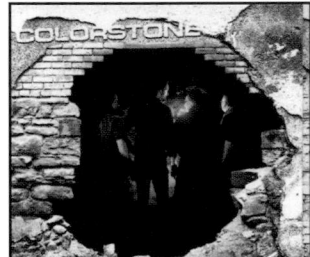

2011 CD+DVD - SE26E11001

COLOSSUS
Niklas Eriksson: v/g, Peter Berg: b, Thomas Norstedt: d

Stockholm - A Stockholm-based trio with their roots in the stoner/doom/sludge genre. The band recorded the demo *The Mechanical Engineering Of Living Machines* which gave them some well-deserved attention. Not your traditional stoner/sludge band, as **Colossus** has a more progressive twist to their music which makes it a bit more interesting. The vocals are more in the thrash/death-ish vein. Great stuff! On *Wake* Berg (ex-**Machinery**) had replaced Jonathan Näslund.
Website: www.colossus.se/

2011 ■	Spiritual Myasis...MCD 3tr	Dark Matter dmrcd001	
	Tracks: Parasite/The Gnawing/Eternal Return		
2013 □	WAKE..CD	Perennity Records ....PRCD 002	

2011 MCD - dmrcd001

COLOURDREAM
Joachim Walter: v/g, Jonas Larsson: g, Nicklas Silfverin: b, Daniel Alfredsson: d

Smedjebacken - 70s-infused hard rock, influenced by bands like **Trouble** and **Danzig** as well as some grungier overtones. High-quality stuff.

1995 ■	COMING SOON..CD	Steppinstone .... STEP 001	

COLT 45
**Leif Goldkuhl: v/g, Kjell Jennstig: g, Per-Åke Persson: g,
Michael Lagesson: b, Per Andersson: d**

Örebro - *Kärlek* is a poppy, almost countryish tune, while *Jag ger inte upp* is decent, straight hard rock, but with quite thin production. The second single is most interesting, and in particular *Kom tillbaka*, which is a great melodic hard rock with nice harmony guitars. The A-side is however more of a disco-rock type song. **Colt 45** is really on the verge of entering the book.

1995 CD - Step 001

158

The band changed their style to straight boogie rock 'n roll and changed their name to **Kenneth & The Knutters**. The track *Fortsätt framåt* is also featured on the compilation *Svensk Rock* (1981 Sonest). Not to be confused with the Bollnäs punksters.

1979 ■	Kärlek/Jag Ger Inte Upp	7"	private	RR 01
1980 ❑	Fortsätt Framåt/Kom Tillbaka	7"	Sonet	T 10014

COLT 45

KÄRLEK
JAG GER INTE UPP

1979 7" - RR 01

COMANDATORY
Andreas Blomberg: v/g, Niklas Lundgren: g, Anders Falestål: b, Andreas Melander: d

Västerås - The band was formed already in 1992. After recording some demos they were spotted by Italian label Garden Of Grief. **Comandatory** play quite melodic death metal, a bit reminiscent of **Entombed** at times, not especially well produced though. Melander is now in the band **Seventribe** and **Slick**. Blomberg also appears in the latter.

1996 ❑	COMANDATORY	CD	Garden Of Grief	GGP 003

COMATOSE
Ulf Stöckel: v, Peter Laestadius: g, Kim Lantto: b, Peter Tavér: d

Kiruna/Göteborg - Quite close to **Waving Corn** with occasional death vocals, thrown in pop-harmonies mixed with serious shit-heavy guitar-riffs. The weird album title was inspired by Swedish comedian Henrik Schyffert who made an entire monologue in Swenglish (I guess you've heard the Swedish chef in the Muppet show). As drummer Hans Carlsten wouldn't move from Kiruna, he was replaced by Peter Tavér (**Legion**) on the second release. This multischizo-union was formed in 1992 as a hobby project besides the punk, AOR and grunge bands they originally played with. They are also found on the compilations *Phased Out* and *Bästa Plattan*.

1998 7" - - -

1993 ❑	FNÖL PUT A RÖCK FROM THE KNUCK	CD	TT Records	LHM 0187
1998 ■	Shellbreak	7" 4tr	Major Label	- -

Tracks: Shellbreak/Cruising/Punkrockrevolution/Eyes Of Death. Clear vinyl.

COME SLEEP
Misha Sedini: v/g, Thomas Henriksson: g, Anders Carlström: b, Patrik Juutilainen: d

Stockholm - **Come Sleep** was created as an outlet for ideas that the members couldn't use in their other projects, alternative rockers **Lingua** and punk/hardcore band **Rövfitta** (Ass-pussy). The band was initially called **I Am Ahab**. Heavy emo-oriented doom/stoner in the vein of **Sleep** meets **Cult of Luna**. Carlström is also found in **Lingua** and guests with **Swarm Of The Sun**. In 2005 they recorded their first demo *The Skull Of Ahab*, released on CD-R.

come sleep

2007 CD - VSCD 002

2007 ■	THE BURDEN OF BALLAST	CD	Version Studio	VSCD 002

COMECON
Pelle Ström: g, Rasmus Ekman: b, Fredrik Pålsson: d

Stockholm - Formed in 1990. This was a project born from the minds of Rasmus and Pelle, former members of **Omnitron**. Pelle was also in **Agony**. On the first album L-G Petrov from **Entombed** guests on vocals, on the second it was Dutchman Martin Von Druinen (ex-**Asphyx**) and on *Fable Frolic* the band was assisted by **Morgoth**-singer Marc Grewe. On the second album Fredrik replaced Anders Green on drums. Musically this band delivers well-played fast death metal. All albums were recorded in the Sunlight studio and produced by Tomas Skogsberg.

1991 ■	Branded By Sunlight (split)	7"	CBR	CBR S 134
	Split with Merciless. Promo.			
1992 ❑	MEGATRENDS IN BRUTALITY	CD	Century Media (Germany)	849735-2
1993 ❑	CONVERGING CONSPIRACIES	CD	Century Media (Germany)	77057-2
1995 ❑	FABLE FROLIC	CD	Century Media (Germany)	77094-2
2010 ❑	MEGATRENDS IN BRUTALITY	LPg	Svart Records	SVR029

1991 7" - CBR S 134

CONCRETE STUFF
Tony Jelencovich: v, Stefan Thuresson: g, Lars Häglund: b, Staffan Johansson: d

Göteborg - Sleaze/funk-oriented hard rock, pretty good at that. On the subsequent three track demo with *Power Ranger/Under My Nails/Headkick Revolution*, recorded in 1992 they became much heavier. After this they changed drummer and also changed their name to **B-Thong**. The tracks on the *Rockslaget 1991*-compilation are *Little Teaser* and *Dog On The Run*. Tony later formed **Transport League** and is today found in **Massive Audio Nerve** (aka **M.A.N**).

1992 ■	Demo CD-Single	MCD 3tr	Exit	C.C.S 0102 $

Tracks: Rocket Angel/Little Teaser/Dog On The Run

1992 MCD - C.C.S 0102

CONFESS

Elliot Hofvander: v, Johan Blom: g, Daniel Sundberg: g,
Sebastian Sjöström: b, Samuel Olofsson Jonsson: d

Stockholm - Confess is a young Stockholm based band formed late 2007. In 2008 they released their first 4-track demo. Initially Elliot also played guitar, but decided to concentrate on the vocals. The debut was ranging from decent punkish/sleaze to *Metallica*-influenced metal, while the MCD is all sleaze. *Flickorna på TV2* is a sleaze-version of popsters *Gyllene Tider*.

2010	■	LIGHTS OUT	CD	Sliptrick	SLP021.010
2013	□	The Gin Act	MCD 5tr	Sliptrick	SLP012.034

Tracks: Divine 69/Delightful Love/Flickorna på TV2 (Gyllene Tider cover)/Get Wasted/
Sin & Tonic

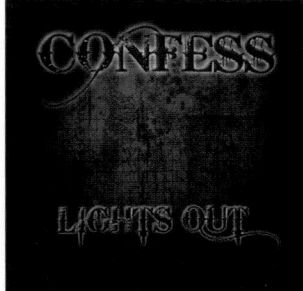

2010 CD - SLP021.010

CONFIDENCE

Emil Kyrk: v, Per-Owe "Ewo" Solvenius: g, Clas Sjöstrand: k,
David Lecander: b, Janne Jaloma: d

Stockholm - Confidence was formed in 2009 with members being switched around the first couple of years, before finding a steady line-up. The band sounds very much like orchestrated *Gutter Ballet*-era *Savatage* with former *Hell N' Diesel* singer Kyrk possessing the same vocal range as Jon Oliva. A great-sounding, very promising band, indeed. The band are only releasing their songs digitally and the MCD is only a promo release.
Website: www.confidenceofficial.com

2012	■	Prelude	MCDp 4tr	private	DT 1312-696

Tracks: Flesh And Skin/WarTorn Skies/Never Meant To Be/Poison Lies

2012 MCDp - DT 1312-696

CONQUEST

Mikael Sundkvist: v/b, Johnny Georgsson: g, Per Karlsson: g, Bo Georgsson: d

Sundsvall - Conquest was formed already in 1986 and recorded several demos such as *Glory Of Death* (1997), *Vengeance Of Our Gods* (1998) and *Only The Strong* (1999). The band has had several songs featured on American compilations. True heavy metal with guitar playing behind the neck and the works. The *Bad Girls* single was recorded already in 1990. Karlsson was also in *Blot Mine* and *Setherial*. The last line-up featured Johnny, singer Denny Edström, guitarist Daniel Sahlin-Nilsson (*In Aeternum, Setherial*), bassist Daniel Ljung (*Valkyrja*) and drummer Johan Brändström. In 2001 the band became *Inferiah*, but only one demo has surfaced.

2001	■	Bad Girls/Gambling Man	7"	Metal Fortress	MFE 002

300 copies.

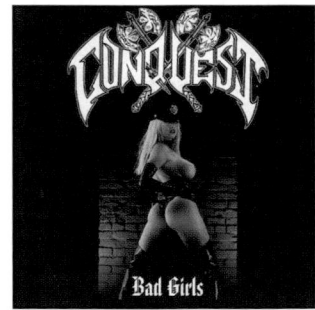

2001 7" - MFE 002

CONSTANCIA

David Fremberg: v, Janne Stark: g, Mikael Rosengren: k,
Michael Mueller: b, Peter "TrumPeter" Svensson: d

Stockholm/Mörrum/Malmö/Karlshamn/Hamburg - It all started in 2007 when the former *Scudiero/Token* keyboard player asked Stark (*Locomotive Breath, Overdrive, Mountain Of Power* etc) to lay down some guitars on a demo. It evolved into a band and more members were added to the line-up. Janne had previously played together with drummer Peter in *Overheat, Locomotive Breath* and *Mountain Of Power* and Rosengren knew *Jaded Heart* bass player Mueller from the time they were on the same label. After trying out various singers, *Andromeda* singer David Fremberg was asked and fit right in. David also sings on Janne's *Mountain Of Power* albums, while Peter is in doom/folk rockers *Faith*. At first the band tried out various producers who did test mixes, including Beau Hill (*Europe, Bon Jovi, Ratt* eyc), Pelle Saether, Pontus Norgren and Pontus Lindmark, but opted for Fredrik Folkare (*Unleashed, Scudiero*) to mix the album. Stark is also in *Grand Design, Zoom Club* and *Overdrive* while Rosengren has recorded an, as yet, unreleased album with *Skarr*, which also features Folkare. The band's second album is written and being recorded for a release in 2014. The Japan only track *Wasted* is also featured on the Melodicrock.com 15 year anniversary compilation (2012 Melodic Rock Records).
Website: www.constancia.se

2009	□	LOST AND GONE	CD	Frontiers Records	FR CD 417
2009	□	LOST AND GONE	CD	Irond (Russia)	CD 09-DD751
2009	■	LOST AND GONE	CD	King (Japan)	KICP-1398

Bonus: Wasted. Different artwork.

2009 CD - KICP-1398

CONSTRUCDEAD

Jens Boman: v, Rickard Dahlberg: g, Christian Ericson: g,
Thomas Fällgren: b, Niklas Karlsson: d

Enskede - *Construcdead* was formed in 1999 by Christian, Rickard and Erik Thyselius (also in *Terror 2000*). They drafted former *Face Down* bassist Joakim Harju and finally found singer Jonas Sandberg. After just a few months the band was already playing festivals and even supported *Soilwork* on a Japan tour. In 2002 Sandberg left the band and was replaced by former *Dog Faced God* singer Peter Tuthill. After a couple of demos the band was signed by Black Lodge and recorded the debut with producers Peter Wichers (*Soilwork*) and Richard Larsson. In 2004 Joakim left to spend more time with the family and reform *Face Down*. He was replaced by Johan Magnusson, formerly of *Carnal Forge* and the band entered the studio to record the *Wounded* EP, adding another grade of aggressiveness to the sound. In April 2005, just before entering the studio, Peter and Johan decided to part ways with the band. Jens Boman (*The Defaced*) came in as singer on short notice and recorded *The Grand Machinery*, produced by Jocke Skog (*Clawfinger*). Viktor Hemgren took over the bass after the album was recorded. In 2007 Erik and Viktor left the band. Niklas Karlsson entered the drum stool and the bass duties are taken care of by Thomas Fällgren (*Sins Of Omission*). After the recording of *Endless Echo*, Niklas was out of the band again and replaced by *Face Down* drummer Chris Barkensjö. Thyselius is now found in *Scarpoint*. *Construcdead* play high-quality Bay Area oriented thrash. In April 2010 the band parted ways with founding member Christian Ericson.

2002 CD - COLD 001

2005 CD - BLOD006CD

2002	■	REPENT	CD	Cold Records	COLD 001
2002	☐	REPENT	CD	Irond (Russia)	CD 02-356
2005	■	VIOLADEAD	CD	Black Lodge	BLOD006CD
2005	☐	VIOLADEAD	CDd	Black Lodge	BLOD006DG
		Different artwork.			
2005	■	Wounded	MCDd 4tr	Black Lodge	BLOD021CD
		Tracks: Wounded/Human Harvest/Misery/Save Me/Woulded (video).			
2005	☐	THE GRAND MACHINERY	CD	Black Lodge	BLOD026CD
2009	☐	ENDLESS ECHO	CD	Black Lodge	BLOD062CD
		Patch.			

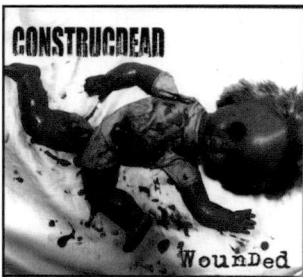

2007 MCDd - BLOD021CD

CONVICTION

José Gomez-Sanchez: v, Niclas Karlsson: g,
Fredrik Jordanius: g, Lars Rapp: b, Martin Tilander: d

Borås - The band was previously known as *Fierce Conviction*, Tight power metal with a touch of *Metallica* meets *Pantera*. After the album was recorded singer José left the band and Daniel Heiman joined. The band split when Daniel left to join *Lost Horizon*. Fredrik later joined *Raising Faith* and José, who was previously in *Empire Saint*, has his own band *Sanchez*.

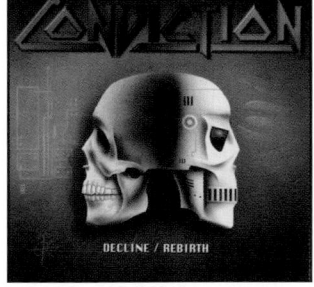

1999	■	DECLINE/REBIRTH	CD	ABS	TODAY 215

1999 CD - TODAY 215

CONVINCED, (THE BAND)

Jessica Johansson: v, Johan Gärdt: g, Joakim Johansson: g,
Amir Tehrani: b, Martin Magnusson: d

Karlstad - The band, which is actually called *The Band Convinced*, started out as a hard-core band but as they learned to handle their instruments more skilfully, they changed to 80s-influenced melodic metal. Pretty decent band, but the vocals can get a bit tedious. The album *In The Process Reach Forever Lost* was supposed to be released on CD in 2002, but it never happened and the band broke up.

1999 CD - GEN 1232 CD

1996	☐	A Dream Of Reality	7" 4tr	Words Of Wisdom	Words 001
		Tracks: To a friend/How long can live?/Believe/Unwanted knowledge. 525 copies.			
1997	☐	Convinced	7" 4tr	Words Of Wisdom	Words 002
		Tracks: Will I Ever?/Nice Try/Raped Soul/It's Your Game. 535 copies.			
1998	☐	IN THE PROCESS REACH FOREVER LOST	LP	Words Of Wisdom	Words 005
1999	☐	Silence	7"	Words Of Wisdom	Words 008
		Tracks: In Silence I Scream (7" version)/The Rain Will Remain. Avalable in transparent, orange and black vinyl with various colour splatter.			
1999	■	LIFE IS MY ENEMY	CD	Genet	GEN 1232 CD
1999	☐	LIFE IS MY ENEMY	LP	Genet	GEN 1232 LP
		Available in black, purple and white vinyl.			
2000	☐	The Way Of Life / Crash & Fall	7"	Stick To The Core	STTC 006
		Available in black and solid burgundy vinyl.			
2000	■	THE CARNIVAL	CD	Genet	GEN 1241 CD
2000	☐	THE CARNIVAL	LP	Genet	GEN 1241 LP
2001	☐	2001	MCD 4tr	Positivi Outlook	POSITIVE9
		Tracks The Invitation/ Hold Me Close/ Weak Spot/ You Let Me Follow			

2000 CD - GEN 1241 CD

COOL FOR CATS

Arnold Compier: v, Tommy Denander: g/k, Kent Kroon: g/programming

Stockholm - Well-played and well-produced AOR, similar to an up-tempo *Toto*. Arnold is a very good singer quite close to Tommy Nilsson of *Horizont*/*Easy Action*/solo-fame. Guitarist Tommy Denander has since become a household name in the melodic rock business.

1989 ■ Talking In Your Sleep/Stop Playing With Fire....................................7" private.............................CFC 001

1989 7" - CFC 001

CORE OF NATION

Andreas Hedman: v/b, Anders Dahm: g, Rickard Westerberg: g, Henrik Gustafson: d

Stockholm - *Core Of Nation* was formed in 2002 by Dahm and Henrik under the name *Distorted Nation*. Singer Rolf Berg joined and with various other members they recorded three demos, *Distorted Nation*, *Watch Your Back* and *Urban War*. The trio wanted to go for a heavier sound and formed a side-project, which soon meant the the end of *Distorted Nation* and the beginning of *Core Of Nation*. In 2005 Westerberg joined, initially playing lead guitar, but switched to bass. In 2007 they recorded the demo *Behind Enemy Lines*. Now lead guitarist Ricardo joined and the band was signed by UK based Rocksector Records. After the release of the album, Ricardo left, Westerberg switched to guitar and former bass player Ola Nilsson joined the camp. Now Rolf Berg left and was replaced by former *Soul Source* singer Kjell Holboe, who only made some live shows with the band before leaving. In February 2010 Hedman joined the gang, taking over the vocal duties and also replacing Nilsson on bass. The *Septor Of Doom* MCD was recorded. *Core Of Nation* play doom-oriented metal quite close to vintage *Candlemass*. *Website: www.coreofnation.com*

2008 CD - RSRCD 1200

2008 ■ MACHINE WORLD ....CD Rocksector Records ....RSRCD 1200
2011 ■ Septor Of Doom ....MCDp 6tr Dwarf Doom Records DDR666
    Tracks: Black Temple/Eye Of The Serpent/Dawn/Electric Funeral (Black Sabbath cover(/
    Septor Of Doom/Two Suns

2011 MCDp - DDR666

CORNEL BAND

Grigoriou Cornel: v/g, Anders Tönnäng: k, Paul Börjesson: b, Göran Alnestrand: d

Göteborg - Really good driving melodic metal. The B-side is a power ballad.

1988 ■ I Gonna Live Forever/All That I Need...7" private ....CM 001

198? 7" - CM 001

CORNERSTONE

Kent Franklin: v/g/h, Mattias Holm: g, Samuel Gustafsson: b, Fredric Josefsson/Käld: d

Jönköping - Formed in 1989. This is a Christian heavy gauge blues oriented hard rock band that should appeal even to fans of classic hard rock. In songs like *Doing My Best* from the debut they are quite reminiscent of Finnish rockers *Peer Günt*. On *Jesus Rides Harley Too* they took a step towards the heavier riff-oriented 70s hard rock. The band split, but re-united in 2006 under the name *Stonefuze*, now featuring Franklin, Gustafsson, Holm and Mick Nordström (*Modest Attraction, Spearfish*). The style was now heavier and slightly more stoner-oriented. The band released a CD in 2008. *Cornerstone* are also found on compilations such as *Resurrection Blues* on *Shades Of Blues* (96 Spark Music), *Jesus Is Coming* on *The House Of Dot* (98 Feedback Records), *Little Prayer* on *Treff CD #2 94* (94 Treff), *Ton Of Led* on *Treff CD #2 95* (95 Treff) and *What Is Happening* on *ACM Journal* (92 ACM).

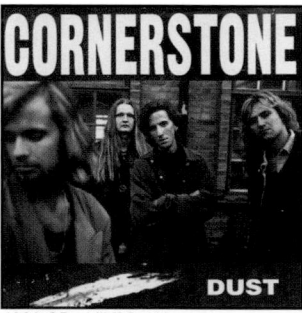

1993 CD - VIVAD 112

1993 ■ DUST ....CD Viva ....VIVAD 112
1995 ■ FLYIN' GASOLINE ....CD Megaphone ....MCD 04
1999 □ JESUS RIDES HARLEY TOO ....CD Feedback ....FBRCD 304

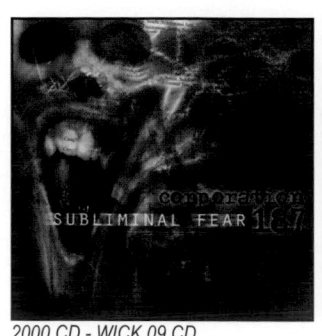

1995 CD - MCD 04

CORPORATION 187

Filip Leo (Carlsson): v, Olov Knutsson: g,
Magnus Pettersson: g, Viktor Klint: b, Robert Eng: d

Linköping - *Corporation 187* was formed in the beginning of 1998 by Pettersson, Knutsson and Eng. They actually started out as a *Slayer* cover band already in 1995, under the name *Divine Intervention*, then also featuring singer Pehr Severin (ex-*Daisy Chain*) and Filip (Carlsson) Leo (*Thornclad, Satanic Slaughter*) on bass for a period of time. They recorded the *Promo '98* demo. In 1999 Johan Ekström joined on bass and the first album was recorded featuring Pehr, Olov, Magnus, Johan and Robert. The album was recorded at Studio Underground by Pelle Saether. After the album they changed singer and Pehr was replaced by Filip. After a European tour, bass player Johan was replaced by Viktor Klint (*Thornclad*). *Perfection In Pain* was again recorded at Studio Underground and mixed by Peter Tägtgren at Studio Abyss.

2000 CD - WICK 09 CD   *2002 CD - WICK 14 CD*

The band toured with *Arch Enemy* in 2002-2003. After the last album singer Filip left the band for medical reasons, suffering from extreme headaches. The band announced they were taking a break after this. Eng is also found in *Statanic Slaughter*.

2000	■	SUBLIMINAL FEAR	CD	Wicked World	WICK 09 CD
2002	■	PERFECTION IN PAIN	CD	Wicked World	WICK 14 CD
2008	■	NEWCOMERS OF SIN	CD	Anticulture	ACCD 24

2008 CD - ACCD 24

CORRODED
Jens Westin: v/g, Peter Sjödin: g, Tommy Rehn: g, Bjarne Elvsgård: b, Per Soläng: d

Ånge - The band started out in 2004, initially as a four piece featuring Jens, Peter, bassist Nicke Källström and drummer Martin Källström. Soon second guitarist Fredrik Westin was added to the line-up. In 2005 they recorded their first demo *Heart Of The Machine*. In 2007 the self-financed album *Sessions – Ward 22* saw the light of day. In 2008 a three track CD-R entitled *III* was released and now they were picked up by Ninetone Records. In the fall of 2008 the Källström brothers left and were replaced by Bjarne and Per. Platinum selling producer Patrik Frisk collaborated with the band on the single *Time And Again* and it received some heavy rotation. The track was later picked to be the theme song for national TV show *Expedition: Robinson* (Swedish equivalent of "Survivor") and the debut album reached number two in the charts. *Corroded* play heavy, modern metal, a bit reminiscent of *Shinedown* and *Alter Bridge* in their heavier moments. Great razor sharp vocals by Westin, a fat, heavy mix and killer song material. Guitarist Tommy Rehn (*Moahni Moahna, Angtoria* etc) replaced Fredrik Westin in 2011.
Website: www.corroded.se

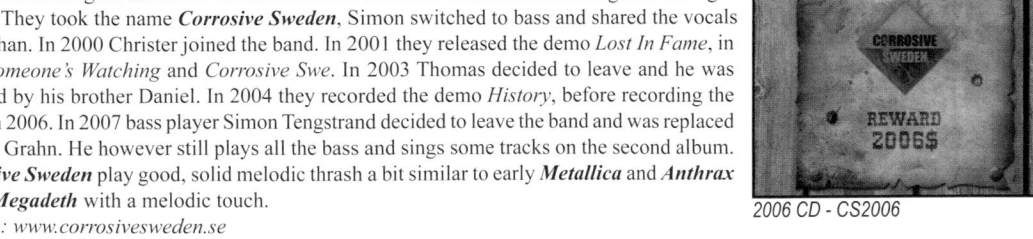
Five shades of black

2007 CD - - -

2007	■	SESSIONS – WARD 22	CD 7tr	private	--
2009	□	Time And Again	CDSp 1tr	Universal	NRCDS 012
2009	□	ELEVEN SHADES OF BLACK	CD	Ninetone	NRCD104
2009	□	ELEVEN SHADES OF BLACK	CDd	Ninetone	NRCD104X
		Bonus: Time And Again (Radio Edit)/Alpha & Omega			
2010	■	EXIT TO TRANSFER	CD	Ninetone	NRCD109
2010	□	Piece By Piece	CDSp 1tr	Ninetone	NRCDS019
2012	□	STATE OF DISGRACE	CD	Ninetone	NRCD116

2010 CD - NRCD 109

CORROSIVE SWEDEN
Johan Bengtsson: v/g, Christer Ulander: g, Lars Grahn: b, Daniel Hedin: d

Stockholm - It all began in 1997, in Iggesund, when Johan felt his two bands weren't enough and started looking for some new talents. He found drummer Thomas Hedin and guitarist/singer Simon. They took the name *Corrosive Sweden*, Simon switched to bass and shared the vocals with Johan. In 2000 Christer joined the band. In 2001 they released the demo *Lost In Fame*, in 2002 *Someone's Watching* and *Corrosive Swe.* In 2003 Thomas decided to leave and he was replaced by his brother Daniel. In 2004 they recorded the demo *History*, before recording the debut in 2006. In 2007 bass player Simon Tengstrand decided to leave the band and was replaced by Lars Grahn. He however still plays all the bass and sings some tracks on the second album. *Corrosive Sweden* play good, solid melodic thrash a bit similar to early *Metallica* and *Anthrax* meets *Megadeth* with a melodic touch.
Website: www.corrosivesweden.se

2006 CD - CS2006

2008 CD - CS2008

2006	■	WANTED	CD	private	CS2006
2008	■	FROM THIS DAY TO ETERNITY – THE 3RD CHAPTER	CD	private	CS2008

CORRUPT
Joseph Tholl: v/g, Olof Wikstrand: g, Tobias Lindquist: b, Micael Wennbom: d

Arvika - The band was formed in 2002 by Joseph and Micael under the name *Corrupted*. Inspired by bands like *Sepultura, Kreator* and *Sodom* they soon went into Wikstrand's studio Hvergelmer to record the *Lethal Anger* demo with, then session bassist, Tobias. In 2003, with Tobias now being a full time member, they recorded the demo *Shotgun Death*. Soon after, studio owner Wikstrand stepped in as second guitarist, and the line-up was complete. In 2004 the name was shortened to *Corrupt* and they recorded the demo *Born Of Greed* (at first released under the old banner). Wikstrand is also found in thrashers *Oppression* and heavy metal band *Enforcer*, where Tholl and Lindquist are also found. Tholl is also in *Black Trip*.
Website: www.shotgundeath.tk

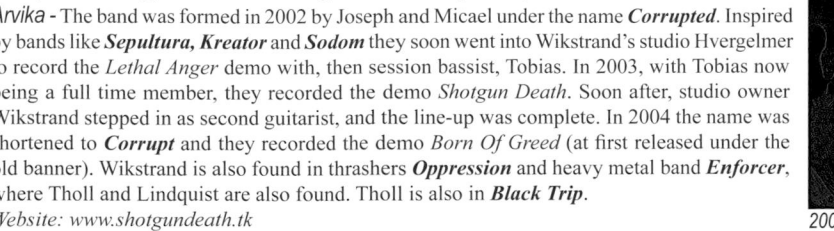
2005 7" - YOTZ#4

2005 7" - YOTZ#5

2005	■	Curse Of The Subconscious (split)	7" EP	Blood Harvest	YOTZ#4
		Split with Necrovation. Tracks: Chain Of Command/Curse Of The Pharaohs (Mercyful Fate cover). 500 copies.			
2005	□	Silence Equals Death	7" 4tr	Blood Harvest	YOTZ#5
		Tracks: Silence Equals Death/State of Fear/Profit's Prevailed/Modern World Hypocrisy. 500 copies.			

COSMIC JUNK

Ola Mohlin: v/g/k, Christer Paulstrup: g, Björn Danielsson: d

Malmö - This is actually the band *Dark Continent* that sacked their keyboard player and changed style from depressive *Sisters Of Mercy*-influenced rock to really good slightly grungy heavy riff oriented hard rock. Ola is the type of singer you probably either love or hate, and I like him.

1994 ■ COSMIC JUNK ....CD XTC ....LHM 0229

1994 CD - LHM 0229

COUNT RAVEN

Dan Fondelius: g/v/k, Fredrik Jansson: b, Jens Bock: d

Stockholm - Formed already in 1987 under the name *Stormvarning*, they recorded one track for the compilation *Storstadsrock*. In 1989 they changed their name to *Count Raven*. The band was picked up by German doom label Hellhound, and the first release under the new name was instead entitled *Storm Warning*. After the debut, singer Christian "Chritus" Lindersson left the band for a short career with *Saint Vitus* and later recorded with *Terra Firma* and Dan took over his task. The style is very similar to old *Black Sabbath* and *Saint Vitus*, with heavy, searing riffs and slow pounding rhythms. The vocals from both Christian and Dan are very influenced by *Ozzy Osbourne*, but unfortunately the early releases lack in tightness from the rhythm section. After the split in 1998 Dan formed *Doomsday Government*. *Count Raven* reformed in 2003, now with former *Doomsday Government* drummer Jens Bock replacing Christer Petersson and *Abramis Brama/Witchcraft* bassist Fredrik Jansson replacing Tommy "Wilbur" Eriksson, who is now found in doomsters *Semlah*. *Wolfmoon* was a non-album bonus track from the recording of *Mammon's War*, which is an excellent doomster.

1990 LP - ATV 16

1993 CD - HELL 026

1990	■	STORM WARNING	LP	Active	ATV 16
1990	□	STORM WARNING	CD	Hellhound	H 009
1990	□	STORM WARNING	LP	Hellhound	H 009
		Blue vinyl.			
1992	□	DESTRUCTION OF THE VOID	LP	Hellhound	HELL 019
1992	□	DESTRUCTION OF THE VOID	CD	Hellhound	HELL 019
1992	□	DESTRUCTION OF THE VOID	CD	Nuclear Blast (USA)	NBA RED 6092-2
1993	■	HIGH ON INFINITY	CD	Hellhound	HELL 026
1993	□	HIGH ON INFINITY	LP	Hellhound	HELL 026
1996	■	MESSIAH OF CONFUSION	CD	Hellhound	H0042 2
2006	□	STORM WARNING	CD	Irond (Russia)	CD 06-1110
		Bonus: High Beliefs/Frightened Eyes Never Lie			
2006	□	DESTRUCTION OF THE VOID	CD	Irond (Russia)	CD 06-1113
		Bonus: Point Of Youth/Sworn To Fun			
2006	□	HIGH ON INFINITY	CD	Irond (Russia)	CD 06-1114
		Bonus: Chritte's Triumph			
2006	□	MESSIAH OF CONFUSION	CD	Irond (Russia)	CD 06-1111
		Bonus: Regression			
2006	□	STORM WARNING	CD	Cyclone Empire	CYC 0032
		Bonus: High Beliefs/Frightened Eyes Never Lie			
2006	□	DESTRUCTION OF THE VOID	CD	Cyclone Empire	CYC 0042
		Bonus: Point Of Youth/Sworn To Fun			
2006	□	HIGH ON INFINITY	CD	Cyclone Empire	CYC 0052
		Bonus: Chritte's Triumph			
2006	□	MESSIAH OF CONFUSION	CD	Cyclone Empire	CYC 0062
		Bonus: Regression. New artwork.			
2009	■	MAMMON'S WAR	CD	I Hate Records	IHRCD 065
		Bonus: Regression			
2010	□	Wolfmoon (split)	7"	Ván Records	Ván 41
		Split with Griftegård.			
2010	□	Wolfmoon (split)	CD+7"g	Ván Records	Ván 41
		Split with Griftegård. Lavish version with CD listening copy in gatefold cover.			
2010	□	MAMMON'S WAR	2LPg	Ván Records	Ván 042
		Double LP recorded on 3 sides. Bonus: Regression			

1996 CD - H0042 2

2009 CD - IHRCD 065

COVERED CALL

Göran Edman: v, Joel Carlsson: g, Morgan Rosenquist: g,
Anders "Andy" Loos: b, Ronny Svanströmer: d

Stockholm - Quite an interesting combination of members featuring *Spearfish* bassist Thomas Thulin and *Talk Of The Town/Candlemass/Dark Illusion* singer Thomas Vikström. *Covered Call* was formed in 2006 by Svanströmer who re-connected with former jamming buddy and *Spearfish* guitarist Ola Johansson, Joel Carlsson and bassist/singer Johan Palmberg. They started writing and came up with a bunch of songs. Palmberg decides to take a break, enter Thulin. They got in touch with multi-faceted singer Vikström to take care of the vocal duties. In the autumn of 2008 Ola was replaced by Morgan Rosenquist. Highly interesting classic AOR album influenced by the likes of *Journey* and *Bon Jovi*. The debut was recorded by Fredrik

Rockers under cover

Nordström (**Dream Evil**). On the foillow-up Andy Loos (**Lion's Share**) and Göran Edman entered the ranks, both ex-**Glory**.

2009 CD - BR 019

2009 ■	MONEY NEVER SLEEPS	CD	Blistering Records	BR 019
2013 □	IMPACT	CD	Metal Heaven	00079

COWBOY PROSTITUTES
Luca "Isabelle" D'Andria: v/b, Tobbe Johansson: g, LAO: g, Jonas Lewen: d

Örebro - **Cowboy Prostitutes** came to life in 2003 when Italian-born Luca moved from London to Sweden. He put up a note in the local music store and got a call from a guitarist named Anders Wickström, who also had a drummer friend and an idea for a rock band. They started writing and recorded the demo *Take No Shit!*. The drummer was fired and Per "Pistolper" Widell was drafted. So was keyboard player Andreas Strömbäck. They recorded and released the debut single themselves, but it caught the attention of US label Retrospect. Enter second guitarist Martin Wilhelmsson. They recorded the debut album, after which Anders and Martin left and guitar slingers Tobbe Johansson and Simon Solomon came in. They also had a falling out with the label, left and recorded a new demo, *New Bullets* in 2006 and were signed by Nicotine Records. *Swingin' At The Fences* was mixed and mastered by Dan Swanö. On *Let Me Have Your Heart* guitarist Simon Solomon had been replaced by LAO and drummer Per Widell by Jonas. Sleazy hard rock in the same region as **Faster Pussycat** meets early **Skid Row** and **Junkyard**. Well-played, well-sung and with nice lead guitars. The debut suffers from bad production, but the follow-ups makes up for it. In December 2010 the band announced they will stop releasing CDs and only release digital singles. In 2011 Per Bjelovuk became the band's drummer.
Website: www.cowboyprostitutes.net

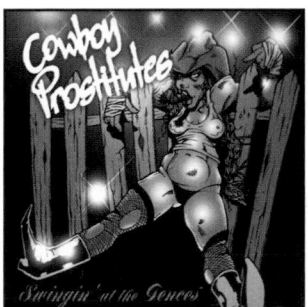
2008 CD - SBCD 045

2009 7" - TRR 011

2004 □	Over The Top/Downtown	CDS	private	COW 001
2005 □	COWBOY PROSTITUTES	CD	Retrospect	- -
2008 □	SWINGIN' AT THE FENCES	CD	Nicotine Records	NIC 047
2008 ■	SWINGIN' AT THE FENCES	CD	Sunny Bastards	SBCD 045
2009 □	LET ME HAVE YOUR HEART	CD	Sunny Bastards	SBCD 059
2009 ■	Pirate Town/Just As Long	7"	Tornado Ride Records	TRR 011
	Red vinyl. 500 copies.			

CRAFT
Mikael Nox Pettersson: v, John "Doe" Sjölin: g, Joakim Karlsson: g, Phil Alex Cirone: b

Mora - The band was formed under the name **Nocta** and changed their name to **Craft** in 1998. The band's first release was the demo *Total Eclipse* 1999. Sjölin is also found in **Twin Earth**. The core of the band is Nox, John (also in **Shining** and **Watain** live) and Joakim. On the first three albums the band also featured Daniel Halén (**Twin Earth**) on drums until 2005. Norwegian Per "Dirge Rep" Husebö (**Gorgoroth**, **Enslaved**) plays drums with the band live. Uncompromising old-school black metal, similar to a primitive **Marduk**. Despite such great musicians it's actually mindboggling how they can sound as bad at times, while some songs are quite enjoyable in some moments. Should appeal to fans of **Armagedda** and **Avsky**. On *Void* Joakim concentrated on guitar and Phil Alex Cirone (**Shining**) was added on bass.

Craft nox you out!

2000 CD - LEGION 001

2002 CD - MONUMENT 009

2005 CD - CR 006

2000 ■	TOTAL SOUL RAPE	CD	The Black Hand	LEGION 001
2002 □	TOTAL SOUL RAPE	LP	Selbstmord Services	MONUMENT 007
	200 copies. Poster.			
2002 ■	TERROR PROPAGANDA	CD	Selbstmord Services	MONUMENT 009
2002 □	TERROR PROPAGANDA	LP	AIDS Productions	HIV 001
	200 copies. Poster.			
2003 □	TOTAL SOUL RAPE	CD	Selbstmord Services	MONUMENT 007
	Re-issue with silver letters.			
2003 □	TOTAL SOUL RAPE	CD	Selbstmord Services	MONUMENT 007
	Re-issue with blue letters. Features a hidden track.			
2003 □	TOTAL SOUL RAPE	LP	Perverted Taste	CELLAR 006
2004 □	TOTAL SOUL RAPE	CD	Moribund	DEAD 058
2005 ■	FUCK THE UNIVERSE	CD	Carnal	CR 006
2005 □	FUCK THE UNIVERSE	CD	Southern Lord (USA)	SUNN 54CD
2005 □	FUCK THE UNIVERSE	2LPg PD	Southern Lord (USA)	SUNN 54
	Mail order version: one LP on red vinyl, and one is a picture disc. Regular version: one Lp black vinyl and on picture disc.			
2005 □	FUCK THE UNIVERSE	2LPg	Blut & Eisen/Carnal	- -
	100 in grey splatter die hard vinyl + 400 black vinyl. Bonus: 3 untitled rehearsal tracks.			
2006 □	TOTAL SOUL RAPE	CD	Unexploded	UER 009
2011 □	VOID	CD	Carnal Records	CRCD 012
2011 □	VOID	2LPg	Carnal/Trust No One	CRLP012/TNO036
	100 clear + 400 black vinyl.			
2011 □	VOID	CD	Southern Lord (USA)	LORD 145
2011 □	VOID	2LPg	Southern Lord (USA)	LORD 145
	Clear black splatter or black vinyl.			

CRANIUM

Fredrik "Chainsaw Demon" Söderberg: v/g, Philip "Grave Raper" Von Segebaden: b/v, Johan "Necro Nudist" Hallberg: d

Stockholm - The band was formed in 1985 under the name *Legion* and the subsequent year they recorded the demo *The Dawn*. They broke up, but reformed in 1996 as *Cranium*. The debut album featured drummer Joakim Pettersson (*Niden Div. 187, Regurgitate, Thy Primordial, Unmoored, Dawn* etc), guitarist Gustaf von Segebaden (*Legion*), Fredrik and Philip. On the second album Pettersson was replaced by Hallberg (*Utumno*) and on the third release the band was a trio with Gustaf out of the band. In 2001 Hallberg committed suicide. Fredrik is also found in *Dawn* and *Legion*, while Philip has played with *Afflicted, Legion, Defender* and *Dawn*, where he's still a member. German-sounding speed metal á la *Destruction* or *Exodus* with a tongue in cheek approach. Really fast and tight. The lyrics really take the piss out of the genre with nice lyrics and song titles like *Dentist Of Death, Lawnmower Lover* and *Slaughter On The Dance Floor*.

1997 MCD - NR 6669

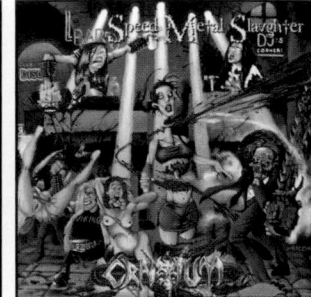

1998 CD - NR 033

1997 ■	Speed Metal Satan	MCD 5tr	Necropolis	NR 6669	

Tracks: Lucifer's Breath (The Storm To Come)/Storms Of Steel And Hate/Riders Of Damnation/Bestial Butcher/Raped By Demons

1998 ■	SPEED METAL SLAUGHTER	CD	Necropolis	NR 033	
1999 ☐	SPEED METAL SENTENCE	CD	Necropolis	NR 039	

CRASH

Michael Erlandsson: v/k, Jan Eliasson: g/k, John Melander: b, Lars Eliasson: d

Alingsås - High-class melodic hard rock with great guitars and vocals. Michael Erlandsson started a solo career in late 1994, but in a much softer AOR-direction. He has also recorded with *Last Autumn's Dream*. The album contains a very good cover of *Led Zeppelin*'s *Rock And Roll*. In 2006 an Italian bootleg label "released" the CD as a CD-R, sold on Ebay. The Eliasson brothers has recorded an outstanding album under the name *Born Electric*.

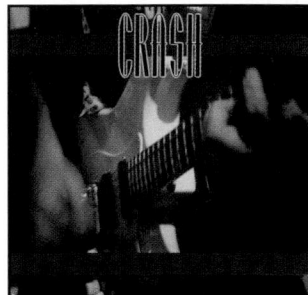

1992 CDS - EMCDS 9210-1

1992 ■	Eyes Don't Lie/Six Strings And A Highway	CDS 2tr	EMP	EMCDS 9210-1	
1993 ■	CRASH CRASH CRASH	CD	EMP	EMCD 9303-1	$

CRASHDÏET

Simon Cruz: v, Martin "Sweet" Hosselton: g, Peter "London" Lundén: b, Eric "Young" Gjerdum: d

Stockholm - Formed in 2000 by David "Dave Lepard" Hellman, at first named *Crash Dïet* and featuring drummer Dennis Ekdahl (*Raise Hell, Rutthna, Sins Of Omission, Siebenbürgen* etc), guitarist Tobias Forge (*Repugnant, Ghost, Subvision*) and bassist Gustav Lindström (*Repugnant*, ex-*Ghost, Iron Lamb*). The style was then classic metal. It however changed to sleaze and in 2002 the first recording line-up, featuring Lepard, Sweet, London and Young (ex-*Pandemonic*) was formed, now named *Crashdïet*. The first single was produced by Ulf "Chris Laney" Larsson. Quite a hyped glam/sleaze band that even had a major ad campaign on national Swedish TV, which was quite unheard of in this genre, however not for the band but for phone operator 3. Original singer David "Dave Lepard" Hellman took his life January 20, 2006. The band decided to continue, despite having said in interviews that the band would rest with Dave. However six months later, in 2007, the band returned with new Finnish singer Olli "H. Olliver Twisted" Herman Kosunen (ex-*Restless Love*) and recorded the album *The Unattractive Revolution*, which featured guest spots from *Mötley Crüe*'s Mick Mars. The video for the single *In The Raw* was recorded by the former singer's grave. In 2009 Olliver was replaced by Simon Cruz (ex-*Foxy*, the band that became *Dynazty*) who made his debut on *Generation Wild*.

2004 7" - RRR001

1993 CD - EMCD 9303-1

2004 ■	Riot In Everyone/Out Of Line	7"	Rabid Rednecks Records	RRR001	$
2005 ■	Riot In Everyone/Riot In Everyone (demo)	CDS	Stockholm Records	986 888-9	
2005 ☐	Knokk 'Em Down/Tikket	CDS	Stockholm Records	987 185-4	
2005 ☐	Breakin' The Chainz/Tomorrow (demo)	CDS	Stockholm Records	987 324-5	
2005 ☐	REST IN SLEAZE	CD	Stockholm Records	987 234-5	
2005 ☐	REST IN SLEAZE	CD	Universal (Japan)	UICO-1090	

Bonus: Tomorrow (Demo)/Riot In Everyone(Demo) + videos: Riot In Everyone/Private Shit

2005 ☐	It's A Miracle/Out Of Line	CDS	Stockholm Records	987 487-0	
2007 ☐	In The Raw/In The Raw (Instrumental)	CDS	Stockholm Records	0602517-47122	
2007 ■	THE UNATTRACTIVE REVOLUTION	CD	Universal Records	0602517-47146	
2010 ☐	Generation Wild/One Of A Kind/Fear Control	MCDpg 3tr	Gain	GPCD 75	
2010 ☐	GENERATION WILD	CD	Gain	GPCD 76	
2010 ☐	GENERATION WILD	LP	Gain	GPCD 76V-L	
2010 ☐	GENERATION WILD	CD	King (Japan)	KICP-1482	

Bonus: Sick Mind

2012 ☐	THE SAVAGE PLAYGROUND	CD	Gain	8876544-0292	
2012 ☐	THE SAVAGE PLAYGROUND	2LP	Back On Black	RCV094LP	

1000 copies. Bonus: Liquid Jesus

2012 ☐	THE SAVAGE PLAYGROUND	CD	Icarus Music (Argentina)	ICARUS 1087	
2012 ☐	GENERATION WILD	LPg	Nuclear Blast	NB 2838-1	

300 hand-numbered copies. Red vinyl. Poster.

2005 CDS - 986888-9

2007 CD - 0602517-47146

CRASH THE SYSTEM

Sören Kronkvist: k/b/g, Daniel Flores: d/b/g/k

Stockholm - Crash The System is one of the numerous bands/projects involving drummer/ multi-instrumentalist/producer Flores (*The Murder Of My Sweet, Mind's Eye, Tears Of Anger* etc). The band is a collaboration between Flores and former Finnish hurdle champion Kronqvist that came about in 2008. The album is a nice mix of AOR and hard rock/metal. It also features guest spots from numerous musicians, such as singers Göran Edman, Thomas Vikström, Mats Levén, Björn Jansson (*Tears Of Anger*) and Angelica Rylin (*The Murder Of My Sweet*), guitarists Johan Niemann (*Therion, Mind's Eye, The Murder Of My Sweet*), Daniel Palmqvist (*The Mudrer Of My Sweet*), Manuel Lewys (*Machinery*) and keyboardist Andreas Lindahl (*The Murder Of My Sweet*).

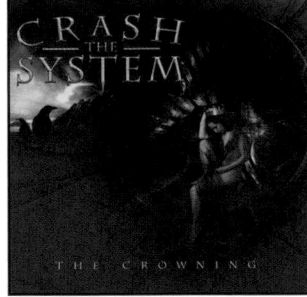

2009 CD - FR CD 418

2009	■	THE CROWNING	CD	Frontiers Records	FR CD 418
2009	□	THE CROWNING	CD	King Records (Japan)	KICP-1397
		Bonus: Dangerous Game			
2009	□	THE CROWNING	CD	Irond (Russia)	CD 09-DD750

CRAWLEY

Joel Andersson: v/b, Lawrence West: g , Perra Johansson: d

Uppsala - It started in 1987, when Lawrence and Joel played in the band *Vital Signs*. After having spent some time in the US they returned to Sweden in 1992 and formed *Crawley*. On the band's debut the bass was handled by Matte Järnil and rhythm guitarist Jonas Ragnarsson was also part of the band. *Addiction* is not as heavy as the follow-up, but more influenced by bands like *Extreme* and *King's X*, while *Supersonic* is far heavier, more guitar-oriented and shows more traces from the heavier sides of *Alice In Chains* and *Soundgarden*. The album also meant a switch from Matte to new bass player Sampo Axelsson. Late 1994 the band started receiving great recognition in Europe. The *Soundfront Releases Spring 95* three band split contains demo-versions of *N.N.P.W* and *TV Screen*. In 1995 the band split, but reformed with bass player Christer "Chris Goldsmith" Goldschmidt replacing Sampo. He was however not part of the band on the third album. Matte was later found in labelmates *Lost Souls*. Lawrence has previously recorded an MLP with the band *Damien*. *Territorial* shows an even heavier and more brutal side of the band, with Joel's singing transforming into the barbwire type of vocal treatment and a musical direction approaching a ton of bricks. Sampo later joined *Road To Ruin* and *Lion's Share*, while Goldsmith can be found in *Full Strike, Hellinor* and *Scarpoint*.

1992 CD - FRONTCD 2

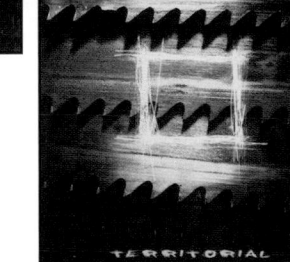

1994 CD - FRONTCD 6

1996 CD - RR 8884 2

1992	■	ADDICTION	CD	Soundfront Records	FRONTCD 2
1994	■	SUPERSONIC	CD	Soundfront Records	FRONTCD 6
1994	□	Soundfront Releases 94 (split)	CDSp	Soundfront Records	FRONTPR 1
		Split with Lost Souls. Track: Wrecking Crew. Promo.			
1996	■	TERRITORIAL	CD	Soundfront/Roadrunner	RR 8884 2

CRAZE

Apollo Papathanasio: v, Patrik Holmgren: g, Christian Lecaros: k,
Ricki Aresu: b, Christof Jeppsson: d

Halmstad - Melodic, keyboard-based good AOR featuring a young Apollo Papathanasio. Formed in 1986 and split in 1989. Drummer Christof was only 13 years old. The band also recorded a 4-track demo which was never mixed. Apollo was later in bands like *City People, Majestic* and is now in *Spiritual Beggars* and *Firewind*. The cover was painted by Lecaros mother.

1988	■	Living In Sin/Too Hot Loving	7"	Sting Records	STS 8848 $

1988 7" - STS 8848

CRAZY LIXX

Danny Rexon: v, Andy Dawson: g. Loke "Luke" Rivano: b, Joél "Joey" Cirera: d

Lund - This sleaze-unit was formed in 2002 by singer/guitarist Danny and guitarist Vic Zino. They later found former *Omnious/Enshrined* drummer Joél. All three had actually played together in the band *Blindead* prior to this. They drafted guitarist Max Flamer and recorded a three-track demo (*Death Row/Bad In A Good Way/Love On The Run*). As Danny skipped playing guitar they also drafted second guitarist Calle "Krizzy Field" Fäldt (later in *Pretty Wild*). A second demo, entitled *Do Or Die* was finished in 2004. After a fistfight between Max and Krizzy in Kalmar, Sweden, they were both fired. In May 2005 they did another recording, the *Do Or Die* CDS, with a different line-up featuring Danny, Vic, Joél and stand-in bassist John Huldt. In the summer of 2005 they finally found Luke. After working their way up playing shows and recording demos they were now finally signed by Swedmetal Records. In 2006 the label also released the CD-R promo *Want It (Radio version)* in 100 copies.. In 2008 the band supported *Hardcore Superstar*, when their guitarist announced he was leaving. Vic was asked to stand in on the tour, and was consequently asked to join the band leaving *Crazy Lixx* guitarless again

Ready for some rioting?

in April the same year. They however soon found Stockholm based, former *Sharp* guitarist, Andy Dawson who soon relocates to the south and makes his debut on the *Make Ends Meet* single. In 2009 the band was picked up by Italian label Frontiers, who released the album *New Religion* in 2010. A great album, where the band has become more hard rock in their sound, even though there are some strong hints of *Poison* and *Skid Row* in some tracks. Before the recording of the follow-up drummer Cirera declared this would be his last album with the band. Furthermore, right after the recording of *Riot Avenue*, on February 14, 2012, Loke announced he was leaving the band. Edd Liam replaced him.
Website: www.crazylixx.com

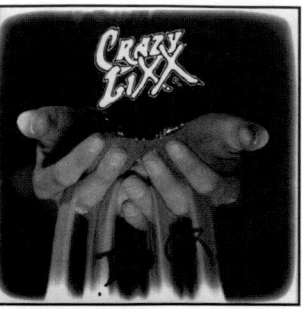

2005 CDS - DR009

2005	■ Do Or Die/Death Row (demo)	CDSp 2tr	private	DR009
	1000 copies.			
2006	■ Heroes Are Forever/On Your Marks, Get Set, Rock!	CDSp 2tr	Swedmetal	SM-03-CDS
	1000 copies.			
2007	☐ LOUD MINORITY	CD	Swedmetal	SM-014-CD
2007	☐ LOUD MINORITY	CD	Stay Gold (Japan)	ARTSG-025
	Bonus: Bad In A Good Way/No Guts, No Glory			
2008	☐ Make Ends Meet/Want It (Radio Edit)	CDS	Swedmetal	SM-04-CDS
	1000 copies.			
2010	☐ NEW RELIGION	CD	Frontiers Records	FRCD 452
2010	☐ NEW RELIGION	CD	Stay Gold (Japan)	ARTSG-030
	Bonus track: Lights Out			
2012	☐ RIOT AVENUE	CD	Frontiers Records	FRCD 551
2012	☐ RIOT AVENUE	CD	Icarus Music (Argentina)	ICARUS 972
2012	☐ In The Night/Riot Avenue/Fire It Up	MCDpg 3tr	Frontiers Records	334 42976
	Came with Sweden Rock Magazine #91, 2012.			

2006 CDS - SM-03-CDS

CRAZY VISIONS

Thomas Olofsson: g/v, Leif Starck: g, Morgan Mathiasson: k,
Stefan Olofsson: b, Tony Johansson: d/v

Kungälv - Morgan, Tony, Leif and Thomas recorded a poppy single under the name *Tencider* in 1979. The same line-up changed the name to *Crazy Vision*. Semi-heavy melodic hard rock, like a mix of *Kiss* and *Magnum Bonum*, with some ballads. The song *The War Is Coming* was used as a background song for the Swedish political election. On the single Morgan switched to keyboard and Stefan was added on bass. When the band had just released the last single the distribution company SOS went bankrupt. The last release was actually released under the name *Richard Hallifax & Crazy Vision*, with UK DJ Richard handling the vocals. The band then changed their name to *Tiffany* and did a 180 degree musical turn to pure dance-pop.

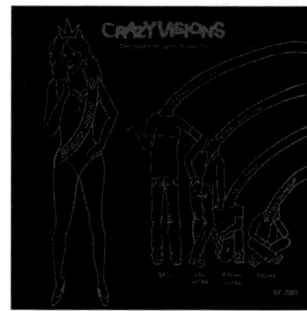

1982 7" - SF 2002

1982	■ Beauty Queen/Back To Rock 'N Roll	7"	Superfax	SF 2002
1982	○ Crazy Nights/Let's Make Love	7"	Superfax	SF 2003
1983	■ The War Is Coming/Let's Make Love	7"	Superfax	SF 2004
1984	○ Mr. Man In The Moon/(instrumental)	7"	Superfax	SF 2005

CREMATORY

Stefan Harrvik: v, Urban Skytt: g, Johan Hansson: b, Mats Nordrup: d

Stockholm - Crematory started out in 1989. Guitarist Micke Lindvall (*Proboscis*) and drummer Mats were ex-*Afflicted Convulsion/Afflicted*, while bass player Johan was ex-*Megatherion*. They recorded their first demo *Metal Torment* the same year. In the fall of 1989 Urban joined the band and shortly after Micke left. The second demo (actually named *Demo 1* on the cassette) *The Exordium* was recorded in 1990. In 1991 the follow-up demo *Wrath From The Unknown* was recorded and the band was offered a deal by M.B.R Records. *Denial* contains two new songs and one song from each demo (not counting the first). Urban designed the cover and he actually drew the *Dark Funeral* logo, too. As a coincidence Johan is also an excellent logo-designer responsible for the logos of bands like *Unleashed, Unanimated, Dawn* etc. After the release of *Denial,* Stefan lost interest and they went on as a three-piece for some time. In 1992 they recorded another demo, *Netherworlds Of The Mind*, but the band was highly dissatis-fied with the studio and the outcome of the recording. Mats was also playing with grind band *Regurgitate*, which also caused some friction in the band. Stefan had left and the band wasn't satisfied with the label, so when questions of a full length album came up in 1993, the band instead split. Ironically Mats was fired from *Regurgitated* and Urban (who works as a science and math teacher) replaced him. Mats was ex-*General Surgery*. Urban and Johan continued in *Regurgitate* and Stefan was also part of *Necrophobic* for some time. High-speed, quite technical at times, old-school-oriented death metal, well-played, with traditional death type vocals. The 2009 CD is a compilation of all demos.

1983 7" - SF 2004

1992	☐ Denial	MLP 4tr	M.B.R. Records	MANGLED 4
	Tracks: Into Caliphates/Chunks Of Flesh/Denial/On Concreted Ground			
1992	☐ Denial	MCD 4tr	M.B.R. Records	MANGLED 4
2009	■ DENAIL	CD	Necroharmonic	SLEAZY 025
	First pressing (matrix: CREMATORY - 35842) made from incorrect master.			

2009 CD - SLEAZY 025

CREOZOTH

Michael Storck Uppman: v, Lars "Lasse" Johansson: g,
Torbjörn "Tobbe" Moen: b, Jan Lindh: d

Stockholm - In 2004, when *Candlemass* was having a break, members Johansson (ex-*Macbeth*) and Lindh (ex-*ATC*), who had earlier also recorded an album together in the band *Zoic* in 1996, started a new band. They teamed up with former *Rising Force/Paradise/Explode* singer Uppman and *Red Fun/Oz/Gotham City/Silent Call* bass player Moen and formed the band *Tarmac*, which later became *Creozoth*, named after a *Monty Python* character. The style was as heavy as *Candlemass*, but more up-tempo and almost a bit thrashy, sounding a bit like *Destiny* in their almost Wagnerian metal vein. An outstanding album well worth checking out.

2005 ■ CREOZOTH...CD Escapi...EMS20027

2005 CD - ESM20027

CRIER

Björn Svensson: v, Thomas Axelsson: g, Jonas Hellström: g,
Anders Olinder: k, Mats Svensson: b, Mikael Gustavsson: d

Sölvesborg - It all actually started back in 1982 when the band was called *Metal Muthaz*, which later became *Sacrifice*, who recorded one single. In 1986 the name was changed to *Crier* and Rikard "Rille" Larsson (later in *Mercy, Supreme Majesty* etc.) handled the vocals. The track *Fantasy World* was featured on the compilation *The Metal Collection* (1986 Ebony Records). In 1987 the band entered the Rock SM competition, now featuring Anders Strengberg on vocals, Axelsson and Henrik "Stanley Hawk" Lindén on guitars, Svensson on bass and Gustavsson on drums. In 1988 the band changed singer to Björn Svensson and Benny Lundgren replaced Stanley. When the band released their single *Bad Booze* (a song originally recorded by *Metal Muthaz*), the line-up featured keyboard player Olinder and guitarist Hellström. The A-side is actually a ballad, while the B-side is a melodic hard rocker. Mid-league stuff. The band folded in 1990. In 2009 they made a first re-union attempt, but the chemistry wasn't there. In 2011 Mats and Thomas decided to resurrect *Crier* with original singer Björn and new members, drummer Jimmy Ek and guitarist Andreas Klügel. A new digital album was recorded in 2012. *Website: www.crier.se*

1989 7" - HSP 2075

1989 ■ Bad Booze/Running In The Night ....7" Hellrec... HSP 2075 $

CRIMSON MOONLIGHT

Simon "Pilgrim" Rosén: v, Erik Tordsson: g, Per Sundberg: g,
Johan Ylenstrand: b, Gustav Elowsson: d

Nässjö - Keyboard-driven Christian black metal, or as the band calls it; "sophisticated black metal". The band was formed in 1997 with the aim of playing old-school black metal and do one show before breaking up. However, they decided to continue. In 1997 they recorded an 11-track demo entitled *The Glorification Of The Master Of Light*. The band was featured on the compilations *In The Shadow Of Death* (Endtime 00), *Twisted Sounds From The Swedish Underground* (Topsound 99) and *Power From The Sky* (02 C.L. Music & Publishing). The line-up on the first MCD featured Simon, Gustav, guitarists Jonathan Jansson and Petter Stenmarker (ex-*Oblivion*), bassist Simon Lindh and keyboardist Alexander Orest (ex-*Sanctifica*). In 2000 Jonathan left to concentrate on his other band *Sanctifica* and was replaced by Samuel Lundström. Around this time the band also switched bass player to David Seiving. When the band recorded *The Covenant Progress*, Hubertus Liljegren (*Pantokrator, DivineFirand, Sanctifica, Audiovision*) had replaced Seiving, and Per Sundberg replaced Samuel. *Songs From The Archives* features various old recordings. On *Veil Of Remembrance* Hubertus had switched to guitar, excluding

2003 CD - RRCD 013

2005 CD - RRCD 022

keyboardist Orest and adding new bass player Erik Tordsson. Jonathan was also replaced by Jani Stefanovic (*DivineFire, Sins Of Omission, Miseration* etc). On the *In Depths...* MCD, mixed by Pelle Saether, sold on the US tour, Jani and Hubertus were out of the band. Erik had switched to guitar and new bass player Ylenstrand (*Exhale, Miseration, Sordid Death*) was in. *Crimson Moonlight* play old-school-sounding death metal, quite technical and well-played, with screeching growling vocals, sounding like any other black metal band with the exception of the Christian lyrical content.
Website: www.crimsonmoonlight.com

1999 ☐ Eternal Emperor...MCD 5tr private ....-
     Tracks: Intro-Preludium/Where Darkness Cannot Reach/Symphony Of Moonlight/Final
     Battle/Eternal Emperor
2003 ■ THE COVENANT PROGRESS...CD Rivel Records ....RRCD 006
2003 ■ SONGS FROM THE ARCHIVES ....CD Rivel Records ....RRCD 013
2005 ■ VEIL OF REMEMBRANCE ....CD Rivel Records ....RRCD 022
2007 ■ In Depths Of Dreams Unconscious.....................................MCD 4tr Endtime..ENDCD15
     Tracks: In Depths Of Dreams Unconscious/The Advent Of The Grim Hour/Shiver Of Fear/
     Alone In Silence

2007 MCD - ENDCD15

CRIPPLE

Daniel Ruud: v/g, **Anton Renborg:** g, **Mattias "Lurgo" Fransson:** b, **Daniel Berg:** d

Örebro - Formed in 1988, with the same members. Quite an interesting technical thrash band with some nice musical twists and turns. The music contains elements of traditional thrash as well as the more progressive techno-metal. The vocals are a bit closer to death metal though. The band made their first demo, *No More Living* in 1990 and the follow-up, *Independent Luminary*, came the year after. After the CD the band recorded some demos and the style turned a bit more psychedelic, also with cleaner vocals. Guitarist Anton was also lead singer in rap-metal band *Waving Corn*. Ruud is now in post-grunge band *Honk The Horn* and Berg is in punk bands *My God The Sound* and *Leatherboys*.

1993 CD - 8213-2

1993 ■ GREEN PILLOW..CD Crypta/Inline..8213-2

CROC

Tomas Jonasson: v/g, **Christoffer Seidbo:** g, **Anders Nilsson:** k,
Christofer Olofsson: b, **Mikael Hurtig:** g

Göteborg - Great melodic hard rock with a touch of pomp. Not really AOR either. The vocals are a bit weak, but the song material rocks. Seidbo later formed *Faster Fuel* and is now found in folk-rockers *Black Magic Fools*.

1997 CD - EVER001

1997 ■ COUGH IT UP...CD Everest...EVER001

CROMLECH

Fredrik Arnesson: v, **Jonas Eckerström:** g, **Henrik Meijner:** g,
Dick Löwgren: b, **Mattias Bäck:** d

Varberg - In 1994 Meijner and, at the time drummer, Eckerström formed the band *Delirium*. After some line-up changes Bäck joined as drummer and Eckerström returned to his main instrument, guitar. Bassist Anders Lundin joined, so did singer Arnesson and *Cromlech* was born. In 1996 the recorded the first demo, *...And Darkness Fell*. The subsequent year the track *My Entombment In The Desolate Shade Of Bereavement* was featured on the *Near Dark Compilation Vol 1*. A deal was offered the band, but they put it on hold for a while. Meijner joined *Eucharist* and Arnesson joined *Ablaze My Sorrow*, which later on Lundin also joined. In 1999 the decided to pick up the pieces and the band now recorded a new three track demo entitled *Promo '99*. In the fall of 1999 Lundin left and was replaced by former *Eucharis/Arch Enemy* player Löwgren. They were signed by Italian label Beyond Productions who released the MCD. It was also planned to be released as a 10" vinyl, which never happened. The band broke up in 2001. Löwgren can also be found in *Meshuggah*, *Last Tribe*, *Time Requiem* and *Armageddon*. Not to be confused with the US band that released the album *Reconsciousness*.

2000 MCDd - BEY.0016

2000 ■ The Vulture Tones...MCDd 4tr Beyond... Productions....................BEY.0016
Tracks: A Clarity Denied/The Bleeding/The Vulture Tones/Garden of Sin

CROSS

Hansi Cross: v/g, **Göran Johnsson:** k, **Lollo Andersson:** b, **Tomas Hjort:** d

Stockholm - *Cross* started out in 1987 as Hansi's solo project. Hansi and drummer Benny Hadders were previously in *Blåeld*, with whom they released one single and in *Von Lyx*, who released two singles. On the first MLP the members were Cross, Hadders and bass player Jonas Olson (*Talk Of The Town*). On *Uncovered Heart* the band also had some help from keyboard player Christian André and singer Pär Villsé. On *Second Movement* the band featured Cross, Hadders, Olson, André and singer Jock "Tai/Russel" Millgård (ex-*9T9*, later in *Russel*). On *III – Changing Poison Into Medicine* only Jock and Hansi are depicted, but the musicians also include Villsé, Hadders, drummer Per Liljefors, bass player Johan Nordenfeldt (ex-*Von Lyx*) and guitarist Kent Kroon among others. *Paradox* is an 18 minute "miniature symphony for sampler and electric guitar" not close to the other releases in style. *Gaze* saw a completely different line-up featuring Hansi, bass player Tomas Christensen, keyboardist Joachim Floke and drummers Tomas Hjort (who left when half the album was recorded) and Rickard Stenmark. *Dream Reality* is a compilation of songs from the earlier albums, re-mastered, re-mixed and some even rerecorded. Some new names popped up here as well, such as keyboardist Olle Siljeholm and drummer Robert Iversen. Secrets featured a major trio consisting of Hansi Cross, bassist Lollo Andersson and drummer Tomas Hjort. Guest appearances were performed by keyboardist Olov Andersson (*Grand Stand, Audiovision*), Millgård, singer Lizette von Panajott (*Spektrum*) and cellist Lars Borgström. The line-up was actually the same on the subsequent release *Playgrounds*. At the time Hansi was also part of the prog-project *Spektrum*, also featuring members from *Grand Stand* and *Galleon*. The long gap until the new release is due to Hansi having problems with tinnitus and sensitivity to sound preventing him from listening to music for over a year.

1988 LP - LVLP 1

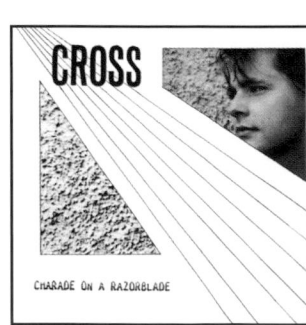
1987 MLP - LVS 2

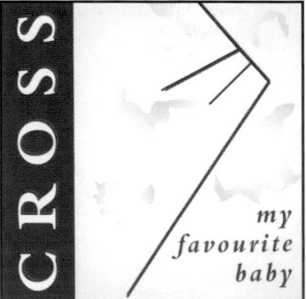
1990 7" - LVS 4

1993 CD - LVCD-3

The Thrill Of Nothingness features Hansi, Lollo, Thomas and newcomer Göran Johnsson (*Grand Stand*) on keyboards. There are also guest spots from Kent Kroon, Tomas Bodin (*The Flower Kings*) and Bruno Edling. The constellation *Cross-Nordenfeldt* also has two tracks on the compilation *Fyra Singlar Vol 1* (Lyxvax 88). *Cross* play intricate progressive/symphonic hard rock at times sounding a bit like the missing link between *Saga*, *Yes* and *Anekdoten*, while in other moments they are almost close to vintage *Styx* mixed with *Marillion*. An outstanding band that any prog-fan should check out.

1987	■	Charade On A Razorblade	MLP 3tr	Lyxvax	LVS-2
1988	■	UNCOVERED HEART	LP	Lyxvax	LVLP-1
1988	□	UNCOVERED HEART	CD	Lyxvax	LVCD-1
		Re-mixed. Bonus: Time Waves			
1990	□	SECOND MOVEMENT	LP	Lyxvax	LVLP-2
1990	□	SECOND MOVEMENT	CD	Lyxvax	LVCD-2
1990	■	My favourite baby/Break Every rule	7"	Lyxvax	LVS-4
		Break Every Rule is previously unreleased.			
1993	■	III - CHANGING POISON INTO MEDICINE	CD	Lyxvax	LVCD-3
1995	■	Paradox	CDSd 1tr	Lyxvax	LVCD 4
1996	□	GAZE	CD	Lyxvax	LVCD 5
1997	□	GAZE	CD	Cyclops	CYCL 039
1997	□	DREAM REALITY	CD	Cyclops	CYCL 054
		Compilation featuring re-mixed and rerecorded versions of old songs.			
1998	□	VISIONARY FOOLS	CD	Progress	PRCD 001
1999	□	GAZE	CD	Progress	PRCD 004
		Remastered. Different artwork.			
1999	□	Halfway To Somewhere	CDS	Lyxvax	- -
2000	□	SECRETS	CD	Progress	PRCD 007
2004	■	PLAYGROUNDS	CD	Progress	PRCD 013
2008	□	SECRETS	CD	Progress	PRCD 030
		Reissue.			
2009	□	THE THRILL OF NOTHINGNESS	CD	Progress	PRCD 038
2009	□	THE THRILL OF NOTHINGNESS	2CDd	Progress	PRCD 038LTD
		Bonus Love/Superstition/Bläckfisken/Nothing Yet Something/Shake Your Enslaver/Fulmi-nation/Rhinnanian Daëy			
2012	□	WAKE-UP CALL	CDd	Progress	PRCD 048
		Bonus: Now			

1995 CDSd - LVCD 4

2004 CD - PRCD 013

CROSS BOW
Peter Svensson: b/v, David Stranderud: g, Christian Lindell: g, Ola Fröjd: d

Malmö - *Cross Bow* (also called *X-Bow*) was formed in 2000 and recorded their first demo in 2002. They released the single in 2003 and at the time the line-up featured Peter Svensson (*Devil Lee Rot*) on bass and vocals, David Stranderud and Christian Lindell on guitars and Ola Fröjd on bass. In 2005 they recorded the demo *Warzone*, where Peter was the only remaining member, now only playing bass. The rest of the line-up featured singer Lena Persson, guitarist Malte Nordström and drummer Tomas "Sagittarius" Hedlund (*The Ancient's Rebirth, Autopsy Torment, Entity, Karnarium*). In 2007 they changed their name to *Cult Of The Fox*. Lena had now been replaced by Magnus Hultman. *Cult Of The Fox* has recorded some demos and two albums to date.

2003	■	Priestkiller/Walking Through Hell	7"	Monster Nation	MN-07
		500 copies, the first 100 with extra fold out sleeve			
2003	□	Strhána Tvár/Priestkiller (split)	MCD	Monster Nation	- -
		Split with Puls. Same tracks as on the single. Promo.			

2003 7" - MN-07

CROSSING OCEANS
Johan "Joe" Ling: v/g, Stefan Bellnäs: b, Kim Gabrielsson: d

Göteborg - Formed in 1990. Kim has previously worked with *Sky High* and *Jonas Hellborg*, while Stefan has played with bluesman *Peps Persson*. Johan has also recorded the excellent track *My Woman* with the band *Hypocondria*, released on the *Rockbox* compilation. On *Live Acid Blues* Patrik Öblad plays bass. The first album and live-CD contains good, solid heavy blues in the traditional vein, while on *Straight Lines* they are closer to 70s hard rock in the vein of *Jericho* and *Demian*. Check them out!

1992 CD - CO 2

1992	□	CROSSING OCEANS	LP	private	CO 1 $
		A shipment of 500 copies was stolen and never found, which makes this album a rarity.			
1992	■	LIVE ACID BLUES	CD	private	CO 2
1992	■	Straight Lines	MCD 3tr	Noveaux	CO 3
		Tracks: Straight Line/God Don't Like Ugly/Where The Angel's Talking			

1992 MCD - CO 3

CROSSROAD JAM

Roland Chantre: v, Fredric Norburg: g, Peter Emilsson: k,
Matt Vereez: b, Johan "Joje" Lindskoog: d

Örebro - In 1986 Joje, Matt and Fredric were all playing in a fusion rock band called *Madrigal*. Two years later, Joje and Peter played in the band *Be Bop Bandit* who moved to Los Angeles to find stardom. They recorded some demos with Cary Sharaf (*Wasa Express, Under Fire*) and Jeff Scott Soto did some backing vocals, but they moved back to Sweden a year later to form *Crossroad Jam*. The line-up on the first MCD featured Joje, Peter, Matt, Fredric and singer Kent Paul Svensson. Due to personal problems Kent left the band and Robert took his place. Solid Rock Records signed the band and *Raw Brew* was released. It was a great CD but it contained both new tracks with Robert and tracks from the debut with Kent, making it feel kind of split. *From Within*, featuring Robert only on vocals, is a true gem in the old 70's vein with an early *Purple*-sound, mixed with hints of *Black Crowes*. Kent Paul went on to *Under The Sun* with whom he only did some demos. Joje (who played with punk band *Perversa Individer* in the early 80s) was also part of *Waving Corn*. The band split in 1995. A re-union featuring Kent-Paul took place in 1996, but nothing came out of it. Fredric started studying law and today has his own law firm Norburg Avokatbyrå.

1992 CD - SPR 2003

1992 MCD - CDM 01

1994 CD - MRRCD-013

1992 ■	Crossroad Jam	MCD 7tr	private	CDM 01	$
	Tracks: On Way Train/Raw Brew/Time Is Turning/Back To You/Six String Shock/Fighting				
	The Will To Change/Time Is Turning (Slight Return)				
1992 ■	RAW BREW	CD	Solid Rock	SPR 2003	
1994 ■	FROM WITHIN	CD	Megarock	MRRCD-013	

CROW

Tomas Vasseur: v/g, Christian Lundh: g, Dennis B Nagy: b, Glenn Eriksson: d

Katrineholm - Formed in 1991 under the name *Indomitus*, under which name they recorded a four-track MCD in 1995. The music was then varied and well-played progressive doom-oriented thrash metal. The same line-up emerged in 1996 under the new name *Crow*, playing post-grunge alternative hard rock with some heavy riffing. At times reminiscent of *Alice In Chains*. The label had an idea of incorporating a big multimedia section on their releases, containing not only an interview and pictures of the band, but also test versions of software from Adobe, Microsoft etc. Not sure how well it worked out though. Nagy was later playing in *Iron Maiden* cover band *Moonchild* and Glenn was later in *Vise*.

1996 ■	CROW	CD	Download Records	DLR 002

1996 CD - DLR 002

CROWN, THE (aka CROWN OF THORNS)

Jonas Stålhammar: v, Marko Tervonen: g, Marcus Sunesson: g,
Magnus Olsfelt: b, Janne Saarenpää: d

Trollhättan - The band was formed in 1990 as *Crown Of Thorns*, and recorded their debut demo *Forever Heaven Gone* in 1993. Before the second demo, *Forget The Light*, original guitarist Robert Österberg left the band to be replaced by Marcus. Singer Johan Lindstrand has previously recorded some demos with the band *Impious*, as drummer. Due to confusion with the US melodic rockers, in 1999, the band had to shorten their name to *The Crown*, and the third album was released under the new banner. On *Deathrace King* the band was guested by Tomas Lindberg (*At The Gates, Lock Up*) and Mika Luttinen (*Impaled Nazarene*) on backing vocals. On *Crowned In Terror* Lindberg took over the microphone after Johan Lindstrand (later in *One Man Army And The Undead Quartet*). The band appears on a number of compilations, such as *Power From The North*, *Slatanic Slaughter* (95 Black Sun), *Sepultural Feast* (98 Black Sun). *The Crown* split in 2004, because of bad touring arrangements. Marko was later in *Angel Blake*. In 2008 Tervonen, Sunesson, Olsfeldt and Saarenpää joined forces under the name *Dobermann*. They drafted *Deathstars* singer Andreas Bergh, who was sacked in 2009. The band play technical death metal from mid-tempo to ultra-speed stuff. High-quality musicianship and growling death style vocals. In the vein of *Slayer*. After *Crowned Unholy* the band went on hiatus. In December 2009 they however made it official they would return to using the old name – *The Crown*. The return saw former *Utumno/God Macabre* vocalist Jonas Stålhammar replacing singer Tomas Lindberg. *The Crown* returned with the album *Doomsday King*, which was as heavy and brutal sounding as vintage releases. Stålhammar sang on the album, but in September 2011 the band announced he had been replaced by original singer Johan Lindstrand. The band also announced a new album, *Nemesis 8 - Death Is Not Dead*, was to be released late 2013.
Website: www.thecrownofficial.com/

The Crown Of Thorns

1997 CD - BS 10

Year		Title	Format	Label	Catalog
1995	□	THE BURNING	CD	Black Sun	BS 05
1997	■	ETERNAL DEATH	CD	Black Sun	BS 10
1998	□	THE BURNING	LP PD	Black Sun	BSLP 05
1998	□	ETERNAL DEATH	LP PD	Black Sun	BSLP 10
1998	■	HELL IS HERE	CD	Metal Blade	3984-14193-2
2000	□	DEATHRACE KING	CD	Metal Blade	3984-14296-2
2002	□	THE BURNING	CD	Century Media (USA)	7838-2

Bonus video: Of Good And Evil

| 2002 | □ | ETERNAL DEATH | CD | Century Media (USA) | 7839-2 |

Bonus video: Angels Die

2002	□	CROWNED IN TERROR	CD	Metal Blade	3984-14394-2
2002	□	CROWNED IN TERROR	LP	Metal Blade	3984-14394-1
2002	□	CROWNED IN TERROR	CD	JVC Victor(Japan)	VICP-61827

Bonus track Burnin' Leather (Bathory cover).

| 2003 | □ | POSSESSED 13 | CD | Metal Blade | 3984-14446-1 |
| 2003 | □ | POSSESSED 13 | 2CDd | Metal Blade | 3984-14446-0 |

Ltd ed featuring the band's 1993-1994 demos plus Burning Leather (Bathory cover)/Rebel Angel (demo) as bonus.

| 2004 | □ | CROWNED UNHOLY | CD | Metal Blade | 3984-14497-2 |
| 2004 | □ | CROWNED UNHOLY | CD | Metal Blade | 3984-14497 |

Featuring bonus live-DVD

2010	■	DOOMSDAY KING	CD	Century Media	998037-2
2010	□	DOOMSDAY KING	LP+CD	Century Media	998037-1
2010	□	DOOMSDAY KING	2CDd	Century Media	998037-8

Bonus: Die Before Dying/In Bitterness And Sorrow/Kill 2010/Falling 'neath The Heaven's Sea

| 2010 | □ | DOOMSDAY KING | CD | Marquee Avalon (Japan) | MICP-10954 |
| 2010 | □ | HELL IS HERE | LP | Night Of The Vinyl Dead | NIGHT 073 |

500 hand numbered. Red/black splatter vinyl.

1998 CD - 3984-14193-2

2010 CD - 998037-2

CROWPATH

Henrik Ivarsson: v, Patrik Lundh: g, Dan Bengtsson: b, Erik Hall: d

Malmö - **Crowpath**, formed in 1997, plays a furious mix of extreme technical metal, death and grindcore, at times with a pinch of sludge for good measures. Music that makes you feel like you've just been run over by a rhinoceros… and enjoyed it. On the debut split the bass was handled by Björn Kvalvik, and on the following two singles by Thomas Jansson. Dan Bengtsson (**Deranged, Murder Corporation, Inverted**) took over the bass duties in 2001. *Old Cuts And Blunt Knives* is a compilation with the tracks off the first singles, a compilation and two song later on *Red On Chrome*. In 2008 Dan Bengtsson parted ways with the band and Henrik took on the task besides singing.
Website: www.myspace.com/crowpath

1999 7" - #12

2005 LP - WT-030-2

| 1999 | ■ | Crowpath/Drown In Frustration (split) | 7" EP | Pateline Industries | #12 |

Split with Drown In Frustration. Tracks: As Our Chapter Itself Was Dying/Empty Souls. In black or orange vinyl.

| 2001 | □ | Crowpath | 7" 4tr | Scorched Earth Policy | SEP #17 |

Tracks: I, The Arsonist/20 Years Delayed Abortion/We All Missed The First Episode/Among Cards And Pawns

| 2001 | □ | 5" | 7" | Pillowscars | 001 |

Tracks: Knives And Sharpened Scissors/The Silhouette Of A Bastard

2004	□	OLD CUTS AND BLUNT KNIVES	CD	Robotic Empire	ROBO 035
2005	□	RED ON CHROME	CD	Willowtip Records	WT-030
2005	■	RED ON CHROME	LP	Willowtip Records	WT-030-2

150 copies in transparent purple vinyl. Different artwork.

2005	□	RED ON CHROME	CD	Earache	MOSH 309CD
2005	■	SON OF SULPHUR	CD	Willowtip Records	WT-041
2006	□	SON OF SULPHUR	CD	Earache	MOSH 342 CD
2006	□	Crowpath/Swarrrm (split)	7"	Crucificados pelo Sistema	024

Split with Japanese band Swarrrm. Track: Cleansed In Chlorine

| 2006 | □ | Crowpath/Submerge (split) | 7" | Abstraction/Shogun | - - |

Split with Submerge. Track: Thieves

| 2008 | □ | ONE WITH FILTH | CD | Willowtip Records | WT-067 |
| 2008 | □ | ONE WITH FILTH | CD | Candlelight | CANDLE 247 CD |

2005 CD - WT-041

CRUCIFIED BARBARA

Mia "Coldheart" Karlsson: v/g, Klara "Force" Rönnqvist Fors: g, Ida "Evileye" Stenbacka: b, Jannike "Nicki Wicked" Lindström: d

Stockholm - The seed to **Crucified Barbara** was sown by Ida and Klara already in 1995 in Tyresö, a suburb to Stockholm. Members came and went, but in 1998 the band came together when they found drummer Nicki. At the time singer Joey Nine was fronting the band.
Last in was Mia Coldheart, at the time called Mia Madcrap. They recorded the demo *Fuck You*

2004 MCDp - BECDS 001

Motherfucker. When the band was signed by GMR after a live show at the club Tre Backar in Stockholm in 2003, Joey left the band. A few singers were auditioned, but instead Mia decided to take on the vocals, which was a good choice. The first recording was produced by Conny Bloom (**Electric Boys**). The single *Loosing The Game* was recorded by Mankan Sedenberg (**Baltimoore, Silver Seraph**). After the highly acclaimed debut album, they toured the UK supporting **Motörhead**. Cold weather and a broken down van made it an interesting experience for the band, who didn't succumb. The album showed a highly promising hard rock/metal band, with slightly punkish overtones, especially in the vocal department. However, these had vanished on the outstanding follow-up, *Til Death Do Us Party*. Powerful hard rock/metal with fat and heavy riffing and killer performance. Highly recommended. Early on, Nicki was hosting the TV show *MTV Fuzz* in Sweden. In 2012 the band again returned with another metal brick, now showing some crude **Motörhead** overtones mixed with powerful riffing metal. Killer stuff! Mia has also made guest appearances with bands like **The Bones, Bonafide, Babylon Bombs, Mind's Eye** and **Teenage Rampage**.
Website: www.crucifiedbarbara.com

2004 ■	Losing The Game	MCDp 3tr	Black Egg/GMR	BECDS001

Tracks: Losing The Game (Edit)/Killed By Death (Motörhead cover)/Losing The Game

2004 □	IN DISTORTION WE TRUST	CD	Black Egg/GMR	BECD002
2004 □	IN DISTORTION WE TRUST	CD	Liquor & Poker (USA)	LP 6021-2
2004 □	IN DISTORTION WE TRUST	CD	Bad Reputation (France)	310281-2
2004 □	IN DISTORTION WE TRUST	LP PD	GMR	VMLP 031

500 copies

2004 □	IN DISTORTION WE TRUST	CD+DVD	GMR	GMRCD9005

Bonus: My Heart Is Black (Acoustic)/Killed By Death/Shout It Out Loud (Kiss cover) + bonus DVD with documentary and videos. Slipcase.

2004 □	IN DISTORTION WE TRUST	CD+DVD	Woodbell (Japan)	WBEX 28021/2

Slipcase.

2004 ■	IN DISTORTION WE TRUST - SPECIAL EDITION	CD+DVD	Woodbell (Korea)	WBEX 28021-2

Different artwork.

2005 □	Rock 'N Roll Bachelor	CDS	Black Egg/GMR	BECDS005
2006 □	Play Me Hard	MCD 3tr	Black Egg/GMR	BECDS006

Tracks: Play Me Hard/My Heart Is Black (Acoustic)/Play Me Hard (Video)

2006 □	IN DISTORTION WE TRUST	LP	Vinyl Maniacs	WMLP 031
2009 □	TIL DEATH DO US PARTY	CDd	GMR	GMRCD9013
2009 □	TIL DEATH DO US PARTY	LP	GMR	GMRLP9013

500 copies. Different artwork.

2009 □	TIL DEATH DO US PARTY	CDd	Bad Reputation (France)	BAD 090202
2009 □	TIL DEATH DO US PARTY	CD	Bickee Music (Japan)	HMCX-1054

Bonus: Fire

2009 ■	Jennyfer/Fire	CDS	GMR	GMRCDS9018
2010 □	TIL DEATH DO US PARTY + Heaven Or Hell	CD+CDS	GMR	GMRCD9013LTD
2012 □	THE MIDNIGHT CHASE	CD	GMR	L30681
2012 □	THE MIDNIGHT CHASE	CD	Verycords (France)	6022046003
2012 □	THE MIDNIGHT CHASE	CD	Bickee Music (Japan)	BKMA-1002

Bonus: Miss Sunshine/Heaven Or Hell

2012 □	THE MIDNIGHT CHASE	LP	Vinyl Maniacs	VMLP 040

2004 CD+DVD - WBEX 28021-2

2009 CDS - GMRCDS9018

CRUCIFYRE

Erik Sahlström: v, **Thorbjörn "TG" Gräslund:** g, **Urban Skytt:** g,
Henrik Doltz Nilsson: d, **Yasin Hillborg:** d

Stockholm - Old-school death metal influenced by bands like **Bathory, Slayer, Celtic Frost** and **Venom**, but sounding better than their influences. The band was formed in 2006 by Yasin Hillborg (ex-**Afflicted**). He drafted Patrik Nilsson (**Concrete Sleep**) and TG. After some rehearsals they recorded the *Thessalonian Death Cult* demo the same year. In 2008 Sahlström joined the band and the demo *Hellish Sacrifice* was recorded, with Tobias Sillman (**Vicious Art**) as session guitarist. In 2009 the band got their current line-up, adding Nilsson and Skytt. Sahlström is also found in **Serpent Obscene, Maze Of Torment, General Surgery**, Skytt in **Crematory, Nasum** and **Regurgitate**, TG is also in **Morbid** and **The Sun**. In 2011 Hillborg made and directed the movie *Så Jävla Metal* (So Fucking Metal) about the history of Swedish hard rock.

2010 ■	INFERNAL EARTHLY DIVINE	CD	Pulverised	ASH 074 CD
2011 □	INFERNAL EARTHLY DIVINE	LPg	Blood Harvest	YOTZ #68

2010 CD - ASH 074 CD

CRUSH ON YOU

Håkan Karlsson: v, **Dag Carlsson:** g, **Olof Karlsson:** b, **Danne Roos:** d

Uppsala - **Crush On You** play really good melodic hard rock, with a strong touch of early **Van Halen** meets **Extreme**, or later days Uppsala-fellows **Spellbound**. Nice guitar-playing, but a bit "Swenglish" vocals. The track *She Left Me* also appears on the compilation *15 on 1* (Soundfront 92). Quite cool gimmicky artwork, which folds out.

1993 ■	Let There Be Rock/Guider/She Left Me	MCDp 3tr	Prime Time	PTR 001

1993 MCDp - PTR 001

CRUT

Mats Danielsson: v/g, Staffan Hagberg: g, Staffan "Abbe" Schön: b, Björn Hansson: d

Jönköping - *Crut* (gunpowder) was formed in 1976. After the first 7" drummer Mikael Gustafsson was replaced by Björn Hansson and guitarist Christer Nilsson was added to the line-up. After the first album "Abbe" replaced bass player Janne Buchar. The song *HååVee* is actually a song dedicated to the local hockey team. The band split in 1983, but has made several reunions since. The CDs were recorded during the last reunion, and then Christer was replaced by Staffan Hagberg. They had a very strong local following. The first single is very good 70s hard rock, like a more straight, hard-rocking kid brother of *November*. On the second single and the LP they had turned into a more pop-influenced hard rock band, in the same style as *Magnum Bonum* and *Snowstorm*. The MCD and CD are similar to the LP, but with an up-dated and somewhat heavier sound. *Efter 5 Långa År* is however a gem for fans of solid 70s hard rock.

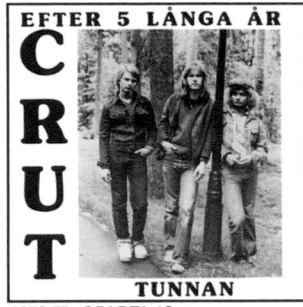

1978 7" - SPARTA 1S

1980 7" - SBS 003

1978 ■	Efter 5 Långa År/Tunnan	7"	Ljudbarrikaden Spartacus	SPARTA 1S	$
1980 ■	Jönköping/Puben lyckan	7"	Skivbolaget Sjöbo	SBS 003	
1980 ■	VÄRLDSPREMIÄR	LP	Sjöbo Påpp Records	SPR 1001	
1981 □	HååVee/Grand Finale	7"	Sjöbo Påpp Records	SPR 011	
1992 □	HååVee/Jönköping/Kom Och Rör Mig	MCD 3tr	Match Town Records	MTR 4002	
1993 □	ABSOLUT SLUT, ABSOLUT CRUT	CD	Match Town Records	MTR 4005	

1980 LP - SPR 1001

CRYONIC

Mikael "Bigswede" Löfqvist: v, Henrik "Henke" Karlsson: g,
Fredrik "Freddy" Elemalm: g, Patrik "Sico" Byström: b, Simon Hardell: d

Piteå/Luleå - Bigswede and Freddy was previously in a pop/rock band called *Madigan* (not to be confused with the hard rockers from Eskilstuna). When the band was put on hold as the singer was entering Swedish Fame Factory, Bigswede took up singing, as well as playing rhythm guitar, and the two decided to form a true metal band. They started recording some songs, met up with bass player Sico and were after a while joined by Digger when he laid down some keyboards for what was to become the *Evil Mind* CD. Bigswede decided to drop the axe and they soon found Henke. They recorded the demo *Rising* in 2006, and were soon signed by Swedmetal, who released their debut. The album featured drummer Dennis Bobzien, singer Mikael Löfqvist, keyboardist Daniel Gustafsson, guitarists Fredrik Elemalm and Henrik Karlsson and drummer Micke Öberg (also in *B-Low*). After the album, drummer Öberg quit for time reasons and Hardell replaced him. In 2009 the band was featured on the Canadian *Downtown Metal Vol 1* compilation with the previously unreleased track *Avalon* and another track is featured in the game *Shadowcastle MU*. *Cryonic* play major-key melodic power metal, sounding a bit like a mix of *Dragonforce* (although not as fast) and *Running Wild*.

2007 CD - SM-10-CD

2010 LP - HHR 094

2007 ■	EVIL MIND	CD	Swedmetal	SM-10-CD	
2010 ■	KINGS OF AVALON	LP	High Roller Records	HHR 094	
	200 in blue/white splatter vinyl, 300 in black. Lyric sheet.				
2010 □	KINGS OF AVALON	CD	Attack (Canada)	??	
2013 □	KINGS OF AVALON	CDd	Battlegod Productions	??	

CRYONIC TEMPLE

Magnus Thurin: v, Esa T "Freewheeler" Ahonen: g, Leif "Gülf Tysk" Collin: g,
Janne "Evil J" Söderlund: k, Stefan Eriksson: b, Hans Karlin: d

Borlänge - Formed in 1997 by Johan "Glen Metal" Johansson and guitarist Esa Ahonen. They recorded the first demo, *Season In Hell* the same year. All three tracks were featured on the local *Nerved* compilation (Rockvaka Records). In 1998 they recorded the demo *Before The End*, produced by Fred Estby. They were reinforced by guitarist Leif Collin and keyboardist Janne Söderlund. In 2000 they recorded the 5-track demo *Warsong*, which awoke the interest of Italian label Underground Symphony. They now completed the line-up with bass player Jan J. Cederlund and drummer Sebastian "Gert Steelheart" Olsson (both later in *Thalamus*). The debut album was recorded at Studio Underground by Pelle Saether (*Zeelion, Locomotive Breath, Diabolical* etc.). The band did a cover of *Heavy Load*'s *Stronger Than Evil* as bonus, where Lasse Bäcke guests on drums. *Cryonic Temple* is more traditional NWoBHM than the new era of German-style metal, more akin to *Saxon* and early *Iron Maiden*, even though the album has some exceptions. The vocals are not of the traditional, melodic, high-pitched and clean sort, but more harsh and almost semi-spoken at times. For the second album they were signed by German label Limb Music and went back into Studio Underground with Pelle Saether to record. The tradition was kept for the follow-up in 2005. Before the 2008 album the band went through some line-up changes. Singer Johansson had been exchanged for Magnus Thurin (ex-*Mindscape*), who is more in the traditional power metal vein. Bass player Cederlund was replaced by Eriksson and drummer Olsson for Karlin. The new album also showed a slightly heavier musical approach and is more akin to bands like *Dragonforce*. In 2009 bass player Eriksson was replaced by Björn Svensson. Cederlund is now found in *Sky Of Rage* (as guitarist).

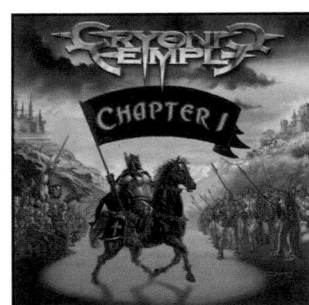

2002 CDd - USCD 056

2003 CD - LMP 0310-063 CD

2005 CD - LMP 0505-079 CD

2002 ■	CHAPTER 1	CD	Underground Symphony	USCD 056

2002	☐	CHAPTER 1	CDd	Underground Symphony	USCD 056
		Cover in A5 format.			
2002	☐	CHAPTER 1	CD	CD-Maximum (Russia)	CDM 1102-1241
2002	☐	CHAPTER 1	LP PD	Underground Symphony	USPD 002
2003	■	BLOOD GUTS & GLORY	CD	Limb Music	LMP 0310-063 CD
2003	☐	BLOOD GUTS & GLORY	CD	Spiritual Beast (Japan)	SBCD-1012
		Bonus: Metal No 1/Swords And Diamonds (video)			
2005	■	IN THY POWER	CD	Limb Music	LMP 0505-079 CD
2005	☐	IN THY POWER	CDd	Limb Music	LMP 0505-079 DP
2005	☐	IN THY POWER	CD	CD-Maximum (Russia)	CDM 0406-2496
2005	☐	IN THY POWER	CD	Spiritual Beast (Japan)	SBCD-1028
		Bonus: Empire/Redeemer/As I Slowly Die			
2008	■	IMMORTAL	CD	Metal Heaven	00061

2008 CD - 00061

CRYPT OF KERBEROS

Christian Eriksson: v, **Peter Pettersson (now Bjärgö):** g, **Jonas Strandell:** g, **Jessica Strandell:** k, **Stefan Karlsson:** b, **Mattias Borgh:** d

Eskilstuna - Formed in October 1990. The band recorded a demo under the name ***Macrodex***, before they changed their name. However, they did release one track on the compilation *Projections Of A Stained Mind* (91 CBR). Death metal with lots of ideas and tempo changes. After the first 7" guitarist Johan Lönnroth was replaced by Jonas. The band recorded a new demo, entitled *Promo 91*. The band was contacted by French label Adipocere who signed them for a single and an album. After the recording of the EP drummer Mikael Sjöberg left the band, and was replaced by Mattias. In September 1992 Jessica Strandell joined the band. After the album was recorded Jonas and Jessica left the band because of musical differences. Soon after, Karlsson also decided to leave. In May 1993 guitarist Jonas Hallgren and bass player Marcus Pedersen, both ex-***Infester***, joined the band. In October 1993 the new line-up played their final live show with singer Christian. He left during the recording of the band's next demo, which was in a much more progressive style. The style and line-up now changed radically and in 1994 the band featured singer Daniel Gildenlöw (***Pain Of Salvation***), guitarists Peter Pettersson and Johan Hallgren, keyboard player Peter Jansson (***Maze Of Torment***) bass player Stefan Källarström and drummer Mattias Borgh. As the style had become so different from the original sound, they decided to change their name to ***Stigmata Martyr*** in December 1994. ***Crypt Of Kerberos*** was officially gone. In 2005 Australian label Bleed Records got in touch with the band to re-release the band's old demos and recordings, which became *The Macrodex Of War*. In 2006 the band decided it was time to make a revival. New songs have been written and made official on the band's MySpace. In 2009 the line-up featured guitarists Jonas Strandell and Peter Pettersson, now named Peter Bjärgö, singer Christian Eriksson, bass player Stefan Källarström and drummer Borgh. The style is a return to the band's old style technical death metal. Peter has also recorded with his solo project ***Arcana***, which has one track on the Cold Meat Industry compilation. ***Arcana*** is in a totally different musical area, soft and atmospheric mood music. Borgh was also part of this band. Jonas has been found in ***Eternal Darkness***. In 2012 *World Of Myths* was re-issued with previously unreleased rehearsal demos as bonus.

1991 7" - SUNABEL 001

1993 CD - CDAR 013

1992 7" - AR 004

2005 CD - BLEED 009

1991	■	Visions Beyond Darkness/Darkest Rites	7"	Sunabel	SUNABEL 001
		500 copies.			
1992	■	Cyclone Of Insanity/The Ancient War	7"	Adipocere Records	AR 004
1993	■	WORLD OF MYTHS	CD	Adipocere Records	CDAR 013
2005	■	THE MACRODEX OF WAR	CD	Bleed Records	BLEED 009
2010	☐	MCMXCI/MCMXCIII	3LP Box	The Crypt	CRYPT10
		Box set featuring: Demo I, Demo II, World Of Myths, Cyclone Of Insanity, Visions Beyond Darkness + rehearsal tracks. 500 hand numbered.			
2012	☐	Into The Ruins/And Our Dying Sun	7"	Temple Of Darkness	TOD 031
2012	■	WORLD OF MYTHS	CDd	Pulverised	ASH 087 CD
		New artwork. Bonus: The Canticle/World Of Myths/World Of Myths/The Canticle/Nocturnal Grasp/Stroembringer/Ancient War/Cyclone Of Insanity/Dream…			

2012 CDd - ASH 087 CD

CRYSTAL AGE

Oscar Dronjac: v/g, **Moses Jonathan Elfström:** g, **Fredrik Larsson:** b, **Hans Nilsson:** d

Back in the crystal age

Göteborg/Onsala - Heavy and technical death metal with brutal black metal parts, slighty similar to ***Dark Funeral***. Oscar has previously played with ***Ceremonial Oath*** and is now found in ***Hammerfall*** (a band he actually formed already back in 1993 as ***Highlander***). Fredrik is also in ***Hammerfall*** and has also played with ***Cans*** and ***Evergrey***. Drummer Nilsson has later been found in ***Dimension Zero***, ***Diabolique***, ***Liers In Wait*** and ***Luciferion***.The track *Son Of Time* is featured on the local compilation *Best Of West* (95 SV) and a cover of *Damage Inc.* was recorded for the ***Metallica***-tribute *Metal Militia* (94 Black Sun).

1995	■	FAR BEYOND DIVINE HORIZONS	CD	Vic Records	VIC 2

1995 CD - VIC 2

CRYSTAL BLUE

Thomas Lassar: v/k, Ove Lundquist: g, Dave Persson: b, Micke Palmström: d

Örebro - Hailing from one of Sweden's No 1 rock cities Örebro, *Crystal Blue* play top notch melodic hard rock. The band was formed by guitarist Lundquist in 1989. The 6-track is well worth investing in, even though it's today a highly priced item. The full-length is even better. Former *Bedroom Love* singer Stephen Nykvist replaced Morgan Johansson before the recording of the album. The band split after the second album, but reformed in 2002 after being persuaded by UK music journalist Nicky Baldrian to pick up the pieces. The re-union saw singer Nykvist out of the band and Lassar taking over the vocal duties, proving he has a killer AOR voice not too far from Joey Tempest in style. The album is a highly recommended guitar driven AOR rocker, quite close to what Europe did on *Out Of This World* or *Prisoners In Paradise*. Lassar has since also written songs for bands like **Last Autumn's Dream** and he is today playing with cover band **Watchie's Orkester**.

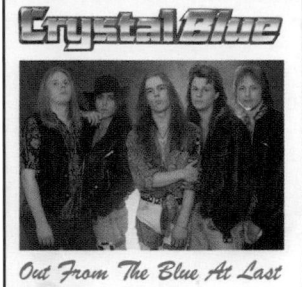
Out From The Blue At Last
1993 MCD - NRCDL-002

1995 CD - SMCCD 20161

2003 CD - 0681-71

1993 ■ Out From The Blue At Last	MCD 6tr	Nice Records	NRCDL-002	$

Tracks: Mind And Heart/Missing You/Prisoner Of Love/Time Is All We Need/There's No High/Break Down The Walls

1995 ■ CAUGHT IN THE GAME	CD	SMC	SMCCD 20161	
2003 ■ DETOUR	CD	MTM	0681-71	

CRYSTAL EYES

Søren Nico Adamsen: v, Mikael Dahl: g/v, Paul Pettersson: g,
Claes Wikander: b, Stefan Svantesson: d

Borås - Formed in 1992 by Mikael Dahl and guitarist Niclas Karlsson (later in *Fierce Conviction, Conviction, Zonata, Freternia, Rising Faith*). The two were joined by bassist Christian Gunnarsson, but having problems finding a drummer, they initially programmed the drums. They constantly recorded demos and the line-up changed quite a bit during the years. Members that passed through were for instance drummers like Fredrik Gröndahl and Martin Tilander (*Fierce Conviction*), while Gunnarsson was replaced by Mikael Blohm. In 1994 the first official, self-titled, demo was recorded. In 1995 drummer Kujtim Gashi joined the ranks and in 1996 the band recorded the second official demo, entitled *The Shadowed Path*. The band now featured Dahl, Gashi, guitarist Jukka Kaupaamaa and bass player Marco Nicolaidis. In 1996 they were one of the first Swedish bands to actually have a website. More members changes, but in 1997 the line-up finally had found a more solid form, consisting of Dahl, Jukka, Kujtim and bass player Claes Wikander. A new demo, *The Final Sign*, was recorded. In October the same year Jukka was replaced by Jonathan Nyberg. In May 1998 the demo *The Dragon's Lair* was recorded and finally the band was picked up by German label Crazy Life Music. However, the band was very displeased with both the labels mix of the album and their promotion. Despite this, they gave Crazy Life Music a second chance on *In Silence They March*, which unfortunately proved to be a mistake. In May 2001 Gashi decided to leave the band to take care of his daughter

"Just look into our crystal eyes"

who had caught ill, and was replaced by *Freternia*'s Stefan Svantesson. *Vengeance Descending* was the first release on the new label, Heavy Fidelity, with the band now being in control of production from start to finish. This album saw guest vocals from Daniel Heiman (*Conviction, Lost Horizon*). On the follow-up, *Confessions Of The Maker*, the band again wanted Heiman to provide some guest vocals. As he had just quit **Lost Horizon** the band asked him to join as a permanent member. However, he agreed to join as a session singer on the album and subsequent gigs. The track *The Wizard's Apprentice* appears on the *Sweden Rock Festival DVD 2005*, the only show Daniel actually did with the band. The band now found permanent singer, Danish Søren Nico Adamsen, who made his debut on *Dead City Dreaming*. During the recording of this album guitarist Jonathan Johnsson decided to leave the band, and only provided one guest solo. After the album the band was completed by returning guitarist Niclas Karlsson. However in 2007 he was again out of the band, and soon replaced by Paul Pettersson, who also appears on *Chained*. In 2009 Nico decided he didn't have enough time for the band, meaning Dahl went back to handling the vocals again. Classic eighties heavy metal with a touch of the new German-oriented vein, with touches of **Helloween, Rhapsody Of Fire** and of course in the company of Swedish colleagues **Hammerfall, Insania (Stockholm)** and **Zonata**. Trivia: Members/former members Dahl, Tilander, Karlsson, Koivo and bass player Stefan Fors are playing in **Judas Priest** tribute band **Defenders Of The Faith**.

Website: www.crystaleyes.net

1999 CD - a.b.s today 214

2003 CD - DMP7350013660016

2000 CD - SHARK 200010

2005 CD - DMP7350013660023

1999	■	WORLD OF BLACK AND SILVER	CD	Crazy Life Music	a.b.s today 214
1999	□	WORLD OF BLACK AND SILVER	CD	Rock Brigade Records (Brazil)	RBR/LCR1850
1999	□	WORLD OF BLACK AND SILVER	CD	NEMS (Argentina)	NEMS 135
		Bonus: Another Race			
1999	□	WORLD OF BLACK AND SILVER	CD	Heavy Fidelity	DMP7350013660030
2000	■	IN SILENCE THEY MARCH	CD	Crazy Life Music/Shark	SHARK 200010
2000	□	IN SILENCE THEY MARCH	CD	Rock Brigade Records (Brazil)	RBR/LCR2720
		Bonus: Mindtraveller			
2003	■	VENGEANCE DESCENDING	CD	Heavy Fidelity	DMP7350013660016
2003	□	VENGEANCE DESCENDING	CD	CD maximum (Russia)	CDM 0304-1710
2005	■	CONFESSIONS OF THE MAKER	CD	Heavy Fidelity	DMP7350013660023
2005	□	WORLD OF BLACK AND SILVER	CD	Heavy Fidelity	DMP7350013660030
2005	□	IN SILENCE THEY MARCH	CD	Heavy Fidelity	DMP7350013660047
2005	□	CONFESSIONS OF THE MAKER	CD	Arise	ARISE068
2006	□	CONFESSIONS OF THE MAKER	CD	CD Maximum (Russia)	CDM 0805-2363
2006	□	DEAD CITY DREAMING	CD	Heavy Fidelity	DMP7350013660054
2008	■	CHAINED	CD	Metal Heaven	00060
2008	□	CHAINED	CD	Soundholic (Japan)	YZSH-1006

2008 CD - 00060

CRYSTAL OCEAN
Fredrik "Ztikkan" Blomberg: v/g, Erik "Svajjen" Fernold: g,
Dennis "Dempa" Johansson: b, Jörgen "Pastor" Ek: d

Strängnäs - The band started off as a trio, featuring Ztikkan, Dennis and Jörgen, under the name *Rojnes* in 1987. As *Rojnes* they released one 7", *Rojnes käkar bananer eller...?*, in a punk style. They added Fernold, who had previously played bass in Ztikkan's band *Wild Youth*, and changed the name to *Crystal Ocean* in 1987. Mid-range hard rock with Swedish vocals, except for the track *Angels In The Sky*. A bit similar to early *Jerusalem*, but with a punkish touch. The band only lasted for about a year. Ztikkan later joined punk band *Strebers* as bass player, plus recorded a couple of singles with offspring band *Sixguns*. When drummer Johhny Rydh died in a car crash he formed *Dia Psalma*, together with *Merciless* drummer Stefan "Stipen" Carlsson.

1988	■	Part 1	7"4tr	Studiefrämjandet	88 CRYSTAL

Tracks: Schakalernas Natt/Själlös/Angels (In The Sky)/Slutet Är Nära

1988 7" - 88 CRYSTAL

CRYSTAL PRIDE
Susanne Christensen (now First): v/k, Krister Taimi: g,
Michael Lundberg: g, Peter Kvick: b, Johnny Mattsson: d

Eskilstuna - This excellent melodic hard rock band was formed in 1981 out of the remains of *Voodoo* and released the self-financed 7"-EP the year after. It has become a sought-after item and considering the musical qualities of the band, it's no wonder. The 7" led to a deal with Mill Records and the band released one album and a 12" in 1984. After the 7" drummer Johnny replaced Fredrick Lindquist. Nothing was heard from the band until 1990, when the band recorded a great 4-track demo. They kept playing, but now consisting of Susanne, Peter and the two ex-*Torch* members Christer First on guitar and Håkan Hedlund on drums. They continued recording demo material but no new deal was ever secured. Original drummer Fredrick is now a famous TV/radio-personality with comedy as a main-subject and has even written scripts and books. Since Susanne Christensen and Christer First got married, Susanne is now Susanne First. The previously unreleased track *Find The Way* can be found on the compilation-CD for my first book. The band has recorded several new and highly interesting demos, but nothing has been released so far. It's not too late for a re-union and new album!

Lookin' proud in the 80s! / *The 1995 line-up.*

1981	■	Sharon/Song For Jeanne d'Arc/Silverhawk	7" 3tr	private	811101-1 $
1984	■	Knocked Out	MLP 3tr	Mill	MMS2001

Tracks: Knocked Out/Venus (Shocking Blue cover)/Magic Man

1984 ☐ CRYSTAL PRIDE	LP	Mill	MILL 5024	

10 copies in clear vinyl also exists.

| 1985 ☐ CRYSTAL PRIDE | LP | Nexus (Japan) | K25P-554 | $ |

Bonus: Venus/Magic Man.

| 1997 ☐ CRYSTAL PRIDE | CD | King Records (Japan) | KICP 2625 | $ |

Bonus: Magic Man/Venus

Unofficial releases:

| 1994 ☐ CRYSTAL PRIDE | CD | Thunderload | TLCD-8840 | |

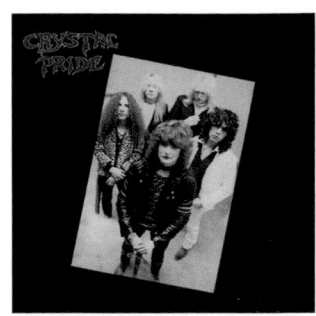
1981 7" - 811101-1

CULT DISCIPLES

Marcus "Demigorgon Bile" Lindelöf: v/b, Richard "Ritchie La Roux" Riekwel: g, Valbon "Bonnie" Gurmani: g, Mattias Schlyter: k, Carl-Mikael Hildesjö: d

Malmö - Judging from the cover and the band's thanks to The Church Of Satan, I was convinced this was a death/black metal band. Wrong was I, as the band sound a lot closer to the melodic doomy hard rock similar to **King Diamond** or **Mercyful Fate** (without the King Diamond falsetto vocals). OK, they do come across as Satanists, too. The lyrics are very anti-Christian and anti-American. It says 1997 on the cover, but it was not released until 1998. In 1995 the band also recorded a demo, entitled *Do What You Wilt*. The keyboards were later handled by Annika Argerich (later in **Stonelake**) In 2002 Annika and Ritchie formed metal band **Veritate**, while Lindelöf and Gurmani was later in **Benevolence**, the latter as drummer. Hildesjö has also recorded an album with hard rockers **From Behind**.

1998 CD - SONCD 013

1984 MLP - MMS2001

| 1998 ■ HANG BY THE CROSS | CD | Sonus | SONCD 013 | |

CULT OF LUNA

Klas Rydberg: v, Johannes Persson: v/g, Erik Olofsson: g, Fredrik Kihlberg: g, Magnus Lindberg: k, Anders Teglund: k/s, Andreas Johansson: b, Thomas Hedlund: d

Umeå - The band was formed by guitarist Johannes Persson and singer Klas Rydberg in 1998 when their hardcore band **Eclipse** split (not the Stockholm AOR band). They started out playing quite traditional hardcore oriented sludge with touches of **Bolt Thrower**, **My Dying Bride** and **Neurosis**. The initial line-up featured bass player Fredrik Rehnström, while on the debut album the line-up consisted of featured Klas, Johannes, guitarist Erik Olofsson, keyboardist Magnus Lindberg (ex-**Lineout**) bass player Alex Stattin (**Separation**) and drummer Marco Hildén (ex-**Broken Trust**). In 2002, after the recording of *The Beyond*, Andreas Johansson replaced Stattin and the band supported **The Haunted** and **Isis** on tours. They were soon picked up by Earche, who also re-issued the debut CD. The band's third album, *Salvation* saw a couple of line-up changes. Drummer Hildén had been replaced by Thomas Hedlund and Anders Teglund had been added handling keyboards and samples. The 2006 singles featured two covers, *Bodies* of **Smashing Pumpkins** and *Recluse* of **Unbroken**. The first 1000 copies of the single was given away as a freebee with the 2LP *Somewhere Along The Highway*. The single actually features Hildén on drums, while the album featured Hedlund. The album also saw the addition of guitarist Kihlberg, who joined the band on the *Salvation* tour. In 2005 the band supported **Bleeding Through** on an extensive US tour. As Thomas was busy with other bands (such as indie rockers **The Perishers**), Lindberg took over the drums on tour. They also supported **Mastodon** on tour after this. In November 2005 the band recorded the conceptual album *Eternal Kingdom* in an octagonal barn (?!). Persson is also found in **Plastic Pride**. The band is also found on numerous compilations. In 2009 the live DVD *Fire Was Born*, was released.

2003 CD - ILLIAD 12

2006 CDd - MOSH 344 CDL

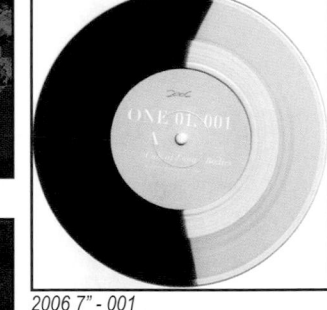
2006 7" - 001

2008 CD - MOSH 359 CD

2000 ☐ Switchblade/Cult Of Luna (split)	7"	Trust No One	TNO 012	

Split-single with Switchblade. Ttrack: Beyond Fate

| 2001 ■ CULT OF LUNA | CD | Rage Of Achilles | ILLIAD 12 | |

2000 copies.

| 2001 ☐ Unfold The Inside/The Art Of Self-extermination | 7" | Hydrahead | HH666-57 | |

220 white, 270 marble purple, 330 transparent/opaque orange, 460 opaque orange

| 2003 ☐ THE BEYOND | CD | Earache | MOSH 263 CD | |
| 2003 ☐ CULT OF LUNA | CD | Earache | MOSH 271 CD | |

Reissue. First pressing with slipcase.

2004 ☐ SALVATION	CD	Earache	MOSH 283 CD	
2004 ☐ SALVATION	CDd	Earache	MOSH 283 CDL	
2004 ☐ SALVATION	2LP	Earache	MOSH 283 LP	
2006 ● Bodies/Recluse	7"	One 01	001	

Half clear/half black vinyl. 1000 copies. No artwork

| 2006 ☐ Bodies/Recluse | 7" | One 01 | 001 | |

500 copies.

2006 ☐ SOMEWHERE ALONG THE HIGHWAY	CD	Earache	MOSH 344 CD	
2006 ■ SOMEWHERE ALONG THE HIGHWAY	CDd	Earache	MOSH 344 CDL	
2006 ☐ SOMEWHERE ALONG THE HIGHWAY	2LP	Earache	MOSH 344 LP	
2006 ☐ SOMEWHERE ALONG THE HIGHWAY	CD	Icarus (Argentina)	ICARUS 242	
2008 ■ ETERNAL KINGDOM	CD	Earache	MOSH 359 CD	
2008 ☐ ETERNAL KINGDOM	CDd	Earache	MOSH 359 CDL	

2008 CD+DVD - MOSH 359 CDX

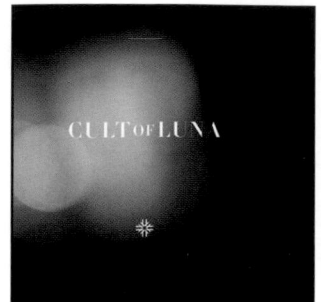

2008	■	ETERNAL KINGDOM	CD+DVD	Earache	MOSH 359 CDX

Features the "Fire Was Born" live-DVD as bonus. Different artwork.

2008	☐	ETERNAL KINGDOM	LPg	Earache	MOSH 359 LP

Different artwork than CD. Printed in black, orange, red and transparent vinyl.

2008	☐	ETERNAL KINGDOM	LP PD	Earache	MOSH 3591
2010	■	CULT OF LUNA	2LP	Earache	MOSH 271 LP

Reissue with new artwork.

2010	☐	THE BEYOND	2LP	Earache	MOSH 263 LP

Reissue with new artwork.

2013	☐	VERTIKAL	CD	Indie Records	INDIE 09 4CD
2013	☐	VERTIKAL	CDd	Indie Records	INDIE 09 4CDL
2013	☐	VERTIKAL	2LP	Back On Black	BOBV 354

2010 2LP - MOSH 271 LP

CULT OF THE FOX
Magnus Hultman: v, Per Persson (now Pilhjerta): g,
Erika Wallberg: g, Peter Svensson: b, Daniel Fritze: d

Malmö - The band was formed in 2007, formerly known as *Cross Bow*, originally featuring guitarist Malte Nordström and drummer Thomas Hedlund (*Void Moon, Autopsy Torment* etc). As *Cross Bow* they released the single *Priestkiller*. *Cult Of The Fox* recorded the demo *Kitsunetsuki* in 2007. In 2008 Fritze replaced Hedlund and the band recorded the demo *The Power We Serve* as a trio completed by Nordström and Svensson. They were completed by Persson (*Nexus*) and recorded the demo *The Sea Beneath The Sand* in 2010. Later the same year Wallberg (*Void Moon*) replaced Nordström and the band recorded the debut. Mid-quality classic Euro metal similar to *Iced Earth* meets early *Manowar*.

2011	■	A VOW OF VENGEANCE	CD	Metalbound Records	MBR003CD
2013	☐	ANGELSBANE	CD	Rock It Up Records	RIUCD-201340

2011 CD - MBR003CD

CURSE
Kai "Ishtar" Partanen: v/g, Sami Karppinen: d

Spånga - *Curse* existed between 1986-1993. The first release featured basist Ralf Söderström and drummer Brajan Månsson, besides Kai.Dark, thrashy death metal.

2013	☐	Ad Futuram Rei Memoriam	10" 4tr	To The Death	TTD 010

Tracks: Morbid Death/Inner Memoir/Forbidden Prophecy/Reign Of Regret.

2013	■	Integumentum De Tenebrae	10" 6tr	To The Death	TTD 011

Tracks: Intro: Aegus Animus/Beyond The.../Infernal Gate/Subconscious Thought/Theme Underground/Funebris Dolore. 100 black + 400 grey vinyl.

2012 10" - TTD 011

CURTAIN, THE
Stefan Juhlin: v, Daniel Carlsson: g, Oscar Olsson: b,
Johan Carlsson: d, Jan Mårtensson: d

Enköping - This is quite a hard band to describe in a simple way. The music is a bit proggy, but definitely not prog. It has some hardcore elements, but it's not hardcore either. There's a bit of *Cult Of Luna*, a bit of *King Crimson*, touches of nu-metal, heavy rock, 70s prog, jazz, space rock and lots of other bits and piece that makes it a really interesting album. The band was formed in 1997 as a trio influenced by *Primus* and *King Crimson*, which is actually a bit evident when listening to the album. Quirky, but great!

2004 CDd - WOOR0104-2

2004	■	NEW SOUND MADE	CDd	Dogbreath	WOOR0104-2

CUT 4
Anders Engberg: v, Mattias Schyberg: g, Sixten Jaskari: b, Sammy Carpenter: d

Stockholm - *Cut 4* was a short-lived but highly interesting melodic hard rock band featuring *Lion's Share* singer Anders Engberg and *Mandala* bass player Sixten. Besides this outstanding gem of a melodic hard rocker this band produced some unreleased demos. Sadly obscure and forgotten, a must for any fan of Swedish melodic hard rock.

1992	■	A Lesson In Selfindulgence	MCD 4tr	private	PROMOCD CUT4	$$

Tracks: Crazy Love/9.1.1/Eyes/Dreams

1992 MCD - PROMOCD CUT4

CUT OUT
Börje Westberg: v, Anna-Karin Nylén: v, Lars Johansson: g, Olov Ericsson: k,
Mikael Johansson: b, Fredrik Lindgren: d

Umeå - A rare single by a really high class keyboard-oriented, but still guitar driven AOR band in the vein of *Alyson Avenue*, *Broke [N] Blue* or US band *Shanghai*, with mainly male vocals.

1988	■	For The Night/Heart Of Steel	7"	CUF Skivklubb	CUF 010	$

1988 7" - CUF 010

D.I.Y.
Patrik Björklund: v/k, Per Hesselrud: g, Olle Bergqvist: b, Mikko Karvonen: d

Stockholm - The letters, of course, stand for Do It Yourself. Slick AOR with biting guitars and nice keyboards in the heavier ***Magnum Bonum***-vein. The band recorded a full-length album that was never released. The single was out in December 1988 and was badly promoted, which resulted in it selling only 79 (!) copies. It however has nothing to do with the quality. Per later formed wacko hard rockers ***Bosse*** and played in even funnier ***IFK Doom***, who did ***Black Sabbath*** songs in Swedish. He is now also in ***Eddy Malm Band***.

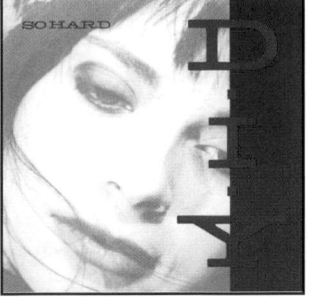

1988 ■ So Hard/Heaven Can Wait...7" Make................................. MR 8802

1988 7" - MR 8802

DA PRESIDENT
Markus Östman: v, Martin Östman: v, Christer Pettersson (Levell): g, Thomas Elmberg: b, Petri Kinnunen: d

1996 CD - CDA 005

Stockholm - Formed 1991-92 by all members, except Martin. In 1993 they went to Los Angeles to study at M.I and then became ***Mr President***, which was changed to ***Da President***. They returned to Sweden after 15 months and were signed by Nylon. Around 1994-95, Markus younger brother Martin joined the band. The band then recorded the demo *Dinnermusic* at Thunderload Studios (by Ragne and Styrbjörn Wahlquist), and a couple of the tracks ended up on the album, which was released in 1996. Thomas left, and later joined ***Sensor***, which turned into ***Stolen Mondays***. Christer joined hard rockers ***T-Bag***. ***Da President*** should also appeal to fans of ***Clawfinger***.

1996 ☐ Mr. Cleverman.. CDS 1tr Nylon................................. CDS 004
1996 ■ GLUE .... CD Nylon................................. CDA 005

DAEMONICUS
Stefan Hagström: v, Per-Olof Wester: g, Jörgen Persson: g, Martin Pudas: b, Johan Hallbäck: d

2009 CD - VSP 005

Umeå - ***Daemonicus*** was formed in February 2006 with the goal to create old-school death metal. In June, specifically 060606, the first demo *Demon Inside* was released and in 2007 second demo *Swarm Of Death* saw the light of day. In 2008 the band was picked up by ViciSolum Productions who released their debut in 2009. On *11th Hour* Martin Pudas (***Hate Ammo***) had replaced Tommi Kuno and Johan Hallbäck had replaced Magnus Boström. Good, solid classic death metal in the vein of ***Desultory***, ***Bolt Thrower*** or ***Grave***.

2009 ■ HOST OF ROTTING FLESH ....CD ViciSolum Productions ....VSP 005
2010 ☐ 11th Hour...MCD 4tr ViciSolum Productions Vici01
　　　 Tracks: 11th Hour/Crystal Mountain(Death cover)/Rotten Sky/Falling Forever (Paradise Lost cover). 333 copies.
2012 ☐ DEADWORK..CD Abyss Records.........................ABYSS 028 CD

2013 7" - HRR 318

DAGGER
Jani Kataja: v, David Blomqvist: g, Tobias Christiansson: b, Fred Estby: d

Stockholm - Formed 2009, initially featuring Erik "Tyrant" Gustavsson (***Nifelheim***). Classic hard rock/metal. The A-side is a ***Quartz*** cover. Jari is also in ***Sideburn*** and ***Mangrove***, while the others are ex-***Dismember***, ***Necronaut*** etc. An album is in the making.

2013 ■ Mainline Riders/Dark Cloud ....7" High Roller Records............................HRR 318
　　　 300 gold, 700 black vinyl copies.

DAISY CHAIN
Pehr Severin: v/g, Daniel Castman: g, Erik Birgersson: b, Tobias Nyström: d

1995 MCD - DC-01

Linköping - Aggressive metal of medium quality and below average vocals. The band only made one MCD and a subsequent demo before they split in 1997. Castman later joined ***Vindra***, while Severin started the band ***Corporation 187*** (actually at first as ***Slayer*** cover band ***Divine Intervention***), which he left in 2000, after one album.

1995 ■ Daisy Chain..MCD 4tr private DC-01
　　　 Tracks: Total Increase/Aimed For A Change/Passing Breath/Hate In Me

DAKKS
David Taylor: v/k, Steve Ruprecht: g, Keijo Ruprecht: b, Kaj Mattsoff: d

Stockholm - *Änglarna* is quite good hard rock with a 70s touch, *Tema för säsongen* is more poppy and *Metallmani* is a weird thing, like a heavier ***Factory***.

1981 ■ Änglarna/Tema för säsongen/Metallmani.............................7" 3tr private .... K. 025

1981 7" - K.025

DALTON

Bo Lindmark: v, **Leif Westfahl:** g, **Ola Lindström:** k,
Anders Lindmark: b, **Mats "Dalton" Dahlberg:** d

The Dalton Brothers waiting for the race.

Stockholm - After Mats Dahlberg (ex-**Highbrow**) left **Treat** he formed **Dalton**, in a more melodic hard rock vein. The single *Heartbroken* was re-mixed into total wimpiness and released after Mats had left the band. After **Dalton** split Mats recorded a demo (later issued on CD) with the Judas Priest-influenced band **Speedy Gonzales**, also featuring Tommy Denander (**ATC,** **Rdioactive**, solo) and Thomas Vikström (**Candlemass, Talk Of The Town**, solo etc). Bo and Anders later joined **R.A.W**, who released two albums. Mats left the music business, but made some attempts at restarting the engine. **Dalton** was an excellent melodic hard rock band in the same vein as **Glory**. Both CDs became highy priced rarities. In 1994 EMI re-issued both CDs, and a lot of copies were sold on Ebay as originals. The track *You're Not My Lover* from *The Race Is On* was written by John Bon Jovi/Desmond Cild/Richie Sambora, and recorded the year before by American band **Witness**. In 2011 the original line-up reunited and did some shows.

1986 ☐	Can't Stop Loving You Now/The Race Is On	7"	EMI	136 232-7	
	Poster cover				
1987 ☐	Loving You/We're Into Rock	7"	EMI	136 258-7	
	Poster cover				
1987 ☐	Loving You/We're Into Rock	12" 2tr	EMI	PRO 4079	
1987 ☐	You're Not My Lover/No Reason	7"	EMI	136 286-7	
1987 ☐	THE RACE IS ON	CD	EMI	136 263-2	
1987 ☐	THE RACE IS ON	LP	EMI	136 263-1	
1988 ☐	I Think About You/Gimme Gimme	7"	EMI	136 302-7	
1989 ■	Like An Angel/Wake You Up	7"	EMI	136 339-7	
1989 ☐	Like An Angel	12"	ParlophoneAudiodisc	PRO 4103	
	One-sided test pressing				
1989 ☐	Love Injection/Breakin' Away	7"	EMI	136 356-7	
	The B-side is non-LP				
1989 ☐	INJECTION	CD	EMI	792 398-2	
1989 ☐	INJECTION	LP	EMI	792 398-1	
1989 ☐	INJECTION	CD	Toshiba (Japan)	TOCP-6178	
1990 ■	Heartbroken/Comin' On Strong	7"	EMI	136 376-7	
1994 ☐	THE RACE IS ON	CD	EMI	475 105-2	
1994 ☐	INJECTION	CD	EMI	792 398-2	
2012 ☐	BEST OF	CD	EMI	5099 94334402 4	

1989 7" - 136 339-7

DAMIEN

Thomas "Tommie Agrippa" Eriksson: v, **Lawrence West:** g,
Mats "Marre Martini" Eriksson: b, **Mikael "Mike Thorn" Lundholm:** d

Uppsala - Formed in 1982 by Mats and guitarist Andreas "Rick Meister" Palm. They split, and then reformed in 1984 with Thomas "Tommie Agrippa" Eriksson on vocals. Andreas left for **Maninnya Blade** and later **Hexenhaus**. He was replaced by Lawrence West. The line-up featuring West, Martini, Agrippa and drummer Gareth Brandt recorded their first demo, *Egypt Eyes*, in 1985, followed by *Hammer Of The Gods* and *Onslaught Without Mercy*, both in 1986. In 1987 Gareth was replaced by Mike Thorn, and two more demos were recorded before the MLP. **Damien** was a very powerful and competent thrash band. Agrippa later joined **Hexenhaus** and West was found in **Crawley**. Mats went to **Lost Souls** and later **Misery Loves Co**. The outstanding track *Knights Of The Realm* appears on the Azra Records compilation *Iron Tyrants III*. The track *Hide And Seek* is found on the 7" split *Is This Heavy Or What* (1988 ITHOW Records). If you listen to Lawrence's subsequent band **Crawley** you can hear that the sound and direction was set already in '88. Not to be confused with hardcore band **Damien** from Karlstad or the melodic nu-oriented rockers from Lund. *Memorandum* is a compilation of the band's five demos and *Requiem Of The Dead*.

1990 7" - 136 376-7

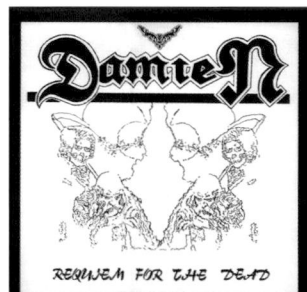

1988 MLP - 001

2012 2LPg - TTD 015

1988 ■	Requiem For The Dead	MLP 3tr	Gothic Records	001	$$
	Tracks: Not A Pleasant Way To Die/Death Is A Part Of The Process/Knights Of The Realm				
2012 ■	MEMORANDUM	2LPg	To The Death	TTD 015	
	100 hand-numbered copies in splatter vinyl + 400 in black.				
2012 ☐	SHADES FROM THE PAST (THE LOST TAPES)	2LPg	To The Death	TTD 022	

DAMN DELICIOUS

Kristofer Greczula: v, **Samuel Berg:** g, **Charlie Johansson:** g,
Christoffer Johansson: b, **Tim Hallerhed:** d

Falkenberg/Stockholm - Formed in 2006. A young band (17-18 years old) that won the Ginza Metal Battle in 2009. The first prize was the recording of a CD single. The single was produced by Matti Alfonzetti and Ronny Lahti. Modern melodic hard rock with the obvious pop-overtones.

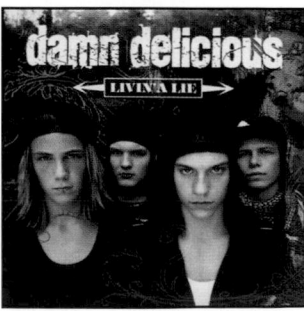

2010 CDSp - LHICDS0149

2010 ■	Livin' A Lie/Can't You See	CDSp	Lionheart	LHICDS0149	

DAMNATION

Richard "Daemon" Cabeza: v/g, Björn "Churchburner" Gramell: b, Peter "Insulter" Stjärnvind: d

Stockholm - Despite the band making their first release in 2004 and the members being foremost known for other acts, **Damnation** started out already in 1989 as a **Bathory** tribute band. They released the demo *Divine Darkness* in 1994, which included a cover of **Bathory**'s *The Return Of Darkness And Evil*. The demo was release as a 7" EP in 2004 and suddenly the band came to life again. They even do a cover of **Bathory**'s *Armegeddon* on the album and their sound is very true to their source of inspiration. The album also features guest appearances from **Watain** members Yonas "Mörk" Lindskog and Erik "E" Danielsson. Cabeza is also found in bands like **Dismember, Unanimated, Murder Squad, Born Of Fire, Dark Funeral, Carbonized** etc., while Stjärnvind is found in **Nifelheim, Merciless, Unanimated, Regurgitate, Face Down** etc.

2004 7" EP - IFPEP 011   *2004 CD - TRECD 012*

2004 ■	Divine Darkness	7" EP	Iron Fist		IFPEP 011

Tracks: Eternal Black/The Dark Divine/The Mistress – Queen Of Sin/The Return Of Darkness And Evil (Bathory cover)

2004 ☐	Insulter Of Jesus Christ	7" EP	Iron Fist		IFPEP 010

Tracks: Insulter Of Jesus Christ/Bloody Vengeance (Vulcano cover)/Night Eternal

2004 ■	DESTRUCTO EVANGELICA	CD	Threeman		TRECD 012
2004 ☐	DESTRUCTO EVANGELICA	LP	Threeman		TRELP 012

DAMNATION ARMY

Thomas Nyholm: v/g/b/d

Borgholm - **Damnation Army** is a solo project by multi-instrumentalist and growler Nyholm. This is really well-played and well-produced black metal with not so interesting type of growl. The last two albums were produced by Tore Stjerna in Necromorbus Studio. Great songs, though. In 2003 the EP *Towards Damnation* was released, followed by the album *Misanthropic Satanarchy*, both released as CD-R:s in 150 copies each, both released by God Is Myth. After this *The Art Of The Occult* was finally the band's first CD release. Nyholm has also made demos with bands like **Blaspheminator, Night Spawn** and **Rotten Minds**.

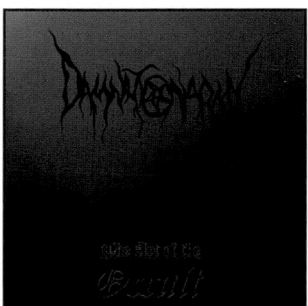

2004 CD - GIM 009

2004 ■	THE ART OF THE OCCULT	CD	God Is Myth		GIM 009
	500 copies.				
2006 ■	TYRANT	CD	Mascot		M 7200 2
2006 ☐	TYRANT	CD	Irond (Russia)		CD 06-DD437
2009 ☐	CIRCLE OF THE BRAVE	CD	Mascot		M 7249 2
2009 ☐	CIRCLE OF THE BRAVE	CD	Irond (Russia)		CD 09-DD737

2006 CD - M 7200 2

DAMNATORY

Babis "Argati" Tasiopoulos: g/v, David Nowén: g, Kim Salmi: b, Kujtim Gashi: d

Borås - Doom-oriented thrash with a progressive touch. At times quite similar to **Testament**. One of the better Büms-releases. Kujtim was later found in **Crystal Eyes** and Babis in **Brainwave**. Before the album the band made a three track self-titled demo in 1990. Babis and Kujtim today have a dark and quirky acoustic heavy rock band called **Argashi**. Babis has recorded some heavier demos with **Divine Recharge**, a bit in the vein of **Psychotic Waltz** with a death twist.

1991 ■	THE MADNESS NEVER ENDS	LP	Büms Records		27123

1991 LP - 27123

DAMNED NATION

Matti Alfonzetti: v, Robert Warnqvist: g, Magnus Jönsson: b, Roger Jern: d

Degerfors - The band started out in 1993 under the name **Easy Street** and released two singles, but with different singers. The first line-up featured Robert, Magnus, drummer Leif Erixon and after some auditions they found former **Powerhouse** singer Thomas Thorsén. Two songs on *Just What The Doctor Ordered* were written by James Christian (**House Of Lords**). Robert was one of the finalists of the 1992 *Guitar Battle* lead guitar competition. *Just What The Doctor Ordered* also featured keyboardist Anders Andersson (later in **Pantheon**), who was only in the band for that album. This album was quite **Van Halen**-influenced, while the follow-up is a true AOR-gem with hints of **Whitesnake**, especially when it comes to Thomas strong and powerful vocals. Between the first and second album, the band shopped around a six-track CD-R with *When Truth Becomes A Lie, The Damage Is Done, Coming Home* and three tracks off the first album. The backing-vocals on the second album were arranged by Pär Edwardsson (ex-**Biscaya**) and it also featured new drummer Roger Jern (**Dead End Street**) and keyboard player Anders Lindén recorded the keyboards for the album, but quit shortly after. The band now featured **Scudiero/Token/Constancia** keyboard player Mikael Rosengren live and in his absence **Dreamhunter** player Thomas Lassar stepped in. A live-album was recorded in 2000, but never released. In 2001 Thomas decided to leave the band and he was soon replaced by Matti Alfonzetti (**Alfonzetti, Bam Bam Boys, Skintrade, Red White & Blues** etc.). The band's fourth album *Sign Of Madness* was recorded with Tomas Skogsberg at the helm and the style was now a couple of notches heavier. After the last album the band sadly vanished.

1999 CD - ZR 1997014

2000 CD - ZR 1997028

Year		Title	Format	Label	Cat. No.
1995	☐	JUST WHAT THE DOCTOR ORDERED	CD	UFO	UFOCD 2013
1995	☐	JUST WHAT THE DOCTOR ORDERED	CD	Pony Canyon (Japan)	PCCY-00773
1999	☐	ROAD TO DESIRE	CD	Pony Canyon (Japan)	PCCY 01379
		Bonus: The Damage Is Done			
1999	■	ROAD TO DESIRE	CD	Z Records	ZR1997014
2000	■	GRAND DESIGN	CD	Z Records	ZR1997028
2000	☐	GRAND DESIGN	CD	Pony Canyon (Japan)	PCCY 01451
		Bonus: Love And Devotion (live)/Are You Willing To Forget (live)			
2004	■	SIGN OF MADNESS	CD	Scarlet	SC 095-2

2004 CD - SC 095-2

DANGER

Janne Risberg: v, Magnus Hälleblad: g/v, Anders Jonsson: b, Sam Nilsson: d

Västervik (Blankaholm) - Danger were formed around 1980-81. They won the recording of the 7" in a rock band competition. The A-side is straightforward boogie-oriented hard rock with mid-range vocals and the B-side is a traditional hard rock/metal number. *Danger* split around 1986. Sam joined *Top Dog Blues Band* in 91 and they have also released a blues album.

1983	■	Night Man/Crazy Town	7"	Soundservice	EDA 6313

1983 7" - EDA 6313

DANGER

Jens "Jesse Kid" Kemgren: v, Robert "Rob Paris" Lilja: g,
Johan "J.J. Glitter" Jonasson: g, Togge Rock: b, Danny Cräsh: d

Växjö - Lilja and Jonasson were previously in *Dethronement* and drummer Jonas Hallberg was ex-*Mindcollapse*. *Danger* were formed in 2003. The vocals were handled by Kristian Wallin (*Rising Faith, Morifade*) and the bass by Mathias Nilsson (*Mindcollapse, Skogen, Entrails*). In 2004 they recorded the self-financed CD *Keep Out*. The style was classic, great sounding metal in the vein of *Iron Maiden*. In 2006 they also released the CD *In Control* before switching singer from Wallin to former *Vulture Cavalry* vocalist Kemgren and bass player to Togge Rock and they now switched into a full blown 80s glam unit with the big hair and outfits to go with it. The music of course also changed with the image and *Danger* became a sleaze/glam rock band in the vein of *Poison* and *Faster Pussycat*. The band has released a number of 2-3 track demos. *Playing The Game* (2006, DCD 003), *Shove It Up Your Azz* (2007) and *First Touch* in 2008. Togge left the band in 2009. In 2008 Jonasson released his solo CD *All That Glitters*. In 2011 the band reportedly started changing their style a bit, going for a bluesy seventies hard-rocking sound more akin to Kemgren's old band *Vulture Cavalry*.

2004	■	KEEP OUT	CD	private	- -
2006	☐	IN CONTROL	CD	private	DCD 002
2007	☐	Spread Your Legz/Rock And Roll	CDS	private	DCD 004
2007	☐	California Red	MCD 3tr	private	DCD 005
		Tracks: California Red/Remedy To My Energy/Midnight Teaser			

2004 CD - - -

DANGER AVENUE

Jimmie "Lee Cooper" Rudolfsson: v, Victor "DiCola" Kinnhammar: g,
Thomas "Van Shaw" Bokgren: g, Viktor "O'Malley" Skatt: b, David "Criss David" Hult: d

Göteborg - Danger Avenue were formed in 2004, but in 2006 the recording line-up was completed. A great sounding AOR band in the vein of *H.E.A.T*, maybe not in the same league, but well worth checking out. A good live act as well.

2008	■	Danger Avenue	MCD 5tr	private	DACD 01
		Tracks: West Coast Angel/The Distance/Boarding Pass/Beat The Night/Avenues & Boulevards			
2010	☐	The Guilty & The Innocent	MCD 3tr	private	DACD 02
		Tracks: The Guilty & The Innocent/Bigger Than All Of Us/The Distance + video			
2010	■	LONG OVERDUE	CD	private	DACD 03
2011	☐	LONG OVERDUE	LP	private	(110068)

2008 MCD - DACD 01

DARK FUNERAL

Magnus "Emperor Magus Caligula" Broberg: v, Bo "Chaq Mol" Karlsson: g, Micke "Lord Ahriman" Svanberg: g, Bennie "B-Force" Fors: b, Matte "Dominator" Modin: d

Stockholm - Dark Funeral were formed in 1993 by Micke Svanberg and David "Blackmoon" Parland (R.I.P 2013). The band was completed by drummer Joel "Draugen" Andersson (later in *Svartsyn*) and bass player/singer Paul "Themgoroth" Mäkitalo. In 1994 they made their debut EP, which was also released on cassette by Carrion Records in Poland, under the name *Open The Gates* (CRR 029), which initially was supposed to be the title. Very brutal black metal and technically very competent. Very strong anti-christian hype with slogans such as "*Support the war against Christianity*", "*The black hordes of Satan*" and "*Remember... only death is real*". The band was picked up by Swedish No Fashion Records and the debut was first recorded with Dan Swanö, but not satisfied with the result the band entered The Abyss Studio with Peter Tägtgren

2010 CD - DACD 03

Teach your children to worship Dark Funeral.

and rerecorded the entire album. The new track *When Angels Forever Die* was also added to the new recording. The band was now completed by singer Magnus "Emperor Magnus Caligula" Broberg and Paul could concentrate on his bass playing. The album says 1995, but wasn't released until January 1996. Tomas "Alzazmon" Asklund (*Infernal*) now took over the drum stool and with this line-up the band recorded two covers of *Bathory*'s *Call From The Grave* and *Equimathorn* for the tribute album *In Conspiracy With Satan*. Now Parland left the band and was replaced by guitarist Henrik "Typhos" Ekeroth. The band returned to The Abyss to record *Vobiscum Satanas*, again with Peter Tägtgren at the helm. Matti "Dominion" Mäkelä entered the band as session bassist, but soon took over as guitar player and replaced Typhos, leaving Caligula to again take over the bass duties. Alzazmon was now replaced by Robert "Gaahnfaust" Lundin. In 1999 they recorded the MCD *Teach The Children To Worship Satan* featuring one new track and four cover tracks. After a show with *Deicide*, *Immortal* and *Cannibal Corpse* Lunding left the band and was replaced by Matte "Dominator" Modin (*Defleshed*). Dominion and Caligula recorded their side project *Dominion Caligula*, while Lord Ahriman formed *Wolfen Society*. In 2001 the band again entered The Abyss with Peter Tägtgren to record what was to become the album *Diabolis Inferium*. On this album the band rerecorded *An Apprentice Of Satan* from the previous MCD. The subsequent tour saw *Hypocrisy*'s Mikael Hedlund as live bassist and after this *Dismember*'s Richard "Daemon" Cabeza took on this task. After the next tour Dominion left the band and was replaced by Bo "Chaq Mol" Karlsson (*Ludichrist*). Gigs from the band's subsequent tour were recorded which resulted in the live album *De Profundis Ad Te Domine*. After taking legal actions against their former label they went to Regain Records, who released the live album in 2004. In 2005 the band started recording their next album with new producers Örjan Örnkloo and Daniel Bergstrand (*Devin Townsend, Crawley*). Bass on the album was played by *Meshuggah*'s Gustaf Hielm. October 24 *Attera Totus Sanctus* was released and even entered the Swedish charts at #35. In 2007 the first albums were re-issued with bonus material. *The Secret Of The Black Arts* featured the entire scrapped first recording by Swanö. They also released the live DVD *Attera Orbis Terrarum Part 1*, with a *Part 2* following in 2008. In 2009 the band's new album *Angelus Exuro Pro Eternus* was unearthed. *Dark Funeral* now featured Bennie "B-Force" Fors, formerly in *The Hymans* and *Epitaph*, on bass. He joined already in 2005 and left the band in 2010 to reform *Epitaph*. *Dark Funeral* have been featured on numerous compilations. For instance the track *My Dark Desires* is found on the compilation *Independent Music For Independent People Vol 1* (HOK '95) and that song plus *In The Sign Of The Horns* are also found on the compilation *Black End* ('95 Plastic Head). They also have tracks on compilations such as *A Tribute To Mayhem: Originators Of The Northern Darkness* (Avantgarde), *Code Red* (Drakkar), *King Diamond Tribute* (Necropolis) etc. Even though the band's sound and musical abilities have clearly developed through the years, and the later albums have showed a more technical side of the band, the sound and style is still as heavy, fast and brutal as ever. In 2011 Magus Caligula surprisingly decided to step down from the *Dark Funeral* throne. His replacement was German *Negator/ Sanguienus* singer Nachtgarm. Now B-Force had also been replaced by Tomas "Zornheym" Nilsson (*Aktiv Dödshjälp, Devian, Suicide Seduction*). In May 2012 the band made it official they had signed with Century Media.
Website: www.darkfuneral.se

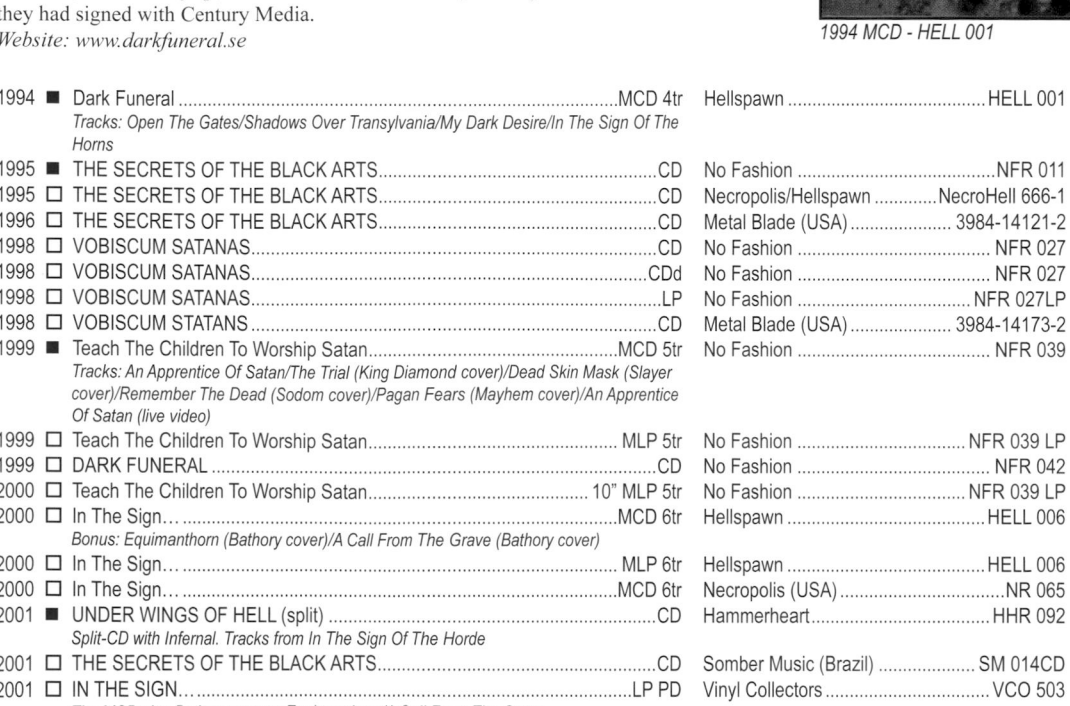
1994 MCD - HELL 001   1995 CD - NFR 011

1994 ■	Dark Funeral	MCD 4tr	Hellspawn	HELL 001
	Tracks: Open The Gates/Shadows Over Transylvania/My Dark Desire/In The Sign Of The Horns			
1995 ■	THE SECRETS OF THE BLACK ARTS	CD	No Fashion	NFR 011
1995 ☐	THE SECRETS OF THE BLACK ARTS	CD	Necropolis/Hellspawn	NecroHell 666-1
1996 ☐	THE SECRETS OF THE BLACK ARTS	CD	Metal Blade (USA)	3984-14121-2
1998 ☐	VOBISCUM SATANAS	CD	No Fashion	NFR 027
1998 ☐	VOBISCUM SATANAS	CDd	No Fashion	NFR 027
1998 ☐	VOBISCUM SATANAS	LP	No Fashion	NFR 027LP
1998 ☐	VOBISCUM STATANS	CD	Metal Blade (USA)	3984-14173-2
1999 ■	Teach The Children To Worship Satan	MCD 5tr	No Fashion	NFR 039
	Tracks: An Apprentice Of Satan/The Trial (King Diamond cover)/Dead Skin Mask (Slayer cover)/Remember The Dead (Sodom cover)/Pagan Fears (Mayhem cover)/An Apprentice Of Satan (live video)			
1999 ☐	Teach The Children To Worship Satan	MLP 5tr	No Fashion	NFR 039 LP
1999 ☐	DARK FUNERAL	CD	No Fashion	NFR 042
2000 ☐	Teach The Children To Worship Satan	10" MLP 5tr	No Fashion	NFR 039 LP
2000 ☐	In The Sign…	MCD 6tr	Hellspawn	HELL 006
	Bonus: Equimanthorn (Bathory cover)/A Call From The Grave (Bathory cover)			
2000 ☐	In The Sign…	MLP 6tr	Hellspawn	HELL 006
2000 ☐	In The Sign…	MCD 6tr	Necropolis (USA)	NR 065
2001 ■	UNDER WINGS OF HELL (split)	CD	Hammerheart	HHR 092
	Split-CD with Infernal. Tracks from In The Sign Of The Horde			
2001 ☐	THE SECRETS OF THE BLACK ARTS	CD	Somber Music (Brazil)	SM 014CD
2001 ☐	IN THE SIGN…	LP PD	Vinyl Collectors	VCO 503
	The MCD plus Bathory-covers: Equimanthorn/A Call From The Grave			

1999 MCD - NFR 039

2001 CD - HHR 092

Year		Title	Format	Label	Catalog
2001	☐	UNDER WINGS OF HELL (split)	CD	Somber Music (Brazil)	SM 015CD
2001	■	DIABOLIS INTERIUM	CD	No Fashion	NFR 066
2001	☐	DIABOLIS INTERIUM	CDd	No Fashion	NFR 266 0
2001	■	DIABOLIS INTERIUM	CDd	No Fashion	NFR 366 7

Different artwork. 6666 copies.

2001	☐	DIABOLIS INTERIUM	LP	No Fashion	NFR 166 3
2001	☐	DIABOLIS INTERIUM	CD	Soundholic (Jap)	TKCS 85021

Bonus: The Trial/Dead Skin Mask/Remember The Fallen/Pagan Fears

2001	☐	DIABOLIS INTERIUM	CD	Hellion (Brazil)	n/a
2001	☐	DIABOLIS INTERIUM	CD	S. Stack Co. (Thailand)	n/a
2001	☐	DIABOLIS INTERIUM	CD	Irond (Russia)	01-102
2001	☐	DIABOLIS INTERIUM	CD	Magnum (Thaiwan)	NFR 066
2002	☐	In The Sign…	MCD 4tr	Necropolis (USA)	NR 065
2002	☐	VOBISCUM SATANAS	CD	Irond (Russia)	CD 02-241
2002	☐	DIABOLIS INTERIUM	CD	Irond (Russia)	CD 02-402
2002	☐	THE SECRETS OF THE BLACK ARTS	CD	No Fashion	NFR 011
2002	☐	IN THE SIGN…	LP	Hammerheart	HHR 092

The MCD plus three Bathory-covers. Repress on blue vinyl.

2002	☐	THE BLACK MASSACRE	LP	Demonic Freak	DRF 01

210 black vinyl, 98 brown. Live.

2003	☐	DE PROFUNDIS CLAMAVI AD TE DOMINE	CD	Candlelight (USA)	CDL 021 CDD
2004	☐	AGOIS A BAPHOMET – LIVE IN CALI	CD	Hell Attacks	HA 006

666 copies.

2004	☐	DE PROFUNDIS CLAMAVI AD TE DOMINE	CD	Regain Records	RRCD 0403-051

Slipcase.

2004	☐	DE PROFUNDIS CLAMAVI AD TE DOMINE	2LP	Regain Records	RRLP 0403-051
2004	☐	DE PROFUNDIS CLAMAVI AD TE DOMINE	2LP PD	Regain Records	RRPLP 0403-051
2004	☐	DEVIL PIGS (split)	CD	Karmageddon	KARMA 057

Split with Von. Tracks: Open The Gates/Shadows Over Transylvania/My Dark Desires/In The Sign Of The Horde/Equimanthorn (Bathory cover)/A Call From The Grave (Bathory)

2004	☐	DEVIL PIGS (split)	CD	Candlelight (US)	CDL 0132 CD
2005	☐	In The Sign …	MCD 6tr	Karmageddon	KARMA 097
2005	☐	In The Sign …	MLP PD 6tr	Vinyl Collectors	VC 0503
2004	☐	DE PROFUNDIS CLAMAVI AD TE DOMINE	CD	Regain Records (USA)	REG-CD-1051
2005	■	ATTERA TOTUS SANCTUS	CD	Regain Records	RRCD 070
2005	☐	ATTERA TOTUS SANCTUS	CDd	Regain Records	RR 070

3000 copies.

2005	☐	ATTERA TOTUS SANCTUS	LP	Regain Records	RRLP 070
2005	☐	ATTERA TOTUS SANCTUS	LP PD	Regain Records	RRPLP 070
2005	☐	ATTERA TOTUS SANCTUS	CD	Candlelight (USA)	CDL 0249 CD
2005	☐	ATTERA TOTUS SANCTUS	CD	Hellion (Brazil)	HEL 0531
2005	☐	ATTERA TOTUS SANCTUS	CD	CD Maximum (Russia)	CDM 2470
2005	☐	ATTERA TOTUS SANCTUS	CD	Soundholic (Japan)	TKCS-85133

Bonus: Atrum Regina/Open The Gates (2005)

2005	☐	ATTERA TOTUS SANCTUS	CD	Icarus Music (Argentina)	ICARUS 265
2005	☐	DE PROFUNDIS CLAMAVI AD TE DOMINE	CD	Icarus Music (Argentina)	ICARUS 267
2007	☐	THE SECRET OF THE BLACK ARTS	2CDd	Regain Records	DF 001/REG-CD-1013

Bonus CD: Shadows Over Transylvania/The Dawn No More Rises/The Secrets Of The Black Arts/Satans Mayhem/Bloodfrozen/My Dark Desires/Dark Are The Part To Eternity/The Fire Eternal

2007	☐	VOBISCUM SATANAS	CDd	Regain Records	DF 002/REG-CD-1014

Bonus live tracks: Enriched By Evil/Thy Legions Come/Vobiscum Satanas/Ineffable King Of Darkness

2007	☐	VOBISCUM SATANAS	LP	Regain Records	DF 002
2007	☐	DIABOLIS INTERIUM	2CD	Regain Records	DF 003/REG-CD-1015

Reissue with bonus disc featuring the tracks from "Teach The Children…"

2009	■	ANGELUS EXURO PRO ETERNUS	CD	Regain Records	RRCD 168
2009	☐	ANGELUS EXURO PRO ETERNUS	LPg	Regain Records	RRLP 168

500 copies.

2009	☐	ANGELUS EXURO PRO ETERNUS	CD	Avalon Marquee (Japan)	MICP-10839

Bonus: 666 Voices Inside (live)/Godess Of Sodomy (live)

2009	☐	ANGELUS EXURO PRO ETERNUS	CD+DVD	Regain Records	RRCD 172

First edition with live DVD recorded at Peace & Love Festival 2008. Slipcase.

2010	☐	ANGELUS EXURO PRO ETERNUS	CD	Soyus (Russia)	RR 168
2010	☐	ANGELUS EXURO PRO ETERNUS	CD	Icarus Music (Argentina)	ICARUS 582
2010	☐	ANGELUS EXURO PRO ETERNUS	CD+DVD	Regain Records (USA)	REG-CD-9008
2011	☐	ATTERA TOTUS SANCTUS	LP	Regain Records	BOBV175LP
2011	☐	DIABOLIS INTERIUM	2LP	Back On Black	BOBV176LP
2011	☐	In The Sign …	MCD 6tr	Hammerheart	HHR2011-23

Unofficial releases:

2001	■	Equimathorn/Call From The Grave	7"	SatanSpawn (Japan)	SPAWN 0600
2001	☐	THE SECRETS OF THE BLACK PAST	CD	Diabolis Interium	DIR 001
2002	☐	THE BLACK MASSACRE	LP	Demonic Freak	DFR 01
2002	☐	LIVE HULTSFRED SWEDEN	LP	Imperial Creations (UK)	IF4

2001 CD - NFR 066

2001 CDd - NFR 366 7

2005 CD - RRCD 070

2009 CD - RRCD 168

2001 7" - SPAWN 0600

DARK ILLUSION

Thomas Vikström: v, Tomas Hultqvist: g, Pontus Egberg: b, Johan Kullberg: d

Stockholm - The band was formed already back in 1982 by a couple of school mates, but split after only three years of existence. In 2003 they felt it was time to blow some life into the old beast again… Now here's a band that went through an earthshaking transformation from the 4-track debut MCD until the first album. The first MCD was a project by guitarists Hultqvist and Tengblad with Vikström guesting on vocals. The keyboards and drum programming were handled by Ulf "Chris Laney" Larsson (*17, Kyss, Chris Laney* etc) and the style was classic melodic hard rock, sort of *Kiss* goes AOR. A great platter well worth looking for. On *Beyond The Shadows* the style was suddenly melodic power metal, the cover depicted the classic ancient power metal warrior and the lyrics were the traditional, clique-filled nonsense. However, I shall be fair and say the band doesn't fall into the power metal traps, but leans more on classic 80s heavy metal with a touch of classic neoclassical melodies. On this album the "band" featured, besides Hultqvist, Tengblad and Vikström, bass player Pontus Egberg (*Lion's Share, The Poodles*) and drummer Jonas Östman (*Gotham City, Mogg, Malmsteen*). Some keyboards were also provided by original *Dark Illusion* keyboard player Ola Jansson. The second album, *Where The Eagles Fly* saw Tengblad only acting as co-producer with Ulf "Chris Laney" Larsson guesting on keyboards, besides handling recording and engineering. The drums were here handled by *Lion's Share/Talk Of The Town* drummer Kullberg. *Where The Eagles Fly* provides more of the same style and sound-wise. A sure buy for fans of neoclassically oriented power metal.
Website: www.darkillusion.se

2003 MCD - BRCD 001

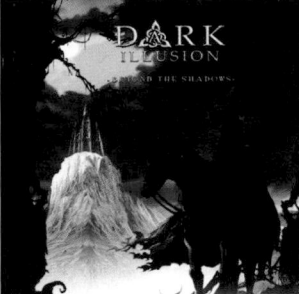

2006 CD - MYST CD 095

2008 CDS - BRCD 008

2003 ■	For Just Another Night	MCD 4tr	Battlefield Records	BRCD 001
	Tracks: For Just Another Night/Outlaw/Close To Me/Battlefield			
2005 ○	Night Knight/Weeper Deeper	CDS	Battlefield Records (promo)	BRCD 003
2005 □	BEYOND THE SHADOWS	CD	Battlefield Records	BRCD 004
2005 □	BEYOND THE SHADOWS	CD	Stay Gold (Japan)	ARTSG-008
	Bonus: Mysterious			
2006 ■	BEYOND THE SHADOWS	CD	Mystic Empire (Russia)	MYST CD 095
2008 ●	Running Out Of Time/Only The Strong Will Survive	CDS	Battlefield Records (promo)	BRCD 008
2009 □	WHERE THE EAGLES FLY	CD	Battlefield Records	BRCD 009
2010 □	WHERE THE EAGLES FLY	CD	Avalon Marquee (Japan)	MICP-10916
	Bonus: Destiny's Call (Piano & Vocals)			

DARK LEGIONS

Pest: v, Dark: g, Vomit: b, Legion: d

Luleå/Stockholm/Finland - Thrashing old-school-type black metal in the vein of *Wargasm*. The album features lots of name guests such as Nicke Johansson (*Hexenhaus, Maninnya Blade*), Jonas Isacsson (*Roxette*), Erik Blodyx (*Lethal*), Hell Mike Motorbike (*Lethal*) etc. The band made their debut with the demo *Awakening The Legions* in 2005. Finnish singer/basist Kutchek Gorealis was a guest, but later replaced Pest and Vomit. He is also found in *Tyranny, Misanthropical Painforest* and *Legacies Unchain*. The band made a second demo in 2008, entitled *Metal Special Forces*.

2006 ■	SATÄNIC DESTRÖYER	CD	Pestilence	PEST 006

2006 CD - PEST 006

DARK TRANQUILLITY

Mikael Stanne: v, Niklas Sundin: g, Martin Henriksson: g,
Martin Brändström: k, Daniel Antonsson: b, Anders Jivarp: d

Calm guys in the light

Billdal/Stockholm - The band was formed in 1989 under the joke moniker *Sceptic Boiler*, under which name they released the demo *Enfeebled Earth*. They soon changed their name to *Dark Tranquillity* and were at the time quite unaware they would be one of the founders of the Gothenburg Sound. The line-up consisted of Niklas Sundin (g), Martin Henriksson (b), Anders Jivarp (d), Mikael Stanne (g) and Anders Fridén (v). In 1993 Polish label Carnage Records released a special cassette with both the first singles. I initially described them as "well-arranged heavy/speed death metal, at times reminiscent of *At The Gates*". *Skydancer* was produced by Dragan Tanacovic and Stefan Lindgren, who also produced the bands earlier work. Anna-Kaisa Avehall lended her voice to one of the tracks. After the debut, Fridén left the band to devote his time to *Ceremonial Oath*. Stanne took over the vocals and guitarist Fredrik Johansson was added to the line-up and made his debut on the *Of Chaos…* MCD. . The *Metallica* cover *My Friend Of Misery* was featured on the tribute album *Metal Militia* (94 Black Sun). For the next album, *The Gallery*, the band entered Studio Fredman with producer Fredrik Nordström (*Dream Evil*). Here Eva-Marie Larsson added some female vocal flare. The band's next album, *The Mind's I*, showed a bit more diversity and even featured some clean vocals by Stanne. On this album former singer Fridén guested, together with Sara Svensson. In 1998 Fredrik Johansson left the band and bass player Henriksson switched to six strings. Enter new bass player Michael Nicklasson and keyboard player Martin Brändström. On *Projector* (which was initially going to be released on Osmose, as #OPCD 078), the band started experimenting with their sound, moving from the more traditional death genre towards a more symphonic sounds and style. Adding more keyboards and strings. The female vocals were provided by Johanna Andersson.

© Photo by Kenneth Johansson

This album, along with the subsequent *Haven,* was produced by Nordström. On *Haven* they broadened their sound even more and even included some elements of goth and more keyboards, at times slightly reminiscent of **Children Of Bodom**, with whom they toured Japan. The album was also released on cassette by Metal Mind in Poland and Atlantis Muzik in Turkey. 2002 saw the release of *Damage Done*, an album that even entered the Swedish charts. The band actually made a club gig in Seoul, Korea under the pseudonym **Damage Done**. The following year also saw a release of the live-DVD *Live Damage*. The album *Character* (2005) was the first album to be produced by the band themselves, an album that was even heavier, faster and more aggressive than its predecessor. This didn't scare the Swedish buyers and the album entered at #3 in the Swedish charts. For the next album, *Fiction*, the band collaborated with Danish producer Tue Madsen, who brought out both new sides and old elements from the band. The band toured quite extensively and visited places like USA, Finland, Germany, Greece, China, Taiwan, Japan and Latin America. During the year bass player Nicklasson left the band for personal reasons and the autumn tour was performed with **Engel** bassist Michael Håkansson as a temporary replacement. The band however settled for new stringsman Daniel Antonsson, formerly of **Dimension Zero** and **Soilwork**. In 2009 the band released the live-DVD *Where Death Is Most Alive*, the first since 2002. On the first screening of the DVD the spectators were given a limited edition CD (333 copies) entitled *The Dying Fragments*, featuring ultra-rare live recordings made between 1991 and 1997. The DVD entered at #1 on the Swedish charts in November 2009. The album *We Are The Void* was released in 2010. The non-CD track *Punish My Heaven* appears on the *W.A.R* compilation (Wrong Again Records). They also have track *Yesterworld* on the German death-compilation *Requiem* (94 Exhumed Productions) and some live-tracks can be found on *World Domination Live* (98 Osmose).

Young and dark: L-R: Sundin, Jivarp, Fridén, Stanne and Brandström.

1992 7" - - -

1992 ■	Trial Of Life Decayed	7" 3tr	Guttural	- -
	Tracks Midvinter (intro)/Beyond Enlightenment/Void Of Tranquillity 1000 copies.			
1992 □	A Moonclad Reflection	7"	Slaughter/Exhumed Prod	CORPSE 001
	Tracks: Unfurled By Dawn/Yesterworld. 500 copies.			
1993 ■	SKYDANCER	CD	Spinefarm	SPI 16 CD
1993 □	SKYDANCER	LP	Spinefarm	SPI 16
1993 □	SKYDANCER	CD	Toys Factory (Japan)	TFCK 88771
	Bonus: Of Chaos And Eternal Night/With The Flaming Shades Of Fall/Away Delight Away/ Alone			
1995 □	Of Chaos And Eternal Night	MCD 4tr	Spinefarm	SPI 23 CD
	Tracks: Of Chaos And Eternal Night/With The Flaming Shades Of Fall/Away Delight Away/Alone			
1995 ■	THE GALLERY	CD	Osmose	OPCD 033
1995 □	THE GALLERY	LPg	Osmose	OPLP 033
	Also available in red vinyl in 300 copies.			
1995 □	THE GALLERY	CD	Osmose	OPCDL033
	Bonus: Sacred Reich (Sacred Reich cover)/Bringer Of Torture (Kreator cover). 3000 copies in 10" sleeve.			
1995 □	THE GALLERY	CD	Toy's Factory (Japan)	TFCK 88769
	Bonus: My Friend Of Misery			
1996 □	SKYDANCER & OF CHAOS AND ETERNAL NIGHT	CD	Spinefarm	SPI34CD
1996 □	Enter Suicidal Angels	MCD 4tr	Osmose	OPMC 049
	Tracks: Zodijackal Light/Razorfever/Shadowlit Façade/Archetype			
1997 ■	THE MIND'S I	CD	Osmose	OPCD 052
1997 □	THE MIND'S I	CD	Osmose	OPCDL 052
	Limited edition in 10"vinyl sleeve, 3000 copies.			
1997 □	THE MIND'S I	LP	Osmose	OPLP 052
1997 □	THE MIND'S I	CD	Toy's Factory (Japan)	TFCK-87107
	Bonus: Razorfever/Shadowlit Facede/Archetype			
1998 □	THE GALLERY	LP PD	Osmose	OPPIC 057A
1996 □	SKYDANCER & OF CHAOS AND ETERNAL NIGHT	CD	Century Media (USA)	7986-2
1999 □	PROJECTOR	CD	Toy's Factory (Japan)	TFCK 87186
1999 □	PROJECTOR	CD	Fono (Russia)	FO 209 CD
1999 □	PROJECTOR	CD	Century Media	77285 2
1999 □	PROJECTOR	LP	Century Media	77285 1
1999 ■	PROJECTOR	CDd	Century Media	77285 2D
	Bonus: Exposure			
1999 □	PROJECTOR	CD	Century Media (USA)	7985 2
2000 □	HAVEN	CD	Toy's Factory (Japan)	TFCK 87235
	Bonus: Cornered, plus enhanced track: Therein			
2000 □	THE MIND'S I	CD	Dream On (South Korea)	DOR 43341-2
2000 □	HAVEN	CD	Century Media	77297-2
2000 □	HAVEN	CDd	Century Media	CM1113-2
2000 □	HAVEN	CD	Century Media (USA)	7997 2
	Bonus: Therein (video)			
2000 □	HAVEN	LP	Century Media	77297-1
2000 □	HAVEN	LP PD	Century Media	77297-1P
2000 □	HAVEN	CD	Fono (Russia)	FO 172CD
2000 □	HAVEN	CD	Century Medi (Brazil)	77297-2
2001 □	SKYDANCER & OF CHAOS AND ETERNAL NIGHT	CD	Fono (Russia)	FO 031CD
2002 □	DAMAGE DONE	CD	Century Media	77403-2

1993 CD - SPI 16 CD

1995 CD - OPCD 033

1997 CD - OPCD 052

1999 CDd - 77285 2D

| 2002 | ☐ DAMAGE DONE | LP | Century Media | 77403-1 |

Bonus: I, Deception. Different artwork. 1000 copies.

| 2002 | ☐ DAMAGE DONE | CDd | Century Media | 77403-8 |

Bonus: I, Deception + Monochromatic Stains (video)

| 2002 | ■ DAMAGE DONE | CD | Toy's Factory (Japan) | TFCK-87288 |

Bonus: The Poison Well + Monochromatic Stains (video)

| 2002 | ☐ DAMAGE DONE | CD | Century Media (USA) | 8103-2 |

Bonus: I, Deception

2002	☐ THE GALLERY	CD	Fono (Russia)	FO 152CD
2002	☐ THE MIND'S I	CD	Fono (Russia)	FO 117CD
2002	☐ HAVEN	CD	Fono (Russia)	FO 172CD

Bonus: Therein (video)

| 2003 | ☐ PROJECTOR | CD | Fono (Russia) | FO 177CD |

Bonus: Monochromatic Stains (video)

| 2003 | ☐ DAMAGE DONE | CD | Fono (Russia) | FO 209CD |

Bonus: Exposure

| 2004 | ■ Lost To Apathy | MCD 4tr | Century Media | 77585-2 |

Lost To Apathy/Derivation TNB/The Endless Feed (Chaos Seed Remix)/Undo Control
(live)/Lost To Apathy (video)

2004	☐ Lost To Apathy	MCD 4tr	Century Media (USA)	8285-2
2004	☐ Lost To Apathy	MCD 4tr	Fono (Russia)	FO 421 CD
2004	☐ CHARACTER	CD	Century Media	77603-2
2004	■ CHARACTER	LP	Century Media	77603-1
2004	☐ CHARACTER	CDd	Century Media	77603-8

Bonus videos: Lost To Apathy/Damage Done/The Wonders At Your Feet/Final Resistance/
The Treason Wall

2004	☐ CHARACTER	CD	Icarus Music (Argentina)	ICARUS 093
2004	■ EXPOSURES IN RETROSPECT AND DENIAL	2CD	Century Media	77503-2
2004	☐ EXPOSURES IN RETROSPECT AND DENIAL	2CD	Century Media (USA)	8203-2
2005	☐ SKYDANCER & OF CHAOS AND ETERNAL NIGHT	CD	Del Imaginario Discos (Argentina)	003
2005	☐ CHARACTER	CD	Fono (Russia)	FO 455 CD
2005	■ THE GALLERY	CD	Century Media (USA)	8260-2

New artwork. Bonus: Bringer Of Torture (Kreator cover)/Sacred Reich (Sacred Reich
cover)/22 Acacia Avenue (Iron Maiden cover)/Lady In Black (Mercyful Fate cover)/My
Friend Of Misery (Metallica cover)

2005	☐ THE GALLERY DELUXE EDITION	CD	Osmose	OPCD 033
2005	☐ THE GALLERY	CD	Icarus (Argentina)	ICARUS 104
2005	☐ THE MIND'S I	CD	Century Media (USA)	8261-2

New artwork. Bonus: Razorfever/Shadowlit Façade/Archetype/ + videos

2005	☐ THE MIND'S I	CD	Osmose	OPCD 052
2005	☐ THE MIND'S I	CD	Icarus (Argentina)	ICARUS 105
2005	☐ PROJECTOR	CD	Icarus (Argentina)	ICARUS 173
2005	☐ HAVEN	CD	Icarus (Argentina)	ICARUS 174
2005	☐ DAMAGE DONE	CD	Icarus Music (Argentina)	ICARUS 175
2007	☐ CHARACTER	CD	Toy's Factory (Japan)	TFCK-87380

Bonus: Derivation TNB/Endless Chaos (Chaos Seed Remix)

| 2007 | ☐ FICITION | CD | Century Media (USA) | 8315-2 |
| 2007 | ☐ FICITION | CD | Century Media | 77615-2 |

Bonus: Winter Triangle + videos: Focus Shift/Focus Shift (Rehearsals)/The New Build

| 2007 | ☐ FICITION | LPg+CD | Century Media | 77615-1 |

Special edition with the album on CD as bonus. Poster.

2007	☐ FICITION	CD	Icarus Music (Argentina)	ICARUS 366
2007	☐ FICITION	CD	Mystic Empire (Russia)	MYST CD 200
2007	☐ FICITION	CDd	Mystic Empire (Russia)	MYST CD 200 LTD
2007	☐ FICITION	CDd	Toy's Factory (Japan)	TFCK-87415

Bonus: A Closer End

| 2007 | ☐ Focus Shift/Terminus (Where Death Is Most Alive) | CDS | Century Media | 7508-2 |
| 2008 | ☐ FICITION – EXPANDED EDITION | CD+DVD | Century Media | 77615-8 |

Different artwork. Bonus: A Closer End/Winter Triangle/Below The Radiance/Silence In
The House Of Tongues (Instrumental)/Terminus (live)/The Lesser Faith (live) + DVD.

| 2008 | ☐ SKYDANCER | CD | Toys Factory (Japan) | TFCK 87426 |

Bonus: Tracks from the Of Chaos And Eternal Night MCD.

| 2008 | ☐ THE MIND'S I | CD | Toys Factory (Japan) | TFCK 87428 |

New artwork. Bonus: Razorfever/Shadowlit Façade/Archetype/Zodijackyl Light (video)/
Hedon (video)

2008	☐ EXPOSURED IN RETROSPECT AND DENIAL	2CD	CDNet Music (Taiwan)	CLSA 003
2008	☐ PROJECTOR	CD	Magnum Music (Taiwan)	CM77852-2
2008	☐ HAVEN	CD	Toy's Factory (Japan)	TFCK-87430

Bonus: Therein (video)

| 2008 | ☐ HAVEN | CD | Magnum Music (Taiwan) | CM77297-2 |

Bonus: Therein (video)

| 2009 | ☐ PROJECTOR | CD | Mazzar Records (Russia) | MZR CD 443 |
| 2009 | ☐ PROJECTOR | CD | Century Media (USA) | 8618-2 |

New artwork. Bonus: Asleep In The Bandaged Light/No One/Exposure/Therein (live)

| 2009 | ☐ PROJECTOR | CD | Century Media | 997918-2 |

New artwork. Bonus: (same as 8618-2). Slipcase.

2002 CD - TFCK-87288

2004 MCD - 77585-2

2004 LP - 77603-1

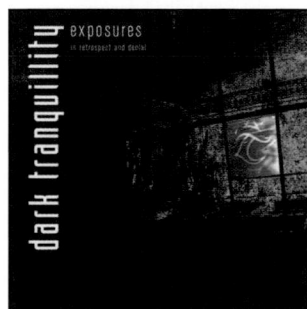

2004 2CD - 77503-2

2005 CD - 8260-2

2009	☐	HAVEN	CD	Century Media (USA)	8619-2

New artwork. Bonus: In Sight/Misery In Me/Cornered/The Wonders At Your Feet (live). Slipcase.

2009	■	DAMAGE DONE	CD	Century Media	997920-2

Bonus: I, Deception/Static/The Poison Well/The Treason Well (live). Slipcase. New artwork.

2009	☐	DAMAGE DONE	CD	Century Media (USA)	8620-2
2009	☐	HAVEN	CD	Mazzar Records (Russia)	MZR CD 445
2009	☐	HAVEN	2LPg	Back On Black	BOBV208LP

Blue vinyl.

2009	☐	DAMAGE DONE	2LPg	Back On Black	BOBV209LP
2009	■	MANIFESTO OF DARK TRANQUILLITY	CD	Century Media	997887-2
2009	■	YESTERWORLDS (THE EARLY DEMOS)	CD	Century Media	997917 2

Slipcase.

2009	☐	YESTERWORLDS (THE EARLY DEMOS)	CDd	Scarecrow Records (Mexico)	SR0469-LTD
2009	☐	WHERE DEATH IS MOST ALIVE	2CD	Century Media (USA)	8613-2
2009	☐	WHERE DEATH IS MOST ALIVE	2CD	Century Media	997913 2
2009	☐	WHERE DEATH IS MOST ALIVE	2CD+2DVD	Century Media	997913 9
2009	☐	THE DYING FRAGMENTS	CD	private	- -

333 copies.

2010	☐	WE ARE THE VOID	CD	Century Media	997955 2
2010	☐	WE ARE THE VOID	LP	Century Media	997955 1
2010	■	WE ARE THE VOID	CDd+DVD	Century Media	997955 8

Bonus: Star Of Nothingless/Out Of Gravity

2010	☐	WE ARE THE VOID (TOUR EDITION)	CDd+DVD	Century Media	997955 0

A5 cover. Bonus: Zero Distance/Star Of Nothingness/Out Of Gravity/To Where Fires Cannot Feed/The Bow And The Arrow

2010	☐	WE ARE THE VOID	CDd+DVD	Century Media (USA)	8608-2
2010	☐	WE ARE THE VOID	CD	Century Media (USA)	8655-2
2010	☐	WE ARE THE VOID	2LPg	Century Media (USA)	8608-1

Bonus: Star Of Nothingness/Out Of Gravity. 1000 copies.

2010	☐	WE ARE THE VOID	CD	Trooper (Japan)	XNTE-00005

Bonus: Star Of Nothingness/Out Of Gravity

2010	☐	WE ARE THE VOID	CDd	Mazzar Records (Russia)	MZR CD 452 D
2010	☐	WE ARE THE VOID	CD	Icarus Music (Argentina)	ICARUS 625
2010	☐	WHERE DEATH IS MOST ALIVE	2CD	Trooper (Japan)	XNTE-00006-7
2010	☐	Enter Suicidal Angels	MLP 4tr	Night Of The Vinyl Dead	NIGHT 088

500 numbered copies.

2010	☐	Of Chaos And Eternal Light	MLP 4tr	Night Of The Vinyl Dead	NIGHT 067

500 numbered copies.. Etching on B-side.

2010	☐	PROJECTOR	2LPg	Back On Black	BOBV207LP

Grey vinyl.

2012	☐	WHERE DEATH IS MOST ALIVE	3LPg	Floga Records (Greece)	FL 37

150 copies in black/white splatter vinyl, plus on black vinyl.

2012	☐	THE GALLERY	2LPg	Century Media	998237-3
2013	☐	CONSTRUCT	CD	Century Media	998337-0
2013	☐	CONSTRUCT	2CDd	Century Media	998337-2
2013	☐	CONSTRUCT	LPg+7"	Century Media	998337-1

Transparent red (limited CM Distro version) or black vinyl.

2009 CD - 997887-2

2009 CD (slipcase) - 997920-2

2009 CD (slipcase) - 997917 2

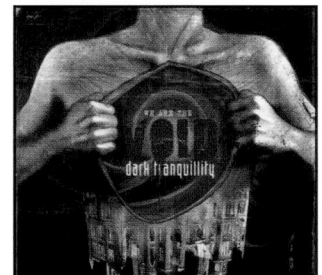

2010 CDd - 997955 8

DARKANE

Lawrence Mackrory: v, Christofer Malmström: g, Klas Ideberg: g, Jörgen Löfberg: b, Peter Wildoer: d

Helsingborg - Formed in 1998, by Wildoer and Malmström out of the ashes of *Agretator*. They teamed up with Ideberg (later in *Terror 2000* and *The Defaced*) and Löfberg (also in *Agretator* and later in *The Defaced*). The name, *Darkane*, is a combination of the words "dark" and "arcane". On the band's first demos the vocals were handled by Björn "Speed" Strid (*Terror 2000, Soilwork, Dog Faced Gods* etc). They found singer Lawrence Mackrory and recorded the debut *Rusted Angel*. On the second album Mackrory (later in *Andromeda*, *The Duskfall*, *Scarve*, *Scavenger*, *Forcefeed*, *Seethings*, *Sportlov* (as Thermoss) and *F.K.Ü* (as Larry Lethal)) was replaced by Andreas Sydow. *Insanity* was produced by Daniel Bergstrand. Highly technical, aggressive thrash with great musicianship. Brutal, with Anselmo-style vocals. *Expanding Senses*, was produced by Daniel Bergstrand and Örjan Örnkloo. After *Layers Of Lies* the band went into a three year hiatus. In 2008 they returned with a vengeance and with new singer Jens Broman (*The Defaced, Construcdead*) at the helm. Malmström also released his solo project *Non-Human Level* in 2005, a project that included Wildoer. Sydow guested as guitarist on Spanish thrashers *Legen Beltza*'s album *Dimension Of Pain*. Wildoer has been and is found in numerous bands and projects, such as *Dawn Of Oblivion, Majestic, Silver Seraph, Armageddon, Arch Enemy, Time Requiem, Grimmark, Pestilence* etc. The band can be found on compilations, such as *Wardance 1* (WAR 1998), *A Tribute To The Beast* (Wicked World), where they do a cover of *Powerslave*, *A Tribute To Accept* (Nuclear Blast), where they do *Restless And Wild*.The album *The Sinister Supremacy* saw Mackrory returning to replace Jens Broman.

Darkane and mysterious

1998	■	RUSTED ANGEL	CD	WAR	WAR 0009
1999	☐	RUSTED ANGEL	CD	Relapse Records	RLP 6430

1983 ■	Jenny's Out Tonight/Well, It's The Last Time	7"	VCM	VCM 102
1983 ☐	YOURS SINCERELY	LP	Shooting Star	SSRLP 1
1983 ■	JENNY'S OUT TONIGHT	LP	Epic (Canada)	FZ 39320

Same as above, but without First Time and with new artwork.

1983 LP - FZ 39320

DAVE NERGE'S BULLDOG
Dave Nerge: v, Benny Jansson: g, Jens Johansson: k,
Per Stadin: b, Anders Johansson: d

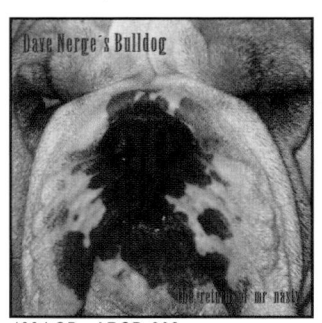

Malmö/Stockholm - This album was originally written for Glenn Hughes vocals, but as he got involved with his own solo-project the offer went to former *Highbrow/Dave & The Mistakes* singer Dave Nerge. He accepted. The backing-band, or the actual band, are three quarters *Silver Mountain* (Johansson, Johansson, Stadin). The style is straight-ahead, slightly *Purple*-influenced solid hard rock. One of the tracks, *If You Don't Want Me To*, was also recorded by Glenn Hughes on his album *From Now On...* (1994 Empire). Dave was a radio-DJ on the Bandit Radio (Stockholm), hosting the show *Dave In The Morning*. Stadin has later recorded with *Snake Charmer*, Anders is today found in *HammerFall* and *Fullforce*, Jens in *Stratovarius* and Benny has recorded with bands like *Two Rocks*, *Snake Charmer*, *Avenue*, *Trail Of Tears* etc.

1994 CD - ARCD-003

1994 ■	THE RETURN OF MR NASTY	CD	Arctic	ARCD-003
1994 ☐	THE RETURN OF MR NASTY	CD	Zero (Japan)	XRCN-1183

DAVID HARLEYSON POWERTRIO
Lasse Gidbo: v/b, Håkan Goldbeck: g, Håkan Rangemo: d

Stockholm - *David Harleyson Powertrio* has made quite a name of themselves in Sweden as a full-bearded *ZZ Top* cover band. The album features only one original track and the rest are covers of *ZZ Top*, *Black Sabbath*, *Motörhead*, *Deep Purple*, *AC/DC* etc. What they do, they do well.

2008 ■	PROBABLY THE HEAVYMOST ROCK 'N ROLL ALBUM!	CD	private	TDHP200801

2008 CD - TDHP200801

DAWN
Henke Forss: v, Andreas Fullmestad: g, Fredrik Söderberg: g,
Lars Tängmark: b, Jocke Pettersson: d

Linköping - It started back in 1990, when founder Fredrik Söderberg left the band *Obduracy*. Between 1985-86 he was also a member of *Cranium* (formerly known as *Legion*). *Seance* colleague Patrik Jensen (now *The Haunted/Witchery*) recommended former *Morgue* guitarist Fullmestad and the duo was later joined by former *Mortified* members Karsten Larsson (d) and Dennis Larsson (b). The band was completed by singer Henke Forss, formerly of *Funeral Feast*. In 1991 they took the name *Dawn* from an old *Legion* song. In 1992, they recorded their first two-track demo, *Demo 1*, which sold in 150 copies. Shortly after, Dennis left to be replaced by *Mortified* bassist Lars Tängmark. The second demo, recorded by Dan Swanö, was entitled *Apparition*. It caught the attention of Mexican Bellphegot Records promising the band a CD, which became a split with Mexicans *Pyphomgertum*, much to the band's dissatisfaction. In 1993 they entered Unisound Stuios with Swanö to record the *Promo '93* tape. *Dawn* now played black metal with fast and heavy, as well as soft, parts all topped with hysterical vocals. Actually he doesn't sing. It says on the cover "nocturnal vampyric chantings". In 1993 Forss also started his side project, grindcore band band *Retaliation*. The promo caught the attention of Necropolis Records. The debut album was again produced by Swanö and two songs, including the title were translated to medieval Swedish by Johan "Shamaatae" Lagher (*Arckanum*). The band suffered a setback in 1994 when guitarist Söderberg injured his hand in an accident at the butchery where he worked. He could not play guitar for a year and the band was put on hold awaiting his recovery. Finding their way back in 1995 the band again wanted to work with Swanö, but as he was heavily booked, the band turned to Peter Tägtgren and his, at the time relatively humble, Studio Abyss. The band recorded the MCD, including a cover of *Infernal Majesty*'s *Night Of The Living Dead*. Another setback hit the band when drummer Karsten Larsson left the band to concentrate on his other band *Mithotyn* and later *Falconer*. The band however found skinsman Jocke Pettersson, who is also found in *Niden Div. 187* (where Forss has also been a member) and *Thy Primordial*. The band continued their hard work and in 1997 they again entered Studio Abyss to record the album *Slaughtersun*. They also made a video for the track *The Knell And The World*. The new album was in English only and some of the lyrics were written by former *Cranium/Afflicted/Defender* main man Philip Von Segebaden. In 1998 Söderberg and Pettersson moved to Stockholm, where the latter started working in the famous Sunlight Studio. Finding less time for the band he finally had to leave. Because of the band's relocation Fullmestad and Tängmark (later in *The Wounded Meadow*) also left the band, leaving Söderberg to spend 1999 finding himself a new Stockholm based line-up. First one in was drummer Tomas "Alzazmon" Asklund, who had left *Dark Funeral* in 1998 after some extensive touring. The two started working on new material. Söderberg also laid down some guest vocals for US band *Dekapitator*'s debut album. The line-up kept growing and the earlier mentioned Philip Von Segebaden joined on bass. In 2000 the band was completed when former *Necromicon* guitarist Stefan Lundgren entered. In 2001 the band recorded a new 4-track promo which caught the attention of Nuclear Blast. The negotiations didn't work out as planned

Dawn, awaiting the slaughtersun

1994 CD - BELLCD 94010

1995 CD - NR 006

and no other label managed to meet the band's expectations, leaving the band stranded... until a new Swedish label signed the band in 2002. The new album was written, the recording was supposed to be made during 2003... and the label went bust. Between 2004-2006 Tomas worked with **Dissection**, and not until 2007 the band started working again. In 2008 the recordings of a new album, entitled *The Fourfold Furnace*, was underway. The most current line-up features Söderberg, Forss, Asklund and von Segebaden.

1996 MCD - NR 6664

1994	■	THE ETERNAL FOREST (split)	CD	Bellphegot (Mexico)	BELLCD 94010

Split with Pyphomgertum. Tracks: In The Depths Of My Soul/Incantation Of Unholyness/ Spawn Of Evil/Thirst Of The Dead

1995	■	NÆR SÓLEN GAR NIÞER FOR EVOGHER	CD	Necropoilis Records	NR 006

Repress has different artwork.

1996	■	Sorgh pa svarte vingar flogh	MCD 4tr	Necropolis Records	NR 6664

Tracks: Vya Hal/Sorrow Flew On Black Wings/Soil Of Dead Earth/Night Of The Living Dead (Inernal Mäjesty cover)

1998	■	SLAUGHTERSUN (CROWN OF THE TRIARCHY)	CD	Necropolis Records	NR 021
1998	□	SLAUGHTERSUN (CROWN OF THE TRIARCHY)	CDd	Necropolis Records	NR 021
1998	□	SLAUGHTERSUN (CROWN OF THE TRIARCHY)	LP PD	Necropolis Records	NR 021

500 hand-numbered copies. Poster.

2004	□	SLAUGHTERSUN (CROWN OF THE TRIARCHY)	2CD	Century Media	CM 44021-2

Bonus on CD 1: In The Depths Of My Soul/Incantation Of Unholyness/Spawn Of Evil/ Thirst Of The Dead. CD 2 contains the 12 tracks from "Nær solen.." and "Sorgh..."

1998 CD - NR 021

DAWN OF DECAY

Tomas Bergstrand: g, Johan Carlsson: b/v, Mikael Birgersson: d

Karlstad - Powerful death metal with variations from really slow and doomy parts to high-speed parts. Some tracks, like *I Fear* and *Hell, Raising Hell!* show influences of up-tempo **Motörhead**, while for instance *The Sunlight Slaying* is more akin to the 80s thrash-scene and bands like **Agony**. Of course with the guttural vocals from Hell. Mid-quality production on the single, while the album is provided with a fat and heavy mix. Before *New Hell* singer/guitarist Rickard Löfgren left to join **Bay Laurel**. Mikael is also found in **Gehennah**, where he is known as "Hellcop". Johan was later found in **Moaning Wind**, **Sparzanza** and also recorded a demo with the death metal band **Capricorn** in 1997. Bergstrand is now found in **Switch Opens** (earlier **Fingerspitzengefühl**) and earlier **Rise And Shine**, **Moaning Wind** and also **Capricorn**.

1994 7" - DOG 001 EP

1994	■	Into The Realm Of Dreams/Grief/As Darkness Falls	7" 3tr	Delusion Of Grandeur	DOG 001 EP

500 copies.

1998	■	NEW HELL	CD	Voices Of Death	VODCD 004

1998 CD - VODCD 004

DAWN OF OBLIVION

Victor Fradera: v, Stefan Rosqvist: g, Jonas Nilsson: b

Helsingborg - The band was formed in 1992 by Victor and guitarist/keyboard player Per Broberg. Two demos were recorded using a drum machine. After this they recruited bass player Jesper Rydberg and drummer Andreas, and recorded the first album. The band split in 1994, to be resurrected with a new line-up consisting of Victor (v), Jimmy Lee Lou (g), Jonas Nilsson (b) and Andreas (d). After *Haunted* Jimmy left the band and he was replaced by Stefan. Heavy and melodic goth/hard rock, like a mix of **Paradise Lost** and **Sisters Of Mercy** with deep goth-oriented vocals. Victor is now found in **Tenebre**. In December 2001 drummer Andreas Båge left the band and was replaced by **Darkane** drummer Peter Wildoer. Before the last album they also released the digital EP *Ikaros* with non-album tracks. The last album features no drummer, but a drum machine they named Miss Decibel. Båge is today in metal band **Mindfuel**. Stefan has since released the solo album, *The Guitar Diaries*, and plays in **Cloudscape** and **FullForce**.

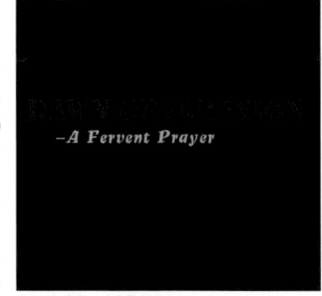
1994 CD - ASP 004

1994	■	A FERVENT PRAYER	CD	Strontium	ASP 004
1997	■	YORICK	CD	M&A	MACDL 951
2000	□	Haunted	MCD 4tr	M&A	MACD 505

Tracks: Haunted/The Hellfire Sermon/Illusions (Infernal version)/November (full version)

2001	■	MEPHISTO'S APPEALING	CD	M&A	MACDL 666
2009	□	THE FINAL CHAPTER	CD	M&A	MACDL 972
2013	□	A FERVENT PRAYER	CD	M&A	MACDL 974

Bonus: Ikaros '94/My Vision

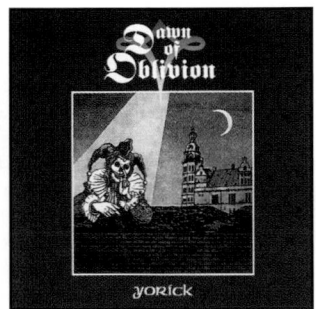
1997 CD - MACDL 951

DAWN OF SILENCE

Patrik Johansson: v/g, Mats Johansson: g, Pelle Johansson: b, Torbjörn Edqvist: d

Finspång - The band was formed in 2000 when Patrik, Mats and Torbjörn met at school when their common interest in metal brought them together. They started out as an **Iron Maiden** cover band, but soon wrote original material. They added Mats' younger brother Pelle to the line-up and took the name **Dawn Of Silence**. They recorded their first demo in 2002, *World Of Lies*, then, *Follow Your Heart* (2003), *Fear Of Life* (2004) and *Lost All Hope* (2005). In 2006 they entered the Black Lounge Studio with Jonas Kjellgren (**Centinex, Scar Symmetry**) and started recording their own album. German label Metal Heaven found it good enough to licence and

2001 CD - MACDL 666

onward it went. In February 2008 they again entered the Black Lounge Studio to record a new album, again searching for a new label since they had separated from Metal Heaven. This time Swedish label GMR picked up the ball. *Dawn Of Silence* play melodic metal bringing influences from bands like *Gotthard* and *Shakra* as well as *Helloween, Iron Maiden* and Swedish fellows *Wolf*. Good classic metal with a slight let down in the vocal department. The tracks *Seven Seas* and *Born Out Of Grief* are featured on *Platinum Compilation Vol 1* (05 Pregal).

2009	☐	MOMENT OF WEAKNESS	CD	Metal Heaven	00029
2010	■	WICKED SAINT OR RIGHTEOUS SINNER	CD	GMR	GMRCD 9017
2010	☐	WICKED SAINT OR RIGHTEOUS SINNER	CD	Spiritual Beast (Japan)	IUCP-16081

2010 CD - GMRCD 9017

DAWN OF TIME
Johan Wiberg: v, Toni Korhonen: g, Rune Foss: g,
Pasi Jaskara: b, Marek Dobrowolski: d

Göteborg - Powerful thrash in the vein of early *Anthrax, Metallica* and Swedish forerunners *Agony*. Tight as a rat's ass with great powerful riffing and raw vocals, at times with a growling attitude. Great band. They also recorded a 4-track CD-R featuring the tracks on the single plus two more. In February 2000 they started recording the album *Shell Of Pain*, but due to financial problems the label folded. They changed their name and continued as *Reclusion*. Rune is also found in *Killaman* and Marek was in *One Man Army And The Undead Quartet*.

| 2000 | ■ | A Force Of One/The Quest | 7"g | Underground Loudness | UGL 008 |

2000 7" - UGL 008

DAYDREAM
Olle Carlsson: v/g, Jörgen Hallberg: b, Torgil Sturesson: d

Klippan/Ängelholm - Formed in 1981, split around 1985-86. Straightforward, melodic hard rock. The four tracks ranges from balladry to pretty good kind of *Gaskin*-sounding hard rock. The latter applies to the track *Play Your Cards Well*, which is the highlight of the EP. Not to be confused with *Day Dream* (*Dagdrömmar*). After the EP, Niklas Ekelund was added on guitar. Torgil is now in heavy metal band *Blacksmith Legacy*, which initially also featured Jörgen.

1983	■	Daydream	7" 4tr	Hönsbodens Röst	DRO 1	$
		Tracks: I Don't Wanna Be There/Misunderstood Tonight/I'll Stay With You/Play Your Cards Well.				
		300 copies.				

1983 7" - DRO 1

DAYS OF ANGER
Alex Jonsson: v/b, Alf Johansson: g, Kristian Houtari: d

Eskilstuna - Formed in 2010, started jamming and only a few months later recorded the debut album. The members have previously been in bands like *Rejected, Tough Trade, Scaar* and *Torch*. *Days Of Anger* plays high-class classic Bay Area thrash.

| 2011 | ■ | DEATH PATH | CD | Massacre | MAS-CD 0711 |

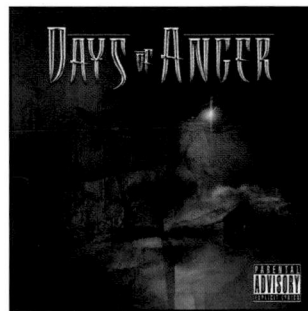

2011 CD - MAS-CD 0711

DE TVEKSAMMA
Albin Gillgren: v, Thomas von Wachenfeldt: g/v, Anders Olsson: g/violin,
Daniel Lindström: b, Matias Klint: d

Bergsjö - The band was formed in 1992 by Klint and Wachenfeldt under the name *Maim*. The line-up also featured Erik Lööv and Anders Åhslund. They were influenced by bands like *Entombed, Sepultura* and *Gorefest*, but also the Swedish hardcore scene. In 1996 they released the 4 track cassette *Hail The End*. In 1999 they were down to Wachenfeldt and Klint again, but they were soon joined by Lindström. In 2000 guitarist Bo-Eric Hellman joined and they recorded the debut. In 2006 Hellman left and they continued as a trio. A new album, entitled *The Battle In Grensforce* was recorded in 2007, but it took five years to release. Even though the name *De Tveksamma* (the doubtful) sounds like it would be an 80s punk band, they produce surprisingly great technical and diverse death-oriented metal which sometime switches into pure *Otyg*-oriented folk metal, unfortunately with quite uninteresting vocals. In 2007 Thomas wanted to concentrate on his guitar playing and new singer Albin Gillgren and fiddler/banjo player/harmonica player Anders Olsson were added to the line-up. Trivia: Thomas has a Masters Degree in teaching Baroque violin and composition. He is also a doctoral student in Music Pedagogy. Thomas and Bo-Eric Hellman also have the folky/ambient project *Lodge Doom*, with whom they have made two releases. Thomas also released an EP with the band *The Hallians*.

1997 CD - HUMCD 001

1997	■	JULIE LAUGHS NOMORE & DE TVEKSAMMA (split)	CD	Humla Productions	HUMCD 001
		Split with Julie Laughs No More. Tracks: Trollens brudmarsch/ Tattered (in Bergsjö)/				
		Baobhan-Sith/ The Dead Leaves/ S.I.M.O.N.S./ We Are the Tweckksamma/ Bitchshaped				
		Box/ And I'll See				
2001	☐	PERFORMS SONGS ABOUT NICK AND OTHER FRIENDS	CD	Hanndom	CD 01
2012	■	THE BATTLE OF GRENSFORCE	CD	Senza Vib	CD 06

2012 CD - CD 06

DEACON STREET

Chris Demming: v, Tommy Denander: g

Göteborg/Stockholm - Deacon Street are something of a "who-is-who" in AOR. The first album features musicans such as Sayit Dölen, Geir Rönning (*Radioactive*) Marcus Liliequist, Marcel Jacob (*Talisman*), Lars Chriss (*Lion's Share*), Magnus Weidenmo (*Spin Gallery*) and Jan Johansen (*Ignition*), while the follow-up states Peter Sundell (*Grand Illusion*),Thomas Vikström (*Talk Of The Town, Candlemass*) Johan Fahlberg (*Scudiero, Jaded Heart*), Andreas Novak (*Novak*), Chris Antblad, Daniel Flores (*Mind's Eye, The Murder Of My Sweet* etc.) and Rönning together with international artists like Steve Morse, Reb Beach, Bruce Gaitch, Tony Franklin, Jeff Watson and Stan Bush. The first album was a project where guitarist Tommy Denander (*Radioactive, ATC, Sayit* etc) and singer Chris Demming (*Spin Gallery, AOR*) opened their drawers and unearthed all the old unused AOR ideas that were too good to be shelved. Both album contain high class classic 80s sounding AOR, somewhere in-between *Journey* and *Toto*.

2004 CD - 00007

2006 CD - 0681-164

| 2004 | ■ | DEACON STREET PROJECT | CD | AOR Heaven | 00007 |
| 2006 | ■ | II | CD | MTM | 0681-164 |

DEAD, THE

Linus "Mr. Jones" Nirbrant: v/g, Tobbe "Necrobarber" Sillman: b,
Fredrik "Fred The Dead" Andersson: d

Stockholm - Old-school death metal with grind tendencies in the vein of *Napalm Death* and *Exhumed*. Formed by three members formerly of the band *Guidance Of Sin*. The debut however only states Nirbrant and Sillman as members. Fredrik is also found in *Amon Amarth*, and together with Nirbrandt in *A Canorous Quintet* and *This Ending*. Sillman is also in *Vicious Art*.

| 2001 | ■ | THE DEAD/BIRDFLESH (split) | CD | Nocturnal Music | NMCD 028 |

Split with Birdflesh. Tracks: Rotten Corpse/Mr. Murder/Urge To Kill/We Are The Dead

| 2002 | □ | Real Zombies Never Die | MCD 6tr | Nocturnal Music | NMCD 042 |

Tracks: There Is Only Flesh/Eat You When You're Dead & Rotten/Zombies Arise/One By One/I Spit On The Cross As I Rise/Another Useless Life

2001 CD - NMCD 028

DEAD AWAKEN

Jörgen Kristensen: v/g/b, Mats Blyckert: d

Västerås - Both Jörgen and Mats were previously in the bands *Abhoth* and *Suffer*. *Dead Awaken* was formed out of the band *Abyssal Chaos*. The first demo, *Death Before Dishonour* was recorded in 2002 and four more were recorded before the debut album. Brutal death metal in the vein of *Sodom* or *Bolt Thrower*.

| 2013 | ■ | WHEN HOPE TURNS DRIPPING RED | CD | Abyss Records | ABYSS 040 CD |

2013 CD - ABYSS 040 CD

DEAD BY APRIL

Jimmie Strimell: v, Zandro Santiago: v, Pontus Hjelm: g/v,
Johan Olsson: g, Marcus Wesslén: b, Alexander Svenningsson: d

Göteborg - In early 2007 the embryo of *Dead By April* started taking shape, when *Nightrage*'s singer Strimell felt he needed an outlet for his melodic side. He started collaborating with guitarist Hjelm and soon *Dead By April* were born. The line-up also featured former *Nightrage* colleagues, bass player Henric Carlsson (*Cipher System, Lavett*) and drummer Svenningsson. The first line-up also featured guitarist Johan Eskilsson (*Cipher System*). The band's first tracks, *Lost* and *Stronger* were recorded and posted on the band's MySpace site and suddenly the interest for the band started growing. Hjelm refused to play live because of severe stage fright, but as an interest for the band to play live started growing he simply had to snap out of it. When looking for a producer they found Henrik Edenhed (*Downstroke, Teddybears* etc). The band's first single, *Losing You* was also the theme song for the trailer of TV show *Robinson 2009* ("Survivor"). The single even reached a #1 position in the Swedish singles chart. Just like a lot of their American colleagues, *Dead By April* mix pop and metal in a highly successful way. In April 2010 Hjelm stepped down from his vocal duties, enter new vocalist Zandro Santiago. Wesslén is also in *By Night*. In 2011 they recorded the digital single *Dancing In The Neon Light*, together with original artist Lena Philipsson. In 2012 the band, quite surprisingly, entered the Swedish qualification heats of the Eurovision Song Contest with the song *Mystery*, and they went straight to the finals. *Stronger* is an extended MCD also containing alternate mixes, acoustic versions and a demo track. In 2012 Strimell left *DeathDestruction* to join the band full time.

2009 CDS - 0602527-03184

2011 CD - 0602527-591964

2012 CD - 0602527-96821

2009	■	Losing You	CDSp 1tr	Universal Music	0602527-03184
2009	□	DEAD BY APRIL	CD	Universal Music	0602527-02091
2009	□	DEAD BY APRIL	CDd+DVD	Universal Music	0602527-03350

Bonus DVD featuring video blog, interviews, Losing You (Karaoke)/Losing You (Video)

| 2009 | □ | What Can I Say/What Can I Say (radio Version)/My Saviour | MCDp 3tr | Universal Music | 0602527-15812 |
| 2009 | □ | Angels Of Clarity | MCDp 4tr | Spinefarm Records | SFCCDP 17 |

Tracks: Angels Of Clarity/Angels Of Clarity(remix)/Losing You (acoustic)/Promise Me (acoustic)

2011	☐ INCOMPARABLE	CD	Universal Music	0602527-76322
2011	☐ INCOMPARABLE	LPg	Universal Music	0602527-79043
	Red vinyl.			
2011	☐ INCOMPARABLE	CD	Universal Music (Japan)	UICO-9057
	Bonus: Painting Shadows			
2011	■ STRONGER	CD	Spinefarm Records	0602527-591964
2012	■ INCOMPARABLE - MYSTERY VERSION	CD	Universal Music	0602527-96821
	Bonus: Mystery/Painting Shadows/Unhateable			

DEAD END STREET

Johnny Engström: g/v, Niklas Högberg: b, Roger Jern: d

Degerfors - Johnny and Niklas knew each other since first grade in school and started playing together at the age of 12 (!). They drafted drummer Jan-Ove "Galle" Johansson, played for a year and then took a break when Johnny moved to the US. In 1984 he returned and the trio formed *Dead End Street*. Galle left the band in 1986 and was replaced by Roger Jern. The style was really good, but quite soft AOR with a touch of 90s *Rush*. The band split in 1992. Jern joined *Damned Nation* and Johnny started writing other type music. He released his first album, *Analyse My Dream*, in 2007 and then formed the *Johnny Engström Band*, who has released two more albums, before changing the name to *Dead End Space* in 2013 and releasing another CD.

1988	■ Sheila/Penicillin Girl	7"	private	DES 0988

1988 7" - DES 0988

DEAD SILENT SLUMBER

Jens Rydén: v/g/b/k

Holmsund - **Dead Silent Slumber** is a solo-project by *Naglfar*-singer Jens, initiated in 1997. He produced the first official four-track demo in 1999, simply entitled *Promo 1999*. It received great response and Hammerheart soon signed him. Highly orchestrated and melodic death metal, with guttural screeching vocals, mixed with the odd female vocals and majestic choirs, adding brutal guitars and well-arranged keyboards. Jens also used to run *Dusk Zine* and has designed logos for bands like *Setherial* and *Naglfar*, as well as highly impressive cover-layouts for *Otyg*, *Vintersorg* and his own project. The album features guest appearances from people like guitarists Ulph Johansson, Andreas Johansson, Christer Bergqvist (*Auberon, Sadistic Grimness*) and singers Jensa Carlsson, Ann Åkerman and Mattias Holmgren. Jens has also been a member of *Thyrfing* and acted as a session member of *Ancient Wisdom*.

1999	■ ENTOMBED IN THE MIDNIGHT HOUR	CD	Hammerheart	HHR 051 CD
1999	☐ ENTOMBED IN THE MIDNIGHT HOUR	LP	Hammerheart	HHR 051 LP

1999 CD - HHR 051 CD

DEADMARCH

Mikael Öberg: v, Mia Ståhl: v, Kentha "Lord K" Philipsson: g/b/d/programming

Örebro - **Deadmarch** was the embryonic version of what was to become *The Project Hate MCMXCIX*. The band is the brainchild of Kentha Philipsson, formerly of *Leukemia*, *House Of Usher*, *Odyssey*, *God Among Insects* etc. The album was recorded back in 1998 by Tomas Skogsberg at Sunlight Studios. Shortly after the recording Kenta teamed up with *Grave* singer/ *Entombed* bassist Jörgen Sandström (who did backing vocals on the album). The plan was for Jörgen to rerecord some parts on the album, but strangely enough Skogsberg said he had lost the recordings, why the release was put on ice. Moving on to 2007, Dan Swanö gave a tip to Vic Records that *The Project Hate* were looking for a new label. The first release would be the legendary, and now unearthed *Deadmarch* album, now remastered by Swanö. The style shows the direction in which *The Project Hate* later headed. Quite heavy, orchestrated and atmospheric, at times even slightly folkish, death metal mixing the clean vocals of Ståhl with the growls of Öberg. Despite having been recorded in 1998 the album sounds nowhere near dated. Both Kentha and the aforementioned Jörgen are today found in the death metal trio *Torture Division*.

2007	■ THE PROJECT HATE: MCMXCIX: INITIATION OF BLASPHEMY	CD	Vic	Vic 008

2007 CD - Vic 008

DEADWOOD

Daniel "Nekro" Jansson: g/b/d/k

Göteborg - **Deadwood** was a solo project created by Daniel to satisfy his lust for "filthy black industrial music", initially under the name **Deadwood Murder**. After recording one demo he was offered a deal with Cold Spring Records. The first release was however a split-tape with *Blodulv* in 2004, entitled *The Havoc We Seek (Forgotten Wisdom)*. The debut CD was released in 2005, delayed by some problems with the printwork coming out in the wrong colours. The second album features guest vocals from *Mayhem*'s Maniac. In 2009 Daniel uploaded the 35 minute drony dark ambient track *Tombs, Confinement And Absolute Silence* for free download on his website. Daniel is also involved with *Blodulv*, the metal project *Culted* and project *The Ritual Inclusion Of Code*. **Deadwood** is also featured in the compilation box *Black Industrial Grimoire* (2009 Radical Matters). Industrial, experimental death noise, not for the faint-hearted.

2005 CD - CSR 53 CD

2008 CD - CSR 104 CD

2005 ■	8 19	CD	Cold Spring Records	CSR 53 CD
2008 ■	RAMBLACK	CD	Cold Spring Records	CSR 104 CD
2008 □	RAMBLACK	LPg	Cold Spring Records	CSR 104 LP

Bonus: Cell Of Sirclin. 300 copies in coloured vinyl.

DEAR MUTANT

**Thomas "Sluggo" Eriksson: v/g, Magnus "Devo" Andersson: g,
Asko Nisula: b, Jens Gustavsson: d**

Norrköping - It all started in 1997. Sluggo and Jens were previously playing in retro-grunge band *K9 Corpse*, bass player Asko were in *Dagon* and "Devo" was also found in *Marduk* and *Overflash*. They were signed by Wet Paint Music already in 1998. The recording took longer than expected because of problems with the label and a break-in at the studio. After the debut "Devo" left the band and was replaced by Fredrik "Lillis" Johansson. The band also recorded the four track demo *Satanic* in 2003 before breaking up. The album also goes under the title *Electric Illusion*. Seventies-influenced stoner-ish hard rock with its roots in bands like *Black Sabbath* and *Led Zeppelin*, but even with a touch of *Hawkwind* in one end and *Entombed* in the other. The track *In Space* is found on the compilation *Molten Universe Volume Two* (2000 Molten Universe). The same track was later featured on *Burn The Street V: The Last Chapter* (2005 Daredevil Records). Eriksson was later in *Bokor* and has been a member of *House Of Aquarius*. Jens passed away in July 2013 after recently having joined *Saturnalia Temple*.

2002 CD - Dream 001

2002 ■	DEAR MUTANT	CD	Wet Paint	Dream 001
2002 □	ELECTRIC ILLUSION	CD	Kozmic Artifact	KA 2

Same as above with different title.

DEATH BREATH

Robert Pehrsson: v/g, Nicke Andersson: d/g/b

Stockholm - After many years of absence from the metal scene, former *Entombed/Hellacopter/Nihilist* drummer Nicke Andersson formed the death metal band *Death Breath* in 2005 together with *Thunder Express/Dundertåget* guitarist Robert Pehrsson (formerly of *Runemagick, Deathwitch*) and bassist Magnus Hedquist. This line-up with additions of guest appearances from singer Jörgen Sandström (*Grave, Entombed, Vicious Art*), American basist Scott Carlson (*Repulsion, Death*) and drummer Fred Estby, recorded the debut album *Stinking Up The Night*. On the subsequent release, *Let It Stink*, the band was decimated to Robert and Nicke, with the vocal additions of Scott and Erik Sahlström (*Serpent Obscene, Maze Of Torment, General Surgery*). The cover and title is a pun on *The Beatles' Let It Be*. Late 2009 the band started recording their third album and the line-up now featured Nicke (g/d), Robert (g/v), Scott (b/v) and guitarist Erik Wallin (*Merciless, Harms Way*). *Death Breath* play death metal with a nod to the old school, at times similar to *Bathory* and *Venom* (but way better musicians).

2006 7" - BLOD 7002

2006 LP PD - BLOD 044PD

2006 CD - BLOD 047CD

2006 ■	Death Breath/Corpses Of Death/Matricide	7" 3tr	Black Lodge	BLOD 7002
2006 □	STINKING UP THE NIGHT	CD	Black Lodge	BLOD 044CD
2006 ■	STINKING UP THE NIGHT	LP PD	Black Lodge	BLOD 044PD
2006 □	STINKING UP THE NIGHT	CDd	Black Lodge	BLOD 044CDL
2006 □	STINKING UP THE NIGHT	CD	Relapse Records (USA)	RR 6745-2
2006 □	STINKING UP THE NIGHT	CD	Relapse Records (Japan)	YSCY-1062
2006 ■	LET IT STINK	CD	Black Lodge	BLOD 047CD
2006 □	LET IT STINK	10" LP	Black Lodge	BLOD 047LP

Also available in burgundy red vinyl.

2006 □	LET IT STINK	CD	Black Lodge	BLOD 047CD
2006 □	LET IT STINK	CD	Relapse (USA)	RR 6749-2

DEATH ORGAN

**Patrik Schultz: v, Jocke "Jox" Sjöström: v, Per "Wibärj" Wiberg: k,
Klas Hägglund: b, Marcus Källström: d**

Borlänge - This is really a weird project featuring two singers and no guitarist. The style is a combination of the great 70s music with bands like *ELP*, *Deep Purple* and *Atomic Rooster* and the 90s sounds of *Faith No More* and *Entombed*. The platter is filled with distorted Hammond organ, heavy riffs and musical twists. Actually it's brilliant and very original. Klas was ex-*Stonecake*, Wiberg had previously also been found in *Boom Club*, *Sky High*, later in *Spiritual Beggars*, *Opeth* and is today in *Mojobone* and *King Hobo*, while Marcus was previously also found in *Stonecake* and has previously played with *Six Feet Under*, *Jammer* and *Sky High*. Joachim was in *Buckshot O.D.* and Patrik is originally with thrashers *Coffinmen* (ex-*Enslavement*). If you're an open-minded prog-metal-fan – Check this out! On the second album they do a pretty good cover of *Rush*'s *Tom Sawyer*.

1995 CD - APM9506 AT/ADINFEROS1

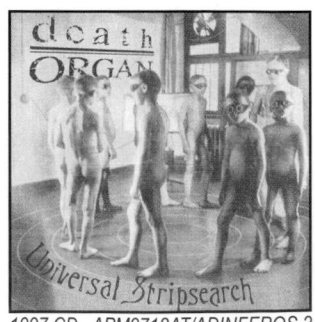

1997 CD - APM9718AT/ADINFEROS 2

1995 ■	9 TO 5	CD	APM	APM 9506 AT/AD INFEROS 1
1997 ■	UNIVERSAL STRIPSEARCH	CD	APM	APM 9718 AT/AD INFEROS 2

DEATHBOOT

Erik Billing: v, Henrik Wendel: g/v, Ludvig "Ludde" von Sersam: b, Viktor "El Gordo" Forss: d

Malmö - Deathboot was formed in 1999 with the members initially fooling around with different instruments (not necessarily the ones they play today) and the initial line-up of Billing, Wendel and Forss was formed. Billing and Forss were into punk, while Wendel was a death metal fan. They found an intersection at crust and also a bassist in Ludvig. Two demos were recorded in 1999; *Deathboot* and *In Käng We Crust*. 2001 saw another two demos; *GrindPusher* and *Ha-gridden* and another one entitled *Ballcrusher* came in 2002. The band slowly evolved, detuning their guitars, slowing down the slow parts and speeding up the fast parts, and it all evolved into a mix of death metal and grindcore. The sound is very much death metal, while the speed in some parts and the length (shortness – mostly 1-2 minutes) of the tracks is definitely grindcore. *Even though You Scream…* is regarded an EP, it has 12 tracks. Wendel is also found in *Vandöd*. After the MCD Forss was replaced by *Viceral Bleeding* drummer Tomas "Rotten Boy" Persson.

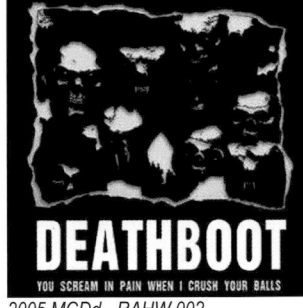

2005 MCDd - RAHW 002

2005 ■ You Scream In Pain When I Crush Your Balls ....MCDd 12tr RAHW..RAHW 002
    Tracks: You Scream In Pain When I Crush Your Balls/Bitch-Ass Motherfucker/Carrocide/
    Clint Eastwood!/I Hate Those Fucking Bastards!/Inside You/Give Him All Your Beer!/Nightmare I/Nightmare
    III/Ode To Oranjebom-Under The Bass/Stryp Mor/Troop 666

2011 10" - 8869790615-1

DEATHDESTRUCTION

Jimmie Strimell: v, Henrik Danhage: g, Fredrik Larsson: b, Jonas Ekdahl: d

Göteborg - A new, brutal and highly-interesting powerful thrash/death unit from Göteborg, sounding a bit like a death-influenced *Pantera*. The track *Fuck Yeah* is a classic to be. Danhage and Ekdahl are ex-*Evergrey*, Larsson is also in *Hammerfall* and Strimell is also in *Dead By April* and formerly in *Nightrage*. The band is produced by Roberto Laghi (*LOK, Transport League*) and recorded in *In Flames'* studio. The debut MLP was actually recorded live in the studio and was released digitally and in a limited vinyl edition. In 2012 Strimmel left to devote his time to *Dead By April*, and was replaced by Tony Jelencovich (*Transport League, M.A.N*)

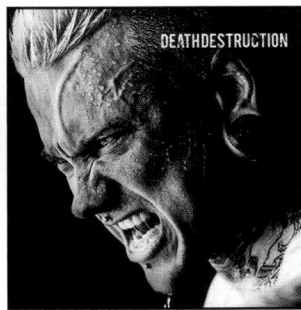

2011 CD - 8869790599-2

2011 ■ Fuck Yeah – Live EP.. 10" MLP 3tr Columbia.................................8869790615-1
    Tracks: Fuck Yeah/Crank It Up/Never Again
2011 ■ DEATHDESTRUCTION ....CD Columbia.................................8869790599-2
2011 ☐ DEATHDESTRUCTION ....LP Columbia.................................8869790599-1

DEATHENING

Kalle Nimhagen: v, Pål Callmer: g, Niklas Fridh: g, Pär Hallgren: b, Arnold Lindberg: d

Malmö/Göteborg - Deathening were formed in 2007 by Pål Callmer and Arnold Lindberg, who have played together in various bands, such as *Murderplan* and *Supraload*. The subsequent year they drafted former *Embraced* singer Kalle Nimhagen, *Muderplan* and *Supraload* colleague Niklas Fridh and surprisingly enough bass player Pär Hallgren from progsters *The Carpet Knights*. Pål also embraced his proggy side in the band *Wraptors*. As they name may suggest *Deathening* play death metal with a strong thrashy side. The band has a great quirky yet melodic touch to their sound. Great musicians, brutal vocals and cool arrangements.

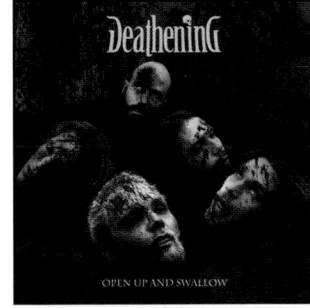

2011 CD - RAKREC 001

2011 ■ OPEN UP AND SWALLOW ....CD Rakamarow.................................RAKREC 001
2013 ☐ CHAINED IN BLOOD...CD Rakamarow.................................RAKREC 031
2013 ☐ CHAINED IN BLOOD...LP Rakamarow.................................RAKREC 032

DEATHSTARS

Andreas "Whiplasher Bernadotte" Bergh: v, Eric "Cat Casino" Bäckman: g, Emil "Nightmare Industries" Nödtveit: g, Jonas "Skinny Disco" Kangur: b, Oscar "Vice" Leander: d

Göteborg/Strömstad - Three quarters of the line-up previously recorded a bunch of albums under the name *Swordmaster*. Late 2001 they decided to change their name, style and approach. The fourth member, Niklas Rudolfsson, left for *Runemagick/Sacramentum* and drummer Ole "Bone W Machine" Öhman took his place. The music was now more in the vein of *Rammstein* meets *Kovenant* with a touch of *Nine Inch Nails*, and with an image quite close to *Marilyn Manson*. The line-up featuring Bergh, Nödtveit, Öhman and bass player Erik Halvorsen recorded the debut album. On the second album Halvorsen had been replaced by *Revolution Riot* bassist Jonas "Skinny Disco" Kangur. In 2009 the band had added a second guitar player; Eric "Cat Casino" Bäckman, who made his debut on *Night Electric Night*. *Deathstars* also uses backing singer Ann Ekberg on several recordings. In 2009 Öhman was replaced by Oscar "Vice" Leander (*Crescendolls*) who made his debut in the song *Metal* on the 2012 compilation.

Stars on the rise

2002 CD - 017 335-2

2001 ☐ Synthetic Generation ....CDSp 1tr LED recordings ....LED PRO CD 4
2001 ☐ Synthetic Generation/Synthetic Generation (video)..........................CDSp 2tr Universal Music 015 505-2
2002 ☐ Syndrome/Genocide/Our God The Drugs.................................MCDp 3tr Universal Music 015 840-2
2002 ■ SYNTHETIC GENERATION ....CD LED Recordings...............................017 335-2

2003 ☐	Synthetic Generation (Club EP)..MCD 4tr	Nuclear Blast	NB 1194-2

Promo. Tracks: The Rape Of Virtue/Synthetic Generation/Syndrome/White Wedding (Billy idol cover) + videos: Synthetic Generation/Syndrome

2003 ☐	SYNTHETIC GENERATION ....CD	Nuclear Blast	NB 1209-2

Second edition with slipcase and bonus tracks: White Wedding (Billy Idol cover)/Our God The Drugs + videos: Synthetic Generation/Syndrome

2003 ☐	SYNTHETIC GENERATION ....CD	Nuclear Blast	NB 1210-2

(NB 1188-2 on the cover.) Bonus videos: Synthetic Generation/Syndrome

2003 ☐	SYNTHETIC GENERATION ....CD	Irond (Russia)	CD 03-690
2005 ☐	Cyanide/Mother Zone ....CDSp 2tr	Nuclear Blast (promo).......................	NB 1598-2
2005 ■	Cyanide/Termination Bliss (Piano Version) ....CDS 2tr	Nuclear Blast	NB 1599-2
2006 ☐	Blitzkrieg/Play God ....CDS 2tr	Nuclear Blast (promo).......................	NB 1630-2
2006 ☐	TERMINATION BLISS ....CD	Nuclear Blast	NB 1450-2
2006 ■	TERMINATION BLISS - EXTENDED ....CD+DVD	Nuclear Blast	NB 1450-0

Slipcase. Bonus DVD including "The making of". Bonus: Termination Bliss (Piano Version)/Blitzkrieg (Driven On Remix)

2006 ☐	TERMINATION BLISS ....CD	Irond (Russia)	CD 06-1122

Bonus: Termination Bliss (Piano Version)/Blitzkrieg (Driven On Remix)

2006 ☐	TERMINATION BLISS - EXTENDED ....CD+DVD	Irond (Russia)	CD 06-1122DL

Slipcase. Bonus DVD including "The making of". Bonus: Termination Bliss (Piano Version)/Blitzkrieg (Driven On Remix)

2006 ☐	TERMINATION BLISS ....CD	Avalon Marquee (Japan).............	MICP-10576

Bonus: Termination Bliss (Piano Version)/Blitzkrieg (Driven On Remix)

2007 ☐	Virtue To Vices (Censored)/Virtue To Vices/Tongues............................MCD 3tr	Nuclear Blast	NB 1980-2
2008 ☐	Blitzkrieg/Cyanide ....7" PD	Nuclear Blast	NB 2180-9

500 copies

2009 ☐	NIGHT ELECTRIC NIGHT ....CD	Nuclear Blast	NB 2107-2
2009 ☐	NIGHT ELECTRIC NIGHT ....LP PD	Nuclear Blast	NB 2107-9
2009 ☐	NIGHT ELECTRIC NIGHT - GOLD EDITION ....CDd+DVD	Nuclear Blast	NB 2107-0

Bonus: Night Skinny Night (Skinny Remix)/Via The End (Piano Version)/Night Electric Night (feat. Daniel Erlandsson) + DVD with videos + "making of". Slipcase

2009 ☐	NIGHT ELECTRIC NIGHT ....CD	Irond (Russia)	CD 09-1563

Bonus: Night Skinny Night (Skinny Remix)/Via The End (Piano Version)/Night Electric Night (feat. Daniel Erlandsson)

2009 ■	Mark Of The Gun ....CDSp 1tr	Nuclear Blast	NB 2490-2
2009 ☐	NIGHT ELECTRIC NIGHT ....CD	Bieler Bros. (USA)	874007 003025
2010 ☐	NIGHT ELECTRIC NIGHT - PLATINUM EDITION .... (Box) CDd+DVD	Nuclear Blast	NB 2665-0

Box set in slipcase, including 17 track bonus CD "Decade Of Debachery".

2009 ☐	DECADE OF DEBAUCHERY ....CD	Nuclear Blast	NB 2665-2
2011 ☐	THE GREATEST HITS ON EARTH ....CD	Nuclear Blast 2736128-082
2011 ☐	THE GREATEST HITS ON EARTH ....CD	Incubator (Japan).......................	COCB-60042

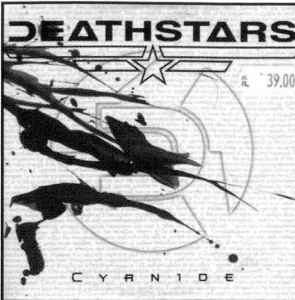
2005 CDS - NB 1599-2

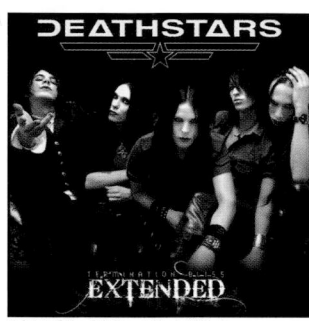
2006 CD+DVD - NB 1450-0

2009 CDS - NB 2490-2

DEATHWITCH

Niklas "Terror" Rudolfsson: v/g/b, "Slade Doom": g, "Morbid Juttu": d

Stockholm - The band was formed in 1994, and the line up settled in 1995 featuring Niklas, guitarist Fredrik "Af Necrohell" Johnsson (*Runemagick*), bassist Emma "Lady Death" Karlsson (now mrs Rudolfsson) (*Runemagick, Dracena*) and drummer/singer Robert "Reaper" Pehrsson. Before the second album Emma and Fredrik left the band, leaving Niklas and Robert to record the album on their own. Rudolfsson is also found in *Runemagick/Sacramentum/Swordmaster*. On *The Ultimate Death* the line-up had again changed, now featuring Rudolfsson, bassist Peter "Carnivore" Palmdahl (*Dissection*) and drummer "Corpse". This album, as well as the band's *Monumental Mutilations* were mixed by Andy LaRoque (*King Diamond*) and mastered by James Murphy. The latter is a collection of various recordings from 1997-1999, containing covers of *Sepultura* and *Quorthon*, plus rerecordings of old tracks. Now Palmdahl and "Corpse" decided to leave the band. On *Deathfuck Rituals* the drums were handled by Daniel "Dan Slaughter" Moilanen and "Slade Doom" took care of the guitar. On *Violent Blasphemt Sodomy* Morbid Jutto temporarily stepped in to record the drums for the album. The band split in 2005. Straight ahead aggressive death metal in the *Slayer*/early *Entombed* vein.

1999 CD - NR 035

1996 ☐	TRIUMPHANT DEVASTATION...CD	Desecration Records	001
1997 ☐	DAWN OF ARMAGEDDON ....CD	Necropolis...	NR 002
1998 ☐	THE ULTIMATE DEATH...CD	Necropolis...	NR 028
1999 ■	MONUMENTAL MUTILATIONS ....CD	Necropolis...	NR 035

Pop-sticker with members

2002 ■	DEATHFUCK RITUALS ....CD	Hellspawn	HELL 009
2003 ☐	VIOLENT BLASPHEMY SODOMY ....CD	Wicked World..............................	WICK 16CD

2002 CD - HELL 009

DEBASE

Micke Hansson: v, Jonas Karlgren: g, Micke Riesbeck: g,
Micko Twedberg: b, Johan Helgesson: d

Malmö - The band was formed in 1996 by Karlgren, Riesbeck and Tweedberg, who started writing songs together. The band was soon completed by Hansson and former/current *Silver*

1999 CD - KICKCD 105

Mountain drummer Mårten Hedener. In 1999 they recorded a the promo *It's Time – 1999*. After the debut Hedener was replaced by Johan Helgesson (*The Drugs, Wit, The Itch*). In 2000 they supported *Alice Cooper* on his European *Brutal Planet* tour. Second album, *Domination,* was well-received and earned the band an opening position for *Judas Priest* on their Scandinavian dates. After this they went on a 30 gig tour around Europe together with Canadians *Annihilator*. It was now time for their third album *Unleashed*, released in 2004. Micko, Jonas and Johan are today also found in the band *Nation Beyond*. Powerful metal with influences from *Danzig*, as well as *Black Sabbath* and *Pantera*, but with less aggro vocals. A nice slab of metal!

2001 CD - KICKCD 132

1999	■	THE WORLD IS LISTENING	CD	Kick	KICKCD 105
2001	■	DOMINATION	CD	Kick	KICKCD 132
2004	☐	UNLEASHED	CD	Noise	LC 09066

DEBBIE RAY
Reine Heyer: v/g, Andreas "Andy" Heleander: g,
Manx Gustafsson (Tummalid): b, Håkan "H-Can" Strind: d

Herrljunga (Göteborg) - *Debbie Ray* is not, as I first thought, any new Swedish dance chick, but a bunch of down-and-dirty gritty sleaze rockers in the vein *Hardcore Superstar*, *Crazy Lixx* etc. The band was formed out of the ashes of two other bands, where some of the members went together to form *Debbie Ray*. Manx Gustafsson (Tummalid) is also found in *Baby Jane*. After the first album Manx was replaced by Martin Söderqvist (*Hostile Cell*).

2009 CD - CSPCD 003

2009	■	ARTIFICIAL MISERY	CD	Coreshot Records	CSPCD 003

DECADENCE
Kitty "Metallic Kitty" Saric: v, Kenneth Lantz: g,
Simon Galle: g, Joakim Antman: b, Erik Röjås: d

Stockholm - The origin came about in 2003 by singer and manager Kitty after a concept idea to go for Bay Area thrash, when her former melodic death metal project *Dekapitera* didn't fly. She auditioned for a band founded by guitarists Christian Lindholm and Niclas Råberg, who had just quit the band *Devastator* to form a new band with drummer Peter Lindqvist. Kenneth Lantz, guitarist of *Demented*, came in as session bassist. The band initially took the name *Ravenous*, which only lasted for two gigs. After this they went by Kitty's old idea, to call the band *Decadence*. Peter (ex-*Chainsaw*) now left to devote his time to his other bands *Canopy* and *A-Bros*. He was soon replaced by Peter Frögéli (*Bloodshed, Rev 16:8*). The band had also just recorded their first demo *Land Of Despair*, which still featured Peter. Lindholm left the band, Lantz stepped up to play guitar and Roberto Vacchi Segerlund took over the four-string, while Mikael Sjölund joined on rthythm guitar in the fall of 2004. This line-up recorded the self-titled debut album. After problems within the band Kittie decided to make some changes in the summer of 2005. Sjölund, Segerlund and Frögéli had to go and were replaced by Daniel Green, Joakim Antman (*The Ugly*) and Erik Röjås (*Sterbhaus, Netherbird*). The new line-up recorded the second album *The Creature*. After still not finding the right chemistry in the band, Green was replaced by session player Ulf Sörman (*Castillion*) in the middle of 2006. In October *Decadence* were officially signed to Kitty's own label HTI and the album *3rd Stage Of Decay* was released. The guitar spot was finally filled in July 2007, when Simon Galle took over after Sörman. The band owes its influences to the Bay Area thrash scene and they do their best to keep it alive. Great technical and really well played thrash. The track *Corrosion* (featuring Chris Astley from *Xentrix*) can be found on *Thrashing Like A Maniac* (2008 Earache), a compilation featuring new school thrash metal bands. In 2009 *Decadence* released their fourth full-length album *Chargepoint* again through Japanese label Spiritual Beast. The track *Corrosion* was used as a Japanese bonus track. *Decadence* play excellent hard hitting thrash in the true Bay Area vein. Kitty has quite an extreme voice a bit in the vein of *Arch Enemy*'s Angela Glossow without the deathiness. Great, tight sounding band that should appeal to fans of bands like *F.K.Ü* etc. It's quite hard to recommend a single album, as the band has kept a high standard and quality ever since the debut, only sharpening the sword slightly from album to album. In 2012 the line-up featured new drummer Marcus Jonsson (*Insision, Pandemonic, Flagellation, Spazmosity*) and guitarist Kristian Järvenpää. Website: www.decadence.se

The decadent creatures of thrash

The Creature

2005 CD - - -

2005 CD - - -

2005	■	DECADENCE	CD	private	- -
2005	■	THE CREATURE	CD	private	- -
2006	■	3RD STAGE OF DECAY	CD	HTI Records	MKR-01
2006	☐	3RD STAGE OF DECAY	CD	Massacre	MAS CD 0605
2006	☐	3RD STAGE OF DECAY	CD	Spiritual Beast (Japan)	POCE-16003
		Bonus: Corrosion			
2009	☐	CHARGEPOINT	CD	Spiritual Beast (Japan)	IUCP-16065
		Bonus: The Demons Run (Instrumental)			

2006 CD - MKR-01

DECAMERON

Johannes Losbäck: v/g, Jonny Lehto: g, Alexander "Alex" Losbäck: v/b, Tobias "Tobbe" Kellgren: d

Hard hitting death metal boys

Hunnebostrand (Göteborg) - Formed in 1991, initially as **Necrofobic**. In 1992 the band recorded their first demo *My Grave Is Calling*. A single was also meant to be released by Corpse Grinder Records but the deal fell though. The band originally featured guitarist Johan Norman, but he left the band in 1994 to join **Dissection** (later also in **Soul Reaper, Sacramentum**). He was replaced by Thomas "Dark" Backelin (ex-**Satanized**, later in **Lord Belial**), who in his turn was replaced by Jonny Letho (**Grief Of Emerald**). Brutal, yet melodic death metal in the vein of **Dissection** and **At The Gates**. After the album was recorded Tobbe left the band to join **Dissection**. Jonny also left after a while. The Losbäck's made another attempt with drummer Adrian Erlandsson who also left the band in 1997. After this things slowly folded. Alexander later made a half hearted attempt to resurrect the band, but nothing happened. Johannes, previously in **Power Unit**, later joined **Seventh One** and **Wolf**, while his brother Alexander, later joined **Cardinal Sin** and is today found in **Despite** (where he replaced **Dead By April** singer Strimmel). Tobias was also part of **Seventh One** and did some live drumming for **In Flames** in Daniel Svensson's temporary absence. Not the band that recorded the album *Mammoth Special*.

1996 ■	MY SHADOW	CD	No Fashion	NFR 013	

1996 CD - NFR 013

DECEIVER

Peter "Pete Flesh" Karlsson: v/g, Crille Lundin: b, Magnus "Flingan" Flink: d

2005 CD - IFPCD 013

2006 CD - IFPCD 018

Strängnäs - The band was formed in 2004 by Karlsson, Lundin and Flink. They were completed with singer Erik "Destormo" Sahlström and recorded their first demo in May of 2004 in Studio Abyss. The demo was however never made public as a demo, but instead the band was signed by Iron Fist, who released it as the self-titled debut EP. Ten months after the release of the MCD the band again entered The Abyss to record the debut album – *Riding With The Reaper*. Shortly after the release of the album Destormo left the band because of his commitments to his other bands **Maze Of Torment** and **Serpent Obscene** (later in **General Surgery** and guest in **Death Breath**). He was however still active in the band, doing layout for their album artwork. Not able to find a replacement Karlsson took over as singer. The band returned to The Abyss in the end of 2005 to record the follow-up *Holov Posen Tro May Trot*, which was released in 2006. This album sounded even tighter and better played than the debut, plus it was a notch more aggressive. The band returned in 2008 with yet another Abyss Recording entitled *Thrashing Heavy Metal*, a title which very well describes what **Deceiver** is all about. If you're into bands like **Exodus**, **Kreator** or **Sodom** you should check them out. Lundin and Karlsson have also recorded with the band **Thrown**. Flink is also found in **Flesh**, which is the brainchild of Peter Karlsson. Trivia: According to an interview in Metal Nightmare, December 2005, Peter took the stage name "Pete Flesh" the day he heard Chuck Shuldiner (of **Death**) had passed. He was drinking beer and listening to **Death** and when hearing the track *Flesh And The Power It Holds* and came up with the name "Pete Flesh" and thus he called his own band **Flesh** as a tribute to Shuldiner. In 2013 Pete returned under the name **The Peter Flesh Deathtrip**.

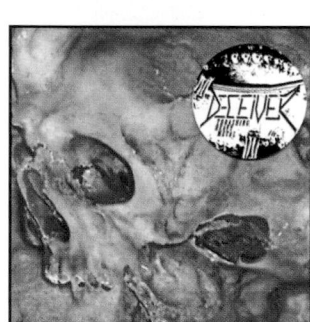

2004 ☐	Deceiver	MCD 5tr	Iron Fist	IRPCD 009	
	Tracks: Deceiver/Hey Woman/Ironsweet/Blessed With A Lust For Blood/Cold Sweat, Shaking Bones				
2005 ■	RIDING WITH THE REAPER	CD	Iron Fist	IFPCD 013	
2005 ☐	RIDING WITH THE REAPER	LP	Iron Fist	IFPLP 013	
2006 ■	HOLOV POSEN TRO MAY TROT	CD	Iron Fist	IFPCD 018	
2008 ■	THRASHING HEAVY METAL	CD	Pulverised	ASH 053 CD	

2008 CD - ASH 053 CD

DECEPTION

Tomas Åberg: v/g, Richard Larsson: g, Mats Pettersson: b, Jimmy Svensson: d

Karlskrona - Formed in 1980. The single features two hard rock ballads, however the band was far heavier live. Strained and slightly out of pitch vocals makes it even less interesting. After the band split Jimmy played with folkrockers **Sinn Fenn** until 1994. Mats was the live bass player for **Locomotive Breath** in 2005-2007 and he played in **Black Sabbath** cover band **Headless Cross** (also featuring Per "PerilOz" Lengstedt (Karlsson) of **Overdrive/Unchained/Portrait**).

1984 ■	Night After Night/Way Of Life	7"	private	DEC 0455	$$	

1984 7" - DEC 0455

DECHAS

Ib Odd Vegger: v, Jakob Asp: g, Joel Edegran: g, Johan Söderberg: b, Martin Franzén: d

Huddinge (Stockholm) - Rap-metal in the vein of **Clawfinger** meets **Korn** with hip-hop influences. Well, they do sound a bit like **Limp Bizkit** with a slight touch of **Red Hot Chili Peppers** (in the

vocal department) at times. On the album the vocals went a bit more melodic with a little less emphasis on the rap. Formed by Ib and Jakob when they were in the sixth grade. **Dechas** has of course also recorded a bunch of demos; *Circle* (1998), *Around* (1999) and *Real Shame* (1999). The band was later signed by Australian Shutdown Recordz and released the album. After the album Vegger and Söderberg were replaced by singer Hakim Hietikko and bass player Georgios Karvelas. The band split in 2004 when Hakim decided to move to Finland to start the band **April**. The remaining members continued with new singer Alex Frigren under the name **Microtone** until 2006, when they split. In **Microtone** the style had changed closer to US nu-pop/metal and they made no releases. Edegran and Karvelas continued in the melodic punk band Mike.

1999 ■ Dechas..MCD 6tr   DayGlo...DGR 14
    Tracks: Getting' Power/Real Shame/Direction/To Blame/Mind Revolution/Behind
2002 □ REBORN..CD   Shutdown Recordz ....n/a

1999 MCD - DGR 14

DECOLLATION
Johan "John Lesley" Österberg: g/v, Jon Jeremiah: g, Niklas "Nick Shields" Sköld: k, Thomas "Charles Von Weissenberg" Johansson: b, Kristian "Chris Steele" Wåhlin: d
Göteborg - Progressive thrash with a razor sharp guitar sound. Well-played and well-arranged, however the vocals are unmelodic and more or less spoken. Thomas was originally found in **Ceremonial Oath**, later in **God Macabre** and **Macabre End**. The band folded not long after the release of the MCD. Kristian Wåhlin later made recordings with **Grotesque, Liers In Wait** and **Diabolique**, all three also featuring Österberg.

1992 ■ Cursed Lands..MCD 4tr   Listenable ....POSH 0004
    Tracks: Dawn Of Resurrection/Point Of No Return/The Godborn/Cursed Lands

1992 MCD - POSH 0004

DEDICATION
Patrik Nyström: g/v, Frank Inered: g, Peter Axelsson: b, John Pååg: d
Avesta - **Dedication** was formed back in 1999 by Nyström and Pååg. They drafted bass player Bosse Eriksson and started out playing heavy metal covers. As they wanted to play covers by **Thin Lizzy** and **Judas Priest** they needed a second guitarist and hired Tommy Fluhr. They also recorded a demo with covers of **Kiss**, **Priest** and **Lizzy**. In 2000 the band parted ways with Fluhr and continued as a trio. In 2002 Bosse left because of problems with Tinnitus and the band got in touch with Axelsson, with whom the boys had been playing back in 1988. Again a second guitarist was required and this time he was named Frank Inered. They now wanted to step it up, write their own music and get a singer. The band drafted former **Blacksmith**/**Motherlode** vocalist Per Englund and soon recorded an eight-track demo. In 2004 they were signed by Italian label Underground Symphony who released the debut album *Reflections Of Time*. The album was basically the demo with two extra tracks. In the summer of 2005 the band parted ways with Englund and Nyström again took over the vocal duties. In 2006 the band entered the studio with producer Jonas Kjellgren (**Scar Symmetry, Katatonia, Centinex** etc) and recorded the album *The Enemy Within*. The album marked a nice step up. The band plays classic heavy metal with a strong 80s footprint and with a powerful twin guitar attack. Well-played, well-sung and highly recommended for fans of bands like **Wolf**, **Dream Evil** etc.
Website: www.myspace.com/dedicationmusic

2004 CDd - US-CD 073

2004 ■ REFLECTIONS OF TIME ....CDd   Underground Symphony................ US-CD 073
2007 ■ THE ENEMY WITHIN ....CD   Sleazy Rider SR-0067

2007 CD - SR-0067

DEED
Emma Fredriksson: v, Carl Åbjörnsson: g, Olof Gustafsson: g, Mikael Carling: b, Mathias Roitto: d
Stockholm - **Deed** were formed in the spring of 2007. Initially the vocals were handled by Daniel Saidi, who was replaced by Emma. Outstanding groove-oriented modern metal with fat riffing. Carling is also found in **Undecimber**.
Website: www.deedband.com

2010 ■ Starfucker...MCDp 4tr   private ....DEEDSTAR 001
    Tracks: Beg For It/Bend's End/Get To It/Lost Opportunities (And Bitter Goodbyes).

DEEP DIVER
Lars "Fubbe" Furberg: v, Jan-Egil Bogvald: g, Janne Blom: b, Kenneth Pettersson: d
Nynäshamn - This line-up, plus keyboard player Anders Uddberg recorded two pop/rock albums under the name **The Radio**. Uddberg sadly died in an accident and the band reformed as **Deep Diver**. The style is ballsy melodic hard rock with catchy songs á la **Kiss**. They actually recorded

2010 MCDp - DEEDSTAR 001

a complete album that was never released due to the record company going bust. Jan-Egil also made the single *Without A Little Bit 'Love* with the band *Cargo*, however it was in a far poppier vein. Lars is also found in 70s glam rockers *Tears*, a band that still exists. He has also played with pop/rockers *Terraneans* and together with Bogvald in cover band *All 4 Fun*.

1984 ☐	Deep Diver	MLP 4tr	Grand Slam	....	GSSM 1101

Tracks: Hey I Like It/Fire/We Wanna Rock You/Can I Touch You.
Also released in a limited edition on red vinyl.

1984 ■	Hey I Like It/fire	7"	Grand Slam	....	GSS 1101

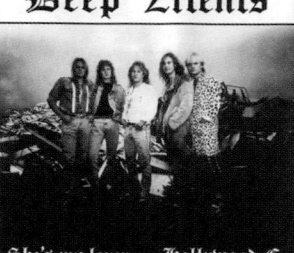
1984 7" - GSS 1101

DEEP ZILENTS
Janne Henriksson: v, Pekka Similä: g, Arto Jetsonen: g,
Harri Sillsten: b, Peter Olsson: d

Karlskoga - Great melodic hard rock in the vein of *Treat*. High-class vocals and nice harmony guitars. *Deep Zilents* were formed already in 1981 when the youngsters were still in school. They recorded some demos before finally recording the single. Since three of the members were hailing from Finland they played some dates in the country and also received some airplay. They split in 1990. Pekka played with the soulband *Dr Deo And His Soul Lotions* for some time, Peter joined a hardcore band in Stockholm, Arto moved to Motala and Janne is a stage manager.

1989 ■	She's My Lover/Hollywood C.	7"	Rox	.... KUL 8909

1989 7" - KUL 8909

DEFACED, THE
Jens Broman: v, Klas Ideberg: g, Mattias "Swaney" Svensson: g,
Mattias Andersen: b, Henrik Pommer: d

Helsingborg - Formed by former *Cul De Zac* singer Henrik Sjöwall and guitarist Klas Ideberg in 1995 as *Rehab*, but changed their name to *The Defaced* in 1999. The line-up featured Henrik Sjöwall, Mattias Svensson (later in *Kayser*), Klas Ideberg (*Darkane*, *Terror 2000*), Jörgen Löfberg (*Darkane*, *Agretator*) and Henry Ranta (*Soilwork*). The band recorded a four track demo that caught the attention of Italian label Scarlet. Musically slightly reminiscent of *Machine Head* or *The Haunted*. Very heavy twin-guitar grinding power-thrash. Great shit! In August 2002 the band again entered the studio to record the follow-up, "Karma In Black", which brought things up a notch. The album also featured guest spots from Peter Wichers (who also co-produced the album), Ulrika Bornemark and Richard Larsson. In 2004 Jörgen Löfberg left the band and was replaced by Mattias Andersen. In 2005 drummer Ranta and singer Sjöwall left the band. Enter former *Soilwork*/*Construcdead* singer Jens Broman and drummer Henrik Pommer. The band entered Ceasar Studio and Palace Of Noise to record the latest album *Anomality*. Trivia: The artwork for *Anomality* was created by Carlos Del Olmo Holmberg (*Construcdead*, *Soilwork*). *Website: www.defaced.com*

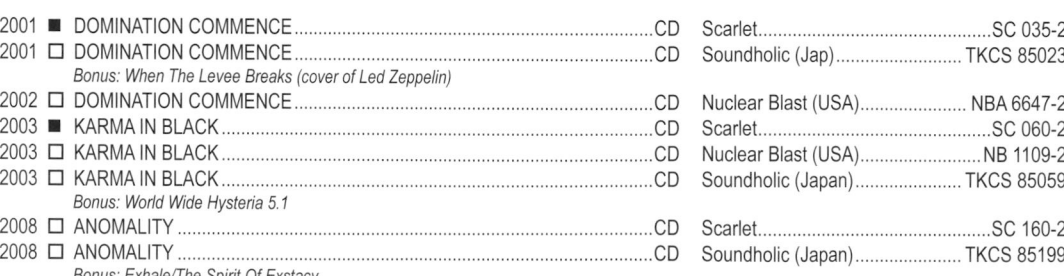
2001 CD - SC 035-2

2001 ■	DOMINATION COMMENCE	....	CD	Scarlet	.... SC 035-2
2001 ☐	DOMINATION COMMENCE	....	CD	Soundholic (Jap)	.... TKCS 85023
	Bonus: When The Levee Breaks (cover of Led Zeppelin)				
2002 ☐	DOMINATION COMMENCE	....	CD	Nuclear Blast (USA)	.... NBA 6647-2
2003 ■	KARMA IN BLACK	....	CD	Scarlet	.... SC 060-2
2003 ☐	KARMA IN BLACK	....	CD	Nuclear Blast (USA)	.... NB 1109-2
2003 ☐	KARMA IN BLACK	....	CD	Soundholic (Japan)	.... TKCS 85059
	Bonus: World Wide Hysteria 5.1				
2008 ☐	ANOMALITY	....	CD	Scarlet	.... SC 160-2
2008 ☐	ANOMALITY	....	CD	Soundholic (Japan)	.... TKCS 85199
	Bonus: Exhale/The Spirit Of Exstacy				

2003 CD - SC 060-2

DEFACED CREATION
Tommy Dahlström: v, Zeb Nilsson: g, Jörgen Bylander: g,
Johan Hjelm: b, Arttu Malkki: d

Östersund - *Defaced Creation* was formed in 1993 under the name *Unorthodox*, but changed due to another band with the same name. Guitarist Stefan Dahlberg (*Equinox Ov The Gods*) was in the line-up in 1994. They initially used a drum machine, as they couldn't find a drummer good enough. The first demo, *Santeria*, was recorded in 1994 and the follow-up in 1995 gained the band a deal with Paranoia Syndrome. On the split-single bass-player Hjelm had replaced Jocke Wassberg, who later turned up in *Souldrainer* and *Equinox Ov The Gods*, together with Arttu. The band "split", or rather all members except Bylander went on to form *Aeon* in 1999. Jörgen started putting together a new line-up. Zeb and Tommy are also found in *Diabolicum*. Bylander was later found in *Deranged*, *Sanctification* and *Celeborn* (who only recorded some demos and appeared on the compilation *Metal North*). *Defaced Creation* play death metal with a nod to the old school, even though they are more technical and has a better sound. Should appeal to fans of *Dismember*.
Fan website: www.myspace.com/defacedcreation666

1996 7" - PS 004

1996 7" - PS 011

1996 ■ Resurrection	7" 5tr	Paranoia Syndrome	PS 004

Tracks: Devastation/Ghoul's Attack/Resurrection/Entering The Gates/Stillborn. 300 copies, hand numbered.

1996 ■ Defaced Creation/Aeternum (split)	7"	Paranoia Syndrome	PS 011

Split single with Swiss band Aeternum. Tracks: Fall/Bloodwar. 1000 numbered copies on clear vinyl.

1998 ☐ Split	7" EP	Rockaway	001

Split with the band Standing Out. Tracks: Victorious Underworld/Infernal

1999 ☐ SERENITY IN CHOAS	LP	Paranoia Syndrome	PS 018

300 hand numbered copies

1999 ■ SERENITY IN CHOAS	CD	Voices Of Death	VODCD 005

1999 CD - VODCD 005

DEFENDER

Philip Von Segebaden: g/b

Stockholm - When his former band *Afflicted* broke up after two albums in 1994, Philip went solo. *Afflicted* were a death-oriented band with strong influences of *Iron Maiden* and *Manowar*, while this project is a purification of the later influences. Classic and good sounding 80's influenced melodic heavy metal with a strong touch of NWoBHM. The *Iron Maiden* influences are quite obvious. As session-drummer we find Peter Nagy-Eklöf (*Mörk Gryning*) and on vocals Michael Van de Graaf, who was also found in *Afflicted*. Peter is also found in *Cranium* and *Dawn*.

1999 ■ THEY CAME OVER THE HIGH PASS	CD	Necropolis	NR 043

1999 CD - NR 043

DEFLESHED

Gustaf Jorde: v/b, Lars Löfven: g, Matte Modin: d

Uppsala - High speed death metal with lyrics that would be more suitable in a morgue, sung with a voice taken from the depths of Hell. The band was formed in 1991 by Lars Löfven, Kristoffer Griedl and Oskar Karlsson, from the two speed metal bands *Inanimate* and *Convulsion*. The band recorded their first, self-titled (aka *Rotten Inflictioner demo*), demo in 1992 with singer Robin Dohlk. Later the same year they recorded their second demo *Avrah Kadavrah*, now with singer Johan Hedman. Now Gustaf Jorde had also joined and the band released the *Phlegm* EP. The EP contains two tracks taken from *Avrah Kadavrah* demo and the track *Obsculum Obscenum* was featured on the compilation *Grindcore* (Nuclear Blast). In 1993 the band recorded the demo *Body Art* that caught the attention of Invasion Records. On the first album the band changed drummer from Oscar Karlsson (later in *Gates Of Ichtar*, *The Duskfall*, *The Everdawn*, *Scheitan*, *Rasied Fist*) to Matte (*Dark Funeral*, *Sportlov*, *The Hidden*). *Abrah Kadavrah* could be described as progressive death metal. After the first album second guitarist Kristoffer Griedl left the band. *Fast Forward* was recorded at Unisound, with Dan Swanö at the helm. Not only is the sound so much better than the previous recordings, the band has gone through a musical metamorphosis bringing interesting tempo changes into the music. Berno Paulsson (*Spiritual Beggars, The Quill* etc.) produced the album. *Death…* is a limited edition live EP. Gustaf is ex-*Crematorium* (released one track on the *Uppsala* compilation single). *Reclaim The Beat* contains a cover of *Mötley Crüe*'s *Red Hot*. In 2005 Jorde announced the band's official split-up. Website: www.defleshed.com

Death metal boys in the flesh

1993 ☐ Phlegm	7" 3tr	Miscarriage Records	MS 002

Tracks: Obsculum Obscenum/Satanic Source/Phlegm

1994 ☐ Ma Belle Scalpelle	MCD 5tr	Invasion	I.R 009

Tracks: Gathering Flies/Morbidiance Blue Café/Simply Fall Towards/Many Mangled Maggots/Ma Belle Scalpelle

1995 ☐ ABRAH KADAVHRAH	CD	Invasion	I.R 019
1997 ■ UNDER THE BLADE	CD	Metal Blade	14157-2
1998 ☐ UNDER THE BLADE	CD	Invasion	I.R 032
1998 ☐ UNDER THE BLADE	LP PD	Invasion	I.R 040

Bonus: Beneath The Remains (Sepultura cover). 1000 copies.

1999 ☐ FAST FORWARD	CD	W.A.R.	WAR 011
1999 ☐ FAST FORWARD	2CD	Pavement Music (USA)	32340-2

The first 1000 copies contains a live bonus-CD

1999 ☐ Death… The High Cost Of Living	MCD 7tr	W.A.R.	RAW 003

Tracks: Entering My Yesterdays/Mary Bloody Mary/Metallic Warlust/Under The Blade/Walking The Moons Of Mars/In Chains & Leather/Thorns Of A Black Rose. 1500 copies.

1999 ☐ Death… The High Cost Of Living	MCD 7tr	Pavement Music (USA)	332363-2
1999 ☐ PERFECT WORKS: FAST FORWARD + 7 LIVES	2CD	Soundholic (Japan)	SHCDI 0032

Fast Forward + Death… The High Cost For Living

2000 ■ UNDER THE BLADE	CDd	Hammerheart Records	HHR 081

Bonus: Entering My Yesterdays (live)/Metallic Warlust (live)/Under The Blade (live)/Walking The Moons Of Mars (live)/Thorns Of A Black Rose (live)/Beneath The Remains (Sepultura cover)/Obsculum Obscenum/Satanic Source/Phlegm. New artwork.

2000 ■ FAST FORWARD	CD	Pavement Music (USA)	32340-2

Bonus: Under The Blade (Live)/Thorn Of A Black Rose (Live)

1999 CD - 14157-2

2000 CDd - HHR 081

2000	☐	FAST FORWARD + 7 LIVES	...CD	Soundholic (Japan)......................	SHCD-0032
		Seven live tracks as bonus.			
2001	☐	ABRAH KADAVRAH/Ma Belle Scalpelle......................................	CDd	Hammerheart.................................	HUW 001
2002	☐	ROYAL STRAIGHT FLESH...	CD	Soundholic (Japan)....................	TKCS-85050
2002	☐	ROYAL STRAIGHT FLESH...	CD	Regain Records	RR 0211-019
		Slipcase.			
2002	☐	ROYAL STRAIGHT FLESH...	LP	Regain Records	RRLP 0211-019
2002	☐	ROYAL STRAIGHT FLESH...	LP PD	Regain Records	RRPLP 0211-019
		500 copies.			
2002	☐	FAST FORWARD: THE SPECIAL EDITION	CD	Regain Records	RR 0305-031
		Bonus: Fast Forward (2002 version)/Radiation Sickness (Nucleas Assault cover)/Beneath The Remains (Sepultura cover)/Curse Of The Gods (Destruction cover). Slipcase			
2003	☐	ROYAL STRAIGHT FLESH...	CD	Regain North America (USA)...........	RNA 1019
2004	☐	DEATH – THE HIGH COST OF LIVING	CD	Crash Music..............................	CSME 61051
2004	☐	ABRAH KADAVRAH..	CD	Karmageddon	KARMA 073
		Bonus: the tracks from Ma Belle Scalpelle +Mary Bloody Mary (live)/In Chains And Leather (live)			
2004	☐	ABRAH KADAVRAH..	CDd	Fono (Russia)	FO246CD
		Same as KARMA 073.			
2004	☐	UNDER THE BLADE	CD	Karmageddon	KARMA 074
		Bonus: the tracks from Phlegm, Beneath The Remains (Sepultura cover) and 5 live tracks: Entering My Yesterdays/Metallic Warlust/Under The Blade/Walking The Moons Of mars/Thorns Of A Black Rose. Different artwork.			
2002	☐	FAST FORWARD...	CD	Crash Music (USA)	61046-2
		Bonus: Under The Blade (live)/Speeding The Ways (live)			
2005	☐	ABRAH KADAVRAH/UNDER THE BLADE	2CD	Candlelight (USA)	CDL 0165 CD
		Bonus: The tracks from "Death…" and "Phlegm" plus Beneath The Remains.			
2005	■	RECLAIM THE BEAT..	CD	Regain Records...........................	RR 051
2005	☐	RECLAIM THE BEAT..	CD	CD-Maximum (Russia)	CDM 0705-2341
2005	☐	RECLAIM THE BEAT..	CD	Candlelight (USA)	CDL 0217 CD
2005	☐	RECLAIM THE BEAT..	CD	Soundholic (Japan).....................	TKCS-85116
		Bonus: Needless To Pray			

2000 CD - 32340-2

2005 CD - RR 051

DEFUELD

Christoffer "Chris" Wetterström: v/g, Alexander "Alex" Ånfalk: g, Fredrik "Fredde" Hedberg: k, Emil Bygde: b, Patrik Jansson: d

Stockholm - Defueld were formed in 2003 by Wetterström and Ånfalk, both formerly in *Darkmoon Ritual*. The year after drummer Viktor Eklund (ex-*Shadows Past*, later in *Slavegrind*), keyboard player Ludde Siggelin and bass player Benny Strålberg joined them. The band recorded the six track demo, *Vs. Yourself*, in 2005. In 2005 Jerry Östman replaced Eklund and the subsequent year Emil Bygde (ex-*Encounter Darkness*) took over the bass, Fredrik Hedberg the keyboards and Johan Sundborger became the band's drummer. In November 2007 the band went to Senegal, Africa, a country well known for its many thrash bands (well, not really…). They played for over 6000 people in Dakar. They also held workshops and got to play for VIP guest including embassy personnel (a well know rowdy metal crowd). Sunborger was now replaced by Patrik Jansson and in January 2008 the band entered the studio to record their debut album. A first track, *Forever*, was featured on the compilation *Mama Trash Family Artists Vol 2* (2008 Mama Trash). It's hard to categorise *Defueld* with just one term. I'd say they come across like the missing link between *Metallica* and *Evanescence*. Chris sure has his James Hetfield moments and Hedberg's colourful keyboard playing over the crunchy riffing bears resemblance of *Evanescence*. Nice production, too. Patrik is also found in country-rockers *Hellsingland Underground*.
Website: www.defueld.com

2008 CDd - SEYAX08001

2008	■	DEFUELD	CDd	Short Wave Records..................	SEYAX08001
2008	○	Spawn..	CDS	Triada Promotion	- -
		Promo single without artwork			
2013	■	RORSCHACH..	CD	Short Wave Records.......................................	-

2013 CD -

DEGIAL

Hampus "Hampe Death" Eriksson: v/g, Rickard "R. Meresin" Höggren: g, Joel "J. Megiddo" Lindholm: b, Emil "Forcas" Svensson: d

Uppsala - Formed in 2004 under the name *Degial Of Embos*, under which name they recorded three demos before dropping *Of Embos* in 2005. Recorded the demo *Awakening From Darkness* in 2006. Produced by Fred Estby, cover by Erik Danielsson (*Watain*). Old-school death in the vein of *Morbid Angel* and *Possessed*. Joel Lindholm (*Undergång*, *Patronymicon*, *Shining*) joined after the debut 7". Emil is also found in *Die Hard* and Hampus in *Unpure*.

2010	■	Death And Darkness Buries All	7"	Blood Harvest	YOTZ#43
		500 copies. Tracks: Chaos Chant/To Darkness/Death In Heaven			
2012	☐	DEATH'S STRIKING WINGS...	CD	Supulchral Voice	SVRCD 07

2010 7" - YOTZ#43

DEGRADE

Manne: v, Victor Nordström: g, Andreas "Söder" Söderlund: g, Emanuel Odh: g, Kristian Carlin: b, Berto Hjert: d

Lidköping - When the band **Holocaust** disbanded in 2000, Victor (**Battered Bowels**) approached Carlin and Hjert and started talking about forming a new band. The three started jamming late 2001. In 2002, they were joined by Söder, and later on singer Manne completed the line-up. The subsequent year saw the release of their first demo *Feasting On Bloody Chunks*, having set the musical and lyrical direction. The band now recorded the MCD for one label, but due to problems they went for Permeated instead. With some more gigs under the belt the band recorded their debut album and in 2006 they played NRW Deathfest. **Degrade** play ultra-fast death/grind with totally indecipherable distorted growling vocals in the vein of **Cannibal Corpse** or Swedish colleagues **Severe Torture**. Söder was later out of the band.
Website: www.degrade.se

2005 MCD - PR 003

2006 CD - PR 008

2005	■	Hanged And Disemboweled	MCD 6tr	Permeated Records	PR 003

Tracks: Repulsive Gore/Covered With Stabwounds/Hanged And Disemboweled/Remnants Of Mutilated Bodies/Cleansed By Sin/The Dead Will Roam The Earth

2006	■	LOST TORSO FOUND	CD	Permeated Records	PR 008

DEGRADEAD

Mikael Sehlin: v, Anders Nyström: g, David Szücs: g, Michel Bärzén: b, Kenneth Helgesson: d

Stockholm - A young band that caught the attention of **In Flames**' Jesper Strömblad, calling the band "the future of metal". It all begun already back in 2000 in the thrash oriented band **Septima**, formed by Szücs. After a bunch of demos and several member changes, the last one being Anders Nyström (not the same person as "Blackheim"), who joined in 2004. They had to change their name in 2007, due to legal reasons, and **Degradead** was born. The band had however already recorded three demos with this line-up, as **Septima**. It was actually the demo *Death Row* that impressed the aforementioned Strömblad, who ended up co-engineering the debut album. The follow-up was recorded by Jonas Kjellgren at Abyss/Black Lounge Studios and mixed by Daniel Bergstrand at Dugout Studios. In July 2012 drummer Helgesson announced he was leaving the band, later replaced by Amit Mohla.
Website: www.degradead.com

2008 CD - DY10062-2

2009 CD - DY10077-2

2008	■	TIL DEATH DO US PART	CD	Dockyard 1	DY10062-2
2008	□	TIL DEATH DO US PART	CD	Locomotive Records	LM 592
2009	■	OUT OF BODY EXPERIENCE	CD	Dockyard 1	DY10077-2
2011	■	A WORLD DESTROYER	CDd	Metalville	MV 015
2013	□	THE MONSTER WITHIN	CDd	Metalville	MV 038

2011 CDd - MV 015

DEGREED

Robin Ericsson: v/b, Daniel Johansson: g, Jesper Adefelt: g, Micke Jansson: k, Mats Ericsson: d

Kopparberg/Älvsjö - The band was originally formed back in 1998, but after various member changes they became **Degreed** in 2006. They made one promo called *These Black Eyes*, which featured the last three songs later released on the 2007 MCD, plus the tracks *Arms Of Misery* and *My Fall*. In 2008 singer Robin Ericson entered the Swedish Idol and finished at a 6th place. In 2009 the band started recording the debut album, Guitarist Jonas Erkers had now been replaced by Jesper Adefelt. Outstanding AOR with a touch of prog. Some tracks are close to symphonic rockers **A.C.T** but with less quirkiness and prog-influences. Highly recommended. The debut album was released in 2010 by Australian Melodic Rock Records. Robin also plays bass, and Mats drums, in sleazy hard rockers **Angel King**.

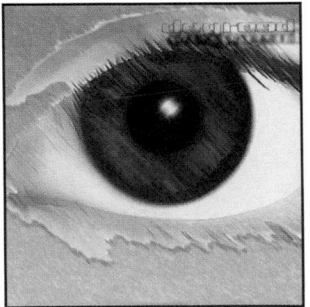
2007 MCDp - 40671

2010 CD - MRR 004

2007	■	Degreed	MCDp 5tr	private	40671

Tracks: Story Of Life/Here I Am/Catch The Feeling/The Less The Better/Human Being

2010	■	LIFE LOVE LOSS	CD	MelodicRock Records (Australia)	MRR004
2010	□	LIFE LOVE LOSS	CD	Spinning (Japan)	SPIN 23

Different artwork. Bonus: Constant/Bark At The Moon (Ozzy cover)

2011	□	LIFE LOVE LOSS	CD	Rambo	MRR004
2013	■	WE DON'T BELONG	CD	Spinning (Japan)	SPIN-052
2013	□	WE DON'T BELONG	CD	AOR Records	AOR 014

DELETION

Patrik Mattsson: v, Jonas "Lindblood" Lindblad: g, Johan Norman: g, Mathias Rosén: k, Andreas Niemi: b, Johan Forsberg: d

Mölndal (Göteborg) - Quite a young band, but with highly merited members. Formed in 2005 by Johan Norman (**Dissection, Decameron, Soulreaper, Runemagick**). Mattsson is ex-**Forsaken**/

2013 CD - SPIN-052

Thornium, Lindblad is ex-*Teatre*, *Putreaeon*, *Thorium*, Niemi is ex-*Akilles*, now in *Opera Diabolcus* and Rosén is ex-*Jaggernaut*. The band recorded a demo in 2006, which lead to a deal with Belgian label Painkiller. Unfortunately it took almost two years before the album was released, in which time founder Norman and drummer Forsberg left the band. *Deletion* play quite melodic and well-arranged death metal ranging from almost symphonic passages to raging blast beats. The album only has six tracks, but they are long and quite varied.
Website: www.deletion.se

2008 CD - PKR 071

2008 ■ DELETION	CD	Painkiller Records	PKR 071

DELLAMORTE

Jonas "The Box" Kjellgren: v/g, Mattias "The Crypt" Norrman: g/v,
Johan "Chainsaw" Jansson: g/v, Daniel "Death" Ekeroth: b, Kennet Englund: d

Stockholm - The band was formed in 1990 under the name *Interment* and recorded three demos under this name, but two recordings have been posthumously released on CD. Jonas Kjellgren and Kenneth Englund were part of this constellation. Around 1993 they changed name to *Moondark*, where Johan Jansson and Mattias Norrman entered the line-up, and in 1994 they became *Dellamorte* and Daniel Ekroth (*Insision, Tyrant, Diskonto*) completed the line-up. Johan was at the time also playing guitar in *Fulmination* in 94. Somewhere along the line Eklund was replaced by Sonny "Sick" Svedlund (who has also been in *Interment*). The band recorded their first demo *Drunk In The Abyss* in 1995 at the Abyss Studio. They were soon picked up by Finn Records who released their debut. The subsequent split-single on Yellow Dog lead to a deal with Osmose. They again entered Abyss Studios to record *Uglier And More Disgusting*. In 1997 they went out on the *World Domination Tour* together with *Enslaved* and *Dark Tranquility*. During this tour they recorded the live album and video for the *World Domination Live*. The band could be described as a mix of *Discharged*, *Motörhead* and *Slayer*. Old-school death metal with punk/grind influences. The band revisited Abyss Studio to record the *Home Sweet Hell* album in 1999. The album proves to be a musical step-up for the band. Heavy and really good production with fat detuned guitars, sounding a bit like *Entombed*. Musically the album is also a really hard-hitting slab of metal, at times a bit reminiscent of *Entombed* in their *To Ride…* era. *Dellamorte* left Osmose and recorded a 4-track MCD which was also released as a 7" on Elderberry Records. On this recording drummer Sonny "Sick" Svedlund was out of the band and replaced by former drummer Kennet (also found in *Centinex, Subdive, Uncanny*). *Dellamorte* also recorded a single and an album together with Dick Lundberg (ex-*Crystal Agony*) entitled *Århundradets Fest* (Party of the century) (01 Birdnest) after Daniel had parti-ciaped in the reality show Baren (The bar), where he came at second place. Daniel is also found in *Insision* and *Tyrant*, Mattias in *Subdive* and *Katatonia*, Jonas was later in *Carnal Forge*, *Centinex, Sideburners* and is now in *Scar Symmetry* and *World Below*. Johan recorded with various bands like *Centinex, Fleshrevels, Fulmination, Panzerfaust, Uncurbed, Demonical* and *Regurgitate*. Some live-tracks can be found on the compilation *World Domination Live* (98 Osmose OPCD 068). After the *Fuck Me Satan* single the intensity of the band slowed down as the members were busy in their other bands. They however did what they called a re-union gig in 2004. Since then there's been silence… Trivia: Daniel is the author of the fantastic Swedish death metal encyclopedia *Swedish Death Metal*.
Website: www.dellamorte.tk

1996 CD - FINN REC 016   1997 CD - KRON-H 09 CD

1996 ■	EVERYTHING YOU HATE	CD	Finn Records	FINN REC 016
1997 □	Dirty (split)	7" EP	Yellow Dog	YD 006
	Split with the band Corned Beef. Tracks: Dirty/Plug Me In/Suchastupid Disgustingfucke-dupfuck			
1997 ■	UGLIER AND MORE DISGUSTING	CD	Osmose/Kron-H	KRON-H 09 CD
1997 □	UGLIER AND MORE DISGUSTING	LP	Osmose/Kron-H	KRON-H 09 LP
1999 ■	HOME SWEET HELL	CD	Osmose/Kron-H	KRON-H 14 CD
2001 □	Fuck Me Satan	7"	PAS-83/Elderberry	013001
	Tracks: A Sure Shot/1000 Dead/Hellhole/I Am King. 666 copies.			

1999 CD - KRON-H 14 CD

DELVE

Linus "Germaniac" Björklund: v/g, Johan Skough: g,
Måns "Manster" Welander: b, Andreas "Agge" Johansson: d

Åhus - A mere bunch of kids, around 14 when they started the band. In 2001 Nuclear Winter released the 4-track cassette *Sentenced By The Unknown*. The band also featured guitarist Jonas Juhlin. In 2002 the band, at the time featuring Linus, Andreas and guitarist Per Melander (brother of *Kaamos* drummer Christofer "Chris Piss" Barkensjö) folded, so they started a new band under the name *Verminious*, and have kept recording under this name. *Delve* plays old school oriented death metal in the vein of *Grave*, *Kaamos* etc.

2003 ■	The Dead Amongst	MCD 5tr	Nuclear Winter Records	NWR 005
	500 copies. Tracks: Intro/Of Evil Blood/The Devil Amongst/Blasphemic Wartorture/Odour Of Decay			

2003 MCD - NWR 005

DEMENTAL

Linus Melchiorsen: v/g, Andreas Gustafsson: g,
David Henriksson: b, Magnus Hultgren: d

Linköping - **Demental** was founded by former *Isengard* singer/*Powerdise* drummer Linus Melchiorsen in 2001. The band's first release was quite a decent platter. The title track sounds like something that could have been on **Black Sabbath**'s *Mob Rules* album, while there are hints of vintage **Priest, Deuce, Fifth Angel** etc. The CD is actually really good when it comes to the songs and performances, but the mix, and especially the guitar sound, is plain horrible. Former **Mindless/Mindless Sinner/Powerdise/Skinny Horse** vocalist Christer Göransson, who sang on the album, still has his voice in order and does a killer job. The remaining line-up featured guitarist Andreas Gustafsson, bassist David Henriksson and drummer Linus Melchiorsen. The album also featured guest appearances from guitarist Jerker Edman and former **Mindless Sinner** guitarist Magnus Dannerblad. The album even features a re-make of **Mindless Sinner**'s track *Mystery*. In 2003 the band recorded a 5-track demo CD-R entitled *High Times*. It was planned to be released by JPL Music, but as Gustafsson left the band it never happened and the band folded in 2004. On the demo the line-up had been changed. Göransson was out of the band and Melchiorsen took over the vocals. He, in his turn, left the drum work over to Hultgren. Melchiorsen went to the band *Maitreya*. In 2013 the band reunited and the tracks from *High Times*, plus new material is planned to be recorded and released.

2002 CD - JPL 2002-1

2002 ■ MENTAL ED...CD   JPL Music ....JPL 2002-1

DEMIURG

Roger "Rogga" Johansson: g/v

Gamleby - **Demiurg** started as a solo-project by **Carve/Paganizer/Edge Of Sanity/Deranged/Ribspreader** guitarist Rogga in 2006 as an outlet for his interest in primitive black metal. However, it evolved into something more with more intricate twists and turns. On the first album he drafted session musicians: Johan Berglund (**This Haven**) on bass and drummer/singer Dan Swanö (**Bloodbath, Edge Of Sanity, Nightingale** etc). The second album also featured bass player Berglund, now guitarist/keyboardinst Dan Swanö, while the drums were handled by Dutchman Ed Warby (**Elegy, Gorefest, Valkyrie, Ayreon**) and clean vocals by Pär Johansson (**Satariel, The Duskfall, Torchbearer**). **Demiurg** started becoming more of a band than a project. In 2009 the band left Mascot Records for Cyclone Empire. *Slakthus Gamleby* (means Slaughterhouse Gamleby) shows a more diverse side of **Demiurg**. It also showcases the talents of some guests. To handle the more complex bass playing of the new album Rogga again invited Johan Berglund from **This Haven**, Dan Swanö was supposed to handle the drums as well as production. To complete the more complicated drum parts Ed Warby was again drafted, and Swanö handled guitars and keyboard arrangements. Warby also handles some clean vocals together with Dutch Marjam Welman (**Autumn**). Trivia: *The Demiurg* is a Gnostic idea of the entrapping physical being, much akin to Jean-Paul Sartre's idea of being, causing anguish by limiting our infinite mind (nothing).

2007 CD - M 7208-2

2008 CD - M 7238-2

2010 CD - CYC 050 CD

2007 ■ BREATH OF THE DEMIURG...........................CD   Mascot ....M 7208-2
2008 ■ THE HATE CHAMBER.....................................CD   Mascot ....M 7238-2
2010 ■ SLAKTHUS GAMLEBY.....................................CD   Cyclone Empire ....CYC 050 CD

DEMON CLEANER

Martin Stangefeldt: v, Rickard "Snicken" Ny: v/g, Kimmo Holappa: g,
Daniel Jansson: b/v, Daniel Lidén: d

Borlänge - Formed in 1996 by Martin Stangefeldt, Kimmo Holappa and Daniel Lidén as an instrumental trio, named after a song by **Kyuss**. They made their first commercial debut with the track *Kickback*, featured on the *Welcome To Meteor City* compilation. Singer Daniel Söderfeldt joined before the first single, but left the band after the CD. His only recording footprint was the track *Pathfinder* found on the compilation *A Fist Full Of Freebird*. After this Stangefeldt resumed his position as singer. The band's first three releases were all splits with fellows **Dozer**, while the debut album *The Freeflight* was a band only effort. A cover of *Graven Images* was also found on the **Misfits** tribute *We Are 138* (2000 Freebird). In 2000 Lindén and Holappa formed the side project **Greenleaf**. In March 2000 Rickard Ny was drafted as second guitarist and Daniel Jansson took over the bass from Stangefeldt. The band's second album was released in 2002 and not long after the band split, their last show being at *Stoned From The Underground* in Erfurt, Germany September 14, 2002. Fuzzed out, chord-oriented garagey stoner-rock with an almost punkish overtone and quite "non-melodic" vocals. After the band split Ny and Jansson went on to form **The Stonewall Orchestra** and Lidén joined **Dozer** as well as running his own post-metal-emo-soundtrack-piano-dominated band **Vaka** (where also Holappa is found). The song *Center Of The Universe* can be found on the compilations **Molten** *Universe Volume One* (1999 MU), *Damned Dodge* on *Molten Universe Volume Two* (2000 MU). Trivia: Bass player Martin is actually the man behind the Molten Universe label.
Website: www.myspace.com/demoncleanerrocks

1998 7" - MOLTEN 001

1999 7" - MOLTEN 002

1999 7" - MOLTEN 003

1998 ■	Demon Cleaner vs Dozer (split)	7"	Moltenuniverse	MOLTEN 001

Split with Dozer. Tracks: Barracuda/Redlight. 300 copies in black vinyl + 200 copies in transparent vinyl.

1999 ■	Hawaiian Cottage (split)	7" 4tr	Molten Universe	MOLTEN 002

Split with Dozer. Tracks: Heading Home/Megawheel. 400 copies in orange transparent vinyl + 100 in purple

1999 ■	Domestic Dudes (split)	7" 4tr	Molten Universe	MOLTEN 003

Split with Dozer. Tracks: Tanglefoot/Centerline. 500 copies.

2000 ■	THE FREEFLIGHT	CD	Molten Universe	MOLTEN 007
2002 ☐	DEMON CLEANER	CD	Molten Universe	MOLTEN 017

2000 CD - MOLTEN 007

DEMON SEED

Fredrik Karlsson: v, Mathias Söderström: g, Håkan Holmström: g, Michael Daxberg: b, Dennis Nilsson: d

Nyköping/Stockholm/Åker Styckebruk - Death metal with a strong melodic touch mixed with straight-ahead metal and also some slightly progressive moments, a bit reminiscent of **The Crown**-meet-**Entombed** with a touch of **In Flames**. Great stuff. Produced by Nicko DiMarino (**Steelwing**). The band was formed in 2004 over a couple of beers. The demo single *Mr. Anderson* was recorded with a slightly different line-up. In 2008 former **Dispatched** singer Karlsson took over the mike, and soon after his former colleague Nilsson also joined.

2011 ■	WORLDTHRASHER	CD	Rambo Music	DSCD 01

2011 CD - DSCD 01

DEMONICAL

Sverker "Widda" Widgren: v, Johan Jansson: g, Martin Schulman: b, Ronnie Bergerståhl: d

Avesta/Stockholm - **Demonical** was formed in 2006 by former **Centinex** members Jansson, Schulman and Bergerståhl with a mission to return to the roots of death metal. They recorded the four track promo *Blodspell Divine* at Necromorbus Studio the same year. In November they added singer Ludvig Engellau (**Remasculate, Unchaste**) as Johan wanted to concentrate on his guitar playing. The debut album, *Servants Of The Unholy Light*, recorded at Black Lounge and Necromorbus Studio, was released in 2007. The label Temple Of Darkness also released a split with **Absu** featuring one track from the aforementioned promo. The band toured Europe twice, also in 2007. However, at the end of the year the band parted ways with singer Engellau due to musical and personal reasons. After using some session singers the band finally in March 2008 they found new vocalist Sverker "Svedda" Widgren (**Diablocal**). Between December 2008 and February 2009 the band recorded the follow-up album, *Hellsworn*, again at Necromorbus. Jansson has also been found in **Interment, Beyond, Regurgitate** and **Dellamorte**, Bergerståhl in **World Below, Amaran** and **Grave**, while Schulman is a previous member of **Centinex** and **Interment**. In the last couple of years the band has also featured Fredrik Widigs and Johan Jansson.

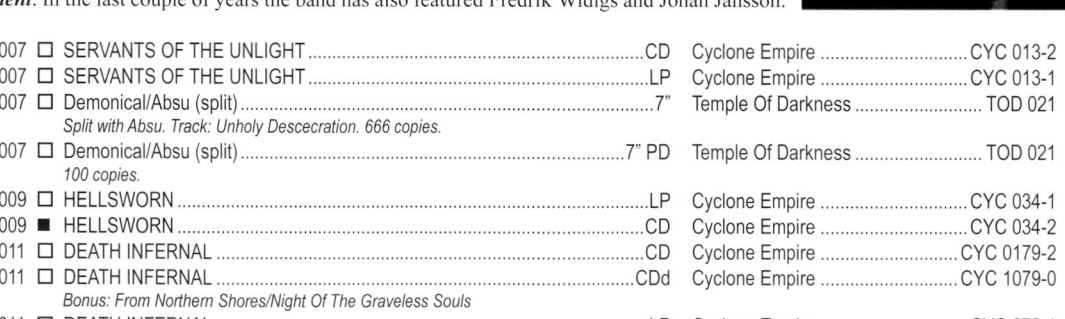

Demonical servants

2007 ☐	SERVANTS OF THE UNLIGHT	CD	Cyclone Empire	CYC 013-2
2007 ☐	SERVANTS OF THE UNLIGHT	LP	Cyclone Empire	CYC 013-1
2007 ☐	Demonical/Absu (split)	7"	Temple Of Darkness	TOD 021

Split with Absu. Track: Unholy Descecration. 666 copies.

2007 ☐	Demonical/Absu (split)	7" PD	Temple Of Darkness	TOD 021

100 copies.

2009 ☐	HELLSWORN	LP	Cyclone Empire	CYC 034-1
2009 ■	HELLSWORN	CD	Cyclone Empire	CYC 034-2
2011 ☐	DEATH INFERNAL	CD	Cyclone Empire	CYC 0179-2
2011 ☐	DEATH INFERNAL	CDd	Cyclone Empire	CYC 1079-0

Bonus: From Northern Shores/Night Of The Graveless Souls

2011 ☐	DEATH INFERNAL	LP	Cyclone Empire	CYC 079-1

Bonus: From Northern Shores

2009 CD - CYC 034-2

DEMONOID

Christofer Johnsson: v, Kristian Niemann: g, Johan Niemann: b, Richard Evensand: d

Stockholm - **Demonoid** is a side-project formed by **Therion** guitarist Kristian in 2002. He had made earlier attempts to produce more brutal music together with his brother Johan, but nothing appeared on record. The project was now revamped and soon reinforced by **Therion** fellows, singer Christofer Johnson and drummer Richard Evensand (also in **Dog Faced Gods, Soilwork, Southpaw, Ebony Tears, Sorcerer**, now in **Toehider**). The band was originally supposed to be using aliases to see if it was possible to make a name of themselves without riding on the **Therion** wave. The label however decided to play it safe and spill the beans, which is why there were no names on the CD-cover, but in the promo material. After the release of *Riders Of The Apocalypse*, Christofer left the band and was replaced by Masse "Emperor Magus Caligula" Broberg (**Dark Funeral, Dominion Caligula, Hypocrisy** etc). Johan has also been found in **Mind's Eye, Afterglow, Tears Of Anger, The Murder Of My Sweet** and is today found in **Evergrey**.

2004 ■	RIDERS OF THE APOCALYPSE	CD	Nuclear Blast	NB 1314-2

2004 CD - NB 1314-2

DEMONS OF DIRT
Mikael Widmark: v, Mikael Eriksson: g, Pontus Jonsson: b, Magnus Olsson: g

Sveg - The two Mikael's formed the band in 1999, which then went by the name *Engraved*. They recorded two demos in 2000-2001, which were put together on a promo-CD and sent out to labels. It caught the attention of several labels, where Hammerheart won the battle. The band describes their style as "death n' roll", and they are in the vein of *Vermin*, *The Haunted* or *Entombed* on *To Ride…*. The band also recorded a four-track demo in 2003. Eriksson and Nilsson were later found in *Grindnecks* and *Slaughtercult*.
Website: www.demonsofdirt.net

2001 ■ KILLER ENGINE ....CD Hammerheart..................................HHR 107
2002 ☐ Demonblues..MCD 3tr Hammerheart..................................HHR 117
Tracks: Repetitions/In Dreams/Demonblues

2001 CD - HHR 107

DEMORIAN
Tony "Satanic Tony" Sundstrand: v/g/b/k, Micke "Bullen/Bullf@n/Alltears": g/b/k

Sala - It started back in 2001 when the band *Curse* was formed out of the ashes of *Tragic Serenade*. Some songs were written, but it didn't last. In January 2007 Tony and Bullen reunited *Curse*. They released the demo *Wintercold* in 2007. As the name *Curse* was already taken they changed their name to *Demorian* and recorded the demo *Christ of Evil*, also in 2007. In 2009 the band appeared on the pro-printed CD-R compilation *Unholy Trinity – Thy Gathering I* (KVLT 666), with three tracks. After this they got a deal with Mexican label Azermedoth and released the debut *Back To The Glorious Past*. The two track demo *Before All Ends*, can also be downloaded from the band's website, and was released on tape, in 40 copies (Obscuration Productions). The band states they play a mix of old-school black metal, death, pagan, doom and goth. Well, after listening I do agree there are all sorts of elements in the band's music, which is pretty interesting and even new for the genre. However the Gollum-like vocals and the fact that they dominate the mix, are very disturbing factors. The band is also found on compilations *Beheaded By Evil* (Salute Records) and *This Black Abyss Vol. 1* (Dark Art). Tony is also found in his pagan/gothic/doom-solo project *Wintercold*, while Bullen has been found in *Corpestor*, *Killteam* and *Obey*. In 2010 the band was featured on the CD-R split *Indonesian Swedish Brotherhood* (Salute Records), followed by the download/tape release *For The Glory And Our Time* (2010). Not to be confused with the German band. During 2011 the band released numerous digital/cassette/CD-R singles and splits and in 2012 the CD-R album *Excerpts From A Diary* was released on Satanica Productions. Later the same year the digital/CD-R single *Frost* was also released. The track *My Beloved My Beheaded* was featured on the *The Legion Of TchorT - #2* compilation, released by TchorT Magazine.

2008 ■ BACK TO THE GLORIOUS PAST ....CD Azermedoth AZH-CD-20
1000 copies

2008 CD - AZH-CD-20

DENANDER, TOMMY
Tommy Denander: g/k/b/d

Stockholm - Tommy has quite a long and interesting history. He started out at the age of 13 in the band *ATC*, which also featured Mappe Björkman (*Candlemass*). When Mappe joined *Candlemass*, *ATC* changed some members and became *Downtown*. *Downtown* later changed into the band *Cheese*, which also recorded a single in 1987. In 1989 Tommy recorded another single with the AOR-band *Cool For Cats*. He also worked as session-guitarist with numerous musicians of various styles, like Dag Finn, Buster, Janne Dahlin etc. He also engineered albums by *Unanimated*, *Morpheus*, *Earthquake* and several others. At the time, a diamond in the rough. *Less Is More* is quite laid back, while *Skeleton* is a lot heavier. Both albums are instrumental with Tommy's excellently technical, yet highly sensitive guitar playing as a main feature. If you're into instrumental music with the emphasis on songs and melodies, not just flashy finger-work, you should check it out. Buy 'em! *Limited Access*, which is a 500 copies limited edition intermediate release, featuring some tracks from the first two album, unreleased tracks from those sessions and new demo-recordings. *Counterparts* is not really hard rock, but soft guitar-oriented melodic rock, one song featuring Bill Champlin on vocals. It says 1998 on the cover, but was not actually released until 1999. A cassette-album entitled *Guitar Czar* was released by Rockris Disc (001-13) in Romania. It's a compilation of the first two albums, plus some unreleased tracks. In 1996 the plans to release the long awaited album with his project *Radioactive*, entitled *Ceremony Of Innocence* started moving again. The album was finally released in 2001. Other musicians that appeared on the album were Jeff, Mike and Steve Porcaro, David Paich and Steve Lukather of *Toto* fame, plus session guitarist Michael Landau, Bill Champlin and Simon Phillips. Quite an impressive line-up. The track *5495* from that session also appears on *Less Is More* and the track *Remember My Conscience* is found on the compilation-CD for my first book. Tommy also released a CD together with blues-singer/guitarist David Book at the same time, *Tied To The Blues* (D&W, BOOK 002). In 2000 he released two brilliant pomp-albums together with Ricky Delin (Björn Rickard Lindbom) under the moniker *Prisoner* and he has released two albums with *Sayit*. In 2000 he was part of *Talk Of The Town*, as well as the

Tommy Denander - gazing in the spotlight

outstanding *Rainmaker*. Other bands where Tommy has made guest appearances include Fee Waybill, Bruce Gaitch, Fergie Fredrickson, *Locomotive Breath*, *Street Talk*, *Lec Zorn*, Chris Catena etc. He also organised the Swedish contribution to the anti-terrorist project-DVD where he gathered more or less the entire Swedish hard rock/metal-elite on the track *Where Is The Fire*, written by him and Ricky Delin. In 2003 Tommy released a second album with *Radioactive*. He also co-wrote a song for the Swedish Eurovision Song Contest that earned him his first gold and platinum awards. In 2006 Tommy added some guitars on a track on Paul Stanley's solo album *Live To Win*. He also laid down some guitars for albums by Kelly Keagy, *AOR*, David Readman, Cleo, Dalida, Sofia Draco, Jim Jidhed, Michael Bormann, *Mountain Of Power* etc. In 2009 he was part of *Spin Gallery*, who released the return album *Standing Tall*. Tommy is also involved in numerous song-writing and production projects, frequently travelling between Sweden and USA. In 2009 he backed US singer Mitch Malloy on UK festival Firefest and in 2010 he backed Jimi Jamison at the same festival, plus some further shows. A new Radioactive album is in the making and in 2012-13 he has toured with *Legends Voices Of Rock*.
Website: www.tommy-denander.com

1995 CD - LHM 0416

1995 CD - LHM 0417

1995 ■	LESS IS MORE	CD	Local Dealer	LHM 0416	$
1995 □	SKELETON	CD	Local Dealer	LHM 0417	$
1995 ■	Less Is More & Skeleton	MCDpg 6tr	Local Dealer	LHM 0421	$
	A promo-CD featuring three tracks from each album.				
1997 □	LIMITED ACCESS	CDp	Noble House	NH9705	
	500 copies.				
1998 □	COUNTERPARTS	CD	Angelynn	ANG 003	
	This is actually a collaboration with Tommy and Bruce Gaitch released under the name Denander/Gaitch.				

1995 MCDpg - LHM 0421

DENATA

Tomas Andersson: g/v, Roger Blomberg: b, Åke Danielsson: d

Linköping - Shortly after the breakup of the band *Skullcrusher* in 1998, Tomas formed *Denata* together with former *Total Death* drummer/singer Pontus Sjösten (brother of Patrik Sjösten of *Raped Teenagers, Satanic Slaughter*). In 1999 they recorded the first EP as a tribute to the old-school thrash scene. This year Tomas also released his solo project *Screams Over Northland*. After this the band hooked up with bass player Blomberg.They now entered Guja Studio in Linköping to record the debut album, which was an album of true eighties-influenced old-school thrash in the vein of *Hellhammer*. They changed label to Arctic, who released the faster and heavier follow-up. In 2002 Pontus unfortunately had to leave the band due to severe ear problems. They found replacement Åke Danielsson and Tomas now took over the vocals. On *The Art Of The Insane* they even took the rawness up another notch. The album also contains a cover of *Celtic Frost*'s *Morbid Tales*. The band was put on hold in 2003, but they do still exist. Tomas and Roger are now found in *Freevil*, who made their debut album in 2007. Roger is also in melodic metal band *Sins IV Ages*. *Departed To Hell* has also been re-issued as a digital release only, featuring two bonus tracks. If you're into bands like *Witchery* or *The Crown*, check this out.
Website: www.denata.com

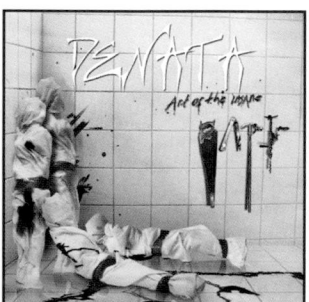

2002 CD - 80501-91011-2

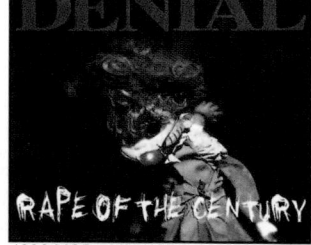

2003 CD - 80501-98104-2

1999 □	Denata	7" 4tr	Ghoul Records	GR 002
	Tracks: Necro Erection/Stench In My Throat/The Ape At The Right Shelf/Man On The 3rd Floor			
2000 □	DEPARTED TO HELL	CD	Ghoul Records	GR 003
2002 ■	DEATHTRAIN	CD	Arctic Records	80501-91011-2
2003 ■	ART OF THE INSANE	CD	Arctic Records	80501-98104-2
2003 □	ART OF THE INSANE	CD	Frozen North	FZN 81042
2009 □	DEATHTRAIN	CD	Frozen North	FZN 10112

DENIAL

Kristoffer Hessö: v, Marcus Bressler: g, Ola Håkansson: g/b, David Augustsson: d

Vallda (Göteborg) - This band melts concrete. Fast, ultra-heavy hardcore/metal. Mikael Stanne of *Dark Tranquillity* helps out on the track *Animal Roots* and the MCD was produced by Fredrik Nordström (*Dream Evil* etc).

| 1996 ■ | Rape Of The Century | MCD 4tr | MNW Zone | MNWCDS 222 |
| | *Tracks: Nature Abused/Animal Roots/Hate The Police/Humanity Fails.* | | | |

1996 MCD - MNWCDS 222

DENIED

Johan Fahlberg: v, Andreas Carlsson: g, Chris Vowden: g,
Fredrik Isaksson: b, Pete Dolls: d

Upplands Väsby - Heavy melodic metal band *Denied* were formed in 2003 by guitarist Andreas Carlsson. In 2005 the debut album saw the light of day. The line-up featured Andreas, fellow guitarist Benny Persson, bass player Henrik Westerlund, drummer Tomas Holtinkoski and former *Human Rage* singer Jari Salonen. For the second album the line-up changed a bit, now

2005 CD - RWR 001 00

featuring Andreas, Jari, former **Human Rage** bass player Robert Stellmar and former **Make Me Sick** drummer Pete Dolls. Former member Westerlund produced the album. Jari had actually left the band when the album was released. His replacement was none less than **Jaded Heart** singer Johan Fahlberg. In 2009 they released the three track demo *III*, now with Johan handling the vocals. The debut was a pretty decent album that suffered from a pretty weak mix and not really any killer tracks. Heavy and powerful metal with a touch of a more melodic **Pantera** with a hint of **Priest** at times. The follow-up showed a lot more promise, a notch in the sound department (horrible drum sound, though) but with a real killer track in *The Black Room*. The 2009 demo featured three tracks, where one was a remake of the aforementioned *The Black Room*, now with Johan on vocals. Nothing wrong with Jari, but *Let Them Burn* is a cut above the predecessors. It also features new bassist Isaksson (**Therion, Grave**) and guitarist Chris Vowden (**Expulsion, Hydrogen**). Micke Jacobsson and René Sebastian adds some extra guitars. Jari is now in **13 Chaos St.**

2008 CD - RWR 002 00

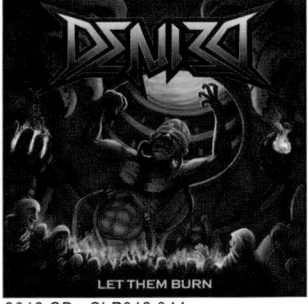

2005 ■	7 TIMES YOUR SIN	CD	Ravenwood	RWR 001 00	
2008 ■	NEW ARMY FOR THE OLD REVOLUTION	CD	Ravenwood	RWR 002 00	
2013 ■	LET THEM BURN	CD	Sliptrick Records	SLP013.044	

2013 CD - SLP013.044

DEPZON

Michael Svensson: v, Peter Wingård: g, Stefan Nilsson: g.
Peter Månsson: b, Per-Owe "P-O" Johansson: d

Norrköping - **Depzon** was the spin-off of fusion band **Casiopeia**, featuring Månsson, Wingård and Johansson. Månsson and Johansson were earlier also in **Crash Boom Band**. Great metal in the NWoBHM-vein with nice **Thin Lizzy**:ish guitar harmonies and good vocals. One of the best Platina-releases. Highly recommended and very rare! Månsson was later playing in **Åke Borts Orkester**. Johansson was in **Per de Flon**, which also features **Pole Position/Reptilian** singer Jonas Blum.

1985 ■	Flying On The Sundown/Lost In The Forest	7"	Platina	PL 6	$$

1985 7" - PL 6

DERANGED

Martin Schönherr: v, Thomas Ahlgren: g, Andreas Johansson: b, Rikard Wermén: d

Hjärup - Formed early 1991. The first demo *...The Confessions Of A Necrophile* (1992) sold 700 copies in 6 months. Brutal old-fashioned death metal with quite weird vocals. One thing worth noticing is that Mike Amott (ex-**Carcass**, now **Spiritual Beggars/Arch Enemy**) plays lead guitar on the *Architects Of Perversion* MCD. The band had great problems with the release of the new album. The CD was totally x-rated in Germany because of the explicit lyrics and no printer wanted to press the new album. Which lead to the title. The band claims the printers can't see the irony in the lyrics. Quite a good hype though... After the second 7" bass player Jean-Paul Asenov was replaced by Mikael Bergman, who was fired in January 1995. Johan plays bass on *Rated X* and Dan Bengtsson (ex-**Inverted**) joined after the recording. The CD has been compared to bands like **Suffocation** and **Cannibal Corpse**. The track *In League With Satan* was featured on the **Venom**-tribute *Promoters Of The Third World War* (92 Primitive Art) and *Hammer Cottered Rectum* was featured on *Sometimes... Dead Is Better* (93 Shiver) and the band also had a track on the compilation *A Repulsive Assault* (95 Repulse). *III* contains a cover of **The Doors**' *Break On Through* and **Mötley Crüe's** *Knock 'em Dead*. The album was produced by Berno Paulsson. Singer Per Gyllenbäck (also co-owner of Wrong Again Records) was not part of the band after the 1995-release. Singer Fredrick Sandberg joined in 1997 and the line-up on *High On Blood* featured Sandberg (v), Axelsson (g), Bengtsson (b) and Wermén (d). Bass-player Dan Bengtsson was fired in November 1998 and Anders took over his task until Johan Anderberg (**Murder Corporation**) joined in 1999. The self-titled 2001 release featured Johan Anderberg (v/b), Johan Axelsson (g) and Wermén (d), as did the 2006 *Obscenities In B Flat*. On the band's 2001 European tour the vocals were handled by Roger "Rogga" Johansson (**Paganizer, Demiurg, Edge Of Sanity** etc). On the subsequent *Plainfield Cemetery* Anderberg had been replaced by bassist/singer Calle Fäldt (**Feared Creation**). In 2007 the line-up once again changed when bass player Anderberg was replaced by Thomas Ahlgren (**Pandemonium, End, Monolith**) and the band was reinforced with singer Martin Schönherr (**Splattered Mermaids, Virgin Sin**). After the album the band split, but reunited in 2009, now without original member Axelsson and a line-up featuring Schönherr (v), Ahlgren (g), Wermén (d) and new bassist Andreas Johansson. Axelsson is today found in Danish band **Thorium**. The bonus tracks on the 2008 re-issue of *High On Blood* were recorded in 2003. The new line-up was first featured on the 2011 album *Cut, Carve, Rip, Serve*.

The deranged architects of perversion

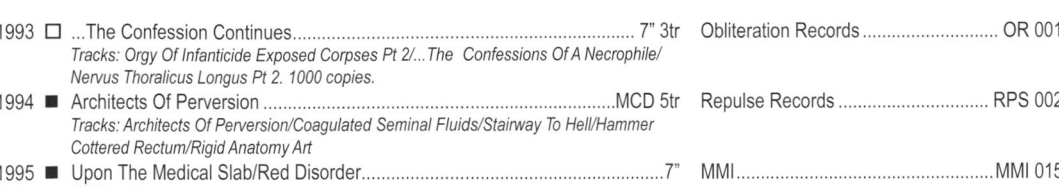

1994 MCD - RPS 002

Architects Of Perversions

1993 ☐	...The Confession Continues	7" 3tr	Obliteration Records	OR 001	

Tracks: Orgy Of Infanticide Exposed Corpses Pt 2/...The Confessions Of A Necrophile/ Nervus Thoralicus Longus Pt 2. 1000 copies.

1994 ■	Architects Of Perversion	MCD 5tr	Repulse Records	RPS 002	

Tracks: Architects Of Perversion/Coagulated Seminal Fluids/Stairway To Hell/Hammer Cottered Rectum/Rigid Anatomy Art

1995 ■	Upon The Medical Slab/Red Disorder	7"	MMI	MMI 015	

1000 copies.

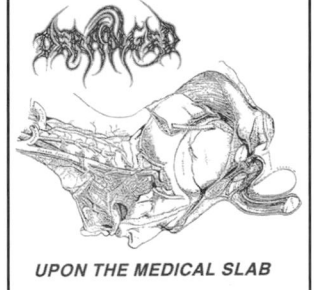

UPON THE MEDICAL SLAB

1995 7" - MMI 015

Year		Title	Format	Label	Catalog
1995	☐	Sculpture Of The Dead	MCD 4tr	Repulse Records	RPS 010B

Tracks: Internal Vaginal Bleeding/The Bowels Of My Dismay/Majestic Hole/Sculptures Of The Dead

| 1995 | ☐ | RATED X | CD | Repulse Records | RPS 010 CD |

The first 2000 copies featured the Sculpture Of The Dead MCD tracks as bonus.

1998	☐	HIGH ON BLOOD	CD	Regain Records	9803-001
1999	■	III	CD	Listenable Records	POSH 018
1999	☐	III	CD	Soundholic (Jap)	SHCD1-0031

Bonus: Relentless (Pentagram cover)/Stagnant Pool (LeafHound cover)/Icon Of Murder/Vermin Of A Sewer World

| 2000 | ☐ | III | LPg+7" | Merciless Records | MR SRLP 018 |

Features red vinyl single with: Hammer Cottered Rectum/Raised On Human Sin/Razor Divine/Some Kinda Hate. Bonus: Stagnant Pool (Leafhound cover)

| 2000 | ☐ | RATED X | 2LPg | Perverted Taste | PT 030 |

With the Sculpture Of The Dead and Archetects Of Perversion MCDs as bonus.

2001	☐	DERANGED	LP	Merciless Records	MRSRLP 028
2001	☐	DERANGED	CD	Listenable Records	POSH 028
2001	☐	DERANGED	CD	Irond (Russia)	01-141
2001	☐	DERANGED	CD	Soundholic (Japan)	TKCS 85019

Bonus: Straight Razor/Injected

| 2001 | ☐ | ABSCESS/DERANGED (split) | 10" MLP | Listenable Records | POSH 029 |

Split with Abcess. Tracks: Vermin Of A Sewer World/Relentless/Stagnant Pool (Leafhound cover)

| 2001 | ☐ | RATED X | CD | Listenable Records | POSH 033 |

Re-issue with Sculpture Of The Dead and Architects Of Perversion as bonus.

| 2002 | ☐ | PLAINFIELD CEMETARY | CD | Listenable Records | POSH 040 |
| 2002 | ☐ | PLAINFIELD CEMETARY | LP | Listenable Records | POSH 040 LP |

500 copies.

2002	☐	PLAINFIELD CEMETARY	CD	Irond (Russia)	02-388
2006	■	OBSCENITIES IN B FLAT	CD	Listenable	POSH 083
2007	☐	OBSCENITIES IN B FLAT	CD	CD-Maximum (Russia)	CDM 1206-2635
2008	☐	HIGH ON BLOOD	CD	Regain	RR 0304-021

Bonus: Razor Divine/By Knife

| 2008 | ■ | THE REDLIGHT MURDER CASE | CD | Regain | RR 139 |

Slipcase with different artwork.

| 2011 | ☐ | CUT, CARVE, RIP, SERVE | CD | Sevared Records | SR-160 |

1999 CD - POSH 018

2006 CD - POSH 083

2008 CD - RR 139

DESERT RAIN

**Brian "Bee" Frank: v, Mats Byström: g, Leif Ehlin: k,
Anders "L.A." Rönnblom: b, Steve "A.J" Ranzow: d**

Örnsköldsvik - "Bee", formerly a Canadian resident, met "L.A." and moved to Sweden. He has previously recorded two albums with Canadian metal band *Rapid Tears*. Mats had previously recorded with *Sergeant* and *Boogietryck*. The record feels very split, with some AOR-songs, some sleaze, some ballads and some poppy FM rock. Bee, Byström and "L.A" went on to form *Killer Bee*. Ranzow later joined *Espinoza* and *Original Sin*. In 2007 Frank was back in business with his new project *Planet B.* Rönnblom is playing in heavy rockers *Absorbing The Pain* and *Killer Bee* has reformed.

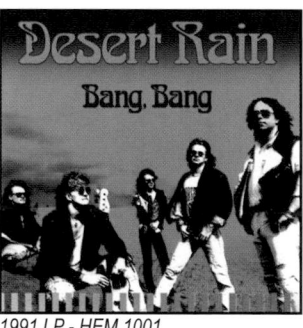
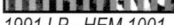
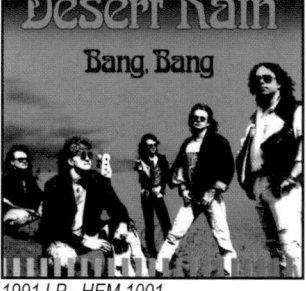

1991 LP - HEM 1001

1991	☐	BANG BANG	CD	HEM	HEM 1001
1991	■	BANG BANG	LP	HEM	HEM 1001
1991	☐	Bang, Bang/In Love (live)	7"	HEM	HEMS 101

DESPITE

**Alex Losbäck Holstad: v, Timmy Leng: g,
Jonatan Larsson: g, Matte D: b, Oscar Nilsson: d**

Göteborg - *Despite* was formed in 1998 by Leng and bassist Fredrik Meister. In 2007 singer Jimmie Strimell, who went to *Dead By April*, was replaced by *Decameron/Cardinal Sin/Runemagick* Losbäck. The debut was a well-produced affair ranging from hardcore style metal to crushing heavy death metal with heavy detuned guitar riffs. A piece of trivia is that Göteborg comedian Knut Agnred (*Galenskaparna*) makes a guest appearance on the album. In 2009, after the release of the album, the band went through some changes as drummer Jesper Astorga and guitarist John Lidén were replaced by drummer Oscar Nilsson and former *Marionette* guitarist Johan Sporre. Astorga is now found in *Minora*. Before the release of the second album Sporre was replaced by Jonatan Larsson and Meister was replaced by Matte D. *Clenched* was produced by Alex Losbäck Holstad, who was replaced by Peter Tuthill in 2012, while André Gonzales replaced Jonatan. New CD *EPic* is being recorded.

Brutal dudes, despite the stonery looks

DESPITE
clenched
2011 CD - DR10101

| 2009 | ☐ | IN YOUR DESPITE | CD | Tractor | TRPR 93001 |
| 2011 | ■ | CLENCHED | CD | Dozer Records | DR10101 |

DESTINY

Kristoffer Göbel: v, Janne Ekberg: g, Stefan Björnshög: b, Birger Löfman: d

Göteborg - Formed in 1980, but didn't really get going until 1982.
The band's first singer was 18 year old Therese Hanseroth, who sang
on the band's first six track demo and the band's first gig. She left the
band a year later and was replaced by Håkan Ring. The first album
is totally different from the band's following recordings. It contains
slightly **Iron Maiden**-influenced heavy metal with awful castrate-
vocals. The line-up on the debut featured Håkan Ring (v), John
Prodén (g), Magnus Österman (g), guest drummer Peter Lundgren
and founding member Stefan Björnshög. On *Atomic Winter* the band
changed quite dramatically and it contains some great fatal tracks like
Bermuda and *Living Dead*. Their music could in a way be described
as Wagner-goes-heavy-metal. On *Atomic Winter* the band consisted of
new singer Zenny Hansson (later Gram) (ex-**Faith**, **Metal Muthaz**),
Stefan, Peter, and guitarists Jörgen Pettersson and Floyd Konstantin,
the latter of **King Diamond/Geisha** fame. The album-cover was made
by Derek Riggs (**Iron Maiden**). On *Nothing Left To Fear* the line-up
was Zenny, Stefan, Gunnar Kindberg (g), Knut Hassel (g) and Håkan
"Kane" Svantesson (d). Zenny left the band for a while to record an
album with **Treasure Land**, but came back in the ranks and now he
had changed his last name to Gram. Knut Hassel and Peter Lundgren
later recorded one album with the band **7th Planet** in 1995. Today,
Hassel is in **Gudars Skymning**. Drums on *The Undiscovered Country*
were played by Svantesson, although he was not in the official line-

The 2013 incarnation of Destiny

up. The band featured Zenny (v), Knut (g) and Stefan (b). The album was produced by Jörgen
Cremonese (**Whipped Cream**). In 1999 **Destiny** started rerecording the first three albums.
Future Of The Past saw a new and pretty drastic change in the line-up, featuring Stefan, singer
Kristoffer Göbel, guitarists Janne Ekberg and Niclas Granath (**Sabbtail**) bass player Stefan and
former **Biscaya** drummer Birger Löfman. The album shows a refreshing and heavy **Destiny** with
a bright future for the dark music. After the album Granath was out of the band. In 2005 the
rerecorded *Beyond All Sense* was finally released, proving the vocal shortcomings of the first
version could easily be fixed by Göbel making this a highly current album. In 2005 Michael
Åberg (**Nostradameus**) was added on guitar. After the album Göbel however left the band and
in 2010 the band announced the new album *Global Warning* was recorded and ready for a new
singer to step in and finish the album. The line-up now featured Björnshög, Löfman and Åberg.
On January 17, 2012 **Destiny**'s original singer and Stefan Björnhög's fiancée Therese Hanseroth
sadly died. This put the plans for a 30th Anniversary **Destiny** album on a hiatus, as well as the
Global Warning album. The band was again back on path in August 2012 and the anniversary
album will be entitled *The Incompatibility of Philosophical Terminology*, set for release late
2013. Late 2012 Löfman was replaced by Roger Christiansson (**Solid, Rampage, Attrapp** etc),
who was replaced by the returning Svantesson in 2013.
Website: www.destinymetal.com

1985 LP - M506

1988 LP - US 141991

1985	■ BEYOND ALL SENSE	LP	Musikbolaget		M506
1988	☐ ATOMIC WINTER	CD	US Metal Records		US 141991
1988	■ ATOMIC WINTER	LP	US Metal Records		US 141991
1991	☐ NOTHING LEFT TO FEAR	CD	Active Records		ATV-18
1991	■ NOTHING LEFT TO FEAR	LP	Active Records		ATV-18
1991	☐ NOTHING LEFT TO FEAR	CD	IRS (Germany)		IRS 985418
1999	☐ THE UNDISCOVERED COUNTRY	CD	GNW		GNW 01
2004	☐ FUTURE OF THE PAST	CD	Powerline		PLRCD 011
	Slipcase.				
2005	☐ BEYOND ALL SENSE 2005	CD+DVD	Powerline		PLRCD 015
	Rerecording with bonus tracks: Ode To You/No Way Out				

1991 LP - ATV-18

DESTYNATION

Anders Häggkvist: v, Ronny Blylod: g/k, Daniel Niemann: g,
Patrik Nordendahl: b, Magnus Larsson: d

Örnsköldsvik - The band rose up from the ashes of the band **Eternia** in February 2005. They
recorded a demo the same year and a deal with Greek label Sonic Age was penned. With new
singer Häggkvist they became **Destynation**. The band plays high class melodic power metal
in the same vein as **Nocturnal Rites** or **Morifade**. They also recorded a cover of *Time Has
Come* for the **Europe** tribute *Heading For Venus* that unfortunately was only released as a
digital download. In 2006 Blylod, who is a very talented guitarist, initiated the project **Planet
Storm** and recorded a demo. After this he has recorded an album with melodic hard rockers
Justaquickstop in 2009, which transformed into **Blackrain** and another album was released
in 2011. A second **Destynation** album entitled *No Tomorrow* was recorded and planned to be
released in 2010, but the band split before its release.

2006 CD - SARECD 011

2006	■ RISING UP	CD	Sonic Age		SARECD 011

DESULTORY

Klas Morberg: v/g, Håkan Morberg: g, Johan Bolin: b, Thomas "Snake" Johnsson: d

Södertälje - Formed in 1989 and recorded their first demo *From Beyond* in 1990. The band's second demo *Death Unfolds* (1990), which sold around 1500 copies, and the third entitled *Visions* (1991) were compiled and released as their debut mini-LP *Forever Gone*. In January 1992 bass player Jens Almgren quit and was replaced by Håkan. In August 1992 the band once again entered Sunlight Studios together with producer Tomas Skogsberg, now to record their debut album *Into Eternity*, a pretty intense thrash metal affair. They also have a track on the compilation *Against All Odds* (95 Displeased). *Bitterness*, also produced by Skogsberg, was another brutal thrash/death metal album. They claimed to be unique in the death genre as they only detune a half-step. Guitarist Stefan Pöge wasn't happy with the change of musical direction on the last album, so he left before it was recorded. *Swallow The Snake* sees the band entering a more melodic, slightly goth-oriented side of death metal. The band later changed its name to **Zebulon**, continued their musical transformation and made a few releases in a more sludge/doom/stoner approach more akin to **Mustasch**. Lo and behold, in 2010 **Desultory** announced their comeback, signed by Pulverised and with a new album being recorded. The trio had now been reinforced by new bassist Johan Bolin (**Unanimated, Zebulon**), while Morberg switched to guitar.

1993 CD - CD ZORRO 52

2007 CD - - -

2011 CD - ASH 079 CD

1992	☐	Forever Gone	MLP 6tr	House Of Kicks	HOK LP 002

Tracks: Forever Gone/Depression/Visions/Passed Away/The Chill Within/Death Unfolds. 1000 copies.

1993	■	INTO ETERNITY	CD	Metal Blade	CD ZORRO 52
1993	☐	INTO ETERNITY	CD	Metal Blade (USA)	3984-14008-2
1994	☐	BITTERNESS	CD	Metal Blade	CD ZORRO 77
1994	☐	BITTERNESS	CD	Metal Blade (USA)	3984-14070-2
1996	☐	SWALLOW THE SNAKE	CD	Metal Blade (USA)	3984-14109-2
2007	■	FROM BEYOND THE VISIONS OF DEATH	CD	- - (bootleg?)	- -
2010	■	COUNTING OUR SCARS	CD	Pulverised	ASH 079 CD

Slipcase. Super jewel box.

2011	☐	COUNTING OUR SCARS	LP	Temple Of Darkness	TOD 036

500 copies.

2011	☐	INTO ETERNITY	CD	Pulverised	ASH 077 CD

Bonus: Eternal Darkness/The Awakening/Cease To Exist/Insanity

2011	☐	INTO ETERNITY	LP	War Anthem Records	WAR 043LP
2011	■	BITTERNESS	LP	War Anthem Records	WAR 044 LP
2011	☐	BITTERNESS	CD	Pulverised	ASH 078 CD

Bonus: Passed Away/The Chill Within/Death Unfolds/Forever Gone/Depression/Visions

2011 LP - WAR 044 LP

DETEST

Micke Därth: v/g, Janne Johansson (now Ström): g, Jörgen Svahn: b, Nicke Landin: d

Skövde - **Detest** was formed in 1988 with members of the band **Coma**. They only played live once in 1990 at Skövde Stadsteater. The first line-up featured Micke Därth (g/v), Ermin Mujnovic (g), Jörgen Svahn (b) and Niklas Landin (d). The first three-track demo, *The Masterpiece* was recorded already in 1988 and so was the second, *The Meaning Of Pain*. On this one Ermin had left to work with Mika Korpi (**Cosmic Zoo**) and he was replaced by Yngve Frank. In 1989, on the third demo *Killer On Halloween*, Ermin was back again, but with Landin out of the band Därth handled the drums here. The second 1989 demo *Death Dance* saw a vast change of personnel leaving only Därth and Svahn doing all the work, plus guest solos from Yngve Frank and Jocke Därth. The 1990 demo *Thundersteel* saw the return of drummer Landin and the addition of guitarist Janne Johansson (now Ström), formerly of **Trace** and later in **Slug**. The band now decided it was time to make a proper impact and the MLP was recorded, som of the tracks were earlier found on the last demo, but re-recorded. After the MLP the band recorded the demo *The Shambles Of Styx* in 1991 after which the band split. What actually happened was that the band met Danish guitarist Finn Zierler, who drafted Micke, Niklas and Janne for his band **Twilight** (later **Beyond Twilight**). Micke Därth is now in progressive metal band **Nocturnal Alliance**. **Detest**'s MLP is a classic metal collector's wet dream. Classic **Metal Church** style power metal. The track *Killer On Halloween*, from the 2CD, was later re-written for **Nocturnal Alliance**, and on the demo, plus on some other tracks, features Thomas G.Son (**Masquerade**) on lead guitar.

1990 MLP - DT-01

1990	■	Thundersteel	MLP 5tr	private	DT-01	$$$

Tracks: Thundersteel/Chains Of Hell/Cold Steel Tears Your Flesh/Steinhurst Chainsaws/Oblivion (outro). 300 copies.

2012	☐	THUNDERSTEEL	2CD	Stormspell/Red White Heävy	SSR-RWH-87

23 demo bonus tracks.

DETHRONEMENT

Jörgen Örnhem: v/b, Johan Orre: g, Johan Jonasson: g, Andreas Mitroulis: d

Växjö - The band was formed in 1993 by Jonasson and Örnhem as a project under the name **Bacon Warriors**. Add Mitroulis (later in **Birdflesh, Overdeth, General Surgery, Jigsore Terror, Sayyadina**) on drums. In 1996 they changed their style from food metal to death, and their

1999 CD - LNP 088

name to the slightly cooler **Dethronement**. The first four track promo was recorded in 1997, and a second, nine track entitled *Astral Serenity*, released later the same year. The latter was issued on CD in 2008 on Jonasson's own label Narcism Records. With the addition of guitarist Johan Orre they released their third demo *Breeding The Demonseed* in 1998, a demo also issued on CD in 2008. In 1999 the band was signed by the short-lived Loud 'N Proud Records, who released the band's debut album *Survival Of The Sickest*. The album suffers from quite poor production and it's quite a thrashy death metal album with simple and primitive melodies with hints of **Dissection**. After the album Orre left the band and later joined **Hypnosia**. He was replaced by Robert Lilja in 2000. For a period of time singer Kristoffer Svensson (**Tears Of Grief, Exanthema**) was in and out of the band. In 2000 the band also recorded the album *World Of Disgust* that is still unreleased due to Loud 'N Proud going bust. In 2002 the band recorded their last demo, entitled *Steel Manufactured Death*. The band split in 2003. Jonasson (as J.J. Glitter) and Lilja (as Rob Paris) went on to form metal band (later glam/sleaze) **Danger**. In 2008 Jonasson released the solo MCD *All That Glitters* and later became a member of the band **Redlight Attraction**. The album contains a cover of **Massacre**'s *Dawn Of Eternity*. If the last two albums actually do exist is a bit uncertain. Noone seems to know, not even the members...

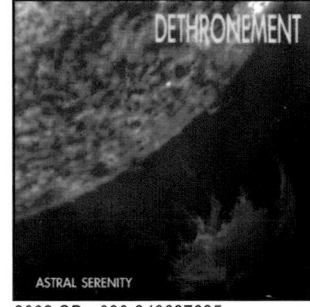
2008 CD - 030-240687625

1999 ■ SURVIVAL OF THE SICKEST	CD	Loud 'N Proud	LNP 008
2008 ■ ASTRAL SERENITY	CD	Narcism Records	030-240687625
2008 ☐ BREEDING THE DEMONSEED	CD	Narcism Records	030-272880645

DeVAN
Eric "De Van" Nytomt: v, Mikael "Mike" Lavér: g, Greg Andersson: g,
Johan Adler: k, Simon "Cee" Algesten: b, Bjarne Gudmundsson: d

Arvika - The journey started when singer Eric met producers Tord Bäckström and Stefan Åberg in 2007. Eric had been hired to lay down vocals for an MTV theme song. A first digital EP was released under Eric De Van's name. In 2008 bass-played Cee joined the singer. He was followed by Andersson, Lavér, Adler and drummer Joakim Janthe, later replaced by Gudmundsson. *DeVan* played its first gig in the spring of 2009, only three weeks after the line-up had been solidified. Lavér is also found in **Dynazty**. Modern, pop-oriented melodic metal with plenty of synths and loops. In 2012 Eric participated in the Swedish version of takent show *The Voice*. Keyboardist Adler was replaced by Joan Ericsson in 2012. Bjarne was formerly in punksters **The New Wind**.

2010 CD - JSM 052510

2010 ■ PLANET BOTOX	CD	JamSync Music	JSM 052510

DEVELOP
Lars Ståhl: v, Martin Kronlund: g/v, Mats Bostedt: b, Aki Järvinen: d

Göteborg - The band was formed in 1978, then also featuring guitarist Paolo Mendonca, who later reached bigger stardom on his own before he vanished from the stage and started writing music for other bands/artists, such as Jeff Scott Soto. The band's only claim to fame is however this single. *Develop* produces traditional 80s metal with a strong touch of NWoBHM, but with Swedish vocals. Not bad, at all. After the band split, Martin formed the band **Gypsy Rose**, who were close to being signed by both Geffen and Mausoleum, but it fell through on the finish line. **Gypsy Rose** also featured Mats. Martin was also later found in **Dogface**, who released two albums. **Gypsy Rose** finally reformed and released a long lost album in 2005 and later delivered a follow-up. Kronlund has since also appeared in Canadian rockers **White Wolf, Lover Under Cover** and **Reece Kronlund**, and he runs JM Recording Studio outside Göteborg.

1981 7" - CFR-S-7022

1981 ■ Säg Mej/Vad Vill Du?	7"	CFR	CFR-S-7022

DEVIAN
Erik "Legion" Hagstedt: v, Jonas "Joinus" Mattsson: g,
Tomas Nilsson: g, Roberth Karlsson: b, Emil Dragutinovic: d

Norrköping/Jönköping - Originally formed in 2006 under the name **Rebel Angels**, which soon changed to **Elizium**. After finding other bands of the same name and being signed by Century Media the name was changed to **Devian**. The founders are former **Marduk** members Hagstedt (also in **Ophthalamia**) and Dragutinovic (also in **Nominon, The Legion**). The band was completed by Mattsson (**Sargatana's Reign, Rise And Shine, Nominon**), initially on bass, and Nilsson (**Aktiv Dödshjälp, Suicidal Seduction**). The band claims to be influenced by bands like **Slayer, Iron Maiden, Possessed, Dissection** etc. Quite an accurate description even if I think **Devian** sounds way better, heavier and more interesting than several of the aforementioned. Musically this feels closer to heavy thrash oriented metal than death metal. Great sound, great songs, great arrangements and (to me) acceptable growl makes this a very interesting band in my opinion. *Ninewinged Serpent* was mixed by Fredrik Nordström (**Dream Evil** etc). The debut album featured Legion (v), Joinus (g), Nilsson (b), Dragutinovic (d) and Marcus Lundberg (g). Lundberg, who was also in **Sargatanas Reign** left in 2007 just after the recording. Now Nilsson switched to guitar and Roberth Karlsson (**Pan Thy Monium, Incapacity, Facebreaker, Solar Dawn, Scar Symmetry, Darkified, Edge Of Sanity** etc) was added on bass. Karlsson was out of the band only a year later and was replaced by session bassist Carl Stjärnlöv (**Diabolical, Abscentia**).

2007 CD - 8425-2

2007 ■	NINEWINGED SERPENT	CD	Century Media (USA)	8425-2
2007 ☐	NINEWINGED SERPENT	CD	Century Media	997725-2
2007 ☐	NINEWINGED SERPENT	CD	Century Media	997725-0
	O-card. Bonus: Burning Daylight/Jackal			
2009 ■	GOD TO THE ILLFATED	CD	Century Media	997824-2
2009 ☐	GOD TO THE ILLFATED	CD	Century Media	997824-0
	O-card,sticker. Bonus: Reap The Storm/Raison D'etre			
2009 ☐	GOD TO THE ILLFATED	CD	Century Media (USA)	8524-2
	O-card,sticker. Bonus: Reap The Storm/Raison D'etre			

2009 CD - 997824-2

DEVIANT

Alex: v, Johan Wikmark: g, Magnus Wikmark: g,
Fredrik Holmqvist: b, Erik "EB" Björkegren: d

Uppsala - Deviant released their first four-track demo in 2003, at the time without Fredrik in the line-up. The demo was issued on cassette in 2004, under the name *Tools Of Termination*, by Nuclear Winter Records. The debut CD featured guest spots from *Defleshed* man Gustaf Jorde and *21st Impact* man Ronnie. *Deviant* play high-speed hardcore-oriented death metal, at times quite close to *Repugnant* or *Nasum*. The band was put on ice in 2009. Magnus and EB were also found in sludge/doom band *St. Erik*. EB is also in hardcore/thashers *Always War*, *Inception* and *Valley Of The Dead*. Holmqvist is also in *Inception* and in grindcore band *Splitter*.

2005 ■	LARVAEON	CD	The Spew Records	TS11
2007 ☐	Apathyphus	MCD 4tr	Nuclear Winter Records	NWR 021
	Tracks: Apathyphus/To Give Ends/Weak And Withered/Inhale Exhale (Nasum cover). 500 copies.			

DEVIANT
L A R V A E O N

2005 CD - TS11

DEVIL'S WHOREHOUSE

Valentin Maelstrom: v, Marcus "Markko" Bäckbrant: g,
Morgan "Mogge/Steinmeyer" Håkansson: b, Mikael "Hrafn" Karlsson: d

Norrköping - Side-project of *Marduk*-founder Morgan "Mogge/Steinmeyer" Håkansson initiated in 2000. This is not close to his ordinary territory, but a more punk-oriented installation closer to *Misfits*, which is not so strange since the band started out as a *Misfits/Samhain* coverband. The name was actually taken from a song by *Misfits*. The line-up on the debut featured Zwedda (v), Morgan (g), Roger "B War" Svensson (b) and Mikael "Hrafn" Karlsson (d). One side of the debut album is only *Misfits* covers, while the other is originals. Produced by Magnus "Devo" Andersson. *Revelation Unorthodox* contains a cover of *Christian Death*'s *Deathwish*. After the second album the band took a long break and when returning singer Zwedda Svedbo (*Nifters*, also guitarist in punk bands *Absolute Bastards*, *Acursed*) was replaced by Maelstrom (*Rumur*, *Deadpulse*) and Markko (*Brewmaster*) was added on guitar. *Werewolf* showed a heavier side of the band with some surprising and highly interesting hints of *Mustasch* and *The Cult*, not least in Maelstrom's Glen Danzig meets Ralf Gyllenhammar vocals. On *Blood & Ashes* the line-up had changed with bass player Roger "B War" Svensson out of the band and Morgan had taken over the bass. The last two releases are highly recommended. Hrafn is also found in *IXXI*. In 2011 the band changed its name to *Death Wolf* and have since released two albums.

Werewolf now gone Death Wolf

2000 ☐	The Howling	10" MLP 8tr	Blooddawn	BLOODLP 002
	Tracks: The Howling/Blood Nymphoman/Erotikill/We Live Again/Halloween (Misfits cover)/Black Dream/All Hell Breaks Loose (Misfits cover)/Moribound			
2000 ☐	The Howling	MCD 8tr	Blooddawn	BLOOD 004
2000 ☐	The Howling	MLP PD 9tr	Blooddawn	BLOODPLP 002
	1000 copies. Bonus: We Bite			
2003 ☐	REVELATION UNORTHODOX	CD	Blooddawn	BLOODCD 015
2003 ☐	REVELATION UNORTHODOX	LP	Blooddawn	BLOODLP 015
2003 ☐	REVELATION UNORTHODOX	LP PD	Blooddawn	BLOODPLP 015
	Special edition available through Ginza Records with PD in frame.			
2003 ☐	REVELATION UNORTHODOX	CD	Regain Records(USA)	BLOODNA 1016
2004 ☐	THE HOWLING	CDd	Blooddawn	BLOOD 016
	Bonus: Bullet/Children In Heat/Halloween 2. All Misfits covers. Different artwork			
2008 ☐	Werewolf	MCD 3tr	Regain Records	BLOOD 039
	Tracks: Werewolf/Mouth Of Hell/Pentagram Murderer			
2008 ☐	Werewolf	7" 3tr	Regain Records	BLOODEP 039
2008 ☐	Werewolf	MLP PD	Regain Records	BLOODPLP 039
2009 ■	BLOOD & ASHES	CD	Regain Records	BLOOD 042 CD

DEVILS WHOREHOUSE
· Blood & Ashes ·

2009 CD - BLOOD 042 CD

DEVILICIOUS

Mikael Jacobsson: g/v, Martin Olsson: g, Carl Paulsen: b, Stefan Jansson: d

Göteborg - Devilicious was formed by Jacobsson and Paulsen in 2005. The band's second outing, *Samsara*, was voted EP of the month in Close-Up Magazine. In 2009 guitarist Martin Olsson (ex-*Nevärlläjf*) and drummer Stefan Jansson joined. In 2009 they released the digital album *Constructing Hell*. *Develicious* play stoner-oriented heavy rock, at times with a touch of *Volbeat*. Quite catchy, but still heavy.

DEVILICIOUS
the asylum gospels

2011 CD - DTM 027

Website: www.devilicious.se

2006 ☐	The Haunt Of Fear	MCD 5tr	Micxter Records		MJ07

Tracks: I Sold My Soul To The Devil/Bride Of Satan/Panda/Misery/Welcome Sinners

2007 ☐	Samsara	MCD 6tr	Micxter Records		n/a

Tracks: Torch/The Perverted/Jesus/And Let The Devil Ride/Finders Fee/Days Like Cocaine

2011 ■	THE ASYLUM GOSPELS	CD	Dead Tree Music		DTM 027
2012 ■	THE ESOTERIC PLAYGROUND	CD	Rambo		FLP 001

2012 CD - FLP 001

DEVILLE

Andreas Bengtsson: v/g, Martin Hambitzer: g, Markus Åkesson: b, Markus Nilsson: d

Malmö - *Deville* were formed in 2003 when Åkesson returned from Australia and Hambitzer gave up playing soulless pop and they joined the duo Bengtsson and Nilsson to form a heavy stoner band. *Deville* are one of Sweden's numerous stoner bands, with the significant detuned heavy muffled Les Paul riffs borderlining on a *Black Sabbath* touch, plus some influences of *Kyuss* and *Fu Manchu* here and there. *Hydra* saw the band stepping it up a bit. Killer album!

2005 ■	SERGEJ THE FREAK MEETS DEVILLE (split)	CD	Darevedil		DD 032

Split with Sergej The Freak. Tracks: Hands Of Mine/From Below/Devola/The Wreck The You Make/Seven/Lowride/Get It Right/Thorn In My Side

2007 ☐	COME HEAVY SLEEP	CD	Buzzville		BUZZCD 024
2009 ☐	HAIL THE BLACK SKY	CD	Buzzville		BUZZCD 032
2013 ☐	HYDRA	CD	Small Stone		SS-137
2013 ☐	HYDRA	LP	Small Stone		SS-137-LP

100 black, 100 gold, 100 blue, 100 green and 100 white/gold/blue marble vinty.

2005 CD - DD 032

DEVLIN

Lexi: v, Marcus Ehlin: v/g/b/d

Stockholm - *Devlin* is a side-project initiated by *Siebenbürgen* man Marcus formed already back in 1994. However, it was not until 2001 Marcus decided to take action. Early 2002 he recorded a first 3-track demo that found its way to Napalm Records, who offered Marcus a deal. Just before the recordings of the album he split with the singer, but soon found then 24 year old singer Lexi, who started recording two weeks later. The result speaks for itself. The style is way more melodic than Marcus' other bands, goth-influenced melodic rock with hints of *Within Temptation*, mixing clean female vocals from Lexi with the occasional growls from Marcus. A really great album. They also do a really cool version of Billy Idol's *White Wedding*. Marcus is also found in *A Canorous Quintet* and *Maledictum*.

2002 ■	GRAND DEATH OPENING	CD	Napalm Records		NPR 114
2002 ☐	GRAND DEATH OPENING	CD	Irond (Russia)		02-402

2002 CD - NPR 114

DEVOURMENT

Johan Axelsson (Liiva): v/b, Anders Gyllensten: g, Ramon Novak: g, Max Thornell: d

Växjö - *Devourment* were formed in 1990 influenced by bands like *Master, Death Strike* and *Repulsion*. They recorded a three-track rehearsal demo in August 1990. The band however dissolved, and Liiva and Thornell went on to form *Furbowl*. The single (initially an unauthorised release) was recorded live in 1990. Liiva/Axelsson has later been found in bands like *Arch Enemy, Nonexist, Hearse* and *Carnage*, Gyllensten in *Violent Work Of Art* and *Thrashholes*, Thornell in *Satanarchy, Hearse* and *Wonderflow*.

2007 ■	Shallow Grave/Too Late	7"	Ancient Enemy Records		002
2010 ☐	Shallow Grave/Too Late	7"	Detest/Me Saco Un Sojo		DR015/MSUO-11

2007 7" - 002

DEXTER JONES' CIRCUS ORCHESTRA

Tia Marklund: v/g, David Israelsson: g, Mathew Bethancourt: g,
Fredrik Jonsson: b, Daniel Israelsson: d

Umeå/Stockholm - This strangely named unit was formed in Umeå in 2000, but later relocated to Stockholm. The debut single and album featured Tia, David, Daviel, Fredrik and guitarist Magnus Bergqvist. The album is a pretty good, quite riff oriented, slightly progressive album in a groovy seventies vein with hints of vintage *Granmax*, *Epitaph* and *Blue Öyster Cult*. Interestingly enough, despite being on two stoner labels, on none of the bands albums there are any heavily distorted guitars. The sound is quite clean, yet heavy. On the excellent album *Side By Side* the line-up had changed, now featuring Tia (v/b), David (g), Håkan Dalsfelt (g), Kent Jonsson (g), Björn Billgren (g), Daviel (d). The last album has taken a slightly more rock/pop-oriented vein more akin to bands like *Mando Diao*, which is not quite as interesting in my opinion.

2003 ☐	The Losers Are Back In Town/I Should Have Known	7"	Freebird		FRV 015
2004 ☐	DEXTER JONES' CIRCUS ORCHESTRA	CD	Freebird		FRC 018

2007 CD - FUZZCD 007

| 2006 ☐ | Morbyn Outtakes | MCD 4tr | Freebird | FRC 022 |

Tracks: In Front Of You All/A Dirty Thing/I Do My Best/Expectations

2007 ■	SIDE BY SIDE	CD	Fuzzorama	FUZZCD 007
2010 ■	IF LIGHT CAN'T SAVE US, I KNOW DARKNESS WILL	CDd	Fuzzorama	FUZZCD 011
2010 ☐	IF LIGHT CAN'T SAVE US, I KNOW DARKNESS WILL	LPg	Fuzzorama	FUZZLP 004

500 copies.

2010 CDd - FUZZCD 011

DIABLO SWING ORCHESTRA

Annlouice Lögdlund: v, Daniel Håkansson: g/v, Pontus Mantefors: g/k, Johannes Bergion: cello, Anders "Andy" Johansson: b, Petter Karlsson: d

Stockholm - It all began in 1501… or rather 2003, when two young men, descendants of the original members of **The Devils Orchestra**, decided to blow new life into the band that had been in a deep sleep for centuries. Extremely extreme and unconventional music without any boundaries. They mix everything from heavy driving metal to jazz, swing and Mariachi style music with trumpets, cello, violin, flute, heavy drums, thumping bass and driving heavy guitar work, topped with high-pitched opera style female vocals. Extremely well-produced debut by Pelle Saether at Studio Underground, which came as a musical shock to the market, but a positive one as such. It was initially released by the band, but soon picked up by Candlelight Records. The second album was recorded by Roberto Laghi (**Mustasch, Freak Kitchen, LOK**) and shows yet another highly exciting and even more playful musical journey. In 2010 Petter Karlsson (**Therion, Master Massive, Conspiracy, Distorted Wonderland, Holocaster**) replaced Andreas Halvarsson as their new full time drummer.

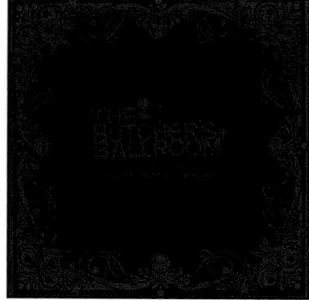

2007 CD - CANDLE195CD

2009 CDd - ASC2301-3CD

2006 ☐	THE BUTCHER'S BALLROOM	CDd	Guillotine Grooves	GILDSO2006
2007 ■	THE BUTCHER'S BALLROOM	CD	Candlelight	CANDLE195CD
2007 ☐	THE BUTCHER'S BALLROOM	CD	Sirenette Music Industry (USA)	DSO0601
2007 ☐	THE BUTCHER'S BALLROOM	CDd	MALS (Russia)	MALS 192
2009 ■	SING ALONG SONGS FOR THE DAMNED & DELIRIOUS	CDd	Ascendance Records	ASC2301-3CD
2009 ☐	SING ALONG SONGS FOR THE DAMNED & DELIRIOUS	CD+DVD	Ascendance Records	ASC2301-3CDSP

Tin box also featuring postcards, pewter pendant, sticker.

2009 ☐	SING ALONG SONGS FOR THE DAMNED & DELIRIOUS	CDd	Sensory (USA)	SKU SR3050
2011 ☐	THE BUTCHER'S BALLROOM	LP	Ascendance Records	ASC23014LPSP
2011 ☐	SING ALONG SONGS FOR THE DAMNED & DELIRIOUS	LP	Ascendance Records	ASC2301-3LPSP
2012 ■	PANDORA'S PIÑATA	CD	Candlelight (USA)	CANDLE 362 CD
2012 ☐	PANDORA'S PIÑATA	CDd	Candlelight (USA)	CANDLE 363 CDSE

Digi book with different artwork.

| 2012 ☐ | PANDORA'S PIÑATA | LP | Back On Black | BOBV 345 LP |

2012 CD - CANDLE 362 CD

DIABOLICAL

Sverker "Vidar" Widgren: g/v, Tobias Jansson: g, Dan Darforth: g, Carl Stjärnlöv: b, Pär Ivy: d

Sundsvall - Vidar formed the band in 1995 under the name **Misanthropic Orchestra**. The first line-up featured Vidar, Jens "Agilma" Blomdal (v), Phamarus (b) and Kim "Keuron" Thalén (d). The track *Natural Selection* was featured on the first *Voices Of Death*-compilation under this name. In 1998 the band changed its name to **Diabolical**. The first split with **Blazing Skies**, *Northern Triumphators* (MC, Cadla 1998) was recorded with Vidar (g), Lars Söderberg (b/d, later in **Maitreya**) and singer Blomdal (later in **Haimad**, died of a GHB overdose in 2007). Söderberg was later in **Maitreya** and Thalén in **Haimad**. On the first MCD the line-up featured Vidar, guitarist Hans Carlsson (**Odhinn, Horde Of Hel, Valkyria, In Battle**), singer Magnus "Infaustus" Ödling (**Setherial, Blackwinds, Fenria**) and bassist/drummer Söderberg (**Maitreya**). The band was initially using the services of bassplayer Jonas Berndt (**Mörk Gryning, Wyvern**) for live-gigs. They did a cover of *No Remorse* on the **Metallica** tribute *Metal Militia Vol 3* (2001). Both *Synergy* and *A Thousand Deaths* are highly accomplished and really well-played death-oriented thrash metal albums, a bit in the vein of **Slayer**, but better in my opinion. Lots of nice twists and turns, cool riffs and tempo changes. Well-played and well produced (by Pelle Saether, Studio Underground). The band did some tours with **Amon Amarth**, **Vomitory** and **Defleshed**. In 2002 the band recruited bassist Roger Bergsten (**Hectorite, Syn:drom**), but after the tours a new rhythm section was drafted and the band now consisted of Vidar, Hans, Magnus, plus new bassist Rickard Persson and drummer Henric Ohlsson (**Theory In Practice**). Some shows were played in 2002, but soon the clashes in schedules meant Ohlsson had to leave and after several months of auditions the band finally found Carl Stjärnlöv (**Devian, Absentia**) in 2003. Due to Vidar's heavy work schedule at Necromorbus Studio the work was however put on hold for several years, before they returned with a vengeance with *The Gallery Of Bleeding Art* in 2008. Vidar has also recorded with **Demonical**. *Ars Vitae* contains both new material and older unreleased stuff, plus some live tracks. The line-up had again changed. In August 2010 bass player Rickard Persson was replaced by Dan Darforth. On the latest recording the members have been switched around and exchanged, where Carl plays bass, Darforth is on guitar, Widgren handles vocals and guitar, Tobias Jansson has taken over Hans Carlsson's duties and new drummer Pär Ivy has been added to the line up. In July 2012 the band entered Necromorbus Studio to record their fifth album *Neogenesis*.

Diabolical guys who left misanthropia behind

2001 CD - SC 026-2

2002 CD - SC 044-2

Year		Title	Format	Label	Catalog
2000	☐	Deserts Of Desolation	MCD 4tr	Cadla Communications (W EuR)	CADLA 008

Tracks: Ashes/Guidance Of Sins/Deserts/The Dreaming Dead

2000	☐	Deserts Of Desolation	MCD 4tr	Guano (Estonia)	GR003MCD
2000	☐	Deserts Of Desolation	MCD 4tr	Civilian Death Network (USA)	CDN 002
2001	■	SYNERGY	CD	Scarlet	SC 026-2
2001	☐	SYNERGY	CD	World War III (USA)	CD 71175
2001	☐	The Misantropis Ceremonies	MCD	Spikekult	012

Split with Watain. Tracks: Wartide (All Out Genocide), demo version. 300 copies.

2002	■	A THOUSAND DEATHS	CD	Scarlet	SC 044-2
2002	☐	A THOUSAND DEATHS	CD	CD-Maximum (Russia)	CDM 1314
2002	☐	A THOUSAND DEATHS + SYNERGY	2CD	Zenor Records (Brazil)	ZENOR 03
2008	☐	THE GALLERY OF BLEEDING ART	CD	ViciSolum	VSP 002
2010	■	ARS VITAE	CD	ViciSolum	VSP 015
2013	☐	NECROGENESIS	CD digi book	ViciSolum	VSP 042

2010 CD - VSP 015

DIABOLICAL MASQUERADE

Anders "Blackheim" Nyström: v/g/k/b/d

Stockholm - This is the solo-project from *Katatonia*/*Bewitched* guitarist Andreas Nyström initi-ated in 1993. Like his other projects, this one is of course also an out and out death metal band. *Nightwork* and *Death's Design* were produced by Dan Swanö, who also contributed with some keyboards. *Death's Design* actually has 61 (!) songs and was composed as theme-music for a movie with the same title. It's of course more symphonic with lots of different moods and twists. Drums on most of the albums were played by Sean C. Bates. The project was laid to rest in 2004. *Website: www.diabolicalmasquerade.com/*

1996	☐	RAVENDUSK IN MY HEART	CD	Adipocere	CD AR 036
1997	☐	THE PHANTOM LODGE	CD	Adipocere	CDAR 039
1999	■	NIGHTWORK	CD	Avantgarde	AV 033
1999	☐	NIGHTWORK	LP	Avantgarde	AV 033

Bonus: Cryztalline Fiendz. 500 copies.

2001	■	DEATH'S DESIGN - THE LOST SOUNDTRACK	CD	Avantgarde	AV 055
2001	☐	DEATH'S DESIGN - THE LOST SOUNDTRACK	LP	Avantgarde	AV 055
2001	☐	DEATH'S DESIGN - THE LOST SOUNDTRACK	CD	Olympic	OLY 2020-2
2001	☐	RAVENDUSK IN MY HEART	LP PD	Vinyl Collectors	VC 014
2002	☐	DEATH'S DESIGN	CD	Irond (Russia)	02-217
2003	☐	NIGHTWORK	CD	Irond (Russia)	CD 03-441
2004	☐	RAVENDUSK IN MY HEART	CD	Irond (Russia)	CD 04-417
2004	☐	THE PHANTOM LODGE	CD	Irond (Russia)	CD 04-718
2005	☐	RAVENDUSK IN MY HEART	LP	Profound Lore (Canada)	PFL 004-04
2006	☐	RAVENDUSK IN MY HEART	CDd	Peaceville	CDVILED 159
2007	☐	THE PHANTOM LODGE	CDd	Peaceville	CDVILED 160
2007	☐	NIGHTWORK	CDd	Peaceville	CDVILED 161

Bonus: Cryztalline Fiends.

2007	☐	DEATH'S DESIGN	CDd	Peaceville	CDVILED 162

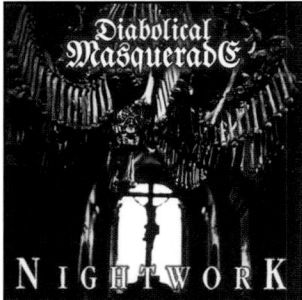

1999 CD - AV 033

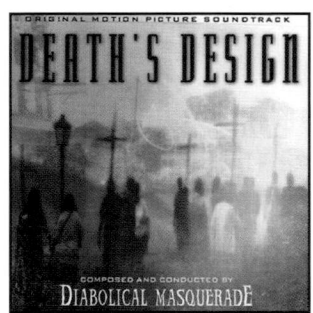

2001 CD - AV 055

DIABOLICUM

Tommy "Blackblood" Dahlström: v, Björn "Sasrof" Holmberg: g,
Zeb "Nathzion" Nilsson: g, Kalle "Gorgorium" Antonsson: b, Arttu "Amath" Malkki: d

Sundsvall - In December 1994 Sasrof and Daniel "Thorne" Edström formed *Imperial*. The first two track demo, recorded in a mental hospital, was entitled *Mori Volunatia*. Blackblood provided vocals for the demo. Thorne left the band and drummer Amath (later in *Equinox Ov The Gods*, *Souldrainer*, *Aeon*) and bass player Kalle "Gorgorium" Antonsson joined. Thyrfing provided vocals and lead guitar on the 1996 demo *The Imperial Darkness*. Amanth left and was replaced by Håkan "Myseriis" Sjödin (*Setherial*) and Thyrfing was replaced by the returning Blackblood. The demo *De fördömdas legion* was released. In 1997 the members from *Imperial* formed *Helvete* together with Per "Kraath" Hellqvist (*Setherial*). As Sasrof joined *Setherial* on bass in 1998 the band was put on hold. In 1999 *Imperial* changed their name to *Diabolicum*. In 1999 the debut album was recorded featuring Blackblood (v), Sasrof (g), Nathzion (g) and Gorgorium (b). *The Dark Blood Rising* featured guest spots from singers Caroline Darkness, John Odhinn Sandin, Elena Schirenc and Martin Schirenc. The drums were programmed by Amath. *The Killing Spree 1.5* features five new tracks, a demo track from 1999 and the remastered *Imperial* demos *De fördömdas legion* and *The Imperial Darkness*. Arttu, Zeb and Tommy are also found in *Aeon* and *Defaced Creation*, while Sasrof handled the bass and synth in *Setherial*. Some of the lyrics on *The Dark Blood Rising* were written by the late Jon Nödtveit (*Dissection*) while he was still in jail. In 2004 the band recorded the album *Vengeance (The Matricide)* for Code 666 Records, but not happy with the result is has remained unreleased. In 2005 Niklas "Kvarforth" Olsson of *Shining* joined on vocals and guitar and the bass was handled by Daniel "D.D. Executioner" Johansson (*Angst, Kill, Sadistic Grimness*). Gorgorium is now found in *Assassins* and Sasrof in *The Bloodline*. After some years of silence Sasrof, Gorgorium and Niklas Kvarforth gathered forces and a new album, entitled *In The Night Of The Scarecrow*, was in the works. Fast and brutal industrial style black metal, quite straight-ahead and with semi-growling *Venom* style vocals.

1999 CD - NPR 095

2001 CDd - CODE 008

2001 CDd - CODE 005

2001 7" - SPK EP 012

1999 ■	GRANDEUR OF HELL	CD	Napalm Records	NPR 065
2001 ■	THE DARK BLOOD RISING (THE HATECROWNED RETALIATION)	CDd	Code666	CODE 005
2001 □	THE DARK BLOOD RISING (THE HATECROWNED RETALIATION)	CDd	Irond (Russia)	01-124
2001 □	THE DARK BLOOD RISING (THE HATECROWNED RETALIATION)	CDd	Mercenary Music (USA)	WAR 033
2001 ■	THE KILLING SPREE 1.5	CDd	Code666	CODE 008

666 copies.

2001 ■	The Misantropis Ceremonies (split)	7"	Spikekult (France)	SPK EP 012

Split with Watain. Track: Wartide (All Out Genocide). 300 hand numbered copies.

2002 □	My Way Is The Way Of The Axe	7" PD	Mester Productions	MP 008
2002 □	THE DARK BLOOD RISING (THE HATECROWNED RETALIATION)	LP PD	Mester Productions	MP 011

500 copies.

2005 ■	Hail Terrror (split)	7"	Eerie Art	EAR 006

Split with Angst. Track: Weaving Fate. 500 copies.

2005 7" - EAR 006

DIABOLIQUE

Kristian Wåhlin: v/g, Johan Österberg: g, Christian "Bino" Carlsson: b, Hans Nilsson: d

Göteborg - Diabolique was founded in 1995 by former *Decollation* drummer Kristian Wåhlin (where he was known as Chris Steele). Kristian, foremost known as Necrolord (also ex-*Grotesque, Liers In Wait*) is foremost known as an outstanding painter, who's made covers for bands like *Mercyful Fate, Bathory, Morgana Lefay, Tad Morose, Narnia* and his own band of course. He was joined by former *Decollation* colleagues Österberg and bass player Alf Svensson (also in *Grotesque, Liers In Wait, Midvinter, Oxiplegatz, At The Gates*) and drummer Daniel Erlandsson (*Liers In Wait, Armageddon, Eucharist, Arch Enemy* etc). When *The Diabolique* was recorded, before the first album in 1996, the line-up featured Wåhlin, Österberg, drummer Nilsson (ex-*Liers In Wait, Ludiferion, Crystal Age, Dimenzion Zero*) and *Seance* man Carlsson. They started out quite doomy and heavy, but already on the the second album they evolved to doomy goth, quite similar to *Paradise Lost*, not at all as metal as you may expect. It also has an extremely beautiful cover, of course painted by Kristian. *The Green Godess* also features guest spots from Jaime Salazar (d), Henrik Larsson (k) and Berno Paulsson (k), who also produced the album. After the release of *The Green Godess* the band immediately started working on the follow-up. 22 songs were recorded and a rough mix was made, but never finished, which finally lead to the decline of the band. In November 2007 Kristian and Johan started writing material for a new *Diabolique* album, at first set to be released in 2009, but later postponed. Kristian, Johan and Hans are also found in *The Great Deceiver*.
Website: www.diabolique.se

1997 CD - BS 11

1999 CD - BS 18

2005 2CD - BLACK 093 DCD

1997 ■	WEDDING THE GROTESQUE	CD	Black Sun	BS 11
1997 □	WEDDING THE GROTESQUE	LP PD	Black Sun	BSLP 11
1998 □	The Diabolique	MCD 5tr	Listenable Records	POSH 11

Tracks: Stealing The Fire From Heaven/Blood Of Summer/Beggar Whipped In Whine/ Sorrow Piercing Art/Deep Shame Of God

1999 ■	THE BLACK FLOWER	CD	Black Sun	BS 18
2000 □	Butterflies	MCD 6tr	Necropolis	NFR 044

Tracks: Rain/Losing You/Butterflies/Summer Of Her Heart/Stolen Moments/Beneath The Shade

2001 □	THE GREEN GODDESS	CD	Necropolis	NR 060
2001 □	THE GREEN GODDESS	CD	Orion Music (Argentina)	OME 001
2005 ■	THE BLACK SUN COLLECTION	2CD	Blackend	BLACK 093 DCD

Re-issue with the two first albums in one pack.

DIARY

Ulrik Arturén: v, Pierre Östh: g, Per Rylander: b, Hans Tanska: k/b/g/d

Borås - Diary was more or less Tanska's solo project, where he drafted the other musicians to help out. He was in the band *Black Rose* between 1984 and 1987, but only some demos came out of this. *River Styx* contains great melodic hard rock, at times similar to 80s *Rainbow*. Arturén is a shamelessly unnoticed singer, who in 2011-2012 started recording a highly promising solo album in the vein of *Yes* and *Anyone's Daughter*.

1998 MCD - HTPE 5792

1998 ■	River Styx	MCD 6tr	private	HTPE 5792

Tracks: Lie To You/Asylum/Give It Up/Diary/Hey You/River Styx

DIAVOX

Håkan Norgren: v/g, Tony Eriksson: g, Stefan Göransson: b, Kari Sävelää: d

Storvik - Good, straight melodic hard rock. The vocals may not be that exiting, but they're not too bad. Similar to the first single by *Highbrow* in style. Well worth checking out. The band later reformed and became *Arizona*. They recorded a demo in 1985, after which they split. Tony is now found in *Morgana Lefay*.

1983 ●	Angel Eye/Black Heart	7"	Pang	PSI 067

1983 7" - PSI 067

DIBBUKIM

Ida Olniansky: v, Niklas Olniansky, Magnus Wohlfart: g, Jacob Blecher: d

Lund - Progressive folk metal with vocals in Yiddish. Musically it's good, but the mix leaves a bit more to be desired, with quite weak vocals overpowering the music. The band was formed in 2009 by the Olnianskys. They drafted Wohlfart (***Anti-Christian Assault, Nae'blis, Vanmakt, Yggdrasil, Wohlfart***). After the single, drummer Blecher was drafted.

2010 ■	Oyfn veg shteyt a boym/(video)	CDS	Grand Master Music	GMM 008
2011 ☐	AZ A FOYGL UN A GOYLEM TANTSN	CD	Grand Master Music	GMM 012

2010 CDS - GMM 008

DIE HARD

Simon Wizén: v/g, Mattias "Harry" Åhrman: b, Per "Perra" Karlsson: d

Uppsala - In 1995 bass player Harry formed a band with its goal to play old-school thrash. The name was also taken from an old **Venom** song. A year later a band featuring Mattias "Harry" Åhrman (b), Andreas "Hasse" Hansson (g/b), Micke (g) and Nicke (d) started rehearsing. **Die Hard** finally took shape in 2005. In 2007 they entered the studio to record their first demo, *Emissaries Of The Reaper*, limited to 200 copies. In January 2008 Micke and Nicke left the band. **Watain** drummer Håkan Jonsson took over the sticks and the band recorded the debut MCD *Evil Always Return*. The track *Die Hard* is a **Venom** cover. Hasse is also in **Searing I.** Ronnie "Ripper" Olsson (**Gehennah/Turbocharged**) guests on the *Thrash Them All* 7", where the line-up featured Hasse, Harry and session drummer Emil "E Forcas" Svensson of **Degial**. Before this drummer Martin Karlsson (**Bloodshed, Mykorrhiza**) made a short stint with the band. *The Hatred's Black Flame* single features some guest vocals from Teddy Möller (**F.K.Ü/ Loch Vostock**) and the B-side is a cover of **Venom**. In 2012 the line-up featured Harry on bass and vocals, Simon Wizén (**Ondskapt, Valkyrja**) on vocals and guitar and Per "Perra" Karlsson (**Nominon, Nex, In Aeternum, Serpent** etc) on drums.

2008 MCD - SMP002

2009 CDd - ARcd068d

2007 ☐	Emissaries Of The Reaper	7"	Angel Of Metal	AOM 009
	Tracks: Pestilent/Necromantic Action/Emissaries Of The Reaper/The Hate Within. 500 numbered copies.			
2008 ■	Evil Always Return	MCD 6tr	S.M.P Records	SMP002
	Tracks: Evil Always Return/Black Mass/Emissaries Of The Reaper/The Weak Lead The Blind/Necromantic Action/Beneath Pain And Death			
2008 ☐	Evil Always Return	MCD 6tr	EMF Records (Mexico)	SMP002
	500 copies			
2008 ☐	Evil Always Return	MCD 6tr	Abyss Records (USA)	ABYSS004CD
2009 ☐	Evil Always Return	MLP 6tr	Agonia Records	Armlp 014
	500 copies.			
2009 ☐	Mercenarys Of Hell/Die Hard (Venom cover)	7"	Agonia Records	AREP 017
2009 ☐	NIHILISTIC VISION	LP	Agonia Records	ARlp065
	500 copies. Poster.			
2009 ☐	NIHILISTIC VISION	CD	Agonia Records	ARcd068
2009 ■	NIHILISTIC VISION	CDd	Agonia Records	ARcd068d
	1000 copies, cover folds out to a cross. Patch. Different artwork.			
2010 ☐	Thrash Them All/Sadistic Pleasure	7"	Agonia Records	ARep019
	Transparent red vinyl and black vinyl.			
2011 ☐	Hatred's Black Flame/Countess Bathory (Venom cover)	7"	Agonia Records	ARep020
	500 copies, 100 dark blue including patch + 400 black.			
2011 ☐	EVIL ALWAYS RETURN/EMISSARIES OF THE REAPER	CDd	Abyss Records	ABYSS 016 CD
	Bonus: The Weak Lead The Blind (rehearsal 2007)/Emissaries Of The Reaper (rehearsal)			
2012 ■	CONJURE THE LEGIONS	CD	Agonia Records	ARCD 104
2012 ☐	CONJURE THE LEGIONS	LPg	Agonia Records	ARLP 101
	434 black + 66 copies in yellow splatter vinyl.			
2012 ☐	Antichrist/Bloodlust (Venom cover)	7"	Agonia Records	AREP 021
	300 copies.			

2012 CD - ARCD 104

DIESEL

Thomas Irgard: v/b, Sten Gustavsson: g, Kalle Stridh: d

Göteborg - Straight hard rock with a bluesy base, quite similar to **Motvind** in their heavier moments. Tomas was ex-**Thunderhog**. One of the few releases on the short lived Ewita-label.

1982 ■	Feber/Rock 'N Roll Lady	7"	Ewita	LSPS 112

1982 7" - LSPS 112

DIESEL DOWN

Thomas Selander: v, Johan Blomdahl: g,
Joakim Eriksson: d, Joakim "Lahger" Lahgerkranser: d

Stockholm - This Stockholm unit was formed in 2005 and slowly built a good local following. Great sounding heavy melodic metal with a singer similar to **Rush**'s Geddy Lee.

2009 ■	DIESEL DOWN	CD	Blue Topaz Records	BTR CD 56

2009 CD - BTR CD 56

DIESELKOPF

Peter Carlfors: v, Ronny Rasmusson: g/b, Ola Lindström: k

Gävle - Initiated in 1993 by former *Twang* guitarist Rasmusson, but things didn't start happening until singer Carlford joined in 1996 and the band's debut was released the year after. Industrial metal in the vein of *Die Krupps*, *Nine Inch Nails* and *Ministry*. Lindström previously recorded with punk band *Lars Langs*. The band now consists of Ronny and singer Pierre Knutsson. Bassist Christian Smedlund and drummer David Lindqvist has also been in the line-up.

1997 ■ USE THE MACHINES FOR YOUR OWN SICK PURPOSE ....CD   private ....CD-BAR 022

1997 CD - CD-BAR 022

DIMENSION ZERO

Jocke Göthberg: v, Daniel Antonsson: g/b, Jesper Strömblad: b/g, Hans Nilsson: d

Göteborg - **Dimenzion Zero** was formed in 1995 as a side-project for *In Flames* members Glenn Ljungström and Jesper Strömblad. They created a band that took the style of their original band a step further when it came to brutality and speed. They were initially called *Agent Orange*, but found out it was already taken. In 1996 the line-up was completed by Göthberg and Hansson and the first MCD was recorded. Jocke had previously played with *Marduk*, *Darkified* and *Cardinal Sin* while Hans was ex-*Diabolique*, *Luciferion* and *Crystal Age*. The line-up on the first MCD also featured guitarist Fredrik Johansson (also in *Chameleon*). In 1997 the band also recorded the track *My Demon* for the *Mercyful Fate Tribute* (Listenable Records) and in 1998 they did *Troops Of Doom* for the *Sepultura* tribute *Sepultural Feast* (Black Sun). The band split in 1998, to reform two years later. Daniel Antonsson (*Pathos*) was part of the line-up, too, but was not on the album. He became a member of the band in 2002. *Silent Night Fever* was mixed by Anders Fridén (*In Flames*). During the recording of *This Is Hell* bass player Glenn Ljungström divorces the band and Antonsson also took care of the bass duties. *He Who Shall Not Bleed* shows a slightly more melodic but also heavier side of the band and it features a guest solo by *Annihilator*'s Jeff Waters. High-class, well-produced, tight and aggressive melodic death metal. *Website: www.dimensionzero.se*

1997 MCD - 97929-3

2002 CD - RR 111010

1997 ■	Penetrations From The Lost World ....MCD 4tr	WAR Music 97929-3

Tracks: Through The Virgin Sky/Dead Silent Shriek/Forgotten But Not Forgiven/Everlasting Neverness

1997 ☐	Penetrations From The Lost World ....MCD 5tr	Toy's Factory (Japan)................. TFCK 87151

Bonus: Troops Of Doom (Sepultura cover)

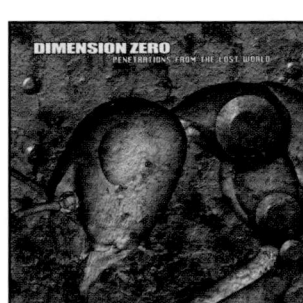

2003 CD - RR0305-028

2002 ☐	SILENT NIGHT FEVER ....LP	Regain Records ....RRLP 111010
2002 ☐	SILENT NIGHT FEVER ....LP PD	Regain Records ....RRPLP 111010
2002 ■	SILENT NIGHT FEVER ....CD	Regain Records ....RR 111010

Bonus: Helter Skelter (Beatles cover)

2002 ☐	SILENT NIGHT FEVER ....CD	Toy's Factory (Japan)................. TFCK 87274

Bonus: Helter Skelter (Beatles cover)

2002 ☐	SILENT NIGHT FEVER ....CD	Century Media (USA)...........................7876-2
2002 ☐	SILENT NIGHT FEVER ....CD	CD-Maximum (Russia) ....CDM 1494
2003 ■	PENETRATIONS FROM THE LOST WORLD....................CD	Regain Records RR0305-028

Bonus: Condemned/Helter Skelter (Beatles cover)/Silent Night Fever (live)/Not Even Dead (live)/The Murder-In (live)/They Are Waiting To Take Us (live)/Through The Virgin Sky (live). New artwork.

2008 CD - VIC005CD

2003 ☐	PENETRATIONS FROM THE LOST WORLD....................CD	CD-Maximum (Russia) ....CDM 2164
2003 ☐	THIS IS HELL...CD	Century Media (USA)...........................8117-2
2003 ☐	THIS IS HELL...CD	Regain Records RR0308-032
2003 ☐	THIS IS HELL...CD	CD-Maximum (Russia) ....CDM 2116
2008 ☐	HE WHO SHALL NOT BLEED.......................................CDd	Vic Records.................................VIC005CD

First edition. Bonus: Stayin' Alive/Rövarvisan

2008 ■	HE WHO SHALL NOT BLEED.......................................CD	Vic Records.................................VIC005CD

DIMHYMN

Jonas "Nattdal" Bergqvist: v/g/b, Alex "Nordsjäl": d

Stockholm - The band was formed in 2003 and released their first demo *Darkened Bleeding Journey* in 2004 and a second followed later the same year, entitled *Det enda eviga*. *Fördärvets maskineri* was also released in 222 cassette copies on the Insikt label. On *Djävulens tid är kommen* *Hypothermia*'s Kim Carlsson provided some additional vocals. The band never gave any interviews. Split late 2006. Lars Jonas "Nattdal" Bergqvist was also found in *Lifelover* (as B), *IXXI* and *Ondskapt*. He was reported dead on September 9, 2011 and the band has also been put to rest. Raw, primitive, old-school black metal.

2005 ■	FÖRDÄRVETS MASKINERI...CD	private .... - -

1000 hand-numbered copies.

2005 ☐	DJÄVULENS TID ÄR KOMMEN ....CD	Insikt Insikt-25-
2006 ☐	DJÄVULENS TID ÄR KOMMEN ....LP	Turannum............................ TUIRANNUM 001

Poster.

2005 CD - - -

| 2006 | ■ SJUKLIG INTENSION (split) | CD | Eerie Art | EAR 011 |

Split with Hypothermia. Tracks: Drakoforism/The City/Projektil

| 2006 | □ SJUKLIG INTENSION (split) | LP | Obscure Abhorrence | OAPDHLP2007 |

500 copies, of which 100 hand numbered in black/red splatter vinyl

DIMMA
Richard Jennische: g/v, Jakob Jennische: b, Olle Nilsson: d

Uppsala - *Dimma* were formed in 1999 and influenced by bands like **Blue Cheer** and **November**, they dug deep in the vaults of the primevil 70s hard rock sounds. Just like forefathers **November** the lyrics are in Swedish. *Pengar i sjön* also featured singer Albert Gustavsson. On *På grund av dimma* Richard had taken over the vocals, which is actually the weak side of an otherwise great band. The album also featured guest solos from Johan Haag and Jakob Orzechowski (**Mugwums**). The latter also helps out on the follow-up. Jakob Jennische also plays drums in the band **454**, bass in **Fuzzdevil**, while he handles vocals and guitar in the band **Mugwupms**, where Olle is also behind the drums. Dimma is fog in Swedish.
Website: www.myspace.com/dimmasweden

2006 CD - EAR 011

2004 CD - GS 010

2000	□ Ingen bur/Skärseld/Mitt regn/Levande bomb	7" 4tr	Group Sounds	- -
2004	■ PENGAR I SJÖN	CD	Group Sounds	GS 010
2008	■ PÅ GRUND AV DIMMA	CD	Group Sounds	GS 012
2011	□ TREDJE DIMMA	LP	Group Sounds	GS 014

2008 CD - GS 012

DIMMZ
Sonny Andersson: g/v, Andreas Eriksson: g,
Jens Åkesson: b, Andreas Karlsson: d

Kristianstad - The foundation of **DimmZ** was made back in 2003 under the name **Mizery**, but shortly after changed their name to **DimmZ**. A demo was recorded in 2006 and the current formation took shape in 2007, when they also released the second demo *Ways In Life*. The debut was released by Blue Topaz and the band played support for **Dead By April**, **Deathstars** and **Lillasyster**. In 2010 the band were picked up by US label Sliptrick who released their second album. Straight-ahead quite melodic metal with a touch of **Metallica** at times.

| 2008 | □ THIS IS LIFE | CD | Blue Topaz | BTRCD 21 |
| 2010 | ■ STILL HUMAN? | CD | Sliptrick | SLP010.022 |

2010 CD - SLP010.022

DIONDA
Nicke Wadström: g/v, Isse Isaksson: b, Mika Kahilainen: d

Stockholm - The band was formed in 1986 and recorded a punk-single under the name **Dacke**. It was an on and off operation during the years up until they became **Dionda** in 2001. The album was recorded at Studio Sunlight. The title *Dockhusdocka* means "Doll house doll". Mika was also in reggae-group **Tom Bombadill** and Nicke has been in hardcore bands **Karoshi** and **Farbror Arg** (aka **Svart Snö**). He also runs B-Head Records. **Dionda** is very similar to **LOK** or **Rage Against The Machine**, dead heavy and crunchy rap-core with Swedish vocals. High-quality stuff!
Website: www.dionda.org

| 2002 | ■ DOCKHUSDOCKA | CD | B-Head | BHR 05 |

2002 CD - BHR 05

DIONYSUS
Olaf Hayer: v, Johnny Öhlin: g, Kaspar Dahlberg: k,
Magnus "Nobby" Norberg: b, Ronny Milianowicz: d

Bålsta - In the autumn of 1999 Ronny (ex-**Sinergy**) and Johnny (ex-**Nation**, **Sinergy** touring guitarist) formed a band they named after the Greek wine God. Johnny called his former **Nation** colleague Nobby and in 2000 Ronny drafted German singer Olaf (ex-**Chrystyne**, **Luca Turilli**) and Kaspar (ex-**Treasure Land, Stormwind**). The three track demo *Paradise Land* (2001) lead to a deal with AFM. The debut album was recorded in Rhön Studio (**Edguy, Avantasia**), produced by Tobias Sammet and mixed by Tommy Newton (**Helloween, Victory** etc). The style is classically influenced melodic power metal, in the same musical region as Italian band **Rhapsody**, **Edguy** or **Avantasia**. *Keep The Spirit* is a compilation with some unreleased bonus tracks. *Tales Of Dionysus* is a two CD package of *Anima Mundi* and *Fairytales And Reality*. In 2007 Ronny left the band, shortly after followed by Kaspar. The band recruited new members Joakim Floke (k) and Johannes Berg (d), but was permanently put to rest in 2008 as both Ronny and Nobby devoted their time to their new career in the band **Saint Deamon**.

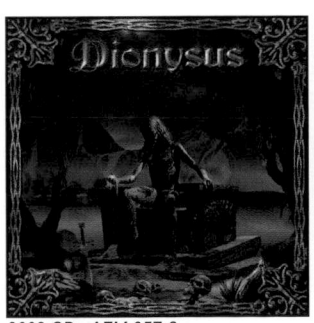

2002 CD - AFM 057-2

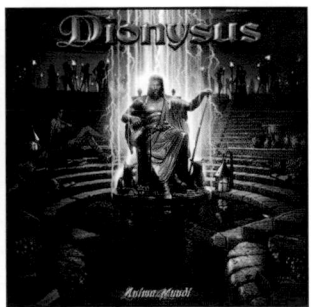

2004 CD - AFM 074-2

225

2002	☐ SIGN OF TRUTH	CDp	Painful Lust	PL CD 006-2
	Paper pocket promo. Bonus: Loaded Gun			
2002	■ SIGN OF TRUTH	CD	AFM	AFM 057-2
2002	☐ SIGN OF TRUTH	CD	CD-Maximum (Russia)	CDM 1262
2002	☐ SIGN OF TRUTH	CD	Avalon Marquee (Japan)	MICP-10331
	Bonus: Key Into The Past			
2003	☐ TOUR PROMO 2003 (split)	CD	AFM	AFM Tour Promo 2003
	Split with Axxis. Promo in paper pocket. Tracks: Anima Mundi/March For Freedom/Divine/			
	Bringer Of War			
2004	■ ANIMA MUNDI	CD	AFM	AFM 074-2
	Bonus: March for Freedom (radio edit)			
2004	☐ ANIMA MUNDI	CD	AFM	AFM 074-2
	Limited edition with different track order. Bonus: Closer To The Sun/Holy War (pre-produc-			
	tion, 2001)+ video Time will Tell. as bonuses instead of "March for Freedom" (radio edit)			
2004	☐ ANIMA MUNDI	CD	Avalon Marquee (Japan)	MICP-10422
	Bonus: Closer To The Sun (demo)			
2006	■ FAIRYTALES AND REALITY	CD	AFM	AFM 105-2
2006	☐ FAIRYTALES AND REALITY	CDd	AFM	AFM 105-9
	Bonus: Time Will Tell (demo)/Bringer Of Salvation (demo)/Videoclip and making of			
2006	☐ FAIRYTALES AND REALITY	CD	CD-Maximum (Russia)	CDM 1794
	Bonus: Time Will Tell (demo)/Bringer Of Salvation (demo)/Videoclip and making of			
2006	☐ FAIRYTALES AND REALITY	CD	Victor (Japan)	SRCD-2890
	Bonus: Time Will Tell (demo)/Bringer Of Salvation (demo)/Videoclip and making of			
2006	☐ FAIRYTALES AND REALITY	CDd	CD-Maximum (Russia)	CDM 2660
	Bonus: Videoclip and making of			
2008	■ KEEP THE SPIRIT	CD	AFM	AFMCD 226-2
2009	☐ TALES OF DIONYSUS	DCD	AFM	AFMCD 276-3

2006 CD - AFM 105-2

2008 CD - AFMCD 226-2

DIPLOMA

Tom Åsberg: v, Frank Thunström: g, David Funck: g, Emil Wigelius: b, Olle Karvonen: d

Falun - *Diploma* were formed in the winter of 2006. This young unit produces high-class seventies influenced heavy rock with a modern touch. Nice heavy riffing and great musical qualities and they put their own personal twist to the style and sound. Their debut album was released in 2008, but already in May 2009 the band put up five new tracks on MySpace, demo versions from a forthcoming second album. In December 2009 singer Tom left the band in the middle of the recordings of the new album. After this the band changed their name to ***Blind By Attraction*** and the line-up now features Frank on guitar and vocals, David, Emil and Olle. The band's debut under the new name has the working title *Fors Fortuna* and was set to be released in 2010, but still hasn't been released. The style of the new tracks promises more of the same as the excellent *Diploma* album. Frank has also recorded some solo stuff under the name Franky Zak. Emil and Frank have also recorded an album with the band ***Mozkovitch***, also on BLP.

| 2008 | ■ AI | CD | BLP | BLP 2008-01 |

2008 CD - BLP 2008-01

DIRTY OLD MEN, THE

Tony Carlsson: v/b, Olle Boson: g, Janne "Jie" Zelf: d

Stockholm - Tony was formerly in garage-rockers ***The Nomads***. The ***D.O.M.***'s first release is also more of a garage-rock type thing, while the second album was pure hard rock with influences from the old 70s school as well as traditional hard rock with a bluesy touch. After these releases guitarist, Mr. South left the band. *Reflections Of..* is a true ***Cream*** meets ***Hendrix*** piece. The albums are only out on vinyl and have yet to be re-issued on CD.

1987	☐ Need Love Too	MLP 4tr	Swingin Zombie Productions	SZS 101
	Tracks: Female Animal/Big Black Coon/Making Time/How To Ride			
1988	☐ FERTILIZATION	LP	Swingin Zombie Productions	SZS 212
1992	■ REFLECTIONS OF	LP	Swingin Zombie Productions	SZS 323

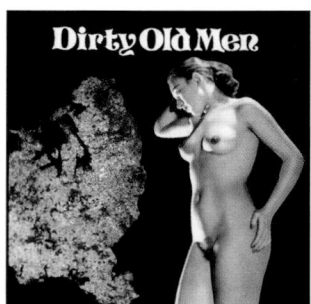

1992 LP - SZS 323

DIRTY PASSION

Emil Ekbladh: v, Christoffer Lohikoski Svensson: g,
Björn Wilander: b, Markus Wiberg: d

Stockholm/Hässleholm - *Dirty Passion* are a classic melodic hard rock band, drawing their influences from the 70s and 80s. The band was formed in 2006, recorded some demos before being signed by Transubstans sub-label Denomination Records. Christoffer is also found in ***Sleazy Joe***.
Website: www.dirtypassion.net

| 2010 | ■ DIFFERENT TOMORROW | CD | Denomination Records | DEN 002 |
| 2012 | ■ IN WONDERLAND | CD | Denomination Records | DEN 004 |

2010 CD - DEN 002

Year		Title	Format	Label	Cat. No.
2005	☐	LIKE AN EVER FLOWING STREAM	CD	Karmageddon	KARMA 092

Bonus: Deathevocation (demo)/Defective Decay (demo)/Torn Apart/Justifiable Homicide

| 2005 | ☐ | PIECES | CD | Regain Records | RR 062 |

Bonus: Torn Apart, plus 9 tracks live in Stockholm 1993.

| 2005 | ☐ | PIECES | CD | CD-Maximum (Russia) | CDM 2343 |
| 2005 | ■ | INDECENT AND OBSCENE | CDd | Regain Records | RR 063 |

Bonus: Hill 112/Beyond The Unholy Grave (Death cover)

| 2005 | ☐ | INDECENT AND OBSCENE | CD | Candlelight (USA) | CDL 0229 CD |
| 2005 | ☐ | MASSIVE KILLING CAPACITY | CD | Regain Records | RR 064 |

Bonus: Justifiable Homicide/Collection By Blood (demo)/Life – Another Shape Of Sorrow (demo)/On Frozen Fields-Shadowlands (demo)

| 2005 | ☐ | MASSIVE KILLING CAPACITY | CD | Candlelight (USA) | CDL 0231 CD |
| 2005 | ☐ | DEATH METAL | CDd | Regain Records | RR 065 |

Bonus: Pagan Saviour (Autopsy cover)/Shadowlands/Afterimage/Shapeshifter

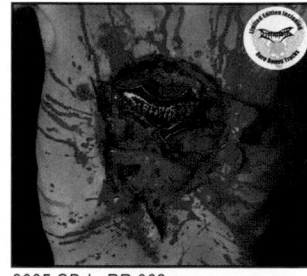

2005 CDd - RR 063

| 2005 | ☐ | HATE CAMPAIGN | CD | Regain Records | RR 067 |

Bonus: Live To Hate/Unhealing Scars

| 2005 | ☐ | HATE CAMPAIGN | CD | Candlelight (USA) | CDL 0234 CD |
| 2005 | ☐ | HATE CAMPAIGN | LP | Night Of The Vinyl Dead | NIGHT 006 |

Bonus: Live To Hate/Unhealing Scars. Yellow splatter vinyl. 500 numbered copies.

2006	■	THE GOD THAT NEVER WAS	CD	Regain	RRCD 083
2006	☐	THE GOD THAT NEVER WAS	LP	Regain	RRLP 083
2006	☐	THE GOD THAT NEVER WAS	LP PD	Regain	RRPLP 083
2006	☐	THE GOD THAT NEVER WAS	CD	Candlelight (USA)	CDL 0255 CD
2006	☐	THE GOD THAT NEVER WAS	CD	CD-Maximum (Russia)	CDM 1006-2601
2008	■	DISMEMBER	CD	Regain	RR 118

Slipcase.

2006 CD - RRCD 083

| 2008 | ☐ | DISMEMBER | LPg | Regain | RRLP 118 |

500 copies.

2008	☐	DISMEMBER	LP PD	Regain	RRPLP 118
2008	☐	DISMEMBER	CD	Regain	REG-CD-1019
2008	☐	DISMEMBER	CD	Avalon Marquee (Japan)	MICP-10732

Bonus: Trail Of The Dead (live)

2008	☐	DISMEMBER	CD	Sylphorium (Colombia)	SR 020
2008	☐	DISMEMBER	CD	CD-Maximum (Russia)	CDM 0208-2819
2010	☐	LIKE AN EVER FLOWING STREAM	2LPg	Back On Black	BOBV 186 LP

1000 copies transparent blue vinyl. Bonus: Deathevocation/Defective Decay/Torn Apart/Justifiable Homicide

| 2010 | ☐ | INDECENT AND OBSCENE | LP | Back On Black | BOBV 182 LP |

Bonus: Hill 112/Beyond The Unholy Grave (Death cover). 1000 copies, red vinyl.

| 2010 | ☐ | MASSIVE KILLING CAPACITY | 2LPg | Back On Black | BOBV 183 LP |

Bonus: Justifiable Homicide/Collection By Blood (demo)/Life – Another Shape Of Sorrow (demo)/On Frozen Fields-Shadowlands (demo). 1000 copies, clear vinyl.

2008 CD - RR 118

| 2010 | ☐ | DEATH METAL | 2LP | Back On Black | BOBV 180 LP |

Bonus: Pagan Saviour (Autopsy cover)/Shadowlands/Afterimage/Shapeshifter. Grey vinyl.

| 2010 | ☐ | THE GOD THAT NEVER WAS | LPg | Back On Black | BOBV 185 LP |

1000 copies. Purple vinyl.

| 2010 | ☐ | DISMEMBER | LPg | Back On Black | BOBV 181 LP |

1000 copies. White vinyl.

| 2010 | ☐ | PIECES | LPg | Back On Black | BOBV 184 LP |

Bonus: Torn Apart, plus 9 tracks live in Stockholm 1993. Red vinyl.

| 2010 | ■ | COMPLETE DEMOS | LP | Back On Black | BOBV 179 LP |

Red vinyl.

| 2012 | ☐ | LIKE AN EVER FLOWING STREAM | CD | Hammerheart | HHR 2012-08 |

Bonus: Deathevocation/Defective Decay/Torn Apart/Justifiable Homicide

2010 LP - BOBV 179 LP

DISPATCHED

Fredrik "Mussla" Karlsson: v/k, Daniel "Garion Blackwater" Lundberg: g, Emil Larsson: g, Fredrik Larsson: b, Dennis Nilsson: d

Gnesta/Södertälje - Formed new years eve 1991/92. The initial line-up featured singer Krister "Chris Reeve" Andersson, guitarist Daniel Lundberg, bassist Jonas Kimbrell and drummer Fredrik Larsson. Shortly after Larsson was replaced by Emanuel Åström. They made their first six-track demo *Dispatched Into External* in July 1992, a second two-track in 1993 and another four-track the same year. The first 7" was originally going to be an album, entitled *Blackshadows*, and 11 tracks were recorded, but Exhumed decided to make it a 7" EP instead. Five more tracks were released in 1996 as the *Blackshadows* MCD. After the record Kimbrell (**The Marble Icon, Cryptic Art**) was replaced by Fredrik Larsson (**Dark Edge**) and drummer Emanuel Åström by Dennis Nilsson. On *Returned To Your Mind,* Dennis Hultin was credited for playing guitar, but never did. On *Promised Land* they became slightly more melodic. On *Motherwar* singer Andersson was replaced by Fredrik Karlsson. On this album they do a death-slaughter of **Europe**'s *The Final Countdown. Promised Land* and *Motherwar* were recorded at The Abyss and produced by Tommy Tägtgren. When the album *Terrorizer* was finalised, Music For Nations dropped the band and Khaosmaster licensed it for a limited edition, with the subtitle *The Last Chapter.* As they sold out, Rising Realm Records signed the band and the album was rerecorded, since Music

Dispatched, back in the day

229

For Nations owned the rights. During the recording, Rising Realm bought the rights from MFN and the new recording was never finished. Death metal with a touch of traditional heavy metal and quite warped vocals. Heavy and great production.
Website: www.dispatched.nu

1995 ■	Awaiting The End	7" 4tr	Exhumed	CORPSE 06	

Tracks: Blue Fire/...Is Born/Awaiting The End/Red Zone

1996 □	Blackshadows	MCD 4tr	TCR/Black Wolf	TCR 002/BWP 001	

Tracks: You Only Know Life/Ghastly Gates/Blackshadows/Act Of Resurrection

1998 □	Returned To Your Mind	MCD 4tr	TCR/Black Wolf	TCR 003/BWP002	

Tracks: Restless Mind/Like A River Of Sand/Hate My Life/Canis Lupus

1998 ■	Promised Land	MCD 6tr	Kshatryas Productions	KSP 007	

Tracks: A Griffin Banner/Ravenous Men/Promised Land/Grant Me Rest/The Revealing/Fallen Wind

2000 □	MOTHERWAR	CD	Music For Nations	CDMFN 259	
2000 □	Motherwar/Down	CDS	Music For Nations	DISP1	

Different mixes than the album.

2003 □	TERRORIZER – THE LAST CHAPTER	CDd	Khaosmaster	MP/DD 006	
2003 □	TERRORIZER	CD	Crash	CMU 61137 CD	
2003 □	TERRORIZER	CD	Hellion (Brazil)	HEL 0387	
2004 □	TERRORIZER	CD	Soundholic (Japan)	TKCS-85098	

Bonus: A Trail Of Fear

2007 □	MOTHERWAR	CDd	Metal Mind	MASS CD DG 1096	

2000 hand numbered copies.

1995 7" - CORPSE 06

1998 MCD - KSP 007

DISRUPTION

**Jonas Renvaktar: v, Mikael Lundqvist: g, Peter Eriksson: g,
Daniel Sköld: b, Jonatan Forssander: d**

Karlskrona - **Disruption** were formed in 1999 by five young music students and recorded their first five-track demo *A Soul Full Of Hate* the same year. The demo *Bitch On The Cross*, recorded by Magnus Sedenberg (**Baltimoore, Sins Of Omission**), came the subsequent year and the unreleased album *Behind The Trigger* in 2001. In 2001 Peter (**Unchained**) replaced Tom Persson. In 2003 Sedenberg and the band released the *Demolisher Pack* multimedia CD-R in 100 copies, a collection of live tracks, videos and the 2001 unreleased album. It was sent out to various labels and a licence deal was inked with UK based Copro Productions. The band now recorded their debut album *Face The Wall*. The track *Behind The Trigger* was featured on the *Hordes Of Darkness* compilation (Unexploded 2003). Jonas, also known as Mordechai, has also been a member of **Spawn Of Possession, Istapp** and is today in rockers **Jack Daw**.

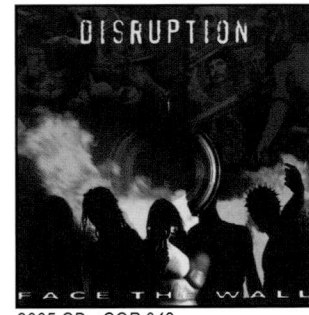

2005 ■	FACE THE WALL	CD	Copro	COP 042	

2005 CD - COP 042

DISSECTION

Jon Nödtveidt: v/g, David "Set/Sethlans Teitan" Tataro: g, Tomas Asklund: d

Strömstad/Göteborg - Not to be confused with Canadians **Dissection** who made an album in '88-89. Jon Nödtveit, bassist Peter Palmdahl and drummer Ole Öhman had a long history together in different thrash-oriented bands before getting **Dissection** together in Strömstad in 1989. The band's first release was the self-released cassette *The Grief Prophecy* (1990). This demo also featured rhythm guitarist Mattias "Mäbe" Johansson (**Third Stone From The Sun, Ophthalamia, Mäbe, Nifelheim, Sarcastic, Nosferatu, Mäbe**). He was replaced by John Zwetzloot (**The Haunted, Cardinal Sin, Nifelheim**), who made his debut on the *Into Infinite Obscurity* EP . Furious black speed metal with Satanic lyrics, double bass drums and intense guitars. Produced by Tomas Skogsberg. In 1991 Nödtveit also recorded a demo with the band **Satanized**. In 1992 the band recorded the demo *The Somberlain* and the year after *Promo '93*, containing a cover of **Tormentor**'s *Elisabeth Bathori*. The demos lead to a deal with No Fashion Records and the debut *The Somberlain* was recorded by Dan Swanö. The album is a black metal milestone, but with a variety in the sound with even some acoustic passages. The band now left Strömstad for Göteborg, where they shared rehearsal space with **At The Gates**. This also lead to the project band **Terror**, featuring Nödtveit and **At The Gates** musicians Jonas and Anders Björler and Adrian Erlandsson. Only a demo came out of this. In 1994 Nödtveit joined Tony "It" Särkkä's band **Ophthalamia**, which also featured Mäbe and Öhman. In 1995 Zwetzloot was replaced by Johan Norman (**Satanized, Decameron, Soulreaper, Runemagick**) who made his debut on *Storm Of The Light's Bane*. Öhman played on the album, but Tobias Kellgren (**Satanized, Decameron, Swordmaster, Soulreaper** etc) made the subsequent tour. After the *Gods Of Darkness* tour in 1997 Palmdahl and Norman left the band. Jon's brother Emil Nödtveit (**Deathstars**) temporarily stepped in on drums. In December 1997 Jon Nödtveit was arrested and convicted of the murder of a homosexual Algerian man in Keillers Park in Göteborg. He was sentenced to eight years imprisonment for assisting of murder and posses-sion of an illegal weapon. The band was now put to rest. The album *The Past Is Alive* contains old recordings plus two tracks by **Satanized**. A live album was released in 2003 and Nödtveit actually wrote some lyrics for the band **Diabolicum** during his imprisonment. When he was

Children of the grave

released in September 2004 a new incarnation of **Dissection** was already formed, featuring Nödtveit, bassist Brice Leclercq (*Nightrage, Satyricon*), guitarist David "Set/Seithan Teitan" Tataro (*Aborym, Bloodline, Watain*) and drummer Tomas Asklund (*Dark Funeral, Dawn, Necronomicon, Infernal*). 2004 saw the first recording of the new **Dissection**, the single *Maha Kali*. The band was supposed to play the Metalist Festival in Israel, but had to pull out because reformed Christian **Megadeth** frontman Dave Mustaine refused to share stage with the band because of their satanic messages. The band's live show in Stockholm in 2004 was recorded and released as the *Rebirth Of Dissection* DVD and *Live In Stockholm 2004* and *Live Rebirth* CDs. Leclercq left the band and they continued as a trio. **Watain** bassist Erik Danielsson stepped in as the band's live bassist. In April 2006 the band's new studio album *Reinkaos* was released. All their previous albums were reissued. On June 24 2006 **Dissection** made their last live show at the Midsummer Massacre. August 16 2006 Jon Nödtveit was found dead in his home. Death cause: suicide by gun. The band was now permanently dissolved. In 2007 Black Horizon reissued all of **Dissection**'s work with loads of bonus tracks. The album *Live In Stockholm* was recorded at Arenan, Stockholm October 30, 2004 and the line-up featured Set Teitan, Jon Nödtveit, Brice Leclercq and Tomas Asklund. **Dissection** is featured with two non-CD tracks on two Wrong Again compilations. The tracks are *Where Dead Angels Lie* (demo version) and *Elisabeth Bathori*. They also recorded the track *Anti-Christ* that appears on the **Slayer**-tribute (95 Black Sun) and another track that featured on the **Bathory** tribute. A demo version of *Nightblood* is found on *Death Is Just The Beginning Part 3* (Nuclear Blast).

1991 7" - CGR 003   *1993 CD - NFR 006*

1997 CDd - NR 017

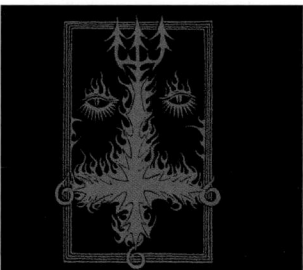

1998 CD - NR 017

2001 CD - NR 076

2003 CD - CD 03-475

1991	■	Into Infinite Obscurity	7" 3tr	Corpse Grinder Records	CGR 003	
		Tracks: Shadows Over A Lost Kingdom/Son Of The Mourning/Into Infinite Obscurity. 1000 copies.				
1993	■	THE SOMBERLAIN	CD	No Fashion Records	NFR 006	$
1993	□	THE SOMBERLAIN	CD	Somber Music (Brazil)	SM 018CD	
1994	□	THE SOMBERLAIN	CD	Victor (Japan)	VICP 5491	
		Bonus: Son Of The Mourning				
1995	□	STORM OF THE LIGHT'S BANE	LPg	Nuclear Blast	NB 129 1	$$
		1000 black, 500 blue vinyl.				
1995	□	STORM OF THE LIGHT'S BANE	LP PD	Nuclear Blast	NB 129 1	
		1000 copies.				
1995	□	STORM OF THE LIGHT'S BANE	CDd	Nuclear Blast	NB 129 2	
		15 000 copies.				
1995	□	STORM OF THE LIGHT'S BANE	CD	Nuclear Blast	NB 129 2	$
1995	□	STORM OF THE LIGHT'S BANE	CD	Nuclear Blast America (USA)	NBA 6129 2	
1995	□	STORM OF THE LIGHT'S BANE	CD	Victor (Japan)	VICP 5636	$
		Bonus: Feather's Fell				
1996	□	THE SOMBERLAIN	LP PD	Nuclear Blast	NFR 006 1A	
		1000 copies.				
1996	□	Where Dead Angels Lie (Tormentor cover)	MCD 6tr	Nuclear Blast	NB 167-2	
		Tracks: Where Dead Angels Lie (demo)/Elisabeth Bathori/Antichrist/Feather's Fell/Son Of The Mourning/Where Dead Angels Lie (album)				
1996	□	Where Dead Angels Lie	MCD 6tr	Victor (Japan)	VICP 15065	
1996	□	Where Dead Angels Lie	MCD 6tr PD shaped	Nuclear Blast	NB 167-2	
		3000 copies.				
1996	□	STORM OF THE LIGHT'S BANE	CD	JVC Victor (Japan)	VICP-5636	
1997	■	THE PAST IS ALIVE	CDd	Necropolis	NR 017	
1998	■	THE PAST IS ALIVE	CDd	Necropolis	NR 017	
		Different artwork.				
1997	□	THE PAST IS ALIVE	LP PD	Necropolis	NR 017 PD	
1998	□	STORM OF THE LIGHT'S BANE	LPg	Nuclear Blast	NFR 129	
		500 copies, blue vinyl.				
2001	■	THE PAST IS ALIVE	CD	Necropolis (USA)	NR 076	
		Different artwork. Slipcase.				
2002	□	STORM OF THE LIGHTSBANE + WHERE ANGELS DIE	CD	Nuclear Blast	646-2	
2002	□	STORM OF THE LIGHTSBANE + WHERE ANGELS DIE	CD	Nuclear Blast (USA)	6646-2	
2002	□	STORM OF THE LIGHTSBANE + WHERE ANGELS DIE	CD	Irond (Russia)	CD 02-275	
2002	□	STORM OF THE LIGHTSBANE + WHERE ANGELS DIE	CD	Somber (Brazil)	SM 024 CD	
2002	□	STORM OF THE LIGHTSBANE + WHERE ANGELS DIE	CD	Seoul (Korea)	CM 0237	
2003	□	LIVE LEGACY	CDd	Nuclear Blast	NB 650-2	
2003	□	LIVE LEGACY	CD	Nuclear Blast	NB 650-2	
2003	□	LIVE LEGACY	LPg	Nuclear Blast	NB 650-1	$
2003	□	LIVE LEGACY	CD	Victor (Japan)	VICP-62271	
2003	■	LIVE LEGACY	CD	Irond (Russia)	CD 03-475	
2003	□	THE SOMBERLAIN	CD	Century Media	CMR 8031-2	
2003	□	THE SOMBERLAIN	CD	Irond (Russia)	CD 03-560	
2004	□	Maha Kali/Unhallowed (Rebirth Version)	CDS	Escapi	AUD 008x	
		1000 copies.				
2004	□	THE PAST IS ALIVE	CD	Hammerheart	HHR 158	
		Different artwork. Bonus: Where Dead Angels Lie/Elizabeth Bathory (Tormentor cover)				
2005	□	THE PAST IS ALIVE	CD	Candlelight (USA)	CDL 205CD	
2005	□	THE PAST IS ALIVE	CD	Karmageddon	KARMA 082	
2005	□	THE SOMBERLAIN	CDd	Black Lodge	BLOD 018 DG	
2005	□	THE SOMBERLAIN	CD	Black Lodge	BLOD 018CD	

231

| 2005 | ■ | THE SOMBERLAIN | CDd | Black Lodge | BLOD 018DG | |
| 2005 | ■ | THE SOMBERLAIN | CD box | Black Lodge | BLOD 018WB | $ |

Wooden box including CD, t-shirt and sticker. 666 copies.

| 2006 | □ | Starless Aeon | CDS | The End (USA) | TE 071 | |

Tracks: Starless Aeon/Xeper-I-Set/Starless Aeon (Instrumental/Starless Aeon (video). 1000 copies.

| 2006 | □ | THE SOMBERLAIN | 2CD | Black Horizon Music | BHM 002 | |

Bonus: Frozen (Live '95)/The Somberlain (Live '95)/Shadow Over A Lost Kingdom (Demo '91)/Son Of The Mourning (Demo '91)/Into Infinite Obscurity (Demo '91)/Frozen (Demo '92)/Into Cold Winds Of Nowhere (Demo '92)/Feathers Fell (Demo '92)/Mistress Of The Bleeding Sorrow (Demo '92)/The Call Of The Mist (Demo '90)/Severed Into Shreds (Rehearsal '90)/Satanized (Rehearsal '91)/Born In Fire (Rehearsal '91)

2005 CD box - BLOD 018WB

2006	□	THE SOMBERLAIN	2LPg	Black Horizon Music	BHM 002	$
2006	□	THE SOMBERLAIN	2CD	The End (USA)	TE 072	
2006	□	THE SOMBERLAIN	CD	Irond (Russia)	CD 06-1189	
2006	□	THE SOMBERLAIN	2CD	Seoul (Korea)	SRCD-2854	
2006	□	STORM OF THE LIGHTSBANE (ULTIMATE REISSUE)	2CD	Black Horizon Music	BHM 003	

Slipcase. Bonus-CD: Night's Blood)/Unhallowed/Retribution – Storm Of The Light's Bane/ Where Dead Angels Lie/Feathers Fell/Thorns Of Crimson Death/Soulreaper/No Dreams Breed In Breathless Sleep/Night's Blood (demo)/ Retribution – Storm Of The Light's Bane/ Where Dead Angels Lie (Demo)/Elisabeth Bathory/Antichrist /Son Of The Mourning

| 2006 | □ | STORM OF THE LIGHTSBANE (ULTIMATE REISSUE) | 2CD | Icarus Music (Argentina) | ICARUS 216 | |

Slipcase.

2006	□	THE SOMBERLAIN (ULTIMATE REISSUE)	2CD	Icarus Music (Argentina)	ICARUS 217	
2006	□	STORM OF THE LIGHTSBANE (ULTIMATE REISSUE)	2LPg	Black Horizon Music	BHM 003	
2006	■	STORM OF THE LIGHTSBANE (ULTIMATE REISSUE)	2CDd	The End (USA)	TE 073	
2006	□	STORM OF THE LIGHTSBANE (ULTIMATE REISSUE)	2CD	Seoul (Korea)	SRCD 2855	
2006	□	STORM OF THE LIGHTSBANE	CD	Irond (Russia)	CD 06-1190	

2005 CDd - BLOD 018DG

Bonus: Night's Blood (Demo '94)/Retribution – Storm Of The Light's Bane (Demo '94)/ Elisabeth Bathory ('96)/Where Dead Angels Lie (Demo Version)/Antichrist ('96)/Son Of The Mourning ('96)

| 2006 | □ | REINKAOS | CD | Black Horizon Music | BHM 001 | |

First edition 1001 copies. Slipxase and sticker. Second edition with red star slipcase and patch in 999 copies. Third edition with slipcase.

| 2006 | □ | REINKAOS | LPg | The End (USA) | TE 067 | |
| 2006 | □ | REINKAOS | CD | The End (USA) | TE 067 | |

Slipcase (different from Europe).

2006	■	REINKAOS	LP	Black Horizon Music	BHM 001	
2006	□	REINKAOS	CD	Irond (Russia)	CD 06-1171	
2006	□	REINKAOS	CD	Pulverized (Singapore)	ASH 018	
2006	□	REINKAOS	CDd	Seoul (Korea)	SRCD-2116	

Bonus: Starless Aeon (instrumental)

2006 2CDd - TE 073

| 2006 | □ | REINKAOS | CD | Scarcrow (Mexico) | SR 06264 | |

Slipcase.

| 2006 | □ | REINKAOS | CDd | Seoul (Korea) | SRCD-2116 | |
| 2006 | □ | REBIRTH OF DISSECTION | CD+DVD | Escapi | EMUS 20074 | |

1000 copies.

| 2007 | □ | STORM OF THE LIGHTSBANE (ULTIMATE REISSUE) | 2CD | Trinity Records (Hong Kong) | TRHKO 13 | |
| 2008 | □ | LIVE LEGACY | LPg | Back On Black | BOBV 081 LP | |

Blue vinyl.

| 2009 | ■ | LIVE IN STOCKHOLM | LP | Escapi Music | EMUS 390 | |
| 2010 | □ | LIVE REBIRTH | 2LPg | High Roller | HRR 105 | |

First press. 100 clear 900 in red, clear or black vinyl. Poster.

| 2011 | □ | LIVE REBIRTH | 2LPg+MLP PD | High Roller | HRR 105 | $ |

Second press. 250 red + 250 gold vinyl + picture disc. New poster. Bonus: At The Fathomless Depths/Black Horizons + interview. 3rd press 250 clear/red+250 black. Poster.

2006 LP - BHM 001

| 2013 | □ | LIVE REBIRTH | 2LPg | High Roller | HRR 105 | |

Third press. 250 black + 250 clear/red splatter vinyl.

Unofficial releases:

| 1996 | □ | CHAOSATANIST LIVE | CD | n/a | n/a | |

Recorded at The Witchwood, Ashton, UK, 19960205.

| 1997 | □ | FROZEN IN WACKEN | CD | Headache | - - | |
| 1998 | □ | Sacrifice (split) – Live In Stockholm | 7" | n/a | n/a | |

Split with Immortal. Recorded live in Stockholm February 25, 1995.

| 1999 | □ | Into Infinite Obscurity | 7" 3tr | Nuclear Boom | CYW666-9902 | |

Bootleg w different artwork

| 19?? | □ | Into Infinite Obscurity | 6" 3tr flexi | n/a (Russia) | n/a | |
| 1999 | □ | NIGHTS BLOOD | CD | Headache | - - | |

Live-bootleg recorded in Oslo 1994.

| 1999 | □ | NIGHTS BLOOD | LP | Headache | - - | |
| 1998 | □ | Dissection/Immortal (split) | 7" | - - | Benov 003 | |

Split with Immortal. Track: Sacrifice

| 1999 | □ | FROZEN IN WACKEN | CD | Darkness | H 021 | |
| 2005 | □ | The Grief Prophecy – Demo '91 | 7" | - - | DISSECTION A/B | |

Tracks: Intro/Severed Into Shreds/The Call Of The Mist

2009 LP - EMUS 390

DISTORTED WONDERLAND
Olof Lindgren: v, Fredrik Lundstedt: g, Axel Karlsson: b, Petter Karlsson: d

Göteborg - **Distorted Wonderland** started out as a side-project by members Karlsson and Lindgren of **Overnight Sensation** (who actually sang some backing vocals on the first **Hardcore Superstar** album), but came into focus when this band split. **Distorted Wonderland** play high-class sleazy yet heavy rock in the vein of **Hardcore Superstar**. Well worth checking out.

2010 ■ DISTORTED WONDERLAND ....CD JamSynch ....JSM 071310

2010 CD - JSM 071310

DIVA (aka DEEVA)
Krister Boquist: v/b, Anders Lundquist: v/g, Christian Nielsen: g, Kent Nordström: d

Jokkmokk - Formed in 1986. In 1988 guitarist Bengt Anders Lundmark was replaced by Christer Nielsen. The single is a great and very obscure melodic hard rock platter. In 1990 Nielsen moved to Göteborg. In 1991 they changed name to **Deeva**, and the style was more melodic rock. The CD *No Tour* was released in 1996. In 2004 Jerry Rutström (**Maninnya Blade/Slowgate**) joined.

1989 ■ All My Love/Eternal Peace ....7" Platina ....PL 63 $$
1994 ☐ NO TOUR ....CD Mosquito Productions ....DEVCD 137
    As Deeva.

1989 7" - PL 63

DIVINE BAZE ORCHESTRA, THE
Alexander Frisborg: v/g/k, Oliver Eek: g, Tobias Pettersson: b,
Daniel Karlsson: b, Christian Eklöf: d

Uddevalla - This interestingly named eccentric band was formed by Eek and Eklöf in 2003. Frisborg and Petterson joined and the band started writing and gigging. In 2006 Karlsson completed the line-up. The band recorded their debut album *Once We Were Born…* in 2007, but it took a while before its release. After the album Tobias left the band. He was replaced by former **Gryningstid**/**Nangiala** bassist Joel Berntson. The band was now also reinforced by keyboardist and former **Gryningstid** member Mattias Johansson. In 2008 Daniel left the band and was later replaced by Joel Lööf (**The Hazeflower Experiment**). The band themselves describes their sound accordingly: *"As if Uriah Heep and King Crimson were having a bar brawl and the guys in Yes step in between, while in the other end of the bar Miles Davis and John Mclaughlin enter the bar stage and start jamming..."*. Well, I won't argue.

2008 CD - TRANS 036

2008 ■ ONCE WE WERE BORN ....CD Transubstans ....TRANS 036
2010 ■ DEAD BUT DREAMING ....CD Transubstans ....TRANS 074

2010 CD - TRANS 074

DIVINE SIN
Fredde Lundberg: v, Micke Andersson: g, Peter Halvarsson: g,
Bubby Goude: b, Martin Knutar: d

Söderhamn - **Divine Sin** recorded their first demo *Dying To Live* in 1990, the second, *Years Of Sorrow* followed the year after *Resurrection* in 1993, after which the band was picked up by Black Mark. They mix elements of death, thrash and pure heavy power metal with lots of tempo-changes and heavy yet melodic riffs. The vocals are dark and rough-edged, but not death-oriented. Recommended. The band disbanded after the second release. Fredde was found in bands like **Incarnated**, **Fantasmagoria**, **Lefay** and **Morgana Lefay**, Knutar in **Incarnated** and Micke in **Moribund**. Knutar and Goude are today found in pop/rock band **Seven Days**. In 2009 the band reformed and according to their MySpace a new album is to be expected.

1995 CD - BMCD 83

1995 ■ WINTERLAND ....CD Black Mark ....BMCD 83
1997 ■ THIRTEEN SOULS ....CD Black Mark ....BMCD 121

1997 CD - BMCD 121

DIVINE SOULS
Mattias Lilja: v, Mikael Lindgren: g, Stefan Högberg: g,
Daniel Lindgren: b, Daniel Sjölund: d

Kramfors - The band was formed in 1997, rising from the ashes of defunct band **Cromlech**. The old band was more of a traditional death band, while **Divine Souls** owes more to the technical and more melodic side of brute metal. They recorded their first self-entitled demo in 1997, second *Astraea* in '98 and a third, entitled *Devil's Fortress* the year after. The track *The Eve Of The Serpent* was featured on *Voices Of Death Part III* (00 VOD) and the 2000 demo *Erase The Burden* caught the attention of Scarlet Records. **Divine Souls** could be compared to bands like **In Flames** and **Sentenced**. The band split in 2004 when Lindgren (**Setherial**, **Apostacy**) left the band.

2001 ■ EMBODIMENT ....CD Scarlet ....SC 034-2
2002 ☐ THE BITTER SELFCAGED MAN ....CD Scarlet ....SC 055-2

2001 CD - SC 034-2

DIVINEFIRE

Christian Liljegren (aka Rivel): v, German Pascual: v, Jani Stefanovic: g/v/d,
Andreas Passmark (formerly Olsson): b

Stockholm - *Divinefire* is a side project instigated by *Narnia/Modest Attraction/Wisdom Call/Audiovision* singer Liljegren together with *Crimson Moonlight/Am I Blood/Sins Of Omission* musician Stefanovic in 2004. *Narnia/Wisdom Call/Stormwind* bassist Andreas Olsson (now Passmark) completed the band. A variety of guests appear on the bands albums, including people like Carl Johan Grimmark (*Narnia, Grimmark*), Eric Clayton (*Saviour Machine*), Torbjörn Weinesjö (*Veni Domine, Audiovision*), Pontus Norgren (*Great King Rat, Hammerfall, The Poodles, Talisman*), Fredrik Sjöholm (*Veni Domine*) and Thomas Vikström (*Talk Of The Town, Candlemass, Stormwind* etc). The album *Hero* features a cover of *Queen*'s *The Show Must Go On* where Liljegren shares the vocals with *One More Time/Misth* singer Maria Rådsten and Thomas Vikström. The band's live line-up was completed by guitarist Patrik Gardberg (*Ammotrack*), keyboardist Anders Berlin (*Street Talk, Bloodbound*) and drummer Andreas Johansson (*Narnia, Rob Rock*). *Divinefire* play hard-driving metal, verging on melodic death metal, but with clean vocals and a strong Christian message. Well-played and well-produced! In 2009 Andreas Passmark (Olsson) left the band. The same year the band also drafted Christan's replacement in *Narnia*, German Pascual (*Mind's Eye/Afterglow*), who appears on *Eye Of The Storm*.

2006 CD - RRCD 025

2005 CD - RRCD 020

2004	☐	GLORY THY NAME	CD	King Records (Japan)	KICP-1040
		Bonus: Free Like An Eagle			
2005	■	GLORY THY NAME	CD	Rivel Records	RRCD 020
2005	☐	GLORY THY NAME	CD	Metal Heaven	00008
2006	■	HERO	CD	Rivel Records	RRCD 025
		Bonus: Cryptic Passages			
2006	☐	HERO	CD	Metal Heaven	00013
		Bonus: Cryptic Passages			
2006	☐	HERO	CD	King Records (Japan)	KICP-1097
		Bonus: Masquerade			
2006	■	INTO A NEW DIMENSION	CD	Rivel Records	RRCD 029
		Bonus: Free Like An Eagle			
2006	☐	INTO A NEW DIMENSION	CD	King Records (Japan)	KICP-1192
		Bonus: Masters & Slaves/Special message to Japan			
2008	☐	FAREWELL	CD	Rivel Records	RRCD 037
2008	☐	FAREWELL	CD	King Records (Japan)	KICP-1311
		Bonus: Close To The Fire			
2011	■	EYE OF THE STORM	CD	Liljegren Records	LRCD 005
2011	☐	EYE OF THE STORM	CD	King Records (Japan)	KICP-1540
		Bonus: Forever One			

2006 CD - RRCD 029

2011 CD - LRCD 005

DIZZINESS

Tomas Naeslund: v, Lars Boquist: g, Stefan Wallman: g,
Lars Hultman: b, Daniel Gese: d

Norrköping - This band dropped guitarist Stefan, changed singer and later became *Pole Position*. The 12" is a very high prized and rare collector's item. Good solid melodic hard rock. They also have a track on the compilation *Swedish Metal* (Pang) and the song *Stå på* was a split single taken from the local musical *Trigger*. A good solid hard rocker with great guitar playing. The single was later re-released on Polar with new artwork. They recorded a full-length album that wasn't released due to the record company going bust. Boquist was later in *Neondaze* and today in *Fair Of Freaks*. In 2013 Greek label No Remorse released the album plus single.

1982	☐	Ur Musikalen Trigger (split)	7"	Trigger	S&M 8202
		Split with SamBand. Track: Stå på			
1982	☐	Trigger (split)	7"	Polar	POS 1309
		Same as above on deifferent label and with different artwork.			
1985	■	Playing With Fire/Take It Or Leave It	12" 2tr	Björnspår	BJS 005 $$$
2013	☐	ON THE ROCKS	CD	No Remorse	NRR 040

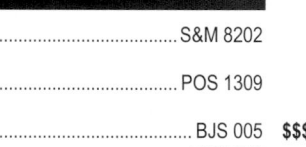

1985 12" - BJS 005

DOCTOR WEIRD

Björn Persson: v, Patrik Svärd: g, Björn Eliasson: g,
Anders Johansson: b, Roger "Mini" Landin: d

Helsingborg - High-quality classic melodic hard rock. These boys mix influences of progressive oriented rock with classical *Dokken*:ish hard rock from their old days and even some touches of old *Rainbow*. Great stuff, well worth checking out. After the MCD the band started writing for their debut album, but they soon took another turn. With new singer Mike Andersson and bassist Hans Persson the band became *Cloudscape* in 2001, a band with a history of its own.

1995	■	Doctor Weird	MCD 4tr	Pama Records	PACD 95042
		Tracks: In Vain/Treason/Lost Again/Liar			

1995 MCD - PACD 95042

DOG FACED GODS

Johnny Wranning: v, Conny Jonsson: g, Peter Tuthill: b, Rickard Evensand: d

Norrtälje (Stockholm) - Brutal and gut ripping like a battering ram, the **Dog Faced Gods** album slashes the air into pieces. Could be compared to **Illwill**, **Slapdash** or **Transport League** and is highly recommended. Pelle Sather, who does guest-vocals on one track, accompanied by Mats Olsson and Lennart Glenberg, also from **Zello**, produced the album in Studio Underground. Evensand is ex-**It's Alive**/**Sorcerer**, later in **Southpaw**, **Therion** and now in Australian band **Toehider**. Wranning is ex-**Miscreant** and was now also found in **Ebony Tears** together with Conny.

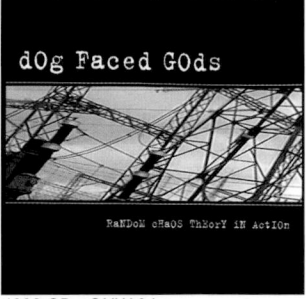

1998 CD - GNW 04

1998 ■	RANDOM CHAOS THEORY IN ACTION	CD	GNW	GNW 04

DOGFACE

Mats Levén: v, Martin Kronlund: g, Anders Skoog: k,
Stefan Egeman: b, Patrik Engelbrektsson: d

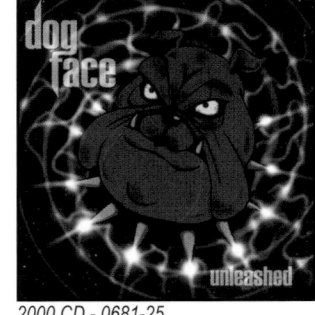

Göteborg - It all started in the late eighties when Martin, Anders and Patrik were playing in the band **Gypsy Rose**. The band was on the verge of being signed by Geffen and later Mausoleum, but both deals fell through. Patrik is ex-**Tai Rose** and **Earthquake**, while Anders and Mats were once partners in **Capricorn**. Martin previously recorded a single with **Develop**. Of course, Mats has a rap-sheet longer than a flagpole. Guitar-dominated melodic hard rock with an edge. The first album contains a cover of **The Sweet**'s *Set Me Free*. **Gypsy Rose** actually reformed and released their long awaited debut in 2005. Martin has since also recorded with **White Wolf**, **Reece/Kronlund**, **Lover Under Cover** etc. and written songs for Joe Lynn Turner, as well as recorded and produced numerous bands, including **Hammerfall**, **Lotus**, **Mass** and **Lost Weekend**.

2000 CD - 0681-25

2002 CD - 0681-50

2000 ■	UNLEASHED	CD	MTM	0681-25
2002 ■	IN CONTROL	CD	MTM	0681-50

DOGMAN

Frasse Franzén: v/g/b/d

Malmö - Frasse is foremost known as one of Sweden's prime rock photographers, but he is also a multi-talented musician. Between 1998 and 2001 he recorded his solo album *Reeact* under the **King's X** inspired name **Dogman**. The music also bears traces of **King's X**, or rather Ty Tabor's more low-key melodic rock material. There are however some pretty nice heavy riffing thrown in there as well. In 2007 Frasse was launched by Roastinghouse as the quirky singing chef Sven in Japan…

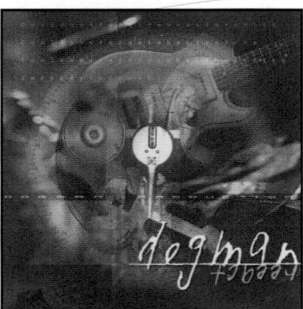

2001 CD - Dogman001

2001 ■	REEACT	CD	private	Dogman001

DOGPOUND

Henrik "Hea" Andersson: v, Mikael Dahlqvist: g,
Fredric "Figge" Danielsson: b, Calle "Tuka" Boman: d

Will this dog have its day?

Karlstad - Mikael and Henrik grew up together playing anything from badminton to hard rock. Along the line they teamed up with Calle and in 1999 they became **Dogpound**. In 2001 they released their first baby, entitled *Demo # 1 2001*, a seven track recording. One of the tracks, *When The World Comes Down* found its way to the compilation *Rock The Nations II* (02 Z Records) and a deal with Z Records. Unfortunately the label failed to live up to its promise and just locked the band up. In the autumn of 2002 the band recorded a new demo and in 2003 another two tracks were recorded. These final tracks lead to a deal with Finnish label Lion Music and the debut was released in November 2003. Unfortunately the cartoon style cover made most people mistake the album for a punk or hip hop act. The cover for the band's second album was not much better received, but luckily the bands great musical qualities more than made up for the artwork. On the band's third effort all the pieces however came together, both artwork and music. **Dogpound** is a very consistent band that have released one killer album after another. Great melodies, killer guitar work and high-class vocals. Heavy and melodic with a touch of **King's X** at times and with a great sound.
Website: www.dogpound.da.ru/

2005 CD - LMC 154

2007 CD - LMC 213

2003 □	THE HELLBUM	CD	Lion Music	LMC 082
2005 ■	A NIGHT IN THE GUTTER	CD	Lion Music	LMC 154
2007 ■	III	CD	Lion Music	LMC 213
2007 □	III	CD	Soundholic (Japan)	TKCS-85169

235

DOM DRACUL

Lord Therramon: v/g/b/d

Göteborg - Badly mixed old-school style death, except for the very strange vocals, not always growl, but often just strange deep-voiced, really bad vocals. The demo *Genocide In The Name Of Satan* was released in 2004, followed by *Devil Dedication* in 2006. The band was also featured with *Unleashed From The Abyss* on the EP *Satanic Butchery* (2006 Horned, HR 004).

2006 ■ ATTACK OF THE CRUCIFIED...CDd Blasphemous Undeground BUP-08L

2006 CDd - BUP-08L

DOMGÅRD

**Jonas "Grim Vindkall" Almen: v/g/k, Andreas "Heljamadr" Vingbäck: g,
K. "Hraegelmir" Fjällbrandt: b, Patrick "Hrimner" Kullberg: d**

Göteborg/Jönköping - Formed in 1997 by Vindkjall and Trollheim. Drummer Lars "Orm" Adolfsson (aka Lord Thurisaz) was added to the line-up and later on Ulv joined. Old-school black metal a bit similar to **Shining**. A first rehearsal demo from 1997 can be downloaded from the band's website. The demo *Blodskald* was recorded in 2004. Trollheim left and was replaced by Illbrand (who committed suicide in 2007). The band took 13 years to record the debut, a lot of it because the band members frequently visited the halls of justice. Vindkall, Illbrand and Orm were sentenced to several years in prison for church burning. In 2008 Hrimner (*Nox Aurea*) and Mörkestöl joined Vindkall in a new incarnation of the band. Enter Hraegelmir (*Nox Aurea, Panphage, Panzerkampf*). In 2009 Mörkestöl again left and the remaining trio entered the studio to record *Svartsejd*. The band is working on their second album, supposed to be entitled *Nekromantisk trolldom*. Grim is also found in **Cursed 13**, **Nox Aurea** and as session member in **Svartrit**. Also Heljamadr has joined **Cursed 13**. Grim is the only original member remaining. He was also one of the members convicted for burning some churches around Jönköping, which fits the bands hedonistic, aggressive, fairly old-school black metal, a bit similar to early **Satyricon**-meet-**Dissection**.

2009 CD - GPCD001

2010 CD - FS57

2009 ■ SVARTSEJD/TEARING THE WORLD ASUNDER (split) ....CD Ginnung Productions GPCD001
    Split with Cursed 13. Tracks: Svartsejd/Fimbulvetr/Ginnungs kall/Etterblod/Griftefärd
2010 □ I NIFELHELS SKYGD..CD Frostscald Records..................................FS45
2010 ■ MYRKVIðR...CD Frostscald Records..................................FS57

DOMINION

Victor Brandt: v/g/b, Jocke Olofsson: d/v

Gävle - Formed in 2004. The duo's debut wasn't even preceded by a demo, they went straight for a debut album. Victor is also found in **Necrocide**, **Aeon**, **Entombed** and **Totalt Jävla Mörker**, plus he's played with **Satyricon** live. Jocke is also in **In Aeternum**. *Dominion* (not to be confused with the **Dominion** that appears on a split with **Nae'blis**) plays technical death metal.

2006 ■ BORN GOD AND AWARE ....CD Unique Leather Records............. ULR 60035-2

2006 CD - ULR 60035-2

DOMINION CALIGULA

**Masse "Magus Caligula" Broberg: v, Matti "Dominion" Mäkelä: g, Lars Johansson: g,
Jocke Widfeldt: b, Robert Lundin: d**

Stockholm - Formed in 1998. Quite interesting mix of music. Musically the band owes a lot to the likes of **Tool** and **Biohazard**, while the vocals are out and out death metal style. Outstandingly fat riffing and nice chord-progressions, with a heavy de-tuned and poweful sound. Recorded at Abyss Studios by Tommy Tägtgren. The cover was made by Micke "Lord Ahriman" Svanberg (**Dark Funeral**). Masse is ex-**Hypocrisy** and Matti is ex-**Obscurity**. Both were formerly in **Dark Funeral**, where Robert was a session-drummer. Robert was formerly in popsters **Midnight Roses** and also session-drummer in Christian band **Heaven**.

2000 CD - NFR 045

2000 ■ A NEW ERA RISES ....CD No Fashion Records .... NFR 045
2000 □ A NEW ERA RISES ....LP No Fashion Records .... NFR 045 LP
2001 □ A NEW ERA RISES ....CD Irond (Russia) 01-122

DON PATROL

**Dille Diedricson: v/g, Peter Nordholm: g, Dan Helgesen: k,
Henkan Thomsen: b, Imre Daun: d**

Göteborg - Dille recorded some singles and albums with hard pop/rock band **Snowstorm**, but quit in 1983. He worked as a producer and technician and formed **Don Patrol** in 1989. The first release is more AOR-ish and OK, while the second is a great piece of **Deep Purple**-influenced hard rock with Dille's rough edged vocals. After the second album the band went through some changes and in 1995 a new album was recorded. Now the band had dropped the keyboards, changed drummer and the sound has become rougher. It was however never released.

1990 7" - TATI 48

Daun and Thomsen also backed singer Michael Erlandsson. Daun also recorded albums with
Arose, *Kharma*, *Alien*, *Gypsy Rose*, *Hope*, *White Wolf* etc. The band reformed in 2013.

1990	■	I'll Be Coming Around/Make It Through The Night	7"	The Record Station	TATI 48
1990	☐	All Night Long/Hard Time City	7"	The Record Station	TATI 50
1990	☐	All Night Long	MCD 4tr	he Record Station (promo)	PROMCD 4
		Tracks: All Night Long/I'll Be Coming Around/Fire With Fire/No Time To Fight			
1990	■	DON PATROL	LP	The Record Station	STAT 22
1990	☐	DON PATROL	CD	The Record Station	STAT 22
1992	☐	A WIRE, A DEAL AND THE DEVIL	LP	The Record Station	STAT 36
1993	☐	A WIRE, A DEAL AND THE DEVIL	CD	BMG Victor (Japan)	BVCP-672
1993	☐	Fire In The Night/Don't Wait Too Long	CDS 2tr	The Record Station	TATI 83

1990 LP - STAT 22

DOOM DOGS
Thomas "GG" Eriksson: v, Christer Cunat: g,
Patrik Andersson Winberg: b, Anders "Nanne": d

Göteborg - Formed in 2006 by Cunat, when he and his drummer Thomas left the cover band they
were in. They shared a love for *Black Sabbath*. Drafted singer Thomas Eriksson (ex-*Intoxicate*,
Valedictory, *Runemagick* and drummer of *Grotesque*) and bass player Viktoria Larsson (ex-*Ice
Age*) and formed *Dogs Of Doom*. After six months Patrik replaced Viktoria and they changed
their name to Doom Dogs. After a while drummer Thomas also left and after trying out a bunch
of different sticksmen, in 2008 Anders was in. Excellent, riff-oriented slow stoner/doom with
a strong touch of vintage *Black Sabbath* with rough-edged vocals more in the vein of Lemmy.

2010	☐	DOOM DOGS	CD	Doomentia	DOOM021CD2
2010	☐	DOOM DOGS	CDd	Doomentia	DOOM021CD1
		Cross–shaped digipack. 500 copies.			
2010	■	DOOM DOGS	LPg	High Roller Records	HHR 103
		150 black vinyl and 350 clear vinyl. Poster.			
2011	☐	UNLEASH THE TRUTH	CD	Doomentia	DOOM049CD2
2011	☐	UNLEASH THE TRUTH	2LPg	Doomentia	DOOMLP 49
2011	☐	UNLEASH THE TRUTH	CDd	Doomentia	DOOM149CD1

2010 LPg - HHR 103

DOOM:VS
Johan Ericson: v/g/b/d

Säffle - This is the solo project from *Draconian*/*Shadowgarden* member Ericson. Late
2004 he recorded the demo *Empire Of The Fallen*. The vocals on the demo were handled
by *Draconian/Scorched* singer D Arvidsson, which lead to a deal with Finnish label
Firebox's sub label Firedoom. On the album Johan handles all instruments and vocals.
The style is slow, searing funeral doom mixed with old-school doom, with growling vocals
and with some slightly atmospheric touches.
Website: www.myspace.com/doomvs

2006	■	AETERNUM VALE	CD	Firedoom Music	Fdoom013
2008	☐	DEAD WORDS SPEAK	CD	Firedoom Music	Fdoom025

2006 CD - Fdoom013

DORIAN GRAY
Per Anders Sahlström: v, Mikael Sahlström: g, Ted Stenlöv: b,
Jan Söderholm: k, Anders Oredsson: d

Vetlanda - A high-quality AOR band that has only released this 4 track CD. The CD sounds
quite slick, but the band claims they are indeed rougher live. I believe them. Anders Oredsson, who also produced the CD was the man who discovered *Neon Rose* and has since mixed/
produced over a hundred albums. Per Anders is ex-*Priority* and was later in the first line-up of
Silver Seraph, but was sacked during the recording. Mikael recorded an album with AOR-band
Unicorn in 1988 that was never released. Ted was ex-*Long John* and is now in *Mancamp*.

1994	■	Dorian Gray	MCD 4tr	private	AMOSCD 001
		Tracks: Sexomania/It Was Your Sister/Loved And Lost/I'm Alive.			

1994 MCD - AMOSCD 001

DOUBLE DEUCE
Anders Hammarström: v, Mathias Samuelsson: g,
Hans Forsman: g, Mikael Ericsson: b, Rickard Armén: d

Eksjö - Musically this is actually really good classic eighties heavy metal, but the vocals are the
big let-down. Actually it's very similar to early *Gotham City* in style and sound, also the vocals.
Apparently the artwork was misprinted and only about a hundred copies survived.

1992	■	Soldier In The Sun	MLP 4tr	Opus 1	OPUS 005	$
		Tracks: Soldier In The Sun/Emptiness/Time's Out/The Best.				

1992 7" - OPUS 005

237

DOUBLE DIAMOND

**Conny Höök: v, Peter Björklund: g, Peter Ytterman: g, Mats Svensson: k,
Lars-Åke Eriksson: b, Thomas Gustavsson: d**

Varberg - High-quality AOR with strong chorus-parts and a big chunk of melodies. Highly recommended.

1986 ■ Internal Heat/Back To Paradise ....7" private .... DDS 861 **$**

1986 7" - DDS 861

DOUBLE TROUBLE

(See Bai Bang)

DOWNBOUND TRAIN

**Morgan "MC Hellbound" Hellman: v/g, Richard Warldén: g,
Magnus Hedin: b, Mikael Thomsen: d**

Norrköping - Morgan has a past in garage rock bands like **Lowriders**, **Bad Bones** and **Gypsy Rockers**, while Hedin was formerly in metal band **Axewitch** and Thomsen has been in **Sonic Surf City** and **Great Gypsy Rockers**. After the band split Morgan and Magnus joined country rockers **Nashville Neurotics**. The band was also featured on the compilation *SnD Records Vol. 1* (1990 SnD). **Downbound Train** play decent sleaze.

1991 ■ If You Say You're Mine/Lucie Loves The Loser/Like A Heatwave .... 7" 3tr SnD Records SND010

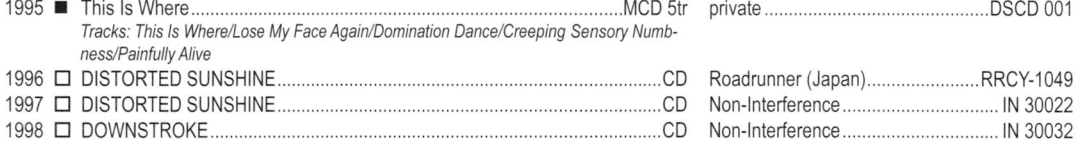

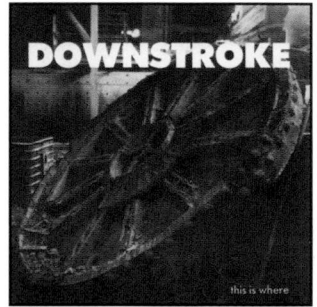
1991 7" - SND010

DOWNSTROKE

Henrik Edenhed: v, David Andersson: g, Per Fällström: b, Andreas Westerling: d/k

Lidköping - Formed in 1992. Outstanding heavy rock with great vocals, nice harmonies and shit-heavy guitars. Sounds as they have been listening quite a lot to bands like **King's X**, **Galactic Cowboys** and similar. The first album is an outstanding heavy rocker while the second CD was far more indie-rocking than the debut. As this was however not so successful, the band recorded a new 4-track demo in 1999, which is style-wise close to the MCD and the first album. Edenhed also recorded an outstanding, as yet unreleased, album under the name **Edenhed**. He has also recorded and produced numerous bands and artists.

1995 ■ This Is Where..MCD 5tr private ....DSCD 001
     Tracks: This Is Where/Lose My Face Again/Domination Dance/Creeping Sensory Numbness/Painfully Alive
1996 ☐ DISTORTED SUNSHINE..CD Roadrunner (Japan)......................RRCY-1049
1997 ☐ DISTORTED SUNSHINE..CD Non-Interference............................... IN 30022
1998 ☐ DOWNSTROKE..CD Non-Interference............................... IN 30032

1995 MCD - DSCD 001

DOWNTOWN CLOWNS, THE

Thomas Wallén: v, Patrik Larsson: g, Jonas Reingold: b, Johan Folker: d

Malmö - A great band with one or two hints of **Van Halen** and **Extreme**. Thomas actually used to sing in **Van Halen** cover band **Fan E´ De**' and he sure has a voice quite close to Mr. Lee Roth. The band's second album was due to be released in 1996, said to be heavier and with a more live-feeling, but unfortunately never surfaced. Worth checking out! In 1995 Jonas released a bass-album and he has since been found in bands like **The Flower Kings**, **Midnight Sun, Reingold** and **Karmakanic**. He now runs his own label Reingold Records.

1994 ☐ THE DOWNTOWN CLOWNS.....................................CD private/Local Hero...... CLOWNS 13/LHM 0223
1994 ■ Reachin' Up/Day Off ....CDS 2tr Local Hero .... LHM 0225

1994 CDS - LHM 0225

DOZER

Fredrik Nordin: v/g, Tommi Holappa: g, Johan Rockner: b, Olle Mårthans: d

Borlänge - The band was formed in 1995. Original bass player Magnus Larsson left in 1997 and was replaced by Johan. The first single became "Single Of The Week" in UK magazine Kerrang! Heavy stoner rock with hints of **Nebula**, **Mushroom River Band** etc. The track *Cupola* can be found on *Molten Universe Volume One* (1999 MU) and *Thunderbolt* on *Molten Universe Volume Two* (2000 MU). They also did a cover of **DEVO**s *Mongoloid* on *Sucking In The Seventies* (2007 Small Stone). Johan and Erik are also found in punk rock band **The Sick**, while Tommie is in **Greenleaf**. On *Call It Conspiracy* the band worked with **Sator** man Chips Kisbye (**Bonafide**) and its release Erik Bäckwall left and was replaced by Daniel Lidén (**Demon Cleaner, Greenleaf, Vaka**). **Mastodon** singer Troy Sanders makes a guest appearance on *Through The Eyes Of Heathens*. Early 2006 Daniel left the band and was replaced by Olle. In 2009 the band played their last show.

1998 ■ Demon Cleaner vs Dozer (split).........................7"	Molten Universe..........MOLTEN 001

Split with Demon Cleaner. Tracks: Tanglefoot/Centerline. 300 copies in black vinyl + 200 copies in transparent vinyl.

1999 □ COMING DOWN THE MOUNTAIN (split).........CD	Meteor City..........MCY-005

Split with Unida. Tracks: Twilight Sleep/Calamari Sidetrip/From Mars/Overheated

1999 □ COMING DOWN THE MOUNTAIN (split).........LP	Meteor City..........MCY-003

Red vinyl.

1999 □ COMING DOWN THE MOUNTAIN (split).........LP	Cargo Records (Germany)..........CAR 002

Black/white splatter vinyl.1000 copies.

1999 □ Hawaiian Cottage.........7" 4tr	Molten Universe..........MOLTEN 002

Split with Demon Cleaner. Tracks: Riding The Machine/Silverball. 400 copies in orange transparent vinyl + 100 in purple.

1999 □ Domestic Dudes (split).........7" 4tr	Molten Universe..........MOLTEN 003

Split with Demon Cleaner. Tracks: Octanoid/Hail The Dude. 500 copies in black vinyl.

2000 □ IN THE TAIL OF A COMET.........CD	Man's Ruin..........MR 134 CD
2000 □ Supersoul.........10" 4tr	Man's Ruin..........MR 135

Tracks: Supersoul/Lightyears Ahead/Speeder/Inside The Falcon. 1500 copies in semi-transparent green vinyl.

2000 □ The Phantom Tour Single.........7"	Molten Universe..........MOLTEN 009

racks: The Phantom/Sub Etna. 500 copies.

2000 □ DOUBLE EP (split).........MLP	Subway Records..........CAR 002

Split with Unida. Tracks: Headed For The Sun/Calamari Sidetrip/From Mars/Overheated. 1000 copies in white marbled vinyl.

2000 □ COMING DOWN THE MOUNTAIN (split).........LP	People Like U..........PRISON 997-1
2000 □ COMING DOWN THE MOUNTAIN (split).........CD	People Like U..........PRISON 997-2
2001 □ MADRE DE DIOS.........LP	Molten Universe..........MOLTEN 013

Bonus: Rings Of Saturn. First edition 1000 copies in black vinyl, second 1000 copies in orange transparent vinyl.

2001 ■ MADRE DE DIOS.........CD	Man's Ruin..........MR 2010 CD

Different artwork.

2002 □ Day Of The Rope/The Electrocuter.........7"	World Records..........WORLD 004

500 copies.

2002 □ Dozer/Los Natas (split).........7"	Black Ju Ju/45 Records..........JUJU 1

Split with Los Natas. Track: Sonic Reducer (Dead Boys cover). 1000 copies.

2003 ■ CALL IT CONSPIRACY.........CD	Molten Universe..........MOLTEN 019
2003 □ CALL IT CONSPIRACY.........2LPg	Molten Universe..........MOLTEN 019
2005 □ COMING DOWN THE MOUNTAIN (split).........CD	Meteor City..........MCY-997
2003 □ Rising/The Wreck.........7"	Molten Universe..........MOLTEN 020
2005 □ THROUGH THE EYES OF HEATHENS.........LP	Molten Universe..........MOLTEN 022
2005 □ THROUGH THE EYES OF HEATHENS.........CD	Molten Universe..........MOLTEN 022
2005 □ THROUGH THE EYES OF HEATHENS.........CD	Small Stone..........SS-061
2008 □ BEYOND COLOSSAL.........CD	Small Stone..........SS-087
2009 □ BEYOND COLOSSAL.........LP	Vinyl Maniacs..........VMLP 034
2011 □ IN THE TAILOF A COMET/MADRE DE DIOS.........2CD	Meteor City..........MCY063DCD
2011 □ IN THE TAILOF A COMET/MADRE DE DIOS.........3LPg	Headspin Records..........HSLP 319

200 copies.

2011 □ IN THE TAILOF A COMET/MADRE DE DIOS.........3LPg	Headspin Records..........HSLPC 319

200 copies. LP1: black/white, LP2: blue, LP3: orange.

2013 □ The Impostor (split).........7"	Transubstans..........TRANSV 706

Split with Nymf. Black vinyl + 100 copies white vinyl.

1998 7" - MOLTEN 001

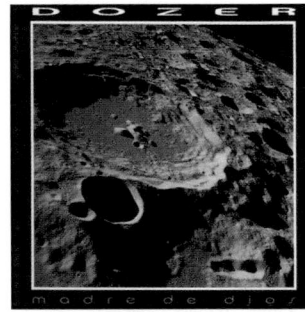

2001 CD - MR 2010 CD

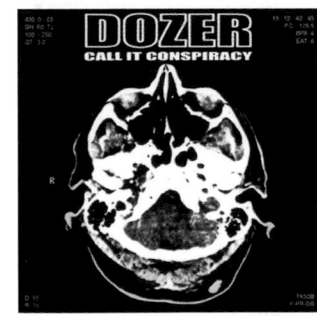

2003 CD - MOLTEN 019

DR BOOSTER

Peter Degerfelt: v/g, Jens Westin: v/g, Pelle Rönningås: b, Lennart Salthammer: d

Ånge - **Dr. Booster** started out in 1990 as a cover band. They later began writing their own material and when Jens and Lennart had completed the band they recorded the MCD. **Dr Booster** play basic **AC/DC** influenced bluesy hard rock with a touch of Johnny Winter. In 1995 Jens and Peter went their own way and recorded some new material in a more hard rocking direction. Jens is now in heavy rockers **Corroded**.

1992 ■ The First 4 Songs.........MCD 4tr	private..........DB 01

Tracks: Rock 'N Roll Woman/Don't Talk/Me And My Friends/Sky High.

1992 MCD - DB 01

DR DREAM

José "Joe Canner" Gomez-Sanchez: v, Mikael Vaarala: g/k,
Thomas Johansson: b, Yari Säisä: d

Borås - José was ex-**Empire Saint**. The A-side is a semi-heavy ballad, while the B-side is a good, melodic hard rocker quite close to early **Treat**. Well worth checking out. José later recorded a CD with **Fierce Conviction** and is today fronting his own band **Sanchez**.

1991 ■ Secrets/Side By Side.........7"	City Records..........UNI 2465

1991 7" - UNI 2465

DR. LIVING DEAD!

Andreas "Dr. Ape Grüber" Sandberg: v, Johannes "Dr. Toxic" Wanngren: g
Dr. Rad: b, Thomas "Dr. Dawn" Daun: d

Stockholm - New thrash/crossover band **Dr. Living Dead**, formed in 2007, influenced by bands like **Suicidal Tendencies**, **D.R.I** and **S.O.D**, have already toured Brazil and supported **Slayer**. The band went through a couple of drummer changes before finding Dr. Dawn and recorded the album, produced by Fred Estby. Wanngren is also found in **Undergång** and **Leprosy**. Great, high-speed melodic thrash well worth checking out. On the band's first demo, *Thrash After Death* (2007) they were a trio featuring Rad, Toxic and Ape, but on the 2008 effort *Thrashing The Law*, Dawn was added to the line-up. In 2013 Sandberg launched his solo band **Ouijabeard** and in later the same year he was replaced by Love "Dr. Mania" Utterström.

2010	■	DR. LIVING DEAD	LPg	High Roller Records	HRR 179

First pressing 150 green vinyl, 350 black. Poster. Second pressing 250 pink + 250 black vinyl.

2010	□	DR. LIVING DEAD	CD	High Roller Records	HRR 179 CD
2010	□	DR. LIVING DEAD	CD	Tribunal Records (USA)	TRB 111
2012	□	RADIOACTIVE INTERVENTION!	CD	High Roller Records	HRR 271 CD
2012	■	RADIOACTIVE INTERVENTION!	LPg	High Roller Records	HRR 271

100 yellow, 300 mustard and 350 black vinyl. Poster.

2010 LPg - HRR 179

2012 LP g - HRR 271

DRABNESS

Sinisa Krnjaic: v/b, Morgan Gottfridsson: g, Anders Tillaeus: g, Martin Lundgren: d

Motala - **Drabness** were formed in 1994. The band recorded the five-track demo *Trapped* the same year. In 1995 they recorded a second self-titled six track demo and the third six track, entitled *Mask Of Silence*. **Drabness** only released one EP, did some shows and then split up in 1998. After the EP the band added bass player Nader Moini with whom they recorded the demo *Dramiticly Uninspired*. In 1998 Moini was replaced by Jimmy Öster and the band recorded the last nine-track untitled demo. Anders, Sinisa and Martin moved to Malmö and started the alternative rock band **LeGrand**. Imagine a mix of **Pantera**, **Entombed** and **Breach**. Heavy hardcore with death influences.

1996	■	Affliction	MCD 5tr	TPL Records		TPL 003

Tracks: You/Won't Let You Fall/A Million Lies/Tears Of Bitterness/Footsteps

1996 MCD - TPL 003

DRACENA

Mia Larsson: v/g/b, Daniel "Mojjo" Moilanen: d

Göteborg - Old-school death-thrash. The band was formed in 1994 by Mia Larsson, initially an all-female band also featuring Emma Karlsson (now Rudolfsson) on guitar, Åsa Pettersson on bass and Karin Blomqvist (**Deathwitch**) on drums. They recorded their first demo in 1997, but as Karin quit they used Nicklas "Terror" Rudolfsson as session-drummer before finding Daniel Moilanen. Brutal music and guttural vocals. Sweden's heaviest all-girl band. Niclas "Pepa" Andersson (**Vassago, Lord Belial**) contributes with a solo. The band recorded a three-track CD-R demo in 1999 entitled *Demonic Women*. The band also recorded a three-track demo in 2002, entitled *Labyrinth Of Darkness*, before Mia put the guitar on the shelf to go for all vocals. Mia is also found in **Deathwitch**, while Emma and Daniel are found in **Runemagick**. After some years of silence the band returned as a duo. Chris Loud added lead guitar on the CD. Trivia: Daniel Moilanen is half-brother of Harry "Cody" Kemppainen of **Shotgun Messiah**. *Website: www.dracenaonline.com*

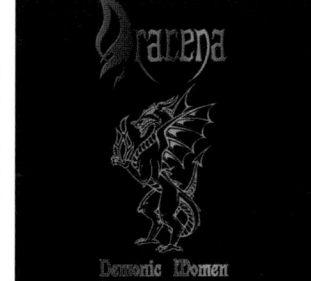

2001 7" - BLOOD 004

2001	■	Demonic Women	7" 4tr	Bloodstone		BLOOD 004

Tracks: Preludium Infernal/Demonic Women/The Hounds Of Hell/Realms Of Dragons. 300 copies in bloodred vinyl.

2006	■	INFERNAL DAMNATION	CD	private		DRAC 001

2006 CD - DRAC001

DRACONIAN

Anders Jacobsson: v, Lisa Johansson: v, Johan Ericson: g,
Daniel Arvidsson: g, Fredrik Johansson: d, Jerry Torstensson: d

Säffle - The origin of **Draconian** dates back to May 1994, when Johan Ericson (d/v), Andy Hindenäs (g) and Jesper Stolpe (b/v) formed **Kerbero,** a melodic heavy/death metal ensemble with black metal influences. Seven months later, lead vocalist and poet Anders Jacobsson joined the band, which then changed its name to **Draconian**. Their first demo, *Shades of a Lost Moon,* was released in February 1996. End of January 1997, **Draconian** recorded their second demo, *In Glorious Victory*. Not happy with the sound quality of the recording it was never released. August 1999, the band entered Studio Kuling to record *The Closed Eye of Paradise*. Unfortunately, the recording, suffering from a bad production, was not released until 2000, after various improvements. On their next two track promo *Frozen Features*, the sound had become slower and doomier. A final demo, *Dark Oceans We Cry,* was recorded in the summer of 2002, now featuring the vocal talents of Lisa Johansson. The demo lead to a deal

with Napalm Records, and the band recorded the debut album, *Where Lovers Mourn* in Studio Mega under the supervision of Chris Silver (*Sundown, Cemetary*) in July 2003. The line-up on the debut consisted of Johan, Anders, Lisa, Jerry, Magnus Bergström (g) and Thomas Jäger (b) and Andreas Karlsson (k). Two years later the band entered Studio Underground with Pelle Saether to record *Arcane Rain Fell*. Jäger, now in *Marulk* and *Monolord*, was replaced by the returned Stolpe. In 2006 *Draconian* began working on their third release. But the band decided to first deliver a bonus album to include remakes of old tracks from *The Closed Eyes of Paradise* demo. *The Burning Halo* would also include three new tracks and two covers of *Ekseption* and *Pentagram*. The album was delayed, completed in June and released in September 2006. In September 2007, *Draconian* recorded their fourth album *Turning Season Within*, and as well as the follow-up *A Rose For The Apokalypse*, with producers Jens Bogren and David Castillo (*Opeth, Katatonia*). Ericson is also found in *Doom:VS* and *Shadowgardens*, where Lisa has also did a stint. Arvidsson is also in *Scorched* and Torstensson is also found in folk rockers *Paganus*. In 2013 Lisa was replaced by South African singer Heike Langhans.

2003 CD - NPLM 232294 2   2006 CD - NPR 196

2003	■	WHERE LOVERS MOURN	CD	Napalm Records	NPLM 232294.2
2003	☐	WHERE LOVERS MOURN	CD	Irond (Russia)	CD 03-712
2005	☐	ARCANE RAIN FELL	CD	Napalm Records	NPR 158
2005	☐	ARCANE RAIN FELL	CD	Irond (Russia)	CD 05-959
2006	☐	THE BURNING HALO	CD	Irond (Russia)	CD 06-1218
2006	☐	THE BURNING HALO	CD	Napalm Records	NPR 196
2008	☐	TURNING SEASONS WITHIN	CDd	Napalm Records	NPR 234
2008	☐	TURNING SEASONS WITHIN	CD	Irond (Russia)	CD 08-1419
2011	■	A ROSE FOR THE APOKALYPSE	CDd	Napalm Records	NPR 376

2011 CDd - NPR 376

DRAGONLAND

Jonas Heidgert: v, Nicklas Magnusson: g, Olof Mörck: g, Elias Holmlid: k, Anders Hammer: b, Martin Löwe Sörensen: d

Göteborg - The band was formed in 1999 by Nicklas and Jonas. Nicklas is also found in *Nightshade, Prophanity* and *Rapture*, where Olof is also found. Christer is also ex-*Nightshade/Moonlight Agony*. The first line-up of the band also featured guitarist Daniel Kvist (*Sacrilege, Taetre*), who was replaced by Olof in 2000. In 2000 they recorded their first demo *Storming Across Heaven*. Elias toured with *King Diamond Band* in 2001 and has also recorded with *Falconer* and *Iron Ware*. Produced by Andy La Roque. In 2002 Heidgert, who previously handled both drums and vocals, left the sticks and concentrated on the vocals. Enter drummer Robert Willstedt (*Moonlight Agony*), who was soon replaced by *Nostradameus/Dreamland* drummer Jesse Lindskog. *Starfall* was produced by *Evergrey*'s Tom Englund and Arnold Lindberg. *Astronomy* features guest spots from Jimmie Strimmel (*Nightrage/Dead By April*), Marios Iliopolous (*Nightrage*) and Elsie Ryd. *Dragonland* play melodic power metal in the vein of *Lost Horizon, Rhapsody Of Fire, Supreme Majesty* etc. Great musicianship and great vocals. Musically the band follows the path of the aforementioned. Elias is also in *Disdain*. On *Under the Grey Banner* the band returned to the chronicle about the fantasy realm *Dragonland*, which was brought to life on the band's first two albums. On this album the band explored the sounds and sounds from various fantasy movies. The line-up had also changed featuring drummer Morten Löwe Sörensen, replacing Lindskog. Bass player Christer Pedersen had also been replaced by Anders Hammer. The album also features vocal guest spots from *Amaranthe* members Elize Ryd, Joakim "Jake E" Lundberg and Andy Solveström. Heidgert is now found in *Destiny*.

Gates of the Dragonland?

2001	■	THE BATTLE OF THE IVORY PLAINS	CD	Black Lotus	BLRC 025
2001	☐	THE BATTLE OF THE IVORY PLAINS	CD	Black Lotus	BLRC 025
		Bonus: World's End			
2001	☐	THE BATTLE OF THE IVORY PLAINS	CD	Hot Rockin' Records (Japan)	HRHM 2001
		Bonus: World's End			
2001	☐	THE BATTLE OF THE IVORY PLAINS	CD	CBS (Taiwan)	MMMF2004
		Bonus: World's End			
2002	☐	HOLY WAR	CD	Black Lotus	BLR CD 036
2002	☐	HOLY WAR	CD	Hot Rockin' Records (Japan)	HRHM 2002
		Bonus: The Never Ending Story			
2004	☐	STARFALL	CD	Century Media	77512-2
2004	☐	STARFALL	CD	Century Media (USA)	1512-2
2004	☐	STARFALL	CD	King Records (Japan)	KICP-1024
		Bonus: Rusty Nail (X-Japan cover)/Sole Survivor (Helloween cover)			
2004	☐	STARFALL	CD	Dope Entertainment (Korea)	DE17036
		Bonus: Rusty Nail (X-Japan cover)/Illusion			
2004	☐	STARFALL	CD	CBS (Taiwan)	MMMF 2122
		Bonus: Rusty Nail (X-Japan cover)/Illusion			
2006	☐	ASTRONOMY	CD	Century Media	77579-2
2007	☐	ASTRONOMY	CD	King Records (Japan)	KICP-1214
		Bonus: Intuition (TNT cover)/The Last Word			
2011	■	UNDER THE GREY BANNER	CD	AFM	AFMCD 359
2011	☐	UNDER THE GREY BANNER	CD	King Records (Japan)	KICP-1562
		Bonus: At The Inn Of The Eamon Bayle			

2001 CD - BLRC 025

2011 CD - AFMCD 359

DRAIN (S.T.H)

Maria Sjöholm: v, Flavia Canel: g, Anna Kjellberg: b, Martina Axén: d

Stockholm - It all started in the band *Livin' Sacrifice*. They were initially a punk band, but when Martina and Flavia joined in the mid-80s the style changed to genuine melodic hard rock. The band also changed its name to *Aphrodite* and recorded an MLP, after which they changed their name to *Afrodite* and released another single. As some of the members wanted to go into a more pop-oriented direction Flavia, Martina and singer Malin Ekholm left to form *Rag Doll*. Anna was recruited. Just when they received great interest from several record companies, the singer suddenly left. Martina got fed up and went to Musicians Institute in the US. In 1993 she received a call from old mate Anna asking her to come home as they were about to get signed. Unfortunately there was no deal and still no singer. After a long search they found Maria, previously a guitarist in *Necronancy* and *Gudars Skymning* (not the current band of the same name). Things started rolling and soon they had signed to MVG Records. The name *Rag Doll* was changed to *Drain* and in the late summer of '95 the debut MCD was released. In 1996 the band toured as support for *Clawfinger*. *Drain* produced great, grinding, dark hard rock with a hint of Seattle, or "horror metal" as the band described it. Influences can be traced from bands like *Alice In Chains*, *Skintrade* and similar, but with a personal touch. Will hit you like a ton of bricks! In 1997 the band participated on the Ozzfest tour and continued with *Corrosion Of Conformity*. In 1999 singer Maria Sjöholm got engaged to, and later married *Black Sabbath*'s Toni Iommi, who also co-wrote the track *Black* on *Freaks Of Nature*. In 1999 the band also participated on the Ozzfest tour. In 2000 the band split. Anna (now on guitar) and Martina (who now handled the vocals) started a new band called *Superfix*. They recorded some demo material in 2002, but got no deal. Flavia first formed the US based band *Anotherday*, which never lifted off. She then returned to Sweden and in 2003 she formed *Blowsight*, where she played bass, but later ended up managing the band, and also *Sonic Syndicate*. Kjellberg has played with *Revolting Cocks* and *Opiate For The Masses*, Axén, now residing in California, did a short stint with *Snake River Conspiracy* before going solo in a nice heavy vein not too far from what *Drain* probably would have done today. The style is also more industrial-oriented. *Drain* can also be found on compilations like *Ozzfest* (tracks *Enter, Down*), *Ozzfest 97* (track: *I Don't Mind*), *Detroit Rock City Soundtrack* (track: *20th Century Boy*). The band is known as *Drain* in Europe and *Drain S.T.H* in the US. S.T.H stands for "Stockholm".

Freaks in the nature

1996 MCD - EW033CD

1999 CDS - MECD 1016 2

Year		Title	Format	Label	Cat. No.
1995	☐	Serve The Shame	MCD 5tr	MVG	MVGCDS 32
		Tracks: Serve The Shame/Unreal/Klotera/So I Will Burn(Alone)/To Be Continued..			
1995	☐	HORROR WRESTLING	CD	MVG	MVG 122
1996	☐	I Don't Mind	CDS	MVG	MVGCDS 37
1996	☐	I Don't Mind	MCD 4tr	MVG (promo)	SAM 1790
		Tracks: I Don't Mind/Serve The Shame/Stench/Crack The Liars Smile			
1996	☐	I Don't Mind	MCD 3tr	The Enclave (USA)	11705
		Tracks: I Don't Mind/Serve The Shame/Stench			
1996	☐	I Don't Mind	MCD 3tr	MVG/WEA (Germany)	0630-13775-2
		Tracks: I Don't Mind/Someone/So I Will Burn (Alone)			
1996	☐	I Don't Mind	MCD 4tr	MVG/WEA (Germany)	0630-14611-2
		Tracks: I Don't Mind/Someone/So I Will Burn (Alone)/I Don't Mind (Remix)			
1996	■	I Don't Mind	MCD 4tr	EastWest (UK)	EW033CD
		Tracks: I Don't Mind/Someone/So I Will Burn (Alone)/I Don't Mind (Remix)			
1996	☐	Crack The Liars Smile	MCD 3tr	MVG	MVGCDS 38
		Tracks: Crack The Liars Smile/Without Eyes/Klotera			
1996	☐	Crack The Liars Smile	MCD 5tr	EastWest (USA)	EW057CD
		Tracks: Crack The Liars Smile/Ace Of Spades (Motörhead cover)/I Don't Mind (Clawfinger remix)/Klotera (live)/Serve The Shame (acoustic)			
1996	☐	HORROR WRESTLING	CD	The Enclave (USA)	54971
		Bonus: Someone/Klotera			
1996	☐	HORROR WRESTLING	CD	MVG /WEA(Germany)	0630-13774-2
1997	☐	Serve The Shame	CDS	The Enclave (USA)	- -
		Acoustic version made for promotion in the USA.			
1997	☐	HORROR WRESTLING	CD	Metronome (Japan)	AMCE 961
		Bonus: (So I Will Burn) Alone/Someone/I Don't Mind (remix)			
1997	☐	HORROR WRESTLING	CD	The Enclave (USA)	314 558 459 2
		Bonus: Ace Of Spades/Serve The Shame (acoustic)/(So I Will Burn) Alone			
1997	☐	HORROR WRESTLING	LP PD	The Enclave (USA)	54971
1997	☐	Ace Of Spades	CDS 1tr	The Enclave (USA)	MECP 448
1999	■	Enter My Mind/Down	CDS 2tr	The Enclave (USA)	MECD 1016 2
1999	■	FREAKS OF NATURE	CD	MVG	MVG 139
1999	■	FREAKS OF NATURE	CD	Mercury (USA)	314 546 262 2
		Different artwork.			
1999	☐	FREAKS OF NATURE	CD	MVG/WEA (Germany)	3984-27719-2
1999	☐	Simon Says (Radio Edit/Simon Says (Album Version)	CDS 2tr	Mercury (USA)	MVGCDS 59
1999	☐	Simon Says (Radio Edit/Simon Says (Album Version)	CDS 2tr	Mercury (USA)	MECD 1034-2

1999 CD - MVG 139

1999 CD - 314 546 262 2

DRAMA

Helena Pettersson: v, Peter Franzén: g, Håkan Oksanen: k,
Lars Lindgren: b, Tomas Oksanen: d

Kumla - *Drama* were formed in 1986. In 1987 they entered the Rock SM, and actually won the finals in the below 20 age group. The band awaited stardom, but nothing happened. They finally recorded a four-track MLP of their own, but still nothing happened. They were influenced by bands like **Toto**, **Chicago**, **Saga** and **Rush**, but the sound was a bit more soul-influenced. On the second single they had taken on more influences from melodic bands like **Bon Jovi** and **Europe**. After some personnel changes, the band finally folded. Some of the members continued as cover-band, later dance band, *Nova*. Tomas now plays in cover/show band *Janssons Frestelse*.

1987 ■ Opening .... MLP 4tr   Rolab .... RM 1201
    Tracks: Carefully/So Far Away/Find Yourself/Am I To Blame?
1990 □ Hold On The Night/Never Stop Believe In Love ....7"   Rolab .... RM 1105

1987 MLP - RM 1201

DREAM

Kenny Lindal: v, Kennth Holmberg: g, Claes Hedlund: g,
Mikael Gustafsson: b, Bo Stenlund: k, Lars-Göran Persson: d

Skellefteå - Really good, 70s-sounding hard rock, a bit similar to **Neon Rose**, but with a more commercial touch. The band can also be found on the compilation *Musik i Skellefteå 2* (1982).

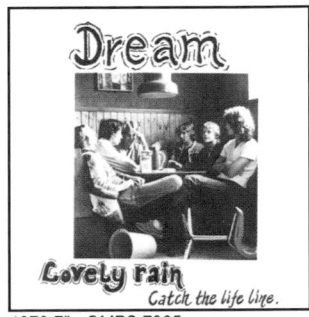

1979 ■ Lovely Rain/Catch The Lifeline ....7"   Great Music Production .... GMPS 7905

1979 7" - GMPS 7905

DREAM BANK

Tony Hellander: v, Göran Elmquist: g/b, Niclas Sigevall: d

Stockholm - When **Trash** broke up, singer Tony kept writing material. He got together with guitarist and producer Göran (**Erika, Bam Bam Boys**) and they recorded the 12". The style is very varied, from mellow **Zeppelin**-influenced hard rock to **Zappa**:ish fusion. After the 12" former **Electric Boys** drummer Niclas joined the band, but the band only lasted for another CDS, which is quite anonymous AOR. Tony later joined forces with Conny Bloom's *Titanic Truth* and recorded one CD. Göran is a highly skilled pedal board builder at Sound Of Silence.

1991 □ Leave The Lights On/Watson .... 12" 2tr   New Republic NR-100-10
1993 ■ Don't Stand In The Rain ....CDS 1tr   New Republic NR-100-11

1993 MCD - NR-100-11

DREAM EVIL

Niklas Isfeldt: v, Fredrik Nordström: g, Daniel "Dannee Demon" Varghamne: g,
Peter Stålfors: b, Patrik "Pat Power" Jerksten: d

Göteborg - Something of a metal all-star band formed in 1999 when Fredrik was on a vacation in Greece and met up with **Mystic Prophecy**/**Firewind** guitarist Kostas "Gus G." Karamitroudis. Gus made a visit to Göteborg later the same year. Fredrik is the owner of Studio Fredman, and the two ended up working on some song ideas. Fredrik also wrote one of the tracks on the debut by **Hammerfall**, which was recorded in his Fredman Studio, and where Niklas did the backing vocals. Remembering Niklas' vocals they drafted the high-pitched metal singer. Niklas was in the coverband **The Jericho Brothers** together with Peter and suggested him as bassist. A demo later they were signed by Century Media, without even having a name. Now they needed a drummer and Fredrik knew former **Mercyful Fate**/**Notre Dame** drummer Tommy "Snowy Shaw" Helgesson, who was perfect for the job, at first just as a session member, but ending up permanent after a few gigs. They now took the name off the classic **Dio** album. Fredrik has, by the way also produced and recorded numerous bands like **Dimmu Borgir, In Flames, Hammerfall, Arch Enemy** etc. The band's first official show was at the 2000 Decibel Show in Bengtsfors May 2002. *Dream Evil* play outstanding melodic metal, not the major-scale German-style sing-along power metal, but more in the vein of Swedish colleagues **Lost Horizon, Nocturnal Rites** etc. There's even a metal shuffle on the album **H.M.J** (Heavy Metal Jesus). They are incredibly tight, with top notch musicianship and killer vocals. The song titles are however total wonderfully clichéd - *Heavy Metal In The Night, Kingdom Of The Damned, Hail To The King* etc. Despite this... highly recommended! After *The Book Of Heavy Metal* Gus left the band and was replaced by Markus "Mark Black" Fristedt (**Illwill, Dragonord**, now in **Massive Audio Nerve**). In January 2006 Snowy also left the band to work on his glam/slease project **XXX**, who released one album before they folded, plus he is a member of **Therion**. They now found drummer Pat Power, practically in their own living room, since he had worked as an engineer in Studio Fredman for several years. In 2007 Markus decided to leave the band as he needed more time for his family life and the band found Daniel "Dannee Demon" Varghamne to replace him. In 2009 Gus replaced Zakk Wylde as Ozzy's guitarist. *Dreamland* guitarist Joakim "Jake E" Lundberg was also in the band briefly during 2005.

2002 CD - 77322 2

2002 CD - 77426-2

2003 MCD - 77522 2

2004 CD - 77526 2

2002 ■ DRAGONSLAYER ....CD   Century Media 77322 2
2002 □ DRAGONSLAYER ....CD   King Records (Japan) KICP-878
    Bonus: Dragon Heart/Losing You

| 2002 | ■ | EVILIZED | CD | Century Media | 77426 2 |
| 2003 | ■ | Children Of The Night | MCD 4tr | Century Media | 77522 2 |

Tracks: Children Of The Night (Edit)/Dragon Heart/Betrayed/Evilized (unplugged)+ video
Children Of The Night

2004	■	THE BOOK OF HEAVY METAL	CD	Century Media	77526 2
2004	■	THE BOOK OF HEAVY METAL	CD+DVD	Century Media	77526 0
2004	□	THE BOOK OF HEAVY METAL	CD	King Records (Japan)	KICP-996

Bonus: The Enemy/Chapter 6

| 2004 | □ | THE BOOK OF HEAVY METAL | CD+DVD | King Records (Japan) | KICP-9996 |

Bonus: The Enemy/Chapter 6

| 2004 | ■ | The First Chapter | MCD 3tr | Century Media | 77525 3 |

Tracks: The Book Of Heavy Metal/Tired/Point Of No Return

| 2006 | ■ | UNITED | CD | Century Media | 77570 2 |
| 2006 | □ | UNITED | 2CD | Century Media | 77570 0 |

Bonus: Calling Your Name/Dynamite/Into The Unknown/I Will Never/Vengeance. Slipcase.

| 2006 | □ | UNITED | 2CD | King Records (Japan) | KICP-91208 |

Bonus: Pain Patrol/Lady Of Pleasure + bonus CD: Calling Your Name/Dynamite/Into The
Unknown/I Will Never/Vengeance. Slipcase.

2006	□	UNITED	CD	King Records (Japan)	KICP-1208
2006	□	UNITED	CD	Fono (Russia)	FO636CD
2006	□	United	MCD 3"	Century Media	77570-0

Tracks: Calling Your Name/Dynamite/Into The Unknown/I Will Never/Vengeance

2008	□	GOLD MEDAL IN METAL	2CD	Century Media	997666-2
2009	□	GOLD MEDAL IN METAL	2CD	King Records (Japan)	KICP-1328/9
2010	□	IN THE NIGHT	CD	Century Media	997968-2
2010	□	IN THE NIGHT	CDd	Century Media	997968-0

Bonus Good Nightmare/The Return

| 2010 | □ | IN THE NIGHT | CD | King Records (Japan) | KICP-1460 |

Bonus Good Nightmare/The Return/Save Yourself/Black Hole

2010	□	IN THE NIGHT	CD	Century Media (USA)	8868-2
2010	□	IN THE NIGHT	CD	Mazzar Records (Russia)	MZR CD 447 D
2013	□	THE BOOK OF HEAVY METAL	2CD	Century Media	998279-0

Slipcase. Bonus live CD from Gold Medal In Metal.

2004 MCD - 77525 3

2006 CD - 77570 2

DREAM POLICE

(See Snakepit Rebels)

DREAMHUNTER

Stig Gunnarsson: v, Olle Zimmerman: g, Thomas Lassar: k,
Peter Otterborg: b, Perry Karlsson: d

Örebro - The band was previously known as *Lifeline* and recorded two 7" singles and the MCD *Anyway You Want It* under that name. When *Lifeline* didn't work out as planned, despite the band's high musical quality, Olle and drummer Per Karlsson formed pop-band *Vibe*. Finally Z Records heard the old *Lifeline* recordings and blew life into the band again. New name and a new outstanding heavy AOR-album. Thomas Lassar also recorded three albums with *Crystal Blue* and has also played with *Damned Nation* for a brief period. He has also written some tracks for *Last Autumn's Dream*, plus he has his own cover band *Watchie's Orkester*.

2000 CD - ZR 1997025

2001 CD - ZR 1997046

| 2000 | ■ | KINGDOM COME | CD | Z Records | ZR 1997025 |
| 2000 | □ | KINGDOM COME | CD | Pony Canyon (Japan) | PCCY-01465 |

Bonus: The Confessions Of An Ordinary Man

| 2001 | ■ | BAD ATTITUDE | CD | Z Records | ZR 1997046 |

DREAMLAND

Joakim "Jake E/Jake Steel" Lundberg: v, Eric Rauti: g,
Nils Olsson: g, Mats Rendlert: b, Alexx Hedlund: d

Göteborg - The band was formed in 1997, initially called *Infinity*, under which name they released the CDS *The Call/Hercules* (2002 private). In 2002 the band split, but reformed as *Dreamland* when Rauti replaced guitarist Fredrik Josefsson. On the band's debut album the line-up featured Joacim, Erik, Mats, guitarist Johan Eriksson and drummer Marcus Sköld. In 2006 Sköld had been replaced by Jesse Lindskog (*Dragonland*). After *Eye For An Eye*, in 2008, the band again changed drummer to Alex and Eriksson was replaced by Nils Olsson. Jake has also lent his voice to backing vocals on albums by bands like *Hammerfall*, *Dragonland*, *Cans* and *Dignity*. Mats is also found in Spanish/Swedish band *Sandlinas*, Rauti is a member of the resurrected *Torch* and Joakim is found in *Amaranthe*.

2005 CD - DY10020-2

2006 CD - DY10028-2

2009 CD - DY20085-2

| 2005 | ■ | FUTURE'S CALLING | CD | Dockyard 1 | DY10020-2 |
| 2005 | □ | FUTURE'S CALLING | CD | Avalon (Japan) | MICP-10556 |

Bonus: Masquerade/Fade Away (video)

| 2006 | ■ | EYE FOR AN EYE | CD | Dockyard 1 | DY10028-2 |
| 2009 | ■ | EXIT 49 | CD | Dockyard 1 | DY20085-2 |

1995 MCD - - -

DREAMLINE
Andreas Michols: v/g, Kenth Lindh: g, Kjell Haraldsson: k, Kenneth Sundqvist: b, Fredrik Nilsson: d

Uppsala - Formed in 1993. *Dreamline* are a good melodic hard rock band. The verses are straight, heavy AOR, but they tend to throw in some progressive sections in between to make it all a bit more interesting. The track *Chains Of Freedom* is quite close to *Talisman*. Good stuff, but with low budget production. Good vocals and good musicians. Kenth was previously drummer of *Tony Barrera Band*. After the MCD Andreas was sacked.

1995 ■ Land Of Love ....MCD 4tr   private .... - -
    Tracks: Feel The Heart/Dreamline/Chains Of Freedom/Land Of Love.

1994 MCD - PLC 2001

DRIVER
Peter Arvidsson: v/g, Jimmy Pinaitis: g, Patric Carlsson: b, Jörgen Björk: d

Växjö - A very good melodic hard rock band with emphasis on heavy guitars and good vocals. In the vein of old *Dokken*. Unfortunately nothing more came out of this promising band. Jörgen and Peter later recorded an album with the more industrial band *Dumper*.

1994 ■ Driver ....MCD 4tr   private ....PLC 2001
    Tracks: By The River's Edge/Back In Your Arms/Kick In The Groin/Wind Cries

1998 MCDp - Drugs 98001

DRUGS, THE
Nils Lindström: v, Orvar Wennström: g, Martin "Bollack" Wezowski: b, Johan Helgesson: d

Malmö - Killer seventies-tinged hard rock with a strong touch of *Badlands*. Killer vocals. Bass player Martin previously recorded some demos with *Booze Brothers* and was later in *Majestic* and *Merrygold*. Orvar was also found in *Reptilian* and Helgesson in *Pete Sandberg's Jade* and *Wit*. Orvar, Martin and Johan later also recorded an album with *Original Sin*.

1998 ■ Bottom Of The Sea ....MCDp 4tr   private .... Drugs 98001
    Tracks: Bottom Of The Sea/Evil On/ Outside Your Door/ Couldn't Be Better

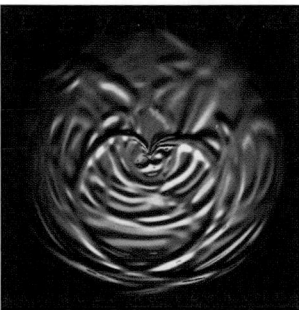

1995 CD - DDCD 001

DRY DIVE
Thomas Rehn: v, Allan Sundberg: g, Henric Von Boisman: b, Marcus Von Boisman: d

Huddinge (Stockholm) - Formed in December 1993. Rather quirky hard rock with influences from grunge, *U2* and... you name it. No quality problems though. Good vocals and good musicianship. Fans of *Pearl Jam* and similar should check it out. Quite witty title.

1995 ■ ASS HOLE AS POSSIBLE...CD   ReSuBo Productions .... DDCD 001

2010 CD - FS46

DRÅPSNATT
Vinterfader: v/k, Narstrand: g/b/d

Skellefteå - The band was formed in 2005 by Vinterfader (*Maleficium*) and Narstrand (*Sangre*, *Maleficium* as Charot) influenced by bands like *Mayhem*, *Old Mans Child*, *Månegarm* and *Dark Funeral*. Really interesting and varied, almost progressive folk-oriented death metal with a touch of *Vintersorg* and *Kampfar*, with high-pitched, *Burzum*-style screeching vocals in Swedish. Very competent musicians. *I denna skog* is a bit faster and more brutal than the follow-up. Dråpsnatt means "manslaughter night". The band also recorded two, as yet unreleased, full albums before the debut. *Skelepht* means Skellefteå. Drums on this album were played by Blotgast and the style and sound had a more metal approach and also with a more melancholic touch. Not a Satanic band, but dealing more with dystopia, armageddon and current worldly problems.

2009 ☐ I DENNA SKOG ....CD   Frostscald Records................................FS32
2010 ■ HYMNER TILL UNDERGÅNGEN..CD   Frostscald Records................................FS46
2012 ☐ SKELEPHT ....CD   Frostscald Records................................FS58

2002 CDSp - BMCD 162

DUMPER
Peter Arvidsson: v/g/k, Eric Johansson: g/v, Jörgen Björk: d

Eksjö/Nässjö - Heavy, industrially-oriented metal with a strong glam-ish attitude, quite similar to late *Shotgun Messiah* or try to imagine a mix of *Peace Love & Pitbulls* and *Nasty Idols*. The singer sounds slightly influenced by Billy Idol. Jörgen and Peter are ex-*Driver*.

2002 ■ X-teen Revolution/Pick Your Poison .... CDSp   Black Mark .... BMCD 162

DUNDER

Franco Mavica: v/h, **Kent Spjuth:** g, **Dick Karlsson:** g,
Stephan Anderzon: b, **Carl Moser:** d

Västerås - Quite straight and bluesy hard rock. Formerly known as *Dunder Å Snus*. The album is not as heavy as they were live. This band was actually offered, but rejected, the song *Skateboard* before it was picked up by *Magnum Bonum*, who had a huge hit with that song... Carl Moser later joined *Pegasus* and he also recorded one album with *Lynx*. He is now breeding pigs (not that far from the music business, eh...).

1978 ○ Struggle/Misery ....7" private FIX-1
    White label test pressing without sleeve.
1978 ■ DUNDER...LP Mercury..6363 014

1978 LP - 6363 014

DURANGO RIOT, THE

Fredrik "Fred" Andersson: v/g, **Håkan Ficks:** b, **Erik Sjökvist:** d

Karlskoga - **The Durango Riot** were formed by a bunch of childhood friends in 2005. They started mixing the finesse of **Queens Of The Stoneage** with the energy of **The Stooges** and thereby did stick out a bit compared to a lot of the stoner acts on the Fuzzorama label. The band is also featured on the soundtrack of the game *Pro Evolution Soccer*. On the second album the band became a trio dropping second guitarist Jakob "Jake" Martinsson. The album was produced by Joe Barresi (**Kyuss, QOTSA**).

2007 ■ TELEMISSION..CD Fuzzorama.................................FUZZCD 008
2009 □ TELEMISSION..CD Universal (Japan)...........................UICE-1152
    Bonus: Burn The House. Different artwork.
2012 □ BACKWARDS OVER MIDNIGHT ....CD NineTone...NRCD 114

2007 CD - FUZZCD 008

DURTHANG

Archaic: v/g, **"Henrik Nachtzeit/Norden" Sunding:** d/b/g

Östersund - **Durthang** existed between 2004 and 2005. The band recorded the demo *Passage Beyond The Cold Vales Of Desolation* in 2004, released on pro CD-R in 100 copies. The name was taken from the castle in the land of Mordor (*Lords Of The Ring*). Nachtzeit (aka Norden) is also found in **Nihilium**, **Hypothermia** and **Life Neglected**. Horribly recorded, depressive, more or less emo-oriented black metal, which sounds more like a rehearsal recording. Sunding has also recorded with **Hypothermia**, **Life Neglected**, **Lustre** and **Mortem Parto Humano**.

2005 ■ LEAD YOURSELF TO FAILURE (split).....................................LP Old Ruin...ORR 001
    Split with Hypothermia. Tracks: Chamber Of Rape And Ruin/Silence. 111 copies

2005 LP - ORR 001

DUSKFALL, THE

Kai Jaakkola: v, **Mikael Sandorf:** g, **Antti Lindholm:** g, **Matte Järnil:** b, **Oskar Karlsson:** d

Luleå - In 1999 the band, initially named **Soulash**, rose from the ashes of death metal band **Gates Of Ishtar**, initially featuring Sandorf, bass player Tommi Kuno (later in **Daemonicus**, **Hellmaster**) and drummer Urban Carlsson. The band recorded their first demo in 1999, at the time with singer Per Johansson (later in **Hel**, **Torchbearer**, **Satariel**) and guitarist Jonny Ahlgren. It was followed by *Tears Are Soulash* in 2000 and the addition of new singer Kai (**Necromicon**, **Deathbound**). After this they changed their name to **The Duskfall** and went through another member change when Kuno was replaced by Kai Molin and Carlsson by Oskar Karlsson. The first demo under the new name was *Deliverance* (2001). The line-up on the debut album featured Jaakkola, Sandorf, Karlsson, Molin and guitarist Glenn Svensson. It was produced by Daniel Bergstrand and featured guest appearances by backing singer Lawrence Mackrory (**Damien, Andromeda, Darkane, F.K.Ü**) and guitarist/keyboardist Örjan Örnkloo (**Misery Loves Co.**). After the album Svensson was replaced by Joachim Lindbock. Second album *Source* was also recorded at the Dug Out by Bergstrand. *Lifetime Supply Of Guilt* saw another change in line-up with Molin being out of the band with Marco Eronen (**Raised Fist**) stepping in and Antti Lindholm replaced Lindblock. For the band's last album Eronen had left to devote his time to **Raised Fist** and his replacement was none less than former **Crawley**/**Lost Souls** member Matte Järnil. In 2008 Sandorf decided to leave and by this the band folded. In 2009 former **Duskfall** members Sandorf, Järnil and Karlsson formed the band **Helltrain**. Powerful thrash-infused death metal, quite close to early In Flames, Dark Tranquillity and Soilwork. Great production. Highly recommended.
Website: www.myspace.com/theduskfall

Duskfall at daybreak

2002 □ FRAILTY..CD Black Lotus ....BLRCD 041
2003 □ SOURCE...CD Black Lotus ....BLRCD 060
2005 □ LIFETIME SUPPLY OF GUILT...CD Irond (Russia) ....CD 05-1049

2005 CD - NB 1491-2

...

<table>
</table>

Year		Title		Format	Label	Catalog
2005	■	LIFETIME SUPPLY OF GUILT	CD	Nuclear Blast	NB 1491-2	
		Slipcase				
2005	□	FRAILTY & SOURCE	2CD	Nuclear Blast	NB 1499-2	
		Bonus: Unspoken/The Light (Demo)/None (Demo)/Dawn Skies (Demo)/Take Control (Demo)/Tune Of The Slaughtered Hearts (Demo)				
2005	□	FRAILTY & SOURCE	DCD	Irond (Russia)	CD 05-1050	
		Same as NB 1499-2				
2006	□	LIFETIME SUPPLY OF GUILT	CD	Metal Mind	MASSCDDG1299	
		2000 copies.				
2007	■	THE DYING WONDERS OF THE WORLD	CD	Massacre	MAS CD 0578	
2011	□	FRAILTY/SOURCE	2CDd	Metal Mind	MASS CD 1394 DGD	
		Double pack re-issue. Bonus: Tune Of Slaughtered Hearts/The Light/None/Dawn Strikes/ Taking Control/Unspoken. 2000 numbered copies.				

2007 CD - MAS CD 0578

DUST

Henrik Wenngren: v/g/b, Joakim Jonsson: d/b/k

Västerås - The band was formed in 1996 when the duo decided to start a side-project to their original band **Mornaland**. They recorded their first demo the same year, but under the name **Nerghal**. Late 1996 they became **Dust** and recorded the demo *A Wander Through The Dark Realm*. The demo was released by Mester and sold in 300 copies. After a short break they recorded the demo *The Third Convention* in 1999 and later the 7" was released by Mester. A new four track demo-CD was supposed to be recorded in 2002. Black/death metal with a touch of **Amon Amarth**. The members are also found in **Skyfire** and Joakim has also recorded with numerous other bands like **Axenstar**, **The Mist Of Avalon**, **Skinfected** and he is also found in **Assailant**. Wenngren is also found in **Autumn Dweller**. The band has now changed its name to **Favilla** and a demo was recorded in 2007.
Website: http://dust.vze.com/

2001 7" - MP 005

2001	■	The Endless Fall	7" 3tr	Mester Productions	MP 005
		Tracks: The Prophecy/Chosen One/Endless Fall For Humanity. 500 copies.			

DUST BOWL JOKIES

Alexander "Alex" Brorsson: v, Victor Karlsson: g,
Niklas "Nicke" Nilsson: g, Hampus "Action" Södergren: d

Sölvesborg - **Dust Bowl Jokies** are a young sleaze-oriented band with a hint of vintage **Guns 'N' Roses** mixed with **Quireboys** as well as a southern-ish touch. Decent. Stepped it up on the CD.

2011	□	Hoodoo Voodoo Allstar/Burlesque	CDSp 2tr	private	DBJ01
2013	□	COCKAIGNE VAUDEVILLE	CDd	Rambo Music	MES 001

2013 CD -??

DYNAMITE

Mattias Karlsson: v/g, Sebastian Hed-Pikas: g, Adam Butler: b, Jonas Hagström: d

Växjö - When I first heard **Dynamite**, I was blown away by their stage presence and by their genuine old-school **AC/DC** sound, even down to the Bon Scott-style vocals. The band recorded their first demo in 2012. They also made a big impression on the local police when staging a bank robbery for their video, but forgot to let them know beforehand...

2013	■	LOCK 'N LOAD	CD	Denomination	DEN006

2013 CD - DEN006

DYNAMITE WASTELAND

Jarmo Mäkkeli: v/g, Trond Vinje: g, Magnus Engdahl: b, Patrik Johansson: d

Västerås - The band was formed in 1990. The line-up on the flexi was Jarmo, Patrik, Janne (g) and Kenneth (d). The follow-up saw the change from Patrik to Nicky on bass. On the CD the line-up was as above. **Dynamite Wasteland** could be described as adrenaline-reinforced sleaze-tainted hard rock 'n roll. You can find similarities to bands like **Hanoi Rocks**, **Faster Pussycat** etc. Bass-player Magnus was later found in hard rockers **Schizophrenic Circus**.

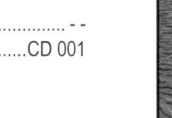

1990	□	A F**king Christmas/Sad 'N Blue/Restless	7" 3tr flexi	private	SF1 896
		Flexidisc with a low budget cover.			
1992	■	THIS WASN'T SUPPOSED TO HAPPEN	LP	Manland Records & Productions	- -
1993	□	Yellow House Rock	MCD 5tr	Legit Music	CD 001
		Tracks: Lay Your Eyes/Take My Soul/She Comes Down/Come Back/She's A Clown.			

1992 LP - - -

DYNAZTY

Nils Molin: v, "Rob" Love Magnusson: g, Mikael Lavér: g,
Joel "Joey Fox" Apelgren: b, Georg "Egg" Härnsten: d

Stockholm - Formed in 2007 by Love Magnusson and John Berg, soon accompanied by Härnsten and Apelgren. In 2008 they found singer Molin on MySpace. Great, well-played, well-produced

heavy sleaze in the vein of **Hardcore Superstar** meets **Nasty Idols** with a high pitch-singer in Nils. Great guitarist, too! Fits like a glove on the Perris label. The debut was produced by Chris Laney. In 2010 the band was signed by movie star Peter Stormare for his Stormvox label (**H.E.A.T**) and in 2011 they recorded their first album for the new label in Stormare's own studio Sherman Oaks in California. Before this release guitarist John Berg was out of the band, and later replaced by Mikael Lavér (**DeVan**). Drummer George was part of the Swedish **Queen** musical *We Will Rock You*. In 2012 the band participated in the Eurovision Song Contest with the song *Land Of Broken Dreams*, written by Thomas G:son (**Masquerade**) and Thomas "Plec" Johansson. The song is found on the compilation *Melodifestivalen 2012* (2012 M&L). *Website: www.dynazty.com*

2009 CD - PER 2172

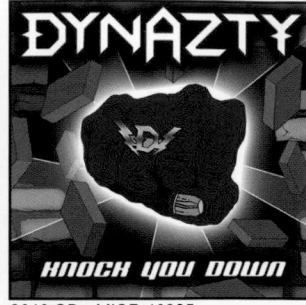

2010 CD - MICP-10985

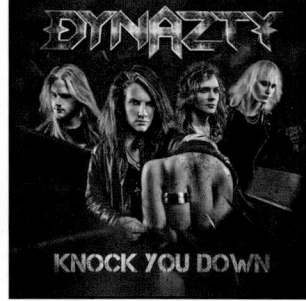

2010 CD - SVXCD 7007

2012 CD - SoFoCD 004

Sultans bringing the thunder to knock you down

2009 ■	BRING THE THUNDER	CD	Perris	PER 2172
	Bonus: Sail Away			
2010 ■	KNOCK YOU DOWN	CD	Stormvox	SVXCD 7007
	Bonus: This Is My Life/A Girl Like You			
2010 ■	KNOCK YOU DOWN	CD	Avalon Marquee (Japan)	MICP-10985
	Bonus: Too Much Is Not Enough/One In A Million/Stand As One. Different artwork.			
2012 ■	SULTANS OF SIN	CD	SoFo Records	SoFoCD 004

DYNGRAK
Crax: v, Teijo Järvinen: g, Martin Stenquist: g, Thomas Netzler: b, Pelle Ekman: d

Göteborg - Straight blues-oriented hard rock with whiskey-stained vocals. Quite close to Finnish band **Peer Günt** or like a hard rock version of **Count Bishops**. Not bad at all. *Dyngrak* is Swedish for "shitfaced". Netzler and Ekman have previously recorded with folk-rockers **Kebnekajse**. The simple design cover seems to be stamped by hand as they all look a little different.

1987 ■	Gambler/One More Line	7"	Rockland Scandinavia	Z-1002

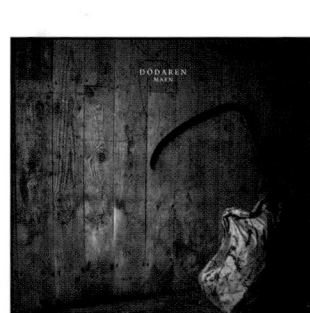

1987 7" - Z-1002

DÖDAREN
Martin Claesson: v/g, Fredrik Boulund: g, Eric Rådegård: b, Jon Solheim: d

Göteborg - Another new, young addition to the ever growing Swedish retro scene, also singing in Swedish like colleagues **Abramis Brama**, **Horisont** and **Mårran**. **Dödaren** (approximately "the killer"), play outstanding, quirky retro-oriented groovy riff-oriented hard rock. Killer!

2012 ■	MAEN	CDd	Transubstans	TRANS 105

2012 CDd - TRANS 105

DÖDFÖDD
Emil "Atum" Lundin: v/d, Filip: g/k, Johannes "Tehôm" Kvarnbring: b

Borlänge - The band was formed in 2001, featuring Atum and guitarist Filip, and recorded their first two demos the same year, *Livlös massa, dödfödd själ* and *Förfall, undergång och död*. In 2002 Total Holocaust released the band's two demos on one cassette in 666 copies and the same year Orderless Evil Productions released the demo *Besvärjelser för omvänd rekreation* on tape. The line-up now featured Atum, Kvarnbring and Filip. The album is the band's old demos released on vinyl. Melancholic black metal. Kvarnbring is also found in **Mortuus** and **Ofermod**, while Lundin was found in the latter and **Reverborum Ib Malacht**. The band has also featured Sir N (**Kaos Sacramentum**, **Grifteskymfning**, **Svartrit** etc). Dödfödd means stillborn in Swedish.

2012 ■	DEMO10	LP	Ancient Records	AR 029
	250 copies.			

2012 LP - AR 029

EF BAND

Roger Marsden: v, Bengt Fisher: g/v, Anders "Andy LaRocque" Allhage: g, Pär Ericsson: b, Dag Eliason: d

Göteborg - In 1976 Pär Ericsson and Bengt recorded the album *Daybreak* with heavy fusion-unit *Epizootic*, an expensive item today. *EF Band* were formed in 1978. The line-up on the first two singles featured guitarist Bengt Fisher, bassist/singer Pär Ericsson and drummer Christer Jönsson. After an ad in Melody Maker, Scotsman Andy Goodwyn became the band's manager. *EF Band* was the only Swedish band to appear on the first *Metal For Muthas* compilation album, probably because they were more well-known in the UK than in Sweden and because the band's drummer at that time was Dave Dufort (**Steve Gibbons Band,** Mike Oldfield, *Angelwitch*). In time for the debut-album young skinsman Dag Eliasson took over after DuFort. *Last Laugh Is On You* was produced by Derek Lawrence (**Deep Purple, Wishbone Ash, Legs Diamond**), but due to an untrimmed studio, the album didn't come out sounding too well. *Alien* guitarist Tony Borg appeared with the band on a TV-show but he was never a member of the band. On *Deep Cut* the band was completed with former *Picture* singer John Ridge (aka John Boutkam), but he left just after its release. New singer was Roger Marsden (*Angelwitch*, **Deep Machine**) and another guitarist was added to the band, Anders Allhage a.k.a Andy LaRocque. The band's last album was no big hit and they disbanded in 1987. Anders has later been found in **King Diamond Band, Illwill** and is now a well-reputed producer with his own studio Los Angered, later renamed Sonic Train Studios. Dag moved to Los Angeles where he sold used cars, Per quit music and Bengt had his own studio and was active as a musician working with childrens music. Bengt Fisher sadly passed away from lung cancer in April 2001. *EF Band* played high-quality powerful hard rock with a touch of the 70s, as well as the traditional 80s metal sound. The vocals on the early recordings were quite "Swedish", but still good. Recommended. Dave Dufort has now changed name to Gerian Germaine Dufort. The songs *Another Day Gone* and *Night Angel* can be found on the compilation *British Steel Vol 2* (Metal Rarities). *Their Finest Hours* is a tribute in the memory of Bengt, containing all the band's material plus bonus-tracks. Long-time friend and manager Andy Goodwyn pulled the strings on this one. In 2003, also Ridge passed away from brain cancer. The 2005 live album, is also a posthumous release, originally recorded in 1983.

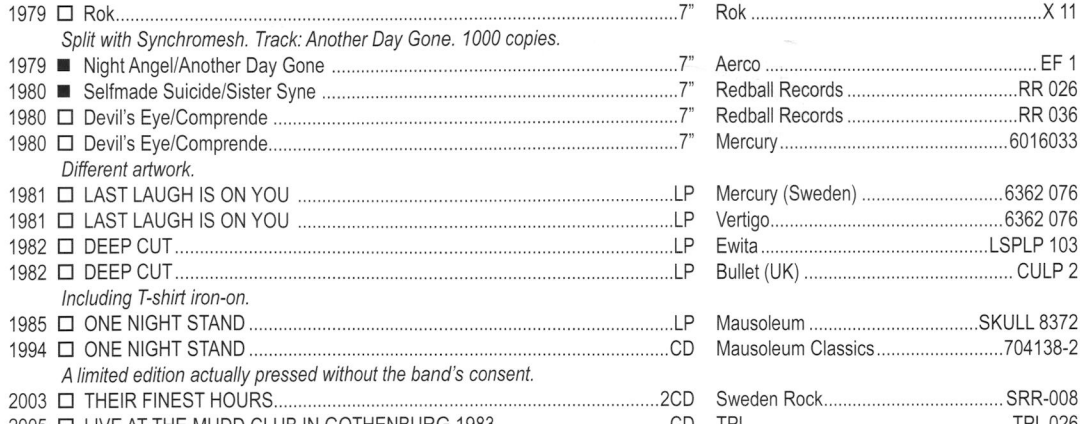
Who's laughing?

1979 7" - EF 1

Year		Title	Format	Label	Cat. no.
1979	□	Rok	7"	Rok	X 11
		Split with Synchromesh. Track: Another Day Gone. 1000 copies.			
1979	■	Night Angel/Another Day Gone	7"	Aerco	EF 1
1980	■	Selfmade Suicide/Sister Syne	7"	Redball Records	RR 026
1980	□	Devil's Eye/Comprende	7"	Redball Records	RR 036
1980	□	Devil's Eye/Comprende	7"	Mercury	6016033
		Different artwork.			
1981	□	LAST LAUGH IS ON YOU	LP	Mercury (Sweden)	6362 076
1981	□	LAST LAUGH IS ON YOU	LP	Vertigo	6362 076
1982	□	DEEP CUT	LP	Ewita	LSPLP 103
1982	□	DEEP CUT	LP	Bullet (UK)	CULP 2
		Including T-shirt iron-on.			
1985	□	ONE NIGHT STAND	LP	Mausoleum	SKULL 8372
1994	□	ONE NIGHT STAND	CD	Mausoleum Classics	704138-2
		A limited edition actually pressed without the band's consent.			
2003	□	THEIR FINEST HOURS	2CD	Sweden Rock	SRR-008
2005	□	LIVE AT THE MUDD CLUB IN GOTHENBURG 1983	CD	TPL	TPL 026

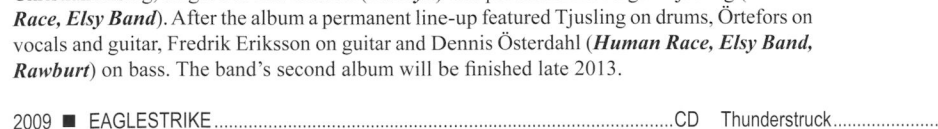
1980 7" - RR 026

EAGLESTRIKE

Christer Örtefors: v/b/g, Shara Peterson: g, Björn Fryklund: d

Göteborg - Solo project from *Freak Kitchen* (formerly *Road Ratt*) singer/bassist Örtefors. Really good melodic hard rock, not as quirky as *Freak Kitchen*, but with some hints of the songs Örtefors writes for his ordinary band. The album also features appearances from guitarist Christian Alsing, singer Pär Edvardsson (*Biscaya*) and percussionist Jörgen Tjusling (**Human Race, Elsy Band**). After the album a permanent line-up featured Tjusling on drums, Örtefors on vocals and guitar, Fredrik Eriksson on guitar and Dennis Österdahl (**Human Race, Elsy Band, Rawburt**) on bass. The band's second album will be finished late 2013.

Year		Title	Format	Label	Cat. no.
2009	■	EAGLESTRIKE	CD	Thunderstruck	TSP 5109 2210

2009 CD - TSP 5109 2210

EARTHQUAKE

Peter Arnildstam: v/g, Olton: b, Thorbjörn Andersson: g, Pontus Lundström: d

Vänersborg - Formed in 1985. Sweden's answer to *Metallica*. *The Truth* is poorly produced, but musically the band is strong. The album was originally mixed by Tommy Denander, but as the band and record company (run by the late *Mercy* guitarist Andrija Veljaca) were not satisfied with his job, they re-mixed it... into a total disaster. Before the second album was recorded, drummer Patrik Engelbrektsson was replaced by Pontus and Niklas Hultman was replaced by Thorbjörn (ex-*Rising*). On *Theatricals* they do a metal-version of *Bee Gees Stayin' Alive*. The band split and Peter was later found in *NME Within*. They recorded a third, still unreleased album.

1992 ■ THE TRUTH..CD Euro ERCD922
Released with two different artworks. "bleeding rose" and "scull".
1993 □ THEATRICALS..CD Euro ....EURO 935/SPV 084-24832

1992 CD - ERCD922

EAST END

Richard Davidsson: v, Peter Tillgren: g, Paul Eriksson: k,
Tomas Nielsen: b, Daniel Fredriksson: d

Jönköping - *East End* rose out of the ashes of *Wild Frontier* in 1989 and folded around '93. They also recorded some demos and entered the Musik Direkt bandstand. Great melodic hard rock! Peter is today in cover band *Why Not*.

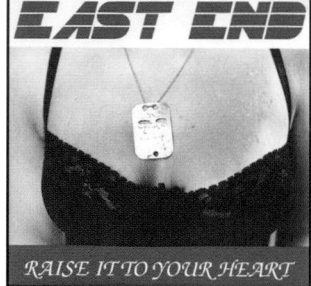

1991 ■ Raise It To Your Heart .... 7" 3tr   private ....EE 001
Tracks: Raise It To Your Heart/Coming Home/The Way I Feel For You.

1991 7" - EE 001

EASY ACTION

Bo "Zinny Zan" Stagman: v, Kjell "Kee Marcello" Lövbom: g, Simon "Roxx"
Karlsson: g, Micael "Grimm" Magnusson: b, Björn "Grizzly" Höglund: d

Stockholm - The band sprung out of Kee and Peo "Alex" Tyrone's collaboration *Kee & Alex*, under which name they recorded a 12". Zinny and Dan also had a band called *Zinny & Danny*, who had recorded a demo that caught the attention of Tandan owner Sanji Tandan. Zinny had a past as a punk rocker in bands like *Belsen Boys* and new wave band *Easy Action* (as drummer), but let his old *Sweet* influences take over and asked if he could use the name. The first constellation of *Easy Action* consisted of Kee, Freddie von Gerber (d), Bo "Zinny Zan" Stagman (v), Dan "Danny Wilde" Segerstedt (g) and Peo "Alex" Tyrén (b). Dan was previously in *Roadrats*, together with Conny Bloom (later *Electric Boys*). He was replaced by former *B-Films* guitarist Kristopher "Chris Lynn/Linn" Lind (son of Magnus Lind of *Aston Reymers Rivaler*, not to be confused with synth/disco artist Chris Linn) and the album was rereleased with new artwork. The song *Turn Me On* was also replaced with *Rock On Rockers*. They had a minor hit with *We Go Rockin'*, a song that was later "borrowed" by US glamsters *Poison* in their song *I Want Action*, which ended up in *Poison* having to pay a settlement to *Easy Action*. Zinny left to form *Dream Police*, then *King Pin*/*Shotgun Messiah* with whom he recorded one album. He was sacked/left and formed *Grand Slam*, and later his own band *Zan Clan*. Former *Horizont* singer Tommy Nilsson replaced Zinny and soon after Björn "Nalle" Påhlsson (*AB/CD, Do-In-It, Treat, Therion*) took over Peo's task as he had left for glam band *Sha-Boom*. *That Makes One* is considered one of Sweden's AOR-classics. On the 7" *Teachers Do It With Class* (quite witty, eh...) Gunnar Hallin (*Neon Rose, Bam Bam Boys*) is also found on the cover but never appeared on record. The band lost their deal. In October 1986 Kee joined *Europe* and the band fell apart. Freddie then formed *Bam Bam Boys* with Matti Alfonzetti (*Jagged Edge, Skintrade*) and later *Rat Bat Blue*. Later on, he founded *Red Fun*, where Marcello was also a member, as well as touring with different acts. Zinny had gone to Los Angeles, while Tommy returned to singing top-40 pop and has had great success doing so. Freddie and Peo toured with their reformed teen pop/punk band *Noise* in 1995, a band that gained major success in the late 70s/early 80s. They even released a new album in 1995. *Easy Action* was not only a rock band but also a bunch of actors (well...). They played the suitable role of a rock band in a blood dripping thriller entitled *Blood Tracks*, one being the track *In The Middle Of Nowhere* with Zinny on vocals. The band actually wrote two songs for the soundtrack as well. Kee released some solo albums in various styles and also produced several other artists. In 2002 Zinny released a solo album entitled *City Boy Blues* (Fastlane Records). He later reformed *Zan Clan* (with Nalle Pålsson on bass) and recorded a new studio album and a live release. In 2005 the band was approached by several festivals with a request to reform. Zinny contacted the former members. Kee and Peo were on, while Chris and Freddy weren't available. After a few rehearsals Peo had to leave and the boys now found new members, Björn "Grizzly" Höglund on drums, Micael "Grimm" Magnusson (ex-*Glanzig*) on bass and Simon "Roxx" Karlsson on guitar. The band also found it was time to reissue the debut, which came in 2007, with several bonus tracks. In 2010 the band started working on a new studio album, which was set for relase in the fall of 2011, but never came out. Kee wrote his autobiography and released the albums *Europe:Redux* (rerecordings of Europe songs), *Melon Demon Drive:Redux* and *Shine On:Redux* in 2011. Grimm sadly died in May 2011 (diabetes related).

Then...

...and now

1983 ☐	We Go Rockin'/Turn Me On	7"	Tandan	EASY 001
1983 ☐	Easy Action	MLP 4tr	Tandan	EASY ML-001
	Tracks: Number One/We Go Rockin'/Don't Cry/Turn Me On			
1983 ☐	Round Round Round/Rock On Rockers	7"	Alpha	ONESIN 003
1983 ■	EASY ACTION	LP	Tandan	TAN LP-007
	First press with Danny Wilde and the track Turn Me On.			
1984 ☐	We Go Rockin'/Turn Me On	7"	Sire (UK)	W9299
1984 ■	EASY ACTION	LP	Tandan	TAN LP-009
	Second press with Chris Lynn and the track Rock On Rockers.			
1984 ☐	The End Of The Line/Another Saturday Night	7"	Tandan	TAN SIN 031
1985 ☐	EASY ACTION	LP	Sire (Japan)	923973-1
1985 ☐	Round, Round, Round/Rock On Rockers	7"	Alpha	ONESIN 003
	White vinyl.			
1986 ☐	Rosie/Partners In Crime/ +1	MLP 3tr	Alpha	ONEMAX 013
1986 ■	Rosie/Partners In Crime	7"	Alpha	ONESIN 013
	Clear or black vinyl.			
1986 ☐	THAT MAKES ONE	LP	KGR	KGRCD 03
	Released in two versions. Second press has the names of the members on the front cover.			
1986 ☐	THAT MAKES ONE	CD	KGR	KGR 03 $
1986 ☐	In The Middle Of Nowhere/Eye For An Eye	7"	KGR	S-005
1986 ☐	Talk Of The Town/There Is A River	7"	KGR	S-008
1986 ☐	Talk Of The Town/Talk Of The Town (Instrumental)	MLP 3tr	KGR	MS-08
	Tracks: Talk Of The Town/Talk Of The Town (instrumental)/Talk Of The Town (Another Swemix Remix)			
1986 ☐	Teachers Do It With Class/One In A Million	7"	KGR	S-010
1988 ☐	Only Love/Teachers Do It With Class	7"	KGR	S-020
1992 ☐	THAT MAKES ONE	CD	WEA	90046-2
	New artwork.			
1994 ☐	THAT MAKES ONE	CD	WEA (Japan)	WMC5-679 $$
	Bonus: There Is A River. New artwork.			
2007 ☐	EASY ACTION	CD	Diesel & Glory	DG 004
	Bonus: Round Round Round/Drop The Bomb (live)/In The Middle Of Nowhere/Roll baby Roll (live)/The End Of The Line/Round Round Round (live)/Don't Cry Don't Crack (live)/Number One (live)/We Go Rockin' (live)			
2007 ☐	EASY ACTION	CD	3D Japan (Japan)	XQAN-1058
	Same as DG 004 plus bonus: Sweet Sangria (live 2006)			
2008 ☐	We Go Rockin' (2008 Re-make)/Jack's Back	CDS	Diesel & Glory	DG 005

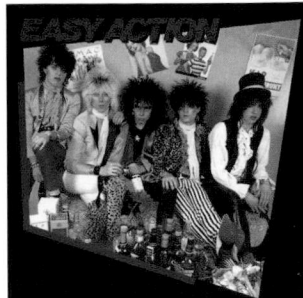
1983 LP - TAN LP-007

1984 LP - TAN LP-009

1986 7" - ONESIN 013

EASY-STREET
Mikael Carlsson: v, Robert Warnqvist: g, Magnus Jönsson: b, Leif Erixon: d

Degerfors - The first single featured singer Ove Jonsson and was an attempt to make a commercial breakthrough. *This Must Be Love* was OK, but not more. *Everybody Want Some* on the other hand was a great single in the vein of *Van Halen*. After the second release the band changed singer and name to *Damned Nation*, and released a number of albums under this name.

| 1989 ■ | With You/This Must Be Love | 7" | Platina | PL 69 |
| 1992 ☐ | Everybody Want Some/High On Emotion | 7" | H.E.M. | HEMS 102 |

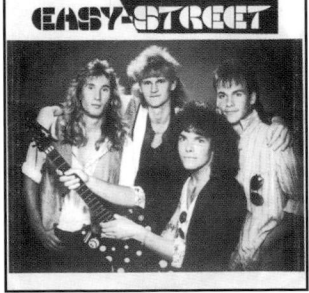
1989 7" - PL 69

EBONY TEARS
Johnny Wranning: g, Conny Jonsson: g, Peter Kahm: b/k, Richard Evensand: d

Stockholm - Powerful death/power metal with touches of goth and traditional metal, featuring former members of *Miscreant* and *Memorium*. Guest violin on the first album by Lennart Glenberg (*Zello*). The album was recorded by Tomas Skogsberg. Peter and Conny has played together in various bands like *It's Alive, Southpaw* and *Dog Faced Gods*, where Wranning was also found on the latter. On *Evil As Hell* bass player Thomas Thun was replaced by Peter and drummer Iman Zolgharnian (*Cauterizer, Dog Faced Gods*) by Richard. The album was recorded in Studio Underground by Pelle Saether (who also does guest vocals on one track) and Lasse Lindén (who also did the artwork). This album owes more to traditional power metal in the *Pantera/Machine Head*-vein. Great stuff. Evensand was also in *It's Alive* and is now living in Australia playing with *Toehider*.

1997 LP PD - BSLP12

1997 ☐	TORTURA INSOMNIA	CD	Black Sun	BS12
1997 ■	TORTURA INSOMNIA	LP PD	Black Sun	BSLP12
1998 ☐	TORTURA INSOMNIA	CD	Toy's Factory (Japan)	TCFK 87147
1999 ☐	A HANDFUL OF NOTHING	CD	Toy's Factory (Japan)	TCFK 87182
	Bonus: Forbidden Thoughts			
1999 ☐	A HANDFUL OF NOTHING	CD	Black Sun	BS 17
2001 ☐	EVIL AS HELL	CD	Black Sun	BS 23
2001 ■	EVIL AS HELL	CD	Black Sun	BS 23 LTD
	Slipcase. Bonus: Bloodsucker			

2001 CD - BS 23 LTD

ECLIPSE

Erik Mårtensson: v/b/g, Magnus Henriksson: g, Johan Berlin: k, Robert Bäck: d

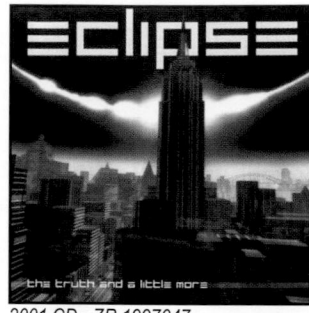

2001 CD - ZR 1997047

2008 CD - FRCD 377

Stockholm - The band was formed in 2000, but prior to this Erik had recorded several first rate demos under his own name, from which some of the tracks appeared on the debut-album. The demos landed Erik a deal with UK based Z Records. He found himself some band members and *Eclipse* was born. High class AOR with vocals pretty reminiscent of Joey Tempest. The debut featured Erik on vocals, bass and guitar, Magnus on guitar and Anders Berlin (*Timescape*) on keyboards and drums. Not satisfied with the infamous label, the band moved on to Frontiers Records. The second album also saw a change in personnel. Berlin was out and in came bass player Fredrik Folkare (guitarist in *Scudiero*, *Unleashed*) and drummer Magnus Ulfstedt (*Torch*). Keyboardist Mats Olausson also makes guest appearance on the album. The album saw the band step it up both in the songwriting and production department. A great piece of melodic metal. The band now took a time out due to some personal problems. In 2007 Erik and Magnus Henriksson returned with some new compadres. The third album, appropriately entitled *Are You Ready To Rock*, saw the return of Anders Berlin and the addition of drummer Robert Bäck (*BALLS, Baltimoore, Sabaton, Billion Dollar Babies*). Kee Marcello also guests on the album. Anders is also found in *Street Talk* and *Bloodbound*. Erik recorded the debut album with the all-star trio *W.E.T* in 2010, where Robert and Magnus Henriksson also lend their helping hands. He has also produced and recorded various bands, as well as lent his vocals as backing singer for bands like *Golden Resurrection*. When *Eclipse* returned in 2012 Anders Berlin had been exchanged for his brother Johan Berlin (*Timescape*). *Bleed And Scream* is yet another high class hard rockng AOR-platter.The 2012 MCD contains two exclusive tracks.
Website: www.myspace.com/eclipsemania

2012 MCDpg - 334 43031

Year		Title	Format	Label	Cat.No.	
2001	■	THE TRUTH & LITTLE MORE	CD	Z Records	ZR 1997047	$$
2004	☐	SECOND TO NONE	CD	Frontiers	FRCD 183	
2004	☐	SECOND TO NONE	CD	Crown Nippon (Japan)	CRCL-4597	
		Bonus: Masterpiece Girl				
2008	■	ARE YOU READY TO ROCK	CD	Frontiers Records	FRCD 377	
2008	☐	ARE YOU READY TO ROCK	CD	Blistering Records (USA)	BR 007	
2008	☐	ARE YOU READY TO ROCK	CD	Irond (Russia)	CD 08-DD681	
2008	☐	ARE YOU READY TO ROCK	CD	King Records (Japan)	KICP-1339	
2012	■	Bleeed And Sceam/Come Hell Or High Water/Into The Fire	MCDpg 3tr	Cosmos Music Group	334 43031	
2012	■	BLEED AND SCREAM	CD	Frontiers Records	FRCD 563	

2012 CD - FRCD 563

EDGE OF SANITY

Robert Karlsson: v, Andreas "Dread/Drette" Axelsson: g,
Sami Nerberg: g, Anders Lindberg: b, Benny Larsson: d

1991 LP - BMLP 10

Finspång/Stockholm - Hard driving death metal with growling vocals, except on some songs where original vocalist Dan Swanö actually sings with a clean voice. The band was formed in 1989 out of the two punk bands *F.Z.Ö.* (Sami, Benny, Dread) and *Ulan Bator* (Dan, Anders). Both bands made vinyl recordings. The demo *Kur-Nu-Gi-A* (the Sumerian word for hell) was the opening key for the band and led to a deal with Black Mark. The debut was recorded at Montezuma Studio (*Candlemass*). Andreas "Drette" Axelsson was the singer in *Marduk* on their first album and later had his pop/rockband *Lucky Seven* on the side, in which Benny was also found. On *The Spectral Sorrows* they do a cover of *Manowar*'s *Blood Of My Enemies* and on *Until Eternity Ends* they surprisingly do a cover of *Police*'s *Invisible Sun*. *Edge Of Sanity* is one of the few bands that never changed any members, like Dan says "It's the five of us, or no one". Benny has also recorded two albums with *Ophthalamis* under the name "Winter". Dan Swanö is involved in production, mixing and has also played in a zillion other bands including the symphonic *Unicorn, Pan-Thy-Monium, Nightingale, Subway Mirror, Ulan Bator, Godsend, Infestdead, Karaboudjan, Bloodbath* etc. etc. He is also singing on Danish band *Macreation*'s album *A Serenade Of Agony* ('93 Progress Red Labels - CD 7913004), but under the name Day Disyraah. The MLP *When All Is Said* that has been seen for sale in lists, was recorded and ready, but never released. A cover of *Slayer*'s *Criminally Insane* is found on the Black Sun Records *Slayer* tribute. In 1997, after *Crimson*, Dan left the band and was replaced by Roberth Karlsson (*Devian, Facebreaker, Scar Symmetry, Pan-Thy-Monium* etc), Dan's old band-mate from *Pan-Thy-Monium* (meaning they did actually change members...).. But after *Cryptic* the band disbanded. *Evolution* is a ten years anniversary CD featuring re-mastered, re-mixed, rerecorded and previously unreleased tracks only. *Evolution* is a double-CD monument of the band, featuring loads of previously unreleased tracks, version, re-mixes etc. *When All Is Said* is another best of. In 2003 Dan revived the band on his own and released the *Crimson* sequel. After this it went quiet.

1993 CD - BMCD 37

1992 CD - BMCD 18

1994 CD - BMCD 61

Year		Title	Format	Label	Cat.No.
1991	■	NOTHING BUT DEATH REMAINS	LP	Black Mark	BMLP 10
1991	☐	NOTHING BUT DEATH REMAINS	CD	Black Mark	BMCD 10
1991	☐	NOTHING BUT DEATH REMAINS	CD	JVC Victor (Japan)	VICP 231 08
		Bonus: Pernicious Anguish (rerecorded)			
1992	☐	UNORTHODOX	CD	JVC Victor (Japan)	VICP 231 09
		Bonus: Human Abiration (rerecorded)			

1992 ☐	UNORTHODOX	LP	Black Mark	BMLP18
1992 ■	UNORTHODOX	CD	Black Mark	BMCD18
1993 ☐	Sanctified	CDS 1tr	Black Mark	BMCD 37-P
	One track promo single.			
1993 ☐	THE SPECTRAL SORROWS	LP	Black Mark	BMLP 37
1993 ☐	THE SPECTRAL SORROWS	CD	Black Mark	BMCD 37
1993 ☐	THE SPECTRAL SORROWS	CD	JVC Victor (Japan)	VICP 231 10
	Bonus: Bleed			
1994 ☐	Until Eternity Ends	MCD 4tr	Black Mark	BMCD 58
	Tracks: Bleed(Until Eternity Ends/Eternal Eclipse/Invisible Sun (Police cover)			
1994 ■	PURGATORY AFTERGLOW	CD	Black Mark	BMCD 61
1994 ☐	PURGATORY AFTERGLOW	CD	JVC Victor (Japan)	VICPS 5453
	Bonus: Until Eternity Ends/Eternal Eclipse			
1996 ☐	CRIMSON	LP	Black Mark	BMLP 68
1996 ☐	CRIMSON	CD	Black Mark	BMCD 68
1996 ☐	CRIMSON	CD	Victor (Japan)	VICP-5683
	Bonus: Murder Divided			
1997 ■	INFERNAL	CD	Black Mark	BMCD 108
1997 ☐	INFERNAL	CD	Victor (Japan)	VICP-5859
1997 ☐	CRYPTIC	CD	Black Mark	BMCD 125
1997 ☐	CRYPTIC	CD	Victor (Japan)	VICP-60165
1999 ■	EVOLUTION	2CD	Black Mark	BMCD 140
2003 ☐	CRIMSON II	CD	Black Mark	BMCD 168
2003 ☐	CRIMSON II	CDd	Black Mark	BMDP 168
2003 ☐	PURGATORY AFTERGLOW	CD	Irond (Russia)	CD 03-430
2003 ☐	CRIMSON	CD	Irond (Russia)	CD 03-435
2003 ☐	THE SPECTRAL SORROWS	CD	Irond (Russia)	CD 03-436
2003 ☐	INFERNAL	CD	Irond (Russia)	CD 03-645
2003 ☐	CRYPTIC	CD	Irond (Russia)	CD 03-646
2003 ☐	UNORTHODOX	CD	Irond (Russia)	CD 03-647
2003 ☐	NOTHING BUT DEATH REMAINS	CD	Irond (Russia)	CD 03-648
2003 ☐	UNORTHODOX	LP	Black Mark	BMLP18
2003 ☐	PURGATORY AFTERGLOW	LP	Black Mark	BMCLP61
2003 ☐	CRIMSON I & II	2LP	Black Mark	BMLP 168
2006 ☐	WHEN ALL IS SAID	2CDd	Black Mark	BMCD 186

1996 CD - BMCD 68

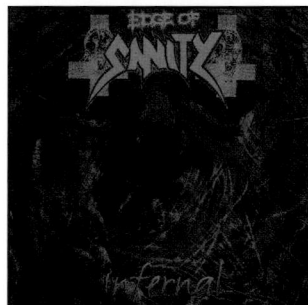

1997 CD - BMCD 108

1999 2CD - BMCD 140

EDLING, LEIF

Leif Edling: v/g/b

Stockholm - Leif Edling is the Swedish forefather doom. Born August 6, 1963. He started his career as singer of the band *Toxic* (the embryo of *Trilogy*, featuring Ian Haugland). In the early eighties he formed the band *Witchcraft*, where he also sang. The style was *Black Sabbath*-influenced doomy metal. The band changed into *Nemesis*, where Leif still handled the vocals. Let's just say, doomy riffs and heavy bass were definitely his stronger side. *Nemesis* released the MLP *Day Of Retribution*, now an expensive classic. *Nemesis* turned into *Candlemass* and in 1986 they released the classic doom album *Epicus Doomicus Metallicus*. Edling has been a consistent member of the band since and also made some side-steps with bands like *Krux* and *Abstrakt Algebra*. In 2003 Edling released a compilation of demos and unreleased tracks from various parts of his career and in 2008 he released his first real solo album. Besides Leif the musicians include guitarists Ulf "Chris Laney" Larsson and Björn Eriksson (*The Cold Existance*), keyboardist Carl Westholm (*Krux, Abstrakt Algebra, Jupiter Society*) and *Tiamat* drummer Lars Sköld. The albums do not stray too far away from the doom of *Candlemass*, although Leif handles the vocals here, himself and he doesn't really measure up to his fellow *Candlemass* singers. Although, it does ad a certain dimension to the music. Besides his bass playing Leif has also been a successful radio host and magazine writer.

Cheer up, Leif!

2003 ☐	THE BLACK HEART OF CANDLEMASS – DEMOS & OUTTAKES	2CD	Powerline	PLRCD 008
2003 ☐	THE BLACK HEART OF CANDLEMASS – DEMOS & OUTTAKES	2CD	CD-Maximum (Russia)	CDM 0403-1361/2
2008 ■	SONGS OF TORMENT, SONGS OF JOY	CDd	GMR	GMRCD 9012
2008 ☐	SONGS OF TORMENT, SONGS OF JOY	CDd	Candlelight	CDL 457 CD

2008 CDd - GMRCD 9012

EGGS ON LEGS

Greta Zackrisson: v, Per Axelsson

Stockholm (?) - Great melodic hard rock. The vocals give it a strong touch of Alannah Myles. Weird name though… Greta had earlier reached some minor stardom when she participated in the 1977 *Eurovision Song Contest* together with Malou Berg. She also sings on the Tom Zacharias' albums *Belinda* and *Till frukost* and has lent her voice to recordings with Bo Hansson and *Gin & Grappo*.

1985 ■	Maggi Said I'm A Prostitute/Nothing Left	7"	Double You	WS 002

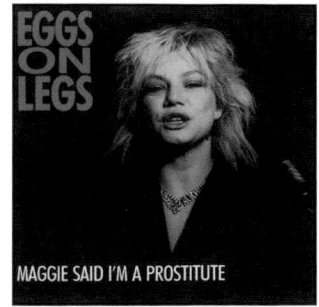

1985 7" - WS 002

EGONAUT

Fredrik Jordanius: v/g, Dennis Zielinski: k, Mikael Bielinski: b, Markus Johansson: d

Borås - Take an ounce of stoner, two ounces of vintage classic hard rock with distorted Hammond organ to spice it up and a touch of sleazy rock 'n roll and you get **Egonaut**. Some tracks are pure 70s hard rock, some have a stoner touch and some are almost sleazy. A great mix indeed! The band labels it "bastard rock". Formed in 2005 by Fredrik (also in *Lake Of Tears*) and Markus. In 2010 the band also released the pro-printed four-track CD-R *N-Pire*.

2011 CD - BRR 004

2009 □	Soundtrack To A Fistfight	MCD 4tr	Bastard Rock Records	- -
	Tracks: 33MPH/Turn/We've Come For You All/Nowhere Bound			
2009 □	Circus Egonaut	MCD 4tr	Bastard Rock Records	BRR 002
	Tracks: I, Me Mine/Bulletproof/Quicksand/A.W.S			
2011 ■	ELECTRIC	CD	Bastard Rock Records	BRR 004
2013 □	MOUNT EGONAUT	CD	Transubstans	TRANS 107

EIDOMANTUM

Christian "Tyrann/S.S. Sexual Death" Andreasson: v,
Richard "St. Erben" Lagergren: g/b, Joel "Ace Tormenta" Pälvärinne: d

Linköping - The band was formed under the name *Lukemborg* in 1998 by Joel and Richard, put on ice for two years, and then reformed with Tyrann on vocals. They recorded the demo *From The Tomb Of All Evil* in 2000 and later got in touch with German label Sombre Records. Musically the band produces fast and furious, but pretty technical death metal, like a mix of early **Bathory** and **Dark Tranquillity**. However, the problem is the utterly awful sound. Not even an old **Nifelheim** live-bootleg would probably sound this bad. In 2003 they recorded the demo *Old Blood* and in 2006 they released a new and better effort. In 2004 Witchhammer Records released the band's first two recordings as a cassette album entitled *At War With Eidomantum*. Lagergren is now found on guitar in **Portrait**.

2001 7" - - -

2006 7" - IHR 017

2001 ■	The Death/Perfection Of Death	7"	Sombre	- -
	333 hand-numbered copies.			
2006 ■	Fear The Master/Black Aura	7"	I Hate	IHR 017

EKLUNDH, MATTIAS "IA"

Mattias IA Eklundh: g/v/d/b/k

Härryda - When **Freak Kitchen** guitar virtuoso Bernt Johannes Mattias "Ia" Ekludh goes solo, he leaves no stone unturned. He not only turns them, he juggles, he throws, he eats and he probably shits them, too. Total guitar-weirdness with guitars, remotes and dildos and with titles that speak for themselves. He also showed a different side on the **Mr Libido** project... but that's another story. The Thunderstruck/Victor-versions of *Freak Guitar* contain a cover of Frank Zappa's *The Black Page*, but Frank's widow did not allow the label to include this on the USA release. Mattias also appears as guest on albums by **Pagan, Locomotive Breath, Evergrey, Pagan, Bumblefoot, Soilwork, Urbandux** etc., plus he has produced, recorded and plays all instruments besides lead-guitar on the first solo album by young guitar-wizz Johan Randén. Non-album tracks can also be found on compilations, *Lydia's House* on *Warmth In The Wilderness* (Lion Music 01) and *Yngwie 2000* on *A Guitar Odyssey – Tribute To Yngwie Malmsteen* (Black Sun 99). The second album contains more guitar virtuoso madness, with a highly unorthodox cover of **Deep Purple**'s *Smoke On The Water*. A highly entertaining and talented guitarist who can put a smile on anyone's face. Mattias has also recorded a more eastern oriented album with the band **Art Metal**, together with bass virtuoso Jonas Hellborg and drummer Anders Johansson. 2013 saw the third crazy venture of Mattias Ia Eklundh, this time songs featuring comb, balloons and alarm clocks. In 2012 Mattias has also released three digital tuition "albums" with play along tracks from his Guitar Camp, entitled *Grow Your Own Mustache*. *The Smorgasbord* features mind-blowing covers of *Hell's Bells, Mah Na Mah Na* and *That's Amore* plus original tracks. If you've never been to an Ia clinic, go se one!!!
Website: www.freakguitar.com

1999 - TSP 2163992

2005 CD - NTS 3093202

2013 2CD - TSP 53131006

1999 ■	FREAK GUITAR	CD	Thunderstruck	TSP 2163992
	Bonus: The Black Page			
1999 □	FREAK GUITAR	CD	JVC Victor (Japan)	VICP 60925
	Bonus: Our Man In Beijing, The Black Page			
1999 □	FREAK GUITAR	CD	Magnum (Taiwan)	VICP 60925
	Same as JVC Victor, but with Taiwanese OBI.			
2001 □	FREAK GUITAR	CD	Nothing To Say (France)	NTS 3068712
2001 □	FREAK GUITAR	CD	Favored Nations (USA)	FN 2210-2
	Bonus: Faith In Chaos/Our Man In Beijing			
2005 ■	FREAK GUITAR – THE ROAD LESS TRAVELLED	CD	Nothing To Say (France)	NTS 3093202
2004 □	FREAK GUITAR – THE ROAD LESS TRAVELLED	CD	Favored Nations (USA)	FN 2500-2
2004 □	FREAK GUITAR – THE ROAD LESS TRAVELLED	CD	JVC Victor (Japan)	VICP-62833
2005 □	FREAK GUITAR – THE ROAD LESS TRAVELLED	CD	Replica (France)	RPL 028
2013 ■	FREAK GUITAR – THE SMORGASBORD	2CD	Thunderstruck	TSP 53131006

EL CAMINO

Daniel Ridell: v, Jimmy Sjöqvist: g, Niklas Hanell: g/k,
Timmy Persson: b, Mattias Johansson: d

Nässjö - **El Camino** were formed in the winter of 2002/2003 with the ambition to create their own style. The first demo was recorded in 2003 and a second in 2006. In 2008 original drummer AR left to pursue other projects, and he was replaced by Johansson (also in **Karnivore** and **Fear The Future**). **El Camino** play heavy stoner rock in the vein of bands like **Electric Wizard** mixed with **Danzig**, but with quite strange vocals. Persson and Sjöqvist are both ex-**Vermin** and also in **Karnivore**.

2013 CD - NTRCD013

2010	☐ Satanic Magiik	MCDd 4tr	Triangular Chaoz	NTR002CD
	Tracks: Prelude To The Horns/Hail The Horns/Mountain Man/Satanic Magiik			
2011	☐ THE SATANIC MAGIIK	LP	Night Tripper	NTR002
2011	☐ THE SATANIC MAGIIK	CD	Night Tripper	NTRCD002
2012	☐ Swedish Assault (split)	7"	Night Tripper	NTR 007
	Split with Rise And Shine. Track: In League With Satan (Venom cover)			
2013	☐ Småland	MLP 3tr	Night Tripper	NTR 012
	Tracks: Småland/I lag med Satan (Venom cover)/Daemonangel			
2013	■ GOLD OF THE GREAT DECEIVER	CD	Night Tripper	NTRCD013

EL GORDO

Filip Fransson: v/b, Joel Pettersson: g, Jens Björk: d

Kungsör - **El Gordo**, formed in 2002, play fuzzed-out stoner similar to **The Graviators**.

2007	■ THE MAN BEHIND THE MACHINE	CD	Glen Ghost	GHOSTCD 001

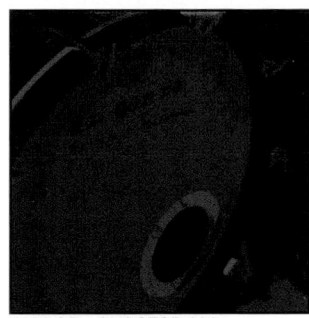
2007 CD - GHOSTCD 001

ELDRIMNER

Alexander Andersson: v, Martin Tjusling: g, Robin Holgersson: g,
Otto Halling: b, Robert Johansson: d

Göteborg - Formed in 2006, originally as a black metal band, but later changed into a more experimental, almost screamo-influenced death metal. On the first demo, *Frusen*, the drums were handled by Oscar Petterson. On the second demo, *Sorg*, he had been replaced by Robert. As Alexander wanted to concentrate on singing the band drafted bass player Otto Halling after the release of the MCD. Alexander is also found in **Marionette**.
Website: www.eldrimner.net

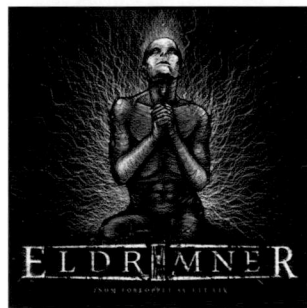
2012 CD - ELD 001

2010	☐ I mitt jag	MCDp 4tr	private	W20852
	Tracks: Ett nytt kapitel/Självförakt/I mitt jag/Sinnets ljuva brott			
2012	■ INOM LOPPET AV ETT LIV	CD	private	ELD 001

ELECTRA TOP RAIDERS (aka ETR)

Åke Reinholtz: v/b, Jerry Nilsson: v/h, Göran Larnö: g, Magnus Birgersson: d

Växjö - The band was formed just for a party gig in 1978 as **Elriders**, playing mostly 60s rock. The original line-up featured singer Jerry Nilsson, guitarist Jan-Erik Andersson, bassist Åke Reinholtz and drummer Sven Kihlström. After about a year they reunited now taking on the name **Electra Top Raiders**, and adding Göran Lärnö on guitar. The band continued playing covers, but started writing their own material in a heavier vein. Jan-Erik quit and Magnus Birgersson took over the drums. In the 1988 the band recorded the album, which contains really great, quite raw and boogie-based hard rock in the vein of early **Foghat**. The band quit in the early nineties, also having keyboardist Stefano Moggia in the line-up the last couple of years. Jerry and Åke had previously released two albums with folkband **Knoa**. Jerry and Göran also released a record with **Kardus**.

1988 LP - SSETR 8801

1988	■ ELECTRA TOP RAIDERS	LP	private	SSETR 8801
	Printed in clear and black vinyl.			

ELECTRIC BOYS

Conny "Bloom" Blomquist: v/g, Franco Santunione: g,
Anders "Andy" Christell: b, Niclas Sigewall: d

Stockholm - Conny and Andy had been playing together since their childhood. The first recording was made with the band **Roadrats**. However Andy had left before the singles were recorded. The two were however reunited in the band **Rolene**. The band made an extensive tour with Finnish glamsters **Hanoi Rocks** in Finland and ironically the guitarist in **Rolene** was none other than Gyp Casino, ex-**Hanoi Rocks**. **Rolene** actually made their farewell-gig as support to the Finns, who also made their last gig that night. Conny was later asked to join a re-union of the band as replacement for Razzle, who was killed in a car crash caused by an intoxicated Vince Neil. He turned it down and later made a short career with the re-united **Neon Rose**. After they split he joined forces with Andy and they took the name **Electric Boys**. The first single, *All Lips 'n*

Hips, was recorded as a duo. This song has actually been considered a classic by influential persons such as **Alice Cooper**, Wizzard (**Mother's Finest**) and not forgetting **Mötley Crüe**, who actually used the band's video as introduction for their show. The song also became a great hit in Sweden. The band was now completed with drummer Niclas Sigewall and former **Glory Bell's Band**-guitarist Franco Santunione. The debut album was produced by the band themselves, but the year after they went to the US to record five new tracks with Bob Rock as producer. The tracks *Freaky Funksters, Hallelujah!, Get Nasty, Party Up* and *Funk-O-Metal Carpet Ride* are not on the US-release. On *Groovus Maximus* the music took a more heavy yet funky turn and the band had a great hit with the **Beatles**-sounding *Mary In The Mystery World*. Vertigo Records also released a cassette called *The Abbey Road Jams* (1992) featuring three previously unreleased tracks. After *Groovus Maximus,* Niclas and Franco left the band and the bands future was uncertain. However at the Zeppelin-awards in 1993 the "new" *Electric Boys* made their first official performance. The new boys were ex-**Great King Rat** drummer Tomas Broman and guitarist Martin "Slim" Tomander, previously with **Grand Slam** (Zinny Zan's band). *Freewheelin'* was never the success they hoped and in 1994 Conny felt he couldn't take the band any further and therefore quit to start a solo-career or form a new band. Franco joined **Reptile Smile**, where Niclas was found as a session-player. In 1995 Conny was writing and recording with the aid of drummer/Singer Tony "Roy Taylor" Hellander (**Trash, Dream Bank**) and bassist Anders "Nippe" Nilsson (now Fästader) (**Advice, Great King Rat**, later **Southfork, John Norum**). The project later became **Titanic Truth** which was a bit different from *Electric Boys*, but still sounding like Conny. Andy made a tour with ex-**Hanoi Rocks** man Andy McCoy. In 1999 Conny released his first solo-album *Psychonaut* which however flunked and in 2000 he joined UK outfit **Silver Ginger 5** where Thomas Broman was also found. Thomas has also been found in bands like **Firebird, John Norum Band, Michael Schenker Group** etc. The previously unreleased track *Shake That Rattle* is found on the bonus-CD for the first encyclopaedia. In 2005 Conny and Andy joined their old friends in **Hanoi Rocks**, with whom they toured and recorded a studio album, before the band folded Christmas 2008. In 2006 Franco joined straight-ahead rockers **Loco Motive**, but nothing has come out of it except some good demos. In 2009 *Electric Boys* once again decided to re-unite with the original line-up. The same year the compilation *Now Dig This!* was released, featuring a 2009 remix of *All Lips N' Hips,* and the recordings of a comeback album commenced. The band made numerous live shows and seemed to be back in their prime. In 2010 the band was picked up by Swedish label Supernova. The return album *And Them Boys Done Swang*, released in 2011, shows a band that had returned to the peak of their sound and style. A killer funk 'o metal album. The track *King Kong Song* was recorded for the **ABBA** tribute *ABBA: The Tribute* (Polar 1992). A new album is set for release in 2014.

Damn, the finger's stuck again!

1987 7" - 888 885-7

1988 7" - 870 586-7

1987 □	All Lips 'N Hips	7"	Mercury	888 865-7	
1987 ■	All Lips 'N Hips/Cheesecake Funk	7"	Mercury	888 885-7	
1987 □	Get Nasty/Get Stoopid (nasty mix)/Get Nasty	MLP 3tr	Mercury	870 586-1	
1988 □	All Lips 'N Hips/Cheesecake Funk	7"	Amulet (Finland)	HOPE 49	
1988 ■	Get Nasty/In The Ditch	7"	Mercury	870 586-7	
1989 □	Electrified/Do The Dirty Dog	7"	Mercury	872 618-7	
1989 □	FUNK 'O METAL CARPET RIDE	CD	Mercury	836 913-2	
1989 ■	FUNK 'O METAL CARPET RIDE	LP	Mercury	836 913-1	
1989 □	Electrified/All Lips 'N Hips (bat mix)	12"	Mercury	VERXDJ 50	

Advance DJ copy. No picture cover.

1989 □	Hallelujah! I'm On Fire/Freaky Funksters	7"	Mercury	874 498-7	
1989 □	Hallelujah! I'm On Fire	CDS 4tr	Mercury	874 499-2	

Tracks: Hallelujah!/Freaky Funksters/Into The Ditch/Do The Dirty Dog

1989 □	För Fet För Ett Fuck/Svullo On Acid	7"	Mercury	SVULLO 1	

Electric Boys backing comedian Svullo, under whose name it is released. The title translated is - Too Fat For A Fuck.

1989 □	För Fet För Ett Fuck/Svullo On Acid/För fet - fetmix	12"	Mercury	SVULLO 112	
1990 ■	För fet... Rappa själv	7"	Mercury	SVULLO FREE	

Single-sided instrumental version of "För fet"

1989 □	All Lips 'N Hips/Hallelujah! I'm On Fire	7"	Vertigo	875 452-7	
1989 □	All Lips 'N Hips/All Lips 'N Hips/Get Nasty (Dance Mix)	MLP 3tr	Mercury	E BOYS 112	
1989 □	All Lips 'N Hips/All Lips 'N Hips	12"	Mercury	EBDJ 1 12	
1990 □	All Lips 'N Hips/All Lips 'N Hips	CDS	Vertigo	EBCDJ 1	
1990 □	Electrified/Who Are You	7"	Vertigo	878 454-7	

Tracks: Electrified + live tracks Funk-O-Metal Carpet Ride/Psychedelic Eyes/Into The Ditch recorded in Eskilstuna June 1990.

1990 □	All Lips 'N Hips	MLP 3tr	Vertigo	VERX 48	

Tracks: All Lips 'N Hips, Hallelujah!/Funk 'O Metal Carpet Ride. Also available in white vinyl w/out picture sleeve.

1990 □	All Lips 'N Hips	MLP PD	Vertigo/Phonogram	VERXP 48	

Tracks: All Lips & Hips/Hallelujah (I'm On Fire)/Get Nasty (Dance Mix). Picture disc with insert.

1990 □	All Lips 'N Hips/Captain Of My Soul	7" PD	Mercury	EB 7	

Limited edition.

1990 □	Electrified/Who Are You	7"	Vertigo (UK)	VER 50	
1990 ■	Electrified	MLP 4tr	Vertigo (UK)	VERX 50	

Tracks: Electrified/Who Are You/All Lips 'N Hips (The Bat Mix)/Freaky Funksters

1990 □	Electrified	MLP 4tr	Vertigo (UK)	VERXR 50	

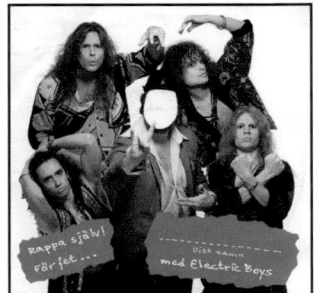

1989 LP - 836 913-1

1990 7" - SVULLO FREE

1990 MLP - VERX 50

Year		Title	Format	Label	Catalogue No.
1990	☐	Electrified	MLP 4tr	Mercury	872 618-7
1990	☐	FUNK 'O METAL CARPET RIDE (US-version)	CD	ATCO (US)	7 91337 2
1990	☐	FUNK 'O METAL CARPET RIDE (US-version)	CD	Columbia (US)	A2 91337 2
1990	☐	FUNK 'O METAL CARPET RIDE (US-version)	LP	ATCO (US)	7 91337 1
1990	☐	FUNK 'O'METAL CARPET RIDE (US-version)	CD	Vertigo	846 055 2
1990	■	FUNK 'O'METAL CARPET RIDE (US-version)	LP	Vertigo	846 055 1
1990	☐	FUNK 'O'METAL CARPET RIDE (US-version)	LP	Vertigo (Japan)	PHCR-1014
1990	☐	All Lips 'N Hips	MCD 3tr	Vertigo	EBCDJ 1

1990 LP - 846 055 1

Tracks: All Lips 'N Hips/Hallelujah!/Funk 'O Metal Carpet Ride

| 1990 | ☐ | Excerpts From The Funk O' Metal Carpet Ride | MCD 3tr | Vertigo (UK) | EBCDJ 1 |

Tracks: All Lips 'N Hips, Rags To Richies/Into The Woods.Was released as promo only.

| 1990 | ☐ | All Lips 'N Hips-edit/LP-version | CDS 2tr | ATCO (US-promo) | n/a |
| 1990 | ☐ | WESTWOOD ONE | 2LP | WW1 | HV-90 |

Live radio promo also featuring Steve Vai, Living Colour and Mother Love Bone. Tracks: If I Had A Car/Into The Woods/The Change/Cheek To Cheek/All Lips 'N Hips

| 1992 | ☐ | Four Tracks From The New Allbum Groovus Maximus | MCD 4tr | Vertigo (UK) | BOYCD1 |

Promo sampler. Tracks: Mary In The Mystery World/Groovus Maximus/Knee Deep In You/ Bed Of Roses

1992	☐	GROOVUS MAXIMUS	LP	Vertigo	512 255 1
1992	☐	GROOVUS MAXIMUS	CD	Vertigo	512 255 2
1992	☐	GROOVUS MAXIMUS	CD+MC	Vertigo (UK)	512 255 2

1992 7" - 866764-4

Initial pressint featuring a bonus-cassette (EBMC 1) with: Wake Up Judge/Bloom's Blues/ Space Jam

| 1992 | ☐ | GROOVUS MAXIMUS | CD | ATCO (USA) | 7 92143-4 |
| 1992 | ☐ | GROOVUS MAXIMUS | CD | Vertigo (Japan) | PHCR-41 |

Bonus: Bloom's Blues

1992	■	Mary In The Mystery World/Why Don't We Do It In The Road?	7"	Vertigo	866764-4
1992	☐	Mary In The Mystery World/Why Don't We Do It In The Road?	7"	Vertigo (UK	VER 65
1992	☐	Mary In The Mystery World/Why Don't We Do It In The Road?	12"	Vertigo (UK)	VERX 65

Clear etched vinyl.

| 1992 | ☐ | Mary In The Mystery World | MLP 3tr | Vertigo | VERXP 65 |

Tracks: Mary In The Mystery World/Knee Deep In You/Why Don't We Do It In The Road. Clear vinyl. Numbered. 7500 copies.

| 1992 | ☐ | Mary In The Mystery World | CDS | Vertigo | VERCDJ 65 |

Promo single.

| 1992 | ☐ | Mary In The Mystery World | MCD 4tr | Vertigo | VERCD 65 |

Tracks: Mary In The Mystery World, Knee Deep In You, Why Don't We Do It In The Road/ All Lips 'N Hips

ARE YOU READY TO BELIEVE

1994 CDS - EBOYSPROMO 1

| 1992 | ☐ | Knee Deep In You/Groovus Maximus | 12" | Vertigo (promo) | VERXDJ 65 |
| 1992 | ☐ | Groovus Maximus | MCD 4tr | Vertigo | 864 397-2 |

Tracks: Groovus Maximus/Knee Deep In You(live)/Rags To Richies(live)/The Change(live)

1992	☐	Groovus Maximus/March Of The Spitrits	7"	Vertigo	864 396-7
1992	☐	Dying To Be Loved/Black Betty	7"	Vertigo	864732-7
1992	☐	Dying To Be Loved/Black Betty/The Sky Is Crying	MCD 3tr	Vertigo	864 732-2
1992	☐	WESTWOOD ONE - IN CONCERT (split)	2CD	WW1	92-48

Live radio promo with Electric Boys, Hardline and Mr Big.

| 1994 | ■ | Are You Ready To Believe | CDSd 2tr | Polar | EBOYSPROMO 1 |

Tracks: Ready to Believe/My Knuckles Your Face. Promo.

1994	☐	FREEWHEELIN'	LP	Polar	521 722 1
1994	☐	FREEWHEELIN'	CD	Polar	521 722 2
1994	☐	FREEWHEELIN'	CD	MFN (UK)	CDMFN 164

Bonus: Some Kind Of Voodoo/Freewheelin'/Black Betty (Lead Belly/Ram Jam cover)

1994 MCD - 855 405-2

1994	☐	FREEWHEELIN'	CD	Polydor (Japan)	POCP 1415
1994	☐	Are You Ready To Believe	CDS 1tr	Polar	855 296-2
1994	☐	Mountains And Sunsets/Some Kind Of Voodoo	CDS 2tr	Polar	855 402-2
1994	■	Groover	MCD 4tr	Polar	855 405-2

Tracks: Groover/Some Kind Of Voodoo/Black Betty/Freewheelin'

| 2001 | ☐ | FUNK-O'-METAL CARPET RIDE | CDd | Universal/Sweden Rock | 981 940-1 |

Bonus: Rags To Richies/The Change/If I Had A Car/Captain Of My Soul/Into The Woods/ Psychedelic Eyes (live)/Into The Ditch (live)/All Lips N' Hips (drum machine version)

| 2001 | ☐ | FREEWHEELIN' | CDd | Universal/Sweden Rock | 986 664-6 |

Bonus: Some Kind Of Voodoo/Freewheelin'/Mountains And Sunsets (demo)/Messin' With Voodoo (demo)/The Groover (demo)/Down At The Bottom (demo)

| 2001 | ☐ | GROOVUS MAXIMUS | CDd | Universal/Sweden Rock | 982 058-2 |

Bonus: Trouble In Paradise (demo)/Love's Kickin' In (demo)/Dying To Be Loved (demo)/ Why Don't We Do It In The Road/Space Jam/

2009	☐	NOW DIG THIS! THE BEST OF	CD	Universal	600753 19269
2011	■	AND THEM BOYS DONE SWANG	CD	Supernova	SUPERCD034
2011	☐	AND THEM BOYS DONE SWANG	CD	Victor (Japan)	VICP-64937

Bonus: Chickalicious/Down On Shakin' Street/Nowhere To Go But Up

2011	☐	AND THEM BOYS DONE SWANG	CD	Escape	ESM 226
2013	☐	GROOVUS MAXIMUS	CD	Southworld	SW0078CD
2013	☐	FUNK-O'-METAL CARPET RIDE	CD	Southworld	SW0079CD

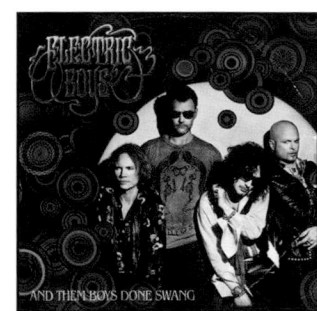

2011 CD - SUPERCD035

Unofficial releases:

| 199? | ☐ | WE'RE GONNA GROOVE (BAD MOTHERFUNKERS) | CD | Mixing Records | MX 004 |

E

ELECTRIC EARTH
Peter Gottlieb: v/g, Tommy Scalisi Svensson: g,
Lyris M. Karlsson: b, Lars "Draken" Berger: d

Trollhättan - Electric Earth were formed in 2001, influenced by bands like **Stone Temple Pilots,**
Soundgarden and **Black Sabbath**. All members, except Peter came from the band **Rat Salad**. The
band's second release was produced by Roberto Laghi (**Mustasch, LOK, Hardcore Superstar**
etc). The limited edition CD EP *Selling Souls* features guest apperances from **Clawfinger**'s Zak
Tell and guitarist Mattias Ia Eklundh, who lends a hand in a cover of **Kiss**' *I Want You*. Before
the release of Vol II, drummer Magnus Olsson replaced Lars Berger. After a hiatus they entered
the studio in 2010 for the recordings of a new album, which in my opinion has turned out to
be their best effort ever. The band had now dropped the grungy influences and deliver a great
retro-oriented hard rock album. Scalisi and Berger have also made recordings with the band
Gooseflesh. The song *Free Fall* from the 2011 album was also released digitally in a different
version mixed by Beau Hill. A cover of *Young Blood* will be featured on the **Whitesnake** tribute
album *Still Of The Night: A Millennium Tribute To Whitesnake* (2011 Versailles).

2007 CDd - 251091

2004 CDd - PM 7001

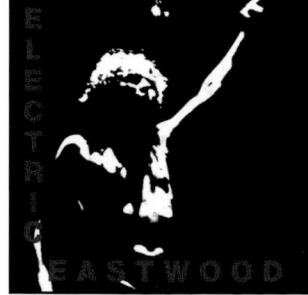

2011 CDd - TYSS 7016

2004 ■	ORGANIC SONGS VOLUME ONE	CDd	Phantom Music	PM 7001
2007 □	Selling Souls	MCD 4tr	Phantom Music	PM 9488
	Tracks: Bring On The Storm/Unicorn/I Want You (Kiss cover)/Heartbreaker (Led Zeppelin cover)			
2007 ■	VOL II – WORDS UNSPOKEN	CDd	Mausoleum	251091
2011 ■	TOUCHING THE VOID	CDd	TySS Music	TYSS 7016
2011 □	D.D.T (DELIBERATE DISTORTION OF THE TRUTH)	CD	TySS Music	n/a

ELECTRIC EASTWOOD
Karl "Charlie" Granehed: v, Ronnie Hassleqvist: g, Per Andersson: g,
Tobbe Larsson: b, Robert Eklundh: d

Falköping - Formed in 1988 as an **AC/DC** cover band, which shows in their original material.
Good, solid stomping hard rock. Charlie, who went to Hollywood and became an actor, and
Ronnie have also been part of 60s rockers **The Mop Tops**. Ronnie later played in retro rockers
Volume Unit, and Robert is in Ska-band **The Liptones**. Karl now releases solo material and
does Elvis Presley impersonations. Per sings in cover band **Jam Pack** and in **The Scapegoats**.

1989 ■	Party Around The World/Fire With Fire	7"	private	P 1

1989 7" - P 1

ELEVEN PICTURES
Martin Emil: v, Johan "Ewan" Wallqvist: g, Christian Jansson: b, Patrik Herrström: d

Göteborg - The first album was quite reminiscent of what **Alice In Chains** did on their debut.
Heavy, really powerful and with slightly grunge-oriented touches. Great vocals, well played
and a very powerful production. Highly recommended. On the second release they turned a bit
more pop-oriented and "twangy", while on the third album they kept the same style, but added
more heaviness. The third album also saw the change from drummer John Lindén to Patrik
Herrström (ex-**Road Ratt**) and also bass-player Gurkha was sacked. In 2001 Christian, who
was ex-**Pagandom**, left to join **Transport League**. In 2009 Johan Wallquist and original drummer Lindén released a digital EP with their new band **Dakota Project**, something for **Eleven**
Pictures fans to check out.

1995 CD - M 7011 2

1988 7" - MR 8802

1995 ■	FLOWERLAND	CD	Mascot	M 7011 2
1995 □	FLOWERLAND	CD	FEMS (Japan)	APCY-8230
1997 ■	INITIALS	CD	Mascot	M 7022 2
1997 □	INITIALS	CD	Pony Canyon (Japan)	BLCK-85963
1997 □	All I Want/Anywhen	CDS	Mascot	M 2002 3
2000 □	SUPERFICIAL TO THE CORE	CD	Mascot	M 7041 2
2000 □	Little Killer (radio version)/(album version)	CDS	Mascot	M 2041 3

ELEVENER
Pierre Wensberg: v, Johan Bergquist: v/b/k, Magnus Lindqvist: g,
Robert Garnold: b, Anton Roos: d

Göteborg/Stockholm - Childhood friends Johan Bergquist (v/b/k) and Andreas Brodén (g/d)
have been keeping in touch during the years, recording the odd demo until they finally in 2005
decided to take the project to a new level. Johan was also handling the keyboards in hard rockers **Million**, at the time. In 2009 Johan decided to take a break from music and the band was
put on hold. In January 2010 guitarist Magnus Lindqvist approached Johan and the two started
jamming. The band was soon revived and drummer Anton Roos (**Saffire**) was added to the
line-up. The line-up kept growing and was completed when renowned singer Pierre Wensberg
(**Prisoner, Heartbreak Radio**) and bass-player Robert Garnold (**Roach, Heartbreak Radio**)
entered. The new line-up started recording a new album at JM Studio together with Martin
Kronlund (**Phenomena, Gypsy Rose** etc). The summer of 2011 saw the release of *Symmetry*

2008 CD - 00035

2011 CD - AORH 00055

In Motion. **Elevener** is a high class AOR band in the vein of **Journey**. The band now features bassist Urban Fermdal (**Adams Eve, Gung**), who was actually up for the vocal spot before Pierre. Johan has, also played on albums by **Hammerfall, Full Strike** and was a member of **Eden's Curse**, besides **Million.**

2008	■	WHEN KALEIDOSCOPES COLLIDE	CD	AOR Heaven	00035
2008	□	WHEN KALEIDOSCOPES COLLIDE	CD	Avalon (Japan)	MICP-10766
2008	□	WHEN KALEIDOSCOPES COLLIDE	CD	Irond (Russia)	CD 08-DDD
2011	■	SYMMETRY IN MOTION	CD	AOR Heaven	AORH 00055

2012 CD - UER 044

ELIMI

Tobias "Rogirrek Garm" Eriksson: v, Kim "Maturz" Löfstrand: g/b,
Mattias "Perish" Svensson: d

Nybro/Kalmar - Formed in 2004 and in 2006 the band released its first demo *Slutet, Mörkret & Tystnaden*. Bass player Adam "Verrot" Aronsson, who played on the debut, committed suicide October 3, 2008. Maturz is also the man behind the band **Snötårar**, plus he has his solo project **Mahapralaya**. Melancholic, well-played and varied old-school black metal with desperate screeching vocals. A bit reminiscent of old **Dark Funeral** at times. Session bassist Karl Alling also plays bass in **Misfits** influenced band **138**. *The Seed* and *King Of The Red Desert* clocks at 9.41 and 12.27 respectively. In 2012 Svensson had to leave because of personal matters.

2008	□	SUMMONED FROM ASHES	CD	Death Dealers Association	DDA-004
2010	□	ASYLUM	CD	Eerie Art Records	EAR 026
2012	■	ASYLUM	CD	Unexploded Records	UER 044
2012	■	The Seed/King Of The Red Desert	CDS 2tr	Obscure Abhorrence	OAP 024

2012 CD - OAP 024

ELLEN B

Lasse Nilsson Wihk: v, Lasse Olsson: g, Johan Lyander: k,
Kenneth Eriksson: b, Per Hedtjärn: d

Tureberg - Melodic slimline hard rock with Christian lyrics. Quite close to **Time Gallery** and **F.R.E.E.** in style and approach. The band also have three tracks on the compilation *We Will Stand* (86 Leon). *Två* was actually the first CD-release on the Christian record market. On the first single Christer Axelsson played drums. He was replaced by Johan Fransson, who left in 1986. On the first album the line-up was Lasse, Lasse, Kenneth, Johan and keyboardist Robert Wirensjö (Mikael Rickfors).

1983	□	Confession	7"	S&A	SAMS 5210
1985	□	ATTACHÉ	LP	Leon Music	LMP 836
1987	□	Bra karl/Water Into Wine	7"	Cantino	CS 023
1987	■	TVÅ	LP	Cantino	SLP 571
1987	□	TVÅ	CD	Cantino	SCD 571
1988	□	PRINCE OF PEACE	CD	Edge	ECD 7010
		English version of "Två".			

1987 LP - SLP 571

ELSESPHERE

Johnny Berntsson: v, Mikael Lindahl: g, Joakim Floke: k,
Sven-Olof "Lollo" Andersson: b, Mikael Kvist: d

Stockholm - Formed by Kvist in 1995 they went through several line-up changes before becoming a steady unit a few years later. In 2000 they recorded the demo, *Last Night On Earth*. The band produces outstanding melodic progressive metal with killer-vocals from Johnny. Musically very intricate, but without getting lost in the maze of odd times, complex patterns and musical somersaults. Highly recommended! After the album Floke (later in **Meduza** and **Dionysus**) was replaced by Andreas Kronqvist (**Eventide**). In 2004 singer Berntsson was replaced by Andi Kravljaca (**Seventh Wonder, Vindictiv**). Kvist and Kravljaca are now in **Silent Call**. The band sadly split.

2002	■	BLIND LEADING THE BLIND	CD	Lucretia	LU 20013 2

2002 CD - LU 20013 2

ELSY BAND

Christer Jarefäll: v, Marcus Berndtsson: g, Christer Persson: g,
Anders Mossberg: b, Pär Berndtsson: d

Göteborg - Christian melodic straight hard rock in the vein of early **Jerusalem**. Maybe not that surprisingly as bass-player Anders Mossberg was previously in **Jerusalem**. He had also earlier played with bluesy hard rockers **Vatten**. Anders has also been found in the band **Korsdrag**, which also featured Jörgen Tjusling (**Human Race, Lommi, Eaglestrike**), Dennis Österdahl (**Human Race, Eaglestrike, Lommi, Big Easy**) and Håkan Fransson.

1983	■	Vart är du på väg/Vilse	7"	private	Elsy 001

1983 7" - Elsy 001

ELVIRA MADIGAN

Marcus Hammarström: v/g/k/b/d

Stockholm - In 1988 Marcus did the first recording session, which ended up as the demo *Varsel*. In 1999 he recorded another album, which was never released, but ended up as bonus tracks on his first album. Founding his own label Northlore Records, Marcus released the first album *Black Arts* in 2000. The album has a highly impressive packaging, with a recording quality that unfortunately doesn't live up to it. Musically the band has been described as a mix of **Blind Guardian** and **Emperor**, which pretty much sums it up. **Elvira Medigan** however falls quite short of these bands in comparison when it comes to sound quality. Musically it's quite decent, though. The subsequent year the follow-up *Witches* was released. The mix is a bit better on this one, even though programmed drums always sound like… programmed drums. This album had more of a movie score type of style with long instrumental songs, quite atmospheric at times. In 2003 and 2004 the albums were re-mixed and re-released by Black Lodge. *Angelis Deamonae* is a cover album featuring black/death metal covers of artists like Tori Amos, Chris DeBurgh, **Nordman** and **Scorpions**. Marcus is also found in **Ethnocide** and **Andalucia**, but mainly in the killer band **Sterbhaus**.

2000 CD - LORECD 001

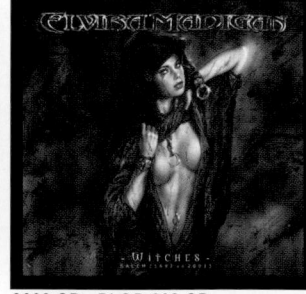
2003 CD - BLOD 002 CD

2000 ■	BLACK ARTS	CD	Northlore Records	LORECD 001
2001 ☐	WITCHES – SALEM (1692 vs 2001)	CD	Northlore Records	LORECD 002
2003 ■	WITCHES – SALEM (1692 vs 2001)	CD	Black Lodge	BLOD 002 CD
2004 ☐	BLACK ARTS	CD	Black Lodge	BLOD 003 CD
2005 ■	ANGELIS DEAMONAE – WICCAN AFTERMATH	CD	Black Lodge	BLOD 012 CD
2008 ☐	REGENT SIE: SHEDEVILS OF DEMONLORE, OF BLOOD CROSSES AND BIBLE WARS	CD	Black Lodge	BLOD 035 CD
2008 ☐	REGENT SIE: SHEDEVILS OF DEMONLORE, OF BLOOD CROSSES AND BIBLE WARS	CDd	Black Lodge	BLOD 035 CDL
2008 ☐	REGENT SIE: SHEDEVILS OF DEMONLORE, OF BLOOD CROSSES AND BIBLE WARS	CD	Irond (Russia)	CD 08-1432

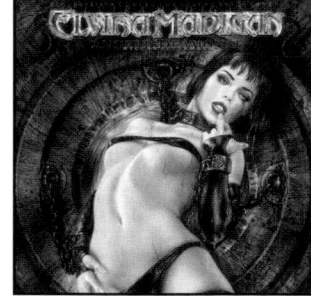
2005 CD - BLOD 012 CD

EMBODIED, THE

Marcus Thorell: v, Chris Melin: g, Jon Mortensen: g, Agust Ahlberg: b, Axel Janossy: d

Jönköping - The Embodied were formed in 2005 by Melin and Mortensen with the aim of playing metal with an innovative touch. In 2006 the band recorded their first demo, *Relativity Fade*. In 2008 Janossy joined and the band recorded their second demo *Chapter One*. When recording their debut album, they used the services of name producer Andy LaRocque. **The Embodied** play an interesting mix of classic power metal and melodic death metal, but with clean, great vocals. Well worth checking out.
Website: www.theembodied.com

2011 ■	THE EMBODIED	CD	Pre Legend Records	PLRCD 002

2011 CD - PLRCD 002

EMBRACED

Kalle Johansson (now Nimhagen): v, Davor Tepic: g, Peter Mårdklint: g, Sven Karlsson: k, Julius Chmielewski: k, Michael Håkansson: b, Thomas Lejon: d

Malmö - Formed in 1993 by Peter and Kalle. They started out as a more thrash-oriented band, but when drummer Daniel Lindberg and keyboard-player Sven joined in the mid-nineties they had become a bit more progressive. In 1997 they recorded the demo *A Journey Into Melancholy* which lead to the deal with Regain Records. Now second keyboardist Julius and guitarist Davor joined. After the album was recorded Daniel left the band and was replaced by Andreas Albihn, who in his turn only lasted for four months. His successor was Thomas Leijon. Melodic death-oriented and pretty progressive metal with lots of keyboards, they actually have two keyboard-players. Death-ish vocals and a goth-touch. The band has now folded. Peter and Andreas later joined **Tenebre**, Thomas is in **A.C.T** and **Andromeda,** Sven joined **Evergrey**, Julius went to **Misteltein** as drummer, Håkansson has played with **Evergrey** and **Engel**, Kalle (now Kalle Nimhagen) joined **Burning Engines** and is now in **Deathening**, while Mårdklint is found in **All Ends**. Not to be confused with the Norwegian namesakes on Aftermath Records.

1998 CD - 9803-002

1998 ■	AMOROUS ANATHEMA	CD	Regain	9803-002
2000 ■	WITHIN	CD	Regain	RR 0008-007
2001 ☐	WITHIN	CD	King Records (Japan)	KICP 792
	Bonus: Big In Japan (Alphaville cover)/Book Of Keys			

EMBRACING

Mattias Holmgren: v/d/k, André Nylund: g, Ola Andersson: g, Mikael Widlöf: b

Umeå - The band was formed in 1992 under the name **Beyond**, influenced by brutal bands such as **Bolt Thrower**, **Unleashed** and **Grave**. The line-up featured singer Henrik Nygren,

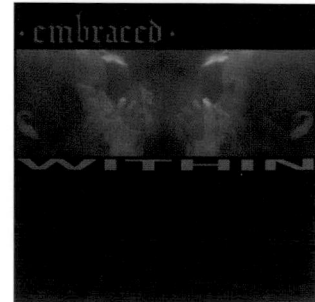
2000 CD - RR 0008-007

guitarists André Nylund and Johan Westerlund, bass player Peter Lundberg and drummer Mattias Holmgren. In 1994 they released their first demo *Of Beauty Found In Deep Caverns*, at the time they were called **Mishrak**. After this Mattias joined **Naglfar**, but returned after *Vittra*. Original guitarist Johan Westerlund left to join **Oberon** (not the recording band) and was replaced by Rickard Magnusson, also Peter Lundberg decided to leave the band leaving Nylund to also handle the bass. In 1995 they recorded the demo *Winterburn*, introducing their newfound name **Embracing**. They were signed by Invasion and the first album was recorded by Jens Kidman of **Meshuggah**. After the album, Rickard left and bass player Ola Andersson changed from bass to guitar, furthermore bass player Mikael Widlöf joined. Just before the recording of the second album Henrik quit and the vocal duties were taken over by Mattias. After this the band went through another change of line-up. They recorded a new demo in 1998, entitled *Inside You*, now with a more progressive touch and yet another demo in 1999 entitled *Rift*. On this demo the band featured Mattias and Mikael, guitarists Ulph Johansson and Markus Lidström. In 2001 Markus and Mikael left the band and was replaced by Ronnie Björnström and Peter Ulvén. Mattias also has his solo side-project **Tired Tree** and his first solo-album *Changing Sides* was released on Musea 2002. He also guests on albums by **Azure**, **Dark Side Cowboys** and **Dead Silent Slumber**, plus he has also been a member of **Supreme Majesty**. In 2002 Mattias' brother Nicklas joined for a tour, but became a permanent member. The band's last demo, *The Dragon Reborn*, was recorded in 2003. In 2004 *Dreams Left Behind* was re-issued also featuring some tracks from the *Inside You* and *Rift* demos. In 2008 the band became a trio featuring Mattias, Ronnie and Peter Ulvén. In 2009 the line-up consisted of singer/guitarist Mattias Holmgren, guitarist Ilmo Venja, bassist Mikael Bauer and drummer Nicklas Holmgren. In 2009 the band also uploaded the rerecorded song *Hit Me Hard* to their MySpace.

1996 CD - IR 022 CD

1997 CD - IR 031 CD

1996	■	I BEAR THE BURDEN OF TIME	CD	Invasion	IR 022 CD
1997	■	DREAMS LEFT BEHIND	CD	Invasion	IR 031 CD
2004	■	DREAMS LEFT BEHIND	CD	Thrashcorner	TH CD 014

Bonus: Sunrise At Lauras Shore/Stranger/Chased By A Shadow/Precious Discovery/Rift. New artwork.

2004	☐	I BEAR THE BURDEN OF TIME	CD	Khaosmaster Productions	KMP 006

Bonus: My Dragon banner/Emerald Eyes/Stop Crying/Inside You/Dragon Rage/Heroes Die In Battle/Winterburn. New artwork.

2004 CD - TH CD 014

EMERALD
Robert "Bobby" Vargkvist: v, Timo Nilsson: g,
Magnus Trulsson: b, Pavel: k, Johan Hansson: d

Trelleborg - Quite good melodic hard rock in the vein of **Treat** with high-pitch vocals. Bobby later joined sleaze/glam band **Bewarp** and metal band **Espinoza**. At the time, his main project was the powerful hard rock band **D-Dust**, but they only recorded some demos. Timo was later in the band **Wizard** and is today in **Lovehandles** where former **Emerald** members Mikael Delén and Johan Widerberg are also found.

1988	■	She Is A Rock 'N Roll Star/Never Alone	7"	private	UNI 1013	$

1988 7" - UNI 1013

EMMAS BOOGIE BAND
Tomas Ernvik: v/g, Mats Öhlen: b, Matte Marklund: d

Stockholm - The A-side is a cover of the old Robert Johnson-song (quite similar to the version recorded by **Mountain**) and the B-side was written by John Mayall. Tomas and Matte were also found in **Vatten**. 70s influenced bluesy hard rock. Good stuff worth looking for.

1983	■	Crossroader/Television Eye	7"	Gutta	GUTS 1006

1983 7" - GUTS 1006

EMOTION
Mikael Lägermo: v/g, Jan Samefors: k/v, Ingemar Mårtensson: b, Pelle Petersson: d

Nässjö - This is a high-class Christian melodic hard rock band with some influences from **Deep Purple**. On the debut 7" Patrik Lägermo was handling the keys. On *Taste Of Grapes* the style was a bit more rough-edged than the MCD. It was however a pretty big disappointment. The band recorded a second album in 1998 which still hasn't been released. It is however way better than *Taste Of Grapes*. Samefors previously recorded a 7" with the band **Disciple**. The 2006 self-titled album was a re-mastered re-release of *Taste Of Grapes* and *Tip To Toe* on one album and with new artwork.

1991	■	Right On Time/Can't Hold Back My Tears	7"	private	MM 1001
1994	☐	Tip To Toe	MCD 5tr	private	E-OPUS 103

Tracks: Tip To Toe/Wholeness & Holyness/Rendez-Vous/Fakin' My Face/Way Over Jordan

1997	☐	TASTE OF GRAPES	CD	Massive Music	MASS 506
2006	☐	EMOTION	CD	Retroactive	RAR 7830

1991 7" - MM 1001

EMPIRE

**Lars Gunnar Selinder: v/k, Björn Nygren: k,
Thomas Nordmark: g, Per Lundh: b, Per Lundgren: d**

Söderhamn - *Empire* were a pretty decent, slightly amateurish, hard progressive act that only released this 7", which was actually recorded live.

1975 ■ Stop This Merry-Go-Round/Oriental Blind ....7" Splash... PLA 103
300 copies.

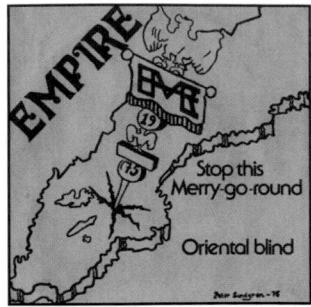

1975 7" - PLA 103

EMPIRE SAINT

**José "Joe Kanner" Gomez-Sanchez: v, Peter Johansson: g,
Tomas "John Raymore" Ferm: g, Kim "Caine" Kajjuuti: b,
Mikael "Mike Randle" Dimle: d**

Borås - High-quality 80s melodic metal with great vocals. After this, José recorded a single with *Dr Dream* and later went on to *Lies*, *Dye Vest* and recorded with the more powerful metal band *Fierce Conviction*. In 2009 he formed his own band *Sanchez*, which has made a couple of releases so far.

1989 ☐ Broken Dreams/Shout It Out...7" Platina......................................PL 67
1990 ■ R "N" S .... MLP 5tr NBV .... NBV 01
Tracks: Sometimes/Looking For Some Love/Hot Lips/Don't Treat Me Like A Fool/Watch The Sky Falling Down

1990 MLP - NBV 01

EMPTY GUNS

**Henrik Klefbäck: v, Daniel Bertilsson: g, Tobias Bertilsson: g,
Andreas Wiberg: b, Mattias Jonsson: d**

Norrköping - Formed in 1991 and split in 1994. Raunchy sleaze/glam with a punkish attitude in the vein of *Faster Pussycat* with a touch of early *Guns 'N Roses*. Good sound and high-quality. Should appeal to the fans of the 90's US-glam metal wave. The songs were co-written by Claes Wållberg (*Axewitch*, *Marshal Kane*). The band later changed their name to *Saw*, but has now split.

1993 ■ Causeless Rebel Without A Clue/Downward Voices.......................................7" private .... EGS 9304

1993 7" - EGS 9304

ENBOUND

**Lars "Lee Hunter" Säfsund: v, Martin "Marwin Flowberg" Floberg: g,
Sven "Swede" Odén: b, Mikael "Mike Cameron Force" Hörnqvist: d**

Borås - The band was formed by guitarist Jonathan Nyberg and drummer Mikael "Mike Cameron Force" Hörnqvist (*IronWare, Ablaze, Zonata, Axenstar*) in 2006. Jonathan was at the time playing with *Crystal Eyes*, while Mike previously had played with Jonathan's younger brothers in the band *Zonata*. Because of personal reasons Jonathan had to leave *Crystal Eyes* during the recordings of their fifth album, but only after a few days he got in touch with Mike to form a new band. They now drafted former *Stentorian* singer Marcus Nygren (also in *8-Point Rosie*) and *Ibidiah* bassist Sven Odén. In 2008 they released their first four-track MCD. In the summer of 2008 they parted ways with guitarist Jonathan. He was soon replaced by Martin "Marvin Flowberg/The Butcher" Floberg (*Mezmoria*). Now Marcus left the band, but was soon replaced by *Work Of Art* singer Lars "Lee Hunter" Säfsund. The band play classy melodic power metal in the vein of *Nocturnal Rites*, *Zonata* etc. Killer vocals and great musical performance. In 2010 the band was picked up by Inner Wound Records and the album *And She Says Gold* was released early 2011.

2008 MCD - ENB 001

2008 ■ You Are Now Forever Enbound...MCD 4tr private .... ENB 001
Tracks: Under A Spell/Running Free/Death Is Dawning/Noiseless Bullet
2011 ■ AND SHE SAYS GOLD...CD Inner Wound IW83012
Slipcase. 2 stickers. Bonus: Beat It
2011 ☐ AND SHE SAYS GOLD...CD Spiritual Beast (Japan) IUCP-16103
Bonus: Frozen To Be

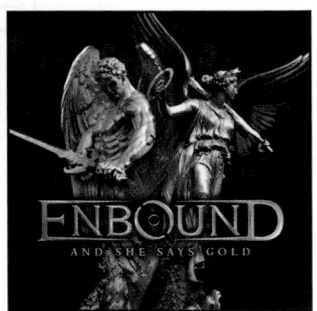

2011 CD - IW83012

END, THE

**Janne Hansen: v, Mats Olsson: g, Mikael Nilsson: g, Per-Ove Nilsson: k
Nils Ingvar Ekholm: b, Christian Lauritson: d**

Landskrona - Janne had previously recorded an album with *Grassroots*, Mats recorded a single with rock-pop group *Heavy Station* and was later in *Etra Band*, who can be found on the *Skånsk Rock* compilations. In 1995 they formed *The End*. Mikael and Per-Ove came from the band *Oxid*, who had recorded one album. In 1992 Janne (who was then the band's drummer) left to

join **U.L.C** as lead singer. He however returned later the same year... as lead singer. The albums were produced by Berno Paulsson (**Espinoza, WET, Spiritual Beggars** etc.). After the first album they changed drummer from Magnus Andersson to Christian (ex-**Wat 69, Wooden Jesus**). **The End** produces straight hard rock, with the second album showing a nice improvement.

1996 CD - TE566062636374

1996 ■	IT'S MORE THAN ROCK 'N ROLL	CD	private	TE566062636374
2001 □	A KEY TO THE SEVENTH FLOOR	CD	private	TE566062636365

THE, *END
Tobias Gustafsson: b/v, Matti Almsenius: g, Daniel Erlandsson: d

Karlstad - When **Eucharist** split in 1994 Matti at first re-united with his former band **Revengia**, but after a while former band-mates Daniel and Tobias got in touch with Matti and they started elaborating on a new project. As the name **The End** was taken, they called themselves **The*End** (notice the *). They recorded a couple of demos, which were finally compiled into the debut-album. After the album Daniel went to **Arch Enemy**, Matti joined cover-band **Ace Of Spades** and later on **Järnet** and Tobias went to what was to become **Unborn**. In 1997 the band finally broke up. Daniel went to record a new album with **Eucharist**, while Tobias and Matti found drummer Niclas Jernberg and formed **Croam**. The previously unreleased track *Mourn* is found on the compilation CD for the second encyclopedia (2002). **The*End**'s effort is a very mixed platter ranging from heavy, quite doomy metal with a touch of death to high speed blast beat hardcore influenced metal. Nevertheless it's a really great CD, well worth checking out.

1996 ■	The* End	MCD 5tr private		AGE 001

Tracks: Lamentation/They/With Pain/Picture/Legend

1996 MCD - AGE 001

ENEMIES SWE
Rickard Andersson: v, Simon "Roxx" Karlsson: g, Andreas Lagerin: g, Daniel "Bevis" Bivensjö: b, Marko Siila: d

Skövde/Göteborg - **Enemies Swe** were formed by Marco and Rickard in October 2001. The band was soon completed by Simon, Andreas and Bevis. Their secret plan was to create a dangerous rock 'n roll band in the true spirit of **AC/DC, Kiss, Aerosmith** and **Guns 'N Roses**. The supported colleagues like **Hardcore Superstar** and played several festivals before being picked up by Plugged Records who released a first single featuring a cover of **Alice Cooper's** *Is It My Body*. The debut album followed in 2004. After the album Andreas was replaced by former **Shotgun Messiah** guitarist Jukka "JK Knoxx" Kemppainen and bass player Bevis by Pontus Carmbrandt. Simon was later drafted by **Easy Action** and in 2006 the band folded. Rickard, Jukka and Marko formed high energy rockers **Volume Unit** in 2007.

2004 CDS - PLUCD 002

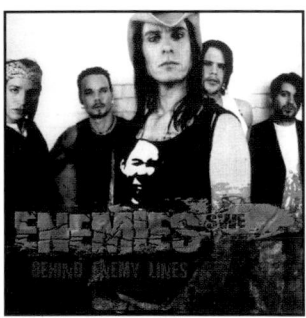
2004 CD - PLUCD 003

2004 ■	Enemy/Is It My Body	CDSp 2tr	Plugged	PLUCD 002
2004 ■	BEHIND ENEMY LINES	CD	Plugged	PLUCD 003

ENEMY IS US
Ronnie Nyman: v, Peter Lindholm: g, Staffan Winroth: g, Lawrence Mackrory: b/v, Olle Ferner: d

Uppsala - It all started out as a fun project in 2003, but soon turned into something more than the boys had expected. Late 2003, after putting up their first demo *Ashes To The World* on mp3.com, they were offered a three-album deal with Finnish Rising Realm Records. This lead to the release of their debut *We Have Seen The Enemy... And The Enemy Is Us* in 2004, but no-one, not even the band, has seen the release on the Rising Realm label, only on Crash Music. **Defleshed**'s Gustaf Jorde does some guest vocals on the album. In 2006, before starting the recording of the follow-up, their label folded and the band went ahead to record without a label. The production was taken care of by bass player Mackrory and producer Daniel Bergstrand (**Crawley, Soilwork, In Flames** etc). The recording resulted in the album *Venomized*. Before the second album drummer Magnus Ingels had been replaced by **21 Lucifers**' drummer Ferner. **Enemy Is Us** play high energy death metal with a touch of hardcore, in the vein of **Soilwork** and **Dark Tranquillity**. Mackrory can also been found in **Darkane, Andromeda, The Duskfall, F.K.Ü, Scarve** etc. The band has now folded.
Website: www.enemyisus.com

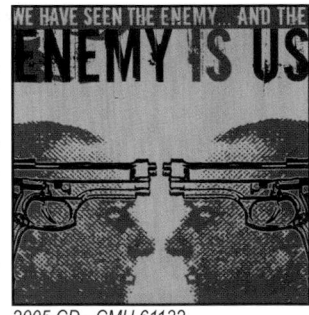
2005 CD - CMU 61132

2008 CD - BE032

2005 ■	WE HAVE SEEN THE ENEMY... AND THE ENEMY IS US	CD	Crash Music (USA)	CMU 61132
2005 □	WE HAVE SEEN THE ENEMY... AND THE ENEMY IS US	CDd	Scarecrow (Brazil)	SC 05188
2005 □	WE HAVE SEEN THE ENEMY... AND THE ENEMY IS US	CD	Soundholic (Japan)	TKCS-85102
	Bonus: Tonight We Murder			
2008 □	VENOMIZED	CD	Tribunal Records (USA)	TRB 095
2008 ■	VENOMIZED	CD	Bastardized Recordings	BE032

ENFORCER

Olof "Enforcer" Wikstrand: v, Joseph Tholl: g, Tobias Lindqvist: b, Jonas Wikstrand: d

The evil attackers!

Arvika - Enforcer were formed in 2004 as Olof's solo project. In 2005 he recorded the demo *Evil Attacker*. In 2006 Olof's brother Jonas joined on drums and Adam Zaars (*Tribulation*) on guitar. The subsequent year the line-up was completed by Joseph Tholl on bass and they recorded the debut album. The band plays furious, class A, classic heavy metal with a strong touch of NWoBHM and some speed metal overtones, similar to bands like *Riot*, *Agent Steel* and *Exciter*. Great guitar work with tons of harmonies. In 2008 Tholl switched to guitar and Tobias Lindqvist joined on bass. Before *Death By Fire* Olof started playing guitar, releaving guitarist Adam Zaars of his duties. Olof, Tobias and Joseph are ex-*Corrupted*. Olof has also been a member of *Leprosy*, *Oppression*, *Hazard* and *Caustic Strike*. Highly recommended.

2008 LP - HA5-5007-2-1

Year		Title	Format	Label	Cat. No.
2007	☐	Evil Attacker/Mistress From Hell	7"	Iron Pegasus	I.P.S 11
		100 copies in red/white vinyl, 400 in black vinyl.			
2008	☐	INTO THE NIGHT	CD	Heavy Artillery	HA5-5007-2-2
2008	■	INTO THE NIGHT	LP	Heavy Artillery	HA5-5007-2-1
		First 100 copies in clear/blue vinyl, 100 in purple, all including poster, sew-on patch.			
2008	☐	INTO THE NIGHT	LP PD	Heavy Artillery	HA5-5007-PD
		500 copies.			
2008	☐	INTO THE NIGHT	CD	Spiritual Beast (Japan)	IUCP-16084
2008	☐	DIAMONDS	CD	Earache	MOSH399-CD
2008	■	DIAMONDS	LPg	Earache	MOSH399-LP
		200 clear vinyl, 300 white, 400 black, 100 half/half coloured and retro album cover. Re-press: 100 black/white, 200 red/black, 300 red/yellow and 400 black.			
2008	☐	DIAMONDS	CD	Heavy Artillery (USA)	HA5-5013-CD
2008	☐	DIAMONDS	LP PD	Heavy Artillery (USA)	HA5-5013-PD
		500 copies.			
2008	☐	DIAMONDS	CD	Spiritual Beast (Japan)	IUCP-16083
2010	☐	DIAMONDS	CDd	Earache	MOSH399CDL
2011	☐	Bullet/Enforcer (split)	7"	Black Lodge	BLOD 7004
		Split with Bullet. Track: High Roller.			
2012	☐	INTO THE NIGHT	CD	Earache	MOSH 462
2012	☐	INTO THE NIGHT	LP	Earache	MOSH 462 LP
2013	☐	DEATH BY FIRE	CDd	Nuclear Blast	NB 3034-0
2013	☐	DEATH BY FIRE	LPg	Nuclear Blast	NB 3034-1
		Patch. Black + 250 red numbered vinyl.			
2013	■	Mesmerized By Fire/You Can Be	7"	Nuclear Blast	NB 3046-1
		250 clear, 250 red vinyl.			

2008 LPg - MOSH399-LP

2013 7" - NB 3046-1

ENGEL

Magnus Klavborn: v, Niclas Engelin: g, Marcus Sunesson: g, Steve Drennan: b, Jimmy Olausson: d

Göteborg - Engel were formed in 2004 by Engelin (ex-*Passenger, Gardenian, Sarcazm*) and Sunesson (*The Crown*). The line-up was completed by *Evergrey*/*The Project Hate* bass player Michael Håkansson, former *Lord Belial*/*Runemagick*/*Dracena* drummer Daniel "Mojjo" Moilanen and *Headplate*-singer Magnus Klavborn. In 2005 the band recorded their first four track demo and a second in 2006. The band's debut album, *Absolute Design*, had a really cool fold-out gimmick cover and was produced by Daniel Bergstrand. After the release, in 2008, Håkansson left the band and was replaced by Steve Drennan. In 2009 Engelin temporarily replaced Jesper Strömblad in *In Flames* on tour 1997-98, 2006-7 and 2009-10 and he's still out there. The band's second album *Threnody* was released in 2010 and produced by Tue Madsen, who has also worked with *Dark Tranquillity*. In August 2010 Moilanen left the band and was replaced by former *Marionette* drummer Jimmy Olausson. In 2012 Mikael Sehlin (*Degradead*) replaced Klavborn. The debut album is a piece of brutal, death-oriented melodic metal, while the follow-up is more melodic and the third album even a step further. All albums are high quality stuff.

2007 CDd - SPV 98362 CD

Year		Title	Format	Label	Cat. No.
2007	■	ABSOLUTE DESIGN	CDd	Steamhammer	SPV 98362 CD
2008	☐	Next Closed Door/Casket Closing	MCD	Steamhammer	SPV 80001249 CDS
2010	■	THRENODY	CDd	Seasons Of Mist	SOM 226
2010	☐	THRENODY	CD	Trooper (Japan)	XNTE-00003
		Bonus: Fearless			
2012	☐	BLOOD OF SAINTS	CDd	Seasons Of Mist	SOM 260

2010 CDd - SOM 226

ENGLUND, THORBJÖRN

Thorbjörn Englund: g/b/d

Kalix - This is the solo project of *Winterlong* guitarist Thorbjörn. The album, of course an instrumental one, features a variety of styles, from Satriani/MacAlpine style shredding to flamenco style playing and even a piano tune. Great player, indeed. Thorbjörn also plays on the albums by *Star Queen*, a Bulgarian band formed by Thorbjörn's girlfriend Stella Tormanoff.

Year		Title	Format	Label	Cat. No.
2006	■	INFLUENCES	CD	Lion Music	LMC174

2006 CD - LMC 174

ENIGMATIC

Stefan Karlsson: v/k, Peter Jonsson: g, Per Ryberg: g,
Tommie Eriksson: b, Magnus Lövgren: d

Bollnäs - Formed in December 1990, under the name **Limited Knowledge** and recorded the demos *Location Hell* ('91) and *Skulls Of Pain* ('92). They switched drummer from Peter Andersson to Lövgren and changed their name before releasing the MCD. They were signed by Euro Records, but nothing happened due to the company going bust. Death metal with keyboards and where you can actually hear the words! Quite heavy and varied, but the sound could be better. On the second MCD they have taken a few steps in the right direction. Slightly clearer vocals and a change towards a more and better, heavy progressive metal sound, with the addition of acoustic guitar and piano. The last release also features a metallised cover of Kim Wilde´s *Cambodia*.

1993 ■ Two Days Of April ....MCD 4tr Enigmatic ....LR CD1
      Tracks: The Tabular Bells Symphony/Fear Of The Dead/The Master Of Dreams/Dishonest
      Belief
1996 □ The Tranquilled Icy Water ....MCD 4tr Enigmatic ....LR CD2
      Tracks: A Way To Eternity/Violence Without Permission/Where Only Death.../Cambodia

1993 MCD - LR CD1

ENJOY THE VIEW

Johan Martinsson: v, Max Olsson: g/v, Håkan Almbladh: g,
Dennis Sand: b, Markus Ekborg: d

Osby - A young, great metal core unit mixing screamo and clean vocals. Tight, powerful and great sounding, also live. The band made their first digital EP, *Dreams To Remember*, in 2010, followed by *Guided By Lights* the year after. The band's debut album *We Curse The Day You Were F*****g Born* is due to be released through Panic & Action.

2011 ■ Guided By Lights...MCD 5tr private .... - -
      Tracks: Once We Named A Song Twice/Dreamer/A Story/We'll Make It Happen/Lights

2011 MCD - - -

ENSHRINED

Dejan Milenkovits: v, Martin Germ Bermheden: g, Benjamin Koverman: g,
Anders Nauclér: b, Henrik Schönström: d, Joél Cirera: d

Malmö - Not to be confused with the Karlskoga band that recorded a demo in 1991. This band recorded their first demo *Abyssimal* in 2003 and made a follow-up two years later, entitled *Spawn Of Apathy*. Nauclér is ex-**Misteltein**, Bernheden is also found in **Visceral Bleeding** and Cirera is ex-**Omnious** and was also part of slease rockers **Crazy Lixx**. High-speed, technical, well-played, thrash-oriented death metal. Cirera was later replaced by Henrik Schönström. *Website: www.enshrined.net*

2006 ■ DEREVELATION...CD Unexploded Records ....UER 010

2006 CD - UER 010

ENTER THE HUNT

Krister Linder: v, Björn Flodkvist: g, Mats Ståhl: g,
Ulf "Rockis" Ivarsson: b, Stefan Kälfors: d

Stockholm - **Enter The Hunt** were formed in 2002 by former **Gone** members Kälfors, Ståhl and Flodkvist. Kälfors was formerly in **Omnitron/The Krixhjälters**, while Ståhl and Flodkvist both did a short stint with classic doom band **Candlemass** in the late 90s. The subsequent year bass player Pontus Lindqvist, former **Omnitron/The Krixhjälters** colleague of Kälfors, completed the line-up. They recorded two three-track demos, before more pop-oriented singer Krister Linder (ex-**Grace, Dive**, solo) joined ranks in 2004. Krister actually made some demo attempts with **Talisman**, but never joined the band. In 2005 they recorded a new three-track demo and after this Krister became a permanent member of the band. The band was picked up by Sony BMG and Jacob Hellner (**Rammstein**) produced the bands first MCD and album. In 2006 Lindkvist left the band and was replaced by Joen Carlstedt (**Infinite Mass**), who in his turn was replaced by **Sky High** bassist Ivarsson. **Enter The Hunt** play quite heavy, yet melodic nu-breed metal with a progressive touch. Linder has a quite personal voice, rather thin and fragile, which you may like or not. The MCD *Become The Prey* contains two non-album tracks. In 2007 the band released the digital single *Go* and in 2009 the digital single *Fighters* followed. *Website: www.enterthehunt.com/*

2006 CDS - 82876 88297 2

2006 MCD - 82876 85072 2

2006 ■ One (Edit)/True Love...CDS 2tr Sony BMG 82876 88297 2
2006 ■ Become The Prey ....MCD 3tr Epic...82876 85072 2
      Tracks: Never Stop/No Return/Now Or Nowhere
2006 ■ FOR LIFE. 'TIL DEATH, TO HELL WITH LOVE...........................CD Epic...82876 85071 2

2006 CD - 82876 85071 2

ENTITY

Dan-Ola "Danne" Persson: v, Jimmy Svensson: g,
Tomas "Tompa" Gustafsson: b/k/v, Tomas Hedlund: d

Falkenberg - They claim to be a doom band... Personally I would categorise the music as soft, atmospheric, symphonic rock with the addition of screaming death style vocals. The band was formed by Gustafsson (editor of *Falken Zine*) early 1991 and recorded their first demo, *The Sad Fate*, in 1992, followed by *The* in 1993, and the more official *Demo #1* in 1994. Persson and Hedlund are also found in **The Ancient's Rebirth** and **Fall From Grace**. Hedlund has also been found in numerous other bands like **Cross Bow**, **Autopsy Torment**, **Pagan Rites** etc. Persson has been in **Pagan Rites**, **The Ancient's Rebirth**, **Fall From Grace** and **Cardinal Sin**.

1995 年 2024

1995 ■ The Lasting Scar.. 7" 3tr Megagrind... - -
     Tracks: My Inner War/The Lasting Scar/Leave The Kiss To Die
1995 ☐ The Payment... 7" 3tr Megagrind..................................MGREP 004
     300 copies. Tracks: The Payment (intro)/Storms Of Bitterness And Blood/My Dream Is Bleeding

1995 7" - - -

ENTOMBED

Lars-Göran "L-G" Petrov: v, Alex Hellid: g, Nico Elgstrand: g,
Victor Brandt: b, Olle Dahlstedt: d

The serpet saints of the uprising inferno

Stockholm - **Entombed** started out in 1987 in the same mind-squeezing manner as **Cannibal Corpse** and **Beherit** under the name **Nihilist**, when they also recorded some demos of which *Only Shreds Remain* caught the attention of Earache Records. **Nihilist** split and about a week later L-G, Ulf, Nicke and Alex formed **Entombed**, basically the old band minus Johnny Hedlund. They recorded the legendary demo *But Life Goes On* (on which David Blomqvist handled the bass) and Earache signed the band. They made their debut gig in Rinkeby November 4, 1989. The band actually had no bass-player when they recorded *Left Hand Path*. The style was the same as in the former constellation, but changed on *Hollowman*, where they put more heaviness and variety into the songs. On *Clandestine* Johnny Dordevic (ex-**Carnage**) had joined the band as L-G had left for **Comecon**, with whom he recorded one album. The vocals on *Clandestine* and *Stranger Aeons* were handled by Nicke Andersson and Uffe Cederlund. L-G was also in **Morbid** but later returned to **Entombed**. On *Crawl* they used session singer Orvar Säfström from **Nirvana 2002**. Lars is also found in **Carbonized** who recorded a split-CD with Dutch band **Monastery**. Nicke has also played in **Clint Eastwood Experience** and **Corrupt** and together with Ulf, Nicke (**Nomads**) and Jocke (**Nomads**) had the hobby project **Ledfoot** on the side. They recorded a MCD that has not yet been released, however one track is found on the **Hüsker Dü**-tribute. Ulf has also played in **Morbid** and **Corrupt**. Drummer Nicke formed his punkish side project **The Hellacopters**.. and we all know where that little side-project went. All the early **Entombed** albums were produced by Tomas Skogsberg. Late 1995 Lars Rosenberg left to join **Therion**. He was replaced by Jörgen Sandström, also in **Grave**. The band's next album saw the light of day in 1996 and had the working-title *DCLXVI* (666 in Roman numbers). It became *To Ride, Shoot Straight And Speak The Truth* and showed an even more heavy rocking side of **Entombed**, more towards ex-member Lars Rosenberg's band **Serpent** or **Transport League**. Heavy grinding power-boogie doom, with vocals closer to **Motörhead** or **White Zombie** than growl. Brilliant! In late 1997 drummer Nicke Andersson left the band to devote more time to **The Hellacopters** and was replaced by Peter Stjärnvind. *Same Difference* showed a brand new side of the band, with clean vocals and a much garagey musical approach. *Monkey Puss* (Live In London) was also released as a video. Jörgen was also found in **Project Hate MCMXCIX**, while Ulf is found in the far more pop-oriented **Washoe** as well as heavies **Murder Squad**. Peter is also found in bands like **Murder Squad, Loudpipes, Born Of Fire, Merciless, Nifelheim, Krux** and **Unanimated**. *Morning Star* shows the band is back to the powerful riffing of *To Ride...* once again. Heavy as lead! In 2002 the band provided the music for the 45-minute ballet *Unreal Estate* together with **The Swedish Royal Ballet Ensamble**. In 2005 Sandström and Andersson formed death metal band **Death Breath**. Before the release of *When In Sodom* Uffe Cederlund left the band. Later on Jörgen Sandström left the ranks and so did Peter Stjärnvind, to be replaced by drummer Olle Dahlstedt (**Misery Loves Co**). *The Serpent Saints – The Ten Amendments* album features a line-up consisting of L-G Petrov (v), Alex Hellid (g), Nico Elgstrand (b) and Olle Dahlstedt (d). In 2010 Nico Elgstrand switched from bass to guitar and the band has used Viktor Brandt (**Aeon, Totalt Jävla Mörker, Necrocide**) live. In 2012 the band signed a new deal with Ninetone Records. Some exclusive tracks can be found on compilations, for instance: *Vandal-X* on *Backstage presenterar: Garanterat Ipluggat-95* (95 Backstage), *Rearache* (Earache CD/video-compilation 95), *One Track Mind* on *Motörhead Tribute* (95 Rosa Honung), *March Of The S.O.D/Sargeant 'D' And The S.O.D* on *Swedish Sins* (Jazz '96). The band is also featured on *Power From The North* (Digital Dimension) where they do a cover of **Stillborn**'s *Albino Floged In Black*. They also appear on several other compilations such as: *Grindcrusher II, Earplugged, Gods Of Grind* and *Projections Of A Stained Mind*.

1989 LP - MOSH 21 LP

1991 7" - MOSH 38 S

1991 LP - MOSH 37 LP

1992 MLP - MOSH 52

1989 ■ LEFT HAND PATH...LP Earache ....MOSH 21 LP **$**
     2000 black + 1000 red splatter vinyl copies.
1989 ☐ LEFT HAND PATH...CD Earache ....MOSH 21 CD
1990 ☐ LEFT HAND PATH...LP PD Earache ....MOSH 21 P

Year		Title	Format	Label	Catalog
1990	☐	LEFT HAND PATH	CD	Combat (USA)	88561-2021-2
1990	☐	LEFT HAND PATH	CD	Toy's Factory (Japan)	TFCK 88579
		Bonus: Crawl			
1991	☐	LEFT HAND PATH	LP	Rock Brigade (Brazil)	RBR 360
1991	■	CLANDESTINE	LP	Earache	MOSH 37 LP $
		Also released in a limited edition with embossed cover.			
1991	☐	CLANDESTINE	CD	Earache	MOSH 37 CD
1991	☐	CLANDESTINE	CD	Relativity (USA)	88651-1095-2
1991	☐	CLANDESTINE	CD	Toy's Factory (Japan)	TFCK 88578
		Bonus: Forsaken/Bitter Loss			
1991	■	Crawl/Forsaken/Bitter Loss	7" 3tr	Earache	MOSH 38 S $
1991	☐	Crawl/Forsaken/Bitter Loss	MLP 3tr	Earache	MOSH 38 T
1991	☐	Crawl/Forsaken/Bitter Loss	MCD 3tr	Earache	MOSH 38 CD
1992	■	Stranger Aeons/Dusk/Shreds Of Flesh	MLP 3tr	Earache	MOSH52
1992	☐	Stranger Aeons/Dusk/Shreds Of Flesh	MCD 3tr	Earache	MOSH52
1992	☐	Stranger Aeons/Dusk/Shreds Of Flesh	MCD 3tr	Relativity (USA)	88561-1111-2
1993	☐	CLANDESTINE	LP	Back 2 Basics (Brazil)	BTB 090/93
1993	■	Hollowman	MLP 6tr	Earache	MOSH 94 T $
		Tracks: Hollowman/Serpent Speech/Wolverine Blues/Bonehouse/Put Off The Scent/Hellraiser			
1993	☐	Hollowman	MCD 6tr	Earache	MOSH 94CD
1993	☐	Hollowman	MCD 6tr	Columbia (USA)	CK 57504
1993	☐	Full Of Hell/God Of Thunder/State Of Emergency	MCD 3tr	Columbia (USA)	CSK 6407
1993	☐	WOLVERINE BLUES	LP	Earache	MOSH 82 LP
1993	☐	WOLVERINE BLUES	CD	Earache	MOSH 82 CD
		A misprinted version with the artwork of Napalm Death's From Enslavement To Obliteration exists.			
1993	☐	WOLVERINE BLUES	CD	Columbia (USA)	CK 57593
1994	■	Wolverine Blues	CDS 1tr	Columbia (USA)	CSK 5565
1993	■	WOLVERINE BLUES	CD	Columbia (USA)	CK 57542
		Limited edition with Marvel cover, includes 10 page comic book. Some changes, censored words in songs.			
1993	☐	WOLVERINE BLUES	CD	Toy's Factory (Japan)	TFCK 88618
		Bonus: State Of Emergency (Stiff Little Fingers cover)			
1993	☐	State Of Emergency (split)	7"	King Kong	KK 004
		Split with Doll Squad and Teddybears STHLM, enclosed with King Kong Magazine.			
1994	■	Out Of Hand/God Of Thunder/Black Breath	MLP 3tr	Earache	MOSH114
		God Of Thunder (Kiss cover) and Black Breath (Repulsion cover) are non-LP.			
1994	☐	Out Of Hand/God Of Thunder/Black Breath	MCD 3tr	Earache	MOSH114 CD
1994	☐	Out Of Hand/God Of Thunder/Black Breath	7" 3tr	Earache	7MOSH114
1994	☐	Full Of Hell/God Of Thunder/State Of Emergency	MCD 3tr	Earache (USA)	CSK 6407
1994	☐	OUT OF HAND	CD	Toys Factory	TFCK 88673
		10 track Japanese release featuring the tracks from Out Of Hand, Hollowman (except the title track), Dusk and Shreds Of Flesh.			
1995	☐	Night Of The Vampire (split)	7"	Earache	7MOSH132
		Split with New Bomb Turks. Track: Night Of The Vampire (Roky Erikson cover)			
1995	☐	Out Of Hand/God Of Thunder/Black Breath	7" 3tr	Earache	7MOSH114
1996	☐	WOLVERINE BLUES	CD	Earache	MOSH 82
1996	☐	Hollowman	MCD 6tr	Earache	MOSH 94CD
1997	●	Like This With The Devil/Damn Deal Done	CDS 2tr	Music For Nations	ENT1
		Promo single without artwork.			
1997	☐	TO RIDE, SHOOT STRAIGHT AND SPEAK THE TRUTH	CD	Music For Nations	CDMFN216
1997	☐	TO RIDE, SHOOT STRAIGHT AND SPEAK THE TRUTH	2CDd	Music For Nations	CDMFNX216
		Contains bonus-MCD featuring covers.			
1997	☐	TO RIDE, SHOOT STRAIGHT AND SPEAK THE TRUTH	2LPg	Music For Nations	MFN 216
		Bonus: Tear It Loose (Twisted Sister cover)/Satan (The Dwarves cover)			
1997	☐	TO RIDE, SHOOT STRAIGHT AND SPEAK THE TRUTH	CD	Pony Canyon (Japan)	PCCY 01099
		Bonus: Lost and Ballad Of Hollis Brown (Bob Dylan/Nazareth cover)			
1997	☐	ENTOMBED	CD	Earache	MOSH 125CD
		13 track best of.			
1997	☐	ENTOMBED	CD	Toy's Factory (Japan)	TFCK-87109
		17 track best of.			
1998	☐	Wreckage	MCD	Music For Nations	CDNFNM 233
		Tracks: Wreckage/Reckage (Indy Cart)/Tear It Loose (Twisted Sister cover)/Lost (Jerry's Kids cover)/The Ballad Of Hollis Brown (Dylan cover)/Satan (The Dwarves cover)			
1998	☐	MONKEY PUSS (LIVE IN LONDON)	CD	Earache	MOSH 213 CD
1998	☐	MONKEY PUSS (LIVE IN LONDON)	LP	Earache	MOSH 213 LP
1998	☐	SAME DIFFERENCE	CD	Music For Nations	CDMFN 244
1998	☐	SAME DIFFERENCE	CD	Avex/Bareknuckles (Japan)	AVCB-66063
		Bonus: Vices By Proxy			
1998	☐	SAME DIFFERENCE	LP	Music For Nations	MFN 244
1999	☐	LEFT HAND PATH	CD	Combat	88561-2021-2
		Bonus: Camal Leftovers/Premature Autopsy			
1999	☐	CLANDESTINE LTD VERSION	CD	Earache	MOSH 037 CDL
		Remastered and with new artwork with yellow text.			

1993 MLP - MOSH 94 T

1994 CDS - CSK 5565

1993 CD - CK 57542

1994 MLP - MOSH 114

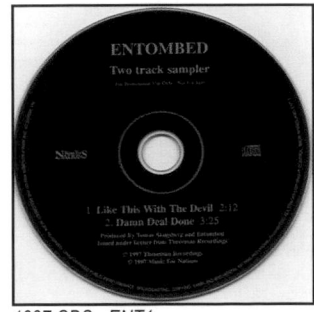

1997 CDS - ENT1

E

| 1999 ☐ | LEFT HAND PATH LTD VERSION | CD | Earache | MOSH 021 CDL |

1999 ☐ LEFT HAND PATH LTD VERSION ....CD　Earache ....MOSH 021 CDL
Re-mastered with new artwork.
1999 ☐ Black JuJu.................. 10" 4tr　Man's Ruin (USA) ....MR 099
Tracks: Mesmerization Eclipse (Captain Beyond cover)/Vices By Proxy/Black Juju (Alice Cooper cover)/Sentimental Funeral (Hey On Glue cover)
1999 ☐ BLACK JUJU ....CD　Man's Ruin (USA) ....MR 119
1999 ☐ BLACK JUJU ....CD　Man's Ruin (USA) 751 014-2
2000 ☐ UPRISING ....CD　Music For Nations ....CDMFN 257
2000 ☐ UPRISING ....CD　Threeman ....TRECD 005
2000 ☐ UPRISING ....LP　Threeman ....TRELP 005
2000 ■ UPRISING ....CD　Metal-Is (USA) ....NR 4534
Bonus: Superior/The Only Ones/Words

2000 CD - NR 4534

2001 ■ MORNING STAR ....CD　Threeman ....TRECD 006
2001 ☐ MORNING STAR ....LP　Threeman ....TRELP 006
2001 ☐ MORNING STAR ....CD　Music For Nations ....CDMFN 265
2001 ☐ MORNING STAR ....CD　Victor (Japan) ....VICP 61485
2001 ☐ MORNING STAR ....CD　Koch (USA) KOC-CD-8357
2001 ☐ WOLVERINE BLUES LTD VERSION ....CD　Earache ....MOSH 082 CDL
Re-mastered with new artwork.

2002 ☐ LEFT HAND PATH ....LP　Earache ....MOSH 021
1000 copies in black vinyl, 300 white and 700 in orange vinyl.
2002 ☐ LEFT HAND PATH (LIMITED EDITION) ....CD　Earache ....MOSH 021 CDL
2002 ☐ CARNAGE IN WORLDS BEYOND ....LP　Displeased D-00112
2002 ☐ CARNAGE IN WORLDS BEYOND ....LP PD　Displeased D-00112
2002 ☐ SONS OF SATAN PRAISE THE LORD ....2CD　Music For Nations ....CDMFN 293
2003 ☐ INFERNO ....CD　Music For Nations ....CDMFN 295
2003 ☐ INFERNO ....CD　Threeman ....TRECD 009
2003 ☐ INFERNO ....CD　Threeman ....TRECDX 009
2003 ☐ INFERNO ....2LPg　Threeman ....TRELP 009
2003 ☐ INFERNO ....CD　JVC Victor(Japan) VICP-62399
Bonus: Albino Flogged In Black (Stillborn cover)/Some Velvet Morning

2001 CD - TRECD 006

2004 ☐ INFERNO/AVERNO ....2CD　Candlelight (USA) CANUS0124CD
Second disc contains When Humanity's Gone/There Are Horrors Of 1000 Nightmares/ Random Guitar/Retaliation (video)/Albino Flogged In Black (video). Slipcase.
2004 ■ UNREAL ESTATE ....CD　Threeman ....TRECD 015
2004 ☐ UNREAL ESTATE ....CDd　Candlelight (USA) ....CDL 0174CD
2006 ■ When In Sodom ....MCD 5tr　Threeman ....TRECDEP 022
Tracks: When In Sodom/Carnage/Thou Shalt Kill/Heresy/Amen

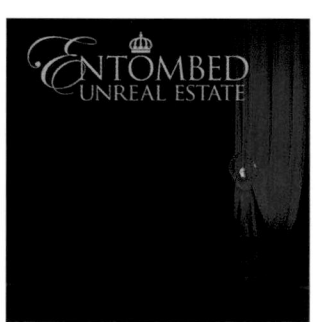

2007 ☐ SERPENT SAINTS ....CD　Threeman ....TRECD 021
2007 ☐ SERPENT SAINTS ....LP　Back On Black ....BOBV 067 LP
Red vinyl.
2007 ☐ SERPENT SAINTS ....CD　Threeman ....TRECD 021
2007 ☐ SERPENT SAINTS/THE TEN AMENDMENTS ....CD　Candlelight ....CANDLE 183 CD
2007 ☐ SERPENT SAINTS/THE TEN AMENDMENTS ....CD　Candlelight (USA) ....CDL 0175CD
2007 ☐ SERPENT SAINTS/THE TEN AMENDMENTS ....LP　Back On Black BOBV067LP
Red vinyl.

2004 CD - TRECD 015

2003 ☐ INFERNO ....CD　Earache ....MOSH 0821 CD
Bonus: State Of Emergency
2007 ☐ INFERNO ....CDg　Metal Mind ....MASSCD 1006DG
2007 ☐ SONS OF SATAN PRAISE THE LORD ....2CDd　Metal Mind ....MASSCD 1007DG
2007 ☐ MORNING STAR ....CDd　Metal Mind ....MASSCD 1008DG
2007 ☐ TO RIDE, SHOOT STRAIGHT AND SPEAK THE TRUTH ....CDd　Metal Mind ....MASSCD 1009DG
2008 ☐ CLANDESTINE ....CD+DVD　Earache ....MOSH 037 CDV
Includes a DVD containing 5 videos and Live In London. Slipcase.

2012 ■ When In Sodom Revisited ....7" 3tr　WHTtRfS ....Reason 009
Tracks: When In Sodom/Welcome Home/Sodom Revisited. 475 silver, 475 gold, 25 black in denim sleeve plus 30 copies test press in folded paper sleeve.
2013 ☐ Candlemass vs. Entombed ....CDSg　Sweden Rock Magazine ....(12-12/0446-4689)
Track: Black Dwarf (Candlemass cover)
2013 ☐ BACK TO THE FRONT ....CD　Century Media ....n/a

2006 MCD - TRECDEP 022

Unofficial releases:
1991 ☐ Live! (Holland 11/11-90) ....7"　Distorted Harmony ....- -
Tracks: Drowned/But Life Goes On/Sentenced To Death recorded live + Forzaken (studio version). First pressing had black labels and the second had white.
1991 ☐ TWILIGHT OF THE GODS ....LP PD　Headache ....HR 009
A live picture disc bootleg.
1992 ☐ THE TRUTH BEYOND ....CD　Northwind 001
Recorded at Den Haag 920319.

ENTRAILS
Joakim Svensson: v/b, Jimmy Lundqvist: g, Mathias Nilsson: g, Adde Mitroulis: d

Linneryd/Växjö - Death metal in the vein of early *Entombed*. The band was initially formed already in 1991, but was soon put on hold. In 2008 Lundqvist resurrected the beast. Mitroulis

2012 7" - Reason 009

2011 CD - DDR 040 CD

(as Smattro Ansjovis) and Svensson (as Panda Flamenco) are also found in **Birdflesh**. Nilsson and Svensson are also in death metal band **Skogen**. Mitroulis has also played with bands like **General Surgery**, **Jigsore Terror** and **Overdeth**. The drums on the debut were handled by Fredrik Widings. The band recorded two demos in 2009, *Reborn* and *Human Decay*.

2010	☐	TALES FROM THE MORGUE	CDd	FDA Rekotz	FDA 25
2010	☐	TALES FROM THE MORGUE	LP	FDA Rekotz	FDA 25
2011	☐	THE TOMB AWAITS	CD	FDA Rekotz	FDA 33 CD
2011	■	THE TOMB AWAITS	CD	Dark Descent (USA)	DDR 040 CD
2011	☐	THE TOMB AWAITS	LP	FDA Rekotz	FDA 33 LP
		100 yellow, 400 black vinyl.			
2013	☐	RAGING DEATH	CD	Metal Blade	15192-2
2013	☐	RAGING DEATH	CD+DVDd	Metal Blade	15192-2LTD
2013	☐	RAGING DEATH	LP	Metal Blade	15192-1

ENTRENCH

Fredrik Pellbrink: v/g, Joel E. Sundin: b, Victor Holmström: d

Västerås - Very crude old school thrash in the vein of **Kreator** or **Slayer**. The band was formed in 2005, originally featuring bassist Hannes Lindkvist.

2011 CD - ABYSS 025 CD

2011	■	INEVITABLE DECAY	CD	Abyss Records	ABYSS 025 CD
2011	☐	INEVITABLE DECAY	LP	Blood Harvest	YOTZ #79

ENTROPY

Christian "Norsken" Knudsen: v/g, Andreas "Ankan" Alriksson: g, Henrik "Mange" Brun: b/v, Henrik "Henke" Borg: d

Strängnäs - The band started out in 1991 and the same year they recorded the demo *Trust Is Out Of Question*, at the time featuring singer/guitarist Norsken, guitarist Ankan, bassist Pontus Andersson and drummer Henke. Pontus later appeared in **Cipher System**. Powerful metal in the vein of **Pantera**. In 2002 **Merciless** singer Roger "Rogga" Pettersson did a guest appearance on a demo by **Entropy**. The demo went well and it instead resulted in Henke and Norsken leaving the band to form **Satureye** together with Rogga in 2000. After this the band folded.

1997 MCD - 96010

1997	■	First Ascent	MCD 4tr	private		96010
		Tracks: Drain/Name/Stuck/Not For Me				

EPEDEMIC

Carl-Johan Wictor: g, Mikko I. Petersen: g, Henrik Karlsson: b, Jeppe Wihlborg: d

Väckelsång/Växjö - Power metal with lots of musical variations. At times similar to **Anthrax**, with a guesting singer Torbjörn Wahrotén in the vein of Dan Dark (**Torch**). Great quality and sound. The band unfortunately split shortly after the record was released. Carl-Johan changed direction and is today playing up-right bass in rockabilly band **Willie And The Ramblers**, plus he runs his own vinyl pressing plant Vic Tone. The story behind the vocals is that the band hadn't really heard how bad their original singer was until they hit the studio, when they fired him on the spot. Wahrotén was a local pop singer who accepted to record the songs in just a matter of days. He however had no idea what musical style the band had and was shocked at what he heard. He however did an amazing job considering the circumstances.

1989 MLP - EPE 001

1989	■	Futuredoom	MLP 4tr	Sin City		EPE 001
		Tracks: Futuredoom/Radioactive/Epedemic/Rest In Peace				

1991 LP - INF 002

EPITAPH

Manne Svensson: g, Nicke Hagen: b/g, Johan Enocksson: d/v

Sollentuna - The band was formed in 1992 when the members were only around fifteen years old. They recorded the demo *Blasphemy* under the name **Dark Abbey** before changing to **Epitaph** (not to be confused with the Ludvika band or German hard rockers). The band also recorded the demo *Disorientation* in 1991. Death/power metal with tempo-changes from ultra speed to almost melodic parts. Thrash-type vocals. *MCMXC – MCMXII* is a compilation box set featuring the remixed *Seeming Salvation* plus demos.

1992 CD - THR 017

1991	■	EPITAPH/EXCRUCIATE (split)	LP	Infest Records	INF 002	$
		Split with Excruciate. Tracks: Cannibalized/Bloodstained Visions/Disorientation/Seeds Of Hypocrisy				
1992	■	SEEMING SALVATION	CD	Thrash Records	THR 017	
2009	☐	SEEMING SALVATION	CD	Konqueror (Singapore)	KR011 CD	
		The tracks from the split as bonus.				
2010	☐	MCMXC – MCMXCII (1990-1992 DISCOGRAPHY)	2LP box	The Crypt	CRYPT 07	
		500 copies. Orange+black vinyl.				

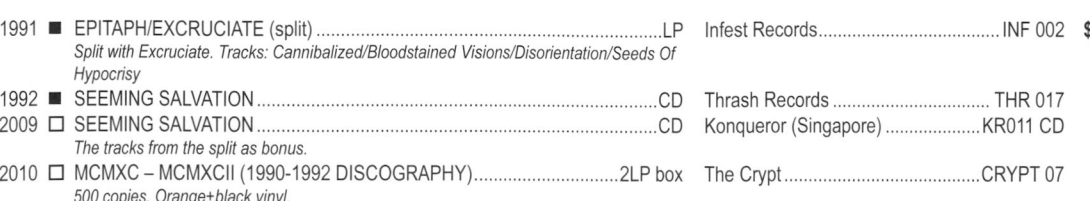

EPITAPH

Jonas Österberg: g/v, Matthias Segerström: g, Bennie Fors: b, Lars Szöke: d

Ludvika - **Epitaph**, not to be confused with the above band and the German hard rockers, were formed around 1986/87. The line-up featured singer/guitarist Österberg, drummer Szöke, guitarist Jonas Tornemalm and bassist Tolan. Shortly after, Tornemalm was replaced by Segerström. After a couple of demos, in 1990, Bennie Fors replaced Tolan. The same year the band recorded a highly acclaimed demo that lead to a deal with World Fluid Records and the recordings of *Tranquillity*, which was released in 1500 copies on CD and as many on vinyl. When Österberg and Szöke went to **Hypocrisy** in 1992 the band folded. Fors started playing guitar in punksters **The Hymans** and during 2005-2010 he played bass in **Dark Funeral** under the moniker "B- Force". In 2010 the recording line-up finally decided to reunite. Killer classic death-infused thrash.

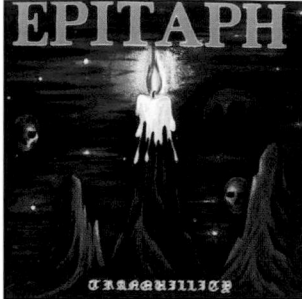

1992 ■ TRANQUILLITY ....LP World Fluid.....................................WRFD502 $
1992 ☐ TRANQUILLITY ....CD World Fluid.....................................WRFD502 $

1992 LP - WRFD502

EQUINOX OV THE GODS

Fredrik Wallin: v, Morgan Svedlund: g, Joakim Wassberg: b, Arttu Malkki: d

Östersund - The band was formed in 1990 by singer Wallin and bass player Melker Ryymin. They released their first demo *Songs From The Hill Of The Heartless Giant* two years after. Some members came and went during the first years. They released two more demos (*Watch The Shadows Dance* and *This Sombre Dreamland*) before being signed by Unisound and at first appearing on the compilation *Into The Cathacthonium*. Daniel Dlimi (ex-**Divine Desecration)**, joined the band in 1998 to replace Joakim Bylander (**Harassed**). The third album *Where Angels Dare To Tread* was supposed to be released by Heathendoom in 1999, but due to various reasons it wasn't. It was then supposed to be issued by Italian label Black Widow, but it wasn't released until 2002 on Virusworx. Daniel Dlimi left in 2001, joined **Aeon** and is also found in **Sanctification** and **Souldrainer**. Morgan Svedlund replaced him in 2002. Ryymin left the band in 2003 and was replaced by Joakim Wassberg. The line-up was also completed with drummer Arttu Malkki (**Souldrainer, Aeon, Sanctification, Defaced Creation**). In 2004 the band recorded a new four-track promo. In 2010 **Equinox Ov The Gods** collaborated with artist Björn Öberg and the two made a joint release, where Björn's 40 page book accompanies the bands two track single *Nemesis/Finis Malorum*. It was released in only 100 copies. Keyboard-based, pretty cool and orchestrated metal with a touch of **Cradle Of Filth**. On the early recordings the vocals were of the death-oriented guttural type, but with the desperation and dramatic touch of some of the goth-oriented bands. On the later recordings the band has become quite theatrical and intricate in its musical forms and the vocals are low range, but clean and raw, more in the vein of Jocke of **Sabaton**. At times with the addition of clean female vocals.

Gods in the garden

1996 ■ IMAGES OF FORGOTTEN MEMORIES....................................CD Unisound...USR 024
1996 ☐ IMAGES OF FORGOTTEN MEMORIES....................................CDd Unisound...USR 024
1997 ☐ IMAGES OF FORGOTTEN MEMORIES....................................LP PD Unisound...USR 24
1997 ☐ FRUITS AND FLOWERS OF THE SPECTRAL GARDEN............CD Unisound...USR 027
2002 ☐ WHERE ANGELS DARE NOT TREAD.....................................CD Virusworx Records.........................WORX003
2007 ☐ FRAGMENTS OF LUST & DECAY...CDpg Burning Star (promo) B12229
2007 ☐ FRAGMENTS OF LUST & DECAY...CD Burning Star.................................BSRCD027
2010 ☐ THE END OF DAYS...MCD 5tr private .... - -
    Tracks: The End Of Days/Gothic Lullaby/Anarchos/The Way Of The Serpent/The Gallows Lord
2010 ■ Nemesis/Finis Maorum .... CDS private ....M 80 GL 113763
    100 copies with 40-page book.

1996 CD - USR 024

2010 CDS - M 80 GL 113763

EREB ALTOR

Crister "Mats" Olsson: v/b/g/d, Daniel "Ragnar" Bryntse: v/g/b/d/k

Gävle - Formed in the early 90s by **Isole** members Olsson and Bryntse, with **Bathory** as their guiding star. They however took a decade-long break before returning. The band recorded the four-track demo *The Awakening* in 2003, which was made in 100 copies with colour artwork. Bryntse is also found in **Sorcery**, **Withered Beauty**, **Windwalker** and **Forlorn**. Both members are also in **February 93**. The first album had a lot of traces from **Bathory** with its epic Viking metal, while the follow-up sounded much cleaner in its approach, much more similar to **Quorthon**'s solo material with clean vocals. The band also uses Jonas Lindström as live session drummer, and he also played keyboards on the first album as well as produced it. Well worth checking out. *Website: http://hem.bredband.net/criols/ea.htm*

2010 LP - NRR 002

2008 ☐ BY HONOR...CD I Hate....................................... IHR CD 052
2010 ■ THE END ....LP No Remorse.....................................NRR 002
    500 numbered copies.
2010 ☐ BY HONOR...LP No Remorse.....................................NRR 003
    350 numbered copies.
2010 ☐ THE END ....CD Napalm..NPR 329
2012 ■ GASTRIKE...CD Napalm..NPR 432

2012 CD - NPR 432

EROTTICA

David Gabrielsson: v, Torgny Johansson: g, Torbjörn Skogh: b, Henrik Petersson: d

Ljungby - The band was formed and released their first demo in 1999 and a second entitled *Inside A Blackened Heart* in 2001. *Iron Maiden*-influenced heavy metal. Petersson is now found in **Screamer**, while Gabrielsson and Johansson formed **By My Fear**.

2005 ■	ERROTICIZM	CD	Swedmetal	SM-04-CD

2005 CD - SM-04-CD

ESPINOZA

Robert "Bobby" Vargkvist: v, Peter Espinoza: g, David Delring: b, Steve Ransow: d

Malmö - After **Nasty Idols** split, guitarist Espinoza went solo showing some different colours, far from the sleaze rock of his other band. *Espinoza* is instead quite close to **Pantera**. Peter actually had another, much more melodic, band named *Espinoza* in the late 80s. Their only vinyl effort was the AOR:ish *Without You* on the compilation *Rock Of Sweden* (89 Hex). The members back then were Peter, singer Anders Strengberg (**Why, Crier, Mercy, Gerfast**), keyboardist Nicklas Brant (dance band **Grönwalls**), bassist Roger Munch and drummer Bengt Johnsson. Ranzow is ex-**Desert Rain** and **Gerfast**. Bobby, who left in 1995, was ex-**Bewarp** and **Emerald**. He was later replaced by American Paul Allen, formerly with **Original Sin**, but nothing more came out of it. *Espinoza* is also found on the compilation *The Lizzy Songs* (95 SMC). In 2006 Peter Espinoza was in the reunited **Nasty Idols**. In 2013 he was again working on new solo material.

1995 ■	SOUL DECAY	CD	SMC	SMCCD 20171

1995 CD - SMCCD 20171

ETERNAL

Christer Gärds: v, Bosse Gärds: g, Pontus Lekaregård (aka Larsson): k,
Anders Sandström: b, Pelle Hindén: d

Björbo/Nås/Gagnef - Drummer Hindén and Pontus (then named Larsson) recorded a single with the band **Aquila** in 1988. The members have played together in various constellations since the 80s, and the band actually recorded a CD-R demo in 1992 under the name **B Gärds Project**. Bosse, Christer and Anders were in the band **High Tension** for quite some time. Hindén also made a stint with **Keen Hue** between 1995 and 2000. *Eternal* was then re-formed in 2007. Pontus, Christer and Anders were also part of party band **Jämnt Skägg** at the time. The CD was produced by Peter Tägtgren. Great-sounding melodic metal in the same vein as **Nocturnal Rites** with a touch of **Europe**. In 2009 the band again visited Tägtgren and recorded the demo *Dalecarlian Metal*, which was followed by the album *Chapter 1*, also recorded in The Abyss.

2008 MCD - Eternal 666

2008 ■	Start Of A New Era	MCD 4tr	private	Eternal 666
	Tracks: The Thing/Cross The Line/Stay The Night/Face The Truth			
2012 ■	CHAPTER 1	CD	HGM	HGM 013

2012 CD - HGM 013

ETERNAL AUTUMN

John Carlsson: v/g, Sami Nieminen: b, Thomas Ahlgren: g

Töreboda - *Eternal Autumn* recorded their first demo in 1994 and another in 1996. On the first album the band only consisted of John and Thomas, sharing the bass duties. The band mixes old fashioned metal with a big chunk of death metal. The first album was mixed by Daniel Bergstrand, while the second was produced by Rickard Sporrong. In 1999 the band also did a cover of *Return Of The Vampire* for *The Unholy Sounds Of The Demons Bells – Tribute To Mercyful Fate*. The band split in 2001. John and Thomas formed the band **Oath**.

1998 ■	THE STORM	CD	Black Diamond	BDP 005
2000 ☐	FROM THE EASTERN FOREST	CD	Soundholic (Japan)	SHCD1-0037

1998 CD - BDP 005

ETERNAL DARKNESS

Janne Heikkinen: v, Jarmo Kuurola: g, Tony Pietilä: g,
Tero Viljanen: b, Make Pesonen: d

Eskilstuna - This unit was formed in 1990 under the name **Necropsy**, by Make Pesonen and Rokki Toni Pietilä. They were soon joined by Janne Heikkinen, Tero Viljanen and Jonas Strandell. The latter left to join **Crypt Of Kerberos** and was replaced by Jarmo Kuurola. Several demos were recorded during 1991-1992. Necropolis Records were supposed to release an album in 1992, but this never happened. In 1993 Rokki left the band and they took a break. In 1994 Strandell put the band together again and recorded the album. On June 12 1995 guitarist Jarmo was unfortunately killed and the band put to rest. The LP and CD have different track lists and feature the unreleased album plus the demos. Slow death metal with very detuned guitars and a singer whose vocal chords probably have been detuned as well. Make is also found in black metal band **The Black**.

1992 7" - DH 006

1992 ■	Doomed/Psycopath	7"	Distorted Harmony (Mexico)	DH 006
	1000 copies.			

2006 LPg - TOD 016

| 2006 ☐ TOTAL DARKNESS | CD | Morbid Wrath/Necroharmonic | MWR004 |
| 2006 ■ TOTAL DARKNESS | LPg | Temple Of darkness | TOD 016 |

999 white vinyl, 200 die hard with patch.

1998 MCD - TLSCD 3398

ETERNAL DESIRE

Anders Olsson: v, Daniel Strid: g, Fredrik Eriksson: b, Carl Olsson: d

Östersund - Traditional eighties influenced melodic heavy metal. Really good vocals, but the production is a bit lacking. Well worth checking out if you're into bands like *Enforcer* etc.

| 1998 ■ THE SECOND RISING | MCD 5tr | TL Studio | TLSCD 3398 |

Tracks: Crimson Rain/The Emperor's Fall/Transylvanian Freeway/Edge Of Tomorrow/The Dream Of Death. 300 copies.

ETERNAL FEAR

Ove Jonsson: v, Daniel Henriksson: g, Mattias Thomasén: g, Mattias Lövdahl: b, Stefan Almqvist: d

2007 CDd - EF 001

Karlskoga - The band was formed already in 1988, they however didn't actually become *Eternal Fear* until 1995. The first line-up featured Henriksson, Thomasén and Jonsson. On the first release the band had been completed with Lövdal and Almqvist. The band has recorded six demos; *Break Down The Wall* (1996), *Look Inside* (1997), *Away* (1998), *The Lost Tracks* (1998), *Emptiness* (1999) and *Solitude* (2000). In 2002 they released the CD-R album *Never Ending Existance* and in 2007 the first printed album, *Evil Deeds*, arrived. The first two albums are great-sounding doomy hard rock with hints of *Spiritual Beggars* as well as *The Sword*, while *Eternal Damnation* saw the band upgrade the style more akin to heavy-edge *Savatage*.

2013 CD - SLP012.038

2007 ■ EVIL DEEDS	CDd	Noréen Production	EF 001
2010 ☐ EMBRACED IN DARKNESS	CD	private	EF 002
2013 ■ ETERNAL DAMNATION	CD	Sliptrick Records	SLP012.038

ETERNAL LIES

Tommy Grönberg: v, Björn Johansson: g, Martin Karlsson: b, Conny Pettersson: d

2002 CD - AMG 91012

Veddinge - *Eternal Lies* were formed in 1998 by guitarist Björn Johansson and drummer Conny Pettersson. In 1999 Jocke Ludwigson joined on guitar and later that year former *Fatal Embrace* singer Tommy Grönberg joined. Bass player Martin Karlsson, who had previously recorded with metal band *Parazite* and death metal band *Eucharist*, was the last man in. The band recorded a demo in 2000, but the engineer disappeared (?) and the recording with him. After this, Ludwigson left the band. In December 2000 *Eternal Lies* made another, now much more successful attempt. The new demo was voted best demo in Close-Up Magazine and in 2001 they were signed by Arctic Music Group for four albums. The first one (and only one so far), was *Spiritual Deception*. After the album Martin left the band and was soon replaced by Marcus Wesslén from *Aggressive*. The band also drafted second guitarist Erik Månsson, also ex-*Aggressive*.

| 2002 ■ SPIRITUAL DECEPTION | CD | Arctic Music Group | AMG 91012 |

ETERNAL OATH

Joni "Gösta" Mäensivu: v, Petri Tarvainen: g, Peter Nagy-Eklöf: g/b, Johan Adler: k, Ted Jonsson: d

1999 CD - ASH 010 CD

2005 CD - BLOD 022 CD

Södertälje/Tumba - Formed in 1991. After recording some demos, the band was signed by Rat Pack Records. *Eternal Oath* play heavy doom/goth-oriented yet melodic and progressive/symphonic death, where the only thing that really differs from other prog/symph-bands is the guttural vocals. High-quality sound and music. Peter Nagy (now Nagy-Eklöf) is ex-*Mörk Gryning/Hypocrite/Wyvern/Defender*. Martin Viklander played bass on the first MCD. The second album *Righteous* was set for release in 2001, but didn't hit the streets until two years later. On *Wither* keyboard player Per Almquist had been replaced by Stefan Norgren (*Lion's Share*). The album *Re-releasd Hatred* features the first two releases. *Ghostlands* saw Peter taking over the bass from Peter Wendin and Adler (*De Van*) replacing Stefan Norgren.

| 1996 ☐ So Silent | MCD 6tr | Rat Pack Records | NWM 01001 |

Tracks: The Dawn/Harmonic Souls Departed/So Silent/Insanity/Eternal Rest/Dream Of Rising

1999 ■ THROUGH THE EYES OF HATRED	CD	Pulverised	ASH 010 CD
2003 ☐ RIGHTEOUS	CD	Greater Art Records	GREAT 08001 CD
2003 ☐ RIGHTEOUS	CD	Black Lodge	BLOD 009 CD
2003 ☐ RIGHTEOUS	CD	Irond (Russia)	CD 03-515
2005 ■ WITHER	CD	Black Lodge	BLOD 022 CD
2006 ■ RE-RELEASED HATRED	CD	Black Lodge	BLOD 010 CD
2013 ☐ GHOSTLANDS	CD	Black Lodge	BLOD 090 CD

2006 CD - BLOD 010 CD

ETERNIA

Mats Dahlberg: v, Ronny Blylod: g, Daniel Niemann: g,
Patrik Nordendahl: b. Magnus Larsson: d

Örnsköldsvik - The band was formed in 1996 by Daniel, Patrik and Magnus. Ronny was also found in **Nypon & Blylod**. The song *Spiritual Advisor* can be found on the American compilation *Original Sin*. In 2000 the band recorded the five track demo-CD-R The Guardian Of The Treasure. It sold very well in the undeground metal circuit in Germany, USA and Japan. The debut album was released on the same label as the first **Damned Nation**, their only two heavy rock releases. Another illegitimate Swedish German metal offspring, with the warrior-theme, the double bass-drums, twin guitars and the **Hammerfall:**ian metal riffing. Not bad at all, just one of many in a genre with limitations. In 2003 they also recorded a three track demo entitled *Shadow Gate*, produced by Anders Zackrisson (former **Gotham City** singer). In 2005 the band changed its name to **Destynation**, now featuring singer Anders Häggkvist replacing Dahlberg. Blylod is also in **Planet Storm**, **Blackrain** and **Justaquickstop**.
Website: http://welcome.to/eternia

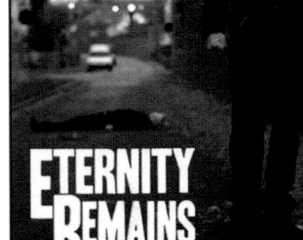

2002 CD - UFOCD 2030

2002 ■	TALES OF POWER	CD	UFO	UFOCD 2030

ETERNITY REMAINS

Jensen: v, Patrik Bolwede: g, Tim Öhrström: g,
Pelle Andreasson: b, August Holmgren: d

Göteborg - *Eternity Remains* were formed in 2005. Quite clever, technical death metal with more screamo-oriented vocals. In 2009 the band also released the single *Don't Forgive Don't Forget/Monkey Syndrome*, where Andreasson had been replaced by Thomas Lundell and Bolwede by Jonathan Thorpenberg (**Anubis, Crash**). In May 2010 they however decided to call it a day. Thorpenberg, also in **Ruined Soul**, joined **Faithful Darkness** in 2013 and will release his solo project **Clouds In Retreat** digitally later the same year.

2009 CDS - - -

2008 □	UNCURBED	CD	private	- -
2009 ■	Don't Forgive Don't Forget/Monkey Syndrome	CDS 2tr	private	- -

ETOS

Nils-Åke Andersson: v, Sören Karlsson: g, Kenneth Lindberg: g,
Mikael Sundh: k, Håkan Hammarström: b, Anders Jansson: d

Kristinehamn - Boogie-based hard rock with Swedish lyrics. Recorded on the workers movement's own label. The band has several unreleased songs on their MySpace.
Website: www.myspace.com/etossweden

1981 7" - BS 810815

1981 ■	Den Nakna Sanningen/Skulden	7"	A-Disk	BS 810815

EUCHARIST

Markus Johnsson: v/g, Thomas Einarsson: g,
Tobias Gustafsson: b, Daniel Erlandson: d

Karlstad/Veddinge - *Eucharist* were founded around 1989 in the small town Veddinge outside Göteborg. They recorded their first demo *Greeting Immortality* in 1992, which was released as a vinyl single by Obscure Plasma, without the band's consent. In 1993 the song *The View* was featured on a Peaceville-compilation *Deaf Metal Sampler*. They split, but were talked into re-uniting by Wrong Again Records. In 1994 guitarist Matti Almsenius was briefly part of the band. Quite high-quality technical death metal with a touch of thrash. The production could however be a lot better. Daniel, who is actually brother of Adrian in **At The Gates**, also appears on the *Subterranean* MCD by **In Flames** and was later found in the bands **Liers In Wait** and **Diabolique**. In 1995 they split up again and Daniel and Tobias formed **The*End**, together with former colleague Matti Almsenius. A second re-union in 1996 and Daniel Erlandsson and Markus Johnsson were the only original members remaining from before the band's four years of silence. Two tracks can also be found on the *WAR* Compilation.
Website: http://www.metalprovider.com/eucharist/

1992 7" - 92006

1997 CD - 971005-2

2002 LP RRLP 004 AS

1992 ■	Greeting Immortality/Into The Cosmic Sphere	7"	Obscure Plasma	92006
1993 □	A VELVET CREATION	CD	Wrong Again Records	WAR 001
1997 ■	MIRRORWORLDS	CD	WAR	971005-2
2002 □	A VELVET CREATION	CD	Regain Records	RR 004 AS
	Bonus: Wounded And Alone/The Predictable End			
2002 ■	A VELVET CREATION	LP	Regain Records	RRLP 004 AS

EUROCK

Jan Morge: v/g, Michael Jönsson: g, Lars "Quast" Dahlqvist: k,
Janne Blondell: b, Anders "Theo" Theander: d

Malmö - Formed in 1977, split in 1985. This is a really high class late 70s, early 80s-style
AOR-band with touches of *Morningstar*, *Trillion*, *707* and such. *Eurock* unfortunately never
received the recognition they deserved. Theo was later in *Bewarp* and had previously played
with rock 'n roller *Kal P Dal*, where Morge was also found. Morge had also played with the hard
blues-rocking band *Skåne* that never emerged on record. *Eurock* were approached by manager
Thomas Ertman, who wanted to buy the name and the song *Heloise* for his band *Force*. They
however turned him down and Thomas' band got the name… *Europe*. *Eurock* tried to stop
them but the lawyers found the names too different to make a case of it. Unfortunately *Eurock*
were later accused by media for trying to take advantage of the far more well known *Europe*.
Today Theo is running Roastinghouse Studios and Morge is in the rock band *Pedalens Pågar*.

1984 7" - EUS 575

1984 ■ The Loner/Stenblomma	7"	Eutone	EUS 575
1984 ■ EUROCK	LP	Eutone	EULP 675

1984 LP - EULP 675

EUROPE

Joakim "Joey Tempest" Larsson: v/g, John Norum: g, Gunnar "Mic" Michaeli: k,
John Levén: b, Håkan "Ian" Haugland: d

Upplands Väsby - It all started in Upplands Väsby, north of Stockholm, in the seventies. Young
guitar player John Norum, born February 24, 1964 in Vardö, Norway decided he would become
a rock star around the age of 10. In 1976 he formed his first band, *Dragonfly*, which also featured
singer/guitarist Stefan Kéry (who later played with Haugland in a punk band) and drummer
Tony "Reno" Niemistö. John's mother's boyfriend was a man named Thomas Witt. Thomas
was a music producer and he was working with classic vulgo-rocker *Eddie Meduza*. At the age
of 14, in 1978, John was offered the chance to play guitar with Eddie, live and on the single
Punkjävlar (which became a huge hit). John was ironically enough into punk like *Sex Pistols*
and at the time had a band called *Dog Wayst*, where he was called Johnny Fuckfaster. The feeling for hard rock and *Thin Lizzy* in particular however took over and he formed the band *WC*
(…yes indeed) where he now started playing covers of *UFO*, *Thin Lizzy* etc. The band also
featured Jan-Erik Bäckström, Mikael Kling (later in *Universe*) and his old friend, drummer Tony
Niemisö. Only one song was ever recorded, a live recording of the song *In My Head* found on
the compilation *Musikfest med sångare & musker i Väsby 78* (79 Upplands Väsby Kommun).
Joey Tempest has said he was actually in the audience at that particular gig. In 1979 John did
two guest solos on the album *Eddie Meduza & The Roaring Cadillacs*. John became friends
with Joakim Larsson. He reformed *WC* with bass player Peter Olsson and drummer Ulf "Bo
Werner" Sundberg (later in *Mogg*, *Rising Force*, *Steamroller*). Ulf left and John drafted his old
friend Tony. John was singing at the time, but soon asked his friend Joakim (at the time singer/
bass player in the band *Roxanne*) if he would sing. He would, and the band now changed its
name to *Force*, taken from the *UFO* album *Force It*. They started writing their own material
with songs like *Give Me A Break*, *Mystery*, *Midnight Show*, *Black Rose* and *Rock On*, which
was later re-written and featured on the Europe debut as *Farewell*.

Young boys on the road to stardom

In 1981 Peter quit (as Joey stole his girlfriend). Joey, who took his stage name from *The Tempest*
by Shakespeare, handled the bass in the meantime, also on some demo recordings. Norum knew
guitarist John Levén, asked him to join and he did, switching to bass. In April 1981 Levén was
asked to join *Yngwie Malmsteen*, a local guitar hero who had just landed a deal with CBS. As a
result Norum asked Yngwie's former bass-player Marcel Jacob to join, which he did. Even though
he only did two shows with the band, he was quite influential in the song writing and co-wrote
some tracks that would later appear on the first two *Europe* albums, such as *Scream Of Anger*
(at the time called *Black Journey For My Soul*) and *The King Will Return*. However after just
three months Marcel and Levén traded bands once again. Joey's girlfriend Anita Katila (sister
of Power-drummer Jari) sent a rehearsal demo to enter the band to the Rock-SM competition,
against the band's will, I may add. The songs on the demo were *Rock On*, *Paradize Bay*, *The
King Will Return*, *Children Of This Time* and *Seven Doors Hotel*. Since Yngwie Malmsteen had
his band *Rising Force* they felt there might be some confusion. Joey came up with the name
Europe from the Deep Purple album *Made In Europe* (According to the Swedish band Eurock
they were approached by *Force/Europe* manager Thomas Erdtman, who wanted to buy the
name *Eurock*, but they wouldn't sell it). Joakim now officially went by the name Joey Tempest
and drummer Niemistö became Reno. So *Force* now changed their name to *Europe* and they
won the Swedish Rock-SM in 1982. This led to the recording of the first album, which is actually more of a traditional hard rocker influenced by bands like *Thin Lizzy*, *UFO* and *Rainbow*.
They also got a manager in Thomas Erdtman, who even tried to make the band sing in Swedish
and become a bit more commercial, which they luckily rejected, of course. The album set the
beginning of what was to be Swedens no. 1 melodic hard rock band. The budget was quite slim,
it was recorded quite rapidly and the production may not be the best, but it's still become quite
the classic. The sales weren't bad either. It sold in the excess of 35 000 copies in just a few weeks
after its release. Thanks to Japanese metal journalist Masa Itoh at *Burrn!!* Magazine, who found
the album on a trip to the UK and brought it back to Japan, the band was contacted and finally

So, can we agree on which finger to flip?

Slightly older boys on the road to stardom

contracted by Victor Records in Japan. Actually, before all of this, in 1982, John recorded the *Eddie Meduza* live album *Dåren 'e lös – The Roaring Cadillacs Live*. Maybe not the proudest of moments for John, but Eddie Meduza (Errol Norstedt, died in January 2002) became a legend and the album actually features the song *Boyazont*, which later would appear on *Europe*'s debut album. In 1984 John actually recorded two more solos for Eddie Meduza. The songs were *Hold Your Fire* and *California*, found on the album *West A Fool Away*. February 23, 1984 *Europe*'s second album *Wings Of Tomorrow* continued in the vein of the debut, but saw the band adding a bit more keyboard into the mix. Gunnar "Mic" Michaeli, previously with the bands *Avalon* (only demos) and *Universe*, was at this stage hired as a tour keyboardist. After some tours on the second album Tony was given the boot, by Erdtman, by letter and without the band knowing it. In August 1984, ex-*Trilogy* drummer Håkan "Ian" Haugland took his place and at the same time Mic became a full-time member. In 1985, the new line-up recorded the track *Rock The Night* for the movie *On The Loose*, sponsored by the industrial workers union, LO. The songs *On The Loose* and *Broken Dreams*, on that EP, were actually recorded by Joey only, with the aid of a drum-machine. The band also participated in the movie. Later the same year, in August 1985, Joey was asked by journalist and project manager Stefan Johansson (OKEJ magazine) to write the song for *Swedish Metal Aid*, a benefit project helping the starving people of Ethiopia. Joey wasn't interested at first, but when Stefan said he'd use a composition from rivals *Treat*, Joey delivered. The result was the amazing ballad *Give A Helping Hand*. The lead vocals of the song were shared between Joey, Tommy Nilsson (*Easy Action/Horizont*), Malin Ekholm (*Aphrodite*), Björn Lodin (*Six Feet Under/Baltimoore/BALLS*), Robert Ernlund (*Treat*) and Joakim Lundholm (*220 Volt*). The chorus vocals from all the 120 musicians posing on the cover, were actually recorded by the lead vocalists the day before. All according to Kee Marcello and journalist Jörgen Holmstedt in the fantastic book *OKEJ* (Premium Publishing).

In 1986 *Europe* recorded the song that would forever define the band. One simple musical phrase on keyboard, just as defining as the first guitar chords of *Smoke On The Water*, set the band on the world map forever. The album and the song was of course *The Final Countdown*. This album meant a world breakthrough for the band, and their biggest commercial success ever. The peak of their career, if you will. It also meant the end of a musical relationship. John Norum felt the album was way too commercial and he didn't buy the poodle look, the playback TV shows etcetera, so after the release of *The Final Countdown*, early 1986, Norum decided to leave the band (or was sacked depending on who you believe). Former *Easy Action*-guitarist Kjell "Kee Marcello" Lövbom was drafted. Joey had previously met Kee when he produced the *Swedish Metal Aid* single. For dedicated Kee-fans, he has previously made recordings with *Stetson Cody* (7"), *D'Accord* (7"), *Kee & The Kick* (7" - note that Kee in the name is the female singer), *Silver* (7"– En Gång Till, 1980 Planet) and *Easy Action*. It however came as a surprise to the rest of the band that manager Ertman had promised Kee to share writing credits and co-producing the next album (Kee's version of these events can be found in his autobiography *The Rock Star God Forgot*). Norum's musical career continued and can be found under John's name in this book. In 1986 the soundtrack compilation *World Grand Prix Pride One* (Victor Japan, VIP 28137) featured two exclusive instrumental versions of *Carrie* and *Love Chaser*. Kee's first recording with the band was the album *Out Of This World*, which showcased a heavier, bluesier side of the band. The album did however not reach the sales level of *The Final Countdown*. In 1989 the band parted ways with manager Thomas Erdtman, whose tax planning had made the band members tax exiles with heavy tax debts when they returned from a stint at the Bahamas. This was actually one of the reasons it took so long for the band to finally reunite. But, things were not over yet. In 1991 *Prisoners In Paradise* continued showing some heavier sides of *Europe*, but the heaviest moments unfortunately never appeared on the album. The band recorded several songs that never made it on record because the label found them a bit too heavy. This is what's referred to as *Le Baron Boys Session*. The Japanese version did contain one of the heaviest and best songs this band has ever produced, entitled *Yesterday's News*, as bonus track. Another highlight, even heavier, is entitled *Rainbow Warrior* and can be found on the compilation-CD for the first encyclopedia and a second one entitled *Blame It On Me* in the second book. For interested fans there are of course video's available with the band. *The Final Countdown Tour '86"* ('86, Japanese), *The Final Countdown Tour* (Hammersmith Odeon '87 - 56 min.), *Europe In America* ('87, 56 min.) and *The Final Countdown Video Singles* ('87 - 4 tracks). In 1992 the members had a break that seemed to last. Kee recorded an instrumental album with jazz-fusion guitarist Ulf Wakenius and joined the band *Red Fun*, after at first only being the producer. They only released one album before splitting. Kee later toured and recorded with pop/rocker Michael Rickfors in the summer of 1995. He also released his solo album *Shine On* (95 CNR). It's not hard rock, but west coast oriented music inspired by the likes of Don Henley and *Eagles*. Ian reformed his old band *Trilogy* and they released one album in 1995. Ian also did a cover of *Changes* for an Ozzy Osbourne tribute. A second *Trilogy*-album was supposed to be recorded, but things were put on hold. Ian also recorded and toured together with Glenn Hughes. So did John and Mic, however due to the former *Purple* hero's inability to pay his musicians as agreed, the collaboration took a hault. Levén became a member of the band *Damage Done*, which later turned in to Pontus Norgren's solo-project, however without Levén. A brilliant demo was recorded, and current big pop-star Patrik Isaksson handled the vocals. Joey released some solo-contributions to the westcoast/pop scene, which was a minor hit in Sweden. Mic was working with production and song writing and was involved with the blues-project *Walking Heads*, also featuring Kee, while Mic and Ian were working with Finn-

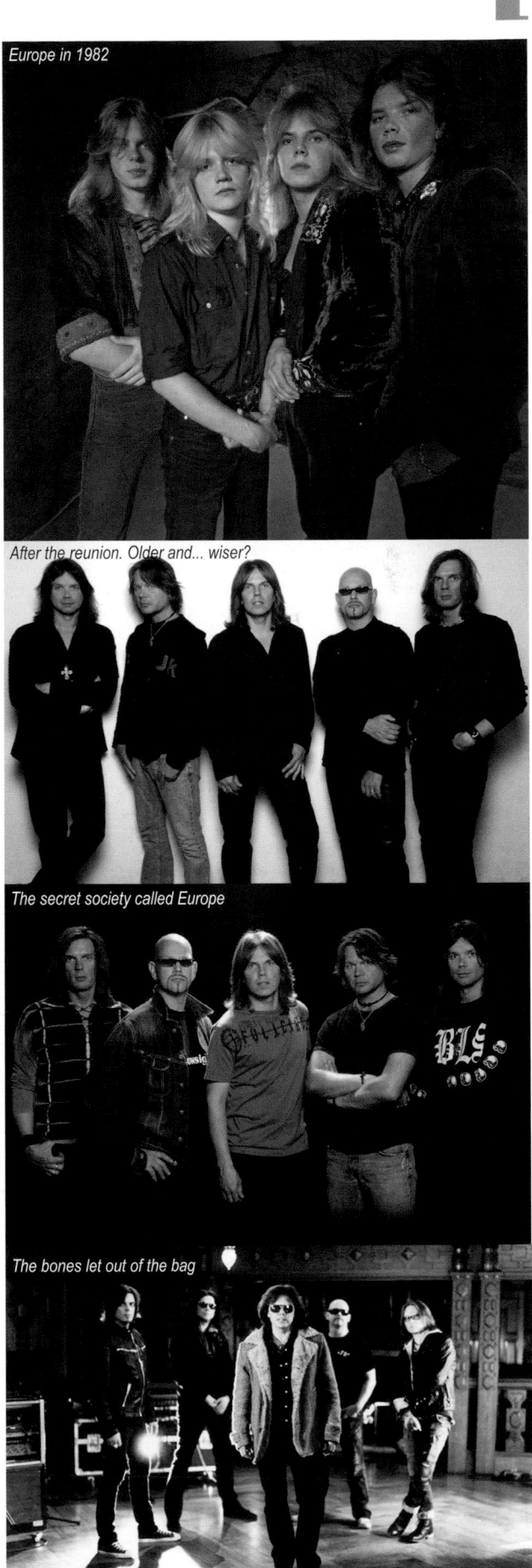

Europe in 1982

After the reunion. Older and... wiser?

The secret society called Europe

The bones let out of the bag

ish band **Brazen Abbot** and blues guitarist Tommy TC Carlsson. Tony Niemistö recorded an album with sleaze-rockers **Geisha** and in 1993 he worked with Danish hard rockers **=Y=** (featuring Yenz from **Brats/Geisha**, Oliver Steffensen and Hal Patino). John Norum pursued a quite successful solo career and recorded an album with **Don Dokken**. There was by the way also an Italian band called **Europe** that released a self-entitled album on the Chord-label in 1986. A live recording from Solna 1986 was bought by Empire records, but as the band didn't feel it was good enough to be released it wasn't until much later. In 1996 Ian started a pop-project together with ex-**Visitors** man Göran Danielsson under the whitty name **Brains Beat Beauty** (First Came Moses Victor VICP-60173). What was to be the second **Trilogy**-album, changed into **Haugland-Hofgard**, as the bass-player/singer was sacked and Ian took over the vocal task. An album however never saw the light of day. Ian also played with cover-band **Let's Party** together with Peo Thyrén and Dag Finn (both ex-**Sha-Boom**). In '97 Levén and Haugland backed ex-**Fortune** singer Benny Söderberg in his project **Clockwise**. Levén, Haugland and Micaeli were also involved in the rock 'n roll project by Swedish singer Thore Skogman. In 1998 Levén joined the band **Eyeball**, together with Mats Levén (Yngwie, **Abstrakt Algebra** etc and Fredrik Åkesson (**Talisman**). However, they changed their name to **Southpaw** and released one album. Ian and Mic were also part of cover band **White Purple**, lead by **Alien**-guitarist Tony Borg.

Joey and John rockin' the night in Karlshamn

In 1999 **Europe** finally re-united to do a one-off performance on the millennium New Years Eve. The line-up featured Joey Tempest, John Norum, Kee Marcello, John Levén and Ian Haugland. The band played *The Final Countdown* live on national television when 1999 became 2000 in the blistering cold. The 1999 re-release of *The Final Countdown* is a horrible dance-version, where some blasphemic person has more or less removed the heavy guitars and put progammed drums all over the place. The first pressing actually had a Freudian misprint... it lacked the first "o" in the last word... In 2002 Ian started working as a radio DJ at Radio Rockklassiker in Stockholm and was playing with the resurrected **Sha-Boom**, Joey released his third solo album in 2002, Kee was producing and working on solo-material which later surfaced as the **K2** band, Norum was again recording and touring with **Don Dokken**. Some buzzing began about a possible **Europe** re-union, once the tax debts had been written off... Finally, October 2, 2003 **Europe** announced their comeback. The band was recording a new album. Initially the line-up was going to feature both Kee and John, but that idea didn't really work out, leaving the strongest player standing. The band's debut live show was recorded for Swedish radio and the band performed the title track of the forthcoming album, *Start From The Dark*, showing a more modern and heavier side of the band. The album, along with John and Michelle Norum's son Jake, arrived on September 22, 2004. The song *Hero* was a tribute to John and Joey's hero Phil Lynott. John also released his solo album *Optimus* on his birthday the subsequent year, February 23, 2005. There are several similarities between the album and the style in which **Europe** went. John also made some guest appearances and recorded a tribute to Frank Marino on the album *Second Hand Smoke*.

"Hey, isn't that Kee in the audience?"

In October 2006 the **Europe** album *Secret Society* was released, continuing on the same path as *Start From The Dark*. The first single off the album being *Always The Pretenders*. The band recorded a semi-acoustic show in January of 2008, released on vinyl, CD and DVD as *Almost Unplugged*. John also started recording the follow-up to *Optimus*, which was supposed to be released in 2008, but tragedy struck with the sudden demise of John's ex-wife, and mother of his son Jake, Michelle and it was postponed. In 2009 **Europe** recorded the album *Last Look At Eden*, using new producer Tobias Lindell. The album showed a bluesier **Europe**, with a retro-touch leaning more towards classic **Deep Purple** style hard rock, still with some modern heavy riffing. The title track, and first single, however bears some traces of bands like **Coheed And Cambria**. In 2009 John recorded a three minute long, retro, spaced out guest solo on the Frank Marino cover *Talkin 'Bout A Feelin* on the album *Volume Two* by **Mountain Of Power**, released in 2010 on Grooveyard Records. 2010 also saw the release of John's long-awaited solo album *Play Yard Blues* (Mascot Records), which also had a retro style hard rock feel to it. In 2011 Ian Haugland played on the solo album *Diamonds And Dirt* (SPV) by former **Thin Lizzy** guitarist Brian "Robbo" Robertson, with whom Norum has played on several shows. In 2011 Kee Marcello also released his revealing autobiography, plus an album featuring his version of some **Europe**-tracks, entitled *Europe: Redux*. The Europe autobiography *Only Young Twise*, by Mattias Kling, was also released this year. In 2012 **Europe** returned with yet another slab of music, *Bag Of Bones*, this time taking it to yet another heavier level, more classic seventies hard rock. The album was produced by Kevin Shirley (**Iron Maiden**, Joe Bonamassa, **Black Country Communion** etc) and featured guest spots from guitarist Joe Bonamassa and drummer Anton Fig. The first single off the new album was *Not Supposed To Sing The Blues*. Late 2012 Norum started working on a new solo album.
Website: www.europetheband.com

The power of 2013!

Year		Title	Format	Label	Catalog	
1983	☐	EUROPE	LP	Hot Records	HOTLP 83001	
1983	■	EUROPE	LP	Victor (Japan)	VIL-6067	
		Different artwork.				
1983	☐	EUROPE	CD	Epic (Japan)	ESCA 5623	
1983	☐	Seven Doors Hotel/Words Of Wisdom	7"	Hot Records	HOTS 834	
1983	☐	Seven Doors Hotel/Words Of Wisdom	7"	Victor (Japan)	VIPX 1725	$
1983	■	Lying Eyes/Dreamer	7"	Hot Records	HOTS 8312	$$
		Never officially released..				
1984	☐	EUROPE	LP	Jigu CBS (Korea)	KJPL-0521	
1984	☐	EUROPE	LP	Epic (Holland)	EPC 463084 1	
		Different artwork.				
1984	☐	Dreamer/Lying Eyes	7"	Victor (Japan)	VIPX 1756	
1984	☐	WINGS OF TOMORROW	LP	Hot Records	HOTLP 84004	
1984	☐	WINGS OF TOMORROW	LP	Victor(Japan)	VIL-6095	
		Japanese press with lyrics.				
1984	☐	WINGS OF TOMORROW	LP	Victor(Japan)	VDP-29	
1984	☐	WINGS OF TOMORROW	LP	Epic (Holland)	2638 4	
1984	☐	WINGS OF TOMORROW	LP	Epic (UK)	460213 1	
1984	☐	WINGS OF TOMORROW	LP	Epic (USA)	PC-40049	
1984	☐	WINGS OF TOMORROW	LP	Epic (Greece)	EPC 26384	
1984	☐	WINGS OF TOMORROW	LP	New Aspect	CR 8005	
1984	☐	WINGS OF TOMORROW	LP	Jigu CBS (Korea)	KJPL-0441	
		Red label. Korean insert.				
1984	☐	WINGS OF TOMORROW	LP	Chin Shiang (Taiwan)	HQ-1114	
1984	■	Stormwind/Dreamer	7"	Hot Records	HOTS 8313	
1984	☐	Open Your Heart/Wings Of Tomorrow	7"	Hot Records	HOTS 8417	
1984	☐	Open Your Heart/Wings Of Tomorrow	7"	Epic (Holland)	A-6077	
1985	☐	WINGS OF TOMORROW	LP	Epic	CBS 263 84	
1985	☐	WINGS OF TOMORROW	CD	Epic (Japan)	ESCA 5624	
1985	☐	WINGS OF TOMORROW	CD	Epic	CDEPC 26384	
1985	☐	WINGS OF TOMORROW	LP	Epic	RK 056	
1985	☐	WINGS OF TOMORROW	LP	Epic (South Africa)	NIC 012	
1985	☐	EUROPE	LP	Epic	CBS 263 85	
1985	☐	Open Your Heart/Wings Of Tomorrow	7"	Epic	CBS 6077	
1985	☐	Open Your Heart/Wings Of Tomorrow	7"	Epic (Holland)	A 6077	
1985	☐	Rock The Night/Seven Doors Hotel (new version)	7"	Epic	EPCA 6166	
1985	☐	Rock The Night/Rock The Night/Seven Doors Hotel	MLP 3tr	Epic	CBS12 6166	
1985	☐	Rock The Night/On The Loose/Broken Dreams	7" 3tr	CBS	ML-LO	
		This is a special edition soundtrack from the film On The Loose where Joey has a part. Different recording than on the LP.				
1985	☐	Rock The Night/Seven Doors Hotel	7"	Epic (Spain)	EPC 650171 7	
		Poster.				
1985	☐	Rock The Night/Seven Doors Hotel	7"	Epic (Spain)	EPC 650171 7	
		Yellowish cover, no poster.				
1985	■	Rock The Night/Seven Doors Hotel	7"	Epic (Australia)	650171 7	
1985	☐	Rock The Night/Seven Doors Hotel	7"	Epic (Portugal)	EPC 650171 7	
		Blue cover.				
1985	■	Rock The Night/Seven Doors Hotel	7"	Epic (UK)	EUR 1	
1985	☐	Rock The Night/Seven Doors Hotel	7"	Epic (UK)	EURQ 1	
		Sew-on patch				
1985	☐	Rock The Night/Seven Doors Hotel	7"	Epic (UK)	EURP 1	
		Gold vinyl.				
1985	☐	Rock The Night/Seven Doors Hotel	7"	Epic	EPCA 6166	
1985	☐	Rock The Night/ (remix)Rock The Night (single)/Seven Doors Hotel	12"	Epic	A 12.6166	
		Cover w live pic of Joey .				
1986	☐	Rock The Night/Rock The Night	7"	Epic (USA-promo)	34-07091	
1986	☐	Rock The Night/Ninja	7"	Epic (South Africa)	EN 6007	
1986	☐	Rock The Night/Seven Doors Hotel	7"	Epic (Holland)	EPC 650 171 7	
1986	☐	Rock The Night/Seven Doors Hotel	7"	Epic (New Zealand)	650 171 7	
1986	☐	Rock The Night	MLP 4tr	Epic (Spain, Holland)	EPC 650 171 6	
		Tracks: Rock The Night/Seven Doors Hotel/Stormwind/Wings Of Tomorrow.				
1986	☐	Rock The Night	MLP 4tr	Epic (Holland)	EPC 650171 6	
		Group cover.				
1986	☐	Rock The Night/Seven Doors Hotel	7"	Epic (Spain)	EPC 650 171 7	
		Group cover.				
1986	☐	Rock The Night	MLP 4tr	Epic (Australia)	EURT 1 7127	
1986	☐	Rock The Night	MLP 4tr	Epic (UK)	EURT 1	
1986	☐	Rock The Night	MLP 4tr	Epic (UK)	EURQT 1	
		Poster.				
1986	☐	Rock The Night	MLP 4tr	Epic	LC-0199	
1986	☐	Rock The Night	2MLP 5tr	Epic (UK)	EURD 1	
		Double MLP with same as above + The Final Countdown.				
1986	☐	Rock The Night/Rock The Night	12"	Epic	EAS 02665	
		Promo in white carton stand.				
1986	☐	The Final Countdown/Carrie	7"	Old Gold	OG 9946	

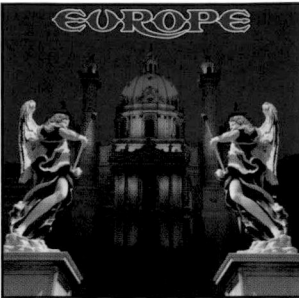

1983 LP - VIL-6067

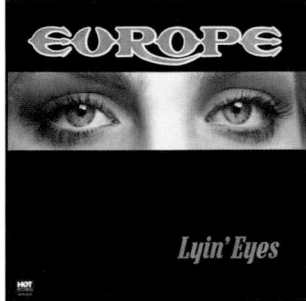

1983 7" - HOTS 8312

1984 7" - HOTS 8313

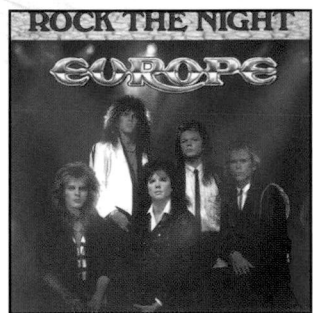

1985 7" - 650171 7

1985 7" - EUR 1

E

Year		Title	Format	Label	Cat. No.

1986 ● Rock en la noche/Rock en la noche ....7" Epic (Argentina) ....ASS 8741
No artwork.
1986 ☐ The Final Countdown/On Broken Wings ....7 Epic ....EPC A 7127
1986 ☐ The Final Countdown ....MLP 3tr Epic CBS12 7127
Tracks: The Final Countdown/On Broken Wings/Heart Of Stone
1986 ■ The Final Countdown/On Broken Wings ....7" Epic ....A 7127
Different artwork with/without tour dates on back cover. Same catalogue number.
1986 ☐ The Final Countdown/On Broken Wings ....7" Epic (UK) ....A 7127
1986 ☐ The Final Countdown/On Broken Wings ....7" Epic (UK) ....QA 7127
Poster.
1986 ■ The Final Countdown ....MLP 3tr Epic (UK) ....TA 7127
Tracks: The Final Countdown/On Broken Wings/Heart Of Stone
1986 ○ La ultima cuenta regresiva/La ultima cuenta regresiva ....7" Epic (Argentina) ASS8428
No artwork.
1986 ☐ The Final Countdown/On Broken Wings ....7" Epic (Spain) ....EPC A 7127
Different back cover.
1986 ☐ The Final Countdown/On Broken Wings ....7" Epic (Portugal) ....EPC A 7127
Different back artwork.
1986 ☐ The Final Countdown/On Broken Wings/Heart Of Stone ....MLP 3tr Epic (Holland) ....A 12.7127
Different back artwork.
1986 ☐ The Final Countdown/On Broken Wings ....7" Epic (Canada/USA) 34-06416
1986 ☐ The Final Countdown/The Final Countdown (re-mix) ....7" Epic (USA promo) 34-06416
1986 ☐ The Final Countdown ....7" Epic (USA promo) 34 06146
1986 ☐ The Final Countdown ....7" Epic (Portugal) ....EPCA 7127
1986 ☐ The Final Countdown/Carrie ....12" 2tr CBS Brasilia (Brazil) ....EPC 52103
Different artwork.
1986 ☐ The Final Countdown/Carrie ....7" CBS (Jukebox-single) 15-69126
1986 ○ The Final Countdown/Carrie ....7" Epic Collectables (Jukebox-single) 15-69126
No artwork.
1986 ☐ The Final Countdown ....7" Epic (Australia) ....ES 1199
1986 ☐ The Final Countdown/On Broken Wings ....7" Epic (Australia) ....ES 1199
Different artwork "No 1 band in Europe & UK". Kee on cover picture.
1986 ☐ The Final Countdown/On Broken Wings ....12" Epic (Australia) ....ES 12205
1986 ☐ The Final Countdown/On Broken Wings ....7" Epic (South Africa) ....EN 5990
1986 ○ The Final Countdown(long)/The Final Countdown (short) ....12" 2tr Epic (USA) ....EAS 2533
No artwork. Promo.
1986 ○ The Final Countdown ....7" Epic (USA) ....EAS 2533
No artwork. Promo.
1986 ○ The Final Countdown/Rock The Night ....12" 2tr Epic (USA) ....EAS 2351
No artwork. Promo.
1986 ☐ The Final Countdown (split) ....7" Epic (Jukebox-single) ....JC 15190
Split with James Brown.
1986 ■ The Final Countdown/On Broken Wings ....7" Victor (Japan) VIPX-1848
1986 ☐ THE FINAL COUNTDOWN ....LP Epic ....CBS 268 08
On the back of the cover there's a small printed ring. The pressing with no 57 has raised logo and triangle plus a poster, while the cover with no 58 does not
1986 ☐ THE FINAL COUNTDOWN ....CD Epic ....CBS 268 08
1986 ☐ THE FINAL COUNTDOWN ....CD Epic ....CDEPC 268 08
Different artwork.
1986 ☐ THE FINAL COUNTDOWN ....LP Epic (Australia) ....ELPS 4584
Different artwork.
1986 ☐ THE FINAL COUNTDOWN ....LP Victor (Japan) VIL-28019
Different artwork. Some with tour book.
1986 ☐ THE FINAL COUNTDOWN ....LP Epic 466328 1
1986 ☐ THE FINAL COUNTDOWN ....CD Epic 466328 2
1986 ☐ THE FINAL COUNTDOWN ....LP Epic (USA) ....ELPS 4584
1986 ☐ THE FINAL COUNTDOWN ....LP Epic (Australia) ....ELPS 4584
1986 ☐ THE FINAL COUNTDOWN ....LP Epic (Can) ....FE 402 41
1986 ☐ THE FINAL COUNTDOWN ....LP Epic (USA) ....BFE 402 41
1986 ☐ THE FINAL COUNTDOWN ....CD Epic (USA) ....EK 40241
1986 ☐ THE FINAL COUNTDOWN ....CD Epic (USA) ....EM 40241
Longbox.
1986 ☐ THE FINAL COUNTDOWN ....LP Gong (Hungary) ....SLPXL 371 22
1986 ☐ THE FINAL COUNTDOWN ....CD Epic (Brazil) 700.110
1986 ☐ THE FINAL COUNTDOWN ....CD CBS Discos (Brazil) 144909
1986 ☐ THE FINAL COUNTDOWN ....CD Epic (Israel) 26808
Title printed in Hebrew on front cover.
1986 ☐ THE FINAL COUNTDOWN ....LP Epic (UK) ....EPC 26808
Group cover + insert. Poster in some.
1986 ☐ THE FINAL COUNTDOWN ....LP Epic (Spain) ....EPC 26808
Group cover + insert.
1986 ☐ THE FINAL COUNTDOWN ....LP Epic (Taiwan) ....AR 5188
Group cover + insert.
1986 ■ THE FINAL COUNTDOWN ....LP NEO Record & Tape (Taiwan) VIL-28019
1986 ☐ THE FINAL COUNTDOWN ....LP Jigu (Korea) KJPL-0482

1985 7" - ASS 8741

1986 7" - A 7127 (tour edition)

1986 7" - A 7127

1986 MLP TA 7127

1986 7" - VIPX-1848

1986	☐	THE FINAL COUNTDOWN	LP	Discos (Argentina)	120.000.867
1986	☐	THE FINAL COUNTDOWN	LP	Epic (Mexico)	LNC 17507
1986	☐	THE FINAL COUNTDOWN	LP	Supraphon (Checz Rep.)	11 0265-1 311
1986	☐	THE FINAL COUNTDOWN	CD	One Music (Korea)	CPK 1054
1986	☐	THE FINAL COUNTDOWN	LP	One Music (Korea)	CPL 1054
1986	☐	THE FINAL COUNTDOWN	LP	Epic (Zimbabwe)	KSF 3132
1986	☐	THE FINAL COUNTDOWN	LP	Victor (Japan)	VIL 28019
1986	☐	EUROPE	CD	Victor (Japan)	VDP 1147
1986	☐	PRIDE ONE	CD	Victor (Japan)	VIP-28137

Japanese white label promo.

1986 7" - VIPX 1849

1986	☐	THE FINAL COUNTDOWN	CD	Victor (Japan)	VDP 1083
1986	☐	THE FINAL COUNTDOWN	CD	Victor (Japan)	VDP-28055
1986	☐	THE FINAL COUNTDOWN	CD	Epic (Japan)	ESCA 5625
1986	☐	THE FINAL COUNTDOWN	CD	Epic	EPC CL 136 879

Special club-edition.

1986	☐	THE FINAL COUNTDOWN	CD	Epic (France)	H 663282
1986	☐	THE FINAL COUNTDOWN	CD	Epic (Columbia)	KSF 3132
1986	☐	THE FINAL COUNTDOWN	CD	Epic (Peru)	S.E 3416
1986	☐	THE VERY BEST OF EUROPE	LP	T.F.C Music Design Records	MDRC-1071

Compilation (Korea).

1986	■	Love Chaser/Carrie	7"	Victor	VIPX 1849

Soundtrack with "Grand Prix"-cover.

1986 7" - 650 179 7

1986	■	Cherokee/Love Chaser	7"	Epic	650 179 7
1986	☐	Cherokee/Danger On The Track	7"	Epic (Spain)	EPC 651135 7

Group front, different back.

1986	☐	Cherokee/Heart Of Stone	7"	Epic (Canada/USA)	34-07638
1986	☐	Cherokee/Danger On The Track/Stormwind	MLP 3tr	Epic	EPC 651135 6
1986	■	Cherokee/Danger On The Track	7"	Epic (Holland)	EPC 651135 7

Group front artwork.

1986	☐	Cherokee/Danger On The Track	7"	Epic (Holland)	EPC 651135 7

Pattern front artwork.

1986	☐	Carrie/Carrie	7"	Epic (USA promo)	34-07282
1986	☐	Carrie/Love Chaser	7"	Epic (Canada)	34-07282
1987	☐	Carrie/Love Chaser	7"	Epic (USA)	34-07282

Group front artwork.

1986 7" - EPC 651135 7

1986	☐	Rock En La Noche/Rock En La Noche	7"	CBS (Argentina)	ASS-8741
1987	☐	Carrie/Love Chaser/Danger On The Track	MLP 3tr	Epic	EPC 650 354 6
1987	☐	Carrie/Love Chaser	7"	Epic	EPC 650 354 0

Poster.

1987	☐	Carrie/Love Chaser	7"	Epic	EPC 650 354 7
1987	☐	Carrie/Love Chaser	7"	Epic (UK)	EUR 2
1987	☐	Carrie/Love Chaser	7"	Epic (UK)	EURQ 2

Poster.

1987	○	Carrie/Love Chaser	7"	Epic (UK silver vinyl)	EURP 2

Silver vinyl. No artwork.

1987	☐	Carrie	2x7" 4tr	Epic (UK)	EURD 2

Tracks: Carrie/Love Chaser/Dance The Night Away/Open Your Heart

1987	■	Carrie/Love Chaser	7"	Victor (Japan)	VIPX-1849

Group front.

1987 7" - VIPX 1849

1987	☐	Carrie/Love Chaser	7"	Victor (Japan)	VIPX-1849

World Grand Prix version w different artwork

1987	☐	Carrie/Love Chaser/Danger On The Track	MLP 3tr	Epic (UK)	EURT 2
1987	☐	Carrie	7"	Epic (Spain)	EPC 650 354 7

One-sided promo.

1987	☐	Carrie (split)	7"	Epic (Italy)	JC 15203

Special Jukebox-promo with Tracy Spencer on the flip-side. No artwork.

1987	☐	Love Chaser/Drum Drum	7"	Technology (Italy)	TECHNO 12.02

Note, this is NOT a Europe release, but a disco re-mix that only says "Written by Joey Tempest" on the cover.

1987	■	Rock The Night/Seven Doors Hotel	7"	Victor (Japan)	VIPX 1862
1987	☐	Rock The Night/Seven Doors Hotel	7"	Epic (US)	34-07091
1987	☐	Rock The Night/Seven Doors Hotel	7"	Epic (Canada)	34-07091
1987	☐	Rock The Night/Ninja	7"	Epic (Zimbabwe)	EN 6007
1987	○	Rock The Night	7"	Epic (Argentina promo)	DEP 590

No artwork.

1987	○	Rock The Night (split)	7"	JC	JC 15199

Special Jukebox-promo with Paul Young on the flip-side. No artwork.

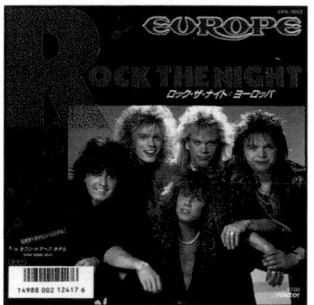

1987 7" - VIPX 1862

1987	☐	Cherokee/Cherokee	7"	Epic (USA promo)	34-07638
1987	☐	Cherokee/Heart Of Stone	7"	Victor (Japan)	VIPX 1881
1987	☐	EUROPE	LP	Epic	CBS 263 85-1
1987	☐	EUROPE	CD	Epic	CBS 263 85-2
1987	☐	EUROPE	LP	One Music (Korea)	KJPL 0521
1987	☐	WINGS OF TOMORROW	CD	Epic	CBS 263 84
1987	☐	WINGS OF TOMORROW	LP	Epic	460 213 1
1987	☐	WINGS OF TOMORROW	CD	Epic	460 213 2

1987	□	WINGS OF TOMORROW	CD	Epic (Japan)	ESCA 5624
1987	□	PERFECT LIVE	LD	Sfinx (Japan)	S-1021
1987	□	IN CONCERT (split)	2LP	In Concert (USA)	-

Set of 2LPs with Europe and The Cure (1 live LP each) for radio broadcast.

| 1987 | □ | IN CONCERT (split) | 2LP | In Concert (USA) | - |

Set of 2LPs with Europe and Robert Cray (1 live LP each) for radio broadcast.

| 1987 | □ | The Final Countdown/On Broken Wings | 7" | Epic (Australia) | ES-1199 |

Different artwork.

1987	□	LIVE IN JAPAN	2LP	HE	86 EV
1988	□	Open Your Heart/Towers Calling	CDS 3"	Victor (Japan)	VDPS 1024
1988	■	The Final Countdown/Carrie	CDS 3"	Victor (Japan)	VDPS 1002

Also available in snap-pack version.

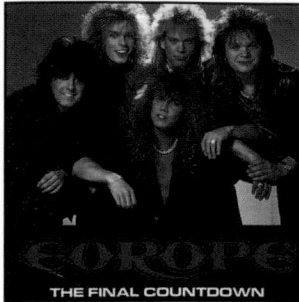

1988 3" - VDPS 1002

1988	□	You & I/We Are The Love/Superstitious	7"	Victor (Japan promo)	YPS-024
1988	□	Superstitious/Lights And Shadow	CDS 3"	Victor (Japan)	VDPS 1014
1988	□	Superstitious/The Final Countdown	7"	Victor (Japan promo)	SEP 20
1988	□	Open Your Heart/More Than Meets The Eye	7"	Victor (Japan promo)	SEP 29
1988	□	Superstitious/Superstitious	CDS	Epic (USA promo)	ESIC 1225
1988	□	Superstitious/Lights And Shadow	7"	Epic (UK)	EUR 3
1988	□	Superstitious/Lights And Shadow	7"	Epic (UK)	EURC 3

Silver vinyl.

| 1988 | □ | Superstitious/Lights And Shadow | 7" | Epic (UK + poster) | EURQ 3 |
| 1988 | ■ | Superstitious | MLP 4tr | Epic (UK) | EURT 3 |

Tracks: Superstitious/Lights And Shadow/Towers Calling/The Final Countdown

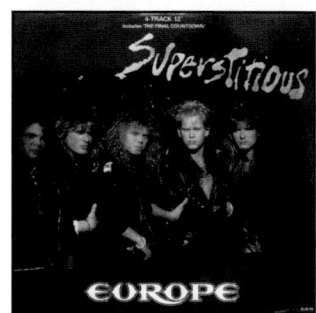

1988 MLP - EURT 3

| 1988 | ○ | Superstitious (split) | 7" | Epic (Italy) | JC 15237 |

Jukebox single. Split with Sade. No artwork.

1988	□	Superstitious/Lights And Shadow	7"	Epic	EPC 652 879 0
1988	□	Superstitious/Lights And Shadow/Cherokee	MLP 3tr	Epic	EPC 652 879 6
1988	□	Superstitious/Lights And Shadow/Cherokee	MLP 3tr	Diski CBS (Greece)	EPC 652 879 6
1988	□	Superstitious/Lights And Shadow/Cherokee	CDS 3tr	Epic	EPC 652 879 3
1988	□	Superstitious/Lights & Shadow	7"	Epic (Australia)	652879 7
1988	□	Superstitious/Lights & Shadow	7"	Epic (Spain)	652879 7
1988	□	Superstitious/Lights & Shadow	3" CDS 2tr	Epic (USA)	49K-08129
1988	□	Superstitious/Lights And Shadow	7"	Epic (Canada/USA)	34 07979
1988	■	Superstitious (long)/Superstitious (short)	CDS 2tr	Epic (USA promo)	ESK 1225
1988	○	Superstitious/Superstitious	12" 2tr	Epic (USA)	EAS 1204

No artwork.Promo.

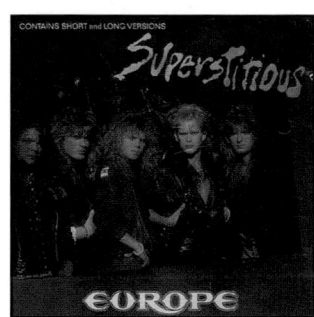

1988 CDS - ESK 1225

| 1988 | ● | Superstitious/Superstitious | 12" 2tr | Epic (Brazilian-promo) | 52.126 |

White label promo. Also says Amostra Invendável and no ITS-1377 on the label.

| 1988 | □ | Supersticioso | 7" | Sony (Mexico) | CBS PR-653226 |

Promo with same song on both sides.

| 1988 | □ | Supersticioso | 7" | CBS (Argentina) | DEP 669 |
| 1988 | ○ | Superstitious | 7" 1tr | Epic (Spain-promo) | EPC 652 879 0 |

No artwork.

| 1988 | ■ | OUT OF THIS WORLD- PREMIERE WEEKEND | 2LP | Epic | A2S 1230 |

Special promo. Extra disc with collage, promos, intros, interviews and instrumental clips.

1988 12" - 52.126

1988	□	OUT OF THIS WORLD	LP	Epic	EPC 462 449 1
1988	□	OUT OF THIS WORLD	CD	Epic	EPC 462 449 2
1988	□	OUT OF THIS WORLD	LP	Epic (USA)	BL 44 185 1
1988	□	OUT OF THIS WORLD	LP	Epic (Canada)	OE 44 185 1
1988	□	OUT OF THIS WORLD	CD	Epic (Canada)	OE 44 185 2
1988	□	OUT OF THIS WORLD	LP PD	Epic (USA)	462 449 0
1988	□	OUT OF THIS WORLD	LP PD	Epic (UK)	462 449 0
1988	□	OUT OF THIS WORLD	LP PD	Epic (Australia)	462 449 0
1988	□	OUT OF THIS WORLD	LP	Suzy (Yugoslavia)	462 449 1
1988	□	OUT OF THIS WORLD	LP	Epic (UK)	462 449 1

Printed in two versions, silver or red vinyl.

1988	□	OUT OF THIS WORLD	LP	Epic (Israel)	EPC 462449 1
1988	□	OUT OF THIS WORLD	LP	Victor (Japan)	VILB 2300 1
1988	□	OUT OF THIS WORLD	CD	Victor (Japan)	VICB 2300 2
1988	□	OUT OF THIS WORLD	CD	Victor (Japan)	VDPB 2500 1

Picture disc + picture card.

| 1988 | □ | BEST OF EUROPE | CD | Victor (Japan) | VICP-98 |
| 1988 | □ | OUT OF THIS WORLD | LP | Jigu/CBS (Korea) | KJPL-0590 |

Korean insert.

1988	□	OUT OF THIS WORLD	CD	Epic (Japan)	ESCA 5626
1988	□	OUT OF THIS WORLD	CD	Epic (Austria)	467 393 2
1988	□	OUT OF THIS WORLD	CD	Epic (Brazil)	700 152
1988	□	OUT OF THIS WORLD	CD	CBS Discos (Brazil)	231139
1988	□	OUT OF THIS WORLD	LP	Sony (Mexico)	LNS 462449

Song titles in Spanish.

| 1988 | □ | OUT OF THIS WORLD | CD | Epic (USA) | EK 44185 |

Best value series.

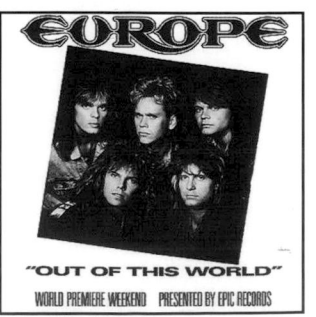

1988 2LP - A2S 1230

| 1988 | □ | OUT OF THIS WORLD | CD | Epic (USA) | 44185 |

Longbox.

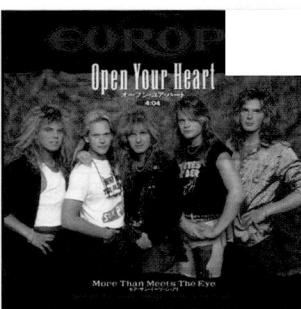

1988 7" - SEP 29

1988 7" - EUR 4

1988 7" - ARI-2099

1989 MCD - 654 564 3

1990 MCDp - 655 573 3

1988	☐	OUT OF THIS WORLD	CD	CBS (Russia)	14384
1988	☐	OUT OF THIS WORLD	LP	One Music (Korea)	KJLP 0590
1988	☐	OUT OF THIS WORLD	LP	Epic (Australia)	462 449 1
		Poster.			
1988	☐	FUERA DE ESTE MONDO	LP	Epic (Argentina)	70-020
1988	☐	Open Your Heart/Towers Calling	7"	Epic (USA)	34-08102
1988	☐	Open Your Heart/Towers Calling	7"	Epic (Australia)	653178 7
1988	☐	Open Your Heart/Tower's Calling	3" CDS 2tr	Epic (Japan)	VDPS-1024
		Snap pack.			
1988	■	Open Your Heart/More Than Meets The Eye	7"	Hot Records (Japan)	SEP 29
1988	☐	Open Your Heart/Just The Beginning	CDS 2tr	Epic	653 097 3
1988	☐	Open Your Heart/Just The Beginning	12"	Epic	653 097 6
1988	☐	Open Your Heart/Just The Beginning	7"	Epic	653 097 7
1988	■	Open Your Heart/Just The Beginning	7"	Epic (UK)	EUR 4
1988	☐	Open Your Heart/Just The Beginning/Rock The Night/Lyin' Eyes	MCD 4tr	Epic (UK)	CD EUR 4
1988	☐	Open Your Heart/Just The Beginning/Rock The Night/Lyin' Eyes	MLP 4tr	Epic (UK)	EUR T4
1988	☐	Open Your Heart/Just The Beginning	7"	Epic (UK)	EUR Q4
		Poster.			
1988	☐	Open Your Heart/Just The Beginning	7"	Epic (UK)	EUR B4
		Badge.			
1988	☐	Open Your Heart (Edit)/Open Your Heart (Album)	CDS 2tr	Epic (USA)	ESK 1325
		DJ promo.			
1989	☐	Let The Good Times Rock/Never Say Die	7"	Epic (UK)	EUR 5
1989	☐	Let The Good Times Rock/Never Say Die	7"	Epic (UK)	EUR Q5
		Poster.			
1988	☐	Let The Good Times Rock	MLP 4tr	Epic (UK)	EUR T5
		Tracks: Let The Good Times Rock/Never Say Die/Carrie/Seven Doors Hotel			
1988	☐	Let The Good Times Rock	MLP 4tr	Epic (UK promo)	EURTS 5
1988	○	Let The Good Times Rock	7" 1tr	Epic (Spain)	654 573 7
		No artwork. Promo.			
1988	☐	Let The Good Times Rock/Carrie/Superstitious	7" 3tr	Epic (Spain)	ARIE 2099
		Spanish tour dates on back			
1988	■	Let The Good Times Rock	7" 4tr	Epic (Spain)	ARI-2099
		Tracks: Let The Good Times Rock/Open Your Heart/Superstitious/The Final Countdown. *Special release for tour of Spain 1989. Promo.*			
1988	☐	Tomorrow (split)	7"	CBS (Brazil)	52.135
		Split with Bangles. No artwork, white label promo. It also says Amostra Invendavel and no ITR-1392.			
1988	☐	Carrie/Love Chaser	7"	Victor (Japan)	VIPX 1849
		Not to be confused with the 1986-version with "Grand Prix"-cover.			
1988	☐	Special Fan Club Edition	7" flexi	Flexi Records	- -
		Greeting + Dreamer acapella. Including fanclub book "Euro Press".			
1989	■	Carrie/Rock The Night/Open Your Heart (Solid Gold)	MCD 3tr	Epic	654 564 3
1989	☐	Let The Good Times Rock	CDS 1tr	Epic (USA promo)	ESK1428
1989	☐	Let The Good Times Rock/Let The Good Times Rock	7"	Epic (USA promo)	34-68547
1989	☐	Let The Good Times Rock/Never Say Die	7"	Epic (USA)	34-68547
1989	☐	Let The Good Times Rock/Dreamer	7"	Epic	654 573 7
1989	☐	Let The Good Times Rock/Dreamer	CDS 2tr	Epic	654 573 3
1989	☐	Let The Good Times Rock	MLP 3tr	Epic	654 573 6
		Tracks: Let The Good Times Rock/On The Loose/Dance The Night Away			
1989	☐	EUROPE	LP	Epic	463 084 1
		Different artwork.			
1989	☐	EUROPE	CD	Epic	463 084 2
		Different artwork.			
1989	☐	EUROPE	LP	Epic (Canada)	VFE 45093-1
1989	☐	EUROPE/WINGS OF TOMORROW	2LP	Epic (Germany)	EPC 465 210-1
1989	☐	EUROPE/WINGS OF TOMORROW	2CD	Epic (Germany)	EPC 465 210-2
1989	☐	More Than Meets The Eye/Let The Good Times Rock	CDS 3"	Victor (Japan)	VDPS 1031
1989	☐	More Than Meets The Eye/Let The Good Times Rock	7"	Victor (Japan promo)	SEP 37 $
1989	☐	More Than Meets The Eye	MLP 3tr	Epic (France)	654 652 6
		Tracks: More Than Meets The Eye/On The Loose/Dance The Night Away			
1989	☐	More Than Meets The Eye/Dreamer	7"	Epic	654 652 7
1989	☐	More Than Meets The Eye	7"	Epic (Spain promo)	ARIE 2130
1989	☐	Open Your Heart	7"	Epic (Spain promo)	EPC 653 097 7
1990	☐	EUROPE	CD	Columbia (USA)	450 093-2
1990	☐	The Final Countdown/Carrie	7"	Old Gold (UK)	OG 9946
1990	■	Solid Gold	MCDp 3tr	Epic (Germany)	655 573 3
		Tracks: The Final Countdown/Cherokee/Superstitious			
1990	☐	EUROPE/WHAM (split)	2LP	Il Rock De Agostini (Italy)	IGDA 1189/190
		Split with Wham. One band on each album.			
1990	☐	BEST OF EUROPE	CD	Victor (Japan)	VICP-98
		Japan only compilation plus picture booklet. 18 tracks. Slipcase.			
1990	☐	IL ROCK	CD	CBS (Italy)	IGDA 1189
1991	☐	WINGS OF TOMORROW	CD	Epic Collectors Choise (UK)	982650 2
1991	☐	PRISONERS IN PARADISE	LP	Epic	EPC 468 755 1

| 1991 | ☐ | PRISONERS IN PARADISE ....CD | Epic.. | EPC 468 755 2 |

Available with the same catalogue number pressed in Spain, Holland and Austria.

| 1991 | ☐ | Prisoners In Paradise/Seventh Sign ....CDS 3" 2tr | Epic (Japan) .... | ESDA 7078 |
| 1991 | ☐ | Prisoners In Paradise(single edit)/Seventh Sign.............7" | Epic .... | EPC 657 441 7 |

Some covers have photo on both sides, some o one side.

1991	■	Prisoners In Paradise/Seventh Sign ....12"	Epic	EPC 657 441 6
1991	■	Prisoners In Paradise/Seventh Sign ....CDS 2tr	Epic	EPC 657 441 2
1991	☐	Prisoners In Paradise/Break Free/Yesterday's News ....MCD 3tr	Epic (Japan)	ESCA 5460
1991	☐	Prisoners In Paradise ....MCD 3tr	Epic (USA)	ESK 4179

Prisoners In Paradise in three different versions. Promo.

| 1991 | ● | Prisoners In Paradise ....7" | Epic (Spain) .... | AIRE 3050 |

One-sided promo. No artwork.

| 1991 | ☐ | Prisoners In Paradise ....MCD | Epic (UK promo) .... | XPCD-157 |

Tracks: Prisoners In Paradise/Halfway To Heaven/I'll Cry For You/Talk To Me. Different artwork.

| 1991 | ○ | Prisoneros En El Paraiso ....7" | Sony (Mexico) .... | CBS 95562 |

White label promo. Same song on both sides.

| 1991 | ☐ | PRISONERS IN PARADISE ....CD | Epic (Japan) .... | ESCA 5460 |

Bonus: Break Free/Yesterday's News.

1991	☐	PRISONERS IN PARADISE ....LP	One Music (Korea).....................	CPL 1207
1991	☐	PRISONERS IN PARADISE ....CD	CBS (Russia)	14382
1991	☐	PRISONERS IN PARADISE ....LP	Epic (Brazil)	188.208/1
1991	☐	PRISONERS IN PARADISE ....CD	Epic (Brazil)	752.075/2
1991	☐	PRISONERS IN PARADISE ....CD	Spitfire (USA)	SPT 15190-2
1991	☐	PRISONIEROS EL PARAISO ....LP	Epic (Argentina)........................	50016
1991	☐	PRISONERS IN PARADISE ....LP	CBS (Mexico)............................	DMI-468755
1991	☐	PRISONERS IN PARADISE ....LP	Epic (Greece)...........................	EPC 468755 1

Grey label.

1991	☐	PRISONERS IN PARADISE ....CD	Epic..	468 755 1
1991	☐	PRISONERS IN PARADISE ....CD	Epic..	468 755 1
1991	☐	PRISONERS IN PARADISE ....LP PD	Epic (UK)	468 755 0
1991	☐	PRISONERS IN PARADISE ....CD	Epic (UK)	468 755 9

English tour picture CD edition.

| 1991 | ☐ | PRISONERS IN PARADISE ....CD | Columbia (USA) .... | 453 28 |
| 1991 | ☐ | PRISONERS IN PARADISE ....CD | Epic (USA) .... | EK 453 28 |

Best Value series.

| 1991 | ☐ | SNEAK PREVIEW ....CD | Epic.. | SAMPCD 1549 |

CD sampler with pre-release excerpts from Prisoners In Paradise

| 1991 | ☐ | I'll Cry For You...7" | Epic (Spain promo) .... | ARIE-3072 |

Different artwork.

1991	☐	Halfway To Heaven/Break Free/I'll Cry For You ....MLP 3tr PD	Epic..	657 851 6
1991	☐	Halfway To Heaven ....CDS 1tr	Epic (USA promo)	ESK 74117
1991	☐	I'll Cry For You/Break Free..................................7"	Epic..	657 630 7

Some copies had an info sheet in German.

| 1991 | ☐ | I'll Cry For You/Break Free/I'll Cry (acoustic) ....MCD 3tr | Epic.. | 657 630 2 |

Break Free is non-LP.

| 1991 | ☐ | I'll Cry For You/I'll Cry For You (acoustic)............. 12" 2tr | Epic.. | 657 630 6 |

Blue vinyl.

| 1991 | ☐ | I'll Cry For You..MLP 4tr | Epic (UK) .... | XPR 1722 |

Tracks: I'll Cry For You/Break Free/I'll Cry For You (acoustic)/Seventh Sign. Promo in blue vinyl.

1991	☐	I'll Cry For You/Break Free/I'll Cry For You (acoustic).........MLP 3tr	Epic..	657 697 6
1991	☐	I'll Cry For You/Break Free/I'll Cry For You (acoustic)....... MLP 3tr PD	Epic (UK)	657 697 6
1991	☐	THE BEST ....CD	Music Design Records (Korea).........	DRC 307
1991	☐	THE BEST ....LP	Music Design Records (Korea).....	MDRC 1071
1991	☐	THE VERY BEST 1983-1991 ....CD	K&J (Bulgaria)...........................	IC 4468

17 track compilation. Made with two different front covers.

| 1991 | ☐ | EUROPE JOHN NORUM ....CD | Columbia (Italy)........................ | CDDEA 2284 |
| 1991 | ☐ | Mystery Disc ....MCD 4tr | Epic (USA-promo)...................... | EFK 4195 |

Tracks All Or Nothing/Got Your Mind In The Gutter/Little Bit Of Lovin'/Halfway To Heaven. Promo sampler.

| 1991 | ☐ | STORMWIND: THE BEST OF EUROPE ....CD | Epic (Spain) .... | RCD0 14 2 |

Rare Spain-only 9 tracks compilation.

1991	■	I'll Cry For You (edit)/Seventh Sign ....7"	Epic..	657 697 7
1991	☐	I'll Cry For You..7"	Epic (Spain promo)	ARIE 3072
1992	☐	I'll Cry For You..MCD 4tr	Epic (Austria)	657 697 2

Tracks I'll Cry For You/Break Free/I'll Cry For You (acoustic)/Prisoners In Paradise

| 1992 | ☐ | I'll Cry For You..MCD 4tr | Epic (Japan)............................. | ESCA 5628 |

Tracks: I'll Cry For You/I'll Cry For You (acoustic)/Sweet Love Child/Long Time Comin'

| 1992 | ☐ | Halfway To Heaven ....MCD 4tr | Epic (UK) .... | 657 851 1 |

Tracks: Halfway To Heaven/Yesterday's News/Got Your Mind In The Gutter/Superstitious

| 1992 | ■ | Halfway To Heaven .... MLP 4tr PD | Epic.. | 657 851 6 |
| 1992 | ☐ | Halfway To Heaven/Open Your Heart ....CDS 2tr | Epic.. | 657 851 2 |

Open Your Heart was recorded live at BBC January 20, 1992.

| 1992 | ☐ | Halfway To Heaven/Yesterdays News ....7" | Epic (UK) .... | 657 851 7 |

1991 12" - EPC 657 441 6

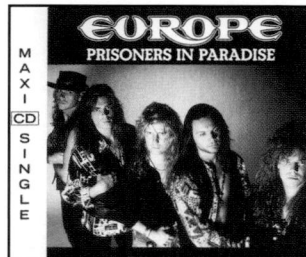

1991 CDS - EPC 657 441 2

1991 7" - AIRE 3050

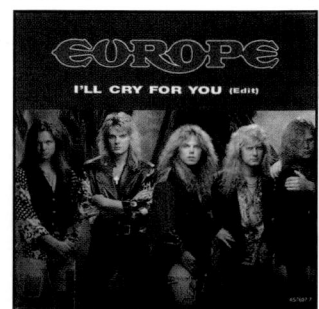

1991 7" - 657 697 7

1992 MLP PD - 657 851 6

Year		Title	Format	Label	Catalog
1992	☐	Halfway To Heaven/Yesterdays News	7"	Epic (Holland)	EPC 657 851 7
1992	☐	Halfway To Heaven	MCD 4tr	Sony (Austria)	657 851 2

Tracks: Halfway To Heaven/Yesterday's News/The Final Countdown/Open Your Heart

Year		Title	Format	Label	Catalog
1992	☐	Halfway To Heaven	MCD 4tr	Epic	657 859 2
1992	☐	Halfway To Heaven	MLP 4tr	Epic	657 859 6
1992	■	Halfway To Heaven/Long Time Comin'	7"	Epic (Holland)	657 859 7
1992	☐	Halfway To Heaven	CDS 1tr	Epic (USA promo)	EFK 74117
1992	○	A La Mitad De Camino Al Cielo	7"	Sony (Mexico)	PR 95581

Mexican promo-pressing of Halfway To Heaven. Same song on both sides. No artwork.

Year		Title	Format	Label	Catalog
1992	☐	OUT OF THIS WORLD + THE FINAL COUNTDOWN	2CD	Epic	471605 2
1992	☐	THE FINAL COUNTDOWN	CD	Epic Sony (Japan)	ESCA-5625

Tempest liner notes.

Year		Title	Format	Label	Catalog
1992	☐	PRISONERS IN PARADISE	LP PD	Q Sound (UK)	4687550B

For 1992 UK tour. Tour schedule on back.

Year		Title	Format	Label	Catalog
1992	☐	A La Mitad De Camino Al Cielo	CDS 1tr	Sony (Mexico)	PR 95581

Halfway To Heaven

Year		Title	Format	Label	Catalog
1992	☐	A La Mitad De Camino Al Cielo/ A La Mitad De Camino Al Cielo	7"	Sony (Mexico)	PR 95581

Halfway To Heaven

Year		Title	Format	Label	Catalog
1993	☐	Sweet Love Child/Stormwind/The Final Countdown	MLP 3tr	Epic	EPC 659 113 6
1993	☐	Sweet Love Child/Stormwind	7"	Epic	EPC 659 113 7
1993	☐	Sweet Love Child/Stormwind	CDS 2tr	Epic	659 149 1
1993	☐	Sweet Love Child	7"	Epic (Spain promo)	ARIE 3178
1993	☐	Sweet Love Child/Stormwind/The Final Countdown	MLP 3tr	Epic	659 149 6
1993	☐	Sweet Love Child/Stormwind/The Final Countdown	MCD 3tr	Epic (Austria)	659 113 2
1993	☐	1982-1992	CD	Epic (Japan)	ESCA 5798

Compilation featuring non-album tracks Sweet Love Child, Yesterday's News, I'll Cry For You (acoustic) and Prisoners In Paradise (single edit).

Year		Title	Format	Label	Catalog
1993	☐	1982-1992	CD	Epic	473 589 2
1993	☐	1982-1992	CD	Epic (Austria)	EPC 473589-3
1993	☐	1982-1992	2LP	Epic	473 589 1
1993	☐	1982-1992	CD	Epic (USA)	EK 57445

Not the same as 473 589 2. Diffent tracks.

Year		Title	Format	Label	Catalog
1993	☐	1982-1993	2x7" promo	Epic (Spain)	ARIE-3193

Tracks: The Final Countdown/Carrie/Sweet Love Child/I'll Cry For You (acoustic)

Year		Title	Format	Label	Catalog
1993	☐	1982-1992	2LP	- (Korea)	MDRC 1071
1993	☐	1982-1992	CD	Sony (France)	476 562 2

Different artwork with frame.

Year		Title	Format	Label	Catalog
1993	☐	1982-1992	CD	Sony (USA/Can)	EK 57445
1995	☐	The Final Countdown/Superstitious	CDS 2tr	Sony	655 573 3
1995	☐	The Final Countdown/Cherokee/Superstitious	MCD 3tr	Sony (Austria)	655 573 3
1995	☐	I PIU GRANDE SUCCESS	CD	Sony	n/a
1995	■	1982-1993	2x7"g	Epic (Spain)	AIRE 3193

Tracks: The Final Countdown/Carrie/Sweet Love Child/I'll Cry For You (acoustic)

Year		Title	Format	Label	Catalog
1996	☐	BEST BALLADS	CD	Sony (Bulgaria)	K-9796003
1996	☐	THE FINAL COUNTDOWN	CD	Epic Sony (Japan)	ESCA 7629
1996	■	ROCK THE NIGHT AWAY	CD	Sony Music Special Products	A 26749

Compilation 10 tracks.

Year		Title	Format	Label	Catalog
1997	☐	DEFINITIVE COLLECTION	CD PD	Epic (Austria)	486 576 0
1997	☐	DEFINITIVT COLLECTION	CD	Sony BMG (Japan)	486 576 2
1997	■	DEFINITIVT COLLECTION	CD	Epic (Germany)	486 576 2
1997	☐	DEFINITIVE COLLECTION	2CD	Epic (Austria)	486 576 9

Contains bonus CD with five extra tracks.

Year		Title	Format	Label	Catalog
1997	☐	DEFINITIVT COLLECTION	2CD	Epic (Germany)	486 576 9
1997	☐	THE BEST	CD	Sony	
1997	☐	THE FINAL COUNTDOWN	CD PD	Epic (Germany)	CBU 67518

Compilation. Picture CD.

Year		Title	Format	Label	Catalog
1997	☐	EUROPE	CD	Sony (Italy)	488 806 2

Compilation 14 tracks.

Year		Title	Format	Label	Catalog
1998	☐	SUPER HITS	CD	Sony/Legacy (USA)	A 65440

Compilation compiled by Bruce Dickinson (Iron Maiden).

Year		Title	Format	Label	Catalog
1998	☐	SUPER HITS	CD	Epic (Austria)	498633 2
1998	☐	SUPER HITS	CD	Sony BMG	SBMK 705460 2
1998	☐	MUSICA PIU	CD	Epic (Italy)	EPC 491 018
1998	☐	MUSICA PIÚ	CD	Sony (Colombia)	COL 491018 9
1999	☐	EUROPE 1982-2000	CD	Epic (UK)	473 589 9

Compilations, same as 1982-1992, but also featuring The Final Countdown 2000.

Year		Title	Format	Label	Catalog
1999	☐	EUROPE 1982-2000	CD	Epic (Japan)	ESCA 7816
1999	☐	The Final Countdown 2000/The Final Countdown 2000 (edit)	12"	Epic (UK promo)	XPR 3368
1999	☐	The Final Countdown 2000	CDS 1tr	Epic (UK promo)	XPCD 2430
1999	☐	The Final Countdown 2000/The Final Countdown	CDSp 2tr	Epic	668 504 1

1:st pressing had a misspelling of the word "countdown", which became "cuntdown".

Year		Title	Format	Label	Catalog
1999	■	The Final Countdown 2000	MCD 3tr	Epic	668 504 2

Tracks: The Final Countdown 2000 (Edit)/The Final Countdown/ The Final Countdown (Original Radio Edit)

Year		Title	Format	Label	Catalog
1999	☐	The Final Countdown 2000	MLP 3tr	Epic	668 504 6

1992 7" - 657 859 7

1995 2x7"g - AIRE 3193

1996 CD - A 26749

1997 CD - 486 576 2

1999 MCD - 668 504 2

Year		Title	Format	Label	Catalogue
1999	☐	SIMPLY THE BEST	CD	Sony (UK)	EPC 493 427 2
1999	☐	SIMPLY THE BEST	CD	Sony (Austria)	493 427 2
1999	☐	SIMPLY THE BEST	CD	Sony	SME 493 427 2
2000	■	FOREVER GOLD	CD	Diamond (Germany)	731453335523
2001	☐	THE FINAL COUNTDOWN	CD	Legacy	EK 85757
		Bonus: The Final Countdown (live)/Danger On The Track (live)/Carrie (live)			
2001	☐	PRISONERS IN PARADISE	CD	Spitfire	SPT 15190-2
		Bonus: Government Man/A Long Time Comin'. New foreword.			
2001	☐	CARRIE	CD	Epic	493 427 9
		13 track compilation.			
2001	☐	THE FINAL COUNTDOWN	CD	Sony	SNY 85757.2
		Bonus live: The Final Countdown/Danger On The Track/Carrie			
2001	☐	THE FINAL COUNTDOWN	CD	Portrait/Legacy (USA)	EPC 504492 2
		Bonus live: The Final Countdown/Danger On The Track/Carrie			
2002	☐	THE FINAL COUNTDOWN	CD	Sony Music (Japan)	EICP-7050
		Bonus live: The Final Countdown/Danger On The Track/Carrie			
2002	☐	ROCK COLLECTION	CD	Warner (Russia)	WB325982CD
		Limited edition double pack.			
2002	☐	FINAL BALLAD – THE BEST BALLADS	CD	Epic	WDA-324
		Compilation in steel box			
2004	☐	START FROM THE DARK	2CDd	Epic	EPC 517751 9
		Limited edition double pack.			
2004	☐	START FROM THE DARK	CDd	Epic	EPC 517751 9
2004	☐	START FROM THE DARK	CD	Epic	EPC 517751 2
2004	■	START FROM THE DARK	CD	T&T	TT0064 2
2004	☐	START FROM THE DARK	CD	T&T	TT0067 2
2004	☐	START FROM THE DARK	CD	T&T	TT0067 0
		Promo.			
2004	☐	START FROM THE DARK	CD	T&T (Russia)	TT00642
		Russian counterfeit.			
2004	☐	START FROM THE DARK	CD	JVC Victor (Japan)	VICP-62832
		Bonus: Seven Doors Hotel (Live)/Wings Of Tomorrow (live)			
2004	☐	START FROM THE DARK	CD	Seoul Records (Korea)	SLRK-2751.2
		Bonus: Seven Doors Hotel (Live)/Wings Of Tomorrow (live)/Documentary (enhanced CD)			
2004	☐	ROCK THE NIGHT – THE VERY BEST OF	2CD	Sony	SME 5160542
		Compilation 32 tracks.			
2004	☐	THE BEST OF EUROPE	CD	Sony	519567 2
2004	☐	ROCK THE NIGHT	2CD	Epic	516 054 2
		Compilation.			
2004	☐	ROCK THE NIGHT – THE VERY BEST OF EUROPE	2CD	Sony (Japan)	MHCP-414/5.2
		Bonus: Ninja (Live)/On The Loose (live).			
2004	☐	Got To Have Faith	CDS 1tr	Epic	SAMPCD 14295 2
		Got To Have Faith + medley of Start From The Dark/Wake Up Call/Spirit Of The Under-dog/America			
2004	■	Got To Have Faith/Settle For Love	CDS 2tr	Epic	EPC 675157 1
2004	☐	Got To Have Faith/Settle For Love/Got To Have Faith (video)	CDS 2tr	Epic	EPC 675157 2
2004	☐	Got To Have Faith/Settle For Love/Got To Have Faith (video)	CDS 2tr	JVC Victor (Japan)	VICP-62817
2004	☐	Hero	CDS 1tr	Epic	n/a
		Promo.			
2004	■	Hero (Radio mix)/Hero (album version)/Reason	MCDd 3tr	T&T	TT00643
2004	☐	EUROPE	CD	JVC Victor (Japan)	MHCP-431
		Remastered.			
2004	☐	WINGS OF TOMORROW	CD	JVC Victor (Japan)	MHCP-432
		Remastered.			
2004	☐	THE FINAL COUNTDOWN	CD	JVC Victor (Japan)	MHCP-434
		Remastered.			
2004	☐	OUT OF THIS WORLD	CD	JVC Victor (Japan)	MHCP-433
		Remastered. Bonus: The Final Countdown (live)/Danger On The Track (live)/Carrie (live)			
2004	☐	PRISONERS IN PARADISE	CD	JVC Victor (Japan)	MHCP-435
		Remastered.			
2004	☐	FINAL COUNTDOWN TOUR 1986	CD	JVC Victor (Japan)	VICP-62914
2004	☐	LET THE GOOD TIMES ROCK	CD	Delta No 1	23317
		Re-issue. Compilation 10 tracks.			
2005	☐	START FROM THE DARK	CD	Friday Music	FRIM1018.2
2005	☐	Live From The Dark	MCD 4tr	Warner Bros.	WHVPROMOCD2005-1
		Tracks: Got To Have Faith/Flames/Superstitious/Start From The Dark. Promo sampler			
2005	☐	ALL OR NOTHING	CD	Sony/BMG (USA)	A 92999
		Compilation.			
2005	☐	1982-2000	CD	JVC Victor (Japan)	MHCP-173
		Compilation 18 tracks.			
2006	☐	BEST OF THE BEST GOLD	CD	Sony (Japan)	EPC 486576-2
		Compilation.			
2006	■	COLLECTIONS	CD	Sony BMG	82876 718452
		Compilation 10 tracks.			
2006	☐	EUROPE	2CD	Fback (Italy)	82876 807932
		Compilation 20 tracks.			

2000 CD - 731453335523

2004 CD - TT0064 2

2004 CDS - EPC 675157 1

2004 MCD - TT0643

2006 CD - 82876 718452

2006 ■	SECRET SOCIETY	CDp	Sanctuary	LC04700/TT 00660

Promo in paper pocket with different artwork.

2006 ☐	SECRET SOCIETY	CD	Sanctuary	TT 00660
2006 ☐	SECRET SOCIETY	CD	JVC Victor (Japan)	VICP-63631

Bonus: Start From The Dark (live)

2006 ☐	SECRET SOCIETY	CD	Sanctuary (USA)	SANY 34113.2
2006 ☐	SECRET SOCIETY	CD	BMG (Russia)	017-0231 057

Bonus: The Final Countdown (live). Counterfeit?

2006 ■	Always The Pretender	MCD 4tr	T&T	TT 00673

Tracks: Always The Pretender (radio edit)/Always The Pretender (album edit)/Flames (live)/Superstitious (live)

2006 ☐	LIVE FROM THE DARK	2DVD/CD	T&T	MVD4490DVD
2006 ☐	DEFINITIVE COLLECTION	CD	Epic	486576 2
2006 ☐	HIT COLLECTION	CD	SBC	886 97195772
2006 ☐	HIT COLLECTION	CD	DJ's Club Records	BRONS 1099
2007 ☐	EXTENDED VERSIONS	CD	Sony BMG	A706233.2

Live at Hammersmith Odeon + Solna Stadium.

2007 ☐	SUPER HITS	CD	Sony BMG (USA)	A 705460

Compilation.

2008 ☐	ROCK THE NIGHT – THE VERY BEST OF	CD	Sony	SME 5195672

Compilation.

2008 ☐	ROCK THE NIGHT	2CD/DVD	Epic (Japan)	EICP-1135-7

Compilation.

2008 ☐	ALMOST UNPLUGGED – LIVE AT NALEN	CD	Hell & Back	HBCD100
2008 ☐	ALMOST UNPLUGGED – LIVE AT NALEN	CD+DVD	Hell & Back	HBDVD002
2008 ☐	ALMOST UNPLUGGED – LIVE AT NALEN	2LP	Hell & Back	HBLP100

100 copies in orange vinyl.

2008 ☐	ALMOST UNPLUGGED – LIVE AT NALEN	CD	CDNET Music (Taiwan)	MMMF-2301
2008 ☐	ALMOST UNPLUGGED – LIVE AT NALEN	CD/DVD	Magnum Music (Taiwan)	MVP-100201
2008 ☐	THE FINAL COUNTDOWN	CDd	Epic/Espresso (Greece)	466328 2
2009 ☐	Last Look At Eden/U Devil U/Last Look At Eden (Radio Edit)	CDS	Universal	06025 270 985-0
2009 ☐	Last Look At Eden	MCD 5tr	Universal	06025 270 985-0

Tracks: Last Look At Eden/U Devil U/Superstitious (live)/Start From The Dark (live)/Since I've Been Loving

2009 ☐	Last Look At Eden	MCD 5tr	EAR Music (UK)	0198162ERE
2009 ■	LAST LOOK AT EDEN	CDd	EAR Music (Germany)	0198172ERE

Bonus: Yesterday's News (live)/Wake Up Call (live)t

2009 ☐	LAST LOOK AT EDEN	CD	Linfair (China?)	0198172ERE

Bonus: Yesterday's News (live))

2009 ☐	LAST LOOK AT EDEN	CD	Universal	060252709851
2009 ☐	LAST LOOK AT EDEN	CD	Victor (Japan)	VICP-64772

Bonus: Scream Of Anger (live)

2009 ☐	LAST LOOK AT EDEN	CD	Decca Records (Taiwan)	IP042

Bonus: Yesterday's News (live)

2009 ☐	LAST LOOK AT EDEN	CD	Universal (Russia)	46012-503649-6

With green strip.

2009 ☐	LAST LOOK AT EDEN	CD	Mnet Media (Korea)	809231-38685-1

With green strip.

2009 ☐	LAST LOOK AT EDEN	CDd	Love-da-records	LOVECD70

Bonus: Yesterday's News (live)/Wake Up Call (live). Orange strip.

2009 ☐	LAST LOOK AT EDEN	CDd	EAR Music (UK)	0197847ERE
2009 ■	LAST LOOK AT EDEN	CD+7"	EAR Music (UK)	019784ERE

Bonus 7" red vinyl: Sign Of The Times/Start From The Dark

2009 ☐	LAST LOOK AT EDEN	CD	PT Indo Semar Sakti (Indones.)	MCD3720909

Slipcase.

2009 ☐	LAST LOOK AT EDEN	CD	Icarus (Argentina)	ICARUS 699

Yellow/orange strip.

2009 ☐	FLASHBACK	2CD	Venus	886974352921

Compilation.

2009 ☐	PLAYLIST – THE VERY BEST OF EUROPE	CD	Legacy/Epic	88697-41347 2
2009 ☐	THE FINAL COUNTDOWN – THE BEST OF EUROPE	2CD	Sony BMG	8869753657-2
2009 ☐	ROCK THE NIGHT – THE VERY BEST OF EUROPE	CD+DVD	Sony Music Japan (Japan)	EICP-1135

Vinyl replica.

2009 ■	GREATEST HITS	CD box	Sony Music	88697458642

Compilation in steel box.

2009 ☐	OUT OF THIS WORLD/PRISONERS IN PARADISE	2CD	Iron Bird	IBIRD2 0001CD

Two albums in one box.

2009 ☐	THE COLLECTION	CD	Sony Music	8869761-8732

Compilation.

2009 ☐	WINGS OF TOMORROW	CD	Wounded Bird	WOBR 404-9
2009 ☐	EUROPE	CDv	Sony Music Japan (Japan)	EICP-1247
2009 ☐	WINGS OF TOMORROW	CDv	Sony Music Japan (Japan)	EICP-1248
2009 ☐	THE FINAL COUNTDOWN	CDv	Sony Music Japan (Japan)	EICP-1249

Bonus: The Final Countdown (live)/Danger On The Track (live)/Carrie (live)

2009 ☐	OUT OF THIS WORLD	CDv	Sony Music Japan (Japan)	EICP-1250
2010 ☐	THE FINAL COUNTDOWN - THE BEST OF EUROPE	2CD	Sony (Taiwan)	88697536572

2006 CDp - LC04/00/TT 00660

2006 MCD - TT 00673

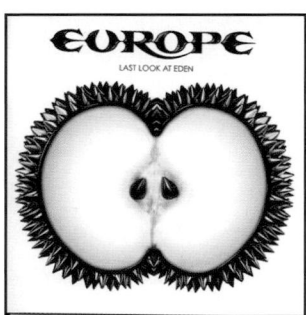

2009 CDd - 0198172ERE

2009 CD+7" - 019784ERE

2009 CD box - LC 00316

2010	☐	WINGS OF TOMORROW...CD	Cherry Red ....CDLEM 152
		Remastered reissue with extended sleeve notes.	
2011	☐	LIVE LOOK AT EDEN ....2CD+DVD+Book	Ear Music.................................. 0209649ERE
2011	☐	LIVE AT SHEPHERD'S BUSH, LONDON.....................CD+DVD	Victor (Japan)...............................VIZP-106
		Recorded live 2011.	
2012	☐	BAG OF BONES...CD	Gain 88691956201
2012	☐	BAG OF BONES...LP	Gain 88691956202
2012	☐	BAG OF BONES...CD	Victor (Japan)........................... VICP-65047
		Bonus: Beautiful Disaster	
2012	☐	LIVE IN STOCKHOLM 2008 ....2CDd	Immortal Music ....IMA 104258
2012	☐	GREATEST HITS 3CD	Columbia....................................8725473982

1987 LP PD - - -

Unofficial releases:

1986	☐	LIVE IN JAPAN 2LP	private ....HE 86 EV
		Recorded in Umeå in September 1986, Sweden, which is quite far from Japan…	
1986	☐	JOHN NORUM'S LAST STAND.................................2LP	private (Japan) E-6981/2
1986	☐	LIVE IN JAPAN SEPTEMBER 86 ....2LP	private (UK).....................................HE 86 EV
		Recorded in Stockholm.	
1987	☐	TALKING PICTURES...LP PD	Bakta Bak (UK) BAK-2041
		Interview record.	
1987	■	THE LIVE COUNTDOWN ....LP PD	Merry (Holland) .... - -
		Recorded in Bologna March 2, 1987.	
1987	☐	TALKING PICTURES...LP PD	Music & Media .... CT 1002
		Interview record.	
n/a	☐	THE KING WILL RETURN......................................CD	Bondage (Japan) BON083
		2 tracks live at Rock SM in Stockholm, Sweden on 12/12/1982 + 6 tracks live in Jönköping, Sweden on 28/08/1983 + 7 tracks live in Trollhättan, Sweden on 20/06/1984.	
n/a	☐	FIRST COUNTDOWN '86 ....CD	Gryphon (Japan)..........................Gryphon-002
		The cover says "Osaka 09/86" but this is live in Los Angeles,California on 04/1987.	
n/a	☐	NORTHERN NOBLESSE ....CD	Excalibur (Japan) EXC-07
		Live at Hammersmith Odeon in London, England in 1987 + 1 acoustic medley.	
1987	☐	ROCK SAGAS ....LP PD	Spartan (UK) .... CT 1002
		Chris Tetley interview.	
1992	☐	FINAL COUNTDOWN FAREWELL TOUR.....................LP	Patty (Germany) ....n/a
1992	■	ROCK THE NIGHT ....CD	private (Holland) ....LLRCD 155
		Recorded at Whilton Theatre, Los Angeles, USA 1987.	
1992	☐	METALLIC FJORD..CD	Buccaneer Records (Italy) .... BVC 054
		Recorded at Whilton Theatre, Los Angeles 1987.	
1997	☐	IN CONCERT ....CD	BIO (Japan) BIO-104
		Live at BBC in London, England on 04/08/1989.	
1987	☐	LIVE IN EUROPE ....LP	Juke Box Records (Switzerland).......... MS 102
1987	■	LIVE IN ITALY 2LP	European Music (Canada).................. MS 201
1987	■	MUSIC MACHINE 1987 - RADIO SHOW ....LP	7-UP AE/CPL/7UP
n/a	☐	STORMWIND...CD	Epic (Spain) ....RCD 0142
n/a	☐	LIVE IN CONCERT ....CD	n/a (Taiwan) ....n/a
n/a	☐	SWEDEN 86 WITH JOHN NORUM ....CD	n/a...n/a
n/a	☐	SWEDEN 86 WITH JOHN NORUM ....CD	n/a...n/a
2000	☐	TORONTO LIVE PRESENTS EUROPE ....CD	Blaze Music Production Ent........................ - -
2001	☐	EUROPE..CD-ROM	Домашняя Коллекция (Russia)........... - -
		MP3 compilation with all albums.	
2004	☐	EUROPE..CD-ROM	Фонотека В Кармане (Russia) 5P178
		MP3 compilation with all albums.	
2007	☐	ROCK THE NIGHT ....CD	Living Legends.............................LLRCD 155
		Recorded at Whilton Theatre, Los Angeles 1987. Same as Metallic Fjord.	
2008	☐	EUROPE..2CD	MP3Service (Russia) .... - -
		Bootleg featuring all of Norum's and Tempest's solo albums plus Start From The Dark as mp3 files.	

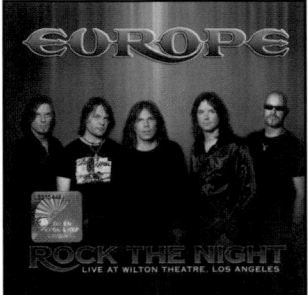
1992 CD - LLRCD 155

1987 LP - MS 201

1987 LP - AE/DPL/7UP

EVENTIDE

Jacob Magnusson: v/g, Sebastian Olsson: g, Thomas Magnusson: b, Max Seppälä: d

Stockholm - The band was formed in 1988 featuring Magnusson, Seppälä, guitarist Niclas Linde and bassist Åke Walleborn. In 1999 the first demo CD, *Caress The Abstract*, was recorded. It was followed by *Promo 2000*. In 2001 bassist Walleborn left the band. In 2004 Jacob and Max recorded another **Eventide** demo and in the following year Jacob's brother Thomas joins on bass. They also drafted guitarist Johan Sjölin, who unfortunately quit shortly after. In 2006 guitarist Sebastian joined and the band started recording the debut. They were soon picked up by Cartel Media, who released the debut, which was produced by Andy LaRoque. The label went bust, so in 2008 the band recorded a new four-track demo entitled *Planet Plague*. In 2010 the band again recorded an album at their own expence. The band was put on hold in November 2011. Max stepped in to play with **Degradead** on tour in 2012. **Eventide** play excellent progressive, riff-oriented death-ish metal, a bit similar to **Assailant**.

2006 CD - CM 007

2010 CDp - RU 4260

| 2006 | ■ | DIARIES FROM THE GALLOWS ....CD | Cartel Media .... CM 007 |
| 2010 | ■ | THE BEAST AND THE MACHINE ....CDp | private ....RU 4260 |

EVERCRY

Johan Wadelius: v/b, Niklas Brodd: g, Martin Boman: g, Petter Ter-Borsh: d

Bollnäs - The band was formed in 1994. The first MCD was recorded as a trio with the aid of
a drum machine. The band drafted drummer Jonas Renöfeldt, but on *Gnome* the drums were
handled by Petter. Doomy goth in the vein of **Anathema, Cemetary** or **Tiamat**. The MCD *Focus*
caught the attention of Century Media, who signed the band in 2001, and they now changed
their name to **Marble Arch** and in 2002 released *Another Sunday Bright*. Singer Wadelius
concentrated on singing and left the bass duties to new bass player Jesper Bagge.

1996	■	Demise Of The Crown...MCD 4tr	Heathendoom	.................................LR CD 3
		Tracks: The Stream Of A Dark River/A Silhouette Of Silence/Ethereal Company/Behind		
		A Sorrow Veil		
1997	☐	Gnome ....MCD 3tr	Cry Production	001
		Tracks: The Passion/The Sin/The Punishment		
1999	☐	Focus ....MCD 4tr	Cry Production	002
		Tracks: Disguise/Never Mind/Angeldust In Midnight Blue Part 1/Angeldust In Midnight		
		Blue Part 2		

1996 MCD - LR CD 3

EVERDAWN, THE

Pierre Törnkvist: v/g, Patrik Törnkvist: g, Niklas Svensson: b, Oskar Karlsson: d

Luleå - Oskar and Niklas are ex-**Gates Of Ishtar**, while Pierre has previously played with
Schietan. Oskar has also recorded with the band **Sarcasm**. On the first release the band was a
trio featuring Oskar, Patrik and Pierre (who also handled the bass). *The Everdawn* produce fast,
yet melodic death metal in the vein of **Dark Tranquillity** meets **At The Gates**.

1997	☐	Opera Of The Damned ....MCD 4tr	Black Diamond................................ B.D.P 001
		Tracks: The Everdawn/Nightborn/The Silent Winter Sky/Opera Of The Damned	
1997	■	POEMS - BURN THE PAST ....CD	Invasion .... IR 029
1997	☐	POEMS - BURN THE PAST ....CD	Metal Blade (USA)................... 3984-14153-2
1998	☐	POEMS - BURN THE PAST ....CD	Avalon Marquee (Japan)................MICY-1014
		Bonus: The Everdawn/Nightborn/The Silent Winter Sky/Opera Of The Damned	
2003	☐	POEMS - BURN THE PAST ....CD	Hammerheart Records .... HHR 137
2012	☐	Opera Of The Damned ....7" 4tr	Century Media 998260-1
2012	☐	POEMS - BURN THE PAST ....CD	Century Media 998249-2
		Opera Of The Damned EP as bonus. 500 copies. Remixed and remastered.	
2012	☐	POEMS - BURN THE PAST ....LP	Century Media 998249-1

1997 CD - IR 029

EVERGRACE

Johan Falk: v, David Ohlsson: g, Jon Bålefalk: g, Jonathan Stenberg: k,
Martin Davidsson: b, Josef Davidsson: d

Edsbyn - Because of mix-ups with the band *Evergrey*, the band changed their name to *Incrave*
and the album was re-issued under the title *The Escape* with the bonus track *The Masquerade*.
They have since released a second album. Semi-progressive, melancholic power metal, like
a mix of **Kamelot**, **Tad Morose** and **Evergrey**. A band well worth checking out. See *Incrave*.

2006	■	EVERGRACE ....CD	Ulterium Records ....ULTCD 001

2006 CD - ULTCD 001

EVERGREY

Tom S Englund: v/g, Marcus Jidell: g, Rickard Zander: k,
Johan Niemann: b, Karl-Hannes Van Dahl: d

Göteborg - Evergrey started out in the vein of **Paradise Lost** or **My Dying Bride**, but on the first
album they had adopted a sound closer to **Savatage**. The line-up then featured singer/guitarist
Tom S Englund, guitarist Dan Bronell, keyboardist Will Chandra, bassist Daniel Nöjd and drummer Patrick Carlsson. Mattias "IA" Eklundh (**Freak Kitchen**) did a guest solo on one track. On
Solitude Dominance Tragedy Will was out of the band and Zachary Stephens was hired to do the
keyboards. On *In Search For Truth* the line-up went through another drastic change. Keyboard
player Sven Karlsson (**Soilwork**) was added to the line-up, Michael Håkansson (**Engel, Dark
Tranqullity, Embraced** etc) replaced Daniel Nöjd on bass and Henrik Danhage replaced Dan
Bronell on guitar. The first two albums are killer, but the third release took it all a step further
and they added an even more progressive touch to their slightly **Savatage**-ish sound. Highly
recommended for fans of melodic, yet intricate progressive hard rock with a melancholic touch.
The band also did a cover of Yngiwe's *Rising Force* on *A Guitar Odyssey - Tribute To Yngwie
M*. In 2001 Sven Karlsson left and was briefly replaced by Christian Rehn (who was replaced
by Rickard Zander in 2002). *Recreation Day* was another milestone for the band, a very dark
and heavy album. Now drummer Carlsson had been replaced by Jonas Ekdahl. *Monday Morning Apocalypse* continued in the same vein. The big difference here was that the band now
used outside producer Sanken Sandquist and Stefan Glaumann (**Rammstein, Bon Jovi** etc).

Early grey

On the follow-up, *Torn*, the line-up changed slightly when **Stratovarius'** Jari Kainulainen handled the bass duties. After this things changed drastically, not because of animosity but because of a sensation of the members not being able to take the ship any further. Danhage, Ekdahl and Kainulainen left the band. When Tom called his friend Pontus Norgren of **Hammerfall/The Ring/Talisman/Great King Rat** to ask if he knew a suitable guitar player, he simple recommended the guy sitting next to him in the studio, Marcus Jidell, also a former member of **The Ring**, as well as **Jekyll & Hyde**, **Royal Hunt**, **Punchline** and **Kreegah**. Next up were drummer Karl-Hannes Van Dahl and former **Therion/Murder Of My Sweet** bassist Johan Niemann. *A Decade And A Half* is a greatest hits collection featuring the two unreleased tracks *Wrong* (live unplugged) and *Frozen* (live unplugged). Danhage and Ekdahl are now in brutal metallurgists **DeathDestruction**. Niemann is also in **Evil Masquerade**.
Website: www.evergrey.net

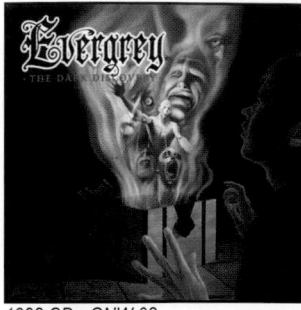
1998 CD - GNW 02

1998 ■	THE DARK DISCOVERY	CD	GNW	GNW 02
1998 ☐	THE DARK DISCOVERY	CDd	GNW	GNW 02
1999 ☐	SOLITUDE, DOMINANCE, TRAGEDY	CD	GNW	GNW 05
1999 ☐	SOLITUDE, DOMINANCE, TRAGEDY	CD	Nothing To Say (France)	NTS 3084012
1999 ☐	SOLITUDE, DOMINANCE, TRAGEDY	CD	Hall Of Sermon (Switzerland)	HOS 7111
2001 ☐	IN SEARCH FOR TRUTH	CD	InsideOut	IOMCD 081
2001 ☐	IN SEARCH FOR TRUTH	CD	Soundholic (Japan)	TKCS 85029
	Bonus: Trilogy Of The Damned/For Every Tear That Falls(video)/The Masterplan (video).			
2003 ■	Recreation Day	MCD 3tr	InsideOut (USA)	IOMACD 2051
	Tracks: The Great Deceiver/End Of Your Days/Recreation Day			
2003 ☐	RECREATION DAY	CD	InsideOut	IOMCD 117
2004 ☐	THE DARK DISCOVERY	CD	InsideOut (USA)	IOMACD 4044
	Bonus: For Every Tear That Falls(video). Slipcase.			
2004 ☐	SOLITUDE, DOMINANCE, TRAGEDY	CD	InsideOut (USA)	IOMACD 4045
	Bonus:The Masterplan (video).			
2004 ☐	THE INNER CIRCLE	CD	InsideOut	IOMCD 165/SPV 60732
2004 ☐	THE INNER CIRCLE	CDd	InsideOut	IOMSECD 165/SPV60730
	Bonus: I'm Sorry (live)/Recreation Day (live)/Madness Caught Another Victim (live)			
2004 ☐	THE INNER CIRCLE	CD	InsideOut (USA)	IOMACD 2079
2005 ☐	A NIGHT TO REMEMBER	2CD	InsideOut	IOMSECD 203/40842 DCD
2006 ☐	MONDAY MORNING APOCALYPSE	CD	InsideOut	IOMSECD 240
2006 ☐	MONDAY MORNING APOCALYPSE	CD	Soyus (Russia)	SPV 48882 CD
2006 ☐	Monday Morning Apocalypse	MCD 3tr	InsideOut	SPV 48953
	Tracks: Monday Morning Apocalypse/Rulers Of The Mind (live)/Monday Morning Apocalypse (karaoke)			
2010 ☐	RECREATION DAY	CD	Steamhammer	SPV65530
	Bonus: Trilogy Of The Damned			
2010 ☐	RECREATION DAY	CD	Steamhammer	SPV 65532
2010 ☐	TORN	CDd	Steamhammer	SPV 92840
	Bonus: Caught In A Lie			
2010 ■	TORN	CD	Steamhammer	SPV 92842
2010 ☐	TORN	CD	Hellion (Brazil)	HEL 0807
	Bonus: Caught In A Lie			
2011 ☐	Wrong (single version)/Wrong (Extended Album Version)	CDS	Steamhammer	SPV 309143-CDS
2011 ☐	GLORIOUS COLLISION	CD	Steamhammer	SPV 308762
2011 ☐	GLORIOUS COLLISION	CDd	Steamhammer	SPV 308760
	Bonus: ...And The Distance (Alternate vocals)			
2011 ☐	A DECADE AND A HALF	2CD	Steamhammer	SPV 30932 2CD

2003 MCD - IOMACD 2051

2010 CD - SPV 92842

EVIL MASQUERADE

Apollo Papathansaio: v, Henrik Flyman: g, Artur Meinild: k, Johan Niemann: b, Dennis Buhl: d

*Halmstad/Stockholm - **Evil Masquerade** were formed in the summer of 2003 by former **ZooL/Moahni Moahna** guitarist Flyman. He teamed up with drummer Dennis Buhl, singer Henrik Brockmann and bass player Kasper Gram. On the band's third album, *Third Act*, Brockmann was replaced by Apollo Papathanasio (**Craze, Majestic, Firewind, Spiritual Beggars**), while Gram was replaced by Thor Jeppesen. The album also saw a guest appearance from former **Rainbow/Malmsteen** keyboardist David Rosenthal. The line-up once again changed for the fourth album, when Jeppesen was replaced by Niemann (**Therion, Evergrey, Murder Of My Sweet** etc). The album also features a guest appearance by another **Rainbow** keyboardist, Tony Carey. On *Pentagram,* the line-up again changed seeing the return of Dennis Buhl and Thor Jeppesen, plus the addition of keyboard player Artur Meinild. **Evil Masquerade** play great-sounding melodic metal with strong hints of classic **Rainbow**.*
Website: www.evilmasquerade.com

Unmasked!
2004 CD - FRCD 186

2004 ■	WELCOME TO THE SHOW	CD	Frontiers Records	FRCD 186
2004 ☐	WELCOME TO THE SHOW	CD	Avalon Marquee (Japan)	MICP-10426
2004 ☐	WELCOME TO THE SHOW	CD	CD-Maximum (Russia)	CDM0604-1879

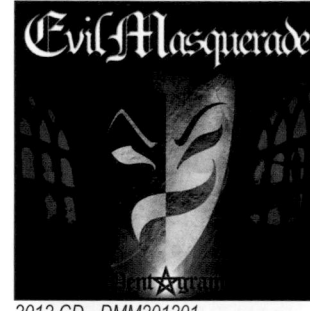

2005 ☐	THEATRICAL MADNESS	CD	Frontiers Records	FRCD 238
2005 ☐	THEATRICAL MADNESS	CD	Avalon Marquee (Japan)	MICP-10505
2005 ☐	THEATRICAL MADNESS	CD	Irond (Russia)	05-DD265
2006 ☐	THIRD ACT	CD	Escape	ESM 134
2006 ☐	THIRD ACT	CD	Avalon Marquee (Japan)	MICP-10594
2006 ☐	THIRD ACT	CD	AMG (Russia/CIS/Baltic)	n/a
2006 ☐	THIRD ACT	CD	Nightmare (USA)	NMR-322

Bonus: The Wind Will Rise/Bozo The Clown

2009 ☐	FADE TO BLACK	CD	Avalon Marquee (Japan)	MICP-10805
2009 ☐	FADE TO BLACK	CD	Escape	ESM 182
2012 ■	PENTAGRAM	CD	Dark Minstrel	DMM201201

2012 CD - DMM201201

EVIL'S EVE

Olof "Puss Packard" Lönnroth: v, Freddy "Johnny Schlong" Sövik: g, Per "S:t Caramel Jr III" Sparring: g, Mattias "Krs Krstal" Tranberg: b, Håkan "Kane Insane" Svantesson: d

Göteborg - Gimmicky melodic metal with a touch of **Steel Panther**. Drummer Håkan recorded the album *The Undiscovered Country* with **Destiny** and has played on record with **Dreamland**. Per "Billie/St Caramel Jr III" Sparring has his weird death/folk project **Ambugaton** and the acoustic **Millie & Billie**. The band also released a promo single with the tracks *Incompetence Is Bliss* and *Never Turn Your Back On Love*.
Website: http://evilseve.com/

2010 ■	DON'T FALL ASLEEP... IT'S EVIL'S EVE	CDp	Manora Records	MRCD 007

2010 CDp - MRCD 007

EVILDOER

Andreas "Andy" Sölveström: v, Martin Bergman: g, Johan Olsson: g, Simon Frödeberg: b, Andreas "Agge Bones" Johansson: d

Kristianstad/Hässleholm - The band recorded their first demo in 2004. Andreas is also found in **Within Y, Cipher System**, etc. The album was produced by Berno Paulsson. Heavy and fast, great-sounding, death/thrash in the vein of **The Haunted** and **Wicthery**. In 2006 the band recorded a new three-track demo entitled *The New Empire*. Sölveström has been replaced by Lucas Jeansson. Olsson is ex-**Blinded Colony**, later in **Dead By April**, while Fröderberg has been found in **Sgt. Carnage** and **Verminious**. Johansson is also in **Vermonious** and **Delve**.
Website: www.evildoer.se/

2005 ■	TERROR AUDIO	CD	Scarlet	SC107-2

2005 CD - SC 107-2

EVOCATION

Thomas Josefsson: v, Marko Palmén: g, Vesa Kenttäkumpu: g, Martin Torsson: b, Janne Kenttäkumpu Bodén: d

Borås/Göteborg - Death metal band **Evocation** were formed in 1991 in Borås by bass player Thomas Josefsson, singer Jani Karvola, drummer Janne K. Bodén and guitarists Marko Palmén and Vesa Kenttäkumpu. Jani parted ways with the band shortly after and Thomas switched to vocals. In 1992 the band recorded two demos, the first one with death metal producer Tomas Skogsberg, entitled *The Ancient Gate*. Before the second four track demo the line-up was reinforced by bass player Christian Saarinen. The band's sound mixed the Gothenburg and Stockholm-style death metal. In 1993 the band took a time-out, which lasted until 2004. After returning they recorded two demos, which were released as the debut album. In 2005 the band started working again, but now bass player Saarinen left and was replaced by Torsson. They recorded another demo in 2006. *Tales From The Tomb* was released by Cyclone Empire in 2007 and the subsequent year, the follow-up *Dead Calm Chaos* saw the light of day. The latter featured guest spots from Andreas Björler (**At The Gates, The Haunted**) and Dan Swanö. Early 2010 the band started recording their next album *Apocalyptic* working with Roberto Laghi (**In Flames, Freak Kitchen, LOK**). The collaboration continued on the follow-up *Illusions Of Grandeur*, which also featured a guest spot from **Amon Amarth** singer Johan Hegg. **Evocation** play death metal with an old-school touch similar to bands like **Grave** and **Dismember**, but also touches of **At The Gates**.
Website: www.evocation.se

Dead calm tell no tales

2004 ☐	EVOCATION	LP	Merciless Records	M.R BON 13LP
2004 ☐	EVOCATION	CDd	Merciless Records	M.R BON 13CD
2007 ■	TALES FROM THE TOMB	CD	Cyclone Empire	CD CYC 014-2
2007 ☐	TALES FROM THE TOMB	LP	Cyclone Empire	CD CYC 014-1
2008 ☐	DEAD CALM CHAOS	CD	Cyclone Empire	CD CYC 028-2
2008 ☐	DEAD CALM CHAOS	LP	Cyclone Empire	CD CYC 028-1

2007 CD - CD CYC 014-2

289

2010	☐	DEAD CALM CHAOS	CD	FONO (Russia)	FO 806CD
2010	☐	APOCALYPTIC	CDd+DVD	Cyclone Empire	CYCCD 065-0
		Bonus DVD Live in 2009.			
2010	☐	APOCALYPTIC	CD	Cyclone Empire	CYCCD 065-2
2010	☐	APOCALYPTIC	LP	Cyclone Empire	CYCCD 065-1
2010	☐	APOCALYPTIC	CD	Metal Blade (USA)	3984-1-14965-2
2012	☐	ILLUSIONS OF GRANDEUR	CDd	Century Media	998257-8
		Bonus: Shades Of Shame/Dark Day Dawn/Dead Without A Trace			
2012	■	ILLUSIONS OF GRANDEUR	CD	Century Media	998257-2
2012	☐	ILLUSIONS OF GRANDEUR	LP	Century Media	998257-1
		Poster.			

2012 CD - 998257-2

EVOLUTION

Tony Lindberg: v/g, Martin Hamrén: g, Mats Andersson: k, Roland Josefsson: k, Jonas Hellgren: b, Ulf Johansson: d

Alingsås - *Evolution* play quite solid melodic hard rock with nice guitars, a bit like the missing link between *Treat* and *Thin Lizzy*. Not bad at all.

1987	■	We Can Do It/Stay Close Together	7"	Platina	PL22	$

1987 7" - PL22

EXANTHEMA

Tero Viljanen: b/v, Fredrik Carlsson: g, Jörgen "Jögge" Persson: b, Adam Grembowski: d

Eskilstuna - This quite primitive run-of-the-mill death metal band's only release is a split-MCD with *Chronic Decay*. However, the band has recorded numerous demos, such as *The Dead Shall Rise* (1992), *Follow The Path Of Life* (1993), *Lunacy* (1994) and *Dream World* (1995). Split in 1995, reformed in 2007, but split again in 2009. *Exanthema* have featured a variety of members through the years, such as singer Kristoffer Svensson (*Dethronement*), Jacek Kedzierski (g) and Oliver Mets (b/v/g). The last line-up featured Adam and *Tears Of Grief* members Mattias Arreflod (b), Janne Röök (g/v) and Mattias Björklund (g). Viljanen is also found in *Eternal Darkness*. Several of the members ended up in Björklund's solo project *Tears Of Grief*.

1993	■	Exanthema/Chronic Decay	MCD 5tr	Studiefrämjandet	SFRCDS 9305
		Split with Chronic Decay. Tracks: Return To Heaven/Silent Prayer/Visions Of A Madman			
2011	☐	Exanthema/Chronic Decay	MLP5tr	Me Saco Un Ojo	MSUO 026
		New artwork.			

1993 MCD - SFRCDS 9305

EXCESSUM

Daniel Contagion: v/g/b, Erik Dahlström: g, Lars Broddesson: d

Smögen - The band was formed in 2001 by Contagion and keyboard player Arvid Hammar. In 2002 the line-up was completed by Dahlström, bass player Henrik Johansson (*Bloodlust*) and drummer Kim Gustavsson (*Blut, Human Death*), but he was soon replaced by Pontus Norman (*Blut, Bloodlust, Human Death, Holocaustia*). Hammar left the same year. Contagion is also found in *Matricide, Blut, Human Death* and *Absurdeity*, Dahlström in *Human Death* and *Bloodlust*, while Broddesson is ex-*Marduk* and *Descending*. In 2003 bass player Kaj Palm (*Descending, Matricide*) replaced Henrik Johansson, but was himself replaced by Andreas Hedström (*Grief Of Emerald, Mastema, Descending, Sadistic Grimness*) in 2004. When the band's first and only album was released the line-up featured Contagion, Dahlström and Broddesson. The band also released a cassette demo entitle *Bleeding Eternally*.

2005 CD - DR 041

2005	■	DEATH REDEMPTION	CD	Deathstrike	DR 041

EXCITERS

Mats Rambin: v/g, Sven-Inge Nilsson: g, Torgny Pettersson: b, Per Elmquist: d

Linköping - A typical Pang Records release. Amateurish heavy metal. Not that exciting, despite the name. Released in a very limited edition with artwork.

1983	■	My Bad Stars/Metal Man	7"	Pang	PSI 083	$$
		Most copies without artwork (plain Xeroxed sheet).				

1983 7" - PSA 083

EXCRETION

Thomas Wahlström: v/b, Christoffer Holm: g, Anders Hanser: g, Tommy Ottemark: d

Rönninge (Stockholm) - Formed in the spring of 1990. Fast, but well-played death metal with dual high speed guitars. Loaded with double bass-drums and with real chord-killer screamy vocals. After having recorded two demos, they had one song featured on the Nuclear Blast Grindcore compilation in 1994. The album was produced by Berno Paulsson.

1995	■	VOICE OF HARMONY	CD	Wrong Again	WAR 007

1995 CD - WAR 007

EXCRUCIATE

Lars Levin: v, Hempa Brynolfsson: g, Johan Rudberg: g, Fredrik Isaksson: b, Per Ax: d

Upplands Väsby/Årsta (Stockholm) - Death/thrash metal. Formed in 1989 by Hempa, Per and guitarist Johan Melander. Just before their first demo *Mutilation Of The Past* in 1990, the band was completed with Fredrik and singer Christian "Crippa" Carlsson. The band is featured with four songs on the split-LP together with *Epitaph*. In 1991 former Mastication singer Lars Levin replaced Crippa. In 1992 Johan left the band and was replaced by Janne Rudberg (also ex-*Mastication*). The album was recorded in 1991 but wasn't released until 1993. By that time the band had already split. Part of this band later reformed and became *Rosicrucian*. *Excruciate* reformed for a short period in 2001, after which Hempa formed *Mykorrhiza*. The lyrics for the song *Eternal Incubation* on the album was written by Christofer Johnsson (*Therion*). Per Ax is also the son of AOR-singer Anette Ax. *Beyond The Circle* is a compilation including both previous releases plus unreleased demo tracks.

1991 LP - INF 002

1993 CD - 852 314

1991 ■	EXCRUCIATE/EPITAPH (split)	LP	Infest	INF 002	$

Split with Epitaph. Tracks: Intro/Sickness Hate/Hymn Of Mortality/Sign Of Suffer/I Pray For Infinity. 3000 copies.

1993 ■	PASSAGE OF LIFE	CD	Thrash	852 314	
1993 □	PASSAGE OF LIFE	LP	Thrash	852 314	
2003 □	BEYOND THE CIRCLE	2CD	Konqueror	KR 004	

EXHALE SWE

Peter Andersson: v, Johan Ylenstrand: g/v, Andreas Allenmark: g, Johan Fogelberg: b, Gustav "Gurra" Elowson: d

Jönköping/Skövde/Göteborg - Death-grinders *Exhale* were formed in 2004 by guitarist Ylenstrand and drummer Elowson (*Crimson Moonlight, Ancestor*). They recorded the first demo, *Die Inside*, using studio engineer Ulf Blomberg on vocals and Karl Hannus on bass. Later 2004 Fogelberg (*Inevitable End, Crimson Moonlight, Miseration, Sordid Death, Vital Decision*) was added to the line-up. The band was picked up by Acoustic Trauma, but they soon left and was picked up by Emetic, who released the band's debut album. After the album Ulf quit and Peter stepped in. In 2007 Andreas joined on second guitar. In October 2011 Peter announced he was leaving the band. He was later replaced by Martin Brzinski. *Exhale Swe* play a mix of death metal and grindcore in the vein of *Napalm Death*.
Website: www.exhaleswe.com

2006 CD - EME 20

| 2006 ■ | PROTOTYPE | CD | Emetic | EME 20 | |
| 2006 □ | PROTOTYPE | LP | Emetic | EME 20 | |

Green splatter vinyl.

| 2010 ■ | BLIND | CD | Dark Balance | DB 014 | |
| 2010 □ | BLIND | LP | Dark Balance | DB 015 | |

300 red + 200 white vinyl.

2010 CD - DB 014

EXPLODE

Michael "Mike Lestadt" Uppman: v, Anders "Andy Kentacky" Arstrand: g, Jan "Rio Sunwill" Walles: b, Conny "C.B. Carella" Bevelius: d

Stockholm - The band was formed in 1996, initially called *Xplode*. They recorded a great demo, from which the track *Live Forever* was featured on a compilation released by Dzynamite. For the album, the name was changed to *Explode*. Highly-potent, first-rate, ballsy, melodic hardrock with loud guitars. Kentacky is also found in country-dance-hitmakers *Rednex*. Michael Uppman has previously sung with *Yngwie Malmsteen*, *Paradise*, *Autocrash* and *Critical Mass*. He later joined *Candlemass* guitarist Lars Johansson's band *Tarmac*, with whom he recorded a demo. The band later evolved into *Creozoth*, who released one album. In 2013 Uppman, now named Michael Storck Uppman launched his new melodic hard rock band *BaRock*.

1997 CD - DZRCD 013

| 1997 ■ | LIVE FOREVER | CD | Dzynamite Records | DZRCD 013 | |

EXPORT

Lars-Henry " Lasse" Karlsson: v, Niklas "Nicke" Andersson: g, Mac: k, Ron: b, Magnus: d

Göteborg - *Export* play really good melodic hard rock in the same vein as *Europe* and *Treat*, and with quite biting guitar work, a bit similar to *White Lion*. Upper mid-class vocals. Both tracks are mid/up-tempo melodic rockers. Not to be confused with the Lund or Katrineholm popsters.

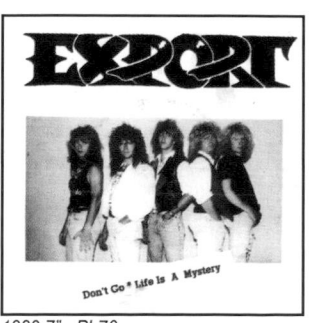

| 1989 ■ | Don't Go/Life Is A Mystery | 7" | Platina | PL70 | $ |

1989 7" - PL70

EXPULSION

**Fredrik Thörnqvist: v, Stefan "Emetic" Lagergren: g, Chris Vowden: g,
Anders Holmberg: b, Calle Fransson: d**

Täby (Stockholm) - Formed in 1988, as *River's Edge*, by ex-*Treblinka*/*Tiamat* members Stefan and Anders together with Calle. They recorded the demo *Mind The Edge* in 1988. The band changed name to *Expulsion* and released two demos in 1989; *Cerebral Cessation* and *Veiled In The Mists Of Mystery*. In 1991 they recruited Fredrik and Chris and recorded the self-financed MCD. The band plays skilled and brutal death metal. In 1994 the band was featured with six tracks on the four-way split *Vociferous & Machiavellian* (1994 Evil Omen). Vowden has also been in *Denied*, *Absurd*, *Hydrogen*, *Stressfest* and *Abnormity*.

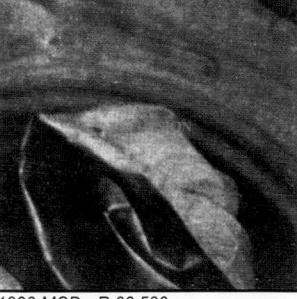

1993 ■ A Bitter Twist Of Fate ....MCD 3tr   private ....R 33 599
    Tracks: With Aged Hands/Lain Hidden/In Whirling Dust
1994 ☐ OVERFLOW ....CD   Godhead GOD011CD
1996 ☐ MAN AGAINST ....CD   Godhead .... GOD 027 CD

1993 MCD - R 33 599

EXTASY

**Peter Åhs: v/k, Lars Hallbäck: g, Jörgen Andersson: k,
Mikael Andersson: b, Thorbjörn "Tobbe" Persson: d**

Skövde - When the excellent band *Rhapsody* (aka *Rhapsody Sweden*) split, Peter and Thorbjörn formed *Extasy*. This album is an outstanding piece of well-played and well-arranged AOR/pomp, quite close to early *Toto*. There are some really nice guitar/keyboard interplays here. Producer is Tommy Folkesson, foremost known as the amp-wizard who customizes guitar-amps for guys like John Norum, Frank Marino and Kee Marcello. The album was recorded in 1980 but not finished until 1983. It's a rarity but also a must for all fans of AOR/pomp.

1983 ■ EXTASY ....LP   Artist... ARLP 10831 $

1983 LP - ARLP 10831

EXTAZ

**Patrik Jemteborn: v, Jens Johansson: g, Andreas Jonasson: k,
Mikael Jonsson: b, Pär Lundgren: d**

Östersund - These melodic rockers were formed in 1985 and they were 17 years old when the single was recorded. They won some local talent shows and first prize of the *1989 Expo Norr Talangen* competition, was the recording of a single at Tommys Musik Lab in Östersund. In the summer of 1989 they went on a peace and environment tour in the Nordic countries and even in Murmansk in Russia. The music is really decent AOR, while the vocals are in Swedish and with a slightly poppier attitude. Well worth checking out anyhow.

1989 ■ Visa vad jag vill/Jag vill ha mer ....7"   private ....JMP 8912

1989 7" - JMP 8912

EYE

**Ivan Höglund: v, Oscar "Oz Osukaru" Petersson: g,
Mathias Rosén: k, Daniel "Daco" Svensson: b, Matt Schelin: d**

Göteborg - The members have previously been found in bands like *Katana*, *Sharp*, *Damaged Dolls*, *Rattlesnake* and *Deletion*. After the MCD, Oscar (also in *Osukaru*) was replaced by Martin Danstål. *Eye* play high-quality AOR in the vein of *H.E.A.T.* The vocals are not as strong as the aforementioned, but fine enough. A second 8 track CD entitled *Second To None* was recorded and supposed to be released in 2010, but the release was cancelled and the band split. The album was shelved. The band however re-united again in 2012, with the same line-up and a new album is in the making, planned to be released in 2013. Ivan is also found in *Pretty Wild* and Oz is also in *Panorama*.
Website: http://eyeofficial.info.se/

We've got our eye on YOU!

2009 ■ 2 Hearts ....MCD 7tr   Blue Topaz BTRCD32
    *Tracks: Lovers Apart [intro]/2 Hearts (Lovers Apart)/Without You/Restless Dreams/These
Tears/How Many Roads (demo)/Without You (acoustic)*

2009 MCD - BTRCD32

F.K.Ü

Lawrence "Larry" Mackrory: v, Peter "Pete" Hägglund (now Lans): g, Patrik "Pat" Sporrong: b, Teddy "Ted" Möller: d

Uppsala - A totally far-out, old-school thrash-project in the vein of early **Anthrax** meets **Stormtroopers Of Death**. Tight as a rats ass and with enough energy and intensity to invade a small nation. The band recorded their first demo *Beware (Of The Evil Underwear)* in 1998, a classic to be! Killer stuff, indeed! *F.K.Ü* actually stands for Freddie Krueger's Ünderwear. Theo Savidis (**Lost Souls**) played drums on the debut. Lawrence has recorded with **Andromeda**, **Sportlov**, **Enemy Is Us**, **The Duskfall** etc., Patrik was in **Midas Touch**, **Kapoor**, **Lost Souls**, Teddy in **Mayadome**, **Loch Vostok** and **Flagellation**. *Space Beer* is a **Tankard** cover. As a side comment, singer Lawrence also dubs voices in movies and does the panda Po in *Kung Fu Panda*, where American actor Jack Black does the original. The first version of *4: Rise Of The Mosh Mongers* was released as a digipack with two bonus tracks. http://www.moshoholics.com/

Beware of Freddie's ünderwear!

Year		Title	Format	Label	Cat. No.
1999	☐	METAL MOSHING MAD	CD	Black Diamond	BDP 007
2003	☐	A Mosh Under Pressure/Maniac Cop	7"	Nitskivor	NIT 2
2005	■	SOMETIMES THEY COME BACK... TO MOSH	CD	Head Mechanic	NAWHMCD008
2007	■	METAL MOSHING MAD	CD	Razorback	RRA42
		Reissue featuring the 1998 18 track demo as bonus. New artwork.			
2008	☐	Twitch Of The Thrash Nerve (split)	7"	Deep Six	DS-93
		White vinyl. Split with Hirax.			
2008	☐	Horror Metal Moshing Machine/Space Beer	7"	Torture Garden	TG 210
		Grey vinyl.			
2009	☐	WHERE MOSHERS DWELL	CD	Metal On Metal	MOMR09009
2012	☐	WHERE MOSHERS DWELL	LP	TPL	TPL 028
		500 copies. With magazine.			
2013	☐	4: RISE OF THE MOSH MONGERS	CD	Napalm Records	NPR 474
2013	☐	4: RISE OF THE MOSH MONGERS	CDd	Napalm Records	NPR 474
		Bonus: Mirrors Painted Black/The New Flesh/(untitled). Sew-on patch.			
2013	☐	4: RISE OF THE MOSH MONGERS	LP	Napalm Records	NPR 474
		200 copies gray/blue vinyl. Bonus: We're Evil			
2013	☐	4: RISE OF THE MOSH MONGERS	CD	Spiritual Beast (Japan)	IUCP-16166
2013	☐	WHERE MOSHERS DWELL	CD	Napalm Records	NPR 482

2005 CD - NAWHMCD008

2007 CD - RRA42

FACE DOWN

Marco Aro: v, Joacim Carlsson: g, Joakim Hedestedt (aka Harju): b, Peter Stjärnvind: d

Stockholm - The band was formed under the name **Machine God** in 1993 by bass player Joakim Harju and drummer Richard Bång, who also plays on the first album. The first album also featured Henrik Blomquist on "audio hardware". The first two albums were produced by Daniel Bergstrand (**Crawley, Devin Townsend** etc.). Joacim Carlsson was ex-**Afflicted** and **Proboscis**, while drummer Peter Stjärnvind was ex-**Entombed, Unanimated, Merciless** etc. **Face Down** delivers raw, aggressive and brutal metal in the vein of **Slayer** and early **Voi Vod**. On the reunion album in 2005 the line-up had changed. Stjärnvind (now in **Krux**) had been replaced by Erik Thyselius and bass player Harju had changed his name to Hedestedt. The album was produced by **Clawfinger**'s Jocke Skog. In 2006 Thyselius was replaced by Christofer Barkensjö (**Repugnant, Carnal Forge, Serpent Obscene**) and in 2007 Joacim Carlsson was replaced by Rickard Dahlberg from **Construcdead**.

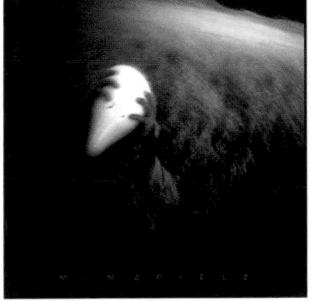

1995 CD - RR 8902 2

Year		Title	Format	Label	Cat. No.
1995	■	MINDFIELD	CD	Roadrunner	RR 8902 2
1997	☐	TWISTED RULE THE WICKED	CD	Nuclear Blast	NB1942
2005	■	THE WILL TO POWER	CD	Black Lodge	BLOD 069 CD
2005	☐	THE WILL TO POWER	CD+DVD	Black Lodge	BLOD 069 CDL
		Bonus DVD featuring live videos + My Sacrifice/Strife			
2006	☐	THE WILL TO POWER	CD	Soundholic (Japan)	TKCS-85136
		Bonus: Demon Seed (rerecorded)/Be My Enemy			
2008	☐	THINK TWICE (split)	CD	Unexploded	UER 028
		Split with Remasculate. Tracks: Lost Cause/Indifference/Irreversible/White Trash God			

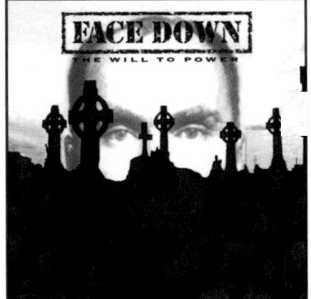

2005 CD - BLOD 069 CD

FACE OF EVIL

J. Wildfire: v/g, Destructo: b, Mats "Mad Witchburner" Wikberg: d

Stockholm - Wikberg is also found in **Bloodstone** and **Bifrost**. The band released their first demo in 1994. Black metal/thrash similar to **Sodom** and **Nifelheim**. Thrash-oriented death metal in the vein of **Sadus** and **Nifelheim**. It was scheduled to be re-issued with new artwork, by Invictus in 2011, but this never happened and the band has since folded.

Year		Title	Format	Label	Cat. No.
2004	☐	FACE OF EVIL	CD	Metalblood Music	strike 003
2004	■	FACE OF EVIL	LP	Metalblood Music	strike 003
		333 copies.			

2004 LP - strike 003

FACEBREAKER

Roberth Karlsson: v, Janne Ivarsson: g, Mika Lagreen: g,
Jonas Magnusson: b, Mikael Wassholm: d

Finspång - *Facebreaker* were formed in 1999 by Janne, Roberth, Mikael and Jonas. The band was soon completed by guitarist Janos. The subsequent year they recorded the demo *Use Your Fist*. In 2002 the second demo *Hate And Anger* was released and caught the attention of UK label Rage Of Achilles, who featured the band on the compilation *Conquest For The Empire*. Now Janos left and was replaced by Mika. In June 2003 the demo was released as a vinyl single, followed by the debut album *Bloodred Hell* in 2003. When Rage Of Achilles went belly-up the band was picked up by Pulverised who released the follow-up: *Dead, Rotten And Hungry*, which was given a vinyl release by Cyclone Empire, who later re-issued *Bloodred Hell* with a bonus track and took over the band for their latest release, *Infected*. Heavy, crushing death metal in the vein of early *Entombed* or *Edge Of Sanity*. Roberth is ex-*Edge Of Sanity* and also found in *Solar Dawn*, *Scar Symmetry* and *Tormented*.

2004 CD - ILIAD 047

2008 CD - ASH 039 CD

2011 CD - 3984-14964-2

2003	☐ Hate And Anger	7" 4tr	Rage Of Achilles	ILIAD 036
	Tracks: Hate And Anger/Me (Mean)/Beyond Redemption/Death			
2004	■ BLOODRED HELL	CD	Rage Of Achilles	ILIAD 047
2008	■ DEAD, ROTTEN AND HUNGRY	CD	Pulverised	ASH 039 CD
2008	☐ DEAD, ROTTEN AND HUNGRY	LP	Cyclone Empire	CYC 024-1
	Red vinyl. 500 copies.			
2009	☐ BLOODRED HELL	CD	Cyclone Empire	CYV 038-2
	Bonus: Bring Out The Gimp (Dontcares cover)/Hate And Anger/Me (Mean)/Beyond Redemption/Death			
2010	☐ INFECTED	CDd	Cyclone Empire	CYC 060-0
	Bonus: The Return			
2010	☐ INFECTED	LP	Cyclone Empire	CYC 060-1
	Transparent red with black smoke. 500 copies.			
2011	■ INFECTED	CD	Metal Blade	3984-14964-2

FACEQUAKE

Sarah Kreft: v/k, Martin Hållqvist: g, Janne Svensson: b, Tony Elfving: d

Gävle - The first CD is melodic Seattle-stained hard rock with great female vocals and heavy guitars. Recommended. On the second CD, also self-titled, drummer Fredrik Hamberg had been replaced by Elfving. The second release was produced by Pelle Saether and follows in the same style as the debut, only a bit elevated. The tracks on the CDS are found on the second album. Well worth checking out! Hållqvist is now in *The Hellfire Club*. In 2011 Kreft participated in the Swedish TV show *True Talent*.

1996 CD - FACE 001

1996	■ FACEQUAKE	CD	private	FACE 001
2000	☐ Shoeshine/Changed My Mind	CDSp 2tr	Maxi 2000	LC03219.32
2004	☐ FACEQUAKE	CD	Maxi 2000	LC 033

FACESHIFT

Timo Hovinen: v, Petri Tarvainen: g, Peter Nagy-Eklöf: g/b, Stefan Norgren: d

Stockholm - In 2005, the band *Eternal Oath* decided to call it a day. However, feeling they had more to give, guitarists Tarvainen and Nagy-Eklöf formed the band *Faceshift* together with keyboardist Stefan Norgren (*Lion's Share*). Norgren however returned to his main instrument, drums and singer Hovinen was drafted. On the debut album Nagy (*Mörk Gryning, Wyvern*) also handled the bass work. In 2008 he left the band and after a hiatus Mika Kajanen (*Godphobia*) joined on bass and David Bertilsson took over the guitar. *Faceshift* play great, melodic, slightly progressive metal, at times similar to band like *Cloudscape* and *Evergrey*. Highly recommended. The band has also released the digital single *A New Beginning* in 2012.

2007 CD - BLOD 058 CD

2007	■ RECONCILE	CD	Black Lodge	BLOD 058 CD

FAFNER

Peter Nilsson: v/g/b/d

Jönköping - *Fafner* is the black metal brainchild of former *Nominon* member Nilsson, initiated already in 1992. The first three track demo *Stycken Mörkre* was recorded in 1993 and the second, *Stycken hata Kristers blo* came the following year. A compilation tape of the two was released in 1995 under the name *Trolskust*, the same recording that appears on the only CD release from the band.

2004 CD - NSP 006

2004	■ DAEMONS FROM THE PAST (split)	CD	Northern Silence	NSP 006
	Split with Nominon. Tracks: Upon a Throne of Thorns/Doomed to Wander Alone/Han Som Drogs I Djupet/Han Som Drogs I Djupet (instrumental)/Att Dricka Mörkret/Skymning			

1978 7" - BRIS-100

FAGIN

Berne Svanberg: v/d, Michael Winkler: g, Magnus Rosén: g,
Mats Ringström: k, Peter Jacobson: b/k

Kungälv - The band was formed in 1973. Like **Uriah Heep** they took their name from a character in *Oliver Twist* by Charles Dickens. The band built their own studio, Nigaf Demo Studio, at Berne's parents' house. They acted as backing band for singer Zein Ayari. **Fagin** play decent straight-ahead, boogie-oriented hard rock, quite similar to early **Status Quo**.

1978 ■ I'd Better Go/Rocksymphony ....7" Bauta BRIS-100

FAIR CHILD

Stefan Borg: v, Jonas Kjell: g, Tony Hadarsson: g,
Stefan Lekström: b, Johan Andersson: d

Eksjö - The band was formed as a quartet in 1983 under the name **IQ-Zero**, who had the track *Murder And Evil* featured on the compilation *Pang I Bygget* (83 Pang). The line-up then featured Tony (v/g), Jonas (g), Glenn Stenlöf (b) and Johan (d). The line-up changed to the above in 1984 and the single was recorded. Sleaze/glam-oriented hard rock, quite similar to **Reptile Smile** and **Tornado Babies**. However, the singer sounds like a mix of Brian Johnson and Vince Neil but with severely squeezed balls. They also recorded a demo. After the single a manager showed interest in the band, fired the singer and things slowly fell apart until the end in 1988-89. Stefan is found in the band **Tumbleweed**, Tony was in the field group **Dessertörerna** and Jonas in the band **Stefan Herde & His Broomdusters**.

1986 ■ Take On Me/On The Run ....7" Team Lucas ....LUC 001

1986 7" - LUC 001

FAIRNESS

Peter Kihlberg: v, Thord L. Steen: g, Urban Larsson: b, Fredrik Johansson: d

Säffle - A band in the traditional 80's NWoBHM vein, mid-quality, but good vocals.

1989 ■ Live For Rock 'N Roll/Darling Of My Heart ....7" private ....FAIR 01 $

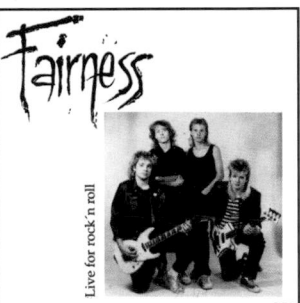

1989 7" - FAIR 001

FAITH

Christer Nilsson: b/v, Roger Johansson: g, Peter "TrumPeter" Svensson: d

Karlshamn - Formed under the name **Stormbringer** in 1984, featuring Roger, Christer, Peter and second guitarist Jörgen Thuresson (brother of **Overdrive** singer, now bassist Pelle Thuresson). They recorded some demos and in 1985 they changed their name to **Faith**. Before the recording of the 7" Jörgen left the band and singer Roger Berntsson was added to the line-up. The style of the first single is heavy, doomy metal. Berntsson left the band after just a few months and Zenny Hansson (now Gram) took his place. Shortly after, he received an offer he couldn't refuse, and moved to Göteborg to join **Destiny**. **Faith** went on in the trio-format with Christer handling the vocals again. They recorded the demo *Insanity*. Second guitarist Peter Zwieniger was added to the line-up, but in 1987 they finally broke up when drummer Peter Svensson moved to Göteborg where he joined melodic rockers **Globe** with whom he recorded some demos and two tracks for the 1993 *Rockslaget* compilation. Fed up with Göteborg he moved back after just a few years to join doomsters **Mercy**, with whom he recorded the album *King Doom* (without getting credited as he left before its release). He then teamed up with **Overdrive** members Janne Stark and Pelle Thuresson in the band **Overheat** in 1989 and also recorded two tracks with Janne for the *Guitar Heroes Of Sweden* compilations. In 1995 Christer, Roger and Peter resurrected the band. They recorded the demo *In The Twelfth Hour*, but the progress was slow because of family and work reasons. However in 2003 the band entered Studio Sound Palace to record again. The style now took a more folk-influenced doom metal turn, which shows on the return album *Salvation Lies Within*, where Stark appears as guest on one track as well as old colleague Jörgen Thuresson. The CD bonus tracks are rerecordings of the tracks from the first single. *Sorg* and *Blessed?* follows in the same style and a new album is in the making. Peter has also recorded several songs and albums with **Locomotive Breath**, **Mountain Of Power**, **Constancia** and Chris Catena. The last album features a Louis Armstrong cover!
Website: www.faitharmy.com

1986 7" - HSP 2060

2003 LPg - SKULL 9814

2005 CD - DS CD-006

2008 CD - TRANS 039

1986 ■	Hymn Of The Sinner/Possession	7"	Hellrec	HSP 2060	$$
2003 ■	SALVATION LIES WITHIN	LPg	Stormbringer	SKULL 9814	
	100 yellow + 400 black vinyl copies, numbered.				
2005 □	SALVATION LIES WITHIN	CDd	Doom Symphony	DS CD-004	
	Bonus: Possession/Hymn Of The Sinner				
2005 ■	SORG	CD	Doom Symphony	DS CD-006	
2008 ■	BLESSED?	CD	Transubstans	TRANS 039	
2013 □	DECADES OF DESPAIR	CD	Transubstans	TRANS 110	

FAITH TABOO

**Apollo Papathanasio: v, Jonas Ström: g, Ola Svensson: k,
Patric Brundin: b, Tomas Persson: d**

Malmö - Formed in 1993. *Faith Taboo* is a great melodic band that balances between AOR and funkish hard rock. Great vocal and instrumental qualities. Drummer Tomas, who has a past with thrashers *Exile*, joined after the recordings of the album. Drums on the album were played by Ludwig Witt from *Spiritual Beggars/Firebird*. Singer Apollo (ex-*Craze*, *City People*) later joined and recorded with *Majestic*, *Meduza* and is now a member of *Firewind*, *Evil Masquerade* and *Spiritual Beggars*. The Long Island version of the debut is very scarce since the label went bust just as it was released.

1996 ■ PSYCHOPATH	CD	Long Island	35637
1996 □ PSYCHOPATH	CD	Semaphore	SM 9601
1997 □ PSYCHOPATH	CD	Avalon Marquee (Japan)	MICY-1021
Bonus: Perfect Man			

1996 CD - 35637

FAITHFUL DARKNESS

**Erik Nilsson: v/g, Jimmy Persson: g/v, Johan Aldgård: g, Andrea Green: k,
John Svensson Rehnström: b, Martin Langen: d**

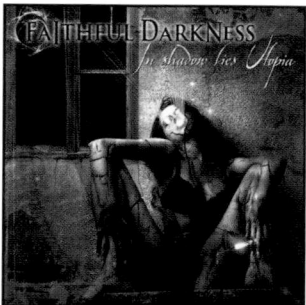

Höganäs - *Faithful Darkness* was formed by former *Soilwork* drummer Jimmy Persson, who quit playing drums and instead picked up the guitar. He started collaborating with drummer Martin Langen and the band started taking shape. They recorded their first demo *Evil Game* in 2005. It was followed by *Alive* and *Fields Of Yesterday* in 2006 and soon the band started working on their debut with producer Pontus Lindmark (*Cloudscape*, *Planet Alliance*) who had also produced two of the demos. In 2010 Erik Nilsson was replaced by Richard Sjunnesson (*Sonic Syndicate*) and drummer Joakim Strandberg-Nilsson replaced Langen (also in *Undecayed*). *Faithful Darkness* delivers well-played, great-sounding melodic death metal with a progressive touch, mixing growl and clean vocals. In 2013 Jonathan Thorpenberg (*Eternity Remains*, *Ruined Soul* etc) replaced Jimmy.

2008 ■ IN SHADOW LIES UTOPIA	CD	Golden Core	GCR 20032-2

2008 CD - GCR 20032-2

FAKE

**Tony Wilhelmsson: v, Ulrika Örn: v, Mikael Ohlsson: g,
Jan Fagerberg: k, Stefan Bogstedt: b, Stefan Sverin: d**

Stockholm - *Fake* were formed in 1977 by composer Erik Strömblad and Stefan Bogstedt under the name *Size 46*. The line-up was completed by Stefan Sverin (*Glory Bells Band*), Tony Wilhelmsson and singer Ulrika Örn. The first single is the only thing worth checking out for fans of melodic hard rock/AOR. After this they transformed into a horrible synth pop band in the vein of *Depeche Mode*, had a big hit with the song *Donna Rouge* and recorded numerous singles and the album *New Art*. Strömblad later formed *Walk On Water* and Wilhelmsson his solo project *Pillow Parade*. Ulrika appeared in the movies *G* and *Splittring* and today works as a music journalist at Swedish Television. She also released a solo pop single. The listed single is the only thing worth checking out.

1981 ■ Dreamgirl/Warlord	7"	Lacerate Music	WHIP 01

1981 7" - WHIP 01

FALCONER

**Mathias Bladh: v/k, Stefan Weinerhall: g, Jimmy Hedlund: g,
Magnus Linhardt: b, Karsten Larsson: d**

Waiting for the birds to return?

Mjölby - In 1999 Stefan started writing new material and left his former death metal band *Mithotyn*. Karsten soon followed. Falconer instead delivered medieval metal with powerful, yet soulful vocals from Mathias, who is actually a musical-singer originally. This line-up recorded the debut album. In 2002 they were completed by session-guitarist Anders Johansson and bass player Peder Johansson and *Chapters Of The Forlorn* followed. The second album featured even more elements of medieval music and quite a few overtones of Swedish folk music. Killer-band!! In 2003 Blad decided to leave the band because of time issues. He was replaced by *Destiny* singer Kristoffer Göbel. At this point Anders and Peder also became full part members. The album *The Scepter Of Deception* followed showcasing the new line-up. Andy LaRocque and former singer Blad guests on the album. However only a year later Anders and Peder left the band because of musical differences. Enter bass player Linhardt, formerly of *Choir Of Vengeance*. In 2004 the band finally found a new lead guitarist in Jimmy Hedlund. The new line-up entered Studio Los Angered to record *Grime Vs Grandeur*. It also features guest drums from Snowy Shaw (*Dream Evil*, *Therion*, *XXX*,

Notre Dame etc.) on one track. When the material for its follow-up was written and ready, original singer Blad decided to return to the ranks. The first edition of *Northwind* featured bonus songs in the form of Swedish traditional songs. *Among Beggars And Thieves* saw another return to Los Angered. Stefan is also found in **Indungeon** and had the dance/death/techno-band **Atryxion** on the side. Karsten is ex-**Dawn** and **Choir Of Vengeance**. On *Armod* the band took their Swedish folk roots to a new level incorporating cello, flute, fiddle etc., a one-off thing.
http://www.falconermusic.com/

2001	■	FALCONER	CD	Metal Blade	3984-14355-2
2001	□	FALCONER	CD	Fono (Russia)	FO59CD
2002	□	CHAPTERS FROM A VALE FORLORN	CD	Metal Blade	3984-14397-2
2002	□	CHAPTERS FROM A VALE FORLORN	CD	Fono (Russia)	FO143CD
2002	□	CHAPTERS FROM A VALE FORLORN	CD	Soundholic(Jap)	TKCS 85036
		Bonus: En Kungens Man			
2004	□	THE SCEPTER OF DECEPTION	CD	Metal Blade	3984-1447-2
2004	□	THE SCEPTER OF DECEPTION	CD	Fono (Russia)	FO289CD
2004	□	THE SCEPTER OF DECEPTION	CD	Soundholic (Japan)	TKCS-85076
2005	□	GRIME VS GRANDEUR	CD	Metal Blade	3984-14532-2
2005	□	GRIME VS GRANDEUR	CDd	Metal Blade	3984-14532-0
		Bonus: Wake Up			
2005	□	GRIME VS GRANDEUR	CD	Fono (Russia)	FO486CD
2005	□	Rock 'N'Roll Devil (split)	7"	Swedmetal	SM-02-7
		Split with Nocturnal Rites.			
2006	□	NORTHWIND	CD	Metal Blade	3984-14588-2
2006	□	NORTHWIND	2CD	Metal Blade	3984-14588-0
		Bonus: Kristallen den fina/Ridom Ridom/Liten vätte/Vårvindar friska			
2006	□	NORTHWIND	CD	Fono (Russia)	FO627CD
2008	□	AMONG BEGGARS AND THIEVES	CD	Metal Blade	3984-14688-2
2008	□	AMONG BEGGARS AND THIEVES	CDd	Metal Blade	3984-14688-0
		Bonus: Dark Ages/Vi sålde våra hemman/Carnival Of Disgust (video)			
2008	■	AMONG BEGGARS AND THIEVES	LP PD	Metal Blade	3984-14688-1
2008	□	AMONG BEGGARS AND THIEVES	CD	Avalon Marquee (Japan)	MICP-10804
		Bonus: Dark Ages/Vi sålde våra hemman			
2008	□	AMONG BEGGARS AND THIEVES	CD	Fono (Russia)	FO752CD
2011	□	ARMOD	CDd	Metal Blade (UK)	MTB15030-2
		Bonus: Black Widow/Grimborg/By The Roses Grave/O, Silent Solitude			
2011	■	ARMOD	CD	Metal Blade	MTB15030-2

2001 CD - 3984-14355-2

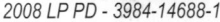
2008 LP PD - 3984-14688-1

2011 CD - MTB15030-2

FALL OV SERAFIM

Ville "Skorrgh" Kemi: v/b, Varg "Aldrathan" Strand: g, John "K" Huldt: g, Julius "Farnargh" Chmielewski: k, Thomas "Nirag" Lejon: d

Malmö - In 2005 Malmö-based death metal band *Misteltein* set out to record their new album, but early 2006 some member-changes took place. As one of the former members owned the rights to the name *Misteltein*, the band now became *Fall Ov Serafim*. Kemi is also found in **Obscure Divinity**, **Twilight Orchestra**, **Life Illusion** and **Vandöd**, Strand in **Ishtar** and **Blind**, Huldt in **Feared Creation**, **Dymanic** and he has released two solo CDs, Lejon also plays with **A.C.T** and **Andromeda**. Chmielewski and Lejon are also ex-**Embraced**. The latest know line-up featured Kemi, Chmielewski, Lejon and Strand.

2006	■	NEX JEHOVAE	CD	Regain	RR 088

2006 CD - RR 088

FALLEN ANGEL

Johan Bülow: v, Joacim Persson: g, Mattias Hedenborg: b, Fredrik Lindén: d

Örebro - The band was formed in 1984 and two years later they took the name *Fallen Angels*, but dropped the "s". They recorded their first demo in 1988 and a follow-up came the year after. On the debut the bass was handled by Gustaf Ljungström and the guitar by Fredrik Hänhel, who shortly after was replaced by Kent Engberg. He only recorded one demo in 1988, before he was replaced by Joacim Persson. Bass player Gustaf left and Mattias took over his task. The band now recorded the track *Etanolic Intoxication* for the compilation 7" EP *Opinionate* (1990 Opinionate - OP/002). *Fallen Angel* produce powerful thrash of high quality, but they are rather weak in the vocal department. Joacim and Mattias went on to form the brilliant band *Under The Sun*, now sadly defunct. In 1994 Joacim recorded a MCD with the band *Tyburn*. Mattias later formed *Cripple* and both members were later found in rap-metal band *Waving Corn* who recorded one album. Bülow has also been found in *Altar*, *Wolf* (2000-2002) and *Chain Of Hate*.

1987 MLP - UNI 2474

1987	■	Fallen Angel	MLP 7tr	private	UNI 2474
		Tracks: Spectacle Of Fear/Ice/D.F.H/Injection – Overdose/Another One/Visions Of Terror/ Trapped In Siberia			
1992	■	FAITH FAILS	LP	Massacre Records	MASS LP 003
1992	□	FAITH FAILS	CD	Massacre Records	MASS CD 003

1992 LP - MASS LP 003

F

FANTASMAGORIA

Peter Grehn: v/g, Rickard Harrysson: g, Micke Åsentorp: b, Robin Engström: d

Bollnäs - Heavy and uncompromising heavy/power metal in the true *Pantera*-vein. The album contains a cover of *Judas Priest*'s *The Rage*. In 2000 Lefay split and the boys went for *Fantasmagoria* full-time... until *Lefay* reformed and Peter, Micke and Robin returned to the *Lefay*-ranks.

1998 ■ FUCK YOU ALL ....CD Trudani...FYA 666

1998 CD - FYA 666

FANTASY

**Tomas Bergsten: v/g, Micke Friman: g, Göran Greus: k,
Ekko Karttunen: b, Arto Karttunen: d**

Hällefors - Quite poppy AOR with slightly weak vocals, but quite decent anyway. Think *Time Gallery* meets *Alien*. The band was formed in 1987 and the members had earlier on played in local bands like *Miztrezz*, *Worship* and *Unicorn*. In 1989 they participated in the *Talang 1989* bandstand in Örebro. Ekko and Tomas, who has become a better singer through the years, later played in *Aristokraterna*, Friman in folk band *Kuntera*, Arto in *Wet Bandits* and *Payback*. In 2013 Thomas released the album *Caught In The Dark* under the *Thomas Bergsten's Fantasy* moniker, also featuring a guest appearance from Friman.

1989 7" - APTMG 1

1989 ■ The Wand/Only Your Love ....7" private ....APTMG 1

FAR NORTH

**Patrick Jonsson: v, Peter Karlsson: g, Jan Andersson: g, Tobias Öhman: k,
David Nyström: b, Svenne Schönfeldt: d**

Skellefteå - *Far North* are another high-class AOR band. Good songs, nice arrangements, great vocal harmonies and a nice, juicy sound. Very strong influences from mid-80's *Europe*. The *Thin Lizzy*-cover *Heart Attack* is also found on the compilation *The Lizzy Songs* (95 SMC).

1995 CD - SMC CD 2015-1

1995 ■ WHAT?!..CD SMC ....SMC CD 2015-1
2003 ☐ WHAT?!..CD MTM Classix 0681-86
          Bonus: Heartattack

FAT NELLY

Jocke Olsson: v, Jane Björck: g, Tony Eriksson: g, Henrik Lindberg: b, Pete Peeters: d

Helsingborg - The band was formed in 2007 and recorded their first demo in 2008. This lead to a deal with Forest Records in 2009 and in 2010 the debut saw the light of day. *Fat Nelly* play decent melodic hard rock with a seventies touch, sounding a bit inspired by *Thin Lizzy* and a bit reminiscent of *Pole Position*. In 2012, singer Jocke left the band and a replacement has not been found as yet.

2010 CD - FRS 003

2010 ■ WAKE UP...CD Forest Records ....FRS 003

FATAL ATTRACTION

**Anders Fältsjö: v, Thomas Nilsson: g, Patrik Eriksson: k,
Magnus Pettersson: b, Per Sandlund: d**

Mönsterås - Formed in late 1993. In 1995 they were featured on the American compilation *Best Unsigned European Acts* (Showcase Rec). Their style is symphonic sounding melodic AOR, quite close to early *Asia* with some hints of *Toto* and *Grand Prix*. A great band!

1996 ■ END OF REGULATION TIME..CD High Rock Records HRR960905
1997 ☐ END OF REGULATION TIME..CD Sound Treasure (Japan)................STCD-004
2003 ☐ SIMPLICITY RULES ....CD Adrenalin Records ....ADR 0022

1996 CD - HRR960905

FATAL EMBRACE

Tommy Grönberg: v/b, Manne Engström: v/g, Andreas Johansson: g, Henrik Serholt: d

Varberg - Melodic death metal in the vein of *Dark Tranquillity*. Mattias Lodmalm guests on *Shadowsoul's Garden*. Grönberg are also found in *Eternal Lies*, Engström in *Beseech, Cemetary 1213, Sundown, Those We Don't Speak Of* and is now in *Lavett*. Johansson is also found in *Auberon* and *Sundown* and Serholt in *Lothlorien*. A demo entitled *Scars In Dismal Icons* was also recorded in 1995. On the album the band are reinforced by Mathias Lodmalm and Daniel Heiman (*Lost Horizon, Heed* etc). A second album, entitled *Hail Down Deep* was recorded in 1998, but never released. Not to confused with the German thrashers.

1997 ■ SHADOWSOULS' GARDEN..CD Candlelight............................CANDLE 018 CD

1997 CD - CANDLE 018 CD

FATAL SMILE

Bassel Elharbiti: v/g, Fredrik Emneus: g, Johan Folke: k,
Robert Krook: b, Peter Hedberg: d

Uppsala - Good, solid melodic hard rock in the vein of *Europe* and *Bon Jovi*. Formed in 1989. The band had minor success in Finland, but internal conflicts and an overdose put an end to the band. They attempted a reunion, but it fell apart. Bassel was later found in *Mayadome*. Peter and Fredrik formed the band *Bulldog* in 2002, and Peter is now in *Freedom Bleeder*.

1993 ■ Left In A Shadow..MCD 4tr   Uppsala Musikfabrik ....TRY 69
    Tracks: Falling In Love/Left In A Shadow/Calling You/Fire Walk With Me

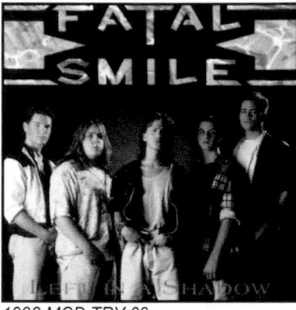

1993 MCD TRY 69

FATAL SMILE

Thomas "Blade" Emblad: v, Yüksel "Y" Unutmaz: g,
Alexander "Alx" Jonsson: b, Steff "Philty": d

Katrineholm/Stockholm - Formed in 1991 by guitarist Yüksel. The band was first featured with the tracks *Silver Moon* and *Mad Dog Fury* on the *Under Development* (95 Ironbeard) compilation, then featuring Unutmaz, bassist Mattias Eliasson, drummer Magnus Gustavsson and guest singer Classe Byström. This band has really been working hard for their deal! Not to be confused with *Fatal Smile* from Uppsala. I personally received at least four demos between 1999 and 2002. The 1999 demo featured Unutmaz, singer Nicklas Jonsson, bassist Markus Johansson and drummer Rickard Johansson. The demos were pretty decent, but what made the real change, was when *Scudier/Token/Mindsplit*-singer Hasse "H.B" Andersson joined the ranks. The debut album was way better than the demos and the band belongs to the same genre as *Lynch Mob* or *Slaughter*, at times with a heavier edge. The line-up now featured Andersson, Unutmaz, Markus Johansson and drummer Robin Lagerqvist (*Six-Pack Solution*). Quite predictable, but worth checking out. Before the next album Lagerqvist was replaced by Tomas Lindgren. On the first single for Locomotive Music the line-up had again changed, now featuring Yüksel, bass player Alx (also lead singer of *Scaar*, *Tough Trade*), drummer Steff "Philthy"and new singer Thomas "Blade" Emblad. The track *Pissed Off* was written by Paul Sabu. In 2010 the band also recorded a tribute to Ronnie Dio, entitled *For The Last In Line*, which was co-written by Mikael Rosengren (*Constancia*, *Token*, *Scudiero*).
Website:www.fatalsmile.com/

2002 CD - SOTRCD 003

2008 CD - LM 576

2002 ■ BEYOND REALITY ....CD   Stars On The Rise/GMR.............SOTRCD 003
2005 □ Learn-Love-Hate/(video)..CDS   GMR FS1654
2006 □ NEO NATURAL FREAKS ....CD   GMR ....FS 1971
2006 □ NEO NATURAL FREAKS ....CD   Spiritual Beast (Japan) SPCD-1035
    Bonus: Learn-Love-Hate (video)
2008 □ S.O.B ....CDS   Locomotive ....n/a
2008 ■ WORLD DOMINATION ....CD   Locomotive ....LM 576
2008 □ WORLD DOMINATION ....CD   Spiritual Beast (Japan) POCE-16021
    Bonus: Six String Gun
2009 □ Run For Your Life ....MCD 3tr   FS Productions FSP001CDS
    Tracks: Run For Your Life (Radio edit)/Run For Your Life/Pissed Off
2009 ■ WORLD DOMINATION - SPECIAL EDITION ....CDd   FS Productions FSP001CD
    Bonus: Six String Gun/Pissed Off/S.O.B (video)/Run For Your Life (video)
2012 □ Welcome To The Freakshow ....MCDpd   FS Records........................... FS1655
    Tracks: Welcome To The Freakshow/Judgement Day/Run For Your Life (2012 remix)/Hip MF
2012 ■ 21ST CENTURY FREAKS...CDd   FS Productions FS999

2009 CDd - FSP001CD

2012 CDd - FS999

FATAL TABASCO

Svante Wickström: v, Robert Nilsson: g, Niklas Thorn: g,
Simon Lindholm: b, Torbjörn Haraldsson: d

Alingsås - Happy metal? Well, at least heavy metal/hard rock with a lot of riffs in the major scale. As the name suggests they are a bit odd. Could be described as a slower cousin of *Scatterbrain*. Upper mid-league, with strained, slightly out of tune vocals that at times make it unbearable to listen to. A pity.

1995 ■ MOUSE CAFÉ ....CD   private .... - -

FEAR THE FUTURE

Johan "Nephete": v, Tobbe "Ash" Gustafsson: g, Luna: k,
Björn "Azazel/Folkilsk" Thorup: b, Mattias "Panzer" Johansson: d

Nässjö - *Fear The Future* were formed in 2002 by Ash, guitarist Grim and Luna, with the goal of making aggressive metal drawing from both the Scandinavian and international metal legacy. Ash and Nephete had played together in different bands since 1992. The band recorded their first demo in 2003, simply entitled *Demo 1: 2003*. It was printed in 100 copies on CDR. After

1995 CD - - -

the release drummer Viper left the band and was replaced by Spawn. The band was approached by New Aeon/Karmageddon Media who offered the band a deal. Now Thorup was added to the line-up and the recording commenced in 2004 in Studio Sunlight with classic death metal producer Thomas Skogsberg. Unfortunately the deal with Karmageddon didn't work out as the label went bust, so two years later the CD was released by Ninth Gate. Tobbe and Johan are also found in **Benighted**. Johan is also in **Netherbird** and Mattias in **Karneywar**. **Fear The Future** could be compared to bands like **Cradle Of Filth** or **Dimmu Borgir**. Unfortunately the mix leaves a lot more to be desired.

2006 ■ The Bloody Beginning...MCD 4tr Ninth Gate...NGR 001
    Tracks: This World's Bane To Be/The Escalation Of Self/The Bitter Fall/This Flare Will Fade

2006 MCD - NGR 001

FEBRUARI 93
Daniel Bryntse: v/b, Josefin Qvarnström: flute, Crister Olsson: g, Magnus Björk: d

Gävle - Folk-progg with occasionally heavy guitars. Partly reminiscent of **Kebnekajse** and **Vintersorg**. Olsson, Bryntse and Björk are all ex-**Forlorn** (which later became **Isole**). Bryntse is also found in **Withered Beauty**, **Windwalker**, **Ereb Altor** etc., Björk in **The Storyteller**, **Withered Beauty** and **Nightchant**, Olsson in **Ereb Altor**. Despite the name, the band was formed in... 1994, but named after a project-name for a **Forlorn**-song. Started out as a fun project but caught the attention of German Solistitium Records. The album contains nine originals and four reworked lullabies. The band recorded the demo *Kapitel II* in 2004 and now features Bryntse and Olsson only, plus the style has become less folky and dreamier.

1997 ■ FEBRUARY 93..CD Solistitium...SOL 016

1997 CD - SOL 016

FEED
Rickard Jonsson: v, Jocke Olsson: g, Mathias Hellström: b, Janne Spanedal: d

Stockholm - Formed in 1993. Aggressive crossover, like **Clawfinger** meets **Faith No More**. Jocke is ex-**Mary's Operation** and **Wild Blue Yonder**. Rickard has previously recorded with **Dom Där** and played drums with popsters **Fläskfarmen**, where Mathias was also found. Janne has a past in the death-tango band **Heavy Tangobendi** (sounds like an interesting musical mix). The band has written and recorded material for a second release, but they started looking for a new deal in the end of 1995 and since then nothing has happened.

1995 ■ 25 DOWNINSTREET...CD Lost & Found.....................................LF108CD

1995 CD - LF108CD

FENRIA
Magnus "Necroghoul" Ödling: v/g, Hornaeus Nebelhammer: g,
Joel "Terrorgoat" Viklund: b

Sundsvall - Ödling is also found in **Setherial**, **Sorghegard**, **Blackwinds**, **Diabolical** and **Cavevomit**. Viklund is also found in the latter. Very low-fi (= horrible thin mix) old-school black metal with spoken, screeching growling which sounds like it's been recorded in a garage with a boom box. The album features three tracks only where the title track is 38 minutes long.

2006 □ DE ÅT DÖDEN VIGDA..CDd Hell Attacks......................................HA 013
    333 copies.
2006 ■ DE ÅT DÖDEN VIGDA..LP Hell Attacks......................................HA 013
    500 copies.

2006 LP - HA 013

FERAL
David "Hook" Nilsson: v, Petter "Svarte Petter" Nilsson: g,
Markus "Big Mac" Lindahl: g, Viktor "Valmer" Eriksson: b,
Rickard "Damien" Lundmark: d

Norsjö - **Feral** were formed in 2003. It was initially not intended to be a serious band and started out as **Valmer & Hook**, under which name they recorded the demo *Black Death* in 2004. In 2005 they drafted live guitarist Joel "Johell" Holmström. Valmer now switched from playing drums to handling the bass and new skinsman Damien entered. In 2006 they recorded the demo *Grim Winternight!* and realised it was time to change the name of the band, which is when they became **Feral**. In 2007 the demo *Graverobber* was recorded and the band's musical style became more focused. After the release of *Graverobber* Johell left the band and was replaced by Sebastian Westermark. In 2009 the track *Altar Of Necromancy* was featured on the compilation *Resurrected In Festering Slime* (2009 Soulseller/Iron Fist). Great, heavy death metal in the vein of **Grave**.

2009 MCD - - -

2009 ■ Welcome To The Graveyard ....MCD 5tr private..- -
    Tracks: Once Inside The Tomb/The Deathbog/Welcome To The Graveyard/The Curse Of The Casket/Behead The Crucifix
2011 ■ DRAGGED TO THE ALTAR...CD Ibex Moon..MRI5580

2011 CD - MRI5580

FIELD, FREDDIE

Fredrik "Freddie Field" Feldt: g, Andreas "Andy Clarke" Claesson: b,
Jakob "Jake Samuel" Samuelsson: d/v

Lidingö (Stockholm) - A badly produced recording, although the single was highly acclaimed by some American magazines. The B-side is an instrumental that shows influences of Steve Vai and Eddie Van Halen. Andy was previously in *Yale Bate*. Jake is ex-*Yale Bate*, *Talisman*, *Totem*, *Jekyll And Hyde*, *The Ring* and is now fronting popular melodic rockers *The Poodles*. *Freddie Field* also recorded a great AOR-influenced demo in 1990.

1989 7" - PL 64

1989 ■ Losing In Communication/Drop Dead ....7" Platina ....PL 64

FIERCE CONVICTION

José Gomez-Sanchez: v, Niclas Karlsson: g, Jocke Puuraid: g,
Robert Larsson: b, Martin Tilander: d

Borås - *Fierce Conviction* were formed by Niclas Karlsson after he left *Crystal Eyes* in 1995. José was ex-*Empire Saint* and now does his own thing under the name *Sanchez*. Karlsson is also found in *Zonata* and *Freternia*, while Tilander is in *Freternia*, *Soul Source* and *Crystal Eyes*. In 1999 the band shortened their name to *Conviction* and released the album *Decline/Rebirth* in 1999. See *Conviction* for further information. Great US-style power metal.

1996 ■ Time ....MCD 4tr private .... kftcds 196
       Tracks: Tell Me Who You Are/Crimson Red Rain/In Your Mind/Time
1998 ☐ THE REQUIEM OF A MOURNER ....CD a.b.s .... a.b.s today 206

1996 MCD - kftcds 196

FI5TH REASON

Kristian Andrén: v, Simon Johansson: g, Marco A. Nicosia: g,
Mårten "Marty Marteen" Sandberg: b, Martin Larsson: d

Stockholm - The band was formed by Simon already in 1992 and on the first demo *Stranded*, Thomas Lundin (ex-*Hexenhaus*) provided the vocals. Simon joined *Abstrakt Algebra* in 1994 and put the band on ice. After one album the band split and Simon picked up the pieces, so with Kristian Andrén (ex-*Tad Morose*, later *Memento Mori*, *Bloodbound*, *Wuthering Heights*), Marco (*Hexenhaus*, *Memento Mori*), bassist Oscar Tillman and Martin Larsson he recorded the debut album. Simon has previously been playing with *Memento Mori* and *Memory Garden*. In 1998 the band took a time-out. Simon devoted some time to *Memory Garden* and Kristian recorded an album with Danes *Wuthering Heights*. On the second album Mårten (ex-*Hexenhaus*, now in *Lizzy Borden*) had replaced bass-player Oscar Tillman. The band plays progressive and slightly doom-oriented power-metal in the vein of *Hexenhaus*, *Abstrakt Algebra* or *Psychotic Waltz* and actually describes it as Psychotic metal. The first album was really good, nevertheless the second effort blew it away completely. Both albums were produced by Mike Wead. Today, Simon is playing in Mike Wead's band *Bibleblack*. He has also been playing in *Steel Attack* and *Wolf*.

1997 CD - HDMCD 004

2001 CD - SC 028-2

1997 ■ PSYCHOTIC ....CD Heathendoom .... HDMCD 004
2001 ■ WITHIN OR WITHOUT ....CD Scarlet .... SC 028-2

FIMBULTYR

Christofer Bergqvist: v, Oskari Katainen: g, Niclas Boman: g, Dag Kristoffersson: k,
Fredrik Joelsson: b, Jonas Arnberg: d

Borlänge - Bergqvist and Arnberg are also found in *Hell Patrol*. According to the band's MySpace they are writing material for a new album. Well-played black metal with folkish influences. Formed in 2005 and in 2006 the band released their first demo *Ändlösa frågor*. *Website: www.fimbultyr.nu*

2008 CD - UER 022

2008 ■ GRYENDE TIDEVARV ....CD Unexploded .... UER 022

FINGERSPITZENGEFÜHL

Jesper Skarin: v/b, Mikael Touminen: g, Tomas Bergstrand: g, Anders Bartonek: d

Stockholm - The band was formed in 2000. *Fingerspitzengefühl* ("fingertip feeling" in German, meaning to have great sensitivity) play highly interesting versatile metal drawing influences from anything from *Pantera* to *System Of A Down* to *Alice In Chains* to *Queens Of The Stoneage*. Touminen has also been a member of *General Surgery* and *Nice Idiot*, while Bartonek also recorded with *Forkeyed*. In 2008 they recorded the demo *Pyramids/Express Death*, They changed the name to *Switch Opens* in 2008 and have made more releases under this name.

2004 CD - KOOL CD 0600505

2004 ☐ FINGERSPITZENGEFÜHL ....CD Kooljunk ....KOOL CD 0400105
2006 ■ HAPPY DOOMSDAY ....CD Kooljunk ....KOOL CD 0600505

FIRE

Christer Ankarlid: v, Bo Persson (now Hoflin): g, Yngve Hammervald: g,
Leif Jergefeldt: b, Arne Öhrström: d

Stockholm - *Fire* existed between 1969 and 1972. Considering the song titles the band members seem to love the summer... There were some rumours about this band being *November* under different names, which was not true. It however gives you an idea of their musical direction. Fuzz-oriented hard rock in the vein of the aforementioned band. They also have the song *Nu Är Det Sommar* on the compilation *Festen På Gärdet* (71 Silence).

1971 ■ Sommaren Är Förbi/Sommaren Är Skön ....7" Marilla ....MAS 88 $

1971 7" - MAS 88

FIRE & ICE

Hasse Andersson: v, Örjan Gill: g, Ola Hellström: b, Göran Fagerli: d

Hudiksvall - Great melodic hard rock with prominent guitars and great vocals. After the CDS the band recorded some demos. They were also active as a cover-band. Hasse later joined *Scudiero*, *Fatal Smile* and *Token* and is now fronting prog metal band *Mindsplit*. The band still exists, now called *Fire & Bajs* (Fire & Poop).

1995 ■ One More Try/Right Between The Eyes.............................CDS 2tr Azora ....AZRCDS 0595

1995 CDS - AZRCDS 0595

FIRECRACKER

Tommy Karevik: v, Stefan Lindholm: g, Pontus Larsson: k,
Fredrik Folkare: b, Hasse Worzel: d

Stockholm - *Firecracker* is the brainchild of *Vindictiv* guitarist Stefan. Before *Vindictiv* he was working with keyboardist Larsson and did some recordings. With the addition of Folkare (*Unleashed*, *Scudiers*) and Worzel the rhythm section was complete. The band finally completed the line-up with singer Karlevik from *Seventh Wonder*. The album also features additional keyboards from Henrik Mawe. *Firecracker* is a bit more progressive than *Vindictive*, but should appeal to the same fans. *Born Of Fire* was more or less an unreleased album realised after Lindholm's *Vindictiv* release.

2010 ■ BORN OF FIRE ....CD Escape...ESM 208

2010 CD - ESM 208

FIRESTONE

Mathias Gustaffsson: v, Oskar Cedermalm: g, Andreas Sonderlid: g,
Winfred Kennerknecht: b, Andreas Wiil: d

Örebro - *Firestone* were a great, pretty short-lived heavy and groovy stoner band that only released two MCDs and a split. Formed in 1999 and split in 2005. The debut featured bass player Kristina Johansson, who was replaced by Winfred. Oscar, who was the founder of *Firestone* also started the band *Truckfighters* on the side and where Winfred was also a member. Unfortunately two bands take too much time and one had to go. The two continued with *Truckfighters*.

2002 ■ Stonebeliever ....MCD 4tr Fuzz Production.....................(FIRESTONE 2)
Tracks: Nigel Mansel/Stonebeliever/Kaleidoscope Eyes/Experience '79
2002 □ Mexicon EP ....MCD 5tr Fuzz Production............................ - -
Tracks: Grand Prix/Riot Sensation/Mexicon/Everybody's Got A Hold (On You)/One Take Mamboo/Inside Out
2003 □ FUZZSPLIT OF THE CENTURY (split).............................CD Fuzzorama Records ....FUZZ CD 001
Split with Truckfighters. Tracks: Code To Destroy/Megalomania/Planet Remover/High Ride/Let The Sky Fall
2003 □ FUZZSPLIT OF THE CENTURY (split)...............................LP Fuzzorama Records ....FUZZ LP 001 $
Yellow vinyl.

2002 MCD - (FIRESTONE 2)

FIREWORK

Thomas Åhman: v/g, Lars Nilsson: g, Kent Hedlund: b, Christer Nordlander: d

Sollefteå - *Firework* were formed in 1978, split in 1982 and reformed in 1991. The style on the first 7" is at times similar to early *Thin Lizzy*, while the second is still hard rock but a bit more straight. The line-up on the first recording was Thomas, Christer, Lars Holmlund (g), Mats Flodin (g), and Henry Lampeinen (b). On the follow-up Lars and Mats were replaced by Stefan Edlund. In 1991 the band reformed with the above constellation. Today they survive on playing covers, like so many others. They however have the two originals, *Play The Game* and *Smalltown City*, on the compilation *Promotionmusic '92* (92 Hillson). Christer is also found in the grunge-oriented band *Sunflower*.

1979 7" - CFR-S-7011

1982 7" - PSI 033

1979 ■ Victim To Death/Queen Of Fashion..7" CFR CFR-S-7011
1982 ■ Ohlalala My Baby/Bring Me Love...7" Pang ....PSI 033

FISSION
Andreas "Vintersorg" Hedlund: v/g/k, Benny Hägglund: g/b/d

Skellefteå - *Fission* started out as Benny's brainchild in 2002. He drafted Hedlund of the band *Vintersorg*, with whom Hägglund is playing drums live. A two-track demo was recorded which lead to a deal with Napalm Records who released the debut *Crater* in 2004. *Fission* is a mixed bowl of musical fruit, at times thrashy and at times quite symphonic and melodic with mixed growl and clean vocals. Not bad at all. Very nice clean vocals, but the growl is not of the more exciting type. Hedlund is also in Norwegian death metal band *Borknagar* and has his own bands *Otyg*, *Vintersorg* and *Waterclime*. Hägglund is also in *TME* and Hedlund has also been found in *Havayoth*, *Cosmic Death* and *Cronian*.

2004 ■ CRATER ....CD Napalm .... NPR 150
2008 □ PAIN PARADE ....CD Aphotic Records .... - -

2004 CD - NPR 150

FISTFUNK
Lasse Mårtén: v, Kristian Åkesson: v/scratch, Marcus Klack: g,
Pierre "P-Air" Carnbrand-Lindsjöö: b, Antonio "Julle" Juhlin: k, Joel Uhr: p,
Erik Soukkan: p, Richard Netterman: d

Stockholm - Formed in 1992. Even though the band hates the word "crossover", it's actually a good way to describe them. *Fistfunk* is a hybrid of *Biohazard* and *Snoop Doggy Dogg*, a mix of pure hip-hop and bonehard metal. They are however more hip-hop than *Clawfinger* (with whom Richard is also working). Netterman has also played and recorded with *John Norum*, *Rammstein* and *Plankton*.

1995 ■ System ....MCD 3tr Stockholm Recording........................579 145-2
     Tracks: System (sidestep re-mix)/System (12" version)/Can I Let It Out.
1995 □ TOTALMASSCONFUSION ....CD Stockholm Recording........................527 673-1
1995 □ Bob Your Head ....MCD 5tr Stockholm Recording........................579 785-2
     Tracks: Bob Your Head/Take It From The Top/Blues On Lipovitan/Slapstick Theme (vocal mix)/It's Madness

1995 MCD - 579 145-2

FJELLTRONE
Markus "Fjelltrone" Sjökvist: v/g/b/d

Karlshamn - Dark ambient black/death metal in the vein of *Mysteeris*. Solo project of Markus Sjökvist, brother of Nicklas Sjökvist (*Dampungarna*). Both were also found in the band *Setback*.

1999 ■ SKOGENS ANDE ....CD Dark End....................................DREND 001
2002 □ Vinterriket/Fjelltrone (split) ....7" Neodawn/Dark End.........................NDP 015
     Track: Nattens barn. 500 copies.
2006 □ Trollskog...MCD 5tr Dark End....................................DREND 002
     Tracks: Trollskog/Dödens änglar/Krigets fält/Nattens barn/Han som reiste (Burzum cover)

1999 CD - DREND 001

FLAGELLATED SERAPH
AsO (aka A. Death/Casket): v/g/b/d

Järfälla - Raw black metal in the vein of *Craft* and *Watain*, but quite strange desperate screaming punkish vocals and some quite unusual musical influensed for the genre, ranging from doomy riffs to almost punkish twists. Mixed by Magnus "Devo" Andersson (*Marduk*). AsO is also found in *Putrified* and *Infuneral*, and he also made the artwork.

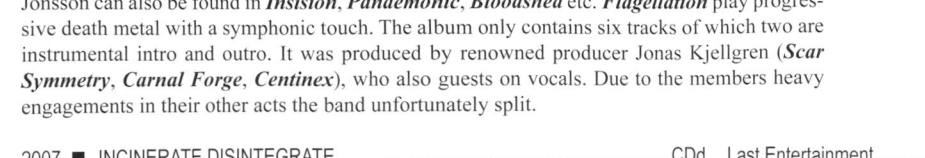

2012 ■ BEYOND SALVATION ....CDd Hellthrasher Productions ....HT 019

2012 CDd - HT 019

FLAGELLATION
Per Lindström: v/b, Teddy Möller: g/v, Daniel Cannerfelt: g, Fredrik Klingwall: k,
Jacob Andersson: b, Marcus Jonsson: d

Stockholm - *Flagellation* were formed in 1997 and recorded their first demo, *Spineless Regression* in 1998. This is a definition of an all-star band indeed with Lindström being ex-*In Grey* and ex-*Machinery*, Möller is also in *Loch Vostock* and *FKÜ*, Cannerfelt is also in *In Grey*, Klingwall in *Loch Vostock*, *Anima Morte* and *Machinery*, Andersson is in *Plague Divine* and Jonsson can also be found in *Insision*, *Pandemonic*, *Bloodshed* etc. *Flagellation* play progressive death metal with a symphonic touch. The album only contains six tracks of which two are instrumental intro and outro. It was produced by renowned producer Jonas Kjellgren (*Scar Symmetry*, *Carnal Forge*, *Centinex*), who also guests on vocals. Due to the members heavy engagements in their other acts the band unfortunately split.

2007 ■ INCINERATE DISINTEGRATE ....CDd Last Entertainment............................LAST 007

2007 CD - LAST 007

FLAGSHIP

Christian Liljegren (aka Rivel): v, Carl Johan Grimmark: g, Linus Kåse: k, Kristofer Eng: b, Mikael Nordström: d

Stockholm - The fact that **Narnia/DivineFire/Modest Attraction** singer Christian is a big fan of progsters **Kansas** is no big secret. Together with **Narnia** keyboard player Linus Kåse he made this clear in the **Flagship** project, formed in 2002, embracing his love for seventies-influenced pomp rock. The album also features a guest solo from former **Kansas** guitarist Kerry Livgren on the track *Ground Zero*, which was also composed by Livgren. A great album.

2005 ■ MAIDEN VOYAGE ....CD Rivel Records RRCD023
2005 ☐ MAIDEN VOYAGE ....CD Metal Heaven.. 00011
2005 ☐ MAIDEN VOYAGE ....CD Stay Gold (Japan)......................... ARTSG-007

2005 CD - RRCD023

FLAME

Åke Sold: g/v, Leif Westergren: k, Erik Arvidsson: b, Bengt Almquist: d

Märsta (Stockholm) - The band was formed in 1979 and were called **Shining** for some years. In 1982 they recorded a single under the name **Flame**, but due to the popularity and similarity of the musical *Fame*, they changed it to **Taroc**. Basic **Purple**-influenced hard rock. A high-quality band, well worth checking out. They dissolved in 1985 after having recorded some demos. Bengt has since worked as a songwriter for some female artists. He is now an airline-pilot and lives in France. Åke has also released a single with the Euro-disco type band **Mostly Men**. Trivia: Bengt went to school together with Ian Haugland (**Europe**) and they were the first in Märsta to play with double bass-drums. Also featured on the *Pangkaka* (82 Pang) compilation.

1982 ■ No Road To Heaven/Lonewolf Song..7" Pang Records ....PSI 053

1982 7" - PSI 053

FLASH

Bengt Sandblom: v/g, Ralf: g, Mackan: b, Mats: d

Göteborg - **Flash** play decent blues/boogie-based melodic hard rock. *Vintermorgon* is a pretty good boogie-style hard rocker quite similar to seventies **Status Quo**, while *Mörkret igen* is more straight-ahead similar to **Ocean** and **Dunder**. Guitars on the first single were handled by Krook. Sandblom is currently in pop/rock band **Bas Edit**.

1979 ☐ Förortsmiljö/Hemlängtan...7" private F-1
1980 ■ Vintermorgon/Mörkret igen...7" Nacksving 45-8

1980 7" - 45-8

FLEGMA

Kalle Metz: v, Jörgen Lindhe: g, Martin Olsson: g, Richard Lion: b, Martin Brorsson: d

Malmö - Formed in 1988. Shortly after the release of the 7" they broke up, but reformed with Kalle and Martin replacing former members Ola Püschel (**Doodles**) and Rother. The initial style was pure hardcore, but the last album shows a more mature band with some serious power metal riffing. Fans of early **Metallica** as well as death metal should lend an ear to this fivesome. One description I overheard was "a crueller version of **Autopsy**". On *Flesh To Dust* Jörgen (ex-**Obscurity** - the mid 80's demo-death-band) was added to the line-up. On the album there is also a cover of **Kiss**' *I Stole Your Love*. **Flegma** has contributed to the **Venom**-tribute *Promoters Of The Third World War* (93 Primitive Art) with the cover *Leave Me In Hell* as well as on the **Metallica**-tribute *Metal Militia* (94 Black Sun) with the track *The Thing That Should Not Be*. Lindhe is today fronting brutal hard rockers **S.K.U.R.K** (aka **S.K.U.R.K 666**), as singer.

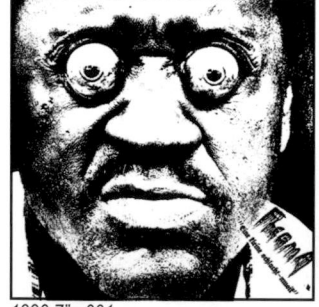

1990 7" - 001

1990 ■ Eine Kleine Schlachtmusik.. 7" 7tr Insane 001
   Tracks: Tune In, Turn On Drop Out/Wasted Life/I'm OK/Fiend Of The State/Lovetrap/Ultra Bizarre/Armageddon. 1150 copies.
1992 ■ BLIND ACCEPTANCE ....CD Black Rose....................................... BRR 001
1994 ☐ FLESH TO DUST...CD Black Rose....................................... BRR 002

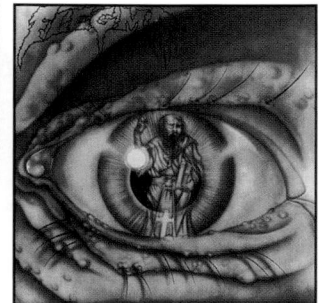

1992 CD - BRR 001

FLESH/THE PETE FLESH DEATHTRIP

Peter "Pete Flesh" Karlsson: v/g/b

Strängnäs - **Flesh** is the brain child of **Maze Of Torment/Deceiver/Thrown** member Peter Karlsson. He took the moniker Pete Flesh in tribute to the late Chuck Schuldiner of US metal band **Death** and the track *Flesh And The Power It Holds*. In 2001 he decided to go solo. The result was **Flesh**. The first two albums were recorded and mixed by Tommy Tägtgren and feature session drums by former **Deceiver**-colleague Magnus "Flingan" Flink. For live shows bass player Chrille Lundin (also **Deceived** and **Thrown**) was used. In 2010 the fourth album *Mortui Vivos Docent* was recorded, now using the drum talents of Andreas Jonsson (**Tyrant, Crypt Of Kerberos**). **Flesh** play old-school death metal in the vein of **Maze Of Torment**. In 2013 Pete returned with a new album, now also under the new name The Pete Flesh Deathtrip. The album features guest spots from Peter (**Tyrant, Crypt Of Kerberos**) and Cecilia Bjärgö.

2005 CD - IRPCD016

2006 CD - ASH 034 CD

2005 ☐	DÖDSÅNGEST	CD	Iron Fist	IRPCD016
2005 ☐	DÖDSÅNGEST	CD	Pulverised	ASH 033 CD
	Different artwork.			
2006 ☐	TEMPLE OF WHORES	LP	Iron Fist	IRPCD020
2006 ■	TEMPLE OF WHORES	CD	Pulverised	ASH 034 CD
2008 ☐	WORSHIP THE SOUL OF DISGUST	CD	Pulverised	ASH 040 CD
	Super jewel box.			
2013 ■	MORTUI VIVOS DOCENT	CD	Pulverised	ASH 093 CD
	As The Pete Flesh Deathtrip.			

2013 CD - ASH 093 CD

FLESHCUT
Pate Lundberg: v, André Nilsson: g, Jimmie "Knudan" Ogefalk: b, Padde Holmgren: d

Malmö - Formed in 2006. In 2007 Goregeous released the band's first five track demo *Machine Driven Crushing* (GORE 006) as a pro-printed CD-R in 100 copies. Martin Schönherr (**Deranged, Splattered Mermaids, RazorRape**) guests on the debut MCD. Right after *Gruesome And Vile* bass player Jarlau Wiahl left the band. *Evil Unfolds* was only supposed to be a demo as CD-R, but Goregeous released it as a black 3" MCD. On this disc guitarist Slurge was out of the band and Wiahl's empty spot had been filled by Jimmie. Padde is also found in grindcore band **DPOS!!!**. *Fleshcut* play old-school death metal.

2011 ■	GRUESOME AND VILE	CD	Goregeous	GORE 014
2011 ☐	Evil Unfolds	3" MCD 5tr	Goregeous	GORE 021
	Tracks: Plutoon Of The Abyss/Ghouls Of The Graveyard/Evil Unfolds/Mourning (Nirvana 2002 cover)/Helvete			

2011 CD - GORE 014

FLINTSTENS MED STANLEY
Ajax Stargazer: g, Billy Svinto: b, Hilding Marshmallow: g, Hempo: d

Skövde - This was a hype that just happened in the beginning of 1995. The band **Black Ingvars** started doing covers of old and new Swedish dansband/easy-listening songs, mixing them with heavy metal classics and suddenly there was a big boom. So when the almighty record-boss Bert Karlsson couldn't sign the founders, **Black Ingvars**, he gathered a bunch of Swedish top musicians and created **FlintStens Med Stanley**. The musicians on the record are actually singer Göran Edman (**Madison, Glory, Malmsteen** etc.), singer/bassist Thomas Vikström (**Candlemass, Stormwind**, solo etc.), singer Mika Korpi (**Cosmic Zoo**), singer Peo Pettersson (**Axia, Leviticus**), guitarist Jan Strandh (**Zanity, Master Massive**), drummer Marco Tapani (**Masquerade**). The project was led by Patrik Tibell (**Trace, T'Bell**). As this was more of a project than a band they were "dead" only a few weeks after the record was released. Drummer Hempo Hildén was only featured on the cover, not on the recording.

1995 MCDp - HRRCDS 001

1995 CD - HRCD 1001

1995 ■	Inatt inatt	MCDp 4tr	Hard Rock Records	HRRCDS 001
	Tracks: Inatt inatt/Hallå, du gamle Indian/Mälarö kyrka/Dagny			
1995 ■	FLINTSTENS MED STANLEY	CD	Hard Rock Records	HRCD 1001

FLOOD
**Alexander "Alex" Nilsson: v/g, Mattias Bergkvist: g,
Patrik Holmström: b, Mattias Lundberg: d**

Ulricehamn - Heavy grunge-oriented hard rock with hints of **Stone Temple Pilots**, but pretty limited vocals, horrible guitar solos and mid-range song material.

1996 ■	Savior	MCD 6tr	private	FDCDS-1096
	Tracks: Fall/Weakness/Mother Sweet/667/River Drown/Saviour			

1996 MCD - FDCDS-1096

FLOWER KINGS, THE
**Hasse Fröberg: v, Roine Stolt: v/g, Tomas Bodin: k/v,
Jonas Reingold: b, Felix Lehrmann: d**

Uppsala - Roine has recorded numerous albums with a big variety of artists and styles, including Åsa Jinder, Zia Lindberg, **Triangulus**, Wennman, **Flumorkestern, Sirius, Pekis** and others. He has also made some albums with his own bands **Kaipa, Fantasia** and **Stolt**. He was later found in all-star international band **Transatlantic**. The album *The Flower King*, actually released under his own name, is a concept album hailing beauty, peace and freedom. Musically it was mostly long flowing pieces of music, but at times a heavy guitar riff flashes by. Definitely not hard rock, but well worth checking out for fans of the more progressive side of hard rock. On the second album **The Flower Kings** project started to take shape and on *Retropolis* it was clear this was a serious band. The style could be compared to a heavier and more progressive version of **Kaipa** with slightly more edge. Even though Hasse Fröberg (ex-**Spellbound, Solid Blue** now also **Hasse Fröberg & Musical Companion**) had been adding vocals on the first albums, it wasn't until on *Stardust We Are* he became a firm member of the band. On *Space Revolver*, which

F

showed a slightly heavier side of the band and now bass player Michael Stolt (ex-*Desperados*/*Fantasia*) had been replaced by ex-*Downtown Clowns*/ *Reingold*/*Sand & Gold*-player Jonas. Hasse Bruniusson, who played on the first albums, was ex-*Zamla Mammas Manna*. The album *The Rainmaker* is an excellent intriguing musical journey. Theatrical symphonic rock, which spans from heavy crunchy riffs to soft swirling keyboards. It also saw the change of drummer from Jaime Salazar (*Midnight Sun, Bad Habit* etc.) to Zoltan Csösz. The band also does a very different version of *Captain Beyond*'s *Raging River Of Fear* on the tribute *Thousand Days Of Yesterdays* (1999 Record Heaven). Roine also released a solo-album entitled *Hypo-dromia* in 1998. *Road Back Home* is a compilation compiled and re-mixed and re-worked by Roine Stolt. On *Unfold The Future*, Bruniusson was only listed as a guest, together with Daniel Gildenlöw (*Pain Of Salvation*) and Ulf Wallander. *Betchawannadancestoopid!!!* is a live improvisation album recorded in New York. No vocals, very jazzy and quite uninteresting to be honest. The subsequent *BrimStoned In Europe* is another instrumental live album, this time featuring Reingold, Bodin, Stolt and drummer Marcus Liliequist. Marcus also plays on the *Harvest Fan Club* and *Carpe Diem* CDs. *Tour Kaputt* was recorded live in Holland 2007 and features Fröberg, Stolt, Bodin, Reingold and guest Pat Mastelotto (*King Crimson, Mr. Mister*). The band has also released several live DVDs such as *Instant Delivery* and *Tour Kaputt*. On *Banks Of Eden* drummer Zoltan Czösz had been replaced by Felix Lehrmann and Hasse Bruniusson was no longer in the line-up.
Website: *www.flowerkings.com*

Flower power!

Year		Title	Format	Label	Catalogue
1994	☐	THE FLOWER KING	CD	Foxtrot	FOXCD 011
1994	☐	THE FLOWER KING	CD	InsideOut America (USA)	IOMA 4013-2
1995	■	BACK IN THE WORLD OF ADVENTURES	CD	Foxtrot	FOXCD 015
1995	☐	BACK IN THE WORLD OF ADVENTURES	CD	InsideOut America (USA)	IOMA 4012-2
1996	■	RETROPOLIS	CD	Foxtrot	FOXCD 016
1996	☐	RETROPOLIS	CD	InsideOut America (USA)	IOMA 4010-2
1996	☐	BACK IN THE WORLD OF ADVENTURES	LP PD	Record Heaven	RHPD 6
1997	☐	STARDUST WE ARE	CD	Foxtrot	FOXCD 018
1997	☐	STARDUST WE ARE	CD	InsideOut	IOMCD 048
1997	☐	STARDUST WE ARE	CD	InsideOut America (USA)	IOMA 4011-2
1998	☐	SCANNING THE GREENHOUSE	CD	Avalon Marquee (Japan)	MICY-1076
		Bonus: Cinema Show			
1998	☐	SCANNING THE GREENHOUSE	CD	Musea	FGBG 4384.AR
1998	☐	SCANNING THE GREENHOUSE	CD	Outer Music (USA)	OM 2008 CD
1998	☐	SCANNING THE GREENHOUSE	CD	Rock Sym (Brazil)	- -
1998	☐	Edition Limitee Quebec 1998	MCD 6tr	IpsoFacto (Canada)	IF 9802
		Tracks: Kite/Piece Of Nizzmo (live)/The Flower King (re)/Duke Of Nuke (live)/Garden Of Dreams Pt 1/Buffalo Man			
1999	☐	FLOWER POWER	2CD	Avalon Marquee (Japan)	MICY-9001/9002
		Bonus: She Carved Me A Wooden Heart/Space Revolver/Jupiter Backwards			
1999	☐	FLOWER POWER	2CD	Foxtrot	FOXCD 020
1999	☐	FLOWER POWER	CD	InsideOut	IOMCD 046
1999	☐	FLOWER POWER	CD	InsideOut America (USA)	IOMA 2003-2
2000	☐	ALIVE ON PLANET EARTH	2CD	Avalon Marquee (Japan)	MAR-00543/4
2000	☐	ALIVE ON PLANET EARTH	2CD	InsideOut	IOMCD 054
2000	☐	ALIVE ON PLANET EARTH	2CD	InsideOut America (USA)	IOMA 2007-2
2000	■	SPACE REVOLVER	CD	InsideOut	IOMCD 062
2000	☐	SPACE REVOLVER	CD	InsideOut America (USA)	IOMA 2014-2
2000	☐	SPACE REVOLVER - SPECIAL EDITION	2CD	New Mellotron	-
2000	☐	FANCLUB CD 2000	CD	Foxtrot	FOX CD 021
2001	☐	THE RAINMAKER	CD	InsideOut	IOMCD 085
2001	☐	THE RAINMAKER	CD	InsideOut America (USA)	IOMA 2027-2
2001	☐	THE RAINMAKER - SPECIAL EDITION	2CDd	InsideOut	IOMLTDCD 085
		Limited edition featuring an extra disc containing bonus-tracks and live video footage.			
2001	☐	THE RAINMAKER	CD	Avalon Marquee (Japan)	MAR 01683
2002	☐	UNFOLD THE FUTURE	2CD	InsideOut	IOMCD 112
2002	☐	UNFOLD THE FUTURE	2CD	InsideOut	IOMCD 112
		Bonus: Too Late For Tomatos. Slipcase.			
2002	☐	THE FAN CLUB CD 2002	CD	Foxtrot	FOX CD 022
2003	☐	LIVE IN NEW YORK: OFFICIAL BOOTLEG	CD	Foxtrot	FOX CD 023
2004	☐	MEET THE FLOWERKINGS – LIVE 2003	2CD	InsideOut	IOMCD 142
2004	☐	MEET THE FLOWERKINGS – LIVE 2003	2CD+2DVD	InsideOut	IOMLTDDVD 005
2004	☐	ADAM & EVE	CD	InsideOut	IOMCD 174
2004	☐	ADAM & EVE	2CD	Avalon Marquee (Japan)	MICP-90017
2005	☐	THE FLOWER KINGS FAN CLUB CD 2004	CD	Foxtrot	FOX CD 024
2004	☐	BETCHAWANNADANCESTOOPID!!!	CD	Foxtrot	FOX CD 025
2005	☐	BRIMSTONED IN EUROPE	CD	Foxtrot	FOX CD 026
2005	☐	HARVEST FAN CLUB CD 2005	CD	Foxtrot	FOX CD 027

1995 CD - FOXCD 015

1996 CD - FOXCD 016

2000 CD - IOMCD 062

2006 2CD - SPV 48072

2006 ■	PARADOX HOTEL	2CD	InsideOut	SPV 48072
2007 ☐	ROAD BACK HOME	2CD	InsideOut	IOMCD 276/SPV 79532
2007 ☐	THE SUM OF NO EVIL	CD	InsideOut	IOMCD 285/SPV 79622
2007 ■	THE SUM OF NO EVIL	2CD	InsideOut	IOMSECD 285/SPV 79620
2008 ☐	CARPE DIEM – LIVE IN USA	CD	Foxtrot	FOX CD 028
2011 ☐	TOUR KAPUTT	2CD	Rheingold Records	RRCD 0006
2012 ☐	BANKS OF EDEN	CD	InsideOut	5052250-5862
2012 ☐	BANKS OF EDEN	2CDd	InsideOut	5052250-5868

Bonus: Fireghosts/Going Up/Illuminati/Lo Lines

2012 ☐	BANKS OF EDEN	2LP + 2CDd	InsideOut	5052250-5861
2013 ☐	DESOLATION ROSE	CD	InsideOut	n/a
2013 ☐	DESOLATION ROSE	LP	InsideOut	n/a

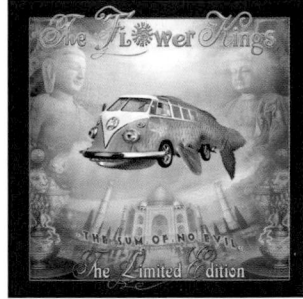

2007 2CD - IOMSECD285/SPV 79620

FOOBAR THE BAND

Jonny Zasella: v, Anders Karlsson: g, Dennis Brandeby: g,
Janneck Larsson: b, Tim Ferm: d

Göteborg - *Foobar The Band* were formed in 2005 by four Göteborg boys, of which two were actually living in the rehearsal room. The debut, *Hellride*, was released in 2007 and featured guitarist Robert Kulka, who was replaced by Brandeby before the second album. Peter Korsgard handled the drums on the debut, but he was later replaced by Ferm. In 2010 the band also released a digital only EP entitled *Grand Theft Audio*. A bit of *Backyard Babies*, a bit of *Danko Jones*, a bit of *Motörhead* and all of it thrown into a stoner rock blender.

2007 ☐	HELLRIDE	CD	Daredevil	DD 041
2009 ■	YOUR FRIEND, MY FRIEND	CDd	Reside Records	RR 004

2009 CDd - RR 004

FOR YOU (4U)

Elin Melgareijo: v, Christian Selan: g, Eric Jonasson: k,
Daniel Bergenbrandt: b, Fredrik Lindholm: d

Norrköping - The band was formed 1988. Fredrik was also found in the band *Thinker*. High-class melodic hard rock, influenced by bands like *Toto* and *Heart*. Good female vocals. After the single, Elin was replaced by Jens Axnér.

1990 ■	I Won´t Go Back/Tell Me	7"	Jet Set	- -

1990 7" - - -

FORCEFEED

Lawrence Mackrory: v, Dennis Olsson: g, Ronnie Nyman: g,
Ted Mattson: b, Simon Wettervik: d

Uppsala - The band was formed in 1995 by Lawrence, Dennis and Simon. Lawrence is now found in *FKÜ*, *Darkane* and *Enemy Is Us* and sang on first version of *Andromeda*'s debut. The band recorded a new demo in 1999 with the tracks *Shed The Clouds* and *Tonight*. Ronnie was later replaced by Peter Waites. In 2002 the band changed their name to *Seethings* and Ted was also out of the band. Produced by Daniel Bergstrand. *Forcefeed* played great, aggressive, brutal metal in the vein of *Deftones* and early *Korn* with a touch of *Tool*.

1998 ■	Forcefeed	MCD 3tr	Nature Always Wins	NAWCD 004

Tracks: Soil/In Tongues/Pressure

1998 MCD - NAWCD 004

FOREST

Christer Olsson: v, Terje Hjortander: g, Lars Monat: g,
Hans Bergqvist: b, Robert Lendahl: d

Göteborg - Another typical 80's band mixing pop harmonies, Swedish lyrics and hard rock. Similar to *Snowstorm*. Terje is ex-*Quinzy*. After the second single the band changed their name to *Heaven Next*, but split when Terje went to join *Leviticus*. He later joined the excellent band *The Jet Circus*.

1980 ☐	Nattens Kung/Lång Väg	7"	private	FRTS 101
1981 ■	Våga Säga Nej/Här Igen	7"	Mercury	6016 038

1981 7" - 6016 038

FOREST OF SHADOWS

Niclas Frohagen: v/g/k, Micce Andersson: g/b/k/d

Stockholm - *Forest Of Shadows* were formed in 1997 by Niclas Frohagen, initially intended to be a solo-project. However, when finding guitarist/bassist/keyboardist/violinist Micce Andersson in 1998 thoughts of a full band started growing and also became a reality. The two were however

the only firm ,consistent members, at least until after the debut MCD. Before this, the band had recorded five demos. After the MCD, Frohagen returned to the solo-format. The debut is slow, doom-oriented ambient metal with growling or death-oriented vocals, while the full album has clean vocals and a less distorted sound. Frohagen is also found in *Ningizzia* and *Shubend*. The band can also be found on the compilations *Conquest For The Empire* (2002 Rage Of Achilles) and *December Songs – A Tribute To Katatonia* (2007 Northern Silence).
Website: www.forestofshadows.com/

2001 MCD - ILIAD 017

2001 ■	When Dreams Turn To Dust	MCD 3tr	Rage Of Achilles	ILIAD 017
	Tracks: Eternal Autumn/Wish/Of Sorrow Blue			
2004 ☐	DEPARTURE	CD	Firedoom	FDOOM 002
2004 ☐	DEPARTURE	CD	CD-Maximum (Russia)	0605-2309
2005 ☐	When Dreams Turn To Dust	MCDd 5tr	Firedoom	FDOOM 009
	Tracks: Eternal Autumn/Wish/Of Sorrow Blue/Under The Dying Sun/The Silent Cry			
2007 ☐	SIX WAVES OF WOE	CD	Firedoom	FDOOM 022

FORKEYED
Björn Wahlström: v, Love Florgård: g, Andreas Åkerlund: b, Anders Bartonek: d

Sollentuna/Stockholm - The band started in 1993/94 under the name *Clench* (not to be confused with *Clench* from Enköping). The initial line-up featured Andreas Åkerlund (b), Björn Wahlström (g), Felix Reinhard (v) and Anders Bartonek (d). A couple of demos were recorded before the band changed their name to *Forkeyed* in 1995 and the MCD was recorded. In 1996 Reinhardt left the band. Now Wahlström took over the vocals and Florgård entered as guitarist. The band emigrated to Berlin in 1997, but split in the end of that year. Anders is also found in *Fingerspitzengefühl*, now *Switch Opens*. *Forkeyed* play quite wacky rap funk metal, like a mix between *24/7 Spys*, *Scatterbrain*, *Primus* and *Fistfunk*.

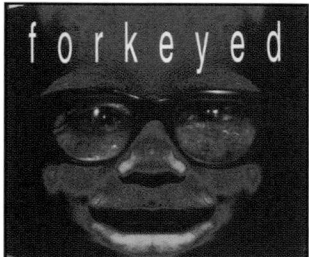

1995 MCD - FECDS 01

1995 ■	Forkeyed	MCD 6tr	private	FECDS 01
	Tracks: Land Of Peanuts/Monkey/Collecting The Cream/Magic Earmuffs/Leaking Functions/Cancelling My Strategy			

FORSAKEN, THE
Anders Sjöholm: v, Patrik Persson: g, Stefan Holm: g,
Michael Håkansson: b, Nicke Grabowski: d

Landskrona - Formed in 1997 as *Septic Breed*. The first demo was entitled *Patterns Of Delusive Design* and after this they found former *Omnious*/*Massgrav*-singer Anders and bassist Michael (*Evergrey*, *Engel*, *Mortum* etc). Recorded by Tommy Tägtgren. *Arts Of Desolation* was recorded at Studio Abyss, also by Tägtgren. Mikael left the band in 2002 to concentrate on *Evergrey* and he later joined *Engel*. Death metal influenced by Swedish colleagues like *At The Gates*, *Grave* and *Hypocrisy*. After some years of silence the band returned in 2010, now featuring guitarist Calle Fäldt (*Deranged*, *Feared Creation*) replacing Stefan Holm. The band returned with the album *Beyond Redemption*, showing the band was still able to deliver top-notch death metal in the vein of the old stuff.
Website: www.theforsaken.net

2001 CD - 77318 2

2002 CD - 77418 2

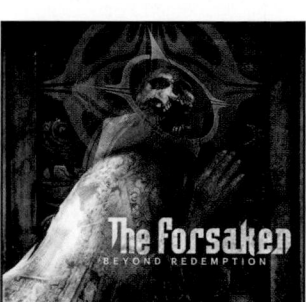

2012 CD - MAS CD 0767

2001 ■	MANIFEST OF HATE	CD	Century Media	77318 2
2001 ☐	MANIFEST OF HATE	CD	Century Media (USA)	8018 2
2001 ☐	MANIFEST OF HATE	CD	King Records (Japan)	KICP 822
	Bonus: Project: The New Breed 666			
2002 ■	ARTS OF DESOLATION	CD	Century Media	77418 2
2002 ☐	ARTS OF DESOLATION	CD	Century Media (USA)	8118-2
	Bonus: Human Prey			
2002 ☐	ARTS OF DESOLATION	CD	King Records (Japan)	KICP 886
	Bonus: Human Prey/Creeping Death (Metallica cover)			
2003 ☐	TRACES OF THE PAST	CD	Century Media	77518-2
	Bonus: Creeping Death (Metallica cover)/Spirit In Black (Slayer cover)/You'll Never See (Grave cover)/Project: The New Breed 666			
2004 ☐	TRACES OF THE PAST	CD	King Records (Japan)	KICP-984
	Bonus: Shredding My Skin/Counteract The Dead			
2012 ■	BEYOND REDEMPTION	CD	Massacre Records	MAS CD 0767

FORTUNA
Jörgen Westerberg: v, Jan Minolf: g, Mikael (Bennich) Pergel: k,
Håkan Stolt: b, Thomas Lundeskog: d

Stockholm - Really good melodic hard rock that lacks a bit from weak vocals.

1988 7" - MZRC-7

1988 ■	Key To My Heart/You Took Me By Surprise	7"	Montezuma Recording	MZRC-7 $

FORTUNE

**Hans Dimberg: v, Magnus Olsson: g, Jan Johannesson: k,
Magnus Pettersson: b, Claes Magnusson: d**

Jönköping - Formed in 1983, split in 1993. Quite mellow melodic rock with hints of *Saga*. The single features high-quality AOR-ballads, with some distorted guitars though. The LP shows a slightly heavier side, still within the AOR genre. Dimberg, Olsson and Magnusson later reappeared in the high class AOR band *Blind Alley*.

1989 ☐ Land Of Lounge Lizards/Fight It	7"	MTR	MTR 1002
1990 ■ TURNING POINT	LP	MTR	MTR 2001

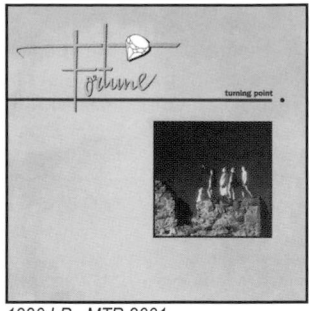
1990 LP - MTR 2001

FORTUNE

**Benny Söderberg: v, Henrik Bergqvist: g, Emil Fredholm: g,
Janne Lund: b, Sebastian Sippola: d**

Stockholm - The first *Fortune* album shows a melodic hard rock band at times reminiscent of *Madison* but lacking their quality. The second album was a slight improvement. Emil joined before the third album, where original drummer Thomas Hauk was replaced by Sebastian. If this is the reason I don't know, but it shows a whole new and improved band producing a bunch of great, well written, melodic hard rockers. Benny's voice shows traces of Göran Edman, who actually sings back-up on the latest album. After the band split Benny formed his own band *Clockwise*, Henrik and Sebastian recorded with *Four Sticks*, Sebastian has also recorded with *Southfork* and *Grand Magus*, and Janne with *Sabbtail*. Emil and Sippola have recorded several albums with the instrumental band *Plankton*, while Henrik is found in *The Poodles*.

1992 CD - DINCD 5

1992 ■ MAKING GOLD	CD	Dino	DINCD 5
1992 ☐ MAKING GOLD	CD	Zero (Japan)	XRCN-1043
1992 ☐ Life Goes On/Eyes Of Ice/Mindreader	CDS 3tr	Dino	DINCSG 5-1
1992 ☐ Life Goes On/Eyes Of Ice	7"	Dino	DINSG 5-1
1994 ☐ CALLING SPIRITS	CD	Zero (Japan)	XRCN-1115
1995 ■ LORD OF FLIES	CD	Zero (Japan)	XRCN 1245
1996 ☐ CALLING SPIRITS	CD	Empire	ERCD 1019
New artwork.			
1996 ☐ LORD OF FLIES	CD	Empire	ERCD 1024
Bonus: Intoxication			

Unofficial release:
1998 ☐ SOLDIERS OF FORTUNE	CD	- -	FOJP-52194
Recorded 21/5-94 live in Osaka.			

1995 CD - XRCN 1245

1996 CD - ERCD 1019

FOUR STICKS

**Stefan "John Stefan" Berggren: v, Henrik Bergquist: g,
Tomas Thorberg: b, Sebastian Sippola: d**

Stockholm - Outstanding 70s meets 90s melodic, yet riff-oriented hard rock. Some funky overtones. The name came from the old *Led Zeppelin* song. Stefan has a strong hint of David Coverdale, which might be one of the reasons why he was later fronting *Company Of Snakes*. Stefan and Thomas are also members of *Snakes In Paradise*, while Henrik and Sebastian are ex-*Fortune*. Sebastian was later in *Southfork* and *Grand Magus* and today he and Thorberg are found in instrumental band *Plankton*. Henrik is today found in melodic rockers *The Poodles*. The album was produced by Pontus Norgren (*Humanimal*/*Talisman*/*The Poodles*/*Hammerfall*) and it is a very pricy and sought after item today.

1997 ■ ELECTRIC CELEBRATION	CD	private	FSCD 9703	$$

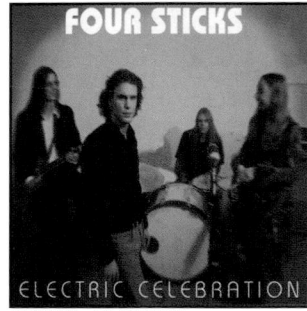
1997 CD - FSCD 9703

FOUREVER

Mia Moilanen: v/g/b, Majja Persson: b, Nina Moilanen: d

Olofström - *Fourever* were formed in 2000 as a four-piece, hence the name, initially featuring singer Matilda Persson and bassist Malin Karlsson. In 2006 they recorded their first demo, but later the same year singer Matilda left and Mia took over the vocals, making the band a trio. Later the same year, the demo *New Era* was released as a pro-printed CDR. The band played shows in Finland, the Czech Republic, Holland and even Egypt. In 2008 Malin Karlsson left the band and was replaced by Lisa Bouvin, but after a year she left and was replaced by seventeen year old Maja Persson. Since the recording of the album had already begun, Mia plays both bass and guitar. The band plays a variety of metal, ranging from *Iron Maiden* style plodding, to some doomy stuff to straight-ahead sing-along *Kiss* style anthems. A great band, and a great live-act.
Website: www.fourever.com

2012 ■ SOLITARIUM	CD	Fastball	FB11C899

2012 CD - FB11C899

FRAISE

Ola Hedman: v, Christian Doyle: g, Svante Widerström: b, Patrik Fransson: d

Alingsås - The band was formed by drummer Fransson, initially as a studio project beside his original band *Velvet Crash* in 2003. When *Velvet Crash* was put on ice later the same year the first *Fraise* album was recorded and ready for release, which happened in February 2004. Guitarist Anders Karlsson and bass player Simon Lindholm (*Fatal Tabasco*, *Mellowdrome*) now left the band and their replacements were Christian Doyle and *Arbogast*/*Fatal Tabasco* bassist Svante Widerström. The band now started working on the follow-up, but when they were about to enter the studio, singer Jesper Max decided to leave. Several auditions later they found Ola Hedman. In 2009 the work on a new album commenced. However Doyle now left because of a muscle problem and Widerström decided to devote all his time to *Arbogast*. As the band had also gone for a heavier and more brutal sound, keyboard player Håkan Ivarsson got the boot. With only Ola and Patrik left in the band new members were required. Guitarist Gunnar Hård af Segerstad (*Disdain*) was drafted and the bass was taken care of by temporary replacement André Westerberg. The band's third release was planned to be released in 2012. *Fraise* play high-class power metal, at times sounding like a mix of *Savatage* and *Nocturnal Rites*.

2004 CD - PF-003

2007 CD - PF 004

2004 ■ HELLCORNIA	....	CD	private	PF-003
2007 ■ A NEW BEGINNING	....	CD	private	PF-004

FRAME

Robert Westin: v, Kristian Kallio: g, Christian Svensson: b, Andreas Ragnarsson: d

Mölndal - The band was formed in 1997 by Kristian, Robert and Andreas. They released their first demo-album *Framing Our Audience* in 1998 and the demo-single *A Sonic Sensation* in 2000. Christian was added to the line-up in 2001. *Frame* play rough-edged heavy rock, similar to Finnish colleagues *Peer Günt*, but with a slightly stoner-oriented touch. Great phat ass riffing, indeed!
Website: www.kickass.at/frame

2002 MCD - PB 919

2002 ■ A Loco Motive	....	MCD 5tr	Perpetual Burn	PB 919

Tracks: Hell And Back/Wrong Or Right/Whatever Blues/Place To Call Home/Sonic Wall

FREAK KITCHEN

Mattias "Ia" Eklundh: v/g, Christer Örtefors: b, Björn Fryklund: d

Göteborg - *Freak Kitchen*'s debut was one of the most interesting releases of '94, with its dead heavy yet melodic power hard rock. Mattias is also one helluva guitar-player, with hints of Steve Vai... on acid. Early on he lent a helping hand to several recording bands such as *Croming Rose*, *Pagan*, *Tornado Soup*, *Road Ratt* etc. Mattias recorded an album with the band *Frozen Eyes* in 1988. They split when he was offered to join Danes *Fate*. He recorded the album *Scratch And Sniff* and made several tours before he quit to form his own band. Mattias called old *Frozen Eyes*-drummer Joakim Sjöberg who was at the time working with *Jethro Tull* drummer Mark Craney in the USA. He went home, they found Christian Grönlund (ex-*Lazy Bones*) and in 1992 *Freak Kitchen* was a reality (name inspired by Mattias' idol Frank Zappa). They received the award of *Best hard rock band of 1994* at the Zeppelin Awards, for the debut *Appetizer*. *Spanking Hour* continued in the same hard hitting, yet melodic, tongue in cheek kinda way, while the self-titled *Freak Kitchen* showed quite a different side of the band. On this album they decided to explore more melodic and quirky pop-rock-oriented rhythms, still quite heavy though. The instrumentation was a bit different, adding banjo, accordion etc to the music. On *Dead Soul Men* they however returned to heaviness with killer-tracks like *Shithead* and *Ugly Side Of Me*. In 2000 the band released a digital album entitled *Junk Tooth*, which was a collection of unreleased tracks. The fans could download one new track each week in mp3-format and there was an artwork competition (and I made the winning cover!). It contains classics like *Excuse me, I Am Swedish* and *The Man Who Taught His Asshole To Play The Flute*. A must for die-hard Freak-fans. Mattias is furthermore guesting on albums by *Locomotive Breath*, *Evergrey*, *Soilwork*, *Mister Kite*, *Chris Catena*, *Urbandux* etc. In 1999 Mattias also released his first guitar solo-album entitled *Freak Guitar*, released on Steve Vai's label Favoured Nations in 2002. In November 2000 Christian and Joakim both decided to leave Mattias stranded. Those of you who thought this would kill the band are wrong. Mattias went on a quest and found drummer extraordinaire Björn Fryklund.

Organic freaky dead soul men on the move.

1994 CDS - TSCDS 942

1996 CD - TSCD 941962

The bass was taken over by a newcomer in the bass-world, namely Christer Örtefors, former singer of *Road Ratt*. After having witnessed the new line-up live a first time, one can only establish the fact that *Freak Kitchen*, no disrespect to the former members, have never been better and more vital. They kill with a smile! This shows on the live-track on the CD for my first encyclopaedia book, the first official track by the new line-up. Fryklund also plays on the solo-project by former *Hammerfall*-guitarist Stefan Elmgren, *Full Strike*. Material for a live album, was recorded at the 2001 Sweden Rock Festival and the French Tour of the same year. This has however not yet been released. The band's fifth official album was released in October 2002. Mattias has also recorded a very quirky, non-guitar, solo-effort entitled *Sensually Primitive*, under the name *Mr. Libido*. Far from the heavy style of *Freak Kitchen*, but still quite fun. In 2004 Mattias released his second guitar album *The Road Less Travelled*. In 2007 he also also appeared in the band *Art Metal*. Örtefors also plays guitar and sings in his side-project *Eaglestrike*. 2013 will see the release of the new Freak Kitchen album *Cooking With Pagans*, where Mattias plays with a comb and his son's birthday balloons. Weird, wicked and highly intriguing music mixed with simple, catchy melodies and lyrics that will make you think. Also a killer live act.
Website: www.freakkitchen.com

Aaaaaaaa: Freak out!!

Year		Title	Format	Label	Catalogue
1994	☐	APPETIZER	CD	Thunderstruck	TSCD 941
1994	■	Raw	CDS 1tr	Thunderstruck	TSCDS 942
1994	☐	APPETIZER	CD	Victor (Japan)	VICP-5463
1996	■	SPANKING HOUR	CD	Thunderstruck	TSCD 941962
1996	☐	SPANKING HOUR	CD	Victor (Japan)	VICP-5762
1997	☐	SPANKING HOUR	CD	Seoul (South Korea)	SRCD 2350
1998	■	FREAK KITCHEN	CD	Thunderstruck	TSP 2162982
1998	☐	FREAK KITCHEN	CD	Victor (Japan)	VICP 60405
		Bonus: Also Sprach Catachea			
1998	☐	FREAK KITCHEN	CD	Favored Nations (USA)	FN 2210-2
		Bonus: Also Sprach Catachea			
1999	☐	FREAK KITCHEN	CD	Seoul (South Korea)	SRCD 2464
2000	☐	DEAD SOUL MEN	CD	Thunderstruck	TSP 4440072
2000	☐	DEAD SOUL MEN	CD	Victor (Japan)	VICP-61070
2000	☐	DEAD SOUL MEN	CD	Magnum (Taiwan)	MVP 61070
2001	☐	Compilation Promo	MCDp65tr	Nothing To Say (France)	Promo 015
		Tracks: Gun God/Walls Of Stupidity/See You In Pittsburg/My New Haircut/Apparatus/Jerk			
2001	☐	APPETIZER	CD	Nothing To Say (France)	NTS 3068722
2001	☐	SPANKING HOUR	CD	Nothing To Say (France)	NTS 3068732
2001	☐	FREAK KITCHEN	CD	Nothing To Say (France)	NTS 3068742
2001	☐	DEAD SOUL MEN	CD	Nothing To Say (France)	NTS 3068752
2001	☐	MOVE	CD	Nothing To Say (France)	NTS 3079292
2001	☐	MOVE	CD	Thunderstruck	TSP 00644132
2002	☐	MOVE	CD	Victor (Japan)	VICP-62064
2002	☐	MOVE	CD	Magnum (Taiwan)	MVP 62064
2002	☐	Vaseline Business/Vibrato Masseur Samba From Hell	CDS 2tr	Nothing To Say (France)	NTS 3080415
		2500 copies. Also released as a special French tour-package together with Move.			
2002	■	Nobody's Laughing/Move (promo medley)/video	CDSp 2tr	Nothing To Say (France)	NTS 3080425
2005	☐	ORGANIC	CD+DVD	Thunderstruck	TSP 982892 8
		The first 1000 copies only with DVD containing live + promo videos.			
2005	☐	ORGANIC	CD+DVD	Victor (Japan)	VICP-63101
		The first 1000 copies only with DVD.			
2005	☐	ORGANIC	CD	Thunderstruck	TSP 982892 8
2005	☐	ORGANIC	CD	Replica (France)	RPL 004
2005	☐	APPETIZER	CD	Replica (France)	RPL 022
2005	☐	FREAK KITCHEN	CD	Replica (France)	RPL 024
2005	☐	DEAD SOUL MEN	CD	Replica (France)	RPL 025
2005	☐	MOVE	CD	Replica (France)	RPL 026
2009	■	LAND OF THE FREAKS	CD	Thunderstruck	TSP 51091208
2009	☐	LAND OF THE FREAKS	CD	Roadrunner (France)	RR 7796-2
2013	☐	COOKING WITH PAGANS	CD	Thunderstruck	n/a

1996 CD - TSP 2162982

2002 CDS - NTS 3080425

2009 CD - TSP 51091208

FRED'S FUEL
Göran Böwing: v, Fredrik Heghammar: g, Jonas Lembke: b, Jonas Heghammar: d
Stockholm - Today *Fred's Fuel* is a seven-piece funk and soul band, but things used to be different… The band was formed in 1990 and when the CD single was recorded the band had a heavier edge, with a strong touch of *Black Crowes* meets *Hendrix*. May not be metal, but definitely hard rock. In 1995 they released the EP *Snow Clean Fleet Magic*, which was funk and in 2000, the EP *Bring Out Da Boost*, which was total soul/funk.

1990	■	Castle Of Dreams/Right Through	CDS	private	FFCDS-004

1990 CDS - FFCDS-004

FREDRIK THORDENDAL'S SPECIAL DEFECTS

Fredrik Thordendal: v/g/b/k

Umeå - This is definitely music for people with a steel-reinforced nervous system. At times, it's in the vein of Fredrik's original band *Meshuggah*, but with lots of weird ingredients, such as primal screams, spaced-out sounds, spoken voices and lots of other oddities. Fredrick, born February 11, 1970, has also produced bands like *Emotion*, *Blacksmith* etc., plus guested on recordings by *Blender*, *Mats/Morgan*, *XXX Atomic Toejam*, *Memorandum* and Mattias Ia Eklundh's third *Freak Guitar* CD. Other musicians appearing on the album are for example: drummer Morgan Ågren, keyboardist Mats Öberg, singer Tomas Haake and bassist Jerry Ericsson. On the first version of the album the 29 musical pieces are not divided into separate tracks, but as one 40 minute track. This was however changed on the *Version 3.33*, which was also re-mastered.

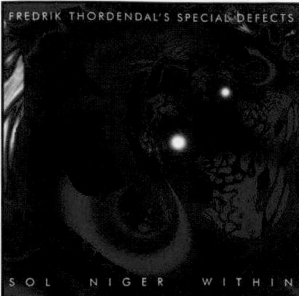

1997 CD - NB 271 2

1997 ■	SOL NIGER WITHIN	CD	Nuclear Blast	NB 271 2
1997 ☐	SOL NIGER WITHIN	CD	UAE	UAE DISC 4
1997 ☐	SOL NIGER WITHIN	CD	Avalon Marquee (Japan)	MICY-1001
	Bonus: Missing Time			
1999 ■	SOL NIGER WITHIN VERSION 3.33	CD	Relapse Records	RR 6417

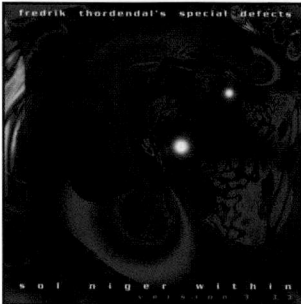

1999 CD - RR 6417

FREEDOM BLEEDER

Henrik Renström: v, Johan Haag: g, Gustav Grusell: b, Peter Hedberg: d

Uppsala - Heavy stoner rock in the vein of *Spiritual Beggars* with a touch of *Monster Magnet*. Driving and groovy, but not as riff-oriented as *Beggars*. The singer is at time reminiscent of John Bush (*Armoured Saint/Anthrax*). A very promising act! The band was formed in 1995 by Renström, Grusell and Haag with the intention to play heavy rock in the vein of *Kyuss* and *Monster Magnet*. The band soon recorded a demo, featuring drummer Kim Norberg. After a while Kim was replaced by Johan Hedman, who was soon replaced by Andreas Wiil (*Firestone*). In 1999 the band was picked up by UK label Yperano for two albums, but the band left the label in 2001 before releasing anything. In the fall of 1999 drummer Hedberg replaced Wiil. The band started recording their debut album in 2001, but it wasn't released until 2005. The band is also found on a couple of compilations. *Freerider* can be found on *Fistfull Of Freebird* (1998 Freebird Records), *A Million Times* can be found on *Molten Universe Volume One* (1999 MU), *Ghouls Night Out* can be found on *Graven Images – A Tribute to The Misfits* (2000 Freebird) and *Breathing* can be found on *Molten Universe Vol 2* (2001 Molten Universe).

1997 7" - FRV 974

1997 ■	Freedom Bleeder/Mugwumps (split)	7"	Supercharger Recordings	SCR 666
	Split with Mugwumps. Tracks: Third Day/Frazzle			
2000 ☐	Breathing/Redemption Song/Away From The Sun	MCD 3tr	Molten Universe	MOLTEN 010
	500 copies.			
2005 ☐	10 OUT OF 10	CD	Freebird	FRC 0505

FREEWAY

Thomas Englund: g/v, Roger Helj: g/v, Tomas Westerlund: b/v, Ricard Andersson: d

Avesta - *Status Quo*-inspired boogie hard rock of mid-class.

| 1985 ■ | Looking For A Way/Soul On Fire | 7" | Aktiv Musik Productions | S 011 |

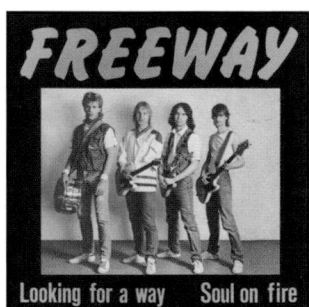

1985 7" - S 011

FREEVIL

Mique Flesh: v/d, Tomas Andersson: g, Roger Blomberg: b

Linköping - Fast and furious, but highly accomplished death metal with screeching vocals. Former *Denata* members Tomas Andersson and Roger Blomberg teamed up with *Seance/Witchery/Satanic Slaughter* singer/drummer Mique Flesh to form this evil trio. Session drums have also been played by Fredrik Andersson (*Marduk*, *Allegiance*, *Triumphator*).

| 2007 ■ | FREEVIL BURNING | CDd | Frozen North | AMG 63632 |
| 2009 ☐ | FREEVIL BURNING | CDd | Nastified productions | NSP 666-4 |

2007 CDd - AMG 63632

FREKVENS

**Peter Danielsson: v, Tapio Flink: g, Tony Lindberg: g,
Raimo Flink: b, Mikael Wängkvist: d**

Alingsås - *Frekvens* were formed in 1979 from the local bands *Ozborn* and *Nattfrost*. They were influenced by bands like *Thin Lizzy* and did some gigs, but broke up not long after the single. *Revolver* is great seventies sounding melodic hard rock, like a mix of *Wildmarken* and *Neon Rose*, while *Respekt* is a bit more funky. Well worth checking out. The band made a re-union show in 2012, now with guitarist Henrik Claesson replacing Tapio.

| 1981 ● | Revolver/Respekt | 7" | Troll-music | TROLL 20 | $ |
| | *500 copies* | | | |

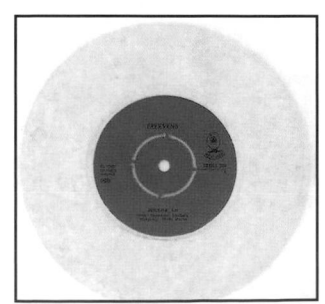

1981 7" - TROLL 20

FRENZY

Lisa Svanström: v/k, Johan Jansson: g, Andreas Brattlund-Klein: g/b,
Mattias Kindberg: b, Ronnie Eriksson: d

Kristinehamn - Frenzy were formed in 1986. The recording of the single was a school project for young entrepreneurship, and they drafted Lisa just for the single, as they needed a good singer. The band only lasted a year and broke up due to personal differences. Johan continued with his band *Lucy*, while Andreas and Mattias formed the band *Big Kick*. The A-side is a pretty good melodic rocker with nice guitar-playing, and OK vocals. The B-side is a pretty wimpy ballad.

1987 7" - FM 001

1987 ■	Point Of No Return/I Don't Wanna Lose You	7"	private	FM 001
	300 copies.			

FREQUENCY

Rick Altzi: v, Linus Wikström: g, Tobias Birgersson: g,
Mats Halldin: b, Daniel Hannedahl: d

2006 CD - SC 117-2

Varberg - Formed in 2002 by former *Lothlorien* members Wikström, Birgersson and Hannedahl. The trio was completed by singer Glenn Laurén and bass player Mats Halldin. In 2003 they recorded the first demo *Disengage Powers*, where tracks also landed on the compilations *Metal Ostenation Vol. 5* and *DEMOlition Vol 1*. The band's 2004 studio session *Oblivion/Time* resulted in a deal with Italian label Scarlet Records and the debut *When Dream And Fate Collide*. After the debut album Laurén was replaced by Rick Altzi (*Sanity*/*At Vance*/*Thunderstone*). *Frequency* play melodic power metal in the vein of colleagues *Dreamland*.

2008 CD - SC 152-2

2006 ■	WHEN DREAM AND FATE COLLIDE	CD	Scarlet	SC 117-2
2006 □	WHEN DREAM AND FATE COLLIDE	CD	King Records (Japan)	KICP-1168
	Bonus: Oblivion/Time (demo)			
2008 ■	COMPASSION DENIED	CD	Scarlet	SC 152-2

FRETERNIA

Pasi Humppi: v, Tomas Wäppling: g, Tommie Johansson: k,
Peter Wiberg: b, Martin Tilander: d

2000 CD - LNP 013

2000 CD - LNP 019

Borås - Freternia were formed in 1998. The line-up on the band's first demo-CDR, *The Blood Of Mortals,* featured Wäppling (v), Patrik Lund (g), Bo Pettersson (g), Wiberg (b) and Svantesson (d). After this, Johansson was recruited. In 1999 Wiberg and Pettersson left. Second guitarist Mikael Bakajek was recruited and Wäppling took over the bass. They recorded the demo *Somewhere In Nowhere* which lead to a deal with Loud 'N Proud and the release of *Warchants And Fairytales*. Shortly after the recording and before the release, Patrik Lund (now von Porat) left and was replaced by Andreas Helander. Loud 'N Proud folded, but the band recorded a new demo in 2001. Now Helander was out and Wäppling took over the guitar, while drummer Stefan Svensson was replaced by Tilander (*Fierce Conviction, Crystal Eyes, Soul Source*). The band was signed by Spanish Arise Records and *A Nightmare Story* was recorded. Traditional power metal with that German touch. Svantesson is now found in *Crystal Eyes* while Humppi and Wiberg are found in *Ironware*. Pettersson and Lund (von Porat) are also found in *Cremonic*. After the second album guitarist Niclas Karlsson (*Zonata, Crystal Eyes, Fierce Conviction*) was added.
Website: www.freternia.com

2002 CD - ARISE 036

2000 ■	WARCHANTS AND FAIRYTALES	CD	Loud N' Proud	LNP 013
2000 ■	Swedish Metal Triumphators Vol 1 (split)	CD	Loud N' Proud	LNP 019
	Split with Persuader. Tracks: The Worst Of Enemies/Guardians Of The Night/Two Friends In Enemyland (demo)/Guardians Of The Night (demo)			
2002 ■	A NIGHTMARE STORY	CD	Arise	ARISE 036
2002 □	A NIGHTMARE STORY	CD	Sail Production (Korea)	SPCD 0020
	Bonus: Grimbor The Great (demo version)			

FRETLESS

Patrik Carlsson: v/g, Dennis Forsberg: b, Reine Dahlström: d

Göteborg - Fretless were formed in 2009 by former *Aquila* guitarist Patric Carlsson. The debut featured Patrik, bassist Dennis Forsberg and drummer Birger Löfman (*Biscaya, Destiny*). Classic melodic metal in the vein of *Saxon*, *Accept* and a touch of *Running Wild*, with the crude vocals being the Achilles heel. Good song material and well played. In July 2011 Löfman left the band. The second release features Adde Larsson on drums, but at the time of the release the band had found a permanent replacement in Reine Dahlström. Löfman joined *Motvind* in 2012.
Website: www.fretless.se

2011 CD - DRR003

2011 ■	LOCAL HEROES	CD	Dusty Road Records	DRR003
2012 □	Ride/Stand & Deliver	CDS	E.L.T Records	ELTCD 004

FROM BEHIND

Nicky Moore: v, Manny Charlton: g, Mikael Fässberg: g, Fredrik Borg: g, Andreas Grufstedt: b, Carl Michael Hildesjö: d

Malmö/UK/US - *From Behind* started out as a combination of two bands with former *Samson/ Hackensack/Mammoth* singer Nicky Moore as front man. The band initially featured *Locomotive Breath* members: Janne Stark (g), Mattias Osbäck (v) and Ted Wernersson (d) combined with *Burning Engines* members Mikael Fässberg (g), Martin Wezowski (b) and Carl Mikael Hildesjö (d). An eight-track demo was recorded in 2004. Shortly after the recording the band started falling apart, mainly for management reasons. Stark, Osbäck and Wernersson jumped ship. Shortly after, Wesowski (*The Drugs, Majestic, Merrygold*) also left. To up the stardom status former *Nazareth* guitarist Manny Charlton was drafted. Unfortunately he was also put in charge of the production, which is lacking, to say the least. A pity since a lot of the songs are really good and Moore is an outstanding singer. One album and some shows was all that came out of the band. The demo-drums of Wernersson was actually re-used for the track *Play Dirty*, which was also arranged by Stark. Fässberg is now in *Bonafide*. Good solid bluesy hard rock, but probably the worst band name ever... try Googling it!

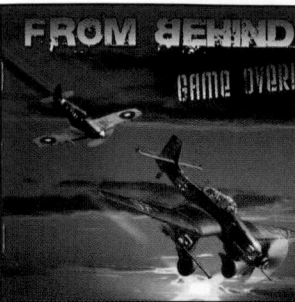
2006 CD - LMC 176

2006 □	GAME OVER	CD	Sweden Rock Records	SRR 666	
2006 ■	GAME OVER	CD	Lion Music	LMC 176	
2006 □	GAME OVER	CD	Irond (Russia)	CD 06-DD387	

FRONTIERS

Tony Brorsson: v, Hans Asp: g, Peter Söderström: g/k, Peo Gaasvik: k, Patrik Söderström: b, Johan Kullberg: d

Avesta - This is a high-quality melodic hard rock/AOR band that unfortunately never made it big. They sure had the qualities. Johan later joined *Talk Of The Town* and *Lion's Share*. In 2003 Peter Söderström recorded a great AOR album with singer Jan Johansen in the band *Ignition* and he is also part of quirky rockers *Bosse*. Check this out!

1986 MLP - FT-19861104

1986 ■	Frontpage	MLP 4tr	Frontattack	FT-19861104	$

Tracks: Time Will Tell/Help Me Now/This Feeling/Separate Worlds

FROZEN EYES

Aulis Hultin: v, Mattias "Ia" Eklundh: g, Leif Larsson: b, Jocke Sjöberg: d

Göteborg - Formed in 1986. After some demos the song Intruder was featured on the collection *Metal Collection 3* (1987 Ebony Records). In December 1987 Danish company Büms Records wanted the boys to record an album on their label (at their own expense, of course...). They did and the result is, well... not that bad, but not really good either. Ia later joined Danish band *Fate* and in 1992 formed *Freak Kitchen*, where also drummer Jocke Sjöberg was found. Leif Larsson later recorded with the band *NME Within* and was part of *Black Ingvars*.

1988 LP - 78901

1988 ■	FROZEN EYES	LP	Büms	78901
1995 □	FROZEN EYES	CD	Büms	67890

FROZEN FIRE

Dan Nordell: v, Tommy Nordell: g, Mikael Ross: g, Bert Bratén: b, Sten Nordell: d

Degerfors - On the first singles these guys look so incredibly heavy on the cover that it just has to be heavy. Well, it is heavy regarding sound and attitude; however the music is built around the traditional rock/blues scale and offers no greater surprises. Quite a fun one though. In 1982 Mikael left to play with numerous well-known Swedish pop and rock-artists. Dan and Bert then formed the band *Succé* with whom they recorded one single. *Frozen Fire* reformed again and in 1993 they rerecorded the 1982-single and added some tracks recorded in 1978. In 1998 they also recorded the live-CD and the band still shows its face now and then. On the live-CD back-up singers Monica Blom and Monica Falk also assisted the band. The live-CD is actually the heaviest offering from this band with some pretty edgy guitar work even though musically, it still stays within the borders of the traditional 12 bar blues-rock genre. The first line-up consisted of Dan, Bert, Mikael, bassist Sten-Olof "S-O" Björk and drummer Rolf Heische. The band has also featured two other drummers; Göran Persson and Sven Lanz, not at the same time, though. *Frozen Fire* has recorded lots of unreleased material.

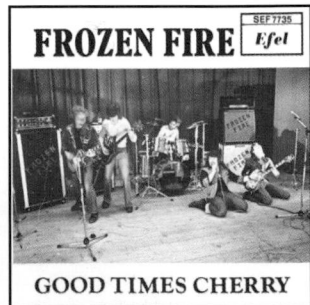

1976 7" - SEF 7430

1977 7" - SEF 7735

GOOD TIMES CHERRY

1976 ■	Det Enda Som Får Mig Att Tända/I Call Him "Rocky"	7"	Efel	SEF 7430
1977 ■	Good Time Cherry/I Got A "Roadrunner"	7"	Efel	SEF 7735
1978 ■	KÄNN DRAGET	LP	Scranta	BOLP 002
1982 ○	Den Mogna Kvinnan/Eller Hur	7"	Pang	PSI 011
1993 □	Den Mogna Kvinnan	MCD 4tr	private	FFCDS 9301

Tracks: Den Nakna Kvinnan/Lita På Mej/Svarta Pantern/Festen Är Över

1998 □	ON THE ROAD AGAIN	CD	private	FFCD 9809

1978 LP - BOLP 002

FRUITCAKE

Niklas "N. Carrot" Börjesson: v/g, Tomas "T. Cucumber" Modig: b/v, Hans "H Asparagus" Eriksson: d

Göteborg - Formed in 1990 by Modig after he came out of his punk era. He recorded with bands like **P-Nissarna**, **Likbas**, **Kachina Dance** and **Overland Stage Riders**, who all recorded demos, except **P-Nissarna** who made some vinyls, too. A nutty three-piece that almost only wrote songs about fruits, like *Happy Apple, Fructify* and *Citric Acid*. The style varies from song to song, from clean laid back rock, to funk and Hendrix-influenced 70's hard rock. Truly weird, but still classy. They also have the previously unreleased track *Ain't Worth A Fig* on the compilation *Backstage: En Himla Massa Oväsen* (93 Backstage), which is their best track ever. They are not to be confused with the Norwegian band on Cyclops Records. Drums on the MCD are actually played by Hans "B Broccoli" Bruhn who left in 1997. The band later changed their name to **Lotus** and recorded several albums under this name. After **Lotus** called it a day, Tomas recorded some demos with **The White Negroes**, an album with **Skyron** and is now in hard rock 'n rollers **Speedfreaks**.

1995 MCD - NSM 45-49

1995 ■ Freaks .... MCD 4tr   Nonstop .... NSM 45-49
    Tracks: Happy Apple/Fructify/Citric Acid (In Lake Placid)/Dog Rose Hip

FUCK BITCH

Jon Rekdahl: v/g, Simon Grenehed: g, Markus Linfeldt: b, Richard Netterman: d

Stockholm - Totally fucked up, weird and brutal metal. The whole thing started in 1991, when Jon teamed up with Richard and Erlend Ottem (**Clawfinger**) to get some of his ideas out. He went through several line-ups before he, in 1997, was doing a production at Polar Studios for an Ericsson commercial and at the same time started recording an album under the moniker **Fuck Bitch**. He recorded a complete album, but just when it was to be released the record label changed shape and it was put on hold. The album has now been refined with new bass and guitars added by George Bravo (**Skintrade**/**Roachpowder**), who also produced it. **Fuck Bitch** is an old, pissed-off cleaning woman, according to Jon, who is foremost known for being a jazz-trumpet player in **Jon Rekdahls Orkester** (at the TV-show *Baren* among others) and composer of music for TV-shows like *Expedition Robinson* etc. He also recorded a sleazy pop-single under the name Juan Ramos. The song *War* is found on fashion magazine Fjord's sample CD for the April 2002 issue. A second, entitled *Don't Fuck*, was supposed to be released. Guitarist Simon is also found in **Blindside** and Netterman, aka Hux, has recorded and played with **John Norum**, **Rammstein**, **Fistfunk** and **Plankton**.

1999 MCD - OSP 005

1999 ■ 1999 .... MCD 4tr   Outside Society .... OSP 005
    Tracks: 1999/Shut The Fuck Up/In Flux/Bite Me

FUELHEAD

Andréas Henemyr: v/b, Ulf "Palle" Hammarlund: g, Jimmie Svensson: d

Uddevalla - **Fuelhead** were formed in 1999 and released their first self-titled three track demo the same year. Another four-track followed the year after and four more demos emerged before the band was finally picked up by Plugged Records who released the outstanding debut album in 2006, with a single teaser the year before. Really great groovy heavy rock with a touch of **Freak Kitchen**, but without the wackiness, a bit similar to **Dogpound**. Svensson was formerly in the band **Wildness**. Liv Jagrell (**Sister Sin**) guests on the album.

2005 CDS - PLUCD011

2006 CD - PLUCD015

2005 ■ Little Ones/Both Hands Tied .... CDS 2tr   Plugged Records PLUCD011
2006 ■ FUELHEAD .... CD   Plugged Records PLUCD015

FULL METAL JACKETZ

J.C. Petersson: v, Sverrir Marinosson: g, Christian Smedström: g, Christian "Crippa" Odin: b, Martin H-Son: d

Göteborg - Formed in 1988. The members have a past in punk bands like **Attentat**, **Troublemakers** and **Anti-Cimex**. It's actually only **Full Metal Jacketz** last record that fully qualifies into this book. *Finger Lickin' Good* contains powerful straight biker metal in the vein of **Motörhead** meets **AC/DC**, but with clean vocals, while the earlier recordings are closer to **Ramones**. The non-CD track *One Time* can also be found on the compilation *Backstage: Högtalarterror '94*. After the *Rock 'N Roll* album they changed guitarists to Christian and Sverrir, who brought the hard rock sound into the band. *Eat The Rich* on *Finger Lickin' Good* is a **Motörhead** cover. It's also available on *Motörhead Tribute* (95 Pink Honey). Smedström later joined stoner rockers **The Awesome Machine**.

1989 7" - FMR 001

1989 ■ Full Metal Jacketz .... 7" 4tr   private .... FMR 001
    Tracks: Vi Ska Va Glada/Up Against The Wall/Ge Mig En Öl/Dö För Dig.

1990 7" - FMR 002

1990 ■	I Want Your Body/Keep On Rockin'	7"	private	FMR 002
1990 ☐	AIN'T GOT THE BLUES	LP	Arda	REX 104
	Also released on red and clear vinyl.			
1990 ☐	AIN'T GOT THE BLUES	CD	Arda	REX 104
	Bonus: It's Alright/Keep On Rockin'.			
1992 ☐	ROCK `N´ ROLL	CD	Helikopter	HELCD-06
1994 ■	Finger Lickin' Good	MCD 4tr	Helikopter	HELCD-14
	Tracks: Feel It Kickin'/Flesh And Bone/Eat The Rich/Nanana (nanananana).			

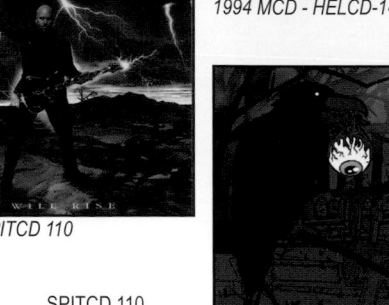

1994 MCD - HELCD-14

FULL STRIKE, Stefan Elmgren's

Niclas Johnsson: v, Stefan Elmgren: g,
Christer "Chris" Goldsmith: b, Björn Fryklund: d

Göteborg - When *Hammerfall*-guitarist Stefan went solo, what would you expect? Well, I actually expected something completely different from his ordinary band, but wrong was I. *We Will Rise* contains out-and-out melodic power metal in the same vein as *Hammerfall*, with a different and possibly more technical vein, at least guitarwise. He has also drafted helpers Björn (*Freak Kitchen*) Chri (*Crawley, Scarpoint, Hellinor*) and Niclas (*Mentor's Wish*). Björn was later replaced by former *Hammerfall*-colleague Patrik Räfling. The band folded and Stefan finally also left *Hammerfall*. In 2011 he released the debut album with his new band *FullForce*.

2002 CD - SPITCD 110

2002 ☐	We Will Rise/Force Of The World	CDS	Spitfire	
(promo)	SPITCD 110P			
2002 ■	WE WILL RISE	CD	Spitifre	SPITCD 110
2002 ☐	WE WILL RISE	CD	CD-Maximum (Russia)	CDM 1003-1530
2002 ☐	WE WILL RISE	CD	Victor (Japan)	VICP-62039
	Bonus: Ghost Traveller			
2010 ■	WE WILL RISE	CD	Store For Music	SRFMCD 157
	New artwork.			

2010 CD - SRFMCD 157

FULLFORCE

Mikael "Mike" Andersson: v/k, Stefan Elmgren: g, Stefan Rosqvist: g,
Tommy Larsson: b, Anders Johansson: d

Helsingborg/Göteborg - *Fullforce* were formed early 2009 by Andersson (*Cloudscape, Planet Alliance*) and former *Hammerfall* members Elmgren and bass player Magnus Rosén. Elmgren had previously also released an album with his solo project *Full Strike*. Magnus and Mike had already played together on the *Planet Alliance* album. Anders Johansson (*Hammerfall, Silver Mountain, Rising Force* etc) joined on drums and guitarist Carl Johan Grimmark (*Narnia, Grimmark*) was also drafted. Late 2009 Rosén decided to leave and was replaced by former *Heed* bassist Larsson. *Fullforce* is a quite natural continuation on what the boys did in *Hammerfall*, *Full Strike* and *Cloudscape*. High-class melodic metal. In 2011 Carl Johan decided to leave the band and Stefan Rosqvist (*Cloudscape, Dawn Of Oblivion, Stefan Rosqvist Band*) replaced him.

May the Full Force be with you!

2011 CD - SPV 309432

2011 ■	ONE	CD	Steamhammer	SPV 309432
2011 ☐	ONE	CD	Avalon Marquee (Japan)	MICP-11008
	Bonus: Best Of Times			
2012 ■	NEXT LEVEL	CD	Steamhammer	SPV 260572 CD

2012 CD - SPV 260572 CD

FULLMAKT

Johan Wahlström: v/k, Jana Persson: g/v, Tore Nylund: g,
Håkan Ståhl: b, Janne Jernestrand: d

Stockholm - Good, straightforward, melodic hard rock with great vocals and biting guitars. A band with a Christian message. The track *Skrämmer Mig* is an up-tempo prime hard rocker. Jana was also in funky band *Licence*.

1982 ■	Mästerkatten/Hej Du/Skrämmer Mig	7" 3tr	Prim	PRS 9002

FUNERAL

Mikael "Cab" Castervall: v/g, C.S Johansson: b, Lenny "Blade" Bladh: d

Växjö - Formed in 2002. Castervall is also found in bands like *Hypnosia*, *Unreal* and *Bird-flesh*, Johansson in *Pagan Rites*, *Karnarium* and Blade is ex-*Bullet*, *Pagan Rites*, *Nominon* and *Hypnosia*. Doom-laden death metal. Not to be confused with the Norwegian doomsters.

1982 7" - PRS 9002

| 2004 | ☐ | Forgotten Abominations | 7" 3tr | Pentagram Warfare | - - |

Tracks: Funeral/Forgotten Abominations/Sacramental Blasphemy. 500 copies, first 100 numbered + badge.

| 2011 | ■ | Forgotten Abominations | MLP 3tr | Nuclear War Now | NWR 044 |

500 copies. Different artwork.

| 2011 | ☐ | Forgotten Abominations | MCDg 4tr | Pentagram Warfare | NWR 044 |

500 copies.

2011 MLP - NWR 044

FUNERAL DIRGE

Niklas "Kvarforth" Olsson: v/b, Fredrik "Missfall" Karlsson: g/b

Upplands Väsby - *Funeral Dirge* is the now cult declared project of *Shining* persona Kvarforth. The CD features Kvarforth in three of his bands, *Funeral Dirge*, *Shining* and the industrial project *Mrok* (which also features Orias), two tracks each. *Funeral Dirge* played raw black metal with an industrial touch and with very warped vocals. Kvarforth has also recorded with bands like *Diabolicum*, *Skitliv*, *Bethlehem*, *Shining* and *Den Saakaldte*. The song *Alpha Sans Omega* is found on Niklas' solo album *Fifteen Years Of Absolute Darkness*.

| 1999 | ■ | The Silence Ebony | 7"g | Selbstmord Services | - - |

Tracks: The Black Breath/Livsleda. 200 copies hand numbered.

| 2007 | ☐ | THE SINISTER ALLIANCE (split) | CD | Old Temple | OLD 12 |

Split with Shining. Tracks: The Black Breath/Livsleda. In a 7" cover, stickers. 666 copies, hand numbered.

1999 7"g - - -

FUNERAL FROST

Forn Paananen: v/b, Pasi "Izaph" Viitasalo: g, Ångest: g, Fullmåne: d

Västerås - The band was formed in 1993 originally featuring Paananen, Viitsalo and drummer Corpse. In 1994 the demo *Midnight Speeches* was unearthed, followed by another demo the subsequent year. In 1997 Ångest entered as second guitarist and later the same year *Watch Them Burn* was recorded. It however took ten years for it to be released. In 2001 Fullmåne (also known as F.M in *Jotunheim* and Schattenführer in *WOD*) replaced Corpse on drums. Viitsalo is also a member of *WOD*. *Funeral Frost* was also featured on a couple of cassette compilations. Martin Axenrot (*Bloodbath*, *Morgue*, *Nifelheim*, *Triumphator* etc) has also been part of the band.

| 1996 | ■ | QUEEN OF FROST | CD | Wolfnacht Domain | FF9603 |

500 copies

| 2007 | ☐ | Watch Them Burn | 7" 4tr | Raging Bloodlust | - - |

666 copies. Tracks: Millennium of Conquering/ Bringer of War/ Watch Them Burn/ Unleashed Is Our Hidden Wrath

1996 CD - FF9603

FUNERAL MIST

Daniel "Arioch/Mortuus" Rostén: v/g/b

Stockholm - The band was formed in 1993. Before this Daniel had his own band *Winds*. In 1995 they recorded the demo *Darkness* and the year after *Havoc*. The first two releases features Daniel "Arioch" Rostén (v/g), Tobbe "Nachash" and Tore "Necromorbus" Stjerna (d). Daniel is also found in *Triumphator* and Tore, who owns Studio Necromorbus, was in *Watain*. Tobbe was not really a member, but did the bass-track for one song on the first album. *Salvation* was initially supposed to be released on Svartvintras in 2001, but as it was extremely delayed the release was taken over by Norma Evangelium Diaboli. On *Maranatha* it had turned into Arioch's solo project, using an unknown session drummer. Old school death metal in the vein of *Watain* and *Ondskapt* with very disturbing vocals. Daniel has also been fronting *Marduk* as *Mortuus* since 2004.
Website: www.funeralmist.cjb.net/

1998 MCD - SHADOW 003

2003 CD - NED 002

| 1998 | ■ | Devilry | MCD 5tr | Shadow | SHADOW 003 |

Tracks: The Devil's Emissary/Bringer Of Terror/Nightside Phantom/Funeral Mist/The God Supreme. 1000 copies.

| 1998 | ☐ | Devilry | MLP 6tr | Shadow | SHADOW 003 |

Tracks: The Devil's Emissary/Bringer Of Terror/Nightside Phantom/Funeral Mist/The God Supreme/Hellspell 2

| 2003 | ■ | SALVATION | CD | Norma Evangelium Diaboli | NED 002 |
| 2003 | ☐ | SALVATION | DLP | Norma Evangelium Diaboli | NED 002 |

500 copies.

2003	☐	SALVATION	CD	The Ajna Offensive (USA)	FLAME 37
2005	☐	DEVILRY	CD	The Ajna Offensive (USA)	FLAME 38
2005	☐	DEVILRY	CD	Norma Evangelium Diaboli	NED 009
2005	☐	DEVILRY	LP	Norma Evangelium Diaboli	NED 009
2009	■	MARANATHA	CD	Norma Evangelium Diaboli	NED 014
2009	☐	MARANATHA	LP	Norma Evangelium Diaboli	NED 014

2009 CD - NED 014

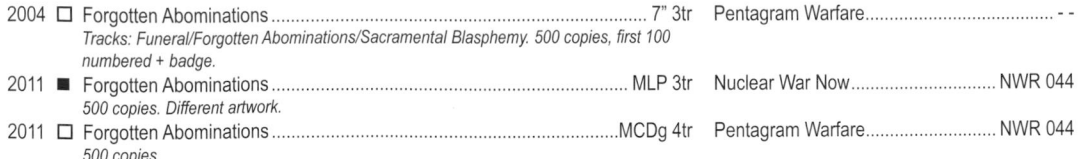

FUNERAL ORCHESTRA, THE

"Priest 1": v/g, "Priest 2": g, "Priest 3": b, Nicklas "Priest 4" Rudolfsson: d

Göteborg - *The Funeral Orchestra*, abbreviated *TFO*, were formed in 2002 by *Runemagick/ Swordmaster/Sacramentum* member Rudolfsson. They recorded the demos *Necronaut* and *SSBTWOTL* the same year. The latter was released on CD by Aftermath in 2006. The CD-R album *We Are The End* was released by Eternal Dark in 2003. Quite dissonant slow horror drone/ doom with death-oriented growling vocals. The *ODO* single was recorded in 2004 during the *Necro Occult* session and completed in 2008.

Website: www.funeralorchestra.com

2003 CDd - Chapter XXIII

2008 7" - Chapter 57

Year		Title	Format	Label	Cat. no.
2003	■	FEEDING THE ABYSS	CDd	Aftermath	Chapter XXIII
		999 hand numbered copies.			
2005	□	FEEDING THE ABYSS	2LP	Parasitic Records	Parasitic 12
2006	□	SLOW SHALT BE THE WHOLE OF THE LAW	CDd	Aftermath	Chapter 46
		999 hand numbered copies.			
2008	■	ODO	7" 3tr	Aftermath	Chapter 57
		Purple-red vinyl. Tracks: Pentagram Shock/Opium De Occulta/Drug Trance			
2010	■	THE NORTHERN LIGHTS II (split)	LP	Aftermath	Chapter 60
		Split with Ocean Chief. 250 copies. Track: Den mörka shamanens glöd			
2011	□	SLOW SHALT BE THE WHOLE OF THE LAW	2LP	Darkland	DARK 017
		444 copies			

2010 LP - Chapter 60

FURBOWL

Johan Axelsson: v/b, Nicke Stenemo: g/k, Max Thornell: d/k

Växjö - Formed in 1991. Johan is ex-*Carnage*. The band got a deal with Step One through their 1991-demo *The Nightfall Of Your Heart*, produced by Mike Amott (*Carcass, Spritual Beggars, Arch Enemy*), who also plays lead guitar on two of the tracks. Before the recordings of *The Autumn Years* guitarist Nicke joined the band. The style is well-played death metal with a touch of goth. Max was ex-*Jesusexercise*, *Max & The Chainsaws*, *Dom Där* and has also recorded a solo-cassette entitled *Sole Child*. He has also recorded with the band *Satanarchy*. After the album, Johan was replaced by Per Jungberger. In 1995 they changed name to *Wonderflow*, as they wanted to leave Black Mark for MNW, and made a new recording under this name.

1992 CD - SOR004

Year		Title	Format	Label	Cat. no.
1992	■	THOSE SHREDDED DREAMS	CD	Step One	SOR004
1994	■	THE AUTUMN YEARS	CD	Black Mark	BMCD 47
1994	□	THE AUTUMN YEARS	CD	Victor (Japan)	VICP-5466
2010	□	THOSE SHREDDED DREAMS	3LPg	The Crypt	CRYPT 12
		500 hand numbered. Box containing demos, live, Those Shredded Dreams and unreleased tracks. White vinyl.			
2011	□	THOSE SHREDDED DREAMS	CD	Vic Records	VIC 031 CD

1994 CD - BMCD 47

FUROR

Christoffer Jonsson: v, Petter Adsten: g, Kalle Kjellberg: g, Viktor Kröger: b, Joel Widegren Lundström: d

Umeå - Formed in 2008 when the members were only 13-14 years old. They released their first digital EP No End in 2011. Despite their (still) young age *Furor* is a tight, technical and highly competent melodic mix of death metal and metal core. Like a mix of *Meshuggah*, *Avatar* and *In Flames*.

Year		Title	Format	Label	Cat. no.
2013	■	SYSTEM ANNIHILATED	CD	Discouraged Records	MMI 23

2013 CD - MMI 23

FUZZDEVIL

Henrik Lindahl: v, Martin Öhman: g, Fredrik "Frasse" Welin-Berger: g, Jakob Jennische: b, Peder Clevberger: d

Uppsala - Heavy stoner-rock with a touch of *Kyuss, Fu Manchu* and *Motörhead*. Highly energetic! The band rose from the ashes of *Six Pack Sonic*, which featured Henrik, Fredrik, Peder and Jakob. The latter is also drummer of *454*, has been a member of *Spacebone* and is now in the band *Dimma*.

Year		Title	Format	Label	Cat. no.
2000	■	THE MAN	10" 8tr	Group Sounds	GS 001
		Tracks: Alright/The Man/Keeper Of The Worldpeace/City Of Silver/I'm On The Move Now, Brother/Manfighter5/Steve II/Burning Wheels			

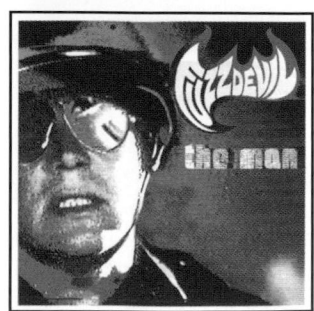

2000 10" - GS 001

G.O.L.D.

Per Svensson: v/g, Magnus Paulsson: g, Mårten Eriksson: b, Johan Holmberg: d

Stockholm - *G.O.L.D* play straightforward, biker-style hard rock, influenced by a band like *MC 5*. A more straight hard rock version of *The Leather Nun* with a singer at times sounding like Billy Idol. The follow-up album *Inner Space Highway* was supposed to be released in 1996 on Thunderload Records, but it never happened. The band disappeared into obscurity.

1992 ■ MAGIC POWER...CD   Psychick Release .... Psyche C004

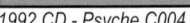
1992 CD - Psyche C004

GRK

Rolf Hellmark: v/g, Björn Hellmark: g, Göran Sonesson: k,
Peter Andersson: b, Richard Lundgren: d

Malmö - Brothers Rolf and Björn have previously recorded a single with the band *Hellmark*. *GRK* play quite good melodic hard rock, slightly bluesy at times. Today Rolf plays with the hard rock band *Rock 'N Roll Boys*.

1995 ■ TIMEWARP...CD   private GRKCD-001

1995 CD - GRKCD-001

GSO

Lasse Holmgren: g/v, Jonas Nordqvist: g, Janne Skärming: b, Patrik Jonsson: d

Västerås - *GSO* were formed in 1998 and the name stands for *Gary Springfeldt Orchestra*. Holmgren was formerly in *Ten Foot Pole* and later in *Bullhorn*, where Jonsson was also found. Skärming had previously played with punksters *T.S.T*. The band made their debut recording, *Singing Super, Super Songs*, in 2000, which featured a cover of *The Runaways*' *Queens Of Noise*. On the second release they shortened their name to *G.S.O* and on this album they made a cover of *Blur*'s *Song Two*, in Swedish. In 2008 the band announced a new album was ready and that Rainbow keyboardist Tony Carey would guest. The band was also cut down to a trio excluding Nordqvist. Some songs recorded after the second album are up on the band's MySpace page, but no new album has been released as yet. *GSO* play heavy, riff-oriented rock with a touch of *Black Label Society*, but with vocals closer to sleaze.

2001 ☐ JAZZ & DISTORTION..CD   October Fist .... - -
2004 ■ HOW TO GET AHEAD IN LIFE..CD   GMR/Powerline............................PLRCD 013

2004 CD - PLRCD 013

GABRIA

Rick Evans v/b, Johnie Wilde: g, Hank Black: d

Sölvesborg - *Gabria* started out as a cover band paying tribute to the 80's full on! It's wigs, leather, lace and the complete package. The band mostly plays covers, but started writing their own material in the same vein and made an album with originals in the same vein, and pretty good, too! They were actually way before *Steel Panther*, but not as explicit. Rick has previously recorded with *Headline* and also appears on the single by *The Kaars*. It should also be noted that the name... is actually the word "airbag" backwards.
Website: www.gabria.net

2008 ■ GABRIA..CD   private ....GAMC 0010807

2008 CD - GAMC 0010807

GALAXY

Jonas Sköld: v, Niklas Ahlin: g, Eric Jexén: g, Håkan Henriksen: k,
Mats Dahlberg: b, Daniel Svensson: d

Mariestad - Mid-heavy keyboard driven AOR, quite predictable but still good. The B-side is a traditional 80's ballad. The band's weak link is in the vocal department. It's not out of key, merely lacking in power and professionalism. Produced by Peo Pettersson (*X-Ray, Leviticus, Axia*, solo).

1989 ■ Stronger Than Ever/Two Of A Kind ....7"   private ....GA 001 $

1989 7" - GA 001

GALAXY SAFARI

Jesper Nyberg: v, Macke Strandberg: g, Andy Söderström: b, Alexander Malmström: d

Nyköping - After having been part of the Swedish hardcore/punk band *Victims* for some years Söderström and Strandberg decided to switch genre. In 2002 bands like *Stone Temple Pilots*, *Queens Of The Stone Age*, *Kyuss* and *Masters Of Reality* influenced them. They drafted singer Nyberg and drummer Micke Blomberg (ex-*Voice Of A Generation*). In 2006 Blomberg left the band and was replaced by Malmström. *Galaxy Safari* play high-octane hard rock at times similar to *The Hellacopters* but with a more stoner-oriented sound and attitude.

2009 ☐ STAR OF THE MASQUERADE	CDd	Granat Records	GRA 006
2009 ☐ Save Me	CDS	Granat Records	GRA 005
2010 ■ Pretend	CDS	Granat Records	GRA 008
2010 ☐ IT'S TIME FOR YOU TO LEAVE	CDd	Granat Records	GRA 009

2010 CDS - GRA 008

GALLANTRY
Tommy: v, Johnnie: g, Thomas: g, Conny: k, Jesper: b, Michael Stark: d

Stockholm - Quite good power metal with some folky influences, a bit similar to *Nostradameus*, but with mid-league vocals. No info on the band, but the song writers are Janewall, Smith, Perkins and Meier.

| 2000 ■ Stormbringer | MCD 5tr | private | POLYVOX 991033 39297 |

Tracks: Stormbringer/Silent Skies/Bound To Nowhere/Dreams Of A Youthful Youth/The Old Mansion

2000 MCD POLYVOX 991033 39297

GALLEON
Göran Fors: v/b, Sven Larsson: g, Ulf Pettersson: k, Dan Fors: d

Ljusdal - Formed in 1981 under the name *KG 200*, became *Aragon* in 1985 and changed it to *Galleon* around 1989. *Helium Head*-singer Esbjörn Johansson was originally in the band, but he quit early on. The first album was a good, symphonic rock album in the vein of *Saga*, while *Heritage & Visions* is a killer album sounding a bit like *Saga* meets *Kansas*. On this album the band had also been reinforced by Ulf Pettersson (*Lotus*). Guitarist Sven Larsson replaced Micke Värn in 2000. The band's only weakness are (were, actually) the vocals, while the songs on the other hand are top notch. However Göran's vocals have gradually improved and *In The Wake...* is an excellent album, musically and vocally, in the vein of *Ayreon*. Göran is also found in the band *Spektrum*. Sven has since recorded solo albums and played in various bands. In 2006 drummer Dan Fors left and was replaced by Göran Johnsson (*Cross, Grand Stand, Spektrum*).

1992 CD - VF 001

1992 ■ LYNX	CD	VF Productions	VF 001
1992 ☐ LYNX	CD	Zero (Japan)	XRCN-1100
Bonus: Astonished			
1994 ☐ HERITAGE & VISIONS	CD	VF Productions	VF 002
1994 ☐ At This Moment In Time	MCD 3tr	VF Productions	VF 003
Tracks: Crimewave /Illusive Exhibition/King Of Aragon. All tracks are non-CD.			
1994 ☐ HERITAGE & VISIONS	CD	Zero (Japan)	XRCN-1116
Bonus: King Of Aragon (instrumental version).			
1995 ☐ KING OF ARAGON	CD	Zero (Japan)	XRCN 1256
Bonus: Eternal Shadows			
1996 ■ THE ALL EUROPEAN HERO	CD	VF Production	VF 004
1996 ☐ THE ALL EUROPEAN HERO	CD	Zero (Japan)	XRCN 1277
1998 ☐ MIND OVER MATTER	CD	VF Production	VF 005
1999 ☐ LYNX	CD	Progress	PRCD 002
1999 ☐ KING OF ARAGON	CD	Progress	PRCD 003
2000 ☐ HERITAGE & VISIONS	CD	Progress	PRCD 005
2000 ☐ BEYOND DREAMS	CD	Progress	PRCD 006
2003 ☐ FROM LAND TO OCEAN	2CD	Progress	PRCD 011
2005 ☐ MIND OVER MATTER	CD	Progress	PRCD 017
2007 ☐ ENGINES OF CREATION	CD	Progress	PRCD 029
2010 ■ IN THE WAKE OF THE MOON	CD	Aerodynamic	AEROCD 02

1996 CD - VF 004

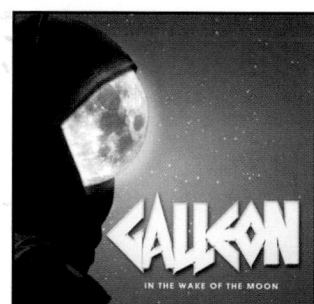

2010 CD - AEROCD 02

GALLERY (aka [GÆLERI])
Anders Bengtsson: v/g/k, Niklas Rollgard: g, Jonas Andersson: b, Patrik Borgkvist: d

Helsingborg - The band was founded in 1992, initially called *Shooting Gallery* under which name they recorded some pretty impressive melodic hard rock demos. They changed the name to *Gallery*, but their logo was the name in phonetics, i.e *[Gæləri]* and became their official spelling. Killer melodic hard rock with hints of *Led Zeppelin* and *Whitesnake*. There are some really devastating riffs on *Still Here*, where the backing vocals are handled by Thomas Vikström (*Talk Of The Town, Candlemass* etc.), Lena Vikström and Pontus Norgren (*Hammerfall, Talisman* etc), who also does a guest-solo on one track. Anders has previously recorded with the band *Seventeen* (*17*) and Jonas was also found in *Scratch* and *Unameus*. A third album, with the working-title *Stand Aside*, was recorded late 2001 and was supposed to be released in 2002. It was re-titled *A Brighter Day*. The band had by this time turned more commercial and almost pop-oriented. In 2001 Jonas left the band and was replaced by Jokke Rosén.

1999 CD - KICK 102 CD

1996 ☐ (GAELERI)	CD	Dream Circle	531 212-2
1999 ■ STILL HERE	CD	Kick Music	KICK 102 CD
2000 ☐ Maybe My Eyes	CDS 1tr	Kick Music (promo)	KICK PROSCS 106
2002 ■ A BRIGHTER DAY	CD	Kick Music	KICKCD 180

2002 CD - KICKCD 180

GALLERY

**Benny Ahlquist: v, Åke Wallin: g, Dan Klasson: k,
Hans Lagerström: b, Mikael Ellgren-Svensson: d**

Lidköping - When symphonic rockers *Ambra* were reinforced with former *Rhapsody* singer Benny, they changed their name to *Gallery*. The style is great well played AOR, with a touch of early Russ Ballard. The music stretches from total wimp to great ballsy AOR. The track *Trance* is quite close to Pat Benatar's *Treat Me Right*. When the band split, Mikael joined pop/rockers *Shanghai* and later formed *Trixi*. Benny then teamed up with Tony Borg and Jimmy Wandroph (both later in *Alien*) and formed *Cheap Thrill* in 1982. *Gallery* were offered deals with both Virgin and Polydor, but turned them down as they were aiming world-wide. On the demo I've heard, you can definitely hear this is where *Alien* was born. Benny and Mikael, who is a great drummer who has picked up a trick or two from Neil Peart, were later working on a duo project, but nothing has emerged so far. Benny was later in the reunited *Rhapsody*.

1980 7" - 7C-006-35724

1980 ■	En Del Av Mig/Inte Bara Jag	7"	EMI	7C-006-35724
1980 □	Sköt Dig Själv/Du	7"	EMI	7C-006-35801
1981 ■	Jag Kommer I Natt/Trance	7"	Epic	1711

1981 7" - 1711

GALLOWS END

Thord Klarström: v/g, Peter Samuelsson: g, Niklas Nord: b, Mikael Karlsson: d

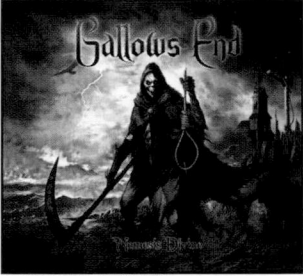

Arvika/Karlstad - *Gallows End* were formed in 2007 by Klarström and was initially intended to be a solo project between bands. In September the same year he recorded three tracks and immediately caught the attention of several labels. This resulted in Klarström getting a full band together in 2008 and signing a deal with Ohio based Farvahar Records, who released the debut *Nemesis Within* in 2010. The music is a mix of classic heavy metal and German power metal - fast and melodic.

2010 ■	NEMESIS WITHIN	CDd	Farvahar Records	SHE 119

2010 CDd - SHE 119

GARDENIAN

Jim Kjell: v/g, Niclas Engelin: g, Håkan Skoger: b, Thim Blom: d

The two feet gardeners

Göteborg - The band saw the light of day in April 1996 by Jim and Thim. They were soon accompanied by Niclas and Håkan and a rehearsal-tape found its way to Listenable Records, who signed them on the spot. They started recording the debut already in December the same year. The band also recorded a cover of *A Dangerous Meeting* for the compilation *A Tribute To Merciful Fate* (98 Listenable). The album went well, but the label did not have the financial possibilities to put the band on the road, so they left. Niclas joined *In Flames* for the *Whoracle*-tour. This however put him in touch with Nuclear Blast, who signed the band. For the new album Jim's lacking vocal capacity (when it came to clean vocals) made them recruit Icelandic/Norwegian singer Eirikur "Eric Hawk" Haukson (*Artch, Skarr*) who helped put a clean touch to four songs on the *Soulburner* album. Another guest was Sabrina Kihlstrand (*Ice Age*). In 1998 bass-player Håkan Skoger left to dedicate his time to *Headplate*, but still did the bass-tracks for the second album. After the album, the band found bass-player Krister Albertsson. Krister was ex-*Sarcazm*, just like Niclas. *Sindustries* was recorded at Studio Abyss. Influenced by bands like *At The Gates* and *Entombed*, but with lots of fast and melodic parts. On *Sindustries*, produced by Peter Tägtgren, Jim stepped up to the task and made his clean voice be heard, this time with much better success. The album also showed a bit more melodic feel than the debut, but it was still death metal. Not long after its release the band however went through a pretty vast line-up change, when both Kjell and Albertsson decided to leave the band. Replacements were singer Apollo Papathanasio (*Craze, Majestic, Meduza, Spiritual Beggars* etc.) and the bass was taken over by Robert Hakemo (*Engel, Gooseflesh*). Unfortunately this new line-up didn't last long and the group disbanded in 2004, before making a recorded statement. Engelin later formed the band *Engel*. The band also covers *Cut Throat* on *Sepultural Feast* (1998 Black Sun), *A Dangerous Meeting* on *Mercyful Fate: Tribute* (1998 Listenable) and *Got To Give It Up*, by *Thin Lizzy*, on *Emerald – A Tribute To The Wild One* (2003 Nuclear Blast).
Website: http://sindustries.cjb.net/

1997 CD - POSH 07

2000 CD - NB 533-2

1997 ■	TWO FEET STAND	CD	Listenable	POSH 07
1997 □	TWO FEET STAND	CD	Avalon Marquee (Japan)	MICY-1034
	Bonus: Ecstacy Of Life			
1999 □	SOULBURNER	CD	Nuclear Blast	NB 397-2
1999 □	SOULBURNER	LP	Nuclear Blast	NB 397-1
1999 □	SOULBURNER	CD	Nuclear Blast America (USA)	NBA 6397-2
1999 □	SOULBURNER	CD	JVC Victor (Japan)	VICP 60874
2000 ■	SINDUSTRIES	CD	Nuclear Blast	NB 533-2
2000 □	SINDUSTRIES	CD	Nuclear Blast America (USA)	NBA 6533-2
2008 ■	SOULBURNER/SINDUSTRIES	2CDd	Metal Mind	MASSCD 1146 DGD
	2000 copies, numbered.			

2008 2CD - MASSCD 1146 DGD

GAS
Barbro: v, Stiffe: v, Frille: g, Tobbe: g/v, Homping: g, Erik: b, Nylle: d
Stockholm - Slightly proggy, seventies-influenced melodic rock. Nice guitar playing.

19?? ■ En gång till!/Hjälp mej...7" private .... GAS 1

19?? 7" - GAS 1

GASOLINE QUEEN
Dennis "Dee Fearless" Hoffman: v, Martin "Mart Wildheart" Unosson: g,
Mikael "Mike Spider" Bäcklin: g, Per-Ola "MadDog" Embretsén: b,
Anders "Andy McQueen" Unoson: d
Söderhamn - *Gasoline Queen* play, not surprisingly, sleazy hard rock in the vein of vintage *Crüe* or Swedish colleagues *Loud 'N Nasty, Crazy Lixx* etc. Highly competent and good-sounding. The band was formed in 2000 and made their last show in 2010. The tracks *Restless Kid* and *Gasoline Queen* are found on the compilation *Swedish Sleaze & Rock 'N' Roll* (2006 Swedmetal). *Website: www.gasolinequeen.com*

2008 ■ Gas For The Underclass...MCD 4tr private .... FUELCD 001
      Tracks: Down All Around/Young Man Burning/Broke, Cursed And Damned/Stalker

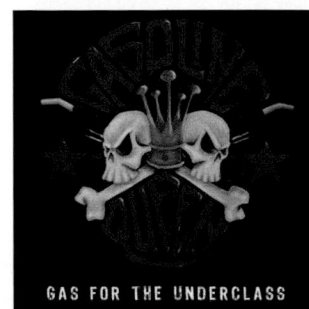

2008 MCD - FUELCD 001

GATES OF ISHTAR
Mikael Sandorf: v, Tomas Jutenfaldt: g, Andreas Johansson: g,
Niklas Svensson: b, Oskar Karlsson: d
Umeå - *Gates of Ishtar* were formed by Sandorf, Johansson, guitarist Stefan Nilsson and bassist Henrik Åberg, in 1992. They recruited second guitarist Tomas Jutenfäldt. When the first demo, *Seasons Of Frost* in 1995, the line-up featured Sandorf, Johansson, Jutenfäldt, Svensson and Karlsson. The band was soon picked up by Finnish label Spinefarm, who released their debut *A Bloodred Path* in 1996. Recorded at Studio Unisound and produced by Dan Swanö. In fact *The Dawn Of Flames* was the last album to be recorded at the classic Unisound studio. *A Bloodred Path* contains a cover of *W.A.S.P*:s *I Wanna Be Somebody*. Varied and quite melodic death metal with elements of traditional metal, as well as high speed thrashing. Nice dual *Iron Maiden*:esque guitar work, great production and lots of time-variations make this quite an interesting band. Sandorf is also found in *The Duskfall*, *Deathbound* and *Agroth*, Karlsson in *Defleshed*, *Scheitan*, *Helltrain*, *The Duskfall* and *The Everdawn*, while Svensson is in *The Everdawn*, *Throne of Ahaz* and *The Moaning*.

1996 CD - SPI 31

1996 ■	A BLOODRED PATH	CD	Spinefarm	SPI 31
1997 □	THE DAWN OF FLAMES	CD	Invasion	IR 027
1997 □	THE DAWN OF FLAMES	CD	Metal Blade (USA)	3984-14156-2
1997 □	THE DAWN OF FLAMES	CD	Avalon Marquee(Japan)	MICY-1019

    Bonus: Where The Winds Of Darkness Blow/A Bloodred Path/The Dreaming Glade/The Silence

1997 □	THE DAWN OF FLAMES	CD	Avalon Marquee(Japan)	MICP-10019
1998 □	AT DUSK AND FOREVER	CD	Avalon Marquee(Japan)	MICY-1045

    Bonus: Red Hot (Mötley Crüe cover). 1000 copies.

1998 ■	AT DUSK AND FOREVER	CD	Invasion	IR 035
1998 □	AT DUSK AND FOREVER	LP PD	Invasion	IR 041

    Bonus: Red Hot (Mötley Crüe cover). 1000 copies.

2001 ■	THE DAWN OF FLAMES/ AT DUSK AND FOREVER	2CD	Unveiling The Wicked	HUW 013

    Bonus: Where The Winds Of Darkness Blow/A Bloodred Path/The Dreaming Glade/The Silence

2007 □	A BLOODRED PATH	CD	Fono (Russia)	FO 673 CD

1998 CD - IR 035

2001 2CD - HUW 013

GEFF
Göran Edman: v, Ralf "Geff" Jedestedt: g, Mats Olausson: k,
Per Stadin: b, Anders Johansson:d
Klågerup - *Geff* was a project initiated by guitarist Ralf Jedestedt. The background is that Ralf, an old time friend of Anders and Per, asked Per if he would record and album in his studio and play bass on it. They gathered some more friends to complete the line-up and the musicians arranged the songs together. Anders' brother Jens (*Silver Mountain*, *Stratovarius* etc.) also guests on the album. Anders is also in *Hammerfall* and *Fullforce*, Göran is found in *Glory*, *Mårran* etc., Olausson is ex-*Rising Force* and Per plays in *Silver Mountain* and *Snake Charmer*. A second album is also in the making.
Website: www.geff.se

2009 ■	LAND OF THE FREE	CD	Metal Heaven	MHV00073
2009 □	LAND OF THE FREE	CD	Bickee Music (Japan)	HMCX-1064

    Bonus: Loup-Garou

2009 CD - MHV00073

GEHENNAH

Stefan "Mr. Violence" Mithander: v, Robert "Garm Stringburner" Fjällsby: g, Ronnie "Ripper" Olsson: b, Mikael "Hellcop" Birgersson: d

Forshaga/Karlstad - The band started out as a *Venom*-cover band in 1992. Very fast, straight and punkish metal/hardcore with death-oriented vocals. The band calls it "blood metal". The lyrics are about beer, whores, horror and violence. "Genuine metal lyrics and no atmospheric bullshit", to quote Mr. Violence. Musically quite close to early *Venom*. Hellcop is also found in *Dawn Of Decay*, while Ronnie is in *Vomitory* and his side project *Turbocharged*. Not to be confused with the Norwegian black metal band. The band made their first demo *Kill* in 1993, followed up by *Brilliant Loud Overlords Of Destruction* the subsequent year. Before the recording of *Hardrocker*, Hellcop replaced first drummer Captain Cannibal. Robert also did a side-project on his own under the name *Rob Coffinshaker* and Mithander has been found in *Satanarchy*. The 10 year anniversary 7" was only sold at the band's anniversary show, and later reprinted by Bad Taste Records.

A decade of hard rock!

1995 CD - PAR 004

1995 7" - PAR 005

1995 ■	HARDROCKER	CD	Primitive Art	PAR 004
1995 ■	No Fuckin' Christmas	7"	Primitive Art	PAR 005
	Tracks: Satana Claus/Merry Shitmas. 500 copies. Gold vinyl Christmas single.			
1996 ☐	KING OF THE SIDEWALK	CD	Osmose	OPCD 046
1996 ■	KING OF THE SIDEWALK	LP	Osmose	OPLP 046
1997 ☐	Jackson/Deadringer (For Love) (split)	7"	Private Art	PAR 015
	Gehennah and Rise & Shine together on both songs.			
1997 ☐	No Fuckin' Christmas	12"	Primitive Art	PAR 00512
	Tracks: Satana Claus/Merry Shitmas. 1000 numbered copies.			
1997 ☐	DECIBEL REBEL	CD	Osmose	OPCD 065
1997 ☐	DECIBEL REBEL	LP	Osmose	OPLP 065
	Bonus: Discodeath			
1998 ☐	HARDROCKER	LP	Primitive Art	PAR 004 LP
	1000 numbered copies.			
2002 ☐	10 Years Of Fucked Up Behaviour	7" 4tr	private	- -
	Tracks: Intro/Obsculum Obscenum/Burning Strings/Bleed You Bastards/Drink, Fight And Fuck (G.G. Allin cover). 50 copies.			
2003 ■	10 Years Of Fucked Up Behaviour	7"g 4tr	Bad Taste Entertainment	BTE 01 EP
	500 copies. First 100 die hard edition with badge and sew on patch. New artwork.			

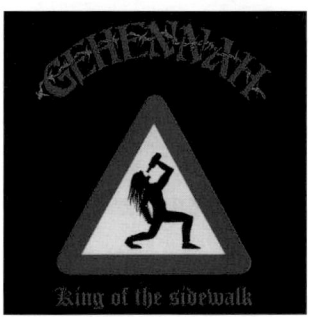
1996 LP - OPLP 046

GEISHA

Yenz "Cheyenne/Leonhardt" Arnsted: v, Peter "Pete Black" Jacobsson: g/v, Joel Starander: b, Tony Nemistö: d

Göteborg/Köpenhamn - Formed in 1984. For some strange reason this band has been labelled as Danish. *Geisha* were formed in Göteborg by Peter, Joel, drummer Mikkey Dee (*King Diamond, Motörhead*) and Danish singer Yenz. Yenz was previously in *Brats*, the band that became *Mercyful Fate*, and later formed his own band *=Y=*. Peter had previously recorded a 7" with the band *Trazer* and also joined *EF Band* for a short period in 1982. He left *Geisha* to join *King Diamond Band* and later released a MCD and full album with the band *Blakk Totem*. Mikkey Dee left to join *King Diamond* and he was replaced by former *Europe* skinsman Tony "Reno" Nemistö (later in *=Y=*). Shortly after *Geisha* was formed they moved headquarters to Copenhagen, Denmark. The CD-version of the album is rare. *Geisha* play good, melodic hard rock with a touch of sleaze. Yenz has later been in *Kingdom Come, Iron Saviour, Stormwarrior* and *Savage Circus*. Peter is now backing *Alice Cooper* style rocker *Maryann Cotton*.

1987 LP - HMI LP 88

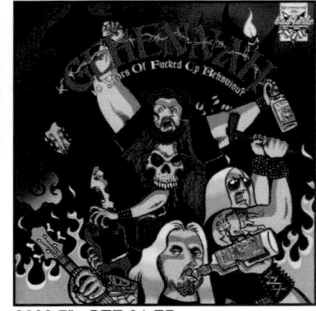
2003 7" - BTE 01 EP

1987 ■	PHANTASMAGORIA	LP	FM Revolver	HMI LP 88	
1987 ☐	PHANTASMAGORIA	CD	FM Revolver	HMI CD 88	$

GEMINI FIVE

Stefan "Tin Star" Molander: v, Mikael "Snobben/Snoopy" Jonasson: g, Roger "Hot Rod" Teilmann: b, Peter "Slim Pete" Henriksson: d

Göteborg - Gemini Five (named after a song by Teilmann's old band *The Jet Set*) were formed in 2001 embracing all the antics from 80s *Mötley Crüe*, both musically and image-wise. A first demo, entitled *Let's Go Starstrippin' In The Blow Zone* was recorded the same year. They were soon picked up by Swedish label Wild Kingdom. In 2009 Snoopy was replaced by Örebro based guitarist Tom Wouda. Molander and Henriksson have previously recorded with *Jekyll & Hyde* and pop band *Plaster*, while Theilmann was previously a member of US bands *Beautiful Creatures* and *The Jet Set*, but immigration problems sent him home again. *You Spin Me Round* is a *Dead Or Alive* cover. Drummer Henriksson is now in *Slingblade*.
Website: www.gemini5.net

Looking for gemini number five?

2003 ☐	BABYLON ROCKETS	CD	Wild Kingdom	KING 002 CD
2003 ■	You Spin Me Round (Like A Record)/Automaticool	CDS	Wild Kingdom	KING 003 CD
2004 ☐	BABYLON ROCKETS	CD	Spiritual Beast (Japan)	SBCD-1007
	Bonus: Cherry Koolaid/You Spin Me Round (Like A Record) + video			
2004 ☐	Babylon Rockets	MCDp 3tr	Wild Kingdom	KING 006 CD
	Tracks: Babylon Rockets/Suicide Tuesday/Get It Off (demo) + Babylon Rockets (video)/ Babylon Rocks (video)			
2005 ☐	BLACK: ANTHEM	CD	Wild Kingdom	KING 019 CD
2005 ☐	BLACK: ANTHEM	CD	Spiritual Beast (Japan)	SBCD-1026
	Bonus videos: When The Body Speaks/Babylon Rockets (live)/Babylon Rockets			
2006 ☐	Black: Anthem/Black: Anthem (video)	CDS	Wild Kingdom	KING 024 CD
2008 ☐	SEX DRUGS ANARCHY	CD	Wild Kingdom	KING 052 CD
2008 ☐	SEX DRUGS ANARCHY	CD	Spiritual Beast (Japan)	POCE-16033
	Bonus: I Hollow (demo)			

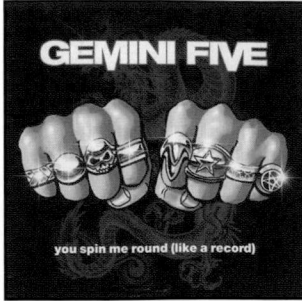

2003 CDS - KING 003 CD

GEMINI SOULS

Roger "Spy-T" Albinsson: v, George "Georg Allen" Wallen: g, H. Sebastian: b, Jonas "J.R" Östman: b

Stockholm - **Gemini Souls** are a bit hard to pinpoint style-wise. They have a bit of post-grunge blended into their heavy melodic hard rock. Not bad at all. The album also features guests like bass player Chris Goldsmith (**FullStrike, Scarpoint, Hellinor**), keyboard player Ulf Wahlberg (**Baltimoore**) and backing singer Thomas Vikström (**Talk Of The Town, Candlemass** etc). The album was produced, arranged and engineered by Jan Granvik (**Glory, Grave**). Östman has also been in **Gotham City, Mental Hippie Blood** and **Yngwie Malmsteen's Rising Force**.

1997 ■	GS	CD	Local Hero	LHM 0520

1997 CD - LHM 0520

GENARO *(See Talisman)*

GENERALS, THE

Rickard Hednar: v/b, Rickard Bengtsson: g, Rickard "Dick" Johansson: g, Martin "Metal" Svensson: d

Karlstad - Formed in 2002 in a rehearsal studio in Åmål, but the band now has its base in Karlstad. The members' wide array of influences reflects in their music which is a sort of death 'n roll a bit reminiscent of classic **Entombed** mixed with **Motörhead**. The debut was produced by Tomas Skogsberg in Sunlight Studios and the follow-up by Rikard Lövgren at Leon Music.

2009 ■	STAND UP STRAIGHT	CD	Metalcentral	MCRCD 003
2013 ☐	BLOOD FOR BLOOD	CD	Lightning Records	LIR 010

2009 CD - MCRCD 003

GENEROUS MARIA

Göran Florström: v, Lars Elf: g, Dan Johansson: g, Jesper Klarqvist: b, Mats Ohlsson: d

Göteborg - Formed in 1998. The demo *Strict Nurse* was released as a split with **Skua** on Spanish label Alone. Heavy, stoner-oriented and slightly psychedelic hard rock, like a stoner-version of **The Cult**. Fat, slow-pace riffing and good vocals. Mats was formerly in horror rockers **Mobile Mob Freakshow** and Dan was previously in **Mary Beats Jane**. They are also found on compilations like *Sacred Groove* (Monstruo De Gila), *Rock N Roll Blvd Vol 1* (Buzzville), *Burn The Street Vol 5* (Daredevil), and *New Rays From A Rising Black Sun* (Dirt Culture), plus the split 2x7" *Swedish Rock 'N' Roll Dammit* (Game Two Records). The band also does a cover of *Wild Child* on the **Zodiac Mindwarp** tribute *Snake Oil Supercharm* (Sleazegrinder). After *Electricism* guitarist Ulrik Nilsson was out of the band, replaced by Lars Elf. On III the band showed a more garagy musical side, closer to colleagues **Graveyard**.

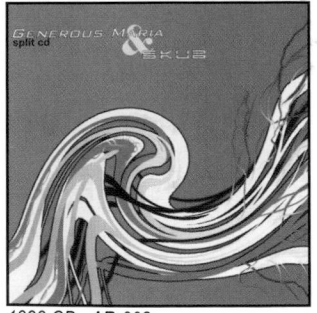

1999 CD - AR-002

2002 CD - LUNA 009 CD

1999 ■	GENEROUS MARIA VS. SKUA (split)	CD	Alone/Custom Heavy Records	AR-002
	Tracks: Strict Nurse/Like A Dog With A Frisbee/Lack Of Faith/Brother Pain			
2002 ■	COMMAND OF THE NEW ROCK	CD	Lunasound	LUNA 009 CD
2004 ☐	Crawl Back In/Daddy Rattlesnake	7"	private	GM001
	500 copies hand numbered.			
2005 ☐	COMMAND OF THE NEW ROCK – 2005 EDITION	CD	Buzzville	BUZZCD 014
	Bonus: Crawl Back In/Daddy Rattlesnake/Devil's Brood/Wild Child			
2005 ■	ELECTRICISM	CD	Buzzville	BUZZCD 016
2008 ☐	COMMAND OF THE NEW ROCK – 2005 EDITION	LP	Tornado Ride	TRR 036
2008 ☐	ELECTRICISM	LP	Tornado Ride	TRR 037
2008 ☐	ELECTRICISM	LP+7"	Tornado Ride	TRR 037+GM 0018
	With bonus 7": Crawl Back In/Daddy Rattlesnake. 500 copies, numbered on the single.			
2008 ☐	Crawl Back In/Daddy Rattlesnake	7"	private	GM 0018
	500 copies, hand-numbered. The majority delivered with the above LP.			
2012 ☐	III	CDd	Transubstans	TRANS111

2008 CD - BUZZCD 016

GENESARET

Mats Danielsson: v/g, Kjell-Arne Lindvall: g, Carl-Johan Kvaldén: k,
Tom Gustavsson: b, Bengt Danielsson: d/v

Åmål - Christian rockers singing in Swedish. Based on the A-side, the band wouldn't be featured anywhere near this book. Lame pop with a 70s disco touch. However the B-side is a really good guitar-oriented melodic hard rocker.

1983 ■ Tro och tvivel/Säg ja till livet...7"   Stanley & Andrew Music ....SAM 5207

1983 7" - SAM 5207

GENIE

Ulf Forslund: v, Krister Pirkkanen: g, Leif Laestander: g,
Peter Jakobsson: b, Hans Andersson: d

Kalix - Formed in 1987 and split in 1991. The members are still active as musicians, but merely playing covers. The band seems to have picked up one or two influences from bands like **Yes**, **Toto** and **Saga**. Well-played and well-sung AOR with a symphonic touch. Well worth checking out.

1987 ■ Power/Never Give Up ....7"   Platina...PL 30 $

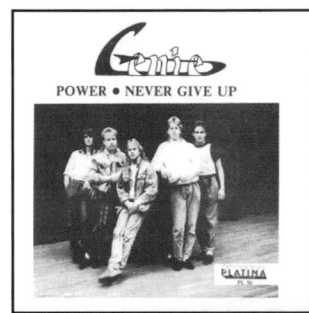

1987 7" - PL 30

GENOCRUSH FEROX

Thorbjörn "Toob" Brynedal: v/g, Per Eriksson:g,
Marcus "Mackan" Jonsson: b, Henrik "Henke" Östensson: d

Borlänge - The band was formed in 1997 by Toob, Danne and Henrik. They recorded their first demo the same year. In 1998 Mackan completed the band and they recorded the demo *The Sepulchure Devastation* late 1998. After the demo *Wappatrax,* Danne left the band. Per now entered and with the new reinforcement, the band recorded the new demo *Glory Glory Strangulation* in 1999, actually the same tracks as on the previous one, plus one extra track. In the end of 2000 the band finally split and the *Sepulchure Devastation* and *Glory Glory Strangulation* demos were released on one CD. High-speed, blastbeat death metal. Very well played and tight.

2003 ■ THE SEPULCHRE STRANGULATION...CD   Escorbuto Recordings ....SYMPTOM 01

2003 CD - SYMPTOM 01

GHAMOREAN

Andreas Båtsman: g/v, Samuel Wistemar: b/v, David Ekevärn: d

Umeå - **Ghamorean** were formed already back in 1997. The original line-up featured the only remaining original member Andreas Båtsman plus singer Jonas Ahlmark, guitarists Daniel Eriksson and Ulrik Bjuhr, bass player Siavosh Bigonah (**Slumber, Ondskapt**) and drummer Patrik Öberg. Singer Henrik Sundström replaced Ahlmark in 1998. Eriksson left in 1999 and in 2001 Johan Nilsson replaced Bjuhr, but he only lasted for a year. In 2001 Öberg was replaced by Peter Widding who in his turn was replaced by Bergström in 2003. After the first album Gandal was replaced by Ludvig Johansson (**Apostasy, Knife Of Christ**) and Samuel Persson was added on second guitar. **Ghamorean** play death/black metal. The band's second effort showed a more aggressive approach. For fans of bands like **Mayhem** and **Bloodbath**. On the band's third effort they had become a trio with a completely new line-up, where Båtsman was the only remaining member, now also handling the vocals. Drummer Jimmy Bergström had been replaced by Ekekvärn (**Those Who Bring The Torture**) and bass player Johansson by Wistemar.

2005 CD - KARMA 096

2005 ■ PLAGUEMPIRE..CD   Karmageddon ....KARMA 096
2008 ☐ EON ESCHATOS...CD   Ge Hinnom Music ....GHM 001
2011 ■ TERRA RUINA..CD   Discouraged......................................MMI 12

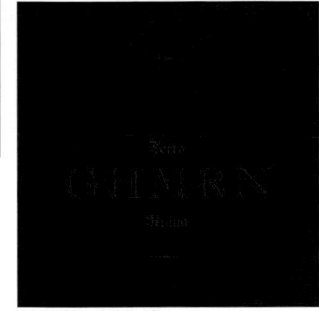

2011 CD - MMI 12

GHOST (aka GHOST B.C)

Papa Emiritus II: v, Nameless Ghouls: g/b/k/d

Linköping - **Ghost** is one of the most successful hypes of the new millennium. Secrecy and Satanism coupled with catchy songs. The band is portrayed through spokesperson Papa Emeritus I (now II), aka Tobias Forge (first officially revealed by mistake by Classic Rock magazine). The first demo was recorded by **Repugnant/Subdive/Magna Carta Cartel** singer/guitarist Forge himself, but it soon became a band. The image was created to give the band a clean slate and to avoid any misconceptions regarding music and message. If you knew it was the people from **Repugnant** you would most likely be disappointed by the musical deliverance. **Ghost** plays really great, seventies-influenced, melodic hard rock, sounding like a mix of **Demon**, **Blue Öyster Cult** and **Mercyful Fate** with clean and very retro-sounding vocals. The debut was recorded as a trio, by Forge, bassist Gustaf Lindström and drummer Thomas Daun, but live Forge handles the vocals and his guitar duties were taken over by two of his former **Magna Carta Cartel** colleagues. The first single was soon sold out and became a collectors' item in no time. Lindström and Daun are no longer in the band, but are now in punkish rockers **Iron Lamb**. As a matter of fact, no one can really be sure who is actually in the band now since the members have been changed around… *Infestissumam* proved it was not just a hype. After making a highly interesting minor-key interpretation of **The Beatles'** *Here Comes The Sun* on the Japanese press, the B-side

Papa and the ghouls

of *Secular Haze* features Papa Emiritus II and his face- (and name-) less ghouls giving Swedish pop icons *ABBA* the same nice treatment. Bootlegs have now also started flooding the market.

2010 ■	Elizabeth/Death Knell	7"	Iron Pegasus	I.P.S 014	$$$

300 copies. Available in black, red, red/black and clear vinyl.

| 2010 □ | OPVS EPONYMVS | CD | Rise Above | RISECD1-24 | |
| 2010 □ | OPVS EPONYMVS | LP | Rise Above | RISELP1-24 | $($)$ |

First press: 300 purple, 400 blue, 400 clear/speckled, 300 tri-coloured, 300 green/black, 300 clear, 500 black/purple, 500 transparent blue, 500 clear/blue splatter. Second press: 500 black/purple, 500 clear/blue splatter, 500 transp. blue, 500 transp. red/blue, 500 clear/trans. purple, 500 white/black/blue splatter. Third press: 500 clear/purple splatter, 500 blue/clear, 300 black/clear. 2012 re-issue in gold vinyl and red vinyl.

| 2010 □ | OPVS EPONYMVS – DELUXE EDITION | LP box | Rise Above | RISELP124 | $$$ |

300 copies, black audiophile vinyl.

2010 7" - I.P.S 014

| 2010 □ | OPVS EPONYMVS | CD | Trooper (Japan) | XNTE-00035 | |

Bonus: Here Comes The Sun (Beatles cover)

2011 □	OPVS EPONYMVS	CD	Metal Blade (USA)	3984-14967-2	
2011 □	OPVS EPONYMVS	LP PD	Metal Blade (USA)	3984-25005-1	
2013 □	Secular Haze/A Marionette	10"	Universal	060253722432	$

200 copies clear or black vinyl. The B-side is an ABBA cover.

2013 □	Secular Haze	CDSp 1tr	- - (UK promo)	HAZECD 001	
2013 □	INFESTISSUMAM	CD	Universal/Sonet	060253731913	
2013 □	INFESTISSUMAM	LPg	Universal	060253734016	

2000 clear vinyl.

| 2013 □ | Secular Haze/A Marionette | CDS 2tr | Republic Records (USA) | 0253734778 | |
| 2013 □ | INFESTISSUMAM | CD | Republic Records (USA) | B0018321-02 | |

As Ghost B.C. Secret bonus tracks: La Mantra Mori/A Marionette (ABBA cover)

2013 □	INFESTISSUMAM	CDd	Republic Records (UK)	602537331246	
2013 □	INFESTISSUMAM	LPg	Republic Records (UK)	602537343737	
2013 □	Year Zero/Orez Raey	10" 2tr	Universal	060253734993	$

1500 green vinyl. Also available as picture disc.

2012 MLP - 666

Unofficial releases:

| 2012 ■ | The Early Rituals | MLP PD 3tr | - - | 666 | $ |

Tracks: Ritual/Prime Mover/Death Knell. One-sided PD. Demos.

| 2012 □ | Live Ceremony (Con Clavi Con Dio/Elizabeth) | 7" | - - | - - | $ |

66 numbered black, and 66 numbered clear vinyl copies.

| 2012 □ | Con Clavi Con Dio | 7" PD | - - | - - | |

20 numbered copies. Live at Hellfest, France 2011.

| 2013 □ | Until The Satan's Dawn | 10" 4tr Box | - - | - - | $$$ |

Tracks: Con Clavi Con Dio/Satan Prayer/Here Comes The Sun/Ritual. Live in Oregon 2012. Box with poster, pin, certificate. 10 numbered copies (acc to the disc).

GIANT
Karl Åke Wallin: g, Johan Evertsson: b, Knut Owe Wallin: d

Frövi - Outstanding, professional high-quality melodic metal with great vocals and musicians. Well worth looking for! Örebro based singer Roland "Rolle" Rosenqvist was used for the recording. After the band split the Wallin brothers played with the band *Taste*, not hard rock, who made a recording in Thunderload Studios which unfortunately didn't lead anywhere. Karl Åke sadly took his own life. Evertsson later joined *Motherlode*.

1989 7" - PL 67

| 1989 ■ | Got To Get Out/London Street | 7" | Platina | PL 67 | $ |

GILT
**Annica Jensen: v, Jörgen Holmberg: g, Svante Lundin: k,
Håkan Stiernström: b, Mikael Lundgren: d**

Sundsbruk - High-quality AOR with plenty of keyboard/guitar. At times reminiscent of Canadians *Wrabit*. Great female singer. Well worth searching for. They also have the two excellent tracks *Still Alive And Sane* and *I'm Beggin' You For It* on the *Promotion Music '92* compilation.

1991 7" - CUF 016

| 1991 ■ | Looking For An Alibi/Slippin' Away | 7" | CUF:s Skivklubb | CUF 016 | |

GIN LADY
**Magnus Kärnebro (aka Lindgren): v, Joakim Karlsson: g, Klas Holmgren: k,
Anthon Johansson: b, Fredrik Normark: d**

Skellefteå - In 2012 the band *Black Bonzo* died and was resurrected as *Gin Lady*, releasing their self-titled debut in 2012. The sound now became less progressive, leaning more towards classic hard rock such as seventies *Lucifer's Friend*, *Atomic Rooster* and *Uriah Heep*, with the occasional *Humble Pie* moment. A killer band with the perfect retro hard rock touch.

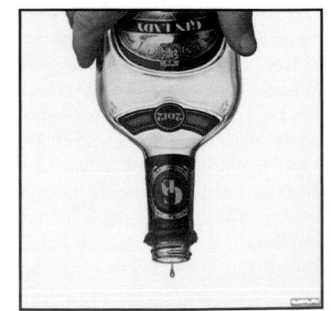

2012 □	GIN LADY	LPg	Transubstans Records	TRANSV 12	
2012 ■	GIN LADY	CD	Transubstans Records	TRANS 096	
2013 □	MOTHER'S RUIN	2CD	Transubstans Records	TRANS 117	

2012 CD - TRANS 096

GIN N' IT
Mike: v, Magnus "Nasty" Arens: g

Malmö - This is overblown, hyped out glam metal with a punkish attitude. The vocals are horrible, but the sound is really powerful. The two sleaze-boyz are backed by Robert (g), Robin (b) and Martin (d). Peter Espinoza (**Nasty Idols, Espinoza**) plays a guitar solo on one track.

1995 ■ STORIES OF A SAD SAD MAN...CD   HSM...HSMCD 014

1995 CD - HSMCD 014

GINGER TREES
Rasmus Blomqvist: v/g, Jonte Johansson: b, Johan Magnberg: d

Borås - The band was formed in 2007 by Rasmus Blomqvist and Henri Gylander in southern town Ronneby. In 2007 Rasmus relocated to Borås and original bassist Fredrik Hugosson was replaced by Jonte Johansson. Early 2009 Henri left the band, which now became a trio. Psychedelic rock, at times a bit too 60s to be hard rock, but they throw in the occasional heavy riff that should appeal to fans of early 70s hard rock. The Russian release is a paper sleeve version.

2008 ☐ CAME THE MORNING ....CD   Blue Topaz....................................BTRCD 29
2010 ■ ALONG WITH THE TIDE ....CDd   Transubstans ....TRANS 077
2011 ☐ ALONG WITH THE TIDE ....CDp   MALS (Russia)................................MALS 371

2010 CDd - TRANS 077

GLANZIG
Tony Jelencovich: v, Peter "Krist" Hynyadi: g,
Micael "Vån" Magnusson: b, Morgan "Cake" Pettersson: d

Göteborg - The band is more or less **Transport League** members under another name doing **Danzig**-covers, except for Magnusson who is originally found in **Supergroupies**. When the label wanted another album they suggested they would do a **Danzig**-tribute under their cover-band name and the label agreed. The cover is a based on **Danzig**'s *Lucifuge*-album.

1999 ■ GLANZIG 1 - GLANZIFUGE...CD   Mascot ....M 7040 2

1999 CD - M 7040 2

GLOOMY SUNDAY
Jari Kuittinen: v, Denis Boardman: g, Pär Boberg: b, Stefan Joansson: d

Göteborg - Heavily distorted stoner sludge with quite bad vocals. The band was formed in 2002.

2007 ■ BEYOND GOOD AND EVIL..CD   Solitude Productions..........................SP.011-0

GLORIA STORY, THE
Joan "Kid" Sallrot: v/g, Filip Rapp: v/g, Carl Ahlander: g,
Joakim Ståhl: b, Henrik Siberg: d

Skövde - The Gloria Story start off their debut album sounding like **Thin Lizzy** rip-offs of the worst kind, even the lyrics. It however does become better. The band released their first single track, *Oh No*, in 2010. The album was produced by former Hellacopter Anders "Bobba Fett" Lindström and it does show. The band wanders between the musical shores of **The Hellacopters**, **Thin Lizzy** and **The Ark** with some **T Rex** and vintage **Kiss** for good measures. Very 70s glamish and with a strong poppy vein on the melodic side. **The Gloria Story** was formed in 2009 and on stage they do act like the big rock stars they aim to be. The first single went platinum.

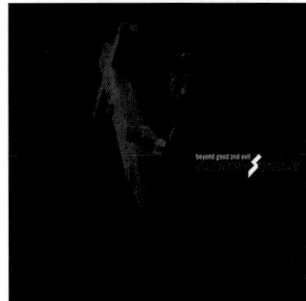

2007 CD - SP.011-0

2011 ■ SHADES OF WHITE..CD   Rambo Music.....................................TGS002
2012 ☐ Out Of The Shade ....MCD 4tr Wild Kingdom.............................KING 061 CD
　　　　Tracks: Adore/Tennis Is Nice/Oh No (EP remix)/Lacie Heart
2013 ☐ BORN TO LOSE ....CD   Wild Kingdom.............................KING 063 CD
2013 ☐ BORN TO LOSE ....LP   Wild Kingdom.............................KING 063 LP

GLORIOUS BANKROBBERS
Olle Hillborg: v, Jonas Petersson: g, Lake Skoglund: b, Anders "Oden" Odenstrand: d

Stockholm - One of Sweden's first sleaze bands, in the vein of **Hanoi Rocks**, formed in 1983. The initial line-up featured Olle, Jonas, guitarist Mikael Jansson, bassist Staffan Björkman and drummer Jörgen. Before the first album Mikael left and the two latter were replaced by bassist Pelham Söderström and drummer Anders Odenstrand. Before the second album Mikael was in again. In 1990 the band made a promotion tour in the USA, playing clubs like Cat Club, Red Spot and CBGBs. In 1992 Jonas, Mikael, Anders and Lake went on to form **Mental Hippie Blood** while Olle ended up in Norwegian band **Backstreet Girls**. The first album is a sought after item out on vinyl only. In 1987 Pelham left and was replaced by Lake. On the debut they did a cover of **Sex Pistols** *Did U No Wrong* and on *Dynamite Sex Doze* they did **Alice Cooper**'s *I'm Eighteen*. The band re-united in 2006, but without guitarist Mikael Jansson and released the album *The Glorious Sound Of Rock 'N Roll*, featuring new recorded songs, both unreleased and previously released ones. Jonas Petersson also released an album with rockers **Greed**.

2011 CD - TGS002

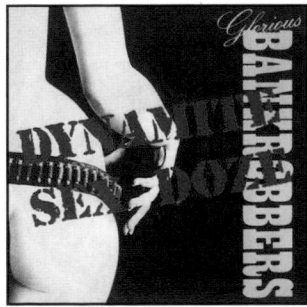

1989 7" - MOP 148

1984	☐	GLORIOUS BANKROBBERS	LP	Planet	MOP 3033
1989	☐	DYNAMITE SEX DOZE	CD	Planet	MOPCD 3052 $
1989	☐	DYNAMITE SEX DOZE	LP	Planet	MOPLP 3052
1989	○	Dynamite Sex Doze/Spitfire	12"	Planet	MOP 12/148
1989	■	Dynamite Sex Doze/Spitfire	7"	Planet	MOP 148
1991	☐	Live at CBGB's N.Y.C.	MCD 7tr	Planet	MOP 2003

Tracks: Crazy Sioux/Ridin' Down The Highway/Young Alcoholic/Dynamite Sex Doze/We Will Rock You/Spitfire/Hair Down To His Knees

1991	☐	Live at CBGB's N.Y.C.	MLP 7tr	Planet	MOP 2003
2001	☐	DYNAMITE SEX DOZE	CD	Musidisc (France)	MCD107012
2007	■	THE GLORIOUS SOUND OF ROCK 'N ROLL	CD	Swedmetal	SM-11-CD

Unofficial recordings:

| 2006 | ☐ | GLORIOUS BANKROBBERS | CD | Time Warp | - - |

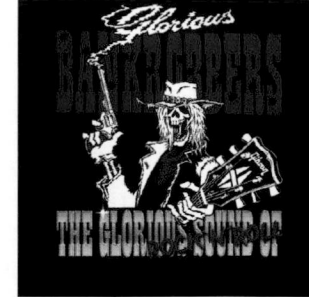

2007 CD - SM-11-CD

GLORY

Göran Edman: v, Jan "Granwick" Granvik: g, Mats Olausson: k, Johan Granström: b, Jonas Östman: d

Stockholm - Jan, who was born in Kiruna, recorded a single with the band *Grave* in 1984. He and drummer Mats "Matt Driver" Förare then recorded several demos with the band *Neptune*, which became *Glory North*, fronted by *Glory Bell's Band* singer Göran "Glory" Nordh, later replaced by Pelle Saether (*Unchained, Zeelion, Zello, Grand Design* etc), who recorded an album that was never released because the label went bust. In 1985 *Glory* was a reality. The first recording constellation featured Jan, Matt, singer Reine "Ray Alex" Alexandersson (ex-*Warreins*), keyboardist Jonas Sandkvist and bassist Anders Loos, but it only lasted for one single. Before the debut album Ray Alex was sacked and the new singer was Peter Ericson. Jonas was out of the band on the second album. In 1990 Granvik released a solo-single and started working on a solo-album, which never happened. Mats had to quit because of hearing problems. Now former *Madison*/*Malmsteen* singer Göran Edman joined the band and the album *Positive Buoyant* was a mix of instrumental guitar music, classical guitar and hard-edged AOR. Some of the material was actually written for Jan's solo-album. The members on this album were Göran, Jan, Anders Loos and drummer Jonas Östman (ex-*Gotham City*, *Mogg*, later with *Mental Hippie Blood*, *Malmsteen*). The 1994 line-up that recorded *Crisis vs Crisis*, the most complex and well-written album in the band's history, featured Göran, Jan, Mats, bassist Svante Henrysson and drummer Morgan Ågren. Olausson has also played with Malmsteen, *Motvind* and has worked as session musician on numerous albums. Svante played with Malmsteen and Morgan has played with *Mats & Morgan*, Dweezil and Frank Zappa among others. On *Wintergreen* the bass work was handled by Johan Granström and Östman was back on drums. The band sadly folded after this. Göran has since fronted various bands like *Kharma*, *Street Talk*, *Vindictiv*, *Mårran* etc.

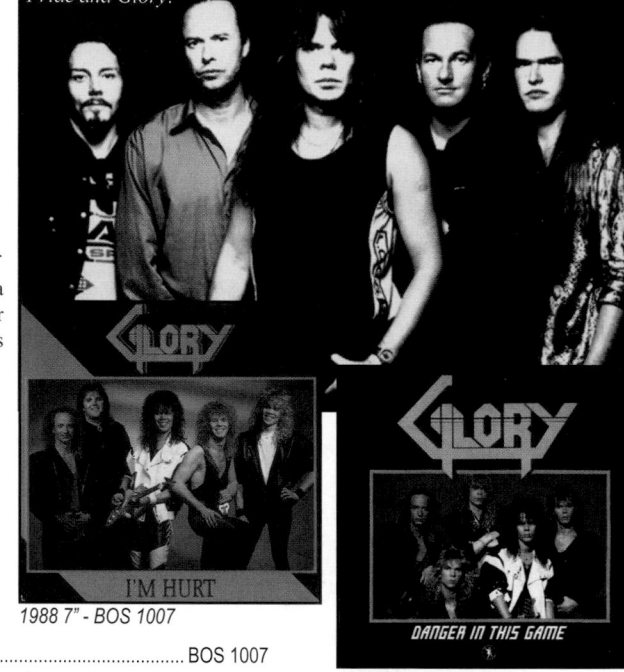

Pride and Glory!

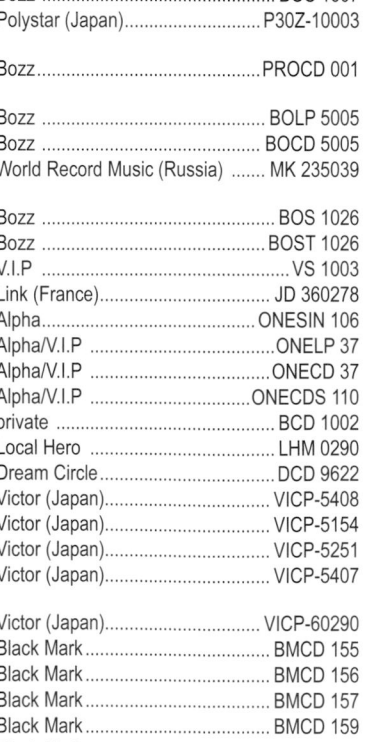

1988 7" - BOS 1007

| 1988 | ■ | I'm Hurt/Burning For You | 7" | Bozz | BOS 1007 |
| 1988 | ■ | DANGER IN THIS GAME | CD | Polystar (Japan) | P30Z-10003 |

Different artwork.

| 1989 | ☐ | Feel The Fire | MCD 4tr | Bozz | PROCD 001 |

Tracks: Feel The Fire/This Is The Love/Danger In This Game/Like An Eagle. Promo.

1989	☐	DANGER IN THIS GAME	LP	Bozz	BOLP 5005
1989	☐	DANGER IN THIS GAME	CD	Bozz	BOCD 5005
1989	■	DANGER IN THIS GAME	LP	World Record Music (Russia)	MK 235039

Different artwork.

1989	☐	Feel The Fire/Runaway	7"	Bozz	BOS 1026
1989	☐	Feel The Fire (single)/Feel The Fire (LP)/Runaway	12" 3tr	Bozz	BOST 1026
1989	☐	This Is The Love/Exhibition	7"	V.I.P	VS 1003
1990	☐	DANGER IN THIS GAME	LP	Link (France)	JD 360278
1991	☐	Love Never Lasts/Can't Hide Your Tears	7"	Alpha	ONESIN 106
1991	☐	2 FORGIVE IS 2 FORGET	LP	Alpha/V.I.P	ONELP 37
1991	☐	2 FORGIVE IS 2 FORGET	CD	Alpha/V.I.P	ONECD 37
1992	☐	Dr Of The Blues/Tonight	CDS 2tr	Alpha/V.I.P	ONECDS 110
1993	☐	POSITIVE BUOYANT	CD	private	BCD 1002
1994	☐	CRISIS VS. CRISIS	CD	Local Hero	LHM 0290
1996	☐	CRISIS VS. CRISIS	CD	Dream Circle	DCD 9622
1996	☐	DANGER IN THIS GAME	CD	Victor (Japan)	VICP-5408
1996	☐	2 FORGIVE IS 2 FORGET	CD	Victor (Japan)	VICP-5154
1996	☐	POSITIVE BUOYANT	CD	Victor (Japan)	VICP-5251
1997	☐	CRISIS VS CRISIS	CD	Victor (Japan)	VICP-5407

Different artwork. Also available as counterfeit without OBI.

1998	☐	WINTERGREEN	CD	Victor (Japan)	VICP-60290
2000	☐	WINTERGREEN	CD	Black Mark	BMCD 155
2000	☐	POSITIVE BUOYANT	CD	Black Mark	BMCD 156
2000	☐	CRISIS VS. CRISIS	CD	Black Mark	BMCD 157
2000	☐	Kite Of Love	CDS	Black Mark	BMCD 159
2000	☐	Blue Heaven	MCD 3tr	Black Mark	BMCD 160

Tracks: Blue Heaven (radio mix)/Kite Of Love (radio mix)/Blue Heaven (album mix)

1989 LP - BOLP 5005

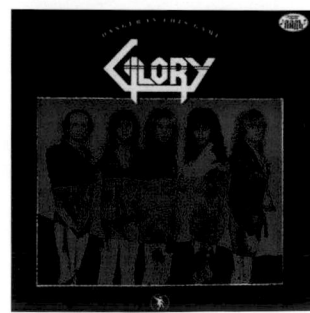

1989 LP - MK 235039

GLORY BELLS/GLORY BELL'S BAND

Göran "Glory North" Nordh: v, Miguel Santana: g, Franco Santuione: g,
Mats Andersson: g/k, Bo Andersson: b, Peter "Udd" Sandberg: d

Stockholm - Before joining *Glory Bell's Band* in 1980, singer Göran Nordh released the solo single under his own name, *Die In Two Different Countries*, where the song *Oh I Am The Captain* was later rerecorded for the first album. *Dressed In Black* features some good 80's hard rock songs but the vocals and in particular the English, is appalling. Franco later joined *Electric Boys* and Peter was ex-*Råg I Ryggen* and *Rising Force*. On *Century Rendez-Vous* the band shortened their name to *Glory Bells*, but the style is the same. In January 1985, the band broke up and singer Glory North formed the band *Glory North* with guitarist Jan Granvik, Björn Melander (*Gotham City, Neptune, Mogg*), Franco Santuione (*Electric Boys, Reptile Smile*) and Mats "Matt Driver" Förare. They recorded the album *National Force* but the band split and the label went bust. Göran was replaced by Pelle Saether (ex-*Unchained*, now *Grand Design*) and the band later evolved into *Glory*. Göran himself was still out rockin' in 2002 (a one-off reunion was made), trying to get a new band together, but in 2008 he sadly passed away.

1982 LP - SOSLO 068

1982 ■	DRESSED IN BLACK	LP	SOS	SOSLP 068
	Released as Glory Bells Band.			
1984 ■	CENTURY RENDEZ-VOUS	LP	SOS	SOSLP 119
1984 □	CENTURY RENDEZ-VOUS	LP	Bellaphon	260.07.071
1984 □	CENTURY RENDEZ-VOUS	LP	Nexus (Japan)	K25P486
1985 □	CENTURY RENDEZ-VOUS	LP	Thunderbolt (UK)	THBL 023
1994 □	CENTURY RENDEZ-VOUZ	CD	King Records (Japan)	KICP 2624

Unofficial releases:

n/a □	DRESSED IN BLACK/CENTURY RENDEZ-VOUZ	CD	Sound Of Scandinavia	SOSCD 068/119

1984 LP - SOSLP 119

GOD AMONG INSECTS

Magnus "Emperor Magus Caligula" Broberg: v, Kenta "Lord K" Philipson: g,
Tomas Elofsson: b, Tobias Gustafsson: d

Stockholm - God Among Insects were formed in 2004 and features part of the "who's who" of Swedish death metal. Caligula is found in *Dark Funeral, Dominion Caligula, Hypocrisy*, Philipson is *Dark Funeral, House Of Usher, Leukemia, The Project Hate, Torture Division* etc., Elofsson is in *Sanctification* and *Divine Descecration* and Gustafsson is in *Torture Division, Vomitory* and *Syrus*. The band plays sludgy death metal and tuned down 11 half steps to make a heavy impact. The second album showed a slightly faster side of the band. In 2007 the band announced they would exit the scene and made their last performance at the House Of Metal Festival in 2008. Caligula also plays a part in the German movie *Die Zombiejäger* (the zombie hunter).

2004 CD - TRECD 013

2004 ■	WORLD WIDE DEATH	CD	Threeman	TRECD 013
2006 ■	ZOMBIENOMICON	CD	Threeman	TRECD 020

2006 CD - TRECD 020

GOD B.C.

Magnus "Manuck" Nilsson: g, Jesper "Ratt B" Granath: b, Thomas "Tom" Hallbäck: d

Helsingborg - The band was formed in 1986, initially called *God*, and at the time featuring singer/guitarist Pierre Richter (*Agretator, Demise*) and singer Fredrik Elander. They recorded the demos *God* (1987) and *Four Wise Men* (1988), before being picked up by Wild Rags Records. When recording the album, the trio had no permanent singer, but borrowed Jocke Warneryd for the album. Together with some members from *Hyste'riah* they later turned into *Hyste'riah G.B.C.* Granath was later in *Agretator* and guitarist Nilsson in *Time Requiem* and *Space Odyssey*. Fast, furious and quite good thrash with quite melodic vocals, similar to early *Metallica* and *Anthrax*.

1989 □	EARGASMS IN EDEN	CD	Wild Rags Records	WRR 013
1989 ■	EARGASMS IN EDEN	LP	Wild Rags Records	WRR 013
1989 □	EARGASMS IN EDEN	LP PD	Wild Rags Records	WRR 013

1989 LP - WRR 013

GOD KILLS

Phil Levy: v, Richard Sjöberg: g, Magnus Wikholm: g,
Magnus Malte Olsson: b, Robert "Robban" Eriksson: d

Frösön (Östersund) - Formed late 1991 and in 1993 they relocated to Stockholm. Low-budget production, but well-played promising raunchy hard rock. In 1993 Robert was also a roadie for *Entombed* and also played in punksters *Sexationals* (later *The Killbillies*). In 1994 he joined *The Hellacopters, The Sewergrooves* and in 2004 he joined *Midlife Crisis*. God Kills band split in 1994. Wikholm is now in *Maxwell Jackson*.

1993 ■	God Kills	MCD 5tr	Local Hero	LHM 0181
	Tracks: I/Mayor/Kick Out The Trash/To Young/Dreams			

1993 MCD - LHM 0181

GOD MACABRE

Per Boder: v, Ola Sjöberg: g, Jonas Stålhammar: g, Thomas Johansson: b

Karlstad - Formed in 1988 as *Botten på Burken* (the bottom of the can) playing grindcore and changed their name to *Macabre End* in 1989. In 1990 they recorded the demo *Consumed By Darkness*, which was slightly altered and then released by Corpse Grinder Records as a 7" EP under the name *Macabre End*. One of the pioneers in the Swedish death metal scene. After this they changed their name to *God Macabre*. The album was actually recorded already in December 1991, but wasn't released until 1993, when the band had already split. On the CD they used session drummer Niclas Nilsson. *God Macabre* is a tight and technical death metal band with the traditional low pitch vocals. *The Winterlong* is recorded at Sunlight Studios and engineered by Tomas Skogsberg. Sjöberg and Boder went on to form *Snake Machine* which later turned into stoner band *Space Probe Taurus*. Stålhammar has also been found in *Abhoth*, *The Crown* and *Utumno*. *Eve Of Souls Forsaken* was recorded live at Forshaga Folkets Hus in 1991. The "re-issue" by Strike Force Records is a CD-R bootleg.
Website: www.myspace.com/godmacabreend

1991 7" - CGR 001

1993 CD - MANGLED 6

2002 CD - RR 6843-2

1991 ■ Consumed By Darkness ....7"	Corpse Grinder Records...................CGR 001
Tracks: Consumed By Darkness/Cease To Be/Spawn Of Flesh. Released as Macabre End		
1993 ■ THE WINTERLONG ....CD	MBR Records .... MANGLED 6
2002 ■ THE WINTERLONG ....CD	Relapse Records .... RR 6483-2
Re-issue featuring the tracks from Consumed By Darkness as bonus.New artwork.		
2008 □ THE WINTERLONG ....LP	Blood Harvest YOTZ20
2010 □ Eve Of Sould Forsaken...............................MLP 6tr	HMSS (Japan) HMSS-CD-099
Tracks: Spawn Of Flesh/Into Nowhere/Ashes Of Mourning Life/The Day Man Lost (Carnage cover)/Lost-Consumed By Darkness/In Grief		

GODDAMNED, THE

Teo Dahnberg: v, Joakim Widén: g, Dennis Widén: b, Henrik Allbjer: d

Falkenberg - After death metal band *Moria* recorded their last demo, *K.I.A*, in 2001 they reformed as *The Goddamned*, with Teo switching from bass to vocals. The style had now changed into *Motörhead*-style hard rock/metal. Recorded their first 8-track demo in 2002, followed by the 4-track *Damned* in 2004, the 5-track *It Takes A Good Horse* in 2006, 3-track *Head First* in 2007 and the 3-track *Disaster Comes Along* in 2008. After this bass player Fredrik Johansson (*Draconian*) left and was replaced by Fredrik Pettersson. Before the album guitarist Kim Gustafsson was replaced by Joakim and bass player Fredrik Pettersson by Dennis. In 2011 the band released another three-track demo entitled *General Bad Luck*.
Website: www.thegoddamned.com

The Goddamned

2009 ■ THE GODDAMNED ....CD	private .... GDMND

2009 CD - GDMND

GODDEFIED

Janne Arvidsson: v/g, Rickard Eriksson: g/b

Karlskoga - Fast death metal quite similar to early *Ceremonial Oath*. Formed in 1989 as thrash band *Hymen Imperforatus*, but changed their style and name the following year. They went through *Assembly* and *Enshrined* before they settled for *Goddefied* in 1991. Only Arvidsson and Eriksson remained from the first line-up and they were flanked by guitarist Jonas Aneheim and drummer Mattias Pettersson. In 1992 they entered Studio Sunlight to record a three-track demo. Wild Rags Records showed immediate interest in the band and three more tracks were recorded and released as the MCD *Abysmal Grief*. In 1995 the band split up because of internal problems. Janne has been and Jonas is found in the industrial/synth band *Pouppée Fabrikk* that has released two albums. Before the band split, Mattias was replaced by Felipe Queiroz. Jonas, Janne and Rickard later formed hardcore band *Lame*, with the addition of Marcus Tjernström. Mattias was later in crust band *Mörder* and hardcore band *Misconduct*. However, in 2007 things started happening again. Arvidsson and Eriksson resurrected the beast, now playing a more modern type of death metal. Session drummer Magnus "Dirk" Hellman (*Pure Massacre*) is also part of the plan. In 2008 *Abysmal Grief* was reissued on vinyl and a 7" EP featuring two new tracks and a rerecorded oldie, was unearthed. Material for a new release was being recorded in 2009, but nothing has happened since.
Website: www.goddefied.com

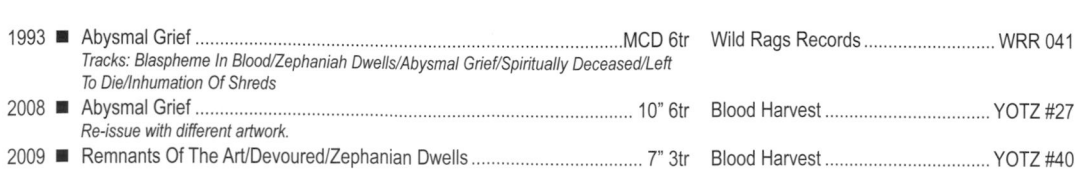

1993 MCD - WRR 041

2008 10" - YOTZ #27

2009 7" - YOTZ #40

1993 ■ Abysmal Grief ....MCD 6tr	Wild Rags Records .... WRR 041
Tracks: Blaspheme In Blood/Zephaniah Dwells/Abysmal Grief/Spiritually Deceased/Left To Die/Inhumation Of Shreds		
2008 ■ Abysmal Grief ....10" 6tr	Blood Harvest .... YOTZ #27
Re-issue with different artwork.		
2009 ■ Remnants Of The Art/Devoured/Zephanian Dwells .... 7" 3tr	Blood Harvest .... YOTZ #40

GODGORY

Matte Andersson: v, Erik Andersson: d

Karlstad - **Godgory** were formed in August 1992 by Matte and Erik (not related despite the same last name). They soon recruited guitarists Stefan Grundel/Olsson and Mikael Dahlquist and bass player Fredrik Danielsson. They started out playing covers by **Entombed**, **Grave**, **Unleashed** and **Napalm Death** before writing their own material. In 1994 they entered Dan Swanö's Unisound to record their first demo simply entitled *Demo 94*. Invasion Records showed interest and the recordings of the debut started. In 1996 it was finally released. Death metal with a gothic touch. Varies from acoustic guitar parts to really heavy doom-oriented music and the odd fast track. The title track on the debut is an orchestrated song with high-class arrangement and highly interesting guitar work. The vocals are of the growling death type. Recorded at Unisound and produced by Dan Swanö. Matte has also recorded a demo with his depressive, doom-oriented, solo project **Grave Flowers** and is also found in punksters **Mantaray-K.D**. On the first two releases the line-up was Matte, Erik, Stefan Grundel/Olsson (g), Mikael Dahlquist (g), Thomas Hedner (k) and Fredrik Danielsson (b). Mikael, Fredric and Thomas were involved in their prog-metal band **World Of Silence**, which is why on the last album Mikael and Thomas acted as session musicians. The band does a cover of *Princess Of The Dawn* on A *Tribute To Accept Vol II* (02 Nuclear Blast).

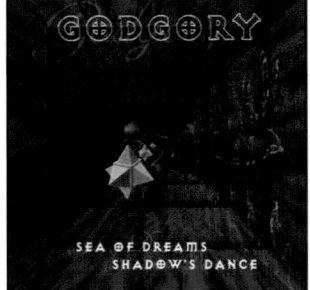

1995 CD - IR 017

1996 CD - NBCD 371-2

1995 ■	SEA OF DREAMS	CD	Invasion		IR 017
1996 ☐	SHADOW'S DANCE	CD	Invasion		IR 021
1999 ■	RESURRECTION	CD	Nuclear Blast		NBCD 371-2
1999 ☐	RESURRECTION	CD	Nuclear Blast America (USA)		NBA 6371-2
2001 ☐	SEA OF DREAMS/SHADOW'S DANCE	2CD	Hammerheart		HUW 014
2001 ■	WAY BEYOND	CD	Nuclear Blast		NB 534-2
2001 ☐	WAY BEYOND	CD	Nuclear Blast America (USA)		NBA 6534-2
2001 ☐	WAY BEYOND	CD	Irond (Russia)		01-93
2002 ☐	RESURRECTION	CD	Irond (Russia)		02-343
2009 ☐	WAY BEYOND	CDd	Metal Mind		MASS CD 1330 DG

2000 hand numbered copies.

2001 CD - NB 534-2

GODHATE

Tony Freed: v/g, Björn "Chris" Johansson: g, Björn Eriksson: b, Roger Sungquist: d

Västerås - **Godhate** started out as **Mysterion** in 1991, later **Beyond Black Horizon** and in 1995 **Thronaeon**, under which name they made several recordings. The line-up then featured Tony Freed (v/g), Roger Sundquist (d), Göran Eriksson (g) and Andreas Dahlström (b). Jens Klovegård (Abhoth) handled the bass in 1993, left and returned in 1998. In 2003 the band changed name to **Godhate** after releasing an album by this title, but as **Thronaeon**... On the last **Thronaeon** album the bass was handled by Magnus Wall, who was replaced by Claes Ramberg (**Abhoth, In Aeternum**). In 2005 the band released the Anguish demo on CD-R, officially released in 2008. Dahlström returned for a short stint as temporary tour replacement. In 2006 Clas left the band. In 2008 Tony declared that he had formed a new project called **Innersane** and considered putting **Godhate** to rest. However, he changed his mind and returned with a new line-up, which made its debut on the 2010 release. A cover of *Kingdom Gone* can be found on *Slaughterous Souls: A Tribute To At The Gates* (2004). In 2012 the Thronaeon recordings were released by Metal Fortress, however, under the **Godhate** banner (see **Throneaeon** for further info).
Website: www.godhate.com

2008 MCD - МГЕ 014

2008 ■	Anguish	MCD 4tr	Metal Fortress		MFE 014
	Tracks: In Fear Of God/Anguish/Promethean Ascension/With Might And Main				
2010 ■	EQUAL IN THE EYES OF DEATH	CD	Metal Age Productions		MAP 080

2010 CD - MAP 080

GODPHOBIA

Robin Westlund: v/b, Linus Nylen: d/v, Mika Kajanen: g, Niklas Liliengren: g

Stockholm - **Godphobia** were formed in 2006 from the remains of **Torture Eternal**. After the split, a new band, named **Chaos**, was formed by Tobbe (g), Linus (d) and Johan (g). They changed their name to **Godphobia** and entered Necromorbus' Studio to record a demo in October the same year. The band was now completed by singer Robin. The demo lead to a deal with Cutting Edge Records who released the debut. Prior to the album bass player Richard joined. He however left in 2007 and was replaced by Mika, also in modern melodic rockers **Faceshift**. In January 2008 a new album entitled *As Maggots Crawl* was recorded, but during the recording guitarist Johan left the band. He was replaced by Paul, who was sacked not long after. After using some session members Niklas Liliengren filled the guitar slot. In 2010 the band was signed by Noise Head and on Friday the 13th *Necrolust Madness* was released. **Godphobia** play a mix of grindcore and death metal.

2007 CD - - -

2007 ■	ON YOUR KNEES	CD	Cutting Edge		- -
2010 ■	NECROLUST MADNESS	CD	Noise Head Records		NHR 1510

2010 CD - NHR 1510

GODS INCORPORATED

Eddie Nilsson: v, Per Gustavsson: g/k/v, Mats Holm: b, Niklas Lövgren: d

Fagersta - In 1994 Eddie and Mats joined forces. It wasn't until three years later, when Per and Niklas joined things started happening. The band released two albums and then disappeared in 2001. *Gods Incorporated* play quite dark, almost goth-influenced heavy rock.

1998	☐	BULLET FROM INSIDE	CD	EPR	CD 02
1999	■	THIS HEAVEN'S HELL	CD	private	- -

1999 CD - - -

GOLDEN DAWN

Jonas Tropp: g/v, Mats Tropp: g/v, Roger Lindbladh: b, Raymond Henning Lindblad: d

Pjungserud (Töreboda) - Great classic eighties heavy metal with a NWoBHM touch. Started out in 1986/87 doing covers of *Moxy, Priest, Nugent* etc. Split in 1990.

1988	■	Cold Hearted Woman/So Far Away	7"	Platina	PL 48 $

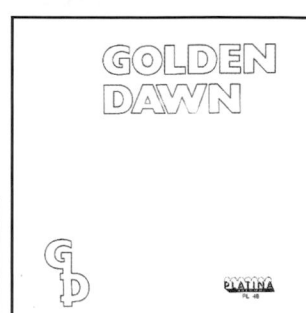

1988 7" - PL 48

GOLDEN RESURRECTION

Christian Liljegren: v, Tommy Johansson: g/v, Svenne Jansson: k,
Stefan Käck: b, Alfred Fridhagen: d

Stockholm - In 2008 former *Narnia/Modest Attraction/Audiovision/DivineFire* singer Christian Liljegren joined forces with *ReinXeed* singer/guitarist Tommy Johansson and formed the band *Golden Resurrection*. The aim was to bring back the neoclassical metal of the late 80s to life. The band was completed by bass player Stefan Käck, keyboardist Olov Andersson (*Grand Stand/Audiovision*) and former *Pantokrator* drummer Rickard Gustafsson. In 2011 the band also recorded the song *Pray For Japan*. *Golden Resurrection* continued on the early path of Narnia, neo-classic melodic metal which should appeal to fans of Mr Malmsteen, *Impellitteri* etc. Great guitar playing from the swift-handed Tommy Johansson. Liljegren is also the man behind Rivel Records and Liljegren Records. On the second album keyboardist Andersson was replaced by Kenneth Lillqvist. On the album *One Voice For The Kingdom* the line-up had again changed featuring new keyboardist Svenne Jansson and drummer Alfred Fridhagen. Musically the album offers yet another slab off well-played melodic power metal with a neoclassical touch.

2011 CDS - DOOCD002

2010	☐	GLORY TO MY KING	CD	Liljegren Records	LRCD 003
2010	☐	GLORY TO MY KING	CD	King Records (Japan)	KICP-1498
		Bonus: Metal Praise			
2011	☐	MAN WITH A MISSION	CD	Liljegren Records	LRCD 008
2011	☐	MAN WITH A MISSION	CD	King Records (Japan)	KICP-1591
		Bonus: Point Of Know Return (Kansas cover)/The End Of The World/Pray For Japan			
2011	■	Pray For Japan/(Radio edit)	CDS 2tr	Dolittle Group	DOOCD002
2012	■	ONE VOICE FOR THE KINGDOM	CD	Liljegren Records	LRCD 0014

2012 CD - LRCD 0014

GONDOLINE

Robert Hoffman: v, Johan Bäckström: g, Anders Levander: k,
Andreas Bonnevier: b, Henrik Nilsson: d

Sollentuna (Stockholm) - Formed January 1st 1986. High-quality mid-soft AOR with a sound quite reminiscent of *Saga*. Great vocal capacity. Johan left and was replaced by Håkan Olsson, and the band changed musical direction towards softer pop/rock. Anders was later replaced by Peter Nylén and the band changed their name to *Hoffman's Circus*. In 1995 they released their debut, entitled *Just Around The Hill*. Andreas also played with pop singer Roger Rönning.

1988	■	Madman/Standing In The Rain	7"	Wire & Wood Records	GOS 001

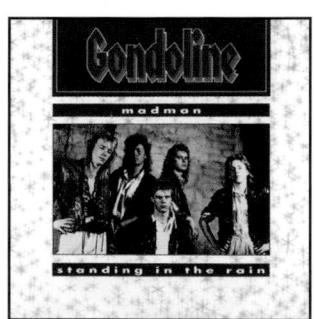

1988 7" - GOS 001

GONE

Björn Flodkvist: v, Mats Ståhl: g, Måns P. Månsson: g/k,
Peter Hellström: b, Stefan Kälfors: d

Stockholm - Stefan is ex-*Krixhjälters/Omnitron*, Björn was previously in punksters *Rolands Gosskör* and Måns has played in *Crimson Shadow* and *Zonk*. This band has a very heavy and powerful sound, yet they blend the heaviness with odd twists and nice melodies. Interesting. A cover of *Die You Bastard* is featured on the compilation *Motörhead Tribute* (95 Pink Honey) and they have also recorded the soundtrack to a snowboard movie. *Demology* contains demos recorded between 1991-1995, also featuring Lars Andersson on drums and guitarist Daniel Frödén guitar on some tracks. *Into The Bright…* only contains Björn, Stefan, Mats and Peter. Flodkvist was later in *Candlemass* and *Enter The Hunt*.

1994	■	NOTHING	MCD 6tr	Frisbee	FBEE 1001
		Tracks: Nothing/Clodmasher/Pus/Brain/Radiant/Gonejah			
1997	☐	INTO THE BRIGHT OXYGEN OF MY NOD	CD	Pink Honey	ROSACD 73
1997	■	DEMOLOGY	CD	Pink Honey	ROSACD 74

1994 MCD - FBEE 1001

GOOSEFLESH

Kristian Lampila: v/g, Tommy Scalisi Svensson: g, Robert Hakemo: b, Lars Berger: d

Trollhättan - Formed in 1995. Dead heavy hard rock/metal, quite similar to what *Entombed* did on *To Ride, Shoot Straight...* High-quality heavy stuff. After having made four highly-acclaimed demos, the last one was finally released as a MCD by Spanish label Goldtrack Records. The High Gain release was only available as a paper-sleeve promo and did not reach the market before the label went bust. The official release on Digital Dimension was re-mastered. The band is featured on the compilation *Powers From The North* with a cover of *Trash*'s *Boogie Woogie Man*. The band folded in 2000. Lampila was also in *Relevant Few* and Scalisi has his own band *Electric Earth*. Hakemo has also been found in *Ton Of Bricks*, *Gardenian*, *Relevant Few* and *Engel*.

1997 CD - ROSACD 74

1998	☐	Welcome To The Suffer Age ....MCD 5tr	Goldtrack	.....................................GT 006 MCD	
		Tracks: Suffer Age/Blinded/Killing Stone/Seeds Of Terror/Fine Tuned War Machine			
1999	☐	CHEMICAL GARDEN ....CDp	High Gain	..........................0055332HGR-ACY	
		Never officially released. Only available as cardboard cover promo.			
1999	■	CHEMICAL GARDEN ....CD	Digital Dimension	.......................0060072 DDE	
		Bonus: Thin Skinned Jesus			
1999	☐	CHEMICAL GARDEN ....CD	Dolphin (Japan)	...........................BLCK-86035	
		Bonus: Black/Eyes Sewn Shut			
1999	☐	CHEMICAL GARDEN ....CD	Digital Dimension (USA)	.................DD7003-2	
		Different track order.			

1999 CD - 0060072 DDE

GORDON FIGHTS

Viktor Balkewitsch Persson: v/g, Tobias Alpadie: g,
Anders Carlsson: k, Patrik Engström: b, Rasmus Söderling: d

Stockholm - *Gordon Fights* is one of Sweden's numerous retro bands. Formed in 2008 and made their first recording later the same year. In 2009 the CD-R EP *Vol 1* was released. The band owes a lot to the likes of *Humble Pie*, *Free*, *Led Zeppelin* and newer acts like *The Answer*, *Graveyard* and *Wolfmother* with a southern touch and a true 70s sound. Very strong song material performed really well. A great band! The album features a guest spot by classic Swedish singer Cyndee Peters. Alpadie has also been found in *Insision* and *Jesaiha*.
Website: www.gordonfights.se

Gordon may fight but these guys seem peaceful

2011	■	GORDON FIGHTS...CD	Transubstans	...............................TRANS 084	

2011 CD - TRANS 084

GOREMENT

Jimmy Karlsson: v, Patrik Fernlund: g, Daniel Eriksson: g,
Nicklas Lilja: b, Mattias Berglund: d

Nyköping - *Gorement* were formed in 1990, from the remains of *Sanguinary*. Heavy mid-tempo death metal in the vein of *Carcass* with growling pitched-down vocals. The band relies on heavy riffs and a doom-oriented touch, even though there are faster moments. The band's first three-track demo *Human Relic* was recorded by Dan Swanö at Gorysound in 1991. Vocals on the demo was handled by Micke, who was soon replaced by former *Mortified Flesh* singer Jimmy. The second demo, *Obsequies,* was recorded later the same year. This was later released as the first 7". In 1995 the band recorded another three-track demo simply entitled *Promo '95*. Now drummer Mattias left and was replaced by Robin Bergh (*October Tide, Amaran*), but the band folded later the same year. However, they reformed with different members and a new melodic style under the name *Pipers Dawn* in 1996. Guitarist Patrik is now in *Meshuggah*-style staccato-metallurgists *Genuflection To Limbo*, whose demo *Demo 2001* is a hard-hitting and interesting installment. *Darkness Of The Dead* is a retrospective compilation of *The Ending Quest, Human Relic* demo, *Obesequies, Into Shadows* and one track from the *Promo '95*. Eriksson has also been found in *Moribund*, Karlsson in *Grief Of Emerald* and *Cretoria*. The 2012 release is a compilation of the complete demo/7"/CD works remastered by Dan Swanö.

1994 CD - DA 8207-2

1992	☐	Obsequies.. 7" 4tr	After World	....AWR 005	
		Tracks: Intro/Process Of Cent/Gruesome Modification Of Form/Obsequies Of Mankind. Red marbled vinyl.			
1992	■	Into Shadows/The Memorial ....7"	Poserslaughter	....................................PSR 007	
		White vinyl.			
1994	■	THE ENDING QUEST..CD	Crypta	....DA 8207-2	
2004	☐	DARKNESS OF THE DEAD ....CD	Necroharmonic	...........................SLEAZY 010	
2012	■	WITHIN THE SHADOW OF DARKNESS 2CD	Century Media	9982552	
2012	☐	WITHIN THE SHADOW OF DARKNESS ....2LPg+2CD	Century Media	9982551	

1992 7" - PSR 007

2012 2CD - 9982552

GORMATHON

Tony Sunnhag: v, Stefan Jonsson: g, Peter Sonefors: g,
Thomas Hedlund: b, Tony Sandberg: d

Bollnäs - The origin of this band stretches all the way back to 1987, when they started out under the name *Overload* (featuring Tony, Stefan and Tony), under which name they made several recordings (see *Overload*) in a classic hard rock/metal direction. In 2006 they started to change musical direction towards melodic death metal and decided to change their name to *Gormathon*. In 2009 the band was reinforced by bass player Thomas Hedlund and guitarist Peter Sonefors. A three-track demo was recorded, which lead to a deal with Supernova. After the album Hedlund was replaced by Kalle Svedåker.

2010 CD - SUPERCD 003

2010 ■ LENS OF GUARDIAN...CD Supernova .... SUPERCD 003

GOSH!

Anders Johansson: v, Patrik Heath: v, Dan Ryteniemi: g,
Marcus Mustafa: g, Jonaz Lindgren: b, Jens Heath: d

Göteborg - Formed in 1992 by Jonas and Dan. The line-up on the two first releases were Anders, Patrik, Jonaz, Dan, Jens, Henke Karlsson (v) and Jörgen Larsson (k). The members have quite colourful backgrounds. Dan is ex-*Cloud Catchers* and also drummer in *The Pogues*-style band *Bad Liver*, Jonaz played keyboards on *Submachines* mini-CD and even on some cassettes Volvo produced for their employees. He also handled the bass on *Mary Beats Jane*'s debut, Mustafa was previously in popsters *Mystery* and Henke recorded two albums with doom-rockers *Stillborn*. The band mixes all kinds of styles from rap and hip-hop to out and out metal. The band also have the non-LP track *No Deposit* on the *Backstage '95* compilation. A great band!

1994 MCD - NSM 4540

1994 CD - NSM 3319

1994 ■ Shaved/Shaved (remix)/Party Prople (live)...........................MCD 3tr Nonstop ....NSM 4540
1994 ■ PEACE THRU SUPERIOR FIREPOWER ....CD Nonstop ....NSM 3319
1994 ○ Hard Fist/Hard fist (live)/Jesus Loves A Prostitute ....MCD 3tr Nonstop (promo)............................NSM 4546

GOTHAM CITY

Anders Zackrisson: v, Mårten Edlund: g, Björn Erik Melander: b, Jonas Östman: d

Umeå - Formed in 1980. This band started out as a pretty simple metal band with quite bad vocals. Despite this the debut single is a highly priced item. Singer on the single and first MLP was Ola Ohlsson, who was replaced by Anders in 1983. *The Unknown* is a great piece of vinyl in the style of *Tygers Of Pan Tang*, well worth checking out. The band split in 1987. Björn quit in 1984 and went on to *Mogg, Glory North, Neptune* and now has his own studio, producing relaxing music. He was replaced by Torbjörn "Tobbe" Moen (*Red Fun, Creozoth, Oz*). Jonas also left in 1984 and later joined *Mogg, Glory, Mental Hippie Blood, Yngwie Malmsteen* and *Dark Illusion*. He was replaced by Frank Stenbom (*Oz, Witch*), who was shortly after replaced by Lars-Åke Edström. The band also drafted second guitarist Michael Lundholm (*Oz*) in 1986. The band split in 1987. Anders was later found in power metal band *Nocturnal Rites*, with whom he recorded three albums. In the late 90's he joined the band *Born Bandit* that recorded some pretty interesting demo material. He was also a member of *Planet Storm* and is today fronting *Shade Of Grey*. *The Legend Of Gotham City* is a compilation of all the band's releases.

1982 7" - BFR 004

1983 MLP - BFR 009

1984 LP - FING 006

1982 ■ Gotham City/Killer Angels ....7" Brute Force Records.........................BFR 004 **$$$**
1983 ■ Black Writs ....MLP 6tr Brute Force Records.........................BFR 009 **$**
       Tracks: Monsters Of Rock/1995/The Coven/Black Writs/Born To Rock Hard/In Vino
       Veritas
1984 ■ THE UNKNOWN...LP Fingerprint Records .... FING 006 **$**
2005 □ THE LEGEND OF GOTHAM CITY ....CD Metal Crusade .... METCRU 00143

Unofficial releases:
1995 □ Gotham City/Killer Angels ....7" New Wave Of Swedish Heavy Metal 002
       Counterfeit in clear vinyl.

GRACE

Bernt Ek: b/v, Jan Morin: g, Dick Greuz: g, Henrik Thall: k,
Mikael Junell: k, Janne Lundberg: d

Luleå - *Grace* was formed in 1976 and recorded their debut two years later. The style is high-quality symphonic rock in the vein of *Blåkulla* or early *Marillion* sung in Swedish. Bernt later joined *Wildliw, Bedlam, Wizz* and *The Station/House Of Shakira*. Janne Lundberg was previously in the band *Marathon*. Thall, who later recorded with bands *Vision* and *Grave*, sadly died of a heart attack in June 1995. He was said to be more or less a musical genius.

1981 LP - MAN 20

1981 ■ BLIND ....LP Manifest...MAN 20

GRAND DESIGN

**Pelle Saether: v, Dennis Vestman: g, Janne Stark: g,
Mats Vassfjord: b, Peter Hermansson: d**

Västerås - *Grand Design* started out as a brainchild of former *Unchained/Schizophrenic Circus/Zello/Zeelion* singer Pelle, to create a new band in the vein of classic *Def Leppard*. He drafted former *Vanessa* guitarist Peter Ledin, *Steel Attack* guitarist Dennis Westman, *Wolf* members Anders Mood on bass and Holmgren on drums and *Grand Design* was a reality. Holmgren was, by the way, also in *Vanessa*. The band is a true nod to the English Leppards with the same type of song style, sound and big harmony vocals. Great-quality stuff indeed. Tommy Denander and Janne Stark also guest on lead guitar (trivia: Stark also actually came up with the band name, first album title and made the logo). In 2011 the band recorded the exclusive track *Love Will Shine The Way* for AOR Heaven's *Rock For Japan* compilation, where Stark also does a guest solo. The second album saw the band elevate the *Leppard*-infused melodic hard rock even further. Denander does a guest solo on this one as well. In January 2012 the band announced a vast line-up change, where Ledin, Mood and Holmgren were out of the band, replaced by guitarist Janne Stark (*Overdrive, Constancia, Locomotive Breath, Zoom Club, Mountain Of Power, BALLS* etc), bass player Mats Vassfjord (*Chris Laney's Legion, Scaar, Pink Panther*) and drummer Peter Hermansson (*220 Volt, Talisman, Norum, Zoom Club*). The new line-up released a digital single, a cover of the eighties bands *Promises'* hit *Baby It's You* in May 2013, featuring guest vocals from pop singer Susie Päivärinta (*Lili & Susie*). Early 2013 Peter Hermansson was replaced by Magnus Ulfstedt (*Torch, Eclipse, Jimi Jamison* etc), who made his debut on the new video.

The grand 2013 design

2009 ■	TIME ELEVATION	CD	Metal Heaven	MHV 00077
2011 ☐	IDOLIZER	CD	Metal Heaven	AORH00065

2009 CD - MHV 00077

GRAND ILLUSION

Per Svensson: v, Peter Sundell: v, Anders Rydholm: k/b

Nässjö - The band was initially known as *Promotion* with the alteration that backing singer Per Svensson became lead singer and the horn section was dropped. The music is a bit heavier and more guitar-oriented than *Promotion*. High-quality AOR indeed. *In The Beginning* is actually a double-CD re-issue of both *Promotion*-albums including four previously unreleased tracks, and one mistakenly left out. The Japanese version is the Escape pressing, repacked with a Japanese insert and OBI. On *Brand New World* guitarist Ola "Alo" Karlsson (*Killbilly 5'ers*) and drummer Christian Sundell were out of the band. Instead they used session musicians such as guitarists Danny Jacob, Ola Af Trampe (*Killbilly 5'ers*), Roger Ljunggren and Kjell Klaesson, plus guest spots from Mike Slamer (*City Boy, Streets*) and Tim Pierce. The drums were handled by Gregg Bisonette. Peter has also been found on albums by bands like *Code, Decoy, Overland* and *Heartland*, plus he has previously released two singles with *Wulcan* and one solo single. The 25th anniversary album *Prince Of Paupers* features guest spots from people like Steve Lukather, Jay Graydon and Tim Pierce.

No ordinary band at all

2001 ☐	THE BOOK OF HOW TO MAKE IT	CD	Avalon Marquee (Japan)	MICP 10235
	Bonus: The Desperate Man's Plea/The Hardest Part			
2001 ☐	THE BOOK OF HOW TO MAKE IT	CD	Escape Music	ESM 063
	Bonus: Death Of Me			
2001 ☐	IN THE BEGINNING	2CD	Escape Music	ESM 068
2001 ☐	IN THE BEGINNING	2CD	Avalon Marquee (Japan)	MAR 01666/7
2002 ☐	VIEW FROM THE TOP	CD	Avalon Marquee (Japan)	MICP-10305
	Bonus: Don't Hurt Yourself			
2002 ☐	VIEW FROM THE TOP	CD	Escape Music	ESM 076
	Bonus: Itch In My Brain			
2004 ☐	ORDINARY JUST WON'T DO	CD	Avalon Marquee (Japan)	MICP-10451
	Bonus: Forever And Always			
2004 ☐	ORDINARY JUST WON'T DO	CD	Escape Music	ESM 103
2010 ■	BRAND NEW WORLD	CD	AOR Heaven	AORH00045
2010 ☐	BRAND NEW WORLD	CD	Avalon Marquee (Japan)	MICP-10915
	Bonus: Search For Light			
2011 ■	PRINCE OF PAUPERS	CD	AOR Heaven	AORH00068
2011 ☐	PRINCE OF PAUPERS	CD	Avalon Marquee (Japan)	MICP-11022
	Bonus: Not For Sale			

2010 CD - AORH00045

2011 CD - AORH00068

GRAND MAGUS

Janne "JB" Christoffersson: v/g, Mats "Fox" Hedén: b,
Ludwig Witt: d

Three wise men

Stockholm - In 1999 this trio recorded a highly promising three-track demo under the name *Smack*. Drummer Fredrik "Trizze Trash" Liefvendahl was ex-*Backdraft* and Janne, previously of *Cardinal Fang*, was also found in *Spiritual Beggars*. They changed their name to *Grand Magus* and recorded another three-track demo in 2000. The tracks *Glow* and *Mountain Of Power* can be found on the compilation *Greatest Hits Vol. 1* (Water Dragon 00). *Grand Magus* is the prime example of the power-trio concept. They're a trio and they've got power! Then add the term "groove" and you've got *Grand Magus*! In 2006 Liefvendahl left to join *Abramis Brama* and he was replaced by Sebastian "Seb" Sippola (*Plankton, Southfork*). *Iron Will* is in my opinion the band's best effort ever, perfectly mixing 70s influenced riffs with classic metal power. An outstanding band. In 2010 JB left *Spiritual Beggars* to devote all his time to *Grand Magus*. In 2011 the band had to pull out of a tour with *Grave Digger* due to drummer Seb having a leg problem. In March 2012 he finally announced he was leaving the band for family reasons. He was replaced by Ludwig Witt (ex-*Spiritual Beggars, Firebird, Shining*), who made his debut on *The Hunt*. The band started out as a retro seventies sounding band, but has gradually become more influenced by classic metal. A killer band!
Website: www.grandmagus.com

2001	■	Spiritual Beggars/Grand Magus (split)	7"	Southern Lord	SUNN10.5

Split with Spiritual Beggars. Track: Twilight Train. 1000 copies in black, 100 green and 100 clear vinyl.

2001	□	GRAND MAGUS	CD	Rise Above	RISE 34
2001	□	GRAND MAGUS	CD	The Music Cartel (USA)	TMC 55 CD
2001	□	GRAND MAGUS	CD	Victor (Jap)	VICP 61569

Bonus: Tales Of The Unexpected/Grand Magus

2002	□	GRAND MAGUS	CD	The Music Cartel (USA)	TMC55CD
2003	□	MONUMENT	CD	Rise Above	RISECD44
2003	□	MONUMENT	LPg	Rise Above	RISELP44

Also in blue vinyl.

2003	□	MONUMENT	CD	Victor (Japan)	VICP-62718
2005	□	WOLF'S RETURN	CD	Rise Above	RISECD 060
2005	□	WOLF'S RETURN	LPg	Rise Above	RISELP 060

500 black vinyl, 500 silver/grey

2005	□	WOLF'S RETURN	CD	Victor (Japan)	VICP-63052

Bonus: Brotherhood Of Sleep (live)

2005	□	WOLF'S RETURN	CD	Candlelight (USA)	CDL 201 CD
2006	□	GRAND MAGUS – EXPANDED VERSION	CD	Rise Above	RISECD069

Bonus: Tales Of The Unexpected/Grand Magus. Brown cover.

2008	□	IRON WILL	CD	Rise Above	RISECD113
2008	□	IRON WILL	LP	Rise Above	RISELP113

200 clear, 200 white, 300 black sparkle, 400 pale blue and 400 transparent black vinyl. Poster.

2008	□	IRON WILL	CD	Victor (Japan)	VICP-64178

Bonus: Mountain Of Power (demo)

2008	□	IRON WILL	CD	Candlelight (USA)	CDL 409
2009	□	GRAND MAGUS	LP	Rise Above	RISELP069
2009	□	HAMMER OF THE NORTH	LP	Roadrunner/Cargo	RRCAR 7788-1
2009	□	HAMMER OF THE NORTH	CD	Roadrunner	RR 7788-2
2009	□	HAMMER OF THE NORTH	CD+DVD	Roadrunner	RR 7788-5

DVD featuring videos, behind the scenes and track by track.

2009	□	HAMMER OF THE NORTH	CD	Roadrunner Japan (Japan)	RRCY-21372
2010	■	Hammer Of The North (edit)/I, The Jury	CDS	Roadrunner (promo)	RR PROMO 1201
2010	■	At Midnight They'll Get Wise	CDS	Roadrunner (promo)	RR PROMO 1224
2010	□	GRAND MAGUS	LP+7"	Rise Above	RISElp069

Contains bonus 7": Tales Of The Unexpected/Grand Magus. Brown cover, gold vinyl.

2010	□	GRAND MAGUS	CD	Rise Above	RISE CD 069
2010	□	MONUMENT	CD	Metal Blade (USA)	3984-14952-2
2012	□	WOLF'S RETURN	CD	Metal Blade (USA)	3984-15103-2
2012	■	THE HUNT	CD	Nuclear Blast	NB 2901-2
2012	□	THE HUNT	2LPg	Nuclear Blast	NB 2901-1

250 copies blue+yellow, 250 copies dark red and 150 copies white vinyl. Poster.

2012	□	THE HUNT	CD	Nuclear Blast America (USA)	NB 12901SP

Bonus: Silver Moon (demo)/Storm King (demo)/Sword Of The Ocean (demo). Patch.

2012	□	THE HUNT	CD	Nuclear Blast America (USA)	NBA 12901-2

Bonus: Silver Moon (demo)/Storm King (demo)/Sword Of The Ocean (demo)

2001 7" - SUNN 10.5

2010 CDS - RR PROMO 1201

2010 CDS - RR PROMO 1224

2012 CD - NB 2901-2

GRAND SLAM

Lars "Slarre" Landegren: v, Mats Lindfors: g, Johan Pettersson: g, Jan Bergström: b, Sigge Frenzel: d

Stockholm - A good solid mid-paced hard rock band. Mats has worked with many Swedish bands like *Talisman*, *Angeline* and John Norum, both as session musician and producer. In 1995 he started his own label Clone Records & Tapes. *Grand Slam* recorded a five-track demo in 1983, from where the two single tracks were picked.

1984 ■ Telephone/Strong Together ....7" Duran ....GSS 001

1984 7" - GSS 001

GRAND STAND

Göran Johnsson: v/g, Olov Andersson: k, Leif Isberg: b, Tomas Hurtig: d

Upplands Väsby/Sollentuna - Hurtig and Andersson started out in local band *Big Blue* back in 1987. When the band split up they became a duo rehearsing *Genesis* songs. They soon started writing original material and the project turned into the band *Marble Stains*. In 1995 they added a singer to the band, but he only lasted until 1998. After his departure the debut album was recorded. In August 1998 Michael Rank Jensen entered on guitar, but he also handled the vocal parts. Now Leif Isberg entered on bass. The band also collaborated with symphonic colleagues *Cross* on a *Pink Floyd* tribute. December 23, 2000 singer and multi-instrumentalist Göran Johnsson joined the ranks. The band now started writing what became *Tricks Of Time*. Göran and Olov also played in side project *Spektrum*, where Göran handled the drums. Late 2002 Göran decided to devote his time to drumming and he left the band, to be replaced by singer Daniel Groth. Olov also played in *Audivision* and *Golden Resurrection*. In 2009 the band resurrected, now featuring Olov, Tomas, Klasse Sundberg (b) and guitarist/singer Torbjörn Weinesjö (*Veni Domine*, *Audiovision*). *Grand Stand* play high-quality symphonic rock in the vein of *Cross* etc.

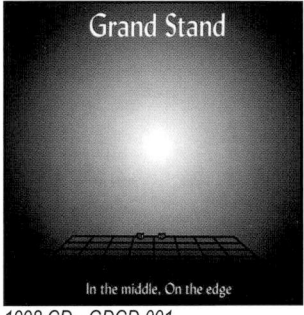

1998 CD - GDCD 001

2002 CD - PRCD 009

1998 ■ IN THE MIDDLE ON THE EDGE ....CD GSE ....GDCD 001
2002 ■ TRICKS OF TIME ....CD Progress Records ....PRCD 009

GRAND TRICK, THE

Kalle Sellbrink: v, Stefan Johansson: g/k, Jonas Malmqvist: b, Daniel Larsson: d

Linköping - The band was formed by *Bones* members, bass player Jonas Malmqvist and drummer Daniel Larsson in 2003, influenced by classical hard rock bands like *Deep Purple* and *Led Zeppelin*. Michael Karlsson entered on guitar and *Bones* became *The Grand Trick*. On the first EP Karlsson handled the vocals. Now former *Satanic Slaughter* guitarist Stefan Johansson joined the ranks and he knew singer Daniel Sandberg who completed the line-up. The band now rerecorded the EP, which was now picked up and distributed by Transubstans, who signed the band for an album. In the middle of the recording singer Sandberg had to move abroad for six months and Johan Dahnberg stepped in, re-recorded and finished the vocal parts on the album. *The Decadent Session* was finally unearthed in 2005. Waiting to record the second album, the band entered the studio again and released the MCD *She's On The Run*. Unfortunately Dahnberg now left because of family matters. He was soon replaced by Kalle Sellbrink. More bad news came when guitarist Karlsson left in 2007. He was replaced by Erik Kurtsson, who later left. Dahnberg returned to the ranks in 2008. In 2009 keyboard player Magnus Nilsson entered the ranks. In 2011 Dahnberg left and was replaced by Johan Hallendorf in June the same year. *The Grand Trick* also does a cover of Bo Hansson's *The Black Rider* on the *Rökstenen* compilation (2009 Collossus Projects). *The Grand Trick* play quite decent 70s-influenced hard rock. In 2011 the digital only album *Reminence Boulevard* was finally released. Singer Toby Poynter replaced Sellbrink and guitarist Karlsson returned in 2013.

2005 CD - TRANS 010

2004 MCD - - -

2006 MCD - - -

2004 ■ The First Trick ....MCD 4tr private .... - -
    Tracks: Black Hills/Rollercoaster Ride/The Grand Trick/Never Felt So Good
2005 ■ THE DECADENT SESSION ....CD Transubstans ....TRANS 010
2006 ■ She's On The Run ....MCD 3tr private .... - -
    Tracks: She's On The Run/Daddy Mac The Knife/The River Queen

GRAND VISION

Mikael Fredriksson: v, Krister Björkholm: g, Mikael Lövdal: k, Lars Hultman: b, Daniel Gese: d

Norrköping - Formed in 1985. *Grand Vision* was actually Krister's own project that turned into a band. Top-quality melodic hard rock/AOR in the vein of *Treat* and *Europe* with great vocals, nice arrangements and quality production. Daniel was later found in *Dizziness*, *Pole Position* and *Reptilian*. The band existed for some time as a cover band (doing mostly *Led Zeppelin* songs) featuring Niclas Hedenström on keyboards and Tommy Eklund on drums. Fredriksson (ex-*Sleazy Roze*) is now fronting a *Journey* cover band and sings in *Big Hoss And The Animal*.

1988 7" - CWC 034

1988 ■ Honor And Glory/Too Late ....7" CWC ....CWC 034
    1000 copies.

GRANWICK, JAN

Jan "Granwick" Granvik: g

Stockholm/Haparanda - When *Glory* were having a break, Jan decided to do a single with instrumental guitar music. There was a follow-up on the *Glory*-album *Positive Buoyant*. Jan was also part of the band *Grave* (not the death metal band, though).

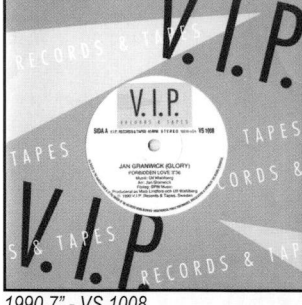

1990 ● Forbidden Love/Bourrée ....7" VIP ....VS 1008

1990 7" - VS 1008

GRAVE

Dan Wande: v, Jan "Granwick" Granvik: g, Jussi Pöysälä: g,
Henrik Thall: k, Kari Korkala: b, Tomas Tornefjell: d

Haparanda - A great single in the same vein as *Deep Purple* featuring Jan Granwick, later *Glory*. A collector's item. Henrik was earlier found in symphonic rockers *Grace* and *Vision*. He sadly passed away in 1995.

1984 ■ Screaming From The Grave/Dreamer..7" private ....GS 001 **$$**

1984 7" - GS 001

GRAVE

Ola Lindgren: g/b/v, Fredrik Isaksson: b, Ronnie Bergenståhl: d

Visby/Stockholm - Not to be confused with the 80s heavy metal band featuring Jan Granwick. This band was formed late 1986 under the moniker *Corpse*, but already back in 1984 they started playing heavy metal and went under names like *Anguish*, *Destroyer* and *Rising Power*. In 1988 they changed their name to *Grave* and also changed style from speed metal to death metal, making them one of the pioneers in the Swedish death metal scene. Before the first record they made three demos: *Sick, Disgust, Eternal* (1988), *Sexual Mutilation* (1989) and *Anatomia Corporis Humani* (1989). The latter was released on vinyl in 1991. The line-up on the first demo featured Ola Lindgren (g), Jörgen Sandström (v/g/b) and Jensa Paulsson (d). The first album line-up also featured bass player Jonas Torndal. Ola, Jensa and Jonas were also involved in the side project *Putrefaction*, who released the demo *Painful Death*. On *You'll Never See* Jonas left and Jörgen took over the bass, too. This album is a bit more polished than its predecessor. Very well played death metal with a touch of power metal. Lots of tempo changes and the traditional growls. In 1995 Jörgen Sandström (v/b) left to join *Entombed* and Ola took over the vocal duties. They now released two albums as a trio before taking a time out until 2001. The line-up now featured Ola, Jensa, Jonas (now handling the guitar) and bass player Fredrik "Fredda" Isaksson (*Therion*). The return album *Back From The Grave* was also released as a double CD version with a bonus CD containing old demos. After the album Jensa was temporarily replaced by Pelle Ekegren, but early 2003 he left permanently and was replaced by Christofer Barkensjö (*Kaamos, General Surgery, Repugnant*). However, in 2004 Barkensjö left again and was replaced by the returning Ekegren who made his debut on *Fiendish Regression*. After the release of *Burial Ground*, in 2010, Isaksson was replaced by *Dismember* bassist Tobias Christiansson. *As Rapture Comes* features a cover of *Alice In Chains*' *Them Bones*. On *Dominion VIII* the line-up had once again changed and the band was back to being a trio featuring Lindgren, Isaksson and drummer Ronnie Bergenståhl. A classic high-class death metal band.
Website: www.intothegrave.com

Grave - The band that won't die

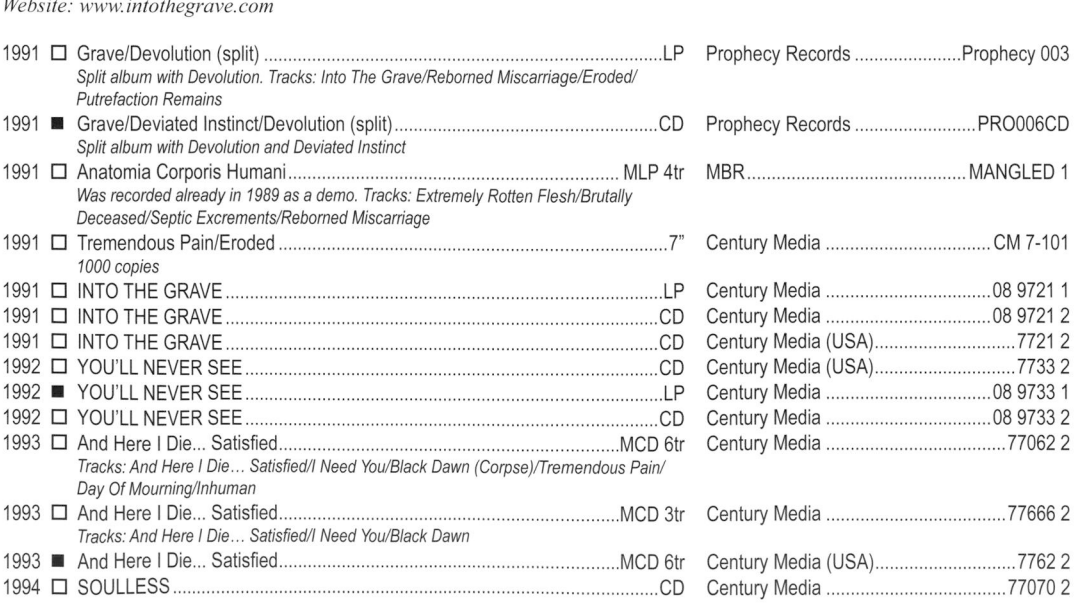

1991 □ Grave/Devolution (split) ....LP Prophecy Records ....Prophecy 003
    Split album with Devolution. Tracks: Into The Grave/Reborned Miscarriage/Eroded/
    Putrefaction Remains
1991 ■ Grave/Deviated Instinct/Devolution (split)..CD Prophecy Records PRO006CD
    Split album with Devolution and Deviated Instinct
1991 □ Anatomia Corporis Humani.. MLP 4tr MBR..MANGLED 1
    Was recorded already in 1989 as a demo. Tracks: Extremely Rotten Flesh/Brutally
    Deceased/Septic Excrements/Reborned Miscarriage

1991 □ Tremendous Pain/Eroded ....7" Century Media ....CM 7-101
    1000 copies
1991 □ INTO THE GRAVE ....LP Century Media 08 9721 1
1991 □ INTO THE GRAVE ....CD Century Media 08 9721 2
1991 □ INTO THE GRAVE ....CD Century Media (USA)............................7721 2
1992 □ YOU'LL NEVER SEE ....CD Century Media (USA)............................7733 2
1992 ■ YOU'LL NEVER SEE ....LP Century Media 08 9733 1
1992 □ YOU'LL NEVER SEE ....CD Century Media 08 9733 2
1993 □ And Here I Die... Satisfied ....MCD 6tr Century Media 77062 2
    Tracks: And Here I Die... Satisfied/I Need You/Black Dawn (Corpse)/Tremendous Pain/
    Day Of Mourning/Inhuman
1993 □ And Here I Die... Satisfied ....MCD 3tr Century Media 77666 2
    Tracks: And Here I Die... Satisfied/I Need You/Black Dawn
1993 ■ And Here I Die... Satisfied..MCD 6tr Century Media (USA)............................7762 2
1994 □ SOULLESS ....CD Century Media 77070 2

1991 CD - PRO006CD

1992 LP - 08 9733 1

338

1994 ☐	SOULLESS	CD	Century Media (USA)	7770 2
1994 ☐	SOULLESS	CD	Century Media	77070 2
1996 ☐	HATING LIFE	CD	Century Media	77106 2
1997 ☐	INTO THE GRAVE	CD	Century Media	77136 2

Bonus: Tremendous Pain/Putrefaction Remains/Haunted/Eroded/Day Of Mourning/Inhuman/Obscure Infinity/Soulless (video)

1997 ☐	HATING LIFE	CD	Century Media (USA)	7806-2
1997 ☐	EXTREMELY ROTTEN LIVE	CD	Century Media	77162 2
2000 ☐	YOU'LL NEVER SEE/AND HERE I DIE... SATISFIED	CD	Century Media (USA)	7733-2
2001 ☐	INTO THE GRAVE	CD	Century Media	77388 2

Bonus: Tremendous Pain/Putrefaction Remains/Haunted/Eroded/Day Of Mourning/Inhuman/Obscure Infinity/Soulless (video)

2001 ☐	INTO THE GRAVE/TREMENDOUS PAIN	CD	Century Media (USA)	7721-2
2002 ■	BACK FROM THE GRAVE	2CD	Century Media (USA)	8111-2
2002 ☐	BACK FROM THE GRAVE	LP	Century Media	77411-1
2002 ☐	BACK FROM THE GRAVE	LP PD	Century Media	77543-076

2000 copies

2002 ☐	BACK FROM THE GRAVE	CD	Century Media	77411-2
2002 ☐	BACK FROM THE GRAVE	2CD	Century Media	77411-2A
2003 ☐	YOU'LL NEVER SEE/ANATOMIA CORPONS HUMANI	LP PD	Century Media	77543-072

2000 copies.

2003 ☐	AND HERE I DIE SATISFIED/SEXUAL MUTILATION	LP PD	Century Media	77543-073

2000 copies.

2003 ☐	HATING LIFE/SICK DISGUST ETERNAL	LP PD	Century Media	77543-075

2000 copies.

2003 ☐	INTO THE GRAVE/TREMENDOUS PAIN	LP PD	Century Media	77543-071

2000 copies.

2004 ☐	FIENDISH REGRESSION	CD	Century Media (USA)	8211-2
2004 ☐	FIENDISH REGRESSION	CD	Century Media	77511-2
2004 ☐	FIENDISH REGRESSION	CD	Century Media	77511-0

Bonus: Burial At Sea (St Vitus cover)/Autopsied (rerecording)

2006 ■	MORBID WAYS TO DIE	6LP PD Box	Century Media	77543-0

6LP box with picture discs of Grave/You'll Never See/And Here I Die/Soulless/Hating Life/Back From The Grave. 2000 copies. Numbered.

2006 ☐	YOU'LL NEVER SEE	CD	Century Media	77612-2

Re-mastered with new artwork. Bonus: songs from And Here I Die Satisfied

2006 ☐	SOULLESS	CD	Century Media	77613-2

Re-mastered with new artwork. Bonus: Soulless (video)

2006 ☐	AS RAPTURE COMES	CD	Century Media	77611-2
2006 ☐	AS RAPTURE COMES	CD	Century Media (USA)	8311-2
2006 ☐	AS RAPTURE COMES	LP	Animate Records	AR 016

Bonus: Autopsied. 799 black, 100 clear yellow, 100 clear blue vinyl.

2008 ■	DOMINION VIII	CD	Regain	RRCD 140
2008 ☐	DOMINION VIII	LP	Regain	RRLP 140
2010 ☐	BURIAL GROUND	CD	Regain	RRCD 171
2010 ☐	BURIAL GROUND	LPg	Regain	RRLP 171

500 copies.

2010 ☐	EXHUMED: A GRAVE COLLECTION	CD	Animate Records	997809-2
2010 ☐	EXHUMED: A GRAVE COLLECTION	2LP	Animate Records	50836

566 black, 100 in red/yellow vinyl.

2011 ☐	NECROPSY - THE COMPLETE DEMO RECORDINGS 1986-1991	3LPg	Century Media	998080-1

150 clear, 100 brown/black, 100 red/black, 100 green and 500 black vinyl.

2012 ☐	ENDLESS PROCESSION OF SOULS	CD	Century Media (USA)	8910-2
2012 ☐	ENDLESS PROCESSION OF SOULS	2CD box	Century Media	998210-0

Bonus Covered In Blood CD. Poster, patch.

2012 ☐	ENDLESS PROCESSION OF SOULS	2LP	Century Media	998210-1

Red vinyl + 185 copies green vinyl.

2013 ☐	Morbid Ascent	MLP 5tr	Century Media	n/a

Tracks: Venial Sin/Morbid Ascent/Possessed (Satyricon cover)/Epos/Reality Of Life

1993 MCD - 7762 2

2002 CD - 8111-2

2006 6LP PD Box - 77543-0

2008 CD - RRCD 140

GRAVE FLOWERS

Matte Andersson: v/d, Jan "Jason" Jansson: g/b

Karlstad - The band is former **Godgory** member Matte's own project and was realised in 1993. In 1995 a 3-track demo was recorded and the track *Emotionally Paralized* appears on the compilation *And The Ravens Left The Tower* (Teutonic Existence Rec). In 1997 Matte recorded a second demo entitled *Garmonbozia* with the aid of Jan Jansson from **Mental Crypt/Loss**. Musically it's pretty good symphonic doom, though lacking a bit in the vocal department. Matte also plays bass in the punk/hardcore band **Mantaray K-D**. Erik Andersson (**Godgory**) plays keyboard on the recordings.

2000 ■	SOLACE ME	CD	Serenades	SR 030
2001 ☐	SOLACE ME	CD	Irond (Russia)	01-53
2002 ☐	SOLACE ME	LP PD	Painkiller	-

300 copies.

2000 CD - SR 030

Graveyard - still got the blues.

GRAVEYARD
Joakim Nilsson: v/g, Jonathan Larocca Ramm: g, Rikard Edlund: b, Axel Sjöberg: d

Göteborg - *Graveyard* were formed in 2007 out of the ashes of Örebro-based retro rockers *Norrsken*, who split up in 2000. After they split up, Magnus Pelander formed *Witchcraft*, while Nilsson and Edlund went to blues rockers *Albatros*. When *Albatros* finally folded they drafted drummer Sjöberg and guitarist/singer Truls Mörck and formed *Graveyard*. Mörck however soon left and was replaced by Ramm. *Graveyard* play 60s-influenced, hippie-ish 70s hard rock. Very groovy, very jamming and really great stuff indeed, like the missing link between *MC5* and *Mountain*. The band became extremely hyped in 2010 and was soon picked up by Universal/Nuclear Blast. A very intense live band.
Website: www.graveyardmusic.com

2009 7" - VEVC 0012

2007	☐	GRAVEYARD	CDd	Transubstans	TRANS028
2008	☐	GRAVEYARD	LPg	Tee Pee (USA)	TPEE90081-1
2008	☐	GRAVEYARD	CDd	Tee Pee (USA)	TPEE90081-2
2009	■	Graveyard/Ancestors (split)	7"	Volcum Ent. Vinyl Club	VEVC 0012
		Track: As The Years Pass By/The Hours Bend (live). 1000 numbered. Turquoise vinyl.			
2011	☐	Hisingen Blues/Granny And Davis	7"	Stranded	REK 085/060252755678 $
		500 copies.			
2011	☐	Hisingen Blues/Granny And Davis	7" PD	Nuclear Blast	NB 2717-7
		500 copies.			
2011	☐	HISINGEN BLUES	LP	Stranded/Universal	EKO143/060252761388 $$
2011	☐	HISINGEN BLUES	CDd	Stranded/Universal	EKO143/060252760324
2011	☐	HISINGEN BLUES	CDd	Nuclear Blast	NB 2716-0
		Bonus: Cooking Brew			
2011	■	HISINGEN BLUES	LPg	Nuclear Blast	NB 2716-1
		500 copies green vinyl.			
2011	☐	HISINGEN BLUES	CD	Nuclear Blast	NB 2716-2
2011	☐	HISINGEN BLUES	LPg	Nuclear Blast	NB 2716-5
		500 copies bronze vinyl.			
2011	☐	HISINGEN BLUES	LPg	Nuclear Blast	NB 2716-7
		Beige vinyl. 500 copies.			
2011	☐	HISINGEN BLUES	LPg	Nuclear Blast	NB 2716-8
		500 Clear w white/blue splatter. 500 white.			
2011	☐	HISINGEN BLUES	LPg	Nuclear Blast	NB 2716-9
		Blue vinyl. 100 copies. Hand-numbered.			
2011	☐	HISINGEN BLUES	CDd	Stranded/Universal	060252760324
2011	■	HISINGEN BLUES	LP	Stranded/Universal	060252761388
		500 copies. Green vinyl. Sold at Bengans exclusively.			
2011	☐	HISINGEN BLUES	CD	Avalon Marquee (Japan)	MICP-10989
2011	☐	HISINGEN BLUES	LP	Nuclear Blast	NB 2768-9
		500 copues, 180g black vinyl.			
2011	☐	HISINGEN BLUES	LPg	Nuclear Blast	NB 2768-9
		100 copies, numbered, 180g blue vinyl.			
2011	☐	GRAVEYARD	LPg	Nuclear Blast	2767-1 $
		100 black, 300 blue, 300 orange vinyl. Poster.			
2011	☐	GRAVEYARD	LPg PD	Nuclear Blast	2767-4
2012	☐	HISINGEN BLUES	5x10" box	Nuclear Blast	NB 2768-5 $$
		500 copies. Poster. Bonus: Cooking Brew.			
2012	☐	HISINGEN BLUES	LPg	Nuclear Blast	NB 2768-4
		150 copies, multi-colour splatter vinyl, 500 blue/clear/green vinyl.			
2012	☐	HISINGEN BLUES	LPg	Nuclear Blast	NB 2768-6
		150 five-colour splatter vinyl, 500 red, 500 bi-coloured vinyl.			
2012	☐	GRAVEYARD	LPg	Nuclear Blast	2767-5 $
		150 green + clear vinyl. Poster.			
2012	☐	GRAVEYARD	LPg	Nuclear Blast	2767-9
		500 copies.			
2012	☐	Goliath/Leaving You	7"	Stranded Rekords	0602537-16966-5
		Green sleeve.			
2012	■	Goliath/Leaving You	7"	Stranded Rekords	REK096/0602537-16474-5
		Black and white sleeve.			
2012	☐	Goliath/Leaving You	7"	Nuclear Blast	NB 2964-9
		Green sleeve + green vinyl. 250 copies.			
2012	☐	Goliath/Leaving You	7"	Nuclear Blast	NB 2964-8
		Yellow sleeve + yellow vinyl. 250 copies.			
2012	■	Goliath/Leaving You	7"	Nuclear Blast	NB 2964-7
		Blue sleeve + blue vinyl. 250 copies.			
2012	☐	Goliath/Leaving You	7"	Nuclear Blast	NB 2964-1
		Black/white sleeve + white vinyl. 250 copies.			
2012	☐	LIGHTS OUT	CD	Stranded Rekords	0602537-16183
2012	☐	LIGHTS OUT	CDd	Stranded Rekords	0602537-17074
2012	☐	LIGHTS OUT	LP	Stranded Rekords	0602537-16473
		Also 300 copies in red vinyl. Poster.			
2012	☐	LIGHTS OUT	CDd	Nuclear Blast (USA)	NBA 29632-2

2011 LP - NB 2716-1

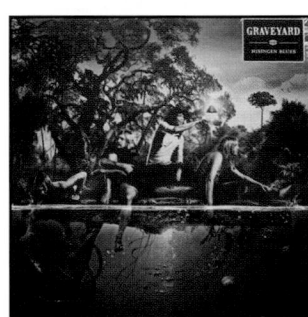

2011 LP - 060252761388

2012 7" - REK096/0602537-16474-5

2012 7" - NB 2964-7

GRAVIATORS, THE

Niklas Sjöberg: v, Martin Fairbanks: g, Johan Holm: b, Henrik Bergman: d

Karlshamn - The band was formed in the outskirts of Karlshamn in 2008 and recorded their debut in Studio Sound palace with Johan Blomström (*Blinded Colony, Overdrive, Spice And The RJ Band*) at the helm. *The Graviators* play 70s influenced stonerish heavy rock. A bit of vintage *Black Sabbath* meets *Pentagram* meets *Saint Vitus*. Great stuff, indeed! Sjöberg is also found in *Nymf*. In 2012 the band was picked up by Napalm Records.

2010 2LPg - HSLPC00318

2009 ☐	THE GRAVIATORS	CD	Transubstans	TRANS 052
	Released with two different covers. Original was dark brown.			
2010 ☐	THE GRAVIATORS	2LPg	Headspin	HSLP000318
	Different artwork. Poster			
2010 ■	THE GRAVIATORS	2LPg	Headspin	HSLPC000318
	Different artwork. Poster. 200 copies marble olive green.			
2011 ☐	The Graviators-Brutus (split)	12"	Transubstans	TRANSV01
	Split with Brutus. 200 coloured + 300 black vinyl. Track: Druid's Ritual			
2012 ☐	Häxagram/Big Bust	7"	Napalm Records	NPR 430
	150 purple + 150 green vinyl. Hand numbered. Big Bust is non-album.			
2012 ☐	EVIL DEEDS	CD	Napalm Records	NPR 424
2012 ☐	EVIL DEEDS	2LPg	Napalm Records	NPR 424 LP
	100 purple + 100 orange.+ black vinyl. Posters in some.			

GREASY SADDLES

Peter Beckman: v/g, Hans Rosander: g, Per Lefvert: b, Jens Rosander: d

Stockholm - *Greasy Saddles* came out of cover band *Million Dollar Quartet*. Beckman and Rosander were also in *The Primitives*. In 1989, they changed their name to *Greasy Saddles*. Greasy, sleaze-influenced, southern-sounding hard rock, quite similar to *Havana Black*, *Gringos Locos* or a mix of *Molly Hatchet* and *AC/DC*. Nice stuff, well-recorded and well-performed. In 1991 Pete was sacked and replaced by singer/songwriter Christoffer Tideström. The band continued in silence but popped up again in 2011, now in a more southern-sounding, almost country-rock influenced vein. The line-up still features Hans, Jens and Per, now reinforced with Matte Norberg (g/v), Patrik Lindqvist (k) and Niklas Böhme (g/v and accordion). Beckman is now found in *Beatles* cover band *The Repeatles*.

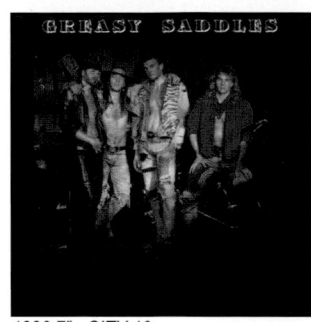

1990 7" - CITY 10

| 1990 ■ | Breakin' Your Chains/Crankshaft Sprocket | 7" | City | CITY 10 |

GREAT AD

Peter Ekström: v, Johan Borelius: g, Edward Nyström: g,
Claes Andersson: b, Stefan Bergh: d

Malmö - Great 70s hard rock on the same label as *Solid Ground*. The first single was instrumental, heavy progressive hard rock and the line-up consisted of Johan, Claes and Stefan. The boys were around 17 years old. Johan is brother of the renowned guitarist Eric Borelius. Before the second release Nyström (age 15) and Ekström (age 18) had joined. The second single is killer 70s heavy rock similar to bands like *Teargas* and *Bang* with outstanding guitar playing and great vocals. A 30 minute live-show was also recorded by the Swedish national radio. Stefan later joined the far poppier *Sing Sing & The Crime*.

1975 7" - SS 009

| 1975 ■ | Great Ad.../Borne, Andy, Mountain | 7" | Scam | SS 009 | $ |
| 1976 ■ | She's Got The Fire/You'll Never Believe | 7" | Scam | SS-023 | $ |

GREAT DECEIVER, THE

Tompa Lindberg: v, Kristian Wåhlin: g, Johan Österberg: g,
Matti Lundell: b, Hans Nilsson: d

Göteborg - The band was actually formed already in 1996 and recorded an album under the name *Hide*. It was however never released and in 1998 they became *The Great Deceiver*. Dark and heavy doom/hardcore. Desperate and aggressive vocals. Kristian, Johan and Hans are also found in *Diabolique*. Tompa is also found in *At The Gates* and he and Kristian are both ex-*Grotesque*. Recorded at Berno Studios.

1976 7" - SS-023

1999 ☐	Cave In	MCD 5tr	Bridge	BOC 013
	Tracks: Cornered Rat/Jet-Black Art/Suffering Redefined/The End Made Flesh And Blood/ Desperate & Empty			
1999 ■	Cave In	10" 5tr	Bridge	BOC 013 LP
2000 ☐	JET BLACK ART	CD	Trustkill Records	TRUSTKILL 30
2002 ☐	A VENOM WELL DESIGNED	CD	Peaceville	CDVILE 118
2004 ☐	TERRA INCOGNITO	CDd	Peaceville	CDVILEF 120
2007 ☐	LIFE IS WASTED ON THE LIVING	CD	Deathwish Inc.	DW 60

1999 10" - BOC 013 LP

GREAT KING RAT

Leif Sundin: v, **Pontus Norgren**: g, **Anders "Nippe" Fästader (aka Nilsson)**: g/k, **Mikael Höglund**: b, **Thomas Broman**: d

Stockholm - This band could've made it really big with the proper backing. One of Sweden's most underrated bands. The first album is a first-class study of classic hard rock with influences from **Bad Company** as well as more AOR:ish stuff. Leif is one of Sweden's No. 1 singers, with a voice quite similar to Paul Rodgers and Eric Martin. He replaced Conny Lind (**State Of Mind, Raceway**) and was previously bass player/singer in the band **Circus**. Mikael and Tomas were ex-**Tryckvåg** (where Lind was once a member, too) and later on **Bang Bang**, where they met Anders, who had recorded a single with the band **Advice**. After the album, the band made some great demos, one featuring a cover of **Free**'s *Be My Friend*. In 1993 the band sadly split. Leif recorded some solo material under a different moniker and in a more soul-pop vein, plus some demos in the band **Earth Revival**, also featuring Thomas Broman, in a more grunge-oriented style. He has also sang with **The Johansson Brothers** on their first album and fronted **Michael Schenker Group** on the album *Written In The Sand* 1996, later **John Norum Band** on stage and on the live album *Face It Live '97*. He returned to John on several occasions and sings on his solo album *Playyard Blues* (2010 Mascot Records). Pontus joined **Monica Maze Band**, who only recorded some excellent demos, later **Damage Done** (also featuring John Levén and Patrik Isaksson) and made two releases with **Jekyll 'N Hyde**, but left in 1999. In 2000 he made the solo-release *Damage Done* under his own name, joined **Talisman** and recorded the album *Truth* plus a live-album. In 2001 **Talisman** became **Humanimal**, where Thomas was also found. Höglund made some records with UK band **Thunder** and Broman recorded the album *Freewheelin* with **Electric Boys** before they split. He has later been found behind Conny Bloom, John Norum, Pontus Norgren and in **Send No Flowers** (UK), **Silver Ginger 5** (UK), **Firebird** (UK), among others. In 1998 Z Records persuaded the boys to clean up the old unreleased demo material and make a reunion. Even though *Out Of The Can* is the old demos, it sounds almost as good as the first album. A safe buy! The reunion was however very short-lived. Pontus Norgren later recorded an album with **Jekyll 'N Hyde** singer Jakob Samuelsson in the band **The Ring**. The two later reunited in **The Poodles**, before Pontus decided to go metal with **Hammerfall**, a band he's still playing in. Sundin sang on former **Thin Lizzy** guitarist Brian Robertson's solo album *Diamonds And Dirt* in 2011 and released a great solo album under the moniker **House Of Leaf** in 2012, in a more singer/songwriter-oriented style. Fästader and Höglund also appeared in melodic rockers **Beautiful Grey**, while Broman is in **Bridge To Mars**.
Website: http://listen.to/greatkingrat

Rattus Swedicus

1992 ■	GREAT KING RAT	LP	Planet	MOPLP 3055
1992 □	GREAT KING RAT	CD	Planet	MOPCD 3055
1992 □	Woman In Love/One By One	CDS 2tr	Planet	FOP 200
1992 ■	Take Me Back	CDS 1tr	Planet	FOP 201
1993 □	BRIGHT LIGHTS BIG CITY	CD	Fandango (Japan)	FRML 9001
	Same as the self-entitled debut			
1999 □	OUT OF THE CAN	CD	Z Records	ZR1997012
1999 □	OUT OF THE CAN	CD	Pony Canyon (Japan)	PCCY 01388
	Bonus: Can You Feel It			

1992 CDS - FOP 201

1992 LP - MOPLP 3055

GREED

Danne Andersson: v/g, **Jonas Petersson**: g, **Fredrik Söderström**: b, **Tomas Nordin**: d

Stockholm - When **Glorious Bankrobbers** split Jonas later went on to form **Greed**. Musically they feel like the bastard child of **Glorious Bankrobbers** and **The Hellacopters**. Rough-edged punkish biker rock with a strong scent of glam rock. Not bad at all actually. The album was recorded already back in 1996, but later released by Swedmetal Records.

2010 ■	BURN IT DOWN	CD	Swedmetal	SM-23-CD

2010 CD - SM-23-CD

GREEN SLEEVES

Anders Johansson: v/g, **Peter Ottosson**: g, **Ulf Magnusson**: b, **Pelle Petersson**: d

Vetlanda - **Green Sleeves** were originally formed way back in 1979 and did some gigs during the 80s, but never released anything on their own. They guys were only 16-18 years old. They recorded some demos, and the tracks *The Evil* and *Fire* were featured on the *Rock 82 Vetlanda* (1982 Music 66 Club) compilation. At the time the band was a trio featuring Johansson, Magnusson and Petersson. They finally split up in 1984. Johansson has made several releases with his own band **Heartcry**, a band which also featured Petersson on one album. In September 2005, they finally decided to re-unite the band and record the long lost debut album. **Green Sleeves** play traditional heavy metal, influenced by bands like **Judas Priest** and **Accept**. Not original, but decent.
Website: www.greensleeves.nu

2006 ■	GREEN MACHINE	CD	Vital Music	VTM 007 GS

2006 CD - VTM 007 GS

GREENLEAF

Oskar Cedermalm: v, Tommi Holappa: g/k, Johan Rockner: g,
Bengt Bäcke: b, Olle Mårthans: d

Borlänge - Stoner-oriented, seventies-influenced hard rock. Influences can be heard from various direction, **Black Sabbath** and the early doom-bands, as well as **Spiritual Beggars**. It all started out in the end of 1999 as a side project for Tommi Holappa and drummer Daniel "Danny" Lidén. Bäcke was added on bass and Peder Bergstrand from **Lowrider** handled the vocals on the first 10". This is more or less an "all-star-stoner-band". Fredrik and Tommi are from **Dozer**, Daniel from **Demon Cleaner** and Bengt is more-or-less a stoner super-producer. The track *Sold My Lady* can be found on *Molten Universe Volume One* (1999 MU). On the second release, **Dozer**-vocalist Fredrik Nordin took over. On *Secret Alphabets* the band was reinforced by second guitarist Daniel Jansson (**Demon Cleaner**, now in **Stonewall Noise Orchestra**). As the members were quite busy with their other bands, **Greenleaf** took a backseat ride for a while and when *Agents Of Ahriman* saw the light of day in 2007 the band was back to being a quartet, now featuring new singer Oskar Cedermalm (**Truckfighters**) and new drummer Erik Bäckwall, formerly of **Dozer**. The album also features guest spots from singer Peder Bergstrand and John Hermansen, guitarist John Hoyles (**Spiders**) as well as keyboard player Jocke Åhslund (**Payback**). On Nest Of Vipers the line-up had changed again, seeing Bäckwall replaced by Olle Mårthans (**Dozer, Chainwreck**) and Johan Rockner (**Dozer**) added on second guitar.

2001 CD - MOLTEN 014

2000 10" - MOLTEN 008

2000 ■	Greenleaf	10" 6tr	Molten Universe	MOLTEN 008

Tracks: Get Your Love Outta Here/Sold My Lady/Kvinna du ger mig ingen kärlek/Smell The Green/Land Of Lincoln/Status: Hallucinogenic. 500 copies

2001 ■	REVOLUTION ROCK	CD	Molten Universe	MOLTEN 014
2001 □	REVOLUTION ROCK	LP	Molten Universe	MOLTEN 014

1000 copies.

2003 □	SECRET ALPHABETS	CD	Small Stone	SS-038
2007 □	AGENTS OF AHRIMAN	CD	Small Stone	SS-074
2012 □	NEST OF VIPERS	CD	Small Stone	SS-125
2012 ■	NEST OF VIPERS	LP	Small Stone	SS-125

150 black, 150 clear green and 150 white/gren/black swirl vinyl.

2012 LP - SS-125

GREGOR SAMSA

Anders Jacobsson: v, Magnus Qvist: g, Lars Risberg: k,
Daniel Minton: b, Pierre Erixon: d

Stockholm - An odd band indeed. The music is a mix of traditional, quite melodic hard rock and vocals in the vein of Iggy Pop with a goth-oriented feel to it. The band also recorded a cassette album in 1986. The name was taken from Franz Kafka's novel *Die Vervandlung*.

1986 ■	Sexplosion/Nu ringer stormklockorna igen	7"	private	GRE 6012
1987 □	Captain Mission/I Stand Proud	7"	Pet Sounds	GS 27

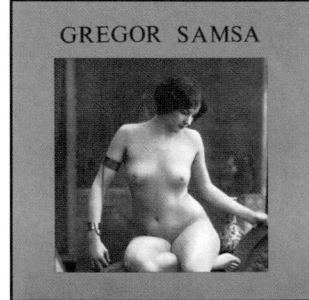

1986 7" - GRE 6012

GREYHATE

John Hermansen: v/g, Hasse Hermansen: g,
Marcus Jäderholm: b, Mattias Åström: d

Fjärdhundra - After releasing one MCD, melodic hard rockers **Staiger** changed style and name. As **Greyhate** they picked up more of **Alice In Chains**' grungy heaviness. The band split in 1997 and John and Marcus later reappeared in **Mother Misery.**

1996 ■	Greyhate	MCD 6tr	private	GHCD 001

Tracks: Lowlife/Rusty Soul/Stretchuntilyoubreak/Stronger/Silver/Vacum

1996 MCD - GHCD 001

GRIEF OF EMERALD

Johnny Lehto: v/g, Christer Bergqvist: g, Johan Havås: k,
Andreas Hedström: b, Carl Karlsson: d

Uddevalla - **Grief Of Emerald**, originally **Emerald Grief**, was formed in the early 90's by former **Mandatory** members Lehto and Hedström. Robert Bengtsson (k) joined in 1995 and recorded the demo *The Beginning*, later released as an MCD. The band was picked up by Listenable Records and the debut was released in 1998. Drummer Fredrik Helgesson (**Obligatorisk Tortyr/Dawn**) was replaced by Jonas Blom before *Malformed Seed*. The band recorded a tribute to **Celtic Frost**. Blom suffered from houlder problems and was replaced by Carl Karlsson (**Author Of Pain/ Third Stone From The Sun/Mäbe/Mastema**). Robert Bengtsson quit and Jonas Blom, (**Trident, Azazeron**) temporarily helped out. He was replaced by Lena Hjalmarsson from **Cyphoria**, who was later replaced by Havås. Anders Tång was also handling the bass for a short period. Bassist Andreas Hedström (**Descending**) joined. Johnny has also been found in **Decameron** and **Oderu**, while Hedström is ex-**Necrofast**. Quite pompous and progressive, yet very brutal black metal, similar to a heavier **Dimmu Borgir**. Great and very intricate arrangements with lots of tempo-changes. Traditionally brutal death-vocals. In 2009 the band recorded the demo *Holocaust*.

1998 CD - POSH 013

2000 CD - POSH 021

1997 ☐	The Beginning	MCD 3tr	Spellcast	SPELL 001
	Tracks: ...And The War.../Mystic Silence/The Forgotten Lies			
1998 ■	NIGHTSPAWN	CD	Listenable	POSH 013
2000 ■	MALFORMED SEED	CD	Listenable	POSH 021
2002 ■	CHRISTIAN TERMINATION	CD	Listenable	POSH 037
2002 ☐	CHRISTIAN TERMINATION	CD	Irond (Russia)	02-284

2002 CD - POSH 037

GRIFFEN

Jörgen Söderberg: v,
Stefan Törnblom: g,
Tomi Peltonen: g,
Harri Tuovila: b,
Kristian Huotari: d

2010 CD - STH 1024

Eskilstuna - Griffen were formed in 2006 and made two promos before being picked up by Italian label Steelheart. The album was mixed by Pelle Saether (*Grand Design, Zello* etc). Peltonen is ex-*Madigan/Torch*, Houtari has previously been in *Torch* and *Scaar*, Törnblom in *Madigan* and *Metalorgy* and Söderberg was also in the latter. *Griffen* is an excellent classic hard rock/metal band with both feet in the 80s. A second album has been recorded.
Website: www.griffen.se

2010 ■	LIFE – A WAY TO DIE	CD	Steelheart	STH 1024

GRIFTEGÅRD

Thomas Eriksson (now Sabbathi): v, Ola Blomqvist: g, Per Broddesson: g,
Thomas Jansson: b, Jens Gustafsson: d

Stockholm - Formed in 2005 by Blomqvist, when his former band *The Doomsday Cult* folded. He drafted former band mates Broddesson and bassist Dennis Olsson and formed *Griftegård*. *Griftegård* (meaning a graveyard without a church) play doom so slow you can go out and have a smoke between the snare beats. What set them apart from several other bands in the genre are the excellent vocals of Eriksson. I hear a slight touch of Messiah Marcolin at times. Ola was previously co-owner of I Hate Records. On *Solemn. Sacred. Severe* bass player Dennis Olsson had been replaced by Thomas Jansson (*Wolverine*). Eriksson and Gustafsson are ex-*Dear Mutant*. Blomkvist is also found in *Spetälsk*, Eriksson in *Bokor* and *Year Of The Goat*, Broddesson in *Wolverine* and *Absurdeity*. *Psalmbok* was also released in 80 copies as a CD-R in a digipack. The track *Pagan Altar Cometh* can be found on the *Knock 'Em Down To Size* 7" sampler. Jens (*Dear Mutant, Saturnalia Temple, K9-Corpse* etc) sadly died in July 2013.

2007 12" - NACHT 002

2009 CDd - Ván32C

2007 ■	Psalmbok	12"	Nachtgnosis	NACHT 002
	Tracks: Charles Taze Russell/Paul Gustave Dore. 500 copies.			
2009 ☐	Psalmbok	MCDd	Ván	Ván24
	Different artwork.			
2009 ■	SOLEMN. SACRED. SEVERE	CDd	Ván	Ván32C
2009 ☐	SOLEMN. SACRED. SEVERE	CDd	Ván	Ván32C
	A5 die hard digi-pack with gold printing.			
2009 ☐	SOLEMN. SACRED. SEVERE	LP	Nachtgnosis	NACHT 009
2009 ☐	SOLEMN. SACRED. SEVERE	LP	Nachtgnosis	NACHT 009
	200 copies. Red marble vinyl. Bronze metal seal.			
2009 ☐	SOLEMN. SACRED. SEVERE	LP	Nachtgnosis	NACHT 009
	100 copies. Red marble vinyl. Bronze metal seal. Slipcase, black leather, gold foil + linen.			
2010 ☐	Wedded To Grief (split)	7"	Ván	Ván41
	Split with Count Raven			
2010 ☐	Wedded To Grief (split)	7"+CD	Ván	Ván41
	Special packaging, 3-panel gatefold, CD listening copy. Sealed with wax.			
2011 ■	Griftegård/Lord Vicar (split)	7"	Ván	Ván48
	Split with Lord Vicar. Track: A Deathbed For All Holy			

2011 7" - Ván48

GRIFTESKYMFNING

Sir N: v/g/b, Sir J Marklund: d

Dalarna - The first demo is horrible, badly recorded instrumental black metal. The second album is equally horribly recorded (almost no drums), this time with strange whispering "vocals". JM is also found in *LIK*, *Sorgedom*, Both Sir N and Marklund are also in **Kaos Sacramentum**.

2008 ☐	DEMO 08	CD	Mystery Of Death	Mystery 001
2009 ☐	DJÄVULENS BONING	CD	Mystery Of Death	Mystery 002
2012 ■	LIKPSALM	2LP	Mordgrimm	GRIM 33
	300 copies.			
2012 ☐	DEMO 08	LP	Ancient Records	AR 035
2012 ☐	DJÄVULENS BONING	LP	Ancient Records	AR 036

2012 2LP - GRIM 33

GRIMMARK

Carl-Johan "CJ" Grimmark: v/g/k/b, Jan S Eckert: b, Peter Wildoer: d

Jönköping - Carl-Johan Grimmark is foremost known as the guitarist of **Narnia**, but when he made a solo album, it showed he was also an outstanding singer! Besides his work with **Narnia**, Grimmark has made guest spots with **Locomotive Breath**, **Hero**, **Planet Alliance**, **Saviour Machine** and **Divinefire**. He was also part of the band **FullForce** and is now in **Empire 21**. The *Grimmark* CD is a great, heavy instalment, more in the vein of **Black Label Society** musically. Wildoer is also found in **Arch Enemy**, **Armageddon**, **Agregator** and **Dawn Of Oblivion**.

2007 ■	GRIMMARK	CD	Rivel Records	RRCD 035

2007 CD - RRCD 035

GROTESQUE

Tomas Lindberg: v, Alf Svensson: g/b/k, Kristian Wåhlin: g/k

Billdal (Göteborg) - Black/death metal with lots of tempo changes from doomlike heavy riffing to ultra-speed parts. Really heavy and detuned guitars. Traditional death-vocals. After the release of the Mini-LP the band split. Tomas and Alf then formed **At The Gates**. Alf, who was in punk-band **Oral** before **Grotesque**, now has his own band **Oxiplegatz** and also runs a renowned tattoo-shop in Göteborg. Kristian, a.k.a Necrolord, is a phenomenal artist and has made lots of great album covers for bands like **Lake Of Tears**, **Morgana Lefay** and **Tad Morose**. The MLP was later released as a full album completed with tracks from the unreleased demo *In The Embrace Of Evil*. Two of the tracks features bass player David Nuctemeron.

1990 ■	Incantation	MLP 5tr	Dolores	DOL 004
	Tracks: Incantation/Spawn Of Azaroth/Nocturnal Blasphemies/Submit To Death/Blood Runs From The Altar			
1996 ☐	IN THE EMBRACE OF EVIL	CD	Black Sun Records	BS 007
2001 ☐	GARDENS OF GRIEF/IN THE EMBRACE OF EVIL (split)	CD	Century Media	8040-2
	Split with At The Gates.			
2002 ☐	IN THE EMBRACE OF EVIL	LP	Black Sun Records	BS 07LP
	Red vinyl.			

1990 MLP - DOL 004

GROUND MOWER

Magnus Arnar: v, Jonas Wigstad: g, Tomas Marklund: b, Richard Bång: d

Stockholm - Formed in 2004 when drummer Bång heard Arnar perform with the band **Soul 78** at a summer festival and decided he was going to form a new band. Awesome, heavy yet melodic metal in the vein of **Disturbed**. Arnar joined **The Quill** in 2010 and was previously in **King Chrome**. Bång is also in **Face Down**, and together with Wigstad and Marklund he was also part of metal band **Mosez**, who made two releases in 1992-93. In the fall of 2009 former **Subculture** guitarist Jonathan Granlund Pennheim replaced Wigstad.

2008 ■	GROUND MOWER	CDd	Casket	CSK 144

2008 CD - CSK 144

GUARDIAN ANGELS

Fredrik Jernberg: v, Anton Solli: g, Lasse Lekberg: b

Stockholm - They started out under the name *IQ*, as a pure hard rock band. They later became a pretty slick and commercial AOR band. High-quality and all. Sadly, they never really broke through and never got to record a full length album. Buy all four singles and you've got almost an album. Fredrik later joined **Rat Bat Blue** while Anton and Lasse joined **Snakepit Rebels**, later **Blind System**. On the last single the band was only a trio with Fredrik, Anton and Lasse. Up until the last single the band was completed with Thomas Anderberg (k) and Dennis Camenborn (d).

1987 ■	Every Piece Of You/One By One	7"	Sonet	T-10228
1987 ☐	When I'm Back.../Fire's Burning	7"	Sonet	T-10245
1988 ☐	Every Situation/Dreamer	7"	Sonet	T-10263
1989 ☐	Two Of A Kind/Silent Light	7"	Sonet	T-10290

1987 7" - T-10228

GUDARS SKYMNING

Kenny-Oswald Sjödin: v/g, Knut Hassel: g, Magnus Hasselstam: b, Anders Olofsson: d

The grass is always greener...

Backe (Strömsund) - Another great player in the Swedish retro hard rock league together with colleagues like **Magnolia**, **Abramis Brama**, **Svarte Pan**, **Skånska Mord** etc. Hassel is ex-**Destiny** and **7th Planet**, while Sjödin and Hasselstam played with progressive rockers **Hatt**, who released a digital-only album called *Watch Out For Naughty George* (Turmic Records). On the debut Dennis Sjödin played keyboards. *Gudars Skymning* play great 70s hard rock with strong influences from heavier bands like **Black Sabbath**, **Mountain** and **Led Zeppelin** as well as some more proggy bits thrown in. Ulf Torkelsson from **Abramis Brama** guests on *Mörka vatten*.
Website: www.gudarsskymning.se

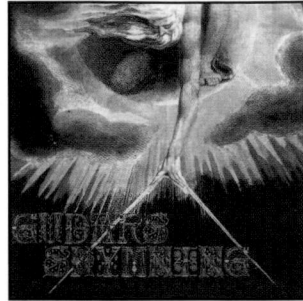

2008 CD - GS-01

2010 CDd - BRR 005

2008	■	DANSA TILLBAKS TILL DIN GRAV	CD	private	GS-01
2010	■	MÖRKA VATTEN	CDd	Bloodrock	BRR 005
2010	☐	MÖRKA VATTEN	LP	Black Widow	BWR 126

GUIDANCE OF SIN

Leini: v, Jesper Löfgren:g, Linus Nirbrant: g, L-E Limnell: b, Fredrik Andersson: d

2000 CD - PMZ 012-2

Stockholm - Formed as a side project by Linus and Jesper of *A Canorous Quintet* in 1994. In 1995 singer Leini from **Sanguinary** joined. In 1997 Fredrik Andersson, also from *A Canorous Quintet /Marduk/Allegience*, joined on drums. In 1997 they recorded the demo *Soul Disparity*, which sold over 500 copies. In 1998 they entered the Sunlight studio to record two tracks, of which one is found on the compilation *Voices Of Death Part 2*. In 1998 they were signed by Mighty Music. Linus and Jesper now left *A Canorous Quintet*, who consequently split. Fredrik was now replaced by Tobbe Sillman and L-E (also ex-**Sanguinary**) joined. The first release is a collection of all the demo-material the band had recorded up until this. The album also contains a cover of **Motörhead**'s *Killed By Death*. The band folded in 2001. Linus and Tobbe are now found in **Dead**.

2000 7" - NMEP 017 EP

2000	☐	SOULSEDUCER	CD	Mighty Music	PMZ 006-2
2000	■	6106	CD	Mighty Music	PMZ 012-2
2000	☐	6106	CDd	Mighty Music	PMX 012-2
2000	■	Acts/In The Hour Of Peril	7"	Nocturnal Music (Italy)	NMEP 017 EP
2000	☐	6106	CD	Irond (Russia)	01-58

GUILLOTINE

Fredrik "Spider" Mannberg: v/g, Daniel Sundbom: g, Nils "Snake" Eriksson: b, Efraim Juntunen: d

1997 CD - NR 020

Umeå - 80s style thrash, influenced by bands like **Kreator**, **Razor** and **Whiplash**. Mannberg is ex-**Ligament** and **Nocturnal Rites**, where Eriksson was also a member. The band was formed by the two under the name **Holocaust** and as a side-project to **Nocturnal Rites**. Fredrik Degerström (**Auberon**, **Naglfar**, **Bewitched**) tried out as singer for the group but never recorded anything. Rumors has it that drummer Cobra is actually not playing on the first album, only participated in the band photo. *Guillotine* was reactivated in 2007 drafting **Persuader** members Daniel Sundbom and Efraim Juntunen. *Guillotine* play old-school thrash, fast and furious like vintage **Anthrax** and a fine competitor alongside current Swedish thrashers **F.K.Ü**, but without the tongue-in-cheek factor. Tight, powerful and really great! The second album is a nice improvement when it comes to production. Highly recommended!
Website: www.myspace.com/251759960

2008 CD - ASH 052 CD

1997	■	UNDER THE GUILLOTINE	CD	Necropolis	NR 020
1997	☐	UNDER THE GUILLOTINE	LP PD	Necropolis	NR 020-P
		500 hand numbered copies.			
2008	■	BLOOD MONEY	CD	Pulverised	ASH 052 CD
2008	☐	BLOOD MONEY	CDd	Pulverised	ASH 052 DG
		Bonus: I Hate Society			
2008	☐	BLOOD MONEY	CD	Toy's Factory (Japan)	TKCS-85211
		Bonus: Fool's Paradise			

GUNGFLY

Rikard Sjöblom: v/g/b

Gävle - Solo project by **Beardfish** frontman Rikard. Seventies-sounding progressive rock, similar to **Bearfish**. Also influenced by **Them Crooked Vultures**, **Foo Fighters** as well as **Jethro Tull** and **Opeth**. Quite interesting stuff indeed.

2009 ☐	PLEASE BE QUIET	CD	Gungfly Productions	JSM 005
2011 ■	LAMENTATIONS	CD+DVD	Progress Records	PRCD 044

Live bonus DVD recorded 2009.

2011 CD+DVD - PRCD 044

GUNS 'N' HORSES

Anders Almgren: v, Niklas Brevestedt: g, Niklas Ekander: g, Henrik Lovén: k, Johan Rylander: b, Anders Westring: d

Nybro - Sleazy hard rock similar to **Bad Business**. In 1994 the band was picked up by party fixer Brinkenstjärna who wanted to make the band more disco, following the success of the band **Rednex**. Unfortunately Brinkenstjärna went bankrupt and they never signed. Shortly after, the band folded. Brevestedt plays with the band **Rekyl** (not the seventies rock band). Quite a witty name... Stop the presses! In 1995 the band returned with the single *I Shot The Sheriff* (yes, the Bob Marley song) and a CD entitled *Lucky Days* (both on C&R Music), where the band made an 180 degree turn and play hillbilly country!! Fiddels, yodels, banjo etc. Avoid at all cost!!

1991 ■	Roadhouse Lisa/My Horse's On Fire	7"	private	BLÅ II
1992 ☐	Roadhouse Lisa/No One Knows	7"	Tonophone	TNPS 003

19?? 7" - BLÅ II

GYPSIES, THE

Emil Wållberg: v/g, Mikael Sundvisson: v/b, Jonas Höglund: v/d

Nykvarn - The Gypsies were a very young trio who won the 2001 edition of the Spinnrock bandstand, with recording of a CD was first prize. When you see the cover and the young age of the members, don't be mistaken. This is a really good one! If you're into the heavy Hendrix-style power-trio-vibe, this is a disc to check out. Two years later **The Gypsies** recorded their second album, *Rhythmic Expression*, which was more of the same. Unfortunately the album has remained unreleased. Emil is now in the **Blue Wild Angels**, while Mikael has been in **Jane Gulliou** and **D Major Seven**.

2002 ■	LAND OF COLOR	CD	Spinnrocken	SPCD 001

2002 CD - SPCD 001

GYPSY

Stefan Johansson: v/b, Anders Karlsson: v/g, Anders Carolusson: g, Mikael Börjesson: d

Tanum - When the intro starts with highly out of tune guitars it definitely made me wonder. Well, it does get a bit better. The A-side is a pretty good NWoBHM style track similar to **Trespass**.

1982 ■	III World War/Explosive Hangover	7"	private	RR-001

1982 7" - RR-001

GYPSY ROSE

Dave Reece: v, Martin Kronlund: g, Rikard Quist: k, Mats Bostedt: b, Imre Daun: d

Mölnlycke (Göteborg) - Gypsy Rose were originally formed in 1981 inspired by the classic hard rock of the seventies. In 1984 they were picked up by a Belgian label, that unfortunately went out of business before the release of the debut album. In 1989 they received interest from American producer Taavi Mote who wanted to record the band, but things slipped out of their hands again and the band folded. In 2004 the idea of re-uniting sprung to life. As the original drummer hadn't touched his drums since 1991, former **Don Patrol**/**Alien**/**Kharma** drummer Daun was drafted. Håkan Gustafsson handled the vocals on the debut, and they also had Mats Leven (**Swedish Erotica, Abstrakt Algebra, Malmsteen** etc) on backing vocals. On the follow-up *Another World* these duties were handled by American Dave Reece (**Bangalore Choir, Accept, Sircle Of Silence**), with whom Kronlund has made several recordings, one being the duo **Reece Kronlund**, where Quist added his flare as well. The album also features guest spots from keyboard player Mats Olausson (**Malmsteen**) and guitarists Danny Gill (**Speak No Evil**) and Peter Svensson. *Gypsy Rose* play high-quality heavy melodic rock/AOR. Both albums are well worth checking out, but the second one stepped it up quite a bit. Kronlund and Daun have also recorded two albums together in the band **Dogface**.

2005 CD - ESM 120

2005 ■	GYPSY ROSE	CD	Escape	ESM 120
2005 ☐	GYPSY ROSE	CD	Avalon Marquee (Japan)	MICP-10535
	Bonus: Solitude			
2008 ■	ANOTHER WORLD	CD	Escape	ESM 171

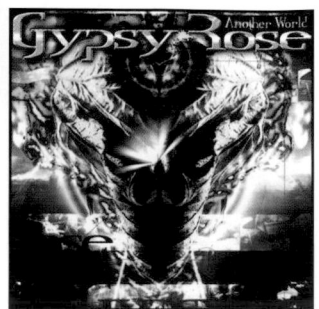

2008 CD - ESM 171

H.E.A.L
Christian Sture: v/g, Jonas Ygnell: g, Wolfgang Kempfel: b, Adrian Erlandsson: d

Göteborg - Formed in 1993. Outstanding shit-heavy *Danzig*-influenced heavy rock. The guitar sound is like a ton of bricks and the singer sounds like a more varied version of Glenn Danzig. Adrian was also in *At The Gates*. On the second release the band had no firm drummer but the job was done by Adrian and Fredrik Sandsten (*Whipped Cream*). Highly recommended. A full length album *Shivas Ohm* (Classical Music Prod. CMP 7), was recorded and ready in January 1996. However it was never released, as the singer fired the rest of the band. Erlandsson later played in *Decameron*.

1994 MCD - CMP 1

1994 ■ There Can Be Only One ....MCD 6tr   Classical Music Productions ....CMP 1
  Tracks: I Don't Know My World/She Calls My Name/There Can Be Only One/I Know.../
  Gather Around Me/Look At Yourself

H.E.A.T
Erik Grönwall: v, Erik "Eric Rivers" Hammarbäck: g, David "Dave Dalone" Axelsson: g, Jonas "Jona Tee" Thegel: k, Jimmy "Jay" Johansson: b, Lars "Crash" Jerkell: d

Upplands Väsby - The band was formed out of the ashes of young melodic metal bands *Trading Fate* (Jimmy, Erik H, Lars, Kenny) and *Dream* (Jona, Dave and Kenny) in 2007. The denominating factor was singer Kenny Leckremo, who handled the vocals in both bands. *Dream* was more AOR, while *Trading Fate* had a more metal attitude in the vein of *Iron Maiden*. The merger resulted in the high-class AOR band *H.E.A.T.* After some great-sounding demos they signed a deal with actor Peter Stormare's label Stormvox, who released the self-titled debut in 2008. The band received rave reviews and played quite a lot of festivals and support shows. The album contains high-class melodic hard rock in the vein of bands like *Giant*, *Bad English* etc. The band also entered the Eurovision Song Contest with the song *1000 Miles* in 2009, where they ended up at a seventh place in the Swedish finals. The second album, *Freedom Rock*, was released in 2010. Unfortunately the album didn't live up to the expectations, neither song nor sound-wise. In 2010 some big changes took place. The band left their old label, management as well as their singer. Kenny moved to London, and was replaced by Swedish Idol winner Erik Grönwall. Jona Tee and Jimmy Jay were also backing former *Target/Cobra/Survivor* singer Jimi Jamison on a tour. In 2012 *H.E.A.T* returned with a vengeance, sending out the digital teaser *Living On The Run* before the album release. The album was produced by Tobias Lindell (*Europe, Mustasch*) and shows the band returning to their melodic glory. The exclusive track *Fill Your Head With Rock* is found on the *Sweden Rock Festival 2008* compilation. In July 2013 Dave Dalone left the band, who will continue as a five-piece.

The HEAT is on!

2010 MCDpg - SVXCDS 1002

2010 CD - SVXCD 7006

2008 ☐ H.E.A.T ....CD	Stormvox.....................................	SVXCD 7004
2008 ☐ H.E.A.T ....CD	Avalon Marquee (Japan)...............	MICP-10811
Bonus: Stay (2008 version)		
2009 ☐ 1000 Miles/1000 Miles (Karaoke Version) ....CDSp 2tr	Stormvox.....................................	SVXCDS 1000
2009 ☐ H.E.A.T 2CD	Stormvox.....................................	SVXCD 7004X
With bonus CDS containing the 1000 Miles CDS.		
2009 ☐ Keep On Dreaming (Radio edit)/(album version)/(live) ....CDSp 3tr	Stormvox.....................................	SVXCDS 1001
2010 ■ Beg Beg Beg..MCDpg 3tr	Stormvox.....................................	SVXCDS 1002
Tracks: Beg Beg Beg/Tonight/Living In A Memory		
2010 ■ FREEDOM ROCK...CD	Stormvox.....................................	SVXCD 7006
2010 ☐ FREEDOM ROCK...CD	E.A.R (Germany)	0204732EREP
2010 ☐ FREEDOM ROCK...CD	Avalon Marquee (Japan)...............	MICP-10900
Bonus: Tonight/Living In A Memory		
2010 ☐ FREEDOM ROCK...CD	Magnum (Taiwan)	AVA 100601
Bonus: Tonight/Living In A Memory		
2010 ☐ FREEDOM ROCK (COLLECTOR'S EDITION)................2CD	Avalon Marquee (Japan)...............	MICP-20001
Bonus: H.E.A.T/High On Love (5 different mixes). SHM-CD.		
2012 ■ ADDRESS THE NATION ....CD	Gain	8869195-2132

2012 CD - 8869195-2132

H2O
Thomas Augustsson: g/v, Thomas Magnusson: g, Urban Engström: g, Juha Koikeroinen: b, Jimmy Johansson: d

Karlskoga - The A-side on the first single was good solid hard rock with some nice *Thin Lizzy*-inspired guitar harmonies, while the B-side was a ballad. The follow up was a bit more radio-shaped, closer to early *Snowstorm* (and on the same label, too). Now singer Jan Carlsson was no longer in the band. The last single was made as a promo for a local football club. The A-side (in Swedish) is crap while *The Game* (in English) is quite good. They also had a song on a *FIB Aktuellt* (Swedish men's magazine) compilation cassette. Not to be confused with the English band on RCA.

1980 ○ Lyftet/Just Nu Idag ....7"	Mariann.......................................	MAS 2293
No artwork.		
1982 ■ Håll I Mej/Ingenting Alls......................................7"	Mill	MRS 1003
1985 ☐ IBK-Visan/The Game ....7"	Modern Music Production	IBK 101

1982 7" - MRS 1003

HADES

dB: v, Erik "Sigge" Danielsson: g, Jerker: b, Olov: k, Ivar Katranka: d

Umeå - I really don't know how to categorise this band. At times they feel like a pop-punk band with a hard rock sound, at times they are pure hard rock/metal. The vocals are quite horrible. On the same label as *Gotham City*.

1982 ■ Flickor Är Blinda..7" 4tr   Brute Force..BFR 005 **$$**
  Tracks: Flickor Är Blinda/Legoknekt/Friklandet/Kaijsa.

1982 7" - BFR 005

HAGEN

Michale Ohlsson: v, Per Nilsson: g, Anders Rosén: violin, Hans Lundin: k, Hasse Rosén: b, Patrik Jansson: d

Uppsala - Michael is ex-*Zircus*, *Zeit* and *New Clear Daze*, Hasse is also ex-*Zircus* and *New Clear Daze*, Hans is also found in *Kaipa*, Per is ex-*Legia* and Patrik has previously banged the drums for *Arcana Major*. This is an outstandingly interesting bunch that mixes Swedish folk-music with highly intricate hard rock, prog and AOR, featuring distorted violin, fat Hammond and heavy guitars, similar to a heavier *Hoven Droven*. Great vocals and great song material makes this a safe buy!

Website: www.hagen.nu

2001 ■ CORRIDORS OF TIME..CD   Angular ....SKAN 8220.AR

2001 CD - SKAN 8220.AR

HALF MAN

Janne Bengtsson: v/g, Peter Lilja: g, Patric Carlsson: b, Roger Bengtsson: d

Örkelljunga - *Half Man* were formed in 1986 and originally consisted of Bengtsson, Carlsson, Gunnar Kastman (Andersson) on guitar and Mats Nilsson on drums. The band folded in 1988, but was resurrected two years later with the above line-up. A demo was recorded in 1994, but nothing really happened until the debut was recorded four years later. Very 70's inspired blues-based hard rock with touches of *Cream*. Good stuff, indeed! On *Red Herring* they do an excellent cover of Zappa's *Willy The Pimp*. In 2000 the band recorded a cover of *Aerosmith*'s *Round And Round* for the tribute album *Right In The Nuts* (Small Stone). *Half Man* sort of withered away, but in 2006 a new band appeared - *Skånska Mord*. The band features Bengtsson and Carlsson plus former *Mothercake* members Patrik Berglin, Petter Engström and Tomas Jönsson.

1999 CD - HMCD 001

1999 ■ THE COMPLETE FIELD GUIDE FOR CYNICS ....CD   private ....HMCD 001
  Bonus: Rodney's Song. 500 copies.
1999 □ THE COMPLETE FIELD GUIDE FOR CYNICS ....LP   private ....HMLP 001
  500 copies.
1999 □ THE COMPLETE FIELD GUIDE FOR CYNICS ....CD   Skivfabriken ....SFAB 001
1999 □ Vol 1 ....7» EP   private ....HM&M 001
  Split with Mothercake. The Half Man-tracks are Red Herring/Acid Park
2002 ■ RED HERRING..CD   Beard Of Stars .... BOS 23
2002 □ RED HERRING...2LPg   Beard Of Stars .... BOS 23
  Bonus: Red Herring

2002 CD - BOS 23

HALLONBOMB

Bonde Svedberg: v, Christer Nilsson: g, Kenneth Forsell: b, Håkan Nilsson: d

Ljusdal - *Hallonbomb* (raspberry bomb) started out in 1986 as a blues-oriented pop-band, but on their third album *Tung Medicin* they recruited singer Bonde (who replaced Ulf Hagberg) and turned into a mid-weight hard rock band, still with a bluesy touch though. They sing in Swedish.

1995 □ TUNG MEDICIN..CD   Bombolaget .... BCD 1
1995 ■ Hallonbomb...MCDp 4tr   Bombolaget BCDS-4
  Tracks: Anna/TV-Man/Gift/Spring För Ditt Liv.

1995 MCDp - BCDS-4

HAMMERFALL

Joacim Cans: v, Oscar Dronjac: g, Pontus Norgren: g, Fredrik Larsson: b, Anders Johansson: d

Göteborg - Formed in 1993 by Oscar Dronjac (ex-*Ceremonial Oath* and *Crystal Age*) who teamed up with drummer Jesper Strömblad. The initial line-up also featured singer Mikael Stanne (*Dark Tranquillity*), guitarist Niklas Sundin and bassist Johan Larsson. In 1994 Fredrik Larsson replaced Johan Larsson and the year after Glenn Ljungström replaced Sundin. Despite some of the initial members having a death metal back ground, *Hammerfall* is pure, classic heavy metal inspired by 80s bands like *Saxon*, *Accept* and *Judas Priest*. Quality stuff indeed with great vocals, lots of guitar twiddling and double bass drum playing. Before the debut album

Backed by the big hammer

Strömbland left and was replaced by Patrik Räfling (ex-*Mega Slaughter*). Strömblad however continued writing for the band. The debut album contains a cover of *Warlord*'s track *Child Of The Damned*, a band singer Joacim would later come to front. This was the band that made Nuclear Blast broaden their musical spectrum and include melodic metal in their catalogue. The first album reached to number 38 in the German charts. After the debut, the line-up changed. Ljugström was replaced by Stefan Elmgren and Fredrik Larsson (ex-*Crystal Age*) was replaced by Magnus Rosén (ex-*Keegan, Von Rosen* etc). *At The End Of The Rainbow* on the second album features a guitar solo by ex-*Warlord*-guitarist Bill Tsamis. The album also contains a cover of *Pretty Maids*' *Back To Back*. In 1999 the home video - *First Crusade* (Nuclear Blast VHS NB 413-6) was released and later the same year Anders Johansson (*Silver Mountain, Malmsteen, Johansson* etc) replaced drummer Räfling. On *I Want Out*, Kai Hansen (*Gamma Ray*) guests. Joacim also recorded a CD with side project *Mrs. Hippie*. In 2000 Magnus released his first solo effort in a totally different direction. It's entitled *Imagine A Place* and is jazz record featuring saxophonist Biggi Vinkeloe. His second album was released in 2002. *Renegade* was recorded in Nashville at Wolf Hoffman's (*Accept*) studio and produced by Michael Wagener (*Accept, Dokken* etc). In 2001 the band toured excessively through Europe and South America. With *Renegade* they managed to do something that had not been done since the days of Europe, go straight in to number 1 on the Swedish sales-chart! Stefan also unleashed his first solo-release *Full Strike*, using the services of *Freak Kitchen*-drummer Björn Fryklund and bass player Chris Goldsmith. In 2001 *Hammerfall* covered the song *We're Gonna Make It* on the *Twisted Forever* (Victor Japan) *Twisted Sister*-tribute, as the only Swedish act. In November 2001 *Renegade* was certified gold in Sweden, 40 000 copies. The 2005 release *Chapter V: Unbent, Unbowed, Unbroken* is a best of, also featuring some new material. In 2007 Magnus Rosén and the band parted company. He was replaced by long lost *Hammerfall* bassist, also formerly in *Evergrey*, Fredrik Larsson, who returned in glory. The 2008 album *Masterpieces* features covers only by bands like *Pretty Maids, Picture, Rainbow, Helloween, Riot* etc. Now Stefan Elmgren made his exit and was replaced by former *The Poodles/The Ring/Great King Rat/Talisman* guitarist Pontus Norgren. The 2009 release *No Victory, No Glory* features a cover of *The Knack*'s 80s hit *My Sharona*. The album also features guest spots from Jens Johansson (*Stratovarius, Silver Mountain* etc), Stefan Elmgren, Nicky Moore (*From Behind, Samson* ect), Biff Byford (*Saxon*), Dave Hill (*Demon*), Billy King and Mats Rendlert (*Dreamland, Infinity*). In 2009 former guitarist Elmgren and bassist Rosén announced they were in the new formed band *FullForce* together with *Cloudscape* singer Mike Andersson, and where Anders Johansson also handles the drums. The band's debut was unearthed in 2011. The song *Glory To The Brave* (radio edit) is featured on the *Metal Dreams* (Nuclear Blast, 1999) compilation. A cover of *Head Over Heels* (featuring Udo) can be found on the *Tribute To Accept* (Nuclear Blast 99) and a cover of *Man On The Silver Mountain* on *Holy Dio* (Nuclear Blast/Victor Japan '99). They do a cover of *Heavy Load*'s *Run With The Devil* on *Power From The North* (Digital Dimension), which later appeared as bonus on the *Renegade* MCD. The band's answer to *Iron Maiden*'s Eddie, their mascot, is named Hector. In 2012 the band took a break. To be continued... Website: www.hammerfall.net

1, 2, 3 POOOOSE!

1997 CD - NB 265-2

1998 CD - NB 335-2

1997 ■	GLORY TO THE BRAVE	CD	Nuclear Blast	NB 265-2
1997 □	GLORY TO THE BRAVE	LP	Nuclear Blast	NB 265-1
	Also available in a limited edition in orange vinyl.			
1997 □	GLORY TO THE BRAVE	LP PD	Nuclear Blast	NB 265-0
1997 □	GLORY TO THE BRAVE	CD shape	Nuclear Blast	NB 265-6
	3000 copies. Shaped disc.			
1997 □	Glory ToThe Brave	MCD 4tr	Nuclear Blast	NB 299-2
	Tracks: Glory To The Brave/Ravenlord (Stormwitch cover)/The Metal Age (live)/Glory To The Brave (live). Withdrawn press.			
1997 □	Glory ToThe Brave	MCD 4tr	Nuclear Blast	NB 299-2
	Re-press with I Believe instead of The Metal Age			
1997 □	Glory To The Brave	MCD 4tr	Nuclear Blast America (USA)	NBA 6299-2
1997 □	GLORY TO THE BRAVE	CD	Nuclear Blast America (USA)	NBA 6265-2
1997 □	GLORY TO THE BRAVE	CD	Victor (Japan)	VICP-60135
1998 ■	LEGACY OF KINGS	CD	Nuclear Blast	NB 335-2
1998 □	LEGACY OF KINGS	LP	Nuclear Blast	NB 335-1
1998 □	LEGACY OF KINGS LTD BOX	CD box	Nuclear Blast	NB 335-9
	Cardboard box. Including guitar pick, sticker and autographed cards.			
1998 □	LEGACY OF KINGS	LP PD	Nuclear Blast	NB 335-1
1998 □	LEGACY OF KINGS	CD shape	Nuclear Blast	NB 335-6
1998 □	LEGACY OF KINGS	CD	Nuclear Blast America	NBA 6335-2
1998 □	LEGACY OF KINGS	CD	Seoul Records (North Korea)	SRCD-2445
1998 □	LEGACY OF KINGS	2CD	CNR (France)	3043245
	Bonus-CD contains: The Metal Age (live)/Glory To The Brave/Ravenlord			
1998 ■	Heeding The Call	MCD 5tr	Nuclear Blast	NB 333-2
	Tracks: Heeding The Call (edit)/Eternal Dark (Picture cover)/The Metal Age (live)/Steel Meets Steel (live)/Stone Cold (live)			

1998 MCD - NB 333-2

| 1998 ☐ | Heeding The Call | 7" 4tr shape | Nuclear Blast | NB 333-1 |

Tracks: Heeding The Call/Eternal Dark (Picture cover)/The Metal Age/Steel Meets Steel

| 1998 ☐ | Heeding The Call | MCD 4tr | Nuclear Blast America (USA) | NBA 6333-2 |
| 1998 ☐ | LEGACY OF KINGS | CD | Victor (Japan) | VICP-60456 |

Bonus: Stone Cold (live)/Eternal Dark (Picture cover) (live)

| 1999 ☐ | I Want Out | MCD 3tr | Nuclear Blast | NB 414-2 |

Tracks: I Want Out (Helloween cover)/At The End Of The Rainbow/Man On The Silver Mountain (Rainbow cover)/Glory To The Brave (video)

| 1999 ☐ | I Want Out | 7" 3tr | Nuclear Blast | NB 414-1 |

Tracks: I Want Out (Helloween cover)/At The End Of The Rainbow/Man On The Silver Mountain (Rainbow cover)

1999 ☐	I Want Out	MCD 3tr	Nuclear Blast America (USA)	NBA 6414-2
1999 ☐	I Want Out	MCD 3tr	Nothing To Say (France)	3052335
2000 ■	Renegade	MCD 3tr	Nuclear Blast	NB 530-2

Tracks: Renegade/Run With The Devil (Heavy Load cover)/Head Over Heels (Accept cover)

2000 MCD - NB 530-2

| 2000 ☐ | Renegade/Head Over Heels | 7" | Nuclear Blast | NB 530-7 |

Red vinyl.

2000 ☐	Renegade	MCD 3tr	Nuclear Blast America (USA)	NBA 6530-2
2000 ☐	Renegade	7"	Nuclear Blast America (USA)	NBA 6511-7
2000 ☐	RENEGADE	CD	Nuclear Blast	NB 511 2
2000 ☐	RENEGADE	LP PD	Nuclear Blast	NB 511 1
2000 ☐	RENEGADE	CDd	Rock Brigade (South America)	NB 511-0
2000 ☐	RENEGADE	CD	Nuclear Blast America	NBA 6511-2
2000 ☐	RENEGADE	LPg	Nuclear Blast America	NBA 6511-1
2000 ☐	RENEGADE	LP PD	Nuclear Blast America	NBA 6511-9
2000 ■	Always Will Be	MCD 4tr	Nuclear Blast (Sweden)	NB 620-2

Tracks: Always Will Be/The Fallen One/Always Will Be (acoustic)/Breaking The Law (Judas Priest cover)

2000 MCD - NB 620-2

2000 ■	Always Will Be/The Fallen One	CDS	Nuclear Blast (Sweden)	NB 620-2
2000 ☐	Always Will Be/The Fallen One	7" PD shape	Nuclear Blast	NB 620-7
2000 ☐	Always Will Be/The Fallen One	7" PD shape	Nuclear Blast America (USA)	NBA 0649-1
2000 ☐	Always Will Be	MCD 4tr	Nuclear Blast America (USA)	NBA 6620-2
2000 ☐	RENEGADE	CD	Victor (Japan)	VICP 61183
2000 ☐	RENEGADE	CD	Irond (Russia)	00-12

Bonus: Run With The Devil (Heavy Load cover)/Head Over Heels (Accept cover)

| 2000 ☐ | Renegade/Head Over Heels | 7" | Nuclear Blast | NB 511-7 |

Red vinyl.

| 2000 ☐ | LEGACY OF KINGS | CD | Irond (Russia) | 00-45 |

Bonus: Stone Cold (live)/I Want Out/Man On The Silver Mountain (Rainbow cover)/The Metal Age

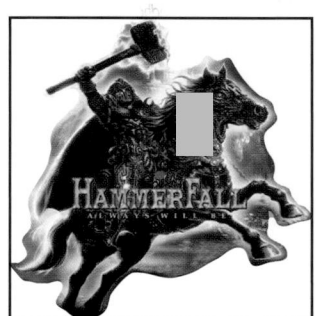

2000 7" PD shape - NB 620-7

| 2000 ☐ | RENEGADE | LP | Nuclear Blast | NB 511 9 |

Blue vinyl. Second press: 100 yellow, 200 black, 200 clear vinyl.

| 2001 ☐ | RENEGADE | CD shape | Nuclear Blast | NB 511 8 |
| 2001 ☐ | GLORY TO THE BRAVE | CD | Irond (Russia) | 01-165 |

Bonus: Always Will Be (acoustic)/Breaking The Law (Judas Priest cover)/Steel Meets Steel (live)

| 2002 ☐ | GLORY TO THE BRAVE + RENEGADE | CD | Nuclear Blast | NB 2655 |

Re-issue of the debut plus the tracks from the Renegade EP.

| 2002 ☐ | LEGACY OF KINGS + ALWAYS WILL BE | 2CD | Nuclear Blast | NB 3355 |

Re-issue plus the tracks from the Always Will Be EP.

| 2002 ☐ | RENEGADE | LP | Nuclear Blast | NB 511 9 |

Available in black or blue vinyl.

| 2002 ☐ | HEARTS ON FIRE | CD | Victor (Japan) | VICP-62038 |
| 2002 ☐ | Hearts On Fire | MLP 3tr | Nuclear Blast | NB 1030-1 |

Orange vinyl. Tracks: Hearts On Fire/We're Gonna Make It (Twisted Sister cover)/Heeding The Call (live)

2002 MCD - NB 1030-2

| 2002 ■ | Hearts On Fire | MCD 3tr | Nuclear Blast | NB 1030-2 |

Same tracks as vinyl plus Heeding The Call (live video)

| 2002 ☐ | Hearts On Fire | MCD 6tr | Victor (Japan) | VICP-62038 |

Tracks: Hearts On Fire/We're Gonna Make It (Twisted Sister cover)/Rising Force/Templars Of Steel (live)/Heeding The Call (live)/Let The Hammer Fall (live)/Heeding The Call (video)

| 2002 ☐ | Crimson Thunder | MCD 4tr | Nuclear Blast | NB 1066-2 |

Promo sampler. Tracks: Riders Of The Storm/Hearts On Fire/Crimson Thunder/Dreams Come True

| 2002 ☐ | CRIMSON THUNDER | CD | Victor (Japan) | VICP-62063 |

Bonus: Crazy Nights (Loudness cover)

| 2002 ■ | CRIMSON THUNDER | CD | Irond (Russia) | 02-342 |

Bonus: Rising Force (Malmsteen cover)

| 2002 ☐ | CRIMSON THUNDER | CDd | Nuclear Blast | NB 1031-0 |

Bonus: Rising Force (Malmsteen cover)

| 2002 ☐ | CRIMSON THUNDER | CDd | Nuclear Blast | 27361 10372 |

Bonus: Rising Force (Malmsteen cover). A4 size cover with comic book.

| 2002 ☐ | CRIMSON THUNDER | 3CD box | Nuclear Blast | NB 1031-2 |

CD+2 CDS in A4 size hardback leather comic book. 1000 copies. Bonus: Rising Force (Malmsteen cover)/Crazy Nights (Loudness)/Detroit Rock City (Kiss)

2002 CD - 02-342

2002 ☐	CRIMSON THUNDER – SPECIAL COMIC EDITION	CD	Nuclear Blast	NB 1031-2
	Bonus: Rising Force (Malmsteen cover)			
2002 ☐	CRIMSON THUNDER	LP	Nuclear Blast	NB 1031-1
	Bonus: Rising Force (Malmsteen cover)			
2002 ☐	CRIMSON THUNDER	LP PD	Nuclear Blast	NB 1031-9
	Bonus: Rising Force (Malmsteen cover)			
2002 ☐	CRIMSON THUNDER	CDd	Nuclear Blast America (USA)	NB 1031-0
	Bonus: Detroit Rock City (Kiss cover)			
2002 ☐	CRIMSON THUNDER	CD	Nuclear Blast	NB 1113-2
	Bonus: Rising Force (Malmsteen cover)/Heeding The Call (live)/Hearts On Fire (video)			
2003 ☐	GLORY TO THE BRAVE – DELUXE EDITION	CD	Nuclear Blast	NB 1018-2
	Bonus: Ravenlord (Stormwitch cover)/Glory To The Brave (video) + photo gallery, etc.			
2003 ■	ONE CRIMSON NIGHT	2CD	Nuclear Blast	NB 1196-2
2003 ☐	ONE CRIMSON NIGHT	3LP	Nuclear Blast	NB 1196-1
2003 ☐	ONE CRIMSON NIGHT	2CD	Victor (Japan)	VICP-63569-70
	Bonus: The Dragon Lies Bleeding/Stronger Than All/A Legend Reborn			
2003 ☐	ONE CRIMSON NIGHT	3CD+DVD box	Nuclear Blast	NB 1212-2
	Box with live DVD+DCD+bonus CD. Swedish flag, backstage pass replica. 1000 copies. Bonus: Dreamland (live) + messages.			
2004 ☐	ONE CRIMSON NIGHT	2CD	Irond (Russia)	04-723
	Bonus: The Dragon Lies Bleeding/Stronger Than All/A Legend Reborn			
2005 ☐	GLORY TO THE BRAVE	CD	Nems (Argentina)	NEMS 349
	Bonus: Ravenlord (Stormwitch cover)			
2005 ☐	LEGACY OF KINGS	CD	Nems (Argentina)	NEMS 350
	Bonus: The Metal Age (live)/Steel Meets Steel (live)			
2005 ■	CHAPTER V: UNBENT, UNBOWED, UNBROKEN	CD	Nuclear Blast	NB 1375-2
2005 ☐	CHAPTER V: UNBENT, UNBOWED, UNBROKEN	LP PD	Nuclear Blast	NB 1375-1
2005 ☐	CHAPTER V: UNBENT, UNBOWED, UNBROKEN	CDd	Nuclear Blast	NB 1375-0
	Bonus: Bloodbound (video)			
2005 ☐	CHAPTER V: UNBENT, UNBOWED, UNBROKEN	CDd	Sacarecrow (Mexico)	SC05178
2005 ☐	CHAPTER V: UNBENT, UNBOWED, UNBROKEN	CD box	Nuclear Blast	NB 1375-5
	Bonus:Bloodbound (video) Making Of Bloodbound (video). In metal box. 10 000 copies.			
2005 ☐	CHAPTER V: UNBENT, UNBOWED, UNBROKEN	CD	Nuclear Blast America	NBA 1375
2005 ☐	CHAPTER V: UNBENT, UNBOWED, UNBROKEN	CD	Avalon Marquee (Japan)	MICP-10496
	Bonus:Bloodbound/The Metal Age (live)			
2005 ☐	CHAPTER V: UNBENT, UNBOWED, UNBROKEN	CD	Nems (Argentina)	NEMS 355
	Bonus:Bloodbound/The Metal Age (live)			
2005 ☐	CHAPTER V: UNBENT, UNBOWED, UNBROKEN	CD	Irond (Russia)	05-962
2005 ☐	LEGACY OF KINGS – DELUXE EDITION	CD	Nuclear Blast	NB 1382-2
	Bonus: The Metal Age (live)/Steel Meets Steel (live)/Let The Hammer Fall 8video) + multimedia			
2005 ■	Blood Bound/Blood Bound (karaoke)/The Metal Age (live)	MCD 3tr	Nuclear Blast	NB 1355-2
2006 ☐	LEGACY OF KINGS	CD	Nuclear Blast	NB 1752-2
2006 ☐	LEGACY OF KINGS	CDd	Nuclear Blast	NB 1752-0
	Gimmick digi-cover.			
2006 ☐	LEGACY OF KINGS	CD+DVD	Nuclear Blast	NB 1752-8
	In 7" gatefold cover. Bonus: Natural High (video)/The Fire Burns Forever (video)/The Making Of Natural High (video)			
2006 ☐	THRESHOLD	CDd	Nuclear Blast	NB 1752-0
	Sticker.			
2006 ☐	THRESHOLD	CD	Nuclear Blast	NB 1762-2
	Promo with voice-overs.			
2006 ■	THRESHOLD	CD	Nuclear Blast	NB 1752-2
	Sticker.			
2006 ☐	THRESHOLD	CD	Avalon Marquee (Japan)	MICP-10615
	Bonus: The Fire Burns Forever/Raise The Hammer (live)			
2006 ☐	THRESHOLD	CD+DVD	Nuclear Blast	NB 1752-8
	Bonus: Natural High (video) + DVD with Natural High/The Fire Burns Forever/Making Of Natural High. In 7" gatefold. Mail-order edition.			
2006 ☐	THRESHOLD	CD	Nems (Argentina)	NEMS 394
	Bonus: Natural High (karaoke)/The Fire Burns Forever/Raise The Hammer			
2006 ☐	THRESHOLD	CD	Irond (Russia)	06-1213
2006 ☐	Natural High	MCD 4tr	Nuclear Blast	NB 1730-2
	Tracks: Natural High/Natural High (karaoke)/The Fire Burns Forever/Raise The Hammer (live)/The Fire Burns Forever (video))			
2006 ☐	Natural High	10"g 4tr	Nuclear Blast	NB 1730-1
	Tracks: Natural High/Natural High (karaoke/The Fire Burns Forever/Raise The Hammer (live)			
2006 ☐	RENEGADE	CD	Nems (Argentina)	NEMS 407
	Bonus: Run With The Devil (Heavy Load cover)/Head Over Heels (Accept cover)			
2007 ☐	STEEL MEETS STEEL – TEN YEARS OF GLORY	2CDd	Nuclear Blast	NB 1935-0
2007 ☐	STEEL MEETS STEEL – TEN YEARS OF GLORY	2CDd	Avalon Marquee (Japan)	MICP-90032
	Bonus: The Metal Age (live)/Stone Cold (live)/Hammerfall v2.0.07 (video)			
2007 ☐	STEEL MEETS STEEL – TEN YEARS OF GLORY	2CDd	Irond (Russia)	07-1343
2007 ■	Destined For Glory/Glory To The Brave/Heeding The Call	MCDp 3tr	Nuclear Blast	NB-1772-2
2008 ☐	REBEL WITH A CAUSE + MASTERPIECES	CD+DVD	Nuclear Blast	NB 2120-0

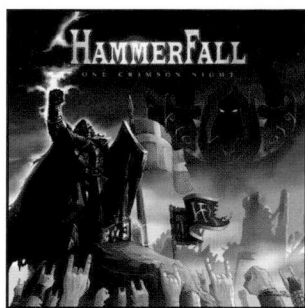

2003 2CD - NB 1196-2

2005 CD - NB 1375-2

2005 MCD - NB 1355-2

2006 CD - NB 1752-2

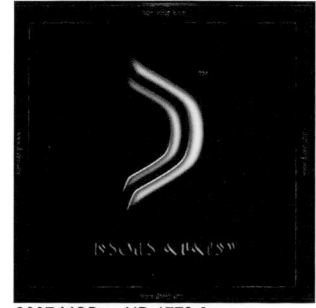

2007 MCDp - NB-1772-2

2008 ☐	The Vinyl Singles Collection	4x7" PD box	Nuclear Blast	NB-2103-5

4 singles: Last Man Standing/The Abyss/Restless Soul, Hammerfall v2.0.07/Heeding The Call/Renegade/Hearts On Fire/Blood Bound/Natural High

2008 ☐	MASTERPIECES	CD	Avalon Marquee (Japan)	MICP-10740
2008 ☐	MASTERPIECES	CD	Nuclear Blast America (USA)	NBA 1824
2008 ■	MASTERPIECES	CD	Nuclear Blast	NB 1824-2
2008 ☐	MASTERPIECES	2LP	Nuclear Blast	NB 1824-1
2008 ☐	MASTERPIECES	CD	Irond (Russia)	08-1483
2009 ☐	NO SACRIFICE, NO VICTORY	CD	Nuclear Blast	NB 2266-2
2009 ☐	NO SACRIFICE, NO VICTORY	CDd	Nuclear Blast	NB 2266-0

3D cover.

2009 ☐	NO SACRIFICE, NO VICTORY	2LP	Nuclear Blast	NB 2266-1
2009 ☐	NO SACRIFICE, NO VICTORY	CD	Irond (Russia)	09-1572
2009 ☐	NO SACRIFICE, NO VICTORY	CD	Avalon Marquee (Japan)	MICP-10825
2009 ☐	NO SACRIFICE, NO VICTORY	CD	Avalon Marquee (Japan)	MICP-30005

SHD CD with bonus video of Any Means Necessary.

2009 ☐	NO SACRIFICE, NO VICTORY	CD	Magnum Music (Taiwan)	NB226662
2009 ☐	Any Means Necessary/My Sharona	7" PD	Nuclear Blast	NB 2354-9

500 copies.

2009 ☐	Any Means Necessary	MCD	Nuclear Blast (promo)	NB 2331-2
2011 ☐	One More Time/Trailblazer (live)/Blood Bound (live)	MCDpg 3tr	Nuclear Blast	NB 2743-2

Free bonus CD for Sweden Rock Magazine #81, 2011.

2011 ■	INFECTED	CD	Nuclear Blast	NB 2692-2

Slipcase.

2011 ☐	INFECTED	CDd+DVD	Nuclear Blast	NB 2692-0

Bonus: DVD live in the studio.

2011 ☐	INFECTED	2CD box	Nuclear Blast	NB 2692-?

Mail-order edition incl. bonus karaoke CD. 500 copies.

2011 ☐	INFECTED	CD	Warner Music (Japan)	WPCR-14136

Bonus: Blood Bound (remix)/Send Me A Sign (Hungarian version)/Let's Get It On (instrumental)

2011 ☐	INFECTED	CD+DVD	Warner Music (Japan)	WPZR-30401

Bonus: as above + DVD.

Unofficial releases:

1998 ☐	NEW SWEDISH LEGACY	CD	Highland (Japan)	H 018

Recorded in Sundsvall 980124.

2008 CD - NB 1824-2

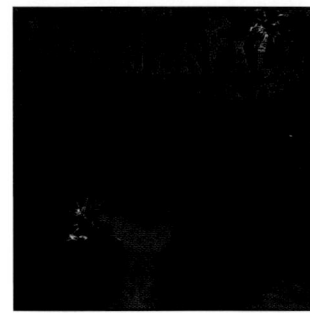

2011 CD - NB 2692-2

HANSSON, JONAS

Jonas Hansson: v/g/b/k/d

Malmö - Silver Mountain guitarist gone solo. *Classica* also features singers Chrisse and Fiama Fricano. It is, as the title suggests, Jonas doing an "Yngwie", i.e. playing classical metal guitar, but without the full orchestra. Great guitarist, decent album. *Valhallarama* is a more of a traditional melodic heavy rock album with Jonas handling all the instruments and vocals. Much better songs on this one! Well worth checking out (despite the programmed drums)!

1999 ☐	CLASSICA	CD	Avalon Marquee (Japan)	MICY 1120

Bonus: Acoustix/Electrix

1999 ☐	CLASSICA	CD	Hex Records	HRCD 981
2006 ■	VALHALLARAMA	CD	Hex Records	HRCD 0501
2006 ☐	VALHALLARAMA	CD	Avalon Marquee (Japan)	MICP-10606

2006 CD - HRCD 0501

HANGOVER

Lars Noren: v/g, Stefan Hellspong: g, Per Blomgren: g,
Kurt-Ove Åhs: b, Patrik Fryklund: d

Ljusdal - Good, basic hard rock, a bit like *Motvind* meets *Wildmarken*. Quite horrible lyrics at times. The lyrics for *Esplanaden* is actually the poem *Esplanadsystemet*, by author August Strindberg. The tracks *Sick Society* and *Goodbye* are also found on the compilation *Swedish Tracks '79* (1979 Sonet).

1977 ●	Hangover/Esplanaden	7"	Wig Wam	WS 04

No artwork. 500 copies.

1977 7" - WS 04

HAPPY CAKES

Micke Jansson: v/g, Reino Naatikka: b, Magnus Gustavsson: d

Hofors - A bit reminiscent of *The Quill* at times, Seventies-influenced hard rock with funky interludes and at times even close to *Living Colour*. Interesting band! Magnus had previously recorded with the band *Zeit*.

1995 ■	Brandcore	MCD 4tr	Mtone Production	M 22525

Tracks:TV-Reality/Brandcore/Justified/Trust. 500 copies.

1995 MCD - M 22525

HAPPY HOUR

Louise Eriksson, Anna Hellgren, Michael Hedlund, Christian Iwung, Christian Rosen

Norrköping - **Happy Hour** is another borderline band. The B-side is pretty good AOR with female vocals. Poppy overtones, but biting guitars. However, the A-side is quite crappy pop.

1992 ■ Why Is Everything I Do So Wrong/Paradise ....7"   private ....HAPPY 001

1992 7" - HAPPy 001

HARDCORE CIRCUS

Jörgen "Jojje" Bolmstad: v/g, Carl-Johan "CJ" Grimmark: g,
Nalle Påhlsson: b, Joakim Bloohm: d

Stockholm - **Hardcore Circus** started out as a project in 2009, formed by **Mötley Crüe** fans Bolmstad (**Surround**) and Bloohm (**Randy Piper's Animal**). They started writing and finally recorded a sixteen track demo. They now needed a steady line-up and drafted Bloohm's former **Piper**-colleague Nalle Påhlsson (**Treat, Vindictive, Therion** etc) and finally former **Narnia** guitarist Grimmark. The band also used the talents of **Malmsteen/Treat/Therion** singer Mats Levén as backing singer on the album. **Hardcore Circus** play melodic hard rock with a sleazy touch, in the vein of Corabi era **Motley Crüe**. Heavy and riff-oriented, high-quality stuff.

2010 ■ WAKE UP CALL..CD   Silverside Records..........................SRCD 001

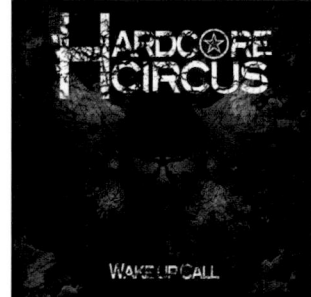

2010 CD - SRCD 001

HARDCORE SUPERSTAR

Jocke Berg: v/g, Vic Zino: g, Martin Sandvik: b, Magnus "Adde" Andreasson: d

Göteborg - It all started with the band **Link**, formed by Jocke and Adde. They were joined by guitarist Fredrik "Fidde" Johansson and bassist Martin Sandvik. They recorded a couple of demos before Adde went to seek fame and fortune elsewhere. They recruited drummer Mika "Dyna Mike" Vainio and kept on until the fall of 1997, when Fredrik left to play psychedelic rock. The remaining trio now adopted the name **Hardcore Superstar** and finally found guitarist Thomas "Silver" Livenborg, who had just left **Green Jesus Saviours**. They started out musically somewhere between **Faster Pussycat/Mötley Crüe** and **Sex Pistols** with a touch of **AC/DC**. Glammy hard rock with a punkish attitude. Through the years they have evolved and are today still a sleazy/glammy, but way heavier band, and the punk attitude has worn off. Jocke and Thomas had also previously played in **Glamoury Foxx**, while drummer Magnus "Adde" Andreasson was in the heavier **Dorian Gray**. Thomas later recorded some demos with the band **Lazy Bones**. The songs *Hello/Goodbye* and *Someone Special* were featured on a compilation and Gain offered the band a deal resulting in the debut *It's Only Rock 'N Roll* in 1998. After the release of the album Vainio left the band because of lack of interest and old friend Adde, who had studied at MI, joined. Mika has later been found in **Brassmonkey** and **Mrs Hippie**. A deal with Music For Nation was now inked and the new label wanted to reissue the debut. As the band wanted to rerecord the old tracks with Adde on drums it resulted in the album *Bad Sneakers And A Piña Colada*, which featured some old songs rerecorded plus some new written stuff. The band does a cover of *Don't You Ever Leave Me* on the **Hanoi Rocks** tribute *11th Street Tales* (00 Feedback Boogie) and the interest for the band started growing in Sweden as well as in Japan. **Thank You** was produced by Roberto Laghi (**B-Thong, Transport League** etc.). In 2006 the band released a live DVD recorded at Sticky Fingers in Göteborg. In January 2008 Thomas Silver left the band. The band quickly drafted Bosnia born **Crazy Lixx** guitarist Vic Zino, who went on tour in Australia and Japan just two weeks after joining the band. *Lovin' The Dead* on the *Moonshine* MCD is an exclusive track. *The Party Ain't Over* is a 10-year anniversary compilation featuring the non-album track *We Don't Need A Cure*.

1999 MCD - CDKUT 180

Year		Title	Format	Label	Cat. No.
1998	☐	IT'S ONLY ROCK 'N ROLL.....................................CD		Gain	GPCD 007
		Contains a secret track: Fly Away			
1998	☐	Hello Goodbye/Right Through Me..................... CDS		Gain	GPCD 008
1999	☐	Someone Special/So Deep Inside/Send Myself To Hell..........	MCD 3tr	Music For Nations	CDKUT 180
2000	■	Someone Special/So Deep Inside/Send Myself To Hell..........	MCD 3tr	Music For Nations	CDKUT 180
2000	■	Someone Special/Don't You Ever Leave Me/Fly Away..........	MCD 3tr	Music For Nations	CDXCUT 180
2000	☐	Someone Special.................................... CDS		Koch (USA)	KOC-DS-8221
2000	☐	BAD SNEAKERS AND A PINA COLADA............CD		Music For Nations	CDMFN 256
2000	☐	BAD SNEAKERS AND A PINA COLADA.............LP		Music For Nations	MFN 256
2000	☐	BAD SNEAKERS AND A PINA COLADA.............LP		Pinnacle	11112561
2000	☐	BAD SNEAKERS AND A PINA COLADA............CD		JVC Victor (Japan)	VICP 61025
		Bonus: Don't You Ever Leave Me. (Hanoi Rocks cover)			
2000	☐	Liberation/Come Along/You Say You Want Me (demo)..........	MCD 3tr	Music For Nations	CDKUT 181
		Available with two different artworks (pink or black).			
2000	☐	Have You Been Around/Long Way To Go/Have You Been (live)......	MCD 3tr	Music For Nations	MNWCDS 294
2001	☐	Shame/Things On Fire/They Are Not Even A New Bang Tango	MCD 3tr	Music For Nations	CDKUT 187
2001	☐	Shame/Things On Fire........................	CDS 2tr	Music For Nations	CDXKUT 187
2001	■	BAD SNEAKERS AND A PINA COLADA............CD		Koch (USA)	KOC-CD-8221
2001	☐	THANK YOU (FOR LETTING US BE OURSELVES) ....CD		Music For Nations	CDMFN 268
2001	☐	THANK YOU (FOR LETTING US BE OURSELVES) ....LP		Music For Nations	MFN 268
2001	☐	Staden Göteborg..........................	MCD 3tr	MVG	MNWCDS 302
		Recorded together with LOK. HCS also performs Hello/Goodbye			

2000 MCD - CDKUT 180

2000 MCD - CDXKUT 180

2001 ☐	THANK YOU (FOR LETTING US BE OURSELVES)	CD	JVC Victor (Japan)	VICP 61498
	Bonus: Long Way To Go (Alice Cooper cover)			
2001 ☐	THANK YOU (FOR LETTING US BE OURSELVES)	CD	Sony BMG (Austria)	88697066192
2002 ■	Mother's Love/Significant Other	MCD 4tr	Gain/Zomba	GPCD 12
	Tracks: Mother Love/Significant Other/Heaven Sent (INXS)/Don't You Ever Leave Me			
2002 ■	Mother's Love/Significant Other	MCD 6tr	JVC Victor (Japan)	VICP-61599
	Bonus:Things On Fire/A Long Way To Go (Alternate Version)			
2003 ☐	Honey Tongue/You Know Where We All Belong/Need No Invitation	MCD 3tr	Music For Nations	CDKUT 202
2003 ☐	Honey Tongue/You Know Where We All Belong/Need No Invitation	MCD 3tr	Victor (Japan)	VICP-35092
2003 ☐	Still I'm Glad/Who-Who	CDS	Music For Nations	CDKUT 207
2003 ☐	NO REGRETS	CD	Music For Nations	CDMFN 296
2003 ☐	NO REGRETS	CD	JVC Victor (Japan)	VICP-62415
	Bonus: Who (The Who cover). Different artwork.			
2005 ■	Wild Boys/Wild Boys (pre-production)	CDS	Gain	GPCD 024
2005 ☐	We Don't Celebrate Sundays/We Don't (rehearsal take))	CDS	Gain	GPCD 026
2005 ☐	HARDCORE SUPERSTAR	CD	Gain	GPCD 027
2005 ☐	My Good Reputation	CDS	Gain	GPCD 029
2005 ☐	HARDCORE SUPERSTAR	CD	Victor (Japan)	VICP-63216
	Bonus: GTO			
2005 ☐	HARDCORE SUPERSTAR	CD	Seou Records (Korea)	SRCD-2811
2007 ☐	Bastards	CDS	Gain	GPCD 037
2007 ☐	BAD SNEAKERS AND A PINA COLADA	CD	Sony BMG (UK)	88697066182
2007 ☐	NO REGRETS	CD	Sony BMG (UK)	88697066362
2007 ☐	DREAMIN' IN A CASKET	LP	Cargo	CARLP 084
2007 ☐	DREAMIN' IN A CASKET	CD	Gain	GPCD 044
2007 ☐	DREAMIN' IN A CASKET	CDd+DVD	Gain	GPCD 044L
2007 ☐	DREAMIN' IN A CASKET	CD	Victor (Japan)	VICP-64007
	Bonus: Bastards			
2007 ☐	DREAMIN' IN A CASKET	CD	Sony BMG (UK)	88697066192
2007 ☐	DREAMIN' IN A CASKET – SPECIAL EDITION	CD+DVD	Victor (Japan)	VIZP-56
	Bonus: Bastards + DVD			
2008 ☐	DREAMIN' IN A CASKET	CD	Irond (Russia)	08-1481
2009 ☐	BEG FOR IT	CD	Gain	GPCD 68
	Bonus: Bastards			
2009 ☐	BEG FOR IT	CD	Victor (Japan)	VICP-64709
	Bonus: Silent For The Peacefully (live)			
2009 ☐	BEG FOR IT	CD	Scarecrow (Mexico)	SR 0495
2009 ☐	BEG FOR IT	CD	Icarus (Argentina)	ICARUS 558
2009 ☐	BEG FOR IT	CDd	Nuclear Blast (USA)	NB 2380-2
	Bonus: Welcome To Your Own Death (demo)/When I Glow (demo)			
2009 ☐	BEG FOR IT	LPg	Nuclear Blast (USA)	NB 2380-1
	Green vinyl. 500 copies.			
2009 ☐	BEG FOR IT	CD	Irond (Russia)	09-1606
2009 ☐	Beg For It	7"	Gain	GP 67
	100 copies.			
2009 ☐	Beg For It	CDS	Gain	GP 67
2009 ☐	HARDCORE SUPERSTAR - RELOADED	CD	Nuclear Blast	NB 2467-2
	Bonus: Kick On The Upperclass/We Don't Celebrate Sundays (rehearsal))/Wild Boys			
2009 ☐	HARDCORE SUPERSTAR - RELOADED	CD	Icarus Music (Argentina)	ICARUS 574
2009 ☐	HARDCORE SUPERSTAR	CD	Irond (Russia)	09-1652
2009 ☐	DREAMIN' IN A CASKET - RELOADED	CD	Nuclear Blast	NB 2468-2
	Bonus: Dreamin' In A Casket (demo)/Sophisticated Ladies (demo)/This Is For The Mentally Damaged			
2009 ☐	DREAMIN' IN A CASKET - RELOADED	CD	Scarecrow (Mexico)	SR 0505-0
2009 ☐	DREAMIN' IN A CASKET - RELOADED	CD	Icarus Music (Argentina)	ICARUS 575
2010 ☐	SPLIT YOUR LIP	CDd	Nuclear Blast	NB 2671-2
2010 ☐	SPLIT YOUR LIP	CD	Gain	GPCD 78
2010 ☐	SPLIT YOUR LIP	CD	Victor (Japan)	VICP-64907
	Bonus: Medicate Me (live)			
2010 ☐	SPLIT YOUR LIP	LP	Night Of The Vinyl Dead	NIGHT 093
	Blue vinyl. 333 copies, numbered.			
2010 ☐	Moonsine/Guestlist	CDS	Nuclear Blast	NB 2684-2
2010 ☐	Moonsine/Lovin' The Dead/Guestlist	MCDd 3tr	Gain	GPCD 79
2011 ☐	THE PARTY AIN'T OVER 'TIL WE SAY SO	CD	Gain	GPCD 89
2011 ☐	THE PARTY AIN'T OVER 'TIL WE SAY SO	2LP	Gain	GPCD 89VL
	Bonus: We Don't Need A Cure			
2011 ☐	THE PARTY AIN'T OVER 'TIL WE SAY SO	CD	Victor (Japan)	VICP-75031
2011 ☐	HARDCORE SUPERSTAR	LP	Night Of The Vinyl Dead	NIGHT 099
	333 hand-numbered copies. Star center piece.			
2011 ☐	HARDCORE SUPERSTAR	CD	Victor (Japan)	VICP-65123
2012 ☐	BAD SNEAKERS AND A PINA COLADA	CD	The End (USA)	TE 244-2
2012 ☐	THANK YOU (FOR LETTING US BE OURSELVES)	CD	The End (USA)	TE 245-2
2012 ☐	NO REGRETS	CD	The End (USA)	TE 246-2
2013 ☐	C'MON TAKE ON ME	CD	Victor (Japan)	VICP-65136
2013 ■	C'MON TAKE ON ME	CD	Gain	8876544-3802

2001 CD - 8221

2002 MCD - GPCD 12

2002 MCD - VICP-61599

2005 CDS - GPCD 024

2013 CD - 8876544-3802

2013	☐	C'MON TAKE ON ME	LP	Gain	8876544-3801
2013	☐	C'MON TAKE ON ME	LP	Nuclear Blast	NB 3036-1

Different artwork. Black, 250 pink, 100 green numbered (Firepower Records). Poster.

HARM'S WAY

**Pedro "Mr. Dim" Pico: v/b, Fredrik "Freddie/Eugene" Lindgren: g,
Erik Wallin: g, Stefan "Stipen" Carlsson: d**

Stockholm - Pedro and Fredrik had previously recorded a single with the band **Born Of Fire**, while Wallin and Carlsson were ex-**Merciless**. Carlsson has also played with **Transport League**, **Blackshine** and has also been a member of punkish rockers **Dia Psalma**. Wallin is also in **Death Breath** and Fredrik has been found in **Terra Firma** and **Unleashed**. On the first release the drums were handled by Mike. In 2010 Fredrik formed the new band **Atlantic Tide**. **Harm's Way** play heavy stoner-oriented rock with a very strong classic 70s touch. At times reminiscent of early **Grand Magus** mixed with **Terra Firma**. Well worth checking out. In 2011 Pedro, Erik and Stefan released the debut by their new thrash band **Thrash Amigos**.

2004 10" - IFP 072

2006 CDS - BLODPR 038CDS

2004	■	Harm's Way	MLP 10" 3tr	Iron Fist	IFP 072
		Tracks: High Becomes Low/Went Wrong/Hocus Pocus			
2006	☐	OXYTOCIN	CDd	Black Lodge	BLOD 038CD
2006	■	Move Your Face	CDS 1tr	Black Lodge (promo)	BLODPR 038CDS

HARMONY

Pehr Larsson: v/b, Peter Karlsson: g, Kjell Enblom: d

Strängnäs - Formed in 1993 by Kjell and Peter, initially also featuring singer/bassist Odd Larsson, singer Ingela Ehrenström and guitarist Thomas Fyrebo. The same year, they made their first demo *Blood Angels*, followed by *Until I Dream*. In 1994 they recorded their third demo, *The Radiance From A Star* and later released as the split. After this the band changed its name to **Torment**, but when signing a deal with Corrosion Records they became **Maze Of Torment**. Larsson has also been in **Vinterland** and Karlsson in bands like **Deceiver**, **Flesh** and **Thrown**. Not to be confused with Borås progsters. *Summoning The Past* is a posthumous compilation.

1996 CD - SERE 008

1996	■	THE RADIANCE FROM A STAR (split)	CD	Arctic Serenades	SERE 008
		Split with Serenade. Tracks: Cold Atmosphere/The Radiance From A Star/The Lonely Kingdom/Conjuration/Mountains Of Frost/Mysterious			
2006	■	Summoning The Past	MCD 6tr	Conqueror Records	KR005MCD
		Tracks: The Sinking/Wasteland/Duke Of Grief Part I/Duke Of Grief Part II/Mountains Of Frost/The Lonely Kingdom			

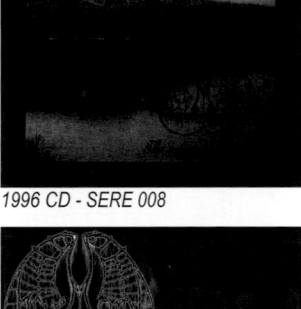

2006 CD - KR005MCD

HARMONY

**Henrik Båth: v, Markus Sigfridsson: g, Magnus Holmberg: k,
Andreas Olsson: b, Tobias Enbert: d**

Borås - Christian progressive metal band **Harmony** were formed in 2000 by guitarist Sigfridsson and drummer Enbert. They were soon joined by singer Båth. After recording a demo in 2001, they were signed by Massacre Records. Bass player Andreas Olsson (**Narnia, Stormwind, Wisdom Call, DivineFire, 7days**) and keyboardist Holmberg completed the line-up. Pelle Saether at Studio Undeground produced the band's second effort and features guest spots from Daniel Heiman (**Lost Horizon**) and Daniel Gildenlöw (**Pain Of Salvation**), who handle the bass playing on the entire album, since Olsson was out of the band. Båth, Holmberg, Sigfridsson and Enbert are all also found in prog metal band **Darkwater**. A great melodic power metal band with prog-influences well worth checking out.

2003 CD - MAS PC 0350

2003	■	DREAMING AWAKE	CD	Massacre	MAS PC0350
2008	☐	End Of My Road	MCD 5tr	Ulterium Records	ULTCD 008
		Tracks: End Of My Road/Prevail/Alone/Enter The Sacred/Rain			
2008	■	CHAPTER II: AFTERMATH	CD	Ulterium Records	ULTCD 009
2008	☐	DREAMING AWAKE	CD	Ulterium Records	ULTCD011
2008	☐	CHAPTER II: AFTERMATH	CD	King Records (Japan)	KICP-1351
		Bonus: Alone/End Of My Road (acoustic)			

2008 CD - ULTCD 009

HARVEY WALLBANGER

**Fritz Quathoff: v, Magnus Hansson: g, Daniel Sören: g,
Johan Feldtmann: b, Jonas Wincent: d**

Sala - Quite technical thrash with a personal touch, including a harmonica solo. The vocals are quite demonic. They later became **Chickadickadeekcheez** (eeeh??), but shortened it to **Chikadee**.

1991	■	Irrevocable Act	7" 3tr	Active Music	HEJ S-038
		Marbled vinyl. Tracks: Dead Fruits Of Love/Up Against The Wall/Ein Reich (Ein Volk, Ein Führer)			
1992	☐	SICK JAR OF JAM	LP	Frisk Fisk	FISH 016

1991 7" - HEJ S-038

HASSE FRÖBERG & MUSICAL COMPANION
Hasse Fröberg: v/g, Anton Lindsjö: g, Kjell Haraldsson: k,
Thomas Thomsson: b, Ola Strandberg: d

Uppsala - Hasse Fröberg was first recognised as lead singer of eighties hard rockers *Spellbound*, but he had actually recorded a single with bluesy hard rockers *Barrelhouse* before this. He also later recorded an album with popsters *Solid Blue* and later ended up in *The Flower Kings*. He then returned with his own prog/symph rock/metal project *Hasse Fröberg & Musical Companion*. The albums stretch from pure *Genesis* style symphonic rock to heavy riff oriented proggy hard rock with outstanding musicianship, at times flirting with seventies bands like *Styx* and *Kansas*. Thomsson and Strandberg are also former *Spellbound* members.

2010	■	FUTURE PAST	CD	Reingold Records	RRCD 004
2012	□	POWERPLAY	CDd	Reingold Records	RRCD 007

2010 CD - RRCD 004

HATE AMMO
Peder Sundqvist: v, Ronnie Björnström: g, Henrik Mikaelsson: g,
Olov Norberg: b, Peter Morgan Lie: d

Umeå - *Hate Ammo* were founded in 2008. After the album bassist Olov Norberg was replaced by Martin Pudas (*Daemonicus*). In 2011 singer Sundqvist (*Assailant, Lesra, Dead Street Journal*) was fired. *Feared*-singer Mario Santos Ramos from South America replaced him. Well-played, fast and furious high-energy thrash in the vein of *Machine Head*, *Sepultura* and *Testament*. Drummer Lie is also found in *Auberon*, *Naglfar* and *Bone Gnawer*. Björnström is also in *Bone Gnawer*, *Ribspreader*, *Embracing*, *Scumkill* and *Knife In Christ*, while Mikaelsson is in *Live Elephant*. A new album is in the making.

2010	■	BOUND BY HATE	CD	Supernova	SUPERCD 001

2010 CD - SUPERCD 001

HATE GALLERY
Janne Jarvis: v/b, Petja Lepola: g, Rille Lundell: g, Freddie "Cocker" Kvarnebrink: d

Stockholm/UK - *Hate Gallery* were formed in London in 2006 and later developed in Stockholm. Lundell, Jarvis and Kvarnebring are also found in *Warrior Soul*. The EP *Dead Celebrities* was released in 2009, but only as a digital release. *Hate Gallery* does definitely not sound as heavy as the name may suggest. Sleazy hard rock with a punkish touch, but still some heavy riffing.

2008	□	COMPASSION FATIGUE	CD	The Unit	UNIT60-4
2011	■	VIVA LA RESISTANCE	CD	North & South	NORTH 59

2011 CD - NORTH 59

HATERUSH
Stefan Embretsson: v, Jan Sandberg: g, Carl Berglund: g,
Magnus Wall: b, Richard Holmgren: d

Västerås - The band was formed by Sandberg (ex-*Bullhorn*, *Ten Foot Pole*) and Embretsson. The band's first demo soon elevated to a full album. After the first album Carl Berglund joined as second guitarist. Holmgren is also found in *Soulskinner*, *Blackworld* and *Wolf,* and has previously played with bands like *Vanessa*, *Apostasy* and *Scaar*. The name may suggest a band playing hardcore or death metal, but *Haterush* play melodic power metal in the vein of *Gamma Ray*, *Hammerfall* and *Edguy*. Bass player Wall is also found in *Thronaeon*, *Abhoth*, *Soulbreach* and *Septic Breed*.

2004	□	MARK OF THE WARRIOR	CD	Black Lotus	BLRCD 074
2004	□	MARK OF THE WARRIOR	CD	Soundholic (Japan)	SHCD1-0061
		Bonus: Fly Or Die			
2007	■	BAPTISED IN FIRE	CD	Black Mark	BMCD 188

2007 CD - BMCD 188

HAUNTED, THE
Marco Aro: v, Anders Björler: g, Patrick Jensen: g,
Jonas Björler: b, Per Möller Jensen: d

Göteborg - Jensen (ex-*Seance*, later in *Witchery*, *Satanic Slaughter* and *Orchriste*), Jonas Björler and drummer Adrian Erlandsson, the core-duo from *At The Gates*, formed the band in late 1996 together with *Dissection*'s John Zwetsloot. Their first musical contribution was the song *Undead* on the *Earplugged 2* compilation. At this point Peter Dolving (ex-*Mary Beats Jane*) handled the vocals and Anders Björler had replaced Zwetsloot. A demo-version of *Shattered* was also featured on the *Statements Of Intent* (Wicked World '99) compilation. Peter left after the first album and was replaced by Marco Aro, who was previously in *Face Down*. In 1999 drummer Adrian Erlandsson left the band to join *Cradle Of Filth* and was replaced by Per. In 2001 they won the Swedish Grammy for best Hard Rock. In 2001 they were the head act of a power-trio-pack also featuring *Nine* and *Nasum*. It went under the name *Close-Up Made Us Do*

1998 CD - MOSH 197 CD

2000 CD - MOSH 241 CD

The photograher made us do it!

It and was also promoted with a CD featuring the three bands. In 2001 Anders Björler left the band and Mike Wead joined, but was temporarily replaced by **The Crown**'s Marcus Sunesson for the 2001 US-tour. Björler then returned in 2002 before the recording of **One Kill Wonder**, which was the last album featuring Marco Aro on vocals. He was replaced by the returning Dolving in 2003. The early albums are heavy melodic death metal, while on the 2008 album *Versus* some more melodic touches could be heard. *Warning Shots* is a compilation. *Roadkill* contains a live-show from Amsterdam and rare/unreleased tracks from the *Versus* sessions. On *Unseen* the band presented quite a new sound, adding clean vocals and a much more varied musical landscape. A great band! In February 2012 Dolving quit and In October Per Möller Jensen and Anders Björler announced they were leaving the band. In June 2013 a new line-up was presented, featuring Jensen, Jonas Björler, Erlandsson, Aro and guitarist Ola Englund.

2000 CD - MOSH 241 CDL

2002 CD box - MOSH 265 CDL

1998	■	THE HAUNTED	CD	Earache	MOSH 197 CD
1998	□	THE HAUNTED	CD	Toy's Factory (Japan)	TFCK-87157
2000	■	THE HAUNTED MADE ME DO IT	CD	Earache	MOSH 241 CD
2000	■	THE HAUNTED MADE ME DO IT	CD	Earache	MOSH 241 CDL
		5000 copies. In black jewel case.			
2000	□	THE HAUNTED MADE ME DO IT	LP	Earache	MOSH 241 LP
2000	□	THE HAUNTED MADE ME DO IT	CD	Koch (Poland)	52283-2
2000	□	THE HAUNTED MADE ME DO IT	CD	Toy's Factory (Japan)	TFCK 87231
		Bonus: Eclipse			
2001	□	THE HAUNTED MADE ME DO IT + LIVE ROUNDS IN TOKYO	2CD	Earache	MOSH 241 CDB
2002	□	LIVE ROUNDS IN TOKYO	CD	Toy's Factory (Japan)	TFCK-87284
		Bonus: Blinded By Fear (At The Gates cover)			
2002	□	ONE KILL WONDER	CD	Earache	MOSH 265 CD
2002	□	ONE KILL WONDER	CD	Earache	MOSH 265 CDX
		Bonus: Creed/Ritual/Well Of Souls (Candlemass cover)			
2002	■	ONE KILL WONDER	CD box	Earache	MOSH 265 CDL
		In a box with six photo cards.			
2002	□	ONE KILL WONDER	LP PD	Earache	MOSH 265 LP
2003	□	ONE KILL WONDER	CD	Toy's Factory (Japan)	TFCK-87304
		Bonus: Creed/Ritual/Well Of Souls			
2003	□	ONE KILL WONDER	CD	Soyus (Russia)	MOSH 265 CD
2003	□	THE HAUNTED	CD	Soyus (Russia)	MOSH 197 CD
2004	■	REVOLVER	CD	Century Media	77488-2
2004	□	REVOLVER	CDd	Century Media	77488-8
		Bonus: Fire Alive/Smut King. Red artwork.			
2004	□	REVOLVER	CD	Century Media (USA)	8188-2
2004	□	REVOLVER	CDd	Century Media (USA)	8188-8
2004	□	REVOLVER	LP	Century Media	77488-1
2004	□	REVOLVER	CD	Fono (Russia)	FO416CD
2004	□	REVOLVER	CD	Century Media (Australia)	CM77488-8
2006	□	The Medicateion/The Drowning	CDS 2tr	Century Media (promo)	777588-3P
2006	□	THE DEAD EYE	CD	Century Media	77588-2
2006	□	THE DEAD EYE	CD	Century Media (USA)	8288-2
2006	□	THE DEAD EYE	CD+DVD	Century Media	77588-0
2006	□	THE DEAD EYE – LIMITED EDITION	CD+DVD	Century Media (USA)	8288-0
		Bonus: The Highwire/The Program + DVD			
2006	□	THE DEAD EYE	LP	Century Media	77588-1
2006	□	THE DEAD EYE	LP	Century Media (USA)	8288-1
2006	□	THE DEAD EYE	CD	Mazzar (Russia)	MYST CD 162
2007	□	THE HAUNTED MADE ME DO IT (EARACHE CLASSIC METAL)	CD+DVD	Earache	MOSH 2411-2
		DVD featuring "Caught On Tape" live 2002. Slipcase.			
2007	□	THE HAUNTED MADE ME DO IT	CD+DVD	Earache	MOSH 241CDV
2008	□	VERSUS	CD	Century Media (USA)	8444-2
2008	□	VERSUS	LP	Century Media (USA)	8444-1
		1000 copies in red vinyl.			
2008	■	VERSUS	CD	Century Media	77444-2
2008	□	VERSUS	CD	Mazzar (Russia)	MYST CD 380
2008	□	VERSUS	LP+CD	Century Media	74444-1
2008	□	VERSUS	2CD	Century Media	74444-2
		Bonus CD: Seize The Day/Narcotic/Versus/Devolve. Plus poster, patch, pic. Yellow cover.			
2008	□	VERSUS	2CD	Toy's Factory (Japan)	TFCK-87449
		Bonus CD: Seize The Day/Narcotic/Versus/Devolve/Meat Wagon			
2009	■	WARNING SHOTS	2CD	Earache	MOSH 374 CD
2009	□	WARNING SHOTS	2CD	Earache (USA)	EAC 60374-2
2010	■	ROADKILL	CD	Century Media	997991-2
2011	□	UNSEEN	CD	Century Media	998020-2
2011	□	UNSEEN	CDd	Century Media	998020-8
		Bonus: Attention/Just Asking/The Reflection (live)/The Fallout (live)			
2011	□	UNSEEN	LP+CD	Century Media	998020-1
2011	□	UNSEEN	CD	Trooper (Japan)	XNTE-00032
		Bonus: Attention/Just Asking/The Reflection (live)/The Fallout (live)			
2011	□	UNSEEN	CD	Mazzar (Russia)	MYST 482

2004 CD - 77488-2

2008 CD - 77444-2

2009 2CD - MOSH 374 CD

2010 CD - 997991-2

HAVAYOTH

Andreas "Vintersorg" Hedlund: v, Marcus E "Vargher" Norman: g, Morgan Hansson: b

Umeå - Andreas is also found in *Otyg/Vintersorg*, Marcus in *Ancient Wisdom/Bewitched* and Morgan in *Naglfar*. *Havayoth* produce melodic, yet heavy, goth-influenced symphonic hard rock with influences from *Paradise Lost* and *Fields Of The Nephilim*. At times quite reminiscent of Dan Swanö's *Nightingale*. A highly recommendable band. The band's second album was recorded in 2001, for release in 2002 and is entitled *Sinvocation*. It's however not yet surfaced.

2000 □	HIS CREATION REVERSED	CD	Soundholic (Japan)	TKCS-85002
2000 ■	HIS CREATION REVERSED	CD	Hammerheart	HHR 065
2000 □	HIS CREATION REVERSED	LP	Hammerheart	HHR 065 LP

2000 CD - HHR 065

HAVOK

Johan Bergström: v, Mahan Ahmadi: g, Simon Dahlberg: g,
Andreas Johansson: b, Johan Cronqvist: d

Lund - *Havok* were formed in 2003, when guitarists Mahan Ahmadi and Miguel Cabrera formed technical thrash band *Ecliptica*. In 2004 they switched drummer to Johan Cronqvist and also changed their name to *Havok*. In 2005 singer Bergström entered and soon after Johansson (*Deranged*) completed the band. The band recorded the first demo, *Realms Of Reverie*, in 2006, which was soon followed up by the two-track demo *World Shroud*. In 2008 Miguel Cabrera left the band and was replaced by Dahlberg. After this the band recorded the six-track CD-R *Apathy Esplanade*. *Havok* play US-style death metal.
Website: www.havok.se

2009 ■	BEING AND NOTHINGNESS	CD	ViciSolum	VSP 004
2012 □	STATUES OF SISYPHUS	CD	ViciSolum	VSP 040

2009 CD - VSP 004

HAWK

Per-Håkan Skånberg: g

Limmared - This is actually Per-Håkan Skånberg's solo-project. Quite standard hard rock. The first single features singer Per Edwardsson (*Biscaya, Time Code Alpha*), bassist Johan Strömberg and drummer Jonas Lundberg. The second single features *Biscaya* session members, singer Pär Edwardsson, bassist Martin Hedström and drummer Birger Löfman (*Fretless, Destiny*). Nothing too exciting, though. Per-Håkan was said to be writing material for a full-length album and trying to put a permanent band together, but nothing came out of it.

1991 □	Just A Little Boy/Dangerous Man	7"	private	PHS 91
1993 □	The Truth Is A Lie/Rollercoaster	CDS 2tr	Compact Records & Music	CRM 001

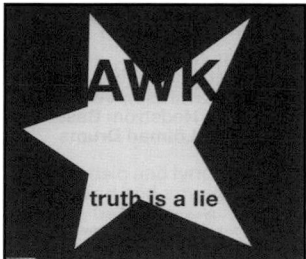
1993 CDS - CRM 001

HAYSTACK

Ulf "Uffe" Cederlund: v/g, Johan Blomqvist: b, Jonas Lundberg: d

Stockholm - *Haystack* were formed in the mid-90s as a result of Uffe not getting some of his song ideas to work in *Entombed*. *Haystack* a punk-metal side-project that may attract fans of bands like *The Melvins* and *Unsane*. Uffe is also a former member of *Nihilist*, *Murder Squad* and *Morbid*, while Blomqvist was in *Backyard Babies* and Lundberg ex *A-Bombs*.

1996 □	RIGHT AT YOU	CD	Outside Society	OSP 001
1998 ■	SLAVE ME	CDd	Threeman	TRECD 003
1998 □	SLAVE ME	CD	Music For Nations (UK)	CDMFN 240

1996 CDd - TRECD 003

HAZE

Martin Johansson: v/g, Peter Ehlebrink: g, Niklas Laihanen: k
Claes Johansson: b, Håkan Andersson: d

Trollhättan - Formed in 1987. Lightweight, funky, medium-quality hard rock.

1991 ■	Make Me Explode!/Blood Ran Cold	7"	private	HZ 001

1991 7" - HZ 001

HAZY

Lollo Öberg: v/g, Tony "Odin" Ulvan: v/g, Tommy Brage: b, Leif Fors: d

Linköping - Formed in 1984 by former *Axewitch* bass player Brage. On the second recording Lollo Öberg replaced Conny Lindblom and keyboard player Mia Von Barde was no longer in the band. Lollo is also in *W.E.T.* They made their last gig in the summer of 1989. Tony was later in the cover-band *Vakant* and he has also done session jobs as lead-singer, and was later

found in *Isengard*. *Hazy* produced melodic upper mid-class hard rock in the vein of *Crystal Pride*. Dolphin was Brage's own label. The band was also featured on *Double Up* (Rock SM 87).

1986	■ A Sight Of Action	MLP 5tr	Dolphin	DLRM 8601	$
	Tracks: On The Run/Fredman´s Epistle No 48/Rock Tonight/A Sight Of Action/Ballad To Life.				
1987	□ King Of The Universe	MLP 4tr	Dolphin	DLRM 8701	$
	Tracks: King Of The Universe/Captive Of The Law/Polar Knight/Scientist.				

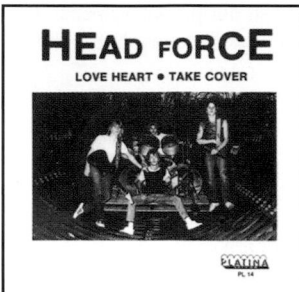

1986 MLP - DLRM 8601

HEAD FORCE

Mikael Holmberg: v, Per Almgren: g, Thomas Pålsson: k,
Peter Olsson: b, Thomas Karlsson: d

Linköping - **Head Force** were formed in 1984, initially featuring Mikael "Räven" Holmberg on vocals, Pelle Almgren and Roger Claussen on guitars, Peter "Skinnet" Olsson on bass and Thomas "Massi" Karlsson on drums. Claussen left quite early on. In 1985 the band opened up for **Europe**. Mid-quality melodic hard rock in the vein of Canadian band **Fist** (a.k.a **Myofist**). In 1987 singer Roger "Lolle" Samuelsson replaced Holmberg, and Claussen returned on guitar. However, he left after a couple of months, and Stefan "Gubben" Karlsson replaced him. During this time the band recorded a demo. After this Samuelsson left, and was replaced by original singer Holmberg. Later on Olsson and Holmberg left again and were replaced by singer Tommy Adolfsson and bassist Janne Olsson. The band split around 1989. A reunion took place in 2009.

| 1986 | ■ Love Heart/Take Cover | 7" | Platina | PL 14 | $ |

1986 7" - PL 14

HEADACHE

Micke Strömberg: v, Frank Stenbro: g, David Andersson: g, Gösta Eliasson: k,
Michael Stenbom: b, Fredrik Lindgren: d

Vilhelmina - **Headache** were formed already in 1974. The sound has traces of bands like **Bon Jovi** and **Europe** as well as more laid-back Tom Petty-style rock. The vocals are slightly weak. On the first single the line-up featured Strömberg on guitar/vocals, Eliasson on keyboards, Stenbom on bass and Egon Danielsson on drums. For collectors only.

| 1990 | □ Paradise/Calling | 7" | private | UNI 2354 | |
| 1994 | ■ -53,3 | CD | Headache Prod | HEADCD 01 | |

1994 CD - HEADCD 01

HEADLINE

Ingvar Bengtsson: v, Mats Flygelholm: g, Anders Nilsson: k,
Fredrik Svensson: b, Jesper Andersson: d

Kristianstad - The first single, which was not released until 1989, featured bass player Richard Persson and drummer Magnus Nordlund. Very well-played AOR with great vocals... but with severe problems in the handling of the English language on the 1993 release. I quote "*I was hunted like a fox with a gun... I took me to the street... the worstest day in my life...*" Get it?! Apart from that this band is well above average and both releases are well worth checking out. The singer is now a vocal instructor and after having spent a few years in the US his English is probably much better. However, the band is since long, sadly defunct. A piece of trivia: After having searched for information about the band for quite some time, without luck, I later ended up working for the same company as the bass player. Svensson is also found in **Gabria**. There is also another band called **Headline** from the same city, who released the singles *Storstadssnack* and *Miljonärer*. This band however plays punk/pop.

1988 7" - Head 100

1988	■ Love Lies/I Wish You Here Forever	7"	Polar Head	Head 100	
1993	■ Headline	MCD 4tr	private	HEAD 200	
	Tracks: You Can Have It All/Hide & Lie/Fallin' In Love/Sister Sister				

1993 MCD - HEAD 200

HEADLINE

Clas Idéhn: v/g, Mikael Hermansson: g, Lasse Hermansson: b,
Mikael Eklöv: k, Mikael Falk: d

Huskvarna/Jönköping - The members later formed **Racoon**, a more pop-oriented band that has released two CDs on Büms Records. This band however had more of a boogie-based hard rock approach on the first single, and even more hard rock on the second effort. The tracks *Come On Sharon* and *I'm Walking Away* are featured on the compilation *Vätterzound* (1986 Zound).

| 1987 | □ I'm Gonna Give It/Up/Rock Yourself To Sleep | 7" | Zound | Z.R 1005 | |
| 1987 | ■ Mutual Friends/Painkiller | 7" | Zound | Z.R 1006 | $ |

1987 7" - Z.R 1006

HEADPLATE

Magnus Klavborn: v, Daniel Granstedt: g, Håkan Skoger: b, Niklas Österlund: d

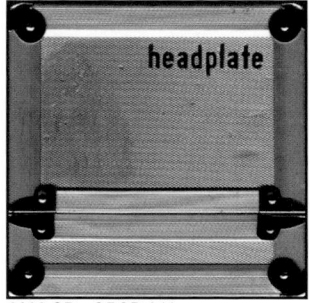

2000 CD - GPCD 010

Göteborg - The basics were set already back in 1993 when Niklas, Daniel and bass player Marcus formed a band. The name *Headplate* was however not found until 1997. Klavborn joined the crew in 1998. Their demo *Sleepy* (1998) lead to the deal with Gain Productions. *Headplate*, from the home region of *Transport League*, *LOK*, *B-Thong* and *Mustasch*, produces heavy, bone-crushing but still groovy metal in the vein of *Biohazard* and *Machine Head*, whom they have also supported on tour. At times with a touch of *Rage Against The Machine*. The vocal style range between rap-oriented, brutal and melodic. Great band! Roberto Laghi co-produced both albums assuring a bull size sound. The band has also featured bass player Johan Andreassen (*All Ends, Hostile Cell, Amaranthe*).
Website: www.headplate.com

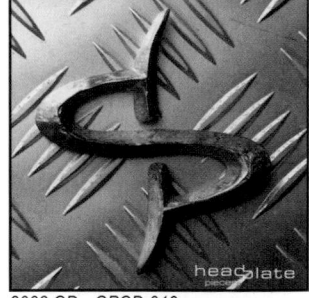

2003 CD - GPCD 019

2000 ■	BULLSIZED	CD	Gain	GPCD 010
2002 □	DELICATE	CD	Gain	GPCD 014
2003 ■	PIECES	CD	Gain	GPCD 019

HEADS OR TALES

Robert Forse: v, Mikael Lindkvist: g, Jonas Sjöholm: g,
Torbjörn Brogren: b, Marcus Nowak: d

Karlskoga - Formed in 1993. Outstanding prog metal in the true *Dream Theater* style, but without keyboards. Incredible song material, first-class arrangements and top-notch vocals. Could have been huge with the right backing. A sure buy! Markus is also working as session drummer and has appeared on numerous albums. He was also in *CC Rock*. Robert left the band late 1995 and was in *Mind's Eye* for a while. Unfortunately the band folded.

1995 CD - BMCD 69

1995 ■	ETERNITY BECOMES A LIE	CD	Black Mark	BMCD 69
1995 □	ETERNITY BECOMES A LIE	CD	Victory (Japan)	VICP-5661

HEARSE

Johan Liiva: v, Mattias Ljung: g, Max Thornell: d

2003 CD - HHR 130

2004 CD - KARMA 031

Stockholm/Helsingborg - Max Thornell and Johan Liiva played together in various bands between 1984-1994, such as *Furbowl* and *Devourment*. In 2001, Max decided to form a new band and Liiva again came to mind. As Liiva had just left *Arch Enemy* the timing was perfect. When looking for a new guitar player, Max came across Mattias Ljung, who actually hadn't played metal for years. The trio was completed and a first demo was recorded. This lead to a deal with Hammerheart Records, who later regrouped as Karmageddon. The song *Cambodia* is a cover of Kim Wilde. This is an EP, but with enough songs to make it a full album. *Single Ticket To Paradise*, as well as its predecessor were mixed by Dan Swanö. The bonus DVD features a live show recorded in Holland in 2004. Hearse plays heavy, driving old-school thrash/punk-oriented metal with a touch of *Motörhead*.
Website: www.hearse.se

2005 CD - KARMA 085

2009 CD+DVD - VIC 024 CD

2001 □	Torch/Avalon	7"	Hammerheart	HHR 129
2003 ■	DOMINION REPTILIAN	CD	Hammerheart	HHR 130
2003 □	DOMINION REPTILIAN	CDd	Hammerheart	HHR 130
	Bonus: The Unknown/Avalon			
2003 □	DOMINION REPTILIAN	LP	Hammerheart	HHR 130
	Bonus: The Unknown/Avalon			
2004 ■	ARMAGEDDON, MON AMOUR	CD	Karmageddon	KARMA 031
2004 □	ARMAGEDDON, MON AMOUR	CD	Candlelight (USA)	CANUS 0092 CD
2004 □	ARMAGEDDON, MON AMOUR	CD	Irond (Russia)	04-758
2004 □	ARMAGEDDON, MON AMOUR	CD	Spiritual Beast (Japan)	SBCD-1016
	Bonus: Avalon/Torch – 7" versions			
2005 □	Cambodia	MCD 9tr	Karmegeddon	KARMA 077
	Tracks: Cambodia (Kim Wilde cover)/The Accused/Wheel Of Misfortune/Torch/Avalon/			
	Well Of Youth/Raptured In Twilight/Dominion Reptilian/So Vague			
2005 ■	THE LAST ORDEAL	CD	Karmageddon	KARMA 085
2005 □	THE LAST ORDEAL	CD	Spiritual Beast (Japan)	SBSL-1002
2005 □	DOMINION REPTILIAN	CD	Candlelight (USA)	CDL 0135 CD
2006 □	IN THESE VEINS	CD	Dental Records	DR 190310
2006 □	IN THESE VEINS	CD	Candlelight (USA)	CDL 381
2006 □	IN THESE VEINS	CD	Soundholic (Japan)	85155
	Bonus: In These Veins			
2009 ■	SINGLE TICKET TO PARADISE	CD+DVD	Vic Records	VIC 024 CD

HEARTBREAK RADIO

Pierre Wensberg: v, Mikael Erlandssson: v, Mats Johansson: g,
Johan Axelsson: k, Berra Holmgren: b, Peter Strandberg: d

Göteborg/Stockholm - *Heartbreak Radio* were a project initiated by the producer team behind *Last Autumns Dream*, Claes Andreasson and Torbjörn Wassenius (both ex-*Talent*) and Mikael Erlandsson. The vocals on the album are shared between Erlandsson and Wensberg (*Prisoner*). The debut featured a backing band featuring *Motörhead* drummer Mikkey Dee, former *HammerFall* bass player Rosén and the highly gifted "I'm-on-all-albums" guitarist Tommy Denander. Among the guests are, Joel Starander (ex-*Geisha*), Robert Garnold (*Elevener*, *Roach*) and Jim Jidhed. High-class melodic hard rock/AOR. Well worth checking out. *On Air* saw a totally new crew. Henrik Båth (Darkwater) guests on the second release.

2005 CD - 00012

2005 ■	HEARTBREAK RADIO	CD	AOR Heaven	00012
2013 ☐	ON AIR	CD	AOR Heaven	00077

HEARTCRY

Anders Johansson: v/g, Dan Tibell: k, Björn Klingvall: b, Anders Köllerfors: d

Jönköping - Anders Johansson, Pelle Pettersson and bass player Mikael Hed were previously known as Christian hard rockers *Johannes*, under which name they recorded a single. They changed line-up, style and name to *Heartcry*, still with a Christian message. The first album is half pop-oriented AOR, and half heavier and guitar-based. Then featuring Anders, keyboardist Dan Tibell (*Jerusalem, Agape*) bassist Jerry Grimaldi, drummer Jack Kelly and drummer Pelle Pettersson. The second album is heavy-edged AOR sung in Swedish. The line-up now featured Anders, Anders Tingsvik (k), Jörgen Olausson (b) and Christian Eidevald (d). You can also find the track *Going Home* on the *Twisted Sounds* compilation. On the third album, also sung in Swedish, the band was a trio with keyboard player Tingsvik out of the band. After some years of silence the band was suddenly resurrected and released through the label owned by *Narnia* singer Christian Liljegren (aka Rivel). The line-up offered some new changes with Anders still in the lead, Dan Tibell back on keyboards and now backed up by bass player Björn Klingvall and drummer Anders Köllerfors. The album had a more metal approach at times with a touch of *Rainbow*, all in English and with an absolutely horrible production. The subsequent album *Firehouse* contains six tracks from the first LP only release and six new songs, actually sounding really consistent anyway, which also goes for the mix. The musicians on the album were a mix of earlier members such as all three drummers and both bass players besides Anders and Dan. However, this is the band's best effort. Anders later formed metal band *Green Sleeves*.

1990 LP - VT 002

2005 CD - RRCD 021

1990 ■	COME BACK TO ME	LP	Vital Music	VT 002
1997 ☐	HEARTCRY	CD	Vital Music	VT 003
1997 ☐	HEARTCRY	CD	Sound Treasure (Japan)	STCD-007
1997 ☐	ÖKENLAND	CD	Vital Music	VTM 004
2005 ■	LIGHTMAKER	CD	Rivel Records	RRCD 021
2006 ■	FIREHOUSE	CD	Rivel Records	RRCD 026

2006 CD - RRCD 026

HEARTS ALIVE

Jesper Persson: v, Daniel Wallenborg: g, Dan Svensson: g,
Alexander Kirst: b, Jonatan Östling: d

Helsingborg - *Hearts Alive* is a brutal riff-oriented hardcore/thrash/metal band, formed in mid-2005. After *The Tragedy In Us* the band released the five-track EP *The Black Sheep* as a free digital release. In 2011 the band was signed to Rising Records, but they parted ways and the second album, *He Who Has The Gold Makes The Rules*, was self-released. After the album bass player Kirst was temporarily replaced by Peter Valefors. Svensson also plays bass in *Terror 2000*.

2007 ■	THE TRAGEDY IN US	CD	Dead Vibrations Industry	DVI 014
2012 ☐	HE WHO HAS THE GOLD MAKES ALL THE RULES	CD	Hearts Alive Music	#002
	300 copies.			

2007 CD - DVI 014

HEAVE

Per Richard: v, Patrik Stoor: g, Pasi J Lappi: b, Patrik Nikolic: d

Sundbyberg (Stockholm) - Formed in 1994 by drummer Patrik Nikolic. The band released the demo *Beguile* in 1997. The vocals on the debut were handled by Per Richard. They also recorded a demo-CD entitled *Lies* in 1999. Heavy, slightly *Metallica*-influenced metal, but with cleaner vocals. In 2002 the band released a five track CD-R entitled *Time*, now featuring singer Andi. In 2005 the band recorded yet another demo entitled *Fear Comes Alive*, now with new singer Anna Olsson. A new attempt was made with the album *Final Day*, now produced by Mike Wead. In 2009 singer Per Richard returned and Stoor was replaced by Marcus Sundqvist.

1998 ■	Self Destruction	MCD 5tr	private	HECD 9802
	Tracks: Never Fall/Insanity/Why/Die 4 Your Sins/Never Fall (Laid back version)			

1998 MCD - HECD 9802

HEAVY CARGO

Miqael Persson: v/b, Mikael Nilsson: g, Pelle Persson: k/g, Glenn Borgquist: d

Helsingborg - Heavy Cargo were formed in 1974 and kept going until late 1980. Miqael had some songs featured on the *W.E.T* (Jeff Scott Soto's band) album, Nilsson has played with *Nasty Idols* and *Bai Bang* while Glenn found a home in popsters *Brandsta City Släckers*. Today, Persson and Nilsson are found in cover band *Seven*. Quite lightweight, but good, melodic hard rock.

1980 ■ Ensam/Sommartid ....7" private .... HO 180
   500 copies.

1980 7" - HO 180

HEAVY LOAD

Ragne Wahlquist: v/g, Eddy Malm: v/g, Andreas Fritz: b, Styrbjörn Wahlquist: d

Stockholm - Heavy Load were formed already in 1976 featuring the Wahlquist brothers plus Michael Backlund on bass. Before this Ragne Wahlquist released the very rare funkish pop/rock single *It's A Dream/Everything Or Nothing* (1976 Universum) with the band *Tommy Mac Frees*. It's definitely not hard rock, but the B-side contains some pretty fierce solo riffing from Wahlström. The year after the formation of *Heavy Load*, Michael was replaced by Dan Molén and the debut *Full Speed At High Level* was recorded. The style was heavy riff-oriented seventies-style hard rock. Heavy Sound Records went bust and the band started their own Thunderload Records. In 1979 Dan was replaced by Thorbjörn Ragnesjö and guitarist/singer Eddy Malm was added to the line-up. Eddy had previously recorded two singles with *Highbrow*. The band's image was the Vikings at large, well-chosen with their music in mind. The album *Stronger Than Evil* features the song Free with *Thin Lizzy*'s late Phil Lynott on bass. The band's last single featured new bassist Andreas Fritz who was formerly in *Wisdom* and was an attempt to put some commerciality into the band, which failed. In 1987 the band reunited with former *UFO*-bass-player Paul Gray, guitarist Patrik Karlsson and the Wahlquist brothers. An album was recorded but never released. In 1988 the brothers built their own recording studio and started working with their record company Thunderload Recordings. The exclusive track *I Am Me* is featured on *Rocket - Caught In Steel* (85 Virgin). In 1999 *Hammerfall* recorded a cover version of *Run With The Devil* for the *Power From The North* compilation in the Thunderload Studio with the Wahlquist brothers behind the desk. Eddy also recorded a 4-track demo in 2000 under the name *Eddy Malm Band* (also featuring the members of the band *Bosse*), in the true 80s vein with a strong touch of his former band *Highbrow*. The Wahlquist brothers have recorded and produced several bands such as *Veni Domine*, *G.O.L.D* and *Isengard*. The brothers are a true enigma. Lots of labels have contacted them trying to get the rights to re-issue the albums on CD, but none have succeeded. The result? Well, there are plenty of bootlegs out there!

Full speed with heavy load!

1978 ■	FULL SPEED AT HIGH LEVEL	LP	Heavy Sound	HSLP 03	$$
1981 ■	Metal Conquest	MLP 5tr	Thunderload	TMP 811	
	Tracks: You've Got The Power/Dark Nights/Heavy Metal Heaven/Hey/Heathens From The North				
1982 ☐	DEATH OR GLORY	LP+7"	Thunderload	TMP 822	
	Also released with the bonus single Take Me Away/Trespassser as bonus. Poster.				
1982 ☐	Take Me Away/Trespasser	7"	Thunderload	TSP 823	
	This single was actually released as a bonus 7" with Death Or Glory. Pressed in red vinyl.				
1982 ☐	DEATH OR GLORY	LP	King Records (Japan)	K28P-401	
1982 ☐	DEATH OR GLORY	LP	Corona Music Company	CMC 013007	
1983 ☐	STRONGER THAN EVIL	LP	Thunderload	TLP 834	
1983 ☐	STRONGER THAN EVIL	LP	King Records (Japan)	K25P-497	
1983 ☐	Free/Run With The Devil	7"	Corona Music Company	CMC 009001	
1984 ☐	Free/Run With The Devil	7"	Thunderload	TSP 835	
1984 ■	Monsters Of The Night/I'm Alive	7"	WEA	248 983 7	
1996 ☐	DEATH OR GLORY	CD	Nexus (Japan)	KICP 2621	$$
1996 ☐	STRONGER THAN EVIL	CD	Nexus (Japan)	KICP 2622	$$

1978 LP - HSLP 03

Unofficial releases:

1991 ☐	METAL ANGELS IN LEATHER	CD	Laserlight	- -
n/a ☐	Free/Run With The Devil	7"	New Wave Of Swedish Heavy Metal	004
	Clear vinyl. Swedish bootleg.			
1999 ☐	FULL SPEED AT HIGH LEVEL	CD	- -	003
n/a ☐	DEATH OR GLORY	CD	Thunderload	(Heavy Load-Death Or Glory)
n/a ☐	DEATH OR GLORY	CD	Thunderload	TLCD 8822
n/a ☐	DEATH OR GLORY	CD	Nexus (Greece)	KICP 2621
	Counterfeit copy.			
n/a ☐	STRONGER THAN EVIL	CD	Thunderload	TLCD-8834
n/a ☐	STRONGER THAN EVIL	CD	Nexus (Greece)	KICP 2622
	Counterfeit copy.			
2000 ☐	STRONGER THAN EVIL & MONSTERS OF THE NIGHT	CD	Rock Guitar Heroes	- -
2000 ☐	FULL SPEED AT HIGH LEVEL & METAL CONQUEST	CD	Rock Guitar Heroes	- -
2009 ☐	FULL SPEED AT HIGH LEVEL	CD	Flawed Gems	GEM 1
2000 ☐	SWEDISH CONQUEST	CD	- -	
	Greek bootleg of two radio shows.			

1981 MLP - TMP 811

1984 7" - 248 983 7

HEBRON
Peder Borgemo: g/v, Daniel Svensson: b, Kjell Adolfsson: d

Kalmar - Well played Christian AOR. Apart from the single, they have also recorded some highly acclaimed demos.

1987 ■ Dance/Hearts Of Desire...7"   private ....HS 001

1987 7" - HS 001

HEED
Daniel Heiman: v, Fredrik Olsson: g, Martin Nadersson: g,
Tommy Larsson: b, Ufuk Demir: d

Göteborg - Heed was formed in the fall of 2004 after Heiman and Olsson decided to leave their former band **Lost Horizon**. They were also joined by **Last Horizon** stand-in drummer Mats Karlsson. In December 2004 they recorded a two-track demo. A few months later bass player Jörgen Olsson joined and they recorded some further demo tracks. However the musical visions of four members didn't go hand in hand, resulting in Mats and Jörgen being asked to leave. Enter Ufuk and Tommy. Shortly after, second guitarist Martin joined and the band was complete. The debut album was recorded by renowned producer Tobias Lindell (**Mustasch, Europe**) at Bohus Sound Studios in 2005. **Heed** play high-quality melodic metal, not too far from Heiman and Olsson's former band, but with fewer power metal overtones and more metallic heaviness.

2005 CD - MICP-10545

2005 ■ THE CALL...CD   Avalon Marquee (Japan)...............MICP-10545
    Bonus: The Flight/Heed The Call (hidden track). Different artwork.
2006 ■ THE CALL...CD   Metal Heaven.......................................00021

2006 CD - 00021

HEEL
David Henriksson: v, Marcus Eliasson: g, David Jonasson: k,
Magnus Öberg: b, David Jonasson: d

Bjurholm - The embryo of **Heel** was formed already in 2003 when Henriksson and Eliasson started collaborating on a demo. The band name was comprised of the first two letters of the members' names **HE-EL**. Henriksson had previously sung on a couple of releases by power metal band **Insania (Stockholm)**, while Eliasson had recorded a single with the band **Ramm** in 1989. The duo recruited **Ramm** members Rikard Öberg (k) and Magnus Öberg (b). The first Heel album featured three drummers: Gothard Stenlund, Per Mikaelsson and Anders Jansson. The backing vocals were handled by Leif Grabbe (**Angeline, Shade Of Grey, Ramm**) and Anders Zackrisson (**Gotham City, Norcturnal Rites, Born Bandit**). After the album the two wanted to get a full line-up and drummer Alexander Gustavsson (**Riveria**) was drafted. Rikard however decided he didn't have the time and departed (but still contributes to the songwriting). The band instead found David Jonasson (**Riveria**) to fill his spot and the new line-up recorded the follow-up *Chaos And Greed*, released in 2009. In 2010 the band started writing a new album. **Heel** play melodic power metal in the vein of **Mr. Big** meets **Narnia**, at times with a neoclassical feel. Unfortunately the albums suffer from quite weak production, especially the drum sound on the second album is totally powerless. The debut is slightly better, but not great. Great guitar playing from Eliasson, though, and the song material is quite decent.
Website: www.heelsite.com

2007 CD - RRCD 033

2009 CD - RRCD 041

2007 ■ EVIL DAYS...CD   Rivel Records .... RRCD 033
2009 ■ CHAOS AND GREED.....................................CD   Rivel Records .... RRCD 041

HELGEDOM
Vanskapt: v/g/b/d, Svartedöden: v/k/d

Nyköping/Norrland - *Svartkonst* (black arts) is really badly recorded black metal. It sounds like it's been recorded with a boom box in a rehearsal space. The music is slow, quite well-played old-school black metal with desperate, crying "vocals". There are seven tracks, where one is called *Intro*, one *Outro* and the rest *Rehearsal*. Seems quite fitting. The recording featured Lik (session vocals on *Svartrit*) on vocals, Vanskapt a.k.a Sir N (**Grifteskymfning, Vanskapt, Svartrit, Grav**) on vocals, guitar, bass and drums, while vocals, keyboard and drums were handled by Svartedöden a.k.a Swartadauþuz (**Svartrit, Grav, Urkaos, Balwezo Westijiz**), who also runs Ancient Records. The second album featured only Vanskapt and Svartedöden. **Helgedom** means sanctity in Swedish. A new album was being recorded in late 2012.

2010 MCD - Mystery 004

2010 ■ Svartkonst ....MCD 8tr   Mystery Of Death.......................... Mystery 004
    Tracks: I – Intro/II/III/IV/V (Rehearsal)/VI/VII/VIII-Outro. 500 copies
2011 ☐ DEN MÖRKA SKOGEN AF ONDO.................................LP   Ancient/Mystery Of Death.....................AR 011
    Demo-LP. 250 copies, 50 with A3 poster.

HELIUM HEAD

Esbjörn Johansson: v, Anders Wallin: g, Lasse Hägg: b, Peter Lundell: d

Ljusdal/Yxbo - Quite good for being a Pang-recording. The band plays quite standard heavy metal/hard rock with decent vocals and mid-league song quality. They later disbanded. The drummer moved to Norway, Anders and Lasse started making their living as troubadours and Esbjörn is doing some odd jobs in local bands.

1982 ● In The Sky/Take Me Home...7" Pang...PSI 040

1982 7" - PSI 040

HELL N' DIESEL

Emil Kyrk: v, Martin Carlsson: g, Martin Joelsson: g,
Andreas Sundh: b, Mojje Andersson: d

Falköping - Rough-edged, dirty and low-down biker-rock. De-tuned and fat riffing with raw vocals. The missing link between **Motörhead**, **Entombed** and **Backyard Babies**. Today, Kyrk is fronting **Savatage** style metal band **Confidence**.

1999 □	And Away Goes The Dust....................................MCD 6tr	private.................................	HnD 007

Tracks: Fuck It/Damnation Song/Bury Me Slowly/Spank The Monkey/Batman/My Porch

2002 □	Asphalt Supreme ....MCD 6tr	Shuffle Recordings	SHRCD 001

Tracks: Strap On Your Leather/Ten Dollar Ride/Devil's Path/Blame It All On Me/Angel/Lickin' My Wounds

2003 □	Tears For The Wicked/Rebel/Speed Devil ....MCD 3tr	Shuffle Recordings	SHRCDS 001
2007 ■	PASSION FOR POWER ....CD	Smilodon	SMILCD 7109
2007 □	Sweet Sister/Freak City Blues ....CDS	Smilodon	SMILCDS109
2007 □	PASSION FOR POWER ....CD	Locomotive (USA)................................	LM 631

2007 CD - SMILCD 7109

HELLBELLY

Jon Agrell: v, Oskar Forsberg: v/g, Andreas Nilsson: b, Johan Wickenberg: d

Lund - **Hellbelly** was formed in 2004 and made their debut in 2006 with the self-financed *What Would Satan Do?* **Hellbelly** play ballsy and groovy heavy rock with a really heavy sound, a bit reminiscent of **Black Label Society** meets **Metallica** with a stonery touch. Singer Jon is no longer in the band and he has been temporarily replaced by Vincent Daly.

2006 □	WHAT WOULD SATAN DO?..CD	private	- -
2008 ■	Fields Of Blood ....MCD 5tr	private	- -

Tracks: Capital Whiplash/Run Hide Or Die/Fields Of Blood/Emptiness/Voodoo Love

2008 MCD - - -

HELLENNIUM

Khaled El Tayara: v, Martin Lindberg: g, David-Borg Hansen: g,
Linus Palmqvist: b, Dave O'Neil: d

Unndevalla - Formed in 2004 and recorded two demos before the album. Very classic, decent **Manowar** style heavy metal. The band are currently looking for a new singer.

2011 ■	HELLENNIUM...CD	Rambo Music................................	HEKCD 01

HELLFIRE

Horribly badly recorded old-school black metal, like a bad offspring of early **Bathory**. They even use the same font and a similar goat on the cover. No information about the band whatsoever. Not to be confused with the death metal band from Strängnäs, which later became **Merciless**. This band is rumoured to be a German band with the guys from **Falkenbach** taken from a demo recorded in the late eighties/early nineties, but this is unconfirmed. The LP (single sided) has a "sermon" cover and the CD a "goat" cover.

Website: www.myspace.com/hellfiresweden

2011 CD - HEKCD 01

2000 ■	INTO FIRE ....CD	No Colours..	NC 027
2003 □	INTO FIRE ....CD	No Colours..	NC 027

Re-issue with new artwork.

2009 □	INTO FIRE ....LP	No Colours..	NC 027

99 copies.

HELLFUELED

Andy Alkman: v, Jocke Lundgren: g, Henke Lönn: b, Kent G Svensson: d

Huskvarna - The band took shape in 1998, but childhood friends Jocke and Kent had been jamming together since 1990. In high school Jocke met singer Andy and they shared the common interests of beer drinking and heavy metal. They drafted Henke, then to play rhythm guitar. Andy handled bass and growls. They were influenced by bands like **Entombed** and **Cathedral** and went under the names **Below** and **Firebug**, but had to change name in 1999, due to threats of lawsuits from American namesakes. They recorded a demo under the name **Below** in 1998,

2000 CD - NC 027

one as *Firebug* in 1999, and the first demo under the new name *Hellfueled*, was unearthed later in 1999. Here Andy's vocals had changed from growling to a more rough-edged style similar to Rob Zombie meets Zakk Wylde. In 2002 the band went through a drastic change. Andy handed over the bass to Henke and adopted his very Ozzy-like clean vocals register. The demo *The Red One* (2002) even contains a cover of *Black Sabbath*'s *Children Of The Grave*. The demo lead to a deal with Black Lodge and the debut *Volume One* in 2004. The first three albums were all recorded at Studio Fredman and produced by Fredrik Nordström. All three albums are high-class, guitar-driven hard rock with very Ozzy-like vocals from Andy and the occasional Zakk-overtones from guitar wiz Jocke. On *Emissions Of Sins* the band used the services of producer Rikard Löfgren (*Sparzanza, Deathstars* etc) and the sound took a slightly heavier turn, still within the boundaries of heavy rock though. A band well worth checking out. Alkman and Lundgren are now also found in heavy rockers *Firegod Mountain*.

Only memories remain...

2004 □	VOLUME 1	CD	Black Lodge	BLOD 008 CD
2004 □	VOLUME 1	CD	Soundholic (Japan)	TKCS-85090
	Bonus: Endless Work/Big Fat Eight			
2005 □	Midnight Lady	MCD 4tr	Black Lodge	BLOD 020 CD
	Tracks: Midnight Lady/Endless Work (demo)/Big Fat Eight (demo)/Midnight Lady (video)			
2005 □	Look Out/Look Out (video)	CDS	Black Lodge (promo)	BLODPRO 028CDS
2005 □	BORN II ROCK	CD	Black Lodge	BLOD 028 CD
2005 □	BORN II ROCK	CD box	Black Lodge	BLOD 028 CDL
	Metal box. 3000 copies.			
2005 □	BORN II ROCK	CD	Soundholic (Japan)	TKFC-85129
	Bonus: *			
2006 □	Look Out/Look Out (video)	CDS	Black Lodge	BLOD 042 CD
2007 □	MEMORIES IN BLACK	CD	Black Lodge	BLOD 059 CD
2007 □	MEMORIES IN BLACK	CDd	Black Lodge	BLOD 059 CDL
	Bonus: Song For You/5 AM			
2007 □	MEMORIES IN BLACK	CD	Soundholic (Japan)	TKCS-85176
	Bonus: Song For You/5 AM			
2009 ■	EMISSIONS OF SINS	CD	Black Lodge	BLOD 061 CD

2009 CD - BLOD 061 CD

HELLMARK
Rolf Hellmark: v/g, Björn Hellmark: g, Kalle Magnusson: k/b, Richard Lundgren: d
Svedala - Good melodic hard rock. The band also recorded several demos. The band does the way heavier track *Get Up And Get Wild* on the compilation *Skånsk Rock III* (CS Music '82). Rolf, Björn and Richard were later found in the band *GRK*, with whom they recorded the album *Timewarp* in 1995. Today Rolf plays with the hard rock band *Rock 'N Roll Boys*.

1986 ■	Nobody But You/Spell In Your Eyes	7"	private	HMK 002 $

1986 7" - HMK 002

HELLSPELL
Chrille Andersson: v/d, Daniel Andersson: g/b
Malmö - Brutal and quite primitive, but nevertheless technical and at times innovative death/black metal. They've even thrown in clean goth-oriented vocals at times. Both members are also found in *Non Serviam* and *Supreme Majesty*.

1999 ■	DEVIL'S MIGHT	CD	Invasion	I.R. 050

1999 CD - I.R. 050

HELLSPRAY
Anders Moberg: v, Janusz Fursa: g, Mattias Rydell: g, Nilo Kovacic: b, Johan Häll: d
Jönköping - The band was formed in 2005 by, Fursa, Rydell, bass player Janne Rehnquist and drummer Magnus Persson. In 2006 Rehnquist left and was replaced by Kovacic (*Stone Free, Layout, Hair Of The Dog*). In 2007 the band was completed with former *Renegade/Arrow* singer Magnus Tallåker, who handled the vocals on the band's first release. He was replaced by Anders Moberg in 2008. The band recorded the demo-CD *Pandemonium* in 2009. Early 2010 drummer Persson left and was replaced by Johan Häll (*Shivering Spines, Layout*). Fursa has previously played with bands like *Metal Mercy*, *Colorblind* and *Piece Of Clay*, while Rydell was found in *Big Thing*, *Venture* and *Antarctica*. *Hellspray* play great sounding powerful yet melodic metal with a heavy approach, at times similar to *Black Label Society*. *Part Of The Solution* contains a cover of *The Cardigans*' *Favourite Game*.

2008 CD - - -

2008 ■	FULL MOON IN PLAINFIELD	CD	private	- -
2011 ■	PART OF THE SOLUTION	CD	Perris	MA2011917

2011 CD - MAS2011917

HELLTRAIN
Pierre Törnkvist: v/b, Patrik Törnkvist: g/k, Mikael Sandorf: g,
Mats "Matte" Järnil: b, Oskar Karlsson: d
Luleå - Formed in 2002 as a trio featuring Pierre Törnkvist, Patrik Törnkvist and Oskar Karls-

son. This is a band with members that have been in quite a lot of interesting bands. Pierre and Patrik have been in **Scheitan**, **The Moaning**, **The Everdawn**, **Gilgamosh** and **Decortication**, plus Patrik was also in **Incinerator**, while Karlsson is ex-**Gates Of Ishtar**, **Sarcasm**, **Scheitan**, **The Duskfall**, **The Everdawn**, **Raised Fist** and **Defleshed**. Quite the busy bunch. A three-track demo was recorded early 2003, and soon released by Heathendoom as the band's first EP. When it was time for the debut, the band entered Dug-Out Studio with producer Daniel Bergstrand (**Meshuggah**, **In Flames**, **Crawley** etc.). The band also recorded a three-track demo in 2006. In 2009 Pierre quit playing bass and concentrated on the vocals. The bass was now taken over by Matte Järnil (**Inrage**, **Lost Souls**, **Crawley**, **The Duskfall**). At this point second guitarist Mikael Sandorf (**Gates Of Ishtar**, **The Duskfall**, **Twilight** and **Agroth**) was also added to the line-up. **Helltrain** plays, what they refer to as, rot 'n roll. Almost industrial-sounding, straightforward rocking death metal, almost in the vein of **Deathstars** with a touch of **Entombed** at times.
Website: mediakonsult.net/helltrain/index.asp

2004 CD - NB 1312

2012 CD - TPL 029

2004 ☐	The 666 EP	7" 3tr	Heathendoom	HDMEP 001	
	Tracks: Rot 'N Roll/Route 666/Helltrain. 500 copies.				
2004 ■	ROUTE 666	CD	Nuclear Blast	NB 1312	
2004 ☐	ROUTE 666	CD	Irond (Russia)	CD 04-892	
2006 ☐	ROUTE 666	CD	Jimmy Franks Recording (USA)	JFRCD 0601	
2008 ☐	ROCK 'N' ROLL DEVIL	CD	Jimmy Franks Recording (USA)	JFRCD 0801	
2009 ☐	ROUTE 666	CDd	Metal Mind	MASS CD 1329 DG	
	2000 numbered copies.				
2012 ■	DEATH IS COMING	CD	TPL Records	TPL 029	

HELS
Stefan Lindahl: v, Fredrik "Gädda": g, Kent Nei: b, Åberg: d

Oxelösund - A young and very amateurish doom band, deserves no greater attention. They also appear on the local compilation **Klipprock** (1987) with the tracks *Chaos On Earth* and *Living Dead*. Despite the quality, it is a highly prized collector's item.

1985 7" - DS S-001

1985 ■	Birth/Death	7"	Dead Sound Records	DS S-001	$$

HELSEFYR
Mathias: v/g/b, Patrik: d

Övertorneå - Formed in 1999. **Helsefyr** is another old word for Hell in Swedish. Old-school, bad-sounding, fast and quite badly mixed black metal. Recorded their first demo *The Land Of No Return* in 2004, followed by *Deadly Black I Am* later the same year. The recordings also features some covers of **Sodom**, **Mayhem** and **Bathory**. The demos were released as one cassette by Total Holocaust in 2005 and as the CD *Witches Sabbath* in 2006. The band split up in 2009. The posthumous split cassette *Aquilonious Frigus Vorago* was released by Rotting Grave in 2010 and as a limited CD-R in 50 copies on Svartgalgh (VBFR0127/SV073) in 2009. The band was anti-fascist and anti-racist, and appeared with the track *Frozen Soul*, on the compilation *Burning Roots: Anti-NSBM* (2007 Eronydead Records).

2006 CD - SMR 001

2006 ■	WITCHES SABBATH	CD	Summon Malum	SMR 001	

HELVETETS PORT
Tomas "Witchfinder" Ericson: v/g, Dag-Erik "Kongo/ K.Lightning " Magneli: g,
Philip "Inquisitor" Svennefeldt: b, Oscar "O. Thunder" Rolfsson: d

Göteborg/Kristianstad/Karlshamn - Helvetets Port (the gate of hell) sound just like the 80s heavy metal on all those old demo cassettes from 1982 by Swedish bands like **Gotham City**, **Donnerblitz**, **Steelwings**, **Axewitch** etc. Raw, crude, quite amateurish at times, but with a big heart and songs that rock. The band was formed around 2001 as **Brute Force**, by Tomas and Erik Sjödin, in their home town Skellefteå. The guitars were handled by Christian Lindell, who left in 2003 to form **Portrait**. As a coincidence, current bass player Svennefeldt was the former singer of **Portrait**. The band recorded their first six track demo *Metal Strike* in 2004, where three of the tracks were released as a vinyl single in 2006. Magneli was also found in **Necrogay**.
Website: www.myspace.com/helvetetsport

Stairway to heaven?

2006 7" - AOM 005

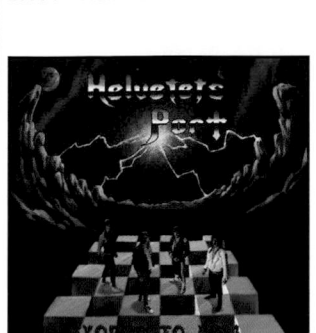

2009 LP - HHR 042

2006 ■	Metal Strike	7" 3tr	Anger Of Metal	AOM 005	
	Tracks: Swing The Studded Mace/Heavy Metal Night/Hårdrockens Förkampe. 500 copies, first 100 with woven patch.				
2009 ■	EXODUS TO HELL	LP	High Roller	HHR 042	
	100 green+patch, 200 clear, 450 back vinyl. A2 poster.				
2009 ☐	EXODUS TO HELL	CD	Pure Steel	PSRCD 030	
	Contains the tracks from LP, the single and a video.				
2010 ☐	Man With The Chains	MLP 3tr	High Roller	HHR 151	
	Tracks: Crusaders Must Die/Man With The Chains/Lightning Rod Avenger. Ltd ed 350 copies black vinyl + 150 in yellow.				

HEMLIGT UPPDRAG

Stefan Zeylon: v, Kjell Johansson: g, Ulf Wessman: g,
Jonny Gustavsson: b, Jonas "Jonkan" Andersson: d

Gamleby - *Hemligt Uppdrag* (secret mission) play punkish metal. A bit similar to *Turbo*, while the vocals are more punk style Swedish chanting. Well, at least they play guitar solos!

1983 ■ Svarta natter/Född rik ....7" Gamleby Screen 1

2006 CD - STF046CD

HER WHISPER

Magnus Af Nestergaard: v/g, Christian Widen: g, Marcus Christensen: k,
André Samuelsson: b, Kenneth K Gilbert: d

Lysekil - The band was formed in 2004, initially known as *Dragonfly*. After recording a demo in Studio Fredman in 2005 the band secured a deal with German label STF Records, who released the debut in 2006. The band describes their music as dark symphonic heavy metal, which is a pretty good description. At times a bit reminiscent of *Memento Mori* meets *Tad Morose*. Singer Magnus sounds very influenced by Messiah Marcolin when he hits the higher and cleaner notes. Well worth checking out. On the second album guitarist Christian Widén was added to the line-up. Mike Wead adds a guest solo on the album. In 2009 Widén left *Her Whisper* and with this the name was changed to *Sinners Paradise*, but the band split in March 2010.

2006 ■ CHILDREN OF THE BLACK SOIL.............................CD STF Records................................STF046CD
2008 ■ THE GREAT UNIFIER ....CD STF Records................................STF067CD

2008 CD - STF067CD

HERESI

Skamfer: v/g/k/b

Stockholm - *Heresi* is the solo project of Skamfer (founder of the band *Ondskapt*) formed in 2004. An unnamed session drummer was used during the recordings. Black metal similar to *Mayhem* meets early *Satyricon*. Decent production and vocals from the depths of Hell. "A misanthropic worship of darkness and death".

2005 ☐ Psalm I ....MCD 3tr Total Holocaust ....THR 80
  Tracks: Civitate Dei - Ondskans Hov/ Deus Absconditus/ Efter Själens Stympning
2005 ☐ Psalm I .... MLP 3tr W.T.S Productions .... - -
  300 copies black, 100 red vinyl.
2006 ☐ Psalm II – Infusco Ignis.................................MCD 5tr Total Holocaust ....THR 66
  Tracks: Liothe/ Bevingad Och Försedd Med Horn/ Dionyssosinitiationen/ Prosairesis/ Infusco Ignis.
2006 ☐ Psalm II – Infusco Ignis.................................MCDd 5tr Hydra Head (USA)..........................HH666-119
2006 ■ Psalm II – Infusco Ignis................................. MLP 5tr End All Life (France) ....EAL 046
  Poster
2008 ☐ HERESI...2MLP Viva Hate VHR-45-010
  Contains Psalm I+II on MLP+picture disc and t-shirt. 150 copies.

2006 MLP - EAL 046

HERO

Michael "Hero" Hjelte: g/v, Björn Sundström: g/v,
Henrik Deleskog: b, Daniel "Dannie Boy" Mouton: d/v

Stockholm - Hjelte (hero in English), born in the cold part of Sweden, moved to Stockholm, formed *Sons Of Thunder* with whom he made two half-decent recordings in 1998 and 2000. He then teamed up with Björn Sundström and the Weinesjö brothers, guitarist Torbjörn and drummer Thomas (*Veni Domine*) in 2003 and *Hero* was born. In 2006 they recorded the self-financed debut *Bless This Nation*. In 2007 former *Sons Of Thunder* drummer Mouton replaced Tomas. Before *Immortal,* Torbjörn was replaced by Mauritz Vetterud. *Immortal* showed a big step forward compared to the first release. On *Afterlife,* a gothy heavy rocker, Henrik replaced Vetterud. Olov Andersson (*Audiovision, Grand Stand*) play keyboards on *Afterlife.*

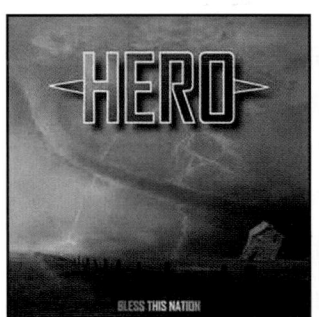

2006 CD - GNMCD 200501

2009 CD - RAR 7872

2006 ■ BLESS THIS NATION ....CD Good News Music.................. GNMCD 200501
2009 ■ IMMORTAL ....CDd Retroactive Music .... RAR 7872
2013 ☐ AFTERLIFE...CD Blood Red Music............................. BRM 0113

HETSHEADS

Anders "Atte" Strokirk: g/v, Joakim Stabel: g,
Fredrik "Fredda" Holmberg: b, Anders "Freiman" Freimanis: d

Stockholm - This band delivers, despite a nice keyboard intro, high-speed death metal with very fuzzed-out guitars and the typical death-like vocals. The album was already recorded in May and December 1991, but not released until four years later. Anders is also a member of *Nechrophobic*. The band changed name to *Blackshine*.

1995 ■ WE HAIL THE POSSESSED ....CD Repulse.......................................RPS003CD

1995 CD - RPS003CD

HEXAGON

Christer Wikström: v, Fredrik Karlsson: g, Sten Widhman: g,
Urban Åhden: b, Gunnar Green: d

Skellefteå - Great melodic 80s hard rock, similar to early *Europe*. Good, powerful vocals and good production. Anders Wallentoft (*Axewitch*) guests on keyboards.

1988 ■ Pieces Of A Crime .... MLP 5tr   W.M.R .... W.R.M.H.B 02 $
        Tracks: On The Rodeo/I Got Love/Pieces Of A Crime/Drifters/Love Eases The Pain

1988 MLP - W.R.M.H.B 02

HEXENHAUS

Thomas "Lyon/Jaeger" Lundgren: v, Mikael "Mike Wead" Wikström: g,
Marco A. Nicosia: g, Mårten "Marty Marteen" Sandberg: b,
Johan "Billy St. John" Billerhag: d

Stockholm - The band was originally known as *Maninnya Blade*, later *Maninnya*. In 1987 they changed their name to *Hexenhaus* and the line-up on the first album featured guitarist Mikael "Mike Wead" Wikström, singer Nicklas Johansson, bassist Jan "Blomman" Blomquist, guitarist Andreas "Rick Meister" Palm (ex-*Damien*) and drummer Ralph "Raideen" Rydén (ex-*Mercy*). In 1990 Nicklas quit. On the second album Thomas "Lyon/Jaeger" Lundgren (*Keegan, Destiny*) handled the vocals. On *Awakening* bassist Mårten "Marty Marteen" Sandberg (ex-*Nagazaki*) was replaced by Conny Welén (ex-*Mezzrow*, later *Dry Dead River*, *Speaking To Stones*). Ralph was later found in *Keegan*, *Keehole* and is now in *Lizard Eye* and Mikael later formed the band *Memento Mori*, where Marco and Mårten were also found, and it was more of a continuation of *Hexenhaus*. He was also part of ex-*Candlemass* bass-player Leif Edling's project *Abstrakt Algebra*, *King Diamond Band* and *Illwill*. Thomas was also found in goth rock band *The Saviours*. *Hexenhaus* is high-quality progressive thrash, sounding a bit like *Psychotic Waltz* at times, but will also attract fans of *Memento Mori*. Billerhag is ex-*Parasite*/*Memento Mori*. The "reunion" album from 1997 is a slab of high-class, powerful progressive metal, and happened when *Memento Mori* called it a day, the band reformed into *Hexenhaus*. The re-union started happening in 1995, but the album took two years, but it was well worth waiting for. A killer-version of *Cream*'s *Sunshine Of Your Love* can be found on *Black Mark Tribute Vol 2*. Watch out for Russian/Greek counterfeits of the band's CDs.

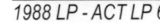

Hexen in da haus!

1988 ■	A TRIBUTE TO INSANITY	LP	Active	ACT LP 6
1988 □	A TRIBUTE TO INSANITY	CD	Active	ACT CD 6
1990 □	A TRIBUTE TO INSANITY	LP	Metal Blade (USA)	7 72422 1
1990 □	A TRIBUTE TO INSANITY	CD	Metal Blade (USA)	7 72422 2
1990 □	THE EDGE OF ETERNITY	LP	Active	ATV 13
1990 □	THE EDGE OF ETERNITY	CD	Active	ATV 13
1991 ■	AWAKENING	LP	Active	ATV 19
1991 □	AWAKENING	CD	Active	ATV 19
1997 □	DEJA VOODOO	CD	Black Mark	BMCD 98

1988 LP - ACT LP 6

1991 LP - ATV 19

HIGHBROW

Dave Nerge: v, Staffan Persson: g, Lasse Wahlman: k,
Bo "Bobo" Andersson: b, Mats "Dalton" Dahlberg: d

Stockholm - On the first single the singer was Eddy Malm, who later joined *Heavy Load* and now has his own band *Eddy Malm Band*. He was replaced by Dave Nerge. Dave, Staffan and Mats later formed pop/rockers *Dave & The Mistakes* and Dave himself returned in 1994 under the name *Dave Nerge's Bulldog* with the album *The Return Of Mister Nasty*, together with the guys from *The Johansson Brothers*. Mats left *Dave & The Mistakes* in 1980 and reformed *Highbrow* together with Christopher Ståhl (*Power, Talisman*), Michael Uppman (*Rising Force, Paradise, Explode*) and Eero Koivisto. In 1981 the line-up changed, Marcel Jacob replaced Eero who left to form *Red Baron* and for a short period, Yngwie Malmsteen replaced Christopher, but the band split. Keyboard player Patrik Appelgren (*Treat, State Of Mind*) was also found in the last line-up. They later changed their name and became *Power*. Bo was later found in *Glory Bell's Band*. The first single contains pure dual-guitar hard rock of prime quality. Highly recommended. The second effort is a bit more commercial but still a great piece of vinyl. *Lucille* is of course a cover of the old Chuck Berry tune. Both releases are very rare.

1978 7" - TBS 171

1978 ■	A Loser/Roumers	7"	T-Bone	TBS 171 $
1980 ■	Love Light/Lucille	7"	SOS	SOS 1002 $

1980 7" - SOS 1002

HIGHER GROUND

Peter Lundberg: v, Niklas Hammarberg: g, Ulf Merkell: k,
Petter Eriksson: b, Erik Pettersson: d

Sandviken - The band started out as a cover band around 1994 and later started writing original material. *Higher Ground* produces high-quality AOR, which varies from guitar-driven powerful stuff like *Ghost In My Head* to some softer, almost westcoast-ish moments. A great band! In 2002 the band recorded a new demo and in 2005 AOR Heaven picked them up.

1997 ☐ Keep On Walkin' ....MCD 6tr ProActive ....PROCD 2011001
    Tracks: Keep Walking/Make It Right/Through The Eyes Of Love/Dangerous Game/Reasons/The Big Lie
2000 ☐ Ghost In My Head ....MCD 3tr ProAcive ....PROCD 2011005
    Tracks: Ghost In My Head/Everlasting Love/Keep Walking (acoustic)
2000 ☐ PERFECT CHAOS...CD ProActive ....PROCD 2011004
2004 ■ A THOUSAND PIECES...CD AOR Heaven....................00011
2009 ☐ 13 TRACKS ....CD Speechless Music.......SPMCD0901

2004 CD - 00011

HIGHWAY

Thomas Engström: v, Tony Borg: g, Janne Borg: b, Torbjörn Tarrach: d

Göteborg - The band was formed in 1978 and only existed for one year. Actually, on the A-side the band was called *Karl Brun & Highway*. *I kväll* is straight-ahead boogie hard rock similar to *Motvind*, while *My Love Is Burning* is more 70s-influenced hard rock, similar to *Elf* with Tony Borg sounding as Blackmore as can be. Thomas was ex-*Shaggy* and later appeared in *Lady Jane* (featuring Ralph Peeker from *Vivaldi Group*) and *The Army*. Tony (ex-*Viki Vaki*) later joined *EF Band* and *Alien* and has also recorded a solo-album. Tarrach was ex-*Spectrum* and later also found in *Alien*. Janne later played with *Snake Hips*.

1979 ■ I kväll/My Love Is Burning ....7" private ....THANX 2840 $

1979 7" - THANX 2840

HIN HALEY

Yoga Andersson: v, Morgan Svedlund: g, Mats Öhr: g,
Malin Almén: b, Mattias Andersson: d

Östersund - Heavy, detuned and brutal metal slightly reminiscent of *Entombed* in the *To Ride, Shoot Straight...* era. Founded in 1995 featuring guitarist Morgan Svedlund, drummer Mattias Andersson and guitarist Mats Öhr. A year later the band was completed by singer Yoga Andersson and bassist Malin Almén. The band recorded the first EP and released it themselves. The second effort was a very simple promo-style release, also a bit rougher in the style and mix. *Hin Haley* is most likely a play with words referring to Hin Håle, a Swedish name for the devil.

1996 ■ Electric Boladuster ....MCD 4tr God Damn Records ....GDR 001
    Tracks: I Boogie... You Die/New Orleans Woman/Twin Graves/Upside Down. 300 numbered copies.
1998 ☐ Transylvanian Pig..MCD 5tr GDR/TL Studio.........GDR001/TLSCD 34-98
    Tracks: Rock And Roll/Thalidomide/Slow Coffin/Saturday Night Hog/I Boogie – You Die

1996 MCD - GDR 001

HIROSHIMA

Tony "Hanover" Hedin: v, Ismo "Hero O'Hara" Varonen: g,
Kari "Luke Powerhand" Varonen: g, Juoko "Jake Killer" Kinnunen: b,
Raimo "Quick" Pikanen: d

Stockholm - Formed in 1982 under the name *Target*, split in 1987. Hyped-up looks and hyped stage names, fortunately the music was a lot better. Great classic 80's metal/hard rock with some 70's influences released on a Finnish label. Albert Järvinen from Finnish rockers *Hurriganes* guests on one track. After the album they recorded several demos. Jouko later joined sleaze-rockers *Pussy Galore*. In 1988 singer Tony moved to the USA. This band is not to be confused with the punk band on Pink Honey/Rosa Honung Records.

1983 7" - HIRS 830901

1984 LP - KRÄLP 16

1983 ■ Soldier Of The World/Nuclear Night........................7" Pirate ....HIRS 830901 $
1984 ■ TASTE OF DEATH...LP Kräk! ....KRÄLP 16 $
1985 ☐ Rock `N´ Roll Priest/Touch Me ....7" Kräk! ....KRÄKS 45 $

HJÄRTER SEX

Janne Söderberg: v/g, Björnsson

Stockholm - The A-side may be a pretty meek Rolling Stones cover, but the B-side shows this band could really rock it out similar to bands like *Teargas* and early *Uriah Heep*. Awesome acidy guitar playing on this one.

1974 ● Star, Star, Star/Listen..7" Philips ....6015 012 $$

1974 7" - 6015 012

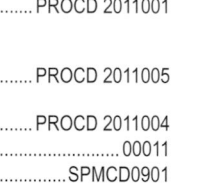

HOLLOW

Andreas Stoltz: v, Marcus Bigren: g, Thomas Nilsson: b, Urban Wikström: d

Umeå - Great semi-progressive hard rock influenced by bands like **Queensrÿche** and **Crimson Glory** with a touch of **Helloween**. Top-class, high-pitched vocals and great song material. Highly recommended. The private release of *Modern Cathedral* was made just before the band was signed by Nuclear Blast and is available in a very limited edition with totally different artwork than the NB-release. The band still exists, more or less as Andreas' solo project, but no new records have come out of it, only MySpace demos.

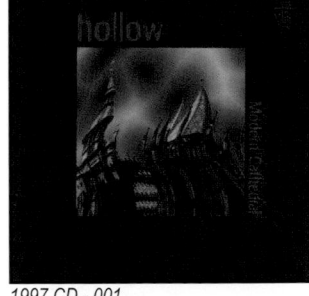

1997 CD - 001

1995 ☐	Hollow	MCD 4tr	Zakana	ZRCD005
	Tracks: Stand Or Fall/My Vision Fails/Break The Chains/When The Night Is Over			
1997 ☐	Hollow	MCD 4tr	Sound Treasure (Japan)	STCD 003
	Same as above with OBI and Japanese booklet.			
1997 ■	MODERN CATHEDRAL	CD	private	001
1998 ☐	MODERN CATHEDRAL	CD	Nuclear Blast	NB 291-2
	New artwork.			
1998 ☐	MODERN CATHEDRAL	CD	Nuclear Blast America (USA)	NBA 6291-2
1999 ☐	ARCHITECT OF THE MIND	CD	Nuclear Blast	NB 358-2
1999 ☐	ARCHITECT OF THE MIND	CD	Nuclear Blast America (USA)	NBA 6358-2
2010 ☐	MODERN CATHEDRAL/ARCHITECT OF THE MIND	2CDd	Metal Mind	MASS CD 1396 DGD
	2000 numbered copies.			

HOLLOW BREED

Petrus Lindström: v/b, Björn Gottfridsson: g, Andreas Antonsson: g, Oskar Höglund: d

Torsby - Formed in 2005-2006. Highclass melodic power metal, at times with a darker edge, that should appeal to fans of bands like **Masterplan**, **Nocturnal Rites** and **Tad Morose**. The band has also released some demos on Facebook after the album.

2009 CD - HBR 701188 9

2009 ■	HOLLOW BREED	CD	private	HBR 701188 9

HOLM, MATHIAS

Mathias Holm: g/k/b, Thomas Bäckman: b, Mats Eriksson-Wigg: d

Hudiksvall - Instrumental guitar-oriented music in the vein of Vinnie Moore. Good stuff. In 2009 he did a guest solo on the CD *Lost And Gone* by **Constancia**. In 2011 Mathias made his first album with the progressive metal band **Mindsplit**.

1996 CD - MH 701007-4

1996 ■	PICTURES OF A DREAM	CD	private	MH 701007-4
1996 ☐	PICTURES OF A DREAM	CD	Sound Treasures (Japan)	STCD 011
	Same as above but with extra booklet			

HOLOCAUST

**Andreas "Metalwarrior" Söderlund: v/g, Kristian "Gutsfucker" Carlin: b,
Berto "Drumtormentor" Hjert: d**

Lidköping - The band was formed in 1994, recorded the demo *Eternized Death* in 1996, followed by *Gloom* in 1998. Söderlund is not the same person as in **Abyssos** and **Insalubrious**. The track *Straight From Hell* is featured on the compilation *From The Underground* (X-Treme). **Holocaust** plays blast beat, old-school death metal, quite well-produced and well-played. More grunting than actual growling vocals. Not to be confused with the UK heavy metal band. Disbanded in 2000. Singer/gitarist Victor Nordström approached Carlin and Hjert, and they started up as **Degrade**, adding Söderlund and lead singer Manne. See **Degrade** for further information.

2000 MCD - SRP 04

2000 ■	Hellfire Holocaust	MCD 7tr	Sound Riot	SRP 04
	Tracks: Hellfire Holocaust/I Gut You Baby/Feel The Pain/Nuclear Hell/Straight From Hell/ Skull Implosion/The Necrosearch			

HOLOCAUSTIA

Oskar Fredén: v/g, Simon Karlsson: b, David Rosén: d

Ljungskile - Formed in May 2002 by Fredén and Rosén. **Holocaustia** made their first demo, *Order Of Terror*, in September the same year, followed by *Tyranny Through Honour* two years later, released on cassette by Death Propaganda. In 2006 Unholy Horde released the band's first MCD *The Sacrement Seed*. Oskar is also found in **Alvsvart** and Rosén in **Sworn**. Three tracks are also found on the *Assault Webzine Compilation #1*. **Holocaustia** play old-school-sounding black metal with hints of **Watain**, **Funeral Mist** and **Dark Funeral**. Lots of blast beats and a pretty thin sound. In 2007 Oskar and David formed the melodic punk/glam unit **Kendolls** with whom they have made several recordings.

2006 MCD - UHR 003

2006 ■	The Sacrement Seed	MCD 5tr	Unholy Horde	UHR 003
	Tracks: Into The Chamber/ Sword Of Azazel/ The Sacrament Seed/ Temple Of Flesh/ Gospel Macabre. 1000 copies.			

HOPE

Henrik Thomsen: v/b, Mats Johansson: g, Imre Daun: d

Göteborg - Daun has been found in numerous bands like **Snowstorm, Don Patrol, Alien, White Wolf, Phenomena, Salute** and **Gypsy Rose**. He was also on stage, playing congas, when pop artist Lotta Engberg won the Swedish qualification round to the Eurovision Song Contest with *Fyra Bugg och en Coca Cola*, in Hawaii shirt and a true 80s look. All three are also found in cover band **Partypatrullen**. Henrik was also in **Don Patrol** and Mats and Henrik were also in **ABBA** metal cover band **The Black**. **Hope** play quite slick AOR, like a mix between Bryan Adams and **Def Leppard**. Henrik actually sounds like a mix between Joe Elliott and Bryan Adams.

2009 ☐ ALL OF MY DAYS ....CD   Escape Music ....ESM 181

2009 CD - ESM 181

HORDE OF HEL

John "Odhinn" Sandin: v

Lillström (Sundsvall) - The band initially wanted to be anonymous and secret, but it was revealed some of the members have been found in **In Battle** and **My Own Grave**. On the first album guitars were played by Hans Carlsson (**In Battle, Diabolical, Valkyria**), bass by Stefan Kihlgren (**My Own Grave**) and vocals by John Sandin (aka Östlund) (**Abyssos, In Battle, Valkyria**). The album was produced by **Marduk**'s Devo Andersson, and musically there are some similarities between the **Horde** and **Marduk**, but with some strange industrial additions and some quite dark passages. The second album featured only Sandin.

2009 ☐ BLODSKAM...CD   Blooddawn.................................. BLOOD 043
2009 ☐ BLODSKAM...CD   Moribund (USA) ....DEAD 129 CD
2010 ☐ BLODSKAM II...CD   Moribund (USA) ....DEAD 151 CD
  *Bonus: Leave Life Behind/Honor Of Death/Visdomen kallas döden/Legacy Of Vengeance/
  Ashborn See All/Proud Shall Die*
2011 ■ LIKDAGG..CD   Blooddawn.................................. BLOOD 050

2011 CD - BLOOD 050

HORISONT

Axel Söderberg: v, Charles van Loo: g, Kristofer Möller: g,
Magnus Delborg: b, Pontus Jordan: d

Göteborg - Formed in 2006. Outstanding seventies hard rock, picking influences from classic bands like **November, Mountain** and **Black Sabbath**. *Två sidor av horisonten* (Two sides of the horizon) mixes songs in Swedish and English. After the first album the band was picked up by UK label Rise Above. The demo track *Road To Cairo* was also featured on a Classic Rock Magazine freebie compilation.

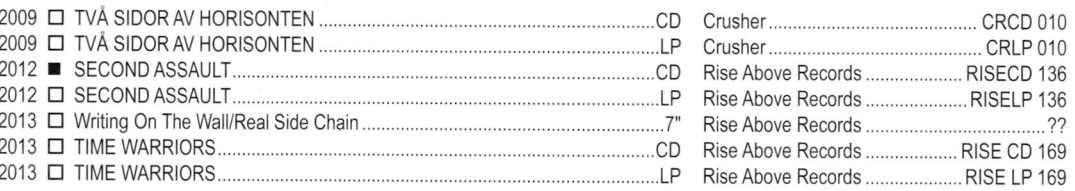

2009 ☐ TVÅ SIDOR AV HORISONTEN ....CD   Crusher..................................... CRCD 010
2009 ☐ TVÅ SIDOR AV HORISONTEN ....LP   Crusher..................................... CRLP 010
2012 ■ SECOND ASSAULT..CD   Rise Above Records .... RISECD 136
2012 ☐ SECOND ASSAULT..LP   Rise Above Records .... RISELP 136
2013 ☐ Writing On The Wall/Real Side Chain ....7"   Rise Above Records .... ??
2013 ☐ TIME WARRIORS..CD   Rise Above Records .... RISE CD 169
2013 ☐ TIME WARRIORS..LP   Rise Above Records .... RISE LP 169

2012 CD - RISECD 136

HORIZON

Joachim Hellström, Christer Johansson

Karlsborg (?) - Quite a strange record. Out of the four tracks, one is outstanding, both musically and vocally, while the other three are quite mediocre. The track *Into The Night* is **Europe**-style hard rock with dual guitars and great, powerful vocals. *Cadillac* is a cover of the old fifties song.

1992 ■ Mystery Ride ....7" 4tr   Amanda .... AMAEP 041
  Tracks: Into The Night/Children Of Tomorrow/Heartbreaker/Cadillac

1992 7" - AMAEP 041

HORIZON

Pär Wennerström: v, Jens Andersson: g, Björn Nilsson: k,
Gert Daun (aka Erikson): b, Michael Levenstad: d

Malmö - Killer melodic hard rock with a touch of heavier **Toto**. On the first single, the band also featured guitarist Stefan Ekström and the drums were handled by Rickard Roskvist. The band unfortunately split in 2000. Pär later joined **Turning Leaf**, who released their debut late 2002 and Gert was also a member of **Andromeda**. Not to be confused with the Helsingborg based **Horizon**, who recorded a split 7" with **Movement**. Both releases are now rare items. Gert and Björn reunited in 2013 under the new name **Daunforce**.

1992 ☐ I've Seen The Light/Here We Go ....7"   Blackbird ....BBS 255 $
1998 ☐ Horizon...MCD 4tr   private .... - - $
  Tracks: I See You See/Sometimes/Sweet Surprise/Walls

1992 7" - BBS 255

HORIZONT

Tommy Nilsson: v, Jonas Isacsson: g, Christian Rosenberg: k,
Tommy Gällhagen: b, Thomas Löfgren: d

Stockholm - *Horizon* were formed in 1977. *Horizont*, and play outstanding symphonic rock/ pompy AOR with a great proggy touch, in the vein of *Styx*, *Asia* and a touch of *Kansas* and even *Toto*, with plenty of keyboards and great, biting guitar work by Isacsson (later in *Roxette*). Some songs had a poppy touch. Unfortunately the band split in 1979, when Tommy was offered a solo deal in France. He made quite a successful solo career, which later continued in Sweden. In 1984 he returned to melodic hard rock in the band *Easy Action* and he also did some cover gigs together with John Norum back in the nineties under the name *The Boys Are Back In Town*. Gällhagen was in *7:e Himlen*. A live radio recording was made in 1979 in the Tonkraft show, but hasn't been made official yet. One live song, *Delirium fetisch* is found on the compilation *Tonkraft 1977-1982* ('82 Tonkraft, TLP-5-6).

1978 LP - CBS 83114

1979 12" - DW-2

1979 ○	Samtal vid horisonten	7"	CBS	DW-1	
	One-sided promo. Different version from LP.				
1978 ■	HORIZONT	LP	CBS	CBS 83114	
1979 ■	Förlorar igen	12" 1tr	CBS (promo)	DW-2	
1979 □	Förlorar igen/Samtal vid horisonten	7"	CBS	CBS 7472	
1979 □	Tänk om du visste/Angela	7"	CBS	CBS 8519	
1979 □	Medley	7"	CBS	PROM 7	
	One sided promo with a medley from Andra vyer.				
1979 ■	ANDRA VYER	LP	CBS	CBS 83592	

1979 LP - CBS 83592

HOROSCOPE

Andrija Veljaca: v/g, Tommy Wirén: g, Anders Olsson: b, Olle Olausson: d

Sölvesborg - The band was originally signed to Nacksving Records, but as they went bust, *Horoscope* released the 7" themselves. The band split in 1981 and Andrija joined hard rockers *Turbo*, a band that later turned into *Mercy*. Wirén later teamed up with *Ocean* and now plays country music. The single is quite far from the heaviness of *Mercy*, rather weak hard rock, but funny in its own way, especially the lyrics. Sadly, on August 25, 2005 Andrija died of a brain haemorrhage.

1978 ■	Come To Me/Gryningen	7"	private	HSP 1008	$

1978 7" - HSP 1008

HOROSCOPE

Mikael Andersson: g/v, Anders Janocha: b, Olof Larsson: d

Trollhättan - The band was formed by Anders and Mikael around 1977, initially as *TV3*, but changed it to *Backstage* and in 1979 they became a trio and the name was *Horoscope*. They found a mentor in popster Peter Fransson (aka Peter Le Marc) who helped them record some demos. They all had different inspirations, from *Rush* and *Deep Purple* to *Hendrix* to *Blondie* and *Television*, which made the musical style quite wide. The single is however good poppy hard rock with nice guitar playing. Pretty decent. The second single was released as *Stonte Kramer With Horoscope* and was actually singer Lennart "Stonte Kramer"'s solo project, but he wanted *Horoscope* to back him. In 1983-84 the style became a bit more complex, but finally military service made the boat sink. After this, Janocha joined the band *Catwalk*, but left before they recorded anything, while Anders formed his own *Horoscope*. In 2004 the band reunited for a show (with both line-ups). Nowadays, Larsson is in the rock group *Astrolites*.

1981 7" - OMAS 8101

1982 7" - OMAS 8102

1981 ■	Inte ensam/Det vågade jag inte säga	7"	OMA Records	OMAS 8101	
	2000 copies				
1982 ■	Green Light/Have A Nice Day	7"	OMA Records	OMAS 8102	$
	As Stonte Kramer With Horoscope. 1000 copies.				

HOSTILE CELL

Martin Söderqvist: v/g, Johan Svensson: g, Per Romwall: b, Eric Olausson: d

Göteborg - *Hostile Cell* were formed in 2006 by Romwall, Söderqvist and Olausson. Second guitarist Svensson was drafted in 2007. However, he was not featured on the artwork of the first version of the CD, while on the second Svensson was in the pictures. The first version was redrawn due to the band not getting the rights to use the artwork. It's the same album, but just with different artwork. Early 2009 former *Headplate*/*All Ends*/*Engel* bassist Johan Andreassen replaced Romwall. *Hostile Cell* play aggressive, yet quite melodic metal. As they did not gain the attention they wished for the band split to regroup after the second release. In 2011 a new reunion featuring the original line-up announced they would record under a new name. In 2010 Söderqvist joined sleaze rockers *Debbie Ray*. Tony Jelencovich guests on *The Deafening*.

2007 CD - CSPCD 001

2007 CD - CSPCD 002

2007 ■	HOSTILE CELL	CD	Coreshot Productions	CSPCD 001	
2008 ■	HOSTILE CELL	CD	Coreshot Productions	CSPCD 002	
2010 □	THE DEAFENIING	CDd	Coreshot Productions	CSPCD 003	

HOUSE OF HEAVY

Mattias Wellhag: v/g/k/d, Henrik Lundberg: g/b

Skövde/Trollhättan - House of Heavy is a duo featuring old friends Wellhag (*Preserved In Grace*) and Lundberg (*Masquerade*), who had talked about forming a band for a long time. They recorded an outstanding, sadly unreleased, album with the band *Straitjackets* in 1995. *House Of Heavy* has also used former *Shotgun Messiah* man Pekka "Stixx" Ollinen for some intense drumming, but not on the album. The band produces very heavy and grinding, yet highly melodic hard rock/metal. The album also features a heavy version of *Def Leppard*'s *Billy's Got A Gun*.

2008 ■ HOUSE OF HEAVY ....CD   Spiritual Beast (Japan) POCE-16045
    Bonus: Digital Heartbeat

2008 CD - POCE-16045

HOUSE OF SHAKIRA

Andreas Novak: v, Mats Hallstensson: g, Anders Lundström: g/k,
Basse Blyberg: b, Martin Larsson: d

Angry tennants tired of paying to play

Stockholm - Anders Lundström and drummer Henrik Andreasson first teamed up in the band *Spray*, which later lead to the two joining guitarist Mats in the melodic rock band *Vision*. In 1985 the three formed the band *The Avenue* in their home town Luleå. They recorded some demos, but no labels were interested. In 1986 they packed up and moved to Stockholm. Mats was briefly a member of the band *Macbeth*, but left for *The Station*, which was formed in 1989. They recorded some demos, but in 1991 they had to change their name, due to similarities with the record label The Record Station and another Swedish band. At that point Bernt Ek (*Grace, Wildliw, Bedlam*) handled the bass, and singer Mikael "Zifa" Eriksson had also completed the band. They recorded an album for Planet Records in 1993, but the company went bust just before it was to be released. *House Of Shakira* play outstanding mid-heavy AOR with strong hints of *Journey* and an occasional African feel on the early recordings, which gave them a very personal sound. One song found its way to a compilation released by Frontiers Magazine. Bernt Ek was replaced by bass player Per Schelander. Per was also found in space rock act *Spyke* between 1998-2002 and was also a member of Danes *Royal Hunt*. Drummer Andreasson was replaced by Tony Andersson (*Sin City*), who had spent some years in the US, and had there met Schelander at the Musician's Institute. *House Of Shakira* were later spotted by another record company, which only resulted in them stealing singer Mikael "Zifa" Eriksson, who went on to doing a solo career singing African-sounding dance-pop under the name *Zifa*. Mikael was however still participating on some songs on the band's early albums. He was replaced by Andreas Eklund, who had also recorded an album with the band *Sabbtail*, as a guest vocalist. The band's first two albums were released by German BlueStone Records, who unfortunately didn't last too long. However, they were soon picked up by MTM, who released *Best Of Two,* a compilation of the first two albums plus previously unreleased tracks: *Susan, You Touched Me* and *Antelope* from the Planet Records sessions. They also released the third album, entitled *III*. The album features a guest solo from Pontus Norgren (*Hammerfall, Talisman, The Poodles, Great King Rat* etc.). The band made a tour with *Royal Hunt*, where Schelander would later end up. Eklund guests on the *Radioactive*-album *Ceremony Of Innocence*. He has also recorded an as-yet unreleased solo-album. *Live +* contains 10 tracks recorded live plus three studio covers. In 2010 Andreas Novak (*Mind's Eye, Novak*) replaced singer Andreas Eklund. In 2011 the band also announced the replacement of Per Schelander by Basse Blyberg and Tony Andersson by Martin Larsson. The band's sixth studio album, entitled *HoS*, shows a slightly heavier and more rough-edge side of the band. Still as melodic, though. A great band! The non-album track *Black Is White* is found on the compilation *MRCD9 – 15 Years Later* (2012 MelodicRock Records) and *Shell Shock* on *MRCD11 - This One Goes To... Eleven* (2013 MelodicRock Records). Website: www.houseofshakira.com

1997 CD - BSM 1010   *2001 CD - HOS 001*

2007 CD - LMC 216

Year		Title	Format	Label	Cat. No.
1997	■	LINT	CD	Bluestone Music	BSM 1010
1998	□	LINT	CD	Avex/Bareknuckles (Jap)	AVCB-66023
		Bonus:Stone In Love (Journey cover)			
1998	□	LINT	CD	Pulse (USA)	n/a
1998	□	ON THE VERGE	CD	Bluestone	BSM 1018
2000	□	BEST OF TWO	CD	MTM	0681-14
2000	□	III	CD	MTM	0681-16
2000	□	III	CD	Avalon Marquee (Japan)	MICP 10209
2001	■	LIVE +	CD	private	HOS 001
2004	□	FIRST CLASS	CD	Lion Music	LMC 110
2005	□	LINT	CDd	Lion Music	LMC 129
		Bonus: On The Green/Heroes			
2007	■	RETOXED	CD	Lion Music	LMC 216
2007	□	RETOXED	CD	Irond (Russia)	CD07-DD561
2007	□	RETOXED + LIVE AT FIREFEST 2005	CD+DVD	Soundholic (Japan)	TKCS-85182
		Bonus: Demonica/Escape			
2008	□	RETOXED + LIVE	2CD	Lion Music	LMC 234
2008	□	III + LIVE AND SWEDEN ROCK	CD+DVD	Lion Music	LMC 240
2012	■	HOS	CD	Lion Music	LMC 315
2013	□	PAY TO PLAY	CD	Melodicrock Records	MRR013

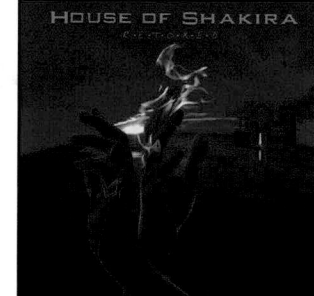

2012 CD - LMC 315

HOUSE OF USHER

Jani Ruhala: v, Mattias Kennhed: g, Martin Larsson: g,
Stefan Källarsson: b, Jani Myllärinen: d

Eskilstuna - Furious death metal, although with a thrashy feel and interesting musical variations. Well-played and with slightly cleaner vocals than "normal".

1991 ■ On The Very Verge ....7" Obscure Plasma Record.......................911002
    Tracks: Revengeance/Rather Black.

1991 7" - 911002

HOUSTON

Hampus "Hank" Erix: v, Björn "Ricky Delin" Lindbom: k, Freddie Allen: d

Stockholm - Following in the footsteps of Swedish melodic rock sensation **H.E.A.T** came a new wave of Swedish AOR. **Houston**, consisting of the duo of Hampus and Freddie, managed to strike the melodic rock world with wonder with their self-titled debut album, preceded by the single *Hold On*. However, they did have some help, namely Thomas Vikström (**Talk Of The Town**), Mats Olausson (**Malmsteen**), Tommy Denander, Ricky Delin (**Prisoner**), Lasse Falck, Johan Kronlund and Krille Eriksson. If you're into the slicker side of AOR bands like **Journey**, **Starship** and **Survivor**, this is a band to check out. *Relaunch* features covers, acoustics and one new track and was initially sold exclusively at the 2011 UK Firefest festival, but was later made public. For *Houston II*, Delin became a permanent member of the band.

2010 CDS - 350052 670014

2010 ■	Hold On...	CDS	Rocket Songs	350052 670014
2010 □	HOUSTON.......................................	CD	Rocket Songs	ROCKET 002
2010 □	HOUSTON.......................................	CD	Spinefarm (UK)	0602527587011

    Bonus: Under Your Skin/Chasing The Dream

2011 ■ RELAUNCH..MCD 9tr Spinefarm ....SPINE 786962
    Tracks: Runaway (Dakota cover)/Carrie (Michael Bolton cover)/Brief Encounter (Airrace cover)/Don't You Know What Love Is (Touch cover)/Don't Ever Wanna Lose You (New England cover)/Didn't We Almost Win It All (Laura Brannigan cover)/Without Your Love/ Truth Slips (acoustic)/1000 Songs (acoustic)

2013 □ HOUSTON II......................................CD Livewire...............................HOUSTON 2

2011 MCD - SPINE 786962

HULDT, JOHN

John Huldt: g

Staffanstorp/Los Angeles - Swedish guitar virtuoso was born in 1981 and started his career in various thrash and death metal bands such as **Feared Creation**. He also recorded several demos with the more progressive band **Dynamic**. He relocated to Los Angeles in 2006. *Rules Do Not Apply* is a versatile album ranging from almost jazzy parts to heavy progressive metal and should appeal to fans of Joe Satriani, Steve Vai etc. A great guitarist indeed. In 2012 the digital album *A Permanent State Of Transformation* was released.

2008 ■ RULES DO NOT APPLY ....CD private .... - -

2008 CD - - -

HUMAN CLAY

Jeff Scott Soto: v, Marcel Jacob: g/b/d

Stockholm/LA - When **Talisman** fell apart (the first time) Jeff and Marcel made a new album under the name **Human Clay**. The album sounds like any **Talisman** album, only a bit rougher, like a good **Talisman** demo. The song *Holdin' On* was even found on **Talisman** album *Life* under the title *Body*. The first album also features Fredrik Åkesson (**Talisman, Opeth, Arch Enemy**) and Brian Young (**Talisman, Jeff Scott Soto Band**) on guitars. Yngwie Malmsteen is also a guest on one track. The second album also featured drummer Jamie Borger (**Talisman, Treat**). Sadly, Marcel took his own life July 21, 2009. *Closing The Book* contains both albums plus bonus tracks.

1996 ■	HUMAN CLAY.....................................	CD	Seagull Int.	35434
1996 □	HUMAN CLAY.....................................	CD	Pony Canyon	PCCY-00978

    Bonus: In The Line Of Fire/Eternal Flame

1997 □	U4IA...	CD	Music For Nations	CDMFN 227
1997 □	U4IA...	CD	Pony Canyon (Japan)	PCCY-01140

    Bonus: Boy On The Golden Hill

2004 ■ CLOSING THE BOOK ON HUMAN CLAY.....................2CD Rock Treasures..............................RTCD 014
    Bonus: In The Line Of Fire/Eternal Flame/Boy On The Golden Hill

1996 CD - 35434

HUMAN COMETH

Kaj Roth: v, Steve Gardner: v, Morgan Pettersson: g, Jan Schankman: k,
Björn Pehrson: b, Jon Robbins: d

Örebro - Guitarist Morgan Pettersson started out as a rocker-gone-jazz for a period of time, but for some time now he has been working on the online collaboration project **Human Cometh**. After some demos, the first album was finally a reality. In 2010, *Evolution* was released, but only

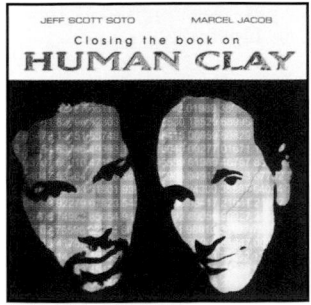

2004 2CD - RTCD 014

as a pro-printed CD-R. A slab of powerful melodic metal with great guitar playing by Pettersson. In 2011 the follow-up was released, taking the sound even further. The vocals are handled by Kaj Roth, who has sung and played with numerous bands, such as *Clown Eraser*, *A-Team*, *Shooz* etc., but had never made it to an album. About time, and well done! Morgan also made a guest appearance on *Odyssey*'s album *Reinventing The Past*. The name was taken from a line uttered by hard boiled cop Mac Taylor in CSI NY :"Like a human cometh". In 2011 the band welcomed new singer Eric Johns and drummer Walter Kelleher to the line-up.
Website: www.humancometh.com

2011 ■ HCII...CD   private.. - -

2011 CD - - -

HUMAN RACE
Stefano Marcesini: v, Robert Hansson: g, Mats Lilienberg: k,
Dennis Österdahl: b, Jörgen Tjusling: d

Göteborg - First-class hard rock with influences from early *Rainbow*, as well as 90s progressive hard rock. Lots of distorted Hammond and guitars. Great vocals in the vein of Graham Bonnett. The first album was produced by Pär Edwardsson (*Biscaya, Million*) and is quite a step above the MCD. Outstanding, melodic thinking man's metal. The band recorded a second album for Z Records, but the deal was ended before its release. *Dirteater* contains the heaviest tracks from *For The Sake*.. and the heaviest from the unreleased second album. The result is a great heavy, yet melodic hard rocker. Robert also had his weird side/solo-project *Bonkyman*, that features some mean guitar playing. He has also released an instrumental solo-MCD. The Rainbow covers are probably a result of Robert playing in *Rainbow* tribute band *Ritchie's Rainboots*. The non-album track *Weary Eyes* is also found on the *Hard Roxx Taster Vol. 5* compilation. In 2010 Robert formed his new band *Rawburt*, which also featured Stefano and Jörgen. Several outstanding demos have been released so far and the band is working on getting a deal. Österdahl was also found in *Elsy Band*, *Big Easy* and is now in *Eaglestrike*, while Tjusling is ex-*Elsy Band* and also in *Eaglestrike*.

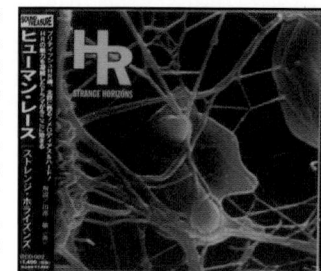

1997 MCD - STCD 002

1998 CD - ZR 1997003

2001 CD - MAS CD 0274

1997	□	Strange Horizons	MCD 4tr	Trebor	STCD 002
		Tracks: Lost In The Shadow/All The Moments/So Good/So Fine/Stargazer (Rainbow cover)			
1997	■	Strange Horizons	MCD 4tr	Sound Tresures (Japan)	STCD 002
		Same as above, but with Japanese booklet + OBI.			
1998	■	FOR THE SAKE OF YOUR SOUL	CD	Z Records	ZR1997003
1998	□	FOR THE SAKE OF YOUR SOUL	CD	Teichiku (Japan)	TECW-25722
		Bonus: Weary Eyes/All The Moments/So Good So Fine			
2001	■	DIRTEATER	CD	Massacre	MAS CD 0274
		Bonus: Tarot Woman (Rainbow cover)			

HUMAN RAGE
Erik Petschler: v, Danjel Södervall: g, Robert Stellmar: b, Stefan Olsson: d

Upplands Väsby/Stockholm - *Human Rage* were formed back in 1990. The debut was a more or less out-and-out blast of heavy power metal, influenced by the likes of *Pantera*, with a mix of brutal and clean vocals from singer Johan Thosell. The second album shows a whole new side of the band. It's still very heavy and de-tuned, but far more experimental and with the addition of programmed sounds. *Wormwood* also saw the change of singer from Johan Thorsell to Jari Salonen and keyboardist/guitarist Fredric Ryttergård was also out of the line-up. In 2003 the band also recorded the 6-track demo *Four Seasons Parade*. Two years later *Human Rage* was back with the MCD *Values* and some more changes in the line-up, where Jari had been replaced by Erik Petschler. The sound was also a bit more laid-back, still very heavy, but more post-grunge-oriented. Erik was also quite a different singer, not as aggressive in his approach. Stefan is also a session member of death metal band *Mordichrist* while Jari and Stellmar are found in *Denied*. Jari is now also a member of *13 Chaos St*. In 2011 the band decided to reunite the line-up from *Birth* for some shows in 2012, to celebrate 15 years since its release.

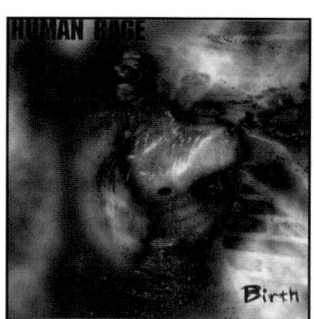

1997 CD - AXCD 009

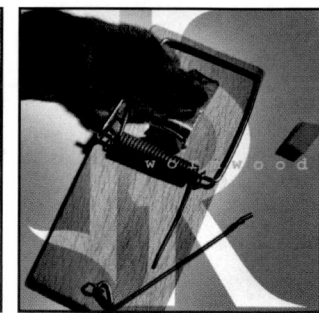

2001 CD - SUB 01

1997	■	BIRTH	CD	Sonus	AXCD 009
2001	■	WORMWOOD	CD	private	SUB 01
2005	□	VALUES	MCDp 5tr	Subsonic	SUB 03
		Tracks: Knifework/Silent/Values/Indulgent/Angel			

HUMANIMAL
Jeff Scott Soto: v, Pontus Norgren: g, Marcel Jacob: b, Thomas Broman: d

Stockholm - To get out of a lousy deal with the infamous Z Records label, *Talisman* (officially, for the second time) called it a day, after the semi-interesting and semi-heavy album *Truth*.3/4 of the line-up from the final album (not counting the live re-union album), with the addition of *Great King Rat/Norum/Electric Boys*-drummer Broman, regrouped as *Humanimal*. The band is named after a *Talisman*-album and as you might have guessed it the name-change didn't fool anyone. The sound was back to the good old *Talisman*-days, with great melodies, heavy riffs and great songs. Well, since *Humanimal* was only a way for the band to get out of the

2002 MCD - ZR CDS1

lousy deal, they went back to the name **Talisman**, and returned with the album *7*, after doing some battling with Z Records, who also reissued the album in 2012, without the band's consent.

2002	☐	HUMANIMAL	CD	Z Records	ZR 1997048
2002	☐	HUMANIMAL	CD	Avalon Marquee (Japan)	MICP 10284
		Bonus: Love's Dominion			
2002	■	Find My Way Home	MCD 3tr	Z Records	ZR CDS1
		Tracks: Find My Way Home/Love Dominion/Turn Away			
2002	☐	HUMANIMAL	CD	Front Line Rock (Brazil)	FLA 1008
2012	■	HUMANIMAL	CD	Z Records	ZR 04970-161
		Bonus: Love's Dominion. New artwork.			

2012 CD - ZR 04970-161

HUMBLE BEE
Linus Pilebo: v, Johannes Sande: g, Mikael Thorne: b, Henrik Börjesson: d

Romelanda - Heavy rock with a slightly grunge-oriented touch, a bit reminiscent of **Downstroke**, both musically and vocally. Good production, too. A great band, that unfortunately disappeared off the radar.

1996	■	Humble Bee	MCD 4tr	Musikanten	ROBCD 004
		Tracks: Shades/Games Of Today/I'm A Kid/Don't Blame Me			

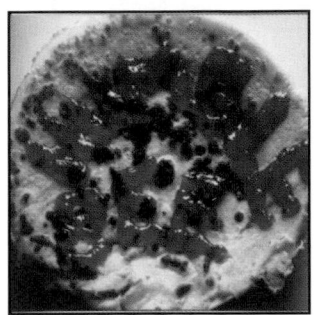

1996 MCD - ROBCD 004

HUNGRY HEAD HUNTERS
Håkan "E.Zee Lynn" Linn: b/v/h, Mårten "Rigor Martini" Wanning: g,
Erik "Eric Richards" Öster: d

Sollentuna/Täby - (The name kinda puts you off, doesn't it?) Straightforward metal with a sleaze feel to it. Not bad, just a bit average. The band was formed in 1985 and kept going until 1993. Öster has also played in **Rockheart**, **Kinky Case** and cover band **The Holy Divers**. Håkan runs Stone Studio and also plays in the band **Gudibrallan**. He is also found in **Uncle Sid And The Piranhas**. In 2012 the original line-up reunited to record new material.

1987	■	Down In The Dumps/I Want You	7"	Singapore Singles	0007

1987 7" - 0007

HYDRA
Patrik Andersson: v, Stefan Gustafsson: g, Christer Andersson: k,
Jonas Eliasson: b, Tony Svensson: d

Gagnef (Borlänge) - A really high-class AOR band with sharp guitars, prominent keyboards and very good vocals. It seems they've picked up one or two influences from acts like **Saga** and **Toto** as well. The band has now split but Christer, Stefan and Jonas are still a unit. Patrik is now making a living imitating Elvis Presley.

1990	■	Forever A Day/Dangerous Game	7"	Hydra	Hydra 01

1990 7" - Hydra 01

HYDRA
Dennis "Erebus" Carlin: v, Anders "Flame" Eriksson: g/b,
Alexis "Titan" Xanthopolous: g, Karl "Thunder" Tunander: d

Stockholm - **Hydra** were formed in 1995 as Titan's own project, playing old-school, primitive black metal. Due to problems, the band was put on hold until 1999, when Titan recruited guitarist Flame (also in **Satan's Penguins**) and singer Erebus. The band now recorded a bunch of demos, *Polemos* (1999), *Cursed Battlegroups* (2000), *To Aima Emon* (2000) and *Tantalus* (2000). In 2002 drummer Tornado was replaced by Karl (**Bloodbanner, Impyreal, Talion**) and Maugrim (**Vargagrav**) was added on bass. The band recorded some tracks for a planned split-album with *Unholy Angel*, but this was never released. In 2003 the band was picked up by Portuguese label Heretic Sounds, who released the album *Phaedra*. The band started working on a follow-up, but was put on hold in 2005. In 2009 things started happening again, now without Erebus, but Flame taking care of the vocals as well, and in 2010 the band recorded a new three-track demo entitled *Grown From The Cold*. **Hydra** play primitive, but quite decently-produced black metal in the vein of **Dissection**, **Watain** or **Dark Funeral**. The band also features Linus "Lord Khazad" Ekström (**Siebenbürgen, Pandemonic, Dimness**) on bass. He was also a member in 1995, but then playing drums. Titan is also found in **Bloodbanner** and **Dimness**.

2003	■	PHAEDRA	CD	Heretic Sounds	HS 004

HYDROGEN
Niclas "Nicke" Olsson: v, Björn "Ace" Kromm: g, Paul Flensby: b, Martin Karlsson: d

Stockholm - **Hydrogen** were formed in 2002, released the demo *Devastating Matters* in 2004, *II* in 2006 and finally an album the year after. The band has also featured Ralph Rydén (**Keegan, Mercy, Shock Tilt, Hexenhaus**, now **Lizard Eye**) on drums and Johan Alinger on guitar. In 2007

2003 CD - HS 004

379

drummer Martin Karlsson (ex-**Cobolt Syndicate**) quit and Tobbe Geson replaced him. 2008 Flensby (ex-**Vulture Cavalry**) was replaced by Oliver Vowden (**Stressfest, Mouthpeace**) and his brother Chris (**Expulsion, Absurd, Denied**) joined on guitar. Oliver however quit later the same year. **Hydrogen** play death-oriented thrash metal with vocals in the vein of Phil Anselmo, but a bit more choked. The band split in 2009 and the last known line-up featured Björn, Niclas, drummer Tobias Gustafsson (**Infernal, Mistweaver, Zombie Autopilot**) and guitarist Chris Wowden (**Denied, Absurd, Expulsion** etc).

2007 ■ NOW IS NO MORE... ....CD   Cutting Edge 320470 080061

2007 CD - 320470 080061

HYENA
Eric "Syre" Massicotte: v, Björn "Sasrof" Holmberg: g/programming

Sundsvall/Quebec - A side project featuring **Diabolicum/Setherial/Bloodline** guitarist Sasrof and Canadian singer Eric Syre. High-speed death metal in the vein of **Diabolicum**, quite lousy, thin production and horrible programmed drums, though the song titles do offer a sense of humour.

2007 ■ Hyena.. 7" 4tr   Obscure Abhorrence.................................... - -

Tracks: Gospel of the Hyena (Intro)/ Little Bobby Brown/ Hymn to Hagamannen/ Lennart the Lycanthrope (Outro).500 copies, first 100 in slimy green vinyl.

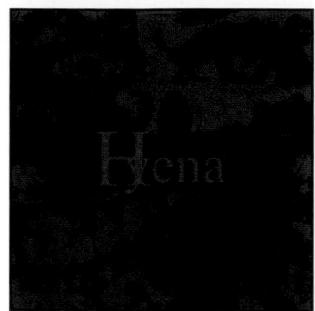

2007 7" - - -

HYPERHUG
Johan Lannering: g/v, Johan Reiven: b, Anders Malmer: d

Göteborg - Previously known as **Wunderbaum**. This band seemed to be highly influenced by the likes of **Soundgarden** and **Korn**, but with a big dose of hardcore. Good vocals. Some heavy riffing but also some clean, twiddling guitars. The band won the 1995 Partillerocken contest. Bassist Johan, formerly with **In A Pigs Eye**, was also found in **Transport League**. The band also does a cover of **Sator**'s *Anxiety, Coke And Chocolate Bars* on the tribute *Guldskivan: Svenska band hyllar Sator och Sator Codex* (1996 Backstage). In 1995 bassist Johan Reiven formed the band **LOK** together with **Psychobetabuckdown** singer Martin Westerstrand. In 1996 drummer Malmer was replaced by Adrian Erlandsson (**Arch Enemy** etc), but the band folded in 1997. Besides **LOK**, Reiven was later found in **Kneget** and **Zen Monkey**.

1995 ■ Hyperhug ....MCD 6tr   private ....PRCD 04

Tracks: Like A God/Seed/Climb/Blame/Modern Society/Killing Time

1995 MCD - PRCD 04

HYPNOSIA
Mikael "Cab" Castervall: v/g, Hampus Klang: g/b, Mikael Sjöstrand: d

Växjö - **Hypnosia** were formed in 1995, inspired by bands like **Slayer** and **Death**. They released two highly acclaimed demos in 1996 (*Crushed Existence*) and 1997 (*The Storms*). A cover of **Sodom**'s *In The Sign Of Evil* is found on a compilation by Putrefaction magazine. The band has no bass player, although Lenny "Blade" Bladh (**Bullet, Pagan Rites, Nominon** etc.) handled the bass with the band after the last record until the band broke up in 2002. Tight and powerful high-speed thrash, still in the vein of **Slayer**, **Dark Angel** and **Kreator**. Lots of nice twin-guitar work. On *Extreme Hatred* guitarist Hampus had replaced Johan Orre. Mange Roos was session bassist on the first release. Hampus is found in **Bullet, Jigsore Terror** and a former member of **Birdflesh**. Castervall is also ex-**Birdflesh** and found in **Funeral** and **Incinerator**. Sjöstrand sadly died of skin cancer in 2004. *Horror Infernal* is a collection of old demos.

1999 MCD - IFP 004

1999 ■ Violent Intensity..MCD 6tr   Iron Fist.. IFP 004
Tracks: Funeral Cross/Haunting Death/Undead/Perpetual Dormancy/Mental Terror/The Storms
1999 ☐ Violent Intensity.. 10" 7tr   Soul Seller .... SSR 001
Bonus: Outbreak Of Evil (Sodom cover). 500 hand numbered copies.
2000 ☐ EXTREME HATRED ....CDd   Hammerheart................................... HHR 053
5000 copies. Contains the tracks from Violent Intensity + My Belief as bonus.
2000 ■ EXTREME HATRED ....CD   Hammerheart................................... HHR 053
2000 ☐ EXTREME HATRED ....LPg   Hammerheart...............................HHR 053LP
Bonus: My Belief (Possessed cover)
2012 ■ HORROR INFERNAL ....CD   I Hate Records.............................. IHRCD 101

2000 CD - HHR 053

HYPOCRISY
Peter Tägtgren: v/g/k, Andreas Holma: g,
Mikael Hedlund: b, Reidar "Horgh" Horghagen: d

Ludvika - Peter and drummer Lars Szöke formed the band **Conquest** in 1984, recorded four demos and split in 1987. Peter went to USA, while Lars and guitarist Jonas Österberg recorded an album with the band **Epitaph**. In 1991 Peter returned to Sweden and recorded two demos under the name **Hypocrisy**. In 1992 he recruited former **Votary**-singer Magnus "Masse" Broberg (later in **Dominion Caligula, Dark Funeral, Sanctification, Demonoid, God Among Insects, Witchery** etc.) and on the first album, Mikael Hedlund (**Repugnant, The Abyss, War**) on bass

2012 CD - IHRCD 101

and drummer Lars Szöke completed the band. A four-way split single entitled *Nuclear Blast Sample 4 Way Split*, was released in 1992 and featured the track *To Escape Is To Die*. On the follow-up Jonas was out of the band and on *The Fourth Dimension* the band featured Tägtgren, Hedlund and Szöke. Mostly slow and heavy **Sabbath** style metal with the traditional death-vocals, while in other moments they can be compared to **Deicide** or **Cannibal Corpse**. *Inferior Devoties* contains a cover of **Slayer'**s *Black Magic*. No lyrics are featured on any of the band's albums. The above constellation also released an album in 1995 under the name **The Abyss**, but the members had then changed instruments. *Abducted* even contains some **Pink Floyd**-ish moments. Peter runs studio Abyss and has recorded acts like **Dark Funeral**, **Naglfar**, **Centinex** and **Algaion**. He has also has a successful solo career under the name **Pain** and in a more industrial vein. *Hypocrisy Destroys Wacken* is a live album, which also contains four studio tracks. In 2004 Reidar "Horgh" Horghagen replaced Lars Szöke and Andreas Holma was added to the line-up, which made its debut on the *Virus Radio* EP. In 2011 the band released the live DVD *Hell Over Sofia – 20 Years Of Chaos And Confusion*.

1992 CD - NB 067-2

1993 CD - NB 080-2

1992	■	PENETRALIA	CD	Nuclear Blast	NB 067-2
1992	☐	PENETRALIA	LP	Nuclear Blast	NB 067-1
		Black or blue vinyl.			
1992	☐	PENETRALIA	CD	Nuclear Blast America (USA)	NBA 6055-2
1992	☐	PENETRALIA	LP PD	Nuclear Blast	NB 067 PD
		Bonus: Lead By Satanism			
1993	☐	Pleasure Of Molestation	MCD 4tr	Relapse Records	RR 6040
		Tracks: Pleasure Of Molestation/Exclamation Of A Necrofag/Necronomicon/Attachment To The Ansester			
1993	☐	OBSCULUM OBSCENUM	LP	Nuclear Blast	NB 080-1
1993	■	OBSCULUM OBSCENUM	CD	Nuclear Blast	NB 080-2
1993	☐	OBSCULUM OBSCENUM	CD	Nuclear Blast America (USA)	NBA 6081-2
1994	■	Inferior Devoties	MCD 5tr	Nuclear Blast	NB 098-2
		Tracks: Inferior Devoties (re-rec)/God Is A Lie/Symbol Of Baphomet/Mental Emotions/ Black Magic (Slayer cover)			
1994	☐	Inferior Devoties	MCD 5tr	Nuclear Blast America (USA)	NBA 6104-2
1994	■	THE FOURTH DIMENSION	CD	Nuclear Blast	NB 112-2
1994	☐	THE FOURTH DIMENSION	CDd	Nuclear Blast	NB-112Digi
		Bonus: The Abyss.			
1994	☐	THE FOURTH DIMENSION	LP PD	Nuclear Blast	NB 112-1 PD
1994	☐	THE FOURTH DIMENSION	CD	Nuclear Blast America (USA)	NBA 6984-2
1995	☐	Maximum Abduction	MCD 4tr shaped	Nuclear Blast	NB-145-2
		Tracks: Roswell 47/Carved Up/Request Denied/Strange Ways (Kiss cover). Shaped disc.			
1995	☐	Maximum Abduction	MCD shaped PD	Nuclear Blast America (USA)	NBA 6145-2
1996	☐	ABDUCTED	LP	Nuclear Blast	NB 133-1
1996	☐	ABDUCTED	LP PD	Nuclear Blast	NB 133-9
1996	☐	ABDUCTED	CDd	Nuclear Blast	NB 133-2
1996	☐	ABDUCTED	CD	Nuclear Blast	NB 133-2
1996	☐	ABDUCTED	CD	Nuclear Blast America (USA)	NBA 6133-2
1996	☐	PENETRALIA	CD	Nuclear Blast	NB164-2
1996	☐	PENETRALIA	CDd	Nuclear Blast	NB164-2
		Bonus: Life Of Filth/Lead By Satanism.			
1996	☐	Carved Up/Beginning Of The End	7"	Relapse	RR 00301
1996	☐	Hypocrisy/Meshuggah	7"	Nuclear Blast	NB 154-7
		1000 copies. Released for the 1996 Hypocrisy/Meshuggah ttour. Track: Roswell 47			
1996	☐	ABDUCTED	CD	Victor (Japan)	VICP 5713
1996	☐	OBSCULUM OBSCENUM	CDd	Nuclear Blast	NB 215-2
		Bonus: Symbols Of Baphomet/Mental Emotions/God Is A Lie/Black Magic (Slayer cover)/ Please Of Molestation (demo)/Exclamation Of A Necrofag (demo)/Necronomicon (demo)/ Attachment To The Ancestor (demo)			
1997	■	THE FINAL CHAPTER	CD	Nuclear Blast	NB 283-2
1997	☐	THE FINAL CHAPTER	LP	Nuclear Blast	NB 283-1
1998	☐	THE FINAL CHAPTER	CD shape	Nuclear Blast	NB 283-2
1998	☐	THE FINAL CHAPTER	CD	Nuclear Blast America (USA)	NBA 6283-2
1998	☐	THE FINAL CHAPTER	CD	Avalon Marquee (Japan)	MICP 10043
1999	☐	HYPOCRISY DESTROYS WACKEN	CD	Nuclear Blast	NB 376-2
1999	☐	HYPOCRISY DESTROYS WACKEN	CD	Nuclear Blast America (USA)	NBA 6376-2
1999	☐	HYPOCRISY DESTROYS WACKEN	CD	Avalon Marquee (Japan)	MICY-1108
		Bonus: Request Denied/Strange Ways (Kiss cover)			
1999	☐	HYPOCRISY	LP	Nuclear Blast	NB 388-1
1999	☐	HYPOCRISY	CD	Nuclear Blast America (USA)	NBA 6388-2
1999	☐	HYPOCRISY	CD	Avalon Marquee (Japan)	MICY 1142
		Bonus: Selfinflicted Overload/Elastic Inverted Visions (demo version)/Falling Through The Ground			
1999	☐	HYPOCRISY	CD	Nuclear Blast	NB 388-2
1999	■	HYPOCRISY	CDd	Nuclear Blast	NB 388-2
		Bonus: Selfinflicted Overload			
2000	☐	INTO THE ABYSS	CD	Avalon Marquee (Japan)	MICP 10210
		Bonus: Roswell 47 (demo)			
2000	■	INTO THE ABYSS	CDd	Nuclear Blast	NB 529-2

1994 MCD - NBA 098-2

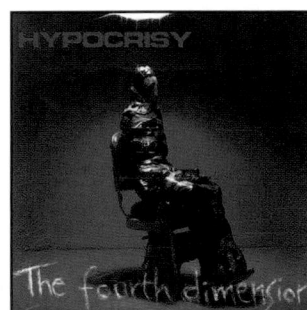

1994 CD - NB 112-2

1997 CD - NB 283-2

1999 CDd - NB 388-2

2000 ☐	INTO THE ABYSS	CD	Nuclear Blast	NB 529-2
2000 ☐	INTO THE ABYSS	CD	Nuclear Blast America (USA)	NBA 6529-2
2000 ☐	INTO THE ABYSS	CD	Irond (Russia)	CD 00-17
2001 ☐	HYPOCRISY	CD	Irond (Russia)	CD 01-67

Bonus: Selfinflicted Overload/Fuck U/Beginning Of The End

2001 ☐	10 YEARS OF CHAOS AND CONFUSION	CD	Nuclear Blast	NB 630-2
2001 ☐	10 YEARS OF CHAOS AND CONFUSION	CD	Irond (Russia)	CD 01-79
2001 ☐	10 YEARS OF CHAOS AND CONFUSION	2CD Box	Nuclear Blast	NB 630-2

Bonus CD with 1991-1992 demos + six videos.

2001 ☐	10 YEARS OF CHAOS AND CONFUSION	2CD Box	Nuclear Blast America (USA)	NBA 6630-2
2002 ■	CATCH 22	CDd	Nuclear Blast	NB 710-2
2002 ☐	CATCH 22	CD	Nuclear Blast	NB 710-2
2002 ☐	CATCH 22	CD	Nuclear Blast America (USA)	NBA 6710-2
2002 ☐	CATCH 22	2LP	Nuclear Blast	NB 710-1

Featuring bonus album Into The Abyss.

| 2002 ☐ | CATCH 22 / INTO THE ABYSS | 2LP | Nuclear Blast America (USA) | NBA 710-1 |

Bonus: Nowhere To Run

2002 ☐	CATCH 22	CD	Avalon Marquee (Japan)	MICP 10288
2002 ☐	CATCH 22	CD	Irond (Russia)	CD 02-192
2002 ☐	ABDUCTED	CD	Irond (Russia)	CD 02-224
2002 ☐	PENETRALIA	CDd	Nuclear Blast	NB 0164-2

Bonus: Satanism/Life Of Filth

| 2002 ☐ | PENETRALIA | CD | Irond (Russia) | CD 02-400 |

Bonus: Life Of Filth/Lead By Satanism

| 2002 ☐ | PENETRALIA | CDd | Nuclear Blast America (USA) | NBA 6164-2 |
| 2002 ☐ | OBSCULUM OBSCENUM | CD | Irond (Russia) | CD 02-406 |

Bonus: Symbol Of Baphomet/Mental Emotions/God Is A Lie/Back Magic Pleasure Of Molestation/Exclamation Of A Necrofag/Necronomicon/Attachment To The Ancestor

2002 ☐	OBSCULUM OBSCENUM	CDd	Nuclear Blast	NB 0215
2002 ☐	OBSCULUM OBSCENUM	CDd	Nuclear Blast America (USA)	NBA 6215-2
2002 ☐	THE FOURTH DIMENSION	CDd	Nuclear Blast	NB 0467-2

Bonus: Request Denied/Strange Ways

2002 ☐	THE FOURTH DIMENSION	CD	Irond (Russia)	CD 02-268
2002 ☐	THE FOURTH DIMENSION	CD	Nuclear Blast	NBA 6894-2
2002 ☐	LIVE AND UNPLUGGED	DVD	Nuclear Blast	NB 0589
2002 ☐	THE FINAL CHAPTER	CD	Irond (Russia)	CD 02-334
2003 ☐	ABDUCTED	CDd	Nuclear Blast	1106-2

Bonus: Drained. New artwork.

2003 ☐	ABDUCTED	CD	Nuclear Blast (USA)	6133-2
2004 ■	THE ARRIVAL	CDd	Nuclear Blast	1230-0
2004 ☐	THE ARRIVAL	CD	Nuclear Blast	1230-2
2004 ☐	THE ARRIVAL	LP	Nuclear Blast	1230-1

1000 copies hand numbered

| 2004 ☐ | THE ARRIVAL | CD+DVD | Nuclear Blast | 1230-5 |

1000 copies. DVD: Live At Summer Breeze. Post cards.

2004 ☐	THE ARRIVAL	CD	Avalon Marquee (Japan)	MICP-10432
2004 ☐	THE ARRIVAL	CD	Irond (Russia)	CD 04-784
2005 ☐	Virus Radio (Split)	MCDp 4tr	Nuclear Blast	NB 1555-2

Split with Exodus. Promo. Tracks: Scrutinized/Compulsive Psychosis

| 2005 ■ | VIRUS | CD | Nuclear Blast | 1141-2 |
| 2005 ☐ | VIRUS | CD+DVD | Nuclear Blast | 1141-0 |

Bonus: Watch Out. DVD live in Strasbourg

| 2005 ☐ | VIRUS | LP | Nuclear Blast | 1141-1 |
| 2005 ☐ | VIRUS | CD | Avalon Marquee (Japan) | MICP-10542 |

Bonus: Watch Out (demo)

2005 ☐	VIRUS	CD	Irond (Russia)	CD 05-1053
2005 ☐	VIRUS	CD+DVD	Irond (Russia)	CD 05-1053 DL
2007 ☐	THE FINAL CHAPTER/HYPOCRISY	2CD	Nuclear Blast	NB 283-5
2008 ☐	PENETRALIA	CD	Metal Mind	CD 1165 DG

Bonus: Life Of Filth/Lead By Satanism. 2000 copies numbered.

| 2008 ■ | CATCH 22 (v 2.0.08) | CD | Nuclear Blast | NB 2067-2 |

Rerecorded, new artwork. Bonus: Nowhere To Run

| 2008 ☐ | CATCH 22 (v 2.0.08) – SPECIAL EDITION | CD box | Nuclear Blast | NB 2067-? |

Rerecorded, new artwork. Bonus: Nowhere To Run. In metal box + postcards + letter of authenticity. 500 copies.

| 2008 ☐ | Don't Judge Me/Nowhere To Run | 7" PD | Nuclear Blast | NB 2151-9 |

500 copies.

2008 ☐	CATCH 22 (v 2.0.08)	LP	Nuclear Blast	NB 2067-1
2008 ☐	CATCH 22 (v 2.0.08)	CD	Irond (Russia)	CD 08-1468
2009 ☐	Valley Of The Damned (split)	7" PD	Nuclear Blast	NB 2513-9

Split with Immortal. 333 copies.

| 2009 ☐ | THE FOURTH DIMENSION | 2LPg | Black Sleeves | BLACK 115 LP |

200 black, 100 orange vinyl.

| 2009 ☐ | HYPOCRISY | 2LPg | Black Sleeves | BLACK 116 LP |

200 black, 100 grey vinyl.

2000 CDd - NB 529-2

2002 CDd - NB 710-2

2004 CDd - 1230-0

2005 CD - 1141-2

2008 CD - NB 2067-2

2009 ☐	A TASTE OF EXTREME DIVINITY	CD	Nuclear Blast	NB 2278-2
2009 ☐	A TASTE OF EXTREME DIVINITY	CD	Nuclear Blast (USA)	NB 2278-2
	Bonus: The Sinner/Taste The Extreme Divinity (demo)/Valley Of The Damned (demo).			
2009 ■	A TASTE OF EXTREME DIVINITY	CDd	Nuclear Blast	NB 2278-0
	Bonus: The Sinner			
2009 ☐	A TASTE OF EXTREME DIVINITY	LPg+7"	Nuclear Blast	NB 2278-1
	Bonus: The Sinner. Numbered.			
2009 ☐	A TASTE OF EXTREME DIVINITY	LP	Nuclear Blast	NB 2278-1
2009 ☐	A TASTE OF EXTREME DIVINITY	CD	Irond (Russia)	CD 09-1646
	Bonus: The Sinner			
2010 ☐	PENETRALIA	LPg	Nuclear Blast	NB 2601-1
2011 ☐	HELL OVER SOFIA	2CD+DVDd	Nuclear Blast	NB 2560-0
2011 ☐	HELL OVER SOFIA	2CD+Blu-Ray	Nuclear Blast	NB 2560-8
2011 ☐	HELL OVER SOFIA	2LPg	Nuclear Blast	NB 2560-1
2011 ☐	Eraser (live)/Killing Art (live)	7"	Nuclear Blast	NB 2802-1
	Brown vinyl.			
2012 ☐	OBSCULUM OBSCENUM	LPg	Floga Records	FL 45
2013 ☐	END OF DISCLOSURE	CDd	Nuclear Blast	NB 3006-0
	Bonus: Living Dead			
2013 ■	END OF DISCLOSURE	CD	Nuclear Blast	NB 3006-2
2013 ☐	END OF DISCLOSURE	CD	Columbia Japan (Japan)	COCB-60090
	Bonus: Living Dead			
2013 ☐	END OF DISCLOSURE	LPg+7"	Nuclear Blast	NB 3006-1
	100 red transparent (SCR), green NB mail order version 300 copies, 300 grey, 250 blue, 250 clear vinyl copies. Also in black vinyl. Poster. Single: Living Dead/They Lie (The Exploited cover)			
2013 ☐	END OF DISCLOSURE	CD Box	Nuclear Blast	NB 3006-0
	500 copies with 3 shot glasses and poster. Bonus: Living Dead			

2009 CDd - NB 2278-0

2013 CD - NB 3006-2

HYPOCRITE

Johan Haller: v/b, Henrik Hedberg: g, Peter Nagy (-Eklöf): d

Stockholm - Formed by Johan and Niclas Åberg in 1989 under the name *Dark Terror*. Quite similar to bands like *Napalm Death* and *Bathory*. Peter (now Nagy-Eklöf) is also found in *Mörk Gryning*, *Eternal Oath*, *Wyvern* and *Defender*. L-G Petrov (*Entombed*) and Thomas Vikström (*Candlemass*, etc.) guests on *Edge Of Existance*. On *Into The Halls Of The Blind* guitarist Nicke Åberg had left the band. Kimera from *Mörk Gryning* guests on that album. The 2000 re-issue of *Edge Of Existence* is a re-mixed (by Fred Estby) and re-mastered version.

1994 ☐	Hypocrite/Electrocution (split)	7" EP	Molten Metal	- -
	Split with Electrocution. Tracks: Heaven's Tears/Genocide			
1996 ■	EDGE OF EXISTENCE	CD	Off World	OW003
1999 ☐	INTO THE HALLS OF THE BLIND	CDd	No Fashion	NFR 032
2000 ☐	EDGE OF EXISTENCE	CD	No Fashion	NFR 047

1996 CD - OW003

HYPOTHERMIA

Kim Carlsson: v/g, Richard Abrams: d

Jönköping - *Hypothermia* were formed in 2001 by *Lifelover/Kyla/Life Is Pain* member Kim. Between 2003 and 2005 the band recorded numerous cassette demos. *Lead Yourself To Failure* was released on cassette in 2005, but later re-issued as a split LP. On the first release the drums were handled by Henrik "Nachtzeit" Sunding (*Durthang, Life Neglected, Nihilum*). He was later replaced by Richard Abrams (*Sitra Ahra, Through The Pain, Iblis Industries*). The split single track *Melankoli* features guest vocals from Ravenlord (*Woods Of Infinity*) and Sara L. *Köld* contains two songs with a total length of 46:15. *Kaffe & Blod* are also one song per side. *Hypothermia* could be described as very badly recorded, mostly improvised and quite disorganised, melancholic, depressing black psychedelic "metal" with only guitars, drums and puke-ish growls and no bass. The current line-up features Kim, Richard and guitarist Patrik. Johannes Abrahamsson (*Sitra Ahra/Kallbrand*) has also been a session guitarist for the band. In 2008 the exclusive track *Julia* was featured on a four-way split LP released by Raging Bloodlust Records.

2006 7"g - FOTA EP 003

2006 CD - TOR 001

2006 ■	Arkha Sva/Hypothermia (split)	7"g	Fog Of The Apocalypse	FOTA EP 003
	Track: Från ett depraverat inre II. 500 hand numbered copies.			
2006 ☐	Hypothermia/Aska (split)	7"	Unjoy	Unjoy 01
	Track: Melankoli. 520 copies.			
2006 ☐	SJUKLIG INTENTION (split)	CD	Eerie Art Records	EAR 011
	Split with Dimhymn. Tracks: Från ett depraverat inre/Hora			
2006 ☐	Undergången (split)	7"	Eternity	ETER 018
	Split with Svartnar. Track: Själavälten. 340 numbered copies.			
2006 ☐	VEINS	CD	Insikt	Insikt 30
2006 ■	KÖLD	CD	Those Opposed	TOR 001
	First copies came with a button.			
2007 ■	RAKBLADSVALSEN	CD	Total Holocaust	THR-09
2007 ☐	RAKBLADSVALSEN	2LP	Aphelion Productions	AP 035
	500 copies. First 100 with patch. One LP in white/red marbled vinyl and one in black.			

2007 CD - THR-09

2008 ☐	LEAD YOURSELF TO FAILURE (split)	LP	Old Ruin	ORR 001

Split with Durthang. Tracks: Lid/Ur ångest född. 111 copies.

2008 ☐	Gråtoner	12"	Turannum	002

Tracks: Gråtoner I & II/Gråtoner Repression. 800 black, 100 green, 100 brown haze vinyl.

2008 ☐	SJUKLIG INTENTION (split)	LP	Obscure Abhorrence	OAPDHLP2007
2008 ☐	KAFFE & BLOD	LP	Turannum	003

100 brown, 100 red. Markes wrong.

2009 ☐	KÖLD	LP	Turannum	004

800 black, 100 blue and 100 white vinyl.

2011 ■	VEINS	LP	Fog Of The Apocalypse	FOTA LP 013

250 red splatter vinyl, 250 black vinyl.

2012 ☐	SJÄLVDESTRUKTIVITET FÖDD AV MONOTONA TANKEGÅNGAR I	LP	Galgenstrang	GS 035

300 copies. Marbled vinyl

2012 ☐	SJÄLVDESTRUKTIVITET FÖDD AV MONOTONA TANKEGÅNGAR II	LP	Galgenstrang	GS 036

300 copies. Marbled vinyl

2011 LP - FOTALP 013

HYSTE'RIAH G.B.C.

Ray Grönlund: v, Klas "Cliff T" Ideberg: g,
Jerry "Läppen/Krown" Kronqvist: b, Tom Hallbäck: d

Landskrona/Helsingborg - Formed out of the two bands *Hyste'riah* (Klas and Jerry) and *God B.C* (Tom). The band recorded a demo tape in 1989. After the demo singer Ray (also in punk band *The Bristles*) was added to the line-up. Klas was later in *Darkane*, *Terror 2000* and *The Defaced*. A bit reminiscent of classic thrash bands like *Death Angel* and *Kreator*.

1991 ☐	SNAKEWORLD	CD	Hellhound	HELL 011
1991 ■	SNAKEWORLD	LP	Hellhound	HELL 011

1991 LP - HELL 011

HYSTERICA

Anni Lovisa "De Vil" Sundqvist: v, Maria "Bitchie" Eriksson: g,
Britt-Marie "Marydeath" Ebbersten: k,
Sara "SatAnica" Leni Englund: b, Elin "Hell'n" Eriksson: d

Stockholm - The all-female metal band *Hysterica* was formed by Hell'n and Bitchie in 2005 and recorded their first demo the subsequent year. After exploring the live scene they finally made their first album in 2009. Most of the lyrics on the album were written by Liv Jagrell (*Sister Sin*), who was the band's former singer, and Peter Tägtgren produced it. Really good heavy rock/metal with a doomy touch. After the debut keyboard player Marydeath joined and guitarist Maria "RockZilla" Tern (ex-*Shalalee*, *Aphrodite*, now *Metalnun*, *Heartattack*) was out. The second album was recorded by Pontus Norgren and Marcus Jidell.

2009 ☐	METALWAR	CD	Crong	hystcd 001
2012 ■	THE ART OF METAL	CD	Black Lodge	BLOD 081CD
2012 ☐	THE ART OF METAL	CD	Rubicon Music (Japan)	RBNCD-1106

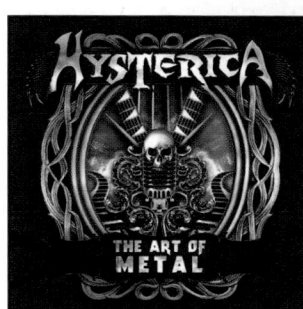

2012 CD - BLOD 081CD

HÅF-BAND

Leif Åhman: v/g, Glenn Fransson: b, Kent Helgesson: d

Uppsala - The band released one single with a good, solid hard-rocking version of the Mikael Wiehe-song *Flickan Och Kråkan* (The Girl And The Crow) on side A and their own 80s metal plodder, *Under Control* on the B-side. In 1991 the band split and Leif formed his own *Leif Åhman Band*, a more commercial-sounding unit.

1989 ■	Flickan Och Kråkan/Under Control	7"	Platina	PL 50

1989 7" - PL 50

HÄDANFÄRD

Sir N: v/g/b

(Norrland) - Solo project by *Grifteskymfning/Svartrit/Vanskapt/Kaos Sacramentum* member Sir N (aka Vanskapt). *Evil-Minded* is a compilation of different recordings, also released on cassette. Hädanfärd is an old word for death in Swedish. *Hädanfärd* play raw, crude, primitively-recorded, old-school black metal with desperate spoken/screamed vocals. Some tracks are more ambient. Musically it's not bad at all.

2012 ☐	Vederstyggelsens uppväckelse	MLP 5tr	Ancient Records/Afgrundsvisioner	AR 026

Tracks: En fördold ohelighet/Bevilja af hans oheliga afgrundsmakt/I skuggan af Kristus rangliga kors/Svurna förbannelser af besvärtade energier/Ändlöshetens helgedom (bonus). One-sided LP. 250 copies.

2012 ☐	EVIL-MINDED	LP	Mystery Of Death	Mystery 012

100 hand-numbered copies. Patch.

2012 ■	SMUTSIGA SINNEN	LP	Ancient Records	AR 024

250 copies.

2012 ☐	VEDERSTYGGELSENS UPPVÄCKELSE PART II	LP	Ancient Records	AR 041

Red/brown vinyl. 250 copies.

2012 LP - AR 024

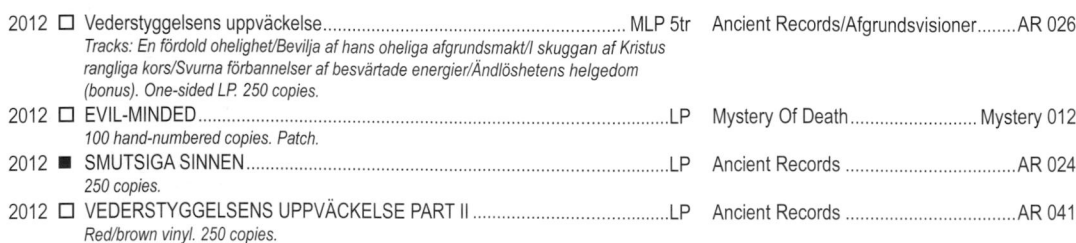

ICE AGE

Sabrina Kihlstrand: v/g, Pia Nyström: g,
Viktoria "Vicky" Larsson: b, Tina Strömberg: d

Göteborg - *Ice Age* is one of the strangest stories in Swedish metal history. This all-female melodic thrash unit could've been big, and I mean really big, if management problems and other business crap, had not fucked it up. The band was formed in 1985, by songwriters Pia and Sabrina, starting out under the name *Rock Solid*. The initial line-up also featured Tina and Sabrina's sister Helena Kihlstrand on bass. They recorded a three-track demo, before Vicky replaced Helena in October 1986. Bands like *Iron Maiden*, but also *Rush* and *Queensryche* initially influenced them. When the sound started being more thrash-oriented, they changed their name to *Ice Age*. The band recorded the demo *General Alert* in 1987, and started gaining interest through the underground media. They played shows in their local area, but were soon invited to play at London's Marquee Club by Mike Shannon, owner of legendary record shop Shades. In 1988 a second demo was recorded and widely spread. The band's third demo *Instant Justice*, 1989, sold in the excess of 1200 copies. *Runaways*' manager Kim Fowley approached the band, but his idea of putting appearance before music didn't go down well with the band and the collaboration ended. *Ice Age* signed a deal with manager Dave Maile, under dubious circumstances. They went on a short tour with *Candlemass*, and were soon headlining their own European tour, after exposure in major magazines like Kerrang! and Metal Hammer. But still no recording deal. During the 1989 European tour Sabrina left the band due to problems with the management, and three months later she was replaced by Debbie Gunn (*Sentinel Beast, Znöwhite*) and Italian guitarist Isabella Fronzoni (*Warhammer*). Vicky left, only to join again soon after. The band recorded a video, and went on MTV's *Headbangers Ball* for a promo spot. The new European tour started with gigs in Britain, and continued in Holland and Denmark. Now management problems truly set in, and two thirds of the band left in late 1989. The final demise was to come in spring 1990. The manager made an attempt to illegally release a record, by forging the band member's signatures on a deal, but this was stopped. Pia, Sabrina and drummer Anders Ström formed the band *Idiots Rule*, where Vicky also came back to the fold. Other members that were in the line-up were Niclas Engelin (*Engel*) and Lori Linstruth (*Stream Of Passion*). The ex-manager made a second attempt to make some cash with an illegal release in 2009, which was stopped by the band's legal advisor. A few copies are still out there. *Ice Age* have since put up most of their recordings on-line for free download. In 2006 Viktoria resurfaced in the band *Dogs Of Doom and* played live with *Notre Dame*. However, she left after six months and the band became *Doom Dogs*.

Unfortunately Hell still hasn't frozen over...

Unofficial release:
2009 ■ A THRASH-METAL FAIRY STORY..CD Nemesis...NICD 666 $

2009 CD - NICD 666

IDIOT

Jim Sundström: v/g, Joakim Jacobsson: g, Viktor Eriksson: b, David Wikberg: d

Norsjö - This is another strange beast in the Swedish metal world. They sound metal and sing about having snow in your shoes. With song titles like *Enter Plantman*, *Semester* ("vacation"), *Pang på pungen i Portugal* (*The Kristet Utseende* cover) and *Snö i skorna* ("snow in the shoes"), what can go wrong? Yes, everything, I know. Well, it's not that wrong actually. *Idiot* play decent metal, at times with a touch of *Metallica*, with silly lyrics and vocals in the vein of *Dia Psalma*. The band was formed in 2002 by Jim and Andreas J (who was supposed to play key harp, but left the band after the demo) and released their first demo later the same year. After a couple of demos they attracted punk label Ägg Tapes & Records, who featured them on two compilations and finally released their only release.

2005 ■ STORVÄRK OCH HUVUDVERK.......................................CD Egg Tapes.....................................ÄGG-59

2005 CD - ÄGG-59

IGNEOUS HUMAN

Andreas Joelsson: v, Ewo Solvenius: g, Daniel Persson: g,
Mikael Gustavsson: b, John Thorner: d

Falköping - During the recordings of the band *Gaphia*'s debut album in 2007, the guitarist quit. Andreas, Mikael and John now teamed up with guitarist Daniel and in 2008 they reformed as *Igneous Human*. In 2009 they were reinforced by second guitarist Ewo and the band was complete. They were picked up by new started German label Tractor Productions who released the band's debut. *Igneous Human* says they have picked their influences from various styles and bands such as *Led Zeppelin, Pantera, Guns 'N Roses* and *Dream Theater*. I do have a hard time finding the *Zeppelin*, *Guns 'N Roses* and *Dream Theater* vibes, but *Pantera*, definitely. They are however not as constantly heavy as *Pantera*, but mix in some melodic moments.
Website: www.igneoushuman.com

2009 ■ PYROCLASTIC STORMS ....CD Tractor.....................................TRPR910-003

2009 CD - TRPR910-003

II SHY

Jannicka Segemark: v, Helena Wahlgren: v, Victor Erdesjö: g, Joakim Söderlind: k, Mikael Andersson: b, Johan Jämtberg: d

Gävle - II Shy were formed in the fall of 1984 as a school project. All members were beginners, but soon caught up. The band went through various line-ups, but the basics featured Joakim, Johan, Micke, Jannicka, Victor and Helena. At some points the band also featured Steven Anderson, Peter Westby and Sebastian Lind. Really good melodic hard rock/AOR with female vocals. The band folded in 1988 and evolved into **Broken Glass** featuring Jämtberg and Erdesjö.

1986 7" - MA-502

| 1986 ■ | Midnight Dream/I Want You Back | 7" | Mamma | MA-502 |
| 1987 ☐ | Voices/Inside Me | 7" | Pappa | PA-503 |

ILL-NATURED

Emil Johansson: v/g/b, Rikard Markusson: d

Uddevalla - Ill-Natured started as Emil's solo project in 1999. Emil is ex-**Azeazeron** and also in **Suicidal Winds**. He started out by recording the very limited demo *Impetuous*. In August 2000 he recruited drummer Rikard "Fleshripper" Markusson (**Sadistic Grimness, Conspiracy, Azeazeron**) and they recorded a new demo entitled *Armed*, featuring a cover of **Bathory**'s *Die In Fire*. 2001 saw a new demo out, this one also featuring a cover of **Celtic Frost**'s *Circle Of The Tyrants*, and in 2002 the demo *Return Of The Lust Murderer* was unearthed.

2005 7" - DR 037

| 2005 ■ | Reject The Living (split) | 7" | Deathstrike | DR 037 |

Split with Axis Powers. 666 copies. Tracks: The Veinslayer/On Master's Command

ILLFIGURE

Max Malmgren: v, Jesper Malmgren: g, Alex Dzaic: g, Tommy Södergren: b, Henric Merkel: d

Norrköping - Illfigure were formed in 2004. *Chaos Tranquillity* is a slab of high-class heavy, driving modern metal with heavy riffing and mixed clean and angry vocals. A great release indeed. The band won the 2006 years *Rockkarusellen* competition. In 2009 Petter Swartz replaced Södergren. The CD was mixed and mastered by Magnus Devo Andersson (**Marduk, Overflash**). Max is ex-**AbuZimbel**, while Alex was earlier in **Breach Point**. *Website: www.illfigure.se*

Illfigure in full figure

2009 MCD - ILL 001

| 2009 ■ | Chaos Tranquillity | MCD 6tr | private | ILL 001 |

Tracks: (Trust No One) One Man Army/Bleed/Home/Warped Mind/Just Want To Know/Exodus

ILLWILL

Jonas Dahlström: v, Anders "Andy La Rocque" Allhage: g, Charles Petter "Sharlee d'Angelo" Andreasson: b, Tommy "Snowy Shaw" Helgesson: d

Göteborg - This is a gruesome bunch. **Pantera** feels like **Back Street Boys** in comparison. Power metal extraordinaire! *Illwill* was formed in 1997 and recorded their first demo, *Revolution*, the same year. Quite a bunch of name musicians, especially Snowy (**Therion, Notre Dame, Dream Evil, XXX** etc), Andy (**Mercyful Fate, EF Band**) and Sharlee (**Arch Enemy, Spiritual Beggars, Withcery, Facelift, Sinergy** etc). Singer Jonas is ex-**Ton Of Bricks**.

1998 CD - AIN 902023

1998 CD - DR 002 CD

1998 ■	EVILUTION	CD	private	AIN 902023
1998 ■	EVILUTION	CD	Diamond	DR 002 CD
1998 ☐	EVILUTION	CD	New Renaissance (USA)	NRCD 107-2

IMMACULATE

Mika Eronen: v, Nino Vukovic: g, Fadi Ghanime: g, Danile Kallin: b, Oscar Moritz: d

Uppsala - Formed in 2004 as the brainchild of Nino Vukovic. *Immaculate* recorded their first demo in 2004. On the first album the line-up featured Mika, Nino, Fadi and drummer Andreas "Skullthrasher" Bolldén. After the album, Joakim Björkelid was added on bass and Mårten Jansson replaced drummer Bolldén. On the second album the two had however been replaced by Kallin and Moritz (**Destrukto, Megalomaniac**). Killer high-speed thrash done the classic mid-80s way, in the vein of **Agent Steel**. Similar to **Destruction** and **Vio-Lence**, but with slightly annoying high-pitched vocals at times. A tight musical unit, with great songs.

| 2007 ☐ | KILL, THRASH 'N DESTRÖY | CD | Witches Brew | BREW 019 |

Bonus: The Burning Of Sodom (Dark Angel cover). First 100 copies with a logo patch

| 2010 ■ | ATHEIST CRUSADE | CD | StormSpell Records | SSR-DL56 |

1000 copies.

2010 CD - SSR-DL56

IMMEMOREAL

Martin "Goatnecro" Qvist: v/g, Christer "Grendel" Olsson: g, Blash: g
Christian Aho: b, Anders "Wouthan" Malmström: d

Alingsås/Falkenberg - *Immemoreal* were founded in 1993 by Blash and Tyr, who left the year after. The first demo, entitled *Winter Breeze* was recorded in 1995 and the song *Under The Depths Of Hell* was featured on the *Voices Of Death Vol 1* compilation. They recorded the second demo *The Age Nocturne* 1998. Christer, Christian and Anders are also found in *Prophanety*. Anders later turned up in *Putreaeon*, *Nominon* and *Inverted*. Death metal in the vein of *Dissection*. Martin is ex-*Ablaze My Sorrow*/*The Ancient's Rebirth* and he is also found in *Fall From Grace* and Anders is ex-*Inverted*. *Immemoreal* play well-produced and well-played death metal in the vein of *Necrophobic*. The album was slated to be released on vinyl by Metal Supremacy in 2001, but it never happened.

2000 CD - BLACK 027 CD

2000 ■ TEMPLE OF RETRIBUTION ....CD   Blackend ....BLACK 027 CD

IMMERSED IN BLOOD

Stefan Lundberg: v, Johan Ohlsson: g, Robert Tyborn Axt: g,
Joel Andersson: b, Jocke Unger: d

Göteborg - When the band *Inverted* folded in October 1998, Johan and Joel (*Nominon*) decided to continue the battle and in an even more brutal way. Stefan, who was also ex-*Inverted* joined the ranks in December the same year, followed by Unger. In February 1999 Axt completed the line-up. Their first demo *Eine Kleine Deathmusik* was unearthed in August 1999. Two new songs were written for the *Sweets For My Sweet Chapter 1* three-way split on Lowlife Records. In 2001 the band recorded a new MCD and a cover of *Dark Angel*'s *We Have Arrived* for a tribute album on Arctic Music Group. In 2002 Arctic Music Group signed the band, and in June the same year the band entered Studio Mega to record the *Killing Season* CD. In June 2003 Unger decided to leave the band and *Imperious* drummer Chris helped out. In June 2004 Lundberg and Axt were relieved from their duties due to lack of commitment. They were replaced by drummer Jonny Bogren and guitarist Christian Strömblad (*Nominon*). In 2005 they also found new singer Fredrik Johnsson (*Hawthorn*). Blast beat filled death metal. Musically the band can be compared to *Cannibal Corpse* or *Deicide*. No news since 2008. Act and Lundberg are also in *Skymning*, while Ohlsson is in *Openwide*.

2001 MCD - FALLMCD 005

2000 CD - LOW 006

2000 ■ SWEETS FOR MY SWEET CHAPTER 1 (split) ....CD   Lowlife..............................LOW 006
    Split-CD with Confessions Of Obscurity and Outcast Tracks: Letum Non Omnia/Finit/Sal-
    vatorian Rape/Immersed In Blood/Pull The Trigger/Breed/Transmutation Emporium.
2001 ■ Relentless Retaliation ....MCD 5tr   Downfall .... FALLMCD 005
    Tracks: Relentless Retaliation/Collector Of Souls/Genuine Suicide Attempt/Celestial
    Carnage/Serpent Of Chaos
2003 ■ KILLING SEASON ....CD   Arctic Music Group ....AMG 81502

2003 CD - AMG 81502

IMPALE

Anders Larsson: v/g, Peter Henningsson: g, Jonas Ydlinger: b, Johan Strende: d

Kristinehamn - The band was formed around 1996. *Impale* produces slightly thrash-oriented metal in the vein of early *Metallica* or *Megadeth*. Erik Jansson played drums on the debut. The second effort shows a great improvement and leans more towards the German-type power metal. Check it out! Strende and Henningsson were also in *Silent Scythe*.

1998 ☐ Illusions Of The Past..MCD 4tr   Zalt...........................ZALTREC 9801
    Tracks: Illusions Of The Past/Silent Eyes/Tell Us/Fight For Your Right
2000 ■ Keeper Of The Flame ....MCD 3tr   private ....IMPALE 02/2000
    Tracks: Keeper Of The Flame/Remember (Fighting The Lord)/Mankind's Call

2000 MCD - IMPALE 0272000

IMPERA

Matti Alfonzetti: v, Tommy Denander: g, Mats Vassfjord: b,
Johan "J.K Impera" Kihlberg: d

Stockholm - *Impera* were formed in 2009, initially with *Mötley Crüe*/*Union* singer John Corabi on board, but as schedules clashed, the vocal duties were taken over by Matti Alfonzetti (*Skintrade, Bam Bam Boys, Red White & Blues* etc). The guitar spot was filled by multi-session musician Tommy Denander and the bass work by *Grand Design*/*Scaar*/*Chris Laney's Legion* man Mats Vassfjord. The secret Mr Impera is really drummer Johan Kihlberg (former president of Kiss Army Sweden). A great, solid melodic hard rock band, indeed.

The Impera empire

2012 ☐ Shadows In Light ....MCDpg 3tr   Escape ....ESM 999
    Tracks: Turn My Heart To Stone/Shoot Me Down/Tell Me (SRM version)
2012 ■ LEGACY OF LIFE ....CD   Escape ....ESM 244
2013 ☐ PIECES OF EDEN...CD   Escape ....ESM 259

2012 CD - ESM 244

IMPERIAL DOMAIN

Tobias Heideman: v, Peter Laitinen: g, Philip Borg: g, Alvaro Romero: d

Uppsala - The band was formed in 1994 and recorded their first four-track demo *The Final Chapter* the following year. In 1996 they recorded their second four-track *In The Ashes Of The Fallen* which received rave reviews and they were soon signed by Pulverized Records. Romero is ex-*Azotic Reign* and later in **Loch Vostok** and **Sandalinas**. The debut album was recorded at Sunlight Studios by Tomas Skogsberg. Erik Wargloo handled the bass duties, while on the second album Borg and Laitinen handled this. *The Ordeal* also featured guest spots from Teddy Möller (**F.K.Ü, Mayadome, Loch Vostock** etc), Sebastian Okupsi and Bassel Elharbiti (ex-**Fatal Smile, Mayadme**).

1998 ☐	IN THE ASHES OF THE FALLEN	CD	Pulverized Records	ASH 006 CD	
2003 ■	THE ORDEAL	CD	Konqueror Records	KR 003 CD	

2003 CD - KR 003 CD

IMPERIOUS

Emil Fredenmark: v, Adam Skogvard: v/g, Johan Thoren: v/g,
Rickard Thulin: b, Christian Nyström: d

Nynäshamn - **Imperious**, featuring Emil, Christian and Johan, was formed under the name **Obscura**, under which name they recorded two demos. They changed their name to **Imperious** and released their only album *In Splendour*. Thulin and Skogvard were also members of **Coercion**. Skogvard has also been found in **Slodust** and progsters **Book Of Hours**. Emil and Johan handled the bass work on the CD recording. **Imperious** play blast-beat-infused, high-speed death metal with alternating deep growls and high pitch screeching. A bit similar to **Morbid Angel** and early **Deicide**. The band has now split up.

2003 ■	IN SPLENDOUR	CD	Retribute Records	RET 015	

2003 CD - RET 015

IMPIETY

Urban Österberg: v/g, Thomas Johnsson: g, Rille Eriksson: b, Benny Åkermark: d

Kramfors - Heavy power metal with a touch of vintage **Metallica**. Urban, who sadly passed away in 2012, was also in the band **Black Web** who released the album *Old Habits Die Hard* (2006). Not to be confused with the Singaporean death metal band. Thomas is now found in **Semlah**.

1996 ■	Impiety	MCD 4tr	private	WEB 0001	
	Tracks: Black Web/Crawling/Your Demon/Flower				

1996 MCD - WEB 0001

IMPIOUS

Martin Åkesson: v/g, Valle Daniel Adzic: g, Robin Sörqvist: g,
Erik Peterson: b, Mikael Norén: d

Trollhättan - **Impious** were formed in 1994 by Valle and Martin. Initially Johan Lindstrand (later in **The Crown, Incapacity, One Man Army And The Undead Quartet**) handled the drums. The song *Dominated By Tales* was featured on the local compilation *Vad Händer?* in 1995. They recorded their first demo, *Infernal Predomination,* in 1995, *The Suffering* in 1996 and *Promo '97* in 1997. They also covered the song *Inner Self* for the **Sepultura** tribute (Black Sun 1997) and *One* for the Black Sun **Metallica** tribute (1998). After *The Killer* album, Robin (also In **Power Supreme**) changed to guitar, Martin concentrated on the vocals and they added Erik Peterson on bass. High-speed technical thrashy death metal in the vein of colleagues **The Haunted** and **The Crown**, where Robin is now found. Drummer Ulf "Wolf" Johansson (**Power Supreme**) left the band in 2002 to join **Tribal Ink**, a band created in a TV-show called *Wannabee*. He was replaced by Mikael Norén (**Enthralled, Conformatory**). *Born To Suffer* was a compilation of demos and cover songs. Valle was also found in **One Man Army And The Undead Quartet**.

1998 CD - BS 14

2000 CD - BS 21

2002 CDd - HHR 121

1998 ■	EVILIZED	CD	Black Sun	BS 14	
2000 ☐	TERROR SUCCEEDS	CD	Black Sun/Century Media	BS 21/8044-2	
2000 ■	TERROR SUCCEEDS	CD	Black Sun	BS 21	
2002 ☐	THE KILLER	LP	Hammerheart	HHR 121	
2002 ■	THE KILLER	CDd	Hammerheart	HHR 121	
	Bonus: Extreme Pestilence (rerecorded)/Trapped Under Ice (Metallica cover)/Soldiers Of Hell (Running Wild cover)/Live Wire (Mötley Crüe cover)				
2002 ☐	The Deathsquad	MCD 7tr	Hammerheart	HHR 128	
	Tracks: The Deathsquad/Extreme Pestilence (rerecorded)/Trapped Under Ice (Metallica cover)/Soldiers Of Hell (Running Wild cover)/Live Wire (Mötley Crüe cover)/Dead Eyes Open (demo)/The Deathsquad (demo). 1000 copies				
2002 ☐	THE KILLER	CD	Karmageddon	KARMA 065	
	Bonus: Extreme Pestilence				
2004 ☐	BORN TO SUFFER	CD	Karmageddon	KARMA 066	
2004 ☐	HELLUCINATE	CD	Metal Blade	3984-14502-2	

2007	☐	HOLY MURDER MASQUERADE	CD	Metal Blade	3984-14592-2
2007	☐	HOLY MURDER MASQUERADE	CD	Metal Blade Japan (Japan)	MBCY-1078
		Bonus: Liberator-Assassinator			
2009	■	DEATH DOMINATION	CD	Metal Blade	3984-14781-2
2009	☐	DEATH DOMINATION	CD	Metal Blade Japan (Japan)	MBCY-1121

2009 CD - 3984-14781-2

IMPLODE

**Johan Ejerblom: v, Viktor Lindqvist: g, Christoffer Knutsson: g,
Victor Danling: b, Henrik Axelsson: d**

Mariestad - Formed in 2006. The band's demo *Memento Mori* (2008) received great reviews. After the demo guitarist Viktor Lindqvist replaced Jon Dehlén. Early 2009 singer Viktor Brunö left the band and was replaced by Axelsson's former *Slug* colleague Johan Ejerblom. The band's music became heavier and more brutal, and when entering the competition *Best Unsigned* they were spotted by Supernova Records. The debut album was mixed by Thomas "Plec" Johansson at Panic Room studios.On the second album Victor replaced bassist Gustav Johansson. High class thrash metal.

2011	■	THE HOUR HAS COME	CD	Supernova	SUPERCD 031
2013	☐	Under A New Sun	MCD 4tr	Cramada	CRA 003
		Tracks: She/We're The Soil/Under A New Sun/A Grim Smile Fades			

2011 CD - SUPERCD 031

IMPULSIA

Johan Längquist: v, Uno Sjöström: g, Marcus Jidell: g/k

Stockholm - *Impulsia* is the project of guitarist Ulf Sjöström and the band came together when Uno started writing songs together with former *Candlemass/Jonah Quizz* singer Längquist. Twelve songs were recorded during 2008-2009, using Marcus Jidell (*Royal Hunt, The Ring*, now *Evergrey*) on guitar and keyboards. The album also featured Marcel Jacob on bass and Tomas Broman on drums, plus guest vocals from pop singer Pandora and female American vocalist Robin Beck. Other musicians appearing on the album include Tommy Denander, Pontus Norgren (*Hammerfall, Great King Rat, Talisman* etc.) and Rickard Hux Flux Netterman (*Plankton*). A second album, tentatively named *Impressions*, is being recorded. The album also features a cover of *Derek And The Dominoes*' monster hit *Layla*. *Impulsia* play high-class AOR/melodic hard rock, a great album well worth checking out. Live, the band features Zalle Salbert on bass, Marika Willstedt on keyboards, Thomas Broman on drums and Tommy Denander on guitar.

| 2009 | ■ | EXPRESSIONS | CD | Riverside | RRCD 133 |

2009 CD - RRCD 133

IN AETERNUM

David "Impious" Larsson: v/g/b, Per "Perra" Karlsson: d

Sandviken - Formed as the duo *Behemoth* already in 1992. They recorded the demos *Domini Inferi* and *The Ancient Kingdom* the year after, before changing their name to *In Aeternum*. The first release was recorded as a duo with David and Paul Mäkitalo (*Infernal, Dark Funeral*). On the first album Paul was out and besides David, there was drummer Paul Johansson (*Sorcery*), bassist Mats Eldblom and drummer Joacim Olofsson. The band went through several line-up changes leaving David as the only remaining member. Black metal with influences from the 80s death/speed/thrash/black metal scene. *Forever Blasphemy* is produced by Fredrik Nordström. David is also found in *Infernal/WAR*. *Past And Present Sins* is a compilation featuring live tracks, covers and old tracks. Guitarist John Falk (*Sorcery*) was briefly in the band. In 2004 drummer Per "Perra" Karlsson (*Nominon, Serpent, Altar, Bergraven* etc) joined. The *No Salvation* MCD features three new tracks and a cover of *Grotesque*'s *Blood Runs From The Altar*, which was initially recorded for the *At The Gates* tribute CD *Slaughterous Souls*. The band was also sued by Mel Gibson for using images from the movie *The Passion Of The Christ* without permission. In 2005 bass-player Claes "Clabbe" Ramberg (*Thronaeon, Godhate, Abhoth*) joined and the year after guitarist Erik Kumpulainen replaced Daniel N Sahlin. The band has also participated on *A Tribute For King Diamond* and *Tyrants From The Abyss – A Tribute To Morbid Angel*. *In Aeternum* plas highly accomplished and technical blast-beat-ridden riff-oriented black metal. A new album was said to be recorded for 2008, but still hasn't been released.
Website: www.inaeternum.com

1998 MCD - FTDP 002

1999 CD - NR 038

1998	■	And Darkness Came	MCD 4tr	From The Darkness Productions	FTDP 002
		Tracks: And Darkness Came/Spawned To Crush/Witches Spell/The Arrival Of The Horde			
1999	☐	FOREVER BLASPHEMY	LP	Merciless Records	M.R SRLP 010
1999	■	FOREVER BLASPHEMY	CD	Necropolis Records	NR 038
1999	☐	Demon Possession/Hellion	7" PD	Metal Supremacy	MS 001
		500 copies. Hellion is a W.A.S.P cover.			
2000	☐	THE PESTILENT PLAGUE	CD	Necropolis Records	NR 052
2000	☐	THE PESTILENT PLAGUE	LPg	Merciless Records	M.R.SRLP 022
2000	☐	THE PESTILENT PLAGUE	LP PD	Merciless Records	M.R.SRPLP 022
2000	☐	THE PESTILENT PLAGUE	LPg	Necropolis Records	NR 052 LP

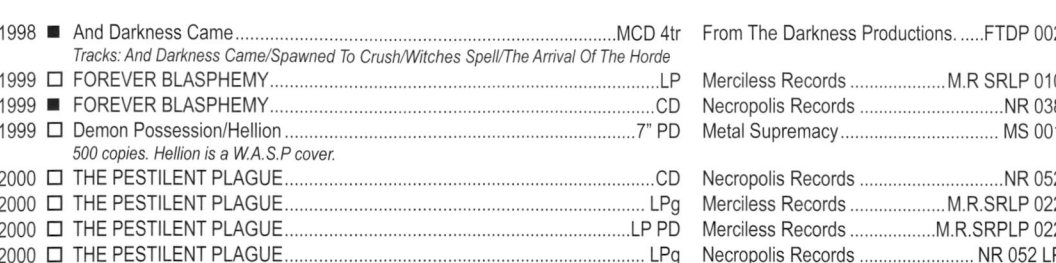

2000 LP PD - NR 052 P

2000 ■	THE PESTILENT PLAGUE	LP PD	Necropolis Records	NR 052 P
2001 ☐	PAST AND PRESENT SINS	CD	Necropolis Records	NR 059
2003 ☐	NUCLEAR ARMAGEDDON	CD	Agonia Records	Arcd 001
2003 ☐	Beast Of The Pentagram	10" 6tr	Supreme Chaos	SCR-VL006

Tracks: Beast Of The Pentagram/Black Funeral/Satanic Lust/By Thy Command/Tormentor (Kreator)/Hades. 333 hand-numbered copies.

2004 ☐	By Thy Command/Tormentor	7" PD	Bloodstone	Blood006

500 copies.

2004 ☐	No Salvation	MCD 4tr	Agonia Records	Armcd 004

Tracks: Poison The Holy/No Salvation/Blood Runs From The Altar (Grotesque cover)/East Of The Pentagram

2005 ☐	DAWN OF A NEW AEON	CD	Agonia Records	Arcd 026
2007 ☐	Curse Of Devastation	MCD 4tr	Pulverised	ASH 027 MCD

Tracks: Curse Of Devastation/Consume/New World Filth/Reaper In Black 2006

2007 ■	Curse Of Devastation/New World Filth	7" 4tr	Blood Harvest	- -

2007 7" - - -

IN BATTLE

John "Fröléti" Frölen: g/b, Otto Wiklund: d

Sundsvall - In 1996, Frölen, John Östlund and Otto Wiklund from **Odhinn** joined forces with Håkan "Mysteriis" Sjödin from **Setherial** and formed **In Battle**. The debut was recorded at Sunlight Studios by Fred Estby and Tomas Skogsberg. Just before the second release Sjödin and Östlund were relieved of their duties. In 1999 the band went through a vast line-up change. *Soul Metamorposis* featured Frölén, singer John Odhinn Sandin (**Odhinn, Valkyria, Horde Of Hel**), guitarist Hasse Karlsson (**Diabolical, Odhinn, Horde Of Hel**), bass player Marcus Edvardsson (**Sanctification, Souldrainer, Chasticement, Endless Torture, Aeon**) and drummer Nils Fjellström (**Dark Funeral, Odhinn, A*Teem, The Wretched End, Aeon, Chastisement, Sanctification, Souldrainer**). *Welcome To The Battlefield* features a guest solo from producer Erik Rutan (**Hate Eternal, Morbid Angel**). Viking-influenced, thrashy, fast and extreme death-oriented metal with hints of **Behemoth** and **Setherial**. August 13, 2006, Otto Wiklund sadly took his own life.

2003 MCD - IDR 001

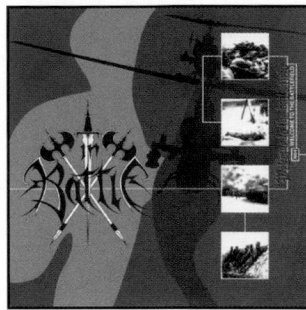

2004 CD - 3984-14504-2

1997 ☐	IN BATTLE	CD	Napalm Records	NPR 031
1998 ☐	THE RAGE OF THE NORTHMEN	CD	Napalm Records	NPR 050
2003 ■	Soul Metamorphosis	MCD 4tr	Imperial Dawn	IDR 001

Tracks: Pioneers Of A Dead Future/Dawn Of Darkness/Soul Metamorphosis/King God

2004 ■	WELCOME TO THE BATTLEFIELD	CD	Metal Blade	3984-14504-2
2004 ☐	WELCOME TO THE BATTLEFIELD	LP	Animate	50239

666 hand numbered copies.

2007 ■	KINGDOM OF FEAR	CD	Candlelight	CANDLE 153 CD
2007 ☐	KINGDOM OF FEAR	CD	Candlelight (USA)	CDLO320 CD

2007 CD - CANDLE 153 CD

IN BLACK

Rikard Larsson: v, Mattias Göransson: g, Anders Nyander: g,
Håkan Nyander: b, Johans Rydberg: d

Kristianstad - **In Black** rose out of the ashes of **Sanzia**. Rikard is ex-**Mercy**, **Magica** and **Supreme Majesty**. *True Darkness* is a nice slab of heavy rock/metal with a touch of vintage **Savatage** meets **Jag Panzer** or Swedish colleagues **Destiny**.

2000 ■	True Darkness	MCD 4tr	private	IBCD 01

Tracks: I'm Charmed/True Darkness/Inside/Born In Sin

2000 MCD - IBCD 01

IN FLAMES

Anders Fridén: v, Niclas Engelin: g, Björn Gelotte: g,
Peter Iwers: b, Daniel Svensson: d

Göteborg/Västra Frölunda - In the first encyclopedia, from 1996 I wrote "*This band mixes traditional death metal with guitar playing a'la early Iron Maiden, folk music and influences from Paradise Lost. Quite innovative.*" Since then this has been labelled "*The Gothenburg sound*". **In Flames** was formed in 1990, when former **Ceremonial Oath** member Jesper Strömblad decided to form a new band. He drafted Johan Larsson and Glenn Ljungström, recorded a demo and was soon signed by Wrong Again Records. The line-up on the first album was Jesper (g/d), Johan Larsson (b), Glenn Ljungström (g), Carl Näslund (g) and Mikael Stanne (v), where the two latter were only hired hands. When *Subterranean* was recorded the line-up featured Jesper, Johan, Glenn and drummer Daniel Erlandsson (ex-**Eucharist, The*End**). Mikael Stanne, singer on the debut concentrated on his other project **Dark Tranquillity** and session singer Henke Fors, originally in **Dawn**, was hired to do the album. At the time Jesper also had a side project together with Niklas Sundin (**Dark Tranquillity**) called **De Vittfarne**, an out-and-out folk music band. Just before the release of *Subterranean* singer Anders Fridén (**Dark Tranquillity, Ceremonial Oath**) joined and Björn Gelotte replaced Daniel Erlandsson. In 1997, during the recording of *Whoracle*, Johan Larsson and Glenn Ljugström decided to leave the band. They drafted bass player Peter Iwers and guitarist Niclas Engelin to finish the album, but they soon became full

1994 CD - WAR 003

1994 MCD - WAR 006

Fire, walk with us!

members. After some touring Engelin decided to leave to focus on his other band **Gardenian**. Before *Colony*, drummer Björn Gelotte switched from being the band's drummer to playing guitar and thus replaced Glenn Ljungström. Daniel Svensson of **Sacrilege** became the band's drummer. Jesper (on bass), Anders and Björn were also found on the debut album by **Sinergy**. On the 2000 tours Dick Löwgren temporarily replaced Iwers, who had just become a father. After a short break during 2001, the band returned with *Reroute To Remain,* and a slightly re-furbished sound, where the addition of synths became more evident. This change continued on the follow-up album *Soundtrack To Your Escape.* The popularity started growing and the band was invited to play *Ozzfest.* The live CD/DVD *Used And Abused... In Live We Trust* featured recordings from Hammersmith Odeon in London and Sticky Fingers in Göteborg. In 2006 the band released their most successful album so far, *Come Clarity*, which peaked at number 1 in the Swedish chart. The fall of 2006 saw the band as part of the tour package *The Unholy Alliance* together with **Slayer**, **Lamb Of God**, **Children Of Bodom** and **Thine Eyes Bleed**. During the tour guitarist Strömblad decided to take a break and Engelin returned to help out. Gelotte was also temporarily replaced by Henrik Danhage (**Evergrey, Deathdestruction**) on tour. In 2008 the album *A Sense Of Purpose* saw the light of day and the band entered the *Gigantour* tour package together with **Megadeth**, **Children Of Bodom** and **High On Fire**. The band toured extensively and in 2009 Strömblad took a time-out to tend to his excessive drinking, temporarily replaced by old friend Engelin. In February 2010 Strömberg made public that he was leaving the band permanently to tend to his problems. Engelin became a permanent replacement, making his debut on the 2011 album *Sounds Of A Fading Playground*, where the melodic side had been taken yet another step, with the vocals being give some clean touches here and there.

In Flames have also recorded the song *Eye Of The Beholder* for the **Metallica** tribute *Metal Militia* (94 Black Sun), then with the aid of **Ancient Slumber**'s singer Robert Dahne. On *Lunar Strain* the band does a great cover of the old Swedish folk song *Hårgalåten* (also recorded by **Kebnekajse**). On *Power From The North* a killing version of **Treat**'s old AOR-song *World Of Fantasy* can be found. Another rare track is *Come Clarity (Remix)*, found on *Sounds From The Underground 2006 – Live & Rare* compilation (2006 SFU).
Website: www.inflames.com

In the days of black and white

1994 ■	LUNAR STRAIN	CD	Wrong Again Records	WAR 003
1994 ■	Subterranean	MCD 5tr	Wrong Again Records	WAR 006

Tracks: Stand Ablaze/Ever Dying/Subterranean/Timeless/Biosphere

1995 ☐	LUNAR STRAIN	CD	Toys Factory (Japan)	TFCK 88737

Bonus: Stand Ablaze/Ever Dying/Subterranean/Timeless/Biosphere/Eye Of The Beholder. Available with various OBIs.

1995 ☐	LUNAR STRAIN	CD	Toys Factory (Japan)	TFCK 87310

Second version. Bonus: In Flames (demo)/Upon An Oaken Tree (demo)/Acoustic Piece(demo)/Clad In Shadows (demo)

1995 ☐	LUNAR STRAIN	CD	Candlelight (USA)	CDLO 218 CD
1996 ■	THE JESTER'S RACE	CD	Nuclear Blast	NB 168-2
1996 ☐	THE JESTER'S RACE	LP PD	Nuclear Blast	NB 168-1
1996 ☐	THE JESTER'S RACE	CD	Nuclear Blast America (USA)	6168-2
1996 ☐	THE JESTER'S RACE	CD	Toy's Factory (Japan)	TFCK 88777

1996 CD - NB 168-2

Bonus: Dead Eternity (demo)/The Inborn Lifeless (demo). Different artwork.

1996 ☐	THE JESTER'S RACE + BLACK-ASH INHERITANCE	CD	Platinum Marketing (Thailand)	NB 616-2
1997 ☐	Black Ash Inheritance	MCD shaped 5tr	Nuclear Blast	NB 251-2 $

Tracks: Goliaths Disarm Their Davids/Gyroscope/Acoustic Medley/Behind Space (live)

1997 ☐	Black Ash Inheritance	MCD 5tr	Nuclear Blast	NB 251-2

Same as the above, but a rare version, without cut out shape.

1997 ☐	Black Ash Inheritance	MCD shaped 5tr	Nuclear Blast America	NBA 6251-2
1997 ☐	THE JESTER'S RACE	CD	Nuclear Blast America (USA)	6168-2

Re-issue with different address.

1997 ■	WHORACLE	CD	Nuclear Blast	NB 284-2
1997 ☐	WHORACLE	LP	Nuclear Blast	NB 284-1

Bonus: Re-cycles (same song as Acoustic Medley on Black-Ash Inheritance)

1997 ☐	WHORACLE	CD	Nuclear Blast America	NBA 6284-2
1997 ☐	WHORACLE	CD	Toy's Factory (Japan)	TFCK-87134

Bonus: Goliath Disarm Their Davids/Acostic Medley/Behind Space (live)

1997 ☐	WHORACLE	CD	Platinum Marketing (Thailand)	NB 284-2
1997 ☐	WHORACLE	CD	Nuclear Blast America (USA)	NBA 6284-2
1999 ☐	SUBTERRANEAN	LP	Regain Records	RR LP002

1997 CD - NB 284-2

Bonus: In Flames/Upon An Oaken Throne/Clad In Shadows. 1000 copies.

1999 ☐	SUBTERRANEAN	LP PD	Regain Records	RRP LP002

1000 copies.

1999 ■	COLONY	CD	Nuclear Blast	NB 399-2
1999 ☐	COLONY	2CD	Nuclear Blast	NB 399-2

Bonus CD "Dr. Blast's Top 20".

1999 ☐	COLONY	CD	Toy's Factory (Japan)	TFCK 87185

Bonus: Clad In Shadows '99/Man Made God. Slipcase, sticker, OBI-sticker. 2nd press without slipcase and with OBI.

1999 ☐	COLONY	CDd	Pony Canyon (Korea)	PCKD-20009

Bonus: Clad In Shadows '99/Man Made God

1999 ☐	COLONY	LP PD	Nuclear Blast	NB 399-1

1999 CD - NB 399-2

Year		Title	Format	Label	Catalog
1999	■	LUNAR STRAIN	LP	Regain Records	RRLP 001
1999	□	LUNAR STRAIN	LP PD	Regain Records	RRPLP 001

1000 copies.

| 1999 | □ | LUNARSTRAIN/SUBTERRANEAN | CD | Regain Records | RR9910-005 |

Released in two versions with different artwork, one original and one with the artwork from the Japanese version of The Jester's Race.

1999	□	LUNARSTRAIN/SUBTERRANEAN	LP	Regain Records	RRLP9910-005
1999	□	LUNARSTRAIN/SUBTERRANEAN	LP PD	Regain Records	RRPLP 005
2000	□	CLAYMAN	CD	Nuclear Blast	NB 499-2

First press with 3D cover. Bonus: World Of Promises (Treat cover)

| 2000 | ■ | CLAYMAN | CD | Nuclear Blast | NB 499-2 |

Second press.

| 2000 | □ | CLAYMAN | CD shaped | Nuclear Blast | NB 499-8 |

1000. Sawblade shaded.

2000	□	CLAYMAN	CD	Nuclear Blast America (USA)	NBA 6499-2
2000	□	CLAYMAN	LP PD	Nuclear Blast	NB 499-1
2000	□	CLAYMAN	CD	Toy's Factory (Japan)	TFCK 87214

Bonus: Strong And Smart. First press with slipcase, family tree and, sticker OBI. Second press without slipcase and with normal OBI.

| 2000 | □ | CLAYMAN | CD | Irond (Russia) | CD 00-15 |

Bonus: World Of Promises (Treat cover)

| 2000 | □ | CLAYMAN | CD | Magnum Music (Taiwan) | TFCK 87214 |

Bonus: Strong And Smart. First press.

| 2000 | □ | CLAYMAN | CD | Magnum Music (Taiwan) | NB 2207-2 |

Bonus: Strong And Smart. Second press.

| 2001 | □ | COLONY | CD | Irond (Russia) | CD 01-11 |

Bonus: Goliath Disarm Their Davids/Acoustic Medley/Behind Space (live)

| 2001 | □ | COLONY | CD | Nems (Argentina) | NEMS 353 |

Bonus: Man Made God

| 2001 | ■ | Bullet Ride/Ordinary Story/Episode 666 | MCD 3tr | Nuclear Blast (USA) | NBA 6499-0 |

Promo compilation.

| 2001 | □ | WHORACLE | CD | Irond (Russia) | CD 01-68 |

Bonus: Clad In Shadows '99/Smart & Strong

| 2001 | □ | THE TOKYO SHOWDOWN – LIVE IN JAPAN 2000 | CDd | Nuclear Blast | NB 636-2 |

Second press in jewelcase.

| 2001 | □ | THE TOKYO SHOWDOWN – LIVE IN JAPAN 2000 | 2LP | Nuclear Blast | NBA 636-1 |

White vinyl.

| 2001 | □ | THE TOKYO SHOWDOWN – LIVE IN JAPAN 2000 | CDd | Nuclear Blast America | NBA 6636-2D |
| 2001 | □ | THE TOKYO SHOWDOWN – LIVE IN JAPAN 2000 | CD | Nuclear Blast America | NBA 6636-2 |

Bonus: Clad In Shadows '99/Strong And Smart/Behind Space (live)/Goliaths Disarm Their Davids. Second press in jewel case.

| 2001 | □ | THE TOKYO SHOWDOWN – LIVE IN JAPAN 2000 | 2LP | Nuclear Blast America | NBA 6636-1 |

Bonus: Clad In Shadows '99/Strong And Smart/Behind Space (live)/Goliaths Disarm Their Davids. White vinyl.

2001	□	THE TOKYO SHOWDOWN – LIVE IN JAPAN 2000	CD	Toy's Factory (Jap)	TFCK 87255
2001	□	THE TOKYO SHOWDOWN – LIVE IN JAPAN 2000	CD	Platinum Marketing (Thailand)	TFCK 87255
2001	□	THE TOKYO SHOWDOWN – LIVE IN JAPAN 2000	CD	Magnum Marketing (Taiwan)	TFCK 87255
2001	□	THE TOKYO SHOWDOWN – LIVE IN JAPAN 2000	CD	Platinum Marketing (Thailand)	NB 636-2
2001	□	THE TOKYO SHOWDOWN – LIVE IN JAPAN 2000	CD	Irond (Russia)	CD 01-78
2001	□	THE TOKYO SHOWDOWN – LIVE IN JAPAN 2000	2CDd	Scarecrow (Mexico)	SC02041

Bonus: Clad In Shadows '99/Strong And Smart/Behind Space (live)/Goliaths Disarm Their Davids.

| 2001 | □ | THE TOKYO SHOWDOWN – LIVE IN JAPAN 2000 | CD | Dream On (Korea) | Park 9008 |

With puzzle.

| 2001 | □ | THE TOKYO SHOWDOWN – LIVE IN JAPAN 2000 | CD | Nuclear Blast (Brazil) | 55636-2 |

Bonus: The Inborn Lifeless (demo)

2001	□	THE JESTER'S RACE	CD	Irond (Russia)	CD 01-128
2002	□	THE JESTER'S RACE/BLACK ASH INHERITANCE	CDd	Nuclear Blast	NB 616-2
2002	□	THE JESTER'S RACE/BLACK ASH INHERITANCE	CD	Nuclear Blast America (USA)	6616-2
2002	□	THE JESTER'S RACE/BLACK ASH INHERITANCE	CD	Nuclear Blast (Brazil)	55616-2
2002	□	THE JESTER'S RACE/BLACK ASH INHERITANCE - DELUXE	CD	Scareceow (Mexico)	WOE005

Different artwork with border.

| 2002 | ■ | WHORACLE – DELUXE EDITION | CD | Nuclear Blast | NB 1063-2 |

Bonus: Clad In Shadows '99. Different artwork with border.

2002	□	WHORACLE – DELUXE EDITION	CD	Rock Brigade (Brazil)	NBR 0019
2002	□	WHORACLE – DELUXE EDITION	CD	Scarecrow (Mexico)	WOE 006
2002	□	WHORACLE	CD	Nems (Argentina)	NEMS 351

Bonus: Clad In Shadows '99

| 2002 | □ | CLAYMAN | CD | Scarecrow (Mexico) | WOE 024 |

Bonus: World Of Promises (Treat cover) + screensavers.

| 2002 | □ | Reroute To Remain – 4 Track Teaser | MCD 4tr | Nuclear Blast | NB 1058-2 |

Tracks: Cloud Connected/System/Reroute To Remain/Dawn Of A New Day. Also available as cardboard promo.

| 2002 | ■ | In Flames/Meshuggah (split) | MCD 4tr | Nuclear Blast (USA) | - - |

Promo split with Meshuggah. Tracks: Reroute To Remain/Cloud Connected

| 2002 | □ | REROUTE TO REMAIN | CD | Rock Brigade (Brazil) | NBR 0041 |

1999 LP - RRLP 001

2000 CD - NB 499-2

2001 MCD - NBA 6499-0

2002 CD - NB 1063-2

2002 MCD - - -

2002 ☐ REROUTE TO REMAIN	CD	Nuclear Blast (Brazil)	55624-2
2002 ☐ REROUTE TO REMAIN	CD	Magnum Music (Taiwan)	NB 624-2
2002 ☐ REROUTE TO REMAIN	CD	Toy's Factory (Japan)	TFCK-87289

Bonus: Colony (live). First pressing has slipcase, 6 postcards and sticker-OBI.

2002 ■ REROUTE TO REMAIN	CD	Nuclear Blast	NB 624-2

On first press sub-title says Fourteen Songs Of Conscious Madness, instead of Insanity.

2002 ☐ REROUTE TO REMAIN	CD	Nuclear Blast	NB 624-2

Slimbox promo.

2002 ☐ REROUTE TO REMAIN	CD	Nuclear Blast	NB 624-2
2002 ☐ REROUTE TO REMAIN	CDd	Nuclear Blast	NB 624-0

Different artwork

2002 ☐ REROUTE TO REMAIN	LP	Nuclear Blast	NB 624-1
2002 ☐ REROUTE TO REMAIN	LP PD	Nuclear Blast	NB 624-9

Different artwork.

2002 CD - NB 624-2

2002 ☐ REROUTE TO REMAIN	CD	Nuclear Blast (USA)	NB 6624-2

Different artwork with black border. Second press has normal artwork.

2002 ☐ REROUTE TO REMAIN	CD	Irond (Russia)	CD 02-315
2002 ☐ REROUTE TO REMAIN	CDd	Dream On (Korea)	Park 9019

Second press has jewel case.

2002 ■ Cloud Connected/Colony (live)	CDS	Nuclear Blast	NB 1083-2
2003 ☐ COLONY	CD	Moon Records (Ukraine)	MNCD-306-2
2003 ☐ CLAYMAN	CD	Moon Records (Ukraine)	MNCD-307-2
2003 ☐ REROUTE TO REMAIN	CD	Moon Records (Ukraine)	MNCD-308-2
2003 ☐ THE JESTER'S RACE	CD	Moon Records (Ukraine)	MNCD-309-2
2003 ☐ WHORACLE	CD	Moon Records (Ukraine)	MNCD-310-2

Bonus: Clad In Shadows '99/Strong & Smart

2003 ☐ Trigger	MCD 5tr	Nuclear Blast	NB 1130-2

Tracks: Trigger (Single Edit)/Watch Them Feed/Land Of Confusion (Genesis cover)/Cloud Connected (Club Connected Remix)/Moonshield (C64 Karaoke Version) + Trigger (video)/Cloud Connected (video)

2002 CDS - NB 1083-2

2003 ☐ Trigger	MCD 5tr	Nuclear Blast (USA)	NB 1130-2
2003 ■ Trigger	10" 5tr	Nuclear Blast	NB 1130-1

Tracks: Trigger (Single Edit)/Watch Them Feed/Land Of Confusion/Cloud Connected (Club Connected Remix)/Moonshield (C64 Karaoke Version). Some copies also had a two track DVD (NB 1142-0) as bonus.

2003 ☐ Trigger	MCD 5tr	Irond (Russia)	03-587
2003 ☐ Trigger	MCD 5tr	Dream On (Korea)	Park 9030
2003 ☐ Trigger	MCDd+DVD	Nuclear Blast	NB 1130-0

Tracks: Trigger (Single Edit)/Watch Them Feed/Land Of Confusion (Genesis cover)/Cloud Connected (Club Connected Remix)/Moonshield (C64 Karaoke Version). On DVD: Trigger (video)/Cloud Connected (video)/Only For The Weak (video)

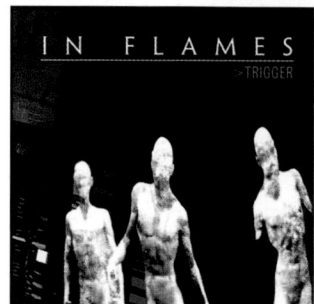

2003 ☐ Trigger	MCDd+DVD	Toy's Factory (Japan)	TFCK-87320
2004 ☐ Soundtrack To Your Escape – Media Market Teaser	MCD 5tr	Nuclear Blast	NB 1288-2

Tracks: The Quiet Place/Borders And Shading/Touch Of Red/In Search For I/My Sweet Shadow. Plus one track each by Mnemic, Raunchy and Ektomorf. Promo..

2003 10" - NB 1130-1

2004 ■ Soundtrack To Your Escape (split)	MCD	Nuclear Blast America	- -

Tracks: The Quiet Place/In Search For I. Split with Mnemic, Raunchy and Ektomorf.

2004 ☐ SOUNDTRACK TO YOUR ESCAPE	CD	Nuclear Blast	NB 1231-2
2004 ☐ SOUNDTRACK TO YOUR ESCAPE	CD	Magnum Music (Taiwan)	NB 1231-2
2004 ☐ SOUNDTRACK TO YOUR ESCAPE	CD	Nuclear Blast (Brazil)	7520019-1

Bonus: Watch Them Feed/Land Of Confusion (Genesis cover)

2004 ☐ SOUNDTRACK TO YOUR ESCAPE	CD	Platinum Marketing (Thailand)	NB 1231-2
2004 ☐ SOUNDTRACK TO YOUR ESCAPE	CD	Nuclear Blast (USA)	NB 1231-2
2004 ☐ SOUNDTRACK TO YOUR ESCAPE	CDd+DVD	Nuclear Blast (USA)	NB 1231-2

Alternate artwork. Bonus DVD feat videos, live and the making of.

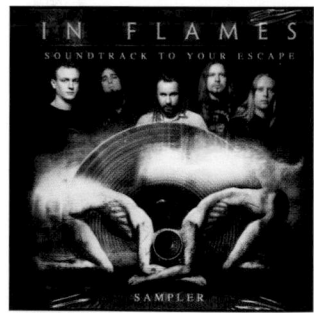

2004 ■ SOUNDTRACK TO YOUR ESCAPE	CDd	Nuclear Blast	NB 1231-0

Alternate artwork. Bonus: Discover Me Like Emptiness

2004 ☐ SOUNDTRACK TO YOUR ESCAPE	CDd+DVD	Nuclear Blast	NB 1231-5

Alternate artwork. DVD: live, videos, the making of.

2004 ☐ SOUNDTRACK TO YOUR ESCAPE	CDd+DVD	Dream On (Korea)	PARK 9040

Bonus: Discover Me Like Emptiness/Clayman (live) + DVD

2004 MCD - - -

2004 ☐ SOUNDTRACK TO YOUR ESCAPE	CDd	Dream On (Korea)	PARK 9041

Bonus: Discover Me Like Emptiness/Clayman (live)

2004 ☐ SOUNDTRACK TO YOUR ESCAPE MAILORDER EDITION	CD+DVD box	Nuclear Blast	NB 1231-5

1000 copies, mailorder version. Bonus: Discover Me Like Emptiness/Clayman (live). DVD Live in Korea 2002.

2004 ☐ SOUNDTRACK TO YOUR ESCAPE	LP	Nuclear Blast	NB 1231-1
2004 ☐ SOUNDTRACK TO YOUR ESCAPE	LP PD	Nuclear Blast	NB 1231-1
2004 ☐ SOUNDTRACK TO YOUR ESCAPE	CDd	Nuclear Blast	NB 1279-2

Bonus: Discover Me Like Emptiness. Different artwork.

2004 ☐ SOUNDTRACK TO YOUR ESCAPE	CD	Icarus (Argentina)	ICARUS 62
2004 ☐ SOUNDTRACK TO YOUR ESCAPE	CD	Irond (Russia)	CD 04-773
2004 ☐ SOUNDTRACK TO YOUR ESCAPE	CD	Toy's Factory (Japan)	TFCK-87346

Bonus: Clayman (live). Slipcase + mouse pad. OBI-sticker. Second press without slipcase.

2004 ☐ SOUNDTRACK TO YOUR ESCAPE	CD	Platinum Marketing (Thailand)	NB 1231-2

2004 CDd - NB 1231-0

Year		Title	Format	Label	Catalog
2004	☐	SOUNDTRACK TO YOUR ESCAPE	CD	Magnum Music (Taiwan)	NB 1231-2
2004	☐	SOUNDTRACK TO YOUR ESCAPE	CD	Nuclear Blast (Brazil)	7520019-1

Bonus: Watch Them Feed/Land Of Confusion

2004 MCD - NB 1272-2

2004	☐	SUBTERRANEAN	CD	Toy's Factory (Japan)	TFCK-87311

Remastered, alt artwork. Bonus: Dead Eternity/The Inborn Lifeless/Murders In The Rue Morgue (Iron Maiden cover)/Eye Of The Beholder (Metallica cover)

2004	☐	SUBTERRANEAN	CD	Regain Records	RR 0304-024
2004	☐	SUBTERRANEAN	CDd	Regain Records	RR 176

Different artwork.

2004	☐	SUBTERRANEAN	CD	Regain America (USA)	REG CD 1071
2004	☐	SUBTERRANEAN	CD	Candlelight (USA)	CDL 0218 CD
2004	☐	SUBTERRANEAN	CD	Irond (Russia)	CD 04-936
2004	■	The Quiet Place	MCD 3tr	Nuclear Blast	NB 1272-2

Tracks: The Quiet Place/Borders And Shading/Touch Of Red. Promotional Club & Radio single. Slimcase.

2004	■	The Quiet Place	MCD 3tr	Nuclear Blast	NB 1249-2

Tracks: The Quiet Place/My Sweet Shadow (remix)/Värmlandsvisan (live) + The Quiet Place (video)/Session video

2004 MCD - NB 1249-2

2004	☐	The Quiet Place	MCD 3tr	Irond (Russia)	CD 04-774
2004	■	The Quiet Place	CDS	Nuclear Blast America (USA)	NB PRO-011
2004	☐	COLONY – DELUXE EDITION	CD	Nuclear Blast	NB 1116-2

Bonus: Man Made God. Different artwork with border.

2004	☐	COLONY – DELUXE EDITION	CD	Nuclear Blast	NBA 6399-2
2004	☐	COLONY – DELUXE EDITION	CD	Rock Brigade (Brazil)	NBR 0026
2004	☐	COLONY – DELUXE EDITION	CD	Scarecrow (Mexico)	WOE 007
2005	☐	SOUNTRACK TO YOUR ESCAPE	CD	Moon Records (Ukraine)	MR 1066-2
2005	☐	USED AND ABUSED... IN LIVE WE TRUST	2CDd	Irond (Russia)	CD 05-1034
2005	☐	USED AND ABUSED... IN LIVE WE TRUST	2CD	Moon Records (Ukraine)	MR 1846-2
2005	☐	USED AND ABUSED... IN LIVE WE TRUST	2CD	Rock Empire (Taiwan)	MMMF 2332
2005	☐	USED AND ABUSED... IN LIVE WE TRUST	2CD+DVD	Dream On (Korea)	Park 9057
2005	☐	USED AND ABUSED... IN LIVE WE TRUST	2CD+DVD	Rock Brigade (Brazil)	NBR 0030
2005	☐	USED AND ABUSED... IN LIVE WE TRUST	2CD+DVD	Toy's Factory (Japan)	TFCK-87392
2005	☐	USED AND ABUSED... IN LIVE WE TRUST	2CD+DVD	Nuclear Blast	NB 661-5
2005	☐	USED AND ABUSED... IN LIVE WE TRUST	2CD+DVD	Rock Empire (Taiwan)	NB 6661-0
2005	☐	LUNAR STRAIN	CD	Regain Records	RR 0304-023

Bonus: In Flames (93 promo)/Upon An Oaken Throne (93 promo)/Acoustic Piece (93 promo)/Clad In Shadows (93 promo)

2004 MCD - NB PRO-011

2005	☐	LUNAR STRAIN	CDd	Regain Records	RR 175

Different artwork. Bonus: In Flames (93 promo)/Upon An Oaken Throne (93 promo)/Acoustic Piece (93 promo)/Clad In Shadows (93 promo). With pin, poster and patch. 3000 copies.

2005	☐	LUNAR STRAIN	CD	Irond (Russia)	CD 04-935
2005	☐	LUNAR STRAIN	CD	Candlelight (USA)	Canus 0218 CD

Different artwork. Bonus: In Flames/Upon An Oaken Throne/Acoustic Piece/Clad In Shadows

2005	☐	LUNAR STRAIN	CD	Dream On (Korea)	Park 9002

Different artwork. Bonus: Dead Eternity/The Inborn Lifeless/Murders In The Rue Morgue (Iron Maiden cover)/Eye Of The Beholder (Metallica cover)

2005	■	CLAYMAN – DELUXE EDITION	CD	Nuclear Blast	NB 1503-2

Bonus: Strong And Smart/World Of Promises (Treat cover). Different artwork with border.

2005 CD - NB 1503-2

2005	☐	CLAYMAN – DELUXE EDITION	CD	Nuclear Blast America (USA)	NB 6499-2
2005	☐	CLAYMAN – DELUXE EDITION	CD	Rock Brigade (Brazil)	NBR 0060
2005	☐	WHORACLE	CD	Nems (Argentina)	NEMS 351

Bonus: Clad In Shadows '99 + enhanced. Different back cover.

2005	☐	COLONY	CD	Icarus (Argentina)	Icarus 509

Bonus: Man Made God + enhanced part.

2006	☐	THE JESTER'S RACE	CD	Dream On (Kores)	43342-1

2nd press hass different artwork on back.

2006	☐	WHORACLE	CD	Dream On (Korea)	43342-2

Bonus: Goliaths Disarm Their Davids/Acoustic Medley/Food For The Gods (live)

2006	☐	COLONY	CDd	Dream On (Korea)	Park 9033

Bonus: Clad In Shadows '99/Man Made God/Murders In The Rue Morgue (Iron Maiden cover). Second press in jewel case.

2006	☐	CLAYMAN	CDd	Dream On (Korea)	Park 9034

Bonus: Strong And Smart. Second press in jewel case.

2006	☐	CLAYMAN	2CD	Dream On (Korea)	DOR 43346-1

Bonus: Strong And Smart. First press in slipcase.

2006	☐	CLAYMAN	2CD	Dream On (Korea)	DOR 43346-2
2006	☐	WHORACLE	CD	Nuclear Blast	NB 284-2

Repress with slightly different insert and smaller CD-print.

2006	☐	Take This Life/Leeches	CDS	Nuclear Blast	NB 1597-2

Radio promo.

2006	■	Come Clarity - EP	CDS	Nuclear Blast	NB 1765-2

Tracks: Come Clarity/Only For The Weak. Promo.

2006	☐	Come Clarity - EP	MCD 3tr	Nuclear Blast	NB 1765-2

Tracks: Come Clarity/Only For The Weak/System

2006 CDS - NB 1765-2

Year		Title	Format	Label	Catalog	
2006	□	Come Clarity (remix) .... CDS		Ferret (USA) FPR012-2		
2006	□	Come Clarity/Only For The Weak .... 7"		Black Lodge .... BLOD 7003		
		White vinyl.				
2006	■	COME CLARITY .... CD		Ferret (USA) F062-2ADV		
		Advance promo. Alternate artwork.				
2006	□	COME CLARITY .... CD		Ferret (USA) F062		
		Alternate artwork.				
2006	□	COME CLARITY .... CDd+DVD		Ferret (USA) F962		
		500 copies were also featured in a special promo pack with shirt, patch and the below 7" Take This Life.				
2006	■	Take This Life/Leeches .... 7"		Ferret (USA) .... FPR07-7 $		
		500 copies. Only with special promo pack.				
2006	□	Take This Life/Leeches .... CDS 2tr		Nuclear Blast .... NB 1597-2		
		Club/Radio promo in slim jewel case.				
2006	□	Take This Life (Radio edit) .... CDS 1tr		Ferret (USA) .... FPRO 10-2		
2006	□	COME CLARITY .... CD		Ferret (USA) F962-8		
		Best Buy version.				
2006	□	COME CLARITY .... CD		Nuclear Blast .... NB 1309-2		
		Cardboard promo with different artwork. Missing the track Your Bedtime Story Is Scaring Everyone				
2006	■	COME CLARITY .... CD		Nuclear Blast .... NB 1309-2		
2006	□	COME CLARITY .... CD		Platinum Marketing (Thailand) .... NB 1309-2		
2006	□	COME CLARITY .... LP		Nuclear Blast .... NB 1309-1		
		Clear vinyl.				
2006	□	COME CLARITY .... CDd+DVD		Nuclear Blast .... NB 1309-5		
2006	□	COME CLARITY .... CDd+DVD		Nuclear Blast .... NB 1309-0		
		Same as above but with different number.				
2006	□	COME CLARITY .... LP		Nuclear Blast .... NB 1309-1		
		Clear vinyl.				
2006	□	COME CLARITY – MAIL ORDER EDITION .... CD Box		Nuclear Blast NB 1643-2/1644-2/1645-2/1637-5		
2006	□	COME CLARITY .... CD		Irond (Russia) .... CD 06-1121		
2006	□	COME CLARITY .... CDd+DVD		Irond (Russia) .... CD 06-1121DL		
2006	□	COME CLARITY .... CD		Moon Records (Ukraine) .... MR 1846-2		
2006	□	COME CLARITY .... CD		Rock Brigade (Brazil) .... NBR 0048		
2006	□	COME CLARITY .... CD+DVD		Magnum Music (Taiwan) .... NB 1309-0		
2006	□	COME CLARITY .... CDd+DVD		Toy's Facory (Japan) TFCK-87399		
		First press.				
2006	□	COME CLARITY .... CD		Toy's Facory (Japan) TFCK-87399		
		Second press.				
2006	□	COME CLARITY .... CD		Nems (Argentina) .... NEMS 381		
2006	□	COME CLARITY .... CDd+DVD		Dream On (Korea) .... Park 9060		
		First press with paper doll set.				
2006	□	COME CLARITY .... CD		Clairvoyant (Singapore) .... NB 1309-2		
2006	□	COME CLARITY .... CD		Platinum Marketing (Thailand) .... NB 1309-2		
2006	□	COME CLARITY .... CD		Nuclear Blast (Taiwan) .... NB 1309-0		
2006	□	COME CLARITY .... CD		Rocris Disc (Romania) .... RD 012-01		
2006	□	COME CLARITY .... CD		Hammer Licence (Hungary) .. HMRCD-NB1309		
2007	■	Black Ash Inheritance .... 10" 4tr PD shaped		Night Of The Vinyl Dead .... NIGHT 009 SH		
		Tracks: Goliaths Disarm Their Davids/Gyroscope/Acoustic Medley/Behind Space (live). 555 copies.				
2007	□	Black Ash Inheritance .... MLP 4tr PD		Night Of The Vinyl Dead .... NIGHT 009 SH		
		Tracks: Goliaths Disarm Their Davids/Gyroscope/Acoustic Medley/Behind Space (live). Same as the above, but not cut out. 20 copies including promo package.				
2008	■	The Mirror's Truth .... MCD 4tr		Nuclear Blast .... NB 2084-2		
		Tracks: The Mirror's Truth/Eraser/Tilt/Abnegation				
2008	□	The Mirror's Truth .... CDSp 1tr		Nuclear Blast .... NB 2135-2		
		Cardboard promo.				
2008	□	The Mirror's Truth .... MLPg 4tr		Nuclear Blast .... NB 2084-1		
		Numbered.				
2008	□	The Mirror's Truth .... MLPg 4tr PD		Nuclear Blast .... NB 2084-9		
		Numbered.				
2008	□	The Mirror's Truth .... CDS 1tr		Koch (USA) KOC-D5-4498		
2008	□	The Mirror's Truth .... MCD 4tr		Koch (USA) KOC-D5-4568		
2008	□	The Mirror's Truth .... MCD 4tr		Dream On (Korea) .... Park 9074		
2008	□	The Mirror's Truth .... MCD 4tr		Nuclear Blast (Sweden) 060251763662		
2008	□	LUNAR STRAIN .... CDd		Regain Records (USA) REG-CD-1070		
		Bonus: In Flames (93 promo)/Upon An Oaken Throne (93 promo)/Acoustic Piece (93 promo)/Clad In Shadows (93 promo)				
2008	□	WHORACLE RE-LOADED .... CD		Nuclear Blast .... NB 2205-2		
		Bonus: Clad In Shadows '99 + enhanced track.				
2008	□	WHORACLE RE-LOADED .... CD		Icarus (Argentina) .... Icarus 508		
2008	□	WHORACLE .... CD		Magnum (Taiwan) .... NB 2205-2		
2008	□	COLONY – RE-LOADED .... CD		Nuclear Blast .... NB 2206-2		
		Bonus: Man Made God/Ordinary (story video)				
2008	□	WHORACLE RE-LOADED .... CD		Magnum Music (Taiwan) .... NB 2205-2		
		Bonus: Clad In Shadows				

2006 CD - F062-2ADV

2006 7" - FPR07-7

2006 CD - NB 1309-2

2007 10" - NIGHT 009 SH

2008 MCD - NB 2084-2

Year		Title	Format	Label	Catalog

2008 ☐ CLAYMAN – RE-LOADED ....CD Nuclear Blast ....NB 2207-2
Bonus: World Of Promises (Treat cover)+ screensavers

2008 ☐ CLAYMAN ....CD Icarus (Argentina) ....Icarus 510
Bonus: World Of Promises (Treat cover) + screensavers

2008 ☐ CLAYMAN – RE-LOADED ....CD Magnum Music (Taiwan)..................NB 2207-2
Bonus: World Of Promises (Treat cover) + screensavers

2008 ☐ COLONY – RE-LOADED ....CD Magnum Music (Taiwan)..................NB 2206-2
Bonus: Man Made God/Ordinary (story video)

2008 ☐ A SENSE OF PURPOSE ....CD Toy's Factory (Japan)..................TFCK-87435
Bonus: Eraser/Tilt/Abnegation. First limited edition with poster and slipcase.

2008 ☐ A SENSE OF PURPOSE ....CD+DVD Toy's Factory (Japan)..................TFCK-87462

2008 ☐ A SENSE OF PURPOSE ....CD+DVD Nuclear Blast ....NB 2083-0
Slipcase.

2008 ☐ A SENSE OF PURPOSE ....CD+DVD+game box Nuclear Blast ....NB 2083-5
Labyrinth game edition with certificate. 1500 copies.

2008 ■ A SENSE OF PURPOSE ....LP PD Nuclear Blast ....NB 2083-9

2008 ☐ A SENSE OF PURPOSE ....LP Nuclear Blast ....NB 2083-1

2008 ■ A SENSE OF PURPOSE ....CD Nuclear Blast ....NB 2083-2

2008 ☐ A SENSE OF PURPOSE ....CD Magnum Music (Taiwan)..................NB 2083-2

2008 ☐ A SENSE OF PURPOSE ....CD Platinum Marketing (Thailand).........NB 2083-0

2008 ☐ A SENSE OF PURPOSE ....CD Koch (USA)..............................KOC-CD 4498

2008 ☐ A SENSE OF PURPOSE ....CD Koch (USA)..............................KOC-CD 4499
Clean "edited" version.

2008 LP PD - NB 2083-9

2008 ☐ A SENSE OF PURPOSE ....CD+DVD Koch (USA)..............................KOC-CD 4502
Slipcase with cardboard pullout.

2008 ☐ A SENSE OF PURPOSE ....LP Koch (USA)..............................KOC-LP 4575

2008 ☐ A SENSE OF PURPOSE ....CD Irond (Russia) .... CD 08-1439

2008 ☐ A SENSE OF PURPOSE ....CD+DVD Irond (Russia) ....CD 08-1439 DL

2008 ☐ A SENSE OF PURPOSE ....CD+DVD Dream On (Korea) ....Park 9075

2008 ☐ A SENSE OF PURPOSE ....CD Dream On (Korea) ....Park 9076

2008 ☐ A SENSE OF PURPOSE ....CDd+DVD Scarecrow (Mexico)....................SC08380-2

2008 ☐ A SENSE OF PURPOSE ....CD Scarecrow (Mexico).....................SC08380-0

2008 CD - NB 2083-2

2008 ☐ A SENSE OF PURPOSE ....CD+DVD Icarus (Argentina) ....Icarus 440

2008 ☐ A SENSE OF PURPOSE ....CD Icarus (Argentina) ....Icarus 440

2008 ☐ A SENSE OF PURPOSE ....CD+DVD Rock Brigade (Brazil)......................NBR 0125

2008 ☐ A SENSE OF PURPOSE ....CD CSA (Indonesia)....................CDCR-003.0909

2008 ☐ A SENSE OF PURPOSE ....CD BMG (USA)......................................D173240
Record club re-issue. Identical to Koch release.

2008 ☐ A SENSE OF PURPOSE ....CD Universal Music (Sweden) 060251764620
First press in special jewel case, second in standard jewel case

2008 ☐ A SENSE OF PURPOSE ....CD+DVD Universal Music (Sweden) 060251764619
Slipcase.

2008 ☐ A SENSE OF PURPOSE + THE MIRROR'S TRUTH.............2CD Nuclear Blast ....NB 2255-2
Tour edition. Slipcase.

2008 CDS - NB 2243-2

2008 ☐ THE JESTER'S RACE/BLACK ASH INHERITANCE.....................CD Nuclear Blast ....NB 2204-2

2008 ☐ THE JESTER'S RACE/BLACK ASH INHERITANCE.....................CD Nuclear Blast America (USA)...........NB 2204-2

2008 ☐ THE JESTER'S RACE/BLACK ASH INHERITANCE.....................CD Magnum (Taiwan) ....NB 2204-2

2008 ☐ THE JESTER'S RACE/BLACK ASH INHERITANCE.....................CD Icarus (Argentina) ....Icarus 507

2008 ■ Alias ....CDS 1tr Nucleast Blast...............................NB 2243-2

2008 ☐ Alias ....CDS 1tr Koch (USA)..............................KOC-DS-4499
Different artwork.

2009 ■ Delight And Anger ....CDS 1tr Nucleasr Blast...............................NB 2377-2

2009 ☐ WHORACLE RE-LOADED ....CD Nuclear Blast America (USA)...........NB 2205-2
Bonus: Clad In Shadows '99

2009 ☐ COLONY RE-LOADED..CD Nuclear Blast America (USA)...........NB 2206-2
Bonus: Man Made God + enhanced part

2009 ☐ CLAYMAN RE-LOADED ....CD Nuclear Blast America (USA)...........NB 2207-2
Bonus: World Of Promises (Treat cover) + screensavers

2010 ■ SUBTERRANEAN ....CD box Regain Records ....RR 176
New artwork. Bonus: Dead Eternity/The Inborn Lifeless/Eye of the Beholder (Metallica cover)/Murders In The Rue Morgue (Iron Maiden cover)

2009 CDS - NB 2377-2

2010 ☐ LUNAR STRAIN..2LP Back On Black ....BOBV 187 LP
Bonus: In Flames (93 promo)/Upon An Oaken Throne (93 promo)/Acoustic Piece (93 promo)/Clad In Shadows (93 promo). Blue vinyl.

2010 ☐ SUBTERRANEAN ....LP Back On Black ....BOBV 188 LP
Bonus: Eye of the Beholder/Murders In The Rue Morgue (Iron Maiden cover). Red vinyl.

2010 ☐ LUNAR STRAIN..2CD box Regain Records ....RR 175
Diff artwork. Bonus: In Flames (93 promo version)/Upon An Oaken Throne (93 promo version)/Acoustic Piece (93 promo)/Clad In Shadows (93 promo)

2010 ☐ LUNAR STRAIN..LP Back On Black ....BOBV 187 LP
Bonus: In Flames (93 promo version)/Upon An Oaken Throne (93 promo version)

2010 ☐ THE JESTER'S RACE ....CD Trooper (Japan) XNTE-00024
Bonus: Moonshield (live)/Artifacts Of The Black Rain (live)/Moonshield (C64 Karaoke version)

2010 ☐ WHORACLE ....CD Trooper (Japan) XNTE-00025
Bonus: Goliaths Disarm Their Davids/Jotun (live)/Food For The Gods (live)

2010 CD box - RR 176

2010	☐	COLONY	CD	Trooper (Japan)	XNTE-00026

2010 ☐ COLONY ....CD Trooper (Japan) XNTE-00026
Bonus: Colony (live)/Ordinary Story (live)/Scorn (live)
2010 ☐ COLONY ....CD Fighter Street (Germany) ....FSR 003
2010 ☐ CLAYMAN ....CD Trooper (Japan) XNTE-00027
Bonus: Only For The Weak (live)/Pinball Map (live)//Strong And Smart
2010 ☐ CLAYMAN ....CD Fighter Street (Germany) ....FSR 004
2010 ☐ SOUNDTRACK TO YOUR ESCAPE ....CD Trooper (Japan) XNTE-00029
Bonus: Discover Me Like Emptiness/The Quiet Place (live)/My Sweet Shadow (remix)
2010 ☐ COME CLARITY ....CD Trooper (Japan) XNTE-00030
2010 ☐ A SENSE OF PURPOSE ....CD Trooper (Japan) XNTE-00031
Bonus: Eraser/Abnegation/Alias (remix)
2010 ■ USED AND ABUSED… IN LIVE WE TRUST ....2CD+2DVD CDNET Records (Taiwan)................NB6661-0

2010 2CD+2DVD - NB6661-0

2011 ☐ Deliver Us ....CDS 1tr Century Media/EMI (UK)..........................- -
Promo.
2011 ■ Deliver Us (Radio Edit)Deliver Us (Album Version) ....CDS 2tr Century Media ....- -
Promo.
2011 ☐ Deliver Us ....7" Century Media 9980871
Transparent red. 500 copies.
2011 ☐ SOUNDS OF A PLAYGROUND FADING ....2LPg Century Media 9977471
2011 ☐ SOUNDS OF A PLAYGROUND FADING ....2LPg Century Media 9977471
Clear vinyl.
2011 ☐ SOUNDS OF A PLAYGROUND FADING ....2LPg Century Media 9977471
333 marbled grey.
2011 ☐ SOUNDS OF A PLAYGROUND FADING ....2LPg Razzia (Sweden) ....Razzia 180
Hand numbered.
2011 ☐ SOUNDS OF A PLAYGROUND FADING ....CDd+DVD Century Media 9977478
DVD featuring "making of".
2011 ☐ SOUNDS OF A PLAYGROUND FADING ....CD Century Media 9977472
2011 ☐ SOUNDS OF A PLAYGROUND FADING .... CDd+DVD box Century Media 9977470
Long box containing CD, DVD, belt, buttons, postcards.
2011 ☐ SOUNDS OF A PLAYGROUND FADING ....CDd+DVD Century Media (USA)............................8804-2
DVD featuring "making of".
2011 ☐ SOUNDS OF A PLAYGROUND FADING ....CD Century Media 8447-2

2011 CDS - - -

2011 ☐ SOUNDS OF A PLAYGROUND FADING ....CD Yoshimoto (Japan) YRCG-90061
Bonus: Deliver Us (instrumental)
2011 ☐ SOUNDS OF A PLAYGROUND FADING ....CD Mazzar (Russia)..........................MZR CD 495
2011 ☐ SOUNDS OF A PLAYGROUND FADING ....CD Del Imaginario (Argentina) ....D.I 198
2011 ☐ SOUNDS OF A PLAYGROUND FADING ....CD Evolution Music (Korea)................L100004309
2011 ☐ SOUNDS OF A PLAYGROUND FADING ....CD OZ Productions (Mexico) SR0663-0
2011 ☐ SOUNDS OF A PLAYGROUND FADING ....CD Razzia (Sweden) ....Razzia 177
2011 ■ SOUNDS OF A PLAYGROUND FADING ....CD Magnum Music (Taiwan)..............CM9977472
2011 ☐ REROUTE TO REMAIN...CD Trooper (Japan) QATE-10002
Bonus: Colony (live)
2011 ☐ THE JESTER'S RACE...CD Evolution Music (Korea)................L100004216
Bonus: Moonshield (live)/Artifacts Of The Black Rain (live)/Moonshield (C64 Karaoke
version)

2011 CD - CM9977472

2011 ☐ WHORACLE ....CD Evolution Music (Korea)................L100004217
Bonus: Goliaths Disarm Their Davids/Jotun (live)/Food For The Gods (live)
2011 ☐ COLONY ....CD Evolution Music (Korea)................L100004218
Bonus: Colony (live)/Ordinary Story (live)/Scom (live)
2011 ☐ CLAYMAN ....CD Evolution Music (Korea)................L100004219
Bonus: Strong And Smart/Only For The Weak (live)/Pinball Map (live)
2011 ☐ REROUTE TO REMAIN...CD Evolution Music (Korea)................L100004220
Bonus: Watch Them Feed/Land Of Confusion/Cloud Connected (Club Connected Remix)
2011 ☐ SOUNDTRACK TO YOUR ESCAPE ....CD Evolution Music (Korea)................L100004221
Bonus: The Quiet Place (live)/My Sweet Shadow (remix)
2011 ☐ SOUNDTRACK TO YOUR ESCAPE ....CD Evolution Music (Korea)................L100004222
2011 ☐ A SENSE OF PURPOSE ....CD Evolution Music (Korea)................L100004223
Bonus: Eraser/Tilt/Abnegation/Alias – Laid Remix
2011 ■ 8 SONGS ....CD FighterStreet ....- -
Promo compilation with Rock Hard Magazine.

2011 CD - - -

Unofficial releases:
2002 ■ Moonshield/Only For The Weak......................................7" - - ....- -
Supposedly 10 copies made. Recorded live at the Denver Fillmore Theater in 2002.
2005 ☐ LUNAR STRAIN...CD Regain (China)..................................CM1534
Chinese counterfeit/bootleg.
2005 ☐ LUNAR STRAIN/SUBTERRANEAN ....CD Regain (Russia) ....-RR 9910-005
Russian counterfeit/bootleg. Says Limited edition on CD.
2011 ☐ THE JESTER'S RACE...CDd Regain (China) CM1531
2 bonus tracks.
2011 ☐ SUBTERRANEAN ....CDd Regain Records (China) CM1532
2011 ☐ SUBTERRANEAN + BLACK-ASH INHERITANCE ....CDd - - (Russia) ....- -
2011 ☐ THE JESTER'S RACE+BLACK-ASH INHERITANCE ....CDd Regain Records (China) CM1533
2011 ☐ THE JESTER'S RACE+BLACK-ASH INHERITANCE ....CDd Asialink Trading (Asia)............5351662808042
2011 ☐ COLONY ....CDd Nuclear Blast (China)......................NB 1231-2

2002 7" - - - -

2011	□	CLAYMAN	CD	Asialink Trading (Asia)	IF 8037
2011	□	COLONY	CDd	Asialink Trading (Asia)	IF 8113
2011	□	COME CLARITY	CD	Asialink Trading (Asia)	IN 8046
2011	□	A SENSE OF PURPOSE	CD	Asialink Trading (Asia)	IN 8120
n/a	■	METALL EMPIRE	2CD	Hi-End Ultra	5625467565
2000	□	LIVE IN FLAMES	2CD	Unreleased File Death	UFD-041

Recorded live in Osaka, Nov 13, 2000.

| 2004 | □ | DESTROYS SRF 2004 | CD | House Of Kicks | HOK-016 |

Recorded live at Sweden Rock 2004.

| 2002 | □ | BEAST TO REMAIN | 2CD | Sylph | SP-121902391 |

Recorded in Japan – Tokyo Shibuya 021219 + Makuhari 021215.

| 2005 | □ | MP3 COLLECTION | 2CD | RMG Records/Irond (Russia) | 601365018554 |

MP3 collection of 9 albums.

| 2005 | □ | IN FLAMES | 2CD | Star Records (Russia) | MP3DM-256/1617-5 |

MP3 collection of all albums, including two live bootlegs.

n/a CD - 5625467565

IN GREY

Joakim Croneström: v, Niklas Axelsson: g, Fredrik Klingwall: k
Per Lindström: b, Dennis Starkenberg: d

Stockholm - Formed in 1992, inspired by the darker sides of life, which shows in the band's melancholic, goth-induced slightly doomy metal. The band recorded their first demo *The Journey* in 1994, followed by *Skydancer* (1995), *Time Circles* (1996), *Seasons Change* (1999), *Mask* (2000) and *Above* (2001) before releasing their first album *Sulphur Tears* in 2003. On the second album, *Liyah*, the line-up had changed quite drastically. Croneström, who was a bit less gothy in his vocal style, had replaced singer Dennis Liljedahl. Guitarist Daniel Cannerfelt had also been replaced by keyboardist Fredrik Klingwall (**Anima Morte, Loch Vostock**), who is also the man behind the Last Entertainment label. However, Klingwall left after the second album and Christian Edström replaced him. Between the albums guitarist Igor Jevtic had been in and out of the band, and the two demos *MMIV* and *XII* were recorded in 2004.

2003 CD - LE002

| 2003 | ■ | SULPHUR TEARS | CD | Last Entertainment | LE002 |
| 2006 | ■ | LIYAH | CD | Last Entertainment | LAST 005 |

2006 CD - LAST 005

IN MOURNING

Tobias Netzell: v/g, Björn Pettersson: g, Tim Nedergård: g,
Pierre Stam: b, Christian Netzell: d

Falun/Vansbro - **In Mourning** were formed in 2000, at the time inspired by **My Dying Bride** and with a more goth-oriented sound which shows on their early demos like *In Mourning* (2000) and *Senseless* (2002). Before the first album, *Shrouded Divine*, singer Jon Solander had left the band. The vocals, now almost only growling, was taken care of by Netzell, changing the band's sound a bit. The first two albums were produced by **Scar Symmetry**'s Jonas Kjellgren, which ensures a great sound. **In Mourning** play an interesting type of progressive death metal, with great arrangements and very intricate riffing, with cool passages inserted here and there. Well-produced and well-played. More aggro-style vocals, than growl. Highly recommended. The Netzell brothers are both ex-**Volturyon**. On The *Weight Of Oceans* the style got even more intricate, blending lots of different musical elements, not as goth-oriented, but more melodic and proggy, also adding some completely clean vocals. A really great album.

2008 CDd - Chapter 55

| 2008 | ■ | SHROUDED DIVINE | CD/d | Aftermath | Chapter 55 |

Jukebox cover or Digipack, 1000 copies each.

| 2010 | □ | MONOLITH | CD | Pulverised | ASH 068 CD |
| 2010 | □ | MONOLITH | LPg | Pulverised | ASH 068 LP |

250 copies.

| 2010 | □ | SHROUDED DIVINE | LP | Kolony | G66503 |
| 2012 | □ | THE WEIGHT OF OCEANS | CD | Spinefarm | SPI 423 CD |

2010 CD - ASH 068 CD

IN SOLITUDE

Pelle "Hornper" Åhman: v, Niklas Lindström: g, Henrik Palm: g,
Gottfrid Åhman: b, Uno Bruniusson: d

Falun/Uppsala - Not to be confused with the Portuguese hard rockers. *In Solitude* was formed in 2002 by Niklas, Uno, Gottfrid and guitarist Henrik Helenius. Pelle, Gottfrid's younger brother, was only 11 years old at the time and didn't join until 2003. They recorded the first demo in 2004. In 2005 Helenius left and was replaced by Mattias Gustafsson. In 2006 the second demo, *Hidden Dangers*, comprising of four tracks, saw the light of day. Two of the tracks were released as a vinyl single by S.M.P, and soon sold out. The band was soon picked up by vinyl label High Roller, who released the debut. In 2009 Mattias Gustafsson left to be replaced by Palm (**Sonic Ritual**) the subsequent year. In 2011 the band's sophomore album was recorded by Fred Estby (**Death Breath, Dismember** etc). *In Solitude* are in the row of the New Wave of Swedish Heavy Metal bands together with **Steelwings**, **Portrait**, **Katana** etc. Great-sounding, retro-influenced classic heavy metal, with influences from **Iron Maiden**, **Mercyful Fate** etc.

2008 7" - SMP 001

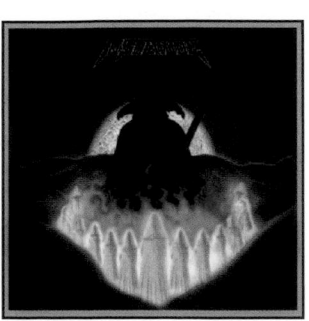

2008 LP - HHR 040

Year		Title	Format	Label	Cat. No.

2008 ■ Hidden Dangers (In The Night)/Kathedral.................................7" — S.M.P .... SMP 001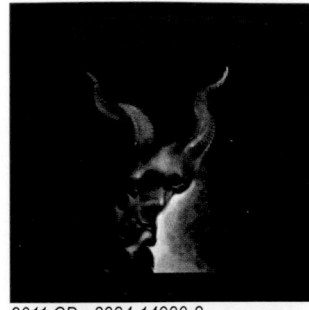
2008 □ IN SOLITUDE ....LP — High Roller .... HRR 040
First press with rough surface, poster, lyric sheet. 700 black, 200 purple and 100 silver/ grey vinyl.
2008 □ IN SOLITUDE .... LP+7" — High Roller .... HRR 040
Second press with embroidered patch, poster, lyric sheet. 300 black, 200 black/blue splatter. Bonus 7" with 7th Ghost/Kathedral/Hidden Dangers in black/blue splatter vinyl.
2008 ■ IN SOLITUDE ....LP — High Roller .... HRR 040
Third pressing 500 gold vinyl (PSM). Fourth pressing 250 purple, 250 black + woven patch, thick cardboard cover. Fifth pressing 200 black + 300 clear + different poster.
2009 □ 7th Ghost/Kathedral/Hidden Dangers (In The Night) ....7" — High Roller .... HRR 040
100 copies. Blue vinyl.
2009 □ IN SOLITUDE ....CD — Pure Steel .... PSRCD 022

2011 CD - 3984-14980-2

2011 ■ THE WORLD. THE FLESH. THE DEVIL ....CD — Metal Blade 3984-14980-2
2011 □ THE WORLD. THE FLESH. THE DEVIL ....2LPg — Metal Blade 3984-14980-1
Red vinyl + 250 dark brown. Poster.
2012 □ Mother Of Mercy ....7" flexi — Decibel Magazine .... DB 017
Came with Decibel Magazine. Red flexi disc. Samhain cover.
2013 □ IN SOLITUDE ....CD — Seasons Of Mist .... SOM 265
2013 □ IN SOLITUDE ....2LPg — Seasons Of Mist .... SOM 265 LP
2013 ■ SISTER ....CD — Metal Blade .... 3984-15251-2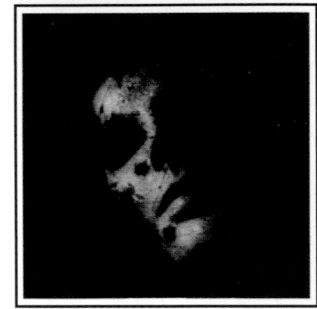
2013 □ SISTER ....CDd — Metal Blade 3984-15251-0
Bonus: Hidden Dangers (In The Night)/Faceless Mistress (demo)
2013 □ SISTER ....LP — Metal Blade 3984-15251-1
Black and coloured vinyl.

2013 CD - 3984-15251-2

IN THE COLONNADES
Johan Pettersson: v/b, Magnus Gehlin: g, Ingemar Sollgard: g,
Olle Borg: k, Olle Pettersson: d

Stockholm - Formed in 1984. Gehlin and Borg recorded a single with the industrial synth band **Plast** in 1979. *In The Colonnades* is a band quite close to **Danzig** in style and sound. Heavy bulldozer rock, with few tempo changes or technical surprises. The first MLP and the single were released together as one album on German label Yellow Records. *Scrap Metal Value* was released in 1991 on CBR, but reissued on Accelerating Blue Fish the year after. In 1990 they recorded a cover of **Black Sabbath**'s *Sabbath Bloody Sabbath* for the compilation *The Legacy* (1990 Sinderella) and the year before the song *Grind 'Em Down* was featured on *The Swedish Stand-In* (1989 Sinderella). In 1994 they were featured on the compilation *The Return Of Yesterday's Tomorrow Part 2* (1994 Accelerating Blue Fish). In 1993 Ingemar joined the band and the year after singer Ulf Lenneman left and bass player Johan took over his task. *Rest And Recreation* shows an even heavier side of the band and the vocals are also almost death-oriented. It was produced by famous metal producer Tomas Skogsberg. Gehlin, born January 30, 1961 sadly passed away from cancer March 10, 2005.

1989 MLP - PCR 001

1991 LP - CBR LP 127

1986 □ In The Colonnades.. MLP 6tr — Joker ....ITC 610
Tracks: Talk For An Hour/Black Soul/Beating/Kill The Sun/Fox Hill/Total Destruction
1987 □ Wheels/Sort Of Heaven ....7" — Joker Music Box .... JOKE 712
1988 □ IN THE COLONNADES ....LP — Yellow (Germany) ....YELLOW 21
1989 ■ Fry Day/War/REPO .... MLP 3tr — Pale & Common................................. PCR 001
1989 □ Fry Day/War/REPO .... MLP 3tr — Yellow (Germany) ....Pale 001
1991 ■ SCRAP METAL VALUE...LP — CBR ....CBR LP 127
1991 □ SCRAP METAL VALUE...CD — CBR ....CBR CD 127
Bonus: Sabbath Bloody Sabbath (Black Sabbath cover)/This 'N That
1991 □ SCRAP METAL VALUE...LP — Accelerating Blue Fish ....CBR LP 127
1991 □ SCRAP METAL VALUE...CD — Accelerating Blue Fish ....CBRCD 127
Bonus: Sabbath Bloody Sabbath (Black Sabbath cover)/This 'N That
1992 □ SCRAP METAL VALUE...CD — Rebel (Germany) .... SPV 084-45292
1995 □ REST AND RECREATION...CD — Accelerating Blue Fish .... ACC CD 25
2008 ■ IN THE COLONNADES ....CD — Playwood ....Playcd 08/8
Different artwork. Bonus: Wheels/Sort Of Heaven/Sexgun (live)/Dropping Acid In A Combat Zone (live)/Dreamland (live)/Ain't Love A Bitch (live)

2008 CD - Playcd 08/8

IN THY DREAMS
Thomas Lindfors: v, Håkan Stuvemark: g, Jari Kuusisto: g,
Petri Kuusisto: b, Stefan Westerberg: d

Sala - The band was formed in 1995 and could be described as a mix of **At The Gates** and **Dark Funeral**. The line-up on the debut MCD featured Westerberg, Jari Kuusisto, Stuvemark, bassist Fredrik Ericsson and singer Jonas Nyrén (**Armageddon**). On *Highest Beauty* (recorded in Studio Underground) Ericsson was replaced by Petri and Nyrén by Lindfors (**Wombbath**). Melodic death metal with twin-guitar attack. Jari and Petri are also found in **Carnal Forge**. Petri has also been found in **Asperity** and **Soulskinner**. Stefan recorded two albums with **Steel Attack** and is now also found in **Carnal Forge**. As Jari and Stefan were concentrating on **Carnal Forge** the band became inactive.

1997 MCD - WAR 014

1999 CD - WAR 008

1997 ■	Stream Of Dispraised Souls	MCD 5tr	Wrong Again Records	WAR 014

Tracks: Fateless/Glistering Truth/Fleeing Illusions/Dreams Within/Stream Of Dispraised Souls

1999 ■	THE GATE OF PLEASURE	CD	WAR	WAR 008
1999 □	THE GATE OF PLEASURE	CD	Soundholic (Japan)	SHCD1-0022

Contains the MCD Stream OF Dispraised Souls as bonus.

2001 ■	HIGHEST BEAUTY	CD	Teichiku (Japan)	TKCS 85012

Bonus: Swirl Chaotically

2001 CD - TKCS 85012

INCAPACITY
Andreas "Dread/Drette/Mourning" Axelsson: v, Christian Älvestam: g, Robert Ivarsson: g, Anders Edlund: b, Henrik Schönström: d

Skövde - In 2002, a phone call came from Cold Records' label manager Omer Akay to Anders Edlund (*Angel Blake, Solution .45, Few Against Many, Solar Dawn*) asking if he would be into forming a death/thrash band was the spark that started *Incapacity*. Anders gathered some quite high-profile musicians. Älvestam is also found in numerous bands like *Unmoored, Solution .45, Miseration* and *Scar Symmetry*, Axelsson in *Tormented, Edge Of Sanity, Marduk, Infestdead, Total Terror* and *The Deadbeats*, Ivarsson has been in *Pan-Thy-Monium, Ophthalamia, Ashes* and Schönström can also be found in *Unmoored, Enshrined, Solar Dawn, Torchbearer, Traumatized* and *Spawn Of Posession*. *9th Order Instinct* was recorded at Soundlab by the late Mieszko Talarzcyk (*Nasum*). After the second album, Edlund was replaced by Jani Stefanovic (*DivineFire, Miseration, Solution .45, Crimson Moonlight*), Axelsson was out and Älvestam took over the vocals, Ivarsson was replaced by Robert Ahrling (*Origin Blood*). The current whereabouts are a bit foggy however. *Incapacity* play brutal, well-produced technical death metal with a touch of thrash. On *Chaos Complete* Tomas Johansson (*Unmoored*) is featured as a guest doing some guitar solos.

2003 CD - COLD 002

2003 ■	CHAOS COMPLETE	CD	Cold Records	COLD 002
2003 □	CHAOS COMPLETE	CD	Soundholic (Japan)	TKCS-85067

Bonus: Hellhearted

2004 ■	9TH ORDER INSTINCT	CD	Metal Blade	3984-14495-2
2005 □	9TH ORDER INSTINCT	LP	Animate	AR 011

Bonus: Fistful Of Satan. 666 hand numbered copies.

2004 CD - 3984-14495-2

INCINERATOR
Lenny "Blade" Bladh: v/b, Daniel Wikstén: g, Jonas Mattson: g, Andreas Nilzon: d

Jönköping - Not to be confused with the Italian band. *Incinerator* was the creation of Lenny Blade, also found in *Bullet, Devil Lee Rot, Nominon, Hypnosia, Pagan Rites* etc. The band's first demo, *Order Of Chaos*, was released in 1996 and the line-up then featured Lenny, Henrik Åberg (*Gates Of Ishtar, Satariel, Battlelust, Necromicon*), Fredrik Andersson (*Satariel*) and Haris Agic, and four years later the first MCD was unearthed. The line-up featured Blade, Nilzon (*Satariel, The Moaning*) and Mattson (*Devian, Nominon*). The tracks *Disciples Of Doom, The Return Of The Thrashing Dead* and *Premeditated Murder* are found on the four-way split cassette *The Cocoon Of Asphyx* (2005 Nihilistic Holocaust). In 2005 The tracks on the from the *Early Thrashings* demo was featured on the CDR 3-way split *Demon Seed Of Thrash* (2005 Northern Warrior). In 2010 Lenny moved to Thailand and formed a new Incinerator with an all-Thai crew. Old-school thrash similar to bands like *Destruction, Slayer* and *Kreator*.

2000 MCD - SRP.05

2000 ■	Thrash Attack	MCD 5tr	Sound Riot	SRP.05

Tracks: Scream Queen/Storm of the Thrasher/The Collapse/Bestial Rage/Hypocritical Convictions

INCINIA
Patrik Muhr: g, Sebastian Olsson: g, Daniel Stenberg: b, Henrik Öhlund: d

Djursholm - Started out as punk band *Ravish* in 1996, changed members and became metal band *Incinia* the year after. Average-quality music and musicians with quite weak production. Mjorga, who sings *Falconer*-ishly soft and melodic, guests on lead vocals.

1998 CD - INCD 666

1998 ■	SAVIOUR	CD	private	INCD 666

INCRAVE
Johan Falk: v, David Ohlsson: g, Jon Bålefalk: g, Jonathan Stenberg: k, Martin Davidsson: b, Josef Davidsson: d

Edsbyn - *Incrave* was initially named *Evergrace*, under which name the first album was originally released in 2006 (ULTCD001). However, as the name caused a lot of confusion and mix up with the band *Evergrey*, they changed their name to *Incrave* and the first album was reissued under the new name, and with the extra track *The Masquerade*. The style is actually

2007 CD - ULTCD 005

not that far from the aforementioned *Evergrey*, only not as melancholy and with singer Falk residing in a higher vocal register. Semi-progressive, melancholic power metal, like a mix of *Kamelot*, *Tad Morose* and *Evergrey*. A band well worth checking out. The track *No One Else* on *The Forgotten* is an exclusive track for this release.
Website: www.incrave.se

2008 CD - ULTCD 007

2007 ■	THE ESCAPE	CD	Ulterium Records	ULTCD 005
2008 □	The Forgotten	MCD 4tr	Ulterium Records	ULTCDS 001
	Tracks: The Forgotten (single version)/The Forgotten (radio edit)/A Shadow In The Dark/ No One Else			
2008 ■	DEAD END	CD	Ulterium Records	ULTCD 007
2008 □	DEAD END	CD	Toy's Factory (Japan)	TKCS-85201

INDIAN RED
Karl-Johan Samuelsson: v/g, Claes Kåge: b/v, Fredrik Dahllöf: d

Stockholm - This band started out as a blues cover band but on the album, developed into some kind of mix between *Red Hot Chili Peppers*/*Megadeth*/*Hendrix*. Very interesting and unusual, though. The song *Dog Food* on the EP features the members from *Stonecake*. Kåge is the brother of Lennart and Sten of *Blues Bag*.

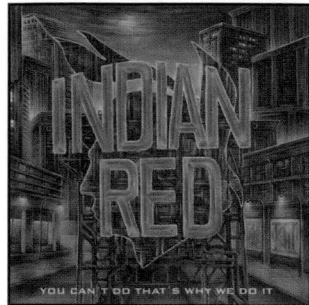
1993 CD - BMCD 31

1993 ■	YOU CAN'T DO THAT'S WHY WE DO IT	CD	Black Mark	BMCD 31
1994 □	Wicked Politician	MCD 4tr	Black Mark	MZCDS 2
	Tracks: Wicked Politician/Metal Window/I've Been Looking/Dog Food			

INDOMITUS
Tomas Vasseur: v/g, Christian Lundh: g, Dennis B Nagy: b, Glenn Eriksson: d

Katrineholm - Formed in 1991. Quite an original band. The music could be described as varied and well-played progressive doom-oriented thrash metal. Really heavy and really good. The band later changed their name to *Crow*, and released a CD in 1997. They also changed style to more post-grunge alternative hard rock with some heavy riffing.

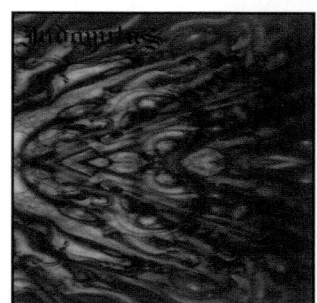
1995 MCD - ICD 95

1995 ■	Indomitus	MCD 4tr	private	ICD 95
	Tracks: 11/Lower/Darkened/Epics			

INDUNGEON
Karl Bäckman: v/d, Stefan Weinerhall: g, Mikael Andersson: g, Jonas Albrektsson: b

Mjölby - The band was formed in 1996 and split three years later. Stefan was later found in *Falconer* and *Atryxion*, while the Mikael and Jonas returned to their main band *Thy Primordial*. Jonas is also found in *Niden Div.187*. Karl and Stefan were previously found in *Mithotyn*. On the first album Albrektsson played guitar and Weinerhall bass, on the second album they switched.

1998 CD - FMP 012

1998 ■	MACHINEGUNNERY OF DOOM	CD	Full Moon	FMP 012
1999 □	THE MISANTHROPOCALYPSE	CD	Invasion	IR 054

INEVITABLE END
Andreas Gerdén: v, Marcus Bertilsson: g,
Johan Wold Ylenstrand: b, Joakim Malmborg: d

Jönköping/Göteborg - *Inevitable End* were formed in 2003, initially leaning more towards thrash. They released the first self-titled demo in 2004 and a second one, *Reversal*, in 2006. On the latter the line-up featured Andreas Gerdén (v), Joakim Malmborg (g), Emil Westerdahl (b) and Christoffer Johansson (d) The band relocated to Göteborg and the line-up changed, now featuring Gerdén (*VIXIVI*), Marcus Bertilsson (*Miseration, The Weakening*), Malmborg (now on drums, ex-*Crimson Moonlight*) and Westerdahl. On the debut the sound had become more aggressive and brutal. Pure, high-class, super-aggressive grindcore-infused death metal. The band's second effort, where Johan Ylenstrand (*Exhale, Sordid, Crimson Moonlight, Miseration, Sordid Death*) had replaced Westerdahl, contains blast-beat-filled technical death metal with a strong touch of grindcore, at an even more furious tempo. In October 2011 Gerdén and Malmborg left the band and were replaced by the line-up featured Bertilsson, Ylenstrand, singer Christoffer Jonsson and drummer Johan "Savage" Olsson.
Website: www.inevitable-end.com

2009 CD - RR 7039

2011 CD - RR 7145

2009 ■	THE SEVERED INCEPTION	CD	Relapse Records	RR 7039
2009 □	THE SEVERED INCEPTION	LP	Relapse Records	- -
	100 copies clear vinyl, 500 clear red, 400 black.			
2009 □	THE SEVERED INCEPTION	CD	Relapse Records (Japan)	YSCY-1140
2011 ■	THE OCULUS	CD	Relapse Records	RR 7145
2011 □	THE OCULUS	CD	Relapse Records (Japan)	YSCY-1217

INFANTICIDE

Daniel Westerberg: v, Michael Löfqvist: g, Andreas Fors: g,
Pelle Öberg: b, Mikael Öberg: d

Piteå - Formed in 1990, soon took the name *Force Majeure* and recorded their first demo, *Disharmony*, in 1991. They changed their name to *Infanticide* and recorded the demo *Obtain And Devour* in 1992, when the 7" was also unearthed. Musically the band delivers high-quality technical power metal with a top-notch sound. However the vocals would fit better in a death metal band. After the third demo, *Infanticidemo* (1993), Niklas decided to leave the band and Michael Löfqvist soon replaced him. The band added some *Slayer* covers to their repertoire and in 1994 the last demo, *Obsolete*, was unearthed. Andreas quit in April 1994 and the remaining members continued under the name *Punishment*. In 1995 the new foursome released the 5-track MCD *Life*. Not to be confused with the grinders from Gävle. Fors was later in *Tundra* and Westerberg in *Necrocide*.

1992 7" - HIT 008

1992 ■ From Tomorrows Past/Confusion (My Internal World) ....7" Hit It Productions .... HIT 008

INFERNAL (aka INFERNAL 666)

David "Blackmoon" Parland: v/g

Stockholm - The band was initiated in 1997, by David "Blackmoon" Parland and Paul "Themgoroth" Mäkitalo (ex-*Dark Funeral,* later in *Obscuratum*) with the goal to create as satanic and uncompromising music as possible. According to themselves they play "Satanic Holocaust Metal" as they feel black metal is too meek a description for their music. The duo recruited drummer Matte Modin (*Defleshed/Dark Funeral*) and bass player David "Impious" Larsson (*In Aeternum*). This line-up entered Dug Out studios together with acclaimed producer Daniel Bergstrand (*Crawley, Meshuggah* etc.) to record the debut. After this, *Infernal* disbanded, but in 2001 David reformed the band featuring Henrik "Typhoz" Ekeroth (g/v) and Tomas "Alzazmon" Asklund (d). Both Henrik and Tomas were also members of *Dark Funeral* on *Vobiscum Satanas*. The band's first full-length album *Hellstorms* was recorded late 2002, but has still not been released. After *Summon Forth The Beast* the band dissolved. In 2008 David reformed the band, now with himself taking over the vocals as well, adding guitarist/singer Martin Halfdan (*Necrophobic*). However, Tomas Askund was soon out of the band, replaced by Norwegian Carl Engström (*Recovery, Astaroth*). In 2010 the band was picked up by Goathorned, who released *The Infernal Return*, recorded in 2009, before the last line-up was set, featuring Parland on vocals, guitars and bass plus Asklund on session drums. A new album was in the making, but on March 19, 2013, Parland, who was an excellent guitarist, sadly ended his own life at the age of 42.

1999 MCDd - HELL 005

2001 CD - HHR 092

1999 ■	666 Infernal ....MCDd 4tr	Hellspawn ....HELL 005
	Tracks: Requiem (The Coming Of The Age Of Satan)/Wrath Of The Infernal One/Storms Of Armageddon/Under The Hellsign	
2001 □	666 Infernal .... MLP 4tr	Vinyl Collectors ....VC 031
2001 ■	UNDER THE WINGS OF HELL (split) ....CD	Hammerheart Records .... HHR 092
	Split with Dark Funeral. Infernal's tracks are the same as on the MCD.	
2002 □	Summon Forth The Beast................................MCD 5tr	Hammerheart Records .... HHR 096
	Tracks: Branded By Hellfire/Infernal Holocaust/Bleed For The Devil (Morbid Angel cover)/ Devil Pig (Von cover)/Of Doom (Bathory cover)	
2010 ■	The Infernal Return .... 7"g 3tr	Goathorned Productions................... Goat 010
	Tracks: The Darkside Calls/Of The Seven Gates/Godforsaken (With Hate I Burn). 500 copies, first 100 in dark purple.	

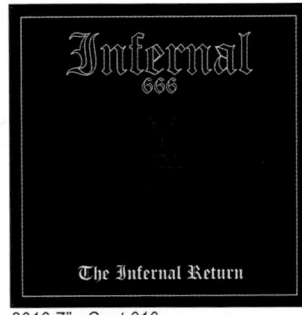
2010 7" - Goat 010

INFERNAL GATES

Stefan Sundholm: v/k, Johan Hedman: g, Jan-Åke Österberg: g,
Anders Hagerborn: b, Jonas Gustafsson: d

Karlstad - *Infernal Gates* were formed already in 1992 by Gustafsson, Sundholm and Hagerborn. The line-up was soon completed by Hedman and Österberg. The band released their first demo *In Sadness...* the year after. The second demo was entitled *The Gathering Of Tears* and released in 1994. Gustafsson is also found in *Souldivider*. In 1999 the band released another 3-track promo entitled *When Angels Fall*. *Infernal Gates* play heavy, doom-oriented death metal.

1997 ■ FROM THE MIST OF DARK WATERS................................CD   X-treme .... X-TR 002

1997 CD - X-TR 002

INFERNAL VENGEANCE

Karl "Bastard" Beckman: v/g, Daniel "Dee" Nilsson: g,
Claes "Anger" Kylemo: b, Karl "Mori" Lindén: d

Vadstena - *Infernal Vengeance* were formed by Beckman after his former band *Mithotyn* split up in 1999. They recorded the first demo in 2004. Bass player Johan Kullander sadly passed away in 2005, the day after the band's second demo *Tremendous Malice*, was released and they took a break. However, they returned with Kim Johansson taking over Johan's tasks.

He departed after a while and was temporarily replaced by **Thy Primordeal/Indungeon** man Jonas Albrektsson until Kylemo came in as a permanent replacement. They recorded the demo *Unleash The Wrath* in 2007 and split the subsequent year. *Dual Mayhem* is a compilation of the first two demos, remastered. **Infernal Vengeance** plays death metal heavily influenced by traditional thrashy metal and with a strong touch of folk.

2006 CD - TRHK 008

2006 ■ DUAL MAYHEM ....CD   Trinity Records (Hong Kong) .... TRHK 008

INFERNO
Tim Norell, Keith Almgren, Mats Gunhamre, Christer Lundh, Niklas Hasselberg

Sundsvall - *Novemberbarn* is quite a poppy song with nice harmony guitars, while *Monopol* is quite a good melodic hard rocker with some biting guitar work. Hasselberg was also in pop band **Rasta Hunden**. Almgren has later been found in bands like **Intact** and **Blåljus**, while Gunhamre was in **GunFire**. The second single is pop. For collectors only. Norell and Almgren have continued writing music for numerous pop artists.

1980 ■ Novemberbarn/Monopol ....7"   New Generation .... MAS 2290
1981 ☐ Du leker med en eld/En hjälpande hand ....7"   New Generation .... MAS 2333

1980 7" - MAS 2290

INFESTDEAD
Andreas "Drette" Axelsson: v, Dan Swanö: g/b/d

Örebro - Multi-musician and producer Swanö, the man behind bands like **Edge Of Sanity**, **Unicorn**, **Nightingale** etc. has yet another solo project on his conscience. This one is far more brutal than the symphonic/progressive **Nightingale**. **Infestdead** is a hybrid of goth, death and black metal. The label went bust in 1999. *JesuSatan* contains a black metal version of **Deep Purple**'s *Black Night*. Most of the guitar solos on *Jesusatan* were played by Robert "Marcello" Wendelstam (**Danger Danger, Chris Laney's Legion**).

Wrrrroaarrghhhhh

1997 ☐ Killing Christ ....MCD 4tr   Invasion Records .... I.R. 020
     Tracks: I'll Be Black/In The Spell Of Satan/Save Me From The Hands Of Christ/Fucked By Satan
1997 ☐ HELLFUCK ....CD   Invasion Records .... I.R. 026
1997 ☐ HELLFUCK ....LP PD   Invasion Records .... I.R. 026
1999 ☐ JESUSATAN ....CD   Invasion Records .... I.R. 047
1999 ☐ HELLFUCK/KILLING CHRIST ....CD   Unveiling The Wicked .... HUW 019
2000 ☐ JESUSATAN ....CDd   Unveiling The Wicked .... HUW 020
2001 ☐ HELLFUCK/KILLING CHRIST ....CD   Fono (Russia) FO46CD
2007 ■ INFESTDEAD/DARKCIDE (split) ....7"   Ancient Enemy .... AER 001
     Split with Darkcide. Track: Dead Earth. 500 copies.

2007 7" - AER 001

INFINITY
Joacim Lundberg: v, Fredrik Josefsson: g, Eric Rauti: g,
Mats Rendlert: b, Ronny Andersson: d

Mariestad - The band was formed in 1997 under the name **Nazgül**. Fredrik, who initially also handled the vocals, was previously with punksters **Woodchuck**. The band folded, but reformed as **Unchained** which was later changed to **Infinity**. The band recorded their first demo *Crystal Age* in 2000. Rendlert is also found in **Ancient Dreams**, **Rusty Souls** and **Shoeshine Man**. Eric was ex-**NME Within**. The band also recorded the demo *Falling Higher* in 2002, before all except Josefsson went on to form the band **Dreamland**. Lundberg has also played with **Dream Evil** and is today found in **Amaranthe**.

2002 ■ The Call/Herculons ....CDS 2tr   private .... INF 001
     1000 copies

2002 CDS - INF 001

INFRA
Frans Perris: g, Victor Alneng: v/b/k, Michael Ludvigsson: d

Umeå - A new band that sounds as they've been force-fed with early 70s music since birth. Very psychedelic, classic hard rock with long, weird tracks featuring heavy guitars, flute, cello, spoken voices and the odd saxophone. The first three tracks on the MCD are taken from the album. A trip for all you hippies.

1995 ☐ Infrangible time ....MCD 4tr   Mellotronen .... MELLOSING 1
     Tracks: At The Fountain-Head/Cicada/10 Companions/Infrangible Time. 500 copies.
1996 ☐ THE ABOMINABLE STORY OF HAROLD S. WOODHOUSE ....CD   Garageland .... GRCD 19
1999 ■ CREPUSCULE ....CD   The Wild Places .... WILD 007

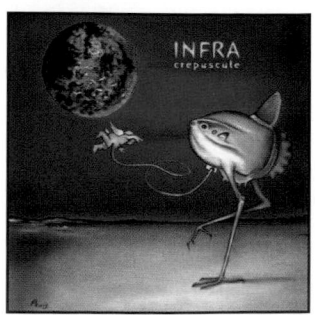
1999 CD - WILD 007

INFUNERAL

Grave: v/g, Casket: d

Järfälla - Formed in 2002. Casket is also found in *Putrified* as A. Death and in *Flagellated Seraph* as AsO, while Grave is in *Dödsfall* and has played live with *Ondskapt*. The band released their first CD-R demo, *A Pile Of Skulls* in 2002. A second demo came in 2003, entitled *Bloodstaind Journey* and a third, *Beneath The False Moon*, came in 2005. The tracks were later found on the debut CD. *Infuneral* play old-school death metal in the vein of *Watain* and *Dissection*.

2011 MCD - Poison 001

Year		Title	Format	Label	Cat. No.
2007	□	SEPULCHRAL MONUMENTS	CD	Iron Fist Productions	IFPCD 023
2011	■	A Scent Of Death	MCD 5tr	Odious Recordings	Poison 001

Tracks: Beyond The Glowing Stars/Änglamakaren/Cloak Of Death/Supremacy/Into Silent Slumber. 500 copies.

2011	■	TORN FROM THE ABYSS	CD	Blackcrowned Records	001

In DVD-box. 200 copies, first 100 hand numbered with black ink, second 100 with gold ink.

2011 CD - 001

INGO & FLOYD

Magnus Carlberg: v/g, Hannu Kiviaho: g, Heikki Kiviaho: b, Jörgen Wall: d

Stockholm - Formed in 1988. This is quite a schizophrenic band that started out with a female singer. The first self-titled album (1990 Virgin) is more or less pop, sung in Swedish. Basically, the band made a few releases before *Highways In Stereo*, which are not even worth noting. *Highways In Stereo* on the other hand, qualifies well into this book and contains some great heavy funky riffing quite similar to *Electric Boys*, mixed with some straight power chord songs and a couple of ballads. The latest album showed a new and even heavier side with some rap-metal tracks. Hannu has previously recorded three albums with the dark-mood-rock band *Memento Mori* (not the band on Black Mark Records). Drummer Jörgen was working with Louise Hoffsten live in 1995. He also plays on *Screaming Mothers* first CD and early '96 he reinforced noise-rockers *Whale* together with Heikki. A cover of *Kiss*' *Parasite* can be found on the compilation *Högtalarterror* (1994 Backstage). Heikki is now found in reformed classic punk-ish rockers *Sator*.

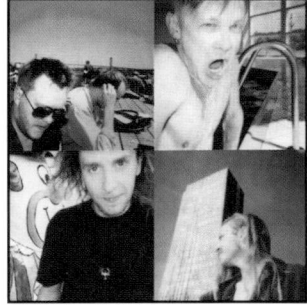

1992 CD - 11401 2

1995 CD - 26142 2

Year		Title	Format	Label	Cat. No.
1992	■	HIGHWAYS IN STEREO	CD	RCA/BMG	11401 2
1992	□	HIGHWAYS IN STEREO	LP	RCA	11401 1
1992	□	Generator/Good Game	7"	RCA	11048 7
1992	□	Generator/Good Game	CDS 2tr	RCA	11048 2
1992	□	Johnny Colours/Let You Ride	CDS 2tr	RCA	11875 2
1993	□	Ghost Town	CDS 1tr	RCA	13693 2
1994	□	Eyes Of The Blind/Apes	CDS 2 tr	RCA	24544 2
1995	■	PEEL	CD	RCA	26142 2
1995	□	Shock You/Sadness	CDS 2 tr	RCA	27422 2

INHALE

**Roland Johansson: v, Jocke de Vil: g, Andreas Olavi: g,
Pelle "DeLuxe" Karlsson: b, Fredrik Gomersson: d**

Varberg - *Inhale*, formed in 1997, play hardcore-influenced metal sung in Swedish. Quite reminiscent of *LOK*, but with slightly more melodic vocals. Olavi and Gomersson later backed up *Fame Factory* singer Sara Löfgren. Gomersson has also been found in *Parallel Universe* and *Project: Voodoo*. In 2007 Olavi joined modern melodic rockers *Lavett*.

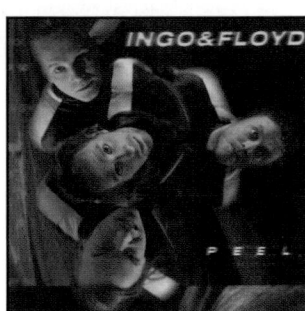

2002 CD - KICKCD 165

2002	■	KÄNN PÅ DET!!	CD	Kick Music	KICKCD 165

INIURIA

**Fredrik Johannesen: v, Stefan Karlsson: g, Henrik Dahlberg: g,
Johan Landhäll: b, Patrik Pelander: d**

Örebro - Formed in 1992. They initially recorded some demos under the name *Immortal Death*. *Iniuria* is a doom-oriented band, musically in the vein of *Solitude Aeturnus* or UK doom band *Cathedral*. When reading the lyrics I get the impression they're a Christian band. The material is quite OK, but the unmelodic vocal work is a really weak link... as well as the English grammar (see MCD-title). Beautiful artwork though. The band recorded their first demo in 1992, followed by *...Forgiveness* in 1993. In 1996 they released the demo *The Red One*, followed by *Empty Words* in 1999. The track *Walk Away* was featured on the compilation *Sometimes... Death IS Better* (1998 Shiver Records). Pelander was later replaced by Johan Jansson.

1995 MCD - CDS 003

1995	■	All The Leaves Has Fallen	MCD 3tr	private	CDS 003

Tracks: The Heavenly Choir/Father Of Heaven/God Of Thunder

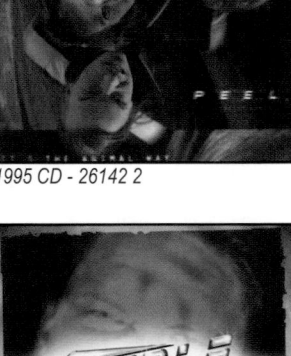

405

INMORIA

Charles Rytkönen: v, Christer "Krunt" Andersson: g, Dan Eriksson: k,
Tommi Karppanen: b, Peter Morén: d

Bollnäs - In May 2008 *Tad Morose* drummer Dan Eriksson left the band and started recording stuff all on his own. He soon asked his former colleague Christer "Krunt" Andersson to listen to some songs he had written. Krunt liked what he heard and joined the band. Next up was drummer Morén (*Tad Morose, Steel Attack*), since Dan had switched to keyboards, and bass player Karppanen (*Tad Morose, God Awful Machine*). Former *Tad Morose* colleague Rytkönen (also in *Morgana Lefay, LeFay*) was asked to try doing some vocals, and soon also he was part of the new band. On the second album Danish singer Sören Nico Adamsen (*Artillery, Crystal Eyes, Twinspirits, Starrats*) had however replaced Rytkönen. *Inmoria* plays melodic power metal in the vein of *Savatage*, not too far from the style of *Tad Morose*.
Website: www.inmoria.com

2009 CD - MAS-CD 0637

2011 CD - RIUCD 20-11

| 2009 ■ | INVISIBLE WOUNDS | CD | Massacre | MAS-CD 0637 |
| 2011 ■ | A FAREWELL TO NOTHING – THE DIARY PART 1 | CD | Rock It Up | RIUCD 20-11 |

INNOCENT ROSIE

Oscar Kaleva: v, Joel Eiasson: g, Dick Börtner: g, Olof Oljelund: b, Benjamin Boräng: d

Falkenberg - *Innocent Rosie* were formed in 2006 by guitarist Skid "Sadde" La'Russo and drummer Benjamin. They added Olof and Oscar to the line-up and soon recorded their first five-track demo. In 2007 guitarist Eliasson was also drafted and they started recording the demos for what was to become the debut album. In 2008 they recorded a video for the track *Knock Me Out* and went on a trip overseas to play Cruefest in Los Angeles. After this, Skid left the band and he was replaced by former *Boulevard/The Ungrateful* member Börtner. *Bound To Fuck Up* was recorded live and is also available as DVD. The CD version was however only a pro-printed CD-R (2009 Swedmetal SM012CD). *Innocent Rosie* play hard-edged, eighties-influenced sleazy metal in the same league as Swedish colleagues *Gemini Five* and *Hardcore Superstar*.

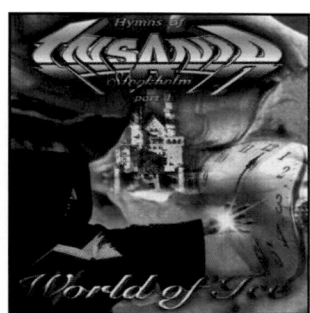
2009 CD - SM015CD

| 2009 ■ | BAD HABIT ROMANCE | CD | Swedmetal | SM015CD |
| 2009 □ | BAD HABIT ROMANCE | CD | Stay Gold (Japan) | ARTSG -028 |

INRAGE

Christer Salling: v, Magnus Söderman: g, Peter Lans (ex-Hägglund): g,
Matte Järnil: b, Perra Johansson: d

Uppsala - Another band with well-known faces. When *Lost Souls* called it a day *Inrage* rose from the ashes, featuring former members Salling, Johansson, Lans (Hägglund) and Järnil. Söderman is also found in *Zeelion* and was formerly with *Rosicrucian* and *Slapdash*. Järnil and Johansson are both ex-*Crawley* and the latter has also been found in *Lafayette*. Recorded at Studio Underground/Dug-Out. Raw thrash with a touch of the eighties (in a positive way!). Lans is today found in *F.K.Ü* under the name Pete Stooaahl.

2002 CD - SC 049-2

| 2002 ■ | BUILT TO DESTROY | CD | Scarlet | SC 049-2 |

INSANIA (STOCKHOLM)

David Henriksson: v, Henrik Juhano: g, Niklas Dahlin: g,
Patrik Västilä: k, Tomas Stolt: b, Mikko Korsbäck: d

Stockholm - Might this band be a change of direction for the death-oriented No Fashion Records? *Insania* follows in the footsteps of *Helloween*, *Edguy* and of course fellow Swedes *Hammerfall*. High-class, melodic German-tinged metal with high-pitched vocals and a powerful dual guitar-attack. If the debut felt a bit anonymous, the second album really makes up for it. Not to be confused with the German namesakes, who actually recorded their first album in 1993, thus the addition of "(Stockholm)". The band was formed in 1992 by Korsbäck and guitarist Henrik Juhano. They were completed by bassist Tomas Stolt, guitarist Niklas Dahlin and keyboard player Patrik Västilä. The band recorded two demos before signing with No Fashion. On *Fantasy - A New Dimension* the line-up had changed, where Ola Halén (*Shadows Past*) had replaced singer David Henriksson (later in *Heel*). After *Fantasy* the band recorded two demos, before recording a new album in 2005 (not released until 2007) with an updated line-up. Now guitarists Henrik Juhano and Niklas Dahlin were out of the band, replaced by Peter Östros (*Jaded Heart*). The keyboard duties had also been switched from Patrik Västilä to Dimitri Keiski. Johano, Dahlin and Stolt later formed the band *Disdained*. After a long pause Korsbäck and Juhano met to see if they could still write together. It worked and the band now had two guitarists again. As singer Halén was busy with his solo project *Shadows Past*, Östros' *Jaded Heart* colleague Johan Fahlberg was brought in. He finally dropped out, not finding the time and Keiski now stepped up as singer/bass player instead of keyboard player, bringing in old colleague Västilä again. The new line-up has played several shows and are planning a new album. In 2011 Dimitri entered Sweden's TV show True Talend where he did very well. Mid-2013 the band announced they were working on a new album with a new line-up, now

2001 LP - NFR 050 LP

1999 CD - NFR 035 CD

2002 CD - NFRCD 60

featuring singer Dimitri Kieski, guitarists Peter Östros and Niklas Dahlin, bassist Tomas Stolt and drummer Mikko Korsbäck.

1999	■	WORLD OF ICE	CD	No Fashion Records	NFR 035 CD
1999	□	WORLD OF ICE	LP	No Fashion Records	NFR 035 LP
1999	□	WORLD OF ICE	CD	Avalon Marquee (Japan)	MICY-1125
		Bonus: The Abyss Of The Morningstar/Fire In The Sky			
2001	□	SUNRISE IN RIVERLAND	CD	Avalon Marquee (Japan)	MICP 10233
		Bonus: The Right To Be Free			
2001	□	SUNRISE IN RIVERLAND	CDd	No Fashion Records	NFR 050 CD
2001	■	SUNRISE IN RIVERLAND	LP	No Fashion Records	NFR 050 LP
2001	□	SUNRISE IN RIVERLAND	CD	Irond (Russia)	01-121
2002	■	FANTASY - A NEW DIMENSION	CD	No Fashion Records	NFRCD 60
2002	□	FANTASY - A NEW DIMENSION	CD	Avalon Marquee (Japan)	MICP-10339
		Bonus: St. Patriks Lyrics			
2003	□	FANTASY - A NEW DIMENSION	CD	Irond (Russia)	CD 03-479
2007	■	AGONY - GIFT OF LIFE	CD	Black Lodge	BLOD 057 CD
2007	□	AGONY - GIFT OF LIFE	CD	Avalon Marquee (Japan)	MICP-10667
		Bonus: Gypsy Heart			
2008	□	AGONY - GIFT OF LIFE	CD	Irond (Russia)	CD 08-1391

2007 CD - BLOD 057 CD

INSISION

Carl Birath: v, Roger Johansson: g, Joel Andersson: b, Marcus Jonsson: d

Stockholm - The band was formed in 1997 out of the remains of **Embaler** and **Ildoor**. The first demo, *Meant To Suffer* was recorded in 1998 and later the same year the second effort, *Live Like A Worm* was unearthed. In 1999 the first MCD was released and the line-up featured singer Johan Thornberg, Joonas Ahonen and Roger Johansson (**Disfigured**) on guitars, Janne Hyytiä on bass and Thomas Daun (**Ghost, Repugnant, Dismember, Iron Lamb, Crashdïet**) on drums. Death metal with low-range growling vocals in the vein of **Vomitory**. Late 1999 Thornberg and Ahonen left the band for personal reasons. Singer Carl Birath (**Azatoth**) entered and soon after, Daniel Ekeroth (**Dellamorte, Diskonto**) replaced bass player Hyytiä. In 2000 they recorded a new promo. In 2001 the band was reinforced by guitarist Tobias "Toob" Brynedal (**Genocrush Ferox**). This year, they also recorded the demo *Revelation Of The Sado God*, which featured a cover of **Death**'s *Zombie Ritual*. The track was also found on the 10" split with Greek band **Inveracity**. Earache Records picked the band up, and they released *Beneath The Folds Of Flesh* on the sub-label Wicked World. The album was produced by Berno Paulsson. In 2003 the band was featured with four tracks on the four-way split *Supreme Brutal Legions Volume 1* (Vrykoblast). In 2004 they released *Revealed And Workshipped*, produced by the late Mieszko Talarczyk (**Nasum**). After the album, Brynedal left and Daun was replaced by Marcus Jonsson (**Pandemonic, Genocrush Ferox, Remasculate, Flagellation**). In 2009 Ekeroth left the band to concentrate on finishing his excellent encyclopedia of Swedish death metal. He was replaced by Joel Andersson (**Immersed In Blood, Inverted, Nominon**). **Insision** play fast and furious death metal with a touch of thrash. Well-produced and well-played, with some quite technical twists. *Website: www.insision.com*

1999 MCD - HDMCD 010

REVELATION OF THE SADOGOD

2002 10" - NWR 004

2004 CD - WICK 17CD

1999	■	The Dead Live On	MCD 5tr	Heathendoom	HDMCD 010
		Tracks: Corridors Of Blood/Paedophilia Cum Sadissimus/The Dead Live On/She Speaks No More/Exaggerated Torment			
2002	□	The Dead Live On	MCD 5tr	Immortal Sould Productions	ISP 034
2002	■	Revelation Of The Sado God (split)	10" MLP	Nuclear Winter	NWR 004
		Split with Inveracity. Tracks: Intro/Before My Altar/SadoGod/Trapped Within/Zombie Ritual/The Revelation (outro). Limited edition 500 copies.			
2002	□	BENEATH THE FOLDS OF THE FLESH	CD	Wicked World	WICK 13CD
2004	■	REVEALED AND WORSHIPPED	CD	Wicked World	WICK 17CD
2004	□	REVEALED AND WORSHIPPED	CD	Soyuz Music (Russia)	WICK 17CD
2007	■	IKON	CDd	Dental Records	DR 190510
2011	□	End Of All	MCD 5tr	Sevared Records	SR-148
		Tracks: Expire/Curvature/Descend/Beckoning/Ex Oblivione			

2007 CDd - DR 190510

INSULT

Johan Svensson: v, Erik Gärdefors: g, Johan Thorstensson: b, Karl "Kalle" Wahllöf: d

Stockholm - **Insult** were formed in 2004, influenced by old-school Swedish death metal. They recorded their first demo, *Decree*, in 2005, at which time the band featured Erik, Kalle and Johan T. Before the second demo, Erik left the vocal duties to new singer Johan and they recorded the second demo *Axiom* between 2006-2007. In August 2009, Daemon Worship Productions released both demos as one CD. Old school-oriented death metal in the vein of **Vomitory** or **Kaamos**. After the release, session player Henke G replaced bass player Johan Thorstensson. Gärdefors has also played in **A-Bomb** and **Heresy**, the latter also featured Wahllöf.

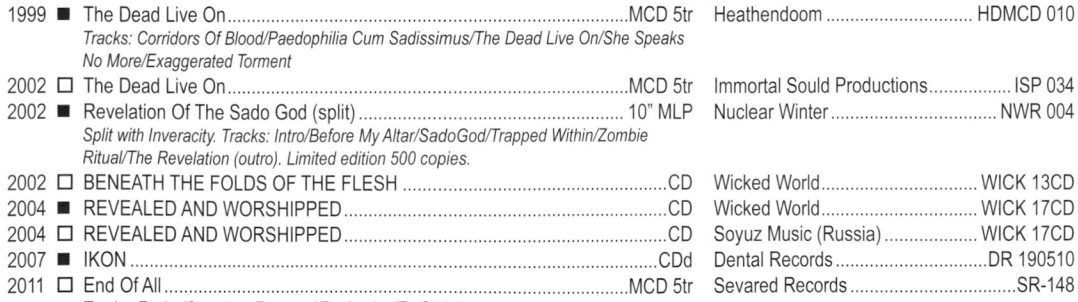

2009	■	ABYSMAL INCANTATIONS	CD	Daemon Worship	DWP 008

2009 CD - DWP 008

INTERACTION

Peter Lindskog: v/g, Jim Johnsson: g, Johnny Granström: b, Roger Karlsson: d

Karlshamn - Formed in 1979 by Peter, Jim and Roger. They started out sounding quite reminiscent of *Scorpions*, something that can be heard on the two tracks featured on the compilation-3LP *Rockslaget* (80 SOS). The band has recorded tons of demos and the single *Silver Lady* was only pressed as a promo-single in 6 copies. On the 7" Håkan Windahl was the lead singer. He left before the MLP was recorded and joined *Overheat*. Johnny was ex-*Ocean* and he replaced Kenth Eriksson, who had previously recorded two albums and an MLP with *Overdrive*. The band existed for a few years after the MLP, but went on playing cover-gigs and unplugged shows, which is a pity. *Interaction* was an excellent melodic hard rock band with great vocals and the talents of lead guitarist Jim (who actually is left handed and lost half his right hand ring-finger in an accident - guitarists should be banned from workshops). Jim is today found in the tribute band *AC/DC Jam*. Today Roger and Johnny play in country band *One 58*, while Håkan has released two solo albums ranging from pop and singer/songwriter stuff to melodic rock.The track *It's A Game* is also found on *Karlshamns Musikforum 15 år* (89 Musikforum).

1990 MLP - INT 002

1987	○	Silver Lady/It's A Game	7"	Sonet	- -	$$
		Test pressing, 6 copies without artwork.				
1990	■	Interaction	MLP 6tr	Tekla	INT 002	
		Tracks: Warrior/Go Man Go/Confession/Today/Pay With Rock/Shadow				

INTERMENT

Johan Jansson: v/g, John Forsberg: g, Martin Schulman: b, Kennet Englund: d

Avesta - Formed under the name *Beyond* already back in 1988. Two years later they released the rehearsal demo *Birth Of The Dead*. The line-up then featured singer Dan Larsson, guitarists Johan Jansson and John Forsberg, bass player Tomas Ängstgård and drummer Sonny Svedlund. In 1990 Larsson and Ängstgård jumped ship, while Jansson also took care of the vocals and they added Michael Gunnarson on bass. They now decided to change their name to *Interment*. In 1991 they entered Sunlight Studios to record the demo *Where Death Will Increase*. Sonny left and was replaced by Kennet Englund (*Centinex, Uncanny*). In 1992 they recorded the new demo *Forward To The Unknown* under the supervision of Dan Swanö. In 1994 they recorded the demo *The Final Chapter*, with Jens Törnroos (*Uncanny*) on vocals. After this, the band split. Johan went to *Uncurbed* and *Moondark* (later *Dellamorte*), where Kennet was also found. John went to *Astma* and *Morgue*. In 2002 Johan decided to blow new life into *Interment*. However nothing happened until 2006 when Michael Norrman became the band's new bass player and Conqueror Of Thorn Records wanted to release some of the old demos on a CD, plus some new songs for a split. This became the *Conjuration Of The Sepulchral* split CD. A few months later, Norrman (later in *Katatonia*) left and was replaced by Martin Schulman. They signed a new deal with Pulverised in 2008 and two years later the compilation CD *Where Death Will Increase* was released. The band also recorded their first album ever, entitled *Into The Crypts Of Blasphemy*. On tour, as John and Kennet couldn't make it, guitarist Tobias "Toob" Brynedal (*Insision, Genocrush Ferox*) and drummer Perra Karlsson (*Nominon, In Aeternum*) helped the band out. Jansson has been found in *Regurgitate, Demonical, Uncanny, Dellamorte* and *Centinex*, the two latter also featured Schulman.
Website: www.interment.se

Interment in front of the crypts

2007 CD - COT 006

2010 CD - ASH 070

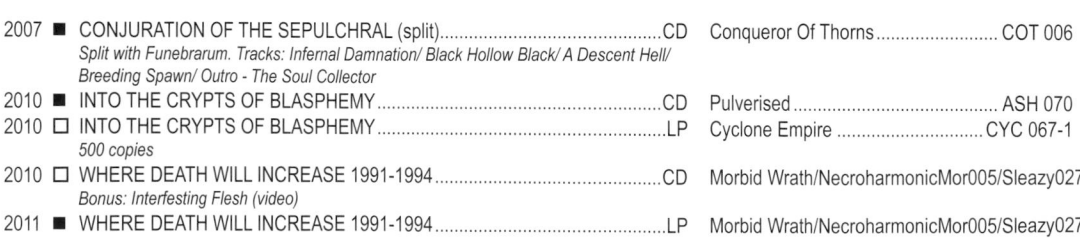

2011 LP - Mon005/Sleazy027

2007	■	CONJURATION OF THE SEPULCHRAL (split)	CD	Conqueror Of Thorns	COT 006
		Split with Funebrarum. Tracks: Infernal Damnation/ Black Hollow Black/ A Descent Hell/ Breeding Spawn/ Outro - The Soul Collector			
2010	■	INTO THE CRYPTS OF BLASPHEMY	CD	Pulverised	ASH 070
2010	□	INTO THE CRYPTS OF BLASPHEMY	LP	Cyclone Empire	CYC 067-1
		500 copies			
2010	□	WHERE DEATH WILL INCREASE 1991-1994	CD	Morbid Wrath/NecroharmonicMor005/Sleazy027	
		Bonus: Interfesting Flesh (video)			
2011	■	WHERE DEATH WILL INCREASE 1991-1994	LP	Morbid Wrath/NecroharmonicMor005/Sleazy027	

INTERNAL DECAY

Kim Blomqvist: v, Micke Jacobsson: g, Hempa Brynolfsson: g,
Karim Elomary: k, Kenny Lundstedt: b, Thomas Sjöblom: d

Upplands Väsby - Formed in 1987 under the name *Critical State*, which was changed into *Subliminal Fear*. They released the first demo under the name *Internal Decay* in 1991. A few weeks after the release of the album, guitarist Willy Maturana was replaced by ex-*Excruciate* man Hempa Brynolfsson. Their style is thrash with a touch of death metal. The CD was recorded at Sunlight Studios. The band split in 1994. Kenny and Micke have later been part of *Ad Infinitum* and *Deformity*.

1993 CD - EURO0934CD

| 1993 | ■ | A FORGOTTEN DREAM | CD | Euro Records | EURO934CD |

INTO THE VOID
Ola Wentrup: v/g, Joakim Bröms: k, Ola Svensson: b, Per Olofsson: d

Lund - Formed at the Roskilde festival in Denmark in 1993. A heavy 70s-oriented hard rock band that have also picked up one or two influences from bands like **Faith No More** and **Soundgarden**. Nice heavy riffing going on. Actually quite reminiscent of **Monster Magnet** but with the addition of a Hammond organ and not as depressing in their attitude. The band recommended *Facelift* should be filed under: EXPLOSIVE... and they are by no means out of line. Highly recommendable for fans of the early 70s heavy rock.

1995 ■ FACELIFT ....CD   M&A MACDL947

1995 CD - MACDL947

INVERTED
Patrik Svensson: v, Johan Ohlsson: g, Joel Andersson: b, Kristian Hasselhuhn: d

Alingsås - Formed in 1991. The band recorded their first demo, *Tales Of Esteban*, the same year, followed by *Heaven Defied* the year after. Quite varied high-speed death metal with warped low-key guttural vocals. Tight and powerful with a thrashy touch. The line-up featured Henric Heed (v), Mats Blomberg (g), Lars-Håkan "Larsken" Svensson (g) and Dan Bengtsson (b). On *Empire Of Darkness* Joel Andersson handled the bass duties. On *There Can Be Only One* the line-up had changed drastically and only Hasselhuhn and Andersson remained. The band split in 1998 and Johan and Joel were later found in **Immersed In Blood**. Hasselhuhn is the owner of Voice Of Death Records. Andersson was later to become a member of **Insision** and **Nominon**, while Ohlsson has been in **Blessed** and **Openwide**.

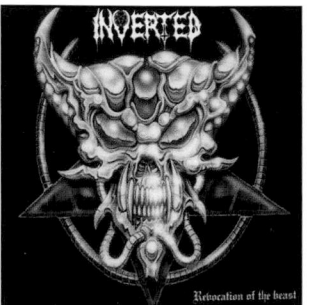
1994 MCD - WRR 046

1994 ■	Revocation Of The Beast	MCD 4tr	Wild Rags	WRR 046

Tracks: Revocation Of The Beast/Beyond The Holy Ground/Lost/Into The Sign Of Chaos

1995 ■	Empire Of Darkness/Crawling Underlies	7"	Regress Records	BTT 004
1995 ☐	THE SHADOWLAND	CD	Shiver Records	SHR 016
1996 ☐	Diabolical Ceremonies (split)	7"	Voice Of Death	VOD 003
	Split with Centinex. 600 copies.			
1997 ☐	THERE CAN BE ONLY ONE	CD	Shiver Records	SHR 025

1995 7" - BTT 004

INZIGHT
Anders Öhman: v, Peter Gidlund: g, Mikael Stålberg: g,
Peter Eriksson: b, Tommy Mattsson: d

Brunflo - Good, solid 80s melodic metal in the vein of **Judas Priest**. After the single, singer Öhman left and was replaced by former/later **220 Volt/Magic** singer Christer Åhsell. In 1991 the band split. However in 2005 Peter Eriksson decided to reunite the band. Besides old colleague Stålberg, he drafted former **220 Volt** guitarist Thomas Drevin, singer Stefan Sedvalsson and **Blackshine** drummer Håkan Eriksson. In 2008 Drevin left and was replaced by Mats Sannetorp. The band has played quite a few gigs since, mostly playing covers. Sannetorp has also released two solo albums in a heavy, bluesy vein and is now in the band **Zpeedfreak**.
Website: www.inzight.se

1989 7" - HEJ S-034

1989 ■ Lay Down Stay Down/We Are Gonna Be In Town Tonight ....7"   Active Music.................................. HEJ S-034
1000 copies.

ION OLTEANU BAND
Ion "Nutu" Olteanu: v/g, Petrus Kukulski: k, Kjell Allinger: k,
Ken Sundberg: b, Christer Karlsson: d

Stockholm (Botkyrka) - Great melodic hard rock/AOR similar to early **Toto**. Great guitar playing from Romanian-born guitarist Ion "Nutu" Olteanu, who had a prospering career in his home country before moving to Sweden (ex-**Iris**, **Titusi**) in 1990. He also released an eleven-track cassette album entitled *Olteanu* (AMP). The band reformed in 2008. Ion was also part of the outstanding band **Lead Boots** (also featuring Ken Sundberg). Ion also imitated Billy Gibbons in the Swedish TV show Sikta mot stjärnorna (aim at the stars). He has also been in **Bejerstrand Band** and **Sabbtail**. Ken Sundberg was also in **Stitch** and later in **Wasa Express**, while Allinger has been involved in lots of bands like **Kaargo** and **Tuk Tuk Rally**.

1991 7" - LAGRET 001

1991 ☐ Signs Of Reason/Love, Hope And Failure ....7"   Lagret............................LAGRET 001

IRON LAMB
Gustaf "Grga" Lindström: v, Johan Wallin: g, Jens Bäckelin: g,
Daniel Ekeroth: b, Thomas Daun: d

Stockholm/Linköping - **Iron Lamb** were formed in 2009 featuring some well-known names in the Swedish death metal scene. Lindström and Daun were both ex-**Repugnant** and Lindström

2009 7" - - -

was also in *Ghost* on the first single and album, Ekekroth was also in *Insision* and Wallin has played with *General Surgery* and *Repugnant*. The band, as they say themselves, is closer to *Motörhead* than *Iron Maiden*. Quite punkish hard rock. After *The Original Sin*, Jens (*Sanctuary In Blasphemy*) was added to the line-up. In 2013 Grga was out of the band.

2011 CD - ASH 085

2009	☐	Iron Lamb	7" 4tr	Nuclear Winter	NWR 033

Tracks: Suicide/Beamed Away/Dead Inside/Parasites. 500 copies.

| 2009 | ☐ | A Motorlamb With An Ironbreath (split) | 7" EP | Hellrocker Records | 001 |

Split with Motorbreath. Tracks: I Don't Like You/Fuck Off/We Murder. 300 copies.

| 2009 | ■ | Peskycostal Preaching | 7" 3tr | Soulseller | - - |

Tracks: Dubious Preacher/One Eyed Jack/Iron Lamb. 476 copies.

| 2011 | ■ | THE ORIGINAL SIN | CD | Pulverized | ASH 085 |
| 2011 | ☐ | THE ORIGINAL SIN | LPg+7" | High Roller Records | HHR 162 |

1st press: 150 bone/red splatter + woven patch + 350 black, poster, bonus 7" with Another Miserable Day/T.B.C.

| 2011 | ☐ | THE ORIGINAL SIN | LPg | High Roller Records | HHR 162 |

2nd press: 150 white/black splatter + 350 black. No bonus 7".

| 2013 | ☐ | Iron Lamb/Motorbreath (split) | MLP | High Roller Records | HHR 283 |

Split with Motorbreath. Tracks: Center Of The Universe/M.M.A. 500 copies.

| 2013 | ■ | Rip It Up/Mental Hell (Ramones cover) | 7"g | Craneo Negro Records | - - |

2013 7" - - -

IRON SHIT SNAKES
Tony Jelenkovich: v/g, Patrik Ljungblad: b, Peter Thorne: d

Partille (Göteborg) - This band is actually on the verge of punk and metal, but qualifies for this book mostly because of the more metallic approach and because of singer Tony Jelenkovich. Tony was also found in power metal band *B-Thong*, later heavy rockers *Transport League* and is now in *Massive Audio Nerve,* while Patrik and Peter joined *Teacher's Pet*. *Iron Shit Snakes* was just a side project for the guys to do something different. The lyrics are quite explicit, mildly speaking. They also have the song *Lars* on the local compilation *Greatest Hits Of Partille Rocken 1993*. A follow-up to *Syfilisation* was supposed to be released. It had the working-title *Goonoreation (An Ocean Of Diarrhea)*...eh?! But it was (fortunately?) never released.

| 1994 | ■ | Syfilisation | MCD 8tr | Noble Art | NARCDS 002 |

Tracks: Treklöver/Messed Up Fuck/Mayonarsch/Suck My Pink Pong/Whore: Pillu/Fuck To Please/Bullshit/Fuck U Eat Shit

1994 MCD - NARCDS 002

IRONWARE
Pasi Humppi: v/k, Niklas Möller: g, Stefan Andersson: g, Freddy Zielinsky: b, Håkan Strind: d

Borås - *IronWare* were formed in 1998 by Humppi and Möller with the aim to make easily listenable melodic metal in their own style. They found drummer Benny Eriksson and guitarist Stefan Andersson. Zielinsky (*Ablaze*) soon completed the line-up and later the same year they recorded their first demo, *Tales From A World Twisted*. As they needed a keyboard player, Dan Ljungdahl was recruited. Now Eriksson decided to leave and Strind entered. In 2000 the MCD *Return To The King* was unearthed. Shortly after Zielinsky and Ljungdahl decided to leave. Peter Wiberg (*Freternia*) filled the bass spot, but soon left to be replaced by the guy he replaced. The album was recorded by the above-listed line-up. Humppi has also been found in bands like *Freternia* and *Ablaze*. Zielinsky was also found in the latter plus *Fierce Conviction/Conviction*. Break Out was produced by Andy LaRoque and Pelle Saether. *IronWare* play melodic power metal in the vein of *Lost Horizon* and *Nocturnal Rites*. The band split after the album.

2000 MCD - THEKING 1187

| 2000 | ■ | Return Of The King | MCD 4tr | private | THEKING 1187 |

Tracks: Man Of Hope/Sanctuary/Return Of The King/From Deep Inside

| 2003 | ■ | BREAK OUT | CD | Limb Music | LMP 0309-058 |

2003 CD - LMP 0309-058

IRRBLOSS
Irrbloss: v, Vettfall: g, Alexander Wik "Frid" Fridén: g, Vrind (Tunnan): b, Isojärvi: d

Göteborg - The band initially started as singer Irrbloss' solo project, but he felt he needed better musicians backing him and drafted guitarist Fridén. Singer Irrbloss is also found in *Hvergelmer* and *Minionslayer*, while Fridén is ex-*It Will Come* and *Masugn*. In 2004 they recorded the track *Vandringssägen från skogs rike*, but the band was put on hold for a while before re-emerging in 2006. The line-up had now been completed with Isojärvi and Vettfall. They recorded the demo *Hymn* in 2007. Old-school, high-speed death metal. Well-played and better produced than many other bands in the old-school genre.

| 2008 | ■ | BLOODLINE | CD | Twilight Vertrieb | Twilight 784-1488 |

2008 CD - Twilight 784-1488

ISCAROTH

Vilhelm Bladin: v, Erik Söderlund: g, Erik Norbeck: b, Jonathan Hjalmarsson: d

Hudiksvall - The band was formed under the name *Enter The Core*, but in 2008 they changed their name to *Iscaroth*. The band plays high-speed, old-school death metal with a technical touch. The MCD was co-produced by Daniel Bergström (*Vildhjärta*).
Website: www.iscaroth.se/

2010 ■ Era Of The Cadaver..MCD 5tr   privat.................................EOTC 01
     Tracks: 1340 A.D/Bringers Of Disease/Sadistic Addiction/As Thou Come Forth/Era Of
     The Cadaver

2010 MCD - EOTC 01

ISENGARD

Linus Melchiorsen: v, Ronnie Andréson: g, Janne "Goat" Tillman: b, Ulf Tillman: d

Linköping - *Isengard* were formed in 1991 by Ronnie, Ulf and Jan. They released their first demo in 1992. On the first album Ronnie handled the vocals, and after this Tony "Odin" Ulvan (ex-*Hazy*) took over the task. The track *The Fire Of Isengard* is featured on the Büms compilation *Scandinavia Calling 2* and another track is found on the local compilation *Projekt Demokrati* (95 Studiefrämjandet). Ronnie has also recorded several solo demos. The early albums were mid-league, straightforward metal in the vein of *Vicious Rumors*. In 1998 Linus took over the vocal tasks. *Enter The Dragon Empire* owes more to the new German-style power metal genre with dragons, swords and the traditional paraphernalia. The English sure has its flaws with lines such as "Running so fast you can... the nightmares has open wide... or The dawn has spoke/ we standing here again". The latest album was produced by one of the forefathers of Swedish metal, Ragne Wahlquist (*Heavy Load*). Linus has later been found in bands like *Demented, Los Sin Nombre, Maitreya* and *Powerdise*.

1996 CD - SSCD-6001

2001 CD - SPHERE 001

Year		Title	Format	Label	Cat. no.
1994	□	FEEL NO FEAR	CD	EMP	49123
1995	□	Under The Dragons Wing	MCD 4tr	private	ISENCD-1
		Tracks: Under The Dragons Wing/Mirror Of Sadness/The Cold Dream/Final Journey			
1996	■	ENTER THE DRAGON EMPIRE	CD	Sound Hills (Japan)	SSCD-6001
2001	■	CROWNLESS MAJESTY	CD	Hemisphere	SPHERE 001

ISHTAR

Varg "Ahldrathan" Strand: v/g, Kaiserin: k/v, Troll: b, Agatash: d

Malmö - Formed in 1998 named after the Babylonian goddess of evil. Epic black metal with traces of *Dimmu Borgir* and *Siebenbürgen*. Varg is ex-*Misteltein* and *Fall Ov Seraphim* and is also in *Blind*. Artwork on the *Krig* reissue was made by Andreas Söderlund (*Abyssos, Insalubrious*).

2005 CD - IDR-666

Year		Title	Format	Label	Cat. no.
1998	□	Diabolical Hymns	MCD 3tr	Unv. The Wicked/Hammerh.	HHTUTW 001
		Tracks: Mörkrets Furste/Damnation/Dismal Paradise. 1000 copies.			
1999	□	KRIG	CD	Hammerheart	HHR 035
		1000 copies.			
2005	■	KRIG	CD	Imperial Dawn (Japan)	IDR-666
		999 copies. New artwork. Bonus: Damnation			

ISILDUR

Fredrik: v/b, Totte: g, Tom: v/k, Mange: d

Uppsala/Avesta - Straight ahead black metal with a thin sound and out of key vocals.

1998 ■ Isildur .... 7" 3tr   WSR .... WSR 001
     Tracks: Retarded/Remains To Be Seen/A Small Apartment:

1998 7" - WSR 001

ISOLE

Daniel Bryntse: v/g, Crister Olsson: g, Henrik Lindenmo: b, Jonas Lindström: d

Gävle - Formed in 1990 by Bryntse and Olsson under the name *Forlorn*, and recorded several demos with various other members in the line-up. The band took a break in the late nineties, until 2004, when I Hate Records contacted the band. Since they weren't the only band using the *Forlorn* moniker, they decided to rename themselves *Isole*. Bryntse is ex-*Withered Beauty, Windwalker, February '93, Sorcery, Theory In Practise, Ereb Altor* and *Morannon*, Lindenmo is ex-*Outremer* and *Morannon*, Olsson is ex-*Ereb Altor* and *February '93*, while Lindström is ex-*Demonical, Undivine* and *February '93*. The track *The Punishment* on the 2010 split-single was written during the early *Forlorn* days. *Isole* play slow melancholic doom metal, slightly reminiscent of *Solstice* and at times similar to *Griftegård*, but not as slow.
Website: www.forevermore.se/

2005 CD - IHR 010 CD

2005 ■ FOREVERMORE..CD   I Hate Records............................ IHR 010 CD

2006 CD - IHR 022 CD

2006 ☐	The Beyond/Beyond The Black II	7"	I Hate Records	IHR 018
	500 copies.			
2006 ■	THRONE OF VOID	CD	I Hate Records	IHR 022 CD
2007 ☐	FOREVERMORE	CD	I Hate Records	IHR 034 CD
	Re-issue with new artwork. Bonus: Tears Of Loss			
2007 ☐	BLISS OF SOLITUDE	CD	Napalm Records	NPR 232
2009 ☐	SILENT RUINS	CD	Napalm Records	NPR 279
2009 ☐	SILENT RUINS	2LPg	Cyclone Empire	CYC 037-1
	Bonus: Forevermore (demo)/Tears Of Loss (demo)/A Wish (demo)/Autumn Leaves (demo). 500 copies. Poster.			
2010 ☐	FOREVERMORE	LP	No Remorse Records	NRR 004
	Bonus: Tears Of Loss. 250 copies.			
2010 ☐	THRONE OF VOID	LP	No Remorse Records	NRR 005
	Bonus: Moonstone (live). 250 copies.			
2010 ■	Imperial Anthems 4 (split)	7"	Cyclone Empire	ANTHEM 004
	Split with Semlah. Track: The Punishment. 500 hand-numbered copies. Red/black splatter vinyl.			
2011 ☐	BORN FROM SHADOWS	CD	Napalm Records	NPR 394
2011 ☐	BORN FROM SHADOWS	2LPg	Napalm Records	NPR 394LP
	Bonus: Towards The Abyss/Waves Of Sorrow/No Return/Moonstone			

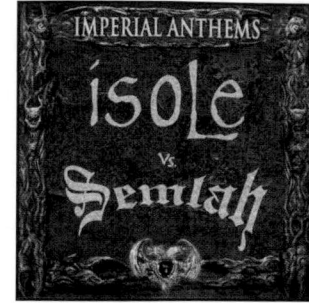

2010 7" - ANTHEM 004

ISTAPP

**Jonas "Mordechai" von Renvaktar: v/g,
Christoffer "Ashuck" von Renvaktar: b,
Martin "Fjalar" Michaelsson: d**

Has Hell finally frozen over?

Nättraby - **Istapp** play death metal with a lyrical theme about the wish for eternal winter (istapp means icicle in English), mixing old-school blast-beats with modern and quite melodic parts. Well-played and well-produced. A great band! **Istapp** was formed in 2000 by Michaelsson and recorded the first demo *Må det aldrig töa* (May it never thaw) in 2004 as a duo featuring Michaelsson (**Unchained, Nepharitus, Stacy's Inn**) and singer Erik "Erkblerk den Förskräcklige" Wulff. Christoffer (**Nepharitus, The Shattering**) and Tommy Carlsson (**Abomination, Devoured**) were drafted they released and a second demo, entitled *Ljusets förfall*, two years later. After this, Wulff was out of the band and so was Carlsson. In November 2007 Jonas (**Spawn Of Posession, Disruption**) was drafted and the band recorded a new demo as a trio. *Köldens union* is a compilation of the first two demos plus bonus tracks. Jonas is also found in rock 'n roll band **Jack Daw**. Late 2011 Michaelsson made **Istapp** his solo project again, and a new album is in the making.
Website: istappofficial.com/

2008 CD - SOL 02 CD

2010 CD - 3984-14872

2008 ■	KÖLDENS UNION	CD	Sol Invictus	SOL 02 CD
2008 ☐	KÖLDENS UNION	LPg	Sol Invictus	SOL 02 LP
	500 copies. White vinyl.			
2008 ☐	KÖLDENS UNION	LPg	War Anthem Records	WAR 020 LP
	Bonus: Köldens union (rehearsal demo)			
2010 ■	BLEKINGE	CD	Metal Blade	3984-14872
2010 ☐	BLEKINGE	CD	Fono (Russia)	FO832CD

IT WILL COME

Louise Halldin: v/b, Jonas Jörgensen: g, Mats Dacke: g, Christian Martinsson: d

Göteborg - The band name, strange as it seems, was taken from a song by *My Dying Bride*. The band made their first demo in 2004, made a follow-up in 2005, which was later released as a proper CD by Trinity Records, featuring some bonus material. A song was also released on the compilation *Entering The Levitation: A Tribute To Skepticism* (2007 Foreshadow). Another promo was recorded in 2008, entitled *Truth Is Nothing But Deceit*. *It Will Come* play quite melancholic, slightly goth-influenced but still melodic heavy rock. Previous members include guitarists Alexande Wik Fridén (*Irrbloss, Masugn*) and Linus Pilebrand (*Beneath The Frozen Soil*).

2007 CD - TRHK 012

2007 ■ 47 ....CD   Trinity Records (Hong Kong) .... TRHK 012

IT'S ALIVE

Martin "Max Martin/White" Sandberg: v, Per Aldeheim: g, Joakim "Kim" Björkegren: g, Peter Kahm: b, John Rosth: k, Rickard Evensand: d

Stockholm - Formed in 1987. Kim was ex-*Shed* while Per, Kim and John played in the band *Lazy*. The first 7" is a very rare item and the style is more soul/pop-oriented. After this the band went for a more heavy yet melodic and funky hard rock style. At times in the vein of *Dan Reed Network* at their heaviest. The first CD was only released as a promo. The single *Metalapolis* was never officially released due to the band landing a deal with Cheiron Records. There was also a cassette album enclosed with an issue of the English metal magazine *Metal Forces*. In 1994 *It's Alive* pursued an European-tour as support for *Kingdom Come*, after which drummer Anders "Gus" Gustafsson quit the band. He was replaced by ex-*Sorcerer/Manic Depression* drummer Rickard Evensand. Unfortunately, late 1994 the charismatic singer Martin decided to leave the band for a career as songwriter for Cheiron Records. The band recorded some demos with singer Anders Jansson (ex-*Mother Groove*) but later settled for former *Black Dog* singer Henrik "Baffe" Olsson. The new material had a much heavier approach, but still in the good old *It's Alive*-vein. The band however split in 1995. All singles contain non-CD tracks. Per Alderheim has contributed to the songwriting for *Def Leppard* and *Scorpions*, while Max Martin is a household name in the circuits of *Back Street Boys*, *Céline Dion*, *Westlife*, Pink, Britney Spears etc. Evensand is today living in Australia, playing with progressive rockers *Toehider* and Björkegren is in heavy rockers *Chosen By Gods*.

1988 7" - ILR 001

1992 MCD - CDATV 103

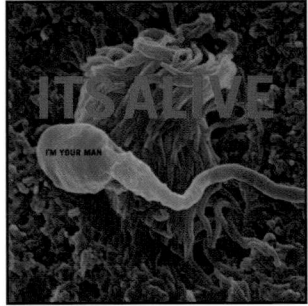
1993 CDS - CHC-6

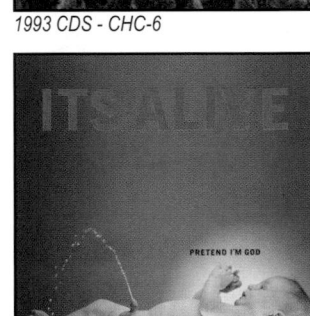
1994 CDS - CHC-22

1988 ■	Time Waits For No One/You ....7"	private	ILR 001	$
	The single was released with a transparent plastic cover with the band's name on it. 1000 copies.			
1991 ☐	IT´S ALIVE ....CD	Megarock Records..........MRR 001		
	1500 copies.			
1992 ■	Metalapolis/Face To Face/Funky Time ....MCD 3tr	Active ....CDATV 103		
1992 ☐	Metalapolis/Face To Face ....7"	Active ....ATV 103		
1993 ■	I'm Your Man/Parasite ....CDS 2tr	Cheiron CHC-6		
1993 ☐	News From The Swedish Rock Scene (split)..........MCDp 4tr	Cheiron ....PROMO CHC2		
	Promo split with Red Fun. Tracks: I'm Your Man/Pain			
1993 ☐	Sing This Blues ....MCD 3tr	Cheiron CHC-11		
	The tracks are Sing This Blues/Damnation/Sing This Blues (powerfailure version).			
1993 ☐	EARTHQUAKE VISIONS..........CD	Cheiron 74321 16144 2		
1993 ☐	EARTHQUAKE VISIONS..........CD	BMG Victor (Japan) MVCP-741		
1994 ■	Pretend I'm God/Play That Funky Music..........CDS 2tr	Cheiron CHC-22		

ITCH, THE

Lukas Landerö (aka Sunesson): v/g, Magnus Wahlberg: g, Tobbe Skogh: b, Johan Helgesson: d

Malmö - *The Itch* were formed during a night of alcohol splendour, when Magnus and Lukas were at a show. The original line-up featured Lukas (ex-*Booze Brothers*), Magnus, drummer Thomas Helgesson and bass player Conny Andersson. Because of obligations to his other bands *Svarte Pan* and *Babian*, Conny soon left the band. While in the studio they called Tobias (ex-*Carnival Sun*) to record some bass, and soon he was drafted. The songs were released as the first MCD. After this drummer Thomas (now in *Grand Rezerva*) left over to his brother Johan, who took over. Johan has previously played with *The Drugs*, *Original Sin* and *Pete Sandberg's Jade*. *The Itch* play great retro-oriented bluesy hard rock with a touch of bands like *Badlands*.
Website: www.theitch.se

2007 MCD - ITCH 0001

2007 ■	The Itch..........MCDp 4tr	private ....ITCH 0001	
	Tracks: Action/If You Could See/Get Me Started/Sold My Soul		
2011 ☐	SPREADING LIKE WILDFIRE..........CD	Rambo TI-SRV-1101	

ITCHY DAZE

Tomas Andersson: v/g, Mattias Klein: g,
Mattias "Dogge" Johansson: b, Patrik Nyman: d

Hofors - Formed in 2005 by Andersson, Klein, Nyman and Tomas Snellman. Snellman however left and was replaced by Mattias Heldevik, who was replaced by Johansson before the second album. The first album was more neo-punkish and influenced by bands like **Hoobastank** and **Green Day**, while the follow-up contains great melodic quirky hard rock, a bit reminiscent of **Galactic Cowboys** with a touch of **Foo Fighters**. On the verge of book entry.

2011 CDS - NRCD 110

2008	☐	I Never Work On Mondays/I Never Work On Mondays (acoustic)	CDS 2tr	Ninetone	NRCDS 008
2009	☐	DAZE OF OUR LIVES	CD	Universal	0602517-95722
		Bonus: I Never Work On Mondays			
2011	☐	Halo	CDS 1tr	Ninetone	NRCDS 022
2011	■	PROMISE LITTLE RUIN MUCH	CD	Ninetone	NRCD 110

IVORY

Janne Berggren: v, Mikael Sjöbom: g, Mats Olsson: g,
Kent Johansson: b/k, Håkan Wedin: d

Sundsvall - The A-side starts off with a nice keyboard intro and the rest is even more interesting. Well-played AOR, in the early and heavier **Alien** vein. Well worth looking for. Janne later formed the band **Europunch**, now known as **B 'N J**, which also features Thomas Nesslin (**Roulette, Cherry Red**) and Stefan Johansson, who were also found in **Snakes In Paradise**.

1987 7" - IV-001

1987	■	Find My Way/Hold On To The 80's	7"	private	IV-001

IXXI

Totalscorn: v, Axel "Acerbus" Axelsson Johnsson: g,
Jonas "Nattdal" Bergqvist: g, Avsky: b, Smoker: d

Stockholm - **IXXI** means 911 in Roman numbers. Formed in February 2006 by Axel "Acerbus" Axelsson Johnsson (**Ondskapt**) and Jonas "Nattdal" Bergqvist (**Dimhymn, Lifelover**). They drafted **Zavorash** singer Totalscorn, bassist Avsky and drummer Selin. Acerbus is also found in **Ondskapt**. The first album featured Selin (**Lifelover, Libricum**) on drums and Magnus "Devo" Andersson (**Marduk, Oxiplegatz**) handled "electronics". In 2008 guitarist Tommy "Talon" Åberg (**Rev 16:8, Bloodshed**) was added to the line-up. During the recording of *Assorted Armament*, Selin left and was replaced by Smoker. Mikael "Hravn" Karlsson of **Devil's Whorehouse** also added some drums. In 2009 Totalscorn suddenly left the band and attempts to find a replacement failed. In February 2010 the band finally folded. In 2011 the band was resurrected and the line-up changed drastically. Avsky and Talon were dismissed and Smoker was added. Elias "Core" Niemi was drafted on bass and Andreas "Stigmata/Non" on second guitar. They wrote new material, and Acerbus handled the vocals, but soon Stigmata was forced to leave and in the end of July founder Nattdal left the band. In August 2011 Adrian "Outlaw" Lawson (**Angrepp**) was drafted as singer. In September 2011, Jonas "Nattdal" Bergqvist, who was also found In **Lifelover, Dimhymn, Ondskapt** and **Woundism**, sadly committed suicide. **IXXI** labels their music death 'n roll and I do agree. It's not your typical death metal, but more groove-oriented in the musical department, with quite different growling style vocals. A bit similar to **Satyricon**, at times. Pretty good stuff well worth checking out.
Website: reverbnation.com/ixxi

IXXI in a darker shade of grey

2007 CD - THR 102

2007 CD - VOID 04

2009 CD - CANDLE 190 CD

2007	■	IXXI	CD	Total Holocaust	THR 102
2007	■	ASSORTED ARMAMENT	CD	Sigilla Malae	VOID 04
2009	■	ELECT DARKNESS	CD	Candlelight	CANDLE 190 CD

JACKWAVE

**Janne Persson: v, Janne Grunditz: g, Johan Petersson: g,
Björn Holstensson: b, Stefan Axelsson: d**

Boxholm - The A-side is a classic NWoBHM A-string pumping metal number, while the B-side is a semi-heavy power-ballad. Good vocals and a single well worth looking for! After the single Persson was replaced by Abbe and Grunditz by Toni Lindgren (*Transylvania*). The band recorded a demo in 1987 where the bass was handled by Tommy. A live video from Stenbocken Sporthall, recorded in January 1987 also exists. Now Toni handled both guitar and lead vocals. In 1988 the band recorded the songs *Rising Star* and *Release Me*, which were supposed to be the band's second single. Five test press copies are said to exist. Axelsson was also in *Airborne*, *Eisst* and *Transylvania*. Petersson was also ex-*Transylvania*.

1986 7" - PL 19

1986 ■	King Of The Sea/I'll Be There	7"	Platina	PL 19	$$
1988 ○	Rising Star/Release Me	7"	- -	- -	$$$
	Test press. Five copies.				

JADE, PETE SANDBERG'S

(See Pete Sandeberg's Jade)

JAGUAR

Rolf Scherrer: g/v, Per Ousbäck: g/v, Per Bruun: b/v, Håkan Höglund: d

Stockholm - Not sure how to categorise this. *Here To Live* mixes straight-ahead bluesy biker rock with some heavier guitars and brutal slide-work. *Southwind* is a pretty slick AOR-track, with some biting guitars however. Scherrer is also in *Kebnekajse* and Bruun is in *Fläsket Brinner*.

1986 7" - Z-1001

1986 ■	Here To Live/Southwind	7"	Rockland	Z-1001
	Red vinyl.			

JAMMER

**Erik Hjalmarsson: v, Thomas Larsson: g, Jocke Larsson: b,
Michael Rodin: k, Marcus Källström: d**

Borlänge - Originally known as *Jämmer Och Elände* they shortened their name to *Jammer*. Thomas recorded this when he was also in *Six Feet Under*. He later joined *Yeah Bop Station*, Glenn Hughes and has also recorded solo-CDs. Marcus was also in *Six Feet Under*, later *Sky High*, *Stonecake* and *Death Organ*. When Björn Lodin left *Six Feet Under*, Tomas, Jocke and Erik continued and recorded some great demos. They were actually just about to sign with EMI when they broke up due to internal disagreements. The demos, recorded under the names *Six Feet*, *Jammer* or *Tuppjuck Rock* are great and one contains the hit *My Blue Moon* later recorded by both *Baltimoore* and *Yeah Bop Station*. The 7" is great melodic hard rock! Jocke, who is Thomas' brother, later joined *Treat*.

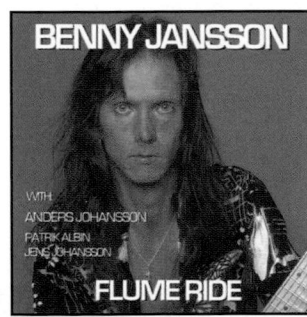

1983 7" - S-8301

1983 ■	Take Me Higher/Overlord	7"	Limelite	S-8301	$

JANSSON, BENNY

Benny Jansson: g

Stockholm - Benny is ex-*Avenue*, *Two Rocks*, *Power United*, *Mind Crime*, *Racketeer* etc. The last three bands however only recorded demos. *Racketeer* actually recorded a full-length album for Montezuma Records, but it was never released. Benny also plays on the albums by *The Johansson Brothers*, *Erika*, *Snake Charmer*, *Xaviour* etc. The solo albums are great instrumental pieces with Benny's highly sensitive but yet raw guitar playing. The music ranges from traditional Tony MacAlpine-type songs to more fusion-coloured numbers. The musicians on the first album were, besides Benny (g), Jens Johansson (k), Patrik Albin (b) and Anders Johansson (d). On the second they were a trio consisting of Benny, Anders and bass-player Fille Lindström (*Blacksmith*). *Save The World* saw Benny moving to Lion Music, and it also includes a couple vocal tracks. The album features some great guests, such as Göran Edman (v), Jens Johansson (k), Mathias GarGarnas (b) and Daniel Flores (d). Benny has also recorded an album together with Svullo.

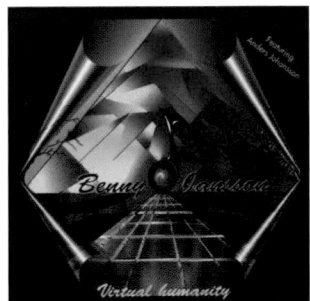

1995 CD - HECD 009

1999 CD - HECD 024

2002 CD - LMC 2226 2

1995 ■	VIRTUAL HUMANITY	CD	Heptagon	HECD 009
1999 ■	FLUME RIDE	CD	Heptagon	HECD 024
2002 ■	SAVE THE WORLD	CD	Lion Music	LMC 2226 2
2004 □	SAVE THE WORLD	CD	Irond (Russia)	CD 04-DD160

J

JAR

Reine "Ray Alex" Alexandersson: v, Anders Olsson: g/k,
LE Ericsson: g, Jan Andersson: d/b/k

Stockholm - **JAR** came together as a project in the 90s when Andersson and Olsson started recording their songs. They needed a singer and found former **Glory** vocalist Ray Alex. The name was simply made up of their initials. The recording took years, as they only used off-time in a studio. In 2000 they uploaded some songs on MP3.com, which became their one and only album, *In Truth We Trust*. The album was very limited and is a true collectors' item today. **JAR** produced some fine AOR, a bit thin on the production side, but a CD well worth looking for.

2000 ■ IN TRUTH WE TRUST...CD   mp3.com .... -- $$

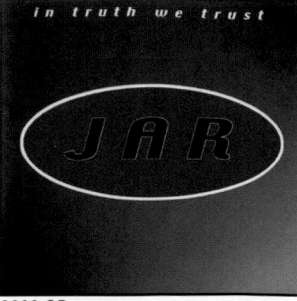

2000 CD - - -

JEANNE D'ARC

Björn Jönsson, Ulf Andersson

Hällevadsholm - Really good AOR in the vein of **Alien**. The B-side is a power ballad. Not to be confused with the Finnish namesakes.

1989 ■ Love Story/We All Know..7"   private ....JDS 1

1989 7" - JDS 1

JEKYLL & HYDE

Jakob "Jake Samuel" Samuelsson: v, Pontus Norgren: g,
Marcus Yidell: g, Mikael Höglund: b, Rickard Evensand: d

Stockholm - Jakob has quite a long and intriguing history, from being the drummer in AOR-band **Yale Bate**, singer of the band **Totem** (with Pete "Blakk" Jacobsson), drummer in **Talisman** and singer of **Jekyll & Hyde**. Of course, he has come quite a bit since, but let's stop here for a while. This is a great, powerful melodic hard rock band with Jake's vocals a' la James Neal (**Malice**). The band was formed in 1993 by bassist Stefan Molander, drummer Peter "Henrix" Henriksson (both later in **Gemini Five**) and Marcus Jidell. They later recruited singer Jacob Samuelsson. The first life sign was the track *Carry My Cross* on the *Peppes Album* (94 Peppes) compilation. After the first album was recorded the band was reinforced with former **Great King Rat** guitarist Pontus Norgren. On *Fallen Angel* bass player Molander was replaced by Mikael Höglund (ex-**Great King Rat**, **Thunder**, later in **Audiovision**) and drummer Henriksson by Rickard Evensand (**It's Alive, Southpaw** etc.). The band split in 1999. Jacob was also singing in the prog-metal band **Treasure Land** on their second album and in 2001 he replaced Pete Sandberg in **Midnight Sun**. He later joined forced with Norgren and Yidell in power metal band **The Ring**. He and Norgren were also in the first recording line-up of **The Poodles**, whom Jakob is still fronting. Norgren is found in **Hammerfall**. Evensand is living in Australia and plays with progressive band **Toehider**. Yidell was a member of Danish band **Royal Hunt** for several years and plays with rock 'n rollers **The Chiefs** and **Punchline**. In 2012 Jacob release his first solo album, in a westcoast/singer songwriter style.

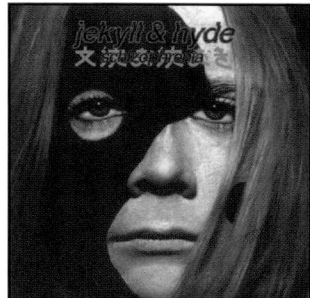

1995 CD - ERCD 1028

1998 CD - ZR 1997001

1995 ■ SCHIZOPHRENIA...CD   Empire ....ERCD 1028 $
1998 ■ HEAVENLY CREATURES................................CD   Z Records ZR1997001
1998 ☐ FALLEN ANGEL...CD   Z Records ZR1997009

JENNIE TEBLER'S OUT OF OBLIVION

Jennie Tebler: v, Fredrik Rhodin: g, Kent Jädestam: g/b, Tony Baioni: d

Stockholm - Jennie is the sister of legendary **Bathory** founder and Swedish death metal forefather, the late Ace "Quorthon" Forsberg. In 2006 Jennie also released two CD singles under her own name (see **Tebler, Jenny**), where *Silverwing* was a tribute to her late brother. *Till Death Tear Us Apart* was mixed by Pelle Saether. Surprisingly far from the style of Quorthon, more modern-sounding almost emo-oriented metal with a folky touch.

2008 ■ TILL DEATH TEAR US APART ....CD   Black Mark .... BMCD 190

2008 CD - BMCD 190

JEREMIAH

Göran Bengtsson: v/g, Thomas Jacobsson: b, Kjell Nilsson: d

Varberg - Pretty decent straight-ahead hard rock/metal. Despite the English title, both songs are sung in Swedish.

1980 ■ Rock à strul?..7"   KAP Records .... KAPS-8001 $
    Tracks: Bluff-Stop/Lost In (Lund)

1980 7" - KAPS-8001

JERUSALEM

Ulf Christiansson: v/g, Peter Carlsohn: b, Michael Ulvsgärd: d

Göteborg - Jerusalem have to be one of Sweden's first Christian hard rock bands. Although they were far heavier live than on vinyl, the albums contain some really powerful tracks, especially the early ones. On *Vi kan inte stoppas/Can't Stop Us Now* they became more symphonic and softer. *Klassiker 1* is a compilation of *Jerusalem* and *Volym 2*, while *Klassiker 2* contains *Krigsman* and *Vi kan inte stoppas*. The early albums were released in one English and one Swedish version. Up until *Live In USA*, Dan Tibell played keyboards and on *Dancing...* Reidar I Paulsen took over. Michael Ulfsgärd replaced Klas Andelhell on *Vi Kan Inte Stoppas*, Peter Carlsohn replaced Anders Mossberg on *Krigsman*. On the debut the bass was handled by Bertil Sörensson and drums by Dan Gansmoe. *Prophet* sounds a bit like *U2* goes AOR and featured the following personnel: Ulf, Peter, Reidar and Mikael. Ulf Christiansson has also released the solo album entitled *The Lifestyle From Above* (91 Pierced Records - JMRCD/LP 55006/-4). The musicians on that album are, besides Ulf, Peter Carlsohn, Reidar Paulsen and Mikael Ulfsgärd. Almost makes it a ***Jerusalem***-album, doesn't it? Another album that featured Christiansson, Carlsohn, Ulvsgärd and Paulsen was *Kom loss* by Jonnie Slottheden (1986 JS Förlag). Dan Tibell was later found in **Agape** and **Heartcry**. *Volym Tre* was recorded in 1996, but with the 1978 line-up. The songs were written between 1974 and 1983 and were originally meant to be the third ***Jerusalem***-album. The line-up split and new material was written. The album is actually a gem, with great guitar-oriented hard rock in the vein of the first two albums. In 1997 the band released the live album *Live på ren svenska* and after that they took a long break. In 2006 they returned with the thirty-year anniversary live CD and DVD, feauring Mossberg, Carlsohn, Anderhell, Ulvsgärd, Tibell, Paulsen and Christiansson. In 2010 they returned as a trio with the new, quite heavy, studio album *She*.

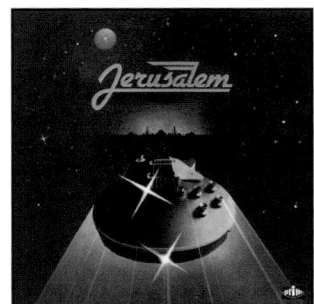

1978 LP - LP 570 430

1980 LP - LP 570 680

1981 LP - PRL 5004

Year		Title	Format	Label	Catalog
1978	■	JERUSALEM (Swedish)	LP	Prim	LP 570 430
1978	□	JERUSALEM (English)	LP	Prim	LP 570 550
1978	□	JERUSALEM (English)	LP	Lamb & Lion (USA)	LL 1049
1979	□	JERUSALEM (English)	LP	Praise Records (UK)	PLP 4
1980	□	VOLYM 2 (Swedish)	LP	Prim	LP 570 650
1980	■	VOLUME 2 (English)	LP	Prim	LP 570 680
1980	□	VOLUME 2 (English)	LP	Myrhh (UK)	MYR 1097
1981	■	KRIGSMAN (Swedish)	LP	Prim	PRL 5004
1981	□	WARRIOR (English)	LP	Prim	PRL 5006
1982	■	It's Mad/Nu Skall Jag Lita På Jesus	7"	Prim (promo)	PRS 9001
		B-side taken from Ulf Christiansson's solo album.			
1981	□	WARRIOR (English)	LP	Myrrh (UK)	1113
1983	□	VI KAN INTE STOPPAS (Swedish)	LP	Royal Music	RMLP 012
1983	□	Vi kan inte stoppas/Regn	7"	Royal Music	RM 012
1983	■	CAN'T STOP US NOW (English)	LP	Refuge Records (USA)	RO 3862
1985	□	IN HIS MAJSETYS SERVICE - LIVE IN USA	LP	Refuge Records (USA)	R 84026
1985	□	IN HIS MAJSETYS SERVICE - LIVE IN USA	LP	World Record Music	WRMLP 03
1986	□	10 YEARS AFTER	LP	Refuge Records (USA)	7900603905
1987	■	Dancing On The Head Of The Serpent/Listen To Me	7"	JM Records	JMRS 55004
1987	□	DANCING ON THE HEAD OF THE SERPENT	LP	JM Records	JMRLP 5500
1987	□	DANCING ON THE HEAD OF THE SERPENT	CD	JM Records	JMRCD 55003
1988	□	DANCING ON THE HEAD OF THE SERPENT	CD	Refuge Records (USA)	7900603018
1988	□	DANCING ON THE HEAD OF THE SERPENT	LP	Refuge Records (USA)	7900602984
1993	□	KLASSIKER 1	CD	Fruit Records	FRCD 55009
1993	□	KLASSIKER 2	CD	Fruit Records	FRCD 55010
1993	□	Tomorrow/Coming Down	CDS 2tr	Viva	VIVADS 10
1994	□	PROPHET	CD	Viva	VIVAD 124
1994	□	PROPHET	CD	R.E.X (USA)	REW 41010-2
1994	□	PROPHET	CD	Zero (Japan)	XRCN-1138
1994	□	The Waiting Zone/Berlin 38	CDS 2tr	Viva	VIVADS 12
1996	□	CLASSICS 1	CD	Jerusalem Music International	JMI-CD 7700
1996	□	CLASSICS 1	CD	Fruit Records	FRCD 55012
1996	□	CLASSICS 2	CD	Jerusalem Music International	JMI-CD 7701
1996	□	CLASSICS 2	CD	Fruit Records	FRCD 55013
1995	□	CLASSICS 3	CD	Jerusalem Music International	JMI-CD 7702
1995	□	CLASSICS 3	CD	Fruit Records	FRCD 55011
		Compilation of In His Majesty's Service and Dancing On The Head Of The Serpent.			
1996	□	VOLYM TRE	CD	Fruit Records	FRCD 55014
1997	□	THOSE WERE THE DAYS (VOLYM TRE)	CD	Alliance	ALD 125
1997	□	THOSE WERE THE DAYS (VOLYM TRE)	CD	Jerusalem Music (USA)	JMI-CD 7703
1997	□	VOLYM FYRA	CD	Fruit Records	FRCD 55015
1998	□	R.A.D (VOLYM FYRA)	CD	Jerusalem Music (USA)	JMI-CD 7704
1998	□	LIVE PÅ REN SVENSKA	CD	Fruit Records	FRCD 55016
1999	□	VOLUME FOUR	CD	Alliance	50285 1901912 7
2006	□	TRETTI	2CD	Pierced Records	PCD 011
2006	□	GREATEST HITS	CD	Pierced Records	PCD 012
2010	□	SHE	CDd	Pierced Records	PCD 014

1982 7" - PRS 9001

1983 LP - RO 3862

1987 7" - JMRS 55004

J

JESUSEXERCISE
Ulrika Karlsson: v, Max Thornell: g, Jan-Olof Karlsson: b, Magnus Svensson: d

Växjö - Formed in 1989, split in 1992. Heavy and slow gothy thrash in the vein of *Paradise Lost*. Max was later found in *Furbowl* (later *Wonderflow*) and has previously recorded with doomsters *Dom Där* and his own punk/hard core project *Max & The Chainsaws*. The previously unreleased track *Silent Spring* can be found on the local compilation *Café Kristina* (92 Växjö 650 dB). Thornell is also found in *Satanarchy*.

1990 7" - JESUS

1990 ■	The Voice Of Profit, The Sound Of Poverty	7" 3tr	private		JESUS
	Tracks: The Voice Of Profit/Revenge/Sick & Holy				
1990 □	The Voice Of Profit, The Sound Of Poverty	7" 3tr	PAS-83		0081/291
	Re-issue. 500 copies.				

JET
Elinor Hasson: v, Janne Wännström: g/k/b, Tobbe Sandström: d/k

Skellefteå - Ok, this one is definitely on the edge. I entered the band before hearing the entire album, which contains only four really good AOR songs, while the rest is pop. For fans of *Time Gallery* etc. Formed in 1980, split in 1983. Janne Wännström, who was also a hockey player in Mörrums GoIS, continued in the band *Twice* and now runs production company Voicemedia.

1983 LP - KNLP 004

1983 ■	MIXED EMOTIONS	LP	KN	KNLP 004
	1000 copies.			

JET AIRLINER
Andreas Aspell: v/b/g/k/d, Åke Noreen: v/g

Karlskoga - *Jet Airliner* play melodic light weight AOR with a strong 80s touch. Some tracks have pretty strong pop overtones with a touch of *The Cars*, while the track *Heaven's Waiting* sounds quite similar to *Starz*'s *Fallen Angel*. Well-played and well-sung. Should appeal to fans of bands like Brett Walker, *Bad Habit* and *Alien*. Noreen has played in various bands like *Bloomingdays*, *Wood*, *Flames* and *De Nadas*.

2007 CD - SBSR 09

2007 ■	PUSH ON THRU' TIL DAWN	CD	Side By Side	SBSR 09

JET CIRCUS (THE)
Sven "Ez" Gomér: v/b

Göteborg - *The Jet Circus* is a great hard rock band with various influences, one being early *Van Halen*. Lots of melody, great guitar-work and high-class vocals. *Victory Dance* should appeal to fans of *Electric Boys*. Before they formed *The Jet Circus*, bass player Sven "Ez" Gomér and singer/guitarist Terje "Terry Haw" Hjortander recorded the album *Setting Fire To The Earth* with Christian hard rockers *Leviticus*. The band was completed with drummer Jörgen "Little George Gustavsson" Tjusling (*Elsy Band, Human Race, Eaglestrike*). *Step On It* was supposed to be released on vinyl, but due to incorrect mastering it never officially happened. It was however released on cassette by Wonderland. A second album was recorded and set for release late in 1996, but it didn't happen. They also shortened the name to *Jet Circus*. The album featured Gomér, Hjortander and drummer Michael Ulvsgärd (*Jerusalem*). It was also scheduled for 2012, under the name *No Mercy For The Living Dead*. They were sponsored by Harley Davidson, even though Terje didn't even have a driver's license! In 2005 the band resurfaced with the album *Look At Death Now*, but was now more or less Ez Gomer with friends, including people like drummers Mikkey Dee (*Motörhead, Nadir*) and Michael Ulvsgärd (*Jerusalem*), guitarists Tommy Denander, Sayit Dölen and Stefan Elmgren (*Hammerfall, Full Force, FullStrike*) and keyboardists Dan Helgesson, Ulf Vinyl Stenberg and Joakim Holgersson. The album is a strange mishmash of heavy, modern riffs, poppy melodies and Ez vocals which is not bad, but not really up-to-par, which also applies to the messy production. The album is scheduled to be reissued as *Dance Or Die* with heavy dance remixes of the songs. Hypersonic Records will also reissue of *Step On It* with bonus material. Gomér has also planned a solo release for 2013, entitled *Vegas Overdose*, containing Elvis Presley covers.
Website: www.jetcircus.com

Ez Rider
1990 CD - 60101

1989 □	Victory Dance/Rocking Horse	7"	Eurozont	EZS 013
1989 □	Be-Bop-A-Lula/Ghosttown	7"	Eurozont	EZS 018
1990 ■	STEP ON IT	CD	Wonderland (USA)	7013000655
1990 □	STEP ON IT	CD	Epic	EK 47 802/468831
	With Let's Dance (Jim Lee cover) instead of Be Bop A Lula (Gene Vincent cover).			
1991 □	STEP ON IT	CD	Pony Canyon (Japan)	PCCY 00280
	Same songs as above, but with a different booklet.			
1990 ■	STEP ON IT	CD	Pila (Germany)	60101
	With Be Bop A Lula (Gene Vincent cover) instead of Let's Dance (Jim Lee cover)			
1990 □	STEP ON IT	LP	Pila (Germany)	LP 20157 $
	Around 120 copies exist, as the release was stopped by the band.			
2005 □	LOOK AT DEATH NOW	CD	Hypersonic	HRCD 001

1990 CD - 7013000655

418

JET TRAIL

Carolina Lindwall: g, Jon Stavert: g, Johan Holst: b, Christian Sundell: d

Växjö - Jet Trail play high-class ballsy AOR/melodic hard rock, produced by Martin Kronlund (*Dogface, Gypsy Rose* etc). Sundell has also played with *Grand Illusion*, while guest bassist Tommy Braic is ex-*Mandrake Root* and Stavert is ex-*Promotion*.

2007 ■	EDGE OF EXISTANCE	CD	Escape	ESM 158
	Bonus: Why			

2007 CD - ESM 158

JEZIDER

Sebastian Lind: v/g, Fredrik Nilsson: v/g, Stefan Nordström: b, Henrik Lingman: d

Gävle - Jezider were formed in 1984. *Don't Beat My Friend* is a decent hard rock/metal tune, while the B-side is a horrible rap with metal guitars halfway through the song. The band never considered themselves being hard rock, even though they were influenced by *Kiss*, *Anthrax* and *Beastie Boys*. In 1988 Stefan Norström sadly died in a biking accident and he was replaced by Valle Magnusson. The band was also reinforced by keyboardist Rikard Eriksson. Today Fredrik is a music journalist, Magnusson a bass teacher, Lind is head of BSS Marketing at Ericsson and Eriksson a frame maker.

1987 ■	Don't Beat My Friend/Rock 'N Roll Rap	7"	private	CAP 087
	500 copies.			

1987 7" - CAP 087

JIDHED, JIM

Jim Jidhed: v

Göteborg - Just when *Alien* had made their big break with the old *Marbles*-cover *Only One Woman*, Jim decided to leave the band. However, he went solo, and in 1989 he recorded the album *Jim* which is a highly acclaimed album among AOR-lovers. Later on he was more into making poppy hit-music and started to sing in Swedish. He recorded more things in this vein, not worth mentioning. A new album was set to be released in 1996, but nothing happened, until 2003, when Atenzia Records finally convinced Jim to get back in action. This resulted in the 2003 album *Full Circle*, an excellent AOR album featuring an array of high-class musicians such as Tommy Denander (g), Sayit Dölen (g), Bruce Gaitch (g), Marcel Jacob (b), Henrik Thomsen (b) and Marcus Liliequist (d). In 2007 he recorded the Swedish pop album *Reflektioner* and in 2005 Jim made a comeback with the reunited *Alien*.

1989 LP - 210 290

1989 CDS - 662 788

1989 □	JIM	CD	Virgin	260 290
1989 ■	JIM	LP	Virgin	210 290
1989 □	Silence Is Golden/Mirror	7"	Virgin	112 163-7
1989 □	Silence Is Golden/Mirror	CDS 3" 2tr	Virgin	112 163-2
1989 □	Woman Is The Hunter/(extended re-mix)	12" 2tr	Virgin	612 231-1
1989 □	Wild Young And Free/You Must Tell Her	7"	Virgin	112 788-7
1989 ■	Wild Young And Free/You Must Tell Her	CDS 2tr	Virgin	662 788
1990 □	Oh, Girl/Two Cold Hearts	7"	Virgin	113 140-2
1990 □	Love Spins/Heart To Heart	7"	Virgin	114 117-7
1990 □	Love Spins/Heart To Heart	CDS 2tr	Virgin	114 117-2
1990 □	JIM	CD	Virgin Japan (Japan)	VJCP-71
2002 □	I'll Be Ready Then	CDS 1tr	Atenzia (promo)	ATZPROM1
2003 ■	FULL CIRCLE	CD	Atenzia	ATZ02006
2003 □	Full Circle	CDS 1tr	Atenzia (promo)	ATZPROM2
2008 □	JIM	CD	AL!VE	10050
	Bonus: Heartbreak/Miss Lovin' You/Love Spins/Woman Is The Hunter			

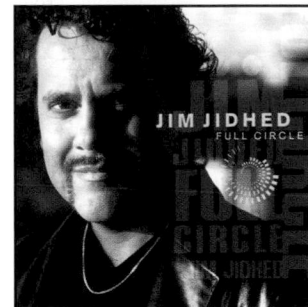

2003 CD - ATZ02006

JIGSORE TERROR

Tobbe Ander: g, Hampus Klang: b/v, Adde Mitroulis: d

Växjö - Jigsore Terror were formed in 2001 as an outlet for the members' love of death/grind. Klang is also in *Bullet* and *Birdflesh*, formerly with *Hypnosia*, Mitroulis is also in *Birdflesh*, *Dethronement*, *General Surgery* and grind band *Sayyadina*, while Ander is ex-*Leukemia*. *Jigsore Terror* play quite streamlined blast-beat-filled death/grind in the vein of *Carcass*.

2004 □	WORLD END CARNAGE	CD	Listenable	POSH 062
2005 ●	Jigsore Terror/Suppository (split)	7" PD	Power It Up	P.I.U 35
	Split with Suppository. Tracks: Rotten Heads/Reeking Death/Feast Of Dismembered Limbs. 500 copies.			
2005 □	WORLD END CARNAGE	LP	Power It Up	P.I.U 48
	Bonus: The Needle (Furbowl cover).			
2005 □	WORLD END CARNAGE	LP	Power It Up	P.I.U 48
	Bonus: The Needle (Furbowl cover). 100 copies in blue vinyl.			

2005 7" PD - P.I.U 35

J

JIMMY NIELSEN & BAND
Jimmy Nielsen: v, Magnus Jonsson: g, Jan Hotverber: b, Erik Amkoff: d

Umeå - The A-side is a great, raw, bluesy, seveties hard rocker, while the B-side is an up-tempo proto metal rocker. Decent vocals with a Christian message. Nice biting guitar work. Well worth looking for!

1982 ■ Heroin där fick du tji/Fort fort springer du.......................................7" Karamel Musikproduktion .... JN 777

1982 7" - JN 777

JOHANNES
Anders Johansson: v/g, Mikael Hed: b, Pelle Pettersson: d

Jönköping - Christian melodic hard rock/metal with prominent guitars. The band is good, but the production leaves a lot more to be desired. Vocals in Swedish. They later added a keyboard player, a chorus girl, switched bass player, changed their style to more AOR-oriented hard rock and changed their name to **Heartcry**. Anders and Pelle are also in **Green Sleeves**.

1984 ■ Röst I Öknen/Kärlekens Pansar...7" Vital Music.. VT 001 **$**
       Some copies came with a slightly different brown-ish artwork.

1984 7" - VT 001

JOHANSSON (BROTHERS, THE)
Jens Johansson: k, Anders Johansson: d

Anderslöv/Los Angeles - This is more of a project of Jens and Anders Johansson. The story actually starts in the late 70s when Anders and Jens formed the fusion-jazz-rock trio **Slem** together with guitarist Erik Borelius. They later joined **Silver Mountain** and did their first show with the band on January 10, 1981 and recorded a song for the compilation album *Skånsk Rock*. The **Silver Mountain** debut *Shaking Brains* was recorded for Ewita Records, who sold the rights to Roadrunner. In 1984 the brothers joined **Yngwie Malmsteen's Rising Force**, but left in 1989 after the live album *Trial By Fire*. They joined forces with Swedish bass virtuoso Jonas Hellborg and spontaneously recorded two albums under the names **RAF** (*Ode To A Tractor*) and **Shining Path** (*No Other World*). The last one being a great heavy death/progressive record, also made in another (initially) unreleased version under the name **Bakteria** – it became the ultimate cult tape with totally unprintable lyrics! It was finally released in CD in 2010, on Anstalt Records, but no one really got it at all. At least not the attorneys, who forced the label to destroy the pressing of 3000 copies (a few promos were saved). At the same time Anders did tons of studio jobs for numerous unnamed bands and musicians in Los Angeles, until the spring of 1991 when he joined **Blue Murder**. He played with John Sykes for 12 hours a day for 6 months until he was sacked, asked to rejoin the band and then finally left. Some of the drum tracks actually ended up on John Sykes' solo album *Nuclear Cowboy*. In 1991 Jens released his strange solo effort *Fjäderlösa Tvåfotingar* on Amigo Records. In the fall of 1991 Anders recorded the debut album with **Billionaires Boys Club** (*Something Wicked Comes*) as well as the debut by **Snake Charmer** (*Smoke And Mirrors*), in 1993 Anders released his solo album *Shu-Tka* and then the first **The Johansson Brothers** platter was recorded. The bass was handled by the late Marcel Jacob (**Yngwie Malmsteen, Talisman, Humanimal**), guitar by Benny Jansson (**Two Rocks, Avenue**, solo) and the vocals by Leif Sundin (**Great King Rat, Norum, MSG**). Anders also helped out on **Keegan**'s debut, **Racketeers** (featuring Benny Jansson), Jonas Hellborg (**E**), Benny Jansson's solo CDs, **Power United**, **Quadruple**, Svullo, Robban Blennerhed's debut, **Mountain Of Power, Seven** etc. Jens was part of the backing band on the album *Smoke On The Water - A Tribute* on Shrapnel Records and has also recorded with **Dio, Deadline**, Steve Ross, Ginger Baker, Tony MacAlpine, Roland Grapow, **Blackmore's Night** and is now a member of Finnish metallurgists **Stratovarius**. The above line-up minus singer Leif also backed Dave Nerge on the album *The Return Of Mr. Nasty* in 1994, an album originally written for Glenn Hughes (who even recorded some of the tracks). Anders and Jens also released the album *Heavy Machinery* together with Allan Holdsworth (96 Heptagon /97 Shrapnel), which was in a fusion-oriented style. *Sonic Winter* and *The Last Viking* were released under the name **Johansson**. In 1999 Anders joined heavy metal band **Hammerfall**, where he is still found. He was also a member of **Aces High** and is now in the band **FullForce**. On *The Last Viking* Leif Sundin was replaced by Göran Edman and Benny Jansson by Michael Romeo (**Symphony X**) and the band had no bass-player, whereas the bass work was handled by Marcel Jacob on the first two albums. The first two albums owe a bit more to **Deep Purple**, while *The Last Viking* is high-quality, neoclassical metal. *The Johansson Brothers/Sonic Winter* is a double-CD package of the first two albums at single CD price. In 2000 Anders released an album together with Jakob Hydén under the name **Elvis Pelvis**, doing only 50s covers in the true 50s vein. Truly odd. In 2001 he and Jens were reunited with **Silver Mountain** for the one album *Breaking Chains*.

Brothers in arms... and legs

1994 CD - ARCD-002

1999 CD - HECD 23

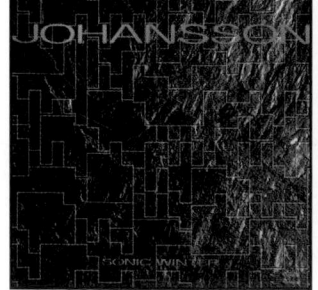
1996 CD - PCCY-00970

1998 CD - NEMS 107

1994	■	THE JOHANSSON BROTHERS	CD	Arctic Records	ARCD-002
1994	☐	THE JOHANSSON BROTHERS	CD	Zero (Japan)	XRCN-1127
		Different artwork.			
1996	■	SONIC WINTER	CD	Pony Canyon (Japan)	PCCY-00970
1998	☐	THE LAST VIKING	CD	Pony Canyon (Japan)	PCCY-01340
		Bonus: Samurai			
1998	☐	THE LAST VIKING	CD	Laser Company (Brazil)	RBR/LCR 1690
1999	■	THE LAST VIKING	CD	Heptagon	HECD 23
1999	■	THE LAST VIKING	CD	NEMS (Argentina)	NEMS 107
		Bonus: Samurai. Different artwork with Viking.			
2000	■	THE JOHANSSON BROTHERS/SONIC WINTER	2CD	HMG	HECD 21/22
2000	☐	THE JOHANSSON BROTHERS/SONIC WINTER	2CD	NEMS (Argentina)	NEMS 200
		Different artwork with Viking.			

2 CDs for the price of one!
JOHANSSON
FEATURING
YNGWIE MALMSTEEN
JOHN LEVÉN
LEIF SUNDIN

The Johansson Brothers / Sonic Winter

2000 2CD - HECD 21/22

JOHNNY ENGSTRÖM BAND
Johnny Engström: g/v, Niklas Högberg: b, Jan-Ove "Galle" Johansson: d

Örebro/Karlskoga - Johnny and Niklas started playing together at the age of 12 (!). They drafted drummer Galle, played for a year and then took a break when Johnny moved to the US. In 1984 he returned and the trio formed **Dead End Street**. Galle left the band in 1986 and was replaced by Roger Jern. In 1988 they recorded the single *Sheila* (1988, DES 0988), but split in 1992. Jern joined **Damned Nation** and Johnny started writing music. He put up some of his songs on MySpace and in 2007 he was contacted by Blue Topaz who wanted to release his music. He compiled some of his finished songs and released the debut album under his own name. The recordings featured Anders Lindén (k), Henrik Randén (b) and drummers Galle and Erik Lindstedt. The album was a mixed bag of tricks ranging from **Rush**-style semi-progressive hard rock to AOR to almost pop-oriented melodic rock. When it was time to start promoting the album Johnny drafted his old friends Niklas and Galle and the band became the **Johnny Engström Band**. On the second album, *From Birth To Chaos*, the style had become more refined progressive hard rock ranging from heavy riffing in the vein of **Dream Theater** mixed with **Rush**, to serene symphonic parts similar to **The Flower Kings**. On *Magnetic Force* the sound had become even heavier, leaning more towards **Dream Theater** and **Rush**, but with a darker edge. A great band! Changed their name to **Dead End Space** and released the killer album *Distortion Of Senses* in 2013, with the same line-up.

A band of many names but few faces

2008 CD - BTRCD 31

2007	☐	ANALYSE MY DEAM	CD	Blue Topaz	BTRCD 13
		Released under Johnny Engström's name.			
2008	■	FROM BIRTH TO CHAOS	CD	Blue Topaz	BTRCD 31
2011	■	MAGNETIC FORCE	CD	Alienation Records	ARCD 0111
2013	☐	DISTORTION OF SESES	CDd	Alienation Records	ARCD 0313
		Released as Dead End Space.			

2011 CD - ARCD 0111

JOKE
Susanne "DesDemona" Pecovnik: v, Tirre "Dione" Bendroth: v, Valentine "Charon" Pecovnik: g/b/v, Fredrik "Phobos" Norlander: g/b/v, Daniel "Io" Pecovnik: d/v

Malmö - **Joke** were formed in 1994, dressing up in harlequin costumes. Robert "Triton" Pecnovnik played bass on the debut. After the first album Tirre Bendroth replaced Anna "Pandora" Wallenborg. The band played around fifty shows and ironically enough, split just as *Colonize* was released. Musically **Joke** really didn't make up for the name. Biting guitar work, great vocals and harmonies. Imagine a mix between early **Kiss**, **Girlschool** and early **Mötley Crüe** and you'll come close to what the band sounded like. Well worth checking out. Susanne also recorded some demos under the name DesDemona and Valentine has also recorded with **Renegades** and is today found in the project **Hellvalla Burn**.

1996 CD - 2K-AACF2001

2001 CD - 20110121

1996	■	TOUCHDOWN	CD	Vacant Music	2K-AACD2001
2001	■	COLONIZE	CD	Vacant Music	20110121

JONAH QUIZZ
Johan Längquist: v, Anders Bergman: g, Tony Bohman: g, Kenth Edvardsson: b, Anders Lindgren: d

Stockholm - **Jonah Quizz** was the band of the first classic **Candlemass** singer Johan Längquist. The band only made some demos between 1980-82, but finally these demos have been available for fans by Stormspell Records. Johan appeared at the **Candlemass** reunion show in 2007 and is part of the AOR project **Impulsia**. He also sings on some demos with the re-united band **Notorious**. **Jonah Quizz** play classic eighties heavy metal influenced by the NWoBHM, but sung in Swedish. For fans of bands like **Onyx**, **Nattsvart**, **Detest** etc.

2009 CD - SSRDY 29

2009	■	ANTHOLOGY 1980-1982	CD	Stormspell Records	SSRDY 29

Jonas Hansson - The man of Silver Mountain (...and Jonas Hansson Band)

JONAS HANSSON BAND

David Swan Montgomery: v, Jonas Hansson: g/v, Mårten Andersson: b, Jan Uvena: d

Malmö/Los Angeles - After Jonas had made numerous releases with **Silver Mountain** he packed his bags and moved to the US where he formed a new band. The line-up on the first album consisted of singer Mike Stone, Jonas Hansson, bassist Gary Shea (**New England**) and drummer Jan Uvena (**New England**). Jan and Gary also used to be in **Alkatrazz** (featuring Yngwie Malmsteen), a band with which **JHB** has many similarities. However, this record is not the best that has come out of Jonas. On *Second To None,* Stanley Rose handled the vocals. In 1998 Jonas released an album with the band **Legacy** and in 2001 **Silver Mountain** reunited for an album. He moved back to Sweden and in 2010 permanently reformed **Silver Mountain**, who has now started working on new material.

1996 CD - RRCY 1002

1994	☐	NO. 1	CD	Arctic/Hex	HRCD 941
1994	☐	NO. 1	CD	FEMS (Japan)	APCY 8172
1996	■	SECOND TO NONE	CD	Roadrunner (Japan)	RRCY 1002
1999	☐	THE ROCKS	CD	Avalon Marquee (Japan)	MICY-10119
		Bonus: Stratovarius/Classica			
2003	☐	THE ROCKS	CD	CD-Maximum (Russia)	CDM 0203-1308

JONNY CARTONG

Christer Bergman: g/v, Anders Rothman: g, Urban Mattsson: b, Peter Diephuis: d

Älvdalen - **Jonny Cartong** were formed in 1979 and took the name from a local "raggare" saying, meaning when a party was great. The early stuff is straight-ahead biker style **Status Quo**-oriented boogie hard rock, while *III* is melodic pop/rock. *Give The Iron*, which was recorded in 29 hours, was produced by Leif Walter. The debut also featured second guitarist Per Elberg.

1981 LP - JCB 1001

1981	■	GIVE THE IRON	LP	private	JCB 1001
		The track Lonely Man is not on the CD reissue.			
1982	☐	ÄH, VI SPELAR JU BARA ROCK	LP	private	JCB 2002
2004	☐	III	CD	XTC Productions	XTC A 006
2004	☐	Tusen eldar	CDS	XTC Productions	XTC-S 015
2005	☐	GIVE THE IRON	CD	private	JCB 5005
		Bonus: Gummimadrass/What Did I Do/Big Brown Eyes/Hembrännarrock/Jut Johan Persson/It's Hard To Find The Words			

JONNY'S BOMB

Johnny Lindquist: v, Henrik Kjellberg: g, Johannes Nordström: g,
Fredrik Fagerlund: g, Stefan Sandberg: b, Olle Lingwall: d

Umeå - Formed and split in 1992. Fredrik, Owe and Johannes had previously recorded a single with the poppy band **Änglarna**. Still up for playing, they recruited Stefan and Henrik (**Witch**), with whom Johannes had played in punksters **Nasses Dieselknappar**. Jonny and Stefan were also in the band **Ten Toes Up**. Jonny was ex-**Mogg**. The band played two gigs. **Jonny's Bomb** play really good melodic hard rock mixing in some bluesy moments as well as classic AOR. Jonny and Owe went to **Nocturnal Rites**, while Fredrik has played with artists like **The Facer**, **Diamond Dogs**, Ulf Lundell and Titiyo. Henrik was also in **The Facer** plus **Doq Squeeze** and **Catch**.

1992 CD - SID 001

1992	■	ENOUGH AS IT IS	CD	Sids Music	SID 001	$$

JOTUNHEIM

S.E (aka Böödhel), F.M (aka Shattenführer/Fullmåne)

Västerås - Both members are also in the band **Wod**. F.M has also played with **Funeral Frost**. The band was formed already in 1997. They released two demos in 1998 (*Aldagautr*) and 1999 (*Hoght Blaesir Heimdallr*). Chaotic, high-speed, badly-mixed black metal with totally indecipherable screeching "vocals". **Jotunheim** is the land of giants and evil spirits in the Norse mythology.

2007 LP - (70462E)

2007	■	JOTUNHEIM	LP	Raging Bloodlust	(70462E)
		500 copies.			

JULIE LAUGHS NOMORE

Daniel Carlsson: v, Thomas Nilsson: g, Benny "Blomman" Halvarsson: g,
Thomas "TH" Olsson: b, Ronnie Bergerståhl: d

Ljusdal - The band was formed in 1995, at first under the name **Die Laughin**. In 1996 they also recorded a live demo CD-R entitled *Live In The Studio 5/5/96*. The track *Crescent Moon* appears on the local compilation *Hälsingerock* (Studiefrämjandet 97). In 1999 bass player Babbaen was replaced by TH. A mix of goth metal, death and German-sounding stuff, melodic death metal if you will. Bergerståhl has later been found in bands like **World Below, Amaran, Grave, Centinex** and **Demonical**. Olsson is also found in **Unleashed**. The band split in 2005.

1999 CD - SE 012 CD

| 1997 ☐ Julie Laughs Nomore | MCD 4tr | private | BCDS 03 |

1997 ☐ Julie Laughs Nomore ....MCD 4tr   private ....BCDS 03
Tracks: Into Eternity/Dying Years/Hate/Bleeding Inside. 500 copies.
1997 ☐ JULIE LAUGHS NOMORE/DE TVEKSAMMA (split) ....CD   Humlan .... HUMCD 001
Split with De Tveksamma. Tracks: Another Illusion/Crescent Moon/You're Nothing/Emptiness/Melting Sky/Decay/Pure Sadness
1999 ■ WHEN ONLY DARKNESS REMAINS ....CD   Serious Entertainment ....SE 012 CD
2000 ■ FROM THE MIST OF THE RUINS ....CD   Vile Music..VM 2002

2000 CD - VM 2002

JUNCTION

Jan-Erik Liljeström: v/b, Patrick Salin: g, Håkan Bengtsson: k, Lars-Göran Siljeholm: d

Borlänge - A good 70s-sounding hard rock band that showed great promise. They unfortunately split and Jan-Erik formed prog rock group *Anekdoten* with whom he has released numerous albums. The band recorded some demos that were even better than the 7". Two tracks from a late demo appears on the compilation *Eleven-On-A-One-To-Ten* ('93 Meantime).

1989 ■ Living Without You/Flying High ....7"   Junk Records......................................JR 001

1989 7" - JR 001

JUPITER SOCIETY

Carl Westholm: k

Stockholm - Carl Westholm is the man behind the symphonic band *Carptree* and he has also played in *Abstrakt Algebra*. Here he has compiled a nice collection of people helping him create a really heavy, progressive monster. The list of musicians includes names like Leif Edling (*Candlemass, Abstrakt Algebra, Krux*), Mats Levén (*Treat, Abstrakt Algebra, Krux*), Sven Lindvall (*Nord, Bronk*), Lars Sköld (*Tiamat*) and Jonas Källbäck etc. The second album offers more, and better, in the same musical direction. The outstanding, heavy, doomy, proggy 2013 release also features Levén, Fredrik Åkesson, Edling, Marcus Jidell, Dirk Verbeuren, Peter Söderström, Björn Eriksson, Stefan Fandén, Cia Backman, Sebastian "Basse" Blyberg and Pål Olofsson.

2008 ■ FIRST CONTACT – LAST WARNING ....CD   Fosfor Creation CWJS1
2009 ☐ TERRAFORM ....CD   Progrock Records ....PRRS 31
2013 ☐ FROM ENDANGERED TO EXTINCT..CDd   Fosfor Creation ....CWJ 53

2008 CD - CWJS1

JUPITER, IODINE

Viktor "Iodine Jupiter" Wennerkvist: v/g, Erik Likagod (Björkman): g, Niklas Rundqvist: k/sampl, Rickard Donatello: b, Anders Åström: b, Mårten Tromm: d

Stockholm - "Stephen King meets Jaques Brel who shake hands with *Black Sabbath* at David Lynch's party" This is actually Sony Music's description of the mysterious rock poet/writer Iodine Jupiter. Well, try mixing heavy rock in the vein of *Mental Hippie Blood* with poetic recitals. Weird indeed, but still not bad. The vocals are in Swedish and they are very dark and strange. Donatello and Likagod are also found in *Screamin´ Mother*. The album was produced by Sank (*Clawfinger, Shotgun Messiah, Screamin´ Mother* etc.) Likagod later changed his name to Björkman. Tromm was also found in *Baby Jesus*. Viktor was also in *Zzzang Tumb* and *Iodine Jupiter och Hororna från Helvetet*.

IODINE JUPITER

1995 ☐ Vilda Lilla Blomma / Naken I Dom Dödas Rum... CDS   Starton/Sony ....09 - 661468 - 17
The second track is a non-CD demo version.
1995 ☐ Tomma Boots På Väg Ut.. CDS   Starton/Sony ....09 - 662551 - 17
Tracks: Tomma Boots På Väg Ut (radioversion)/Night Of The Living Dead (skräckballad). The second track is non-CD.
1995 ■ LILLA FLICKA ZOMBIE...CD   Starton/Sony ....09 - 478398 - 10

1995 CD - 09 - 478398 - 10

JUSTAQUICKSTOP

Daniel Söderberg: v, Ronny Blylod: g, John Vigebo: b, Henrik "Honken" Söderqvist: d

Örnsköldsvik - The band initially started as Ronny's solo project, where he played all instruments. He drafted singer Söderberg and in 2009 the two recorded the CD *One Week Notice* under the name *Justaquickstop*. Shortly after, bass player Vigebo joined and finally drummer Söderqvist completed the line-up. After a few gigs with the new line-up and the adoption of a slightly heavier sound they decided to change the name to *Blackrain*, and in 2011 they recorded the first album under the new name. Great modern-sounding melodic hard rock with great vocals and high-class musicians. Söderberg and Vigebo have previously played with *Freelancer*, while Blylod has been found in bands like *Destynation*, *Engine No 9*, *Planet Storm* and *Eternia*.

2009 ■ ONE WEEK NOTICE ....CD   JAQS Production ....JAQSCD 001

2009 CD - JASQSCD 001

KAAMOS

Karl Envall: v/b, Konstantin Papavassiliou: g,
Nicklas Eriksson: g, Christofer "Chris Piss" Barkensjö: d

Haninge (Stockholm) – In the summer of 1998, four fifths of ***A Mind Confused*** reformed as ***Kaamos***. Ultra-speed death metal similar to early ***Unleashed***. The first single was quite badly recorded and not very exciting musically either. After the single singer/bassist Johan Thörngren left and was replaced by Karl Envall (***Revokation, Repugnant***). In 2000 drummer Thomas Åberg also quit and Christofer Barkensjö (***Carnal Forge, Blackshine, Repugnant, Face Down, Grave, Serpent Obscene***) replaced him. The band recorded the demo *Curse Of Aeons* in 2001 and was soon picked up by Candlelight, who released their self-titled debut in 2002. Nuclear Winter Records released the demo on vinyl in 2001. In 2004 they recorded the second album with Berno Paulsson at the helm, but in 2006 they announced they were breaking up. *Scales Of Leviathan* was released as a last farewell. Konstantin is also in ***Saturnalia Temple***.

2004 10" - NWR 666

2005 CD - CANDLE 091 CD

1999	☐	Desecration/Blood Of Chaos	7"	Dauthus 1899	D/1
		Released in 397 numbered copies.			
2002	☐	KAAMOS	CD	Candlelight	CANDLE 073 CD
2002	☐	KAAMOS	CD	Candlelight (USA)	CANUS 006 CD
2004	■	Curse Of Aeons	10" 5tr	Nuclear Winter Records	NWR 666
		Tracks: Prophesies/Curse Of Aeons/Khem/Mass Of The Dead/Descent. 666 hand			
		numbered copies. Poster and sticker.			
2005	☐	KAAMOS	LPg	Imperium Productions	IMP 003-1
		500 copies. Poster.			
2005	■	LUCIFER RISING	CD	Candlelight	CANDLE 091 CD
2005	☐	LUCIFER RISING	CD	Candlelight (USA)	CANUS 0154 CD
2005	☐	LUCIFER RISING	LPg	Imperium Productions	IMP 004-1
		1000 copies.			
2007	☐	Scales Of Leviathan	MCDd 5tr	Nuclear Winter Records	NWR 020
		Tracks: Scales Of Leviathan/Darkness Awaits/Blood Has Stained The Cross/Seven			
		Demons/Spiritual Funeral. 666 copies			
2008	■	Scales Of Leviathan	MLP 5tr	Imperium Records	IMP 005-1
		105 red, 100 red/black and 302 black copies. Poster.			

2008 MLP - IMP 005-1

KAARS, THE

Fredrik Svensson: v, Roger Mattsson: narrator, Janne Stark: g/b, Peter Svensson: d

Mörrum/Karlshamn/Sölvesborg – This was just a one-off project where Janne was asked to write and record a heavy metal anthem for local soccer team Mjällby AIF. He chose old drummer pal Peter Svenson (***Locomotive Breath, Constancia, Mountain Of Power***) and ***Headline/Gabria*** singer/bass player Fredrik. The track is a typical straightforward hard rock anthem. The MCD features bonus tracks by Kim Mitchell, ***From Behind*** and ***Locomotive Breath***.

2007	■	Göra maul kaa (split)	MCDp	Sweden Rock Records	SRR 888
		Numbered. Tracks: Göra maul kaa			

2007 MCDp - SRR 888

KAIPA

Patrik Lundström: v, Aleena Gibson: v, Per Nilsson: g,
Hans Lundin: k/v, Jonas Reingold: b, Morgan Ågren: d

Uppsala – Hans, Tomas and Gunnar released an album under the name ***San Michaels*** in 1971, but the style was very poppy. The first single was recorded by Leif Mases already in 1972, but released two years after under the name Ura Kaipa. The members on the single were Hans Lundin (k/v), Jan "Nane" Kvillsäter (g, later in ***Good Clean Fun***), Tomas Eriksson (b) and Gunnar Westberg (d). Guitarist Roine Stolt joined after the 7" was released and the band shortened their name to Kaipa. The three first albums are filled with classic 70s-sounding atmospheric progressive/symphonic rock, not that heavy but with great keyboard/guitar interplays. Similar to ***ELP/YES*** and also Swedish band ***Dice***, although ***Kaipa*** has a higher musical level. The debut album featured Hans Lundin (k/v), Roine Stolt (g), Tomas Eriksson (b) and Ingemar Bergman (d). On *Solo*, Mats Lindberg replaced Tomas and Mats Löfgren was added on vocals. In 1979, after the release of *Solo*, Roine quit and was replaced by Max Åhman. The band then went in a much poppier direction with vocals in Swedish. The last two albums are strictly for collectors. On *Nattdjurstid*, Ingemar was replaced by former ***Dice*** drummer Pelle Andersson. Bass player Mats Lindberg was replaced by... Mats Lindberg. Yes, it's true, same name, different guy. The band split in November 1982. When ***Kaipa*** split Roine formed what was to become ***The Flower Kings***, where he still is found. He has also done tons of session jobs for artists of various musical directions and is part of the multinational project ***Transatlantic***. Hans Lundin has recorded three solo albums in a direction similar to ***Kaipa***, but much softer and with the emphasis on keyboards. The titles are *Tales* (84 Örat Rec. - RAT 1), *Visions Of Circles Of Sounds* (86 Örat - RAT 2) and *Houses* (89 Örat - RATCD 3). Roine and Hans reformed ***Kaipa*** and new material was recorded and supposed to be released in 1996. It however didn't surface until 2002. The line-up on *Notes From The Past* features drummer Morgan Ågren (***Mats & Mor-***

Kaipa, back in 1976, a little soft around the edges

gan, *Glory* etc.), singer Patrik Lundström (*Ritual*), bassist Jonas Reingold (*The Flower Kings, Karmakanic, Reingold, Downtown Clowns*), singers Aleena and Tove Thörn Lundin. The same line-up recorded *Keyholder* and *Mindrevolutions*, while on *Angling Feelings* founder Stolt was out of the band and Per Nilsson had taken his place. The latter day albums have a heavier edge than the early works and should appeal to fans of bands like *Porcupine Tree*, *Karmakanic* etc.

1978 7" - FM 44598

1974 ☐	För Sent/Bay-E Bay-O	7"	Four Leaf	EFG-1013 089
	Released under the name Ura Kaipa.			
1975 ☐	KAIPA	LP	Decca	SKL 5221
1976 ☐	INGET NYTT UNDER SOLEN	LP	Decca	SKL 5260
1978 ■	Sen Repris/Visa I Sommaren	12"	Decca	FM 44598
1978 ☐	SOLO	LP	Decca	SKL 5293
1980 ☐	Äntligen/Staden Lever	7"	Polar	POS 1264
1980 ☐	HÄNDER	LP	Polar	POLS 311
1982 ☐	NATTDJURSTID	LP	Piglet	PR 2006
1982 ☐	Cellskräck/Blandad Kväll	7"	Piglet	PR 201
1993 ☐	KAIPA	CD	Musea	FGBG 4091AR
1993 ☐	INGET NYTT UNDER SOLEN	CD	Musea	FGBG 4098
	Bonus: Skenet bedrar (live)/Från det ena till det andra			
1994 ☐	KAIPA	LPg	Si-Wan (Korea)	SRML-3017
	Bonus: Awaking-Bitterness			
1994 ☐	SOLO	CD	Musea	FGBG 4128AR
	Remixed re-issue. Bonus: Visan I sommaren (live)/En igelkotts död – Ömsom sken medley (live)/Live In An Elevator (jam)/Från det ena till det andra/Karavan/Awakening Bitterness/How Might I Say Out Clearly/The Gate Of Day/Blow Hard All Tradewinds			
1997 ☐	SOLO	CD	2000 Fruitgum (Australia)	FCCD 200345-2
	Bonus: Visan I sommaren/En igelkotts död-Ömsom sken medley/Live In An Elevator			
2002 ☐	NOTES FROM THE PAST	CD	InsideOut	IOMCD 097
2002 ☐	NOTES FROM THE PAST	CD	InsideOut America (USA)	IOMACD 2035
2002 ☐	NOTES FROM THE PAST	CD	Marquee (Japan)	MAR-02722
2003 ☐	KEYHOLDER	CD	InsideOut	IOMCD 132
2003 ☐	KEYHOLDER	CD	InsideOut (USA)	IOMACD 2064
2005 ☐	THE DECCA YEARS 1975-1978	5CD box	Inside Out	IOMCD 234
	Contains the first three albums, plus Kaipa Live 1976-78 and Unedited Master Demo Recording 1974.			
2005 ☐	MINDREVOLUTIONS	CD	InsideOut	IOMCD 208
2007 ☐	ANGLING FEELINGS	CD	InsideOut	IOMCD 275
2009 ☐	KAIPA	2CDp	Belle Antique (Japan)	BELLE 091605-6
	Bonus CD is the Unedited Master Demo Recordings 1974, plus Från det ena till det andra/Karavan. Two separate paper sleeve replicas.			
2009 ☐	SOLO	2CDp	Belle Antique (Japan)	BELLE 091609-10
2009 ☐	INGET NYTT UNDER SOLEN	2CDp	Belle Antique (Japan)	BELLE 091607-8
	Bonus CD.			
2010 ■	IN THE WAKE OF EVOLUTION	CD	InsideOut	IOMCD 0519-2
2012 ■	VITTJAR	CD	InsideOut	50522 -505978
2012 ☐	VITTJAR	2LP+CD	InsideOut	50522 -505971

2010 CD - IOMCD 0519-2

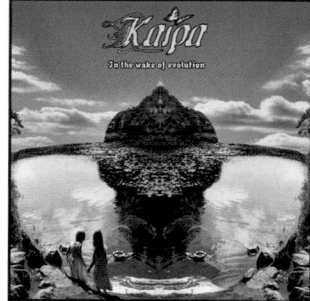

2012 CD - 50522-505978

Unofficial releases:

1993 ☐	STOCKHOLM SYMPHONIE	CD	- - -	ED-010
	This is a Japanese live session bootleg, recorded at Swedish radio 1974. Great quality.			

KALAJS

Lasse Nordström: v, Hans Schakonat: g, Jan-Olof Jansson: g, Ulf Ahlberg: b, Micael Stålbom: d

Falkenberg - The A-side is a bluesy hard rocker with biting guitar work, while the B-side is quite light-weight proggy hard rock. Schakonat has been an incredibly active musician through the years playing with artists and bands like Totta Näslund, *Power Unit*, Robert Wells, *Shine On* etc.

1982 ■	Kom igen kom igen/Asocial	7"	CWC	CWC 015

1982 7" - CWC 015

KAMASUTRA

Tomas Antonsson: v, Erik Carling: v, Eric Björner: g, Fredrik Persson: b, Johannes Sundblad: k, Hampus Grönberg: d

Lund - *KamaSutra* play excellent seventies-oriented heavy rock with a strong touch of stoner, like a mix of *Spiritual Beggars* and *Deep Purple*. Singer Antonsson (*Supraload*) sounds very close to Eric Moore of US band *The Godz*. Fredrik played with progressive retro rockers *Wraptors*, while Björner is in modern melodic hardcore band *The Apollo Program*. The band also recorded the Mission Hall Studios five-track demo in 2005.

2003 ■	Moonbound	MCDp 5tr	Revolver	RRCH 02-2
	Tracks: Standing Ground/Yellow Lights/Need To Get/Silver Man/Moonbound			

2003 MCD - RRCH 02-2

KAMCHATKA

Roger Öjersson: v/b, Tomas "Juneor" Andersson: g/v, Tobias Strandvik: d

Varberg - **Kamchatka** were formed in 2001, influenced by the sixties and seventies heavy bluesy rock. The band made their debut in 2005, showcasing a power trio with heavy seventies riffing and a great melodic sense. At times close to **Mahogany Rush**, at times in the heavier Robin Trower vein and at times quite close to fellows **Mojobone**. Heavy, groovy and riff-oriented. Before the second album, Juneor also recorded an album with retro rockers **King Hobo**, featuring keyboardist Per Wiberg (**Opeth, Mojobone, Spiritual Beggars, Death Organ** etc.) who also lent a helping hand to some **Kamchatka** songs, plus he is the band's official cover artists. Andersson also lays a guest solo on the **Mahogany Rush** cover *Talkin' Bout A Feeling* on *Volume Two* by **Mountain Of Power** (Grooveyard Records 2010). In 2012 the band announced bassist/singer Roger Öjersson (ex-**Vildsvin**) had been replaced by Linus Carlsson.
Website: www.kamchatka.se/

2009 CDd - SPR 005

2011 CD - GMRCD 9028

2005	☐	KAMCHATKA	CD	Grooveyard	GYR 016
2007	☐	VOLUME II	CD	Grooveyard	GYR 033
2009	■	VOLUME III	CDd	Superpuma Records	SPR 005
2011	■	BURY YOUR ROOTS	CD	GMR	GMRCD 9028
2011	☐	BURY YOUR ROOTS	LP	GMR	GMRLP 9028
		500 copies.			

KANSAS CITY ROLLERS

Oskar Fjäll: v/g, Fredrik: g, Marcu Lehto: b, Kristian: d

Norrköping - The band was formed late 1991. They recorded the CD and a demo, entitled *Never Comin' Home*, with the above line-up. After this Fredrik has been replaced by Håkan Fried and Kristian by Andreas Wahlberg, who was actually in the band from the start. Håkan and Andreas are also found in **Cherokee**. Andreas was previously in the band **Epidemic**, before they released the MLP. **Kansas City Rollers** sound quite close to early **D.A.D.** in style and approach, meaning: no-nonsense, heads-down, hands-up, mindless party sleaze hard rock 'n roll.

1994 MCD - KCRCDS

1994	■	Kansas City Rollers	MCD 4tr	Taltratten	KCRCDS
		Tracks: Indian Tribe/Oversleeping/Dancing At The Gallows End/Hangover.			

KAOS SACRAMENTUM

Erik "E" Sundén: v, Sir N (aka Vanskapt): g/b, J "JM" Marklund: d

Norrland - The band was formed by Sir N and E in the autumn of 2007. They had a full line-up until the first demo *Triumph In Depravation* was recorded in February 2008. After this they continued as a duo again. *Förneka den fysiska lekamen* and *Bloodcurse Stigmata* (recorded in 2009) only featured E (aka Dr. Sundén) and Sir N. Sir N is also found in **Grifteskymfning, Helgedom, Hädanfärd, Svartrit, Vanskapt** and **Grav**. JM is also in **Grifteskymfning, LIK, Sorgeldom** and **Whirling**, while E is in **Blodskald** and **Sorgeldom**. All the band's albums were released in 500 copies each. In early 2011 E was fired and shortly after the band split up. **Kaos Sacramentum** play fast black metal in the vein of **Lord Belial**. Great production and very well-played.

2010 CD - AR 003

2010 CD - AR 004

2010	■	FÖRNEKA DEN FYSISKA LEKAMEN	CD	Ancient Records	AR 003
2010	■	SCARS OF REVELATION	CD	Ancient Records	AR 004
2010	■	AVGRUNDENS KONST	CD	Ancient Records	AR 005
2010	☐	BLOODCURSE STIGMATA	CD	Ancient Records	AR 006
2012	☐	SCARS OF REVELATION	LP	Ancient Records	AR 037
2012	☐	AVGRUNDENS KONST	LP	Ancient Records	AR 038
2012	☐	BLOODCURSE STIGMATA	LP	Ancient Records	AR 039
2012	☐	FÖRNEKA DEN FYSISKA LEKAMEN	LP	Ancient Records	AR 043

2010 CD - AR 005

KAPTAIN SUN

Anders "Andy" Håkansson: v/g, Andreas "Andrey" Svensson: g, Rickard "Richie" Gustafsson: b, Marcus "Mackie" Hamrin: d

Karlshamn - This unit was formed in 1998 from the ashes of **Clandestine**. Stoner-type hard rock, but with a more traditional metal-touch. The missing link between **Sleep** and **Iron Maiden** with rough growling vocals. The band received rave reviews in Kerrang and Classic Rock. *Trip To Vortex* was first released as a CDR with proper artwork (different from the 2000 release) in 1999, but mainly for promotional purposes. Both have the same tracks.
Website: www.kaptainsun.cjb.net

2000	☐	TRIP TO VORTEX	CD	Rage Of Archilles	ILIAD 004
2004	■	RAINBOWRIDE	CD	Rage Of Archilles	ILIAD 040
2005	☐	BLOOD, ROCK 'N ROLL & BLACK ANGELS	CD	Metal Breed	KSUN 01

2004 CD - ILIAD 040

KARABOUDJAN

Dan Swanö: v/g/b/d, Dag "Tom Nouga" Swanö: g/sax, Jimmy Thunlind: sax

Örebro - Yet another project of the Swanö brothers. Despite the line-up stated on the cover, featuring people like Wolf, Abdallah, General Alcazar and Serafim Svensson among others, the above trio are the performing artists. Innovative avant-garde metal, very dark and doomy with lots of strange noises and almost frightening moods. The album was recorded already in 1996. The song titles are actually all taken from books featuring Tintin.
Website: www.swano.com

2001 ☐ SBRODJ ....MCD 3tr   Relapse.. RR 6498-2
    Tracks: Plan 714 Till Sydney/Den Svarta Ön/Den Mystiska Stjärnnan

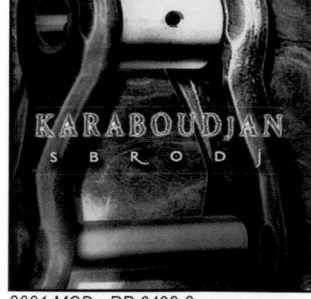
2001 MCD - RR 6498-2

KARLBERG, HASSE

Hasse Karlberg: v/g/b/d/k

Upplands Väsby - The single is quite a strange one. The A-side is a really good hard rock, while the B-side is a remake of the Swedish national anthem. Hasse also recorded a 4-track demo with the band *Lorraine* in Decibel Studios, but nothing was ever released. He played some blues and was also in *Bekantas Bekanta*. Furthermore Hasse had a band called *Big Frame* together with Thomas Váradi (Pernilla Wahlgren, *Sussies Orkester*), who wrote the A-side of the single.

1980 ■ A Little Claim/Du unga, du fängslande ....7"   BMB .... BMB 106
    1000 copies

1980 7" - BMB 106

KARMA

Mats Karlsson: v/b, Reine Johansson: g, Anders Jansson: g, Fredrik Bergener: d

Uddevalla (?) - The A side is a really good melodic hard rocker with a boogie touch, while the B-side starts out like a ballad, but becomes heavier in the middle.

1983 ■ Dreams/Forgotten Hero ....7"   Liphone ....LiSi 1027

KARMAKANIC

Göran Edman: v, Nils Erikson: v/k, Krister Jonsson: g,
Lalle Larsson: k, Jonas Reingold: b, Marcus Liliequist: d

Malmö - In the autumn of 2000 bass player Jonas Reingold (*Downtown Clowns, The Flower Kings, The Tangent*) wrote a couple of progressive songs and decided to form a new musical unit. The name was actually selected through a name competition on *The Flower Kings'* website and picked out of 200 suggestions. He had previously worked with singer Göran Edman (*Madison, Kharma, Mårran* etc) and invited him to sing on his new concept album *Entering The Spectra*. Jaime Salazar (*Bad Habit* etc) handled the drums, and among the other musicians there were Johan Glössler, Robert Engstrand and Tomas Bodin. On the follow-up, *Wheel Of Life*, *Flower Kings* skinsman Zoltan Csörcz took over, and the guitars are handled by Krister Jonsson. Lots of guests here, as well, such as Richard Andersson, Roine Stolt, Hasse Bruniusson, Tomas Bodin etc. The album *The Power Of Two* was a musical joint venture between *Karmakanic* and *Agents Of Mercy*. Both bands, together as one big prog unit, on stage playing songs from both band's repertoire. At the time *Karmakanic* had Nick d'Virgillo handling the drums. *Karmakanic* is in a way comparable to *The Flower Kings*, but here he takes the prog to totally different directions. Some tracks are way heavier, with more brutal guitar work, at times it's also wackier, with more of a Zappa attitude, plus it's way more intense. Imagine a mix of *Dream Theater*, Zappa, *The Flower Kings*, *It Bites* and *Yes*.

2002 CD - RR 0209-013

2002 ■ ENTERING THE SPECTRA...CD   Regain .... RR 0209-013
2004 ☐ WHEEL OF LIFE..CDd   Regain .... RR 0405-045
2008 ☐ WHO'S THE BOSS IN THE FACTORY ....CD   InsideOut ....IOMCD 304
2010 ☐ THE POWER OF TWO – KARMAKANIC & AGENTS OF MERCY ....CD   Reingold Records .... RRCD 003
2011 ■ IN A PERFECT WORLD ....CDd   InsideOut ....IOMCD 0505568
    Bonus: Turn It Up (Radio edit)/Send A Message From The Heart (video)

2011 CDd - IOMCD 0505568

KARNARIUM

Funeral Whore: v/g, Jimmy "Jim Voltage" Edström: b,
C.S "Perversion Trauma/CJ Sodomizer)" Johansson: d

Göteborg - Formed in 1998 and split in 2004. *Karnarium* play quite badly recorded, fast, old-school death metal, decently played though. At times similar to *Morbid Angel* and *Immolation*. They recorded their first demo *Demo #1* in 2000 and the second one, *Breaking The Manacles Of Mankind* later the same year. *Tänk på döden* is a compilation of demo recordings and odd

2005 CD - EMF 008

tracks recorded between 2000 and 2004. Jim is also in **Cross Bow**, **Kill**, **Devil Lee Rot** and **Pagan Rites**. CJ Sodomizer was also in the latter. Among the former members, one is Christian Aho (**Prophanity, Immemoreal**).

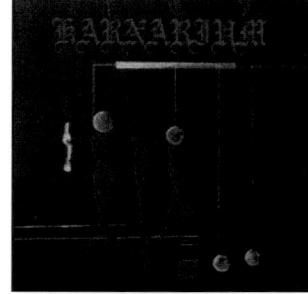

2006 7" - YOTZ 09

2004 ☐ Karnarium	7"	Nuclear Abominations Records	NA 003
Tracks: Averse Incantation (Ode To The Queen Of Beasts)/ Post Coitum Assimilabar Ab Familia Dulci			
2005 ■ TÄNK PÅ DÖDEN	CD	Embrace My Funeral	EMF 008
2006 ■ Deity Of Opposites	7" 3tr	Blood Harvest	YOTZ 09
Tracks: Deity Of Opposites (An Ever-Swinging Pendulum)/Yearning Dissolution/Deconstructing The Structure (Intelligence Burns Between Its Horns). 500 copies.			
2008 ☐ KARNARIUM	CD	Blood Harvest	YOTZ #30
2008 ☐ KARNARIUM	LP	Blood Harvest	YOTZ #30
2008 ☐ Hail Occult Masters (split)	7" 3tr	Hells Headbangers	HELLS EP 028
Split with Bestial Mockery. Tracks: Watching The Watchers			
2009 ☐ Karnarium/Defiler	7"	Nuclear Winter	NWR 027
Split with Defiler. Track: Nihiliphobia. 500 copies.			
2012 ■ OTAPAMO PRALAJA	CD	Nuclear Winter	NWR 057 CD
2012 ☐ OTAPAMO PRALAJA	LP	Nuclear Winter	NWR 057 LP
500 copies			

2012 CD - NWR 057 CD

KAROSS

Magnus Knutas: v, Fredrik Lösnitz: g, Mikael Berggren: b, Markus Neuendorf: d

Skövde/Falköping - Formed in the winter of 2000, by Mikael, Fredrik and Isaac Ingelsbo. They were completed by drummer Daniel Green and later on singer Magnus. In 2002 the band recorded the demo *The Denim Demo*. Soon Daniel left, enter Markus and later on Issac Ingelsbo left and the band was a four-piece. In 2004 they recorded the second demo, *Hell Yeah*. The subsequent year, they won the Partillerock competition. This resulted in a deal with Eastground Records. In 2009 they added second guitarist Kalle Sjöstrand (**Slug, Hatebox**). In 2010 Fredrik left and was replaced by Björn Midborg. **Kaross** play really outstanding groovy heavy stoner-oriented hard rock with a singer reminiscent of Ian Astbury with a touch of Lane Staley. A new album is in the making planned to be released in 2012-2013. Kaross means car body in Swedish. A new album is in the making.
Website: www.myspace.com/kaross

2007 ■ MOLOSSUS	CD	Eastground	EGR 001

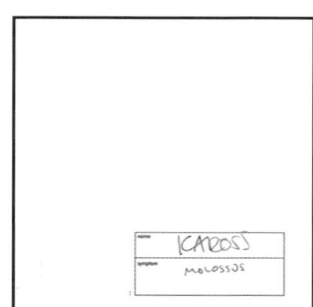

2007 CD - EGR 001

KATANA

Johan Bernspång: v, Tobias Karlsson: g, Patrik Essén: g, Susanna Salminen: b, Anders Persson: d

Göteborg - Between 2006-2008 Sweden started pouring out new promising classic heavy metal bands. Names like **Steelwing**, **RAM**, **Helvetets Port** and **Portrait** started competing with established bands like **Hammerfall** and **Wolf**. In 2005 Göteborg produced another high-class heavy metal band, trading the same musical patterns as classic **Maiden**, **Judas Priest** and **Accept**. Completely authentic 1985-style heavy metal with all the necessary attributes. Great singer, great songs and a great band. The band recorded its first demo, *Night Avengers*, in 2005, at the time featuring Karlsson, Samninen, Oscar "Oz Osukaru" Petersson (**Osukaru, Eye**) on guitars and Dan Bäck (**Disdain**) on vocals and Christian Börjesson on drums. On the band's second recording, *Heart Of Tokyo* (2006) Bäck had been replaced by Bernspång. In 2008 the demo *Rock 'N Roll Disaster* was released. After this Persson replaced Börjesson and Essén replaced Osukaru and in 2011 the current line-up made their debut on the three-track demo *Heart Of Tokyo* (which featured a rerecording of the title track of the 2006 demo). The band was picked up by Rambo/Avalon Marquee and the debut saw the light of day. *Storms Of War* was produced by Andy LaRocque (**King Diamond**).
Website: www.myspace.com/bladeofkatana

Hold on, the storms are coming!

2011 ☐ HEADS WILL ROLL	CD	Rambo Music	KACD 001
2011 ☐ HEADS WILL ROLL	CD	Avalon Marquee (Japan)	MICP-10988
Bonus: When You're Gone			
2012 ■ STORMS OF WAR	CD	Gain	8869196-2452

2012 CD - 8869196-2452

KATATONIA
**Jonas "Lord Seth" Renkse: v, Anders "Sombreius Blackheim" Nyström: g,
Fred Norrman: g, Mattias Norrman: b, Daniel Liljekvist: d**

Stockholm - The band was formed in 1987 by Nyström and Renkse (who then also handled the drums), initially inspired by **Bathory** and **Celtic Frost**, why the band's early sound would qualify into the brutal death metal genre. After a split they reunited in 1991 and with bass player Guillaume "Isphael Wing" Le Huche they recorded the debut album, now with a more doom-oriented death touch and Jonas' growling vocals. The song *Without God* appeared on the first *Extreme Close-Up* compilation. Their music turned more gothic and by the time they recorded *Brave Murder Day* their sound had matured and was closer to **Paradise Lost**. The vocals on this album were handled by **Opeth**'s Mikael Åkerfeldt, and Fred Norrman had now been added on guitar, Le Huche was out and the production was made by Dan Swanö. Tomas Skogsberg produced the subsequent MCD, as was the album *Discouraged Ones*. Now Åkerfeldt became a vocal producer and Renkse change from growling to traditional melodic vocals, which changed the band's sound dramatically. On the album Micke Oretoft was added on bass. The band's next release, *Tonight's Decision*, is an excellent goth-inspired melodic doom album with a strong symphonic touch. On this album they were a trio consisting of Renkse, Nyström and Fred Norrman. In 2011 the band was reinforced by bassist Mattias Norrman and drummer Daniel Liljeqvist. *Last Fair Deal Gone Down* is yet another step up in the goth-inspired symphonic staircase. An excellent album which might mean a bigger breakthrough for this band, if they manage to wash off the death metal-mark from their name. *Last Fair Deal...* and the EP features the above line-up. *Brave Yester Days* is a best of. Anders and Jonas also have a side-project called **Diabolical Masquerade**. Jonas and Fredrik are also found in **October Tide** and Anders in **Bewitched**. Through the years **Katatonia** has been leaning more and more to the **Opeth**-style prog and on *Night Is The New Day*, they sound very much like **Opeth**, with all clean vocals, very melancholic and symphonic, but still heavy and doomy. It's in my opinion the band's best effort so far.
Website: www.katatonia.com

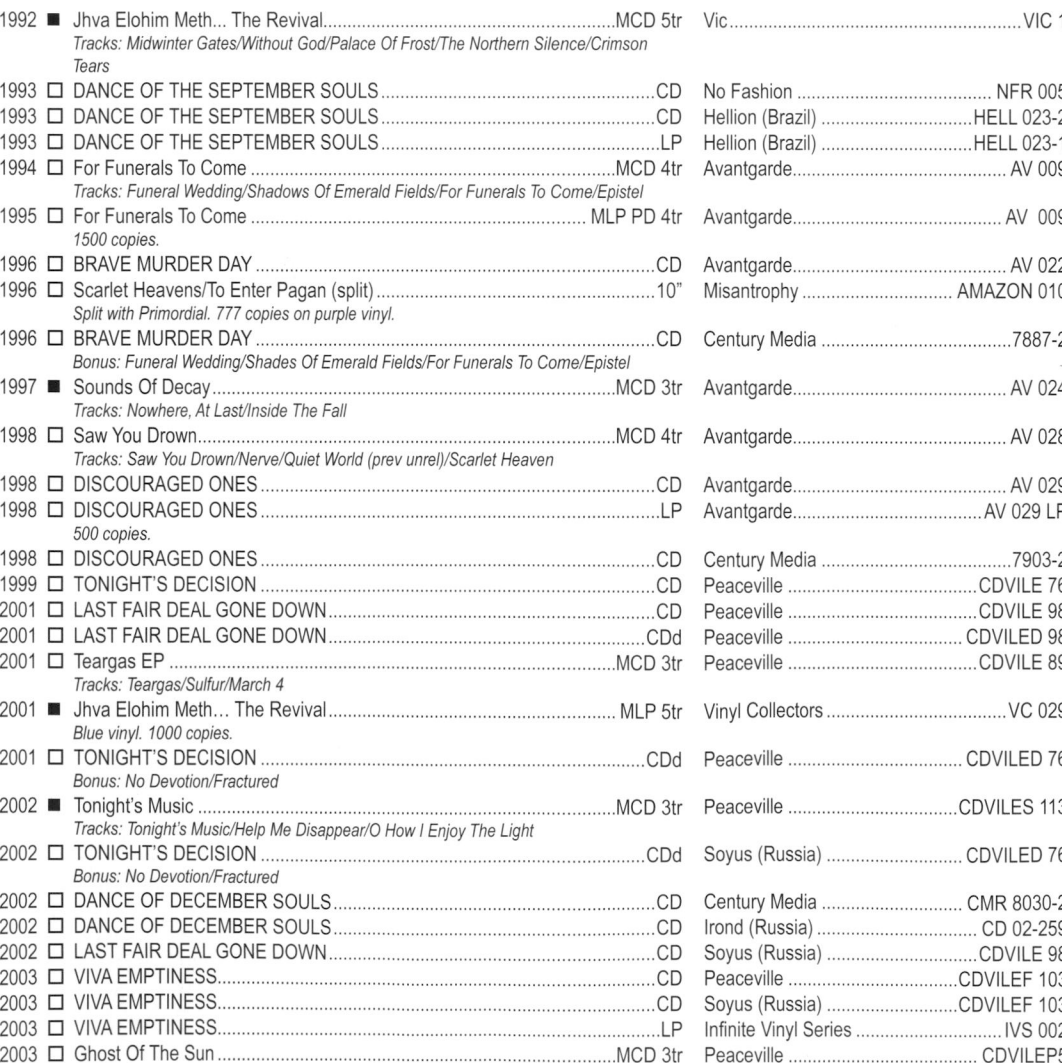
The dead end kings

1992 ■	Jhva Elohim Meth... The Revival	MCD 5tr	Vic	VIC 1
	Tracks: Midwinter Gates/Without God/Palace Of Frost/The Northern Silence/Crimson Tears			
1993 ☐	DANCE OF THE SEPTEMBER SOULS	CD	No Fashion	NFR 005
1993 ☐	DANCE OF THE SEPTEMBER SOULS	CD	Hellion (Brazil)	HELL 023-2
1993 ☐	DANCE OF THE SEPTEMBER SOULS	LP	Hellion (Brazil)	HELL 023-1
1994 ☐	For Funerals To Come	MCD 4tr	Avantgarde	AV 009
	Tracks: Funeral Wedding/Shadows Of Emerald Fields/For Funerals To Come/Epistel			
1995 ☐	For Funerals To Come	MLP PD 4tr	Avantgarde	AV 009
	1500 copies.			
1996 ☐	BRAVE MURDER DAY	CD	Avantgarde	AV 022
1996 ☐	Scarlet Heavens/To Enter Pagan (split)	10"	Misantrophy	AMAZON 010
	Split with Primordial. 777 copies on purple vinyl.			
1996 ☐	BRAVE MURDER DAY	CD	Century Media	7887-2
	Bonus: Funeral Wedding/Shades Of Emerald Fields/For Funerals To Come/Epistel			
1997 ■	Sounds Of Decay	MCD 3tr	Avantgarde	AV 024
	Tracks: Nowhere, At Last/Inside The Fall			
1998 ☐	Saw You Drown	MCD 4tr	Avantgarde	AV 028
	Tracks: Saw You Drown/Nerve/Quiet World (prev unrel)/Scarlet Heaven			
1998 ☐	DISCOURAGED ONES	CD	Avantgarde	AV 029
1998 ☐	DISCOURAGED ONES	LP	Avantgarde	AV 029 LP
	500 copies.			
1998 ☐	DISCOURAGED ONES	CD	Century Media	7903-2
1999 ☐	TONIGHT'S DECISION	CD	Peaceville	CDVILE 76
2001 ☐	LAST FAIR DEAL GONE DOWN	CD	Peaceville	CDVILE 98
2001 ☐	LAST FAIR DEAL GONE DOWN	CDd	Peaceville	CDVILED 98
2001 ☐	Teargas EP	MCD 3tr	Peaceville	CDVILE 89
	Tracks: Teargas/Sulfur/March 4			
2001 ■	Jhva Elohim Meth... The Revival	MLP 5tr	Vinyl Collectors	VC 029
	Blue vinyl. 1000 copies.			
2001 ☐	TONIGHT'S DECISION	CDd	Peaceville	CDVILED 76
	Bonus: No Devotion/Fractured			
2002 ■	Tonight's Music	MCD 3tr	Peaceville	CDVILES 113
	Tracks: Tonight's Music/Help Me Disappear/O How I Enjoy The Light			
2002 ☐	TONIGHT'S DECISION	CDd	Soyus (Russia)	CDVILED 76
	Bonus: No Devotion/Fractured			
2002 ☐	DANCE OF DECEMBER SOULS	CD	Century Media	CMR 8030-2
2002 ☐	DANCE OF DECEMBER SOULS	CD	Irond (Russia)	CD 02-259
2002 ☐	LAST FAIR DEAL GONE DOWN	CD	Soyus (Russia)	CDVILE 98
2003 ☐	VIVA EMPTINESS	CD	Peaceville	CDVILEF 103
2003 ☐	VIVA EMPTINESS	CD	Soyus (Russia)	CDVILEF 103
2003 ☐	VIVA EMPTINESS	LP	Infinite Vinyl Series	IVS 002
2003 ☐	Ghost Of The Sun	MCD 3tr	Peaceville	CDVILEP5
	Promo. Tracks: Ghost Of The Sun/Criminals/Evidence			

1992 MCD - VIC 1

1997 MCD - AV 024

2001 MLP VC 029

2002 MCD - CDVILES 113

2004	■	DANCE OF DECEMBER SOULS	CDd	Black Lodge	BLOD 017 CD

New artwork.

2004 ☐ BRAVE MURDER DAY ..... CD — Irond (Russia) ..... CD 04-730
Bonus: Nowhere/At Last/Inside The Fall/Funeral Wedding/Shades Of Emerald Fields/For Funerals To Come/Epistel

2004 ☐ BRAVE MURDER DAY ..... LPg — Northern Silence ..... NSP 009
Numbered. 444 black, 333 purple vinyl.

2004 ☐ Saw You Drown ..... MLP — Avantgarde ..... AV 028
Blue vinyl.

2004 ☐ BRAVE YESTER DAYS ..... 2CDd — Century Media (USA) 8152-9
2004 ☐ BRAVE YESTER DAYS ..... 2CDd — Avantgarde ..... AV 075
2004 ☐ BRAVE YESTER DAYS ..... 2CDd — Irond (Russia) ..... CD 04-877
2004 ☐ DISCOURAGED ONES ..... CD — Irond (Russia) ..... CD 04-731
Bonus: Saw You Drown/Nerve/Quiet World/Scarlet Heavens

2004 ☐ DISCOURAGED ONES ..... CD — Shock (Australia) ..... CM 8159-2
2004 ☐ LAST FAIR DEAL GONE DOWN ..... CDd — Peaceville ..... CDVILED 98
Bonus: Sulfur

2004 ☐ VIVA EMPTINESS ..... CDd — Infinite Vinyl Series ..... IVS 003
2004 ☐ VIVA EMPTINESS ..... LPg — Peaceville ..... CDVILED 103
2005 ☐ BRAVE MURDER DAY ..... CD — Woongjin Entech (South Korea) ...WPOC 0036
Bonus: Nowhere/At Last/Inside The Fall/Untrue

2005 ☐ DISCOURAGED ONES ..... CD — Woongjin Entech (South Korea) ...WPOC 0037
Bonus: Quiet World/Scarlet Heavens

2005 ☐ VIVA EMPTINESS ..... CD — Moon (Ukraine) ..... MR 1290-2
2005 ■ THE BLACK SESSIONS ..... 2CD+DVD box — Peaceville ..... CDVILEB 129
2005 ☐ Saw You Drown ..... 10" MLP 4tr — Infinite Vinyl Series ..... IVS 010
Blue vinyl. 1000 copies.

2006 ☐ BRAVE MURDER DAY ..... CDd — Peaceville ..... CDVILED 154
Bonus: Nowhere/At Last/Inside The Fall

2006 ☐ BRAVE MURDER DAY ..... CD — Icarus (Argentina) ..... ICARUS 252
Bonus: Funeral Wedding/Shades Of Emerald Fields/For Funerals To Come/Epistel

2006 ☐ DANCE OF DECEMBER SOULS ..... CDd — Mystic Empire (Russia) ..... MYST CD 030
New artwork. The Jhva Elohim Meth MCD as bonus.

2006 ☐ THE GREAT COLD DISTANCE ..... CD — Peaceville ..... CDVILEF 128X
Bonus: My Twin (video)

2006 ☐ THE GREAT COLD DISTANCE ..... 2LPg — Peaceville ..... CDVILELP 128
Red vinyl. 2000 copies. Bonus: Displaced/Dissolving Bonds/In The White (Urban Dub)/Code Against The Code

2006 ☐ THE GREAT COLD DISTANCE ..... CD — Peaceville ..... CDVILEF 128
2006 ☐ THE GREAT COLD DISTANCE ..... CD — Soyus (Russia) ..... CDVILEF 128
2006 ☐ THE GREAT COLD DISTANCE ..... CD — Moon (Ukraine) ..... MR 1633-2
2006 ☐ My Twin ..... MCDd 4tr — Peaceville CDVILES138
Tracks: My Twin (single ed)/My Twin (Opium Dub)/Displaced/Dissolving Bonds

2006 ☐ Deliberation ..... MCDd 3tr — Peaceville CDVILES140
Tracks: Deliberation/In The White (Urban Dub)/Code Against The Code

2007 ■ July ..... MCDd 3tr — Peaceville ..... CDVILES 172
Tracks: July/Soil's Song (Krister Linder 2012 Remix)/Unfurl + July (video)

2007 ☐ DANCE OF DECEMBER SOULS ..... CD — Century Media ..... CEN 8030-2
2007 ☐ DANCE OF DECEMBER SOULS ..... CDd — Peaceville ..... CDVILED 175
New artwork. The Jhva Elohim Meth MCD as bonus.

2007 ☐ BRAVE MURDER DAY ..... CD — Soyus (Russia) ..... CDVILED 154
New artwork. Bonus: Nowhere/At Last/Inside The Fall

2007 ☐ DISCOURAGED ONES ..... CD — Soyus (Russia) ..... CDVILED 155
New artwork. Bonus: Quiet World/Scarlet Heavens

2007 ☐ TONIGHT'S DECISION ..... 2LPg — Peaceville ..... VILELP 76
1500 numbered. Bonus: No Devotion/Fractured

2007 ☐ LAST FAIR DEAL GONE DOWN ..... 2LPg — Peaceville ..... VILELP 89
1500 numbered. Bonus: Sulfur/March 4/Help Me Disappear

2007 ☐ THE GREAT COLD DISTANCE – 5.1 MIX SPECIAL EDITION ..... CDd+DVD — Peaceville ..... CDVILEF 176X
New artwork. Bonus: Displaced/Dissolving Bonds

2007 ☐ LIVE CONSTENATION ..... CD+DVD — Peaceville ..... CDVILEF 179X
2007 ☐ LIVE CONSTENATION ..... CDd+DVD — Peaceville ..... CDVILEF 206X
2007 ☐ DISCOURAGED ONES + BRAVE MURDER DAY ..... 2CD — Shock (Austraila) ..... CMKAT 001-2
2009 ☐ Forsaker/Evidence ..... CDS — Peaceville CDVILEF271TP
Promo freebee.

2009 ■ NIGHT IS THE NEW DAY ..... CDd — Peaceville ..... CDVILEF 271
Bonus: Ashen. Digibook.

2009 ☐ NIGHT IS THE NEW DAY ..... CD — Peaceville ..... CDVILEF 271
Slipcase.

2009 ☐ NIGHT IS THE NEW DAY ..... CD — Soyus (Russia) ..... CDVILE 271
2009 ☐ NIGHT IS THE NEW DAY ..... LPg — Peaceville ..... VILELP 271
Bonus: Ashen. Digibook.Also 1000 copies on white vinyl.

2009 ☐ THE GREAT COLD DISTANCE ..... CDd+DVD — Peaceville ..... CDVILED 264X
2010 ■ The Longest Year ..... MCD 4tr — Peaceville ..... CDVILES 282
Tracks: The Longest Year/Sold Heart/Day And Then The Shade (remix)/Idle Blood (remix)

2010 ☐ LIVE CONSTENATION ..... LP — Night Of The Vinyl Dead ..... NIGHT 061
500 hand numbered copies.

2004 CDd - BLOD 017 CD

2005 2CD+DVD box - CDVILEB 129

2007 MCD - CDVILES 172

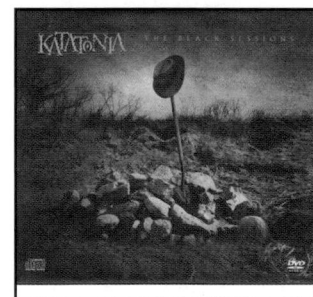
2009 CDd - CDVILEF 271

2010 MCD - CDVILES 282

| 2011 ☐ | DISCOURAGED ONES | LP | Svart Records | SVR 037 |

Bonus: Quiet World/Scarlet Heavens. 550 copies in orange vinyl.

| 2011 ☐ | LAST FAIR DEAL GONE DOWN – 10TH ANNIVERSARY EDITION | 2CD | Peaceville | CDVILED 335X |

New artwork. Bonus: Help Me Disappear/Oh How I Enjoy The Light/Sulfur/March 4

| 2011 ☐ | NIGHT IS THE NEW DAY | CD | Peaceville | CDVILED 332 |

Slipcase. New artwork. Bonus: Ashen/Sold Heart/Day And Then The Shade (Frank Default Mix)/Idle Blood (Linje 14)

2012 ☐	DEAD END KINGS	CD	Peaceville	CDVILEF-403
2012 ☐	DEAD END KINGS	CD+DVD	Peaceville	CDVILEF-402X
2012 ■	Buildings/Hypnone	7"	Peaceville	VILES 413

Clear vinyl.

2012 7" - VILES 413

KAYSER

Christian "Spice/Kryddan" Sjöstrand: v, Mattias Svensson: g/b, Jokke Pettersson: g/b, Bob Ruben: d

Helsingborg - *Kayser* were formed in 2004 when Spice, Ruben, Svensson and Spice's former *Aeon* colleague Fredrik Finnander (also in *Rise And Shine*) decided to join forces. On the debut album Richard Caesar, who produced the album, also played organ. In 2005 Finnander left the band and was replaced by Jokke Pettersson, who together with Svensson also handled bass on *Frame The World*. In 2006 bass player Emil Sandin joined the band. Spice is ex-*Spiritual Beggars*, *The Mushroom River Band*, *Aeon*, *Spice & The RJ Band* and is also in *Band Of Spice*. Bob has been in all except *Aeon*, Svensson is ex-*The Defaced* and Sandin is ex-*Chaostribe* and *Poseidon*, while Pettersson was also in the latter. *Kayser* play bone-hard thrash metal similar to *Slayer* and *Sepultura* with a heavier touch at times, and with Spice sounding surprisingly similar to Tom Araya. Some songs are however a bit heavier and more melodic drawing on *Pantera*.

2005 CD - SC 103-2

2006 CD - SC 125-2

| 2005 ■ | KAISERHOF | CD | Scarlet | SC 103-2 |
| 2005 ☐ | KAISERHOF | CD | Gencross (Japan) | GCCY-1012 |

Bonus: Lost Cause (demo)/Noble is your blood (demo/Rafflesia (demo)/The Waltz (demo)/Perfect (demo)/Good Citizen (video)

| 2006 ☐ | The Good Citizen | MCD 4tr | Scarlet | SC 123-2 |

Bonus: Good Citizen/Lost In The Mud/Fall/Propaganda/Good Citizen (video)

| 2006 ■ | FRAME THE WORLD .... AND HANG IT ON YOUR WALL | CD | Scarlet | SC 125-2 |
| 2008 ☐ | KAISERHOF – SPECIAL EDITION | 2CD | Scarlet | SC 154-2 |

Re-issue featuring the tracks from The Good Citizen on a separate CD.

KAZJUROL

Henrik "Gator" Ahlberg: v/b, Tommie "Tban/Rayban" Petersson: g, Pontus "Chris/Kong" Ekwall: g, Ulf "Udo" Larsson: d

Fagersta - Formed in 1986 as a "fun-project" by the members in hardcore band *Rescues In Future*. In 1986 they recorded the track *Breaking The Silence* for a 7" compilation-EP released by German Artcore Records. In 1987 they recorded two two-track demos and in 1988 they recorded the demo *A Lesson In Love* that sold about 2500 copies. On the first 7" the line-up featured Pontus, Tommie, Håkan (b), Kjelle (v) and Bonden (d). On *Dance Tarantella*, Tomas "Bäsan" Bengtsson replaced Kjelle and Ulf replaced Bonden. On *Bodyslam*, the above line-up was formed. They also contribute with a *Discharge*-cover on the thrash compilation *A Tribute Of Memories* ('91 Burning Heart) and the *Venom* cover *Countess Bathory* on *Promoters Of The Third World War* ('93 Primitive Art) which is also found on the *Bodyslam*-EP. Musically the band is in the same territory as early *Megadeth* or *Metallica* with vocals at times reminiscent of Cronos (*Venom*). The band has split and Tommie and Pontus were later found in the far more punk/hardcore-ish band *Bad Dreams Always*.

1996 7" - UPROAR 004

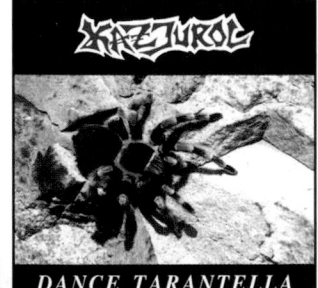

DANCE TARANTELLA
1990 LP - ATV 12

1991 7" - Heartcore 001

1991 7" - Heartcore 002

| 1986 ■ | Messengers Of Death | 7" 3tr | Uproar Records | UPROAR 004 |

Tracks: Messengers Of Death/Stagedive To Hell/Who Needs You?2100 copies

| 1990 ■ | DANCE TARANTELLA | LP | Active | ATV 12 |
| 1990 ☐ | DANCE TARANTELLA | CD | Active | ATV 12 |

Bonus: Cocaine (JJ Cale cover)/The Human Force

| 1991 ■ | Bodyslam | 7" 4tr | Burning Heart | Heartcore 001 |

Tracks: We Gotta Know (Cro-Mags cover)/United Forces (S.O.D cover)/Pay To Cum (Bad Brains cover)/Countess Bathory (Venom cover).

| 1991 ■ | Concealed Hallucinations | 7" 3tr | Burning Heart | Heartcore 002 |

Tracks: Hallucinations/Dance Tarantella/Blue Eyed Devils (Crude SS cover).

| 1991 ☐ | Toothcombing Reality's Surroundings | MCD 4tr | Burning Heart (promo) | BHP 101 |

Tracks: Hallucinations/Dance Tarantella/The Unholy War/Deathcon 5. 300 copies.

KEEGAN

Per "Jeff Keegan" Lindstedt: v/g, Thomas "Jaeger/Lyon" Lundgren: g, Magnus Rosén: b, Ralph "Rydeen" Rydén: d

Hässleholm - *Keegan*'s first album can be described as a cross between *Megadeth* and *Crimson*

Glory with **King Diamond**-influenced vocals. On the debut album Anders Johansson (*Silver Mountain, Malmsteen, HammerFall* etc) played drums and Pete Sandberg (*Jade, Madison, Alien* etc) handled the backing vocals. Jeff then played guitar, bass and handled the lead vocals. Before the second album, *Keegan* was a complete band with the former **Hexenhaus**-boys Ralph (formerly Lindgren) and Thomas (**Destiny**) and ex-**Von Rosen/Billionaires Boys Club** bassist Magnus. The band's second album was released in April '95 and showed a nicely upgraded band. Jeff made his first vinyl attempt with *Arrowz* in 1983. Magnus later went to **Hammerfall** and is now a bass solo artist. Rydén is playing in **Lizard Eye**.The track *Back To The Wall* is featured on the *Dzynamite Records Promotion Only* (96 Dzynamite Records) compilation.

1993 ■	AGONY IN DESPAIR	CD	Aprobo		621027
	Also released in a limited promo-edition in the shape of a book.				
1995 ☐	MIND NO MIND	CD	Aprobo		CD 556507

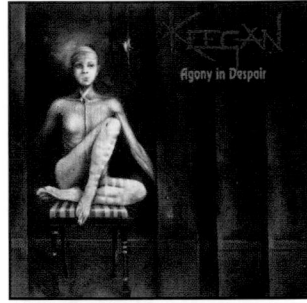

1993 CD - 621027

KEEHOLE

Kee Bergman: v, Björn "Ace Chrome" Kromm: g, Mikael "Edgy Led" Pireng: b

Bålsta - **Keehole** play heavy melodic power metal with quite dramatic vocals. The overall quality is quite good, while the production leaves a bit more to be desired. The first album featured Bergman, Kromm, bass player Andreas "Andy" Mallander and former **Keegan**/**Mercy** drummer Ralph Rydén (now in **Lizard Eye**). On the second release Rickard Johansson (**Twilight Illusion**) was a hired drummer. The band has recorded further material, but is currently on hold. Kromm now has his own band **Crometone** and he is found in **Cellout**.

2003 ■	REALM OF KEEHOLE SAVING PLANET EARTH EPISODE 1	CD	Label Of Heaven		LoH2003-03
2006 ☐	The Code Of Life, Epizode Zero	MCD 3tr	Label Of Heaven		LoH2006-03
	Tracks: The Guest/Heeron Is Dying/The Return				

2003 CD - LoH2003-03

KEEN HUE

Mats Frimodigs: v, Stefan Morén: g, Per Andersson: k,
Kent Jansson: b, Peter Eriksson: d

Vansbro - This band has almost turned into an institution. They started out with a single on Pang Records, followed by an album on Ebony Records' sub label Criminal Response. They then recorded some great demos with titles like *Fishing For A Deal* and *Horny Dick Has No Eyes* and had the song *Fly Away Honey* featured on the *Rockbox* compilation in 1989, but didn't settle a real deal until 1993 when Black Mark took the band under their wings. On the debut album the line-up featured guitarist Åke Nyström, bassist Lars-Åke Nilsson, Stefan Morén and Peter Eriksson. Patrik Silén was the singer on the compilation track. Mats, who replaced Patrik in 1991 was previously in **One Way Street**. The last album is a fine piece of melodic hard rock, however I personally think the band had some greater moments on some of the demos. Kent is ex-**Six Feet Under**, while Stefan recorded a 7" with the band **United** in 1988. He also released a solo-CD in 1996 and has recorded demos after this. Stefan has also produced a number of bands. In the mid-nineties they changed their concept and became a cover band playing anything from hard rock to reggae and pop. The current line-up features Morén, Jansson, drummer Christer Persson and singer/keyboardist BJ Lindström.
Website: www.keenhue.nu

1982 7" - PSI 052

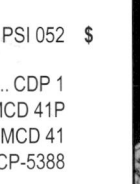

1985 LP - CDP 1

1982 ■	One Of Two/Spread Your Wings Of Fire	7"	Pang		PSI 052	$
	A very limited edition was available with artwork.					
1985 ■	OGRE KING	LP	Criminal Response		CDP 1	
1993 ☐	Coming Home/Into The Night	CDS 2tr	Black Mark (promo)		BMCD 41P	
1993 ☐	JUICYFRUIT LUCY	CD	Black Mark		BMCD 41	
1995 ■	JUICYFRUIT LUCY	CD	Victor (Japan)		VICP-5388	
	Different "censored" artwork.					

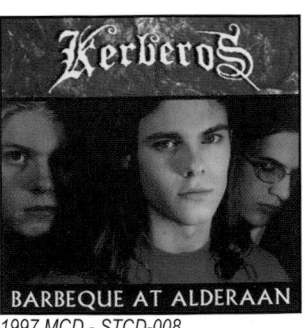

1995 CD - VICP-5388

KERBEROS

Lesli Liljegren: g/k/v, Fredrik Bergenstråhle: b, Oskar Kvant: d

Stockholm - A very young and very promising trio that produces high-class progressive metal. All three versions of the MCD have the same tracks, only the covers and label varies. The full-length album *Heart Jar Cabinet* was never officially released. The band had a long hiatus but in 2000 they changed their name to **Random Hope** and also changed their style to more straightforward melodic rock. Bergenstråhle has later played with **Chris Laney** and **Loud**. Leli has recorded several acoustic albums under his own name.

1995 ☐	Barbeque At Alderaan	MCD 5tr	Powerpuke Productions		ID1
	Tracks: Silhouette/Seaside Death/Contribute/Misjudged/Chewie Tells His Story (part I to X)				
1996 ☐	Barbeque At Alderaan	MCD 5tr	Mellotronen		MELLOSING 02
1997 ■	Barbeque At Alderaan	MCD 5tr	Sound Treasure		STCD-008
	Japanese press with different artwork.				
1999 ☐	HEART JAR CABINET	CD	private		Kerberos #5

1997 MCD - STCD-008

KEYSTONE

Stefan Johansson: v/g, Johan Holmström: g, Roger Karlsson: g, Magnus Lindh: b, Mats Söderbom: d

Ronneby - Quite amateurish melodic hard rock, similar to early *Ocean*, but with a thin sound. For collectors only. The single was recorded at Starec in Växjö already in 1981.

1984 ■ The Robber .... 7" 4tr   private KSEP-111
    Tracks: The Robber/Burnflame/Chicago/Boostramper

1984 7" - KSEP-111

KHARMA

Göran Edman: v, Dragan Tanaskovic: g, Atilla Szabo: k, Joel Starander: b, Imre Daun: d

Göteborg - A highly interesting combination of people producing a highly interesting platter. Try mixing influences from *Kansas*, *Styx* and *Journey* and you'll get *Kharma*. Göran is also found in *Glory*, *Vindictive*, *Malmsteen*, *Mårran* etc. Joel was found in the band *Geisha* in the 80's and Imre is ex-*Don Patrol*, *The Black* etc.

2000 ■ WONDERLAND ....CD   MTM..0681-13

2000 CD - 0681-13

KILL

Carl "Warslaughter" Wochatz: v, Jimmy "Jim Voltage" Edström: g, Kalle "Gorgorium" Antonsson: b, Lawen "Getaz" Palmgren: d

Göteborg - Formed in 1998 by Lawen "Getaz" Palmgren (*Likblek, Necroplasma, Stykkmord*) and Martin "Black Curse" Solymar. The duo was reinforced by bassist Assassmon. They recorded the demo *Nocturnal Death* in 1999, released in 100 copies. A second printing, featuring the bonus track *Satanic Chaos*, was released in 243 copies. *Necro* was produced by Onkel (*Nifelheim*) and Witchhammer Productions also released it on cassette. In 2001 Assassmon left the band and Carl "Warslaughter" Wochatz (also drummer in *Bestial Mockery*) joined. They recorded the debut album, after which Warslaughter left the band. Enter singer Jens "Killheiler" Pedersen (*Church Bizarre, Cerekloth, Undergang* (DK), *Ad Noctum*) and bassist Hellthrasher. They recorded a second demo, *Morbid Curse*, 2003, released in 100 copies and later released on vinyl. In 2004 Hellthrasher and Black Curse parted ways with the band. Bassist Kalle "Gorgorium" Antonsson (*Diabolicum, Tehom, Divine Desecration*) and guitarist Daniel "DD Executioner" Johansson (*Diabolicum, Sadistic Grimness, Angst*) joined in 2005. The latter however left later the same year. The year after, guitarist Hellheiler and Jimmy "Jim Voltage" Edström (*Devil Lee Rot, Pagan Rites, Autopsy Torment, Cross Bow, Church Bizarre, Karnarium* etc) joined. In 2007 Warslaughter returned as the band's new singer and Hellheiler was kicked out. *No Catharsis* featured Voltage, Gorgorium, Getaz and Warslaughter. On the 2010 split the line-up featured Wochatz, bassist/guitarist Gorgorium, guitarist Jim Voltage and drummer Getaz. *The Necrofiles* is a compilation of the *Nocturnal Death* demo and the *Necro* EP. *Kill* play primitive old-school black metal in the vein of *Bathory*.
Website: www.kill.nu

2001 7" - - -

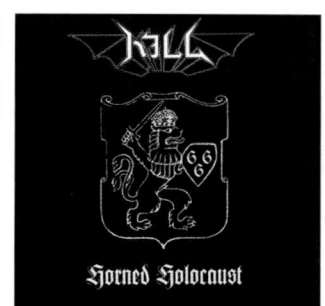

2002 LP - WORSHIP 001

2007 CD - THR 107

Year		Title	Format	Label	Cat.No.
2001	■	Necro .... 7" 4tr	Evil Never Dies		- -
		500 hand-numbered copies. Tracks: Necro 1/Infernal Slaughter/Necro 2/Fields Of Devastation			
2002	■	HORNED HOLOCAUST ....LP	Worship Him Records	WORSHIP 001	
		666 copies.			
2004	□	HORNED HOLOCAUST ....CD	Invictus Productions	IP 008	
2005	□	Morbid Curse .... 7" 4tr	Apocalyptor/Pentagram W.	AREP05/PWR003	
		Tracks: Vomit Of Heaven/Below/Morbid Curse/Unleash The Fury Of Abyss Flames			
2007	■	INVERTED FUNERAL ....CD	Total Holocaust	THR 107	
2007	□	INVERTED FUNERAL ....LP	Obscure Abhorrence	- -	
		500 copies, first 111 in splatter vinyl.			
2009	□	NO CATHARSIS ....CD	Worship Him	WORSHIP 016	
		500 copies, first 111 in splatter vinyl.			
2010	□	UNITED IN HELL'S FIRE (split) .... 10" MLPg	Burning Churches	- -	
		Split with Thornspawn. Tracks: Unlight Ritual/Let Hell Reign/Nails Of Cursed Steel/Necro 2. 500 copies. Poster.			
2010	□	UNITED IN HELL'S FIRE (split) ....CD	Morbid Metal Records	- -	
2010	□	THE NECROFILES ....CD	Dybbuk Records	DKR 010	
2012	■	BURNING BLOOD ....CD	BlackSeed Productions	SEED 23	
2012	□	BURNING BLOOD ....LP	Burning Churches		

KILLAMAN

Rune Foss: v, Roger Johansson: g, Johan Axelsson: g, Rikard Wermen: d

Hjärup/Göteborg - Formed out of the ashes of *Murder Corporation*. The band recorded the first demo in 2002 which lead to a deal with Displeased Records. Foss is also in *Dawn Of Time*, *Reclusion* and *Exempt*, Wermén and Axelsson are also found in *Deranged* and *Murder*

2012 CD - SEED 23

Corporation. The album was produced by Berno Paulsson. Roger Johansson was part of the line-up when the album was released, but Axelsson played all the guitars on the album. After the album the band was completed by bassist Kaspar Larsson (*Withering Surface*). The band has now split. *Killaman* play high-speed death metal with a strong thrashy touch.

2003 ■ KILLAMAN ....CD   Displeased D-00122

2003 CD - D-00122

KILLBILLY 5'ERS, THE
Ola "Alo" Karlsson: v, Ola Af Trampe: g, Wincent Persson: g,
Daniel Tegnvallius: b, B-O Kjellsson: dd
Växjö - Formed in 2009 on a night of drinking, when former *Violent Work Of Art* guitarist Persson persuaded singer Alo (*Grand Illusion, My Curse, Picassos Äventyr*) to form a country metal band. The style is down and dirty, shitkickin', hillbilly southern heavy rock in the vein of *Texas Hippie Coalition*, Killer stuff!! Trampe is also in *Code*, *Grand Illusion* and *My Curse*, while Daniel plays guitar in *Soulcreek* and B-O is in *Rhino As A Pet* and *Bellybuster*. Ola, Ola and B-O is also in country band *Stray Dawgs*.
Website: www.killbilly5.com

2012 ■ WELCOME TO TOWN NOW GET THE HELL OUT ....CDd   private ....- -

2012 CD -

KILLER BEE
Brian "Bee" Frank: v, Jimmy DeLisi: g, Denny DeMarchini: k/g,
Anders "L.A" Rönnblom: b, Morgan Evans: d
Örnsköldsvik/USA/Canada - When the band *Desert Rain* started to disband, Bee and L.A formed *Killer Bee*, completed by drummer Magnus Grundström, keyboardist Mattias Bylund, guitarists Peo Hedin and Mats Byström. Bee is actually from Canada where he recorded two albums with the band *Rapid Tears*. *Killer Bee* had some great success in Norway with the first single, however the Swedish audience has been quite reserved. Singles contains the bonus track *You Think You're Hot*, a sneak preview from the second album. *Killer Bee* play good solid sleaze-oriented hard rock with a touch of *Van Halen*. *World Order Revolution* was produced by Kee Marcello. Hedin has previously recorded a solo-track for the first *Guitar Heroes Of Sweden* compilation, and is today found in heavy rockers *Absorbing The Pain*. In 2011, the band re-united with new guitarists P-O Sedin and Rolf "Trazan" Nordström (ex-*Limit*) and Canadian drummer Morgan Evans (*Juliet, Lee Aaron*). Brian has also recorded some solo material. L.A previously recorded an EP with melodic rockers *Romance* and Mats Byström had recorded with the band *Sergeant* and *Boogietryck*. *Almost There* is a compilation album. Before the album *From Hell And Back*, the band also announced the departures of Byström, P-O and Trazan, who were replaced by Denny DeMarchini (*The Cranberries, Alias*) on keyboard/guitar and Jimmy DeLisi (*Julliet, Brian Johnson*) on lead guitar, making LA the only Swede.

1997 CD - FRCD 9701

1993 ☐	RAW ....CD	Freedom	....................................FRCD 9301
1994 ☐	Singles ....MCD 3tr	Freedom	...................................FRCDS 9401
	Tracks: Piece Of My Heart/The Count/You Think You're Hot non-LP.		
1994 ☐	Take Me Home..CDS 1tr	Freedom	...................................FRCDS 9402
1995 ☐	Singles 3 ....MCD 3tr	Freedom	...................................FRCDS 9501
	Tracks: You Think You're Hot/Word To The Wise/Free Rides.		
1995 ☐	Singles 4 ....MCD 4tr	Freedom	...................................FRCDS 9502
	Tracks: Hey Hey/Cracked Up/Everything Everytime/Gonna Do It.		
1995 ☐	Singles 5 ....MCD 4tr	Freedom	...................................FRCDS 9504
	Tracks: All I Need (piano mix)/Whispers In The Dark (acoustic mix)/All I Need (rcok mix)/		
	Whispers In The Dark (instrumental)		
1995 ☐	CRACKED UP..CD	Freedom	....................................FRCD 9501
1997 ■	WORLD ORDER REVOLUTION ....CD	Freedom	....................................FRCD 9701
2011 ■	ALMOST THERE (1990-1998)....................................CDd	UFO Records	...........................UFOCD 2044
2012 ■	FROM HELL AND BACK...CD	Z Records	.................................ZR0497165
2013 ☐	EVOLUTIONARY CHILDREN......................................CD	Target Distribution	...............TARGETCD1333

2011 CDd - UFOCD 2044

2012 CD - ZR0498165

KING & ROZZ
Göran "George King" Kunstbergs: v/b/k/d, Peter "Rozz" Rosenbach: g/h
Eskilstuna - Mid-quality melodic hard rock. The debut was a bit heavier, while *Bleeding Feelings* was quite radio-oriented. Göran is ex-*Wizz* and *Treasure*. He was later in the weirdo-folk-rock band *Urban Turban* and has recorded a strange album under the moniker *Icon X*. Peter, who also owned the record label, has released a 7" with *Rozz The Boss*.

1987 ☐	CAUGHT IN THE ACT ....LP	Backstage Music	...........................BSM 001
1987 ■	Bleeding Feelings/Judge...7"	Backstage Music	...........................BSM 765
1988 ☐	Leaving With You/The Rebel Rocker ....7"	Backstage Music	...........................BSM 767
1988 ☐	GUIF Eskilstuna/Street Of Love ....7"	Backstage Music	...........................BSM 789
1990 ☐	BLEEDING FEELINGS ....LP	Backstage Music	...........................BSM 995

1987 7" - BSM 765

KING CHROME

Magnus Arnar: v/g, Andreas Vaple: g, Aaron Coombs: b, Mats Lingman: d

Gävle - A highly interesting band that mixes old-school thrash with **Spiritual Beggars** type stoner and some touches of **Backyard Babies** as well as **Entombed**. Great stuff! Vaple is also found in **In Aeternum** and **Azotic Rain**. Arnar is also found in **Ground Mower** and is today fronting **The Quill**. Not to be confused with the German band.

2002 ■ Ache City Sessions ....MCD 5tr   private .... - -
   Tracks: Badass Bitchcraft/Hatred/Love You As You Are/Spacecake/Hotter Than Me

2002 MCD - - -

KING HOBO

Tomas "Juneor" Andersson: v/g, Per Wiberg: v/k,
Ulf "Rockis" Ivarsson: b, Jean Paul Gaster: d

Borlänge/Göteborg/USA - **King Hobo** is an all-star project formed in 2005 by keyboardist/ singer Per Wiberg (**Mojobone, Opeth, Spiritual Beggars**) and drummer Jean Paul Gaster, from American stoner rockers **Clutch**. They invited **Kamchatka** guitarist/singer Andersson and former **Sky High** bassist Ivarsson to join and recorded the album in a week. Anyone being familiar with and liking **Mojobone** and **Kamchatka** will definitely appreciate **King Hobo**. Seventies-oriented heavy rock leaning on heavy riffs and groovy rhythms.

2008 ■ KING HOBO..CDd   Hippodrome Music............................HM0208

2008 CDd - HM0208

KING KOOLE

Magnus Ekberg: v/g, Krister Karlsson: g/v, Sven Johansson: g,
Magnus Karlsson: b, Peter Karlsson: d

Klippan - **King Koole** were formed in 1981 also featuring keyboard player Mats Bengtsson (**Wilmer X**). The band initially featured bassist Karl-Otto Ahlberg, who was replaced by Karlsson in 1989. The band kept going until 1993, when Ekberg sadly died. The band continued as a cover band going through various members. The A-side is a great straight-ahead **AC/DC** style hard rocker with great balls, while the two tracks on the B-side are a bit more pop-oriented, almost in the vein of **Heavy Metal Kids**. In 2012 the band is still going as a cover band (playing anything from pop to hard rock), now featuring Krister, Peter, Magnus and bassist Göran Sjöberg.

1991 ■ Hot Love/Come Back/Can't Put Out The Fire ....7" 3tr   Svenska Popfabriken..............KK 01

1991 7" - KK 01

KING OF ASGARD

Karl Bäckman: v/g, Lars Tängmark: g, Jonas Albrektsson: b, Karsten Larsson: d

Mjölby - **King Of Asgard** were formed in 2008 by former **Mithotyn** members Bäckman and Larsson. Larsson has also been a member of **Dawn**, **The Choir Of Vengeance** and **Falconer**, while Bäckman has been in **Indungeon** and **Infernal Vengeance**. In 2009 the duo recorded the seven-track demo *Prince Of Märings*. Later the same year they were reinforced by Albrektsson (**Indungeon, Niden Div. 187, Thy Primordial**) and a year later Tängmark (**Dawn, The Choir Of Vengeance**) joined. **King Of Asgard** play high-quality folk-influenced Viking theme black metal. Great production on both albums by Andy LaRocque.

2010 ■ FI'MBULVINTR...CD   Metal Blade.................................3984-14921-2
2010 □ FI'MBULVINTR...CD   Metal Blade Japan (Japan)............MBCY-1140
2012 □ TO NORTH ....CD   Metal Blade.................................3984-14921-2

2010 CD - 3984-14921-2

KING PIN

Bo "Zinny Zan" Stagman: v, Harry "Kody" Kemppainen: g,
Tim "Skold" Skjöld: b, Pekka "Stixx" Ollinen: d

Skövde - The band was originally formed in the early 80s as **Shylock**. Singer back then was Jukka "J.K Knox" Kemppainen (no relation to Harry) and the drummer was Krister Rispling. They recorded a great demo in 1983. In 1984, they changed name to **King Pin** and recorded some more demos, from which some of the songs would appear on the debut *Welcome To Bop City*. Pekka "Stixx" Ollinen now handled the drums. Before the album was recorded, Bo "Zinny J. Zan" Stagman (ex-**Easy Action**, later in **Zan Clan**) replaced J.K. The style was guitar-dominated sleazy hard rock. *Welcome To Bop City* was first released under the **King Pin**-banner, but in 1988 the band moved to the US. The album was reissued the year after by Relativity under the band's new name **Shotgun Messiah**. (See **Shotgun Messiah** for further details). The instrumental track *The Explorer* was highly acclaimed by U.S metal-guru Mike Varney. Harry has worked with, among others, bass player Stuart Hamm. Bootleg label Time Warp Records has also released an unauthorised version of the album on CD.

1987 7" - CMM 008

1987 ■ Shout It Out/I Don't Care 'Bout Nothin' ....7"   CMM ....CMM 008
1988 ■ WELCOME TO BOP CITY..................................LP   CMM ....CMLP 105

1988 LP - CMLP 105

KING SIZE

**Crille Pettersson: v, Niclas Flodberg: g, Tomas Musial: g,
Larsy Sundberg: b, Ulrik "Urkke" Thunman: d**

Gävle - Upper-class glam metal with mid-class vocals. A third single recorded, featuring the songs *Mercedes Benz* (Joplin cover) and *Joe, Let's Go* was only released as a cassette single. Ulrik (aka Urrke) was previously in punk band **Bizex-B** and later in the band **Maryslim**.

| 1987 ■ I Love London/Nightlife Living | 7" | private | KSPHB 001 |
| 1987 □ I Love You/No No No | 7" | Westbell Sinclaire | WBS 0008 |

1987 7" - KSPHB 001

KINGSIZE

Dougie Lawton: v, Coste Apetrea: g, Anders Henriksson: k

Stockholm - There's not much information to find about this release on the record, besides the song was written by Coste Apetrea, Anders Henriksson and Dougie Lawton. Synchro Sound Music was a studio and production company run by Coste and Anders. The single is high-quality AOR with keyboards sounding similar to *The Final Countdown*. According to Apetrea, the song was ordered for Joe Weiders' *Mr. Olympia* contest in 1987. The band also played the song live, using drummer Magnus Persson, during the contest and on American television.

| 1987 ■ Mr O/Clash Of The Nations | 7" | Synchro Sound Music | SSRS 100 |

1987 7" - SSRS 100

KINGS N' FOOLS

**Mikael Löfgren: v, Perti Hellala: g, Gunnar Johansson: k,
Thomas Andersson: b, Janne Fernström: d**

Köping - Formed in 1988. **Kings N' Fools** is a very good, melodic hard rock band, slightly reminiscent of early **Magnum**. Well worth looking for. The band still exists, but with Janne as the only remaining member. The style has also changed towards the heavier thrash vein. Janne is related to famous rocker Erik "Jerry Williams" Fernström.

| 1989 ■ Former Life/Early Dawn | 7" | SGV | S 9011 $ |

1989 7" - S 9011

KINGS OF MODERN SWING

Sonny Larsson: v, Jörgen Lejon: g, Rolle Larsson: b, Peter Olsen: d

Örebro - Bluesy hard rock in the vein of late David Lee Roth. High-quality musicians indeed. Singer Sonny has previously recorded with **Leviticus**, **Motherlode**, **XT** and Björn Stigsson.

| 1996 □ CURSING IN THE SHADOWS | MCD 4tr | private | KINGSCD 9601 |

Tracks: Turn Me On/The Channel Club/Far Away/The Power

KISS OF THUNDER

Mackan Andersson: b/v, Matz Matsson: g/v, Håkan Frisk: g, Dan Barrling: d

Borlänge - As you might suspect, this is a true **Kiss**-cover band. They dress like **Kiss**, look like **Kiss** and sound like **Kiss**. They do it very well indeed. The band does classics like *Deuce, Strutter, Hotter Than Hell* and *Firehouse* with pure energy.

| 1997 ■ LIVE AT COZMOZ | CD | Tribute Records | TRO 15 |

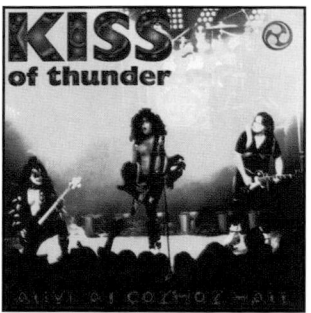

1997 CD - TRO 15

KISSES FROM THE PAST

**Johan Rosenberg: v, Urban Fagerholm: g, Pelle Wilhelmsson: g,
Anders Hagerborn: b, Jörgen Ekener: d**

Karlstad - Just like **Kiss Of Thunder** and **Kyss**, here's a CD with **Kiss**-covers only. This band has concentrated on the early **Kiss**-years and cover songs like *Cold Gin, Black Diamond, Strutter* and *Deuce*. **KFTP** actually manage to recreate the old sound and style of the masters quite well. Good performance, but like any other cover band - they don't match the originals. Parts of the band also have another cover band, doing Hendrix tunes. Urban has played with Zia Lindberg. Ekener previously recorded a single with the band **Shee**.

| 1995 ■ A TRIBUTE TO KISS | CD | private | KFTP 01 |

1995 CD - KFTP 01

KLICHÉ

**Janne Nilsson: g/v, Tommie Johansson: g/v, Ronnie Biveland: b/v,
Christer Lorichs: k, Benny Johansson: d**

Linköping - Quite amateurish AOR, even though the band saw themselves as pop/rockers. The band was formed in 1979-80 and split only three years later. None of the members pursued any musical career. The band also saw renowned jazz/blues/country singer Lana Brunell in the line-up for some time. For collectors only. Trivia: Christer Lorichs' daughter Nathalie is engaged to *Opeth*'s Martin Axenrot and sang a duet on the *Opeth* song *Coil*. She has also made guest appearances with Jon Lord (R.I.P) and Glenn Hughes.

1981 ■ Beach Avenue/Night Train ....7" AVD Records AVD81011

Beach Avenue / Night Train

1981 7" - AVD81011

KNOCKOUT

**Simon "Tapani" Asikainen: v, Paul Fernandez: k,
Jesper Kviberg: g, Mats Ymell: g, Daniel Grüter: b**

Stockholm - *Knockout* represent the wimpier side of the AOR-genre, in the same league as *Guardian Angel* and late *Easy Action*. Mats was later found in melodic rockers *Planet Waves*, *Rossall & The Gang* and *J.R:s Glitter Band*. Simon also recorded an album with Danish band *Naked Rain* in 1996.

1989 ■ Yesterday Night/Faces (Without Names)..7" V.I.P..VS 1001

1989 7" - VS 1001

KONGH

David Johansson: g/v, Oscar Ryden: b, Tomas Salonen: d

Nässjö - In 2004 Johansson and Salonen decided to form a loud and heavy band. After jamming and starting to write, they became *Kongh* in 2006. With a 45 minute four-track demo under the belt they were soon picked up by Stockholm label Trust No One. They rerecorded two songs from the demo and wrote two new tracks, which became the *Counting Heartbeats* MCD. The split with *Witchlord* was part of a 5-single box set entitled *Pharmacopoeia*, but 50 copies were also sold separately. *Kongh* play detuned heavy, almost drone-style stonerish doom with growling vocals. *Sole Creation* features a guest spot from John Doe (*Craft*).
Website: www.kongh.net

2007 □	COUNTING HEARTBEATS	CD	Trust No One	TNO 031
2008 □	Kongh/Ocean Chief (split)	LP	Land O Smiles	LOS 15
	Split with Ocean Chief. Track: Drifting On Waves. 500 copies.			
2008 □	COUNTING HEARTBEATS	2LP	Sound Devastation	SD 01 LP
	270 green/black, 519 brown.			
2008 □	Kong/Witchlord (split)	7"	Land O Smiles	LOS 14 GH
	Track: Turn Into Dust.			
2009 ■	SHADOWS OF THE SHAPELESS	CD	Trust No One	TNO 035
2009 □	SHADOWS OF THE SHAPELESS	2LP	Music Fear Satan	MUF 005
	200 red, 1300 black.			
2010 □	SHADOWS OF THE SHAPELESS	CD	Seventh Rule (USA)	SRULE018
2011 □	COUNTING HEARTBEATS	2LP	Music Fear Satan	MUF 017
	150 clear, 150 pink swirl, 700 black.			
2013 □	SOLE CREATION	CD	Agonia Records	ARcd108

2009 CD - TNO 035

KOREA

Michael Ehrnstén: v, Mats Karpestam: g, Robert Bunke: b, Dennis Ehrnstén: d

Solna - *Korea* were formed in 2003 and soon discovered by American producer Blake Althen. Brothers Dennis and Michael formed the band together with Robert. Later on Mats replaced the band's first, unnamed, guitarist. They claim to be inspired by bands like *Carpark North*, *NIN* and *Mew*, which should put them outside the book, but when listening there are enough metal elements to keep them in. It's melodic and melancholic yet quite heavy and at times quite close to *Takida*.

2008 □	Above/Rebound	CDS	ViciSolum	VSPS 001
2008 □	FOR THE PRESENT PURPOSE	CD	ViciSolum	VSP 003
2010 ■	THE DELIRIUM SUITE	CD	ViciSolum	VSP 011

2010 CD - VSP 011

KORP

**Erik Hillströms: v, Fredrik Lundberg: v, Tommy Mattsson: g/k,
Henrik Westin: g/k, Olsson: b, Peter Andersson: d/v**

Bollnäs - *Korp* were founded already in 1995, initially under the name *Nocturnal*, changed the name to *Demogorgon* and recorded *Döden förde dem till sitt rike* in 1996. As there was a Greek

1999 CD - VODCD 006

band with the same name they changed it to **Korp** (meaning "raven" in Swedish) and recorded the demo *Utvald* later in 1996. The full-length album *Until Eternity Calls* was recorded for Craziness Music in 1997, but was never released. High-speed death/black metal with elements of thrash. They rely more on speed and power than progressive twists. No symphonic keyboard-nonsense, just a pedal to the metal wall of guitars. Traditional screeching guttural vocals. The lyrics on the debut was in Swedish, while they had changed to English on the follow-up. On the second album Mattsson had replaced Jonsson on guitar and Lundberg was added to the line-up. Andersson and Westin have also played with **Blazing Skies** and the latter was also in **Inmoria**.

1999 ■	DEMON – REBORN	CD	Voices Of Death	VODCD 006	
2001 ■	THORNS OF CENTURIES UNFOLD	CD	Voices Of Death	VODCD 009	

2001 CD - VODCD 009

KREMLIN'S INN
Susanne Johansson: v, Janne Wernersson: g, Kalle Carlsson: k,
Janne Lidström: b/v, Lasse Korhonen: d

Bålsta - **Kremlin's Inn** were a continuation of hard rockers **Zonic Attack** (1976-1985), which at one time featured Johnny Öhlin, later in **Nation**. The band recorded a couple of demos, entered the *Rock SM* in 1987, but only made it to the local final. The single was released after the band split (in October 1988). Really good **Van Halen**-influenced hard rock. Great singer and great guitarist. The B-side is a power ballad, but with really great guitars. In 2011 **Zonic Attack**, featuring Lidström, re-united for some new metal adventures.

1989 ■	Tunnel Of Love/Shooting For The Moon	7"	Get Inn Records	INN 014	$
	500 copies.				

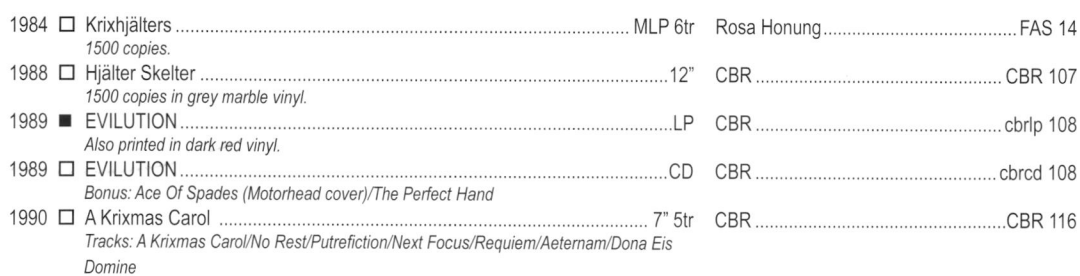

1989 7" - INN 014

KRIXHJÄLTERS, THE
Pontus Lindqvist: v/b, Pelle Ström: g, Rasmus Ekman: g, Stefan Kälfors: d

Stockholm - Formed around 1980-81. On the first MLP the style was more pure hardcore, but that later changed to a more original type of technical power metal. When the band was formed Pelle was also found in thrashers **Agony**. In 1990 the band changed their name to **Omnitron**. Stefan was later found in **Gone**. The band has several tracks on compilations, such as *The Swedish Stand-In* (89 Sinderella). Pelle and Rasmus were also in **Comecon** and Pontus was in **Rubbermen**.

1984 ☐	Krixhjälters	MLP 6tr	Rosa Honung	FAS 14	
	1500 copies.				
1988 ☐	Hjälter Skelter	12"	CBR	CBR 107	
	1500 copies in grey marble vinyl.				
1989 ■	EVILUTION	LP	CBR	cbrlp 108	
	Also printed in dark red vinyl.				
1989 ☐	EVILUTION	CD	CBR	cbrcd 108	
	Bonus: Ace Of Spades (Motorhead cover)/The Perfect Hand				
1990 ☐	A Krixmas Carol	7" 5tr	CBR	CBR 116	
	Tracks: A Krixmas Carol/No Rest/Putrefiction/Next Focus/Requiem/Aeternam/Dona Eis Domine				

1989 LP - cbrlp 108

KRUX
Mats Levén: v, Fredrik Åkesson: g, Jörgen Sandström: g,
Carl Westholm: k, Leif Edling: b, Peter Stjärnvind: d

Stockholm - When **Candlemass** split/took a break in 2002, after their reunion tour, Edling decided to get a new thing going. He recruited his former **Abstrakt Algebra** colleague Levén (also in **Therion, Amaseffer, Malmsteen, Sabbtail** etc), guitarist Sandström (**Entombed, Grave, The Project Hate, Vicious Art**) and drummer Stjärnvind (**Unanimated, Entombed, FaceDown, Merciless, Regurgitate, Nifelheim** etc) and formed **Krux**. On the first album the guitar solos were handled by Fredrik Åkesson (**Talisman, Opeth, Arch Enemy**) and Nico Elgstrand (**Entombed, Terra Firma**), while Leif's former **Abstrakt Algebra** colleague Carl Westholm (also in **Jupiter Society** and **Carptree**) played keyboards. On the second album Åkesson and Westholm were members of the band. **Krux** is all about simple melodic riffing with doom written all over it, but without becoming drony and boring, despite the songs being quite long. Plus, Mats' voice really fits this genre. *III* features a guest solo from **Trouble**'s Bruce Franklin.
Website: www.kruxdoom.se/

2003 CD - M 7072-2

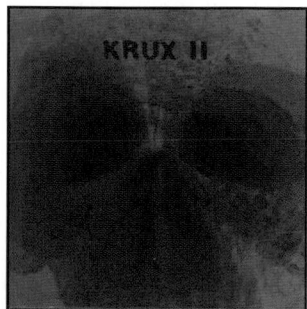

2006 CD - GMRCD9001

2003 ■	KRUX	CD	Mascot	M 7072-2	
2006 ■	KRUX II	CD	GMR	GMRCD9001	
2012 ☐	KRUX III – HE WHO SLEEPS AMONG THE STARS	CD	GMR	GMRCD9030	
2012 ■	KRUX III – HE WHO SLEEPS AMONG THE STARS	LPg	High Roller Records	HRR 210	
	100 blue/white, 300 blue and 600 black vinyl.				
2012 ☐	KRUX II	LPg	High Roller Records	HRR 221	
	100 orange, 500 red, and 400 black vinyl.				

2012 LPg - HRR 210

No sleep for the wicked! Jörgen and Leif of Krux.

KYLA
Kim Carlsson: v/g/b/d

Jönköping - The solo project of *Hypothermia*/*Lifelover*/*Life IS Pain* man Carlsson, who also runs the Insikt label. Not surprisingly, *Kyla* (chill/cool in Swedish) is musically quite close to *Hypothermia*'s depressive low-fidelity, buzz saw-guitar, primal scream "vocals", badly-mixed, old-school black metal. The first demo was recorded in 2004, followed by the debut album. The self-titled 2005 demo was also released as a single, but without the outro track. In 2005 a split tape with *Life Neglected* was also released on Northern Sky.

2005 ■ GLORY OF NEGATIVITY ....CD Eternity Records ....ETER 013
        300 copies. Insert smeared with Kim's blood.
2009 ☐ Into The Depths/Blood ....7" Turannum Records ....Turannum 005

2005 CD - ETER 013

KYRKSTÖT
Hans Isaksson: v, Göran Karlsson: g, Håkan Nordell: g,
Thomas Rydfeldt: k, Peter Årnes: b, Matz Mjörnheim: d

Göteborg - Formed in 1976. A Christian band in the same vein as mid 70s *Status Quo*. Despite the English song titles the lyrics are in Swedish. They also have the track *Deus Ex Machina* on the compilation *Rock Plock* (81 Talking Music). The band is on the same label as *Leviticus*. Before they split in 1983 the line-up had changed featuring Ken Wennerholm (*Sidewalk*) and Inga-Lill Nyström. Thomas is now a piano teacher, Hans is working with theatre, Göran is working with a music school for children. Matz later played with *Vatten*, *Sidewalk* and pop-band *Salt*. A "kyrkstöt" is a pole they were using to wake people up who fell asleep in church.

KYRKSTÖT

1980 ■ No Smoking/Dr. Jekyll...7" Talking Music ....KRF 001

1980 7" - KRF 001

KYSS
Thomas "Demon" Vikström: b/v, Ulf "Starchild" Larsson: g/v,
Lars "Spaceman" Christmansson: g, Johan "The Cat" Koleberg: d

Stockholm - Yet another *Kiss* tribute band. This one however consists of more name-musicians, such as *Lion's Share*-members Lars and Johan and of course Thomas Vikström (*Talk Of The Town, Candlemass, Stormwind*). Ulf, today more known as Chris Laney, is ex-*Seventeen*, now solo and in *Chris Laney's Legion*. They do the originals justice. The band still reforms from time to time.

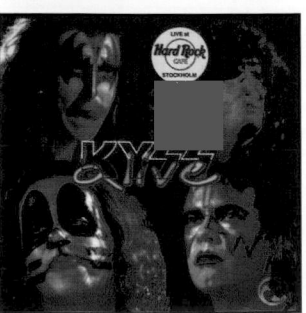

1997 ■ ALIVE...CD Tribute...................................... TRO23

1997 CD - TRO23

LACK OF FAITH

Ronny Hemlin: v, Andreas Silén: g, Johan Löfgren: b, Tony Elfving: d

Stockholm - *Lack Of Faith* came together in 1997. Hemlin has previously been found in *Arcana Major*, *Tad Morose* and *Planet Storm*. The band recorded the 8-track pro-printed CD-R *Act Of Perfection* in 2001. At the time the band featured Silén, Hemlin, bass player Mikael Hallberg, keyboardist Daniel Forslund (*Steel Attack*) and drummer Ronnie Lundqvist. The style was quite heavy, progressive metal, more in the vein of *Arcana Major*. The demo also featured a cover of *Deep Purple*'s *Stormbringer*. On *Aeternus Caligato,* Forslund was out and the style was a lot heavier, less progressive and more aggressive. Silén is ex-*Two Moon Junction*. After the album, Lundqvist was replaced by Tony Elfving (*Conspiracy, Facequake, Arcana Major*) and Hallberg by Johan Löfgren. In 2004 Hemlin became the new singer of *Steel Attack* with whom he has recorded three albums so far. The band has split.

2003 ■ AETERNUS CALIGATO...CD   Rivel Records .... RRCD 010

2003 CD - RRCD 010

LAETHORA

Jonathan Nordenstam: v, Joakim Rosén: g, Niklas Sundin: g,
Jonnie Tell: b, Joel Lindell: d

Göteborg - *Laethora* is the side project of *Dark Tranquillity* guitarist Niklas Sundin (also a renowned graphic designer/artist). Niklas has also been part of *Hammerfall* and *Septic Boiler*. Lindell, Tell and Rosén were all ex-*The Provenance*. *Laethora* play heavy death metal, ranging from almost melancholic parts to full on blast beats, more aggressive than his ordinary band.
Website: www.laethora.com/

2007 □	MARCH OF THE PARASITE	CD	Unruly Sounds	US003-2
2007 ■	MARCH OF THE PARASITE	CD	Osmose	OPCD 193
2010 □	THE LIGHT IN WHICH WE ALL BURN	CD	Unruly Sounds	USTE007-2

2007 CD - OPCD 193

LAFAYETTE

Stefan Lönnhagen: v, Peter Lindh: g, Patrik Selén: k,
Danne Pettersson: b, Perra Johansson: d

Uppsala - *Lafayette* play high-quality AOR in the same vein as *Treat*. Two well-played and well-arranged songs with above-average vocals. Produced by *Kaipa*/*The Flower Kings* guitarist Roine Stolt. Perra later joined *Crawley*, while Peter, Danne and Patrik formed *Three Mile Smile* together with singer Anders Jansson (later in *It's Alive*) and recorded a track for the *15 On 1* compilation. This band later changed their name to *Mother Groove* and has an outstanding track on the compilation *15 On 1 Twice*.

1990 ■ The Mirror/Chasin' The Wind ....7"   Studio 55... ST 55-512

1990 7" - ST 55-512

LAKE OF TEARS

Daniel Brennare: v/g, Magnus Sahlgren: g, Mikael Larsson: b, Johan Oudhuis: d

Borås - Formed in May 1992 by members Daniel Brennare, Jonas Eriksson and Mikael Larsson from *Carnal Eruption* and *Forsaken Grief*. Oudhuis was soon drafted. After recording the first three track demo, *Demo 1 '93,* they were soon picked up by Black Mark. *Lake Of Tears* produces music in the vein of *Black Sabbath*, but with growl. The debut album was produced by Tomas Skogsberg and Mathis Lodmalm (*Cemetary*), while the follow-up was recorded at Wave Station by Ulf Petersson (*Galleon*). The result was a change of sound and style like a mix of *Sabbath* and *Paradise Lost* with a touch of goth. Daniel had also changed his vocals more towards James Hetfield's rough but somewhat melodic way of singing. Guitarist Jonas Eriksson was part of the line-up on the first two albums. He was replaced by Ulrik Lindblom. Christian was added to the line-up on *Forever Autumn*. The track *Devil's Diner* was found on a compilation-CD that came with German *Rock Hard* magazine in March 97. The band split up in 1999, but recorded *The Neonai* as a contractual obligations album, which actually brought the band together again in 2003. The comeback album, *Black Brick Road* saw the band as a trio, featuring Brennare, Larsson and Oudhuis. In 2004 Magnus Sahlgren joined on guitar. Christian Saarinen was part of the band briefly during the recording. On *Illwill* they took the tempo up a few notches on some tracks and added more of a metal touch.
Website: www.lakeoftears.net/

1994 CD - BMCD 49

1995 CD - BMCD 72

1997 MCD - BMCDS 97

1994 ■	GREATER ART	CD	Black Mark	BMCD 49
1994 □	GREATER ART	CD	Victor (Japan)	VICP-5465
1995 ■	HEADSTONES	CD	Black Mark	BMCD 72
1995 □	HEADSTONES	CD	Victor (Japan)	VICP-5654
1997 ■	Lady Rosenred	MCD 3tr	Black Mark	BMCDS 97

    Tracks: Lady Rosenre/ Devil's Diner/A Crimson Cosmos

1997	☐	Lady Rosenred	MCD 3tr	Black Mark	BMCD 106
1997	☐	A CRIMSON COSMOS	CD	Black Mark	BMCD 97
1999	☐	FOREVER AUTUMN	CD	Black Mark	BMCD 132
1999	☐	FOREVER AUTUMN	CD	One Music (South Korea)	ERCD 314
2000	☐	FOREVER AUTUMN	CD	Nippon Crown (Japan)	CRCL-4749
2001	☐	FOREVER AUTUMN	CD	NEMS (Argentina)	NEMS 151
2001	☐	FOREVER AUTUMN	CD	Irond (Russia)	CD 01-23
2001	☐	HEADSTONES	CD	Irond (Russia)	CD 01-34
2002	☐	A CRIMSON COSMOS	CD	Irond (Russia)	CD 02-225
2002	☐	GREATER ART	CD	Irond (Russia)	CD 02-228
2002	☐	THE NEONAI	CD	Black Mark	BMCD 153
2002	☐	THE NEONAI	CD	Irond (Russia)	CD 02-351
2002	■	Sorcerers (single mix)/Nathalie And The Fireflies	CDS 2tr	Black Mark	BMCDS 164
2003	☐	FOREVER AUTUMN	CD	Moon Records (Ukraine)	MNCD 314
2004	☐	GREATEST TEARS VOL 1	CD	Black Mark	BMCD 174
2004	☐	GREATEST TEARS VOL 2	CD	Black Mark	BMCD 175
2004	☐	BLACK BRICK ROAD	CD	Sanctuary/Noise	N 0388-2
2004	☐	BLACK BRICK ROAD	CD	Soyus (Russia)	N 0388-2
2007	☐	MOONS AND MUSHROOMS	CD	Dockyard 1	DY 100302
2007	☐	MOONS AND MUSHROOMS	CDd	Dockyard 1	DY 100309
2007	☐	MOONS AND MUSHROOMS	CD	Locomotive Records (USA)	LM 485
2007	☐	MOONS AND MUSHROOMS	CD	Scarecrow (Mexico)	SC 07320
2011	☐	ILLWILL	LP	AFM	AFMLP296-1
2011	■	ILLWILL	CD	AFM	AFMCD296-2
2011	☐	ILLWILL	CD	Soyus (Russia)	AFMCD296-2
2011	☐	ILLWILL	CDd	AFM	AFMCD296-9
		Bonus: As Daylight Yields (live)/Demon You-Lily Anne (live)/Crazyman (live)			
2011	☐	ILLWILL	CDd	AFM (Japan)	XQAN-1081
		Bonus: As Daylight Yields (live)/Demon You-Lily Anne (live)/Crazyman (live)			

2002 CDS - BMCDS 164

2011 CD - AFMCD296-2

LANCER

Isak Stenvall: v, Peter Ellström: g, Fredrik Kelemen: g,
Emil Öberg: b, Sebastian Pedernera: d

Arvika - The band was formed at the Music Academy in Arvika in 2009 and recorded their first demo *Reaching Higher* in 2010. The EP *Purple Sky* (2012), lead to a deal with Dolittle Group. *Lancer* plays classic *Iron Maiden* style heavy metal with a strong touch of melodic power metal.

2012	☐	Purple Sky/Dreamchaser/Mr. Starlight	MCDp 3tr	private	(4608)
2013	■	LANCER	CD	Dolittle Group	DOOCD 004

2013 CD - DOOCD 004

LANDBERG, JAYCE

Göran Edman: v/k, Erik Jayce Landberg: g/k, Christian Pettersson: b, Jens Bock: d

Stockholm - Guitarist Erik Jayce Landberg was born in Stockholm, studied music at a conservatory in Switzerland and went back to Sweden as a great guitarist, influenced by the likes of Malmsteen, Steve Vai and Joe Satriani. In 2007 he released his first EP, featuring one AOR track, one power ballad and one acoustic instrumental track. Armed with the vocal force of Göran Edman he secured a deal with UK label Escape. The musicians on the first release were, besides Jayce, Göran Edman (*Madison, Malmsteen, Vindictive, Kharma, Mårran* etc), bass player Carl Manstrand, keyboard player Charlie Arvstrand and drummer Michael Storm. The line-up on the second album was, besides Jayce and Göran, bass player Christian Pettersson and drummer Jens Bock. *Good Sleepless Night* featured guest appearances from singer Marc Boals (*Malmsteen, Codex*) and bass player John Leven (*Europe*). Both albums contain high-class heavy, yet melodic metal, at time reminiscent of *Dio* mixed with *Dokken*.

2008 CD - ESM 178

2007	☐	Lost Without You/Marilyn/Lullubuy	MCD 3tr	Victoria Records	- -
2008	☐	BREAK THE SPELL	CD	Avalon Marquee (Japan)	MICP-10724
2008	■	BREAK THE SPELL	CD	Escape	ESM 178
		Bonus: Dance Of The Borderline (demo)/Lost Without You/Caprice No 25. Re-mastered.			
2010	■	GOOD SLEEPLESS NIGHT	CD	Escape	ESM 203

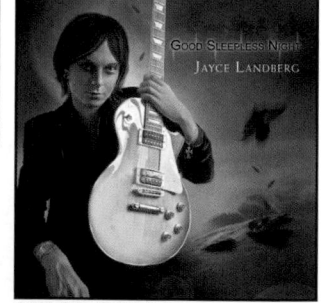

2010 CD - ESM 203

LANEY, CHRIS

Ulf "Chris Laney" Larsson: v/g/k/b

Stockholm - Chris made his first recording with the band *Unameus* in 1987, a second one with *Scratch* in 1988 and made three releases with *Seventeen (17)* between 1990-1992 in Helsingborg. He relocated to Stockholm, played with *Kiss* tribute band *Kyss* and got into producing and engineering, where he has put his stamp on releases by bands like *Gaeleri, Randy Piper's Animal, Easy Action, Crucified Barbara, Candlemass, Crazy Lixx* etc. He also wrote lots of songs for Swedish dance bands. Chris then joined forces with Zinny Zan in the band *Zan Clan*, where he has played on the later releases. He has also played guitar on albums by Leif Edling, *Randy Piper's Animal* etc. In 2009 he made his solo debut, rocking out in a true melodic sleaze-

2007 CD - MH 00065

oriented rock manner, sounding a bit like mix of **Def Leppard** and **Skid Row**. His debut album featured Johan "Koleberg" Kullberg (*Talk Of The Town, Lion's Share, Kyss* etc.) on drums and Nalle Påhlsson (*Treat, Therion*, etc.) on bass with a multitude of other musicians contributing. Among the names there's Vic Zino, Zinny Zan, Rob Lowe, Mats Leven, Lennart Östlund and Anders Ringman. On the follow-up the drums were handled by Ian Haugland (*Europe, Trilogy*) and George "Egg" Härnsten, bass by Påhlsson and Fredrik Bergenstråhle. Conny Bloom and Brian "Robbo" Robertson (ex-*Thin Lizzy*) also added their flare. In 2011 he formed the **Chris Laney's Legion**, featuring guitarist Robert "Marcello" Wendelstam (*Danger Danger, Ironhorse*), bassist Mats Vassfjord (*Pink Panther, Grand Design, Scaar*) and drummer Patrik Jansson.

2007 ■	PURE	CD	Metal Heaven	MH 00065
2010 ☐	ONLY COME OUT AT NIGHT	CD	Metal Heaven	MH 00083
2010 ☐	ONLY COME OUT AT NIGHT	CD	Bickee Music (Japan)	HMCX-1096
	Bonus: Fire & Ice/Make You Cry			

LARSSON, THOMAS

Thomas Larsson: g/v,

Borlänge - Thomas is ex-*Jammer, Six Feet Under, Baltimoore, Yeah Bop Station*, Glenn Hughes and is also found in locals *Bocca Bandet*, who was featured on a *Grand Funk*-tribute. In 2000 *Baltimoore* reformed and Thomas has been in and out of the line-up since. Clas Yngström from *Sky High* makes a guest appearance on *Freeride*. Thomas is also the man behind the infamous Gaywhore guitar amp. The 2000-release of *Freeride* was remastered and given new artwork. The first album also featured singers Göran Edman and Erik Hjalmarsson (*Jammer*), bass player Weine Johansson and drummer Eiron Johansson. In 2002 Thomas started working on a new album showing a direction leaning more towards a more atmospheric, yet melodic side. It took until 2006 when *Harmonic Passion* was released. This album was all instrumental, and showed a more ambient and soft side of Thomas, but of course it's filled to the brim of his fantastic guitar playing. Harmonic Passion featured old fellows Weine and Eiron, but also bassist (and his brother) Jocke Larsson (*Treat*), keyboardists LO Johansson, Clas Hägglund and Pierre Swärd.

1996 CD - XRCN 1265

2000 CD - ADR 100

1996 ■	FREERIDE	CD	Zero (Japan)	XRCN 1265
2000 ■	FREERIDE	CD	Border Music	ADR 100
	New artwork.			
2006 ☐	HARMONIC PASSION	CD	Grooveyard Records	GYR 023

LAST AUTUMN'S DREAM

Mikael Erlandsson: v, Andy Malaecek: g, Nalle Påhlsson: b, Jamie Borger: d

Göteborg/Stockholm/Germany - **Last Autumns Dream** were formed in 2002 by singer Mikael Erlandsson (*Crash, Salute*) and German guitarist Andy Malaecek (*Fair Warning*). On the first album they used the talents of 3/5 of *Europe*; Ian Haugland, John Leven and Mic Michaeli as backing musicians. When *Europe* reunited they however had to go. For the second album they found a new, steady line-up featuring bassist Marcel Jacob (*Talisman, Malmsteen*), drummer Jamie Borger (*Talisman, Treat*) and keyboardist Thomas Lassar (*Crystal Blue, Dreamhunter*). Thomas however left after the second album and the band continued as a quartet. July 21, 2009 Marcel Jacob sadly took his own life and *Dreamcatcher* was his last album. The band brought in *Treat/Therion* bassist Nalle Påhlsson as replacement. **Last Autumns Dream** play classic high-class Swedish AOR in the vein of *Talisman* meets *Treat*.

2005 CD - ESM 129

2003 CD - FRCD 173

2009 CD - ESM 183

2003 ■	LAST AUTUMNS DREAM	CD	Frontiers Records	FRCD 173
2003 ☐	LAST AUTUMNS DREAM	CD	Avalon Marquee (Japan)	MICP-10402
	Bonus: Pictures Of Love			
2005 ☐	II	CD	Frontiers Records	FRCD 226
2005 ☐	II	CD	Avalon Marquee (Japan)	MICP 10476
	Bonus: Fire With Fire			
2005 ■	WINTER IN PARADISE	CD	Escape Music	ESM 129
2005 ☐	WINTER IN PARADISE	CD	Avalon Marquee (Japan)	MICP 10560
	Bonus: 'Til The End Of Time			
2006 ☐	SATURN SKYLINE	CD	Escape Music	ESM 145
2006 ☐	SATURN SKYLINE	CD	Avalon Marquee (Japan)	MICP 10625
	Bonus: Skyscraper			
2008 ☐	BEST OF & MADE IN GERMANY	2CD	Escape Music	ESM 165
2008 ☐	LIVE IN GERMANY	CD	Avalon Marquee (Japan)	MICP-10716
	Bonus: When You Love Somebody/You Won't See Me Cry			
2008 ☐	IMPRESSIONS: THE VERY BEST OF LAD	CD	Avalon Marquee (Japan)	MICP-10663
2008 ☐	HUNTING SHADOWS	CD	Escape Music	ESM 166
2008 ☐	HUNTING SHADOWS	CD	Avalon Marquee (Japan)	MICP-10704
	Bonus: Match Made In Heaven			
2009 ☐	DREAMCATCHER	CD	Escape Music	ESM 183
2009 ☐	DREAMCATCHER	CD	Avalon Marquee (Japan)	MICP 10800
	Bonus: Hello, Hello, Hello			
2010 ■	A TOUCH OF HEAVEN	CD	Escape Music	ESM 201

2010 CD - ESM 201

2010 ☐	A TOUCH OF HEAVEN	CD	Avalon Marquee (Japan)	MICP 10885
	Bonus: Running On Like Water			
2010 ■	YES	CD	GMR	GMRCD9026
2010 ☐	YES	CD	Avalon Marquee (Japan)	MICP-10965
	Bonus: I Forgive You			
2011 ☐	NINE LIVES	CD	Avalon Marquee (Japan)	MICP-11030
	Bonus: Waited A Long Time			
2011 ☐	NINE LIVES	CD	GMR	GMRCD9031
2013 ☐	TEN TANGERINE TALES	CD	Bad Reputation	BAD130101
2013 ☐	TEN TANGERINE TALES	CD	Avalon Marquee (Japan)	MICP-11070
	Bonus: Rebel Rouser (Sweet cover)			

2010 CD - GMRCD9026

LAST LAUGH

Daniel "Östnytt" Karlsson: v, Pontus Wallin: g,
Marcus "Stene" Pehrsson: b, Dennis "Damp" Strömberg: d

Sparreholm/Nyköping - This band is completely impossible to musically categorise. Weird, weirder… *Last Laugh*. They could be described as the missing progressive link between **Primus** and **King's X** with a touch of general madness. Well, it's highly interesting and musically very competent. A nice little treat. In 2001 they recorded a 3-track demo-CDR entitled *Count To One*, and in 2003 another three-track demo entitled *Shapes*, was unearthed. The band was now a trio featuring Wallin, Pehrsson and Strömberg. Marcus is also found in progsters **Darxtar**.

1996 ☐	Our Spot On The Planet Earth	MCD 4tr	private	Laugh 01
	Tracks: Peace/Busy/Exhausted/My Spot			
1998 ■	MEET US WHERE WE ARE TODAY	CD	Record Heaven	RHCD08

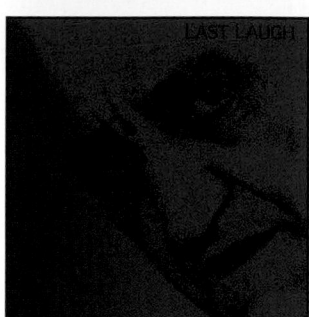

1998 CD - RHCD08

LAST LAUGH

Peder Karlsson: v/g, Peter Fjällström: g, Anton Östergren: b, Fredrik Edholm: d

Tärnaby - These youngsters probably didn't know about the above **Last Laugh**. They however did know about **Freak Kitchen**. A rip-off of the highest order. The guitarist has tried to pat down more or less all the tricks of Mattias Ia Eklund, without success, I should add. They even used the same title as one of **Freak Kitchen**'s – *Raw*. Badly-produced and not very well-conceived.

2005 ■	RAW	CD	private	- -

2005 CD - - -

LAST TEMPTATION

Lars "Lerta" Palmqvist: v, Roger Svensson: g,
Kennet Jansson: g, Classe Johnson: b, Michael "Micki" Pihl: d

Norrköping - The embryo of **Last Temptation** was spawned already in 1999 by **Seven** bassist Kennet Jansson. In 2002 he joined forces with Roger Svensson, Classe Johnson and drummer Magnus Lind. They recorded their debut album the same year. Right after the recording Lind left the band and was soon replaced by Michael "Micki" Pihl. Since no label showed interest they released it on Kennet's own label Regal. Kennet handled the vocals on the debut, but since the general response was that a new, better, singer would raise the band's level They drafted Lerta (**Backwardness, Borelia**) in 2005. In 2006 the new line-up recorded a new four track pro-printed CD-R demo entitled *In Memoriam*. In 2008 another six track demo, entitled *Back'In Vocals* was recorded. Palmqvist has also been in **Scar Symmetry**. The tracks *Alone* and *In Memoriam* are found on *Platinum Compilation Vol 1* (05 Pregal).

2002 ■	LAST TEMPTATION	CD	Pregal Records	RMR 1145080303

2002 CD - RMR 1145080303

LAST TRIBE

Rickard Bengtsson: v, Magnus Karlsson: g, Dick Löwgren: b, Jaime Salazar: d

Malmö/Halmstad - Guitarist Magnus Karlsson was asked to record guitar solos "like Yngwie" for the band **Midnight Sun**. He then got drafted and was asked to write the band's next album as founder Jonas Reingold didn't have the time or energy. Magnus did, but in the end Reingold did write the album himself (*Mean Machine*) and Magnus had an entire album worth of material. He decided to record it himself and it soon evolved into a great band. Magnus is an astounding guitarist, technical but with great feeling and a solid neoclassical touch, which he has later proved in bands like **Allen Lande**, **Starbreaker**, **Planet Alliance** and **Primal Fear**. The first album was a good slab of solid melodic metal. The line-up initially featured bass player Pär Wallmark and drummer Kristoffer Andersson. On the second album the music had turned more progressive and it is truly a brilliant piece of melodic prog-oriented metal, like **Majestic** meets **Evergrey** at times with almost AOR:ish choruses. Rickard and Dick have previously been working together in the band **Armageddon**. Dick has also toured with **Arch Enemy** and **In Flames**. Jaime is also found in bands like **The Flower Kings**, **Bad Habit**, **Bai Bang**, **Midnight Sun**, **Kaipa** etc. The band has split up. In 2013 Magnus released his first solo album **Magnus Karlsson's Freefall**, which also features Rickard on vocals.

The first of the last

2001	☐	THE RITUAL	CD	Frontiers Records	FR CD 085
2001	☐	THE RITUAL	CD	Avalon Maruqee (Japan)	MICP 10249
		Bonus: Take It Away (And Don't Bring It Back)			
2002	☐	WITCH DANCE	CD	Avalon Marquee (Japan)	MICP 10292
		Bonus: Tell Me More			
2002	☐	WITCH DANCE	CD	Frontiers Records	FR CD 116
2003	■	THE UNCROWNED	CD	Frontiers Records	FR CD 72
2004	☐	THE UNCROWNED	CD	CD-Maximus (Russia)	CDM 0104-1663

2003 FR CD 72

LAST VIEW

Jakob Reinhard: v, Sebastian Kellgren: v, Erik Sundquist: g,
Tobias Ericson: g, Viktor Alasalmi: b, Robin Duvfors: d

Stockholm - **Last View** was formed in 2008 in Stockholm. They recorded their first EP, *Seven,* the same year and it was also accompanied by a video. They recorded another digital EP, entitled *Become The Storm*, in 2009, which lead to a tour with **Yersinia** and **Sanctum**. In 2010 they started recording their debut album together with producer William Blackmon (**Gadget**) and struck a deal with ViciSolum Records. **Last View** play quite intense, riff-oriented and well-produced metalcore, at times with a touch of old **The Haunted**. The band has two singers, but unlike most other bands, both singers are aggro vocalists.
Website: www.lastview.se

2011	■	HELL IN REVERSE	CD	ViciSolum	VSP 022CD
2011	☐	HELL IN REVERSE	LP	ViciSolum	VSP 022LP
		Bonus: Liaisons/Anastacia			

2011 CD - VSP 022CD

LATEX

Micke "Sin" Backelin: v/b, Mattias "Ardias" Danielsson: g, Martin Bullit: b,
Niclas "Pepa" Andersson (now Green): b, Robert "Bobbo" Hansson: d

Trollhättan - **Latex** was formed in 1997, as an **Impaled Nazarene** cover band by **Lord Belial/ Vassago** members Micke and Pepa. Their own material continued in the same raw punkish death metal manner. The band recorded a demo, which then became the *Hammerfuck* EP. The release had its problems because of the explicit cover art. Despite the EP having eight tracks, it's only 13 minutes long. In 2010 the original line-up of **Lord Belial** reunited, but in 2011 they had split again. Micke has also previously played with **Hellgoat**, **Altus Ultionis**, **Them** and is now drummer in the band **Hex** and **Lord Belial**. A reunion was planned, also featuring Micke's brother Thomas Backelin, but nothing came out of it..

1998	■	Hammerfuck	10" MLP	Metal Fortress	MFE 001 $
		Tracks: Hammerfuck/Suicide/Hail To The Hard Drugs/Rape/Sodomaniac/Leather Weapon/Sado/Kill All The Women. 300 copies.			

1998 10" MLP - MFE 001

LAUDAMUS

Peter Stenlund: v/g/k, Jonas Stenlund: b, Jonas Cederteg: d

Piteå - The Christian melodic hard rock band **Laudamus** was formed around 1988. The single line-up featured Peter, Anneli Storå (k), Pelle Johansson (b) and Anders Sandlund (d). Guitarist Stefan Berg joined after the first single and Fredrik Burström replaced Pelle. In December 1993 the band made a demo with *Realize* and *Until The End,* and the same year Peter and Anneli got married. After this they quit and Peter formed his own and heavier-sounding project, called **Reach Out**, later **Meduza**. The band has picked up a thing or two from the more melodic side of Yngwie Malmsteen, with great guitar playing and good vocal capacities as a bonus. **Laudamus** later reformed with the above line-up and on *Unlimited Love*, which was recorded in 1999 and released in the dawn of the new millennium, the sound is far heavier. Before the band returned with the album *Lost In Vain*, produced by Ken Tamplin, they released a two-track CD-R entitled *Promotion CD 2001* containing the songs *I Am* and *Salvation*. The album featured guests Mattias Is Eklundh, Jeff Scott Soto, Rob Rock and Marty Friedman. The self-titled 2006 release is a compilation of rerecorded songs from the first album and single, plus the *Ready Or Not* MCD as bonus. The band is still active as a live band and the latest known line-up featured, besides Peter and Jonas Stenlund, keyboardist Elinor Stenlund and drummer Anders Wigestam.
Website: www.laudamus.se

1992 7" - HIT 006

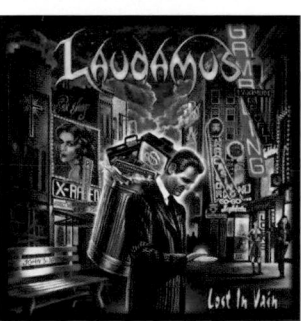

2003 CD - ESM 088

2006 CD - RRCD 027

1992	■	Be There Forever/Overlord	7"	Hit It Productions	HIT 006
1993	☐	Ready Or Not	MCD 4tr	private	LDS 001
		Tracks: Ready Or Not/He Will Be There/Healed By God/In Christ (We Are Strong)			
2000	☐	UNLIMITED LOVE	CD	private	CLCD20001
2003	■	LOST IN VAIN	CD	Escape Music	ESM 088
2006	■	LAUDAMUS	CD	Rivel Records	RRCD 027
		Bonus: Ready Or Not/He Will Be There/Healed By God/In Christ			

L

LAVA ENGINE

Magnus Florin: v/g, Ronnie Jaldemark: g, Simon Dahlström: b, Mick Nordström: d

Göteborg/Jönköping - *Lava Engine* were formed under a different name back in 2006, then featuring Florin, drummer Christian Karlsson, bassist Tomas Carlström and keyboardist Daniel Bentzer. The music was very different, more in the vein of *The Beatles*, *Jellyfish* or *Crowded House*. In 2007 they took the new name *Lava Engine* and adopted a heavier sound. They also recorded a new demo. Bentzer left the band and Jaldemark replaced him. In 2008 Carlström fled the ship and was temporarily replaced by Ian Varjanne, who also played on the band's four-track self-titled demo CD-R. Now the band was approached by drummer Mick Nordström (*Modest Attraction, XT, Flagship, Spearfish* etc.), and as a stroke of luck Karlsson decided to leave the band. Vanja Hadzic (*Matreya, Ten Feet High*) handled the bass duties, before Dahlström (*Beyond Known*) joined as permanent bass player. In 2010 they recorded the self-financed MCD *In Limbo*. *Lava Engine* play highly interesting powerful proggish melodic metal, at times similar to *Pain Of Salvation* with a touch of *Porcupine Tree*. Great vocals, great musicians and powerful production.

2011 MCD - LENCD 001

2011 ■ In Limbo ....MCD 5tr private ....LENCD 001
    Tracks: Drain Your Soul/In Limbo/Common Ground/Ctrl Z/Windows Closed

LAW, THE

Tobias "Toby Jay" Jansson: v, Björn Larsson: g,
Peter Östlund: g, Kristian Karlsson: b, Johan Rudberg: d

Karlstad/Göteborg/Falun - *The Law* is a great hard-hitting thrash unit with a fat sound, similar to *F.K.Ü* and *Anthrax* at their best. Jansson is also found in *Angel Blake* and was briefly in *Treasure Land*, Östlund is also in *Vomitory*, Karlsson in *Neodawn* and *Inferior*, Rudberg in *Horned, Karensdag* and death-punksters *Mordbrand*. The band, not to be confused with Paul Rodgers' band of course, recorded their first demo in 2004, followed by the *Dudes Of Darkness* demo in 2006.

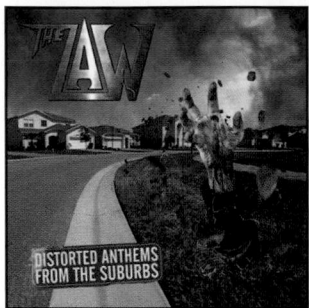
2008 CD - MCRCD 002

2008 ■ DISTORTED ANTHEMS FROM THE SUBURB ....CD Metalcentral ....MCRCD 002

LAYOUT

Marika Andersson: v, Björn Göransson: g, Nilo Kovacic: b, Daniel Wickström: d

Jönköping - *Layout* were formed by 14 year old class mates Marika, Nilo, Daniel and guitarist Johan Häll in 1984. They started out playing hard rock, both their own material and also covers by bands like *Status Quo*. When Björn replaced Johan they became a bit heavier. The single is classic NWoBHM-style with driving guitars and great female vocals. Well worth trying to find! Around 1987-89 Marika also sang backing vocals in the band *Venture*, which was fronted by Christian Liljegren (later in *Narnia, Golden Resurrection* etc). The band recorded some demos only. Around 1988-89 *Layout* folded. Marika left, as she had no time. They found a replacement (who was later married to Nilo), but it didn't lift off again. Marika quit music, but later returned singing salsa in *Östvalls Trio*. Björn works for the tax authorities in Göteborg and Daniel quit music. Kovacic continued and is today in metal band *Hellspray*, which also features Mattias Rydell, who was also in *Venture*. The band made a one-off reunion gig about ten years after the split.

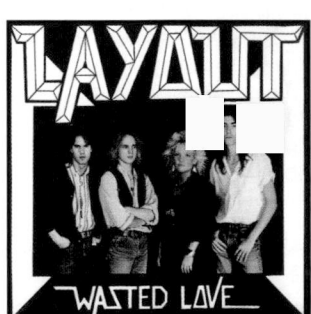
1987 7" - MTR 002

1987 ■ Wasted Love/Fight Back ....7" MTR ....MTR 002
    500 copies.

LAZY

Roger Johansen: v, Jari Forsman: g, Leo Hed: b, Thorbjörn Löfgren: d

Eskilstuna - A good, hard-rocking album with some bluesy overtones. They also recorded a 4-track video with tracks from the LP. *Lazy* also recorded a great demo after the album was released. The band went through some changes in the line-up and featured Joakim Björkegren and Per Ahlström (both ex-*Shed*). Björkegren later ended up in *It's Alive*. The tracks *Darkness* and *Mountains* are found on the compilation *Rock On, Roll On* (1983 Pang).

1984 LP - MILL 5023

1984 ■ CREATURE...LP Mill ....MILL 5023

LEASH

Martin Scherman: v, Thomas Lindberg: g, Dan Lindberg: b, Anders Östman: d

Göteborg - The band was formed in 1990 by Anders and Thomas. *Leash* was among the early bands to let people download their music from their website, starting already back in 1996. After years of demos and live shows the band signed a production deal with Roastinghouse and Danish Kick Music. A second album was supposed to be recorded late 2002, but never happened. Hard rock with a strong touch of *King's X* meets *Pearl Jam*. The band reformed as *Frankly*.

1999 CD - KICK 101 CD

1999 ■ GENERATION X-LARGE...CD Kick ....KICK 101 CD

LECHERY

Martin Bengtsson: v/g, Fredrik Nordstrandh: g/k,
Martin Karlsson: b, Kristian Svensson: d

Halmstad - *Lechery* came together in 2004, but the idea had been spawned several years earlier by Bengtsson, when he left *Arch Enemy* to create his own music. Karlsson and Persson are both ex-*Dragonthrone*, while Bengtsson has also been found in *Armageddon*. *Lechery* recorded their first demo in 2005, followed by a self-released promo in 2006. This lead to a deal with AOR Heaven. The band play high-octane classic heavy metal in the vein of *Judas Priest*, *Saxon*, *Primal Fear* or Swedish colleagues *Bloodbound*. On *In Fire* drummer Robert Person had been replaced by Svensson.
Website: www.lechery.se

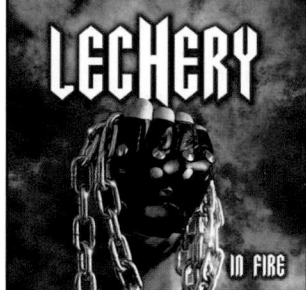

2011 CD - MH 00092

2008 ☐	VIOLATOR	CD	Metal Heaven	MH 00045
2008 ☐	VIOLATOR	CD	Spiritual Beast (Japan)	POCE-16017
	Bonus: On And On			
2011 ■	IN FIRE	CD	Metal Heaven	MH 00092
2011 ☐	IN FIRE	CD	Avalon Marquee (Japan)	MICP-11031
	Bonus: Fail And Fall			

LEFAY

Charles Rytkönen: v, Tony Eriksson: g, Peter Grehn: g,
Micke Åsentorp: b, Robin Engström: d

Bollnäs - Formed in 1998, when *Morgana Lefay* took a halt and Charles and Tony continued under the name *Lefay*. The music is not too far from *Morgana Lefay*'s territory. *Symphony Of The Damned* is a rerecording of *Morgana Lefay*'s debut-album from 1990, as bonus it features covers of *Crazy* (*Nazareth*), *Captain Howdy* (*Twisted Sister*), *Strange Ways* (*Kiss*) and *Cocaine* (*JJ Cale*). Rytkönen guests on the 2002-release of *Tad Morose* and later joined *Inmoria*. Peter, Micke and Robin also had their side project *Fantasmagoria*, with whom they recorded one album. After *S.O.S* the band left Noise and returned in 2004 with the old *Morgana Lefay* name.

1999 CD - N 0312-2

1999 ○	The Boon He Gives	CDS 1tr	Noise	N 0312-3
	Promo. No artwork.			
1999 ■	THE SEVENTH SEAL	CD	Noise	N 0312-2
1999 ■	SYMPHONY OF THE DAMNED	CD	Noise	N 0317-2
2000 ☐	S.O.S	CD	Noise	N 3312-2

1999 CD - N 0317-2

LEFT HAND SOLUTION

Mariana Holmberg: v, Janne Wiklund: g, Peter Selin: b, Erik Barthold: d

Sundsvall - The band was formed in 1991 by guitarist Jocke Mårdstam, singer/bassist Jörgen Fahlberg and drummer Liljan Liljekvist, and recorded their first demo, *Dwell*, in 1992. It sold over 1000 copies. In 1992 the line-up changed, when Peter Selin took over the bass, since Jörgen wanted to concentrate on vocals, but left the band altogether after a few months. They now went for a female singer and drafted Kicki Höijertz. A while later Erik Bartold replaced Liljan. They entered the studio and recorded two tracks for the compilation *Metal North* (93 Massproduktion). In 1994 they recorded the third demo *Falling* and were soon signed by Massproduktion, who released their debut MCD in 1994. Slow, searing doom in the style of *Count Raven* with clean laid-back female vocals. After the debut, singer Kicki Höijertz (later in *Sibenbürgen*) was replaced by Mariana. In 1995 they recorded a promising 3-track demo entitled *The Wounds Of Bitterness*. In 1997 guitarist Jocke Mårdstam left the band and was replaced by Wiklund, who had previously played with *Unholy* and punkish band *The Kristet Utseende*. They now also changed from the doom-goth concept to a slightly more rocking attitude, which showed when the band covered *Eurythmics*' *Missionary Man*. In 2004 the band started recording demos for a new album, but the success of *The Kristet Utseende*, featuring Erik and Janne, put the band on hold in 2005. In 2009 the band reunited for a one-off show featuring Höijertz, Mårdstam, Barthold and Selin. *Left Hand Solution* also appears on the compilation *Call Of The Dark* (98 Nuclear Blast) with the non-album track *Worn Away*, a cover of *Mine*'s *Nowhere To Go* on *We're Only In It For The Money* (01 Massproduktion) and they did two *Misfits* covers, *She* and *Hybrid Moments*, on the tribute *Hell On Earth... Hail To Misfits* (96 Tribute Records).

If the right don't get you, the left one will...

1994 MCD - MASS-CDS 63

1994 ■	Shadowdance	MCD 6tr	Massproduktion	MASS-CDS 63
	Tracks: Shroud/Infernal/Solitary Fallen Angel/Nightbloom/Final Withering/Shadowdance			
1996 ☐	FEVERED	CD	Massproduktion	MASS CD 74
1997 ☐	FEVERED	CD	Nuclear Blast	NB 239-2
1999 ☐	Missionary Man (Eurythmics cover)	MCD 3tr	Massproduktion	MASS CDS 81
	Tracks: Missionary Man/The Enemy Within (non-album)/Missionary man - The Video			
2001 ☐	LIGHT SHINES BLACK	CD	Massproduktion	MASS CD 84
	Bonus: video of Missionary Man (Eurythmics cover)			
2003 ☐	SHADOWDANCE	CD	Massproduktion	MASS CD 63
	Bonus: Menlösa brudjävel/Dwell/Master Of Disaster/Sinister/To Walk The Night (Danzig cover)			

LEGBONE

Otto Almqvist: v/g, Henrik Wetterholm: b, Tomas Sjölander: d

Borås - Otto and Tomas joined forces already in 1979, as punksters *High Level*. The trio then became *Legbone* in 1986. Good, bluesy, sleazy hard rock. The track *Brainghost*, which is a bit more garagy/punkish, is found on the compilation *Det hjälper inte att ropa på mamma... och inte pappa heller* (97 Brosk). Otto is now in *Drool* and Tomas played with *Vrävarna*.

1994 ■ Legbone ....MCD 5tr   Local Hero ....LHM 319
    Tracks: Too Bad/Mr Jack/Life Express/Dance On The Clouds/Hangover

1994 MCD - LHM 319

LEGIA

Anton Strömberg: v/b, Krisse Lenmark: g, Per Nilsson: g, Henrik Ohlsson: d

Sandviken - A high-quality private release, produced by Tomas Skogsberg and Fred Estby (*Dismember*). The band's musical spectrum ranges from pure thrash to almost death-style metal. However the vocals are more "ordinary". The band also recorded the demo *Depose The Tyrants* in 1992. Ohlsson is also found in bands like *Theory In Practice*, *Black Dog*, *Altered Aeon*, *Diabolical*, *Scar Symmetry* and *Mutant*, while Nilsson has been in *World Below*, *Kaipa*, *Altered Aeon*, *Scar Symmetry*, *Thrawn* and *Adversary*.

1993 ■ LEGIA...CD   private ....HYR LEG 001

1993 CD - HYR LEG 001

LEGION, THE

Lars "Lazr" Martinsson: v, David Svartz: g, Rikard "Tiwaz" Kottelin: g/k, Kristoffer Andersson: b, Emil Dragutinovic: d

Jönköping - The band was formed in 1996 under the name *Tyrant*. In 1997 they recorded the song *Northern Wisdom* for a compilation and in 1998 they released the first demo *Rise Of The Fallen*. The changed their name to *The Legion*, and in 1999, to at least differ slightly from the others, they added *The* in front of *Legion*. In 2000 they recorded demo *Bloodaeons* (Downfall). Sune Hammerström joined on vocals in 2001, but on *Unseen To Creation* he had been replaced by Anders Fäldt. He is however featured on two of the tracks on the *Awakened Fury* MCD. Lars "Lazr" Martinsson handled the bass. On *Revocation* the line-up featured Kottelin, Svartz, Dragutinovic, Kjetil Hektoen on vocals and Kristoffer Andersson on bass. On *A Bliss To Suffer*, Martinsson took care of the vocals. Dragutinovic and Svartz are ex-*Nominon*. Emil is also in *Marduk* and *Devian*. *The Legion* play modern death metal with some technical riffing going on, a bit similar to *Dissection*.

2003 CD - POSH 052

2003 ■ UNSEEN TO CREATION ....CD   Listenable Records ....POSH 052
2003 □ UNSEEN TO CREATION ....LPg   Listenable Records ....POSH 052
    Bonus: Havoc/C.O.T.L.O.D. 500 copies.
2003 ■ Awakened Fury .... 7" 3tr   Neodawn productions ....NDP 016
    Tracks: Knee Deep In Blood/Retribution/Legion. 666 copies in orange vinyl. Different artwork.
2005 □ Awakened Fury ....MCD 5tr   Deepsend Records ....DSR 006
    Tracks: Knee Deep In Blood/Retribution/Torment Divine/Legion/On Swift Wings
2006 □ REVOCATION...CD   Listenable Records ....POSH 078
2006 □ REVOCATION...CD   CD-Maximum (Russia) ....CDM 2638
2009 □ A BLISS TO SUFFER ....CD   Listenable Records ....POSH 116

2003 7" - NDP 016

LEMON BIRD

Daniel Axelsson: v, Johan Runesson: g, Rikard Borginger: b, Anders Jonasson: d

Växjö - *Lemon Bird* is a strong player in the new wave of Swedish seventies hard rock. The band plays great energetic retro hard rock with strong hints of classic *Led Zeppelin*. Axelsson was ex-*Muddy Road*.

2008 □ RARA AVIS ....CDd   Yellow Note ....YNLBCD 01
2010 ■ HANGMAN AND THE JURY..................................CD   Yellow Note ....YNLBCD 02

2010 CD - YNLBCD 02

LETHAL

Mikael Markström: v/b, Bobbe Nordin: g, Jonathan "Jonte" Jonsson: g , Emil: d

Umeå - *Lethal*, not to be confused with the American band, recorded their first demo, *Demolition*, in 2004 and in 2005 they had four tracks on the compilation tape *The Cocoon Of Asphyx* (Nihilistic Records). On the first single second guitarist Erik Grahn (*Nasheim*) was in the band. Markström is also in *Nasheim* and Nordin in *The Ugly*.

2006 ■ Deliverance/Fire Reigns The Sky/Through Your Flesh .... 7" 3tr   Blood Harvest ....YOTZ #6
    500 copies.
2007 □ ANNIHILATION AGENDA ....CD   Iron Fist Productions.......................IFPCD 015
2007 □ ANNIHILATION AGENDA ....LP   Blood Harvest ....YOTZ #18

2006 7" - YOTZ #6

LEUKEMIA

Joakim "Jens-Ove/Jojje" Granlund: v, Tobias Ander: g, Kent-Åke "Kentha" Philipsson: b/g/programming

Malmköping - Formed in 1989 by Kentha and Joakim. They received a great underground following through their first demo *Innocence Is Bliss* (1991). In the beginning the band contained Benke (b) and Bernst-Gunnar (g). *Suck My Heaven* was produced by Tomas Skogsberg and the follow-up by Dan Swanö. On December 5th 1994 the band changed their name to *Lame* and recorded the album *Love*, which was never released, not until it was re-mastered by Dan Swanö and released under the **Leukemia** banner, in 2012. The style is quite hard to describe, besides being brutal and with unmelodic vocals. I guess it would fit into the grungy death/thrash/pop/hardcore/metal genre. Granlund still records but in a totally different genre. Philipsson is still highly active and is/has been in bands like **The Project Hate**, **Torture Division**, **Odyssey**, **House Of Usher** etc. Ander is also in **Jigsore Terror**, **Witchgrave** and **Slingblade**.

1993 CD - BMCD 29

1994 CD - SOR 008

1993	■	SUCK MY HEAVEN	CD	Black Mark	BMCD 29
1994	■	GREY-FLANNEL SOULED	CD	Step One	SOR 008
2012	☐	LOVE	CD	Vic Records	CSR 004 CD

LEVIATHAN

Roger "Phycon" Markström: v/g/b/d, "Sir" A. Pettersson: g

Skellefteå - **Leviathan** is another name quite widely-used, so they are not to be confused with the US band. **Leviathan** play raw old-school death metal, but with a more modern production. Musically they are quite similar to **Burzum**. Sir A is also found in **LIK**, **Volkermord**, **Lönndom** and **Armagedda**, while Markström is found in the two latter plus **Maleficium**.

2002 CD - CELLAR 009 CD

2002	■	FAR BEYOND THE LIGHT	CD	Selbstmord Services	CELLAR 009 CD
2002	☐	FAR BEYOND THE LIGHT	LP	Selbstmord Services	CELLAR 009
		Released in 500 copies, the first 100 with poster.			

LEVITICUS

Björn Stigsson: g, Peo Pettersson: v/k, Niklas Edberger: k, Niklas Franklin: b, Kjell Andersson: d

Skövde - The band started out as a trio with Björn, Kjell and Håkan Andersson on bass and vocals. The first EP was in a more synth-based mode and sung in Swedish, while the more metallic first album was released both in English and Swedish. On *Setting Fire To The Earth* former **Quinzy**/**Forest**-singer Terje "Terry H" Hjortander and bassist Sven "Ez" Gomér, replaced Håkan. In the summer of 1987 they left to form their own band, **The Jet Circus**. Sonny Larsson (**Motherlode**) took over the mike, but left after a year to join a bible study. Björn recorded a solo-album the same year. It was entitled *Together With Friends* and also featured Sonny. The two would later meet again. New singer was former **Axia**-man Peo Pettersson and Niklas Franklin (**Two Franklin Grove**) took care of the bass. In 1989 they released the last **Leviticus** album, entitled *Knights Of Heaven* and is the one I consider to be their top album with some great melodic hard rockers. Maybe it's because it was produced by Dino and John Elefante, the latter of **Kansas** fame. Peo released his first solo album late 1995. Björn formed the band **XT** together with Sonny Larsson. The 1994 *Best Of* contains no previously unreleased material. In 2003 the band, reinforced by keyboardist Niklas Edberger, reformed for a live show at Bobfest, and the subtitle of the CD recorded at this event is "after thirteen years of silence".

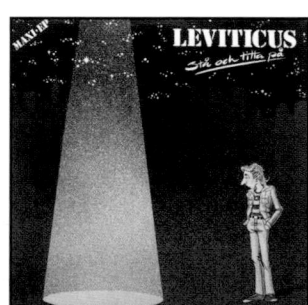
1982 MLP - SAMLP 52 00003

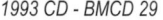

LET ME FIGHT - DAY BY DAY
1984 7" - SAM 5213

1984 LP - TALKLP 1016

1985 LP - TRLP 851

1982	■	Stå Och Titta På	MLP 4tr	Stanley&Andre	SAMLP 52 00003 $
		Tracks: Stå Och Titta På/Följ Mej/Leva Som Man Lär/Min Mästare			
1983	☐	JAG SKALL SEGRA	LP	Stanley&Andre	SAMLP 5209
1984	■	Let Me Fight/Day By Day	12"	Stanley&Andre	SAM 5213
1984	☐	Let Me Fight/Day By Day	12"	Talking Music	TALKS 1014
1984	■	I SHALL CONQUER	LP	Talking Music	TALKLP 1016
		Jag Skall Segra in English.			
1984	☐	I SHALL CONQUER	LP	Shadow	LS 5899
		The US-version with different artwork.			
1985	■	THE STRONGEST POWER	LP	Twilight	TRLP 851
1985	☐	THE STRONGEST POWER	LP	Pure Metal	SPCM 79006 00566
		The US-version with different artwork.			
1987	☐	SETTING FIRE TO THE EARTH	LP	Royal Music	RMLP 027
1987	☐	SETTING FIRE TO THE EARTH	CD	Pure Metal (USA)	SPCM 790060411
1987	☐	Love Is Love/Flames Of Fire	7"	Royal Music	RMS 023
1987	☐	Love Is Love/Flames Of Fire	12" 2tr	Solid Rock	43495-3
1989	☐	KNIGHTS OF HEAVEN	LP	Royal Music	RMLP 040
1989	☐	Isn't It Love/Born Again	7"	Royal Music	RMS 033
1994	☐	THE BEST OF LEVITICUS	CD	Viva	VIVAD 132
1995	☐	THE BEST OF LEVITICUS	CD	Zero (Japan)	XRCN-1206

2000 ☐ I SHALL CONQUER	CD	Magdalene	M8D-1035	

Bonus: Följ mig/Leva som han lär/Min mästare. 2500 copies.

2000 ☐ THE STRONGEST POWER	CD	Pure Metal	SPCM 7900600566	

Bonus: Följ mig/Leva som han lär/Min mästare.

2003 ☐ LIVE AT BOBFEST	CD	BTS Records	BTSCD1001	

1983 7" - PSI 074

LEZLIE PAICE

Tony Tillerås: v, Håkan Ljunggren: g, Mikael Mörk: g,
Lars Andersson: b, Niklas Jerberg: d

Varberg - One of all the young Pang-bands, playing typical 80s NWoBHM, a bit similar to early *220 Volt*, but with mid-quality vocals. Jerberg later resurfaced in *Livin' Parazite*.

1983 ■ Fighting Man/People Wanna Know	7"	Pang	PSI 074	$

LICK THE DOG

Tomas "Tosse" Gustafsson: v/b, Peter "Pedda" Westman: g, Kai: g, Richve: k, Uffe: d

Fagersta - One of the first records to come out of the now legendary Studio Underground and to be produced by Pelle Saether. Sounds like a band that doesn't consider their musical mission a serious affair, but a band out to have fun and make a record. I'm not saying it's bad, not at all. In fact, songs like *Horny But…* and *Not So Sure* are great powerful classic hard rockers with a sleazy attitude. Westman was also in *Sex Sex Sex* and *Bokassa Brothers*.

1993 - MCD - LTD 001

1993 ■ Universal Joint	MCD 5tr	private	LTD 001	$

Tracks: Know Your Head/Bits And Pieces/Horny But…/Dog Time/Not So Sure

LIERS IN WAIT

Kristian "Bullen/Necrolord" Wåhlin: g, Mattias Gustavsson: b, Hans Nilsson: d

Göteborg - Ultra-technical death metal in ultra-speed tempo. At times reminiscent of US band *Death*. Outstanding drum work. Kristian is ex-*Grotesque* and he is also a phenomenal artist who has made several beautiful cover paintings for bands like *Dismember*, *Lake Of Tears*, *Memory Garden* etc. On the MCD, *Therion* singer/guitarist Christofer Johnson has lent his voice. Hans was also found in the bands *Crystal Age* and *Luciferion*, so was singer Micke Nicklasson, who was in the band temporarily. As Hans was highly involved with his other bands they were going to use the talent of *Eucharist*-drummer Daniel Erlandsson on their new album, which was set for release in 1996. However in 1995 the group disbanded and Wåhlin and Nilsson formed *Diabolique*. A cover of *Angel Of Death* is also found on the *Slayer* tribute *Slatanic Slaughter II*. Hans Nilsson has later been in *Dimension Zero*.

1992 MCD - DOL 7

1992 ■ Spiritually Uncontrolled Art	MCD 5tr	Dolores	DOL 7	

Tracks: Overlord/Bleeding Shrines Of Stone/Maliphisent Dreamvoid/Liers In Wait/Gateways.

LIFE

Anders Nordh: g/p, Paul "Palle" Sundlin: b, Thomas Rydberg: d

Stockholm - In the late 60s Anders and Palle made some recordings with the pop/rock band *Trolls* and around 1968-69, they made an album with the Hendrix-influenced band *King George Discovery.* That band also recorded a second album that only exists in four test press copies. In 1969 Anders recorded some guitar solos on the album by *Blond*, appeared on the cover but was never really a member. *Life* was formed in 1970. The band produces top league 70s hard rock in the vein of *Tear Gas*, *Leafhound* etc., but with some progressive and mellow pieces in between. The track *Living Is Loving* makes the first single well worth looking for, but it also appears on the English version. The album was released in two versions, one sung in Swedish and one in English. The track *Tro På Vår Värld* also appears on the compilation *Musik Från Frihamnen* (1972) and the non-LP track *Life* is featured on the compilation *Resan* (1973 CBS). The band split in late 1972. Anders, Palle, Peter Lundblad, Tommy Andersson and Lasse Tenander formed the band *Duga*, that released one album in 1974 that varied from symphonic rock to poppy ballads. Late 1974 Lasse quit and the band changed their name to *Figaro*. The band had a hit with the song *Framåt*. Anders Nordh also appeared in the band *Bättre Lyss*.

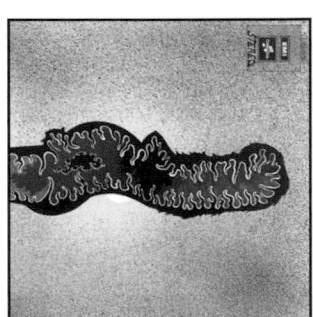

1970 LP 062-342 63

1970 7" - 006-341 96

1970 ■ Jag Färdas/Living Is Loving	7"	Columbia	006-341 96	$
1970 ■ LIFE	LP	Columbia	062-342 63	$$$
1971 ☐ LIFE	LP	Odeon	062-343 66	$$$

English version of the above. 800 copies.

1972 ■ Tro På Vår Värld/To The Country	7"	Columbia	006-345 56	$
1997 ☐ LIFE	CD	Mellotronen	MEL 007	

CD re-issue featuring the 7" tracks as bonus.

2011 ☐ LIFE	LP	Golden Pavillion	GP1010LP	

English version. Coloured vinyl. 500 copies.

2013 ☐ LIFE	2CD	RPM	RETROD929	

Contains both Swedish and English version plus single tracks. Remastered.

1972 7" - 006-345 56

LIFE ILLUSION

Gustav "Golgara" Grenstam: v/g/b/d

Malmö - Life Illusion is the solo project of *Prosecutor* member Golgara, where he handles the clean vocals and Ville "Skorrgh" Kemi (*Fall ov Serafim, Misteltein, Vandöd, Obscure Divinity*) handles the growling. The music is old-school-style black metal. They recorded a demo in 2007 and after the album new songs have been posted on *Life Illusion*'s MySpace.

2008 ■ INTO THE DARKNESS OF MY SOUL..CD Black Saw........................ Brack Saw Recs 001

2008 CD - Brack Saw Recs 001

LIFELESS IMAGE

Magnus Törnkvist: v, Kennet Berggren: g, Magnus Brolin: b, Jocke Eriksson: d

Arboga - Formed in 1990. Very heavy and powerful metal in the vein of *B-Thong* and *Stoneflow*. Well-played and well-produced. Worth checking out. They also have a track on the compilation *CD Icing* (1995 Wounded Records) and another on *Deaf & Wounded* (1995 Wounded Records).

1995 ■ Sidetracked ....MCD 5tr Wounded..WR 10
    Tracks: Steppin' Out/Without Exceptions/Just One Justice/Funeral Of Brains/Loss For Words

1995 MCD - WR 10

LIFELINE

Stig Gunnarsson: v, Olle Zimmerman: g, Johan Lindström: k,
Peter Otterborg: b, Per "Perry" Karsson: d

Örebro - This band have made tons of great demos but their only releases are two singles and the 4 track CD *Anyway You Want It*, which is a hard-rocking AOR platter well worth investing in. Great vocals, songs and musicians. The first single was produced by Tommy Nilsson (*Easy Action*) and with the right backing it could have been a great hit. The band actually recorded three songs for the compilation album *Alsterett* (Aktiv Ungdom) already in 1978, then under the name *Gain*. On the first 7" the line-up featured Olle, Perry, Lena Johansson (v/k), Janne Hedström (b), Mats Lindström (g), and on the second Ulrica Carnell (k/v) joined. In 1994 *Lifeline* received great interest from a Japanese label. Everything was set and ready... until the record company found out the members had just passed 30. Too old to rock 'n roll, they thought, and told them - no thanks. Per and Olle were later working as a duo under the name *Vibe* and the music became a bit more pop-oriented. In 2000 the *Lifeline* returned with almost the same line-up, except Lindström had been replaced by Thomas Lassar. They took the new name *Dreamhunter*, and recorded new albums. See *Dreamhunter* for further information.

1986 7" - HEJ S 009

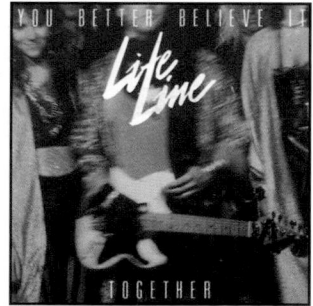
1986 7" - 136 239-7

1986 ■ Love On The Line/Win Or Lose ....7" Active Music....................................HEJ S 009
1986 ■ You Better Believe It/Together..7" EMI 136 239-7
1993 ☐ Anyway You Want It ....MCD 4tr Kuling..KULCD 9305
    Tracks: Anyway You Want It/Money Loves Hate/My Days Are Counted/Lean On Me

LIFELOVER

Kim "( )" Carlsson: v/g, Jonas "Nattdal/B" Bergqvist: v/g/k,
Johan "1853" Gabrielsson: v, Henrik "H." Huldtgren: g, Felix "Fix" Öhlén: b

Stockholm/Jönköping - Lifelover were formed by Carlsson (*Hypothermia, Kyla, Life Is Pain*) and Bergqvist (*Dimhymn, IXXI, Ondskapt*) in 2005, and released their first demo the same year. They released their first album already the subsequent year. I'm not sure what to call their style, but to me it sounds more like *Joy Division* trying to play some weird death metal with a crazy singer desperately screaming to get the message through. At times a bit reminiscent of *Shining*. The lyrics are all about anxiety, drugs, hate and the society, which sort of makes sense. Main member Bergqvist died on September 9, 2011 and after this the band split. *Pulver* featured Carlsson, Bergqvist, Gabrielsson and lyricist Rickard "LH" Öström, while on *Erotik* Huldtgren was added to the line-up. On *Konkurs* Öhlén completed the line-up. Live, the band used the services of drummer Andreas "Stigmata/S" (*IXXI*).

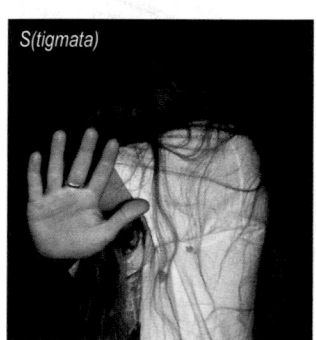
S(tigmata)

2006 CD - SDL027

2007 CD - THR 105

2006 ■ PULVER..CD GoatowaRex..SDL027
    The first 500 copies were released with different artwork.
2006 ☐ PULVER..LP Northern Sky... - -
    300 copies. Different artwork.
2007 ■ EROTIK...CD Total Holocaust .... THR 105
2007 ☐ EROTIK..2LP Eternity...ETER 026
    500 copies, first 100 in red vinyl.
2008 ☐ KONKURS ....CD+CDR Avantgarde... AV 103
    100 copies in cotton bag with poster, sticker and the first demo on pro-printed CD-R.
2008 ☐ KONKURS ....CD Avantgarde... AV 103
2009 ☐ PULVER..CD Osmose .... OPCD 213
2009 ☐ EROTIK...CD Osmose .... OPCD 214

2009 ☐	Dekadens	MCD 7tr	Osmose	OPCD 231

Tracks: Luguber framtid/Myspys/Major Fuck Off/Lethargy/Androider/Visdomsord/Destination: Ingenstans

2010 ■	KONKURS	2CDd	Prophecy Productions	PRO 111LU
2010 ☐	KONKURS	CD	Prophecy Productions	PRO 111
2011 ☐	SJUKDOM	CDd	Prophecy Productions	PRO 113
2011 ☐	SJUKDOM	LP	Prophecy Productions	PRO 113 LP
2011 ☐	SJUKDOM	CDd box	Prophecy Productions	PRO 113 BOX

1000 copies in tin box. With syringe, razorblade, barbed wire, torn piece of cloth, postcard

2010 2CDd - PRO 111LU

LIGHTS OUT

Viveca Bjerselius: v, Angela Esposito: g, Jenny Back: k,
Therese Runsö: b, Malin Andersson: d

Norrköping - Formed in 1987. The single recording was first prize in a bandstand. The record is well worth checking out. *Lights Out* is a great melodic metal band in the vein of *Vixen*. Therese Runsö was replaced by Heidi Lehmus.

1991 ■	Seriously/Fire Of Love	7"	KFUM	KFUM 02

300 copies.

1991 7" - KFUM 02

LIK (LEKAMEN ILLUSIONEN KALLET)

Stefan "Graav/Stoif" Sandström: v/g/b/d, Andreas Pettersson: g/b

Boliden - The band was formed in 2003, also known as *LIK* (corpse). The self-titled release *Lekamen Illusionen Kallet* (the body, the illusion, the calling) is labelled as an album despite it only has four songs and a total length of 24 minutes. The band took a time out in 2007, but returned in 2010 to record *The Second Wind*, on which the drums were played by J. Marklund. I'm not really sure what to call this, style-wise. It's definitely not traditional black or death metal, but closer to doomy goth with a touch of folk and with Graav singing low and clean, more in the vein of Glenn Danzig. Both Sandström and Pettersson are also found in *Armagedda*, *Lönndom* and *Volkermord*. Pettersson is also in *Leviathan*.

2003 CD - - -

2003 ■	MÅ LJUSET ALDRIG NÅ OSS MER	CD	W.T.C/Blut & Eisen	- -
2005 ☐	MÅ LJUSET ALDRIG NÅ OSS MER	LPg	Blut & Eisen	- -
	400 hand-numbered copies.			
2005 ■	BESVÄRTADE STROFER	CD	Agonia Records	ARCD 030
2005 ☐	BESVÄRTADE STROFER	LPg	Agonia Records	ARLP 026
	Poster.			
2007 ☐	MÅ LJUSET ALDRIG NÅ OSS MER	CD	Agonia Records	ARCD 054
2007 ☐	LEKAMEN ILLUSIONEN KALLET	CD	Agonia Records	ARCD 043
2007 ☐	LEKAMEN ILLUSIONEN KALLET	LP	Agonia Records	ARLP 040
2010 ☐	MÅ LJUSET ALDRIG NÅ OSS MER	CD	Frostscald/Silenced Voices	FS42/Deadmoon03
2010 ☐	BESVÄRTADE STROFER	CD	Frostscald/Silenced Voices	FS43/Deadmoon04
2010 ☐	LEKAMEN ILLUSIONEN KALLET	CD	Frostscald/Silenced Voices	FS44/Deadmoon05
2011 ☐	THE SECOND WIND	CD	Nordvis Produktion	NVP 005
2011 ☐	THE SECOND WIND	2LP	Eisenwald Tonschmeide	EISEN 056

500 copies. With poster. Wine red. Different artwork.

2005 CD - ARCD 030

LIKBLEK

Dennis "L. Svartvén" Larsson: g/v, Daniel "DK" Kvist: g,
Kenneth "Thunderbolt" Gagner: b, Lawen "Getaz" Palmgren: d

Göteborg - Fast and primitive black metal with a touch of thrash and a punkish simplicity. Quite monotonous and uninteresting. Recorded their first demo, *Deathgod Serpent*, in 2009. Kvist is also in *Sacrilege*, *Taetre*, *Dragonland* and *Immemoreal*, Palmgren in *Kill* and *Necroplasma*, Gagner is *Swordmaster* and *Mastema* and finally Larsson is in *Styggelse*. Likblek means pale (or rather pale as a corpse) in Swedish.

2010 ■	LIKBLEK	CD	Daemon Worship Productions	DWP 011

2010 CD - DWP 011

LILLASYSTER

Martin Westerstrand Skans: v, Max Flövik: g, Andy "Oh My God": b, Ian-Paolo Lira: d

Göteborg - When classic metalcore band *LOK* decided to call it quits, singer Westerstrand and bass player Daniel Cordero returned under new flag. In the form of *Rallypack*. The band was completed by drummer Lira and electric cellist Flövik. They recorded one album, in English, called *Sod Off, God!! We Believe In Our Rockband*. In 2006 Martin again started writing in Swedish and the band changed their name to *Lillasyster* (little sister). Flövik now switched to guitar. The style is the same vein as *LOK*, but with slightly more melodic vocals. In 2007

Twisted little sister...

Lillasyster had a huge hit with a heavy cover of Rhianna's song *Umbrella*. In December 2010 Cordero left the band and was later replaced by Andy. *Hjärndöd kärlek* is a compilation of the first two album for the Norwegian market. The album *3* features guest spots from **Mustasch**, Henrik Danhage (**Deathdestruction, Evergrey**) and Tommy Rehn (**Moahni Moahna, Zool, Corroded**).

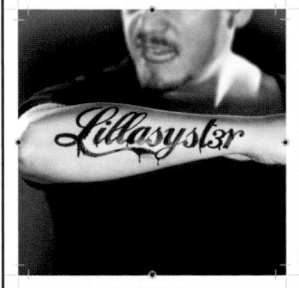

2007 □	Berätta det för Lina	CDS	Gain	GPCD 34
2007 □	HJÄRNDÖD MUSIK FÖR EN HJÄRNDÖD GENERATION	CD	Gain	GPCD 38
2007 □	Umbrella	MCD 4tr	Cargo Records	D99955
	Tracks: Umbrella/Hårdrock + Umbrella (video)/Berätta det för Lina (video)			
2009 □	DET HÄR ÄR INTE MUSIK, DET HÄR ÄR KÄRLEK	CD	Tjockis Records	TJOCKCD2-1
2009 □	HJÄRNDÖD MUSIK FÖR EN HJÄRNDÖD GENERATION	CD	Tjockis Records	TJOCKCD 03
	Bonus: Umbrella			
2009 □	Jag är här nu	CDS	Tjockis Records	TJOCKCD-S002
2010 □	HJÄRNDÖD KÄRLEK	CD	Universal (Norway)	N501022
2011 ■	3	CD	Ninetone	NRCD 113

2011 CD - NRCD 113

LIMIT
Mårten Eriksson: b/v, Rolf "Trazan" Nordström: g, Anders Svedberg: k, Peter Olsson: d

Örnsköldsvik - Outstanding Christian melodic hard rock in the vein of **Treat**. Trazan was previously in **Romance** and later joined the reunited **Killer Bee**. Eriksson has participated in the Eurovision Song Contest, for Ireland. Not the same band that release the single *Put The Engine On*.

1988 ■	WHEN THE CLOCK STRIKES	LP	private	19.88

1988 LP - 19.88

LIMITLESS
Johan Hansson: v, Mikael Johannesson: g,
Martin Danielsson: b, Mikael Wennergrund: d

Stockholm - The band was first formed under the name **Retro Pak**. Johan and Mikael have previously recorded with the bands **Tippen Ruda** and **Mandala**. Mikael is also found in the English melodic hard rock band **Double Trouble** and Johannesson is playing with the band **Lovehandles**. The band only plays covers and is not a all hard rock, but more the 70s blues-oriented type. The MCD however contains an explosive version of the old **Allman Brothers Band** tune *Whipping Post*, where the drums are handled by Frank Roleau.

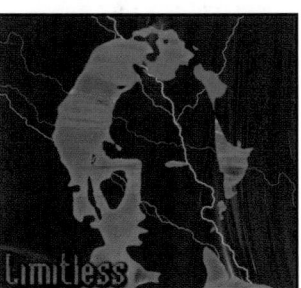

1999 ■	Limitless	MCDd 4tr	private	- -
	Tracks: Southbound (Allman Bros cover)/Love Is A Beautiful Thing (Al Green cover)/Whipping Post (Allman Bros cover)/Lennie (Stevie Ray Vaughn cover)			

1999 MCDd - - -

LINDBERG, ZIA (aka CIA)
Zia Lindberg: v

Uppsala - Melodic hard rock/AOR. This lassie won the soloist-class in the 1991 Rock-SM competition, and no wonder. Zia has a great voice in the neighbourhood of Alannah Myles or Tamara Champlin. She worked as backing-singer for Roine Stolt and lead singer with the all-girl band **Miss Tress**, before pursuing a solo career. The album is OK, but would need a bit more balls (sorry girls). Check out the cover of **Lynyrd Skynyrd**'s *One Good Man*, though. There is also some nice guitar work from Roine Stolt (**Kaipa, The Flower Kings, Stolt**). On the first single she spelled her first name with a C instead of Z and the guitar work was then handled by Göran Elmquist (**Dream Bank, Bam Bam Boys**).

1993 CDSp - ONECDS 129

1991 □	Like The Way I Do/I Should've Told You	7"	Alpha	ONESIN 109
1993 □	I'll Be The Only One	CDSp 1tr	Alpha	ONECDS 119
1993 ■	Piece Of My Heart/You're So Good (At Being Bad)	CDSp 2tr	Alpha	ONECDS 129
1993 □	Still On My Mind	CDSp 1tr	Alpha	ONECDS 136
1993 ■	ZANINESS	CD	Alpha	ONECD 045

1993 CD - ONECD 045

LINE UP
Patrick Axelsson: v, Björn Åsander: k, Peter Jones: b

Stockholm - This was a band among many that managed to get disillusioned by the dubious Büms Records. **Line Up** delivers high-quality melodic hard rock in the vein of Canadian rockers **Wrabit**. Well-produced with quite dominating and fat guitars. Great singer in the traditional AOR-mode. Guitarist Tony Nyberg and drummer (drum machine) A. Lesis are stated as additional musicians on the album. They changed some members and their name to **Reckless** and later made more releases under the new moniker. In 1994 Büms re-issued the *Lucky One* album because of interest from the Japanese market.

1992 ■	Lucky One	CD	Büms	CD 39 123
	The CD was reissued in 1994 with a different back-cover.			

1992 CD - CD 39 123

LINEHOUSE

Niklas Dernebo: v, Jonas Öhlund: g/k/b/programming

Örnsköldsvik - The duo of Dernebo and former *Pride* guitarist Öhlund got together in 2005. In 2007 they released the three track EP *First Love*, and were featured on the compilation *Munich's Hardest Hits – Melodic Rock Is Back Vol. 9* with the track *Stormrider*. After this they were picked up by BLP Music, who released the debut album *Take One*. **Linehouse** plays quite slick but solid AOR in the vein of *Stage Dolls* and Swedish colleagues *CC Rock* or *T'Bell*.
Website: www.linehouse.se

2009 CD - BLP 2009-05

2009 ■ TAKE ONE ....CD BLP Music....................................BLP 2009-05

LINEOUT

**Jerker Avander: v, Andreas Lindmark: g, Fredrik Lindqvist: g,
Henrik Wiklund: b, Samuel: d**

Skellefteå - Heavy, brutal metalcore/screamo metal. Drums on the single were played by Magnus Lindberg (*Cult Of Luna*). Avander and Lindqvist are now in *Totalt Jävla Mörker*.

2001 ■ Drowning Face/Break The Day..7" Rage Of Achilles ....ILIAD 008

2001 7" - ILIAD 008

LINGUA

Thomas Henriksson: g, Misha Sedini: g, Anders Calström: b, Patrik Juutilainen: d

Stockholm - The band was formed by former *Arize* members Henriksson and Sedini. The drafted drummer Juutilainen and guitarist Carlström (*A Swarm Of The Sun, Come Sleep, Rövfitta*) and **Lingua** was born. The band describe themselves as "not metal, not hard rock, not rock, but alternative and pretentious". They are often compared to bands like *Cult Of Luna* and *Tool*, which I definitely agree with. Modern, heavy detuned rock with a strong alternative, emo and at times almost doom/goth-oriented touch. A really good band.
Website: linguamusic.blogspot.com/

2010 CD - AURA 010

2006 □ THE SMELL OF A LIFE THAT COULD HAVE BEEN....................................CD Rebel Monster ....RMR 7183 2
2010 ■ ALL MY RIVALS ARE IMAGINARY GHOSTS ....CD Aural ....AURA 010

LION'S SHARE

Nils Patrik Johansson: v, Lars "Chriss" Christmansson: g, Sampo Axelsson: b

Stockholm/Sundsvall - Formed in 1987, in Sundsvall, by Lars and keyboardist Kay Backlund, and released their debut single the year after. The band then consisted of Lars, Kay, singer Marcus Nordenberg, bassist Mikael Hansson and drummer Jauni Niemi. The style on the single was pure keyboard-dominated AOR with catchy choruses. In 1989 they won the recording of yet another single that never saw the light of day due to line-up problems. In 1992 Lars recorded the song *Nothing's Free* for a Belgian compilation-CD. As **Lion's Share** was more a solo-project then he invited Thomas Vikström (*Talk Of The Town, Candlemass, Stormwind* etc) and Conny Lind (*State Of Mind, Raceway, Amaze Me*) on vocals, the late Marcel Jacob (*Rising Force, Talisman, Humanimal* etc.) on bass, P A Danielsson (*Veni Domine, Tiamat*) on keyboards and Johan Kullberg (*Talk Of The Town*) on drums. In March 1993 the line-up featured Lars, Johan, Kay, former *Glory* bass-player Anders Loos and *Sorcerer*-singer Anders "Andy" Engberg. In the beginning **Lion's Share** was more or less a traditional AOR-band, but with the new line-up the style started changing towards a more progressive, yet heavy and melodic style. They recorded some highly acclaimed demos before signing to XTC Management, which lead to a deal with Japanese label Zero and German Long Island Records. The first album was recorded in the super hot summer of 1994 and it is an absolute must for fans of well-played progressive yet melodic hard rock. The European versions on Local Hero and Long Island were re-mastered and have a heavier sound than the Japanese version. The artwork is also a bit different. In 1996 the band was signed to Century Media and on the second album, *Two*, the line-up consisted of Engberg, Chriss, Backlund, Kullberg and bass player Pontus Egberg (now in *The Poodles*). In 1999 the band was on the bill of the *Monsters Of The Millenium* tour together with *Manowar*, *Dio* and *Motörhead*. In 2000 singer Anders Engberg decided to leave the band and Tony Niva (*Tracy Goes Crazy, Swedish Erotica, Niva, Oxygen*) joined. Also keyboard player Kay Backlund left the band before the recording of *Entrance*, and keyboards on the album were played by Mats Olausson (*Malmsteen, Motvind* etc). After *Entrance* the band went into a long hiatus, and returned in 2007 with a completely new line-up and new sound. Lars Chriss was the only remaining member, now reinforced with singer Nils Patrik Johansson (*Astral Doors, Wuthering Heights*) and bass player Sampo Axelsson (*Crawley*). The album also showcased a more metal-oriented side of the band, moving from their proggier style to classic heads down *Priest*-influenced metal. *Dark Hours* was an even heavier instalment. Richard Evensand (*It's Alive, Soilwork, Therion, Chimaira, Toehider*) played drums on the album. It also featured guest spots from Michael Romeo (*Symphony X*) and Conny Pettersson (*Anata*). The production

Trillion (get it?)

was handled by Jens Bogren (**Opeth**, **Amon Amarth** etc). After the album Axelsson left the band and the line-up currently only features Lars and Nils Patrik. A new album is being written. Nils Patrik joined **Civil War** in 2012 (the new band with former **Sabaton** members).
Website: www.lionsshare.org

1988 7" - CUF 008

1988 ■	Ghost Town Queen/I'm On A Roll	7"	CUF Skivklubb	CUF 008
1994 □	LION'S SHARE	CD	Zero/Japan	XRCN-1170
1995 □	Sins Of The Father/Scarecrow/Just In Time To Be Late	CDS 3tr	Local Hero (promo)	LHM 0365
1995 □	LION'S SHARE	CD	Local Dealer	LHM 0407
1995 □	LION'S SHARE	CD	Long Isand	LIR 00080
1997 □	TWO	CD	Century Media	CD 77154-2
1997 □	TWO	CD	Victor (Japan)	VICP-60005
1997 □	LION'S SHARE	CD	Century Media	CD 77153-2
	This version does not include Taking On The World and Nothing's Free.			
1997 □	Flash In The Night(radio edit)/Don't Come Easy/Shadows	MCD	Century Media	CD 77155-2
1999 □	FALL FROM GRACE	CD	Bareknuckles (Japan)	AVCB-66060
	Bonus: Lion's Share			
2000 □	PERSPECTIVE	2CD	Massacre	MAS CD 0268
	The two first albums in a 2-CD set. Bonus: I Don't Believe In Love/Lion's Share/Nothing's Free			
2001 □	ENTRANCE	CD	LCM Production	LCM 4001
2001 □	ENTRANCE	CD	Toxic (South America)	4624-2
2007 □	EMOTIONAL COMA	CD	AFM	AFM 171-2
2007 □	EMOTIONAL COMA	CDd	AFM	AFM 171-9
	Bonus: Ring Of Stupidity			
2007 □	EMOTIONAL COMA	CD	Spiritual Beast (Japan)	POCE-16014
	Bonus: Ring Of Stupidity/The Edge Of The Razor (video)			
2008 □	EMOTIONAL COMA	CD	Locomotive Music (USA)	LM 559
2008 □	EMOTIONAL COMA	CD	CD-Maximum (Russia)	CDM 1107-2756
	Bonus: Ring Of Stupidity/The Edge Of The Razor (video)			
2009 ■	DARK HOURS	CD	Blistering Records	BR 020
2009 □	DARK HOURS	CDd	Blistering Records	BR 020DLTD
	Bonus: King Of All The Kings/Judas Must Die (video)			
2009 □	DARK HOURS	CD	King Records (Japan)	KICP-1366
	Bonus: King Of All The Kings + video			
2009 □	DARK HOURS	CD	Soyus (Russia)	BR 020

2009 CD - BR 020

LIPKIN
Rauno Luoto: v, Joakim Svedlund: g, Patrik Zakrisson: b, Mats Hillström: d

Sandviken - Out of nowhere this band came with the excellent contribution entitled, *Seduced*. Though there are elements of bands like **Soundgarden** and **Alice In Chains**, they don't sound especially grungy, but more 70s influenced with some great guitar riffs. The Step One release is a reissue of the debut with a new cover and three extra tracks. Recommended. Luoto later returned with the band **Bablefish**, but only recorded some demos.

1994 CD - ZCD 301

1994 ■	SEDUCED	CD	private	ZCD 301
1995 □	LIPKIN	CD	Step One	SOR CD9

LIPSTIXX 'N' BULLETS
Anders "Andy Lipstixx" Arvidsson: v/g, Per "Rikki Bullet" Olsson: g,
Jörgen "Jamie Tease" Arvidsson: b, Johan "Johnny Wizzer" Voxberg: d

Stockholm - **Lipstixx 'N' Bullets** play, yes you guessed it right, eighties-sounding glam/sleaze. The band started out with two demos in 2006, at the time with Ondahl on drums, and released their debut in 2009. Arvidsson previously played guitar in **Evilution** and **Cesar Nero**. After the album Voxberg (ex-**Demonia**, **Detox**) left and was replaced by Michael "Sweet" Hosselton, brother of Martin Sweet of **Crashdïet**. Andy and Michael are now found in **Toxic Rose**.

2009 CD - SR-0096

2009 ■	BANG UR HEAD	CD	Sleazy Rider	SR-0096

LIQUID PHASE
Johan Pettersson: v, Björn Schagerström: g, Per-Erik Thorp: g,
David Zackrisson: b, Kristian Zackrisson: d

Dals Långed - Powerful and heavy thrash/hardcore with brutal and quite indecipherable vocals.

2000 7" - Take 006

2000 ■	Liquid Phase/Aspected (split)	7"	TakeA Stand/No Appearance	Take 006
	Split with Aspected. Tracks: Intro-Coldstare/Questionmark/Dark Chronicles. Red vinyl.			

LIQUID SCARLET

Markus Fagervall: v/g, Olov Andersson: g, Frida Lundström: k,
Joel Lindberg: b, Johan Lundström: d/g/k

Stockholm - *Liquid Scarlet* were formed in Kalix in 1996. The line-up was set in 2000 and the debut came in 2004, followed by the *Killer Couple* EP and a second album, the subsequent year. After the debut, Olle Sjögren replaced keyboardist Frida Lundström. In 2006 singer Fagervall won the Swedish Idol, resulting in a solo record, which made the future of the band a bit uncertain. A few scandals and a life-crisis later he made public he was back in the band in 2009, but since then nothing has happened. *Liquid Scarlet* play really good progressive rock in the vein of *Trettioåriga Kriget* meets *Anekdoten* with a touch of *The Mars Volta*. The second album is a bit more straightforward.

2005 MCD - PREP 001

2004 ☐	LIQUID SCARLET	CD	Progress Records	PRR 165
2005 ■	Killer Couple Strikes Again	MCD 5tr	Progress Records	PREP 001
	Tracks: Killer Couple Strikes Again/This Might Be The Last Time/Staden rämnar vid fågelns skri/Heading For Golgata/All That Is Grey			
2005 ☐	II	CD	Progress Records	PRO PRCD 016

LIQUIDUST

Kiana Svalold: v, Tobbe "Toby" Höckert: g, André Skaug: b, Lacki Miliadis: d

Stockholm - *Liquidust* were formed as a trio in 2001. Bass on the MCD was handled by André Skaug (*Clawfinger*), who was replaced by Magnus Östborg (*Reckless*). The production may not be stellar, but the quality of the music makes up for it. Great, groovy modern heavy rock with a post-grunge vibe. Magnus left in 2006 and the band folded shortly after.

2002 MCDp - LIQUIDIST 001

2002 ■	Denied/Hypotalamus/My Ground	MCDp 3tr	private	LIQUIDUST 001

LISA GIVES HEAD

John Wreibo (now Lindqwister): v, Jari Tissari: g, David Andersson: g,
Jarmo Vehmanen: b, John Lillestrand: d

Malmö - On the first two recordings they were called *Lisa G Head*, but on *A Closer Look At The Ground* they returned to their original full name *Lisa Gives Head*. Formed in 1989, but the present set-up wasn't final until 1992. The band received great recognition in 1994 with their aggressive heavy sound á la *Pantera* and *Helmet* meets *Megadeth*. The track *Someone Else Will* on the *Everlost* MCD is a cover of the old *Sweet*-song. Renowned producer Tomas Skogsberg produced *A Closer Look*. David and Jarmo were previously in the punk band *Puke*, which recorded the album *Back To The Stoneage* (CBR Records) and John Lillestrand recorded an album with *Black Uniforms*. The last official track was a cover of *Metallica*'s *The Four Horsemen* on the *Metal Militia* compilation in 1996. Andersson recorded a demo with the band *Murinus* in 2004. In 1997 Wreibo (now Lindqwister) joined the band *Cat Rapes Dog*, later *Basswood Dollies* and now sings alternative pop in Swedish.

1993 CD - ACC CD 22

1995 CD - ACC CD 26

1993 ■	GIVE THE IRON	CD	Accelerating Blue Fish	ACC CD 22
1994 ☐	Everlost/Chill Out In Hell(cool)/Someone Else Will (Sweet cover)	MCD 3tr	Accelerating Blue Fish	ACC CD 24
1995 ■	A CLOSER LOOK AT THE GROUND	CD	Accelerating Blue Fish	ACC CD 26

LITHANY

Jonas: v, Nicklas Bäckström: b/v, Markus Lindström: g, Mattias: k, Jakob Burstedt: d

Umeå - Really interesting technical, heavy, proggish metal with a wacky touch, a bit similar to *Tool* with the crazy rhythmic patterns of *Meshuggah* and even a touch of *The Mars Volta*. Great production, too! *Lithany* was formed in 2000, released their first demo *For You Alone* in 2003 and the second, *Devilbox*, the year after. Burstedt and Bäckström went on to form *Moloken*. *Website: www.lithany.net*

2006 CD - MMICD 02

2006 ■	LITHANY	CD	Discouraged	MMICD 02

LITHIUM

Carl Larsson: v, Johnny Hagel: b

Stockholm - *Lithium* were originally comprised by former *Tiamat/Sorcerer/Cemetery 1213/ Sundown* bassist Hagel, *Moth*-singer Larsson and guitarist Nico Pedersen, who left before the album. For live work Hagel used the services of Johan and Kristian Niemann, both on guitar, and drummer Sami Karppinen. *Lithium* play industrial metal in the vein of *Pain*, *Misery Loves Co* and *Tiamat* with a goth-touch in the vocals.

2002 CD - NFR 61

2002 ■	COLD	CD	No Fashion	NFR 61

456

LITTLE YANKEES

Paul Dexter: v/g/k, Tobias Wernersson: g/k, Eddie Persson: b, Frederik Björling: d

Malmö - Melodic hard rock/AOR, like a mix of *Toto* and *Van Halen*, with a westcoast-ish touch. High-quality, but a bit lacking in originality. It all started when Englishman Paul Dexter toured Sweden with his cover band *Obsession*. He met a Swedish girl and finally moved to Sweden in the late eighties. Paul found bass-player Eddie and later Tobias and Fredrik from the band *Perfect Remedies*. The last CDS was recorded as a hymn for the C4 Lions football-team. The team participates as choir.

1997 CD - MASS 508

1995	☐	Wanna Go To America	MCD 5tr	private	PDCD 001
		Tracks: Go To America/The Power/I'll Be There/Nowhere To Run/Yankees			
1997	■	ALL OR NOTHING	CD	Massive Music	MASS 508
1997	☐	ALL OR NOTHING	CD	Ursa Major (Asia)	n/a
1997	☐	Mighty Lions/Mighty Lions (Remix)	CDS 2tr	private	CDM 01

LIVE ELEPHANT

**Morgan Eriksson: v/d, Henrik Mikaelsson: g,
Mathias Nylén: g, Olov Norberg: b, Olov Nilsson: d**

Umeå - Formed in 1995. The first release was powerful, heavy riffing, hard rock with occasional hints of *Megadeth*, *Rage Against The Machine*, *Pantera* and... well Frank Zappa. *Masterhead* on the other hand is an extremely heavy and powerful album, like a doom-oriented version of *Pantera*. Killer stuff indeed! They also do a cover of *Black Sabbath*'s *Symptom Of The Universe* on the first release and *Sweet Leaf* on the second. On the first release Anders Hellman handled the vocals. In 2006 *Live Elephant* returned with another slab of metal, where drummer Eriksson had also taken over the lead vocals, taking the vocals to a more aggressive style. As a result Mikael Ludvigsson handled the drums live, until Olov Nilsson became the permanent drummer. The band had also switched guitarist Jörgen Lindgren for Henrik Mikaelsson.

1996 CD - ZRCD 009   *2000 CD - LECD 002*

1996	■	SKIN N' BONE	CD	Zakana	ZRCD 009
2000	■	MASTERHEAD	CD	private	LECD 002
2006	☐	INTO THE MACHINERY	CD	private	LECD 003
2011	■	SPEAK THE TRUTH OR DIE ALONE	CD	Rockfall	RRCD 137
2011	☐	SPEAK THE TRUTH OR DIE ALONE	LP	Rockfall	RRLP 137

2011 CD - RRCD 137

LIVIN' PARAZITE

**Larsa Bertilsson: v, Ola Renkse: g, "Linkan" Andersson: g,
Martin Karlsson: b, Niklas Jerberg: d**

Varberg - Formed in 1989 under the name *Parazite* as a more traditional hard rock band with the addition of keyboards. In 1990 the keyboards were out and the music took a heavier approach. In 1992 they recorded their first three track demo, at the time featuring Andersson, Renkse, Karlsson, Fritiofsson and singer Tomas. Later the same year Bertilsson had taken over the vocals and they recorded a second demo. The first release is great high-class metal/thrash, quite close to *Anthrax* on *Spreading The Disease*. The vocals are also in the vein of Joey Belladonna (*Anthrax/Belladonna*). After the MCD they recorded another demo, before adding some *Livin'* into the band name. *Paranoia Chaos* is a full-blown power pack with tons of energy taking the style of the MCD a step further. Highly recommended for fans of power metal loaded with a wall of guitars, great vocals and a tight and driving rhythm unit. In 1998, the band recorded a second album in the same killer vein, but it was for some unimaginable reason not released until 2002. Tracks like *Hell Of An Angel*, *More Haste Less Speed* or *Nothing Better To Do* should definitely have be brought to the public sooner. On this album Niklas Jerberg (ex-*Lezlie Paize*) had replaced drummer Geron Fritiofsson. Three of the members are also found in cover band *The Beerbelly Boys*. Linkan and Martin have also been playing on albums by *The Andersson Mills Project* and *Acid For Blood*, together with former *Quiet Riot* drummer Franki Banali. Karlsson has also played with *Eucharist*, *Eternal Lies* and *Revengia*. The band split in 1998 and *Down* was released posthumously.

Now dead livin' parazite

1998 CD - USG 1915-2

2002 CD - KICKCD 179

1994	☐	Consider It Done	MCD 4tr	private	PZCD 001
		Tracks: Live In Pain/A Different Kind Of Livin'/Bastard/Cry Baby. Released under the name Parazite.			
1998	■	PARANOIA CHAOS	CD	USG	USG 1915-2
2002	■	DOWN	CD	Kick	KICKCD 179

LIVSNEKAD

Ulf Nylin: v, **Christian Larsson:** g, **Andreas Larsen:** g/b/v,
Seiya Ogino: k, **Richard Schill:** d

Halmstad/Halland - In 2007 the band released the three-track demo EP *Köttet och sinnets bi-ografi* in 50 copies, only featuring Nylin and Larsen. On the album the band had a full line-up. Niklas Kvarforth (*Shining*) also appears on the album as session singer. *Livsnekad* play doomy, gloomy, desperate doom/death metal, with very long songs, at times reminiscent of *Shining*. Christian is also found in *Svart* and *Shining*, Schill is ex-*Shining* and *Spawn Of Possession*, while Nylin has been in bands like *Skendöd*, *Korpblod*, *Level Above Human* and *Rådare*. The second album *Tills döden skiljer oss åt* was recorded in 2010, but the *Nostalgisk katarsis* was released before, containing rerecorded versions of two older tracks, and only featuring Nylin, Larsen and Larsson. Livsnekad means life denied.

2009 CD - Misstag 1

2011 MCD - X62221

2009 ■ DEN SOCIALA VANFÖRHETEN ....CD Katastrophy Records .... Misstag 1
2011 ■ Nostalgisk katarsis ....MCD 4tr Art Of Propaganda X62221
    Tracks: Bered mig den väg/Jag är levande död/En färgad kärlek; en vissnad begivenhet/ Fobisk sälta

LIZARD EYE

Lasse Gudmundsson: v, **Patrik "PM" Saari:** g, **Fredrik Thörnblom:** b, **Ralph Rydén:** d

Stockholm - *Lizard Eye* started as former *Whimzy*-singer Gudmundsson's solo project, where he drafted various members through the years. Several demos were recorded between 2001 and 2009, when the band finally got a steady line-up featuring Saari, Thörnblom (ex-*Oz*, *Jack Of All Trades*) and Rydén (ex-*Mercy, Hexenhaus, Keegan* etc). In 2011 the band finally released the debut *Flames Of The Sun*. Lasse is also now fronting the band *Angel King*.

2011 CD - LECD001

2011 ■ FLAMES OF THE SUN...CD private LECD001

LOADED

Johan Öberg: v, **Marcus Palm:** g, **Michael Karlsson:** b, **Marcus Fritiofsson:** d

Strömsnäsbruk - Formed in 1999 under the name *Troubled Wine*, but changed to *Loaded* the year after. Good solid hard rock with a seventies-touch and some nice riff-work.

2000 MCD - - -

2000 ■ First Brew..MCD 6tr private .... - -
    Tracks: Where Is The Sun/Why/Needle Cry/The Dream/Leave/Hell Yeah

LOBOTOMY

Max Collin: v, **Etienne Belmar:** g, **Lars Jelleryd:** g,
Patric Carsana: b, **Daniel "Dudde" Strachal:** d

Stockholm - Formed from the ashes of *Rapture*. Recorded their debut demo *When Death Draws Near* at Sunlight Studios 1990, followed by *Instinct Of Brutality* (1991), *Against The Gods* (1992) and *Nailed In Misery* (1993). They label their music "Go-go-death", well... they are not a typical death band, as they blend their music with elements of thrash, doom and traditional metal as well as some non-traditional rhythms. Musically the band will probably appeal to the wider metal-audience, while the vocals are of the classical growling death-type. The first 7" was released by a Finnish label and the debut album was recorded and ready early 1995, but the Austrian record company Leathal who was supposed to release it, went bust. The album was later released by Chaos. US-label Thrash Corner Records released a compilation of two demos *Against The Gods* and *Nailed In Misery*. The latter was also released as a cassette-EP by Obscure Plasma in 1993. On the 1992 recording the line-up consisted of Lars (v/g), Patrik (b) and Daniel (d), and the following year the band was reinforced with guitarist Fred. *Born In Hell* was produced by Jocke Pettersson (*Dawn, Regurgitate*) and *Holy Shit* by Pettersson in co-operation with Tomas Skogsberg and the band. In 2001 Lars Jelleryd left the band and was replaced by former *Messanine*-member Jakob Lecinzky. Daniel has his metal band *Tongue Twister* on the side, where Lecinzky is also found. Daniel has also recorded some demos with his other current side-project *Blindfold*, a doom/sludge-unit showing his passion for *Pentagram*. Collin and Belmar were also in the band *Votary*. Belmar was later in German band *Buried In Black*. *Website: www.lobotomy.nu*

1995 CD - THCR007CD

1997 CD - NFR 023

1993 ☐ Hymn...7" 3tr Rising Realm Records RRR001
    Tracks: Flowertrip Pt 1/ In Bloodstained Green/Turmoil
1995 ☐ LOBOTOMY...CD Chaos ....CD 04
1995 ■ AGAINST THE GODS/NAILED IN MISERY ....CD Thrash Corner............................THCR007CD
1997 ■ KILL..CD No Fashion Records .... NFR 023
1999 ☐ BORN IN HELL...CD No Fashion Records .... NFR 036
2000 ☐ BORN IN HELL...CD Metal Blade (USA/Can) 3984-14291-2
2000 ■ Holy Shit...MCD 5tr No Fashion Records .... NFR 048
    Tracks: Porno For The Wicked/Invite The Needle/Sunblind/Divination/Blood Angel (remix)

2000 MCD - NFR 048

LOCH VOSTOK

Teddy Möller: v/g, Niklas Kupper: g, Fredrik Klingwall: k, Jimmy Mattson: b, Lawrence Dinamarca: d

Uppsala - When **Mayadome** disbanded in 2001, drummer Teddy Möller (**F.K.Ü, Vivaldi's Disciples, Mellow Poetry, Wuthering Heights, Flagellation** etc.) decided to get heavy again. He drafted keyboardist Sebastian Okupski and bassist Erik Grandin and **Loch Vostok** was a reality. At the arrival of drummer Alvaro Svanerö (**Imperial Domain, Azotic Reign**) and guitarist Niklas Kupper (**El Presidente, Searing I**), Möller took on the task of vocals and guitar. When Grandin relocated to the US, former **Mellow Poetry** guitarist Tomas Jonsson stepped in to fill the bass spot. Using the services of renowned producer Daniel Bergstrand, they recorded the debut album *Dark Logic*, which was picked up by Russian label CD-Maximum. After the album Okupski left to play covers, and he was replaced by **Platitude/Audiovison/Zool/Wuthering Heights** keyboardist Andreas Lindahl. He only lasted for one album and was replaced by Fredrik Klingwall (**Anima Morte, Flagellation**). After some touring the band recorded the third album, *Reveal No Secrets*.

The children of the sea

Since Escapi went belly-up, they were picked up by US label Nightmare Records. In 2009 Svanerö was replaced by Lawrence Dinamarca and bassist Jonsson by Jimmy Mattsson. In 2011 the new line-up delivered *Dystopium*. Loch Vostok is an subterranean lake in the Antarctica.
Website: www.lochvostock.com

2003	☐	DARK LOGIC	CD	CD-Maximum (Russia)	CDM0403-1366
2004	☐	DARK LOGIC	CD	Magnetism (Portugal)	MGR 001
2006	☐	DESTRUCTION TIME AGAIN	CD	Escapi Music	EMUS 20057
2009	■	REVEAL NO SECRETS	CD	Nightmare (USA)	NMR-502
2009	☐	REVEAL NO SECRETS	CD	Silverwolf	SWP0015LV
2011	☐	DYSTOPIUM	CD	ViciSolum	VSP 024
2012	■	V: THE DOCTRINE DECODED	CD	ViciSolum	VSP 034

2009 CD - NMR 502

LOCOMOTIVE BREATH

Mattias Osbäck: v, Janne Stark: g, Marcel Jacob: b, Ted Wernersson: d

Mörrum/Karlskrona - **Locomotive Breath** were founded in 1995 by Janne Stark and Kjell Jacobsson, both ex-**Overdrive**. The band was completed by bass player Ulf Kronsell (ex-**Blue Town, E-Type, Solid Flow**), drummer Mats Brandström (ex-**T For Trouble**) and singer Herman Saming (**A.C.T**). At the time of recording of the debut, Kjell was no longer in the line-up. *Train Of Events* features guest spots from Micke "Nord" Andersson (**Nord, Roxette, BALLS**), Mattias Ia Eklundh (**Freak Kitchen**), Tommy Denander, Calle CJ Grimmark (**Narnia, Fullforce**), Anders Altzarfeldt (**Zello**) and Kjell Jacobsson. The Japanese bonus-track *Captured* was originally written in 1984 for the third **Overdrive**-album. In 1998 a heavy **King's X**-influenced version of the classic Christmas-carol *Silent Night* was released on the compilation *Released By X-mas*. In 1999 Mats left the band and was replaced by Peter "TrumPeter" Svensson (ex-**Mercy, Faith, Constancia**), and the band was featured on the **Captain Beyond**-tribute *Thousand Days Of Yesterdays* (99 - Record Heaven), covering *I Can't Feel Nothing Part 1 and Part 2*. A cover of **Europe**'s *Scream Of Anger* was also featured on the *Power From The North* (99 Digital Dimension) compilation. In June 2000 drummer Peter left and was replaced by 20-year-old Jimmy Lexe (son of Kjell Jacobsson!) and the band recorded a cover of **Thin Lizzy**'s *Warriors* for *The Spirit Of The Black Rose – A Tribute To Phil Lynott* (01 Record Heaven). In September 2001 singer Herman Saming was replaced by the more rough-edged Mattias Osbäck. *Heavy Machinery* contains guest-spots from Nord, Denander, Eklundh, Roland Grapow (ex-**Helloween, Masterplan**) and Pontus Norgren (**Humanimal, Talisman, Great King Rat, Hammerfall**, solo etc.). A cover of **Target**'s *Can't Fake It* was also recorded for bonus-purposes. In reviews *Train Of Events* was described as a "straight **Dream Theater** meets **Thin Lizzy**", while *Heavy Machinery* is far heavier, with a more **King's X**-ish vibe. A demo version of *Sacred Alien* with Herman on vocals can be found on the bonus-CD for the second Encyclopedia. In 2003 Rivel Records reissued *Train Of Events*, but removed the **Jethro Tull** cover in favour of four demo-tracks from the *Heavy Machinery* pre-production, featuring Herman Saming. In 2003 Kronsell left the band and drummer Lexe was replaced by Ted Wernersson (**Mandrake Root, Groover**). When it was time to record the *Change Of Tracks* album, no permanent bass player had been found so Marcel Jacob (**Talisman, Humanimal, Rising Force** etc) stepped in to record bass for the album. *Change Of Track* was a more straigh- ahead melodic metal album compared to bands like **Talisman**. The album features guest spots from Mattias Ia Eklundh, Hank Shermann (**Fate, Mercyful Fate**), Lars Eric Mattsson and Tommy Denander. The band made some live shows featuring bassist Mats "Staa" Petersson (**Deception**) and second guitarist David Blomé (**Unchained, Stacy's Inn**). In 2011 the band regrouped, featuring Janne, Mattias and drummer Peter "TrumPeter" Svensson, to record the track *Rise Up* for the Japan benefit album *Embraced By The Sun*. New material is in the making, planned to be released in 2014... or -15.

The final four trainees

2012 CD - VSP 034

459

1997 ☐	TRAIN OF EVENTS	CD	Bluestone Music	BSM 1012
1998 ☐	TRAIN OF EVENTS	CD	Avex (Japan)	AVCB-66030
	Bonus: Captured			
2002 ☐	HEAVY MACHINERY	CD	Record Heaven	RHCD 64
	Slipcase.			
2002 ■	HEAVY MACHINERY	CD	Sweden Rock Records	SRR001
	Bonus: Can't Fake It (Target cover)			
2003 ☐	TRAIN OF NEW EVENTS	CD	Rivel Records	RRCD 011
2005 ☐	CHANGE OF TRACK	CD	Lion Music	LMC 153
2005 ☐	CHANGE OF TRACK	CD	Irond (Russia)	CD 05-DD328

2001 CD - SRR001

LOHENGRIN

Ulf Thunberg: v, Svante Stenberg: g, Jonte Eliasson: g,
Jan Bengtsson: b, Maths Sundwall: k, Lasse Eliasson: d

Halmstad - Lohengrin play symphonic rock, where the B-side is a pretty heavy rocker and the A-side much mellower. Jan Bengtsson was later in progg/punksters *Unos Kanoner*.

1980 ■	En ny vision	7"	KAP Records	KAPS 8002
	Tracks: A New Vision/Opiumrökarens sista cigg			

1980 7" - KAPS 8002

LOK

Martin Westerstrand: v, Thomas Brandt: g, Daniel Cordero: b, Johan Reivén: d

Göteborg - The band was formed in 1995 by Westerstrand (ex-*Psychobetabuckdown*) and former *Hyperhug* bassist Reivén. Brutal powerful metal with hardcore energy in the vein of *B-Thong* meets *Rage Against The Machine* with rap-oriented vocals in Swedish. Bloody great! Reivén has also previously recorded with *Transport League*. The first two albums were produced by Roberto Laghi (*B-Thong, Transport League* etc) which guarantees a lead heavy sound. The first release was the first price of the Partille Rocken competition. It was recorded at Studio Fredman. Thomas has previously been found in *Judas Priest* tribute band *Just As Priest*. The title of the debut (translates to naked, blastered and pissed off), was decided through a competition. The band's second album, *Sunk 500*, was not as strong as the debut, while the band's last album *Ut ur discot och in i verkligheten* (out of the disco and into reality) is their best album. When the live album *Blästrad levande* was released the band had already decided to call it quits. Westerstrand and Cordero went on to form the band *Rallypack*, singing in English. After one album, the band changed name to *Lillasyster* and now returned to the style of *LOK*. Reivén was later in the bands *Kneget* and *Zen Monkey*. A cover of punksters *Bumsen Muss Man*'s *Lärarjävlar* is featured on the compilation *Äggröran 5*, while a cover of *Nationalteaterns* song *Lägg av* is found on the tribute album *National Sånger*.

1996 MCD - PRCD 006

1996 ■	Ord och inga visor	MCD 6tr	private	PRCD 006
	Tracks: Experiment/Som nn hund/Rosa/Natten till i morgon (Den här är till fig)/Plyschbeklädd/Rosendröm. 500 copies.			
1998 ☐	Lokpest/Bygg din båt/Jätteklen	MCD 3tr	Sonet	567 038-2
1998 ☐	LOK står när de andra faller/re-mix	CDS 2tr	Sonet	563 056-2
	Bonus: Videos of Lokpest and LOK står när de andra faller			
1999 ☐	Skrubbsår/Plyschbeklädd/Rosa	MCD 3tr	Sonet	567 780-2
1999 ☐	Ensam gud	MCD 5tr	Sonet	561 110-2
	Tracks: Ensam gud/Rosendröm (live)/Lokpest (live)/Skrubbsår (live)/LOK står när de andra faller (live)			
1999 ■	NAKEN, BLÄSTRAD OCH SKITSUR	CD	Sonet	555 908-2
2000 ☐	Stänkskärmar och sprit	MCD 3tr	Stockholm	156 735-2
	Tracks: Stänkskärmar och sprit/Kompanjoner/Blästrad Levande 1999: Del 1 Stelopererad Frihetsrörelse (MPEG)			
2000 ☐	Bedragaren i Murmansk	MCD 3tr	Stockholm	156 967-2
	Tracks: Bedragaren i Murmansk, plus two videos: Stänkskärmar och sprit and Sommar, Lång från Murmansk (Del 2)			
2000 ☐	SUNK 500	CD	Stockholm	157 474-2
2001 ☐	Staden Göteborg (split)/Stänkskärmar och sprit (live)	MCD 3tr	MNW	MNWCDS 302
	LOK+ Hardcore Superstar recorded this together.			
2002 ☐	Sug min (radio edit)/Sug min (folkets)/Blästrad levande 2002 (video)	CDS	Stockholm	015 733-2
2002 ☐	Pyromandåd i ponnyslakteriet/16007340/Tommys ponny	MCD 3tr	Stockholm	019 106-2
2002 ■	UT UR DISCOT OCH IN I VERKLIGHETEN	CD	Stockholm	017 147-2
2003 ☐	BLÄSTRAD LEVANDE	CD	Stockholm	067 748-2

1999 CD - 555 908-2

2002 CD - 017 147-2

LOMMI

Jens Florén: v/g, Dennis Österdal: b, Jörgen Tjusling: d

Göteborg - Lommi is a power trio featuring Österdal and Tjusling who have played together in bands like *Elsy Band*, *Human Race* and are both also in *Eaglestrike*. *Lommi* plays detuned riff metal with a touch of *Black Label Society*. Good stuff!

2012 ■	LIFE IN SEPIA	CDp	private	LOMMI001

2012 CDp - LOMMI001

LONELY HEARTS

Göran Werner: v/g, Christer Ericsson: v/b, Torbjörn "T.L" Lindberg: g, Per Stappe: d

Borås - A young band with quite big potential formed in 1982 and split in 1986. The A-side is a traditional up-tempo eighties metal song with good vocals from Göran. Keyboard player Håkan Werner, brother of Göran (married to singer Jill Jonsson) was only a session musician on the 7". Stappe later played in **Loud** and works as a sound engineer with John Norum, among others. Christer passed away of cancer from 1987.

1984 ■ Lonely Heart/One More Night ....7" Hard Rock Café .... HRC 001

1984 7" - HRC 001

LONG JOHN

Johan Söderman: v/g, Ted Stenlöv: b, Patrik Andersson: d

Eksjö - Johan and Ted started playing in 1979, and Patrik joined in 1983. **Long John** play blues/boogie based hard rock, like **Status Quo**-meet-**ZZ Top**, and the single was recorded by the Wahlquist brothers (**Heavy Load**) in Thunderload Studios. Patrik sadliy died of cancer in 2008. Johan and Ted are today in **ZZ Top** cover band **Mancamp**. Ted also played with **Dorian Grey**.

1985 ■ Ready To Rock/Let It Be ....7" private .... (501)

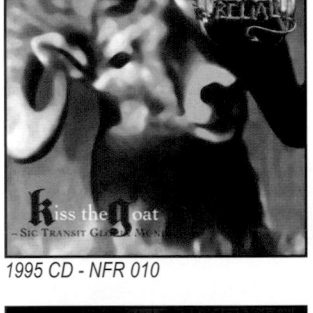

1985 7" - (501)

LORD BELIAL

Thomas "Dark" Backelin: v/g, Niclas "Pepa/Vassago" Andersson: g/v, Anders "Bloodlord" Backelin: b, Mikael "Sin" Backelin: d

Hedekas (Trollhättan) - It all started already back in 1989 when Mikael, Thomas and Anders formed a band. They went under several names, but in December 1992, with Niclas also in the line-up, they became **Lord Belial**. Mikael and Niclas were in the band **Sadist** around 1987 and Thomas was in **Satanized**, together with Jon Nödtveit around 1991, and he was also previously in **Decameron**. **Lord Belial** recorded their first demo *The Art Of Dying* in 1993 and the follow up, *Into The Frozen Shadows* in 1994. This is very black metal with highly satanic lyrics. One odd thing compared to other black metal/death metal bands at the time was the use of flute, even though it's hardly ever heard. Fredrik "Plague" Wester, who is also found in **Mastema** together with Thomas, joined in 2000. He replaced Niclas, who joined the band again one month after *Angelgrinder* was recorded. *Angelgrinder* is a pretty diverse album ranging from ultra-speed to doom and even symphonic passages. Niclas and Mikael are also found in **Vassago**. A cover of **Bathory**'s *Massacre* is found on *In Conspiracy With Satan – Tribute To Bathory* and **Iron Maiden**'s *The Trooper* was featured on the Japanese tribute *Made In Tribute*. The song *Purify Sweden* was removed from the album by the label as they figured it was a racist song. According to Thomas it is not racist at all, but deals with the multitude of religions that poisons the country. "We are not a political band", as he says. Even though he sent the lyrics to the label, they felt the title was a bit too provocative. On *The Seal Of Belial* the line-up featured Thomas, Anders, guitarist Hjalmar Nielsen and drummer Daniel "Mojjo" Moilanen (**Engel, Runemagick, Dracena, Relevant Few, Sandalinas**). In 2006, and subsequently on *Revelation The 7th Seal*, Pepa was back in the line-up, and the album also featured guests like Tony Jelencovich, Daniel "DD Executioner" Johansson (**Diabolicum, Angst, Kill Sadistic Grimness**), Jonas "Yonas Af" Dahlström (**Illwill**) and Andy LaRoque. *Ancient Demons* is a compilation containing the first two demos. On *The Black Curse* the band was again a foursome. In January 2009 **Lord Belial** officially split up, mainly because Mikael had a tinnitus problem. The band however reunited in mid-2010, but in August 2011 they again announced the band was now on hold. Mikael Backelin is today in the band **HEX**.

1995 CD - NFR 010

1997 CD - NFR 020

1999 CD - NFR 033

2003 MCD - MFE 006

Praise the lords!

Year		Title	Format	Label	Cat. No.
1995	■	KISS THE GOAT	CD	No Fashion Records	NFR 010
1995	□	KISS THE GOAT	CD	Metal Blade (USA)	3984-14287-2
1995	□	KISS THE GOAT	CD	Toy's Factory (Japan)	TFCK 88752
		Bonus: Bleed On The Cross (demo)			
1997	□	ENTER THE MOONLIGHT GATE	CDd	No Fashion Records	NFR 020
1997	■	ENTER THE MOONLIGHT GATE	CD	No Fashion Records	NFR 020
1997	□	ENTER THE MOONLIGHT GATE	CD	Metal Blade (USA)	3984-14160-2
1999	■	UNHOLY CRUSADE	CD	No Fashion Records	NFR 033
1999	□	UNHOLY CRUSADE	CD	Metal Blade (USA)	3984-14286-2
2002	□	Doomed By Death (split)	7"	Aftermath Music	Chapter XVII
		Split with Runemagick. Track: Scythe Of Death. 666 numbered copies.			
2002	□	ANGELGRINDER	CD	No Fashion Records	NFR 058
2002	□	ANGELGRINDER	LP	No Fashion Records	NFRLP 058
2003	□	Purify Sweden/Come To The Sabbath (Mercyful Fate cover)	7" PD	Metal Fortress	MFE 004
		300 copies.			
2003	■	Scythe Of Death	MCD 4tr	Metal Fortress	MFE 006
		Tracks: Scythe Of Death/Black Void/Possessed Of Fire/Purify Sweden (bonus)1666 copies.			
2003	□	ENTER THE MOONLIGHT GATE	CD	Irond (Russia)	CD 03-423
2004	■	THE SEAL OF BELIAL	CD	Regain Records	RR 049
2005	□	THE SEAL OF BELIAL	CD	CD-Maximum (Russia)	CDM 1204-2165
2005	□	THE SEAL OF BELIAL	CD	Candlelight (USA)	CDL 024 CD
2006	■	NOCTURNAL BEAST	CD	Regain Records	RR 075
2007	□	REVELATION – THE 7TH SEAL	CD	Regain Records	RR 114
2007	□	REVELATION – THE 7TH SEAL	CD	Regain Records (USA)	REG-CD-1006
2007	□	REVELATION – THE 7TH SEAL	CD	CD-Maximum (Russia)	CDM-0707-2727
2008	□	ANCIENT DEMONS	CD	Regain Records	RR 084
2008	□	THE BLACK CURSE	CD	Regain Records	RR 146
2008	□	THE BLACK CURSE	CD	Regain Records (USA)	REG-CD-1986
2008	□	THE BLACK CURSE	CD	Paranoid Records (Brazil)	??

2004 CD - RR 049

2006 CD - RR 075

LORÉNE

Jari Laakso: g, Anders Kiel: g, Jocke Andersson: b, Micael Lundberg: v/d

Göteborg - Decent AOR. The first single is up-tempo poppy hard rock quite reminiscent of **Snowstorm**, while the second is a bit similar to heavier **Saga** at times. Very traditional 80s sound and style.

Year		Title	Format	Label	Cat. No.
1981	■	Nattrock/Tina	7"	Mariann	LSPS 102
1983	○	Sommardagar/Häxor	7"	private	LE 1002
		Promo. No artwork.			

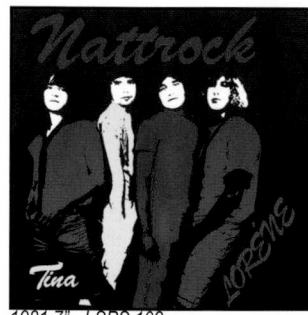

1981 7" - LSPS 102

LOS BOHEMOS

Perre Lindberg: v/g, Peter Kvist: g, Peter Lundström: b, Mikael Forsberg: d

Gävle - The band started out as a punk band and released a couple of singles, but the latest releases are in the vein of early **Soundgarden**. The album *Into Dreamland* contains a cover of **Cheap Trick**'s *He's A Whore*.

Year		Title	Format	Label	Cat. No.
1991	■	INTO DREAMLAND	LP	Birdnest	BIRD 026
1993	□	SOULSURFER	CD	Arda	REXCD 115
1993	□	BOSS DRUM EP	MCD 5tr	Arda	CDTAR 025
		Tracks: Boss Drum/Naked Man/Reactivate/Shower At 5000/Overdrive At 5000			

1991 LP - BIRD 026

LOS SIN NOMBRE

Pär Palm: v, Jack Karlsson: b, Saul Camara: g,
Martin Fogander: g, Linus Melchiorsen: d

Linköping - **Los Sin Nombre** were formed by Saul, Jack, drummer Steve Mills and guitarist Arvid Sjögedahl in 2002. They started out playing **Entombed** covers, but successively started writing their own material. In September 2002 they recorded their first four-track demo *Tate Murders*. After this guitarist Jimmie Fornel replaced Arvid. The demo was followed by *Down With Pressure* in 2004, *Demo '05* in 2005 and *Another Dark Place Of Hate* in 2007, before being signed by ViciSolum. In 2006 Olle Dickson had replaced drummer Mills. The last demo was recorded in Studio RecLab, owned by Melchorisen and Fogander. When Dickson and Fornell left after the demo, the studio owners replaced them, putting a halt to their former band **Maitreya**. The debut is a well-produced melodic death metal power pack in the vein of **Soilwork**, **Lamb Of God** or **Dark Tranquillity**. Melchiorsen is ex-**Isengard**, **Demented** and **Powerdise**. The demo track *Chain Reaction* can be found on the *Demobanken 2006* (06 Studiefrämjandet) compilation.
Website: www.lossinnombre.se

Year		Title	Format	Label	Cat. No.
2009	■	BLIND LEADING BLIND	CD	ViciSolum	VSP 008

2009 CD - VSP 008

LOSS

Matte Andersson: v, Jan Jansson: g, Ulf "Blappan" Jansson: b, Kjell Elmlund: d

Karlstad - Formed in September 2000. Death metal with a touch of early *Entombed*. Their demo CD-R *Human Decay* was demo of the year in Close Up Magazine in 2000 and the track *Enclosure* was featured on Close Up Magazine's *Soundcheck #43* compilation. On the 2004 promo, *No Sanity Left* Matte Andersson (*Godgory, Grave Flowers*) had replaced singer Hugo Bryngfors and on *Hateinfected* guitarist Sven-Erik "Fritte" Fritiofsson was out of the band. Matte is also president of Khaoz Star Records. *Loss* is not to be confused with the US doom band. Elmlund, Jansson and Jansson are also in *Mental Crypt*. The two latter were also in *Fester Plague*, and Jan is also in *Grave Flowers*. The band has also been featured on the compilations *The Iron Force*, *Metal Ostenation* and *The Iron Force 2*.

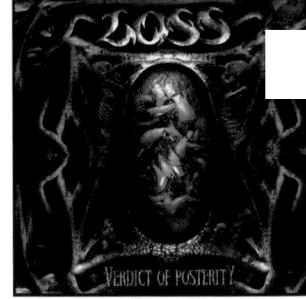
2001 CD - SC 029-2

2001 ■	VERDICT OF POSTERITY	CD	Scarlet	SC 029-2
2007 □	HATEINFECTED	CD	Khaoz Star Records	KSR 003

LOST HORIZON

Daniel Heiman: v, Wojtek Lisicki: g, Fredrik Olsson: g,
Attila Publik: k, Martin Furängen: b, Christian Nyqvist: d

Göteborg/Borås - The band was formed in 1990 under the name *Highlander*, also featuring Michael Nicklasson (*Dark Tranquillity*), Joacim Cans, Patrik Räfling and Stefan Elmgren later in *Hammerfall*, and Niclas Lideskär Johnsson (*Full Strike, Jaggernaut*). In 1993 the band was put on hold, but resurrected in 1998, at first under the *Highlander* banner, but soon changed to *Lost Horizon* due to ideological reasons. The band takes the genre a step further with great arrangements and some original ideas. Highly recommended. On *A Flame To The Ground Beneath*, Fredrik Olsson joined on second guitar and keyboardist Attila Publik was added to the line-up. The album really showcases the band's great potential. Great song material, well-played and performed. After the second album Lisicki left the band, but returned after one year. Heiman and Olsson left and formed *Heed* and the band went into a state of limbo. Heiman has also been in *Conviction*, *Crystal Eyes* and is today found in *Lavett*. Furängen and Lisicki are ex-*Luciferion*. Lisicki is also known from *Against The Plagues* and *Jaggernaut*.

2001 CDS - LH 1

2001 CD - CDMFN 261

2001 ■	Awakening The World – The Sampler	CDSp 2tr	Music For Nations	LH 1
	Promo. Tracks: Heart Of Storm/Welcome Back			
2001 ■	AWAKENING THE WORLD	CD	Music For Nations	CDMFN 261
2001 □	AWAKENING THE WORLD	CD	Victor (Japan)	VICP 61274
2001 □	AWAKENING THE WORLD	CD	Koch Records (USA)	KOCCD 8261
2002 □	Cry Of A Restless Soul	CDSp	Music For Nations	LH2
	Promo.			
2003 ■	A FLAME TO THE GROUND BENEATH	CD	Music For Nations	CDMFN 289
2003 □	A FLAME TO THE GROUND BENEATH	CD	Victor (Japan)	VICP 62040
2003 □	A FLAME TO THE GROUND BENEATH	CD	Koch Records (USA)	KOCCD 8656
2007 □	A FLAME TO THE GROUND BENEATH	CD	Zomba Music	88697066382

2003 CD - CDMFN 289

LOST SOULS

Christer Salling: v, Peter Hägglund (now Lans): g,
Michael Hahne: g, Mats "Matte" Järnil: b, Theo Savidis: d

Uppsala - Formed in 1991. Their first recording was the track *Powermad* on the *15 On 1* compilation (Soundfront 91) after which they recorded the 1992 demo. The band then drafted ex-*Damien* bassist Mats "Marre Martini" Eriksson (later in *Misery Loves Co*) and the style was far more melodic than later on. The album contains powerful high quality thrash-core similar to *Ministry* and *Pantera*. On the debut ex-*Midas Touch/Kapoor*-man Patrik Sporrong handled the bass, but in 1995 he was replaced by Matte Järnil, ex-*Crawley*. *Soundfront Releases 95* contains two non-CD tracks. The *Motörhead*-cover *Sweet Revenge* is featured on the compilation-CD *Motörhead Tribute* (95 Pink Honey). *Fracture* was produced by Daniel Bergstrand (*Crawley, Meshuggah* etc.) and on this album guitarist Michael Hahne was out of the band. The album was also more mallcore metal and received some pretty bad reviews. After having been a techno metal-oriented band, they used live drums on the third album. Savidis and Hägglund later joined thrashers *F.K.Ü.* Järnil, who was also in *The Duskfall*, is today found in *Helltrain*, while Hägglund also plays in *Valley Of The Dead*. The last known line-up featured Salling, Järnil, Hägglund (now Lans), guitarist Magnus Söderman (*Slapdash, Rosicrusian, Leech, Zeelion*) and drummer Perra Johansson (*Crawley, Lafayette*). The band folded in 2000 and went on to be resurrected as *Inrage*, featuring Järnil and Salling.

1994 CD - FRONTCD 7

1996 CD - RR 8883 2

1994 ■	Never Promised You A Rosegarden	CD	Soundfront	FRONTCD 7
1994 □	Soundfront Releases 94 (split)	CDSp	Soundfront	FRONTPR 1
	Split with Crawley. Track: Lost Found Lost			
1995 □	Soundfront Releases Spring 95 (split)	MCD	Soundfront	FRONTPR 2
	Split with Crawley and Buckshot OD. Tracks: Close Your Mind/Life Beyond Flesh			
1996 ■	CLOSEYOUREYESANDITWONTHURT	CD	Soundfront/Roadrunner	RR 8883 2
1998 ■	FRACTURE	CD	Nuclear Blast	NB 294-2

1998 CD - NB 294-2

LOTHLORIEN

Henrik Serholt: v, Tobias Birgersson: g, Linus Wikström: g,
Tobias Johansson: b, Daniel Hannendahl: d

Varberg - Heavy progressive metal with furious growling death vocals. Interesting songs with lots of harmony guitars and well-arranged keyboards. Produced by Chris Silver. The band also recorded the demo *In The Depth Of Thee Mourning* in 1996. Singer Serhold was also in **Fatal Embrace**. Hannendahl, Birgersson and Wikström formed melodic power metal band **Frequency** in 2002, with whom they have made several releases.

1998 ■ THE PRIMAL EVENT..CD   Black Mark .... BMCD 133

1998 CD - BMCD 133

LOTUS

Anders Åhlund: v, Kjell Danielsson: g, Ulf Pettersson: k,
Göran Hansson: b, Lasse Vänngård: d

Söderhamn - The band was formed in 1987 and made a few demos before recording the single. Great melodic hard rock with high-pitched vocals. Ulf is now found in **Galleon** and Lasse is in cover band **Rocktools**. Anders plays in the soul band **Grooveyard** and recorded a single with **Nasty Groove** and an album with **Saigon**. Not to be confused with the below band or another **Lotus** that released a single on the same label, entitled *Lotus Part 1&2*.

1988 ■ She Don't Want You Anymore/Love The Way..7"   Platina..PL 36

1988 7" - PL 36

LOTUS

Niklas Börjesson: v/g, Tomas Modig: b, Hans Eriksson: d

Göteborg - This band previously released a MCD under the name **Fruitcake**. Modig hasd also previously recorded with punk bands like **P-Nissarna**, **Likbas**, **Kachina Dance** and **Overland Stage Riders**, who all recorded demos, except **P-Nissarna** who made some vinyls, too. **Lotus** plays heavy, psychedelic, riff-oriented 70s hard rock with hints of **Led Zeppelin**, **Mountain** etc. Power trio is a highly suitable description. Brian "Robbo" Robertson (ex-**Thin Lizzy**) guests on all but the first album. A cover of **Captain Beyond**'s *Mesmerization Eclipse* can also be found on *Thousand Days Of Yesterdays - A Tribute To Captain Beyond* (99 Record Heaven). On *Quartet Conspiracy* "Robbo" appears as a special guest member on the entire album. The co-operation was however a bit strained towards the end of the recording sessions. *Complete Fruitage* is a reissue of *Fruitage* with 8 previously unreleased bonus tracks – a gem! *Roots* contains covers of **Blue Öyster Cult**, **Kiss**, **Deep Purple**, **Led Zeppelin** etc. and it was produced by Martin Kronlund (**Dogface**) at JM Studio. After **Lotus** called it a day, Tomas recorded some demos with **The White Negroes**, an album with **Skyron** and is now in hard rock 'n rollers **Speedfreaks**.

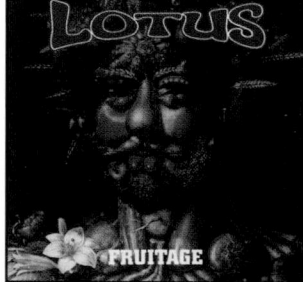

1997 CD - RHCD4

1997 ■	FRUITAGE	CD	Record Heaven	RHCD4
1997 □	FRUITAGE	LP PD	Record Heaven	RHPD11
1999 ■	A TASTER FOR THE BIG ONE	CD	Record Heaven	RHMCD 1
1999 ■	Mesmerization Eclipse/Orange Sunshine	7"	Record Heaven	RH7 2
	Red vinyl.			
2000 □	QUARTET CONSPIRACY	CD	Record Heaven	RHCD 27
2000 □	Butterfly Effect	MCD 3tr	Record Heaven	RHCDM 10
	Tracks: Butterfly Effect/Granny Smith & Wesson/Green Power			
2000 □	COMPLETE FRUITAGE	CD	Record Heaven	RHCD 37
2001 □	ROOTS	CD	Record Heaven	RHMCD 2

1999 CD - RHMCD 1

1999 7" - RH/ 2

LOUD

Karin Sjögren: v, Fredrik Åberg: g, Lennart Östlund: g,
Fredrik Bergenstråhle: b, Peer Stappe: d

Boden/Stockholm - Karin started writing pop songs in the 90s and wrote her first rock song as late as 2003. Two years later she went **Loud**! **Loud** play quite commercial, but heavy modern rock/hard rock. Some tracks are a bit too close to modern dance for comfort, but some tracks rock pretty good with a heavy vibe to them. Great powerful singer, too. After the album the band changed singer to Linnea Helgé (aka Liny Wood) and their name to **1 Louder**. A new album was recorded with Linnéa, but hasn't been released so far. Karin is now in acoustic popsters **Blue Utopia**. A second album with **Loud** featuring Karin has also been recorded and finished, just waiting to be released. Bergenstråhle is ex-**Kerberos**, while Stappe has played with **Lonely Hearts**, **Rydell & Quick**, plus he is working with John Norum.

2005 CDS - NATCDS 105

2005 ■	Enemy/To Myself	CDS	National	NATCDS 105
2005 □	Selected/Safe And Sound	CDS	National	NATCDS 106
2005 ■	QUICK FIX	CD	National	NATCD 053

2005 CD - NATCD 053

LOUD 'N' NASTY

Robban "Rob Nasty" Jonasson: b/v, Kristoffer "Chris Loud": g,
Tommy "Tommie Rocker/T-Bone" Svanbo: d

Tanumshede - Rob and Chris were previously playing in a *Kiss*-cover band called *Kissin' Time*. Rob was also in *Mötley Crüe* cover band *Bastards*, punksters *Kokt Grus* and later formed *Sin On Skin*. He is also a tattoo artist. This band evolved into *Loud 'N' Nasty* in 1998. The same year they recorded their first 12-track self-entitled demo CD-R, and the following year they unearthed the 2-track demo CD *Hellbound/Sweet Sixteen*. The band is very close to early *Mötley Crüe* in style, sound and looks for that matter. True glam-metal, loud and raunchy, as it's supposed to be. The last MCD was produced by Snowy Shaw and mixed by Kee Marcello. After this, Snowy Shaw replaced drummer Svanbo and bassist Micael Grimm joined. The band later evolved into *XXX*, now featuring Shaw, Robban and Kristoffer.
Website: www.loudnnasty.com

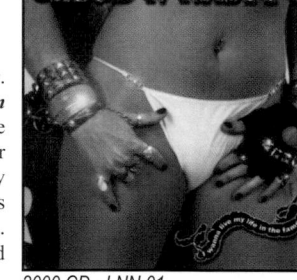

2000 CD - LNN 01

2000	■	I WANNA LIVE MY LIFE IN THE FAME	CD	private	LNN 01
2002	■	Too Much Ain't Enough	MLP 6tr	Hellbound Recordings	LNN 02
		Tracks: Too Much Ain't Enough/Me And The Boys/You Better Run/Little Miss Pretty/Clown Of The Town/Leave Me Alone			
2002	■	Too Much Ain't Enough	MLP 6tr PD	Hellbound Recordings	LNN 02
		Poster.			
2004	□	TEASER TEASER	CD	Perris Records	PER 01392
2005	□	TOO MUCH AIN'T ENOUGH	CD	Perris Records	PER 01552
		Bonus: Sweet Sixteen/Hellbound			
2007	□	No One Rocks Like You	MCDp 3tr	Swedmetal	SM-02-CDS
		Tracks: No One Rocks Like You/Nasty Girls/You Make My World Go Around			

2002 MLP - LNN 02

LOUDHELL

Daniel Holmgren: g/v, Björn Hansén: g/v, Fredrik Lind: b, Björn Stenmark: d

Vuollerim - Slow and heavy rock in the vein of *Danzig* with a singer reminiscent of Jim Morrison. On the cover it says "The biggest thanks to Daniel Holmgren 1974-1995 for our years together", which leads to believe he is no longer with us.

1995	■	Loudhell	MCD 5tr	private	LHCDS 395
		Tracks: End Of Discussion/Heroin-A/Walk Away/Aerie Collapse/XS Cumosity.			

1995 MCD - LHCDS 395

LOVE CHILD

Tomas Hermansson: v, Anthony Cedergren: g, Tony Westgård: b, Jens Persson: d

Karlskoga - *Love Child* were formerly known as *Trazy*, under which name they contributed with the track *See The Light* on the *Rock Of Sweden* compilation in 1989. They changed their name to *Love Child* just before the release of the CD. At that time they were a five-piece also featuring second guitarist Mikael Folkesson. The album contains some high-class sleaze-tainted AOR in the vein of *Skid Row*. The album was only released in Japan. Tony later formed the band *Seven Wishes* and also played in cover band *Loud Inc.* together with Pete Blakk.

1994 CD - ALCB-3014

1994	■	LOVE CHILD	CD	Brunette/Alfa (Japan)	ALCB-3014

LOVE INJECTION

Helen Polstam: v, Seppo (Räftegård) Toivanen: g,
Thomas Johansson: b, Stefan Tyresten: d

Kristinehamn - *Morning Train* is standard rock while *City Hall* is more punkish hard rock/metal. Weak vocals and definitely only for completists. Seppo is now playing in a blues band and a pop duo.

1989	■	Morning Train/City Hall	7"	private	TJS 8911

1989 7" - TJS 8911

LOVEBONE

Roger Lindroth: v, Janne Lenéll: g, Conny Kokkonen: g,
Peder Skoglund: b, André Nyvoll: d

Sundsvall - This band was formed in 1987 under the name *Mystery*. The style was AOR and the sound was really professional. They recorded a 7" in 1988. As the style, sound and drummer had changed they decided to change their name to *Lovebone* just before the release of this CD. Powerful sleaze rock quite similar to *Skid Row* and *Mötley Crüe*, but with "cleaner" vocals. Contains some great tracks. Check it out. The MCD has become quite a collector's item.

1994 MCD - LBCDS 9404

1994	■	Shit Happens When You Party Naked	MCD 5tr	private	LBCDS 9404	$$
		Tracks: Ain't Your Business/Living In The Shades/Be My Downfall/Crazy Spin/10 Sec Love				

LOVEHANDLES

Johan Widerberg: v, Mikael Johannesson: g,
Timo Nilsson: g, Mikael Delén: b, Jens Frank: d

Malmö - The idea for *Lovehandles* was conceived already in 1995 by former *Emerald* members Delén and Widerberg, who drafted drummer Frank (*Sloppy Baboons, Noble Life*). In 2003 Mikael Johannesson (*Tippen Ruda, Mandala, Sloppy Baboons, Double Eclipse*) moved back to Malmö after some years in Stockholm, and he was in. In 2006 guitarist Timo Nilsson approached Johan asking if he was interested in resurrecting their old band *Emerald*, but the project crashed before departure. Instead Timo was asked to join *Lovehandles* and the band was complete. They now went from playing covers to writing their own material. They made their debut in 2008. *Lovehandles* play heavy riff-oriented metal with a touch of *Black Label Society*, or as they label it themselves – Sumorock! Mikael is now also in UK hard rockers *Evilyn Strange*. *www.lovehandles.se*

2008 MCD - - -

2010 CDd - BADASS 1

2008 ■	… To Do Before We're Dead	MCD 5tr	Love Music		- -
	Tracks: Scared/Save Your Soul/B-Tune/Backstabber/Can't Go On				
2010 ■	LOVEHANDLES	CDd	Lipservice	BADASS1	

LOVER UNDER COVER

Mikael Erlandsson: v, Martin Kronlund: g, Mikael Carlsson: b/k, Perra Johansson: d

Göteborg - Band or project? Well, today there's a fine line. Let's say these boys do appear in other bands, too. Erlandsson in *Last Autumn's Dream*, ex-*Crash*, Kronlund in *Reece Kronlund*, *Gypsy Rose, Salute* etc and Johansson in *Coldspell*. The album also features guest spots from *Coldspell* colleague Michael Larsson, Ged Rylands and *Jorn* guitarist Tor Erik Myhre. *Set The Night On Fire* is a nice slab of melodic hard rock, placing themselves somewhere in-between *Coldspell*'s 70s sounding hard rock and the AOR of *Last Autumn's Dream*. In the vein of *Bangalore Choir*, actually.

2012 CD - ESM 246

2012 ■	SET THE NIGHT ON FIRE	CD	Escape	ESM 246

LOWRIDER

Ola Hellquist: g/v, Niclas Stålfors: g, Peder Bergstrand: b/v, Andreas Eriksson: d

Karlstad - Stoner rock in the vein of *Kyuss* or Swedish colleagues *The Awesome Machine* and *The Mushroom River Band*. Heavy and nice. The band was formed in the mid-nineties. The song *Saguaro* can be found on two compilations on Molten Universe and High Beam/Freebird Records. A new album was due in 2003, but hasn't appeared yet.

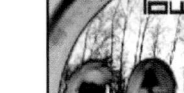

2000 CD - PRISON 996-2

1999 ☐	DOUBLE EP (split)	CD	People Like You	PRISON 995-2
	Split with Nebula. Tracks: Lameneshma/The Gnome The Serpent The Sun/Shivaree/ Upon The Dune. Picture-CD.			
1999 ☐	DOUBLE EP (split)	LP	People Like You	PRISON 995-1
1999 ☐	DOUBLE EP (split)	CD	Meteor City	MCY 004
1999 ☐	DOUBLE EP (split)	LP	Meteor City	MCY 004
	Poster.			
1999 ☐	DOUBLE EP	MLP 4tr	Cargo	CAR 001
	Tracks: Shivaree/Ol Mule Pepe/Upon The Dune/The Gnome The Serpent The Sun. Yellow/red marble vinyl.			
2000 ■	ODE TO IO	CD	People Like You	PRISON 996-2
2000 ☐	ODE TO IO	2LP	People Like You	PRISON 996-1

LUCID LEGEND

2010 MCD - LL2010

Daniel Johansson: v/g, Martin Nilsson: g, Filip Karlsson: b, Frans Karlsson: d

Vara - Formed in 2007, influenced by 70s and 80s hard rock and metal. The band recorded their first demo in 2007 and the track *Bottom Of The Swamp* was featured on the compilations *Kill City Vol. 9* (272 Records) and *Metal Downtown International Vol. 1* (Quick Star Productions). Late 2009, the band took a break as singer/guitarist Daniel moved to Los Angeles to study at MI in Hollywood. Upon his return in 2010 the band released their self-financed debut and also signed a deal with Record Union for digital releases.
Website: www.myspace.com/lucidlegend

2010 ■	Lucid Legend	MCD 7tr	private
	Tracks: Wasteland/Call Of The Wild/Demon Seed/My Heresy/Crumblin' Castle/Lovin' You Up/Lights Out. 400 copies.		

LUCIFER

Lars Thorsén: g, Mikael Andersson: g, Mikael Fasth: b, Johnny Fagerström: v/d

Mjölby - Death metal with a technical touch and very "evil" vocals. Johnny was also in *Belsebub*, but when they split he put his effort into *Lucifer*. At one time Mika Savimäki, also in *Belsebub* was in the line-up. They recorded an album in 1993, but split before its release. Johnny, Mikael and Mika formed the surf-punk band *Valium*. The band also appeared on *Phased Out* (94 BlackBoone Music). Johnny and Mikael were also in the band *Salvation*.

1993 ■	The Dark Christ	7"	Bellphegot (Mexico)	BELL 93002

Tracks: No Return/Endless Journey.

1993 7" - BELL 93002

LUCIFERION

Wojtek "Isko" Lisicki: v/g/k, Michael Nicklasson: v/g,
Martin Furängen: b, Hans Nilsson: d

Göteborg - Formed 1992 by guitarist/singer Lisicki, guitarist/singer Nicklasson and drummer Peter Andersson Weiner. Johan Lund played keyboards on the debut album. After the release of the debut, they were reinforced by bass-player Martin Furängen, while Peter was replaced by Liers In Wait/Crystal Age drummer Hans Nilsson. Michael and Peter were ex-*Sarcazm* and Michael was also briefly lead-singer in *Liers In Wait*. Wojtek and Michael were previously in the 80's metal band *Highlander* that only released two demos. The debut album contains high-speed death metal, quite close to *Deicide* and *Morbid Angel* in sound and style. In 1996 the band folded, mainly because of lack of the members' interest. Nicklasson joined *Dark Tranquillity*, while Lisicki and Furängen resurrected *Highlander*, changed the name to *Lost Horizon* and made several releases. Nilsson has been found in bands like *Dimenzion Zero*, *The Great Deceiver* and *Diabolique*. In 2002 the band was again resurrected, at first only to release some old unreleased demo material, but creativity prevailed and the result was an album that mixed the old demo and completely new compositions. The style is still high-speed death metal, but with a bit more finesse and a bit more use of keyboards. However Wojtek, with age, became opposed to all religious affiliation and therefore ended the band shortly after *The Apostate* was released. *Luciferion* covers *Fight Fire With Fire* on the *Metallica* tribute *Metal Militia* (94/04 Black Sun/Blackend). They also recorded *Blasphemer* for the *Sodom* tribute *Homage To The Gods* (99 Drakkar), *Chemical Warfare* for the *Slayer* tribute *Slatanic Slaughter II* (96/04 Black Sun/Blackend) and *Bramy Żądz* for the *KAT* tribute *Czarne Zastępy W Hołdzie KAT* (98 Pagan Records), featuring Snowy Shaw (*King Diamond*) and Sharlee D'Angelo (*King Diamond*) as guests. They also recorded a cover of the *Celtic Frost*-track *Circle Of The Tyrant* for a tribute that was never released. It later appeared on *The Apostate*.

1995 CD - POSH 007

2003 CD - POSH 049

1995 ■	DEMONICATION (THE MANIFEST)	CD	Listenable		POSH 007
2003 ■	THE APOSTATE	CD	Listenable		POSH 049
2003 □	THE APOSTATE	CD	Soundholic (Japan)		TKCS-85077

LUCKY STIFF

Torsten "Tott" Jacobsson: v, Dan Eriksson: g, Hans Diechle: b, Johan Mossberg: d

Göteborg - The first album was a weak and quite boring metal product, while the single was more up to date power metal, but weird. *Yahozna* is a Zappa-cover and *Simple Song* was written by *The Residents*, see... The album *E.Z.*, shows a band that has turned into *Pantera* meets *Biohazard* meets *Devo*. Actually it sounds great.

1988 □	Telephone To Nowhere/Fall Down	7"	Nonstop	NSM 4519
1991 □	D'ya Gotta Problem? Dance/The Night	7"	Nonstop/WEA	NSM 4529/9031-73945-7
1991 □	HEY MR BORING	LP	Nonstop/WEA	NSM 3311/9031-73740-1
1991 ■	HEY MR BORING	CD	Nonstop/WEA	NSM 3311/9031-73740-2
1994 □	Autonal Song/Hairy Organism/Yahozna/Simple Song	CDS 4tr	Helikopter	HELCD 16
1995 □	E.Z.	CD	Helikopter	HELCD 23

1991 CD - NSM 3311/9031-73740-2

LUCY

Torbjörn Enberg: v, Johan Jansson: g, Johnny Pettersson: g,
Mikael Brunzell: b, Fredrik Frykman: d

Kristinehamn - A mix of *Crimson Glory*, *Fifth Angel* and at times early *Dream Theater* played very well. The 5 track MCD *Fear* is well worth searching for. Witty title, huh? *Lucy - Fear*. Geddit? On the MCD singer Patrik Hjalmarsson had replaced Antti Mäkinen and bass player Marcus Calmborg had replaced Thomas Persson. The band is also featured with two tracks on the compilation-CD *Zalt* as well as the track *Abyss Of Despair* on the compilation *Jukebox Collection* (95 RFM). In 1995 singer Patrik Hjalmarsson was replaced by Torbjörn and bass-player Marcus Calmborg by Mikael. Before the last album they also changed guitarist from Tony Isaksson to Johnny. The last album can also be found as a demo-CD under the name *Moonshine*. The style was now closer to the likes of *Vicious Rumors* or early *Savatage*, unfortunately with rougher and not as precise vocals. Frykman later appeared in *Sabbtail* and in Alice Cooper cover band *Alice Troopers*. Johan Jansson was also in *Frenzy*.

1990 7" - NOVA S 190

1993 MCD - FEAR 03

| 1990 ■ | You're Gone/Unfaithful | 7" | Nova | NOVA S 190 |
| 1993 ■ | Fear | MCD 5tr | private | FEAR 03 |

Tracks: Fear/Nevertheless/On Fire/Dancing On A Minefield/Crawl To The Cross

| 1999 ■ | FRUITS FROM A POISONED TREE | CD | private | TLSCD 6499 |

1999 CD - TLSCD 6499

LUGNORO

Björn Hansson: v, Emil Rolof: g, Mikael Edebro: k, Filip Lange: b, Carl Baumann: d

Göteborg - Retro rockers *Lugnoro* ("peaceandcalm") were formed in 2007 by Rolof and bassist Antti Remes after their previous band *The Earth Machine Band* folded. Singer Hansson joined ranks and they tried various drummers before Antti took care of the drums for recording of the first demo in 2008. In May the same year Antti emigrated to Finland to build boats and the band recruited Edebro, Baumann and bassist Kim Stockfelt. In 2009 they released the pro-printed CD-R demo *Tellus*. Before the album Stockfelt was replaced by Lange. *Lugnoro* plays high-quality seventies-oriented progressive, riff-oriented hard rock similar to Swedish colleagues *Siena Root* and *Three Seasons*.
Website: www.lugnoro.com

2012 CDd - OZIUM 001

| 2012 ■ | ANNORSTÄDES | CDd | Ozium Records | OZIUM 001 |

LYNX

Mats Eriksson: v, Per Larsson: g, Mats Hermansson: k,
Kauno Vaattovaara: b, Carl Moser: d

Eskilstuna - This band hails from Eskilstuna, just like *Torch*, *Wizz*, *Lazy* and *Crystal Pride*. Some of the members were previously found in the band *Pegasus* who only recorded a demo. Carl had also recorded an album with *Dunder* in 1978. *Lynx* plays great *Purple*-influenced hard rock. Not to be confused with the Canadian pomp-rockers. In 1988 Imtrat/Rival Music released the compilation *Metal Hammer From Scandinavia* where *Lynx* are featured with five tracks.

1985 LP - MILL 5029

| 1985 □ | Caught In The Act/Kiss And Tell | 7" | private | n/a |
| 1985 ■ | CAUGHT IN THE TRAP | LP | Mill | MILL 5029 |

LÅNGFINGER

Victor Crusner: v/b/k, Kalle Lilja: g, Jesper Pihl: d

Göteborg - *Långfinger* (index finger) is a young trio formed in January 2008 on the shores of Göteborg. Influenced by the likes of *Mountain*, *Grand Funk*, *Captain Beyond* and *West Bruce & Laing*, they are rocking out in the true seventies manner. A great and very authentic band, despite their young age.

2010 CDd - BED001

| 2010 ■ | SKYGROUNDS | CDd | Beduin | BED001 |
| 2011 □ | Stare Me Blind | 10" 4tr | Beduin | ALC 033 |

Tracks: No Surrender/Slow Rivers/One Track Mind/Stare Me Blind

| 2012 □ | SLOW RIVERS | LP | Beduin | ALC035 |

LÖNNDOM

Andreas Petterson: v/g/b, Stefan Sandström: v/g/d

Boliden - Petterson is also found in *Armagedda*, *Volkermord*, *Leviathan* and *Whirling*. Sandström is in *LIK*, *Armagedda* and *Volkerrmord*. *Lönndom* (meaning secretly in Swedish) are quite far from all their other bands. This band nurtures the Swedish folk music inheritance and some tracks are just two acoustic guitars, while others are melancholic folk-oriented hard rock (not really metal) with deep folkish vocals. *Hågkomster från nordliga nejder & Norrskensritual* is a re-issue of the vinyl EP with the unreleased *Norrskensritual* recording.

2007 CD - NORDVIS 001

| 2007 ■ | FÄLEN FRÅN NORR | CD | Nordvis Produktion | NORDVIS 001 |
| 2008 □ | FÄLEN FRÅN NORR | LP+7" | Eisenwald Tonschmeide | EISEN 032 |

Bonus: 7" Hågkomster från nordliga nejder (below). Die hard edition 100 copies.

| 2008 □ | Hågkomster från nordliga nejder | 7" | Nordvis Produktion | - - |

Tracks: Smell mot det förmultnande/Omhuld av de underjordiska. 100 handnumbered copies available together with the above LP.

2008 □	FÄLEN FRÅN NORR	CD	Eisenwald Tonschmeide	EISEN 032
2010 □	VIDDERNAS TOLV KAPITEL	CD	Eisenwald Tonschmeide	EISEN 047
2010 □	Hågkomster från nordliga nejder & Norrskensritual	MCDdg 5tr	Those Opposed Records	TOR 025

Tracks: Intro/Smell mot det förmultnande/Omhuld av de underjordiska/Andlig själ utan kropp/Norrskensritual. Hand made embossed digipack.

| 2012 ■ | VIDDERNAS TOLV KAPITEL | 2LPg | Eisenwald Tonschmeide | EISEN 047 |

White vinyl. Poster.

| 2012 □ | Till Trevaren | MLP 3tr+MCD | Eisenwald Tonschmeide | EISEN 061 |

Tracks: I fallet/En stillastående vandring/Bårgå. Grey vinyl. Poster.

2012 2LPg - EISEN 047

M.A.C
Ola Wikström: v, Markus Gunnarsson: g, Andreas Holmberg: k,
Tomas Lundin: b, Krille Johansson: d
Ullared - **M.A.C** stands for Musical Art Creators, a name well suitable for this high-quality progressive, late *Yes*-meets-*Dream Theater*-sounding unit. A really interesting band with well-arranged and very well-played songs, however they initially had the same problem as for instance prog-fellows *Galleon* - the vocals is a weak link. On the second album the band had switched singer from Jörgen Carlsson to Ola and keyboardist from Andreas Holmberg to Jörgen. Markus is an outstanding guitarist. Unfortunately the band folded.

1995 □	ANOTHER PIECE OF ART	CD	private	MAC9495
1999 ■	FRAGMENTS OF LIFE	CD	private	MAC9798

1999 CD - MAC9798

M.A.D
Susanne Gillberg: v, Stefan "Stuk" Rådlund: g, Peo Olofsson: k,
Matti Larsson: b, Thomas "Nibbe" Nilsson: d
Umeå - Formed in 1993 with Leif Grabbe (*Ramm, Angeline, Shade Of Grey*) on vocals. This is highly-interesting, really heavy, yet melodic prog-metal with the talent of amazing singer Susanne Gillberg. Great songs, great arrangement and all of it well-played. A definite check-out. The band recorded a full length album in December 1995, but it was unfortunately never released.

1995 ■	Amusement Land	MCD 4tr	private	- -

Tracks: Woman On Parade/Part Of You/Built On A Lie/Amusement Land.

1995 MCD - - -

M.O.B
Fredrik Notling: v, Peter Gustafsson: g, Conny Goldschmidt: b, Richard Averdahl: d
Stockholm - A straightforward, powerful hard rock band in the upper middle class. They were big fans of *Kiss*, which shows in their style and sound, especially on the first two albums. Richard is a cousin of Roger in the band *Atlantis*. In 1996 Patrik Reimers was replaced by ex-*Candy Roxx/Ban-Zai* man Goldschmidt (brother of Chris Goldsmith of *Slodust/FullStrike/Scarpoint*). On *Merrie Melodies* they turned a bit heavier and the album is an excellent platter. On *The Greatest Enemy* Notling does a vocal duet with *The Ark* singer Ola Salo, and Janne Stark does a guest solo, and it feels as though the band stepped up their game yet a notch on this album. Website: www.mobrockz.com

1992 CDS - HAWKPROM 007

1990 ■	READ MY HIPS	LP	private	AIRMOB 001
1992 ■	High On Emotion	CDS 1tr	Hawk	HAWKPROM 007
1998 □	LOONY TUNES	CD	private	MOB 004
2001 □	MERRIE MELODIES	CD	private	MOB 005
2001 □	LOONY TUNES	CD	private	MOB 004
	Re-issue with new artwork and one extra secret track.			
2007 □	READ MY HIPS	CD	private	AIRMOB 001
	Bonus: High On Emotion/Who's To Blame/Rock 'N Roll Demon/(hidden track)			
2008 □	THE GEATEST ENEMY	CD	private	MOB 007
2008 □	THE GEATEST ENEMY LIVE IN STOCKHOLM	CD	private	MOB 008

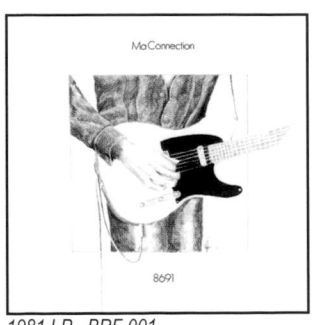
1990 LP - AIRMOB 001

M-TRAIN
Hans Nilsson: v/h, Conny Wendel: g, Magnus Lundin: b, Andreas Krenz: d
Tingsryd - The first album is straightforward blue-rock, while *Drivin' South* has a far heavier edge similar to *Sky High*. Conny was one of the finalists of the national Guitar Battle in 1990. He is also "Angus" in *AC/DC* tribute band *Hazy/Dizzy*. On *Alligator* drummer Jonas Persson was replaced by Krenz.

1995 □	SCRAMBLE	CD	Midnight	MT 01
1998 ■	DRIVIN' SOUTH	CD	Midnight	MT 02
2003 □	ALLIGATOR	CD	Midnight	MT 03

1998 CD - MT 02

MA CONNECTION
Ola Sundqvist: v/h, Janne Buhr: g/k, Heino Särkioja: g,
Håcan Åström: b, Åke Borgström: d
Umeå - **Ma Connection** was formed in May 1979. Bluesy, boogie-based hard rock. Similar to *Crut, Frozen Fire* and *Dunder*. Pretty good with some flaws in the vocal department. Released on the same label as *Gotham City*. In 1980 they also released a live cassette. The band folded in 1982, when Ola and Åke quit the band.

1981 ■	8691	LP	Brute Force	BRF 001	$$

1981 LP - BRF 001

MAC & PLOIDS

Peter Olsén: v/h, Fredrik Forssblad: g, Johan Nilsson: g,
Niklas Boström: b, Magnus Lund: d

Borås - Great boogie/blues-infused hard rock produced by Kenneth Fahlman (*Empire Saint*, *Orient*). Boström also played with punksters *Vrävarna*. The B-side is a *Rolling Stones* cover.

1992 ■ Good Times Comin'/19th Nervous Breakdown ....7" private .... - -

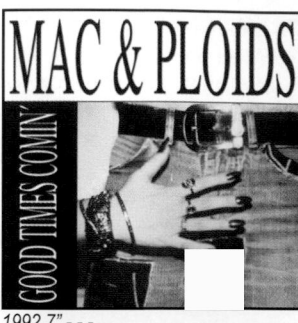

1992 7" - - -

MAC BLAGICK

Martin "Marino Funketti" Wiberg: v, Nils "Sledge Nelson" Ekblad: g,
Karl "Clarious Thump" Sjöblad: b, Kristoffer "Snipe/Viking Slammer" Widman: d

Uppsala - It all started back in the nineties when Ekblad and Sjödin were playing in the band *Aska*. In 2002 they relocated from Eskilstuna to Uppsala because of studies. They then teamed up with drummer Ingo Blomqvist and *Aska* became *The Boom Boom Band*. Along the line Ingo was replaced by Kristoffer Widman (*Mac Attack*) and early 2006 they changed the name to *Mac Blagick*. In May the same year, singer Wiberg joined in and in 2007 they released the debut. Primitive, slightly psychedelic hard rock with a 60s touch.
Website: www.macblagick.com

2007 □ MAC BLAGICK ....CD Glen Ghost..............................GHOSTCD 02
2009 ■ RAMADAWN..CD Glen Ghost..............................GHOSTCD 03

2009 CD - GHOSTCD 03

MACABRE END

Per Boder: v, Ola Sjöberg: g, Jonas Stålhammar: g,
Thomas Johansson: b, Niklas Nilsson: d

Vålberg/Karlstad - Formed in late 1988 under a different name and playing in a more grindcore-oriented style. In 1990 they changed the name to *Macabre End* and style to death metal. The EP was recorded at Studio Sunlight, produced by Tomas Skogsberg. Dark death metal in the traditional style. They also made a recording in December 1991, for Relapse, but it was never released. The band had then changed their name to *God Macabre* and Johansson had left the band. Stålhammar has also been in bands like *Utumno*, *The Crown*, *Abhoth*, *Darcreed* and *Bombs Of Hades*. See *God Macabre* for further information.

1991 ■ Consumed By Darkness/Ceased To Be/Spawn Of Flesh ....7" 3tr Corpse Grinder ....CGR-001 **$**

1991 7" - CGR-001

MACHINAE SUPREMACY

Robert "GAZ" Stjärnström: v/g, Jonas "GIBLI" Rörling: g,
Andreas "GORDON" Gerdin: k, Johan "Dezo" Hedlund: b,
Tomas "TOM" Nilsén: d

Luleå - Ever heard of SID metal? Well, here's *Machinae Supremace*! The term comes from the use of a SidStation which features the SID chip (used in Commodore 64). The band was formed in 2000 by Stjärnström, Rörling and bass player Kahl Hellmer. The trio was completed by keyboardist Gerdin and drummer Tobbe. They immediately started giving away their music for free, through their website. They even had something of a hit with a cover of the theme of *Great Gianna Sisters*, released onto several Commodore 64 remix sites. In 2001 Hellmer and Stjärnström spent some time with their punk side project *Flak*. In 2002 Tobbe left and Nilsén replaced him. At the time of the release of the debut, the band had already recorded two albums worth of material for free download. After the first official album Hellmer relocated and was replaced by Johan Palovaara. They continued releasing a lot of material online, before the second album in 2006.
Website: machinaesupremacy.com

Viewing the overworld or the end of it?

2004 □ DEUS EX MACHINAE ....CD MbD Records............................MBD0008MS
2005 □ DEUS EX MACHINAE ....CD Hubnester Records............................HUB 002
　　　Bonus: Soundtrack To The Rebellion. New artwork.
2006 □ REDEEMER...CD Hubnester Records............................HUB 001
　　　Bonus: Fury/Kaori Stomp/The Cavern Of Lost Time/Prelude To Empire/Empire
2006 □ REDEEMER...CD Spinefarm ....SPI280 CD
　　　Bonus: Ghost (Beneath The Surface). New artwork.
2008 □ OVERWORLD..CD Spinefarm ....SPI 328 CD
2010 ■ A VIEW FROM THE END OF THE WORLD..................................CD Spinefarm ....SPI 379 CD

2010 CD - SPI 379 CD

MACHINEGUN KELLY

Anders "Andy Pierce" Persson: v, Clifford "Cliff" Lundberg: g,
Robert "Lefty" Jörgensen: b, Jörgen "Stanley" Olsson: d

Malmö - This is a side project featuring *Nasty Idols* members Andy and Stanley and former *AntiCimex/Black Uniforms/DrillerKiller* guys Cliff and Lefty. *Machinegun Kelly* is out-and-out sleazy, shit-kicking hard rock 'n roll with 110 % attitude. Stanley has also recorded a 7" with the band *Wizzy Blaze*. The video for the song *Whiteline Offside* was banned on MTV, since it shows scenes of the members snorting cocaine. The band however claims it's supposed to turn people off drugs, as it shows the bad sides of the addiction (...are there any good ones?).

1995	■	WHITELINE OFFSIDE	CD	Megarock	MRRCD 019
2004	□	WHITELINE OFFSIDE	CD	Perris Records	PER 01442
		Re-issue with new artwork.			

1995 CD - MRRCD 019

MACHINERY

Michel Isberg: v/g, Manuel Lewys: g, Fredrik Klingwall: k,
Peter Berg: b, Johan "Vebba" Westman: d

Saltsjö-Boo - On the first album the line-up featured Michel, Fredrik, Johan, guitarist Markus Isberg and bass player Per Lindström. The band recorded the first demo, *A Part Of Steel In An Endless Machinery* in 2002, followed by *Rising* and *The Beginning* in 2005, from which about half the songs were later recorded for the CDs. Klingwall is also in *Anima Morte*, *Flagellation* and *Loch Vostok*, while Lindström is ex-*In Grey* and *Flagellation*. *Machinery* play really good, quite melodic and dynamic thrash-oriented metal in the vein of *Nevermore*. Mostly clean, melodic vocals, but the occasional growling thrasher spices things up. The second album totally outshines the debut, especially in terms of production, where the debut is quite thin sounding. The band announced they split in June 2011.

2006	□	DEGENERATION	CD	Fast Entertainment	LAST 005
2007	■	THE PASSING	CD	Regain Records	RR 142

2007 CD - RR 142

MACROCOSMIC EMOTIONS

Andreas Risberg: v/k/d, Mathias Karlsson: b, Kristian Möllerström: g

Jönköping - The band started under the name *Xymothra* and recorded a demo in 1993, but in 1994 the name was changed to *Macrocosmic Emotions* and on the first record Daniel Barkman was hired to play guitar. In December 1996 Möllerström joined the band and recorded the MCD, before he also left the band to seek different musical adventures. However, he was back in the line-up later again. Death-oriented progressive thrash/metal, where the songs go from mellow symphonic parts to double bass drum thrashing. Warped, weird, spoken vocals, mixed with pretty awful clean semi-spoken monotonous vocals. This would maybe have changed to the better as Andreas was not meant to do the vocals and they drafted former hired hand guitarist Daniel as lead singer. It would hopefully also have changed the mid-quality song material and below-average sound with programmed drums for the next album. However, the band split. The final 8-track demo *The Third Explosive Announcement* was recorded in 2000, with Risberg still handling the vocals. Kristian and Daniel also play in heavy/power metal band *Cartagrian*.

1995 CD - MACROCD 01

1995	■	THE CONTEMPORANEOUS EXPLOSIVE ATMOSPHERE	CD	private	MACROCD 01
1998	■	Her Soft Emotional Announcement	MCD 5tr	private	MACROCD 02
		Tracks: When All Realize That We Need Each Other/I Can See Fear And Uncertainty In Her Eyes/Unique Future Thought Wakes Her/Psychological Key Find Her Well/Her Soft Emotional Announcement			

MADIGAN

Mikael Lejon: v/k, Stefan Thörnblom: g, Tomi "Tommy Martell" Peltonen: g,
Tommy Pettersson: b, Kimmo "Kim Wyn" Värynen: d

Eskilstuna - *Madigan* was formed in 1989 featuring Kent Österlöv on keyboards and Conny Hall on rhythm guitar. They quit in 1990, and were replaced by Stefan Thörnblom. An above-average melodic hard rock/AOR band whose album is only to be found on vinyl. The album was originally sold for 1 SEK (about 0.13 €) as a gimmick. They can musically be placed somewhere between *Baltimoore* and *Treat*. Well worth checking out. Stefan quit during the mixing of the album. The band split in 1993, but recorded some really outstanding and heavier demos after the album. Peltonen has later played with *Torch* and is together with Thörnblom today in metal band *Griffen*. Leijon and Värynen formed cover band *Lacy Lucy* and Pettersson is in the band *Vita Vatten*.

1998 MCD - MACROCD 02

1992	■	SHADES OF YOUTH	LP	Backstage	BSM 980

1992 LP - BSM 980

MADISON

Pete Sandberg: v, Mikael Myllynen: g, Anders Karlsson: g,
Conny (Sundqvist) Payne: b, Peter Fredricksson: d

Hudiksvall/Göteborg - The band **Regent**, featuring Conny and Dan Stomberg won the recording of a 7" in a local bandstand. The single (*Lay Down Your Arms/Changes*) caught the attention of Rixi Records. Conny and Dan convinced Anders and Peter from local band **Destiny** (not the Göteborg band) to join. They also recruited singer Göran Edman and **Madison** was born. Both **Regent** songs were rerecorded for the debut, which is a great piece of melodic hard rock that suffers from bad production. After this album, Mikael Myllynen replaced guitarist Dan Stomberg. The second album is a true gem. After *Best In Show* Göran left the band to join Yngwie Malmsteen. Pete Sandberg (**Alien, Snake Charmer, Bewarp**, solo) replaced him. Peter record several demos, but the only thing released was the very AOR-ish single *Northern Light*. Actually, before this, the new line-up recorded the unreleased single *Don't Close Your Eyes*. This was only made as a test pressing as they were not on terms with the songwriter. A late incarnation also featured bassist Johan Strömberg and keyboardist Calle Engelmarc (**Turbo, Mercy**). Conny later joined cover band **Riff Raff**, which was reformed into **Big Easy** (also featuring Calle). He later joined **Alien** and is today in prog metal band **Mindsplit**. Anders moved to the US where he went to theatre school. Pete was later in **Bewarp, Jade, Silver Seraph** and has also released solo albums. Mikael Myllynen took the last name Moon and joined **King Diamond Band** for a period. Göran Edman was later in **Glory, Kharma, Vindictiv, Mårran** and has recorded with several other acts such as Jayce Landberg, **Kharma, Geff, Stratosphere** etc. **Madison** also have two tracks on the Japanese soundtrack CD and laser disc *Pride One*. A great high-quality melodic hard rock band in the vein of **220 Volt** and early **Europe**.

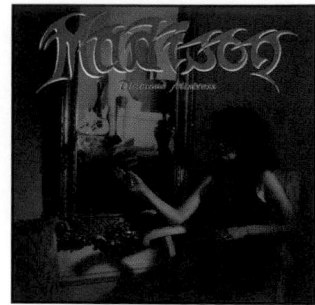

1984 LP - TRIX-LP 111

1986 LP - VIL-28036

1986 7" - SON 2305

Year		Title	Format	Label	Cat.No.
1984	■	DIAMOND MISTRESS	LP	Rixi	TRIX-LP 111
1984	□	Lay Down Your Arms/Pictures Return	7"	Rixi	TRIX 025
1986	□	DIAMOND MISTRESS	CD	Victor (Japan)	VDP-1073
1986	□	DIAMOND MISTRESS	LP	Victor (Japan)	VIL 28013
1986	□	DIAMOND MISTRESS	LP	Roadrunner	RR 9766
1986	□	DIAMOND MISTRESS	LP	Roadrunner (Korea)	0106
		Same as RR 9766 with "0106" added on the label.			
1986	□	BEST IN SHOW	LP	Sonet	SNTF 960
1986	■	BEST IN SHOW	LP	Victor (Japan)	VIL-28036
1986	□	BEST IN SHOW	CD	Victor (Japan)	VDP-1106
		Bonus: Look In Your Eyes			
1986	■	Give It Back/The Tale	7"	Sonet	SON 2305
1986	□	Give It Back/Shine/The Tale	MLP 3tr	Sonet	
1986	○	Shine (re-mixed)/Out Of The Bunker	7"	Sonet	T-10221
		The B-side is non-LP.			
1987	■	The Tale	MLP 4tr	Victor (Japan)	VIP-5122
		Tracks: Give It Back (single version)/Shine (re-mixed)/Look In Your Eyes/The Tale			
1989	○	Don't Close Your Eyes/Don't Close..(instrumental)	7"	Sonet (test pressing)	- - $$
		Test pressing of 5 copies.			
1989	□	Northern Light/Northern Light (instrumental)	7"	Sonet	T-10271
1993	□	DIAMOND MISTRESS/BEST IN SHOW	CD	Rock Star	04312
		Slipcase.			
2008	□	DIAMOND MISTRESS	CD	Victor Metal 80 (Japan)	VICP-64507
2008	□	BEST IN SHOW	CD	Victor Metal 80 (Japan)	VICP-64508

1987 MLP - VIP-5122

MADRIGAL

Martin Karlsson: v/g, Kristoffer Sundberg: g, Linda Emanuelsson: k,
Lukas Gren: b, Marcus Bergman: d

Göteborg - **Madrigal** was formed in 1998 and released their debut demo *Enticed* the same year. The band play melodic goth-oriented metal and has often been compared to **Paradise Lost** and **Anathema**. Karlsson avoids the deep goth vocals and I feel they are more similar to **Evergrey**.

Year		Title	Format	Label	Cat.No.
2001	■	I DIE YOU SOAR	CD	Nuclear Blast	NB 655-2
2001	□	I DIE YOU SOAR	CD	Nuclear Blast America (USA)	NBA 6655-2
2009	□	I DIE YOU SOAR	CD	Metal Mind	MASS CD 1332 DG
		2000 copies			

2001 CD - NB 655-2

MAEDAY

Jörgen "Jamie" Anderson: v, Lasse "Lace" Malmberg: g,
Rolph Van Royce: b/k, Tom Lind: d

Stockholm - Jamie, Tom and Lace were previously in locals **Balticum**. In 1984 they were reinforced by Rolph (half-brother of Dan Fondelius of **Count Raven**), and **Maeday** was born. The album was produced by Ragne Wahlqvist (**Heavy Load**). **Maeday** play quite decent AOR in the vein of early **Alien**. Keyboards, guitar-harmonies, good vocals and a good sound.

Year		Title	Format	Label	Cat.No.	
1988	■	MAEDAY	LP	private	M1-88	$

1988 LP - M1-88

MAGIC
Christer Åsell: v, Leif Carlsson: g, Torgny Östlund: b, Dan Hellström: k, Sigge Kron: d

Östersund - It all started back in 1985 as the band **Backstreet Blue**, initially featuring Carlsson, Östlund, Kron (ex-**Central**), singer Morgan Eklöv and guitarist Mats Norberg. Around 1989 Eklöv and Norberg quit the band, and they were replaced by former **220 Volt** singer Åhsell and keyboardist Hellström. Because of name similarities with **Backstreet Boys**, they changed it to **Magic**. They recorded the MCD in 1993. *Shadows On The Wall* is a high class guitar driven AOR/Melodic hard rock platter well worth looking for. Hellström is now found in **Turkey Twisters**, Carlsson is a producer, Östlund a teacher and Åhsell was in the reunited **220 Volt** for a while.

1994 ■ Shadows On The Wall ....MCD 5tr   John's Records ....JCD 9432
Tracks: Just Another Fool/Shadows On The Wall/Never Too Late/Hard Days/What Do
We Do

1994 MCD - JCD 9432

MAGNOLIA
Ronny Eriksson: v/b/g, Mark Tholin: g/k, Anders Hedström: d

Åmål - Power trio **Magnolia** was formed already in 1994 and took their name from the **Blue Cheer** song *Magnolia Caboose Babyfinger*, which will also give you a hint of their style. Take a big chunk of **November**, mix it with some **Mountain**, some **Cream** on top and a piece of **Blue Cheer**, and you've got **Magnolia**. A killer band indeed. On the first album the drum duties were shared between Hedström and Ronny's younger brother Tomas Eriksson. In June 2011 drummer Anders Hedström played his last gig with the band. Ronny is also in **My Brother The Wind**.

2006 ☐ MAGNOLIA..CD   Transubstans ....TRANS 022
2008 ☐ FALSKA VÄGAR...CD   Transubstans ....TRANS 038
2010 ■ STEG FÖR STEG...CDd   Transubstans ....TRANS 058
2013 ☐ TÄNK SJÄLV...CDd   Transubstans ....TRANS 116
2013 ☐ TÄNK SJÄLV...LP   Transubstans ....TRANSV 17

2010 CDd - TRANS 058

MAIM
Rikard Ottosson: v/b, Christian Sandberg: g, Scott Andersson: g, Henric Ottosson: d

Åtvidaberg/Linköping - The band was formed early 2006, initially with a more thrash-oriented death metal sound similar to **Entombed** and **Defleshed**, but gradually took a path down old-school lane. Sandberg is also found in **Ocean Chief** and Andersson in **Morbus Chron** as live guitarist.

2009 ■ FROM THE WOMB TO THE TOMB ....CD   Soulseller ....SSR 015
2009 ☐ FROM THE WOMB TO THE TOMB ....LPg   Soulseller ....SRR 015
500 copies. Patch.
2011 ☐ DECEASED TO EXIST..CDd   Soulseller ....SSR 033
2011 ☐ DECEASED TO EXIST..LP   Soulseller ....SSR 033
300 copies.

2009 CD - SSR 015

MAINLINE
Ernesto Grande: v/b, Mats Andersson: g, Thomas Wikblad: d

Västerås - Good, solid hard rock with a sound and style quite reminiscent of UK hard rockers **Mama's Boys** early material. Definitely worth checking out.

1990 ■ The Pieces Of A Broken Heart/Back To Me ....7"   SGV SGV-S9014

1990 7" - SGV-S9014

MAITREYA
Linus Melchiorsen: v, Martin Fogander: g/v/k, Enes Sabanovic: g,
Vanja Hadzic: b, Jonas Olofsson: d

Linköping - Linus, Martin and Nils Holmqvist, all three ex-**Powerdise**, discussed building a studio. Linus (ex-**Isengard**), was at the time singer in the band **Demented**. The studio plans started in 2004 and around that time **Demented** folded. In 2005 Martin, Linus and engineer Johan "Goomba" Nilsson started working on what was to become *New World Prophecy*. They were also using the talents of former **Spiritual Beggars** man Stefan Isebring for some odd instrumentation such as hurdy gurdy, citter etc. On the album Martin handled all guitars, keyboards and clean vocals, while Linus took care of the drums, bass and growls. After the album the line-up was completed by guitarist Mikael Almgren and drummer Lars Söderberg. They however didn't last long and soon Vanja Hadzic took over the bass, Enes Sabanovic was added on second guitar and Jonas Olofsson (**Conformatory**) was brought in on drums. This line-up started gigging in 2007. **Maitreya** plays very accomplished, quite melodic and dynamic progressive metal, with a touch of death metal, mixing clean vocals and growl. There are definitely hints of **Opeth**. In 2007 the band **Los Sin Nombre** recorded in Linus' and Martin's studio, and it ended with the band drafting them both, and **Maitreya** sadly withered away.

2006 ■ NEW WORLD PROPHECY ....CD   private ....MNWP 06

2006 CD - MNWP 06

MAJESTIC

Apollo Papathanasio: v, **Magnus Nordh:** g, **Richard Andersson:** k,
Martin Wezowski: b, **Peter Wildoer:** d

Malmö - Here's a band that changed its line-up to 60 % between the first and second album. On the debut the band featured founder Richard on keyboard and Martin on bass, while Peter Espinoza (**Nasty Idols, Espinoza**) handled the guitar playing, Jonas Blum (**Pole Position, Reptilian**) took care of the vocals and the Joel Linder (**Tenebre, Reptilian**) played drums. Martin has previously recorded with **Original Sin** and **The Drugs**. Both albums were recorded at Roastinghouse by Theo Theander. After the second album Andersson drafted most of the members for his own band **Time Requiem**. Apollo, who was ex-**Faith Taboo/Craze**, is also found in **Evil Masquerade**, **Firewind** and **Spiritual Beggars**. Peter Wildoer has also recorded with **Agretator, Arch Enemy, Armageddon, Darkane, Grimmark** and **Silver Seraph**, where Richard was also found. **Majestic** plays high-quality neo-classic power metal, not too far from **Time Requiem**.

1999 CDd - MASDP 0185

1999	☐	ABSTRACT SYMPHONY	CD	Zero (Japan)	XRCN-10027
1999	☐	ABSTRACT SYMPHONY	CD	Massacre	MASCD 0185
1999	■	ABSTRACT SYMPHONY	CDd	Massacre	MASDP 0185
		Bonus: Abstract Symphony			
1999	☐	ABSTRACT SYMPHONY	CD	Toshiba (Japan)	TOCP 65292
		Bonus: Silence			
1999	☐	ABSTRACT SYMPHONY	CD	Rock Brigade (Brazil)	RBR/LCR 1470
1999	☐	ABSTRACT SYMPHONY	CD	NEMS (Argentina)	NEMS 98
		Bonus: Abstract Symphony			
2000	■	TRINITY OVERTURE	CD	Massacre	MASCD 0245
2000	☐	TRINITY OVERTURE	CDd	Massacre	MASDP 0245
		Bonus screensaver			
2000	☐	TRINITY OVERTURE	CDd	EMI Toshiba (Japan)	TOCP-65456
		Bonus: Cadenza Op. 1 In A Minor			

2000 CD - MASCD 0245

MAJESTIC DIMENSION

Göran Nyström: v, **Magnus Mild:** g, **Robin Högdahl:** g, **Ulrik Zander:** b, **Johan Rask:** d

Göteborg - Great-sounding proggy melodic metal in the vein of **Cloudscape** or **Darkwater**, with a touch of classic power metal. The band was formed in 2009, by Robin and Magnus. Zander is ex-**Metal Mercy/Colorblind.**
Website: www.majesticdimension.com

| 2013 | ■ | BRINGERS OF REVOLUTION | CD | private | - - |

2013 CD - - -

MAJESTIC VANGUARD

Peter Sigfridsson: v, **Johan Abelsson:** g, **Andreas Andersson:** b,
Samuel Fredén: k, **Daniel Eskilsson:** d

Falköping - The foundation of **Majestic Vanguard** was laid already in the early nineties when Andreas Andersson and his brother Samuel Andersson (later Fredén) played in a band with drummer Daniel Eskilsson. The band folded in 1995, but some years later it was resurrected, not really putting great effort into it though. In the spring of 2003 singer Peter Sigfridsson was drafted and they now formed **Divine Disciples**. A demo was recorded in 2004. A copy was sent to Rivel Records, who responded immediately. Now second guitarist Abelsson completed the line-up and the name was changed to **Majestic Vanguard**. In 2005 the debut was released. In 2007 singer Sigfridsson had to leave because of problems with his vocal cords. Andreas switched to second guitar and bass player Lars Walfridsson was drafted. The band plays melodic power metal in the same vein as **Stratovarius**, early **Narnia** or **Royal Hunt** with a strong Christian message. Tommy Johansson (**ReinXeed, Golden Resurrection**) was also in the band for two gigs, but it didn't work out as planned.

| 2005 | ■ | BEYOND THE MOON | CD | Rivel Records | RRCD 025 |

2005 CD - RRCD 025

MAJOR N.A.

Daniel Magnusson: v, **Manuel Korsoski:** h, **Rasmus Andersson:** g,
S.O. Anda: b, **Mattias Starander:** d

Majorna (Göteborg) - The name was taken from a place in Göteborg called "Majorna", the members' home town. Like fellow Swedes **Tornado Babies** and **Straight Up** there's a lot of **AC/DC** in the band's music, as well as in the vocal department. Actually they are at times very reminiscent of **Trash**, both regarding music and vocals. Powerful and stompin'. Mattias was later found in **Transport League**.

1993	■	MAJOR N.A.	CD	Radium	RACD 92
1993	☐	MAJOR N.A.	LP	Radium	RA 91382
1993	☐	Angel/Back In The Rock/Hard Times	MCD 3tr	Radium	RAPRCD 93-1

1993 CD - RACD 92

MAKE UP

Hans-Olof Childs: v, Tomas Engberg: g, Ulf Mellander: g,
Leif Persson: b, Peter Sandqvist: d

Matfors - Pretty straight-ahead melodic poppy hard rock in the vein of *Magnum Bonum*, *Nadir* and *Ocean*. Swedish lyrics except for two tracks.

1980 ☐	My First Love/Hot Love Street	7"	Wave	WAVE S 003
1981 ■	NATTLIV	LP	Wave	WAVE LP 8003

1981 LP - WAVE LP 8003

MALAISE

Martin Danielsson: v, Fredrik Leijström: g

Uppsala - Formed in 1989 by singer Martin as a one-man all-electronic project, influenced by *Front 242, Frontline Assembly* etc. In 1993 guitarist Robert Svärdh and drummer Johan Linder joined and they released the MCD. In 1994 Juho Korhonen replaced Robert Svärdh, and bass player Kim Boman was added to the line-up. In 1997 Nicklas Bergström replaced Johan Linder. Early 1998 Juho and Kim were replaced by Jim Edwards (ex-*Misery Loves Co*) and Fredrik Leijström, and Peter Waites (*Forcefeed*) joined on bass. On *A World Of Broken Images* they became heavier and more gothic. Industrial Goth metal might be one description. Stefan Väisinen replaced Peter, and before the last MCD Jim and Nicklas left. They were replaced by Jimmy Värn, Jimmy Widegren and programmed drums. The MCD *Re-assimilated* was recorded already in 2000, but was delayed due to line-up changes and technical difficulties. On the last recording the line-up was again different, now featuring only Martin Danielsson and Fredrik Leijström. Guitars on the recording were handled by Tobias "Tobbe" Sidegård (*Necrophobic, Therion*) and the bass duties were shared between Stefan Väisinen and Kim Blomkvist (*Therion*).

1993 MCD - MEMO 006

1993 MCD - CCP 009

1993 ■	Secession	MCD 6tr	Memento Materia	MEMO 006
	Tracks: Something Else/Faraway Garden/Submissive/Scenes From The Past/We Are Colliders/Gods Of War			
1993 ■	Secession	MCD 6tr	Celtic Circle	CCP 009
1996 ☐	52 WAYS	CD	Memento Materia	MEMO 015
1999 ☐	A WORLD OF BROKEN IMAGES	CD	Memento Materia	MEMO 025
2003 ☐	Re-assimilated	MCD 6tr	Memento Materia	MEMO 049
	Tracks: Walk Through The Wonderland (2K2 Remix)/Dead I Walk/Narrow Line/Hollow Dream/We Are Colliders (2K2 Remix)/Assimilate (Skinny Puppy cover)			
2006 ☐	Hypnotized By Forgotten Lies	MCDd 5tr	Ultrachrome	ULTRA 003 CD
	Tracks: This Is For A Friend/In Your Dreams/No Confusion/Little Girl Of Mine/Paradox			

MALEFICIO

Daniel Johannesson: v, Mikael Fredriksson: g, Erik Gustafsson: b, Peter Derenius: d/k

Lerum - *Maleficio* was formed by Johannesson (*Mnemonic*) and Derenius in 1990 and between 1991-2004 they recorded eighteen demos. The track *Pain To Desecration* was featured on the *Voices Of Death (Part III) – In Death We Trust* (2000 VOD) compilation. The line-up featured Johannesson, Gustafsson, Derenius and guitarist Jimmy Hitula (*Sister Sin, Archangel*). *Under The Black Veil* was produced by Pelle Saether. In 2008 former *Grief Of Emerald* guitarist Tore joined the band and the year after the CD-R album *Go To Hell* (Apollon) was released in 66 copies. *Maleficio* plays high-quality well-produced quite technical death metal.

2008 CD - HWS 22 CD

2008 ■	UNDER THE BLACK VEIL	CD	Hateworks	HWS 22 CD

MALIGN

Jonas "Nord" Tengner: v, Yonas "Mörk" Lindskog: g/d, Mikael "Mist" Schelén: b

Stockhom/Spånga - *Malign* have been around since 1994 and recorded several demos. The music is, according to the band, "deeply religious black metal". According to an early statements from Mörk (aka Rev Worthodox aka Yonas, also in *Watain*, *Svartsyn* and *Werewolf*), "Anything people need to know about us is found in our lyrics. We as individuals are not important, it's what we preach that mean something. If we have anything to add we will include it on future releases". Tengner, also in *Ofermod* between 1998-2011, is a younger half-brother of highly acclaimed former metal journalist Anders Tengner. Mist is also found in *Ophthalamia* and *Ofermod*. In 2011 the band, (Mörk, Nord, guitarist H Death and drummer E Forcas), did a one-off show, their first in ten years, supporting *Watain* at their 13 year anniversary show. *Malign* plays simple straight-ahead, almost punkish old-school black metal. The early stuff is much cruder and not that well-played, while the later material has improved both in sound and quality.

2002 10" - EAL 033

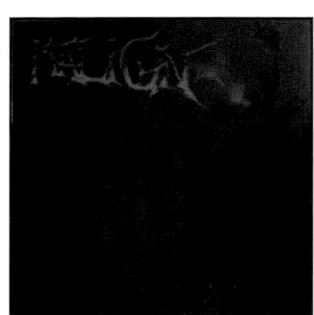

1999 7" - SHADOW 007

2011 LP - NED 004

1999 ■	Fireborn/Entering Timeless Halls	7"	Shadow	SHADOW 007
	300 copies.			
2002 ■	Divine Facing	10" 4tr	End All Life	EAL 033
	Tracks: Sinful Fleshpear/Divine Facing/Ashes And Bloodstench/Entering Timeless Halls			
2005 ■	DIVINE FACING AND FIREBORN	CDd	Norma Evangelium Diaboli	NED 004
2011 ☐	DIVINE FACING AND FIREBORN	LP	Norma Evangelium Diaboli	NED 028
	Red vinyl.			

MALISON ROGUE

Sebastian "Zeb" Jansson: v, Jonatan "Bjoerkborg" Björkborg: g, Petter "Pete Fury" Furå: b, Jens "Doc" Vestergren: d

Nyköping - **Malison Rogue** is yet another strong competitor in the New Wave of Swedish Heavy Metal together with bands like **Enforcer, Steelwings, Portrait** etc. The band started out under the moniker **Ashes**, but changed it to **Malison Rogue** in 2010. They were picked up by Inner Wound and entered the studio with singer Mats Levén as producer, to record their debut. In 2011 the band was reinforced by second guitarist Mats Johansson, who had already been a session member for six months.

2011 ■ MALISON ROGUE...CD   Inner Wound Recordings IW83011

2011 CD - IW83011

MALMSTEEN, YNGWIE (RISING FORCE)

Yngwie Malmsteen: g/b/v/d

Los Angeles/Stockholm - Besides **Europe** and **ABBA**, Yngwie Malmsteen is one of the names that put Sweden on the worldwide music map. The guitar-wiz from Stockholm was born June 30, 1963 as Lars Johan Yngve Lannerbäck. At the age of five his mother Rigmor gave him a guitar and two years later he saw Jimi Hendrix on TV, setting fire to a guitar, which made him actually start playing the six-string. He came from a very musical family. His mother sang jazz and in a choir, his father played guitar and sang, his grandfather played drums and his brother, Björn, played drums, violin and flute. What made the biggest impact on the young Yngwie was when his sister Lollo played **Deep Purple**'s *Fireball*. This album made him realise he wanted to play hard rock. At the age of 10 he took his mother's maiden name Malmsten. Another highlight was **Genesis'** *Selling England By The Pound*, which made him discover inverted chords and the symphonic side of rock, which lead him to the classical masters. He even brought the guitar to school (when he was actually there). On one side he was into the gimmicky and heavy hard rock sound and on the other side he wanted to infuse the classical music, which early on formed his unique sound and style, later on named "neoclassical". Around this time he also discovered Paganini, who made a huge impact on him. His goal was to play all those fast violin runs, on guitar. In 1977 he formed the band **Powerhouse**, which was renamed **Rising Force** (after the cover painting on Uli Jon Roth's album *Eathquake*) around two years later. The live debut took place in 1981.

Yngwie in Malmö in 1983, with Anders, Jens and Per.

Lots of members came and went, like John Levén (**Europe, Glenn Hughes, Southpaw** etc), Marcel Jacob (**Power, Talisman, Humanimal** etc), Peter "Udd" Sandberg (**Råg I Ryggen, Glory Bell's Band**), Michael Uppman (now Storck) (**Paradise, Explode, Autocrash**), Sepp "Zepp" Urgard, Thomas Hultmark, Kjell (Nietzche) Eriksson (**Paradise**), Eero Koivisto (**Red Baron**), Mats "Dalton" Dahlberg (**Dalton, Treat**) and more. **Europe**'s Ian Haugland tried out for the band, but decided not to join. According to Anders Tengner's unofficial biography on Yngwie, *Såsom i himmelen, så ock på jorden*, Ian was scared by Yngwie and Marcel Jacob's brutal fighting and said he couldn't join as he had been offered a job as delivery boy. When Yngwie was around fourteen his uncle had a studio at Zinkensdamm, where he started rehearsing and recording. He spent most of his days in the studio until he was around seventeen. Yngwie claims he taught himself to become faster and faster because of a tape recorder which was a bit slow. What happened was, he recorded the song at rehearsal, but when listening at home, on another tape recorded, the song went slightly faster, which forced him to constantly up his game. He was at the time working in a guitar shop, as he had quit school at fifteen. In the guitar shop he had the possibility to explore the instrument even more and he discovered the beauty of playing with a scalloped neck (carving the guitar's neck between the frets).

Jimi Hendrix is dead??!! .

Around 1980 demo tapes of the fast-playing young guitarist started surfacing and eyebrows were lifted wherever they were played. Tracks such as *Anguish & Fear, Merlin's Castle* and *Speed & Action* became tape-trader classics. Yngwie's talent was finally discovered by CBS Records' Jan Askelind who wanted to sign him. **Rising Force** recorded three songs in July 1982, as a single for CBS that was never released. The songs were *You Got The Force* (also known as *You're Going To Break Them All*), *Horizon* and *Unresting Place*. CBS finally rejected the recording because the vocals were not in Swedish. Years later, when Yngwie's status had grown considerably, he was approached by the label again, but he now told them to shove it. On that recording the band consisted of Yngwie, singer Michael Uppman, bassist John Levén and drummer Peter Sandberg. Yngwie also went to Malmö in January 1983 where he teamed up with the Johansson brothers Anders and Jens and bass player Per Stadin (all three from **Silver Mountain**). Some demos and live recordings were made, all of them found on various bootlegs. As nothing happened in Sweden, Yngwie started sending his material overseas. He was finally discovered by Mr US Metal, Mike Varney of *Guitar Player Magazine*, who brought him to the US in February of 1983. Mike lured him into singer Ron Keel's band **Steeler** with whom he recorded one self-titled album (in one day). Rumours spread fast and comments like "Yngwie is God" could be read in various fanzines. It only lasted for four months, though, as he was very displeased with not having any input in the band, plus he didn't like the vocals (even calling singer Ron Keel "Wrong Key"). After only six weeks he was approached by both Phil Mogg and Graham Bonnet about forming bands. He then took quite a big step upwards

Listen to this new biting lick!

when he decided the join what became *Alcatrazz* featuring Graham Bonnet (*Rainbow*), Jan Uvena, Jimmy Waldo and Gary Shea, the two latter were ex-*New England*. He recorded two albums with this band, *No Parole From Rock And Roll* and *Live Sentence*, before starting his own band and returning to the *Rising Force* moniker in 1984. The deal for the solo album was set whilst on tour with *Alcatrazz* in Japan and finally lead to him leaving the band. The classic solo debut album *Rising Force* is a true masterpiece where the fresh talent of Yngwie really shows. The album actually made it to #60 on the Billboard chart, which was quite remarkable for an instrumental album with no airplay. The musicians were drummer Barriemore Barlow (*Jethro Tull*), keyboard player Jens Johansson (*Silver Mountain*) and singer Jeff Scott Soto (*Talisman, Eyes, Skräpp Mettle* etc). According to Yngwie this was never really meant to be an album. On his second album things started falling into place and he was now reinforced by his old companions Marcel Jacob on bass and Anders Johansson on drums. In 1985 singer Soto left. However, he started a co-operation with former *Fandango/Rainbow/Deep Purple* singer Joe Lynn Turner, but this came to a halt. On June 22, 1987 many thought Yngwie's career was over when he crashed his Jaguar into a tree. He was unconscious for five days and woke up with a useless right hand. However, he managed to recover with therapy and incredible will-power. Around Christmas he went back to Sweden, as his mother was ill. Shortly after, she passed away and Yngwie played a musical piece at her funeral. At the same time he found out his manager had ripped him off. On the album *Odyssey* the members had changed again and the band now consisted of Yngwie, Jens, Anders and singer Joe Lynn Turner (*Rainbow, Mother's Army, Hughes Turner* etc). New bass player was ex-Pat Travers man Barry Dunaway, but the bass on the album was recorded by Bob Daisley (*Ozzy, Wild Horses, Dio, Planet Alliance* etc) and Yngwie himself. In 1990 Yngwie recorded the album *Eclipse* with a totally new line-up. This time he brought in Göran Edman on vocals (*Madison, Norum, Glory* etc.), Svante Henrysson on bass, Mats Olausson (ex-*Motvind*) on keyboards and Michael Von Knorring (*Norden Light*) on drums. Michael unfortunately had to leave the band and Ulf "Bo Werner" Sundberg (*Mogg, Steamroller*) took his place on the 1992 release *Fire And Ice*. Yngwie also recorded his first guitar instruction video at this point. It's only for dedicated fans though as he does not seem very willing to teach what he knows. The line-up on *The Seventh Sign* consisted of Yngwie, Mats Olausson, singer Michael Vescera (ex-*Obsession, Loudness, MVP*) and drummer Mike Terrana (*Rage, Axel Rudi Pell* etc).

On *Magnum Opus,* Terrana was replaced by Shane Gaalaas (*MSG, Cosmosquad, Vinnie Moore*) and bass player Barry Sparks (*Dokken, Ted Nugent, Vinnie Moore, MSG, B'z*) was added to the line-up. Yngwie had a short and intense marriage with AOR singer Erika Norberg (now Evenlind). He even co-wrote some of the songs and played guitar on her album at the time. They divorced and in 1996 he married model Amber Dawn, to whom he dedicated several songs. Regarding the J in Yngwie's name a member of *Spinal Tap* once said, -"I like the way he puts Yngwie J Malmsteen on his albums, so you don't confuse him with all the other Yngwie Malmsteens in the business". The album *Inspiration* contains covers of some of his early favourites, including *Kansas*, *Rush*, *Deep Purple* etc. The musicians on the album were Yngwie, Marcel Jacob, Anders Johansson, Mats Olausson, Mark Boals, Joe Lynn Turner, Jeff Scott Soto, Jens Johansson and David Rosenthal (*Rainbow*). The artwork says it's Rosenthal playing keyboards on *Gates Of Babylon*, but it is actually Jens. In 1997 Yngwie released *Facing The Animal* featuring Mats Levén on vocals and Cozy Powell on drums. Cozy was supposed to tour with Yngwie, but cancelled due to an injury and Jonas Östman (*Gotham City, Mental Hippie Blood*) was brought in. Fate had it Cozy died in a car crash April 5, 1998. The line-up on *Live!* consisted of Yngwie, bassist Barry Dunaway, singer Mats Levén, keyboardist Mats Olausson and drummer Jonas Östman. On *Concerto…* Yngwie played together with the *Czech Philharmonic Orchestra*. In 1999 he also recorded a heavy and outstanding version of the *ABBA*-song *Gimme Gimme Gimme*, with Marc Boals on vocals, meant for the compilation *Powers From The North*. However, his manager talked him out of it (after the master was ready and all), as he thought it was too good, and it ended up on the *Anthology 1994-1999*. Another story behind that song is that Yngwie was initially going to record *Seven Doors Hotel* by *Europe*, but the studio he was in didn't have a turn-table and they were running out of time to record the drums. He then found a tape with the *ABBA*-song which he thought would be cool to do. It's quite funny considering album it was supposed to be on was a tribute to Swedish heard rock/heavy metal, which is a genre *ABBA* have never been deeply involved in, or even remotely considered belonging to. Marc also refused to sing "gimme gimme gimme a man after midnight", why they changed it to "gimme gimme gimme, your love after midnight". Around this time Yngwie used the talents of young drummer John Macaluso (*Ark*). *Anthology 1994-1999* also contains the previously unreleased tracks *Flamenco Diablo* and *Amadeus Quattro Valvole*.

In 2000 Yngwie was signed to US label Spitfire, who reissues his back catalogue with new artwork. On *Asylum* Yngwie returned to using the *Rising Force* moniker, partly because this album is the closest to that era he had done. The title track is a 15 minute, trilogy masterpiece. The line-up featured Yngwie, Mark Boals, Mats Olausson, Barry Dunaway and John Macaluso. On *War To End All Wars* it was only Yngwie, Mark, Mats and John. On the subsequent tour Mark was replaced by Jörn Lande (*The Snakes, Vagabond, Ark, Jorn*), who left amidst a lot of commotion, and was later replaced by Doogie White (*Rainbow, Tank*). The live line-up of 2001 also featured drummer Patrik Johansson (*Stormwind*) and keyboard player Derek Sherinian (*Speedway Blvd, Dream Theater, Planet X*, solo, now *Black Country Communion*), whom

You don't remember?

Tapping away at Göta Lejon in 1985

Yngwie had helped out on his solo albums. Despite rumours, *Birth Of The Sun* is no bootleg (even though the release caused a never-ending bitter argument between Marcel and Yngwie). The recording (made in 1980) was, according to Marcel, owned by his mother. It was remixed (the bass beefed up) and properly mastered. As a result Yngwie himself released the CD *The Genesis*, with more or less the same songs. Line-up on this recording featured Yngwie, Marcel Jacob and drummer Zepp Urgard. However Yngwie replaced all the bass on the recording, excluding Marcel from it. In early 2002 Yngwie recorded the new studio album, *Attack*, which also features drummer Patrik Johansson, now as an integral part of the band. Initially Swedish keyboard-ace Richard Andersson (**Majestic, Silver Seraph, Time Requiem**) was drafted, but he turned the offer down after some rehearsals. Instead the keyboard spot was filled by Derek Sherinian, who was also on the previous tour. This was the first album with new singer Doogie White. *Attack* was in the classic Yngwie vein, but the production was quite below par. In 2005 Yngwie released the album *Unleash The Fury*. The title came from an air plane incident that took place on a flight to Tokyo in 1988, where another passenger was so provoked by the band's behaviour (which involved dipping a sanitary pad in Bloody Mary and throwing it in other people's food), she threw a glass of water over his head and shouted "Cool down boys". Yngwie responded by shouting the now-immortal words "You've released the fucking fury", which was recorded by a member of the band (read: Jens). The recording wasn't "released" until some twenty years later, and became big news. The commotion almost resulted in the plane landing in Anchorage. The album features Yngwie, Doogie, Patrik and keyboard player Joakim Svalberg (**QOPH, Opeth, El Gamo**). In 2003, after having a bad infection Yngwie decided to quit smoking and drinking. In 2004 he participated on the *G3* tour together with Joe Satriani and Steve Vai, resulting in the three-way split album *G3 Live: Rockin' In The Free World* (2004 Epic). In 2007 Yngwie was featured on the Xbox game *Guitar Hero II*. In early 2008 Doogie White was replaced by former **Judas Priest** singer Tim "Ripper" Owens (also found in **Iced Earth, Beyond Fear**), together with whom Yngwie had recorded a cover of *Mr Crowley* for the Ozzy Osbourne tribute *Bat Head Soup*. Later the same year Yngwie returned with the album *Perpetual Flame*, mixed by Roy Z (**Fight, Tribe Of Gypsies, Bruce Dickinson**). This is his best effort in years, proving he still had his great chops intact. In 2009 Yngwie finally gave in to his wife's request to record an acoustic all instrumental album in her honour (and with her on the cover), called *Angels Of Love*. The album features Yngwie and keyboardist Michael Troy Abdallah only. The album features all rearranged old material, except for the track *Oceana Sonata*. The album *High Impact* is a compilation of instrumentals only, with the bonus track *Beat It*, a Michael Jackson cover sung by Owens.

In 2010 Yngwie returned with a new album, the title reflecting his relentless pursuit in the name of neoclassical shredding, simply entitled *Relentless*. The keyboards were now handled by Nick Marino, while Patrik and Tim were still in the band. Live bass duties were handled by Björn Englén (**Soul Sign, Quiet Riot, Robin McAuley**) - a role he had played for several years. On **Spellbound** singer Tim "Ripper" Owen was out of the band and Yngwie now decided to take on the vocal task as well as all the other instruments. Unfortunately the album doesn't live up to the expectations. The **Queen** cover *Keep Youself Alive* is found on the compilation *Dragon Attack: A Tribute To Queen* (Victor - Japan: VICP-5832). Guest-appearances from Yngwie can be found on albums like *Windows* (**MVP**), *Third Stage Alert* (**Third Stage Alert**), *Sonic Winter* (**Johansson**), *Holy Dio* (tribute-compilation), *This Time Around* (**Carmine Appice's Guitar Zevs**), *Tribute To Van Halen* (tribute-compilation, 2000 Triage) and *Bat Head Soup – Tribute To Ozzy*. The albums *The Young Person's Guide To The Classic Vol. 1* and *Vol. 2* do not include any perfomances by Yngwie himself, but contains classical pieces selected by Yngwie Malmsteen. It however says "Yngwie Malmsteen" on the covers. In 2006 Yngwie also participated on the **Beatles** tribute CD *Butchering The Beatles* (2006 Restless).
Official website: www.yngwiemalmsteen.org

In front of the wall of Marshalls in Göteborg, 2008

1984 LP - 28MM0400

1984 ■	RISING FORCE	LP	Polydor (Japan)	28MM0400
	Poster.				
1984 ☐	RISING FORCE	LP	Polydor (USA)	825 324-1 Y-1
1984 ☐	RISING FORCE	LP	Polydor (Canada)	PDS-1 6409
1984 ☐	RISING FORCE	LP	Polydor Sung Eum (Korea)	SEL-RG 770
1984 ☐	RISING FORCE	LP	Polydor/RTB (Yugoslavia)	RTB 221864
1984 ☐	RISING FORCE	LP	Polygram (Mexico)	825324 1
	Song titles in Spanish.				
1984 ☐	RISING FORCE	LP	Polygram (Argentina)	835405
	Song titles in Spanish.				
1984 ☐	SPECIAL EDITED VERSIONS	LP	Polydor K.K (Japan)	M14137
	Promo-LP containing Black Star/As Abobe, So Below/Evil Eye/Icarus' Dreaming Suite				
	Opus 4/Far Beyond The Sun plus 5 tracks containing Tak Yonemochi interviewing Yngwie				
1985 ☐	RISING FORCE	LP	Polydor	825324 1
1985 ☐	RISING FORCE	CD	Polydor	825324 2
1985 ☐	RISING FORCE	CD	Polydor (Japan)	POCP-2309
1985 ■	I Am A Viking/Don't Let It End	7"	Polydor K.K (Japan)	7 DM 0130
1985 ☐	Studio/Live '85	MLP 3tr	Polydor	883 073-1
	Tracks: I'll See The Light Tonight/Far Beyond The Sun (live)/I'm A Viking (live)				
1985 ☐	Studio/Live '85	MLP 3tr	Polydor (Japan)	12MM 7015
1985 ☐	MARCHING OUT	LP	Polydor	825 733 1

1985 7" - 7 DM 0130

Year		Title	Format	Label	Catalog
1985	☐	MARCHING OUT	CD	Polydor	825 733 2
1985	☐	MARCHING OUT	LP	Polydor (Japan)	28MM 0420
		With girl and guitar cover, lyrics and a poster.			
1985	☐	MARCHING OUT	CD	Polydor (Japan)	POCP-2310
1985	☐	MARCHING OUT	CD	Polydor (Japan)	POCP-1838
1985	■	MARCHING OUT	CD	Polydor (Japan)	P33P 20002
		With girl and guitar cover.			
1985	☐	MARCHING OUT	LP	Polydor (USA)	825 733 1 Y-1
		Available with two different covers. The track Prelude is missing.			
1985	■	Black Star	7" flexi	Guitar Player EVA Tone	#7 – 850370XS
1985	☐	You Don't Remember, I'll Never Forget	12"	Polydor (USA)	PRO 439
		Radio promo, same track on both sides.			
1985	○	I'll See The Light Tonight/Don't Let It End	12"	Polydor (USA)	PRO 372-1
		Promo without artwork.			
1985	☐	MARCHING OUT	LP	Polydor (Uruguay)	825.733-1
1985	☐	MARCHING OUT	LP	Kolin/Polydor (Taiwan)	825.733-1
		Insert in Chinese.			
1985	☐	MARCHING OUT	LP	Polydor (Canada)	PDS-1-6424
1985	☐	MARCHING OUT	LP	Polydor (UK)	POLD 5183
1985	☐	MARCHING OUT	LP	Polydor Sung Eum (Korea)	SEL-RG 798
1985	☐	MARCHING OUT	LP	MJS (Korea)	MJ 1014
		Green cover promo (bootleg?). Different track order plus bonus tracks: Disciples Of Hell/ On The Run Again			
1985	☐	You Don't Remember, I'll Never Forget (split)	7"	Polygram (Italy)	AS 5000764
		White label promo. Split with Styper.			
1986	☐	You Don't Remember, I'll Never Forget/Fury	7"	Polydor (Japan)	7DM 0164
		Also available as white label promo.			
1986	○	You Don't Remember I'll Never Forget/Crying	7"	Polydor (Spain)	n/a
		Promo.			
1986	☐	You Don't Remember, I'll Never Forget/Fury	7"	Polydor (Spain)	885 431 7
1986	○	You Don't Remember, I'll Never Forget/You Don't Remember	12"	Polydor (USA)	PRO 439-1
		Promo without artwork.			
1986	○	Fire/Cryin'	12" 2tr	Polydor	PRO 486-1
		Promo without cover.			
1986	☐	TRILOGY	CD	Polydor	831073 2
1986	☐	TRILOGY	LP	Polydor	831073 1
1986	☐	TRILOGY	LP	Polydor (USA)	831 073 1 Y-1
1986	☐	TRILOGY	LP	Polydor (Japan)	28MM-0515
1986	☐	TRILOGY	LP	Polydor (Japan)	POLD 5204
1986	☐	TRILOGY	CD	Polydor K.K (Japan)	POCP 9172
1986	☐	TRILOGY	LP	Polydor (Mexico)	831073-1
		Song titles in Spanish.			
1986	☐	TRILOGY (TRILOGIA)	LP	Polydor (Argentina)	29072
		Song titles in Spanish.			
1986	☐	TRILOGY	LP	Polydor Discos (Brazil)	8310731
1986	☐	TRILOGY	LP	Polydor Sung Eum (Korea)	SEL-RG 882
1986	☐	Save Your Love (edit)/Motherless Cild	7"	Polydor	877 598 7
1988	☐	Heaven Tonight/Riot In The Dungeons	7"	Polydor	887 518 7
1986	☐	Heaven Tonight/Rising Force/Riot In The Dungeons	MLP 3tr	Polydor	887 518 2
1986	☐	Heaven Tonight	MCD 4tr	Polydor (UK)	887 518 2/YJMCD1
		Tracks: Heaven Tonight/Rising Force/Riot In The Dungeons/Trilogy Suite Op. 5			
1986	■	Heaven Tonight/Riot In The Dungeons	7"	Polydor (UK)	YJM 1
1988	☐	Heaven Tonight/Rising Force/Riot In The Dungeons	MLP 3tr	Polydor (UK)	887 518-1/YJMX 1
1988	■	Heaven Tonight/Rising Force/Riot In The Dungeons	MLP 3tr PD	Polydor (UK)	YJMX P1
1988	☐	Heaven Tonight/Riot In The Dungeons	7"	Polydor (Spain)	887 518-7
1988	☐	Heaven Tonight/Riot In The Dungeons/Trilogy Suite Op:5	MLP 3tr	Polydor	887 614-1
1988	☐	Heaven Tonight/Riot In The Dungeons	7"g	Polydor (UK)	YJMG-1
1988	○	Heaven Tonight/Heaven Tonight	12»	Polydor (USA)	PRO 582-1
		Promo without artwork.			
1988	■	Heaven Tonight	MCD 4tr	Polydor (USA)	870 731-2
		Tracks: Riot In The Dungeons/Faster Than The Speed Of Light/Krakatau/Heaven Tonight/ Heaven Tonight (video)			
1988	☐	Heaven Tonight/Riot In The Dungeons	7"	Polydor (Spain)	887518-7
		Different artwork.			
1988	☐	ODYSSEY	CD	Polydor	835 451 2
1988	☐	ODYSSEY	LP	Polydor	835 451 1
1988	☐	ODYSSEY	CD	Polydor (Japan)	POCP-2312
1988	☐	ODYSSEY	CD	Polydor (Brazil)	835451-1
1988	☐	ODYSSEY (ODDISEA)	CD	Polydor (Argentina)	29128
		Song titles and additional cover text in Spanish.			
1988	☐	ODYSSEY	CD	Polydor K.K (Japan)	P32P 20150
1988	☐	ODYSSEY	LP	Polydor (Japan)	28MM 0625
1988	☐	ODYSSEY	LP	Polydor Sung Eum (Korea)	SEL-RG 1124
1988	☐	ODYSSEY	LP	Polydor/RTB (Yugoslavia)	RTB PGP 221864
1989	☐	TRIAL BY FIRE - LIVE IN LENINGRAD	LP	Polydor	839 726 1

1985 CD - P33P 20002

1985 7" flexi - #7 850370XS

1986 7" - YJM 1

1988 MLP PD - YJMX P1

1988 MCD - 870 731-2

479

| 1989 | ☐ | TRIAL BY FIRE - LIVE IN LENINGRAD | LP | Polydor (Australia) | 080 998 2 |

1989 LP - C60 27355 005

1989 ☐ TRIAL BY FIRE - LIVE IN LENINGRAD ....LP — Polydor (Australia) 080 998 2
1988 ☐ ODYSSEY.................LP — BTA (Bulgaria)................BTA 12581
    Song titles in Bulgarian.
1989 ☐ TRIAL BY FIRE - LIVE IN LENINGRAD ....LP — Polydor (Korea)............MT-35
    Has grey back cover and label.
1989 ☐ TRIAL BY FIRE - LIVE IN LENINGRAD ....LP — Sonografika/Polydor (Venezuela) 30.590-L
1989 ☐ TRIAL BY FIRE - LIVE IN LENINGRAD ....LP — Polydor 422 839 726-1 Y-1
1989 ☐ TRIAL BY FIRE - LIVE IN LENINGRAD ....LP — Polydor Sung Eum (Korea)....... SEL-RG 1466
1989 ☐ TRIAL BY FIRE - LIVE IN LENINGRAD ....CD — Polydor 839 726 2
1989 ☐ TRIAL BY FIRE - LIVE IN LENINGRAD ....CD — Polydor K.K (Japan)............POOP-20280
1989 ☐ TRIAL BY FIRE - LIVE IN LENINGRAD ....CD — Polydor K.K (Japan)............POCP-1887
1989 ☐ TRIAL BY FIRE - LIVE IN LENINGRAD ....CD — Polydor (Japan) ....POCP 2313
    Bonus: Spanish Castle Magic
1989 ○ Live In Leningrad ....MCD 6tr — Polydor (USA) .... CDP 126
    Tracks: Spanish Castle Magic (Radio Edit)/Heaven Tonight (live)/Dreaming (live)/Guitar Solo (Sapcebo Blues) (live)/Black Star (live)/Spanish Castle Magic (LP version). Promo.
1989 ■ Трилогия (TRILOGY) ....LP — Polydor (Russia) C60 27355 005
1989 ☐ TRILOGY ....LP — Polydor (Russia) 5289-88
    Track listing in Russian.
1989 ☐ TRILOGY ....LP — Polydor (Argentina)............831 073-1
    Track listing in Spanish.
1989 ☐ EN VIVO EN LENINGRAD ....CD — Polydor (Argentina)............29229
1990 ☐ TRILOGY ....CD — Polydor K.K (Japan)............POCP-1839
    Re-issue without bonus tracks, but with a dedication to the late Prime Minister Olof Palme.

1990 7" - PO 79

1990 ☐ Makin' Love/Eclipse ....CDS — Polydor 877 122 1
1990 ☐ Makin' Love/Eclipse ....7" — Polydor 877 122 7
1990 ☐ Makin' Love/Eclipse ....7" — Polydor (Australia) 877 122 7
    Different artwork.
1990 ☐ Makin' Love ....MCD 4tr — Polydor (USA) .... CDP 238
    Tracks: Makin' Love/Makin' Love (edit)/Makin' Love(LP-version)/Eclipse. Promo.
1990 ○ Makin' Love/Eclipse (Instrumental)/Save Our Love ....MLP 3tr — Polydor (UK) ....YNG 1 DJ
    Promo without artwork.
1990 ☐ Makin' Love/Makin' Love (extended guitar mix)/Eclipse.................MLP 3tr — Polydor (UK) .... PZ 79
1990 ■ Makin' Love/Eclipse ....7" — Polydor (UK) ....PO 79
1990 ☐ Makin' Love/Makin' Love (extended guitar mix)/Eclipse.................MCD 3tr — Polydor (Germany) 877123-2/PZCD 79
1990 ☐ Makin' Love/Makin' Love (extended guitar mix)/Eclipse.................MLP 3tr — Polydor ....INT 877 123-1
1990 ○ Bedroom Eyes ....CDS 1tr — Polydor (USA)............ CDP 284
    Promo. No artwork.

1990 CD special - SACD 178

1990 ■ YNGWIE MALMSTEEN ON GUITAR ....CD special — Polydor (USA)............SACD 178 **$**
    Best of promo, with guitar-shaped paper sleeve.
1990 ☐ ECLIPSE.................LP — Polygram 843361 1
1990 ☐ ECLIPSE.................CD — Polygram 843361 2
1990 ☐ ECLIPSE.................CD — Polydor (Japan) ....POCP 2314
1990 ☐ ECLIPSE DOUBLE PACK.................2CD — Polydor (Japan) POCP-9007/8
    Japanese double-CD also featuring MCD with Overture 1383/Krakatau/Far Beyond The Sun (live)/Crying/Eclipse
1990 ☐ ECLIPSE.................LP — Polydor (Argentina)............29254
    Titles in Spanish.
1990 ☐ ECLIPSE.................LP — Polydor Sung Eum (Korea)........ SEL-RG 2027
1990 ☐ ECLIPSE.................CD — Polydor (Japan) POCP-2314
    Bonus: Making Love (extended guitar-solo)

1992 MCD - 66439-2

1991 ☐ YNGWIE MALMSTEEN COLLECTION ....CD — Polydor............849 271 2
1991 ☐ YNGWIE MALMSTEEN COLLECTION ....CD — Polydor (Japan)............POCP-1148
1991 ☐ YNGWIE MALMSTEEN COLLECTION ....CD — Polydor (Japan)............ POCP-2559
1991 ☐ YNGWIE MALMSTEEN COLLECTION ....CD — Polydor (Brazil)............849 271 2
1991 ☐ YNGWIE MALMSTEEN COLLECTION ....CD — Polydor (Argentina)............29387
    Titles in Spanish.
1991 ☐ THE YNGWIE MALMSTEEN COLLECTION ....CD — Polydor (USA)............849 271 2
1992 ○ Teaser (Single version) ....CDS — Elektra (USA)............PRCD 8514-2
    Promo.
1992 ☐ Teaser/Perpetual.................3" CDS — WEA (Japan)............WMD5 4092
1992 ■ Teaser/Perpetual/Broken Glass ....MCD 3tr — Elektra............66439-2
1992 ☐ No Mercy/All I Want Is Everything.................3" CDS — WEA (Japan)............WMD5 4104
1992 ○ Dragonfly.................CDS — Elektra (USA)............PRCD 8570-2
    Promo without artwork.
1992 ☐ FIRE AND ICE ....CD — Elektra (Japan) WMCS-479
    Bonus: Broken Glass. Slipcase

1992 LP - 7559 61137 1

1992 ☐ FIRE AND ICE ....CD — Elektra (Japan) WMCS-480
1992 ☐ FIRE AND ICE ....CD — EastWest (Japan) AMCY-3084
    Bonus: Broken Glass
1992 ☐ FIRE AND ICE ....CD — Elektra 7559 61137 2
1992 ■ FIRE AND ICE ....LP — Elektra 7559 61137 1
1992 ☐ FIRE AND ICE ....LP — Elektra (USA)............61137
1992 ☐ FIRE AND ICE ....LP — Elektra (Korea)............EL-036

1994	☐	TRILOGY	CD	Polydor (Japan)	POCP 2311
1994	☐	THE SEVENTH SIGN	CD	Pony Canyon (Japan)	PCCY-00531
		Bonus: Angel In Heat. Slipcase. Different artwork.			
1994	☐	THE SEVENTH SIGN	LP	MFN (UK)	LPMFN 158
1994	☐	THE SEVENTH SIGN	CD	MFN (UK)	CDMFN 158
1994	☐	THE SEVENTH SIGN	LP	Polydor (Korea)	R-1185
1994	☐	Forever One/Brothers	3" CDS 2tr	Pony Canyon (Japan)	PCDY 00122
1994	■	I Can't Wait	MCD 5tr	Pony Canyon (Japan)	PCCY-00629
		Tracks: I Can't Wait/Aftermath/Rising Force (live)/Far Beyond The Sun (live)/Power And Glory. Contained three tattoos.			
1994	☐	Power And Glory: Takada's Theme	3" CDS 3tr	Pony Canyon (Japan)	PCDY 00127
		In 3" long-box. Tracks: Power And Glory/Power And Glory (Stadium edit)/Seventh Sign			
1995	☐	MAGNUM OPUS	CD	MFN (UK)	CDMFN 188
1995	■	MAGNUM OPUS	CD	Pony Canyon (Japan)	PCCY-00772
		Bonus: Cantabile. Slipcase.			
1995	☐	MAGNUM OPUS	2CD	Pony Canyon (Korea)	PCKD-00030
		Contains the "I Can't Wait" EP as a separate bonus-disc.			
1995	☐	MAGNUM OPUS	CD	Viceroy Architect (USA)	VIA 8026-2
1995	○	No Love Lost	CDS 1tr	Viceroy Archetect (USA)	9/95 1da2
		Promo without artwork.			
1995	☐	The Only One	CDS 1tr	Canyon Int. (Japan)	DSP-1134
		Promo.			
1996	☐	Carry On Wayward Son	CDS 1tr	Canyon Int. (Japan)	DSP-1234 $
		Promo.			
1996	☐	INSPIRATION	LP	Music For Nations	MFN 200
1996	☐	INSPIRATION	CD	Music For Nations	CDMFN 200
1996	☐	INSPIRATION	2CD	Music For Nations	CDMFNX 200
1996	☐	INSPIRATION	CD	Foundation (USA)	720907-1401-2
1996	☐	INSPIRATION	CD	Pony Canyon (Japan)	PCCY-01009
		Bonus: Spanish Castle Magic. Different artwork.			
1996	☐	INSPIRATION	2CD	Spitfire (USA)	5137-2
		Bonus: Merlin's Castle/interview/Soft Prelude In G Minor/Hunted/Evil/Voodoo. Different artwork.			
1996	☐	INSPIRATION	CD	Magnum Music (Taiwan)	PCCY-01009
1996	☐	YNGWIE MALMSTEEN (BEST BALLADS)	CD	Best Ballads	08051996ZP
		Bonus: Suffer Me (by Alcatraz)			
1997	☐	FACING THE ANIMAL	CD	Pony Canyon (Japan)	PCCY-01154
		Bonus: Casting Pearls Before Swine			
1997	☐	Facing The Animal/Facing The Animal (Album version)	CDS 2tr	Mercury (USA)	MECP 362
		Promo.			
1997	○	Alone In Paradise/Another Time	CDS 2tr	Canyon International (Japan)	DSP-1313
		Promo without artwork.			
1998	☐	FACING THE ANIMAL	CD	Mercury (US)	536 737 2
1998	☐	FACING THE ANIMAL	CD	Samphony (Korea)	D 1397
		Bonus: Casting Pearls Before Swine			
1997	○	Facing The Animal Promo CD	MCD 4tr	Mercury (USA)	568 473-2
		Promo. Tracks: Facing The Animal (Radio edit)/Alone In Paradise/Like An Angel/Facing The Animal (Album version). No artwork.			
1998	☐	CONCERTO SUITE FOR ELECTRIC GUITAR AND ORCHESTRA IN E FLAT MINOR OP. 1 - MILLENIUM	CD	Pony Canyon (Japan)	PCCY-01211
1998	☐	CONCERTO SUITE FOR ELECTRIC GUITAR AND ORCHESTRA IN E FLAT MINOR OP. 1 - MILLENIUM	CD	Canyon Classics (Japan)	PCCI-00424
		Released in the Canyon Classics series.			
1998	■	LIVE!!	2CD	Pony Canyon (Japan)	PCCY-01277
1998	☐	LIVE!!	3CD	Pony Canyon (Japan)	PCCY-01278
		Also features a 3 track CD with opening act Dr Sin.			
1998	☐	LIVE!!	3CD+VHS box	Pony Canyon (Japan)	PCCY-01279
		Also features 3 track CD with opening act Dr Sin, plus a 12 track live video.			
1998	☐	LIVE!!	3CD+VHS box	Pony Canyon (Korea)	PCKD-00028
1998	☐	LIVE!!	2CD	Dream Catcher	CRIDE 8
1998	☐	LIVE!!	2CDd	Dream Catcher	CRIDE 8X
1999	☐	CONCERTO SUITE FOR ELECTRIC GUITAR AND ORCHESTRA IN E FLAT MINOR OP. 1	CD	Dream Catcher	CRIDE 16R
1999	☐	CONCERTO SUITE FOR ELECTRIC GUITAR AND ORCHESTRA IN E FLAT MINOR OP. 1 - MILLENIUM	CD	Dream Catcher	CRIDE 16C
		Different artwork than CRIDE 16R and has "Millenium" added to the title. Dream Catcher Classics series.			
1999	☐	ALCHEMY	CD	Dream Catcher	CRIDE 20
		First press with slipcase and poster.			
1999	☐	ALCHEMY	CDd	Dream Catcher	CRIDE 20X
1999	☐	ALCHEMY	2LP	Dream Catcher	CRIDE 20
1999	☐	ALCHEMY	CD	Pony Canyon (Japan)	PCCY 01409
		Bonus: God Is God			
1999	■	DOUBLE LIVE	2CD	Spitfire (USA)	SPIT 5134-2
1999	☐	THE SEVENT SIGN	CD	Spitfire (USA)	SPIT 5135-2
		Different artwork than the European release.			

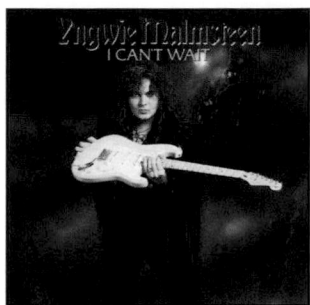

1994 MCD - PCCY-00629

1995 CD (slipcase) - PCCY-00772

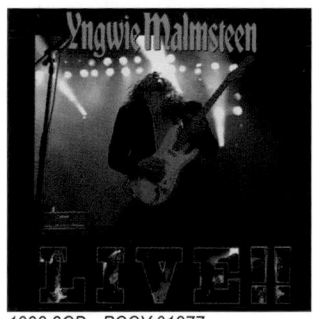

1998 2CD - PCCY-01277

1999 2CD - SPIT 5134-2

1999 CD - SPIT 5136-2

1999 ■	MAGNUM OPUS	CD	Spitfire (USA)	SPIT 5136-2
	Different artwork than the European release.			
1999 □	CHASING YNGWIE - LIVE IN TOKYO '85	LD	Polygram (Japan)	POLV 1601
1999 □	COLLECTION	LD	Polygram (Japan)	POLP 1605
1999 ■	CONCERTO IN E FLAT MINOR FOR ELECTRIC GUITAR AND ORCHESTRA			
		CD	Spitfire (USA)	SPIT 5138-2
1999 □	ALCHEMY	CD	Spitfire (USA)	SPIT 5139-2
	Different artwork than the European release.			
1999 □	FACING THE ANIMAL	CD	Spitfire (USA)	SPIT 5140-2
	Different artwork than the European release.			
1999 □	BEST OF 1990-1999	CD	Spitfire (USA)	SPIT 5141-2
1999 □	RISING FORCE	CDv	Pony Canyon (Japan)	POCP 9170
	Original cardboard jacket series, digitally remastered.			
1999 □	MARCHING OUT	CDv	Pony Canyon (Japan)	POCP 9171
	Original cardboard jacket series, digitally remastered.			
1999 □	TRILOGY	CDv	Pony Canyon (Japan)	POCP 9172
	Original cardboard jacket series, digitally remastered.			
1999 □	ODYSSEY	CDv	Pony Canyon (Japan)	POCP 9173
	Original cardboard jacket series, digitally remastered.			
1999 □	TRIAL BY FIRE: LIVE IN LENINGRAD	CDv	Pony Canyon (Japan)	POCP 9174
	Original cardboard jacket series, digitally remastered.			
1999 □	ECLIPSE	CDv	Pony Canyon (Japan)	POCP 9175
	Original cardboard jacket series, digitally remastered. Bonus: Making Love (extended)			
2000 □	ANTHOLOGY 1994-1999	CD	Pony Canyon (Japan)	PCCY-01446
2000 □	THE BEST OF 1990-1999	CD	Dream Catcher	CRIDE 25
2000 □	WAR TO END ALL WARS	CD	Dream Catcher	CRIDE 32
	Bonus: Black Sheep Of The Family			
2000 □	WAR TO END ALL WARS	CD	Spitfire (USA)	ADV 171
	Promo.			
2000 □	WAR TO END ALL WARS	CD	Spitfire (USA)	SPI 5171-2
	Bonus: Black Sheep Of The Family. Different artwork.			
2000 □	WAR TO END ALL WARS	CD	Spitfire (USA)	STE2EA077
2000 □	WAR TO END ALL WARS	CD	Pony Canyon (Japan)	DSP 1567
	Bonus: Treasures From The East/Requiem			
2000 □	WAR TO END ALL WARS	CD	Pony Canyon (Japan)	PCCY 01483
	Bonus: Treasure From The East/Requiem. Different artwork + guitar pick.			
2001 ■	YNGWIE MALMSTEEN ARCHIVES	8CD+2DVD Box	Pony Canyon (Japan)	PCCY 01501 $$
	Contains 8 CDs plus "Live At Budokan 1994" and "Live In Brazil 1998" on 2 DVD:s, 24 page booklet, silver cross pendant, card.			
2001 ■	CONCERTO SUITE FOR ELECTRIC GUITAR AND ORCHESTRA IN E FLAT MINOR – LIVE WITH THE NEW JAPAN PHILHNIC			
		CD	Pony Canyon (Japan)	PCCY 01551
2001 □	CONCERTO SUITE FOR ELECTRIC GUITAR AND ORCHESTRA IN E FLAT MINOR			
		CD	Pony Canyon (Japan)	PCKD-00101
	Bonus: Black Star Overture/Trilogy Suite, Op 5: The First Movement/Brothers/Blitzkrieg/ Far Beyond The Sun			
2002 □	CONCERTO SUITE FOR ELECTRIC GUITAR AND ORCHESTRA IN E FLAT MINOR			
		CD	Pony Canyon (Japan)	PMDI 01551
2002 ■	BIRTH OF THE SUN	CD	Powerline	PLRCD 006
2002 □	ATTACK	CD	Steamhammer	085-74602
2002 □	ATTACK	CD	Spitfire (USA)	SPIT 5139-2
	Different artwork. Bonus: Dreaming (live)/Battlefield			
2002 □	ATTACK	CD	Pony Canyon (Japan)	PCCY-01582
	Bonus: Nobody's Fool			
2002 □	ATTACK	CD	Pony Canyon (Japan)	PMDI-01582
	Bonus: Nobody's Fool			
2002 □	ATTACK	CD	Pony Canyon (Korea)	PCKD-00111
	Bonus: Nobody's Fool			
2002 □	ATTACK	CD	Universal (China)	HDCD 329
	Bonus: Nobody's Fool			
2002 □	RISING FORCE	CD	Universal (Korea)	DG-8774
2002 □	BIRTH OF THE SUN	CD	Powerline	PLRCD 006
	Bonus: Nobody's Fool			
2002 □	THE GENESIS	CD	Universal (Japan)	UICY-1137
2002 □	RISING FORCE	CD	Universal (Japan)	UICY-2343
2002 □	MARCHING OUT	CD	Universal (Japan)	UICY-2344
2002 □	TRILOGY	CD	Universal (Japan)	UICY-2345
2002 □	ODYSSEY	CD	Universal (Japan)	UICY-2346
2002 □	TRIAL BY FIRE – LIVE IN LENINGRAD	CD	Universal (Japan)	UICY-2347
2002 □	ECLIPSE	CD	Universal (Japan)	UICY-2348
2002 □	THE GENESIS	CD	Pony Canyon (Japan)	PCCY-01627
	Bonus: Heloo/On A Serious Note (1997)			
2003 ■	MAGNUM OPUS	CD	Steamhammer	076-74762
	Bonus: Tournament. Blue frame on artwork.			
2003 □	INSPIRATION	CD	Steamhammer	076-74772
	Artwork with face and guitar.			
2002 □	ATTACK	CD	Epic (USA)	EK75421

1999 CD - SPIT 5138-2

2001 8CD+2DVD - PCCY 01501

2001 CD - PCCY 01551

2002 CD - PLRCD 006

2003 CD - 076-74762

Year		Title	Format	Label	Catalog	
2003	☐	SEVENTH SIGN	CD	Steamhammer	076-74752	

Different artwork.

2004	☐	OUYA RESSOU - INSTRUMENTAL BEST	CD	Pony Canyon (Japan)	PCCY-01689	
2004	☐	RISING FORCE	CD	Ukrainian Records (Ukraine)	986657	
2004	☐	MARCHING OUT	CD	Ukrainian Records (Ukraine)	988273	
2004	☐	ECLIPSE	CD	Ukrainian Records (Ukraine)	991879	
2004	☐	G3 LIVE: ROCKIN' IN THE FREE WORLD (split)	2CD	Epic	EPC 515 021 2	

Split with Joe Satriani and Steve Vai. Tracks: Blitzkrieg/Trilogy Suite Op. 5 The First Movement/Red House/Fugue/Finale. Three additional tracks were recorded by all three: Voodoo Chile/Little Wing/Rockin' In The Free World

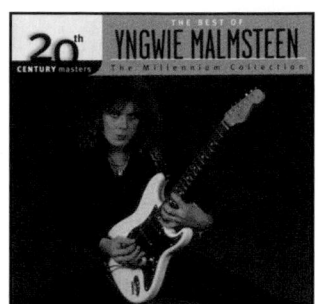

2005 CD - AAB000406202

| 2005 | ■ | 20th CENTURY MASTERS – THE MILLENNIUM COLLECTION | CD | Polydor (USA) | AAB000406202 | |
| 2005 | ☐ | UNLEASH THE FURY | CD | Universal (Japan) | UICE-1078 | |

Slipcase. Bonus: Special lesson Insight #1

2005	■	UNLEASH THE FURY	CD	Spitfire	SPITCD 258	
2005	☐	UNLEASH THE FURY	CD	Steamhammer	SPV 99592 CD	
2005	☐	FACING THE ANIMAL	CDd	Dream Catcher	CRIDE 2X	
2005	☐	ODYSSEY	CD	Universal (Japan)	UICY-90052	
2005	☐	ECLIPSE	CD	Universal (Japan)	UICY-6411	

Bonus: Making Love (Extended guitar solo)

| 2006 | ☐ | COMPLETE BOX POLYDOR YEARS | 6CDv box | Universal (Japan) | UICY-90273/--8 | $$ |

Cardboard jacket sleeves, special booklet, family tree and stickers.

| 2006 | ☐ | COMPLETE BOX POLYDOR YEARS | 6CDv box | Universal (Japan) | UICY-93547/--52 | $$ |

2005 CD - SPITCD 258

2007	☐	FIRE & ICE	CD	Notable Rot	NOT 5006-2	
2007	☐	THE YNGWIE MALMSTEEN COLLECTION	CD	Universal (Japan)	UICY-90230	
2007	☐	RISING FORCE	CD	Universal (Japan)	UICY-90050	
2007	☐	RISING FORCE	CD	Universal (Japan)	UICY-6407	
2007	☐	TRILOGY	CD	Universal (Japan)	UICY-6409	
2007	☐	ODYSSEY	CD	Universal (Japan)	UICY-6410	
2007	☐	ODYSSEY	CDv	Universal (Japan)	UICY-93355	
2007	☐	RISING FORCE	CDv	Universal (Japan)	UICY-93352	
2007	☐	MARCHING OUT	CDv	Universal (Japan)	UICY-93553	
2007	☐	TRILOGY	CDv	Universal (Japan)	UICY-93554	
2007	☐	ECLIPSE	CDv	Universal (Japan)	UICY-93557	
2008	☐	TRIAL BY FIRE – LIVE IN LENINGRAD	CDv	Universal (Japan)	UICY-93556	
2008	☐	THE YNGWIE MALMSTEEN COLLECTION	CD	Universal (Japan)	UICY-90896	
2008	☐	2 ORIGINALS OF YNGWIE MALMSTEEN	2CD box	SPV	SPV 98820 2CD	

Double pack containing Attack and Unleash The Fury in hard slip-cover.

2008	☐	PERPETUAL FLAME	CD	Rising Force	RFR-CDEU 01	
2008	☐	PERPETUAL FLAME	CD	CDNet Music (Taiwan)	MMVT 1134	
2008	☐	PERPETUAL FLAME	CD	Universal (Japan)	UICE-1139	
2008	☐	PERPETUAL FLAME	CD+DVD	Universal (Japan)	UICE-9076	

Bonus DVD with track-by-track comments by Yngwie. SHM-CD.

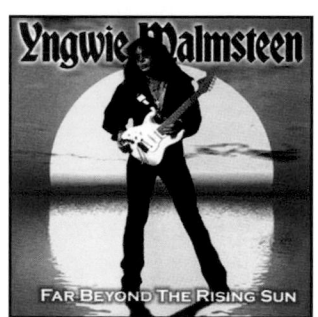

2008 CD - RFR-CDEU 03

| 2008 | ■ | FAR BEYOND THE RISING SUN | CD | Rising Force | RFR-CDEU 03 | |

Compilation of bonus tracks and unreleased songs.

| 2009 | ☐ | ANGELS OF LOVE | CD | Rising Force | RFR-CD 2 | |
| 2009 | ☐ | ANGELS OF LOVE | CD | Universal (Japan) | UICE-1149 | |

SHM-CD.

| 2009 | ■ | THE GENESIS | CD | Rising Force | RFR-CD 3 | |

Different artwork than the Japanese version. Bonus: Merlin's Castle (video)

| 2009 | ■ | HIGH IMPACT | CD | Rising Force | RFR-CD 4 | |

Bonus: Beat It (Michael Jackson cover)

| 2010 | ☐ | THE YNGWIE MALMSTEEN COLLECTION | CD | Universal (Japan) | UICY-91464 | |
| 2010 | ☐ | RISING FORCE | CDv | Universal (Japan) | UICY-93547 | |

SHM-CD.

| 2010 | ☐ | MARCHING OUT | CDv | Universal (Japan) | UICY-93548 | |

SHM -CD.

| 2010 | ☐ | TRILOGY | CDv | Universal (Japan) | UICY-93549 | |

SHM -CD.

2009 CD - RFR-CD 3

| 2010 | ☐ | ODYSSEY | CDv | Universal (Japan) | UICY-93550 | |

SHM -CD.

| 2010 | ☐ | TRIAL BY FIRE – LIVE IN LENINGRAD | CDv | Universal (Japan) | UICY-93551 | |

SHM -CD.

| 2010 | ☐ | ECLIPSE | CDv | Universal (Japan) | UICY-93552 | |

SHM -CD.

| 2010 | ☐ | RELENTLESS | CD | Universal (Japan) | UICE-1170 | |

SHM-CD.

2010	☐	RELENTLESS	CD	Rising Force	RFR CD 6	
2010	☐	THE YNGWIE MALMSTEEN COLLECTION	CD	Universal (Japan)	UICY-91733	
2011	☐	CONCERTO SUITE FOR ELECTRIC GUITAR AND ORCHESTRA IN E FLAT MINOR	CD	Steamhammer	089 745 72	

Bonus: Broken Glass

| 2010 | ☐ | RISING FORCE | CD | Universal (Japan) | UICY-20246 | |

SHM-CD.

| 2010 | ☐ | MARCHING OUT | CD | Universal (Japan) | UICY-202047 | |

SHM -CD.

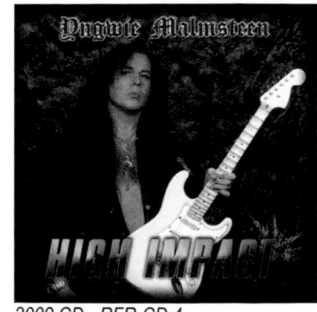

2009 CD - RFR-CD 4

2010 ☐	TRILOGY	CD	Universal (Japan)	UICY-20248
	SHM -CD.			
2010 ☐	ODYSSEY	CD	Universal (Japan)	UICY-20249
	SHM -CD.			
2010 ☐	TRIAL BY FIRE – LIVE IN LENINGRAD	CD	Universal (Japan)	UICY-20250
	SHM -CD.			
2010 ☐	ECLIPSE	CD	Universal (Japan)	UICY-20251
	SHM -CD.			
2011 ☐	FIRE & ICE	CD	Warner (Japan)	WPCR-14257
2012 ■	SPELLBOUND	CD	Universal (Japan)	UICN-1024
2012 ☐	SPELLBOUND	CD+DVD	Universal (Japan)	UICN-9008
	Bonus DVD with interview and photo session.			
2012 ☐	SPELLBOUND	CD	Rising Force Records	RFR CD6

2012 CD - UICN-9024

Unofficial releases:

1980 ☐	BLACK STAR	LP	private	603
	Early demos. Line-up Yngwie: g/v, John Levén: b, Peter Udd: d.			
1984 ☐	LIVE FORCE – THE GREAT TASTING SWEDISH SMORGASBOARD	2LP	Matrix Records	- -
	Recorded at The Country Club, Los Angeles, December 1984.			
1985 ☐	HERO'S RETURN	LP	Roxy	RF8505YM
	Recorded at Göta Lejon, Stockholm in May 1985.			
1985 ☐	TORONTO 23/9-85	LP	Metalworks	HW 003
n/a ☐	FIRE IN THE SKY	2CD	private	8 8251 55-52
	Japanese bootleg recorded 88-08-23+25.			
1985 ☐	A SIGN OF TRILOGY	CD	Eclipse (Japan)	EC 007
	Recorded in Oakland Coliseum, Oakland 85-08-31 + Seattle Centre, Seattle 85-12-13.			
1985 ■	SVENSK METAL	2LP	- -	- -
	Recorded at Pomona Valley Auditorium, CA. 1985-05-11. White label.			
1985 ☐	A SIGN OF VIKING OPUS 1	2CDR	Metal Sword	MS CD 029
	Recorded at Pomona Valley Auditorium, CA 85-05-11.			
1985 ☐	A SIGN OF VIKING OPUS 2	2CDR	Metal Sword	MS CD 030/031
	Recorded at Hollywood palladium, CA 85-06-07.			
1985 ☐	TRANSONIC PLANET	CD	Planet X	PLAN 035
	Recorded in Miwaquee, WI 85-07-06.			
1985 ☐	ENSLAVING TONIGHT	2CD	- -	- -
	Recorded at Yubin Chockin Hall, Tokyo, 85-01-27.			
1985 ☐	NASVILLE	CD	- -	- -
	Recorded at Nashville Municipal Auditorium 85-11-15.			
1985 ☐	FIRST GIG IN CANADA	CDR	Langley	050
	Recorded Maple Leafs Garden, Toronto 85-09-23.			
1985 ☐	1985: GONNA BLOW YOUR FACE OFF	LP	n/a (Sweden)	n/a
	Demos.			
1985 ☐	THE TALES OF THE VIKING	CD	Aces High	AH CD 030
	Recorded at The Forum, LA 85-10-18.			
1985 ■	KNOXVILLE	CD	- -	- -
	Recorded in Knoxville 85-11-05.			
1985 ☐	MARK ON BALLS	2CD	D.A.T	- -
	Recorded at Center Coliseum, Seattle, 85-12-31 + Toledo, Ohio, 85-09-07.			
1986 ☐	Rising Force	MLP 4tr	private	RF-1 $
	No cover or label. It contains old re-mixed Rising Force demos and was released by Marcel Jacob as an attempt to get back some of the money he felt Yngwie owed him. Tracks: Merlins Castle/Birth Of The Sun/Dyin' Man/Suite Opus No 3. Later officially released on the CD Birth Of The Sun in 2002. Same as bootleg CD Something Else.			
1986 ■	1985	LP 6tr	WSR	Q 9024
	Same as above in different version. On the cover it says "Limited edition fan club release", but it most surely is a bootleg. Tracks: Chops City/Little Savage/Black Star/Far Beyond The Sun/Anguish & Fear/Disciples Of Hell.			
1986 ■	SPLITTING IMAGES - MAY THE RISING FORCE BE WITH YOU	2LP	Wonderwall (Canada)	- -
	Recorded at Summerfest Milwaquee 1985-07-07.			
1986 ☐	THE VIKINGS ARE BACK	2LP	YJM	YJM1/2/2/4
	Recorded at NHK Hall, Tokyo 1986-11-09.			
1986 ☐	YOU DON'T REMEMBER, I'LL NEVER FORGET	2LP	Bench Records	8614191
	Recorded at Festival Hall, Osaka 1986-11-14.			
1986 ☐	ALPINE VALLEY 1986	CD	Aces High	AHCD 004
	Recorded in Alpine Valley, Wisconsin 86-09-20.			
1986 ☐	MARK ON BALLS	2CD	D.A.T (Japan)	008/009
	Toledo, Ohio 95-09-07 and Seattle, WA 85-12-31.			
1986 ☐	THE VIKING AGES	2CD	Metal Sword	MSCD 046/047
	Recorded at NHK Hall, Tokyo, Japan 85-11-09.			
1986 ☐	VISIONS OF THE FIRE	2CD-R	No Limit (Japan)	023/024
	Recorded at Shibuya Kokaido, 86-1--07.			
1986 ☐	TEXAS REMEMBER	CD	Jailbait (Japan)	JBCD 035
	Recorded Dallas, Texas, 86-09-14.			
1986 ☐	NIGHT OF TRILOGY	2CD	Shades	057
	Recorded at NHK Hall, Tokyo, 86-11-09. Evening show.			
1987 ☐	THE VIKING'S DREAM OPUS	CD	YMCD (Japan)	YMCD 001
	Featuring 12 tracks from various dates and places.			

1985 - - -

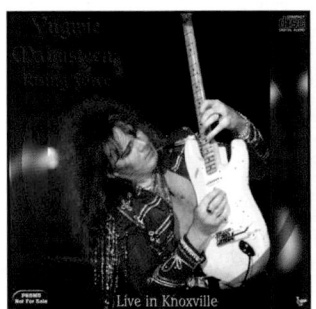

1985 CD - - -

1986 LP - Q 9024

1986 2LP - - -

Year		Title	Format	Label	Catalog
1987	☐	AS ABOVE SO BELOW	2LP	Keri Records/Megafarts	HE 1620R

Recorded at Sun Plaza Hall, Tokyo 85-01-24.

1987 ☐ BY REQUEST ....CD 8-Ball (Japan) 8-Ball 004
Studio outtakes 1987 + Studio rehearsal 1987-09-29.

1987 ☐ I SURRENDER ....CD-R TMOQ (Japan) ....TMOQ
1987 Odyssey Tour instrumental rehearsals. Same as "By Request".

1987 ☐ FAR BEYOND THE USA.....................CD Bondage (Japan) ....BON 060
Troy, NY, 87-01-11 + San Fransisco with Anvil Chorus 83-11-19.

1988 ☐ THE SUITE OF SOULMATE ....2CD Firefall FF-002-03
Recorded Festival Hall, Osaka 88-08-17 and Minneapolis 85-10-29.

1988 ☐ DREAMING.....................CD Music House ....HD 22
Recorded at Tower Theatre Upper Darby, PA, 88-07-10.

1998 ☐ THE VIKING'S DREAM OPUS 2 ....2CD-R Vikingdom (Japan)......... VIKINGDOM 039/040
Unreleased demos + Guitar clinic in Akasaka Blitz, Japan 98-04-07.

1988 ☐ HEAVEN TONIGHT IN JAPAN.....................2CD Heaven Tonight (Japan)..............- -
Recorded at Kyoto Kalkan Daichii Hall, Kyoto 88-08-20.

1988 ☐ HIGHWAY STAR ....2CD - - 8 8171/8172
Recorded at Festival Hall, Osaka 88-08-17 and Yokohama 88-08-23

1988 ☐ 1988: AN AXE ODYSEEY ....2CD Langley 036
Recorded Dominion Theatre, London 88-11-20.

1988 ☐ STREET OF DREAMS.....................2CD Jailbait (Japan) ....JBCD 042/043
Recorded at Toads Place, New Haven, Connecticut 88-07-21.

1988 ☐ ODYSSEY TOUR.....................2CD Paradise (Japan) ....YJM 823
Recorded in Yokohama, Japan 88-08-23.

1988 ☐ I SURRENDER 1988 ....2CD Langley 026
Recorded at Lisebergshallen, Göteborg 88-12-18.

1990 ☐ YING YANG'S FIRST STAND ....2LP Bud Records ....Y 1013
Recorded in Lund, Sweden 1990-04-05. The first gig with Yngwie, Göran, Mats, Svante and Michael in the line-up.

1990 2CD - YM 2161/2162

1990 ☐ SWEDISH ALCHEMY ....2CD Metal Sword ....MSCD 069/070
Recorded at Nakano Sun-Plaza, Tokyo, 90-06-22.

1990 ☐ KISS THE SKY ....2CD YM (Japan) ....YM 2061/2062
Recorded at Nakano Sun-Plaza, Tokyo, 90-06-21.

1990 ■ KISS THE SKY 2 ....2CD YM (Japan) ....YM 2161/2162
Recorded at Koseinenkinkaikan, Osaka, 90-06-20.

1990 ■ DOUBLE ECLIPSE ....CD Jailbait (Japan) ....JBCD 044
Recorded at The Ritz, New York 90-08-21.

1990 CD - JBCD 044

1991 ☐ I'M A VIKING ....2LP Taurus 0049111
199? ■ SWEDISH DEVIL ....CD Crystal Sound ....CS 006
A collection of old demos with made of 3rd generation copies.

1991 ☐ JAPAN LIVE PRESENTS.....................CD Blaze Music (Malaysia)................BM 0069
Great sound board recording w Mats Levén, making 1991 impossible as release year.

1991 ■ AS ABOVE SO BELOW ....2LP Golden Stars (Italy)................GSLP 2040 BS
Recorded at Tokyo Sun Plaza, Tokyo 85-01-24.

1991 ☐ AS ABOVE SO BELOW ....CD Golden Stars (Italy)................GSCD 1040
Recorded at Tokyo Sun Plaza, Tokyo 85-01-24.

199? CD - CS 006

1992 ☐ KISS THE SKY ....LP Hee Jee U(Korea)................HJLR 0042
Featuring Yngwie, Edman, Jens, Svante Henrysson and Pete Barnacle.

1992 ☐ SOMETHING ELSE.....................CD Crystal Sound ....CS 013
Contains demos + live-tracks from Nagoys, Osaka, Hyogo and Tokyo.

1992 ☐ NO MERCY ....2CD No Mercy (Japan) 2 3141/3142
Recorded at Budokan, Tokyo, 92-03-14.

1992 ■ ATTACK OF THE VIKING CHIEF ....2CD Meteorite ....MR 05-1/2
Recorded in in Montral 1992-05-18 and Budokan, Tokyo 1992-03-14.

1992 ☐ VIKING AXE.....................CD Stay Sharp ....STS 70505
Recorded in Milan, Italy (says Switzerland on the cover) 1992.

1992 ☐ MIAMI VICE.....................CD Jailbait (Japan) ....JBCD 052
Studio rehearsals 1992 for "Fire & Ice" tour in Maiami, FL + early demos.

1992 ☐ MIAMI VICE.....................CD-R Jailbait (Japan) ....-
Studio rehearsals 1992 for "Fire & Ice" tour in Maiami, FL + early demos. Second press.

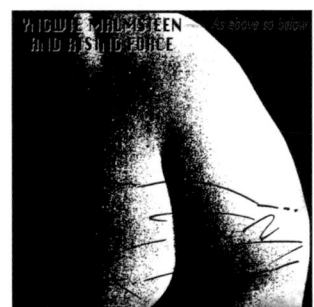
GSLP 2040 BS

1994 ☐ PYRAMID OF CHEOPS ....2CD Sonic Boom SH-3181-82
Japanese bootleg recorded at Omiya Sonic City 94-03-18.

1994 ☐ HIGHWAY STAR ....2CD-R Nightlife (Japan)................N-030-31
Recorded at Festival Hall, Osaka 86-11-14.

1994 ☐ REHEARSALS '83 ....2CD Nightlife ....N 018/019
1994 ☐ HEAVEN TONIGHT ....2CD PD Wyvern.....................WYM 35 F1/2
Recorded at Festival Hall, Osaka, 94-03-14.

1994 ☐ TOKYO NIGHT ....2CD Tube................TUCD 007/008
Recorded at Budokan, Tokyo, March 16, 1994-03-16.

1994 ☐ CLASH AND BURN ....2CD Sonic Boom ....SH 943161/2
Recorded at Budokan, Tokyo, March 16 and Omiya 94-03-18.

1994 ☐ EARLY DEMO'S VOL. 1 ....CD Nightlife N-012
Japanese bootleg featuring demo's from 1981-82.

1994 ☐ EARLY DEMO'S VOL. 2 ....CD Nightlife N-016
Japanese bootleg featuring 1982-demos.

1994 ☐ EARLY DEMO'S Vol. 1+2+3 ....3CD Nightlife N-012--016-017
CD box with sticker and photo.

1992 2CD - MR 05-1/2

1994 ☐	TOKYO NIGHT	2CD	Tube (Japan)	TUCD 007/8

Recorded at Budokan, Tokyo, 94-03-14.

1994 ■	ROUGH CUT	CD 7tr	Crystal Sound	CS 23

Japanese bootleg featuring rough mixed demos from Seventh Sign.

1994 ■	PYRAMID OF CHEOPS	2CD	Spider Glass (Italy)	SGCD 016/17

Recorded in Palasesto, Milan, Italy 94-05-23.

1995 ☐	Y MALMSTEEN ON VOCAL 1995	2CD-R	Magnum (Japan)	11/12

Recorded in Schuner, Switzerland, 95-12-10.

1995 ☐	THE REAL VIKING	CD	YM	YM 2256-2

Compilation of B-sides and rare tracks.

1995 ☐	LAST SWEDISH HERO	CD	Bondage (Japan)	BON 066

Recorded in Sundsvall, Sweden, 95-11-17.

1995 ☐	LIVE OPUS	2CD	My Phenix Co. (Japan)	BS 8/9

Recorded in Koseinenkin Hall, Sapporo, Japan, 95-09-22.

1995 ☐	EUROPEAN MAGNUM	CD-R	Shelter (Japan)	- -

Recorded in Kristianstad, Sweden, 95-11-21.

1995 ☐	MAGNUM SIGN	2CD-R	- -	- -

Recorded in Kyusyu, Fukuoka 1995-09-09.

1995 ☐	THE MAGNUM OPUS TOUR 1995	2CD	YM	YM-509111/-112

Recorded in Yubinchokin Hall, Hiroshima, 95-09-11.

1995 ☐	INSIDE OF YOU	2CD-R	Sylph	SP 91595215

Recorded at Festival Hall, Osaka, 95-09-15.

1995 ☐	FORBIDDEN KNOWLEDGE	2CD-R	Sylph	SP 91895216

Recorded at Alcaic Hall, Osaka, 95-09-18.

1995 ■	FOREVER ONE	CD	Kobra (Germany)	KRHM 09

Recorded in Sundsvall, Sweden 95-11-17 + Budokan, Tokyo 94-03-16

1995 ☐	SWEDISH MAGNUM IN JAPAN 1995	2CD-R	Jailbait (Japan)	JBCD 009/010

Recorded in Kyoto Japan, 95-09-16, Osaka, Japan 95-09-15, Hyogo, Japan 95-09-18.

1996 ☐	THE VIKING'S DREAM OPUS 1	CD	- -	YM 001

Various recording from USA and Japan 1984-1994, plus one track with Ronnie J Dio.

1996 ☐	INSPIRE MYSELF	2CD	Warheads (Japan)	WAR 003/004

Recorded in Osaka Festival Hall 96-11-04.

1996 ■	FIRST NIGHT INSPIRATION	2CD box	8-Ball (Japan)	014/015

Recorded in Birch Hall Night Club, New Jersey, 96-08-16.

1996 ☐	REGAL	2CD-R	Shelter (Japan)	- -

Recorded in Tilburg, Germany, 96-11-26.

1996 ☐	SHACHIHOKO TAPE	2CD-R	Shelter (Japan)	- -

Recorded in Nagoya, Japan, 96-02-11.

1996 ☐	TOO YOUNG TO DIE, TOO DRUNK TO LIVE	2CD-R	Shelter (Japan)	- -

Recorded in Nagoya, Japan, 95-09-19.

1996 ☐	LONDON '96	2CD-R	- -	- -

Recorded at Astoria, London, 96-11-26.

1996 ☐	DANVILLE FORCE	2CD	8-Ball (Japan)	012/013

Danville, Illinpois, USA, 88-06-24. Soundboard.

n/a ☐	BURNING OF LOVE '85	2CD	Neptune (Japan)	NT 53221/2

Recorded in Osaka 85-01-22.

1996 ☐	BURN BITCH BURN	2CD-R	Bio (Japan)	- -

Recorded in Shaunberg, Illinois, USA, 96-09-20

1996 ☐	ALIVE	2CD-R	- -	- -

Recorded in Shikokaido, Nagoya, Japan, 96-11-02.

1996 ☐	EDGE OF INSPIRATION	2CD	Zkaraztsmhgkaz	SB 001/002

Live 96-11-04 + 86-10-21 sound check.

1996 ☐	IN THE DEAD OF LAST NIGHT	2CD	Pour The Soul (Japan)	TCD 009/010

Recorded at Nakano Sun Plaza, Tokyo, 96-11-07.

1996 ☐	FAR BEYOND SWEDEN	2CD-R	Shelter (Japan)	- -

Recorded in Malmö, Sweden, 96-11-10.

1996 ☐	FIRST NIGHT INSPIRATION	2CD	- -	014/015
1996 ☐	PLAYING IN PARADISE	2CD	- -	- -

Recorded In Amsterdam 96-11-27.

1996 ■	GATES OF INSPIRATION	2CD	YM	YM 002/-3

Recorded in Detroit, USA, 96-09-14.

1998 ☐	FACING THE ANIMAL 1998 JAPAN TOUR	2CD-R	Reality	- -

Recorded Shibuya, Tokyo, Japan, 98-04-05.

1997 ☐	HOME SWEET HOME	2CD	Ascap	YJM 612141/2

Live in Longbeach Artena, CA 1986-12-14.

199? ☐	I'LL SEE THE LIGHT IN THE VEGAS DESERT	2CD	Demon's Eye (Japan)	DE-018-19

Recorded Las Vegas 86-01-10, Minneapolis 85-10-29, Pink Pop Holland 85-05-27 and Hollywood palladium, CA 85-01-07.

1998 ☐	FACING THE ANIMALMSTEEN	2CD-R	Facing (Japan)	n/a

Recorded in Nagoya, Japan, 98-04-17 + 2 bonus-tracks.

1998 ☐	FACING THE PARADISE	2CD-R	Sylph (Japan)	n/a

Recorded in Osaka, Japan, 98-04-21.

1998 ☐	BEAST IN PARADISE	2CD-R	Vikingdom (Japan)	VIKINGDOM 001/2

Recorded in Kurashiki, Japan, 98-04-18.

1998 ☐	LAST SHOW IN HEAVEN	2CD-R	Vikingdom (Japan)	VIKINGDOM 003/4

Recorded in Fukuoka, Japan, 98-04-24.

1998 ☐	LIVE IN SHEFFIELD 1988	2CD-R	HSD (Japan)	HSD-003

1994 CD - CS 23

1994 2CD - SGCD 016/17

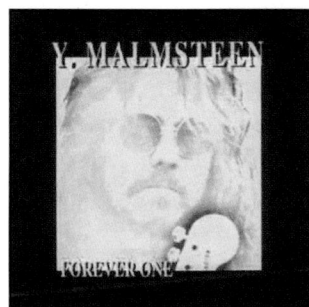

1995 CD - KRHM 09

1996 2CD box - 014/015

1996 CD - YM 002/-3

Year		Title	Format	Label	Catalog
1998	☐	OUT IN THE LIGHT	2CD-R	Vikingdom (Japan)	VIKINGDOM 015/016

1998 ☐ OUT IN THE LIGHT .... 2CD-R — Vikingdom (Japan) .... VIKINGDOM 015/016
   Recorded in Kawaguchi, Japan, 98-04-12.
1998 ☐ LIVE ON THE EDGE .... 2CD-R — Vikingdom (Japan) .... VIKINGDOM 005/6
   Recorded in Sapporo, Japan, 98-04-15.
1998 ☐ ETERNAL BURNING .... 2CD-R — Vikingdom (Japan) .... n/a
   Recorded in Osaka, Japan, 98-04-20.
1998 ☐ LIKE AN ANGEL .... 2CD-R — Gold&Platinum (Japan) .... n/a
   Recorded in Osaka, Japan, 98-04-20.
1998 ☐ HIROSHIMA MON AMOUR 94 .... 2CD-R — Vikingdom (Japan) .... VIKINGDOM 017/018
   Recorded in Hiroshima, Japan, 94-03-11.
1998 ☐ KING OF THE ANIMAL .... CD-R — Vikingdom (Japan) .... VIKINGDOM 013/014
   Recorded in Tokyo, Japan, 98-04-10.
199? ■ PERPETUAL PRODIGY .... 2CD-R — Lost And Found LAF1617/1618
   Recorded in Paris, France 92-04-14 and Tokyo, Japan, 92-03-14. 100 copies.

199? 2CD-R - LAF1617/1618

1998 ☐ LOVE IS BLUE 98 .... 2CD-R — - .... - -
   Recorded at Koseinenkin Hall, Nagoya 98-04-17.
1998 ☐ DOUBLE ECLIPSE .... CD-R — Jailbait (Japan) .... JBCD 044
   Recorded at Ritz, New York, 90-08-21. Second press.
1998 ☐ CRYSTAL EYES .... 2CD — Vikingdom (Japan) .... VIKINGDOM 019/020
   Recorded in Hiroshima 90-06-18.
1998 ☐ SOLDIER OF THE VIKING 85 .... 2CD-R — Vikingdom (Japan) .... VIKINGDOM 021/022
   Recorded at Municipal Auditorium, Nashville 85-11-15 and Coliseum Oakland, 85-10-19.
1998 ☐ FOURTH NIGHT .... 2CD-R — Vikingdom (Japan) .... VIKINGDOM 011/012
   Recorded in Yokohama, Japan, 98-04-09.
1998 ☐ LOVE ME OR LEAVE ME .... 2CD-R — TMOQ (Japan) .... - -
   Recorded at Akazaka Blitz, Tokyo, Japan, 98-04-07.
1998 ☐ WILD, YOUNG & FREE .... 2CD-R — TMOQ (Japan) .... - -
   Recorded at Akasaka Bllitz, Tokyo, Japan, 98-04-06.
1998 ☐ HEAVEN TONIGHT - LIVE AT UMEDA HIGH BEAT .... 2CD-R — No Limit Production (Japan) 11/12
   Recorded at Umeda High Beat, Osaka, 98-04-22.

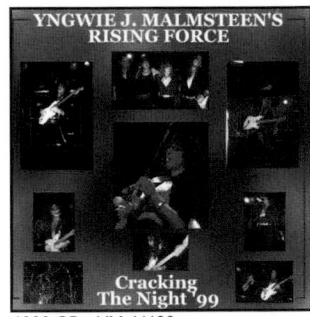

1999 CD - YM 41199

1999 ☐ PLAYING IN ASYLUM .... 2CD-R — Vikingdom (Japan) .... VIKINGDOM 023/024
   Recorded in Fukuoka, Japan, 99-11-24.
1999 ☐ LIVE REGION IN ASYLUM .... 2CD-R — Vikingdom (Japan) .... VIKINGDOM 025/026
   Recorded at Koseinenkin Kaikan, Osaka, Jaoan, 99-11-25.
1999 ☐ HANGER K.N.K AREA OSK .... 2CD-R — Sylph .... SP 251-42
   Recorded at Koseinenkin Kaikan, Osaka, Japan, 99-11-25.
1999 ☐ LIGHTNING BLITZKRIEG .... 2CD-R — Vikingdom (Japan) .... VIKINGDOM 029/030
   Recorded Shibuya-Kokaido, Tokyo, 99-11-29.
1999 ☐ SOLDIER OF HELL .... 2CD-R — Vikingdom (Japan) .... VIKINGDOM 031/032
   Recorded at Civic Coliseum, Knoxv 85-11-09 and Wings Stadium, Kalamazoo 86-09-19.
1999 ☐ PLAYING WITH BOALS. .... 2CD-R — - .... - -
   Recorded at Shikokaido, Nagoya, Japan, 99-11-26.
1999 ■ CRACKING THE NIGHT 99 .... CD — YM .... YM 41199
   Recorded at Birch Hill Night Club, Old Bridge, NJ, USA, 99-11-04.
1999 ■ GALAXY GUITAR GOD .... 2CD — Shout To The Top .... STTP 069/070
   Recorded at Galaxy Theatre, Costa Mesa, CA 99-11-10 and at The Country Club,
   Reseda, CA, 84-03-29.

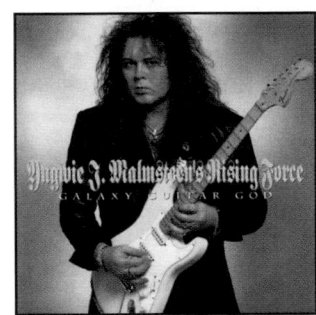

1999 2CD - STTP 069/070

1999 ☐ BURN 1999 IN JAPAN .... 2CD-R — Mobile Reality Sound Lab .... - -
   Recorded at Kanagawa Kenmin Hall, Yokohama, 99-12-02.
n/a ☐ THE REAL VIKING .... CD — Ym Records (Japan) .... - -
n/a ☐ BIRTH OF THE RISING FORCE .... CD — Mother Earth (Japan) .... ME 020
   Demo recorded 81-11-16 + Rising Force demo.
n/a ☐ THE RISING FORCE UNRELEASED TRACKS .... CD — Black Ghost (Japan) .... BGRGH 002
n/a ☐ STEELER EXCITED '83 .... 2CD — 33 (Japan) .... ST 355/RH 51018
   1 CD Steeler live at Perkin's Palace 83-05-05 + 1 CD Rising Force live at The Forum,
   Inglewood 1985-10-18.
n/a ☐ LITTLE SAVAGE .... CD — YMS (Japan) .... YMS 0524
   Contains demo 85-05-24, RISING FORCE demo + 1 track live Manchester, UK 88-11-17.
n/a ☐ SWEDISH GOD .... CD — Bondage (Japan) .... BON 011
   Live in Milwaukee 1985-07-06.
n/a ☐ PLAY LOUD .... CD — - .... RF 85 YM
   Recorded at Metro Centre, Minneapolis 85-10-29, Pink Pop, Holland 85-05-27, Hollywood
   Palladium 85-06-07.

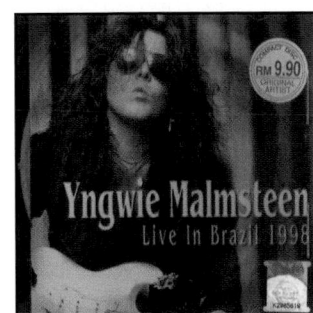

2000 CD - JDP 12

2000 ☐ FATAL ALUMNI .... CD — Bondage (Japan) .... BON 222
   Recorded at Universal Amphitheatre, LA, 00-11-18 and Music Fair, Frankfurt, Germany
   99-03-06.
2000 ☐ JORN LANDE ON VOCAL .... 2CD-R — Vikingdom (Japan) .... VIKINGDOM 033/034
   Recorded at Ogden Theatre, Denver Nov 25, 2000 and House Of Blues, Chicago 00-11-
   28.
2000 ■ LIVE IN BRAZIL 1998 .... CD — JD Records (Brazil) .... JDP 12
   Recorded in Brazil 1998.
2001 ☐ PHILHARMONIC ORCHESTRA 2001 .... 3CD-R — N.N .... N.N 01615176
   Recorded at Sumida Triphony Hall, Tokyo, 01-06-05 and Bunkamura Hall, Tokyo, 01-06-
   17.
2001 ■ SWEDISH ALCHEMY .... 2CD-R — Metal Sword .... MS CD 069/70
   Recorded at Yokohama Bay Hall, Kanagawa, 01-06-13.
2001 ☐ JACKPOT BABY .... 2CD-R — Sylph SP-71301218
   Recorded at Yokohama Bay Hall, Kanagawa, 01-06-13.

2001 2CD-R - MS CD 069/70

2001	☐	CATCH THE DREAMING	2CD-R	Sylph	SP-71401217

Recorded at Shibuya Kokaido, Tokyo, 01-07-14.

2001	☐	ANCIENT INCANTATION	2CD-R	Sylph	SP-71601221

Recorded at Koseinenkin Kaikan, Osaka, 01-07-16.

2001	☐	HIROSHIMA MON AMOUR 2001	2CD-R	Vikingdom (Japan)	VIKINGDOM 035/036

Recorded at Aster Plaza, Hiroshima, 01-07-17.

2001	☐	FUKUOKA MON AMOUR 2001	2CD-R	Vikingdom (Japan)	VIKINGDOM 037/038

Recorded at Skaraespashio, Fukuoka 01-07-18.

2001	☐	THE TALES OF THE VIKING	CD	Aces High Sound Production	AH CD 030

Recorded at The Forum, LA, USA, 85-10-18. 300 copies.

2001	☐	WE ARE ONE	2CD-R	Sylph	SP-71901230

Recorded at Club Diamond Hall, Nagoya, 01-07-19.

2001	☐	RUNNING WILD	2CD-R	Sylph	SP-72201229

Recorded at Akasaka Blitz, Tokyo, 01-07-22.

2002	☐	TIME FOR ME TO RISE	2CD-R	Sylph	0462

1978 demos by Powerhouse.

2003	■	YNGWIE MALMSTEEN'S POWERHOUSE	CD	Hit & Run	- -

1978 demos by Powerhouse.

2003 CD - - -

2007	☐	THE REAL VIKING	CD	YM Records	YM 2256-2

B-sides and rare.

2008	☐	RETURN OF ROCK STAR	2CD	Invisible Works	5843-72453-4

Recorded in Göteborg 08-07-16.

2008	☐	RIPPER RISING	2CD-R	Lost And Found	LAF 577/578

Recorded in Göteborg 08-07-16. 100 copies.

2008	■	AGORA THEATER 2008	2CD	Moon Callf Disc	MCD-006

Recorded at Agora Theater, Cleveland, 08-10-18.

2008 2CD - MCD-006

MAMA KIN

Kristian Ward: v/g, Elias Håkansson: g, Jon Stinnerbom: b, Edvin Norrman: d

Karlstad - In 2001 a bunch of guys, Ward (ex-***Ben Dover***), Stinnerbom and Norrman (ex-***Havoc***), during a drinking night on the town, decided they would form a band and rehearse the next day. Well, as it happens they actually did and they had soon recorded their first demo. The name was of course taken from the old ***Aerosmith*** song. In 2005 Håkansson (ex-***Havoc***) completed the line-up. Style-wise, they do have a few similarities, although ***Mama Kin*** is quite cliché-filled sleazy hard rock with hints of ***Crüe***, ***Poison***, ***Kiss*** etc.

2009	☐	Superman/One Of A Kind	CDS	Leon Music	LEON 001
2009	■	IN THE CITY	CD	Leon Music	LEON 004
2010	☐	IN THE CITY	CD	Jamsync (USA)	JSM 042710

2009 CD - LEON 004

MAMMOTH VOLUME

Jörgen Andersson: v, Daniel Gustafsson: g/k, Kalle Berlin: b, Nicklas Andersson: d

Lysekil - ***Mammoth Volume*** was formed in 1996 by Nicklas and Daniel. The band plays seventies hard rock, mixing influences from the traditional hard rock bands like ***Budgie*** and ***Deep Purple*** with more psychedelic and spacey stuff like ***Mahavishnu Orchestra***. A Great band! The album *The Early Years* contains demo songs recorded between 1997-1998.

1999	☐	MAMMOTH VOLUME	CD	The Music Cartel (USA)	TMC 22 CD
2000	☐	NOARA DANCE	CDd	The Music Cartel (USA)	TMC 35 CD
2000	☐	NOARA DANCE	LP	The Music Cartel (USA)	TMC 35 LP
2001	☐	A SINGLE BOOK OF SONGS BY	CDd	The Music Cartel (USA)	TMC 49 CD
2002	■	THE EARLY YEARS	CD	The Music Cartel (USA)	TMC 58 CD

2002 CD - TMC 58 CD

MAMMUTH

Daniel Jakobsson: v, Mikael Larsson: g, Carl-Magnus "Calle" Palm: g, Samuel Larsson: b, Daniel Backman: d

Jönköping - Christian rockers ***Mammuth***, of course hailing from Jönköping, were formed in August 2000. Two years later they were signed by Christian label Talking Music, who released their debut in January the following year. ***Mammuth*** plays heavy, riff-oriented hardcore-infused modern metal, at times with a touch of ***Rage Against The Machine***, but with melodic vocals. On *Die To Rise In Spring* the style was more hardcore-influenced and the vocals took on a more aggressive edge. On *The Cardiac Defect* they changed bassist from Henrik Olofsson to Samuel. This album took the band even closer to the almost emo-influenced modern nu-metal genre, not at all as interesting as the previous, and especially first, album.

2005 CD - TALKCD 1049

2003	☐	SHINE	CD	Talking Music	TALKCD 1027
2004	☐	Embraced	MCDd 4tr	Talking Music	TALKCD 1038

Tracks: Embraced/Graceland/Du är mitt ljus/Star Of Hope

2005	■	DIE TO RISE IN SPRING	CD	Talking Music	TALKCD 1049
2008	■	THE CARDIAC DEFECT	CD	Talking Music	TALKCD 1073

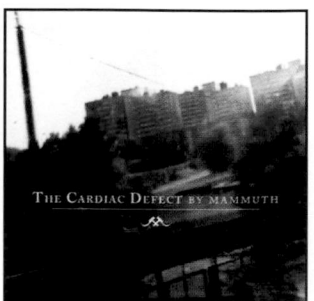

2008 CD - TALKCD 1073

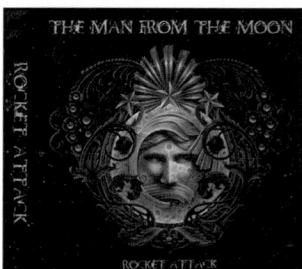

MAN.MACHINE.INDUSTRY (aka M.M.I)

Jhonny "Berget" Bergman : v, Jimmy "Car Crash Jim" Bergman: g,
Sulan "13" Von Zoomlander: b, Albin Bennich: d

Stockholm - *Man.Machine.Industry*, sometimes referred to as *M.M.I*, was formed in 2000 as a
solo project by *Rosicrucian/Slapdash/Mr:Hangpike And Adams Leaf*-singer Berget, influenced
by early *Ministry* and *Front Line Assembly*. In 2004 he brought in some friends to help out,
bass player Nalle and drummer Dennis "DNA". The second album also featured guest spots
from Gustaf Jorde (*Defleshed*) and Patrik Wirén (*Misery Loves Co*.). In 2010 Dennis abruptly
left the band, and was instantly replaced on tour by Adde Larsson (*Engel, Urbandux*). A permanent drummer was found in Thomas Manell (*Pronoid*) in 2011 and a permanent guitarist
in Jimmy Bergman. The band was also completed on stage by bassists Misha Sedini (*Come
Sleep, Lingua*) and David Wiltz. The third album, *Lean Back, Relax And Watch The World
Burn*, features guest vocals from *Corroded*'s Jens Westin. The band then saw new bassist 13
(*Nothing Divine*) and drummer Bennich (*Centicore*) in the line-up.

2001 □ MENTION	CD	Hi-Tech Music Design	H.T.M.D 001
2004 □ Be Like The Dog You Are And Enter The Circle	MCD 6tr	Hi-Tech Music Design	H.T.M.D 002
Tracks: Enter The Circle/The Devil IS A Liar/Escape The Good/Hard Core Criminal/What He Said/Dei Grata			
2010 □ WHITE TRASH DEVIL IN A JESUS POSE	CD	GMR	GMRCD 9020
2012 ■ LEAN BACK, RELAX AND WATCH THE WORLD BURN	CD	GMR	GMRCD 9032

2012 CD - GMRCD 9032

MAN FROM THE MOON, THE

Micke "Mimo" Moberg: v/g/b/d

Nacka - Micke Moberg has previously made numerous recordings with bands like *Zeta, Moberg-
Talton, Garvin, The Voice, 2001* etc. In 2007 he started his solo project *The Man From The
Moon*. *The Man From The Moon* plays melodic hard rock with a strong eighties touch with
programmed drums. Moberg helped record the last five *Bathory* albums, which explains why
the album was out on Black Mark. In 2011 the new album *Instrumental Injection* was recorded,
only released as a digital album. He also plans to launch his new project *Luna Metusa*.
Website: www.mimosound.com

2007 □ My Home Town/Warmblooded Woman	CDS 2tr	Black Mark	BMS 189
2008 ■ ROCKET ATTACK	CDd	Black Mark	BMDP 189
2009 □ I'm Going Home/Let Us Fly In The Night/The Happy Hooker	MCD 3tr	MIMO	MIMO-CDS-012

2008 CDd - BMDP 189

MANDALA

Johan Hansson: v, Mikael Johannesson: g, Sixten Jaskari: b, Ulf Johansson: d

Stockholm - This band's only release was a 4-track promo-CD, but it's well worth searching
for. *Mandala* produces great powerful grungy heavy rock quite reminiscent of the first *Alice
In Chains*-album. Johan and Mikael previously recorded a MCD under the name *Tippen Ruda*
and Jaskari was in the band *Cut 4*. They recorded a new 2-track demo in March 1995 and it
showed great promise. Unfortunately the band folded. Michael moved to England, but returned
to Sweden and joined cover band *Lovehandles*, which started writing their own material and
have now made several releases. He is also in UK band *Evilyn Strange*.

| 1994 ■ Mandala | MCD 4tr | private | MACDS 001 |
| *Tracks: Esoteric Song/Ace Of Grace/Mandala/My Intestinals.* | | | |

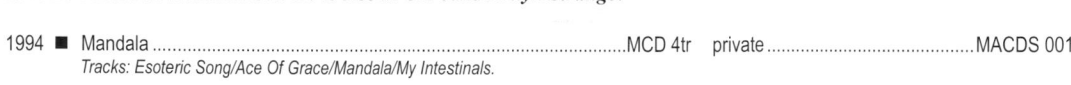

1994 MCD - MACDS 001

MANDRAKE ROOT

Per Englund: v, David Braic: g, Staffan Stavers: k, Tommy Braic: b, Hempo Hildén: d

Växjö - The debut is a bit too varied, but contains some great *Deep Purple*-influenced hard rock.
The full length is a great effort in the traditional guitar/keyboard-oriented *Purple*-vein, but was
initially only released in Japan. Per is also found in *Blacksmith, Garbo* and *Motherlode* and has
also worked with the *220 Volt* boys in the band *Voltergeist*. Hempo (*John Norum, Trash* etc)
joined the band in 1996. On the Swedish version of the album Stefan Nilsson, Ted Wernersson
(later in *Locomotive Breath*) and Hempo Hildén play drums. Stefan was the band's drummer on
the first release. The Swedish version contains a cover of Holland/Holland/Dozier's *You Keep
Me Hangin' On*. The band recorded material for a new album, but it was unfortunately never
released. In 2001 the band picked up where they left off and the second album was supposed to
be recorded, possibly with a different singer, but nothing surfaced. Braic is now in *Blackmore's
Night* soundalikes *Minstrel Spirit* playing renaissance music with bells and whistles.

1993 MCD - PR 001

1993 ■ Waves In Motion	MCD 5tr	Pama Records	PR 001
Tracks: Inside Information/Speed Trippin'/Waves In Motion/Strange Walkin'/March Of The Immaculate			
1994 ■ TALES OF THE SACRED	CD	Zero (Japan)	XRCN-1172
Bonus: Movin' On Home/You Keep Me Hangin' On			
1996 □ TALES OF THE SACRED	CD	Local Dealer	LHM 0496
Bonus: Solitary Traveller/I Can't Stop Believin'			

1994 CD - XRCN-1172

MANGROVE

Jani Kataja: v/b, Magnus Jernström: g, Fredrik Broqvist: d

Stockholm - Power trio *Mangrove* plays retro hard rock, quite close to *The Quill*, and the singer sounds quite similar to former *The Quill* singer Magnus. The band was formed in 2006 and recorded their first demo a year later. It lead to a deal with Swedish retro label Transubstans and in 2009 the excellent debut *Endless Skies* was released. It was followed by the equally great *A Distant Dream Of Tomorrow*. Broqvist was also in *Sideburn*, where Kataja is still found.

2009 ■	ENDLESS SKIES	CDd	Transubstans	TRANS 045	
2010 □	A DISTANT DREAM OF TOMORROW	CDd	Transubstans	TRANS 070	

2009 CDd - TRANS 045

MANIAC

Fredrik Jansson: v/k, Lasse Hallin: g, Anders Hallin: g,
Robert Franck: b, Tobbe Broström: d

Piteå - The A-side starts out with a nice piano/vocal intro, but soon rips out into the old 80's metal style. The band does have quite a high degree of melodic feeling as well as good vocal qualities. Quite reminiscent of late *Gotham City*, with nice guitar work in the vein of John Norum. Well worth looking for. Broström is now in *Coldspell*.

1985 ■	(Grief) Beauty Queen/Take It Away	7"	private	TIN-S 003	$

1985 7" - TIN-S 003

MANIMAL

Samuel Nyman: v, Henrik Stenroos: g, Pether Mentzer: b, Rickard Mentzer: d

Kungsbacka (Göteborg) - Henrik and Rickard met already in their teens and then formed the band *Wildness*. In 2001 the band was completed where singer Nyman entered. The Mentzer brothers' uncle is none less than Christer "Chris" Mentzer (*Norden Light, Silver Mountain, Mentzer*). *Manimal* plays high-class melodic metal mixing more prog-oriented metal with classic power metal and Nyman's high-pitched vocals. Reminiscent of *Masterplan* and *Eden's Curse* with an additional touch of *Helloween*. The debut album was initially self-released. *Website: www.manimal.se*

2009 ■	THE DARKEST ROOM	CD	MMM	MMMCD 001	
2009 □	THE DARKEST ROOM	CD	AFM	AFMCD 292	

2009 CD - MMMCD 001

MANINNYA BLADE

Leif Eriksson: v, Nicklas "The Ripper" Johansson: g, Jerry Rutström: g,
Jan "Blomman" Blomqvist: b, Ingemar Lundberg: d

Boden/Stockholm - The band was formed around 1980, at first under the name *Fair Warning*. They recorded their first demo in 1982, under the old moniker, before changing the name to *Maninnya Blade*. Inbetween, Leif and Jan also recorded a couple of tracks with the band *Kamax*, which are found on the compilation *Kommersiell kultur* (1983 Pang). The first *Maninnya Blade* single featured Leif, Nicklas, Jan and Ingemar. After its release, Mikael "Mike Wead" Wikström joined. They recorded two demos with this line-up, but in 1985 they decided to move from the northern town of Boden, to Stockholm. However Mikael decided to stay and Jerry Rutström (*Diva/Deeva*) later replaced him. The first album contains a lethal dose of 80's heavy metal, not that well-played and produced but it was quite good for that time... Jerry was later replaced by ex-*Damien* guitarist Andreas "Rick Meister" Palm and Ingemar by Martin Eriksson. They then shortened their name to *Maninnya*. Leif was asked to leave and Nicklas took over his task. Wead, who had also moved to Stockholm, joined again and Martin left. Martin later found great international success as a rapper under the moniker *E-Type*. In 1987 the band changed their name to *Hexenhaus*. In 1990 Nicklas quit and moved back to Boden to start working in the theatre. He then reformed the band with Jerry, Jan and new drummer Johan Henriksson. On the bands 1995 demo Leif Eriksson sings, but he was soon sacked (for the second time) and his replacement was supposed to be *Diva/Deeva*-singer Christer Boquist. The new material showed the band still had a lot to offer the prog-thrash-doom-metal scene. *A Demonic Mistress...* contains the previously unreleased demos recorded after the first album, as well as the tracks off the first single. I however do prefer the 1995-demos. The band finally made an attempt to resurface in 2002. They did some live shows, but nothing really came out of it. In 2005 the band was contacted by Brazilian label Marquee, who released *Undead, Unborn, Alive...*, a collection of demos and live material from the 2002 re-union. The band recorded some new songs in 2007, but nothing was released. The last line-up featured singer Leif Larsson, guitarists Nicke Johansson and Jerry Rutström, bassist Jan Lindberg and drummer Andreas Lindmark.

1984 7" - PL 02

E-Type, being kicked out

1986 LP - KILP 4005

1984 ■	The Barbarian/Ripper Attack	7"	Platina	PL 02	$$
1986 ■	MERCHANTS IN METAL	LP	Killerwatt	KILP 4005	
2001 □	A DEMONIC MISTRESS FROM THE PAST	LP	Stormbringer	SKULL 9808	
	500 numbered copies in clear vinyl.				
2006 ■	UNDEAD, UNBORN, ALIVE	2CD	Marquee (Brazil)	MR 026	

2006 2CD - MR 026

MANSSON

Edde Weile: v, Jocke Sandberg: g, Michael "Manson" Månsson: g,
Richard Andersson: k, Michael Borup: d, Anders Johansson: d

Malmö - Quite an impressive line-up featuring Jocke Sandberg (*Aces High*), Anders Johansson (*Malmsteen, Hammerfall, FullForce, Aces High* etc), Richard Andersson (*Majestic, Time Requiem, Silver Seraph*) etc. The guest-list features even more: for example Peter Espinoza (*Nasty Idols, Espinoza*), Jonas Reingold (*Downtown Clowns, Reingold, The Flower Kings* etc) and Pete Sandberg (*Alien, Midnight Sun, Jade, Madison* etc). *Mansson* play classic melodic hard rock in the same category as *Scorpions*, with a singer reminiscent of Udo Dirkschneider. Unfortunately the musicians are better than the actual album. Main man Månsson is today working as a dentist in Germany.

1999 ■ ARCH OF DECADENCE ....CD   Point Music 10080

1999 CD - 10080

MANTICORE

Kjell Jansson: v, Ulf Holmberg: g, Erik Olsson: k,
Göran Holmberg: v/b, Putte Eriksson: d

Uppsala - A high-quality symphonic rock band that is influenced by *Kansas* and *Marillion*. The band was formed in 1986 by Ulf, Göran, Putte and former *Mirage* member Kjell. In 1992 the song *Time To Fly* was featured on the compilation *15 On 1* and the 4-track demo that followed caught the attention of US-label Lazers Edge who signed them. The band featured keyboard player Pär Lindh (*Pär Lindh Project*) in an early constellation.

1994 ▢ TIME TO FLY ....CD   Lazers Edge... LE 1020

1994 CD - LE 1020

MARAMON

Peter Ristiharju: v, Christer Karlsson: g, Henrik Tranemyr: g,
Denny Axelsson: b/v, Pär Hjulström: d

Lindesberg (Örebro) - *Maramon* was formed in 2001 when the boys were still in high school. The band recorded their first demo *Sömn* in 2002 and the follow-up *Dödens rike* the subsequent year. The band went through an array of member changes before recording the first album in 2006. Tranemyr has also played with *The Bereaved* and *Clone*, Axelsson has been in *Calm*, *The Bereaved* and *Blinded Colony*, while Hjulström is also found in *Amaran*. *Maramon* plays high-quality death-infused technical powerful metal with some thrash influences, mixing growl and clean vocals. The band has now split up.

2006 ■ ME, MYSELF, I...CD   Cyniscope ....CYNIREC 001

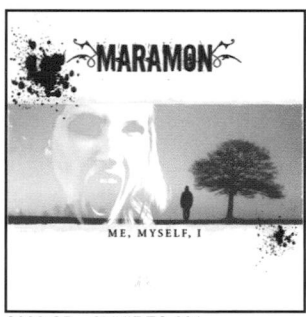
2006 CD - CYNIREC 001

MARC QUEE

(See Quee, Marc)

MARCELLO, KEE (aka KEE MARCELLO'S K2)

Kjell "Kee Marcello" Lövbom: g/v

Stockholm/Göteborg - Kjell "Kee Marcello" Lövbom started his career already in the late seventies and the jazz-rock band *Stetson Cody*. He then went into a pop era with bands like *D'Accord*, *Silver* and the slightly more rockier *Kee & The Kick* (where "Kee" was actually the female lead singer). In the early eighties he entered the genre that would change his life – glam! After a single with the band *Alex & Kee*, he joined *Easy Action* with whom he recorded and toured a lot. He then replaced John Norum in Europe in 1986 and recorded the albums *Out Of This World* and *Prisoners In Paradise* before the band folded. He then went solo, but unfortunately for the fans of the heavier *Europe* stuff, *Shine On* is pure AOR/westcoast rock. However, it's a style known to have been closest to Kee's heart for a long time, something you can hear on his early recordings. Unfortunately former *Europe* colleague Joey Tempest released a solo album in the same vein shortly before him, causing writers to accuse Kee of copying Joey. Kee's album is however musically different from Joey's and they complement each other quite well. His previous recording career goes as follows: *Stetson Cody* (7" - 1979 - jazz rock), *D'Accord* (7" - 1979 - West coast/AOR), *Silver* (7" - 1980 - guitar-oriented synth-pop), *Kee & The Kick* (7" - 1982 - AOR), *Alex & Kee* (12" - 1983 - glam rock), *Easy Action* (several recordings), *Europe* (several recordings) and *Red Fun* (several recordings). He has also did session work for Michael Rickfors, Ulf Wakenius and others. In 2004 Kee returned to heavy modern rock with the album *Melon Demon Drive*, now under the moniker *Kee Marcello's K2*. The band now featured drummer Snowy Shaw (*Dream Evil, Therion, Notre Dame* etc) and bass player Klatau (which was actually Kee himself). This was a low-down and dirty but very melodic modern rocker, quite weak and badly mixed, with song material all over the place. The band's live shows featured bassist Ulf "Ken" Sandin (*Alien, Transport League*). In 2005 he recorded the anthem for ice hockey team the Frölunda Indians, under the name *Stark* and together with

1995 CD - 955 031-2

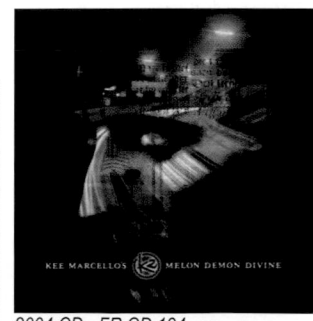
2004 CD - FR CD 194

2005 CDS - stark 001

Mikael Wikström. Kee has been frequently playing live with a rock band, performing *Europe* songs etc. In 2011 he released his autobiography, revealing his side of the Europe business. As part of the package he also released the album *Redux: Europe*, where he rerecorded some of the *Europe* tracks "the way they were meant to be". Funnily enough some of the tracks, such as *The Final Countdown*, *Rock The Night* and *Carrie* were written and recorded long before he even joined the band. The music is quite decent, but Kee's singing leaves a bit more to be desired, I'm afraid, at least comparing to the original versions. The musicians on the album are guitarist Jonny Scaramanga, keyboardist Tim Moore, bass player Ken Sandin and drummer Zoltan Csörcz (*The Flower Kings, Art Metal*). Another album entitled *Redux: Dog Eat Dog*, is also planned seeing Kee pay homage to his early hard rock influences. As the icing on the cake Kee announced 2012 would see the first big rock festival in Kee's name, *Keefest*. Well, the festival never happened, and the tour that was supposed to support his autobiography and Redux album was indefinitely postponed. However, he did some shows with a line-up featuring Kee, guitarist Magnus Scharin, keyboardist Lalle Larsson, bassist Richard Lindén and drummer Mats Cristiansson. Kee's autobiography *The Rock Star God Forgot* is well worth reading.

1988 7" - MR 8802

2011 CD - GPM 002

2011 CD - GPM 003

1995 ☐	Shine On/Call Me	CDS 2tr	CNR	188 073-3
1995 ■	SHINE ON	CD	CNR	955 031-2
1996 ☐	Sweet Little Sister/Together Alone	CDS 2tr	CNR	178 079-3
2004 ■	MELON DEMON DRIVE	CD	Frontiers	FR CD 194
	As Kee Marcello's K2			
2005 ■	Do It Again	CDS 1tr	STARK	stark 001
	As Stark			
2011 ■	KEE MARCELLO EUROPE	CD	TMS Artist & Media (promo)	- -
2011 ☐	REDUX. SHINE ON	CD	GPM Management	GPM 001
2011 ■	REDUX. MELON DEMON DRIVE	CD	GPM Management	GPM 002
2011 ■	REDUX. EUROPE	CD	GPM Management	GPM 003
2013 ☐	JUDAS KISS	CD	7Hard	7H 099 2

MARCUS BRUTUS BAND

Christer Johnsson: v/k, Janne Sjödin: g, Peter Carlberg: g/k, Björn "Rolle" Persson: b, Bo Thörnhult: d

Gävle - Formed in the late seventies. Traditional mid-league 80's heavy metal in the NWoBHM-vein with a touch of *Thin Lizzy*. Good but not very original. They later became the more AOR-oriented band *Wildborn*. Thomas Musial (*King Size*) has also been in and out of the band. Peter and Janne were later found in *Bigfoot*.

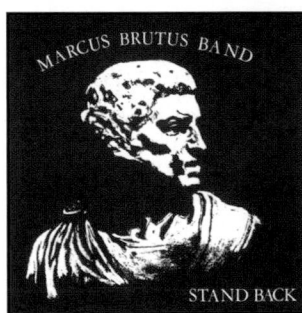

1983 ■ Stand Back/Pictures Of My Mind .... 7" Pang .... PSI 077 $

1983 7" - PSI 077

MARDUK

Daniel "Mortuus" Rostén: v, Morgan "Mogge/Steinmeyer" Håkansson: g, Magnus "Devo" Andersson: b, Lars Broddesson: d

Norrköping - Formed in September 1990 by Morgan. The name was taken from the Babylonian god who created earth and sky from the dragon Tiamat (the mother of all). One of Sweden's blackest metal bands, meaning they are incredibly evil in their approach. *Fuck Me Jesus* was actually the band's first demo, recorded in June 1991. Singer on the demo was Andreas "Dread/Drette" Axelsson, previously with pop/punksters *Lucky Seven* and later in *Edge Of Sanity*, Rickard Kalm played bass, Joakim "af Gravf" Göthberg handled the drums and Morgan guitar. In 1991 the band also recorded the single *Here's No Fucking Silence*, which was not released until six years later. On *Dark Endless* the line-up was Andreas, Mogge, guitarists Joakim and Magnus "Devo" Andersson and bassist Roger "Bogge/B-War" Svensson (although Rickard Kalm plays on the album). On *Those Of The Unlight* Andreas had left to play with *Edge Of Sanity* and Göthberg handled the vocals, while Fredrik Andersson played drums. Magnus later had his own band *Overflash* as well as being in bands like *Allegience* and *Cardinal Sin*. On that album Jocke Göthberg (later in *Grave, Dimension Zero* etc.) handled drums and vocals. Morgan himself has previously played with punksters *Moses*, who also made a demo entitled *I vassen* (In the weed). In 1994 they also recorded the *Black Flag*-cover *Drinkin' And Driving* that appears on the 7" compilation-EP *King Kong* (94 King Kong - KK 005). In 1995 Göthberg left the band to join *Cardinal Sin*. He later formed *Dimenzion Zero*. On *Opus Nocturne* singer Erik "Legion" Hagstedt (*Ophthalamia*) was added to the line-up and so was guitarist Kim Osara (*Overflash*). Morgan is also found in the black metal band *Abruptum*. Roger was previously in the *Rush*-inspired demo-band *Chained* and the two have also joined forces in the band *The Devil's Whorehouse*, now *Death Wolf*. Fredrik has recorded with the band *Triumphator*. In 1997 the band went on tour, reinforced with guitarist Peter Tägtgren (*Pain, Abyss, Hypocrisy*), which resulted in the live album *Live In Germania*. *Nightwing* was recorded and mixed by Peter Tägtgren. Morgan now formed the label Blooddawn, which reissued some of the older material. Early 2002 the band parted company with drummer Fredrik, who was replaced with Emil Dragutinovic

The panzer division

(*Nominon, Spawn Of Possession*). *Blackcrowned* is a box set featuring re-recordings, demos, rehearsals and also covers of *Misfits* and *Rolling Stones*. After this Hagstedt and Svensson left the band. *Infernal Eternal* was a double CD recorded live in France on the *World Panzer Battle Tour* in 1999. In 2004 the band released the DVD *Funeral Marches & War Songs*. Singer Legion was replaced by Daniel "Mortuus/Arioch" Rostén (*Funeral Mist, Triumphator*) and Magnus "Devo" Andersson returned, now as bassist. *Plague Angel* was the first album featuring the new line-up. In 2006 the band released the live DVD *Blood Puke Salvation* recorded in The Netherlands and Belgium. During the recordings of *Rom 5:12* Dragutinovic left the band, and was replaced by Lars Broddesson after recording most of the album. Göthberg adds some guest vocals on the album. 2009 saw the release of the band's album *Wormwood*, followed by the EP *Iron Dawn*. In 2011 the band was picked up by Century Media who released the MLP *Iron Dawn* in 2012, followed by the album *Serpent Sermon* later the same year. *Marduk* is one of the early very influential black metal bands alongside and in the same vein as *Dissection* and *Dark Funeral*. The style and sound has been refined over the years, but without losing the aggressiveness and primeval anger.

1992 CD - NFRCD 003

Year		Title	Format	Label	Cat. No.	
1992	☐	DARK ENDLESS	LP	No Fashion	NFR003	
1992	■	DARK ENDLESS	CD	No Fashion	NFRCD 003	
1993	☐	DARK ENDLESS	CD	Necropolis (USA)	NR 005	
1993	☐	THOSE OF THE UNLIGHT	CD	Osmose	OPCD015	
1993	☐	THOSE OF THE UNLIGHT	LP	Osmose	OPLP 015	
1994	☐	OPUS NOCTURNE	CD	Osmose	OPCD 028	
		Also released in a limited promo versdion with blue cover.				
1994	■	OPUS NOCTURNE	LP	Osmose	OPLP 028	
1994	☐	Fuck Me Jesus	MCD 5tr	Osmose	OPCD 030	
		Tracks: Intro-Fuck Me Jesus/Departure Of The Mortals/The Black.../Within The Abyss/ Outro.-Shut Up And Suffer				
1995	■	Fuck Me Jesus	7" 5tr	Osmose	OPEP 006	$
		700 hand-numbered copies.				
1996	☐	HEAVEN SHALL BURN... WHEN WE ARE GATHERED	CD	Osmose	OPCD 040	
1996	☐	HEAVEN SHALL BURN... WHEN WE ARE GATHERED	LPg	Osmose	OPLP 040	
1996	☐	HEAVEN SHALL BURN... WHEN WE ARE GATHERED	LP PD	Osmose	OPPIC 040	
1996	☐	HEAVEN SHALL BURN... WHEN WE ARE GATHERED	LP PD	Shadow	SHADOW 001	
		1000 copies.				
1996	☐	GLORIFICATION	MCD 5tr	Osmose	OPCD 043	
		Tracks: Glorification Of The Black God (re-mix)/Total Desaster (Destruction cover)/ Sex With Satan (Piledriver cover)/Sodomize The Dead (Piledriver cover)/The Return Of Darkess And Evil (Bathory cover)				
1996	☐	GLORIFICATION	MLP 5tr	Osmose	OPMLP 043	
1997	☐	GLORIFICATION	MLP PD 5tr	Osmose	OPPIC 043	
1997	☐	Here's No Peace	MCD 3tr	Shadow	SHADOW 002	
		Tracks: Here's No Peace/Still Fucking Dead/Within The Abyss				
1997	☐	THOSE OF THE UNLIGHT	LP PD	Osmose	OPPIC 015	
		300 copies.				
1997	■	LIVE IN GERMANIA	CD	Osmose	OPCD054	
1997	☐	LIVE IN GERMANIA	2LP	Osmose	OPLP054	
1997	☐	NIGHTWING	CD	Osmose	OPCD 064	
1997	☐	NIGHTWING	LPg	Osmose	OPLP 064	
		500 copies.				
1998	☐	Here's No Peace	MCDd 5tr	Blooddawn	BLOOD 009	
		Bonus: In Conspiracy With Satan (Bathory cover)/Woman Of Dark Desires (Bathory cover). 5000 copies				
1998	☐	Here's No Peace	10" MLP 5tr	Blooddawn	BLOODLP 009	
		500 copies				
1998	☐	Here's No Peace	MLP 5tr PD	Blooddawn	BLOODPLP 009	
		500 copies				
1998	☐	NIGHTWING	LP PD	Osmose	OPPIC 064	
1999	☐	Fuck Me Jesus	10" MLP PD 8tr	Osmose	OPPIC 030	
		Bonus: Dark Endless/In Conspiracy With Satan/Woman Of Dark Desires (Bathory covers)				
1999	☐	Fuck Me Jesus	MCD 8tr	Osmose	OPCD 030	
1999	☐	DAY OF DARKNESS	CD	Darkness	H 020	
1999	☐	PANZER DIVISION MARDUK	CD	Osmose	OPCD 080	
1999	☐	PANZER DIVISION MARDUK	CDd	Osmose	OPCDL 080	
1999	☐	PANZER DIVISION MARDUK	LP	Osmose	OPLP 080	
1999	☐	PANZER DIVISION MARDUK	LP PD	Osmose	OPPIC 080	
2000	☐	Obedience	MCDd 3tr	Blooddawn	BLOOD 003	
		Tracks: Obedience/Funeral Bitch/ Into The Crypts Of Rays(Celtic Frost cover)				
2000	■	Obedience	10" MLP 3tr	Blooddawn	BLOODLP 002	
		500 copies				
2000	☐	Obedience	MLP PD 3tr	Blooddawn	BLOODPLP 001	
		500 copies				
2000	☐	Obedience	MCD 3tr	Century Media (USA)	8034-2	
2000	☐	INFERNAL ETERNAL	2CD	Blooddawn	BLOOD DCD 007	
2000	☐	INFERNAL ETERNAL	2LPg	Blooddawn	BLOODLP 007	
		1000 copies				

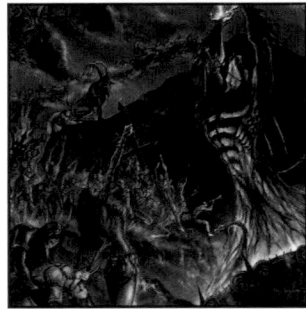

1994 LP - OPLP 028

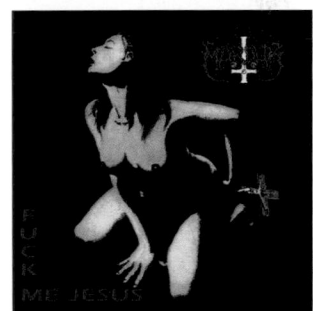

1994 7" - OPEP 006

1997 CD - OPCD 054

2000 10" - BLOODLP 002

2000	☐	INFERNAL ETERNAL	2LP PD	Blooddawn	BLOODPLP 007
		500 copies			
2000	☐	INFERNAL ETERNAL	2CD	Century Media (USA)	8035-2
2001	☐	PANZER DIVISION MARDUK	CD	Fono (Russia)	FO111CD
2001	☐	INFERNAL ETERNAL	2LPg PD	Blooddawn	BLOOD PLP 007
2001	■	LA GRANDE DANSE MACABRE	CD	Blooddawn	BLOOD 008
2001	☐	LA GRANDE DANSE MACABRE	CD	Blooddawn	BLOOD 008
		Slipcase. Bonus: Samhain (Samhain cover). 10 000 copies.			
2001	☐	LA GRANDE DANSE MACABRE	LP	Blooddawn	BLOODLP 008
		1000 copies.			
2001	☐	LA GRANDE DANSE MACABRE	CD	Century Media (USA)	8036-2
2001	☐	LA GRANDE DANSE MACABRE	LP PD	Blooddawn	BLOODPLP 008
		1000 copies.			
2001	☐	Here's No Peace	10" 5tr	Blooddawn	BLOOD 009
		Tracks: Here's No Peace/Still Fucking Dead/Within The Abyss			
2001	■	Here's No Peace	MCDd 5tr	Bloodbdawn	BLOOD 009
		Bonus: In Conspiracy With Satan (Bathory cover)/Woman Of Dark Desires (Bathory cover). 5000 copies.			
2001	☐	Here's No Peace	MLP 5tr	Blooddawn	BLOOD 009
		500 copies. Poster.			
2002	☐	BLACKCROWNED	2CD+VHS Box	Blooddawn	BLOOD 011
		10 000 copies. Rare, unreleased and re-recorded material, video, biography and photos.			
2002	☐	BLACKCROWNED	2LP	Bloodbdawn	BLOOD 011
2002	☐	BLACKCROWNED	2LP PD	Bloodbdawn	BLOODPLP 011
2002	☐	HEAVEN SHALL BURN... WHEN WE ARE GATHERED	CD	Pony Canyon (Japan)	PCKD-20049
		Bonus: Glorification Of The Black God (remix)/Total Desaster (Destruction cover)/Sex With Satan (Piledriver cover)/Sodomize The Dead (Piledriver cover)/The Return Of Darkness And Evil (Bathory cover)			
2002	☐	LA GRANDE DANSE MACABRE	CD	Sail Productions (Korea)	SPCD 00004
		Slipcase.			
2002	☐	LA GRANDE DANSE MACABRE	CD	Mystic Productions (Russia)	MYST 270
2002	☐	NIGHTWING	CD	Fono (Russia)	FO133CD
2002	☐	Slay The Nazarene/Of Hell's Fire	7"	Warlock Records	WREP 07
		1500 copies.			
2003	☐	Hearse/Phantasm (Possessed cover)	CDS	Blooddawn	BLOOD 013
		5000 copies.			
2003	☐	Hearse/Phantasm (Possessed cover)	7"	Blooddawn	BLOODEP 013
		500 copies on black and 200 on white vinyl.			
2003	☐	Hearse/Phantasm (Possessed cover)	7" PD	Blooddawn	BLOODPEP 013
		500 copies.			
2003	■	WORLD FUNERAL	CD	Blooddawn	BLOOD 012
2003	☐	WORLD FUNERAL	LP	Blooddawn	BLOODLP 012
		1500 copies.			
2003	☐	WORLD FUNERAL	LP PD	Blooddawn	BLOODPLP 012
		1500 copies.			
2003	☐	WORLD FUNERAL	CD	Blooddawn (USA)	BLOODNA 1012
2003	☐	WORLD FUNERAL	CD	CD-Maximum (Russia)	CDM 0803-1478
2003	☐	LA GRANDE DANSE MACABRE	CD	CD-Maximum (Russia)	CDM 0803-1479
2004	■	PLAGUE ANGEL	CD	Blooddawn	BLOOD 018
2004	☐	PLAGUE ANGEL	CDd	Blooddawn	BLOOD 018
		Bonus: Steel Inferno (video)			
2004	☐	PLAGUE ANGEL	LP	Blooddawn	BLOODPLP 018
		500 copies on black and 500 on red vinyl.			
2004	☐	PLAGUE ANGEL	LP PD	Blooddawn	BLOODPLP 018
2004	☐	PLAGUE ANGEL	CD	Candlelight (USA)	CDL0167CD
2004	☐	PLAGUE ANGEL	CD	CD-Maximum (Russia)	CDM 0805-2348
2004	☐	PLAGUE ANGEL	CDd	CD-Maximum (Russia)	CDM 0805-2348/d
		Bonus: Steel Inferno (video)			
2004	☐	PLAGUE ANGEL	CD	Del Imaginario Discos (Argentina)	n/a
2004	☐	THOSE OF THE UNLIGHT	CD	CD-Maximum (Russia)	CDM 0304-1755
2004	☐	OPUS NOCTURNE	LP	Regain Records	BLOODLP 026
2004	☐	HEAVEN SHALL BURN... WHEN WE ARE GATHERED	CD	Blooddawn	BLOOD 028
2004	☐	HEAVEN SHALL BURN... WHEN WE ARE GATHERED	CD	CD-Maximum (Russia)	CDM 0304-1756
2004	☐	Deathmarch Tour EP	MCD 4tr	Blooddawn	BLOOD 020
		Tracks: Steel Inferno (alternate version)/Tod Und Vernichtung/The Hangman Of Prague (Rehearsal)/Throne Of Rats (rehearsal)			
2004	☐	Deathmarch Tour EP	7"g 4tr	Blooddawn	BLOOD 020
2005	☐	DARK ENDLESS	CDd	Black Lodge	BLOD 024DG
		Reissue made without the band's consent.			
2005	■	WARCHAU	CD	Blooddawn	BLOOD 032
2005	☐	WARCHAU	CD	Blooddawn	BLOOD 032
		Slipcase. 10 000 copies.			
2005	☐	WARCHAU	2LPg	Blooddawn	BLOODLP 032
		500 copies. With poster.			
2005	☐	WARCHAU	2LPg+7"	Blooddawn	BLOODLP 032/020
		Warchau LP + Deathmarch Tour 7". Patch, guest pass, poster, in special sack. 50 copies.			

2001 CD - BLOOD 008

2001 MCD - BLOOD 009

2003 CD - BLOOD 012

2004 CD - BLOOD 018

2005 CD - BLOOD 032

Year		Title	Format	Label	Catalog
2006	☐	THOSE OF THE UNLIGHT	CDd	Regain Records	BLOOD 025

New artwork. Bonus: Darkness Breeds Immortality/A Scupiture Of The Night/The Funeral Seemed To Be Endless

2006	■	THOSE OF THE UNLIGHT	LPg	Regain Records	BLOOD LP 025
2006	☐	WORLD FUNERAL – LIMITED EDITION	2CD+DVD box	Regain (Roadrunner)	SMBLOOD 029

3 000 copies. Contains World Funeral, Hearse and Live Party San Festival 2003 DVD, photod, in clap box.

2006	☐	LA GRANDE DANSE MACABRE	CD+DVD box	Blooddawn	BLOOD 030

Bonus: Samhain (Samhain cover). DVD recorded live in Germany 2001. 3000 copies. Pin.

2006	☐	Fuck Me Jesus	10" MLP 8tr	Osmose	OPLP 030

Bonus: Dark Endless/In Conspiracy With Satan (Bathory cover)/Woman Of Dark Desires (Bathory cover)

2006	☐	LIVE WARCHAU	CD	Blooddawn	BLOOD 032
2007	☐	Here's No Peace	MCDd 5tr	Blooddawn	REG-CD-1038

New artwork.

2007	☐	HEAVEN SHALL BURN... WHEN WE ARE GATHERED	CDd	Blooddawn	BLOOD 028

Bonus: Beyond The Grace Of God/Glorification/Black Tormentor-Shadow Of Our King/ Infernal Eternal-Towards The Land Of. New artwork.

2007	☐	HEAVEN SHALL BURN... WHEN WE ARE GATHERED	LP PD	Blooddawn	BLOODPLP 028

500 copies.

2007	■	HEAVEN SHALL BURN... WHEN WE ARE GATHERED	LP	Blooddawn	BLOODLP 028
2007	☐	HEAVEN SHALL BURN... WHEN WE ARE GATHERED	CD	Del Imaginario Discos (Argentina)	D.I.106
2007	☐	DARK ENDLESS	CDd	Blooddawn	BLOOD 024DG

Live-Bonus: Departure From The Mortals/Within The Abyss/Still Fucking Dead/The Black Goat/Evil Dead

2007	☐	DARK ENDLESS	LP	Blooddawn	BLOODLP 024
2007	☐	DARK ENDLESS	LP PD	Blooddawn	BLOODPLP 024
2007	■	ROM 15:2	CD	Blooddawn	BLOOD 034
2007	☐	ROM 15:2	2LPg	Blooddawn	BLOODLP 034

500 copies. Poster.

2007	☐	ROM 15:2	LP PD	Blooddawn	BLOODPLP 034

500 copies.

2007	☐	ROM 15:2	CD	CD-Maximum (Russia)	CDM 0707-2726
2007	☐	ROM 15:2	CD	Avalon Marquee (Japan)	MICP-10684

Bonus: Wolves (video)

2007	☐	OPUS NOCTURNE	CD	Mutilation (Brazil)	MUT 039
2007	☐	OPUS NOCTURNE	CD	Regain Records (USA)	REG-1004
2007	☐	OPUS NOCTURNE	LP PD	Blooddawn	BLOODPLP 026

Bonus: Sulphur Souls/Materialized In Stone/Opus Nocturne

2007	■	OPUS NOCTURNE	LP	Blooddawn	BLOODLP 026
2007	☐	OPUS NOCTURNE	CDd	Blooddawn	BLOOD 026DG
2007	☐	Here's No Peace	MCD 5tr	Regain (USA)	REG-CD-1038

Different artwork.

2007	☐	THOSE OF THE UNLIGHT	LP PD	Blooddawn	BLOODPLP 025
2007	☐	WARCHAU	CD+DVD	Regain (USA)	REG-CD-008

Live DVD.

2008	☐	NIGHTWING	CD+DVD	Blooddawn	BLOOD 036

Re-issue with new artwork and bonus DVD.Slipcase.

2008	☐	NIGHTWING	CD+DVD	Regain (USA)	REG-CD-1045
2008	☐	PANZER DIVISION MARDUK	CD	Regain (USA)	REG-CD-1049
2008	☐	PANZER DIVISION MARDUK	CD	Blooddawn	BLOOD 038
2008	☐	PANZER DIVISION MARDUK	LPg	Blooddawn	BLOODLP 038

500 copies.

2008	☐	THOSE OF THE UNLIGHT	LP PD	Regain Records	BLOOD PLP 025

500 copies.

2008	☐	PLAGUE ANGEL	CD+DVD box	Blooddawn	BLOOD 041 CDB

Bonus: The Deathmarch Tour MCD + Live on Party San 2006. Patch. 3000 copies

2008	☐	Obedience	MCD 3tr	Blooddawn	BLOOD 031
2009	☐	WORMWOOD	CDd	Blooddawn	BLOOD 044
2009	☐	WORMWOOD	LP	Blooddawn	BLOODLP 044

700 copies.

2009	☐	WORMWOOD	LP	Blooddawn	BLOODLP 044

500 copies red vinyl. 32-page booklet.

2009	☐	WORMWOOD	LP PD	Blooddawn	BLOODPLP 044

500 copies.

2009	■	WORMWOOD	CD	Regain (USA)	REG-CD-9003
2009	☐	WORMWOOD	CD	Icarus (Argentina)	ICARUS 581
2010	☐	NIGHTWING	LP	Blooddawn	BLOODLP 036
2011	☐	PANZER DIVISION MARDUK	LP PD	Blooddawn	BLOODPLP 038
2011	☐	PANZER DIVISION MARDUK	4x7" PD Box	Regain Records	BLOOD 049

Box set featuring four pic disc 7": Panzer Division Marduk/Baptism By Fire, Christcaping Black Metal/Scorched Earth, Beast Of Prey/Blooddawn, 505/Fistfucking Gods Planet. 666 copies

2011	☐	Iron Dawn	MCDd 3tr	Blooddawn	BLOOD 051

Tracks: Warchau 2: Headhunter Halfmoon/Wacht Am Rhein: Drumbeats Of Death/ Prochorovka: Blood And Sunflowers

2006 LPg - BLOOD LP 025

2007 LP - BLOODLP 028

2007 CD - BLOOD 034

2007 LP - BLOODLP 026

2009 CD - REG-CD-9003

2012	☐	Iron Dawn	MLP 3tr	Century Media	998187-1	
		600 black + 300 white vinyl copies. One-sided.				
2012	■	Iron Dawn	MLP 3tr	Blooddawn	BLOOD 053	
		Yellow vinyl. One-sided.				
2012	☐	SERPENT SERMON	LPg	Century Media	998160-1	
2012	☐	SERPENT SERMON	LPg	Blooddawn	BLOOD 055 LP	
2012	☐	SERPENT SERMON	CD	Century Media	998160-2	
2012	☐	SERPENT SERMON	CDd	Century Media	998160-0	
		Digibook 40 pages. Bonus: Coram Satanae				
2012	☐	SERPENT SERMON	CD	Blooddawn	BLOOD 055	
2012	☐	SERPENT SERMON	CDd	Blooddawn	BLOOD 055L	
		Digibook 40 pages. Bonus: Coram Satanae				
2012	☐	SERPENT SERMON	LPg+7"	Century Media	998160-1	
		Dark red vinyl + 7" on dark-red vinyl featuring Coram Satanae. 300 copies				
2012	☐	Souls For Belial/Oil On Panel	CDSd	Blooddawn	9981643/BLOOD 054	
2012	☐	DARK ENDLESS	LPg	Century Media	998160-1	
		Available in black, white or clear vinyl.				

2012 MLP - BLOOD 053

MARIONETTE

Alexander Andersson: v, Aron Parmerud: g, Anton Modig: g, Linus Johansson: k, Mikael Medin: b

Göteborg - **Marionette** was formed in 2005 by high-school friends Aron Parmerud, Mikael Medin and Linus Johansson, with an average age of 16. In 2006 they recorded the first demo *Terror Hearts*. In 2008 they released the debut *Spite*, produced by Christian Silver (**Sonic Syndicate**). The line-up then featured singer Axel Widén (**Mindfall, Poem, Zombiekrieg**), guitarist Johan Sporre and drummer Jimmy Olausson (not the same person as in **The Cold Existence**). For the second album, *Enemies*, they teamed up with producers Åke Parmerud and Pontus Hjelm (**Dead By April**). The line-up had now changed and Sporre had been replaced by Modig and the band used Robin Jensen as live drummer. In 2010 the band entered Studio Fredman together with producer Fredrik Nordström (**Dream Evil, Dimmu Borgir, Bring Me The Horizon**) to record the third album, *Nerve*, the first to include new singer Alexander Andersson (**Eldrimner**). **Marionette** plays well-produced technical and melodic death metal with quite prominent keyboards, in the vein of **Dead By April**, but a bit more metal. Powerful delivery and great songs. *Nerve* was also released digitally by Pivotal Recordings.

2008 CD - POSH 104

2009 CD - POSH 123

2008	■	SPITE	CD	Listenable	POSH 104
2009	■	ENEMIES	CD	Listenable	POSH 123
2011	■	NERVE	CDd	private	(MARIONETTE01)
		Bonus: Overdose			

2011 CDd - (MARIONETTE01)

MARSH, JJ

Joakim "JJ" Marsch: v/g/b

Uppsala - Jocke "JJ" Marsh, or Kurt Joakim Ellner Juno Marsh, born February 16, 1966, made his debut with the outstanding melodic hard rock band **Spellbound** in the eighties, where Marsh proved to be a great **Van Halen**-influenced bluesy shredder. He also laid down guitars with **Marc Quee**. From 1996 and on he was the right-hand man of former **Trapeze/Deep Purple** singer/bassist Glenn Hughes, with whom he has recorded numerous albums. He also recorded the more prog-oriented album *The Simon Lonesome Combat Ensemble* (1994 Musea) with Simon Steensland. *Music From The Planet Marsh* is his first solo album. The album also features drummer Thomas Broman (**Electric Boys, Great King Rat** etc), keyboardists Kjell Haraldsson and Tomas Bodin (**Kaipa, The Flower Kings**). The style is quite bluesy, retro-oriented hard rock, at times similar to what he does with Glenn Hughes. He also proves he can sing, besides being an outstanding guitarist. Trivia: JJ was also in **Van Halen** cover band **HanValen** (male whale). Today JJ is playing in **Bridge To Mars** together with the aforementioned Thomas Broman.

2006	■	MUSIC FROM THE PLANET MARSH	CD	private	JJCD 01

2006 CD - JJCD 01

MARSHAL KANE

Michael Ahlström: v, Claes Wållberg: g, Patrik Strömberg: k, Johan Helander: b, Morgan Kane: d

Norrköping - Formed in 1986, split in 1992. **Marshal Kane** should attract fans of mid-weight AOR, in the vein of Bryan Adams. Good-quality musicians, songs and vocals. The 7" is heavier, while they have more synthesizers and syn-drums on the MLP. Claes was later in **Axewitch**, while Ahlström was in **Violent Divine**. At some point **Violent Divine** members Mikael Qvist and Gustaf Liljenström were also part of **Marshal Kane**.

1987	■	Sucker For Love/Hired Heart	7"	Active Music	HEJS 020
1989	☐	Bubblegum/Diana/Human Target	MLP 3tr	Active Music	HEJMAXI 002

1987 7" - HEJS 020

MARULK
Danne Palm: v/b, Thomas B. Jäger (aka Jaeger): g, Esben Willems: d

Göteborg - Marulk (monkfish in English) was formed in 2007 and plays high-quality retro hard rock which should appeal to fans of *Blue Cheers, Grand Funk* or fellow Swedes *Abramis Brama, Svarte Pan* and *Magnolia*. Jäger has also played in bands like *Draconian* and *Keegan*.
Website: www.marulk.net

2010 ■	MARULK	CD	Transubstans	TRANS 055
2010 ☐	MARULK	LP	private	ULK 001
2010 ☐	Devil's On A Stroll/Tvåhundra	7"	private	ULK 002
	250 copies. Signed.
2011 ☐	Devil's Boogie	10" 4tr	Lightning Records	LIR 006
	Tracks: The Devil's Boogie/Jumpsuit Elvis/Headless Rider/Blodsmak

2010 CD - TRANS 055

MARY MAJOR, THE
Erik Molarin: v, Lotta Höglin: v, Daniel Elofsson: g,
Jörgen Ström: b, Jonas Strömberg: d

Göteborg/Borås - The Mary Major rose out of the ashes of goth-oriented rockers *Beseech* in 2006. The four Beseechers added Jörgen Ström and *The Mary Major* was born. The band's own musical description says they play "heavy, straight-to-the-point, kick ass rock 'n' roll". That would at least lead me into thinking they sound like *The Hellacopters*, which they do not. It's definitely heavy and not very complicated, but there's some really heavy and detuned riffing going on. Nice mix of male and female vocals, which puts them apart in this genre. The debut was distributed with the help of Rambo Music, who signed the band for their second effort.

| 2010 ■ | 04:13 | CD | TMM Production | TMM 001 |
| 2012 ☐ | GRINDING TEETH, GUARD DOWN | CD | Rambo | TMM 002 |

2010 CD - TMM 001

MARYSCREEK
Mats Nilsson: v, Bobby "Ho" Holmberg: g, Robert Möller: b, Stefan Halldin: d

Linköping - MarysCreek was formed by Mats and Stefan in 2004 with the ambition to combine the melodic hard rock of the nineties with the heavy and aggressive riffing of today. Robert was drafted on bass and they recorded the demo *Bedroom Eyes* in 2005. It was followed by a couple of demos later the same year, and after which Bobby "Ho" Holmgren (*Blacksmith*) replaced guitarist Peter Björkman and they were picked up by MTM. In 2009 Jonas Hallberg (*Simon Says, Superset*) took on the lead guitar parts, replacing Bobby. Peter Bergkvist was also added on guitar. Roger Blomberg (*Denata, Freevil*) replaced Möller. *MarysCreek* play good, solid melodic hard rock. A new-track EP was recorded in 2013, but has yet to be released.
Website: www.maryscreek.com

2007 CD - MTM 0681-182

| 2007 ■ | SOME KIND OF HATE | CD | MTM | MTM 0681-182 |

MASCOT PARADE
Henrik Bringås: v, Staffan Andersson: g/k, Daniel Engström: b, Carl Ottosson: d

Västerås - Mascot Parade plays great riff-oriented groovy heavy rock with a stonerish touch. The band was formed under the moniker *The Buck* back in 2003, featuring Bringås, Andersson and drummer Christer Teglund. Just two weeks after forming they recorded their first demo, which was crowned *Surprise of the Month* of Close-Up magazine. In 2004 they signed a deal with a UK label, but only a year after they parted ways. In 2007 they changed their name to *Mascot Parade* and signed a deal with Swedish label Alabama. The debut *Deathmatch* was released in 2008 featuring the above line-up. In January 2011 they released the new digital single *The Uninvited Guest*, produced by Chips Kisbye (*Sator, Bonafide, Dozer* etc.) and a new album is in the making.

2008 CD - ALAB010

| 2008 ■ | DEATHMATCH | CD | Alabama Records | ALAB010 |

MASON
Örjan Armgren: v, Pelle Höglund: g, Lars-Åke Löwin: g,
Gabriel Axelsson: k, Mats Johansson: b, Tony Jansson: d

Gävle - The A-side is pretty decent semi-heavy eighties power ballad, while the B-side is an up-tempo melodic metal track. The vocals may not be very exciting, especially not the backing vocals, but for fans of *Treat, 220 Volt* and *Glory* it is well worth checking out. The music rocks. Tony was ex-*Slam*.

| 1989 ■ | Tears/Running In The Shadows | 7" | Far-Out | FOR 001 $ |

1989 7" - FOR 001

MASQUERADE

Tony "Yoanson" Johansson: v, Thomas "G:son" Gustafsson: g,
Henrik Lundberg: b, Marco Tapani: d

Skövde - The first single and album are mid-weight AOR in the vein of *TNT*, well-played and well-sung but lacking a bit in originality. The band's new sound, starting off with the three-track single, was quite different. Later day's *Masquerade* was heavy 90s-sounding power hard rock but still with melodic feeling. Great band! The first single also contained Ulf "Wolf" Andersson on guitar. In 1995 the bands second album was picked up by Metal Blade, who released it with a different cover. In Europe it was released by RMG, who also made a new cover. The songs are the same on all pressings. Henrik also played with the excellent power metal band **Straightjackets** (later known as **Booster**), **Vollster** and he is today in heavy rockers **House Of Heavy**. Marco played drums on the **Flinstens Med Stanley** album. Tony recorded some great demos with the Skövde band **Act** (featuring Tim Sköld, Jan Strandh and Christer Rispling) in the eighties. The 2004 release *In Disguise* contains unreleased demos recorded during the early AOR days. Thomas G:son is, besides his heavy rock persona, a highly acclaimed pop/dance song writer. The track *Love Is A Runaway* was featured on the compilatiuon *MRCD7* (Melodicrock).

1991 7" - TJ 6602

1994 CD - ERCD 1007

1995 CD - 3984-14099-2

1991 ■	Dancin' On The Edge/Stop	7"	private	TJ 6602
1992 ☐	MASQUERADE	CD	Dino	DINCD 15
1992 ☐	MASQUERADE	CD	Zero (Japan)	XRCN-1011
1992 ☐	Sudden Love Affair/Justice	CDS 2tr	Dino	DINCSG 15-1
1993 ☐	Dancing On The Edge	MCD 3tr	Dino	DINCSG 15-2
	Tracks: Dancing On The Edge/Give It A Shot/Lonely World			
1994 ☐	Suffering/Say Your Prayer/America	MCD 3tr	Empire	ERCDS-1007-1
1994 ■	SURFACE OF PAIN	CD	Empire	ERCD 1007
1994 ☐	SURFACE OF PAIN	CD	Zero (Japan)	XRCN-1133
1995 ☐	SURFACE OF PAIN	CD	RMG	009708-2 RMG
	"Hurting face" cover.			
1995 ■	SURFACE OF PAIN	CD	Metal Blade (USA)	3984-14099-2
	"Hands and cross" cover.			
1999 ☐	MASQUERADE	CD	Empire	W-CD 2044
	Bonus: Stop and Main Attraction			
1999 ☐	Wish/Freedom	CDS 2tr	Empire	W-CDS 2045-1
2000 ☐	FLUX	CD	Metal Blade	3984 14200 2
2001 ■	FLUX	CD	Metal Blade	3984 14200 2
	New "brown/white" artwork.			
2004 ☐	IN DISGUISE	CD	Sorcery Studios/Razar	090904 SSMASQ
2005 ☐	IN DISGUISE	CD	Spiritual Beast (Japan)	SBCD-1022
	Bonus: My Dying Days			
2008 ☐	MASQUERADE	CD	Yesterrock	NL 10054
	Bonus: Feels Good (live video)/Our Time Has Come (live video)/Gimme All Your Love (live video)/Sudden Love Affair (video)			

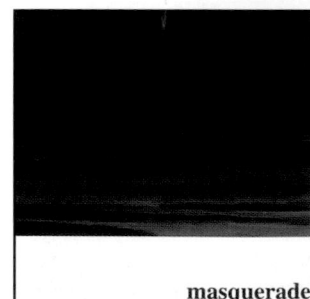

2001 CD - 3984 14200 2

MASS MURDER AGENDA

Tristan Agdler: v, Martin Sundberg: g, Joakim Hedestedt: b,
Henrik Blomqvist: sampl, Christofer Barkensjö: d

Stockholm - Formed in 2009 by Hedestedt (**Construcdead, Face Down** etc), who drafted Tristan (**NIL**) and his former **Face Down** colleagues Barkensjö and Blomqvist to form this industrial monster. Sundberg (**Sexy Death**) completed the band. Similar to **Ministry** and **Nine Inch Nails**. The name was originally meant for **Face Down**'s last album.

2012 ■	BRING THE VIOLENCE	CD	Black Lodge	BLOD 083

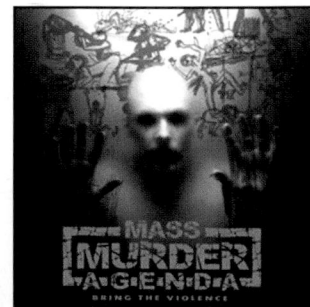

2012 CD - BLOD 083

MASSIVE AUDIO NERVE (aka M.A.N)

Tony "JJ" Jelencovich: v, Rob Guz : g, Robert "Rob" Hakemo: b, Andreas Engberg: d

Göteborg - Formed in August 2005 from the ashes of **Transport League** featuring singer Tony Jelencovich (**Mnemic, Icon In Me, B-Thong, Angel Blake,** etc). The line-up on the debut featured Tony, guitarist Martin Meyerman (**Zombiekrieg**), Fredrik "Stitch" Blomkvist (b) and Magnus 155 (d). In November 2011 the band started using the full name: **Massive Audio Nerve**. M.A.N sounds like the missing link between **Soulfly, Korn** and **Machine Head** with a touch of **Rob Zombie** and **Pantera**, mixing growl and clean vocals. A funny detail is that the guitarist plays on a quarter note guitar (one extra fret between each "normal" fret), which gives it a cool sliding touch. After **Massive Audio Nerve** Nils Olsson replaced Rob, and late 2011 Markus "Mark Black" Fristedt (**Dream Evil, Dragonlord, Illwill**) replaced Nils and Adde Larsson (**Engel, Urbandux**) replaced Andreas Engberg. In 2011 the band also released the digital EP *Massive Audio Outtakes*. The band's fourth album will be entitled *Cancer Vulgaris*.

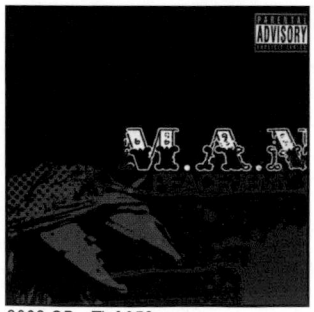

2008 CD - Tief 059

2010 CDd - Tief 075

2007 ☐	OBEY CONSUME REJECT	CD	Gain	GPCD 35
2008 ■	PEACENEMY	CD	Tiefdruck Musik	Tief 059
2008 ☐	My Own Sickness/Body Sewer/Kill It	MCD 3tr	Tiefdruck Musik	Tief 061
2010 ■	MASSIVE AUDIO NERVE	CDd	Tiefdruck Musik	Tief 075

MASTER PIECE
Tomas: v, Robert: g, Mattias: k, Patrik: k, Öyvind: b, Magnus: d

Örnsköldsvik - Really good Christian AOR-sounding a bit like a mix of ***Bad Habit*** and ***Time Gallery***.

1989 ■ Don't Walk Alone/Come To Him ....7" private MPS-01

1989 7" - MPS-01

MATRICIDE
**Carl "Tiburtius" Nordblom: v/d, Daniel "Contagion" Abrahamsson: g/b,
Kaj "Gimbrynjer" Palm: g/b**

Uddevalla - The band was formed in 2002 as ***Pagan Ritual***, under which name they soon released the demo tape *Blasphemic Fire* (NUN 001). Later the same year they changed their name to ***Matricide***, the term meaning "the act of murdering one's mother". They now recorded *St. Lucia Was A Fucking Bitch* (NUN 0029), released as a CDR-S by Nun Violence later in 2002. In 2003 the CDR *Beyond The Plague Of Light* (NUN 003) was released. *Black Mass Gathering* was a slab of blast beat-filled, old-school-style black metal in the vein of ***Watain*** or ***Mayhem***. The song *Nocturnal Necromancy* can be found on the *Assault Webzine Compilation #1*, released in 100 numbered copies. Nordblom and Palm are ex-***Descending***. Palm and Abrahamsson were both in ***Excessum***. Nordblom is currently the only member left in the band.

2004 CD - MNR 006

2004 ■ BLACK MASS GATHERING ....CD Northern Sky/Meurtre Noir ....MNR 006
    666 copies
2006 ☐ Holy Virgin...MCD 4tr Unholy Horde ....UHR 005
    Tracks: Demonseed/Black Funeral Poison/Perditoir/Holy Virgin
2006 ■ Holy Virgin.. MLP 5tr Obscure Abhorrence.................................. - -
    Tracks: Demonseed/Black Funeral Poison/Perditoir/Holy Virgin/The Era Of Satan Rising
    (The Art Lord cover). 500 copies, first 60 with patch.

2006 MLP - - -

MAYADOME
**Bassel Elharbiti: v, Fredrik Kjörling: g, Sebastian Okupski: k,
Erik Grandin: b, Teddy Möller: d**

Uppsala - It actually started when the band ***Mellow Poetry*** changed their name and style around 1995. When they released the MCD *Welcome To The Surreal World* they had changed from a melodic hard rock band, to a progressive power-pack. The name ***Mayadome*** felt more appropriate. They recorded a killer-demo, which finally lead to a deal with Mike Varney's Shrapnel Records. The band also contributed on the *Released By X-mas* compilation with their highly progressive version of *When You Wish Upon A Star*, as well as their interpretation of *Disciples Of Hell* for the Yngwie Malmsteen tribute *A Guitar Odyssey*. In 2001 the band split due to internal controversies. Teddy is now found in ***F.K.Ü*** and his main band ***Loch Vostock***, where Sebastian is also found. Vocals on the debut were handled by Björn Homquist and keyboards by Jonas Hägg. Both albums are well worth looking for if you're into powerful progressive metal in the vein of ***Fates Warning*** meets ***Fear Factory***. Due to lousy promotion work from the label the second album only sold around 500 copies. Elharbiti previously recorded a single with the Uppsala band ***Fatal Smile***.

1996 CD - SH 10982

1999 CD - SR-0013

1996 ■ PARANORMAL ACTIVITY ....CD Shrapnel ....SH 10982
1996 ☐ PARANORMAL ACTIVITY ....CD Roadrunner (Japan)......................RRCY-1029
1999 ■ NEAR LIFE EXPERIENCE ....CD Siegen Records SR-0013

MAZE OF TIME
**Jesper Landén: v, Robert I Edman: v/g, Axel Jonsson: k,
Jan Persson: b, Thomas Nordh: d**

Stockholm - ***Maze Of Time*** was founded in 2001 by Robert I Edman. He drafted bassist Persson and drummer Nordh to further developed some songs he had written. Now keyboardist Jonsson and singer/guitarist Christer Lindström were added to complete the line-up. In 2003 the three track demo *Under The Sun* was released, and is now long out of print. In 2006 the debut album was recorded after which Lindström left the band and was replaced by singer Jesper Landén. ***Maze Of Time*** plays mostly quite subtle symphonic rock, but suddenly some heavy guitar riffs enter the musical brew and things start to happen. A bit reminiscent of ***Galleon*** and ***Twin Age***. The new digital single Mile By Mile was released in 2012, and a new album is in the making. *Website: www.mazeoftime.com*

2007 CD - ArtP003

2008 CDd - ArtP010

2007 ■ TALES FROM THE MAZE ....CD Art Performance...................................ArtP003
2008 ■ LULLABYE FOR HEROES ....CDd Art Performance...................................ArtP010

MAZE OF TORMENT

Erik Sahlström: v, Rickard Dahlin: g, Magnus Lindvall: g,
Cloffe Caspersson: b, Kjell Enblom: d

Strängnäs - Formed in 1995 from the ashes of *Harmony*, initially as *Torment*. The band changed line-up a number of times until 1995, when the band changed its name to *Maze Of Torment* and featured Pehr Larsson (v/b), Peter "Pete Flesh" Karlsson (g) and Kjell Enblom (d). After a three-tracks demo they were signed to German We Bite/Corrosion and recorded the debut at Unisound. On the second album Pehr had quit playing bass and now concentrated on the vocal duties, while the bass-work was handled by Peter Jansson (*Crypt Of Kerberos*). The album lacked from bad distribution and the band went on to Necropolis. New line-up change, as Pehr was replaced by Erik Sahlström (*Serpent Obscene, General Surgery, The Marble Icon*) and Peter (later in *Deceiver, Flesh, Thrown, Embryo*) by Kalle Sjödin. The album was recorded at Sunlight Studios. Thrash-oriented black/death metal similar to *At The Gates* and *Dissection* or early *Slayer*. Pehr was later found in *Vinterland*. The song *Maze Bloody Maze* is actually a *Black Sabbath* medley. In 2004 the line-up changed drastically when Sjödin and Karlsson were replaced by Caspersson (*Quilmess*) and Dahlin (*Sorg*). In 2005 Lindvall (*Soils Of Fate*) reinforced the guitar department. The band split in 2007.

1998 CD - IFP.003

2005 CD - BLOD 016 CD

1997	☐	THE FORCE	CD	We Bite/Corrosion	CR 6503
1998	■	FASTER DISASTER	CD	Iron Fist Productions	IFP. 003
2001	☐	DEATH STRIKES	CD	Necropolis	NR 056 CD
2001	☐	DEATH STRIKES	LP PD	Merciless	MRLP 024
		500 copies.			
2002	☐	THE UNMARKED GRAVES	CD	Necropolis	NR 075
2002	☐	Maze Bloody Maze/Death Orientated/Sea Of Madness	7" 3tr	Merciless	MRE 013
		500 copies			
2002	☐	THE UNMARKED GRAVES	LP	Black Lodge	BLOD 011
2003	☐	THE UNMARKED GRAVES	CD	Hellspawn	HELL 010
2003	☐	THE FORCE	CD	Iron Fist Productions	IFP 006
2004	☐	Brave The Blizzard	7" 3tr	TPL	TPL 018
		Tracks: Brave The Blizzard/Eclipse The Night/Land Unknown. 545 copies.			
2005	■	HAMMERS OF MAYHEM	CD	Black Lodge	BLOD 016 CD
2007	☐	HIDDEN CRUELTY	CD	Black Lodge	BLOD 048 CD
2009	■	THE UNMARKED GRAVES	CD	Black Lodge	BLOD 011 CD

2009 CD - BLOD 011 CD

MEADOW

Anders Einarsson: v, Ted Larsson: g, Glenn Larsson: k,
Peter Johansson: b, Lars Isaksson: d

Målilla/Hultsfred - Slick AOR, in the vein of *Alien* and *Skagarack*. Average, quite traditional songs and OK in the vocal department. The second release showed a big improvement. The members on the first singles were Anders, Glenn, Peter, Johan Nyström (g) and Hasse Johansson (d). They later started playing dance music under the name *Bröderna Elmrots* (The Elmrot Brothers) and backed female dance-pop singer Lotta Engberg on tour. The band recorded a third 7" entitled *Unstable*, however it never came further than a test press in 3 - 4-copies.

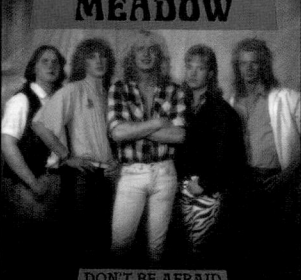

1986 7" - PLC 0001

1986	■	Stay Alive/Eyes In The Sky	7"	PLC Studios	PLC 0001	$
1987	■	Don't Be Afraid/Love To Survive	7"	private	M-001	

MEADOW IN SILENCE

Micke Karlsson: v/g, David L: g/k, Anders Göth: b, David: d

Linköping - The band recorded their first demo *Far Beyond The Stars* in 1995, the year they were formed. *Meadow In Silence* plays old-school-oriented death metal, actually with a hint of traditional melodic metal and, at times, even a folkish touch. Göth also recorded a demo with the band *Erug* and he was the editor of the zine *Sorrow Mag*. Göth and Karlsson also recorded a demo with the band *Ferocity*. Some references claim Weinerhall, Karl, Schutz and Karsten were members of the band, but I believe this is a mix-up with the band *Mithotyn* and their demo of the same title (the members of Mithtyn were Weinerhall, Schütz, Larsson and Bäckman).

1987 7" - M-001

1996	■	THROUGH THE TIDES OF TIME AND SPACE	CD	Garden Of Grief	GGP 004

MEADOWS END

Anders Rödin: v, Jan Dahlberg: g, Henrik Näslund: k, Mats Helli: b, Daniel Tiger: d

Örnsköldsvik - Formed under the name *Genocide* in 1993, featuring Daniel Nordlund, Magnus Olsson, Roger Engvik and Björn Johansson. Björn was replaced by Mats Helli and the band started rehearsing. Next up was Magnus, who was replaced by Jan Dahlberg. The band went through several name-changes such as *Thorns Of Desolation* and *Dawn Of Flames*, before finding *Meadows End* in 1997. Now the band was reinforced by singer Anders Rödin and keyboardist Henrik Näslund. In 1998 they recorded the demo *Beyond Tranquil Dreams* and a cover of the song *Crystal Mountain* for a *Death* tribute. After this Roger left the band and was replaced by

1996 CD - GGP 004

Björn Rydman, who recorded the *Everlasting* demo in 1999, but was asked to leave after this. Singer Anders Rödin also left. After this, private matters slowed the band down. However about a year later life was brought back to the band and new songs were written. Now drummer Daniel Tiger (**Amethyst**) entered the ranks and the band recorded the demo *Sombre Nation's Fall*. A new attempt was made with the CDR *Dead Calm Rise* in 2006. After this Henrik left the band and was replaced by Robin Mattsson (**Zealotry**). Second guitarist Joakim Rönström was added. Since Anders had lost the interest, they drafted new singer Anton Eriksson. The band's first full length album, *Ode To Quietus* featured Mats, Jan, Tiger, Robin, Joakim and Anton. After this, Anton and Joakim left for various reasons. They were replaced by **Soul Decay** singer Johan Brandberg and guitarist Stefan Sjölander. Great-sounding progressive and quite orchestrated death metal, at times almost like if Evergrey would have drafted a growler on vocals.

2010 ■ ODE TO QUIETUS ....CD private ....MEADOWS 001

2010 CD - MEADOWS 001

MEAN STREAK

Andy La Guerin: v, David Andersson: g, Thomas "Plec" Johansson: g,
Peter Andersson: b, Jonas Källsbäck: d

Skara - Great classic **Accept**-style heavy metal, but with a singer that sounds quite a lot like Biff Byford, but not really at his level. Well worth checking out, though. The band was formed in 2009 by former **Axia** man Andersson and singer La Guerin. The line-up was reinforced by **Jupiter Society** drummer Källsbäck, plus guitarists Thomas "Plec" Johansson and Yngve Frank. On the second album the band was equipped with two new guitarists in Patrik Gardberg (**Ammotrack, Solution .45, Torchbearer**) and David Andersson (**Soilwork**). The first two albums were mixed by Fredrik Nordström, and *Trial By Fire* by returning guitarist Thomas "Plec" Johansson.

2009 ■	METAL SLAVE	CD	Download Music	DMCD 002
2010 □	METAL SLAVE	CD	Bickee Music (Japan)	HMCX-1084
	Bonus: Shattered Soul			
2011 □	DECLARATION OF WAR	CD	Black Lodge	BLOD 077 CD
2011 □	DECLARATION OF WAR	CD	Bickee Music (Japan)	HMCX-1107
	Bonus: The Hunter And The Prey			
2013 ■	TRIAL BY FIRE	CD	Black Lodge	BLOD 087 CD

2008 CD - DMCD 002

MEDUZA

Apollo Papathanasio: v, Stefan Berg: g, Jan Larsson: k,
Jonas Edström: b, Ola Grönlund: d

Piteå - The band was formed in 2000 by the highly skilled and technical guitarist Stefan, who was previously a member of Christian band **Laudamus**. He quit to form his own band in 1994, initially called **Mind's Eye**, but later changed it to **Autumn Lords** four years later, under which name he recorded some demos. The style was then a bit more doom-oriented. The demo *Now And Forever* caught the attention of Danish agency Intromental who helped the band to a deal. They initially helped engage **Street Talk**/**Memento Mori**-singer Kristian Andrén to do the vocals for the next demo. They however found a very suitable permanent replacement in Apollo (**Craze, Faith Taboo, Majestic, Spiritual Beggars**). After the debut Joakim Floke (**Dionysus, Elsesphere, Memento Mori**) replaced keyboardist Jan Larsson. *Meduza* produces high-class melodic metal with a neo-classic touch and incredible guitar-work from Stefan, topped by Apollo's first-rate vocals. Not to be confused with Swedish Eddie Meduza cover band **Meduza**. In 2006 drummer David Wallin (**Blacksmith, Pain, Stormwind**) replaced Ola. Edström and Grönlund are ex-**Savage Skülls** and now in the promising heavy metal band **Alloy**.

2002 CD - MASCD 0328

2002 □	NOW AND FOREVER	CD	EMI/Toshiba (Japan)	TOCP-66076
	Bonus: Incarnation			
2002 ■	NOW AND FOREVER	CD	Massacre	MASCD 0328
2002 □	NOW AND FOREVER	CD	Sail Productions	SPCD 2018
2004 □	UPON THE WORLD	CD	Massacre	MASCD 0412
2004 ■	UPON THE WORLD	CD	Art Music Group (Russia)	AMG 167
2004 □	UPON THE WORLD	CD	Soundholic (Japan)	TKCS-85081
	Bonus: Saviour Of The Damned/Forzafurioso			

2004 CD - AMG 167

MEFISTO

Sandro Cajander: b/v, Omar Ahmed: g, Roberto "Thord" Granath: d

Stockholm - This cult-proclaimed old-school death metal band only has two demos (*Megalomania* and *The Puzzle*) to their claim to fame. The demos were recorded in 1986, which makes them one of the first bands to follow in the footsteps of masters **Bathory**. They were formed in 1984, initially as **Torment**, but quite soon changed their name to **Mefisto**. These 8 demo-tracks were later released as **The Truth**. Early brutal death in the vein of **Bathory, Obscurity** etc.

2001 ■	THE TRUTH	CD	Blooddawn	BLOOD 005
	Released with a black CD tray with goat embossing on front. 500 copies.			
2001 □	THE TRUTH	LP	Blooddawn	BLOODLP 005

2001 CD - BLOOD 005 (booklet)

MEGA SLAUGHTER

Emil Ilic: v, Kenneth Arnestedt: g, Alex Räfling: b, Patrik "Putte" Räfling: d

Göteborg/Malmö - Formed in 1986 under the name *Dinloyd*, but changed it the year after. In 1989 they recorded their first demo, entitled *Death Remains* and later that year they were signed to the new French Thrash-label. In 1991 they recorded a demo entitled *Demo 91* that sold quite well. They however split in 1992. Violent death-metal with satanic lyrics, at times similar to *Morbid Angel*. After the album they recorded a demo that´s supposed to be even better. They were actually changing their style into more progressive type metal. Putte later reappeared in *Aeon*, *Hammerfall*, *Lost Horizon* and *Full Strike*. Patrik, Alex and Emil were all found in *Jaggernaut*, who only made it to the demo stage. Emil later appeared in *Murder Corporation* and *Concrete Mass*. The latter also featured Arnestedt. *Death Remains* is a demo compilation.

1991 LP - THR 010

1991 ■	CALLS FROM THE BEYOND	LP	Thrash Records	THR 010	$
2010 ☐	DEATH REMAINS - THE DEMOS 1990-1991	LP	To The Death	TTD 002	
	300 hand-numbered copies.				
2012 ☐	CALLS FROM THE BEYOND	LP	To The Death	TTD 018	

MELDRUM

Moa Holmsten: v, Michelle Meldrum (Norum): g, Frida Ståhl: b

Stockholm - If you recognise the name Michelle Meldrum, it's probably because of her background in US metallurgists *Phantom Blue*. She later married John Norum and moved to Sweden. In 1998 she formed *Meldrum*, initially featuring Michelle, bass player Frida Ståhl, drummer Åsa Person and singer Janet Simmonds (later in *Siena Root*). Musically it's several tons heavier than her previous band. It's detuned, power chords, heavy throbbing riffs and Moa Holmsten's brutal vocals as the icing on the cake. Highly recommended! The debut featured drummer Fredrik Haake, who is ex-*God Is My Co-Pilot* and *The Vanity Set*, and is also found in *Sideburn* and punk-blues band *Badge*. He is also cousin of drummer Fredrik in *Meshuggah*... it runs in the family! *Meldrum* toured a lot with bands like *Motörhead*, *Black Label Society* and *Nashville Pussy*. Michelle also guested on John Norum's shows. In 2004 the band recorded a cover of *Motörhead*'s *No Class* for a tribute album. The band's second effort featured guest spots from Lemmy Kilmister (*Motörhead*), Gene Hogland (*Strapping Young Lad, Dark Angel*) and Linda McDonald (*Phantom Blue*) and Haake was not part of the line-up. It was a bit more experimental, incorporating more modern touches. On May 21, 2008 disaster struck when Michelle sadly passed away from a cystic growth in her brain. The band's third album, *Lifer* (2012 Reversed) was in the making and was completed, after her passing. Since the album features a line-up consisting of Michelle Madden (v), Laura Christine (g/b) and Gene Hogland (d) and no Swede's, I don't consider them a Swedish band anymore, hence it's not listed in the discography. Moa has since release a solo album in a more punk-oriented vein, where Haake handles the drums.

Michelle rockin' it out in 2001

2001 CD - RHCD 52

2001 ■	LOADED MENTAL CANON	CD	Record Heaven	RHCD 52
2007 ■	BLOWIN' UP THE MACHINE	CD	Frontiers Records	FR CD 334
2007 ☐	BLOWIN' UP THE MACHINE	CD	Locomotive Records (USA)	LM 518

2007 CD - FR CD 334

MELEK TAUS

Melek Taus: v/g/b

Sundsvall - A musically varied journey that ranges from soft piano music to thrash-oriented death metal and quite bad growling. *Melek Taus* (the benevolent Peacock Angel in the Yazidi faith) recorded the demo *We Unite* in '94. According to the label Melek was comatose after an overdose in 2001. Nils Johansson did keyboards and programming on the album and *Midvinter* member Kristeian played drums.

1997 ■	Expulsions From The Realm Of Light	MCD 4tr	Near Dark	NDP 005
	Tracks: We Unite/Encircled By Fire/Where The Forest Never Ends/A Dedication To The Northern Nature			

1997 MCD - NDP 005

MELISSA

Stezzo: g, Paranoya: g, Trauma: b, Tobbe "Schizo" R: d

Vittsjö - *Melissa* were formed in Markaryd in 1985, named after a *Mercyful Fate* song. initially playing in a more hardcore style. Recorded their first demo in 1986. Schizo initially handled the vocals. In 1987 bassist Paranoya joined. He later switched to guitar. Great enthusiasm but poor production and untight performance. The vocals are closer to death metal than traditional thrash. The band also made a demo, entitled *Garage Demo*, in 1988, where the members were named: Stefan (v/b), Patrik S (g), Tobbe R (d), and another one, *Welcome*, in 1989, before recording the single. On the single Trauma handled the bass. The band actually recorded an album, entitled

To Be Born In The Gutter, but the studio messed the tapes up, ruining four songs, and it was never released. For the last two gigs the band changed its name to **Decubitus**.

1989 ■ A Flight To Insanity ....7" Underground....................................U.G.R 01
    Tracks: No Rest For The Dead/Corpsacrations Death.

1989 7" - U.G.R 01

MELLOW POETRY
**Björn "Bobo" Holmquist: v, Fredrik Kjörling: g, Jonas Hägg: k,
Erik Grandin: b, Teddy Möller: d**

Uppsala - Top-notch progressive metal with an equal doze of power and melody. Great harmonies and well-written song material. They have been called a cross between *Fates Warning* and *Fear Factory*... well if you pick the vocal capacity and melodies from the first and the power from the second it sounds right. Besides the MCD they recorded a great amount of demo material. The band later became a bit more progressive and changed their name to *Mayadome*, under which name they released two albums. Möller is now in *F.K.Ü* and *Loch Vostock*. *Mellow Poetry* are also found on the compilation *15 On 1* (1992 Soundfront).

1995 MCD - PFG 952

1995 ■ Welcome To The Surreal World ....MCD 4tr Prime Familia....................................PFG 952
    Tracks: Wait A Minute...Who Am I Here?/Copper Colored/Primal Secrets/New Way Of Existence.

MEMENTO MORI
**Eddie "Messiah" Marcolin: v, Mikael "Mike Wead" Wikström: g, Nickey Argento: g,
Mårten "Marty Marteen" Sandberg: b, Miguel Robaina: k, Tom Björn (Johansson): d**

1994 CD - BMCD 51

Stockholm - It started out as a project, based around Mike Wead. Mike had previously recorded three albums with *Hexenhaus* and wanted to record some material that wasn't right for his previous band. Mårten has previously recorded a 7" with the band *Nagasaki* and an album with *Hexenhaus*. On the first two albums the bands figurehead and lead singer was the huge Jan Bror Alfredo "Eddi/Eddy/Eddie/Messiah" Marcolin, previously in *Candlemass* and *Mercy*. After the second album Eddie left the band to join doomsters *Stillborn* (re-named *Colossus*). Nothing however ever came out of it. His replacement, Stefan Karlsson was ex-*Neocori*. He actually sounds a lot like Eddie, but he only lasted for one tour. Wead was ex-*King Diamond Band/Hexenhaus*, later in *Mercyful Fate*, *Illwill* and *Abstrakt Algebra*. The music is doomy progressive hard rock in the vein of *Candlemass*-meet-*Psychotic Waltz*. The albums are all excellent. On the third release singer Kristian Andrén (ex-*Tad Morose*) replaced Stefan and Johan "Billy St John" Billerhag (*Parasite, Hexenhaus*) replaced Tommy "Snowy Shaw" Helgesson (*Dream Evil, Therion, XXX, Notre Dame* etc.). *Songs From The Apocalypse* saw the return of singer Marcolin and a change from drummer Billerhag to Tom Björn (later in *Memory Garden*). The album contains a cover of *Scorpions'* *Animal Magnetism*. After the release keyboardist Miguel Robana left the band and his spot was filled by Joakim Floke (*Elsesphere, Dionysus, Meduza*).

1993 LP - BMLP 32

1996 CD - BMCD 71

1993 ☐ RHYMES OF LUNACY ....CD Black Mark ....BMCD 32
1993 ■ RHYMES OF LUNACY ....LP Black Mark ....BMLP 32 $
1994 ■ LIFE, DEATH AND OTHER MORBID TALES ....CD Black Mark ....BMCD 51
1994 ☐ LIFE, DEATH AND OTHER MORBID TALES ....LP Black Mark ....BMLP 51
1996 ■ LA DANSE MACABRE..CD Black Mark ....BMCD 71
1996 ☐ LA DANSE MACABRE..LP Black Mark ....BMLP 71
1996 ☐ LA DANSE MACABRE..CD Teichiku (Japan)..............................TECW-25195
1997 ■ SONGS FROM THE APOCALYPSE VOL. IV ....CD Black Mark ....BMCD 124

MEMFIS
**Mattias Engström: g/v, Johan Boqvist: g/v, Christian Öberg: b/v,
Carl-Johan Lindblad: d**

1997 CD - BMCD 124

Kristinehamn/Göteborg - *Memfis*, the name taken from the Egyptian city, started out in Kristinehamn in 2003. The first line-up featured Engström, Lindblad (*Moonville*), guitarist/singer Johan Boqvist and bass player Christian Öberg. During 2004 they recorded two demos, *The Judgement* and *Breathless*, which caught the attention of new label Dental Records. After the single and debut were recorded in 2006, Boqvist was replaced by Daniel Göstedt and Öberg by Henrik Hedelund. The track *Breakdown* on the single is non-album. In 2008 *Memfis* recorded their second album, *Vertigo* in Bohus Sound Studio. Later the same year Dental Records sued the band, but after two years, the day before the trial the label pulled out. As a result the band released the album digitally through their website (pay what you want). *Memfis* play modern, aggressive, yet progressive and technical metal, mixing growling vocals with some clean vocals. Some tracks are even silimar to *Opeth* during the *My Arms Your Herase* era. Great stuff, indeed!

2006 CDd - DR 190110

2006 ■ THE WIND-UP ....CDd Dental Records ....DR 190110
2006 ■ The Wind-Up/Breakdown...7" Futhermocker....................................MOCK 07
    220 hand-numbered copies.
2006 ☐ THE WIND-UP ....CD Candlelight (USA) ....CDL 357 CD

2006 7" - MOCK-07

MEMORIA
Ludvig Friberg: v, Josef Torvaldsson: g, Jens Englund: g,
Martin Rydin: b, Patrik Johnsson: k, Johan Rydin: d

Nässjö - **Memoria** were formed in 1997 when Friberg, Torvaldsson and guitarist Erik Persson decided to form a black metal band. Johansson and Martin Rydin were drafted and shortly after Martin's older brother Johan entered on drums. Persson left and the band made their debut gig in 2000. The band recorded the first MCD and shortly after the band was completed by guitarist Jens Englund. Another MCD was recorded, from which the track *Man In Disguise* was featured on the compilation *Hordes Of Darkness* (2003 Unexploded). Excellent progressive metal with growling vocals. With clean vocals they would be a regular prog metal band. In August 2001 the band folded. Englund is today **Karnivore** (formerly known as **Karneywar**). Split-up.

2000 MCD - MEMCD 01

2001 ■	Memoria	MCD 3tr	private	MEMCD 01
	Tracks: Pure White/In Search For Tranquillity/Blackened Souls			
2002 ☐	Memoria 2	MCD 3tr	private	MEMCD 02
	Tracks: The Dawn Of Day/Man In Disguise/Insane.			

MEMORIUM
Fredrik Strömkvist: v, Markus Görsch: g, Daniel Andersson: k, Joel Görsch: b

Horred - Formed in 1992. Very slow and melodic death/black metal with spoken vocals, programmed drums and prominent keyboards. Released two demos in 1992 (*The Oak Of Memories* and *Enlightenment*) and two in 1993 (*At The Graveyard* and *Deepest Woods*). Quite strange but also quite interesting. Not the same band that released the demo tape *Eons In Slumber* in 1993.

1994 ■	Memorium	MCD 4tr	Local Hero	LHM 0220
	Tracks: Black Roses/Gods Of Frozen Water/Dance With Death/A Girl			

1994 MCD - LHM 0220

MEMORY GARDEN
Stefan Berglund: v, Simon Johansson: g, Andreas Mäkelä: g,
Johan Fredriksson: b, Tom Björn (Johansson): d

Kumla - Formed in 1992 and recorded their first demo in 1993. This band produces some very doom-laden riffs and slow, searing songs. They should attract fans of bands like **Solitude Aeternus** and **Candlemass**. Dan Swanö produced the first single. The 1995 EP *Ta någon hårt i hand så åker vi till tomteland* is **Memory Garden** playing Christmas songs in a **Memory Garden** way. The last song *Jultomten är faktiskt död* means "Santa Claus is really dead". Cuddle up and listen, children. On *Verdicts Of Posterity* the band changed guitarist from Rick Gustafsson to Anders Looström. *Mirage* was produced by Mike Wead (**King Diamond, Memento Mori** etc). Tom is also found in **Memento Mori** and **Nightingale**. The band is also featured on a **Black Sabbath** tribute with *Country Girl*, on a **Queensryche**-tribute with *The Needle Lies* and on the **Mercyful Fate** tribute *Curse Of The Demon* (2000) with *Nightmare Be Thy Name*. In 2007 bass player Ken Johansson quit and was replaced by Johan Fredriksson. In 2008 Andreas Mäkelä (**Evil Conspiracy**) replaced Looström. Simon is also found in **Abstrakt Algebra, Fifth Reason** and **Bibleblack**.
Website: www.memorygarden.net

1994 7" - MGREP 002

1996 CD - HDMCD 003

2004 7" - HDMEp 02

1994 ■	Blessed Are The Dead/Badlands	7"	Megagrind/Immortal Underground	MGREP 002
1995 ☐	Forever	MCD 4tr	Heathendoom	HDM 001
	Tracks: Warlord/Inarticulo Mortis/Forever/Autumn Anguish			
1995 ☐	Ta någon hårt i hand så ger vi oss av till tomteland	7" 4tr	private	- -
	Tracks: Mössens julafton/Tomtarnas julnatt/Stilla natt/Jultomten är faktiskt död			
1996 ■	TIDES	CD	Heathendoom	HDMCD 003
1996 ☐	TIDES	CD	Hellion (South America)	n/a
	Contains the tracks from the MCD Forever as bonus.			
1998 ☐	VERDICT OF POSTERITY	CD	Metal Blade	3981-14191-2
2000 ☐	MIRAGE	CD	MetalBlade	3984-14337-2
2004 ■	Nameless/Marion	7"	Heathendoom	HDMEP 002
2007 ☐	CARNAGE CARNIVAL	CD+DVD	Vic Records	VIC 006
	First edition with bonus DVD			
2007 ■	CARNAGE CARNIVAL	CD	Vic Records	VIC 006 CD
2009 ☐	TIDES	CD	Vic Records	VIC 023 CD
	Bonus: Genesis (demo)/Rhyme Of The Elder (demo)/A Dark Embrace (reh). New artwork.			
2013 ☐	DOOMAIN	2CD	Metal Blade	3984-15205-2
2013 ☐	DOOMAIN	LP	Metal Blade	3984-15205-1

2007 CD - VIC 006 CD

MENTAL CRYPT
Hugo Bryngfors: v, Jan Jansson: g, Sven-Erik Fritiofsson: g,
Ulf "Blappan" Jansson: b, Kjell Elmlund: d

Karlstad - Formed in 1993 by Jansson and Elmlund. They recorded their first demo, *Black Hole*,

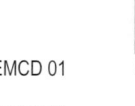

later the same year, with another singer. Hugo joined and the second demo, entitled *Aimless* was recorded in 1994 and the third demo, *Sects Of Doom*, was unleashed in 1996. The band was featured on a number of compilations such as *Frykenrock*, *Out Of The Box* (Black Mark), *Black Mark Attack II* and *A Black Mark Tribute*. The band left Black Mark and recorded a three-track demo entitled *Ground Zero* in 1999, after which nothing has happened. In 2000 they changed their name to **Loss** and are still active. **Mental Crypt** plays old-school death metal. Elmlund was also found in **Feral** and **Fester Plague**, Jansson in **Grave Flowers** and **Fester Plague**.

1998 ■ EXTREME UNCTION ....CD   Black Mark .... BMCD 134

1998 CD - BMCD 134

MENTAL HIPPIE BLOOD
Michael Oran: v, Mikael Jansson: g, Anders "Gary" Wikström: g,
Lake Skoglund: b, Jonas Östman: d

Stockholm - **Mental Hippie Blood** derived out of the ashes of sleaze rockers **Glorious Bankrobbers** with Michael Oran as their new singer. After the first album drummer Anders Odenstrand left the band to join **Manic Depression** and his place was filled by Jonas Östman, ex-**Gotham City/Glory/Yngwie Malmsteen**. Guitarist Jonas Pettersson (later in **Greed**) was replaced by former **Treat** string-bender Anders "Gary" Wikström and in 1994 the band pursued a successful European tour supporting **Accept**. The debut was good even though there were some ups and downs, while *Pounds* was a strong and heavy steamroller with hints of **Soundgarden** and **Alice In Chains** in their heavier moments. In 1995 the band unfortunately split and singer Michael Oran later replaced his own brother in **Albatross**, previously known as **Manic Depression**, but nothing came out of it.

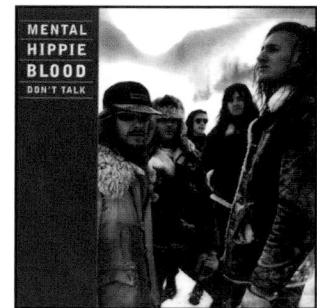

1993 MCDp - MVGCDS 5

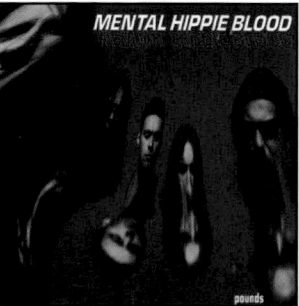

1994 CD - MVG 118

1992 □	MENTAL HIPPIE BLOOD ....CD	MVG..MVG 110
1993 ■	Don't Talk ....MCDp 3tr	MVG..MVGCDS 5
	Tracks: Don't Talk/Psychopathic Mind/Don't Talk (full length version)	
1994 □	MENTAL HIPPIE BLOOD ....CD	Steamhammer (Germany) ...... SPV 084-76892
1994 ■	POUNDS..CD	MVG..MVG 118
1994 □	POUNDS..CD	Metal Blade (USA)..................... 3984-14100-2
1994 ■	Chosen/Golden Sun/Save Me ....MCD 3tr	MVG..MVGCDS 24
1995 ○	Still Pounds - Zorbact Mix/Still Pounds (album version) ....CDS 2tr	MVG..MVGPROM 30
	Radio promo. No artwork.	

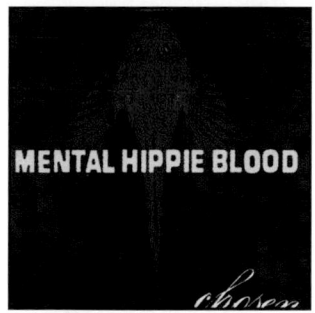

1994 MCD - MVGCDS 24

MENTOR'S WISH
Johan Engström: v, Johan Wikström: g, Eric Liljeros: k,
Christer Wiik: b, Fredrik Scherman: d

Stockholm - The band was formed in 1994 under the name **Crime Of Passion**, but changed to **Mentor's Wish** in 1996. The album contains outstanding progressive melodic hard rock with a very personal touch. The band implement totally unexpected tempo and harmony changes without making it sound over-arranged. A great surprise and highly recommended. After the album they went through some member changes. Engström (later in **Masque**) was replaced by Nicklas Johnsson, who also sang on **Hammerfall**-guitarist Stefan Elmgren's solo project **Full Strike**. In 2001 Bengt Weber replaced Eric and Fredrik Larsson replaced Christer. The band had material written for a second album and in 2002 negotiations were taking place with a label for a future second release. It however never surfaced. Christer was later involved with his own band that went under the working name **Catch 22**.

1998 ■ THE FINE THREAD OF SANITY ....CD   Sonus.. SONCD 011

1998 CD - SONCD 011

MERCENARY MUSTANGS
Ove Wulff: v/g, Micke Jönsson: b. Pär Norén: d

Östersund - It all started around 1979-80, when Ove formed the band **Mighty Riff**. In 1980 Pär Norén replaced drummer Lars Westerlund. In 1982 they recorded ten songs. They split later the same year, but reunited in 1983 under the name **Intruder**. The song *Intruder* was also released on the compilation *Mixed Music For Lonely Nights* (1984 Pang). The band split, but some year later Ove formed **Roadhouse**, which in 1990 became **Mercenary Mustangs**. They released one single and the demo *On The House*. The song *Judy Go Round* was also featured on the *Nordic Sounds* compilation released by Joker Records in 1991. In 1992 they changed into **Orange Disaster** and then played more grunge-oriented hard rock. The band split in 1993. In the late nineties they changed name and style to country rock. They have released an album entitled *The Sun Never Shines On Frank's Backdoor* under the name **Enzendoh**. The **Mercenary Mustangs** single is really good melodic **Purple**/**Heep**-influenced hard rock. Micke is today playing in **The Humbuggers**, Per in **JB:s Wiretag Band** and Ove has released some solo stuff, more in the vein of Steve Earle.

1990 ■ Some Kind Of Madness/Run And Hide...7"   John's Records .... JSR 9008

1990 7" - JSR 9008

MERCILESS

Roger "Rogga" Pettersson: v, Erik Wallin: g, Fredrik Karlén: b, Peter Stjärnvind: d

Strängnäs - Starting out as a punk/metal band in 1985, *Merciless* are among the veterans of Swedish death metal. Drummer Stefan "Stipen" Carlsson was replaced by Peter Stjärnvind in 1991. Stjärnvind is also a member of *Unanimated* and *Loudpipes*, where also Fredrik was found (under the name Carl Leen). Peter is also found in metal band *Face Down*, who released their debut on Soundfront Records early 1996. *Merciless* folded in 1994, to reunite five years later. Stipen later joined punk rockers *Dia Psalma*, and was also found in *Harm's Way*, *Transport League* and *Trash Amigos*. *The Awakening* was the first release on Norwegian Deathlike Silence, run by the late Eronymous from *Mayhem*. Wallin is now found in *Trash Amigos* and *Death Breath*. *Merciless* play thrash/death a bit reminiscent of bands like *Kreator* and *Sodom* with a touch of classic *Bathory*. Fast and brutal, but with quite melodic guitars.

1989 LP - ANTIMOSH 001

1991 7" - CBR S 134

1989	■	THE AWAKENING	LP	Deathlike Silence	ANTIMOSH 001	$$
1989	□	THE AWAKENING	CD	Deathlike Silence	ANTIMOSH 001	$$
1991	■	Branded By Sunlight (split)	7"	CBR	CBR S 134	
		Split with Comecon. Promo.				
1992	□	THE TREASURE WITHIN	LP	Active	ATV 26	
1992	□	THE TREASURE WITHIN	CD	Active	CDATV 26	
1994	□	UNBOUND	CD	No Fashion	NFR 007	
1994	□	UNBOUND	LP	No Fashion	NFR 007	
1997	■	Behind The Black Door (Demo Tape 1987)	7" 4tr	Iron Fist	IFPEP 01	
		Tracks: Total Destruction/Bestial Death/Satanic Slaughters/Behind The Black Door				
1997	□	Realm Of The Dark (Demo Tape 1988)	7" 4tr	Iron Fist	IFPEP 02	
		Tracks: Realm Of The Dark/Souls Of The Dead/Nuclear Attack/Dreadful Fate				
1999	□	THE AWAKENING	LP+7"	Osmose	OPLP 087+OPEP 087	
		Re-issue featuring bonus live single: Bestial Death/The Awakening/Nuclear Attack/Pure Hate. 500 hand-numbered copies.				
1999	□	THE AWAKENING	CD	Osmose	OPCD 037	
		Bonus: Bestial Deat/ The Awakening/Nuclear Attack/Pure Hate				
2002	□	MERCILESS	CD	Black Lodge	BLOD001CD	
2002	□	MERCILESS	LPg	Black Lodge	BLOD001LP	
2003	□	THE TREASURE WITHIN	CD	Black Lodge	BLOD005CD	
		Re-mastered. Bonus: Book Of Lies (demo)/Nuclear Attack				
2006	□	UNBOUND	CD	Black Lodge	BLOD25CD	
2007	□	UNBOUND	LPg	War Anthem Records	WAR 005 LP	
		500 copies. Embossed cover.				
2011	□	THE AWAKENING	LP	Temple Of Darkness	TOD 033	
		Bonus: Bestial Death/The Awakening/Nuclear Attack/Pure Hate. Poster. 500 copies. New artwork.				
2011	□	THE AWAKENING	LP PD	Temple Of Darkness	TOD 033	
2011	■	THE TREASURES WITHIN	LP	Temple Of Darkness	TOD 038	
2011	□	UNBOUND	LP	Temple Of Darkness	TOD 039	
2011	□	UNBOUND	LP PD	Temple Of Darkness	TOD 039	

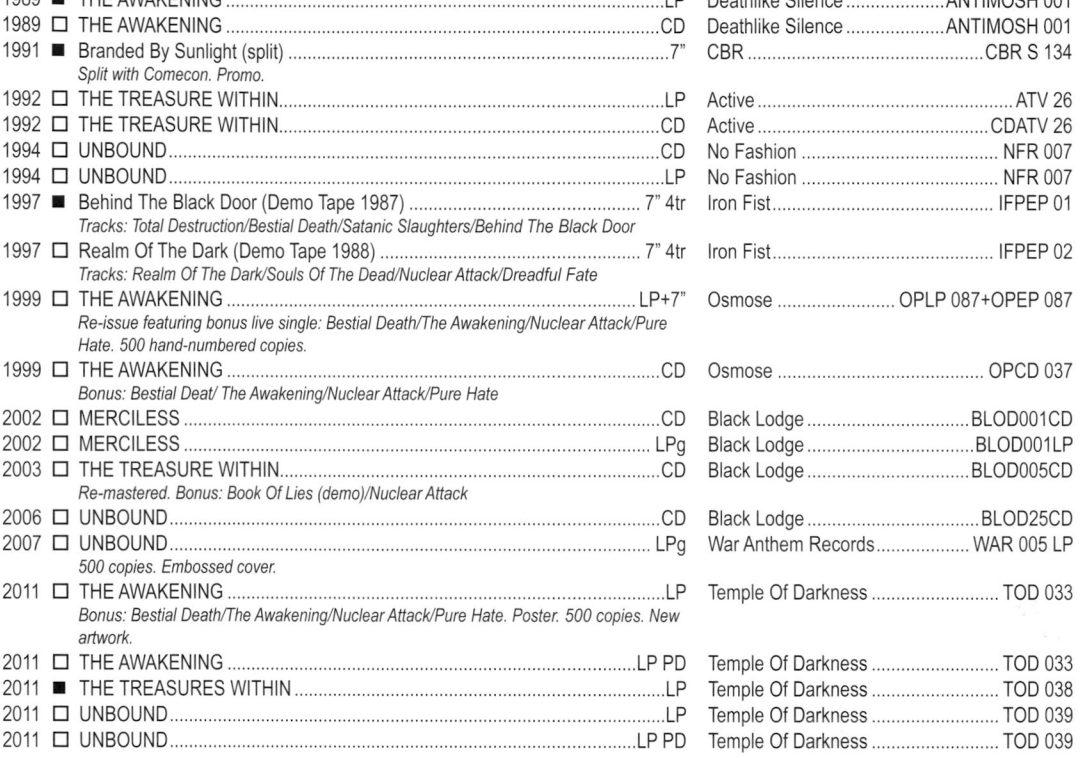

1997 7" - IFPEP 01

2011 LP - TOD 038

MERCURY FANG

Fredrik Glimbrand: v/g, Håkan Granat: g, Jörgen Schelander: k,
Olle Bodén: b, Martin Larsson: d

Stockholm - *Mercury Fang* started out as a co-operation between Bodén and drummer Ken Savefjord in 1999. The band was completed with Granat, Glimbrand (ex-*Atlantis*) and Schelander (also in *Audivision*). In 2000 the band recorded a four-track demo, followed by another ten-track outing. On *Ignition*, which was produced by Pontus Norgren (*Hammerfall, Talisman* etc), drummer Ken Savefjord had been replaced by Martin Larsson (*Stabb*). In 2004 the band did a cover of *Identity Crisis* for the *Sweet* tribute *The Sweet According To Sweden* (2004 Rivel). *Mercury Fang* plays high-class, melodic, guitar-dominated hard rock with a twist. *Ignition* even has a *King's X* twist in some songs, while others have a slightly proggy touch. In 2010 the band decided to make a drastic change when they added female singer Maria Rådsten (*One More Time*, guest on *Mountain Of Power*) to the line-up. They also changed their name to *Misth*. A new album, under the new moniker, was released in 2012. *Misth* has taken the style even a step further when it comes to musical drama and complexity. A great band!

2003 CD - RRCD 008

2007 CD - RRCD 034

2003	■	LIQUID SUNSHIN	CD	Rivel Records	RRCD 008
2007	■	IGNITION	CD	Rivel Records	RRCD 034

MERCY

Andrija "Weechking" Veljaca: v/g/b, Adam Pavlovic: d

Sölvesborg/Karlshamn - Formed in 1980 from the ashes of heavy metal band *Turbo*, who released one single. *Turbo* featured singer/guitarist Ola Persson (now Calle Engelmarc), guitarist Håkan Jacobsson (brother of Kjell Jacobsson in *Overdrive*), bassist Christian Karlsson and drummer Paul Gustafsson. Håkan left to join *Hatchet* and Andrija came into the band, which now became *Mercy*. Some demos were recorded when Ola was still in the band, handling guitar

1982 MLP - MCI 111 (bw)

and vocals, but the members on the first MLP were Andrija on guitar and vocals, Paul on drums and vocals and Christian on bass. The band also had two songs on the *Rockslaget* compilation (82 SOS). The EP is a "charming" piece of vinyl while *Mercy* is a quite acceptable platter in the **Judas Priest**-vein. The reason is that Eddie "Messiah" Marcolin (ex-**Rough Lizard**, later in **Candlemass**, **Memento Mori**) had joined on vocals and Magnus Klintö on rhythm guitar. Magnus later left the band, and so did Paul and Christian. Paul later joined **High Voltage**, **Overheat** and is now playing in a cover band (now with last name Bergholtz) while Christian played with **Ocean** for a while. New bassist Jörgen Holst was recruited and on *Witchburner* both drums and vocals were handled by Eddie (he was actually a drummer/singer in **Rough Lizard**). *Witchburner* is doom at its slowest pace. A demo, featuring *Black Death*, was recorded in 1986 with Ralph Rydén on drums. Eddie left to join **Candlemass** and drummer Peter "TrumPeter" Svensson (also in **Faith**, later **Overheat**, **Locomotive Breath**, **Constancia** etc.), bassist Tom Mitchell and high-pitched singer Rikard "Rich Wine" Larsson (**Supreme Majesty, In Black**) joined. After the recordings of *King Doom* Peter left the band and Johan Norell replaced him. The album actually states Norell as the drummer, although Peter plays on it. The band was defunct for several years, although Andrija constantly claimed a new album unexpectedly could turn up. *Black Magic* is a CD-reissue of *Witchburner* plus two demo tracks with singer Anders Strengberg (ex-**Sacrifice, Metal Muthas, Wham Glam Boys**). Andrija was actually the man behind the Euro Records label and he had previously recorded a single with the band *Horoscope*, a dire effort though. *Victory March* is a previously unreleased album, recorded in 1987, featuring Veljaca, Norell, Strengberg and guitarist Roger Johansson (**Faith**). On some recordings the track *Black Death* is called *Black Dead*. In 2003 the unexpected expected album suddenly turned up! The album featured drummer Adam Pavlovic (**Zap Yankeefy**) and Andrija handled all guitars, bass and vocals. It's an extremely detuned album, doomy and not exactly any of the band's finest work. Andrija handled the vocals doing his best to try to emulate Messiah Marcolin's vocals, without succeeding. The album also featured three bonus tracks: *H.M Warriors, Black Death* and *Bangers Of Destruction*, recorded in 1983-1985. On August 25, 2005 Andrija unexpectedly died of a brain haemorrhage. The 2007 7" *Session 1981* was originally a demo with the very first line-up featuring Ola on vocals/guitar, Andrija, Christian and Paul. Ola (Calle) was later working with **Madison**.

Mercy me - It's the black magic witchburners!

1982 ■	Swedish Metal ...... MLP 5tr	Metal Shock ...... MCI 111	$($)$	
	Tracks: State Of Shock/Don't Stop Heavy Guitar/Heavy Sound/Lost In Time/Stranger From The Dark. Released in two versions,the original version with b/w artwork, and the second pressing with red print.			
1984 ■	MERCY ...... LP	Fingerprint ...... FINGLP 008	$	
1985 ■	WITCHBURNER ...... LP	Fingerprint ...... FINGLP 013	$$	
1989 ☐	KING DOOM ...... LP	Euro Records ...... MCY 112		
1990 ☐	BLACK MAGIC ...... CD	Vivo ...... IMT 555.006		
	Same as King Doom, but with the two bonus tracks Mercy and Black Death, sung by Anders Strengberg.			
1990 ■	BLACK MAGIC ...... LP	Electrecord (Romania) ST-ELE04080	$$	
1992 ☐	WITCHBURNER ...... CD	Euro Records ...... ERCD 921	$	
2002 ☐	Black Death/Bangers Of Destruction ...... 12"" PD	Stormbringer ...... SKULL 9813P		
	333 copies.			
2002 ☐	VICTORY MARCH ...... LP	Stormbringer ...... SKULL 9809		
	100 red + poster and 400 black vinyl copies.			
2003 ☐	VICTORY MARCH ...... CD	TPL ...... TPL 014		
2003 ☐	UNDERGROUND ...... CD	TPL ...... TPL 105		
2006 ☐	WITCHBURNER/MERCY ...... CD	Keltic ...... KELTIC 007		
2007 ☐	Session 1981 ...... 7" 4tr	Nuclear War Now ...... ANTI GOTH 059		
	Tracks: Beggin For Mercy/Shadow Woman/Dreams/Stranger From The Dark. 500 copies			
2013 ☐	WITCHBURNER ...... LP	Svart Records ...... SVR 193		
	200 silver, 300 black vinyl copies.			

1984 LP - FINGLP 008

1985 LP - FINGLP 013

MERRYGOLD
Greta "Gosia" Zachoszcz: v, Staffan Österlind: g, Per Berglund: g, Martin "Bollack" Wesowski: b, Markus "Mackan" Persson: d

Malmö/Hörby - **Merrygold** were formed in 2001 when former punk guitarist Berglund (ex-**Moderat Likvidation**) and Staffan Österlind (ex-**DiAnno**) joined forces. The initial line-up featured singer Selma Liljenberg and drummer Andreas "Adde" Larsson (**Urbandux, MMI, M.A.N**), who also guests on drums on one track on the album. The band went through some tough times recording the debut album, as the studio burned down and all the hard drives were destroyed. It's quite hard to pinpoint the band's style, as it goes from poppy hard rock to *Evanescence*-ish heavy melodic metal with a touch of **Foo Fighters** in some places. Wesowski was also found in **Original Sin, Booze Brothers** and **Majestic**. Österlind now lives in the USA and has recorded an album with hard rockers **Black Robot**.

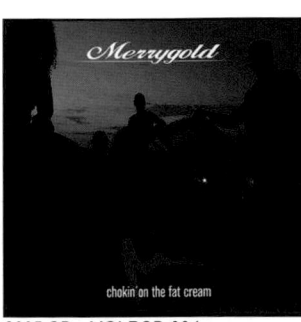

2005 CD - MGLRCD 004

1990 LP - ST-ELE04080

2005 ■	CHOKING ON THE FAT CREAM ...... CD	Mangalore ...... MGLRCD 004	

MESHUGGAH

Jens Kidman: v, **Mårten Hagström:** g, **Fredrik Thordendahl:** g,
Dick Löwgren: b, **Tomas Haake:** d

Umeå - Originally formed by Thordendahl in 1985 as **Metallien**, and changed their name to **Meshuggah** in 1987. The name means "crazy" in jiddish. The first line-up featured Jens Kidman, Fredrik Thordendahl, Johan Sjögren (g), Jörgen Lindmark (b) and Per Sjögren (d). Niclas Lundgren handled the drums on the first 12", and at that time Jens also played guitar. Later the same year, they recorded the demo *Ejuculation Of Salvation*. On *Contradictions Collapse* Tomas had replaced Niclas and the remaining members were Jens, Fredrik and Peter Nordin (b). The first EP, often referred to as "*Psykisk testbild*", was tight and technical thrash with hints of hard core, while *Contradictions Collapse* had some jazzy influences. The reason there was a gap between the '91 and '94 releases is because of some misfortune... First Fredrik cut off his left hand index fingertip and then Tomas caught his fingers in a lathe at work. They returned in 1994 with the self-produced EP *None*, where Mårten was added to the line-up and Jens concentrated on singing. The band toured Europe with **Machine Head** in the spring of 1995. *Destroy Erase Improve* is a really heavy, yet highly technical thrasher produced by the young knob wizzard Daniel Bergstrand (**Crawley, Lost Sould, Devin Townsend** etc). In 1997 they changed bass player from Peter Nordin to Gustaf Hielm (ex-**Charta 77**, now in **Badge**), whose first appearance was a live track on the *The True Human Design* MCD. This year Thordendahl also released his solo album *Sol Niger Within*, under the moniker **Fredrik Thordendahl's Special Defects**. Peter had to leave because of stress-related illness. Fred Estby (**Dismember**) often reinforced the band live and as a producer. The song *Unanything* was recorded for *Chaosphere* and even included on an early promo, but never issued. Fredrik Thorendahl has also guested on tracks and albums by bands like **Blacksmith, Memoranum, XXX Atomic Toejam, Blender** etc. In 2001 Gustaf left the band and on *Nothing* Thordendahl also handled the bass. The album also features Thordendal for the first time using his 8-string guitar, and Haake handling the lead vocals on a couple of tracks. In 2004 Dick Löwgren (**Dark Funeral, Arch Enemy**) was used as live bassist. *Rare Trax* is a compilation of rare tracks and MPEG videos. The single *I* contains just one 21-minute-long track, a concept they continued using on the subsequent album *Catch Thirtythree*, where the entire album is one track divided into thirteen parts. On this album the bass duties were shared between Thordendahl, Kidman and Hagström, while the drums were programmed. On the follow-up, *ObZen*, the real drums were back and the bass was handled by former live bassist Löwgren. In 2010 the live DVD/CD *Alive* was released. The band can be found on numerous compilations. Some of the non-album recordings include, a live-recorded cover of **Whimzy**'s *Attacked By A Shark* on the *Power From The North*-compilation, *Sickening* live on *Death Is Just The Beginning* IV (97 Nuclear Blast), *Soul Burn* live on *Noise From Umeå Vol 1* (96) and *We'll Never See The Day* on *Ich Zahl Nicht Mehr Vol 1* (92 SPV).
Website: www.meshuggah.net

Then...

...and now!

Year		Title	Format	Label	Cat. No.	
1989	■	Meshuggah	MLP 3tr	Garageland	BF 634	$$
		Tracks: Cadaverous Mastication/Sovereigns/Morbidity/The Depth Of Nature. 1000 copies				
1991	■	CONTRADICTIONS COLLAPSE	LP	Nuclear Blast	NB 049 1	
1991	□	CONTRADICTIONS COLLAPSE	CD	Nuclear Blast	NB 049 2	
1991	□	CONTRADICTIONS COLLAPSE	CD	Victor (Japan)	VICP 5660	
		Bonus: Sickening/Gods Of Rapture/Aztec Two-Step				
1994	□	None	MLP 5tr	Nuclear Blast	NB 102 1	
		Tracks: Humiliative/Sickening/Ritual/Gods Of Rapture/Aztec Two-Step				
1994	□	None	MCD 5tr	Nuclear Blast	NB 102 2	
1994	□	None	MCD 5tr	Nuclear Blast America (USA)	NBA 6119 2	
1995	□	Selfcaged	MCD 4tr	Nuclear Blast	NB 132 2	
		Tracks: re-arranged pre-album versions of Vanished/Suffer In Truth/Inside What's Within Behind/Gods Of Rapture(live)				
1995	□	Selfcaged	MCD 5tr	Nuclear Blast America (USA)	NBA 6132 2	
		Bonus: re-arranged pre-album versions of Gods Of Rapture				
1995	□	DESTROY ERASE IMPROVE	CD	Nuclear Blast	NB 121 2	
1995	□	DESTROY ERASE IMPROVE	CDd	Nuclear Blast	NB 121 2	
1995	□	DESTROY ERASE IMPROVE	CD	Nuclear Blast America (USA)	NBA 6874 2	
1995	□	DESTROY ERASE IMPROVE	CD	Victor (Japan)	VICP 5659	
		Bonus: Humiliative/Ritual/Gods Of Rapture				
1996	□	Hypocrisy/Meshuggah (split)	7"	Nuclear Blast	NB 154-7	
		1000 copies. 1996 tour edition. Track: Future Breed Machine				
1997	□	The True Human Design	MCDd 7tr	Nuclear Blast	NB 268 2	
		Tracks: Sane/Future Breed Machine (live)/Future...(Mayhem version)/Futile Breed Machine(campfire vers)/Quant's Quantastical Quantasm/Friend's Breaking And Entering/ Terminal Iluusions (video).				
1997	□	The True Human Design	MCD 7tr	Nuclear Blast America (USA)	NBA 6268 2	
1998	■	CONTRADICTIONS COLLAPSE/NONE	CDd	Nuclear Blast	NB 292 2	
1998	□	CONTRADICTIONS COLLAPSE/NONE	CDd	Nuclear Blast America (USA)	NBA 6292 2	
1998	□	CHAOSPHERE	CD	Nuclear Blast	NB 336 2	
1998	□	CHAOSPHERE	CD	Nuclear Blast America (USA)	NBA 6336 2	
1999	□	CHAOSPHERE	CD	Avalon/Marquee (Japan)	MICY-1095	
		The catalogue number on the OBI reads: MICP-10095				
2001	■	RARE TRAX	CD	Nuclear Blast	NB 605 2	

1989 MLP - BF 643

1991 LP - NB 049 1

1998 CDd - NB 292 2

2001	☐	RARE TRAX	CD	Nuclear Blast America	NBA 6605 2
2001	☐	Meshuggah	MCD 3tr	Nuclear Blast	n/a

Tracks: Cadaverous Mastication/Sovereigns Morbidity/The Depth Of Nature.

2001	☐	RARE TRAX	CD	Avalon/Marquee (Jap)	MICP 10259
2002	■	NOTHING	CD	Nuclear Blast	NB 542 2
2002	☐	NOTHING	CD	Nuclear Blast (USA)	NB 6542 2
2002	☐	NOTHING	CD	Avalom Marquee (Japan)	MICP-10309
2003	☐	CHAOSPHERE	CD	Irond (Russia)	CD 03-570
2004	☐	I	CDS	Fractured Transmitter	FTRC-001
2004	☐	I	CDS	Fractured Transmitter (USA)	HA-001
2005	☐	CATCH THIRTYTHREE	CD	Nuclear Blast	NB 1311-2
2005	☐	CATCH THIRTYTHREE	CD	Nuclear Blast (Australia)	RIOT 004 CD
2005	☐	CATCH THIRTYTHREE	CD	Avalon Marquee (Japan)	MICP-10506
2005	☐	CATCH THIRTYTHREE	CD	Irond (Russia)	CD 05-1016
2005	☐	CATCH THIRTYTHREE	2LPg	Back On Black	BOBV 036DPD

2000 copies

| 2006 | ■ | NOTHING | CD+DVD | Nuclear Blast | NB 1729-2 |

Live bonus DVD.

| 2006 | ☐ | NOTHING | CD+DVD | Irond (Russia) | CD 06-329 DL |
| 2007 | ☐ | NOTHING | LP | Night Of The Vinyl Dead | NIGHT 017 $ |

333 copies. Poster.

| 2007 | ☐ | OBZEN | CD | Nuclear Blast | NB 1937-2 |

Limited edition also in slipcase

| 2007 | ☐ | OBZEN | LP | Nuclear Blast (USA) | NBA 11937-1 |
| 2007 | ☐ | OBZEN | LP | Nuclear Blast | NB 1937-1 |

Red vinyl

| 2007 | ☐ | OBZEN | CD | Nuclear Blast (USA) | 2010-2 |
| 2007 | ☐ | OBZEN | LP | Back On Black | BOBV 079 LP |

1000 copies

| 2007 | ☐ | OBZEN | CD | Avalon Marquee (Japan) | MICP-10692 |
| 2007 | ☐ | OBZEN | LPg | Back On Black | BOBV 079 LP |

Grey vinyl

2007	☐	OBZEN	CD	Irond (Russia)	CD 08-1430
2007	☐	OBZEN	CD	Icarus (Argentina)	ICARUS 436
2007	☐	CHAOSPHERE	LP	Night Of The Vinyl Dead	NIGHT 021

333 numbered copies in grey splatter vinyl.

| 2007 | ☐ | DESTRORY ERASE IMPROVE | LP | Night Of The Vinyl Dead | NIGHT 025 |

333 numbered copies in "Swedish flag" coloured vinyl.

| 2008 | ☐ | CONTRADICTIONS COLLAPSE/NONE | CD | Nuclear Blast | NB 2202 2 |

In super jewel case

| 2008 | ☐ | DESTROY ERASE IMPROVE | CD | Nuclear Blast | NB 2192-2 |

Bonus: Vanished (demo)Suffer In Truth (demo)/Inside What's Within Behind (demo)/Gods Of Rapture (live)/Aztec Two Step

| 2008 | ☐ | CHAOSPHERE | CD | Nuclear Blast | NB 2203-2 |

Bonus: Sane (demo)/Future Breed Machine (Mayhem version)/ Future Breed Machine (Campfire version)/ Future Breed Machine (Quant's Quantastical O La La)/Future Breed Machine (Remix)

| 2008 | ☐ | NOTHING | CD | Nuclear Blast | NB 1729-0 |
| 2009 | ☐ | The Singles Collection | 3MLP | Night Of The Vinyl Dead | NIGHT 060 $ |

450 copies. Contains: Selfcaged (10", 4tr), None (11", 5tr) and The True Human Design (12, 6tr")

2010	■	ALIVE	CDd+DVD	Nuclear Blast	2527-0
2010	☐	ALIVE	CDd+DVD	Nuclear Blast (USA)	2388-9
2010	☐	ALIVE	CDd+DVD	Icarus (Argentina)	ICARUS 597
2010	☐	ALIVE	2LPg	Back On Black	BOBV 225 LP
2010	☐	ALIVE	CD	Avalon Marquee (Japan)	MICP-10894
2010	☐	ALIVE	CD+DVD	Avalon Marquee (Japan)	MIZF-70011
2010	☐	ALIVE	CDd+DVD	Evolution Music (Korea)	L100004016
2011	☐	CONTRADICTIONS COLLAPSE/NONE	2LPg	Nuclear Blast	NB 2732-1

150 hand-numbered copies in red/yellow marble vinyl. Embossed cover. Second pressing 300 copies in yellow vinyl.

| 2012 | ☐ | I Am Collossus/I Am Collossus (remix) | 7" | Scion Audio/Visual (USA) | SA/V 23-12 |

Available in black, blue/green and clear/black marbled vinyl. Free concert give away.

2012	■	KOLOSS	CD	Nuclear Blast	12388-2
2012	☐	KOLOSS	CDd	Nuclear Blast	12388-8
2012	☐	KOLOSS	CDd+DVD	Nuclear Blast	12388-0
2012	☐	KOLOSS	2LPg	Nuclear Blast	12388-1

METAL MERCY
Bengt "Boogi" Igefors: v, Nicklas Arvidsson: g, Leif Andersson: b, Basse Norberg: d

Jönköping - Formed in 1986. The reason the title of the MLP was *The Unborn Child* is because all the members in the band had got their girlfriends pregnant at around the same time. So when it was recorded there were four unborn children. They later had to change their name for legal reasons and took the moniker Anona. They recorded the track *Dark Life* for the compilation

2001 CD - NB 605 2

2002 CD - NB 542 2

2006 CD - NB 1729-2

2010 CDd+DVD - 2527-0

2012 CD - 12388-2

Loud 'N Proud (91 Planet Records/M&M) and after that Leif was replaced by Ulrik Zander, Mikael Hilmersson (ex-*Twilight Project*) was replaced by Basse and later on Nicklas was replaced by Mathias Persson. The band now changed their name to **Ten Feet Tall** and recorded a track for the '93 Close-Up compilation. Mathias quit and was replaced by Mattias Henriksson. The name was changed to **Colorblind** and their debut was released in 1995. **Metal Mercy** is a solid, powerful heavy rock/metal band quite close to **Destiny** and **Mercyful Fate** in style and approach. Boogi is a good, powerful metal singer. Well worth looking for. In 2000 Stormbringer released the picture disc *Liferide*, originally recorded as a demo in 1987.

1989 MLP - MRC 101

1989 ■ The Unborn Child	MLP 4tr	private	MRC 101	$

Tracks: In Total Rage/Who's In The Dark/The Unborn Child/Rendez Vouz With Death.
600 copies.

2000 □ Liferide	7" 3tr PD	Stormbringer	SKULL 9810P

Tracks: Liferide/Between Life & Death/Two Time Loser. 400 copies

MEZZROW

Ulf Pettersson: v, Zebba Karlsson: g, Staffe Karlsson: g,
Conny Welén: b, Steffe Karlsson: d

Nyköping - **Mezzrow** were formed and recorded the demo *Frozen Soul* in 1988, followed by *The Cross Of Torment* in 1989. These Bay Area style thrashers sound quite reminiscent of bands like **Testament** and the demos were highly rated in tape-trading circuits. After the album, the band also recorded the demo *Demo 91*. After this they sadly just vanished. The album was a great slab of classic thrash done the Bay Area way Conny later joined **Hexenhaus**, **Dry Dead River** and retro rockers **Galaxy Safari**. He also went into production and has written material for a **Sorcerer** reunion album, plus he has released solo material in a different vein. Ulf joined **Rosicrucian**, but later on became a high-profile soccer trainer. In 2005 the band reunited for a one-off show, which was also videotaped and sold by the band as the video *Then Came The Video*.

1990 LP - ATV 11

1990 ■ THEN CAME THE KILLING	LP	Active	ATV 11
1990 □ THEN CAME THE KILLING	CD	Active	CD ATV 11

Bonus: Inner Devastation

2011 □ THEN CAME THE KILLING	LP	JDC (USA)	39011

MIASMAL

Pontus Redig: v/g, Magnus: g, Ruben: b, Micael: d

Göteborg - Formed in 2007. Made a four-track demo in 2008, which was later released by Detest Records. They 2011 release is a compilation of the demo and the 7". Later theat year, drummer Björn replaced Micael. **Miasmal** plays decent death metal, mixing old-school with some doomy parts. Pontus and Björn are found in **Agrimonia** and Pontus is ex-**Martyrdöd**. In May 2012 the band was picked up by Century Media.

2009 MLP - DR004/ANTI-GOTH123

2009 ■ Demo	MLP 4tr	Detest/Nuclear War Now	DR004/ANTI-GOTH123

Tracks: Abduction Of The Soul/Kallocain/Apocalypse Legion/Anima Sola. 500 copies.

2009 □ Demo	MLP 4tr PD	Detest/Nuclear War Now	DR004/ANTI-GOTH123

250 copies

2010 □ Creation Of Fire/Bionic Godhead Erase	7"	Detest/Me Saco Un Ojo	MSUO 04

150 red, 600 black copies

2011 ■ MIASMAL	CD	Dark Descent Records	DDR025CD

Bonus: Demo + the 7"

2011 □ MIASMAL	LP	Detest/Me Saco Un Ojo	DR020/MSUO 16

100 grey + 900 black copies

2011 CD - DDR025CD

MIDAS TOUCH

Patrik Wirén: v, Rickard Sporrong: g, Lasse Gustavsson: g,
Patrik Sporrong: b, Bosse Lundström: d

Uppsala/Björklinge - Formed in 1985, **Midas Touch** were one of the early Swedish thrash bands that landed a deal outside of Sweden. Their style could be described as technical speed/thrash. In 1987 they recorded their first demo, entitled *Ground Zero*, and the year after they signed to German Noise Records. When **Midas Touch** split, Patrik and Patrik formed **High Tech Junkies**, a band that never made it on record. Rickard recorded a track for the compilation *Guitar Heroes Of Sweden Part 2* in 1992 and then joined the cyber-power-rockband **Peace, Love And Pittbulls**, with whom he recorded two albums. Both Sporrongs are also found in the band **Karma Kain**, who were supposed to release their debut on Soundfront Records in 1996. Patrik is also found in **Alpha Safari** and **Misery Loves Co**.

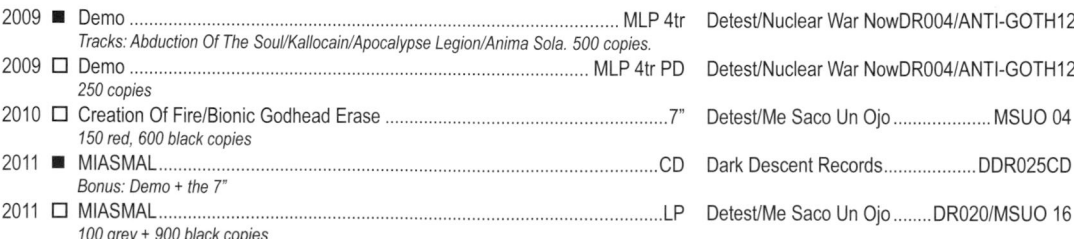

1989 ■ PRESAGE OF DISASTER	LP	Noise Records	NO 124
1989 □ PRESAGE OF DISASTER	CD	Noise Records	NO 124-2
2012 □ PRESAGE OF DISASTER	2CD	Divebomb Records	DIVE032

Bonus: 18 demo tracks (Ground Zero, The Deliberate Stranger, Noise Demo)

1989 LP - NO 124

MIDDLEAGE
Freddie Rein: v, Mike Szymanski: g, Rasmus Weinheim: b, Fredrik Flink: d

Stockholm - **Middleage** were formed in 2002 and the style is great-sounding modern metal in the vein of **Papa Roach**, **My Chemical Romance** and **P.O.D.** Pelle Saether produced the debut. On the second album drummer André Andersson who wrote all the lyrics on the debut, had been replaced by Fredrik Flink and bass player Johan Andersson by Rasmus Weinheim.

| 2007 | ■ | DIFFERENT VIEW | CDd | Hot Wheel Records | (DR 088) |
| 2009 | □ | MOREISMO | CD | private | n/a |

2007 CDd - (DR 088)

MIDNIGHT BLUE
Roy El Hoshy: v, Lennart Widegren: g/b, Morgan Pettersson: d

Göteborg - This was a laid-back AOR-oriented side project by three **Boulevard** members. The single was even recorded on the same label as **Boulevard**. Lennart later joined **The Ungrateful**, with whom he recorded one CD before he went to Los Angeles to study at Musicians´ Institute. Morgan later joined **B-Thong** and Roy was in the **Sisters Of Mercy**-sounding **Gift**.

| 1988 | ■ | Together/Streets Of Fire | 7" | Norman Musik | NLJ-S 130 |

MIDNIGHT BLUE
1988 7" - NLJ-S 130

MIDNIGHT SUN
Jakob "Jake Samuel" Samuelsson: v, Magnus Karlsson: g,
Jonas Reingold: b, Jaime Salazar: d

Malmö - Former **Alien/Madison/Snake Charmer/Silver Seraph** etc etc. vocalist Pete Sandberg put this melodic hard rock band together. Initially they were quite similar to **Whitesnake** or early **Glory**. *Above & Beyond* and *Nemesis* feature guest appearances from John Norum. On *Nemesis*, Jonas at first drafted shredder Magnus Karlsson (later in **Last Tribe**, **Starbreaker**, **Primal Fear** etc) to lay down some Yngwie-style solos, while Hal Jonston/Marabel (**Bad Habit**, **Bai Bang**) handled the rhythm guitars. Magnus subsequently became the band's permanent guitarist. Drummer Jaime Salazar (**Bad Habit**) also replaced Hempo Hildén (**Norum, Thrash**). Jonas, formerly in **Downtown Clowns** also had his side-project **Reingold** and was later in **The Flower Kings**, while Pete had a solo career, as well as **Pete Sandberg's Jade**. Before *Metal Machine* Pete decided to go for his other projects and was replaced by Jake (ex-**Yale Bate/Jekyll & Hyde/ Treasure Land/The Ring**, now **The Poodles**). Jonas asked Magnus to write material for the album, which he did. He however changed his mind and wrote the album himself. The style was also now a bit heavier and darker; almost in the vein of late **Helloween** meets **Queensryche**, especially in tracks like *Dungeons Of Steel*. Since Magnus had an album worth of material he formed **Last Tribe** and recorded what was supposed to be the *Metal Machine* album as **Last Tribe**'s debut. *Days Of Heaven* is a hidden bonus track on the European *Metal Machine* release.

1997 CD - ALCB-3180

2001 CD - LMP 0109-034 CD

1997	■	ANOTHER WORLD	CD	Alfa/Brunette (Japan)	ALCB-3180
		Bonus: Deep In My Heart (instrumental version)/Fire Still Burns			
1997	□	ANOTHER WORLD	CD	Point Music	- -
		Bonus: Name Of Love (hidden track)			
1997	□	ABOVE & BEYOND	CD	Bluestone	BSM 1019
1997	□	ABOVE & BEYOND	CD	Point Music	(CD991021)
1998	□	ABOVE & BEYOND	CD	Avalon Marquee (Japan)	MICY-1061
		Bonus: Scream & Shout			
1999	□	NEMESIS	CD	Avalon Marquee (Japan)	MICY 1138
		Bonus: Nightfall			
1999	□	NEMESIS	CD	Rock Brigade (Brazil)	RBR/LCR 2200
1999	□	NEMESIS	CD	NEMS (Argentina)	NEMS 175
2000	□	NEMESIS	CD	Point Music	- -
2001	■	METAL MACHINE	CD	LMP	LMP 0109-034 CD
2001	□	METAL MACHINE	CD	Avalon Marquee (Japan)	MICP 10260
		Bonus: Genesis			
2001	□	METAL MACHINE	CD	Rock Brigade (Brazil)	RBR/LCR 2980
2001	■	ANOTHER WORLD	CD	CD-Maximum (Russia)	CDM 1001-730

2001 CD - CDM 1001-730

MIDVINTER
Tobias "Kheerot" Fjällström: v, Mikael "Damien Midvinter" Lindberg: g/b/k,
Anders "Zathanel" Löfgren: d

Umeå/Karlskrona - The band was formed in 1993 by Björn "Vlad Morbius" Magalhaes, Mikael "Damien Midvinter" Lindberg and guitarist Kalle, all from the band **Apollgon** residing in Karlskrona. When the band became **Midvinter**, the core consisted of Vlad and Damien. The first demo *Midvinternatt* featured Damien (g/b), Vlad (v) and drummer Kristian "Krille/Kristeian" Terävä (ex-**Mephitic**, also in **Melek Taus**). Björn was, according to the band's website, later admitted to a mental hospital. According to the label's biography Damien and Kristeian got into a fight where Kristian broke three ribs. To avoid prosecution, Damien fled to Greece... where he got into a motorcycle accident and had to return three months later. Some of the members

1997 CD - BDP 002

were also part of the Satanic order MLO (Misanthropic Luciferian Order). Björn and Kristian were replaced by Kheerot (**Setherial**) and Zathanel. Real black metal, majestic and symphonic. Great production by Andy La Roque (**King Diamond Band**). Rumours had it that Alf Svensson (**Oxiplegatz**) and Jon Nödtveidt (**Dissection**) were participating on the album, which was not true, even though they did help out. Damien and Nödtveit were however room mates and created the electronica project **De Infernali**, with whom they released one album. According to the band's MySpace they returned in 2006, now featuring only Damien and Kheerot. Reasons for the downtime were, Mikael had to leave the country for several years for "various reasons". A new album, entitled *Harmagedo*, was supposed to be released in 2007, but hasn't happened. Fjellström is the owner of Metal Fortess.

1997 ■	AT THE SIGHT OF THE APOCALYPSE DRAGON	CD	Black Diamond	BDP002
1997 □	AT THE SIGHT OF THE APOCALYPSE DRAGON	CD	Metal Blade (USA)	3984-14155-2
2009 ■	AT THE SIGHT OF THE APOCALYPSE DRAGON	CD	Frostscald	FS 27

2009 CD - FS 27

MILKY

Luciano Peirone: v, Sotiris Geveniotis: g, Peter Füle: b, Joakim Olofsson: d

Lund - Strong, powerful bluesy melodic rock/hard rock with influences from **Led Zeppelin** and Jimi Hendrix as well as **Beatles** and **Red Hot Chili Peppers**. On the verge, but still interesting. They supported **Ritchie Blackmore's Rainbow** on their 1995 Sweden tour.

1995 □	Love/Fill Me	CDS 2tr	The Record Station	TATI 123
1995 □	Majestic Heights (radio edit)/Majestic Heights	CDS 2tr	The Record Station	TATI 126
1995 ■	MILKY WAY	CD	The Record Station	STAT 51

1995 CD - STAT 51

M.ILL.ION

Ulrich Carlsson: v, Andreas Grövle: g, Angelo Modafferi: k,
BJ "Berra" Laneby: b, Per Westergren: d

Göteborg - Quite the institution in melodic Swedish hard rock. The band was first featured on the *Rockslaget 1990* compilation with the tracks *Fire* and *Hold On*. The line-up here featured Hans Johansson (now Dalzon) on vocals, Stefan Wetterlind and Carl Thore "C.Tee" Rohdell (ex-**Panama**) on guitars, Anette Wigenius on keyboards, BJ "Berra" Laneby on bass and Roland Christoffersson on drums. The debut was a traditional heavy AOR-platter with the required choirs, catchy choruses, keyboards etc, while *We, Ourselves And Us* is a prime example of powerful melodic hard rock with elements of **Biscaya**. Incidently the album was produced by Pär Edwardsson, ex-**Biscaya**. The band was now featured with a cover of *Deuce* on the *Kissin' Time: A Tribute To Kiss* (1996 Tribute Records) compilation. The second album is highly recommended. The debut was first released on the dubious label Büms, but the band managed to buy the rights and reissued it on their own label. After the second album the band changed style to a more straightforward 80s-influenced type of hard rock, similar to a mix of **Dio** and **AC/DC**. On this album keyboard player Mikael Böhnke had replaced Markus Ydkvist and Per Westergren had replaced Roland Christoffersson. *Get Millionized* is a compilation of the three first album, also featuring two tasters from the new line-up where singer Hasse Johansson (Dalzon) had been replaced by Ulrich and guitarists Rohdell and Wetterlind by Jonas Hermansson. *Detonator* is closer to the heavy, yet melodic hard rock the band produced on the second album. Great production, great performance and simply the best of the lot! This album also featured new keyboard player Johan Bergquist replacing Böhnke. In 2004 the band was picked up by UK label Majestic Rock and the band's previous releases remastered and re-issued. The band's new debut for the new label, *Kingsize*, proved the band was still keeping the melodic metal flag flying. On the band's 2011 release, *Sany & Insanity*, the line-up had again changed and guitarist Hermansson had been replaced by Andreas Grövle, while keyboard player Bergquist had been replaced by Angelo Modafferi. After the album, drummer Westergren was replaced by Johan Häll. The album is yet another solid melodic hard rocker. The band's two latest efforts are in the same vein and class. High-class melodic hard rock! After *Sane & Insanity* drummer Westergren left the band and was replaced by Johan Häll (**Layout, Hellspray**).

The M.EMB.ERS

1992 CD - CD36123

1994 CD - MM94200

1992 ■	NO. 1	CD	Büms	CD36123
1993 □	NO. 1	CD	K.M.C.	CD93001
1993 □	NO. 1	CD	Zero (Japan)	XRCN-1077
1994 □	Judgement Day	CDS 1tr	K.M.C.	MM 941
1994 ■	WE, OURSELVES & US	CD	K.M.C.	MM94200
1995 ■	WE, OURSELVES & US	CD	JVC Victor (Japan)	VICP-5627
1998 □	ELECTRIC	CD	Bluestone	BSM 1016
2001 □	GET MILLIONIZED	CD	A2	A2CD 06
2001 □	DETONATOR	CD	A2	A2CD 11
2001 □	DETONATOR	CD	3D (Japan)	n/a
2002 □	THE FIRST TWO MILLION	CD	A2	A2CD 08
2004 □	NO. 1	CD	Majestic Rock	MAJCD 045
2004 □	2004	MCD 5tr	Majestic Rock	MAJSCDS 003

Tracks: On And On/What I Want/Fight You Forever/Sign Of Victory (unplugged)/In Your Dreams (unplugged)

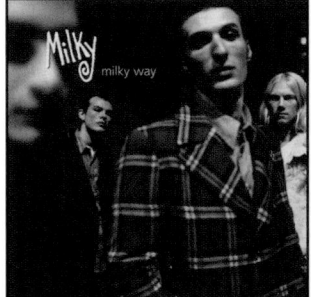

1995 CD - VICP-5627

2004 ☐ WE, OURSELVES & US	CD	Majestic Rock	MAJCD 046
2004 ☐ ELECTRIC	CD	Majestic Rock	MAJCD 047
2004 ☐ ELECTRIC	CD	Majestic Rock Japan (Japan)	ARMJ 022
Bonus: Deuce (Kiss cover)			
2004 ☐ DETONATOR	CD	Majestic Rock	MAJCD 048
2004 ☐ KINGSIZE	CD	Majestic Rock	MAJCD 049
2006 ☐ 1991-2006 THE BEST OF SO FAR	CD	Majestic Rock	MAJCD 081
2008 ☐ THRILL OF THE CHASE	CD	Metal Heaven	00053
Slipcase			
2008 ☐ THRILL OF THE CHASE	CD	Avalon Marquee (Japan)	MICP-10752
Bonus: The Godbye Song			
2011 ■ SANE & SANITY	CD	Metal Heaven	MHV 00091
2011 ☐ SANE & SANITY	CD	Rubicon (Japan)	RBNCD-1061
Bonus: Sign Of Victory (unplugged)			

2011 CD - MHV 00091

MIND'S EYE
Andreas Novak: v, Johan Niemann: g/b, Daniel Flores: d

Stockholm - Formed in 1992 when bass player Johan Niemann teamed up with drummer Daniel Flores and guitarist Fredrik Grünberger. They took the name *Afterglow* and after a year singer Germán Pascual was added to the line-up. In 1995 the band released a self-financed MCD, which contains top-notch progressive hard rock/metal with outstanding musical skills from a pretty young band. When Pascual left, he was replaced by Robert Forse (*Heads Or Tales*), but only recorded a demo. After that Thomas Vikström (*Talk Of The Town, Candlemass, Stormwind*, etc) sung on one of the band's demos. They later found singer Johan Persson and changed the name to *Mind's Eye* as a German death metal band was also using this name *Afterglow*. Unfortunately Johan came in just in time to put the vocals on the finished album *Into The Unknown*, why the result could have been better. In 1999 Andreas Novak replaced Johan, who was later found in *Scudiero*. *Waiting For The Tide* showed a more melodic and symphonic side of the band, yet without losing the progressive technicalities. They took this side even further on *A Work Of Art*. Great band with outstanding musicians! Niemann is also touring with *Therion* and in 2011 he joined *Evergrey*. Flores has recorded with numerous bands and projects such as *Eclipse, The Murder Of My Sweet, Crash The System, Fatal Force, Mindcage, Tears Of Anger, Speedy Gonzales, Cortex, Frozen Rain* etc. After *A Work Of Art* the band took a break. When returning to make another album, Fredrik Grünberger, who was working as a stockbroker, decided not to return. The band's new album *Walking On H2O* featured Niemann taking care of both guitars and bass. The band has since continued as a trio. *A Gentleman's Hurricane* is a conceptual album featuring numerous guests, such as Mia Coldheart (*Crucified Barbara*), Tommy Denander and Chris Catena. The album also took the heaviness to a new level. The album *1994/The Afterglow* features the band's debut under the name *Afterglow* plus some of the previously unreleased demo tracks featuring singer Germán Pascual (later in *Narnia*, now solo). Novak has released two solo albums and is today fronting melodic rockers *House Of Shakira*.

1998 CD - SR-3002

2001 CDS - - -

2000 CD - RR 001

2002 CD - RS 312.5004-2

1998 ■ INTO THE UNKNOWN	CD	Sensory	SR-3002
2000 ■ ...WAITING FOR THE TIDE	CD	Round	RR 001
2001 ■ Calling (Father To Son)	CDS 1tr	Round	- -
2002 ■ A WORK OF ART	CD	Rising Sun	RS 312.5004-2
2005 ☐ A WORK OF ART	CD	Lion Music	LMC 139
Bonus: I Will Remember (Queensryche cover)/End Of The Line			
2006 ☐ WALKING ON H20	CD	Lion Music	LMC 162
2006 ☐ WALKING ON H20	CD	Mellow Music (Japan)	MWCD 0003
2006 ☐ ...WAITING FOR THE TIDE	CD	Lion Music	LMC 181
Bonus: Endless Passages (demo)/Spellbound			
2006 ■ A GENTLEMAN'S HURRICANE	CD+DVD	Mellow Music (Japan)	MWCD 0005
2007 ☐ A GENTLEMAN'S HURRICANE	CD+DVD	Lion Music	LMDVD 214
2007 ☐ A GENTLEMAN'S HURRICANE	CD	Irond (Russia)	CD 07-DD563
2008 ☐ 1994/THE AFTERGLOW	CD	Lion Music	LMC 231
2008 ☐ ...WAITING FOR THE TIDE	CD	Irond (Russia)	CD 08-DD624
2008 ☐ A WORK OF ART	CD	Irond (Russia)	CD 08-DD625

2006 CD+DVD - MWCD 0005

MINDBLASTER
Per-Olof Hogebrandt: b/v, Olof Martinsson: g, Martin Hogebrandt: d

Tanumshede - The band was formed in 1994 and recorded two demos before the first release. The first single was death-punk-metal, or crust if you wish, with death-hard-core-screaming vocals. Untight as hell and shitty mix. Musically like a more metal-oriented cousin of *Disfear*. What more can I say... well, both sides start off with sounds from a porn-movie. Martin is ex-*Suicidal Winds* and also found in the excellent thrash band *Conspiracy*.

1999 ☐ Days Of Coma	7" 4tr	Genocidal	001
Tracks: Final Day/Bloodfight/Wasted/Days Of Coma			
2001 ■ Losers – Unite! (split)	7" EP	Genocidal	002
Split with Hathor. Tracks: Chemical Lobotomy/Alcohol And Anguish. 500 copies.			

2001 7" - 002

MINDCOLLAPSE

Johan Kaiser: v, Mathias Nilsson: g, Eddie Partos: g,
Tobias Nilsson: b, Jonas Hallberg: d

Växjö - Technical death-oriented power metal, at times similar to early *In Flames* and early *Meshuggah*. Varies from doomy stuff like *Forbidden Land* and *God Abandoned* to high-speed thrashers like *Forever Lost* and *Fear Of Heaven*. Always relying on an in-your-face twin guitar action with lots of *IronMaiden*-esque harmony work. Thrash-oriented and brutal vocals and tight musicianship. The non-CD track *Santa Claus Is Coming To Town* can also be found on the compilation *Released By X-mas 98 Sin City)*. *Vampires Dawn* is highly recommended.

2000 CD - VODCD 007

1998 ☐	LIFELESS	CD	Dark Past	DPP 004
2000 ■	VAMPIRES DAWN	CD	Voices Of Death	VODCD 007

MINDFUEL

Magnus Westman: v, Markus Kinell: g/k/b, Magnus Göransson: d

Åstorp/Helsingborg - *Mindfuel* started as a project in 2008 when Magnus (ex-*Red Dawn*) agreed to lay down some vocals on a track Markus had written. They drafted drummer Magnus Göransson and recorded the debut. After the recording of the debut Göransson was replaced by Andreas Båge (ex-*Dawn Of Oblivion*). *Mindfuel* plays melodic metal with a German touch. The album *Time For A Change* was released digitally in 2013. Båge is now in *Scandal Circus*. Website: www.mindfuel.se

2009 ■	IN YOUR MIND…	CD	Blue Topaz	BTRCD 35

MINDJIVE

Tobias Danielsson: v, Erik Engström: g, Magnus Zotterman: b, Christian Gabel: d

Karlstad - Shows clear influences from bands like *Rage Against The Machine* and *Red Hot Chili Peppers*, but the debut lacks the power and energy of the two. The latest release however shows great improvement and has a lot more power, also thanks to the great production from Pelle Saether. They also have a track on the compilation *Rock Around The Clock* (94 G-Spot).

2009 CD - BTRCD 35

1993 ■	Green Grass	MCD 4tr	Burning Heart	BHR 005
	Tracks: My Way/Jive/Another View/Digging Up.			
1994 ☐	Mindjive	MCD 5tr	Burning Heart	BHR 020
	Tracks: Spotless/Chicken/Thirst/Green Grass/Fresh Fruit.			
1996 ☐	Package Design	MCD 3tr	Burning Heart	BHR 037
	Tracks: Package Design/Bug To You/The Virus (remix)			
1996 ☐	CHEMICALS	CD	Burning Heart	BHR 040

1993 MCD - BHR 005

MINDLESS SINNER/MINDLESS

Christer "Chris G-son" Göransson: v, Magnus "Dan Blade" Danneblad: g,
Jerker "Jee Eden" Edman: g, Christer Carlsson: b, Tommy "McJo" Johansson: d

Linköping - **Mindless Sinner** started out in 1981 featuring guitarists Magnus Danneblad and Anders Karlsson, bass player Magnus Van Wassenaar and drummer Tommy Johansson, as **Purple Haze** (not the band on Plebb Records). Later the same year, singer Christer Göransson joined. They changed the name to **Genocide** and in September 1981 supported local metal heroes **Axewitch**. In 1982 Wassenaar left and Anders Karlsson switched from guitar to bass. Late 1982 they also changed their name to **Mindless Sinner**. In April 1983 the band recorded their first five-track demo. After this they added second guitarist Jerker Edman. After winning a local bandstand they made enough money to record the *Master Of Evil* demo, which attracted Web Records who released the demo as the band's first MLP in 1984. The style was quite average **Tygers Of Pan Tang**-sounding heavy metal. The band had a fit when they saw the record cover with the misspelled name (**Mindless SinnerS**) and the awful cover. When it was time to record the first album, in October 1984, Anders had an accident and cut his hand so bad, he could not play anymore. Göransson took care of the bass parts on the album instead and after the album Christer Carlsson was added to the line-up. Despite his face being on the cover, he only contributed with some "horror" vocals on one track. Web Records went bust shortly after the release, but in 1986 the band made a deal with local Delta Records and started recording the follow-up. In 1987 they finished the recordings and also shortened their name to **Mindless**. The album was finished in 1988, but released just after the New Year, in 1989. They also have a track on the *Great Metal Attack* compilation. Twelve new tracks were recorded in 1989, but when Tommy left in 1990 **Mindless** disbanded. However only a month later the remaining foursome reformed the band with former **Axewitch** skinsman Mats Johansson. They changed the name to **Skinny Horse** and released the CD *No Pain No Gain*. Christer, Danne and also drummer Tommy were later found in the **Wildhearts**/**Green Day** influenced band **Fluff**, who changed their name to **Everlone**, released an album and split in 2001. The same year the band reunited for a gig at a local biker club. They also played the Motala Metal Festival 6, which was recorded. In 2003 German label High Vaultage reissued the band's albums on their sub-label Metal For Muthas, packed with bonus material and a lengthy biography from where most information was taken.

1983 MLP - FINGMLP 002

1986 LP - FINGLP 014

1989 7" - DELTAS 001

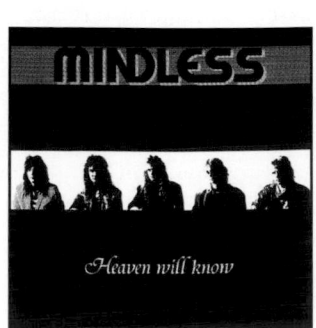

1989 7" - DELTAS 001

1983 ■	Master Of Evil	MLP 4tr	Fingerprint	FINGMLP 002

Tracks: Broken Freedom/Key Of Fortune/Master Of Evil/Screaming For Mercy.

1986 ■	TURN ON THE POWER	LP	Fingerprint	FINGLP 014
1989 ☐	MISSIN´ PIECES	LP	Delta	DELTALP 001
1989 ■	Heaven Will Know/Caught Up In The Action	7"	Delta	DELTAS 001

Released as Mindless. Cover available in normal and inverted version.

2003 ■	MASTER OF EVIL	CD	Metal For Muthas	MM 1007

Bonus: Broken Freedom (live)/Key Of Fortune (live)/Screaming For Mercy 8live)/Master
Of Evil (live)/Taking My Life Away/Mindless Sinner/Higher And Higher/We All Go Back/
Heavy Metal Will Never Die/City Games/Master Of Evil (live)/Broken Freedom (live)/
Screaming For Mercy (live)/Mindless Sinner (live)/City Games (live)

2003 ☐	TURN ON THE POWER	CD	Metal For Muthas	MM 1008

Bonus: Rock And Roll Man/A Long Time Ago/Time Of Pleasure/Step Into The Fire/Point
Below Zero/We Go Together/Turn On The Power (live)/Here She Comes Again (live)/Live
And Die (live)/Voice Of The Doomed (live)

2003 ■	MISSIN´ PIECES	2CD	Metal For Muthas	MM 1009

As Mindless. Bonus: A Dream Of A Dream/Hold On/Run Away/Reflections Of Fantasia/
End Of The Road/Missin' Pieces (live)/Rockin' In The Heat Of The Night (live)/Heaven Will
Know (live)/Caught Up In The Action (live)/Love No Limit/Head High Who's Shy/Over The
Edge/Human Race Habit/Life In A Legend/Give A Little Heart And Soul/If Every Eye Could
See/I Guess We Never Made It/Famous And Rich/Reach Out/Lack Of Image/Living It Up/
Over The Edge (live)/Life In A Legend (live)/Reach Out (live)/Famous And Rich (live)/Give
A Little Heart And Soul (live)/End Of The Road (live)/Heaven Will Know (live)/I'm Gonna
Have Some Fun (live)/Rock And Roll Man Ulive)

2003 CD - MM 1007

2003 2CD - MM 1009

MINDSPLIT

Hans HB Andersson: v, Mathias Holm: g, Jonas Lidström: k,
Conny Payne: b, Jon Skäre: d

Gävle - The story dates back to the late 80s when Hans and Mathias played in the same band, **The 'N Sin**, a glam/sleaze unit that never made it on record. Hans, formerly in **Fire & Ice**, later recorded with bands like **Scudiero** and **Fatal Smile**, while Mathias went solo. Around 2002 the two joined forces again as Hans had a new idea after discovering his grandfather's old therapy notes (he was a respected therapist). This became the foundation for the concept of **MindSplit**. They asked former **Madison**/**Pete Sandberg's Jade** bassist Conny to join, which he did. Lidström and Skäre were also added to the line-up and the recording of *Charmed Human Art Of Significance* was recorded. **MindSplit** plays highly interesting progressive melodic metal, not too far from what Hans did in **Scudiero**.
Website: www.mindsplit.se

2010 ■	CHARMED HUMAN ART OF SIGNIFICANCE	CD	Lion Music	LMC 292

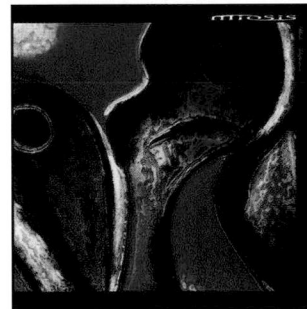

2010 CD - LMC 292

MIOSIS

Erik Skoglund: v, Henrik von Harten: g, Mårten Bergkvist: g/k,
Mikael Mangs Edwardsson: b, Mattias Axelsson: d

Göteborg - *Miosis* was formed in the late summer of 2005. The members were fans of melancholic bands like **Radiohead** and **Massive Attack**, but also liked heavier bands like **Tool, Isis** and **The Mars Volta**. This made up the foundation of **Miosis**. In 2007 they released the self-financed demo EP *Konvolut*, which lead to a deal with Finnish label Lion Music. The album proves the influences from bands like **Tool** is quite evident. There are also some traces of **Porcupine Tree** here and there. After *Abedo Adaption* the band has gone through some changes and the 2011 line-up features only Axelsson and Edwardsson from the album line-up. New members are: Michael Andersson (v), Fabian Ericson (g) and André Robsahm (b).

2007 ☐	Konvolut	MCD 4tr	private	n/a

Tracks: Our Floods/Flow/Without The Scars/The Lucid

2009 ■	ALBEDO ADAPTION	CD	Lion Music	LMC 254

2009 CD - LMC 254

MIRADOR

Jakob Forsberg: v/g, Erik Mjörnell: g, Olof Gardestrand: d

Finspång - *Mirador* were formed back in 1991 by Forsberg and Mjörnell, together with drummer Kalle Santana. Many members have come and gone and the band has been unproductive for many years. The band **Veni Domine** made a great impact on the young guys and reinforced with singer Isak they recorded their first demo. The drums were handled by Lars Palmquist (**BackWardness**). In 1997 the band had a blow when an interested label went bust and singer Isak left the band. That is until 2003 when Christian label Rivel Records helped revive the band. Kristian Niemann also plays a guest solo. The influences from **Veni Domine** sure shows. If you are into said band's first two releases, you should definitely check out Mirador. Great progressive, **Quennsryche**-style melodic metal with great musicians and a singer that can hit the high notes. Mjörnell has also played in Carola Häggkvist's backing band.

2005 ■	THE AZRAEL TALES	CD	Rivel Records	RRCD 018

2005 CD - RRCD 018

MIRAGE
John L. Swedenmark, Michael Ahlander

Sundsvall (?) - Quite a tough one. Quite amateurish and weak, but still an attempt to play melodic hard rock. For collectors only.

1980 ● In The Winter/Utrangerad..7"   private..Mirage 1
No artwork.

1980 7" - Mirage 1

MISANTHROPIAN
Daniel Lundh: v, Johan Adamsson: g, Janek Hellqvist: g,
Andreas Lundin: b, Jaanus Kalli: d

Stockholm - Formed in Stockholm in 2001 and has kept the original line-up. In 2005 the band recorded the CD-R EP *Dead Silence*. Five years later the band made their debut album, a slab of uncompromising death metal similar to bands like **Cannibal Corpse** and **Behemoth**.
Website: www.misanthropian.com

2010 ■ A TORTURE OF YOUR OWN DESIGN..CD   Supernova Records.................SUPERCD 013

2010 CD - SUPERCD 013

MISCELLANY
Jenny Persson: v, Henrik Nygren: g, Thobias Wall: g, Henrik Christensson: k,
Magnus Hansson: b, Patrik Olsson: d/v

Lund - **Miscellany** were formed in the summer of 2003 by Thobias and Henrik (ex-**Blackshift**). They started out playing covers, but soon started writing their own material and began searching for more members. Jenny joined and late 2003 the first demo was recorded. Patrik (ex-**Thoron**) and Magnus (ex-**Power Unit**) joined and in the summer of 2004 they recorded their first official demo. They now started mixing Jenny's clean vocals and Patrik's growl, and found their own sound. They now booked Studio Roasting House and producer Pontus Lindmark (**Cloudscape, Planet Alliance**) and recorded their first MCD. **Miscellany** plays operatic power metal quite close to bands like **Within Temptation** or a heavier **Nightwish** with growl as a spice.
Website: www.miscellanyonline.com

2006 MCD - SM-01-CDS

2006 ■ Catch-22 ....MCD 3tr   Swedmetal....................................SM-01-CDS
Tracks: Catch-22/Sorrow And Fear/My Solitude

MISCREANT
Johnny Wranning: v, Peter Kim: g, Peter Johansson: g,
Magnus Ek: b/k, Johan Burman: d

Västerås - Formed in 1992. "Atmospheric death metal with symphonic pieces" is how it was described to me... I'd call this band the missing link between death and prog-metal. If **Dream Theater** would get a death metal singer and inject influences from **Morbid Angel**, this would be it. Not bad at all. On the demo *Promo-93* Jocke "Grave" Göthberg (**Darkified, Dimenzion Zero, Marduk, In Flames, Cardinal Sin**) was in the band. After the album the band changed drummer to Pontus Jansson (ex-**Utumno**). No news on the band since 2007.

1994 CD - WAR 004

1994 ■ DREAMING ICE..CD   Wrong Again ....WAR 004

MISDEMEANOR
Vera Olofsson: v, Sara Fredriksson: g, Jenny Möllberg: g,
Jenny Lindahl: b, Mia Möllberg: d

Stockholm - Formed in the early nineties by Jenny, Jenny and drummer Mia Möllberg as *Miz'Dmeaner*. In 1994 the band was completed by Vera and Sara. The debut single was mixed by Fred Estby. The *Five Wheel Drive* MCD was produced by Dave Catching (**Queens Of The Stoneage**) and Brant Bjork (**Fu Manchu**) and the second 7" by Chips Kisbye (**Sator**). On *Five Wheel Drive* Mia was temporarily replaced by drummer Rikard. **Misdemeanor** is a heavy stonerish band, influenced by bands like **Kyuss** and **Black Sabbath**, but on the latest MCD, *Stay Away*, the sound had become a bit more sixties retro, but still quite heavy.

2002 CD - MERCD 002

1997 ☐ Misedemeanor ....7" 4tr   Psychout.......................................PSYCH 004
Tracks: Sub.Way/Drill Thrall/Doomsday Machine/No Alteration. Also in purple vinyl.
1998 ☐ You're Nothing (And You Know It)/Y.S.B.T.................7"   Freak Scene ....FREAK 8
1000 copies
1999 ☐ Five Wheel Drive..MCD 4tr   Meteor City ....MCY 006
Tracks: Snowballing/Gizmo/Venom/Love Song
2002 ☐ Let Me Know/The Hard One ....7"   Muse Entity ....MERSP 001
2002 ■ MISDEMEANOUR ....CD   Muse Entity.....................................MERCD 002
2004 ■ HIGH CRIMES AND MISDEMEANOR ....CD   Muse Entity ....MERCD 005
2006 ☐ Stay Away ....MCDd 3tr   Shedevil recordings ....shevil 1
Tracks: Stay Away/The Symptom/Throw Things

2004 CD - MERCD 005

MISERATION

Christian Älvenstam: v, Jani Stefanovic: g/b/d, Marcus Bertilsson: g/b, Oscar Nilsson: d

Jönköping/Skövde - *Miseration* started out in 2006 as a project between Älvestam (*Scar Symmetry, Solar Dawn, Torchbearer, Quest Of Aidance, Zonaria, Angel Blake, Unmoored, Syconaut, Solution .45* etc) and Stefanovic (*DivineFire, Sins Of Omission, Am I Blood, Crimson Moonlight, Essence Of Sorrow, Mehida* etc). Several of the songs were actually written by Stefanovic for his band **Renascent**, but since Älvestam is not, unlike Stefanovic, a practising Christian, these themes were more toned down in the lyrics. On the first album the musicians only featured Christian and Jani. The band was later reinforced by drummer Rolf Pilve (**Astral Sleep, Essence Of Sorrow, Status Minor**), bass player Johan Ylenstrand (**Sordid Death, Exhale, Crimson Moonlight**) and guitarist Marcus Bertilsson (**Inevitable End**). After the second album Stefanovic left and was temporarily replaced by Tobias Alpadie, but he returned in 2011. Ylenstrand left in 2011, and Rolf Pilve was replaced by Oscar Nilsson (**Despite, X-Rated, Saint Deamon**). *Tragedy Has Spoken* is a concept album dealing with the major tragedies of mankind. The lyrics were written by Pär Johansson (**Satariel, Torchbearer, The Few Against Many**). In 2012 the bass spot was filled by Christian Lundgren (**Vomitous, Quest Of Aidance, Carnalized**).

2007 CD - RRCD 030

2009 CD - LFR 100-2

2007	■	YOUR DEMONS – THEIR ANGELS	CD	Rivel Records	RRCD 030
2008	□	YOUR DEMONS – THEIR ANGELS	CD	Lifeforce	LFR 087-2
2008	□	YOUR DEMONS – THEIR ANGELS	CD	King Records (Japan)	KICP-1212
		Bonus: Free From Light, Devoid Of Fire			
2009	■	THE MIRRORING SHADOW	CD	Lifeforce	LFR 100-2
2012	■	TRAGEDY HAS SPOKEN	CD	Lifeforce	LFR 126-2

MISERICORDIA

Don-Allan "Deobrigula" Palmroos: v/g, Robert "Kail" Karlsson: g,
Bard: b, Fredrik "Endymion" Nilsson: d

Norrköping - Formed in the winter of 1998 with the intention of spreading dechristianizing black metal. They started proving it already on their first two demos *I Love Jesus Ripped To Pieces* (1998) and *Delenda Caeli* (1999). They were picked up by Downfall Records and released their first MCS *Erase The Skies* in 2002, produced by Magnus "Devo" Andersson (**Marduk**). After the album bass player Deumus Silent decided to leave the band, and was replaced by Rius as a session player. In 2010 they announced Bard as the permanent replacement. **Misericordia** plays old school sounding, blast beat filled black metal metal with a touch of vintage **Dark Funeral**. A second album was planned for 2007, but as yet hasn't been released. However a four-track demo was released in 2010 as a taster for the forthcoming album. Endymion joined **Satanic Slaughter** in 2006, and he is also found in **Spetälsk** and **Deadpulse**. Deobrigula and Endymion are also found in the band **Throne Of Kasdeya**.

2012 CD - LFR 126-2

2002 MCD - FALLMCD 011

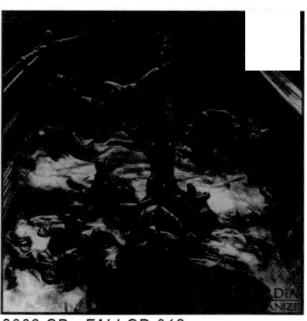

2003 CD - FALLCD 013

2002	■	Erase The Skies	MCD 5tr	Downfall	FALLMCD 011
		Tracks: Satans's Servant/Delenda Caeli/God Sent/Von Cosel/ Torture Be Thy Name			
2003	■	DECHRISTIANIZE	CD	Downfall	FALLCD 013
2010	□	Misericordia	MCD 4tr	private	MCDS 1002
		Tracks: The Art Of Perfection/Throne Of Existence/Bleak/The Righteous Order. Promo.			

MISERY

Rafael Martinez: g, Mikael Johansson: g, Christer Sundell: k,
Göran Sten: b, Peter Andersson: v/d

Karlskoga - Good, solid melodic hard rock with lots of guitar. Formed in 1978 when the guys were in their mid-teens. The band later became **Stallion**.

1979	■	Restless Strategi/If I Won't Come	7"	private	REF 080	$
		500 copies.				

1979 7" - REF 080

MISERY LOVES CO.

Patrik Wirén: v, Örjan Örnkloo: g/programming, Michael Hahne: g, Olle Dahlstedt: d

Uppsala - Industrial metal band **Misery Loves Co.** were formed in 1993 and made their debut later the same year on a compilation issued by Close-Up magazine. Patrik was ex-**Midas Touch** and **High Tech Junkies** and Örjan had been working with Graham Lewis. **Misery Loves Co.** is in the same style as **Ministry** and **Nine Inch Nails**, brutal and heavy with sequencers and drum machine. On stage the band also included guitarist Jim Edwards (from **Kharma Kain**), bassist Marre Eriksson (ex-**Lost Souls, Damien**) and drummer Bosse Lundström (ex-**Midas Touch, High Tech Junkies**). The band was really hyped in the English metal magazine Kerrang! in the beginning of 1995 and took part on the Kerrang! Tour in March 1995, together with **Warrior Soul, Clawfinger** and **Headswim**. Michael and Olle were added to the line-up on the last album. Olle was later in **Entombed** and Wirén was in **Alpha Safari** and did a guest spot with **Man.Machine.Industry**. The band has been featured on numerous compilations, such as: *Sonic Attack* on *Extreme Close-Up* (93 Close-Up/JIGU Records Korea), *Private Hell* on *MNW*

1994 MCD - MNWCD 182

1994 CD - MNWCD 259

Zone (94 MNW), *My Mind Still Speaks* on *Huh Music Service Vol. 5* (95 Huh Music) *Faith No More Q&A* (Interview-CD mixed with tracks), *Honour Code Loyalty* on *Corporate Rock Wars* (95 Earache), *Happy?* on *Huh Music Services Vol. 7* (Magazine-promo CD 1995), *Kiss Your Boots - NancySinatratakemine mix* on *Fuckin Hardfloor Vol 1-2* (95 Atom). On *Not Like Them* the band left the more techno-influenced side for a more traditional power metal vein.

1994 ■	Private Hell/This Is No Dream/Honour Code Loyalty	MCD 3tr	MNWZone	MNWCD 182
	Honour Code Loyalty is non-CD.			
1994 ■	MISERY LOVES CO.	CD	MNW Zone	MNWCD 259
1995 □	MISERY LOVES CO.	CD	Toy's Factory (Japan)	TFCK-88738
	Bonus: Honor Code Loyalty			
1995 □	My Mind Still Speaks	MCD 3tr	Earache	MOSH 1995
	Tracks: My Mind Still Speaks/Need Another One/Happy?			
1995 □	Kiss Your Boots – DJ Mix CD Promo	MCD 4tr	Earache	DJ MOSH 135 CD
	Tracks: Kiss Your Boots - four different mixes: Open Your Mind mix/NancySinatraketamine mix/Industriual Hazard mix/Urban Jungle mix			
1995 ■	Need Another One	MCD 5tr	Earache	MOSH 135 PRO
	Tracks: Need Another One/Honour Code Loyalty/Kiss Your Boots (Kiss My Black Sabbathy Ass Mix)/(Open Your Mind Mix)/Nancysinatraketamine Mix). DJ Promo.			
1995 □	Need Another One	MCD 3tr	MNW Zone	MNWCDS 202
1995 □	MISERY LOVES CO.	CD	Shock (Australia)	MOSH 133 CD
1995 □	MISERY LOVES CO.	LP	Earache	MOSH 133
1995 □	MISERY LOVES CO.	CD	Earache	MOSH 133 CD
	Bonus: re-mixes of Sonic Attack and Kiss Your Boots			
1996 ■	HAPPY?	CD	Earache	MOSH 151 CD
	Contains live/unreleased tracks, plus a CD-ROM track for MAC and Windows.			
1997 □	Blinded/Kiss Your Boots (Urban Jungle Mix)	7"	Earache	7 MOSH 203
	Five different covers, which together forms the album cover.			
1997 □	NOT LIKE THEM	CD	MVG	MVG 132
1997 □	NOT LIKE THEM	CD	Shock (Australia)	MOSH 184 CD
1997 □	NOT LIKE THEM	CD	Earache (UK)	MOSH 184 CD
1997 □	NOT LIKE THEM	CDd	Earache (UK)	MOSH 184 CDL
	Bonus: Nothing Remains			
1997 □	NOT LIKE THEM	CD	Toy's Factory (Japan)	TFCK-87136
1997 □	Prove Me Wrong/A Million Lies/Feed The Creep	MCD 3tr	Earache	MOSH 184 DJ PRO
	DJ promo.			
1998 □	A Million Lies	MCDp 4tr	Earache	MOSH 184 CDT
	Tracks: A Million Lies (live)/Not The Only One (Ultraviolence Mix)/Submit (demo)/Nothing Remains. Bonus for the tour version of Not Like Them.			
2000 ■	YOUR VISION WAS NEVER MINE TO SHARE	CD	Earache	MOSH 231
2000 □	YOUR VISION WAS NEVER MINE TO SHARE	CD	Toy's Factory (Japan)	TFCK 87205

1995 MCD - MOSH 135 PRO

1996 CD - MOSH 151 CD

2000 CD - MOSH 231

MISFORTUNE

**Daniel Saidi: v, Peter Ruhdberg: g, Martin Unosson: g,
Henrik Wiklund: b, Marcus Losbjer: d**

Söderhamn - The band was formed early 1995, inspired by the likes of **Carcass** and **At The Gates**. Their first demo, *Midnightenlightening*, was recorded in 1997. They were signed to Blackend, but it took some time for the debut to see the light of day as they lost their drummer Mattias Sundberg and later also their rehearsal-facilities. Losbjer (**Wolverine**) took over the drum-stool. The demo was re-mastered and released as an MCD.

1998 □	Midnightenlightened	MCD 3tr	Blackend	BLACK 015 MCD
	Tracks: The Prophecy/Midnightenlightened/Pain Unbearable			
1999 ■	FORSAKEN	CD	Blackend	BLACK 023 CD

1999 CD - BLACK 023 CD

MISS BEHAVIOUR

Sebastian Roos: v, Erik Heikne: g, Henrik Sproge: k, Anders Berlin: d

Kalmar - **Miss Behaviour** were formed by Sproge and Heikne in 2003, when they studied Music Management in Kalmar. Late 2003 the demo *Give Us The World* was recorded. The band went through a lot of member changes before the debut, where the band featured Heikne, Sproge, singer Mattias Wetterhall, bass player Sebastian Gustafsson and drummer Hampus Landin. Since the full commitment wasn't there, members once again changed. On *Last Woman Standing* the line-up featured the founders, plus singer Sebastian Roos (**Shineth**) and drummer Anders Berlin (**Shineth, Street Talk**). On this album the band really stepped things up! Guest solo is also provided by **Masterplan**/ex-**Helloween** guitarist Roland Grapow and additional drums by Daniel Gese (**Pole Position**). After the album, in January 2011, drummer Magnus Jacobsson replaced Berlin and bass player Niclas Lindblom was added to the line-up. Both releases are classy pieces of AOR, well worth checking out.
Website: www.misbehaviour.se

2006 CD - MISS 001

| 2006 ■ | HEART OF MIDWINTER | CD | private (MTM) | MISS 001 |
| 2011 ■ | LAST WOMAN STANDING | CD | Avenue Of Allies | Avenue 11010021 |

2011 CD - Avenue 11010021

MISS WILLIS
Uffe Andersson: v/b, **Hante Andersson:** g, **Jimmy Högfeldt:** k, **Mats Berggren:** d

Trollhättan - The band was originally formed 1986 under the name *Twilight Zone* and later on reformed into **Miss Willis Flowerchild**. They recorded a number of killer demos under this name, before dropping the *Flowerchild*-monicker. **Miss Willis** plays outstanding seventies-influenced hard rock.

2011 ■ Rewolf ....MCD 6tr   private .... MW 001
  Tracks: Spirit/Do You See?/Bad Day/Alpha Male/One Night In Nice/Heavens Gate

2011 MCD - MW 001

MIST OF AVALON, THE
Aram Yildiz: v, **Erik Sjölander:** g, **Malin Yildiz:** k,
Magnus Ewald: b, **Andreas Hermansson:** d

Uppsala - **Sisters Of Mercy**-meet-**Type O Negative**. Goth-oriented dark metal with a folkish touch. Formed in 1994. Made their first demo *Silent Souls* in 1995, which was very **Sisters Of Mercy** influenced. On their second demo they adopted a slightly heavier sound. Before the album they had a track on *New Alternatives III* compilation. The first album featured Yildiz, Sjölander, Yildiz, Hermansson and bass-player Andreas Winkler. On *Here And After*, Magnus had replaced Andreas. *Some Kind Of Stranger* was also featured on a **Sisters Of Mercy** tribute. *On Tears*, which was produced by Daniel Bergstrand, they have adopted a much heavier sound picking influences from **Black Sabbath** and **Fields Of Nephilim**. The current line-up features Aram, Erik, Malin, Magnus, Juho Korhonen (g) and the drum machine "Frau Roland". After years of silence the promo-CDR *The Mist Of Avalon Limited Edition Promo* appeared in 2007. In 2010 the band returned with the new album *Dinya*. The sound had now become less metal and more pop/rock, still with the addition of heavy guitars, but not really interesting for metal fans, more like a mix of **Tiamat** and **Simple Minds**. The line-up had also changed where Joakim Jonsson had replaced guitarist Erik Sjölander and Tony Lind drummer Andreas Hermansson. After the album guitarist Staffan Winroth had also been added to the line-up.
Website: www.mist-of-avalon.com

2000 CDd MACDL 962

2001 MCD - MACDL 963

1998 □	THE MIST OF AVALON ....CD	M&A .... MACDL 957
1999 □	Sleepless ....MCD 4tr	M&A .... MACD 506
	Tracks: Sleepless/Belthana/We Are 138 (Misfits-cover)/Belthana (RBC version)
2000 ■	HERE AND AFTER ....CDd	M&A .... MACDL 962
2001 ■	Tears ....MCD 6tr	M&A .... MACDL 963
	Tracks: Tears/This Time (v2.02)/The Witch/Follow Me/Some Kind Of Stranger (Sisters Of Mercy cover)/Follow Me
2010 ■	DINYA ....CD	Echozone EZ10C479

2010 CD - EZ10C479

MISTELTEIN
Seron (aka Morgh): v, **Magnus "Nagrinn" Gillberg:** g,
Sven "Mishrack" Karlsson: g, **Ivana "Hel" Baukart:** k,
Anders "Karagat" Nauclér: b, **Julius "Farnargh" Chmielewski:** d/k

Malmö - Melodic and fast black metal in the vein of **Dimmu Borgir**. The band was formed in 1996 by Seron, Magnus "Nagrinn" Gillberg, Anders "Karagat" Nauclér and drummer Alex. Alex was soon replaced by Julius "Farnargh" Chmielewski and the line-up was completed by Hel and guitarist Patrik "Baalzephon" Mårtensson (later in **Karneywar/Karnivore**). In 1998 they released their first demo *Spawn Of The Phantom Moon* that received rave reviews. *Rape In Rapture* was recorded in Underground Studios and Divine in Berno Studio. Johan Axelsson (**Deranged, Murder Corporation**) guests on the second album. After the first album Patrik "Baalzephon" Mårtensson was replaced by Sven "Mishrack" Karlsson (**Embraced, Evergrey, Soilwork**). A shorter version of the track *Inquisition Of The Bleeding God* can be found on *Soundcheck #20*. *Divine.Descecrate.Complete* also features a guest solo from Johan Axelsson (**Murder Corporation, Deranged**). On the 2001 tour Varg "Ahldrathan" Strand (ex-**Ishtar**) covered up for Mishrack. After the tour Karagat left the band and in 2002 Mishrack left to devote his time to **Soilwork**. The latter was replaced by Ahlrathan. In April 2004 Ville "Shorrgh" Kemi was drafted as the band's new singer. Now Hel and Nagrinn left and took the name, leaving former Mistelteiners Chmielewski (**Embraced, Tenebre**) and Kemi (**Life Illusion, Vandöd, Obscure Divinity**) forming the band **Fall Ov Serafim**. Ivana is ex-**Tenebre**. Mårtensson passed away of cancer in 2009.
Website: www.misteltein.cjb.net/

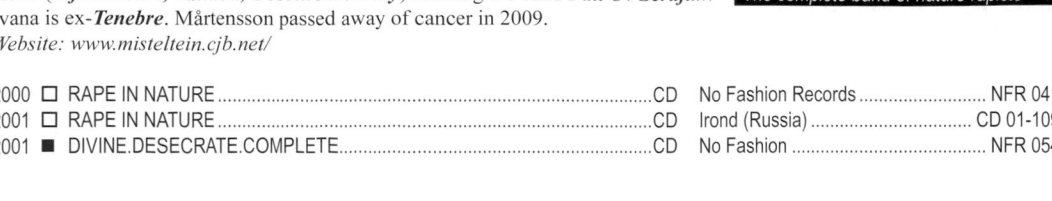
The complete band of nature rapists

2000 □	RAPE IN NATURE ....CD	No Fashion Records .... NFR 041
2001 □	RAPE IN NATURE ....CD	Irond (Russia) .... CD 01-109
2001 ■	DIVINE.DESECRATE.COMPLETE ....CD	No Fashion .... NFR 054

2001 CD - NFR 054

MISTER KITE

Alf Wemmenlind: v, Magnus Kristensson: g, Tomas Djurfeldt: k/g, Anton Johansson: b, Mats Bergentz: d

Trelleborg (Malmö) - The band was formed in 1999 and the name was taken from the *Beatles* song *Being For The Benefit Of Mr. Kite*. Mats was found in the early years of *Silver Mountain*. Magnus is also found in pop bands *S.P.O.C.K* and *Page*. Before they were signed by guitar hero Lars-Erik Mattsson on his Lion Music label, the band recorded some highly acclaimed demos. Mattias Ia Eklundh guests on the debut album and as usual he blasts out an incredible and highly personal solo. The album was produced by Björn Dahlberg (*Pete Sandberg, Bad Habit* etc). *Mister Kite* produces a highly interesting mix of melodic hard rock and killer-heavy riffing at times with a modern touch, like a heavier and up dated cousin of *Hardline* or *Harem Scarem*. Some songs even have a modern touch. Great, ballsy production. Highly recommended! A cover of *Deep Purple*'s *Bloodsucker* can be found on the compilation *Blackmore's Castle* (05 Lion Music). In 2005 Djurfeldt and Johansson left the band. Linus Abrahamsson (*Visceral Bleeding*) took on the bass parts and Robert Ahrling (*Origin Blood*) stepped in as guitarist. The song *Won't Go Away* was written and recorded for the book *Stigma* by Åsa Schwartz in 2006. On June 10, 2013, guitarist Magnus Kristensson, born 1975, sadly lost the battle against cancer.

2002 CD - LMC 2201 2

2003 MCD - LMC 088

2002	■	ALL IN TIME	CD	Lion Music	LMC 2201 2
2003	■	The Hunger	MCD 3tr	Lion Music	LMC 088
		Tracks: The Hunger (radio edit)/How Long/Bloodsucker (Deep Purple cover)			
2004	■	BOX OF FEAR	CD	Lion Music	LMC 090
2004	□	ALL IN TIME	CD	Tokuma (Japan)	TKCA-72669

MISTH

Maria Rådsten: v, Fredrik Glimbrand: g/v, Håkan Granath: g, Jörgen Scelander: k, Olle Bodén: b, Martin Larsson: d

Stockholm - The story of *Misth* goes back to 1999, when Bodén and bass player Ken Savefjord formed the band *Mercury Fang*. The band was completed with Granat, Glimbrand (ex-*Atlantis*) and Schelander (also in *Audivision*). The band recorded two albums, but in 2010 the band decided to make a drastic change when they added female singer Maria Rådsten (*One More Time*, guest on *Mountain Of Power*) to the line-up. They also changed their name to *Misth*. They have now taken the style even a step further when it comes to musical drama and complexity. A great band!

2004 CD - LMC 090

2012 CD -

2012	□	ALL IN TIME	CD	private	- -

MISTIE

Magnus Mets: v, Mattias Kun: g, Robert Peterzon: b, Krister Angelovski: d

Eskilstuna - It all started in 1998 when the band *Divine* decided it was time for a style change and went from vocals in Swedish, to English and changed the musical path to a more brutal one. It all started with the song *The Survivor*. I'd put this bunch in the same slot as *Deftones*, *Sevendust*, *Creed* or Swedish colleagues *Downstroke*. Who said nu-metal? Well, nice pop-oriented melodies mixed with brutal power-chords, detuned guitars and heavy chunky rhythms. Great band, ideed! In 2000 guitarist Johannes Johsson left the band and was replaced by Morgan. In 2001 they also released a 4-track demo-CDR. The first two records are even heavier than the more commercial, but still dead heavy *10 Times Guilty*, where guitarist Morgan and keyboardist Niklas Mets were out of the band. The band reissued all albums digitally in 2004. The band played their last show in December 2005 and in 2008 they finally, sadly called it quits.

1999 MCDd - 19112504

1999	■	Emotional Hangover	MCDd 6tr	private	19112504
		Tracks: Love At First Sight/Use U/Para Noid/Modern Hate/You Adore/Blow Job			
2002	□	SURVIVAL SKILLS	CD	MM Records	001 (Mistie_003)
2003	■	10 TIMES GUILTY	CD	Dogbreath Entyertainment	DOGGY 008
		500 copies.			

2003 CD - DOGGY 008

MITHOTYN

Richard Martinsson: v/b, Stefan Weinerhall: g, Karl Bäckman: g/k, Karsten Larsson: d

Mjölby - Formed in 1992 as *Cerberus* and became *Mithotyn* in 1993. The early releases were heavy, gothic-sounding Viking metal with big female choirs. In 1999 guitarist Stefan Weinerhall (*Indungeon, Genetic Mutation*) started writing music for a new project. This ended in both him and drummer Karsten Larsson leaving *Mithotyn* for the new band *Falconer*. *Rape In Rapture* is an up-tempo symphonic black metal-platter with screeching vocals, a bit reminiscent of *Celtic Frost* at times. On the first album Karl and Stefan shared the vocal duties. *Rape...* was recorded by Pelle Seather at Studio Underground. Between 1994-95 the band also had a female keyboard player named Helene Blad, sister of *Falconer*-singer Mathias Blad. *Gathered Around...* was the last album to be released on Invasion. The label folded only a few months after its release. The band's three albums were all reissued by Karmageddon in 2004. Martinsson and Larsson were both found in *The Choir Of Vengeance*. The latter has also played with *Dawn* and *Genetic Mutation*. Beckmann is also in *Infernal Vengeance* and *Indungeon*.

1997 CD - IR 034

1999 CD - IR 048

Year		Title	Format	Label	Cat.No.
1997	☐	IN THE SIGN OF THE RAVENS	CD	Invasion Records	IR 028
1997	☐	IN THE SIGN OF THE RAVENS	CD	Metal Blade (USA)	3984-14154-2
1997	■	KING OF THE DISTANT FOREST	CD	Invasion	IR 034
1997	☐	KING OF THE DISTANT FOREST	CDd	Invasion	IR 034-2

Bonus: Ragnarokk/Wisdom/In The Bower Of Shawods/Meadow In Silence/As Brothers Now Bonded

| 1997 | ☐ | KING OF THE DISTANT FOREST | CD | Metal Blade (USA) | 3984-14190-2 |
| 1997 | ☐ | KING OF THE DISTANT FOREST | LP PD | Invasion | IR 034 |

1000 copies.

| 1997 | ☐ | IN THE SIGN OF THE RAVEN | LP PD | Invasion | IR 043 |

1000 copies.

| 1999 | ■ | GATHERED AROUND THE OAKEN TABLE | CD | Invasion | IR 048 |
| 1999 | ☐ | GATHERED AROUND THE OAKEN TABLE | CD | Soundholic (Japan) | SHCD1-0025 |

Bonus: Bland vargars yl

| 1999 | ☐ | IN THE SIGN OF THE RAVENS | CD | Soundholic (Japan) | SHCD1-0034 |

Bonus: As Brothers Now Bonded/In The Bower Of Shadows

| 1999 | ☐ | KING OF THE DISTANT FOREST | CD | Soundholic (Japan) | SHCD1-0035 |

Bonus: Ragnarokk/Wisdom/Meadow In Silence

| 2002 | ☐ | IN THE SIGN OF THE RAVENS | CD | Unveiling The Wicked | HUW 021 |

New artwork.

| 2002 | ☐ | KING OF THE DISTANT FOREST | CD | Unveiling The Wicked | HUW 022 |

New artwork.

| 2002 | ■ | KING OF THE DISTANT FOREST | CD | Karmageddon Media | KARMA 071 |
| 2002 | ■ | GATHERED AROUND THE OAKEN TABLE | CD | Unveiling The Wicked | HUW 023 |

New artwork.

2003	☐	GATHERED AROUND THE OAKEN TABLE	CD	Fono (Russia)	FO 218 CD
2003	☐	KING OF THE DISTANT FOREST	CD	Fono (Russia)	FO 233 CD
2004	☐	IN THE SIGN OF THE RAVEN	CD	Karmageddon	KARMA 070
2004	☐	KING OF THE DISTANT FOREST	CD	Karmageddon	KARMA 071
2004	☐	IN THE SIGN OF THE RAVENS	CD	Karmageddon	KARMA 072
2005	☐	KING OF THE DISTANT FOREST	CD	Nordic Media (Russia)	NMK 0013
2013	☐	CARVED IN STONE	3CD	Hammerheart	HHR2013-02

2002 CD KARMA 071

2002 CD - HUW 023

MOAHNI MOAHNA

Martin Häggström: v, Tommy Rehn: g/trumpet , Henrik Flyman: g/flute

Sundsbruk/Stockholm - This is a very interesting band with strong influences from old **Rainbow** and **Deep Purple**, but they also display a lot of influences from Swedish folk music into the songs. Long, epic songs with some serious harmony guitars and long instrumental parts. Highly recommended. Martin, Tommy and Henrik are the band and the other instruments are played by session musicians (Jaime Salazar, Richard Andersson, Fredrik Burstedt, Johan Bobäck etc). Tommy and Henrik also had a side project in the straightforward metal vein called **Give The Iron** (it's actually "pedal to the metal" translated to Swedish and word by word back to English). They have recorded the track *Santa Claus Clothes Of Course* for the local compilation *Om En Timrå Jul*. In 1995 the band left SMC and a new album was released on their own label. On the second album the band had changed into a more **Queen**-flavoured act, with highly intriguing songs with lots of quirky ideas. It also features a cover of **ABBA**'s *King Kong Song*. Singer Martin and guitarist Henrik later formed the band **Zool**. Rehn later formed the band **Angtoria**, which he left in 2011 to join metal band **Corroded**. He also runs NineTone Records. Henrik recorded two albums with Danish band **Wuthering Heights** and is now found in **Evil Masquerade**.

| 1992 | ■ | Face the light | MCD 3tr | Give The Iron | DDD 12b |

Tracks: Face The Light/The Quest For The Unholy Sword/Eternal Slaves

1994	☐	Queen Shamar/Day Tripper (Beatles cover)	CDS 2tr	SMC	91181
1994	■	TEMPLE OF LIFE	CD	SMC	90181
1995	☐	TEMPLE OF LIFE	CD	Victor (Japan)	VICP-5520

Bonus: Day Tripper (Beatles cover)

1997	☐	WHY	CD	Santa Claus Prod	SC001MM201
1997	☐	WHY	CD	JVC Victor (Japan)	VICP-5836
1998	☐	WHY	CD	Rising Sun	35895
1998	☐	TEMPLE OF LIFE	CD	Rising Sun	007291 2 RS

1992 MCD - DDD 12b

1994 CD - 90181

MOANING, THE

**Pierre Törnkvist: v, Patrik Törnkvist: g, Mikael Grankvist: g,
Niklas Svensson: b, Andreas Nilzon: d**

Luleå - Fast and powerful, yet quite intriguing death metal with elements of traditional metal. Nice twin-guitar work. Screeching vocals. The band recorded their first demo, *Promo 94*, in 1994. The album was recorded at Studio Abyss by Peter Tägtgren. Pierre and Patrik are also in **Helltrain**, **Scheitan** and **Everdawn**, Niklas in **Gates Of Ishtar**, **Throne Of Ahaz** and **Everdawn**, Mikael and Andreas in **Incinerator** and **Satariel**.

| 1997 | ■ | BLOOD FROM STONE | CD | No Fashion | NFR 018 |
| 2013 | ☐ | BLOOD FROM STONE | LP | Century Media | 998315-2 |

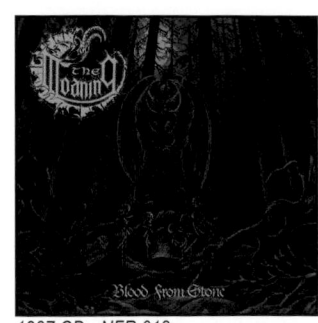

1997 CD - NFR 018

MOANING WIND

Johan Carlsson: v/b, Tomas Bergstrand: g, Magnus Eronen: g

Karlstad - Black metal with dual guitars and great production. The band recorded three demos; *In My Forest* and *Demo 2*, in 1994 and *Demo 3* in 1995. Johan, Magnus and Tomas later joined rockers *Tailpipe*. Johan is also part of *Sparzanza* and death metal band *Dawn Of Decay*. Tomas is now found in *Switch Opens* and has also been found in *Dawn Of Decay* and *Rise And Shine*. Eronen is also in *Sparzanza*. In 1997 they recorded a demo under the name *Capricorn*.

1997 ■ VISIONS IN FIRE...CD   Corrosion CR6502

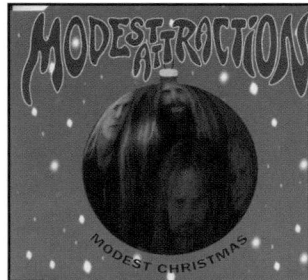

1997 CD - CR6502

MOBERG-TALTON

Mikael Moberg: v/g/k, Wes Talton: v

Nacka - High-quality AOR. Moberg recorded two singles with the band *Zeta* in the late seventies and he has made several recordings with various bands such as *Garvin*, *2001* and *The Voice*. He has also released solo recordings as *The Man From The Moon*. Moberg also helped record three *Bathory* albums. American, Talton was ex-The Radio. Formed 1984, split in 1987.

1986 ■ MOBERG-TALTON .... MLP 4tr   Freelance....................................Freemx 203
Tracks: Bringing Back/My Woman/Pictures/Sandy

1986 MLP - Freemx 203

MODEST ATTRACTION

Christian Liljegren (aka Rivel): v, Stephan Mohlin: g,
Simeon Liljegren: b, Mick Nordström: d

Jönköping - The band was formed under the name Borderline, and recorded two singles. A very good 70s-sounding *Christian* hard rock band, influenced by bands like *Deep Purple*, *Uriah Heep* and *The Sweet*. The second album features a killer version of *The Sweet's Burn On The Flame*. Thanks to the success of singer Christian Liljegren's subsequent band Narnia's, a best of from the two albums was released in Japan. The band also reformed, but soon split again. In 2002 the band once again reformed with the original line-up and there were also plans for a live-album and a video. Mick has produced a number of bands such as *Cornerstone* and *Sanctifica*. Liljegren runs Rivel/Liljegren Records and sings in *DivineFire*, *Audiovision*, *Wisdom Call*, *Flagship* and currently in *Golden Resurrection*. Mick has played on albums by *Wisdom Call*, *Narnia*, *Bengalen*, *Charizma*, *Flagship*, *Stonefuze*, *XT*, *Spearfish* and he is currently a member of *Lava Engine*. Simeon Liljegren (brother of Christian) is found in *Audivision*.

1994 MCD - VIVADS 16

| 1994 □ THE TRUTH IN YOUR FACE | CD | Viva | VIVAD 122 |
| 1994 ■ Modest Christmas | MCD 4tr | Viva | VIVADS 16 $ |

Tracks: Modest Christmas/Christmas Time/Feed Your Fire (live)/Give You My Song (live)

| 1996 ■ DIVINE LUXURY | CD | private | MACD 74001 |
| 1999 □ MODEST ATTRACTION | CD | Pony Canyon (Japan) | PCCY-01349 |

1996 CD - MACD 74001

MOGG

Mats "Matt Attaque" Håkansson: v/g, Thomas Carfors: g,
Janne Eklund: b, Ulf "Bo Werner" Sundberg: d

Umeå/Stockholm - *Mogg* was formed in 1981 by Eklund and Carfors. They drafted bass player Robert "Bobby" Eriksson (now Valerie) and took the name *Mogg*, inspired by the names *Mud* and *Mott*. After a year, they drafted singer Jonny Lindqvist from locals *Arrows*. The band was soon completed by second guitarist Patrik Andersson. In 1983 the song *Lose You* was featured on the *Universe Records* 7" four-track compilation. They recorded a zillion demos, getting better and better. After having won a bandstand in 1985, Thomas and Jonny moved to Stockholm. In Stockholm they teamed up with former *Gotham City* boys, bassist Björn Melander and drummer Jonas Östman. In 1987 they released their first single, *In And Out Of Love*. Melander later played with *Neptune*, *Glory North*, *Bernie/Melander* and *Liar's Dice*. He now runs a recording studio in Stockholm. Jonas Östman was later in *Glory*, *Mental Hippie Blood* and Yngwie Malmsteen's band. After a while Björn and Jonny left the band. The latter would later play with *Jonny's Bomb* and *Nocturnal Rites*. Former bassist Janne Eklundh moved to Stockholm and rejoined the band. They drafted singer Thomas Persson, who was soon replaced by Mats Attaque (Håkansson) (ex-*Tryckvåg*). Early 1990 they moved to Los Angeles, all except Östman, who was replaced by Bo Sundberg (Werner). In the US they didn't accomplish much except being ripped off by managers, work as studio musicians and record music for X-rated movies. In 1994 they recorded the CD *From The Icefields*, but in 1995 the members, except Bo, moved back to Sweden. Bo would later appear on Yngwie Malmsteen's *Fire & Ice* album and he recorded a CD with the band *Steamroller*. The 7" is Van Halen-esque AOR while the CD shows an updated and much more brutal style, more in the vein of *Alice In Chains*. In 1995 the band folded. However in January 2012 the line-up featuring Attaque, Carfors, Lindqvist, Andersson, Eklund and Valerie made a one-off reunion gig.

Van... who?

1987 7" - AIRS 044

| 1987 ■ In And Out Of Love/Please Don't Call | 7" | Air | AIRS 044 |
| 1994 ■ FROM THE ICEFIELDS | CD | GMR (USA) | GMR 1/S20 |

1994 CD - GMR 1/S20

MOJOBONE
Per Wiberg: k/g/v/b, Markus Källström: d

Borlänge - The band was previously known as *Foodbox*, initially featuring Per Wiberg, guitarist Per Mårtensson (*The Morning After, Stonecake*), bass player Marcus Aldén (*Stonecake, Sky High*) and drummer Eiron Johansson (Thomas Larsson). Wiberg has also been found in *Death Organ, Sky High, Spiritual Beggars, Opeth* and is also in *King Hobo*. *Mojobone* produces outstanding riff-oriented hard rock in the true seventies vein. Phat guitar-based riffage reminiscent of a wide musical spectrum including influences from old *Black Sabbath*, *Deep Purple* and even *Electric Boys* around the *Freewheelin'* era. Killer band!! Only half the tracks from the 10" were rerecorded for the album. After nine years of silence Wiberg returned with a new slimlined band featuring himself and Marcus Källström (*Stonecake*) plus guest performances by Mike Amott (*Spiritual Beggars, Carcass*), Christopher Shoori (Little Mike) and Petra Kvännå (*Sky High*). Now Wiberg also handled the bass work. *Crossroad Messages & Tales From The Bone* is a compilation of the first two releases plus ten previously unreleased demo tracks.

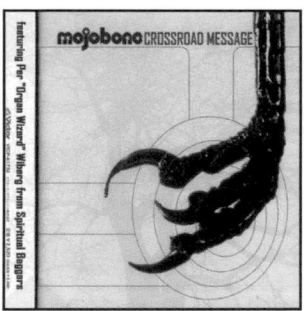
2001 CD - VICP 61732

2011 2CD - HM0410

1999	☐	Tales From The Bone	10" 6tr	Hippodrome	HR 199

Tracks: Walking Level/Sure/Can't Hurt Me/Knowledge Is Power/Southpaw/Brother

2001	■	CROSSROAD MESSAGE	CD	Victor (Japan)	VICP 61732
2010	☐	COWBOY MODE	CDd	Hippodome Music	HM0310
2011	■	CROSSROAD MESSAGE & TALES FROM THE BONE	2CD	Hippodome Music	HM0410

MOLLY'S GUSHER
Simon Vegas: v/g, Billy Eriksson: g, Jonas Lewén: b, Alex Wehlin: d

Örebro - After recording some demos and playing lots of gigs, *Molly's Gusher* decided to take things in their own hands and record an album at their own expence in November 2005. The band plays great, heavy, yet melodic modern metal at times similar to *Shinedown* and *Alter Bridge*. Just before the release of the album guitarist Lars Wadström left the band and was replaced by Billy Eriksson.
Website: www.mollysgusher.net

2007 MCD - ALAB 008

2005	☐	MOLLY'S GUSHER	CD	private	- -
2006	☐	Indestructible	CDS	private	- -
2007	■	Pick Your Poison And Form A Tragedy	MCD 4tr	Alabama	ALAB 008

Tracks: Indestructible/Dead Inside/Bulletproof/Carved In Stone. A video-CD accompanies the MCD

MOLOKEN
Kristoffer Bäckström: v/g, Nicklas Bäckström: b/v,
Patrik Ylmefors: g, Jakob Burstedt: d

Umeå - *Moloken* were formed in 2007 by the Bäckström brothers and Burstedt. They wrote and recorded one fifteen minutes long track, after which guitarist Johan Öman was drafted. The band now released the long track as its first MCD on Kristoffer's own label, Discouraged. Moloken now recorded two album demos after which they felt confident enough to record their first full length album, *Our Astral Circle*. After the album Öman left the band and was soon replaced by Patrik Ylmefors, formerly in *Overlord Industries*. Influenced by progressive bands like *Rush, Porcupine Tree* and *King Crimson* mixed with death metal like *Opeth* and *Katatonia*, the band produces a hybrid style of music.
Website: www.moloken.net

2008 MCD - MMICD 004

2009 CD - MMICD 018

2008	■	We All Face The Dark Alone	MCD 3tr	Discouraged Records	MMICD 004

Tracks: We All Face The Dark Alone/Part 1: Lost Saviour/Part 2: Dual Core Friction/Part 3: Paranoia

2009	■	OUR ASTRAL CIRCLE	CDd	Discouraged Records	MMICD 018
2010	☐	OUR ASTRAL CIRCLE	LP	Discouraged Records	MMI 018 LP
2011	■	RURAL	CDd	Discouraged Records	MMICD 013

2011 CDd - MMICD 013

MOMENT MANIACS
Tomas Jonsson: v, Alho: g, Jocke Göthberg: g,
Roger "Bogge" Svensson: b, Fredrik Andersson: d

Stockholm - Ultrafast death/hardcore/punk with screeching vocals. Some songs are closer to punk than metal, while some are slightly reminiscent of *Entombed*. There's even wah-wah on some of the solos. Pretty tasteless pics of the "members", taken from corpses. Svensson and Andersson are also found in *Marduk* and *Allegiance*, while Jonsson is in *Wolfpack/Wolfbrigade*. Jonsson also played bass and sang in punk/crust band *Anti-Cimex*. Andersson has also played with *Triumphator, Skullcrusher* and *Freevil*. Göthberg was found in *Darkified, Dimenzion Zero, Marduk, In Flames* and *Cardinal Sin*.

1999 CD - DISTCD 51

1999	■	TWO FUCKING PIECES	CD	Distortion	DISTCD 51

MOONDARK

Johan Jansson: v/d, Kennet Englund: g,
Mattias "Cryptan" Norrman: g, Mats "Mabbe" Berggren: b/v

Avesta - *Moondark* were formed in the beginning of 1993. Norrman was ex-*Dellamorte* and *Katatonia*, Englund was ex-*Dellamorte*, *Uncanny*, *Centinex* and *Interment*, Berggren was ex-*Fulmination* and *Entrails* and Jansson was formerly with *Dellamorte*, *Centinex*, *Regurgitate*, *Demonical*, *Beyond*, *S.G.R* and *Interment*. The album was recorded as a demo back in 1993 and has become somewhat mythical, before its release in 2007. Slow, heavy and brutal death metal in the vein of *Crypt Of Kerberos*.

2007 ☐ THE SHADOWPATH	CD	Dreamtide	n/a
299 copies, numbered.			
2007 ☐ THE SHADOWPATH	CDd	No Colours	NC 130
1000 copies			
2008 ■ THE SHADOWPATH	LP	Temple Of Darkness	TOD 022
500 copies			

2008 LP - TOD 022

MOONLIGHT AGONY

David Åkesson: v, Karl Landin: g, Rikard Petersson: g, Martin Mellström: k,
Christer "Zigge" Pedersen: b, Robert Willstedt: d

Kungsbacka - Symphonic metal band *Moonlight Agony* were initially formed in 1999, under the name Thorum. They started out covering *Helloween* and *Blind Guardian* material as a trio featuring Willstedt, Landin and drummer Christofer Starnefalk. In 2000 second guitarist Andreas Lindvall and keyboard player Mellström joined. Later the same year singer Christian Karlzon was found. The first demo, *Dust*, was released in 2001 and a second self-titled one later the same year. In 2002 Karlzon left and was replaced by Simon Hermansson. Second guitarist Rikard Petersson was also added, and the demo *Echoes Of A Nightmare* was recorded. In 2003 singer Hermansson left and the band drafted *Firewind/Faro/Avalon* singer Chitral "Chity" Somapala to record the band's debut album, which was released in 2004. Kristian Niemann guests on the album. In 2005 the band and Somapala went separate ways because of geographical difficulties, and David Åkesson joined. After the recording of second album *Silent Waters* bass player Sternefalk left and was replaced by Christer "Zigge" Perdersen, who had previously already been involved in mixing the band's earlies demos. *Evergrey*'s Tom Englund is credited for co-production and a guitar solo. A third album is in the making. The band plays highly interesting symphonic power metal with high-class, high-pitched vocals and great musicianship, at times similar to *Rhapsody In Fire* meets *Thunderstone*, but with a dark side lurking.
Website: www.moonlightagony.com

Moonlight in daylight

2004 ☐ ECHOES OF A NIGHTMARE	CD	Massacre Records	MAS PC0435
2004 ☐ ECHOES OF A NIGHTMARE	CD	Nightmare (USA)	NMR-00032
2004 ☐ ECHOES OF A NIGHTMARE	CD	King Records (Japan)	KICP-1020
2007 ■ SILENT WATERS	CD	Dockyard 1	DY100460
Bonus: Erlkönig			
2007 ☐ SILENT WATERS	CD	Soyus (Russia)	DY100460

2007 CD - DY100460

MOONSHINE

Tomas Skoog: v/g, Fredrik Håkansson: g, Bjarne Elvsgård: b, Ulf "Knirk" Johansson: d

Bispgården (Jämtland) - Formed in 1995 when Ulf and Fredrik's former band had split. *Moonshine* plays mid-class melodic hard rock with elements of *Metallica* as well as *Mötley Crüe* and more AOR-oriented bands. A hard rock version of the Swedish folk-song *Jämtlandssången* puts a nice ending to the CD. Not bad actually. The band also recorded another 10-track demo, which is even better than the album. The band folded in 2000. Johansson and Håkansson are now in the band *Zpeedfreak*.

| 1996 ■ 3 DAYS & 1 AFTERNOON | CD | Audiomix Produktion | UJCD 9610 |
| 1998 ☐ AND ALL YOUR ANGELS | CD | private | MOONCD 98 |

1996 CD - UJCD 9610

MOONSTRUCK

Fredrik Sandberg: v/g, Jonas Forsen: g, Magnus Persson: b/k, Per Telg: d

Bjärred - Formed in 1993 and recorded their first demo, *Under Her Burning Wings* in 1996. The album, released on Italian label Dragonheart, contains well-played melodic death metal with nice guitar harmonies more akin to power metal. The only thing that makes this band sound death metal is actually the growling vocals. The band has now split up.

| 1999 ■ FIRST LIGHT | CD | Dragonheart | CHAOS 006CD |

1999 CD - CHAOS 006CD

MOONVILLE

Pierre Oxenryd: v/k, Jimmy Gunnarsson: g, Jonas Ydlinge: b, Carl-Johan Lindblad: d

Kristinehamn - Great melodic power metal with a symphonic touch. High-class, high-pitched vocals and a great, tight band. Something for fans of ***Avantasia***, ***Edguy*** etc. Ydlinger is ex-***Impale*** and ***Brimstone***, while Lindblad is also found in ***Memfis***. The first demo, *Claws In The Dark* was released in 2002, *Fool's Victory* in 2003 and the seven-track demo *Silver Screen* in 2004, before the debut album was released in 2006. The band is currently on hold.
Website: www.moonville.se

2006 CD - 814350

2006 ■ SILVER SCREEN........CD Risestar Music........814350
2006 □ SILVER SCREEN........CD Avalon Marquee (Japan)........MICP-10697
Bonus: 8mm Goddess

MOOSTERS

Dave Nerge: v, Kjell Segebrant: g/v, Hasse Derestam: b, Pelle Alsing: d

Stockholm - Great heavy blues rock in the vein of ***Sky High*** and ***Blues Bag***. Derestam is ex-***Blues Bag***, while Dave Nerge has appeared in bands like ***Highbrow***, ***Dave & The Mistakes*** and ***Dave Nerge's Bull Dog***. The band was initially called ***Moose***, but lengthened the name a bit.

2006 ■ EXECUTIONER........CD TMC........TMC 103710

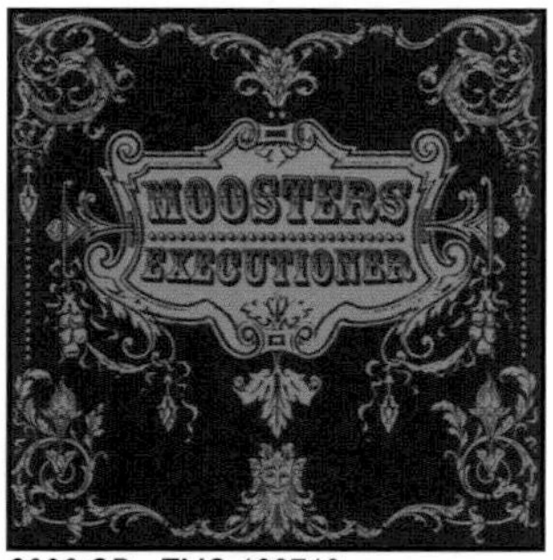

2006 CD - TMC 103710

MORBID

Per Yngve "Dead" Ohlin: v, Uffe "Napolean Pukes" Cederlund: g, John "Gehenna" Berger: g, Jens "Dr. Schitz" Näsström: b, Lars-Göran "L-G/Drutten" Petrov: d

1994 LP - - -

Stockholm - ***Morbid*** are most likely the biggest cult band in Sweden. The band was formed in 1987 and recorded the demo *December Moon* the same year. The demo was recorded in Thunderload Studios and produced by Ragne Wahlquist (***Heavy Load***). The band reached its cult status, not only because of some of the members later achievements, such as Petrov in ***Entombed***, ***Nihilist***, ***Comecon***, ***Hypocrite*** and ***The Project Hate*** and Cederlund's history in ***Nihilist***, ***Entombed***, ***Haystack*** and ***Murder Squad***. No, I guess the biggest reason was singer Ohlin's Norwegian stint in ***Mayhem*** and the fact that he committed suicide on April 8, 1991. Before his they wouldn't get the time of day from the labels, but suddenly everyone and his mother wanted to release the demos, rehearsals and live recordings, no matter the quality. Raw and aggressive proto-death metal.

1994 MLP - RR-002

1994 ■ December Moon........MLP 5tr Reaper Records........RR-002
Tracks: Tragic Dream/My Dark Subconscious/Wings Of Funeral/From The Dark/Disgusting Semla - Deathexecution (trailer). 650 copies in black vinyl, 350 red and 2-4 red/black marble. 300 wth poster. There are also 25 promo copies in white jacket.
1996 □ DEATH EXECUTION........CD Reaper Records........
500 copies.
1997 □ DEATH EXECUTION........LP Holycaust Records........SIN-004
100 hand numbered copies.
2000 □ My Dark Subconscious........6" flexi Body Snatcher........- -
100 copies.
2000 □ December Moon........MCD 4tr Reaper Records........RR 002-CD
Tracks: My Dark Subconscious/Wings Of Funeral/From The Dark/Disgusting Semla - Deathexecution. 1000 copies, first 300 with poster. Different artwork.
2001 □ Death Execution III........7" 3tr PD Reaper Records........RR 004
Tracks: Disgusting Semla/Deathexecution/From The Dark. Recorded live in Handen, Norway, in 1988. 300 copies.
2010 ■ Ancient Morbidity........MLP 3tr Nuclear War Now!........ANTI-GOTH 169
Tracks: Tragic Dream - From The Dark/Wings Of Funeral/Necrodead. Came with issue #20 of Slayer Magazine. 2000 copies
2012 □ YEAR OF THE GOAT........2CD box Century Media........998081 8
2012 ■ YEAR OF THE GOAT........3LPg Century Media........998081 1
500 black, 100 grey, 100 gold, 200 transparent green, 100 red/black marble vinyl.

2010 MLP - ANTI-GOTH 169

Unofficial Recordings:
1994 ■ TRIBUTE TO THE BLACK EMPERORS (split)........LP Land Of The Rising Sun........(MM 25006)
Split with Mayhem. 1000 copies. Tracks: My Dark Subconscious/Wings Of Funeral/From The Dark/Disgusting Semla/Deathexecution
1994 □ TRIBUTE TO THEBLACK EMPERORS (split)........CD Warhammer........666 Hell 666
Split with Mayhem.
1997 □ LIVE FROM THE PAST........CD From The Past Production........n/a
666 copies. Bootleg.
1997 □ TRIBUTE TO THE BLACK EMPERORS (split)........CD Warhammer (USA)........Lust 3
1998 □ TRIBUTE TO THEBLACK EMPERORS (split)........LP PD - -........- -
1000 copies
2000 □ LIVE IN STOCKHOLM........CD Reaper Records........RR005-CD
500 copies.

2012 3LPg - 998081 1

2005 ■	December Moon	MLP PD 4tr	Hellslaughter	HRS 001

Tracks: same as Reaper MCD. 500 copies, numbered. Bootleg

2005 ☐	DEATH EXECUTION	LP	Hellslaughter	- -

300 copies. Bootleg

2005 ☐	LIVE IN STOCKHOLM	LP	Hellslaughter	HRS 002

500. Numbered. Bootleg

2005 ☐	MORBID/MORTEM (split)	CD	Heritage	666 hell 666

500 copies.

2007 ☐	CRUCIFIX MASTURBATION	CD	Beyond Of Death	1

333 copies. Contains December Moon and Live In Stockholm.

2008 ☐	STORM IN STOCKHOLM	LP	- -	- -

311 copies on black and yellow vinyl. Numbered. Bootleg

n/a ☐	December Moon/Deathcrush (split)	LP	Asian Hordes (Phillipines)	- -

156 copies. Bootleg. Split with Mayhem.

2005 MLP PD - HRS 001

MORBID INSULTER

Erik "Expulser" Skogberg: v/g, Carl "Conjurer/Tiburtius" Nordblom: b, Alex "Aids": d

Hönö - Morbid Insulter were formed in 2004 and released their first demo *Strike From The Grave* the subsequent year and a second outing in 2006, entitled *From The Womb Of Pestilence – Second Strike*. A deal was made with I Hate Records, who released the MLP *Thundering Evil*. Carl, who replaced Pontus "Penetrator" after the first release, is also found in **Matricide**, **Nightbringer**, **CON**, **Descending** and **Acrimonious**. **Morbid Insulter** plays quite messy, horribly produced old-school death metal. A CD-version containing both MLPs is planned to be released by Chilean label Proselytism Records. Frontman Erik (born in 1987) took his own life on November 9, 2011.

2008 ☐	Thundering Evil	MLP 5tr	I Hate Records	IHR 053

Tracks: The Abomination Curse/Thundering Evil/Breaking The Cross/Take Me To Hell/
Black Fate. 500 copies

2010 ☐	Antichrist Blasphemies	MLP 4tr	I Hate Records	IHR 082

Tracks: Antichrist Blasphemies/Poison Of God/Extol Sathanas/Raped Graves

2012 ■	FUNERAL MYSTICISM	2CD	I Hate Records	IHR 098

2012 CDd - IHR 098

MORBUS CHRON

Robert "Robba" Andersson: v/g, Edvin "Edde" Aftonfalk: g,
Dag "Dagge" Landin: b, Adam Lindmark: d

Kungsängen (Stockholm) - The initial line-up was formed in 2007, by three schoolmates sharing the same morbid musical interests. They recorded their first demo in 2009 and in 2010 the cassette album *Splendour Of Disease* was released by Dibbuk Records and the 7" came out the same year. The demo caught the attention of Pulverised Records, who signed the band and released the first full length album. **Morbus Chron** plays quite competent death metal, mixing thrashy elements with heavier moments. Should appeal to fans of **Autopsy** and **Slayer**. In 2012 the band signed a deal with Century Media. *A Saunter Through The Shroud* was produced by Fred Estby.

2010 ☐	Creepy Creeping Creep/The Hallucinating Dead	7"	Me Secon Un Ojo/Detest	MSU-10/DR014

First 150 in yellow vinyl, the rest in black.

2011 ■	SLEEPERS IN THE RIFT	CD	Pulverised	ASH 082 CD
2012 ■	A Saunter Through The Shroud	10" 3tr	Century Media	998213 1

Tracks: Channeling The Numinous/Black Orb Reverence/The Place Of The Four Hundred
Volcanoes. 700 black 200 volcanic red and 100 electric red vinyl.

2011 CD - ASH 082 CD

MORDANT

Peter "Bitchfire" Karlsson: v, Jimmy "Soulmolester" Nilsson: g,
Lars "Angelreaper" Karlsson: g, Jonny "Carnage" Nielsen: b,
Dan "Necrophiliac" Andersson: d/g

Dals Långed - A band from the same small town as **Nifelheim**, which shows quite well in their style and sound. Also, Hellbutcher from **Nifelheim** made the art cover for the debut and his band mate Demon took care of the second release. The band was formed in 1997. In 2001 they recorded the demo *Die!.* Between 2002 and 2004 the band featured guitarist Leatherdemon. A few years later they found guitarist Soulmolester, but now drummer Marcus "Hell" Häll left the band and with Necrophiliac also handling the drums they recorded the demo *Back From Hell* (**Death Invocation**) in 2008, plus a song for the **Sabbat** tribute album on Iron Pegasus. The band also used drummer Nils "Chaos" Lindroth for a while.

2002 MCD - Armcd 002

2002 ■	Suicide Slaughter	MCD 6tr	Agonia	Armcd 002

Tracks: Ex Inferis/Pestilent/Suicide Slaughter/Horde Of Satan/Whores Of Destruction/
Eternal Damnation

2004 ☐	MOMENTO MORI	CD	Agonia	Arcd 021
2011 ■	BLACK EVIL MASTER	CD	Night Tripper	NTRCD 005
2011 ☐	BLACK EVIL MASTER	LP	Night Tripper	NTRLP 005

400 blue + 100 black hand-numbered.

2012 10" - 998213 1

2011 CD - NTRCD 005

MORDBRAND

Per Boder: v, Björn Larsson: g, Johan "Skuggan" Rudberg: d

Karlstad - Formed by **The Law/Karensdag/Horned** members Larsson and Rudberg. In 2010 former **God Macabre/Macabre End** singer Boder joined the ranks. **Mordbrand** (arsin in Swedish) plays classic Swedish death metal with hints of early **Entombed**, **Grave** and **Desultory**. *Necropsychotic* has been slated to be rereleased by Chaos Records, but it hasn't been seen as yet.

2006 ☐	EVOKE/MORDBRAND (split) ....LP	Me Saco Un Ojo	..............................MSUO-07
	Split with Evoke. 100 copies in green vinyl.		
2011 ■	Necropsychotic ....MCD 6tr	Deathgasm Records	..............................DG 63
	Tracks: Eaters Of The Void/Graveyard Revisited/Skärseld (Return Of The Unholy)/The Fall Of Flesh/Deathbound/Deliverance.		
2012 ☐	No Life ....10" EP	Carnal/Bifrost	..............BRLP001/CRBRLP001
	Split with Bombs Of Hades. Tracks: Idol Of The Abbatoir/The Eternal Feast Of Annihilation/With Lidless Eyes. 800 black and 200 black/white splatter vinyl copies.		
2012 ☐	Kolumbarium ....7"	Deathgasm Records	..............................DG 71
	Tracks: Consume Them/Let Them Slumber. 200 white and 300 black vinyl copies.		

2011 MCD - DG 63

MORDGRIM

Martin "Grimner" Eversholt: v/b, Joachim "Gwahlar" Eversholt: d/b/g

Landskrona - The band was initially called **Burning Legion**, but when the Eversholt brothers decided to continue on their own, they changed the name to **Mordgrim**. Recorded the demo *Pestens år* in 2004 and a split-cassette with **Blasphemy** in 2005. A self-titled demo was also released in 2005 and *Dead World* in 2006, before they recorded the debut album. Raw sounding old-school black metal. The band changed their name to **Old Bones** and recorded a demo in 2008 and a split album in 2010.

2007 ■	FLESH AND THE DEVIL...CD	Funeral Moonlight......................FMP-CD 002

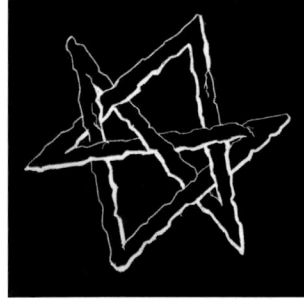

2007 CD - FMP-CD 002

MORDICHRIST

Nenia: k/v/b, Bo "Chaq Mol" Karlsson: g/b/k

Stockholm - Formed in 2000. Chaq Mol was also found in **Dark Funeral** and **Nefarium** and has previously played with **Skellington**. Before the first 10" the band recorded several demos; *The Root Of The Embryo* (2001), *Hatred On Repeat* (2002) and *The Blood Rise* (2003). The 10" is actually a collection of tracks from the demos. Fast and dark black metal with Nenia sounding more evil than Angela Gossow! The band announced they would be using drummer Erik Sayenga (**Laceration, Witchhunt, Dying Fetus**), bassist Lix Tetrax and drummer Af Dictator. The band's website hasn't been updated since 2007.
Website: www.mordichrist.com

2005 ■	Mordichrist .... 10" MLP 4tr	Danza Ipnotica Records ....................D.I. 012
	Tracks: Invocation/Nemesis(Goddess Of Revenge)/Immemorial/World Of Shades. 500 copies.	
2006 ☐	Dressed In Menace...7"	Danza Ipnotica Records ....MOR 013
	Tracks: Villainy/The Fallen. 500 copies.	

2005 10" MLP - D.I. 012

MORÉN, STEFAN

Stefan Morén: v/g/b/d

Vansbro - **Keen Hue**-guitarist Stefan released his first solo-album in 1996. A very good piece of melodic hard rock. No guitar-wanking or overblown progressive complexities, just plain guitar-oriented melodic hard rock. Stefan also played lead-guitar and has recorded songs with the highly popular Swedish duo **Hjalle & Heavy**. Almost ten years later Stefan found it was time for another outing, *The Last Call*. On this album Stefas plays all instruments. It also featutres a cover of **The Sweet**'s *Wig Wam Bam*. This album has a far more modern touch. Stefan still plays in **Keen Hue**, which is now a cover band. Stefan made a new video/single in 2013.

1996 ☐	YIPPIE YA YA...CD	private ....SMCD 96
2005 ■	THE LAST CALL...CD	Swedmetal......................................SM-02-CD

2005 CD - SM-02-CD

MORGAN MASTLING BAND

Morgan Mastling: v/g, Jörgen Carlsson: g, Mats Hagman: g, Conny Mattsson: k, Gunnar Wiklund: b, Dan Olandersson: d

Torsby - Tough one. The A-side is classic Swedish progg/pop similar to Ulf Lundell, while the B-side is definitely a piece of classic seventies-sounding hard rock with some cool biting licks. However, Mastling sounds very inspired by Sweden's Bob Dylan; Ulf Lundell. For completists only.

1989 ■	Tangerine/Kyss mej..7"	Platina PL59

1989 7" - PL 59

MORGANA LEFAY

Charles Rytkönen: v, **Tony Eriksson:** g, **Peter Grehn:** g,
Fredrik Lundberg: b, **Pelle Åkerlind:** d

The damned

Bollnäs - Formed in 1986 under the name *Damage*, featuring Jonas Söderlind (d), Joakim Lundberg (b), Tony Eriksson (g) and Stefan Jonsson (g). In 1988 they were reinforced by former *Sepher Jezirah* singer Rytkönen and they finally changed their name to *Morgana Lefay* in 1989. Jonsson left the band and was replaced by Tommi Karppanen (also ex-*Sepher Jezirah*) and the band recorded their debut album in 1990 (pressed in only 537 copies). In 1991 the band recorded the demo *Rumours Of Rain*, during which recording bass player Lundberg left and was replaced by Joakim Heder. The tape lead to a deal with Black Mark in 1992. A great band in the vein of early *Savatage* with elements of *Testament*, heavy and powerful with lots of musical twists and turns. In 1994 guitarist Tommi Kappanen left the band and during the recordings of *Sanctified* they found a replacement in Daniel Persson (ex-*Shotgun Alley*). Peter Grehn (*Fantasmagoria*) was actually Tommi's first replacement, but left after a short while. In 1998 Joakim Heder (b), Thomas Persson (g) and Jonas Söderlind (d) moved to Stockholm, leaving singer Charles Rytkönen and guitarist Tony Eriksson, who continued under the name *Lefay*, for legal reasons (see *Lefay* for further information). *Lefay* released the album *The Seventh Seal* and a rerecording of the album *Symphony Of The Damned* in 1999 and the album *...---... (S.O.S)* in 2000. In 2004 Lefay took the old name back and returned to Black Mark. The line-up now featured Rytkönen, Eriksson, Grehn, Lundberg and drummer Robin Engström. In 2006 Engström left and was replaced by Pelle Åkerlind (*Bloodbound, Lednote, Rocktools*). All albums are well worth checking out. Past Present Future features covers of *Voulez Vous* (*ABBA*) and *Lost Reflection* (*Crimson Glory*). *Morgana Lefay* features a cover of Prince's... sorry the song by "The artist formerly known as Prince, and now again called Prince", *Darling Nikki*. In January 2012, singer Charles Rytkönen annouced he was fronting new band *Cibola Junction*. The band was on an "indefinite hiatus", but did some live shows in 2013.

1990 LP - JOMES BAND 007

1996 CD - BMCD 86

Year		Title	Format	Label	Cat No	
1990	■	SYMPHONY OF THE DAMNED	LP	Fata Morgana Music	JOMES BAND 007	$$$
		537 copies.				
1992	□	KNOWING JUST AS I	LP	Black Mark	BMLP 28	
1992	□	KNOWING JUST AS I	CD	Black Mark	BMCD 28	
1993	□	THE SECRET DOCTRINE	LP	Black Mark	BMLP 42	
1993	□	THE SECRET DOCTRINE	CD	Black Mark	BMCD 42	
1994	□	THE SECRET DOCTRINE	CD	Victor (Japan)	VICP-5370	
1992	□	KNOWLING JUST AS I	CD	Victor (Japan)	VICP-5371	
1995	□	SANCTIFIED	LP	Black Mark	BMLP 63	
1995	□	SANCTIFIED	CD	Black Mark	BMCD 63	
1995	□	SANCTIFIED	CD	Victor (Japan)	VICP-5511	
		Bonus: Voulez Vouz (Abba cover)/Fatal Illusions secret tracks.				
1995	□	PAST PRESENT FUTURE	CD	Black Mark	BMCD 84	
		This is a Best Of, with 4 new tracks				
1995	□	Symphony Of The Damned	CDS 1tr	Black Mark	BMCD 89	
1996	■	MALEFICIUM	CD	Black Mark	BMCD 86	
1996	□	MALEFICIUM	CD	Victor (Japan)	VICP-5816	
1998	■	FATA MORGANA	CD	Black Mark	BMCD 128	
1999	□	MORGANA LEFAY	CD	Black Mark	BMCD 147	
2000	□	MORGANA LEFAY	CD	Nippon Crown (Japan)	CRCL-4762	
2000	□	MORGANA LEFAY	CD	Nems (Argentina)	NEMS 176	
2005	□	GRAND MATERIA	CD	Black Mark	BMCD 179	
2005	■	GRAND MATERIA	CDd	Black Mark	BMDP 179	
		Bonus: Sangreal				
2005	□	GRAND MATERIA	2LP	Black Mark	BMLP 179	
		Bonus: Sangreal				
2007	□	Over And Over Agaiin/Face Of Fear	CDS	Black Mark	BMCDS 183	
2007	□	ABERRATIONS OF THE MIND	CD	Black Mark	BMCD 183	
2007	□	ABERRATIONS OF THE MIND	CDd	Black Mark	BMDP 183	
		Bonus: Nightmares Made In Hell				

1998 CD - BMCD 128

2005 CDd - BMDP 179

MORIA

Dennis Widén: v, **Joakim Widén:** g, **Christian Bengtsson:** g,
Christoffer Rudbeck: b, **Johan Kuurne:** d

Falkenberg - Another band that has taken its name from *The Lord Of The Rings*, *Moria* (Not to be confused with the Stockholm band). Recorded the demo *Death & Destruction* in 1998 in 100 copies, appeared on the split-MLP together with *Blood Storm* and recorded the demo *In The Trenches* in 2000 and *K.I.A* in 2001. Black metal. Dennis is also in *Pagan Rites* and *The Ancient's Rebirth*, while Kuume and Rudbeck are ex-*Dynamic*. K.I.A featured the Widéns, Teo Dahnberg (b) and Henrik Allbjer (d), who all later formed *The Goddamned*.

Year		Title	Format	Label	Cat No
1999	■	Evil Rapid Death (split)	MLP	Hellflame Productions	HFP 016
		Split with Blood Storm. Tracks: Evil Rapid Death/Death And Destruction. 500 hand numbered copies. Stickers.			

1999 MLP - HFP 016

MORIFADE

Stefan Petersson: v, Jesper Johansson: g, Adrian Kanebäck: g, Fredrik Eriksson: k, Henrik Weimedal: b, Kim Arnell: d

Linköping - The band was formed in 1992 under the name *Gothic*. In 1995 they released their first demo *The Hourglass*. On the first MCD the band was a quartet featuring Christian Stinga-Borg (v/k), Fredrik Johansson (g), Jesper Johansson (g), Henrik Weimdal (k) and Kim Arnell (d). The debut album saw the band as a quartet featuring new singer Stefan Petersson (ex-*Savage Skülls*), Jesper, Henrik and Kim. The album also features a guest-solo by *Master Massive*-guitarist Jan Strandh, who also co-produced it. Melodic metal with strong influences of *HammerFall*, *Gamma Ray* and *Rhapsody In Fire*. High-quality stuff. The band also contributes with the song *Walk Against The Wind* on the *Born To Walk Against The Wind* (98 Loud 'N Proud) compilation. Unfortunately Loud 'N Proud crashlanded. The band contributed on the *Helloween* tribute *Walls Of Jericho – A Tribute To Helloween* (2000 Arise). On *Cast A Spell* the band had become reinforced by guitarist Adrian Kanebäck (*Nephenzy/Nephenzy Chaos Order*), but on *Imaginarium* Robin Arnell had replaced him and the band had been reinforced with former *Tad Morose* keyboardist Fredrik Eriksson. The same line-up recorded the subsequent album *Domi<>Nation*, but in 2004, Kristian Wallin (*Rising Faith, Meadow, Danger*) replaced singer Stefan Petersson the band recorded two new promo recordings in 2005. The new album was long awaited, but nothing happened until September 2011 when the band returned with the album *Empire Of Souls*, now featuring new guitarist Mathias Kamijo (*Algaion, Pain, Sinergy, Vergelmer, Hypocrisy* etc), replacing Jesper Johansson.
Website: www.morifade.com

1998 MCD - LNP 001

1999 CD - LNP 010

2000 MCD - 3063032

2003 CD - Karma 005

1998 ■	Across The Starlit Sky	MCD 4tr	Loud 'N Proud	LNP 001
	Tracks: Enter The Past/Tomorrow Knows/Starlit Sky/Distant World			
1999 ■	POSSESSION OF POWER	CD	Loud 'N Proud	LNP 010
1999 ☐	POSSESSION OF POWER+ACROSS THE STARLIT SKY	2CD	Nothing To Say (France)	NTS 3056272
2000 ☐	POSSESSION OF POWER+ACROSS THE STARLIT SKY	CD	Pony Canyon (Korea)	PCKD 20047
	Bonus: Walk Against The Wind			
2000 ■	Cast A Spell	MCD 5tr	Nothing To Say	3063032
	Tracks: Cast A Spell/As Time Decide/Tomorrow Knows/Dance With The Devil (Phenomena cover)/Walk Against The Wind			
2002 ☐	IMAGINARIUM	LP	Hammerheart	HHR 106
2002 ☐	IMAGINARIUM	CD	Hammerheart	HHR 106
2002 ☐	IMAGINARIUM	CD	Fono (Russia)	FO149CD
2002 ☐	IMAGINARIUM	CD	King Records (Japan)	KICP-871
2003 ☐	DOMI<>NATION	CDd	Karmageddon	Karma 005X
	Bonus: Cast A Spell/As Time Decides/Tomorrow Knows/Dance With The Devil (Phenomena cover)/Judas (Helloween cover)/Lost Within A Shade (video). 5000 copies.			
2003 ■	DOMI<>NATION	CD	Karmageddon	Karma 005
2011 ☐	EMPIRE OF SOULS	CD	IceWarrior Records	IWR11

MORNALAND

Henrik Wenngren: v/g, Tommy Öberg: g, Jacob Alm: b, Joakim Jonsson: d

Västerås - It all started in 1995 when Henrik and Joakim founded the band. They recorded three demos as a duo, (*Deyond The Dreamers Labyrinth, Origin Land* and *The Journey*) before being reinforced by Tommy (g). In 1997 the track Land *Of Dreaming* was featured on the *Voices Of Death* compilation. Another track, *In Dead Skies Looms Tranquillity*, was featured on *From The Underground* (99 X-treme). After this bass-player Jacob joined. In 1998 *Sore Lies* and a cover of *Metallica*'s *Seek And Destroy* appeared on the compilation *Metal Militia III*. The band has now split. Henrik and Joakim were later found in death metal band *Dust*. Joakim is also found in *Skinfected* (as lead-guitarist), *Axenstar*, *The Mist Of Avalon*, *Ecliptica*, *Autumn Dweller* and is now in *Assailant*. Joakim, Jacob and Tommy are also found in *Slumber* and Henrik was also in *Skyfire*. The tracks from the 2002 Mester release was taken from the 1998 cassette *In Dead Skies…*, which in its turn was taken from several demos. The band made their last demo, *Feathers Of Rapture* in 2000.
Website: http://come.to/mornaland

1996 CD - PTE 002

1996 ■	PRELUDE TO THE WORLD FUNERAL (split)	CD	Path To Enlightenment	PTE 002
	Split with Abominator. Tracks: Invert/Floating Semblance/Fallen Angels/Mournful Secrets, Part 1/Silent Forest/…Then Came The Dawn/Voice In The Wind			

MORNING AFTER, THE

Per Mårtensson: v/g, Ove Jansson: g, Per Holmstedt: b, Johan Sjöström: d

Borlänge - A great hard rock band with some great riffs and nice 70's influences. Per is also found in *Stonecake* and was in the first line-up of *Mojobone*. The band had the intention of recording a full length CD, but unfortunately it never happened.

1994 MCD - MORCD 01

1994 ■	Confessions Of A Loony/Dancin' With Ghosts	CDS 2tr	private	MORCD 01

MORPHEENA

Adam Gilderstam: v/b, Tony Lang: v/g, Ioan Nuca: g, Niclas Persson: d

Kristianstad/Hässleholm - **Morpheena** were formed in 2005 out of the ashes of Kristianstad band **Mite** and Hässleholm band **Leech**. The style became a mix of **Mite**'s Seattle rock and the **Helmet** style brutality of **Leech**. The band's first demo recordings *Rocknrollpunkmetal* and *El Duce* (2005) proved the band was a perfect musical mix. It all continued on the debut album *Headshot Blues*, which was a killer platter full of modern post-grunge heaviness in the vein of colleagues **CellOut** or Americans **Sevendust**. The band also had two great lead singers. Niclas and Adam were also playing in the same cover band, **Laxton Band**. In December 2008 the band unfortunately split. Niclas and Tony formed the band **Unsolved**, who released their debut in 2010 and continued in the same style as **Morpheena**.

2006 ■ HEADSHOT BLUES ....CD private RNRPM-200666

2006 CD - RNRPM-200666

MORPHEUS

David Brink: v, Sebastian Ramstedt: g, Stefan Ekström: g,
Johan De Daux (Bergebäck): b, Markus Rüden: d

Farsta/Enskede (Stockholm) - A death metal band formed in 1991 from the ashes of **Exhumed** and **Carbonized**. The style is technical death metal with lots of tempo changes, even though it's mostly speed that counts. The production could be better. On the first release guitarist Janne Rudberg (now Björkenfjäll) was in the band, but didn't play on the album. He later formed **Excruciate** and is today in **Birch Mountain**. Ramstedt has later been found in **Necrophobic** and is now in **Nifelheim**. Bergebäck (named De Daux during this time) was later in **Nifelheim** (as Apocalyptic Desolator) and previously also in **Dismember** and **Necrophobic**.

1991 ■ In The Arms Of... MLP 4tr	Opinionate ....OP 003	$
Tracks: No Mans Land/Among Others/The Third Reich 3979 A.C/Thoughts Of Distraught		
1993 ☐ SON OF HYPNOS ....CD	Step One.. STEP 005	
2012 ☐ IN THE ARMS OF...CD	Temple Of Darkness .... TOD 040	
The entire Exhumed demo Obscurity as bonus.		
2012 ☐ IN THE ARMS OF ....LP	Temple Of Darkness .... TOD 040	

1991 MLP - OP 003

MORT

Andreas "Mort" Stahre – v/g/b/d

Stockholm - The idea of **Mort** was brought to life in 2001-2001 but nothing really happened until 2005 when Andreas "Mort" Stahre finally got his ideas down on a demo. This lead to the debut album, where Andreas handled all the instruments and vocals. When he started writing for the second album, *Zombiefication*, he started searching for a band to back him up. Early 2008 he had gathered Malmö-based guitarists Martin Bermheden (**Enshrined, Visceral Bleeding**) and Ville Kemi (**Life Illusion, Obscure Divinity, Vandöd, Fall ov Serafim** etc), bass player Divina Korhonen and Magnus Löfgren entered. Unfortunatey it all fell apart, Andreas was again alone, but soon found new partner, bass player-gone-guitarist Johan Klevenskog (ex-**Godphobia**), bass player Hjalle Klitse Kyrö and drummer Nicke Olsson. The latter left the band in 2011. **Mort** plays quite strange industrial death metal. The second album is still in production.

2006 CD - JAS 001

2006 ■ TILL DEATH DO US PART...CD Nightrose .... JAS 001

MORTALICUM

Henrik Högl: v/g, Mikael Engström: g,
Patrick Backlund: b, Andreas Häggström: d

Sundsvall - **Mortalicum** were formed in 2006 by **Quicksand Dream** mastermind Backlund, initially as a studio project with himself handling all instruments. He drafted singer Robert Wiklander to add vocals on the demos. He also played drums on the initial jams and writing sessions. End of 2007 guitarists Henrik Högl and Mikael Engström joined. The final piece of the puzzle came when drummer Andreas Häggström joined in 2008. In the spring of 2009 the band and singer Robert parted ways, and Henrik took over the vocal task and in November 2009 the band recorded the debut album *Progress Of Doom*, which was released in 2010. **Mortalicum** plays great melodic doomy hard rock/metal with a hint of bands like early **Trouble**, **Black Sabbath**, **Grand Magus** and **Spiritual Beggars**. Henrik's clean, bright, high-class vocals give the package a new twist. Killer band!
Website: www.mortalicum.com

The prophets of doom

2010 ☐ PROGRESS OF DOOM ....CD	Metal On Metal .... MOMR 10016	
2012 ■ THE ENDTIME PROPHECY...CD	Metal On Metal .... MOMR 12033	

2012 CD - MOMR 12033

MORTHIRIM
Mats: v, Roger Johansson: g, Ole: g, Nicklas Sundqvist: b, Robert "Zoid" Sundelin: d

Luleå - The band was formed in 1994 and featured *Necromicon* members Robert, Roger and Nicklas. They release the first demo, *Pure Fucking Metal*, the same year. The MCD was originally recorded as a split with the band *Anateus*, but due to some problems it became a release for *Morthirim* alone. The recording also featured a guest solo by Robert's *Satariel* band-mate Magnus Alkangas (also in *Incinerator, Hel*). Robert and Nicklas were also found in *Hellmasker* and *Deathbound*. Quite strangely produced black metal, musically a bit reminiscent of early *Marduk*.

1998 ■ Morthirim ....MCDd 4tr   Spikekult Records..............................SPK 001
Tracks: Introduktion/The 7th Knife/Cold And Gold/Desolate World

1998 MCDd - SPK 001

MORTUM
Chrille Andersson: v/g, Anna Carlsdotter: v, Rille Svensson: g,
Michael Håkansson: b, Bartosz Nalezinski: d

Kristianstad - Melodic death metal with female choirs and melodic keyboard parts. The first demo, *The Everlasting* was recorded in 1997 and a second outing, *The Goddess Of Dawn*, was released the same year. The album was produced by Andy LaRocque. Not to be confused with the Stockholm-based black metal band. A third demo was recorded in 1998 after which the band broke up. After *Mortum* split up Chrille, Bartek and Rille formed melodic power metal band *Supreme Majesty*. Håkansson has also appeared in *Evergrey, Embraced, The Project Hate MCMXCIX, The Forsaken* and *Incapacity*, while Andersson has fronted *Hellspell, Non-Serviam, The Darksend* and *Infernal*.

1998 ■ DRUID CEREMONY ....CD   Invasion .... IR 038
1998 □ DRUID CEREMONY ....LP PD   Invasion .... - -

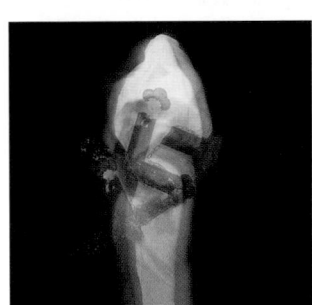
1998 CD - IR 038

MORTUUS
J "Tehôm" Kvarnbrink: v/g/b, Marcus Hinze: d

Umeå - Formed in 2003. Quite old-school low-fi black metal with agonizing vocals. Kvarnbrink is also found in *Dödfödd, Shade Of Black* and *Ofermod*, while Hinze is in *Ondskapt, Lepra* and also in *Shade Of Black*.

2005 □ Silence Sang The Praise Of Death/All Dead.....................7"   The Ajna Offensive....................FLAME 22 EP
2007 ■ DE CONTEMPLANDA MORTE: DE REVERENCIE LABORIUS AC ADORATIONIS
....CD   The Ajna Offensive..........................FLAME 40
666 copies.
2008 □ DE CONTEMPLANDA MORTE: DE REVERENCIE LABORIUS AC ADORATIONIS
....LP   The Ajna Offensive..........................FLAME 40

2007 CD - FLAME 40

MOSEZ
Tomas Marklund: v/b, Jonas Wigstad: g, Urban Robertsson: d

Stockholm - The debut is an OK CD with some influences of bands like *Motorhead*, while the 4-track is a far more interesting installment with more heaviness and a better sound. Worth checking out. Marklund and Wigstad were later found in excellent heavies *Ground Mower*.

1992 □ NO SOUL..CD   private ....MOSEZ 001
1993 ■ In The Flesh ....MCD 4tr   private ....MOSEZ 002
Tracks: Great Burden/In The Flesh/All Gone/Partypig.

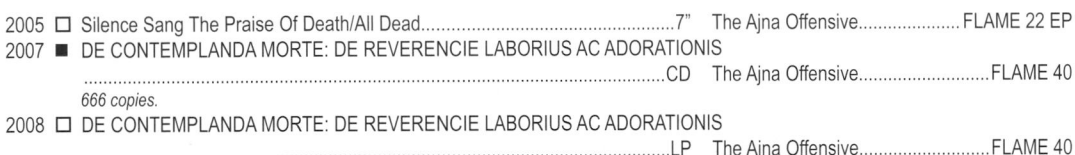
1993 MCD - MOSEZ 002

MOTHER ICE DOG
Jan "Auwa" Altsjö: v/g, Magnus "Bonum" Hedin: b, Bumpa: d

Linköping - Formed in 1995 by Auwa and Bumpa. Great seventies-oriented hard rock with an Ozzy:ish touch on the vocals. Highly recommended. The members have previously recorded with *Bubblegum Justice, Downbound Train* and *Nashville Neurotics*. Hedin was also found in *Axewitch* and *Overflash*.

1998 ■ First..MCD 4tr   Blind Dog ....BDCD 009
Tracks: Come In/Barbecue Night/Undressed/Back To Nature

MOTHER MISERY
John Hermanssen: v, Thomas Piehl: g,
Stefan "Stiff Hell" Hellström: b, Jimmy Lindbergh: d

Enköping - The beginning of the band dates back to 2002, and it was initiated by former *Grey-hate/Awesome Machine/Stonewall Noise Orchestra* singer/guitarist Hermansson who teamed up with guitarist Thomas Piehl under the name *Nosedive*. They appeared on some compilations

1998 MCD - BDCD 009

and started working on the debut, before which they changed their name to *Mother Misery*. After the debut, drummer Jens Wide and bassist Örjan Baudin (*Clench*) left the band and were replaced by drummer Jimmy Lindbergh and bass player Marcus Jäderholm. The MCD *For The Crows* was released as a teaser for the new album. Three of the tracks were later rerecorded for the album, while two are non-CD. On the second album *All Eyes On You* the sound changed slightly going from stoner to more classic heavy rock. In January 2008 Jäderholm left and was replaced by Stiff. In 2010 the band entered Studio Underground with producer Pelle Saether to record *Standing Alone*, which was released by Transubstans.

| 2004 | ☐ | GRANDIOSITY | CD | Greyhate | MMCD2004 |
| 2006 | ☐ | For The Crows | MCD 5tr | Daredevil | DD 0034 |

Tracks: My Soul/Take A Good Look/I Will Never Learn/For The Cows/Pray For Them Pigs

2008	☐	ALL EYES ON YOU	CD	Alabama/Daredevil	ALAB005/DD042
2010	■	STANDING ALONE	CDd	Transubstans	TRANS 069
2012	☐	STANDING ALONE	LPg	Transubstans	TRANSV03

2010 CDd - TRANS 069

MOTHER OF GOD
Daniel Nygren: v/g, Johan Kvastgård: g, Carl Lindblad: b, Jimmy Hurtig: d

Morgårdshammar - Formed in 2008 these four young gentlemen took their influences from seventies hard rock and blended with their love for grungy bands like *Alice In Chains* and *Soundgarden* and came up with a nice and heavy stoner blend. The first sign of life was the five track self titled demo, released in 2009, followed by the, now sold-out, debut MCD *Forging A New Path*. After being picked up by Small Stone, the debut *Anthropos* was released, proving the band was a solid powerful unit fitting well alongside bands like *Dozer* and *Lowrider*, and at time sounding like a mix of *Graveyard* and *Alice In Chains*. Good stuff!

| 2010 | ■ | Forging A New Path | MCD 4tr | Man Make Fire Records | MMF 001 |

Tracks: Four Wanderes/Ancient Tracks/Blind Monkey/Into The Unknown

| 2012 | ■ | ANTHROPOS | CD | Small Stone Records | SS 134 |
| 2012 | ☐ | ANTHROPOS | LP | Small Stone Records | SS 134 LP |

150 black, 150 red and 175 green vinyl copies.

2010 MCD - MMF 001

MOTHER SUPERIOR
David Berlin: v, Sölvi "Silver" Blöndal: g, Per Ellwerson: g,
Fredrik Cronsten: b, Anders Stub: d

Uppsala - Loud, loud, loud! Would be the closest description of this fivesome. With the roots in the 70's and the feet buried in the Woodstock-mud these lads carry on the most hippish *MC5*-tradition with a stoner touch. Groove to the max. One of the four nominees in the 1996 Grammis awards in the hard rock category. Not to be confused with the Los Angeles bunch.

2012 CD -

1996	☐	THE MOTHERSHIP HAS LANDED	CD	Velodrome	RACE 7
1998	☐	THE MOTHERSHIP MOVEMENT	CD	Loudsprecher	LSD 024
2000	☐	3 Song EP	7" 3tr	Bad Afro	FRO 019

Tracks: Have You Seen That Cat/You Gotta Gotta/Good Is Good

| 2003 | ☐ | SIN | CD | Fargo | FA 20325 |

MOTHER'S HOPE
Markus "El Barkus" Berglund: v, Håkan "Hawkan" Englund: g, John Lindholm: k,
Jörgen "Jukken" Lindhult: b, Håkan "Bronco" Brunnkvist: d

Sala/Västerås - It all actually started with the band *Mouth Of Clay*, that later turned into *Josh's Appletree*, both bands recording a multitude of demos. In 2009 they changed their name to *Mother's Hope* and finally got a deal and an album out. Great 70s-influenced hard rock. In 2010 guitarist Hawkan (now in *Concrete Gypsy*) left the band and was replaced by Uffe Andersson.

| 2010 | ■ | NEVERENDING HIGHWAY | CD | Mangora Spiderrecords | MNGS 001 |

2010 CD - MNGS 001

MOTHERCAKE
Martin Ohlsson: v, Lars Jönsson: g, Patrik Berglin: g,
Henrik Paulsson: b, Thomas Jönsson: d

Örkelljunga - Outstanding heavy stoner-oriented hard rock in the vein of *Spiritual Beggars*, *Spirit Caravan* etc. The band can also be found on the compilations: *Burned Down To Zero* (00 Daredevil), *Doomed* (00 The Dark Reign), *Sacred Groove* (00 MDG) and *The Mighty Desert Rock Avengers* (2002 People Like U). Lars Jönsson was later replaced by Patrik "Petter" Englund. Ohlsson and Englund are now in stoner band *The Firm Hand*. Berglin, Jönsson and Englund are now found in stoner band *Skånska Mord*.

| 1999 | ■ | Vol 1 | 7" EP | private | HM&M 001 |

Split with Half Man. The Mothercake-tracks are: Fists Of Fury/Baglady. 400 copies.

| 2003 | ☐ | MOTHERCAKE | LP | El Huevo | MCLP 001 |

1999 7" - HM&M 001

MOTHERLODE

**Sonny Larsson: v, Tom Nilsson: g, Fredrik Beckmann: k,
Johan Evertsson: b, Pär Hjulström: d**

Örebro - *Motherlode* are a top-class melodic band with great complex song, nice keyboard/guitar interludes and great vocals. Kit Woolven mixed the debut album and there was also *Magnum*'s Mark Stanway guesting on keyboards. The cover was made by renowned artist Rodney Matthews. Besides the records listed the band appears on the compilation album *Swedish Metal* (86 Sonet) and on an official compilation cassette entitled *Hårdrock* (Aktiv Musik, 500 copies). On the first album keyboard player Johan Lindström was also part of the band. After the album Sonny quit and was replaced by Per Englund (*Mandrake Root, Blacksmith* etc). The second single features Sonny on vocals, although Per is on the cover-photo. After recording a five-track demo in 1989 they disappeared for quite a while but never really disbanded. They contributed on tributes to *Thin Lizzy*, where they do *Killer Without A Cause* and *Grand Funk Railroad*, where they interpret *People Let's Stop The War*. As a taster for what was to become the band's second album, the non-album track *Rabiatha*, can be found on the bonus CD for the second encyclopedia in 2002. The line-up had now changed. On the old recordings the bass was handled by Peter Rundström and the drums by Martin Hedberg. It however took until 2010 before the second album was unearthed. The line-up had now changed again, where drummer Patrik Nordlander had been replaced by Hjulström and Beckmann added to the line-up. However, Rikard Nilsson plays keyboards on most parts of the record and Nordlander did actually play the drums on the album. The style had now become a bit heavier and modern.

1986 LP - HEJLP 017

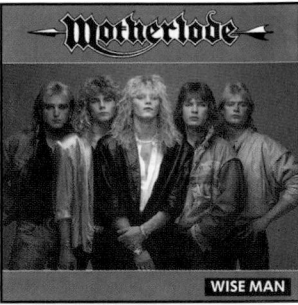
1987 7" - HEJ-S 027

2010 CD - 329470 120095

1986 ☐	Downtown/Live It Out	7"	Active Music	EJ-S 017	
	1000 copies				
1986 ■	THE SANCTUARY	LP	Active Music	HEJLP 017	
	2055 copies				
1987 ■	Wise Man/Moving Emotions	7"	Active Music	HEJ-S 027	
	505 copies				
1991 ☐	THE SANCTUARY	CD	Metalmania (Germany)	16 350	
1995 ☐	THE SANCTUARY	CD	Naxos	CCD 9509	
	Bonus: The Tide Is Turning/On The Run/Summerdreams/When Autumn Fell/Fantasy Child				
2010 ■	TOMORROW NEVER COMES	CD	Bold Stroke	329470 120095	

MOTHERPEARL

Oscar Olandersson: v, Birger Wikström: g, Daniel Sjöstrand: b, Gustaf Hedtström: d

Göteborg - Great bluesy, slightly funky hard rock with biting guitar work, at time similar to *Extreme*. Unfortunately on the first release, the singer Oscar Oldanersson is not up to par with the rest of the band. Could have been one killer of an album as the song material really rocks. In 2010 the band switched singer to Martin Brisshäll, who lifts the band to a new dimension. The current line-up features Wikström, Sjöstrand and Brishäll. In 2011 the band recorded the digital EP *Bend Over Here It Comes Again*, which is a killer. In June 2012 the second album was recorded and ready, but would only be released through digital media.

2009 CD - MPCD 01

2009 ■	LONG TIME COMIN'	CD	private	MPCD 01	

MOTHERS PRIDE

**Jonas Pålsson: v, Christoffer Silverberg: v, Simon Rue Hallén: v/g,
Björn Sjöblom: b, Jon Grinde: d, Daniel Blomstrand: sampler**

Kirseberg (Malmö) - Rap-metal in the vein of *Mindjive* or *Clawfinger*, but a little more light-weight. More melodic chord changes than fat angry riffing. Split in 1997. Jon now plays jazz

1995 ■	Mothers Pride	MCD 7tr	private	MOTHERSPRIDE 1	
	Tracks: See My Will/Peter Parker/She/Dizzy/La Coueleue De Betty/Mr Presley/No Coke				
1996 ☐	Sour Face Ep	MCD 5tr	private	CDM 01	
	Tracks: Intro/See My Will/KB Fire/Sour Little Dipper/Sourface + nameless				

1995 MCD - MOTHERSPRIDE 1

MOTORCITY MADHOUSE

**Steven Williams: v, Håkan Tyresten: g, Johan Nääs: g,
Jarle Strand: b, Stefan Tyresten: d**

Kristinehamn - Formed in 1989. Quite garagey hard rock with influences from *Motorhead*, Hendrix and *Soundgarden*. Singer on the MLP was Christer Tångring. The CDS was recorded at Sunlight Studios. The band has now changed their name to *Suborn* and a demo was recorded in 1995. By the way "Tünt Säu" means "bullshit" in Norwegian. A video was recorded for *Wirehead*.

1991 ☐	What's Buggin' You?	MLP 6tr	Tünt Säu	TS-001	
	Tracks: Madman Blues/Lowrider/Liars/Pretty Trigger/Fire/Last Night				
1993 ■	Wirehead/Putrefy	CDS 2tr	Tünt Säu	TS-002	

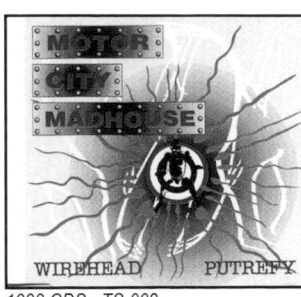
1993 CDS - TS-002

MOTVIND

Juris Salmins: g/v, Tommy Johannesson: g, Olle Nyberg: k,
Johan Strömberg: b, Leif Mårtensson: d

Göteborg - A very politically-oriented, angry hard rock band. On the debut the band featured Juris, Göran Ekstrand (v), Jan Brynsten (g), Krister Jacobsson (b) and Leif Mårtensson (d). The next album saw the addition of keyboard player Olle Nyberg and the album contained the song *Lära För Livet*, which was the theme song for a youth TV-series. They had a big hit with the song, but due to the record company's strong left-wing political beliefs it was never released as a single. The albums contain some serious hard rockers as well as mainstream material. *Lära För Livet* and the non-LP track *Bakfull* are also found on the compilation *Fristil* ('77 Nacksving). Göran left the band and the members on the '78-release were: Juris, Olle, Mikael Gyllenstig (d) and Anders Rundblad (b). Now the band became more slick musically and on the next LP consisted of Juris, Mikael, Per Giöbel (g), Matts Tohver (b) and Anders Söderberg (k). In 1981 Per and Matts left and bassist Johan Strömberg joined. The last and the band's least interesting effort had the ironic title *Kamikaze (*produced by Börje "Boss" Forsberg (***Bathory***)), and saw the addition of keyboard player Mats Olausson (Malmsteen, ***Glory*** etc.). Olle later joined ***Sky High*** for a period. The band split in 1984. When the compilation *Stormvarning* was released, the band also reunited and released a MCD also featuring re recordings of some old songs with a slight change of line-up, now featuring drummer Leif Mårtensson and guitarist Tommy Johannesson. In 2012 Leif left and was replaced by Birger Löfman (***Biscaya, Fretless, Destiny***). A mixed bag of tricks, ranging from straightforward rock to great bluesy hard rock to melodic rock.

Plockepinn-Törst

1979 7" - 45-6

1976 LP - 031-5

1983 LP - PL 40266

1976 ■	KÄNN DIG BLÅST	LP	Nacksving	031-5
1977 ☐	JO JO, JA JA	LP	Nacksving	031-12
1978 ☐	MOTVIND	LP	Nacksving	031-18
1979 ■	Plockepinn/Törst	7"	Nacksving	45-6
1980 ○	Mr X/Som i en dimma	7"	Nacksving	PRS 05
	Promo. No artwork.			
1981 ☐	Tilt/Som i en dimma	7"	Nacksving	45-07
1981 ☐	SNACKA GÅR JU	LP	Nacksving	031-34
1981 ○	Nu vill jag leva/Spökskeppet	7"	Affection Records	AFS 001
	No artwork			
1981 ☐	HJÄRTA AV STÅL	LP	Affection Records	AFF 001
1983 ■	KAMIKAZE	LP	RCA	PL 40266
1983 ■	Kamikaze/Zombie	7"	private	PB 60055
1996 ☐	STORMVARNING 1976-1983	CD	Stormy Records	001
1996 ☐	Bara en sommar/Stormvarning/Mr X/Zombie	MCD 4tr	Stormy Records	002

1983 7" - PB 60055

MOUNTAIN OF POWER

Janne Stark: g/b

Mörrum - ***Mountain Of Power*** is more of a solo project initiated by Grooveyard Records' owner Joe Romagnola and guitarist Janne Stark (***Overdrive, Constancia, Locomotive Breath, Zello, Zoom Club, BALLS*** etc). Janne was asked to do a cover album of unsung seventies hard rockers and agreed with the only demand it should be songs he loved and that had rarely been covered before. The first effort featured songs by bands like ***Neon Rose, Captain Beyond, Stray Dog, Mountain, Wireless, Moxy, Goddo*** etc. The guest list was also quite impressive, featuring singers David Fremberg (***Andromeda, Constancia***), Björn Lodin (***Baltimoore, BALLS***), Mikael Nord Andersson (***Nord, Roxette, BALLS***), Dan Swanö (***Nightingale, Edge Of Sanity*** etc), Chris Catena, Mike Andersson (***Cloudscape, Fullforce***), Roger Holegård (***Neon Rose***), drummers Peter "TrumPeter" Svensson (***Faith, Locomotive Breath***) and Anders Johansson (***HammerFall***, Yngwie), bass players Nalle Påhlsson (***Treat, Therion***), Mårten Andersson (***Lizzy Borden***) and Björn Englén (Yngwie, ***Soul Sign***) plus fellow guitarists Sven Cirnski (***Bad Habit, Truth***), Thomas Larsson (***Baltimoore, Yeah Bop Station***), Tommy Denander, Lars Erik Mattsson, Hank Shermann (***Mercyful Fate***), Jocke Sandberg (***Aces High***) and Jonas Hansson (***Silver Mountain***). The second release took it all even a step further now featuring international musicians such as Paul Shortino (***Rough Cutt, Quiet Riot***), Ty Tabor (***King's X***), Jarrod England (***Rufus Huff***), Greg Martin (***Rufus Huff***), Craig Erickson, Martin Andersen (***Blindstone***), Cindy Weichmann (***Nail, Helix***), Rusty Burns (***Point Blank***) and James Collins (***Pod***), beside Swedish guests like John Norum (***Europe***), Tomas "Juneor" Andersson (***Kamchatka***), Christian Liljegren (***Narnia, DivineFire*** etc), Mikael Nord Andersson, David Fremberg, Maria Rådsten (***Misth, One More Time***), Conny Bloom (***Electric Boys***), Clas Yngström (***Sky High***), Pontus Snibb (***Bonafide, PS3***), Kjell Bergendahl (***Thalamus, Renaissance Of Fools***), Tommy Denander. This time covering bands and artists like Sammy Hagar, ***Leslie West Band, Pat Travers, Rory Gallagher, ZZ Top, Blackfoot, Ozz, Y&T*** etc. The band actually played live once featuring Stark, Nord, Catena, Fremberg, Osbäck, Påhlsson and drummer Peter "TrumPeter" Svensson.
Website: www.mountainofpower.com

2010 CDd - GYR 060

2006 ■	MOUNTAIN OF POWER	CD	Grooveyard Records	GYR 025
2010 ■	VOLUME TWO	CDd	Grooveyard Records	GYR 060

2006 CD - GYR 025

MOURNING SIGN

Robert Pörschke: v, Petri Aho: g, Thomas Gardh: b/k,
Kari Kainulainen: g/b, Henrik Persson: d

Hallstahammar - Well-played death metal with plenty of tempo changes and interesting guitar parts, at times closer to technical power metal than death. In the same league as *Entombed*. There are actually even some parts with clean vocals. Keyboards on the album were played by Petri Kähäri. They also have the track *Redeem* on the compilation *Extreme Close-Up II* and *En To Pan* is found on *W.A.R* (Wrong Again). The band has split and guitarist Kari is now found in *Aamaran* who recorded an oustanding demo in 2001.

1995 ■	Alienor	MCD 4tr	Godhead	GOD 15
	Tracks: Redeem/Desert Sun/Godsend/No Paradise			
1995 ☐	MOURNING SIGN	CD	Godhead	GOD 16
1996 ☐	MULTIVERSE	CD	Godhead	GOD 22

1995 MCD - GOD 15

MOVIN' GLOBE

Janne Rosenholm: v/k, Johan Englund: g/k, Roger Englund: g,
Peter Ljungberg: b, Lasse Johansson: d

Stockholm - Formed in 1984, influenced by bands like *Boston, Europe* and *Rush*. A good melodic hard rock single. Engineered by Christer Åkerberg (*Trettioåriga Kriget*). Split in 1987. Ljungberg is now in metal band *Eterno* and *Rough Rockers*.

1986 ■	I'll Be Fine/Wasted Summer	7"	CTR	CTR-686

1988 7" - MR 8802

MOZKOVITCH

Arvid Jonsson: v, Erik Wallberg: g, Frank Thunström: g,
Eric Nilsson: b, Andreas Sandberg: d

Falun - Named after a Russian car, *Mozkovitch*, this young five-piece won a contest as Sweden's best unsigned band in 2005, the same year they were formed. After recording a demo in 2006 they were picked up by BLP Records. The album is a killer recording filled with seventies sounding hard rock like a perfect mix of *Deep Purple* and *Thin Lizzy*. After the album the band found it impossible to co-operate with the label and the band started working on their own. The sound changed towards doomy psychedelic heavy rock. Now Thunström and keyboard player Marcus Olsson left the band. In 2009 they started writing more material, now leaning more towards the seventies progressive rock. Some great unreleased demos have been recorded. The track *Addiction Song* is featured on the *Demobanken 2006* (06 Studiefrämjandet) compilation.

2007 ■	MOZKOVITCH	CDd	BLP	BLP2007-04

2007 CDd - BLP2007-04

MR. DEATH

Jocke Lindström: v, Alex Stjärnfeldt: g, Stefan Lagergren: g,
Jörgen "Juck" Thullberg: b, Jonas Ohlsson: d

Stockholm - The band was formed in 2007 and made their first demo, *Unearthing*, in 2008. Only after having been up on MySpace for three days, the band was contacted by labels. Lagergren and Thullberg are both ex-*Treblinka*, *Tiamat* and *Expulsion*, Ohlsson is ex-*Septic Grave* and Lindström was previously in *Digression Assassins*. Old-school death metal.

2009 ☐	DETACHED FROM LIFE	CD	Agonia	ARcd065
2009 ☐	DETACHED FROM LIFE	CDd	Agonia	ARcd065d
	A5 size digi book. 1000 copies			
2010 ■	Death Suits You	MCD 6tr	Agonia	ARmcd014
2010 ☐	Death Suits You	10" 6tr	Agonia	ARmlp014
	300 copies			
2011 ☐	DESCENDING THROUGH ASHES	CD	Agonia	ARcd086
2011 ☐	DESCENDING THROUGH ASHES	LP	Agonia	ARlp080
	400 copies			
2011 ☐	DESCENDING THROUGH ASHES	LP	Agonia	ARlp080d
	100 copies inred vinyl.			

2010 MCD - ARmcd014

MR QUINN

Johan Paavola: v, Christer Lundgren: g, Urban Lundgren: k,
Jonas Wiik: b, Dag Holmgren: d

Skellefteå/Burträsk - Formed in 2008. However, Christer, Johan and Urban started playing together already in the 80s, in the band *Borderline*, who released one single. Johan and Dag played in colleagues *Ride The Sky* at the time. Great, classic hard rock quite similar to *Rhapsody (Sweden)*, or *Deep Purple* with a touch of *Asia*.

2013 ■	DREAM ON	CDp	private	(MRQ 001)

2013 CDp - (MRQ 001)

MR. TIGER

Börje Reinholdsson: v, Ulf Larsson: g, Fredrik Lindvall: k,
Mikael Reinholdsson: b, Lars Öhman: d

Umeå - Great high class AOR with slight influences of *Dan Reed* as well as traditional AOR. The vocals are in Swedish. The band later changed its name to *X-Union*. They dropped the keyboard player, turned a bit heavier and started singing in English. In 2004 Mikael Reinholdsson made his first release with solo-project *Balthazars Machine*, and a second one came in 2006. Also well worth checking out.

1992 ■ IDENTITET...ROCK `N ROLL ....CD Büms....................................... CD-34123

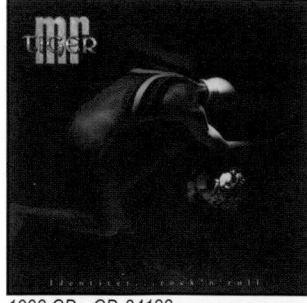

1992 CD - CD-34123

MRS. HIPPIE

Joacim Cans: v, Christian Smedström: g, Mika Vai: d

Göteborg - This is a side project by three guys way more known for their other bands, Joacim in *HammerFall*, Christian in *The Awesome Machine* and Mika in *Hardcore Superstar* and *Brassmonkey*. In 1994 Christian and Mika started writing and playing together. Joacim joined on vocals and they were helped out by Peter Iwers (*In Flames*) on bass. The album is a studio session made in 1996. The music is outstanding heavy stoner-oriented hard rock with Joacim's clean vocals as the icing on the cake.

2000 □ LOTUS ....CDd HF Records.............................HFCD-01
2000 ■ LOTUS ....CD Metal Blade (USA) 14332-2

2000 CD - 14332-2

MUD & BLOOD

Conny Lind: v, Christoffer Hofgaard: g, Michael Lundholm: g/b,
Tapio Kariranta: k, Jari Katila: d

Upplands Väsby - Christoffer and Jari found each other back in the 80s in the band *Vision*. Many stories later, *Mud & Blood* started taking form around 2010. Michael is ex-*OZ*, Conny has been in *Amaze Me* and *State Of Mind*, Jari in *Power* and Christoffer in *Trilogy*. Great heavy melodic hard rock with a seventies-meet-the eighties sound.

2013 ■ HIPPOPHONIC...CDp Hippo Records ....MnBC 001

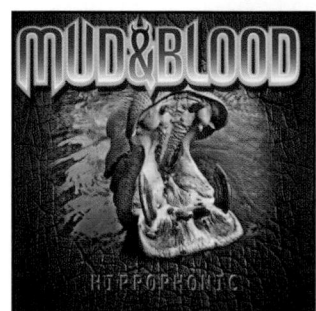

2013 CDp - MnBC 001

MUDDY ROAD

Daniel Axelsson: v, Björn Lindqvist: g, Magnus Danielsson: b, Ronny Lindqvist: d

Växjö - An interesting band with influences from the good old 70's hard rock. Magnus is also part of the band *Pyramid* that mostly play *Deep Purple* covers. Well worth checking out. Axelsson is today found in retro-rockers *Lemon Bird*.

1995 ■ Introspective..MCD 4tr Art Of Sound ....AOSP 101
    Tracks: Wild Rose/Seasons In Hell/Melody Rag/Days Of Hell.

1995 MCD - AOSP 101

MURDER CORPORATION

Johan Anderberg: v/b, Johan Axelsson: g, Rikard Wermén: d

Hjärup - The band was formed in 1995 when *Deranged* members Axelsson, Bengtsson and Wermén joined forces with *Mega Slaughter* singer Jens Johansson. After *Kill* Jens left and was replaced by Anderberg. In 1997 bass player Dan Bengtsson was relieved of his duties and Anderberg took over the bass, too. Death metal that flirts with traditional power metal and thrash. The first released was recorded only three weeks after the band was formed. *Whole Lotta Murdering Goin' On* is a compilation featuring tracks from their singles, compilations, covers and some previously unreleased material. After being picked up by Necropolis the band split and reformed with a new singer under the name *Killaman*, featuring Axelsson and Wermén.

2002 CDd - PSDL 9061-2

1996 □ Blood Revolution 2050...MCD 5tr Quabalah ....QAB 003
    Tracks: Bulls Eye Eight In The Head/Cybergenocide/Blood Revolution 2050/Point Blank
    Range/I Am In Hell
1998 ■ Kill ....MCD 6tr Planet End ....PE 001
    Tracks: Violated (Only Rage Remains)/9mm Lobotomy/Squeeze The Trigger/...Nameless/
    Die Laughing/Dog Heaven
1998 □ Retract The Hostile/Forced Into Regression ....7" Stormbringer ....SKULL 9802
1999 ■ Procreate Insanity/Vomitory Goes Pugh (split) ....7" 4tr Hangnail.............................HANGNAIL 001
    Split with Vomitory. Tracks: Procreate Insanity/Hostage Situation
1999 □ MURDER CORPORATION...CD Regain ....CDRR 9910-003
2000 □ SANTA IS SATAN (split)..CD Psychic Scream ....PSDL 9045-2
    Split with Grind Buto. Tracks: Fooled By The Fools/Muscle Of Madness/Predator/Children
    Of The Grave (Black Sabbath cover)/Out Of Bullets/12-Gauge Retaliation.
2000 □ WHOLE LOTTA MUDERING GOIN' ON ....CD Psychic Scream ....PSDL 9040-2
2001 □ TAGGED & BAGGED ....CD Displeased ....D 00087

1998 MCD - PE 001

| 2002 ■ | TAGGED & BAGGED | CDd | Psychic Scream (Malaysia) | PSDL 9061-2 |
| 2003 □ | MURDER CORPORATION | CD | CD-Maximum (Russia) | CDM 1103-1544 |

Bonus: Kill At Will/Breed Me. 2000 copies.

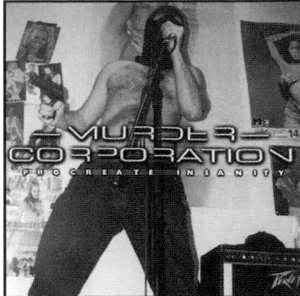

1999 7" - HANGNAIL 001

MURDER OF MY SWEET, THE
Angelica Rylin: v, Christopher Vetter: g, Teddy Westlund: b, Daniel Flores: d

Stockholm - Formed by Daniel Flores (*Mind's Eye, Cortex* etc). At first featuring singer Maria Rådsten (*Misth, One More Time*), who was replaced by Angelica. *The Murder Of My Sweet* sounds very much like *Within Temptation* meets *Evanescence*, poppy modern melodic metal with lots of keyboards. The second album saw guitarist Daniel Palmqvist replaced by Christopher Vetter and bass player Johan Niemann (*Evergrey, Therion*) replaced by Teddy Westlund. Furthermore keyboardist Andreas Lindahl was out of the band. In November 2012 Angelica announced she was recording a solo album pursuing her passion for AOR, to be released in 2013.

2009 □	Bleed Me Dry/(instrumental)/Sands Of Time	MCDp 3tr	Frontiers	FRPRCD 013
2009 □	DIVANITY	CD	Frontiers	FR CD 442
2009 □	DIVANITY	CDd	Frontiers	FR CD 442

Bonus: Bleed Me Dry (video)

| 2009 □ | DIVANITY | CD | Avalon Marquee (Japan) | MICP-18090 |

Bonus: Death Of A Movie Star

| 2012 ■ | BYE BYE LULLABY | CD | AFM Records | AFMCD 3989 |
| 2012 □ | BYE BYE LULLABY | CDd | AFM Records | AFMCD 3989 |

2012 CD - AFMCD 3989

MURDER SQUAD
Matti Kärkki: v, Ulf Cederlund: g, Richard Cabeza: b, Peter Stjärnvind: d

Stockholm - The band was already formed in 1993 under the name *Bonesaw*, covering old *Autopsy* tunes. The band took a break between 1996 and 1999. Matti is also found in *Dismember*, Richard was also a member of *Dismember* and ex-*Unanimated*, while Peter and Ulf were also found in *Entombed*. Musically this band produces music close to *Motörhead*-goes-death metal.

2001 ■	UNSANE, INSANE AND MENTALLY DERANGED	CD	Pavement Music	PVMT 32375
2003 □	RAVENOUS MURDEROUS	CD	Threeman Records	TRECD007
2013 □	Human Genocide (Autopsy cover)/Blackness Within	7"	Wolfsbane Records	WOLF 004

384 black and 116 copies on red vinyl. Numbered.

2001 CD - PVMT 32375

MURDERPLAN
Fredrik Söderlund: v, Pål Callmer: g,
Niklas Fridh: b Arnold Lindberg: d

Malmö - A short-lived death metal band in the vein of *Dismember* and *Carnage*. Söderlund is also in *Parnassus, Puissance, Algaion, Octinomos, Worshipper* and *Dismal*, while Callmer has been in *Supraload*. Lindberg has been in *Supraload* and *Jaggernaut*. Pål and Arnold started the band *Deathening* on the side, which finally took over.

| 2008 ■ | LET'S ROLL | CDd | Ascent | ASC 003 |

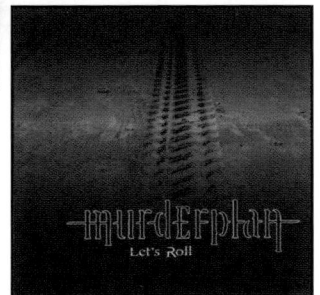

2008 CDd - ASC 003

MUSHROOM RIVER BAND, THE
Christian "Kryddan/Spice" Sjöstrand: v, Anders Linusson: g,
Alexander "Saso" Sekulovski: b, Christer Rockström: d

Värnamo - The band was founded in 1996 by Anders, Saso and Christer. Christian was first asked to guest on the first demo, but things went well and he was asked to join. The band recorded the demo *Rocketcrash* in 1998, later pressed on a 10". The second demo, entitled *No Quarter Recordings* was not made public. Great and heavy stoner-oriented hard rock. Christian is ex-*Spiritual Beggars* and later in *Spice & The RJ Band/Band of Spice*. Fredrik Finnander guests on lead-guitar on the first album. The song *Twin Lyrics#1* can be found on *Molten Universe Volume One* (1999 MU). In 2002 Christer left the band and was replaced by Robert Hansson.

| 1999 □ | Rocketcrash | 10" | Tea Pot | TPR 001 |

500 copies. Tracks: Lyrics #1/Super Insomnia/B.M/Loser's Blues

2000 □	MUSIC FOR THE WORLD BEYOND	CD	Meteor City (USA)	MCY 013
2000 □	MUSIC FOR THE WORLD BEYOND	CD	People Like You	PRISON 998-2
2000 □	MUSIC FOR THE WORLD BEYOND	LP	People Like You	PRISON 998-1
2001 □	MUSIC FOR THE WORLD BEYOND	CD	Victor (Japan)	VICP-61293

Bonus: Loser's Blues

2002 □	SIMSALABIM	CD	Century Media	77347 2
2002 □	SIMSALABIM	CD	Victor (Japan)	VICP 616178
2002 □	SIMSALABIM	CD	Meteor City (USA)	MCY 24

2002 CD - 77347 2

MUSTAIN

Johan Lindström: v/g, Marcus Stark: g, Johan Danielsson: b, Frank Kooistra: d

Falun - Formed in 2001, initially featuring drummer Patrik Blomström, who was replaced by Kooistra in 2002. Split in 2005, and Kooistra formed ***Billion Dollar Babies***. **Mustain** plays really high-quality, powerful thrash, quite similar in sound and style to Bush-era ***Anthrax***. A CD-R promo split, *The Clown Show*, together with ***Chainwreck***, was released in 2005. Lindström now sings in his brother's band ***Svarti Loghin***.

2003 ■	Dead Alive	MCD 4tr	Zombie House	ZH 01 DA 03	
	550 copies. Tracks: Dead Alive/I'm Within/Slowburn/Undone				

2003 MCD - ZH 01 DA 03

MUSTASCH

Ralf Gyllenhammar: v/g, David Johanesson: g,
Mats "Stam" Johansson: b, Danne McKenzie: d

Göteborg - On the island of Orust, outside of Göteborg, in 1998, that's when the band ***Mustasch*** started out. Singer Ralf (ex-***B-Thong***) actually started as an accordion player and was asked to join Swedish rock legend Rock Olga on tour at the age of fourteen, but his mother said "no". The initial line-up featured Ralf, Mats, guitarist Hannes Hansson and drummer Mats Hansson (ex-***Sonic Walthers***). Before the debut the band recorded a 5-track demo containing *Homophobic/Alcoholic, Coomber, Log, Muddy Waters* and *6:36*. Heavy stoner-ish power hard rock with grinding detuned guitars. The first album was similar to the heavy side of ***B-Thong***, while the second was a bit more diverse, ranging from almost ***Black Sabbath***-type riffs to ***The Cult***-influenced groove. A killer band, indeed! Trivia: The band appears in the commercials for Toyota Avansis and Ralf's uncle was the CEO of Volvo in Sweden. The song *Muddy Waters* can be found on *Burn The Streets Vol 1* (01 Daredevil) and *Taunus* on *Burned Down To Zero* (01 Daredevil). The unreleased track *Log* can be found on the bonus CD for *The Encyclopedia Of Swedish Hard Rock Vol 2*. After the album *Latest Version Of The Truth* Hannes Hansson left and was replaced by David Johannesson (ex-***Sparzanza***). In 2008 the live DVD *In The Night* was released. *Lowlife Highlights* is a compilation. *Singles A's & B's* is a collection of single tracks. In 2009 drummer Mats Hansson left for medical reasons, and Danne McKenzie stepped in. The band also switched label to Regain and the self-titled album received a Swedish Grammy award. *The New Sound Of The True West* contained rerecordings of old songs. In 2011 Ralf also made a guest appearance on the album *3* by ***Lillasyster***. In December 2011 drummer Danne McKenzie announced he was leaving the band. He was replaced by Jejo Percovic (ex-***Abstrakt Algebra, Candlemass, Brick***). In 2013 Ralf made his first solo release.
Website: www.mustasch.net

Sounds like Hell, but looks like... well...

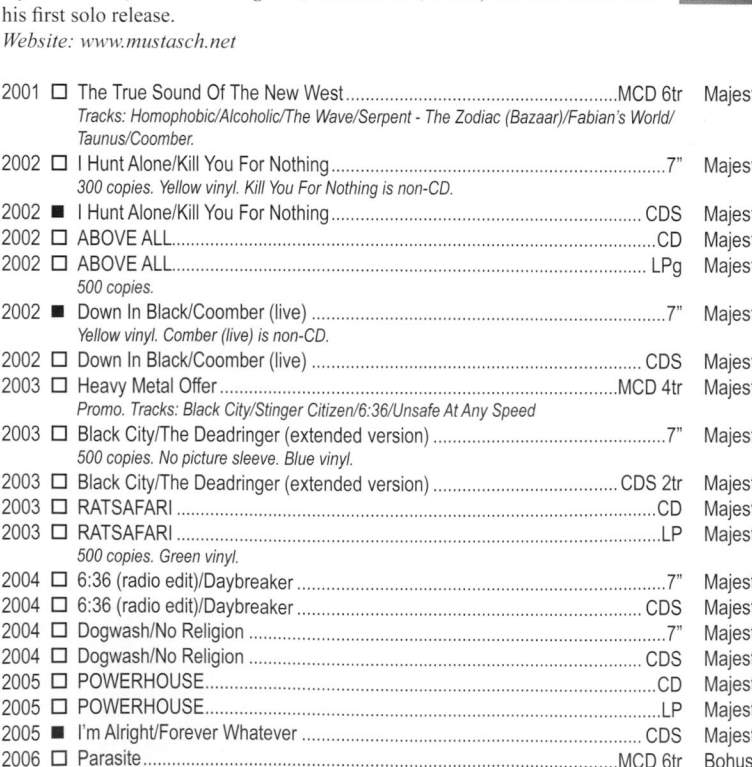

2001 □	The True Sound Of The New West	MCD 6tr	Majesty/EMI	7243 5 30866 2	
	Tracks: Homophobic/Alcoholic/The Wave/Serpent - The Zodiac (Bazaar)/Fabian's World/ Taunus/Coomber.				
2002 □	I Hunt Alone/Kill You For Nothing	7"	Majesty/EMI	MA 306	
	300 copies. Yellow vinyl. Kill You For Nothing is non-CD.				
2002 ■	I Hunt Alone/Kill You For Nothing	CDS	Majesty/EMI	7243 5 50297 2	
2002 □	ABOVE ALL	CD	Majesty/EMI	7243 5 38038 2	
2002 □	ABOVE ALL	LPg	Majesty/EMI	7243 5 38038 1	
	500 copies.				
2002 ■	Down In Black/Coomber (live)	7"	Majesty/EMI	MA 307	
	Yellow vinyl. Comber (live) is non-CD.				
2002 □	Down In Black/Coomber (live)	CDS	Majesty/EMI	724355 04832 5	
2003 □	Heavy Metal Offer	MCD 4tr	Majesty/EMI	CDPRO 4331	
	Promo. Tracks: Black City/Stinger Citizen/6:36/Unsafe At Any Speed				
2003 □	Black City/The Deadringer (extended version)	7"	Majesty/EMI	MA 314	
	500 copies. No picture sleeve. Blue vinyl.				
2003 □	Black City/The Deadringer (extended version)	CDS 2tr	Majesty/EMI	7243 5 52962 2	
2003 □	RATSAFARI	CD	Majesty/EMI	94188 2	
2003 □	RATSAFARI	LP	Majesty/EMI	MA 315	
	500 copies. Green vinyl.				
2004 □	6:36 (radio edit)/Daybreaker	7"	Majesty/EMI	94188 2	
2004 □	6:36 (radio edit)/Daybreaker	CDS	Majesty/EMI	7243 548512 2	
2004 □	Dogwash/No Religion	7"	Majesty/EMI	??	
2004 □	Dogwash/No Religion	CDS	Majesty/EMI	7243 8 72909 2	
2005 □	POWERHOUSE	CD	Majesty/EMI	3 30719 2	
2005 □	POWERHOUSE	LP	Majesty/EMI	3 30719 1	
2005 ■	I'm Alright/Forever Whatever	CDS	Majesty/EMI	0946 344627 2 3	
2006 □	Parasite	MCD 6tr	Bohus Entertainment	BE 002	
	Tracks: Nailed to pain/My Disorder/Do Or Die/Parasite/Kill The Light/The Dagger (live)				
2006 □	Parasite	MCD 6tr	Regain Records	RR 110	

2002 CDS - 7243 5 50297 2

2002 CDS - MA 307

2005 CDS - 0946 344627 2 3

Year		Title	Format	Label	Cat. No.
2006	☐	THE LATEST VERSION OF THE TRUTH	CD+DVD	Regain Records	RR 113-1
		Bonus DVD containing video clips and the making of			
2006	☐	THE LATEST VERSION OF THE TRUTH	CD	Avalon Marquee (Japan)	MICP-10688
		Bonus: Once A Liar			
2006	☐	THE LATEST VERSION OF THE TRUTH	CD	Regain Records	RR 113
2007	☐	Double Nature/(radio edit)	CDS	Regain Records	RR 123
2007	☐	Bring Me Everyone (radio edit)/Forever Begins Today (radio edit)	CDS 2tr	Regain Records	0701
2008	☐	LOWLIFE HIGHLIGHTS	CD	Regain Records	RR 131
2008	☐	Spreading The Worst/Once A Liar/Double Nature	MCD 3tr	Regain Records	RR 152
2008	☐	Spreading The Worst/Once A Liar/Double Nature	MCD 3tr	Phantom (UK)	797451
2009	☐	SINGLES A'S & B'S	CD	Majesty	5099 6 95033 2
2009	☐	I'm Frustrated (radio edit)/The Audience Is Listening	CDS	Nuclear Blast (promo)	NB 2538-2
2009	☐	Mine/Mine (instrumental)	CDS	Regain Records	5051865-621324
2009	☐	MUSTASCH	CD	Regain Records	7320470-116395
2009	■	MUSTASCH	CD	Nuclear Blast (USA)	873247
		Bonus: Mine (instrumental). Different artwork.			
2011	☐	THE NEW SOUND OF THE TRUE WEST	CD	Gain	GPCD 80
2011	☐	THE NEW SOUND OF THE TRUE WEST	LP	Gain	GPCD 80VL
2012	☐	SOUNDS LIKE HELL, LOOKS LIKE HEAVEN	CD	Flying Dolphin (Germany)	FDDL 0006
2012	☐	SOUNDS LIKE HELL, LOOKS LIKE HEAVEN	LPg	Gain	8869193-1271
2012	☐	SOUNDS LIKE HELL, LOOKS LIKE HEAVEN	CD	Gain	8869193-1272

2009 CD - 873247

MUTANT
Henrik Ohlsson: v, Peter Lake: g/b

Sandviken - **Mutant** were formed in 1998 as a dark and evil side project from their main band **Theory In Practice**. Their first demo was entitled *Eden Burnt To Ashes*. Style-wise the band could be labeled as black metal, but without the satanic lyrics, corpse paint and devilry.

Year		Title	Format	Label	Cat. No.
1998	☐	Eden Burnt To Ashes	MCD 5tr	private	H3
		Tracks: Demon World/Beyond Bet Durrabia/Eden Burnt To Ashes/Dark Spheres/Abduct To Mutate			
2000	■	THE AEONIC MAJESTY	CD	Listenable	POSH 019

2000 CD - POSH 019

MY DEAR ADDICTION
Kim Lindstén: v, Varg Strand: g, Jonas Paulsson: g,
Daniel Forsén: b, Peter Karlsson: d

Älmhult - Who knew the change of name would make such a difference? After ten years of rehearsals and struggling, original members Lindstén and Parkeborn finally had some results when changing the name from **Blind** to **My Dear Addiction**. They also changed guitarists from Sven Wolf and Magnus Larsson to Varg Strand (ex-**Misteltein, Fall Ov Serafim**) and Jonas Paulsson. In 2009 they were picked up by Supernova Records and finally recorded their debut. Melodic death metal mixing growl and clean vocals, a bit similar to **Scar Symmetry** and **Blinded Colony**. Karlsson is ex-**Sanzia** and **Zap Yankefy**.

Year		Title	Format	Label	Cat. No.
2010	■	NEW BLOOD	CD	Supernova	SUPERCD14

2010 CD - SUPERCD 14

MY ENDLESS WISHES
Frida Viberg: v, Martin Viberg: g, Fredrik Pernros: g,
Magnus Källström: b, Erik Ekestubbe: d

Lindesberg (Örebro) - Formed in 2005 by the Viberg's, influenced by bands like **Within Temptation** and **Evanescence**. The line-up was however not final until 2009. Decent, but quite anonymous modern melodic metal. Some slight flaws in the production, but not bad. The track *Never Walk Alone*, from the band's 2009 demo, was featured on the *Ultra Pop Overdose* compilation in the US. Pernros was also found in **Azure**.

Year		Title	Format	Label	Cat. No.
2013	■	MY ENDLESS WISHES	CD	Dolittle Group	DOOCD 008

2013 CD - DOOCD 008

MY OWN GRAVE
Mikael Aronsson: v, Anders Härén: g, Stefan Kihlgren: g,
Max Bergman: b, John Henriksson: d

Sundsvall - **My Own Grave** were formed in the northern town Timrå in April 2001 by Härén, Bergman and Henriksson. The band released four demos before being picked up by Karmageddon Media in 2004. The debut, *Unleash*, was recorded at Necromorbus Studio by Sverker "Widda" Widgren (**Demonical, Diabolical**). When Karmageddon folded the band was picked up by Pulverised who released the next outing, *Unholy*, which proved to be a darker more death metal-oriented platter. The band's next album was produced by Dan Swanö. Aronsson is also found in **Cavevomit** and Henriksson was part of **Angtoria**. The track *My Own Grave* is also featured on the compilation *Hordes Of Darkness* (03 Unexploded Records).

2006 MCD - ASH 028

2006 □	UNLEASH	CD	Karmageddon		KARMA 099
2006 ■	Unholy	MCD 5tr	Pulverised		ASH 028

Tracks Buried/Above The Weak/Beneath Dark Waves/God Forbid/Cross After Cross. First version in slipcase, 200 copies.

2007 □	Unholy	MCDd 5tr	Pulverised		ASH 028
2009 ■	UNLEASH - EXTENDED & REMASTERED	CD	Pulverised		ASH 058 CD
2009 □	NECROLOGY	CD	Pulverised		ASH 059 CD

2009 CD - ASH 058 CD

MYKORRHIZA

Henrik "Hempa" Brynolfsson: g/b, Martin Karlsson: d

Stockholm - It all started in 2001, when Hempa tried to resurrect his old band *Excruciate*, but the rest weren't committed. Instead he drafted drummer Karlsson (*Sin, Stairland, Bloodshed, Blackshine, The Cauterized*) and started *Mykorrhiza*, initially as a grind core band, but going into the death metal mode instead. The vocals on the first two releases were handled by *Blackshine/Necrophobic* singer Anders Strokirk, while on the third release the band used Lars Levin (*Excruciate, Mastication*), Tor Adolfsson (*Encined*), Matilda Karlsson and Siri Hagfors. *Mykorrhiza* produces a nice mix of death metal, heavy metal and thrash, even with some proggy moments. The band's third album Immortal Blood is recorded and ready, now featuring Strokirk and Paul "Themgoroth" Mäkitalo (Dark Funeral) on vocals.

2002 □	Mykorrhiza	MCD 5tr	Konqueror		KR 001

Tracks: Going Away/Consume/Another Dimension/Into War/No Resurrection

2003 ■	SHATTERED DREAMS	CD	Konqueror		KR 002
2006 □	NORTHERN REMEMBRANCE	CD	Konqueror		KR 009

2003 CD - KR 002

MYRAH

Patrik Essman: v/g, Tobias Lepistö: g, Josefin Berg: k,
Micael Svan: b, Natalie Duarte: d

Östersund - *Myrah* were formed in 2005, originally named *Myra*, under which name they recorded the single *Smelling Your Fear*. In 2007 they changed their name to *Myrah*, drafted a new drummer and recorded the EP *Death & Despair*. In 2010, they released their first album *Six Feet Down*. After this drummer Joakim Granvold was replaced by Duarte. The band produces heavy goth in the vein of *Amorphis* and *Paradise Lost*.

2010 □	SIX FEET DOWN	CD	private		MP 001
2012 ■	MY DELIVERANCE	CD	Rambo		MM 001

2012 CD - MM 001

MYSTERY

Roger Lindroth: v, Janne Lenell: g, Conny Kokkonen: k,
Peder Skoglund: b, Stefan Svensson: d

Sundsvall - This is a good, solid melodic AOR/hard rock band with strong guitars and plenty of keyboards. Not bad at all. This band is not to be confused with the pop band with the same name. In 1990 they started playing covers, but returned to writing their own material. Stefan was replaced by André Nyvoll and Conny switched his keyboards for a guitar. The style changed towards powerful sleazy hard rock and in 1993 they recorded a 5 track CD. They released it in 1994 under the new name *Lovebone*.

1988 ■	Do You, Do I/Two Hearts	7"	Active Music		HEJ S 031

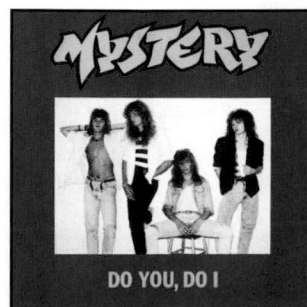
1988 7" - HEJ S 031

MÅNEGARM

Erik Grawsjö: v/b/d, Markus Andé: g, Jonas Almquist: g, Jacob Hallegren: d

Norrtälje - Formed in 1995, initially featuring singer Svenne Rosendahl and guitarist Mårten Matsson (ex-*Scab*). They first went by the name *Antikrist* and changed it to *Månegarm* (a wolf in the old Norse mythology) in time for the first demo *Vargaresa*, where Matsson had been replaced. The line-up featured Rosendahl, Almquist, Andé, Pierre Wilhelmsson and Grawsjö. In 1997 a second demo, *Ur nattvindar*, was recorded. The demo contains the first song they ever recorded in English, entitled *Daughters Of Eve* and can be downloaded from the band's site. Now Johnny Wranning (*Miscreant, Ebony Tears, Dog Faced Gods, Eyetrap*) replaced Rosendahl. The first album was recorded in Studio Sunlight and the vocals were now handled by Viktor Hemgren (*Construcdead, Sorg, Maze Of Torment*). On *Havets Vargar*, recorded in Studio Underground, the line-up featured Almquist, Grawsjö, Andé and Wilhelmsson. Musically the band produces ultra speed death metal with Swedish vocals and a strong asgard/viking theme. The EP *Ur-minnes hävd*, featuring Janne Liljeqvist on cello and violin, was recorded together with folk band *Två Fisk Och En Fläsk*. Janne was a member of *Månegarm* on *Nordstjärnans tidsålder*. On the 2013 release Jacob Hallegren (*Angrepp*) was added on drums and Pierre Wilhelmsson was out of the band.

1998 CD - D 00057

1998 ■	NORDSTJÄRNANS TIDSÅLDER	CD	Displeased		D 00057
2000 □	HAVETS VARGAR	CD	Displeased		D 00069

2004 LP - D 00137-1

2003 ☐	NORDSTJÄRNANS TIDSÅLDER	CD	Irond (Russia)	CD 0703-1443	
2003 ☐	DÖDSFÄRD	CD/d	Displeased	D 00116	
2004 ☐	VARGRESA – THE BEGINNING	CD	Displeased	D 00137	
2004 ■	VARGRESA – THE BEGINNING	LP	Displeased	D 00137-1	
2005 ☐	VREDENS TID	CD/d	Displeased	D 00140	
2006 ☐	Urminnes hävd – The Forest Sessions	MCD 7tr	Displeased	D 00148	

Tracks: Intro/Himmelsfursten/Utfärd/Älvatrans/Hemkomst/Döden/Vaggvisa

2007 ☐	Genom världar nio	CDS 1tr	Black Lodge (promo)	BLODPR45CD	
2007 ☐	VARGSTENEN	CD	Black Lodge	BLOD 045 CD	
2007 ■	VARGSTENEN	CDd	Black Lodge	BLOD 045 CDL	

Bonus: Tba

2007 ☐	VARGSTENEN	LP PD	Black Lodge	BLOD 045 PD	
2007 ☐	VARGSTENEN	CD	Mutilation Records (Brazil)	MUTP 018	
2008 ☐	VARGSTENEN	CD	Irond (Russia)	CD 08-1393	
2009 ☐	NATTVÄSEN	CD	Regain Records	RR 159	
2013 ☐	LEGIONS OF THE NORTH	CD	Napalm Records	NPR 486	

2007 CDd - BLOD 045 CDL

MÅNLJUS
Å Haglund, P Selin, C Andersson, K D Davidsson

Edsbyn (?) - The A-side starts out as an uptempo AOR-track, to suddenly change tempo into a heavier but still very melodic rocker. The B-side starts off with keyboards similar to *Hold The Line* but the rest offers very little resemblance. Very melodic rock with a strong Christian message. Vocals below average. The names are of the composers.

1981 ■	Stopp! Stanna!/Tiden	7"	Rondo	RON 101	

1981 7" - RON 101

MÅRRAN
Göran Edman: v, Ludwig Larsson: g, Morgan Korsmoe: b,
Max Lorentz: k, Björn "Binge" Inge: d

Dark and mysterious

2012 CDd - MÅRR 001

2012 MCDpg MarrEP001

2012 CDd - MÅRR 002

2013 7" - MÅRRAN 7001 (#173)

Stockholm/Älvdalen - *Mårran* are a new retro band that builds on the legacy of Swedish heavy rock forefathers *November*. Even though Larsson and Korsmoe are young guys, they are surrounded by guys that have been there and done that. Göran (here singing in Swedish) is ex-*Malmsteen*, *Madison*, *Glory*, *Norum*, *Kharma* etc., Björn is ex-*November*, while Max has played with Swedish pop/rockers like Pugh Rogefeldt, Mats Ronander and Ulf Lundell. *Mårran* plays vintage, dynamic, analogue-sounding riff-oriented retro hard rock with big drums, cool guitars and great vocals. Highly recommended. The single version of *Gärdesbrud* is a different mix than on the album. *Mårran - Vid liv* is a live recording, where the band was also reinforced by former *November* colleague Rickard Rolf. The band released the second album within the same year and when released, *Mårran 3* was already halfway written!
Website: www.marran.se

2011 ☐	Gärdesbrud	CDS	private	mårrprom 001	
2012 ■	MÅRRAN	CDd	S-Rock	MÅRR 001	
2012 ■	Mårran - Vid liv	MCDpg 4tr	S-Rock	MarrEP001	

Tracks: Roadie/Kom i in min värld/Med Lena/Ensamma stränder

2012 ■	MÅRRAN 2	CDd	S-Rock	MÅRR 002	
2012 ☐	MÅRRAN	LPg	S-Rock	MÅRR LP-001	

500 hand numbered copies.

2013 ■	Skasilverland/Nattens kristall	7"	S-Rock	MÅRRAN 7001	

300 copies with unique hand painted sleeves. (Number 173 and 203 are depicted)

2013 7" - MÅRRAN 7001 (#203)

MÖRK GRYNING

Johan Ljung: v, Jonas "Goth Gorgon" Berndt: b/g/k,
Peter "Draakh Kimera" Nagy: v/g/k/d, Fredrik Boëthius: g,
Henrik Hedberg: g, Johan Larsson: k, Carl-Gustav "C-G" Bäckström: d

Stockholm - Formed by Jonas "Goth Gorgon" Berndt and Peter "Draakh Kimera" Nagy in 1994 and recorded a first demo in 1994. Very fast, but still pompous black metal with lots of variations. Light-weight death metal if you will. On the debut some of the lyrics are in English, but most of them are written in mediaeval Swedish. Very "evil" vocals, more or less indecipherable. Production by Dan Swanö. Peter was also found in **Hypocrite**, **Eternal Oath** and **Wyvern**. *Return Fire* contains a cover of **Slayer**'s *Necrophiliac*. The band recorded a cover of **Venom**'s *Leave Me In Hell* for the tribute album *In The Sign Of The Horns: A Tribute To Venom* (2000 Dwell Records) and **Kreator**'s *Storming The Menace* for *Under The Guillotine: Tribute To Kreator* (2001 Dwell Records). On *Pieces Of Primal Expressionism* the band became a trio, adding keyboard player Johan "Aeon" Larsson. In 2005 the band recorded the final demo, before disbanding. The band however soon reunited without Nagy, but with a full line-up to record the final self-titled album. Now adding singer Johan Ljung (**Blackmoon**, as Hellterror), guitarist Henrik Hedberg, bass player Fredrik Boëthius and drummer Carl-Gustaf Bäckström (**Sectu, Amarath, Hypocrite, Wyvern**). After the album Ljung, Hedberg, Larsson, Bäckström and Boëthius (now on guitar) formed the band **C.B. Murdoc**, who have recorded two albums.

How dark is the dawn

1995	☐	1000 ÅR HAR GÅTT	CD	No Fashion	NFR 012
1997	☐	RETURN FIRE	CD	No Fashion	NFR 022
2001	☐	MAELSTROM CHAOS	CD	No Fashion	NFRCD 53
2001	☐	MAELSTROM CHAOS	CDd	No Fashion	NFRDG 53
2003	■	PIECES OF PRIMAL EXPRESSIONISM	CD	No Fashion	NFR 062
		Slipcase			
2005	☐	MÖRK GRYNING	CD	Black Lodge	BLOD 034 CD
2005	☐	MÖRK GRYNING	CDd	Black Lodge	BLOD 034 DG
		Different artwork.			

2003 CD - NFR 062

MÖRKER

Andreas "Ascaroth" Axelsson: v, Grimner: g/b,
Tommi "Larssa" Larsson : k, Niklas "Nicke" Pelli: d

Örebro/Degerfors/Haparanda - Formed under the monicker **Bloody Scream**. Musically well-played and quite melodic black metal with screeching Norwegian-style growls. Larsson (**Darkness Falls, No Armor**) and Pelli (**Nordic Necropolis**) are also in **Cryptic Death**. Axelsson also runs Ancient Path Records. The band has previously also featured guitarist David "Natt" Larsson (ex-**Självmord**). In 2005 the demo *Den sista utfärden* followed up the untitled 2004 debut demo.

2007 CD - NSP 035

2006	☐	DEN SISTA UTFÄRDEN/SEIL PÅ SKYGGANS HAV (split)	LP	Northern Silence	NSP 023
		Split with Draugsang. 500 copies, first 100 with patch.			
2007	☐	SKUGGORNAS RIKE	CDd	Northern Silence	NSP 035
		200 numbered.			
2007	■	SKUGGORNAS RIKE	CD	Northern Silence	NSP 035
2008	☐	HÖSTMAKTER	CDd	Northern Silence	NSP 070
		1000 in A5 size cover			
2008	☐	HÖSTMAKTER	LPg	Northern Silence	NSP 070
		300 black+ 200 splatter, 66 splatter+CD. Poster.			
2008	■	HÖSTMAKTER	CD	Northern Silence	NSP 070

2008 CD - NSP 070

MÖRRUM'S OWN

Mattias Osbäck: v, Janne Stark: g/b, Peter "TrumPeter" Svensson: d

Mörrum - This was just a one-off project created to write and record a song for local hockey team Mörrum's GoIS. The heavy metal version of the Swedish national hymn *Du gamla du fria* came about when Janne was given the task to arrange a heavy metal version to be performed at a rock festival. The result was **Locomotive Breath** backing Swedish drummer/comedian/singer Janne "Loffe" Karlsson (**Hansson & Karlsson**). A studio version featuring Janne and drummer Peter Svensson from **Locomotive Breath**, plus "Loffe" was recorded as a bonus track. "Loffe" also does some chanting in the track *Mörrum Ka'*, where **Locomotive Breath** singer Mattias Osbäck handles the lead vocals. Backing vocals were provided by Håkan Windahl (**Interaction**) and Mikael Loorenz (**Killerhawk**).

2007	■	Mörrum Ka'	MCDp 4tr	Sweden Rock Records	MCD1
		Tracks: Mörrum Ka'/Du gamla du fria + two tracks by Hockeybandet/Nöjeskompaniet.			
		Numbered			

2007 MCDp - MCD1

N.J.B.

Urban Henriksson: v, Peter "P-Son" Andersson: g,
Stefan Johansson: g, Lars Dannesäter: b, Roger Gustafsson: d

Mönsterås - Formed under the name *Night Jamming Band* in 1983, then shortened it to *N.J.B.* the year after. P-son also played with the band *Meadow* for two four-month periods at a bar in Puerto La Cruise and in 1989 he quit *N.J.B.* The cover states Roger Gustafsson as drummer, but it was actually George "Jolle" Atlagic (*The Quill*) who played on the recording. The band folded in 1990. The recordings contain high-quality melodic hard rock/metal, similar to early *Europe*. Good vocals, high-quality musicianship and a fat sound make this a safe buy. In 2013 Greek label No remorse released the *Anthology* CD featuring all the *N.J.B* recordings.

1986 ■ Soldier Of Love/Runaway ....7" private ....S 001
1988 ☐ HEROES..LP Büms...101 23
2013 ☐ ANTHOLOGY ....CD No Remorse................................n/a

1986 7" - S 001

NADIR

Gunnar Janupe: v, Roger Kääpää: g, Håkan Olofsson: g,
Kristian Östergren: b, Micael "Mikkey Dee" Delaoglou: d

Göteborg - This might not be one of the heaviest bands this country has produced, although the guitar work is biting at times. I guess I'd describe them as the missing link between *Magnum Bonum* and *Thin Lizzy*. They were formed in 1980. Keyboards on the second single were played by Mats Olausson (*Motvind, Yngwie Malmsteen, Glory* etc). The band split in 1984, when Micael (later known as Mikkey Dee) moved to Denmark to join *Geisha*. He joined *King Diamond Band* later the same year and stayed with them until 1988, when he went to *Dokken*. He was then a member of *Dokken*, *WWIII* and *Motörhead* at the same time, before joining the latter full time, where he is still found. He was also a member of *W.A.S.P* (with Blackie, Johnny and Chris) for a few chaotic months. Roger is found in dance band *Miami*. Janupe later joined *Snowstorm* and he is found in cover band *Partypatrullen* together with Imre Daun (*Don Patrol, The Black* etc).

1982 7" - NADS 001   *1983 7" - PTS 326*

1982 ■ Snön Faller Ner/Ett Nytt Försök ....7" private ....NADS 001
1983 ■ Frusna Tårar/Sommar......................................7" Protape ....PTS 326

NAE'BLIS

Magnus Wohlfart: v/g/b/d

Höör - This is the solo project of *Yggdrasil*-man Wohlfart, initiated in 2004. Wohlfart is also found in bands like *Dibbukim, Broken Dagger, Anti-Christian Assault* and *Folkearth*. The name, *Nae'blis*, comes from the description of evil in Islam. It's also found in author Robert Jordan's series *The Wheel of Time*. The first two albums were depressing, quite varied black metal, ranging from soft piano pieces to full on quite (as should be?) badly mixed old-school black metal with screeching vocals quite far in the background, while the latest album was all acoustic and more ambient.

2004 CD - NC 086

2004 ■ BEYOND THE LIGHT ....CD No Colours.............................NC 086
2004 ☐ BEYOND THE LIGHT ....LP No Colours.............................NC 086
  Bonus: A Sign Of Things To Come. 200 copies. Different artwork.
2006 ☐ DEATH OF MANKIND... A DREAM (split) ....CD Northern Silence .... NSP 037
  Split with Dominion. Tracks: The Death Of Mankind Part I/Part II/Part III/Lost And Forgotten
2006 ☐ DEATH OF MANKIND... A DREAM (split).................CDd Northern Silence .... NSP 037
  200 copies.
2007 ■ SKETCHES OF REALITY.......................................CD Northern Silence .... NSP 048
  Available as regular CD and 100 numbered copies in metal case including patch.
2008 ☐ SKETCHES OF REALITY.......................................LP Northern Silence .... NSP 048
  250 black, 250 clear, 100 clear with patch.
2010 ☐ CONFUSION AND APATHY – IN A FOG OF SURREAL DAYDREAM..........CD Grand Master Music ....GMM 007

2007 CD - NSP 048

NAGAZAKI

Lars Hjelm: v, Tomas Ylivaimo: g, Bernt Olovsson: g,
Mårten Sandberg: b, Staffan Ström: d

Piteå - Great self-financed single in the style of early *Silver Mountain*, with slight hints of *Maiden*-esque twin-guitar work. Mårten later moved to Stockholm and played with *Hexenhaus, Fifth Reason* and *Memento Mori*, then under the name "Marty Marteen". Tomas recorded an album with the band *Burn* and Hjelm has been found in *Phoenix* and *Autumn Lords*.

1986 ■ You Can Be/Nobody..7" MS ....NAGA 001

1986 7" - NAGA 001

NAGLFAR

Kristoffer "Wrath" Olivius: v, Marcus E. "Vargher" Norman: g, Andreas Nilsson: g

Umeå - Not to be confused with German band *Nagelfar*. The band name comes from the ship in the Norse mythology made out of human fingernails and toenails of the dead. The band was formed in 1992 by Jens Rydman (ex-*Ancient Wisdom*) and Kristoffer Olivius under the name *Uninterred*. The first demo *Stella Trajectio* was recorded in 1994. It was followed by the demo *We Are Naglfar - Fuck You!* in 1995, which resulted in a deal with Wrong Again and the debut album *Vittra*. Drums on the first demo were supposed to be played by Ulf Andersson of *Nocturnal Rites*, but he couldn't do the job and a drum machine was used. The line-up on the debut featured Jens, Kristoffer, Andreas (ex-*Ancient Wisdom*), guitarist Morgan Hansson (*Havayoth*) and drummer Mattias Holmgren (later in *Embracing Shadows*, *Tired Tree*, *Azure*). The album was recorded at Studio Abyss and produced by Peter Tägtgren. Featuring new drummer Mattias, they recorded the 7" in 1997, and the year after, the second and more intense *Diabolical* was released. In 2000 guitarist Morgan Hansson left the band and was replaced by ex-*Bewitched* man Vargher. The band contributes on an *Iron Maiden* tribute with the track *The Evil That Men Do*. A demo version of *12th Rising* can be found on the *Statements Of Intent* compilation (Wicked World '99). In 2005 founder Rydén left the band to study in Stockholm, and Olivius, who also handled lead vocals in *Setherial*, took over the vocals. Peter Morgan Lie entered on bass on *Harvest*. On *Téras* the line-up only features Norman, Olivius and Nilsson, seeing drummer Mattias Grahn out of the band. Unlike many other death metal bands *Naglfar* have not become more melodic or proggish through the years. The band still delivers uncompromising, fast and furious death metal the same way they always have.
Website: www.naglfar.net

1995 CD - WAR 008

1998 CD - WAR 005

2002 MCD - NewH 002-2

2003 CD - NewH 005-2

2007 CD - 8277-2

2012 7" - 998182-1

Year		Title	Format	Label	Catalogue
1995	■	VITTRA	CD	Wrong Again Records	WAR 008
1995	□	VITTRA	LP PD	Wrong Again Records	- -
		1000 copies.			
1997	□	When Autumn Storms Come/The Brimstone Gate	7" PD	War	W1
1998	□	VITTRA	CD	Toy's Factory (Japan)	TCFK-87159
		Bonus: 12th Rising (demo)			
1998	■	DIABOLICAL	CD	WAR	WAR 005
1998	□	DIABOLICAL	LP PD	WAR	WAR 005
1998	□	DIABOLICAL	CD	Relapse Records (USA)	RR 6412-2
1998	□	DIABOLICAL	CD	Toy's Factory (Japan)	TFCK-87158
2002	■	Ex Inferis	MCD 5tr	New Hawen	NewH 002-2
		Tracks: Of Gorgons Spawned Through Witchcraft/Emerging From Her Weeping (rerecorded)/Dawn Of Eternity (Massacre cover)/When Autumn Storms Come/The Brimstone Gate			
2002	□	Ex Inferis	MCD 5tr	Century Media (USA)	8003-2
2002	□	VITTRA	CD	Regain Records	RR 001-AS
		Bonus: 12 Rising/The Evil Thas Men Do (Iron Maiden cover)/Pleasure To Kill (Kreator cover)			
2002	□	VITTRA	LP	Regain Records	RRLP 001-AS
		Bonus: 12 Rising			
2003	□	SHEOL	CD	Toy's Factory (Japan)	TFCK-87299
2003	□	SHEOL	CD	Century Media (USA)	8014-2
2003	□	SHEOL	LP	New Hawen	NewH 005-1
2003	□	SHEOL	LP PD	New Hawen	NewH 005-1
		500 copies. In sleeve.			
2003	■	SHEOL	CD	New Hawen	NewH 005-2
2005	□	PARIAH	CD	Century Media (USA)	8314-2
2005	□	PARIAH	CD	Fono (Russia)	FO506CD
2005	□	PARIAH	CD	Century Media	77502-2
2005	□	PARIAH	CDd	Century Media	77502-8
2005	□	PARIAH	LP	Century Media	77502-1
2007	■	HARVEST	CD	Century Media (USA)	8277-2
2007	□	HARVEST	CD+DVD	Century Media (USA)	8277-2
2007	□	HARVEST	CD	Century Media	77577-2
2007	□	HARVEST	LPg	Century Media	77577-1
		500 copies red + 500 black vinyl. Poster.			
2007	□	HARVEST	CD+DVD	Century Media	77577-0
2007	□	DIABOLICAL	CD	Regain Records (USA)	REG-CD-1025
2007	□	VITTRA	CD	Regain Records (USA)	REG-CD-1026
		Bonus: 12th Rising/The Evil Thas Men Do (Iron Maiden cover)/Pleasure To Kill (Kreator cover)			
2007	□	HARVEST	CD+DVD	Toy's Factory (Japan)	TFCK-87413
		Bonus: Necrospiritus			
2007	□	DIABOLICAL	CD	Regain Records (USA)	REG-CD-1025
2011	□	VITTRA	LPg	Floga Records	FL 35
		100 clear/black splatter + 400 black vinyl. Bonus: 12th Rising (demo)			
2012	■	An Extension Of His Arm And Will/As Long as They Fear	7"	Century Media	998182-1
		300 black, 100 transparent red and 100 white vinyl (exclusive for North America). Hand numbered.			
2012	□	TÉRAS	CD	Century Media (USA)	18796-2

2012 ☐	TÉRAS	.CD	Century Media	998096-2
2012 ☐	TÉRAS	.2LP	Century Media	998096-1

Bonus: Tired Bones. Red/black marbled vinyl and black vinyl.

2012 ☐	TÉRAS	.CDd	Century Media	998096-8

Bonus: Tired Bones. Patch.

2007 CD - NAKD 6603

NAKED

Petri Vehviläinen: v, Mats Stattin: g, Ronny Zander: g/b, Mike Roos: d

Stockholm - *Naked* started out as a studio project by Stattin, but evolved into a full line-up. The band made one live show, then featuring Vehviläinen, Stattin, guitarist Daniel Nellänge, bassist Anders Nyberg and drummer Anton Klaesen. The album was produced by Tony Borg (*Alien*). Petri participated in the Swedish Idol in 2010. Eighties-style melodic hard rock in the vein of *Europe* and *Bonfire*.

2007 ■	GET NAKED	.CD	Stattin Music & Design	NAKD 6603

NARDUZ

Christer Lindgren: v/g, Tomas Jonsson: g, David Larsson: b, Jan Lindh: d

Edsbyn - One side is decent rocking hard rock with quite weak vocals, while the second side is a ballad. Lindh later joined *Candlemass*.

1983 ■	Vägar utan slut/Hur ska jag få dig att förstå?	.7"	private	UAs 001

1983 7" - UAs 001

NARNIA

Germán Pascual: v, Carl Johan Grimmark: g/b/k. Martin Claesson (Härenstam): k. Andreas Olsson: b. Andreas Johansson: d

Christian (and) rockers.

Jönköping/Stockholm - *Narnia* were formed in 1996 by former *Borderline* and *Modest Attraction* singer Christian Liljegren (aka Rivel) and guitarist Carl Johan "CJ" Grimmark. The latter was ex-*Sentinel* and was also found in a late version of *Modest Attraction*, where he temporarily replaced Stephan Molin on tour. The initial line-up featured Christian, CarlJohan, bass player Jakob Persson, keyboardist Linus Kåse and drummer Fredrik Junhammar. The latter was replaced by Andreas Johansson in 1997. *Awakening* is a platter in the true *Dio*-meets-Malmsteen-vein, with Carl Johan showing he's learned from the master. Janne Stark is doing a guest solo on the track *Shadows From The Past* on the album, while Carl Johan was returning the favour on Janne's band *Locomotive Breath*'s album *Train Of Events*. The second album was still in the same vein, while *Desert Land* was a bit more straight metal, still with a neoclassical touch though. In my opinion this was their best effort so far. In 1999 Christian started working on a solo-project called *Wisdom Call*, while Calle recorded a song for the Yngwie Malmsteen-tribute with a different singer, both now found in Calles *Dio/Sabbath*-sounding side-project *System Breakdown*. In 2001 bass player Andreas Olsson (also in *Wisdom Call, Stormwind*) replaced Jacob Persson. *Desert Land* was also released on tape in Malaysia (Pony Canyon Malaysia - PMCI 01486). Christian runs his production company/label CL Production that has released albums by *Sanctifica, Oblivion* etc. He has also recorded an album with hymns and ballads in Swedish. The band has had songs on several compilations such as *Stahlmaster*, *Rock Hard*, etc and a cover of *Sunrise* was recorded for the *Uriah Heep*-tribute *A Return To Fantasy* (03 Century Media). In 2004 the band recorded the live DVD *At Short Notice... Live In Germany*. Now keyboardist Linus Kåse (*Flagship*) had replaced Martin Claesson (now Härenstam). *Decade Of Confusion* is a compilation with rare, unreleased and live tracks. In April, 2008 singer and founder Christian decided to leave the band because he needed a rest. He was later replaced by former *Afteglow* (pre-*Mind's Eye*) singer Germán Pascual and the band recorded the heavier more metal-oriented *Curse Of A Nation*. April 15, 2010 the band announced its break-up. Rivel, who went back to his unmarried name, Liljegren, runs Rivel/Liljegren Records and sings in various bands such as *Divine Fire, Flagship, Audiovision* and *Golden Resurrection*. Grimmark was later in all-star band *FullForce* and now has a new project named *Empire 21* where Germán handles the vocals. A *Narnia* resurrection may actually happen in 2013/14. In 2012 Germán released his first solo album *A New Beginning*.
Website: www.narniaworld.com

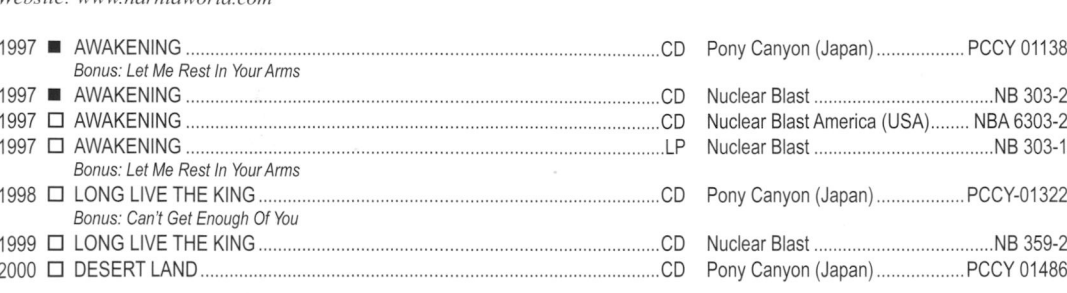

1997 CD - PCCY 01138

1997 CD - NB 303-2

2001 CD - NB 514-2

1997 ■	AWAKENING	.CD	Pony Canyon (Japan)	PCCY 01138

Bonus: Let Me Rest In Your Arms

1997 ■	AWAKENING	.CD	Nuclear Blast	NB 303-2
1997 ☐	AWAKENING	.CD	Nuclear Blast America (USA)	NBA 6303-2
1997 ☐	AWAKENING	.LP	Nuclear Blast	NB 303-1

Bonus: Let Me Rest In Your Arms

1998 ☐	LONG LIVE THE KING	.CD	Pony Canyon (Japan)	PCCY-01322

Bonus: Can't Get Enough Of You

1999 ☐	LONG LIVE THE KING	.CD	Nuclear Blast	NB 359-2
2000 ☐	DESERT LAND	.CD	Pony Canyon (Japan)	PCCY 01486

2001	■	DESERT LAND	CD	Nuclear Blast	NB 514-2
2001	☐	DESERT LAND	CD	Nuclear Blast America (USA)	NBA 6514-2
2006	☐	ENTER THE GATE	CD	Massacre	MAS CD 0517
2006	☐	ENTER THE GATE	CD	Gencross (Japan)	GCCY-1018
		Bonus: Hymn To The North			
2007	☐	DECADE OF CONFESSION	2CD	NL Records	NL 563
2007	☐	DECADE OF CONFESSION	CD	Massacre	MAS CD 0563
2009	■	CURSE OF A GENERATION	CD	Massacre	MAS CD 0636
2009	☐	CURSE OF A GENERATION	CD	Nightmare (USA)	NMR-532
		Bonus: Master Of Lies			

2009 CD - MAS CD 0636

NASHEIM

Erik Grahn: v/d, Andreas Wikström: g, Mikael Markström: v/b, Nicklas Holmgren: d

Umeå - Atmospheric and epic black metal, where some songs are around 25 minutes. Grahn and Markström are also in **Lethal**, Holmgren in **Embracing** and Wikström in **Cruoris**. The exclusive song *Leda* can be found on the compilation *Tormenting Legends II* (Blut & Eisen). The band was formed in 2001 and recorded their first demo *Evighet* in 2003, followed by *Undergång* in 2004. These two, plus a cover of **Bathory**'s *Blood Fire Death* were released as the first album. *Nasheim* is, according to nordic mythology, the great hall containing the least heroic souls. Their style is old-school black metal, in the vein of **Bathory**.

2004	☐	EVIGHET & UNDERGÅNG	CD	Northern Silence	NSP 010
2004	■	EVIGHET & UNDERGÅNG	LPg	Northern Silence	NSP 010
		999 copies			
2007	☐	NASHEIM – ANGANTYR (split)	CD	Northern Silence	NSP 057
		Split with Danish band Angantyr. Track: Sövande mjöd vill jag tömma			
2007	☐	NASHEIM – ANGANTYR (split)	LP	Northern Silence	NSP 057

2004 LPg - NSP 010

NASTY GROOVE

Anders Åhlund: v, Steven Kautzky Andersson: g,
Bino Rindestig: k, Christer Lövgren: b, Jonas Carlsson: d

Gävle - The A-side is actually very reminiscent of John Norum's *Let Me Love You*. Very high-class melodic hard rock with impressive guitar work by Steven and also great vocals. Steven recorded a solo album in 1994, on which Bino also appears. He has also appeared in other bands and projects such as psychedelic rockers **Iubar**. Jonas was later in **Turning Point**. Åhlund was ex-**Lotus**.

1991	●	Bad Habits/Street Of Dreams	7"	Heavenly Project Production	MP 101
		No artwork.			

1991 7" - MP 101

NASTY IDOLS

Anders "Andy Pierce" Persson: v, Peter Espinoza: g,
Dick Qwarfort: b, Richard "Rikki" Dahl: d

Malmö - **Nasty Idols**, named after a **New York Dolls** song, were started by Andy and Dick around 1987 as a punk band, initially featuring guitarist Chris Vance, who was replaced by Jonas "Johnny Wee" Westerlund before the first release. On the debut they had transformed into a quite average glam/sleaze act. The line-up was comprised of singer Andy, guitarist Johnny, bass player Dick (ex-**Syron Vanes**), keyboardist Roger "White" Grönberg and drummer George "Swanson" Svensson (d). On the second album things started happening. The attitude sharpened and the sound became much heavier, probably because of the change of guitarist from Westerlund to Peter Espinoza (ex-**Sad Wings**). The video on *Cool Way Of Living* was played several times on MTV's *Headbangers Ball*. On *Vicious* Svensson was replaced by Jörgen "Stanley" Olsson (ex-**Wizzy Blaze**, later in **Heed**). The third album was by far the band's heaviest and the video on *Head's Down (In Tinseltown)* was also aired on the *Headbanger's Ball*. In 1994 second guitarist Mikael "Mikkie Nielsen" Nilsson (**Bai Bang, Sapphire Eyes, Pierce, Alyson Avenue**) was added to the line-up. Andy and Stanley went on to the band **Machinegun Kelly** who released one album. Peter joined **Bai Bang** for a while, before forming his own band **Espinoza**, who also released one album. He was later in **Majestic** (originally known as **Lab Rat**) and **Reptilian**. Pierce also released a solo album. A new album, initially entitled *The Fourth Reich*, but renamed *Heroes For Sale* was planned to be released in 1996, but the band split in 1995. In 2002 Perris Records re-issued the old **Nasty Idols** albums, including a new compilation and finally the *Heroes For Sale* album saw the light of day. The band finally reformed for a show in 2006 and later the same year the live video *Rejects On The Road* was recorded at KB in Malmö. In 2009 the new album *Boys Town* was released. The band now features new drummer Dahl (ex-**Bewarp**, also in **StarRats** and **69-Hard**). In 2012 the band released the album *Kalifornia*, still keeping it true. Website: *www.nastyidols.com*

Still doing the nasty!

1988	☐	Don't Walk From Love/Easy Come Easy Go	7"	CRN	66 0316
		1000 copies			
1989	■	GIGOLOS ON PAROLE	LP	HSM	HSMLP 004

1989	☐	GIGOLOS ON PAROLE	CD	HSM	HSMCD 004
1990	☐	Alive N' Kickin/B.I.T.C.H	7"	HSM	HSM 006
1991	☐	CRUEL INTENTION	CD	HSM	HSMCD 007
1991	☐	CRUEL INTENTION	LP	HSM	HSMLP 007
1991	☐	CRUEL INTENTION	CD	Zero (Japan)	XRCN-1031
1993	☐	VICIOUS	CD	HSM	HSMCD 010
1993	☐	VICIOUS	LP	HSM	HSMLP 010
1993	☐	VICIOUS	CD	Zero (Japan)	XRCN-1047
2002	☐	THE BEST OF NASTY IDOLS	CD	Perris Records (USA)	PER 10128
2002	☐	VICIOUS	CD	Perris Records (USA)	PER 10326
		Bonus: Hurt Me/Forest Of Cries			
2002	☐	CRUEL INTENTION	CD	Perris Records (USA)	PER 10425
		Bonus: Sex Shooter/Electric Wonderland			
2005	☐	THE SWEDISH SLEAZE COLLECTION	CD	Swedmetal	SM-07-CD
2005	☐	HEROES FOR SALE	CD	Perris Records (USA)	PER 10227
2006	☐	CRUEL INTENTION	CD	Swedmetal	SM-08-CD
2006	☐	VICIOUS	CD	Swedmetal	SM-09-CD
2006	☐	HEROES FOR SALE	CD	Swedmetal	SM-10-CD
2009	■	BOYS TOWN	CD	Metal Heaven	MH 00066
2012	☐	KALIFORNIA	CD	Perris Records	PER 4112

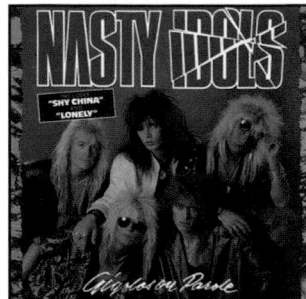

1989 LP - HSMLP 004

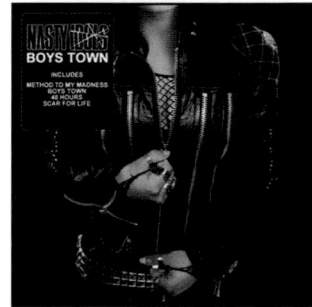

2009 CD - MH 00066

NATION

**Isaac Isaacson: v, Johnny Öhlin: g/k, Kalle Carlsson: k,
Magnus "Nobby" Noberg: b, Anders Wallberg: d**

Bålsta - Formed in 1990. The debut contained a bunch of well-played and well-sung 80s melodic metal songs with lots of melody and impressive Yngwie:esque guitar work. Great vocals. Very well received in Japan. Johnny has previously done studio jobs for some pop bands. In 1995 they changed label to Septima and the second album is even better than the debut. They actually do a stunning hard rock cover of *ABBA*'s *Waterloo*. Highly recommended. The band split in September 2000. Johnny and Nobby were later found in *Dionysus*. The *Nation* line-up minus the keyboard player was also active as a cover band under the name *King Cash*. Nobby is now found in Norwegian/Swedish prog/power metal band *Saint Deamon*. The band reunited in 2012 and in June 2013 the first new song *Throw The Dice* was unleashed. Better than ever!

1994 CDS - SMC 21121

1994	■	Hang Him High/Way Of Love	CDS 2tr	SMC	SMC 21121
1994	■	CHASED BY TIME	CD	SMC	SMC 101201
1994	☐	CHASED BY TIME	CD	JVC Victor (Japan)	VICP-5418
1995	■	WITHOUT REMORSE	CD	Septima	SEP 195 1003
1995	☐	WITHOUT REMORSE	CD	JVC Victor (Japan)	VICP-5672
		Bonus: Just Before			
1995	☐	Waterloo/Just Before	CDS	Septima	SEP 295 1004
1997	☐	WITHOUT REMORSE	CD	Now & Then	NTHEN 38
		Bonus: Destiny/Hang Him High/Just Before			
1997	☐	FALL OF AN EMPIRE	CD	Shrapnel (USA)	SH 11142
		Compilation of first and second album.			

1994 CD - SMC 101201

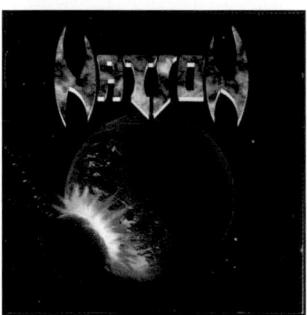

1995 CD - SEP 195 1003

NATION BEYOND

**Nielz Lindström: v, Sara Heurlin: v, Jonas Karlgren: g/k,
Micko Twedberg: g, Joakim "Harju" Hedestedt: b, Johan Helgesson: d**

Malmö - Formed in 2006 by Karlgren and Hedestedt. Karlgren and Twedberg are also in *Debase*, Hedestedt in *Face Down* and *Construcdead*, while Heurlin used to front funky hard rockers *Come Alive* and Helgesson is ex-*Original Sin/The Itch*. *Nation Beyond* plays high-class ultra ballsy semi-progressive melodic metal with a heavy edge, at times reminiscent of a mix between *Evergrey* and vintage *Queensryche*.
Website: www.myspace.com/nationbeyond

2007 CDd - BSRCD 0030

2007	■	THE AFTERMATH ODYSSEY	CDd	Burning Star	BSRCD 0030
2007	☐	THE AFTERMATH ODYSSEY	CDd	Sensory (USA)	SR 3040

NATTAS

**Kacper "Mickey Mouth" Rosanski: v, Johan "Meanos" Murmester: g,
Jonas "Evil Ed Engine" Bülund: b, Conny "Demonizer" Bevelius: d**

Stockholm/Örnsköldsvik/Falun - Great *Pantera*-style thrashy metal with a minimal touch of black metal! Anselmo-style vocals and killer guitar work. Bevelius is ex-*Explode*. The band was initially featured on several compilations, such as *Metal Reigns Supreme*, *Beloved Apocalypse* and *Atomic Annihilation*. In 2003 Kiravilu Records released a 6-track CDR entitled *Salvation* (KV-R 001). Before the recording of the album, drummer Bevelius joined, while Murmester

2004 CD - ARcd 024

joined after its release. The band's second outing was produced by Mike Wead (*Mercyful Fate*, *Abstrakt Algebra*) and Simon Johansson (*Memory Garden, Abstrakt Algebra*). A second version of the album (only digitally released so far) was mixed by Fredrik Groth (*Storyteller*) and mastered by Göran Finnberg. Murmester is also found in *Clairvoyant Seed*.
Website: www.nattas.se

2007 CDd - E0701

2004	■	AT EASE WITH THE BEAST	CD	Agonia	ARcd 024
		Bonus video Hatred			
2004	☐	AT EASE WITH THE BEAST	LP	Agonia	ARlp 024
		Bonus: Believer (live)			
2007	■	INDE DEUS ABEST	CDd	Emrinc	E0701

NATTFROST

Hasse Gustafson, Micke Johansen, Lennart Blomqvist, Bosse Westerlund, Toyyi Sjöqvist

Huddinge - *Nattfrost* (night frost) plays pretty good melodic hard rock with Swedish lyrics and some poppy overtones in the chorus, similar to early *Magnum Bonum*, but a bit heavier. Worth checking out.

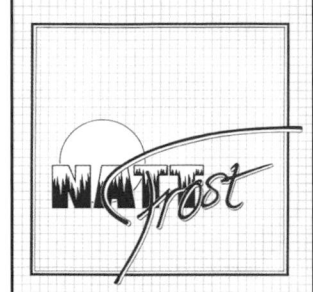
1981 7" - SOS 1064

1981	■	Vad gör vi för fel/Nu är det helg	7"	SOS	SOS 1064

NATTSMYG

Dan Heikenberg: v/g/b/k, Linn Carlshaf: v, Adam Nilsson: g/b

Malmö - *Nattsmyg* is a project formed by *Frostnatt* member Dan Heikenberg in 2005. The albums have featured musicians such as guitarist Martin Albinsson, keyboardist Sandra Bergman, bassist Robin Fors, drummer Jacob Bramsell and Anton Hinterlach. Heikenberg, Bergman and Fors are ex-*Frostnatt*. Quite epic folkish death metal with added female clean vocals.
Website: www.nattsmyg.com

2006 CD -

2006	☐	NÄR SOLEN SLOCKNAR	CD	private	n/a
2007	☐	FÖDD ATT HÄRSKA	CD	private	n/a
2011	☐	FYLGJA	CD	Unexploded Records	UER 040

NATTSVART

Mikael "Ludde" Svennberg: v/b, Kjell Svensson: g, Per Forsell: g, Johan Thörn: d/v

Upplands Väsby - Formed in 1981 as a trio under the name *Coop*. *Nattsvart* (pitch black in Swedish) only existed between 1982-1983. They were actually support act for *Europe* on their first gig after they won the *Rock SM* in 1982. The band plays straightforward metal in the true English vein. At times also reminiscent of *Onyx*. Lyrics in Swedish. The B-side starts out almost identical to *Iron Maiden*'s *The Ides Of March*. Great metal and a rare item.

1983 7" - PSI 069

1983	■	Vargarna/Drakens Öga	7"	Pang	PSI 069	$$

NAUGHTY BOYS

Mikael Sandvik: v, Hans Olsson: g, Morgan Valentin: k, Robert Norberg: b, Jonas Ludvigsson: d

Hagfors - *Naughty Boys* started out back in 1989. After some member changes the line-up featured singer Mikael Persson, guitarist Hans Olsson, keyboardist Morgan Sjöberg, bass player Peter Sandberg and drummer Jonas Ludvigsson. The first release was a decent AOR album, but with big problems in the vocal department. The band split in 1994, but reunited in 2002, now updating the sound and giving it a heavier touch. The line-up now featured original members Olsson and Ludvigsson. Norberg was also in *SugarGlider*, while Morgan is also in *Vision* and coverband *Värmlänningarna*. The last two recordings are pretty decent melodic hard rock with a touch of *White Lion*, especially singer Mikael Sandvik has a touch of a Mike Tramp in the rough. Nice production and quite ok song material.
Website: www.naughtyboys.se

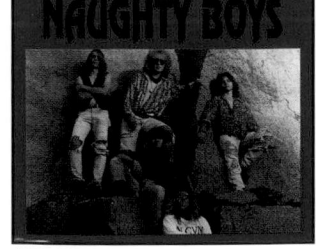
1993 MCD - - -

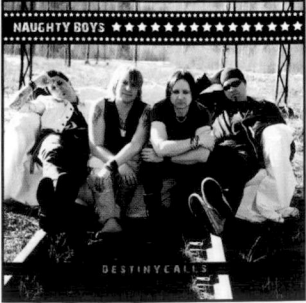
2009 CD - CD 6044

1993	■	Naughty Boys	MCD 5tr	private	- -
		Tracks: Fallen Angel/Love For A Lifetime/Straight From My Heart/Stay The Night/Believe In You.			
2003	☐	XTen	MCD 3tr	private	- -
		Tracks: I Will/Believe/Crazy World			
2007	☐	R U NAUGHTY ENOUGH?	CDd	N Records	CD 6006
2009	■	DESTINY CALLS	CDd	N Records	CD 6044

NEBULOSA

Roger Johansson (Pontare): v, Thomas Fransén: g,
Thomas Kacso: k, Lennart Usterud: b, Bengt Skarin: d

Stockholm - This is a scarce one. Very high-quality symphonic rock with interesting tempo-changes, great vocals and wailing guitar-solos. Skarin, Usterud and Fransén was previously in the band *Yama*. *Nebulosa* was formed in 1977. The album tells about the situation in Hungary at the time, in the form of a trilogy. The band split in 1979. Lennart became a Mormon, Fransén a boss at JVC, Kasco moved back to Hungary, Skarin became a music teacher and Roger pursued quite a successful solo career under the name Roger Pontare, known for his personal haircut and folk-inspired clothing style. Highly recommended.

1977 ■	NEBULOSA	LP	private	NB 1	$$
	1000 copies.				
2011 ☐	NEBULOSA	LP	private	NB 1	$
	Re-press with hand painted red cover. 198 copies.				

1977 LP - NB 1

NECROMICON

Kai Jaakkola: v, Nicklas Sundqvist: g, Stefan Lundgren: g,
Patrik Sundkvist: b, Tomas "Alzazmon" Asklund: d

Luleå - In 1993 Nicklas, Robert "Zoid" Sundelin and Henrik Åberg formed the band *Leprechaun*. Singer Daniel Björkman came into the band and they soon changed their name to *Necromicon*. The first demo, *When The Sun Turns Black*, was recorded in 1994. Now bass player Jonas Mejfeldt was added to the line-up and the second effort, *Through The Gates Of Grief*, came later the same year. Åberg left the band and Mejfeldt took over the guitar, leaving the bass duties to Nicklas younger brother Patrik. Keyboardist Roger Johansson was also added to the line-up. The band was picked up by Impure Creations to record a split, which was later changed to become the band's debut. Before it was finished Mejfeldt however left the band to be replaced by Stefan Lundgren (*Sombre Nocturn, Sectu*), who plays on three tracks. The band now changed label to Hammerheart who released the second album. After *Sightveiler* the band took a break. The line-up then drastically changed. Robert left to join *Satariel*, Daniel was replaced by Kai (ex-*Twilight, Deathbound, The Duskfall, Dawn Of Relic*), singer Sara Näslund was replaced by Ann-Sofi Elert and Robert with Tomas "Alzazmon" Asklund (ex-*Dark Funeral*). Patrik, Nicklas and former member Åberg are also found in the band *Hellmasker*, whose demo *Probably The Best Band In The World* can be found on mp3.com. Stefan is also found in *Sobre Nocturn, Dawn* and *Mörk Gryning*. Jaakkola was fired in 2004 and the band changed their name to *Cimmerian Dome* in 2004. *Necromicon* plays quite generic and uninteresting black/death metal with a symphonic touch at times and not very well-produced. Patrik is also found in *Morithrim, Hellmasker* and *Depraved*.

1996 CD - IRC003

2000 CD - HHR 046

1996 ■	REALM OF SILENCE	CD	Impure Creations	IRC003
1998 ■	SIGHTVEILER	CDd A5	Hammerheart	HHR 014
2000 ■	PECCATA MUNDI	CD	Hammerheart	HHR 046
2000 ☐	PECCATA MUNDI	LPg	Hammerheart	HHR 046 LP

1998 CDd - HHR 014

NECRONAUT

Fred Estby: v/g/b/d

Stockholm - Solo project of former *Dismember* member and producer Fred Estby. In 2007 he left his former band to go solo. Fred is foremost the drummer, but also handles guitars and even vocals in one song. The album features guest performances by Tomas Lindberg (*At The Gates*), Erik Danielsson (*Watain*), Erik "Tyrant" Gustavsson (*Nifelheim*), Janne "JB" Christoffersson (*Grand Magus*), Andreas "Drette" Axelsson (*Tormented, Edge Of Sanity*), Nicke Andersson (*Entombed, Hellacopters, Imperial State Electric*), Per "Hellbutcher" Gustavsson (*Nifelheim*), David Blomqvist (*Dismember*), Tobias Christiansson (*Dismember, Grave*) and Robert Pehrsson (*Death Breath, Dundertåget*). The multitude of guests makes the album almost sound like a compilation, but it's kept together pretty well. Since Estby was the main song writer in *Dismember*, the album does have a strong hint of his former band.

2010 CD - RR CD 178

2010 ■	NECRONAUT	CD	Regain Records	RR CD 178
2010 ☐	NECRONAUT	LP	Regain Records	RR LP 178

NECRONY

Anders Jakobsson: g/b/v, Rickard Alriksson: d/v

Örebro - The band was formed in 1990 under the name *Necrotomy*. After changing name twice, they went for *Necrony*. The band recorded their first demo, *Severe Malignal Pustule*, shortly after. Drummer Jakobsson had reportedly never held a guitar before he started this band. When listening to the lyrics on the debut 7", I wonder what type of dictionary they've been using.

1991 7" - PSR 001

How about "Corrosive digestion of embryonic corpus, slow decomposing of verrucos amorphus..." or "With a straw in your rectum, sucking out enormous excrements..." Yuck! Medical digest, eh! Musically the band plays heavy death metal with warped vocals, sounding a bit like **Carcass**. Dan Wall plays guitar on the first 7". All songs on *Necronycism* are covers of **Carcass**, **Repulsion, Bolt Thrower, Napalm Death** and **Carnage**. Dan Swanö (**Edge Of Sanity, Nightingale** etc.) sings on some tracks and plays guitar solos on five of them. The duo started the side-project **Nasum**, which soon became a full time band and **Necrony** folded. Anders, Rickard and Dan are also found in punksters **Genocide SS** together with Matte Borg (**2 Ton Predator**). Alriksson can also been found in **Hellchamber** and Jakobsson in **Masticate, Coldworker** and **Route Nine**. The 2005 compilation was released without the band's consent.

1991 ■	Mucu-Purulent Miscarriage/Multiocular Merphea-Sakroblaster ....7"	Poserslaughter..................................	PSR 001	
	1:st edition in yellow vinyl 1000 copies, 2:nd in orange 1500 copies.			
1993 ☐	PATHOLOGICAL PERFORMANCES ....CD	Poserslaughter..................................	WIMP 001	
1994 ■	Necronycism: Distorting The Originals...................................MCD 12tr	Poserslaughter.......................PSR-WIMP 009		
	Tracks: Fermenting Innards/Swarming Vulgar Mass Of Infected Virulency/Die In Pain/Mucupurulence Excretor/Dis-Organ-Ized/Bodily Dismemberment/Festering Boils/Cenotaph/Lucid Fairytale/The Kill/Deceiver/The Day Man Lost			
2000 ☐	Under The Black Soil/Forensickness ....10" PD	Hangnail.....................................	AS 21985	
	500 copies.			
2005 ☐	POSERSLAUGHTER CLASSIC REMASTERS..CD	Poserslaughter..........................	PSR-WIMP098	

1994 MCD - PSR-WIMP 009

NECROPHOBIC

Tobias Sidegård: b/v, Sebastian Ramstedt: g,
Johan Bergebäck: g, Joakim Sterner: d

Johanneshov/Stockholm - The band was formed already in 1989 by guitarist David Parland and drummer Joakim Sterner, initially under a different moniker. Well-played and varied black metal, at times reminiscent of **Unleashed**. The band's description is "Pure Bloody Antichrist Mangle". The band's first official demo, *Slow Asphyxiation*, was recorded in 1990. One song can also be found on a compilation released by Witchhunt Records. The second demo, *Unholy Prophecies*, was released in 1991. The 7" was recorded at Sunlight Studios. The debut featured singer Stefan Harrvik, guitarist David "Blackmoon" Parland (**Dark Funeral**), Tobias and Joakim. On *The Nocturnal Silence* Anders Strokirk had taken over the vocals. *Spawned By Evil* saw another change. Tobias took over the vocals and Anders was out. They had also added Martin Halfdan on guitar. On *Darkside* the band was a trio featuring Tobias, Martin and Joakim. *The Third Antichrist* saw the addition of guitarist Sebastian, who was also found in **Nifelheim**. On *Bloodhymns* Martin was out and Johan took his place. Tobias also played keyboards in **Therion**. The 2012 line-up features guitarist Fredrik Folkare (**Unleashed, Hellinor**). The album *Womb Of Lilithu* is slated for a 2013 release.
Website: www.necrophobic.net

Evil and nocturnal

1993 ■	The Call...7" 3tr	Wild Rags	WRR-NEC	$
	Tracks: Shadows Of The Moon/The Ancient Gate/Father Of Creation. With poster.			
1993 ☐	THE NOCTURNAL SILENCE ....CD	Black Mark	BMCD 40	
1993 ☐	THE NOCTURNAL SILENCE ....LP	Painkiller	PKR 034	
1996 ☐	Spawned By Evil ....MCD 4tr	Black Mark	BMCD 60	
	Tracks: Spawned By Evil/Die By The Sword (Slayer cover)/Nightmare (Venom cover)/Enter The Eternal Fire (Bathory cover)			
1997 ☐	DARKSIDE ....CD	Black Mark	BMCD 96	
1999 ☐	THE THIRD ANTICHRIST...CD	Black Mark	BMCD 146	
1999 ☐	THE THIRD ANTICHRIST...CD	Nippon Crown (Japan)..................CRCL-4748		
2002 ☐	BLOODHYMNS ....CD	Hammerheart................................	HHR 098	
2002 ☐	THE NOCTURNAL SILENCE ....CD	Hammerheart................................	HHR 138	
2002 ☐	DARKSIDE ....CD	Hammerheart................................	HHR 139	
2002 ☐	THE THIRD ANTICHRIST...CD	Hammerheart................................	HHR 140	
2003 ☐	THE NOCTURNAL SILENCE ....LP	Painkiller Records	PKR 034	
2003 ■	Tour EP ....MCD 9tr	Hammerheart................................	HHR 133	
	Tracks: Before The Dawn/Spawned By Evil/Into Armageddon/Dreams Shall Flesh/Die By The Sword (Slayer cover)/Nightmare (Venom cover)/Enter The Eternal Fire (Bathory cover)/Ridden With Disease (Autopsy cover)/Moon Child (Iron Maiden cover). 1000 copies.			
2006 ☐	BLOODHYMNS ....CD	Karmageddon	KARMA 100	
2006 ☐	HRIMTHURSUM ....CD	Regain Records	RR 093	
2006 ☐	HRIMTHURSUM ....CD	Candlelight (USA) ....CDL 311 CD		
2007 ☐	HRIMTHURSUM ....LP	War Anthem Records...................	WAR 004LP	
2009 ■	SATANIC BLASPHEMIES....................................CD box	Regain Records	RR 122	
	With patch and poster in a box.			
2009 ☐	SATANIC BLASPHEMIES....................................CD	Regain Records	RR 122 CD	
	Different artwork.			
2009 ☐	SATANIC BLASPHEMIES....................................LP	Regain Records	RRLP 122	
	Different artwork. 500 copies.			
2009 ☐	DEATH TO ALL ....CD	Regain Records	RR 116 CD	
	Slipcase.			

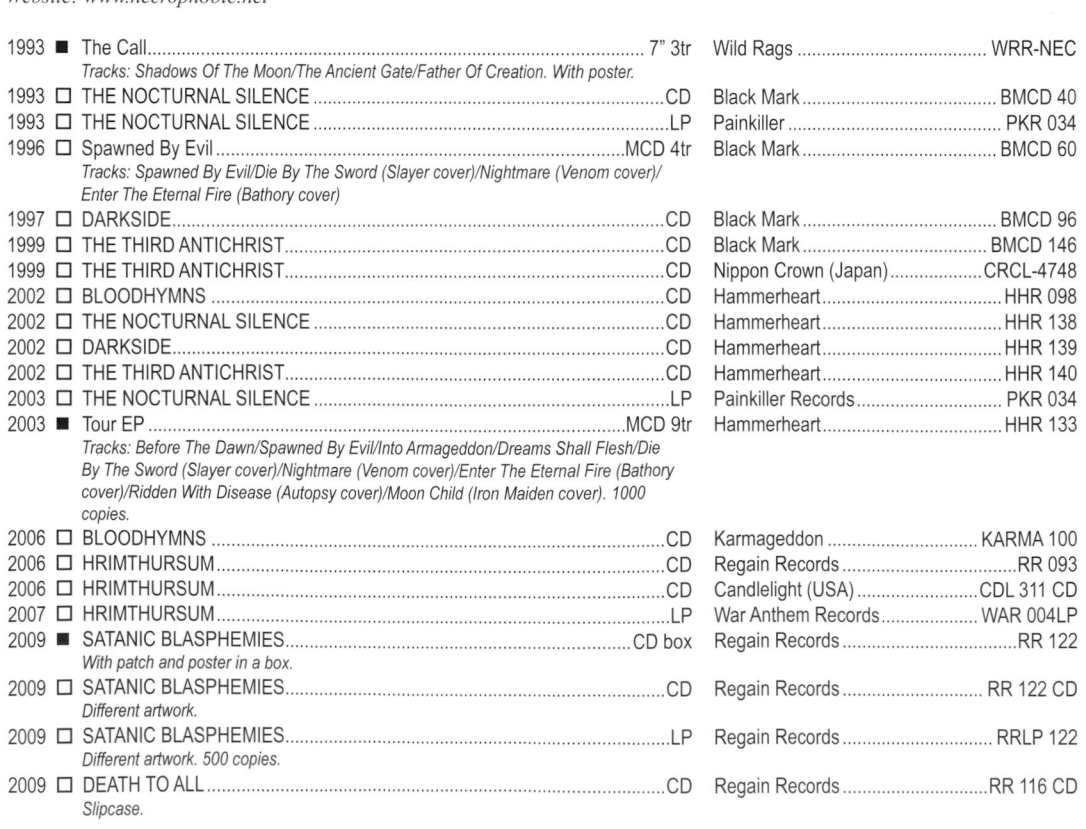

1993 7" - WRR-NEC

2003 MCD - HHR 133

2009 CD box - RR 122

550

2009 ☐	DEATH TO ALL	LPg	War Anthem	WAR 028 LP
	With A1 poster.			
2009 ■	DEATH TO ALL	LP	Regain Records	RRLP 116
2011 ☐	DARKSIDE	CD	Hammerheart	HHR 201004
2011 ☐	DARKSIDE	LP	Hammerheart	HHR 201004
	Blue vinyl.			
2011 ☐	DARKSIDE	LP	Hammerheart	HHR 201004LP
2011 ☐	BLOODHYMNS	CD	Hammerheart	HHR 201002CD
2011 ☐	BLOODHYMNS	LP	Hammerheart	HHR 201002LP
2011 ☐	BLOODHYMNS	LP	Hammerheart	HHR 201002LP
	Purple vinyl.			
2011 ☐	THE NOCTURNAL SILENCE	CD	Hammerheart	HHR 201008
2011 ☐	THE NOCTURNAL SILENCE	LP	Hammerheart	HHR 201003
2011 ☐	THE THIRD ANTICHRIST	CD	Hammerheart	HHR 201005
2011 ☐	THE THIRD ANTICHRIST	LP	Hammerheart	HHR 201005LP
2012 ☐	SATANIC BLASPHEMIES	LPg	Floga Records	FL 30
	400 white + 600 black vinyl.			
2012 ☐	SPAWNED BY EVIL	LP	Hammerheart	HHR 201217LP
	Bonus: Ridden With Disease (Autopsy cover)/Moonchild (Iron Maiden cover)/Black Moon Rising/The Call			
2012 ☐	SPAWNED BY EVIL	CD	Hammerheart	HHR 201217

2009 LP - RRLP 116

NECROPLASMA

Judas "Priestor Af Hellgoat" Isaksson: v/g, Tobias "Deathslaughter" Söderström: d

Köping - Formed in 1996 and recorded their first demo *The Cold Of The Uncaring Moon* in 1999. Their second demo, *Black Funeral Horns* was recorded the year after and a third self-titled demo was released in 2001. All demos were released by Neodawn. Evil and fast underground black metal with a thrashy touch. After *My Hearse, My Redemption* bass player Spinegrinder de Sate was out of the band. In 2005 Satanic Propaganda released the cassette album *X Corona Bestia Vox Vovis*. The 2006 release *Gospels Of Antichristian Terror* contains early demos including a cover of **Venom**'s *Witching Hour*. Isaksson sadly passed away in June 2008. The track *Grave Dark Journey* is found on the compilation EP *Satanic Butchery* (7" Horned, HR 004)

2001 7" - NDP 010

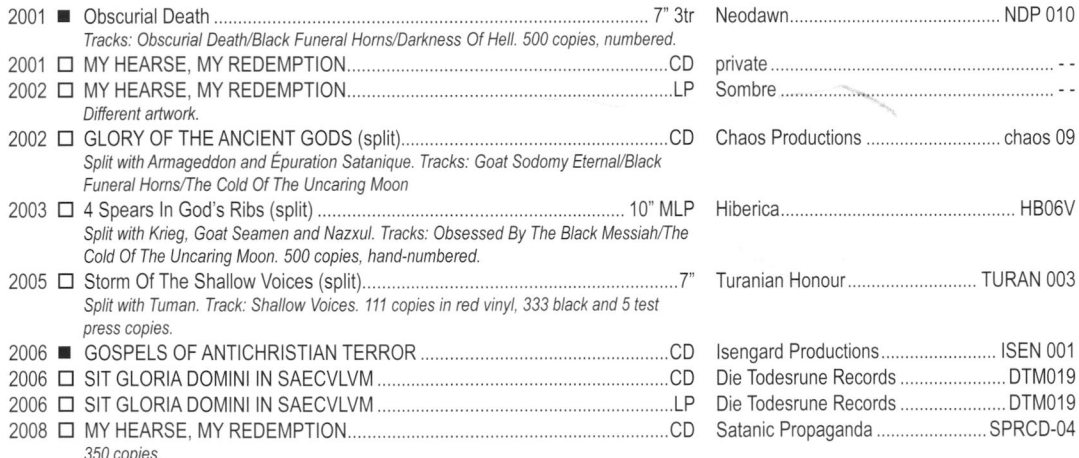

2001 ■	Obscurial Death	7" 3tr	Neodawn	NDP 010
	Tracks: Obscurial Death/Black Funeral Horns/Darkness Of Hell. 500 copies, numbered.			
2001 ☐	MY HEARSE, MY REDEMPTION	CD	private	- -
2002 ☐	MY HEARSE, MY REDEMPTION	LP	Sombre	- -
	Different artwork.			
2002 ☐	GLORY OF THE ANCIENT GODS (split)	CD	Chaos Productions	chaos 09
	Split with Armageddon and Épuration Satanique. Tracks: Goat Sodomy Eternal/Black Funeral Horns/The Cold Of The Uncaring Moon			
2003 ☐	4 Spears In God's Ribs (split)	10" MLP	Hiberica	HB06V
	Split with Krieg, Goat Seamen and Nazxul. Tracks: Obsessed By The Black Messiah/The Cold Of The Uncaring Moon. 500 copies, hand-numbered.			
2005 ☐	Storm Of The Shallow Voices (split)	7"	Turanian Honour	TURAN 003
	Split with Tuman. Track: Shallow Voices. 111 copies in red vinyl, 333 black and 5 test press copies.			
2006 ■	GOSPELS OF ANTICHRISTIAN TERROR	CD	Isengard Productions	ISEN 001
2006 ☐	SIT GLORIA DOMINI IN SAECVLVM	CD	Die Todesrune Records	DTM019
2006 ☐	SIT GLORIA DOMINI IN SAECVLVM	LP	Die Todesrune Records	DTM019
2008 ☐	MY HEARSE, MY REDEMPTION	CD	Satanic Propaganda	SPRCD-04
	350 copies.			

2006 CD - ISEN 001

NECROVATION

Sebastian Gadd: v/g, Anton Wanstadius: b, Andreas Bünger: d

Kristianstad - *Necrovation* were formed in 2002 as **Das Über Elvis** (under which name they recorded the demo *Bratwürst Terror*), but soon changed it to **Necrovation**, and in 2004 the four track demo *Ovations To Putrefaction* was released. It was also released by Japanese Deathrash Armageddon. The band was picked up by Blood Harvest and have since stayed true to the label. The band plays quite crude old-school-sounding black metal in the vein of **Grave** and early **Entombed** with a touch of vintage Sunlight Studios.
Website: www.necrovation.com

2004 7" - YOYZ #1

2004 ■	Chants Of Grim Death	7" 4tr	Blood Harvest	YOTZ #1
	Tracks: Beyond Possession/Rigormortic Mind/Carnal Bleeders/Pure Hate (Merciless cover). 500 copies. Green vinyl.			
2005 ☐	Curst Of The Subconscious (split)	7" 4tr	Blood Harvest	YOTZ #4
	Split with Corrupt. Tracks: Black Spree/My Dark Subconscious (Morbid cover)			
2008 ☐	BREED DEADNESS BLOOD	CD	Blood Harvest	YOTZ #23
2008 ☐	BREED DEADNESS BLOOD	LP	Blood Harvest	YOTZ #23
	500 copies.			
2010 ■	Gloria Mortus/Otherside	7"	Blood Harvest	YOTZ #65

2010 7" - YOTZ #65

NECTARIS

Stefan Larsson: v, Thorbjörn Holm: g, Ola Lugner: k, Christer Hjort: b, Jonas Lugner: d

Lidköping - Melodic hard rock, quite wimpy, but slightly heavier than *Magnum Bonum* or *Snowstorm*. Stefan, Christer and Ola later formed the excellent hard rock band *Bad Business*.

1980 □	NÄSTA DRAG	LP	Marilla	MALP 1053
1980 □	Sebastian B/Allt Mellan Himmel Och Jord	7"	Marilla	MA-S 168
1981 ■	EN GALEN VÄRLD	LP	Svenska Media	SMTE 5002
1981 □	Heta kyssar/En galen värld	7"	Svenska Media	SMTE 502

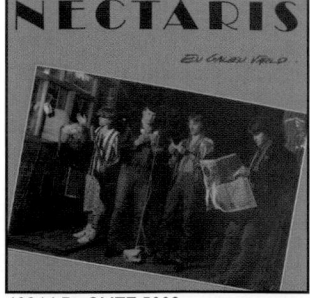

1981 LP - SMTE 5002

NEFANDUS

Tony "Blackwinged/Demogorgon": v/g, Mika "Michayah/Belfagor" Hakola: v/g/b/d, Kristoffer "Ushatar" af Dolphins Andersson: b/g

Norrköping - *Nefandus* were formed in 1993 by Blackwinged and Belfagor and used various names before recording the demo *Behold The Hordes* in 1995, and settling for the name *Nefandus*. By that time drummer Ushatar was also a member.. The debut was produced by Magnus "Devo" Andersson (*Marduk*), however not to the band's (read: Blackwinged) satisfaction, as stated in an interview with the singer. In 1996 the band broke up due to internal disagreements. Belfagor joined *Ofermod* and Ushatar went to *Sargatanas Reign* and later *The Legion*, while Blackwinged/Demogorgon (same person) left the music business. Blackwinged and Belfagor also had the side project *Hellsent*, with songs that didn't fit the *Nefandus* format. In an interview with tiagoblackmetal Blackwinged said he was not a Nazi, but he did support them together with other acts that are considered evil and sick. In 2008 Belfagor and Ushatar reformed the band, now as a side project and returned with a new release in 2009. It also featured a track written my *Marduk*'s Morgan Håkansson and one by Thomas "Daemon Deggial" Karlsson (*Shadowseeds*). The band's second album is a piece of well-produced black metal with a touch of *Marduk*.

1996 CD - NEX-003

2004 CD - THR 45

1996 ■	THE NIGHTWINDS CARRIED OUR NAME	CD	Secula Delenta	NEX-003
2004 ■	THE NIGHTWINDS CARRIED OUR NAME	CD	Total Holocaust	THR 45
	Different artwork. 1000 copies. Bonus: Intro-Behold The Hordes/In The Moonlight/On The Path To The Other Side/Death's Beauty I Met - Outro			
2004 □	THE NIGHTWINDS CARRIED OUR NAME	LP	W.T.C Records	- -
	Different artwork. 400 copies black + 100 gold vinyl.			
2009 □	DEATH HOLY DEATH	CD	Left Light Emanations	Emanation 001
2010 □	DEATH HOLY DEATH	LPg	Blut & Eisen	- -
	400 black + 100 red vinyl copies.			
2012 ■	Your God Is A Ghost	MCD 4tr	Daemon Worship Productions	DWP 026
	Tracks: Crown Of Labour And Strength/Temptress Of Thantifaxath/This One Is For God/ Your God Is A Ghost (Come Into My Light)			

2012 MCD - DWP 026

NEGRO

Marita Vikström: v, Mathias Wendt: g, Niclas Rundkvist: k, Lars Gabrielsson: b, Pär Lindholm: d

Västerås - Negro means black in Spanish, so the name is not as provoking as it may seem today. The band was not influenced by any hard rock bands at all, but instead wanted to sound like *Noice* and *Blondie*, which they actually do on the A-side. However, the B-side, sung in Engligh, is quite decent AOR, musically quite ok but with a wimpy sound and fragile vocals. The song is great, though. Lindholm and Wendt now play in dance band *Frontline*.

1986 7" - PL 13

1986 ■	Varför gör du så här/Love Is A Bird	7"	Platina	PL 13
	500 copies.			

NEMESIS

Leif Edling: b/v, Anders Wallin: g, Christian Weberyd: g, Anders Waltersson: d

Upplands Väsby - This is the embryo of what later became *Candlemass*. Some of the *Nemesis* songs were even played under *Candlemass* banner. Leif, formerly in *Witchcraft*, which he left in 1981, handled the vocals, which maybe wasn't such a good idea. Wallin and Waltersson were ex-*Surgery*. The band came together in 1982. *Day Of Retribution* was originally only meant to be a demo. The MLP was re issued with a new cover (the logo in red on a black background) and with the two bonus tracks *Demon's Gate* and *Blackstone Wielder*, both taken from the first *Candlemass*-demo (1985-86). At that time the members were Leif, Mats "Mappe" Björkman (g) (ex-*ATC*), Klas Bergwall (g) and Matz Ekström (d). And it's very heavy! Edling then recorded the demo *Tales Of Creation* together with Johnny Reinholm. After this *Nemesis* became *Candlemass*, for legal reasons, because of a chain store. Messiah Marcolin joined and the rest is… *Candlemass*. The double LP *The Demos 1983/84* contains demo tracks from 1983-84, some of which are also found on the High Roller re-issue of *The Day Of Retribution*.

1984 MLP - MLP 003

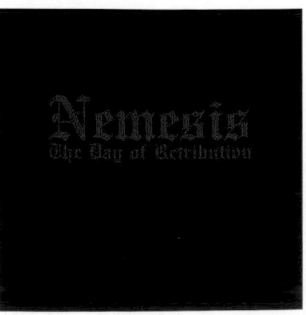

1990 CD - ATVCD 15

1984 ■	The Day Of Retribution	MLP 5tr	Fingerprint	MLP 003	$
	Tracks: Black Messiah/In God We Trust/Theme Of The Guardians/The King Is Dead/ Good Night. 495 copies.				

1990 ■	THE DAY OF RETRIBUTION	CD	Active	ATVCD 15	

1990 ■ THE DAY OF RETRIBUTION ....CD Active ....ATVCD 15
Bonus: Demon's Gate/Blackstone Wielder.
1990 □ THE DAY OF RETRIBUTION ....LP Active ....ATVLP 15
1990 □ THE DAY OF RETRIBUTION ....CD Metal Blade (USA) 773441-2
2007 □ THE DAY OF RETRIBUTION ....CD GMR ....GMRCD 9006
Bonus: In God We Trust (demo)/Theme Of The Guardian (demo)/Black Messiah (demo)/ The King Is Dead (demo)/Burn The Witch (demo)/The Act (demo). Slipcase
2009 □ THE DEMOS 1983/84 ....2LP Doom ....DOOM 1/2
107 copies
2010 ■ THE DAY OF RETRIBUTION ....2LPg High Roller Records ....HHR 158
150 milky clear vinyl, 250 red, 600 black. Bonus: In God We Trust/Theme Of The Guardians/Black Messiah/The King Is Dead/Burn The Witch/Nemesis/Lucifer/The Act/Black Messiah/Lucifer (live). Lacking the track Goodnight.

2010 2LPg - HHR 158

NEOCORI
Stefan Karlsson: v, Magnus Ludvigsson: g, Michael Christmansson: g, Mikael Höglund: b, Stefan Suomalainen: d

Sundsvall - Formed in 1993. Great progressive doom metal with strong and clean vocals. At times in the vein of **Candlemass** with a singer quite reminiscent of Bruce Dickinson. Great stuff! Stefan later joined **Memento Mori** for one tour in 1995 and was later in **Pathos**. The track *Into The Flesh* is found on the American compilation-CD *Best Unsigned European Band* ('94 Showcase). The band also recorded the two track demo *Make Way/Green World* in 1985.

1994 ■ Purgatory Dreams ....MCD 4tr private ....EVIL 007 $
Tracks: Purgatory Dreams/Invite Reality/Feet Of The Liar/Into The Flesh

Purgatory Dreams

1994 MCD - EVIL 007

NEOFIGHT
Roger Ekelund: v/g, Göran Berg: k, Jan Nilsson: b, Micke Danielsson: d

Perstorp - Formed in 1982, split in 1986. Seventies-style melodic hard rock where the B-side also has a touch of **The Spotnicks**. Guitarist Bo Nilsson was also in the band. Roger has made several records with relaxing music. Neofight also recorded several demos and radio live recordings.

1985 ■ Gipsy Woman/Someone To Love ....7" private ....RJGM 001

1985 7" - RJGM 001

NEON
Kenneth Asplund: v/g, Peter Lindström: g, Jonas Falk: b, Kenth Sandell: d

Kristianstad - A-side is straightforward boogie-style hard rocker with **Thin Lizzy**-inspired guitar harmonies, like the heavy side of **Magnum Bonum**. The B-side is a melodic, almost pop-oriented hard rocker. Pretty good vocals and musicianship, much better than the singer's English.

1981 ■ Everybody Want's/It's All That They Can ....7" private ....HSP 2026

1981 7" - HSP 2026

NEON ROSE
Roger Holegård: v, Pierro Mengarelli: g, Gunnar Hallin: g, Benno Megarelli: b, Thomas Wiklund: d

Stockholm - In 1969 Roger, Pierro and Benno formed the band **Spider**. In 1973 drummer Kenta Krull was replaced by Stanley Larsson and **Neon Rose** were born. The name came from the fact that they wanted to mix something that sounded hard with something that sounded soft, a bit like **Iron Butterfly** – **Neon Rose**. Their debut gig was to open up for **Dr. Hook**. **Neon Rose** is considered to be one of Sweden's best seventies hard rock bands. The first single was only released in 500 copies and is a very sought after item that gains a high price. On the debut album Gunnar was not a member of the band, but a guitar roadie. *A Dream Of Glory And Pride* is a true gem with the classic *Love Rock* and the brilliant *Julia's Dream*. On *Two* the style was a bit more powerful with songs like *Waiting For The Train* and *False Star*. After the second album Stanley had quit to join the blues rockers **Nature**. His replacement was Thomas Wiklund, who in 1971 recorded a single with the excellent hard rock band **Uppåt Väggarna**. Now Roger too left the band, but was persuaded to return. *Reload* contains some serious heavy rockers such as *A Man's Not A Man, Tears Of Pain* and *Too Long*. After the album however he quit to join **Wasa Express**. He later formed **Truck** where Thomas Wiklund also played. Gunnar was offered the job as Manny Charlton's co-guitarist in **Nazareth**, but surprisingly turned down the offer. Now Thomas left the band. In 1987 Pierro made another attempt to get the band rolling. **Neon Rose** now consisted of Pierro on vocals and guitar, drummer Joaquin Calafell, keyboardist Erik Svensson and bassist Lasse Byström (ex-**Wildmarken, Circus** and later in **Dave And The Mistakes**). They recorded some demos but it never took off. The band again split... to reform in 1981. The band now featured Pierro, Benno, Joaquin, Erik and new guitarist/singer Conny "Bloom" Blomquist. Yes, the guy that was previously in **Roadrats** and **Rolene**, and later in **Electric Boys/Titanic Truth/Hanoi Rocks**. Demos were once again recorded and the bands style was now more polished melodic hard rock. They actually recorded a 7" for Rosa Honung Records, but it never made it past the test-press stage. The single was however made in three copies.

Dreaming of glory and pride!

Neon Rose ready to reload with some dedicated... ehhh... fans?

Carola Häggkvist/Söögard, who is now a very famous pop singer, was supposed to sing back-up on the recording, but her band **Stand By** had a gig that night. In 1982 the band finally split. Roger later recorded with **Micke Andersson's Dropouts**. Benno made two albums with pop/rockers **Internezzo**, then he joined **Magnus Lindberg Band** (about as heavy as Springsteen). Stanley made some tours and recordings with **Nature**, Pugh Rogefeldt, rock-poet Ulf Lundell and popster Magnus Uggla (where Gunnar Hallin was also found). Thomas made two singles with **Truck**, some tours and albums with **Magnum Bonum**. Gunnar joined Magnus Ugglas's backing band and later recorded the bass tracks for both **Trash** albums, recorded a single and an album with AOR band **Bam Bam Boys**. In 2000 the compilation *Dust And Rust And* was released. It actually also contains two new tracks with the reunited band. Yepp, in 1998 the original line-up reformed and recorded material for an album. The two songs are *Schizo Love* and *The Last day On Earth*. The flip side of the first single, a cover of *Come On Everybody*, can also be found on the bonus-CD with the first Encyclopedia Of Swedish Hard Rock And Heavy Metal and another new song, *Woman From My Tribe* is featured on the CD in the second encyclopedia. In January 2007 Stanley Larsson (born November 20, 1953) sadly passed away.

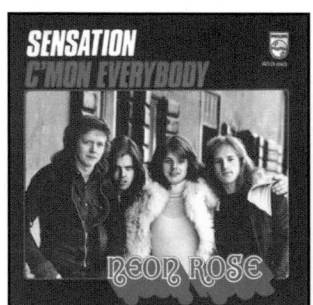

1974 7" - 6015 083

1074 LP - 6316 250

1974 ■	Sensation/Come On Everybody	7"	Phillips	6015 083	$
	Come On Everybody is a non-LP track. 500 copies.				
1974 ■	A DREAM OF GLORY AND PRIDE	LP	Vertigo	6316 250	
1974 □	TWO	LP	Vertigo	6316 251	
1975 □	A DREAM OF GLORY AND PRIDE	LP	Yum Yum (Germany)	89260 OT	
1975 □	TWO	LP	Red Point (Germany)	89079 XOT	
1975 ■	RELOAD	LP	Vertigo	6316 252	
1975 □	A Man's Not A Man/Dead Eyes	7"	Vertigo	6015 156	
1975 ○	A Man's Not A Man (edited)/Dead Eyes	7"	Philips	6015 156	
	Promo-copy w/out picture sleeve.				
1981 ○	Whatever Happened To Rock & Roll/I Saw Her Standing There	7"	Rosa Honung	ROSA SP 4	$$
	This is an extremely rare test-pressing made in a limited edition of 3 copies, of which one has been destroyed.				

1975 LP - 6316 252

| 2000 ☐ | DUST AND RUST AND… | CD | Vertigo | 548325-2 |
| 2005 ☐ | A DREAM OF GLORY AND PRIDE | CDd | Vertigo | 210361-7 |

Bonus: C'mon Everybody/War Song/Julia's Dream (live)/Love Rock (live)

| 2005 ■ | TWO | CDd | Vertigo | 2103620 |

Bonus: Sister (I'm An Entertainer)(live)/Roll Me Over (live)/C'mon Everybody (live)

| 2005 ☐ | RELOAD | CDd | Vertigo | 2103621 |

Bonus: A Man's Not A Man (single edit)/Dead Eyes (video)

Unofficial releases:

| 1994 ☐ | TWO | CD | Limited Records | LMTRCD09 |

Italian bootleg made from a vinyl copy

2005 CDd - 2103620

NEONDAZE

Marcus Lundgren: v, Lars Boquist: g, Jesper Malm: b, Hampus Landin: d

Norrköping - Former *Dizzinezz/Pole Position/Reptilian* guitarist Lars Boquist was planning on putting together a new band when he saw singer Marcus Lundgren on TV, imitating Bon Scott. The members Boquist had already gathered were former *Miss Behaviour* drummer Hampus Landin and bassist Jesper Malm. They all felt Lundgren was the man to front the band. If you were into Boquist's previous band *Pole Position* you'll recognise the sound. The style is still melodic hard rock, with a touch of *Def Leppard* in the choruses, but with way more dynamite in the sound. There's also a bit of vintage *TNT* in the mix. A great rocker indeed! In 2012 Lars launched his new band *Fair Of Freaks*, which followed in the same style, but a bit more quirky and melodic at times.
Website: www.myspace.com/neondaze

| 2008 ■ | NEONDAZE | CD | Music Buy Mail | MBM CD 6034 |

2008 CD - MBM CD 6034

NEPHENZY (CHAOS ORDER) (aka N.C.O)

Martin "Khaos" Hallin: v/g, Mathias "M Flatline" Kamijo: g, Tobias "T Nails" Leffler: g, Simon "S Demon" Axenrot: b, Martin Axenrot: d

Linköping - Formed in 1994 under the name *Nephenzy*. In 1996 the tape *Stolen Blessing* was recorded, followed by *Worshipped By The Mass* in 1997. The first album featured Hallin (ex-*Blasphemous, Dismal*), guitarist Adrian Kanebäck (later in *Morifade*), bass player Mattias Fredriksson and drummer Kim Arnell (later in *Morifade, Sombre Nocturne*), who had replaced a drummer named Fredrik earlier. Well-played death metal in the old-school vein, similar to early *At The Gates*, *Swordmaster* or a less evil sounding *Dark Funeral*. The band split in 1999, but two years later original members Hallin resurrected the band with a new line-up. *Chaos Order* was added to the name and the music took a more brutal touch. The return album *Pure Black Disease* was recorded in two different studios with Tommy Tägtgren and Magnus "Devo" Andersson. The band says they're not a black metal band, but plays "infected mental metal". Kamijo can also be/has been found in bands like *Hypocrisy, Pain, Abemal, The Abyss, Vergelmer* and *Algaion*, while Leffler is also found in the last two. Martin Axenrot has played with numerous bands like *Witchery, Bloodbath, Nifelheim, Triumphator, Opeth, Satanic Slaughter* and he also played with Hallin in *Blasphemous* in 1991.

1998 CD - BDP 004

1999 7"g - UGL 006

1998 ■	WHERE DEATH BECOMES ART	CD	Black Diamond	BDP 004
1999 ■	In Anguish And Furious Pain/Gathered And Mighty	7"g	Loud 'N Proud	UGL 006
2003 ■	PURE BLACK DISEASE	CD	Baphomet	BAPH 120

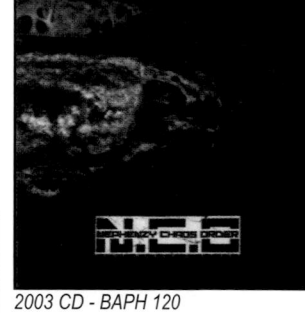

2003 CD - BAPH 120

NERVED

Johan Ekelund: v, Marcus Hanser: g, Magnus Stenvinkel: b, Björn Lundberg: d

Stockholm/Falun - Nerved were formed in late 2000, originally featuring singer Emil Gammeltoft (ex-*Burn, Squeeler, Rampant, Manny Charlton*). After only six months the band had a nice break when the Tenants Association wanted to use that band's song *Believe In Me* in their commercial on TV and movies. This gave the band the financial resources to build their own studio and record the debut album. In October 2005 Gammeltoft left the band to pursue a different musical career in the folk rock band *Some Kind Of Robus*. Johan Ekelund later replaced him. The band had a second go at making music for a commercial, this time it was the power ballad *I Love You*, featuring Anna Hanser that was used by the organisation *Rädda Barnen* (Save The Children). In September 2011 the band searched for a new singer on Facebook. The band had also replaced drummer Lundberg with Joacim Brunnberg. *Nerved*'s style is not that easy to describe as they mix a lot of styles from poppy melodies to heavy melodic hard rock to industrial sounding songs. In 2012 the band drafted outstanding female singer Petra Kvännä (*Sky High*) and the bass was now handled by Elias Modig. A third album was slated for 2012. Website: www.nerved.com/

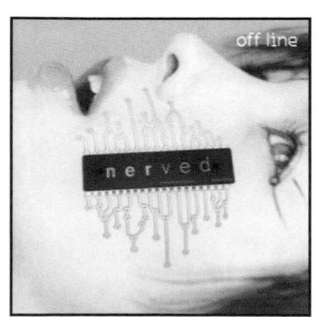

2004 CD - MMSCD009

2004 ■	OFF LINE	CD	Sphére De Feu	MMSCD009
2008 ■	FINALLY NERVED	CD	Sphére De Feu	MMSCD016
2008 ☐	I Love You	MCD 4tr	Sphére De Feu	MMSCDS032

Four different mixes of the same song, by Dumb Dan.

2008 CD - MMSCD016

NESTOR

Tobias Gustafsson: v, **Jonny Wemmenstedt:** g, **Martin Johansson:** k,
Marcus Åblad: b, **Mattias Carlsson:** d

Göteborg - *Nestor* were good solid hard rock with a melodic AOR:ish touch, while *Insane* was much heavier. Well worth checking out. Not to be confused with the stoner band from Borlänge.

1993 ■	Nestor	....MCD 4tr	private	....MUV 01
	Tracks: Life Is/Mice 'N Men/Love Soul 'N Pride/Second Of September.			
1996 ☐	Insane	....MCD 5tr	private	....NESTCD 9603
	Tracks: Insane/Pain/Cover 95/SweetHeart/I Am One.			

1993 MCD - MUV 01

NETHERBIRD

Johan "Nephente": v, **"Bizmark":** g/k, **Johan Nord:** g,
Tobias Gustafsson: b, **Erik Röjås:** d

Stockholm - Formed in 2004 and initially featured only Nephete and Bizmark. In 2005 the promo *Boulevard Black* was released in 100 copies. This year Janne Saarenpää handled the drums and Brice Leqlerc the bass, and the year after Daniel "Mojjo" Moilanen took over the drums and Jonas "Skinny" Kangur (*Deathstars*) the bass. In 2007 the demo EP *Blood Orchid* was released, followed by *Lighthouse Eternal* later the same year. *The Ghost Collector* contains all previous promo/EP tracks. The albums have also featured guest musicians such as Kitty Saric, Klara Gripe, Ivar Edding and Valkyria. In 2009 the band recorded another three-track promo entitled *Promo 2009*. On *Monument Black Colossal* the band had been expanded with guitarist Johan Nord, bass player Tobias Gustafsson (*Eucharist, Revengia*) and drummer Adrian Erlandsson (*At The Gates, The Haunted, Paradise Lost* etc). The artwork was made by Kristian Wåhlin (*Grotesque, Diabolique*). In 2010 Erlandsson was replaced by Erik Röjås. The band has also made all their recordings available for free download. In 2011 *Shadow And Show* saw the light of day, followed by the demo *Abysmal Allure* later the same year. *Netherbird* play great-sounding orchestrated death metal, at times similar to *Therion*, but without the opera vocals and clean male vocals. Nephete is also found in *Fear The Future*, and was previously in *Sickness/Benighted*.

2008 CDd - ASH 042 CD

2010 CD - SR 001 CD

2008 ■	THE GHOST COLLECTOR	...................................CDd	Pulverised	....................ASH 042 CD
2010 ■	MONUMENT BLACK COLOSSAL	.......................CD	Scarecrow	.....................SR 001 CD
2011 ■	Shadows And Snow	......................................MCD 4tr	Scarecrow	....................SCR 004 EP
	Tracks: Shadows And Snow/Twilight Gushes Forth…/Nightwards/Ode To The False. 500 copies, hand numbered.			
2012 ☐	Abysmal Allure	....MCD 4tr	Scarecrow	....................SCR 007EP
	Tracks: Myosotis Scorpioides/Abysmal Allure/Swedish Sadness/Born Defiant			
2012 ☐	Boulevard Black/Blood Orchid/Ashen Nectar	.....MLP PD 3tr	Scarecrow	....................SCR 010 PD

2011 MCD - SCR 004 EP

NEW BRAND

Daniel Taylan: v/b, **Thomas Jörlöv:** g, **Stefan Roxenby:** b, **Frank Roxenby:** d

Malmö - *New Brand* stem from the band *Stormbringer*, also known as *Phoenix*. They recorded the track *Let Me Know* for the Ebony Record's compilation *Metal Killers*, then featuring later highly acclaimed rapper Stakka Bo (Bo Johan Renck). *New Brand* was also featured on the compilation *Rock Of Sweden* (89 Hex). The band produced good solid melodic hard rock. Daniel moved to Australia and worked as background singer for John Farnham. He later returned to Sweden and sang with pop-group *Big Area*.

1990 ■	High On Feelings/Vertigo	...................................7"	private	....................UNI-2321

1990 7" - UNI-2321

NEW BREED

Marcus Andersson: v, **Andreas Tönnerheim:** g,
Johan Nyman: g, **Peter Andersson:** b, **Tobias Wiik:** d

Alingsås - Formed in October 1993. *New Breed* produce heavy, guitar-dominated grungy hard rock with the emphasis on strong melodies. "Heavy *Beatles*-grunge", could be one description. High-quality stuff indeed. Should attract fans of bands like *Alice In Chains* and *Pearl Jam*. The non-CD track *77 Weeks* is also found on the compilation *Best Of West* (95 SV) and four live-tracks are found on *Jubileums Rock* (94).

1995 ■	LOVE FOR POETS	...................................CD	EMP	....................EMCD95062

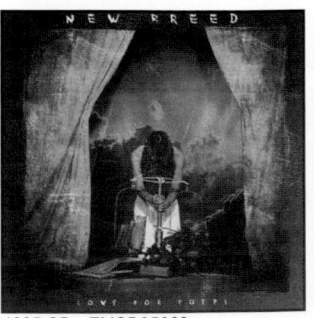

1995 CD - EMCD95062

NEW BULSARA

Jari Kujansuu: v/b, **Peder Lindblom:** g, **Mats Johansson:** k, **Martin Lindberg:** d

Tomelilla - Kujansuu started his career in the band *Heroes* that transformed into *Laroche*, who had two tracks on the Pang compilation *Heavy Metal* (1982). The band became *Cheers* and recorded the single *Run Down/Loose Control* (Studio 55, ST 55-511) in 1989. *Cheers* dissolved and in 1993 Jari formed *New Bulsara*. An dubious video was made for the song *The Thing*, but the music is really good. The album, *Monday*, is AOR, ranging from almost westcoast/poppy things to really good guitar-dominated rockers. After problems with the label the band changed

its name to **Seven Days** and released another single, *So Right*, in 1998. **Seven Days** split in 1999 and Jari wrote music, played bass in American band **Ten Jinn** and in 2006 he released his first solo album, *Silverbutton*. He is now found in pop band **Ronja** and in cover band **Too Much Monkey Business**, together with Lindberg. The track *Another Day* is found on the *15 On 1 Twise* (93 Soundfront) compilation, the featuring drummer Alexandra Isberg.

1995 □	MONDAY	CD	LiquiDisc	LCD 001
1995 ■	Right Or Wrong/Good Dreams	CDS	LiquiDisc	LCD 001P
1995 □	Pleasure & Lies/So Right/Burning	MCD 3tr	LiquiDisc	LMD 001

1995 CDS - LCD 001P

NEW KEEPERS OF THE WATER TOWERS
Rasmus Booberg: v/g, Victor Berg: g, Robin Holmberg: b, Tor Sjödén: d

Stockholm - The strangely named quartet from Stockholm was formed in 2006 by Rasmus and Tor, inspired by the Swedish doom and stoner scene. Broberg and Berg are also in **Vexation** and the latter is also in **Divider**. The band's first two EPs were merged together and released as the album *Chronicles*. The band was actually only called **New Keepers** on the original releases. Albin Rönnblad Ericsson played bass on these recordings. On the second album Edvard Hansson handled the lower frequencies, while Karlskrona son Robin Holmberg replaced him for the 2011 release. The band plays great-sounding heavy, crunchy stoner in the vein of **Kaross** mixed with **Mastodon**.

2008 MCD - - -

2007 □	CHRONICLES OF THE MASSIVE BOAR	MCD 8tr	Toraz	- -
	Tracks: Enter The Great Forest/Giant Subway Beast/The Strafing Lobster/The Three-headed Cow/The Knowledgeable Kangaroo/The Monument/Fall Of The Massive Boar Pt.1/Fall Of The Massive Boar Pt.2			
2008 ■	CHRONICLES OF ICEMAN	MCD 7tr	Toraz	- -
	Tracks: Awrecktion/Masterclaw/Persuit Of Yeti/Scientists And The Man Of Ice/Rise Of The Lizard King/Flight Of The Reptilians/New Sleepers			
2009 □	CHRONICLES	CD	Meteor City (USA)	MCY-048
2010 □	CHRONICLES	LP	Meteor City (USA)	MCY-048
2010 □	CHRONICLES OF ICEMAN	MLP 7tr	High Roller	HHR 107
	200 white, 200 black/orange splatter + 100 black vinyl. Poster.			
2011 ■	CALYDONIAN HUNT	CDp	Meteor City	MCYCD 60
2013 ■	THE COSMIC CHILD	CD	Listenable	POSH 213
2013 □	THE COSMIC CHILD	LP	Listenable	POSH 213
	150 black + 150 blue vinyl copies.			

2011 CDp - MCYCD 60

2013 CD - POSH 213

NEX
Tore Stjerna: v/g/b, Pär Gustafsson: g, Per "Perra" Karlsson: d

Stockholm - Tore Stjerna, who also runs Necromorbus Studio, is for today's death metal what Tomas Skogsberg and his Sunlight Studio was in the nineties. He has also played with numerous death/black metal bands such as **Funeral Mist, Watain, Zavorash, In Aeternum, Blackwitch, Necromorbus, Chaos Omen, Ofermod** etc. Here he however goes in a different direction playing slow searing doom metal sounding a bit like a mix of **Candlemass** and **Entombed** on *To Ride, Shoot Straight...* meets **Katatonia**. Great heavy stuff indeed. Drummer Karlsson is/has also been found in numerous bands such as **Nominon, Serpent, T.A.R, In Aeternum, Bergraven, Suffer, Dion Fortune** and **Altar**, while Gustavsson is also in **Bergraven**. Highly recommended.

2007 ■	ZERO	CD	Next Horizon	NHZCD 002
2007 □	ZERO	CD	Deathgasm (USA)	DG 042

2007 CD - NHZCD 002

NIDEN DIV. 187
Henke Forss: v, Leo Pignon: g, Jonas Albrektsson: b, Jocke Pettersson: d

Mjölby - The band was formed in 1995 as a trio. 187 is the American police term for murder, while Niden was just "a name". Jonas joined the band after the MCD on which Leo handled all the strings. Henke and Jocke are also found in **Dawn** and Leo in **A Canorous Quintet**. Jocke and Jonas are found in **Thy Primordial** and in grind-core band **Retaliation**, who has made several releases. **Niden Div. 187** didn't officially die, but has only been resting... for a long time. The band produces black metal mixed with melodic grindcore similar to **Zyklon B**. Forss has also been found in **Funeral Feast, Circle Six** and **In Flames**, Pettersson in **Ocean Chief, Regurgitate, Unmoored, Cranium, Traumatic, Carcaroth** and is now in **Bloodshield Nihil**. Pignon was previously in **The Plague, This Ending, A Canorous Quintet, Curriculum Mortis** and is now in **This Ending**. Albrektsson has been in **Ceremonial Execution, Thy Primordial, Indungeon, Carcaroth** and is found in **Retaliation, Bloodshed Nihil** and **King Of Asgard**.

1996 MCD - NR 6665

1996 ■	Towards Judgement	MCD 4tr	Necropolis Records	NR 6665
	Tracks: Black Water/Renitence/A View In The Mirror Black/Towards Judgement			
1997 □	IMPERGIUM	CD	Necropolis Records	NR 016
2004 ■	IMPERGIUM/TOWARDS JUDGEMENT	CD	Barbarian Records	BARB 606
2004 □	IN THE TWILIGHT OF WAR	LP	BBSA	BBSA 3
	Same as the above CD with new title and artwork.			

2004 CD - BARB 606

NIDRIKE
Henrik "Gjallar" Kindvall: v, Mattias "Gorgoth" Svensson: v/g/b, Liedheim: d

Karlskrona - Not to be confused with the Karlshamn band, even though both bands are from the same region. Kindvall is also found in folk band **Skald**, while Gorgoth and Liedheim reside in **Vanmakt**. *Nidrike* signed a new deal with Undead Propaganda Records from Sweden and recorded tracks for a MCD in 2009. It has however not been released and the label is no more. The name means approximately "country of scorn" in old Swedish.

2008 ■ BLODSARV ....CD Black Plague.....................................BPR 014

2008 CD - BPR 014

NIDSANG
Amducious: v/g, Blodshird: b/g, Korpr: d

Sundsvall - The name means something similar to "song of scorn". Formed in 2004 under the name **Lammoth** and recorded two demos, *Silent On Their Thrones* and *Rehearsal Tape* under this name. They changed their name and recorded their first demo under the new name the year after. After this they parted ways with guitarist Erik "Hat" Nyberg. The band previously featured bassist Joel "Terrorgoat" Viklund (**Fenria, Cavevomit**). All three members are also found in **Lammoth**. Old-school black metal, like a mix of **Darkthrone**, **Bathory** and **Rotting Christ**.

2007 ☐ THE MARK OF DEATH..CD Drakkar ....DKCD 056
2008 ■ Streams Of Darkness...7" Drakkar ....DK EP 011
    500 copies. Tracks: Come Darkness, Come/Drinking The Serpents Venom

2008 7" - DK EP 011

NIFELHEIM
Per "Hellbutcher" Gustavsson: v, Erik "Tyrant" Gustavsson: b,
Sebastian Ramstedt: g, Johan Bergebäck: g, Peter Stjärnvind: d

Dals Långed/Göteborg - *Nifelheim* means "the dark hell" in the Nordic realm of death. On the first albums Per handled bass and vocals, Erik played guitar and by Martin "Demon" Hansén played rums. Per and Erik were also part of **Pagan Rites**. *Unholy Death/The Devastation* is a 10-year anniversary release that was recorded already in 1993 and has, as the cover states, "worst possible sound-quality guaranteed". Per and Erik are known to the Swedish people as "Bröderna Hårdrock" (The hard rock brothers), as they appeared in a documentary and later in a commercial on national broadcast. They are extreme collectors of **Iron Maiden** and have an impressive collection of records and paraphernalia. However, *Nifelheim* are far from **Iron Maiden**'s finesse and refinery. They spew brutal, uncompromising death metal with gargling, warped and utterly evil vocals. In 2002 the line-up also featured guitarists Mikka "Sadist" and Sebastian "Vengeance Of Beyond" Ramstedt, but in the past people like John Zwetzloot, Emil Nödtveit and Adrian Erlandsson have been in and out of the band. In 2006 drummer Martin "Devastator" Axenrot was replaced by Peter Stjärnvind (**Krux, Unanimated, Born Of Fire, Face Down, Regurgitate** etc) and guitarists Sebastian Ramstedt (**Morpheus, Necrophobic, Exhumed**) and Johan Bergebäck (**Morpheus, Necrophobic, Exhumed, Dismember**) were added to the line-up. The band also appears on various compilations, such as *Gummo Soundtrack* (97 London, featuring T Kjellgren on drums), *In Conspiracy With Satan - Tribute To Bathory* (98 HOK), *Riff Vol 2* (00 Riff), *Headbangers Against Disco Vol 2* (96 Static Age). Per and Erik are now flanked by Eric Ljung (**Ondskapt**), Tamás Buday (**Tormentor**) and Felipe Plaza Kutzbach.

The devil's servants of the force of darkness

1995 ☐	NIFELHEIM..CD	Necropolis Records	NR 007 CD
1995 ☐	NIFELHEIM..LP	Necropolis Records	NR 007 LP
1998 ☐	DEVIL'S FORCE..CD	Necropolis Records	NR 022 CD
1998 ☐	DEVIL'S FORCE..LP	Necropolis Records	NR 022 LP
2000 ■	SERVANTS OF DARKNESS..........................CD	Black Sun	BS 22
2000 ☐	SERVANTS OF DARKNESS..........................LP	Black Sun	BS 22
2000 ☐	SERVANTS OF DARKNESS..........................CD	Black Sun	BS 22
	Slipcase.		
2000 ☐	Unholy Death/The Devastation.....................7"	Primitive Art	PAR 021
2003 ☐	MCMXC - MMIII..LP	I Hate	IHATE 005
	1000 copies in clear vinyl.		
2006 ☐	Thunder Metal (split)..................................7"	I Hate	IHATE 026
	Split with Volcano. Tracks: Raging Flames/Sepulchral Fornication. 900 black.		
2006 ☐	Thunder Metal (split)..................................7" PD	I Hate	IHATE 026
	100 copies.		
2006 ☐	Thunder Metal (split)..................................MCD 3tr	I Hate	IHATE 026
	Split with Volcano. Tracks: Raging Flames/Sepulchral Fornication/Insulter Of Jesus Christ.		
2006 ☐	Tribute To Slayer Mag (split).......................7"g	Nuclear War Now	ANTI GOTH 049
	Split with Sadistik Exekution. Track:Gates Of Damnation 200 copies in red vinyl. Poster.		
2008 ■	ENVOY OF LUCIFER.....................................LPg	Regain Records	RR 128
2008 ☐	ENVOY OF LUCIFER.....................................CD	Regain Records	RR 128
2009 ☐	NIFELHEIM..CD	Regain Records	RR 150 CD
2009 ☐	NIFELHEIM..LP	Regain Records	RR 150 LP
2009 ☐	DEVIL'S FORCE..CD	Regain Records	RR 151 CD

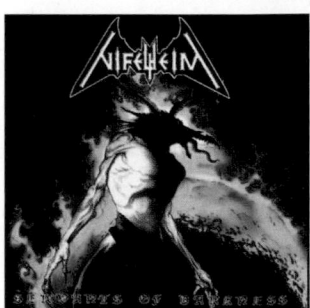

2000 CD - BS 22

2008 LPg - RR 128

2009 ☐	SERVANTS OF DARKNESS	LP	Back On Black	BOBV 102 LP
2010 ■	DEVIL'S FORCE	LP	Regain Records	RR 151 LP

Altered artwork.

2010 LP - RR 151 LP

NIFTERS

**Mats Larsson (now Seiterö): v/g, Johan Söderhielm: g,
Christoffer "Zwedda" Svedbo: g, Martin Thornell: b, Jocke Göthberg: d**

Norrköping - In 1999 Mats Larsson (now Seiterö) and Johan Söderhielm formed the band *Nifters* and drafted bassist Robert Breiner and drummer Mattias Svensson.. The first MCD was produced by Jocke Göthberg (*Marduk, In Flames, Dimenzion Zero*). Svensson left and was replaced by Tommy Storback. The band had a minor hit with the song *074-830622 Phonecall To God*. Shortly after the release, Göthberg joined the band as drummer. From the second release on the band has been using producer Peter Samuelsson, surprisingly enough he's the bass player of dance band *Barbados*. On *If This One Becomes A Hit*, Breiner was out and the bass on the recording was played by Joakim Samuelsson. Christoffer "Zwedda" Svedbo was added as second guitarist in 2004, which enabled Larsson to focus on the vocals. In 2007 Martin Thornell replaced the departed Joakim Samuelsson. Great-sounding modern melodic metal hardcore/mallcore.

2003 MCDd - JUJU6

2003 ■	Cognitive Eclipse	MCDd 5tr	Black JuJu	JUJU6
	Tracks: It's Not Me It's You/074-830622 Phonecall To God/Schlaraffenland/Spir Fortis/ Lackadaisical			
2004 ☐	Allein/Reality Will Kill Me	CDS 2tr	Black JuJu	JUJU13
2004 ☐	If This One Becomes A Hit I Swear I Am Going To Kill Myself	CDS 2tr	NZW	NZW 003
	Tracks: If This One Becomes A Hit I Swear I Am Going To Kill Myself/A Favour In Vain			
2007 ☐	Genesis Apocalypse/A Cut Smile/Genesis Apocalypse (video)	CDS 2tr	NZW	NZW 005
2008 ☐	INVISIBLE CAINE	CD	NZW	NZW 006
2011 ■	ZALVATORE CAINE INCORPORATED	CD	Killer Caine	KCR 110

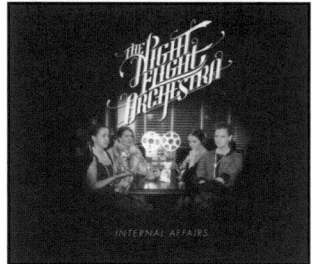

2011 CD - KCR 110

NIGHT FLIGHT ORCHESTRA, THE

**Björn "Speed" Strid: v, David Andersson: g, Richard Larsson: k,
Sharlee d'Angelo: b, Jonas Källsbäck: d**

Glumslöv/Göteborg/Helsingborg - Quite a surprising project. With people like *Soilwork* members Strid and Andersson and d'Angelo (*Arch Enemy, Spiritual Beggars*) you'd expect a heavy affair. Well, This band is quite close to *Asia*, with Strid singing cleanmand very melodic. Great melodic pomp hard rock with a strong seventies touch. Highly recommended.

2012 ■	INFERNAL AFFAIRS	CDd	Coroner Records	CR 023

2012 CDd - CR 023

NIGHTFALL

A Lindén, A Hallgren

Good-quality melodic hard rock in the vein of early *Treat* or *Alien*. Recorded at Studio Largen.

1987 ■	Hold On To Love/Don't Stop The Feeling	7"	Platina	PL 25	$

NIGHTINGALE

Dan Swanö: v/g, Dag "Tom Nouga" Swanö: g/k, Erik Oskarsson: b/v, Tom Björn: d

Örebro - The first *Nightingale* song *Time To Die* was recorded way back in 1978. However, it took a few years until the project became a reality. Dan was also in *Edge Of Sanity/Unicorn*. The style was quite far from his work with death metal band *Edge Of Sanity*, but closer to his symphonic band *Unicorn*. *The Breathing Shadow* contains quite mellow progressive/symphonic rock, like a heavier version of *Marillion*. The first two albums featured Dan Swanö on all instruments and vocals, while his brother Dag "Tom Nouga" Swanö handled guitars, bass and keyboards on I. Tom Björn is also found in *Memory Garden* and ex-*Memento Mori*, and bass player Erik Oskarsson is ex-*Blackbird*. *Nightingale* evolved and the later releases are outstanding symphonic/progressive hard rock, ranging from softer parts to heavy melodic rockers, not too far from bands like *Ayreon* and *Star One*. Dan continued this musical path in *Witherscape*.

1987 7" - PL 25

1995 CD - BMCD 66

1995 ■	THE BREATHING SHADOW	CD	Black Mark	BMCD 66
1996 ☐	THE CLOSING CHRONICLES	CD	Black Mark	BMCD 90
2000 ☐	I	CD	Black Mark	BMCD 135
2001 ☐	LIVE AT THE METALFEST	CD	Spam	SPAM 000
	Limited fan club edition.			
2002 ☐	ALIVE AGAIN: THE BREATHING SHADOW PART IV	CD	Black Mark	BMCD 165
2002 ☐	ALIVE AGAIN: THE BREATHING SHADOW PART IV	CD	The End Records	TE 030
2003 ☐	THE CLOSING CHRONICLES	CD	Irond (Russia)	CD 03-422
2003 ☐	I	CD	Irond (Russia)	CD 03-426
2004 ☐	INVISIBLE	CD	Black Mark	BMCD 172
2005 ■	NIGHTFALL OVERTURE	CD	Black Mark	BMCD 184
2007 ☐	WHITE DARKNESS	CDd	Black Mark	BMDP 187

2005 CD - BMCD 184

NIGHTSCAPE
Simon Åkesson: v, Joakim Wiklund: g, Pontus Åkesson: g,
Markus Sundquist: k, Stefan Vidmark: b, Tyler Voelz: d

Skellefteå - Two schoolmates formed *Nightscape* in 2001 and after some collaboration on their own it became a band. Widmark is also found in *Terrortory* and *December Child*. *Nightscape* plays great neoclassical melodic power metal with killer vocals and great guitar work, a bit similar to early Yngwie Malmsteen meets *The Ring*. Great mix by Jonas Kjellgren.

2005 ■ SYMPHONY OF THE NIGHT ....CD Lion Music...LMC 150
2005 □ SYMPHONY OF THE NIGHT ....CD King (Japan) KICP-1086
     Bonus: Merlin (demo)

2005 CD - LMC 150

NIGHTSHADE
Daniel Kvist: v, Stefan "Snake Stevens" Rasmusson: g, Daniel Hjelm: g,
Christer Pedersen: b, Daniel Larson: k, Kristoffer "Kristo Napalm" Palm: d

Kungsbacka (Göteborg) - Formed in 1996 as *Northern Shadow*, initially featuring guitarists Nicklas Magnusson (*Dragonland, Prophanity*) and Daniel Hjelm, drummer Daniel Boström, singer Adam and bass player Sebbe. The band recorded three demos before the album, *Benighted* (1997), *Devil* (1998) and *Astoreth* (1999). On the album Hjelm had been replaced by Stefan Rasmusson and Boström by Palm. Recorded at Studio Underground by Pelle Saether. Try mixing **In Flames, Dimmu Borgir** and **Dark Tranquility**. Really good melodic death metal. The band split in 2003 and the last known line-up featured Kvist, Rasmusson, Magnusson, Pedersen, Larsson and Palm. Christer Pedersen was later in **Apostasy, Alsvart** and is now found in **Dragonland**, while Kvist went to **Taetre, Sacrilege** and **Dragonland**, and Rasmusson is found in **Chilihounds**.

2001 ■ WIELDING THE SCYTHE..CD Scarlet...SC 302

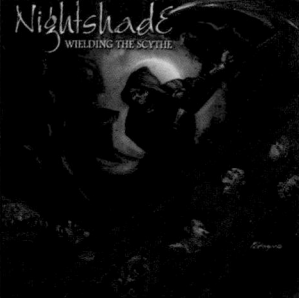
2001 CD - SC 302

NIGHTVISION
Peter Högberg: v, Stefan Fjellner: g, Mårten Sandén: k,
Johan Pettersson: b, Michael Szemler: d

Stockholm - Not to be confused with the UK thrashers. Formed in 2001 and noted by **Fatal Smile/MindSplit** singer Hans Andersson, who recommended MTM to sign the band. Great sounding power loaded eighties-oriented melodic hard rock with a kick-ass, high-pitched singer, a bit similar to later day's **Pretty Maids**. Highly recommended. In 2011 Sandén was out of the band and Pettersson had been replaced by John Egnell.
Website: www.myspace.com/nightvisionsweden

2005 ■ NIGHTVISION...CD MTM...0681-134

2005 CD - 0681-134

NIHILIST
Lars-Göran "L-G" Petrov: v, Alex Hellid: g, Ulf "Uffe" Cederlund: g,
Johnny Hedlund: b, Nicke Andersson: d

Stockholm - *Nihilist* are by many, including Daniel Ekeroth, author of the excellent book *Swedish Death Metal*, said to to be the first 100% death metal band in Sweden. Considering they only lasted for a little over two years, they made great impression. The band was formed in 1987 from the ashes of hardcore band **Brainwarp**, by drummer Nicke Andersson, bassist, later guitarist Leif Cuzner and guitarist Alex Hellid. Andersson's former band mate Johan Edlund was the band's singer for a short period (two days, as they had different musical goals). Edlund would later appear in **Treblinka** and **Tiamat**. Singer Mattias "Buffa" Boström was drafted later the same year, but never sang on any recordings. He was replaced by Lars-Göran "L-G" Petrov (at the time drummer in **Morbid**) in 1988 and the band also drafted Ulf Cederlund (also in **Morbid**) on guitar, but only as a temporary session man. The band recorded the first demo *Premature Autopsy*. Cuzner now concentrated on guitar and bassist Johnny Hedlund was added to the line-up. The band now entered Sunlight Studios together with Tomas Skogsberg and recorded the second demo, *Only Shreds Remain*. The band had a setback when Cuzner's family moved to Canada taking their son with them. Now, as **Morbid** had split up, Cederlund stepped back into the ring as a member. The band was now asked to record a song for a Slayer magazine compilation, which was *Morbid Devourment*. The compilation however never happened. In 1989 CBR Records released a four-track promo MCD featuring the track *Face Of Evil*. It featured bands that were supposed to be released on CBR (**Strebers, D.T.A.L, Cemetarium** and **Nihilist**), but this never happened. In August 1990, the band recorded their third demo, *Drowned*, from which the song *Severe Burns* was later rerecorded by **Entombed** on *Clandestine*. Some extra songs were also recorded, in a more crude format, and would later appear on the bootleg single *Radiation Sickness* (a cover of **Repulsion**). Problems with bass player Hedlund caused the demise of the band. However Andersson, Cederlund, Petrov and Hellid changed their name to **Entombed** and with the aid of **Dismember** bassist David Blomqvist, they recorded the demo *But Life Goes On*,

1989 7" - BRD 001

2005 CD - TRECD 018 (promo)

2005 CD - TRECD 018

again in Sunlight Studios. The rest is history. Johnny later formed *Unleashed*. *Nihilist* sure were pioneers, thrashing out well-played death metal with lots of variations. Definitely interesting for fans of *Entombed*. Cuzner sadly passed away in Montreal in 2006.

1989 ■	Drowned...7"	Bloody Rude Defect Records	BRD 001
	Tracks: Severe Burns/When Life Has Ceased. This was originally the Drowned demo.		
2005 ■	NIHILIST...CD	Threeman Records	TRECD 018
2005 ■	NIHILIST...CD	Candlelight (USA)	CDL 176
2009 □	CARNAL LEFTOVERS...Box 5x7"	Century Media	9979061
2011 □	CARNAL LEFTOVERS...LP+7"	Southern Lord	LORD 12X $
	200 copies in gold, silver and black vinyl.		

Unofficial release:
| 1991 ■ | Radiation Sickness/Face Of Evil/Morbid Devourment...7" | - - ... - - |
| | A bootleg 7". | |

1991 7" - - -

NINE

Johan Lindqvist: v, Benjamin Vallé: g, Robert Karlson: b, Karl Torstensson: d

Linköping - Pretty hard band to describe. *Nine* started out in 1994, originally in the punk-jazzish hardcore-vein, and recorded their first demo, *Sign Of Strength*, the same year. The band was formed out of the ashes of *Gregory's Edge*, *Chopstick* and *Galore Confusion*. The debut album was recorded at Studio Sunlight and produced by Fred Estby (*Dismember*). On *Lights Out* influences from bands like *Motörhead*, *Black Sabbath* alongside with sounds of *Milencollin*, *The Hellacopters* and *Entombed* were found. The album was co-produced by the late Mieszko Talarczyk (R.I.P) (*Nasum*) and Mathias Färm (*Millencollin*). Bass player Oskar Eriksson left after the recording and was temporarily replaced by Martin Lindkvist (*Bombshell Rocks*), later permanently by Robert Karlsson. The album also contains a hidden track called *9 Seconds Of Fame* also featuring Johan's brother Henrik (*Outlast, Dead End*). *Killing Angels* was produced by Daniel Bergstrand (*Crawley, Devin Townsend* etc) and the band's sound had now become even heavier, more akin to classic death metal with a hardcore touch. The album also features guest spots from L-G Petrov (*Entombed*) and Örjan Örnkloo (*Misery Loves Co.*). On *It's Your Funeral* drummer Tor Castensson had been replaced by Karl Torstensson.

Four dressed up as a nine
Photo: Jakob Fridholm

1995 □	To The Bottom...MCD 4tr	No Looking Back	NLB CD 004
	Tracks: To The Bottom/Cold/Miles Apart/Grasp Me		
1997 □	LISTEN...CD	Startracks	STAR 5217-2
1998 □	LISTEN...CD	Sidekicks/Burning Heart	JABSCO 011
1998 ■	KISSED BY THE MISANTHROPE...CD	Sidekicks/Burning Heart	JABSCO 012
1998 □	KISSED BY THE MISANTHROPE...LPg	Bridge Of Compassion	BOC 010
	Purple vinyl.		
1999 □	SPLIT...CD	Outlast Records	OR 001
	Split with Spanish band Like Peter At Home. Tracks: Getting Out/The Wolves Want More/Nothing Will Remain		
2001 □	LIGHTS OUT...CD	Burning Heart	BHR 128
2001 □	LIGHTS OUT...LP	Burning Heart	BHR 128-1
2003 ■	KILLING ANGELS...CDd	Burning Heart	BHR 168
2003 □	KILLING ANGELS...LP	Combat Rock Industry	CRI 020
2003 □	KILLING ANGELS...CD	Deathwish Inc (USA)	DW 40.0
2004 □	KILLING ANGELS...CD	Alliance Trax (Japan)	AT-1013
	Bonus: Ironhead/...And The Wolves Want More/Damnation/Anxiety Report (video)/Euthanasia (video)/Time Has Come (video)		
2006 □	Death Is Glorious...MCD 4tr	Combatrock	CRI 033
	Tracks: Everything Went Black/The Long Sleep/The Day Before The Day/Just To Get Away		
2006 □	Death Is Glorious...7" 4tr	Blacktop Records	BTR 005
2007 □	IT'S YOUR FUNERAL...CD	Spinefarm	SPI 279 CD
2007 □	IT'S YOUR FUNERAL...LPg	Combat Rock Industry	CRI 043

1998 CD - JABSCO 012

2003 CDd - BHR 168

NINGIZZIA

Niclas Frohagen: v/g/k/d, Stéphane Peudupin: g

Malmö/France - Quite atmospheric and orchestrated doomy death metal with the addition of flutes, acoustic guitar, mixing growl, clean vocals and female vocals. You will find a strong folky touch as well. Good stuff! Frohagen and Peudupin are the main persons of the band, one in Sweden and one in France. The songs are written over the internet and the band considers both Sweden and France their homeland. In 1998 the demo-CD *The Dark Path* was recorded, which was later reworked and released as a tape in 1999. The track *Beneath The Silent Moon* was featured on the compilation *The Cold, The Silent* (1999 Dragonflight). A cover of *Freezin' Moon* was also recorded for a *Mayhem* tribute. Dolorus Novella features guest spots from flutist Anna Ekblad, singer Jenny Frohagen and violinist Micce Andersson.
Website: www.ningizzia-doom.com

| 2003 ■ | DOLORUS NOVELLA...CD | Haceldama Productions | HP 03 CD |

2003 CD - HP 03 CD

NINNUAM

Mattias "Matte Hellcore"Johansson: v, Kim Laakso: g, Robert Gustafsson: g,
Robert Johansson: k, Måns Jaktlund: b, Thord Brännkärr: d

Katrineholm - *Ninnuam* were formed late 2001 under the moniker *Yxa* ("axe" in Swedish), featuring Laakso, Gustafsson, Brännkärr and bass player Andreas "Lenny" Jennische. Soon singer Johansson completed the band and they changed name to *Ninnuam*. The name was taken from the book *The Necronomicon* and Ninnuam refers to the power of the demon Marduk. In 2002 Måns Jaktlund replaced Jennische and the four track demo *Scar Salvation* was recorded. In 2003 the band was picked up by Finnish label, Low Frequency Records and the debut album was recorded. In 2007 singer Johansson left the band to focus on his other band *Centicore*. They found replacement Stephanie Rudert, but soon guitarist Gustafsson decided to leave. Thomas Wahlberg (ex-*Julie Laughs No More, Triton Enigma*) replaced him. In 2009 singer Rudert left the band and was replaced by Joakim Gustafsson and the band recorded six new songs for a demo released in 2011. *Ninnuam* plays quite orchestrated, but still brutal, death metal.

2004 CD - 61118

2004 ■ PROCESS OF LIFE SEPARATION ....CD Crash Music..61118

NIRVANA 2002

Orvar Säfström: v/g, Lars Henriksson: b, Erik Qvick: d

Swamp metal?

Edsbyn/Malmö - *Nirvana 2002*, originally named *Prophet 2002* and then *Nirvana* but changed name for obvious reasons, only existed for a brief period between 1988-1992 and only recorded some demos. The band was featured on compilations such as a four band split 7" on *Opinionate* (1990), *Projections Of A Stained Mind*. Säfström also sang in *Entombed* on the *Crawl* EP, but went on to a career in television as host and journalist, still keeping his long hair and musical interest though. The CD is a compilation of the bands demos and unreleased material, and two old songs with new vocals. The band made a reunion gig in 2007 for the released of Daniel Ekeroth's book Swedish Death Metal, after which the band's demos were finally released. *Nirvana 2002* plays old-school-style death metal in the vein of vintage *Entombed* or *Dismember*.

2011 LP - RR 7051-1

2011 □ RECORDINGS 89-91 ....CDv Relapse Records ....RR 7051-2
2011 □ RECORDINGS 89-91 ....CD Relapse Records (Japan)..............YSCY-1165
2011 ■ RECORDINGS 89-91 ....LP Relapse Records ....RR 7051-1
100 clear and 500 black vinyl copies.

NIVA (aka OXYGEN)

Tony Niva: v, Roger Ljunggren: g, Marcus Persson: k,
Peter Andersson: b, Bengan Andersson: d

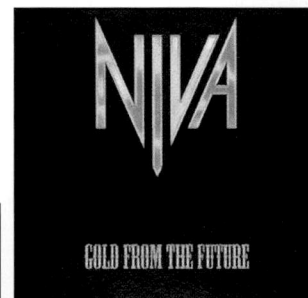
2011 CD - MICP-11014

Skövde - Tony Niva recorded an outstanding demo in 1987-88 with the band *Zanity* before leaving for *Swedish Erotica*. He then recorded a 7" with the band *Tracy Goes Crazy* and also sang in *Malibu Band*. In 1991 he joined *Axia*, a band that later turned into *Niva*. The line-up on the debut features Tony on vocals, guitarist Robert Jacobsson, bass player Peter Andersson and drummer Dan Götestam. The album was produced by Tomas Skogsberg, well known as the death metal producer working with bands such as *Entombed* and *Dismember*. *Europe*'s Ian Haugland played the drums on the album. *No Capitulation* was released in Japan in December 1994. It was also supposed to be issued through Long Island in Europe and Empire in Sweden, but nothing happened. A great band with melody, finesse, power and an outstanding singer. In the end of 1995 they started working on album number two, produced by *Zanity/Master Massive* guitarist Jan Strandh, but the band was put to rest. Tony Niva joined *Lion's Share* in 2000 and recorded the album *Entrance* with the band, and Andersson is today found in *Mean Streak*. However, in 2010 things started happening again. Guitarist Roger Ljunggren (*T'Bell, Grand Illusion*) started writing with keyboard player Marcus and the two were looking for a great singer. They called Tony and they decided to go under the established *Niva* banner. The song *Janitor Of Love* was recorded and sent to Japanese label Avalon Marquee, who loved it and wanted to hear more. Another four tracks were recorded and the deal was sealed. Former *Niva* bassist, Peter Andersson makes a guest appearance on the second album. This one is less metal and more eighties AOR-oriented. In 2012 Escape Music released the album, but the name was now changed to *Oxygen*. In 2013 they went back to using the *Niva* moniker on *Magnitude*.

1994 CD - XRCN-1175

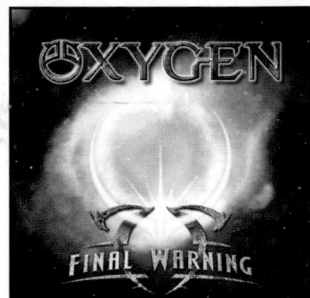
2012 CD - ESM 240

1994 ■ NO CAPITULATION..CD Zero (Japan) XRCN-1175
2011 ■ GOLD FROM THE FUTURE..CD Avalon Marquee (Japan)..............MICP-11014
Bonus: Bring Back The Joy
2012 ■ FINAL WARNING..CD Escape ....ESM 240
Released under the name Oxygen. Bonus: Bring Back The Joy
2013 □ MAGNITUDE ....CD AOR Heaven......................................0085

NME WITHIN

Jonas Andersson (now Beijer): v/g, Leif Larsson: b

Göteborg/Trollhättan - If you like *Helmet* or *Shotgun Messiah*'s *Violent New Breed*, then you should check this band out. Brutal guitars, good vocals and a never ending drum sequencer.

1994 MCD - DOLPH 03

Leif is ex-*Frozen Eyes* and was also in the Danish melodic band *Rhapsody*. On stage and on the second album the band was reinforced by guitarists Niclas Mellander (ex-*Dead End*) and Eric Rauti and drummer Anders Ström (*Idiots Rule, Ton Of Bricks*). The track *In Bloom* is found on the *Nirvana* tribute album on Black Sun Records. On *Utopian Konnektion* the band was joined by *Nordman* singer Håkan Hemlin, Tony Jelencovich (*Transport League, Massive Audio Nerve*) and Johan Ling (*Crossing Oceans*). The band is now defunct and Leif was later found in *Black Ingvars*. Rauti has later been found in *Torch*, *Dreamland* and *Opera Diabolicus*.

1994	■	SON OF A GUN	CD	Dolphin Productions	DOLPH 03
1996	☐	Utopian Konnektion	MCD 3tr	Dzynamite	DzRCD001
		Tracks: Utopian Konnektion/Krucikks Fetishist/Utopian Konnektion(Vogue version)			
1997	■	SCIENCE KRUCIFIKKTION	CD	Dzynamite	DzRCD002
2000	☐	SCIENCE KRUCIFIKKTION (Special Edition The Enigma Paradox)	CD	Diamond Records	DR 004

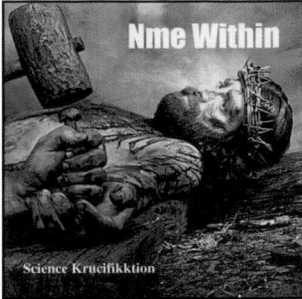
1997 CD - DzRCD002

NO HAWAII
Jamil Pannee: v, Jonas Pannee: g, Carlos Ibarra: g, Erik Ward: b, Gustaf Albinsson: d

Göteborg - *No Hawaii* play quite experimental neo-hardcore infused metal, at times a bit reminiscent of *The Mars Volta* meets *Tool* with a touch of Swedish colleagues like *Cult Of Luna* and *Burst*, mixing growl and clean vocals. The album was produced by Carlos Sepulveda (*Psychore*). Website: www.nohawaii.com/

2007	■	Bruce Lee In Your Brain	MCD 3tr	private	NH 001
		Tracks: Al Final Todos Pagamos/Vessel/Isaul			
2010	☐	SNAKE MY CHARMS	CD	Parallel Music	PM 002

2007 MCD - NH 001

NO RULES
Olof Gustafsson: v, Jens Malmborg: v, Tommy Magnusson: g/k/b,
Johan Augustsson: b, Martin Nilsson: d

Ronneby - The band was founded by Tommy in 2004 and the name stems from the band having no rules or limits on where they pick their influences from. *No Rules* plays quite good symphonic rock in the vein of *Galleon* with a touch of *Asia* and *Pallas* with a heavier touch. Unfortunately the vocals are way below average and the production lacks a bit. Still, it's worth checking out for fans of neo-prog. The band reformed for a new album in 2013.

2006	■	WHERE WE BELONG	CD	No Rules Music	NRM-001

2006 CD - NRM-001

NOCTES
Johan Lönn: v, Holger Thorsin: g, Pasi Lundegård: g,
Åsa Rosenberg: b, Carl Leijon: k, Hugo Thorsin: d

Stockholm - The band was formed under the name *Concealed* in 1992 by Holger and Johan. Their first demo was entitled *Dance Of Dying Dreams*. Åsa joined the band after the first album and took over the bass from Johan. Musically the band range from high-speed to heavy, yet symphonic death metal. Lönn screeches his way through the songs in the traditional manner. Both albums were recorded in Studio Sunlight. After the second album the line-up changed when Johan and Pasi left the band, leaving the vocal duties to Holger and Åsa.

1996 CDd - NFR 025

1996	■	PANDEMONIC REQUIEM	CDd	No Fashion	NFR 025
1999	■	VEXILLA REGIS PRODEUNT INFERNI	CD	No Fashion	NFR 034

1999 CD - NFR 034

NOCTUM
David Indelöf: v/g, Per Wikström: g, Tobias Rosén: b, Gustaf Heinemann Ljungström: d

Uppsala - *Noctum* were formed in 2009 by four school mates influenced by the music created some thirty years ago. Similar to *Witchcraft*, *Witchfinder General* meets *Black Widow*. Good singer, but quite "Swenglish" pronunciation. Tobbe runs the club Oblivion in Uppsala. In August 2011 the band was picked up by Metal Blade Records. The band also announced Per Wikström (ex-*Sweet Danger*) had been replaced by Daniel Johansson. Indelöf is also found in *Veternus*.

2010	☐	THE SÉANCE	CD	Stormspell	SWMR 0087
		500 hand numbered copies.			
2010	☐	THE SÉANCE	LP	High Roller	HHR 137
		First pressing: 100 purple/black splatter, 200 purple, 200 black vinyl copies. Second pressing: 200 special purple, 300 black vinyl copies.			
2011	■	The Fiddler	MLP 3tr	High Roller	HHRB 189
		Tracks: The Fiddler/The Serpent Bride/Lazy Lady (Pentagram cover). 150 pink vinyl, 350 black vinyl.			
2011	☐	THE SÉANCE	CD	Transubstans	TRANS 094
		Bonus: The Fiddler/The Serpent Bride			
2013	☐	FINAL SACRIFICE	CD	Metal Blade	n/a

2011 MLP - HHRB 189

NOCTURNAL ALLIANCE

Henrik Johansson: k/d, Micke Därth: g/b

Skövde - *Nocturnal Alliance* is a co-operation between Henrik Johansson and Micke Därth (*Detest, Twilight, Beyond Twilight*), with guest musicians. Really good heavy melodic power metal. In 2005 the first demo *Dark Voices* was released. The line-up featured, besides Johansson and Därth, Andreas Lagerin on vocals and guitar and Jocke Därth on lead guitar on one track. A second demo, *What Makes Evil Tick*, was released as a pro-printed CD-R in 50 copies in 2007 and featured Johansson, Därth, Lagerin, guitarist Linus Abrahamsson, keyboardist Finn Zieler and singer Mark E. Gunnardo. In 2009 the band's first official album was released. The album also features singers Peo Pettersson (*Leviticus, Axia*, solo) and Michelle, plus guitarists Janne Ström and Linus Abrahamsson. A new album, entitled *Withering*, is said to be finished.

2009 ■ THE 3RD PHASE OF DESTRUCTION ....CD   private ....NA 003

2009 CD - NA 003

NOCTURNAL RITES

Jonny Lindqvist: v, Fredrik Mannberg: g, Nils Norberg: g,
Mattias Bernhardsson: k, Nils Eriksson: b, Owe Lingvall: d

Umeå - The band was formed in 1990 and started out as a three-piece death metal band under the name *Necronomic* and recorded two demos in this style and with Mannberg handling the vocals. The first line-up featured drummer Tommy Eriksson, who was soon replaced by Ulf Andersson. When they added a guitarist and singer Anders Zackrisson (ex-*Gotham City*) in 1993 they also changed their style towards more traditional melodic power metal in the vein of *Helloween*, but with great originality. After the first album guitarist Mikael Söderström was replaced by Nils Norberg, who now took over the lead guitars. On *The Sacred Talisman* drummer Ulf Andersson had to quit because of a leg injury, and was replaced by Owe. Mattias Bernhardsson, who had only been a session player before, was now added to the line-up. Late 1999 Jonny (ex-*Jonny's Bomb, Mogg*) replaced singer Anders Zackrisson, who later recorded some great demos with the band *Born Bandit*. On *Afterlife* the band stepped it all up a notch and the hints of *Dio* and *Rainbow* were a bit more evident, but still with the band's originality. After the album Bernhardsson left and Henrik Kjellberg now handled the keyboards. In 2005 the band's tenth anniversary was celebrated by a double pack reissue of the band's first two albums, under the name *Lost In Time*. The band also performed a live show together with a fifty-five-piece orchestra at the Umeå Opera House, which was televised in Sweden. The album *Grand Illusion* featured guest spots from people such as Jens Johansson (*Malmsteen, Silver Mountain, Stratovarius*), Henrik Danhage (*Evergrey, DeathDestruction*), Kristoffer Olivius (*Naglfar*), Stefan Elmgren (*Hammerfall, FullForce*) and, surprisingly, Swedish skiing champion Per Elofsson. *The 8th Sin* is in my opinion the band's strongest effort, mixing their slightly proggish melodic power metal with almost AOR-infused choruses, but without being cheesy. An outstanding album! In 2008 guitarist Nils Norberg left the band because he lost interest in playing guitar, and he was replaced by Christoffer Rörland (*TME, Sabaton*) in May 2010. A new album is due in 2013. Mannberg and Eriksson are also found in thrashers *Guillotine*. In 2012 Nils Norberg announced he was returning to the scene with his new band *Hellbound*. The exclusive track *Fill Your Head With Rock* is found on the *Sweden Rock Festival 2008* compilation.
Website: www.nocturnalrites.com

1995 CD - MRRCD 032

1999 CD - 77232 2

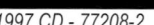

1997 CD - 77208-2

2000 CD - 77292 2

1995 ■	IN A TIME OF BLOOD AND FIRE	CD	Megarock Records	MRRCD 032
1995 ☐	IN A TIME OF BLOOD AND FIRE	CD	Soundholic (Japan)	SHCD1-0012
1997 ☐	TALES OF MYSTERY AND IMAGINATION	CD	Toy's Factory (Japan)	TCFK 87104
	Bonus: The Curse/Live For Today/Burn In Hell			
1997 ☐	TALES OF MYSTERY AND IMAGINATION	CD	Century Media	77208-2
1997 ☐	TALES OF MYSTERY AND IMAGINATION	CD	Century Media (USA)	7908 2
1999 ■	THE SACRED TALISMAN	CD	Century Media	77232 2
1999 ☐	THE SACRED TALISMAN	CD	Century Media (USA)	7932 2
1999 ☐	THE SACRED TALISMAN	CD	Victor (Japan)	VICP-60672
	Bonus: Journey Through Time			
2000 ☐	AFTERLIFE	CD	Victor (Japan)	VICP-61124
	Bonus: Okahoo			
2000 ■	AFTERLIFE	CD	Century Media	77292 2
2000 ☐	AFTERLIFE	LP PD	Century Media	77292 1P
	1000 copies.			
2000 ☐	AFTERLIFE	CD	Century Media (USA)	7992 2
2002 ■	SHADOWLAND	CD	Century Media	77432 2
2002 ☐	SHADOWLAND	CD	Century Media (USA)	8132 2
2002 ☐	SHADOWLAND	CD	Victor (Japan)	VICP-61936
	Bonus: The Iron Force (2002 version)			
2004 ☐	NEW WORLD MESSIAH	CD	Century Media	77532-2
2004 ☐	NEW WORLD MESSIAH	CD	Century Media	77532-?
	Bonus: 15 Minutes Of Strange Behaviour/Eye Of The Dead (video)			
2004 ☐	NEW WORLD MESSIAH	CD	Century Media (USA)	8223 2
	Bonus videos: Eyes Of The Dead/Making of/Live			
2004 ■	NEW WORLD MESSIAH	CD	Victor (Japan)	VICP-62619
	Bonus: Another Storm/Save Us			

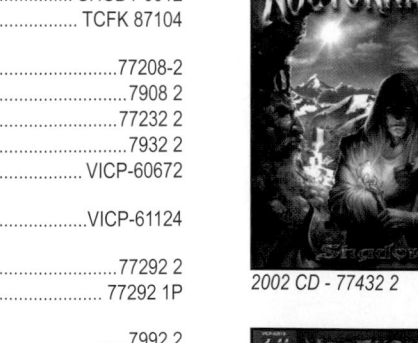

2002 CD - 77432 2

2004 CD - VICP-62619

2004 ☐	NEW WORLD MESSIAH	CD	Fono (Russia)	FO 331 CD
2005 ☐	GRAND ILLUSION	CD	Century Media	77592-2
2005 ☐	GRAND ILLUSION	CD+DVD	Century Media	77592-0

DVD featuring documentary and videos.

| 2005 ☐ | GRAND ILLUSION | CD | Victor (Japan) | VICP-63163 |

Bonus: Fade Away/Under The Ice

2005 ☐	GRAND ILLUSION	CD	Century Media (USA)	8292 2
2005 ☐	GRAND ILLUSION	CD	Fono (Russia)	FO 255 CD
2005 ☐	GRAND ILLUSION	CD	Icarus (Argentina)	ICARUS 164
2005 ■	Okahoo (split)	7"	Swedmetal	SM-02-7

Split with Falconer. Track: Okahoo

| 2005 ■ | LOST IN TIME: THE EARLY YEARS | CD | Century Media | 77623-2 |

The first two albums + bonus: Lay Of Ennui (demo)/In A Time Of Blood And Fire (2004 version)/Winds Of Death (2004 version)/Living For Today (demo) + video

2007 ☐	THE SACRED TALISMAN	CD	Mystic Empire (Russia)	MYST CD 141
2007 ☐	THE 8TH SIN	CD	Century Media	77640-2
2007 ☐	THE 8TH SIN	CDd	Century Media	77640-?
2007 ☐	THE 8TH SIN	CD+DVD	Century Media	77640-0

DVD featuring live and promo videos plus tour documentaries.

| 2007 ☐ | THE 8TH SIN | CD | Century Media (USA) | 8340 2 |
| 2007 ☐ | THE 8TH SIN | CD | Victor (Japan) | VICP-63835 |

Bonus: Coming Home

| 2007 ☐ | THE 8TH SIN | CD+DVD | Victor (Japan) | VIZP-54 |

Bonus: Coming Home + DVD featuring live and promo videos plus tour documentaries.

2007 ☐	THE 8TH SIN	CD	Fono (Russia)	FO 680 CD
2008 ☐	THE SACRED TALISMAN	CD	Victor Metal 90 (Japan)	VICP-64509
2011 ☐	TALES OF MYSTERY AND IMAGINATION	LPg	High Roller Records	HRR 198

150 in clear vinyl, 350 in black vinyl copies.

2005 7" - SM-02-7

2005 CD - 77623-2

NOMINON

Henke Skoog: v, Juha Sulasalmi: g/b, Christian "AntiChristian" Strömblad: g, Alexander Lyrbo: g, Perra Karlsson: d

Jönköping - Nominon were formed in 1993 by Juha and singer Peter Nilsson when their former band *Choronzon* disbanded. The duo released two demos *Daemon 1 & 2*, both in 1993. They also joined the band *Dion Fortune* for some time, but when the band broke up in 1995 Juha and Niklas restarted *Nominon*. They recorded the demo *My Flesh* in 1996 and *Promo 1997* and went through various line-ups before being picked up by X-treme Records and entering Studio Sunlight in 1998 to record the debut-album. The line-up featured singer Niklas Holstensson, guitarists Jonas Mattsson (*Devian, Incinerator, Rise And Shine, Sargatana's Reign*) and Juha Sulasalmi (*Dion Fortune, Chorozon*), bass player Lenny Blade (ex-*Incinerator, Bullet*, solo) and drummer Emil Dragutinovic. On *Blaspheming The Dead* Holstensson was out, while Mattsson handled the vocals, and drummer Dragutinovic had been replaced by Per "Perra" Karlsson (*Die Hard, In Aeternum, Nex, Serpent, Suffer, Altar, T.A.R, Vortox* etc). The tape version also features a cover of *Repulsion*'s *Decomposed*. On *Recremation* the line-up had again changed, seeing Daniel Garpentoft handling the vocals, Christian Strömblad (*Immersed In Blood, RAM*) and Sulasalmi on guitars, Joel Andersson on bass and Karlsson on drums. *Remnants Of A Diabolical History* is a compilation. The band again returned to Necromorbus Studio and Tore Stjerna to record the 2007 album *Terra Necrosis*, a titled suggested by original singer Peter Nilsson (*Fafner*). Also this album saw a change of line-up, where bass player Andersson had been replaced by Anders Malmström. The album saw the band take their old-school-influenced brutal and highly aggressive death metal to a new level. On the 2009 release, *Omen*, a taster for the upcoming album, Sulasalmi handled the vocals and Garpentoft was out. Before this bassist Martin Karlsson (*Zombiekrieg*) had made a short stint with the band. On *Monumentomb* the band also brought in guest singers such as Erik Sahlström and Johan "Barsk" Thornberg. In 2011 the band found new singer Henke Skoog (*Eviscerated*). Now Sulasalmi handled both bass and guitar, drummer Karlsson is still in, but guitarist Strömblad had been replaced by Alexander Lyrbo (*Brutal Noise, Morbid Grin*). On *The Cleansing* Christian Strömblad was back in line.

Diabolical daemons

1999 CD - X-TR 006

| 1999 ■ | DIABOLICAL BLOODSHED | CD | X-treme | X-TR 006 |
| 2004 ■ | Blaspheming The Dead | 7" 3tr | Nuclear Winter | NWR 007 |

500 copies. Tracks: Blaspheming The Dead/Invocations/Blessed By Fire

| 2004 ☐ | DAEMONS OF THE PAST (split) | CD | Northern Silence | NSP 006 |

Split with Fafner. Tracks: Intro: Voice Of The Obscure/My Flesh/Blodsblot/Brinn I Skärseld/Outro: In I Aspen/Intro/Whisters In The Polar Winds/Ur skuggorna/Deep Bogs Of Depression/In This Cold Grave Of Mine/Frozen Mist Over Nordur/Outro: Dress Me In Ice/ Cemetery Of Life/My Flesh/Genocide/Outro

| 2004 ■ | The True Face Of Death | MLPg 5tr | TPL Records | TPL 017 |

Tracks: White Death/Amityville/The Lost Ones/Phantoms/Afterlife Desires

| 2004 ☐ | The True Face Of Death | MCD 5tr | Nuclear Winter | NWR 011 |

725 copies.

| 2005 ☐ | RECREMATION | CD | Konqueror Records | KR 007 CD |

Slipcase.

| 2006 ☐ | RECREMATION | CD | Deathgasm Records | DG-035 |
| 2006 ☐ | RECREMATION | LP | Blood Harvest | YOTZ #3 |

2004 7" - NWR 007

2004 MLP - TPL 017

2006 ☐	REMNANTS OF A DIABOLICAL HISTORY	CD	Pulverised Records	ASH 022
2007 ☐	TERRA NECROSIS	CD	Ibex Moon Records (USA)	MRI1047

Bonus: Condemned To Die (live)

2007 ☐	TERRA NECROSIS	LP	Blood Harvest	YOTZ #14
2008 ☐	DIABOLICAL BLOODSHED	CD	Deathgasm Records	DG 50
2008 ☐	Legiônes Em Portugal	7"	Badger Records	Badger 3.5

Tracks: Hordes Of Flies/Condemned To Die. 520 copies.

2009 ☐	Omen	MCD 4tr	Deathgasm Records	DG 56

Tracks: Omen/Invocations/Through Dead Dreams Door/Submit To Evil (live)

2010 ■	Nominon/Sathanas (split)	7"	Pagan Records	MOON 062

Split with Sathanas. Track: Released In Death. 500 copies.

2010 ☐	MONUMENTOMB	CD	Deathgasm Records	DG 058
2010 ☐	MONUMENTOMB	LP+7"	Blood Harvest	YOTZ #49

Bonus single with the first 100 copies. Tracks: Invocations/Through Dead Dreams Door

2011 ■	Morbid Tunes Of Death (split)	7"	Deathstrike Records	DG 58

Split with Exorcism. Track: Black Chapel. 100 blue, 500 black vinyl copies.

2011 ☐	Manifestations Of Black/Burnt Human Offering	7"	Deathgasm Records	DG 64

300 red, 700 black vinyl copies.

2012 ☐	THE CLEANSING	CDd	Deathgasm Records	DG 72
2012 ☐	THE CLEANSING	LPg	Deathgasm Records	DG 72

Bonus: Slaughter The Imposer. Blue or black vinyl. Patch.

2010 7" - MOON 062

2011 7" - DG 58

NON-HUMAN LEVEL

Peter Wildoer: v, Christofer Malmström: g, Gustaf Hielm: b, Ryan Van Poederooyen: d

Helsingborg - *Non-Human Level* were founded by *Darkane* guitarist as a solo project. He did surround himself with some impressive musicians. Poederooyen is also found in Devin Townsend's band, Hielm is ex-*Meshuggah* and has played with *Pain Of Salvation*, while Wildoer has a rap sheet longer than Manhattan, including *Darkane, Armageddon, Time Requiem, Arch Enemy, Agretator, Grimmark, Electrocution 250* etc, however here as a drummer. *Non-Human Level* plays high energy death-infused thrash metal with ferociously brutal guitar work and a high technical musical level. Killer musicians and great songs.

2005 ■	NON-HUMAN LEVEL	CD	Listenable Records	POSH 076
2005 ☐	NON-HUMAN LEVEL	CD	Soundholic (Japan)	TKCS-85135

Bonus: I Wanna Be Somebody (WASP cover)

2005 CD - POSH 076

NON SERVIAM

Rikard Nilsson: v, Anders Nyander: g, Daniel Andersson: g/b/v, Chrille Andersson: d/v

Malmö - *Non Serviam* is Latin for "I will not serve". It started in 1995 when Chrille and Rikard formed *Carnack*. A year after they became *Non Serviam*. They soon recorded their first demo *Between Light And Darkness* and shortly after Johannes Andersson joined on guitar. In 1997 they recorded the second demo *The Witches Sabbath/The Second Vision*. The band plays eighties-influenced black metal with occasional hints of *Iron Maiden*. *The Witches Sabbath* was recorded at Studio Underground. On the first two albums Chrille played bass and Magnus Emilsson (ex-*Ashes Of Life*) handled the drums. After the first album Johannes Andersson was replaced by Anders (also in *In Black*). *Necrotial* was recorded at Berno Studios. After *Necrotial* Magnus left the band. Daniel (ex-*Ashes Of Life*) and Chrille are now found in *Supreme Majesty* and they have also recorded an album under the name *Hellspell*. *The Witches Sabbath* is the old demos on CD. The band was put on ice in 2000.

1997 CD - IR 030

1997 ■	BETWEEN LIGHT AND DARKNESS	CD	Invasion Records	IR 030
1997 ☐	BETWEEN LIGHT AND DARKNESS	LP	Invasion Records	IR 030
1998 ■	NECROTICAL	CD	Invasion Records	IR 037
1998 ☐	NECROTICAL	LP PD	Invasion Records	IR 037

500 copies.

2000 ■	THE WITCHES SABBATH	CD	Nocturnal Music	NMCD 20
2000 ☐	Play God/With Open Eyes/Satan's Spree/	7" 3tr	Aftermath	CHAPTER V

500 copies.

1998 CD - IR 037

NONEXIST

Johan Liiva: v, Johan Reinholdz: g, Johan Igard: g,
Linus Abrahamsson: b, Joakim Strandberg-Nilsson: d

Helsingborg/Malmö - Johan is ex-*Arch Enemy*, Reinholdz is also found in *Andromeda* and has played with *Widow, Opus Atlantica* and *Skyfire*, while first drummer Matte Modin was in *Defleshed* and *Dark Funeral*. The interesting thing with this band is that none of the members had met until the first photo-session, after the album was recorded and done. The members never met in the studio, but sent tapes and files all across the country. *Nonexist* plays excellent high-quality progressive death metal, like the missing link between *Dream Theater* and early *Arch Enemy*. In 2012 the band released the new, initially digital only, album *From My Cold Dead Hands*, which also featured covers of *Atomic Rooster, Megadeth, Coroner* and *Merciless* as bonus. The line-up now featured drummer Joakim Strandberg-Nilsson replacing Matte Modin,

2000 CD - NMCD 20

bassist Linus Abrahamsson (**Mister Kite, Nocturnal Alliance, Visceral Bleeding**) and guitarist
Johan Igard (**Faithful Darkness**). In 2013 the album was finally given a CD release by Trooper.

2001 ☐	DEUS DECEPTOR	CD	Toys Factory (Japan)	TFCK 87267
	Bonus: Carnage Bloody Carnage			
2001 ☐	DEUS DECEPTOR	CD	Century Media (USA)	8004-2
2002 ■	DEUS DECEPTOR	CD	New Hawen	NewH 001
2013 ☐	FROM MY COLD DEAD HANDS	CD	Trooper (Japan)	QATE-10041

2002 CD - NewH 001

NONWORKINGGENERAION
Jimmy Drexler: v, Jesper Wallgren: g, André Drexler: d

Malmö - Reminiscent of **System Of A Down**, but mixed with some heavy **Black Sabbath** vibes
and a bit of **Faith No More**. A trio that uses programmed drums.

2004 ☐	UNCOVERED AND IGNORED	CD	Orchard	804988
2005 ☐	The Walk Of Ronda K	MCD 4tr	AudioSpot	NWG 002
	Tracks: The Walk Of Ronda K/A Match Did Not Cause This Fire/Home/Paranoid + CD-ROM			
2005 ■	MY MOUTH BELONGS TO YOU	CD	Ant Nest Records	ANRCD 006
2006 ☐	Faces/No Need/Faces (video)	CDS	Ant Nest Records	ANRCDS 001

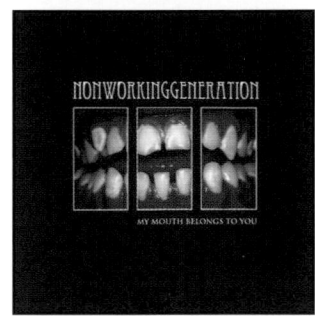

NORD
Micke "Nord" Andersson: v/g, Sven Lindwall: b, Nicci Wallin: d

Stockholm - The band's only release contains covers only, but good ones from **Free**,
Robin Trower and **Fleetwood Mac**, but in really heavy versions and with Micke's
rough-edged outstanding vocals. After the album, Sven left the band and Stefan Olsson
(**House Of Shakira**) took his place. They started recording an album with originals
only, now sounding more like a mix of Robin Trower and **King's X**, but the work was
never finished due to lack of backing from the record company. The musicians are
among the most acclaimed on the Swedish session scene and they have worked with
artists like **Roxette**, Anders Glennmark, Magnus Uggla, Ulf Lundell, **Grymlings** etc.
etc. None of it is hard rock though. Micke also recorded some poppier singles in the
early 80s under the name **Micke Andersson´s Dropouts** where Roger Holegård (**Neon
Rose**) and Hempo Hildén (**Trash, Dokken, Norum**) were among the "drop-outs". He
has also recorded with the Norwegian AOR band **Private Eye** as well as a solo album
under his own name. Nicci was also part of **AC/DC**-clones **AB/CD** and has worked as
a session drummer with a number of artists. In 2008 Micke recorded an album with the
short-lived hard rock band **BALLS**, where the A stands for Andersson. He also wrote
a track on the **Scorpions** album *Evolution v1* and has since produced the last three
2011-2012 *Scorpions* albums, including co-written some songs. In 2013 Mikael will
produce and play live with **Scorpions** on their acoustic return. He has also guested on
both **Mountain Of Power** albums, as singer and guitarist. *Who Do You Love* is a Bo
Diddley cover and *Bridge Of Sighs* a Robin Trower cover.

The power of three

2005 CD - ANRCD 006

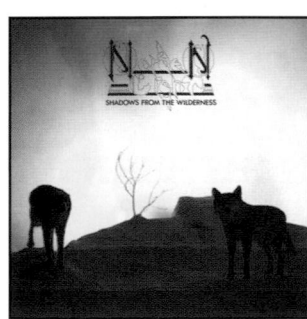

1992 CD - 4509-90369-2

1992 ☐	Who Do You Love/Bridge Of Sighs	CDS 2tr	WEA	4509-90368-2
1992 ■	NORD	CD	WEA	4509-90369-2

NORDEN LIGHT
**Christer "Chris" Mentzer: v, Johan Herlogsson: g, Peter Jeansson: k,
Peter Bodefjord: b, Mikael Von Knorring: d**

Göteborg - In the early 80s Chris lead the band **Mentzer** that, besides some demos, recorded
two tracks for the compilation *Scandinavian Metal Attack II* (RCA 84). Besides Christer and
Johan the band then consisted of former **Snowstorm** drummer Torben Ferm and bassist Nalle
Oskarsson. Chris then joined **Silver Mountain**, sang on the album *Universe* and did a tour of
Japan with the band where he almost cut a deal for his own band. After Jonas Hansson moved
to the US, Chris formed **Norden Light**. The album may not be considered a milestone, but it's
well worth investing in. The style is similar to the **Silver Mountain** album, but the old **Mentzer**
material is heavier. In 1988 the band was going to London to record the second album, but bad
economics put a halt to the plans. Unfortunately the band folded around 1989. Von Knorring
was later with Yngwie Malmsteen, but had to quit due to hearing problems. **Silver Mountain**
made a reunion show and video in 2010, where Mentzer, now residing in Norway, participated.
Mentzer also recorded an album with **Chicago/Santana** style band **Pyramid** in 1978. **Norden
Light** reunited in 2012, but sadly split in 2013 before even playing togther.

1987 LP - SLP 2786

1987 ■	SHADOWS FROM THE WILDERNESS	LP	Sonet	SLP 2786
1987 ☐	SHADOWS FROM THE WILDERNESS	CD	Sonet	SCD 2786
1987 ☐	SHADOWS FROM THE WILDERNESS	CD	FEMS (Japan)	SP25-5319
1987 ■	SHADOWS FROM THE WILDERNESS	CD	RTB/Sonet (Yugoslavia)	RTB-220140
	Different artwork.			
1995 ☐	SHADOWS FROM THE WILDERNESS	CD	Sonet	SLP 2786/527 527-2

1987 LP - RTB-220140

NORDH, GÖRAN

Göran Nordh: v

Stockholm - This was the first release from singer Göran Ove "Glory" Nordh, born 1958. He went through several bands before this, such as **Earth Gravity, Madness Age**, **X-Ray Free** and **Nasty**. In 1980 he joined the band **Glory Bell's Band/Glory Bells**, who also rerecorded both songs. He then took the stage name Glory North and formed a band with the same name. Musicians on the A-side feature guitarist Pekka Adolfsson (later in **Intermezzo**), bassist Micke Johansen and drummer Botte Westerlund. On the B-side there's guitarists Conel Winblad and Kent Karlsson, bassist Jens "J-son" Tillqvist and drummer Sandy B Hansen. He was a hard-working man with a mission, but quite honestly his vocals were not that great, and his English even worse. Göran sadly passed away in February 2008.
Website: www.glorybellsband.com

1981 7" - CTR 381

1981 ■ Die In Two Different Centuries	7"	CTR	CTR 381	$$

Tracks: I Am The Capten/Old Wiking Man

NORGREN, PONTUS

Mats Levén: v, Pontus Norgren: g, Christer "Chris" Goldsmith: b, Thomas Broman: d

Stockholm - This project was initially called **Damage Done** and then featured now famous pop-singer Patrik Isaksson, **Europe/Clockwise/Southpaw** bassist John Levén and drummer Jan Åström (**Syndicate Rag**). A demo was recorded, but Patrik found fame in a different genre and Pontus became heavily involved in **Jekyll 'N' Hyde**. He was finally signed by Z Records and his excellent solo debut saw the light of day. Great guitar-oriented melodic hard rock with Pontus' typical touch, formerly heard in bands like **Great King Rat**. He later joined **Talisman** for the album *Truth* and the subsequent live album, and later **Humanimal**. He has made guest appearances with bands such as **Seventeen, Locomotive Breath** etc. He also made a career as sound engineer touring with bands like **Union, Thin Lizzy** etc and also producing bands like **House Of Shakira, Token, Jekyll 'N' Hyde** etc. The track *Losing My Religion* from the early **Damage Done**-days when Patrik Isakssson was in the band can be found on the bonus-CD for the second Encyclopedia of Swedish Hard Rock And Heavy Metal. Pontus later joined **The Ring, The Poodles** and is today found in **HammerFall**. Goldsmith has played with **Full Strike** and is today in **Scarpoint**. Broman has played with bands like **Great King Rat, Electric Boys, Michael Schenker Group, Tryckvåg, Road To Ruin, Humanimal,** John Norum etc.

2000 CD - ZR 1997032

2000 ■ DAMAGE DONE	CD	Z Records	ZR 1997032

NORRSKEN

Joakim Nilsson: v, Magnus Pelander: g, Rikard Edlund: b, Kristoffer Sjödal: d

Örebro - The band was formed in 1995 under the name **Winter Orb**. Kristoffer was formerly in punk band **Fucking Chaos**. The band recorded its first demo in March 1996 and a second one nine months later. A third demo recording was unearthed in 1997. Seventies hard rock, sounding very seventies, both musically and sound-wise. The single was dedicated to Australian hard rockers **Buffalo**. They also appear on *Blue Explosion - A Tribute To Blue Cheer* (Black Widow) where they do a rendition of the song *The Pilot*. They are also found on *Bastards Will Pay - Tribute To Trouble* (Freedom). The band split late 2000. Magnus is now found in **Witchcraft**, while Joakim and Rikard formed the outstanding and highly hyped retro rockers **Graveyard**.

1999 7" - BTM 004

1999 ■ Armageddon/Little Lady	7"	Swinging Singles Club	BTM 004	$$

NORTHERN DARKNESS

Neanderthal: v/g/b/d

Norrköping - Old-school black metal project influenced by Bathory and initiated in 1996 and the tracks for the split-LP was recorded, quite primitively, already in 1996.

2004 LP - IHR 007

2004 ☐ NORTHERN DARKNESS/DEVIL LEE ROT (split)	LP	I Hate	IHR 007

Split with Devil Lee Rot. Tracks: Northern Shores/At The Battle/In Honour Of The Fallen/ Home Return. 500 copies.

NORUM, JOHN

Leif Sundin: v, John Norum: v/g, Tomas "Pomma" Thorberg: b, Thomas Broman: d

Upplands Väsby/Tyresö - Guitar player John Norum was born February 24, 1964 in Vardø, Norway and at the age of 1 his family moved to Sweden. He decided he would become a rock star around the age of 10. In 1976 he formed his first band, **Dragonfly**, that also featured singer/guitarist Stefan Kéry and drummer Tony Niemistö. John's mother's boyfriend was a man named Thomas Witt. Thomas was a music producer and he was working with classic vulgo rocker **Eddie Meduza**. At the age of 14, in 1978, John was offered the chance to play guitar with Eddie, live and on the single *Punkjävlar* (which became a huge hit). Ironically enough, John was into punk like **Sex Pistols** and at the time had a band called **Dog Wayst**, under the monicker Johnny

Michelle and John flanking Lizzy guitarist Scott Gorham

Fuckfaster. However, his love of hard rock and **Thin Lizzy** in particular took over and he formed the band **WC** (…yes indeed) where he now started playing covers of **UFO**, **Thin Lizzy** etc. The band also featured Jan-Erik Bäckström, Mikael Kling and his old friend, drummer Tony Niemistö. Only one song was ever recorded, a live recording of the song *In My Head* found on the compilation *Musikfest med sångare & musker i Väsby 78* (79 Upplands Väsby Kommun). To make a long story (the rest is found under **Europe**) short, John left/was fired from **Europe** in 1986 because he wasn't happy with the commercial vein the band was heading into. Instead he pursued a solo career. On the first album the musicians included bassist Marcel Jacob (**Talisman, Rising Force** etc), singer Göran Edman (**Madison, Glory, Malmsteen** etc), drummer Peter Hermansson (**220 Volt, Talisman** now **Zoom Club, Grand Design**), keyboardist Per Blom and bass player Mikael Larsson (**220 Volt**). The first live-EP contains the previously unreleased studio track *Free Birds In Flight* (instrumental) and the musicians were John, Marcel, Per Blom, Mats Lindfors (k/g) and drummers Hempo Hildén/Peter Hermansson. Glen Hughes joined on bass and vocals, but was sacked after a month because of his bad habits. The bass work was briefly handled by Torbjörn Larsson (**Macbeth**), before John moved to the US in 1989, to join **Don Dokken** with whom he recorded the album *Up From The Ashes*. In 1993 he landed a deal with US label Shrapnel Records that would release *Face The Truth* in the US as well as a new solo album. In **Dokken** he met Peter Baltes (**Accept**). On *Face The Truth* the line-up featured Glenn Hughes (v), Peter Baltes (b) and Hempo Hildén (d). The album featured the **Thin Lizzy** cover *Opium Trail* and the guest musicians were Mikkey Dee (**Nadir, Geisha, Motörhead**) and Joey Tempest (**Europe**). The musicians on *Another Destination* included singer Kelly Keeling (**Baton Rogue, Blue Murder**), bassist Tom Lilly (**Mick Fleetwood Band**) and drummer Gary Ferguson (**Gary Moore, Hughes Thrall**). A cover of **Thin Lizzy**'s *Massacre* is found on the tribute *The Lizzy Songs* (95 SMC). The line-up featured John on vocals and guitar, bassist John Levén (**Europe, Clockwise**) and drummer Niclas Sigevall (**Electric Boys**). The line-up on *Worlds Away* featured Norum, Keeling, Baltes and drummer Simon Wright (**AC/DC**) and production was handled by Jeff Glixman (**Kansas**). The line-up on *Face It Live* was John on guitar and vocals, singer Leif Sundin (**Great King Rat**), bassist Anders "Nippe" Fästader (formerly Nilsson) (**Advice, Great King Rat, Southfork**) and drummer Hempo Hildén. John also guests on the song *Nothing* on **Carmine Appice's Guitar Zeus** and on the second and third album by **Midnight Sun**. The tour that followed *Slipped Into Tomorrow* saw old friend Marcel Jacob replacing Stefan Rodin on bass. *From Outside In* can be found on MVP Force compilation (98 Zero XRCN-2035). The first pressing of the European version (on Playground) of *Slipped Into Tomorrow* was a mis-press with songs in reversed order. A future collector's item maybe. On the tour for *Slipped…* the line-up featured Marcel Jacob on bass and Thomas Broman on drums, who was later replaced by Hempo Hildén. In 2001 John joined **Dokken** for a gig at the Sweden Rock Festival. Chemistry was created and John went to the US late 2001 to record and tour with the band. In 2000 **Europe** reunited for a one-off show, which lead to the permanent reunion of the band. In 2005 John released the solo album *Optimus*, which showed a heavier, more modern and de-tuned side. When John was working on his follow-up disaster struck in 2008, when his former wife, mother to his son, Jake, Michelle Meldrum Norum died of a cystic growth in the brain. The release was put on hold and the album didn't surface until 2010. This album showed a totally different musical style, back to basic seventies riff-oriented and bluesy hard rock, also containing two covers of **Frank Marino's Mahogany Rush** and **Thin Lizzy**. The boy on the cover is actually John's son. The bass on this album was handled by Tomas "Pomma" Thorberg (**Snakes In Paradise, Plankton**) and Leif Sundin sang on most of the songs. John also laid down a three-minute spaced out guest solo on the **Mahogany Rush** cover *Talking 'Bout A Feeling* on **Mountain Of Power**'s second album *Volume Two*. In 2012 John started working on a new album, which will be released through Gain Music in 2013.

Post show madness with Broman and Marcel

Facing the truth with Glenn Hughes

"Hey sis, I can play this thing, too!"

1987	☐ Love Is Meant.../Don't Believe A Word	7"	CBS	651 047 7
	Don't Believe A Word (Thin Lizzy cover) is non-LP.			
1987	■ Love Is Meant.../Don't Believe A Word	7"	Epic (Japan)	07-5P-488
1987	☐ Love Is Meant...	MLP 3tr	CBS	651 047 6
	Tracks: Love Is Meant (single version)/Love Is Meant (extended version)/Don't Believe A Word (Thin Lizzy cover)			
1987	☐ Love Is Meant...	7" 1tr	Epic (Spain-promo)	651 047 7
1987	○ Let Me Love You/Wild One (Thn Lizzy cover)	7"	CBS (white label)	- -
	White label promo without artwork, but an accompanying promo letter, sent out to radio stations.			
1987	☐ Let Me Love You/Wild One	7"	CBS	651187 7
1987	☐ Let Me Love You/Wild One	12"	CBS	651187 1
	Wild One (Thin Lizzy cover) is non-LP.			
1987	☐ TOTAL CONTROL	LP	CBS	CBS 460 203 1
1987	☐ TOTAL CONTROL	LP	CBS (USA)	EK 44220

JOHN NORUM

Love Is Meant...

1987 7" - 07-5P-488

Year		Title	Format	Label	Catalogue
1987	☐	TOTAL CONTROL	LP	CBS (USA)	EK 44220
1987	☐	TOTAL CONTROL	LP	Epic (UK)	460203 1

With insert, as opposed to printed inner bag line on the CBS version.

1987	☐	TOTAL CONTROL	CD	CBS	460 203 2

Bonus: Wild One (Thin Lizzy cover)

1987	☐	TOTAL CONTROL	CD	Epic (Japan)	ESCA 4245
1987	☐	TOTAL CONTROL	CD	Epic (Japan)	32.8P-230
1987	☐	Back On The Streets	7"	Epic (USA-promo)	n/a
1987	☐	Back On The Streets/Back On The Streets	12"	Epic (USA-promo)	EAS 1154
1988	☐	Back On The Streets/Bad Reputation (live)	7"	CBS	651614-7
1990	☐	Live In Stockholm	MLP 4tr	CBS	467 407-1

Tracks: Eternal Flame/Don't Believe A Word (Thin Lizzy cover)/Blind/Free Birds In Flight

1990	■	Live In Stockholm	MCD 5tr	Epic Sony (Japan)	ESCA 5244

Bonus: Bad Reputation (live) (Thin Lizzy cover)

1990 MCD - ESCA 5244

1990	☐	TOTAL CONTROL	LP	Columbia (USA)	BFE 44220
1990	☐	TOTAL CONTROL	CD	Columbia (USA)	BFE 44220

Bonus: Wild One (Thin Lizzy cover)

1990	☐	TOTAL CONTROL	CD	Epic (USA)	EK 44220
1992	☐	We Will be Strong	CDS	Epic	JNPROMO 1
1992	☐	FACE THE TRUTH	LP	Epic	JNPROMO 2
1992	☐	FACE THE TRUTH	LP	Epic	469441 1
1992	☐	FACE THE TRUTH	CD	Epic	469441 2
1992	☐	FACE THE TRUTH	CD	Shrapnel (USA)	SH 1073 2

Only The Strong Survive was replaced by Free Birds In Flight(live) and Don't Believe A Word (live). Different artwork.

1992	☐	FACE THE TRUTH	CD	Epic (Japan)	ESCA 5574
1992	☐	We Will Be Strong/Free Birds In Flight	CDS 2tr	Epic	657 670 2
1992	☐	We Will Be Strong/Free Birds In Flight	7"	Sony	657 670 7
1992	☐	In Your Eyes/Still The Night	7"	Epic	658 111 7
1992	☐	In Your Eyes/Still The Night/Counting On Your Love	MCD 3tr	Epic	658 111 2
1992	☐	Face The Truth/Distant Voices	7"	Epic	658 132 7
1992	☐	Face The Truth/Distant Voices/Endica	MCD 3tr	Epic	658 132 2
1995	■	Strange Days/Spirit World	CDS 2tr	Sony (promo)	661357
1995	☐	ANOTHER DESTINATION	CD	Epic	EPC 478618 2
1995	☐	ANOTHER DESTINATION	CD	Epic (Japan)	ESCA 6229
1995	☐	ANOTHER DESTINATION	CD	Shrapnel (USA)	SH 1079 2
1996	○	Where The Grass Is Green/Centre Of Balance	CDS 2tr	Zero (Japan)	XRCNS 1
1997	☐	TOTAL CONTROL	CD	Epic (Japan)	ESCA 5245
1997	☐	TOTAL CONTROL	CD	Epic Sony (Japan)	32-8P-230

1995 CDS - 661357

Bonus: Wild One (Thin Lizzy cover)

1997	☐	WORLDS AWAY	CD	Vagabond	- -

Bonus: From Outside In. A promo-release

1997	☐	WORLDS AWAY	CD	Shrapnel (USA)	SH 1106
1997	☐	WORLDS AWAY	CD	Zero (Japan)	XRCN-1289

Bonus: From Outside

1997	☐	FACE IT LIVE '97	CD	Zero (Japan)	XRCN-2011

Bonus: Night Buzz/Where The Grass Is Green/In Your Eyes/Heart Of Stone

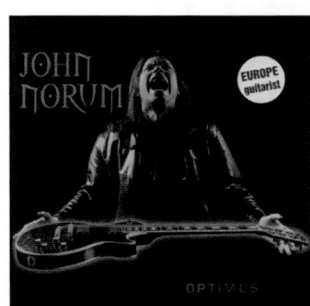

2005 CD - M 7080 2

1997	☐	WORLDS AWAY	CD	Xero/MNW	XRCN-1289

Bonus: From Outside

1998	☐	FACE IT LIVE '97	CD	Shrapnel (USA)	SH 11172
1999	☐	WORLDS AWAY	CD	Toshiba (Japan)	TOCP-50775
1999	☐	FACE IT LIVE '97	CD	Toshiba (Japan)	TOCP-50776
1999	☐	SLIPPED INTO TOMORROW	CD	Toshiba (Japan)	TOCP 65325

Bonus: Centre Of Balance (live)

2000	☐	SLIPPED INTO TOMORROW	CD	Playground (Scandinavia)	TOCP 65325

Bonus: Centre Of Balance (live)

2000	☐	SLIPPED INTO TOMORROW	CD	Shrapnel	SH 1145 2
2000	☐	SLIPPED INTO TOMORROW	CD	Mascot	M 7049 2

Bonus: Centre Of Balance

2001	☐	WORLDS AWAY	CD	Mascot	M 7057 2
2001	☐	FACE IT LIVE '97	CD	Mascot	M 7058 2

Bonus: Night Buzz/Where The Grass Is Green/In Your Eyes/Heart Of Stone

2005	■	OPTIMUS	CD	Mascot	M 7080 2
2005	☐	OPTIMUS	CD	Victor (Japan)	VICP-63289

Bonus: Natural Thing (live)(UFO cover)

2010	■	PLAY YARD BLUES	CDd	Mascot	M 7237 2
2010	☐	PLAY YARD BLUES	CD	Victor (Japan)	VICP-64817
2010	☐	PLAY YARD BLUES	CD	Magnum (Taiwan)	MVP-64817

2010 CDd - M 7237 2

Unofficial releases:

1997	■	HEART OF STONE	2CD	private	JN-6.19.97-1/2

Recorded in Osaka 19/6-97

1995	☐	LIVE IN SWEDEN 1995	CD-R	private	JN-001

Recorded in 12/4-95 in Malmö, 21/5-95 in Göteborg w Glenn Hughes

1997	☐	WORLDS AWAY	CDv	Zero Corporation (Russia)	XRCN-1289

1997 2CD - JN-6.19.97-1/2

NOSTRADAMEUS

Freddy Persson: v, Jake Fredén: g/k, Lennart Specht: g,
Thomas Antonsson: b, Esko Salow: d

Göteborg - Formed in 1998 by Freddy with the aid of members of death metal band *Vapid*, guitarist Jacob "Jake" Fredén, drummer Gustav Nahlin and guitarist Erik Söderman. Late 1998 the band recorded their first demo, first prize in a contest, which lead to a deal with AFM Records. Joacim Cans of *HammerFall* guests on one track on the debut. After the album the temporary line-up was settled when Jake drafted guitarist Michael Åberg, bass player Thomas Antonsson (*Pathos, Fejd*) and drummer Jesse Lindskog (*Dragonland, Dreamland*). *The Prophet Of Evil* contains a cover of *Scream Of Anger* by *Europe*, as a limited bonus-track. After the album Lindskog was replaced by Esko Salow (also in *Lady Mourning*, ex-*Pathos, Fejd*). Freddy and Jake formed side project *Wiz*, with whom they recorded one album. Freddy was also found in punksters *Sten & Stalin*. In 2005 Åberg left to join *Destiny* and the band drafted *Pathos/Fejd* man Lennart Specht. *Nostradameus* plays high-class melodic power metal with a German touch. Like they say in the song *The Untouchables* from the album Pathway: "We know we're not original, but by God we're having fun".

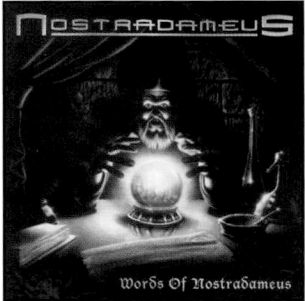
2000 CD - AFMCD 039-2

2001 CD - AFMCD 048-2

2000	■	WORDS OF NOSTRADAMEUS	CD	AFM	AFMCD 039-2
2000	□	WORDS OF NOSTRADAMEUS	CD	Soundholic (Japan)	TKCS 85009
		Bonus: The Oath/Heart Of Stone			
2000	□	WORDS OF NOSTRADAMEUS	CD	Rock Brigade/Laser (Brazil)	RBR/LCR 2570
		Bonus: The Oath/Heart Of Stone			
2001	■	THE PROPHET OF EVIL	CD	AFM	AFMCD 048-2
		Bonus: Scream Of Anger (Europe cover) as a limited edition bonus track.			
2001	□	THE PROPHET OF EVIL	CD	Soundholic (Japan)	TKCS 85022
		Bonus: Son Of A King/Scream Of Anger (Europe cover)			
2001	□	THE PROPHET OF EVIL	CD	Rock Brigade/Laser (Brazil)	RBR/LCR2850
2003	■	THE THIRD PROPHECY	CD	AFM	AFM 062-2
2003	□	THE THIRD PROPHECY	CDd	AFM	AFM 062-9
		Bonus: One For All, All For One (live)			
2003	□	THE THIRD PROPHECY	CD	Soundholic (Japan)	TKCS-85048
		Bonus: One For All, All For One (live)/In Harmony (karaoke)			
2004	□	WORDS OF THE PROPHET	3CD box	AFM	n/a
		Albums: Words Of Nostradameus, The Prophet Of Evil and The Third Prophecy			
2005	■	HELLBOUND	CD	AFM	AFM 082-2
2005	□	HELLBOUND	CDd	AFM	AFM 082-9
		Bonus: I Am Free			
2005	□	HELLBOUND	CD	Rock Brigade/Laser (Brazil)	RBR/LCR3410
2007	□	PATHWAY	CD	AFM	AFM 142-2
2007	□	PATHWAY	CDd	AFM	AFM 142-9
		Bonus: The Untouchables (2004 version)			
2007	□	PATHWAY/HELLBOUND	2CD	AFM	AFM 293-3
2007	□	PATHWAY	CD	Locomotive Music (USA)	LM 439
2009	■	ILLUSION'S PARADE	CD	AFM	AFM 306-2

2003 CD - AFM 062-2

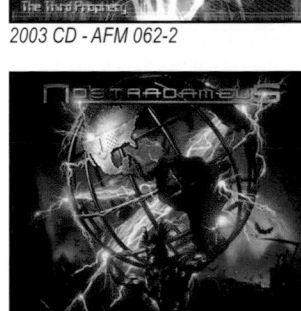

2005 CD - AFM 082-2

NOTORIOUS

Göran Eliasson: v, Johann Nyström: g, Yohann Bohlinder (now Bonér): k,
Duncan "Burberry" Burbury: b, Andy Skinner: d

Stockholm - It all started in 1987, when Johann went to London. There he met bass player Duncan and gave him a demo of his songs. Duncan met a Swedish girl, moved to Stockholm and the two started jamming. They brought over drummer Watashi Nagushi from London, but he had to return for financial reasons. They found fellow countryman Andy Skinner and the trio started rehearsing. They now added a keyboard player and lead singer. Yohann Bohlinder applied as vocalist, but was a better keyboard player and filled that spot instead. They tried out singer Chris Eldblom, who didn't work out and later found frontman Tomas Lewin. The band suddenly had a manager who was paying for a recording and booked a studio. While recording, they suddenly realised Tomas could not deliver in the studio. Studio owner Kent Kroon came up with singer Göran Eliasson (son of opera singer Jan Eliasson), who sang on the recording. Nyström was into a bit more complicated music and did not agree with the bands commercial direction, why he left only a year after he formed the band. The band tried finding a replacement, but finally folded. Nyström recorded some instrumental demo tracks using Andy on drums, but then went to the US to pursue his musical career. Unfortunately to no avail. Skinner went back to the UK and joined *Tigertailz*. He also played with Rory Gallagher and *Vandamne*. Burbury also went back to the UK and did a short stint with *UFO*, before moving to Australia. Lewin went the cover route. In 2010 Johann and Yohann started writing together, invited Andy to join and in 2012 they reunited Notorious. They actually recorded a new demo using singer Johan Längquist (*Candlemass, Jonah Quizz*) and bass player Janne Persson (*Maze Of Time*). Notorius plays pretty good melodic hard rock in the vein of *Treat*, *Dalton* and *Glory*. Nice guitar playing, but the vocals have some flaws. A rarity well worth looking for, though.

2009 CD - AFM 306-2

1988	■	A Taste Of	MLP 4tr	private	P1988	$
		Tracks: Russian Roulette/Cathedral Of Wisdom/A Hundred Souls/Superstition				

1988 MLP - P1988

NOTRE DAME

Melissa "Vampirella" Swan: v, Tommy "Snowy Shaw" Helgesson: v/g/b/d

Göteborg - In 1997 Tommy "Snowy Shaw" Helgesson created his theatrical horror metal solo project *Notre Dame*. Snowy, who is foremost a drummer, had previously played with bands like **Memento Mori, Illlwill, King Diamond, Mercyful Fate**, and later joined **Dream Evil, Therion, XXX** and also made a short stint in **Dimmu Borgir**. He recorded his first demo in 1998. The line-up on the EP was Snowy, Vampirella, Jean-Pierre de Sade on guitars/bass and Snowy's alter ego Mannequin de Sade on drums. *La Theatre Du Vampire* and *Nightmare Before Christmas* both feature a guest spot by Pete "Blakk" Jacobsson (**Geisha, King Diamond, Trazer**). *Coming To A Theatre Near You, The 2nd* is a remixed rerelease with six bonus tracks. On *Demi Monde Bizarros* Jean-Pierre (whomever it was this time) was not out, while he did appear on the *Creepshow Freakshow Peppeshow* live album. The band made its last show on Halloween's Eve in 2004 before being put on hold. A cover of *Into The Coven* is found on a **Mercyful Fate** tribute (1997). In 2012 Snowy joined **Sabaton**. Live, the band has featured people like Daniel Moilanen, Petter Karlsson, Viktoria Larsson, Markus Fristedt and Kristian Niemann.

1999 2LP - OPLP 086

1999 CD - OPCD 091

2000 7" - OP S 096

1998	☐	Coming To A Theatre Near You	MCD	Head Not Found	HNF 060

Tracks: Bells Of Notre Dame/Vlad The Impaler/A Misconception Of The French Kiss/ Daughter Of Darkness/Sisterhood

1998	☐	Hathor's Place (split)	7"	Osmose	n/a

Split with Forgotten Silence. Track: Abbatoir, Abbatoir du Noir

1999	☐	VOL 1: LE THEATRE DU VAMPIRE	CD	Osmose	OPCD 086
1999	■	VOL 1: LE THEATRE DU VAMPIRE	2LP	Osmose	OPLP 086

Bonus: The Day The Virus Diminished Hallelujaville's Population/From The Chronicles: The Rue Morgue. 1000 hand numbered copies.

1999	■	NIGHTMARE BEFORE CHRISTMAS	CD	Osmose	OPCD 091
1999	☐	NIGHTMARE BEFORE CHRISTMAS	LP	Osmose	OPLP 091
2000	■	Abattoir, Abattoir Du Noir/La Croix Rouge	7"	Osmose	OP S 096
2000	☐	La Croix Rouge	MCD 3tr	Osmose	OPCD S 096

Tracks: La Croix Rouge/The Red Cross/Das Rote Kreuz

2002	☐	COMING TO A THEATRE NEAR YOU, THE 2ND	CD	Osmose	OPCD 121
2004	☐	DEMI MONDE BIZARROS	CD	Osmose	OPCD 101

Released with two different artworks.

2005	☐	CREEPSHOW FREAKSHOW PEEPSHOW	CDd	White Trash Records	SSCD001

NOTRE DAME

Lars Karlsson: v, Jan-Olof Sjögren: g, Mats Ångman: g,
Lars Eriksson: b, Stefan Eriksson: d

Örebro - Good solid hard rock with an occasional hint of **Thin Lizzy**. Previously called **Pathfinder**, with the addition of Henrik Lindberg on keyboards. They recorded some killer demo material under that name.

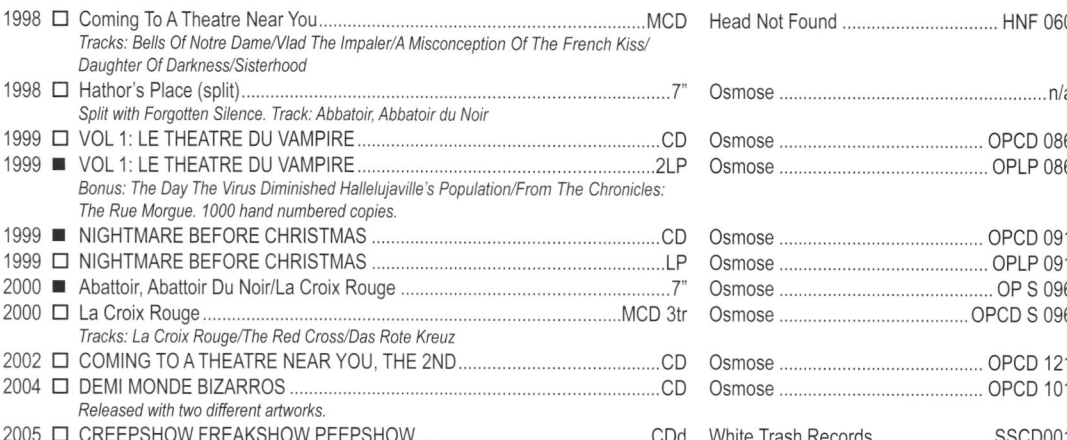
1981 7" - WSR 001

1981	■	Jagad/Ödets timme	7"	West Side	WSR 001

NOVAK (ANDREAS)

Andreas Novak: v, Andreas Passmark: b, Johan Niemann: g,
Mats Hallstensson: g, Jörgen Schelander: k, Daniel Flores: d

Stockholm - Andreas, who found a broader audience in the Swedish version of *Fame Factory*, made his vocal debut with prog metal band **Mind's Eye** on the album *Waiting For The Tide* in 2000. He has also lent his voice to albums by **Deacon Street, Aeon Zen** and **Westlife** (!). In 2005 he recorded his solo album *Forever Endeavour* for German MTM Records and solidified his status as a top-notch AOR singer. In 2011 Andreas made his debut as new front man for melodic rockers **House Of Shakira**. Andreas plays really good, quite ballsy AOR, not too far from the style of **HoS**. The musicians are all well-known people: Passmark (**Stormwind, Narnia, Royal Hunt**), Niemann (**Therion**), Hallstensson (**House Of Shakira**), Schelander (**House Of Shakira**), Flores (**Mind's Eye, The Murder Of My Sweet** etc) and Martina Edoff. Trivia: If you watch an American movie in Sweden the sublines may be written by Andreas Novak. Not to be confused with Swedish pop/rock band **Novak** who released *Perpetual Motion* in 2004.

2005 CD - SPV CD 085-64132

2011 CD - MRR 007

2005	■	FOREVER ENDEAVOUR	CD	MTM Records	SPV CD 085-64132
2005	☐	FOREVER ENDEAVOUR	CD	Avalon Marquee (Japan)	MICP-19495

Bonus: Walking In The Rain

2011	■	NO VAKATION	CD	MelodicRock Records	MRR 007
2011	☐	NO VAKATION	CD	Rubicon (Japan)	RBNCD-1062

NOVEMBER

Christer Stålbrandt: v/g, Rickard Rolf: g, Björn "Binge" Inge: v/d

Stockholm - The foundation was set by Christer and Björn in 1968 under the name **The Imps**. Christer quit to form **Train**. Guitarist back then was none less than Snowy White (**Thin Lizzy**,

NOVEMBER
En ny tid är här...
1970 LP - SLP 2509

solo) and soon Björn replaced drummer Theo Salsberg. Snowy moved back to England and his replacement was Rickard Rolf. On November 1st 1969 they did their first gig under the new name *November*, as opener for *Fleetwood Mac* at the Cue Club in Göteborg. *November* are in my opinion Sweden's first real heavy rock band in the vein of *Mountain*, *Cream* etc. All three albums are absolutely excellent and the vinyls are today collector's items. *2:a November* is the toughest one to find, beside the singles. Even though all lyrics are in Swedish the bands popularity was quite big in England in the early 70's, where the band also toured. The lyrics were actually translated into English but the foreign audience wanted the band to sing in Swedish. The debut album was recorded in only three days. The live CD consists of unreleased recordings from radio and TV shows and it's very heavy! The band made its last gig New Year's Eve 1972 after which they split. Rickard joined Norwegian band *Takt Och Ton* and also recorded with *Jaja Band* in 1979, Christer formed the band *Saga*, whose first and only album consists of songs he never got to do in *November*. Björn went to the heavy progressive band *Energy* and was later more or less a session drummer. Rickard formed the fusion band *Bash* and later joined blues band *Nature*. Björn Inge played with the poppy *Blue Swede/Blåblus* in the mid-seventies and he actually sings lead on the song *Let Your Love Flow* from the album *Better Days Are Coming* (76 EMI). The band reunited for one night in 1993 for the release of *Live*. The gig, that also featured *Trettioåriga Kriget*, was recorded on video and certainly proved the band could still deliver the goods. The video has unfortunately never been released. The song *Cinderella* is also found on the *Jukebox* 7" 4tr (70 Jukebox - JSEP 5601). The English version of *I Sagans Land*, entitled *Nobody's Hand To Hold* is also found on the compilation-CD for *The Encyclopedia Of Swedish Hard Rock And Heavy Metal*. In the nineties several Swedish bands paid homage to *November* by covering their songs, for example *The Quill*, *Abramis Brama* and *November* cover-band *Mouchta*. In 2007 the band once again reunited, on Mellotronen Records twenty year anniversary. The show was filmed and released on DVD. They did several shows, but things later fizzled out. April 16, 2012, on Record Store Day, all three albums were re-issued on vinyl. In 2011 Björn made his debut with the band *Mårran*, following in the tradition of *November*.

1970 7" - T-7805

1971 7" - 006 92842

1971 7" - T-7840

1971 7" - T-7853

1970 ■	EN NY TID ÄR HÄR	LP	Sonet	SLP 2509	$
	Pressed with three different labels depending on year of printing.				
1970 ■	Mount Everest/Cinderella	7"	Sonet	T-7805	
1971 ●	Mitt Hjärta Skall Vara Gjort Av Sten/Mouchta	7"	Sonet	T-7840	
1971 ■	Mount Everest/Cinderella	7"	Stateside (UK)	006-92842	
	Different artwork, with English lyrics.				
1971 □	Mount Everest/Nobody's Hand To Hold	7"	Sonet (France)	T-7842	
	Both sides are in English, the B-side is originally entitled I Sagans Land				
1971 □	Nobody's Hand To Hold/Mount Everest	7"	Sonet (Japan)	UP-298-N	
1971 □	2:A NOVEMBER	LP	Sonet	SLP-2520	$$
1971 ■	Tillbaks Till Stockholm/Sista Reasan	7"	Sonet	T-7853	$
	The A-side is non-LP, produced by Jojje Wadenius.				
1972 ■	6:E NOVEMBER	LPg	Sonet	SLP-2530	$$
1993 □	EN NY TID ÄR HÄR	CD	Sonet	519 679-2	
1994 □	LIVE	CD	Mellotronen	CD 005	
1995 □	2:A NOVEMBER	CD	Sonet	523 112-2	
1996 ■	LIVE	LP PD	Record Heaven	RHPD 5	$
1999 □	6:E NOVEMBER	CD	Mellotronen	MELLO 009	
	Bonus: Cinderella/Tillbaks Till Stockholm/Misstag/Mount Everest (English version)/Nobody's Hand To Hold				
2002 □	6:E NOVEMBER	CDd	Mellotronen	MELLO 009	
	Re-issue in digi pack.				
2012 □	EN NY TID ÄR HÄR	LP	Sonet	060252797980	
2012 □	2:A NOVEMBER	LP	Sonet	060252797979	
2012 □	6:E NOVEMBER	LP	Sonet	060252797975	

Unofficial Releases:
2012 □	2:A NOVEMBER	LP	Sonet	060252797979
	Perfect copy of the vinyl, but with a blue simple cover.			

1972 LPg - SLP-2530

1996 LP PD - RHPD 5

NOX AUREA
Patrick Kullberg: v, Alice Persell: v, Peter Laustsen: g,
Jonas "Grim Vindkall" Almen: g/b/k/v, Roberg Persson: b, Joakim Antonsson: d

Göteborg - Formed in 2005 by *Rimfrost/Ugrinnthul* guitarist Laustsen and Vindkall (*Svartrit, Cursed 13, Domgård, Snakeskin Angels*). In 2007 the line-up was completed. In 2009, after the debut, Patrick (*Domgård, Altar Of Sacrifice*) replaced Jan Sallander. Antonsson is ex-*The Cold Existence* and *Altar Of Sacrifice*, Persson is ex-*Meadow* and *The Cold Existence*. *Nox Aurea* play death-oriented doom metal. *Ascending In Triumph* was mixed by Pelle Saether. Grim, together with three other *Domgård* members was sentenced to jail in 2000, for burning down Bäckaby church in Jönköping and Kulla chapel outside of Eksjö.

2009 CD - SP 030-09

2010 CD - NPR 342

2009 ■	VIA GNOSIS	CD	Solitude Productions	SP 030-09
2010 ■	ASCENDING IN TRIUMPH	CD	Napalm	NPR 342

NUGATORY

Joakim Olsson: v/b, Morgan Johansson: g, Fredrik Gahm: g, Veikko Heikkinen: d

Hallsberg - Nugatory are a young but competent thrashy death metal band with a very heavy approach. They claim to be influenced by bands like *Slayer*, *Death*, *Metallica* and *Black Sabbath*.

1995	■	NUGATORY	CD	Playwood Production	JOKE CD 528

1995 CD - JOKE CD 528

NYMF

Niklas Sjöberg: v, Martin Fairbanks: g, Kristofer Stjernqvist: g,
Robin Ingemansson: b, Thommy Lindskog: d

Karlshamn - Nymf were formed in 2007 by *Graviators* Sjöberg and Stjernqvist, and recorded their first demo in 2008. *Nymf* plays good, solid, doom-oriented stoner, at times quite close to vintage *Black Sabbath* meets *Spiritual Beggars*, with a singer at times similar to *Mustasch*'s Gyllenhammar. Sjöberg and Fairbanks are also found in stoner rockers *The Graviators*. On *Nymf* Pontus Svensson plays bass and Pierre Lopez drums, while Daniel Sköld (*Disruption*) handles the bass on the split. Lindskog is also in *Wulfgar* and Ingemansson in *Unfaithful*.

2010	■	NYMF	CD	Transubstans	TRANS 071
2013	☐	Possessed (split)	7"	Transubstans	TRANSV 706
		Split with Dozer. Black vinyl + 100 copies white vinyl.			
2013	☐	FROM THE DARK	CD	Transubstans	TRANS 115-666
2013	☐	FROM THE DARK	LP	Head Spin	HSLP 328

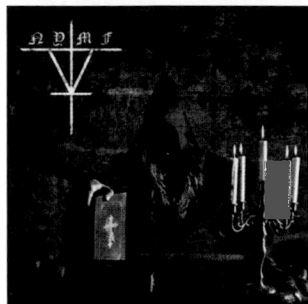

2010 CD - TRANS 071

NÅSTROND

Karl Magnus NE: v/g/b/k, Arganas: d

Göteborg - The band was formed as a trio in June 1993 as *Trident*, but was reduced to a duo in autumn the same year. The changed name to *Nåstrond*, named after the grave land "the beach of corpses" in the Nordic realm of death. Around Christmas they recorded the first rehearsal demo, *The Black Winter*, from which three of the songs were used on the 1994 demo *From A Black Funeral Coffin*, a tape sold in 666 copies and later released on CD/LP. In the winter of 1994-95 they recorded the first single, which featured Draugr on v/g. The single was released as a celebration of the 645 years anniversary of the bubonic plague in Europe. To quote their website: "*Nåstrond* has as always combined their almost absurd interest for blood, sadism, sexuality, Satanism and the question of death for one of the greatest stimulations; Black Metal". *Conquering The Ages* is a compilation. *Toteslaut* was released as a counter reaction towards all "wanna-bee" vampire stories. The band was then also associated with the occult lodge *The Black Order of the Dragon*. On *Age of Fire* the lyrical theme was again the traditional Satanic praises. In 2004 the band released the CD-R album *Celebrating The Four* on their own label, this time celebrating the four elements. The Frostscald reissues have new artworks.

1995 CD - NPR 015

1996 CD - NPR 025

1995	☐	Digerdöden	7" 4tr	Full Moon Production	- -
		Tracks: Hjärulv/Digerdöden/Hanged In An Old Gallow Tree/The Stake Rotten In My Heart			
1995	■	TOTESLAUT	CD	Napalm	NPR 015
1996	■	AGE OF FIRE	CD	Napalm	NPR 025
1996	☐	AGE OF FIRE	CD	Napalm	NPR 025
		100 red spletter vinyl and 400 black vinyl.			
2003	☐	Digerdöden	7" 4tr	Full Moon Production	- -
		166 copies. New artwork.			
2003	☐	FROM A BLACK FUNERAL COFFIN	CD	Cryptia	LCF I
2003	☐	FROM A BLACK FUNERAL COFFIN	LP	Cryptia	LCF I
		300 copies.			
2004	☐	CONQUERING THE AGES	CD	Cryptia	LCF VIII
2005	☐	TOTESLAUT	CD	Cryptia	LCF X
		300 copies.			
2005	☐	Nåstrond/Nocternity (split)	7"g	Debur Morti Productions	DMP 0006
		Split with Nocternity. Poster. Track: Vargtid			
2005	☐	Nåstrond/Nocternity (split)	7" PD	Debur Morti Productions	DMP 0006
2008	☐	MUSPELLZ SYNIR	CD	Debur Morti Productions	DMP 0021
		First edition with black polycarbonate CD + slipcase.			
2008	☐	MUSPELLZ SYNIR	LP	Debur Morti Productions	DMP 0021
2008	☐	MUSPELLZ SYNIR	CD	Moribund Records (USA)	DEAD 112CD
		First edition with black polycarbonate CD + slipcase.			
2007	☐	Nåstrond/Myrkr (split)	10"	Debur Morti Productions	DMP 0025
		Split with Myrkr. Tracks: Intro/Journey Towards Nidafjell/Shores Of Fog & Vermin/Ior Rising			
2010	☐	TOTESLAUT	CDd	Frostscald	FS 49
2010	■	TOTESLAUT	CD	Frostscald	FS 49
2010	☐	AGE OF FIRE	CDd	Frostscald	FS 50
2010	■	AGE OF FIRE	CD	Frostscald	FS 50
2011	☐	AGE OF FIRE	LP	Gineral Industries	FI 026
2010	☐	TOTESLAUT	CD	Galgenstrang/Funeral Industries	GS031/FI025
		100 splatter vinyl and 400 black vinyl copies.			

2010 CD - FS 49

2010 CD - FS 50

OBERON

Bob Rowlands: v, Mika "Robin Nelson" Tikkanen: g

Umeå - Sweden's answer to the *Nelson Brothers*... Musically they're actually quite a bit heavier than the Nelsons. *Oberon* produce melodic hard rock/AOR with incredibly awful vocals. The guest musicians are Magnus Carlsson (k), Magnus Jonsson (b) and Pelle Smuts (d).

1990 ■ They Are Such Fools/I Am Sorry ....7" George Rojo Production .... ROJO 001

1990 7" - ROJO 001

OBITUS

Johan Huldtgren: v, Anders Ahlbäck: g/b/d

Göteborg - Formed in 2000 by Huldtgren and Ahlbäck, both ex-*Vaticide* and also found in the band *Clonaeon*, while the latter is also in *Waning*. The first demo CDR, *Coup De Grace*, was recorded in 2000. The artwork spawned a rumour that the band were Nazis, which they strongly deny. In 2001 the band was then featured with four tracks on the four-way split CD *Gathered Against Humanity* (2001 Christcrusher). The band now started working on the debut, to be entitled *Sonnilon*. Time went and the members' focus was elsewhere. In 2005 the energy was back, but the songs were now old and the recording shelved. However some old songs were rearranged and rerecorded as the *Strategema* MCD. They recorded the debut album *The March Of Drones* already in 2005-06 and it features 45 minutes of uninterrupted music, like one seamless song. Apocalyptic brutal black metal, at times a bit similar to *Waning*.
Website: www.obitus.org

2006 MCD - OBI 001

2006 ■ Strategema ....MCD 3tr   private .... OBI 001
       Tracks: 21st Century Terror State/Breed In Breed Out/Sonnilon
2009 ■ THE MARCH OF THE DRONES ....CD   Eerie Art .... EAR 024

2009 CD - EAR 024

OBLIGATORISK TORTYR

Jens Kjerrström: v/g, Viktor Helge: b, Fredrik Helgesson: d

Göteborg - The name means "compulsory torture" in Swedish. Death metal with a touch of hardcore, or deathgrind if you will, with quite extreme screeching and growling vocals. Incredibly dark, destructive and depressing lyrics. At times similar to *Nasum*. The vocals are in Swedish, but the booklet also includes English translations... but as you can't hear the words anyway it doesn't really matter... The band was formed in 1998. Jens is ex-*Brutaliator* and also found in *Profanity*. On *Återförödelse* (re-devastation) drummer Fredrik Helgesson (ex-*Grief Of Emerald, Dawn*) had been replaced by Stefan Karlsson (*Soulreaper, Brutaliator, Profanity*). The band also recorded the track *I Helvete* for a *Nasum* tribute in 2009.
Website: www.obligatorisktortyr.com

2001 CD - OPCD 107

2001 ■ OBLIGATORISK TORTYR ....CD   Osmose .... OPCD 107
2002 □ OBLIGATORISK TORTYR ....LP   Osmose .... OPLP 107
       500 copies.
2007 ■ ÅTERFÖRÖDELSE ....CD   Power It Up .... PIU 85

OBLIVION

Samuel Emtlind: v, Jimmie Isacsson: g, Johan Isacsson: b, Haakon Sjöquist: d

Jönköping - Brutal hardcore-infused thrash metal. *Oblivion* sound quite influenced by early *Meshuggah*. Tons of staccato riffs and raw growling/screeching vocals. Quite depressing in their approach, both musically and lyrically. A strong Christian lyrical message. The band was formed in 1995 by guitarist Björn, bass player Johan and drummer Franz, starting out playing covers. They went through numerous members changes before finding the line-up that recorded the album. They recorded their first demo, *Faith*, in 1998, at the time with guitarist Petter Stenmarker (*Crimson Moonlight*) and singer Jonas in the band. The band can also be found on *Power From The Sky* (02 C.L. Music & Publishing), *Twisted Sounds From The Underground* (1999 Topsounds) and *Twisted Sounds – The Red One* (2001 Topsound). In 2006 they recorded the demo *Paratorini Muntes Nascetor Ridicolus Mus*.

2007 CD - PIU 85

2002 ■ RENEWAL ....CD   C.L. Music & Publishing .... CLCD 006

OBLIVIOUS

Isak Nordblom: v, Daniel Börefelt: g, Sven: g,
Per Björklund: b, Joakim "Jocke" Svensson: d

Linköping - These stoner rockers from Linköping were formed late 2003/early 2004, by Daniel (also bass/vocals in *Pedro Sanchéz*) and Per, as *Oblivion* and recorded their first demo *Face The Strange* in 2005. Two more demos, *Transparent Man* and *Masters Of Time* were recorded. In March 2009 the band changed their name to *Oblivious*, as there were several bands using

2002 CD - CLCD 006

the same name. The album is an outstanding piece of plastic, drawing influences from bands like **Black Sabbath** and **Bigelf** and mixing it with touches of **Clutch**, **Grand Magus** and **Dozer**. Great authentic late seventies-sounding stoner hard rock.

2009 ■	GOONS AND MASTERS	CD	Transubstans	TRANS 051
2013 ☐	CREATING MEANING	CD	Transubstans	TRANS 114

2009 CD - TRANS 051

OBRERO

Martin Missy: v, Fredrik Pihlström (aka Lundquist): g,
Mathias Öjermark: g, Magnus Karkea: b, Calle Sjöström: d

Stockholm - **Obrero** were formed in 2007 by members of death/thrash bands **Talion** (Karkea, Pihlström, Missy) and **Phidion** (Pihlström, Öjermark, Missy). In 2010 the band, at the time featuring drummer Alex Zaino, recorded the twelve-track demo *Volume 1:Tales From The West And Beyond*. Later the same year Alex went to Colombia and was replaced by Sjöström (**Unchaste**, **Talion**). Öjermark, is ex-**Melting Flesh, Sauron, Total Death, Ruins Of Time**, Lundquist is also in **Bloodbanner**, ex-**Melting Flesh, Lelldorin**, while Missy is ex-**Ruins Of Time, Inzest** and also in **Protector**. Busy boys. **Obrero** play outstanding stoner with very heavy doom-laden riffs, like the perfect mix between **Pentagram** and **Candlemass**. New album, *The Infinite Corridors Of Time*, set for release in 2013/14.

2011 CD - NTR 003 CD

2011 ■	MORTUI VIVOS DOCENT	CD	Night Tripper	NTR 003 CD
2011 ☐	MORTUI VIVOS DOCENT	LP	Night Tripper	NTR 003
	500 copies. Poster.			

OBSCENE

Henrik Olin: v, Mikael Wedin: g, Alexander Andersson: b, Olaf Landen: d

Jönköping - Death metal band **Obscene** recorded their first rehearsal demo in 2001, *Demo '02* the year after and *Laceration Of The Unborn* in 2003. Thrashy and quite original death metal, a bit reminiscent of **Suffocation**. Andersson and Landen are also found in **Svartnar**.

2005 CD - REDRUM 004

2005 ■	LACERATION OF THE UNBORN (split)	CD	Redrum	REDRUM 004
	Split with Bestial Devastation. Tracks: Appetite For The Dead/Consuming Through			
	Disembowelment/Laceration Of The Unborn/Abstract Form Of A Woman/Bonecrusher			
	(Mortician cover)			

OBSCURITY

Daniel Vala: b/v, Jan Johansson: g,
Jörgen Lindhe: g, Valentin Nilsson: d

Växjö/Malmö - The band was formed by Daniel and Jan in 1985 and they were inspired by bands like **Venom**, **Slayer** and **Bathory**. *Ovations To Death* was recorded as a demo in 1985 and contains only Daniel and Jan (guitar and drums). *Damnations Pride* was the band's second demo, recorded in 1986 featuring Valentin Nilsson on drums. Not to be confused with the **Obscurity** that released the MCD *Wrapped In Plastic* in 1992. Jörgen was later found in **Flegma** and is today fronting the brutal Skåne band **S.K.U.R.K**. The Scarlet Records release is a compilation containing old singles, demos and outtakes.

1998 7" - TTD 001

1998 ■	Damnations Pride	7"	To The Death	TTD 001
	Tracks: Graves Of Rebirth/Damnations Pride/Mortal Remains/Demented. Released in			
	666 numbered copies.			
1998 ■	Ovations To Death	7"	To The Death	TTD 002
	Tracks: Intro/Across The Holocaust/Excursion To Eternity/Celestial Conquest/Unblessed			
	Domain. 500 numbered copies.			
1998 ☐	DAMNATIONS PRIDE	CD	Scarlet	SC 001-2
1998 ☐	DAMNATIONS PRIDE/OVATIONS TO DEATH	LP	To The Death	TTD 001
	400 red + 100 black vinyl.			

1998 7" - TTD 002

OBSCURO

Avondo: v/g/b, Tortyr: d

Malmö - Formed in 2001. In 2002 the demo *The Sworn One* was recorded, followed by *När mörkret slukar ljuset* (2005) and *Förintelsen är nära*, which was released on CDR in 2005 by Total Death Production. Quite simple cold and raw old-school black metal with the same blast beat tempo in most of the songs. Long instrumental parts builds up to the desperate screams which feel quite disconnected from the music. A strange beast indeed.

2008 ■	WHERE OBSCURITY DWELLS	CD	Drakkar	DKCD 054

2008 CD - DKCD 054

OCEAN

Stig-Olov Svensson: v/g, Johnny Granström: b/v, Bengt "Kärnkraft" Johansson: d

Karlshamn - Not to be confused with the French hard rockers or the other Swedish band. Formed in the early 70's under the name *Spänn Fläsket* (Strain The Flesh), changed their name to *Brandalarm* (Firealarm). In 1978 they recorded the first self-financed single, got signed by SOS Records who reissued the single with the songs switching sides. The line-up then was Johnny, Kjell Jacobsson (g) and Kenta Svensson (d). Singer/guitarist Stig-Olov Svensson joined the band and the second 7" was recorded in 1980, a weak poppy thing sung in Swedish. Kjell and Kenta joined *Overdrive* in June 1980. Johnny and Stig-Olof recruited Bengt Johansson on drums and they recorded the album *The But*, a collection of straight no-nonsense rock 'n roll tracks with a hard rock attitude. The band also went through some different line-ups featuring Zoltan Djember (ex-*Overdrive*) and Tommy Wirén (ex-*Horoscope*). Johnny later joined *Interaction*, with whom he recorded a MLP. He is now found in country band *One 58*, together with Kjell. Both Kjell and Kenta are still in metal band *Overdrive*.

1978 7" - JG 1004

1980 7" - ONSI 280

1978 ■	Bad Things/See Everybody	7"	private	JG 1004
1978 ☐	See Everybody/Bad Things	7"	T-Bone	TBS 170
1980 ■	Drömmar Om Silver/Dialog På Kungsgatan	7"	private	ONSI 280
1981 ☐	THE BUT	LP	private	DEBUT-LP 180 $

1000 copies hand numbered.

OCEAN

Johan Blidell: v/k, Anders Grönlund: g, Patrik Alfredsson: k,
Claes Axelsson: b, Tomas Fredblad: d

Stockholm - Good, but very slick AOR borderlining on westcoast rock/pop. The B-side is a ballad, while the A-side is an up-tempo AOR offering. Hardly any guitars at all, though. Not to be confused with the Karlshamn band or the French namesakes. The band was formed in 1984 and split ten years later. They started out playing originals, but became more of a pop/rock cover band. Blidell is still highly active as a musician playing pop/rock.

1986 7" - BJS 012

1986 ■	Everything Will Come/I'm Still In Love	7"	Björnspår	BJS 012

OCEAN CHIEF

Tobias Larsson: v/d, Björn Andersson: g, Johan Pettersson: k, Jocke Pettersson: b

Mjölby - Long, slow, stretched-out drone stoner/doom riffing. Similar to *Sleep*. For instance the song *Freja* on the 2008 split is 25 minutes. Pettersson is/was also found in *Niden Div. 187*, *Regurgitate, Retaliation, Thy Primordia, Dawn, Cranium, Unmoored, Traumatic, Funeral Fiest* etc. Andersson is also in *Vanhelgd*. The first demo was recorded in 2002 and a second in 2003. In 2010 the band was reinforced by keyboard player Johan Pettersson and in 2013, after *Sten* was recorded, *Maim* guitarist Christian Sandberg joined.

2004 ☐	The Oden Sessions	MCD 4tr	Church Of Doom	COD-001
	Tracks: Sword Of Justice/Oden/Gates Of Fire/The Ocean Chief Rules My World			
2006 ☐	TOR	CD	12th Records	606041249028
2007 ☐	NORTHERN LIGHTS (split)	CD	Aftermath Music	Chapter 53
	Split with Runemagick. Track: Gathering Souls. 500 copies.			
2008 ☐	OCEAN CHIEF/KONGH (split)	LP	Land Of Smiles	LOS 15
	Split with Kongh. Track: Freja. 100 green/white splatter + 400 black. Poster.			
2009 ■	DEN FÖRSTE	LP	Electric Earth	EARTH 06
2010 ☐	NORTHERN LIGHTS II (split)	12"	Aftermath Music	Chapter 60
	Split with The Funeral Orchestra. Track: Born. 250 copies.			
2013 ☐	STEN	CD	I Hate Records	IHRCD 077

2009 LP - EARTH 06

OCTINOMOS

Fredrik Söderlund: v/g/b/d

Linköping - Black metal in the vein of *Marduk*. Fredrik's one man project, even though Mårten Björkman (*Algaion, Arditi*) sings on the first demo (1994). Fredrik is also the man behind *Puissance* and *Parnassus*. *Fuckhole Armageddon* features Fredrik's manifest in the booklet. The band still exists and in 2008 Björkman rejoined the band, together with bass player Rudra Fjäll (*Angst, Nattstrype, Ofermod*) the year after.

1996 CD - IFR 003

1996 ■	ON THE DEMIURGE	CD	Infortunium	IFR 003
1996 ■	ON THE DEMIURGE	CD	Full Moon	FMP 006
	New artwork and different tracks.			
2000 ☐	WELCOME TO MY PLANET	CD	Baphomet (USA)	BAPH 102-2
2000 ☐	WELCOME TO MY PLANET	CD	Hammerheart	HHR 056
2001 ☐	FUCKHOLE ARMAGEDDON	CD	Baphomet	BAPH 2117 CD
2003 ☐	FUCKHOLE ARMAGEDDON	LP	Miriquidi/City Of Death	MPLP 06
	420 copies.			

1996 CD - FMP 006

OCTOBER TIDE

Alexander Högbom: v, Jonas Kjellgren: g, Jonas Renkse: d/g/v,
Mattias Norrman: g/b, Robin Bergh: d

Stockholm - When *Katatonia* took a break in 1995, Johan and Fredrik formed *October Tide*. The band released two albums before *Katatonia* was resurrected in 1999, which resulted in the band being put to sleep. On the first two albums, the vocals were handled by Mårten Hansen (*A Canorous Quintet, The Plague, This Ending, Sins Of Omission*). The band produces highly intriguing symphonic hard rock but with death-ish vocals. In 2009, after Fredrik Norrman left *Katatonia*, the band was again resurrected. The line-up had now been reinforced with *In Mourning* singer Tobias Netzell, *Scar Symmetry* guitarist Jonas Kjellgren and *Amaran* drummer Robin Bergh. Fredrik was also found in *Uncanny* and *Fulmination*, while Renkse has recorded with *Bloodbath*. The 2008 release of *Rain Without End* was remastered by Dan Swanö. Doomy death with a gothic touch a bit similar to bands like early *Katatonia*, *Swallow The Sun* and *My Dying Bride*. Early 2012 Mattias Norrman (*Katatonia*) repalced Fredrik and Alexander Högbom (*Volturyon, Spasmodic*) replaced singer Netzell.

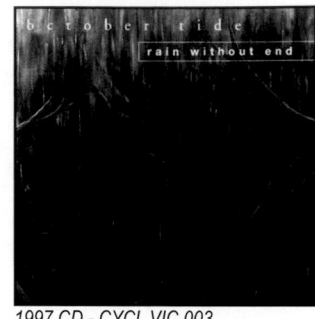

1997 CD - CYCL VIC 003

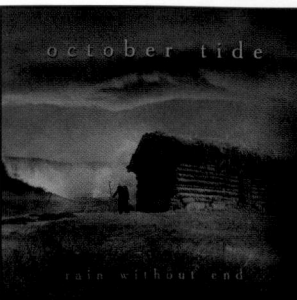

2008 CD - VIC 003

1997 ■	RAIN WITHOUT END	CD	Cyclone Empire/VIC Records	...	CYCL VIC 003
1999 ☐	GREY DAWN	CDd	Avantgarde		AV 037
2008 ■	RAIN WITHOUT END	CD	Vic		VIC 003
2008 ☐	GREY DAWN	CD	Candlelight		CDVILED 163
2009 ☐	RAIN WITHOUT END	CD	Candlelight (USA)		CDL 458 CD
2010 ☐	RAIN WITHOUT END	LPg	Northern Silence		NSP 088
	222 copies in purple/blue, 222 clear/blue and 111 in black vinyl. Different artwork.				
2010 ☐	A THIN SHELL	CD	Candlelight		CANDLE 318 CD
2010 ☐	A THIN SHELL	CD	Candlelight (USA)		CDL 483 CD
2013 ■	TUNNEL OF NO LIGHT	CD	Pulverised		ASH 100 CD

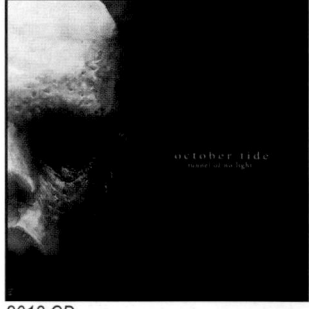

2013 CD -

ODENWRATH

Zach "Odenwrath" Zuchowski: v/g/b, Izzy Stormrider: b,
Eddie Bloodbath: d, Emil P.W.S Holmgren: d

Stockholm - Initially named *Orchards Of Odenwrath*. Zuchowski is ex-*Cauldron*, while drummer Emil P.W.S Holmgren has played with *Chainsaw* and *Illusion Of Clarity*. *Odenwrath* play death metal with thrash/heavy metal infused riffing with quite strange guttural semi-growling vocals. In 2010 the digital EP Braving The Storm was released and in 2011 the band released a new digital album, *Riding The Dragon's Breath*, from which the quite mediocre video *Full Vengeance Rising* was selected. Guitarist Tuho Gutcarver had now joined.

2006 ■	THE RAVENCULT	CD	Ravenpath		RPR 007

2006 CD - RPR 007

ODHINN

John Östlund: v, John Frölen: g/b, Otto Wiklund: d

Sundsvall - The band was formed in 1995 by Östlund and Frölen as a technical death metal band. They later became faster and more brutal. In 1996 the trio formed *In Battle* as a side project. Wiklund was also found in *Setherial*. On *The North Brigade*, Östlund handled all instruments and vocals. The band's last album *The Past Will Rise Again* was supposed to be released in 2000, but the label was put on ice and the album hasn't been released. The album is quite different and features a chamber orchestra. John is also involved with numerous projects such as *Eldkraft*, *Horde Of Hel*, death metal band *Norrsken*, folksy *Valkyia* (one album out), industrial band *Inhuman* and *Rape*. October 13, 2008 Wiklund died of heart failure.

1998 ■	From A Splendorous Battle	MCD 4tr	Napalm		NPR 051
	Tracks: Haunting Winds Over My Grave/From A Splendorous Battle/Pleasure Of Blasphemy/Before Eternal Eyes				
1998 ☐	THE NORTH BRIGADE	CD	Napalm		NPR 054

1998 MCD - NPR 051

ODYSSEY

Jonas Pedersen: v/b, Witold Östensson: g, Jesper Karlsson: d

Helsingborg - The band started out in 2010 as *Bible* and recorded a three-track demo. They changed their name three times before settling for *Odyssey*. In 2011 they recorded their first self-titled four-track demo, also as a digital release. *Odyssey* play heavy riff-oriented loud stoner with a touch of sludge. Very seventies-sounding recording, actually recorded live in the studio.

2012 ☐	Odyssey/Black Pyramid (split)	7"	Transubstans		TRANSV 703
	Split with Black Pyramid. Track: Wicked Witch. 300 black + 200 coloured vinyl.				
2012 ■	ABYSMAL DESPAIR	CD	Transubstans		TRANS 093
2012 ☐	ABYSMAL DESPAIR	CDd	Transubstans		TRANS 093LTD
	Poster				
2012 ☐	ABYSMAL DESPAIR	LPg	Transubstans		TRANSV13
	Green or black vinyl. Different artwork.				

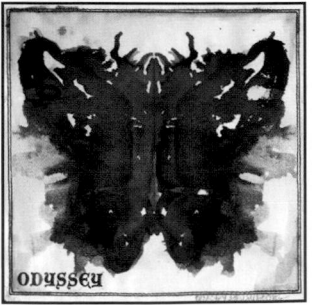

2012 CD - TRANS 093

ODYSSEY

Dan Swanö: v/d/k, Kenth "Kenta" Philipsson: g/k, Rick Gustafson: g

Örebro - Powerful melodic power/speed metal. The record contains three long metal-epics. Dan was a former member of death-acts like *Edge Of Sanity* and *Pan-Thy-Monium*, but here he shows his melodic side and sings with clean voice. All guitar solos on the album were played by Peter Andersson. Kenta is ex-*Leukemia*, Rick is ex-*Memory Garden*.

1999 MCD - UVMCD 006

1999 ■	Odyssey	MCD 3tr	Utopian Vision	UVMCD 006	$

Tracks: I Am Two/I Carry A Secret/Amon-Ra

OFERD

Jocke: g, Raymond Nykvist: b, Emil Tillman: d

Falun - Formed in 2007. No members are stated anywhere. Old-school-sounding primitive black metal. Raymond and Emil are also in *Svarti Loghin*, *Eldrit* and *Död*.

2008 □	OFERD	CD	MiriquidiProductions	MP 046

OFERMOD

Jonas "Leviathan (aka Nebiros/Nord)" Tengner: v,
Mika "Michaya/Belfagor" Hakola: g/b/d

2008 CD - MP 046

Norrköping/Stockholm - *Ofermod*, in old Swedish, means arrogance. The band was formed by Belfagor (*Nefandus, Saturnalia Temple*) in 1996, soon joined by Jonas "Leviathan/Nebiros/Nord" Tengner (*Malign, Superior, Repugnant*). They recorded the first single in 1998 after which it went all quiet. In 1999 bass player Mikael "Mist" Schelén (*Mist, Ophthalamia*) was also in the band, but was out again before the 2004 demo *Netivah Ha-Chokmah* was recorded. At this time the band also featured guitarist Emil "Atum/Abtriakon" Lundin (*Dödfödd*), bass player Johannes "J/Tehôm" Kvarnbrink and drummer Tore "Shiva/Necromorbus" Stjerna (*Nex, Chaos Omen, In Aeternum, Funeral Mist, Corpus Christii*). The 2005 MCD/MLP is actually the single and demo compiled. In 2006 Leviathan served time in prison for assault and robbery. When released he was again imprisoned for further acts of violence. Kvarnbrink, who is also editor of *G'hinnom* zine, has played with *Dödfödd, Mortuus* and *Shade Of Black*. On *Tiamtü* they were back to being a duo featuring Belfagor and Leviathan. Old-school-style black metal similar to *Mayhem* and *Funeral Mist*. On *Thaumiel* the band was picked up by Spinefarm and the music became a bit more varied, with more doomy and almost ambient parts, like *Undead Moon* as well as more classic metal-oriented stuff like *Setnacht*, plus cleaner vocals. Pretty good stuff.

2008 CD - NED 016

2012 CD - SPI 408 CD

1998 □	Mystérion Tés Aniomas/Chained To Redemption	7"	Pounding Metal	PMP 002	
	500 copies.				
2005 □	Mystérion Tés Aniomas	MCD 4tr	Nova Evangelium Diaboli	NED 007	
	Tracks: Mystérion Tés Aniomas/Chained To Redemption/Khabs Am Pekht/Rape The World.				
2005 □	Mystérion Tés Aniomas	MLP 4tr	Nova Evangelium Diaboli	NED 007	
	Poster.				
2008 ■	TIAMTÜ	CD	Nova Evangelium Diaboli	NED 016	
2008 □	TIAMTÜ	LP	Nova Evangelium Diaboli	NED 016	
2009 □	TIAMTÜ	CD	Southern Lord	STHL 985	
2012 ■	THAUMIEL	CD	Spinefarm	SPI 408 CD	

OMNIOUS

Anders Sjöholm: v, Sören Sandved: g, Johan Saxin: g, Johan Lindén: b, Joél Cirera: d

Malmö - *Omnious* were formed in 1991, recorded their first demo in 1994 and their second *Sinister Avocation* the year after. The band is also featured on *Ironic Compilation 1997* (Ironic IRO-001). The first album was produced by Tommy Tägtgren. Cirera, who replaced Thomas Lejon (*Andromeda, ACT*) after the first album, was later in *Enshrined* and *Crazy Lixx*. Bass on the debut was handled by Björn Thunholmer. Sjöholm has been found in *The Forsaken* and *Feared Creation* and Sandved, who replaced Dan Johansson in 2001, is in *S.K.U.R.K*.

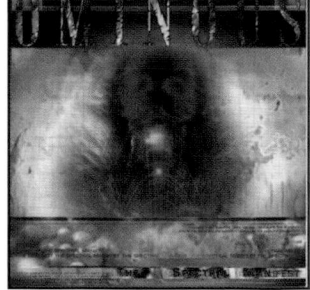

1999 CD - HOLY 56CD

1999 ■	THE SPECTRAL MANIFEST	CD	Holy Records	HOLY 56CD
2002 □	VOID OF INFINITY	CD	Holy Records	HOLY 77CD

OMNISPAWN

John Andersson: v, Markus Harju: g, Rickard Wahlberg: g,
Charlie Persson: b, Daniel Gadd: d

Olofström - *Omnispawn* were formed in 2005, by Harju and Wahlberg . In 2006 Gadd (*Dysmorph*) joined and the year after Persson. Early 2008 singer Andersson completed the band. Melodic death metal in the vein of *Blinded Colony* and *Soilwork*.

2009 ■	DARKNESS WITHIN	CD	private	OMNI 001

2009 CD - OMNI 001

OMNITRON

Pontus Lindqvist: v/b, Rasmus Ekman: g, Pelle Ström: g, Stefan Kälfors: d

Stockholm - Originally formed in 1980-81 under the name *The Krixhjälters*, under which name they recorded some MLP's, singles and an album. In 1989 *The Krixhjälters* changed name to the more international-sounding *Omnitron*. The style is powerful thrash with hints of jazz and influences from bands like *Slayer* and *Faith No More*. The *Motörhead* cover *Ace Of Spades* was featured on *Motörhead Tribute* (95 Pink Honey). However it was recorded already in 1990. The band was also featured on the compilation *The Legacy – A Tribute To Black Sabbath*, where they do a cover of *Symptom Of The Universe*. Ström is ex-*Agony* and has together with Ekman also played in *Comecon*. Lindqvist and Kälfors are now in *Enter The Hunt*.

1990 LP - CBR 123

1990 ■	MASTERPEACE	LP	CBR	CBR 123
1990 □	MASTERPEACE	CD	CBR	CBRCD 123
	Bonus: Ace Of Spades (Motörhead cover)			
1994 □	Somewhere, Sometime, Someone Is Nude You're Dressed	MCD 4tr	Brotherhonkie	PAID 1
	Tracks: Sillyvization/The Man/Rosetta The Stoned/Hell Minus One			

OMNIZIDE

Mikael Nox Pettersson: v, Anders "AE" Pers: g/b, Nicklas "Gaddur" Michaelsson: d

Mora - The band was formed in 1995 as *Belzen*, but split up a few years later. Nox joined the band *Craft* and Anders formed *Avsky*. Later on they crossed paths and decided to start up the *Belzen* machine again. They drafted Gaddur from *Kafziel/Faustus* and changed the name to *Omnizide*. The band recorded a new EP in 2012, now featuring Bennie "B-Force" Fors (*Dark Funeral, Epitaph*) on bass.

2011 ■	Pleasure From Death/Desecration Art	7"	Carnal Records	CREP 020
	100 numbered on black vinyl + 400 on white vinyl.			

2011 7" - CREP 020

ON PAROLE

Tomas Modig: v, Christian Smedström: g, Zvonko Hvizdak: b, Tobbe Bövik: d

Göteborg - *On Parole* was conceived in 2004 by some pretty experienced musicians. Modig is ex-*Lotus*, Smedström and Bövik are ex-*The Awesome Machine*. They recorded the first demo, *Vol 1*, the same year, followed by *Vol 2* and *Vol 3* in 2005. They quite soon signed a three album deal with German label ZYX/Punk 'N Drunk Records and released their debut in 2007. The style draws influences from bands like *MC5*, *New York Dolls*, *Led Zeppelin*, *AC/DC* etc and sound like a mix of *New York Dolls* and *Motörhead*. The band has also been featured on a number of compilations such as *Under The Radar Vol 1* (2006 Antidote), *Hollywood Hairspray Vol 5* (2006 Perris), *A Fistful Of Rock N Roll* (2007 Carbon 14) and *Burn The Street Vol 4* (2005 Daredevil). The band initially featured bass player Zvonko Hvizdak (*Speedfreaks*), who was replaced by Mattias Fredriksson in 2007
Website: www.onparole.net

2007 CD - PND 1011-2

2007 ■	CLASSIC NOISE	CD	Punk 'N' Drunk	PND 1011-2
2007 □	CLASSIC NOISE	LP	Punk 'N' Drunk	PND 1011-1
	Bonus: Hard Rockin' Man			

ON THE ROCKS

Lars-Ola Fritzon: v/g, Kjell-Åke Svensson: g, Anders Zerath: b, Mikael Persson: d

Sölvesborg - Formed by Lars-Ola and Mikael, who had played together since 1984 in various constellations. The A-side is a great melodic hard rocker in the vein of *Treat* or *Power*, while the B-side is a bit more NWoBHM-oriented in its riffing. Both songs are great and the musical abilities leave no complaints. The band changed members several times and in 1992, when entering a talent show, they changed their name to *On The Road*. The band folded in 2000. Zerath and Persson also plays with guitarist Henrik "Stanley Hawk" Lindén.

1990 7" - OTR 1

1990 ■	The Night Is Still Young/Fire In Your Eyes	7"	private	OTR 1
	500 copies.			

ONDSKAPT

Axel "Acerbus" Axelsson Johnsson: v/g, Simon "S.W" Wizén: g, Nabemih: g, Avsky: b, Jocke "J." Wallgren: d

Stockholm - Formed in 2000 featuring Acerbus on vocals, bass and guitar plus Nabemih on drums. The name roughly means "evil-created". *Dödens Evangelium* was recorded at Necromorbus Studio. On *Draco Sit Mihi Dux* the band had become a trio adding Fredric "Wredhe" Gråby (*Chainsaw, Bloodline)* on bass. After the release of *Dödens evangelium* it took five years for the next release. The reason was because Nabemih moved to Landskrona. Shortly after, Wredhe was drafted by *Shining*. Acerbus himself got more involved in *IXXI*, in which Avsky was also part. After the *IXXI Elect Darkness* album the band broke up and Acerbus returned

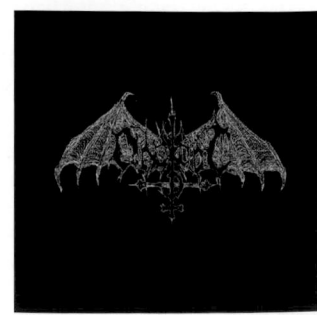

2003 CD - CELLAR 010

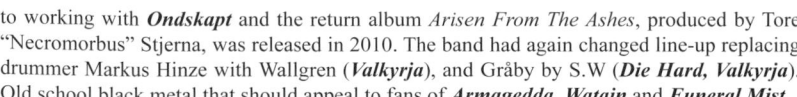

to working with **Ondskapt** and the return album *Arisen From The Ashes*, produced by Tore "Necromorbus" Stjerna, was released in 2010. The band had again changed line-up replacing drummer Markus Hinze with Wallgren (*Valkyrja*), and Gråby by S.W (*Die Hard, Valkyrja*). Old school black metal that should appeal to fans of **Armagedda**, **Watain** and **Funeral Mist**.

2001 ☐	Slave Under His Immortal Will/Dark Path	10" 2tr	Selbstmord Services	MONUMENT 007
	300 copies.			
2003 ■	DRACO SIT MIHI DUX	CD	Selbstmord Services	CELLAR 010
2004 ☐	DRACO SIT MIHI DUX	CD	Oaken Shield	FPG 26
2005 ☐	DRACO SIT MIHI DUX	2LP	The Ajna Offensive	FLAME 23
2005 ■	DÖDENS EVANGELIUM	CD	Next Horizon Records	NHZCD 001
2005 ☐	DÖDENS EVANGELIUM	2LPg	Next Horizon Records	NHZLP 001
2005 ☐	DÖDENS EVANGELIUM	2LPg	Norma Evangelium Diaboli	n/a
2010 ■	ARISEN FROM THE ASHES	CD	Osmose Productions	OPCD 205
2010 ☐	ARISEN FROM THE ASHES	LP	Osmose Productions	OPLP 205
	100 orange, 300 transparent, 515 black vinyl copies.			
2011 ☐	DRACO SIT MIHI DUX	CDd	Osmose Productions	OPCD 244
2011 ☐	DRACO SIT MIHI DUX	2LPg	Osmose Productions	OPLP 244
	520 copies splatter gold/black vinyl.			
2011 ☐	DÖDENS EVANGELIUM	CDd	Osmose Productions	OPCD 245
2011 ☐	DÖDENS EVANGELIUM	2LPg	Osmose Productions	OPLP 245
	525 copies in splatter vinyl.			

2005 CD - NHZCD 001

2010 CD - OPCD 205

ONE CENT
Stefan Berggren: v, Fredrik Åkesson: g, Peter Mikaelsson: k,
Robert Stellmar: b, Glenn Jonsson: d

Stockholm - High-class powerful AOR with nice keyboard arrangements and killing guitar work. Vocals slightly in the vein of Coverdale. Stefan was later found in **Snakes In Paradise**, **Four Sticks** and **Company Of Snakes**, while Fredrik handled the strings in **Talisman** before forming his own band in 1995. The band later reformed under the name **Taurus** with Stefan, Fredrik, Tomas Thorberg (b), who was later in **Snakes In Paradise,** and drummer Zepp Urgard who made some recordings with Yngwie and **Power**. Fredrik also made some recordings with the band **Shock Tilt** before joining **Talisman** in 1992, and he has later been part of bands like **Southpaw**, **Arch Enemy** and is today in **Opeth**. Highly recommended.

1989 ■	Fear Of Time/Falling	7"	private	UVK 1	$
	500 copies.				

1989 7" - UVK 1

ONE HOUR HELL
Micke Hansen: v, Krister "Spud" Andersen: g,
Jompa Nymark: g, Eric Holmberg: b, Matte Ågren: d

Stockholm - Well-produced and well-written high-quality thrashy death metal with a technical twist. Ranges from blast-beats to doomy parts and should appeal to fans of bands like **The Haunted** and **Lamb Of God**. **Carnal Forge** singer Jens C Mortensen guests.

2008 ■	PRODUCT OF MASSMURDER	CD	Twilight Vertrieb	twilight 784-1409

2008 CD - twilight 784-1409

ONE MAN ARMY AND THE UNDEAD QUARTET
Johan Lindstrand: v, Mikael Lagerblad: g, Jonas Blom: g,
Robert Axelsson: b, Marek Dobrowolski: d

Trollhättan - The band was started in 2004 as Johan Lindstrand's (*The Crown, Imious, Incapacity*) solo project. Lagerblad and bassist Valle Adzic (*Impious*) helped out and on the first demo, *When Hatred Comes To Life*, they were a trio with Lindstrand also playing rhythm guitar. Now deciding to make it a band, Lindstrand also drafted Dobrowolski (*Reclusion*) and guitarist Pekka Kiviaho (*Persuader, Auberon, Fraction Of Chaos*) and the band was picked up by Nuclear Blast. The debut was a slab of classic death metal. After the debut Kiviaho was replaced by Mattias Bolander. In December 2006 the anti-Christmas MCD *Christmas For The Lobotomizer* was released and the band embarked on the *X-Mas Mayhem* tour. The follow-up album *Error In Evolution* showed a slightly more experimental and melodic side of the band, while *Grim Tales* went back to basics. The band had now also changed label to Massacre Records. In 2009 Bolander was replaced by Blom, who also plays drums in **Trident** and **Grief Of Emerald**. *The Dark Epic* again sees a change towards a darker, less melodic and more twisted sound. In December 2012 the members announced they were putting the band to rest.

2006 MCD - NB 1793-2

2008 CD - MASCD 0611

2006 ■	Christmas For The Lobotomizer	MCD 4tr	Nuclear Blast	NB 1793-2
	Tracks: Christmas for the Lobotomizer/ Devil on the Red Carpet (live)/ Hell is for Heroes (live)/ Bulldozer Frenzy (live). 500 copies.			
2006 ☐	21ST CENTURY KILLING MACHINE	CD	Nuclear Blast	NB 1551-2

2006	☐	21ST CENTURY KILLING MACHINE	CDp	Nuclear Blast (promo)	NB 1612-2
2006	☐	21ST CENTURY KILLING MACHINE	CD	Irond (Russia)	CD 06-1124
2006	☐	21ST CENTURY KILLING MACHINE	CD	Magnum Music (Taiwan)	NB15512
2007	☐	21ST CENTURY KILLING MACHINE	CD	Paranoid Records (Brazil)	n/a
2007	☐	ERROR IN EVOLUTION	CD	Nuclear Blast	NB 1812-2
2007	☐	ERROR IN EVOLUTION	CDd	Nuclear Blast	NB 1812-0

Bonus: Killing Machine (live)/Public Enemy No. 1/So Grim So True So Real

2007	☐	ERROR IN EVOLUTION	CD	Paranoid Records (Brazil)	n/a
2008	■	GRIM TALES	CD	Massacre Records	MASCD 0611
2008	☐	GRIM TALES	CDd+DVD	Massacre Records	MASDP 0611
2008	☐	GRIM TALES	CD	Locomotive Records	LM 703
2010	☐	21ST CENTURY KILLING MACHINE	CD	Magnum (Taiwan)	NB15512
2011	■	THE DARK EPIC	CD	Massacre Records	MASCD 0704

2011 CD - MASCD 0704

ONE MINUTE LEFT

Fredrik Hansson: v, Calle Fredriksson: g, Johan Forsell: g, CM Häger: b,

Kungsbacka - Formed in 1997 and split in 1999. The recording was first price of the Partille-rocken. Great, heavy, melancholic, almost goth-oriented, screamo hardcore. The band toured with Breached and The Refused. Fredrik is also found in **Boogieman**, **Hurricanez** and **VISE**.

1999	■	Cause Of Aggression From Another View	MCD 5tr	Partillerocker	PROCK 1999

Tracks: Chemical/Cause Of Aggression (From Another View)/Double Standard/Shrink/ Thoughts Of Pain

1999 MCD - PROCK 1999

ONE WITHOUT

Catrin Feymark: v, Kenny Boufadene: g, Joonas Niskanen: g,
Kristofer Bergman: b, Olle Töpel: d

Göteborg - *One Without*, formed by Niskanen in 2003, play classic Gothenburg Metal with new modern melodic elements. The debut was mixed by Mattias Wänerstam (*Within Y, Suicide Nation, Avatar*). *Sweet Relief* is also available as a free digital release.
Website: www.onewithout.com

2009	☐	THOUGHTS OF A SECLUDED MIND	CD	LifeForce	LFR 097-2
2009	☐	THOUGHTS OF A SECLUDED MIND	CD	Avalon Marquee (Japan)	MICP-10879

Bonus: Whispers Of The Voices

2011	☐	SWEET RELIEF	CD	Wormholdeat	WHD 021

ONYX

Kai Nurmi: v, Björn Holm: g, Krister Bengtsson: g,
Pelle Thambert: b, Håkan Kjellberg: d

Stockholm - A good solid hard rock/heavy metal band that sang in Swedish. After the 7" they also recorded a very good demo. A sought after and expensive item today.

1982 7" - CTR 1282

1982	■	Karon/Förlorad Son/Tid Att Dö/Nosferatu	7" 4tr	private	CTR 1282	$$

OPÉRA

Ola: v, Jocke L: v, Bobban: v, John A: v, Martin: g/v, Manfred: b

Rimbo - The name was taken in 2003 and refers to the *Sator Arepo* verse, a verse written on door posts to keep evil away. The band first recorded the seven track CDR demo *First Blood*. The band now features Niklas (g/v), Oskar (b) and Björn (d).

2008	■	A REFILL WITH PAIN AND HATRED	CD	Beyond The Within	BTW 001

500 hand numbered copies.

2008 CD - BTW 001

OPERA DIABOLICUS

Andreas "Adrian de Crow" Niemi: b, David "Grimoire" Asp: g/k

Göteborg - If you can't make it the standard way, try mysterious. Niemi and Aps previously played in straight-ahead hard rockers *Akilles*, but nothing really happened. In 2006 they got themselves some suitable aliases and and changed musical direction. Very orchestrated and operatic heavy power metal. Very epic, but yet very dark and doomy, mixing a variety of singers and voices, but still keeping it together nicely. Success hasn't really found them yet, but this is quite a step in the right direction. The album features numerous name guests, such as Mats Levén (*Malmsteen, Abstrakt Algebra, Therion* etc), Niklas Isfeldt (*Dream Evil*), Snowy Shaw (*Dream Evil, Notre Dame, Therion* etc), Joakim "Jake E" Lundberg, Elias Holmlid and Eric Rauti (*Dreamland, Torch*). Niemi also recorded an album with the band *Deletion* in 2008.

2011	■	1614	CDd	Metalville	MV 0023

2011 CDd - MV 0023

OPETH

**Mikael Åkerfelt: v/g, Fredrik Åkesson: g, Per Wiberg: k,
Martin Mendez: b/v, Martin Axenrot: b/k**

Stockholm - **Opeth** were formed in 1990 by Mikael Åkerfeldt (ex-**Katatonia, Eruption**) and singer David Isberg, named after a Wilbur Smith novel. Drummer Anders Nordin (ex-**Eruption**) joined and the band was soon completed by bassist Nick Döring and guitarist Andreas Dimeo. A year later the two latter left and were replaced by bassist Johan DeFarfalla and guitarist Kim Pettersson. Ken soon left and was replaced by Peter Lindgren, who would stay with the band for many years to come. In 1992 Isberg left and Åkerfeldt took over the vocals as well. DeFarfalla left for a brief period and was temporarily replaced by Stefan Guteklint. Initially **Opeth** played very atmospheric death metal with lots of technical features as well as soft passages. Well-played and well-arranged twin-guitar work brought it a cut above the rest. Furthermore the production was not as compact and detuned as the general death metal records at the time. Produced by Dan Swanö (**Edge Of Sanity, Nightingale, Pan-Thy-Monium** etc.). *Orchid* was a death-oriented platter, while they on *Morningrise* became a bit more progressive and less metal. *My Arms, Your Hearse* showed a mix of the two and here bass-player Johan De Farfalla and drummer Anders Nordin had decided to leave the band. Anders was soon replaced by former **Amon Amarth** drummer Martin Lopez and they continued as a trio. On *Still Life*, where bassist Martin Mendez had helped, the band become a quartet, they developing their style even further letting some of Åkerfeldts seventies-influences come to life. They mix soft symphonic parts and acoustic guitars with bombastic death metal passages. Intricate arrangements and long songs. *Blackwater Park* (title taken from the seventies hard rock band) is a full-blown symphonic/progressive masterpiece. The death-vocals are now very scarce. The album was produced by Steven Wilson (**Porcupine Tree**). The heavy *Deliverance* and the much softer *Damnation* were recorded at the same time, in 2002. Åkerfeldt is a dedicated record-collector, which shows in his own music. He, Peter and Anders are also found in the heavy metal band **Steel** accompanied by Dan Swanö. Åkerfeldt also has another melodic side project together with Dan Swanö called **Sörskogen** and he was also in the death metal side project **Bloodbath**, which he quit in 2012. In 2005 drummer Martin Lopez was replaced by Martin Axenrot. In 2007 guitarist Peter Lindgren left the band and was replaced by Fredrik Åkesson (**Arch Enemy, Talisman, Southpaw** etc). In 2008 the album *Watershed* was released, now bringing forth the symphonic influences even more, leaving out almost all growling vocals. An outstanding album where the bonus DVD features a cover of Robin Trower's *Bridge Of Sighs*. In April 2011 the band announced the departure of keyboard player Per Wiberg, who was relieved of his duties right after the recordings of *Heritage*. The cover actually shows the current members of the band in a tree, past members on the ground and Per is in-between. Per was later replaced by Joakim Svalberg. In 2012 Åkerfeldt joined forces with **Porcupine Tree**'s Steven Wilson in the band **Storm Corrosion**.

Opeth, in Blackwater Park?

1995	■	ORCHID	CD	Candlelight	CANDLE 010
1995	□	ORCHID	CD	Century Media (USA)	7845-2
1996	□	MORNINGRISE	CD	Candlelight	CANDLE 015
1996	□	MORNINGRISE	CD	Century Media (USA)	7849-2
1996	□	MORNINGRISE	LP PD	Candlelight	CVCS 004 PD
1997	□	MORNINGRISE	CD	Avalon Marquee (Japan)	MICY 1022
1997	□	ORCHID	LP PD	Candlelight	CVCS 003 PD
1998	□	MY ARMS, YOUR HEARSE	CD	Candlelight	CANDLE 025
1998	□	MY ARMS, YOUR HEARSE	CD	Century Media (USA)	7894-2
1998	□	MY ARMS, YOUR HEARSE	LP PD	Candlelight	CVCS 005 PD
1999	□	STILL LIFE	CD	Peaceville	CDVILE 78
2000	□	ORCHID	CD	Candlelight (USA)	CANUS 028 CD
		Bonus: Into The Frost Of Winter			
2000	□	MORNINGRISE	CD	Candlelight (USA)	CANUS 032 CD
		New artwork. Bonus: Eternal Soul Torture			
2000	□	MY ARMS, YOUR HEARSE	CD	Candlelight (USA)	CANUS 068 CD
		Bonus: Circle Of Tyrants (Celtic Frost cover)/Remember Tomorrow (Iron Maiden cover)			
2001	■	BLACKWATER PARK	CD	Music For Nations	CDMFN 264
2001	□	BLACKWATER PARK	2CD	Music For Nations	CDMFN 284
		Bonus: Still Day Beneath The Sun/Patterns In The Ivy II/Harvest (video)			
2001	□	BLACKWATER PARK	2LPg	Music For Nations	MFN 264
2001	□	BLACKWATER PARK	CD	Koch (USA)	KOC 8237-2
2001	□	STILL LIFE	CDd	Peaceville	CDVILEM 78
2001	□	ORCHID	CD	Candlelight	CANDLE 053 CD
		New artwork. Bonus: Into The Frost Of Winter			
2001	□	ORCHID	2LP	Displeased	D-00081 LP
		New artwork. Bonus: Into The Frost Of Winter			
2001	■	MORNINGRISE	CD	Candlelight	CANDLE 054 CD
		New artwork. Bonus: Eternal Soul Torture			
2001	□	MORNINGRISE	2LP	Displeased	D-00082 LP
		New artwork. Bonus: Eternal Soul Torture			
2001	□	MY ARMS, YOUR HEARSE	CD	Candlelight	CANDLE 055 CD
		New artwork. Bonus: Circle Of Tyrants/Remember Tomorrow (Iron Maiden cover)			
2001	□	MY ARMS, YOUR HEARSE	2LP	Displeased	D-00083 LP
		New artwork. Bonus: Circle Of Tyrants/Remember Tomorrow (Iron Maiden cover)			

1995 CD - CANDLE 010

2001 CD - CDMFN 264

2001 CD - CANDLE 054 CD

Year		Title	Format	Label	Catalog
2001	☐	BLACKWATER PARK	CD	Victor (Japan)	VICP 61363
2002	☐	STILL LIFE	2LP	Peaceville	DLPVILE 78
2002	☐	The Drapery Falls (single edit)	CDS	Koch	KOCDS8237
2002	☐	Deliverance (radio edit)	CDS	Koch	KOCDS8437
2002	☐	BLACKWATER PARK	2CD	Koch (USA)	KOC-CD-8425

Bonus: Still Day Beneath The Sun/Patterns In The Ivy // + Harvest (video) on separate CD. Slipcase.

2002	☐	DELIVERANCE	CD	Koch (USA)	KOC-CD-8437
2002	☐	DELIVERANCE	LPg	Koch (USA)	KOC-LP-4576
2002	☐	DELIVERANCE	CD	Music For Nations	CDMFNX 291
2003	☐	ORCHID	CD box	Candlelight	CANDLE 053 TIN

In tin box. Bonus: Into The Frost Of Winter

2003	☐	MORNINGRISE	CD box	Candlelight	CANDLE 054 TIN

In tin box. Bonus: Eternal Soul Torture

2003	☐	MORNINGRISE	CD	Irond (Russia)	CD 03-633

Bonus: Eternal Soul Torture

2003	☐	MY ARMS, YOUR HEARSE	CD	Irond (Russia)	CD 03-632

Bonus: Circle Of Tyrants (Celtic Frost cover)/Remember Tomorrow (Iroin Maiden cover)

2003	☐	MY ARMS, YOUR HEARSE	CD box	Candlelight	CANDLE 055 TIN

In tin box. Bonus: Circle Of Tyrants (Celtic Frost cover)/Remember Tomorrow

2003	☐	STILL LIFE	CDd	Peaceville	CDVILED 78
2003	☐	STILL LIFE	CDd+DVD	Peaceville	CDVILED 183X

Bonus DVD with 5.1 surround mix.

2003	☐	BLACKWATER PARK	CD	Monsters Of Rock (Russia)	MOFR 00492
2003	☐	DAMNATION	CD	Koch (USA)	KOC-CD-8652
2003	■	DAMNATION	2LPg	Koch (USA)	KOC-LP-4577
2003	☐	DAMNATION	CD	Music For Nations	CDMFN 294
2003	☐	DAMNATION	CDd	Music For Nations	CDMFNX 294
2003	☐	DAMNATION	LP	Music For Nations	MFN 294
2003	■	Still Day Beneath The Sun/Patterns In The Ivy II	7"	Robotic Empire	ROBO 023

1092 black, 150 opaque grey and 8 test press copies.

2003	☐	LAMENTATIONS – LIVE AT SHEPHERD'S BUSH EMPIRE 2003	2CD	Koch (USA)	KOC-CD-4189
2004	☐	DELIVERANCE	LP PD	Vinyl Maniacs	VMLP 007
2005	☐	The Grand Conjurations	MCD 3tr	Roadrunner	RR PROMO 863

Promo. Tracks: The Grand Conjurations (edit)/Ghost Of Perdition (edit)/ The Grand Conjurations

2005	☐	GHOST REVERIES	CD	Roadrunner (USA)	168 618 123-2
2005	☐	GHOST REVERIES	CD+DVD	Roadrunner (USA)	168 618 123-5

Bonus: Soldier Of Fortune/The Grand Conjuration (video) + documentary

2005	☐	GHOST REVERIES	2LP	Roadrunner (USA)	168 618 123-1
2005	☐	GHOST REVERIES	CD	Roadrunner	RR 8123-2
2005	☐	GHOST REVERIES	2LP	Roadrunner	RR 8123-1
2005	☐	GHOST REVERIES	CD+DVD	Roadrunner	RR 8123-5
2005	☐	GHOST REVERIES	CD	Roadrunner (Russia)	2600765
2005	☐	STILL LIFE	CD	Icarus (Argentina)	ICARUS 132
2005	☐	MY ARMS, YOUR HEARSE	2LP PD	Candlelight (UK)	CVCS 005 PD

2000 copies.

2006	■	ORCHID	CD	Candlelight (Japan)	XQAN-1001
2006	☐	ORCHID	CD	Candlelight/Platinum(Thailand)	CANDLE053CD
2006	☐	MY ARMS, YOUR HEARSE	CD	Candlelight (Japan)	XQAN-1003
2006	☐	GHOST REVERIES	CDd+DVD	Scarecrow	SC6299-2

Alternate artwork. DVD with documentary, video, 5.1 mix of the album.

2006	☐	GHOST REVERIES	CDd+DVD	Roadrunner (USA)	168 618 078-2
2006	☐	DAMNATION	CD	SonyBMG (UK)	82876 82911-2
2006	☐	BLACKWATER PARK	CD	SonyBMG (UK)	82876 82912-2
2006	☐	DELIVERANCE	CD	SonyBMG (UK)	82876 83273-2
2006	■	COLLECTOR'S EDITION SLIPCASE	5CD box	Koch (USA)	KOC-CD-4163 $

Box including Blackwater Park, Deliverance, Damnation and Live Lamentations. Slipcase.

2006	☐	BLACKWATER PARK	CDd	Metal Mind	MASS CD DG 0965
2006	☐	DAMNATION	CDd	Metal Mind	MASS CD DG 0966
2006	☐	DELIVERANCE	CDd	Metal Mind	MASS CD DG 0967
2007	☐	THE ROUNDHOUSE TAPES	2CD	Peaceville	CDVILEF 209X
2007	☐	THE ROUNDHOUSE TAPES	2CD	Soyus (Russia)	CDVILEF 209X
2008	☐	THE ROUNDHOUSE TAPES	2CD	Victor (Japan)	VICP-64100/01
2008	■	Porcelain Heart/The Lotus Eater	CDS	Roadrunner (promo)	RR PROMO 1045
2008	☐	Watershed Radio Sampler	MCD 5tr	Roadrunner (USA)	RDRR 10218-2

Promo. Tracks: Porcelain Heart/(Edit)/The Lotus Eater/(Edit)Heir Apparent

2008	☐	WATERSHED	CD	Roadrunner (USA)	1686-17936-2
2008	☐	WATERSHED	CD+DVD	Roadrunner (USA)	1686-17936-5

Bonus: Derelic Herds/Bridge Of Sighs (Robin Trower cover)/Den ständiga resan (Marie Fredriksson cover). Rehearsal tapes. Video + 5.1 mix.

2008	☐	WATERSHED	2LP	Roadrunner	RR 7962-1

Bonus: Derelic Herds. Poster.

2008	☐	Mellotron Heart	CDS	Roadrunner (USA)	RRDR-10226-2
2008	■	WATERSHED	CD	Roadrunner	RR 7962-2

2003 2LP - KOC-LP-4577

2003 7" - ROBO 023

2006 CD - XQAN - 1001

2006 5CD box - KOC-CD-4163

2008 CDS - RR PROMO 1045

| 2008 ☐ WATERSHED | 2LP+CD | Roadrunner (USA) | 1686 179621 |

Bonus: Derelic Herds + CD. Poster.

2008 ☐ WATERSHED DELUXE	CD+DVD	Roadrunner	RR 7962-8
2008 ☐ WATERSHED	CD+DVD	Roadrunner (Japan)	RRCY-2915
2008 ■ Burning (Radio edit)	CDS	Roadrunner	RR PROMO 1082
2008 ☐ ORCHID	2LPg	Back On Black	BOBV 097 LP

Bonus: Into The Frost Of Winter. Purple, clear, white, burgundy and yellow vinyl.

2008 ☐ MORNINGRISE	CD	Icarus (Argentina)	ICARUS 473
2008 ☐ MY ARMS, YOUR HEARSE	CD	Icarus (Argentina)	ICARUS 474
2008 ☐ MORNINGRISE	2LPg	Back On Black	BOBV 098 LP

Bonus: Eternal Soul Torture. Grey vinyl.

| 2008 ☐ MY ARMS, YOUR HEARSE | 2LPg | Back On Black | BOBV 099 LP |

Bonus: Circle Of Tyrants (CF cover)/Remember Tomorrow (Iron Maiden cover). Blue vinyl.

| 2008 ☐ BLACKWATER PARK | CD | BMG (Japan) | BVCM-35449 |
| 2008 ☐ BLACKWATER PARK | 2LP | Koch (USA) | KOC-LP-4574 |

A limited mis-printed version with the labels on LP1 are switched also exists.

2008 ☐ DAMNATION	LPg	Koch (USA)	KOC-LP-4577
2008 ☐ DELIVERANCE	LPg	Koch (USA)	KOC-LP-4576
2008 ☐ DELIVERANCE	CD	BMG (Japan)	BVCM-35450
2008 ☐ MORNINGRISE	CD	Icarus Music (Argentina)	ICARUS 473
2008 ☐ MY ARMS, YOUR HEARSE	CD	Icarus Music (Argentina)	ICARUS 474
2008 ☐ MORNINGRISE	CD	Avalon Marquee (Japan)	MICP-10808

Bonus: Eternal Soul Torture

| 2009 ☐ THE CANDLELIGHT YEARS | 3CD box | Candlelight (USA) | XQAN 106 678 |

Box with Orchid, Morning Rise My Arms Your Hearse + bonus tracks. 2000 copies..

| 2009 ☐ THE CANDLELIGHT YEARS | 3CD box | Candlelight | CANDLE 273 BOX |
| 2009 ☐ OPETH | 6LP box | Viva Hate | VHR 4515 $$ |

Orchid, Morningrise, My Amrs Your Hearse on 6 LP in a wooden box. 1000 copies.

2008 CD - RR 7962-2

| 2009 ■ THE ROUNDHOUSE TAPES | 3LP | Peaceville | VILELP 268 |

I hard box with poster and booklet. 2000 numbered copies.

| 2009 ☐ THE ROUNDHOUSE TAPES | 3LP+2CD | Peaceville | VILELP 268/CDVILEF209X |

I hard box with poster and booklet. 1000 numbered copies.

| 2010 ☐ BLACKWATER PARK | CD+DVD | Legacy Sony | 88697655822 |

DVD with documentary

| 2010 ☐ BLACKWATER PARK | 2LP+DVD | Music On Vinyl | MOVLP 084 |

DVD with documentary

| 2010 ☐ LIVE AT ROYAL ALBERT HALL | 5CD+DVD | Roadrunner | RRD 177525DVD |

DVD with documentary

| 2010 ☐ IN LIVE CONCERT AT THE ROYAL ALBERT HALL | 4LP+2DVD box | Roadrunner | RRD 09199 |

2000 numbered copies

2008 CDS - RR PROMO 1082

| 2010 ☐ STILL LIFE | 2LPg | Peaceville | VILELP 78 |

2000 numbered copies. Booklet.

2011 ☐ HERITAGE	CD	Roadrunner	RR 7705-2
2011 ☐ HERITAGE	CD	Roadrunner (USA)	1686-177052
2011 ☐ HERITAGE	Box	Roadrunner	1686-177053

2LP+CD+DVD+7" (Pyre/Face In The Snow). Limited version also has postcards.

| 2011 ☐ HERITAGE | CDd+DVD | Roadrunner | RR 7705-5 |

3D cover. DVD with documentary and 5.1 mix.

| 2011 ☐ HERITAGE | CDd+DVD | Roadrunner (USA) | 1686-177055 |
| 2011 ☐ HERITAGE | 2LP | Roadrunner | RR 7705-1 |

Poster. 100 light blue, 100 orange, 100 white, 100 burgundy vinyl.

2011 ☐ HERITAGE	2LP	Roadrunner (USA)	1686-177051
2011 ☐ HERITAGE	LP PD	Roadrunner	RRCAR 7705-1
2011 ☐ HERITAGE	CD	Warner (Japan)	WPCR-14191

Bonus: Pyre/Fave In The Snow

| 2011 ● The Devil's Orchard | CDS | Roadrunner (promo) | PRO 16930 |

Made to look like a vinyl single..

| 2011 ☐ The Throat Of Winter | 7" | Roadrunner | 1686-136677 |

1000 copies. Single sided, etched.

2009 3LP - VILELP 268

| 2011 ■ THE DEVIL'S ORCHARD – LIVE AT ROCK HARD FESTIVAL 2009 | CD | Rock Hard | - - |

Came with Rock Hard magazine #292.

2012 ☐ Slither	7"	Roadrunner (USA) (promo)	- -
2012 ☐ Slither	7" flexi postcard	Roadrunner (USA)	- -
2012 ☐ The Lines In My Hand	CDS	Roadrunner (promo)	- -
2012 ☐ Veri.live (split)	7"	veri.live (Australia)	- - $

Split with Self Is A Seed. With Veri.live magazine #7. Coloured vinyl. Track: Slither

| 2012 ☐ DAMNATION | LP | Music On Vinyl | MOVLP 609 |

1000 copies in clear vinyl.

| 2012 ☐ STILL LIFE | 2LPg | Peaceville | VILELP 78 |
| 2012 ☐ BLACKWATER PARK | CD/DVD | The End Music (USA) | TE 224-2 |

Hybrid-CD/DVD.

| 2012 ☐ DELIVERANCE | 2LPg | Music On Vinyl | MOVLP 608 |

First 1000 copies in marbled white vinyl.

| 2012 ☐ LAMENTATIONS - LIVE - SPECIAL EDITION | 2CD/DVD | The End Music (USA) | TE 227-7 |

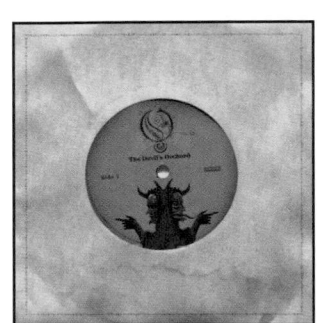

2011 CDS - PRO 16930

Unofficial recodrings:

| 2012 ☐ SONISPHERE | LP | Angst Records | - - |

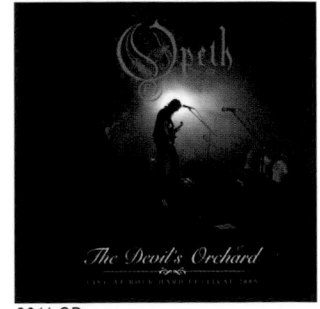

2011 CD - - -

OPHTHALAMIA

**Erik "Legion" Hagstedt: v, Tony "It" Särkää: g,
Emil "Night" Nödtveit: b, Benny "Winter" Larsson: d**

Stockholm - Formed in 1989 under the name *Leviathan*. Death Metal in the slow and heavy category. Standard death vocals, standard sound, standard band. However already the second release is a far better offering. Great production by the band and Dan Swanö, nice heavy riffing and more low-pitch spoken vocals. *Via Dolorosa* is also provided with one of the most beautiful covers I've seen. Tony is also found in *Abruptum* and *Vondur*. The vocals on the debut were cut by the late Jon "Shadow" Nödtveidt from *Dissection/The Black* and the bass work was done by Robert "Mourning" Ivarsson. Benny was also found in *Edge Of Sanity* and *Pan-Thy-Monium*. Emil later formed his own band *Swordmaster*, which became *Deathstars* (under the name Nightmare Industries). He has also worked as session-musician with *Sacramentum*. After *Via Dolorosa* Erik left *Ophthamlamia* for *Marduk* and is now in *Devian*. *Dominion* was recorded in Abyss Studios by Peter Tägtgren. Tracks like *Final Hour Of Joy* are outstandingly doom-oriented with a strong touch of *Trouble*, but with brutal semi-growling vocals. The last known line-up featured Emil, Tony, drummer Ole "Bone" Öhman (now in *Deathstars* as Bone W Machine), singer Jim "All" Berger and bassist Mikael "Mist" Schelén (*Ofermod, Malign*). The 1998 release, *A Long Journey* is a rerecording of *A Journey Into Darkness* featuring a cover of *Venom*'s *Sons Of Satan* as bonus.

1994 CD - AV003

1995 CD - AV013

1994 ■	A JOURNEY IN DARKNESS	CD	Avantgarde Music	AV003	
1995 ■	VIA DOLOROSA	CD	Avantgarde Music	AV013	
1995 ☐	VIA DOLOROSA	CD	Century Media (USA)	7892-2	
1997 ☐	TO ELISHA	CD	Necropolis	NR 013	
1998 ☐	A LONG JOURNEY	CD	Necropolis	NR 026	
1998 ■	DOMINION	CD	No Fashion Records	NFR 024	
1997 ☐	A JOURNEY INTO DARKNESS	CD	Avantgarde	AV003	
	Re-issue with different artwork				
2004 ☐	A JOURNEY IN DARKNESS	CD	Irond (Russia)	CD 04-861	
2004 ☐	VIA DOLOROSA	CD	Irond (Russia)	CD 04-862	
2009 ☐	VIA DOLOROSA	CD	Peaceville Records	CDVILED 226	
2009 ☐	A JOURNEY IN DARKNESS	CD	Peaceville Records	CDVILED 232	
2009 ☐	VIA DOLOROSA	2LPg	Soulseller Records	SSR 014	
	500 copies				
2009 ☐	A JOURNEY INTO DARKNESS	2LPg	Soulseller Records	SSR 013	
	500 copies				
2011 ■	DOMINION	CDd	Soulseller Records	SSR 044	
	Bonus: Great Are The Deeds Of Death/Final Hour Of Joy/Time For War/Sacrifice. New artwork.				

1998 CD - NFR 024

Unofficial releases:
2004 ☐	Ophthalamia/Abruptum (split)	7"			
	Booteg singel. Track: The Eternal Walk				

2011 CDd - SSR 044

OPPRESSION

**Olof Wikstrand: v, Tor Nyman: v/g, Joakim Törnqvist: g,
Fredrik Petersson: b, Jakob Strand: d**

Falkenberg - Formed in 1999, originally featuring bass player Robin Pettersson and drummer Mattias Jakobsen. In 2000 Robin was briefly replaced by Simon Nilsson, before Fredrik stepped in. In 2002 Jakob Strand replaced Jakobsen. Nyman and Petersson are also in *Autopsy Torment*, while Wikstrand is in *Enforcer, Leprosy, Hazard, Corrupted* and *Caustic Strike*. The band has also released several demos and tape-splits. *Oppression* plays tight and powerful old-school thrash in the vein of early *Anthrax* with a singer similar to Joey Belladonna. Really good stuff!

2008 ■	THRASH CLASH VOLUME 2 (split)	CD	Stormspell	SSR DL-13	
	Split with Diamond Plate. Tracks: State of War/ Infected Youth/ Forced Into Fire/ Act of Faith/Visions/ Prophecy of Darkness. 1000 numbered copies				

2008 CD - SSR DL-13

OPTIMYSTICAL

Tommy "Robin Vagh" Silfvenius: g/b/d

Norrköping - Robin Vagh released two albums under his stage name in 2002 and 2004. He started the work on a third album, but lack of funds and a feeling it wasn't up to par put the project to a halt. Instead he decided to change it into the *Optimysical* project in 2006, using a variety of musicians and singers to reach his musical goals. He used the talents of singers Jonas Blum (*Pole Position, Reptilian*) and Ronnie Hagstedt, guitarists Fredrik Fencke, Per Broddesson and Mikael Laver, bassist Johan Sjöberg, drummer Magnus Frid and keyboard player Tom Rask. *Distant Encounters* is a great, melodic hard rocker, way better than the two *Vagh* albums.
Website: www.optimystical.se

2009 ■	DISTANT ENCOUNTERS	CD	Avenue Of Allies	AVENUE 0-9020003	

2009 CD - AVENUE 0-9020003

OPUS ATLANTICA

Pete Sandberg: v, Johan Reinholdz: g,
Jonas Reingold: b, Jaime Salazar: d

Malmö - We're talking quite a name project here. Sandberg is ex-*Alien, Midnight Sun, Madison, Jade* etc, Reinholdz is also in *Andromeda* and *Nonexist*, Reingold is also in *Reingold, Midnight Sun, Time Requiem, The Flower Kings* and ex-*Downtown Clowns*, while Salazar has played on numerous albums by Sandberg, *Bad Habit, Blakk Totem, The Flower Kings, Truth, Midnight Sun* etc. *Opus Atlantica* was another Malmö-based power metal project (and there have been a few). The difference was that there was a progressive touch to this one. However, despite the outstanding quality of the musicians, it fell quite flat.

Busy boys

2009 CD - RR 0211-018

2009	■	OPUS ATLANTICA	CD	Regain	RR 0211-018
2009	□	OPUS ATLANTICA	CD	Regain (USA)	RNA 1018
2009	□	OPUS ATLANTICA	CD	Avalon Marquee (Japan)	MICP-10337

Bonus: Upside Down

ORCIVUS

Mortifier: v, Perditor: g/b/d

Lidköping - *Orcivus* were founded in January 2006 by Perditor. Shortly after, singer Mortifier joined. The band initially went under the name *Haemophilia* and recorded a demo under this name. It caught the attention of Next Horizon Records who signed the band. They now changed their name to *Orcivus* and entered Necromorbus Studio with producer Tore Stjerna to record the debut. The band used two additional session musicians for live shows, one being drummer J Hallbäck (*Daemonicus*). Style-wise *Orcivus* plays old-school style black metal in the same vein as *Dissection* and *Watain*. In 2011 the band posted they would take a break with Perditor continuing with the band *Arfsynd*. They also proclaimed they will never again play live because of the audience being there for the wrong reason, "to drink and look at each other".
Website: www.orcivus.com

2008 CD - NHZCD 003

2010 CD - NHZCD 004

2008	■	CONSUMMATUM ETS	CD	Next Horizon Records	NHZCD 003
2009	□	CONSUMMATUM ETS	LP	Next Horizon Records	NHZLP 003
2010	■	EST DEUS IN NOBIS	CD	Next Horizon Records	NHZCD 004

ORDER OF ISAZ

Tobias Sidegård: v/g, Magnus Barthelsson: g, Johnny Hagel: b, Anders Bentell: d

Stockholm - Quite an all-star line-up featuring *Necrophobic/Trident* man Sidegård, *Therion* man Barthelsson and *Tiamat* man Hagel. Goth-oriented heavy stuff, a bit similar to *Tenebre*.
Website: www.orderofisaz.com

2009 MCD - BFR 001

| 2009 | ■ | Order Of Isaz | MCD 6tr | Blackened Flame | BFR 001 |

Tracks: Drowning/Eternal/Spirit/Corazon/Curse Of The Gypsy/Eternal (Electro remix)

ORIENT

Peder Lundgren: v, Christer Green: g, Pär Alfredsson: g,
Jonas Liberg: k, Dan Wernersson: b, Fredrik Jansson: d

Borås - Melodic hard rock with influences from *Journey*. Christer and Peder are today playing in cover band *Luftens Hjältar*.

| 1987 | ■ | Dying For Love/Heaven | 7" | private | VMA-0 001 |

1987 7" - VMA-0 001

ORIGIN BLOOD

Robert Ahrling: v/g, Robin Sjöstrand: g,
Simon Niklasson: b, Brian Petersen: d

Malmö - Robert (*The Gladiator, Incapacity*) formed *Origin Blood* in 1997 and the recording line-up was set in 1999. They started gigging around and in 2002 they started recording the debut in Robert's studio Flat Pig. Sjöstrand is also found in *Vanity Dies Hard* and Petersen in *Omnious*. High energy death 'n' roll with a touch of thrash as if *Entombed, Pantera* and *The Hellacopters* had a baby. A second album, entitled *After The Storm*, was recorded in 2011, and a pro-printed promo CD-R version is in circulation.

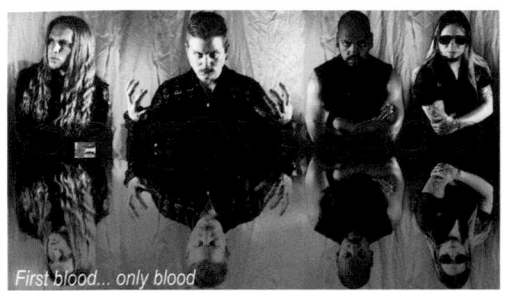
First blood... only blood

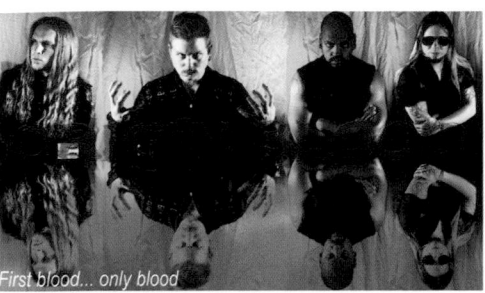
origin blood
mr. Jakker Daw

2004 CDd - rahw 001

| 2004 | ■ | MR. JAKKER DAW | CDd | R.A.H.W Productions | rahw 001 |

ORIGINAL SIN

**Edgar"Paul" Allen: v, Andy Haller: g, Orvar Wennström: g,
Martin "Bollack" Wezowski: b, Johan Helgesson: d**

Malmö - Orvar, Martin and Johan later recorded a MCD with the band *The Drugs*. Orvar later joined *Reptilian* and Martin was found in *Majestic* and *Merrygold*, while Helgesson is now in *Nation Beyond*. Includes guests-spots from Peter Espinoza, Steve Ranzow (*Espinoza, Desert Rain*), David Delring etc. Great heavy rock with a touch of Ozzy Osbourne. The demo tracks *Bough Breaks* and *Pormised Land* is found on *Dzynamite Records* (96 Dzynamite Records).

1997 ■ TEMPTATION ....CD Dzynamlite ....DzRCD 010

1997 CD - DzRCD 010

ORIZ

**Mattias Eriksson: v, Alexander Oriz: g, David Mauritzon: g,
Christopher Davidsson: b, Emil Eriksson: d**

Huskvarna - *Oriz* were formed late 2009, by Alexander (*Sanchez*). The debut was released by Blue Topaz, but due to bad distribution the band started looking for a new label and in 2011 they were signed by *Narnia/Golden Resurrection* singer Christian Liljegren on his Liljegren Records label. *Oriz* play good-quality melodic hard rock, the production being the weak point.

2010 ■ ORIZ ....CD Blue Topaz.........................BTR 61
2011 ☐ II...CD Liljegren Records.........................LRCD 009

2010 CD - BTR 61

ORNIAS

Christer "Pnax" Sverla: v, Aamon (aka Siddtraaharta): v/g/b, Fredrik "Niltor" Romlin: d

Östersund/Härnösand - *Ornias* were the first demon mentioned in the *Testament of Solomon*. The band recorded its first demo, *Förintelse*, in 2004 and the tape/CD-R *Födelse* in 2005. Aamon is ex-*Nidsang*. Niltor is also found in *Psykotisk*, *Vredgad* and formerly in *Azumfard* and *Tyranex*, while Pnax is also in *Vredgad*. In 2009 they also recorded the demo *Känslokall strävan*.

2007 ■ DEATH BRINGER...CD Regimental Records ....REG 039
1000 copies.

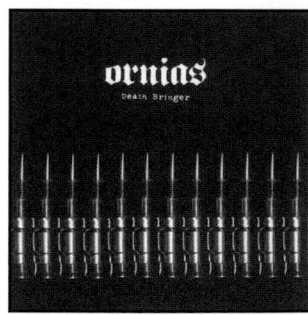

2007 CD - REG 039

ORPHAN GYPSY

**Per Wilhelmsson: v, Mikael Wretfors: g, Woody: g,
Gustaf Malmberg: k, Jonas Asplind: b, Rickard Larsson: d**

Falun - *Orphan Gypsy* have picked one or two inspirational touches from their colleagues in *Helloween* mixing it with *Metallica*. On *Aftermath* the line-up had changed and saw guitarist Per moving on to lead singer, replacing Björn Rydé, *Hostile* member Woody was added on guitar, former *Skyride/Sabaton* drummer Rickard Larsson had replaced Erik Wilhelmsson and Gustaf Malmberg had been added on keyboards. Asplind is also found in *Hostile*.The tracks *The Aftermath* and *Past Time Memories* are found on *Platinum Compilation Vol.1* (05 Pregal).

2000 ☐ The Secret Garden ....MCD 4tr private ....-
Tracks: The Secret Garden/Thorn Of Love/A Thousand Nights/Days Of Sorrow
2003 ■ AFTERMATH ....CD private ....-
2009 ☐ AFTERMATH ....CD Rubicon Music (Japan)..............RBNCD 1006

2003 CD - - -

OSUKARU

**Cecilia Camuii: v, Fredrik Werner: v/g, Oscar "Oz Osukaru" Petersson: g/k,
Adrian Lopez: k, Ryan Coyle: d, Axel Ryberg: d, Jens Björk: sax**

The full triumphant crew

Göteborg - *Osukaru* were formed in 2008 by guitarist Oz Osukaru (ex-*Katana, Eye*). He teamed up with Los Angeles born drummer Coyle and they became a writing team. The first release (an EP with bonus) featured singer Johan Bernspång (*Katana*) and second guitarist Tobias Karlsson (*Katana*). The music was there, but the vocals had its flaws. On the second release new singer Carl "CJ" Johan took the singing to a new level. The band was also reinforced with keyboardist Kristoffer von Wachtenfeldt (*Seven Tears, Platitude*). *Never Too Late* also features guest spots from Kristian Larsen (*Titan*) and David Neil Cline. *Salvation* saw Carl Dahlberg (*Frozen Souls*) taking over the keyboard duties singer CJ being replaced by Christian "Chris Tiann" Thörnlund (*Dirty Dixxx*). Unfortunately he was not on the same vocal level as CJ. Songwise the album is a pretty solid AOR rocker. It however changed on *Triumphant* when Fredrik and Cecilia took over the vocals and bassist Emma Lee Gunnari was out, while Fredrik Svensson handled her task. The band's best effort, hands down. Erik Heikne (*Miss Behaviour*) does a guest solo.

2010 ☐ GBG2LA..CD Dusty Road Records.........................DRR 001
2011 ☐ Never Too Late..MCD 6tr Dusty Road Records.........................DRR 004
Tracks: Never Too Late/City Lights/Whatever It Takes/Driven By Love/City Lights (radio edit)/Never Too Late (karaoke version)
2012 ☐ SALVATION..CD Dusty Road Records.........................DRR 005

| 2012 | ☐ | SALVATION | 2CD | Stay Gold (Japan) | ARTSG-044 |

Bonus: GBG2LA, Never Too Late + Tell Me You'll Stay (2012 version)/Change Of Heart (karaoke)/Tell Me You'll Stay (demo 2010)

| 2013 | ■ | TRIUMPHANT | CD | City Of Lights | COL 03 |

2013 CD - COL 03

OTYG

Andreas "Vintersorg" Hedlund: v/g, Mattias Marklund: g, Cia Hedmark: violin/v, Daniel Fredriksson: b/keyharp/flute, Fredrik Nilsson: d

Skellefteå - *Otyg* were formed in 1995. Starting as a three-piece with members from death metal band ***Blackburning Evening***, they soon became a band hailing the Scandinavian folk music. They recorded their first demo *Bergtagen* in 1995, a second *I Trollskogens Drömmande Mörker* the year after and a third *Gäldersång Till Bergfadern* in 1997. Nordic-sounding folk music mixed with hard rock. Heavy guitars and drums mixed with violins. They also do a personal interpretation of *Dio*'s *Holy Diver*. Daniel has a side project called ***Stures Drömmar***, a pure folk music band that has released the album *Horizonto* (Siljum 2001). The band started recording the third album in 2001, to be entitled *Djävulen* (The Devil), but it was never finished.

1998 CD - NPR 042

1998	■	ÄLVEFÄRD	CD	Napalm	NPR 042
1999	■	SAGOVINDARS BONING	CD	Napalm	NPR 063
2002	☐	SAGOVINDARS BONING	CD	Irond (Russia)	CD 02-368

OUIJABEARD

Andreas Sandström: v/g/b/k

Stockholm - Solo project of ***Dr. Living Dead*** singer Dr Ape. Solid, classic NWoBHM meets ***Kiss***. Guest spots from Johannes Wanngren (***Dr. Living Dead, Undergång***), Blaze Bailey etc.

| 2012 | ■ | DIE AND LET LIVE | LP | High Roller Records | HRR 272 |

150 red + 350 black vinyl. Poster.

1999 CD - NPR 063

OUTREMER

Ola Malmström: v, Henrik Lindenmo: g, Micke Jansson: b, Joacim Olofsson: d

Sandviken - *Outremer* were formed in 2001, however the story dates back to 1985 when guitarist Paul Johansson formed the band ***Acid Queen***. In 1986 they drafted singer Ola Malmström. Later that year Ola, Paul and Magnus Karlsson-Mård formed death metal band ***Sorcery***. Ola also worked on a side project called ***A.S.S*** with bassist Mikael Jansson, who also joined ***Sorcery*** in 1988/89. In 1991 Ola and Mikael formed side project ***Fear My Solitude***, who made around nine demos. Paul was also playing in ***In Solitude***. In 1997 ***Sorcery*** folded. In 2001 Paul and drummer Joacim Olofsson left ***In Solitude***, contacted Mikael Jansson and Ola about forming a new band. ***Outremer*** was a reality. The line-up on the first release featured singer Malmström bassist Jansson, guitarist Paul Johansson and drummer Joacim Olofsson. In 2002 the band also did a live recording. The band started a second studio recording session, during which Paul left and was replaced by Henrik Lindenmo (***Sorcery, Forlorn, Isole***). They finally released the demo *Darkness Falls* in October 2003. Doomy stoner in the vein of ***Cathedral***.

2012 LP - HRR 272

2007 MCDd - ASH 026 CD

| 2002 | ☐ | Outremer | MCD 3tr | Musical Grieves | MUGRI 001 |

Tracks: Funeral Pyre/Outremer/Skeleton Dance

| 2007 | ■ | Turn Into Grey | MCDd 5tr | Pulverised | ASH 026 CD |

Tracks: Turn Into Grey/Twilight Tyrants/Left Unfound/The Undertaker/Outremer.

OUTSHINE

Micke Holm: v, Jimmy Norberg: g, Reine Svensson: b, Fredrik Kretz: d

Göteborg - It all started back in 1998 more or less as a studio project by guitarist Jimmy. Anders Carlberg played drums between 1998 and 2002, then switched to guitar and left the band in 2007. In 2005 the band recorded the demo-EP *Memories* and two years later the debut album came out. The band was switched bass players more often than ***Spinal Tap***'s drummers have disappeared. Between 2004-2009 they went through Thomas Josefsson (***Evocation***), Simon Andersson (ex-***Pain Of Salvation***), Richard Martos (***Urbandux***), Fredrik Carlsson, Per Stenbeck and, playing on *Until We Are Dead*, David Malm. The bass is now handled by Reine Svensson. ***Outshine*** play modern melodic metal, at times similar to ***Paradise Lost***-meet-***Smashing Pumpkins*** with a touch of ***Urbandux***. A cover of Billy Idol's *White Wedding* will also give you a hint of their sound and style. Just after the release of *Addiction* the band announced they were parting ways with singer Jegestad. He was replaced by Micke Holm (ex-***Stagedoor***).

2009 CD - DTM 007

2005 MCD - DTM 005

| 2007 | ☐ | BAD THINGS ALWAYS END BAD | CD | Dead Tree Music | DTM 004 |
| 2005 | ■ | Outshine vs. Carbellion (split) | MCD | Dead Tree Music | DTM 005 |

Split with Carbellion. Tracks: I'm Sorry/Riot

2009	■	UNTIL WE ARE DEAD	CD	Dead Tree Music	DTM 007
2012	■	ADDICTION	CD	Dead Tree Music/Rambo Music	DTM 029
2013	☐	PRELUDE TO DESCENT	CD	Dead Tree Music	DTM 030

2012 CD - DTM 029

OVERDETH

**Mikael Garcia: g/v, Tobias "King Pellinore" Eng: b,
Andreas "Uther Pendragon" Mitroulis: d**

Växjö - Totally horrible, untight metal with a drummer that couldn't even keep the tempo if they put a gun to his head. The vocals, more or less spoken, sound like something taken from Monty Python. Either the members were unbelievably drunk when they recorded this or they were on something... Recorded their first demo in 1994, *King Arthur IS Dead, Alive At Camelot* in 1997 and *No More Tales* in 2002. So bad it's not even funny. Peter Josefsson has also sung with the band. Mitroulis was also found in **Dethronement** and **Jigsore Terror**.

2004 ■ KING ARTHUR'S FINAL BATTLE ....CD   Camelot Records ....CR 001
    550 copies.

2004 CD - CR 001

OVERDRIVE

**Per "Periloz" Lengstedt (aka Karlsson): v, Janne Stark: g,
Kjell Jacobsson: g, Pelle Thuresson: b, Kenta Svensson: d**

Back in 1983

Karlshamn - **Overdrive** were formed in 1980 from the two local bands **Paradize** (recorded one 7") and **Ocean** (recorded two 7"'s and an album). In 1981 the band recorded the self-financed MLP *Reflexions*, and has become quite a collector's item. The non-LP tracks *Tonight* and *Damnation Angel* were released on the local compilation *Rockslaget* (SOS 1982). In the spring of 1985 bass player Kenth Ericsson was replaced by Zoltan Djember (ex-**Ocean**) and in June the same year the band split, partly due to Pelle quit singing and no replacement was found. Janne formed **Overheat** together with singer Pelle, now on bass. Former **Mercy/High Voltage** drummer Paul Gustavsson and ex-**High Voltage** singer Gernot Iversen were drafted and two demos were recorded. Kenta and Kjell continued with the band **Pride**, but also made only demos. Kenta later joined melodic metal band **E-Type**, that appears on a local compilation-CD. Kenth recorded some demos with **Interaction** and **Area**. In 1991 Janne, Pelle and drummer Peter "TrumPeter" Svensson (**Faith, Mercy, Globe, Mountain Of Power**) recorded two instrumental tracks for the compilations *Guitarheroes Of Sweden Part 1* and *Part 2* (G.H.O.S.T Records) under Janne's name. In 1992 **Overdrive** partly reformed with Janne, Pelle (on bass), Kenta and new singer/guitarist Jörgen Aspring (Miller) (ex-**Blue Town, E-Type**). A four-track demo was recorded in 1993 but no records were made. The tracks would later appear on the High Vaultage re-issue of *Reflexions*. In 1994 the band was again dissolved. In 1995 both albums were re-issued on CD with 5 bonus-tracks each. The first MLP was in many reviews compared to early **Def Leppard**, while the albums were heavier. The music was built quite a lot around the twin guitars and amongst the influences you would find bands like **Judas Priest**, **Accept** and **Iron Maiden**. In 1997 the original line-up reunited for a one-off show. The 2000-single (not released until January 2001) is actually the first demo recorded in December 1980. In 2001 Crook'd Records released the 1997 reunion gig, plus live recordings from 1982/1985 as *Mission Of Destructions Live*. Kenta and Pelle later formed **Crosseyed Mary**, while Janne went on to **Locomotive Breath**, that initially also featured Kjell Jacobsson, and later his son, Jimmy Lexe on drums. In 2003 the original **Overdrive** line-up reunited for, what was to be, another one-off show. New offers for gigs poured in and a permanent reunion came about. Original singer, set on playing bass, opted out, and was replaced by former **Unchained** singer Per Karlsson (now Lengtstedt), later also in **Portrait**. In 2006 the MCD *Resurrected* was recorded, featuring rerecordings of four old tracks and one new. A new deal with Lion Music was signed and the album *Let The Metal Do The Talking* (a pun on Joe Perry's *Let The Music Do The Talking*) was recorded by Johan Blomström. It featured half new, half old unreleased and rearranged material. In 2011 the album *Angelmaker* was recorded with all new written material, including a cover of former **ABBA** member Frida's 1982 hit *I Know There's Something Going On*, penned by Russ Ballard. Since 18 songs were written and only 12 were featured on the CD, a vinyl album entitled *The Angelmaker's Daughter* containing the unreleased six tracks, plus three from the CD, was released in a limited vinyl edition. Mixed by Pelle Saether. Non-album track *New Beginning (Anata Na Staato)* was specially recorded for the Japan benefit CD *Embrace The Sun* (2011 Lion Music). In December 2011 internal communication problems between members put a halt to the story and a split was inevitable. However, **Overdrive** reformed in January 2012, without bass player Ericsson, and instead featuring original singer Pelle Thuresson on bass. The first song with the new line-up, entitled *High Roller*, will be featured on the vinyl release *Metal Resurrection*, to be released on vinyl only by High Roller Records in 2014. High Roller will also reissue *Metal Attack* on vinyl as a 2LP with *Reflexions* + demos as bonus.
Website: www.overdrive.se

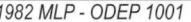

1982 MLP - ODEP 1001

1982 LP - MOP 3025

In 2013, spot the new guy?

Year		Title	Format	Label	Cat. No.	
1982	■	Reflexions	MLP 5tr	private	ODEP 1001	$$

Tracks: Lady Luck/Girls Will Be Girls/High Infidelity/You (Give Me Hell!)/Reflexions. 500 copies.

1983	■	METAL ATTACK	LP	Planet	MOP 3025
1984	☐	SWORDS AND AXES	LP	Planet	MOP 3029
1984	☐	SWORDS AND AXES	LP	Banzai (Canada)	BRC 1910
1995	☐	METAL ATTACK	CD	Rock Treasures	RTCD 01

Bonus: Music For Pleasure/Delusive Heroes/Armed & Ready/Doomwatch (demo-version)/Lost In Time. 1000 copies.

1995	☐	SWORDS AND AXES	CD	Rock Treasures	RTCD 02

Bonus: Lady Luck/Girls Will Be Girls/High Infidelity/You/Reflexions. 1000 copies.

1997	☐	METAL ATTACK	CD	Soundholic (Japan)	SHCD1-007

Same as the Rock Treasures release with OBI, sticker and Japanese booklet.

1995	☐	SWORDS AND AXES	CD	Soundholic (Japan)	SHCD1-008

Same as the Rock Treasures release with OBI, sticker and Japanese booklet.

2000	☐	Overdrive/20th Century	7" PD	Stormbringer	SKULL 9806P

500 hand numbered copies.

2001	■	MISSION OF DESTRUCTION – LIVE	CD	Crook'd	CR 010

1000 copies.

2001 CD - CR 010

2003	☐	REFLEXIONS	CD	Metal For Muthas	MFM-1012

Bonus: Overdrive/20th Century/Damnation Angel/Tonight/Armed & Ready/Delusive Heroes/Music For Pleasure/Doomwatch/Sign On The Line/Lost In Time/Caress Of Steel (by Paradize)/Comin Home (by Paradize)/See Everybody (by Ocean)/Bad Things (by Ocean)

2003	☐	METAL ATTACK	CD	Metal For Muthas	MFM-1013

Bonus: Back On The Hunt (demo)/Sounds Of War (demo)Metal Attack (demo)/Let The Metal Do The Talking (demo)/Heart Of Stone (demo)

2003	☐	SWORDS AND AXES	CD	Metal For Muthas	MFM-1014

Bonus: Die For Love/Mighty Lord/Back To Basics/Lock Of Gold/Trapped Under Ice/Ride The Fire

2006 MCD - ODEP 2002

2006	■	Resurrected	MCDd 5tr	private	ODEP 2002

Tracks: Back On The Hunt/Black Revenge/Ride The Fire/Burn In Hell/Overdrive

2008	☐	LET THE METAL DO THE TALKING	CD	Lion Music	LMC 223

Bonus: Back On The Hunt (video)

2008	☐	LET THE METAL DO THE TALKING	CD	Irond (Russia)	CD 08-DD621

Bonus: Back On The Hunt (video)

2008	☐	LET THE METAL DO THE TALKING	CD	Soundholic (Japan)	TKCS-85189

Bonus: Back On The Hunt/Black Revenge/Ride The Fire/Burn In Hell/Overdrive

2011	☐	ANGELMAKER	CD	Lion Music	LMC 279
2011	☐	ANGELMAKER	CD	Rubicon Music (Japan)	RBNCD-1059

Bonus: Brand New Sinner/Show Your Love

2011	■	THE ANGELMAKER'S DAUGHTER	LP	private	ODLP 2002

120 red, 47 yellow, 94 blue, 10 black, 10 discoloured. Hand numbered. Also 10 black vinyls separately numbered 1-10.

2013	☐	LET THE METAL DO THE TALKING	LP	High Roller Records	HRR 305

150 black, 250 white and 100 clear vinyl.

2011 LP - ODLP 2002

OVERFLASH

Magnus "Devo" Andersson: v/b/g/programming

Norrköping - This one-man-band produced highly mechanical music in the vein of **Pigface**, **Shotgun Messiah** (late) and **NME Within** but with many more death metal influences. Dan Swanö (**Edge Of Sanity**) helped out with the programming and production. Magnus is now (again) in **Marduk** and was also in **Cardinal Sin, Dear Mutant** and **Allegiance**.

1994	■	THRESHOLD TO REALITY	CD	MNW Zone	MNWCD 257

OVERLOAD

Tony Frisk (now Sunnhag): v, Stefan Jonsson: g, Carina Englund: g, Benke Sandberg: b, Tony Sandberg: d

Bollnäs - Biker hard rockers with hints of **Zodiac Mindwarp**. Formed in 1987. On the first album guitarist Hasse Ottosson had been replaced by Stefan and Matte Lindblom by Carina. Between 1994-1995 they recorded several demos, from which the ballad *Age Of Confusion* was released on the compilation *National Confusion*. The demos were later released as the CD-R *Back On Track-2006*. In 2007 they released the CDR album *The Dark Side Of Ambition* and in 2008 the CDR album *The Procession Of Tartaros*. The band now featured guitarist Stefan Jonsson, bassist/singer Tony Frisk (now Sunnhag) and drummer Tony Sandberg. In 2009 the band changed style to more death-oriented metal and name to **Gormathon**. The line-up was completed by bass player Thomas Hedlund and guitarist Peter Sonefors and the debut released in 2010.

1990 MLP - - -

1994 CD - MNWCD 257

1990	■	Overload	MLP 6tr	private	- -

Tracks: Whiskey Drinking Woman/Cold War/Rain/On Stage/Caught In Hell/Touch Of Gold

1991	☐	Second Stroke	7"	private	OLHD 1

Tracks: Motorcycle Man/Ode Of A Biker.

1993	■	DIFFERENCE OF OPINION	CD	Black Mark	BMCD 30

1993 CD - BMCD 30

OVERLORD
Stefan Kuczerski: v/g, Christer Batholdsson: g, Thomas Johansson: b/v, Johan Laux: d

Varberg - Good-quality melodic hard rock, in the vein of early *Jerusalem* or *Leviticus*. Laux was also found in *Spit It Out*.

1982 ■ Vi Kom Vi Sågs Vi Segrade/Kallt Ljus..7" Pang ....PS 041

1982 7" - PS 041

OXAN
Birger Wallsten: v/g/k, Dino "Dynamit" Nicolaides: g,
Henning Eckerborn: b, Lasse Alehag: d/v

Västerås - Straightforward hard rock, based on the blues scale. Quite reminiscent of early *Ocean* (Karlshamn) both in style and name. Lasse later joined Västerås band *Unchained*, who released one single.

1980 ■ Sommarmorgon/Rock 'N Roll Kung .... 7" Gurkas ....OX 001

1980 7" - OX 001

OXID
Mikael Nilsson: g, Daniel Björklund: g/k, Tommy Nilsson: b, Per-Ove Nilsson: v/d

Landskrona - Straightforward simple rock/hard rock in the vein of *Dunder* etc. For collectors only. Per-Ove later joined *The End*.

1981 ■ EKLATANT ....LP private .... SGLP 2

1981 LP - SGLP 2

OXIPLEGATZ
Alf Svensson: g/b/k/v/programming

Göteborg - When Alf got tired of the direction *At The Gates* were heading, he left to do his own thing. *Oxiplegatz* is his solo project. The aim was to create something new and odd. Mix opera, symphonic music and death metal. The songs on the first album were written between 1986 and 1993 and the album was cut between January 1992 - 93. He also has some help in the vocal department by Uno Bjurling (*Oral*), Sara Svensson and Håkan Bjurquist. The style is very technical death metal with a touch of goth and even some folksy tracks with only strings and bright clean female vocals. Strange, but interesting. Alf was previously also in *Grotesque* and punk band *Oral*, with whom he released a 7" in 1993 and the CD *Slagen I Blod* (94 Fairytale). The second album *Worlds And Worlds* takes the symphonic side even further and the third (and last) is just one long track, divided into 33 seamless parts, where Alf explores every crevice of the musical genre (?). It's actually a highly intriguing record with the symphonic and opera-oriented ingredients from the first album taken much further, dropping the death side of it and increasing the goth/folkish-touch in it. The members on the last album are said to be: Sz: bass/vocals, Hy: guitar, z: drums and y: guitar. Yeah, right...

1994 CD - FTCD 001

1994 ■	FAIRYTALE	CD	Fairytale Records............................	FTCD 001
	1000 copies.			
1996 ☐	WORLDS AND WORLDS	CD	Fairytale Records............................	FTCD 003
1998 ☐	SIDERAL JOURNEY..	CDd	Seasons Of Mist	SOM 009

OXYGEN
Tony Niva: v, Roger Ljunggren: g, Marcus Persson: k,
Peter Andersson: b, Bengan Andersson: d

Skövde - The same band as *Niva*. The album was previously released under the *Niva* banner, but reissued by Escape under the new name and with a bonus track. For their 2013 release the band went back to using the *Niva* name. See *Niva* for further information.

2012 ■ FINAL WARNING..CD Escape ....ESM 240
         Bonus: Bring Back The Joy

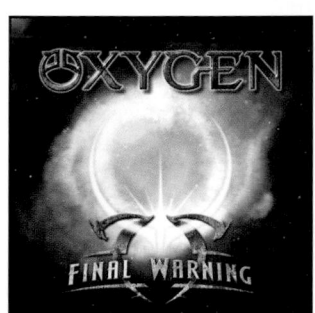

2012 CD - ESM 240

OZIUM
Peter Dahlgren: v/g, Andreas Österlund: g, Thomas Johansson: b,
Jan-Anders "Jompan" Andersson: d

Karlstad - Started out under the name *Tonedeaf* in 1997 and changed their name to *Ozium* in 2000. Straight-ahead traditional doom-oriented heavy rock with a strong seventies-feel and soft melodic vocals. Slightly reminiscent of *Witchfinder General*. Mid-quality league. In 2001 Thomas left the band and the activities went into half-speed after this.

2000 ■ Evolution ....MCD 4tr Hellbilly 001
         Tracks: Out Of My Head/Riding Free/Rage/Insanity

2000 MCD - 001

PAGAN

Olof Lindgren: v, Anders Fagerstrand: g, Ken Olsson: b/k, Björn Öhrfeldt: d

Göteborg - The band was formed in 1987 by Ken, who was previously in the band *Solid*. On the first release Daniel Björnarås (ex-*Solid, DD Band*) did the vocals and the guitars were handled by Rolf Pesonen. On *The Weight* the band used a helping hand from guitarist Mattias "Ia" Eklundh (*Fate, Freak Kitchen*), Martin Hedström (*Biscaya, Magnus Uggla*) and Rolf Pesonen. The debut contains a great original version of *Zeppelin*'s *Immigrant Song* and also a cover of fellow-Göteborgians *Biscaya*'s *Greg's Song*. Olof is ex-*Rampage*. *The Weight* is a prime example of heavy melodic hard rock. In 1995 the band finally got a permanent guitarist in Anders Fagerstrand (ex-*Acheron, Bo Wilson Band*) and they were working on material for the third release, but unfortunately the band folded.

1990 LP - US 18

1990 ■	PAGAN	CD	U.S Metal		US 18
1990 ☐	PAGAN	LP	U.S Metal		US 18
1991 ☐	THE WEIGHT	CD	Meldac (Japan)	MECR-25004	
1993 ■	THE WEIGHT	CD	Brave Records	BRAVE 93001	
2012 ☐	PAGAN	CD	No Remorse Records	NRR 013	
	500 copies.				

1991 CD - BRAVE 93001

PAGAN RITES

Thomas "Unholy Pope/Lee Rot/DevilXXX" Karlsson: v, Simpen "Descecrator" Claezon: g, Björn "Aggressor" Thorup: b, Thomas "Rex-Inferi" Hedlund: d

Halmstad/Göteborg - It all started back in 1989-90, when Thomas and Karl-Jan "Sexual Goatlicker/Karl Vincent" Kristiansson formed the band *Autopsy Torment* in Halmstad. When the band, after a few demos, folded in 1992, they formed *Pagan Rites*. The band also featured former *Ancient's Rebirth* member Dennis Widén, aka Angerbodor. The first single was straightforward, uncomplicated and untight doom/black metal. Guitars slightly out of tune and quite horrible vocals. On the first single the line-up consisted of singer Thomas, guitarist Harri "Sado/Fiend" Juvonen (*Tristitia, Devil Lee Rot*), Adrian "Black Agony" Letelier (g), Rickard "Lord Of The Deeps" (b) and Karl Vincent (d). Thomas and Adrian are also found in *Tristitia*. The band split in 1994, but was reawakened in 1995. On *Bloodlust And Devastation* the line-up had changed featuring Karlsson, Juvonen, Vincent and bassist Per "Tyrant" Gustavsson (*Nifelheim*). Musically they can be compared to *Nifelheim* and *Nunslaughter*. Thomas also has a career under the name *Devil Lee Rot* (see *Rot, Devil Lee*). On *Pagan Metal* the band featured Devil Lee Rot, bass player Lenny "Venom/Blade" Bladh (*Bullet*), guitarist Jimmy "Hora" Edström (*Karnarium, Kill* etc) and drummer C.S "C.J Sodomizer" Johansson (*Funeral, Karnarium, Church Bizarre, Cerekloth*). *Embrace The Torments Of Hell* was recorded as a trio featuring Karlsson, Johansson and Edström. Mia "Necrohell" Larsson (*Dracena*) later replaced Edström. On *Preachers From Hell* Thomas "Rex-Inferi" Hedlund (also in *Zobibor*) had replaced Sexual Goatlicker because of his excessive alcohol consumption. *Hellcome Back To Earth* was recorded live in Denmark. Björn is also in *Karneywar* and *Fear The Future* and Simpen in *Stormdeath*.

1993 7" - 002

2003 LP - I.P 032

1993 ■	Flames Of The Third Antichrist/Sodomy In Heaven	7"	private		002
1994 ☐	Hail Victory!	7"	Molon Lave Records	MLP SP 037	
	Tracks: Intro/Hail Victory/Heathen Land				
2001 ☐	BLOODLUST AND DEVASTATION	LP	Primitive Art	PAR 020 LP	
	666 numbered copies. Purple vinyl.				
2003 ☐	MARK OF THE DEVIL	CD	Primitive Art	PAR 029 CD	
2003 ☐	MARK OF THE DEVIL	LP PD	Iron Pegasus	n/a	
	100 copies.				
2003 ■	MARK OF THE DEVIL	LP	Iron Pegasus	I.P.032	
	666 copies. Different artwork.				
2003 ☐	RITES OF THE PAGAN WARRIORS	CD	Iron Pegasus	I.P.S 028	
	566 copies.				
2004 ☐	Dancing Souls/Moonfog	7"	Monster Nation/STI	MN0666/STI003	
	500 numbered copies.				
2006 ■	Pagan Metal/Pain Of Dagger/Curse From The Grave	7" 3tr	Iron Pegasus	I.P.S 009	
	500 hand numbered copies.				
2006 ☐	PAGAN METAL – ROARS OF THE ANTI CHRIST	CD	Atolinga Records	ATO 20	
	Bonus: Roar Of The Anti Christ/Summon The Power				
2008 ☐	Unholy Ancient War (split)	7"g 4tr	Hells Headbangers	HELLSEP 025	
	Split with Nocturnal. Tracks: The Arrival Of The Beast… 666/Unholy Ancient War				
2008 ☐	Pagan Rites/Evil Wrath (split)	10" 5tr	Nuclear War Now	Anti-Goth 091	
	Split with Evil Wrath. Tracks: Pagan Rites/Lord Of Fire/In The Name Of Darkness				
2009 ☐	HELLCOME BACK TO EARTH	CD	Atolinga Records	ATO 23	
2010 ■	EMBRACE THE TORMENTS OF HELL	CD	Atolinga Records	ATO 26	
	Bonus: Unholy Divine				
2010 ☐	EMBRACE THE TORMENTS OF HELL	LP	Atolinga Records	ATO 26	
	250 copies + 50 die hard with patch and t-shirt.				
2011 ☐	Preachers From hell	MCD 5tr	Unexploded Records	UER 039	
	Tracks: Curse Of Gods/King Of Evil/Catholic Sodom/Vengeance From Hell/Unhallowed Ground				
2013 ☐	BLOODLUST AND DEVASTATION	LP	Lake Of Fire	LOF-LP01	

2006 7" - I.P.S 009

2010 CD - ATO 26

PAGANDOM

Christian Jansson: v/b, **Martin Carlsson:** g, **Johan Zackrisson:** g, **Rickard Ligander:** d

Göteborg - The band recorded the first demo, *Instead Of Watching Your Funeral I Watch You Live,* in 1989 and the follow-up *Hear Your Naked Skin Say Ashes To Ashes* in 1990. In 1990-91 the band was really hot in the Göteborg-area. When they were about to break, guitarist Johan left the band and they had severe problems finding a replacement. When Johan finally returned, they recorded the album. *Pagandom* however were dissatisfied with the label and after a legal dispute they were out of a deal. The *Metallica*-cover *Battery* is found on the tribute-CD *Metal Militia* (94 Black Sun). In 1996 they went under the name *Kung*, and split after recording the demo *Six Specially Blended Songs From Kung.* Carlsson has also played in *Shadowlord* and Jansson in *Transport League. Pagandom* plays quite potent thrash metal.

1994 CD - 8202-2

1994 ■ CRUSHTIME...CD Crypta Records....................................8202-2

PAGANIZER

Rogga Johansson: v/g, **Andreas "Dea" Carlsson:** g,
Dennis Blomberg: b, **Jocke Ringdahl:** d

Gamleby/Västervik - Formed in 1997 from the ashes of *Terminal Grip* by Rogga and drummer Jocke Ringdahl, adding guitarist Andreas Carlsson (*Another Life, Ribspreader*) and bass player Jocke Diener. On *Deadbanger,* the band's only thrash release, Simon Lundin played keyboards. In 2000 Ringdahl left due to a back injury. The second album was recorded for Malaysian Psychic Scream, but because of censorship problems they went to another label. The band also went more old-school thrashy death metal in the vein of *Entombed*, *Grave* and *Carnage*, and changed their name to *Carve* for a period. They recorded a demo under this name, but returned to the original moniker on the second release. The band now featured drummer Mattias Fiebig (*Blodsrit, Portal, Ribspreader*) and additional guitarist F. Pettersson. On the third album the band featured Johansson, Carlsson, Fiebig and bassist Oskar Nilsson. This lasted for another album, while on *No Divine Rapture* the band was a trio seeing Carlsson and Nilsson out of the band, adding new bass player Patrick Halvarsson (*Blodsrit, Ribspreader, Primitive Symphony*). On *Born To Be Buried Alive,* Halvarsson had been replaced by Patrik Myrén, and on *Imperial Anthems No. 1* Rogga handled all instruments and vocals. *Basic Instructions For Dying* is a compilation. On *Carnage Junkie* the line-up again featured Rogga, Myrén and Fiebig. However on *Scandinavian Warmachine* the band was a duo featuring Rogga on vocals, bass and guitar with Brynjar Helgetun handling the drums. The 2011 release saw the return of drummer Ringdahl, guitarist Carlsson with the addition of new bass player Anders Brisheim, who was replaced by Blomberg on the latest album. Rogga has been found in numerous other bands, such as *Demiurg, Edge Of Sanity, Deranged, Ribspreader, Revolting, Bone Gnawer* etc. The band has also featured *Primitive Symphony* drummer Björn Jonsson as a session player.

The deadbangers

2003 CD - XM 006 CD

1999 □	DEADBANGER	CD	Psychic Scream	PSDL 9016
2001 □	PROMOTING TOTAL DEATH	CD	Forever Underground	FUCD 4
2002 □	DEAD UNBURIED	CD	Forever Underground	FU 013
2003 ■	MURDER KILL DEATH	CD	Xtreem Music	XM 006 CD
2004 □	NO DIVINE RAPTURE	CD	Xtreem Music	XM 017 CD
2004 □	DEATH FOREVER – THE PEST OF PAGANIZER	CD	Onslaught	ORCD 004

Bonus: Buried Alive/Skinned/NY Ripper

2005 □	DEADBANGER/PROMOTING../DEADUNBURIED/WARLUST	2CD	Forever Underground	FU 024

1000 copies. The first three albums plus the unreleased EP Warlust.

2006 □	Chapel Of Blood (split)	7" 4tr	Imperium Proiductions	IMP 006-1

Split with Eroded. Tracks: Gasmask Obsession/Hell Is Already Here. Poster+sticker. 500.

2008 □	Unglaube/Split Wide Open (split)	CD	Suffer Productions	Suffer 005-2

Tracks: The Place Is Rot/Untitled 1/Abortion Van/Gasmask Obsession/Hell Is Already Here/Grinded And Exiled v1.0 Exiled/Flashnaut v.10/NY Ripper/Untitled 2/Untitled 3/ Gasmask Obsession.

2008 □	Born To Be Buried Alive	MCD 5tr	Asphyxiate Records	AR 018

Tracks: Flesh Collector/Born To Be Buried Alive/The Morbidly Obscene/Carbonized Resurrection/The Return Of Horror/Erase Humanum Death/Only Ashes Remain - Promoting Total Death (live) + Live In Oskarshamn (video)

2008 □	Paganizer/Sore (split)	7"g 4tr	Bloodred Horizon Records	- -

Split with Sore. Tracks: Only Ashes Remain/Promoting Total Death. 100 copies yellow/ black splatter vinyl.

2009 CD - VIC 008

2009 ■	CARNAGE JUNKIE	CD	Vic Records	VIC 008
2009 □	CARNAGE JUNKIE	CDd	Vic Records	VIC 008

Bonus (all live): Massdeath Maniac/Born To Be Buried Alive/The Morbidly Obscene/Army Of Maggots/The Festering Of Sores

2009 □	BASIC INSTRUCTIONS FOR DYING	CD	Obliteration Records	ORCD 085
2009 □	SCANDINAVIAN WARMACHINE	CD	Cyclone Empire	CYC 032-2
2010 □	Imperial Anthems No 1 (split)	7"	Cyclone Empire	ANTHEM 001

Split with Demonical. Track: The Cyclone Empire. 500 hand numbered copies.

2011 ■	INTO THE CATACOMBS	CD	Cyclone Empire	CYC 082-2
2012 □	CARVE: STILLBORN REVELATIONS IN HUMAN FILTH	CD	Vic Records	VIC 044 CD
2013 □	WORLD LOBOTOMY	CD	Cyclone Empire	CYC 130-2

2011 CD - CYC 082-2

PAGANUS

Johannes "Hampe" Söderqvist: v/g, Maria Larsson: violin/mandolin, Fredrik "Balle" Karlsson: b, Fredrik "Molle" Molin: g, Jolene Fredricson: d

Arvika/Karlstad - Earthy forest rockers *Paganus* were formed in 2004 by Söderqvist and already in the summer of 2005 the band made its first demo recording, entitled *Memento Mori*. Outstanding folk-oriented hard rock in the vein of *Kebnekajse* and *Hoven Droven*, but with a more hard rock-oriented attitude. Great riffs and highly intricate songs. In 2011 Fredricson was replaced by Jerry Torstensson (*Draconian*). Jolene is also in cover band *Dirty Work*.

| 2009 ■ | SKOGSROCK | CDd | Earth N Wood | paganus 01 |
| 2010 ☐ | KALLA | CDd | Earth N Wood | 320470125328 |

2009 CDd - paganus 01

PAIN

Peter Tägtgren: v/g/b/k/d

Pärlby(Ludvika) - This is a solo project by *Abyss/Hypocrisy*-man Peter. The first album is heavy grinding metal, deathish in moods but not with growling vocals. On *Rebirth* the style became more "industrially" oriented, which also meant increasing success. Industrial melodic techno-death, if there is such a term. The song *Just Hate Me* on Nothing Remains... was written by hit maker Max Martin (Martin Sandberg a.k.a Martin White) and his former *It's Alive*-colleague Per Aldeheim. *Nothing Remains The Same* also contains a cover of *The Beatles'* Eleanor Rigby, which was also released as a single. *Pain* had a minor hit with the track *End Of The Line* and has continued making really good, quite disturbing videos for all his singles. German magazine Rock Hard voted Peter one of the world's three most powerful producers. Peter has also written music for movies like *Zero Tolerance* and *Wings Of Glass*. Drums on *Rebirth* were played by Reidar "Horgh" Horghagen. On *Cynic Paradise,* Anette Olzon (*Nightwish, Alyson Avenue*) guests on vocals. Live members included guitarist Marcus Jidell (*The Ring, Royal Hunt, Evergrey*), later replaced by Michael Bohlin (*8th Sin*), bass player Johan Husgafvel (*Plague Divine*) and drummer David Wallin (*Stormwind, Blacksmith*). In 2005 the live DVD *Live Is Overrated*, was released. Tägtgren has also been found in *Bloodbath, War, Dellamorte, Lock Up* and *Algaion*. At the 2009 Sweden Rock Festival Tägtgren celebrated his birthday by throwing a TV and a lamp out of the hotel window. However, as they didn't want to cause too much damage they removed the light bulb. They also wanted a rebate on the invoice for damage, since they had shown good judgement and tried to decrease the damage by removing the bulb.

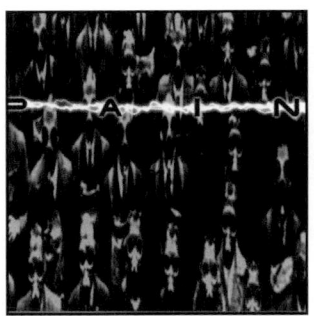

1996 CD - NB 223 2

1999 MCD - 561 472-2

1996 ■	PAIN	CD	Nuclear Blast	NB 223 2
1999 ☐	End Of The Line (radio edit)/Hate Me	CDS 2tr	Stockholm Records	561 471-2
1999 ■	End Of The Line	MCD 4tr	Stockholm Records	561 472-2
	Contains three different versions of End Of The Line and the song Hate Me.			
1999 ☐	REBIRTH	CD	Stockholm Records	542 139-2
2000 ☐	Suicide Machine/Liar	CDS 2tr	Stockholm Records	156 734-2
2000 ■	Suicide Machine	MCD 4tr	Stockholm Records	156 736-2
	Contains three different versions of Suicide Machine and the song Liar.			
2000 ■	On And On	CDS 1tr	Stockholm Records (promo)	- -
2000 ☐	On And On/Langle On And On FT2.08 Remix	CDS 2tr	Stockholm Records	158 000-2
2000 ■	On And On	MCD 4tr	Stockholm Records	158 001-2
	Contains two versions of On And On/End Of The Line (Pinocchio Long Vocoder Remix)/ In Your Knees (Again)			
2000 ☐	On And On/End Of The Line	CDS 2tr	Stockholm Records	158 440-2
2001 ☐	Shut Your Mouth/Give It Up	CDS 2tr	Stockholm Records	015 346-2
2001 ☐	Shut Your Mouth	MCD 4tr	Stockholm Records	015 347-2
	Tracks: Shut Your Mouth/Thru The Ground (demo '96)/Running Out Of Time (demo '97)/ End Of The Line (demo '98)			
2001 ☐	REBIRTH	CD	Renegade (USA)	RENE 7008
2002 ☐	NOTHING REMAINS THE SAME	CD	Stockholm Records	016 095-2
2002 ☐	NOTHING REMAINS THE SAME	CDd	Stockholm Records	016 045-2
	Bonus: Hate Me/Liar/Give It Up			
2002 ☐	Eleanor Rigby (Beatles cover)/Injected Paradise	CDS 2tr	Stockholm Records	015 960-1
2002 ☐	Eleanor Rigby (Beatles cover)	MCD 4tr	Stockholm Records	015 960-2
	Tracks: Eleanor Rigby/Breathe/Breathing In Breathing Out/Injected Paradise			
2002 ☐	Just Hate Me/Don't Waste My Time	CDS 2tr	Stockholm Records	015 674-2
2002 ☐	Just Hate Me	MCD 4tr	Stockholm Records	015 675-2
	Tracks: Just Hate Me/Don't Waste My Time/Mr. Bigmouth/Suicide Machine (demo)			
2002 ☐	Just Hate Me	MCD 4tr	Stockholm Records	015 943-2
	Tracks: Just Hate Me/Shut Your Mouth/Don't Waste My Time/End Of The Line (Pinnochio Long Vocoder Remix)			
2002 ☐	PAIN	CD	Stockholm Records	017 149-2
	Bonus: Hate Me/Liar/Thru The Ground			
2004 ☐	Same Old Song	MCD 3tr	Universal Records	986 898-2
	Tracks: Same Old Song/Trapped/Not Afraid To Die			
2004 ☐	Same Old Song/Trapped	CDS 2tr	Universal Records	986 898-1
2005 ☐	Buy Die (Radio version)/Buy Die (In Your Face version)	CDS 2tr	Stockholm Records	987 039-8

2000 MCD - 156 736-2

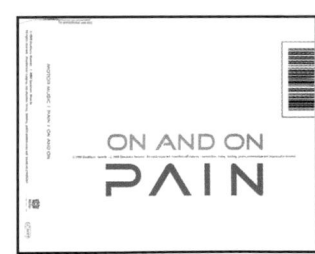

2000 CDS - - -

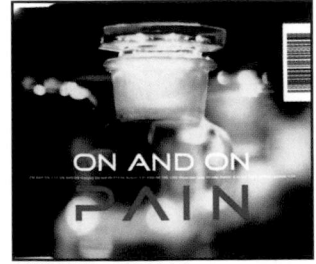

2000 MCD - 158 001-2

Pain, pondering on the psalms of extinction?

2009 CDS - NB 2288-2

| 2005 ☐ | DANCING WITH THE DEAD | CD | Stockholm Records | 986 912-6 |
| 2005 ☐ | DANCING WITH THE DEAD | CD+DVD | Stockholm Records | 986 912-5 |

Bonus: End Of The Line/Suicide Machine/On And On/Shut Your Mouth/Just Hate Me/Same Old Song/Behind The Music

2005 ☐	Nothing (Epic version)/Nothing (album version)	CDS 2tr	Stockholm Records	987 424-2
2007 ☐	PSALMS OF EXTINCTION	CD	Roadrunner	334 41953
2007 ☐	PSALMS OF EXTINCTION	CD	Roadrunner (USA)	RR 7997-2
2007 ☐	PSALMS OF EXTINCTION	CD	Mystic Empire (Russia)	MYST CD 300

Bonus: Behind The Wheel/Here Comes The Hero

| 2007 ☐ | PSALMS OF EXTINCTION | CD | Roadrunner (Japan) | RRCY-21293 |

Bonus: Here Comes The Hero

2008 ☐	I'm Going In/I'm Going In (instrumental)	CDS 2tr	Nuclear Blast	n/a
2008 ☐	REBIRTH	CD	Mystic Empire (Russia)	MYST CD 297
2008 ☐	REBIRTH	CD	Spinefarm	n/a

Bonus: Liar/Suicide Machine (demo)

| 2008 ☐ | CYNIC PARADISE | CD | Irond (Russia) | CD 08-1529 |
| 2008 ☐ | CYNIC PARADISE | 2CDd | Nuclear Blast | NB 2193-0 |

Bonus: Behind The Wheel (Depeche Mode cover)/Here Is The News (ELO cover)/Follow Me (Peter Vox version)/Clouds Of Exstacy (bassflow remix)/Noone Knows (Rectifier remix)

| 2008 ☐ | CYNIC PARADISE | LP | Nuclear Blast (USA) | NB 2193-1 |

Clear vinyl.

| 2008 ☐ | CYNIC PARADISE – DELUXE EDITION | CD+DVD | Nuclear Blast | NB 2192-2 |

Live DVD "What Happened? Official Bootleg"

| 2009 ■ | Follow Me (album version/Follow Me (Anette vox version) | CDS 2tr | Nuclear Blast | NB 2288-2 |
| 2009 ☐ | Follow Me | MCD 3tr | Nuclear Blast | n/a |

Tracks: Follow Me (Album version)/ Follow Me (Peter vox version)/ Follow Me (Anette vox version)

| 2011 ■ | YOU ONLY LIVE TWICE | CD | Nuclear Blast | NB 2694-2 |
| 2011 ☐ | YOU ONLY LIVE TWICE | 2CDd | Nuclear Blast | NB 2694-0 |

Bonus CD containing remixes, live and unreleased.

| 2011 ☐ | You Only Live Twice | MCD 6tr | Nippon Columbia (Japan) | COCB-60021 |

Tracks: You Only Live Twice/Crawling Thru Bitterness/Eleanor Rigby (live) (Beatles cover)/Follow Me (live)/I Don't Care (Live)/Bitch (live)

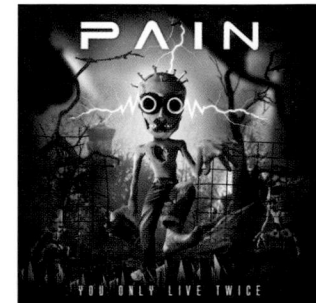

2011 CD - NB 2694-2

PAIN AND PASSION

Björn Asking: v, Roger Ericson: g, Hans Johansson: b, Andre Holmqvist: d

Göteborg - **Pain And Passion** were formed in 1998. Johansson was ex-**Biscaya**, **Moahni Moahna** and **Greyhound**, where he played together with Ericson. Asking was ex-**Punchline**. In 2000 the band recorded their first three-track demo with top-notch producer Fredrik Nordström and a second one followed in 2001. In 2002 drummer Holmqvist entered. After this they entered the studio with Roberto Laghi (**LOK, Freak Kitchen, B-Thong**) to record their debut. In 2004 Ericson left the band and was replaced by Janne Lüthje. The band now changed their name to **Zero Illusions** and has since released two albums under the new name.

| 2003 ■ | DON'T THINK TOMORROW | CD | Escape | ESM 089 |

2003 CD - ESM 089

PAIN OF SALVATION

Daniel Gildenlöw: v/g/b, Johan Hallgren: g, Fredrik Hermansson: k, Léo Margarit: d

Uppsala - This band caught my attention already on their first demo back in 1993. The story however goes way back to 1984, when young Daniel Gildenlöw formed his first band **Reality** at the age of eleven. In 1987 the band entered Rock SM and Daniel won the award for best vocalist. In 1990 the line-up changes and drummer Johan Langell was drafted. The name **Pain Of Salvation**, suggested by Daniel, had the intention of incorporating the notion of balance, e.g. good and bad or light and dark. Bass player Magnus Johansson (later in **The Project Hate MCMXCIX**) replaced Joakim Strandberg, but was replaced by Gustaf Hielm (later in **Meshuggah**) in 1992, who in his turn was replaced by Daniel's brother Kristoffer in December 1994. The first two demos were then released as a cassette album entitled *Hereafter* in 1995. On the demos they were a four-piece, featuring singer/guitarist Daniel Gildenlöw, guitarist Daniel Magdic (later in **Cudfish**, now in **Renaissance Of Fools**), bass player Kristoffer Gildenlöw and drummer Johan

No pain no gain!

Langell (**Crypt Of Kerberos**). On the debut album the band had become reinforced by Hermansson. On the second album Magdic had been replaced by Johan Hallgren. The debut was a pretty heavy and quite intriguing (read: weird) instalment while the second album is an outstanding progressive journey with a more melodic touch. The band has since kept a vey high standard, both musically, vocally and production-wise. Gildenlöw is also found in **Transatlantic**, also featuring Swedish colleague Roine Stolt (**The Flower Kings, Kaipa**) and members from **Dream Theater** and **Spock's Beard**. The 2004 release *12:5* is an acoustic album, while *BE* is a live album recorded with a symphony orchestra. *BE* was also quite different in its musical approach, deeper and less "metal". The band did not play the USA between 2004 and 2009, due to Gildenlöw's contempt for the Bush administration and the US immigration's policy of fingerprinting all foreign visitors. In 2006 Kristoffer (later appearing in **The Consortium Project**) was asked to leave due to missing rehearsals, replaced by Simon Andersson (**Urbandux, Outshine, Johan Randén, Christian Alsing, Thumbrick**) on bass. Bass on *Scarsick* was however played by Daniel. In 2007 Johan Lagnell also left the band. He was replaced by Leo Margarit. In 2009 bass player Andersson was replaced by Per Schelander. The band also released the DVD *Ending Themes: On The Two Deaths Of Pain Of Salvation*. In 2010 the band surprises most people by entering the Eurovision Song Contest with the ballad *Road Salt*. In November 2011 keyboard player Fredrik Hermansson left the band and he was soon replaced by Daniel Karlsson. Early 2012 guitarist Johan Hallgren (**Crypt Of Kerberos, Infester**) was replaced by Icelandic guitarist Ragnar Zolberg. The band has also used old friend and bass player Gustaf Hielm on tour since 2011. In 2013 Kristoffer Gildenlöw released his first solo album, *Rust*, a soft and melancholic musical journey, with Hermansson making a guest appearance.

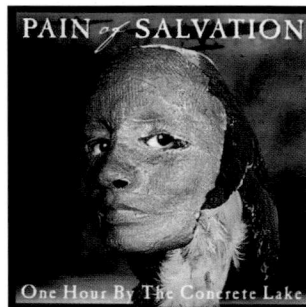

1998 CD - MICY-10066

2002 CD - IOMCD 092

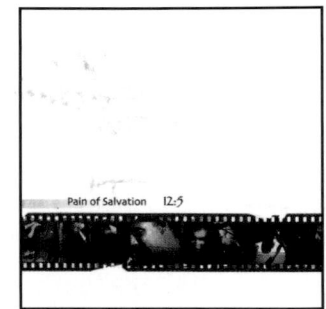

2003 CD - IOMCD 152

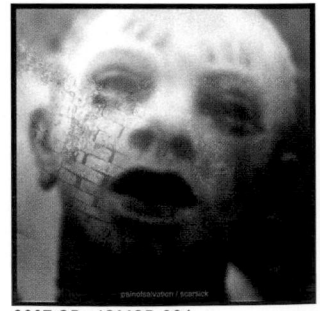

2007 CD - IOMCD 264

| 1997 □ | ENTROPIA | CD | Marquee (Japan) | MICY-10013 |

Bonus: Never Learn To Fly

| 1998 ■ | ONE HOUR BY THE CONCRETE LAKE | CD | Marquee (Japan) | MICY-10066 |

Bonus: Beyond The Mirror and Timeweaver's Tale

1998 □	ONE HOUR BY THE CONCRETE LAKE	CD	InsideOut	IOMCD 030
1998 □	ONE HOUR BY THE CONCRETE LAKE	CD	InsideOut America (USA)	IOMA 2001 2
1999 □	ENTROPIA	CD	InsideOut	IOMCD 040
1999 □	ENTROPIA	CD	InsideOut America (USA)	IOMA 2009 2
1999 □	Painful Chronicles	MCD 6tr	Metal Hammer (Greece)	MHIO 001

Promo. Tracks: !/Oblivion Ocean/Revival/The Big Machine/Inside Out/Black Hills

| 2000 □ | THE PERFECT ELEMENT PART 1 | CD | InsideOut | IOMCD 067 |
| 2000 □ | THE PERFECT ELEMENT PART 1 | CD | Marquee (Japan) | MICP 10208 |

Bonus: Epilogue

| 2000 □ | THE PERFECT ELEMENT PART 1 | 2CD | InsideOut | IOMCD 067 |

Bonus: Beyond The Mirror/Never Learn To Fly/Timeweaver's Tale + videos.

| 2000 □ | THE PERFECT ELEMENT PART 1 | CD | InsideOut America (USA) | IOMA 2019 2 |
| 2000 □ | Ashes | MCD 4tr | Inside Out (Germany) | IOMCD 070 |

Germany only. Tracks: Ashes (radio edit)/Used/The Big Machine/Ashes (album version)

2002 ■	REMEDY LANE	CD	InsideOut	IOMCD 092
2002 □	REMEDY LANE	CD	InsideOut America (USA)	IOMACD 2031 2
2002 □	REMEDY LANE	CD	Avalon Marquee (Japan)	MICP 10282

Bonus: Thorn Clown

| 2002 □ | REMEDY LANE | CD | Avalon Marquee (Korea) | PCKD 20091 |

Bonus: Thorn Clown

2003 ■	12:5	CD	Inside Out	IOMCD 152
2004 □	BE	CD	Inside Out	IOMCD 184
2004 □	BE	CD+DVD	Inside Out	IOMDVD 010
2004 □	BE	CD	Inside Out America (USA)	IOMACD 2094
2007 ■	SCARSICK	CD	Inside Out	IOMCD 264
2006 □	SCARSICK	CD	Inside Out America (USA)	SPV 79202
2009 □	THE SECOND DEATH OF	2CD	Inside Out	IOMCD 298
2009 □	THE SECOND DEATH OF	2CD+2DVD	Inside Out	IOMCD 79980
2009 □	Linoleum	MCD 6tr	Inside Out	IOMCD 323

Tracks: Linoleum/Mortar Grind/If You Wait/Gone/Bonus Track B/Yellow Raven (Japanese "Blue Sky" Version) (Scorpions cover)

| 2009 □ | Linoleum | MCD 6tr | Inside Out (Japan) | MICP-10882 |

Bonus: Idiocrazy (Japanese Scarsicker version)

| 2010 □ | ROAD SALT ONE | CD | Inside Out | IOMCD 349 |
| 2010 □ | ROAD SALT ONE | CDd | Inside Out | IOMLTDCD 340 |

Bonus: What She Means To Me. Extended versions of No Way/Road Salt

| 2010 □ | ROAD SALT ONE | LP | Inside Out | IOMLP 349 |
| 2010 □ | ROAD SALT ONE | CD | Avalon Marquee (Japan) | MICP-10937 |

Bonus: What She Means To Me/Tip Toe Two

| 2011 □ | ROAD SALT TWO | CD | Inside Out | IOMCD 349 |
| 2011 □ | ROAD SALT TWO | CDd | Inside Out | IOMLTDCD 349 |

Bonus: Break Darling Break/Of Salt

| 2011 □ | ROAD SALT TWO | LP | Inside Out | IOMLP 349 |
| 2011 □ | ROAD SALT TWO | CD | Avalon Marquee (Japan) | MICP-11021 |

Bonus: Thirty-Eight/Gone (remix)/Break Darling Break/Of Salt

PAINFIELD
Cain Gordon: v/g, Gabriel Engberg: b, Andreas Engberg: d

Göteborg - Bone hard hardcore-infused modern metal, mixing clean vocals, growl and rap with brutal riffing. The band was formed in 1997 and soon earned the reputation of being a highly intense live act. In 2000 the band released the self-produced EP *Two-Faced*, which was according to the band burned in 10 000 copies given away by the band for fans to duplicate themselves. The album was produced by Christian Silver, but unfortunately the band went shamelessly unnoticed. Andreas is now in **Massive Audio Nerve** (aka **M.A.N**), Cain plays with surf pop band **TCABB** and records his solo stuff, while Gabriel produces movies. However, in November 2011, the band started working on a new album.

2003 ■ THIS TIME ....CD Good Head ....GFD 002-2

2003 CD - GFD 002-2

PALETOE
PH Holgersson, J Hietala, T Malm

Really good early heavy metal with biting guitars sung in Swedish, quite similar to **Onyx**.

1981 ● Erogena zoner/Brooke Shields ....7" Pang ....PSI 020 $

1981 7" - PSI 020

PAINTED MAN, THE
Dennis Carlsson: v, Peter Persson: g, David Persson: b, Jesper "Jeppe" Lindbergh: d

Örebro - **The Painted Man**, formed in 2000, recorded a gazillion demos and when they finally released their first album in 2002, they broke up. Well, at least only a year after. Too bad, since they were a really great band. There's a bit of **Extreme** style funkiness mixed with the powerful hard rock akin to bands like **Dogpound** or **Fatal Smile**. Slightly thin production, but still a really good recording. Lindbergh is ex-**Bedroom Love**.

2002 ■ GET PAINTED ....MCD 6tr TPM TPM-001
Tracks: Liar/Easy Come Easy Go/I Don't Give A Damn/Goodbye For You/Heart To Heart/ In Those Eyes

2002 MCD - TPM-001

PALMQVIST, DANIEL
Daniel Palmquist: g

Stockholm - Daniel is another high-class Swedish shredder in the vein of Lukather, Marcello and Dan Huff. Besides Daniel on guitar, the album features drummer Daniel Flores (**Mind's Eye, The Murder Of My Sweet**) and bass player Johan Niemann (**Evergrey, Therion, The Murder Of My Sweet**), plus two guest spots by bass player Andreas Olsson (**Narnia, Rob Rock**). Daniel is also found in **The Murder Of My Sweet** and **XorigiN**.
Website: www.danielpalmqvist.com

2006 ■ A LANDSCAPE MADE FROM DREAMS....................................CD Lion Music....................................LMC 177

2006 CD - LMC 177

PAN-THY-MONIUM
Robert "Derelict" Karlsson: v, Dag "Aag" Swanö: g/k/sax, Robert "Mourning" Ivarsson: g, Dan "Day Disyraah" Swanö: b/k, Benny "Winter" Larsson: d

Finspång/Örebro - I guess this goes under the death/black metal banner although the music is quite varied with some nice **Sabbath**y riffs and swirling keyboard parts. They have been described as **Black Sabbath**-meet-**Captain Beefheart**. The sound is at times reminiscent of early **Manowar**. The vocals are however of the traditional black/death-type. Some lyrics are in Swedish. The lyrics are based on the tales of the cult of Raagoonshinaah (the God of emptiness and darkness). Dan Swanö and Benny were originally in **Edge Of Sanity**, while Robert Karlsson was found in **Darkified** and Dan's brother Dag records under the moniker Tom Nouga. Recorded at Gory Sound. The track *Klieveage* is also found on the compilation *Pantalgia* (92 Mangled Records - Mangled 2). The track *The Battle Of Geheeb* can be found on *Spectrum Ale Compilation* (Relapse). ...*Dawn* is a remix of the demo, which was originally recorded in 1990. Dag was not in the line-up on this recording.

1992 7" - 92001/AV008

1992 ■ Dream II ....7" 4tr Obscure Plasma 92001/AV008
Tracks: I/II/III/Vvoiiccheeces
1992 □ Dream II ....MCD 5tr Avantgarde....................................AV 008
Tracks: I/II/III/IV/Vvoiiccheeces
1992 □ DAWN OF DREAMS....................................CD Osmose ....OPCD 006
1992 □ DAWN OF DREAMS....................................LP Osmose ....OPLP 006
1993 ■ KHAOOOHS ....CD Osmose ....OPCD 014
1993 □ KHAOOOHS ....LP Osmose ....OPLP 014
1996 □ III: Khaooohs And Kon-Fus-Ion....................................MCD 4tr Relapse....................................RR 6936-2
Tracks: The Battle Of Geheeb/Thee-pherenth/Behrial/In Rememberance

1993 CD - OPCD 014

2001 ☐	...Dawn	MCD 4tr	Spam	SPAM 003

Tracks: Dauwhnh/Zenotaffph/Klieveage/Ekkhoeece

| 2002 ☐ | DAWN OF DREAM / KHAOOOHS | CDd | Osmose | OPCD 115 |
| 2009 ☐ | DAWN | LP | Crypt | CRYPT 009 |

250 gold + 250 in black vinyl.

1987 7" - UNT 48

PANAMA

Charles Lundin: v, Aki Ollila: g, Carl Tore "C.Tee" Rohdell: g,
Morgan Johansson: b, Reine Dahlström: d

Göteborg - Formed in 1985 and split two years later. The A-side is a traditional-sounding 80s hard rock ballad, while the B-side is solid melodic hard rock. Rohdell later joined **Million**.

1987 ■	Stay The Night/Across The Freedom Line	7"	RMA Music	UNT 48

PANAMA RED

Partric Axelsson: v, Alex Kallonas: g, Richard Allercrantz: g,
Jens Cedergren: b, Peter Borg: d

Klippan - The band was formed in 1992. They recorded a demo before the self-financed MCD. The production of the MCD was supposed to recoup by sales, but the members ended up giving more away than selling. The band finally split after only two years due to internal conflicts about style and money. That's rock 'n roll for ya! Their last gig was at Parkfesten in Klippan. Peter was later in the band **Serpentine**. Pretty decent melodic hard rock.

1993 ■	Scream Dream	MCD 5tr	private	EGCD 006 $

Tracks: Freak Behind The Wall/Painter Of Illusions/Who Wanna Believe It/Fools Gold/
Harvester Of Insanity

1993 MCD - EGCD 006

PANDEMONIC

Micke Ullenius: v, Micke Jakobsson: g, Harry Virtanen: b, Niklas Karlsson: d

Upplands Väsby - Formed in the spring of 1998. Jakobsson was ex-**Internal Decay** and Niklas Karlsson was ex-**Soils Of Fate**. Brutal death/thrash metal, at times similar to **At The Gates** and **Slayer**. The band released the three-track demo *Lycantropy* in 1999. The track *Resurgence* is featured on the four way split *Suburban Metal* (7", Denim 1999), after which Virtanen joined the band. In 2002 the band recorded the demo *Ravenous*, which saw drummer Niklas Karlsson replaced by Marcus Jonsson and Eric Gjerdrum added on second guitar. The band's last outing was the 2004 demo *The Art Of Hunting*.

2000 ■	THE AUTHORS OF NIGHTFEAR	CD	private	PAN 001

2000 CD - PAN 001

PANDEMONIUM

Kalle Wallin: v, Thomas Ahlgren: g, Oskar Westesson: g,
Erik Odsell: k, Johan Sånesson: b, Patrik Magnusson: d

Lund - The band was formed in October 1997 by guitarist Thomas "Hellord" Ahlgren (**Arsonist, Deranged, Monolith**) and bassist Oskar Westesson when their old band **End** took an end. They recruited drummer Patrik Magnusson and singer Karl Wallin (**Arsonist**). The band also used temporary keyboard player David J Länne at the time. In 1998 they released their first demo entitled *Emotions...* and later the same year the first MCD was recorded. The band had now drafted keyboardist Erik Odsell. **Pandemonium** mixes death, doom and traditional metal in a pretty original sounding way. Nice production, too. In 2002 the band recorded its second MCD, now taking a bit more experimental musical path. After this Odsell and Magnusson left the band. Late 2001 keyboard player Erik Trazom Olsson joined and later on Jacob Blecher (**Yggdrasil, Dibbukim**) joined on drums. The band entered Berno Studios in Malmö to record the debut album *Insomnia*. The album was also later available for free download on the band's website. *The Autumn Enigma* was actually recorded already in 2003-2004, but due to problems with JCM the release was finally made by Canadian label Prodisk/Profusion in 2006. Stagnation came over the band and in May 2007 guitarist Oskar Westesson left the band, replaced by William "Obizurt" Ekeberg (**Body Core, Broken Dagger, Folkearth, Trymheim, Lodic Severed**) in September the same year. The 2008 album *Whispers* is only available as a free download, as is all the band's releases. The track *The Fire* is featured on the compilation *Profusion Le Metal Store Volume 2* (2004).
Website: www.pandemonium-metal.com

1998 MCD - PANCD 01

1998 ■	...To Apeiron	MCD 3tr	private	PANCD 01

Tracks: Frozen Meadows/Silent Tears/...To Apeiron

2000 ☐	Twilight Symphony	MCD 4tr	private	PANCD 02

Tracks: Promenade Prolusion/Fear Of Denial/Left Behind/Twilight Symphony

| 2002 ■ | INSOMNIA | CD | JCM | JCM 003 |
| 2006 ☐ | THE AUTUMN ENIGMA | CD | Prodisk/Profusion | PR001-2 |

2002 CD - JCM 003

PANIC

Anna-Lena Elfving: v, Lars Johansson: g, Göran Pärnils: k,
Michael Broberg: b, Erik Lindekrans: d

Alfta - Panic were formed around 1981-82. They were initially called *Panik*, but decided English was the way to go to get international stardom. They recorded some demos before releasing the self-financed single. Panic produces great melodic hard rock with femme vocals. Growing tired of only rehearsing and never having the big break, the band folded after a few years. Broberg and Elfving continued and drafted drummer Magnus "Balou" Olsson, keyboardists Anders Westling and Johan Sigfridsson, plus singer Nina Söderqvist. The band went under the name *Earmail* and recorded some demos, but it never took off. Broberg later worked as tour manager for Norwegian hard rockers *Return*, while Erik went on to playing in a local blues band. Nina is now a well-known pop/rock singer.

1984 ■ Nobody Can Stop Me/A Shadow On The Wall.................................7" Unflagging...UNF 011
    1500 copies.

1984 7" - UNF 011

PANNDEADS

Rolle "Rock" Nilsson: v, Johnnie "Colour" Nilsson: g,
Lars "Messias" Andersson: b, Michael Mehler: d

Simrishamn - Good solid basic hard rock with a biker touch. The CD was made with a simple self-made artwork.

1997 ■ PANNDEADS...CD P.D.M...PDCD 01

1997 CD - PDCD 01

PANTHEON

Tomas Edström: v, Sami Tiiainen: g, Anders Andersson: k,
Jarmo Sääskilahti: b, Mats Yngvesson: d

Karlskoga - Pantheon, named after the famous temple in Rome, Italy, built by Marcus Agrippa in 126 AD, however were formed in 2005. Great-sounding melodic power metal with a singer highly reminiscent of *Scorpions*' Klaus Meine. Edström, Sääskilathi and Andersson are today playing in *AC/DC* tribute band *Hells/Bells*. Andersson was previously in *Damned Nation*.

2007 ■ EMPIRE OF MADNESS ....CD Heart Of Steel.................................HOS 0702
    Bonus: Breaking Up Again (Accept cover)

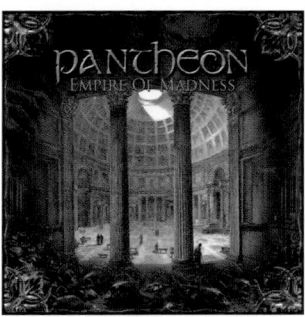

2007 CD - HOS 0702

PANTOKRATOR

Karl Walfridsson: v, Mattias Johansson: g, Jonas Wallinder: b, Rickard Gustavsson: d

Luvehult - Formed in 1996 and recorded their first demo *Ancient Path* the next year. The name means Almightly Lord in Greek. The band initially mixed thrash, doom and death metal, but on the second demo *Ends Of The Earth* they had already become heavier. In 2000 they recorded the third demo *Allhärskare*. In 2001 the band released a self-printed CD-R entitled *1997-2000* containing all three demos. On *Blod* guitarist Jonathan "Steele" Jansson (*Crimson Moonlight, Litania*) had been added to the line-up. Christian death metal with growling, warped vocals, but quite clean guitars for this style. *A Decade Of Thoughs* is a compilation containing seven previously unreleased tracks. *Aurum* was produced by Rickard Bengtsson (*Spiritual Beggars, Arch Enemy*). The tracks *Divine Light* and *Ur Intets Mörker* can also be found on the compilation *Power From The Sky* (02 C.L. Music & Publishing). The song *The Initiation*, a lost track from the *Aurum* sessions, was made official on Pantokrator Day, May 6, 2011. Some of the members are found in side-project *Holy Matrimony*, who recorded the demo *When The Curtains Fall* in 1999.

2001 MCD - PK 004

2001 ■ Songs Of Solomon..MCD 6tr private...PK 004
    Tracks: Ur Intets Mörker/Divine Light/Under Himmelen/Come Let Us Flee/Separated By
    Night/Behind The Veil
2001 □ SANCTIFICA/PANTOKRATOR.......................................CD C.L. Music & Publishing...................CLCD 004
    Split with Sanctifica. Tracks same as on Songs Of Solomon
2003 ■ BLOD ....CD Rivel Records.................................RRCD 005
2007 □ A DECADE OF THOUGHTS 1996-2006......................................CD Momentum Scandinavia.....................MSD 08
    850 copies silver on black embossed booklet.
2007 ■ AURUM ....CD Whirlwind Records............................WW 011

2003 CD - RRCD 005

PANZER PRINCESS

Marcus "Kelly Morgue" Pousette: v, Gustav "Tank Hooker" Bergqkvist: g,
Johan "Sir Alex" Bengs: b, Simon " Simon LaRue" Myrberg: d

Falun - In 1999 Bergqvist and bassist Per Sundström started working on their glam/punk/sleaze band. They drafted drummer Myrberg and went under the name *Nailed*. They recorded one demo, after which Sundström left to devote his time to *Sabaton* and Bergqvist realised his vocal and

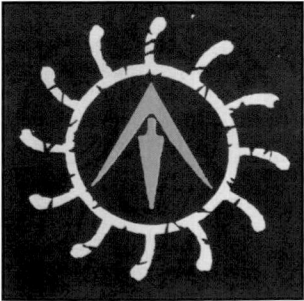

2007 CD - WW 011

guitar talents weren't really up to par. The band split. After about a year they picked it up again, but not until 2003 the pieces started coming together and Pousette joined the band. Now former black metal guitarist Bengs entered the band and the *Moonshine Blues* demo was recorded. One year after, second effort *Legacy Of Ignorance* was recorded by Daniel Beckman. In 2009 they finally made their debut album. **Panzer Princess** plays, as the name may suggest, sleazy glam rock akin to bands like **Hanoi Rocks** meets **Faster Pussycat**. Not the most exciting singer and quite average songs. Not in the same league as **Crazy Lixx** or **Crashdïet**. In 2011 the album *Get Off My Back* was released by Demon Doll Records, it's however a CD-R.
Website: www.panzerprincess.com

2009 ■ OH NO, IT'S PANZER PRINCESS ....CD private ....PPCD 001

2009 CD - PPCD 001

PAPERBACK FREUD
Joakim "Jake The Snake" Jarlsén: v, Jens "Savoy" Storm: g, Jens "Ricki" Gillback: g, Kalle "Yeti" Wanngård: b, Mikael "Mike T Thundersteel" Tanneståhl: d
Stockholm - The boys have played together in different constellations since the 90s, but in 2002 they decided to give it a professional go. **Paperback Freud** play high octane Aussie-style hard rock very similar to early **Rose Tattoo** mixed with newcomers **Airbourne**, at times with a touch of the heavier side of **Backyard Babies** and even some **D.A.D**. Great energy, great vocals and a safe party-mood raiser.
Website: www.paperbackfreud.com

2006 □	Raise Up The Flagpole/Bigger Than God ....CDS	Plugged Records ....PLUCD 017		
	Promo.			
2006 □	ROLLER..CD	Plugged Records ....PLUCD 018		
2009 □	ALL IN A DAY'S WORK..CDpg	Longfellow Deeds ....LDR 014		
2012 ■	HARD ROCK CITY ....CDpg	Longfellow Deeds ....LDR 022		
2012 □	HARD ROCK CITY 2LPg	Longfellow Deeds ....LDR 022		
	250 orange + 50 in back vinyl. Bonus: Song For The Wicked			

2012 CD - LDR 022

PARADISE
Ulla Nordin: v, Mikael Hedström: g, Sune Olsson: k, Tomas Gerdoff: b, Per Eriksson: d
Sundsvall - The A-side is a driving AOR song, while the B-side is a dark ballad. After the band split Mikael continued in the band **Big Prize**, with whom he recorded a single.

1988 ■ Twilight Zone/How Long..7" CUF 007

PARADISE
Michael Uppman (now Storck): v, Tony Nyberg: g, Mats "Matt" Byström: b, Kjell "Shelly" Eriksson (now Nietzche): d
Stockholm - Uppman was previously in **Yngwie Malmsteen's Rising Force** and sang on the unreleased CBS-recording. After this he went to USA and recorded the album *Apathy* with the band **Critical Mass**. In 1986 he returned to Sweden and formed **Paradise**. The guitars on the single were played by Englishman Pete Cockcroft and Tony joined just before the release. Byström had previously recorded with **Sergeant** and **Boogietryck** and later appeared in **Killer Bee** and **Desert Rain**. Kjell was also in (and out of) **Rising Force**. In 1988 the band split. Michael later played with the cover-bands **Playground** and **Sex Shooter**, that featured André Skaug (**Clawfinger**) and Anders Arstrand (**Rednex**). He also sang on the outstanding demo and album by the band **Explode/Xplode** and later appeared in the band **Autocrash** that only recorded a demo. Kjell changed his last name to Nietzsche, after finding out that he was actually related to the German philosopher. **Paradise** is top-notch melodic hard rock in the same category as **Power** and **Talisman**, with great guitar playing and great vocals. Highly recommended.

1987 ■ Breaking Loose/Jennifer ....7" Singapore Singles.............................WBS 0004 $

1987 7" - WBS 0004

PARADISE
Sofia Pettersson: v, Bengt Rönning: g, Stefan Ögren: g, Mats Ögren: k, Gordon Danielsson: b, Urban Greijer: d
Kristinehamn - Formed in 1986. Great high-quality AOR. Well played, well sung and well produced. Well worth investigating. After the single the members changed and at one point the lead singer was Göran Edquist from **Simson**. They recorded a good demo in 1991, but have now split.

1987 ■ Clean My Soul/Take Me Home...7" Active Music..................................HEJ S-025 $

1987 7" - HEJ S-025

PARADIZE
Pelle Thuresson: v/g, Janne Stark: g, Magnus Petersson: k,
Kenth Ericsson: b, Age Karlsson: d

Young and snotty

Mörrum/Asarum - The roots of this band had already grown in around 1975 formed by Janne and Pelle. The band recorded a demo as *TNT* in 1977, featuring drummer Janne Gummesson and singer/guitarist Ola Persson (now Calle Engelmarc, later in *Turbo, Mercy*). Gummesson left and was replaced by Age Karlsson, while Ola was replaced by Kenth. The band started playing covers by *Styx*, *REO Speedwagon*, *New England*, *Goddo* etc. Shortly after the single was recorded, late 1979, Janne, Pelle and Kenth teamed up with Kjell Jacobsson and Kenta Svensson from locals *Ocean*. They formed heavy metal band *Overdrive*, with whom they have recorded numerous albums, and still are. Since the break-up, Age has made recordings with bands like *Tengel*, *Blue Town* and *Something*, bands who have appeared on various compilations. *Paradize* play melodic hard rock. Kenth later joined *Interaction*, *Area* and reunited with *Overdrive* in 2003, but was replaced in 2012. See *Overdrive* for further details. Both tracks appear on the Japanese bootlegged compilation *Swedish Explosion* and were also featured as bonus tracks on the *Overdrive* *Reflexions* CD rerelease (Metal Muthas). ORI (*Turbo, Arsenik*) was not a label, but a studio which helped organize the printing.

1980 7" - ORI 0704 S

1980 ■ Caress Of Steel/Comin' Home .... 7" ORI .... ORI 0704 S **$$**
　　250 copies.

PARADIZE
Jimmy "LJ Roger" Persson: v/g, Fredrik "F. Sunny" Sunnefeldt: g,
Per Ola "F. Fuze" Pettersson: b, U. Jensen: d

1990 7" - MHOS 999

Skövde - Very good traditional-sounding melodic hard rock with powerful guitars, in the same genre as early *Bon Jovi* and Aldo Nova with a touch of *Sinner*. Mid-league vocals. Not to be confused with the Karlshamn band who released a 7" in 1980.

1990 ■ She's Breaking My Heart Again/I Can Hear You Whisper My Name .... 7" Music House Of Sweden .... MHOS 999 **$**

PARAFINE
Björn Wikholm: v, Sven Regner: g, Janne Buckley: g,
Thomas Esteman: b, Miche Johansson: d

1985 7" - PAR-001

Stockholm - Formed in the early 80s and recorded a couple of demos before the single. As bass player Esteman had a French girlfriend they even had a chance to play in France. The band reunited in 2003 and rerecorded the song Fire. Björn has also played with *Rockstone*, *Hope*, *JB Band* and is also in cover band *The Holy Divers*.

1985 ■ Fire/I Want To Hear You Call .... 7" private ....PAR-001 **$$**
　　500 copies.

PARALYCE
Patrik Järlefalk: v, Niklas Sandell: g, Mattias Helmer: k,
Hans Liljegren: b, Rickard Fagerlund: d

Linköping - A mid-quality keyboard-oriented AOR-band with quite weak vocals.

1987 ■ She Loves Another Man/Rock To The End .... 7" Rockkarusellen .... SFSI 4 **$**

PARASITE
Paul Zanichelli: v/b, Bo Petersson: g, Anders Holmström: g, Johan Billerhag: d

1987 7" - SFSI 4

Karlshamn - *Parasite* started out as a trio, influenced by and sounding like *Motörhead*, but with the change into a twin-guitar band, they became more melodic heavy metal in the vein of *Saxon*. A couple of demos were recorded as well. Paul and Anders later recorded a CD with *Rebelene* and Johan (aka Billy St. John) went on to *Hexenhaus* and *Memento Mori*. Paul has been working on and off with bands like *E-Type, Zeven, Crucified Distortion* and solo material, but nothing has happened. In October 2012 Bo sadly passed away from a cardiac arrest.

1984 ■ Parasite .... MLP 5tr Hellrec .... HMAXI 2046 **$$**
　　Tracks: In The Beginning/Burnin'/Nightwinds/Chalice Of The Soul/Lonely Eagle
1984 ☐ Parasite .... MLP 5tr Sword .... SWORD MLP-5
1984 ☐ Parasite .... MLP Roadrunner .... RR 125502
1984 ☐ Parasite .... MLP Banzai (Canada) .... BAM 1008

Unofficial release:
n/a ☐ FORGOTTEN METAL VOL 18 .... CD Forgotten Metal .... n/a
　　Bootleg three-way split with Parasite, Wild Pussy and Widow.

1984 MLP - HMAXI 2046

PARAZITE

**Larsa Bengtsson: v, Ola Renkse: g, "Linkan" Andersson: g,
Martin Karlsson: b, Geron Fritiofsson: d**

Varberg - Formed in 1989 as a more traditional hard rock band with the addition of keyboards.
In 1990 the keyboards were out and the music took a heavier approach. Great high-class hard
rock/thrash, quite close to *Anthrax* on *Spreading The Disease*. Vocals in the vein of Joey
Belladonna (*Anthrax*). Highly recommended. A new demo, even better than the MCD, was
recorded in 1995. The band then changed their name to *Livin' Parazite* and recorded two more
albums. Larsa, Martin and Linkan have also recorded demos with the band *Parallel Universe*.

1994 ■ Consider It Done ....MCD 4tr   private .... PZCD 001
        Tracks: Live In Pain/A Different Kind Of Livin'/Bastard/Cry Baby.

1994 MCD - PZCD 001

PARNASSUS

Fredrik Söderlund: v/g/b/d

Linköping - Fast and symphonic black metal with synth-parts. Prior to the first album the band
recorded two demos, *Receive My Dying Spirit* and *Demo 2*, both released by Infortinum. Fredrik
is also the man behind *Octinomos* and *Puissance* and he initiated this solo project in 1994 to
widen his musical sphere. Atmospheric black metal.

1995 ■ IN DOLORIAM GLORIA...CD   Secula Delena .... NEX 001
1997 ☐ LET THE STARS FALL AND THE KINGDOM COME ....CD   Secula Delena .... NEX 004

1995 CD - NEX 001

PASCUAL, GERMÁN

German Pasqual: v

Swedish, Brazilian, Uruguayan or German?

Stockholm - Germán, born in Uruguay, raised in Brazil and lives in Stockholm since his early
teens, started his career in progressive metal band *Afterglow*, with whom he recorded one
MCD. The band later became *Mind's Eye,* but German had quit before this and disappeared
from the scene for several years. He finally resurfaced as singer for neoclassical metal band
Narnia in 2009, replacing Christian Liljegren. When *Narnia* split he shared the lead vocals
with aforementioned Liljegren in his band *DivineFire*. In 2012 he finally released his first solo
album, actually landing somewhere between *Afterglow* and *Narnia* in style and sound. Melodic
proggy power metal with German's outstanding vocals as the icing on the cake. Musicians on
the album include multi-instrumentalist Jani Stefanovic (*DivineFire*) playing the lion's share
on the album, with addition of CarlJohan Grimmark (*Narnia, FullForce*), bassist Raphael
Dafras, backing singers Andreas Novak (*Mind's Eye, House Of Shakira*) and Erik Mårtensson
(*Eclipse, W.E.T*), and guitarist Thomas Plec Johansson, who also mixed the album. A Japanese
bonus track was recorded, but no Japanese version was ever released.
Website: www.germanpascual.com

2012 CD - NMR-567

2012 ■ A NEW BEGINNING ....CD   Nightmare Records.......................... NMR-567

PASSENGER

Anders Fridén: v, Niclas Engelin: g, Håkan Skoger: b, Patrik J. Sten: d

Göteborg - *Passenger* started as early as 1995/96 with the intention of mixing harder, meaner
and groovy stuff with poppy influences. At the time Engelin was in *Gardenian* and Patrik had
just joined *Transport League*, and the band took a break. In 1997 Engelin played on the *Whoracle*
tour with *In Flames* and there he drafted *In Flames* singer Fridén to his project. The album was
finally released in 2003, recorded in the classic Studio Fredman. *Passenger* have succeeded
in making their goal come through in the music. Heavy, groovy and brutal, yet quite melodic
metal with Fridén singing all clean. A really good album! Too bad nothing more has come out
of this. In 2013 Fridén launched his new band *Port Noir*.

2003 CD - 77415-2

2003 ■ PASSENGER..CD   Century Media 77415-2
2003 ☐ PASSENGER..LP   Century Media 77415-1

PATHOS

**Paul Schöning: v, Lennart Specht: g, Daniel Antonsson: g,
Thomas Antonsson: d, Esko Salow: d**

Trollhättan/Sundsvall - Between 1989-1992, Esko and Lennart played together in the band
Valkyrie, which became *Depict Pathos*. At the same time Daniel and Thomas played in *Judas
Priest* cover band *Desert Plains*, together with *Illwill* singer Jonas Dahlström. Together with
Urna and Leif (later in *NME Within*) Daniel, Esko and Lennart formed a band, which finally
folded. Now *Depict Pathos* were revived, this time featuring Thomas on bass and Daniel on

1997 CD - LiCD 53170

guitar. While trying to find a singer they listened to a demo with the band *Neocori* and heard Stefan Carlsson, whom they immediately drafted. Stefan also sang in *Memento Mori*. *Pathos* was born. They recorded the song *Hoverface*, which ended up on a compilation, and finally Liphone released the debut. Black Mark now picked the band up, and reissued the debut with a better-looking cover. The band recorded the follow-up *Uni Versus Universe*, but split with Black Mark and went back to Liphone. Early 2000 singer Carlsson left the band and after six months the band found the outstanding Paul Schöning. The band's third effort, *Katharsis*, was produced by Anders "Theo" Theander at Roastinghouse, and is an outstanding slab of brutal, yet melodic power metal at time similar to *Memento Mori* and *Hexenhaus*, released by Massacre Records. The band unfortunately split. Daniel has been found in *Dimension Zero*, *Soilwork* and *Dark Tranquillity*, Lennart, Thomas and Esko are all found in *Nostradameus* and *Fejd*, while Schöning is in *Power Plant*. All the albums are killer, well worth checking out!

1997 CD - BMCD 123

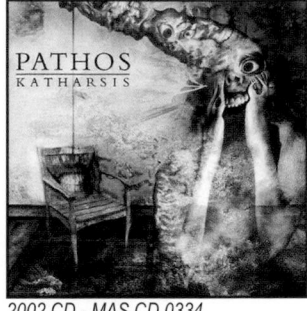

2002 CD - MAS CD 0334

1997	■	HOVERFACE	CD	Liphone	LiCD 53170
1997	■	HOVERFACE	CD	Black Mark	BMCD 123
		Different artwork.			
1999	☐	UNI VERSUS UNIVERSE	CD	Liphone Metall	LiCD 3194
2002	■	KATHARSIS	CD	Massacre Records	MAS CD 0334

PATRONYMICON
Mikael "N. Sadist" Karlsson: v/d/b, Kvist: g, Joel "J Megiddo" Lindholm: g

Sandviken - Formed by Sadist in 2008 and started out as a one-man show for two years. When he entered the studio in 2010 to record the demo *Coldborn* he used the services of his friend and drummer P Sulphur, who became a member of the band. After signing with *Blackcrowned* he also drafted Kvist and Joel "J Megiddo" Lindholm. In 2011 KC and later on J Meddigo left the band. Lindholm is also found in *Degial*, *Shining* and hardcore band *Undergång*. Old-school style black metal in the vein of *Watain* or *Dissection*. In 2012 Kvist quit and in 2013 singer H. Sulphur joined.

2011 CD - 002

2011	■	PRIME OMEGA	CD	Blak Crowned	002

PAX
**Michael Fridh: v, Christian Fridh: g, Stefan Eldevall: g,
SG Petersson: k, Jaime Salazar: d**

Karlskrona - *Pax* were a band formed by the Fridh brothers, who had been playing together since 1989, at the time in the band *Excalibur*. During the years both brothers have been working as hired guns, but in 2000 they felt it was time to do something for themselves and *Pax* was born. For the album, they drafted the best musicians they could come up with and at a great result. Outstanding heavy pompy melodic hard rock. The live line-up featured the Fridh's, keyboard player Oskar Ling, guitarist Adam Grahn and drummer Martin Furst. Christian also plays with punksters *The Bones*.

2005 CD - RHRCD 671-2

2005	■	10 000 WORDS	CD	Roastinghouse	RHRCD 671-2

PAX ROMANA
Stefan Herde: v/g, Leif Ljungkvist: b, Gert-Åke Nilsson: d

Nässjö - The band made its debut on the three-way-split album *Railroad*. At the time the band featured Herde, Anders Karlsson, Jonas Hallström and Gino Renebrandt (*Persons Band*, solo). *Pax Romana* plays really good bluesy hard rock, a bit similar to *Wildmarken*. In 1992 Stefan recorded a great boogie rocking MCD with *Stefan Herde And His Broomdusters*. *Pax Romana* still exists as a party cover band, now featuring Herde, bass player Mats Klang (who was also in *Stefan Herde And His Broomdusters*), guitarist Jan-Erik Falk and drummer Lasse Starö.
Website: www.paxromana.se

1982 7" - RON 102

1978	☐	RAILROAD – BLUES, ROCK & JAZZ FRÅN NÄSSJÖ (split)	LP	Musikfolket	MFP-001
		Split with Armada and Georg Hååred Jazzgrupp. Tracks: Railroad/Sista versen/I'm Only Here For Beer/I'm Moving On			
1982	■	På erotikens tröskel/Du ger mig ljus	7"	Rondo	RON 102

PAYBACK
Demis Skoupras: v, Daniel Paulsson: g, Jonas Wimar: b, Mattias Nilsson: d

Malmö - Brutal rap/metal in the vein of *Biohazard* and *Machine Head*. The band released their first demo, *Paralyzed Emotions,* in 1996 and later the same year their second demo *Perfect World* was unearthed. In 1997 they had a tracks on the *Tomorrow Belongs To Us* compilation and in 1998 on *Promotion 98*.

2000 CD - SEX 666

2000	■	FOR YOUR EYES ONLY	CD	private	SEX 666

PEAK

Anders Gustafsson, Mikael Underdahl, Max Hansen, Adam Pavlovic: d

Kristianstad - Peak's style is quite varied, with elements of grunge, straightforward heavy rock, power metal and 70s-style hard rock. Not bad at all!

1996 ■ Peakmeter - Promotion ....MCDp 4tr   Beagle Music CDM01
Tracks: Blue/Crazy Dream/Garden/Battle

1996 MCDp - CDM01

PEARLY WHITE

Lasse Wester: g/v, Fredrik Bodin: g, Jan-Olov Persson: b, Ronnie Peeters: d

Arvika - This band made two recordings under the name *Thrashon*, but later changed their name to the more suitable *Pearly White*. Jan-Olov switched from guitar to bass and Fredrik joined. This is melodic hard rock with a strong touch of the eighties.

1995 ■ WAY OF LIFE..CD   private ....PWCD 0195

PEJLING

Bert Ringblom: v/g, Mats Wernvall: g, Bo Åberg: b, Lars Hillgren: d

Knivsta - Straightforward, classic hard rock, especially the B-side.

1982 ■ Hjälp mig/Nattens lekar...7"   Pärla Records .... PNLS 014

1995 CD - PWCD 0195

PELLE

Pelle Larsson: v/g/b/d

Jönköping - A solo single by Jönköping boy Pelle Larsson who sings and plays all instruments except keyboards, which are handled by Per Billengren. Magnus Tallåker (*Renegade, Hellspray*) laid down some backing vocals. Pelle plays quite excellent melodic hard rock. The A-side is a rocker, while the B-side is a ballad. Pelle later recorded a CD with melodic hard rockers *Wonderland*.

1990 ■ I Believe/Heaven For Us ....7"   Combra ....UNI 1019

1982 7" - PNLS 014

PEO

Peo Pettersson: v/g/k/bprogramming

Skövde - Peo Pettersson has previously made several recordings with bands like *X-Ray, Axia, Leviticus* and *FlintStens Med Stanley*. When he finally released a solo-album it's was a pure, slick AOR production with some biting guitars, as well as some west coast-oriented tracks. It belongs in the same genre as Jeff Paris, Henry Lee Summer and Brett Walker. High-quality music and vocals that should attract fans of the more commercial side of *Axia*. The debut is actually a collaboration between Peo and Australian songwriter Rod West. Additional musicians on the album are: Bengan Andersson, Marko Grönholm and Per Nordbring on drums, Jan Nordbring and Tomas Varadi on bass, Ivan Persic on guitar and backing singers Tony Niva (*Niva, Swedish Erotica, Zanity*) and Ulf Andersson. Peo's second release was another slick AOR album also featuring musicians such as Bengan Andersson (d), Jonas Källsbäck (d), Stefan Kjällgren, Tomas Varadi (b) and Mathilda Lückner. The NL release features a reissue of Peo's second album as bonus. *Better Not Forget* contained a mix of great, rocking AOR and very slick westcoast. In 2011 Peo returned with a vengeance, releasing his by far heaviest record, which shows in the title. On this album the musicians featured guest spots from guitarists Micke Därth, Dan Boström and Linus Brahamsson and keyboard player Henric Johansson. The title was *The Hardest Rock* (POP CD 1712). It was however only released as a pro-printed CDR in a slightly tacky cover, but is supposed to be released properly.

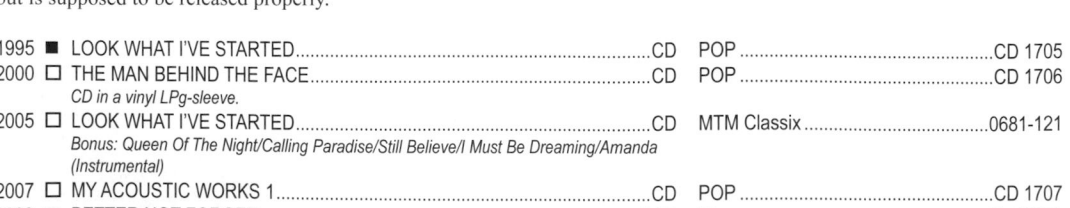
1995 CD - CD 1705

1990 7" - UNI 1019

1995 ■ LOOK WHAT I'VE STARTED...CD   POP ....CD 1705
2000 ☐ THE MAN BEHIND THE FACE...CD   POP ....CD 1706
CD in a vinyl LPg-sleeve.
2005 ☐ LOOK WHAT I'VE STARTED...CD   MTM Classix 0681-121
Bonus: Queen Of The Night/Calling Paradise/Still Believe/I Must Be Dreaming/Amanda (Instrumental)
2007 ☐ MY ACOUSTIC WORKS 1...CD   POP ....CD 1707
2009 ■ BETTER NOT FORGET ....2CD   NL .... NL 10071
1000 copies. Bonus disc: The Man Behind The Face.

2009 2CD - NL 10071

PERSUADER

**Jens Carlsson: v, Emil Norberg: g, Daniel Sundbom: g,
Fredrik Hedström: b, Efraim Juntunen: d**

Umeå - Formed in 1997, and recorded the first demo, *Visions And Dreams* in 1998. In 2000 they were picked up by new Swedish label Loud 'N Proud. Thrash with a touch of German metal, like **Blind Guardian** meets early **In Flames**. The singer is a bit reminiscent of Hansi Küsch. Magnus Lindblom helped out with some guitar solos. In 2001 guitarist Pekka Kiviaho (**Auberon, One Man Army And The Undead Quartet**) was replaced by Emil Norberg (younger brother of **Nocturnal Rites'** Nils Norberg). Jens Ryden from **Dead Silent Slumber** guests. *The Hunter* was recorded for the defunct Loud 'N Proud Records, but was picked up by French label Nothing To Say Records. In 2006 Jens quit playing rhythm guitar and the band drafted Daniel Sundbom. Jens also does clean guest vocals on **Auberon**'s EP *Scum Of The Earth*. Jens and Emil are in German band **Savage Circus**. In 2011 the **Persuader** started recording a new album.

Year		Title	Format	Label	Cat#
2000	□	THE HUNTER	CD	Loud N' Proud	LNP 017
2000	□	SWEDISH METAL TRIUMPHATORS VOL 1 (split)	CD	Loud N' Proud	LNP 019
		Split with Freternia. Tracks: Heart And Steel/Cursed/Escape (demo)/Cursed (demo)			
2000	□	THE HUNTER	CD	NTS	3059932
2004	□	EVOLUTION PURGATORY	CD	Sanctuary Records	823 74140-2
2004	■	EVOLUTION PURGATORY	CD	Noise	N 03820
2004	□	EVOLUTION PURGATORY	CD	King Records (Japan)	KICP-1016
		Bonus: Domination (Pantera cover)			
2004	□	EVOLUTION PURGATORY	CD	Navarre (USA)	74140
2004	□	EVOLUTION PURGATORY	CD	Sauron (Korea)	n/a
		Bonus: Domination (Pantera cover). Slipcase.			
2006	■	WHEN EDEN BURNS	CD	Dockyard 1	DY10012-2
		The paper sleeve promo says DY100120 on the CD and also DY100122 on the cover.			
2006	□	WHEN EDEN BURNS	CD	Avalon Marquee (Japan)	MICP-10598
		Bonus: Align The Heavens			
2006	□	WHEN EDEN BURNS	CD	Locomotive Records (USA)	LM 463
2007	■	THE HUNTER	CD	Dockyard 1	DY10082-2
		Bonus: Escape/Cursed			
2007	□	THE HUNTER	CD	Locomotive Records (USA)	LM 481
		Bonus: Escape/Cursed			
2010	□	THE HUNTER	CD	Soul Thought (USA)	700026

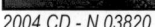
2004 CD - N 03820

2006 CD - DY10012-2

PEST

Martin "Necro" Sällström: v/g/d, Christian "Equimanthorn" Eskilsson: g/b

Stockholm - *Pest* were formed by Martin Sällström and Christian Eskilsson (not the same Equimanthorn as in **Dark Funeral**) already in 1998, the same two people that still form the band. The first four-track demo was recorded the same year, but was never really official. Two tracks were rerecorded for the first official demo *In Eternity Skyless* (1998). Another five-track demo, *Black Thonrs*, was also released this year. The members themselves state influences like NWoBHM, speed and black metal, but they do sound quite similar to **Darkthrone** (even though they do not like the comparison), even though they have spiced things up with some thrash metal influences. On the first release the band used session drummer Hate. The ten-minute *Dauðafærð* (journey of death) is quite different from the band's other songs, a long and slow song sung in old Swedish. The track *Funeral* is also found on the compilation *Tormenting Legends* (2003 Blut & Eisen).

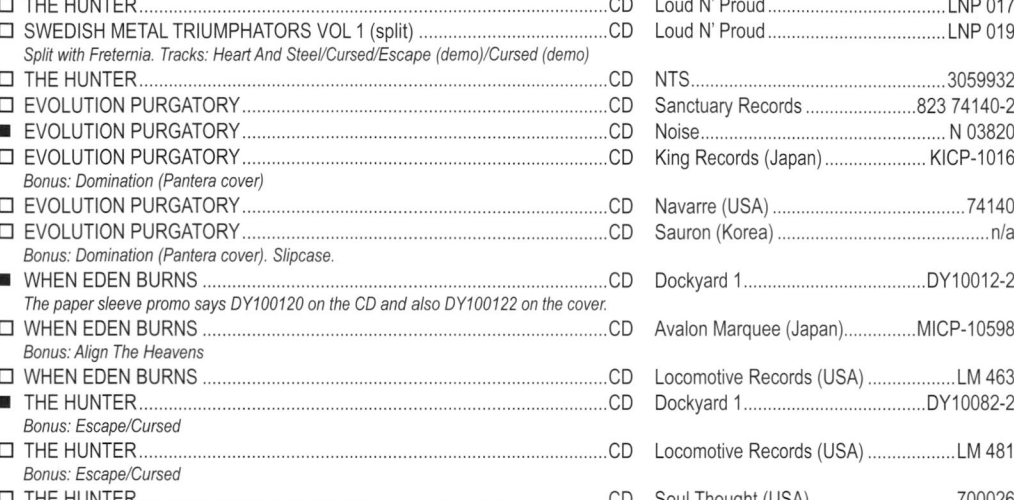
2003 CD - NC 068

2007 CD - DY10082-2

Year		Title	Format	Label	Cat#
2002	□	Blasphemy Is My Throne	MLP 4tr	Bloodstone Entertainment	blood 005
		Tracks: Blasphemy Is My Throne/Along The Path Of The Fallen/Towards Desolation/ Circle Of Damnation's Fire. 300 hand numbered copies.			
2003	□	Blasphemy Is My Throne	MCD 6tr	Bloodstone Entertainment	blood 005SE
		Bonus: When Darkness Is Complete/Thorns From Undead. Different mix than the vinyl. 500 hand numbered copies.			
2003	■	DESECRATION	CD	No Colours	NC 068
2003	□	DESECRATION	LPg	No Colours	NC 068
2004	□	Dauðafærð	CDS 1tr	No Colours	NC 077
		Track: Lifit es dauðafærð			
2004	■	Dauðafærð	12" 2tr	No Colours	NC 077
		Tracks: Lifit es dauðafærðLifit es dauðafærð (English)			
2004	□	Black Thorns	MLP 5tr	Deviant Records	DEV 002
		Tracks: When Darkness Is Complete/Embraced In Grief I Walk/Those Perished/Dead Raven Claws/Thorns From Underneath. 300 copies, first 66 in cloth bag.			
2004	□	IN TOTAL CONTEMPT	LPg	No Colours	NC 092
2004	□	IN TOTAL CONTEMPT	CD	No Colours	NC 092
2006	□	Evil Return/Damnation Until Death	7"	Ironfist Productions	IFPEP 019
2008	□	REST IN MORBID DARKNESS	CD	Season Of Mist U A	SUA 002
2008	□	REST IN MORBID DARKNESS	LP	Ironfist Productions	IFLP 027
2008	□	REST IN MORBID DARKNESS	CD	CD-Maximum (Russia)	CDM 0208-2820
2008	□	Blasphemy Is My Throne	MCD 4tr	Daemon Woship Prod (Russia)	DWP 001
		The original vinyl mix. New artwork. 1000 copies.			
2013	□	Black Oath/Morbid Revelations	7"	Agonia Records	ARep023
		450 black and 50 white vinyl copies.			
2013	□	THE CROWNING HORROR	CD	Agonia Records	ARcd 113
2013	■	THE CROWNING HORROR	LP	Agonia Records	ARlp 106
		Black vinyl + 100 numbered copies purple vinyl.			

2004 12" - NC 077

2013 LP - ARlp 106

PETE SANDBERG'S JADE

Pete Sandberg: v, Jörgen Birch Jensen: g, Joakim Sandin: b, Johan Helgesson: d

Malmö - Being a highly productive dude, Pete found himself having a few minutes off after having recorded the second *Midnight Sun* album and his second solo album *Push*, so he contacted his old buddy Birch (ex-*Bai Bang*) and wrote 18 songs of which 12 ended up on this album. Pete is a man with multiple projects moving side by side. There are usually at least two bands going at the same time as his solo stuff keeps popping out. If it's not *Midnight Sun* and *Jade*, it's *Silver Seraph* and *Jade*. This band is, musically, the missing link between the stuff he did on *Back In Business* and *Silver Seraph* with a touch of *Alien*. Melodic AOR/hard rock with a touch of *Rainbow* at times. Birch has previously also been found in *Silver Seraph*, while Helgesson is ex-*The Drugs/Booze Brothers*. Guests on the second album include Jaime Salazar and Jonas Reingold from... you guessed it - *Midnight Sun*. Sandin is today in *Bai Bang*.

1999 CD - AORH 10096

2000 CD - - -

1999	☐	PETE SANDBERG'S JADE	CD	Avalon Marquee (Japan)	MICY 1157
		Bonus: Illusion			
1999	■	PETE SANDBERG'S JADE	CD	AOR Heaven	AORH 10096
2000	☐	ORIGIN	CD	Avalon/Marquee (Japan)	MICP 10231
		Bonus: Moods (instrumental)/Me And My Piano (acoustic jam)			
2000	■	ORIGIN	CD	Point Music/AOR Heaven	- -

PHOENIX

Larz Hjelm: v, Francisco Lundberg: v, Kenneth Vikland: g, Bernt Olofsson: g, Rob Wikman: k, Patrick Odepark: b, Johnny Dee: d

Piteå - Great high-class melodic hard rock in the vein of *Dokken*. The instrumental track *Wings Of Fire* is in style and sound not too far from the early Yngwie-recordings. There's some serious guitar work going on here. The record was made in memory of late singer Fransisco. Two tracks are with Fransisco on vocals, one is instrumental and one with replacement Larz (who also had made a recording with *Nagazaki*). Well worth looking for.

1989 MLP - HEJ MAXI 001

| 1989 | ■ | Say Goodbye | MLP 4tr | Active Music | HEJ MAXI 001 | $$ |
| | | Tracks: Say Goodbye/Wings Of Fire/Millions For Your Love/Now Is The Time. | | | | |

PHYSICAL ATTRACTION

Anders Palme: v, Peter Lindell: g, Tobbe Nyberg: g, Räven Alisic: b, Martin Palme: d

Kristianstad - The basic elements for this band were laid back in the late 80s - in the band *Refuse*. In 1992 they reformed under the name *Physical Attraction*. (The name *Refused* was well established by another band). This band sounds like a mix of *Suicidal Tendencies* and *Pantera*. Good production and well arranged material. The band's debut on record was with three tracks on the compilation *All Sorts Volume One* (94 Progress). The positive response led to a deal with Danish label Progress. A promising band that have been discovered in Europe as well as in the US. Unfortunately nothing more came out of the band.

2011 CD - - -

| 1994 | ☐ | THE FOOL LEAD THE BLIND | CD | Progress | PCD 15 |

PIHL, FREDRIK

Fredrik Pihl: g/b/d

Helsingborg - Instrumental fusion-oriented hard rock/metal. Quite poorly produced. Guest appearances by Mattias Ia Eklundh (*Freak Kitchen*), Lalle Larsson and Ron "Bumblefoot" Thal.

| 2011 | ■ | SILHOUETTES | CD | private | - - |

PIKE

Robert Kusen: v/g, Pasi Oksa: g, Michael Carlström: b, Mats "Mally" Håxell: d

Södertälje - Powerful and heavy rock with hardcore/death:ish vocals. Closer to *Black Sabbath* than *Entombed*. Nice musical ideas. Mats Håxell is also backing guitarist Steven Andersson (who is guesting on digeridoo) and is now in *Hellinor*.

1996 CD - BMCD 91

| 1996 | ■ | LACK OF JUDGEMENT | CD | Black Mark | BMCD 91 |

PINCH

Frans Mittermayer: v/g, Lars Malmsten: b, Tim Bertilsson: d

Stockholm - Guess these guys have been listening quite a lot to the likes of *Rage Against The Machine* and Swedish colleagues *Refused*. Pinch play angry rap-oriented thrash/hardcore. No quality problems here. Pinch later became *Charcoal*. Tim is now in *Switchblade*.

| 1994 | ☐ | Unsigned | MCD 6tr | private | - - |
| | | Tracks: Full Of Anguish/Deathrow/Graffiti Is For Life/The Pain/Sargent D. Lives/Rootbear Float | | | |

1994 MCD

PINK PANTHER

Michael Garesjö: v, **Harri Touvila:** g, **Mats Vassfjord:** b, **Bosse Lindblom:** d

Eskilstuns - This may sound like a kids' band, but don't be fooled by the name. *Pink Panther* play excellent funky metal with a sleazy touch, a bit like mixing *Extreme* and *Aerosmith*, or close to early *Bewarp*. Well worth looking for! Vassfjord later appeared in *Scaar* and is today playing with *Chris Laney's Legion, Grand Design* and *Impera*, while Touvila is in *Griffen*.

1991 ■ Drunk & Horney/The Dirty Boys Bop ....7" private .... (MU-S 910303)
    Poster cover.

1991 7" - (MU-S 910303)

PIPERS DAWN

Petra Albrecht: v, **Patrik Fernlund:** g, **Daniel Eriksson:** g,
Nicklas Lilja: b, **Robin Bergh:** d

Nyköping - The band was formed in 1996 when the death metal band *Gorement* folded and former members Patrik, Daniel and Nicklas formed *Piper's Dawn*. The band plays great melodic metal slightly reminiscent of *Warlock* and *The Gathering* with really good female vocals. Well worth looking for. Drummer Robin Bergh was later found in *Amaran* and guitarist Patrik in *Meshuggah*-style metallurgists *Genuflection To Limbo*. Bergh is now in *October Tide*.

1996 ■ Moonclad ....MCD 3tr Musikverksta'n .... MV 96015
    Tracks: Moonclad/Wings Of Rage/Seasons Of Ending

1996 MCD - MV 96015

PLAGUE ANGEL

Jörgen Jern: v, **Robert Lundgren:** g, **Kenneth Jern:** b, **Tobias Israelsson:** d

Karlskoga - Death metal band *Plague Angel* were formed in 2005. Tobias (ex-*Butchery, Strangulation*) and Jörgen are also in *Icon Blood*. Lundgren is also ex-*Butchery*. The first demo, *Raped By Lies*, was recorded in 2008. Brutal death metal in the vein of *Malevolent Creation* and *Deicide*. The CD also contains the demo tracks as bonus.

2010 ■ STAGNATION OF CHRIST..CD Severed Records .... SR 106

2010 CD - SR 106

PLAGUE WARHEAD

Martin Gustafsson: v, **Andreas Sjöberg:** g, **Tomas Lindgren:** g,
Mattias Eronn: b, **Benny "Bempa" Larsson:** d

Finspång - *Plague Warhead* were formed in 2008 by Tomas and Benny, with the aim of playing fast and hard thrash metal. Andreas and Mattias (*Allegience, Darkified, Grimorium, Amenophis*, and he was considered for *Entombed* for the *Clandestine* album) were drafted, but they had a hard time finding a singer. On the verge of using a session singer, they found Martin and the pieces fell into place. They recorded the four-track demo *Crypt Of Death,* which lead to the debut EP, which was picked up by Godeater Records. Larsson has played with bands like *Edge Of Sanity, Godsend, Ophthalamia, Pan-Thy-Monium* and *Total Terror*. Sjöberg is ex-*Ashes* and *Deadbeats*, Eronn has been found in *Sorgfaagel, WitchBlack* and *Necrotana*, while Lindgren has played with *Scypozoa, The Black Goat, WitchBlack* and *Disgusting*. In 2011 the band also recorded a new three-track demo. *Whores Of Lücifer* is a slab of fast and furious death-oriented thrash metal, a bit similar to *Slayer* meets *Sepultura*.

2011 MCDd - - -

2011 ■ Whores Of Lücifer ....MCDd 4tr Godeater Records .... - -
    Tracks: Dominate/Forces Of Evil/Blood Messiah/Stench Of Decay

PLAIN ZERO

Lars Bergbom: v, **Emil Malm:** g, **Magnus Windo:** g, **Alexander Gabay:** b, **Erik Fastén:** d

Göteborg - Rap-metal in the vein of *Rage Against The Machine*. The band was previously called *Bubblegum Crisis* under which name they released a CD entitled *Over The Edge*. After the MCD the band also recorded the demo *Violent And Funky*.

2001 ■ Prophets Of Tomorrow ....MCD 5tr private .... - -
    Tracks: The Plague/Rock 'N Roll Rio/ Move Right In /Fake It/Fallen Out

2001 MCD - - -

PLAN 9 (aka PLAN NINE)

Reine Johansson: v/g, **Thomas Hermansson:** g,
Petri "T-Bird" Ranki: b, **Jonny "Superstar" Gustavsson:** d

Herrljunga - Formed in December 1996. The name was taken from the Ed Wood's movie *Plan 9 From Outer Space*. They recorded their first demo *Energy Rock 'N Roll* the year after. Sleaze with the complete concept-package, including make-up, hair and glamour, similar to *Hanoi Rocks* with a punkish attitude. The band has also appeared on several compilations, including tributes to *Hanoi Rocks* and *Dogs D'Amour*. *Generation Action* was produced by Chips Kisbye (*Sator, Bonafide*). After the album, in 2001, guitarist Andreas "Andy" Heleander replaced Tho-

2001 CD - FBR 013

mas Hermansson. In 2004 Ranki left and was replaced by Manx Gustafsson. In 2005, after some member changes, the band changed their name to **Debbie Ray** who made their debut in 2011.

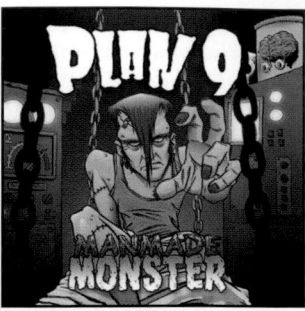

2010 CD - NKDM40011

1999 ☐ Dead Inside	.....MCD 8tr	We Bite	674090
Tracks: Rockaholic/Super Psycho Love/Rock 'N Roll Alcohol/What You Do/Caught In The Act/What You Do/Teenage Lament 99/For You. 500 copies.			
2001 ■ GENERATION ACTION	.....CD	Feedback Boogie	.....FBR 013
2010 ■ MANMADE MONSTER	.....CD	Nickle & Dime Records	.....NKDM40011

PLAN THREE

Jacob Lovén: v, Mathias Garneij: g, Tommie Hammar: g,
David Clewett: k, Peter Kjellin: b, Kristoffer Folin: d

Stockholm - In 2000, out of the remains of two other bands, Lovén, Hammar, Garneij, Andreas Malm and Mattias Willis formed **Plan Three**. The band started out playing soft melodic rock, which developed into alternative metal. The bass player now left to continue playing pop with the band **Mindless** (not the metal band). He was soon replaced by Kjellin and the band also drafted keyboard player Clewett. The band toured with **Takida** and the first single was released. Late 2007 drummer Malm decided to leave and was replaced by Andreas Henriksson. In 2011 Henriksson left, was temporarily replaced by Malm, and permanently replaced by Kristoffer Folin early 2011. Kjellin is a radio host at radio Bandit Rock.

2007 CDS - DODCDS 002

2009 CD - NRCD 105

2007 ■ Achilles Heel/Save Me	.....CDSp 2tr	Dogmatic	.....DODCDS 002
2009 ☐ Still Broken	.....CDSp 1tr	NineTone	.....NRCDS 013
2009 ☐ Brush It Off/The Common Divided	.....CDSp 2tr	NineTone	.....NRCDS 018-1
2009 ■ SCREAMING OUR SINS	.....CD	NineTone	.....NRCD 105
2011 ☐ The Signal - Part One	.....MCDd 5tr	NineTone	.....NRCD 112
Tracks: Chasing Tornados/Soldier/Wake Up/Battle Song/Kill Anyone			

PLANET ALLIANCE

Mikael "Mike" Andersson: v, Magnus Karlsson: g, Janne Stark: g,
CarlJohan Grimmark: g, Magnus Rosén: b, Bob Daisley: b,
Anders Johansson: d, Jaime Salazar: d

Malmö - **Planet Alliance** was a project initiated by AOR Heaven Records together with RoastingHouse Music, and released on the sub label Metal Heaven. The album was centred around singer Mikael "Mike" Andersson (**Cloudscape, FullForce**), who brought in the other musicians. The music was written by Andersson, guitarist Magnus Karlsson (**Last Tribe, Primal Fear, Allen Lande** etc), Bob Daisley (Ozzy, **Widowmaker** etc), Janne Stark (**Overdrive, Locomotive Breath, Mountain Of Power** etc). On the album the rhythm and lead guitars were handled by Karlsson, Stark and Grimmark, with a guest solo by Mattias Ia Eklundh (**Freak Kitchen**), while the bass work was handled by Daisley and Magnus Rosén (**Hammerfall, Von Rosen**). The drum work was handled by Anders Johansson (**Hammerfall, Malmsteen, FullForce**) and Jaime Salazar (**Bad Habit, The Flower Kings, Midnight Sun** etc). **Planet Alliance** play melodic power metal in the vein of **Allen Lande** meets **Cloudscape**.

2006 CD - 00025

2006 ■ PLANET ALLIANCE	.....CD	Metal Heaven	00025
Slipcase.			
2007 ☐ PLANET ALLIANCE	.....CD	Supersonic (Japan)	.....XQA-1012
Bonus: Lights And Shadow/Rise.			
2007 ☐ PLANET ALLIANCE	.....CD	Mystic Empire (Russia)	.....MYST CD 193

PLANKTON

Emil Fredholm: g, Christian Neppenström: g, Tomas "Pomma" Thorberg: b,
Lars Normalm: perc, Sebastian Sippola: d

Stockholm - Instrumental retro rockers **Plankton** were formed in 1998 by guitarists Emil (ex-**Fortune**) and Christian, leaning on the inheritance from bands like **Mahogany Rush**, Hendrix, **Electric Sun**, **Led Zeppelin**, **Cream** etc. ending up with a musical blend which sounds like an instrumental version of **Wishbone Ash** in their prime, actually quite close to **Automatic Fine Tuning**, too. Outstanding band with great songs and killer musicians. Thorberg is ex-**Snakes In Paradise** and also plays with John Norum, Sippola is ex-**Fortune**, **Southfork**, Glenn Hughes and **Grand Magus**. Normalm has worked with Paolo Mendonca. The *Rare Tracks* CD contains the band's first demo, and also a cover of **Wishbone Ash**'s *F.U.B.B.* Emil plays on the 2011 album by **Alfonzetti**. Neppenström and Fredholm also guest on the first album by **Mountain Of Power**.

2004 CD - GYR 012

2009 CDd - BR 001

2002 ☐ PLANKTON	.....CD/d	Grooveyard Records	.....GYR 004
First press in digi pack.			
2004 ■ HUMBLE COLOSSUS	.....CD	Grooveyard Records	.....GYR 012
2004 ☐ PLANKTON	.....CD	Grooveyard Records	.....GYR 004
2006 ☐ 3	.....CD	Grooveyard Records	.....GYR 021
2006 ☐ RARE TRACKS 1998-2005	.....CDp	Grooveyard Records	.....GYR 022
2009 ■ OCEAN TALES	.....CDd	Bulleribock Records	.....BR 001

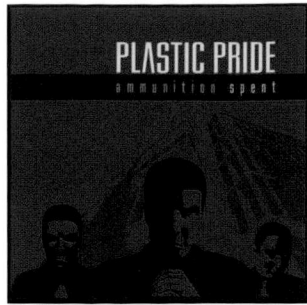

PLASTIC PRIDE

Jan Jämte: v, Magnus Vinblad: g, Johannes Persson: g,
Fredrik Ärletun: b, Thomas Hedlund: d

Umeå - *Plastic Pride* started out more in the hardcore vein, which can be heard on the debut. They have however evolved into a type of crossover, mixing the heavy grunge-oriented style with a hardcore-ish touch. Pretty nice, almost **King's X/Galactic Cowboys**-groove in songs like *Cross* and *The Price For Being Weak*. At times similar to **Eleven Pictures** with a touch of bands like **Fuel** and **Staind**. The lyrics have a strong socialist touch. Johannes is also found in **Cult Of Luna**. According to the site the band is currently in a coma.

1997 ☐	Daredevil I Lost	MCD 5tr	Desperate Fight		DFR 20
	Tracks: Tharaque Means Nothing/Living Machine/Damage/For A Father/In Daredevil I Lost				
1998 ☐	NO HOT ASHES	CD	Desperate Fight		DFR 22
2001 ■	AMMUNITION SPENT	CD	DayGlo		DGR 20
2001 ☐	AMMUNITION SPENT	LP	Black Star Foundation		BSF 004
	Different artwork.				

2001 CD - DGR 20

PLATITUDE

Erik "EZ" Blomkvist: v, Gustav Köllerström: g, Kristofer Von Wachtenfeldt: k,
Patrik Janson: b, Marcus Höher: d

Stockholm - *Platitude* were formed already in 1995, but it didn't take off until the band released their debut in 2002. The album was produced by renowned engineer Tommy Hansen (**TNT, Jorn, Helloween**). After the debut, keyboardist Andreas Lindahl (**Audiovision, Zool, Loch Vostock**) was replaced by Tommie Lundgren, who later left and was replaced by Kristoffer Von Wachtenfeldt. In 2004 the follow-up, *Nine*, was released. After the album, drummer Marcus Höher left and was temporarily replaced by Andreas Brobjer (**Space Odyssey, Angtoria**). Now lead guitarist Daniel Hall (**Rob Rock, Perfect Stranger**) also left and young guitar-wiz Johan Randén temporarily replaced him. In April 2005 the band started recording their third album, *Silence Speaks*. In December 2005 Brobjer moved to California where he toured with synth pop band **Stefy**. The band split in December 2008 and the last known line-up featured Blomqvist, Köllerström, Wachtenfeldt, Janson and drummer Erik Wigelius (now in **Wigelius**). *Platitude* plays high class melodic power metal, at times reminiscent of **Dragonforce** but way better, and with a much proggier touch. Killer vocals by Blomqvist and highly interesting guitar playing from Köllerström. Well, a great band in all! On *Silence Speaks* the style was even more prog-oriented.

2004 CD - SC 081-2

2002 CDd - SC 057-2

2006 CD - 00015

2002 ■	SECRETS OF LIFE	CDd	Scarlet		SC 057-2
2002 ☐	SECRETS OF LIFE	CD	King Records (Japan)		KICP-914
	Bonus: Wings Of Time				
2002 ☐	SECRETS OF LIFE	CD	n/a (Korea)		n/a
	Bonus: Magic				
2003 ☐	SECRETS OF LIFE	CD	CD-Maximum (Russia)		CDM 0403-1372
2004 ■	NINE	CD	Scarlet		SC 081-2
2004 ☐	NINE	CD	King Records (Japan)		KICP-995
	Bonus: Supernova				
2005 ☐	NINE	CD	Plyzen Music (Korea)		0045
	Bonus: Just One Try				
2004 ☐	NINE	CD	NEMS (Argentina)		NEMS 330
2005 ☐	SILENCE SPEAKS	CD	King Records (Japan)		KICP-1119
2006 ■	SILENCE SPEAKS	CD	Metal Heaven		00015
	Bonus: Catch 22 (ballad version)				

PLEASURE AVENUE

Susanne Carlsson: v, Tomas Ahlberg: g, Mats Nilsson: k,
Claas Wallin: b, Jonas Edahl: d

Malmö - **Pleasure Avenue** are, as the name may suggest, one of Sweden's many melodic hard rock bands. Musically this is really good melodic hard rock similar in style to early **Treat**. The B-side is even a bit heavier in some spots, with some double bass drums in the intro. Unfortunately the vocals bring the overall impression down a bit. Well worth checking out anyway.

1989 7" - GOT2CU

1989 ■	Pleasure Avenue/3F	7"	private		GOT2CU

PLEBB

Tommy Gustavsson: v/b, Per-Martin Pettersson: v/g,
Peter Martinsson: v/g, Ronnie Nilsson: d

Mönsterås - The oddly named band **Plebb** was formed in 1976. The initial line-up featured Petersson, Nilsson, guitarist Leif Bergqvist and bass player Tommy Gustavsson. In 1977 Bergqvist left for medical reasons and he was replaced by Peter Martinsson. They recorded a demo tape in 1978 (in 40 copies) and later the same year they recorded the album, on two ¼" reel to reel

1979 LP - TMLP 201

recorders, no mixer just sound-on-sound. Some of the tracks are great seventies hard rock with dual guitars, while some are a bit more standard. The album was only pressed in five hundred copies, so the price is in relation to this if you want a copy... Tommy and Peter later continued under the name *Purple Haze*, and released one album. The band reunited in 2010 and Peter releasied his first solo album in 2012 (Grooveyard Records). Today Pettersson, Martinsson and *Purple Haze* drummer Ulf play in the band *BnBB*. Plebb has also made some reunion gigs.

1979 ■ YES IT IS ISN'T IT ....LP   private ....TMLP-201   **$$$**
     500 copies.

2010 CD - MMI 10

PLECTOR
Erik Engbo: v/g, Patrik Wall: b, Vilhelm Norberg: d

Spice & dartful

Umeå - Formed in December 2006 and made their first demo, *Äkta demo* in 2007. They made a video for the song *Get Drunk Or Die Trying* that was even played in Swedish television. Great sounding technical death metal with strong thrash influences and a progressive twist. Great heavy mix and killer guitar playing. In 2008 the band released their six-track self-financed EP *Suppressed Aggression* as a CD-R. After this they entered the studio with producer Ronnie Björnström (*Hate Ammo, Assailant, Bone Gnawer, Ghamorean*) to record their debut, which was later picked up by Swedish label Discouraged. After the album bassist Björn Anglers left the band and was replaced by Patrik Wall (*Apostasy*).

2012 CDd - MMI 21

2010 ■ DARK & SPITEFUL...CD   Discouraged Records ....MMI 10
2012 ■ PUNISHMENT DAY ....CDd   Discouraged Records ....MMI 21

PLUTONIUM
John Carlsson: v/g/b/d

Karlskoga - *Plutonium* were initiated in 2003 by Carlsson. He teamed up with bassist Lars H and drummer H Fossmo and in 2004 they recorded the demo *Winds Of Change*. Tight, well played death metal with really good production. Some odd industrial-sounding sequences here and there. Definitely not your run of the mill death metal. Carlsson had to pull the heaviest load in the band, which eventually lead to the split between him and the others. *Devilmentertainment Non-Stop* was recorded as Carlsson's solo project in various sessions between 2008-2009. A guest solo was made by T. Ahlgren.

2011 CD - Pu942

2008 □ ONE SIZE FITS ALL ....CD   Khaoz Star Records..........................KSR-002
2011 ■ DEVILMENTERTAINMENT NON-STOP..CD   private Pu942

POINT, THE
Micke Svennerbrandt: v, Jocke Nilsson: g, Richard Ryden: b/g, Mike Down: d

Malmö - In 1998 Mikael Svennerbrandt recorded a power pop single in Swedish with a band named *Point*. When the band folded, he formed *The Point* in 1990 and this band lasted for only a year. He had previously played with pop/rockers *Strike* and was later in *Stinky Toys*. The A-side is more of a ballad, a bit similar to *It Bites*, while the B-side is pretty decent AOR but with some annoying *U2* style guitar twiddling in the chorus.

1990 7" - Point 001

1990 ■ Name Of This Game/When The Light Is Out ....7"   private ....Point 001

POINT OF EXISTENCE
Torbjörn Sandberg: v, Juan Gauthier: g, Stefan Sjöberg: g,
Christer Elofsson: b, Jonas Ohlsson: d

Stockholm - 5-6 years after the band split, former *T.A.R* members Torbjörn, Juan, Stefan and Östen started talking about getting together again. It ended up with Stefan and Östen joining forces and forming *Point Of Existence*. Micael and Christer joined the band and the sound became heavier. Micael however left and again discussions were made with Torbjörn, who weakened and joined the band. Sounds like if *WASP* had an evil cousin with a grudge. Singer Torbjörn sounds very much like Blackie Lawless, but musically the band weaves in a lot more technical and progressive elements. It's very hard to pinpoint the band's style, but I almost hear a bit of Devin Townsend in there as well. Wicked and weird, but interesting.

2009 ■ POINT OF EXISTENCE..CDd   private .... - -

2009 CDd - - -

POLE POSITION

Jonas Blum: v, Lars Boquist: g, Joakim Åberg: b, Hans Persson: d

Norrköping - The band recorded a 12" EP and a split-single under the name *Dizzinezz* before reforming and changing their name to *Pole Position*. Guitarist Lars Boquist has made several highly interesting instrumental guitar demos and he came in third place in the 1991 national lead guitar contest *Guitar Battle*. On the first single keyboard-player Joakim Åberg was also in the band. He returned as a bass player on the second album and replaced Lars Hultman. On the second album Hans had also replaced drummer Daniel Gese. The single and first album is great melodic hard rock with excellent guitar work, a bit like *Vinnie Vincent Invasion* with *Def Leppard* influenced chorus-parts. The second album shows a more modern, alternative but still heavy side of the band. Daniel and Joakim have previously recorded a 7" with the band *Grand Vision* and Jonas recorded a 7" with the band *Rebels*. In 1995 singer Jonas participated in a competition, live on national TV, imitating Axl Rose. A cover of *Paradise City* with Jonas on vocals appears on the compilation-CD *Sikta Mot Stjärnorna 2*. In December bass-player Joakim Åberg sadly passed away after having been seriously ill for six months. He however made the last recording with the band. The album contains a cover of the classic *City Boy* tune *5.7.0.5.* Jonas and Lars later recorded with *Reptilian*, and Lars has also made a CD with *Neondaze* and is now in melodic metal band *Fair Of Freaks*.

1991 7" - PPS 01

1993 CD - MRRCD 004

1991 ■	Call/Love Running	7"	private	PPS 01
1993 ■	POLE POSITION	CD	Megarock Records	MRRCD 004
1993 □	POLE POSITION	CD	Zero (Japan)	XRCN-1101
1994 □	Call/Beautiful Eyes/Rox/Call	MCD 4tr	Megarock Records	MRRCD-S012
	Rox is non-CD and the versions of Call and Beautiful Eyes are different from the CD.			
1998 ■	BIGGER	CD	Analogue/MFN	CDSINE 002

1998 CD - CDSINE 002

POLLUTED INFLUENCE

Mikael Skager: v, Ulf Wedenbrand: g, Johnnie Tiborn: g,
Roberth Steiner: b, Daniel Gustafsson: d

Hisings Backa (Göteborg) - The record was actually the first prize in the *Rockslaget* (The Rock Battle) competition, which they won in 1994. They also contribute with two tracks on the *Rockslaget 94* compilation, *Black Oak* and *Applause*. A solid heavy thrash band in the same vein as *Pantera*. In 1995 the band was signed to Soundfront Records and their first album was supposed to be released in 1996. Skager and Gustafsson later appeared in *Elite*, also featuring former *Soulquake System* members.

1994 ■	Polluted Influence	MCD 4tr	private	PICD 9409
	Tracks: Applause/Try Me/Black Oak/Sandslip			

1994 MCD - PICD 9409

POMPEI NIGHTS

Johan "Joey Eden" Edlund: v, Olle "Olli Cox" Södergren: g, Mathias "Matt Cosby"
Pettersson: g, Rob "Cold" Hammarström: b, Joakim "Devlin" Bengtsson: d

Stockholm - The members first met in 2008 and immediately hit it off. In 2009 *Pompei Nights* was a reality. Pretty good sleazy melodic hard rock. Slightly limited vocals, which pushes it down a few notches. Great mix. The next album is said to be more metal.

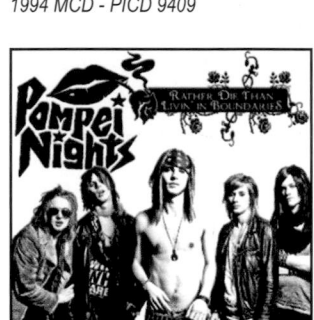

2011 ■	RATHER DIE THAN LIVING' IN BOUNDARIES	CD	Street Symphonies	SSR 008
2011 □	RATHER DIE THAN LIVING' IN BOUNDARIES	CD	Spinning Records (Japan)	SPIN-026
	Bonus: City Of Blinding Lights. Different artwork.			

2011 CD - SSR 008

PONAMERO SUNDOWN

Nicke Engwall: v, Anders Martinsgård: g, Oliver Gille Vowden: b, Peter Eklund: d

Stockholm - "Simplicity, memorable songs, a heavy groove and tons of riff". The band's goal sounds like a winning concept in my book! *Ponamero Sundown* was formed in November 2005, influenced by the seventies riff rock. The result is a dose of classic Swedish stoner in the vein of *Burning Saviour*, *Dozer* etc. Eklund was also in *Dark Funeral* as Equimanthorn.
Website: www.ponamerosundown.com

2009 ■	STONERIZED	CD	Transubstans	TRANS 048
2011 □	RODEO ELÉCTRICA	CDd	Transubstans	TRANS 078

PONTUS SNIBB 3

Pontus Snibb: v/g, Mats Rydström: b, Niklas Matsson: d

Stockholm - Pontus Snibb is a musical institution! Not that he's an old and scarred geezer, he just sounds like one! Pontus has recorded several solo albums in a more traditional blues vein

2009 CD - TRANS 048

under his own name and as **SNiBB**, he's also the drummer of American band **Jason & The Scorchers**, he played guitar in **Brickhouse**, plus he fronts and has recorded several albums with hard rockers **Bonafide**. In 2011 he formed a new power trio featuring the rhythm section of retro rockers **Backdraft**, where Matsson is also the new drummer of **Bonafide**. *Loud Feathers* is an excellent hard rock album, leaning on a fat blues vibe and cool seventies-souding guitar riffing with a hint of **Bonafide**'s *AC/DC* style hard rock. The album also features guest spots from blues man Mats Ronander, **Mustasch**'s Ralf Gyllenhammar and **Electric Boys**' Conny Bloom.
Website: www.ps3rocks.com

2011 CDd - ROOTSY 048

2011 ■	LOUD FEATHERS	CDd	Rootsy	ROOTSY 048
2011 □	LOUD FEATHERS	LP	Rootsy	ROOTSY 048

POODLES, THE

**Jakob "Jake Samuel" Samuelsson: v, Henrik Bergqvist: g,
Pontus Egberg: b, Christian "Kicken" Lundqvist: d**

Stockholm - **The Poodles** were formed already in 1999 by Lundqvist, Tobias Molin and Martina Edoff as an eighties hard rock cover band. Singers Thomas Vikström (**Talk Of The Town, Candlemass, Stormwind** etc), Anton Körberg and Krister Hermansson (**Cleopatra**) were also in the band for some time. So was keyboard player Roger Gustafsson. In 2005 **The Poodles** became a serious band, now featuring singer Jake Samuel and guitarist Pontus Norgren, who had previously played together in the band **The Ring**, plus former **Lion's Share** bassist Pontus Egberg. Only six months after this, they entered the Eurovision Song Contest with the song *Night Of Passion*, and things just exploded. They had to write and record the debut album at the speed of light, also bringing in outside writers such as Matti Alfonzetti, Tommy Denander, Marcel Jacob and Holly Knight. The album also featured a cover of **Ultravox**'s *Dancing With Tears In My Eyes*. The band also did a tour playing 31 gigs in 18 countries in 35 days. The single *Seven Seas* features guest vocals from profile actor (and rocker) Peter Stormare. In April 2008 Pontus left to join **Hammerfall**. He was replaced by Henrik Bergqvist (ex-**Four Sticks**) June 6 the same year. In 2008 the band again entered the Melody Grand Prix, this time together with rapper E-Type (aka Martin Eriksson, former drummer of **Maninnya Blade**) with the song *Line Of Fire*. *Raise The Banner* was the official Olympic song for the national Swedish team. In August 2010 the band was picked up by Italian AOR label Frontiers Records, who released the band's first live CD and DVD, *No Quarter* (CD) and *In The Flesh* (DVD).

Fluffy rockers doin' it doggy style.

2007 CDS - LHICDS 0080

2006 □	A Night Of Passion (radio mix)/ A Night Of Passion (Singback mix)	CDS 2tr	M&L Records	MLCDS0064
2006 □	Metal Will Stand Tall/Number One + video	CDS 2tr	Lionheart	LHICDS 0055
2006 □	METAL WILL STAND TALL	CD	Lionheart	LHICD 0035
2006 □	METAL WILL STAND TALL	CD	King Records (Japan)	KICP-1197
2006 □	Song For You/Echoes From The Past (live)/Song For You (live)	MCD 3tr	Lionheart	LHICDS0063
2007 □	Seven Seas	CDS 2tr	Lionheart	LHICDS 0073
2007 □	SWEET TRADE	CD	Lionheart	LHICD 0052
2007 □	SWEET TRADE	CD	King Records (Japan)	KICP-1270
2007 □	SWEET TRADE	CD	Lionheart	LHICD 0058
	Re-issue with new artwork. Bonus:Street Of Fire/Seven Seas/Line Of Fire			
2007 ■	Streets Of Fire/Seven Seas (video)	CDS	Lionheart	LHICDS 0080
	Available as a gift with Okej magazine. No artwork.			
2008 ■	Line Of Fire (radio version)/ Line Of Fire (singback version)	CDS 2tr	M&L Records	MLCDS0099
2009 ○	I Rule The Night/ I Rule The Night (singback version)	CDS 2tr	Rosehip Alley	RARS 02
	Actually a pro-printed CDR without artwork.			
2009 □	CLASH OF THE ELEMENTS	CD	Rosehip Alley	RARCD 01
2009 □	CLASH OF THE ELEMENTS	CDd	Rosehip Alley	RARCD 01X
2009 □	CLASH OF THE ELEMENTS	CD	King Records (Japan)	KICP-1443
	Bonus: I Rule The Night (Acoustic)/I Rule The Night (Live)			
2009 □	One Out Of Ten/One Out Of Ten (Karaoke)	CDS 2tr	Rosehip Alley	RARS 01
2010 □	NO QUARTER	CD	Frontiers	FR CD 484
2010 □	NO QUARTER + IN THE FLESH	CD+DVD	Frontiers	FR CDVD 484
2011 □	PERFORMOCRAZY	CD	Frontiers	FR CD 511
2011 □	PERFORMOCRAZY	CD	Icarus Music (Argentina)	ICARUS 784
2011 □	PERFORMOCRAZY	CD	King Records (Japan)	KICP-1563
	Bonus: Ship Of Fools (demo)			
2013 □	TOUR DE FORCE	CD	Frontiers	FR CD 602
2013 □	TOUR DE FORCE	CD	Icarus Music (Argentina)	ICARUS 1111

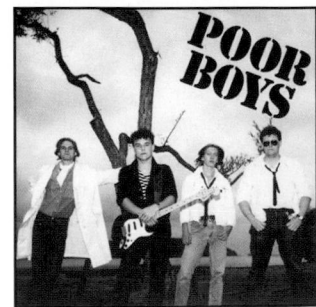

2008 CDS - MLCDS0099

POOR BOYS

Erik Larsson: v/h, Christer Häger: g, Håkan Johansson: b, Hasse Hurnasti: d

Södertälje - Bluesy hard rock with a touch of **Status Quo** or a heavier **Motvind**. Quite raw guitars and ok vocals.

1983 ■	Sol över staden/Bad Time	7"	Södertälje Musikforum	SMF 005

1983 7" - SMF 005

PORKLIFT
Henrik Kihlberg: v, Daniel Hammare: g,
Thomas Hård: b, Johan Hammarlund: sampl/prog
Falun - Totally freaked out mix of hardcore, hip-hop and funk, with an industrial-sounding base. Try mixing **White Zombie**, **Rage Against The Machine** and **Refused**. Started in 1992 as a hobby project for Johan and Daniel. The band was featured on the 1994 *Extreme Close-Up* compilation.

1996 ■ PRIME CUTS..CD MNWZone....................................MNWCD 304

1996 CD - MNWCD 304

PORTAL
Kristian Kaunissaar: v/g, Stefan Johansson: g, Emil Koverot: b, Mattias Fiebig: d
Västervik - The band was formed in 1996 and besides the changing of bass player the line-up is still the same. **Portal** recorded the demo *The Prophet* in 1998 and received great interest from Invasion Records, who unfortunately went bankrupt. The band then entered the crypt of Necromorbus and recorded four new songs which caught the attention of Cadla Records and it finally became a full length album. **Portal** produces melodic death metal with a Norse mythology concept, not unlike **Amon Amarth** mixed with **Gates Of Ishtar**. Koverot and Fiebig are also in **Blodsrit**.

2001 ■ FORTHCOMING...CD Cadla ....CADLA 009
    The spine also says CDN 004 and More Hate MHP 08-008

2001 CD - CADLA 009

PORTRAIT
Per "Periloz" Lengstedt (aka Karlsson): v, Christian Lindell: g,
Richard Lagergren: g, Erik Jansson: b, Anders Persson: d
Kristianstad - **Mercyful Fate**-sounding metal band **Portrait** was formed in 2004 by former **Helvetet's Port** guitarist Lindell. Initially former **Eidomantum** member Lagergren was drafted as bass player, but soon switched to guitar and David Stranderud took the bass spot. Singer Philip Svennefelt was probably the main reason the band was compared to **Mercyful Fate**, as he was treading in the same falsetto-style vocal footsteps. After the first album bass player Stranderud was replaced by Erik Jansson and singer Svennefelt was replaced by **Overdrive** singer Per "Periloz" Lengstedt (aka Karlsson), formerly in **Unchained**. Svennefelt is now handling the bass in **Helvetets Port**. The band's second effort took the sound a bit further from **Mercyful Fate** in is more similar to Swedish colleagues **In Solitude**. In 2012 Lagergren was sacked from the band, David Olofsson took care of his guitar and Cab Castervall (**Hypnosia, Funeral**) entered on bass.

Self Portrait?

2007 7" - NIA 001

2007 ■	Into The Nothingness/His Glowing Eyes	7"	New Iron Age		NIA 001
	500 copies. Sticker.				
2008 □	PORTRAIT	CD	Ironkodex		IK 001
2008 □	PORTRAIT	LP	High Roller Records		HHR 026
	666 copies. Poster.1st press.				
2008 □	PORTRAIT	LP	High Roller Records		HHR 026
	300 copies. Poster, patch, cardboard insert, different artwork. Red vinyl. 2nd press.				
2008 □	PORTRAIT	LP	High Roller Records		HHR 026
	500 copies. Different poster. Cardboard insert. Red/black vinyl. 3rd press.				
2008 □	PORTRAIT	LP PD	High Roller Records		HHR 026
	500 copies. Poster.				
2009 □	PORTRAIT	CD	Holycaust Records (USA)		S810-14
2010 □	The Murder Of All Things Righteous/Son Of All Graves	7"	High Roller Records		HHR 095
	100 gold, 300 clear and 600 black vinyl copies.				
2011 ■	CRIMEN LAESAE MAJESTATIS DIVINAE	CD	Metal Blade Records		3984-15002-2
	666 copies. Poster.				
2011 □	CRIMEN LAESAE MAJESTATIS DIVINAE	LPg	Metal Blade Records		3984-25002-1
	250 blue, 300 grey/blue and 400 black vinyl. Poster.				

2011 CD - 3984-15002-2

POSH FILTH
Anders Nyberg: v, Micke Myhr: g, Johan Berg: g,
Matte Johansson: b, Fredrik Söderström: d
Eskilstuna - Basic, straightforward hard rock with a slightly **AC/DC** influenced sound. *Fever* is a great song.

1990 ■ Whip You/Fever..7" private ....PF 001

1990 7" - PF 001

POUND

Stefan Altzar (aka Gustavsson): v/g , Janne Korpela: g,
Christian Larsson: b/v, Samuel Granath: d

Borlänge - Borlänge-based melodic modern rockers *Pound* were formed in 2004 from the ashes of pop/rock band *Universal Puppies*, singer/guitarist Stefan Altzar (aka Gustavsson), bassist Christian Larsson and drummer Janne Korpela wanted to go heavier. The line-up on the debut EP featured Altzar, Korpela, bass player/keyboardist Mika Itäranta and guitarist/keyboardist Martin Haglund. A few months after the release of *Phantomkiller,* Martin and Mika decided to leave to devote their time fully to their other band, *Astral Doors*. They were replaced by Christian Larsson and Samuel Granath. They started working on the debut album, which was produced by *TNT* singer Tony Harnell. The album was also released digitally by Zia Record Exchange. After the album *Universal Puppies* keyboardist Kalle Sandström joined. Even though they are influenced by bands like *Muse*, *The Killers* and *Tool*, I think they are heavy enough to make it in here. Melodic modern pop-oriented alternative hard rock, at times with a wall of guitars and great vocals, at timed similar to Rick Zander (*Cheap Trick*). In 2013 the band released the digital album *One Of These Days I'm Gonna Bring The Sun In A Box* (Do It Records).
Website: www.poundband.com

Selling Sweden by the Pound

2009 CDd - 320470 114094

2005 ☐	Phantomkiller	MCDp 4tr	Pounding Records	POUND 001	
	Tracks: My Evil Eye/I hate You Too/Fool You/Here All Day				
2008 ☐	Desillusionizer	MCDp 5tr	Pound Music	320470 132913	
	Tracks: Clone/Razorboy/I Hurt You/I'm Holy Man/Not The Man				
2009 ■	STARDUST LIES AND HOLY WATER	CDd	Pound Music	320470 114094	
2009 ☐	STARDUST LIES AND HOLY WATER	CD	Boundee (Japan)	DQC-552	
	Bonus: Radio/Victim Of Science				

2013 CD - - -

POWER

Tomas Jansson: v, Christopher Ståhl: g, Patrik Appelgren: k,
Martin Von Schmalensee: b, Jari Katila: d

Stockholm - *Power* were formed already in the late 70s and in 1983 they recorded a classic demo with the following line-up: Björn Jansson (v) (*Racketeer, Trail Of Tears, Two Rocks* etc), Sepp "Zepp" Urgard (d) (*Rising Force*), Marcel Jacob (b) (*Rising Force, Talisman*), Christopher (*Talisman*) and Patrik (*Treat*). The style was like a more melodic version of *Rising Force*. After the demo, Marcel left to join Yngwie Malmsteen. The band was offered some great deals by big labels but their management managed to scare them off. *Power* made two singles and some great demos before they split in 1990. One track off the 1984-demo, *Let Me Love You*, was later recorded by John Norum. On the first single Peter Olsson played bass. Christopher recorded the first *Talisman*-album and also worked as studio guitarist in England with different bands, one being Canadians *Crystal Eyes*. If you're into bands like *Talisman* and Norum, melodic complex hard rock with astonishing guitar work, you'd better check this band out. At one time the bass was handled by Jocke Larsson, later in *Treat*. Marcel Jacob sadly died in 2009. There are also a couple of really great *Power* demos floating around. Katila is now in *Mud & Blood*.

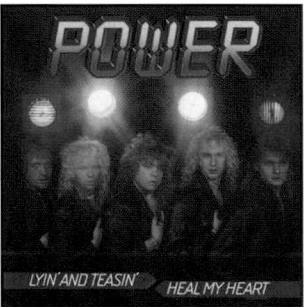

1986 7" - GAS 515

1987 7" - SAS 163

1986 ■	Lyin' & Teasin'/Heal My Heart	7"	Galaxy	GAS 515	
1987 ■	Danger/Love Ain't Meant Forever	7"	Scranta	SAS 163	

POWER UNIT

Yngve Edvardsson: v, Henrik Andersson: g, Johannes Losbäck: g,
Magnus Hansson: b, Jonny Edvardsson: d

Göteborg - Very traditional 80's heavy metal with a melodic feel. In the same league as *220 Volt* and *Crystal Pride*. OK vocals, good songs but quite thin production. Losbäck later played in bands like *Decameron*, *Seventh One* and *Wolf*, Hansson in *Miscellany* and Jonny Edvardsson in *Seventh One*.

1990 LP - 22123

1990 ■	TIME-CHASER	LP	Büms	22123	$

POWERBREEZE

Mikael Nordlander: v, Eric Diurlin: g, Magnus Stenvinkel: b, Pelle Berglund: d

Strängnäs - Magnus, Erik and Pelle previously recorded a demo with the band *Endless Dawn* in 1992. Quite good solid hard rock with some influences from the early 70's type of hard rock as well as *Alice In Chains'* first album. A bit weak in the vocal department though. Drummer Pelle left in 1995.

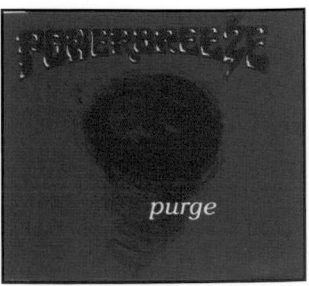

1994 MCD - PB001CD

1994 ■	Purge	MCD 3tr	Underground	PB001CD	
	Tracks: Boy/Blind/My Emptiness.				

POWERDISE

Linus Melchiorsen: v/d, Martin Fogander: g,
Mats Pettersson: k, Janne "Goat" Tillman: b

Linköping - The band was formed in 1997 by Linus (*Hint*) and Martin Fogander (*Lost Divinity*), initially called *Iron Claw*, and then *Powerdice*, then changing the "c" to an "s". Janne and Linus were also found in *Isengard*, while Mats was in sleazy/glam rockers *Rags To Riches* and he also recorded a horrible and very poppy solo MCD entitled *March Into Heaven*. After the MCD Mats was out, Tillman was replaced by Mattias Kindefors (*U.N.IT*), and singer Christer Göransson (*Mindless Sinner, Demental*) was added to the band. Melchiorsen was later in *Demental, Los Sin Nombre* and *Maitreya*, while Fogander was the in the two latter. Death metal.

1999 ■ Shadowland ....MCD 4tr Loud N Proud....................................PDISE 01
    Tracks: Dreams Of A Thousand Lies/Shadowland/Upon A Strar/Last Chapter

1999 MCD - PDISE 01

POWERTRIP

Viktoria Johansson: v, Per Eriksson: g, Peter Uvén: b, Erik Palmqvist: d

Piteå - The band started out under the name *Poue* and recorded their first demo in 2004. They later changed to *Powertrip* and recorded the debut album, in the vein of *Alice In Chains* meets *Soundgarden*. The band is now named *Scars Of Paradise*.

2007 ■ COLD BLACK LIE..CD Sleazy Rider SR-0061

2007 CD - SR-0061

PRESS

Tommy Carron, Marc Cino, Don Ross, Jeff Kaye, Chris Joeney, Toni Lynn

Kalmar - *Press* play really good melodic hard rock/AOR in the vein of early *Treat*.

1986 ■ You And I/On The Line ....7" Platina..PL 15

1986 7" - PL 15

PRETTY WILD

Ivan "Ivve" Höglund: v, Krizzy Field: g,
Kim Chevélle: b, Johan "Johnny Benson" Bengtsson: d

Malmö/Stockholm - Formed in 2006. Ivan, who is the Stockholm part of the band, is also the lead singer of *EYE* and *Shades*. Really good sleazy metal similar to *Crazy Lixx* and *Crashdïet*. After the album guitarist Field was replaced by Axl Ludwig. The band started recording the first full album in 2011 together with Micko Twedberg (*Debase*), to be released late 2012. Bengtsson is also in *Bai Bang*.

2009 ■ All The Way..MCD 8tr Swedmetal...................................SM-016-CD
    Tracks: All The Way/Time/Let The Good Times Roll/Shocking Teen/Dangerous/Take It Off/
    Let The Good Times Roll (-86 mix)/Dangerous (live)

2009 MCD - SM-016-CD

PREY

Thomas Nyström: v/g, Fredrik Plahn: k, Peter Bäcke: b, Robert Bäck: d

Falun - *Prey* play excellent melodic hard rock/metal in the vein of *Eclipse*, but with a slight let-down in the vocal department. Not bad, but lacking in range and power. The band's first drummer was Patrik Johansson, previously with *Without Grief, Stormwind* and *Chainwreck* and has been backing guitar hero Yngwie Malmsteen for several years. The debut was produced by Anders "Theo" Theander at Roastinghouse Studios. Bäck is also found in bands like *Eclipse, Black Ladies, Baltimoore, BALLS* and *W.E.T.*
Website: www.prey-nation.com

2005 ☐ THE HUNTER ....CD Music Avenue/Mausoleum....................251066
2009 ■ KNIGHTS OF THE REVOLUTION...CD GMR .... GMRCD 9015

2009 CD - GMRCD 9015

PRIDE

Dan Kristiansson: v, Jonas Öhlund: g, Stefan Karlström: k
Johan Agerberg: b, Anders Henriksson (now Pellving): d

Östersund - High-class melodic hard rockers *Pride* was formed in 1987, but the story actually begins back in 1984 when the band *Silhouette* was formed. The band featured Öhlund, Karlström, Henriksson and bass player Sven-Olof Nilsson. They had also existed under the name *Grime Crime*, featured on a compilation cassette in 1986. The band was looking for a singer, and finally found former *Transit* singer Dan Kristiansson. In 1988 they took the same *Pride* when entering the competition *Rock SM*. They won and first prize was the recording of a single. Prior to the recording bass player Nilsson left and was replaced by former *Quest* man Agerberg. In

1989 7" - HEJ S-028

July 1989 the band entered Stockholm Recordings and CBS Studios together with *220 Volt*'s Mats Karlsson to record some more songs. A new single was to be released by Lynx Records, but the label went bust. A new EP was planned to be recorded, but drummer problems shelved the plans. Finally they found former *Wilderness* drummer Elinor Mårtensson, but she only lasted for one gig. They used another drummer for a short while but on February 15 1991 the band played its last show. Jonas, Dan and Stefan tried reviving the beast, but things fizzled out. A killer AOR band with a strong U.S. feel. In 2008 AOR-FM Records released the unreleased demos and the single as a CD, later reissued by Yesterrock Records. Öhlund is today found in AOR band *Linehouse*.

2008 CD - AOR-FM 001

1989 ■	You're The Only One/Dreamer In The Night	7"	Active Music	HEJ S-028
2008 ■	PRIDE	CD	AOR-FM	AOR-FM 001
	500 copies.			
2011 □	PRIDE	CD	Yesterrock	Y-2011-7
	Bonus: Heartless Woman/Valkyria. Same artwork as the 7".			

PRIME
Tobias Tybåhl: v/b/k, Tomas Ängshammar: g, Andreas Widén: d

Linköping - High-class melodic hard rock/AOR quite close to *It Bites* in their heavier moments. Outstanding guitar playing from Ängshammar. The band was formed in 1993. Before this Tybåhl, at the time playing drums, and Ängshammar had played together in various prog-oriented bands since 1986, such as *Solitude*, *A.R.E* and *Flight*. Ängshammar went to GIT to study guitar and when he came home Tybåhl had changed to being a singing bass player with keyboard on the side. Initially *Pride* was a quartet, also featuring drummer Marcus Törnquist and keyboard player Tomas Pettersson, but they dropped out because of rehearsal schedules being too heavy. They continued playing as a duo with sequencer and they also had a troubadour cover thing going until Widén joined on drums. In 1996 they recorded the MCD at a friends studio. They only did a handful of gigs but continued writing songs, which actually became a bit heavier, too. Late 1997 the band folded and Ängshammar moved to Göteborg to study journalism. Tybåhl and Widén continued as *Prime II*, with a new keyboard player and guitarist, now more AOR/west coast oriented, but nothing came out of this. Tybåhl later recorded a pop/rock MCD also featuring Morgan "Svisse" Svensson from eighties band *W.E.T*. Ängshammar also made a short stint in *Pär Lindh Project*.

1996 MCD - PRCDS 001

| 1996 ■ | Prime | MCD 4tr | private | PRCDS 001 |
| | *Tracks: The Tales Of Lea/She Ate Her Heart Out/Sleep Tonight/I Know* | | | |

PRIMITIVE SYMPHONY
Jimmie Nyhlén: v, Christian Nordh: g, Rasmus Ström: g/k,
Patrik Halvarsson: b, Björn Jonsson: d

Västervik - Black/death metal. Formed in 1992 and in 1995 the six-track demo *Obscene Sadist* was released. The tracks on the split-CD is more or less the demo *A Last Breath For The Dying*. Nylén is also found in *Blodsrit*, *Wrath* and *Myhrding*, Jonsson in *Paganizer* and Halvarsson has previously played with *Blodsrit*, *Ribspreader*, *Sinners Burn* and *Paganizer*. The track *Left To Bleed* is found on the compilation *Voices Of Death Part III – The Book Of Death* (1998 VOD).

2001 CD - PSOL 9056

2001 ■	Of Satan's Breed (split)	CD	Psychic Scream	PSOL 9056
	Split with German band Bluttaufe. Tracks: Of Satan's Breed/As The Shadows Are Watch-			
	ing Me/Christian Hypocrisy/The Mark Of Darkness/The Last Breath For The Dying/			
	Satanic Hymn.			

PRINT
Martin Schabbauer: v/g, Peter Björklund: g, Niclas Gustavsson: k,
Lennart Johansson: b, Tord Carlsson: d

Norrköping - The A-side is really good melodic hard rock, but the singer is not really up to par on his voice and English pronunciation. The B-side is a pretty useless standard ballad.

1986 7" - S&M 8604

| 1986 ■ | Anguish & Fear/You | 7" | private | S&M 8604 |

PRIORITY
Thomas Thulin: v/b, Morgan Rosenquist: g, Rikard Olsson: d

Lagan - The first single is glam rock in the vein of *Sha-Boom* with quite childish Vince Neil-soundalike vocals. The second 7" however is AOR with great guitar work. The band backed pop singer Svenne Hedlund (*Hep Stars*) on tour and he has also produced their first single. Thulin later formed hard rocker *Spearfish* and recorded several albums. He was also found in *Covered Call*, with whom he released one album.

1990 7" - 90008

| 1989 □ | Undercover/Magic Night | 7" | private | P1 |
| 1990 ■ | In The Mood/Times Of The Past | 7" | Star Music | 90008 |

PRISCA

Andreas Andersson: v, **Jimmy Carlsson (now Svärdhagen):** g, **Johan Broman:** k
Christopher Anderzon: b/v, **Erik Werholt:** d

Tranås - Prisca was a young Roman woman who died as a martyr because of her Christian faith. The band *Prisca*, however, is a really good Christian hard rock band. Formed in 1990 and only lasted until the EP was released. After this the members were geographically scattered. The four songs span from early *Bon Jovi* style AOR to soft balladry. The track *Wake Up* is found on the compilation *Elva till tolv topplåtar* (1995 Toppsound). Andreas is today head of the organisation *Sport For Life*. Christopher has since played with bands like *Meadowland* and *El Corazón*, plus he has backed and recorded with artists like Carola, *A-Teens,* Monica Silverstrand and Thomas Järvheden. Jimmy, now named Svärdhagen, is now foremost a magician.

1995 MCD - ICMA 9501

1995	■	Licence To Save	MCD 4tr	ICMA	ICMA 9501

Tracks: Licence To Save/Wake Up/Amazing/The Only Way

PRISONER

Tommy Denander: g/b, **Björn "Ricky Delin" Lindbom:** k

Stockholm - An outstanding pomp/AOR project initiated by wonder-kid Tommy Denander (solo, *ATC*, *Talk Of The Town*, *Radioactive* etc) and colleague Björn "Ricky Delin" Lindbom. The extraordinary Geir Rönning and Pierre Wensberg handle the vocals on the albums. The drums on the first album were played by Johan Kullberg (*Talk Of The Town, Lion's Share*) and backing vocals provided by names like Thomas Vikström (*Talk Of The Town, Candlemass, Stormwind* etc), Bernt Ek (*Grace, House Of Shakira*), Andreas Eklund (*Sabbtail, House Of Shakira*) and Mikael Eriksson (*House Of Shakira, Zifa*). The project was initially called *Blind*, but the label found the name a bit too "grunge"-sounding.

2000 CD - ZR 1997026

2000	■	BLIND	CD	Z Records	ZR 1997026
2000	□	BLIND	CD	Avalon Marquee (Japan)	MICP-10204
		Bonus: Return My Heart and Susan			
2001	■	II	CD	Z Records	ZR 1997044

2001 CD - ZR 1997044

PROFUNDI

Jens Rydén: v/g/b/d

Tyresö (Stockholm) - *Profundi* is a solo project by former *Dead Silent Slumber*/*Naglfar* singer Jens Rydén, actually not that far from his former band in style and sound. Old-school-style, primitive and evil sounding black metal. Jens is also in *Thyrfing*.
Website: www.profundi.com

2006	□	THE OMEGA RISING	CD	Soundholic (Japan)	TKCS-85153
		Bonus: Pet Cemetary (Ramones cover)/World Wide War			
2006	□	THE OMEGA RISING	CDd	Profound Lore (USA)	PFL 020
		1000 copies.			
2007	□	THE OMEGA RISING	CDd	Viva Hate	VHR 45006 CD
		1000 copies. First press.			
2007	■	THE OMEGA RISING	CD	Viva Hate	VHR 45006
		Second press. Slipcase.			
2008	□	THE OMEGA RISING	LPg	Transcendental Creations	TC 003
		400 black + 100 black/white splatter vinyl. Poster.			

2007 CD - VHR 45006

PROJECT HATE MCMXCIX, THE

Jörgen Sandström: v, **Ruby Roque:** v,
Kenth "Lord K" Philipsson: g/b/d, **Tobbe Gustafsson:** d

Örebro - MCMXCIX is 1999 with Roman numbers, the year the band was formed. Dan Swanö mixed the debut. Kenth has recorded with *Leukemia, Torture Division, God Among Insects* and *House Of Usher*, while Jörgen is ex-*Grave, Entombed, Vicious Art* and also in *Krux*. Dark and heavy metal with an evil streak. A vocal mix of Mia Ståhl's clean voice and Jörgen's brutal growling. On the first two albums the band was a trio with Kenth handling all the instruments. The second album featured guest spots from guitarist Petter S. Freed and singer Morgan Lundin. *Killing Helsinki* is a live album, also featuring three demo tracks with *Entombed*'s LG Petrov on vocals. On *Hate, Dominate, Congregate, Eliminate* the band had been completed with guitarist Petter S. Freed and Mia had been replaced by Jonna Enckell. Magus Caligula guested on backing vocals. On *Armageddon March Eternal* the line-up had been completed with bass player Michael Håkansson (*Evergrey, Embraced, Mortum, Incapacity, The Forsaken*). In *Hora Mortis Nostrae* (means "in the hour of death") features the band's first drummer of flesh and blood: Daniel "Mojjo" Moilanen (*Runemagick, Dracena, Lord Belial, Relevant Few, Sandalinas*). He was however replaced by Thomas Ohlsson on *The Lustrate Process*. The album also features guest spots from Mike Wead, Pär Fransson, L.G Petrov, Christian Älvestam, Johan Hegg, Robban Eriksson and Martin van Drunen. *Initiation Of Blasphemy* was the first album recorded under the old moniker, *The Project Hate*, in 1998. It was supposed to be released with new vocals

2000 CD - MAS CD 0239

2005 CD - TRECD 019

2009 CD - VIC 027 CD

by Sandström, but the original tapes were lost. It later resurfaced and was released under the **Deadmarch** banner. The line-up on this recording features Philipsson, Ståhl and singer Mikael Öberg. On *Bleeding The New Apocalypse (Cum Vitriciis In Marnibus Armis)* the line-up was again changed. Jonna was out and Ruby Roque (**Witchbreed**) had replaced her, drummer Olsson was replaced by Tobbe Gustafsson and guitarist Freed was out. The album featured guest appearances from Wead, Älvestam, Magnus Söderman, Leif Edling and Jocke Widfeldt.

2011 CD - SOM 230

Year		Title		Label	Cat. no.
2000	■	CYBERSONIC CYBERCHRIST	CD	Massacre	MAS CD 0239
2000	□	CYBERSONIC CYBERCHRIST	CD	Pavement (USA)	76962-32349-2
2001	□	WHEN WE ARE DONE, YOUR FLESH WILL BE OURS	CD	Massacre	MAS CD 0284
2003	□	KILLING HELSINKI	CD	Threeman	TRECD 008
2003	□	HATE, DOMINATE, CONGREGATE, ELIMINATE	CD	Threeman	TRECD 010
2003	□	HATE, DOMINATE, CONGREGATE, ELIMINATE	CD	Candlelight (USA)	CDL 123 CD
2005	■	ARMAGEDDON MARCH ETERNAL (SYMPHONIES OF SLIT WRISTS)	CD	Threeman	TRECD 019
2005	□	ARMAGEDDON MARCH ETERNAL (SYMPHONIES OF SLIT WRISTS)	CD	Candlelight (USA)	CDL0257CD
2008	□	IN HORA MORTIS NOSTRAE	CD	Stormvox	SVXCD 7003
2009	■	THE LUSTRATE PROCESS	CD	Vic Records	VIC 027 CD
2011	■	BLEEDING THE NEW APOCALYPSE	CD	Season Of Mist	SOM 230

PROJECT L.E.E

Lasse E. Engström: v, Sven Cirnski: g, Hal Johnson (now Marabel): g, Mats Jeppsson: b, David Brandt: k, Jaime Salazar: d

Trelleborg - **Project L.E.E** was Lasse's solo-project. A great piece of ballsy AOR with a big production by Hal. Mats and Sven were also found in **Raise Cain**, Hal, Sven and Jaime are in **Bad Habit** and David is part of **Aces High**. Great band, great songs and great production. Would have been nice to hear a full-length production. Unfortunately Lasse died of cancer in 2009. Jaime has recorded numerous albums with **The Flower Kings, Truth, Midnight Sun** etc., Cirnski has released an album under the name **Truth** and Jeppsson is in **69 Hard**.

1994 MCD - DEM94004

1994	■	Now Or Never	MCD 4tr	Demolition	DEM94004	$

Tracks: Now Or Never/Don't Stop/Another You/Sweet Little Child

PROJEKT UPA

Erland Wicklund: v, Poa Åhlslund: g, Niclas Nordqvist: k, Mikael Hagberg: b, Rickard Sievert: d

Örebro - Niclas was previously in melodic rockers **Rio**, who released two singles in 1984 and 1985. This single was funded by an anti-drug association. Melodic hard rock in the same vein as **Rio**. UPA means "without personal responsibility".

1985	■	Drag utan drog/Älskade element	7"	DuD	S-001

1985 7" - S-001

PROMILLE

Christer Schill: v/g, Per-Olov Engman: g, Lars-Roland Svensson: b, Leif Jarl: d

Halmstad - Hard rock with a garage touch, but quite a fat sound. Not bad, like a primeval version of **Onyx**. Schill also laid down some guitars on the **Side By Side** single.

1979	■	Promille	MLP 4tr	UFS	UFS 794

Tracks: Tonåring/Tjackpundaren/Låtsasliv/Drömmen

1979 MLP - UFS 794

PROMOTION

Peter Sundell: v, Jon Stavert: g, Anders Rydholm: k/b, Christian Sundell: d

Nässjö - Peter Sundell started his career as lead singer and guitarist in the more metal-oriented band **Wulcan**, with whom he recorded two singles. In 1988 he released the solo single *Serena*, where also Anders and brother/former **Wulcan** colleague Christian participated. **Promotion** plays radio-oriented AOR with strong westcoastish overtones, but the occasional biting guitar, similar to **Toto** or a heavier **Time Gallery**. Great vocals and good melodies. *Not For Sale* was first released as a limited CD-R, featuring the bonus track *Didn't Say Goodbye*, but was in 1997 released as a printed CD. A funny detail is that one member has been erased from the cover painting on the official version. The band later changed their name to **Grand Illusion** and both albums have now been reissued under the new name, as a double-CD entitled *In The Beginning* with some bonus material included. The first **Promotion** album also included guitarist Stefan Johansson, backing singer Per Svensson, sax player Håkan Malmberg and trumpetist Joakim Wikström. Backing singer Per Svensson later became the lead singer in **Grand Illusion**, where the horn section, which plays a minor part on the **Promotion** albums, was excluded.

1997 CD - PR 556

1998 CD - PR 557

1997	■	NOT FOR SALE	CD	Godispåscen AB	PR 556
1998	■	YEAH YEAH	CD	Godispåscen AB/AOR Heaven	PR 557

PROPHANITY

**Mathias "Farbaute" Järrebring: v, Nicklas Magnusson: g,
Christer "Grendel" Olsson: g, Robert Lindmark: b, Anders "Wouthan" Malmström: d**

Alingsås - Formed late 1991 by Farbaute and Grendel, under a different name. Two years later the band was completed with Anders "Woutan" Malmström and Mats "Nauthis" Blomberg (**Nauthis, Inverted**). Mats left before the first demo, *Demo #1* was recorded in 1994. The band's second demo *Messengers Of The Northern Warrior Host* was recorded later the same year and sold around 700 copies. One of the songs can be found on the *Sometime Death Is Better* (Shiver) compilation. In 1996 the band was completed with bass player Robert Lindmark (**Septic Grave**) and guitarist Nicklas Magnusson (**Nightshade/The Rapture**). They recorded the *Battleroar* demo in 1997. The band landed a deal with Blackend and recorded the first album. The track *Walking Through Fire* can be found on a Blackend and a Voices Of Death compilation and *The Battleroar* can be found on *Under The Banners Of Darkness* (Near Dark) In 1999 Mathias and Robert left. Mathias was replaced by Carl-Johan Sörman and Robert by Christian Aho. The band went through some pretty turbulent time when Carl-Johan was later fired, Nicklas left, Mathias rejoined and left. The last line-up before the split in 2001, featured Anders, Christer, Nicklas and new singer/bass-player Patrick "Patsy" Johansson (**The Rapture, Satan's Little Helper**). *Prophanity* plays furious and on the early recordings quite badly produced black metal with Swedish lyrics. Ultra-screamy vocals. The album *Stronger Than Steel* was produced by Anders "Andy LaRocque" Allhage and shows a lot more promise. Anders and Christer are also found in **Immemoreal**, while Anders has also been part of **Putraeon, Nominon, Inverted** and **Absinth**. Nicklas is found in **Dragonland**.
Website: http://prophanity.tripod.com/

Really black metal!

I VARGENS TECKEN

1995 7" - - -

1998 CD - BLACK 010 CD

1995 ■ I Vargens Tecken/Offerkväll	7"	Voice Of Death/Sorrowmoon	- -
500 copies.			
1998 ■ STRONGER THAN STEEL	CD	Blackened	BLACK 010 CD
1999 ☐ STRONGER THAN STEEL	CD	Metal Blade (US)	3984-14199-2

PROSPECT

**Michael Stein: v, Peter Ekman: g, Markus Elfström: k,
Hasse Torensjö: b, Lasse Johansson: d**

Nässjö - The A-side is quite useless disco-funk, while the B-side is a really good AOR track with quite biting guitars and the traditional keyboards. The singer leaves a bit more to be desired and I'd say this is for collectors only.

| 1990 ■ The Difference/Another Woman | 7" | Büms Records | S90111 |

PROSPERITY

Joakim Mikiver: v, Johnny Jonsson: g, Jim Riggo: b, John Aho: d

Mölnbo (Södertälje) - *Prosperity*, formed in August 2004, play quite well-arranged and quite technical, modern brutal death metal, a bit similar to **Slayer** meets **Cannibal Corpse** at times. Riggo and Mikiver were also in **Caliber 666**, while Aho and Jonsson played with **World Battering**. The band had problems keeping members before the release, and after this nothing has happened, so it may be safe to say they have sadly disbanded.

| 2006 ■ Machine Of Terror | MCDp 3tr | private | - - |
| Tracks: Machine Of Terror/Fragile/Hesitant Way Of Living | | | |

PROUD

**Anders Magnell: v, Peter Horvath: g, Magnus Olsson: g,
Bobby Horvath: b, Anders Holmqvist: d**

Landskrona - The band started out in 1982, at first under the name **Burn**, then **Loud & Proud**, but shortened it to **Proud**. Great, powerful hard rock with elements of **Tygers Of Pan Tang** (on *Crazy Nights*) and **Deep Purple**. The album was produced by Kaj Högberg. In 1985 singer Anders left the band and it fell apart. A digital reissue is planned by EMI Music Sweden, for 2013.

1990 7" - S90111

2006 MCDp - - -

1984 ☐ FIRE BREAKS THE DAWN	CD	EMI	1361522
1984 ■ FIRE BREAKS THE DAWN	LP	EMI	1361521
1984 ☐ FIRE BREAKS THE DAWN	LP	EMI Toshiba (Japan)	EMS-91139
1993 ☐ FIRE BREAKS THE DAWN	CD	EMI Toshiba (Japan)	TOCP-8081
2008 ☐ FIRE BREAKS THE DAWN	CD	Old Metal Records	OMR 44

1984 LP - 1361521

PROVENANCE, THE

Emma Hellström: v/k/f, **Tobias Martinsson:** v/g,
Joakim Rosén: g, **Jonnie Täll:** b,
Joel Lindell: d

Göteborg - The band was formed in 1995 by Emma, Tobias and
Joel, initially under the name *Asmodeus*. They recorded the first
demo *Requiems Of Mankind* later the same year. Now Joakim
was added to the line-up and in 1997 the second demo *Endless
Confinement* saw the light of day. While Emma was working
abroad for a year the remaining quartet changed the name to *The
Provenance*, and recorded the demos *Opus Debris* (1998) and
Fervent Regression (1999). In 1999 Emma returned and Jonnie
completed the line-up. The band describes their sound as "a
majestic blend of sophisticated harmonies and pure headbanging
sequences". Goth-oriented hard rock. In 2005 Täll, Lindell and
Rosén joined **Dark Tranquillity** guitarist Niklas Sundin's side
project **Laethoria**, with whom they have recorded two albums
so far. **The Provenance** has split up.

The lens being spat at?

2006 CD - VILEF 146

2001 ☐	25TH HOUR; BLEEDING	CD	Scarlet	SC 038-2
2002 ☐	25TH HOUR; BLEEDING	CD	Irond (Russia)	CD 02-170
2002 ☐	STILL AT ARMS LENGTH	CDd	Scarlet	SC 056-2
2003 ☐	STILL AT ARMS LENGTH	CD	CD-Maximum (Russia)	CDM 0303-1336
2004 ☐	HOW WOULD YOU LIKE TO BE SPAT AT?	CD	Scarlet	SC 100-2
2005 ☐	HOW WOULD YOU LIKE TO BE SPAT AT?	CD	CD-Maximum (Russia)	CDM 0605-2284
2006 ■	RED FLAGS	CD	Peaceville	VILEF 146

PROWOKE

Niklas Wiik: v/g, **Håkan "Fucko" Skoog:** g/v, **Kenneth Hansson:** b, **Robert Karlsson:** d

Gävle - Raw, gritty hard rock with a punkish attitude and horrible vocals and a lead guitarist
that sounds like he's dead drunk. For collectors only.

1992 ■	Listen Up Girls/Drugs 'N' Hookers	7"	private	- -

1992 7" - - -

PSYCHO CIRCUS

Thomas Larsson: v, **Martin Hoväng:** g, **Ola Sjödin:** b, **Magnus Könberg:** d

Östersund - Slightly grunge-stained, melodic mid-league hard rock. Singer Thomas Larsson
was helping out on the MCD, but he's not actually a member of the band. Daniel Eriksson
later joined as lead singer. In 1993 the first demo cassette *Circles* was released. The track *I Am
Tomorrow* was featured on the *Unsigned Artists 1* (96 TBC) compilation.

1995 ■	Turning Into Grey	MCD 4tr	GLB	GLBCD 5-01-95

Tracks: Open Wide/Emptiness/The Ride/I Am Tomorrow

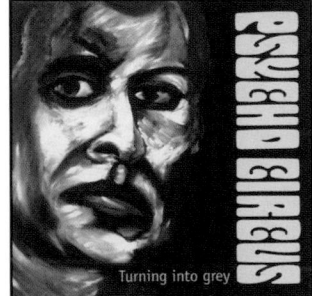
1995 MCD - GLBCD 5-01-95

PSYCHOTIC SUPPER

Patric Fagerberg: v, **Jonas Persson:** g, **Marco Oxala:** g,
Roger Olsson: b, **Lelle Gustavsson:** d

Västerås - The name was probably taken from the album by **Tesla**. However this is traditional-
sounding hard rock/metal with a strong touch of the 80's. Influences from bands like **Kiss**, **AC/
DC** and the mid 80's metal bands. Traditional licks and chord patterns from the beginners book
of metal. Quite disinteresting. Produced by Pelle Saether (**Schizophrenic Circus, Grand Design,
Zello**). A new album was supposed to be released in 1996, but nothing happened.

1995 ■	PSYCHOTIC SUPPER	CD	private	PS CD 001

1995 CD - PS CD 001

PSYCKADELI

Linda Setterborn: v, **Magnus Hansson:** g/k, **Jonas Johansson:** k,
Ulf Hansson: b, **Christian Magnusson:** d

Kristianstad - Formed in 2005. After the CD the band changed line-up, where keyboardist Jonas
was out of the band and drummer Christian had been replaced by Pontus Sköldhammar. In 2012
the band put up new songs on their website, now in a slightly more modern and experimental
vein. Hard rock with a touch of both electronica and goth. Hard to pin-point but it sounds good.
Website: www.psyckadeli.com

2008 ■	CHASING MY SHADOW	CD	ArtShow	ASN/01

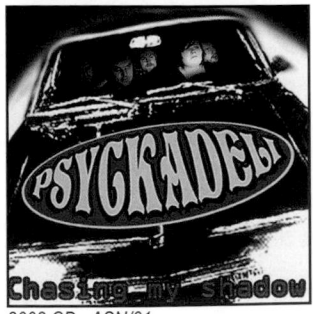
2008 CD - ASN/01

PSYKOTISK

Fredrik "Niltor" Romlin: v/g/b/d

Stockholm - One of the numerous one-man death metal projects, this time by ***Monoscream/ Ornias/Vredgad/Azumfärd*** man Niltor, formed in 2002 and recorded the first demo the same year. In 2003 the demo *Lid* was recorded, followed by *Ångest* in 2004. In 2004 the compilation 2003-2004, featuring the four tracks from *Lid* and *Ångest*, was released in 50 hand-numbered copies on *Cursedcreation*. Jonas "Shugatraa" Mähl (***Torture Eternal, Norrsken, Annihilate, Vituperation***) lays down some guest vocals on some tracks. Niltor also owns Rott Records. Raw and quite badly produced old-school death metal with desperate ***Shining***-style vocals and depressing, suicidal lyrics in Swedish.

2009 CD - REG 050

2009 ■ Psykotisk/Vredgad (split)...CD   Regimental Records ....REG 050
   Split with Vredgad. Tracks: Kallelse/Dödens allians/Anger Of Life/Ge upp ditt hopp. 1000 copies.

PUBLIKFÖRAKT AB

**Mats "Maniac" Ördén: v/k, Janne "Bror Duktig" Ördén: g,
Jesper "Glasse" Arkerud (now Oldberg): b, Pontus Arkerud (now Oldberg): d**

Stockholm - The band was formed late 1979 by the brothers Arkerud (now Oldberg), Pontus (bass) and Jesper (guitar). The name means "Contempt for the audience Inc", a name they took just to make it sound punk, and punk they were. They drafted singer Marie Andersson and her boyfriend Mats Ördén, at first as drummer. Marie was fired and the relationship ended. Mats and Pontus took over the vocal bits, where Pontus handled bass and vocals. The music was punk inspired by ***Stiff Little Fingers***, ***UK Subs*** etc. After a while, Mats' brother Janne learned to play the bass, Pontus took over the drums and Mats went all vocal. Janne got better at playing guitar and took over the guitar parts, while the bass was taken over by Lasse Grönnå, and Jesper got phased out. Now the band had two great guitarists, and Mats took over the bass. The music had now, around 1981, changed to heavy metal, inspired by bands like ***AC/DC*** and ***Iron Maiden***. They now recorded the single, which contained their last punkiest song and their first metal song. After this they found a better singer, named Johnny. The band did some shows, but split late 1983. Johnny later had a career in Italy as a pop singer.

1982 7" - PSI 019

1982 ■ Young rebel/The Night Of Horror ....7"   Pang Records ....PSI 019 $
   500 copies, some with and some without artwork.

PUNISHMENT

Daniel Westerberg: v, Micke Lövquist: g, Pelle Öberg: b, Mikael Öberg: d

Piteå - The band was previously known as ***Infanticide***, then with the addition of guitarist Andreas Fors. ***Punishment*** is out-and-out power thrash with screaming vocals and ripping guitars in the same vein as ***Pantera***.

1995 MCD - DEMOCD 1

1995 ■ Life ....MCD 5tr   private ....DEMOCD 1
   Tracks: Life/Muscle Man/Lust For Pleasure/Erased/Jealousy.

PURPLE HAZE

Peter Martinsson: v/g, Leif Bergquist: g, Tommy Gustafsson: b/v, Ulf Svensson: d

Mönsterås - After the band ***Plebb*** disbanded, Tommy and Peter formed ***Purple Haze***. Quite a mixed bag of sounds. The album starts out rocking and good in the vein of ***Dunder***, but the second track sounds more like ***Dire Straits***. The track *Stad i ruiner* is a killer, though. An uneven ride that costs a fortune today. The vocals are a weak link. In 2010 ***Plebb*** reunited and in 2012 Peter release an outstanding instrumental solo album on Grooveyard Records.

1981 MLP - PLBS 02

1981 ■ Det är så man undrar ....MLP 6tr   private ....PLBS 02 $$
   Tracks:Det är så man undrar/What A Night/Daglig aggression/Stad i ruiner/Linda Eva/ Sommarn 78

PUSSY GALORE

**Anders "Kalkan/Bambi" Glambeck: v, Peter Rode: g, Mikael "Divine" Davidsson: g,
Niklas "Nikki" Bruzell: b, Lars "Lasse Pop" Svensson: d**

Halmstad/Stockholm - This bunch started out as punk band ***Spott*** back in 1977 (featuring stand-up comedian Peter Wahlbeck on vocals), at the time located in Halmstad. Glambeck handled the bass and Svensson drums. Guitarist Peter Rode joined in 1980 and the band became a bit more glam-oriented. Nicki joined and they decided to beef up the sound with Malmö guitarist Fredrik "Feje" Samuelsson. In 1983 they changed the name to ***Pussy Galore*** (after a Bond movie) and the style became glam/sleaze-sounding hard rock with a hint of ***AC/DC***. At times quite close to early ***Easy Action***, with a singer in the same vein as Zinny Zan. Not bad. In 1986 the band imploded due to drug related problems (according to the band's MySpace). Glambeck moved to Stockholm and formed a new line-up featuring guitarists T-Bone and Lou (one of them

1986 MLP - UNT 44

1989 MLP - HIGH 002

named Magnus Bierfeldt), bassist Jukka Vouti and drummer Peter "Perry" Ingman. They now recorded the second effort. Jouko "Jake" Kinnonen (ex-*Hiroshima*) later replaced Vouti. The band broke up. Perry and Jukka later went to *President Gas/Gastones*. T-Bone is now living in the USA. Some of the remaining members from the first line-up formed *Bad Mothers*. In 2009 Anders and Lasse decided to reunite the band. Feje was replaced by Mikael "Divine" Davidsson (ex-*Candystore*). The new songs are in the same style as the old stuff, punkish glam/sleaze.

1986 ■	The Trash Beat `N´ Blues	MLP 4tr	Highscore Records	UNT 44

Tracks: Saturday Night On The Road To Ruin/Climb For The Highscore/C´mon Kiss My Lips (Don´t Mess Up My Hair)/Keep On Lovin´ You. 1000 copies.

1989 ■	Open The Gate	MLP 5tr	Highscore Records	HIGH 002

Tracks: All Night Long/Babylon/Baby Please Don't Go/Share Your Lovin'

2010 □	Red Room Stories	MCD 3tr	Highscore Records	- -

Tracks: God, Jesus Or Pussy Galore/Sometimes Even Rockers Get The Blues/Sweet Angels (I Heard The Sound Of)

2012 ■	THE DIRTY DOWN ADDICTION	CD	Highscore Records	(Y 91965)

2012 CD - (Y 91965)

PUTERAEON

Jonas "Lindblood" Lindblad: v/g, Rune Foss: g,
Daniel Vandija: b, Anders Malmström: d

Alingsås - Puteraeon were formed in 2008 by former *Taetre* guitarist/singer Lindblad. He started recording some demos on his own before he got in touch with Daniel (*13itch*) and Anders (ex-*Nominon, Prophanity, Immemoreal*). In 2008 they recorded the demo *The Requiem*, and soon they were picked up by Cyclone Empire. Guitarist Hasse Sörensen was in the band for a short while, but was replaced by Rune Foss (*Exempt, Reclusion, Aggro*) and the album *The Esoteric Order* was recorded. *Puteraeon* plays hard-edged death metal in the vein of early *Entombed* and *Grave*. The band's second effort was even more dirty and raw in its sound and approach, mixed by Andy LaRocque. Rogga Johansson (*Paganizer* etc.) makes a guest appearance on the album.

2011 □	THE ESOTERIC ORDER	LP	Cyclone Empire	CYC 069 LP
2011 □	THE ESOTERIC ORDER	CD	Cyclone Empire	CYC 069 CD
2012 ■	CULT CTHULU	CD	Cyclone Empire	CYC 091-2
2012 □	CULT CTHULU	LPg	Cyclone Empire	CYC 091-1

500 copies.

2012 CD - CYC 091-2

PYRAMIDO

Ronnie Källback: v, Dan Hedlund: g, Henrik Wendel: g,
Dan Bengtsson: b, Viktor Forss: d

Malmö - Formed in 2006 by drummer Viktor and guitarist Dan. The band aimed at producing sludge metal with the roots in hardcore punk. They were completed by singer Ronnie and bass player Wendel and a first demo was recorded in 2007. The band was picked up by Israeli label Totalrust Music and *Sand* was recorded in 2009. Wendel now switched the bass for a guitar and new bass player Dan entered. Two split records with fellows *Suma* and Germans *Gun Mob* were also unearthed. In 2011 the new album *Salt* was released. Musically they have stuck to their original plan and plays quite slow and very heavy sludge metal with screaming hardcore vocals. The band internally called themselves "AB Långsam Rock" (Slow Rock Inc).
Website: www.pyramido.org

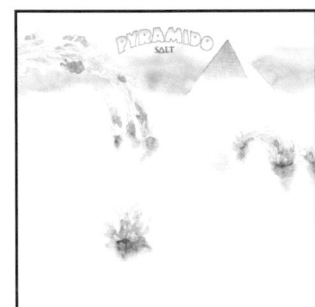

2009 CD - Trust 012

2009 ■	SAND	CD	Totalrust Music	Trust 012
2010 □	Pyramido/Suma(split)	12"	Head Records	HR 015

Split with Suma. Tracks: No Words/I grevens tid

2010 ■	Pyramido/Gun Mob (split)	CD	Ecocentric Records	E.R. 172 CD

Split with Gun Mob. Tracks: In Sovereign Contempt/Our Last Days

2010 □	Pyramido/Gun Mob (split)	LP	Behindf The Scenes	BTS #31
2011 □	SALT	CD	Totalrus Music	Trust 019
2011 □	SALT	LP	Mourningwood Recordings	MWR 004LP
2013 □	Pyramido/Unsurpress (split)	7"	Plague Island	9th Boil

Split with Unsurpress. Track: Serenity. 400 copies.

2013 □	Pyramido/Unsurpress (split) - Wicked Edition	2x7"	Plague Island	9th Boil

Same as above + Bonus single in green or red vinyl, Bonus: Fed Up (Judge cover). 100 copies.

2010 CD - E.R.172 CD

PÄST

Rikard Mårtensson: v, Mattias Jonsson: g, Ulf Andersson: b, Jan Andersson: d

Linköping - AC/DC-influenced hard rock with punkish vocals and very explicit lyrics. The band name is "plague" in English and the title of side A... well I guess you can imagine. The band also featured drummer Stefan Halldin (now in *Maryscreek*). Rikard, Mattias, Ulf and Stefan later formed *The Social Scumbags*, continuing in the same vein.

1990 ■	Hora/Surrounded By Crabs	7"	Rock Karusellen	SFSI 8

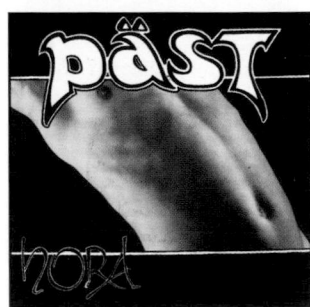

1990 7" - SFSI 8

QOPH
Rustan Geschwind: v, Filip Norman: g, Patrik Persson: b, Federico de Costa: d

Stockholm - The debut album sounds like it was recorded in 1972, which is impossible since the band was formed in 1994. The sound is at times very similar to **November**, but with an even more experimental sort of **King Crimson**:ish touch, at times similar to the more modern **Mars Volta**. The vocals are in Swedish. "*Psychedelic poetry, monotony and dynamic improvising mixed with blues and acid*", is the band's description. Guitarist Jimmy Wahlsteen, who left before the second album, was ex-**Blue Matter**, and is today a renowned acoustic player. They have also recorded a very original version of *Dancing Madly Backwards* for the **Captain Beyond** tribute *Thousand Days Of Yesterdays* (99 Record Heaven). In their Swedish version it's called *Dansar galet bakåt*. When they received more attention from outside Sweden, they changed to English on *Pyrola*. An excellent band well worth investigating. **Qoph** is the nineteenth letter in many Arabic alphabets, similar to Q, K or CK. After seven years of silence the band suddenly unleashed their heaviest album to date, *Freaks*, proving they were definitely back in action. A true masterpiece! The line-up now saw the change from singer Robin Kvist to Rustan Geschwind. *Website: www.qoph.se*

1998 CD - RHCD 11

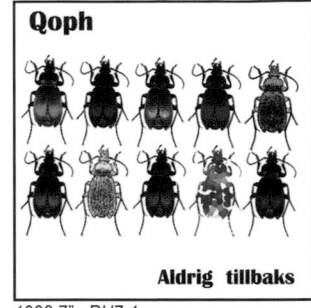

Aldrig tillbaks

1998 7" - RH7-1

Än lyser månen

1999 MCD - RHCDM 6

1998 ■	KALEJDOSKOPISKA AKTIVITETER	CD	Record Heaven	RHCD 11
1998 ■	Aldrig Tillbaks/Månvarv (live)	7"	Record Heaven	RH7-1
	200 orange + 300 black vinyl.			
1999 ■	Än Lyser Månen/Dansar galet bakåt/Ögonblick	MCDp 3tr	Record Heaven	RHCDM 6
1999 ☐	KALEJDOSKOPISKA AKTIVITETER	2LP	Record Heaven	RHLP 1
	Bonus: Kalejdoskopiska aktiviteter			
2004 ☐	PYROLA	CD	Káleidophone	KALCD1
2004 ☐	PYROLA	2LP	Nasoni Records	NASONI 026B
	Black vinyl			
2004 ☐	PYROLA	2LP	Nasoni Records	NASONI 026C
	Coloured vinyl			
2005 ☐	PYROLA	CD	Arcanciel (Japan)	ARC-1087
	Bonus: Resh/Will The Sun Be Back Tomorrow			
2012 ☐	FREAKS	CDd	Nasoni Records	NASONI 126
2012 ☐	FREAKS	LP	Transubstans	TRANS 106

QUADRUPLE
Johnny Lundgren: v/g, Dan Lundgren: g, Danne Johansson: b, Anders Swanholm: d

Malmö - Great heavy rockers with lots of interesting ideas and arrangements. They were formed around 1987 by brothers Johnny and Dan and were previously known as **Sidewinder**. Drummer Mats Björklund from **Aces High** plays on the single. The band later recorded a demo, where they had sharpened their sound and attitude and was more or less a power metal-unit. The cover on the single was made by Dick Qwarforth (**Nasty Idols**' bass-player). After some years of silence the band returned with the self-titled album. The line-up still featured the Lundgrens, while bass player Patrik Bengtsson had been replaced by Danne Johansson and the drums were handled by Anders Swanholm.

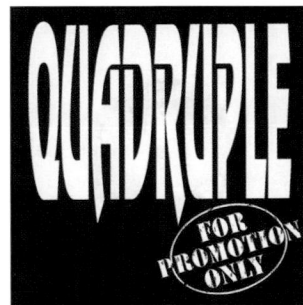

1990 7" - BM1015

1990 ■	Abuse/Your Point Of View	7"	private	BM1015
	The cover is stamped "For Promotion Only" on all copies.			
2004 ☐	QUADRUPLE	CD	Fast Forward	FFR 451

QUARTERBACK BEAT
Sebastian Lilja: v/g, Tobias Holst: k, Fredrik Grähs: b, Fredrik P-zon: d

Höganäs - Formed in 1989 by Sebastian and Tobias. Straightforward basic hard rock with dominating keyboards, quite uncomplicated and with an amateurish feel to it. Good vocals, though. For collectors only. After the EP they have however produced some highly interesting demo-material. The tracks *Me, Myself And I* and *Liquid Lust* are found on the compilation *Malmöhus Landsting* (94 FAB Records) and a live version of *Me, Myself....* can also be found on *Musik Direkt Skånefinal* (94 - MIS 2). The last known line-up featured Sebastian, now mostly on guitar, Tobias (k), Helena and Petra Vadsten (v), drummer Fredrik Eriksson and a new, at the time unnamed, bass player.

1991 7" - UNI 2467

1991 ■	Nasty Fingers/Guilty Of The Crime (split)	7" 5tr	UNI	UNI 2467
	Split with Jonny Batong.			

QUEE, MARC
Marcelo "Marc Quee" Quiroga: v, Quint Starkie: g,
Håkan Sten: k, Björn Melander: b, Peter Lundgren: d

Stockholm - Very FM-oriented AOR, with mid-class vocals. Same track on both sides on the first 7", same track as on the B-side on the second 7"... Björn Melander was previously in **Mogg**, **Neptune** and **Gotham City**. The members from the band **Mogg** handle the backing vocals. Marc tried out for **Talisman**, with a demo as proof, but it didn't work out. He then moved to France,

1989 7" - FLCS 1037

625

joined **Attentat Rock** and sang on their third album, *Strike*. The band turned into **Pink Rose**, who also recorded one album. Marc's vocals had now improved quite a lot. He then relocated to Tenerife, where he has made over one thousand performances in a Freddy Mercury Show and he was also in a **Pink Floyd** tribute. He has now become an outstanding singer.

1989 ■	Queen Of The Night/Queen Of The Night	7"	Four Leaf Clover	FLCS 1037
1989 ■	Till Heaven Calls Our Name/Queen Of The Night	7"	Four Leaf Clover	FLCS 1040

1989 7" - FLCS 1040

QUEEN OBSCENE

Kent Brandin: v/k, Niclas Blomquist: g,
Peter Gustafsson: b, Martin Lous-Christensen: d

Stockholm - Glam rockers **Queen Obscene** were formed in the summer of 1991 by singer Brandin and drummer Peter Gustafsson. They drafted guitarist Anders Hansson and bassist Pontus Norgren (not the **HammerFall** guitarist). In 1993 Hansson and Norgren left and the band was put on hold for a year, until Gustafsson switched to bass and guitarist Blomquist joined. Later the same year Lous-Christensen completed the band. They entered Thunderload Studios and recorded a demo. In 1997 they participated in the commercial for Arla Minimjölk. A record deal was however never signed. In 1999 the band finally recorded their own CD, also recorded at Thunderload Studios. **Queen Obscene** plays glam metal with raw guitars but quite poppy overtones and rather weak vocals, unfortunately not very exciting, even though some tracks will attract fans of bands like **Big Bang Babies** etc.

1998 ■	TO BE CONTINUED…	CD	Glamtastix Records	glamstix 001
	500 copies.			

1998 CD - glamstix 001

QUEENSLAND

Matti Joutsen: v. Lennart "Lello" Gustafsson: g, Kent Gustafsson: b, Örjan Wiberg: d

Askersund - **Queensland** were formed in 1990, featuring former **Adventure** members Joutsen and Gustafsson, and split in 1994. The single is a pretty decent sleazy hard rocker.

1990 ■	Rock 'N Roll Train/Bad Girl	7"	Rolab	RM 1106
	500 copies.			

1990 7" - RM 1106

QUEST OF AIDANCE

Daniel "Daaz" Valström: v, Christian Älvestam: v/g, Christian Lundgren: b

Skövde - **Quest Of Aidance** were formed in 2004 by Älvestam (**Incapacity, Miseration, Solution .45, Torchbearer, Unmoored, Solar Dawn, Angel Blake, Scar Symmetry, Syconaut**) and Lundgren (**Carnalized** and **Vomitus**). After the material for the first demo, *Human Trophy*, had been written, Älvestam switched from drums to guitar and vocals and the duo was completed by bassist Anders Johansson and drummer Henrik Schönström. The quartet now recorded the demo, which later was rereleased with new title and artwork as the *Fallen Man Collection* and contains eight tracks at a total length of just over ten minutes. In 2006 the band was completed with guitarist Jonas Kjellgren, while Johansson was out and Lundgren took over the bass. *The Dark Are The Skies At Hand* EP was now recorded. In 2010 the band announced a new line-up for the recording of the debut album, now featuring Anders Johansson on vocals (low growls), Daniel "Daaz" Valström (**Syconaut**) on vocals (high growls), Christian Älvestam (g/b/k), Christian Lundgren (g) and Jani Stefanovic (**DivineFire**) handling session drums. When the album, *Misanthropic Propaganda*, was finally unearthed in 2013 the line-up was down to a trio featuring Älvestam, Lundgren and Valström. The album features some great guest spots from Johan Randén, Patrik Gardberg (**Ammotrack, Torchbearer, Solution .45**) and Oscar Nilsson (**Miseration, Despite, Saint Deamon**).

2006 MCD . ASH 017M-CD

2006 ■	Fallen Man Collection	MCD 8tr	Pulverised	ASH 017M-CD
	Tracks: Imminence/Distant World Arrival/The Hunter And The Prey/Vanishment/Man In The Harvest/Cranial Works Of Art/7th Target/Yield			
2007 ■	Dark Are The Skies At Hand	10" 5tr	Pulverised	ASH 035 EP
	Tracks: Distant World Arrival/Sirian Breed/Yautjan Overture/Yield/Red Dust/Soundtrack To Hish. 300 copies, hand numbered.			
2013 □	MISANTHROPIC PROPAGANDA	CD	Pulverised	ASH 104 CD

2007 10" - ASH 035 EP

QUICKSAND DREAM

Göran Jacobson: v, Patrik Backlund: g/b/d

Timrå - Formed in 1988, at first as **Epic Irae**. They recorded several demos, but when featured on the *Metal North* (93 Massproduktion) compilation they changed their name to **Quicksand Dream**. The name was taken from a track on a bootleg by the band **Necromandus**. However, it later showed the label had mixed up the titles and it was actually entitled *Orexis Of Death*. *Quicksand Dreams* was a song by **Slowbone**, on the same label. The band split in 1993, but Jacobson and Backlund continued on their own. In 1999 they recorded a concept album, only released as a CD-R in 30 copies. However nearly two decades later they were picked up by Planet

2010 LPg - HRR 099

Metal Records, which gave the album a proper release. Well-played and sung, classic semi-progressive metal in the vein of *Manilla Road*, early *Fates Warning* and Swedish *Behemoth*. Henrik Flyman (*Moahni Moahna*) guests on keyboards. Patrik is also found in *Mortalicum*. The unreleased *Epic Irae* demos were released as a double disc in 2012.

2011 ☐	AELIN – A STORY ABOUT DESTINY	CD	Planet Metal	PM 010	
2010 ■	AELIN – A STORY ABOUT DESTINY	LPg	High Roller Records	HRR 099	
	150 clear + 350 black vinyl.				
2012 ■	DREAMS AND DELUSIONS 1989-1993	2CD	Evil Confrontation Records	EC 02	
	Release as Epic Irae.				

2012 2CD - EC 02

QUILL, THE (aka QUIL)
Magnus Arnar: v, Christian Carlsson: g, Robert Triches: b, George "Jolle" Atlagic: d

Mönsterås - The first two 7"'s and the debut album was recorded under the name *Quil*. On the first single Mats Johansson handled the bass and Tommy Carlsson the vocals. Back then the music was more traditional melodic hard rock with quite mainstream vocal efforts. Mats was then replaced by Peter Karlsson (aka Holm) and Magnus Ekwall replaced Tommy. In 1992 the band changed their name to *The Quill*. This marked a new era for the band, where they had now turned into a fully fledged seventies sounding heavy rock band with top quality songs and performance. Singer Magnus Ekwall has a great bluesy style of singing even though he's got a pretty high pitch voice. The demo that lead to the band's deal with Megarock was entitled *Another Fruitful Day* (1993) but out of the 10 tracks, only one made it onto the album. *The Quill* is an extraordinary productive band and they still keep a high standard. The Megarock-album is a killer for fans of Hammond-stained 70s influenced hard rock with a slightly hippyish feel but still not sounding dated. Bass-player Roger Nilsson replaced Peter Karlsson (Holm) in the beginning of 1994. On *Silver Haze* the band slightly changed their style to even more outstanding heavy stoner-tainted power riffing with strong hints of bands like *Spiritual Beggars* and *Black Sabbath*. This also meant dropping keyboard player Anders Haglund. *Voodoo Caravan* is even more stonerized with totally fuzzed out bass and guitar, not as riff-oriented as its predecessor and a more garagy approach. Still a great album. Roger was also found in *Spiritual Beggars* and Mike Amott guests on the album. In 2005 bass player Roger Nilsson left the band and was replaced by Robert Triches. After the *In Triumph* tours singer Magnus Ekwall and the band also parted ways. *The Quill* was on a hiatus and drummer Atlagic joined *Hanoi Rocks* and also did a stint in *Hanoi Rocks* guitarist Andy McCoy's band *The Real McCoy Band*. In 2010 the band again gathered forces. Now singer Magnus "Magz" Arnar (*Ground Mower*) joined the band and with the new album *Full Circle* the band proved they were back on track with a vengeance, going back to the heavy, riff oriented seventies influenced hard rock. The line-up on this album featured Magnus Arnar, Christian Karlsson, Robert Triches and Jolle Atlagic. In April 2012 Triches parted ways with the band and former bassist Roger Nilsson returned again. Atlagic has also recorded an album with UK retro rockers *Firebird*, while former bassist Nilsson played on the same *Firebird* album, and with bands like *Spiritual Beggars* and *Arch Enemy*. Ekwall later teamed up with former *Treasure Land* guitarist Jonas Hörnqvist in the band *Burning Mustard* and he also did some guest vocals in prog rockers *Ayreon*. The band is also featured on compilations such as; *Thousand Days Of Yesterdays - A Tribute To Captain Beyond* (99 Record Heaven), where they do *Thousand Days Of Yesterdays (intro)* and *Frozen Over*. On the Swedish hard rock tribute, *Power From The North*, they do the English version of *November*'s *Mount Everest*, on *Bastards Will Pay - A Tribute To Trouble* (99 Freedom) they contribute with *A Sinner's Fame* and on the *Iron Maiden*-tribute *Slave To The Power* (00, MCY 009/Victor Japan VICP-61151), they do *Where Eagles Dare*. The previously unreleased track *Unbroken* can be found on the compilation *Judge Not...* (00, Underdogma, UR001-61701). *Website: www.thequill.se*

Hooray, it's The Quill!

1991 7" - QUIL S-01

1986 7" - S 020

1997 MCD - QUILL 001

1986 ■	Read It In Your Eyes/Hiroshima (When Will It End)	7"	Zamba	S 020	$
	500 copies. As Quil.				
1989 ☐	Out Of The Blue Corners	LP	Büms	BR 90123	
	1000 copies. As Quil.				
1991 ■	Good Times/Our Lovin' Is A Funky Thing	7"	private	QUIL S-01	
	As Quil.				

Year		Title	Format	Label	Catalogue
1995	□	THE QUILL	CD	Megarock	MRRCD 023
1997	■	The Quill	MCD 4tr	Warner/Chappell	QUILL 001

Promo. Tracks: Where The Lovelight Shines/Silver Haze/Sparrow/Unbroken (non-album)

| 1999 | □ | SILVER HAZE | CD | Roxon | RX9651.2 |
| 1999 | □ | Evermore | 10" 4tr | Froghouse | FROG 005 |

Tracks Evermore/Silver Haze/The Sparrow/Fairies Wear Boots (Black Sabbath cover). Blue vinyl. 1000 copies.

| 2000 | □ | THE QUILL | CD | Meteor City (USA) | MCY 008 |

Re-issue of the first album with new artwork and minus the songs Jet Of Water and Gleam, but plus A Sinner's Fame (Trouble-cover) and a hidden live-version of I Lost A World Today.

| 2000 | □ | THE QUILL | LP | People Like You | PRISON 993-1 |

Transparent brown vinyl.

| 2000 | □ | THE QUILL | CDd | People Like You | PRISON 993-2 |

Different tracks.

| 2001 | □ | VOODOO CARAVAN | CD | Victor (Japan) | VICP 61504 |

Bonus: Gather Round The Sun/Thousand Years.

2001	■	VOODOO CARAVAN	CD	Steamhammer	SPV 085-72572 CD
2002	□	THE QUILL	CD	CD-Maximum (Russia)	CDM 0903-1486
2003	□	HOORAY IT'S A DEATHTRIP	CD	Steamhammer	SPV 085-69382 CD
2003	□	HOORAY IT'S A DEATHTRIP	CD	CD-Maximum (Russia)	CDM 0903-1861
2006	□	IN TRIUMPH	CD	Steamhammer	SPV 085-99832 CD
2006	□	IN TRIUMPH	CD	Soyus (Russia)	SPV 085-99832 CD
2011	□	FULL CIRCLE	CDd	Metalville	MV 017
2013	□	TIGER BLOOD	CDd	Metalville	MV 037

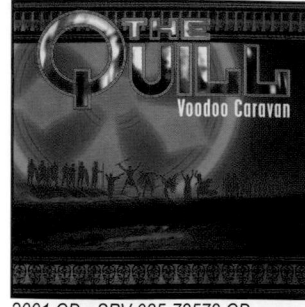

2001 CD - SPV 085-72572 CD

1980 7" - QZS 101

QUINZY
Mikael Lans: v, Terje Hjortander: g, Mikael Lindström: g, Göran Nylén: b, Per Warger: d

Göteborg - *Rosie* is a semi-heavy hard rock ballad with quite interesting guitar work. The B-side is a ballsy boogie-metal tune. Terje later joined and recorded with **Forest**, **Leviticus** and **The Jet Circus**. The band also had the two more commercial tracks *Marie Marie* and *Jessie* featured on the compilation *Made In GBG* (LP 1092 Pang).

| 1980 | ■ | Rosie/Boogie | 7" | private | QZS 101 |

QUIX
Lars Göransson: v, Ulf Wiglund: g, Göran Forssén: b, Thomas Fager: d

Helsingborg - Melodic hard rock of medium-quality. Quite simple songs. **Quix** was formed in 1980 and was disbanded four years later. Lars and Ulf later recorded some demos with the band **Red Hot**. Ulf was later found in the excellent heavy rock band **Dogman** that only made some demo recordings. Göran has played in various band and projects, both rock, jazz and funk.

| 1981 | ■ | Quix | 7" 4tr | Kraftpop | KOP-200 $ |

Tracks: Speed/IT Will Be Alright/Le Me Go With You/Please Don't Go. 100 copies in gold and 400 in silver printing on cover.

1981 7" - KOP-200

QUIZ
Michael Nilsson: v/g, Johan Öhrnell: v/b, Jarmo Miettinen: g, Robert Werngren: d

Karlstad - The band was formed in 1981. The first single is heads-down-no-nonsense-straight-rock-n-roll with Swedish lyrics, while the A-side on the second is more in the vein of **Status Quo**. Nothing special. The band is still around, either as the band **Quiz** or as **Status Quiz**, playing only **Quo**-songs. The members were then Johan, Jarmo, Michael Gustafsson (g) and Christer Lindström (d).

| 1986 | ■ | 8 st. i en Cheva/Digga rock 'n roll | 7" | Aktiv Musik | HEJ 013 |
| 1990 | □ | Come Back To Me/Rock & roll & raggaråk | 7" | Active Music | HEJ S-037 |

1986 7" - HEJ 013

QUOLIO
Michael Carlsson, Ulf Örtensjö

Göteborg - Pretty decent AOR/melodic hard rock. Produced by Jonas Kuling. Örtensjö has also recorded some solo material.

| 1987 | ■ | Girls On My Mind/Waiting For You | 7" | Rox | KUL 8712 |

1987 7" - KUL 8712

QUORTHON

Quorthon, back in the early days of Bathory.

QUORTON

Thomas Ace "Quorthon" Forsberg: v/g

Stockholm - This is **Bathory** main man Quorthon's solo project and it's quite far from the brutal death metal of his main project. *Album* contains great heavy rock with Quorthon actually singing clean. Check out the song *Rain* for heavy riffing, quite close to **Alice In Chains** first album. Quorthon was actually called Ace Shot on the first **Bathory** recordings and he managed to keep his real name a secret all those years. The speculations were many and quite interesting, such as one German magazine claiming it was Runka Snorkråka, (Wank Snot) and a Norwegian encyclopedia revealed it to be Pugh Rogefeldt (a much older Swedish rock/pop singer). He wasn't born Ace, but officially took the name later on. Thomas is the son of Börje "Boss" Forsberg, founder of Black Mark records. On the foreword of the **Bathory** album *Blood On Ice*, he killed all the mythical rumours about the recordings of the early albums. All the blood, guts and satanic mysteries were actually created in an old garage. The drums were partly a drum-machine etc. He also called the whole satanic bit a "fake", which was not very popular in the eyes of all the newborn little metal Satanists who saw Quorthon more or less as the evil one himself. On the website Quorthon himself described the origin of the solo albums like this: "The solo albums were not the true side of me or a reflection of what I really want to do. Not even I had the slightest idea what that would come out as or sound like. I just wrote some material blending **Sex Pistols**, **The Beatles**, Kate Bush, **Mountain** and traditional garage rock and what have you, just to see what that would feel like doing. I would read the newspapers every morning to find ideas for lyrics, trying to land as far away from traditional **Bathory** lyrics as possible." On June 3, 2004 Quorthon (born January 17, 1966) sadly died of heart failure. Early 2004 he and his younger sister Jennie Tebler were making a recording together. It was never finished, but Jennie released this, the single *Silverwing*, as a tribute to her brother.

1994 CD - BMCD 666-9

1997 2CD - BMCD 666-13

1997 MCD - BMCD 666-14

Quorthon 17/1-1966-3/6-2004. R.I.P.

1994 MCD - BMCD 666-9P

2006 2CD - BMCD 666-13

Year		Title	Format	Label	Cat. No.
1994	■	ALBUM	CD	Black Mark	BMCD 666-9
1994	☐	ALBUM	LP	Black Mark	BMCD 666-9
1997	■	PURITY OF ESSENCE	2CD	Black Mark	BMCD 666-13
1997	■	When Our Day Is Through	MCD 4tr	Black Mark	BMCD 666-14
		Tracks: When Our Day Is Through/Cherrybutt & Firefly/An Inch Above The Ground/I've Had It Coming My Way			
1994	●	Single	MCD 3tr	Black Mark	BMCD 666-9P
		Promo. Tracks: No More And Never Again/Feather/Boy In The Bubble			
2002	☐	ALBUM	CD	Black Mark	BMCD 666-9
		Remastered.			
2006	■	PURITY OF ESSENCE	2CD	Black Mark	BMCD 666-13
		Remastered.			

Unofficial releases:
1994	☐	ALBUM	CD	Audi (Russia)	- -

R & R

Mikael "Herman" Long: v, Fredrik "Hilding" Forsén: g,
Jörgen "Holger" Bihagen: k, Thomas "Helge" Carlsson: d

Kiruna - Formed in 1980. The letters do not stand for "Rock & Roll" as might be anticipated, but "Rom & Russin" (Rum & Raisins). They were influenced by bands like *Iron Maiden* and *Europe* and they actually fit in just between. *R & R* had the melodic side of *Europe* and the intensity of *Maiden*. However musically they were more a diamond in the rough. If they hadn't split, they would probably have been a great band today.

1984 7" - CTR-984

1984 ■ Adventures Behind The Eye/The Way Of Evil ....7" private ....CTR-984 $

R.A.W

Bo Lindmark: v, Mikael Larson: g, Anders Lindmark: b, Adam Kårsnäs: d

Uppsala - *R.A.W* stands for "Ready And Willing" and musically the band stands for highly traditional AOR in the same vein as *Snakes In Paradise*. Catchy chorus parts, well-arranged harmonies, rough-edged guitars, quite FM-oriented and very professional. Bo and Anders toured and recorded two albums with *Dalton* between 1986 and 1991. The band originally recorded the album for Soundfront Records in 1994, but the label sadly folded. The album also features guest spots from Ian Haugland (*Europe*), Tommy Nilsson (*Horizont*, solo) and Zia Lindberg. The band split shortly after the release of the second album. Before joining *R.A.W*, Mikael played in the band *Fusion*, who had a song on a compilation 1991. Bo is today playing with cover band *The Playboys* and Mikael is in *Coldspell*. *Dalton* reunited in 2011.

1996 CDS - 29050505

1997 CD - SEP 195 05 07

1994	☐ First time love/Believe	CDS 2tr	Soundfront	FRONTCD 8
1995	☐ FIRST	CD	Septima	SEP 195 050 2
1995	☐ Don't Tell Me Lies/It Just Came Down	CDS 2tr	Septima	SEP 295 050 1
	The track It Just Came Down is non-CD.			
1996	■ I Believe/I Believe (acoustic)	CDS 2tr	Septima	29050505
1996	☐ Everybody/7 Wonders	CDS 2tr	Septima	29050506
1997	■ NOW WE'RE COOKIN'	CD	Septima	SEP 195 05 07
2004	☐ FIRST	CD	MTM Classix	0681-95
	Bonus: It Just Came Down/I Believe. New artwork.			

RFP

Joakim "Jocke" E Ramsell: g/b/h, Marcus Jäderholm: b, Nils "Nisse" Bielfeld: v/d/k

Fjärdhundra - *RFP* was an excellent band/project (that always interacted with the international soccer world cup) with a huge variety of styles represented. Some tracks are heavy blues, some are instrumental heavy rock with outstanding guitar-playing from Jocke and some tracks are power metal. However, the common factor is high quality and despite the varied styles, the albums don't feel split. Highly recommended. Nisse is also found in *Clench* and *Sixcoveredkissongs*. Prog icon Pär Lindh guests on keyboards. For those who wonder, *RFP* stands for "Ramsell For President". Jocke and Nisse have both been members of *Pär Lindh Project* and made their first release with the band *Surrender* in 1991. Jocke has played with poppier acts such as Carola etc. *Minutes* was written and recorded in three days for a USA tour with *Per Lindh Project*.

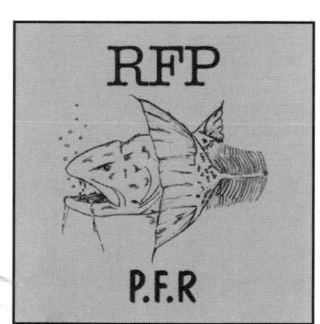

1995 CD - RFPCD 01

1998 CD - RFPCD 03

1995	■ P.F.R	CD	Azora	RFPCD 01
1998	■ MINUTES	CD	private	RFPCD 03

RACEWAY

Patrick Hedqvist: v/g, Lasse Hedlund: b, Conny Lind: v/d

Stockholm - Formed in 1986. An OK southern-sounding band, nothing exceptionally exciting, but still good. The MCD contains covers by *The Sweet*, *AC/DC*, *Grand Funk* etc, and all the albums contain covers of for example *Judas Priest*, *ZZ Top*, *AC/DC*, *The Black Crowes*, *Metallica*, *Status Quo*, *ABBA* etc. After the single singer Conny Lind also took over the drums after Jorma Kytölä. In 1996 they participated in the TV-show Aim At The Stars as *AC/DC* and also backed the late Swedish rockers Svullo and Eddie Meduza on stage. On the second album guitarist Larsa Åström was out of the band, replaced by Micke Nilsson. In 2005 Conny (*Amaze Me*, *State Of Mind*) was out, replaced by drummer Patrik Sviberg and singer Robert Eriksson. Conny is now in the band *Mud & Blood*. On *Decades of Rock,* Conny returned on drums and vocals, adding new guitarist Patrick Hedqvist. The band is still active as a cover band, today featuring Hedlund, guitarist/singer Björn Melin and drummer Mats "Malli" Håxell (*Pike, Hellinor*).

1994 MCD - RACECD 9709

1992 7" - LOL S-92001

2000 CD - CD 2000

1992	■ Lady Of Love/Whisky Retribution	7"	private	LOL S-92001
1994	■ From The Road	MCD 5tr	private	RACECD 9709
	Tracks: Rolling And Tumbling (trad)/High On A Horse (Grand Funk cover)/Manic Depression (Hendrix cover)/Ballroom Blitz (Sweet cover)/Thunderstruck (AC/DC cover)			
2000	■ MILLENJAM	CD	private	CD 2000
2001	☐ ARMED WITH ROCK	CD	private	- -
2008	☐ DECADES OF ROCK	CD	private	- -

RADIOACTIVE

Tommy Denander: g/k

Stockholm - *Radioactive* is the ultimate brainchild of guitarist Tommy Denander, where the debut was in the making for over ten years. The basic tracks were recorded already in 1991 and it was among the latest recordings the original *Toto*-boys did together as a studio-job. The list of musicians playing on this album is like a who's-who of pro studio musicians, including: Jeff Porcaro, Steve Porcaro, Mike Porcaro, Bruce Gaitsch, Fergie Fredriksen, Jason Scheff, Bobby Kimball, David Paitch, Fee Waybill, David Foster, David Hungate, Vince DiCola and Randy Goodrum. Among the Swedish musicians we find Jim Jidhed, Geir Rönning, Kristoffer Lagerström, Marcus Liliequist, Mats Olausson, Pierre Wensberg and Andreas Eklundh. A taster from the album (and now found as bonus-track on the Japanese version) was found on the bonus-CD for the first encyclopedia, *Remember My Conscience*. The song appears in a different version as a hidden track on the album. Musically this is top notch *Toto*:esque, but quite hard-edged AOR. An album well worth waiting for all these years and actually without feeling dated. The second album, *Yeah*, didn't take as long and features an equally interesting bunch of musicians, such as Marcel Jacob, Tony Franklin, Bruce Gaitch, Mikael Erlandsson as well as some from the first album. All three albums are filled with high-class AOR, and were re-issued as a box set in 2013, with six bonus tracks plus a few rerecordings with new singers.

2001 CD - 0681-32

2005 CD - 0681-151

2001 ■	CEREMONY OF INNOCENCE	CD	MTM	0681-32
2001 ☐	CEREMONY OF INNOCENCE	CD	Avalon Marquee (Japan)	MICP 10244
	Bonus: Remember My Conscience			
2003 ☐	YEAH	CD	MTM	0681-61
2003 ☐	YEAH	CD	King Records (Japan)	KICP-938
	Bonus: Somewhere, Someday			
2005 ■	TAKEN	CD	MTM	0681-151
2005 ☐	TAKEN	CD+DVD	MTM	0681-150
2005 ☐	TAKEN	CD	King Records (Japan)	KICP-1123
	Bonus: The Darkness Inside			
2013 ☐	LEGACY	3CD	Escape	ESM 257
	All three albums. Bonus: Shooting Stars/Somewhere, Someday/Juliet/Feel My Heart Again/Remember My Conscience/The Darkness Inside			

RAILROAD

Fredrik Löfdahl: v/g, Anders Granlund: g, Jonas Öhgren: b, Patrik Andersson: d

Tidaholm - *Need Someone* is a great seventies-sounding quite heavy *Status Quo*-inspired hard rocker, while *All Right Now* is a cover of the old *Free* tune. Great singer! Well worth looking for! The record was produced by Patrik Tibell (*T'Bell, CC Rock*).

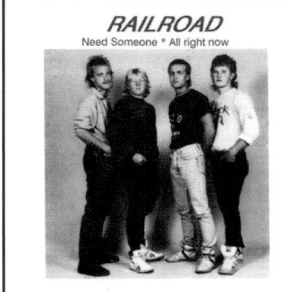

1988 7" - PL 47

1988 ■	Need Someone/All Right Now (Free cover)	7"	Platina	PL 47

RAIN

Tony Westin: v, Claes Edvardsson: g, Ulf Carlsson: g, Eric Asplund: b, Mats Nelin: d

Stockholm - Both songs are straightforward boogie hard rock, and they are actually chants for the local football team Haga Boys, who acts as choir on the single. The B-side is a hard rock version of *When The Saints* with different lyrics. Drummer Mats Nelin was not a member of the band.

1990 7" - HBS 001

1990 ■	Haga Boys/Saints Of Haga	7"	Regn	HBS 001

RAINFALL

Björn Lodin: v/g, Peter Lagestam: g, Lempe Rodin: b, Christer Frost: d

Rättvik - Typical British-sounding 80s heavy metal. Björn recorded the song *Skywalker* with locals *Gathering Freak* in 1981, formed *Six Feet Under* in 1982, and then went on to *Baltimoore*. He has later recorded with *BALLS, H.A.R.D* and as a solo artist. On this single he did not have the same vocal capacity as later in *Baltimoore*.

1980 7" - S-4880

1980 ■	End Of My Love/Laura	7"	Click	S-4880 $
	500 copies.			

RAINMAKER

Geir Rönning: v, Tommy Denander: g, Tony Franklin: b, Walter Dego: d

Stockholm - Yet another brainchild of guitar-wiz Tommy Denander. This time he brought *Prisoner* singer Geir and *Blue Murder*/*The Firm*/*Whitesnake*-bassist Franklin into the line-up. Good, solid melodic hard rock. The band was also featured on various compilations, such as *Sacred Groove, Classic Rock, Musically Correct 4, Musically Correct 5, Rock The Nations* and *Rock The Nations II*.

2000 CD - ZR 1997033

2000 ■	RAINMAKER	CD	Z Records	ZR1997033

RAISE CAIN

Bo Florin: v, Sven Cirnski: g, Mats Jeppsson: b, Bert Lundgren: d

Malmö - The band started when Bo, who wasn't actually a singer, told Mats he wanted to record a single and asked him and the others to back him. Bo paid for the single, and things started evolving from that. Sven is a man of many faces, who has played and is playing with bands like *Bad Habit, Bai Bang, Jet Set Baby, Truth* etc. He has done studio jobs for bands like *Snake Charmer, Project L.E.E, Pete Blakk* and *Pagan. Raise Cain* grew from a sleaze-influenced rock band on the 7", to an aggressive out and out metal-core band. *Stench* is a real kick in the joint that should attract fans of *Helmet, Pantera* and such. Jeppsson today plays in rockabilly punksters *69-Hard*.

1992 7" - DEM 001

1992 ■	Crash 'N Burn/Downtown	7"	Demolition	DEM 001
1994 ☐	Call It Whatever You Want	MCD 6tr	Demolition	DEM 94002
	Tracks: Can't Break Me Down/I Hate!/With A Bullet/Wnough/Taste The Pain/Scumbags			
	Callin'.1050 copies.			
1995 ☐	STENCH	CD	Mascot	M 7012 2

RAISE HELL

Jimmy Fjällendahl: v, Jonas Nilsson: v, Joakim Kulo: g,
Niklas Sjöström: b, Dennis Ekdahl: d

Tyresö (Stockholm) - Raise Hell started out as a young but very competent death-band in the vein of *Dissection*, with an average-age of 18. They were previously called *In Cold Blood*, under which name they recorded their only demo *Nailed*. The first album was recorded at Studio Abyss. Dennis was also found in, at the time, metal side-project *Crash Dïet*, which we all know what happened to. On *Not Dead Yet* the band strayed away from the death metal towards a more thrash-oriented sound. After *Wicked Is My Game,* Jonas Nilsson (*Sins Of Omission, Mortifier, Signo Rojo*) handed the lead vocals over to new singer Fjällendahl and concentrated on playing guitar. In 2004 guitarist Torstein Wickberg left the band and was replaced by Joakim Kulo. Ekdahl is also found in *Rutthna*, and formerly in *Machinery, Mortifier, Siebenbürgen, Mystic Prophecy, Sins Of Omission, Bloodshed* and *Dark Eden*.

1998 CD - NB 339-2

2002 CD - NB 1053-2

1998 ■	HOLY TARGET	CD	Nuclear Blast	NB 339-2
2000 ☐	NOT DEAD YET	CD	Nuclear Blast	NB 443-2
2002 ■	WICKED IS MY GAME	CD	Nuclear Blast	NB 1053-2
2002 ☐	WICKED IS MY GAME	CD	Irond (Russia)	CD 02-348
2002 ■	HOLY TARGET & NOT DEAD YET	CD	Nuclear Blast	NB 1064-2
2002 ☐	HOLY TARGET & NOT DEAD YET	CD	Irond (Russia)	CD 02-407
2006 ■	To The Gallows/Open Your Mind	7"	Black Lodge	BLOD 7001
	300 copies. Red vinyl.			
2007 ☐	CITY OF THE DAMNED	CD	Black Lodge	BLOD 031 CD
2007 ☐	CITY OF THE DAMNED	CDd	Black Lodge	BLOD 031 CDL
2007 ☐	CITY OF THE DAMNED	CD	Mystic Empire (Russia)	MYST CD 177
2008 ☐	HOLY TARGET	CDd	Metal Mind	MASS CD 1196 DG
	2000 copies.			
2008 ■	NOT DEAD YET	CDd	Metal Mind	MASS CD 1197 DG
	2000 copies.			
2008 ☐	WICKED IS MY GAME	CDd	Metal Mind	MASS CD 1198 DG
	2000 copies.			

2006 7" - BLOD 7001

2008 CDd - MASS CD 1197 DG

RALLYPACK

Martin Westerstrand: v, Max Flövik: cello, Daniel Cordero: b, Ian-Paolo Lira: d

Göteborg - In 2004, after the band *LOK* had split, Martin and Daniel formed *Rallypack*. The name was taken from a motor magazine naming the rally accessory package you could purchase for a Ford Mustang in the sixties. The style was quite similar to *LOK*'s bone hard brutal rap-oriented metal, but now the lyrics were in English. The band had a minor hit with the song *Luke Skywalker*. One big difference from *LOK* was that Flövik didn't play guitar, but electrified cello. Honestly, you won't hear the difference. I've never heard such an evil sounding cello. The band however only lasted for one album and in 2006 the band changed its name to *Lillasyster* (little sister), started singing in Swedish again, and Max switched his cello for an electric guitar. They had a big hit with their metal take on Rihanna's *Umbrella*. Still, an album well worth checking out for *LOK* and *Lillasyster* fans.

New band, similar LOK

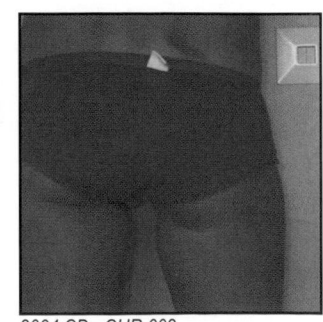

2004 CD - CUR 002

2004 ☐	Luke Skywalker	MCD 2tr	Curling Music	CUR 001
	Tracks: Luke Skywalker/I Love You + Luke Skywalker (video) + Rallyfilm 1 (video)			
2004 ■	SOD OFF GOD! WE BELIEVE IN OUR ROCK BAND	CD	Curling Music	CUR 002

RAM

**Oscar Carlquist: v, Harry Granroth: g, Daniel Johansson: g,
Tobias Pettersson: b, Morgan Pettersson: d**

Göteborg - Sick of the musical misinterpretations that ruled the current scene, Granroth formed classic metal band *RAM* in 1999. He soon found Daniel and the two started collaborating. After some time they drafted singer Oscar and the backbone of *RAM* was now in place. Oscar brought in drummer Morgan and they recruited bass player Leif Larsson (*Frozen Eyes, NME Within, Black Ingvars*). They started rehearsing and in 2003 released the first MCD *Sudden Impact* on their own label. The first pressing of 1000 copies sold out within a month. It was then rereleased with one bonus track. In 2005 the first album saw the light of day, and the band now burst into the classic heavy metal scene like a battering ram. Due to personal differences Leif Larsson was asked to leave in 2007 and *Nifelheim* member Erik "Tyrant" Gustavsson joined as session member. In 2008 the band entered the studio with producer Johan Reivén (*LOK*) to record the album *Lightbringer*. They were picked up by German label AFM, who released the album in 2009. After the album Tobias joined on bass. The band now moved on to Metal Blade Records, who released their latest effort, *Death*, in 2011.

2005 CD - BPMR 03

2003 ☐	Sudden Impact	MCD 6tr	Black Path Recordings	BPMR 01
	1000 copies.			
2005 ☐	Sudden Impact	MCD 7tr	Black Path Recordings	BPMR 02
	Bonus: Disturbing The Priest (Black Sabbath cover)			
2005 ☐	FORCED ENTRY	CD	Black Path Recordings	BPMR 03
2006 ☐	Sea Of Skulls (split)	7"	Metal Coven	MCR 007
	Split with After All. Tracks Sea Of Skulls/In League With Satan (Venom cover)			
2009 ☐	LIGHTBRINGER	CD	AFM	AFM 293-2
2010 ☐	FORCED ENTRY	LP	High Roller	HHR 122
	150 red/black, 350 red and 500 black. Poster + insert.			
2010 ■	LIGHTBRINGER	LPg	High Roller	HHR 126
	250 white, 150 white/silver and 600 black vinyl copies.			
2010 ☐	Under The Scythe/Evil	7"	High Roller	HHR 170
	250 gold + 750 black vinyl. Insert.			
2011 ■	DEATH	CD	Metal Blade	MTB 15073.2
2011 ☐	DEATH	CD+DVD	Metal Blade	MB 15073 LTD
	Bonus live DVD.			
2011 ☐	DEATH	LPg	Metal Blade	3984-15073-1
	200 copies gold vinyl.			

2010 LP - HHR 126

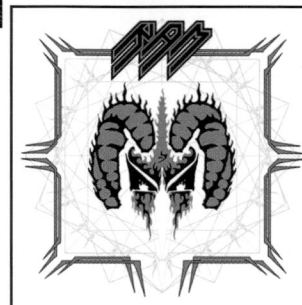

2011 CD - MTB 15073.2

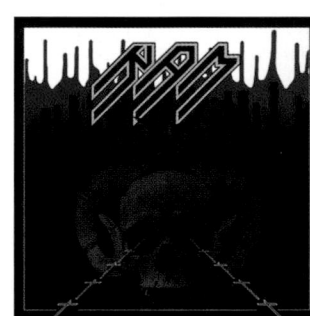

RAMM

**Peter Öberg: v, Marcus Eliasson: g, Richard Öberg: k,
Magnus Öberg: b, Anders Jansson: d**

Umeå - In 1984 Richard Öberg drafted drummer Jansson and together with Eliasson and Öberg they formed an instrumental cover band, which made one gig and called themselves *Victory*, on this gig only. In 1986 they became *RAMM* and Peter Öberg was recruited as singer. They entered and won the Norrlandsrock competition, which resulted in the recording of the single *I Am You Are*. After this, Peter quit and was replaced by Leif Grabbe (later in *Angeline, Shade Of Grey* and now *Turn The Page*). The band did quite a few gigs and radio sessions. In 1991 Marcus went to MI in Hollywood to study guitar. During this time, in 1992, the band recorded a demo, but because of Marcus' absence, the band subsequently split. Leif moved to Stockholm and Richard quit playing. In 1993 Magnus and Marcus were in dance bands *Pererix* and *Boogarts*. Mid-1994 they formed cover band *Freak Out* that features Marcus, Magnus and Anders. In 2003 Marcus, Richard and Magnus formed the band *Heel* together with singer David Henriksson and drummer Alexander Gustavsson. *Heel* has recorded two albums. *RAMM* plays excellent melodic hard rock sounding a bit like Bonnet-era *Rainbow* mixed with early *Europe*. The vocals are unfortunately not on par with the music.

1989 ■	I Am You Are/The Only Way	7"	private	RAMM89

1989 7" - RAMM89

RAMPANT

**Ronny Starborg: v, Urban Nilsson: g, Åke Cromnow: g, Bosse Källström: k,
Juha "Juba" Nurmenniemi: b, Tony K "Shield" Skiöld: d**

Köping - *Rampant* were formed back in 1985, initially featuring Åke, Juba, Tony (ex-*Walkaway*) and Andy Rose. They recorded a demo, and soon drafted Urban. Rose had to quit because of health problems and they recruited Starborg. Keyboard player Kjell Johansson was also added. They recorded a second demo in 1986, and four of the tracks were featured on the split cassette *Hårdrock* (86 Aktiv Musik), together with *Motherlode* and *Holy Message*. Kjell left, and after their third gig, in 1986, they split. In 2001 the band was resurrected and in 2004 the recordings of the first album began. The line-up had now changed slightly (see above). Straight-ahead hard rock, at times a bit similar to eighties *Rainbow*, but unfortunately not even close in quality.

2005 ■	BACK FROM NOWHERE	CD	private	RAMP 001

2005 CD - RAMP 001

RANDÉN, JOHAN
Johan Randén: g

Karlskoga - Johan Randén is a true guitar wiz-kid. He started playing guitar at the age of seven, performed live with *Freak Kitchen* at the Sweden Rock Festival only two years later and the blew the audience away completely. A nine-year-old with such a technique and tone was something completely out of the ordinary. He continued as a guitar student under the guidance of Mattias Ia Eklundh (*Freak Kitchen*) and at the age of thirteen he released his first solo-album. Mattias has written and recorded, plus he plays the backing instruments, but as the title says, it's Johan on lead guitar. Johan's father, Bengt, was once involved in melodic hard rockers *Cicero* as sound engineer. This is a full-blown guitar-album, ranging from heavy power riffing, to soft melodic tracks. As Eklundh has written the tracks it does show traces of *Freak Guitar*, but not as "far out"... all the time. Highly recommended! On the second album Johan used some fellow musicians such as bassist Simon Andersson, guitarist Markus Karlsson, Christian Alsing and drummers Anders Lilja, Preem Sandell and David Flood. Johan has of course continued to develop during the years and is today a totally outstanding guitarist playing in his own trio *Johan Randén 3*. In 2012 he finally released the new album, *Summary*. A great album, but not really your traditional shredder album. Instead Johan has started exploring his fusion, jazzy and countryish sides. Outstanding guitar playing, though. Drums on the album were played by Bengan Andersson and other guests include Staffan Astner, Sven Lindvall and Martin Lindquist.

2008 CD - TSP 987 026 2

2002 CD - TSP 0202/017 823-2

2002	■	JOHAN: LEAD GUITAR	CD	Thunderstruck	TSP 0202/017 823-2
2002	☐	JOHAN: LEAD GUITAR	CD	Victor (Japan)	VICP-61914
2008	■	VERSION 2.0	CD	Thunderstruck	TSP 987 026 2
2012	■	SUMMARY	CDd	Reingold Records	RRCD 008

2012 CDd - RRCD 008

RAT BAT BLUE
Fredrik Jernberg: v, Mats Hedström: g/k/b,
Christoffer "Chris" Lind: g/b, Fredrik "Freddie" Von Gerber: d

Stockholm - *Rat Bat Blue* are an AOR band in the vein of late *Easy Action*, which actually featured Chris and Freddie, while Mats was ex-*Magnum Bonum*/*Major Tom*, and Jernberg was in *Guardian Angel*. Freddie recorded some pop albums in the past, both as a solo artist and in the young and new wave band *Noice*. He also recorded an album with Jean Beavouir's band *Voodoo-X* and a single with *Bam Bam Boys*. In 1991 von Gerber and Hedström parted company, while Tomas Persson replaced Jernberg. Songs for a new album were recorded and they searched for a new deal. Tobbe Moen (ex-*OZ*) replaced Chris Lind. Kee Marcello was drafted to rerecord the guitar solos. Finally, the band then changed its name to *Red Fun* and recorded a new album. All B-sides are non-album. Jernberg has since been involved in *Rednex* and written songs and produced bands like *Back Street Boys* and various Swedish pop/dance artists.

1990 7" - 656 188 7

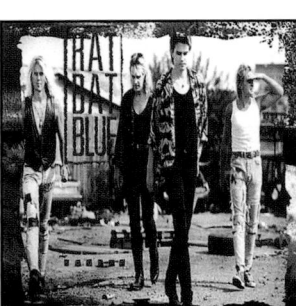
1990 LP - 467 500 1

1990	☐	Saints And Sinners/Long Gone	7"	CBS	651 047 7	
1990	■	Tuned On You/Drive Thru'	7"	CBS	656 188 7	
1990	☐	Gypsy Heart/It Ain't Easy	7"	CBS	656 482 7	
1990	☐	SQUEAK	LP	CBS	467 500 1	
1990	☐	SQUEAK	CD	CBS	467 500 2	
1990	☐	Saints And Sinners/Long Gone	7"	Epic	656 661 7	
1991	☐	Talk To Me/Love Changes Everything	7"	Epic	656 881 7	

RAT PACK
Danny Driver: v/g, Vikki Roxx: g, Zito Ponz: b, Cliff Stiff: d

Uppsala/Tensta - Formed 1998 in Uppsala. Straightforward glam-sleaze metal with a slightly punkish attitude. The band takes it all the way with true sleaze names, make-up and the works. Musically it's no great thrill, especially the guitar solos are quite far off the field... The band also made a split recording with *Twopointeight* entitled *First Class*. Jack Pot replaced Zito. Daniel "Trashcan" Andersson, Olle/Pelle Ferner and Daniel Nyberg are people that have been connected with the band in some way. They also recorded the demo *Ride With Us Or Collide With Us*.

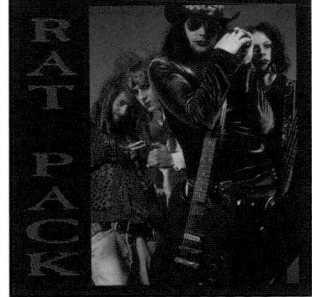
1999 MCD - RAT 666 CD

1999	■	Knee Deep Rockfuck	MCD 5tr	private	RAT 666 CD	$	
		Tracks: Hellraiser/Demons/Martians Juiced My Car/Rubber Fumes/Love Hate					

RAT SALAD
Benny Carlsson: v, Tommy Scalisi Svensson: g, Mikael "Lyris" Karlsson: g,
Micael Larsson: b, Magnus Olsson: d

Trollhättan - A heavy rock band in the same vein as *Mental Hippie Blood*, but with one big problem in the vocal department. The band recorded its first demo in 1990, and two more were recorded in 1991. A non-CD track can be found on the compilation *Backstage: Högtalarterror '94*. A last demo was recorded in 1996. Larsson and Svensson later formed the band *Gooseflesh*. Olsson, Karlsson and Svensson are today found in heavy rockers *Electric Earth*.

1994 CD - DOLPH02

1994	■	THE GOLDEN PLAYGROUND	CD	Dolphin	DOLPH02

RAUBTIER

Payre "Pär" Hulkoff (aka Kankanranta): v/g/k,
Thorbjörn Englund: b, Mattias "Buffeln" Lind: d

Haparanda - Industrial metal band **Raubtier** (predator in German, inspired by the movie *Predator*) were formed in February 2007 out of thrashers **Hunter/Killer**. The band now turned into a Swedish **Rammstein**-style band with vocals in Swedish with a northern accent and a hard-boiled image making Chuck Norris look like Cinderella. Singer Hulkoff spits out the lyrics in a low raspy voice and I wasn't sure if it was actually a joke at first. Well, it sure wasn't. On the second album bass player Peter "Waylon" Kantonmaa was replaced by Hussni Mörsare, who was replaced by Thorbjörn Englund, who was later replaced by Gustaf Jorde (**Defleshed**). The bass is now handled by Jonas Kjellgren (**Scar Symmetry**). Hulkoff (then named Payre Kankanranta) and Mörsare recorded an album with the band **Viperine** in 2004 and in 2012 Hulkoff and Kjellgren released an album with country rockers **Bourbon Boys**.
Website: www.raubtier.se

2009 CD - BDMUSIC 0901

2008 ☐	Kamphund	CDS	DBD Music	BDMUSIC 0810
2009 ■	DET FINNS BARA KRIG	CD	DBD Music	BDMUSIC 0901
2010 ☐	Världsherravälde	CDS	DBD Music	BDMUSIC 1004
2010 ☐	SKRIET FRÅN VILDMARKEN	CD	DBD Music	BDMUSIC 1008
2012 ■	FRÅN NORRLAND TILL HELVETETS PORT	CD	Despotz	DZCD-20
2012 ☐	FRÅN NORRLAND TILL HELVETETS PORT	LP	Despotz	DZLP-3

2012 CD - DZCD-20

RAVING MAD

Peter Andersson: v/g, Stefan Johansson: g, Åke Möller: b, Dennis Enarsson: d

Västervik - Formed in 1984. A great power metal band that recorded three singles, however the second was never released because of problems with the cover (!). It can be found as the demo *Mastermind*. Åke previously recorded some great demos with the band **Orions Sword**. In 1992 **Raving Mad** recruited singer Nicke Ericsson, but nothing was released on record.

1987 ☐	A Dazzling Display/Cryin'	7"	private	RR24017-3	
1990 ■	Lethal Greed	10" PD shaped	AZRA/World Metal	WMR-290	$

Tracks: Lethal Greed/Seduced/Second Hell/Failure. Shaped picture-disc.

1990 10" PD shape - WMR-290

RAZORBLADE

Per Magnusson: v, Jompa Gustafsson: g, Anders Löfgren: g,
Fredrik Gunnarsson: b, Perra Eriksson: d

Söderhamn - Söderhamn-based hard rockers **Razorblade** only released the single and a four-track demo. In 2011 Gunnarsson and Gustafsson started talking about playing together again. They found drummer Pether Svedjewik and formed the band **Afterlife** (www.afterlife.nu), with whom they have released a demo so far.

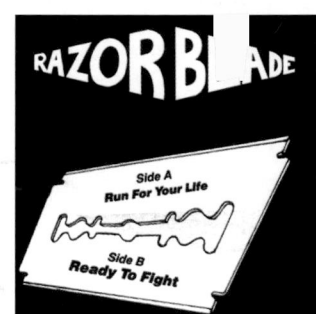

1986 ■	Run For Your Life/Ready To Fight	7"	RC Ljud	RC 102	$

1986 7" - RC 102

REAZON

Magnus Lindqvist: v/k, Staffan Forsell: g/k, Göran Eriksson: g,
Jörgen Ahr: b, Janne Murén: d

Gävle/Valbo - Formed in 1987, split in 1990. Melodic hard rock with a strong 80s touch. In 1989 they won a local band stand and the first prize was to record a single. Murén later played with guitarist Steven Anderson, Lindquist became a magician and the others played in cover bands or quit music. The B-side is a ballad. In 2006 they reformed and rerecorded the songs from the single. These recordings were released as the pro-printed CD-R *Reazon EP* (private, REAZON2). It also contains a cover of **Demon**'s *Night Of The Demon*, some live-tracks and a medley of demos and interviews.

1989 ■	A Woman So Wise/Lost In The Night	7"	CUF	CUF 012

500 copies.

1989 7" - CUF 012

REBELENE

Paul Zanichelli: v, Anders Holmström: g, Lars "Skunken" Gustavsson: g,
Johan Segui: b, Jörgen "George" Gustavsson: d

Stockholm - After eighties metal band **Parasite** split, Paul and Anders moved to different parts of Sweden. In 1993 they teamed up in Stockholm, where they met Larry and George from their mutual hometown Karlshamn. With bassist Johan in the band **Rebelene** was born. They were a straightforward hard rock 'n roll band with a southern feel, reminiscent of bands like **Four Horsemen** and **Georgia Satellites**. They only released one album before they split.

1993 ■	IN THE MIDDLE OF NOWHERE	CD	private	CSA 1

1993 CD - CSA 1

REBELS

Jonas Blum: v, **Krister Jonsson:** g, **Stefan Andersson:** g,
Johnny Eliasson: k, **Patrik Nilsson:** b, **Joel Linder:** d

Norrköping - Great melodic hard rock with quite prominent keyboards and guitars. High-quality vocals, but second rate lyrics. *A Tear In Your Eye* is a typical 80s metal ballad. Jonas later joined *Dizziness*, which became *Pole Position*. He was also later in *Reptilian*, as was Linder.

1986 ■ Never Look Back/A Tear In Your Eye ....7" Chicken.. CRS 001

1986 7" - CRS 001

RECKLESS

Patrik Axelsson: v, **Robert Monegrim:** g, **Johan Romert:** k,
Magnus Östborg: b, **Stefan Orhamn:** d

Stockholm - This band was formerly known as *Line-Up*, and recorded an album for the dubious Büms Records. The MCD features keyboard player Björn Åsander and bassist Robert Fransson. Patrik is vocally quite reminiscent of Klaus Meine but without the German accent. The music also bears traces of mid-80s *Scorpions*, but with a more AOR-ish touch. Great band. The full length version was only out in Japan before it was reissued on the MTM Classix label ten years later.

1993 ■	Curious	MCD 4tr	Rec-Less-Line Up	CDS-01

Tracks: Living Without You/Hot Sweet Lovin'/(Intro) Sally's Rime/Give Her A Sign.

1994 ☐	RECKLESS	CD	Zero (Japan)	XRCN-1152
2004 ☐	RECKLESS	CD	MTM Classix	0681.90

Bonus: Living Without You/Hot Sweet Lovin'/(Intro) Sally's Rime - Give Her A Sign

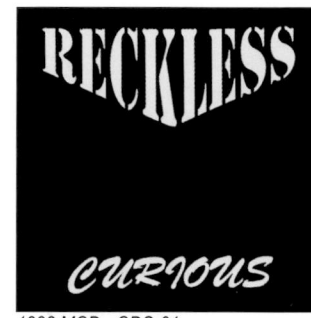

1993 MCD - CDS-01

RECLUSION

Johan Wiberg: v, **Toni Korhonen:** g, **Rune Foss:** g,
Pasi Jaskara: b, **Marek Dobrowolski:** d

Göteborg - The band was formed under the moniker *Dawn Of Time* and in 1999 they recorded the 4-track demo CD-R *A Force Of One*, from which two tracks ended up on a 7". Renamed *Reclusion*, they recorded the album *Shell Of Pain*, but the label went bust and the record was never released. Guitarist Rune also took on the vocal task after singer Johan Wiberg and the band signed to Listenable. Rune now rerecorded the vocals and the album was remixed by Risza (*Hardcore Superstar, Psychore*) and finally released. Heavy thrash with traces of *Anthrax, Pantera* and early *Meshuggah* and a touch of death metal. Tight, powerful and highly recommended.

2001 ■ SHELL OF PAIN...CD Listenable .... POSH 032

2001 CD - POSH 032

RED BARON

Mats Melin: v, **Mats Jonasson:** g, **Jan Petersson:** g, **Eero Koivisto:** b, **Mikael Green:** d

Stockholm - Formed in 1981, by Eero (*Heavy Load, Highbrow, Power*), Mikael (*Rising Force*), Mats and guitarist Henrik Larsson. Singer Lars Axelsson (later in *Black Cat Moan*) joined. In 1982 Green was temporarily replaced by Kjell Eriksson (now Nietzche) (*Rising Force*). The first single is a weak attempt, but the second single shows great improvement. The style is traditional melodic 80s hard rock in the same vein as *220 Volt, Dalton* etc. During the recordings of *R 'N R Power,* guitarist Henrik Larsson left and was replaced by Jan. The recording features guest spots from Pontus Norgren and Mikael Nord Andersson. In 1987 the band started woorking on the debut album, tentatively entitled *Tricolor*, but in the spring of 1988 Melin left for a civil career. In May the same year, Eero also left and the story took an end. Eero since became a well-reputed decorator and left the music business. The band's recordings are planned to be digitally released in 2013, by EMI.

1987 7" - 248 414-7

1985 ☐	Fools Gold/Rock The Highway	7"	Manfred Production	MP07-0185

500 copies in red vinyl. Numbered.

1987 ■	Rock 'N Roll Power/Fools Gold	7"	WEA	248 414-7
1987 ■	R 'N' R Power	MLP 4tr	WEA	242 105-1

Tracks: Rock And Roll Power/Strike A Bad Patch/Razamanaz (Nazareth-cover)/Fools Gold

1987 MLP - 242 105-1

RED FUN

Thomas Persson: v, **Kjell "Kee Marcello" Lövbom:** g,
Tobbe Moen: b, **Fredrik "Freddie" Von Gerber:** d

Stockholm - It all started when the band *Rat Bat Blue* replaced singer Fredrik Jernberg with Thomas and Christopher Lind with Tobbe. What was to be the second *Rat Bat Blue* album was recorded with the aid of Kee Marcello (*Easy Action, Europe, D'Accord*, solo etc). He was only the producer at first but rerecorded the guitar solos, became a member and *Red Fun* was born. Tobbe was an old friend of Kee's and had played with Erika and Finnish hard rockers *OZ* (on *Roll The Dice*). Thomas was a member of *Alien* for a period. Freddie has played with numerous bands like *Noice, Intermezzo, Bam Bam Boys, Rat Bat Blue, Easy Action, Voodoo*

1993 MCDp - PROMO CHC2

X and he's also released some wimpy solo material in the pop/glam manner. **Red Fun**'s music is groovy hard rock 'n roll. The band is now defunct. Freddie also did a revival tour with his resurrected teen band **Noice**.

1993 ☐	Doc. Love (edit)/(album version)/Party	MCD 3tr	Cheiron/BMG	CHC 2/13803-2	
1993 ☐	My Baby's Coming Back/(unplugged)	CDS 2tr	Cheiron	CHC 7	
1993 ☐	RED FUN	LP	Cherion	74321 13775-1	
1993 ■	News From The Swedish Rockscene (split)	MCDp 4tr	Cheiron (Germany)	PROMO CHC2	
	Promo split with It's Alive, Tracks: My Baby's Coming Back/Don't Close Your Eyes				
1993 ■	RED FUN	CD	Cherion	74321 13775-2	
1993 ☐	RED FUN	CD	Music For Nations (UK)	CDMFN 173	
1993 ☐	Don't Close Your Eyes/My Babe	CDS 2tr	Cheiron	CHC 15	

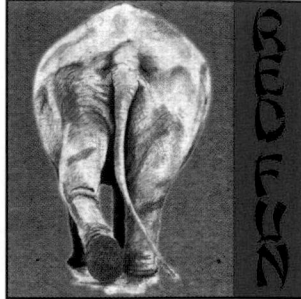

1993 CD - 74321 13775-2

RED ROCKET
Nina Fernandez: v, Pontus Svensson: g/b/d

Stockholm - **Red Rocket** were derived from the melodic metal band **The Buttz**, who recorded the excellent song *Concrete Boots* for the *Rockbox* compilation. Pontus continued with outstanding female singer Nina and recorded the *Red Rocket* CD. Despite the naff-looking cover this is a class A melodic metal album, sounding like an early Ozzy Osbourne album with **Heart**'s Ann Wilson fronting. Killer vocals, killer guitar playing and great songs! The band also recorded heavy metal versions of **Spice Girls**' *Denying* and **Aqua**'s *Barbie Girl* for a tribute CD. The band featured bassist Thomas Berndts and drummer Micke Söderlund on these tracks. Another bunch of demos have been recorded, and the band actually still does exist, but unfortunately nothing more has come out of it. We're still waiting!

1996 ■	RED ROCKET	CD	private	2001	

1996 CD - 2001

RED SURFACE
Magnus "Baus" Skoglind: v, Stefan Svanström: g, Jonas Olsson: b, Mats Bjuhr: d

Kiruna - Formed in 1995. **Red Surface** sounds a bit like early **Metallica**, but with a bit rougher vocals at times.
Website: www.redsurface.com

1997 ■	A Ton Of Bricks	MCD 6tr	private	Red Surface 001	
	Tracks: Burn/2nd Floor/The Day/Hate Song/The Hammer Thrown/Don't Feel				

1997 MCD - Red Surface 001

REDSTORM
Steve Siros Redstorm: v/g/b/k, Jens Jokinen: d

Umeå - The band was more or less Iranian born Siros solo project, but Jens became a part of the band. After the record they had a full line-up, but nothing happened. Jens had earlier recorded some demos with **Wasteland**, later **Stinking Rich** and was then in cover band **Puck**. Siros moved to Stockholm where he ran CSR Studios. He wrote and produced music for artists like **Shy Lovers** and Shawn Leone.

1991 ■	NO EXCEPTION OF A VICTIM OF CRIME	LP	Garageland	BF 641	
	1000 copies.				
2003 ☐	NO EXCEPTION OF A VICTIM OF CRIME	CD	Karthago Records	KR 007	
	Bonus: Take Me Back				

1991 LP - BF 641

REDSUN
Roger Olsson: v, Jonny Rantala: g, Leffe Unnemark: k,
Mattias Svensson: b, Marco Bjurling: d

Stockholm - **Europe** made quite an impact on the Swedish melodic hard rock scene and lot of bands tried to copy Tempest & Co. **Redsun** are definitely in the same musical territory, however calling them **Europe** clones would not be fair. **Redsun** are a classy melodic hard rock band with keyboards á la *The Final Countdown* and great vocals. Well worth looking for.

1988 ■	Eyes Of A Stranger/Wings Of Time	7"	private	RS 100	$
	200 copies.				

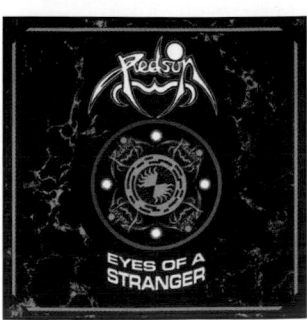

1988 7" - RS 100

REECE/KRONLUND
David Reece: v, Martin Kronlund: g

Göteborg/USA - Martin Krolund is a man who sneaks into just about every second band he can find. He's a gifted producer, songwriter and guitarist who runs JM Studio in Mölnlycke. He also recorded some albums with bands like **Gypsy Rose** and **Dogface**. Lately he has also helped out in bands like Canadians **White Wolf**. In 2007 the two teamed up when Reece was drafted to front **Gypsy Rose**, on the second album *Another World*. In November 2010 the two started working on the joint venture which became the band **Solid** in 2011. Besides David and

Martin the musicians on the album includes Tommy Denander, Rikard Quist, Andy Sushemil, Christian Tolle and drummer Hans Zandt. *Solid* is as the title suggests, a piece of solid melodic hard rock well worth checking out of you like Kronlund's other bands.

2011 ■ SOLID ....CD   AOR Heaven.............................. AORH00058

2011 CD - AORH00058

REENACT

Joakim Bergman: v, Martin Alowerson: v/b, Magnus Edberg: g,
Emil Sjöstrand: g, Johan Edberg: d

Göteborg - Reenact were formed in 2009 influenced by various styles and bands they felt they "re-enacted", hence the name. The band plays modern melodic death metal, mixing growl and clean melodic vocals, a bit in the same vein as *Scar Symmetry* and *Dead By April*, but way more metal than the latter.

2011 ■ Counting The Numbers/My Guilt.. CDSpg   Warner Bros........................ 12-04/00358-3843

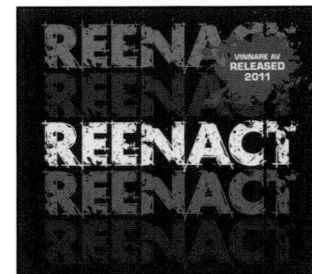

2011 CDSpg - 12-04/00358-3843

REFLEX

Erik Lundberg: v, Rolf "Trazan" Nordström: g,
Mårten Eriksson: g, Erik Häggström: b, Per Öhman: d

Örnsöldsvik/Sundsvall - Reflex were a really good classic guitar-dominated hard rock/metal band in the vein of *Thin Lizzy* that only made one vinyl attempt. Christian lyrics and approach. Erik, Rolf and Mårten later recorded with the band *Limit* and Rolf was later found in the re-united *Killer Bee*.

1983 ■ Dina nya kläder/Diod...7"   Pim Produktion ....PS 1983 $$

1983 7" - PS 1983

REGENT

Peter Nordin: v, Dan Stomberg: g, Ulrik Larsson: g,
Conny Sundquist (now Payne): b, Patrik Holtentjärn: d

Hudiksvall - The band won the recording of the 7" in a band battle. It caught the attention of Rixi Records, who wanted to sign them. Conny and Dan thought *Regent* wasn't strong enough, so they recruited Anders Karlsson and Peter Fredricksson from locals *Destiny* (who actually came in second place in the same competition) and also singer Göran Edman. They changed their name to *Madison* and both tracks on the single was later rerecorded for *Madison*'s debut album *Diamond Mistress*. This single is well worth searching for. Conny later played with *Pete Sandberg's Jade* and is today in prog metal band *MindSplit* and Göran has been found everywhere.

1984 ■ Lay Down You Arms/Changes ....7"   Samdist... FOLS 18 $

1984 7" - FOLS 18

REGURGITATE

Rikard Jansson: v, Urban Skytt: g/b, Johan "Jonken" Jansson: b, Jocke Pettersson: d

Stockholm - Regurgitate were formed by Rikard in 1990. The first demo, recorded in 1991 was 2 minutes long and featured 11(!) songs of pure grind-core. The guitar was then handled by Matte Nordrup (*General Surgery, Crematory, Afflicted*) and the drums by Peter Stjärnvind (*Entombed, Krux, Nifelheim, Face Down, Unanimated* etc). The demo lead to a split with *Vaginal Massacre*, after which Peter left, Matte took care of the drums and guitarist Urban Skytt (*Crematory, Nasum, Crucifyre*) was added. The new line-up recorded the split with *Dead* and was then a pure death metal band, with songs of normal length. *Effortless Regurgitation Of Bright Red Blood* contains 62(!) tracks with nice titles like *Worm Eaten Rectum, Forced Abortion Through The Rectum* and *A Putrid Reek Of The Decomposed Embryos*. Despite the great reviews, the band took a loooong vacation. Rikard and Urban resurrected the band and found drummer Jocke (*Kids Are Sick, Thy Primordial, Retaliation*). The 1999 reissue of *Effortless...* contains a whopping 63 tracks, while *Carnivorous...* contains only 38 tracks, but the lyrics are just as obscene... mildly speaking (kinda brings *Bakteria* to mind). The latter was mixed by the late Mieszko Talarczyk (*Nasum*). The band's music could be labelled noise-oriented splatter-grind metal with "vocals" ranging from guttural growls to primal screams and you can forget about trying to hear the lyrics... The songs are mostly between 30 and 90 seconds, which makes *S.O.D* sound like *Dream Theater* in comparison. The band has also recorded covers of *Psychopathologist* and *Genital Grinder* for a *Carcass*-tribute on Death Vomit Records. The line-up on the 1996 *Fleshmangler* split features Rikard, Urban, Johan and Peter, but after this release Johan and Peter were out of the band, enter drummer Jocke Pettersson, while Skytt handled both guitar and bass. On *Hatefilled Vengeance* the bass was handled by Glenn Sykes. In 2001 Bizarre Leprous Production released a tribute to *Regurgitate* entitled *Comeback Of Goregods*, where 47 bands, including *CSSO, Gore Beyond Necropsy, Haemmorage* and *Inhume* cover the originals. On the *Skullhog* split Johan Jansson had replaced Sykes on bass. Pettersson has also played with bands like *Cranium, Funeral Feast, Niden Div. 187, Bloodshed Nihil, Ocean Chief, Retaliation, Unmoored, Dawn* etc.

Rumination syndrome?

1992 ■ Regurgitate/Vaginal Massacre (split) ....7" EP Poserslaughter.................................. PSR 006
Split with Vaginal Massacre. 1000 copies. Marbled vinyl. Tracks: Morbid Reality/Terror
Reign/Fear?!/Desensitized/Generic Words

1993 □ Psychotic Noise/Regurgitate (split) ....7" EP Glued Stamps ....E.U 008
Split with Psychotic Noise. Tracks: Brainscrambler/Regurgitated Giblets/Internal Bleeding/
Methylated Bile/Liquid Excrements/Carnal Cacophony/Vomit Breath/Suicide

1994 □ Regurgitate/Grudge ....7" EP Obliteration ....OREP 002
Split with Grudge. Transparent vinyl. 1000 copies. Tracks:Corpse Allergy/Sickening
Thoughts/Visceral Organ/Cadaveric Dissolution/Ulcerated Flesh/Deteriorated/Regurgi-
tated Giblets/Matted Fungus/Septicaemic Mutation/Disinterring Urine/Methylated Bile/
Pancreatic Juices/Scorched Entrails

1994 □ Regurgitate/Dead ....MCD 13tr Poserslaughter................. PSR-WIMP CD 010
Tracks:Cyst-Eater/Exhumed Love/Septic Vomit Of Chyme/Cannibalism Misscarriage/
Praedilectio For Menorrhagia/Organic Convulsions/Expelling Pyorrhoea/Purulent Vulvec-
tomy/Morbid Reality/Terror Reign/Fear?!/Desentisized/Generic Words

1994 □ EFFORTLESS REGURGITATION OF BRIGHT RED BLOOD ....CD Lowland ....LOW 007
1996 □ Fleshmangler (split) ....7" EP Noise Variations ....NVEP 002
Split with Infestinal Infection. Tracks: Chronic Lymphatic Leukemie/Meatal Ulcer/Purulent
Discharge From The Uretha/Vaginal Obstriction/Cloudy, Grayish Vomitus/Fleshmangler

1999 □ EFFORTLESS REGURGITATION... THE TORTURE SESSIONS ....CD Relapse Records .... RR 6406-2
Reissue with bonus: Concrete Human Torture demo, Grudge/Regurgitate EP and Psy-
chotic Noise/Regurgitate EP.

2000 □ Regurgitate/Filth (split) ....7" EP Painiac ....PAIN 001
Split with Filth.500 copies, 250 white + 250 black (a few grey). Tracks: Intro/You're About
To Fukkin' Die/Pierced Stiffs/Braindead Amputation/Festering Embryonic Vomit/Relentless
Pursuit Of Rotting Flesh/37 Stabwounds/Stinking Genital Warts/Foetal Putrefaction/No
Fukkin' Title Bitch

2000 ■ CARNIVOROUS ERECTION.................................CD Relapse Records .... RR 6465-2
2001 □ CARNIVOROUS ERECTION.............................LP PD Morbid Records .... MR 084
2001 □ Sodomy And Carnal Assault (split) ....7" EP No Weak Shit...-
Split with Gore Beyond Necropsy. Tracks (9 untitled tracks).

2001 □ Scream Bloody Whore (split) ....7" EP Stuhlgang..................................STUHL 013
Split with Realized. Tracks: Humilated In Your Own Blood/Mayhemic Butchering Abor-
tions/Bloody Pile Of Human Waste/Reek And Decay/Choked In Shit/Just Another
Stillborn/I Wanna Kill/Robbed Of Your Bowels/Funeral Genocide. Dark brown vinyl.

2001 □ CARNIVOROUS ERECTION.............................LP PD Morbid .... MR 084
2003 □ DEVIANT ....CD Relapse Records .... RR 6565-2
2002 □ Cripple Bastards/Regurgitate (split) ....7" E.U '91 Produzioni ....EU 017
Split with Cripple Bastards. Tracks: Obscene Body Slayings/Rape Against Humanity/
Retarded Coprophagist/Ruptured Remains In A Doggybag/Headless She Died/Savaged
Gorewhore/Impaled And Decapitated Fucking Slut/Ferocious Human Body Tormentor/
Smeared With Bloodmixed Semen

2002 ■ Hatefilled Vengeance ....MCD 18tr Relapse Records .... RR 6491-2
All re-recorded tracks.

2002 □ Hatefilled Vengeance ....MLP 18tr Putrid Filth Conspiracy......................PFC 021
2003 ■ Bonesplicer (split) ....5" Tower Violence..- -
Split with Entrails Massacre. Tracks: Powers Of Gore/Bloodspitting/Bonesplicer/Extracting
The Malformed. 5" vinyl.

2003 □ 3-WAY GRINDCORE KNOCKOUT – ROUND 1 (split)................CD Blastwork Records...........................work 001
Split with Supository and Entrails Massacre.

2003 □ Corrupted (split) ....7" R.S. Records .... RSR 039
Split with Noisear. Tracks: Corrupted/Mutinous Tissues/Rifle Surgery/Bad Girls Go To
Hell. Black vinyl + 100 copies clear red vinyl.

2003 □ DEVIANT ....CD Relapse Records .... RR 6565-2
2003 □ DEVIANT ....CD ?? (Japan)...??
2003 □ DEVIANT ....LP Restrain Records ....RR 02
2004 □ REGURGITATE/SUPPOSITORY (split) ....CD Power It Up .... P.I.U 54
Split with Suppository. Tracks: The Ultimate Enslavement/Punish Them With Pain/
Crouching Vomit, Hidden Sniper/Prayers Of Hatred/Ripe For Cruel Mistreatment/Ma-
nipulation Regins Supreme/Embrace Obscenity And Kiss The Eruption Of Destruction/
Dignified Manslaughter

2004 □ REGURGITATE/SUPPOSITORY (split).......................LPg Badger Records ....BADGER 3
525 copies. Bonus: Alles Is Kut

2006 □ SICKENING BLISS...LP Relapse Records .... RR 6592-1
100 clear + 500 red + 600 yellow splatter vinyl. Also available with censored artwork.

2006 ■ SICKENING BLISS...CD Relapse Records .... RR 6592-2
2006 □ SICKENING BLISS...CD Relapse Records (Japan) YSCY-1055
2007 □ SICKENING BLISS...CD Irond (Russia) .... CD 07-1300
2008 □ Regurgitate/Skullhog (split) ....7" R.S Records .... RSR 070
Split with Skullhog. 100 copies with special artwork. Tracks: Colon Collapse Disorder/
Snorting Caustic Vapour/Regurgitated And Humiliated

2009 □ EFFORTLESS REGURGITATION OF BRIGHT RED BLOOD ....2LP+7" Power It Up ....PIU 89+PIU 91
100 numbered coloured vinyl + 7", 400 numbered black vinyl + 7", 500 black vinyl.

2009 □ Yyyaaaaaah (split) ....7" No Posers Please! .... NPP 005
Split with Dead Infection. 1026 numbered copies. Tracks: Excrementality/Massive Vis-
ceral Eruption/Voraginous

2010 □ Imperial Anthems No 3.......................................7" Cyclone Empire ....ANTHEM 003
Split with Atrocity. Tracks: Necrosadistic Cunts/Bloodbath Eruption/I See A Darkness

1992 7" - PSR 006

2000 CD - RR 6465-2

2002 MCD - RR 6491-2

2003 5" - - -

2006 CD - RR 6592-2

REINGOLD

Göran Edman: v, Chris Palm: g, Peter Espinoza: g,
Jonas Reingold: b/k, Jaime Salazar: d

Malmö - A true all-star band featuring Edman (*Glory, Malmsteen, Madison, Kharma* etc etc), Palm (*Midnight Sun*), Espinoza (*Nasty Idols, Espinoza, Majestic*), Reingold (*Downtown Clowns, Midnight Sun, The Flower Kings*) and Salazar (*Bad Habit, The Flower Kings, Truth* etc). Musically the band is pretty close to Malmsteen's neoclassical melodic metal.

1999	■	UNIVERSE	CD	Avalon Marquee (Japan)	MICY 1118
1999	□	UNIVERSE	CD	MTM	MTM 199684
1999	□	UNIVERSE	CD	NEMS (Argentina)	NEMS 165
1999	□	UNIVERSE	CD	Rock Brigade/Lazer (Brazil)	RBR/LCR2170

1999 CD - MICY 1118

REINXEED

Tommy Johansson: v/g, Calle Sundberg: g, Mattias Johansson: g,
Nic Svensson: b, Viktor Olofsson: d

Vindeln - *ReinXeed*, originally Tommy's solo project, play neoclassically-influenced melodic power metal with high-pitched vocals and high-speed shredding, influenced by soundtrack music. The demo *Future Land* was recorded in 2002, followed by *Lionheart* in 2004. The first album featured Johansson, Kerry Lundberg (g), Christer Viklund (b) and Mattias Lindberg (d). On the follow-up Viklund was replaced by Ace Thunder, Lindberg by Erik Forsgren and keyboard player Henrik Fellermark was added to the line-up. On *Majestic* the line-up featured Johansson, Thunder, Calle Sundberg (g), Mattias "Matt Machine" Johansson (g) and Victor Olofsson (d). *Swedish Hitz Goes Metal* was released under the *ReinXeed* banner in Japan only, while it was released as *Swedish Hitz Goes Metal* in Sweden. The album contains metal versions of hits by *ABBA, Roxette, Ace Of Base* etc. and is more of a Tommy Johansson solo thing, but the musicians feature most of the *ReinXeed* line-up: Calle Sundberg and Mattias Johansson, bassist Nic Svensson and drummer Björn Edlund. Tommy is also part of the band *Golden Resurrection*.

Tommy Gun

2010 CD - LRCD 002

2008	□	THE LIGHT	CD	Rivel Records	RRCD 036
2008	□	THE LIGHT	CD	King Records (Japan)	KICP-1290
		Bonus: How Will I Know When I'm Free			
2009	□	HIGHER	CD	Rivel Records	RRCD 040
2010	■	MAJESTIC	CD	Liljegren Records	LRCD 002
2010	□	MAJESTIC	CD	King Records (Japan)	KICP-1468
		Bonus: Forever Carry On			
2011	□	SWEDISH HITZ GOES METAL	CD	King Records (Japan)	KICP-1568
		Bonus: Hooked On A Feeling (B.J Thomas cover)/Listen To Your Heart (Roxette cover)			
2011	□	SWEDISH HITZ GOES METAL	CD	Dolittle Group	DOOCD 003
2011	■	1912	CD	Liljegren Records	LRCD 007
2011	□	1912	CD	King Records (Japan)	KICP-1567
		Bonus: ReinXeed Alliances/Aces High (Iron Maiden cover)/Pray For Japan			
2012	□	WELCOME TO THE THEATER	CD	Liljegren Records	LRCD 012
2012	□	WELCOME TO THE THEATER	CD	King Records (Japan)	KICP-1617
2013	□	A NEW WORLD	CD	Liljegren Records	LRCD 015

2011 CD - LRCD 007

REIZON BAND

Tomas Gustafsson: d, Jocke Reiskog: g, Per J: k, Johan S: b, Jocke Th: g

Floda - Quite decent melodic hard rock. The A-side is sung in English and is not bad at all, while the B-side, sung in Swedish, is not quite as good.

1982	■	Money/Lyftet	7"	Kompass	S 7605

RELENTLESS

Matte Andersson: v/g, Oskar Pålsson: b, Pär Svensson: d

Örebro/Lindesberg - Formed in 1997, initially featuring Matte, Pär, bassist Robban and singer Ducky, and recorded their first demo *Pestilence Of The Undead* in 1999. After this guitarist Gabbe was recruited and Robban replaced by… another Robban. Second demo *Experiment In Excrement* was released in 2000, in 1000 copies by Butchery Music. In 2001 they followed it up with another five-track demo CD, now reduced to a trio featuring Matte, Pär and Robban. The band also made a split cassette with *Enthrallment* in 2001. Around 2003 they found bass player Oskar. Yet another four-track demo was recorded in 2005, which was officially released in 2008 on the split CD. The album was also released on cassette by Butchery Music, in 1000 copies. Matte is also in *Azure*, Oskar in *Coldworker* and Per is ex-*Valkyrja*. *Relentless* play fast and furious death/thrash/grind a bit similar to *Cannibal Corpse*. The band is currently inactive.

1982 7" - S 7605

2005 CD - FNZ 67912

2005	■	TEMPEST OF TORMENT	CD	Frozen North/Arctic Music	FNZ 67912
2008	■	RUIN/RELENLESS (Split)	CD	Relapse Records	RR 61252
		Split with Ruin. Tracks: This Is Where I Burn Them/Perish In Blasphemy/Incarcerated/The Suicidal Dilemma			

2008 CD - RR 61252

RELEVANT FEW

**Johan Karlsson (Carlzon): v, Kristian Lampila: g, Johan Nilsson: g,
Robert Hakemo: b, Daniel "Mojo" Moilanen: d**

Göteborg - Formed in October 2000 and made their live debut opening for *Nasum* after only a few months. The band was previously known as *Mindsnare*, but only recorded a demo in 2001 that was sent out to a few magazines before they were signed by No Tolerance. As there was both an Italian and an Australian band with the same name, they changed it to *Relevant Few*. The band plays death/grind in the vein of *Napalm Death* and *Brutal Truth* with short, intense songs. After the debut was recorded, Johan Karlsson left the band due personal problems and to devote his time to *Abandon*, where Nilsson was previously found. He was replaced by Henke Svensson. Robert is ex-*Ton Of Bricks, Gooseflesh* and *Slavestate*, Kristian had previously recorded with *Gooseflesh* and was part of *Slavestate*. Drummer Daniel "Mojo" Moilanen is/ has been found in numerous bands like *Dracena, Deathwish* and *Runemagick*. During the recording of *The Art Of Today*. Moilanen quit, but returned in December 2003. Late 2005 Svensson left and was replaced by the returning Karlsson. Moilanen (*Engel*) was also out of the band, replaced by Ufuk Demir (*Shadowbuilder*). On the *Afgrund* split the band featured Johan Karlsson on vocals, Lampila on guitar, Hakemo on bass and drummer Demir. In 2008 Johan Karlsson (born 1976) died of a drug overdose. Hakemo was also found in *Engel* and *Massive Audio Nerve* (aka *M.A.N*).

2003 CD - ZERO 007

2008 CD - LSP 003

2002	☐	WHO ARE THOSE OF LEADERSHIP?......................CD	No Tolerance...................ZERO 004
2003	■	THE ART OF TODAY...CD	No Tolerance...................ZERO 007
2004	☐	THE ART OF TODAY...CD	New Hawen Records.............NEWH 006
2008	■	AFGRUND/RELEVANT FEW (split)........................CD	Lifestage Prodctions............LSP 003

*Split with Afgrund. Tracks: Kontra Hegemonic/Everyone Is Judas/Towards The Black
Horizon/Hunting The Architect/Onward/New Age Of Confusion/Three Piece Fascist*

REMO

**Jonas Torrestad: v, David Fridefors: g, Mikael Dahlbom: g,
Lars Mossberg: b, Allan Fredriksson: d**

Vänersborg - Formed in 1983. High-class 80s metal with above-average vocals. At times reminiscent of *Syron Vanes*. Original drummer Andreas Svensson later joined *Rising*. Well worth looking for. David and Mikael were later in *Fleming Bengos*, mostly doing covers.

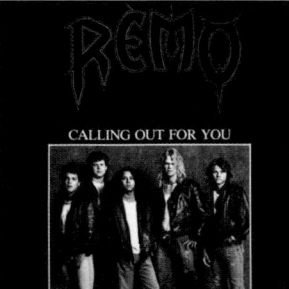

1987 7" - MW 001

1987	■	Calling Out For You/Trueland Dream...............7"	private................MW 001
1988	■	Send In The Clowns........................MLP 3tr	Echoo Production Songs........EPS 1003 $

Tracks: Clown Meets An Angel/Ragged Man Blues/Endless Time?

REMUDA DUST

**Daniel "Jack el Cozmo" Önnerlöv: v/b, Anders "Johnny Fuzz" Östberg: g,
David "James Deerider" Kalitziki: g, Fredrik "Joe Bourbon" Andersson: d**

Karlstad - In 1999 the punk-oriented trio *Grub* were reinforced by local guitar hero Anders and changed their name to *Remuda Dust*. They call their heavy fuzz-oriented music "desert rock". The song *18 Wheeler* can be found on the local *Vol #2* (00 Speedball) compilation, as well as on *Volume One* (00 Molten Metal) and in 2001 *Baby Blue* was featured on *Metalbox* (01 Hellbilly) and *Bleed* on *Mexican Sacred Groove* (01 Monstruo De Gila). Three more songs, as yet unreleased, were recorded at the same session as *Baby Blue*.

1988 MLP - EPS 1003

2000	■	Superhighway EP..................................7" 3tr	Words Of Wisdom............WORDS 006

*Tracks: Superhighway/Facing The Engine/Cactus Canyon. 500 copies, of which 100 were
in white vinyl.*

RENAISSANCE OF FOOLS

**Kjell Bergendahl: v/g, Daniel Magdic: g,
Björn Tauman: b, Magnus Karlsson: d**

Falun/Borlänge - *Renaissance Of Fools* was formed by former *Pain Of Salvation* man Daniel Magdic and drummer Magnus Karlsson (*Leech, Machina*). They teamed up with *Chainwreck/Without Grief* bassist Tauman and singer Mathias Henrysson. The band was then called *Cudfish*. They released a demo, but folded when Magnus and Björn went to Los Angeles for studies. Back home they reunited with Daniel and formed *Renaissance Of Fools*. After some time of writing they drafted *Thalamus* singer/guitarist Kjell and the pieces fell in place. *Renaissance Of Fools* plays excellent high-quality progressive hard rock with a psychedelic touch. The album was mixed by Pelle Saether (*Thalamus, Locomotive Breath, Overdrive, Grand Design* etc) and mastered by *King's X*'s Ty Tabor.

Smart fools!

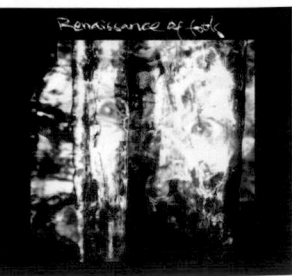

2011 CDd - MV 0020

2011	■	RENAISSANCE OF FOOLS..................................CDd	Metalville..................MV 0020

2000 7" - WORDS 006

RENEGADE

Magnus Tallåker: v, Mats Ottosson: g, Thomas Kullman: g,
Per Billengren: k, Håkan Jardmo: b, Fredde Grahn: d

Jönköping - Magnus and Mats recorded one 7" and a 12" EP with the band *Arrow* and when Håkan joined, this band started reforming into *Renegade* in 1988. Both albums are well worth investing in for true fans of well-played, well-arranged pompy AOR at times reminiscent of American band *Prophet*. The band has sadly split. Tallåker recorded an album with melodic metal band *Hellspray* in 2008, and also contributed on the solo single by Pelle T.

1992 ☐	TIME TO CHOOSE	CD	private	CD2 2	
1992 ☐	TIME TO CHOOSE	CD	Zero (Japan)	XRCN-1032	
1994 ☐	RAVAGES OF TIME	CD	Megarock	MRRCD009	
1994 ☐	RAVAGES OF TIME	CD	Zero (Japan)	XRCN-1124	
1996 ☐	Thousand Miles Away/Com'on Baby	CDS 2tr	RAB	RABCDS01	
1996 ■	III	CD	RAB	RABCD001	
1996 ☐	III	CD	Zero (Japan)	XRCN 1275	
	Different artwork.				

1996 CD - RABCD001

RENEGADE

Björn Petersson: v, Stefan Jonsson: g, Ove Nordin: k,
Patrik Berglund: b, Ulrik Fröberg: d

Sundsvall - Formed in 1979. A band of quite high standard, with good vocals and some nice guitar work. The style is 80s heavy metal with a melodic touch on the first release, while the style turned even more melodic, but still heavy on the second platter. After the debut, guitarist Mikael Swärd (now Carl Lagerholm) quit and keyboard player Ove Nordin filled his spot. Ove was later in popsters *Indy*. Stefan was later found in *Snakes In Paradise*.

1982 7" - PBS 1

1982 ■	Rock 'Til You Die	7" 4tr	Excalibur	PBS 1	$$
	Tracks: Beautiful People/Killer In The Sky/Leviticus/Rock 'Til You Die. 500 copies.				
1986 ■	Mean Streets/Do It	7"	Pan Music	PAS 001	
1986 ☐	Do It (dance mix)/(new 7" version)/Mean Streets	MLP 3tr	Pan Music	PAX 001	

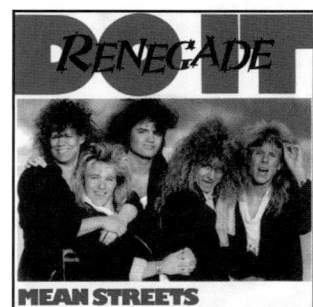

1986 7" - PAS 001

RENEGADE FIVE

David Johansson: v, Per Lidén: g, Håkan Fredriksson: k,
Jimmy Lundin: b, Markus Nowak: d

Karlstad - *Renegade Five* were formed in 2006. In the summer of 2009 bass player Harry Kjövik left and was replaced by David Wilhelmson (*Dave Rock*, *The Trix*). Shortly after, singer Per Nylin and David left to join a new venture with their new band *Dunderman*. Drummer Peter Damin and bass player Harry Kjövik also left the band the same year. In 2010 the band was again complete now featuring new singer Daniel Johansson, drummer Markus Nowak (ex-*Heads Or Tales*, *CC Rock*, *Lambretta*) and bassist Jimmy Lundin. *Renegade Five* is a modern melodic hard rock band, very mainstream and smooth. No sharp edges whatsoever.

2007 ☐	Shadows	CDS	Bonnier Amigo	334 23941	
2008 ☐	Love Will Remain	CDS	Bonnier Amigo	334 42221	
2008 ☐	Darkest Age	CDS	Bonnier Amigo	334 42326	
2008 ☐	Running In Your Veins	CDS	Bonnier Amigo	334 42256	
2009 ☐	Save My Soul	CDS	Bonnier Amigo	??	
2009 ■	UNDERGROUNDED UNIVERSE	CD	Bonnier Amigo	334 42343	
2011 ☐	Life Is Already Fading	MCD 4tr	Bonnier Amigo	060252786050	
	Tracks: Life Is Already Fading/Alive/Bring It On/Lost Without Your Love				
2012 ☐	NXT GENERATION	CD	Universal Music	060252798060	

2009 CD - 334 42343

RENEGADES

Valentine Pecovnik: v/g, Mikael Ahlqvist: g, Pajen Karlsson: b, Richard Svensson: d

Malmö - *Renegades* was formed back in 1984 and recorded their first ten-track demo only a few months later, from which the song *Poison* even topped the local chart. Stardom awaited, but internal conflicts, military service and girlfriends finally put a halt to the story in 1987. In 2004 the members reunited and decided to give it another go and it worked pretty well. In 2006 the long-awaited debut was finally released. The result is not bad at all. Classic-sounding melodic eighties metal with big choruses. If you're into *220 Volt* mixed with *Dokken* and with a touch of *Kiss*, check it out. Pecovnik recorded a couple of albums with the band *Joke* and now has the on-line project *Hellvalla Burn*. Svensson also recorded some solo material.

2006 ■	Knock Yourself Out	MCD 5tr	RG Music	RG 001	
	Tracks: Your Heaven – My Hell/Scream & Shout/Retro Magnetica/This Moment/Wise Ass				

2006 MCD - RG 001

REPTILE SMILE

Peter Shapiro: v, Jan Lissnils: g, Martin Karlegård: g,
Jacob "Jake S:t Snake" Sickenga b, Michelle Maiden: d

The living proof reptiles don't actually smile?

Stockholm - Formed in 1989 by Lissnils and Shapiro who had an *Aerosmith* cover band called *Toys In The Attic*. Karlegård and Maiden joined and they became *Reptile Smile*. Not surprisingly *Reptile Smile* plays sleazy rock 'n roll in the vein of *Aerosmith* or a hard rockin' *Rolling Stones*. The band never got a breakthrough, although they were really good. In '93 Jan and Michelle left. They were replaced by former *Glory Bells/Electric Boys* guitarist Franco Santuione and drummer Peter Nordstedt. The latter quit in 1995 and the new drummer was another former *Electric Boys* boy - Niclas Sigevall. The band recorded a new album and was on the hunt for a record company. According to Peter they had musically gone from black/white to colour, they sure have become heavier. Prior to this band Martin recorded some singles with Luxembourgian *Alderon*. Shapiro made a single with the poppier *Paviljongen* and Jacob had previously made some singles with punk bands *IQ 55* and *Blitzen*. Peter Shapiro was also working for booking agency FTS. The third album has unfortunately never been released. Lissnils is today playing steel guitar in rockabilly band *Fatboy*.

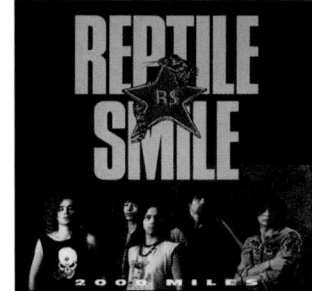

1990	☐	Shove 'Em Down/Loaded Gun	7"	CBS	655 583 7
1990	☐	AUTOMATIC COOL	LP	CBS	466 131 1
1990	☐	AUTOMATIC COOL	CD	CBS	466 131 2
1990	■	2000 miles/Thin Red Line	7"	CBS	655 844 7
1990	☐	Automatic Cool/Gunslinger	7"	CBS	656 282 7
		The A-side is a rerecorded version while the B-side is previoulsy unreleased.			
1991	☐	WHO MAKES THE RULES	LP	Epic	EPC 468748-1
1991	☐	WHO MAKES THE RULES	CD	Epic	EPC 468748-2
1991	☐	WHO MAKES THE RULES	CD	Epic (Japan)	ESCA 5526
		Bonus: Seven Days/Latest Lovin' Voodoo			
1991	☐	Wild Life/Latest Lovin' Voodoo	7"	Epic	657312
1991	☐	I Wanna Be There/Rattlesnake Valley	7"	Epic	657871

1990 7" - 655 844 7

REPTILIAN

Jonas Blum: v, Lasse Boquist: g, Orvar Wennström: g,
Thomas Blum: k, Jonas Reingold: b, Joel Linder: d

Malmö/Norrköping - Quite an interesting constellation, featuring Wennström from *The Drugs* and *Manson*, Blum and Boquist previously in *Dizziness* and *Pole Position*, Linder from *Flegma* and of course Reingold from *Reingold*, *The Flower Kings*, *Downtown Clowns* etc. *Reptilian* produces melodic neo-classic power metal, a style that seems to have made a big impression on the city of Malmö. The city has produced quite a lot of bands in the same genre, such as *Majestic, Silver Seraph, Midnight Sun, Last Tribe* etc. I must however admit they do not sound like clones, but have their own touch and sound. What differentiates *Reptilian* from the others is that they avoid the traditional power metal chord progressions and harmonies. Before the debut they recorded the demo *Skeleton Scales*. Boquist is also a guitarist that digresses from that genre with his personal artful solo-style. A great album! Boquist later recorded with *Neondaze* and is today in the band *Fair Of Freaks*.

2001 CD - RR 0010-008

2002 CD - RR 0209-017

2001	■	CASTLE OF YESTERDAY	CD	Regain	RR 0010-008
2001	☐	CASTLE OF YESTERDAY	CD	Avalon Marquee (Japan)	MICP 10224
		Bonus: Behold Nemesis			
2002	■	THUNDERBLAZE	CD	Regain	RR 0209-017
2002	☐	THUNDERBLAZE	CD	Soundholic (Japan)	TKCS-85052
		Bonus: Demon Wings/Sabre Dance			
2003	■	Demon Wings	MCD 5tr	Regain	RR 310-040
		Tracks: Sleepwalkers/Demon Wings/Raging Storms/Sabre Dance/Behold Nemesis			

REPUGNANT

Tobias "Mary Goore" Forge: v/g, Johan "Sid E Burns" Wallin: g,
Gustav "Carlos Satano" Lindström: b, Thomas "Tom Bones" Daun: d

2003 MCD - RR 310-040

Linköping - The band was formed in June 1998. They recorded their first demo *Spawn Of Pure Malevolence* in 1999. Old-school high-speed death metal in the vein of early *Entombed*, *Dismember* and *Grave*. Fat and heavy sound, tightly performed and overall a pretty good instalment. Produced by Fred Estby. The MCD contains a cover of *Celtic Frost*'s *The Unsurper*. On the first records the bass was handled by Joonas "Roy Morbidson" Ahonen (*Insision*) and the drums by Christoffer "Chris Piss" Barkensjö (*Kaamos, Serpent Obscene, Face Down, Blackshine, Grave*). The band recorded the demo *Draped In Cerecloth* in 2001. Johan is also found in grindcore band *Scurvy*, Tomas in *Insision*. In 2000 Tobias and Gustav were playing in the out-and-out metal band *Crashdïet*, where drummer Dennis Ekdahl (*Raise Hell, Rutthna, Sins Of Omission, Siebenbürgen* etc) was also found. They left in 2002 and the band became sleaze rockers *Crash Dïet*. After some intense touring the band split in 2004, before the release of the debut album, but they partly returned in 2010, as retro Satanists *Ghost*. Lindström is today fronting punkish metal band *Iron Lamb*. Forge was also in rock/popsters *Subvision*.

1999 7" - TTD 005/DMR001

2006 CD - SSR 004

1989 LP - RMLP 8901

REVIVAL BAND

Frövi - The first and only release by this Christian melodic hard rock band, in the vein of colleagues *Jerusalem* and *Leviticus*. Quite varied in style, ranging from melodic metal to straightforward rock 'n roll.

1989 ■ NOW IS THE TIME ....LP   private ....RMLP 8901

REVOKATION

Karl "Drunkschwein" Envall: v/b, "Jonny Putrid": g, "Fred Hellbelly": d

Stockholm - Death metal band *Revokation* (not to be confused with the UK band or the US band *Revocation*) were formed in 1998, and is currently on hold. *Reincarnated Souls Of Hell* was recorded as a cassette demo in 1999, but re-released by Nuclear Winter as a 7" EP in 2004. Envall is also found in *Kaamos* and *Asmodeus*. Jonny is also in *Serpent Obscene*.

2004 7" - NWR 008

2004 ■ Reincarnated Souls Of Hell.. 7" 4tr   Nuclear Winter Records.................... NWR 008
   Tracks: The Old One's Abbey/Sacriligious Copulation/Angel's Bane/Reincarnated Souls
   Of Hell. 550 copies

REVOLTING

Roger "Revolting Rogga" Johansson: v/g, Grotesque Tobias: b, Mutated Martin: d

Gamleby - This nice little horror-inspired death metal combo was formed in 2008 by *Ribspreader/Paganizer/Bone Gnawer/Demiurg/Sinners Burn* etc member Rogga. They recorded the first three-track demo the same year. The tracks from the unreleased MCD *Bonesaw Leftovers* was released as bonus on the second CD. *Revolting* plays well-produced, brutal, yet heavy death metal in the vein of *Grave* and *Unleashed*. The name was chosen by Billy "Grossera" Nocera to reflect the horror films of the eighties.

2009 CD - RR 52

2009 ■ DREADFUL PLEASURES ....CD   Razorback Recordings ....RR 52
2010 □ THE TERROR THRESHOLD..CD   Razorback Recordings ....RR 58
2011 □ IN GRISLY RAPTURE ....CD   F.D.A Rekotz FDA-31
   Sticker.
2011 □ IN GRISLY RAPTURE ....LP   F.D.A Rekotz FDA-31
2012 □ HYMNS OF GHASTLY HORROR.....................................CD   F.D.A Rekotz...FDA-47
2012 □ HYMNS OF GHASTLY HORROR.....................................LP   F.D.A Rekotz...FDA-47
2012 □ Within The Morbid Ossuary (split)..7"   Cyclone Empire CYC-121-1
   Split with Revel In Flesh. Tracks: Operation Razorteeth/The Spawning. 200 red and 300
   in black vinyl.

REVOLUTION RIOT

Per "Glitz" Cederberg: v/g, Jonas "Skinny" Kangur: g,
Wilhelm "Fisch" Fischerström: b, Tommie "Tom-E" Nissilä: d

Stockholm - *Revolution Riot* were formed in the suburbs of Stockholm in 1997 by Glitz and bass player Sleazy Texas. They drafted drummer Nissilä and in 1998 recorded a track for a *Motörhead* tribute. In July the same year they recorded the demo *It's Not A Friend It's A Lifestyle*. In 1999 guitarist Jonas "Skinny" Kangur was added to the line-up. Sleazy left and was replaced by Tobias "Eazy" Danielsson and in January 2000 the demo *Hell Yeah!!!* was recorded. This lead to a deal with Feedback Boogie. Shortly after its release, bassist Danielsson left and Fisch entered. In 2006 guitarist Kangur left to devote his time to *Deathstars*, He was replaced by former *Sister Sin* guitarist Johan "Johnny" Eriksson. Fisch is also handling session bass for *Satariel*. Drummer Nissilä has also been replaced by Simon Becker. Fat and rocking sleaze metal in the vein of classic *Mötley Crüe* or Swedish colleagues *Crazy Lixx*. A new album is in the making.

2005 CD - FBR CD 025

2001 □ OUT OF THE GUTTER, INTO THE LIGHT ....CD   Feedback Boogie...............................FBR 014
2005 ■ BLUES FOR THE SPRITUALLY RETARDED ....CD   Feedback Boogie........................ FBR CD 025

RHAPSODY (SWEDEN)

Benny Ahlkvist: v, Kjell-Åke Norén: g, Peter Åhs: k,
Rudolf Janszky: b, Thorbjörn "Tobbe" Persson: d

Vara/Lidköping - Formed in 1975. This album is a highly acclaimed and sought after item on vinyl. *Rhapsody* are in the vein of *Deep Purple* or *Uriah Heep* with great organ/guitar parts. In 1977-78 they made a 25-gig tour in Hungary, some recorded by radio and TV. Rudolf left and Peter took over the bass. The band split in 1980. Peter and Thorbjörn later formed the excellent AOR/pomp-band *Extasy*. Benny joined the symphonic band *Ambra*, who changed their style into AOR and the name to *Gallery*. They recorded three singles. Kjell-Åke joined "dansband" *Thor-Eriks* and Peter was later found in female dance/popsinger Lotta Engbergs backing group. The album was remixed for Japan, but it was never released there. A rarity worth spending your hard-earned cash on. In 2004 MTM reissued the album, as *Strange Vibrations*, with two new songs, recorded by the reunited band, featuring Ahlqvist, Norén, Åhs and Persson. However,

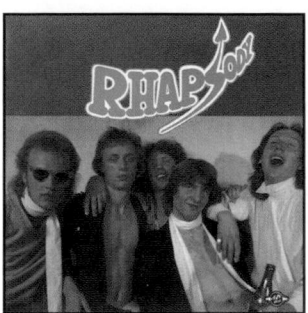

1978 LP - TF 75 609

647

the band name had to be changed due to the Italian namesakes. The new tracks shows great promise and a new album is in the making for a 2013/14 release

| 1978 ■ | RHAPSODY | LP | Tyfon | TF 75 609 | $ |
| 2004 ■ | STRANGE VIBRATIONS | CD | MTM Classix | 0681-118 | |

Bonus: It's Gotta Be Tonight/Sweet Rock 'N Roll.

2004 CD - 0681-118

RIBSPREADER

Roger "Rogga" Johansson: v/g/b, Andreas "Dea" Carlsson: g/b, Brynjar Helgetun: d

Gamleby - Yet another death metal creation of the mighty Rogga (*Paganizer, Demiurg, Carve, Deranged, Edge Of Sanity, Revolting, Sinners Burn, Those Who Bring The Torture* etc.), initiated in 2004. Drums on the debut were handled by Dan Swanö, while Andreas Carlsson (*Another Life, Paganizer, Sinners Burn, Terminal Grip*) played guitar and bass. On the second album, produced by Mieszko Talarczyk, the line-up featured Rogga, Dan, bass player Patrik Halvarsson (*Blodsrit, Paganizer, Sinners Burn, Primitive Symphony*) and drummer Johan Berglund (*Demiurg, This Haven*), while the *Vicar Mortis* EP and *Rotten Rhythms* were recorded by Rogga and drummer Mattias Fiebig (*Blodsrit, Portal, Paganizer*). On *Opus Ribcage* Ronnie Björnström (*Embracing, Bone Gnawer, Knife In Christ, Those Who Bring The Torture, Taedat*) was handling the drums, and Carlsson was back on bass. On *The Van Murders* the line-up had again changed seeing Rogga and Andreas still in the band, while the drums were handled by Brynjar Helgetun (*Paganizer, Crypticus, The Grotesquery, Liklukt, The Skeletal*). *The Kult Of The Pneumatic Killrod* is a tenth anniversary album featuring a bonus CD with much of the old EPs and albums as bonus. Lead guitars are here handled by Patrick Bruss (*Crypticus*). Death metal with a touch of grindcore.

2004 CD - NAM 002

2005 CD - KARMA 083

2004 ■	BOLTED TO THE CROSS	CD	New Aeon Media	NAM 002
2004 ☐	BOLTED TO THE CROSS	CD	Candlelight (USA)	CDL 0115CD
2005 ■	CONGREGATING THE SICK	CD	Karmageddon	KARMA 083
2006 ☐	Vicar Mortis	7" 4tr	Midnight 666	MR666-010

Tracks: Intro/The Day It All Ended/Knee-Deep In Death/Torn To Pieces. Sticker.

| 2006 ☐ | ROTTEN RHYTHMS AND RANCID RANTS | CD | Obliteration Records | ORCD 061 |
| 2007 ☐ | The Monolith | 7" 3tr | Blood Harvest | YOTZ #11 |

Tracks: The Monolith/Trapped In Unhuman Flesh/Domes Of The Ancients. 500 copies.

| 2007 ☐ | Dead As Fuck (split) | MCD | The Spew | TS 15 |

Split with Machetazo. Tracks: The Cryptkeeper/Mortuaty Slut/Repulsed By The Living

2009 ☐	OPUS RIBCAGE: MMVI	CD	Vic Records	VIC 013 CD
2011 ■	THE VAN MURDERS	CD	Vic Records	VIC 039 CD
2012 ☐	THE KULT OF THE PNEUMATIC KILLROD	2CD	Vic Records	VIC 043 DCD

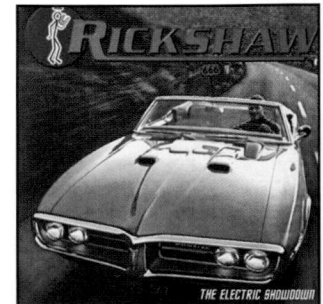

2011 CD - VIC 039 CD

RICKSHAW

Jocke Olsson: v/g, Robert "Bobby Dawn" Nilsson: g, Macke "Machabuzz": d

Göteborg - *Rickshaw* were formed in 1998, initially featuring Jocke, Robert, keyboard player Andreas "Andy Be Bop" Östberg, bass player Magnus Timmerås and drummer Henrik Antonsson. In 2001 the line-up changed now featuring Jocke, Bobby Dawn (*Dorian Grey, Lorilei*), bass player Carl "Carlos Satanos" Linnaeus (*Lucifyre, Abandon*) and drummer Marcus "Machabuzz" in the band and *Double Deluxe* premiered the new band. The 2001 *Adam West* split features Anders Iwers on bass. The 2003 *Down The Road* is a best of. The band has now split. High-octane stoner rock. Linnaeus is today in *Chillihounds* and Macke in straightforward rockers *The Chuck Norris Experiment*.

| 1999 ■ | The Electric Showdown | 7" 4tr | HDP Records | shaw7.001 |

Tracks: Electric Showdown/A.Y.G.T.K/Superfly/Fuel. 1st press: 300 numbered black vinyl. 2nd press: 300 red vinyl.

| 2000 ☐ | One Dollar/Going Down To Hell (split) | 7" EP | HDP Records | shaw7.002 |

Split with Trigger. Tracks: One Dollar/Going Down To Hell/Get It On. 500 copies white.

| 2000 ☐ | TENDER SONGS OF LOVE (THE LP) | LP | Beluga Music | belugalp 010 |
| 2001 ☐ | DOUBLE DELUXE (split) | CD | Beluga/Dare Devil | beluga014/DD0014 |

Split with Hateball. Tracks: Buckle Up!/She Used To Dance/ Tribute To Punk Rock/Life In Hypercolour/Fukk Shitt Up/Only My Soul/Pockets Full Of Sunskine (Lose It)

| 2001 ☐ | Rickshaw/Adam West (split) | 7" | HDP Records | shaw7.003 |

Split with Adam West. Track: Nothing To Lose. 500 copies.

| 2002 ☐ | ACTION... GO (split) | LP | DSB Records | DSB 006 |

Split with Trigger. Clear marble vinyl. Tracks: Actiion... Go/Satellite soul/Temple Of Your Choice/That's Bullshit This Sucks/Enough Is Enough/Perfect Crime/Biker Boy

| 2002 ☐ | ACTION... GO (split) | CD | DSB Records | DSB 006 |

Different artwork.

| 2002 ☐ | Rickshaw/Noise Of Reality (split) | 7" EP | Bootleg Booze | booze 003 |

Split with Noise Of Reality. Tracks: Numbing Fuel/Kick It. 500 copies. 50 ltd edition.

| 2002 ■ | Rickshaw/The Strap-Ons | 7" EP | Bootleg Booze | booze 006 |

Split with The Strap-Ons. Tracks: Hang Tough-Stiff Neck/Bad Breath Baby. 500 copies. 50 ltd ed.

| 2002 ☐ | Rickshaw/The Awesome Machine | 7" EP PD | Daredevil | DD 021 |

Split with The Awesome Machine. Tracks: Fortuneteller/White Light. 500 copies.

1999 7" - shaw7.001

2002 7" - booze 006

2003	■	DOWN THE ROAD & STILL BURNING FUEL	CD	Devil Doll Records	DDR-30
2003	□	SONIC OVERLOAD	CD	Devil Doll Records	DDR-33
2003	□	Rickshaw/Bad Machine (split)	7" EP	Woimasointu	WS 020

Split with Bad Machine. Tracks: Get Your Action/Cry Baby. 500 copies.

| 2003 | □ | I'm Ready/Endless Groove | 7" | Bad Attitude | badat! 010 |

500 copies.

| 2006 | □ | Rickshaw/Duster 69 | MCD | W *Uck Records | n/a |

Split with Duster 69. Tracks: Death:Star/Summer Fun-Part II/Last Man Standing + video

2007 CD - NB 1874-2

RIDE THE SKY

Björn Jansson: v, Benny Jansson: g, Kaspar Dahlqvist: k,
Mathias Garnås: b, Uli Kusch: d

Stokholm/Germany - The basis for **Ride The Sky** was founded in 2006 when **Gamma Ray/ Masterplan** drummer **Uli Kusch** started swapping musical ideas with **Two Rocks** singer **Björn** Jansson. When Uli left **Masterplan**, Björn and his brother Benny Jansson (**Two Rocks, Snake Charmer, Johansson Brothers** etc) asked him to lay down some drums on their new project **Tears Of Anger**. This sparked what would become **Ride The Sky**. They drafted keyboard player Dahlqvist (**Treasure Land, Stormwind**) and bass player Garnås. They were soon picked up by Nuclear Blast Records and recorded their only album to date. The album is very cheesy, ultra-commercial power metal. In 2007 Kaspar left the band and was replaced by **Ram-Zet**'s Henning Ramseth. However in 2008 the band disbanded, due to lacking support from the record label.

| 2007 | ■ | NEW PROTECTION | CD | Nuclear Blast | NB 1874-2 |
| 2007 | □ | NEW PROTECTION | CD | Avalon Marquee (Japan) | MICP-10670 |

Bonus: Make The Spirit Burn/Trail Of Fame

| 2007 | □ | NEW PROTECTION | CD | Irond (Russia) | CD 07-1334 |

RIDGE

Andreas Bergström: v/g, Johannes Svensson: g, Jonas Jönsson: b, Johan Ohlsson: d

Malmö - The band was actually named after Ridge Forrester from the TV-show *Bold And The Beautiful*. The band was formed in 1998. The band claims influences from **Black Sabbath** and Johnny Cash, a mix that reads "stoner". Well, **Ridge** is in the same musical territory as **Kyuss** and **Fu Manchu**. Quite chord-oriented, straightforward stoner rock with a garagey touch and not as fuzzed-out as some of the colleagues. The vocals are more in the semi-spoken vein. The track *Avalanche* can be found on *Molten Universe Volume One* (1999 MU) and *Fuelle* on *Volume Two* (2000 MU). Andreas and Jonas are also in the band **Matadors**. The EP *The Cayuga Sessions* was supposedly released in 2000, but I have found no traces of it in physical form.

| 1999 | □ | Le Rodeo '69 | 7" | Layer Recordings | n/a |

Tracks: Avalanche/Firetruck/The Silver Dragon

| 2001 | ■ | A COUNTRYDELIC AND FUZZED EXPERIENCE IN A COLOMBIAN SUPREMO | | | |
| | | | CD | Molten Universe | MOLTEN 012 |

2001 CD - MOLTEN 012

RIFF, THE

Michael Wedberg: v/g, Göran Pripp, Christer Eriksson

Stockholm - Quite mainstream melodic hard rock in the vein of early **Magnum Bonum** or **Snowstorm** with Swedish lyrics. They look a lot heavier than they sound. Wedberg was later found in cover band **Public Service**.

| 1981 | ■ | Ska Det Va Så Svårt/Leta Guld | 7" | Mercury | 6016 054 |

1981 7" - 6016 054

RIFLES, THE

Mikael Olander: v/g, Gabriel Eskilsson: g, Tomas Nilsson: b, André Swahn: d

Kristianstad - **The Rifles** play straightforward hard rock, at times with a sleazy touch. The singer is not really exciting and the band lacks spark, but they give it a good go.

| 1995 | ■ | GIVE ME SOME ACTION | CD | private | RIF 01 |

1995 CD - RIF 01

RIKSVÄG 77

Ulf Gustafsson: v/g, Åke Svensk: g, Ove Thorell: b/v, Alf Thorell: k, Urban Thorell: d

Rimbo - This band is really on the verge, but since *Klockan* is actually a pretty good hard rocker, I decided to include the band. The overall sound is basic hard rock in the vein of **Dunder** and **Ocean**, but Ulf's punkish, out-of-key, **Noise**-style vocals are quite the turn off. Formed in 1980, when youngest brother Urban was only 13. A few attempts were made to record a full album. Åke and Ulf left in 1986 and the band split in 1996. Urban and Ove today play in **Once Again**.

| 1985 | ■ | Domens murar/Klockan | 7" | Musikimperiet | RV 001 |

1985 7" - RV 001

RIMFROST

Hravn Decmiester: v/g, Peter Laustsen: b, Fredde "Throllv" Hänninen: d

Hagfors/Borås - **Rimfrost** (means rime frost in Swedish), were formed by fourteen-year-old singer/guitarist Hravn in 2002, initially under the name **Mörkrets Furstar** (Lords of darkness) and singing in Swedish. Classmate Throllv joined and they recorded their first self-titled demo in October 2002. The band now started singing in English, went a bit more technical and changed the name to **Rimfrost**. Bassist Sorghim joined and they released the demo *Unredeemed Demons* in 2003. Now bass player Frozthirw joined and they recorded the demo *Winds Of Hostility* with producer Jonas Kjellgren in 2005. There was interest from a label and as they wanted another song, the band went back to Avesta and recorded *At The Mighty Halls They'll Walk*. During the recordings of the debut album the band parted ways with bass player Frozthirw and Beuwolf, who had played guitar live with the band, entered. The album was actually only 37:37 minutes. Throllv now moved to Borås and in 2008 Hravn followed him. Geographical differences made it impossible for Beuwolf to continue and session man Peter Laustsen (**The Cold Existence**, ex-**Nox Aurea**) was drafted for the *Veraldar Nagli* album. **Rimfrost** play well-produced blast beat black metal with a nod to the old school.

The cold lords of darkness

2006 CD - NC 115

2005 ☐	A Journey To A Greater End	MCD 3tr	No Colours	NC 101
	Tracks: At The Mighty Halls They'll Walk/A Frozen World Unknown/Darken			
2006 ■	A FROZEN WORLD UNKNOWN	CD	No Colours	NC 115
2009 ☐	VERALDAR NAGLI	CD	Seasons Of Mist	SUA 007

RIMTHURS

Tommy "Ymer" Holmers: v/g/d

Hudiksvall - Tommy Holmers' solo project **Rimthurs** play ultra-fast old-school black metal with chanted vocals mixed with growl. At times similar to **Vonur**, **Kampfar** and **Enherjer**. The project was initiated already in the mid-nineties and the, still unreleased, demo *Bortom Nidafjäll* was recorded in 1998. The first official demo was however not released until 2004 and the second one, *Ur: Kaos*, in 2005, later officially released by Temple Of Darkness. On *Ur:Kaos* and *Svartnar* the bass work was handled by Mordh. Tommy has also recorded several demos with **Planet Rain**, **Undivide** and **Necrocide**, mainly as a drummer.
Website: www.rimthurs.se/

2010 CD - RITE 002

2006 ☐	Ur: Kaos	MCD 5tr	Temple Of Darkness	TOD 012
	Tracks: Förbannelse/Köld/Ur kaos/Våld/Dreptu allur (Vondur cover)			
2010 ■	SVARTNAR	CD	Archaic Sound	RITE 002
	First press. 500 copies.			
2010 ☐	SVARTNAR	CDd	Archaic Sound	RITE 002
	Second press. 500 copies.			

RING, THE

Jakob "Jake Samuel" Samuelsson: v/d/k, Pontus Norgren: g/b/k, Marcus Jidell: g/b/k

Stockholm - When things don't work one way, try a different one. Before working with fluffy eighties-sounding band **The Poodles**, Jakob and Pontus tried doing it the melodic power metal way. **The Ring** were a fairly short-lived band, also featuring Jidell (now in **Evergrey**). Jakob had previously sung and played drums in bands like **Yale Bate**, **Jekyll 'N Hyde**, **Totem**, **Talisman**, **Trasure Land**, **Punchline** etc., while Pontus had recorded with **Great King Rat**, **Talisman**, **Damage Done** etc. They joined forces in **The Ring** and approached it in a power metal style with a medieval-inspired theme. Not bad at all, a bit like a mix of **Manowar** and **Dream Evil**, at times with a touch of US band **Warrior**. Great production, too. The album also features guest vocals from Doogie White (**Rainbow**, **Tank** etc). Jacob is now fronting **The Poodles**, while Pontus went via **The Poodles** to **HammerFall**.

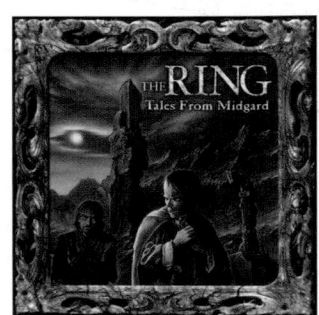
2004 CD - SC 088-2

2004 ■	TALES FROM MIDGARD	CD	Scarlet	SC 088-2
2004 ☐	TALES FROM MIDGARD	CD	King Records (Japan)	KICP-998
	Bonus: Coat Of Many Colours			

RIO

Håkan Hallmén: v/g, Jörgen Berglund: g, Niclas Nordqvist: k,
Christer Linder: b, P Warenmark: d

Örebro - High-quality pomp/AOR with strong influences from **Saga**. Nice melodies and nice guitar/keyboard work. Could have been something. Linder was ex-**Avenue**. On the second single, drummer Peter Axelsson was replaced by Warenmark and keyboard player Johan Lindström (ex-**Avenue**) was out of the band. In 1985 Nordqvist made a single under the name **Project UPA**.

1985 7" - HEJ S-010

1984 ☐	Time Is On The Loose/Surrender	7"	Aktiv Musik	HEJ 003
1985 ■	On My Side/Closer To You	7"	Aktiv Musik	HEJ S-010

RISE AND SHINE

Josabeth Leidi: v, Joakim Knutsson: g, Daniel Josefsson: g, Dennis Pålsson: b, Magnus Rydman: d

Stockholm - **Rise And Shine** were formed in 1993 and is a true doom-band, influenced by the likes of **Black Sabbath**, **Trouble** and **Cathedral**. The powerful vocals of female singer Josabeth give the band a personal touch. The band recorded two demos in 1993 and 1994, before the first EP. The line-up then featured Josabeth, Knutsson, Pålsson and drummer Mattias Värmby. The album also featured guest guitars from Fredrik Gleisner, Fredrik Finnander and Fredrik Lindgren. On *Roadflower*, Tomas Bergstrand was added on guitar and Eric Nordin had replaced drummer Mattias Värmby. On *Ghosts Of The Past*, Magnus Rydman had taken over the drums and Fredrik Finnander guests on two tracks. After a few years of silence the band returned with the album *Empty Hand* and now guitarist Daniel Josefsson (also a writer for Close-Up magazine) was part of the band. **Rise And Shine** can also be found on the compilation *Thousand Days Of Yesterdays – A Tribute To Captain Beyond* (99 Record Heaven), where they do *Armsworth* and on *Bastards Will Pay* (99 Freedom), a tribute to **Trouble**. Josabeth and Joakim are also found in **Satanarchy**.

Roadflowers or couch potatoes?

1996	☐	I'm Sinking/My Day Tomorrow/Home	7" 3tr	Freedom	FRED 701
		Red vinyl.			
1996	☐	Danish Denim/C'mon Cat/Promised Land	7" 3tr	Freedom	FRED 703
		Blue vinyl.			
1997	☐	Deadringer (For Love)	7"	Primitive Art	PAR 015
		Split with Gehennah..Track: Deadringer (For Love) (Meatloaf cover)			
1998	☐	FLOWER POWER METAL	LPg	Black Widow	BWR 023
		400 copies.			
1998	☐	FLOWER POWER METAL	CD	Black Widow	BWR 023-2
2000	☐	ROADFLOWER	LPg	Black Widow	BWR 037
		500 copies.			
2000	☐	ROADFLOWER	CD	Black Widow	BWR 037-2
2006	☐	Break The Chains Of Time/Into The Fog	CDS	Plugged Records	PLUCD 021
2006	■	GHOSTS OF THE PAST	CD	Plugged Records	PLUCD 022
2011	☐	EMPTY HAND	CD	I Hate Records	IHR 103
2012	☐	EMPTY HAND	LP	I Hate Records	IHR 103
		300 copies.			
2012	■	Swedish Assault (split)	7"	Night Tripper	NTR 007
		Split with El Camino. Track: The 7 Gates Of Hell (Venom cover)			

2006 CD - PLUCD 022

2012 7" - NTR 007

RISING

Martin Ramberg: v, Urban Svensson: g, Thorbjörn Andersson: k, Peter "Lato" Andersson: b, Andreas Svensson: d

Vänersborg - Started out as a NWoBHM-influenced band on the first single, recorded a bunch of average metal demos before they recorded a full-length album with producer Göran Elmquist at the helm. He was however so disappointed with the mix that he refused to have his name on it. The album was never even released, only two songs appeared on the *Grampian Heights* single, which was very poppy. The members on the first single were Magnus and Urban Svensson (g), Peter Andersson (b), Paul Utter (v) and Lars Berger (d). In 1994 Urban, who was Andreas and Magnus brother, died of cancer. Urban, Andreas was ex-**Remo**, while Lars was in **Gooseflesh** and **Electric Earth**.

1983 7" - PSI 031

1983	■	Metal Bird/She's Got Bright Eyes	7"	Pang	PSI 031 $$
1990	■	Grampian Heights/Rockin' Horse	7"	Empire	EMPS-030

1990 7" - EMPS-030

RISING FAITH

Kristian Wallin: v, Fredrik Jordanius: g, Jimmie Bergkvist: g, Stefan Englund: b, Tony Gelander: d

Göteborg - Formed in 1999 and recorded their first demo the same year. Thrashy but melodic power metal in the vein of **Megadeth**-meet-**Iron Saviour**. The vocals are the weak link, not bad, but a bit strained. Fredrik joined after *Imagination* was recorded. The band has also recorded a second demo entitled *Promo 2001*. In 2002 drummer Kristian Enkvist was replaced by Gelander. *The Arrival* was mixed by Pelle Saether (**Grand Design, Carnal Forge, Locomotive Breath** etc). The band have now split up.

The arrival of the risen

2000	☐	Imagination	MCD 5tr	private	- -
		Tracks: Marching On/Road To Eternity/Where Sanity Grows/The Other Side/Imagination			
2003	■	THE ARRIVAL	CD	Limb Music	0306-055 CD

2003 CD - 0306-055 CD

RITUAL
Patrik Lundström: v/g, Fredrik Lindqvist: b, Jon Gamble: k, Johan Nordgren: d

Stockholm - A high-class band in the early 70s prog/symph-era. You can hear traces of bands like **King Crimson** and **Yes**, but also **Led Zeppelin** at times. All albums are well worth investigating. Patrik is also found in pop-band **Blond** and he lends his voice to **Kaipa** on the 2002-album.

1995	☐	RITUAL	CD	Musea	FGBG 4158.AR
1996	☐	RITUAL	CD	Belle Antique (Japan)	n/a
		Bonus: Visions Quest (recorded live in Oslo)			
1999	☐	Did I Go Wrong	MCD 4tr	Ritual AB	LOMCDS-1
		Tracks: Did I Go Wrong/Into The Heat/Sadly Unspoken/Breathing			
1999	☐	SUPERB BIRTH	CD	Ritual AB	ROMCD-2
2003	☐	THINK LIKE A MOUNTAIN	CD	Inside Out/Tempus Fugit	035-65602/TF VÖ 12
2004	☐	RITUAL	CD	Tempus Fugit	TF VÖ 13
2004	☐	SUPERB BIRTH	CD	Tempus Fugit	TF VÖ 15
2006	☐	LIVE	2CD	Tempus Fugit	TF VÖ 21
2007	■	THE HEMULIC VOLOUNTARY BAND	CD	Inside Out/Tempus Fugit	TF VÖ 23
2007	☐	THE HEMULIC VOLOUNTARY BAND	CD	Belle Antique (Japan)	MAR-071313

2007 CD - TF VÖ 23

ROACH
Håkan "Gurra" Johnson: v, Pontus Borg: g, Jonas Karlberg: g,
Mats "J.R" Josephson: k, Robert Garnold: b, Stefan Ridderstråle: d

Göteborg - **Roach** were formed in 1983-84 with members spread out in the Göteborg area (Floda, Alingsås, Lindome and Hisingen) influenced by bands like **Rainbow**, **Deep Purple** and **Europe**. They entered several band stands and reached the finals of the 1987 Rock SM. However, the band split a few years later. Robert, Pontus and Stefan formed the new band **Double W Twise**, also featuring singer Pierre Wensberg, more in the vein of **Toto**. The A-side is a great melodic hard rocker with nice guitar harmonies and the B-side is a ballad. Pontus is the nephew of **Alien** guitarist Tony Borg, who also produced the single. Garnold is today in **Elevener**.

1987	■	Time/Last Forever	7"	VMA	WMA-R 002

1987 7" - WMA-R 002

ROACHPOWDER
Fransisco Rencoret: v, George Bravo: g, Lars Rosenberg: b, Håkan Persson: d

Stockholm - When Matti Alfonzetti and Stefan Berggren left **Skintrade** in 1995, George, bass player Håkan Calmroth and Håkan "Måsen" Persson reformed the band under the name **Roachpowder** (the title from **Skintrade**'s last album, taken from William Burrogh's book *Naked Lunch*). Singer Rencoret was added to the line-up. The music is even heavier than **Skintrade**, more like **Black Sabbath** meets **Motörhead** with a psychedelic touch and quite rough vocals. The last track on the debut is entitled *Super Galactic Gargle Blazer*, meaning the boys know their *Hitchhiker's Guide To The Galaxy* (by author Douglas Adams). When the second album was released bass player Håkan Calmroth had been replaced by Lars (**Entombed, Serpent**), but it's also stated on the cover that those duties were actually taken care of by Linus Wiklund on stage.

2001 CDd - TMC 43 CD

1998	☐	VIEJO DIABLO	CD	Outside Society	OSP003
1998	☐	VIEJO DIABLO	CD	The Music Cartel (USA)	TMC 11 CD
2001	■	ATOMIC CHURCH	CDd	The Music Cartel (USA)	TMC 43 CD

ROAD RATT
Christer Örtefors: v, Fredrik Stenberg: g,
Ola Johansson: b, Patrik "PsychoPatrik" Herrstedt: d

Göteborg - A powerful, positive hard rock act with hints of old **Kiss** and **Nazareth** as well as elements of sleaze. **Road Ratt** was highlighted when they won a local bandstand in Göteborg and was featured on the compilation album Rockslaget 1992. After the album, second guitarist Alban Herlitz left the band. After the album the band recorded some new material which showed more power and determination. Christer also sang on a commercial for the Swedish railroad. Patrik left the band to join **Transport League** and Örtefors later joined **Freak Kitchen** handling the bass. He also fronts his own band **Eaglestrike**, who have one album out. The debut CD was supposed to be reissued in 2011, but it hasn't happened yet.

2008 CD - SR 028

1992 CD - REALCD 2

1992	■	RESURRECTION	CD	Reel Records	REALCD 2
1992	☐	Resurrection/I Wish/Use The Lighter	MCD 3tr	Reel Records	REALCDS 2
1992	☐	Itsypooked/Funny People/Itsypooked (acoustic)	MCD 3tr	Reel Records	REALCDS 3
2008	■	YOU LOVE US	CD	Sun City Records (Australia)	SR 028

ROAD II RUIN
Matti Alfonzetti: v, Lars "Criss" Christmansson: g, Sampo Axelsson: b/k

Stockholm - When Lars and Sampo started working together in **Lion's Share** in 2005 they had

2007 CD - 00041

some ideas which didn't fit the metal-oriented style **Lion's Share** was heading towards. Instead of scrapping the stuff, Sampo came up with the idea of doing a full album of the more classic hard rock in the vein of **Rainbow**, **Whitesnake** and **Deep Purple**. They asked Thomas Broman (**Great King Rat**, **Electric Boys**, **Audiovision**, **John Norum** etc.) to lay down drums on the songs. After this, singer Matti Alfonzetti (**Skintrade**, **Alfonzetti**, **Jagged Edge**, **Red White & Blues** etc.) was drafted to the band. Lars Pollack plays keyboards on the album. A great classic hard rock album with great musicianship, killer vocals and great songs.

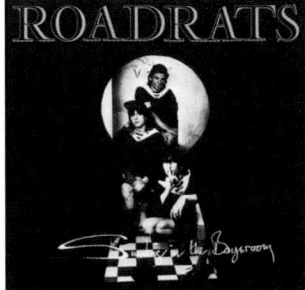
1984 7" - T-20057

2007 ■	RIIR	CD	Metal Heaven	00041	
2008 ☐	RIIR	CD	Locomotive Music (USA)	LM 595	
2008 ☐	RIIR	CD	Avalon Marquee (Japan)	MICP-10717	
	Bonus: Wheels Of The World				
2008 ☐	RIIR	CD	Irond (Russia)	CD 08-DD628	

ROADRATS

Conny "Bloom" Blomqvist: v/g, Dan Lagerstedt: b, Jesper "Gyp Casino" Sporre: d

Stockholm - Formed in 1983 by former **Rex De Rox** drummer Gyp Casino (later in **Hanoi Rocks**) and childhood friends Conny "Bloom" Blomqvist (**Neon Rose**, **Electric Boys**, **Titanic Truth**, **Hanoi Rocks**) and Anders "Andy" Christell (**Electric Boys**, **Hanoi Rocks**). The latter left quite soon, and was replaced by **Easy Action** member Dan Lagerstedt. This is actually closer to rough-edged R&B than hard rock, but still hard enough. *Smokin' In The Boys Room* is a cover of the old **Brownsville Station** tune, later covered by **Mötley Crüe**. The second single had a slight touch of new wave. There were plans for an album, but the band split later 1984. Instead Blomqvist, Casino and Christell joined forces again and formed the band **Rolene**, where Casino switched to guitar/vocals and Anders Bentell was drafted as the new drummer. For collectors only.

1984 7" - BESS 101 A

1984 ■	Smokin' In The Boys Room/Lips That Touch Liquor	7"	Sonet	T-20057	
1984 ■	Satisfaction In Jeans/Pink Satin Cloud	7"	BETA	BESS 101 A	

ROBB AND FRIENDS

Peter Robsahm: v, Roger Nikander: g, Nils Ekholm: b, Mats Hellberg: d

Hjo - **Robb And Friends** was a project initiated by singer Peter Robsahm in 1978. The first single featured bass player Dan Skavhellen. Straight-ahead melodic 70s-sounding hard rock with a touch of **Mott** mixed with early **Foreigner**. Really good stuff! On the second release the band also featured backing singers Helen Froh (now Årjes) and Eva Kemppainen (related to **Shotgun Messiah**'s Jukka Kemppainen). The band recorded enough material for an album, but it sadly fizzled out. In 1984 the band finally folded. Peter went on to write musicals, such as *Notre Dame* and a new rock opera that will be set up in 2013. Nikander went on to form blues band **Roger Nikander Band**, besides being an actor. The second single was second prize in a bandstand.

1979 7" - CFR-S 7007

1982 7" - res 1001

1979 ■	Daydreamer/In The Air	7"	CFR	CFR-S 7007	$
1982 ■	The Adict/Stranger In The City	7"	Studio 66	res 1001	$

ROBEEO

Robin Lundgren: v/g/b/d

Stockholm - Great heavy melodic guitar-dominated metal ranging from almost doomy riffing to metal to rockin' sleaze. Robin is also found in **Powerdrive**, **Scientic** and **The Reckoning** (UK).

2008 ■	FLASHBACK	CD	Goldentouch Productions	rpm 001

2008 CD - rpm 001

ROCK, DAVE

David "Dave Rock" Wilhelmson: v/g/b/d

Rocker Rock

Kil - Hearing **W.A.S.P**'s *I Wanna Be Somebody* at the age of six made Dave want to be a rock star. He recorded his first solo album in 1997, under his real name and together with drummer Christian Jernbro. The album is actually a pretty good instrumental-guitar shredding album, well worth checking out of you're into the Shrapnel Records catalogue of shredding. He later went into band constellations. When his band **Beda** broke up in 2003 he went solo. Dave Rock is quite the gifted musician and when he goes solo he does it all the way, recording and singing every bit on the album. It is actually a really good album as well. Melodic well-played hard rock with a touch of sleaze. After the solo album he formed the sleaze band **The Trix** together with guitarist David Johannesson (later in **Mustasch**), who made some videos and recordings, but broke up in 2009. Later the same year Dave joined **Renegade Five** as their bass player and played on their first singles. After this he started collaborating with **Renegade Five** singer Per Nylin and their new band **Dunderman** was born.

2006 CD - WSONR 001

1997 ☐	BLUE HAPPINESS	CD	private	WCD 9999-1
	Released as David Wilhelmsson.			
2006 ■	LIFE IN FREEDOM	CD	W-son	WSONR 001

ROCK SQUAD

Lars Lagergren: v, Roger Johansson: g, Conny Johansson: g,
Roger Lind: b, Ronny Karlsson: d

Finspång - Really good bluesy hard rock on side A, while the B-side is more melodic rock. The track *The Escape* was also featured on the *Double Up* compilation in 1987.

1983 ■ Enough/Angelica..7" private...RS 007

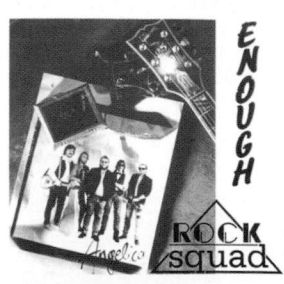
1983 7" - RS 007

ROCKBOX

Urban "Ubbe" Carli: v/g, Rolf "Roffe" Gustafsson: g,
Johan "Joe" Danielsson: b, Urban "Ubbe" Gustafsson: d

Västerås - The band recorded the single *Josefin* in 1984 under the odd name ***Andra Band*** (Other Bands/Second Band). Pretty good melodic (hard) rock with nice twin guitars, unfortunately the vocals are more akin to popster Per Gessle meets Ulf Lundell. On the verge.

1987 ■ Seglar/I dina ögon...7" Sonet...T-10231

1987 7" - T-10231

ROCKVAKTMÄSTARNA

Jonny Andersson: v, Mikael Freij: g, Bertil Harding: g,
Göran Sjöberg: b, Anders Forsse: d

Malmö - Hard rock? Well, some songs are standard rock while others could easily be labelled hard rock. The album features originals, as well as covers of ***Alice Cooper***, ***The Beatles*** and ***The Kinks***.

1979 ■ ROCKVAKTMÄSTARNA..LP Mudist...MUD 501380

ROCKVATTNÄ

Jögge Sundqvist: v/g, Anders Söderström: g, Bengt Mikaelsson: b, Henry Forsén: d

Dorotea - Very left-wing, political, hard rock in the vein of ***Motvind***. M-L in the label name actually stands for "Marxist-Leninists". ***Rockvattnä*** is local slang for "rock water".

1979 ■ ROCKVATTNÄ..LP Ljudbarrikaden (M-L) ....LBLP 502

1979 LP - MUD 501380

ROLENE

Conny Blomquist: v/g, Jesper "Gyp Casino" Sporre: g/v,
Anders "Andy" Christell: b, Anders "Ben Tell" Bentell: d

Stockholm - Late 1984, when the band ***Roadrats*** disbanded Conny and Gyp, reunited with former ***Roadrats*** bassist Christell and formed ***Rolene***. They drafted drummer Bentell. Gyp, who actually played guitar in ***Roadrats***, was later in ***Hanoi Rocks*** and Bentell played with pop-punkster Pelle Almgren (pop band ***Easy Action***, not the sleaze band). ***Rolene*** was a bit more straight-ahead, rock-oriented than ***Roadrats***. The album, which is not really hard rock, but more glammy rock in the vein of ***Hanoi Rocks***, was not as successful as the label had anticipated and the band was dropped. The band split and Conny played with ***Neon Rose*** for a year before he and Andy formed ***Electric Boys***. For completists only.

1986 LP - RAMI 2010

1985 ☐ Rollin' With Rolene/Boys Talk ....7" Pyramid.......................................RAMS 109
1985 ☐ Wouldn't You Like To Know Me/Beep Beep Yeah ....7" Pyramid.......................................RAMS 114
1986 ■ ROLLIN' WITH ROLENE ....LP Pyramid.......................................RAMI 2010

1979 LP - LBLP 502

ROMANCE

Frank Holm: v, Kenneth Olofsson: g, Leif Ehlin: g,
Thomas Widmark: k, Anders "LA" Rönnblom: b, Morgan Höglund: d

Örnsköldsvik - ***Romance*** only existed between 1988-89 and during this time they recorded around 20 songs! They were influenced by bands like ***Journey***, ***Foreigner*** and ***Toto*** and spent a lot of time working on vocal harmonies, which shows on the MLP. Great-sounding melodic hard rock, with great vocals and nice powerful production, quite reminiscent of ***Treat*** and ***Dalton*** at their best. A rarity indeed! After the band split, Rönnblom, Byström and Ehlin formed ***Desert Rain***. Rönnblom and Höglund later went on to form ***Killer Bee***.

1987 ■ Romance... MLP 4tr private...SRHB 001 **$**
    Tracks: Lonely/Hold You/Love's Around/Remember. 1000 copies.

1987 MLP - SRHB 001

ROSICRUCIAN

Ulf Pettersson: v, Lars Lindén: g/k, Magnus Söderman: g,
Fredrik Jacobsen: b, Andreas Wallström: d

Västerås - The band was formed in 1986, at first as *Atrocity*, who were featured on the *Is This Heavy Or What?* split in 1988. They recorded two demos, then changed their name to *Rosicrucian* in 1989 and recorded the demo *Initiation Into Nothingness*. It lead to a deal with Black Mark and the album *Silence*. After the debut, singer Glyn Grimwade and skinsman Patrik Marchente left the band. Glyn was replaced by former *Mezzrow* singer Ulf Pettersson but the drum stool was a hard place to fill and the drum tracks on the second album were played by Jhonny "Bärget" Bergman from *Mr. Hangpike & Adams Leafs*. Permanent drummer Andreas Wallström was finally found in December 1994. *Rosicrucian* are a band with very complex and intelligent songs, at times in the vein of *Candlemass* and *Testament*. They're also not afraid to use odd instruments, like violin. The vocals aren't the most melodic but at least you can hear the lyrics. In 1995 the band changed from Ulf to former death metal guitarist Jens Mårtensson on vocals and "Bärget" returned. They also changed their name to *Slapdash* and label to MNW Zone. Bärget is today running his own show in the band *Man.Machine.Industry*. Lindén is in *Carnal Forge* and Söderman was in *Zeelion*.

1992 CD - BMCD 25

1994 CD - BMCD 57

1992 ■	SILENCE	CD	Black Mark	BMCD 25
1994 ■	NO CAUSE FOR CELEBRATION	CD	Black Mark	BMCD 57
1995 ☐	NO CAUSE FOR CELEBRATION	CD	Teichiku (Japan)	TECX-25985

ROSWELL

Claudio Marino: v, Martin Persner: g, Simon Söderberg: g, Björn Nilsson: b,
Christian "Cribbe" Eriksson: d, Göran Bartol: p

Linköping - The band was formed in 1998 from the ashes of *Both Sides*, and recorded their first two-track demo *Rumours* the year after. After the release of *Whore*, bass player Mathias left the band. While Cribbe was doing his military service the band was on hold. In 2000 they were up and running again, reinforced with new bass player Björn Nilsson. In 2001 they released the three-track demo *Apocalypse Tomorrow* as a CD-R in 200 copies. It was supposed to be released on a 7" by Mäscdunc Records, but nothing happened. In 2002 the MCD *The Nothing* was released. They went through more line-up changes with Martin Persner replacing Jörgen and the addition of percussionist Göran Bartol and sample-guy Björn Nielsen. When the 7" finally arrived in July 2001 the pressing was incorrect and the songs were old, they were scrapped. The band instead recorded new songs and "released" a CD-R in 2001, entitled *Apocalypse*. *Void* is however a nice piece of Gothenburg-sounding death metal, a bit similar to *Soilwork* meets early *The Haunted*. After *Void*, they changed their style to hardcore and name to *TID*. In 2010 *The Nothing* was released digitally on Sounds Of Zilence.

2002 MCDd - RSWL 002

2003 CDpg - RSWL004/NIHIL38CD

1999 ☐	Whore	MCD 4tr	Only Ruins	ORR #001
	Tracks: Whore/Mapping/Copycat/War			
2002 ■	The Nothing	MCDd 6tr	Bridge Of Compaccion Records	RSWL 002
	Tracks: Awaiting Deliverance/Sonic Assault/Ankara Talvi/The New Sun/Queen De Mise/ Unmarked Eclipse. 500 copies.			
2003 ■	VOID	CDpg	Cacophonous	RSWL004/NIHIL38CD

ROT, DEVIL LEE

Thomas "Devil Lee Rot" Karlsson: v

Halmstad - Solo project from *Pagan Rites/Autopsy Torment/Tristitia*-singer Thomas aka Unholy Pope aka Devil Lee Rot. Primitive old-school black metal with a touch of classic heavy metal. *The Devil Has Landed* is a live LP. The band has featured an array of members, such as bass player Lenny "Blade" Bladh (*Bullet, Nominon, Hypnosia, Pagan Rites, Incinerator, Funeral*) and Jimi "The Demon" Fagerstig (*Autpsy Torment*), guitarists Harri "von Hell" Juvonen (*Pagan Rites, Tristitia*), Jimmy "Death" Nilsson, Jimmy "Jim Voltage" Edström (*Kill, Karnarium, Pagan Rites, Cross Bow, Autopsy Torment, Church Bizarre*) and drummer Karl "Sexual Goat Licker" Vincent (*Pagan Rites, Autopsy Torment*). The 2002 split (with *Autopsy Torment*), *Pagan From The Heat*, on Time Before Time (Death 004) is a pro-printed CD-R. After *At Hell's Deep* Devil Lee Rot has released two cassettes: *Devil United With Hellbangers* and *Headbangers In Italy*, both released in 2006. In 2012 Devil Lee Rot started working on the new album *Doom Devilution*, to be released on Atlinga. The style has now changed drastically, sounding closer to bands like *Cathedral* and *Trouble*, but with deep semi-spoken vocals.

2002 CD - BREW 006

2004 7" - MPEP 11

2001 ☐	Explosion From Hell (split)	7"	Iron Pegasus	I.P.S 008
	Split with Flame. Tracks: Beast Infernal Resurrection/Pilgrim In The Age Of Fire. Red splatter or black vinyl.			
2002 ■	HELLSCRAPER/A LITTLE DEVIL AIN'T ENOUGH	CD	Witches Brew	BREW 006
	1000 copies.			
2002 ☐	Hellscraper/A Little Devil Ain't Enough	CDS	Witches Brew	BREW 006
2002 ☐	Pagan From The Heat/The Sky Rained Death	7"	Primitive Art	PAR 028
	First 500 copies come with a free post card.			

2002	☐	A LITTLE DEVIL AIN'T ENOUGH	LP	Miriquidi/City Of Dead	MPLP 05

Bonus: Live Like A Devil. 520 copies.

| 2003 | ☐ | MARK OF THE DEVIL | CD | Primitive Art | PAR 029 |
| 2003 | ☐ | METAL DICTATOR/SOLDIER FROM HELL | CD | Witches Brew | BREW 009 |

1000 copies.

| 2003 | ☐ | SOLDIER FROM HELL | 10" | Miriquidi | MPLP 09 |

520 copies.

| 2004 | ☐ | METAL DICTATOR | LP | Miriquidi | MPLP 14 |

525 copies.

| 2004 | ■ | Infernal Gates | 7" | Miriquidi/City Of The Dead | MPEP 11 |

Split with Grave würm. Tracks: Pirates Of Hell/Roots Of All Evil. 500 hand-numbered copies.

| 2004 | ☐ | METALIZER | CD | Witches Brew | BREW 012 |

1000 copies, first 100 copies with sew-on patch.

| 2004 | ☐ | DEVIL LEE ROT/NORTHERN DARKNESS (split) | LP | I Hate Records | IHR 007 |

Split with Northern Darkness. 500 copies. Tracks Hellmachine/ Metalizer/ Metal Whiplash/ Ride The Beast

| 2005 | ☐ | THE DEVIL HAS LANDED | CD | Atolinga | ATO 05 |

1000 numbered.

| 2005 | ☐ | NORTHERN DARKNESS/DEVIL LEE ROT (split) | LP | Iron Fist | IFPCD 007 |

Split with Northern Darkness. Tracks: Hellmachine/Metalizer/Metal Whiplash/Ride The Beast

| 2005 | ■ | AT HELL'S DEEP | CD | Iron Fist | IFPCD 014 |

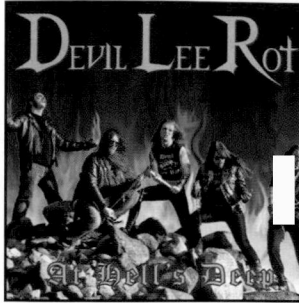

2005 CD - IFPCD 014

ROTEROCK

Janne Apelholm: g, Lennart Nyberg: g, Anders Kritz: b, Parik Wallin: d

Stockholm - The A-side is pretty decent seventies-sounding hard rock with pretty nice *Thin Lizzy*-ish guitars, while the B-side is more pop/reggae-oriented. *Roterock* was formed in 1976 in the Stockholm suburb Rotebro. Wallin, Nyberg and Apelholm later appeared in cover band *Richard Kiel & The Babysharkes*. Wallin also fronted wacky rock band *Tomterockers*.

| 1979 | ■ | Ge och ta/With Or Without You | 7" | Vanity Fair | VF 107 |

500 copies.

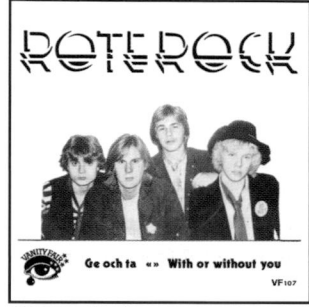

1979 7" - VF 107

ROUGH DIAMONDS

Anders "Al De'Elt" Eltebo: v, Christer "Chris Light" Olsson: g, Claudio Lepori: g, Mats Johansson: b, Anders Borgström: d

Gävle - Formed in 1989, after some demos they had a track on the Büms-compilation *Scandinavia Calling*. This resulted in the recording of *Lost Generation*. **Rough Diamond** is quite a good name for this band. They play rough-edged melodic hard rock/AOR in the vein of early *Glory*. The quality is above average and the record is well worth checking out. The band recorded some promising demos after the album, but nothing happened. After the album Chris was out of the band. Not to be confused with the Stockholm metal band.

| 1992 | ■ | LOST GENERATION | CD | Büms Records | 43 123 |

1992 CD - 43 123

ROULETTE

Thomas Lundgren: v, Magnus Nelin: g, Thomas Nesslin: k, Hansi Fellbrink: b, Mats Nelin: d

Arboga - Very commercial AOR, in the same style as *Guardian Angel* with a singer that's quite reminiscent of Tommy Nilsson. High-quality stuff that definitely will attract fans of well-played and well-produced lightweight AOR. The band changed into *Cherry Red* and recorded an outstanding single. Tomas was later found in the pompy band *B 'N J*. In 2008 AOR-FM Records released the singles plus some demo tracks on one CD.

1988	☐	Hearts Keep On Burning/Call My Name	7"	TAB	TAB-ES-801
1989	■	Fool For Your Love/Face The Music	7"	TAB	TAB-ES-904
2008	☐	BETTER LATE THAN NEVER	CD	AOR-FM	0802

Slipcase

| 2010 | ☐ | BETTER LATE THAN NEVER | CD | Yesterrock | Y-2011-8 |

Bonus: Waiting For A Heartache/Turn Me On

1989 7" - TAB-ES-904

ROUTE NINE

Dan Swanö: v/g/b/k, Anders Jacobsson: d

Örebro/Finspång - This is actually a very interesting band, or rather project. Musically they are a very powerful progressive metal band. Tight and well-played with a great powerful sound. The vocals are of the brutal and death growling kind, but mixed with clean ones. Well, I guess that's what to expect when Dan Swanö is the man behind this project. Dan is/has been found

1993 7" - ORGAN 001

in bands like **Edge Of Sanity, Unicorn, Nightingale, Pan-Thy-Monium** etc. This is however a project that pops up every now and then. The 2001 release is a compilation of demos recorded between 1991 and 1994. Jacobsson was also in **Nasum**.
Website: www.swano.com

1993 ■	Before I Close My Eyes Forever Part 1/Part 2...............................7"	Inorganic.....................................ORGAN 001
2001 ☐	THE WORKS ....MCD 6tr	Spam ....SPAM 006

Tracks: Griefcase/Lifewish/Before I Close My Eyes Part 1/..Part 2/Disruption/The Vacancy

2010 CD - TRG 01

ROYAL GHOST, THE
Norrtälje - This is not really a band, but a symphonic rock opera, written by and under the direction of Teddy Jonasson. The project grew in Teddy's mind for a long time before being realised in 2006. Musically it draws from symphonic rock to quite heavy melodic hard rock, well-played and well-sung. Among the singers and musicians you will find Lasse Gidbo (**The David Harleyson Powertrio**), Jonas Antesten, Emilia Feldt, Andreas Eklund (**House Of Shakira**) and Mio Jäger etc. If you're into stuff like **Ayreon, Nikolo Kotzev's Nostradamus** etc, check this out.

2010 ■ THE ROYAL GHOST ....CD   private .... TRG 01

1991 7" - BSM-996

ROZZ THE BOSS
Kimmo Morja: v, Peter "Rozz" Rosenbach: g, Tommy "Lone Wolf" Zachariasen: k, Håkan "Sueppe" Lindkvist: b, Robert "Rob" Lindell: d
Eskilstuna - Mid-quality AOR/melodic hard rock with an awful guitar sound. Side A is a poppy AOR ballad, while side B is slightly more powerful. Rozz was also found in the band **King & Rozz**, together with Göran Kunstberg from **Wizz**. Kimmo was earlier in **Spitfire**.

1991 ■ Wings Of Words/Miss Lonely...........................7"   Backstage.........................BSM-996

RUBBET
Göran Eriksson: g/v, Mikael Carlsson: g/v, Anders Löfgren: b, Per Johansson: d
Skellefteå - The first album is pretty decent 70s-oriented hard rock similar to **Jerusalem** and **Motvind** in their heavier moments. The vocals are quite weak and they also throw in som funky and poppy bits here and there. The second album contains one heavy metal song, one hard rocker and the rest is horrible funk/pop with lots of horns. For collectors only.

1982 LP - KNLP 002

1982 ■	SKÖRDEN ÄR STOR ....LP	KN..............................KNLP 002
1984 ☐	JOKERMAN...LP	RMP..........................RMLP 021

RUINED SOUL
Johnny Johansson: g/b
Göteborg - Johnny is a member of melodic metal band **Disdain**, and was previously in the band **United Fools**, but went solo to explore his melodic death metal side. The album feature an array of prominent guest musicians and singers: Nils Patrik Johansson (v), Emanuel Johansson (d), Jonas Kjellgren, Benny Jansson, Olof Mörck, Peter Huss, Janne Stark, Tobias Jansson, Eric Rauti, Jonas Hörnqvist, Matias Kupiainen (**Stratovarius**), Niklas Stålvind and Marios Iliopoulos. A great melodic death metal album.

2010 ■ MY DYING DAY ....CD   Suicide Records.............SR 006

2010 CD - SR 006

RUNEMAGICK
Nicklas "Terror" Rudolfsson: v/g/k, Fredrik Johnsson: g, Emma Karlsson (now Rudolfsson): b, Daniel "Mojo" Moilanen: d
Göteborg - The band was formed in 1990 and released their first demo *Fullmoon Sodomy* in 1992. The first line-up featured Nicklas and Robert "Reaper" Pehrsson, as well as Johan Norman of **Dissection/Soul Reaper**-fame. After some line-up changes the band was ready to record. The band then featured Nicklas, Fredrik Johnsson (g), Peter Palmdahl (b) and Jonas Blom (d). Peter however left and Jonas was not prepared, leaving Nicklas to do the works. The debut was actually recorded in less than five days. The second album featured Fredrik on bass and Nicklas on the rest as Jonas was injured. He later left and has since been found in **Grief Of Emerald** and **Azeazeron**. Niclas can also be found in **Sacramentum, Swordmaster** and **Deathwitch**. Old-school death metal with a gothic touch. Emma (also in **Dracena**) was added to the line-up after *Enter The Realm*... and since she and Niclas are now married, her name is also Rudolfsson. Daniel (also in **Dracena, Relevant Few, Deathwish**) replaced Jonas Blom. The band uses the production talent of Andy LaRoque. *Dawn Of The Earth* is a compilation of the first three albums.

The magic trinity

1998 ☐	THE SUPREME FORCE OF ETERNITY	CD	Century Media	77235-2
1999 ☐	ENTER THE REALM OF DEATH	CD	Century Media	77254-2
2000 ☐	RESURRECTION IN BLOOD	CD	Century Media	77307-2
2001 ■	Ancient Incantations	7" 4tr	Aftermath	Chapter IX

Tracks: Ancient Incantations/Funeral Departure/Curse Of The Dark…/Triumph Of The Ancient Death. 500 copies.

2001 ☐	DARK LIVE MAGICK	LP	Bloodstone	BLOOD 002

300 hand numbered copies w poster

2002 ☐	Worshippers Of Death (split)	7"	Bloodstone	BLOOD 006

Split with Soulreaper.500 copies. Track: Death Magick

2002 ☐	REQUIEM OF THE APOCALYPSE	CDd	Aftermath	Chapter XIV

500 copies hand numbered, with A5 digibook.

2002 ☐	REQUIEM OF THE APOCALYPSE	CD	Aftermath	Chapter XIV

Slipcase. 1000 copies.

2002 ☐	REQUIEM OF THE APOCALYPSE	CD	Irond (Russia)	CD 02-267
2002 ☐	REQUIEM OF THE APOCALYPSE	CD	Empire (Poland)	EMP CD 014 L

Bonus: Return Of Darkness And Evil (Bathory cover).

2002 ☐	REQUIEM OF THE APOCALYPSE	LPg	Mester	MP 012

500 copies.

2002 ☐	REQUIEM OF THE APOCALYPSE	LP PD	Mester	MP 012 P

300 copies.

2002 ■	MOON OF THE CHAOS ECLIPSE	CD	Aftermath	Chapter XV

1000 copies.

2002 ☐	Moon Of The Chaos Eclipse	10" PD	Aftermath	Chapter XV

Tracks: Open The Gateway/Grand Sabbath Pact/Revolution Of The Dead/Upon The Red Thrones/The Necro Ambassador/Piece Of Magick. 300 copies.

2002 ■	Doomed By Death (split)	7"	Aftermath	Chapter XVII

Split with Lord Belial. Track: Doomed. 666 hand-numbered copies.

2003 ☐	REQUIEM OF THE APOCALYPSE	LP	Aftermath	Chapter XIV

500 copies. Different artwork.

2003 ☐	DARKNESS DEATH DOOM	CD	Aftermath	Chapter XIX
2003 ☐	DARKNESS DEATH DOOM	2CDd	Aftermath	Chapter XIX

500 copies. Bonus disc: The Pentagram

2003 ■	DARKNESS DEATH DOOM	2CD	Aftermath	Chapter XIX

500 copies.Slipcase. Bonus disc: The Pentagram

2004 ☐	ON FUNERAL WINGS	CD	Aftermath	Chapter XXIX
2004 ☐	ON FUNERAL WINGS	CD	Aftermath	Chapter XXIX

499 copies with slipcase.

2005 ☐	ENVENOM	CDd	Aftermath	Chapter XXXIII

1000 copies.

2005 ☐	ENVENOM	2LPg	Parasitic Records	PR 14

500 copies.Bonus: Claves Inferni/On Funeral Wings. New artwork.

2006 ☐	INVOCATION OF MAGICK	CD	Aftermath	Chapter 44
2006 ☐	INVOCATION OF MAGICK	CDd	Aftermath	Chapter 44

999 numbered copies. Bonus: Conjuration Of The Black Shape/Witchcraft Gateways

2006 ☐	Black Magic Sorceress	10" PD 3tr	Aftermath	Chapter 43

Tracks: Black Magic Sorceress/The Rising/Wizard With The Magic Runes (remix). 300 copies.

2007 ☐	VOYAGE TO DESOLATION/DAWN OF THE END	CD	Enucleation Records	Socket 07
2007 ☐	DAWN OF THE END	CDd	Aftermath	Chapter 52

1000 copies.

2007 ☐	THE NORTHERN LIGHTS (split)	CD	Aftermath	Chapter 53

Split with Ocean Chief. Tracks: Bound In Magic Haze/Chthonic Temple Smoke. 500 numbered + 500 not numbered.

2008 ☐	DARK DEAD EARTH	2CD	Century Media	9978402

Black CD. Death certificate sticker.

2009 ☐	DARK DEAD EARTH	2CD	Mazzar Records (Russia)	MZR CD 436

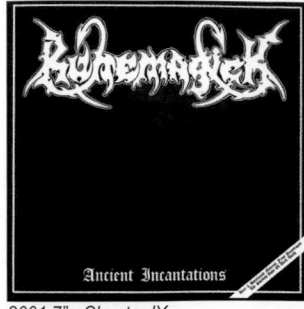

2001 7" - Chapter IX

2002 CD - Chapter XV

2002 7" - Chapter XVII

2003 2CDd - Chapter XIX

RUSSELL

Jock "Russell" Millgård: v, Robert "Scholtz" Scholtyssek: p,
Robert "Foss" Fossengren: g, Christian André: k, Per Hansson: b, Jonas Stadling: d

Stockholm - Formed in 1989. Jock has previously recorded two singles with the melodic band **9T9** and two albums with symphonic AOR-band **Cross** under the name Tai. His new act performs high-quality AOR in the lighter vein, with occasional hints of **Toto** and Bryan Adams. The song *Can't Walk Away* is actually dangerously close to *Hiding From Love* by the latter. At times Jock sounds like a mix of Eddie Money and Mr. Adams. He is originally from Boston, USA and the son of jazz musician George Russell.

1994 ■	1994	MCD 4tr	Warner/Chappell (promo)	- -

Tracks: Summer Nights/Just Between The 2 Of Us (non-CD)/Wall Of Love/World In Pieces (non-CD).

1995 ☐	WALL OF LOVE	CD	Long Island	LIR 0017

1994 MCD - - -

RUTTHNA
Joakim Kristensson: v/b/g, Dennis Ekdahl: d

Tyresö - Atmospheric death metal band *Rutthna* (remove the "h" and it means rot in Swedish) was spawned by *Thyrfing* drummer Kristensson in 2002. A first demo, entitled *Decomposing Eve*, was recorded in Deadbeat Studio, and given to friends. Now drummer Ekdahl (*Raise Hell, Crashdïet, Machinery, Siebenbürgen, Sins Of Omission, Bloodshed, Mystic Prophecy* etc) joined in and the new demo *Doomsdaylight* was recorded in 2004. This demo lead to a deal with Black Lodge who released the first album, consisting of five new songs and a remastered version of *Decomposing Eve*.

2005 ■ DOOMSDAYLIGHT..CD   Black Lodge...............................BLOD 023 CD

2005 CD - BLOD 023 CD

RYDELL & QUICK
Christer Rydell: v/g, Malin Quick: v/sax, Johan Bonnier: b,
Berndt Baumgartner: d, Peer "Zack Booner" Stappe: d

Fristad - *Rydell & Quick* were formed in 1989 and have always been a successful cover band playing an average of 200 shows a year. First single *Stay* was released in 1998, a second one, *Reason To Live* in 1999, followed by the debut album *Nu är det sommar igen* later the same year. The style has been quite uninteresting pop rock, but in 2006 they changed direction with the album *R.O.C.K.O.H.O.L.I.C* which is a guitar-driven and heavy, yet very melodic rocker of really good quality. The follow-up took it all a notch even higher and the band has now become a melodic rock force to be reckoned with.

2006 □	R.O.C.K.O.H.O.L.I.C	CD	RQ	RQCD 0601
2011 □	All In Like A Rock Star	CDS	RQ	RQCDS 1101
2012 ■	R.O.A.D.T.R.I.P	CD	Connection	CD 9911
2012 □	Life IS Just A Dream	CDS	Connection	CCDS 9912
2012 □	Do It Right Now	CDS	Connection	CCDS 9911

2012 CD - CD 9911

RÅG I RYGGEN
Jonas Warnerbring: v, Jan Aggemyr: g, Björn "Nysse" Nyström: g,
Christer Sjöborg: k, Björn "Agge" Aggemyr: b, Peter Sandberg (aka Udd): d

Boys in coallge

Bromma - It all started with the three schoolmates Nysse, Janne and Björn (initially on drums) that put a band together in 1971. The name came from a big box of Wasa hard bread. To have råg i ryggen means to have guts. Björn switched to bass and they drafted drummer Tomas Öndemar. Tomas was later replaced by Kurre Persson and they drafted keyboardist Christer. The band now started finding their style. Nysse was handling the vocals when the band entered a band stand, doing a cover of **Uriah Heep**'s *July Morning*. They won. Another contestant was singer Jonas Warnerbring (ex-**Nederlaget** and son of singer Östern Warnerbring), who was drafted to front the band. Kurre was replaced by Peter Sandberg, who fixed the band a deal by getting severely drunk and being "rescued" by label owner Kjell Gerdin. He helped young Peter get home and their musical chat lead to **Råg I Ryggen** recording a demo for his label, which then lead to the debut album. The album contains great mid-70s hard rock, quite similar to **Uriah Heep**. Great keyboard/guitar arrangements and great vocals. Some songs are in English and some in Swedish. The album is a very sought after item and therefore an expensive one. A true gem! In 1976 Jonas and Peter left to go solo. Singer Bosse Lantz and **Rör inte knappen**-drummer Jonas Hedgren were drafted, but the band finally split in April 1977 after a last gig in Gävle. Nysse later joined pop-rocker Magnus Uggla, **Strix Q** and also recorded the solo album *Ja vill ha mycke pengar* in 1980. Jonas formed pop/rock band **Spray**. Nysse joined rock band **Ja! Ja! Ja!**, later formed **Good Clean Fun**, which also featured Klara Kempff (**Yeah Bop Station**) and did two tours with Pugh Rogefeldt. Peter (now named Udd) later played with **Yngwie Malmsteen's Rising Force** and **Glory Bell's Band**.

Råg i Ryggen in the school of rock!

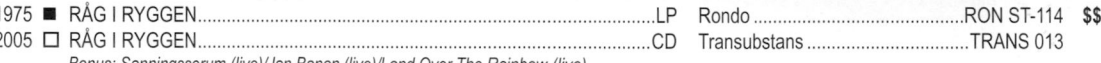

1975 ■	RÅG I RYGGEN	LP	Rondo	RON ST-114	$$
2005 ☐	RÅG I RYGGEN	CD	Transubstans	TRANS 013	

Bonus: Sanningsserum (live)/Jan Banan (live)/Land Over The Rainbow (live)

1975 LP - RON ST-114

RÄVJUNK

Christer Lindahl: g/k/v, **Kenneth Sylwan:** h, **Henrik Lind:** g,
Sören G Andersson: k/v, **Wilhelm Wallin:** b/k, **Peter Eriksson:** d/g/k

Uppsala - The name actually means "fox piss"... **Rävjunk** were formed in 1970 and split in 1981. The LP is a very sought after item, only pressed in 478 copies (+9 test pressings). The album is really strange as it starts out in an almost punkish vein, but suddenly turns into a fully-fledged progressive guitar-dominated hard rocker. It has some long tracks with classic 70s acid guitars that almost give you goosebumps. As soon as the singer opens his mouth you almost want to turn it off though. After the album, they made some demo recordings for a second album, but then changed direction and became an out-and-out punk band. "We just wanted to play and have fun", according to drummer Peter. They had a big hit with the single-track *Bohman Bohman*, but most of the singles are as far from hard rock as possible and are therefore not worth listing. The album and the flip-side of *Bohman Bohman*, which is a heavy cover of *All Along The Watchtower*, are the only recordings that would attract hard rockers. The 95 CD re-issue is a bootleg. Hasse Bruniusson (**Zamla Mammas Manna**) appears as guest on the album. After they split the memebers started playing calypso and **Beatles** covers in punk-tempo (?!). Henrik and Kenneth were added to the line-up on the single. In 2002 the CD-R album *The Freaky Guitar Album* (02 PUKA) was released, featuring Lindahl, Eriksson and Wallin.

1977 LP - JJ-27

1979 7" - Z 100

1977 ■	UPPSALA STADSHOTELL BRINNER	LP	private	JJ-27	$$$
	478 copies.				
1979 ■	Bohman Bohman/All Along The Watchtower	7"	Sub	Z 100	
2008 ■	UPPSALA STADSHOTELL BRINNER	2CDd	Transubstans	TRANS 029	

UNOFFICIAL RELEASES:

1995 ☐	UPPSALA STADSHOTELL BRINNER	CD	Technodisco	JJ27-CD	$$
	This is a Spanish bootleg.				

2008 2CDd - TRANS 029

S.K.U.R.K

Jörgen Lindhe: v, Sören Sandved: g, Francke: b, Martin Brorsson: d

Malmö - **S.K.U.R.K**, previously known as **Skurk 666**, are about as heavy as you get. Brutal metal sung in the "skånska" dialect. The band was formed in 2002. Linhe and Brorsson were ex-**Flegma**, **Obscurity** and **Redrvm**, while Sören was formerly in **Omnious**. In 2002 the band recorded their first demo *666 Personligheter*, followed by *Hedersmord* in 2003. Bass on the debut was handled by Mike Svensson.
Website: www.skurk.eu

2006 ☐	666 PERSONLIGHETER	CD	Tyst Brus Grammofon	TBG666001	
2011 ■	HÄXA	CDd	Denomination	DEN 003	

2011 CDd - DEN 003

S.L.R

Harald Hansen: v, Peder Johansson: g, Micke Ahlquist: b, Lars Danielsson: d

Borås - Formed in 1988 and recorded their first demo, *Controlled By Fear* the year after. Very technical thrash, in the vein of **Onslaught** and **Suicidal Tendencies** but with more powerful vocals. Good stuff. The band later changed their name to **Guineapigs** and switched to playing melodic punk in the vein of **Bad Religion**, however their later material is said to be in a more metallic direction. The tracks *Stimulated Aggression* and *Crusade Of The Cursed* are found on the compilation *Distortion To Hell* (1993 Distortion) and *Mad Man* is featured on *Hardcore For The Masses* (1988 Uproar). A funny detail is that the EP plays on 45 rpm on the A-side and 33 rpm on the B-side. Peder later played with **Falconer**.

1991 ☐	S.L.R/Mögel (split)	7" EP	private		- -
	Split with Mögel. Track: Society Of Lab Rats				
1992 ■	Free From The Cursed At Last	7" 3tr	private	S.L.R 001	
	Tracks: Last Collect/Crusade Of The Cursed/Free From Reality				

1992 7" - S.L.R 001

SABATON

Joakim Brodén: v/g, Rikard Sundén: g, Oskar Montelius: g,
Pär Sundström: b, Daniel Mullbäck: d

Falun - Northern hard rockers **Sabaton** were formed in 1999. Adopting a lyrical war theme initially made for speculations that they were national socialists, which was totally incorrect. "We are just war nerds", the band said. **Sabaton** recorded their first five-track demo in Studio Abyss in 2000, followed by the self-released *Fist For Fight*, which lead to a deal with Italian label Underground Symphony who rereleased it with new artwork. The first album *Metalizer* was recorded, but due to conflicts with the label it was unreleased, until 2007. The band funded the recordings of their first official album *Primo Victoria* themselves, but were soon picked up by Black Lodge. On the second album, *Attero Dominatus*, keyboardist Daniel Myhr was added to the line-up (Brodén played keyboards on the first releases and he was actually originally solely a keyboard player). The band soon became a very strong and popular live act, selling out shows. In 2006 Mullback could not join the band on tour and former member Richard Larsson (**Skyride**) filled in. Sundén is also found in **Deals Death**. The album *Carolus Rex* was released in two versions, with Swedish or English lyrics. On this album the band used renowned historian Bengt Liljegren (former punk drummer in **Garbochock**, **Besökarna** and **Underjordiska Lyxorkestern**). The *Metalus Hammerus Rex* compilation features the exclusive track, *Harley From Hell*. In March 2012 the band declared Rikard, Oskar and Daniel were leaving the band, just before the release of *Carolus Rex*. The new line-up was soon announced, seeing the drum spot taken care of by Robban Bäck (**BALLS, Baltimoore, W.E.T** etc), the guitars by Christoffer Rörland (**Nocturnal Rites, TME**) and Thorbjörn Englund (solo, **Winterlong, Star Queen, Raubtier**), while the keyboards are on backing tracks on the upcoming tour. In May 2012 the remaining members announced they had formed the new band **Civil War**, completed by **Astral Doors**' singer Nils-Patrik Johansson and **Volturyon** bassist Stefan Eriksson (who also was a roadie for **Sabaton**). In November 2012 Robban took a break from the band, to be a father, and was temporarily replaced by Snowy Shaw (**Dream Evil, XXX, Therion** etc) for the tour. Sabaton fits somewhere between **Manowar** and **Rammstein** in style. War metal?

We have this thing for war, you see. Not to worry!

2002 CDd - USCD-061

2001 ■	FIST FOR FIGHT	CD	private		- -	$$$
	600 copies.					
2002 ■	FIST FOR FIGHT	CDd	Underground Symphony	USCD-061		
	Rerelease with new artwork.					

2001 CD - - -

Year		Title	Format	Label	Catalogue
2005	☐	PRIMO VICTORIA	CD	Black Lodge	BLOD 019 CD
2005	☐	PRIMO VICTORIA	CD	Art Music Group (Russia)	AMG 296
2006	■	ATTERO DOMINATUS	CD	Black Lodge	BLOD 037 CD
2006	☐	ATTERO DOMINATUS	LP PD	Black Lodge	BLOD 037 PD
2007	☐	ATTERO DOMINATUS	CD	Locomotive Records (USA)	LM 561
2007	☐	PRIMO VICTORIA	CD	Black Lodge	BLOD 019 CD
2007	☐	METALIZER	2CDd	Black Lodge	BLOD 056 CD

Bonus: Jawbreaker (Judas Priest cover)/Birds Of War + Fist For Fight CD.

| 2007 | ☐ | Attero Dominatus & Primo Victoris Sampler | MCDp 6tr | Black Lodge | BLODPR 037 CD |

Tracks: Attero Dominatus/Primo Victoria/Into The Fire/Rise Of Evil/Light In The Black/Metal Machine. Samples + two full tracks. Promo.

2006 CD - BLOD 037 CD

2008	■	Cliffs Of Gallipoli/Ghost Division	CDS	Black Lodge	BLOD 054
2008	☐	THE ART OF WAR	CD	Black Lodge	BLOD 055 CD
2008	☐	THE ART OF WAR	CD+book	Black Lodge	BLOD 055 CDL

Special edition featuring the book Sun Tzu – Art Ofg War.

2008	☐	THE ART OF WAR	LPg	Black Lodge	BLOD 055 LP
2010	☐	COAT OF ARMS	CD	Black Lodge	BLOD 070 CD
2010	☐	COAT OF ARMS – LIMITED EDITION	CD	Black Lodge	BLOD 070 CDL

Bonus: Coat Of Arms (instrumental)/Metal Ripper (instrumental)

2010	☐	Coat Of Arms	CDS	Black Lodge	BLOD 068 CD
2010	☐	COAT OF ARMS	CD	Nuclear Blast	NB 2541-2
2010	☐	COAT OF ARMS	CDd	Nuclear Blast	NB 2541-0

Bonus: Coat Of Arms (instrumental)/Metal Ripper (instrumental)

| 2010 | ■ | COAT OF ARMS | LP PD+7"g | Nuclear Blast | NB 2541-1 |

Bonus single in orange vinyl featuring: Coat Of Arms (instrumental)/Metal Ripper (instrumental)

2008 CDS - BLOD 054

| 2010 | ☐ | COAT OF ARMS | LP+7" | Nuclear Blast | NB 2541-8 |

Bonus single in red vinyl featuring: Coat Of Arms (instrumental)/Metal Ripper (instrumental). LP in red vinyl. Special edition 100 copies for Supreme Chaos Records.

| 2010 | ☐ | COAT OF ARMS | LP+7" | Nuclear Blast | NB 2541-8 |

Bonus single in featuring: Coat Of Arms (instrumental)/Metal Ripper (instrumental). LP in blue marbled vinyl. 150 copies. Poster..

| 2010 | ☐ | COAT OF ARMS | CD | Spiritual Beast (Japan) | IUCP-16086 |

Bonus: Coat Of Arms (instrumental)/Metal Ripper (instrumental)

| 2010 | ☐ | METALIZER – RE-ARMED | 2CD | Black Lodge | BLOD 072 CD |

Bonus: Jawbreaker (Judas Priest cover)Panzer Batallion (demo)/Hellrider (live) + all tracks from Fist For Fight.

| 2010 | ☐ | METALIZER – RE-ARMED | 2CD | Nuclear Blast | NB 2644-0 |
| 2010 | ☐ | PRIMO VICTORIA – RE-ARMED | CD | Black Lodge | BLOD 073 CD |

Bonus: The March To War/Shotgun/Into The Fire (live)/Rise Of Evil (live)/The Beast (Twisted Sister cover)/Dead Soldiers Waltz

2010 LP PD+7"g - NB 2541-1

| 2010 | ☐ | PRIMO VICTORIA – RE-ARMED | CD | Nuclear Blast | NB 2642-0 |
| 2010 | ☐ | ATTERO DOMINATUS – RE-ARMED | CD | Black Lodge | BLOD 074 CD |

Bonus: Für Immer (Doro cover)/Långa bollar på Bengt (Svenne Rubins cover)/Metal Medley (live)/Nightchild/Primo Victoria (demo)

| 2010 | ☐ | ATTERO DOMINATUS – RE-ARMED | CD | Nuclear Blast | NB 2643-0 |
| 2010 | ☐ | THE ART OF WAR – RE-ARMED | CD | Black Lodge | BLOD 075 CD |

Bonus: Art Of War (demo)/Du gamla du fria (live)

| 2011 | ☐ | THE ART OF WAR – RE-ARMED | CD | Nuclear Blast | NB 2645-2 |
| 2011 | ☐ | PRIMO VICTORIA – RE-ARMED | 2LPg | Nuclear Blast | NB 2642-1 |

350 copies. Silver vinyl. Bonus: same as CD + Dead Soldiers Waltz

2011	☐	Screaming Eagles + video	CDS	Black Lodge	NB 2659-2
2011	■	Screaming Eagles	7" PD	Black Lodge	NB 2659-9
2011	☐	WORLD WAR LIVE	2LPg	Nuclear Blast	NB 2769-1

Grey vinyl.

| 2011 | ☐ | WORLD WAR LIVE - BATTLE OF THE BALTIC SEA | 2LP | Nuclear Blast | NB 2725-1 |

Grey + white vinyl

2011 7" PD - NB 2659-9

2011	☐	WORLD WAR LIVE - BATTLE OF THE BALTIC SEA	2CDd+DVD	Nuclear Blast	NB 2725-2
2011	☐	WORLD WAR LIVE	2CD	Nippon Columbia (Japan)	COCB-60025/26
2012	☐	METALUS HAMMERUS REX	CD	Metal Hammer	- -

Included in Metal Hammer Magazine May 2012.

| 2012 | ☐ | CAROLUS REX | 2CDd | Nuclear Blast | NB 2827-0 |

Swedish and English lyrics versions. Bonus: Twilight Of The Thunder God

| 2012 | ☐ | CAROLUS REX | 2CD book | Nuclear Blast | NB 2827-5 |

Swedish and English lyrics versions. Bonus: Twilight Of The Thunder God/In The Army Now/Feuer Frei. 1000 copies. Mail order version.

| 2012 | ■ | CAROLUS REX | 2LPg | Nuclear Blast | NB 2827-1 |

Bonus: Twilight Of The Thunder God. Blue vinyl + 250 yellow. Poster.

| 2012 | ☐ | CAROLUS REX | CDd | Nuclear Blast | NB 2827-8 |

Swedish lyrics version. Bonus: In The Army Now (Bolland & Bolland cover)

2012	☐	CAROLUS REX	CDd	Nuclear Blast (USA)	NB 2827-2
2012	☐	CAROLUS REX	CDd	High Fidelity LTD (Israel)	D1 3185131
2012	☐	CAROLUS REX (SWEDISH VERSION)	2LPg	Nuclear Blast	NB 2954-9

Bi-coloured (blue/yellow) vinyl. Poster.

| 2012 | ☐ | CAROLUS REX | 2CD | Nuclear Blast | NB 2836-1 |

2012 2LPg - NB 2827-1 (blue)

SABBTAIL

Mats Levén: v, Fredrik Åkesson: g, Jan Bingegård: k,
Janne Lund: b, Håkan Rangemo: b

Stockholm/Kristinehamn - **Sabbtail** were formed in 1996 by Lund and Bingegård. Janne Lund was ex-**Fortune**. Harald Lund played drums and Andreas Eklundh (**House Of Shakira**) handled the vocals on the debut. Original guitarist Frederic Hugues (later in heavy rockers **Blackstone**) was from France. *Otherworlds* contains classic hard rock with a strong touch of late-eighties **Black Sabbath**. Early 2000 the band, featuring Levén, Åkesson, Bingegård, Lund and drummer and Nakko H, recorded a 3-track demo. It took a while but finally the band was picked up by Massacre and the second album *Nightchurch* was released, now featuring drummer Håkan Rangemo. Fredrik Åkesson was later in **Southpaw, Arch Enemy** and today in **Krux** and **Opeth**, while Mats Levén has appeared in **Southpaw, Krux, Therion, Abstrakt Algebra, Yngwie Malmsteen** and various other projects and bands. The second album had a slightly stronger doom-touch and with the power of Levén's vocals the album felt much heavier. A great album, indeed. The band is still active and the last known line-up featured Bingegård, Lund, guitarist Niclas Granath (**Destiny**), singer Kent Ploog and drummer Fredrik Frykman.

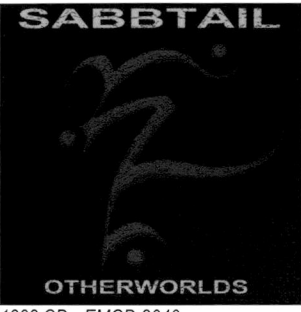

1998 CD - EMCD 2040

2003 CD - MAS PC 0404

1998 ☐	OTHERWORLDS	CD	Pony Canyon (Japan)	PCCY-01235	
1998 ■	OTHERWORLDS	CD	Empire	EMCD 2040	
2003 ■	NIGHTCHURCH	CD	Massacre	MAS PC0404	

SABOTAGE

Anders Johansson: v, Martin Andersson: g, Stefan Olsson: g,
Martin Olsson: k, Mikael Lindbom: b, Stefan Brekh: d

Uddevalla - A very promising band in the vein of **Black Sabbath** during the *Heaven And Hell* era. The single is their only release up to date. A rarity, but well worth looking for! They actually started out as a cover band doing **Black Sabbath** songs, playing mostly at bikers clubs.

1994 ■	Faith Is An Illusion/The Answer	CDS 2tr	private	EGCD 009	$	*1994 CDS - EGCD 009*

SACRAMENTUM

Nisse Karlén: v/b, Anders Brolycke: g, Johan Norrman: g, Niklas Rudolfsson: d

Falköping/Göteborg - Founded by Karlén in 1990 under the name **Tumulus** and changed their name to **Sacramentum** two years later. The first recording, *Sedes Impiorum*, was made in 1992 featuring Karlén on vocals and guitar, Brolycke on guitars and bass and Mikael Rydén on drums. Nisse switched to guitar and Freddy Andersson was added on bass before the next recording. The debut MCD *Finis Malorum* was initially released as a demo-tape. Extremely fast and furious old-school black metal, with some nice guitar harmonies, without wimpy keyboards or choir parts. On the debut album the line-up had again changed, now featuring Karlén on bass and vocals, Brolycke on guitar and new drummer Niklas (**Runemagick, Deathwitch, Swordmaster, Dracena** etc). In 1995 the band was also reinforced with session man Emil "Nightmare" Nödtveidt (**Swordmaster, Ophthalamia**), who also made a guest appearance on *The Coming Of Chaos*. On *The Black Destiny* the band had been reinforced by second guitarist Niclas "Pepa" Andersson (**Lord Belial, Vassago, Latex**). The debut was produced by Dan Swanö and the following albums by Andy LaRocque. In 2001 the line-up changed... or rather the members switched duties. Nisse now only handled the vocals, Niklas took over the bass and Tobias Kellgren (**Soulreaper** etc.) was added on drums. A cover of *Black Masses* was featured on *A Tribute To Mercyful Fate* (1997 Listenable), *The Curse/Antichrist* on *Sepulchral Feast: A Tribute To Sepultura* (1998 Black Sun) and the **Bathory** cover *13 Candles* was featured on the tribute album *In Conspiracy With Satan* (1998 Hellspawn/No Fashion). Karlén was later in **Lord Belial**.

1994 MCD - EVIL 001

1996 CD - CDAR 034

1997 CD - 77178 2

2013 LP - 998244-1

1994 ■	Finis Malorum	MCD 5tr	Northern Production	EVIL 001
	Tracks: Moonfog/Travel With The Northern Winds/Devided Etimpera/Pagan Fire/Finis Malorum			
1994 ☐	Finis Malorum	MCD 5tr	Adipocere	CDAR 023
1996 ■	FAR AWAY FROM THE SUN	CD	Adipocere	CDAR 034
	First pressing in 1000 copies. Second pressing in 1000 copies with misprint in artwork.			
1997 ■	THE COMING OF CHAOS	CD	Century Media	77178 2
1997 ☐	THE COMING OF CHAOS	LP	Century Media	77178 1
1997 ☐	THE COMING OF CHAOS	LP PD	Century Media	77178 1-P
	1500 copies.			
1999 ☐	THY BLACK DESTINY	CD	Century Media	77924 2
1999 ☐	THY BLACK DESTINY	CD	Century Media (USA)	7924 2
2005 ☐	FAR AWAY FROM THE SUN/FINIS MALORUM	CD	Zenor Recordz (Brazil)	ZENOR 004
2008 ☐	ABYSS OF TIME	2CD	Century Media	997839-2
	Two in one containing The Coming Of Chaos and The Black Destiny.			
2013 ☐	FAR AWAY FROM THE SUN	CD	Century Media	998244-2
2013 ■	FAR AWAY FROM THE SUN	LP	Century Media	998244-1

SACRED NIGHT

Micke Green: v, Daniel Bredefelt: g, Henrik Bringås: b, Jonas Lindgren: d

Ludvika - A metal band with strong influences of early *Iron Maiden*. OK vocals. *City Of Dreams* is an instrumental track. The 7" was pressed in 400 copies, all numbered and with handwritten labels. After the release of the EP the band split. Henrik was later working with his *Bad Religion* influenced band *Mayred Right*.

1993 ■ "Demo"-Lishan Project .... 7" 3tr   private .... - -
       Tracks: Victim For Nothing/City Of Dreams/Freeman. 400 copies.

1993 7" - - -

SACRIFICE

Anders Strengberg: v, Thomas Axelsson: g, Thomas Lundgren: g,
Mats Svensson: b, Mikael Gustavsson: d

Hässleholm - It all started in 1982 by Thomas, Mats and drummer Magnus Olsson. Guitarist Thomas Lundgren joined. The band, named *Metal Muthaz*, was completed by singer Jeffrey Branscher. Drummer Olsson left and was replaced by Gustavsson. In 1984 Jeffrey left and singer Zenny Gramm (aka Hansson) replaced him. A demo made EMI interested, but Zenny sadly left the band and it fizzled out. They found singer Anders Strengberg and the name was changed to *Sacrifice*. Only one single (now a mega rarity) was released. Great eighties heavy metal in the traditional NWoBHM-style, with the addition of keyboards. If you like bands like *Mindless Sinner* or *Trespass*, check them out. In 1986 the name was changed to *Crier* and the vocals were handled by Rickard "Rille" Larsson (later in *Mercy, Supreme Majesty* etc.). The track *Fantasy World* was featured on the compilation *The Metal Collection* (1986 Ebony Records). In 1989 *Crier* released the single *Bad Booze* (which was first demoed by *Metal Muthaz* with Zenny on vocals), but folded in 1990. In 2011 Mats and Thomas decided to resurrect *Crier* with original singer Björn and new members, drummer Jimmy Ek and guitarist Andreas Klügel. A new demo was recorded in 2012.

1985 7" - PL 8

1985 ■ Street Fighter/Innocent Victim .... 7"   Platina .... PL 8 **$$$**

SACRILEGE

Daniel Svensson: v/d, Daniel Dinsdale: g, Richard Bergholtz: g, Daniel Kvist: b

Vallda (Göteborg) - The band was formed in 1993 by two of the Daniels (Svensson and Dinsdale). Prior to the albums the band recorded two demos; *To Where Light Can't Reach* and *And Autumn Failed*. Dark metal with a very strong 80s touch, like mixing *HammerFall* and *Dissection*. Daniel Svensson later joined *In Flames* as drummer, which lead to the band's split. He was also part of *Dream Evil* and *Diabolique*, while Kvist has been found in numerous bands like *Dragonland, Taetre, Nightshade, Dragonland* and *Likblek*. Not to be confused with the UK band. In 2006 the band reformed with the original line-up, under the name *Sacrilege GBG*.

1996 CD - BS 09

1996 ■	LOST IN THE BEAUTY YOU SLAY	CD	Black Sun	BS 09	
1996 ☐	LOST IN THE BEAUTY YOU SLAY	LP PD	Black Sun	BSLP 09	
1997 ☐	THE FIFTH REASON	CD	Black Sun	BS 13	
1998 ☐	THE FIFTH REASON	LP PD	Black Sun	BSLP 13	
2001 ☐	THE BLACK SUN COLLECTION	2CD	Black Sun	BLACK 091 DCD	
2001 ☐	LOST IN THE BEAUTY YOU SLAY/THE FIFTH REASON	2CD	Nuclear Blast America (USA)	727701 7841	

SAD WINGS

Tony Ekfeldt: v, Patrick Berg: g, Peter Espinoza: g,
Tommy Persson: b, Magnus Hörberg: d

Malmö - *Sad Wings* were a good band with one or two influences from *Deep Purple*, quite close to *Six Feet Under*. After the album Peter left the band and later joined *Nasty Idols*, with whom he recorded two albums. He was later found in *Espinoza* and *Majestic*. Patrik played with pub rock band *Without Tom*, who released an album on Warner Bros. Peter was later part of the resurrected *Nasty Idols*.

1985 LP - CDP-3

1985 ■	LONELY HERO	LP	Criminal Respose	CDP-3
1985 ☐	LONELY HERO	CD	Criminal Respose	CDP-3CD

SADATRON

Mattias Aurelius: v/g, Anders Johansson: g/v,
Jan Norell: b, Pär "Pärsan" Gunnarsson: d

Linköping - *Sadatron* were formed in 1993 plays heavy metal in the vein of early slow and heavy *Metallica*. Not bad.

1997 MCD - 7 320470 012703

1997 ■ Deep Water, Heavy Rocks .... MCD 4tr   private 7 320470 012703
       Tracks: Untrue/Abused/Lost/Suffer

SADISTIC GRIMNESS

Daniel "DD Executioner" Johansson: v, Christer "C. Carnivore" Bergqvist: g, Rikard "R. Fleshripper" Magnusson: b, J. Demiser: d/g

Stenungsund/Uddevalla - **Sadistic Grimness** were formed in 2000, and recorded the first demo *From Heaven To The Abyss* the same year, followed by *Bleed For The Goat* in 2001. The line-up on *Vicious Torture*, which also contained the tracks from the first two demos, featured Fleshripper, Executioner, guitarist Michael "Nocturnal Skullsodomizer" Carlsson (**Mastema**) and drummer Kemper Lieath. In 2007 the band also released the six-track demo *Rotting In Solitude*. On *Asteni* the line-up had again changed, now seeing Carnivore replacing Skullsodomizer and Demiser replacing Kemper. Fleshripper is also in **Ill-Natured**, **Azeazeron** and **Conspiracy**, Carnivore has been found in **Grief Of Emerald**, **Auberon**, **Disorge** and **Ravaged**. DD Executioner has been a member of **Diabolicum**, **Kill** and **Angst**. The 2012 line-up featured Demiser, Fleshripper and Executioner.

2004 CD - IR 003

2009 CD - DWP 003

2004	☐	Split Cunt Of Virgin Mary (split)	7" EP	Ordealis	OS-EP014
		Split with Dutch band Kerberos. Tracks: IntroRaon Of God's Holy Blood/Unholy Devil Crusade/Split Cunt Of Virgin Mary. 333 hand numbered copies			
2004	■	VICIOUS TORTURE	CD	Infernus Rex	IR 003
2009	■	ASTENI	CD	Daemon Worship	DWP 003

SAFEMODE

Tjet Gustafson (Pipare): v, Robin Ahnlund: g, Juuso Savolainen: g, Sebastian Sander: b, Johannes Karlsson: d

Uppsala - Formed in 2007 and recorded the first demo in 2008 with the help of **Blindside** drummer Marcus Dahlström. **Safemode** won the national Rockkarusellen competition which resulted in a tour of Sweden. During 2009 they recorded two demos; *We're Already Gone* and *Die To Live*, before recording the 37 minute debut album. **Safemode** play quite melodic screamo/metalcore with clean vocals incorporated, at times a bit similar to **HIM** gone metal. In 2011 guitarist Juuso Savolainen left the band.

2010 CD - SMCD 001

| 2010 | ■ | FOR A BETTER TOMORROW | CD | Liljegren Records | SMCD 001 |

SAHARA

Barbro Olsson: v, Mikael Kähäri: g, Sven Olov Wallenstein: g, Tommy Asmola: b, Björn Gustafsson: d

Ludvika - The band was formed early 1981 inspired by bands like **Spliff**, **Blondie** and Robert Palmer. They do however qualify as a hard rock band, albeit not that exciting and I'd say this one is only for collectors. In 1983 Sven Olov moved and Johan Hansson replaced him. The band split in 1984. Barbro went to dance band **Sunshine**, while the others quit playing. In 1998 Kähäri picked it up again and joined blues band **Boogie Doctors**, later **Mojo Docs**, who released the album *Ain't Much To Worry About* in 2001. He later formed **Hound Dog Taylor** (released the CD *Gator's Crossing* in 2006 with Clas Yngström guesting) and later on **Michael K's Rumble Pack**. The latter has released the album *Hands On*.

1981 7" - PSI 013

| 1981 | ■ | Runnin' Around (In Circles)/Want You Tonight | 7" | Pang | PSI 013 |

SAHARA

Ulrick Lönnquist: v/g, Peter Lidström: g

Göteborg - High-quality slightly westcoastish and slick AOR in the vein of **Talk Of The Town** and **Street Talk**. Prominent keyboards, quite a lot of piano, distorted but quite laid back guitars and prominent melodic vocals. Great production and great performance. Should appeal to fans of Mitch Malloy etc. The musicians on the album includes Kaspar Dahlqvist (k) (**Treasure Land**, **Stormwind** etc), Hazze Wazzéen (b), Magnus Eliasson (b) and Fredrik Winero (d).

2001 CD - 4 018996 101799

| 2001 | ■ | SAHARA | CD | AOR Heaven | 4 018996 101799 |

SAIGON

Anders Åhlund: v, Roine Thörnell: g, Stefan Sköld: g, Mikael Berner: b, Daniel Bjerkes: d

Söderhamn - Together with **Sad Wings** the only Swedish bands released on the English Criminal Response label. **Saigon** produces high-quality melodic metal/hard rock with great vocals and classy musical performance. In the same vein as German band **Sinner**, **Proud** and label mates **Sad Wings**. Recommended. Michael and Anders later joined symphonic band **Lotus**.

1985 LP - CDP-5

1985	■	ONE MUST DIE	LP	Criminal Response	CDP-5
1993	☐	ONE MUST DIE (split)	CD	Hot Metal	SPLIT 012
		Split with Wizz. Slipcase.			

SAINT DEAMON

Jan Thore Grefstad: v, Andreas "Toya" Johansson: g, Magnus "Nobby" Norberg: b, Ronny Milianowicz: d

Borås/Bålsta/Norway - *Saint Deamon* (name taken from a fictive ghost rider) were formed by former *Dionysus* drummer Milianowicz in 2006. In 2007 the line-up was completed and then consisted of Norwegian singer Grefstad (*Highland Glory, Wild Willy's Gang, Frostmoon*), guitarist Toya (*Ride The Sky, Sinner*) and former *Dionysus/Nation* bassist Nobby. The second album was produced by Roy Z (*Halford, Bruce Dickinson, Tribe Of Gypsies*) and Jens Bogren (*Opeth, Amon Amarth* etc). Ronny has also played with bands like *Cans, Ride The Sky, Primal Fear, Sinner, Mikeyla, Sinergy* and *Crominic*. *Saint Daemon* play outstanding bombastic melodic power metal with high-pitched vocals, flashy guitar work and memorable songs. In 2011 Ronny left and Oscar Nilsson (*Despite, One Without, Miseration, Ignis*) replaced him. *Website: www.saintdeamon.se*

2008 CD - FR CD 362

2009 CD - FR CD 413

2008 ■	IN SHADOWS LOST FROM THE BRAVE	CD	Frontiers Records	FR CD 362
2008 ☐	IN SHADOWS LOST FROM THE BRAVE	CD	King Records (Japan)	KICP-1297
2009 ■	PANDEAMONIUM	CD	Frontiers Records	FR CD 413
2009 ☐	PANDEAMONIUM	CD	King Records (Japan)	KICP-2318
	Bonus: Pandeamonium (karaoke version)			
2009 ☐	PANDEAMONIUM	CD	Rock Empire (Taiwan)	MMMF-2318
	Bonus: Pandeamonium (video)			

SALTMINE

Mårten Larsson: v, Andreas Magnusson: g, Magnus Sandberg: g, Mikael Elofsson: b, Peter Wikström: d

Östersund - The band was previously known as *Blackwood*, under which name they recorded the MCD *Otherwise* in 1995 (then featuring drummer Tomas Andersson). High-class, heavy, grinding 90s post-grunge with hints of *Tool, Fuel 238* and *Pearl Jam*. Detuned heavy riffing guitars and melodic vocals. Highly recommended. After the first MCD drummer Wikström replaced Peter Limber. The tracks *Kiss My Life Goodnight* and *Pointing Out My Way* were also featured on the compilation *Midwest Vol. 1* (1999 Tilted Records).

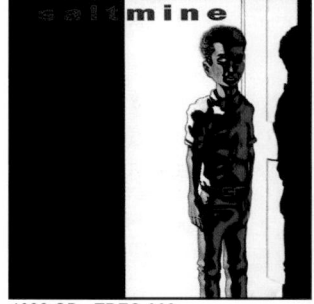
1998 CD - TREC 002

1998 ☐	Rise And Shine/Be Free/Pathetic	MCD 3tr	Tilted Recordings	TREC 001
1998 ■	SALTMINE	CD	Tilted Recordings	TREC 002

SALUTE

Mikael Erlandsson: v, Martin Kronlund: g/b, Dan Helgesson: k, Imre Daun: d

Göteborg - Now here's an AOR-lovers wet dream when it comes to line-up. Erlandsson has recorded with bands like *Crash* and *Last Autumn's Dream*, Kronlund with *Gypsy Rose, Reece/Kronlund, White Wolf* etc and Daun is ex-*Don Patrol* and *Gypsy Rose*. Keyboard player Dan Helgesson also makes a guest appearance on the debut, while the second releases saw Henrik Thomsen playing bass and David Reece on backing vocals. As you may expect, *Salute* is AOR with an edge. Great vocals, fat guitars and great melodies.

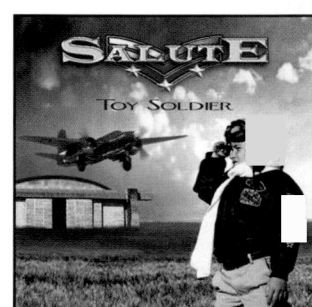
2009 CD - ESM 195

2011 CD - ESM 215

2009 ■	TOY SOLDIER	CD	Escape Music	ESM 195
2009 ☐	TOY SOLDIER	CD	Bickee Music (Japan)	HMCX-1041
	Bonus: No Way Out Of Here			
2011 ■	HEART OF THE MACHINE	CD	Escape Music	ESM 215

SANCHEZ

José Sanchez: v, Kieven Klevmyr: g, Marco "Marc White" Viita: b, Mr. Drumhead: d

Borås - Chilenian-born singer José Sanchez started out in bands like *Empire Saint* and *Fierce Conviction* back in the eighties. In 2007 he made his first release with the band *Sanchez*, now going in a sleaze direction. On the first release the band featured José, guitarists Kenneth Jonsson and Thomas Josefsson, bass player Jörgen Andersson and drummer Martin Tilander. On the second release there was a new band, featuring, besides José, guitarist Pontus Swanberg, bass player Alexander Oriz and drummer Emil Eriksson. So, what happened on the third album? Well, a completely new line-up again. Unfortunately the quality didn't start high on the first album, and it just kept declining with the last album offering standard formula sleaze with quite awful production, below par vocals and quite washed out song material. After the third release the guitar spot was taken over by Andy Blakk. Alexander Oriz formed his own band *Oriz* in 2009 and has released two albums so far. *Sanchez* released a new self-titled digital album in 2013. This time they actually made it! This is their best-sounding effort ever. Hands down.

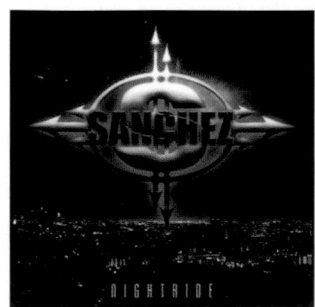
2009 MCD - BTRCD 39

2011 CD - 7H044-2

2007 ☐	SANCHEZ	CD	Artist Service	CD 6001
2009 ■	Nightride	MCD 5tr	Blue Topaz	BTRCD39
	Tracks: Nightride/Lovely/Chasing The Sun/In The Night/Too Bad/Nightride (video)			
2011 ■	RUN THE STREETS	CD	7Hard	7H044-2

SANCTIFICA

Hubertus Liljegren: v/g, Henrik Georgsson: g,
Aron Engberg: k, Jonathan Jansson: b, Daniel Thelin: d

Jönköping - The band was formed in 1996, initially with guitarist Hubertus, drummer Daniel and bassist Alexander Orest. Alexander left and was replaced by Jonathan, but returned, now as keyboard player. This line-up recorded the demo *In The Bleak Midwinter* 1998. The demo was later released on a split-CD with *Pantokrator* in 2001. In 1999 Henrik joined and Alexander was replaced by Aron. The first two releases are Christian death metal, quite close to early *Opeth* with traditional style growling. *Negative B* is quite different. The music was much more diverse, with a more progressive and orchestrated touch, more in the vein of *Pain Of Salvation*. The growls were now reduced and replaced with clean vocals. Highly intricate songs. The album was produced by the band and Calle Grimmark (*Narnia*). Hubertus is the brother of Christian of *Narnia/Widomcall/DivineFire/Modest Attraction/Golden Resurrection* and Simeon (*Modest Attraction*). They also appear on the compilations *In The Shadow Of Death* (Endtime 00) and *Power From The Sky* (02 C.L. Music & Publishing). Aaron was also found in *Ayenna* and Alexander in *Crimson Moonlight*, with whom Jonathan previously recorded a MCD. The band split in 2002.
Website: www.sanctifica.com

2000 CD - LRP 010

2001 CD - CLCD 004

2000 ■ SPIRIT OF PURITY	CD	Little Rose	LRP 010
2001 ■ SANCTIFICA/PANOKRATOR	CD	C.L. Music & Publishing	CLCD 004
Split with Pantokrator. Tracks: Intro/Burial Of The Grave/Blind For Reality/In The Bleak			
Midwinter/Sacrifice To Life/King Of Kings And Lord Of Lords			
2002 ■ NEGATIVE B	CD	C.L. Music & Publishing	CLCD 007

2002 CD - CLCD 007

SANCTIFICATION

Kristoffer Hell: b/v, Tomas Elofsson: g, Marcus Edvardsson: g, Nils Fjellström: d

Östersund - *Sanctification* were formed in 2001 by Elofsson (*In Battle, Divine Descecration, God Among Insects, Those Who Bring The Torture*), drummer Nils Fjellström (*Aeon, A*Teem, Dark Funeral, In Battle, Chasticement, Souldrainer* etc), singer Mathias Mohlin (*Divine Descecration*), guitarist Daniel Dlimi (*Aeon, Souldrainer, Divine Descecration, In Battle, Equinox ov The Gods*) and bassist Peter Jönsson. On the debut album the line-up featured Elofsson, Fjellström, Mohlin and bassist Jörgen Bylander. In 2004 they recorded another four-track demo, entitled *Promo 2004*. The band had now been reinforced by second guitarist Marcus Edvardsson (*Aeon, Endless Torture, Souldainer, Chastisement, In Battle*). Before the second album the band went through more member changes, where bass player Bylander was replaced by Kristoffer Hell, who also took care of the vocals. Mohlin was also out of the band. The album also features guest spots from Peter Tägtgren (who also co-produced the album) and Masse "Magus Caligula" Broberg. After *Black Reign* more member changes took place, where Hell was out of the band and the bass work was taken care of by Andreas Mellkvist, while Jocke Rehnholm handled the vocals. In 2010 Arttu Malkki (*Aeon, Souldrainer, Equinox Ov The Gods, Defaced Creation*) took over the drum stool. *Sanctification* plays American style death metal, quite similar (not surprisingly) to *Aeon* meets early *Morbid Angel*.

2003 CD - RMRCD 006

2009 CD - ASH 06 CD

2003 ■ MISANTHROPIC SALVATION	CD	Remission Records	RMRCD 006
2009 ■ BLACK REIGN	CD	Pulverised	ASH 060 CD

SANCTRUM

Irfan Cancar: v, Viktor Arfwedson: g, Volkan Akol: g, Emil Anter: b, Oskar Odelbo: d

Uppsala - *Sanctrum* were formed in 1999, but up until 2003 they didn't do much in the way of production, but mostly rehearsed covers and made simple garage recordings. They parted ways with the original singer and drafted Irfan and later in 2003 they recorded their first six track demo. In 2005 they recorded the, as yet unreleased, EP *From Ashes To Eternity*. The demo lead to some nice shows and festivals and in 2007 the band recorded some more songs, which along with the unreleased EP, would make up the debut album *In Harm's Way*. The band is working on a second album. *Sanctrum* plays well-produced, great-sounding, heavy, groovy thrash-oriented death metal, not too far from *The Haunted* meets *Machine Head*, but with more screamo-oriented vocals. Guitarist Alex Tollin replaced Volkan after the album.

2008 ■ IN HARM'S WAY	CD	Metalcast	- -

2008 CD - - -

SANCTUARY IN BLASPHEMY

Anton Grönholm: g/v, Micke Kjellman: b/v, Jens Bäckelin: d/v

Stockholm/Göteborg - The name does sound very black metal, but the band sounds a bit like a hardcore band gone doom. Quite screeching desperate vocals, on top of slow, doomy sludge riffing, influenced by bands like *Kyuss* and *Dystopia*. The band actually came out of the Stock-

holm crust punk scene in 2001. After going through some member changes in 2002 drummer Jens (ex-**Martyrdöd**) found two new companions in Micke (ex-**Martyrdöd, Skitsystem**) and Anton (**Sunday Morning Einsteins**). In 2003-2004 they recorded two demos. Six of the demo songs are now featured on the split with their friends in **Sonic Ritual**.

2009 LPg - HRR 059

2009 ■ SANCTUARY IN BLASPHEMY/SONIC RITUAL (split)............................... LPg   High Roller Records........................... HRR 059
    Split with Sonic Ritual. Tracks :Integrity Of Evil/A Lament For A Dying Soul/Wanderer In Darkness/Downwards/The Witch/Rise. 200 black/white splatter + 300 black vinyl.

SANCTUM SANGUIS
Avernus: v, Christian "Draug" Larsson: g/b/d

Fagersta/Västerås - In the middle of 2006, Draug (**Promenia, Shining, Svart, Livsnekad**) initiated his project *Sanctum Sanguis*. After being on hold for a while, he brought in singer Avernus (also in *Apati* as Professor X) in 2007 and the cassette EP *Nothing Prevails* was soon recorded and released by Satanic Propaganda. In 2008 they unearthed the new EP, *Tenebra Perpetua*, this time released on CD. The band (now only featuring Avernus) is currently working on the full length album *DCLXVI*, but no news so far.

2008 MCD - SPRCD-07

2008 ■ Tenebra Perpetua ....MCD 4tr   Satanic Propaganda Records......... SPRCD-07
    Tracks: Wound Of Sacrifice/Djävulens hand/Temptation/The Somberlain (Dissection cover)

SANDBERG, PETE
Peter "Pete" Sandberg: v

Malmö - Peter was born in Norway in 1965, but moved to Göteborg at an early age. He started in the early eighties with bands like **Sir Maxwell**, **Trafalgar** (later **Swedish Erotica**) and various cover bands. He then formed the band **Octagon** with bass player Magnus Rosén (later in **HammerFall**) and guitarist Denny Olsson (later in **Snowstorm**). This band evolved into the duo **Von Rosen**, featuring only Pete and Magnus. They recorded two singles. When Göran Edman left **Madison** for John Norum, Pete took his place. He recorded the single *Nothern Light* (89 Sonet) and an as yet unreleased album, but left when requested to replace Jim Jidhed in the far more commercially successful **Alien**. After this Pete recorded albums with numerous quality acts like **Snake Charmer, Bewarp, Midnight Sun** and the pop duo **Sand & Gold** together with Jonas Reingold (**Downtown Clowns, The Flower Kings, Reingold** etc.). In the eighties he recorded his first solo album, which contains melodic rock in the vein of Brett Walker meets Bryan Adams and with a touch of **Alien**. *Back In Business* is a smooth AOR rocker featuring musicians such as guitarists Henrik "Stanley Hawk" Lindén and Fredrik Bergengren (**Colorstone, Time Gallery**), bassist Patrik Alm, drummer Carl Colt, keyboardists Johan Stentorp and Tommy Falk. *Push*, on the other hand, is an out-and-out heavy riff-oriented power pack with strong hints of **King's X, Eric Gales Band** and **Nicklebag** (NOT **Nickelback**). Musicians on this album were guitarist Sven Cirnski, bassist Jens Lundahl and drummer Jaime, actually the same backing boys that were in **Blakk Totem**. It was later revealed this was actually Sven Cirnski's solo album, but the label though it would be easier to sell with Pete's name fronting. Cirnski later released an album under the name **Truth**, where some of the songs were rerecorded. At the same time as the *Push* album was released, Pete also unearthed an album under the name **Pete Sandberg's Jade** (see separate entry). He also released a disco-pop single under the name Tiko in 1997 together with people from **Basic Element**. The title was *Du Gör Mig Galen* (You drive me crazy) on Level Records (LEVELCDS 001) and is strictly for collectors. In 2000 he decided to leave **Midnight Sun** to go for **Jade**, his solo career. He is also found in **Silver Seraph** as well as **Opus Atlantica**. He was also very active as a troubadour. Did anyone say workaholic? The 2002 release *Reflections* is a bit more laid-back, almost poppy AOR similar to Jim Jidhed's solo albums. Some tracks were actually covers of Hal Marabel's band **Arena Sweden**. The album was listed to be released by Kick Music, but has only been released in Japan. After this it has been quiet, and Pete is mostly doing trobadour gigs. Last minute news. In 2013 Pete recorded an upcoming album with the band **Mad Invasion**, also featuring Mats Berentz (**Silver Mountain**).

Meet the Pete

1998 CD - BSM 1017

2002 CD - MICP-10478

1997 ☐ BACK IN BUSINESS ....CD   Bareknuckle (Japan).................... AVCB-66015
1998 ■ BACK IN BUSINESS ....CD   Bluestone...................................... BSM 1017
1999 ☐ PUSH...CD   Avalon Marquee (Japan)................. MICY 1139
    Bonus: L.O.V.E – A.M.D
2002 ■ REFLECTIONS...CD   Avalon Marquee (Japan)..............MICP-10478
    Bonus: Open Mind

SANDBERG, STEN
Sten Sandberg: g, Kenneth Holmström: b, Martin Fürst: d

Göteborg - Sten has a past in the more jazz and fusion-oriented world, however *Blues Fusion* is like the title suggests a mix of blues and fusion, with Sten's outstanding guitar work. Should appeal to fans of Satriani, MacAlpine etc.

1994 CD - MM10

1994 ■ BLUES FUSION..CD   Musik Musik MM10

SANITY

Ola Wikström: v, Tommie Karlsson: g, Kristofer Samuelsson: g, Tommy Rudak: k, Rickard "Rick Altzi" Thornberg: b, Vladde Labat: d

Varberg - A highly interesting melodic hard rock band with a progressive touch. Great vocals and high-quality musicians. In 1999 the band recorded an outstanding 3-track demo and in 2000 yet another 4-track. When Ola quit, bass player Rickard took over the vocals. They also contributed to the *Released By X-mas* compilation with their version of *We Wish You A Merry Christmas*. In 2002 Rickard joined **Treasure Land** as lead singer, but only some demos came out of it. He later joined **At Vance** under his new alter ego, Rick Altzi and has since sung with **Sandalinas**, **Epysode**, **Frequency** and is now in **Thunderstone**. Tommie and Ola were both ex-**Sign**.

1997 ■	Forgotten World	MCD 6tr	private		SNY 297

Tracks: The Right/Lovin' Tonight/Forgotten World/Find The Way/Lost Forever/Roll The Dice

1997 MCD - SNY 297

SANZIA

Rikard Larsson: v, Jonas Paulsson: g, Marcus Fren: g, Ola Sjöstedt: b, Johan Rydberg: d

Kristianstad - Power metal with a technical touch. Pretty suggestive, intense metal with a touch of **Destiny** mixed with **Death, Pantera, Biohazard** and a touch of the 80s US style metal. The owner of the label was convicted of the murder of **HammerFall's** tour manager Lelle Widén as well as a triple murder, all in the name of money. Rickard is ex-**Mercy** and was also a member of **Supreme Majesty** for a while. **Sanzia** later became **In Black**.

1998 ■	YOU WHIRL WHITHIN IT	CD	Dark Past Productions	DPP 005

1998 CD - DPP 005

SAPFHIER

Mattias "Lord Aganaroth" Björklund: v/g/k/b/d

Eskilstuna - **Sapfhier,** the solo project of former **Exanthema/Tears Of Grief** guitarist Björklund, started in 2001. The first demo *Trollskogen* was initially printed in only 50 copies in 2001, but reissued by God Is Myth in another 150 copies. In 2005 Black Plague gave it a proper release. Lo-fi primitive Norse black metal with guttural vocals and programmed drums, not unlike **Burzum**.

2004 ☐	UNDER ETERNALLY GREAT SKIES	CD	Black Plague	BPR 001
	500 copies.			
2005 ■	TROLLSKOGEN	CD	Black Plague	BPR 009
	500 copies.			

2005 CD - BPR 009

SAPPHIRE EYES

Thomas Bursell: v, Niclas Olsson: k

Malmö - The story actually began already back in 2004 when singer Thomas and keyboardist Niclas played together in the band **Second Heat**. Niclas went to **Alyson Avenue** and the band was put on hold. In 2012 they finally reunited and formed **Sapphire Eyes**. The vocal duties are also shared with Mikael Erlandsson (**Last Autumn's Dream, Lovers Under Cover** etc) and Mike Andersson (**Cloudscape, FullForce**), with backing vocals by **Alyson Avenue** singers Anette Olzon (**Nightwish**) and Arabella Vitanic. The guitar duties were shared between Sven Larsson, Rik Priem (**Frozen Rain**), Emil Knabe, Christopher Dahlmann (**Alyson Avenue**), Mikael Nilsson (**Nasty Idols, Bai Bang, Pierce, Alyson Avenue**), and the bass work by Göran Forssén (**Quix**), Mats Ståhl and Thomas Löyskä (**Alyson Avenue**), while the drums were played by Anders "Theo" Theander (**Bewarp, Eurock**). If you like **Second Heat** and **Alyson Aveue**, as well as **Last Autumn's Dream**, this one's for you. Outstanding melodic hard rock/AOR.

2012 ■	SAPPHIRE EYES	CD	Avenue Of Allies	Avenue 12 09 0047

2012 CD - Avenue 12 09 0047

SARCASM

Heval Bozarslan: v, Henrik Forslund: g, Fredrik Wallenberg: g, Dave Janney: b, Oskar Karlsson: d

Uppsala - Formed in 1990 and recorded their first demo, *Insanity Reborn* in 1992, followed by the *In Hate* and *Soul Enchantment* demos later the same year. At this stage the band featured Janney, Wallenberg, Bozarslan and Forslund. In 1993 they recorded the official demo *Dark* plus another unreleased four-track. Late 1993, Oskar Karlsson was added on drums and the year after they recorded the demo *A Touch Of The Burning Red Sunset*. The band split in 1994 and the first album is a compilation of the demos. Before breaking up they did record an unreleased album. This album, plus all the demos, was finally unearthed in 2011 on the *Never After* album. Henrik is now in sixties-oriented band **Mama Earth**, Oskar is in **Everdawn/Gates Of Ishtar**

1999 7" PD - AO 19640

and Wallenberg formed punksters *Skitsystem*. *Sarcasm* play high-speed death metal in the vein of *Dissection*, with some nice variations thrown in here and there. Not to be confused with the French, German, Polish, Slovenian, Swizz, Ukrainian or American namesakes.

1998	☐ A TOUCH OF THE BURNING RED SUN	CD	Breath Of Night	BOM 4 CD
1999	■ Scattered Ashes/Pile Of Bodies	7" PD	Danse Hypnotica	AO 19640
2011	■ NEVER AFTER – THE COMPLETE RECORDINGS	3LP	To The Death Records	TTD 004
	Red/black splatter. 400 hand numbered copies.			
2011	☐ NEVER AFTER – THE COMPLETE RECORDINGS	3LP+7"	To The Death Records	TTD 004
	Red/black splatter. 100 hand numbered copies.			

2011 3LP - TTD 004

SARCAZM

Krister Albertsson: v/g, Niclas Engelin: g, Michael Nicklasson: b, Peter Andersson: d

Frölunda (Göteborg) - Formed in 1990. They recorded three demos before the MCD was released; *Snaildeath* (1990), *Human Decadence* (1991) and *Jeremiads* (1992). The bass was handled by Bo Falk on the first demo and he was replaced by Michael Nicklasson. The band split in 1992 and bassist Michael Nicklasson went to form *Luciferion*, together with drummer Peter Andersson. The *Metallica* cover *Motorbreath* is found on the tribute CD *Metal Militia* (94 Black Sun). High-quality trash metal, at times similar to *Slayer* and vintage *Metallica*. Engelin was previously in *Idiot's Rule*, later in *Gardenian*, *Engel*, *Passenger* and *In Flames*. Albersson was also in *Gardenian* and Nicklasson in *Lavett*, *Reborn* and *Dark Tranquillity*.

1994	■ Breath, Shit, Excist	MCD 4tr	Deathside	DS10 394
	Tracks: Pure Hate/Covered Again/My Inner Rots/Breathe, Shit, Excist			

1994 MCD - DS10 394

SAREA

Christoffer Forsberg: v, Johan Axelsson: g, Martin Persson: k,
Johan Larsson: b, Calle "Charlie D" Larsson: d

Norrköping - *Sarea* were formed by Johan Axelsson (*Ravenlord, Shineth*), Johan Larsson and singer Mattias Wetterhall in 2005. They recorded their first demo, *Mechanical Prophecy*, in 2006. At this stage the line-up featured Axelsson, Wetterhall and Calle (ex-*Helvete, Kaos Kris*). Keyboardist Henrik Sproge (*Miss Behaviour*) made a guest appearance, as well as guitarists Alexander Lindgren and Johan Lagander (*Taiga, Legionaires*). On the first album the band had been reinforced by Persson. Guest appearances were made by Tomas Lindberg (*At The Gates, The Great Deceiver*), Daniel Heiman (*Lost Horizon, Heed*), Markus Lundberg (*Sargatanas Reign, Devian, Plague Majestic*), Sebastian Roos (*Shineth*), Sigrid Lagander (*Taiga*) and Jocke Göthberg (*Nifters, Dimension Zero*). After the album, singer Mattias was replaced by Forsberg (ex-*Sabotage, Inferior*). *Alive* featured guest appearances from Tomas Lindberg and Sebastian Roos. *Sarea* play bone-hard modern melodic metal with both clean and aggressive vocals.
Website: www.sareamusic.com

2008 CD - - -

2008	■ RISE OF A DYING WORLD	CD	private	- -
2010	■ ALIVE	CD	Supernova	SUPERCD 020

2010 CD - SUPERCD 020

SARGATANAS REIGN

Jonas Matsson: v, Kristoffer "Ushatar" Andersson: g, Markus Lundberg: g,
Niklas Samuelsson: b, Stefan "Vrashtar" Kronquist: d

Norrköping - *Sargatanas Reign* were formed in 1997. The first demo, *Sargatanas* (1998) featured Kristoffer (*The Legion, Nefandus*), Markus, Stefan (*Angst*) and bassist Johan "Jojje" Ericsson. The second and third demos, *The God Below* (1998) and *Satanic Hymns* (1998) featured only Stefan and Kristoffer, now handling vocals, guitar and bass. On the *Euthanasia* album the band was completed with singer Magnus "Devo" Andersson (*Marduk, Allegience, Cardinal Sin, Overflash* etc), Markus (*Sarea, Devian, Plague Majestic, Deadpulse*) and Niklas. Quite technical death/black metal, mixing heavy, riffing parts with high-speed outbursts. The lyrics on the first album were written by Morgan "Steinmeyer" Håkansson (*Marduk*). On the second album, Devo had been replaced by Jonas Matsson (*Nominon, Incinerator, Devian, Rise And Shine*). When Niklas left the band in 2006 singer Jonas added the bass to his tasks. The band is currently working on a new album entitled *Godwork*, and the 2012 line-up features Kristoffer, Marcus and bass player Robert Hylén (*Griftegård, Atom & Evil*).
Website: www.sargatanasreign.com

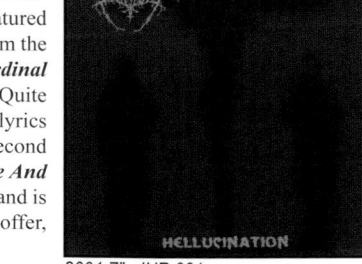

2001 7" - IHR 001

2002 LP - IHR LP 003

2001	■ Hellucination	7" 4tr	I Hate	IHR 001
	Tracks: Hellucination/Amon/Twist The Knife In Christ/Evangelical Clitorial. Pressed in blood red vinyl in 500 numbered copies.			
2002	☐ EUTHANASIA... LAST RESORT	CD	I Hate	IHR CD 003
2002	■ EUTHANASIA... LAST RESORT	LP	I Hate	IHR LP 003
	Bonus: Highest Power (GG Allin cover). 525 copies. Numbered. Different artwork.			
2004	■ BLOODWORK – TECHNIQUES OF TORTURE	CD	Blooddawn	BLOOD 021
2005	☐ BLOODWORK – TECHNIQUES OF TORTURE	CD	CD-Maximum (Russia)	CDM 0805-2350

2004 CD - BLOOD 021

SARGOTH

Fredrik Sundin: v, Patrik Johansson: g, Christian Rehn: g,
Kent Hofling: b, Roger Lagerlund: d

Sundsvall - Formed in 1994 by Fredrik and Patrik. They later recruited drummer Michael Nyström (ex-*Crebain*) and former *Impious* (the Sundsvall demo band, not the Trollhättan band) members, bassist Johan Kempe and guitarist Roger Lagerlund. The two latter left the band shortly after and guitarist Rehn (*Abyssos*) was recruited. They then recorded the demo *Mörkrets Furste*. In 1996 Nyström was replaced by Lagerlund, now on drums. The album was recorded in Dug Out, Uppsala and mixed by Daniel Bergstrand. Shortly after the release, Christian left to concentrate on *Abyssos*. The line-up was later completed with guitarist Olle Jansson (ex-*Impious, Haimad*) while bass player Kent Hofling went from session player to full-time member. The band had a second album (*Under Lucifers Banner*) written and ready, but split before it was recorded. Lagerlund and Jansson are now in *Chaosdaemon*, while Rehn has been a member of *Angtoria*, *Evergrey* and *Insalubrious*. *Sargoth* plays high-quality, fast and furious blast-beat-filled death metal, not too far from *Dissection* and *Dark Funeral*.

1998	■	LAY EDEN IN ASHES	CD	Black Diamond	BDP 006
1999	□	LAY EDEN IN ASHES	CD	Avalon Marquee (Japan)	MICY-1098

Bonus: Under Lucifers Banner/Into Darker Domains

1998 CD - BDP 006

SARTINAS

Patrik Andersson: v/b, Ted Lindström: v/d, Thomas Fredriksson: g, Mathias Bäck: g

Västerås - Formed around 1994 and split around 1999 The track *Threshold To Infinity* was featured on the *Sampler 1* (1997 Shadows Of Michelangelo) compilation. Patrik was later in *The Enthralled* and is now in *WOD Sartinas* plays quite melodic death metal mixing growl and cleaner vocals.

1997	■	Demo CD '97	MCD 4tr	Shadows Of Michelangelo	.- -

Tracks: Thousands Of Tears/Twisted Dreams/Night Warrior/Threshold To Infinity

1997 MCD - - -

SATAN'S PENGUINS

Slayerprincess: v, Albert "Killerpenguin": v/b/g/sax

Stockholm/Karlstad - *Satan's Penguins* were formed by former *Feral* guitarist Albert "Killerpenguin" around 1998 and they recorded the first demo, *Arctic Winter*, the same year. The line-up on the demo was Killerpenguin on guitars and drum programming, Mr. Malice on vocals, Killhammer on drums and Anders "Flame" Eriksson (*Bloodbanner, Nattfrossa, Hydra, Blitzer*) on bass. The name was picked to reflect the band's ambition to depart from old thought patterns that dominated the metal scene. The music on the debut is quite varied folk-inspired black metal with vocals ranging from guttural Gollum-style style and drunken penguin squawks to fair female vocals. Among the weirdest I've heard. The production may not be the most ambient sounding, but it's not all-horrible. On the album the line-up had been reinforced with singer Slayerprincess and drummer Killhammer, besides sax player (??!!) Ludi McSkank. The album also contains an interpretation of the Swedish folk song *Emigrantvisan*. The band went into a long period where nothing happened, but there were difficulties finding musicians since many people didn't consider the band to be serious. With song titles like *An Evil Shade Of Pink*, *The Return Of The Undead Smurfs* and *Mutant Ninja Penguins (From Hell)* I guess it's no wonder. Killerpenguin stated it was by no means a joke band, at least not the music. The lyrical message was neither Satanic, nor in any other form religious. A third recording, initially called *Creatures Of The Ice*, was made 2005-2006, finally named *Bloodlust Of The Warpenguins*, now featuring Killerpenguin, guitarist Geno, percussionist Leppard Seal, sax player Ludi McSkank and singer Razorbeak. The band was finally disbanded because of lack of audience interest.

2001	■	BIRDS OF DARKNESS	CD	Heretic Sounds	HS 001

2001 CD - HS 001

SATANARCHY

Stefan "Mr Violece" Mithander: v, Joakim "Beered" Knutsson: g,
Josabeth Leidi: b, Max Thornell: d

Stockholm - In 2000 they recorded a demo CD-R with four tracks, including a cover of *Motörhead's Killed By Death*. Raw, totally unpolished *Venom* meets *Motörhead*-brutality. Josabeth and Joakim are also found in *Rise And Shine*, Max is ex-*Wonderflow/Furbowl* and Stefan is also in *Gehennah*. The album was produced by Nico Elgstrand (*Entombed, Terra Firma*).

2001	■	DISGRACEFUL WORLD	CD	Primitive Art	PAR 023
2001	□	DISGRACEFUL WORLD	LP	Primitive Art	PAR 023

Bonus: We Are The Undead

2001 CD - PAR 023

SATANIC SLAUGHTER

Stefan "Ztephan Dark" Karlsson: v, Kecke Ljungberg: g, Andreas Deblén: g,
Filip "Fille" Carlsson: b, Robert Eng: d

Linköping - This is really a cult band fronted by (the late) Ztephan Dark. The band was formed in 1985 under the moniker *Evil Cunt*, but soon changed their name. The band has through the years featured more than 22 (!) different members from bands like *Seance*, *Morgue* and *Witchery* etc. In 1988 they recorded their first three-track demo *One Night In Hell*, at the time featuring Ztephan, guitarist Jörgen Sjöström, bassist Ronnie Börjesson and drummer Pontus Sjösten. The band's first appearance on record was in 1995, on a *Slayer* tribute. After numerous member changes the debut album was recorded by Dan Swanö. The line-up now featured Ztephan (on bass), singer Tony "Toxine" Kampner (*Seance, Total Death*, later in *Witchery*), guitarists Patrik Jensen (*Orchriste, Brujeria, Seance*, later in *Witchery, The Haunted* and Rickard "Corpse" Rimfält (*Seance, Morgue*) and drummer Mickie "Mique" Pettersson (*Morgue, Total Death*, later in *Witchery* and *Freevil* as Mique Flesh). The album *Land Of Unholy Souls*, features old demo material. After this album the entire line-up left the band and formed *Witchery*. Ztephan continued with singer Andreas Deblén (*Spiteful, Deranged, Benighted*), who also handled the drums on four tracks on the album, guitarist Kecke Ljungberg (*Morgue*), bassist Filip "Fille" Carlsson (*Spiteful*, later in *Thornclad, Corporation 187*) and drummer Robert Eng (*Corporation 187, Algaion, Höst*). *The Early Years: Dawn Of Darkness* is a compilation of the first two albums. The line-up changed after the recording of *Afterlife Kingdom* and Robban and Kecke were replaced by Martin Axenrot (*Triumphator, Nephenzy Chaos Order, Morgue, Funeral Frost, Blasphemous, Opeth, Witchery, Bloodbath*) and Stefan Johansson (*Morgue, Dismal*). Their style is good, old, well-played death influenced thrash, a bit similar to *Naglfar* meets *Destruction* at times. The band can also be found on compilations such as *Dawning Of Pure Evil* (Necropolis – track *One Night In Hell), Thrashing Holocaust* (Necropolis – track *Mysteries Of Evilness), Legacy Magazine #7* (2000 – track *Through The Dark Profound*) and *Ablaze Magazine #32* (2000 – *track Nocturnal* Crimson Nightmare). In 2005 the band made their last live performance. Ztephan however made one last attempt early 2006, now featuring himself, bassist Simon Axenrot (*Nephenzy Chaos Order*), Stefan Johansson (*Morgue*) and drummer Fredrik Nilsson (*Spetälsk, Miserycordia*). On April 18, 2006, Stefan sadly died of heart failure.

1995 CD - NR 004

1997 CD - NR 014

Afterlife Kingdom

2000 CD - LNP 012

1995	■	SATANIC SLAUGHTER	CD	Necropolis	NR 004
1997	■	LAND OF THE UNHOLY SOULS	CD	Necropolis	NR 014
2000	■	AFTERLIFE KINGDOM	CD	Loud 'N Proud	LNP 012
2001	□	THE EARLY YEARS: DAWN OF DARKNESS	CD	Necropolis	NR 061
2002	■	BANISHED TO THE UNDERWORLD	CD	Black Sun	BS 25

Slipcase with different artwork.

2002 CD - BS 25 *(splicase)*

SATARIEL

Pär "Aemelgoth" Johansson: v, Magnus "Azazel" Alakangas: g, Mikael Granqvist: g,
Mikael "Asael" Granbacke (aka Degerman): b, Robert "Zoid" Sundelin: d

Boden - The band was founded in 1993 by Pär, Magnus and Mikael Granbacke, when the band *Dawn Of Darkness* didn't happen. They were reinforced by drummer Andreas "Astaroth" Nilzon (*Incinerator, The Moaning*). The band recorded the demo *Thy Heaven's Fall* (1993) and *Descecration Black* (1994). In 1995 Fredrik "Thorn" Andersson (*Incinerator, Beyond Dreams*) was added on guitar and they recorded the demo *Hellfuck*. The three-track demo *Promo '96* finally resulted in the deal with Pulverised. Now Fredrik had been replaced by Magnus Granqvist and Robert Sundelin by Andreas. *Lady Lust Lilith* was recorded at Sunlight Studios. Sundelin is ex-*Necromicon*. Messiah Marcolin guests on the second album, which was produced by Daniel Bergstrand (*Crawley, Meshuggah* etc). Techical, powerful and at times melodic death metal like a mix of early *In Flames* and later *Entombed*. The first album was more high-speed, while the second varies from ultra-speed to almost doomy parts. Tight and well-played. Recommended. Sundelin has also been playing in *Hellmasker, Deathbound, Bewitched, Morthirim* and *Zmegma*, Alakangas in *Incinerator, Hel* and *Belsemar*, while Johansson has sung in *The Duskfall, Demiurg, Torchbearer, Hel* and is also in *The Few Against Many*. Pär has also designed artwork for *Satariel*'s and other releases. Satariel was a watcher over leaders of fallen angels in *The Book Of Enoch*.

1998 CD - ASH 005 CD

2002 CD - HHR 089

1998	■	LADY LUST LILITH	CD	Pulverised	ASH 005 CD

First edition was a 24 carat gold disc featuring bonus-track Greeting Immortality (Eucharist cover)

2002	■	PHOBOS AND DEIMOS	CD	Hammerheart	HHR 089
2003	□	LADY LUST LILITH	CD	Hammerheart	HHR 112

Different artwork. Bonus: Violent Dance (demo)/ Yet To Be (demo)/The Great Necropolis

2005	■	HYDRA	CD	Regain	RR 069
2005	□	HYDRA	CD	Candlelight (USA)	CDL 0288CD
2005	□	HYDRA	LP	Animate Records	AR 012

Bonus: Wake Of God. 666 copies.

2007	□	Chifra	MCD 4tr	Pulverised	ASH 019 CD

Tracks: Hogtied Angel/Slitherer/Chifra/Flies Halo + video.

2013	□	WHITE INK	CD	Pulverised	n/a

2005 CD - RR 069

SATAROS GRIEF

Sataros: v/g/b/d

Mora - The solo project of Sataros, brother of Johan "Shamaatae" Lager (*Arckanum, Absorption, Sorhin, Grotesque*). He is also found in *Absorption* and *Arckanum*. Up-tempo melodic death metal with hysteric, desperate vocals. Quite low-budget production.

2008 ■ Älskade min död (split)..7"g Carnal/Blut & Eisen......................................- -
    Split with Arckanum. Track: Älskade min död. 100 green, 600 black vinyl.
2008 □ Älskade min död (split)..7" PD Carnal/Blut & Eisen......................................- -
    300 copies.

2008 7"g - - -

SATELLITE CIRCLE, THE

Jonas Nordin: g/v, Fredrik Holmgren: b, Jonas Ericson: d/v

Umeå - High-quality, heavy riff-oriented stoner. The Jonases have been playing together for about ten years and Fredrik joined the two in 1997. The styles varied and the final name and concept was born in 1999. Even though no releases have been made since 2002, the band still exists.

2001 □ Way Beyond The Portal Of The Bone White Rubber Sun......................MCD 5tr Rage Of Achilles ....ILIAD 006
    Tracks: Kick You Right Back/At The End Of The Day/Reconcile/The More I Drink/ From Where You Stand
2002 ■ THE SATELLITE CIRCLE..CD Rage Of Achilles ....ILIAD 014

2002 CD - ILIAD 014

SATUREYE

Roger "Rogga" Pettersson: v, Christian "Norsken" Knudsen: g,
Joakim "Jocke" Hammare: b, Henrik "Henke" Borg: d

Strängnäs - *Satureye* were formed in the summer of 2000, when *Merciless* singer Rogga made a guest appearance on the band *Entropy*'s demo recording. The band featured Norsken and Henke, and the three decided to form a new band, naming it *Satureye*. They recorded a first unofficial demo as a trio, before Jocke joined in 2001. It was followed by *Silvery Souls*, which was nominated Demo of the year in Close-Up magazine. Another self-titled demo was recorded in 2002 and two more in 2003; *Wither* and *To Nothingness Return*, which lead to the band being picked up by Karmageddon Media who released the debut album. Quite good, well-produced, high-octane thrash in the vein of *Slayer* with Rogga's semi-growling vocals.

2004 ■ WHERE FLESH AND DIVINITY COLLIDE................................CD Karmageddon Media ....KARMA 058
2004 □ WHERE FLESH AND DIVINITY COLLIDE................................CD Nordic Media (Russia) ....NM 020

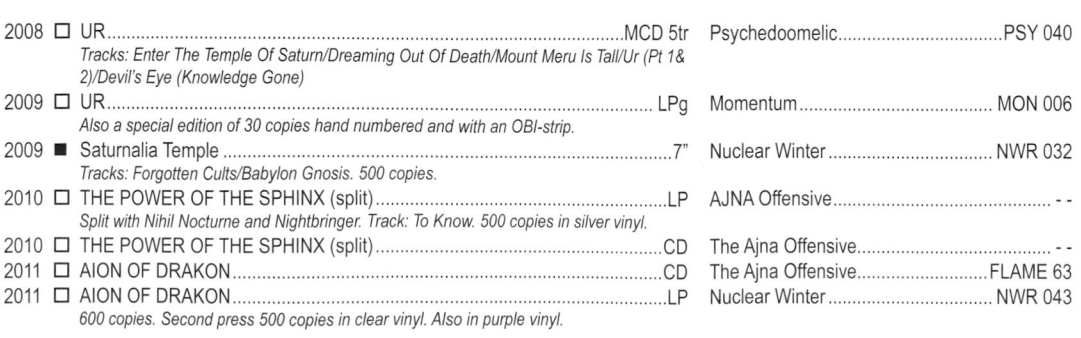

2004 CD - KARMA 058

SATURNALIA TEMPLE

Tommy "Tommie" Eriksson: v/g, Peter Karlsson: b, Paul: d

Stockholm - Formed by Tommie aka Daemon Kajgal (*Lapis Niger, Shadowseeds, Therion, Nocturnal Rites*). On *UR* the band featured Tommie, drummer Paul, guitarist Konstantin Papavassiliou and bass player Ignatius of Loyola. The EP was also released on cassette by Nuclear Winter. On the 2009 7" Peter handled the bass. On *Aion Of Drakon* the band featuried Tommie, Peter and Paul. After the album Paul was replaced by Michael Norrby on 9/11 2011. Simple and basic *Black Sabbath* meets *Hawkwind* meets *Hellhammer*, death doom, with a touch of the British 80s bandwagon. Norrby was replaced by Jens Gustavsson, who sadly died July 15, 2013.

2008 □ UR..MCD 5tr Psychedoomelic................................PSY 040
    Tracks: Enter The Temple Of Saturn/Dreaming Out Of Death/Mount Meru Is Tall/Ur (Pt 1& 2)/Devil's Eye (Knowledge Gone)
2009 □ UR..LPg Momentum.......................................MON 006
    Also a special edition of 30 copies hand numbered and with an OBI-strip.
2009 ■ Saturnalia Temple ....7" Nuclear Winter ....NWR 032
    Tracks: Forgotten Cults/Babylon Gnosis. 500 copies.
2010 □ THE POWER OF THE SPHINX (split)................................LP AJNA Offensive...................................- -
    Split with Nihil Nocturne and Nightbringer. Track: To Know. 500 copies in silver vinyl.
2010 □ THE POWER OF THE SPHINX (split)................................CD The Ajna Offensive...............................- -
2011 □ AION OF DRAKON..CD The Ajna Offensive.........................FLAME 63
2011 □ AION OF DRAKON..LP Nuclear Winter ....NWR 043
    600 copies. Second press 500 copies in clear vinyl. Also in purple vinyl.

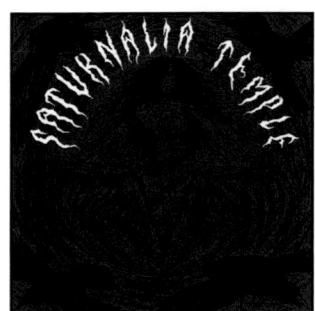

2009 7" - NWR 032

SAVAGE SKÜLLS

Tommy Andersson: v/g, Oskar Wiklund: g, Jonas Edström: b, Ola Grönlund: d

Piteå - 1990 - 1992. Although it looks quite "cheap", the single offers two very good tracks in the style of *Candlemass*, *Trouble* etc. It suffers a bit of poor production, but is well worth looking for. In the end the line-up was re-inforced with singer Stefan Pettersson, however this never emerged on record. They later changed their name to *N.R.G.* and their style to soul-funk.

1991 ■ Lost But Never Found/The Former Things Are Passed Away.........................7" Hit It Productions ....HIT 004

1991 7" - HIT 004

SAVAGERS

Sören "Whitey X'Ero" Lindmark: v/g, Stefan "Steve Thunderhawk" Hozjan: b/v,
Anders "Andy Double-Hammer" Fransson: d

Torup (Hyltebruk) - Savagers were one of those mythical mystery bands, where no one seemed
to know the origin and whereabouts. Well, here it comes. The band was formed in 1980 under
the name *Killers*. In 1983 they changed their name to *Savagers* and recorded their first four-
track demo. In 1984 they went to Nacka to record the MLP. Not satisfied with the mix they
recorded a new five-track demo already in 1985. One of the songs, *Vi är tre* (we are three) is
in Swedish as this was a demand to enter the Rock SM bandstand. After this things was quite
slow, but in 1990 the band was reformed as *X-Eryus*, adding keyboardist Joakim Patsonen and
drummer Patrick Fransson (Anders switched to guitar). The band recorded one LP, now a bit
more commercial-sounding. In 1991 *X-Eryus* also folded. Classic 80s heavy metal. A rarity!

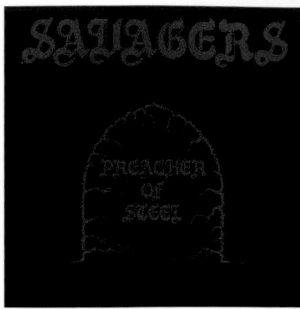

1984 MLP - CTR 1854

1984 ■ Preacher Of Steel .... MLP 6tr CTR .... CTR 1854 $$$
  Tracks: Stormwinds/Preacher Of Steel/Savagers/Crusaders of Fortune/State Of Shock/
  Danger

SAVED BY INSANITY

Emil Näsström: v/g, Johan Lindh: g, Samuel Smitz: b, Simon Holmberg: d

Linköping/Norrköping - Saved By Insanity were formed in 2007, initially named *One Step Ahead*.
The band's first demo, *Stray Dog Society*, was unearthed in 2010. The main part of the drums
on the demo were played by Morgan Lie (*Naglfar*). On the band's second recording, the drum
work was handled by Brynjar Helgetun (*Liklukt, Paganizer* etc). After the recording drummer
Simon Holmberg (*Unlight Order*) completed the line-up. *Saved By Insanity* play powerful
metal, quite goovy and heavy, yet melodic. The EP *Beautifully Disfigured* was released in 2013.

2011 MCD - (114953)

2011 ■ Truth Reborn .... MCD 4tr private .... (114953)
  Tracks: Call To Arms/Sweet Little Slaughter/Bleed/Before The Dawn

SAYIT

Sayit Dölen: g

Stockholm - A solo project by guitarist Sayit (yes that's his name). However, almost all songs
were written by Tommy Denander and most of them in co-operation with Ricky Delin. The
duo also produced the albums. Other prominent musicians found on the albums are Tommy
Denander, Bruce Gaitch, Michael Thompson, Andreas Eklundh, Thomas Vikström, Annika
Burman, Jim Jidhed, Kee Marcello, David Hugate, Mats Olausson etc. The first album is very
slick and almost pop-oriented, mainstream AOR with a strong touch of *Toto*, while the second
album has got a bit more edge to it. Well-recorded, well-written and well-performed.

2001 CD - 4 018996 101881

1999	☐	SAYIT .... CD	Noble House/AOR Heaven NH99
2001	■	AGAIN .... CD	AOR Heaven 4 018996 101881
2004	☐	LOUDER .... CD	MTM 0681-85
2007	☐	SAYIT .... CD	AL!VE 10041

SCAAR

Alex Jonsson: v, Alf Johansson: g, Mats Vassfjord: b, Kristian Huotari: d

Eskilstuna/Västerås - Scaar were formed in 1999, by Alf and Alex (*Tough Trade, Torch, Days
Of Anger*). They were soon joined by Mats (ex-*Pink Pather, Astral Carneval*) and drummer
Richard Holmgren (*Soulskinner, Wolf, Vanessa, Grand Design, Apostasy, Haterus, Black-
world*). On *The Second Insision* Richard had been replaced by drummer Houtari (*Torch, Griffen,
Days Of Anger*). *Next Level Of Torture* was produced by Daniel Bergstrand. Vassfjord is also
found in *Chris Laney's Legion, Impera* and *Grand Design*. Scaar plays high-quality, tight,
hard-edged thrash like a mix of *Pantera* and *F.K.Ü* with powerful production by Pelle Saether.

2005 CD - KARMA 081

2001 ☐ Scarred For Life .... MCD 6tr Private .... - -
  Tracks: Deformed Reality/Evil Strangeland/Shut Up Or I'll Kill Ya/Needle Of Pain/Wood-
  pecker Mosh/Scarred For Life
2005 ■ THE SECOND INSISION .... CD Karmageddon Media .... KARMA 081
2005 ☐ THE SECOND INSISION .... CD Nordic Media (Russia) .... NM 0021
2008 ☐ NEXT LEVEL OF TORTURE .... CD Alabama .... ALAB 009

SCAMPS

Lasse Lundgren: v, Lennart Staaf: g, Ulf Lagestam: g,
Pär Anders "Bajen" Frånberg: b, Bobbe Wallentin: d

Östersund - The A-side is a mid-tempo melodic hard rocker, while the B-side is a bit more
up-tempo. Traditional Swedish 80s hard rock with good vocals. A rarity!

1984 7" - SCR 1001

1984 ■ Love Today Hate Tomorrow/Crystal Night .... 7" private .... SCR 1001 $$
  500 copies.

SCAMS, THE

Daniel Kvist: v/g, Don Krim: g, Kriss Biggs: b, Tobias Ander: d

Växjö - *Scams* were formed in 2003 by Ander and Kvist. The band started out as a psychobilly punk band and released the 7" *Noize, Booze 'N' Tattooz* (2007 Zorch Records, ZR-36) and the CD *One Night Of Mayhem* (2007 Zorch Records, ZR-35) in this style. When guitarist Don entered the band they style changed drastically. The Brylecreem was washed out, the hair got longer and *Rock And Roll Krematorium* is a full-blown hard rocker sounding like a mix of *AC/DC* and *Backyard Babies*. Don has now been replaced by Linus Olsson. A great live act!

2011 ■	ROCK AND ROLL KREMATORIUM	CD	Lightning records	LIR 002
2012 ☐	BOMB'S AWAY	CD	Lightning records	LIR 007

2011 CD - LIR 002

SCAR

Robert Eriksson: v, Joakim Andersson: g,
Tomas Sörlen: g, Mats Demelin: b, Björn Demelin: d

Sollefteå - The band was formed in October 1994. They released a self-financed MCD in February 1995, which lead to a deal with German Massacre Records, which didn't result in anything. *Scar* certainly have a suitable name, as their music is really ripping. It´s heavy as hell, with detuned guitars and raw vocals. Great stuff, quite similar to *Machine Head* and at times *Biohazard*.

1995 ■	Scar	MCD 5tr	private	Scared 1

Tracks: Non Conform/Emptied/Inconsolable/Greed Inc./Punished

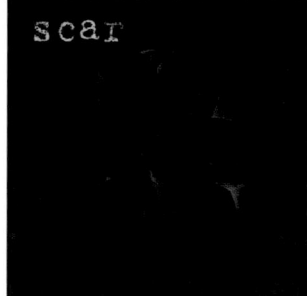

1995 MCD - Scared 1

SCAR SYMMETRY

Lars Palmqvist: v, Roberth Karlsson: v, Jonas Kjellgren: g,
Per Nilsson: g, Kenneth Seil: b, Henrik Ohlsson: d

Don't be afraid, we'll make it symmetric!

Avesta - When Jonas Kjellgren left *Carnal Forge* in 2004, he received an offer from Cold Records to put together a new band, in the vein of *Soilwork*. The band was formed during Henrik and Per's band *Altered Aeon*'s recording session in Kjellgren's studio, Black Lounge. They immediately recorded the demo track *Seeds Of Rebellion*. The initial line-up featured singer Christian Älvenstam (*Incapacity, Solar Dawn, Torchbearer, Solution .45, Unmoored, The Few Against Many, Miseration, etc*), guitarist Per Nilsson (*World Below, Thrawn, Adversary, Kaipa*), bassist Kenneth Seil, drummer Henrik Ohlsson (*Mutant, Thrawn, Theory In Practise, Diabolical*) and guitarist Kjellgren (*Centinex, World Below, Carnal Forge, Dellamorte, Incapacity*). The band was immediately picked up by Metal Blade (EU) and Nuclear Blast (USA) and the debut *Symmetry In Design* was released in 2005. The album showed a band mixing a variety of styles from classic death metal, to more melodic, progressive power metal sounds, clean vocals mixed with growl. Melodic, yet aggressive, a really great musical mix. Great guitar playing and killer production. In 2006 the split-promo *The Neckbreakers Ball* (Nuclear Blast, NB 1660-2) was released, containing three tracks by *Scar Symmetry*. In September 2008, after *Holographic Universe*, singer Älvestam left the band. A month later he was replaced by two singers, clean singer Lars Palmqvist (*Last Temptation, Mirador, Backwardness*) and growler Roberth Karlsson (*Darkified, Incapacity, Solar Dawn, Edge Of Sanity, Aktiv Dödshjälp, Facebreaker, Tormented, Pan-Thy-Monium* etc). Kjellgren is also in *Raubtier*.

2005 ■	SYMMETRY IN DESIGN	CDd	Metal Blade	3984-14524-2
2005 ☐	SYMMETRY IN DESIGN	CDd	Scarecrow Records (Mexico)	SC 05199
2005 ☐	SYMMETRY IN DESIGN	CD	Nuclear Blast	NB 1516-2
2005 ☐	SYMMETRY IN DESIGN	CD	Fono (Russia)	FO469CD
2006 ■	PITCH BLACK PROGRESS	CD	Nuclear Blast	NB1482-2
	Slipcase. Sticker. Bonus: Carved In Stone/Deviate From The Form			
2006 ☐	PITCH BLACK PROGRESS	CD	Irond (Russia)	CD 06-1174
2006 ☐	PITCH BLACK PROGRESS	CD	NEMS (Argentina)	NEMS 382
2008 ■	HOLOGRAPHIC UNIVERSE	CD	Nuclear Blast	NB 2095-2
2008 ☐	HOLOGRAPHIC UNIVERSE	CD	Magnum Music (Taiwan)	AVA 10034
2008 ☐	HOLOGRAPHIC UNIVERSE	CD	Irond (Russia)	CD 08-1487
2008 ☐	Morphogenesis/Artificial Sun Projection	CDS	Nuclear Blast (promo)	2194-2
2009 ☐	DARK MATTER DIMENSIONS	CD	Nuclear Blast	2346-2
2009 ☐	DARK MATTER DIMENSIONS	CDd	Nuclear Blast	2346-0
	Bonus: Pariah			
2009 ☐	DARK MATTER DIMENSIONS	CD	Irond (Russia)	CD 09-1643
2009 ☐	DARK MATTER DIMENSIONS	CD	Avalon Marquee (Japan)	MICP-10858
	Bonus: The Consciousness Eaters (edit)			
2011 ☐	THE UNSEEN EMPIRE	CD	Nuclear Blast	2689-2
	Slipcase.			
2011 ☐	THE UNSEEN EMPIRE	CD	Irond (Russia)	CD 11-1775
2011 ☐	THE UNSEEN EMPIRE	CD	Avalon Marquee (Japan)	MICP-10982

2006 CD - 1482-2

2008 CD - NB 2095-2

SCARPOINT

Henrik Englund: v, Zoran Kukulj: g, Alexander Nord: g,
Chris Goldsmith: b, Erik Thyselius: d

Stockholm - Scarpoint were formed already in 2000 by Englund and Kukulj. They drafted guitarist Nord, bass player Eric Holberg and drummer Thyselius (ex-*Face Down, Construcdead, Arize, Terror 2000*). They recorded their first demo in 2003, followed by *Oblivion* later the same year. The debut, released in 2007, is an outstanding piece of brutal metal produced by Daniel Bergstrand. It featured a surprising guest appearance by singer Martin Westerstrand (*LOK, Rallypack, Lillasyster*). Unfortunately Thyselius had to go through heart surgery in 2008 and the band was put on hold. In 2009 bassist Chris Goldsmith (*Crawley, FullStrike*) replaced Eric Holmberg and the band entered the studio together with Jocke Skoog (*Clawfinger*) to record *The Mask Of Sanity*. In 2010 the band switched guitar player, from Nord to Ola Englund (*Facing Death, Feared, Subcyde*). They also recorded the digital single *Open Your Eyes* as a part of their anti-bullying project *Sweden United*. It features guest vocals from people like Jens Kidman (*Meshuggah*), Jimmie Strimmel (*Dead By April, DeathDestruction*), Anette Olzon (*Alyson Avenue*), Martin Westerstrand, Peter Tägtgren, Tom Englund (*Evergrey*), Zak Tell (*Clawfinger*) and Björn Strid (*Soilwork*). If you're into bands like *Soilwork*, check them out. Great band!

2011 CD - SUPERCD 021

2007 CD - BLIND 01 CD

2007 ■	THE SILENCE WE DESERVE	CD	Blind Prophecy Records	BLIND 01 CD
2011 ■	THE MASK OF SANITY	CD	Supernova Records	SUPERCD 021

SCATCATS

Arne Larsson: v/g, Stefan Jonsson: g, Bosse Falk: b. Sampo Laakkonen: d

Mariestad - Scatcats play quite good melodic hard rock, like a heavier version of early *Magnum Bonum* or *Snowstorm*.

1983 ■	Fru Fortuna/Bara för att få	7"	Hertig Johans Källare	HJK 1001

1983 7" - HJK 1001

SCENTERIA

Stefan Persson: v/g, Carl Bergendahl: g, Niklas Pettersson: g,
Johan Andreasson: b, Daniel Landin: d

Halmstad - Formed in 2002 and recorded their first demo, *Signs Of Hypnotica*, the same year, followed by *Descent From Darkness* later the same year. In 2003 the third demo *Path Of Silence* was recorded. In 2004 the band was picked up by New Aeon Media and the first and only album was released. Guitarist Niklas Pettersson left the band in 2007.

2004 ■	THE ART OF AGGRESSION	CD	New Aeon Media	NAM 010

2004 CD - NAM 010

SCHEITAN

Lotta Högberg: v, Pierre Törnkvist: v/g, Göran Norman: k, Oskar Karlsson: d

Umeå - Scheitan were formed in 1996 and immediately got picked up by Invasion Records. The first album was primitive black metal. Lotta and Göran (also in *Everdawn*) were added to the line-up on the second release which is more gothy, progressive death metal. On *Nemesis* they described their style as "Gothic death 'n roll". Karlsson is now in *Helltrain* and has previously played with *Gates Of Ishtar, Sarcasm, The Duskfall, Decortication, The Everdawn* and *Defleshed*. Törnkvist is also in *Helltrain* and had previously been part of *Decortication, The Everdawn, The Moaning* and *Gilgamosh*.

1996 ■	TRAVELLING IN ANCIENT TIMES	CD	Invasion Records	IR024 CD
1998 □	BESERK 2000	CD	Invasion Records	IR033 CD
	The first edition released in limited edition with an exclusive leather booklet.			
1999 □	NEMESIS	CD	Century Media	77261 2

1996 CD - IR024 CD

SCHIZOPHRENIC CIRCUS

Pelle Saether: v, Sven Jensen: g, Magnus Engdahl: b, Jamil Batal: d

Västerås - In 1986 Pelle recorded a great demo with *Macbeth*, a band that also featured guitarist Lasse Johansson (*Candlemass, Zoic, CreoZoth*). In 1987 he recorded a single with *Unchained* and later on he was also part of *Glory* (ex-*Glory North*). Engdahl previously recorded a MCD with the band *Dynamite Wasteland*, a band that also featured Batal on a single. The band's CD is a great piece of ballsy hard rock with slight feeling of *T Rex* and *Freak Of Nature*. They also have the non-CD *Kiss*-cover *Deuce* on the '95 compilation-CD from Backstage Magazine. Sven Jensen plays on the album *RawChild* by Danes *=Y=* and has previously recorded a 7" with Norwegian band *Astral Sky*. Pelle has his project *Zello* on the side, where Jamil was also found. Pelle owns studio Underground and has produced numerous band. Jamil was later in *Malas Intenciones* and Pelle recorded two albums with *Zeelion* and is now fronting *Grand Design*.

1994 ■	SCHIZOPHRENIC CIRCUS	CD	Megarock	MRRCD 018

1994 CD - MRRCD 018

SCORCHED
Daniel Arvidsson: v/g/b/d

Säffle - *Draconian* guitarist Daniel recorded his first solo demo under the name *Scorched* in 2003, entitled *Forsaken*. In 2004 *Hellspawn* followed and in 2005 he released his first album. Daniel has previously played with **Entity Of Fire** and **Nibdem**, where he handled drums and vocals. Norwegian-style black metal, quite decently-produced as well.

2005	■ FOREVER DYING SUN	CD	Regimental Records	REG 027	
2008	☐ THE 5TH SEASON	CD	Heretic Sounds	HS-2	

2005 CD - REG 027

SCRATCH
Niklas "Nic O'Noon" Olausson: v/g, Anders "Andy T" Folbert: g, Peter "Pete Meat" Vilhelmsson: g, Johan "John Mell" Melin: b, Mats "M.J. Masen" Johansson: d

Karlskrona - This is one of the most sought after items of the eighties, initially because many thought it was a NWoBHM single from the UK. *Before The Rain* is a ballad, while *Metalbreaker* is a classic metal track. Good quality. They later changed their name to **Kazandra**, but never released anything. The band split in 1989. Niklas and Peter also appeared on the *To Africa With Love* project and single.

1985	■ Before The Rain/Metalbreaker	7"	private	SCR 8503	$$$
	1500 copies.				

1985 7" - SCR 8503

SCRATCH
Patrik Schulz: v, Stefan Rosqvist: g/k, Joakim Blomdahl: b, Björn Wijk: d

Helsingborg - The first single was mainstream AOR with quite awful vocals. *F.T.P* (which stands for Fuck That Pussy), however showed an upgraded band in the sleaze rock vein, similar to **Skid Row**. On the first single, Ulf "Chris Laney" Larsson plays keyboards (later **Unameus, 17, Godsache, Zan Clan, Randy Piper's Animal**, now solo) and Jonas Andersson plays bass (later in **Unameus, 17, Shooting Gallery**). Stefan Rosqvist has also recorded a solo CD and he is now in **Cloudscape** and **FullForce**.

1988	☐ I Can Feel My Love For You/No More	7"	Midtown	HSP 8805-002
1990	■ F.T.P (Fuck That Pussy)/Waiting	7"	Hot Spot	103 9004

1990 7" - 103 9004

SCREAMER
Christoffer Svensson: v/b, Anton Fingal: g, Dejan Rosic: g, Henrik Petersson: d

Ljungby - Another highly interesting band in the New Wave of Swedish Heavy Metal with colleagues like **Enforcer, Steelwing** and **Slingblade**. The band was formed in 2009 by Svensson, Fingal, Petersson and guitarist Martin Hallberg. Petersson had just left the band **Erottica** (now **By My Fear**). Two months after forming they recorded the demo *Never Going Down*. They started gigging frequently and late 2010 entered the studio to record the debut. Soon after, Martin Hallberg left the band and was replaced by Dejan. Highly authentic-sounding NWoBHM with killer vocals and a killer sound that brings you back to the tape-trading days.
Website: http://wearescreamer.com/

2011	☐ ADRENALINE DISTRACTIONS	LP	High Roller Records	HHR 206
	100 copies bone white, 350 transparent red/ black splatter vinyl and 550 x black vinyl.			
2011	☐ ADRENALINE DISTRACTIONS	CD	High Roller Records	HHR 206 CD
2013	☐ PHOENIX	LPg	High Roller Records	HRR 285
	100 clear, 300 orange and 350 black vinyl. Numbered.			
2013	■ PHOENIX	CD	High Roller Records	HRR 285 CD

2013 CD - HRR 285 CD

SCREAMIN' MOTHER
Michael Westerlund: v, Michael Svanberg: g,
Eric Björkman (aka Likagod): g, Rickard Donatello: b

Stockholm - Formed in 1993 by Michael and Mikael. The band's first single and album were produced by Sank (**Clawfinger, Mental Hippie Blood** etc.). The style is great heavy rock and their sound is quite original. Singer Michael has a very special relaxed and melodic voice. Drums on the album were played by Jörgen Wall (**Ingo & Floyd**). Rickard and Erik, then by the last name Likagod, have also been working with poetic rocker Iodine Jupiter.

1995	☐ Screamin' Mother	MCD 3tr	Toytown Production	SMCDS 8
	Tracks: Screamin' Mother/Spitzdog/Jesus Without A Cross. Promo.			
1995	☐ SCREAMIN' MOTHER	CD	Soundfront/Roadrunner	RR 89092
1996	■ Jesus With A Cross	MCD 4tr	Soundfront/Roadrunner	RR 2321.3
	Contains four different mixes of the same song.			

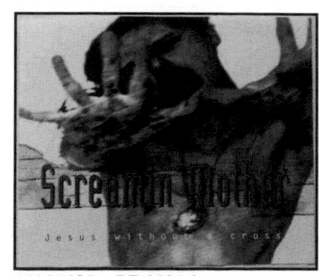

1996 MCD - RR 2321.3

SCREAMS OVER NORTHLAND

Tomas Andersson: v/g/d

Linköping - Atmospheric symph/goth-oriented death metal with a touch of *My Dying Bride*. Screeching spoken vocals. Keyboards were played by Phanatos.

1999 ■ Screams Over Northland ....7" Ghoul 001
    Tracks: Intro/Towards Obargo/The Release/Outro. Red vinyl

1999 7" - 001

SCREWBALL.STHLM

Simon Olsson: v, Fredrik Rhodin: g, Martin Ghaoui: g, Joakim Rhodin: b, Mats Ström: d

Vällingby (Stockholm) - Formed in 1998 by Simon Olsson and Fredrik Rhodin under the name *Screwball*, but when a hip-hop band with a major label backing them took the name in 2000, the Swedes added .sthlm (Stockholm). The band was completed by bass player Joakim Rhodin (a cousin of Fredrik), drummer Mats Ström and when it was time to record they drafted *Ruction* guitarist Martin Ghaoui. In 2002 they took a long break, but the band is now active again and a new album is planned for 2013. Great-sounding, hardcore-oriented metal with a technical touch and rap-oriented vocals, like *Clawfinger* on steroids with a touch of *Rage Against The Machine*.

2000 ■ Screwball.sthlm..MCD 5tr private .... - -
    Tracks: Nothing To Fear/Leave Me Alone/Top Of The World/Bring It/I'm Going Blind.

2000 MCD - - -

SCUDIERO

Johan Persson: v, Fredrik Folkare: g, Mikael Rosengren: k,
Jori Helminen: b, Michael Dahlquist: d

Stockholm - High quality progressive hard rock with lots of melodies. Killer vocals and killer musicians. The band's first demo CD-R *Unknown Utopia* (1996) featured only Jori, Michael and guitarist Magnus Mörth with Jori handling the vocals, too. The second, entitled *Time Will Tell* (1997) saw the above line-up but with Daniel Palmquist (later in *The Murder Of My Sweet*) on guitars. Late 1999 Hans Andersson decided to quit and the vocal duties were taken over by ex-*Mind's Eye* singer Johan Persson. Hans was later found in *Fatal Smile*, the AOR-project *Token*, where Mikael Rosengren is also found, and is now fronting *MindSplit*. In 2001 Patrik Johansson (*Yngwie Malmsteen, Stormwind*) replaced drummer Michael Dahlquist. A second 13 track album was recorded and ready and is just waiting for a deal... and it's killer! It was however never released. Rosengren is now in *Constancia* and *Skarr*. Folkare is also in death metal band *Unleashed* and in melodic metal band *Hellinor*.

1999 ■ WALKING THROUGH MIRRORS ....CD Z Records ZR1997011
1999 □ WALKING THROUGH MIRRORS ....CD Avalon Marquee (Japan)................. MICY-1132
    Bonus: Rising Spirit Of Love

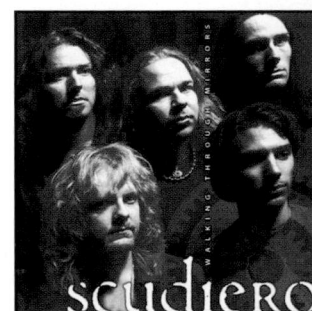
1999 CD - ZR1997011

SCUMKILL

Miika Rudin: v, Christoffer Sandgren: g, Kristoffer Pettersson: g,
Linda Rudin: b, David Lundsten: d

Holmsund/Burträsk (Umeå) - Formed in 2005 as *Dörty Dogs*, but changed it to *Scumkill* in 2008. Sebastian Andersson played bass up until it was time to do the album and Miika's sister took over the four-string. Influenced by bands like *Down* and *Pantera* they call their music "dirtcore". Great sounding thrashy metal in the vein of *Pantera*, but with a bit cleaner vocals, still aggressive though. Great powerful guitar riffing. A great band! Miika is also in *Hellbound*, Kristoffer in *Clark Lane*, while Linda records solo material. In 2011 the band announced Ronnie Björnström (*Hate Ammo*) as their new guitarist. A new album is being recorded for release 2012.

2010 □ DIRTCORE ....CD private .... RPROCD 01
2011 ■ WHAT LURKS BENEATH...CD private .... RPROCD 02

2011 CD - RPROCD 02

SEANCE

Johan Larsson: v, Tony "Toxine" Kampner: g, Rickard "Corpse" Rimfält: b,
Micke "Mique Flesh" Pettersson: d

Linköping - Formed out of the two Linköping-bands *Total Death* and *Orchriste* in 1986. The name was taken from an old *Orchriste* song. *Orchriste* only recorded a demo entitled *Necronomicon* in 1989 and *Total Death*'s track *Has Time Come* appears on the local compilation *Musik För Miljön* (Music For The Environment). *Seance* first demo *Levitised Spirit* made twelve record companies show interest in the band. The band plays aggressive death metal with ultra-brutal vocals, at times similar to *Slayer*. Guitarist Tony Kampner and Micke have a past in the cult band *Satanic Slaughter*. A cover of *Slayer*'s *Post Mortem* is featured on the tribute CD *Slatanic Slaughter* (1996). In 1997 guitarist Patrik Jensen (*The Haunted, Witchery, Brujeria, Orchriste*) and bassist Christian "Bino" Karlsson moved to Göteborg. The remaining members drafted bassist Richard "Rille/Corpse" Rimfält (*Morgue, Satanic Slaughter, Witchery*) and was about to record a new album for Necropolis when Micke left and the band folded in 1998. Ten years

1992 CD - BMCD 17

1993 CD - BMCD 44

later the band picked up where they left off, now featuring Pettersson (also in *Freevil*), Kampner, Larsson and Rimfält. Same style, same sound, same energy, i.e. great high-class technical old-school death metal without gimmicks.

1992 ☐	FOREVER LAID TO REST	LP	Black Mark	BMLP 17
1992 ■	FOREVER LAID TO REST	CD	Black Mark	BMCD 17
1993 ■	SALTRUBBED EYES	CD	Black Mark	BMCD 44
2009 ■	AWAKENING OF THE GODS	CD	Pulverised	ASH 054 CD

2009 CD - ASH 054 CD

SEARING I

Andreas Öman: v, Niklas Kupper: g, Anders Björk: g,
Mattias Hansson: b, Andreas Engman: d

Uppsala - *Searing I* were formed in Uppsala in 1999. The first demo, *Vol. 1* was recorded in 2002, followed by *Vol.2* and *A Treacherous Ride* in 2003. However, it was the 2004 demo *Tons Of Hate* that opened the door to Black Lotus Records. The debut album, *Bloodshred*, was recorded and mixed by Teddy Möller (*F.K.Ü, Loch Vostok* etc.) and Kupper, who is also found in *Loch Vostok*. The second album, *Post Traumatic Death Disorder*, was recorded already in 2007, but only released through CDBaby and iTunes in 2010 as a digital release. Gustaf Jorde (*Defleshed*) guests. The band is now inactive.
Website: www.searingi.com/

| 2005 ■ | BLOODSHRED | CD | Black Lotus | BLRCD 089 |

2005 CD - BLRCD 089

SECOND HEAT

Thomas Bursell: v, Patrik Svärd: g, Niclas Olsson: k,
Thomas Löyskä: b, Roger Landin: d

Helsingborg - It all started already back in 1994 by Thomas and Niclas, but when Niclas got busy with *Alyson Avenue* things fizzled out. However, early 2004 they picked up the thread once again. The basic concept was to play melodic hard rock in the vein of *Giant*, *Firehouse* and *Fair Warning*. As the songwriting began, a slightly different touch was added, but they are still within the high-class heavy AOR boundaries. The duo picked members from their vicinity: Svärd and Landin were in *Alyson Avenue* and *Cloudscape* and Löyskä was also in *Alyson Avenue*, so basically *Alyson Avenue* with a male singer and a heavier edge. The album was produced by Mats Edström (*Shiva*).

| 2004 ■ | SECOND HEAT | CD | AOR Heaven | 00010 |

2004 CD - 00010

SECTION EIGHT

Peter Kronberg: v, Johan Bäckman: g, Jocke Östlund: g,
Robert Smedberg: k, Fredrik Pettersson: b, Patrik Lindqvist: d

Sala - Formed in 1983, split 1988. Despite the somewhat worn-out song titles, this is a really good melodic AOR/hard rock band. Well-played, well-arranged and with strong vocals. Especially the second 7" is highly recommended. All members except Robert continued as a cover band under the name *Nothing Right Now*. Kronberg has recorded a solo CD and was part of *Asperity*. Not to be confused with hardcore band *Section 8*.

| 1985 ☐ | Mr Neighbour/Breakin' Away | 7" | SGV | SGV 8501 |
| 1988 ■ | Bad Girl/Losing You | 7" | Active Music | HEJ S 026 |

1988 7" - HEJ S 026

SECTU

Stefan Lundgren: v/g, Anders Exo Ericson Kragh: g,
Johan Niemann: b, Calle Bäckström: d

Stockholm - The band was formed by Stefan (*Necromicon, Sobre Nocturne, Mörk Gryning*) back in 2005 under the name *Cimmerian Dome*. Early 2006 Peter Nagy-Eklöf (*Mörk Gryning, Eternal Oath*) joined as drummer, but soon switched to playing bass and sharing the vocal duties with Stefan. Later, drummer Calle Bäckström (*C.B Murdoc, Mörk Gryning*) was drafted. The band went through some line-up changes, which saw Nagy out of the band and Angel Dominguez added on guitar. The trio of Lundgren, Dominguez and Bäckström recorded the *Inudate* album. Dominguez had to move back to Spain and was replaced by Anders Exo Ericson (*Argento, Beyond Twilight, Sobre Nocturn*). In the autumn of 2011 Kristofer Elemyr (aka Nilsson) (*Undivine, Machine, Mortellez, Kryptillusion, Rebel Collective*) was added on bass. The album was recorded at Necromorbus Studio. *Sectu* plays excellent technical and quite challenging death metal with cool twists and turns. In 2008 Kristofer was replaced by Johan Niemann (*Therion, Evergrey, Mind's Eye* etc).
Website: www.sectu.se

2011 CD - VSP 018

| 2011 ■ | INUNDATE | CD | Vici Solum | VSP 018 |
| 2012 ■ | GERRA | CD | Vici Solum | VSP 031 |

2012 CD - VSP 031

SEETHINGS

Lawrence Mackrory: v, Dennis Olsson: g, Peter Waites: g,
Lars Söderberg: b, Simon Wettervik: d

Uppsala - Mackrory (***Andromda, F.K.Ü, Darkane, Enemy Is Us, Scarve, Sportlov, Scavenger***) and Wettervik started playing together already back in 1994 and the year after they formed the band ***Forcefeed***, influenced by bands like ***Korn*** and ***Deftones***. They released one EP, but as time went they developed their sound and in 2001 they decided to change their name to ***Seethings***. They started shopping for a deal and landed two, Italian Scarlet Records and Swizz Division. The album, produced by Daniel Bergstrand at Dug Out Studios, was released in 2004. Seethings plays really great, heavy modern nu-metal in the vein of ***Seether, Deftones, Sevendust*** etc. Mackrory sounds very different in this band, now singing clean and very melodic.

2001	■	PARALLELS	CD	Scarlet Records	SC 072-2	
2001	□	Seethings/Unfold (split)	MCD 4tr	Division Records	DR 015	
		Split with Unfold. Tracks: Shed The Cloud/Tonight				
2004	□	PARALLELS	CD	Division Records	DR 022	

2001 CD - SC 072-2

SEKTOR SKANDAL

Johan Andersson, Dennis Berntsson, Kenneth Jonsson

Uppsala - The name sounds like a typical Swedish punk band (sector scandal), but don't let it fool you. The A-side is up-tempo melodic hard rock with a slightly new-wavish touch, while the B-side is a mid-tempo melodic hard rocker. Seems like they didn't know which leg to stand on. Not bad actually. Mats Elf played keyboards on the record.

1985	■	Don't Go To Church/Landscape	7"	Platina	PL 5	$	

1985 7" - PL 5

SELF DECEPTION

Andreas Olsson: v/g, Gabriel Rauhofer: g, Patrik Hallgren: b, Erik Eklund: d

Stockholm - ***Self Deception*** were formed in 2005, and play modern melodic emo-hardcore in the vein of ***Takida, Hoobastank, Breaking Benjamin*** etc. Quite mainstream and without any unique qualities. After the first album bassist Niklas Wester was replaced by Patrik Hallgren.
Website: www.selfdeception.se

2007	□	Relationship Redrum/Postcard (Marked Better Place)	CDS	Roosters Records	RPCDS 01	
2008	■	RESTITUTION	CD	Roosters Records	RPCDS 02	
2011	□	OVER THE THRESHOLD	CD	Ayam Music Group	AMGCD11-001	

2008 CD - RPCDS 02

SEMLAH

Johan "Joleni" Nilsson: v, Thomas Johnson: g,
Tommy "Wilbur" Eriksson: b, Johannes Berg: d

Stockholm - Stockholm based doomsters ***Semlah*** were formed in 2001 by former ***Count Raven*** bassist Eriksson and ***Impiety/Black Web*** guitarist Johnson. After posting ads on the web they found drummer Berg (ex-***Castillion***) and singer Joleni (ex-***Stronghold***). The name actually comes from, either the traditional Swedish pastry (spelled without "h") or an ancient siege ladder, you decide. The first demo, *Ruin*, was recorded in the first year and the second outing *Suffering In Silence* came three years after. Other projects, car accidents and various other projects came in-between and it took until 2009 for the band to finally release their next album. ***Semlah*** play really good riff-oriented doom in the vein of ***Candlemass***-meet-***Count Raven***. Great vocals from Joleni as well.
Website: www.semlah.com

2009 CD - CYC 033-2

2004	□	SUFFER IN SILENCE	CD	Cyclone Empire	SEM 002	
2009	■	SEMLAH	CD	Cyclone Empire	CYC 033-2	
2010	□	SEMLAH	CD	Fono (Russia)	FO 807 CD	
2010	■	Imperial Anthems (split)	7"	Cyclone Empire	ANTHEM 004	
		Split with Isole. Track: Black Flame (Renaissance cover). 500 hand-numbered copies in red/black splatter vinyl.					

2010 7" - ANTHEM 004

SENCELLED

Erik Holmberg: v/g, Fredrik Askenström: g, Mattias Ohlsén: b, Christoffer Ahl: d

Stockholm - ***Sencelled*** play outstanding melodic AOR in the same vein as ***H.E.A.T*** mixed with ***Work Of Art***, produced by Ricky B Delin (***Houston, Tommy Denander***). In 2012 the band changed their name to ***The Spin***.
Website: www.thespin.se

2012	■	SENCELLED	CDd	Rocket Songs	ROCKET 005	

2012 CDd - ROCKET 005

SEPTEKH

Nils Meseke: v, David Wikström: g, Patrik Ström: b, Staffan Persson: d

Järna/Stockholm - *Septekh* released their first demo in 2009. The band plays good-quality thrash metal with some death metal injections and quite tongue-in-cheek lyrics.
Website: www.septekh.com

2012	■	The Seth Avalanche ....MCD 6tr	Abyss Records.........................	ABYSS 034 CD
		Tracks: Fuckslut From Hell/Shoot Them All/Blunt Force To The Hand/Not Quite What I Had In Mind/Eating The Maneater/The Seth Avalanche		
2013	☐	Apolonian Eyes ....MCD 4tr	Abyss Records.........................	ABYSS 050 CD
		Tracks: Apollonian Eyes/Burn It To The Ground/Cursing The Skies/Vlad Tepes		

2012 MCD - ABYSS 034 CD

SEPTIC GRAVE

Daniel Engman: v, Fredrik Hjärtström: g, Robert Lindmark: b, Jörgen Björnström: d

Malmberget - Formed in 1989. Recorded their first demo *Beyond The...* in 1994. After the demo drummer Magnus Olsson was out and Björnström switched from guitar to drums. The tracks *Beyond The...* and *Fallen Angel* were featured on the *Dreams And Illusions* (94 Local Hero) compilation. Engman was later in *Soulquake System*, Lindmark in *Prophanity* and Björnström in *The Embraced*. Brutal, but still somewhat melodic death metal quite reminiscent of *Defleshed*, although *Septic Grave* is a bit slower.

1995	■	Caput Mortuum ....MCD 4tr	Midnight Sun..........................	MSR 3
		Tracks: Spiritual Empire/Blood Red Yashmak/Lust To Dust/Monarch Of Curse		

1995 MCD - MSR 3

SEREMEDY

Seike: v, Kevin Yohio Rehn Eires: g, Ray: g, Jenziih: b, Linder: d

Sundsvall - Formed late 2008. A band going for the visual appearance, mixing really good melodic metal and pop with an emo-touch. Their style and looks have struck well with the Japanese audience who love the band. Yohio is the son of *Moahni Moahna/Angtoria/Corroded* guitarist Tommy Rehn. Yohio also released a solo EP in 2012, and entered the Swedish rounds of the Eurovision Song Contest, where he came in second by a hair. In 2011 the band also released the digital album *Bulletproof Roulette*. The band split early 2013 due to musical differences.

2011	☐	Seasons Will Change...MCD 4tr	Universal.................................	0602527-68455
		Tracks: Bulletproof Roulette/Ideal Enemy/3/Distant Fucker		
2012	☐	WELCOME TO OUR MADNESS...CD	Universal (Japan)...........................	UICN-1012
2012	■	WELCOME TO OUR MADNESS...CD	Universal.................................	0602537-11922

2012 CD - 0602537-11922

SERENADE FOR JUNE

Henrik Hagedorn: v/b, Andreas Olavi: g, Patrik Douglas: d

Varberg - Great modern melodic metal, like a heavier version of *Hoobastank*-meet-*My Chemical Romance*. Andreas Olavi is ex-*Inhale, Dodge, White Silver*, now in *Lavett*. After the album, he was replaced by Jonas Eckerström.

2007	☐	THE EMERGENCY PONCHO ....CDp	Dart Records..........................	0843041052689

SERGEANT

Lars Hägglund: v/g, Peter Östman: g, Nils Berggren: b, Bo Åström: d

Örnsköldsvik - Straightforward melodic metal of high quality. Well worth checking out. Bo, Lars and Peter later formed boogie rockers *Boogietryck* and recorded one album.

1982	■	Doubt/Connection ....7"	Marc Production...........................	Marc.S. 203

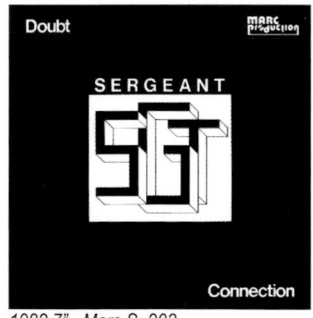

1982 7" - Marc.S. 203

SERGEJ THE FREAK

Niklas Falk: v, Janne Löwstrand: g, Janneck Larsson: b, Tobias "Tobbe" Quick: d

Göteborg - Formed in 1999 by schoolmates Niklas and Tobbe. Recorded their first demo in 2000, the second one, *Crimson Atmosphere*, came later the same year and a third demo was unleashed in 2001, entitled *A Land Called Jojotiro*. Really cool, solid, retro stoner rockers with great fuzzed-out fat and heavy riffing and cool grooves with really good vocals, too.

2002	☐	SERGEJ THE FREAK MEETS THE BURNING ENGINES (split) ....CD	Daredevil...............................	DD 017
		Split with Burning Engines. Tracks: Shedevil Rider/Lady Violent And The Greasing Agent/ The Day The World Forgot Me/A Land Called Jojotiro/Turboville/U Turn		
2005	■	SERGEJ THE FREAK MEETS DEVILLE (split)..CD	Daredevil...............................	DD 032
		Split with Deville. Tracks: The Dark Lodge/Nothing Good/Goliath's Wrath/Shocker/Seth Kill Joy/Dirt Dust Champagne/Follow Shallow/Time Is Mine		

2005 CD - DD 032

SERPENT

Piotr Wawrzeniuk: v/b, Ulf Samuelsson: g, Per Karlsson: d

Stockholm - An excellent band in the doom-oriented vein similar to **Trouble**, **The Obsessed** and **Spirit Caravan**. Piotr's vocals are quite reminiscent of Wino (**The Obsessed**) in the two latter. The band started out more as a side-project of Piotr's, at the time in **Therion**. The first album also featured bassist Lars Rosenberg (**Entombed**) and guitarist Johan Lundell (**The Robots**). Per and Ulf are ex-**Suffer**. Per is also found in **Nominon** and ran HH Promotion (formerly Heathendoom). Johan Lundell is actually cousin of famous Swedish rock-poet Ulf Lundell. Piotr and Lars were also former members of **The Robots**. A new album was due to be released in 2002 on Freedom Records, but unfortunately it never happened. Not to be confuse with the death metal band.

1996 ■ IN THE GARDEN OF SERPENT ....CD Radiation..CAD006
1997 ☐ AUTUMN RIDE ....CD Heathendoom .... HDMCD 005

1996 CD - CAD006

SERPENT OBSCENE

**Erik "Tormentor" Sahlström: v, Johan Thörngren: g, Nicklas Eriksson: g,
Jonny Putrid: b, Christofer "Chriss Piss" Barkensjö: d**

Strängnäs/Rönninge - The band was formed in 1997 and recorded their first demo *Behold The Beginning* the same year. The second one, entitled *Massacre,* was recorded in 1999. The debut was recorded at Berno Studio in Malmö. Drummer Jonas Eriksson left in 2001 and was replaced by drummer Christofer "Chriss Piss" Barkensjö (**Blackshine, Kaamos, Grave, Repugnant, Face Down**). Erik is also found in **Maze Of Torment**, **The Marble Icon** and **General Surgery**, Nicklas in **A Mind Confused** and **Kaamos**. In 2004 bassist Rob Rocker was replaced by Jonny Putrid (**Revokation**). *Chaos Reign Supreme* was also produced by Berno Paulsson (**Spiritual Beggars, Bai Bang** etc). July 19, 2006 Nicklas parted way with the band and the band subsequently folded. **Serpent Obscene** play quite good thrash-oriented death metal. Fast and furious with a primitive touch, but still quite technical. A bit like **Bathory**-meet-**Slayer**-meet-**The Crown**, and a bit similar to **Defleshed** at times.
Website: www.serpentobscene.com/

2000 CD - NR 057

2003 CD - BLOD 004 CD

2006 LPg - BLOD 032 LP

2000 ■ SERPENT OBSCENE...CD Necropolis..NR 057
2000 ☐ SERPENT OBSCENE...LP Necropolis..NR 057
2003 ■ DEVASTATION ....CD Black Lodge ....BLOD 004 CD
2006 ☐ CHAOS REIGN SUPREME ....CD Black Lodge ....BLOD 032 CD
2006 ■ CHAOS REIGN SUPREME .... LPg Black Lodge ....BLOD 032 LP
　　　　500 copies.
2006 ☐ CHAOS REIGN SUPREME .... LPg War Anthem Records.................. WAR 002 LP

SESSION, THE

Peter Johansson: v/g, Tomas Adolfsson: k, Per-Erik "Lillen" Tageson: d

Lidköping - The band's music is pretty hard to box in, but you will find elements of the seventies **Deep Purple**-type style, as well as more contemporary westcoast-oriented rock with some psych-edelic touches. A bit similar to Finnish band **Five Fifteen**. Bass was played by Gustav Jonsson.

2000 ■ Amsterdam Avenue...MCD 4tr Hurricane ....HCD 001
　　　　Tracks: Do You Want Me/Falling In Love/Out In The Cold/The End

2000 MCD - HCD 001

SETBACK

**Johan Gummesson: v, Niclas Sjöquist: g,
Tomas Strömberg: g, Ulf Olsson: b, Markus Sjöquist: d**

Karlshamn - Straightforward hardcore/metal with tons of energy and power. The band recorded the master for a new record in 2000, produced by Berno Paulsson (**The Quill, Spiritual Beggars** etc), which is as yet unreleased. The real setback (excuse the pun) came when they were conned by their label whereby after having received no money, royalties, licence-fees, etc. and they were expected to BUY their own records. **Setback** can also be found on the following compilations: *Distortion To Hell And Back* (95 Distortion), *Things To Do Today* (97 Fetvadd) and *Stand As One* (99 We Bite) *The Punishment Is Here* (00 Bhead/New Noise) with two non-album tracks *Living Hell* and *Don't Wait*. Niclas later recorded a demo with the band **Zeven** (featuring Paul Zanichelli from **Parasite**) and is also in punksters **Dampungarna**, while his brother Markus has released CDs under the name **Fjelltrone**.

Setback sitdown

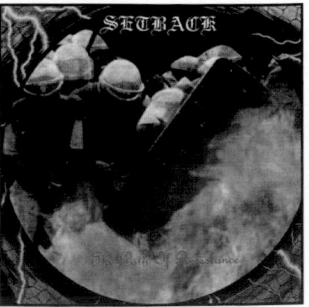

1999 CD - BURN 1999

1999 ■ THE PATH OF RESISTANCE ....CD Burn ....BURN 1999

SETHERIAL

Magnus "Infaustus" Ödling: v, Per "Kraath" Hellqkvist: g/b, Daniel Nilsson-Sahlin: g, Håkan "Alastor Mysteriis" Sjödin: d

Has Hell finally frozen over?

Sundsvall - The band was formed in 1993/94 by Håkan "Alastor Mysteriis" Sjödin (**Blackwinds, In Battle**) and bass player Per-Erik "Devothan" Karlsson. Recorded their first demo *A Hail To The Faceless Angels* in 1994. Singer Tobias "Kheeroth" Fjällström (**Midvinter**) was sacked after the 7". On the debut album the line-up consisted of Sjödin, Karlsson, bassist Daniel "Thorn" Edström (**Blot Mine**), Hellqvist (on vocals) and drummer Anders "Zathaniel" Löfgren (**Blot Mine, Blackwinds, Sorhin, Midvinter**). After the debut the band split, but Håkan and Per continued on their own. On the second release guitarist Göran "Chorozon" Johansson (**Torchbearer, Chaosdaemon**) and drummer Otto "Moloch" Wiklund (**In Battle**) completed the line-up. In 1997 Håkan and Per also formed the band **Helvete** with the members from **Imperial**, but the band was put on hold the year after. They later evolved into **Diabolical**. On *Hell Eternal* Håkan had taken the role of drummer, Per left the vocal duties to new singer Kristoffer "Wrath/ Wrathyr" Olivius (**Bewitched, Naglfar**) and Paul "Themgoroth" Mäkitalo (**Dark Funeral**) guests on vocals. Bassist Björn "Sasrof" Holmberg is also found in **Bloodline**, **Diabolicum** and **Hyena**. *From The Ancient Ruins* was a compilation of demos and unreleased studio sessions. On *Endtime Divine* the line-up had changed, now featuring singer Olivus, guitarists Johansson and Hellqvist, bassist Löfgren and drummer Sjödin. The album also featured backing vocals from Jens Ryden and Erik Bergkvist. August 13, 2006 former drummer Otto Wiklund sadly died of heart failure. The band's next album, *Death Triumphant* saw the bass now being taken over by Daniel "Funestus Inferis" Lindgren (**Apostasy, Divine Souls**). *Ekpyrosis* saw a new incarnation of the band featuring singer Magnus "Infaustus" Ödling, guitarist Daniel Nilsson-Sahlin, guitarist/bassist Hellqvist and drummer Sjödin. The track *Warfare* on the latest 7" is a cover of **Zyklon B**. **Setherial** play intense black metal in the same league as **Marduk** and **Emperor**.
Website: www.setherial.com/

1995 7" - OCCULTA 001

1995 ■	For Dem Mitt Blod/The Blood In Me	7"	Arte De Occulta	OCCULTA 001
	1000 hand-numbered copies.			
1996 □	NORD	CD	Napalm Records	NPR 017
1998 □	LORDS OF THE NIGHTREALM	CD	Napalm Records	NPR 039
1999 □	HELL ETERNAL	CD/d	Napalm Records	NPR 064
1999 □	HELL ETERNAL	CD	Napalm Records (USA)	NPRA 064
2001 □	HELL ETERNAL	LP	Perverted Taste	PT 037
	100 multi colour + 400 black vinyl.			
2003 □	FROM THE ANCIENT RUINS	CD	Napalm Records	NPR 119
2003 □	FROM THE ANCIENT RUINS	LP	Displeased Records	D-00119
2003 □	ENDTIME DIVINE	CD	Regain Records	RR 0304-020
2003 □	ENDTIME DIVINE	CD	Regain Records America (USA)	RNA 1034
2003 □	ENDTIME DIVINE	LP	Regain Records	RRLP 0304-020
2003 □	ENDTIME DIVINE	LP PD	Regain Records	RRPLP 00003
2003 □	NORD	LP	Crypta	LCF II
	300 copies.			
2005 □	HELL ETERNAL	CD	Hellion Records (Brazil)	HEL 215
	Bonus: In The Still Of A Northern Fullmoon/Mörkrets tid/Över det blodtäckta nord			
2006 ■	DEATH TRIUMPHANT	CD	Regain Records	RR 086
2006 □	DEATH TRIUMPHANT	CDd	Regain Records	RR 086
	Bonus: För dem mitt blod. 3500 copies.			
2006 □	DEATH TRIUMPHANT	LP	Regain Records	RLP 086
	Bonus: För dem mitt blod			
2006 □	DEATH TRIUMPHANT	CD	Candlelight Records (USA)	CDL310CD
2008 □	NORD/HELL ETERNAL	2CD	Napalm Records	NPR 264
2010 □	NORD	LPg	Funeral Industries	FI 003
	Different artwork. 100 white + 900 black vinyl.			
2010 □	LORDS OF THE NIGHTREALM	LPg	Funeral Industries	FI 008
	Different artwork. 100 marble vinyl + 900 black vinyl.			
2010 □	EKPYROSIS	CD	Regain Records	RR 170
	Slipcase.			
2010 □	EKPYROSIS	CD	Regain Records (USA)	REG-CD-9037
2011 ■	Treason (A Death That Breeds Through Aeons)/Warfare (God Is Dead)	7"g	Goathorned Productions	GOAT 012
	500 hand-numbered. First 100 in black marble vinyl. Warfare is a Zyklon-B cover.			
2013 □	Firestorms Over Haar-Megiddo/ Neural Cage of Self-infliction	7"	Funeral Industries	FI 051
	400 copies.			

2006 CD - RR 086

2011 7" - GOAT 012

SEVEN

Wiktor Söderström: v, Gabriel Österlund: g, Kennet Jansson: b, Magnus Lindh: d

Norrköping - In 1995 the band **Warhammer** recorded the MCD *Riders*. The band split and three of the members (Gabriel, Kent and Magnus) reformed as **Seven** in the spring of 1998. They were signed by Loud N' Proud and was first featured on the compilation *Born To Walk Against The Wind* (98 LNP). **Seven** have now split. Kennet and Magnus joined **Last Temptation**.

1999 ■	BREAK THE CHAINS	CD	Loud N' Proud	LNP 005

1999 CD - LNP 005

SEVEN TEARS

Zoran Djorem: v, Jonathan Carlemar: g, Kristofer von Wachenfeldt: k, Fredrik Lager: b, Michael Sjöö: d

Vetlanda - **Seven Tears** were formed by Carlemar and Lager out of the ashes of power metal band *Atlantica*, formerly *Demonslave*. During the *Atlantica* period the band picked up drummer Sjöö (*Spearfish, Fantasy Child*) and also featured singer Elin Johansson and keyboard player Martin Rydlund. One demo was recorded under this name. Rydlund was replaced by von Wachtenfeldt (*Platitude, Neon Diver, Fantasy Child*) and they went through singers Tommie Andersson and Madeleine Svensson before finding Djorem. The first demo, *The Story Unfolds*, was recorded in 2006 and lead to a deal with Frontiers Records. **Seven Tears** play excellent melodic hard rock with a slightly proggy touch, a bit like as if *Journey* and *Dream Theater* had a baby.

2007 CD - FR CD 357

| 2007 ■ | IN EVERY FROZEN TEAR | CD | Frontiers | FR CD 357 |
| 2008 ☐ | IN EVERY FROZEN TEAR | CD | Locomotive Music (USA) | 7003475 |

SEVEN WISHES

Pelle Andersson: v, Tobias "Toby" Andersson: g, Tony Westgård: b, Lennart "Leonid" Karlsson: d

Karlskoga - Formed under the name *Trazy*, under which name they recorded the track *See The Light* for the compilation *Rock Of Sweden* (89 Roxx). In 1994 they changed name to **Love Child** and released a self-titled album on Brunette Records in Japan. The style back then was more sleaze-oriented. The line-up on the first **Seven Wishes** album was the same as in **Love Child**, except for the singer Tomas Hermansson who had been replaced by Pelle Andersson. On the second album, drummer Linda Gustafsson replaced Jens Persson. She recorded an album with **The Tuesdays** in 1998 and *Angel* before this. On *Utopia* they do a cover of **Dokken**'s *Unchain The Night* which kinda explains the style of the band. **Seven Wishes** play great-souding, classic eighties melodic hard rock in the vein of **XYZ**, **Dokken** etc. One track on the latest album was co-written by Pontus Norgren. Not satisfied with their former label, they decided to move on. In 2002 the band went through some line-up changes, seeing guitarist Anthony Cedergren replaced by Tobias Andersson and drummer Linda Gustafsson by Lennart "Leonid" Karlsson. Andersson later formed the band **Shadowland**.

1999 CD - ZR 1997018

2001 CD - ZR 1997040

1999 ■	SEVEN WISHES	CD	Z Records	ZR 1997018
1999 ☐	SEVEN WISHES	CD	Bippon Crown (Japan)	CRCL 4513
	Bonus: Prodigal Son			
2001 ■	UTOPIA	CD	Z Records	ZR 1997040
	Bonus: Prodigal Son			
2001 ☐	UTOPIA	CD	Nippon Crown (Japan)	CRCL 4553
	Bonus: Free Your Mind			
2005 ■	DESTINATION: ALIVE	CD	MTM	0681-122

2005 CD - 0681-122

SEVENTH ONE

Rino Fredh: v, Johannes Losbäck: g, Christoffer Hermansson: g, Jörgen Olsson: b, Tobias R Kellgren: d

Göteborg/Uddevalla - **Seventh One**, formed in 1997, play German-style power metal in the same vein as Swedish colleagues **Steel Attack**, **Lost Horizon**, **Nostradameus** etc. In 1999 the first self-titled demo was released, followed by *Through Burning Skies* in 2000 and *The Celestial Prophecy* in 2001. Drums on the debut were played by Jonny Edvardsson. Jonny was replaced by Mats Karlsson, who was replaced by Tobias R Kellgren (**Soulreaper, Dissection, Decameron, Satanized, Swordmaster, Wolf**) before the recording of the album. The line-up on *Sacrifice* featured Fredh, Hermansson (**Decameron, Soulreaper**), Losbäck, Kellgren and bassist Jörgen Olsson (**Heed**) who took over the bass task from Hermansson, who switched to guitar.

2002 CD - MAS CD 0325

1999 ☐	Seventh One	MCD 4tr	Rock Of Bohuslän	ROBCD 008
	Tracks: Intro/Eternally/The Seventh Eye/Shadow Of Your Soul			
2002 ■	SACRIFICE	CD	Massacre	MAS CD 0325
2004 ■	WHAT SHOULD NOT BE	CD	Armageddon Music	AMG 012-0
2004 ☐	WHAT SHOULD NOT BE	CD	Spiritual Beast (Japan)	SBCD-1018
	Bonus: Scattered			

2004 CD - AMG 012-0

SEVENTH PLANET

Kaj Nordstrand: v, Knut Hassel: g, Tomas "Kiwi" Reinersson: b/k, Peter Lundgren: d

Göteborg - Formed in 1994 by former **Destiny** skinsman Peter. The band also features another **Destiny** member, Knut. Knut has previously worked with **Pagan**, while Kaj was in **Dom Andra**. **Seventh Planet** play rough-edged melodic hard rock/metal with clear traces of the eighties. Some tracks are in the vein of **Pagan**, while others show traces of heavier **Destiny**. Good Stuff! Hassel is now found in retro rockers **Gudars Skymning**.

| 1995 ■ | TIME | CD | PLAB | PLABCD 9495/1 |

1995 CD - PLABCD 9495/1

SEVENTH WONDER

Tommy Karevik: v, Johan Liefvendahl: g, Andreas Söderin: k, Andreas Blomqvist: b, Johnny Sandin: d

Stockholm - High-quality progressive metal in the vein of *Evergrey*-meet-*Angra*. The band was formed in 2000 by Blomqvist, Liefvendahl and Sandin. The first demo saw the light of day the year after. Second demo, *Temple In The Storm,* was recorded in 2003. The vocals on the first MCD were handled by hired singer Roman Karpovich (*Proxima*). The band found singer Andi Kravljaca, who was replaced by Karevik (*Vindictiv*) prior to the release of *Become*. After *The Great Escape,* Jonny Sandin left and in 2011 he was replaced by Stefan Norgren (*Lion's Share*)

2001 ☐	Seventh Wonder	MCD 4tr	private		11110308
	Tracks: Premonition/The Seventh Wonder/Blinding My Eyes/Save Me				
2005 ■	BECOME	CD	Lion Music		LMC 132
2006 ☐	WAITING IN THE WINGS	CD	Lion Music		LMC 185
2008 ☐	MERCY FALLS	CD+DVD	Lion Music		LMC 241
2008 ☐	MERCY FALLS	CD	Lion Music		LMC 247
2008 ☐	MERCY FALLS	CD	Bickee Music (Japan)		HMCX-1110
2010 ☐	THE GREAT ESCAPE	CD	Lion Music		LMC 295
2010 ☐	THE GREAT ESCAPE	CD	Bickee Music (Japan)		HMCX-1109
	Bonus: In The Blink Of An Eye 2011				

2005 CD - LMC 132

SEVENTRIBE

Jani Salonen: v, Marco Ayala: v, Marcus Brandel: g, Robert Svensson: g, Dennis Westerberg: g/v, Andreas "Re'carrdo" Sjösted: b, Krister Angelovski: d, Mikael "Mike Thaison" Åhlin: percussion

Västerås - *Seventribe* are a young band consisting of seven people, hence the name, playing metalcore. The band was formed in 1999 and has been described as a flock of beasts in a wild rage on stage. *Comandatory* drummer Andreas Melander was part of the band for some time. *Dream Me* was produced by Pelle Saether. *Seventribe* play modern melodic metalcore, or aggro-metal, similar to *Linkin Park*-meet-*Pantera*.

2007 ■	AGGRO NECESSE EST	CD	Alabama Records		ALAB 004
2011 ☐	Dream Me	MCD 3tr	Supernova Records		SUPERCD 046
	Tracks: Dream Me/WWings Of Belief/Answer				

2010 CD - LMC 295

SGT. CARNAGE

Mats Lyborg: v, Pelle Melander: g, Anders Nyander: g, Simon Frödeberg: b, Jocke Unger: d

Kristianstad - Formed in 2001. Melander and Frödeberg were ex-*Verminious*. The latter has also been in *Evildoer, Internal Hellfire* and *Logic Severed*. Nyander is ex-*Non Serviam* and Unger has been in *Supreme Majesty* and *Immersed In Blood*. The band's first gig, October 26, 2001, was recorded and released as the demo CD *Live Execution*. In 2002 they recorded the first studio demo *Agitation*, followed by *Absolut Carnage* in 2004. In May 2005 the last demo *The Bleeding Ground* was recorded. *Sgt. Carnage* play furious death metal with a touch of Bay Area thrash.

2007 ■	PRIMUS INTER PARES	CD	Cutting Edge Records		- -

2007 CD - - -

2007 CD - ALAB 004

SGT. SUNSHINE

Eduardo Fernandez-Rodrigues: v/g, Michael Mino: b, Robin Rubio: d

Malmö/Lund - *Sgt. Sunshine* are a power trio from Malmö, formed in the late nineties. The style is retro hard rock with some psychedelic touches. The original line-up featured Rodrigues (ex-*The Carpet Knights*), bass player Pär Hallgren (*The Carpet Knights, Hooffoot*) and drummer Christian "Kricke" Lundberg. After recording a couple of demos they recorded the self-titled debut. In 2004 Hallgren was replaced by Michael Mino and Lundberg by Robin Rubio.

2003 ■	SGT. SUNSHINE	CD	Abstract Sounds		ABTS008CD
2003 ☐	SGT. SUNSHINE	LP	Elektrohasch Schallplatten		117
	500 hand-numbered copies.				
2009 ☐	BLACK HOLE	CD	Elektrohasch Schallplatten		118
2013 ☐	III	CD	Elektrohasch Schallplatten		EH 160 CD

2003 CD - ABTS008CD

SHADOWGARDEN

Andreas Hindenäs: g, Johan Ericson: g

Stockholm/Säffle - *Shadowgarden* were formed as a side project of *Draconian* by Hindenäs and Ericson. The album also features *Draconian* members Lisa Johansson on vocals and Jerry Torstensson on drums. Ericson is also in *Doom:Vs. Shadowgarden* plays goth-oriented doom.

2010 ■	ASHEN	CD	Napalm		NPR 337

2010 CD - NPR 337

SHADOWLAND

Robert Forse: v, Tobias Andersson: g, Magnus Jönsson: b, Olle Rodéhn: d

Stockholm - *Shadowland* were formed around 2003 by Forse (**Heads And Tails, Mind's Eye/ Afterglow**) and Andersson (**Seven Wishes**). They drafted bass player Jönsson (**Damned Nation**) and drummer Rodéhn (**Poseidon**). The album contains a cover of **Toto**'s *Don't Chain My Heart*. **Shadowland** plays really good prog-oriented power metal, a bit reminiscent of bands like **Saint Deamon** and **Dionysus**.

2007 ■ FALLING ....CD AL!VE..10037

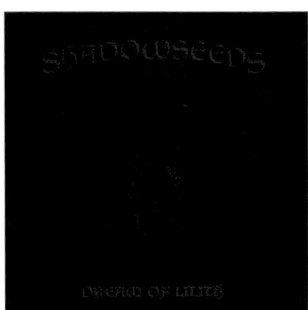

2007 CD - 10037

SHADOWS PAST

Ola Halén: v, Jonatan Berg: g, Staffan Lindroth: k, Patrik Berg: b, Olle Lindroth: d

Karlskoga - Formed in 2005. The band recorded several demos under various constellations. In 2013 the band finally released the debut album. **Shadows Past** plays classy progressive metal with a neo-classic touch, a bit like mixing **Angra** and **Symphony X**. Ola is ex-**Insania**.

2013 ■ PERFECT CHAPTER ....CD Dolittle Group............................... DOOCD 007

2013 CD - DOOCD 007

SHADOWSEEDS

Thomas "Daemon Deggial" Karlsson: v/k,
Tommy (now Tommie) "Daemon Kajghal" Eriksson: g/b/d

Stockholm - This is quite a unique band with an original style. They mix death metal, goth rock, doom and hard rock with folky touches and dark almost preaching vocals, also known as dark wave. The lyrics are quite dark as well, which might have something to do with the two members' involvement in the occult Dragon Rouge sect, where Thomas was actually the leader. Dark Age Music was run by Christofer Johnsson of **Therion**. The band was formed in 1993 by Thomas and Tommy (**Therion**). In 2002, after seven years of silence the project was resurrected, now renamed **Shadowseeds II** to mark the second coming of the band, and only featuring Thomas. He wrote a feature about Swedish seventeenth century occultist Johan Bureus that created the basis for a live performance in Stockholm, and then in Göteborg in March 2003. In 2004 a CD-R release of the live performance was released, entitled *Der Mitternacht Löve* (the midnight lion).

1995 CD - Dark Age 001

1995 ■ DREAMS OF LILITH...CD Dark Age...................................Dark Age 001

SHAGGY

Thomas Engström: v, Jan "Fidde" Rognås: g, Thomas "Tom" Ryan: k,
Janne Gustavsson: b, Kurt Kästner: d

Göteborg - Formed in 1974. Tom was from England and Kurt an Austrian. They supported **The Sweet** on their Swedish tour in 1975. The album actually sold more in Switzerland than in Sweden (!?). Kurt left after the album and was replaced by former **Man** member Julian Hutchings who only lasted a month. The band's last drummer was Magnus "Mackan" Carlsson. In 1976 Ryan left and was replaced by Peter Åhs (ex-**Rhapsody**). After this Engström and "Mackan" left to form **The Army** with guitarist Tony Borg (ex-**Vikivaki**, pre-**Alien**). The band never found a new singer and finally Rognås and Åhs were drafted by **Rhapsody**. Rognås however left the band before they recorded an album. Rognås later recorded a 7" with the poppier **Blacky Band**. Janne and Tom also recorded with AOR band **Darque** in the early 80's. **Nazareth** heard the band's album and wanted to record the song *Destination Nowhere* and Andy Scott (**The Sweet**) was interested in producing the band's next album, which as history shows never happened. This is a top-notch piece of 70's hard rock vinyl. The title track is a long progressive track with an outstanding version of Grieg's *Hall Of The Mountain King* woven into a piece by Brahms. Similar to early **Uriah Heep** and **Lucifer's Friend** with great guitar/keyboard work. This is one of the rarest hard rock records from Sweden, but well worth searching for as it is quite outstanding. Quite strange painted cover with UFO's, a naked woman, the band members standing in water and a big noose in front of it all. Engström later got involved with "dansbands" and even wrote a book about them called *Stora Dansbandsboken*. A reunion was planned, and they even started recording new material, but unfortunately it all fizzled out.

Experienced beginners.

1975 ■ LESSON FOR BEGINNERS...LP Royal..RGLP 80 $$

Unofficial releases:
1998 ☐ LESSON FOR BEGINNERS...CD Re-action ....RECD 005
        Italian bootleg of quite poor quality.

SHAKER

Joel Öhlund: v/g, Kalle Åslund: g, Martin Ericsson: b, Erik Wallin: d

Litslena (Enköping) - **Shaker** were formed in 1997 by Öhlund and Ericsson, influenced by bands like **Foo Fighters**, **Soundgarden** and **Radiohead**. **Shaker** plays modern melodic metal with a

1975 LP - RGLP 80

progressive touch. The first demo, *My Versus Me* was recorded in 2005.
Website: www.shakerband.net

2006 ■ Tight Enough..MCD 3tr   private .... - -
      Tracks: Staying Here No More/Stone Flush/Tight Enough

2006 MCD - - -

SHAKESPEARE
Piotr Jastrzebski: v/b, Niclas Gröndahl: g, Åke Johansson: g, Johnny Darabandt: d
Eskilstuna - Formed in 1980, split in 1984. Quite typical 80s metal/hard rock. Johnny has recorded several demos with the band *Head* that never lift off.

1983 ■ Orphan Devil/Sneakin' Around ....7"   Pang ....PSI 073 $$

Unofficial releases:
2000 ☐ Orphan Devil/Sneakin' Around ....7"   NWOSHM 006
      Swedish bootleg. 500 copies in purple vinyl.

1983 7" - PSI 073

SHALALEE
Maria Landberg (now Tern): g/v, Marianne Hall: b/v,
Agneta "Nulle" Ölund (now Eriksson): d/v
Stockholm - After the band *Revanch* split, Maria joined forces with Marianne from *Livin' Sacrifice* and started *Aphrodite*. After *Aphrodite* split, Maria, Agneta and Rigmor Gustafsson worked with *Åke Erikssons Recept*. The three then started *Shalalee*. Before the single, Rigmor was replaced by Marianne Hall. The B-side is good solid melodic hard rock with vocals not far from Pat Benatar and a nice chorus to go with it. The A-side however is a quite weak version of the old *Sweet*-tune. Well worth checking out, though. Dr Roxx was run by former *Bedlam/ Attack/Wasa Express/Åke Erikssons Recept* drummer Åke Eriksson. Agneta is his wife. Runs in the family, doesn't it? Maria later resurfaced in all-girl metal band *Hysterica* and now plays in cover bands *Metalnun* and *Heartattack*.

1990 ■ Wig Wam Bam/What You See Is What You Get ....7"   Dr Roxx.. PRE 105
      Pink vinyl.

1990 7" - PRE 105

SHAME
Enzo Galione: v, Tobbe Eliasson: g, Mats "Oloph Skam" Grundström: g,
Magnus Rosén: b, Thorbjörn "Turken": d
Göteborg - *Shame* play really good *Thin Lizzy*-ish melodic hard rock, but pretty cheap production. After the band split Magnus Rosen joined 50s rockers *Kung Sune* and recorded the 7" *Sunes Bar & Grill*. He has later been in bands like *Von Rosen, Keegan, Arise* and of course *HammerFall*. Mats later recorded a 7" with popsters *Svart/Vitt*.

1981 ■ Birdie Num Num/On And On...7"   private ....SH 01

1981 7" - SH 01

SHAME
Dag Thornblad: v/g, Johan Rönn: g, Kenth Lindstrand: k,
Hasse Jönsson: b, Jonas Nilsson: d
Helsingborg - Formed in 1985 and split in 1997. The singles were mid-quality AOR, while the CD shows a much greater improvement. High-quality AOR in the vein of *Time Gallery* meets *Alien* with some *Toto*-ish touches. Some of the single tracks were co-written by Jonas Warnerbring (*Råg I Ryggen*). The singles featured keyboard player Lasse Bjarnetoft. He was however replaced by guitarist Johan on the album. Dag later joined cover band *Billy's Jukebox* and Hasse runs the venue Tivoli in Helsingborg. The album was released on the same short-lived label that gave us *W.E.T* and *Nasty Idols*. Cocky title for a debut album!

1989 ☐ Let Me Be The 1/2 Of A Kind ....7"   Rekordia .... ROI 0.4
1991 ■ Don't Break My Heart/It's Not The Same ....7"   Rekordia .... ROI 0.6
1995 ☐ GREATEST HITS..CD   HSM..HSMCD 016

1991 7" - ROI 0.6

SHARP NINE
Jesper Starander: v, Joacim Starander: g, Andreas Jonasson: g,
Dan Hansson: b, Fredrik Lindehall: d
Göteborg - I guess these were the first Swedes on the reborn Mausoleum label. Musically they produce heavy grungy rock in the same vein as *Soundgarden* and *Alice In Chains*. Not too memorable, but still good stuff. Jesper and Joacin are now found in *Blofly*.

1994 ■ UNTIMED...CD   Mausoleum 904153.2
1995 ☐ UNTIMED...CD   Mausoleum (USA) 71278-60010-2
      Same album as above, but with a totally different cover

1994 CD - 904153.2

SHATTERED

Erik Andersson: v/b, **Lars Karlsson:** g, **Jimmy Larsson:** g, **Johan Karlsson:** d

Ed - Formed by Johan and guitarist Jimmy and recorded the CD-R *Serenade Of Sadism* in 2001, followed by *Forgotten* later the same year. The demo *Seductors Manual* was recorded in 2002, and finally *Reckless Aggression*, before the band was picked up by Black Mark, who then released the debut. Jimi Andersson replaced Lars after the release party. Well-produced and well-played death metal a bit similar to early **Entombed** and **Dismember**. The CD was produced by Pelle Saether. Not to be confused with Karlskrona-based death metal band **The Shattered**. Erik was also found in **Skin Infection**. Lars was in **Mordant** and is now in **Evilized** together with Johan. Jimi sadly died in a drowning accident in 2006.

2004 ■ WRAPPED IN PLASTIC ....CD   Black Mark .... BMCD 171

2004 CD - BMCD 171

SHEE

Annika Jansson: v, **Stefan Johansson:** g, **Claes Engberg:** g,
Christer Magnusson: b, **Jörgen Ekener:** d

Karlstad - Medium-weight melodic hard rock with femme vocals. Not especially exciting. The band was formed in the early 80s, originally named **Damnation**. They then changed name to **Shee**, the double "e" because of English band **She**. The highlight was a support gig for German hard rockers **Viva**. **Shee** split around 1986. Engberg started playing in **Permanent Wave** and later recorded an album with **Abacorn**. He also played in **Deep Purple** tribute band **Meat Turtle**, while Ekener recorded a CD with the **Kiss** cover band **Kisses From The Past**.

1985 ■ Amnesia/Don't Want Your Love ....7"   CTR CTR-385

1985 7" - CTR-385

SHEIK AHMEED GROUP

Sheik Ahmeed: v/g, **Johan Åkerman:** v/g, **Kalle Lindström:** k,
Johan Brusell: b, **Simon Steensland:** d

Vallentuna - The A-side is a strange symphonic-sounding ballad with horrible vocals by Johan, while the B-side is slightly progressive, melodic, pompy hard rock with fat guitars and a big ballsy sound, like **Saga** on steroids. Better vocals by Sheik here. Simon has later recorded three solo prog/fusion albums and played with progsters **Landberk**. Brusell is currently found in bluesy psychedelic rockers **Stoneflowers**.

1984 ■ Hello Vacuum/Dark Min Ballad..7"   private .... SAG 001

1984 7" - SAG 001

SHENERAH

Dan Cardesjö: v, **Kenny Bryngelsson:** g, **Gustav Ljungberg:** g,
JörgenThorsson: k, **Marcus Käck:** b, **Ulf Eriksson:** d

Vänersborg - The band was formed in 1997 under the name **Adoration**, later **Gateway** and finally **Shenerah**. They recorded a demo entitled *Morning Light* in 1999. After the MCD Jörgen left the band to study theatre. The song *High Level Of Life* appears on the compilation *Power From The Blade* (JCM 2001). Classic melodic metal influenced by the likes of **Iron Maiden**, promising indeed. Changed their name to **The Breeding** and recorded another demo.

2000 ■ Metal Of Honour..MCD 4tr   private .... - -
　　　　Tracks: The Grim Reaper/Higher Level Of Life/Sacred Forest/Gate To Hell

2000 MCD - - -

SHERE KHAN

Daniel Borch: v, **Kai Lethola:** g, **Thomas "Mowgli" Skogsberg:** g,
Mats Lindbergh: b, **Stephan Knutsson:** d

Eskilstuna - Another band on the Mill label (**Crystal Pride**, **Lynx** etc). **Shere Khan** are an average band on the traditional Swedish 80's melodic metal scene. Singer Daniel later recorded a solo single under the name Danny 'N Rox and later joined **Alien**. Thomas has passed away.

1985 ■ QUITE ENOUGH FOR LOVE ....LP   Mill .... MILL 5030

SHERLOCK BROTHERS

André Andersson: v, **Marcus Hellgren:** g, **Alexander Nordqvist:** g,
Johan Andersson: b, **Andreas Lindqvist:** d

Enköping - **Sherlock Brothers** were formed in 2004, initially just called **Sherlock** under which name they also recorded the three-track demo *This Is The Right Way?* in 2005. On the demo the bass was handled by Fredrik Källberg. In 2009 they released their self-financed debut, produced by Pelle Saether, and was soon picked up by NineTone Records. The band had now

1985 LP - MILL 5030

been reinforced by second guitarist Hellgren. The band was nominated and won "Swedish Breakthrough of the Year" in 2010, by Bandit Rock Radio. **Sherlock Brothers** plays really good solid post-grunge in the vein of **Nickelback** and **Shinedown**, but with a touch of their own. *Website: www.sherlockbrothers.com*

2009 ■ SHERLOCK BROTHERS	CD	privatel	- -
2011 ☐ Stay	CDS	NineTone	NRCDS 107
2011 ☐ BLACK CAT TANGO	CD	NineTone	NRCD 111

2009 CD - - -

SHINETH
Sebastian Roos: v/g/b, Anders Berlin: d/k

Norrköping - **Shineth** were formed in 2002. The duo first met in 1996, while studying music in Norrköping. It however wasn't until 2000 when Sebastian called Anders and asked him to play drums on a demo. They finished the demo, but the year after Anders moved from Stockholm to Norrköping and the two now formed **Shineth**. The debut album was an outstanding melodic hard rocker with a strong touch of AOR, in the same vein as bands like **Giant, Seventh Key** or Swedish colleagues **Eclipse** and **Shiva**. The album also featured lots of guest such as Erik Mårtensson, David Wallin, Alexandra Jardwall, Marcus Sjöwall, Mikael Lindholm etc. The second album offered more in the same sound and direction. Roos is also found in **Miss Behaviour** and Berlin in **Bloodbound, Eclipse** and **Miss Behaviour**. The band started working on a third album in 2011, but the website hasn't been updated since 2009. *Website: www.shineth.se*

2006 CD - MPABCD 001

| 2006 ■ 11 OF 10 | CD | MusikProducenterna | MPABCD 001 |
| 2008 ■ LOST MAGIC PLACE | CD | MusikProducenterna | MPABCD 002 |

2008 CD - MPABCD 002

SHINING
Niklas "Kvarforth" Olsson: v/k, Peter Huss: g,
Christian Larsson: b, Rickard Schill: d

Halmstad - **Shining** were formed in 1997, when Kvarforth was only 14 years old. Initially a traditional black metal band, but soon to become one of Sweden's most controversial, suicidal, depressive and self-destructive bands with a musical landscape that borders on insanity at times, while it's quite beautiful in the next moment. Kvarforth is also a highly theatrical stage persona, where a live show can feature anything from blood and urine to self-mutilation. The first single featured singer Robert, drummer Ted "Impaler" Wedebrand and Kvarforth handling guitars and bass. *Within..* was recorded at Abyss Studios and saw **Bethlehem/Paragon/Belial**-singer Andreas Classen replacing Robert, while Tusk was handling the bass. Kvarforth is also the man behind Selbstmord Services and ran the magazine *Djävulskap*. He has also been part of bands like **Bethlehem, Den Saakaldte, Funeral Dirge, Ondskapt** and **Skitliv**. **Shining** disbanded in August 2004, but reformed later the same year. *VII: Född förlorare* (born loser) features guest spots from Chris Amott (**Arch Enemy, Armageddon**), Erik Danielsson (**Watain**) and Håkan Hemlin (**Nordman**). *Through Years Of Oppression* is a collection of recordings made between 1998-2003 featuring Jan Axel "M Hellhammer" Blomberg (**Mayhem**) on drums. On the third album the line-up had again changed, now featuring drummer Hellhammer, guitarist Håkan "Insis" Ollars and Phil Alex Cirone handling bass and keyboards, while Kvarforth had now taken over the vocals. *The Darkroom Sessions* is a compilation featuring non-album tracks. On the album *Halmstad* the line-up had again changed, now seeing Kvarforth only handling vocals, Fredric "Wredhe" Gråby (**Ondskapt, Bloodline**) and Peter Huss on guitars, Johan Hallander on bass and Ludwig Witt (**Spiritual Beggars, Firebird**) on drums. In 2008 Hallander was replaced by Andreas Larsen (**Livsnekad, Vile Scar**) and Witt was replaced by Rickard Schill (**Livsnekad, Vile Scar, Spawn Of Possession**). In May 2011 Gråby left the band and at the same time Christian Larsson took over the bass duties. The 2011 CDS track *Prince Of Darkness* is a cover of **Alice Cooper**. *Lots Of Girls Gonna Get Hurt* contains covers only, and by pop/goth/punk bands **Kent, Imperiet, Poets Of The Fall** and **Katatonia**. This is by far the most "normal" release by **Shining**, and not at all what I expected. Clean, soft and normal vocals and all songs are very true to the originals, meaning a collection of pop, punk, goth songs. I guess devoted **Shining** fans will either love this or hate it, while death metal fans will probably hate it sincerely. Puzzling... Not to be confused with Norwegian band **Shining**.

Shining in the darkness

2000 CD - MONUMENT 006CD

1998 7" - MONUMENT 002

1998 ■ Submit To Selfdestruction/Endless Solitude	7"	Selbstmord Services	MONUMENT 002
300 copies, hand-numbered.			
2000 ■ I - WITHIN DEEP DARK CHAMBERS	CD	Selbstmord Services	MONUMENT 006CD
2000 ☐ I - WITHIN DEEP DARK CHAMBERS	LP	Selbstmord Services	MONUMENT 006LP
2001 ■ II - LIVETS ÄNDHÅLLPLATS	CD	Selbstmord Services	MONUMENT 008CD
2001 ☐ II - LIVETS ÄNDHÅLLPLATS	LP	Selbstmord Services	MONUMENT 008LP
300 copies marbled vinyl. Catalogue number on the spine says CELLAR 003.			
2002 ☐ I - WITHIN DEEP DARK CHAMBERS	LP	Blut & Eisen	- -
237 hand-numbered copies			

2001 CD - MONUMENT 008CD

Year		Title	Format	Label	Catalog #
2002	☐	III – ANGST, SJÄLDESTRUKTIVITETENS EMMISSARIE	CDd	Avantgarde	AV 066
		A5 size digi pack.			
2002	☐	III – ANGST, SJÄLDESTRUKTIVITETENS EMMISSARIE	LP	Perverted Taste	PT 056
		500 copies.			
2003	☐	I - WITHIN DEEP DARK CHAMBERS	CD	Avantgarde	AV 072
2003	☐	Shining/Dolorian (split)	7"	Perverted Taste/Unpleasant	PT087/UW001
		Split with Dolorian. Track: Through Corridors Of Oppression			
2003	☐	THROUGH YEARS OF OPPRESSION	LP	Unexploded Records	UER 002
		500 copies.			
2004	☐	THROUGH YEARS OF OPPRESSION	CD	Unexploded Records	UER 002
		First 1000 copies with guitar pick			
2004	☐	THE DARKROOM SESSIONS	CD	Perverted Taste	PT 114
		500 copies.			
2004	☐	THE DARKROOM SESSIONS	LP	Perverted Taste	PT 115
		500 copies.			
2004	☐	I - WITHIN DEEP DARK CHAMBERS	CD	Modern Invasion (Australia)	MIM7340-2
		Bonus: Endless Solitude			
2004	☐	II - LIVETS ÄNDHÅLLPLATS	CD	Avantgarde	AV 078
2004	☐	II - LIVETS ÄNDHÅLLPLATS	CD	Modern Invasion (Australia)	MIM7341-2
		Bonus: Manipulation Mass			
2004	☐	III – ANGST, SJÄLDESTRUKTIVITETENS EMMISSARIE	CD	Mercenary Music (USA)	WAR 036
2005	■	I - WITHIN DEEP DARK CHAMBERS	LP PD	Osmose	OVIR 004
		495 copies.			
2005	☐	I - WITHIN DEEP DARK CHAMBERS	CDd	Osmose	OPCD 168
		Bonus: Vargtimmen (Bethlehem cover)			
2005	■	II - LIVETS ÄNDHÅLLPLATS	LP PD	Osmose	OVIR 005
		495 copies.			
2005	☐	II - LIVETS ÄNDHÅLLPLATS	CDd	Osmose	OPCD 169
2005	☐	IV – THE EERIE COLD	LP	Avantgarde	AV 082 LP
		500 copies.			
2005	☐	IV – THE EERIE COLD	CD	Avantgarde	AV 082
2005	☐	IV – THE EERIE COLD	CDd	Avantgarde	AV 082-DIGI
		The promo CD version had a spoken intro which was removed on the official release.			
2007	☐	The Sinister Alliance (split)	CD	Old Temple	OLD.12
		Split with Funeral Dirge. Tracks: Submit To Self-Destruction/Endless Solitude. 7" sleeve, stickers. 666 hand-numbered copies.			
2007	☐	V - HALMSTAD	CDd	Osmose	OPCD 187
2007	☐	V - HALMSTAD	LP	Osmose	OPLP 187
		500 copies. Different artwork.			
2007	☐	V - HALMSTAD	CD	Osmose (USA)	OPCD 2187
2008	☐	Shining/Den Saakaldte (split)	7"g	Temple Of Darkness	TOD 027
		666 black vinyl + 100 copies die hard edition with t-shirt. Track: Ytterligare ett steg närmare total jävla utfrysning			
2008	☐	Shining/Den Saakaldte (split)	7"g PD	Temple Of Darkness	TOD 027
		250 copies. Comes in sleeve.			
2008	☐	III – ANGST, SJÄLDESTRUKTIVITETENS EMMISSARIE	CD	Peaceville (UK)	CDVILED 224
2008	☐	III – ANGST, SJÄLDESTRUKTIVITETENS EMMISSARIE	CD	Avantgarde Music	AV066-JK
		Jakebox reissue.			
2008	☐	IV – THE EERIE COLD	CD	Avantgarde Music	AV082-JK
		Jakebox reissue.			
2008	☐	IV – THE EERIE COLD	CDd	Peaceville (UK)	CDVILED 220
		Reissue with spoken intro.			
2009	☐	V - HALMSTAD	LP PD	Osmose	OVIR 006
		483 copies.			
2009	☐	VI - KLAGOPSALMER	CD	Osmose	OPCD 206
2009	☐	VI - KLAGOPSALMER	2LPg	Osmose	OPLP 206
		First press: 200 white + 500 black vinyl. Second press: 100 gold + 200 blood red vinyl.			
2009	☐	VI - KLAGOPSALMER	LP PD	Osmose	n/a
2011	☐	Förtvivlan, min arvedel/Prince Of Darkness (Alice Cooper cover)	CDSpg	Spinefarm	SPI 397 CD
2011	■	VII – FÖDD FÖRLORARE	CD	Spinefarm	SPI 392 CD
2011	☐	VII – FÖDD FÖRLORARE	LP	Spinefarm	SPI 392 LP
2012	■	Lots Of Girls Gonna Get Hurt	MCD 4tr	Spinefarm	SPINE 70-2346
		Tracks: For My Demons (Katatonia cover)/Utan Dina Andetag (Kent cover)/Kung av jidder (Imperiet cover)/Carnival Of Rust (Poets Of The Fall cover)			
2012	☐	REDEFINING DARKNESS	CD	Spinefarm	SPINE 71-5407
2012	☐	REDEFINING DARKNESS	LP	Spinefarm	SPINE 71-9521
2012	☐	Förtvivlan, min arvedel/Prince Of Darkness (Alice Cooper cover)	7"	Svart Records	SVR 172
		500 copies. Red vinyl.			
2012	■	Tillsammans är vi allt (split)	7"	Svart Records	SVR 173
		Split with Alfahanne. Track: Tillsammans är vi allt. 500 copies. Yellow vinyl.			
2012	☐	Submit To Self Destruction/Endless Solitude	7" PD	Temple Of Darkness	TOD 037
		1000 copies.			
2013	☐	Shining/Momentum(split)	7"	Avantgarde	AV 217
		Split with Momentum. Track: Pale Colours (Bay Laurel cover). 300 copies.			
2013	☐	In The Eerie Cold Where All The Witches Dance (split)	7"	Primitive Art	PAR 034
		Split with Mortuary Drape. Track: Sensommar. 700 black, 300 green, 100 white, 100 purple.			

2005 LP PD - OVIR 004

2005 LP PD - OVIR 005

2011 CD - SPI 392 CD

2012 MCD - SPINE 70-2346

2012 7" - SVR 173

SHINING PATH

Gary "Mudbone" Cooper: v, Jonas Hellborg: b,
Jens Johansson: k, Anders Johansson: d

Lund/Malmö/USA - This is actually a tough one to describe. The music is almost death metal but with great musical skill and with lots of heavy riffs, although there are no guitars on this CD, only distorted bass and keyboards. Anders and Jens were of course in *Silver Mountain, Rising Force, The Johansson Brothers* as well as part of Jonas Hellborg's group. Anders is now in *HammerFall* and *FullForce* while Jens is in *Stratovarius*. Jonas is a very highly-acclaimed bassist that has played with tons of artists including John McLaughlin. Jonas, Jens and Anders have recorded several albums together under different names and with different singers. Many of the backings on the *Shining Path* album are the same as for *Bakteria*, but the lyrics are different... (much different). See *Bakteria* for further insight on that subject. *Shining Path* is the "clean" version with a different singer, but the music is still heavy. It was banned in some countries because it shows the pope wearing a Nazi armband and a helmet. Singer Gary Cooper has been with several well-known American acts. Jonas is today also part of jazz-metal combo *Art Metal* together with Mattias Ia Eklundh (*Freak Kitchen*).

1993 CD - DEM 029

1993 ■ NO OTHER WORLD...CD Day Eight.........................DEM 029

SHIVA

Anette Johansson: v, Mats Edström: g/k

Jönköping - Shiva were formed by Mats and Anette in 2001. Mats was part of the band *Arrow* in the 80s and both Mats and Anette were part of the band *Yankee Heaven*, who released one album. *Shiva* is a lot heavier than their old band. Anette has quite a powerful voice a bit similar to Moa of *Meldrum* mixed with Ann Wilson of *Heart*. Besides Anette and Mats the albums feature bassist Mattias Höijer (ex-*Arrow*), drummer Mikael Malmborg, guitarist Mats Ottosson (ex-*Arrow*) and keyboardist Niclas Olsson (*Alyson Avenue, Second Heat*). The first album was a solid AOR-infused melodic hard rocker, while on the second album they went more metal, picking touches of *Judas Priest* mixed with *Pink Cream 69* and *Phantom Blue*'s second album. On *The Curse Of The Gift* the sound had taken a slightly proggier turn, slightly similar to *Circle II Circle* meets *Masterplan* mixed with the old sound. A great band indeed!

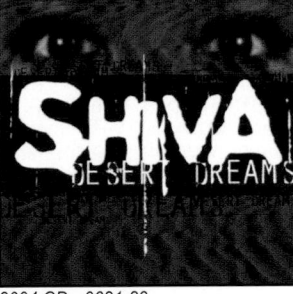

2004 CD - 0681-89

2002 CD - ZR1997077

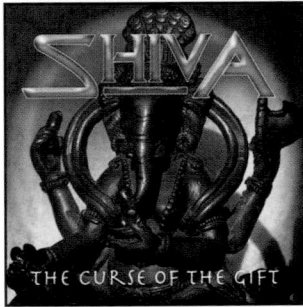

2006 CD - 10020

2002 ■ SHIVA...CD Z Records...................ZR1997077
2004 ■ DESERT DREAMS.................................CD MTM.................................0681-89
2004 □ DESERT DREAMS.................................CD Spiritual Beast (Japan)....SBSL-1013
    Bonus: Dow Jones Index/No Place For The Living
2006 ■ THE CURSE OF THE GIFT.......................CD AL!VE...............................10020
2006 □ THE CURSE OF THE GIFT.......................CD Spiritual Beast (Japan)....SBSL-1006

SHOCK TILT

Per Häggblom: v/g, Jonny Reinholm: g, Rolf Häggblom: b, Thomas Hultmark: d

Stockholm/Finland - Shock Tilt were formed by Finnish brothers Per and Rolf in 1984. They had previously played in the band *Central Heat*. They drafted drummer Hans Montin and guitarist Hannu Rajala and in 1985 they recorded the MLP *Night-Fight*. In 1986 the band relocated to Sweden. The line-up on the 1989 single *Heaven Calls* features Per, Rolf and Thomas. Guest performances were provided by Jonny Reinholm (featured on the *Guitar Heroes Of Sweden* compilation), René Lintunen and Pertti Tikkanen. Good, solid melodic hard rock with excellent guitar work and good vocals. Unfortunately the band is more known for the sad fact that their first guitarist Hannu Rajala was molested, murdered and dismembered by manager Anders Carlsson on November 27, 1987. As Hannu's genitals were missing, Carlsson was suspected of having eaten them... In 1992 the band recorded the demo, *Caliban Demos*. From this demo, the tracks *Heaven Calls* and *I Need Your Love* were featured on the compilation *Coming Up* (1993 Mother Earth). The line-up then featured singer Conny Lind (*Raceway, State Of Mind*), guitarists Fredrik Åkesson (*Talisman, Southpaw, Arch Enemy, Opeth, Krux*), Pär Häggblom, bassist Rolf Häggblom and drummer Hempo Hildén (*Trash, Norum, Dokken, Ball, Sarek* etc). In 1998 the line up featuring Per, Rolf, Jonny Reinholm and drummer Thomas Hultmark, recorded a cover of *Crazy Train* for the tribute album *Ozzified* (1998 Tribute Records). This line-up is still active.

1985 MLP - TR 101

1989 7" - TMS 010

1985 ■ Night-Fight.................................MLP 6tr Tilt Records.....................TR 101 $
    Tracks: Shock Tilt/Check Out Time/Silver Ass/Night Fight/Mr Tilt/Howling Body. 250 copies
1989 ■ Heaven Calls/We Are Crazy.......................7" Top Music.......................TMS 010 $

SHORE

Lena Karlsson: v, Christer Abrahamsson: g, Mikael Edvinsson: b, Thommy Larsson: d

Färgelanda/Mellerud - Basic hard rock with a touch of *AC/DC* and *Rose Tattoo*. High-quality vocals. The members were only 15-16 years old when they recorded the 7".

1989 ■ Hold You/I Just Love You.........................7" Platina.............................PL 56

1989 7" - PL 56

SHOTGUN BLUEZ

Christoffer Antonsson: v, Ronnie "Ronta" Pettersson: g/v,
Danne Neldell, Uffe "Trigger" Johansson: b, Patrick Arnehall: d

Nynäshamn - Raunchy sleaze/glammish hard rock in the vein of *Backyard Babies*-meet-early-*Mötley Crüe* with a punkish sleaze attitude. The band also recorded demo-material after the MCD. In 2000 the 5 track demo CD-R *Final Solution* was produced and in 2001 another 5-track CD-R (with a proper printed cover and all) simply entitled *Promo*, was unearthed. The track *Up On Nine* was featured on the compilation *Riot On The Rocks - Volume 1* (2000 Safety Pin). In 2006 the band reformed under the new name *Sixpack Sinners*.

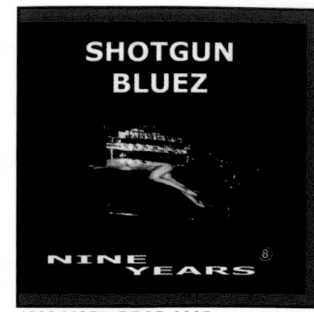

1999 ■ Nine Years..MCD 4tr   private ....RPCD 9905
    Tracks: Up On Nine/My Bitch/Diesel And Power/Who's The King?

1999 MCD - RPCD 9905

SHOTGUN MESSIAH

Tim "Tim Tim/Skold" Sköld: v/b, Harry "Cody" Kemppainen: g

Skövde - The story dates back to the early 80s, when the boys started it all under the name *Shylock*. They recorded some demos, but changed members and also their name, to *Kingpin*. The line-up featured singer Bo "Zinny J. Zan" Stagman, guitarist Harry "Kody" Keppainen, bassist Tim Sköld and drummer Pekka "Stixx" Ollinen. *Kingpin* recorded the album *Welcome To Bop City*. Zinny brought a pack of albums to the USA, kept knocking on doors and finally struck gold with Relativity Records. In 1988 the band moved to the other side of the pond. The album was reissued the year after by Relativity, under the new name *Shotgun Messiah*. Before the release of *Second Coming*, Zinny was sacked and Tim switched from bass to vocals. The bass was now taken care of by American Bobby Lycon. *I Want More* was just an interlude with some covers (*Ramones, The Stooges* and *New York Dolls*) and an alternate semi-acoustic version. Before the recording of *Violent New Breed* drummer Pekka "Stixx" Ollinen and Bobby left the band. Tim and Harry instead transformed the band into a cyber-metal studio project in the vein of *Ministry* and *Nine Inch Nails*. They used drummer Bjarne "BC Strike" Johansson for live shows. *Shotgun Messiah* split and Tim went solo, continuing in the same style as on *Violent New Breeed*. Harry played guitar on Stuart Hamm's album *Kings Of Sleep* and was working with former *Saigon Kick* singer Matt Kramer. The band's first singer Jukka "J.K Knoxx" Kemppainen was later in the highly interesting band *Cosmic Zoo*. Tim released his first solo album under the moniker *Skold* in 1996. He then joined *KMFDM* and ended up backing *Marilyn Manson* between 2002-2008. In 2011 he joined the band *Doctor Midnight & The Mercy Cult*, featuring ex-*Turbonegro* singer Hank von Helvete. Harry sadly vanished into obscurity and is today writing jingles and advertisement music in the USA. In late 2012 the band was partly resurrected, when Zinny and Stixx drafted guitarist Rob "Marcello" Wendelstam (*Danger Danger, Chris Laney's Legion*) and bassist Ulf "Chris Laney" Larsson (*17, Chris Laney's Legion* etc), now using the name *Shotgun*.

Nah, I wouldn't say they look especially violent

1989 LP - 88561-1012-1

1990 7" - BBR 029

1991 CD - 88561-1060-2

1989 ■ SHOTGUN MESSIAH	LP	Relativity (USA)	88561-1012-1
1989 ☐ SHOTGUN MESSIAH	CD	Relativity (USA)	88561-1012-2
1989 ☐ SHOTGUN MESSIAH	LP	Music For Nations (UK)	MFN 105
1989 ☐ SHOTGUN MESSIAH	CD	CBS Sony (Japan)	SRCS-5061
1989 ☐ Shout It Out	CDS	Relativity (USA) (promo)	88561-1021-2
1990 ☐ Don't Care 'Bout Nothin'	CDS	Relativity (USA) (promo)	IRPROCD-0104
1990 ☐ SHOTGUN MESSIAH	LP	Big Bag	BBRLP 116
1990 ■ Shout It Out/The Explorer	7"	Big Bag	BBR 029
1991 ☐ Red Hot	CDS	Relativity (USA) (promo)	IRPROCD-0413
1991 ☐ Hearbreak Blvd	CDS	Relativity (USA) (promo)	n/a
1991 ☐ SECOND COMING	LP	Relativity (USA)	88561-1060-1
1991 ■ SECOND COMING	CD	Relativity (USA)	88561-1060-2
1991 ☐ SECOND COMING	CD	Roadrunner	RR 9239
1991 ☐ SECOND COMING	CD	CBS Sony (Japan)	SRCS-5776
1992 ☐ SHOTGUN MESSIAH	CD	Big Bang	BBRCD 126
1992 ☐ SECOND COMING	CD	Big Bang	BBRCD 116
1992 ☐ I Want More	MCD 5tr	Relativity (USA)	88561-1151-2

    Tracks: I Want More/Search And Destroy/53rd And 3rd/Babylon/Nobody's Home

1993 ☐ VIOLENT NEW BREED	CD	Relativity (USA)	88561-1164-2
1993 ☐ VIOLENT NEW BREED	CD	Roadrunner	RR 9036-2
1993 ☐ VIOLENT NEW BREED	CD	Sony Music (Japan)	SRCS 6980
1993 ☐ Enemy In Me	MCD 3tr	Relativity (USA)	RPRPCD-0215

    Tracks: Enemy In Me/Revolution/Side F/X. Promo.

1993 ☐ Violent New Breed	CDS	Relativity (USA)	RPROCD-0230

SHREDHEAD

Johan Sellman: v, Johan Hörnquist: g, Mikael Olervo: b,
Toft Stade: b, Magnus Egerbladh Öberg: d

Umeå - This is a band with quite a unique touch. They mix metal, punk, funk, hardcore and pure madness. They're like a mix of *Primus*, *Clawfinger* and *Red Hot Chili Peppers* with a touch of jazz and hardcore. There's some seriously heavy guitar riffing going on. Another interesting detail is the unique line-up featuring two bass players. Mikael plays six-string bass with mostly finger picking, while Toft handles the harmonies. Highly original. Jon is also found in *Puffin* and *In The Flesh*, Toft has recorded with *Ray Wonder*, Johan and Magnus have made releases with *Starmarket* and Magnus has also recorded with *Honeymoons* and *Seashells*. However all those bands are more or less pop. The band is also featured on the *Northcore* compilation on Burning Heart Records. *Melting Pot* also featured guest spots from Nina Ramsby, Michael Blair, Pelle Henricsson and MC Tone Capone.

1992 MCD - DOL 010

1993 ■	State Of The Art	MCD 4tr	Dolores Records	DOL 010
	Tracks: Bones Of Contention/Haywire/In The Palm Of The Hand/The Boogeyman			
1993 ☐	PLAYMOBEEL	CD	North Of No South	NONS CD 11
1995 ☐	Dork	MCD 3tr	North Of No South	NONS CD 15
	Tracks: Dork/Slice Of Enrico/Bananas			
1996 ☐	MELTING POT	CD	North Of No South	NONSCD33
1996 ■	MELTING POT	CD	Pioneer (Japan)	PICP-1117
	Bonus: Dog Years			
1996 ☐	Squeezing The Sponge/(radio edit)/Dog Years	MCD 3tr	North Of No South	NONSCD36

1996 CD - PICP-1117

SHUBEND

Niclas Frohagen: v, Dan Lundberg: g/b, Fredrik Linfjärd: g,
Martin Pettersson: b, Martin Eriksson: d

Karlshamn/Malmö - *Shubend* were formed in 1989 by Dan Lundberg (*Emeth, Worst Case Scenario*). In 1999 he recorded the first demo *Hook, Line And Sinker*, now featuring singer Frohagen (*Ningizzia, Forest Of Shadows*). The band was reinforced with bassist Pettersson and drummer Martin Eriksson, and in 2000 the second demo *Singularis*, was recorded. In 2001 guitarist Linfjärd (later in *Stabwound*) was drafted. By the end of 2002 Linfjärd and Pettersson were out again. They also changed their name to *Genesis Of Pain*. High-speed death metal with a technical twist. The album is also known as *Synergism 2.0*, released under the *Genesis Of Pain* moniker.

2002 CD - ILIAD 023

2002 ■	SYNERGISM	CD	Rage Of Achilles	ILIAD 023

SIDE BY SIDE

Christer Schill: v, Marie Melin: v, Conny Lönn: v, Mark Åkerblom: v, Mattias Orre: v,
Michael Johansson: v, Anders "Kalkan" Karlsson: v, Lennart "Ledde" Nilsson: v,
Jörgen Persson: g, Jan Arvidsson: k, Per Wallmark: b, Kenneth Andersson: d

Halmstad - Great melodic hard rock in the vein of *Treat*. A one-sided single with lots of different musicians, released as a benefit project for the Children's Cancer Foundation. Guitar solos were provided by Peter Rhode (*Pussy Galore*), Christer Schill (*Big Talk, Promille*), Bobban Michaljlovic, Thomas Hackberg, Jörgen Persson, Per Ivarsson, Amadou Jobe and Jörgen Nilsson (*Who's Next*). Kalkan was also found in punksters *Spott*.

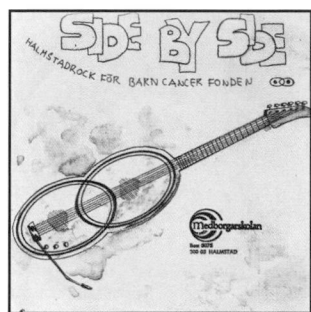
1986 7" - MEDS 861

1986 ■	Side By Side	7"	private	MEDS 861

SIDEBURN

Jani Kataja: v, Morgan Zocek: g, Martin Karlsson: b, Fredrik Haake: d

Stockholm - Swedish retro rockers *Sideburn* were formed in 1997. The track *Rainmaker* was featured on the *Molten Universe Vol 2* (2000 Molten Universe) compilation. On the debut the band was a trio featuring Zocek on guitar, Kataja on bass and vocals and drummer Tor Pentén. After the album, Martin Karlsson was added on bass and keyboards. In 2003 Fredrik Broqvist replaced Pentén. They recorded the demo *I Am King* the same year, followed by *Top Of The World* and the three-track demo *The Newborn Sun* in 2004. It would however take another three years before the album with the same title was released. Kataja and Broqvist are also in *Mangrove*. *Sideburn* plays outstanding stoner-ish, seventies-sounding heavy rock quite similar to early *Grand Magus*-meet-*The Quill* with a touch of *Spiritual Beggars*. Not to be confused with the Swizz band. On *IV Movement* drummer Fredrik Broqvist had been replaced by Fredrik Haake (*Badge, Meldrum*) and the album is an outstanding retro hard rock album.

The newborn suns

2010 CDd - TRANS 053

2001 ☐	TRYING TO BURN THE SUN	CD	Beard Of Stars	BOS CD 17
2007 ☐	THE NEWBORN SUN	CD	Buzzville Records	BUZZCD 022
2010 ■	THE DEMON DANCE	CDd	Transubstans Records	TRANS 053
2012 ■	IV MOVEMENT	CD	Transubstans Records	TRANS 098

2012 CD - TRANS 098

SIEBENBÜRGEN

Marcus Ehlin: v/g/b, Lisa Bohwalli Simonsson: v, Richard Bryngelsson: g,
Joakim Ohlsson: g, Johnnie Gunter: k, Dennis Ekdahl: d

Six forming the seven cities

Stockholm - The band was formed by Marcus and Anders in 1994. The name **Siebenbürgen** (the seven cities) was what the Germans used to call the region of Transylvania. The band's first release was a live demo, released in 1996. The second demo *Ugentum Pharelis*, lead to a deal with Napalm Records. On the first two albums the line-up featured singer Marcus Ehlin (**Devlin**), bass player Fredrik Brockert, drummer Anders Rosdahl, guitarist Linus Ekström and Lovisa Hallstedt, who sang and played violin. On *Delictum* they also switched from Swedish to English lyrics. Pretty interesting mix of death/black metal with a strong folkish touch, especially with Kicki's high-pitched melodic voice. The male vocals are guttural and brutal. In 1999 Lovisa was replaced by Kicki Höijertz (ex-**Left Hand Solution**). **Siebebürgen** can also be found on compilations like *Darkness Is Thy Kingdom I, Darkness Is Thy Kingdom III, Blessed By The Night, From Within The Purgatory I* and various Napalm compilations. Marcus also had his side project **SFX**, but nothing has as yet been released. In 2001 Höijertz was replaced by Turid Walderhaug while Fredrik Folkare (**Unleashed, Scudiero, Incardine, Skarr**) replaced Linus Ekström. In 2002 Turid was replaced by Erika Roos and in 2004 Folkare was replaced by Joakim Ohlsson. The line-up on *Darker Designs & Images* featured Roos, Ehlin, Bryngelsson, Rosdahl and bassist Niklas Sandin (**Amaran, Dark Eden, Shadows Past, Life Eclipse**). Anders Rosdahl was now replaced by Dennis Ekdahl (**Raise Hell, Rutthna, Mortifier, Bloodshed, Sins Of Omission, Mystic Prophecy** etc), Roos by Simonsson, Gunther was added on keyboards, Ohlsson on guitar and Ehlin took over the bass work. The band split in 2009.

1997 ☐	LOREIA	CD	Napalm	NPR 030
1998 ☐	GRIMJAUR	CD	Napalm	NPR 044
2000 ☐	DELICTUM	CD	Napalm	NPR 075
2001 ☐	PLAGUED BE THY ANGEL	CDd	Napalm	NPR 100
	Bonus: Jawbreaker (Judas Priest cover)			
2001 ☐	PLAGUED BE THY ANGEL	CD	Napalm	NPR 100
2005 ☐	DARKER DESIGNS & IMAGES	CD	Napalm	NPR 171
2005 ☐	DARKER DESIGNS & IMAGES	CDd	Napalm	NPR 171
	Bonus: A Night's Eternity/Ute ur graven			
2008 ■	REVELATION VI	CD	Massacre Records	MAS CD0585
2008 ☐	REVELATION VI	LP PD	Massacre Records	MAS PD0585
2008 ■	REVELATION VI	CDd	Massacre Records	MAS DP0585
	Special embossed artwork. Bonus: Enter Omega			

2008 CD - MAS CD0585

2008 CDd - MAS DP0585

SIEBENSÜNDEN

Sveggo: v, Björn: g/b, Klas: g, Simon: g/b, Albin: d, Janne Karlsson: samples

Jönköping - **Siebensünden** (German for "seven sins"), formed after an alcohol binge at the club Lilla Paris in 1997 is an odd sludge-style band. What is surprising is that a band featuring members from bands like **Warcollapse, Counterblast** and **Dom Där**, can sink to such a low musical level. Janne (**Warcollapse, Antabus, Sub Alert, Machindu, Tolshock**) also runs PAS-83 Records. Horrible noise and effect-driven sludge doom with desperately screetching "vocals". The **Siebensünden/Teratologen** co-operation features two songs, over 20 minutes each. The (highly weird and explicit) lyrics were written by the pseudonym Nikanor Teratologen. *Blod, Slem, Galla* (blood, slime, gall) features four songs at 86 minutes. The album was also released as a double CDR (PAS-83, 01403) in 120 copies. This is way past horrible.

1998 ☐	EN KULA TILL TRÖST	LP	Malárie Records	- -
	500 copies.			
2006 ■	BLOD, SLEM, GALLA	2LP	PAS-83	LP 01405
	300 copies.			
2007 ☐	Gläd dig du kristi luder/Herrens djuriska njutning	CDpg	I Hate	I HATE CD 042
	500 copies. Says Siebensünden/Teratologen on the cover.			
2007 ☐	Gläd dig du kristi luder/Herrens djuriska njutning	2LPg	Malárie/Ultra Doom Taliban	LP 01606
	666 copies.Says Siebensünden/Teratologen on the cover.			

2006 2LP - LP 01405

SIENA ROOT

Samir "Sam Riffer" Eriksson: b/v, Karl Gustaf "KG West" Westman: g/k,
Love "Billy" Forsberg: d

Hägersten/Stockholm - Analogue retro rockers **Siena Root** were formed in 1997, taking the name after the "warm, earth colors of the muddy roots of Tuscany". After recording several demos the shortlived UK label Rage Of Achilles signed the band. The line-up on the debut featured singer Oskar Lundström, plus the band's basic stem trio: guitarist KG West, bassist Sam Riffer and drummer Love Forsberg. We're talking primal seventies jam-oriented slightly psychedelic hard rock picking influences from **Deep Purple, Black Widow, Uriah Heep** and the more psychedelic side of the seventies. After the debut album female singer Sanya replaced Oskar. Original member Sartez "Faraj" Abdulrahman left the band during the recording of *Different Realities*. He is now in **Three Seasons**. Janet Jones Simmonds instead handled the lead

2004 CD - ILIAD 055

2005 7" - NASONI 703B

vocals on the album. *Root Jam* is a live album, where the trio was reinforced by Anna Sandberg on vocals, Tängman on hurdy gurgy, Martin Svensson on violin, Jonas Åhlen on vocals, Jonas Myrenberg on mandolin, Sanya on vocals, Maxi Dread on guitar and Stian Grimstad on sitar. An excellent band for retro fans.
Website: www.sienaroot.com

2004	■	A NEW DAY DAWNING	CD	Rage Of Achilles	ILIAD 055
2004	☐	A NEW DAY DAWNING	2LP	Nasoni	NASONI 033B
		Vinyl version contains extended versions of the songs. Colored vinyl			
2004	☐	A NEW DAY DAWNING	2LP	Nasoni	NASONI 033C
		Colored vinyl.			
2004	☐	A NEW DAY DAWNING	CDd	Nasoni	NASONI 033CD
2005	■	Mountain Songs	7"	Nasoni	NASONI 703B
		Tracks: Mountain I/Mountain II			
2005	☐	Mountain Songs	7"	Nasoni	NASONI 703C
		Tracks: Mountain I/Mountain II. Coloured vinyl.			
2006	■	KALEIDOSCOPE	CD	Nasoni	NASONI 049CD
2006	☐	KALEIDOSCOPE	LP	Nasoni	NASONI 049B
2006	☐	KALEIDOSCOPE	CD	Nasoni	NASONI 049C
		Coloured vinyl.			
2008	☐	FAR FROM THE SUN	CDd	Transubstans	TRANS 034
2008	☐	FAR FROM THE SUN	LP	Headspin	HSLP 0000312
2008	☐	FAR FROM THE SUN	CDp	Mals Records (Russia)	MALS 338
2009	☐	A NEW DAY DAWNING	CD	Rockadrome	ROCK 025-2
2009	☐	A NEW DAY DAWNING	CDp	Mals Records (Russia)	MALS 306
2009	☐	DIFFERENT REALITIES	CDd	Transubstans	TRANS 043
2009	■	DIFFERENT REALITIES	LP	Headspin	HSLP 314
2011	☐	A NEW DAY DAWNING	2LP	Root Rock Records	RRR 002
2011	☐	ROOT JAM	2CD	Transubstans	TRANS 088
2011	☐	ROOT JAM	2LPg	Headspin	HSLP 324
2011	☐	ROOT JAM	2LPg	Headspin	HSLPC 324
		Golden vinyl.			

2006 CD - NASONI 049CD

2009 LP - HSLP 314

SIGN

Ola Wikström: v, Tommy Karlsson: g/b, Martin Berg: d

Falkenberg - The single showed quite an OK band in the typical 80s melodic hard rock/metal genre, actually quite close to German melodic bands like **Sinner** and **V2**. The guitar work is excellent while the singer is OK. Worth checking out, though. On the MCD they had stepped up their game a bit more with a nice production, biting guitars, and a style now a bit closer to **Dokken**. Good stuff. Ola and Tommie were later found in the band **Sanity**.

1990	■	Carry Your Cross/Atomic Waste	7"	private	SGN 190
1995	■	Sign Of Time	MCD 4tr	private	SGN 295
		Tracks: Time/Deal With The Devil/Colour Of Truth/No Excuse			

1990 7" - SGN 190

SILENCER

Mikael "Nattramn" Nilsson: v, Leere (aka Casado): g

Växjö/Stockholm - Formed in 1995 as Leere's solo project that became a duo when Nattramn joined. Late 1998 they recorded the one track demo *Death, Pierce Me*, using session drummer Jonas Mattsson (**Nominon**). Black metal ranging from passionate piano passages to brutal growling death metal with quite an uncompromising attitude. Hysterically screaming vocals. Similar to **Burzum**. Anything to shock it seemed. The band's slogan was: "*We promote your death*". On the album they hired **Bethlehem** drummer Steve Woltz. Nattramn (not the same person as in the band **Frostrike**) was institutionalised. Rumour had it he escaped and hit a six-year-old girl in the head with an axe. However, according to locals this was not him, but another person, also institutionalised, who later took his own life because of the event, said to have been caused by a change of his medicines. Nattramn, having problems with himself and being periodically institutionalised, formed therapy side project **Diagnose: Lebensgefahr**, which also resulted in a book. Not to be confused with the US metal band. **Silencer** is no more.

2001	■	DEATH... PIERCE ME	CD	Prophecy Productions	PRO 034
2001	☐	DEATH... PIERCE ME	LP	Prophesy Productions	PRO 034
		200 copies.			
2008	☐	DEATH... PIERCE ME	LP	Autopsy Kitchen Records	AKR 012
		400 copies.			
2008	☐	DEATH... PIERCE ME	LP+10"	Autopsy Kitchen Records	AKR 012
		100 copies in marble vinyl + 10" single featuring the track Death, Pierce Me.			
2008	☐	DEATH... PIERCE ME	LP PD	Autopsy Kitchen Records	AKR 012
		500 copies.			
2009	☐	DEATH... PIERCE ME	CDd	Lupus Lounge	WOLF 009
		Bonus: Death, Pierce Me (demo 1998)			

1995 MCD - SGN 295

2001 CD - PRO 034

SILENT CALL

**Andi Kravljaca: v, Daniel "Danne" Ekholm: g, Patrik Törnblom (formerly Ulfström): k,
Tobbe Moen: b, Micke Kvist: d**

Stockholm - The origin of the band can be traced back to 1990, when founding members Ekholm and Törnblom met and started collaborating, which they did in bands like **Satin 'N Lace** and **Jamback**. In 2006 drummer Kvist (**Elsesphere, Fate**) joined and so did bass player Moen (**Red Fun, CreoZoth, Oz**). Singer Kravljaca (**Elshesphere, Seventh Wonder, Heave, Gryphon**) was drafted later the same year. In 2007 the band recorded the four-track demo *Divided*, which caught the attention of Escape Music. The debut album features guest spots by Daniel Flores (**Mind's Eye, The Murder Of My Sweet** etc) and Göran Edman (**Madison, Malmsteen, Kharma** etc). Both albums were mixed by Martin Kronlund (**HammerFall, Reece/Kronlund** etc). *Silent Call* plays high-class outstanding heavy melodic hard rock with a proggy touch, a bit similar to **Mind's Eye**-meet-**Coldspell**. Killer vocals and great musicians topped with a fat production. Both albums are killer!
Website: www.silentcall.se

2008 CD - ESM 177

2008 ■	CREATIONS FROM A CHOSEN PATH	CD	Escape Music	ESM 177
2010 ■	GREED	CD	Escape Music	ESM 206

2010 CD - ESM 206

SILENT SCYTHE

**Tobbe Jansson: v, Tommi Djukin: g/v, Peter Henningsson: g,
Anders Frykebrant: b, Johan Strende: d**

Karlstad - Formed in 1999 by guitarist Djukin (**Brimstone, Carnal Lust**). They recorded their first demo *Death Is Comin'* in 2002. Henningsson is also found in **Impale**, **Legion** and **Planet Deep**, while Strende was part of **Impale**, **Brimstone** and **Spineless**. *Suffer In Silence* is more or less the same album as *Longing For Sorrow*. The only difference is that the intro was incorporated into the first song on the first release, plus the drunken jam song *Feather* has been added. Before the release of *Suffer In Silence*, Tobbe Jansson was replaced by Fredrik Eriksson (**Crimson Tide**) and bassist Anders Frykebrant by Peter Ogestad (**Twilight Symphony**). This means the booklet states the new line-up, while the old members are mentioned as members during recording session. *Silent Scythe* play really great thrash-oriented metal with a touch of death at times, not too far from **Pathos** or American colleagues **Nevermore**. Good, solid production, too. The band was working on a new album, *Remain Silent*, but nothing came out of it and in 2005 the band split up.

2003 CD - - -

2004 CD - NAM 008

2003 ■	LONGING FOR SORROW	CD	private	- -
2004 ■	SUFFER IN SILENCE	CD	New Aeon Media	NAM 008
2004 □	SUFFER IN SILENCE	CD	Spiritual Beast (Japan)	SBCD-1017
	Bonus: Old World Disorder			

SILICONE VALLEY

Filip Radovic: v/g, Bo Andersson: k, Michael Beck: b, Magnus Anderson: d

Varberg - Really good melodic hard rock with a bit of a gothy touch, but with vocals a bit lacking.

1987 ■	Pictures Of Flowers/Play My Way - Little Lyre	7"	Rookie	001

1987 7" - 001

SILVER MOUNTAIN

Jonas Hansson: v/g, Jens Johansson: k, Per Stadin: b, Kjell Gustafsson: d

Malmö - Jonas is definitely the mastermind behind this band, although this is the group that put the spotlight on two of Sweden's most interesting musicians, Jens and Anders Johansson. *Silver Mountain* were formed in 1978. On the band's debut single the band consisted of Jonas, handling guitars and vocals, second guitarist Morgan Alm, bassist Ingemar Stenqvist and drummer Mårten Hedener. The line-up changed, seeing Mats Bergentz (later in **Mister Kite**) replace Hedener. In 1982 Jens joined on keyboards and Anders replaced Bergentz. They were previously in the fusion band **Slem**, together with guitar ace-to-be, Erik Borelius. Per Stadin replaced Stenqvist on bass. The first recording this line-up did was the song *She Needs* for the compilation album *Skånsk Rock II* (82 GS Music). This line-up unfortunately only lasted for the outstanding debut *Shakin' Brains*. The most hideous front cover, but an outstanding album, influenced by **Rainbow** and **Deep Purple**, but with a heavier edge. After the album Jens and Anders left to join *Yngwie Malmsteen's Rising Force*. There are actually some live demo recordings with Yngwie, Per, Jens and Anders from 1983, before they left. Former **Pyramid** singer Christer Mentzer and keyboard player Erik Björn Nielsen joined and drummer Mårten Hedener returned. The new *Silver*

The resurrected mountain 2013..

Mountain recorded the album *Universe*, which took the band in a more melodic direction. The same line-up also recorded the *Hibiya - Live in Japan*. The LP-version was touched up and "repaired" afterwards, however when the label put out the CD-version they used the original recording for some reason. On the next album, *Roses And Champagne*, Johan Dahlström had replaced Mentzer. Before this they had also recorded some demos with singers Sonny Larsson (**Motherlode/XT**) and Knut Akselsen (from Norwegian band **Road**). Drummer Kjell Gustavsson then replaced Mårten Hedener. The first track from this new constellation was featured on the *Rock Of Sweden* compilation, on which also features Jonas' solo track *Stratovarious*. This album, as well as *Roses And Champagne* were released on Jonas own label Hex. *Universe* and *Roses And Champagne* contain mostly very commercial and slick AOR. There was also a compilation album recorded in 1983 where Jonas was featured on several tracks. It was entitled *Streetwise* and was also financed by himself. There were supposed to be four different volumes, but only two were released. After *Roses And Champagne* Jonas moved to the USA and after several demo recordings he released the CD *No 1* in 1994 (see **Jonas Hansson Band**). The first single and album show the absolute peak of the **Silver Mountain**. I stated in my first book that reliable sources claimed a reunion was supposed to happen in 1996. Well, it actually took some time. In 2001 the original line-up finally rerecorded some of the old tunes. Actually without even getting together. Anders recorded the drums at his home in Anderslöv and Jonas did his parts in Los Angeles and Jens in New York. Modern technology, you know. The result was the album *Breakin' Chains*, which features rerecordings of unreleased demo tracks. A really great album, actually. Jonas plays a guest solo on the **Mountain** cover *Land Of Milk And Honey* recorded by **Mountain Of Power**. He moved back to Sweden in 2008 and after seeing a group on Facebook demanding a reunion, he put on a big reunion show in Malmö in 2010 featuring former members from the various line-ups. The show was filmed and released as the DVD *A Reunion Live*, in 2011. The band also played a number of festivals. The current line-up features Hansson, Stadin, Nielsen and Bergentz. In 2012 the new song, and accompanying video, *Breakin' Brains* was unearthed, proving the band is in serious songwriting mood. A new album should be expected.
Website: www.silvermountainrules.com

Silver Mountain at their peak

1979 ■	Axeman & The Virgin/Man Of No Present Existance	7"	Eutone	EUSM 227	$$
1983 ■	SHAKIN' BRAINS	LP	Roadrunner	RR 9884	
1983 □	SHAKIN' BRAINS	LP	SOS/Roadrunner	SOS-LP 127	
1983 □	SHAKIN' BRAINS	LP	SOS/Roadrunner	RR 9884	
1983 □	SHAKIN' BRAINS	LP	Metal Blade (USA)	MBR 1017	
1983 □	SHAKIN' BRAINS	LP	SMS/FEMS Records (Japan)	SP25-5110	
1985 ■	UNIVERSE	LP	Roadrunner	RR 9800	
1985 □	UNIVERSE	LP	Attic/Roadrunner (Canada)	RRR 213	
1985 □	UNIVERSE	CD	Roadrunner	RR 9800	
1985 □	UNIVERSE	LP	SMS/FEMS (Japan)	SP25-5190	
1986 □	HIBIYA - LIVE IN JAPAN 85	LP	SMSFEMS (Japan)	SP25-5281	
1988 □	ROSES AND CHAMPAGNE	CD	Hex Records	HRCD 881	
1988 ■	ROSES AND CHAMPAGNE	LP	Hex Records	HRLP 881	
1988 □	ROSES AND CHAMPAGNE	CD	Columbia/EMI (Ger)	790731 1	
1988 □	ROSES AND CHAMPAGNE	LP	Columbia/EMI (ger)	790731 4	
1988 □	ROSES AND CHAMPAGNE	LP	Tonpress (Poland)	SX-T 172	
1988 □	ROSES AND CHAMPAGNE	CD	Fun House/H.I.T Avenue (Japan)	28GB 7026	
1988 □	ROSES AND CHAMPAGNE	LP	Fun House/H.I.T Avenue (Japan)	28GD 7026	
1990 □	SHAKIN' BRAINS	CD	Apollon/FEMS (Japan)	APCY 8020	
1990 □	UNIVERSE	CD	Apollon/FEMS (Japan)	APCY 8021	
1990 □	HIBIYA - LIVE IN JAPAN 85	CD	Apollon/FEMS (Japan)	APCY 8022	
1994 □	ROSES AND CHAMPAGNE	CD	Apollon/FEMS (Japan)	APCY 8220	
1996 □	SHAKIN' BRAINS	CD	Roadunner (Japan)	RRCY 2011	
1996 □	UNIVERSE	CD	Roadunner (Japan)	RRCY 2012	
1998 □	SILVER MOUNTAIN BEST	CD	JIGU/Roadrunner (Korea)	JRCD 1143	
2001 □	BREAKIN' CHAINS	CD	Hex Records	HRCD 011	

Bonus: video-clip of Classica by Jonas Hansson.

2001 □	BREAKING CHAINS	CD	Avalon Marquee (Japan)	MICP 10248

Bonus: Resurrection

2002 □	BREAKING CHAINS	CD	Roadrunner (Japan)	RRCY-23049
2002 □	BREAKING CHAINS	CD	Reality Entertainment	RE 100002-2
2003 □	BREAKING CHAINS	CD	Reality Entertainment	RYE 105

Bonus: Prophet Of Doom (video).

2009 □	SHAKIN' BRAINS	CDd	Metal Mind	MASS CD 1256 DG

Bonus: Keep On Keepin' On. 2000 copies.

2009 □	UNIVERSE	CDd	Metal Mind	MASS CD 1257 DG

2000 copies.

2009 □	BREAKIN' CHAINS	CDd	Metal Mind	MASS CD 1258 DG

Bonus: Resurrection/Prophets Of Doom (video). 2000 copies.

2009 □	ROSES AND CHAMPAGNE	CDd	Metal Mind	MASS CD 1259 DG

Bonus: Springtime/Romeo & Juliette (video). 2000 copies.

2009 □	LIVE AT HIBIYA	CDd	Metal Mind	MASS CD 1260 DG

2000 copies.

1979 7" - EUSM 227

1983 LP - RR 9884

1985 LP - RR 9800

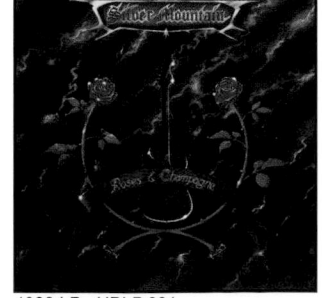
1988 LP - HRLP 881

Unofficial releases:

| 1995 ☐ | Axeman & The Virgin/Man Of No Present Existance | 7" | NWOSHM | NWOSHM 001 |

Bootleg version in red vinyl

| 1996 ☐ | THE LEGEND OF CRYSTALS | CD | Jailbait (Japan) | JBCD 055 |

Japanese bootleg, taken from the band's Swedish 82 radio session - Malmö

| 1997 ☐ | ANTHOLOGY 1 | 2CD | 8-Ball (Japan) | MALMO 001/002 |

Bootleg Live in Malmö 28/5-82 + one disc w DEEP PURPLE-covers

| 1997 ☐ | ANTHOLOGY II | 2CD | 8-Ball (Japan) | MALMO 003/004 |

Bootleg feat 30 prev. unreleased tracks

| 1997 ■ | ANTHOLOGY III | 2CD | 8-Ball (Japan) | MALMO 005/006 |

Bootleg live from Osaka 12/10-85, Malmö 11/6-88 (The band's last gig)

| 199? ☐ | LIVE AT THE WEDNESDAY PIECE | CD | - | - |

From the band's show at the Swedish radio show "Onsdagsbiten".

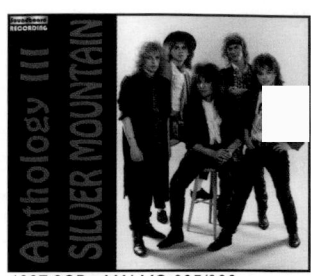

1997 2CD - MALMO 005/006

SILVER SERAPH

Pete Sandberg: v, Jörgen Birch Jensen: g, Richard Andersson: k, Jens Lundahl: b, Peter Wildoer: d

Malmö - Quite an all-star line-up. The band was initially to be called *Silver Serpent*, which it even said in some early ads. Pete, who was ex-*Alien/Madison/Midnight Sun/Snake Charmer/Von Rosen*, was at the time also found in *Pete Sandberg's Jade* and as solo artist. Richard was also in *Majestic*, Jens played on Pete's solo albums, as well as in *Blakk Totem*. Jörgen Birch Jensen was ex-*Bai Bang* and Peter Wildoer was found in *Majestic*, *Darkane* and formerly in *Arch Enemy* and *Armegeddon*. Andersson later formed *Richard Andersson's Odyssey*, *Time Requiem* etc. The lead guitars on the album were played by Magnus Sedenberg (*Painkillaz, Groover, Baltimoore*). The project was initiated by former *Dorian Grey* guitarist Michael Sahlström, who left due to various reasons, which ended up in a bitter fight almost ending in court. Musically very close to early *Rainbow* with a modern neoclassic touch. Great album!

| 2001 ☐ | SILVER SERAPH | CD | Toshiba-EMI (Japan) | TOCP 65929 |

Bonus: Constant Reminder

| 2001 ■ | SILVER SERAPH | CD | Regain | RR 07-AS |

2001 CD - RR 07-AS

SILVER WINGS

Rikard Järlefalk: v, Mikael Hallsten: g, Jonny Birtner: g, Anders Sundelin: k, Peter Johansson: b, Johan Fredriksson: d

Linköping - Formed in 1985. The band won the national final of the *Rockkarusellen* bandstand in 1987 and the week after they were in the finals of *Rock SM*. The single was the first prize in *Rockkarusellen*. After the single Mattias Helmer was added on keyboards. The band finally split because of differences in what style to play. Johnny and Mattias continued playing together, and Rikard (brother of *Taste* singer Patrik) joined cover band *Bröderna Åboys*. The track *Take My Hand* can be found on the compilation *Projekt 12* and *Green Motion* on *Musik för miljön* (1990 Studifrämjandet). *Silver Wings* play really good melodic hard rock in the vein of *Treat*, *Dalton* and *Glory*. The name is written *Silver Wings* on the cover, but *Silverwings* on the label and the compilation album.

| 1987 ■ | What About Love/In The Night | 7" | Studiefrämjandet | SFSI 1/87 |

500 copies.

1987 7" - SFSI 1/87

SILVERDOLLAR

Esa Englund: v, Ola Berg: g, Fredrik Hall: b, Mats Hjerp: d

Nyköping - *Silverdollar* were formed in 1996 as a heavy metal cover band. After playing around Sweden for six years they decided to record some of the covers, which became the album *Covers From Hell*. It features covers by bands like *Iron Maiden*, *Ozzy Osbourne*, *Motörhead*, *Judas Priest*, *Dio* and *W.A.S.P*, plus one original song. In 2005 the band recorded a 3-song demo, now only featuring original music. The style showed great inspiration from the bands *Silverdollar* previously covered, especially Ozzy and *Judas Priest*. The first album featuring all originals, *Evil Never Sleeps*, is a powerful steaming heavy rocker following in the style of the demo. Heavy, guitar dominated and with great vocals from Esa, sounding a bit like if *Priest* would have replaced Tipton and Downing with Zakk Wylde. The album was produced by Marco A. Nicosia (*Memento Mori*). On the 2011 release they continued the beaten path with an ever heavier edge.
Website: www.silverdollar.se

Heavy money!

2002 ☐	COVERS FROM HELL	CD	private	119 415
2007 ☐	EVIL NEVER SLEEPS	CD	Shark Records	SHARK 2035
2011 ■	MORTE	CD	Massacre Records	MASCD 0736

2011 CD - MASCD 0736

SILVERFISH

Markus Sukuvaara: v, Kim "Slim" Bäckström: g,
Robert Johansson: g, Olle Öjebo: b, Magnus Göransson: d

Karlskoga/Degerfors - **Silverfish** recorded their first three-track demo in 2004. The style is grunge-oriented heavy rock, a bit similar to **Soundgarden**-meet-**Pearl Jam** with a touch of stoner. *Feel The Change* was actually a bit heavier than the tracks on the split. Göransson, Johansson and Sukuvaara are also found in acoustic pop/blues band **Suku & The Dobby Mango Band**, while Bäckström is found in hardcore band **Fuck The Fucking Fuckers**. Not to be confused with the UK band.
Website: www.silverfish.se

Year		Title	Format	Label	Cat.no.
2003	■	FEEL THE CHANGE	CD	Red Eye Records	CIN-001
2005	□	SILVERFISH VS. STREETFIGHTERS (split)	CD	Red Eye Records	CIN-002

Split with Streetfighters. Tracks: White Trash/Duff Duff Caff/Action Man/Stealing Bleeding Bones/Backslide/Silence/Give Me Real/Confrontation

2003 CD - CIN-001

SIMSON

Göran Edquist: v, Camilla Cruse: v, Anders Ljunggren: g,
Ola Ruud: k, Jan Nilsson: b, Niclas Cruse: d

Kristinehamn - Formed in 1981. High-quality, guitar-dominated Christian AOR with great vocals, fat Hammond organ and good production. They belong to the same musical segment as **Europe** during the *Final Coundown*-era. Well worth investigating. The album was also released on cassette.

Year		Title	Format	Label	Cat.no.
1986	■	IT'S YOU	LP	private	EXLP 8602

1986 LP - EXLP 8602

SINGER

Andreas Byhlin: v/g, Johan Skugge: g, Joachim Sveder: b, Niklas Jonsson: d

Karlstad - Formed in August 1992 and recorded their first demo in 1993. Their influences ranged from **Kiss** to **Blue** and **Red Hot Chilli Peppers**. On the first CD-singles it was quite hard to determine if **Singer** was a heavy powerful metal band or a pop band, as the song material was very diverse. However on the album they really showed it was heaviness that would rule. Grungy, garagey heavy rock with an almost funk-punkish attitude. Produced by Tomas Skogsberg. The band split in 1996 and Byhlin later formed the garagey rock 'n rollers **Rocket 99**.

Year		Title	Format	Label	Cat.no.
1995	■	Italian Stallion	MCD 4tr	Crank/Virgin	CRANKCD 1

Tracks: Italian Stallion/Broken Bunch/Quicksilver/Stateplay. All are non-album.

Year		Title	Format	Label	Cat.no.
1995	□	Urban Fly/Sunboy	CDS 2tr	Crank/Virgin	CRANKCD 2
1995	□	24/Black Power/Pogokidchase	MCD 3tr	Crank/Virgin	CRANKCD 3
1996	□	FILL IN THE BLANKS	CD	Crank/Virgin	CDCRANK 1

1995 MCD - CRANKCD 1

SINKADUS

Linda Johansson: v/f, Rickard Biström: v/g/b, Robert Sjöbäck: g,
Fredrik Karlsson: k, Lena Pettersson: cello, Mats Svensson: d

Göteborg - A symphonic band which could be compared to **Änglagård**, **Jethro Tull**, **Yes** and **Genesis**. The first album contains only four songs, but they are between 11-18 minutes. The exclusive track *Trubadurens val* is featured on the 3-CD compilation *Kalevala – A Finnish Progressive Rock Opera* (2002 Musea). On this recording the band is only a quartet featuring Rickard, Fredrik, Robert and drummer Mats Segerdahl.

Year		Title	Format	Label	Cat.no.
1996	□	AURUM NOSTRUM	CD	Cyclops	CYCL 048
1998	□	LIVE AT PROGFEST 97	2CD	Cyclops	CYCL 061
1998	■	CIRKUS	CD	Cyclops	CYCL 072
1998	□	CIRKUS	CD	Avalon Marquee (Japan)	MICY 1097

1998 CD - CYCL 072

SINNERS BURN

Marcus Ankarberg: v, Richard "Pinnen" Karlsson: g,
Fredrik Nilsson: b, Jocke Ringdahl: d

Västervik - Well-produced and well-played old-school heavy death metal in the vein of early **Entombed**. High-quality song material. Growling of the raw, but not screeching type. Musically it's at times reminiscent of **Bakteria**, but with slightly better lyrical content. The band was formed in 2007 as a side project of **Pagaziner** members Patrik Halvarsson-Myrén, Jocke Ringdahl and Andreas "Dea" Karlsson, which makes it hardly surprising that they named themselves after a **Paganizer** song, a song they also cover on the debut album. After *Mortuart Rendezvous*, guitarist

2008 CD - NC 142

Halvarsson-Myrén (*Paganizer, Blodsrit, Primitive Symphony, Ribspreader*) was replaced by the band's former bass player Richard "Pinnen" Karlsson and the band brought in new bassist Fredrik Nilsson. Singer Andreas "Dea" Karlsson (*Paganizer, Another Life, Ribspreader, Terminal Grip*) was replaced by Marcus Ankarberg (ex-*Hellification*). Ringdahl was also found in *Blizzard* (only made a demo). The band's mascot goes under the name Mr Fritzl. The new album, entitled *Disturbing Creatures* was due out 2012, but no news on the subject has emerged. Website: www.sinnersburn.com

2008 ■	PRE-MORTAL AUTOPSY	CD	No Colours	NC 142
2008 □	PRE-MORTAL AUTOPSY	CDd	No Colours	NC 142
	99 copies.			
2009 □	MORTUARY RENDEZVOUS	CD	No Colours	NC 147
2009 ■	MORTUARY RENDEZVOUS	CDd	No Colours	NC 147
	50 copies. Different artwork.			
2010 □	INSANITY WARMACHINE	CD	Khaosmaster	KMP 017

2009 CD - NC 147

SINS OF OMISSION
Mårten Hansen: v, Mattias Ekblad: g, Martin Persson: g,
Thomas Fällgren: b, Dennis Ekdahl: d

Stockholm - High-quality, technical death metal. *Flesh On Your Bones* offers a highly intriguing musical mix that features elements of *Iron Maiden*-esque dual guitar-harmonies, as well as powerful early *Anthrax*-meet-*Pantera*-type power metal riffing. The music is however more progressive and challenging than any of the aforementioned bands. The vocals belong to the death metal genre. Highly recommended. The band was formed in 1996 and the initial line-up featured singer Toni Kocmut (*Mournful, Wyvern*), guitarists Johan Paulsson and Jonas Nilsson (*Raise Hell, Mortifier*), bassist Marco Deb (*Mournful*) and drummer Dennis Ekdahl (*Mournful, Mortifier, Raise Hell, Sienbenbürgen, Bloodshed, Rutthna, Mystic Prophecy, In Cold Blood* etc). Before the debut album Thomas Fällgren (*Construcdead*) replaced Marco, while guitarists Johan and Jonas were replaced by Martin (*Mörk Gryning, Dismember, Thyrfing, Beserk*) and Mattias (ex-*Mortifier, Mortum, Mörk Gryning*). On the second album singer Mårten (*A Canorous Quintet, The Plague, This Ending, October Tide, Votur*) had replaced Toni. *Flesh On Your Bones* contains a cover of *Slayer*'s *Angel Of Death*. In 2002 Jani Stefanovic (*Crimson Moonlight, Solution.45, DivineFire, Miseration, Essence Of Sorrow, Am I Blood* etc) replaced Dennis Endahl. Nothing was however recorded with Jani. *The Black Sun Collection* is a two-in-one consisting of both albums.

1999 CD - BS 16

1999 ■	THE CREATION	CD	Black Sun	BS 16
1999 □	THE CREATION	CD	Toy's Factory (Japan)	TCFK-87183
	Bonus: Red Sharks/Maybe The Time			
2001 ■	FLESH ON YOUR BONES	CD	Black Sun	BS 24
2001 □	FLESH ON YOUR BONES	CD	Soundholic (Japan)	TKCS 85032
	Bonus: The Sentinel (Judas Priest cover)			
2005 □	THE BLACK SUN COLLECTION	2CD	Blackend	BLACK 092 DCD

2001 CD - BS 24

SISTER
Jimmy "Jamie" Andersson: v, Gustav "Lestat" Hedlund: g/v,
Rickard "Rikki" Vickhoff: b, Claes "Cari" Fredriksson: d

Stockholm/Jönköping - *Sister* were formed in early 2006 combining punk, glam, rock and metal. During its first year of existence the band made numerous shows around Europe and in 2009 they recorded their first MCD, *Deadboys Making Noise* and a video for the song *Too Bad For You*. *Hated* was mixed by Tobias Lindell (*Mustasch, Hardcore Superstar, Europe* etc). *Sister* plays standard glam/sleaze very similar to *Hardcore Superstar* and *Muderdolls*. In November 2012 guitarist Lestat left the band. Jimmy is ironically boyfriend of *Sister Sin* singer Liv Jagrell. Website: www.sisteronline.net

2011 CD - 3984-14990-2

2009 □	Deadboys Making Noise	MCD 7tr	private	- -
	Tracks: Too Bad For You/D.E.A.D/Crash Boom Bang/When You Fall/Body Blow/Top Of The Line/I Don't Mind If You Die			
2011 ■	HATED	CD	Metal Blade	3984-14990-2

SISTER SIN
Liv Jagrell: v, Jimmy "J Basher" Hiltula: g,
Benton Wiberg: b, David "Dave" Sundberg: d

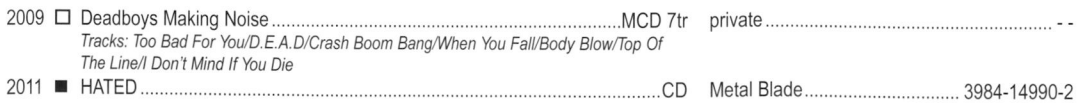

Lerum - *Sister Sin* were formed in 2002. Jagrell was previously in the band *Hystrerica* and is also a fitness instructor. Bassist Christian Bednarz quit in 2009 and was replaced by Benton Wiberg, who quit in 2010 and was temporarily replaced by *Babylon Bombs*' bassist Rickard "Ricky" Harrysson. The spot was finally filled by Andreas Strandh. Hiltula is also found in

2008 CDS - - -

Archangel (as Nightwind) and *Maleficio*. *Sister Sin* plays high-quality, energetic, classic metal quite similar to *Skew Siskin* with a touch of *Warlock*. The band has also featured guitarist Johan Eriksson, now in *Revolution Riot*.

Female finger power!

2003	☐	DANCE OF THE WICKED	CD	Sleazy Rider	SR-0023
2007	☐	Smash The Silence	MCD 5tr	private	- -
		Tracks: Hostile/Breaking New Ground/On Parole/LoveHate/All Systems Go!			
2008	☐	SWITCHBLADE SERENADE	CD	Metal Heaven	00058
2008	■	Switchblade Serenade Sampler	CDS	Victory Records (USA)	- -
		Tracks: One Out Of Ten/On Parole. Promo sampler.			
2008	☐	SWITCHBLADE SERENADE	CD	Victory Records (USA)	VR 482
2010	☐	TRUE SOUND OF THE UNDERGROUND	CD	Metal Heaven	00058
2010	☐	TRUE SOUND OF THE UNDERGROUND	CD	Victory Records (USA)	VR 558
2010	☐	TRUE SOUND OF THE UNDERGROUND	CD	Bickee Music (Japan)	HMCX-1099
		Bonus: On Parole			
2010	☐	TRUE SOUND OF THE UNDERGROUND	CD	Blackstar (Argentina)	STAR 024
		Bonus videos: Sound Of The Underground/Outrage/24/7			
2012	☐	NOW & FOREVER	CD	Victory Records	VR 669
2012	☐	NOW & FOREVER	LP	Victory Records	VR 669 LP

SIX FEET UNDER

Björn Lodin: v, Thomas Larsson: g, Peter Östling: k,
Kent Jansson: b, Marcus Källström: d

Rättvik/Borlänge - Formed in 1982. *Six Feet Under* were at the time as close as you could come to the sound and style of *Deep Purple*. Singer Björn Lodin (ex-*Rainfall, Gathering Freak*) sounded like a cross between Coverdale and Gillan. Thomas has made several recordings with bands like *Jammer*, *Yeah Bop Station*, with Glenn Hughes and has also released solo albums. Marcus was also found in *Jammer*, blues-rockers *Sky High* and *Stonecake* as well as the prog-rockers *DeathOrgan*. Kent Jansson was later in *Keen Hue*. On the first album Claes Annersjö handled the drums. After the second album, around 1985, the band changed their name to *Six Feet*. The line-up featured singer Erik Hjalmarsson (ex-*Jammer*), guitarist Tomas Larsson, bassist Joakim "Joe" Larsson (Tomas' brother, later in *Treat*), keyboardist Boel Lidgren and drummer Jonas Lööf (ex-*Vantage*). They were signed to EMI and recorded an album plus a single. The band however broke up before it was released in mid-1985. The song *My Blue Moon* from these sessions was later recorded by both *Yeah Bop Station* and Lodin's band *Baltimoore*, which also featured Thomas. At one time the band also featured drummer Jamie Borger (*Treat, Talisman*). Lodin has later recorded a CD with hard rockers *BALLS* and is today found in Hungarian band *H.A.R.D*, *Baltimoore* plus he has released solo recordings in Swedish and in a poppier style.

1984 7" - 13 598

1983 LP - ELP 5012

1982	☐	I'm Gonna Win/On The Road	7"	United Records	KJ 001
		500 copies.			
1983	■	SIX FEET UNDER	LP	Europafilm Records	ELP 5012
1983	☐	SIX FEET UNDER	LP	Universe Productions (Holland)	DLS 94
1984	○	Candle In The Dark/Mean Business	7"	Europafilm Records	ES 1031
		No artwork.			
1984	☐	Candle In The Dark/Mean Business	7"	Carrere (France)	13 598
1984	☐	ERUPTION	LP	Europafilm Records	ELP 5024
		The album was released with two different covers: the original with an erupting volcano and the second with smashed up classroom.			
1994	■	SIX FEET UNDER	CD	Zero (Japan)	XRCN-1166
1994	☐	ERUPTION	CD	Zero (Japan)	XRCN-1167

Unofficial releases:

1983	☐	SIX FEET UNDER	CD	Europafilm Records	CDELP 5012-2
		Counterfeit.			
1994	☐	ERUPTION	CD	Europafilm Records	CDELP 5024-2
		Counterfeit.			

1994 CD - XRCN-1166

SIX PACK SONIC

Henrik Lindahl: v, Fredrik "Frasse" Welin-Berger: g,
Martin Öhman: g, Jakob Jennische: b, Anders Stub: d

Uppsala - Formed in 1991. The 7" is quite punk-tainted thrash of medium quality. They are also featured with the track *Me, Superman & Jesus* on the compilation *Meat To Please You* (95 Tango Train). This is a heavier and quite brutal track, more similar to *Kyuss* and *Korn*. In 1995 Anders Stub left to join *Big Fish* as a permanent member. He was replaced by Peder Clevberger. The band recorded new demo material in 1995. The style had now changed into a heavier grunge-oriented vein, in an upgraded class. However, nothing was released. Stub and Jennische was later in the band *454* and Jennische is now found in *Dimma*.

1992	■	Six-Pack Sonic	7" 4tr	private	SPS 01
		Tracks: Suzie/Trip Asleep/Leadhead/Tough Enough			

1992 7" - SPS 01

SIXCOVEREDKISSSONGS

John Hermansson: g/b/v, Nisse Bielfeld: d/v

Stockholm - As the band name suggests this band does six covers by *Kiss*. Nothing to be over-excited about, although their versions are good and personal. The MCD was actually nothing more than a studio project. John was also found in the highly interesting band *Staiger* and Nisse was in *RFP* and *Clench*. John is now fronting *Mother Misery*.

1995 ■ Six Covered Kiss Songs ....MCD 6tr   private ....JNCD 01
    Tracks: Hotter Than Hell/All Hell's Breakin' Loose/Shock Me/I Want You/Warmachine/Not For The Innocent

1995 MCD - JNCD 01

SKALD

Henrik Kindvall: v, David Wiktorsson: g, Daniel Gadd: d

Malmö/Karlshamn - Formed in 2005 by Henrik and David. Musically this band sounds really good, like a mix of *Hoven Droven* and *Otyg*, but the vocals are quite horrible. When clean it's totally out of tune and when growling it just sounds awful. Similar to *Einherjer* but not even comparable on the same day. Before the MCD the band recorded two demos, both in 2006, *Sagor från skogstjärnen* and *Trolska vemodsband*. In 2010 they drafted *Omnispawn* drummer Gadd. The debut features session musicians Mattias Svensson on drums and vocals, Victor Dahlgren on bass plus guest appearances by Emil G. Koverot (violin), Linn De Wilde (vocals) and Pontus Lundin (synth effects). The album actually sounds a bit better than the MCD, but it unfortunately doesn't say much.

2006 MCD - UER 016

2006 ■ I en svunnen tid..MCD 6tr   Unexploded Records ....UER 016
    Tracks: Galdurkonst Och Tusenskrönor (intro)/Dansa Den Ondes Vals/Lindormen/Folksagan/Legenden Om Bergaskatten/När Allt Tystnar. 500 copies.
2011 ■ VITTERLAND..CD   Unexploded Records ....UER 042

2011 CD - UER 042

SKELLINGTON

Jac Rytterholm: v, Joakim Norlander: g, Göran "Guru" Lundgren: g,
Tommy "Jee" Jansson: b, Niklas Öberg: d

Stockholm - The band was formed in 2000 and recorded their first demo, *First Blood, First Demo*, in 2001. At the time the band also featured Bo "Chaq Mol" Karlsson (*Dark Funeral, Mordichrist*). The also did a cover of *Kiss*' *Love Gun*, in Swedish... and with slightly different lyrics, entitled *Stor Kuk* (means "big cock"). In 2004 the band's line-up featured Jac, Göran, Tommy and Andy, and a second demo was recorded. As they wanted to go heavier and darker they drafted second guitarist Jocke and recorded the demo-CD *Demo Diablo*, now sounding more like a bastard child of *Motörhead* and *Mustasch*. Heavy, raunchy and brutal, but still with a melodic touch. On *Professional Anger* drummer Niklas Öberg had replaced Andy K. *Website: www.skellington.org*

2007 CD - BGR-SYCECD 1001   2011 MCD - FILMALIZECD-1002

2006 ☐ Demo Diablo ....MCD 3tr   Syce Enterprises...- -
    Tracks: Ghost/The Unholy/Open The Gate
2007 ■ LAST HUMAN STANDING..CD   BGR ....BGR-SYCECD 1001
2011 ■ Professional Anger..MCD 5tr   Filmalize International...... FILMALIZECD-1002
    Tracks: Professional Anger/Bury My Bones, Bury My Spirit/The Lucifer Files/No One Is Safe/This Damned Love

SKILLER

David "Dave" Sundbom: v, Niclas "Nickrock" Gustafsson: g, Joni Laine: g,
Rikard "Ritchi" Swahn: b, Sebastian "Dihm Rust" Swahn: d

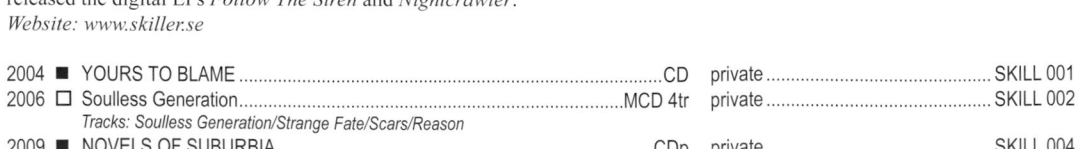

Täby (Stockholm) - *Skiller* were formed in 2003 to "get chicks". The band says they have forged the influences from death metal, hardcore and rock 'n roll, and that sort of makes sense. They sound a bit like if you'd mix *The Haunted*, *Killswitch Engage* and *Disturbed*. They have also released the digital EPs *Follow The Siren* and *Nightcrawler*. *Website: www.skiller.se*

2004 CD - SKILL 001

2004 ■ YOURS TO BLAME ....CD   private ....SKILL 001
2006 ☐ Soulless Generation..MCD 4tr   private ....SKILL 002
    Tracks: Soulless Generation/Strange Fate/Scars/Reason
2009 ■ NOVELS OF SUBURBIA ....CDp   private ....SKILL 004

SKIN INFECTION

David Andersson: v/g, Johan Mellryd: g, Andreas Fäldt: b, Petter Flemberg: d

Vänersborg - *Skin Infection* were created in the spring/summer of 2004 by David Andersson, influenced by the Norwegian black metal scene. The lyrics were however dealing more with sci-fi, sarcasms and dark futuristic pictures, than the classic black metal themes. David recorded the first demo, *Pale Darkness, Dim Lights*, set up a web page and was spotted by Petter Flemberg

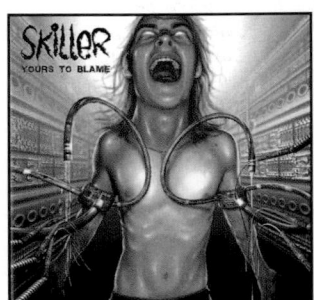

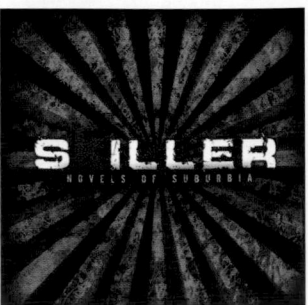

2009 CDp - SKILL 004

who suggested they should team up. They drafted bass player Jerker Johansson and guitarist Jonas Hygren, both in Vänersborg based band **Sacrifice**. After one rehearsal Jonas was out, temporarily replaced by Erik Andersson (**Shattered**), but finally replaced by Johan Mellryd in late spring 2005. Now Jerker was replaced by the aforementioned Erik Andersson, on bass. In the spring of 2006 Andreas Fält (**Sacrifice**, later **Snakestate**) replaced Erik and in the summer of 2006 the band recorded a four track demo. In 2007 they recorded their first self-financed CD, and in 2008 they began recording the follow-up, *Retribution*. The album however didn't see the light of day until February 2010. The album features guest spots from bassist Anders Backelin (who also produced the album), singer Thomas Backelin and former guitarist Jonas Hygren. Andreas and David are also found in death metal band **Them**, together with Backelin-brother Micke. **Skin Infection** plays simple, straightforward death metal.

2007 ☐ NIGHTMARES IN FROZEN SLEEP ....CD private .... - -
2010 ■ RETRIBUTION...CD Undead Propaganda.......................UPCD 003

2010 CD - UPCD 003

SKINFECTED

Fredrik Petersson: v, Joakim Jonsson: g, Andreas Johansson: g,
Daniel Johansson: b, Andreas Edmark: d

Västerås - The band was formed in 1989 under the name **Obnoxious**, under which name they recorded three demos. In 1994 Joakim joined and they changed it to **Side Effects**. Drummer Andeas Hermansson left to join **The Mist Of Avalon** and was replaced by Edmark. They released their first demo under the name **Skinfected** in 1998, entitled *Addicted To Hate*. In November 2002 Joakim (**The Mist Of Avalon, Dust, Mornaland, Autumn Dweller**) left the band. **Skinfected** plays death metal in the vein of early **Entombed**, quite up-tempo, straightforward, brutal vocals and a good, fat sound.
Website: www.skinfected.com

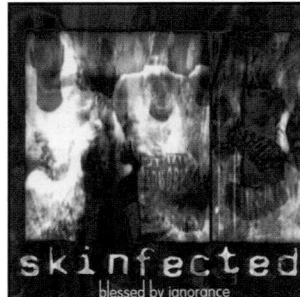

2001 MCD - 003

2001 ■ Blessed By Ignorance ....MCD 6tr King Size..003
   Tracks: Illusions Of Truth/Only Vindictiveness Remains/Addicted To Hate/Sublevels
   Within/Master Of All Lies/The Frame

SKINNY HORSE

Christer Göransson: v, Jerker Edman: g, Magnus Danneblad: g,
Christer Carlsson: g, Mats Johansson: d

Linköping - **Skinny Horse** are a really high-class sleaze-rocking hard rock band in the vein of **Nasty Idols**, but without the characteristic squeaky sleaze vocals. This is actually the band **Mindless** with the addition of Christer Carlsson and former **Axewitch** drummer Mats.

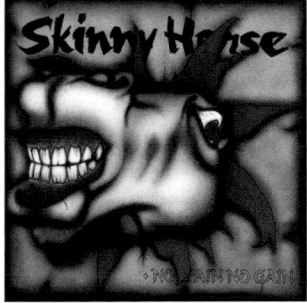

1993 ■ NO PAIN NO GAIN ....CD Delta ....DELCD 6456781

1993 CD - DELCD 6456781

SKINTRADE

Matti Alfonzetti: v, George Bravo: g, Stefan Bergström: g,
Håkan Calmroth: b, Håkan "Måsen" Persson: d

Stockholm - Matti (whose last name was initially Hohilla, after his mother) has been in several interesting constellations and recorded a well acclaimed album with **Bam Bam Boys**, which was however not released until the new century. He later joined UK-band **Jagged Edge** and was at one time member of **Scott Gorham's Western Front**. He returned to Sweden and recorded a great demo with **Talisman**. However, he wanted to get into a heavier band and got in touch with George who had a melodic but heavy hard rock band called **Erratic Tale**. They changed their name to **Skintrade** before Matti joined they recorded an eight track demo, but the style was still melodic Americanised hard rock. At the time the band featured drummer Jonas Östman (**Glory, Mental Hippie Blood, Yngwie, Gotham City**). The line-up then changed and George wrote another bunch of heavy riffing songs more towards more in the vein of US-style power metal. Now they recorded the highly acclaimed debut with slight **Pantera** influences, but more melodic vocals and a bit more varied musically. Renowned death metal producer Tomas Skogsberg produced the second album and the style is even heavier, with more influences of early **Alice In Chains**, but still with more variation. Truly a killer album with awesome tracks like *Can You Spin Me?* and *Motorman*. Late 1995 the band was dropped by Polar. Matti and Stefan also left the band to pursue careers in different musical directions. In 1996 the remains recruited George's brother Francis on vocals and the band was reformed into **Roachpowder**, under which name they recorded two albums. In 2011 **Skintrade** reformed and recorded three new songs (*Falling To Pieces, Back The Hell Up* and *Little Baby*), featured on the compilation *Past And Present*. Matti has also recorded with **Damned Nation, Alfonzetti** and is today in UK band **Red White & Blues** plus Swedish melodic hard rockers **Impera**.

1993 CDS - 859 390-2

1993 CDS - 861 880-2

1993 ■ One By One/Una Tras Otra ....CDS 2tr Polar 859 390-2
   Una Tras Otra is One By One sung in Spanish.

1993 ■	Sick As A Dog/Speak The Truth	CDS 2tr	Polar	861 880-2
1993 □	Sick As A Dog/Speak The Truth/Loco	MCD 3tr	Polar	861 881-2

Loco is the song Sick As A Dog sung in Spanish.

1993 □	SKINTRADE	CD	Polar	519 157-2
1993 □	SKINTRADE	CD	Polydor K.K (Japan)	POCP-9032
1993 □	Soul Sister	MCD 4tr	Polar	859 273-3

Contains the song Soul Sister in 4 versions: Radio re-mix/12" re-mix/12" re-mix instrumental/album version

1994 ■	Fear/Null And Void/War	MCD 3tr	Polar	853 019-2
1995 □	Snap Goes Your Mind	MCD 3tr	Polar	851 443-2

Tracks: Snap Goes Your Mind (edited version)/Can You Spin Me?/Snap Goes Your Mind (album version)

1995 □	ROACHPOWDER	CD	Polar	527 168-2
1995 □	Flies/Silence/Fear (1995 version)	MCD 3tr	Polar	851 445-2
1995 □	SKINTRADE	CD	Polydor K.K. (Japan)	POCP-1389
2011 □	PAST AND PRESENT	CD	Universal	0602527-97073

1994 MCD 3tr - 853 019-2

SKITARG

**Per "Barnet" Rinaldo: v, Daniel "Necrophilip" Lundgren: v, Bob Skurk: g,
Tapio "Doc Tyr" Mäntyranta: g, Niklas "Don Foster" Skogqvist: b,
Sebastian "Kprl. Sigge Hall" Sundqvist: d**

Haninge (Stockholm) - Skitark (means "pissed off") were formed in 2005 when singers Barnet and Necrofilip drank beer in the sunshine, listening to evil black metal. They came up with the idea of forming a recording project, since they wanted to scream their lungs out. The first demo, *Du har keps och knarkar* (You have a cap and do drugs) was recorded with just the two of them. When offers for shows started coming, they drafted people from bands like **Decadencem**, **Sterbhaus**, **The Ugly** and six weeks later they were on stage. The band features clowns in diapers fighting with dildos on stage, extremely silly, but still the band sounds really good. The band calls their style "clown metal". Melodic extreme metal sounding a bit like a mix of **The Haunted**, **The Kristet Utseende** and Bozo The Clown on acid. Lundgren is also in **Sterbhaus**, **Head** and **Septic Boys**. Reinaldo is fronting **The Ugly**, **Painted Devil** and **The Super Orchestra**, while Skogqvist has played guitar in **Decadence** and drums in **Sterbhaus**. On the second album guitarist Jimmy "Mattanten" Ahovalli was replaced by Tapio "Doc Tyr" Mäntyranta (**Kill The Parish**), who has filled in for Mattanten and Bob Skurk before. Bob Skurk has also been replaced by Björn "Varulf" Svensson (**Kill The Parish**). Joakim Antman (**Decadence**) has filled in on bass live. Early 2013 Rinaldo handed in his resignation. The members actually do seem to vary between gigs, so who's actually IN the band, who knows? The digital single *K.E.P.A* was released in 2013.

2011 CD - ARG 002

2010 CD - ARG 001

2010 ■	SKITARG	CD	Ovis Records	ARG 001
2011 ■	DEN HÅRDASTE JÄVELN	CD	private	ARG 002

SKOGEN

Joakim Svensson: v/g/b, Mathias Nilsson: v/g/b/k

Växjö - Skogen (the forest) play atmospheric black metal, old-school sound and style, but at the same time quite melodic and with acoustic parts, mixed clean and growl vocals. A bit similar to **Primordial** and **Ulver**. Nilsson is ex-**Entrails**, **Mindcollapse** and **Danger** (Växjö).

2009 ■	VITTRA	CD	Frostscald	FS38/hammer14
2011 ■	SVITJOD	CD	Frostscald	FS55/hammer22
2012 □	ELD	CD	Frostscald	FS60

2009 CD - FS38/hammer14

2011 CD - FS55/hammer22

SKOGEN BRINNER

Jesper Aronsson: v, David Forsberg: g, Joel Carnstam: b, Jonathan Eriksson: d

Linköping - Skogen Brinner means "the forest is burning". Great retro hard rock sounding a bit like an updated **November** with a touch of **Black Sabbath**. Vocals in Swedish.
Website: http://skogenbrinner.tumblr.com/

2011 ■	Pundarvarning/Svarta skuggor	7"	Gaphals	GAP 006
2013 □	1ST	LP	Subliminal Sounds	SUB-096-LP

200 clear, 200 red, 600 black vinyl.

2013 □	1ST	CD	Subliminal Sounds	SUB-097-CD

2011 7" - GAP 006

SKOGMAN, THORE aka THORE GOES METAL

**Thore Skogman: v, Jonny Reinholm: g, Stefan Karlsson: g, Ulrik Seppänen: g,
Fredrik Ljunge: g, Mic Micaeli: k, John Levén: b, Ian Haugland: d**

Hallstahammar/Stockholm - So, how is this one to be judged? Thore Skogman is sort of the Swedish equivalent of Paul Anka. Kool Kat Club owner Ludde Lindström came up with the clever idea of making hard rock versions of his old songs with the original (60+) singer as the

main artist. The musicians include **Europe** members Haugland, Levén and Micaeli, **Shock Tilt** guitarist Reinholm etc plus backing vocals by Zia Lindberg and Jan Johansen. Good? Funny? Well, maybe if you're Swedish and know the background. *Thore Goes Metal* is a re-mastered re-issue of *Än är det drag* (there's still action) but with a new, more sellable cover and title, released after Thore passed away. For collectors only.

1997 ☐ ÄN ÄR DET DRAG	CD	Music On Line	MOLCD 005
1997 ☐ Dalarock/Fröken Fräken	CDS 2tr	Music On Line	MOLCDS 006
2008 ■ THORE GOES METAL	CD	Rockklassiker	RK 1067

2008 CDd - RK 1067

SKOLD

Tim Sköld: v/g/b

Skövde/Seattle - Tim, born in 1966, is ex-**Kingpin/Shotgun Messiah**. His solo project is in the vein of his former band's last album, **Violent New Breed**. He was also part of German industrial band **KMFDM** and joined **Marilyn Manson** in 2002, with whom he played until 2008. The 2009 album is a collaboration between **Skold** and **KMFDM**. Unfortunately he has been very anonymous in his home country. Paul DeCarli has been handling drums and programming and Neil Taylor did some drumming, but on *Anomie* Tim handled everything himself. In 2011 he joined the band **Doctor Midnight & The Mercy Cult**, featuring **Turbonegro** singer Hank von Helvete.

1995 ☐ Chaos/Neverland (radio edit)	CDS	RCA	RDJ 64613-2
Promo.			
1995 ☐ Neverland	MCD 7tr	RCA	RDJ 64547-2
Tracks: Neverland (edit)/Anything/All Dies/Neverland (Fuzzy Klub Mix I)/Neverland (Fuzzy Klub Mix II)/Anything (Dominatrix mix)/Remember (Dominatrix mix)			
1995 ☐ Neverland	MLP 7tr	RCA	RDAB 64547-1
1995 ☐ Neverland (Remix)/Neverland (LP)	CDS 7tr	RCA	RDJ 64614-2
Promo.			
1996 ☐ SKOLD	CD	RCA	7863-66579-2
1996 ☐ SKOLD	CDd	RCA	RADV-66579-2
1996 ☐ All Dies	CDS	BMG (promo only)	n/a
2009 ■ SKOLD VS. KMFDM	CD	KMFDM Records	KMFDM 029
2009 ☐ SKOLD VS. KMFDM	2LP	KMFDM Records	KMFDM 029
2011 ☐ ANOMIE	CD	Metropolis (USA)	MET 710
2011 ☐ ANOMIE	CD	Dependent/Mindbase	MIND 184
2011 ■ Suck	MCD 8tr	Metropolis	MET 705
Tracks: Suck/Suck (Suck And Mop Up)/Suck (Down On Your Knees)/Suck (Gag It And Tag It)/Suck (My Glock)/I Will Not Forget/Dark Star/Bullets Riccochet			

2009 CD - KMFDM 029

2011 MCD - MET 705

SKOOG, KENNETH

Kenneth Skoog: g/b/k/d

Malmö - Kenneth, born in 1958, studied at the Malmö Institute of Jazz and at MI in Los Angeles. He also played with bands like **Force Majeure**, **Pharamond** and **Touché**. He made his debut single already in 1980 and 13 years later, he released his first instrumental solo album, recorded between 1987-1993. The music is definitely hard rock and even metal at times, instrumental, and very guitar-dominated of course. Kenneth is not really a shredder in the Vai/Satriani sense, but more of a retro melodic player. Decent.

1980 ☐ Moonlight Fantasies/Mechanic Del	7"	Spasmograf	SPAS 00180
1993 ■ DEFLAGRATION	CD	Spektragram	SRCD-001

1993 CD - SRCD-001

SKRÆCKŒDLAN

Robert Lamu: v/g, Henrik Grüttner: g, Tim Ängström: b, Martin Larsson: d

Norrköping - Sweden has produced quite a range of great retro heavy rock bands, *Skrœckœdlan* (Swedish spelling Skräcködlan) being one new great contestant. The band was formed in 2009. In 2010 they released their first EP, *Flykten från Tellus*, which was only sold at gigs. In the summer of 2010 they released their second, only digital, EP *Världarnas fall*. These were later released on cassette. The demos and album were produced by Oskar Cedermalm (*Truckfighters*). A "skräcködla" is a giant, terrifying reptile/lizard/dinosaur. *Mesozoikum* is a vinyl containing the band's first demo and one exclusive track. Well worth checking out for retro fans.
Website: www.skraeckoedlan.com

2010 ☐ Flykten från Tellus	MCD 5tr	private	- -
Tracks: Skräcködlan/Från havet dom kommer/Kaktus Galaxus/Kampen om Tellus/ Sabeltand			
2011 ☐ ÄPPELTRÄDET	CD	Transubstans	TRANS 081
2012 ■ ÄPPELTRÄDET	LP	Transubstans	TRANSV 07
Different artwork.			
2012 ☐ MESOZOIKUM	LP	Walking Lizzy	WL 002
480 copies.			

2012 LP - TRANSV 07

SKUA

Daniel Lind: v/g, Martin Lind: b, Linus Fransson: d

Stockholm - Formed in the autumn of 1998 by Daniel and Linus. On the split, one of the tracks was taken from the band's February 1999 demo *Barracuda*, while the other three were of the third June 1999 demo *The Lotion*. Quite groovy untraditional low-fi stoner. Similar to **Kyuss**. An album entitled *The Trojan Camel* was planned for 2003, but nothing happened.

2001 ■ SKUA/GENEROUS MARIA (split)..CD   Alone/Custom Heavy ....AR 002
    Split with Generous Maria. Tracks: Swirl/Spittin'/Blue Temple/Nitro's Low

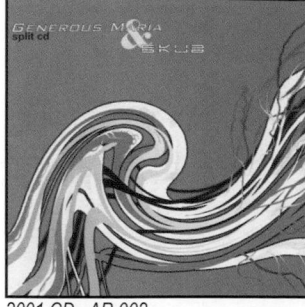

2001 CD - AR 002

SKUGGAN

E "Skuggan" Lundberg: v/g/b/d

Västra Götaland - Cold, raw, high-speed black metal with the odd ambient part. Screeching vocals, sometimes recorded backwards. Similar to **Arckanum**. **Skuggan** means "the shadow".

2013 ■ KEJSAREN AV ETT SVART RIKE ....CD   Ewiges Eis Records..........................EER 053
    500 copies.

2013 CD - EER 053

SKULL PARADE

Erik Anell: v, Magnus Högdahl: g, Magnus Lind: b, Jens Ericson: d

Göteborg - In the beginning of 2009, when **Street Stones** came to an end, Högdahl (ex-**Black Dog, Lizette**) and Lind (ex-**Calilio, Treasure Land, Blue Balls**) decided to form a new unit. They drafted former **Art Rebellion** singer Anell and drummer Mattias Warneflo and named the band **Skull Parade**. Late 2010, Warneflo left the band and after a few months Ericson filled the spot. The band plays excellent post-grunge oriented heavy riff oriented hard rock with Anell's rough edged vocals giving the music a nice touch.
Website: www.skullparade.com

2012 ■ First Four...MCDp 5tr   4 4 Skull Records......................................- -
    Tracks: Killing For Love/The Way We Die/I Rise For No One/Below Hell/I Rise For No One (Radio edit)

2012 MCDp - - -

SKY HIGH (CLAS YNGSTRÖM &)

Clas Yngström: v/g, Ulf "Rockis" Ivarsson: b, James Bradley Jr: d

Falun - This is more or less a band built around the great singer/guitarist Clas Yngström. Before **Sky High** he was in the fusion band **Soffgruppen**, but in March 1979 the band's first release saw the light of day. It was a single with two Hendrix covers, a rarity today. The band then consisted of Clas, Ulf Åhman - drums and Hasse Olausson - bass. The band's self-released debut album was released the year after. Clas has always been considered Sweden's answer to Jimi Hendrix and several of his albums contain Hendrix covers. The debut is sung in Swedish while the other albums are in English. On the debut album Clas was flanked by bassist Börje Olevald and drummer Ulf Åhman (later in **Bite**), while on *Still Rockin'* Åman had been replaced by Kim Gabrielsson. These two albums are semi-heavy blues rock of great quality though. *Freezin' Hot* showed a heavier, yet more commercial side of **Sky High**, quite similar to what **ZZ Top** did at the time mixed with heavy Hendrixy vibes. The album featured Arne Blomqvist on bass (later **Bite**) and Mats Östensson on drums. *Humanizer* saw more changes, where the line-up featured singer Louise Hoffsten, bassist Markus Aldén (**Mojobone**), keyboardist Olle Nyberg and drummer Marcus Källström (**Stonecake, Six Feet Under**). This album also shows an even more commercial side of the band, a bit like **ZZ Top**'s *Eliminator*. *Have Guitar Will Travel* featured Mija and Margaretha Folkesson on vocals, bassist Ross Valory (**Journey**), drummer Prairie Prince (**The Tubes**), Norton Buffalo (**Steve Miller Band**) on harmonica and Tim Gorman (**The Who, Rolling Stones**) on piano. In my opinion Sky High's weakest effort so far. Quite slick commercial hard rock blues. *Safe Sex* was a live album featuring former members Arne Blomquist and Ulf Åhman. This is sheer **Sky High** live power, no holds barred. Hendrix-mania at full throttle! **Sky High** has always been a very active live band and after the live album they toured extensively. They didn't start recording the new album until in 1994. *Fuzzface*, released in 1996, was again back to a heavier edge, featuring bassist Ulf "Rockis" Ivarsson and drummer Christer Björklund. Clas has also produced bands like **Blues Bag, Illbatta Boogie Band** and played on albums by for example **Sator** and **Mountain Of Power**. The two first albums were reissued on CD in 1995. The Hendrix cover *Voodoo Chile* can be found on the compilation *Big Deal!* (1990 Last Buzz). In 1995 he also did a cover of *Supernatural* on the Peter Green tribute *Rattlesnake Guitar*. *Fat Guitar* is the first real solo release from "Mr. Sky High", although since *Have Guitar Will Travel*, the albums have been released under the **Clas Yngström & Sky High** moniker. Fans of Clas previous material won't be disappointed as the album is filled with heavy Yngström-riffing. The bass work was handled by Kenny Aaronson (**Derringer, Dust, Axis**) and the drums by Andy Bigan. Mary Wilson (ex-**Supremes**) guests on vocals and Joy Askew on keyboards. *Purple Haze* was recorded under the name **Clas Yngström's Big Band Experience** and contains Hendrix covers played with a power-trio and a big band with a horn section and the works. Interesting collaboration, some might think. *Highlights* features one CD with

Have band, will travel

previously unreleased material. Per Wiberg from **Death Organ**, **Mojobone**, **Opeth**, **Spiritual Beggars** is guesting on *Bluester*, which carries on the tradition of *Fat Guitar*. *Freedom* was an album featuring live in the studio re-recordings of old tracks. Raw, heavy and brutal. The line-up featured Clas, Arne and drummer Mats Östensson with Thomas Larsson making guest appearances on two tracks. An outstanding album. The album *Live In Stockholm – Tribute To Hendrix*, was released as **Clas Yngström Trio** but features **Sky High** members Klas Hägglund on bass and Ulf Åhman on drums, plus gest appearances from singer Petra Kvännå and bassist Tomas Thorberg (**Plankton**, **Snakes In Paradise** etc). The album contains Hendrix covers only, played in a really heavy and powerful way, live. *Soul Survivor* was an interesting album, fourteen new tracks recorded live, also featuring a horn section and female power package Petra Kvännå on additional vocals. *25 Years Of Madness* was an anniversary album with one best of CD and one CD featuring covers of Hendrix, Vaughan, Clapton etc. *Download* was one of the band's heaviest efforts, featuring some pretty brutal riffing. The line-up had again changed, now featuring Clas, old comrade Ulf "Rockis" Ivarsson on bass and new drummer James Bradley Jr.

1979 7" - SB 103

1980 7" - SB 111

1985 LP - MRLP 3003

1986 MLP - MRCX 122157

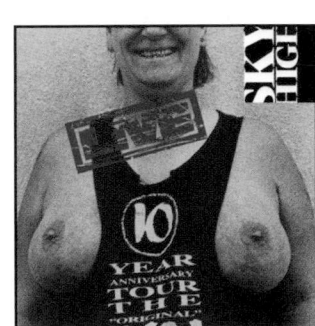

1990 LP - PLP 90101

1999 CD - BLCD 21

Year		Title	Format	Label	Cat No
1979	■	Red House/Stone Free	7"	Sista Bussen	SB 103
1980	■	Säj Nej... Till Kärnkraft/Säj Ja... Till Livet	7"	Sista Bussen	SB 111
		1500 copies.			
1980	□	Sommarvindar/Bidin´ My Time	7"	Good Vibes	GVS-01
1980	□	SKY HIGH	LP	Good Vibes	GV 001
1980	□	STILL ROCKIN'	LP	Good Vibes	GV 002
1983	□	I'll Play The Blues For You/Treat Me Right	7"	Mega	MRCS 2157
1985	■	FREEZIN' HOT	LP	Mega	MRLP 3003
1985	□	FREEZIN' HOT	LP	Pike	PLP 8541
1985	□	FREEZIN' HOT	CD	Pike	PCD 8541
1985	□	I Ain't Beggin'/You Got Me Hooked	7"	Mega	MRCS 2079
1985	□	I Ain't Beggin'/You Got Me Hooked/I Ain't Beggin'	MLP 3tr	Mega	MRCX 2079
1986	□	I'll Play The Blues For You/Treat Me Right	7"	Mega	MRCS 2157
1986	■	I'll Play The Blues For You/I'll Play...(remix)/Treat Me Right	MLP 3tr	Mega	MRCX 122157
1987	□	HUMANIZER	LP	Pike	PLP 8751
1987	□	HUMANIZER	CD	Pike	PCD 8751
1987	□	HUMANIZER	LP	Mega	MRLP 3056
1987	□	Tune Me To Your Station/Dreams	7"	Mega	MRCS 2202
1987	□	Don't Move/Back To The Start	7"	Mega	MRCS 122235
1987	□	Don't Move/(remix)/Back To The Start	MLP 3tr	Mega	MRCX 122235
1987	□	HUMANIZER	LP	PM Records (Spain)	PM 39350005
1989	□	HAVE GUITAR WILL TRAVEL	LP	Pike	PLP 8981
1989	□	HAVE GUITAR WILL TRAVEL	CD	Pike	PCD 8981
1989	□	Get Out Stay Out/Hero	7"	Pike	PS-8911
1989	□	Macho Woman/Jimi	7"	Pike	PS-8961
1990	■	SAFE SEX	LP	Pike	PLP 90101
1990	□	SAFE SEX	CD	Pike	PCD 90101
1995	□	Flower Child/Hold That Note	CDS 2tr	Mega	MRCDS 2700
1995	□	FUZZFACE	LP	Mega	MRLP 3273
1995	□	FUZZFACE	CD	Mega	MRCD 3273
1995	□	Shake Up The House	MCD 3tr	Mega	MRCDS 2718
		Tracks Shake Up The House/Shake Y Pants Mix/Freddie's Shuffle			
1996	□	FAT GUITAR	CD	Borderline	BLCD 11
1998	□	PURPLE HAZE	CD	Last Buzz	BUZZ-8008
		As Clas Yngström & Big Band Experience. Hendrix covers only.			
1998	□	HIGHLIGHTS 1978-1998	2CD	Borderline	BLCD 20
1999	■	BLUESTER	CD	Borderline	BLCD 21
2002	□	FREEDOM	CD	Grooveyard Records	GYR 007
2003	□	Let's Go Crazy	MCD 3tr	Virgin Records	7243 547129 2
		Tracks: Let's Go Crazy/Bad Moon Rising (CCR cover)/The House Is Rockin' (SRV cover)			
2003	□	Can You Forgive Her/Freedom For The Stallion	CDS	Virgin Records	7243 547233 2
2003	□	ON THE COVER - 25 YEARS OF MADNESS	2CD	Virgin Records	7243 581776 2
2004	□	LIVE IN STOCKHOLM – TRIBUTE TO HENDRIX	CD	Grooveyard Records	GYR 011
		Released as Clas Yngstrom Trio.			
2004	□	SOUL SURVIVOR	CD	Virgin Records	7243 473524 2
2005	□	SKY HIGH	CD	Virgin Records	131398 2
		Bonus: Säj ja (till livet/Säj nej (till kärnkraft)/Red House (Hendrix cover)/Voodoo Chile (Hendrix cover)/Little Wing (Hendrix cover)			
2005	□	STILL ROCKIN'	CD	Virgin Records	131674 2
		Bonus: Ramblin' On My Mind/Autumn City Nights/On The Outside Blues/We Ain't Getting' Old			
2005	□	FREEZIN' HOT	CD	Virgin Records	131390 2
		Bonus: I'll Play The Blues For You/Evil Eye/I Want You/Don't Turn Your Back On Me/I Ain't Beggin'/I'll Play The Blues For You/I Ain't Beggin'			
2005	□	HAVE GUITAR WILL TRAVEL	CD	Virgin Records	131391 2
		Bonus: Heavenst/I Sold Your Soul/Mistreated/Blues For The Green			
2005	□	SAFE SEX	CD	Virgin Records	131663 2
		Bonus: Foxy Lady (Hendrix cover)/You Got Me Hooked/Lilla flicka nig å kuta runt.			
2005	□	HUMANIZER	CD	Virgin Records	131673 2

| 2005 ☐ FUZZFACE | CD | Virgin Records | 131392 2 |

Bonus: Once Again/Flowercild/Emptyvision

| 2005 ☐ SKY HIGH | CD | Grooveyard Records | GYR 014 |

Bonus: Hoochie Coochie Man (live)/Fire (live)/Voodoo Chile (demo) (Hendrix cover)

| 2005 ☐ STILL ROCKIN' | CD | Grooveyard Records | GYR 015 |

Bonus: I'm Still Rockin'/On The Outside Blues/Harding Working Man/Danger In The Night/
Autumn City Nights/Love Your Life/Ramblin' On My Mind. All demos. New artwork.

| 2008 ■ DOWNLOAD | CD | Pike | PCD 811 |

2008 CD - PCD 811

SKY OF RAGE

**Staffan Carlsson: v, Joachim Nordlund: g, Janne Cederlund: g,
Mika Itäranta: b, Tomas Friberg: d**

Borlänge - **Sky Of Rage** were formed by **Astral Doors** guitarist Nordlund and drummer Friberg in 2000. They started writing songs together and soon brought in singer Carlsson. They continued writing songs and in 2010 former **Thalamus** guitarist Cederlund joined. After a year, former **Astral Doors** colleague Itäranta completed the band. The debut album was mixed by another former **Astral Doors** members, Martin Haglund. **Sky Of Rage** plays great, classic heavy and quite melodic (not cheesy) metal/power metal with a heavy edge, a bit similar to **Morgana Lefay**-meet-**Cloudscape**. In September 2012 Staffan was replaced by Tony Josefsson.

| 2012 ■ SOR | CDd | Metalville | MV 0033 |

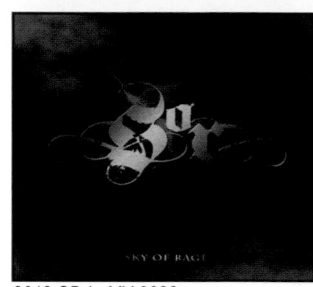

2012 CDd - MV 0033

SKYDIVERSE

Tobbe Damberg: v/g, Jocke Åberg: g, Jonas Eriksson: b, Micke Öster: d

Gävle - Basic melodic hard rock with vocals in Swedish. Sounds a bit like **Motvind** in their heavier moments. After the single, Tobbe and Jocke left. The others continued under the name **Ramlösa**. In 1984 Tobbe and Jocke formed the band **Wang Dang** with whom they recorded some good demos. Tobbe was later in **Zircus** and cover band **Midnight Express**.

| 1982 ■ Ännu Ett Liv/Rör Mig | 7" | private | SRS-001 |

1982 7" - SRS-001

SKYFIRE

**Joakim Karlsson: v, Andreas Edlund: g/k, Johan Reinholdz: g,
Martin Hanner: b, Joakim Jonsson: d**

Höör - The band was formed in 1995 and the line-up on the first MCD featured Martin Hanner, bass player Jonas Sjögren, drummer Tobias Björk, guitarist Andreas Edlund and guest singer Mattias Holmgren (**Embracing, Naglfar**). Henrik Wenngren took on the vocal task shortly after. In 1999 they recorded another 3-track demo entitled *The Final Story* and in August 2000 they entered Abyss Studios with producer Tommy Tägtgren to record their debut. Before *Mind Revolution* drummer Joakim Jonsson replaced Tobias Björk. In 2004 the band released a digital-only four-track EP entitled *Fractal*. The line-up had again changed seeing singer Wenngren replaced by Joakim Karlsson (**Mark:Black**), guitarist Johan Reinholdz (**Andromeda, Nonexist** etc) added on guitar, guitarist Hanner had switched to bass and bass player Jonas Sjögren was out. *Esoteric* was produced by Jonas Kjellgren (**Scar Symmetry**). Musically the band produces quite technical, semi-progressive metal with a neoclassical touch. Add to this traditional non-melodic, screeching death-style vocals. Imagine a mix of **Dark Funeral** and **Rhapsody In Fire**. A great band, with great melodies. Wenngren also sings in the bands **Mornaland** and **Dust**. Jonsson is also in the latter. In 2010 the band also released the digital only album *Fractal*.

2001 CD - HHR 062

| 1998 ☐ Within Reach | MCD 3tr | private | - - |

Tracks: Within Reach/Faces/Open Flower

2001 ■ TIMELESS DEPARTURE	CD	Hammerheart	HHR 062
2001 ☐ TIMELESS DEPARTURE	LP	Hammerheart	HHR 062LP
2001 ☐ TIMELESS DEPARTURE	CD	King Records (Japan)	KICP 821

Bonus: The Final Story (demo)/Skyfire (demo)/By God Forsaken (demo)

| 2003 ■ Haunted By Shadows | MCD 6tr | Hammerheart | HHR 156 |

Tracks: Haunted By Shadows/The Universe Unveils/The Final Story/Skyfire/By God
Forsaken/Free From Torment

| 2003 ☐ MIND REVOLUTION | CD | Hammerheart | HHR 096 |
| 2003 ☐ MIND REVOLUTION | CD | King Records (Japan) | KICP 924 |

Bonus: Free From Torment

| 2003 ☐ MIND REVOLUTION | CD | Dope Entertainment (Korea) | DE 17008 |

Bonus: The Final Story/Skyfire (demo)/By God Forsaken (demo)/Free From Torment

2004 ■ SPECTRAL	CD	Arise	056 CD
2004 ☐ SPECTRAL	CD	CD-Maximum (Russia)	CDM 0704-1922
2004 ☐ SPECTRAL	CD	King Records (Japan)	KICP-1008

Bonus: Skyfire (live)

| 2004 ☐ SPECTRAL | CD | Dope Entertainment (Korea) | DE 17022 |

Bonus:Patterns/Skyfire (live)/Mind Revolution (live)

| 2009 ■ ESOTERIC | CD | Pivotal Rockorddings | PR 005 |

Bonus: Within Reach (demo)

2003 MCD - HHR 156

2004 CD - 056 CD

SKYMNING

Robert "An-ti-christ" Tyborn Axt: v/g/b, Johannes "Architect" Åberg: g,
Stefan "The Mechanic" Lundberg: b, Ola "Machine" Lundberg: d

Alingsås - The band started in 1996 in a traditional death metal vein. *Skymning* is the Swedish word for dusk. The original line-up featured Ola, Johannes, bassist Sebastian Aronsson, singer Kim Andreasson and guitarist Christian Åkerberg (ex-***Throne Of Pagan***). Åkerberg left in 1997. They recorded the first demo in 1998 and were signed by Invasion Records. The style was thrash-oriented death metal. The band also recorded the demo *At The Fields Of Megiddo* in 1999. On this demo Robert (ex-***Immersed In Blood***) had been added on guitar. After the demo Kim was sacked and Robert took over the vocals. *Stormchoirs* was produced by Andy La Rocque. When Invasion went belly up they recorded a new demo in search of a new label. They changed their style and Sebastian was also given the boot. The second album shows a more industrial side of the band, like a mix of the first album and ***Pain*** or ***Deathstars***. After the second album was recorded former ***Immersed In Blood*** bass player Stefan Lundberg took over the bass duties. On *Machina Genova* the band was reinforced with singer "An-ti-christ". In 2006 he was again replaced by former ***Arise*** singer Erik Ljungkvist.

2009 CD - PR 005

1999 CD - IR 046

1999	■	STORMCHOIRS	CD	Invasion Records	IR 046
2002	□	STORMCHOIRS	CD	Blackend	BLACK 046 CD
2002	■	ARTIFICIAL SUPERNOVA	CD	Blackend	BLACK 035 CD
2004	□	MACHINA GENOVA	CD	Blackend	BLACK 067 CD

2002 CD - BLACK 035 CD

SKYWALKERS

Joakim Staaf-Sylsjö: v, Henrik Andersson: g, Johan Haglund: g,
Ragnar Larsson: b, Magnus Sivertsson: d

Östersund - Started under the name ***Clandestine*** playing punk, but later changed name and style. Pretty weird, but really good prog/hardcore/death with screeching vocals. Like a mix of ***Refused*** and ***Primus*** with lots of tempo-changes and breaks. Impossible to box in style-wise. Bass on the first MCD was played by Erik, although he was not in the line-up at the time. Joakim and Henrik have recorded several singles with hard core band ***Human Waste***.

2001	■	Dolor Sufrimiento Odio	MCD 5tr	New Noise/B-Head	NNR 002/BHR 003

Tracks: I Wanna Look Myself Inside/All Alone/ Stars And Dreams/Depression Is Not A Choice/It's All About Life

2001	□	Project: Revolution	7" EP	Mäskdunk	MDR 004

Split with 2 Years After. Green or blue vinyl and fabric-cover or paper cover.

2001 MCD - NNR 002/BHR 003

SKÅNSKA MORD

Jan Bengtsson: v/h, Patrik Berglin: g, Petter Englund: g,
Patric Carlsson: b, Thomas Jönsson: d

Örkelljunga - The name means Skånska murders (Skåne is a county in Sweden) and the name came from a TV series about murders in this region. The band was formed in 2006 as an amalgamation of the defunct bands ***Half Man*** and ***Mothercake***. Bengtsson and Carlsson brought the swampy side of ***Half Man*** and blended it with the more modern side of Jönsson, Berglin and Englund's ***Mothercake***. *Skånska Mord* plays killer riff-oriented, seventie-sounding hard rock with singer Bengtsson sounding a bit like Chris Cornell. I wouldn't call it stoner, but some may. Great band!

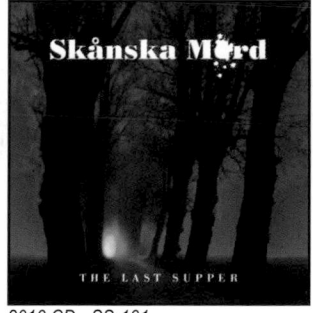
2010 CD - SS-101

2010	■	THE LAST SUPPER	CD	Small Stone	SS-101
2012	■	PATHS OF CHARON	CD	Small Stone	SS-131
2012	□	PATHS OF CHARON	LP	Small Stone	SS-131

150 black, 175 white marble and 175 grey marble vinyl.

2012 CD - SS-131

SLAM

Kenneth "Zone" Nordqvist: v, Thomas Björk: g, Uffe Westberg: g,
Pär Wahlquist: b, Tony Jansson: d

Gävle - *Slam* existed between 1982-1987, formed by five skaters who started up under the name ***Destroy***. They released their first demo in 1983 and their first LP *Ingens slav* in 1984, which was out and out punk. So was the first 7" EP *Welcome Home* (1985). They later adopted a way more hard rock-oriented sound. Up-tempo, straightforward punkish metal with a heavier touch. The band does consider themselves punk and have been featured on numerous punk compilations, but they have too many metal elements to be excluded from this book. Jansson later joined ***Mason***.

1987 LP - SR-007

1985 ☐ Tragedy/Dark World	7"	private	003
1987 ☐ END OF LAUGHTER	LP	Subcore	SR 1987
1987 ■ END OF LAUGHTER	LP	private	SR-007

SLAPDASH

Jens C. Mortensen: v, Magnus "Sudden" Söderman: g, Lars Lindén: g,
Fredrik Jacobsen: b, Jhonny "Bärget" Bergman: d

Västerås - Formerly known as *Rosicrucian*, but in 1996 they changed label to MNW Zone, name to *Slapdash* and singer to Jens (*Carnal Forge, Leech, Revolver*). Not only had these things changed, they had also become an even better unit, producing grade A metal. The *Sator*-cover *Heyday* also appears on the 1996 Backstage Magazine compilation-CD. The album features an incredibly heavy version of *En Vogue*'s *Free Your Mind*. Recommended. Bärget is today fronting his own combo *Man.Machine.Industry* (*MMI*), Söderman has later played in *Zeelion, Axenstar, Powerage* and *Atrocity*, Jacobsen in *Atrocity* and Lindén in *Leech, Carnal Forge* and *Headkillers*.

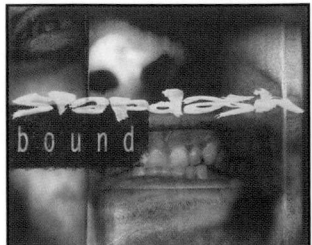

1996 MCD - MNWCDS 219

1996 CD - MNWCD 287

1996 ■ Bound	MCD 3tr	MNW Zone	MNWCDS 219

Tracks: Bound/Unfold/Kill Yourself (S.O.D cover). The two last tracks are non-CD.

1996 ■ 240.25 ACTUAL REALITY	CD	MNW Zone	MNWCD 287

SLEAZY JOE

Conny "Steven Sleaze" Andersson: v/g, Johan "Johnny Sleaze" Åberg: g,
Kim "Kim Sleaze" Turesson: b, Johan "Joe Sleaze" Vegna: d

Hässleholm - Formed in 2004. Good, solid, straightforward hard rock 'n roll in the same vein as *Backyard Babies*, but with another mile to walk before reaching their level, mainly in the vocal department. A live DVD was also recorded and released. The band fizzled out, but reunited in 2010, now featuring lead singer Christoffer "Chris Sleaze" Lohikoski Svensson, also lead singer of *Dirty Passion* and *Unquiet Eden*, plus new bass player Johannes Olsson. Shows good promise.

2007 MCDp - DPRCDM002-2

2007 ■ Rock Star	MCDp 4tr	Display Records	DPRCDM002-2

Tracks: Rock Star/Got Me Goin'/Get Away/Close Enough For Rock N' Roll

SLEAZY ROZE

Mikael Fredriksson: v, Mikael Qvist: g, Stefan Pettersson: b, Per-Olof Johansson: d

Linköping - A top-class powerful AOR band with great vocals, great heavy guitars and classy songs. Great production. Both singles are well worth searching for. Original guitarist Magnus Jarl left the band to join *Straight Up*, with whom he recorded two albums (one as yet unreleased). The band also has a track on the Belgian compilation *Metal Thunder* ('91). Singer Mikael has previously recorded a 7" with the band *Grand Vision* and is today also singing in a *Journey* cover band plus in *Big Hoss & The Animal*. In 1994 they signed to XTC Management and in 1995 they recorded the debut album *Caution! The Filling Is Hot*. On the album guitarist Magnus Jarl was replaced by Mikael and bass player Dennis Printz for Stefan.

1988 7" - CWC 036

1996 CD - SR 01

1988 ■ Only One/She's So Fine/Don't Feed The Animal	7" 3tr	CWC Records	CWC 036
1990 ☐ Caution! The Filling Is Hot	7" 3tr	private	037

Tracks: Hot Woman/Riding High/Snakeskin Boots

1996 ■ CAUTION! THE FILLING IS HOT	CD	private	SR 01

SLEEPING APE

Tomas Strand: v/g, Mats Andersson: b, Tony Fryklund: d

Arvika - A powerful three-piece that owes quite a lot to *Electric Boys*, at least on the track *Black Cat*. The other two tracks are however a bit more funky than the *E-boys*, more towards the heavier *Red Hot Chilli Peppers*-vein. High-quality stuff, though.

1995 MCD - CDZING 008

1995 ■ Sleeping Ape	MCD 3tr	Silence	CDZING 008

Tracks: Black Cat/Barbie Man/We Are.

SLICK STUFF

Janne Skåhlberg: v, Erik Bernholm: g, Johan Sjölin: k,
Niclas Sjölin: b, Patrick Olsson: d

Arboga - As the band name suggests this is a pretty slick AOR band, sounding a bit like *Saga*-meet-*Toto* with a touch of Tommy Nilsson/Jim Jidhed's solo material. Good-quality stuff, but for AOR fans only. The girls on the cover were supposedly two dancers the band used on stage.

1986 7" - TAB-ES-603

1986 ■ I Will Always/Fade Into The Past	7"	TAB	TAB-ES-603

SLINGBLADE

**Kristina Karlsson: v, Johan Berg: g, Tobias "Tobbe" Ander: g,
Niclas Svensson: b, Peter Henriksson: d**

Stockholm - Stockholm based NWoBHM style band *Slingblade* recorded their debut in 2010.
It was soon picked up by German retro label High Roller who gave it its proper push and pres-
entation. Henriksson is ex-*Gemini Five*, *Jekyll 'N Hyde* and was also in eighties demo band
Circus (also featuring Leif Sundin). After the single, guitarist Linnéa Olsson was replaced by
Tobias Ander. The debut is a concept album about a girl in the early eighties. Being abused and
bullied in school she finally flips and murders her class mates. Great eighties-sounding classic
heavy metal a bit reminiscent of *Gaskin*, *Jameson Raid*, vintage *Iron Maiden* with a touch of
Warlock. Really good stuff.

2011 LP - HHR 190

2010 ☐	Can't Get Enough/Until Death Do You Part	7"	High Roller Records	HRR 136
	150 black/white splatter vinyl + 350 black			
2011 ■	THE UNPREDICTED DEEDS OF MOLLY BLACK	LP	High Roller Records	HRR 190
	150 transparent blue + 350 black vinyl copies.			
2011 ☐	THE UNPREDICTED DEEDS OF MOLLY BLACK	CD	High Roller Records	HRR 190 CD

SLIP INTO SILK

Adde Psilander: v/g, Martin Svensson: g, Daniel Samuelsson: v/b, Martin Vangbo: d

Sala - Formed in 1990 by Adde (*Twinball*), Martin and Martin. In 1995 they found former death
metal singer Daniel. The style is nowhere near death metal. *Slip Into Silk* are hard to describe
in short terms, but the elements: melody, hard rock, 70s touch, dual guitars, power and quality
should say at least something. Well worth looking for. A cover of *Charlot The Harlot* is featured
on *Made In Scandinavia - A Tribute To Iron Maiden* (00 Tribute Records).

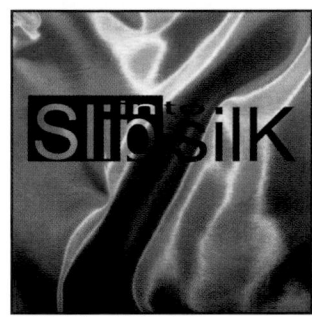

1995 MCD - SISCD-9501

1995 ■	Slip Into Silk	MCD 5tr	private	SISCD-9501
	Tracks: Holy War/Alive/Nothing Revolutionary/Stonewalls/Tree Of Family.			

SLITAGE

Fredrik Muskos, Jocke Mårdstam: g, Tobias Björkman, Fredde Olsson

Sundsvall - Not to be confused with the punksters from Norrtälje. Punkish metal. Mårdstam
was later in *Left Hand Solution* and Muskos in *Subspeed*.

1988 ■	Plastpengar/Livets långa stig	7"	Platina	PL-49 $

1988 7" - PL-49

SLODUST

Niklas Murbäck: v, Niklas "Douglas" Welin: g, Roger Ersson: b, Hugo Tigenius: d

Nynäshamn - *Slodust* stem from the core of rap-core band *Manic Sounds Panic*, founded in
1996 by Roger. After the band folded, he found Hugo and after various line-up changes the
above constellation became *Slodust*. Brutal grinding hardcore/metal with mixed clean and gut-
ripping vocals. Their image is somewhere between *Slipknot* and *Mudvayne* with masks and
the works. Mixed by Janne Lund (*Fortune*, *Sabbtail*). The band recorded a three-track demo
in 2003 and the four-track *Wicked Ahead* in 2006. The latest known line-up featured Ersson,
guitarist Elias Jäderberg Nilsson and drummer Daniel Björklund.

2001 ■	TWISTED AHEAD	CD	Black Mark	BMCD 149

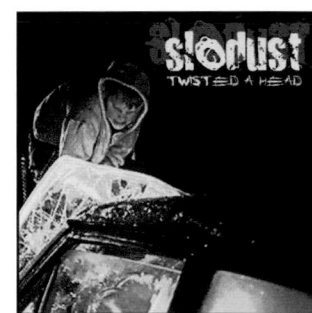

2001 CD - BMCD 149

SLOW TRAIN

Stefan Paparo: v, Andy Andersson: g, Marco Pennbrant: b/k, Daniel Pennbrant: d

Göteborg - Slow Train, formed in the mid-90s, is an outstanding retro hard rock band drawing
sounds and influences from bands like *Foghat*, *Led Zeppelin*, *UFO* and *Thin Lizzy*. Tragically
vanished from the map.

2002 ■	SONG OF THE DAY	CD	Sweden Rock Records	SRR-004

SLOWGATE

**Johan Hedlund: v, Thomas Kraus: g, Nicklas "Nick" Johansson: g,
Peter Uvén: b, Erik Forsgren: d**

Boden - In 1995 Nicklas Johansson formed the band together with fellow *Maninnya Blade*
members Jerry Rutström (g), Jan Blomquist (b), Leif Eriksson (v) and Johan Henriksson (d). They
recorded some songs, but nothing was released. Due to some of the members living far away,
the line-up changed. Jan Lindberg had been in *Dark Opera* together with Kenneth, a band also
Simon Johansson (*Fifth Reason*, *Memento Mori*) and Nikkey Argento (*Memento Mori*) were
part of. In 2000 guitarist Jerry Rutström left and was replaced by Thomas Kraus. The line-up
now featured singer Christoffer Larsson, guitarists Thomas Kraus and Nicklas "Nick" Johans-

2002 CD - SRR-004

son, bass player Jan Lindberg and drummer Kenneth Olofsson. Christoffer has also recorded some solo material under the name Christopher Robin. After *Nordic Rage,* drummer Kenneth left and was replaced by Erik Forsgren. The interest faded and the band took a break. The band was finally restarted with a new line-up (**ReinXeed**). Thomas, Erik and Nicklas drafted new singer Johan Hedlund (ex-**Corrupt**) and bass player Peter Uvén (**Deathchamber, April Divine, Knife In Christ, Blackwater**). Late 2009 they started working on the new album *Day Of Wrath.* The style now changed from the 80s thrash style to more modern heavy groove-oriented metal with screamo-style vocals.

1998 ■	Sick And Confused	MCD 4tr	Dead Raindeer			no2
	Tracks: Confusion/Beast/Sick/Full Of Filth					
1999 □	Confusion/Sick	7"	To The Death			TDD 003
	500 copies.					
2002 □	FORCE OF THE UNKNOWN	CD	Extremity/GMR			EXTREMCD 002
2005 □	NORDIC RAGE	CD	Extremity/GMR			EXTREMCD 003
2012 □	DAY OF WRATH	CD	The Trip Records			n/a

1998 MCD - no2

SLOWLIFE

Kristoffer Österman: v, Mikael Östermalm: g, Johan Flodell: g,
Christian Andolf: b, Carl-Johan Sillén: d

Stockholm - **Slowlife** was formed by Sillén, Andolf and guitarist Waldemar "Walle" Braathen after their band split. They soon recorded their first demo, after which bass player Dan was recruited. After the first MCD Östermalm replaced Walle and Flodell replaced Dan, even though the bass work on the actual recording of *What You Fear* was handled by Jonas Stålne Stensvik. **Slowlife** is quite an interesting crossover band, picking sounds and influences from a variety of styles and bands, mixing the hardcore of **Raised Fist** with the thrash of **Suicidal Tendencies** and the death metal style of bands like **At The Gates**.

2004 □	Slowlife	MCD 5tr	Worston Records		WRMCD 0104
	Tracks: Humiliation/Crawl/The Clown/Walk Away/Liar				
2006 □	WHAT YOU FEAR IS WHAT YOU GET	CD	Worston Records		WRCD 0106
2006 ■	SUICIDE LULLABY	CD	Worston Records		WRCD 0111

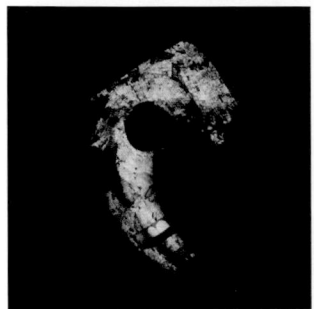

2006 CD - WRCD 0111

SLUDGE

Linus Palmkvist: v/g, Daniel Ovyar-Hosseini: g,
Haraldur "Joe Nebel" Briem: b, Mattias " Moon" Svensson: d

Lund - Heavy 90s **Soundgarden**-meet-**Metallica** with a major touch of **Alice In Chains**. Great sound, great melodies and simply a great band. Singer Linus sometimes sound like a deadringer for Layne Staley. The band changed name and style in the late 90s, but returned to the old style and name again in 2000. After the album Lasse replaced Joe Nebel. The band produced a promising promo CD in 2000 but later reformed under the name **Sunshine Molly**.

1997 □	My Walk/Sail Away	CDS	Septima		SEP 2960408
1997 ■	CRIME, FASHION, IDIOTS AND DUCKS	CD	Septima		SEP 1960409

1997 CD - SEP 1960409

SLUMBER

Siavosh Bigonah: v, Markus Hill: g, Jari Lindholm: g,
Ehsan Kalantarpour: k, Mikael Brunkvist: b, Ted Larsson: d

Skogås/Stockholm - Formed in 2000. The band recorded the demo *Dreamscape* in 2002 and *Seclusion* in 2003. The album, *Fallout,* is basically rerecordings of the demo songs without the song *Labyrinth*, plus the new song *Fallout*. **Slumber** play quite melodic and atmospheric death metal mixed with doom and goth, a bit similar to early **Opeth** and **Katatonia** with a touch of **Paradise Lost**. Keyboard player Daniel Beckman was also a live session member. In 2011 the band split up and reformed under the name **AtomA** and the album *Skylight* is planned.

2004 ■	FALLOUT	CD	Karmageddon		KARMA 062
2004 □	FALLOUT	CD	Nordic Media (Russia)		NMKM 0012

2004 CD - KARMA 062

SLYSIDE

Robban Eriksson: v, Kenny Elfström: g, Andrew Axelsson: k,
Johan Andersson: b, Tommy Palevik: d

Örebro - **Slyside** are a good AOR-ish sleaze band, not among the best but well worth checking out. Richard Söderstedt plays keyboard on both releases, although Andrew Axelsson (ex-**Bedroom Love**) replaced him before the release of the MCD.

1991 ■	Endless Road (Your Song)/Själens Vindar	7"	private		SS 9104-1
1993 □	Slightly Crazy	MCD 5tr	private		BROCD-02
	Tracks: Sweet Obsession/Love Me Angel/Flight 911/Let's Go Crazy/Liar.				

1991 7" - SS 9104-1

SMALL BAND (aka UMEÅ SMALL BAND)

Niklas Munter: v/b, Lars Eklund: g/v, Claes Björnberg: d/k

Umeå - It all started in the late seventies with the pop/symph band *Rikets Affärer*. The band split up and in 1980 three of the members formed *Umeå Small Band*. The band made their debut with the tracks *Kronofogden* and *Det finns ingen hjälp att få* on the compilation *6 x 2* (1981 Polar). The first single, recorded under the name *Umeå Small Band*, was good solid hard rock, a bit similar to *Status Quo*, however not as heavy as the compilation tracks. The second release, with the name now shortened to *Small Band*, the sound was a bit more commercial. After the band split, Lars and Niklas moved to Stockholm.

1983 7" - FEST 011

1982 ☐	Utanför/Nu vill ja vá	7"	Fest	FEST 06
	As Umeå Small Band.			
1983 ■	På väg/Älvornas bal	7"	Fest	FEST 011

SMOKEY BANDITS

Mats Norman: v, Marcus Boholm: g, Jimmy Stridh: b, Benny Eriksson: d

Stockholm - Formed in 1990. Like a rougher *Faster Pussycat* with energy, mean guitars, whiskey voice and a lot of power, this band kicks ass... and members. In January 1995 singer Mats was given the boot. He was replaced by ex-*Stone Free* singer Alex Lycke and the band changed name to *Vicious Tongue*. In late 1995 a new demo was released, but the band was now a trio featuring Marcus, Jimmy (b/v) and Benny. The music has changed to a strange combination of puberty-punk, hard rock, *Nirvana* and Iggy Pop-style. The MCD is a rare and highly prized item today.

1994 MCD - SBCD-394

1994 ■	Won't Lick No Shoe For You	MCD 6tr	Sea Dog	SBCD-394	$($)
	Tracks: Won't Lick No Shoe For You/Backseat Boogie/Whiskey Harmony/Do It Right/				
	Shoot From The Hip/Tattoed Madman				

SNAKE CHARMER

Göran Edman: v, Benny Jansson: g, Per Stadin: b, Anders Johansson: d

Malmö - This is an all-star AOR project formed by Per Stadin of *Silver Mountain*. On the debut the guitar was handled by Sven Cirnski and the vocals by Pete Sandberg (*Silver Seraph, Alien, Madison, Bewarp* etc). Anders is now in *HammerFall/FullForce* and Sven has made numerous recordings with different bands like *Raise Cain, Bad Habit, Truth* etc and he also appears on some of Pete's solo material. On the second album, Sven had been replaced by Benny, who has released several highly acclaimed solo albums and was previously found in *Two Rocks* and *Power Unit*, while Edman is/has been found in *Madison, John Norum Band, Glory, Yngwie Malmsteen, Vindictiv, Mårran* etc. *Snake Charmer* is a true gem for the AOR fans, all pink and fluffy. The non-album track *Cold Hearted Woman* can be found on the bonus-CD for the second encyclopedia.

1993 CD - ARRCD 001

2003 CD - 0681-83

1993 ■	SMOKE AND MIRRORS	CD	Arctic	ARRCD 001
1993 ☐	SMOKE AND MIRRORS	CD	Fems (Japan)	APCY-8121
1998 ☐	BACKYARD BOOGALOO	CD	Avalon Marquee (Japan)	MICY-1070
	Bonus: White Noise Boogie/Heart Of A Demon			
2003 ■	BACKYARD BOOGALOO	CD	MTM Classic	0681-83
	Bonus: White Noise Boogie/Heart Of A Demon/Cold Hearted Woman			

SNAKEPIT REBELS

Ubbe Rydeslätt: v, Anton Solli: g, Kricke Zetterquist: g,
Lasse Lekberg: b, Matte Rydstrand: d

Nyköping - This band recorded the first single under the name *Dream Police*, but had to change it because of some Norwegian colleagues. Ubbe had previously recorded a single with *Steel Arrows* and was also part of *Bang Bang*, the band that later became *Great King Rat*. Anton and Lasse came from the AOR-ish *Guardian Angels*. The first album is a great, riffy, sleazy hard rock platter with plenty of high-class songs, while the second is a weak album with meek sound, even though it's recorded at the famous Abbey Road Studio. *Life On Mars* is a cover of the old Bowie tune. The band later changed drummer, name and style. Ubbe, Kricke, Lasse, Anton and new drummer Staffan Karlsson have become punk rockers *Blind System*. In 1996 the band was accused of being racist and were even banned because of this. This resulted in *Blind System* taking a break and Ubbe recording a solo album.

1990 7" - FLCS 1041

1991 LP - FLC LP 114

1992 CD - FLC CD 122

1990 ■	Sex Booze & Tattoos/Dirty Billy	7"	FLC	FLCS 1041
	Released under the name Dream Police.			
1991 ☐	Sex Booze & Tattoos/Dirty Billy	7"	FLC	FLCS 1044
1991 ☐	SNAKEPIT REBELS	CD	FLC	FLC CD 114
1991 ■	SNAKEPIT REBELS	LP	FLC	FLC LP 114
1992 ☐	Life On Mars/High Heels	CDS 2tr	FLC	FLCSCD 1044
1992 ☐	DUSTSUCKER	LP	FLC	FLC LP 122
1992 ■	DUSTSUCKER	CD	FLC	FLC CD 122

SNAKES IN PARADISE

Stefan Berggren: v, **Thomas Jakobsson:** g, **Stefan Jonsson:** g,
Thomas Jansson: k, **Tomas Thorberg:** b, **Peter Petersson:** d

Stockholm - The band recorded some demos under the name **Jet Lag** before changing it to **Snakes In Paradise**. They started as an out-and-out AOR band with plenty of catchy choruses, nice keyboards and fluffy guitars. They backed Mark (now Marcie) Free on tour and *Play With Fire* on the 4-track was co-written by Glenn Hughes. Fredrik Öberg played drums on the first record. Tomas was earlier in **Wildliw** and **Bedlam** and Stefan Jonsson recorded two singles with the band **Renegade**. *Yesterday And Today* is a best off also featuring a remixed single version of *Book Of My Life* and the previously unreleased *Trail Back Home*. Berggren has also recorded with **Four Sticks** and **Company Of Strangers**, while Thorberg is found in **Plankton**, **Southfork** and **John Norum Band**. A pre-album demo version of *Fire & Rain* can be found on the compilation *MTM Volume 7* (01 MTM). In 2012 Thomas Jakobsson released the debut album with his new band *Angel King*.

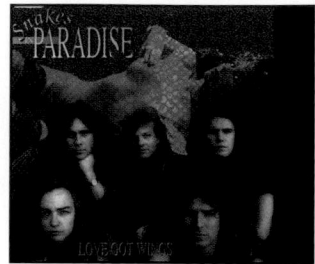
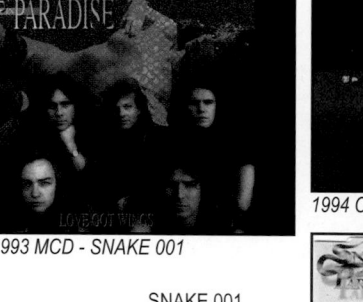

1993 MCD - SNAKE 001

1994 CD - SNAKE 002

1993 ■ Love Got Wings	CDS 4tr	Underground	SNAKE 001
Tracks: Love Got Wings/Heart In Flame/Play With Fire/How Can You Say			
1994 ■ SNAKES IN PARADISE	CD	Underground	SNAKE 002
1994 □ SNAKES IN PARADISE	CD	Zero (Japan)	XRCN-1108
1994 □ Rewrite The Story/Love Got Wings (re-mixed)	CDS 2tr	Underground	SNAKE 003
1994 □ SNAKES IN PARADISE	CD	Long Island	LIR 00021
1995 ■ Book Of My Life/Rather Stand The Rain	CDS 2tr	Warner Chappell	Snake 004
1998 □ GARDEN OF EDEN	CD	Z Records	ZR1992002
1998 □ GARDEN OF EDEN	CD	Pony Canyon (Japan)	PCCY-01295
2001 □ YESTERDAY AND TODAY	CD	MTM	0681-30
2002 □ DANGEROUS LOVE	CD	MTM	0681-49
2003 ■ DANGEROUS LOVE	CD	King Records (Japan)	KICP-873
2007 □ SNAKES IN PARADISE	CD	AL!VE	10039
Bonus: Love Got Wings/ How Can You Say/ Book Of My Life/ Heart In Flame/ Play With Fire.			
2007 □ GARDEN OF EDEN	CD	AL!VE	10040
Bonus: Break The Barriers To A New Dimension/ New York City Sky/ Life's Been Good To U And Me/ If Love Is A Game/ Time To Say Goodbye			

1995 CDS - Snake 004

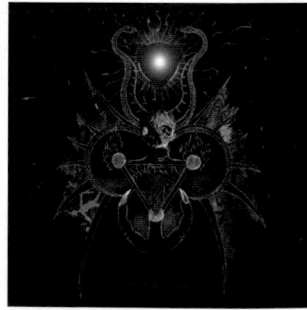

2003 CD - KICP-873

SNAKESKIN ANGELS

Kenneth "Thunderbolt" Gagner: v, **Jonas "Grim Vindkall" Almen:** g, **Daniel "D.K" Kvist:** g, **Gustaf "Kallbrand" Sundin:** b, **Kalle "Graveyard" Pettersson:** d

Göteborg - Formed in 2008 by a bunch of death/black metal musicians who decided to return to their roots and produce some classic metal. They recorded their debut, *Follow The Snake To The Core* in 2010 and released it on CD-R. In 2012 the MCD *Whitechapel* was released and early 2013 the debut was remixed, remastered and given a proper release. Solid-quality classic retro metal with a touch of **Witchfinder General**, but with slightly limited vocals, at times sounding like Ace Frehley. Good stuff, though. Pettersson is ex-**Taetre**, Sundin is also in **Styggelse**, Gagner is ex-**Swordmaster**, **Mastema** and also in **Likblek**, Kvist in **Taetre**, **Nightshade**, **Likblek**, **Sacrilege** and **Dragonland**, while Vindkall is/has been in **Nox Aurea**, **Domgård** and **Svartrit**.

2012 MCD - DWP 022

2012 ■ Witchchapel	MCD 5tr	Daemon Worship	DWP 022
Tracks: The Devil's Thrust/Nightchild/Threefaced Saviour/Beneath Me/Witchchapel. First 100 copies with a woven patch.			
2013 ■ FOLLOW THE SNAKE TO THE CORE	CD	Lake Of Fire	LOF-CD01
2013 □ FOLLOW THE SNAKE TO THE CORE	LP	Lake Of Fire	LOF-LP03
250 copies.			

2013 CD - LOF-CD01

SNAKESTORM

Johan Meiton: v, **Pontus Andersson:** g, **Jesper Heijkenskjöld:** b, **Henke Borg:** d

Göteborg - SnakeStorm were formed by Johan and Pontus, the latter is also found in punksters **Dia Psalma**. They wanted to play metal again and drafted bass drummer Borg. Johan started out playing bass, but as he would become the band's singer, they drafted bass player Jesper. Both Johan and Jesper have worked with **Mustasch**, not as musicians, but as stage techs. **SnakeStorm** play classic heavy metal, influenced by bands like **Accept** and **Judas Priest**, but with a slightly more modern touch in the guitar department. The singer sounds a bit like if you'd merge Lemmy and Axl Rose. Not bad at all.

2010 ■ CHOOSE YOUR FINGER	CD	Kabuki	KR-SE-09

2010 CD - KR-SE-09

SNÖTÅRAR

Kim "Maturz" Löfstrand: v/g/b/d

Nybro - Initiated in 2004. **Snötårar**, means "snow tears" in English. I'm not sure why black metal is the genre where there are so many one-man projects, but here's another one. Pretty well-

played, but badly recorded, cold old-school black metal. Quite melodic though. *Through Time* is a compilation of the 2005 demos *Natt* and *A Path Of Darkness*. Kim is also found in **Elimi**.

2007 ■	VREDESLUSTA	CD	Death Dealers (Poland)	DDA-001
2007 □	VREDESLUSTA	2LPg	Obscure Abhorrence	- -
2008 □	THROUGH TIME... BEHIND LIGHT	CD	Azermedoth Records (Mexico)	AZH-CD-016
	1000 copies.			
2009 □	THROUGH TIME... BEHIND LIGHT	LP	Obscure Abhorrence	- -
	Bonus: Streets Of Blood. 300 copies.			

2007 CD - DDA-001

SOBRE NOCTURNE
Stefan Lundgren: g/v

Luleå - A project initiated by **Necromicon/Dawn**-guitarist Stefan already back in 1996. He put together a line-up and recorded the first four track demo *Mare Cocurbit* in 1997. *Un-named* (three tracks) came later the same year and the two-track *Chapter 3/Rejection* the year after. In 1998 he started recording the debut album. Among the numerous musicians and choir members used on the album we find drummer Kim Arnell (**Morifade, Nephency Chaos Order**), singer Christian Björk, bassist Klaus Gauffin and guitarist Jan Strandh (**Master Massive, Zanity**). Stefan was musically influenced by a variety of bands such as **Samael** and **Morbid Angel**, which shows in the music. In 2002 the band recorded some new material in search of a new deal and the line-up featured Karl Nylin and Petter Karlsson from **Master Massive** and Björn Strandh. *Serpentine Dreamweaver* is a highly interesting album that draws from soft classically-oriented parts with piano, flute and violins to powerful walls of guitars, but highly orchestrated. There are soft choirs and orchestrated passages with a mix of beautiful female and growling male vocals.

2000 CD - LNP 004

2000 ■	SERPENTINE DREAMWEAVER	CD	Loud 'N Proud	LNP 004

SOCIAL SCUMBAGS, THE
Rikard Mårtensson: v, Mattias Jonsson: g, Rami Tainomo: g,
Ulf Andersson: b, Stefan Halldin: d,

Linköping - Rough-edged rock 'n roll/hard rock, like a mix of **Hanoi Rocks** and **Electric Boys**. All except Rami were ex-**Päst** and Stefan is now found in **Maryscreek**.

1996 MCD - 9506009

1996 ■	The Social Scumbags	MCD 4tr	Musikverksta'n	9506009
	Tracks: Misunderstood/Untouchable/Leaving Again/I'm Your Religion			

SOCIETY GANG RAPE (aka S.G.R)
Jens Törnroos: v, Susanne "Sussie" Berger: v/b, Katarina "Kattis" Lammi: g.
Marie-Louise "Mackan" Ehrs (now Gunnarsson): g, Christoffer Harborg: d

Avesta - S.G.R, originally **Sadistic Gang Rape**, started out playing old-school death metal and recorded the demo *Mass Devastation* (1992) in this style. In 1994 they changed their name to **Society Gang Rape** and their style went more towards crust/metal. The boys, Johan (**Interment, Demonical, Uncurbed, Centinex, Dellamorte, Moondark, Beyond**) and Christoffer (**Uncanny**) plus previous drummer Jens Johansson (**Uncanny, Interment, Uncurbed**) were only session members. The MCD *S.G.R* is *More Dead Than Alive* + four tracks. Sussie handled all vocals on this release. Mackan later married **Uncurbed**'s Micke Gunnarsson.

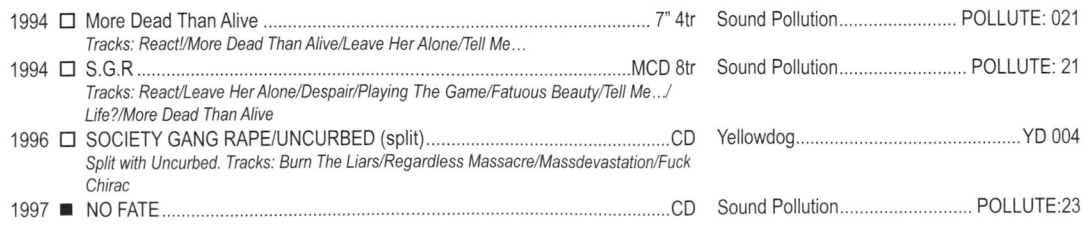

1997 CD - POLLUTE:23

1994 □	More Dead Than Alive	7" 4tr	Sound Pollution	POLLUTE: 021
	Tracks: React!/More Dead Than Alive/Leave Her Alone/Tell Me...			
1994 □	S.G.R	MCD 8tr	Sound Pollution	POLLUTE: 21
	Tracks: React/Leave Her Alone/Despair/Playing The Game/Fatuous Beauty/Tell Me.../ Life?/More Dead Than Alive			
1996 □	SOCIETY GANG RAPE/UNCURBED (split)	CD	Yellowdog	YD 004
	Split with Uncurbed. Tracks: Burn The Liars/Regardless Massacre/Massdevastation/Fuck Chirac			
1997 ■	NO FATE	CD	Sound Pollution	POLLUTE:23

2001 CD - FM 005

SOILS OF FATE
Henrik Crantz: v/b, Magnus Lindvall: g

Knivsta - Formed in 1995 as a duo and recorded their first demo *Pain... Has A Face* in 1997. The second demo, *Blood Serology*, was unearthed a year later. Very brutal, but still quite groove-oriented death/grind in the vein of **Crytopsy** or **Cannibal Corpse**. The band labels their music "Ultra Guttural Blasting Sickness". *Highest Hierarchy Of Blasting Sickness* is a compilation of the first two demos plus bonus tracks. The line-up has also featured drummers Nicke Karlsson and American Kevin Talley (**Misery Index, Dying Fetus**), plus guitarist Henke Kolbjer.

2001 □	SANDSTORM	CD	Retribute	RET 005
2001 ■	GRIME SYNDICATE	CD	Forensick Music	FM 005
2005 ■	HIGHEST HIERARCHY OF BLASTING SICKNESS	CD	Forensick Music	FM 012

2005 CD - FM 012

SOILWORK

**Björn "Speed" Strid: v, Peter Wichers: g, Sylvain Coudret: g,
Sven Karlsson: k, Ola Flink: b, Dirk Verbeuren: d**

Helsingborg - Formed in 1995, initially under the name *Inferior Breed,* featuring singer Björn Strid, guitarist/bassist Peter Wichers and drummer Jimmy Persson (later in *Faithful Darkness*). They changed their name to *Soilwork* a year later. They added second guitarist Ludvig Svartz. Through the 1997 demo *In Dreams We Fall Into The Eternal* they got a deal with Listenable Records. Before the album bassist Ola Flink and keyboard player Carlos Del Olmo Holmberg completed the line-up. Mattias Ia Eklundh (*Freak Kitchen*) makes a guest appearance on one track on the debut. The band was "blessed" by the metal-God himself – Rob Halford, who is an honorary member of their fan club. After the first album, drummer Jimmy Persson was replaced by Henry Ranta and guitarist Ludvig Svartz by Ola Frenning. *The Chainheart Machine* was somewhat of an international break through for the band. Before *Natural Born Chaos,* keyboard player Carlos Del Olmo Holmberg was replaced by Sven Karlsson (*Evergrey*). The first two albums are really powerful and heavy technical up-tempo metal with vocals in the vein of L-G Petrov. Try mixing *In Flames*, *At The Gates* and *Dark Tranquillity* with more traditional metal touch and all of it played tighter than a fly's ass. *Natural Born Chaos*, produced by the one and only Devin Townsend, saw a vast change in style, at least in the vocal department where clean vocals now prevail. Musically the band was now described as a mix of *In Flames* and early *Opeth*, which I agree with. On *Stabbing The Drama*, Henry Ranta had been replaced by Dutch drummer Dirk Verbeuren (*Scarve, Powermad, Devin Townsend* etc). In 2006 Peter Wichers quit the band, as he was tired of touring. He was replaced by Daniel Antonsson on *Sworn To A Great Divide*. In 2008 guitarist Ola Frenning also left the band, and was replaced by Sylvain Coudret (*Scarve, Anaon*). However, late 2008 Peter Wichers returned to the band, and Daniel Antonsson was again out of the band. *The Early Chapters* was an EP with previously unreleased demos and covers. All albums are highly recommended! *The Living Infinite* boasts to be the first double CD in death metal. It's a big chunk of epic, outstanding melodic death metal.

The workin men of soil

Year		Title	Format	Label	Cat. No.
1998	■	STEEL BATH SUICIDE	CD	Listenable	POSH 012
1999	☐	STEEL BATH SUICIDE	CD	Soundholic (Japan)	SHCD1-0021
		Bonus: Disintegrated Skies/Burn (Deep Purple cover)			
1999	☐	THE CHAINHEART MACHINE	CD	Listenable	POSH 17
1999	☐	THE CHAINHEART MACHINE	CD	Teichiku (Japan)	TKCU 77037
		Bonus: Shadow Child			
2000	☐	THE CHAINHEART MACHINE	CD	Century Media (USA)	7966-2
2000	☐	STEELBATH SUICIDE	CD	Listenable	POSH 12A
		Bonus: Sadistic Lullaby (live). New artwork.			
2000	☐	STEELBATH SUICIDE	CD	Century Media (USA)	8051-2
		Bonus: Sadistic Lullaby (live). New artwork.			
2001	☐	A PREDATOR'S PORTRAIT	CD	Nuclear Blast	NB 582-2
2001	☐	A PREDATOR'S PORTRAIT	LP PD	Nuclear Blast	NB 582-1
2001	☐	A PREDATOR'S PORTRAIT	CD	Nuclear Blast (USA)	6582-2
2001	☐	A PREDATOR'S PORTRAIT	CD	Teichiku (Japan)	TKCS 85011
2001	☐	A PREDATOR'S PORTRAIT	CD	Dream On Music (Korea)	PARK 9003
		Bonus: Asylum Dance			
2002	☐	NATURAL BORN CHAOS	CD	Nuclear Blast	NB 581-2
2002	☐	NATURAL BORN CHAOS	CDd	Nuclear Blast	NB 581-2
2002	☐	NATURAL BORN CHAOS	CD	Nuclear Blast (USA)	NB 6581-2
2002	☐	NATURAL BORN CHAOS	CD	Soundholic (Japan)	TKCS 85037
		Bonus: Kvicksilver (Mercury Shadow with Swedish vocals)			
2003	☐	FIGURE NUMBER FIVE	CD	Nuclear Blast	NB 1108-2
2003	☐	FIGURE NUMBER FIVE	2CD	Nuclear Blast	NB 1108-0
		Bonus: Bound To Illusions/My Need/In A Close Encounter/Skin After Skin/Wake Up Call/ Steel Bath Suicide			
2003	☐	FIGURE NUMBER FIVE/NATURAL BORN CHAOS	2LPg	Nuclear Blast	NB 1108-1
		"Figure…" on black vinyl, "Natural…" on white vinyl.			
2003	☐	FIGURE NUMBER FIVE	CD	Irond (Russia)	CD 03-480
2003	☐	THE CHAINHEART MACHINE	CD	Irond (Russia)	CD 03-674
2003	☐	Departure Plan/Rejection Role – Club Single	CDS	Nuclear Blast (promo)	NB 1138-2
2003	☐	Departure Plan/Rejection Role + video	CDSp	Nuclear Blast	NB 1137-2
2003	☐	Light The Torch/Figure Number Five + video	CDSp	Nuclear Blast	NB 1223-2
2004	■	Stabbing The Drama/The Crest Fallen	CDSp	Nuclear Blast (promo)	- -
2004	☐	The Early Chapters	MCD 5tr	Listenable Records	POSH 054
		Tracks: Burn (Deep Purple cover)/Disintegrated Skies/Egypt (Mercyful Fate cover)/ Shadow Child/Aardvark Train (live). Slipcase.			
2005	☐	Stabbing The Drama/Asylum Dance	CDS	Nuclear Blast	NB 1417-2
2005	☐	Stabbing The Drama (edit)/Stabbing The Drama/Nerve	CDS	Nuclear Blast	NB 1418-2
2005	■	STABBING THE DRAMA	CDd	Nuclear Blast	NB 1416-0
		Bonus: Wherever Thorns May Grow. Says NB 1377-0 on spine. Inverted cover artwork. A special edition of 1000 copies in a tin can was also made.			
2005	☐	STABBING THE DRAMA	LP PD	Nuclear Blast	NB 1416-1
2005	☐	STABBING THE DRAMA	CD	Avalon Marquee (Japan)	MICP-10492
		Bonus: Wherever Thorns May Grow/Killed By Ignition			

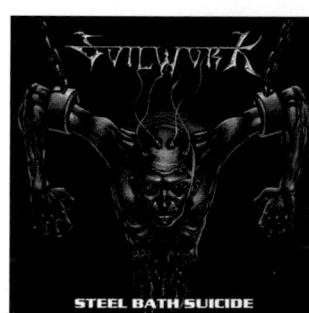
1998 CD - POSH 012

2004 CDSp - - -

2005 CDd - NB 1416-0

2005	☐	STABBING THE DRAMA	CD	Dream On Music (Korea)	PARK 9048
2005	☐	STABBING THE DRAMA	CD	Scarecrow (Mexico)	SC 05179
2005	☐	STABBING THE DRAMA	CD	Nuclear Blast	NB 1377-2
2005	☐	STABBING THE DRAMA	LP	Nuclear Blast	NB 1377-1
2005	☐	STABBING THE DRAMA	CD	Irond (Russia)	CD 05-947
2005	☐	STABBING THE DRAMA	CD	NEMS (Argentina)	NEMS 356
2007	■	SWORN TO A GREATER DIVIDE	CD	Nuclear Blast	NB 1879-2
2007	☐	SWORN TO A GREATER DIVIDE	CD	Icarus (Argentina)	ICARUS 398
2007	☐	SWORN TO A GREATER DIVIDE	CD	Scarecrow (Mexico)	SC 07365-0
2007	☐	SWORN TO A GREATER DIVIDE	CD+DVD	Avalon Marquee (Japan)	MIZP-60007

Bonus: Sovereign/Martyr. Bonus live DVD.

2007	☐	SWORN TO A GREATER DIVIDE	CD	Avalon Marquee (Japan)	MICP-10690
2007	☐	SWORN TO A GREATER DIVIDE	CD+DVD	Nuclear Blast	NB 1879-0
2007	☐	SWORN TO A GREATER DIVIDE	CD+DVD+3" CDS	Nuclear Blast	NB 1879-5

Bonus: Martyr + DVD with live + studio report. Bonus 3" CDS: Overclocked/Sovereign

2007	☐	SWORN TO A GREATER DIVIDE	LP PD	Nuclear Blast	NB 1879-9

1000 copies.

2007	☐	Exile/The Pittsburg Syndrome	CDS	Nuclear Blast	NB 2016-2
2008	■	A PREDATOR'S PORTRAIT	CD	Icarus (Argentina)	ICARUS 489
2008	☐	Exile/The Pittsburg Syndrome	7" PD	Nuclear Blast	NB 2181-9
2009	☐	STEEL BATH SUICIDE	CD	Listenable	POSH 112

Bonus: Sadistic Lullabye (live)/The Aardvark Trail (live)

2009	☐	THE CHAINHEART MACHINE	CD	Listenable	POSH 113

Bonus: Machinegun Majesty (live)/Neon Rebels (live). Different artwork.

2010	☐	STEEL BATH SUICIDE	CD	Avalon Marquee (Japan)	MICP-10941

Bonus: Sadistic Lullabye (live)/The Aardvark Trail (live)/Disintegrated Skies/Burn

2010	☐	THE CHAINHEART MACHINE	CD	Avalon Marquee (Japan)	MICP-10942

Bonus: Machinegun Majesty (live)/Neon Rebels (live)/Shadow Child/Egypt

2010	☐	A PREDATOR'S PORTRAIT	CD	Avalon Marquee (Japan)	MICP-10943
2010	☐	NATURAL BORN CHAOS	CD	Avalon Marquee (Japan)	MICP-10944

Bonus: Quicksilver

2010	☐	FIGURE NUMBER FIVE	CD	Avalon Marquee (Japan)	MICP-10945

Bonus: Downfall 24

2010	■	THE PANIC BROADCAST	CD	Nuclear Blast	NB 2256-2
2010	☐	THE PANIC BROADCAST	CDd+DVD	Nuclear Blast	NB 2256-0

Bonus: Sweet Demise. DVD with studio footage.

2010	☐	THE PANIC BROADCAST - DELUXE	CDd+DVD	Nuclear Blast (USA)	NB 2610-2
2010	☐	THE PANIC BROADCAST	CD	Avalon Marquee (Japan)	MICP-10930
2010	☐	THE SLEDGEHAMMER FILES - BEST OF SOILWORK 1998-2008	CD+DVD	Avalon Marquee (Japan)	MIZP-60020
2013	☐	THE LIVING INFINITE	2CD Earbook	Nuclear Blast	NB 2995-5
2013	☐	THE LIVING INFINITE	2CD	Nuclear Blast	NB 2995-2
2013	☐	THE LIVING INFINITE	2LP	Nuclear Blast	NB 2995-1
2013	☐	THE LIVING INFINITE	2CD	Icarus (Argentina)	ICARUS 1053

2007 CD - NB 1879-2

2008 CD - ICARUS 489

2010 CD - NB 2256-2

SOLAR DAWN

Christian Älvestam: v, Anders Edlund: g, Andreas Månsson: g, Henrik Schönström: d

Skövde - The band was formed in 1997 under the name *Jarawynja*. In '98 they recorded the demo *Festival Of Fools*, with Christian Älvestam (*Unmoored*) only hired to do the vocals. The debut was recorded in Studio Abyss. *Frost-Work* is from the same recording session when the band was called *Jarawynja* and it's actually just a remastering of the demo *Desideratum*. At this point Christian was a permanent member also handling the bass. Drummer Martin Restin (ex-*Enthralled*) left just before the recording of the debut and the band borrowed Jocke Pettersson (*Dawn, Regurgitate, Thy Primordial*) before settling for Henrik, who is also found in *Unmoored*. The band produces what could simply be labelled "melodic death metal". Älvestam is found in bands like *Scar Symmetry, Incapacity, Torchbearer,* and *Quest Of Aidance*.

2001 MCD - PMZ 018-3

2001	■	Frost-Work	MCD 3tr	Mighty	PMZ 018-3

Tracks: Artistic Blasphem/Punished By Silence/Arisen Composure. 1000 copies.

2001	■	EQUINOCTIUM	CD	Mighty	PMZ 20

2001 CD - PMZ 20

SOLEN SKINER

Sven Bjärhall: g/v, Christer Nahrendorf: g, Lennart Holmgren: h, Christer Kilander: b, Håkan Agnsäter: d

Stockholm - *Solen Skiner* (the sun shines) made their first gig at the Gärdet festival in 1970, and was featured on the compilation *Festen på gärdet* (1971 Silence) with the song *Militär*. Participated in the alternative Eurovison Song Contest and toured quite frequently. They were mainly a live band. Split in 1978. Bluesy hard rock with a touch of boogie, quite similar to *Wildmarken* and *Dunder*, with slightly more biting guitars. Political lyrical content. Nahrendorf has made some solo singles and also made an album with rock band *Looping*.

1976	☐	SOLEN SKINER	LP	MNW	MNW-60P
1977	■	STRÅLANDE TIDER	LP	Musiklaget	MLLP-9

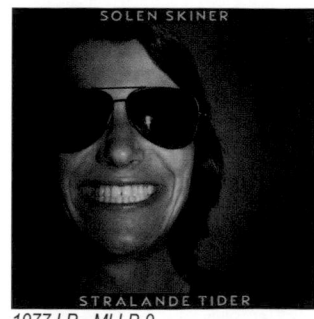

1977 LP - MLLP-9

SOLID

Daniel Björnarås: v, Carino Malmros: g, Claes Lundquist: g,
Ken Olsson: b, Roger Christiansson: d

Göteborg - Daniel and Carino had a band called *Solid* that was disbanded. Roger and Ken had a project and needed assistance. The new *Solid* was founded. They recorded the EP and just when they had signed to Polar/Stranded, the band broke up. Ken and Daniel formed *Pagan*, and recorded their debut. Daniel quit after the album and formed *DD Band*. Carino is now found in *Blobslime*, while Roger was later in *Biscaya*, *Rampage*, *Roxanne* and in 2012 he joined *Destiny*. *Solid* plays pretty solid melodic boogie-style hard rock, similar to *Cheavy* or *Dedringer* with a touch of *Bachman Turner Overdrive*.

1985 ■ Wait N' See/Split Mind/Fly Away/Lifetime...7" 4tr   private ....SOL 001

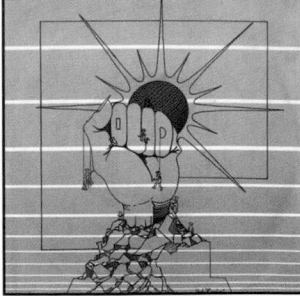

1985 7" - SOL 001

SOLID GROUND

Gösta Hjelmquist: v/g, Björn Uhr: g/v, Peter Eklund: b, Anders Bergé: d/v

Stockholm - This is definitely one of the rarest Swedish albums on vinyl. Only a few copies of the original album exist, as most of the 200 pressed copies were thrown away. In 1992 Mellotronen did a reissue with the first single as bonus. The music is at times great with complex guitar-oriented stuff in the early *Neon Rose*-vein, while some songs are simple amateur-sounding sounding *Status Quo* boogie. When listening to the album you find it is quite overrated. Björn later joined *Tempelrock*, *Attack* and also recorded a solo album in a far poppier vein. Let's say the quality matches the price of a CD reissue rather than an original vinyl.

1975 ☐	My Song/Tell Me	7"	Scam	SS 015	$
1976 ☐	MADE IN ROCK	LP	Scam	LPS-L 007	$$$
	200 copies printed, but only around 30 are said to still exist.				
1992 ☐	MADE IN ROCK	CD	Mellotronen	CD 001	
	Bonus: My Song/Tell Me. 1000 copies.				
1997 ■	MADE IN ROCK	LP PD	Record Heaven	RHPD 7	
2007 ☐	MADE IN ROCK	CD	Mellotronen	MELLOCD-022	
	Bonus: My Song/Tell Me/Inner Sin/Man On The Run/Turkish Delight/Yes, No/Tunnelbane-blues/Vansinniga Berta				
2007 ☐	MADE IN ROCK	CDp	Arcangelo (Japan)	ARC-7243	
	Bonus: My Song/Tell Me/Inner Sin/Man On The Run/Turkish Delight/Yes, No/Tunnelbane-blues/Vansinniga Berta				

Unofficial releases:
1999 ☐ MADE IN ROCK...LP   LPS-L...007
Counterfeit. 500 copies.

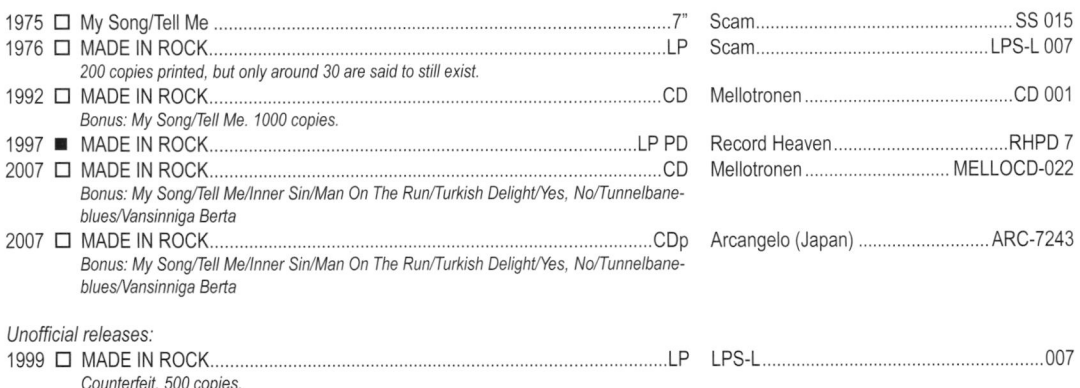

1997 LP PD - RHPD 7

SOLID GROUND

Peter Malmersjö: v/g, Håkan Gustavsson: b,
Johan Clasén: g, Carl-Magnus Petersson: d/k

Linköping - Not to be confused with the Stockholm band. The single was first prize in the Östgötarock bandstand, The band's song *Change* was also featured on the *Musik för miljö* (1990 Studiefrämjandet) compilation and they furthermore recorded the demo *Does Your Mother Know The Devil* in 1993. *Solid Ground* plays quite wimpy melodic hard rock/AOR with below average vocals.

1985 ■ Lonely Rider/Talkin' Bout Love...7"   private .... - -

1985 7" - - -

SOLID ROX

Jane: v, Perlan: g, Skalet: g, Knoven: b, Murre: b

Pretty good Janis Joplin-sounding, seventies-influenced hard rock. B-side is en even better riffy thing. Well worth checking out.

1983 ■ Hela natten/The Traveller...7"   CTR .... CTR 683

1983 7" - CTR 683

SOLITUDE

Andreas "Janos" Lidberg: g, Fredrik "Frippe" Eriksson: k, Magnus Blom: b/d

Bollnäs - Formed in 1988. High-quality instrumental guitar-dominated hard rock. *Echoe* is a cover of the Satriani tune and *Black Star* is a Malmsteen cover. The original track is in the same vein. In my first book I wrote: "Andreas actually knows what he's doing and it would be really interesting to see what would come out if he wrote an album of original material". Well, Andreas later appeared in *Street Talk* and in 2009 he released the excellent solo CD *Russian Tourette*. However, he did not go down the neoclassical route, but it ranges over a variety of styles. Frippe was later in *Tad Morose*.

1989 ■ Solitude Suite 1/Black Star/Echoe ....7"   private ....S 01

1989 7" - S 01

SOLITUDE

Patrik Larsson: v, Dennis Warelius: g/v, Christoffer Apell: g,
Niclas Staberg: b, William Turner: d

Värnamo - *Solitude* were formed in 2006, initially featuring singer Larsson, guitarists Warelius and Henrik Kentsson, bassist Carl Williams and drummer Turner. In 2007 Apell replaced Kentsson, and the year after bassist Staberg replaced Williams. The band recorded two demos at Studio Fredman, before entering again to record the four track MCD *The Revival*. **Solitude** produce well-played metalcore in the vein of **Dead By April**, **Killswitch Engage** mixed with **Avenged Sevenfold**. The digital single *Ricochet* was released in 2011.

2010 ■	The Revival	MCDd 4tr	Dead Tree Music	DTM 017
	Tracks: Last Division/Break Through/The Revival/When Memory Calls			
2012 ☐	TIED TO THE ANCHOR	CDd	Pantherfarm	PFCD 104

2010 MCDd - DTM 017

SOLSTING

Magnus Leijon: v, Pelle Hökengren: g, Mattis Hällström: g,
Tomas Wallin: b, Niklas Brommare: d/k

Härnösand - *Solsting* (sunstroke) started out playing jazz rock, but the single is quite standard, new waveish hard rock of average quality. Singer Leijon later became a radio host on national radio in Sweden, while Hökengren played with party rockers **Trance Dance**. Brommare has later recorded with clarinet player Martin Fröst and is found in jazz band **Trio Trespassing**. The way heavier song *Säj som de é* is also featured on the compilation *Radio Västernorrland 1977-1981* (1982 radio Västernorrland, RVNLP 001). The A-side is a great rocker.

1981 ■	E de' nån skillnad/Andra sidan planeten	7"	Sunshine Productions	SSP 001

1981 7" - SSP 001

SOLUTION

Jonny Wester: g/v, Rune Bertilsson: k, Leif Bertilsson: b, Peter Westin: d

Söderhamn - *Solution* existed between 1986-1990. High-quality melodic hard rock with prominent keyboards. Mid-class vocals, but classy musicianship and good song material. The band split when drummer Peter quit to start training racehorses. Rune (ex-**Air Condition**) and Leif were later in the band **Vital Sign** and the gospel choir **Fresh Air**. Jonny plays in the cover band **Rocktools** as well as doing his solo gigs under the name Ellen Jay.

1990 ■	Foot Prints/Higher Ground	7"	private	UPP 777

1990 7" - UPP 777

SOLUTION .45

Christian Älvestam: v, Patrik Gardberg: g, Tom Gardiner: g,
Jani Stefanovic: g, Anders Edlund: b, Rolf Pilve: d

Söderhamn/Skövde - *Solution .45* were formed by Jani Stefanovic (*DivineFire, Miseration, Essence Of Sorrow* etc) late 2007. The initial line-up also featured singer Christian Älvestam (**Miseration, Scar Symmetry, Torchbearer, Solar Dawn, Syconaut** etc), bassist Anders Edlund (**Angel Blake, Solar Dawn, Incapacity, The Few Against Many**), Finnish drummer Rolf Pilve (**Miseration, Essence Of Sorrow, Megiddon** etc), Finnish guitarist Tom Gardiner (**Essence Of Sorrow, Hateform** etc) and Finnish keyboardist Mikko Härkin (**Essence Of Sorrow, Kotipelto, Kenziner** etc). In 2008 the first demo was recorded. In September 2009 they entered the Panic Room Studios to record the debut. In January 2010 keyboardist Härkin left the band, but is still active as a session member. A few months later Stefanovic left the band, and was replaced by Patrik Gardberg (**Ammotrack, DivineFire, Totchbearer**). However, he returned to the band in 2011, now doing the **Iron Maiden**-three-guitarist-routine. *Solution .45* play killer melodic death metal with mixed clean and growling vocals.

2010 ■	FOR AEONS PAST	CD	AFM	AFM 294-2

2010 CD - AFM 294-2

SOMBER

Pontus Dahlström: v, Carl Fritzell: g, Andreas Henriksson: g,
Björn "Bear" Rehnqvist: b, John Bresäter: d

Göteborg - *Somber* were formed as a high-school band in 2001. The original line-up featured singer Dahlström, guitarists Henriksson and Christoffer Melin, bassist Rehnqvist and drummer Bresäter. They recorded the demos *Oblivion* (2002), *God's Design* (2003) and *Berkley* (2004) before Melin was replaced by Fritzell. The band recorded two more demos, *Name Your Poison* (2004) and *Define: Rend* (2005) before they relocated to California for sixteen months. Back in Sweden they recorded their debut album *The Black Machine*. Great melodic death/thrash.

2008 ■	THE BLACK MACHINE	CD	Suicide Records	SR-003

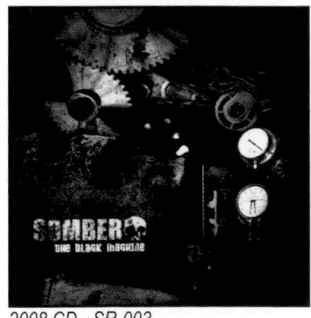

2008 CD - SR-003

SONIC RITUAL

Henrik Palm: v/g, Linnéa Olsson: g, Christoffer Jonsson: b, Viktor Bergman: d

Stockholm - This is pure authentic eighties NWoBHM, very similar to *Paralex* and *Holocaust* with a touch of *Witchfinder General* for good measures. Linnéa, Henrik and guitarist Johan Wallin formed the band in 2007, intending it to be the missing link between *Motörhead* and *Hawkwind*. Christoffer (aka 138 in *DS-13*) joined on bass and they also had a lead singer, but the singer and Wallin left the band. The remaining trio recorded the demo *Rat Eyed Ghoul*, released on cassette in August 2008. Early 2009 drummer Viktor joined and things fell into place. Palm is also found in *In Solitude*.
Website: sonicritual.bandcamp.com

2009	☐	Take The Edge Off	7"	Black Juju	JUJU 16

Tracks: Take The Edge Off/A Silver Express/Vulture Cvlt. 300 copies.

2009	☐	Mother Hearse	MLP 4tr	High Roller Records	HRR 078

Tracks: (Don't Wanna) Feel Alright/Walls/Mother Hearse/Banshee. 150 copies in white vinyl + 350 in black.

2009	■	SANCTUARY IN BLASPHEMY/SONIC RITUAL (split)	LPg	High Roller Records	HRR 059

Split with Sonic Ritual. Tracks: Ritual De La Morte/Rat Eyed Ghoul/Pollituion Tide/Take The Edge Off/A Silver Express/Vulture Kvlt 200 black/white splatter + 300 black vinyl.

2009 LPg - HRR 059

SONIC SYNDICATE

Nathan James Biggs: v, Richard Sjunnesson: v, Roger Sjunnesson: g, Robin Sjunnesson: g, Karin Axelsson: b, John Bengtsson: d

Falkenberg - It all started in 2002, when Sjunnesson brothers Roger and Richard and cousin Robin took a break from their other band *Tunes Of Silence* and decided to form heavy metal band *Fallen Angels*. The band also featured bassist Magnus Svensson, drummer Kristoffer Bäcklund (*Avatar*) and keyboardist Andreas Mårtensson. They entered a bandstand and recorded the demos *Black Lotus*, *Fall From Heaven* and *Extinction*, before being picked up by American label Pivotal Rockordings. However, they decided it was time to change the name, and they now became *Sonic Syndicate*. In 2004 bassist Svensson was replaced by Karin Axelsson and on the first album Roland Johansson (*Dodge*) adds some guest vocals. The style was influenced by bands like *In Flames*, *Dark Tranquillity* and *Soilwork*. After the album, in 2006, the band recorded a new four-track demo, never made official, which lead to a deal with Nuclear Blast. Roland was now a permanent member of the band handling guitar and vocals. Before the second album the line-up changed, seeing Mårtensson out of the band and drummer Bäcklund replaced by John Bengtsson early 2006. In 2007 Richard and Roland made a guest appearance on the *Nuclear Blast Allstars: Out Of The Dark* recording. In 2008 they released the live DVD *Live Inhuman*. It was also included in the CD+DVD tour version of *Only Inhuman*. After a hectic year of touring, singer Roland Johansson left the band in March 2009. In August the same year, he was replaced by UK resident Nathan James Biggs (ex-*Hollow Earth Theory*), who made his debut on the *Rebellion* EP. In October 2010 Richard left the band dissatisfied with the band's musical direction, and later formed *The Unguided*, where John, Roland and Roger are also found. In September 2011 the band decided to take a break.
Website: www.sonicsyndicate.com

The syndicate that rules the night

2005	☐	EDEN FIRE	CD	Pivotal Rockordings	PR-001
2005	☐	EDEN FIRE	CD	Soundholic (Japan)	SHCD-0071
2007	☐	Enclave/Flashback	CDS 2tr	Nuclear Blast	- -
2007	☐	ONLY INHUMAN	CD	Nuclear Blast	NB 1822-0

European bonus: Freelancer

2007	☐	ONLY INHUMAN – TOUR EDITION	CD+DVD	Nuclear Blast (USA)	NB 1822-5
2007	☐	Enclave + video	CDS 1tr	Nuclear Blast (promo)	NB 1898-2
2007	☐	Psychic Suicide/Denied	CDS 2tr	Nuclear Blast (promo)	NB 1905-2
2007	☐	ONLY INHUMAN	CD	Avalon Marquee (Japan)	MICP-10653

My Soul In #000000/Freelancer. Different artwork.

2008	■	ONLY INHUMAN – TOUR EDITION	CD+DVD	Nuclear Blast	NB 1822-2

Bonus: Freelancer. Ltd Tour edition with DVD featuring live-tracks, videos and photo gallery. 5000 copies. Slipcase.

2008	☐	ONLY INHUMAN	CD	Nuclear Blast (USA)	NB 2018-2

Tour edition. Slipcase. Different artwork. European bonus: Freelancer

2008	■	My Escape	MCDp 3tr	Nuclear Blast	NB 2236-2

Three different mixes of My Escape (Radio)/(Video)/(Album version). Promo.

2008	☐	Jack Of Diamonds (Club mix)/(album version)	CDS 2tr	Nuclear Blast	NB 2239-2

Promo.

2009	☐	LOVE AND OTHER DISASTERS	CD	Nuclear Blast	NB 2160-2
2009	☐	LOVE AND OTHER DISASTERS	CD	Avalon Marquee (Japan)	MICP-10760

Different artwork. Bonus: Ruin/Dead Planet

2009	☐	LOVE AND OTHER DISASTERS	CDd+DVD	Nuclear Blast	NB 2160-0

Bonus: Ruin/Dead Planet/Mission: Undertaker. DVD featuring studio report, videos, live.

2009	☐	LOVE AND OTHER DISASTERS	CDd+DVD	Avalon Marquee (Japan)	MIZP-60015
2009	☐	LOVE AND OTHER DISASTERS	2LPg	Nuclear Blast	NB 2160-1

1000 numbered copies in clear vinyl. Bonus: Ruin/Dead Planet

2008 CD+DVD - NB 1822-2

2008 MCDp - NB 2236-2

Year		Title	Format	Label	Catalog
2009	☐	LOVE AND OTHER DISASTERS	CD	Evolution Music (Korea)	SDP-0139

Bonus: Ruin/Dead Planet/Mission: Undertaker

| 2009 | ☐ | LOVE AND OTHER DISASTERS – REBELLION PACK | Box | Nuclear Blast | 2736122-965 |

Contains: Love And Other Disasters CD+DVD and the Burn This City/Rebellion CDS.

| 2009 | ☐ | Burn This City | MCD 4tr | Avalon Marquee (Japan) | MICP-40011 |

Tracks: Burn This City/Rebellion In Nightmareland/Burn This City (radio edit)/The Trailer of We Burn The Night.

| 2009 | ■ | Rebellion | MCD 3tr | Nuclear Blast | NB 2296 |

Tracks: Burn This City/Rebellion In Nightmareland/Burn This City (radio edit).

2010	☐	My Own Life (Radio Edit)	CDSd	Nuclear Blast	NB 2630-2
2010	☐	Turn It Up	CDS	Nuclear Blast	??
2010	☐	Revolution, Baby	CDS	Nuclear Blast (promo)	NB 2610-2
2010	☐	Revolution, Baby	MCDp 4tr	Nuclear Blast	- -

Tracks: Revolution, Baby/Burn This City/Heart Of Eve/We Rule The Night.

| 2010 | ☐ | WE RULE THE NIGHT | CD | Nuclear Blast | NB 2482-2 |
| 2010 | ☐ | WE RULE THE NIGHT | CDd+DVD | Nuclear Blast | NB 2482-0 |

Patch

| 2010 | ☐ | WE RULE THE NIGHT | CD | Avalon Marquee (Japan) | MICP-10920 |

Bonus: Dead And Gone/Perfect Alibi

| 2010 | ☐ | WE RULE THE NIGHT | CD+DVD | Avalon Marquee (Japan) | MIZP-60019 |
| 2010 | ☐ | WE RULE THE NIGHT | CD | EvolutionMusic (Korea) | L100004150 |

Bonus: Dead And Gone/Perfect Alibi

2009 MCD - NB 2296

SONIC TEMPLE

Fredrik "Nellie" Helmersson: v, Martin "Stray" Nilsson: g, Nicklas Lindgren: g, Roger "Mane" Emlid: b, Magnus Strandberg: d

Halmstad - Formed in 1993. Despite the name they don't sound even close to **The Cult**. *Sonic Temple* is an out-and-out thrash band, in the vein of early **Megadeth**. The MCD lacks from an incredibly thin production. Mid-quality stuff. The track *Whore* is about Fredrik's former girlfriend, which she probably feels honoured about...

1995 MCD - ST 001

| 1995 | ■ | Forever | MCD 5tr | private | ST 001 |

Tracks: Fall Through/Doomed Beliefs/I.C.D.I/Whore/Forever

SONIC WALTHERS

Alf Roger Arvidsson: v/g, Johan Andersson: g, Bjarne Olson: b, Paul Sörensson: d

Göteborg - **Sonic Walthers** were formed by two members from the demised punk band *Zäpo*. The line-up on the debut single featured Arvidsson, Andersson, Olson and drummer Paul Sörensson. **Sonic Walthers** is definitely a band worth checking out if you're into the bluesy rock of **The Black Crowes**. On *Medication* the band featured Arvidsson, Olson, Andersson, guitarist Björn Olsson, drummer Mats Hansson. On *Forgot My Name* drummer Mats Hansson (ex- **Grindstone, Mustasch, Tornado Babies**) was out of the band. Bjarne later appeared in **Mary Beats Jane**.

1989 7" - NSM 45-16

| 1988 | ☐ | The Sonic Walthers | MLP 5tr | Pink Honey | ROSAXP 39 P |

Tracks: Don't Lose My Sign/Heart/Price Of Love/Forevermore/God Bless The Child

1989	■	All In The World/No Lies	7"	Nonstop Records	NSM 45-16
1991	■	One The Wall/Time	7"	Radium 226.05	RA 070
1992	☐	MEDICATION	CD	Radium 226.05	RA 9178 2
1993	☐	Election Day/Bottle Of Joy/Election Day (Smile remix)	MCD 3tr	Musik/Musik	MMS 4
1998	☐	Forgot My Name	7" flexi	Torture Entertainment	A.O.I.T 002

Came with the first issue of the magazine Acts Of Interstellar Turture

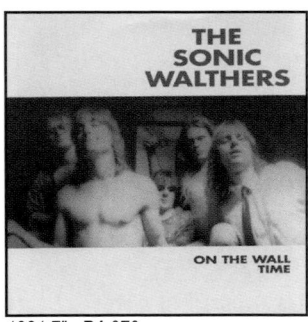

1991 7" - RA 070

SONIQ CIRCUS

Marcus Enochsson: v/g, Marco Ledri: k, Markus Nilsson: b, Christer Ugglin: d

Lund - This history draws back to 1999 when guitarist/singer Enochsson moved to Lund for studies. Later that year he teamed up with drummer Andreas Hanberger and together with singer/guitarist Zache Enochsson they formed a band. They started working on covers and original material in 2000, but a focus on studies made Andreas leave the band. However, things were solved when bassist Ambjörn Furenhed joined in November 2000. They went by the name **Testpilot 380**, later **TP3** and recorded some demos through the years. The band went through several member changes and in 2006 **TP3** became **Soniq Circus**. The debut, which consisted of reworked demo songs as well as new stuff, featured singer Calle Lennartsson and Mathias Beckius handled the keyboards. **Soniq Circus** is also featured on the compilations *Röstenen* (2009) and *A Flower Full Of Stars – A Tribute To The Flower Kings* (2011). The band plays highly intricate and quite heavy progressive/symphonic rock which should attract fans of **The Flower Kings** as well as **Mind's Eye** or **Dream Theater**.

Website: www.soniqcircus.com

2007 CD - PRCD 026

| 2007 | ■ | SONIQ CIRCUS | CD | Progress Records | PRCD 026 |
| 2011 | ■ | REFLECTIONS IN THE HOURGLASS | CD | Progress Records | PRCD 046 |

2011 CD - PRCD 046

SONS OF NEVERLAND
Mike: v, Peter "Pim" Forkelid: g, Rik: b

Tranås - Strange style indeed. Musically, they sound quite a lot like late **Rush** with a goth feeling and with almost death metal-like growling vocals. They are quite influenced by **Fields Of Nephilim**. The music is actually great and could, in my opinion, be really interesting with a more suitable singer. They started out in 1991 as a cover band doing songs by **Sisters Of Mercy**. Peter is also found in punk-band **Rövsvett** (Ass sweat). The band used programmed drums.

1994 ■ SOULKEEPER...CDd   Primitive Art...PAR 003

1994 CDd - PAR 003

SONS OF THUNDER
Michael Hjelte: v/g, Klas Pettersson: b, Daniel Mouton: d

Stockholm - Powerful straightforward metal with tons of heavy power chords, similar to bands like **White Cross** mixed with **Trouble**. I guess they lyrically could also be filed under "Bible-bashers" as they have a very strong Christian message with song titles like *Jesus Jesus Jesus*, *Jesus Viking* and *Lord Take Control*. They also have a track on the 2000 *The Second Coming* compilation. In 2000 Frank Bakken left the band to join Norwegians **Heaven**. He has previously recorded a single with pop band **Midnight Roses**, who gained some success in Norway. On **Sons Of Thunder** Klas replaced him. In 2003 Hjelte teamed up with guitarist Björn Sundström, guitarist Thorbjörn Weinesjö (**Veni Domine, Audiovision**) and drummer Tomas Weinesjö (**Veni Domine**) and the band changed into **Hero**.

1998 □ Metal Praise ....MCD 4tr   private ....TLSCD 5198
       Tracks: Jesus Jesus Jesus/Victorysong/Healing To My Soul/Psalm 151
2000 ■ LOAD AIM FIRE...CD   C.L. Music...................................CLCD 20001
2003 □ CIRCUS OF POWER..CD   Rivel Records .... RRCD 004

2000 CD - CLCD 20001

SORCERER
Anders Engberg: v, Peter Furulid: g/k, Mats Liedholm: g,
Johnny Hagel: b, Tommy Karlsson: d

Kista (Stockholm) - Formed in 1988 by Peter, Johnny and drummer Tommy Karlsson, who was replaced by Rickard Evensand in 1990. This band has sold more demos than some bands have sold albums. They are actually a great progressive doom band in the same vein as **Solitude Aeturnus** and **Candlemass**. Their highly acclaimed demos, *Demo 89* and *The Inquisition* ('92), were released on one CD by John Perez (**Solitude Aeturnus'** guitarist) on his own Brain Ticket Records, some tracks remixed. Anders Engberg was later found in **Lion's Share**, Johnny Hagel joined **Tiamat** in 1992 and Rickard played with **It's Alive** and **Eyeball** (later **Southpaw**). They split in 1993, when Hagel left the band. The song *Born With Fear* is featured on the *Rockbox* compilation. Drummer Tommy replaced Rickard after the first demo. Rickard moved to Australia and was playing with progressive rockers **Toehider**. The CD contains tracks from the band's two demos, where some tracks have been remixed. The band was resurrected in 2010, now featuring Engberg, Hagel, guitarist Kristian Niemann, (**Therion**), Ola Englund and Robert Iversen. A new album is set for release in 2013.

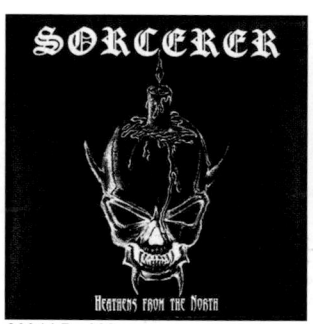

2004 LP - 002

2011 CD - ROCK/BTR033-F-2

1995 □ SORCERER..CD   Brain Ticket...B-001
2004 ■ HEATHENS FROM THE NORTH ....LP   Eat Metal Records 002
       700 copies.
2011 ■ SORCERER..CD   Rockadrome/Brain Ticket...ROCK/BTR033-F-2
       Bonus: Far Beyond. New artwork.

SORCERY
Ola Malmström: v, Fredrik Nygren: g, Magnus Karlsson-Mård: g,
Paul Johansson: b, Jocke Olofsson: d/g

Sandviken - Death metal with a lot of variations, although high speed is quite prominent. *Sorcery* was formed in 1986 as *Acid Queen*, influenced by bands like **Exodus, Slayer** and **Bathory**. The line-up featured guitarists Paul Johansson and Fredrik Nygren, singer Ola Malmström, bassist Magnus Karlsson-Mård and drummer Patrik L. Johansson.They recorded the first demo, *The Arrival*, in 1987, after which guitarist Nygren and drummer Johansson were fired from the band. People came and went, and finally Fredrik was redrafted and they had found drummer Joakim Hansson. Mikael Jansson handled the bass. The music had now become faster and less complicated. In the spring of 1988 they recorded the second demo *Ancient Creation*. After the demo Joakim left. Now Paul switched to drums, Magnus switched to guitar, leaving the bass spot empty. The style had now drawn more towards traditional slow-pace death metal, which showed on the demo *Unholy Crusade*. They were offered a deal with French label Thrash Records, who released the band's debut single. The single also made its way to Underground Records who released the debut album. In November 1991 Mikael left the band and together with singer Ola Malmström he formed **Fear My Solitude**. Guitarist Peter Hedman was drafted to fill the spot and Magnus went back to playing bass. In April 1992 Magnus got the boot and another demo was recorded after this. Shortly after, Fredrik left and later joined the band **Gadget**. The

1991 LP - U.G.R 003

1990 7" - THR 005

2011 3LPg - TTD 003

track *Inhabitants Of The Tomb* was featured on the *Voices Of Death* compilation. At this point the band was just a trio featuring Ola, Paul and Peter. Paul and Magnus went to **In Aeternum**, Peter quit playing and later in 1997 the band split up. In 2001 Paul, Mikael and Ola joined the band **Outremer**. In 2009 **Sorcery** reunited featuring Ola and Paul, and **Outrider** members guitarist Henrik Lindemo and drummer Jocke Olofsson. They recorded the demo *Master Of The Chains* in 2009. Joakim left in 2011 and former **In Aeternum** man John Falk replaced him. Next up, Henrik also left. Paul switched to guitar and they drafted bass player Mikael Carlsson.

Year		Title	Format	Label	Cat#	
1990	■	Rivers Of The Dead/The Rite Of Sacrifice	7"	Thrash Records	THR 005	
1991	■	BLOODCHILLING TALES	LP	Underground	U.G.R 003	$$
		1100 copies.				
1998	□	BLOODCHILLING TALES	CD	No Colours	NC 020	
		Bonus: Rivers Of The Dead/The Rite Of Sacrifice				
2006	□	BLOODCHILLING TALES	CDd	No Colours	NC 020/2006	
		Bonus: Ancient creation demo + Unholy Crusade demo.				
2009	□	BLOODCHILLING TALES	CD	Metal Inquisition	MI 001	
		Bonus: Ancient creation demo + Unholy Crusade demo.				
2009	□	BLOODCHILLING TALES	CDd	Metal Inquisition	MI 001	
		50 hand-numbered copies.				
2011	■	UNHOLY CREATIONS	3LP box	To The Death	TTD 003	
		The band's complete discography on 3 LPs.in a box. 400 copies. 100 copies also in a wooden box with cassette, patch, t-shirt, poster.				
2013	□	ARRIVAL AT SIX	LP	Xtreem Music	XM 120 LP	
2013	■	ARRIVAL AT SIX	CD	Xtreem Music	XM 120 CD	

2013 CD - XM 120 CD

SORDID DEATH
Samuel Johansson: v/g, Johan Ylenstrand: g, Karl Hannus: b, Gustav Karlsson: d

Jönköping - The band was formed in 1999 as a trio, strongly influenced by American death metal. Later the same year Ylenstrand joined. Zombified mangle-death influenced by bands like **Suffocation** and **Cannibal Corpse**, which sounds like it's been recorded in the engine room of a German tank. I swear I've never heard anything like it…

2001	■	Sordid Death	7" 4tr	private	- -
		Tracks: I Dethrone/Inchoating Holocaust/Mouth Of Madness/Of Death			

2001 7" - - -

SOREPTION
Fredrik Söderberg: v, Anton Svedin: g, Rikard Persson: b, Tony Westermark: d

Sundsvall - Intriguing technical death metal, at times a bit similar to **Meshuggah** with deep growling vocals. The band was formed in 2005. Westermark was ex-**Sanctification** and Svedin formerly in **Dragora**. The song 2 is also found on the compilation *Fear Candy 45B* (2007 Terrorizer).

2008	□	Illuminate The Excessive	MCD+DVD 4tr	Cube1 Records	SORE 002
		Tracks: 1/2/3/4 + DVD			
2010	■	DETERIATION OF MINDS	CD	NineTone	NRCD 106
2013	□	ENGINEERING THE VOID	CD	NineTone	n/a

2010 CD - NRCD 106

SORGELDOM
Erik "Dr." Sundén: v, J. Marklund: d/k

Skellefteå - **Sorgeldom** were initiated in 2006, by bassist/guitarist Jodöden as an acoustic solo project. The debut album however sounds closer to **Armagedda** or **Svartsyn**. After the album Jodöden (aka Johdet) left the band. Marklund is also in **Grifteskymfning**, **LIK** and **Whirling**, while Sundén fronted **Blodskald**.

2009	□	INNERLIG FÖRMÖRKELSE	CD	Frostscald Records	FS 33
2010	□	INNER RECEIVINGS	CDd	Nordvis	NVPTOS0-02
2011	■	VITHATTEN	CD	Frostscald Records	FS 53
2011	□	…FROM OUTER INTELLIGENCE	CD	Frostscald Records	FS 54

2011 CD - FS 53

SORHIN
Micke "Nattfursth" Österberg: v, Anders "Eparygon": g/b,
Anders "Zathanel" Löfgren: d

Borlänge - The first sign of life from Borlänge band **Sorhin** was the 1993 demo *Svarta själars vandring*, at the time featuring Johan "Shamaatae" Lagher (**Arckanum**) as session man. It was followed by *I fullmånens dystra sken* in 1995. The members were also found in side project **Fafner**. Brutal death metal. Löfgren is ex-**Setherial** and also found in **Blot Mine** and **Midvinter**. Micke also runs Svartvintras Records. The first album was produced by Peter Tägtgren. The band also used the bass services of Mattias Skoog (**Enslavement, Coffinmen**) on *Apocalypsens Ängel*. The original version of *Skogsgriftens Rike* is a rare item, gaining around 200 USD on Ebay. *Förbannade År* is a box set featuring all songs ever released plus five bonus tracks.

1996 CD - NDP 008

1996	☐	Åt Fanders Med Ljusets Skapelser/Svart Lyser Tronen	7" PD	Near Dark	NDP 006	
		500 copies.				
1996	■	I DET GLIMRANDE MÖRKRETS DJUP	CD	Near Dark	NDP 008	
1996	☐	Skogsgriftens Rike	MCD 4tr	X-Treme	XTR 001	
		Tracks: Svarta själars vandring/Skogsgriftens rike/I Fullmånenes dystra sken/Och om natten min själ dansar				
1996	☐	Skogsgriftens Rike	MLP 4tr	Arte De Occulta	Occulta 002	$$
		300 copies hand-numbered.				
1998	■	Döden MCMXCVIII	MCD 3tr	Near Dark	NDP 013	
		Tracks: Ett sista monument ståtligt/När döden sträcker ut sina vingar/Blott en människa svag. 1998 hand numbered copies.				
1998	☐	I DET GLIMRANDE MÖRKRETS DJUP	LP PD	Mark Of The Devil	DEVIL 003	
		500 copies.				
2001	☐	APOCALYPSENS ÄNGEL	CD	Shadow	SHADOW 007	
2001	☐	APOCALYPSENS ÄNGEL	LP GF	Shadow	SHADOW 007	
		345 copies.				
2001	☐	FÖRBANNADE ÅR 1993-2001	Box	Norma Evangelium Diaboli	NED 015	
		Box with 2LP+2x10"+7".				
2002	☐	To Give Death By The Sword Of Christ! (split)	7"	Svartvintras Productions	SVP 007	
		Split with Puissance. Track: By The Sword Of Christ. 500 hand numbered copies.				
2009	☐	SKOGSGRIFTENS RIKE	CDd	Norma Evangelium Diaboli	NED 015-1	
		Bonus: Svarta själars boning/Enectum/I skuggan af nattens herre/I fullmånens dystra sken/Den mörke härskaren/Ett fornnordiskt rike				
2009	☐	I DET GLIMRANDE MÖRKRETS DJUP	CDd	Norma Evangelium Diaboli	NED 015-2	
		Bonus: Svart lyser tronen				
2009	■	APOCALYPSENS ÄNGEL	CDd	Norma Evangelium Diaboli	NED 015-3	
		Bonus: Blott en människa svag/Att ge död, och att välkomna död				

1998 MCD - NDP 013

2009 CDd NED 015-3

SOULBREACH

Daniel Andersson: v, Per Fransson: g, Dino Medanhodzic: g, Magnus Wall: b, Erik Stenström: d

Arboga - The band was formed in 2003 as *Mausoleum*, and recorded two demos under this name in 2003, *Demo 2003* and *Fluctuating Senses*. In 2004, they changed their name to *Soulbreach*. They were picked up by Mascot Records, who released their debut in 2007. *Soulbreach* play tight and heavy, brutal yet quite melodic metal with a technical twist. Aggressive, but not growling vocals, at times with clean parts. Well played, with killer guitar work and great song material. I'd describe them as *Pantera* mixed with *Soilwork*. Dino has also played in *Septic Breed* and *Carnal Forge*, Wall in *Godhate*, *Haterush*, *Abhothh*, *Septic Breed* and *Thronaeum* and Fransson in *Carnal Grief*. After the album Stenström left the band, and it has been quite since.

| 2007 | ■ | MY DIVIDING LINE | CD | Mascot | M 7207 2 |

2007 CD - M 7207 2

SOULDIVIDER

Jonas Gustafson: v, Andreas Hahne: g, Martin Henricsson: g, Martin Nilsson: b, Claes Lysén: d

Karlstad - Grinding stoner rock with a vibe of *Thin Lizzy*. The band released two demos, *Below The Astral Surface* and *The Big Relax* before being signed. The track *Anymore* was found on *The Mighty Desert Rock Avengers* (2002 People Like U) compilation.

2001	☐	The Big Relax	MCD 5tr	12th Planet Music	TMP 001
		Tracks: A Need To Escape/Anymore/Strange Feeling 4 AM/Inhale Your Destination/Second Ride			
2003	■	SUPERSOUND CITY	CD	12th Planet Music	TPM 005

2003 CD - TPM 005

SOULDRAINER

Marcus Edvardsson: v/g, Joakim Wassberg: b, Arttu Malkki: d

Östersund - Formed in 1999 by guitarist Marcus (ex-*Chastisement, In Battle, Aeon, Endless Torture, Sanctification*), singer Johan Klitkou (ex-*Chastisement*) and drummer Nils Fjellström (*A*Teem, Dark Funeral, Odhinn, Chastisement, In Battle, Aeon, Sanctification* etc) at first as a studio project. Heavy, grinding death metal adding strings and demonic angel choirs. Heavy and fat production and well-played. The band recorded their first demo in 2003, *Everything Ends*, which created a buzz. After this they added second guitarist Daniel Dlimi (*Aeon, Divine Descecration, Sanctification, The Equinox Ov The Gods, In Battle*) and bass player Joakim Wassberg (*The Equinox Ov The Gods, Defaced Creation*). In 2005 a second demo, *First Row In Hell* caught the attention of Mascot Records. After the recording of the debut album *Reborn*, Arttu Malkki replaced Nils. Singer Johan also left the band after the album. They recorded a new demo, *Garage Demo 2008*, with Marcus also taking over the vocals. Before the recording of the second album in 2010 also Daniel parted ways with the band.

2007 CD - M 7216 2

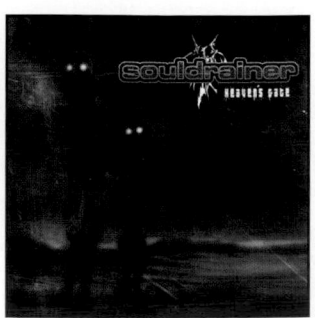
2011 CD - VSP 025

| 2007 | ■ | REBORN | CD | Mascot | M 7216 2 |
| 2011 | ■ | HEAVEN'S GATE | CD | ViciSolum | VSP 025 |

SOULESS

Jenny Bogne: v/g, **Joakim Fasth:** g, **Mattias Fasth:** b, **Peter Persson:** d

Oxelösund - Demo-quality recording, mid-league young band, but with some potential. Slightly grunge-tinged at times out of tune female-fronted hard rock/metal. The title suggests a slightly heavier musical journey. Not to be confused with the US death/grinders.

2001 ■ Songs From The Purgatory...MCD 4tr private .... LRSS 01
    Tracks: One Step Away/All The Same/Leaving/Little Chicago

2001 MCD - LRSS 01

SOULGRINDER

Daniel Lillman: v/g, prog, **Niclas Lillman:** v/b/prog

Västerås - The band was formed in 1993 by the brothers under the name **Grinder**. They immediately added Soul- because of too many namesakes. Between 1994 and 1997 they recorded several demos and changed into a more goth-oriented industrial band. **Soulgrinder** can also be found on the compilations *Extreme Close-Up Vol 2*, *Subreality* and *Subsoil-2*. *The Forgiven Ain't Forgotten* is a ten-track album featuring unreleased **Soulgrinder** demos than can be downloaded from the band's site together with artwork and all. Goth-oriented heavy rock with quite horrible, deep, out-of-pitch vocals, very badly produced, not very well played and generally quite uninteresting. The band was also working on a new album which was to be divided in two parts, one straightforward goth metal part and one very uncommercial part based on occult stories from the band's home town. As the band broke up in 2000 this probably never happened.

1998 ■ ENTER..CD Moriensis .... MORCD 016

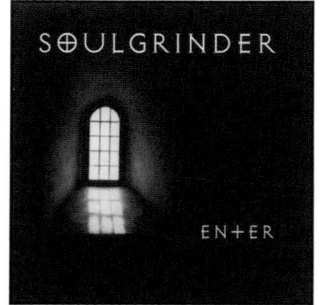
1998 CD - MORCD 016

SOULQUAKE SYSTEM

Daniel Engman: v, **Jocke Persson:** g, **Fredrik Reinedahl:** g,
Johan Nääs: b, **Henrik Bergström:** d

Göteborg - Previously known as *Tyburn*, under which name they released one MCD. Brutal metal/hardcore in the vein of **Biohazard** or **Sick Of It All**. On the second album bass player Nääs (ex-**Suborn**) replaced Jan Lindström and singer Engman replaced Anders Jakobsson. In 1999 they were dropped by the label and the band broke up. The members got involved in the project **Seventy For Nothing**, which was more in the vein of **Foo Fighters**. Fredrik and Johan formed **Elite** together with some former **Polluted Influence** members, but the band soon folded and they are now in the band **Soul Exile**. The track *Lies Shine Through* is found on the *Unsigned Artists 1* (96 TBC) compilation.

1996 CD - BMCD 99

1996 ■ ANGRY BY NATURE - UGLY BY CHOICE.................................CD Strontium/Black Mark........................ BMCD 99
1998 ■ A FIRM STATEMENT..CD Black Mark .... BMCD 126

1998 CD - BMCD 126

SOULREAPER

Christoffer Hjertén: v, **Johan Norman:** g, **Stefan Karlsson:** g,
Mikael Lång: b, **Tobias R Kellgren:** d

Göteborg - When **Dissection** folded due to Jon Nödtveit going to prison in 1997, Kellgren and Norman formed **Reaper**. They were completed with Lång, Hjertén and guitarist Mattias Eliasson, who was soon replaced by Christoffer Hermansson. After a first demo they got a deal with Nuclear Blast and recorded the debut. After the recording Hermansson left to be replaced by Karlsson and the band changed its name to **Soulreaper** before the release. The track *Satanized* from *Written In Blood* is also featured on *The Past Is Alive* by **Dissection**, which is really the only connection to the old band. It's also found on **Decameron**'s *My Shadow*, Norman's old home. **Soulreaper** plays brutal death metal in the vein of **Morbid Angel**. Kellgren is also found in **Seventh One**.

2000 CD - NB 4032-2

2002 7" - HHR 145

2000 ■ WRITTEN IN BLOOD ....CD Nuclear Blast ....NB 4032-2
2000 □ WRITTEN IN BLOOD ....CD Irons (Russia) .... CD 00-9
2002 □ Worshippers Of Death (split)..7" EP Bloodstone................................... BLOOD 006
    Split with Runemagick. Limited edition 500 copies. Track: Blood Boils
2002 ■ Son Of The Dead/Devil's Speech ....7" Hammerheart Records .... HHR 145
2003 ■ LIFE ERAZER...CD Hammerheart Records .... HHR 146
2003 □ LIFE ERAZER..CDd Hammerheart Records .... HHR 146
2004 □ LIFE ERAZER...CD Karmageddon .... KARMA 045
2004 □ LIFE ERAZER..CDd Karmageddon .... KARMA 045
    Bonus: Fall From Grace/Son Of The Dead/Devil's Speech
2004 □ LIFE ERAZER...CD Candlelight (USA) CDL0130CD
2004 □ LIFE ERAZER...CD Nordic Media (Russia) .... NMKM 0016
2006 □ LIFE ERAZER...CD Encore Records (Brazil)..................... ENC 052
2008 □ WRITTEN IN BLOOD ....CDd Metal Mind .... MASS CD 1227 DG
    2000 copies

2003 CD - HHR 146

SOUND EXPLOSION

Fredrika Berggren: v, Mattias Hedberg: g, Jonas Tornemalm: g,
Fredrik Plahn: k, Jens Blylod: b, Daniel Eriksson: d

Falun - This is a really nice, high-quality AOR offering with hints of *Wrabit* and Lisa Price. Lots of keyboard and guitar. Fredrika has a crystal clear and really strong voice. The band has unfortunately split, but the singles are well worth looking for. Jens Blylod is not related to Ronny Blylod (*Destynation, Blackrain*).

1991 ☐ Forget & Forgive/Play By The Rules	7"	Wisa	WISS 27
1992 ■ Bad Seventeen/Save Your Fire	7"	Wisa	WISS 30

1992 7" - WISS 30

SOURCE

Lennart Andersson: k, Thorbjörn Andersson: g, John Miller: b, Håkan Mellquist: d

Västerås - AOR with a strong symphonic touch. Produced by Christer Åkerberg (*Trettioåriga Kriget*).

1988 ■ Domination Of Enterprise/Visions	7"	private	TRAP 1

1988 7" - TRAP 1

SOURCE

Jonathan Blomberg: v, Pierre Andersson: g,
Niklas Fjärve: g, Daniel Fjärve: b, John Gelotte: d

Herrljunga - Formed in the spring of 1998 when the members were in their early teens. Per Korpås inially played bass and Andreas Nilsson guitar. The band recorded their first demo, *Through The Skies Of Destiny*, the year of creation, followed by *Enslaved* in 1998. After this, Pierre Andersson replaced Korpås. Late summer of 2000 Nilsson was out of the band and Pierre took over the guitar, adding Daniel Fjärve as bass player. In 2001 they recorded the demo *Condemnation* and in 2003 the band released their debut. *Source* plays Gothenburg-style death metal, influenced by the masters; *In Flames* and *Dark Tranquillity*.

2003 ■ LEFT ALONE	CD	Goi Music	Goi200315
2003 ☐ LEFT ALONE	CD	Soundholic (Japan)	SHCD-0048

2003 CD - Goi200315

SOURCE OF IGNITION

Andreas Siegrist: v/b, Michael Siegrist: g, Mikael Källgren: d

Stockholm - *Source Of Ignition* grew out of the 90s hardcore and metal scene, building their foundation on aggressive down-to-earth music, drawing influences from bands like *Accept*, *Iron Maiden* and *Mötley Crüe*, as well as the Swedish metal scene. At first they went under the name *Eizenkopf* for about a year and recorded two demos during this time. In 2000 they changed their name to *Source Of Ignition* and recorded their first demo in 2002, followed by a second demo in 2004 and a third in 2005, all self-titled. In 2007 they released their first EP, *What We're Made Of*. Sounds like *Entombed* meets *Transport League* with a touch of *Pantera* for good measure. Great powerful stuff! Guitarist Tomas Karström was added to the live line-up.
Website: www.sourceofignition.com

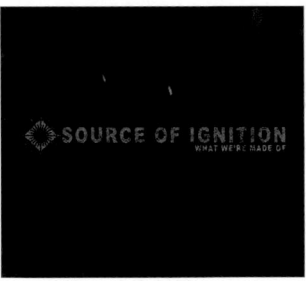
2007 MCDd - HVR 0107

2007 ■ What We're Made Of	MCDd 4tr	Hornvalley Records	HVR 0107
Tracks:Serenity/Dark Signs/Take These Words/Shattered Soul			

SOUTHFORK

Gunnar Lööf: v/g/k, Henrik Bergqvist: g, Tomas Thorberg: b/k, Sebastian Sippola: d

Stockholm - Outstanding, driving seventies hard rock, like a mix of *Mountain*, *Led Zeppelin* and *MC 5*. Henrik and Sebastian have previously played and recorded with *Fortune*. Sippola was also found in *Plankton* and *Grand Magus*. Thorberg is also found in *Plankton*, *Snakes In Paradise* and *John Norum Band* and has also recorded an album with *Four Sticks*, where Bergqvist was also found. He is now in *The Poodles*. Anders Fästader (aka Nilsson) (ex-*Great King Rat, Tryckvåg* etc) handled the bass on the first album.

1999 CD - BMCD 141

1999 ■ SOUTHFORK	CD	Black Mark	BMCD 141
2001 ■ STRAIGHT AHEAD	CD	Black Mark	BMCD 151

SOUTHPAW

Mats Levén: v, Fredrik Åkesson: g, John Levén: b, Rickard Evensand: d

Stockholm - When Fredrik Åkesson left *Talisman* he formed the far heavier instalment *Eyeball*. They recorded an album for Empire Records, but it was never released. The band then changed its name to *Southpaw* and UK label Z Records released it under the new name. It's quite far

2001 CD - BMCD 151

from Åkesson's earlier band and closer to colleagues **Skintrade**. Heavy rock with an alternative/ grungy touch with hints of **Soundgarden** and **Alice In Chains**. A great album indeed, while the band was quite dissatisfied with the mastering and label in general. Mats has recorded with numerous other bands, such as **Therion**, Yngwie Malmsteen, **Dogface, AB/CD, Abstrakt Algebra**, etc etc., John is in **Europe**, while Evensand has recorded several albums with **It's Alive** and **Sorcerer** and is now also found in Australian progsters **Toehider**. A cover of Yngwie Malmsteen's *Disciples From Hell* can be found on the *Power From The North* compilation, but Evensand was not participating on that recording. Åkesson is today found in **Opeth** and **Krux**.

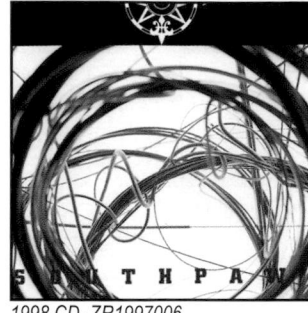

1998 ☐ SOUTHPAW...CD   Dolphin (Japan) BLCK-86016
    Bonus: Spiral
1998 ■ SOUTHPAW...CD   Z Records ZR1997006

1998 CD- ZR1997006

SPACE ODYSSEY (RICHARD ANDERSSON'S)
David Fremberg: v, Magnus Nilsson: g/b, Richard Andersson: k, Jörg Andrews: d

Malmö/Skurup - Richard is the main man behind several neoclassically-oriented bands in the Malmö area. In 1998 he formed **Majestic** and released two albums, in 2001 he recorded an album with **Silver Seraph** and in 2002 he released the first of four albums with the band **Time Requiem**. He has also made guest appearances on a multitude of albums by bands like **Adiago, Zool, Midnight Sun, Mansson, Karmakanic, Evil Masquerade, Angtoria** and **Iron Mask**. Besides working with **Time Requiem**, Richard formed a new band now together with old friend and outstanding neoclassical shredder Magnus Nilsson. He also drafted **Astral Doors/ Road II Ruin/Lion's Share** singer and Dio sound-alike Nils Patrik Johansson, **Talisman** bassist Marcel Jacob and drummer Zoltan Czörsz, who has also played with **The Flower Kings** and **Art Metal**. In 2003 the first album, *Embrace The Galaxy*, was unearthed. If you imagine a mix of Dio-era **Rainbow** and **Rising Force**, I think you're pretty close. On his next release, *The Astral Episode*, Richard used the talents of new seventeen-year-old drummer Andreas Brobjer (**Platitude, Lady Gaga**) and here Magnus also handled the bass work, which he also did on the follow-up, *Tears Of The Sun*. Richard now used the talent of drummer Jörg Andrews and **Andromeda/Constancia/Truth** singer Fremberg, which gave the album a different touch. The music was also less neoclassical and more classic hard rock. According to Richard, it's his most pretentious album, and a great one at that.
Website: www.anderssonmusic.com

You talkin' to ME?!

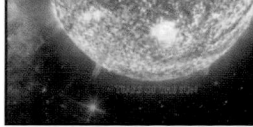
2005 CD - RR 059

2003 ☐ EMBRACE THE GALAXY ....CD   Regain Records ....RR 0309-035
2003 ☐ EMBRACE THE GALAXY ....CD   King Records (Japan) KICP-950
    Bonus: The Finest Of A Good Kind
2005 ■ THE ASTRAL EPISODE ....CD   Regain Records ....RR 059
2005 ☐ THE ASTRAL EPISODE ....CD   King Records (Japan) KICP-1050
    Bonus: The Finest Of A Good Kind
2006 ■ TEARS OF THE SUN ....CD   Regain Records ....RR 111
2006 ☐ TEARS OF THE SUN ....CD   Avalon Marquee (Japan)..............MICP-10622
    Bonus: Jailbreaker

2006 CD - RR 111

SPACE PROBE TAURUS
Ola Sjöberg: v/g, Magnus Eronen: g/v, Per Boder: b, Calle Boman: d

Vålberg/Karlstad - The band was formed in 1992 as **Snake Machine**, featuring Per Boder (**God Macabre, Macabre End**) and drummer Erik Sundler. Former **God Macabre/Macabre End** colleague Ola Sjöberg was drafted. They recorded the demo *Skinned Woman And Mescaline* in 1993, after which singer Enberg was drafted. In 1994 they recorded the second demo *Ride The Wildbeast*, after which the band fell apart. However, they regrouped in 1997 under the new name; **Space Probe Taurus**, with Sjöberg handling the vocals. The style had now become stoner rock and they recorded the three demos *Low On Karma High On Speed, Hallucination Generation* and *Acid Worship* before releasing the 7". The line-up on the single featured singer/guitarist Ola Sjöberg, guitarist Per Boder, bassist Jonas Stålhammar and drummer Erik Sundler. They are also featured on the soundtrack for the movie *I Am Vengeance* (Meteor City), the **Blue Cheer** tribute *Blue Explotion* (99 Black Widow) and the local compilation *Studifrämjandet Vol 2* and *Taurus Rising* is also found on the *Metalbox* compilation (01 Hellbilly). The name came from an old sci-fi movie of the same name. On the album, which was actually recorded already in 2004-2005, Calle Boman (**Dogpound, Tinkerhell**) handled the drums, Magnus Eronen (**Sparzanza, Moaning Wind, Capricorn**) played guitar and the bass was handled by Per Boder. After the album the band went through some line-up changes and recorded the demos *Peace, Love & Satan, Who's Along For The Revolution* and *The Embla Session* before going into hiatus for a couple of years. The last known line-up featured singer/guitarist Sjöberg, guitarist Marius Tömte, bassist Enberg and drummer Boman. A new album is in the making. **Space Probe Taurus** play fuzzed-out, rowdy, garagey stoner with strong hints of **Blue Cheer** and **MC 5**.

2000 7" - SR 03

2000 ■ Insect City/Mescaline/Dirtcult 72..7" 3tr   Slowride/Game Two (USA)....................SR 03
2008 ■ SPACE PROBBE TAURUS...CD   Buzzville Records ....BUZZCD 019

2008 CD - BUZZCD 019

SPACEBONE

Viktor Ahnfelt: v, **Björn Wennås:** g, **Peter Eriksson:** g,
Patrik Thorngren: b, **Mattias Rasmussen:** d

Uppsala/Stockholm - Started out in 1991 under the name *Thog* in a more industrial metal style. On the first demo they were compared to bands like *Jesus And Mary Chain* and *Big Black*. The members were then Jacob Jennische (b), later in *Six Pack Sonic* and *Dimma*, Fredrik Bultmark (g), Mattias and Viktor. The second release shows influences from bands like *Helmet*, *Prong* and *Fudge Tunnel*.

1994 MCDd - TTR 03

1994 ■ Stay Down...MCDd 6tr Tangotrain ....TTR 03
    Tracks: Stay Down/The Fear/Halloween/Wire Mother/Seventy-Seven/Fish Police

SPAPS

Johan Kalin: v, **Nicklas Wintersteller:** g, **Patrik Magnusson:** g,
Björn Follin: b, **Lars Hemlin:** d

Orrefors - Formed in 1991 as a cover band, but started writing original material. They recorded some demos before releasing the MCD. Heavy and grinding detuned metal, a bit reminiscent of *Living Parazite* and *Blakk Totem*. Great, powerful stuff, with a wall of guitars and nice groove. The band was unfortunately put on ice in 1997 due to the members pursuing different other trivial projects such as studies and work.

1997 MCD - SPACD01

1997 ■ Life Lost In Living ....MCD 4tr private SPACD01
    Tracks: Sentenced/Brown Nose/Sleep/Life Lost In Living

SPARZANZA

Fredrik Weileby: v, **Calle Johannesson:** g, **Magnus Eronen:** g,
Johan Carlsson: b, **Anders Åberg:** d

Karlstad - Formed in 1996 by brothers Calle and David (g), Peter Eriksson (v/b) and Anders Åberg (d). They recorded their first demo *Inbetween* under the name *Shallow*. Andreas Kloss joined on bass and the band recorded its first 7". In 1997 he left for his main band *The Hermaphrodites* and Johan Carlsson (*Dawn Of Decay, Tailpipe, Moaning Wind, Capricorn*) replaced him. The first single is a white label with just the name stamped on it and the quality of the pressing is pretty cheap. In 2000 singer Peter was replaced by Fredrik Weileby. The first recording was 70s-influenced riff-oriented hard rock with a spacey touch, like a mix of *Black Sabbath* and *Hawkwind*, while the first album is more akin to the new millennium stoner rock. A great band indeed! On *Into the Sewers* the band's sound went a bit more towards metal. On *Banisher Of The Light* they went into a more modern-metal-influenced style. This one, like the previous was produced by Rikard Löfgren (*Bay Laurel*). The album featured guest spots from Peter Dolving (*The Haunted*) and Ralf Gyllenhammar (*Mustasch, B-Thong*). Early 2008 the band entered the studio, again with Löfgren, to record the album *In Voodoo Veritas*. During the recordings guitarist David Johannesson left the band to join *Mustasch*. He was soon replaced by Magnus Eronen (*Space Probe Taurus, Moaning Wind, Capricorn*). In 2011 the album *Toile Á Cinq* was released. The sound had now completely changed to modern nu-oriented metal similar to bands like *Shinedown* and *Alter Bridge*. The band actually handles both their old and new sound great and very convincingly. The band can also be found on various compilations, such as: *Swallow This* (97 Phyramid, track: *Krakataurus*), *Welcome To Meteor City* (98 Meteor City, track: *Liquid Thoughts*), *A Fist Full Of Freebir*d (98 Freebird, track: *Black Jack Vegas*) and *Metalbox* (Hellbilly 01, track: *Silverbullet*),
Website: www.sparzanza.com

Hangin' in the bars

1999 7" PD - WordS 004

2011 CD - SPI 383 CD

1997 ☐ Wheeler Dealer .... 7" 3tr private ....BON 97-01
    Tracks: Bonanza Justice/Gorilla Circus/Wheeler Dealer
1998 ☐ Sparzanza/Lowrider (split) ....7" private .... - -
    Split with Lowrider. Track: Burnin' Boots. Red vinyl.
1999 ■ Thirteen/Death Trippin' ....7" PD Words Of Wisdom.......................WordS 004
2000 ☐ The Sundancer/Pavement Princess ....CDS 2tr private ....BONO 02
2001 ☐ I Love You Both (split) ....CDS 4tr Water Dragon...............................WDsplit 011
    Split with Superdice. Tracks: Be Myself/Angel Of Vengeance
2001 ☐ ANGELS OF VENGEANCE..CD Water Dragon................................ WDszz 015
2003 ☐ INTO THE SEWER ....CD Water Dragon................................ WDszz 019
2006 ☐ BANISHER OF THE LIGHT ....CD Black Cult Records ....BCR-SZA 001
2009 ☐ IN VOODOO VERITAS...CD Kabuki...KR-SE-07
2009 ☐ Sparzanza/Grand Massive (split) ....7" Kabuki...KR-SE-10
    Split with Grand Massive. Tracks: Dead Red Revolver/Hollow. 500 copies.
2011 ■ FOLIE Á CINQ ....CD Spinefarm ....SPI 383 CD
2012 ■ DEATH IS CERTAIN. LIFE IS NOT..CD Lionheart Records ....LHICD 0148

2012 CD - LHICD 0148

SPAZMOSITY

Peter Emanuelsson: v, Björn Thelberg: g, M. Lamming: g,
Mikael Nordström: b, Dimitri Jungi: d

Stockholm - Formed in 1994 by Thelberg and Lamming, who started out playing covers. Peter Emanuelsson (*Plague Divine*) joined on vocals two years later. The band recorded five demos before the debut album. After the debut album Emanuelsson was replaced by Ola Lindgren (*Grave, Putrefaction*), who made a guest appearance on the debut. The band went through various drummer, such as Marcus Jonsson (*Insision, Pandemonic* etc), Björn Vasseur and Jesper Enander before drafting Jungi (*Cryptic Art, WAN, Cursed 13*) in 2007. The track *Beyond The Gates Of Slumber* was featured on the compilation *From The Underground...* (X-Treme Records).

2010 ■ WELCOME DEATH...CD Khaosmaster.....................................KMP 016

2010 CD - KMP 016

SPAWN OF POSSESSION

Dennis Röndum: v, Jonas Bryssling: g, Christian Müenzner: g
Erlend Caspersen: b, Henrik Schönström: d

Kalmar - **Spawn Of Possession** were formed in 1997 by Jonas Bryssling and Jonas Karlsson, who handled bass and guitar, plus drummer/singer Dennis Röndum (ex-*Visceral Bleeding*). In 2000 they released their first demo, *The Forbidden*. Bass player Niklas Dewerud (former drummer of *Visceral Bleeding*) was soon drafted, and in 2001 the demo *Church Of Deviance* was recorded. The demo resulted in a deal with Unique Leader and they recorded the debut, *Cabinet*, produced by Magnus Sedenberg (*Baltimoore, Groover*). Shortly after the recording singer Jonas Renvaktar (*Disruption, Istapp, Jack Daw*) joined. The band toured with many name bands worldwide. In 2006 the band's second effort, *Noctambulant*, was released. After some time touring and writing the band was picked up by Relapse Records in May 2011. The line-up had again changed seeing Röndum now concentrating on singing, new guitarist Müenzner (*Obscura, Civilization One, Majesty* etc), bassist Caspersen (*Emeth, Apostacy, Vile, Incinerate* etc) and drummer Schönström (*Enshrined, Incapacity, Unmoored, Solar Dawn, Quest Of Aidance, Torchbearer, Traumatized*). *Incurso* saw the band going in a highly interesting ultra-technical direction with lots of cool musical surprises, at times similar to *CB Murdock* and *Calm*.

2002 CD - ULR 60010-2

2012 CD - RR 7184-2

2002	■	CABINET	CD	Unique Leader Records	ULR 60010-2
2006	☐	NOCTAMBULANT	CD	Neurotic Records	NRT 060009
2012	■	INCURSO	CD	Relapse Records	RR 7184-2
2012	☐	INCURSO	CD	Relapse Records (Japan)	YSCY-1238

SPEARFISH

Thomas Thulin: v/b, Peter Lundin: g, Johan Sterner: d

Nässjö - **Spearfish** were formed in 1995 and the name came from the town in Ohio, USA, named after the way the Native American Indians used to catch fish. The first album contains melodic, powerful hard rock with a touch of sleaze. Hints of early *Mötley Crüe*, but with a touch of southern rock as well as traditional hard rock. Thulin (ex-*Priority*) sounds a bit like a mix of Vince Neil and *Rush*'s Geddy Lee. On *Affected By Time* the style changed, now being great seventies-oriented hard rock, with hints of *Zeppelin*. The album also contains a cover of *Rush*'s *Makin' Memories*. The line-up featured Thulin, Lundin and drummer Mick Nordström (*Modest Attraction, Narnia, Lava Engine*), while former rhythm guitarist Ola Johansson was out of the band. The band's next album, *Back For The Future*, was a charity project for the Childrens Cancer Foundation (gained a total of around 300 SEK after Sweden Rock Records' "expenses" had been deducted). Nordström was out and drummer Johan Sterner was in. The album, which is one studio and one live, featured lots of guests such as Mick Box (*Uriah Heep*), Nicky Moore (*Samson, Mammoth, From Behind*), Janne Stark (*Overdrive, Constancia* etc), Manny Charlton (*Nazareth*), Paul DiAnno, Mats Levén, Mick Nordström, Stefan Elmgren etc. CD 1 featured covers of *AC/DC, Thin Lizzy, Free*, Jon English, *Led Zeppelin, CCR* etc. *Area 605* contains a cover of *Rush*'s *Limelight* and the band has actually also appeared as a *Rush* tribute band. Keyboards on the album were played by Björn Gustavsson. Thulin was later in *Covered Call*.

2002 CD - SRR 002

2003 2CD - SRR 011

2005 CD - LMC 127

1996	☐	DIFFERENT ACCESS	CD	Teknik Kompaniet	TKCD003
2002	■	AFFECTED BY TIME	CD	Sweden Rock Records	SRR 002
2003	■	BACK, FOR THE FUTURE	2CD	Sweden Rock Records	SRR 011
2005	■	AREA 605	CD	Lion Music	LMC 127

SPECTRA

Jan Hermansson: v/g/k, Bengt Alexandersson: g, Lasse Olsson: g,
Kenneth Holmström: b, Lennart Andersson: d

Arvika - Not to be confused with the band *Spektra*. Lasse Olsson later played with *Ellen B*. The A-side is pretty good melodic hard rock/AOR. Nice guitars, but the vocals are a bit weak. The B-side is a very *Toto*-ish ballad.

1983 ■ Ensam/Open Your Eyes..7" Stanley & Andrew ....SAM 5205

1983 7" - SAM 5205

SPEEDFREAKS

Roger Crossler: v, Edo Seleskovic: g, Zvonko Hvizdak: b, Uffe "6-10" Speedfreak: d

Göteborg - The band was formed in 1998 and the name was a tribute to **Motörhead**. The present line-up has existed since 2000, when the first 5-track demo CD-R was recorded. Raunchy, rough-edged garagy rock 'n' metal. The missing link between **The Hellacopters** and **Motörhead**. Powerful beer-belly stuff indeed. On the verge of punk, but leaning over on the hard rock side. On the later releases the sound became a bit heavier adding elements of **Black Label Society**. The band has appeared on various compilations, such as *A Collection Of Great Dance Tunes Vol 1* (HDP), *International Punk Box Set* (Meathead Records) and *Röjarskivan 4* (Ägg Tapes & Records). The band split up in 2008.
Website: www.speedfreaks.se

2001 7" - BBR 001

2001	■	Speedfreaks/Sick!Sick!Sick!	7"	Boogiebastard	BBR 001
2001	□	BORN A ROCKER - DIE A ROCKER	CD	Boogiebastard	BBR 003
2001	□	Speedfreaks v/s 69-Hard (split)	7" EP	Beluga	BBR 009
		Split with 69-Hard. Tracks: Not What U Wanted/Leadhelmet			
2003	□	Speedfreaks/Bombäst (split)	7" EP	Bad Reputation Records	BAd REP 002
		Split with Bombäst. White vinyl. Tracks: Ballistic/Devil's Little Helper			
2003	□	Givin' Rock 'N Roll A Bad Name (split)	7"	Zorch Productions	CZ-20
		Split with Electric Frankenstein. Track: Good To Be Alive			
2003	□	Speedfreaks/Powder Monkeys (split)	7"	Bad Attitude Records	Badat! 012
		Split with Powder Monkeys. Tracks: I'm Right, You're Wrong			
2003	■	Starring Your Favourites	7" 4tr	Devil's Shitburner Records	DSB 010
		Tracks: Now It's Tomorrow/Sick! Sick! Sick!/Ballistic/Day By Day. Orange vinyl. 500 copies.			
2003	□	NIGHT RIDING ANTHEMS (split)	CD	Sleazey Records	SLEAZEYSS 007
		Split with We Were Wolves. Tracks: Out For Kicks/Tattooed Beat Messiah/Going Underground/Just A Boy/Somebody To Roll			
2006	□	OUT FOR KICKS	CD	Mondongo Canibale Records	MCR 005

2003 7" - DBS 010

SPEEDNAUTS

Mats Berglund: v/b

Västerås - Quite a strange band. The A-side starts out as a basic 80s metal tune, with a chorus in the true Scotch folk music vein (where are the bagpipes, lads?). The B-side is just generally weird, with thrown in high-pitched vocal parts. Not bad though.

1984	●	Suckers/I Can Dance	7"	Tintagel	TINT. 001
		No artwork.			

1984 7" - TINT. 001

SPEEDY GONZALES

Thomas Vikström: v, Tommy Denander: g, Marcel Jacob: b, Daniel Flores: d

Stockholm - **Speedy Gonzales** were originally founded back in 1990 featuring singer Thomas Vikström (ex-**Talk Of The Town**, later in **Candlemass, Mind's Eye, Stormwind** etc), guitarist Tommy Denander (ex-**ATC**, later in **Radioactive, Prisoner** etc) and drummer Mats "Dalton" Dahlberg (ex-**Treat, Dalton, Highbrow**). The band was heading for greatness, but as they never managed to secure a deal, Tommy left the ship and the band subsequently folded. However, they recorded some highly acclaimed demos that, a decade later, would spawn the interest of German label AOR Heaven. So, in 2004 Denander and Vikström blew new life into the band, engaging bass player Marcel Jacob (**Talisman, Rising Force, Last Autumn's Dream, Humanimal**) and drummer Daniel Flores (**Mind's Eye, The Murder Of My Sweet, 7Days, Zool** etc etc). *Electric Stalker* is probably the most metal album Denander has ever released, aside from his original band **ATC**. The title track sounds like it could have been written for **Judas Priest** with Vikström doing his best Halford falsetto imitation ever. A good, solid melodic metal album, with some songs, of course, leaning on the AOR-ish side.

2005	□	ELECTRIC STALKER	CD	Gencross (Japan)	GCCY-1013
2006	■	ELECTRIC STALKER	CD	Metal Heaven	00014

2006 CD - 00014

SPEKTRUM

Lizette von Panjott: v/k, Hansi Cross: g/k, Olov Andersson: k/g, Göran Fors: b/v, Göran Johnsson: d

Stockholm - Outstanding progressive/symphonic rock, at times sounding like a female-fronted **Saga** mixed with a bit of **Yes**, at times similar to **Mostly Autumn**. The music reaches from quite subtle symphonic passages to full-out heavy riffing and quite proggy drums, making this is a really great album for prog fans. Killer musicians topped with Lizette's quite original voice. Hansi is of course also found in **Cross**, Fors in **Galleon**, Johnsson in **Galleon, Cross** and **Grand Stand**. Olov was also in the latter plus **Audiovision**.

2003	■	SPEKTRUM	CD	Progress Records	PRCD-010

2003 CD - PRCD-010

SPELLBOUND

Hasse Fröberg: v, Jocke JJ Marsh: g, Thomas Thompson: b, Ola Strandberg: d

Uppsala - A great melodic hard rock band that made quite an impact on the English market. In Sweden the albums sold fairly well. After the second album they left Sonet and recorded some songs for another label, but nothing happened. In 1987 guitarist Alf Strandberg left the band, but the others recorded three more outstanding demos. After **Spellbound** split in the fall of 1989, Hasse formed his new band **Solid Blue**, a more pop-oriented band that released their debut in 1994. He also made several appearances with the cover band **Highway Stars**, a 70s cover band with glitter, boots and the works. He was also hired to sing on symph-rocker Roine Stolt's album *The Flower King*. This later evolved into the band **The Flower Kings**, where Hans still is a full-time member. Jocke recorded an instrumental album with drummer Simon Stensland for a French label. Alf has done several session jobs as well as producing his father's jazz records. The first two **Spellbound** albums were reissued on CD in 1995. The band is also featured on the compilation albums *Swedish Metal* on Sonet and the Australian Rockhard. The previously unreleased track *Paradise Ride*, also the band's last studio recording, is found on the bonus CD for the first encyclopedia. In 1996 Jocke joined Glenn Hughes' backing band and was an active part in the recordings, live shows and songwriting of the former **Deep Purple** heroes albums. In 2002 he was also involved in the **Hughes/Turner** album, featuring Glenn Hughes and former **Purple/Rainbow/Fandango** singer Joe Lynn Turner. In 1997 some of the unreleased **Spellbound** demos were finally released. The album was simply entitled *Spellbound* and features the demos recorded between 1987-89 with the above line-up. In 2002 this line-up reunited for some shows and a three-track demo featuring the songs *Drowning*, *Psychonaut* and *My Poor Brain* was recorded. In 2006 Jocke released his first solo album *Music From The Planet Marsh*. Hasse is still in **The Flower Kings** and formed his own progressive melodic band **Hasse Fröberg & Musical Companion**, which also features Thompson and Strandberg. Jocke is now found in the melodic power trio **Bridge To Mars**. The first **Spellbound** album is planned to be reissued with bonus tracks by Liljegren Records. **Spellbound** play high-quality melodic hard rock in the vein of **Madison**, but with a touch of **Van Halen** as well.

Lemmy be in the pic, too!

1984 7" - SON-2294

1985 LP - SNTF-952

1984	☐	BREAKING THE SPELL	LP	Sonet	SMLP 2
1985	☐	BREAKING THE SPELL	LP	Sonet (Japan)	28MM-0461
1984	■	My Kinda Girl/Gone Rockin'	7"	Sonet	SON-2294
1985	■	ROCKIN' RECKLESS	LP	Sonet	SNTF-952
1985	○	Burning Love/Love Taker	7"	Sonet	SMS 1
		The cover was black, thick and with "Swedish Metal" stamped on it.			
1986	■	Rockin' Reckless/I'm On The Prowl	7"	Sonet	SON 2306
		The A-side is a remix while On The Prowl is previously unreleased.			
1995	☐	BREAKING THE SPELL	CD	Sonet	SMCD 2/527 524-2
1995	☐	ROCKIN' RECKLESS	CD	Sonet	SNTCD 952/527 526-2
1997	☐	SPELLBOUND	CD	Rock Treasures	RTCD 003

1986 7" - SON 2306

SPETÄLSK

R. Karlsson: v, Micael Zetterberg: g/b, Fredrik "Endymion" Nilsson: d

Norrköping - **Spetälsk** (leper) were formed in 2000 and recorded their first demo in 2003. Original bass player Deobrugia, was out before the MCD. Zetterberg is also found in **Terrorama**, and Nilsson in **Misericordia** and **Satanic Slaughter**. R. Karlsson has also been in **Nattstrype** (as Osiris). **Spetälsk** plays old-school fast and furious black metal in the vein of **Dark Throne**. After the 2007 album Zetterberg was replaced by Ola Blomqvist (**Griftegård, The Doomsday Cult**).

2005	☐	Perverted Commendment	MCD 4tr	Northern Silence	NSP 015
		Tracks: Your Soul I Will Torture For All Eternity/Perverted Commandment/Invoking/The Pleasure Of Pain			
2005	■	PERVERTED COMMANDMENT	LP	Unexploded Records	UER 006
		Bonus: Christ Fire (Von cover). 300 copies.			
2007	☐	SPETÄLSK	CD	Unexploded Records	UER 012
2007	☐	SPETÄLSK	LPg	Carnal Records/Blut & Eisen	- -
		500 copies. Different artwork.			

2005 LP - UER 006

SPICE AND THE RJ BAND

Christian "Spice" Sjöstrand: v/g, Johann: b, Robert "Bob Ruben" Hansson

Värnamo/Jönköping - **Spice & The RJ Band**, where RJ stands for Ruben and Johann, was formed by former **Aeon, Spritual Beggars, Kayser, The Mushroom River Band** singer/bassist Spice (or Kryddan, as he was initially called). When Anders Linusson joined after the second album, the name didn't feel correct anymore and they became **Band Of Spice**, under which name they now exist. The debut was recorded and produced by Johan Blomström (**Overdrive, Blinded Colony, Faith** etc). If you're into **Spiritual Beggars'** riffy stoner this is a safe buy.

2007	☐	THE WILL	CD	Scarlet	SC 146-2
2007	☐	THE WILL	LP	Night Of The Vinyl Dead	NIGHT 048
		300 numbered copies. White vinyl.			
2009	■	SHAVE YOUR FEAR	CD	Scarlet	SC 173-2

2009 CD - SC 173-2

SPIDERS

Ann-Sofie Hoyles: v, John Hoyles: g, Matteo Gambacorta: b, Ricard Harrysson: d

Göteborg - Formed early 2010. Garagey hard rock with a stroke of punk, reminiscent of *Suffrajett*. After the 10" drummer Axel Sjöberg left to go full on with *Graveyard* and was replaced by Ricard Harrysson (*Fox Machine, The Maharajas*). Formed in Gothenburg in February 2010. John was ex-*Witchcraft* and Matteo was in *Midwest*. The first pressing of the single *Fraction* was sold out before its release. In 2011 The four tracks from the first MLP were released as two singles on different labels. Lies is a *Strollers* cover.
Website: www.wearespiders.com

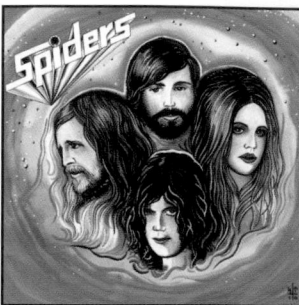

2011 10" - CR 013

2011	■	SPIDERS	10" 4tr	Crusher Records	CR 013
		Tracks: High Society/Gracious Man/Long Gone/Nothing Like You			
2011	□	Fraction/Under My Wheels	7"	De.Nihil Records	NIHIL 006
		1st pressing 500 black vinyl. 2nd pressing 300 copies in green vinyl.			
2011	□	SPIDERS	10" 4tr PD	Crusher Records	CR 013 PD
2011	■	High Society/Gracious Man	7"	Kemado Records	KEM 124
2011	□	Nothing Like You/Long Gone	7"	Valley King Records	VKR 704
		500 copies, hand-numbered.			
2012	□	FLASH POINT	CD	Crusher Records	CR CD 019
2012	□	FLASH POINT	LP	Crusher Records	CR LP 019
2012	□	FLASH POINT	CD	Bickee Music (Japan)	BKMA-1007
2012	□	Weekend Nights/Lies	7"	Crusher Records	CR 018
		500 copies, hand-numbered.			

2011 7" - KEM 124

SPIN AIR

Tony Arnesson: v/g, Joachim Hansson: g, Thomas Kjellsson: g,
Zenny Hansson (now Gram): b, Ralph Rydén (aka Lindgren): d

Kristianstad - This is a very amateurish band in the old *Status Quo* style. The song *Love And Fight* is featured on the compilation *Kristianstadrock Volym 2* (1982 MaNi). Zenny was later found in *Ironside, Arrowz, Treasure Land, Faith* and *Destiny*. Rydén later played with *Hexenhaus*, *Mercy* etc and is now in *Lizard Eye*.

1981	■	We Pray For Rockn´ Roll/The Final Goodbye	7"	Ma-Ni	S 8111-022-02

1981 7" - S 8111-022-02

SPIN GALLERY

Kristoffer Lagerström: v, Tommy Denander: g/b/d

Stockholm - The band initially started in 1997 when multi-instrumentalist Tommy Denander teamed up with singer Kristoffer Lagerström to create some classic AOR influenced by the likes of *Toto* and *Giant,* mixed with poppy influences. Along the way Tommy met singer Chris Antblad through a mutual contact, and the two started writing together. Third singer Magnus Weidenmo was also drafted. They recorded a demo that was picked up by Magnus "Mr. AOR" Söderquist at Atenzia Records. The debut also features musicians such as David Foster, Randy Goodrum, Michael Thompson, drummer Marcus Liliequist and Anders "Theo" Theander, on keyboards. *Spin Gallery* plays very slick AOR with a westcoast touch, and the debut contains two covers of Cliff Magness and *Mr. Mister*. Chris Antblad has also released a solo album in the same style. Some years later Frontiers Records was interested in a follow-up. This time the band only features Tommy and Kristoffer. Drums were handled by Glen Marks and you also find cellist Marika Willstedt, besides guests Robin Beck and Dan Reed. Maybe not as great as the debut, but still a classy AOR album indeed.

2003 MCD - ATZ 02029

2003	■	Am I Wrong (radio)/Trail Full Of Tears/Am I Wrong (album)	MCD 3tr	Atenzia	ATZ 02029
2004	□	STANDING TALL	CD	Atenzia	ATZ 02021
2004	□	STANDING TALL	CD	King Records (Japan)	KICP-1001
		Bonus: Trail Full Of Tears			
2009	■	EMBRACE	CD	Frontiers Records	FR CD 441
2009	□	EMBRACE	CD	King Records (Japan)	KICP-1453

2009 CD - FR CD 441

SPINNING BLACK CIRCLE

Joakim Åström: v, Anders Nyberg: g, Peter Norstedt: g,
Olle Sjölund: g, Dennis Buhr: b, Valter Koivunen: d

Umeå - *Spinning Black Circle*, formed in 2003, play slow emo-oriented post-grunge/metal with a touch of *Cult Of Luna*-meet-*Tool* with a touch of *Katatonia*, but with clean and really great vocals by Åström, quite close to *Tool*'s Maynard. Klas Rydberg (*Cult Of Luna*) adds some guest vocals. In 2008 singer Åström was fired, and things went quiet after this. He later turned up in *April Divine*.

2005	□	Hymnus Ira	MCD 4tr	private	- -
		Tracks: Your Sincerely/Blow/Shortest Path/The Charlatans			
2006	■	SPINNING BLACK CIRCLE	CD	private	PBC 1/1

2006 CD - PBC 1/1

SPINNROCK

Stefan Andersson: v, Göran Andersson: g, Jim Hellström: g,
Bo Svärd: b, Rickard Ozols: d

Landskrona - Side A is straight ahead hard rock/rock, while the B-side is a ballad with quite nice guitar harmonies. On the verge of making it into the book.

1981 7" - HIT-S-1

1981 ■ Nighttime Is The Right Time/I Remember You................................7" Hit-Records.........................HIT-S-1
    Blue vinyl.

SPIRITUAL BEGGARS

Apollo Papathansio: v, Michael Amott: g, Per Wiberg: k,
Charles Petter "Sharlee D'Angleo" Andreasson: b, Ludwig Witt: d

Halmstad - One of Sweden's most interesting bands reproducing good old 70s stuff once produced by bands like *Mountain* and *Montrose* mixed with the heaviness of *Black Sabbath*. The first line-up featured singer/bassist Christian "Kryddan/Spice" Sjöstrand, guitarist Michael Amott and drummer Ludwig Witt. In late 1994 the band recorded four new songs, added them to the first MCD and released it as a full-length in Japan only, at the time. Amott was ex-*Carcass* and *Carnage*. One non-album track was found on the '94 Backstage compilation. Christian has previously recorded a 7" and some demos with the band *Aeon*, and is today in *Band Of Spice* (formerly known as *Spice & The RJ Band*), plus he has recorded with *Kayser* and *The Mushroom River Band*. In 1995 the band signed to Megarock Records and recorded the second album, but before its release they were licensed to Music For Nations. The album, entitled *Another Way To Shine,* showed a step up from the debut. It's packed with heavy 70's riffomania in the old *Sabbath*-vein with a touch of *The Obsessed*. On *Ad Astra* they added Per Wiberg (*Death Organ, Sky High, Mojobone,* later in *Opeth*) on keyboard, as a permanent member. In 2001 "Spice" left the band for *The Mushroom River Band* and was replaced by Janne "JB" Christoffersson from *Grand Magus* on vocals and Roger Nilsson from *The Quill* on bass. On *Demons* Roger Nilsson had been replaced by Sharlee D'Angelo (*Illwill, Witchery, Facelift, Dismember, Mercyful Fate, Arch Enemy, King Diamond*). The album was recorded on analogue tape at Studio Fredman. In June 2010 the band announced Christoffersson would leave because of his commitments with *Grand Magnus*. He was replaced by Apollo Papathanasio (*Craze, Firewind, Evil Masquerade, Meduza, Time Requiem, Gardenian, Majestic*). Witt has also recorded with UK hard rockers *Firebird* and death metal band *Shining*. You will also find *Spiritual Beggars* on compilations like *Burn One Up, Stoned (r)evolution* and the *Trouble* tribute *Bastards Will Pay*, where they do *Manic Frustration*.

1994 MCD - WAR 002

1996 CD - CDMFN 198

1998 10" - FROG 002

2001 7" - SUNN 10.5

2002 CD - RRAS 3

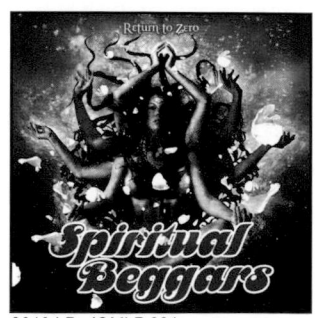

2010 LP - IOMLP 331

1994 ■ Spiritual Beggars..MCD 6tr Wrong Again Records..................WAR 002 $$
    Tracks: Yearly Dying/Pelekas/The Space Inbetween/If This Is All/Under Silence/Magnificent Obsession
1995 ☐ SPIRITUAL BEGGARS..CD Toys Factory (Japan)...............TCFK 88736
    Bonus: Blind Mountain/Nowhere To Go/Sour Stains/If You Should Leave
1996 ■ ANOTHER WAY TO SHINE.................................CD Music For Nations....................CDMFN 198
1998 ☐ MANTRA III..CD Music For Nations....................CDMFN 231
1998 ☐ MANTRA III..CD Pony Canyon..........................PCCY-01196
    Bonus: The Band Is Playing
1998 ■ Violet Karma..10" 3tr Froghouse..................................FROG 002
    Tracks: Euphoria (alternative mix)/If I Should Leave/Mushroom Tea Girl(10 minute jam-version). Violet vinyl.
2000 ☐ AD ASTRA...CD Victor (Japan)..........................VICP-61008
    Bonus: Let The Magic Talk/It's Over
2000 ☐ AD ASTRA...CD Music For Nations....................CDMFN 252
2000 ☐ AD ASTRA..CDd Music For Nations...................CDMFNX 252
    Bonus: Let The Magic Talk
2000 ☐ AD ASTRA...2LPg Music For Nations..........................MFN 252
2000 ☐ AD ASTRA...CD Koch (USA)..........................KOC-CD-8224
2001 ■ Spiritual Beggars/Grand Magus (split)..................7" Southern Lord ....SUNN 10.5
    Split with Grand Magus. Track: It's Over
2002 ☐ SPIRITUAL BEGGARS..LP Regain ....RRLP 003 AS
    Same as the '95 Toy's Factory CD-version. Red vinyl. New artwork.
2002 ■ SPIRITUAL BEGGARS..CD Regain ....RR 003AS
2002 ☐ ON FIRE...CD Music For Nations....................CDMFN 280
2002 ☐ ON FIRE..CDd Music For Nations...................CDMFNX 280
    Bonus: Burden Of Dreams. Different artwork.
2002 ☐ ON FIRE...CD Victor (Japan)..........................VICP-61948
    Bonus: Burden Of Dreams/Blood Of The Sun (Mountain cover)
2005 ☐ DEMONS...CD Inside Out Music.......................IOMCD 214
2005 ☐ DEMONS..2CD Inside Out Music....................IOMSECD 214
    Bonus DVD live in Japan. Slipcase with different artwork.
2005 ☐ DEMONS...CD Toy's Factory (Japan)................TFCK-87379
2007 ☐ AD ASTRA...CD Sony BMG 88697 06642-2
    Bonus: Let The Magic Talk
2007 ☐ ON FIRE...CD Sony BMG 88697 06643-2
    Bonus: Burden Of Dreams

2007	☐	ON FIRE	CD	Metal Mind	MASS CD DG 1010	
2010	☐	RETURN TO ZERO	CDd	Inside Out	0504468/IOMLTDCD 331	

Bonus: Time To Live (Uriah Heep cover)

| 2010 | ■ | RETURN TO ZERO | LP | Inside Out | IOMLP 331 | |

Maroon vinyl.

| 2010 | ☐ | RETURN TO ZERO | CD | Trooper (Japan) | XNTE-00021 | |

Bonus: Time To Live (Uriah Heep cover). Slipcase + poster.

2010	■	RETURN TO LIVE – LOUD PARK 2010	CD	Trooper (Japan)	XNTE-00033	
2010	☐	DEMONS	CD	Trooper (Japan)	XNTE-00034	
2013	☐	EARTH BLUES	CD	Inside Out	50522 -506372	
2013	☐	EARTH BLUES	2CDd	Inside Out	50522 -506370	

Bonus: Return To Live EP.

2013	☐	EARTH BLUES	2LP	Inside Out	50522 -506371	
2013	☐	SPIRITUAL BEGGARS	2CD	Century Media	n/a	
2013	☐	SPIRITUAL BEGGARS	3LPg	Century Media	n/a	

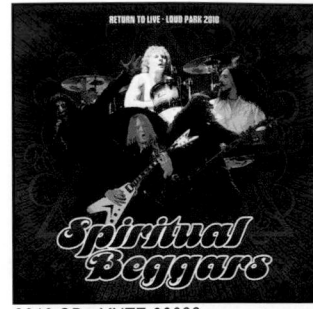

2010 CD - XNTE-00033

SPIT IT OUT
Lars T.C. Anderson: v/b, Carsten Rickerman: g, Michael Persson: k

Varberg - Lars Andersson was ex-*Lezlie Paice*. The line-up on the first 7" also featured guitarist Håkan Ljungtegen and drummer Johan Laux (ex-*Overlord*), who are both listed as guest-musicians on *This Is It*. Around 1994-95 Håkan left the band and they changed their name to **Spit** and recorded a new demo. In 1996 they recorded a video for the song *As I Sit Here And Cry*, still under the name **Spit It Out**, now as a trio featuring Lars, Carsten and new drummer Dennis Jonbarn. In 1997 the band changed their name to **Spank**. They recorded yet another demo with a female singer. A new release was due in 2000, but as the names **Spit** and **Spank** were already taken, they had to find a new name. Nothing ever came out of it, though. **Spit It Out** plays mid-quality melodic hard rock with a strong glam-oriented funk-touch. The vocals that degraded the overall quality of the first 7" are considerably improved on the CD.

| 1991 | ■ | Tied Up (Like A Slave)/H.O.T | 7" | private | S.I.O 001 | |
| 1993 | ☐ | THIS IS IT | CD | private | S.I.O 002 | |

1991 7" - S.I.O 001

SPITFIRE
Kimmo Morja: v, Rauno Morja: g, Reijo Väliaho: g,
Jarmo Heikkinen: b, Jouni Heikkinen; d

Katrineholm - Formed in 1978, split in 1986. Great, powerful 80s metal in the vein of **Parasite**. *In The Night* is a metal ballad, typical for that era. The tracks *Eyes Of Storm* and *Crazy Livin'* can be found on the *Scandinavian Metal Attack* compilation. The single was released in a small edition without cover. Kimmo was also found in **Rozz The Boss**. Jarmo and Jouni later played in the band **Hoboken** and Jouni in **Arcania**. Kimmo had a band called **Fireheart** in the 90s. Rauno and Reijo recorded some demos with the band **Mothergoose**. *Spitfire* also did a reunion in 2005, now featuring keyboard player Charlie Härenvall. In 2010 the band again reunited featuring Kimmo, Rauno, Reijo, plus drummer Lasse Pajula and bassist Tomas Nadersson.

1982 7" - PSI 036

| 1982 | ● | Heavy Rock 'N Roller/In The Night | 7" | Pang | PSI 036 | $ |

No artwork.

SPLASH
Christer Jansson: v/g, Thomas Jutterström: k, Kaj Söderström: b,
Henrik "Hempo" Hildén: d, Christer Holm: sax, Leif Halldén: trumpet,
Torbjörn Carlsson: sax, Lennart Löfgren: trombone

Söderhamn - Even though this band was a jazz rock/folk/brass band it would be wrong of me not to include this outstanding hard rocker in the vein of **Uriah Heep/Lucifer's Friend**. This single was very different from the band's other releases and is on par with the greats of the seventies. Hildén later played with John Norum, **Trash, Dokken**, Glenn Hughes, **Baltimoore, Ball** etc and Söderström also played in **Trash** and **Ball**. The band also recorded numerous albums and singles, but unfortunately none of these are hard rock/metal.

1974 7" - PLA 101

| 1974 | ■ | Orangutang Boomerang/Sunday Ride | 7" | Plask | PLA 101 | $ |

SPLATTERED MERMAIDS
Johan Bergström: v, Johan Hallberg: g, Martin Eklöv: b, Martin Schönherr: d

Malmö/Lund - **Splattered Mermaids** (now there's a name for you!) play furious technical death metal. The first album, *Bloodfreak*, was recorded in 2005, followed by *Creation Of Wounds* in 2006. Both are sold as pro-printed and CD-Rs, where the first one is also hand-numbered (200 copies). Eklöv is also found in **Visceral Bleeding** and **Ignatum**, Schönherr is ex-**Deranged** and also in **RazorRape, Virgin Sin** and **DROPS!!!**.

| 2008 | ■ | STENCH OF FLESH | CD | Bizarre Leprous Productions | BLP 083 | |

2008 CD - BLP 083

SPORTLOV

Stefan "Count Wassberg" Pettersson: v, Kaj "Dubbdäck Doom Culta" Löfven: g,
Lars "Hell Y Hansen" Löfven: g, Lawrence "Thermoss" Mackory: b,
Matte "Fjällhammer" Modin: d

Uppsala - A totally wicked project with several name members. The band's name means "Sports holiday" and they took their name after the band with the "worst name in Germany" *Vintersemestre* (meaning sportlov in Swedish). The album title *Snöbollskrieg* means "snowball war". Masse "Magus Caligula" Broberg guests on vocals. The album was produced by Daniel Bergstrand for the price of one bottle of whiskey and a banana. Of course they had to record a follow up full-length album, *Offerblod I Vallabod* (approximately: sacrificial blood in a shepherds hut). The album also features guest guitarist Jager Frostis. Uncompromising death metal with totally evil lyrics all dealing with holiday subjects such as skiing to Norway and burning Oslo to the ground whilst grilling sausages over the flames.

2002 MCD - NWOHMCD 006

2002 ■	Snöbollskrieg ....MCD 5tr	Head Mechanic..................	NWOHMCD 006	$

Tracks: *Into The Pist/Svarte pisten/Snöbollskrieg/Lady Magda (Satans lönnmördare)/Ur spår.* 500 copies.

2003 ■	OFFERBLOD I VALLABOD ....CD	Head Mechanic..................	NWOHMCD 007	$

500 copies.

2003 CD - NWOHMCD 007

SPOVE, GLEN

Glenn Spove: v, Mats Hedberg: g, Jocke Uddling: k,
Nalle Påhlsson: b, Fredrik von Gerber: d

Stockholm - Glen recorded three quite worthless pop singles 1986-87. He was also a male stripper (which may explain song titles such as *Macho* and *Too Hot*). When he was dropped from Virgin, he thought he'd make a bigger impression on the market by hiring some name musicians and record a more rough-edged AOR single. However, his vocal abilities were somewhat limited and the music is commercial hard rock filled with clichés. Not bad, but very predictable. The backing band also features Matti Alfonzetti (*Skintrade, Bam Bam Boys, Jagged Edge*) on backing vocals. Påhlsson is also found in bands like *Treat, Zan Clan, Therion, AB/CD* etc, von Gerber has been in *Easy Action*, *Red Fun* and *Bam Bam Boys*.

1988 7" - BOSW 1025

1988 ■	Watch Out/Watch Out (instrumental) ....7"	Bozz..............................	BOSW 1025

SQUETTERS

Stefan Öhman: g/v, Jörgen Eriksson: g, Ronny Wikberg: b, Peter "PeeWee" Wikberg: d

Glommersträsk - Formed in 1981. Quite badly mixed, simple, straightforward typical 80s metal, but still quite good. *Squetters* were also featured on the compilation *Heavy Metal* (1982 Pang) with the tracks *Heavy Water* and *Climax*. The band was featured on the TV show *Rakt av* in 1983. They also recorded a five-track demo with the songs *Wicked Boy, Raise Cain, Longing For You, Heavy Water* and *Climax. Squetters* split in 1983, but reunited for a local show in 1988.

1982 ■	Squetters..............................7" 4tr	private.............................. SQ 6969	$$

Tracks: *Paint The Town Red//Not Heading For The Top/Rock In Hell/You Don't Fool Me*

1982 7" - SQ 6969

SRODEK

Jon "Necrofucker" Bäcklund: v/g/b/d

Borås - *Srodek*, formed in 2007, is Polish, meaning center/middle. Jon actually named the band after a song a friend wrote, but it wasn't until afterwards he found out what it meant. *Srodek* plays a pretty strange mix of slightly depressive black metal and goth with an almost indie emo touch, like the bastard child of *Burzum* and *The Jesus & Mary Chain*. Bäcklund is also in *Död, Eldrit* and a live session member of *Svarti Loghin*.

2008 ■	EN HÄLSNING TILL DÖDEN................................CD	Lokisson..............................	LOKI 005
2011 ☐	FÖRFALL................................CD	A Sad Sadness Song............	SSS 005

2008 CD - LOKI 005

S:T ERIK

Erik Nordström: v/b, Tomas Eriksson: g, Magnus Wikmark: g,
Mats Norman: k, Fredrik Aspelin: d

Uppsala - *S:t Erik* were formed in 2006. The name refers to the Swedish king Erik IX (1155-1160). Eriksson is ex-*Devian*. They recorded their first demo, *Uppsala*, in 2007 and two years later the debut album was released. Heavy, sludgy stoner with a psychedelic touch, a bit similar to *Electric Wizard*. Aspelin replaced Erik "EB" Björkregren (*Devian, Always War*) in 2008.

2009 ■	FROM UNDER THE TARN................................CD	Solitude Productions..............	SP.029-09
2012 ☐	FROM UNDER THE TARN................................2LPg	Spora Recordz..............	- -

Clear vinyl. New artwork. 3-sided.

2012 ☐	FROM UNDER THE TARN................................CD	Spora Recordz..............	- -

2009 CD - SP.029-09

STABWOUND

Ulf Nylin: v, Fredrik Linfjärd: g, Per Ahre: g/b, Viktor Linder: d

Göteborg - Stabwound play fast and brutal death metal with vocals that actually sound just a pig being mutilated. Never heard anything like it, I swear! *Stabwound* split in 2005. Nylin is also in *Invocate*, *Neuralgia* and *Cranial Devourment*. The band also recorded the demo *Malicious Addiction* between the MCD and the album. A DVD entitled *Brutal Domination* was also recorded.
Website: www.myspace.com/stabwound

2003 ■ Bloodsoaked Serenades...MCD 6tr   The Flood Records ....TDF 003
    Tracks : Intestestinal Impalement/Red Worms Erected/Bloated Brain Implow/Ancient Art
    Of Gutting/As I Watch You Bleed Again/Kill Your Mother Rape Your Dog (Dying Fetus
    cover) + video of Ancient Art of Gutting
2004 ☐ HUMAN BOUNDARIES ....CD   Brutal Bands ....BB 002

2003 MCD - TDF 003

STAIGER

John Hermanssen (now Hermansen): v/g, Hasse Hermanssen (now Hermansen): g,
Marcus Jäderholm: b, Mattias Åström: d

Fjärdhundra - A highly interesting melodic hard rock band with the emphasis on powerful guitars and great vocals. Could be placed in the same category as *Slaughter*, *Trixter* and *Pretty Maids*. Recommended. John is also found in the *Kiss* cover project *SixCoveredKissSongs*, *Stonewall Noise Orchestra*, *The Awesome Machine* and now in *Mother Misery*. *Staiger* changed their name to *Greyhate* and became way heavier, more similar to *Alice In Chains*. They made one release in 1996, and split in 1997. John and Marcus later reappeared in *Mother Misery*.

1995 ■ Another Worthless Day ....MCD 4tr   Taltratten ....TT CD-S 02
    Tracks: Try Kid/Rainmaker/Another Worthless Day/Fed Up With Monkeys.

1995 MCD - TT CD-S 02

STALLION

Lasse Johansson: v, Michael Johansson: g, Rafael Martinez: g,
Christer Sundell: k, Peter Andersson: b, Kenneth Augustsson: d

Karlskoga - This is a great melodic hard rock/AOR band, with a real professional sound and approach. Musically they are in the same region as early *Treat*. Great arrangements, biting guitars, nice keyboard work and high-class vocals. Too bad they never made it big. Rafael was earlier found in the band *Misery*, with whom he recorded a 7" in 1979. Produced by Ronny Lahti (*Masquerade*, *Saigon Kick* etc.). The track *Echoes Of The Night* is found on the compilation *KURT* (1988 MI Records).

1986 ☐ Helpless/Girls...7"   Alpha...ONESIN 050
1987 ■ ON THE RUN...LP   Alpha..ONELP 020
1989 ☐ Physical/Movin' On..7"   Eurozont ....EZS 005

1987 LP - ONELP 020

STALLION FOUR

Björn Fors: v, Peter Druck: g, Markus Berg: g,
Gustav "Gurra" Ljung: b, Markus Miljand: d

Uppsala - Formed in 2008. Before the single, the band recorded three demos. Actually the last demo featured four songs from which two were released as the single. The song *Sister Mean* was featured on the *Revolver: Hard Rock & Metal Edition: Volume II* (2004 NLP) compilation. Good classic bluesy hard rock in the vein of *Rose Tattoo* and *The Graveyard Train* meets *AC/DC* with singer Björn sounding quite inspired by Angry Anderson. In November 2010 second guitarist Markus Berg joined the band. In 2012 drummer Oscar was replaced by Markus Miljand.
Website: www.stallionfour.se

2009 ☐ Devil In Me/The Train...7"   SMP ....S.M.P 003
    500 copies
2012 ■ ROUGH TIMES..CD   Pure Rock Records ....PRRCD 009

2012 CD - PRRCD 009

Stand by for take off!

STAND BY

Carola Häggkvist: v, Anders Aldrin: g/v, Pontus Holmgren: g,
Benny Andersson: b, Johan Norgren: d

Stockholm - Stand By are a decent melodic rock/hard rock band, with high-quality vocals. The album was recorded in 1981 and 1983, but released after Carola went famous through her victory in the Swedish *Eurovision Song Contest* final. Carola's solo-albums are teen-pop with a touch of gospel and soul, except for the odd AOR-tune. *Stand By* was formed around 1977. They were rehearsing at a daycare centre at Mälarhöjden in Stockholm, when Carola walked in on a Sunday and took the guys by storm. As her pop career started to grow, she and

the band found it best to part ways. Anders took over the mike and the style turned into more slick and pop-oriented rock. The albums are a mix of both. Göran Elmquist (later in *Bam Bam Boys, Dream Bank*) was also in the band for almost a year. Pontus was later in the pop band *Pontus & Amerikanerna*. Johan has been backing bands like *Ace Of Base*, Lena Philipsson and *Legacy Of Sound*. He is brother of Pontus Norgren (*HammerFall, Talisman, Great King Rat* etc). After the album Carola went solo and the last 7" was recorded without her. The band has 5 tracks on the compilation *Vågrätt Samliv* (Vertical Intercourse) and an unreleased track on the compilation *Pärlor*, both on Rosa Honung Records.

1983 ■	STAND BY WITH CAROLA HÄGGKVIST	LP	Rosa Honung	ROSALP 009
1983 □	Boys And Girls/Firescape	7"	Rosa Honung	ROSASP 12
1984 □	STAND BY WITH CAROLA HÄGGKVIST	LP	Rosa Honung	ROSALP 019
	Same LP, but new press in red vinyl and with different artwork.			
1998 □	CAROLA – STANDBY	CD	Pink Honey	ROSACD 29
	Reissue with tracks from LP + others.			

1983 LP - ROSALP 009

STARDOG

Martin Wiklund: v, Niklas Wiklund: g/k, Jon Ericsson: b, Patrik Sundqvist: d

Skellefteå - Formed in 1991 and changed name five times before settling for *Stardog*, taken from the song *Stardog Champion* by *Mother Love Bone*. Great grunge-oriented hard rock. At times similar to *Pearl Jam*, as well as the heavier *Alice In Chains* or *Stone Temple Pilots*. A Great band! Funnily enough *Stardog* backwards is *Godrats*, the title of their second MCD.

1993 □	CHAMPIONS	CD	A Westside Fabrication	WECD 041
1993 □	CHAMPIONS	CD	SPV (Germany)	084-76792
1993 □	All I Want	MCD 3tr	Radium 226.05	RACD 96
	Tracks: All I Want/Wait/I Wonder			
1993 ■	The Godrats E.P	MCD 4tr	A Westside Fabrication	WECD 047
	Tracks: Wait/Alison/I Wonder/If. Same artwork as the above MCD.			
1994 □	STARDOG	CD	A Westside Fabrication	WECD 079
1996 □	Never Be The Same/Five Words Or Less	CDSp 2tr	A Westside Fabrication	WeCD 119
1996 ■	IN ORDER TO DISORDER	CD	A Westside Fabrication	WeCD 122
2000 □	Another Day	CDS	A Westside Fabrication	WeCD 175
	One-track radio promo			
2000 □	RADKO'S MANSION	CD	A Westside Fabrication	WeCD 176

1993 MCD - WECD 047

1996 CD - WeCD 122

STARTERHEAD

Petter Dennevi: v/g/b/d

Örebro - Dark metal band *Starterhead* were formed by Dennevi in the fall of 2002. He recorded two two-track demos in 2004, before releasing the debut *Inside* in 2006. The album was recorded by Jens Bogren (*Katatonia, Opeth*) and at the time Dennevi handled all instruments and vocals. The album was a slab of death metal with hints of early *Opeth*, and Dennevi sounding quite similar to Mikael Åkerfeldt. On the second album Dennevi was also using the talents of guitarist Simon Solomon (*Bloodbath, Flushed*) and *Anata* drummer Conny Pettersson. *Undergrounding* is a much better effort, partly because of the "real" drums and the style is also a bit more metal-infused and even some doomy moments. Great production, too.

2006 □	INSIDE	CD	Indark Music	IND2006
2008 ■	UNDERGROUNDING	CD	Indark Music	IND2008

2008 CD - IND2008

STATE OF MIND

Conny Lind: v, Jörgen Svensson: g, Patrik Appelgren: k,
Johan Larsson: b, Roger Kindstrand: d

Stockholm - A great high-quality AOR band that have backed Jeff Paris on tour. Conny has played in several interesting bands such as *Tryckvåg*, *Sin City* (that became *Great King Rat*), *Unit-X*, *Talk Of The Town*, *Vision* and *Amaze Me*. He was, besides *State Of Mind*, also working with blues rockers *Raceway*. *Mother* is a bit heavier than the debut and was only released in Japan. Patrik Appelgren has appeared in several other bands, such as *Treat* and *Power*. After the second album, Conny was given the boot. A new album was already recorded, but the vocal parts were to be redone by a new singer. The album was due to be released in 1996, but never happened. *State Of Mind* had a track on the compilation album released by the English AOR magazine Frontiers in 1995. *Memory Lane* is a compilation of the MCD and CD plus the previously unreleased tracks *Hang Tough* and *Gypsy Rave*.

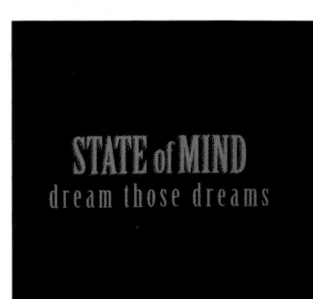

1993 MCD - CD S-001

1993 ■	Dream Those Dreams	MCD 5tr	private	CD S-001
	Tracks: My Kind Of Life/Dream Those Dreams/Sound N' Rhythm/Up On The Top/Cat Walk			
1995 □	MOTHER	CD	Victor (Japan)	VICP-5501
2004 ■	MEMORY LANE	CD	MTM Classix	0681-87

2004 CD - 0681-87

STATUS TWO

Lasse Andersson: v/g, Anders Larsson: g, Hansi Borgström: b, Pelle Andersson: d

Göteborg - For those who haven't already guessed, these guys try to sound like *Status Quo*. Unfortunately, they don't qualify for the higher leagues though. Not to be confused with the *Status Quo* tribute band formed in 1991.

1986 ■ Can't Decide/Take Me ....7" Night Records ....N 003

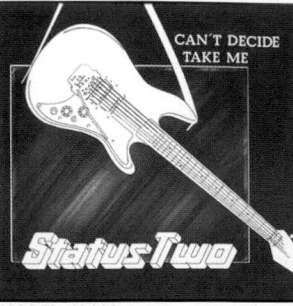
1986 7" - N 003

STEAMBOAT WILLIES

Petrus Engelhart: v, Hans Arleklint: v/g, Jan Mörk: v/g, Thomas Osmark: k, Anders Tibbling: b, Lars Uddberg: d

Stockholm - Anders has previously made recordings of R&B band *Träskmännen* and 60s rockers *Megaflops* with his mobile studio. This is just a bunch of musicians doing a small edition single for fun. Three covers of *Deep Purple*, *ZZ Top* and Jimi Hendrix. I've tried to find some enjoyable moments on this record, but unfortunately they are quite rare. The vocals are quite boring and uninspired, there are tons of bum notes and I quite honestly think Hendrix would spin like a tornado in his grave if he heard the cover of *Purple Haze*. For collectors only.

1991 ■ Back In Line .... 7" 3tr private ....SW 091
    Tracks: Black Night (Deep Purple cover)/Can't Stop Rockin' (ZZ Top cover)/Purple Haze (Jimi Hendrix cover)

1991 7" - SW 091

STEAMROLLER

Fredrik Jansson: v, Paul Humble: g, Pontus Egberg: b, Ulf "Bo Werner" Sundberg: d

Stockholm - High-class melodic hard rock/AOR. The song material varies from pure AOR to riffy heavy melodic hard rock with a touch of *Van Halen*. Bo has previously played with Yngwie Malmsteen and *Mogg*. In 1997 Paul released a soft instrumental guitar album, entitled *Intermission*. Egberg was a member of an early incarnation of *Skintrade*, later joined *Lion's Share*, *Dark Illusion* and is today in *The Poodles* and UK band *Tainted Nation*.

1993 ☐ STEAMROLLER ....CD Steam ....SRCD 3068
1994 ■ DEAD MAN'S TAN ....CD Prestige (UK ....CDSGP 0136
    This is the same album but with a different cover and track order.

1994 CD - CDSGP 0136

STEEL

Dan Swanö: v, Micke Åkerfeldt: g, Anders Nordin: b, Peter Lindgren: d

Örebro - This is more or less Dan Swanö plus three (at the time) *Opeth*-members doing a great fully fledged 80s metal tribute, actually recorded already in 1996, even before *HammerFall* and their followers flooded the metal market. The picture disc is beautiful. The single was only released in 500 copies and is a one-off project. There's however at least one more track recorded, entitled *Say Goodbye (To Love)*. The single is today a rare and high-priced item.

1998 ■ Heavy Metal Machine/Rock Tonight ....7" PD Near Dark ....AH 11932 $$
    500 copies.

1985 7" PD - AH 11932

STEEL ARROWS

Ubbe Rydeslätt: v, Peter Sehlin: g, Mange Ericsson: b, Jocke Fleetwood: d

Nyköping - *Steel Arrows* are 80s metal with a hint of early *Mötley Crüe*. *Loud Guitars* is a great rocker, while the B-side is a ballad. Nothing more came out of this band. Ubbe later joined (*The*) *Case*, *Bang Bang*, (who became *Great King Rat*) then recorded two albums with *Snakepit Rebels* (aka *Dream Police*) and was later found in punk rockers *Blind System*.

1985 ■ Loud Guitars/Lonely Night ....7" private 001

1985 7" - 001

STEEL ATTACK

Ronny Hemlin: v/k, Johan "John Allan" Forssén: g, Simon Johansson: g, Johan Löfgren: b, Peter Morén: d

Sala - The band was formed back in 1995, at the Roskilde Festival, when guitarist Dennis Vestman and basist Stefan "Steve Steel" Westerberg (mainly a drummer in bands like *Asperity, Carnal Forge, In Thy Dreams, World Below, Skineater*) decided to quit their punk band *Hylands Hörna* and form a speed metal band, influenced by *Edguy*. The line-up also featured guitarist Mikael Böhlin. They took the name *Mayer's Eve*, but just before a gig in 1997, changed it to *Steel Attack*. In 1998 they recorded the demo *Mighty Sword Of Steel*. True Swedish German-style metal

in the vein of *Edguy* and *HammerFall*. The debut album was recorded at Studio Underground and co-produced by Pelle Saether (*Zello, Grand Design, Zeelion* etc), who also guests on lead vocals on one track. The line-up now featured Westerberg on bass and vocals, Dennis Vestman, drummer Andreas Vollmer (aka de Vera) (ex-*Nightfall, Kapten Haubits*) and former jazz guitarist Johan "John Allan" Forssén, who had replaced Böhlin. On *Fall Into Madness*, Andreas had been replaced by Roger "Raw" Enstedt (*Wombbath*), who only lasted for the album and a tour, before Andreas returned. On *Predator Of The Empire* singer Dick Johnsson had replaced Stefan, Peter Späth was added on bass and Roger Enstedt had been replaced by Mikael "Mike" Stark (*Into Desolation*). Up until this album Petri Kuusisto had played session keyboards. On *Enslaved* the line-up had again changed, now seeing singer Ronny Hemlin (*Inmoria, Lack Of Faith, Tad Morose, Arcana Major, Planet Storm*) replacing Johnson, guitarist Johan Jalonen Penn (*Asperity, Blackworld*) replacing Westman and bassist Anden Andersson replacing Späth. Guest keyboards were played by Danne Forslund. New album, new line-up. *Diabolic Symphony* saw drummer Stark replaced by Tony Elfving (*Lack Of Faith, Arcana Major, Conspiracy*). The album was produced by Jonas Kjellgren, who also handled keyboards together with Hemlin. In 2008, new album, and guess what? Yes, new line-up. Now bassist Andersson was replaced by Johan Löfgren (*Lack Of Faith*), drummer Elfving by Peter Morén (*Inmoria, Tad Morose*) and guitarist Jalonen Penn by Simon Johansson (*Fifth Reason, Crystal Caravan, Memory Garden, Bibleblack, Satariel, Abstrakt Algebra, Wolf, Dion Fortune*). Former guitarist Dennis Vestman is now found in *Grand Design*. The band no longer exists.

1999 CD - 0046582AFM

2001 CD - 0046762AFM

1999	■	WHERE MANKIND FAILS	CD	AFM	0046582AFM
		Bonus: Holy Sea Of Gold			
1999	□	WHERE MANKIND FAILS	CD	Metal Blade (USA)	14313-2
2001	■	FALL INTO MADNESS	CD	AFM	0046762AFM
		Bonus: Zeelion			
2001	□	FALL INTO MADNESS	CD	Rock Brigade/Laser	RBR/LCS 2860
2003	□	PREDATOR OF THE EMPIRE	CD	Arise	S.L 042 CD
		Bonus: Paradise/Dr. Stein (Helloween cover)			
2003	□	PREDATOR OF THE EMPIRE	CD	King Records (Japan)	KICP-937
		Bonus: Paradise/Dr. Stein (Helloween cover)			
2003	□	PREDATOR OF THE EMPIRE	CD	Sail Production (Korea)	SPCD 0027
		Bonus: Dr. Stein (Helloween cover)			
2004	□	DRAGON'S SKULL	2CD	AFM	AFMCD 0903
		Where Mankind Fails and Fall Into Madness in a double pack.			
2004	□	ENSLAVED	CD	Arise	ARISE 058
2004	□	ENSLAVED	CDd	Arise	ARISE 058
		Bonus: Afraid No More			
2004	□	ENSLAVED	CDd	King Records Japan	KICP-1043
		Bonus: Ease My Pain			
2006	■	DIABOLIC SYMPHONY	CD	Massacre Records	MAS PC 0513
2008	■	CARPE DIEND	CD	Massacre Records	MAS PC 0583
2008	□	CARPE DIEND	CD	Locomotive Music (USA)	LM 618

2006 CD - MAS PC 0513

2008 CD - MAS PC 0583

STEELWING

Riley Ericson: v, Robby Rockbag: g, Alex Vega: g, Nic Savage: b, Oskar Åstedt: d

Nyköping - After their former band *Hellevator* split, Alex, Oskar and Robby joined forces with Riley and bassist Gustav Skürk in 2009, to form *Steelwing*, initially named *Scavenger*. In 2011 bassist Skürk was replaced by Nic Savage. *Steelwing* play classic eighties heavy metal influenced by the NWoBHM and bands like *Raven*, *Grim Reaper* (Riley's vocals sure have a touch of Steve Grimmett at times), *Iron Maiden* and *Saxon*. This is really reinventing the wheel, but since they do it with such conviction you can almost see this as one of those undiscovered hidden gems from 1983. Heavy metal in the niiiiight!!

2010	■	LORD OF THE WASTELAND	CD	NoiseArt Records	NARCD002
2010	□	LORD OF THE WASTELAND	CD	Universal (Japan)	IUCP-16079
		Bonus: Green Manalishi (Fleetwood Mac/Judas Priest cover)			
2010	□	Roadkill (...Or Be Killed)	MCD 4tr	NoiseArt Records	- -
		Tracks: Roadkill (...Or Be Killed)/Sentinel Hill/The Green Manalishi (Fleetwood Mac)/ Judas Priest cover)/Steeler(Judas Priest cover). Last 2 are non-album. Released with Sweden Rock Magazine.			
2012	□	LORD OF THE WASTELAND	LPg	NoiseArt Records	NARLP002
		Bonus: 2097 A.D (extended cut)/Hit 'Em Hard (2010 demo). Clear/white splatter vinyl.			
2012	□	ZONE OF ALIENATION	CD	NoiseArt Records	NARCD016
2012	□	ZONE OF ALIENATION	CDd	NoiseArt Records	NARCD016LTD
		Bonus: 2097 A.D (Extended cut)/Hit 'Em Hard (2010 demo)			
2012	■	ZONE OF ALIENATION	LP	NoiseArt Records	NARLP016LTD
		Bonus: 2097 A.D (Extended cut)/Hit 'Em Hard (2010 demo). Available in green, green/ white splatter, clear/white splatter and black vinyl.			
2012	□	ZONE OF ALIENATION	CD	Universal (Japan)	IUCP-16129
		Bonus: 2097 A.D (Extended cut)/Hit 'Em Hard (2010 demo)/Steeler (Judas Priest cover)			

2010 CD - NARCD002

2012 LP - NARLP016LTD

STEELWINGS

Tommy Söderström: v, Gert-Inge Gustafsson: g, Michael Lindman: g, Krister Andersen: b, Dennis Nybratt: d

Laholm - A great melodic heavy metal band formed in 1982. The year after the song *Live Your Life* was featured on the Ebony Records' compilation *Metal Plated*, but it took another six years before the debut was released. *Steelwings* recorded a 4-track demo in 1990, but they sounded more like *AC/DC* during this period. At one point the guitarist was none less than Peter Espinoza of *Nasty Idols* fame, also in *Espinoza* and *Majestic*.

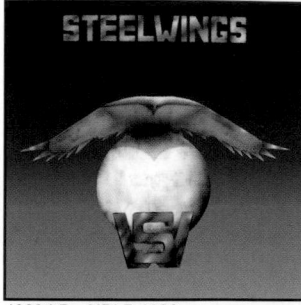

1989 LP - AIRLP 1026

1988 ○	I Wanna Hear You Screaming/Bad Boys	7"	private	LSPS 288
	No artwork.			
1989 ■	STEELWINGS	LP	Air Music	AIRLP 1026
1989 □	STEELWINGS	CD	Air Music	AIRCD 1026

STEFAN HERDE AND HIS BROOMDUSTERS

Stefan Herde: v/g, Anders Karlsson: g/v, Mats Klang: b/v, Richard Ohlsson: d

Eksjö - Straightforward boogie hard rock 'n' roll. Similar to *Status Quo*, *Foghat* and *Jukin' Bone*. The band later featured formed *Fair Child* guitarist Jonas Kjell. Herde was previously in *Pax Romana*, who still exist, and now Klang is also in the line-up.

1992 MCD - OPUS 007

1992 ■	Back To The Roots	MCD 4tr	private	OPUS 007
	Tracks: Wish You Were Here/Down To The Roots/Life Is Strange/Get Yourself A Broom-duster			

STEFAN ROSQVIST BAND

Stefan Rosqvist: g, Bo Eriksson: g, Joakim Attoff: b, Peter Wildoer: d

Helsingborg - Stefan made his first official release with the band sleazy rockers *Scratch* and his second effort playing with death metal band *Dawn Of Oblivion*. However, he is also a fusion-oriented guitarist, which shows when Stefan went solo on *The Guitar Diaries*. The music spans from great shredding, via Eric Johnson-influenced stuff to pure fusion rock. Drummer Wildoer is also found in bands like *Darkane* and *Electrocution 240*. In 2011 Stefan also joined metal bands *Cloudscape* and *FullForce*.

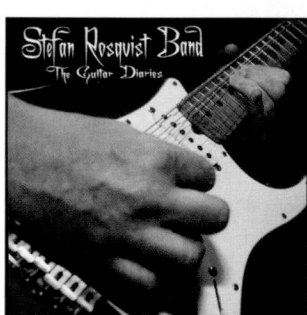

2008 CD - LNR 0007

2008 ■	THE GUITAR DIARIES	CD	Liquid Note Records	LNR 0007

STEN

Maria Weimer: violin, Marcus Weimer: g, Thomas Svensson: d, Magnus Olsson: d

Sundsvall - Folk-rock in the vein of *Hoven Droven*, *Kebnekajse* or Kenny Håkansson with heavy guitars and violin. Or "Härjedalsk folkcore", as the band calls it. *Sten* (stone in Swedish) was formed in 1995, originally featuring Jon Söder on moharp, David Fange on bass, Maria Weimer on violin, Marcus Weimer on guitar and Patrik Israelsson on drums. The band recorded their first four-track demo in 1996. All instrumental. The band also won a contest, where first prize was the recording of an album. So, they recorded a second album in August 1998, all rearranged traditional folk songs. However, the label never released it and the band never received the master. The last line-up featured Maria, Magnus, Marcus, now on bass and new guitarist Tjompen. The band has now folded.

1998 ■	GRÖVRE	CD	TL Studio AB	TLSCD 3598
	500 copies.			

1998 CD - TLSCD 3598

STENCH

Mikael Pettersson: v, Jonathan Hultén: g/b, Johannes Andersson: d

Arvika/Stockholm - *Stench* came about as a beer-drenched idea at the Arvika Festival in 2007. On the first EP the line-up featured Pettersson, Hultén (*Tribulation*) and drummer Jakob Johansson (*Tribulation*). In 2010 the members relocated to Stockholm. *In Putrescence* was mixed by Tore "Necromorbus" Stjerna and drummer Johansson had now been replaced by Johannes Andersson (also *Tribulation*). True Swedish death metal in the vein of *Tribulation* and *Repugnant*. Guitarist Sebastian Gadd and bassist Anton Wanstadius (*Necrovation*) are also added live.

2010 LP - ARLP 071

2009 □	Reborn In Morbidity	7" 4tr	Soulseller Records	SSR 017
	Tracks: Reborn In Morbidity/Through Crypts Of Ghostland/Embodied In Chaos/Stench Of Death			
2010 ■	IN PUTRESCENCE	LP	Agonia Records	ARLP 071
	500 copies.			
2010 □	IN PUTRESCENCE	CD	Agonia Records	ARCD 075

STERBHAUS
Marcus Hammarström: v/b, Simon Olovsson: g, Jimmy Ahovalli: g

Stockholm - Sterbhaus were founded in 2007, playing thrash-infused death metal with a tongue-in-cheek approach (which is also proved by song titles like *Angels For Breakfast, Chili Con Carnage And The Tex-Mexecution* and the outstanding video for the song *House Of The Dead Dwarf*. The band was originally a five-piece featuring singer Daniel "Danne" Lundberg (aka Necrofilip in *Skitarg*), bassist Marcus Hammaström (*Elvira Madigan, Ethocide*), guitarists Robert "Robban" Dunberg and Fredrik Hammar (*Twins Crew*) and drummer Niklas Skogqvist (*Decadence*, aka Don Foster in *Skitarg*). This line-up, minus guitarist Hammar, recorded the first demo CD. Simon Olovsson then replaced Hammar. *Hits For Dead Kids* was recorded late 2008, released as a demo by the band themselves in 2009 and finally officially released in 2011. In 2009 guitarist Robban was given the boot, and was soon replaced by Jimmy Ahovalli (Mattanten in *Skitarg*). In December 2010 singer Lundberg left the band. Instead of drafting a new singer, Hammarström also took over the vocal parts. In 2011 the band started recording their new album, *Angels For Breakfast... And God For Lunch*, in Studio Abyss, together with Tommy Tägtgren. Jimmy cut his finger badly and had to leave for a while. Since Skogqvist had also left the band in 2010, and no new drummer had been found, the band used session drummer Erik Röjås (*Decadence, Netherbird*) for the recording. After this, and before the release, Viktor Bingzelius became the band's new drummer, but he was also out of the band before the album hit the streets. The album features a cover of *Jethro Tull*'s *For A Thousand Mothers*. *Angels For Breakfast...*, produced by Jonas Kjellgren, is a brilliant album, mixing death metal and classic US thrash. *Website: www.sterbhaus.com*

Finished the angels, so where's God??

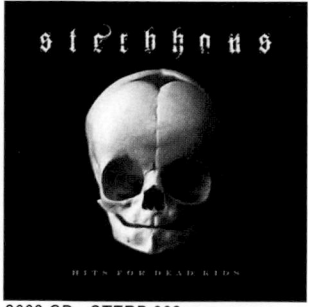

2009 CD - STERB 002

2008 ☐	STERBHAUS	CDp	private	STERB 001	
2011 ■	HITS FOR DEAD KIDS	CD	private	STERB 002	
2012 ■	ANGELS FOR BREAKFAST... AND GOD FOR LUNCH	CD	Killhead	KHCD 001	

2012 CD - KHCD 001

STEREO GENERATOR
Rasmus Bogegård: v/g, Edvin Holm: b, Johan Dahlén: d

Visby - Stereo Generator were formed in 2001, starting out as a stoner band. They recorded their first demo *Insufficient Maña* in 2001, followed by *On Gods Tongue* in 2004 and the first MCD, *Extended Play* in 2006. The line-up now featured singer/guitarist Rasmus Bogegård, bassist Edvin Holm and drummer Johan Dahlén. After this the style took quite a drastic change and on the digital EP *12 Gauges And Coctails* the band is a true heavy southern rock combo in the vein of *Blackfoot*, *Lynyrd Skynyrd* and *Molly Hatchet* with a modern heavy touch. The line-up had also changed seeing drummer Dahlén replaced by Tom Yttergren and keyboardist Jonas Karlsson added to the band. The sounds killer in both styles! *Website: www.stereogenerator.com/*

2006 ■	Extended Play	MCD 3tr	Sandkvie Records	SRCDEP 01	
	Tracks: Drone/Halls Of Deception/Shielded				

2006 MCD - SRCDEP 01

STEVE EASTSIDE BAND
Micke Wickström: v/g, Stefan Englund: g, Lasse Levander: g,
Kent Abrahamsson: b, Mats Blomstrand: d

Uppsala - Heavy blues-oriented rockers, in the vein of *Sky High*. *Backdoor* has a hint of early *Bachman Turner Overdrive*. The band was formed in 1981, initially playing more straight-forward blues. However, they turned a bit heavier on the single. Blomstrand was originally the singer and Jocke Shultz handled the drums, but when Jocke quit, Blomstrand took over the drums and they drafted singer Wickström. Stefan sadly passed away in October 2012.

R.I.P ripper!

BACKDOOR / SILENT

1983 ■	Backdoor/Silent	7"	Studio 55	ST55 503	
1985 ☐	STEVE EASTSIDE BAND	LP	Studio 55	ST55 005	$

1983 7" - ST55 503

STEVE ROPER BAND
Trevor Searle: v, Michael Åhden: g, Samuel Åhden: g,
Magnus M. Jonsson: b, Pär Forsgren: d

Umeå - Existed between 1975 and 1985. Very 70s-sounding powerful rock/hard rock with really biting guitar work. *Betonglåten* should appeal to fans of early 70's bands like *Granmax*, *Bull Angus* and *Demian*. *Fredan är här* is a bit mellower in its approach, but still with great guitars. Described by themselves as "*Motvind* meets *Wishbone Ash*". The line-up on the first single featured Michael and Samuel, who then shared the vocal duties, bassist Frank Granström and drummer Lars Gillén (owner of Garageland and Brute Force). The single was recorded in 1978, but released the year after. The second release, the self-titled MLP was quite a shock, as the band had suddenly taken on a fifties duck tail image and the music had taken the same turn.

1978 7" - ORI

Straight fifties rock 'n roll. I wouldn't say it's horrible, but nothing whatsoever for fans of the band's earlier stuff. After the MLP, in 1983, they recorded the track *On The Telephone* under the name *White Falcons*. It was featured on the 7" 4-track compilation *Universum* (1983 Universum Rec.). However they didn't officially change their name until 1985. Two tracks by *Steve Roper Band* are also found on the compilations *Rätt Till Jobb* (79 Slå Tillbaka) and *Dragonskolan*.

1982 7" - BFR 002

1978 ■	Fredan är här/Betonglåten	7"	Opel	ORI
	Red vinyl.			
1982 ■	Here Comes The Weekend	7" 3tr	Brute Force Records	BFR 002
	Tracks: Here Comes The Weekend/Why Did It have To Be This Way/Another Girl			
1983 ☐	Steve Roper Band	MLP 6tr	Brute Force Records	BFR 011
	Tracks: On The Telephone/My Weekend With You/Out Of My Mind/Respectable Girl/So What/Hot Hot Woman			

STICKY SWEET

Jimmie Olsson: v, Fredrik Jansson: g, Jörgen Engström: g, Andreas Nordkvist: b, Ricky Stahre: d

Skinnskatteberg - **Sticky Sweet** are a young band playing sleazy hard rock, not bad at all. Decent vocals and pretty good performance as well. Well worth checking out.

1989 ■	Freezin' To My Bones/Don't Wanna Wait Until The Next Time	7"	private	SGV-S 9012

1989 7" - SGV-S 9012

STIGSSON, BJÖRN

Sonny Larsson: v, Tina Spångberg: v, Björn Stigsson: g, Dan Tibell: k, Håkan Andersson: b, Kjell Andersson: d

Hjo - Björn recorded his first and only solo album in 1987, while he was still a member of *Leviticus*. Håkan was ex-*Leviticus*, Sonny was a member of *Motherlode* and Kjell was in *Leviticus*. Björn and Sonny later formed the core of the band *XT*. The album is well worth checking out if you like all the aforementioned bands.

1987 ■	TOGETHER WITH FRIENDS	LP	Royal Music	RMLP 031
1987 ☐	TOGETHER WITH FRIENDS	CD	Pure Metal (USA)	SPCM 7900604073

1987 LP - RMLP 031

STILLBORN

Henke Karlsson: v, Ingemar Henning: g, Kim Sandström: g, Sami Miari: b, Peter Asp: d

Göteborg - Formed in 1984. The band recorded their first demo, *Tongue In Thong* in 1985. The debut became quite a classic with its dark moods and the deep vocals from Kari Hokkanen. After the album, Kari quit and rejoined his old band *Dobermanns*. The band consisted of Ingemar, Peter, singer/bassist Sami and guitarist Erik Sandquist. Erik was later replaced by Kim. On *The Permanent Solution* the music was slightly more progressive, in the vein of *Mercyful Fate*. In 1994 Henke quit the band to play country music (?!) and former *Mercy/Candlemass/Memento Mori*-singer Eddie "Messiah" Marcolin took over the microphone. A special recording of the song *Father Of Lies* is featured on the US compilation *Dark Passages*, and another pre-album recording of *Permanent Solution* is found on *In Gold We Trust* (91 Radium 226.05). In 1995 the band, with singer Marcolin at the helm, changed their name to *Collossus* and recorded a couple of demos in 1996, the first one still under the *Stillborn* moniker. Nothing however surfaced on record. Henke was later in funk-rap metal band *Gosh!*. The 2003 single was recorded in 1985, where the B-side was taken from the demo *Tongue in Thong*.

Stillborn, now disconnected

1989 LP - RA 048

1989 ■	NECRO SPIRITUALS	LP	Radium 226.05	RA 048
1991 ☐	THE PERMANENT SOLUTION	LP	Roadracer Records (Holland)	RO 9243-1
1991 ☐	THE PERMANENT SOLUTION	CD	Roadracer Records (Holland)	RO 9243-2
1991 ☐	THE PERMANENT SOLUTION	LP	Radium 226.05	RA 79
1991 ☐	THE PERMANENT SOLUTION	CD	Radium 226.05	RACD 79
1992 ☐	STATE OF DISCONNECTION	LP	Roadrunner Records	RR 9137-1
1992 ☐	STATE OF DISCONNECTION	CD	Roadrunner Records	RR 9137-2
1992 ☐	STATE OF DISCONNECTION	CD	Century Media (USA)	CM 7747-2
1993 ☐	NECRO SPIRITUALS	CD	Radium 226.05	RACD 48
2003 ■	Yesterday's Blood/Son Of Sodom	7"	I Hate Records	IHR 003
	Red vinyl. 500 hand-numbered copies.			

2003 7" - IHR 003

STINGRAY

**Andreas "Andy Stone" Stenfeldt: v, Jonas "Johnny Walker" Svensson: g,
Mikael "Mike Mayson" Palm: g, Marcus "Mack Daniels" Högberg: b,
Daniel "Danny Hitman" Stenå: d**

Uddevalla - Quite honestly, if it was only for the first release only, this band wouldn't be included in this book since the CD is a pro-printed CD-R, even though it's on a "professional" label. *Stingray* play decent melodic hard rock. The band was formed in 2006 under the name *The Starry Red* and recorded their first demo two years later. They were picked up by Blue Topaz and changed their name. After the album guitarist Johan Hedin left the band, and was replaced by Johnny Walker. The band's second album *Further Down* was produced by Jonas Hansson (*Silver Mountain*) and released in 2010. *Further Down* is definitely a step in the right direction. Good solid hard rock. In 2011 the band also switched drummer from Danny to Matt Drumhead (where DO they find all those names??).
Website: www.stingraymusic.se

2009 CD - BTRCD 44

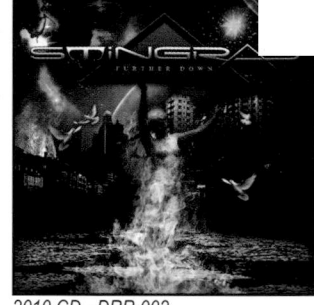

| 2009 | ■ | STINGRAY | CD | Blue Topaz | BTRCD 44 |
| 2010 | ■ | FURTHER DOWN | CD | Dusty Road | DRR 002 |

2010 CD - DRR 002

STITCH

**Sussi Ax: v, Jörgen "Conel" Winblad: g, Lasse Nyström: k,
Ken Sundberg: b, Jörgen Sverin: d**

Södertälje - The first single is average 80s-style NWoBHM with quite monotonous vocals. Musically they were in the vein of *Buffalo*, *Oxym* etc. The line-up was then, besides Ken and Jörgen, singer Bob May, guitarists Leffe Lindström and Jimmy Holmström. Bob later joined the southern-influenced band *Badland*. On the second single guitarist Winblad and keyboardist Lasse Nyström had replaced both guitarists, and singer Sussi Ax (ex-*Revanch*) had taken over the vocals. Style-wise they had now transformed into a mainstream commercial AOR band aiming for the big break. However, they disappeared. Håkan "Ian" Haugland, of *Europe*-fame, was actually in this band for a short period. Bob May later teamed up with former *Parasite*/*Rebelene*-guitarist Anders Holmström in a band mostly doing covers.

1982 7" - SMF 003

| 1982 | ■ | Devil's Deal/Touching The Stars | 7" | SMF | SMF 003 |
| 1988 | ■ | You Light My Fire/Can't Fight This Feeling | 7" | Sonet | T 10253 |

1988 7" - T 10253

STOCKHOLM SHOWDOWN

**Stefan "Sterta" Byrstedt: v/g, Slim Tannberg: g,
Ronnie "Rozen" Johansson: b, Peter Forsberg: d**

Karlskoga - Byrstedt and Johansson were previously in US based sleaze rockers *Princess Pang*. Sleaze oriented hard rock 'n roll, sort of *Aerosmith* meets Chuck Berry.

| 2002 | ■ | LAST CALL TO PARADISE | CD | CCCP Red Records | - - |

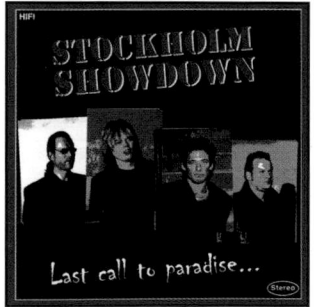

2002 CD - - -

STONECAKE

**Tommy "Stommen" Andersson (now Liljegren): v/g,
Per Mårtensson: b, Marcus Källström: d**

Borlänge - This band is actually quite funny in the way they mix *Beatles* harmonies, psychedelic acid rock, Hendrix riffs and pop melodies. The band labels their music "happy psycho". There are some great tracks on all albums. Marcus is ex-*Six Feet Under/Sky High*. The non-CD track *Who Can Beat That Girl* can be found on the compilation *Backstage: Högtalarterror '94*. The '95 releases saw the change of bass-player from Klas Hägglund to Per (also found in *The Morning After*). Klas was later in *DeathOrgan*, where Marcus also lends a helping hand (or two). *Stonecake* also do occasional gigs where they only play *Beatles* covers in their own heavy versions, but under the name *Birthday Cake*. They also appear on a MCD by the band *Indian Red*. The first album is a great, quite heavy bluesy Hendrixy hard rocker. The "problem" was that the band had a huge hit with the Beatlesque ballad *Tuesday Afternoon*, which made the band become a bit more commercial on the subsequent releases, especially *In The Middle Of Nowhere* is more poppy rock than actual hard rock. *Some People* is even more pop. The band is still active. They also did a cover of *SOS* on the compilation *ABBA – The Tribute* (92 Polar) and a great rendition of *The Sixteens* on *The Sweet According To Sweden* (2005 Rivel).

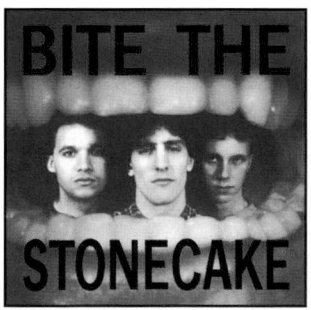

1990 7" - INGY 001

1990	■	Bite The Stonecake/Gunnar	7"	Rock Hard	INGY 001
1991	□	Creatures Of The Factory/Don't Feed The Nasty Dogs	7"	Wire Records	WRS 036
1991	□	Creatures Of The Factory	MCD 3tr	Wire Records	WRCDS 036
		Tracks: Creatures.../Don't Feed The Nasty Dogs/Completely Mad			
1991	□	Nation's On Your Side	MCD 4tr	Wire Records	WRCDS 038
		Tracks: Nation's../Nation's... short version/Completely Mad/Bite The Stonecake (live)			

1992 LP - WRLP 17

1991 ☐	Nation's On Your Side/Bite The Stonecake (Live).................7"	Wire Records.................WRS 038
1992 ☐	UNDER THE BIKETREE....................CD	Wire Records.................WR CD17
1992 ■	UNDER THE BIKETREE....................LP	Wire Records.................WRLP 17
1992 ☐	Under The Biketree/Heartbreak Café.................CDS	Zomba (Holland)....................n/a
1992 ■	Tuesday Afternoon/Under The Biketree.................7"	Wire Records.................WRS 33
1992 ☐	Tuesday Afternoon/Under The Biketree.................CDS 2tr	Wire Records.................WRCD 33
1993 ☐	Sunnier (single edit)/ (fläsk mix)/(album version)/Gunnar.................MCD 4tr	MVG.................MVGCDS 6
1993 ☐	Sunnier (single edit)/(album version).................7"	MVG.................MVG S 6
1993 ☐	Completely Mad.................MCD 3tr	Wire Records.................74321121912

Tracks: Completely Mad/The Nation's On Your Side/Bite The Stoncake (live)

1993 ☐	ACOUSTIC TOILETS.................CD	MVG.................MVGCD 111
1993 ☐	ACOUSTIC TOILETS.................LP	MVG.................MVG 111
1993 ☐	ACOUSTIC TOILETS.................CD	Pioneer (Japan).................PICP-1007

Bonus: Tuesday Afternoon

1994 ☐	Bite The Stonecake.................MCD 6tr	Pioneer (Japan).................PICP-1018

Tracks: The Nation's On Your Side/Bite The Stonecake/Sunnier! (flask mix)/Keep On Despite (unplugged)/Completeluy Mad (unplugged)/Tuesday Afternoon (live)

1995 ☐	Building Castles.................CDS 1tr	MVG (promo).................MVGPROM 25
1995 ☐	IN THE MIDDLE OF NOWHERE.................CD	MVG.................MVG 119
2002 ☐	SOME PEOPLE.................CD	Acoustic Toilets.................CDAT 001

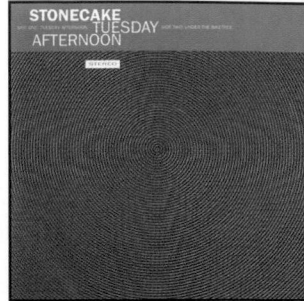

1992 7" - WRS 33

STONECHURCH

Karl-Oskar "Kalle" Wiman: v/b, Ronny Westergren: g,
Pontus Pettersson (now Lennander): g, Jonas Johansson: d

Stenkyrka (Gotland) - Stonechurch (their name of their home town Stenkyrka), from the island of Gotland, were formed in 1999. The band was influenced by bands like **Iron Maiden** and **Metallica**, but they don't really sound like any of them. However we are talking NWoBHM style metal here, actually a bit reminiscent of Swedish colleagues **Destiny** at times. Drummer Johansson was later replaced by Jens Flennemo.
Website: www.stonechurch.se

2001 ☐	VISIONS.................CD	private.................STCD 001
2002 ☐	GOODEVIL.................CD	private.................STCD 002
2006 ■	AMPLIFIED.................CD	Artache.................GA 014

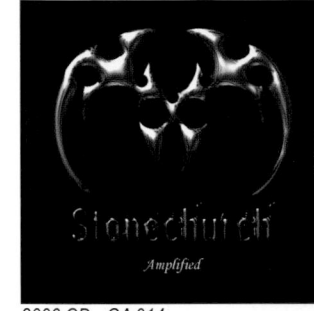

2006 CD - GA 014

STONEFLOW

Lasse Olausson: v, Peter Pohlin: v, Vesa Kenttäkumpu: b, Magnus Persson: d

Borås - Formed in 1992 by former **Kid Vicious** members Peter and Magnus. The album was produced by Roberto Laghi (**B-Thong, Freak Kitchen** etc). This band is almost in the same musical league as their label-mates **B-Thong**, i.e. brutal heavy power metal with tons of heavy power riffs. Although **Stoneflow** is a bit more doomy, with slow and searing riffs that cut steel. Very classy stuff. The band also recorded a **Sator** cover for the compilation *Guldskivan* (96 Backstage Magazine).

1995 ■	SKULLPTURE.................CD	Major Music.................RTD 312.0054-2

1995 CD - RTD 312.0054-2

STONEFUZE

Kent Franklin: v/g, Mattias Holm: g, Samuel Gustafsson: b, Mick Nordström: d

Jönköping - Stonefuze are the continuation of the band **Cornerstone**, formed in 1989. The only difference in personnel is the switch from drummer Fredric Josefsson/Käld to Mick Nordström (**Modest Attraction, Spearfish, Two Franklin Groove** etc). The style also became a bit heavier and more stoner-oriented. A good solid rocker.

2008 ■	STONEFUZE.................CD	Rivel Records.................RRCD 038

2008 CD - RRCD 038

STONEHENGE

Conny Jogander: v, Jens "Dubben" Grundelius: g,
Rolan Wiberg: b/k, Jan Lindekrantz: d

Lidingö (Stockholm) - The band was originally formed by Roland, Jens, Micke "Mike Mocadem" Mujanne and Tony "Roy Taylor" Hellander. All except Roland later formed **Trash**. Well-played hard rock in the same vein as **Deep Purple** but with a slightly bluesier touch. Lots of Hammond and searing bluesy guitar work. A good one.

1985 ■	Oddyse/Have Mercy/Rock Your Heart/White Horse.................7" 4tr	Rosa Honung.................ROS EP 24

1985 7" - ROS EP 24

STONELAKE

Peter Grundström: v, Jan Åkesson: g/k/b/d/v, Annika Agerich: k,
Lasse Johansson: b, Jens Westberg: d

Lund - In 1984 Jan and Peter met after a concert where Jan's band *Ravage* and
Peter's *Whitelight* shared the stage. Later on Jan also joined *Whitelight*. How-
ever, in 1987 he left and the band changed name to *Kee Avenue*. Jan formed
Why Not. Fifteen years later Jan called Peter asking if they should reunite and
StoneLake was formed. The band released their first four-track demo in 2004.
It was followed by the first self-financed album, *Reincarnation* in 2005. At this
point the band featured only Peter and Jan, helped out by drummer Jeremy Child.
They were finally picked up by AOR Heaven, who released the follow-up *World
Entry* on their sub-label Metal Heaven. On this album, the duo used the drum
talents of Jaime Salazar (*Bad Habit, The Flower Kings, Midnight Sun, Truth*
etc). On *Uncharted Souls* the band was back to releasing the album on their
own. The band had now been completed by bassist Lasse Johansson and drummer Jens Westberg. *StoneLake* play melodic metal, sounding a bit like a mix
of *Dokken* and *Judas Priest* with Grundström adding the classic high-pitched
vocals. Quite brutal and guitar dominated mix. The band is good, but a little
rough around the edges sometimes. The 2011 release, *Marching On Timeless
Tales*, was actually the first release where the production sounded professional.
Furthermore the band sounded better than ever. Tommy Denander provided a
guest solo. Keyboardist David Lindell was replaced by Annika Argerich (*Cult
Disciples, Veritate*) in 2011.

Stonelake, impersonating monoliths

2005	■	REINCARNATION	CD	Unlimited Music Productions	Stone 2
2007	□	WORLD ENTRY	CD	Metal Heaven	0037
		Bonus: One Love, One Heart			
2008	□	UNCHARTED SOULS	CD	Unlimited Music Productions	Stone 4
2009	□	SHADES OF ETERNITY	CD	7Hard	7H 008-2
2011	□	MARCHING ON TIMELESS TALES	CD	Massacre Records	MAS-CD 0723
2013	■	MONOLITH	CD	Massacre Records	MAS-CD 0815

2005 CD - Stone 2

2013 CD - n/a

STONELOAD

Andreas Wikström: v, Thomas Isaksson: g, Nitesh Mistry: b, Tobias Oja. d

Umeå - The story actually goes back to 2008 when Tobias and Thomas formed the band *Blackout
Metal*. In 2009 ex-*Nasheim* singer Andreas joined and they recorded an excellent demo in 2011.
In January 2012 they became *Stoneload*. Excellent melodic thrash metal in the vein of *Testament*.

| 2012 | ■ | ADDICT | CD | Sliptrick Records | SLP012.043 |

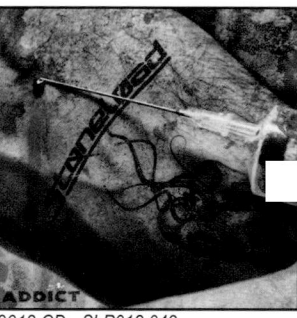

2012 CD - SLP012.043

STONESILK

Johan Sjöberg: v/g, Fredrik Schönbeck: b, Tor Pentén: d

Stockholm - *Stonesilk* were formed around 2004, by producer and former *Token* member
Sjöberg. After having changed members several times, Schönbeck joined in 2007. During the
recording of the album former *Rednex* drummer Pentén replaced Federico da Costa, who plays
drums on six tracks on the debut. *Stonesilk* plays post-grunge in the vein of *Nickelback* and
Creed with Sjöberg at times sounding a bit like Eddie Vedder. In 2010 drummer Pentén was
replaced by Magnus Arndtzen and the sound now became a bit heavier. The singles *Running
From Myself* (2010) and *Falling Down* (2011) were only released digitally. A new album was
set to be released in 2012, but hasn't showed up yet.

2008	□	YOU'RE NOT ALONE	CD	Intravex	INX 001
2008	■	Hold Me Up	CDS	Intravex	INX 002
2009	□	Stop Closing Your Eyes	CDS	Intravex	INX 005

2008 CDS - INX 002

STONEWALL NOISE ORCHESTRA (aka S.N.O)

Lars-Inge "Singe" Strömberg: v, Rickard "Snicken" Ny: g, Viktor Grahnström: g,
Jonas Wahlberg: b, Mathias "Mr. Pillow/Kudden" Adolfson: d

Borlänge - Stonewall Noise Orchestra or *S.N.O*, as they abbreviate the name, were formed in
2004 by Daniel Jansson (*Greenleaf*) and Ny, when their band *Demon Cleaner* split. They were
reinforced by Mr. Pillow (ex-*Unhuman Fear*) and bass player Jonas. In 2006 John Hermansen
(*The Awesome Machine, Staiger, Greenleaf, Mother Misery*) temporarily replaced Singe for
the second album, after which he returned. After the second album Viktor Grahnström replaced
guitarist Daniel Jansson. *S.N.O* play awesome stoner metal in the vein of *Monster Magnet*-
meet-*Queens Of The Stoneage*.
Website: www.snoband.com

2008 CD - DD 049

2005 ☐	VOL.1	CD	DareDevil		DD 030
2008 ■	VOL.1	CD	DareDevil		DD 049

Bonus: Broken Pills/The Practice Of Talking Too Much/Superfortress (live)/Freedom's Prize (live). Different artwork.

2008 ☐	CONSTANTS IN AN EVER CHANGING UNIVERSE	CDd	The Unit		UNIT 603
2010 ☐	SWEET MISSISSIPPI DEAL	CD	Transubstans		TRANS 072
2013 ☐	SALVATION	CDd	Transubstans		TRANS 103
2013 ■	SALVATION	LP	Transubstans		TRANSV 14

100 red + 400 black vinyl.

2013 LP - TRANSV 14

STORM

Lasse Berggrensson: v, Jaques Verup: sax, Bengt "Mulle" Holmquist: g, Rolf Fersam: k, Percy Malmquist: k/horns, Stefan Berggrensson: b, Håkan Nyberg: d

Malmö - This band has never been considered a hard rock band, but especially on *At The Top* they throw in some great progressive and quite heavy passages, quite glam-influenced, sounding a bit like a mix of *Tears* and *Mott The Hoople*. All albums are collectors' items. On the debut, the band consisted of Jan Ek (v), Christer Carlberg (g), Peter Winberg (d) (he died in a car crash in the 80s), Jaques, Bengt and Rolf. On *At The Top*, Lasse replaced Jan, Christer was out and Percy Malmquist, who actually sang one track on the dbut was in on bass. On the last album, Håkan replaced Peter, Stefan Berggrensson was added on bass and Percy switched to keyboards and horns. Jaques is also a well-known poet/writer.

1974 LP - E062 35010

1974 ■	STORMVARNING	LP	Harvest		E062 35010
1975 ■	AT THE TOP	LP	Harvest		E062 35179
1977 ☐	CASANOVA FRÅN MJÖLBY	LP	Harvest		062 35324
2012 ☐	STORMVARNING	CD	Eastworld		EW0090CD
2012 ☐	AT THE TOP	CD	Eastworld		EW0080CD

1975 LP - E062 35179

STORMCROW

Anders Hjärtström: v, Ulf Helander: g, Anders Jonsson: g, Johan Dyyk: b, Daniel Melo: d

Norrköping - *Stormcrow* were formed in 2001 by singer Hjärtström and guitarist Helander. They recorded three demos, *StormCrow* (2003), *Destination Unknown* (2003) and *Million Miles* (2004) before being picked up by Norwegian label Edgerunner after being featured on one of their compilations, and released one album. The style is melodic power metal, reminiscent of bands like *Blind Guardian*, *Tad Morose* and *Nocturnal Rites*. Hjärtström later joined *Miss Behaviour*, Dyyk joined goth rockers *Sabachthani* and Melo progressive band *Bokor*.

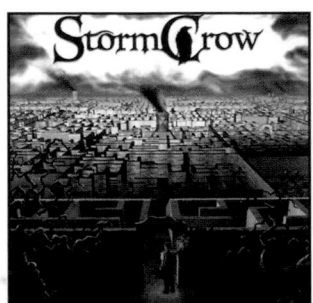

2005 ■	NO FEAR OF TOMORROW	CD	Edgerunner Music		EDGE 013

2005 CD - EDGE 013

STORMRIDER

Henrik "YX" Eriksson: v, Mikael "Strampan" Strandberg: g, Henrik Larsen: g, Morgan Ramstedt: b, Björn Jonsson: d

Bro (Stockholm) - Death/black metal band *Stormrider* were formed in 1999 and recorded their first demo, *Born Of Chaos*, the same year. It was followed by *God Is Dead* in 2000 and *Into Battle* in 2001. A bit similar to *Cradle Of Filth* at times. After the first album Björn Jonsson (*Blodsrit*) replaced drummer Kristoffer Ahlberg.

2003 ☐	FIRST BATTLE WON	CD	Destructive Records		DES 002
2004 ☐	FIRST BATTLE WON	CD	New Aeon Media		NAM 004

Bonus: Burning The Heavens + Completely Dead (video)

2007 ■	LUCIFER RISING	CD	Aural Offerings		offering 001

2007 CD - offering 001

STORMWIND, (THOMAS WOLF'S)

Thomas Vikström: v, Thomas Wolf: g, Andreas Olsson: b, Kaspar Dahlqvist: k, David Wallin: d

Stockholm - Formed in 1995, initially as Thomas Wolf's solo project. He recorded a first eight-track demo in 1995. The style on the debut was highly *Europe*-influenced melodic hard rock with female vocals. The line-up then consisted of singer Tina Leijonberg, Thomas Wolf, keyboard player Per Hallman, drummer Henrik Seeman and bassist Kristofer Eng, who had been added to the line-up after the demo. Tina is foremost known as a TV-hostess and actor, but sure knows how to sing as well, although her vocals were way too soft for this type of music. Thomas was a Swedish Champion in karate in 1993. The band's second release featured singer Angelica Häggström, who had a much rougher edge to her voice. Peter Nilsson (ex-*Glory*) was in the band for a short period in 1997-98, when *Stormwind* played in Cannes, now with a new temporary line-up also featuring drummer Iman Solgarian, bassist Björn and keyboardist Björn Hansson. After this Wolf decided to put together a new line-up. The show was recorded, but never released. Just before the release of *Heaven Can Wait*, High Gain Records went bankrupt

A Wolf in black clothing

1996 CD - MERCD 96001

and the High Gain version was only sent out as a paper-cover promo. The vocals were now handled by former *Talk Of The Town*/*Candlemass*-singer Thomas Vikström and keyboardist Kaspar Dahlqvist (*Treasure Land, Dionysus, Sahara*) was added to the reinforced the line-up. Drummer Patrik Johansson is ex-*Without Grief* and was also working with Yngwie Malmsteen. Andreas was also a member of *Wisdom Call*, *Narnia* and has also been in *7Days, Royal Hunt, Divine Fire, Harmony* and Rob Rock's band. The band has gradually turned better and better, not that they were ever bad though. On the later albums the band went from a more neoclassical touch to slightly prog-oriented, but still melodic high class metal. On *Rising Symphony* drummer Patrik had been replaced by David Wallin (ex-*Blacksmith, Meduza, Pain*). *Legacy* is a compilation with an interactive documentary video, one live-CD and one CD with bonus tracks. *Stormwind* is also featured on the Yngwie Malmsteen tribute *A Guitar Odyssey*, where they do a cover of the *Alkatrazz* song of *Too Young To Die, Too Drunk To Live*. They can also be found on the Lion Music Jason Becker tribute. In 2005 Thomas signed a publishing deal for Scandinavian film and TV companies and put *Stormwind* on hold.

1999 CDp - 0055342HGR

2001 CD - MASCD 0303

1996	■	STRAIGHT FROM YOUR HEART	CD	Mother Earth	MERCD 96001
1998	□	STARGATE	CD	S.M.R.	SMRCD 98-001
1999	□	HEAVEN CAN WAIT	CD	Dreamchaser (Japan)	SCCD-6
		Bonus: Heaven Can Wait (radio edit)			
1999	■	HEAVEN CAN WAIT	CDp	High Gain	0055342HGR
		Promo-CD with card board pocket cover.			
1999	□	STARGATE	CD	Dreamchaser (Japan)	SCCD-7
		Bonus: Satyricon, Heaven Can Wait (radio edition)			
1999	□	HEAVEN CAN WAIT	CD	Digital Dimension	0060062 DDE
1999	□	HEAVEN CAN WAIT	CD	Nems (Argentina)	NEMS 138
1999	□	HEAVEN CAN WAIT	CD	Rock Brigade/Laser (Brazil)	RBR/LSR 1860
2000	□	RESURRECTION	CD	Massacre	MASCS 0250
2000	□	RESURRECTION	CD	Rock Brigade/Laser (Brazil)	RBR/LSR 2340
2001	□	STARGATE	CD	Massacre	MASCD 0275
		Bonus: Too Young To Die, Too Drunk To Live (Alkatrazz-cover)			
2001	■	REFLECTIONS	CD	Massacre	MASCD 0303
2001	□	REFLECTIONS	CD	Avalon Marquee (Japan)	MICP 10261
		Bonus: Venezia/A Little Ain't Enough			
2001	□	REFLECTIONS	CD	Rock Brigade/Laser (Brazil)	RBR/LSR 2900
2001	□	REFLECTIONS	CD	Art Music Group (Russia)	AMG 032
2003	■	RISING SYMPHONY	CD	Massacre	MASCD 0362
		Bonus: Venezia			
2004	■	LEGACY	2CD	Massacre	MASCD 0411

2003 CD - MASCD 0362

2004 2CD - MASCD 0411

STORY

Peter Zyreén: v, Peter Dahl: g, Joakim Westman: k,
Krister Johnsson: b, Mikael Andersson: d

Karlskoga - A good pompy AOR band that sings in Swedish. They also made some good demo-recordings and the tracks *I Don't Wanna Be A Fool* and *Movin' On* are found on the compilation *Skri från vildmarken* (WLP 795).

| 1984 | ■ | Långt In I Framtiden/Ge Dem Allt | 7" | private | VFS 8408 |

1984 7" - VFS 8408

STORYTELLER, THE

L-G Persson: v, Marcus Backlund: g, Jacob Wennerqvist: g,
Henrik Brannerydh: b, Martin Hjerpe: d

Gävle - The band was formed in the summer of 1995 by bassist/singer L-G Persson and guitarist Fredrik Groth, initially intended to be an acoustic folk-influenced duo. Then singer Magnus Björk and guitarist Jocke Lundström were added to the line-up and the first 3-track demo was recorded in 1995, followed by a second demo in 1996. After this, several reasons lead to the group being disbanded. Late 1997 Groth and Persson picked up the pieces, found drummer Martin Hjerpe and reformed the band, now playing power metal with traces of *Blind Guardian* and *Gamma Ray*. A couple of new demos in 1998 lead to interest from some labels. Guitarist Lasse Martinsson was added to the line-up and No Fashion signed the band. The debut was recorded at Studio Fredman and features a appearance by Steven Anderson. After the album, guitarist Erik Gornostajev replaced Lasse. However, Erik left right before the recording of the second album. *Crossroad* was recorded as a trio featuring Persson, Groth and Hjerpe. Some guitar solos were added by Pär Kankanranta (*Raubtier*), while Ronny Hemlin and former member Lasse Martinsson lays down some backing vocals. Fredrik Nordström produced the first two albums. On *Tales Of A Holy Quest* the line-up featured Persson, Groth, Hjerpe and guitarist Jacob Wennerqvist. On the *Seed Of Lies* EP new bassist Johan Sohlberg had been added to the line-up. The band split in 2006, but later reformed, featuring Henrik Brannerydh replacing bassist Johan Solbergh and Marcus Backlund replacing Fredrik Groth. The band returned with *Dark Legacy* .

2002 CD - NFR 056 CD

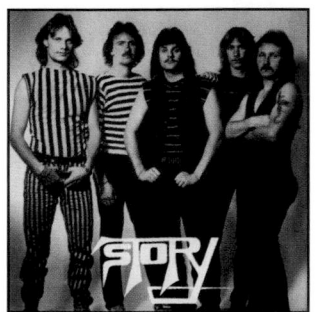

2003 CD - BLOD 007 CD

| 2000 | □ | THE STORYTELLER | CD | Soundholic (Japan) | TKCS 85008 |
| | | Bonus: Chant Of The Thieves | | | |

2000 ☐	THE STORYTELLER	CD	No Fashion	NFR 044	
2001 ☐	CROSSROAD	CD	Soundholic (Japan)	TKCS 85031	
	Bonus: Moonchild (Iron Maiden-cover)				
2002 ■	CROSSROAD	CD	No Fashion	NFR 056 CD	
2002 ☐	CROSSROAD	LP	No Fashion	NFRLP 056	
2003 ■	TALES OF A HOLY QUEST	CD	Black Lodge	BLOD 007 CD	
2004 ☐	Seed Of Lies	MCD 4tr	Black Lodge	BLOD 014 CD	
	Tracks: Seed Of Lies/Bark At The Moon (Ozzy cover)/The Secret's Revealed (live)/Prophets Of Liars (demo) + Seed Of Lies (video)				
2005 ■	UNDERWORLD	CD	Black Lodge	BLOD 030 CD	
2013 ☐	DARK LEGACY	CD	Black Lodge	BLOD 086 CD	

2005 CD - BLOD 030 CD

STRAIGHT FRANK

Tobias Gustavsson: v, Johan Coma Svensson: g,
Henrik Edenhed: b, Kasper Lindgren: d

Stockholm - Straight Frank were formed in 2008 by drummer Lindgren, and the debut album was recorded in 2009. Unfortunately the label went bust before its release. Guitarist Jonny Wemmenstedt was replaced by Johan Coma Svensson. Edenhed is ex-*Downstroke* and also had his own band *Edenhed*. Drummer Lindgren previously played with alternative rockers *Prime Sth* and also plays in *Nordic Shine*. *Straight Frank* plays varied melodic post-grunge quite reminiscent of *Soundgarden*, especially when it comes to Tobias' vocals.
Website: www.straightfrank.com

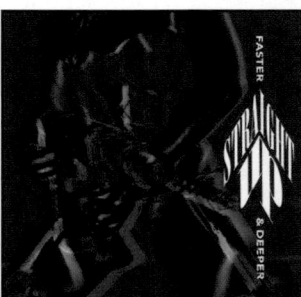

2009 ☐	AND WE WALKED BY WITH A BAG FULL OF MONEY	CDp	Bodog Music	BDMO 149128	
2011 ■	STRAIGHT FRANK	CD	Columbia	8869785-6392	

2011 CD - 8869785-6392

STRAIGHT UP

Jocke Johansson: v, Ralph Pettersson: g, Robban Persson: g,
Lasse Fallman: b, Stephan Engström: g

Linköping - This is straightforward sleazy power rock like early *Nasty Idols* with quite explicit lyrics and song titles like *Straight Up In Your Pussy* and *Fist Fucking Generation*. No wonder the band calls their style "Fuck 'n' roll". After the album rhythm guitarist Robban Persson was replaced by former *Axewitch* bender Magnus Jarl. A second, as-yet unreleased, album was recorded. Robban has released a Johnny Thunders tribute CD under the name Robbie Black.

1991 ■	FASTER & DEEPER	LP	Wire Records	WRLP 016	
1991 ☐	FASTER & DEEPER	CD	Wire records	WRCD 016	

1991 LP - WRLP 016

STRANGULATION

Jonathan O. Gonzales: v, Juha Helttunen: g, John Carlsson: b, Tobias Israelsson: d

Karlskoga - Strangulation were formed in 2001, where all except Carlsson were found in *Butchery*, and released their first demo, *Carnage In Heaven,* in 2002, followed by *Withering Existence* the year after. *Strangulation* play high speed American style death metal similar to *Cannibal Corpse*, with deep mumble-growling vocals, where it sometimes sounds like Swedish actually. The band has split, and Israelsson is now in *Icon Blood*.

2004 ■	ATROCIOUS RETRIBUTION	CD	Retribute Records	RET 019	

2004 CD - RET 019

STREET LEVEL

Eva Beckman: v, Urban Bergman: g, Bo Berggren: g, Kurt Gustafsson: d

Umeå - It all started with the band *Checkpoint Charlie*. After some line-up changes they became *Street Level*. However only Urban and Kurt participated on *Checkpoint Charlie*'s single. *Street Level* delivers straightforward rock & rollin´ hard rock in the mid-quality area. The second release is far more interesting than the first.

1981 ☐	Nattdjur/Naggad I Kanten (Live)	7"	Slam The Ham	SL 75A	
1981 ■	Damned Good Boy/Tonight	7"	Apollo	APS 011	

STREET TALK

Göran Edman: v, Sven Larsson: g, Fredrik Bergh: k,
Björn Lodmark: b, Christian Johansson: d

Bollnäs - On the first album this was more of a project than a band. The members were then, besides founder and main-man Fredrik, guitarist/bassist/keyboardist Andreas Lidberg (ex-*Sacrifice*), bassist Jon Persson and guitarist Tomas Olsson, while the vocals were handled by

1981 7" - APS 011

Göran Edman, Kristian Andrén (*Tad Morose*) and Daniel Jonsson. *Toto*-influenced westcoastish AOR. *Restoration* features both Göran Edman and Hugo Valenti (*Valentine, Open Skys*) on vocals, while the guitars were handled by Sven Larsson, bass by Lodmark, keyboards by Bergh and drums by Johansson. On *Destination* the bass work was shared between Björn Lodmark, Mikael Berner, Tony Franklin (*The Firm, Blue Murder*), while Sven shared his guitar work with Andreas Lidberg. On *V* the line-up was steady again, featuring Edman, Bergh, Larsson, Johansson and Lodmark. The band has actually sharpened their sound by each album and on *V* they have adopted more of a classic AOR sound and style, a bit similar to *Last Autumn's Dream*. A great, solid high-class band. Sven has also recorded an excellent westcoast-oriented solo recordings, and Lindmark has unearthed a more hard rocking solo effort.

2000 CD - 10163

1997	☐	COLLABORATION	CD	USG	USG 1016-2
1997	☐	COLLABORATION	CD	Bareknuckles (Japan)	AVCB 66024
		Bonus: Separate Ways (Worlds Apart) (Journey cover)/Conclusion			
2000	■	TRANSITION	CD	Point Music	10163
2000	☐	TRANSITION	CD	Avalon Marquee (Japan)	MICP-10195
		Bonus: I'll Always Remember (instrumental). Different artwork.			
2002	☐	RESTORATION	CD	MTM	0681-54
2002	☐	RESTORATION	CD	Avalon Marquee (Japan)	MICP-10325
		Bonus: After The Tears			
2004	☐	DESTINATION	CD	MTM	0681-88
2006	■	V	CD	MTM	0681-167

2006 CD - 0681-167

STRIKE
T.C Rundquist: v/g, Alexander Danielsson: g, Eric Losman: b, Stephen Wikström: d

Stockholm - A young, but quite talented melodic hard rock band with sing-along chorus parts and a nice groove. Could be compared to *Kiss* or Swedish fellows *Deep Diver*. There is another band with the same name that has released a single in Swedish, they are a pop band though. The MLP was released on three different labels, but all with the same songs.

1984	■	Strike	MLP 6tr	Tandan	TANMLP 008
		Tracks: I Close My Eyes/We're Bad Boys/Radio Love/Get Out/Feels Like Fire/Loose Trigger			
1984	☐	Strike	MLP 6tr	Sword (UK)	SWORDMLP 002
1984	☐	Strike	MLP 6tr	Banzai (Can)	BAM 1009

1984 MLP - TANMLP 008

STYGGELSE
Dennis "L Svartvén" Larsson: v/g, Gustaf "Kallbrand "Sundin: g,
Björn "Folkilsk" Thorup: b, Mathias "Skadeglade" Svensson: d

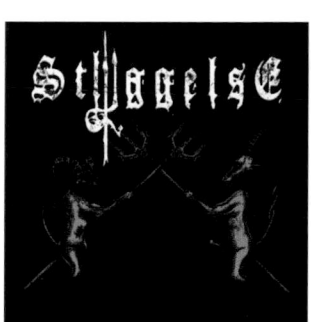

Göteborg - *Styggelse* (abomination in English) were formed in 2003. Larsson went by the moniker L. Svartvén on the first release, but now goes by his last name. Thorup is also found in *Pagan Rites* and has previously played with *Fear The Future* (as Azazel), *Autopsy Torment* and *Karneywar*. Sundin is also in *Snakeskin Angels*, while Larsson is found in *Likblek* and *Hinsides*. After the MCD the band recorded two demos in 2008, *Goatenburg Abominations* and *Mavsoleym Tellvs*. The track *Av äckel* is featured on the compilation *Explicity Intense – Insanity Sampler 13*. *Styggelse* play raw, old-school black metal with touches of thrash and at times almost a touch of *Motörhead*-meet-*Venom*, like in the track *Sadomasochrist*. The digital version of the *Sadomasochrist* EP also contains the bonus track *Born To Bleed*.

2010 CD - UER 034

2005	☐	Bland andlösa fält av snusk och hor	MCD 6tr	Baphomet	BAPH 137
		Tracks: Av äckel/Getsatans svarta podium/Ensamhetens vinter tär/Sjöhäxan/Inter arma silent leges/Styggelse			
2010	■	HEIR TODAY – GOD TOMORROW	CD	Unexploded Records	UER 034
2012	■	Sadomasochrist/Vomit The Cross	7"	Plague Island	7th Boil
		200 black, 100 red (although some were pink) vinyl.			

2012 7" - 7th Boil

SUB SECOND ROCKET
Peter Magnusson: v/g, Patric Ifverson: g, Daniel Melkersson: b, Ola Sundström: d

Malmö - *Sub Second Rocket* were formed in 1998. They recorded a three-track demo in 1999 and a second one followed later the same year. In 2001 the third demo *Horsepower* lead to a deal with Daredevil Records. The demo was completed with three more tracks and released as the band's debut album. One of the numerous bands in the new wave of Swedish stoner rock/metal. Similar to colleagues like *Zebulon* and *Twin Earth*, with some great riffs thrown in and pretty diverse songs.

| 2002 | ■ | HORSEPOWER | CD | Daredevil | DD 016 |

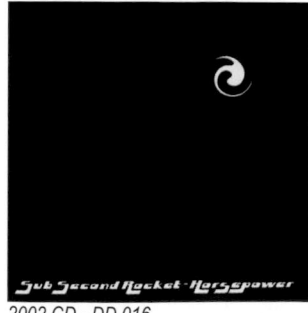

2002 CD - DD 016

SUBCYDE

Antonio Ravina da Silva: v, Ola Englund: g, Martin Anderson: b, Johan Wikforss: d

Stockholm - Not to be confused with the electro band. *Sybcyde* was formed in 1997 by Ola and Johan, at the time playing in a local punk band. Guitarist Martin was asked to play bass and Antonio was asked to add some vocals. Second guitarist Jim was also in the band in the beginning, but left for personal reasons. The first demo was recorded in 2004, followed by a second in 2005 and a third in 2006, before recording the debut album. *Subcyde* plays tight and heavy metal in the vein of **Machine Head** meets **Pantera**. Englund is also found in **Facing Death**, **Feared** and Antonio has been fronting **Circle Of Chaos** and **Barbus**. The track *Breed Of Chaos* was featured on the *Demobanken 2006* (06 Studiefrämjandet) compilation.

2007 ■ SUBCYDE..CD Last Entertainment............................LAST 006

2007 CD - LAST 006

SUBDIVE

Mikael Blixt: v, Johan Ahlgren: g, Fredrik Norrman: g,
Mattias Larsson: b, Kennet Englund: d

Avesta - The band was formed in October 1996. Their first demo, *Walk With Me* was recorded in February 1997 and in June the same year the demo *Born In Vain* saw the light of day. Norrman is ex-**Dellamorte**, **Katatonia** and **October Tide**, while Englund has been found in **Dellamorte**, **Moondark, Uncanny, Centinex** etc. Musically the band is influenced by the New York hardcore scene. In 2002 Johan joined **Centinex**. The MCD was recorded at Studio Underground by Pelle Saether. The band is no longer active.

1999 ■ XXX-Superstars ....MCD 6tr Brickland ....BRICK 001

Tracks: The Perfect Protection/I Won't Surrender/Wasted/Pieces/End Of Time/I Hate

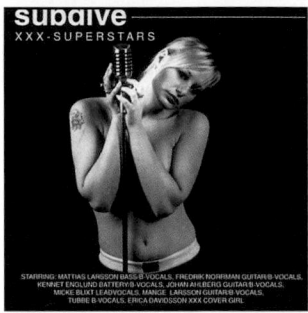
1999 MCD - BRICK 001

SUBTOPIA

Andreas "Antz" Morling: v/b, Peter Blomqvist: g,Tom Berglund: g, Jonne Brolin: d

Upplands Väsby - In the trace of US bands like **Shinedown**, **Hoobastank** and **Nickleback** there are Swedish followers such as **Blindside**, **Takida**, **Stereolith** etc. Well, add the name **Subtopia** to the list. They however do have the additional touch of **Metallica**, **Avenged Sevenfold** and even **Black Sabbath** at times. Great production and strong song material. The band was formed in 2009 by former **Cocoon** member Antz and after the album Jonne was replaced by Mattias Nielsen. In 2011 the band changed its name to **Subztain** because of a company using the same name. The band released the album *Conflict Solution* under the new name, in 2012.

2009 ■ IN WHAT DO WE TRUST ....CD Loud & Clear..................................SUB 0907

2009 CD - SUB 0907

SUBWAY RATS

Zim: v/g, Ollie: g, Stoffe: b, Frille: d

Malmö - Slightly sleaze-oriented hard rock. No information found on this lot.

1995 ☐ Suck On This ....MCD 4tr private ....KOGATI 1000
Tracks: Suck On This/36 Hours/Good Lovin'/Tell Me The Truth

SUBZTAIN

Andreas "Antz" Morling: v/b, Marcus Wahlström: g,
Robin Sandvik: g, Tom Berglund: g, Mattias Nielsen: d

Upplands Väsby - The band **Subtopia** were formed in 2009 by former **Cocoon** member Antz. They recorded one album, *In What Do We Trust* (2011), after which they changed some members and its name to **Subztain** because of a company using the same name. The new album follows in the modern metal trails of the **Subtopia** debut. Good solid modern hard rock/metal in the vein of **Shinedown**, **Alter Bridge** etc.
Website: www.subztain.com

2012 ■ CONFLICT SOLUTION...CD private ....SUB 0212

2012 CD - SUB 0212

SUCCÉ

Dan Nordell: v, Bertil Karlsson: g, Bert Forslund: g,
Bert Bratén: b, Anders "P" Pettersson: d

Degerfors - When **Frozen Fire** took a break Nordell and Bratén formed the more hard rock-oriented **Succé**. *Dom kan dra* is a boogie-oriented straightforward rocker, while *Vilsen i stan* is traditional rocking hard rock more in the vein of the heavier **Frozen Fire** material.

1983 ■ Dom Kan Dra/Vilsen I Stan ....7" private ....SSP 001

1983 7" - SSP 001

SUFFER

Joakim Öhman: v, Ulf Samuelsson: g, Patrik Andersson: b, Per Karlsson: d

Kumla/Fagersta - Formed late 1988 by Joakim, Patrik and drummer Conny Granqvist. In 1990 Norwegian guitarist Ronny Eide (founder of Morbid Magazine) was added to the line-up and later on Conny was replaced by Per Karlsson (*Altar, Wortox, Die Hard, Nominon, In Aeternum, Interment* etc). This line-up recorded the first 7", already in 1991. The song *Wrong Side Of Life* was also recorded for a compilation album that was never released. The album was cut at Sunlight Studios and produced by Tomas Skogsberg. After the release of the album, the band fell apart. Patrik went to rock 'n rollers *In Between Days* and the others quit. The only remaining member, Joakim, tried to resurrect the band with the aid of former *Abhoth*-members Mats Blyckert and Jörgen Kristensen (noth now in *Dead Awaken*), but it seems the band is now put on hold. The style is technical death metal, but nothing out of the ordinary.

1992 7" - NWR EP 039

1992	■	On Sour Ground/My Grief	7"	New Wave	NWR EP 039
1993	☐	Global Warming	MCD 4tr	Napalm Records	NPR CD 002
1993	■	Thrashing The North Away	7"	Immortal Underground	IUP EP 001
		Tracks: Human Flesh/Wrong Side Of Life (live). Available with b/w, red or yellow cover.			
1994	☐	STRUCTURES	CD	Napalm Records	NPR CD 006

SUICIDAL WINDS

Mathias Johansson: v/b, Peter Haglund: g, Emil Johansson: g,
Fredrik Andersson: b, Martin Hogebrandt: d

Uddevalla - The band was formed in 1992 after Mathias and Peter's previous band *Kristos Mortis* had split. At first, they recorded one demo on their own, *The Road To...* (1994) and a second, *Massacre*, after guitarist Andreas Ström (ex-*Conspiracy*, later in *Chtonium*) had joined in 1996. The name was taken from a song by *Celtic Frost*. The line-up was completed in 1996 and the year after they made their first official demo, *Aggression*. The band now consisted of Mathias Johansson on vocals, Peter Haglund on guitar, Andreas Ström on bass and Martin Hogebrandt (ex-*Conspiracy*, *Legions Of War*) on drums. From their 1998 demo *Definitely War*, songs have appeared on various compilation, such as *Sometimes Death Is Better Part 1-5* (98 Shiver, track: *Definitely War*), *From The Underground* (98 X-treme Records, track: *Carnal Lust*) and *No Colours Compilation Vol II* (99 No Colours, track *Rapehammer*). On *Winds Of Death,* Ström had switched to guitar and Johansson handled the bass as well as vocals. In January 2002 the line-up went through a vast change. Guitarist Andreas and drummer Martin Hogebrandt left to concentrate on *Mindblaster* and the new line-up, which premiered on the *Crush Us With Fire* MCD, featured singer Mathias Johansson, guitarists Peter Haglund and Emil Johansson (*Ill-Natured, Azeazeron*, ex-*Distant*), bassist Fredrik Andersson and drummer Thomas Hedgren. In 2004 the cassette *Rarities* was released in 500 copies on Blutveriessen. *Suicidal Winds* plays thrash-oriented, old-school death metal. Johansson, Andersson and Haglund are also found in *Axis Powers*.

1999 CD - NC 028

2003 MCD - NC 061

1999	■	WINDS OF DEATH	CD	No Colours	NC 028
1999	☐	WINDS OF DEATH	LP	No Colours	NC 028
		Bonus: Evil Dreams/Master (Master cover). 300 copies in red vinyl			
2000	☐	Joyful Dying (split)	7"	private	- -
		Split with Bestial Mockery. 300 hand-numbered copies. Tracks: Suicidal Death/Joyful Dying/Supposed To Rot (Nihilist/Entombed cover)			
2001	☐	VICTIMS IN BLOOD	CD	No Colours	NC 047
2001	☐	VICTIMS IN BLOOD	LP	No Colours	NC 047
		The first 100 copies has a different front cover.			
2002	☐	Misanthropic Anger	7" 3tr	Warlord	WREP 10
		Tracks: Misanthopic Anger/Chaotic War/Down There (Beherit cover). 1000 copies.			
2003	■	Crush Us With Fire	MCD 6tr	No Colours	NC 061
		Tracks: Crush Us With Fire/The Beast/Trench Warfare/Burning Inferno Of Death/Submit To Death (Grotesque cover)/Ashes From A Past Life (live). 900 copies.			
2003	☐	Crush Us With Fire	MLP 6tr	No Colours	NC 061
		400 copies.			
2004	☐	WRATH OF GOD	CD	Agonia Records	ARcd 019
2006	☐	FROM CONFLICT TO CONQUEST (split)	CD	Time Before Time	Death 038
		Split with Gravewurm (USA). Tracks: Devil's Doom/Demonic Prayer/The High Priest Of Perversion/Devil's Feast/Malignant Desire/Turn The Cross Upside Down (OZ cover)			
2006	☐	WINDS OF DEATH	CD	No Colours	NC 028
		Bonus: Definitely War/Aggression/Misanthropic Anger/Chaotic War/Down There.../			
2006	■	TOTAL DEATH 'N LIVE	CD	Pulverised	ASH 021 CD
2007	■	CHAOS RISING	CD	Pulverised	ASH 038 CD
2007	☐	CHAOS RISING	CDd	Pulverised	ASH 038 CD
		Bonus: Bass Instrumental (hidden bonus track)			
2008	☐	CHAOS RISING	LP	Cyclone Empire	CYC 025-1
		Clear blue vinyl.			
2010	☐	Necroblasphemies (split)	7"	Iron Bonehead Productions	IBP 087
		Split with Throneum. Tracks: Earth's Last Breath/Void Of Suicide. 500 copies.			

2006 CD - ASH 021 CD

2007 CD - ASH 038 CD

SUICIDE NATION

Daniel Löfgren: v/g, Niklas Johansson: b, Peter Jakobsson: g, Jonas Kronberg: d

Göteborg - In 1999 Daniel, Peter and drummer Matti Lovell formed the band *The Rockateers*. They were later joined by former *Dark Tranquillity* guitarist Fredrik Johansson on bass. They recorded the five track demo *Louder Than Ever* in 2001 and a second, *As Good As It Gets* the subsequent year. The band split, to reunite in 2003, now with Fredrik's younger brother Niklas taking over the bass duties. They started recording *Evilution*, but changed the name to *Suicide Nation* before its release. In 2005 Matti was badly injured when he was run over by a motorbike which forced him to quit the band. He was replaced by Jörgen Fardvik (*Gung*). With this line-up they recorded *Vaya Con Chaos*. In 2007 guitarist Christian Alsing made a stint with the band but he left the following year, as did Fardvik, who was replaced by Jonas Kronberg.. Outstanding heavy powerful melodic metal with touches of *Mustasch* as well as *In Flames*, but with clean and powerful vocals. The debut is a bit more straightforward and melodic, while on *Vaya Con Chaos* (you just gotta love that title!) they have pushed the envelope a bit more, adding a bit more edge. Even though the debut was well produced, the follow-up, mixed by the band and Christian Alsing, also sees an improvement in that area. Both albums are well worth investing in. In 2009 they recorded the third album *Jesus Chrisis*, which took the band yet a few notches up the ladder. This was a heavy rocker in the vein of *Black Label Society*-meet-*Mustasch*-meet-*Soilwork*-meet-*Spiritual Beggars*. Killer stuff!

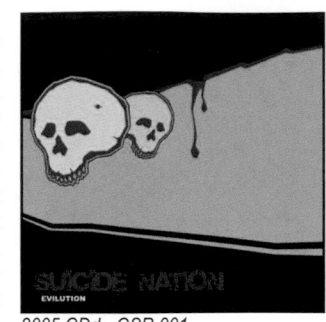

2007 CDd - GSR 002

2005 CDd - GSR 001

2005 ■	EVILUTION	CDd	Godsize	GSR 001
2007 ■	VAYA CON CHAOS	CDd	Godsize	GSR 002
2009 ■	JESUS CHRISIS	CDd	Godsize	GSR 003

2009 CDd - GSR 003

SUMA

Jovan Bojcevski: v, Peter Särnegårdh: g, Johan Westerberg: b, Erik Persson: d

Malmö - *Suma* were formed in 2001. Heavy, slow, drony sludge doom and a wall of sound. Almost desperate screaming vocals. For fans of bands like *Neurosis* with a hint of *Melvins*. Ashes was produced by Billy Anderson (*Melvins, Neurosis, Sleep* etc). Särnegård also plays drums in *Texas Motherfuckers*.

2002 ☐	SUMA	CDp	Speakerphone/Sumamuus	dial025/001
	Only released as a promo-CD.			
2002 ☐	SUMA	2LPg	Speakerphone/Sumamuus	dial025/001
	1000 copies.			
2005 ☐	SUMA	CDp	Speakerphone/Sumamuus	dial025/001
	Bonus: (Still) Doing Nothing (2005 Berlin session). Remastered. Different artwork. 100 copies in screen printed brown fold-out cover and 400 copies in brown or green/gray/ white sleeve.			
2005 ■	By Any Means Necessary #1 (split)	7"	Speakerphone	dial027
	Split with Bastinado. Track: Don't Feed The Pigs. 500 copies.			
2006 ■	By Any Means Necessary #2 (split)	7"	Speakerphone	dial028
	Split with Maufahr. Track: Flood. 500 copies.			
2006 ☐	LET THE CHURCHES BURN	CDd	Speakerphone	dial031
	First edition with silver print, second with white print.			
2007 ☐	By Any Means Necessary #3 (split)	7"	Speakerphone	dial 029
	Split with Texas Motherfuckers. Track: 2$ Haircut. 500 copies.			
2008 ☐	Psychological Operations (split)	10" EP	Speakerphone/Gtimmgrinner	dial033/grimm 2
	Split with Unearthly Trace. Track:This Is My Weapon Of Choice. 500 copies, white vinyl.			
2009 ☐	LET THE CHURCHES BURN	CD	SMD (Japan)	n/a
2010 ☐	LET THE CHURCHES BURN	2LP	Speakerphone	DIAL 031
	500 copies. Red artwork.			
2009 ☐	ASHES	2LPg	Throne Records	throne 05
	Bonus: Wornout… Markes For Death… Burn Your Flag. First press: 400 black + 100 white/grey. Second press: 250 copies black, 50 copies black/white Swirl. Different art-work. Reprinted in black/white splatter, 100 copies in 2012.			
2010 ☐	ASHES	CD	Speakerphone	dial034
2010 ☐	Suma/Pyramido (split)	12"	Head Records	HR 015
	Split with Pyramido. Track: Acidlingren. 500 copies.			
2010 ☐	Suma and Unearthly Trace (collaboration)	12"g+CD	Throne Records	therone 07
	Collaboration with Unearthly Trance. 100 copies grey/white+ 400 black vinyl. Tracks: Sleepwalking Through A Maze/Victim No. 581/Six Months Of Treatmemt			
2012 ☐	Suma/Ultraphallus(split)	7"	Hell Comes Home	HCH 002
	Split with Ultraphallus. Track: Geisteskrank			

2005 7" - dial027

2005 7" - dial028

SUMMONED TIDE

Rickard Thelin: v/g, Mikael Thelin: g, Jimi Toivanen: k,
Jennifer Sikström: b, Nicklas Åström: d

Robertsfors - Great medieval-influenced power metal with a folkish touch. High-pitched classic power metal vocals. Well-played and with a strong bunch of songs.

2010 ■	IF WE FALL WE WILL RISE	CDd	private	- -

2010 CDd - - -

SUN ISLAND

T.J. Johnson: v/b, Neil Detlofson: g, Oggie Jacobi: d

Mora - Quite traditional late 80s melodic metal in the vein of early *Europe*. A bit weak in the vocal department but musically quite nice.

1988 ■	Going On/World In Disaster	7"	Platina	PL 46

1988 7" - PL 46

SUNDELL, PETER

Peter Sundell: v/g, Anders Rydholm: k, Christian Sundell: d

Växjö - After having recorded two singles with melodic metal band *Wulcan*, Peter stood on his own two legs, backed up by his brother and future collaboration partner Anders Rydholm. Already on the second single by *Wulcan* the style was leaning towards AOR and here Peter's melodic side is in full bloom. *Serena* is true AOR in the Bryan Adams vein, while the B-side is a slightly heavier, more or less in the same vein he, Christian and Anders would be heading nine years later in the band *Promotion*, which later turned into *Grand Illusion*, where he is still found, singing better than ever. Well worth checking out!

1988 ■	Serena/Tiden rinner ut	7"	private	8861

1988 7" - 8861

SUNDOWN

Mathias Lodmalm: v, Herman Engström: g, Andreas Karlsson: b, Chris Silver: d

Stockholm - Formed by Johnny Hagel (*Tiamat/Sorcery*) and Mathias Lodmalm (*Cemetary*). Musical references has been made to *Tiamat* and *Sisters Of Mercy*. The sound is very dark. In 1997 they toured with *Paradise Lost*. In 1999 Johnny Hagel was replaced by Chris Silver after the first album, since Hagel was concentrating on his solo project *Cinnamon Spiral*.

1997 ☐	DESIGN 19	CD	Century Media	77161 2
1997 ☐	DESIGN 19 - Special edition	CD	Century Media	77194 2
1999 ☐	GLIMMER	CD	Century Media	77250 2
1999 ☐	Halo	CDS	Century Media	77251 3

SUNFLOWER

Ulf Torkelsson: v, Johan Lundgren: g, Pelle Thörnqvist: b, Christer Nordlander: d

Sollefteå - Christer recorded two singles with the band *Firework* in 1979/-80. *Sunflower* sound like a blend of *Led Zeppelin* and Pearl Jam with a vocal touch of *Soundgarden*. Great stuff. Ulf is now found in seventies rockers *Abramis Brama* and *Atlantic Tide*.

1994 ☐	Even Though I Sleep	MCD 4tr	private	NKCD 002
	Tracks: Even Though I Sleep../Am I Wrong/My Way/Down			
1995 ☐	SUNFLOWER	CD	Borderline	BLCD 06
1996 ■	Flower/My Way/Even Though I Sleep	MCD 3tr	Borderline	BLCDS11
	Contains 2 tracks from the album and one from the first MCD.			

1996 MCD - BLCDS 11

SUNSET BLADE

**Andrea Martinsson: v, Mikael Martinsson: g, Lotta Pettersson: k,
Per Holma: b, Per-Ola "Peo" Vikström: d**

Malmberget - *Nightlife* is a horrible Disney-style ballad, while *Set Me Free* is quite heavy melodic hard rock, still with very thin and "nice" female vocals. Not bad though. Peo later formed the synth/new age band *Aurora*, which soon change name to *Pannoval*.

1989 ■	Night Life/Set Me Free	7"	Sesound	SLS-8901

1989 7" - SLS-8901

SUPERGROUPIES

Kim Simon: v, Andre Daniel: g, Micael "Grimm" Magnusson: b, John Linden: d

Göteborg - Formed in 2001. The album was produced by Kee Marcello. *Supergroupies* play seventies-style glam rock, quite similar to *T-Rex* mixed with *Easy Action* and *Guns 'N' Roses*. After the album lead guitarist Leo Hansson joined the band. However, *Supergroupies* folded in 2006. Bass player Grimm was later in *Easy Action*, but sadly passed away in May 2011. Website: www.supergroupies.com

2005 ☐	SUPERGROUPIES	CD	Victor (Japan)	VICP-63071
	Bonus: I'll Make You Happy			
2005 ■	SUPERGROUPIES – SPECIAL EDITION	CD	Victor (Japan)	VICP-63153
	Bonus I'll Make You Happy/Runaround + Bouncin' (video). Different artwork.			
2006 ☐	SUPERGROUPIES	CD	Livewire	LW018-2

2005 CD - VICP-63153

SUPERSTITION

Alexander Kronlund: v, Valentin Nilsson: g, Patrik Grip: g,
Daniel Lehtihet: k, Kalle Dettner: b, Tobias "Tobbe" Nilsson: d

Stockholm - The A-side is a pretty decent up-tempo melodic hard rocker, a bit weak in the vocal department. The B-side is another up-tempo rocker, actually a bit more metal. The band was formed in 1983, made an appearance on the Swedish television show *Unga Tvåan* and recorded the single. The band split in 1987. Alexander continued working as a producer and songwriter in the pop genre, while Valentin and Daniel played a bit on and off. Tobias is today playing with folkish band *Södervisa*.

1983 ■ Second Life/Uncanny Night ....7" private ....SIS 1

1983 7" - SIS 1

SUPREME MAJESTY

Joakim Olsson: v, Rille Svensson: g, Tobias Wernersson: g,
Christian "Chrille" Andersson: g/k, Daniel Andersson: b, Johan Rydberg: d

Kristianstad/Malmö/Göteborg - The band was formed in 1999. After the MCD drummer Bartek Nalezinski was replaced by Unger and singer Rikard Larsson (ex-*Sanzia, Mercy, In Black*) was replaced by *Deep Quest/The Provenance* vocalist Olsson. Chrille is ex-*Mortum* and was also found in *Non Serviam* together with Daniel. He also ran the metal fanzine *Hellraiser*. The band was also featured on the compilation *10 x Dynamite*. After the album keyboard player Julius Chimelewski reinforced the band. *Supreme Majesty* play outstanding melodic power metal in the vein of Italians *Rhapsody In Fire* meets *Falconer*, but with an strong AOR-ish and at times progressive touch. Joakim is an outstanding singer with a broad range and a strong clear voice. Highly recommended. On *Elements Of Creation* the line-up had changed seeing drummer Jocke Unger replaced by Johan Rydberg and guitarist Tobias Wernersson added to the band. Between 2007 and 2009 the band went through another radical change where singer Olsson was the only remaining member. The guitars were now handled by Jimmy Hedlund (*Falconer*) and Anders Andersson, keyboards by Tommy Fäldt (*Isildurs Bane, Money Joe*), bass by Håkan Nyander (ex-*Sanzia, Cloudscape*) and drums by Linus Pettersson.

1999 MCD - LNP 009

2003 CD - MASCD 0394

1999	■	Divine Enigma	MCD 4tr	Loud 'N Proud	LNP 009
		Tracks: No Farewells/Die In A Dream/King Of Eternity's Dream/The Blood We Spilled			
2001	☐	TALES OF A TRAGIC KINGDOM	CD	Massacre Records	MASCD 0279
2002	☐	TALES OF A TRAGIC KINGDOM	CD	King Records (Japan)	KICP 863
		Bonus: One Step Away			
2003	■	DANGER	CD	Massacre Records	MASCD 0394
2003	☐	DANGER	CDd	Massacre Records	MASCD 0394
		Bonus: One Step Away			
2003	☐	DANGER	CD	AMG (Russia)	AMG 129
2003	☐	DANGER	CD	King Records (Japan)	KICP 965
		Bonus: Never Surrender Alive (acoustic)			
2005	■	ELEMENTS OF CREATION	CD	Massacre Records	MASCD 0457
2005	☐	ELEMENTS OF CREATION	CD	King Records (Japan)	KICP 1070
		Bonus: Far Beyond The Sun (Yngwie cover)/Out In The Fields (Gary Moore cover)			

2005 CD - MASCD 0457

SURRENDER

Nils Bielfeld: v/g, Johan Lindblom, Joakim E Ramsell: g, Ulf Ihrsén

Fjärdhundra - Great party hard rock. The band was formed in 1988/89 and split in 1993 when Nils other band *Thrash Inc.* won the Rock SM. *Thrash Inc* later became *Clench* and Nils was also in *Sixcoveredkissongs*. Joakim has played with popsters Carola, Brolle Jr, Darin, Sanna Nielsen (his fiancée), and both have been in *RFP* and *Pär Lindh Project*.

1991 ■ Let's Get The Party Started/Mystery ....7" private ....FAM 91-01 $

1991 7" - FAM 91-01

SUSPEKT

Lars Crantz: v, Svenne Svensson: g, Ingo Andersson: g,
Esse Swerin: b, Leffe Persson: d

Östersund - A very promising melodic hard rocking band that unfortunately disappeared into obscurity.

1986 ■ Coming Down/Wiseman ....7" private ....MIMM 451
The cover was actually like a small poster. Also released with a black/white cover.

SVART

Christian "Draug" Larsson: v/g/b/d

Fagersta/Halmstad - Solo project by Draug, also in *Livsnekad*, *Shining* and previously in *Apati* (as Patient C), *Sanctum Sanguis* and *Promenia*. Initiated in 2007, solidified by the demo *Då allt upphör* (Livsleda Records) in 2008. *Svart* means "black" in Swedish. *Vanära, vanmakt*

1986 7" - MIMM 451

och avsmak was also released as a cassette version by Livsleda, in 200 hand-numbered copies. Not really sure how to categorise this. Very long tracks, at times with a drone feel to them, but this is more atmospheric, depressive black metal. Desperate screaming vocals. It's not all slow and drony, there are blast beats hiding in the bushes as well. The production is very lo-fi and old-school. At times it's quite similar to *Shining* meets *Burzum*.

2010 CD - FS 40

2009	☐ Våran tid är förbi	MCD 3tr	Frostscald Records	FS 30

Tracks: Den absoluta tomheten/Mot dödens slätter/Dessa kedjor, dessa bojor. 1000 copies.

2009	☐ VANÄRA, VANMAKT OCH AVSMAK	CD	Frostscald Records	FS 31

1000 copies.

2010	☐ Namnlös och bortglömd	MCD 3tr	Frostscald Records	FS 39

Tracks: Den hemlöses klagosång/Den sista droppen utav liv/Namnlös och bortglömd. 1000 copies.

2010	■ FÖRLORAD	CD	Frostscald Records	FS 40

1000 copies

2012	☐ DET PERSONLIGA HELVETETS SPIRAL	CD	Frostscald Records	FS 59

SVARTE PAN

Björn Holmdén: v/h, Conny Andersson: g,
Christian "de Luxe" Norefalk: b, Pelle Engvall: d

Malmö - *Svarte Pan* were formed in 1999 when singer/poet Holmdén (*Strawberry Revolution, Björn Holmdén & Den Dynamiska Trion*) united with riff rockers *The Black Pan* (actually *Svarte Pan* in English) featuring drummer Pelle Engvall (ex-*Tribe*), guitarist Conny Andersson (ex-*Green Hornet, Strawberry Revolution*) and bassist Christian de Luxe (ex-*Miss Ellie*). The band had previously worked with singer Martin Ulvgård. After recording two demos the band was picked up by Ant Nest Records. On the split-single both bands pay tribute to their big source of inspiration – *November*. *Svarte Pan* plays killer riff based seventies hard rock with lyrics in Swedish. Of course *November* comes in mind, but *Svarte Pan* is a bit heavier, reminiscent of bands like *Witchcraft* and colleagues *Abramis Brama*. After *Nattvandring* drummer Engvall was replaced by Hans Månsson. The band sadly parted ways in 2007.

2003 7" - ANR7 001

2002 CD - ANRCD 001

2002	■ SOV GOTT	CD	Ant Nest Records	ANRCD 001
2003	■ Starka tillsammans (split)	7"	Ant Nest Records	ANR7 001

Split with Abramis Brama. Track: Starka Tillsammans (November cover)

2004	■ NATTVANDRING	CD	Ant Nest Records	ANRCD 003

SVARTI LOGHIN

Johan Lindström: v/g/f, Stefan Lindström: g, Raymond Nykvist: b, Emil Tillman: d

Falun - *Svarti Loghin* was founded in 2005 by Stefan as his project. The name was taken from an old *Arckanum* song and means "black flame" in old Swedish. Raymond and Emil are both ex-*Död, Oferd* and *Eldrit*, while Johan is a former member of melodic hard rockers *Black Ladies* and thrashers *Mustain*. *Sea Of Green* is an acoustic EP, which, just like *Empty World*, was also released on cassette in 100 copies, by Total Holocaust Records. *Drifting Through The Void* features a cover of *Black Sabbath*'s *Planet Caravan*. To be honest I don't know where to place this band. At times they play melancholic avant-garde death metal, like a mix of *Shining* and *The Cure* with a touch of folk and screeching desperate vocals, while some recordings are plain melancholic acoustic folk pop/rock with clean vocals. Quite mind-boggling. Total Holocaust has also released the two cassette albums *Luft* and *Skog*. Johan and Stefan are brothers.

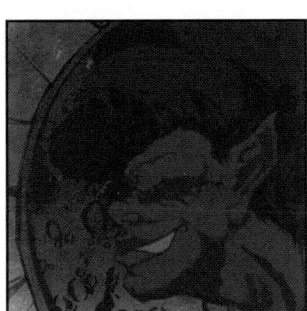

2004 CD - ANRCD 003

2008 MCDd - SSS001

2008	■ Empty World	MCDd 6tr	A Sad Sadness Song	SSS001

Tracks: Karg nordisk vinter/Inner Desolation/Empty World/The Silence Always Returns/ Cold Void/Outro

2010	☐ DRIFTING THROUGH THE VOID	CDd	A Sad Sadness Song	SSS003
2011	■ Sea Of Green	MCD 5tr	A Sad Sadness Song	SSS007

Tracks: Cloud Man/Sea Of Green/Transparent/Celestial Bounds In Cosmic Infinity/Black Moon. 500 copies.

2011 MCD - SSS007

SVARTNAD

Tobias Lindberg: v/g/b, Alexander Larsson: g

Ängelholm - *Svartnad* were formed in 2008 by Lindberg and Karl Hoverman. Lindberg and Larsson are both ex-*Forlorn Remembrance*. In 2008 the band recorded the demo *Days Of Desolation*. Old-school-sounding death rock/metal, mixed with folkish melodic rock. At times, very atmospheric with mainly acoustic instruments. Weird, but unfortunately not really good at all. Metal? On *En studie i ensamhet* (a study in loneliness) drums were played by Pontus Landgren.

2011	■ En studie i ensamhet	MCD 4tr	Downfall Records	FALLCD 022

Tracks: En studie i ensamhet/Vinterriket/Amfetamin/Monotonisk depravering. 1000 copies.

2011 MCD - FALLCD 022

SVARTNAR
Alexander Andersson: v/g/b/d

Jönköping - **Svartnar** (approximately "darkens") is the solo project of *Eldrimner/Marionette/Obscene* singer Andersson, initiated in 2003. Former **Obscene** drummer Olof Landén has played session drums on some recordings. Alexander says the project is a reflection of his own inner struggle and therefore there is no room for other members. Quite depressive and desperate old-school-sounding black metal. Not too far from **Burzum** and **Shining**.

2006	☐	FAILURE OF MANKIND	CD	Eternity Records	ETER 010
		1000 copies			
2006	■	FAILURE OF MANKIND	LP	Blut & Eisen	- -
2006	☐	Undergången (split)	7"	Eternity Records	ETER 018
		Split with Hypothermia. 340 hand-numbered copies. Track: Uppgivenhet.			

2006 LP - - -

SVARTNATT
Hatet: v, Ulv: g/k, Vidunder: k, Liikböhr: b, Kyrkbrand: d

Falköping - Not to be confused with the German band *Svart Natt*. Formed in 2003 and recorded their first demo *Vinterkyla* in 2005. The name means "blacknight". Very simple, old-school, quite punkish black metal with "atmospheric" parts and a singer trying to imitate the desperate vocals of Kvarforth, without succeeding. The band also recorded the demo *Hedniskt krig* in 2009.

2007	■	VARGOLD HAR KOMMIT	CD	Frostscald	FS 07
		1000 copies.			

2007 CD - FS 07

SVARTR STRIJD
Strijd: v/g/b/d

Skänninge - One of Sweden's gazillion black metal solo projects. Started out in 2002, under the name *Strijd*, by Strijd, also in **Black Circle** and **Pagan Winds**. Recorded the first demo, *Dagen då döden kom* in 2002, followed by *Demo #2* in 2003. *En sista vind* was comprised by *Demo #2* and some unreleased songs. **Burzum** style black metal.

2009	■	En sista vind	MCD 5tr	Total Holocaust Records	THR 24
		Tracks: Ford II/Då de sista dropparna blod levrats på min handled/Under den kalla månen/Dödens vind genom natten far/Ford III. 500 copies.			

2009 MCD - THR 24

SVARTRIT
Swartadauþuz: v, Sir. N: v/g/b

Norrland - **Svartrit** (black rite in Swedish) were founded in 2003. Sir N is also found in **Grifteskymfning**, **Helgedom** (as Vanskapt), **Grav**, **Dödfödd**, **Kaos Sacramentum** and **Acerbitas**. In 2009 singer Swartadauþuz (**Grav**, **Helgedom**, **Urkaos**), who also runs Ancient Records, joined. Ancient Records have announced they will release three vinyl albums *IV, V* and *VI* in 250 copies each in 2012, but they are not out as this is written (2013). Old-school black metal sounding a bit like a mix of **Dissection** and early **Satyricon**, at times with **Shining**-style desperate spoken vocals. The first MCD was recorded in 2005, and also featured Ramm on drums plus on two of the tracks E.S played guitar, Vandöd played bass and Asoth sang. On *I* the production was a bit rougher than on the MCD, but the style was the same. The line-up now featured Sir N, singer Swartadauþuz and session musicians, singer Vnkwiz, keyboardist Jonas "Grim Vindkall" Almen and drummer Dogantimur. *II* features the same line-up, except Lik is added on vocals and Grim Vindkall is out. The album was also very different in its approach with several acoustic and almost folky tracks. *III* featured only the duo and drummer Dagantimur. The style was slightly different here as well, more like a mix of *I* and *II*. Well-played and high-quality song material.

2010 CD - Mystery 006

2010	☐	Svarthetens ridå	MCD 4tr	Mystery Of Death	Mystery 005
		Tracks: Bortom ljusets räckvidd/Tronar på mörkrets makter/Funeral Of All Worlds/Deliver My Vile Soul. 500 copies.			
2010	■	I	CD	Mystery Of Death	Mystery 006
		500 copies.			
2010	■	II	CD	Mystery Of Death	Mystery 007
		500 copies.			
2010	☐	III	CD	Mystery Of Death	Mystery 008
		500 copies.			
2012	☐	I	LP	Ancient Records	AR031/LKP001
		150 copies on white vinyl.			
2012	☐	II	LP	Ancient Records	AR032/LKP002
		150 copies on white vinyl.			
2012	☐	III	LP	Ancient Records	AR033/LKP007
		150 copies on white vinyl.			
2012	■	Svarthetens ridå	MLP 4tr	Triumph Of Death	ToD 002

2010 CD - Mystery 007

2012 MLP - ToD 002

SVARTSYN

"Ornias" Sundelin: v/g, Kolgrim: b, Joel "Draugen" Andersson: d

Nynäshamn - Formed in 1991 under the name ***Chalice*** and recorded the first demo, *A Night Created By The Shadows*, in 1995. Grinding black metal in the vein of early ***Bathory***, mixed with more melodic themes. The first album suffers from awful production. Guests include keyboard player Guran and female vocalists Michaela Löfving and Anna Svensson. Surth played bass. Draugen played drums on the first ***Dark Funeral*** recording but he wishes not to be associated with the band. Ornias was actually the singer of ***Dark Funeral*** for two rehearsals in 1993, before he was "let go". Draugen was also in ***Illska***. After ...*His Majesty,* Yonas "Mörk" Lindskog replaced Kolgrim. The tracks on *Skinning The Lamb* are the same as on the ***Arckanum*** split. In 2007 Ornias moved to Belgium and set up a new line-up, replacing bassist Kolgrim with Zoran van Bellegem and drummer Joel "Draugen" Andersson with Baruch van Bellegem, on *Wrath Upon The Earth*. In 2011 Orinias rerecorded the guitars and vocals for *The True Legend*, had Dennis Israel (***Opeth, Katatonia*** etc) do the mix and rereleased the album in 2012 with new artwork. A bit more polished maybe, but still the same old school black metal style in the vein of ***Ofermod*** or ***Funeral Mist***. Not to be confused with the Norwegian namesakes.

1996 CD - FR 007

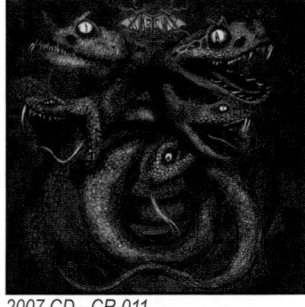
2007 CD - CR 011

2011 CD - ARCD 081

2012 CD - ARcd 089

Year		Title	Format	Label	Cat. No.
1997	☐	Tormentor	7"	Black Militia Productions	BMP 003
		Tracks: Goatthrone/Throne Of The Antichrist. 500 copies.			
1996	■	THE TRUE LEGEND	CD	Folter (Germ)	FR 007
2000	☐	BLOODLINE/HIS MAJESTY	2LPg	End All Life	EAL 021
		500 hand-numbered copies.			
2000	☐	...HIS MAJESTY	CD	Sound Riot (Portugal)	SRP 006
2003	☐	DESTRUCTION OF MAN	CD	Sound Riot (Portugal)	SRP 022
2003	☐	DESTRUCTION OF MAN	LP	Blut & Eisen	- -
		Red vinyl. 1000 hand-numbered copies.			
2004	☐	Skinning The Lamb	MLP 4tr	Blut & Eisen	- -
		Tracks: A Night Created By The Shadows/Furnace In Purgatory/Skinning The Lambs/ Blåkullaförbannelsen. 1000 copies			
2004	☐	Arckanum/Svartsyn (split)	CD	Carnal Records	CR 004
		Split with Arckanum. Tracks: A Night Created By The Shadows/Furnace In Purgatory/ Skinning The Lambs/Blåkullaförbannelsen. 3000 copies.			
2005	☐	BLOODLINE	CD	Sound Riot	SRP 034
2007	■	TIMELESS REIGN	CD	Carnal Records	CR 011
2007	☐	TIMELESS REIGN	LPg	Blut & Eisen	- -
		100 red vinyl + 400 black.			
2007	☐	BLOODLINE	LP+EP	Temple Of Darkness	TOD 013
		500 copies.			
2009	☐	...HIS MAJESTY	CDd	Unexploded Records	UER 029
2009	☐	DESTRUCTION OF MAN	CDd	Unexploded Records	UER 030
2009	☐	BLOODLINE	CDd	Unexploded Records	UER 031
2011	■	WRATH UPON THE EARTH	CD	Agonia Records	ARCD 081
2011	☐	WRATH UPON THE EARTH	LP	Agonia Records	ARLP 076
		500 deep purple with A2 poster + 516 black vinyl copies.			
2012	☐	THE TRUE LEGEND	CD	Agonia Records	ARLP 082
		100 gold, 400 black vinyl. Rerecorded.			
2012	■	THE TRUE LEGEND	CD	Agonia Records	ARcd 089
2013	☐	BLACK TESTAMENT	LP	Agonia Records	ARlp 110
2013	☐	BLACK TESTAMENT	CD	Agonia Records	ARcd 117

SVEN HAHNE & PRÄSTROCK

Sven Hahne: v, Stefan Löwenborg: g, Jonas Sandquist: g,
Kristofer: b, Filip Frostemark: d

Åhus - This is actually a priest that sings hard rock. On the MCD you'll find a good cover of ***Deep Purple***'s *Never Before* as well as a hard rocking version of the old ***Creedence*** number, *Up Around The Bend*. The line-up on the first single featured Sven, Stefan, guitarist Oscar Lindström, bass player Patrik Larsson and drummer Patrik Lundström, and the band was called ***Sven Hahne Med Prästrock***. *Gimme Some Lovin'* is of course a cover of the old ***Spencer Davis Group*** tune.

1991 7" - 9010013

Year		Title	Format	Label	Cat. No.
1991	■	Gimme Some Lovin'/You Leave Your Sunshine Behind	7"	private	9010013
1992	☐	Sven Hahne & Prästrock	MCD 4tr	B.O.R.G	BM 920701
		Tracks: Precious Angel/Never Before/Babe You're So Tough/Up And Around The Bend.			

SWANÖ, DAN

Dan Swanö: v/g/k/b/d

Örebro - This album shows Dan's influences from the 70s progressive/symphonic rock to his musical endeavours with ***Edge Of Sanity***. Death metal as it would have sounded if it had been invented in 1970. A cover of *Lucretia* can be found on a ***Sisters Of Mercy***-tribute and a cover of *Melissa* on a ***Mercyful Fate***-ditto. Dan can also be found in numerous bands, such as ***Edge Of Sanity, Pan-Thy-Monium, Odyssey, Nightingale, Route Nine, Unicorn, Bloodbath*** and now in ***Witherscape***. The version of *Lucretia* found on the bonus-CD for the second encyclopedia is a heavier and different version than on the aforementioned compilation.

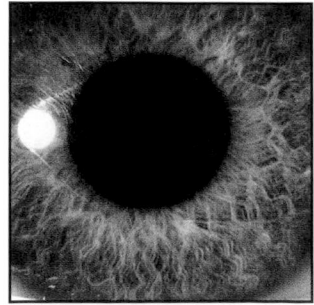
1998 CD - BMCD 129

1998 ☐ Moontower	MCD 3tr	Black Mark	BMCD 129-S

Tracks: Uncreation/Sun Of The Night/Patchworks

1998 ■ MOONTOWER	CD	Black Mark	BMCD 129
1998 ☐ MOONTOWER	CD	Irond (Russia)	CD 03-686

SWEDENS FINEST

Markus Jaan: v, Carlos Sepulveda: g, Jonaz Lindgren: b, Niklas Sposato: d

Göteborg - When hardcore band **Psycore** disbanded, in 2000, Sepulveda and Jaan formed the band **Swedens Finest**. They also formed the electronics band **Mikrotone**, who released one album and is totally irrelevant here. Lindgren was ex-**Gosh!**. *Swedens Finest* released two powerful albums, mixing heavy detuned riffing and their hardcore background into something pretty intense, heavy and cool. The second album had some industrial influences as well. Later on Sepulveda formed the pop/core band **Revenge Of Lorenzo**, which split in 2008. He later formed the band **Magellan Radio** and **God Therapy** and he produced the band **No Hawaii**. In 2006 the digital EP *God Save The Queens* was released, after which the band folded. The EP features covers of **Devo, Robyn, Village People** and **Frankie Goes To Hollywood**.

2003 CD - JAAN 03

2004 CD - JAAN 04

2003 ■ FEEL LIKE MAGNUM, LOOK LIKE HIGGINS	CD	12-51	JAAN 03
2004 ■ LOVE BOMB	CD	12-51	JAAN 04

SWEDES

Leif Alderskanz: v, Roger Nordström: g/v, Christer Nordström: d

Stockholm - The copy I came across was pretty weird. It says on the cover that side B is the same as the A-side, only it's instrumental. However when listening, it's a totally different song, a tribute to the Swedish National Hockey Team. *Don't Break My Heart Again* is AOR-disco with distorted guitars, while the untitled B-side is high-quality up-tempo AOR. The A-side has the number HWO 101 and the B-side HWO 103. A misprint? In the single there were also three photos of a good looking girl, but no name. Leif was ex-**Bubbles** and later recorded with the band **Garvin**. He also appeared in the Swedish Idol in 2009.

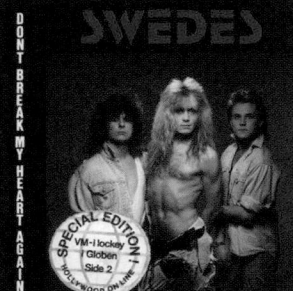
1989 7" - HWO 101

1989 ■ Don't Break My Heart Again/?	7"	Hollywood On-Line	HWO 101

SWEDISH EROTICA

**Anders Möller: v, Magnus Axx: g, Morgan "Lefay" Jensen: g,
Ulf "Ken" Sandin: b, Jamie Borger: d**

Göteborg - The band was formed in the mid-80s under the name **Swedish Beauty**. The line-up was Magnus, Ken, Dan Stomberg (**Madison**), former **TNT** singer Dag Ingebrektsen and drummer Dennis Nybratt. They recorded one track for a Norwegian compilation. Jamie Borger (**Treat, Talisman**) replaced Magnus and Anders "Andy LaRocque" Allhage replaced Dan. At that time Mats Levén (ex-**Capricorn**) did some chorus parts on a demo. *Swedish Beauty* slowly died, but in 1988 Magnus and Morgan formed **Swedish Erotica**. They got their deal through a demo with Göran Edman on vocals, but the singer on the first single was Tony Niva (**Zanity, Master Massive, Niva, Lion's Share, Oxygen**). The song *Break The Walls* is in my opinion one of the best tracks recorded by **Swedish Erotica**. The line-up on the debut album was Mats Levén (v), Magnus and Morgan (g), Jonas "Johnny D'Fox" Tångström (b) and drummer Bjarne "BC Strike" Johansson (**Shotgun Messiah, Skold**). Niva was actually replaced by Levén in the studio during the recording of the album. Jonas had previously recorded an album with the pop/rock band **DD Band**. *Swedish Erotica* is a good, solid band that started out quite sleazy but has on the latest album turned into a more powerful but yet melodic hard rock band. Ken Sandin was in an early line-up of the band but left for **Alien** as well as with Norwegians **Da Vinci**, but later returned. Mats Levén has later appeared in numerous bands like **Treat, Abstrakt Algebra, Dogface, Southpaw, Yngwie Malmsteen, Therion, AB/CD, At Vance, Krux** etc. When the band returned with *Blind Man's Justice,* Anders Möller had taken over the vocals and the album shows a much heavier band in a more hard rock vein. As drummer Bjarne was on tour with **Shotgun Messiah** when *Blind Man's Justice* was recorded, Jamie Borger temporarily occupied his stool. Another problem for the band is the fact that singer Anders Möller was also lead singer/guitarist in the band **Black Ingvars**, who gained great national success in 1995. Their album sold gold and they made a massive summer tour, resulting in an undesired vacation for **Swedish Erotica**, just as the new album was released. The band was put on ice after this. Magnus runs a rock club in Göteborg. Sandin was later in **Transport League**, pop band **Strasse**, plus he has played with Jim Jidhed and Alannah Myles. He is today found in Kee Marcello's band. *Too Daze Gone* was a collection of previously unreleased songs featuring various musicians from the line-ups, even demos featuring Göran Edman and "Deep Throat" on vocals.

The boys you don't wanna google...

1989 7" - 112 166

1989 7" - 112 455

1989 ■ Downtown/Break The Walls	7"	Virgin	112 166
1989 ■ Rock 'N Roll City/Love Hunger	7"	Virgin	112 455
1989 ○ Rock 'N Roll City (7" version)/(re-mix)/Love Hunger	MLP 3tr	Virgin	612 455

The re-mix was made by Swemix and is actually called "Deep Hangover Mix". No artwork.

| 1989 ☐ | We're Wild Young And Free/Loaded Rap | 7" | Virgin | 112 564 |
| 1989 ☐ | We're Wild Young And Free | MCD 3tr | Virgin | 662 564 |

Tracks: We're Wild Young And Free/Loaded Rap/Loaded Gun

| 1989 ☐ | SWEDISH EROTICA | LP | Virgin | 210044 |
| 1989 ☐ | SWEDISH EROTICA | CD | Virgin | 210044 |

Bonus: Break The Walls/Hollywood Dreams (acoustic). Available in two different pressings, one with blue and one with black tray card.

| 1989 ☐ | SWEDISH EROTICA | CD | Virgin (Japan) | VJCP-11 |

Bonus: Break The Walls

1990 ■	Hollywood Dreams/Hollywood Dreams(acoustic)	7"	Virgin	112 789
1990 ☐	Hollywood Dreams/Hollywood Dreams (acoustic)	CDS 2tr	Virgin	662 789
1990 ☐	Hollywood Dreams	MLP 3tr	Virgin	662 789

Tracks: Hollywood Dreams/Hollywood Dreams (acoustic)/She Drives Me Crazy

| 1990 ☐ | KROQ Swedish Eagle Show (split) | MCD | Virgin | 260 260 |

Split with Alien and Bad Habit. Recorded live. Tracks: Rock 'N Roll City/We're Wild Young And Free/Hollywood Dreams

| 1995 ■ | BLIND MAN'S JUSTICE | CD | Empire | ERCD 1014 |
| 1996 ☐ | BLIND MAN'S JUSTICE | CD | Victor (Jap) | VICP-5452 |

Different artwork

| 2005 ☐ | TOO DAZE GONE | CD | MTM | 0681-146 |

Bonus: Break the Walls/Roll Away the Stone (Mott The Hoople cover)/Can you Stand the Beat/Terri/Goodbye to Romance/Open Arms/Love on the Line/Loaded Gun

| 2005 ☐ | TOO DAZE GONE | CD | Spiritual Beast (Japan) | SBSL-1003 |

Bonus: Break the Walls/Roll Away the Stone (Mott The Hoople cover)/Can You Stand the Beat/Terri/Goodbye to Romance/Open Arms/Love on the Line/Loaded Gun

| 2007 ☐ | SWEDISH EROTICA | CD | AL!VE | 10018 |

Bonus: Downtown (Niva version)/Rock 'N Roll City (Deep Hannover mix)/Loaded Rap

1990 7" - 112 789

1995 CD - ERCD 1014

SWEDISH HITZ GOES METAL

See ReinXeed

SWEDISH METAL AID

Joey Tempest: v, Robert Ernlund: v, Björn Lodin: v, Malin Ekholm: v, Tommy Nilsson: v, Joakim Lundholm: v, Kee Marcello: g

Stockholm - This was a one-off project where the royalties were sent to help the people of Ethiopia. It contains a choir with members from numerous known and unknown Swedish bands. The truth is however all the choirs were recorded by the lead singers the day before. There is only one song on the single and the flip side contains the autographs from the lead-singers. The style is the general aid-metal-ballad with a big chorus. It sold over 50 000 copies in Sweden only.

| 1985 ☐ | Give A Helping Hand | 12"g 1tr | Alpha | ONEMAX 017 |
| 1985 ■ | Give A Helping Hand | 7" | Alpha | ONESIN 017 |

1985 7" - ONESIN 017

SWITCH OPENS

Jesper Skarin: v/b, Tomas Bergstrand: g, Mikael Tuominen: g, Anders Bartonek: d

Stockholm - *Switch Opens* was formed in 2000 under the name *Fingerspitzengefühl*, under which name they released two albums, *Fingerspitzengefühl* (2004 Kooljunk) and *Happy Doomsday* (2006 Kooljunk). In 2008 they, not surprisingly, changed their name to *Switch Opens* and were picked up by GMR Records who released the first album under the new name in 2009. *Switch Opens* plays high-class heavy, doomy, stoner-infused heavy rock with a progressive touch. Quite original-sounding. Tuominen has previously played with *General Surgery*, while Bergstrand has been found in bands like *Capricorn*, *Moaning Wind*, *Dawn Of Decay* and stoner rockers *Rise And Shine*.

2009 CDd - GMRCD 9014

| 2009 ■ | SWITCH OPENS | CDd | GMR Records | GMRCD 9014 |
| 2009 ☐ | SWITCH OPENS | LP | Vinyl Maniac | VMLP 037 |

300 copies.

| 2011 ☐ | JOINT CLASH | CDd | Transubstans | TRANS 073 |
| 2011 ■ | JOINT CLASH | LP | Transubstans | TRANSV 08 |

2011 LP - TRANSV 08

SWITCHBLADE

Anders Steen: v/b, Johan Folkesson: g, Tim Bertilsson: d

Stockholm - Formed in 1997. Initially the band played fast and quite chaotic hardcore-influenced strange crossover metal, a bit similar to *Cult Of Luna*. The first 10" was produced by Andreas Ekström (*Breach*). After the second single Henrik Boman was replaced by Henrik Norén. In 1999 the band also parted company with singer/bass-player Norén, who only participated on the 10". Tim is ex-*Pinch/Charcoal* and he runs Trust No One Records. On the first full length album the pace had slowed down and the music was now much more ambient and drony. In 2004 *Switchblade* released a 7" where they were reinforced with *Logh* singer/guitarist Mattias Friberg. The next album, still self-titled, released in 2005 featured both Friberg and Watain singer

The self-titled one is my favourite album!

Erik Danielsson as guests. The subsequent album, released in 2006, was recorded in only three days and features three long tracks, almost hypnotising, drone-style doomy, stonery rock in the vein of *Isis* meets *Melvins* meets *Neurosis*. Not music for the fainthearted.
Website: www.switchblade.se

| 1998 ■ | Switchblade | 7" 7tr | Trust No One | TRUSTNO 05 |

Tracks: A Half Pack Of Morleys/Summoning Of An Escapist/The Grey Zone/He Is One/Troubleshooting/I Know Your Tricks/Fall As August. 500 copies.

| 1999 □ | Switchblade/Last Match | 7" | La Calavera | DISC-S 001 |

Split with Last Match. Tracks: The Plot Thickens/Reduction Into Past Tense/An Eye For Details. 750 copies on black vinyl and 250 on clear vinyl with bloodstains.

| 1999 □ | SWITCHBLADE | 10" | Trust No One | TRUSTNO 10 |

First press 500 copies, second press 300 copies with hand screened covers.

| 2000 □ | SWITCHBLADE | 10" | Blood Of The Young (USA) | YOUNG 008 |

1100 copies.

| 2000 □ | Switchblade/The Jam Session | 7 | Insect | INSECT 5 |

Split with The Jam Session. Tracks: Selfdestruct Schematics/Open Aftermath/Polar Eclipse/Dealing With Rejoice. 1000 copies.

| 2000 □ | Switchblade/Cult Of Luna | 7" | Trust No One | TRUSTNO 12 |

Split with Cult Of Luna. Tracks: Ten Stabs To The Throat/Execution Appendix/T-Minus. 500 copies.

| 2000 □ | SWITCHBLADE | LP | Trust No One | TRUSTNO 13 |

500 copies.

| 2000 □ | SWITCHBLADE | CD | Trust No One | TRUSTNO 13 |

350 copies.

| 2001 □ | SWITCHBLADE | CD | Flower Violence | FLOWER 23 |

Compilation of vinyl tracks.

| 2001 □ | SWITCHBLADE | LP | Trust No One | TRUSTNO 17 |

350 copies from black to clear vinyl. First 50 copies with special design cover.

2001 □	SWITCHBLADE	CD	Trust No One	TRUSTNO 17
2003 □	SWITCHBLADE	CD	Trust No One	TRUSTNO 21
2003 □	SWITCHBLADE	LPg	Trust No One	TRUSTNO 21

Pressed in 12 different colours in different numbers. Totally 517 copies.

| 2003 □ | Switchblade Tour | 7" | Trust No One | TRUSTNO 26 |

Clear or black/white marbled vinyl. Tracks: 07:05/05:52.

| 2003 □ | SWITCHBLADE | CDd | Deathwitch/Icarus (USA) | ICA 01 |

Same as TRUSTNO 26

| 2004 ■ | Switchblade | 7" | Deathwish/Icarus (USA) | Icarus 5.1 |

101 opaque orange + 250 white + 653 clear vinyl. Tracks: 07:05/05:52.

| 2006 □ | SWITCHBLADE | LPg | Trust No One | TRUSTNO 29 |

500 copies in clear vinyl.

2006 □	SWITCHBLADE	CD	Trust No One	TRUSTNO 29
2006 □	SWITCHBLADE	CD	Cyclop Media	C 014
2009 ■	SWITCHBLADE	CD	Trust No One	TRUSTNO 33
2009 □	SWITCHBLADE	2LPg	Denovali Records	DEN 37

180 clear vinyl + 320 black. Fourth side etched.

| 2012 □ | SWITCHBLADE | CD | Trust No One/Denovali | TNO 040/DEN146 |
| 2012 □ | SWITCHBLADE | 2LPg | Trust No One/Denovali | TNO 040/DEN146 |

350 black, 350 black with bag of Switchblade coffee,150 swamp green vinyl copies.

SWORDMASTER

Andreas "Vinnie Whiplasher" Bergh: v, Emil "Naughty Nightmare" Nödtveidt: g,
Erik "Beast X Electric" Halvorsen: g, Kenneth "Thunderbolt" Gagner: b,
Nicklas "Terror" Rudolfsson: d

Göteborg - The band was formed in 1993 by Anders and Emil (brother of Jon Nödtveidt). They were later accompanied by drummer Ole "Inferno" Öhman (*Dissection, Ophthalamia*) and bass player Erik, which formed the line-up on *Wraths Of Time*. When Ole left to join *Dissection* he was replaced by Rudolfsson. In 1996 they recorded the tracks *Claws Of Death* and *Metallic Devastation* for compilations, and they later lead to a deal with Osmose. *Moribund..* was produced by Andy LaRocque. Nicklas was also found in *Sacramentum* and *Runemagick*. Late 2001 they decided it was time for a change, quite a drastic one, too. They changed their name to *Deathstars* and changed their style to something more in the vein of *Marilyn Manson* visually and musically they went industrial, similar to *Pain*. The album *Synthetic Generation* was released early 2002. Rudolfsson was however not into it, so old basher Öhman took his place. *Swordmaster* produced high-quality death metal in the vein of *Bewitched*. Some live-tracks can be found on the compilation *World Domination Live* (98 Osmose).

Deathriders in the night

| 1996 ■ | Wraths Of Time | MCD 3tr | Full Moon | FMP 004 |

Tracks: Wraths Of Time/Upon Blood And Ashes/Conspiracy - Preview. 1000 copies

| 1996 ■ | Wraths Of Time | MLP 5tr | Full Moon | FMP 004V |

Tracks: Wraths Of Time/Upon Blood And Ashes/Metallic Devastation/Conspiracy – Preview/Outro. 1000 copies. Different artwork.

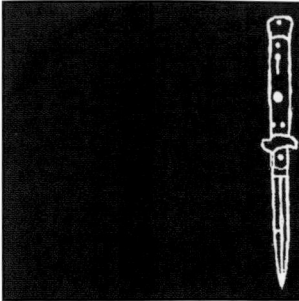
1998 7" - TRUSTNO 05

2004 7" - Icarus 5.1

2009 CD - TRUSTNO 33

1996 MCD - FMP 004

1996 MLP - FMP 004V

1996 ☐	Wraths Of Time	MCD 3tr	Full Moon	FMP 004

New artwork, same as MLP.

1997 ☐	POST MORTEM TALES	CD	Osmose	OPCD 055
1997 ☐	POST MORTEM TALES	LP	Osmose	OPLP 055

1000 numbered copies.

1998 ☐	DEATHRIDER	MCD 5tr	Osmose	OPCD 058

Tracks: Death Rider 2000/Firefall Of The Fireball/Necronaut Psychout/Ironcorpse/Stand For The Fire Demon (Roky Erickson cover)

1998 ☐	DEATHRIDER	LP	Osmose	OPLP 058

Bonus: Whiskey Driver/The Black Ace. 1000 copies.

1998 ■	DEATHRIDER	LP PD	Osmose	OPPIC 058
1999 ☐	MORIBUND TRANSGORIA	CD	Osmose	OPCD 084
1999 ☐	MORIBUND TRANSGORIA	LP	Osmose	OPLP 084

1000 copies, hand numbered.

1998 LP PD - OPPIC 058

SWORN

Emil Abrahamsson: v, Stefan "Steff" Eliasson: g, Peter Wigeborn: g/b, David Rosén: d

Ljungskile - Formed in 2004 and recorded the demo *Global Demise* in 2005. Rosén is ex-**Holocaustia**, while Stefan has been found in **Azeazeron** and **Descending**. After the MCD Daniel Gustavsson (**Kaliber**) was added on bass. Thrash-oriented old-school death metal. The band was also featured on the split CD-R *Sküllcrushing Deströyers* (Grüft Prodüction).

2007 ■	Impious Beast Within	MCD 5tr	Nuclear Winter Records	NWR 019

Tracks: Flesh Desecration/Unleash The Lions/Incite The Impious Beast/Black Death/ Infector Of Souls. 500 copies.

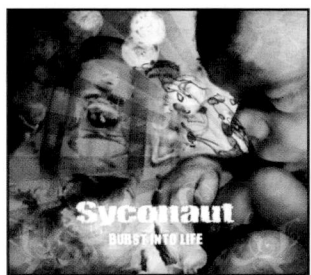

2007 MCD - NWR 019

SYCONAUT

Daniel Valström (aka Nilsson): v, David Holgersson: g, Benny Hagstedt: g, Juha Ojajärvi: b, Daniel Granlund: d

Skövde - *Syconaut* were formed in 199 and recorded the first demo, *March Of A New Division* in 2000, at the time featuring lead singer Christian Älvestam (**Torchbearer, Scar Symmetry, Solution .45, Incapacity, Quest Of Aidance** etc). It was followed by *Shredlust* in 2002 and *Geodesic* in 2004. The band now featured singer Daniel Nilsson (now Valström) (ex-**Quest Of Aidance**), guitarists David Holgersson and Benny Hagstedt, bassist Markus Rytilahti and drummer Daniel Granlund. Two years later the demo *Solace* was recorded and finally, in 2009 the debut album saw the light of day. Juha Ojajärvi now handled the bass work. The album is a powerful punch in the face similar to bands like **Soilwork** meets **Machine Head**, at times with a touch of **Meshuggah**'s chugging. Great production, too. In 2010 they released the four-track digital EP *Fractions*. After this Juha left the band and Johan Fogelberg replaced him.
Website: www.syconaut.com

2009 ■	BURST INTO LIFE	CDd	Ilumni Records	ILUMNICD 006

2009 CDd - ILUMNICD 006

SYN:DROM

Jonny Pettersson: v, David Karlsson: g, Roger Bergsten: g, Daniel Åsén: b, Daniel Mikaelsson: d

Sundsvall - *Syn:drom* were formed in 2002 under the name **Blackbreath**. They recorded their first demo, *Dead Silent Screaming* in 2004, followed by *Promo 2005* the year after. In 2007 they released the self-financed demo EP *Birth Of A Dark Empire*. Death metal in the vein of **Behemoth** and **Hate Eternal** that comes with a nosebleed guarantee.
Website: www.syndromweb.net/

2010 ■	WITH FLESH UNBOUND	CD	ViciSolum	VSP 010
2012 ☐	ICONOCLAST	CD	ViciSolum	VSP 039

2010 CD - VSP 010

SYRON VANES

Rimbert "Rimmy Hunter" Vahlström: v/g, Michel Strand: b, Staffan "Stephen Mavrock" Andersson (now Lindstedt): d

Malmö - *Syron Vanes* were formed in 1980 by guitarist Anders "Andy Seymore" Hahne and drummer Staffan "Stephen Mavrock" Andersson (now Lindstedt). The band was completed by guitarist Ola Pettersson and bassist Anders Lind. A first demo was recorded in 1982, and the track *Violation* found its way to the compilation *Skånsk Rock*. Staffan handled the vocals at this point. Later the same year Ola and Anders Lind left the band. Enter Rimbert "Rimmy Hunter" Vahlström on guitar and new singer Jarmo K. Erik "Rix Volin" Briselius joined on bass. Early 1983 Jarmo left and was replaced by Ola Svedin, but he soon left and the vocals were shared between Rimbert and Erik. A demo was sent to UK label Ebony Records, and the band landed a five-album deal. Erik now took over the vocals permanently and Arne "Ace Greenwood" Sandved was added on bass. The debut *Bringer Of Evil* was released. In 1985 Arne left the band, and was replaced by Dick Qwarfort (**Nasty Idols**). Due to bad quality and lousy distribution

1984 LP - EBON-23

1986 LP - EBON-36

the band left the label in 1987, after two albums. In 1987 Erik and Dick left the band because of musical differences. Rimbert now took over the vocals and bassist Peter Crane was drafted. The style changed from NWoBHM to more melodic metal. In 1988 they recorded a three-track demo, but nothing happened and the band was put to rest. However in 2003 a new life-sign came. On the return album *Insane*, the line-up featured Rimbert Vahlström, Anders Hahne, Staffan Andersson (now Lindstedt) and new bassist Jakob Lagergren. A great powerful heavy metal return, which shows the band still kicks major ass. The style had now been modernised a bit, taking on a heavier edge, at times similar to what *Accept* did on *Deathrow*. Great riffing and a heavy grinding touch. In 2007 the album *Property Of…* was released, now seeing the band reduced to a trio featuring Rimbert, Staffan and new bassist Michel Strand. In 2011 Strand left again and was replaced by the returning Lagergren. Later the same year Staffan suffered a stroke and had to leave the band. He was replaced by Mats Bergentz (*Silver Mountain, Mr. Kite*). *Evil Redux* saw the band returning with yet another top-notch effort of melodic, yet heavy melodic metal that proves they are here to stay.
Website: www.syronvanes.com

2003 CD - CDCR 0011

2007 CD - - -

1984	■	BRINGER OF EVIL	LP	Ebony Records	EBON-23
1986	■	REVENGE	LP	Ebony Records	EBON-36
2003	■	INSANE	CD	Carnival Records	CDCR 0011
2007	■	PROPERTY OF	CD	private	- -
2012	□	BRINGER OF EVIL	CD	Steelheart Records	SMM 1228
		Bonus: Violation/Steal And Run			
2012	□	REVENGE	CD	Steelheart Records	SMM 1229
		Bonus: Lying Again/Taking Over			
2013	□	EVIL REDUX	CD	Denomination Records	DEN 005

SYRUS
Fredrik Persson: v, Daniel Engström: g, Mikael Forsberg: g,
Per Wallgren: b, Tobias Gustafsson: d

Forshaga - Traditional melodic 80s metal of mainstream quality. The B-side is a Top 40 ballad. Tobias later joined death metal band *Vomitory*.

1989 7" - SNP-8904-3

1989	■	Fortune And Fame/The Golden Void	7"	private	SNP-8904-3
		Pink vinyl.			

SYSTEM BREAKDOWN
Pär Hagström: v, Carl Johan "CJ" Grimmark: g, Ronnie Jaldemark: k,
Karl Persson: b, Andreas Johansson: d

Jönköping - **System Breakdown** was a side project of, at the time, **Narnia** guitarist Grimmark initiated late 2001. Jaldemark and Johansson were also in **Narnia** at the time. The band was however quite far from **Narnia**'s neoclassical power metal. Here Grimmark explores darker and heavier territories, at times entering the musical realm of Tony Martin era **Black Sabbath**, while some tracks draws close to the modern vibe of **Skintrade**. This also shows in the artwork, which is pretty dark and gloomy. Grimmark later on took the concept a few steps even further with the project carrying his own name in 2007.

2003 CD - RRCD 009

2003	■	102	CD	Rivel Records	RRCD 009

SYSTEM SHOCK
Dimitris Loakimoglou: v, Lukas Bergis: g, Stathis Cassios: k,
Evan Hensley: b, Kim Gustavsson: d

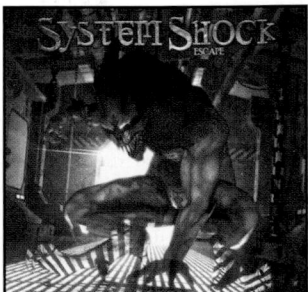

2006 CD - MAU 251079

Norrköping - **System Shock**, being somewhat Swedish/Greek, were formed by guitarist Bergis and had a full line-up early 2004. They immediately started composing and rehearsing. The band was soon picked up by Karmageddon Media, who had heard some demo material. The debut album featured singer Loakimoglou (**Anorimoi, Obscure Natus, Double Square**), guitarists Bergis, keyboardist Stathis Cassios (ex-**Nightfall, Karmic Link**), drummer George Kollias (**Nile, Nightfall, Sickening Horror**) and session bassist Angel M. After this they were picked up by German label Mausoleum, who released the follow-up *Escape*. Now drummer Vagelis Baliousis was in. The line-up saw Cassios out of the band and bassist JB replacing Gustavsson. On *Urban Rage* Gustavsson switched to drums and the bass work was handled by Evan Hensley. The early releases were more melodic death metal while *Urban Rage* is more powerful death metal with a technical twist at times, a bit similar to **Dark Tranquility** and **Mercenary**. A new album is planned for 2013 and the current line-up features Dimitris, Lukas, guitarist John McRis, bassist Joel Kuronen and drummer Toni Paananen.

2004 CD - KARMA 050

2008 CD - SR 0087

2004	■	ARCTIC INSIDE	CD	Karmageddon Media	KARMA 050
2004	□	ARCTIC INSIDE	CD	Nordic Media (Russia)	NMKM 0017
2006	■	ESCAPE	CD	Mausoleum	MAU 251079
2008	■	URBAN RAGE	CD	Sleazy Rider	SR 0087

T.A.R

Torbjörn Sandberg: v, Juan Gauthier: g, Stefan Sjöberg: g,
Östen Johansson: b, Per Karlsson: d

Stockholm - Formed in 1993 by Juan, initially called *Vulture King*. Their first demo was entitled *Baby Inferno* and their second attempt, *Act II*, was recorded at Montezuma by Rex Gisslén (*Candlemass*). For the third demo they changed their name to *T.A.R*. After this Per (ex-*Suffer, Serpent*) joined. Heavy death-ish power metal with influences from *Megadeth*, *Anthrax* etc. and with slightly growling vocals. The band has also recorded a cover of *Torture* for a *Mercyful Fate* tribute.

1998 MCD - TPCD 002

1997	☐	FEAR OF LIFE	CD	Heathendoom	TPCD 001
1998	■	Tar And Feathers For The Millennium	MCD 4tr	Heathendoom	TPCD 002
		Tracks: Burn/Guilty/Countdown To Doomsday/Kiss Of Death			
1998	☐	Tar And Feathers For The Millennium	7" 4tr	Heathendoom	TP 002

TBC

Kenneth Berg: v, L-G Forsman: h, Michael Stattin: g,
Gunnar Jonsen: g, Rune Hellgren: b, Lars Gillén: d

Umeå - The embryo of the band was formed in 1974, as blues rockers *Sex Fördömda Män*, but three years later they became *TBC*. Raunchy, wild hard rock with a touch of blues and an almost punkish attitude. Quite close to *MC5* at times. The band's 5 track 7" was recorded live in October 10, 1978. Two tracks were also found on the compilation *Rätt Till Jobb* (1979 Slå Tillbaka). Lars Gillén was also found in *Steve Roper Band* and later in blues rockers band *Shake Down*. He also runs Garageland Records.

1979 7" - TA 1

1979	■	Musik I Plast/Lillbabs Världens Tråkigaste Kvinna	7"	Mjälthugg	TA 1
1981	☐	TBC Live	7" 5tr	Mjälthugg	TA 4
		Tracks: Nakna Brudar/Lögn Lögn/Lång Väg/Musik I Plast/Rätt Till Jobb.			

T'BELL

Patrik Tibell: v, Roger Ljunggren: g/b, Ola Johansson: d

Skara - The band was known as *Trance* in the eighties, with lots of great demos under their belt, and *Replay* contains rerecordings of some of the old and never before issued tracks. Patrik was also found in the *Flintstens Med Stanley*-project and is now a successful pop/dance composer. Roger co-wrote the song *Don't Close Your Eyes*, later recorded by *Kharma* (although he was never credited for it). He also played guitar on the first *Grand Illusion* album. Tibell and Ljunggren have also written music for *TNT* as well as popsters *Friends*. *T'Bell* was more or less a one-off project and musically it's very slick, almost westcoast-oriented AOR, similar to *Toto*-meet-*Mr Mister*.

2000 CD - 10164

2000	■	REPLAY	CD	AOR Heaven	10164
2000	☐	REPLAY	CD	Avalon Marquee (Japan)	MICP 10213 $
		Bonus: Sorry Elaine/Forever			

TME

Andreas Stenlund: v, Mattias Marklund: g, Johan Lindgren: b, Benny Hägglund: d

Skellefteå - The band was formed in 2002, initially featuring bass player Patrik Pettersson. *TME* is pretty much the members of *Vintersorg* without Mr. Vintersorg - Andreas Hedlund himself. Marklund was in *Vintersorg*, where both Hägglund and Lindgren were session musicians. He is also in *Otyg* and *Casket Casey*, while Hägglund also plays guitar in the band *Fission*. Here they take totally different path far from the folky metal of their other employer. *TME* is sheer brutality in the form of thrashy death metal, a bit like mixing *Machine Head* and *God Dethroned*. After the release of the album Christoffer Rörland was added on second guitar.
Website: www.generation666.com

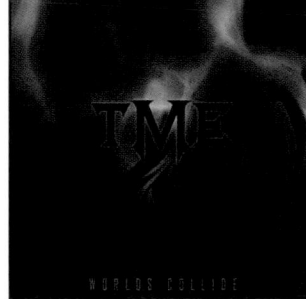

2007 CD - ARCD 001

2007	■	WORLD'S COLLIDE	CD	Aphotic Records	ARCD 001

TNT

Patrik Bergholm: g/v/k, Jonas Hedlund: g/v/k, Ulf Gusatvsson: b, Mathias Ulfheim: d

Umeå - Young and quite amateurish standard hard rock/metal with low rate vocals. *The Brish* is an instrumental track. Needless to say, not to be confused with the Norwegian or German namesakes.

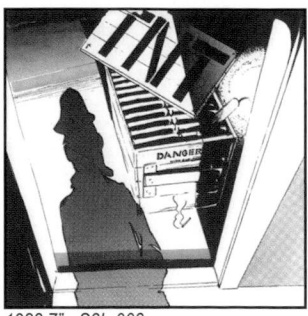

1982 7" - S3L-003

1982	■	The Brish/Flirtin´ With Disaster/Don´t Break My Heart	7" 3tr	Studio 3L	S3L-003 $

TRP
Mikael Jönsson: v/g, Anders Persson: k/v, Eddie Persson: g,
Mats Sundholm: b, Magnus Nyström: d

Fjälkinge/Kristianstad - TRP stands for The Rocking People, which was later (more metal) changed to Tyrannosaurus Rex Prisoners. The band was formed in 1981. The single was quite amateurish metal in the vein of *Lezlie Paice* or *Shakespeare*. They made another recording in 1984, which was never released. Guitarist Eddie Persson was later a member of *Little Yankees*.

1982 ■ My Bike/Lady Of The Night ....7" Pang .... PSI 056
500 copies.

1982 7" - PSI 056

TAD MOROSE
Urban Breed: v, Christer "Krunt" Andersson: g, Daniel Olsson: g,
Anders "Modden" Modd: b, Peter Morén: d

Bollnäs - Originally formed in 1991, split and reformed in 1992 without a singer. During the recordings of their first and only demo, with the witty title *Self Titled Debute Tape*, singer Kristian Andrén joined the band and they were signed by Börje Forsberg to his Black Mark label. Before the recordings of the second album drummer Danne Eriksson decided to leave and Peter Morén replaced him. Right after the album was finished another change of personnel was made. Bass player Per-Ola Olsson was asked to leave due to "communication problems" and Anders Modd soon replaced him. *Tad Morose* are a great, heavy yet melodic band, a bit like *Eternal Idol*-era *Black Sabbath*, but with more musical twists and turns. Highly recommended. On the second album the music took a more progressive, almost symphonic turn, while the subsequent MCD was outstanding powerful and heavy progressive hard rock. In 1998 keyboard player Fredrik Eriksson (ex-*Solitude*) left the band for personal reasons and was replaced by guitarist Daniel Olsson. This line-up took the band's sound to a more heavy ground. *Reflections*, which is a "best of", also contains a cover of *Savatage*'s *Power Of The Night*. On *Undead* the band's sound had evolved into a nice mix between *Crimson Glory* and *Savatage* with a touch of *Jag Panzer*. The vocal task was also passed over from Kristian Andrén to Urban Breed, who is quite reminiscent of Harry Conklin (*Jag Panzer*). *Matters...* features guest vocals from *Morgana Lefay/Lefay*-singer Charles Rytkönen. Since *Modus Vivendi* the line-up has gone through a variety of appearances. Singer Urban Breed left in 2005 and joined *Bloodbound*. He was replaced by American Joe Comeau (*Overkill, Liege Lord, Annihilator*), who only recorded a couple of demos with the band and in 2008 he was replaced by Ronny Hemlin (*Steel Attack*). Guitarist Daniel Olsson left in 2007 to be replaced by Markus Albertsson, who left in 2010. Bass player Modd has been replaced by Tommi Karppanen. In 2012 guitarist Kenneth Jonsson (*Torch, The Citadel*) joined as second guitarist and a new album is in the making. Peter Morén is also found in the resurrected *Torch*. Olsson and Breed are now also found in *Trail Of Murder*.
Website: www.morose.com

The morose bunch dwelling over matters in the dark

© Photo by Benny Backeby

1995 CD - BMCD 62

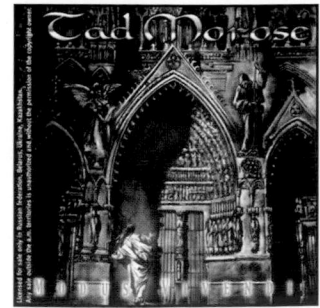

1995 MCD - BMCD 85

2003 CD - FO377CD

1993 □	Voices Are Calling .... MCD 3tr	Black Mark	....	BMCD 39
	Tracks: Voices Are Calling/Leaving The Past Behind/Eternal Lies. Promo.			
1993 □	LEAVING THE PAST BEHIND .... CD	Black Mark	....	BMCD 43
1994 □	LEAVING THE PAST BEHIND .... CD	Victor (Japan)	....	VICP-5363
1995 □	Sender Of Thoughts/Lost In Time/Here After .... CDS 3tr	Black Mark	....	BMCD 56
1995 ■	SENDER OF THOUGHTS .... CD	Black Mark	....	BMCD 62
1995 ■	Paradigma .... MCD 5tr	Black Mark	....	BMCD 85
	Tracks: Stories Around A Tale/Eyes So Tired/Where Dreams Collide/Absent Illusion/ Another Paradigm			
1995 □	SENDER OF THOUGHTS .... CD	Victor (Japan)	....	VICP-5521
	Bonus: Gates Of Babylon (Rainbow cover)			
2000 □	REFLECTIONS .... CD	Black Mark	....	BMCD 154
2001 □	REFLECTIONS .... CD	Irond (Russia)	....	CD 01-24
2000 □	UNDEAD .... CD	Century Media	....	77311 2
2000 □	UNDEAD .... CD	Century Media (USA)	....	8011-2
2002 □	MATTERS OF THE DARK .... CD	Century Media	....	77394 2
2002 □	MATTERS OF THE DARK .... CD	Century Media (USA)	....	8094-2
2003 □	MODUS VIVENDI .... CD	Century Media	....	77494 2
2003 ■	MODUS VIVENDI .... CD	Fono (Russia)	....	FO377CD
2004 □	MODUS VIVENDI .... CD	Crown Nippon (Japan)	....	CRCL-4576
	Bonus: We Watch The Well Die/Devastation			

TAETRE

Jonas Lindblad: v/g, Daniel "Dadde" Nilsson: g,
Daniel Kvist: b, Kalle "Graveyard" Pettersson: d

Göteborg - Taetre means "ugly" in Latin. The band was formed in 1993 under the name *Deformed*, changed their name to *Enthroned* and in 1996 they recorded the demo *Eclipse*. They were also featured on the *Voices Of Death 2* compilation. Melodic and catchy death metal with added flavours from old-school thrash, black metal and traditional heavy metal. In places reminiscent of *Naglfar* and *Dissection*. The first two albums were produced by Andy LaRocque. Jonas is also found in the Danish/Swedish collaboration *Thorium*. In 2001 Conny Vandling left and was replaced by Daniel Kvist. The band's third album features guest vocals from Tony Jelencovich (*M.A.N, Transport League, B-Thong* etc.) and a solo from Andy LaRocque. Kvist and Pettersson are now found in *Snakeskin Angels*.

1998 CD - RRS 963

2002 CD - PMZ 030-2

1998	■	THE ART	CD	Emanzipation Prod.uctions	RRS 963
1999	□	OUT OF EMOTIONAL DISORDER	CD	Diehard	RRS 965
2002	■	DIVINE MISANTHROPIC MADNESS	CD	Mighty Music	PMZ 030-2

TAI ROSE

Magnus "Lillis" Lundbäck: v, Tomas Fredriksson: g,
Morgan Jacobsson: k, Mats Bostedt: b, Patrik Engelbrektsson: d

Göteborg - Tai Rose play quite high-class melodic 80s hard rock with a slightly sleazy touch. The B-side is a bit more commercial, while the A-side is a rocker. Lead singer Magnus was later found in *The Ungrateful*, plus he was the co-founder of Gain Music Entertainment.

| 1989 | ■ | Stay High/Take Me Home | 7" | private | TR-S-1 |

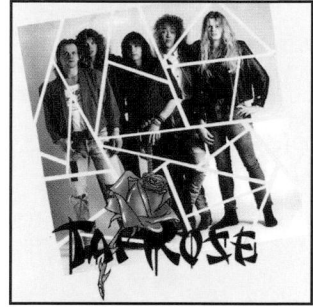

1989 7" - TR-S-1

TAKETH

David Dahl: v, Mikael Lindqvist: g, Lars Walfridsson: b, Johan Dahl: d

Linköping - In 1996 David, Mikael and Johan played under the name *Pergamon* and recorded their first demo, *Forgiven*, in 2000. They also recorded the EP *Breaking An Image* in 2001. In 2000 David and Mikael started *Taketh*. They added David's brother Johan. Twin brothers Jonas and Emil Karlsson completed the band, and in 2002 they recorded their first demo, *His Majesty*. In 2004 the Karlsson twins quit to join *Admonish*. Bass player Lars Walfridsson was now added. In 2005 they were picked up by Fear Dark and recorded the debut album. After the album second guitarist Atahan Tolunay joined. *Taketh* play pretty good Christian melodic death metal, with a Gothenburg-style touch, unfortunately lacking a bit in the mix and the vocals not being up to par. In 2007 Lars left and was replaced by former *System Shock/Deviant Breed* bassist Kim Gustavsson. In 2008 the band also released a three-track preview EP entitled *Minus 24*.

| 2005 | ■ | FREAK SHOW | CD | Fear Dark | FD 021 |

2005 CD - FD 021

TAKIDA

Robert Pettersson: v, Mattias Larsson: g, Tomas Wallin: g,
Fredrik Pålsson: b, Kristoffer Söderström: d

Ånge - Takida were formed in 1999 under the name *Tender*, by former *Sinatra* drummer Fredrik Holm and former *Blowball* guitarist Wallin. Guitarist Roger Olsson, singer Pettersson and bassist Pålsson were added to the line-up. Holm was replaced by Niklas Källström shortly after. In 2000 the band had changed its name to *Takida*, taken after a character in a Japanese manga *Silver Fang*, and recorded their first demo MCD, *Old*, released in 500 copies. It was followed by *T2*, later the same year and a self-titled demo CD in 2001. The band made their debut in 2001, still on their own Diesel Wing label. In 2002 Olsson was replaced by Larsson. In 2008 they had their big break with the single *Curly Sue*, which topped the Swedish charts and stayed in the chart for a staggering 50 weeks, which is a Swedish record. In 2009 the band was signed by Roadrunner (Universal) and *The Darker Instinct* made gold record only three days after its release. The follow-up *The Burning Heart* took two weeks to make it to gold. *Bury the Lies* has reached platinum. In 2011 the band filed a police report against web magazine *Gaffa* after the reviewer had said the singer said he had "Down's Syndrome in his voice" and followed up with the question "I wonder how many years you'd get for premeditated murder in Sweden", considering it a life threat. The song *Jaded* and a cover of *Pet Shop Boys* *It's A Sin* is found on the compilation *Played Out* (2001). *One Of A Kind* and *Evil Eye* are found on *Played Out II* (2002). Takida plays quite well-polished, very pop-oriented, slightly depressive, modern nu-oriented melodic metal. For some reason the press hates them and "true" metal fans hate them, but still they manage to sell gold and platinum, so obviously they're doing something right.
Website: www.takidamusic.com

You can threaten us, but we stand united!

2007 CD - NRCD 102

| 2000 | □ | Old | MCD 5tr | Diesel Wing | TKD01 |

Tracks: Old/Something's On Your Mind/Is It Right?/Have You Waited Long?/Killed By Train. 500 copies.

Year		Title	Format	Label	Catalog	
2000	☐	T2	MCD 5tr	Diesel Wing	TKD02	
		Tracks: Leave Me Alone/It's The Booze Talking/Asleep/Give It To Me/A Point Of View				
2001	☐	TAKIDA	CD	Diesel Wing	TKD03	
2003	☐	Gohei	MCD 5tr	Diesel Wing	TKD04	
		Tracks: Unison/Easy/Snypah/Ponder/Don't Reach Out (The Grand Closure)				
2004	☐	Broken/Tear It Up	CDS 2tr	Diesel Wing	TKD05	$$
2004	☐	Thorns	MCD 6tr	Diesel Wing	TKD06	
		Tracks: Broken/Tear It Up/Another Day/Stay In The Rain/Appreciated/Give Into Me (Ridin' High version)				
2006	☐	...MAKE YOUR BREATHE	CD	NineTone Records	NRCD 100	
2006	☐	Losing (+videos: Losing/live)	CDS	NineTone Records	NRCDS 001	
2006	☐	Reason To Cry	CDS	NineTone Records	- -	
2007	☐	Halo	CDS	NineTone Records	NRCDS 005	
2007	■	...BURY THE LIES	CD	NineTone Records	NRCD 102	
2009	■	Losing	CDS	Roadrunner Records	RR PROMO 1138	
2009	☐	...BURY THE LIES – PLATINUM EDITION	CD	Universal Records	0602517-88481	
		Bonus: Losing/Reason To Cry (2009 Mix)/Jaded/Curly Sue/Handlake Village				
2009	☐	THE DARKER INSTINCT	CD	Universal Records	0602527-12332	
2010	☐	THE DARKER INSTINCT – PLATINUM EDITION	CD	Universal Records	0602527-51785	
		Bonus: Never Alone Always Alone (Box Room Version)/Between The Lines (Orchestral Version)				
2011	■	Deadlock/Evil Eye	7" PD	Universal Records	0602527-59449	
2011	☐	THE BURNING HEART	CD	Universal Records	0602527-74736	
2011	☐	THE BURNING HEART	LP	Universal Records	0602527-77863	
2012	☐	A LESSON LEARNED: THE BEST OF TAKIDA	3LP	Universal Records	0602537-22430	
2012	☐	A LESSON LEARNED: THE BEST OF TAKIDA	2CD	Universal Records	0602537-21027	

2009 CDS - RR PROMO 1138

2011 7" PD - 0602527-59449

TALE

Thomas Thörnblom: v/k, Jonas Andersson: g, Magnus Andersson: b, Jan Dalquist: d

Västervik (?) - Pretty good eighties melodic hard rock with a touch of **Treat**. *Trugania* is an instrumental, while the other two tracks are power ballads. Drummer Dalquist was previously in Västerås band **Unchained** (as Ian Dee Jr). The band's highlight was supporting **Pretty Maids** in Karlskoga.

Year		Title	Format	Label	Catalog
1988	■	Jamie/Love Is All About/Trugania	7" 3tr	SGV	SGV-S 812
		300 copies.			

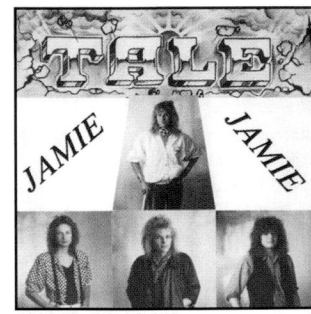

1988 7" - SGV-S 812

TALENT

Mikael "Michael Eden" Erlandsson: v, Claes "Chris Cain" Andreasson, Torbjörn "John Tatum" Wassenius

Göteborg - In 1986 Cain and Tatum formed the duo **Talent**. The first two singles are pop and not worth looking for. *Only You* is closer to synth-pop than hard rock, while *Love Blind* is good-quality, commercial AOR with heavy guitars. This single also featured singer Michael Eden, aka Mikael Erlandssson (**Last Autumn's Dream, Crash, Heartbreak Radio**, solo), which is what makes this release interesting. The last single is also pure pop. The duo of Andreasson and Wassenius has since written numerous songs for pop artists and the Eurovision Song Contest. They also returned into the AOR genre with the bands **Last Autumn's Dream** and **Heartbreak Radio**.

Year		Title	Format	Label	Catalog
1986	☐	Tears/Carolyne	7"	TC Records	TC 001
1987	☐	Love (Don't Hurry!)/Make Her Mine	7"	Grape Garden	GG 011
1988	■	Only You/Love Blind	7"	MR	MR-25
1988	☐	Don't Close Your Eyes/Think About You	7"	Miracle	M-009

1988 7" - MR-25

TALISMAN

Jeff Scott Soto: v, Fredrik Åkesson: g, Marcel Jacobs: b, Jamie Borger: d

Stockholm/Los Angeles - **Talisman** were an excellent, melodic, quite powerful hard rock band lead by the late bass mastermind Marcel Jacob and American singer Jeff Scott Soto. Strong song material and a very international sound were the bands brand marks. Marcel had previously played with bands like **Yngwie Malmsteen's Rising Force, Force, Power, John Norum Band** and later let his bass do the talking on albums by bands like **The Johansson Brothers, Last Autumn's Dream, Locomotive Breath, W.E.T** etc.. He also co-wrote songs like *Scream Of Anger (Europe)*, *Let Me Love You* and *Eternal Flame* (**John Norum**). Jeff has sung with **Yngwie Malmsteen's Rising Force, Skräpp Mettle, Eyes, Takara, W.E.T, Bakteria** to name a few, besides his solo stuff. It started when Marcel had written some songs for the second John Norum album, but they were rejected. He made some demos with Göran Edman (**Norum, Vindictiv, Madison, Kharma** etc.), but also tried various other singers such as Thomas Vikström (**Talk Of The Town, Candlemass, Stormwind** etc), Krister Linder aka Chris

Talismanimals

Lancelot (*Grace*) and Marc Quee, before finding American Jeff Scott Soto (ex-*Eyes*), from a tip by *Wasa Express* guitarist Cary Shafaf. On the first album *Talisman* was not really a band but more a Marcel/Jeff-project + friends. The guitars were played by Christopher Ståhl (*Power*) and Mats Lindfors (Norum, *Grand Slam*), keyboards by Mats Olausson (*Motvind, Malmsteen, Glory* etc etc.) and drums, except where programmed by Marcel, by Peter Hermansson (*220 Volt, Norum, Zoom Club, Grand Design*). The album was recorded for Elektra but they went bust before its release and the master was bought by Vinyl Mania, owned by a former member of the defunct Elektra team, who released it on the new Airplay label. On live gigs the band now featured Jason Bieler on guitar (*Saigon Kick*), former *Yale Bate/Totem* drummer/singer Jakob "Jake Samuels" Samuelsson (later in *Jekyll 'N Hyde, Treasure Land, Midnight Sun, The Ring, The Poodles*) and Tomas Vikström on keyboards. Then Airplay also went bankrupt. In 1992 singer Matti Alfonzetti returned from England after having recorded with *Jagged Edge*. He then joined forces with Marcel, Jakob and new guitarist Fredrik Åkesson (ex-*One Cent*, later in *Southpaw, Arch Enemy, Krux, Opeth* etc.). They recorded a great demo, featuring the song *Angel*. The other tracks turned up on the second *Talisman* album, but this remained unreleased. The band also made some live shows with this line-up. *Talisman* were signed to Dino Music (later renamed Empire) who bought the master and reissued the debut on CD with six badly recorded live tracks as bonus. The band now recorded the follow-up, *Genesis*, where Marcel programmed the drums, since Jakob was in and out of the band within a few months' time. The band also featured live keyboardist Julie Greaux. *Talisman* even had a minor hit with the song *Mysterious*. On the live album the line-up was completed with *Treat* drummer Jamie Borger and the two *Humanimal* albums are classic pieces of melodic well-crafted hard rock. Greaux adds some backing vocals on these recordings. The single *Todo Y Todo* was released in 300 copies for promotion only under the name *Genaro*, as an attempt to break new ground. It is now a collector's item. The *Seal* cover *Crazy*, in a version far more interesting than the original, is found on *Life*. After the release of *Life*, Fredrik left/was asked to leave as he wanted to go in a heavier direction. This shows on the release by his band *Southpaw*, initially named *Eyeball*. Fredrik was temporarily replaced by American guitarist Brian Young, previously with *Beau Nasty*. The band then took a hiatus, where Jeff concentrated on performing in the live show *Boogie Knights* in the US. However during this time Marcel and Jeff recorded two albums under the moniker *Human Clay*, where Yngwie plays lead guitar on one track.

Talisman finally found their way back, reinforced with guitarist Pontus Norgren (*Great King Rat, Jekyll 'N Hyde,* later in *The Ring, The Poodles, HammerFall*). They recorded the album *Truth*, which was a pretty weak effort. It also contained covers of *Frozen* (Madonna), *Let Me Entertain You* (*Queen*) and *Darling Nikki* (Prince). After the album, the band officially split, but did some gigs in the summer of 2001. Jeff, Pontus and Marcel later joined forces with drummer Thomas Broman (*Great King Rat, Send No Flowers, Norum* etc.), but now under the name *Humanimal*. The band released their outstanding album in 2002, an album in the vein and class of classic *Talisman* albums such as *Genesis* or *Humanimal*, but also "borrowing" a lot of riffs from classic hard rock bands like *Rainbow* and *Deep Purple*. A new *Talisman* live album was recorded in 2001, where the gig was almost cancelled due to Marcel forgetting his gear at a previous venue. However, the public demand to see *Talisman* was such that he borrowed gear from *HammerFall*'s Magnus Rosén and the show was even recorded for a live CD (with the guitars and bass being rerecorded afterwards, live in the studio). Unfortunately personal disagreements between Marcel and Pontus made the two go separate ways. To keep the *Talisman* saga going Marcel redrafted former guitarist Fredrik Åkesson and the band also used live guitarist Howie Simon, who had played on some of Jeff's solo material. The result was the album *Cats And Dogs*, another pretty solid, classic *Talisman* album. In 2005 the DVD *World's Best Kept Secret* was released. The band's seventh and final album was simply entitled *7*, but had the working title *BAR*, which stood for Bitter Angry Resentful, because of the members' current outlook on life. As on several of the other albums Marcel played bass and most of the rhythm guitars, with Fredrik only adding the solos. The album was mixed by Pontus Norgren, who also does a guest solo on the Japanese bonus track. Late 2006 Soto was drafted as the new singer of *Journey*. However he was out of the band within six months. July 21, 2009, Marcel Jacob, born January 30, 1964, tragically committed suicide. A new *Talisman* album was in the works. The previously unreleased track *Love's Gone* is found on the bonus CD for the first *Encyclopedia Of Swedish Hard Rock And Heavy Metal* (1996) and another previously unreleased track, *Rainbows End* with a unique line-up featuring Thomas Vikström on vocals and Tommy Denander on guitar, is featured on the bonus CD for the second encyclopedia in 2002.

Sweden's no 1 rock bass player - R.I.P

Marcel, letting the bass do the talking.

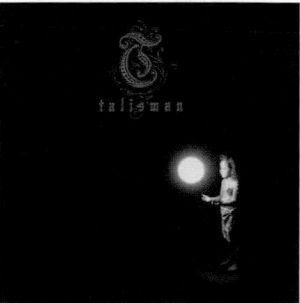

1990 LP - AR 5005

1990 7" - AR 3005

1990	☐ I'll Be Waiting	.........MCD 4tr	Airplay	AIRPRO 001
	Tracks: I'll Be Waiting/Standin' On Fire/Day By Day/Great Sandwich. Promo.			
1990	■ TALISMAN	.........LP	Airplay	AR 5005
1990	☐ TALISMAN	.........CD	Airplay	ARCD 5005
1990	■ I'll Be Waiting/Dangerous	.........7"	Airplay	AR 3005
	Also available with gatefold sleeve.			
1990	■ Just Between Us/Standin' On Fire	.........7"	Airplay	AR 3006
1993	☐ TALISMAN	.........CD	Dino	DINCD 21
	Bonus (live): Just Between Us/Eternal Flame/Scream Of Anger/NJBBWD/Let Me Love You/Ice Cream Man (John Brim/Van Halen cover)			
1993	☐ TALISMAN	.........CD	Zero (Japan)	XRCN-1040
1993	☐ TALISMAN	.........LP	Xero (Korea)	JRPL-5083

1990 7" - AR 3006

| 1993 | ☐ | GENESIS | CD | Dino | DINCD 20 |

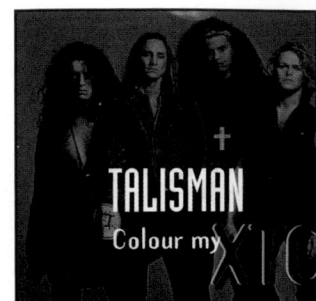

| 1993 | ☐ | GENESIS | CD | Zero (Japan) | XRCN-1039 |

Bonus: Run With The Pack (Bad Company cover)

1993	☐	Mysterious/All Or Nothing/Mysterious	MCD 3tr	Dino	DINCSG 20-1
1993	☐	Time After Time/Comin' Home	CDS 2tr	Dino	DINCSG 20-2
1994	☐	FIVE OUT OF FIVE - LIVE IN JAPAN	CD	Empire	ERCD 1002
1994	☐	FIVE OUT OF FIVE - LIVE IN JAPAN	CD	Zero (Japan)	XRCN-1095
1994	■	Colour my XTC/Blissful Garden/Hypocrite	MCDp 3tr	Empire	ERCDS 5-1
1994	■	Todo Y Todo	CDSp 1tr	Empire	ERCDS 5-2 $

Released under the name Genaro. 300 copies.

1994 MCDp - ERCDS 5-1

| 1994 | ☐ | HUMANIMAL | CD | Empire | ERCD 1005 |
| 1994 | ☐ | HUMANIMAL | CD | Zero (Japan) | XRCN-1122 |

The Japanese pressing contains different tracks.

| 1994 | ☐ | HUMANIMAL | CD | Polydor (Germany) | 523 329-2 |

Bonus: Hypocrite

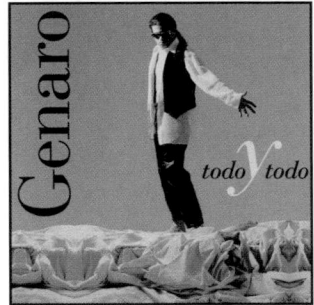

1994	☐	Doin' Time Wit' My Baby/Seasons/Humanimal	MCD 3tr	Polydor	855 303-2
1994	☐	Humanimal Part 2	MCD 7tr	Empire	ERCD 1011
1994	☐	HUMANIMAL PART 2	CD	Zero (Japan)	XRCN 1189

Contains different tracks than the European version, although the tracks on Humanimal and Part 2 are the same all in all. 16 tracks.

| 1995 | ☐ | All + All/Lonely World | CDS 2tr | Empire | ERCDS 1005-3 |
| 1995 | ☐ | LIFE | CD | Zero (Japan) | XRCN 1250 |

Bonus: How Was I 2 Know/Hands Of Time

1994 CDS - ERCDS 5-2

1995	☐	LIFE	CD	Empire	ERCD 1025
1995	☐	Crazy	CDS 1tr	Empire	ERCDS 1-1025
1996	☐	BESTERIOUS	CD	Xero (Japan)	XRCN-1274
1996	☐	BEST OF TALISMAN	CD	Empire	ERCD 1031

Contains nine previously unreleased tracks and demos, some featuring Göran Edman and some Jason Bieler.

| 1998 | ☐ | TRUTH | CD | Pony Canyon (Japan) | PCCY 01321 |

Bonus: T411/2

| 1999 | ☐ | TRUTH | CD | Empire | 10078 |
| 2002 | ☐ | TALISMAN | CD | FrontLine Rock (Brazil) | FLR 1001 |

Bonus: Women, Whiskey And Song/Great Sandwich/Under Fire/Open Your Eyes/Oceans

| 2002 | ☐ | GENESIS | CD | FrontLine Rock (Brazil) | FLR 1002 |

Bonus: Run With The Pack/U Done Me Wrong (demo) + Mysterious (video)

| 2002 | ☐ | HUMANIMAL | CD | FrontLine Rock (Brazil) | FLR 1004 |
| 2002 | ☐ | LIFE | CD | FrontLine Rock (Brazil) | FLR 1005 |

Bonus: How Was I 2 Know/Hands Of Time/Love's Gone

| 2003 | ☐ | CATS AND DOGS | CD | Frontiers | FRCD 146 |
| 2003 | ☐ | CATS AND DOGS | CD | King Records (Japan) | KICP-929 |

Bonus: Time

2005 2CD - RTCD 009

| 2004 | ☐ | TALISMAN | 2CD | GMR/Rock Treasures | RTCD 005 |

Bonus: Break Your Chains (demo)/Under Fire (demo)/If You Need Somebody (demo)/ Dangerous (demo)/Oceans (demo)/Lightning Strikes (demo)/Day By Day (demo)/NJBB-WO (demo)/Just Between Us (live)/Eternal Flame (live)/Scream Of Anger (live)/NJBBWO (live)/Let Me Love You (live)/Ice Cream Man (live). Slipcase.

| 2004 | ☐ | GENESIS | 2CD | GMR/Rock Treasures | RTCD 006 |

Slipcase. Diff tracklisting. Bonus CD with demo tracks: Time After Time/Comin' Home/U Done Mr Wrong/Give Me A Sign/Fighting For Your Life/Time After Time (demo)/Give Me A Sign (demo)/Angel/Lovechild (demo)/Rainbow's End (demo) + video of Mysterious. Slipcase.

| 2004 | ☐ | HUMANIMAL 1 & 2 | 2CD | GMR/Rock Treasures | RTCD 007 |

Slipcase.

| 2004 | ☐ | LIFE & FIVE OUT OF FIVE LIVE | 2CD | GMR/Rock Treasures | RTCD 008 |

Bonus: Tears In The Sky (demo)/ Sympathy (demo)/ Temptation (demo). Slipcase.

| 2004 | ■ | TRUTH + LIVE AT SWEDEN ROCK FESTIVAL | 2CD | GMR/Rock Treasures | RTCD 009 |

Bonus: Pavilion Of Oblivion/T 4 ½ /Heaven's Got Another Hero (demo)/Here 2day Gone 2morrow (demo). Slipcase.

2005	☐	FIVE MEN LIVE	2CD	Frontiers	FRCD 235
2006	☐	7	CD	Frontiers	FRCD 304
2006	☐	7	CD	King Records (Japan)	KICP-1205

2012 CDd - ASHPAB 1007

Bonus: Final Curtain

| 2012 | ☐ | TALISMAN – DELUXE EDITION | CDd | Sun Hill Production | ASHPAB 1006 |

Bonus: MJ solo + live tracks: Just Between Us/Eternal Flame/I'll Be Waiting/Scream Of Anger/NJBBWO/Standin' On Fire/Let Me Love You/Ice Cream Man

| 2012 | ■ | GENESIS – DELUXE EDITION | CDd | Sun Hill Production | ASHPAB 1007 |

Bonus: Give Me A Sign/Comin' Home/U Done Me Wrong/Time After Time

| 2012 | ☐ | LIVE IN JAPAN – DELUXE EDITION | CDd | Sun Hill Production | ASHPAB 1008 |
| 2012 | ☐ | HUMANIMAL – DELUXE EDITION | CDd | Sun Hill Production | ASHPAB 1009 |

17 tracks. Bonus: Hypocrite

Unofficial releases:

| 2007 | ■ | LOST GEMMS | CD-R | AOR Moon (Japan) | - - |

Bootleg featuring demos with various singers.

2007 CDR - - -

TALK OF THE TOWN

Thomas Vikström: v, Antonio Saluena: g, Tommy Denander: g

Stockholm - This is one of Sweden's early US-type AOR bands. They were originally formed in 1987 under the moniker **Scandinavian Dynamite** but when singer Tomas Vikström joined in 1988 they changed their name to **Talk Of The Town**. The line-up consisted of singer Thomas Vikström, guitarist Antonio Saluena, bassist Jonas Olsson, keyboardist Mats Jacobsson and drummer Staffan Scharin. The debut was certified gold and the album sold around 35 000 copies, which is very good in Sweden. They even had a hit with the song *Free Like An Eagle*. The band split in 1990 due to management problems. Tomas and Antonio reformed the band with Johan Kullberg on drums, Joachim Uddling on keyboards and Staffan Linder on bass, but in 1992 Tomas left to join **Candlemass**. He recorded the album *Chapter VI* and the 4 track CD *Sigge Fürst* with the band before he went solo. After Tomas left, Conny Lind took over, but they soon broke up. Conny was later in **State Of Mind, Raceway** and **Amaze Me**. Johan was later in **Lion's Share** and he also backs Tomas on his solo album. Jonas was ex-**ATC** and later backed pop/rocker Mikael Rickfors, Antonio played in a cover band, Staffan joined **Alien** in 1994 and Joachim was in dance/poppers **Suzz**. **Talk Of The Town** recorded a great second album that was never released. However negotiations were taking place. The 1999-release of *Talk Of The Town* is a reissue of the debut also featuring 2 previously unreleased tracks, four tracks from *Reach For The Sky* and two tracks from Vikströms solo release. Also playing on the *Talk Of The Town* 1999 release were drummer Johan Kullberg, bassist Staffan Linder and keyboardist Mats Olausson (**Yngwie, Motvind** etc). Former member Jonas Olsson was later on the Swedish TV show *Gladiators*, known as Titan. The last album featured various musicians besides Thomas and Antonio, such as guitarist Tommy Denander (who also wrote 90 % of the material), bassist Claes "Fille" Lindström (Benny Jansson, **Blacksmith**), drummer Anders Wetterström, keyboardist Mats Jacobsson and backing singer Geir Rönning (**Prisoner**). An OK attempt to resurrect the band.

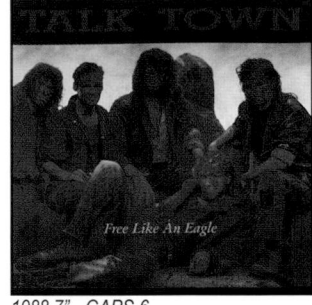

1988 7" - GAPS 6

1989 7" - GAPS 9

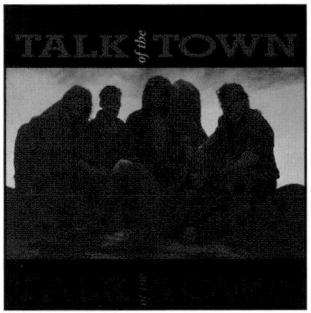

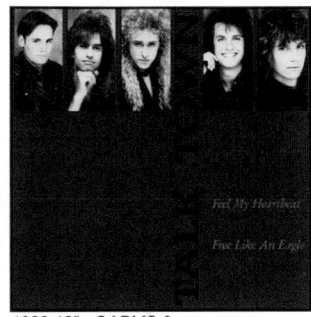

1988 LP - GAP 2

1989 12" - GAPMS 9

Year		Title	Format	Label	Cat. No.
1988	■	Free Like An Eagle/I Love The Look In Your Eyes	7"	Gap	GAPS 6
1988	■	TALK OF THE TOWN	LP	Gap	GAP 2
1988	□	TALK OF THE TOWN	CD	Gap	GAP 2
1989	■	Feel My Heartbeat/Sing To The World	7"	Gap	GAPS 9
1989	■	Feel My Heartbeat/Free Like An Eagle	12" 2tr	Gap	GAPMS 9
1989	□	Sing To The World/The Power inside	7"	Gap	GAPS 17
1999	■	REACH FOR THE SKY	CD	AOR Heaven	4018996 204612
1999	□	TALK OF THE TOWN	CD	Virgin	848046-2
2000	□	THE WAYS OF THE WORLD	CD	AOR Heaven	MSM CD 0137
2000	□	THE WAYS OF THE WORLD	CD	King Records (Japan)	KICP 748

Bonus: Father Of Your Sins

1999 CD - 4018996 204612

TANAQUE

Magnus Lindh: v, Anders Landin: g, Stefan "Steve" Persson: k,
Michael Fantel: b, Nicklas Tärnhamn: d

Jönköping - **Tanaque** were formed in 1985-86 and recorded a demo before the single. They also played the Hultsfred Festival and supported **It's Alive** before calling it a day in 1988. Landin had previously recorded a single with the band **X-Hale**. Lindh later joined folk-rock-punk band **Elvira**, Fantel played in a hard rock cover band, Stefan is a highly acclaimed monitor engineer and Tärnham moved to the US. Great melodic hard rock in the vein of **Alien** with great vocals. Well worth looking for.

Year		Title	Format	Label	Cat. No.
1987	■	Prove It To Ya/Not A Hero	7"	EZ REC	SNRS 021

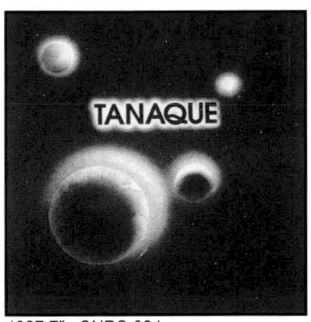

1987 7" - SNRS 021

TASTE

Patrik "Mojen" Järlefalk: v, Magnus Bureteg: g, Fredrik Larsson: g,
Mattias Håkansson: k, Pierre Petterson: k, Mattias Karlsson: b, Robert Kratz: d

Linköping - Pretty good melodic hard rock. Patrik, ex-**Paralyce**, is the brother of **Silverwings** singer Rikard Järlefalk and was later in cover band **Bröderna Åboys**.

Year		Title	Format	Label	Cat. No.
1990	■	Back To The Water/Time Heals All Wounds	7"	Studiefrämjandet	SFS 1790

1990 7" - SFS 1790

TATCH

Janne Andreasson: v, Rainer Fetcher: g, Hans Larsson: k,
Bo Magnusson: b, Lars Eliasson: d

Knippla/Hyppeln (Göteborg) - Melodic rockers **Tatch** were formed around 1975-76, originally as **Nirvana**. The basic line-up featured Rainer, Jan, Bo and Lars. The band landed a deal with Marcello Manci, spent a year recording an album in Vivaldi Studios. The single was released, after which Manci disappeared and the album never came out. 1985-86 the band folded. Janne

is the brother of pop singer Elisabeth Andreasson. Lars runs a studio in Alingsås. The single was produced by Bernard Löhr, who used to work with Björn and Benny of *ABBA* fame. Eliasson later reappeared in *Lothlorien*, *Crash* and *Born Electric*.

1984 ■ Listen To The Radio (Tonight)/She's A Miracle...................................7" VCM...VCMS 110
　　　　1000 copies.

1984 7" - VCMS 110

TAURUS
Per Lundqvist: v, Claes Colbin: g, Anders Lundqvist: k, Ola Colbin: b, Jerker Dahlén: d
Lidköping - Melodic hard rock with a poppy overtone. Could be described as a more AOR-ish version of *Magnum Bonum*. The second release saw an improvement in the vocal department.

1981 ■ Stanna Hela Natten/Efter Vinter Kommer Vår.................................7" Epic..1651
1982 □ Kärleksdrömmar/Franska Kort ....7" Epic..A 2472

TEAM CUSTARD
Magnus Alkarp: v/k, Tomas "Chappe" Lindh: g, Jocke Stoor: b, Jonas Stoor: d
Knutby - *Team Custard* were formed in 1985 out of the remains of the proggier band *Riskzon*. They recorded some demos, and the single track *Local Ulster* was actually an old *Riskzon* song which, through a friend of the band who brought it on cassette to Belfast, was used in a town rally and even got confiscated. The band originally wanted an Irish-sounding singer, but settled for Swede Magnus. However, the higher notes were sung by *Dalton/R.A.W* singer Bosse Lindmark. Magnus later became a renowned archaeologist and writer. He was replaced by Ove Eriksson who only recorded a couple of demos with the band before they disbanded in 1987. They were actually mostly known as *Custard*. Tomas later played with various cover bands and the band *Flame Fiddlers* together with Richard Sporrong and Mats Blomstrand (*Steve Eastside*). *Team Custard* play quite blues-based hard rock with a seventies touch.

1986 7" - ST 55-506

1981 7" - 1651

1986 ■ Loyal Ulster/Seven Blues...7" Studio 55...ST 55-506

TEAMWORK
Ivar Helenius: v/g, Stig Leyonberg: g, Alf Hagström: k,
Hans-Erik Hall: b, Kjell Andersson: d
Hassela - Formed in 1979 under the name *Freaks*, playing covers. They split and reunited in 1981 as *Teamwork*. They entered the Rock SM in 1982 (the same year *Europe* won). Quite meek melodic hard rock that lacks power. The band recorded several way better demos before they finally split in 1989. Strictly for collectors. Helenius also had his one-man band *One & Only*.

1983 ● Hesitation/Wonder ....7" Pang ....PSI 085
　　　　500 copies. No picture sleeve.

1983 7" - PSI 085

TEARS
Lars "Fubbe" Furberg: v, Jan Egil Bogvald: g, Janne Bark: g,
Kenneth Pettersson: b, Janne Blom: d
Katrineholm/Stockholm - *Tears* were formed in Katrineholm back in 1968, inspired by bands like *Small Faces*, *Stones* and *The Beatles*. The first line-up featured Lars Furberg, bassist Matti Vourinen, guitarist Eddi Eriksson, drummer Bengt Walter and Gunilla Ericsson on organ. The two latter quit around 1971 and the new drummer, Tompa Ericsson, was actually Gunilla's brother. He however quit in 1972, replaced by Hans Fogelberg. The first single was on the same label as *Alexander Lucas* and the style was very 60s and poppy with a slight touch of glam. The same goes for *King Of Clowns*. On the debut album they had adopted the style created by the likes of *Gary Glitter* and *The Sweet*. They are considered to be Sweden's first real glam-rock band. After the first album, Tompa returned, replacing his replacement, Hans Fogelberg. The second album, *Rocky-T*, was much heavier and more in the style of *The Sweet* during the *Sweet F.A.* period. After their 1975 tour Tomas and Eddi left the band, and then it was put on hold. In 1976 the band was resurrected. Now Lars and Matti found Norwegian replacements Jan-Egil Bogwald on vocals and guitar and Roald Olsen on drums. Their last LP *Romantic* (1976 Gazell) is a total pop album not worth noticing. Well, to be honest there's actually one good hard rocker entitled *Casablanca Friend* on it. In 1977 Matti left the band. They now brought in bassist Rolle Hermin and also guitarist Janne Bark. After a spring tour Rolle and Roald quit and drummer Janne Blom entered together with bassist Kenneth Pettersson. The band recorded the single *Too Big* and *Tonight, Tonight*, which was also released on the 1979 compilation *Swedish Tracks* (Sonet). After this the band changed their name to *The Radio* and became a pop/rock band. *The Radio* however later transformed in to hard

Swedish prime quality glam of the seventies

rockers *Deep Diver*. In 2000 *Tears* reformed with new bass player Tjaback Holmér and they are actually still alive and do gigs with make-up an all! An out-and-out retro-blast! The 2008 release is a compilation featuring a new rerecording of the track *Rocky-T*, but kinda leaves the feeling that some things should be left undone.

1972	○	Ditt Minne/Anywhere, Any Time, Any One	7"	Efel	SEF 77
		No artwork.			
1973	□	King Of Clowns/Dear Anne	7"	Gazell	C 273
1974	□	TEARS	LP	Gazell	GLP 500
1974	■	Ooh-lah/Messalina	7"	Gazell	C 282
1974	□	Stranger In Town/Ollie	7"	Gazell	C 286
1975	□	ROCKY T	LP	Gazell	GLP 502
1975	○	Raise My Mountain/I Don't Care	7"	Gazell	C 295
		No artwork.			
1976	□	ROMANTIC	LP	Sonet	GLP-503
1978	○	Tonight Tonight/Too Big	7"	Däft	DÄFT 5
		No artwork. Red vinyl.			
1995	□	TEARS	CD	Sonet	GLP 500/523 116-2
2008	□	1973-1978 - WE ALL LIKE MUSIC DON'T WE	CDd	Universal	06025 176562-2

1974 7" - C 282

TEARS OF ANGER

Björn Jansson: v, Benny Jansson: g, Johan Niemann: b, Daniel Flores: d

Stockholm - *Tears Of Anger* are one of many Swedish all-star bands. Formed in 2003 as a continuation on the Jansson brothers' band *Mindcrime*, who recorded some great demos. The Jansson brothers have earlier also recorded with *Two Rocks*, *Avenue*, *The Johansson Brothers*, *Snake Charmer* etc, Niemann is ex-*Therion* and *Mind's Eye*, now in *Evergrey* while Flores has played in/lead numerous bands like *Mind's Eye, Xsaviour, Crash The System, 7Days, The Murder Of My Sweet* etc. *Tears Of Anger* play quite excellent semi-progressive melodic metal, at times with a touch of later day's *Black Sabbath*. Björn sounds very similar to Jorn Lande.

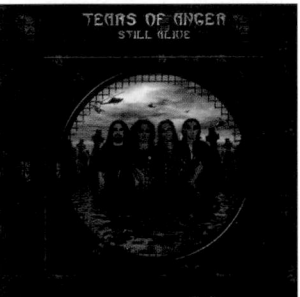

2004	■	STILL ALIVE	CD	Lion Music	LMC 99
2004	□	STILL ALIVE	CD	Avalon Marquee (Japan)	MICP-10443
2005	□	IN THE SHADOWS	CD	Avalon Marquee (Japan)	MICP-10569
2006	□	IN THE SHADOWS	CD	Lion Music	LMC 169

2004 CD - LMC 99

TEBLER, JENNIE

Jennie Tebler: v, Tomas "Quorthon" Forsberg: g/b/d

Stockholm - This was a project where Quorthon recorded the music for the song *Silverwing* in March 2004, only a few months before he died of a heart failure, and where his sister Jennie (ex-*Lake Of Tears*, also in *Jennie Tebler's Out Of Oblivion*) handled the vocals. The recording was then mixed by their father, Börje "Boss" Forsberg between September 2004 and January 2005. *Silverwing* is Jennie's dedication to her brother. The second single was written by Jennie and Kent Jädestam.

2005	■	Silverwing/Song To Hall Upon High	CDSd 2tr	Black Mark	BMDP 181
2006	□	Between Life And Death/Never Stop Crying	CDS	Black Mark	BMDPS 185

2005 CDSd - BMDP 181

TEJP

"Stabben" Wahlman: v/b, Inge Tillberg: g, Thomas Wretman: d

Stockholm - Straightforward hard rock with a touch of rock 'n' roll. Quite close to the first *Ocean* (Karlshamn) single. According to the book *Ny Våg*, the band only existed for the recording of the single. Tillberg later played with *Sky High* and Jukka Tolonen, while Wretman went all reggae.

1979	■	Tung rock/Sanningen	7"	private	A-001	$$

1979 7" - A-001

TEMPELROCK

Sten Tempelman: v/g, Björn Uhr: v/g,
Peter "PJ" Jägerhult: b/v, Werner Lindström: d/v

Stockholm - This is a lightweight hard rock band that could have been a lot heavier with a better production. At times they're quite close to a harder version of *Tom Robinson Band*, but with Swedish lyrics. Björn was ex-*Solid Ground* and later joined *Attack*. PJ was also in *Attack* and later in *Trash*. Sten later produced *Monaco Blues Band* among others and Werner has played in different pop acts.

1979	○	Det stora lyftet/Den första känningen	7"	Planet	MOP 115
		No artwork.			
1979	■	DET STORA LYFTET	LP	Planet	MOP 3009

1979 LP - MOP 3009

TEMPERANCE

Fredrik "Fredde" Erneroth: v/g, Johan "B-Häng" Erneroth: d

Frölunda - Started out in November 1988 as *No Remorse* and changed their name when Danne joined in May 1991. They recorded their first demo *Hypnoparatizt* in 1992. It sold 1500 copies. After the single Danne left and bass on the album was played by Malena Bengtsson, but she was not a permanent member. The band was very active as a live act and played in countries like Poland, Germany, Belgium, France, Slovenia and Lituania. Death metal with quite an untraditional sound, more in the thrash vein. Musically varies from uncontrolled hyper speed to slow doomy parts. The band is also featured on the compilations: *Appointment With Fear Vol 2* and the local *Café Kristina*.

1993 ■	One Grave	7"	Shiver Recrds	SHR 001
	Tracks: One Foot In The Grave/Left Inside. 1000 copies.			
1995 □	KRAPAKALJA	CD	Shiver Records	SHR 015
1999 □	With My Raincoat On/Homagen	7"	Stormbringer	SKULL 9804

1993 7" - SHR 001

TEMPTATION

John Newman: v/b, Pyngas: g, Steve Marlyn: k, Michael Elverson: d

AOR in the vein of early *Alien*, one ballad and one up-tempo track. Quite decent.

1989 ■	Farewell Song/(Prologue op 1) Just One Heart	7"	Platina	PL 53

1989 7" - PL 53

TEN 67

Bo "Ramone" Johander: v, Ina Jönsson: v, Lars Christmansson: g, Peter: b, Håkan "Ian" Haugland: v/d, Örjan "Dr Rock" Englin: d

Stockholm - *Ten 67* is a radio station and the single was a project featuring hosts on the radio station, which happened to be quite famous musicians like Haugland (*Europe*) and Örjan Englin (*Hiroshima, Dust*). The song, which is a really good, solid *Kiss*-style hard rocker, was co-written by Tommy Denander. Lars is also found in *Lion's Share* and *Road II Ruin*.

2003 ■	Rock 'N Roll Alright/Interview	CDSp	Canvas	Canvas 101

2003 CDSp - Canvas 101

TEN FOOT POLE

Lasse Holmgren: v, Jan Sandberg: g/h, Kenneth Olsson: b, Jonas Hollsén: d

Västerås - Straightforward, heads-down, no-nonsense hard rock in the true *AC/DC* vein. Not particularly exciting, but worth investigating. A new album was due to be released in 1996. The demo says "A Band Formerly Known As Ten Foot Pole". The band later changed their name to *Bullhorn* and released the album *(Ladish)* in 1996. Lasse was later found in *G.S.O.*

1994 ■	IN TOO DEEP	CD	Megarock Records	MRRCD 010

1994 CD - MRRCD 010

TENCIDER

Thomas Olofsson: v/g, Leif Starck: g, Morgan Mathiasson: b, Tony Johansson: d

Kungälv - *Tencider* were a young band playing rocking hard rock. Quite amateurish and with quite unexciting and very "Swedish" vocals. The band changed its name to *Crazy Vision* and released four more singles in the eighties, before changing into pop/disco act *Tiffany*. For collectors only.

1979 ■	I Was Lonely/Queen Of Love	7"	Bohus	GBS 527

1979 7" - GBS 527

TENEBRE

Kalle Metz: v, Michael Körner: g, Richard Lion: g/b, Ivana Baukart: k, Jenny Landt: b, Andreas Albihn: d

Malmö - The band was formed by former *Flegma* colleagues Kalle Metz and Richard Lion. The name came from an Italian movie. *Tenebre* started out playing ultra-heavy metal, a bit like *Motörhead*-meet-*Slayer* and with slightly death-ish vocals. Heavy as Hell! The song *No Wrong* on the *Cult Leader* EP was written by Charles Manson. Drummer Joel Linder (*Pole Position*) was later replaced by Andreas (*Embraced*). In 2000 guitarist Lukas Sunesson (now Lanerö) (ex-*Booze Brothers*, now *The Itch*) was replaced by Franco Bollo (*Funhouse*). *Mark Ov The Beast* features singer Kalle Metz, guitarists Fredrik Täck and Franco Bollo, keyboardist Henrik Larsson, bassist Richard Lion and drummer Andreas Albihn. In 2001 singer Kalle Metz quit and was replaced by *Dawn Of Oblivion*-singer Victor Fradera. Next up, Franco quit and was replaced by Peter Mårdklint (ex-*Embraced*). *Electric Hellfire Kiss* is a very goth-oriented metal album. The band is also known for their wild live show including strippers.

1996 CD - RHCD 3

Mark… features guest spot from Italian doom master Steve Sylvester (**Death SS**). In 2005 the band returned with a new album, a new line-up and a new sound. Ivana was also in **Misteltein**. The song *Buried And Forgotten* is found on the compilation *Angel Child III: Belief In Angels* (1998 M&A Musicart). Richard is today playing in punksters **Wolfsblood**.

1996	■	XIII	CD	Record Heaven	RHCD 3
1996	□	XIII	CD	Soundholic (Japan)	SHCD1-0013

Bonus: Not Fragile (Bachman Turner Overdrive cover)

1996	□	Haloween EP	MCD 4tr	Record Heaven	RHCDM 2

Tracks: I, Halloween II (Misfits cover), Dead But Dreaming (unreleased version), Rites Of Passage (unreleased version).

1997	□	Cult Leader	MCD 3tr	Record Heaven	RHCDM 3

Tracks: No Wrong/Skullfuck/Taste My Sin

1998	□	GRIM RIDE	CD	Record Heaven	RHCD10
1998	□	XIII	LP PD	Record Heaven	RECPD 1
1999	□	Tombola Voodoo Master	7"	Primitive Art	PAR 019
2001	■	MARK OV THE BEAST	CD	Regain Records	RR 0010-009
2001	□	MARK OV THE BEAST	CD	CD Maximum (Russia)	CDM 1003-1508
2002	□	Descend From Heaven	MCD 4tr	Regain Records	RR 0209-014

Tracks: Descend From Heaven/Crimson Beast/It's A Sin/In Xanadu

2002	■	ELECTRIC HELLFIRE KISS	CD	Regain Records	RR 0209-015
2002	□	ELECTRIC HELLFIRE KISS	CD	CD-Maximum (Russia)	CDM 0903-1493
2005	□	HEARTS BLOOD	CD	Regain	RR 082
2006	□	HEARTS BLOOD	CD	Candlelight (USA)	CDL0149CD
2006	□	HEARTS BLOOD	CD	CD-Maximum (Russia)	CDM 1006-2609

2001 CD - RR 0010-009

2002 CD - RR 0209-015

TENSION

Johnny Söderkvist: v, Peter Nilsson: g, Magnus Eriksson: k, Radis Davis: b, Christer Wolfbrandt: d

Kungälv - The band was formed in 1986 and split three years later. Their song *Let Me Out* was discovered by Tomas Erdtman (**Europe**'s manager), who promised them stardom... just before they broke up. Christer was later in cover band **Funfair**.

1988	■	Running Away/Fantasy	7"	Triangle	TKIS 8805

Running away

1988 7" - TKIS 8805

TERRA FIRMA

Christian "Chritus" Lindersson: v, Fredrik "Freddie Eugene" Lindgren: g, Nico "Moosebach" Elgstrand: b, Izmo "Ledderfejs" Hedlund: d

Stockholm - In 1995, when Freddie had left **Unleashed** and Christian (**Count Raven, Lord Vicar**) was out of **Saint Vitus**, they formed **Terra Firma**. The subsequent year, they recorded the demo *Rock 'N Roll Superior* that was soon picked up and released as a 7" by Freedom Records. The band's style is pretty close to **Monster Magnet**, **Kyuss** etc. Stoner rock with strong **Black Sabbath**-like overtones, especially Christian's Ozzy-ish vocals. The song *For A Thousand Mothers* is a cover of **Jethro Tull**. Nico is today found in **Entombed**, Izmo and Fredrik in **Atlantic Tide** and Lindersson in **Lord Vicar**.

1998 7" PD - TMC 19

1996	□	Rock 'N Roll Superior	7"	Freedom	FRED702

Tracks: Rainbow Ride/In Orbit

1997	□	Terra Firma/Godscent	7"	Clear Blue Sky	SKY 001

Split with Godscent. Track: Fifth Wheel

1998	■	Spiral Guru/For A Thousand Mothers	7" PD	The Music Cartel (USA)	TMC-19
1998	□	TERRA FIRMA	CD	Steamhammer/SPV	SPV 80000175
1999	□	TERRA FIRMA	CD	Nippon Crown (Japan)	CRCL 4718

Bonus: Sunshine Of Your Love (Cream cover)

1999	□	TERRA FIRMA	CD	The Music Cartel (USA)	TMC 19CD
2001	■	HARMS WAY	CD	Steamhammer/SPV	SPV 085-72322
2001	□	HARMS WAY	LP PD	Sway Records	SR 01

2001 CD - SPV 085-72322

TERRA TENEBROSA

The Cuckoo, Hibernal, Risperdal

Luleå - The band was formed by two of the members from the ashes of post-core band **Breach**, but were using masks to keep their identities under wraps, a bit like **Ghost**. *Terra Tenebrosa* means "the dark earth". The band plays dark, quite abstract, ambient and highly experimental metal with strange whispering vocals. At times it's almost drone-style metal with strange noises. Just plain weird, if you ask me.

2011	■	THE TUNNELS	CD	Trust No One	TNO 037
2011	□	THE TUNNELS	2LPg	Trust No One	TNO 037 LP

100 clear + 400 black vinyl.

2011 CD - TNO 037

TERROR 2000

Björn "Speed" Strid: v/b, Klas Ideberg: g, Nicklas "Nick Sword" Svärd: g, Dan Svensson: b, Erik Thyselius: d

Helsingborg - The band, or actually project, was founded in 1999 by Björn (*Soilwork, Darkane, Dog Faced Gods*) and Klas (*Darkane, Defaced, Hyste'riah G.B.C*), initially named *Killing Machine*. The debut was produced by Pelle Saether at Studio Underground. On the second album drummer Henry Ranta (*Soilwork*) was replaced by Erik Thyselius (*Construcdead, Arize, Face Down, Scarpoint*). The band returned to Studio Underground and Pelle Saether when recording the debut. The band plays tight, heavy, high-speed and uncompromising thrash/power metal, at times similar to *At The Gates* and early *The Haunted*. Highly recommended. By the way, listen to the fading of the track *Infernal Outlaw*... On *Terror For Sale* Björn left the bass playing to new player Dan Svensson (*Hearts Alive*), to concentrate on singing.

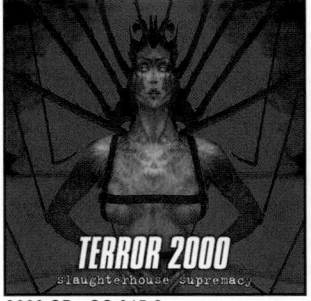

2000 CD - SC 015-2

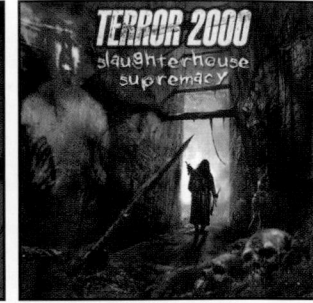

2003 CD - CDM 0303-1334

2000	☐	SLAUGHTERHOUSE SUPREMACY	CD	Soundholic (Japan)	TCFK 77029
		Bonus: The Persuaders Theme			
2000	■	SLAUGHTERHOUSE SUPREMACY	CD	Scarlet	SC 015-2
2000	☐	SLAUGHTERHOUSE SUPREMACY	CD	Pavement (USA)	32357
2000	☐	SLAUGHTERHOUSE SUPREMACY	LP PD	Scarlet	SC 015-1
2002	☐	SLAUGHTERHOUSE SUPREMACY	CD	Scarlet	SC 059-2
		Bonus: The Persuaders Theme/Mental Machinery (live). New artwork.			
2003	■	SLAUGHTERHOUSE SUPREMACY	CD	CD-Maximum (Russia)	CDM 0303-1334
2002	☐	FASTER DISASTER	CD	Scarlet	SC 047-2
2002	☐	FASTER DISASTER	CD	Nuclear Blaster (USA)	NB 1012-2
2002	☐	FASTER DISASTER	CD	Soundholic (Japan)	TKCS-85028
2003	☐	SLAUGHTER IN JAPAN LIVE	CD	Scarlet	SC 076-2
2004	☐	SLAUGHTER IN JAPAN LIVE	CD	Soundholic (Japan)	TKCS-85084
2005	■	TERROR FOR SALE	CD	Scarlet	SC 109-2
		Bonus: Dishwasher Demon			
2005	☐	TERROR FOR SALE	CD	Nuclear Blast (USA)	NB 1647-2
2005	☐	TERROR FOR SALE	CD	Mystic Empire (Russia)	MYST CD 291

2005 CD - SC 109-2

TERRORAMA

Peter Lidén: v, Emil Åström: b, Petter Nilson: g, Mikael Zetterberg: d

Norrköping - Formed in 2001. In 2002 they recorded the demo *Misanthropic Genius* and in 2003 the two-track demo *Promoting The Orthodox*. High-speed, evil death thrash metal. Åström is also in *Bloodride* and *Forgotten Words*. Peter Lidén also runs I Hate Records. In 2006 the demo *The Cleansing* was recorded. In 2008 drummer Petri Pöllänen was replaced by Zetterberg (*Spetälsk, Forgotten Words*).

2004	☐	HORRID EFFACE	CD	Nuclear War Now!	ANTI-GOTH 018
2004	☐	HORRID EFFACE	LPg	Nuclear War Now!	ANTI-GOTH 018
2004	☐	HORRID EFFACE	LP PD	Nuclear War Now!	ANTI-GOTH 018
		200 copies.			
2008	■	OMNIPOTENCE	CD	Nuclear War Now!	ANTI-GOTH 102
2008	☐	OMNIPOTENCE	LP	Nuclear War Now!	ANTI-GOTH 102
		Poster.			
2009	☐	Conceived In Abhorrence (split)	MLP	Nuclear War Now!	ANTI-GOTH 166
		Split with Adorior. Tracks: Conceived In Abhorrence/Of The Three Gunas Tamas (cover of Graf Spee). Gold vinyl. Sew-on patch.			
2012	■	Terrorama/Death Storm (split)	7" flexi post card	To The Death Records	- -
		Split with Death Storm. Promo. Track: Genocide			
2012	■	GENOCIDE	CD	To The Death Records	TTD 014
2012	☐	GENOCIDE	LP	To The Death Records	TTD 014
		200 green, 100 black + postcard flexi			

2008 CD - ANTI-GOTH 102

2013 7" flexi postcard - - -

TERRORTORY

Johan Norström: v, Stefan Vidmark: g, Olov Häggmark: b, Tommy Nilsson: d

Skellefteå/Umeå - *Terrortory* were formed in 2000 by Norström (on bass and vocals), guitarist Michael Bergvall and Vidmark (*Nightscape, December Child*), influenced by *Opeth* and *Dark Tranquillity*. The original drummer left to play pop, and Peter Hägglund (cousin of Benny Hägglund of *Vintersorg/Fission*) joined. In 2004 Johan wanted to concentrate on singing, and bass player Olov Häggmark was drafted. The band recorded the first self-titled demo in 2005 and a second, *One Dead Morning*, in 2006. Late summer of 2006 Bergvall left and was replaced by Marcus Olofsson (*Searing I*). Before the first official album, Tommy Nilsson replaced drummer Hägglund. Heavy death metal with lots of various influences from the chugging guitars of *Pantera* or *Meshuggah* to the symphonic touch of *Opeth* and the harmony guitars of *Dark Tranquillity*. A very versatile, great-sounding band. The track *Reason* was featured on the compilation *Hard Rock & Metal Edition Vol. 2* (2004 NLP, NLPCD 040).
Website: *www.terortory.com*

2011 CDd - MMI17/TER001

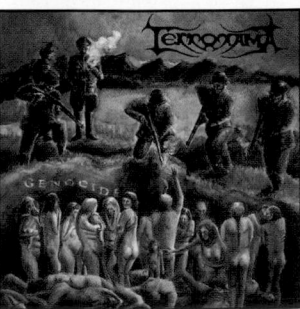

2012 CD - TTD 014

2011	■	THE SEED LEFT BEHIND	CDd	Discouraged Records	MMI17/TER001

TEXAS EGO

Torbjörn Enberg: v/b, Johnny Pettersson: g, Patrik Sjölund: d

Karlstad - Two of the tracks are straightforward garagey rocking metal, a bit like mixing *The Hellacopters* and *Motörhead*, while one has a bit of sleaze thrown in for good measure. Decent.

2002 ■ Blowout ....MCD 3tr private .... - -
    Tracks: Blowout/Crowd Of Fools/Fear No Pain

2002 MCD - - -

THALAMUS

Kjell Bergendahl: v/g, Mats Gesar: g, Joachim Åslund: k,
Peter Johansson: b, Sebastian Olsson: d

Borlänge - *Thalamus* (the main part of the middle brain) were formed in 2006 by Bergendahl (*Kjell-Ronnys Poporkester, Lavskäggä*), Sebastian and Janne Cederlund. The two latter came from power metal band *Cryonic Temple*. Only a month after, they found bassist Peter (ex-*Lavskäggä*). The band recorded an outstanding demo in 2006, and was soon picked up by American riff rock label Grooveyard, who released the debut, produced by Pelle Saether. Janne Stark (*Overdrive, Mountain Of Power, Constancia* etc) does a guest solo. *Beneath A Dying Sun* is an outstanding slab of heavy, groovy seventies-influenced riffy hard rock with a touch of stoner. After the album keyboard player Håkan Danielsson joined. The band played several shows and festivals before again entering the studio. In 2010 guitarist Cederlund (now in *Sky of Rage*) was replaced by Gesar and keyboardist Danielsson by Åslund. As a taster for the second album, the band released their self-financed MCD *Sign Here For Nothing* and was later picked up by Transubstans Records. With some new flavours added, *Subterfuge* is still just more of the same great riff rock. Bergendahl is also found in progsters *Renaissance Of Fools*, and he adds guest vocals and guitar on the second *Mountain Of Power* album. *Soul* was produced by Daniel Bergstrand and takes the band even a step further. In 2013 Magnus Karlsson (*Renaissance Of Fools, Leech*) replaced Sebastian. The jewelbox version of *Subterfuge* is a bootleg. *Website: www.thalamusband.com*

2008 CDd - GYR 047

2013 CDd - TRANS 104

Year		Title		Format	Label	Cat. no.
2008	■	BENEATH A DYING SUN		CDd	Grooveyard Records	GYR 047
2010	□	Sign Here For Nothing		MCDd 5tr	Scoj	SM 001

    Tracks: Hope You Understand/Breathe Easy/Black Day Sunday/New Age Blues/Early Morning Leave

Year		Title		Format	Label	Cat. no.
2011	□	SUBTERFUGE		CDd	Transubstans	TRANS 085
2013	■	SOUL		CDd	Transubstans	TRANS 104

THEE EXPRESSION

Frederik Groove: v, Conleth Hanlon: g, Karl Baker: b, Niklas Kilenstam: d

Lund - With a big dose of the 70s and bands like *MC5*, *Blue Cheer* and *The Stooges,* this band rolls on like a stoned bulldozer. Retro-oriented heavy psychedelia at large. Looking at the cover it could've been recorded back then as well.

1991 ■ Feel It/I'm So Tired...7" Ceilidh Productions............................CEI 020

1991 7" - CEI 020

THEORY IN PRACTICE

Henrik Ohlsson: v/d, Peter Sjöberg (now Lake): g,
Mattias Engstrand: b/k, Patrik Sjöberg: d

Sandviken - Formed in 1995 by guitarist Peter Sjöberg, bassist/keyboardist Mattias Engstrand and drummer Henrik Ohlsson from the ashes of *Rivendell* and *Legia*. Former *Incantation* singer/guitarist Johan Ekman was soon added, but only lasted for one album, after which Daniel Bryntse (*Sorcery, Withered Beauty, Isole, Ereb Altor* etc) did a short stint with the band. On the second album Henrik had taken over the vocals as well as the drums. Their '96 debut demo *Submissive* was highly praised and they were signed by Singaporian label Pulverized Records. Musically the band produces technical death metal with a strong touch of *Meshuggah*. The debut album was recorded by Tomas Skogsberg at Sunlight Studios, while the follow-up was created at The Abyss with Tommy Tägtgren at the helm. Peter and Henrik are also found in *Mutant*. Patrik Sjöberg (Peter's brother, also in *Azotic Reign*) was added to the line-up on the latest album and now plays with *Terminal Conspiracy*. They do a surprising cover of *Sparks'* *This Town Ain't Big Enough For The Both Of Us* on *Colonizing The Sun*.

2000 CD - ASH 009 CD

1997 CD - ASH 003 CD

2002 CD - POSH 035

Year		Title		Format	Label	Cat. no.
1997	■	THIRD EYE FUNCTION		CD	Pulverized	ASH 003 CD
1999	■	THE ARMAGEDDON THEORIES		CD	Pulverized	ASH 009 CD
2000	□	THE ARMAGEDDON THEORIES		CD	Listenable Records	POSH 020
2000	□	THE ARMAGEDDON THEORIES		CD	Soundholic (Japan)	SHCD1-0036
2002	■	COLONIZING THE SUN		CD	Listenable Records	POSH 035
2005	□	THE ARMAGEDDON THEORIES		CD	CD-Maximum (Russia)	CDM 1004-2032
2005	□	COLONIZING THE SUN		CD	CD-Maximum (Russia)	CDM 1004-2034
2006	□	THIRD EYE FUNCTION		CD	Listenable Records	POSH 081

    Bonus: Submissive/Inexplicable Nature/Self Alteration. New artwork.

THERION
Thomas Vikström: v, **Christofer Johnsson:** g/k, **Christian Vidal:** g,
Nalle Påhlsson: b, **Johan Kullberg:** d

Uppland Väsby/Stockholm - It all started back in 1987 in Upplands Väsby, when bassist/ singer Christofer formed the thrash-oriented band *Blitzkrieg* (not the UK band). Guitarist Peter Hansson and drummer Oskar Forss completed the band, which only lasted for a couple of gigs before breaking up. In 1988 Christofer switched to guitar and formed *Megatherion* (taken from a song by *Celtic Frost*). Peter and Oskar joined and so did former *Dismember* bassist Erik Gustafsson. After a while the name was shortened to *Therion*. The band's first 3-track demo was entitled *Paroxysmal Holocaust* also featured singer Matti Kärkki (later in *Carbonized, Carnage, Dismember*). On the second 3-track demo, *Beyond The Darkest Veils Of Inner Wickedness*, Matti was out. This line-up also recorded the first MLP, *Time Will Tell*, originally meant to be just a demo. The MLP was supposed to be printed in 1000 copies, but another 1000 were printed without the band's consent. On the second album Erik was out of the band, as he had to move back to the US, leaving Christofer to handle the bass again. The lyrical content had now also changed and taken on subjects of mysticism and occultism. On *Symphony Masses...* Peter and Oscar had to leave for health and family reasons, and were replaced by drummer Piotr Wawrzeniuk (ex-*Carbonized*, later in *Serpent, Entombed*), guitarist Magnus Barthelsson and bassist Andreas Wahl (*Hexenhaus*), both ex-*Formicide*. The first album is death metal while on the second album they've slowed down and added influences from *Black Sabbath*. Now Magnus and Andreas left the band and the '95 releases showed a completely new line-up featuring Christofer Johnsson, now handling vocals, guitar and keyboards, bassist Fredrik Isaksson and drummer Piotr Wawrzeniuk, as well as a more experimental side of the band, with the use of strings, soprano vocals and other oddities in this genre. The music was also more experimental and influenced by Persian and classical music, with more melodies, quite far from the previous death metal. Tommy Ericsson was hired as second guitarist live and with Isaksson having problems touring, Lars Rosenberg was hired as a session bassist. *Lepaca Kliffoth* was produced by Harris Johns (*Sodom, Tankard, Kreator*) and contains a cover of the old *Celtic Frost*-tune *Sorrows Of The Moon*. On *Lepaca Kliffoth* soprano Klaudia Maria Mohri (*Celtic Frost*) is guesting. Christofer also had a short break from *Therion* to tour and record the album *Underground* ('94 Noise) and the CDS *The Ballad Of Jesus* with Swiss metallurgists *Messiah*. He can also be found in the band *Carbonized*. Count Grisnackh from Norwegian black metal band *Burzum* swore to kill Christofer and a girl saying she was the count's girlfriend even tried to burn down his house. The reason... "Christofer was not a true Satanist"... I don't even dare to comment on that... Magnus Barthelsson was later found in the more grunge-influenced band *Grain*. In late 1995 Jonas Mellberg, formely of *Unanimated* joined on guitar and Tobbe Sidegård, also guitarist in *Necrophobic*, played keyboards. Piotr and Lars were also found in the band *Serpent*, who was signed to Radiation Records late 1995. A previously unreleased version of *The Desert Of Set* can be found on the bonus CD for the first encyclopedia. *Theli* was recorded featuring Christofer, Jonas, Tobbe, Lars and Piotr. Dan Swanö also added some guest vocals.

In 1996 Jonas Mellberg left during a recording and was given the boot and Piotr left because of studies. *Theli* was the band's breakthrough album. A couple of tours followed, but problems with drugs and alcohol resulted in some member changes. *A'arab Zaraq Lucid Dreaming* is a compilation featuring previously unreleased tracks, the soundtrack from *The Golden Embrace* and covers of songs by *Judas Priest, Iron Maiden, Running Wild* and *Scorpions*. On *Vovin Therion* was more Christofer's solo project using musicians like guitarist Tommy Ericsson, singer Martina Hornbacher (*Dreams Of Sanity*), drummer Wolf Simon, bassist Jan Kazda, while Ralph Scheepers (*Primal Fear*) sings on one track, too, plus Sarah from *Cradle Of Filth* helps out with the female vocals. Now Christofer was actually alone without a band. He hired some musicians such as Jan Kazda and Wolf Simons for *Vovin*, which was even more classically influenced and not as doomy as the previous albums. The band now toured using drummer Sami Karppinen and he was offered a place in the band. *Crowning Of Atlantis* contains covers of *Crazy Nights* (*Loudness*), *Thor* (*Manowar*), *Seawinds* (*Accept*), besides three live tracks and some new originals. *Deggial* saw a new line-up featuring Christofer, guitarist Kristian Niemann, bassist Johan Niemann (*Afterglow, Mind's Eye*, now *Evergrey*) and drummer Sami Karpinen. *Secret Of The Runes* had twice the budget of *Theli*, but then Christofer also uses Russian musicians, choirs etc. After the album, Sami left for work reasons and the spot was filled by Rickard Evensand (*It's Alive*, now in *Toehider*). The new line-up recorded the live album, *Live In Midgard*. As the band had enough material to fill three albums, two albums were recorded at once, *Lemuria* and *Sirius B*, released separately and as a double pack. This time Christofer was also using over 170 musicians to fulfil his musical goal. At the same time the Niemann brothers launched their *Demonoid* project. After the album Evensand quit to pursue his other projects and was replaced by Petter Karlsson (*HoloCoaster*). On the 2004-2005 tours Petter handled the drums and Mats Levén was the band's lead singer. *Atlantis Lucid Dreaming* was a compilation featuring B-sides. In 2006 Christofer quit singing. The lyrics were, and have been since the eighties, written by Thomas Karlsson, who has also released some books dedicated to the mysteries and myths of *Therion*. In 2006 the band added drummer/singer Tommy "Snowy Shaw" Helgesson as session singer. The album *Gothic Kabbalah* features Christofer, Johan and Kristian Niemann, drummer/

Back when time should tell...

In the days of Vovin.

singer Petter and the vocals were handled by Mats Levén, Snowy Shaw, Katarina Lilja, Anna Nyhlin and Hannah Holgersson. In 2008 the band and Christofer parted ways. In July 2010 Snowy Shaw left the band to become **Dimmu Borgir**'s new bassist, but he returned to **Therion** more or less as the news was released. The 2010 album, *Sitra Ahra* features Christofer, singer Thomas Vikström (**Candlemass, Stormwind, Talk Of The Town**), guitarist Christian Vidal, bassist Nalle Påhlsson (**Treat, Zan Clan** etc) and drummer Johan "Koleberg" Kullberg (**Talk Of The Town, Lion's Share**). In 2011 opera singer Lori Lewis became a permanent member of the band. Recordings of a new album cemmenced in 2012. A cover of *The King* can be found on *A Tribute To Accept* ('99 Nuclear Blast) and *Polar Nights* on *A Tribute To Scorpions* ('00 Nuclear Blast). *Les Fleurs Du Mal*, which only contains renditions of composers like France Gall, Léonie, and Serge Gainsbourg was released for the band's 25-year anniversary, at first as a special version released by the band, and only sold at shows. The band then decided to take some time off, as Christofer is working on a real rock opera. Snowy Shaw left the band before *Les Fleurs Du Mal*, to concentrate on his own projects, but has still made some shows with the band.
Website: www.megatherion.com

1990 MLP - HOK LP 001   1991 LP - DEAF 6 LP

Year		Title	Format	Label	Catalog	
1990	■	Time Shall Tell	MLP 4tr	H.O.K	HOK LP 001	$

Tracks Time Shall Tell/Dark Eternity/Asphyxiate With Fear/A Suburb To Hell 2000 copies.

1991	■	OF DARKNESS	LP	Deaf Records	DEAF 6 LP	
1991	□	OF DARKNESS	CD	Deaf Records	DEAF 6 CD	
1991	□	OF DARKNESS	CD	Grindcore Records	GC 89808-2	
1991	□	OF DARKNESS	CD	Avanzada Metalica (Mexico)	AMCD 107	
1992	□	BEYOND SANCTORUM	CD	Active Records	CDATV 23	
1992	□	BEYOND SANCTORUM	LP	Active Records	LPATV 23	
1993	□	SYMPHONY MASSES: HO DRAKON HO MEGAS	LP	Megarock Records	MRR 002	
1993	□	SYMPHONY MASSES: HO DRAKON HO MEGAS	CD	Megarock Records	MRR 002	
1993	□	SYMPHONY MASSES: HO DRAKON HO MEGAS	CD	Pavement Records (USA)	76962-32205-2	
1993	□	SYMPHONY MASSES: HO DRAKON HO MEGAS	CD	Toy's Factory (Japan)	TFCK 88770	

Bonus: Enter The Voids/Symphony Of The Dead (demo)/Beyond Sanctorum (demo)

1995 LP - NB 127-1

| 1995 | □ | The Beauty In Black | MCD 4tr | Nuclear Blast | NB 125-2 | $ |

Tracks Arrival Of The Darkest Queen/The Beauty In Black/Evocation Of Vovin/The Veil Of The Golden Spheres. 12 000 copies.

1995	□	LEPACA KLIFFOTH	CD	Megarock Records	MRR 029	
1995	■	LEPACA KLIFFOTH	LP	Nuclear Blast	NB 127-1	
1995	□	LEPACA KLIFFOTH	CD	Nuclear Blast	NB 127-2	
1995	□	LEPACA KLIFFOTH	CD	Nuclear Blast (USA)	NB 6127-2	
1995	□	LEPACA KLIFFOTH	CD	Toy's Factory (Japan)	TFCK 88761	

Bonus: The Veil Of Golden Spheres

| 1996 | □ | Siren Of The Woods | MCD 3tr | Nuclear Blast | NB 178-2 | |

Tracks: Siren Of The Woods/Cult Of Shadow(edit)/Babylon (non-CD)

1996	■	THELI	CD	Nuclear Blast	NB 179-2	
1996	□	THELI	CD	Spurk (Russia)	- -	
1996	□	THELI	CD	Nuclear Blast America (USA)	NBA 6179-2	
1998	□	THELI	LP PD	Nuclear Blast	NB 179-9	
1996	□	THELI	CD	Toy's Factory (Japan)	TFCK-88790	

1996 CD - NB 179-2

Bonus: In Remembrance/Black Fairy/Fly To The Rainbow (Scorpions cover)

| 1996 | □ | LEPACA KLIFFOTH SPECIAL EDITION | CD | Nuclear Blast | NB 216-2 | |

Bonus: Enter The Voids/The Veil Of Golden Spheres

1996	□	LEPACA KLIFFOTH SPECIAL EDITION	CD	Nuclear Blast America (USA)	NBA 6216-2	
1997	□	SYMPHONY MASSES: HO DRAKON HO MEGAS	LP PD	Megarock Records	CPD 005	
1997	■	A'ARAB ZARAQ LUCID DREAMING	CD	Nuclear Blast	NB 249-2	
1997	□	A'ARAB ZARAQ LUCID DREAMING	CDd	Nuclear Blast	NB 249-2	
1997	□	A'ARAB ZARAQ LUCID DREAMING	CD	Nuclear Blast America (USA)	NBA 6249-2	
1998	□	VOVIN	CD	Nuclear Blast	NB 317-2	
1998	□	VOVIN	CD	Nuclear Blast America (USA)	NBA 6317-2	
1998	□	VOVIN	CDd	Nuclear Blast	NB 317-2DP	
1998	□	VOVIN	LP PD	Nuclear Blast	NB 317-9	
1998	□	VOVIN	LP	Nuclear Blast	NB 317-1	
1998	□	VOVIN	CD	Metal Mind (Poland)	MASS CD 0550	
1998	□	VOVIN	CD	Toy's Factory (Japan)	TCFK-87160	

1997 CD - NB 249-2

Bonus: Crazy Nights (Loudness cover)

| 1998 | □ | Eye Of Shiva | MCD 4tr | Nuclear Blast | NB 345-2 | |

Tracks: Eye Of Shiva (radio)/Birth Of Venus Illegitima/The Rise Of Sodom And Gomorrah/ Eye Of Shiva.. Limited radio promo edition.

1999	□	CROWNING OF ATLANTIS	CD	Nuclear Blast	NB 398-2	
1999	□	CROWNING OF ATLANTIS	CDd	Nuclear Blast	NB 398-2	
1999	□	CROWNING OF ATLANTIS	CD	Nuclear Blast America (USA)	NBA 6398-2	
2000	□	LEPACA KLIFFOTH	CDd	Nuclear Blast	NB 216-2	

Bonus: The Veil Of Golden Spheres

| 2000 | ■ | DEGGIAL | CD | Nuclear Blast | NB 442-2 | |
| 2000 | □ | DEGGIAL | CDd | Nuclear Blast | NB 442-9 | |

With special velvet cover

| 2000 | □ | DEGGIAL | CD | Toy's Factory (Japan) | TFCK 87208 | |

2000 CD - NB 442-2

Bonus: To Mega Therion (live)/The Wings Of The Hydra (live)/Black Sun (live)

2000 ☐	DEGGIAL	2LP	Nuclear Blast (Germany)	NB 442-1

Three-sided album with engraving on the fourth side. 1000 copies.

2000 ☐	DEGGIAL	CD	Nuclear Blast America (USA)	NBA 6442-2
2000 ☐	DEGGIAL	CD	Dream On (Korea)	804795006474
2000 ■	OF DARKNESS	CD	Nuclear Blast	NB 580-2

Bonus: A Suburb To Hell (demo)/Asphyxiate With Fear (demo)/Time Shall Tell (demo)/
Dark Eternity (demo). Plus box to include this one + NB 578-2 and NB 579-2

2000 ☐	OF DARKNESS	3CD	Nuclear Blast America (USA)	NBA6580-0

Plus Beyond Sanctorum and Symphony Masses CDs.

2000 ☐	OF DARKNESS	CD	Nuclear Blast America (USA)	NBA 6580-2
2000 ☐	OF DARKNESS	CD	Irond (Russia)	CD 00-21
2000 ☐	THELI	CD	Irond (Russia)	CD 00-16
2000 ☐	BEYOND SANCTORUM	CD	Nuclear Blast (USA)	6578-2
2001 ☐	BEYOND SANCTORUM	CD	Nuclear Blast	NB 578-2

Bonus: Tyrants Of The Damned/Cthulhu (demo)/Future Consciousness (demo)/Sym-
phony Of The Dead (demo)/Beyond Sanctorum (demo)

2001 ☐	BEYOND SANCTORUM	CD	Irond (Russia)	CD 00-20
2001 ☐	SYMPHONY MASSES: HO DRAKON HO MEGAS	CD	Nuclear Blast	NB 579-2
2001 ☐	SYMPHONY MASSES: HO DRAKON HO MEGAS	CD	Irond (Russia)	CD 00-22
2001 ☐	BEYOND SANCTORUM	CD	Nuclear Blast America (USA)	NBA 6578-2
2001 ☐	SYMPHONY MASSES: HO DRAKON HO MEGAS	CD	Nuclear Blast America (USA)	NBA 6579-2
2001 ☐	SECRET OF THE RUNES	LP PD	Nuclear Blast	NB 625 1

1000 copies.

2001 ☐	SECRET OF THE RUNES	CD	Nuclear Blast	NB 625 2
2001 ☐	SECRET OF THE RUNES	CDd	Nuclear Blast	NB 683 2

Bonus: Crying Days (Scorpions cover)/Summernight City (ABBA cover). 2000 copies

2001 ☐	SECRET OF THE RUNES	CDd	Nuclear Blast America (USA)	NBA 6625-2D
2001 ☐	SECRET OF THE RUNES	CD	Nuclear Blast America (USA)	NBA 6625-2
2001 ☐	SECRET OF THE RUNES	CD	Toy's Factory (Jap)	TFCK 87276

Bonus: Crying Days (Scorpions cover)/Summernight City (ABBA cover)/The King (Accept

2001 ■	SECRET OF THE RUNES	CDd	Dream On (Korea)	PARK 9010

Bonus: Crying Days (Scorpions cover)/Summernight City (ABBA cover)/The King (Accept)

2001 ■	BELLS OF DOOM	CD	Therion Fanclub (Croatia)	- -

Special Fan club CD with demo recordings including 2 tracks by Blitzkrieg. 1000 copies.

2001 ☐	LEPACA KLIFFOTH	CD	Irond (Russia)	CD 01-64

Bonus: Enter The Voids/The Veil Of Golden Spheres.

2001 ☐	A'ARAB ZARAQ LUCID DREAMING	CD	Irond (Russia)	CD 01-63
2001 ☐	VOVIN	CD	Irond (Russia)	CD 01-10

Bonus: The King (Accept cover)

2001 ☐	CROWNING OF ATLANTIS	CD	Irond (Russia)	CD 01-18
2001 ☐	DEGGIAL	CD	Irond (Russia)	CD 00-7

Bonus: Polar Nights (Scorpions cover)

2001 ☐	SECRET OF THE RUNES	CD	Irond (Russia)	CD 01-114

Bonus: Crying Days (Scorpions cover)/Summer Night City (ABBA cover)

2002 ■	LIVE IN MIDGARD	2CD	Nuclear Blast	NB 1033-2
2002 ☐	LIVE IN MIDGARD	2CD	NEMS (Argentina)	NEMS 347
2003 ☐	THELI	CDd	Scarecrow (Mexico)	SC 03096

Bonus: To Mega Therion (live)/Black Sun (live)

2004 ☐	SIRIUS B	CD	Nuclear Blast	NB 1252-2
2004 ☐	SIRIUS B	CD	Irond (Russia)	CD 04-810
2004 ☐	SIRIUS B	CD	Icarus Music (Argentina)	ICARUS 067
2004 ☐	LEMURIA	CD	Nuclear Blast	NB 1253-2
2004 ☐	LEMURIA	CD	Irond (Russia)	CD 04-809
2004 ☐	LEMURIA	CD	Icarus Music (Argentina)	ICARUS 066
2004 ☐	LEMURIA/SIRIUS B – DELUXE EDITION	2CD	Nuclear Blast	NB 1295-2
2004 ☐	LEMURIA/SIRIUS B – DELUXE EDITION	2CDd	Nuclear Blast	NB 1295-0
2004 ☐	LEMURIA/SIRIUS B – DELUXE EDITION	2CD	Toy's Factory (Japan)	TFCK-87352
2005 ☐	ATLANTIC LUCID DREAMING	CD	Nuclear Blast	NB 1498-2
2005 ☐	ATLANTIC LUCID DREAMING	CD	NEMS (Argentina)	NEMS 363

Bonus: Black Sun (live)

2006 ☐	CELEBRATIONS OF BECOMING	2CD+4DVD	Nuclear Blast	NB 1677-0
2006 ☐	CELEBRATIONS OF BECOMING	2CD	Nuclear Blast (USA)	NB 1088-9
2006 ☐	CELEBRATIONS OF BECOMING	2CD+4DVD	Irond (Russia)	DVD 06-43
2005 ☐	VOVIN	CD	Scarecrow Records (Mexico)	SC 04118
2007 ☐	LEMURIA/SIRIUS B – DELUXE EDITION	2LPg	Night Of The Vinyl Dead	NIGHT 020

500 copies. Yellow splatter + blue splatter vinyl.

2007 ☐	GOTHIC KABBALAH	2CDd	Nuclear Blast	NB 1780-0
2007 ☐	GOTHIC KABBALAH	2CDd box	Nuclear Blast	NB 1780-0

500 copies in tin box + certificate and photo cards.

2007 ■	GOTHIC KABBALAH	2CD	Nuclear Blast	NB 1780-2
2007 ☐	GOTHIC KABBALAH	2LPg	Nuclear Blast	NB 1780-1

1000 copies.

2007 ☐	GOTHIC KABBALAH	2CD	Toy's Factory (Japan)	TCFK-87412

Bonus: Seven Secrets Of Sphinx (live)/To Mega Therion (live)

2007 ☐	GOTHIC KABBALAH	2CD	Irond (Russia)	CD 07-1233

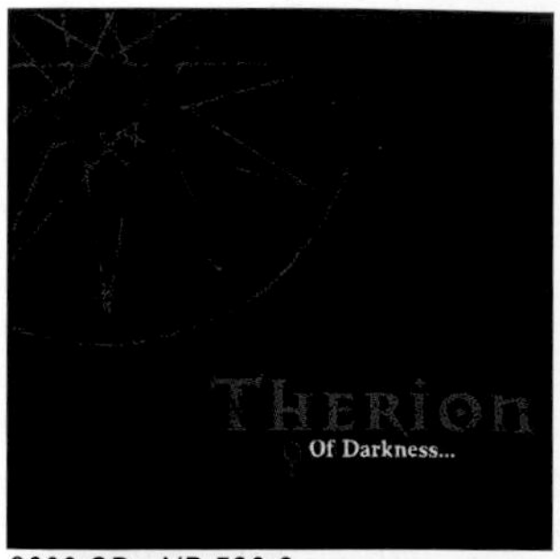

2000 CD - NB 580-2

2001 CDd - PARK 9010

2001 CD - - -

2002 2CD - NB 1033-2

2007 CD - NB 1780-2

Year		Album	Format	Label	Catalog
2007	☐	GOTHIC KABBALAH	2CDd	Irond (Russia)	CD 07-1233D
2007	☐	GOTHIC KABBALAH	2CD	NEMS (Argentina)	NEMS 397
2007	☐	SECRET OF THE RUNES	CD	Icarus Music (Argentina)	ICARUS 371

Bonus: Crying Days (Scorpions cover)/Summernight City (ABBA cover)/The Wings Of Hydra (live)/Black Sun (live)

2007 MCD - NB 1067-2

Year		Album	Format	Label	Catalog
2007	■	Wand Of Abaris	MCD 3tr	Nuclear Blast	NB 1067-2

Tracks: Wand Of Abaris/The Path Of Arcady/T.O.F - Trinity

2008	☐	Wand Of Abaris/Path To Arcady	CDS 2tr	Nuclear Blast	NB 1856-2
2008	☐	LIVE GOTHIC	2CDd+DVD	Nuclear Blast	NB 2118-0
2008	☐	LIVE GOTHIC	2CD+DVD	Nuclear Blast	NB 2162-2
2008	☐	LIVE GOTHIC	2CD+DVD	Nuclear Blast America (USA)	NBA 1216-2d2
2008	☐	LIVE GOTHIC	4LP	Nuclear Blast	NB 2162-1

500 hand-numbered copies.

2009	☐	THE MISKOLC EXPERIMENT	2CDd+DVD	Nuclear Blast	NB 2353-0
2009	☐	THE MISKOLC EXPERIMENT	2CD+DVD	Nuclear Blast	NB 2353-2
2009	☐	THE MISKOLC EXPERIMENT	2CD+DVD	Icarus Music (Argentina)	ICARUS 554
2009	☐	SYMPHONY MASSES: HO DRAKON HO MEGAS	LP	Black Sleeves	BLACK-102LP

Available in red or black vinyl.

| 2010 | ☐ | SITRA AHRA | CDd | Nuclear Blast | 2313-0 |
| 2010 | ☐ | SITRA AHRA | 2LP | Nuclear Blast | 2313-1 |

Clear vinyl.

2012 CD - EOL022-2

2010	☐	SITRA AHRA	CD	Nuclear Blast America (USA)	NBA 12313B-2
2010	☐	SITRA AHRA	CD	Irond (Russia)	CD 10-1728
2010	☐	SITRA AHRA	CD	Icarus Music (Argentina)	ICARUS 669
2010	☐	SITRA AHRA	CD	Trooper (Japan)	XNTE-00022
2010	☐	SITRA AHRA	CD	Scarecrow (Mexico)	SR0584
2010	☐	VOVIN/DEGGIAL	2CD	NEMS (Argentina)	NEMS 404
2010	☐	THELI	CD	NEMS (Argentina)	NEMS 405

Bonus: The Siren Of The Woods (single version)/Cult Of The Shadow (edit)/Babylon

| 2010 | ☐ | THELI | LPg | Nuclear Blast | NB 2667-1 |

200 copies light blue + 200 black vinyl.

| 2010 | ☐ | LEPACA KLIFFOTH | LPg | Nuclear Blast | NB 2596-1 |

Bonus: Enter The Void/The Veil Of Golden Spheres. 200 clear, 100 red, 200 black vinyl.

| 2012 | ☐ | VOVIN | LPg | Floga Records | FL 46 |

500 copies.

| 2012 | ☐ | OF DARKNESS | 2LP | Nuclear Blast | NB 2734-1 |

100 brown/white, 150 brown, 200 white vinyl. 3-sided. Poster

| 2012 | ☐ | LES FLEURS DU MAL | CDd | End Of Light | EOL022L-LTD |

First edition only sold on tour. Different artwork. Poster. Bonus: Les Sucettes

| 2012 | ■ | LES FLEURS DU MAL | CD | End Of Light | EOL022-2 |
| 2012 | ☐ | LES FLEURS DU MAL | CD | Icarus (Argentina) | ICARUS 1061 |

Bonus: Les Sucettes

| 2012 | ☐ | LES FLEURS DU MAL | 2LPg | Adulruna | ADUL 001-1 |

Black vinyl + 500 copies signed + poster.

| 2013 | ☐ | Les Sucettes/Lillith (demo) | 5" | Songs From The Woods | ADUL 002 |

100 copies in clear vinyl, signed. Also in green, yellow, red and blue vinyl.

1995 CD - GKMCD 9504

THIRD STONE

Magnus Leo: v, Mikael Eriksson: g, Klas Lövgren: b, Anders Westman: d

Gagnef - The record starts out in a slightly trippy, late 60s way, but the second half of the CD contains some serious 70s riffing. The album was recorded more as a school project and some of the members even play other instruments now.

| 1995 | ■ | BEYOND SOMEWHERE | CD | private | GKMCD 9504 |

THIS ENDING

Mårten Hansen: v, Leo Pignon: g, Linus Nirbrant: g,
Jesper Löfgren: b, Fredrik Andersson: d

Stockholm - *This Ending* are more or less a continuation of the band *A Canorous Quintet*, originally as *The Plague* in 2005. After *A Canorous Quintet* split in 1998, Pignon played with *Niden Div. 187*, Andersson went to *Amon Amarth*, *Beyond Dreams*, *Alligience* and *Guidance Of Sin*, where Nirbrant was also found. In early 2005 Hansen, Pignon, Nirbrant, Löfgren and Andersson formed *The Plague* and in February 2006 the first demo *Let The World Burn*, was recorded. During this session the band changed its name to *This Ending*. The band plays quite brutal, but great-sounding melodic death metal, actually with indecipherable grunting rather than growling vocals. Great heavy and powerful production. In 2012 the band released the digital three-track EP *Systematic Worship*, one song at a time.

No ending in sight

| 2006 | ☐ | INSIDE THE MACHINE | CD | Metal Blade | MB 14603-2 |
| 2009 | ☐ | DEAD HARVEST | CDd | Metal Blade | MB 14701-2 |

Bonus: Redeemer/First Blood/Parasites (video version) + Parasites (video)

| 2009 | ■ | DEAD HARVEST | CD | Metal Blade | MB 14701-2 |

2009 CD - MB 14701-2

THIS GIFT IS A CURSE

Jonas A. Holmberg: v, Patrik Andersson: v/g, Lars Gunnarsson: b, Johan Nordlund: d

Stockholm - The members of *This Gift Is A Curse* originate from different cities, like Piteå and Gävle, but all ended up in Stockholm. It started in the late summer of 2008, when Holmberg and Nordlund teamed up. The band was soon completed by Andersson and Gunnarsson. With the members' backgrounds in bands like *Seven Nautical Miles* and *Grizzly Twister*, the music became some weird, dissonant hardcore-oriented sludge metal with a touch of death metal. Like mixing *Switchblade* and *Cult Of Luna* with hardcore screaming vocals. After recording five songs in their rehearsal room, the band entered Sunlight Studios together with renowned producer Tomas Skogsberg, to record their debut MCD.

2010 ☐	This Gift Is A Curse	MCDd 4tr	Discouraged Records	MMI 11
	Tracks: The Big Sleep/Death To Your Hometown (Pt. III)/Althea/Voulets Dream			
2012 ■	I, GUILT BEARER	LP	Discouraged Records	MMI 19
2012 ☐	I, GUILT BEARER	LP	Bloated Veins (Denmark)	BV 002
	Red/black splatter vinyl. 500 copies.			

2012 LP - MMI 19

THIS HAVEN

Patrik Karlsson: v, Tobias Jacobsson: g, Johan Berglund: b, Nicklas Keijser: d

Örebro - *This Haven* were conceived in the autumn of 2003 by four old friends. In April 2004 the first demo, *Disexist*, was recorded and mixed by Dan Swanö. The second effort was finished in January 2005, entitled *My Year Zero*, also produced by Swanö and followed by the self-produced *A Soul Wide Open* later the same year. In 2006 they were picked up by Vic Records and Swanö had the honour of producing the bands outstanding debut. *This Haven* play a very unique-sounding heavy prog metal. Adding mellotron to the lead-heavy wall of guitars is not something you hear every day. In October 2010 Keijser left the band and he wasn't replaced until Pär Nilsson (*Asphalt*) joined in November 2011. Berglund is also found in *Demiurg*, *Ribspreader* and *The Grotesquery*.
Website: www.thishaven.com

2008 ■	TODAY A WHISPER, TOMORROW A STORM	CD	Vic Records	VIC 008

2008 CD - VIC 008

THOMSEN, FRANK

Tony Kristiansson: v, Frank Thomsen: g, Martin Sventorp: k,
Fredrik Skoog: b, Patrik Persson: d

Bromölla - This is actually more of a band than the guitarist's solo thing. They were originally known under the name *Purple Rose*. Really good hard rock with strong hints of *Rising Force* and *Silver Mountain*. Great guitars, good vocals and a high-quality sound make this one a sure buy. Shortly after the MCD (same as the 1996 MCD) was released in Japan, Frank sadly died of cancer.

1996 ☐	Frank Thomsen	MCDp 4tr	private	
	Tracks: Open Your Eyes/No More Tears/Living On Borrowed Time/Magic Mirror			
1997 ■	Open Your Eyes	MCD 4tr	Sound Tresures (Jap)	STCD001

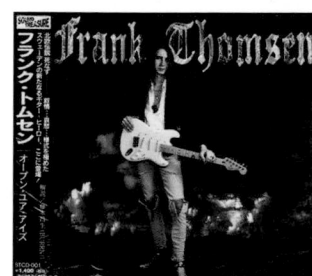
1997 MCD - STCD001

THORNCLAD

Viktor Klint: v/g, Fllip "Fille" Carlsson: g, Jonas Remne: b, Adrian Hörnquist: d

Linghem - Formed as Klint's solo project in 1995. The band recorded the demos *Demonseeds* (1996) and *Ravage* (1997) before the album. Fast and furious thrash in the vein of *Slayer* and *Dark Angel*. Carlsson is also found in *Satanic Slaughter*, *Spiteful*, *Corporation 187* and *Höst*, Remne and Hörnquist in *Nightchant*, while Klint has been in *Corporation 187*, *Nightchant*, and a live musician for *Algaion*. The band split in 2002 and Hörnquist, Carlsson and Klint went on to form *Demons To Prefer*.

1999 ■	CORONATION OF THE WICKED	CD	Loud 'N Proud	LNP 006

1999 CD - LNP 006

THORNIUM

Daniel "Thyphenz/Thyph" Munoz: v/g/b/d,
Anders "Eligor" Lundvall: g, Patrik "Ulverheim": Mattsson g

Mölndal (Göteborg) - The band was formed in 1993 by Thypenz (*Cabal, Cryptic*) on vocals and all instruments. He recorded the demo *North Storms Of The Bestial Goat Sign* in the same year. The demo resulted in a deal with Dutch label Necromantic Gallery, who released the debut, which guitarist Ulverheim had joined. "Raw black metal with melody and mysticism. A travel through death's all kingdoms", is how the bio describes the debut album. Lyrics both in Swedish and English. After this it went all quiet. The band didn't break up, but Thypenz spent

1995 CD - NGP 005

several years in prison, which made recording a bit difficult. In June 2008 Soulseller Records signed the band. On the second album the line-up was completed by Fhurgast on drums and Ulverheims wife, Kali Ma, on bass, while *Fides Luciferius* features Thyph, Eligor (*Descending*) and Ulverheim (*Deletion, Forsaken, Cabal, Cryptic*). Old-school black metal similar to *Marduk* and *Dark Funeral*.

2009 CD - SSR 016

1995	■	DOMINIONS OF THE ECLIPSE	CD	Necromantic Gallery	NGP 005
2010	☐	DOMINIONS OF THE ECLIPSE	2LP	Kneel Before The Master's Throne	Kneel 014

300 black + 100 green. Also 100 clear vinyl including t-shirt, patch and badge. Bonus: North Storms Of The Goat Sign demo.

2009	■	MUSHROOM CLOUDS AND DUSK	CD	Soulseller Records	SSR 016
2010	☐	FIDES LUCIFERIUS	CD	Soulseller Records	SSR 024
2011	☐	DOMINIONS OF THE ECLIPSE	CDd	Soulseller	SSR 043

Re-issue in box. Bonus: Remain In Chaos/Reign Of Terror/In The Depths Of The Northern Darkness/North Storms Of The Bestial Goat Sign/Min vandring till mörkrets fyrste

THOSE WHO BRING THE TORTURE
Roger "Rogga/Crawl" Johansson: v/g/b, Brynjar Helgetun: d

Kiruna - The band was formed in 2007 and after just one week of writing and recording, the debut album was finished. The first two albums featured Roger (as Crawl), Ronnie "Worm" Björnström on lead guitar and drummer David "Maggot" Ekevärn (*Ghamorean, Knife In Christ, Putrevore*). The band officially disbanded in 2010 and the last album was recorded with Rogga and drummer Helgetun (*Ribspreader, Crypticus, Paganizer*) only. *Those Who Bring The Torture* delivers a nice slab of grindcore-infused, quite melodic and very well-played, death metal. Like a mix of *Grave, Exhumed* and *Carcass*.

2012 CD - MI 016

2007	☐	THOSE WHO BRING THE TORTURE	CD	No Colours	NC 126
2008	☐	TANK GASMASK AMMO	CD	Pulverised Records	ASH 046 CD
2012	■	LULLABIES FOR THE DERANGED	CD	Metal Inquisition	MI 016

THRASHON
Lasse Wester: v/g, Jan-Olof Persson: g, Tore Paulsen: b, Ronnie Peeters: d

Arvika - Formed in 1981. Great melodic metal with hints of NWoBHM bands like *Trespass* and *Jameson Raid*. In 1995 they changed their name to the more suitable *Pearly White* and released the album *Way Of Life*. However Tore left the band and Jan-Olof took over his task. The tracks *My Love* and *Annie* are found on the *Coming Up!* (93 Mother Earth) compilation.

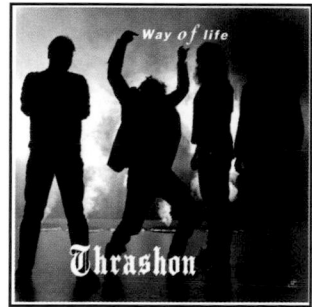

1992 MLP - THRAM 9201

1991	☐	Weird Weird Weird World/Fight 'Em Back	7"	private	UNI 2466
1992	■	Way Of Fire	MLP 4tr	private	THRAM 9201

Tracks: Way Of Life/F.I.L/My Love/Heros

THREE MINUTE MADNESS
Fredrik Norman: v, Henrik Andersson: g, Stefan Vesterberg: g, Peter Åström: b, Gerard Stenlund: d

Umeå/Stockholm - *Three Minute Madness* play modern-sounding melodic, yet heavy and groovy hard rock, mixing touches of *Audioslave* and *Soundgarden* with vibes of *Alter Bridge* and *Shinedown*. Norman is an outstanding singer as well. Vesterberg and Andersson are also found in *Jupither*, while Åström is found in *Clark Lane*.

2010 CD - SUPERCD 006

2007	☐	DISGRACEFUL	CD	Mundo Nuevo	MNR 017
2010	■	DISGRACEFUL	CD	Supernova	SUPERCD 006

THREE SEASONS
Sartez "Faraj" Abdulrahman: v/g, Olle Risberg: b, Christian Eriksson: d

Heby - A new outstanding retro-oriented power trio, featuring former *Siena Root* singer Sartez. Musically in the vein of classic *Uriah Heep*, with a touch of *Night Sun*, especially on the second album where the Hammond organ, played by Malin Ahlberg, gets more space. Highly recommended for retro fans.
Website: www.threeseasonsmusic.com

2012 LP - HSLP 326

2011	☐	LIFE'S ROAD	CDd	Transubstans	TRANS 079
2011	☐	LIFE'S ROAD	CDp	Mals (Russia)	MALS 372
2011	☐	LIFE'S ROAD	2LPg	Headspin	HSLP 320
2011	☐	Escape/Wood To Sand	7"	Transubstans	TRANSV 701

100 red/yellow marble + 400 black vinyl.

2012	☐	UNDERSTAND THE WORLD	CDd	Transubstans	TRANS 101
2012	■	UNDERSTAND THE WORLD	LP	Headspin	HSLP 326

Available in black or red/black marble vinyl.

THRONE OF AHAZ

**Fredrik "Beretorn" Jacobsson: v, Marcus "Vargher" Norman: g,
Kalle "Taurtheim" Bondesson: b, Johan Mortiz: d**

Umeå - The band mixed fast and furious straight death metal in the vein of **Venom** with the melodic style of **Dissection** and vocals that make you wonder when the vocal chords are going to burst. On the first album Johan was not an official member. After the debut guitarist Nicklas "Wortael" Svensson was replaced by Marcus, who was later playing with **Ancient Wisdom** and **Bewitched**. **Ancient Wisdom** also became the new home for Fredrik. **Throne Of Ahaz** also have a track on the compilation *Dark End* (1995 Plastic Head). The band however split in 1995, before the 96-release. *On Twilight...* contains a cover of **Black Sabbath**'s *Black Sabbath*.

1994 CD - NFR 008

1994 ■	NIFELHEIM	CD	No Fashion	NFR 008
1996 ☐	ON TWILIGHT ENTHRONED	CD	No Fashion	NFR 016

THRONEAEON

Tony Freed: v/g, Jens Klovegård: g, Andreas Dahlström: b, Roger Sundquist: d

Västerås - The band was formed in 1991 by Roger, originally as **Mysterion** and later **Beyond Black Horizon**. They went through some changes of personnel and in 1995 took the name **Throneaeon**. They recorded their first demo the same year and were supposed to participate on a split-CD the year after, which however never happened. In 1996 the demo *Carnage* was unearthed and received rave reviews. After *With Sardonic Wrath* Jens Klovegård (**Axenstar, Abhoth, Succumb, Expositor**) replaced guitarist Göran Eriksson. Both releases were recorded at Studio Underground. On the second album bassist Magnus Wall (**Soulbreach, Haterush, Abhoth, Septic Breed**) replaced Andreas Dahlström. Matte Modin (**Defleshed**) also plays session drums on four tracks. In 2003 the band changed its name to **Godhate**. The 2012 releases (says 2011 on the CDs) are re-mastered re-issues containing lots of bonus material and demos. Technical high speed death metal with growling guttural vocals in the vein of **Deicide** with a touch of **Slayer**. Great, powerful production. The last three releases are actually released under the **Godhate** moniker even though they are **Thronaeon** recordings.
Website: www.throneaeon.com

1999 MCD - HEL 001

2001 CD - HH 102

1999 ■	With Sardonic Wrath	MCD 4tr	Helgrind	HEL 001
	Tracks: Despise For God/Sardonic Wrath/Blasphemous Prediction/Entwined To The Lies Of The Light			
2001 ☐	With Sardonic Wrath	MCD 4tr	The Plague	Plague 003
2001 ■	NEITHER OF GODS	CD	Hammerheart	HH 102
2001 ☐	NEITHER OF GODS	LP	Hammerheart	HH 102
2001 ☐	NEITHER OF GODS	CD	Fono (Russia)	FO83CD
2003 ■	GODHATE	CD	Forensick Music	FM 007
2012 ☐	THE THRONEAEON YEARS PART I – WITH SARDONIC WRATH	CD	Metal Fortress	MFE 016
	Bonus: 1995 demo, Carnage demo, Consecration To Satan/Prophet Impaled			
2012 ☐	THE THRONEAEON YEARS PART II – NEITHER OF GODS	CD	Metal Fortress	MFE 017
	Bonus: Dawn Of Eternity (Massacre cover)/Extreme Aggression (Kreator cover)/Where Next To Conquer (Bolt Thrower cover)/Once Upon The Cross (Decide cover)/Lions Den (Morbid Angel cover)			
2012 ☐	THE THRONEAEON YEARS PART III – GODHATE	CD	Metal Fortress	MFE 018
	Bonus: Kingdom Gone/ (At The Gates cover)For Whom The Bell Tolls (Metallica cover)/ Don't Fear The Reaper (BÖC cover)/Fast As A Shark (Accept cover)/The Fight Song (Marilyn Manson cover)/Mandatory Suicide (Slayer cover)			

2003 CD - FM 007

THROUGH TIME TOMORROW

Gunnar Söderström: v/g/k, Mathias Lönngren: b, Tomas Nilsson: d

Södertälje - Hard rock with some fat riffing mixed with pretty mellow ballads, about 50/50. Håkan Hemlin (**Nordman**) has co-written two of the songs. Gunnar and Tomas also played together with Hemlin in "the old days".

1998 ■	THROUGH TIME TOMORROW	CD	private	TTTCD 001

1998 CD - TTTCD 001

THROWN

Peter "Pete Flesh" Karlsson: v/g/d, Crille Lundin: b

Strängnäs - Pete has also been found in **Deceiver, Flesh, Harmony, Torment, Embryo** and **Maze Of Torment** and Crille in **Xenofanes, Deceiver, Flesh, Harmony** and **Maze Of Torment**. Death-oriented doom metal with hints of **Tormentor** and **Bathory** as well as **Pink Floyd**. Peter today has his own project **The Pete Flesh Deathtrip** who released the album *Mortui Vivos Docent* on Pulverised in 2013.

2007 ■	THE SUICIDAL KINGS OCCULT	CD	Iron Fist Productions	IFPCD 022

2007 CD - IFPCD 022

THUNDER

Linus Holgersson: v, Eddie Erixon: g, Mats Pettersson: g,
Henrik Johansson: b, Fredrik Andersson: d

Västervik - *Thunder* were formed as a high school band in 1987 and recorded four demos before the single. The band actually disbanded when the single was released. Eddie went to study at GIT and now plays in cover band *Beeflat*, while Pettersson recorded with *Two Eagles Request* (aka *T.E.R*) and played with metal cover band *Noztalgica*. Linus (also in *Two Eagles Request*) and Fredrik plays in cover band *N.M.A*. Despite having a nice metal edge in the guitar department, Party, is a party rocker with an over-excited lead guitarist, while the B-side is a power ballad with below-average vocals. Rumors of an existing single entitled *Tyrant's Castle* are false.

1989 7" - PLC 910-03

1989 ■ Party/Someone For You..7" PLC...PLC 910-03 $

THUNDERHOG

Tomas Irgard: v/b, Mats Nilsson: g, Lars Wallgren: g, Thomas Hansson: d

Göteborg - Weird, but good hard rock, on the same short-lived label as *EF Band* and *BB Rock*. Irgard later joined *Diesel* and *Crossing Oceans*.

1982 7" - LSPS 110

1982 ■ Sally/Pirahna Faggots..7" Ewita..LSPS 110

THY PRIMORDIAL

Niklas Holstensson: v, Mikael Andersson: g,
Jonas Albrektsson: b, Jocke "Morth" Pettersson: d

Mjölby - The band was formed in 1994 as *Primordial*, and their first demo *De mörka makters alla* was issued the same year, followed by *Svart gryning* the year after. In 1996 the band recorded the demo *Kristallklar vinternatt*, which became the band's first vinyl EP. The line-up featured Albrektsson, Andersson, singer Andreas "Isidor" Karlsson, Morth and guitarist Nisse Nilsson. It lead to a one-album deal with US-label Gothic and the debut, *Under iskall måne*, was recorded already in 1995, but not released until three years after. The band used the services of Sunlight Studios. Jocke is also found in *Regurgitate*, *Dawn*, *Niden Div 187*, *Kids Are Sick* and *Retaliation*. Jonas was also found in *Indungeon* and is also a member of *Retaliation* and *Niden Div 187*. Guitarist Nisse Nilsson left the band in 2000. *Thy Primordial* produce ultra-fast and quite technical, but somewhat chaotic black metal with a wall of twin guitars and screeching vocals, similar to *Dark Funeral*, *Satyricon* and *Dissection*. On *Pestilence Upon Mankind* singer Andreas "Isidor" Karlsson had been replaced by Niklas Holstenson. The band folded in 2005.

1996 7" - PS 009

2002 CD - BLACK 036 CD

1996 ■	Kristallklar vinternatt	7" 5tr	Paranoia Syndrome	PS 009

Tracks: Kristallklar vinternatt/Där blott hat härskar/In i avgrunden/Tronad av natten/Outro. 500 copies.

1997 ☐	WHERE THE ONLY SEASONS MARK THE PATHS OF TIME	CD	Pulverised	ASH 002 CD
1997 ☐	WHERE THE ONLY SEASONS MARK THE PATHS OF TIME	LP	Paranoia Syndrome	PS 015

500 copies.

1998 ☐	UNDER ISKALL TROLLMÅNE	CD	Gothic	GOTHIC 003

1000 copies.

1999 ☐	AT THE WORLD OF UNTRODDEN WONDER	CD	Pulverised	ASH 007 CD
2000 ☐	THE HERESY OF AN AGE OF REASON	CD	Pulverised	ASH 011 CD

1500 copies.

2001 ☐	UNDER ISKALL TROLLMÅNE	CD	WWIII (USA)	CD 71168
2002 ☐	WHERE THE ONLY SEASONS.../AT THE WORLD OF...	2CD	Blackend	BLACK 030 CD

Re-issue of both albums, plus bonus-tracks; Där blott hat härskar/In i avgrunden

2002 ■	THE CROWNING CARNAGE	CD	Blackend	BLACK 036 CD
2002 ☐	THE CROWNING CARNAGE	CD	Candelight (USA)	CANUS 0034 CD
2002 ■	THE HERESY OF AN AGE OF REASON	CD	Blackend	BLACK 042 CD
2004 ☐	PESTILENCE UPON MANKIND	CD	Blackend	BLACK 065 CD

Also released with slipcase.

2002 CD - BLACK 042 CD

THYREOS

Fredrik Nordin: v, Mattias Lilja: g, Daniel Birath: g,
Erik Palmqvist: k, Henrik S Johansson: d

Degerfors - *Thyreos* were formed in 2002 by Nordin. Members changed and in 2007 Palmqvist joined and the demo *Words Of Evil* was recorded. After this Johansson and guitarist Daniel Birath joined. The album was produced by Ronny Milianowicz (*Dionysus*). Stefan Elmgren (ex-*Hammerfall, FullStrike, FullForce*) guests. Really good, melodic metal, sounding a bit like *Nocturnal Rites*-meet-*Tad Morose*. After *I Don't Live To Fail* guitarists Mattias Lilja and Birath were out of the band, and Gianni Bonafedi joined.

2010 CD - SLP10-023-L

2009 ☐	SOUND OF DESTRUCTION	CD	private	THY 124
2010 ■	SOUND OF DESTRUCTION	CD	Sliptrick	SLP10-023-L
2012 ☐	I DON'T LIVE TO FAIL	CD	Sliptrick	SLP012-035

THYRFING

Jens Rydén: v, Patrik Lindgren: g, Peter Löf: k,
Kimmy Sjölund: b, Joakim Kristensson: d

Stockholm - The band was formed in 1995 and the name comes from the cursed sword in the Norse mythology. Death metal with a strong Nordic/Gothic touch and lyrics in Swedish. *Thyrfing* recorded their first demo, *Solen svartnar*, in 1995, followed by *Hednaland* the year after. The first two demos were later released as the CD *Hednaland*. The debut was recorded in Sunlight Studios, while *Valdr Galga* and *Urkraft* were recorded in Abyss Studios. On the digi-pack version of *Urkraft* they do an outstanding version of Gary Moore's *Over The Hills And Far Away*. *Urkraft* was produced by Peter Tägtgren, while *Vansinnesvisor* was done by Daniel Bergstrand. The album was initially supposed to be released on Hammerheart in 2002, but due to the "reformation" of the label it wasn't out until 2004 and on the new label Karmageddon, where the previous albums were also re-issued. On *Hels Vite* singer Thomas Väänänen had been replaced by Jens Rydén (**Naglfar, Dead Silent Slumber, Profundi**) and guitarist Henrik Svegsjö was out of the band. The band can also be found on a number of compilations, such as *Hednaland* (demo) on *Voices Of Death Part 1* (VOD 97), *Storms Of Asgard* on *Victims Of The Bubonic Plague* (Rough Trade 99), *Mjölner* on *Sign Of The Hammer* (Hammerheart 00) and also on *Hammerheart Hails Chaos Magazine* (Chaos Mag 00), *The Breaking Of Serenity* on *Off Road Tracks Vol 35* (Hammer Mag 00) and *Close-Up Soundcheck #41* (Close-Up 00) and some more. Thomas Väänänen, Patrik Lindgren and Joakim Kristensson also had the side-project **Pantheon** between 1995 and 1996.

Swedish Waikings in the dark

1998	■	THYRFING	CD	Hammerheart Records	HHR 016
1998	☐	THYRFING	LP PD	Hammerheart Records	HHR 016PD
1998	☐	VALDR GALGA	CD	Hammerheart Records	HHR 039
1998	☐	VALDR GALGA	CDd	Hammerheart Records	HHR 039
1998	☐	VALDR GALGA	LP	Hammerheart Records	HHR 039LP
1998	☐	VALDR GALGA	LP PD	Hammerheart Records	HHR 039PD
1998	☐	Solen Svartnar	7" 6tr	Grim Rune	GRP 001

Tracks: Intro/Solen svartna I/Solen svartnar II/Slaget/Ty Mörkret Skall Falla/Thyrfing.300 numbered copies.

1999	☐	HEDNALAND	CD	Unveiling The Wicked	HUW 004 $

2000 copies.

1999	☐	HEDNALAND	LP PD	Unveiling The Wicked	HUW 004
2000	☐	URKRAFT	CD	Hammerheart Records	HHR 061
2000	☐	URKRAFT	CDd	Hammerheart Records	HHR 061

Bonus: Over The Hills And Far Away (Gary Moore-cover)

2000	☐	URKRAFT	2LP	Hammerheart	HHR 061
2000	☐	URKRAFT	CD	Soundholic (Japan)	SHCD1 0040
2002	■	VANSINNESVISOR	CD	Hammerheart Records	HHR 083
2002	☐	VANSINNESVISOR	LP	Hammerheart Records	HHR 083
2002	☐	VANSINNESVISOR	CD	Fono (Russia)	FO 147 CD
2004	☐	THYRFING	CD	Karmageddon Media	KARMA 036
2004	☐	THYRFING	CD	Candlelight (USA)	CANUS 0084CD
2004	☐	VALDR GALGA	CD	Karmageddon Media	KARMA 041
2004	☐	VALDR GALGA	CD	Candlelight (USA)	CANUS 0089CD
2004	☐	VALDR GALGA	CD	Fono (Russia)	FO 186 CD
2004	☐	VANSINNESVISOR	CD	Karmageddon Media	KARMA 063
2002	☐	VANSINNESVISOR	CD	Candlelight (USA)	CDL 0173CD
2005	☐	URKRAFT	CD	Karmageddon Media	KARMA 093
2005	☐	URKRAFT	CD	Candlelight (USA)	CDL0295CD
2005	■	FARSOTSTIDER	CD	Regain Records	RR 078
2005	☐	FARSOTSTIDER	CD	Candlelight (USA)	CDL 0289 CD
2005	☐	FARSOTSTIDER	CD	Hellion Records (Brazil)	n/a
2005	☐	FARSOTSTIDER	CD	n/a(Japan)	n/a

Bonus: Järnviljors dans

2006	☐	FARSOTSTIDER	CD	CD-Maximum (Russia)	CDM 1006-2603
2008	■	HELS VITE	CD	Regain Records	RR 155
2008	☐	HELS VITE	LP	War Anthem Records	WAR 019 LP

500 copies.

2008	☐	HELS VITE	CD	Hellion Records (Brazil)	n/a
2008	☐	VANSINNESVISOR	CD	Paranoid Records (Brazil)	n/a
2009	☐	FARSOTSTIDER	CD+DVD	Regain Records	RR 158

DVD featuring live at Party San Open Air 2006.

2008	☐	HELS VITE	CD	Regain Records (USA)	REG-CD 1095
2012	☐	URKRAFT	LP	Hammerheart Records	HHR 201211LP

Bonus: Over The Hills And Far Away (Gary Moore cover)

2012	☐	URKRAFT	CD	Hammerheart Records	HHR 201211

Bonus: Over The Hills And Far Away (Gary Moore cover)

2012	☐	THYRFING	LP	Hammerheart Records	HHR 201201LP
2013	☐	DE ÖDESLÖSA	CDd	NoiseArt Records	NARCD 031 LTD

1998 CD - HHR 016

2002 CD - HHR 083

2005 CD - RR 078

2008 CD - RR158

TIAMAT

Johan "Hellslaughter" Edlund: v/g, Anders Iwers: b, Lars Sköld: d

Stockholm - Formed in 1988 by Johan and Klas "Juck" Wistedt, together with drummer Andreas Holmberg and guitarist Stefan Lagergren, who were later found in **Expulsion, River's Edge** and **Mr Death**. They recorded the 7" *Severe Abomination* in 1989 under the name **Treblinka**. On the debut album the members were Johan, Andreas, Stefan and bassist Jörgen Thullberg (**Mr Death**). *Sumerian Cry* was actually the first album to be recorded in the now mythical Sunlight Studios. On *The Astral Sleep* Holmberg and Lagergren were replaced by Niklas Ekstrand (**Face Down**) and Thomas Petersson. Keyboard player Kenneth Roos joined on *Clouds*. Initially quite innovative death metal with softer classical parts and heavy riffing, but they went more and more goth. The line-up on *The Sleeping Beauty* featured Edlund, bassist Johnny Hagel (**Sorcerer, Sundown**), Petersson, Roos, Sköld, while on *Wildhoney* this was cut down to Hedlund, Hagel and Sköld, plus session guitarist Magnus Sahlgren (**Celeborn, Lake Of Tears, Dismember**). In 1995 the band toured as support to **Black Sabbath** and *Wildhoney* sold well over 100 000 copies. On *Cold Seed* and *A Deeper Kind Of Slumber* the line-up had once again changed. Now the band featured Hedlund, bassist Anders Iwers (**Cemetary, Ceremonial Oath, Descecrator, In Flames**) and drummer Lars Sköld (**Jupiter Society, Leif Edling**), with the addition of guitarist Thomas Petersson, who was out of the band on the 1999 release, but back again on *Judas Christ*. The style had now become softer and goth rock-oriented. On *Amanethes* the band was back to a trio, and the sound had again become a bit heavier. In 2006 the band released the DVD *The Church Of Tiamat*. The box set *The Ark Of The Covenant* contains all albums, the DVD and one CD, *Panopticon*, featuring B-sides, remixes and rarities. The tracks *A Winter Shadow* and *Ancient Entity* appear on the Century Media compilation *In The Eyes Of Death*.

The scarred bunch

A Winter Shadow

Year		Title	Format	Label	Cat. No.	
1991	■	A Winter Shadow/Ancient Entity	7"	CBR	CBR-S 125	$($)$
1991	□	SUMERIAN CRY	LP	Metalcore	CORE 9	
1991	□	SUMERIAN CRY	CD	Metalcore	CORE 9	
1991	□	SUMERIAN CRY	CD	Deadline Music (USA)	CLP 0486-2	
1991	□	THE ASTRAL SLEEP	CD	Century Media	9722 2	
1991	□	THE ASTRAL SLEEP	CD	Century Media (USA)	CM 7722 2	
1992	■	CLOUDS	CD	Century Media	9736 2	
1992	□	CLOUDS	CD	Century Media (USA)	CM 7736 2	
1994	□	The Sleeping Beauty - Live In Israel	MCD 5tr	Century Media	77065 2	

Tracks: In A Dream/Ancient Entity/The Sleeping Beauty/Mountain Of Doom/Angels Far Beyond. Recorded June 3rd 1993 in Tel-Aviv.

1991 7" - CBR-S 125

Year		Title	Format	Label	Cat. No.	
1994	□	The Sleeping Beauty - Live In Israel	MCDd 5tr	Century Media (USA)	7765 2	
1994	□	WILDHONEY	CD	Century Media	77080 2	
1994	□	WILDHONEY	CD	Century Media USA)	CM 7780 2	
1994	□	WILDHONEY	LP	Century Media	77080 1	
1994	□	WILDHONEY	LP PD	Century Media	77080 1P	
1994	□	Gaia	MCD 6tr	Century Media	77089 2	

Tracks: Gaia (video edit)/The Ar(radio edit)/When You're In (Pink Floyd cover)/Whatever That Hurts (video)/Visionaire(remix)/The Ar

| 1994 | ■ | The Tour Sampler | MCDp 5tr | Century Media | 7723-2 | |

Tracks: Gaia(video edit)/The Ar/Whatever That Hurts (video edit)/Visionaire (re-mix)/The Ar(industrial mix)

| 1995 | □ | THE MUSICAL HISTORY OF TIAMAT + WILD-LIVE | 2CD | Century Media | 77059-2 | |
| 1997 | □ | Cold Seed | MCD 3tr | Century Media | 77167-2 | |

Tracks: Cold Seed/Only In My Tears It Lasts (The cat mix)/Three Leary Bisquits

| 1997 | □ | A DEEPER KIND OF SLUMBER | CDd | Century Media | 77180-2 | |
| 1997 | □ | A DEEPER KIND OF SLUMBER | LP | Century Media | 77180-1 | |

3000 copies.

| 1997 | □ | A DEEPER KIND OF SLUMBER | CD | Century Media (USA) | 7880-2 | |

Different artwork.

| 1997 | □ | A DEEPER KIND OF SLUMBER | CD | Victor (Japan) | VICP-60034 | |

Bonus: Only In My Tears It Lasts (the cat mix)/Thee Leary Bisquits

| 1999 | ■ | Brighter Than The Sun | MCD 4tr | Century Media | 77279-3 | |

Tracks: Brighter Than The Sun (radio edit)/Sympathy For The Devil (Stones cover)/Children Of The Underworld/Brighter Than The Sun

| 1999 | □ | SKELETON SKELETRON | CDd | Century Media | 77280-2 | |
| 1999 | □ | SKELETON SKELETRON | LP | Century Media | 77280-1 | |

1000 copies.

| 1999 | □ | SKELETON SKELETRON | CD | Century Media (USA) | 7980-2 | |
| 1999 | □ | SKELETON SKELETRON | CD | Victor (Japan) | VICP 60886 | |

Bonus: Children Of The Underworld

| 1999 | □ | For Her Pleasure | MCD 4tr | Century Media | 77281-3 | |

Tracks: For Her Pleasure/Lucy(demon mix)/Brighter Than The Sun (bullsrun mix)/As Long As You Are Mine (Lodmalm's mix)

2001	□	THE ASTRAL SLEEP/In The Eyes Of Death	CD	Century Media (USA)	7722-2	
2001	□	CLOUDS/The Sleeping Beauty	CD	Century Media (USA)	7736-2	
2001	□	POWERPACK	2CD	Century Media	77350-2	

Double-pack containing A Different Kind Of Slumber and Clouds as a double-CD.

1994 MCDp - 7723-2

1999 MCD - 77279-3

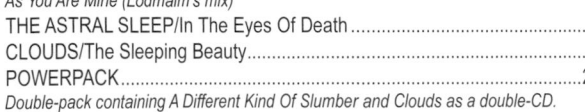

1992 CD - 9736 2

2001 ☐	WILDHONEY/Gaia	CD	Century Media (USA)	7780-2	
2002 ☐	Vote For Love	CDS	Century Media	77379-3	
2002 ☐	JUDAS CHRIST	CD	Century Media	77380-2	
2002 ☐	JUDAS CHRIST	LP	Century Media	77380-1	
	1000 copies				
2002 ☐	JUDAS CHRIST	CDd	Century Media	77380-8	
	Bonus video Vote For Love				
2002 ☐	JUDAS CHRIST	CD	Century Media (USA)	8080-2	
	Bonus: Cold Last Supper				
2002 ☐	JUDAS CHRIST	CD	Century Media (Brazil)	33380-2	
	Bonus: Vote For Love (video)				
2002 ☐	JUDAS CHRIST	CD	Victor (Japan)	VICP 61717	
	Bonus: Vote For Love (video)				
2002 ■	JUDAS CHRIST	CD box	Century Media	77380-0	
	Bonus: Sixshooter/However You Look At It You Lose. Box set with poster + sticker.				
2003 ☐	PREY	CD	Century Media	77480-2	
2003 ☐	PREY	CDd	Century Media	77480-8	
	Bonus: Cain (video)				
2003 ☐	PREY	LP	Century Media	77480-1	
2003 ☐	PREY	CD	Century Media (USA)	8180-2	
2003 ☐	Cain	MCD 3tr	Century Media	77479-3	
	Tracks: Cain (edit)/Sleeping (In The Fire) (W.A.S.P cover)/Love In Chains				
2003 ■	Cain	MCDd 3tr	Century Media	77479-3	
2004 ☐	JUDAS CHRIST	CDd	Fono (Russia)	FO426CD	
2006 ☐	COMMANDMENTS	CD	Century Media	7653-2	
2006 ☐	THE ASTRAL SLEEP	LP	Painkiller Records	PKR 076	
	Different artwork.				
2007 ☐	A DEEPER KIND OF SLUMBER	CD	Century Media	18386B2	
	Bonus: Only In My Tears It Lasts (The Cat Mix) + multimedia track.				
2007 ☐	WILDHONEY	2CD	Century Media	77680-8	
	Bonus: Gaia EP, Live In Stockholm + videos				
2008 ☐	The Temple Of The Crescent Moon	CDSp 1tr	Nuclear Blast	- -	
	Promo				
2008 ☐	THE ARK OF THE COVENANT	13CD/DVD box	Century Media	9977610	
	Solid box with gold foil. Contains: The Astral Sleep/Clouds/Live In Israel/Wildhoney/Gaia/ Wildfire/ A Deeper Kind Of Slumber/Skeleton Skeletron/Judas Christ/Prey/The Church Of Tiamat/Panopticon/The Church Of Tiamat-DVD/Panopticon. 3000 copies.				
2008 ☐	AMANETHES	CD	Nuclear Blast	NB 2013-2	
2008 ☐	AMANETHES	CDd	Nuclear Blast	NB 2013-0	
	Bonus: Thirst Snake				
2008 ☐	AMANETHES	2LP	Black Sleeves	BLACK 106 LP	
	Bonus: Thirst Snake				
2008 ☐	AMANETHES	CD	Icarus Music (Argentina)	ICARUS 443	
2009 ☐	A DEEPER KIND OF SLUMBER	2LP	Black Sleeves	BLACK 130 LP	
	Different artwork. Also in coloured vinyl.				
2009 ☐	SUMERIAN CRY	CD	Candlelight (USA)	CANDLEP234CD	
	Different artwork.				
2012 ■	THE SCARRED PEOPLE	CDd	Napalm Records	NPR 451	
	Also a limited edition with special box and pendant.				
2012 ☐	THE SCARRED PEOPLE	2LPg	Napalm Records	NPR 451 LP	
	100 white, 150 grey, 100 clear, 100 gold, also in red and black vinyl. Bonus: Born To Die/ Paradise/Divided (live)/Cain (live)				

2002 CD box - 77380-0

2003 MCDd - 77479-3

2012 CDd - NPR 451

TIE 28

Olov Öhman: v/b, Johan Eriksson: g/v, Patrik Stenman: g, Andreas Lindqvist: d

Skellefteå - Formed in 1998. Rough edged garage type hard rock like a mix of **The Hellacopters** and **Motörhead** with an occasional touch of **AC/DC** and **Sator**.

1999 ☐	Losing Face	CDS	A Westside Fabrication	SPS 32	
2000 ■	LAGUNA SECA	CD	A Westside Fabrication	SP 34	

2000 CD - SP 34

TIME CODE ALPHA

Mads Clausen: v, Peter Lazar: g/k/v, Ulf "Ken" Sandin: b/k/v

Göteborg - *Time Code Alpha* is a project initiated my Peter Lazar. He drafted singer Clausen (*Biscaya, Empire*) and bassist Sandin (*Alien, DaVinci, Transport League, Kee Marcello's K2*). The album also features session players like drummers Svetlan Råket (*Schizophrenic Circus, Malas Intentiones*) and Anders Josefsson, guitarists Johan Randén, Andy LaRoque, Patrik Hansson and Daniel Gustafsson. *Time Code Alpha* play outstanding proggy and quite epic symphonic hard rock, a bit similar to Swedish colleagues **A.C.T**. In December 2009 the digital single *Try To Make Nice! (It's Christmas Time)* was released. In April 2010 Peter released the digital single *Lucky Me* with the proggy band/project **Fred**, also featuring Ken Sandin.

2009 ■	FREAKSHOW	CD	SpinFox	SRCD01	

2009 CD - SRCD 01

TIME GALLERY

Patrik De Vee: v, Fredrik Bergengren: g, Johan Stentorp: k,
Thomas Nyberg: b, Carl Colt: d

Malmö - Very well-polished, high-class AOR/Westcoast, at times similar to **Toto**. The debut album was the first western album to be released on a Chinese label (Shanghai Audio - cassette only). The album was produced by Keith Olsen (Pat Benetar, **Saga, Scorpions, Europe** etc.). *Kaleidoscope* is more powerful and straightforward. Fredrik has played with various artists mostly in the poppier vein, but in 2011 he joined the outstanding melodic hard rockers **Colourstone**.

1986	☐	Carefree Days/Hearts Of Hunger	7"	Medley	MDS 357	
1987	☐	Carefree Days/Hearts Of Hunger	7"	WEA	WEA 248 353-7	
1988	■	Valerie/Nowhere Land	7"	Medley	MDS 387	
1989	☐	TIME GALLERY	CD	Medley	MD 6325	
1989	■	TIME GALLERY	LP	Medley	MD 6325	
1989	☐	TIME GALLERY	CD	Atlantic (USA)	781868-2	
		Remixed versions of Letter/Valorie.				
1989	☐	Taking The Best/Carefree Days	7"	Medley	MDS 347	
		Carefree Days is non-LP				
1989	☐	Blue Boy/The Letter	7"	Medley	MDS 348	
1991	☐	Love Smash/Gentle Touch	7"	Medley	MDS 494	
1992	☐	Like Summerrain/Merry Go Round	7"	Medley	MDS 501	
1992	☐	Like Summerrain	MCD 3tr	Medley	MDXCD 501	
		Tracks: Like Some Rain/Like Summer (Swaymix)/Merry Go Round				
1992	☐	Like Summerrain	MLP 3tr	Medley	MDX 501	
1992	☐	KALEIDOSCOPE	CD	Blackbird	BBCD-253	
1992	☐	You/Love Smash/Closer To Love	MCD 3tr	Blackbird	BBCDS 256	
2010	☐	TIME GALLERY	CD	EMI Music Denmark	EMI 9182002	
		Bonus: Carefree Days (7")/Gentle Touch (B-side)/Hearts Of Hunger (B-side)/Give It Up (demo)				

1988 7" - MDS 387

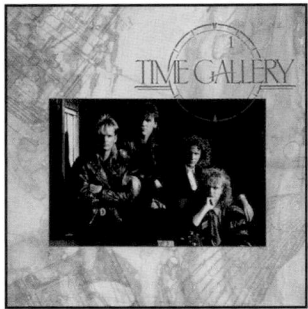

1989 LP - MD 6325

TIME REQUIEM

Göran Edman: v, Magnus Nilsson: g, Richard Andersson: k,
Andy Rose: b, Jörg Andrews: d

Malmö - Main man Richard formed **Time Requiem** in 2001 out of the ashes of the band **Majestic**, with whom he had previously recorded. He has also released albums with **Space Odyssey**, and made guest appearances in **Masson, Adagio, ZooL, Karmakanic, Evil Masquerade, Silver Seraph** etc. The debut features Richard, singer Apollo Papathanasio (**Craze, Spiritual Beggars, Firewind, City People** etc), guitarist Magnus Nordh, bassist Dick Löwgren (**Armageddon, Arch Enemy, Last Tribe** etc) and drummer Peter Wildoer (**Darkane, Grimmark** etc). On the follow-up live album the bass duties were shared between Lögren and Jonas Reingold (who produced the debut), while the drums were shared between Wildoer and Zoltan Csörcz (**The Flower Kings, Art Metal**). The album also features three songs previously recorded by **Majestic**. On *The Inner City Of Reality* Reingold had taken over the bass and Czörcz the drums. On *Optical Illusion* the entire line-up had changed, now featuring singer Göran Edman, guitarist Magnus Nilsson (ex-**God B.C**), bassist Andy Rose and drummer Jörg Andrews. Musically **Time Requiem** is not too far from Andersson's other musical endeavours, such as **Space Odyssey**, meaning high-class, neoclassically infused melodic power metal with great vocals and top-notch musicians.

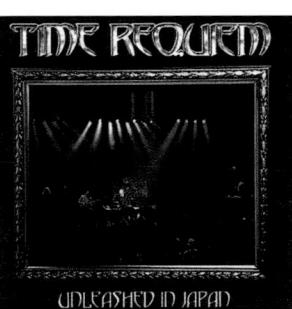

2004 CD - RR 0402-039

2002 CD - RR 016

2002	■	TIME REQUIEM	CD	Regain Records	RR 016
2002	☐	TIME REQUIEM	CD	Avalon Marquee (Japan)	MICP-10328
		Bonus: Losers Shade Of Hell			
2004	■	UNLEASHED IN JAPAN	CDd	Regain Records	RR 0402-039
		1500 copies.			
2004	☐	UNLEASHED IN JAPAN	CD	Avalon Marquee (Japan)	MICP-10394
2004	■	THE INNER CITY OF REALITY	CD	Regain Records	RR 0403-044
2004	☐	THE INNER CITY OF REALITY	CD	Avalon Marquee (Japan)	MICP-10418
		Bonus: Voulez Vous (ABBA cover)			
2006	■	OPTICAL ILLUSION	CD	Regain Records	RR 107
2006	☐	OPTICAL ILLUSION	CD	Candlelight (USA)	CDL 309 CD
2006	☐	OPTICAL ILLUSION	CD	Avalon Marquee (Japan)	MICP-10575
		Bonus: Despair And Pain			

2004 CD - RR 0403-044

TIMELESS MIRACLE

Mikael Holst: v/b, Sten Möller: g, Fredrik Nilsson: k/g, Jaime Salazar: d

Malmö - **Timeless Miracle** were formed in 1995 under the name **Trapped**, but disbanded without releasing anything. Six years later Holst and Nilsson reformed as **Timeless Miracle** and recorded three demos using programmed drums, *In The Year Of Our Lord* (2002), *The Enchanted Chamber* (2003) and *The Voyage* (2004). The line-up was completed with Möller and drummer Jaime Salazar (**The Flower Kings, Bad Habit, Truth** etc) and the band was picked up by Massacre Records in 2005. The debut was released and the band started working on a follow-up, tentatively

2006 CD - RR 107

named *Under The Moonlight*. However problems with the recording pushed the completion date forward and in January 2008 Salazar left due to being fully booked with other bands, and *Trapped* drummer Kim Widfors returned. *Timeless Miracle* play high-speed melodic German style power metal with a touch of folk music, a bit like a mix of *Blind Guardian* and *Falconer*.

2005 ■ INTO THE ENCHANTED CHAMBER ....CD Massacre Records ....MAS CD 0482
2005 □ INTO THE ENCHANTED CHAMBER ....CD Avalon Marquee (Japan)..............MICP-10521
    Bonus: Church Of The Damned
2005 □ INTO THE ENCHANTED CHAMBER ....CD Art Music Group (Russia) ....AMG 270

2005 CD - MAS CD 0482

TIMESCAPE

**Mikael Moberg: v, Kerim Kalkan: g/k, Johan Berlin: g,
Johan Eriksson: b, Anders Berlin: d**

Norrköping - Formed in 1995. The first MCD was a musically good, but vocally very weak effort. The second and especially third release contains highly interesting progressive hard rock. The band is featured on *Ironic Compilation 1997* (Ironic IRO-001). The first release featured singer Robert Haglund. Anders later joined *Eclipse* and has since been found in bands like *Miss Behaviour, Bloodbound* and *Shineth*. The band was preparing the recording of a new album in 2002, but it wasn't released until 2011. *Until Then* is by far the band's best album, where it seems all the pieces fell into place. It's a bit darker than its predecessors, which isn't a bad thing in this genre (just look at *Evergrey*). Great production, strong song material and great musicianship topped with killer vocals from Moberg. Kalkan is ex-*The Waiters*.

1996 MCD - TS 1

1996 ■ Timescape...MCD 3tr private ....TS 1
    Tracks: Silent Room Of Time/Whispering Shadows/My Lonely Stare
1997 □ TWO WORLDS ....CD Nettle-Space Productions ....NSP-AA 001
2000 □ STRANGE ....CD Adrenalin...ADR 0013
2011 ■ UNTIL THEN ....CD Nettle-Space Productions .... NSPCD 004

2011 CD - NSPCD 004

TIPPEN RUDA

Johan Hansson: v, Mikael Johannesson: g, Stefan Olsson: b, Sepp "Zepp" Urgard: d

Stockholm - Johan and Mikael moved from Malmö to Stockholm to start a band, but *Tippen Ruda* was never really a band but more a project. The MCD was recorded with the aid of session bassist Stefan Olsson (*House Of Shakira, Nord*) and drummer Sepp Urgard (*Rising Force*). Early 1993 they changed their name to *High Octane* and in April they recorded 3 new tracks with the help of bassist Anders Moberg and drummer Morgan Ågren. Later that year the band was completed with bassist Sixten Jaskari (*Cut 4*) and drummer Ulf Johansson and they changed name to *Mandala* and released an excellent MCD. Mikael later moved to England, but has since returned and is today in the band *LoveHandles*. Great bluesy riff-oriented hard rock!

1990 MCD - TRP 1

1990 ■ Tippen Ruda...MCD 4tr TR Productions ....TRP 1
    Tracks: Nothing For Your Sweat/The Infant/Doubledealing/Wish To Thank You.

TITAN

**Gustav Larsson: v, Kristian Larsen: g, Christofer Björck: k,
Gustav Bergström: b, Simon Cop: d**

Helsingborg - Formed by a group of schoolmates out of the ashes of the band *Striker*. The average age was around eighteen. The MCD contains slick, well-played AOR in the vein of colleagues like *H.E.A.T, Danger Avenue* and *Houston*. Well worth checking out. A full-length album is in the making.

2009 ■ Steps..MCD 6tr private 320470 122129
    Tracks: Hero/I Want You/When Evening Falls/Steps/Top Of Your World/One More Night

2009 MCD - 320470 122129

TITANIC TRUTH (Conny Bloom's)

Conny "Bloom" Blomquist: v/g, Anders "Nippe" Fästader: b, Tony Hellander: d/v

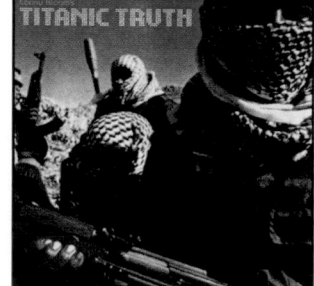

Stockholm - After the (first) split of *Electric Boys*, Conny pursued a solo career that evolved into *Titanic Truth*. Despite this being a good and solid melodic seventies-sounding rocker with the funky swagger of *Electric Boys*, it sank like the famous ship. The band split only a few months after the release as the album did not become the success they had hoped for. Conny then continued under his own name, and recorded a live CD. He was also in *Silver Ginger 5* for a while, before joining *Hanoi Rocks*. When they decided to quit, he reformed *Electric Boys*, who are still highly active. "Nippe" (aka Nilsson) is ex-*Great King Rat, Advice, John Norum Band* and *Southfork*. Tony Hellander (aka Tony Roy Taylor) was once the lead singer of *Trash* and also a member of *Dream Bank*.

1996 CD - 531 573-2

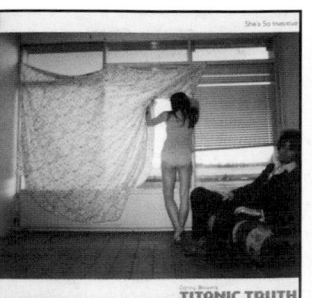

1996 ■ TITANIC TRUTH ....CD Stockholm Records.........................531 573-2
1996 ■ She's So Inventive/Good Time Coming ....CDSp 2tr Stockholm Records.........................576 598-2

1996 CDS - 576 598-2

TO AFRICA WITH LOVE

Johan Olsson: v, Paul Zanichelli: v, Tomas Åberg: v, Niklas "Nic O'Noon" Olausson: v, Håkan Windahl: v, Jay Lee Keen: v, Mats Johansson: g/d, Anders Fernlund: g, Peter "Pete Meat" Vilhelmsson: k, Johan Olsson: b

Karlskrona/Karlshamn - This is a more local version of the *Swedish Metal Aid* project. The single was recorded to raise money for the starving people in Ethiopia. The singers are from the bands *Interaction, Scratch, Parasite/Rebelene, Deception* and *Banzai*. The song is a typical eighties hard rock ballad. Fernlund was also in *Killerhawk*, ex-*Arsenik*, later in *Vekerum Blues Band*.

1985 7" - PL 11

1985 ■ To Africa With Love	7" 1tr	Platina	PL 11
One-sided single.			

TOKEN

Mattias Åhlen: v, Johan Sjöberg: g, Mikael Rosengren: k, Niklas Holmkvist: b, Patrik Johansson: d

Stockholm - *Token* were formed in 1990, but split a few years later. In 2000 Mikael and Niklas decided it was time to re-form the band. They drafted singer Hasse "HB" Andersson (ex-*Fire & Ice*) and in 2001 they landed a deal with MTM. Mikael was also in *Scudiero, Damned Nation* and is now in *Constancia* and *Skarr*. Hasse was also found in *Scudiero, Fatal Smile*, and is now in *MindSplit*. The debut album was mixed by Pontus Norgren (*Talisman, Humanimal* etc). On the second album the line-up had changed seeing singer Mattias Åhlen replacing Andersson and drummer Patrik Johansson (*Yngwie Malmsteen, Stormwind*) replacing Pontus Ågeryd. *Token* produce high-quality melodic guitar driven AOR/hard rock. A notch above the rest as they are quite successful in avoiding the traditional clichés, but still being true to the genre. Great, powerful guitar playing, a driving rhythm section and nice keyboard arrangements. Should appeal to fans of *Eclipse, Damned Nation* and *Dreamhunter*.

2002 CD - 0681-47

2004 CD - 0681-103

2002 ■ TOMORROWLAND	CD	MTM	0681-47
2004 □ PUNCH	CD	Avalon Marquee (Japan)	MICP-10464
Bonus: Tear Down The Walls (video)			
2004 ■ PUNCH	CD	MTM	0681-103

TOM TRICK

Ulf Kjell: v/g, Nisse Carlsson: g, Arne Arvidsson: g, Mikael Carlsson: g/k, Badde Abrahamsson: b, Nils Reuterswärd: d

Stockholm - Formed in 1979. *Tom Trick* is the Swedish name for the comic character Brick Bradford. Basic lightweight hard rock with rough-edged vocals in Swedish. A bit like a hard rock version of the *Tom Robinson Band*. There are a couple of pretty good live recordings from Swedish radio floating around, too. Before the album, Matte Lindgren replaced drummer Gunnar Forselius, and after the album Badde Abrahamsson replaced Roland Sterling and Arne Arvidsson was added on second guitar. On the last MLP Nils Reuterswärd replaced Matte Lindegren and Carlsson was added on keyboard/guitar. The band split in 1983. Ulf is today involved in the ambient pop project *NOW Lab*.

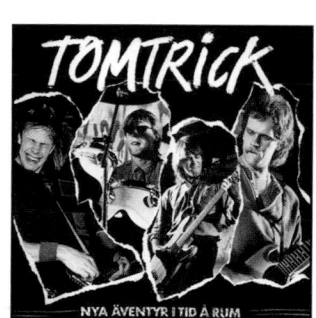

1980 LP - CBS 84857

1981 7" - EPC 1967

1980 □ Suddiga/Profilen/Achtung!	7"	CBS	CBS 9483
1980 ■ NYA ÄVENTYR I TID OCH RUM	LP	CBS	CBS 84857
1981 ■ Reaktioner/Rosita faller!	7"	CBS	EPC 1967
1982 ■ Tom Trick	MLP 7tr	WEA Metronome	MILP 1
Tracks: Det regnar i mitt hjärta/Inte en vinter till/Innan dammet lägger sej/Främmande kroppsspråk/Sista natten/En man utan svindel/Älska mig nu!			

1982 LP - MILP 1

TOMAS BERGSTEN'S FANTASY

Tomas Bergsten: v/g/k/d

Karlskrona - Tomas recorded a single with the band *Fantasy* in 1989 and in 2012 he decided to pick up the pieces and record a solo album. The album features guest appearances from, for instance, Bruce Kulick (*Kiss, Union*), Janne Stark, Per Schelander (*House Of Shakira*), Jörgen Schelander (*Mercury Fang*) and former *Fantasy* colleague Micke Friman. Great melodic hard rock with a strong touch of *Asia* at their heaviest.

2013 ■ CAUGHT IN THE DARK	CD	7Chords	FSY002

2013 CD - FSY002

TOMMY TYSPER & THE KIDS

Tommy Tysper (Pawlicki): v/g, Quint Starkie: g/v, Mark Tysper: b/g/k/v, Niklas Tärnhamn: d

Stockholm - Lightweight melodic hard rock. Tommy was actually a very young man when he recorded this album, 13-14 years old. The quality corresponds with the age... Quint has also worked with *Marc Quee*. Tommy later went into production and songwriting and has had several Billboard top ten hits.

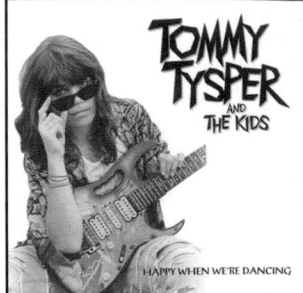

1989	☐	YOUNG AND ROCKIN' CRAZY	LP	Planet	MOP 3053
1989	☐	YOUNG AND ROCKIN' CRAZY	CD	Planet	MOP 3053
1989	☐	Young And Rockin' Crazy/Get It On	7"	Planet	MOP 150
1990	■	Happy When We're Dancing/In My Paradise	7"	Planet	MOP 153
1990	○	Rock The House Down/in The Night	7"	Planet	MOP 154

1990 7" - MOP 153

TOMTEROCKERS

Patrick Wallin: v, Raymond Liljegren: g, Magnus Ählström: g, Anders Romppanen: g, Thomas Wunger: k, John Jacobsson: b, Krister Andersson: d

Sollentuna - Formed in 1980 at a youth club for a Christmas party. Dressed as Santas the guys do songs by *Van Halen*, *ZZ Top*, *Sha-Boom*, *Joan Jett* etc., but with Swedish lyrics all about Christmas. For instance *Sha-Boom*'s *R.O.C.K* became *G.R.Ö.T* (porridge) and *Jump* by *Van Halen* was transformed into *Jul* (Christmas) in the hands of these Santa Rockers. Fun if you understand the language. Singer on the first 7" was Björn Arvidsson. They also did a cover show of *Blues Brothers* material, under the name *Moose Brothers*. For completists only.

1983	☐	God Jul Och Gott Nytt År/Midnatt Råder (Tomtarnas Julnatt)	7"	Mercury	814772-7
1989	☐	G.R.Ö.T/Say Mama!	7"	Eagle Records	ES 10-46
1990	☐	TOMTEROCKERS	CD	Eagle Records	ECD 030
1990	☐	TOMTEROCKERS	LP	Eagle Records	ELP 030
1991	○	Renar/Jag vill ha en gran	7"	Eagle Records	ES 10-57
1993	■	TOMTEROCKERS	CD	EMI	CMCD 6080

1993 CD - CMCD 6080

TON OF BRICKS

Tony Jelencovich: v, Markus Fristedt: g, Martin Andersson: g, Robert Hakemo: b, Anders Blomstrand: d

Uddevalla/Göteborg - The first MCD is really heavy and powerful metal in the vein of *Pantera* or Swedish colleagues like *Livin' Parazite* and *Debase*. Great band with a wall of guitars and great powerful, but melodic vocals. They also do a great cover of *Accept*'s *Fast As A Shark*. Singer Jonas Dahlström, who later joined *Illwill*, was replaced by Tony (ex-*B-Thong*, *Iron Shitsnakes*, *Transport League*, now in *M.A.N* and *DeathDestruction*) on the second release. After the second release Blomstrand left and was replaced by Anders Ström (ex-*NME Within*). Markus left and they drafted Kristian Lampila (ex-*Gooseflesh*). In 1998 they changed their name to *Slavestate* and recorded the track *Roots Bloody Roots* for the Black Sun Records *Sepultura* tribute. They made their last gig May 22nd 1998 together with *The Haunted*, *Destiny* and *Taetre* at Musikens Hus in Göteborg. Martin was later in stonerband *Elixir* and *Black Sabbath* cover band *Sabotage*, who made a CDS in 1994. Robert and Kristian joined *Relevant Few*. The song *Abuse* was supposed to be on the Black Mark compilation *Out Of The Box III*, but it was never released, even though cover and all was finished, due to financial reasons.

1995 MCD - ROBCD 002

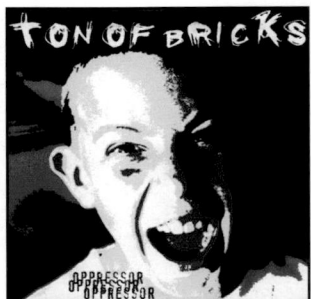

| 1995 | ■ | Blind | MCD 4tr | private | ROBCD 002 |

Tracks: Blind/Outcast/Worst Case Of Weakness/Fast As A Shark (Accept cover)

| 1997 | ■ | Oppressor | MCDp 5tr | private | TOBPR 001 |

Tracks: Abuse/Seven Throats Cut/Within The Chamber/Undying/Oppressor. 500 copies.

1997 MCDp - TOBPR 001

TONVIKT

Michael Ardenheim: v/b, Hans Hogedal: g, Tor Nygård: d

Göteborg - Started in 1975 as *Emphasis*, featuring bassist/singer Michael Ardenheim, drummer Roy Östh and guitarists Hans Hogedal and Anders Mossberg. A year later Mossberg quit and the name was changed to *Tonvikt* (Swedish for emphasis). Anders later played with *Jerusalem*. As Östh quit the band for a period of time, Tor Nygård played drums on the single. In 1981 the band also drafted second guitarist Kurt-Anders Svensson, but six months later *Tonvikt* folded. The band plays quite good seventies-style hard rock quite similar to *Motvind*. The band reunited for some shows in 2008. In 1979-80 the band also played under the name *Gerry & The Moonshiners* featuring Ardenheim, Hogedal, Östh, Gerry Svensson and Sten Sandberg.

| 1979 | ■ | Samma batonger/Morgontankar | 7" | HRM | HRM 1-001 |

1979 7" - HRM 1-001

TOO LATE

André Karlsson: v, Mattias "Lalle" Carlsson: g/k, Carl-Johan "Calle" Lindström: b

Helsingborg (Rydebäck) - Formed in 1992 under the name *Too Fast*, but because they were always too late, this became the new name in 1993. In 1994 Lalle went to the US to study at GIT. When he returned they recorded the MCD. Since they could only fit in 25 minutes, one song had to be shortened when mastering, and in frustration they named it *RÖVEN* (asshole). The band split in 1996. Ballsy hard rock with a seventies touch. Bengt Johansson and Jocke Carlsson played drums on the record, since drummer Peter "Moose" Mosebach, also went to the US.

| 1995 | ■ | Too Late | MCD 6tr | private | TLCD 9509 $ |

Tracks: Going Down/Take It So Bad/Little Bird/Tell Me/She Is Crying/RÖVEN

1995 MCD - TLCD 9509

TORCH

Östen "Dan Dark" Bidebo: v, Tomi Peltonen: g, Alex Jonsson: b, Kristian Houtari: d

Eskilstuna - *Torch* are an out-and-out Swedish FVASHM (First Wave of Swedish Heavy Metal) in the same style and league as *Axewitch* and *Overdrive*. Check out the song *Battle Axe* on the self-titled album. Great powerful stuff. *Torch* was formed in 1980 by guitarist Christer "Chris J" First, drummer Håkan "Steve Streaker" Hedlund and guitarist Claus Wildt. They drafted singer Stefan Wedlund, who was soon replaced by Östen "Dan Dark" Bidebo. Bassist Greger "Ian Greg" Gerlehagen soon completed the line-up. The band did several shows with bands like *Motörhead* and *Warlock* and the albums are classic pieces of Scandinavian 80s metal. The band finally split after *Elektrikiss* and Claus played on *Masi*'s second album, while Christer and Håkan were later in the reformed *Crystal Pride* and Östen in the cover bands *Bläästers* and *Eccept*. The song *Warlock* is found on the compilation *Force Of The Blade* (86 Banzai Records). In 2003 Östen resurrected *Torch*, but with a new recording line-up featuring drummer Kristian Houtari (*Scaar, Griffen, Days Of Anger*), guitarists Tomi Peltonen (*Griffen*) and bass player Alex Jonsson (*Scaar, Days Of Anger*). The album *Dark Sinner* features rerecordings of old songs plus the new tracks *The Dark Sinner* and *We Will Fight*. The band's live line-up has also featured drummer Magnus Ulfstedt (*Grand Design*, live drummer for *Lion's Share, Royal Hunt, Jimi Jamison* etc) and guitarists Eric Rauti (*Dreamland, NME Within, Infinity* etc) and Kenneth Jonsson (*The Citadel, Tad Morose*) plus bass player Jörgen Andersson (*The Citadel, Bloodbound, Soul Source*). All albums have been reissued on CD, except *Elektrikiss* because the record company wouldn't sell Metal Blade the rights. A new album is in the pipeline.

1982 MLP - TEP 001

1983 MLP - MAXI-POOL001

1984 LP - LP-004

1982 ■	Torch .... MLP 5tr	Tandan	TEP 001	
	Tracks: Beyond/Fire Raiser/Pain/Mercenary/Retribution. Aka Fireraiser. First press with blue label, second with pink.			
1983 ■	The Serpent/Cut Throat Tactics/Bad Girls .... MLP 3tr	Record Pool	MAXI-POOL001	
	This is a private press numbered promo, made in 1.500 copies. The Serpent is previously unreleased.			
1984 ☐	TORCH .... LP	Tandan	TAN LP 5	
1984 ■	ELECTRIKISS .... LP	Sword	LP-004	
	Also pressed in red transparent vinyl.			
1985 ☐	Fire Raiser .... MLP 5tr	Mausoleum	BONE 128315	
	Same as the self-titled MLP.			
1985 ☐	TORCH .... LP	Megaton	MEGATON 0006	
1985 ☐	TORCH .... LP	Banzai (Canada)	BRC 1938	
1985 ☐	WARLOCK .... LP	Zyx Metal	45002	
	Same as the self-entitled album.			
1985 ☐	ELEKTRIKISS .... LP	Roadrunner	RR 9812	
1985 ☐	ELEKTRIKISS .... LP	Banzai (Canada)	BRC 1934	
1986 ☐	TORCH .... LP	Nexus (Jap)	K28P-420	
1997 ☐	TORCH .... CD	Nexus (Jap)	KICP 2623	
1990 ■	Fireraiser .... MCD 5tr	Metal Blade	7 73425-2	
1990 ☐	TORCH .... CD	Metal Blade	7 73426-2	
2009 ☐	DARK SINNER .... CD	private	Vincd2002	
2009 ☐	DARK SINNER .... CD	Mausoleum	251194	

1990 MCD - 7 73425-2

Unofficial relases:
2003 ☐	ELEKTRIKISS .... CD	Time Warp	- -	
	Bootleg.			

TORCH BEARER

Pär Johansson: v, Christian Älvestam: g, Patrik Gardberg: g,
Thomas "Plec" Johansson: b, Rolf "Stuka" Pilve: d

Skövde/Boden - High-speed technical death metal in the vein of *Unmoored* and *Satariel* with some nice twists and turns in the arrangements. The line-up on the debut featured Älvestam (*Unmoored, Solar Dawn, Incapacity, Scar Symmetry*), Johansson (*Satariel, Demiurg, The Duskfall*), bassist Mikael Granbacke, guitarist Göran Johansson (*Setherial, Chaosdemon*) and drummer Henrik Schönström (*Unmoored, Solar Dawn, Incapacity, Traumatized*). Tomas "Plec" Johansson provided a guest solo. The album was recorded by Jonas Kjellgren (*Centinex, Carnal Forge, Sonic System*). On the second album Göran Johansson had been replaced by Patrik Gardberg (*Ammotrack, Solution .45*). On *Death Meditation* bassist Mikael Granbacke had been replaced by Thomas "Plec" Johansson and drummer Henrik Schönström was out, while the drums were handled by Rolf "Stuka" Pilve.

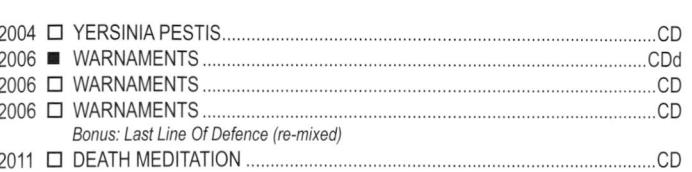

Need a light?

2004 ☐	YERSINIA PESTIS .... CD	Metal Blade	3984-14489-2	
2006 ■	WARNAMENTS .... CDd	Regain Records	RR 106	
2006 ☐	WARNAMENTS .... CD	Candlelight (USA)	CDL 185 CD	
2006 ☐	WARNAMENTS .... CD	Soundholic (Japan)	SHCD-10072	
	Bonus: Last Line Of Defence (re-mixed)			
2011 ☐	DEATH MEDITATION .... CD	Vic Records	VIC 038 CD	

2006 CD - RR 106

TORE AND THE NO SMOKERS

Christoffer Carlsson: v, Robin Larsson: g, Andreas Augustsson: b, Conny Carlsson: d

Stockholm - Tore And The No Smokers are, as you may suspect, not really one of the most serious metal bands. The concept is basically straightforward hard rock/metal with lyrics against smoking aimed for school kids. The album titles are *Rökning dödar* (smoking kills), *Rökfri värld* (smoke free world) and *Nikotinsvin* (nicotine swine). The band mostly plays schools.

2006 ☐	RÖKNING DÖDAR	CD	Artache	GA 016	
2007 ■	RÖKFRI VÄRLD	CD	Artache	GA 018	
2009 ☐	NIKOTINSVIN	CD	Artache	GA 019	

2007 CD - GA 018

TORMENTED

Andreas "Dread" Axelsson: v/g, Claes Holmberg: g,
Roberth Karlsson: b, Jocke Ölund: d

Finspång - Tormented were formed in 2008 with the intention of creating death metal of their own choice. Dread has been found in numerous bands such as *Edge Of Sanity, Infestdead, Total Terror, Incapacity, Marduk* and *Necronaut*, while Roberth is a former member of *Edge Of Sanity, Scar Symmetry, Pan-Thy-Monium, Darkified, Solar Dawn, Facebreaker, Incapacity, Devian* etc. These boys don't fool around with any melodic nonsense. This is pure grinding old-school death metal similar to *Dismember* and *Grotesque*.

2011 CDd - POSH 159

2011 ☐	ROTTEN DEATH	CD	Iron Fist	IFPCD 028	
2011 ■	ROTTEN DEATH	CDd	Listenable Records	POSH 159	
2011 ☐	ROTTEN DEATH	LPg	Nuclear Winter Now!	NWR 036	
	108 red + 393 black vinyl. New artwork.				
2011 ☐	Tormented/Bombs Of Hades (split)	10" EP	War Anthem Records	WAR 041EP	
	Split with Bombs Of Hades. Tracks: Repulsion Fix/Tormentor				
2012 ■	Graveyard Lust	10" 6tr	War Anthem Records	WAR 048 EP	
	Tracks: Graveyard Lust/Revel In Blood/Slowly Twisted To Death/Sacrifice The Dead/Sick In The Head/Horror Of The Faceless Dead				
2012 ☐	Graveyard Lust	MCD 6tr	War Anthem Records	WAR 049 CD	

2012 10" - WAR 048 EP

TORN APART

Christoffer Långström: v, David Eliasson: g, Mikael Sandström: g,
Petter Johansson: b, Alexander Wegebro: d

Umeå - Formed in 2005 by Eliasson, Sandström and Wegebro. A few months later Petter joined and shortly after Christoffer completed the line-up. *Torn Apart* play riff-oriented heavy death metal a bit similar to early *Entombed*. In 2009 singer Långström left the band and it folded.

2007 MCD - - -

2007 ■	Craving Pale Flesh	MCD 4tr	Pathologically Explicit Recordings	- -	
	Tracks: Slaughtered By Hands/The Impaler/Craving Pale Flesh/Morbid Penetration				

TORNADO BABIES

Dan "Harry" Ellström: v, Bertil "Beppe" Nieminen: g,
Kenny Gustavsson: g, Paul Vahala: b, Dan Rigtorp: d

Göteborg - Formed in 1987 by Nieminen, Vahala, Gustavsson, Ellström and drummer Mats Hansson (ex-*Bumsen Muss Man*, later in *Mustasch*). Hansson was soon replaced by Lennart Esbjörnsson (also ex-*Bumsen Muss Man*). However, the albums featured drummer Dan Rigtorp. Sleazy raunchy rock 'n roll with some *AC/DC* hints. The band left Musik Musik and material for a third album was being written, but the band folded. Paul had previously recorded with the punkish band *Nuts*. Beppe and Paul recorded a CD with the grunge/hardcore band *Not Enough Hate*. The song *Razamanaz* is a cover of *Nazareth*.

1991 CD - BAD 18-11

1991 ■	EAT THIS!	CD	Bad & Dangerous	BADCD 18-11	
1991 ☐	EAT THIS!	LP	Bad & Dangerous	BADLP 18-11	
1992 ☐	Instant Fun/Life's A Bitch	CDS 2tr	Musik Musik	MM 03-2	
1993 ☐	Delirious/Another Day In Hell/Razamanaz (live)	MCD 3tr	Musik Musik	MMS 6	
1993 ☐	DELIRIOUS	CD	Musik Musik	MM 7	

TORNADO SOUP

Peter Andersson: g, Johan Lindström: k, Tommy Andersson: b, Martin Hedberg: d

Örebro - Yet another high-class guitarist from Sweden. Peter participated in the Swedish lead guitar competition *Guitar Battle* and reached a final place for the two years it existed on a national basis. He therefore has one track on the compilation CD *Guitar Heroes Of Sweden* Part 2. The CD contains some great guitar wailing that will interest fans of classical lead guitar music from the likes of Satriani, Vai etc.

1994 CD - PA 002

1994 ■	TORNADO SOUP	CD	Navian	PA 002	

TORSTEN

Nicklas: v, Jörgen Månsson: g, Mats Gihl: g, Mikael Östberg: b, Lars Wiklund: d

Löddeköpinge - Below-average standard 80s heavy metal produced by *Heavy Load/Highbrow* guitarist Eddy Malm. The reason was because they had heard the record company was no good at producing. As Mats' mother knew Eddy's mother, she asked her to ask him to help the band during the recording.

1983 ■ King Of The Nest/Are You Ready ....7" Pang ....PSI 086 **$**

Unofficial releases:
2000 ☐ King Of The Nest/Are You Ready ....7" NWOSHM..005
     500 copies bootleg.

1983 7" - PSI 086

TORTURE DIVISION

Jörgen Sandström: v/b, Kenta "Lord K" Philipson: g, Tobias Gustafsson: d

Örebro - Now here's a trio with a lot under their belts. Sandström is/has been in *Entombed, The Project Hate MCMXCIX, Putrefaction, Grave, Vicious Art, Krux, Death Breath* etc., Philipson in *The Project Hate MCMXCIX, Dark Funeral, God Among Insects, Leukemia, Odyssey, House Of Usher* etc. and Gustafsson in *Vomitory, God Among Insects, Syrus* etc. The trio found their common ground in 2007. They were not interested in making albums either, so they just started making demos. This means the CD releases are actually compilations of these demos. The band has recorded eight demos between 2008-2012, all available for download from the band's website. A new demo, *Satan, sprit och våld* (Satan, booze and violence) was recorded in 2012. High-speed, blast-beat, great-sounding death metal in the vein of *Grave* and *Dismember*.
Website: www.torturedivision.net

2008 7" - - -   *2012 CD - P18R 046*

2008 ■ Suffer The Shitmas ....7" private ....- - **$**
    Tracks: The Torture Never Stops (W.A.S.P cover)/The Putrifier. 4 copies. Test press.
2009 ☐ WITH ENDLESS WRATH, WE BRING UPON THEE OUR INFERNAL TORTURE
    ....CDd Abyss Records...........................ABYSS 06 CD
2010 ☐ EVIGHETENS DÅRAR ....CDd Abyss Records........................ABYSS 021 CD
2011 ☐ The Eyes Of The Dead ....MCDpg 3tr Close-Up..CUC 086
    Tracks: Vampire Empire/Through The Eyes Of The Dead/Clark The Monarch. Promo only
2012 ■ WITH ENDLESS WRATH, WE BRING UPON THEE OUR INFERNAL TORTURE
    ....CD Punishment 18 Records P18R 046

TOTAL TERROR

Dan Swanö: v/g, Anders "Drette" Axelsson: b, Benny "Bempa" Larsson: d

Örebro - *Total Terror* is basically a side project of three, at the time, *Edge Of Sanity* members. The trio recorded a demo in 1993. The album was recorded in 1994. The CD is a compilation of all the tracks, mixed and mastered in 2008. Crust core mixed with death metal, sung in Swedish with more punkish lyrics like "to do the dishes sucks dick" and "allow me to puke". Not so evil this time. Nothing for the fainthearted, though!

2009 ■ TOTAL TERROR..CD Vic Records..................................VIC 015 CD

2009 CD - VIC 015 CD

TOUGH TRADE

Patrik "Lind" Lindblom: v, Janne "JJ Taneli" Junttila: g,
Alexander "Alex" Johnsson: b, Johan Sjöberg: d

Eskilstuna - Formed in 1988. High class melodic 80s hard rock in the vein of early *Treat* and *Europe*. Classy vocals, classy musicians and a great sound. Well worth searching for. They also have the song *Put A Li'l Love* on the *Wanted - Hard Rock Compilation*. On the 7", second guitarist Mikael "Mike Wild" Widelund was also in the band and Robert "Geezon" Gustafsson handled the drums. The band split in January 1994. Bass player Alexander Johnsson later became the singer in the far heavier band *Rejected*, where also drummer Johan was found.

1990 7" - TTS 001

1990 ■ Sweet Talkin'/Lost In The Rhythm...7" private ....TTS 001

TOXAEMIA

Stevo Bolgakov: v/g, Linus Olsson: g, Pontus Cervin: b, Emil Norman: d

Motala - Ultra-fast death metal with totally indecipherable vocals. The band was formed in 1989 by Pontus Cervin, Emil Norrman and Stevo Bolgakov, and no-one in the band could play. -"We learned along the way", as one of the members said. Emil was supposed to play guitar but as the drummer had no talent, he took over. They called themselves *O.S.S.* at the time and later went

1990 7" - SCAM 011

through *Mutilator* and *Anguish* before settling for *Toxaemia*, when Stevo and Linus entered the band. In 1990 the band recorded the four-track demo *Kaleidoscopic Lunacy* and printed 200 cassettes. A fifth song, *The Acquisition* was also recorded and featured on the compilation *Rätt i örat* (1991). The song was later renamed *Hate Within* and featured on the demo *Buried To Rot*. Linus had to leave because of military service and the band found no replacement. Despite this they recorded the demo *Buried To Rot* and some songs meant for a second EP, that never happened. The band finally folded in 1992 and all members except Pontus have sold their instruments. *Buried to Rise* is a compilation featuring all the band's recorded material.

2011 2LP - CRYPT 14

1990 ■ Beyond The Realm .... 7" 4tr Seraphic Decay Records .... SCAM 011
  Tracks: Beyond The Realm/Another Lie Another Death/Who Dies/Expired Christianity. Two versions: orange print artwork on purple vinyl (depicted) and b/w on grey marble vinyl.
2010 □ BURIED TO RISE: 1990-1991 DISCOGRAPHY .... 2CD Dark Descent .... DDR 015CD
2011 ■ BURIED TO RISE .... 2LP The Crypt .... CRYPT 14
  300 white and 200 black vinyl copies.

TRACTION
Pontus Pedersén: v/b, Michael Qvarsell: g, Per Blückert: g,
Robert Samuelsson: k, Mattias Pedersén: d
Vretstorp - In 1977 four young guys in Östantorp started the band *The Teenagers*. The members were Pontus and Mattias Pedersén, Robert Samuelsson and guitarist Michael Qvarsell. After a couple of years second guitarist Per Blückert entered the band and the name now felt somewhat out of date, which made them change it to *Traction*. The musical style was also changed to more melodic hard rock. In 1983 the band entered the studio and recorded the single, which was a big hit locally. Pretty decent 70s-oriented melodic hard rock. In 1985 military service was knocking at the door and the band decided to take a break. Mattias later formed the band *Blårock*, which was more sixties-style rock and in 2000 he formed the cover band *Solid*, which also featured guitarist Andreas "Toya" Johansson of *Saint Deamon* fame.

1983 7" - PP 65

1983 ■ You And I/Hopeless End .... 7" private .... PP 65

TRACY GOES CRAZY
Tony Niva: v, Thomas "Paulus" Kilberg: g,
Håkan "Philip Junior" Holmström: b, Michael Alforth: d
Skövde/Skara - Tony was ex-*Swedish Erotica* and *Zanity*, later joined *Axia*, formed his own band *Niva*, which now has become *Oxygen*. Tomas was later in the rock band *Oliver Hardy*. *Tracy Goes Crazy* deliver outstanding AOR with killer vocals, a must for fans of *TNT*, *Treat*, *Dokken* etc. The single was produced by Patrik Tibell (*T'Bell* etc).

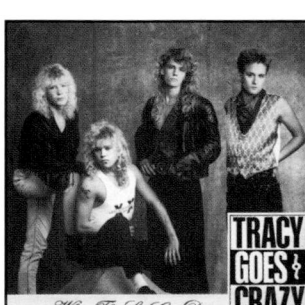

1990 7" - - -

1990 ■ When The Sun Goes Down/Let Me Be The One .... 7" Alexandra Records .... - -

TRAIL OF MURDER
Urban Breed: v, Daniel Olsson: g, Pelle Åkerlind: d
Bollnäs - Another newcomer with skilled musicians. Breed has previously been in *Tad Morose* and *Bloodbound*. The first included Olsson and latter also featured Åkerlind (also in *Morgana Lefay*). Great melodic hard rock in the vein of *Bloodbound*.

2012 CD - MH 00096

2012 ■ SHADES OF ART .... CD Metal Heaven .... MH 00096

TRANSIT
Dan Kristiansson: v, Michael Nilsson: g, Jan Melander: k,
Börje Gyllsén: b, Evert Gyllsén: d
Östersund - Another dark horse. Judging by the cover it might as well be one of those low grade heavy metal dozen bands. However *Transit* play excellent melodic hard rock with some nice keyboard/guitar arrangements and good vocals. Well worth looking for. Singer Dan later recorded a great single with the band *Pride*.

1985 7" - YRA-001

1985 ■ Leaving You/Wait For The Moment .... 7" Trance YRA-001

TRANSPORT LEAGUE
Tony Julien Jelencovich: v/g, Peter Hunyadi: g, Lars Häglund: b, Mattias Starander: d
Göteborg - Formed in 1994 by *Concrete Stuff/B-Thong/Iron Shit Snakes/Ton Of Bricks*-singer Tony. They describe their sound as: "*Black Sabbath* meets *White Zombie* with a hint of boogie", which actually is very close to the truth. Heavy, powerful and as merciless as a raging tank. The line-up on the debut consisted of Tony, drummer Johan Reiven and bassist Lars Häglund. Lars was also found in *B-Thong* and Johan in *Hyperhug*, *Wunderbaum* and later in *LOK*. On the second album Johan was replaced by Ulf "Ken" Sandin (*Alien, Time Code Alpha, Kee*

Marcello's K2). *Superevil*, which featured Tony, Ken, guitarist Peter Hunyadi and drummer Mattias Starander (ex-*Major N.A.*), was also released in a limited edition containing a rusty nail. *Satanic Panic* was produced by Roberto Laghi. The band also have the tracks *Ride Baby* and *Wants You* on the local compilation *Greatest Hits Of Partille Rocken 1994* and they appear on the *Power From The North* compilation, where they cover *Glorious Bankrobbers*' song *Crazy Sioux* and on *Molten Universe Volume Two* (1000 MU), where they do *Speedhead*. The line-up on *Satanic Panic* had changed, now seeing Patrik "J Sten" Jerksten having replaced Mattias Starander. Tony also has his cover-projects *Glanzig*, *Plantera* and *Kriss*, besides the out and out metal band *Commander* (known as Dennis Tomb), which unfortunately only made some demos. After *Satanic Panic* the bass duties were taken over by Fredrik "Stitch" Blomqvist, guitarist Peter Hunyadi was replaced by Adam Magnusson (ex-*Denial*), while drummer Patrik was replaced by Stefan "Stipen" Carlsson (ex-*Merciless/Dia Psalma*, later in *Trash Amigos*). This line-up recorded the excellent bone-crushing and lead-heavy EP *Grand Amputation*. On *Multiple Organ Harvest* guitarist Magnusson had been replaced by Dan "J" Johansson (*Generous Maria, Mary Beats Jane*) and drummer Stitch by Magnus 155. On August 31, 2005, the band split, but continued as M.A.N, later Massive Audio Nerve. In 2009 the *Superevil* line-up reunited for a couple of shows. Tony has also been fronting bands like *Icon In Me, C-187* and *Angel Blake*. In 2011 the single *Speedhead* was released digitally. In 2012 Tony also joined *Deathdestruction*. *Boogie From Hell* saw the returin of Hunyadi, Starander and Häglund.

1995 CD - M7016 2   1997 CD - M 7027 2

1999 CD - RTD 319.5345.2

1995 ■	STALLION SHOWCASE	CD	Mascot	M7016 2
1995 ☐	STALLION SHOWCASE	CD	Marquee (Japan)	APCY 8327
	Bonus: Last Astro Verdict			
1997 ■	SUPEREVIL	CD	Mascot	M 7027 2
1997 ☐	SUPEREVIL	CD	Dolphin Music (Japan)	BLCK-85978
	Bonus: Broken Stitch/Pain For The Pig			
1998 ☐	SUPEREVIL	CD	The Music Cartel (USA)	TMC 3 CD
1999 ☐	SATANIC PANIC	CD	Crash Music (USA)	CMU 061044
1999 ■	SATANIC PANIC	CD	Pavement	RTD 319.5345.2
1999 ☐	SATANIC PANIC	CD	Pavement (USA)	76962-32345-2
2002 ☐	Grand Amputation	MCDd 7tr	Hoffa Communications	TRL 001
	Tracks: Accessus Adligo…/Lobotomico/Disconnect Massconnect/El Gordo/Slack-Wrist-Smack/Safe (Houdini)/Exitus Adligo…			
2003 ☐	Grand Amputation	MCD 5tr	Crash Music (USA)	61071-2
	Tracks: Lobotomico/Disconnect Massconnect/El Gordo/Slack-Wrist-Smack/Safe (Houdini)			
2003 ☐	Disconnect Massconnect	MCD 5tr	Seamiew Records	SMR 41163
	Tracks: Disconnect Massconnect/Never To Burn/The Severed (M15 Sonic remix)/Wrapped Inside (God Inside remix)/The Severed (Dentist remix)			
2003 ■	MULTIPLE ORGAN HARVEST	CD	Seamiew Records	SMR 41172
2013 ☐	BOOGIE FROM HELL	CD	Hoffa Entertainment	HOFFA666

2003 CD - SMR 41172

TRASH

Tony "Roy Taylor" Hellander: v, Mikael "Mike Mocadem" Mujanne: g, Jens "Gene Ball" Grundelius: g, Kaj "Coda" Söderström: b, Henrik "Hempo Hobo" Hildén: d

Stockholm - Tony, Mikael and Jens were previously in the band *Stonehenge*, but only Jens appears on their EP. The first album features Peter PJ Jägerhult (ex-*Attack, Tempelrock*) on bass and Anders "Rudy" Flusch on drums. The bass on the album was however recorded by Gunnar Hallin (*Neon Rose, Bam Bam Boys*). The band's style was in some moments quite reminiscent of *AC/DC*, good stomping classic hard rock. The second album was produced by Max Norman and was a worldwide release. A third album was recorded with Eddie Kramer, but as Atlantic Records thought it was too far from the band's original sound it was never released. The tapes do still exist, so have faith! In 1989 Hempo shortly revived the band, now featuring Tony, Jens and bassist Torbjörn Larsson (*Macbeth*). Tony was later part of *Dream Bank* together with Göran Elmquist and ex-*Electric Boys* drummer Nicklas Sigevall, Mikael had his band *Trash & Passion* in the USA, Jens was in the band *Rain*, Kaj went back to playing with 50s rocker Jerry Williams, PJ runs the booking agency PJP and Hempo has played with numerous acts such as John Norum, Glenn Hughes, *Mandrake Root* etc. The first album was produced by The Boss (Börje Forsberg - the man behind Black Mark Records). Tony was also found in *Titanic Truth* and now plays acoustic country rock. Hempo has been found in numerous bands like *Baltimoore, Dokken, Ball, John Norum Band* etc. The track *Back From The Bottom* from the lost third album can be found on the bonus CD for the first encyclopedia.

Trash metal?

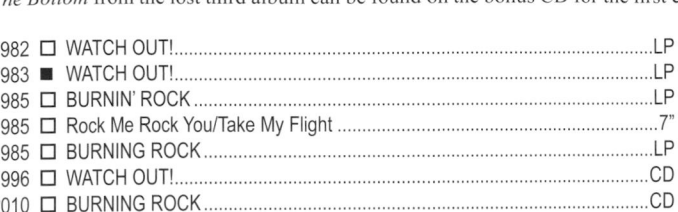

1982 ☐	WATCH OUT!	LP	RCA (Japan)	RLP 8196
1983 ■	WATCH OUT!	LP	RCA	PL 40257
1985 ☐	BURNIN' ROCK	LP	Atlantic	781249-1
1985 ☐	Rock Me Rock You/Take My Flight	7"	Atlantic	789 545-7
1985 ☐	BURNING ROCK	LP	RCA (Japan)	P-13137
1996 ☐	WATCH OUT!	CD	Black Mark	BMCD 113
2010 ☐	BURNING ROCK	CD	Wounded Bird	WOU 1249

1982 LP - PL 40257

TRASH AMIGOS

**Pedro Pico "Mr Dim": v/b, Erik "Pedro el Guero" Wallin: g,
Stefan "Stipen/Pedro Serdito" Carlsson: d**

Göteborg - Early 2009 Pedro pursued his desire to start a thrash band in the old-school vein of *Slayer, Kreator, Sodom* etc. He drafted his former *Harm's Way* colleagues Erik and Stipen (*Transport League, Dia Psalma*). Initially it was only supposed to be a tribute to the old school. After a while the tres amigos teamed up with guitarist Pedro Tacon who joined the band and the *Trash Amigos* was a fact.

2011 ■ HIJOS DE LA CHINGADA ....CD   War Anthem Records.................. WAR 042 CD

2011 CD - WAR 042 CD

TRAUMATIC

Jonas Larsson: v, Pekka Lindqvist: g, Patrik Jonsson: b, Totte Martini: d

Mjölby - The band was formed out of the remains of thrash band *Crab Phobia* but when they went all death metal in 1990 they changed it to *Traumatic*. The first demo, *The Process Of Raping A Rancid Cadaver*, was recorded in 1990, and *A Perfect Night To Masturbate* followed the year after. At the time the band was a trio featuring Larsson, Martini and guitarist/bassist Manuel. High-speed death metal, at times similar to *Morbid Angel*. Nice song-titles... On the 1996 release the style had deviated away from death metal adding more towards crust. Another demo was recorded in 1997.

1991 ■ The Morbid Act Of A Sadistic Rape Incision....................................7"   Distorted Harmony.................................DH 04
      *Tracks: The Morbid Act Of A Sadistic Rape Incision/The Grotesque Mutilation Of Infested
      Organs. 1000 hand numbered copies.*
1996 ☐ SPASMODIC CLIMAX ....CD   Traumatic Entertainment.............................001

1991 7" - DH 04

TRAZER

**Peter "Pete Black/Blakk" Jacobsson: g/v, Magnus Ljungkvist: g,
Jan Karlsson: b, Håkan Fridhagen: d**

Jönköping - The band was formed already in 1979 and recorded the single in 1981. Right after its release Clas Hernegård (later in *Twilight Project*) joined on vocals. Pete, later joined *EF Band, King Diamond, Geisha, Totem* and then formed *Blakk Totem*. *Trazer* play excellent melodic hard rock with a hint of *Thin Lizzy* at times. Pete released the debut album with *Disaster/Peace* in 2010 and is today also found backing Danish rocker *Maryann Cotton*.

1981 ■ Street Fighting Man/Bad Reason...7"   Sjöbo Påpp .... SPR 006 **$$**
      500 copies.

1981 7" - SPR 007

TREASURE

**Göran Kunstberg: v, Per-Erik Karlsson: g, Michael Amberg: g,
Jens Axén: b, Stefan "Allweather" Sundholm: d**

Eskilstuna - One of the few really good singles on the dubious Pang Records. Quite reminiscent of *Torch*. Göran was later in *Wizz* and *King & Rozz*. He was later found in the folkish bands *Urban Turban* and *Dromba* where he plays bagpipe and Moraharp. In 2010 he formed his singing monk style rock project *Icon X*.

1983 ■ Women In Black/Spirit From The North ....7"   Pang ....PSI 070 **$**

1983 7" - PSI 070

TREASURE LAND

**Jakob Samuelsson: v, Jonas Hörnqvist: g, Kaspar Dahlquist: k,
Magnus Lind: b, Magnus Hörnqvist: d**

Stenungsund/Göteborg - *Treasure Land* are one of Sweden's top league progressive bands, but a sadly underperforming band release-wise. The style is somewhere in between *Impellitteri* and *Dream Theater*, with outstanding musicianship. Jonas, Magnus and Magnus have previously recorded a single with the band *Calilio* and original singer Zenny Hansson (Gram) recorded four albums with darksters *Destiny* and previously sung with *Faith, Metal Muthaz, Spin Air, Spitfire* etc. After the first album Zenny was asked to leave the band and he was replaced by Jakob Samuelsson (a.k.a Jake Samuel), who simultaneously released the second album by his own band *Jekyll & Hyde*. In May '98 Kaspar left the band to pursue a career in new age music, but later appeared in *Stormwind, Sahara* and *Dionysus*. Zenny later re-joined *Destiny* for a while, but now mostly does cover gigs. Jonas has previously also recorded some highly acclaimed solo demos. In 2002 the band began working on a new album. The line-up featured Jonas, Magnus L, Magnus H, new singer Rickard "Altzi" Thornberg (ex-*Sanity*) and Italian keyboard player Giulio Capone. It didn't last long and Altzi later joined *At Vance, Thunderstone*

1997 CD - TT 029-2

and is now also in **Masterplan**. In 2005 the band recorded an excellent four-track promo entitled *The Search Has Begun*, but unfortunately the search is not yet over. The line-up on the promo featured Altzi, the Hörnquist brothers and Lind. Lind, who was ex-**Blue Balls**, is now in **Scull Parade** and Jake Samuel is fronting **The Poodles**. The band is currently "resting", while Jonas is active as a guitar teacher and there's still music to be made from the brothers (we hope!).

1997 ■	QUESTIONS	CD	T&T	TT 029-2
1997 □	QUESTIONS	CD	Victor (Japan)	VICP-60119
1998 ■	GATEWAY	CD	T&T	TT 037-2

1998 CD - TT 037-2

TREAT

Robert "Robban" Ernlund: v, Anders Wikström: g, Patrik Appelgren: k, Björn "Nalle" Påhlsson: b, Jamie Borger: d

Stockholm - **Treat** were formed in 1983 by Anders "Gary" Wikström (guitar and keyboards) and Robert "Robban" Ernlund on vocals. They had played together in the band **Sprängdeg** around 78-79 and later recorded an album and a 7" with the pop band **The Boys**. The first line-up featured Robban on vocals Anders Wikström bass, guitarists Stefan Larsson-Almén (ex-**Advice**) and Leif "Lillen" Liljegren (also ex-**The Boys**) on guitar with Mats "Dalton" Dahlberg on drums (ex-**Highbrow, Power, Speedy Gonzales**). Later on Wikström switched to guitar, Stefan was out and Kenneth Siewertsson was added on bass. One of their first gigs was to support **W.A.S.P** in the end of 1984. Late 1985 Dalton quit to form his own band **Dalton**, and he was replaced by Leif Sundin (not to be confused with the singer), who only lasted for a year. Leif was then replaced by ex-**Six Feet Under/Capricorn** drummer Jamie Borger (later in **Talisman**). In December 1988 Liljegren left the band and only two months later so did Kenneth. Their replacements were Joakim "Joe" Larsson on bass and Patrik "Green" Appelgren on keyboards. Patrik was also ex-**Power** and Joe was formerly in **Six Feet Under** (brother of guitarist Tomas Larsson). After *Organized Crime*, Robban Ernlund left and was replaced by Mats Levén (ex-**Capricorn, Swedish Erotica**). The band's last album, before the first break-up, only contained one original member, Anders "Gary" Wikström, but it is by far the best and heaviest album the band ever achieved. Anders later joined **Mental Hippie Blood** and after that he had his own, more alternative-sounding band **Grain**. Since 1997, Anders is also working with Fredrik Thomander (ex-**Vildsvin**) as songwriter duo **Epicentre**. They have written songs for artists such as **N'Sync, A-Teens, Backyard Babies** and Jessica Folker. Mats Levén has since recorded with several bands like **Abstrakt Algebra, Malmsteen, Krux, Therion** etc. Patrik was later a member of **State Of Mind** and later played guitar and sang in his own more pop-oriented band. Robban returned to his previous occupation as sound engineer and producer. The story however did not end here. In 2006 the band was resurrected, now featuring Robban, Jamie, Anders, Patrik and new bass player Nalle Påhlsson (**Therion, Zan Clan, Vindictive, Randy Piper** etc) replacing bassist Joakim "Joe" Larsson. *Weapons Of Choice* is a compilation, featuring the new tracks *Go!* and *Burn For You*. The band again started touring and got a new deal through Italian melodic rock label Frontiers Records who released the excellent come back album *Coup de Grace*. In 2011 Nalle left the band to continue working with **Therion**. The band announced that the last shows would take place in 2013 and then the band would fold. A new compilation is said to be the band's last release.

Waiting to serve the coup de grace

1984 7" - 818 906-7

1984 □	You Got Me/Danger Games	7"	Mercury	272 7
1984 □	You Got Me	MLP 4tr	Mercury	880 272 1
	Tracks You Got Me/Danger Games/Too Wild/On The Outside			
1984 □	Too Wild/On The Outside	7"	Mercury	818 906-7
1984 □	Too Wild/On The Outside	12" 2tr	Mercury	818 906 1
1985 □	We Are One/Hidin'	7"	Mercury	880 577 7
1985 □	We Are One/Hidin'	12" 2tr	Mercury	880 577 1
1985 □	Get You On The Run/Hidin'	7"	Mercury (Japan)	7PP-174
1985 ■	SCRATCH AND BITE	LP	Mercury	824 353-1
	Poster.			
1985 □	SCRATCH AND BITE	LP	Mercury (Japan)	28PP-1007
1985 □	SCRATCH AND BITE	CD	Mercury (Japan)	PPD 3100
1985 □	Ride Me High/Steal Your Heart Away	7"	Mercury	884 375-7
1985 □	Ride Me High	MLP 3tr	Mercury	884 375-1
	Tracks: Ride Me High/Steal Your Heart Away/On The Outside(new version).			
1986 □	THE PLEASURE PRINCIPLE	LP	Mercury	826 918-1
1986 □	THE PLEASURE PRINCIPLE	LP	Mercury (Japan)	25PP-199
1986 □	THE PLEASURE PRINCIPLE	CD	Mercury (Japan)	826 918-2
1986 □	Rev It Up/Fallen Angel	7"	Mercury	888 062 7
1986 □	Rev It Up/Fallen Angel/We Are One	MLP 3tr	Mercury	888 062 1
1986 □	Waiting Game/Strike Without Warning	7"	Mercury	884 839 7

1985 LP - 824 353-1

Year		Title	Format	Label	Catalog
1987	☐	Best Of Me/Tush (ZZ Top cover)	7"	Mercury	870 568 7
1987	☐	DREAMHUNTER	LP	Mercury	832 960 1

1st press with "statue cover", second with "band cover" 1988.

| 1987 | ☐ | DREAMHUNTER | CD | Mercury | 832 960 2 |

1st press with "statue cover", second with "band cover" 1988.

1987	☐	You're The One I Want/Save Yourself	7"	Mercury	888 946 7
1988	☐	World Of Promises/One Way To Glory	CDS 2tr	Mercury (promo)	CDREAM 1
1988	☐	World Of Promises/One Way To Glory	7"	Mercury (promo)	DREAM 1
1988	☐	World Of Promises/One Way To Glory	7"	Mercury	870 159 7
1988	☐	World Of Promises/One Way To Glory/Rev It Up (live)	MCD 3tr	Mercury	870 159 2
1988	☐	World Of Promises/One Way To Glory/Rev It Up(live)	MLP 3tr	Mercury	870 159 1
1988	☐	Treat	CDS 2tr	Mercury (promo)	CDREAM 2

Promo picture disc. Tracks: Best Of Me/Tush(ZZ Top cover)

| 1989 | ☐ | TREAT | LP | Vertigo.(UK) | 836 727-1 |

This is a UK-compilation of the albums Dreamhunter and Pleasure Principle.

1989	☐	TREAT	CD	Vertigo.(UK)	836 727-2
1989	☐	ORGANIZED CRIME	LP	Vertigo	838 929-1
1989	☐	ORGANIZED CRIME	CD	Vertigo	838 929-2
1989	■	Strike Without Warning	MLP 3tr	Vertigo (UK-promo)	TREAT100

Tracks Strike Without Warning/Rev It Up/Fallen Angel

| 1989 | ☐ | Ready For The Takin'/Stay Away | 7" | Vertigo | 876 772 7 |
| 1989 | ☐ | Ready For The Takin' | MLP 4tr | Vertigo (UK-promo) | TRTDJ 112 |

Tracks Ready For The Takin'/Mr Heartache/Hunger/Home Is Where Your Heart Is

1990	☐	Party All Over/Hunger	7"	Vertigo	875 121 7
1990	☐	Party All Over/Party All Over (single version)	MLP 3tr	Vertigo	875 121 1
1990	☐	THE PLEASURE PRINCIPLE	CD	Mercury (Japan)	PPD-3099
1990	☐	DREAMHUNTER	CD	Mercury (Japan)	PPD-3098
1990	☐	ORGANIZED CRIME	CD	Mercury (Japan)	PPD-1120
1992	☐	TREAT	CD	Vertigo	512 818 2
1992	☐	TREAT	CD	Nippon Phonogram (Japan)	PHCR-1185
1992	■	Learn To Fly/We're All Right Now	7"	Vertigo	864 690 7
1992	☐	Learn To Fly/We're All Right Now	CDS 2tr	Vertigo	864 690 2
1992	☐	Learn To Fly (single)/We're All Right Now/Learn To Fly (album)	MCD 3tr	Vertigo	864 691 2
1994	☐	SCRATCH AND BITE	CD	Nippon Phonogram (Japan)	PHCR-4199
2001	☐	DREAM HUNTER	CD	Mercury	832 960 2

Bonus: Tush (ZZ Top cover)

| 2001 | ☐ | THE PLEASURE PRINCIPLE | CD | Mercury | 826 918 2 |

Bonus: Rev It Up (live)

| 2006 | ☐ | WEAPONS OF CHOICE | CD | Universal | 983885-2 |
| 2008 | ☐ | SCRATCH AND BITE | CD+DVD | Universal | 0625 176608-1 |

Bonus: Live at Firefest DVD

| 2010 | ☐ | COUP DE GRACE | CD | Universal | 0602527-32960 |
| 2010 | ■ | COUP DE GRACE | CD | Frontiers | FR CD 453 |

Unofficial releases:

| 2000 | ☐ | MUSCLE IN MOTION | CD | Metal Rendezvous | MRO 010 |
| n/a | ☐ | SCRATCH AND BITE | CD | Mercury | (PPD3100) |

Greek counterfeit. Including OBI. Says: PPD-3100 on matrix.

1989 MLP - TREAT 100

1992 7" - 864 690 7

2010 CD - FR CD 453

TREBLINKA

Johan "Hellslaughter" Edlund: v/g, Stefan "Emetic" Lagergren: g, Klas "Juck" Wistedt: b, Calle "Najse" Fransson: d

Stockholm - Formed in August 1988. A death metal band that later became *Abomination* and after this they changed their name to *Tiamat*. Emetic and Najse were also found in *Expulsion*. The LP is contains demos recorded in 1988 and 1989. Primitive and raw black metal.

| 1989 | ■ | Severe Abomination/Earwigs In Your Veins | 7" | Made In Hell | MHR-S 001 |

Red vinyl.

| 2010 | ☐ | CRAWLING TO THE PENTAGRAM | LP | Made In Hell | MHR 001 |

Purple or yellow vinyl.

1989 7" - MHR-S 001

TREBORIAN

Robert Hansson: v/g/b/d

Göteborg - *Treborian* (Robert backwards, slightly altered) was a solo project by former *Human Race* guitarist Robert Hansson. Great riff-oriented heavy rock, but unfortunately Robert ain't no singer and the vocal parts are more grunting and low range. Robert however developed the concept and returned in 2010 with the outstanding band *Rawburt*, with a great singer, but only two killer demos have come out so far.

| 2002 | ■ | THE PSYCHO MAN | CD | mp3.com | 250646 |

2002 CD - 250646

TRENDKILL

Adrian Westin: v, Andre Gonzales: g, Erik Månsson: g, Marcus Wesslén: b, Conny Pettersson: d

Varberg - **Trendkill** were formed as **Aggressive Serpent** featuring former **Eternal Lies** members Wesslén, Pettersson and Månsson. Before the album, the band recorded the demos *From The Beginning* (2003) and *Break The Silence* (2004). Pettersson was also in **Anata, Revengia, Eternal Lies, Rotinjected, Lion's Share** and **Beseech**, Wesslén, Gonzales and Westin were all in **By Night**. **Trendkill** play bone-hard, thrashy hardcore-influenced metal, a bit similar to **Pantera** meets early **The Haunted**. In February 2007 Erik (**Eternal Lies, Rotinjected**) declared he had run out of inspiration and the band was put on hold indefinitely.

Resurrected metal merchants

2006 CD - RR 080

2006 ■ NO LONGER BURIED	CD	Regain Records	RR 080

TRETTIOÅRIGA KRIGET

Robert Zima: v, Christer Åkerberg: g, Stefan Fredin: b, Dag Lundquist: d

Stockholm - One of Sweden's prime bands in the early symphonic/progressive rock circuit, also known as **Thirty Year War**. This band released some great albums like *Krigssång* and *Trettioåriga Kriget*, quite similar to **Blåkulla**, and also went under the name **Kriget** at times. The band was formed in 1970, but the classical line-up wasn't complete until 1972 when Christer joined. The first two albums are by far the most interesting of the early years. On *Hej På Er*, which was more poppy, keyboard player Mats Lindberg joined. After *Mot Alla Odds* Robert was sacked and *Kriget* became the band's last album. Mats joined **Tredje Mannen**. Stefan recorded some solo material under the name **Fredin Komp**, but the style was quite far from the work **Trettioåriga Kriget** accomplished during their early years. The band reformed in 1992. *War Memories* is an album with great leftovers and previously unreleased live stuff, a CD well worth looking for. All the band's new material was more in the vein of the first two albums. Christer has produced several Swedish hard rock bands like **Unchained** and **Wanton**, while Robert recorded bands like **Blues Bag**. *War Years* is a live album. *Efter Efter* (after after) concluded the trilogy that started with *Elden av år* (the fire of years) and continued on *I början av slutet* (in the beginning of the end). The war is still at large!

1974 LP - EPC 80220

1976 LP - EPC 80900

1998 LP PD - RHPD 3

1974 ■ TRETTIOÅRIGA KRIGET	LP	CBS	EPC 80220	$$
1976 ■ KRIGSSÅNG	LP	CBS	EPC 80900	
1978 □ HEJ PÅ ER!	LP	Mistlur	MLR 4	
1978 □ Rockgift/Hej På Er	7"	Mistlur	MLR-4S	
1979 □ MOT ALLA ODDS	LP	Mistlur	MLR 9	
1981 □ KRIGET	LP	Mistlur	MLR-16	
1981 □ Nya Moderna Tider/En Liten Man	7"	Mistlur	MLRs-21	
1992 □ KRIGSSÅNG	CD	Mellotronen	CD 002	
Bonus: En kväll hos X/Dagspress 76/Moln/Krigssång (Live)				
1992 □ WAR MEMORIES	CD	Mellotronen	CD 003	
1996 □ OM KRIGET KOMMER 1974-1981	CD	MNW	MNWCD 290	
1998 ■ TRETTIOÅRIGA KRIGET	LP PD	Record Heaven	RHPD3	
2004 ■ ELDEN AV ÅR	CDd	Mellotronen	MELLO CD 013	
2004 □ ELDEN AV ÅR	CDp	Arcancelo (Japan)	ARC-2033	
Bonus: Lång historia (live)				
2004 ■ GLORIOUS WAR	CD	Mellotronen	MELLO CD 015	
2004 □ TRETTIOÅRIGA KRIGET	CDd	Mellotronen	MELLO CD 016	
2004 □ KRIGSSÅNG	CD	Mellotronen	MELLO CD 017	
2004 □ KRIGSSÅNG – REMASTERED AND EXPANDED	CDp	Arcancelo (Japan)	ARC-3020	
Bonus: En kväll hos X/Dagspress 76/Moln/Krigssång (Live)				
2005 □ HEJ PÅ ER!	CDd	Mellotronen/MNW	MNWCD 3004	
Bonus: Mot alla odds/Rapport/Hur står det till?/Rockgift				
2005 □ HEJ PÅ ER! – REMASTERED AND EXPANDED	CDp	Arcancelo (Japan)	ARC-3021	
Bonus: Mot alla odds/Rapport/Hur står det till?/Rockgift/Andra sidan (live)				
2007 □ I BÖRJAN OCH SLUTET	CDd	Mellotronen	MELLO CD 023	
2007 □ I BÖRJAN OCH SLUTET	CDp	Arcancelo (Japan)	ARC-3023	
Bonus: Luljuset (live)				
2008 □ WAR YEARS	2CD	Mellotronen	MELLO CD 028/029	
2011 □ EFTER EFTER	CD	Mellotronen	MELLO CD 033	
2011 □ EFTER EFTER	LP	Mellotronen	MELLO LP 10	
Also released on multi colored vinyl.				

Unofficial releases:

1996 □ TRETTIOÅRIGA KRIGET	CD	private	-	

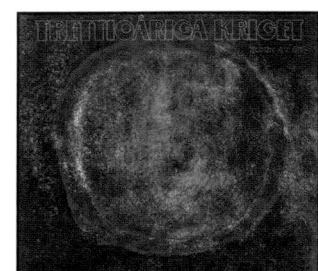
2004 CDd - MELLO CD 013

2004 CD - MELLO CD 015

TRIBAL INK

Dan "Funky Dan" Larsson: v, Lonne Bergman: g, Ulf Johansson: b, Stojan Bdarski: d

Stockholm - *Tribal Ink* were a "band" put together in 2002 by Strix Television as a reality show called *Wannabee*, which also featured Jake Samuel (who auditioned for the band) and Mikkey Dee. Bo "Zinny Zan" Stagman was hired to be the band's manager and auditions were held to get a line-up together, trim the band and make them big stars. Unfortunately it was one big failure. They once supported **House Of Shakira**, but because of the poor attendance at *Tribal Ink*'s performance, they had to "borrow" the audience from **House Of Shakira**. Musically it became some type of rap-core similar to **Linkin' Park**. They did become popular by mistake in 2007, when their song *Refugee* was mislabelled as **Linkin Park**'s single *What I've Done* on several torrents (mistake… yeah, right). It paid off and the band rose high on the MySpace unsigned chart. On the second single guitarist Niels was out of the band. In 2004 the line-up had changed seeing guitarist Rickard Forslund added to the line-up. The singer later appeared in the band **Jupither**. Niels played with pop artist Timo Räisänen. Ulf was also in **Impious**.

2003 CDSp - 334 20851

2003 CD - 334 20903

2002 ☐	To My Face/To My Face (instrumental)	CDSp 2tr	Baseball	334 20611
2003 ■	Don't You Push Me/I Try So Hard	CDSp 2tr	Baseball	334 20851
2003 ■	SURROUNDED BY FREAKS	CD	Baseball	334 20903

TRIBULATION

Mikael "Mike Toza" Tossavainen: g/v, David Sörén: g,
Daniel Hojas: b, Magnus Forsberg: d

Surahammar - One of Sweden's first death metal bands although the music feels more like heavy thrash with some **Maiden**esque metal influences. They were formed in 1986 under the name **Pentagram**, but changed it to **Tribulation** the year after, named after a song by **Possessed**. The vocals aren't of the traditional death growling type, although not exactly melodic. Nice one for power metal/thrash fans. After the album guitarist Stevo Neuman was replaced by Daniel Sörén (ex-**Harvey Wallbanger**) and on *Spicy* they changed style more towards **Bad Religion**-type punk. Not for metal fans. Forsberg was later in **Bombs Of Hades**. The track *Pecuniary Aid* was found on the 7" compilation EP *Is This Heavy Or What?* (1988 ITHOW).

1991 LP - BMLP 16

1994 MCD - BHR 012

1991 ■	CLOWN OF THORNS	LP	Black Mark	BMLP 16
1991 ☐	CLOWN OF THORNS	CD	Black Mark	BMCD 16
1994 ■	Spicy	MCD 7tr	Burning Heart	BHR 012
	Tracks: Cute/Torn To A Puzzle/Strength Into Slime/The Bridge…/Low/Bitter Boy/On The Air			

TRIBULATION

Johannes "Jonka" Andersson: b/v, Adam "D.D. Sars" Zaars: g,
Jonathan "Evil Kid Joe" Hultén: g, Jakob "Bob Gentle" Johansson: d

Stockholm/Göteborg/Årjäng/Arvika - Started out as thrashers **Hazard** in 2001 and recorded the demo *Aggression Within* the same year. However, they started leaning towards death metal within the next couple of years and on the 2004 demo *Agony Awaits* the style was pure death metal. In 2005 they released the demo *The Ascending Dead*, released on Zombie Ritual Tapes. Fast and heavy old-school death metal with a thrashy touch, a bit like **Necrophobic**-meet-**Kreator**. Andersson has also been found in **Non Serviam**, **Stench** and **Sars**, Hultén in **Stench**, Zaars in **Enforcer**, **Repugnant** and **Sars**.

2006 7" - YOTZ #8

2008 CD - ASh 045 CD

2006 ☐	Putrid Rebirth	7" 4tr	private	- -
	Tracks: Dread City Of Death/Zombie Holocaust/Imprisoned In Abhorrence/Churning Sea Of Absu			
2006 ■	Putrid Rebirth	7" 4tr	Blood Harvest	YOTZ #8
2008 ■	THE HORROR	CD	Pulverised	ASH 045 CD
2008 ☐	THE HORROR	CDd	Pulverised	ASH 045 DG
2008 ☐	THE HORROR	LPg	Blood Harvest	YOTZ #32
2013 ☐	THE FORMULAS OF DEATH	CD	Invictus Productions	IP 049
2013 ☐	THE FORMULAS OF DEATH	CD	The Ajna Offensive (USA)	FLAME 77

TRIDENT

Tobias Sidegård: v, Johan Norman: g, Per-Owe Solvelius: g,
Alex Friberg: b, Jonas Blom: d

Stockholm/Göteborg/Uddevalla - Yet another death metal all-star band/project. This one featuring Sidegård (**Necrophobic, Incursion**), Norman (**Satanized, Soulreaper, Azeazeron, Runemagick, Decameron, Dissection, Sacramentum**), Blom (**Azeazeron, One Man Army And The Undead Quartet, Runemagick, Grief Of Emerald**), Friberg (**Necrophobic, Karneyway, Jaggernaut**) and Solvelius (**Darkness, Igneous Human, Epic Future, Power Supreme**). The music is blast-beat-infused furious death metal, technical and well played, but also with a touch of classic metal and even some slow parts here and there, similar to **Necrophobic** and **Unanimated**.

2010 CD - RR 163

2010 ■	WORLD DESTRUCTION	CD	Regain Records	RR 163

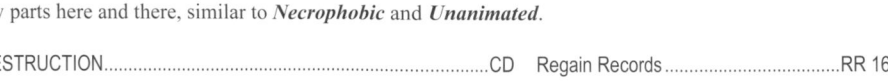

TRILOGY

Marc Gransten: v/b, Christoffer Hofgaard: g, Håkan "Ian" Haugland: d

Stockholm - The band was formed already in 1979/80, initially under the name *Toxic*. The style was inspired by bands like *Rush* and *Budgie*, with lots of instrumental passages. They also had *Candlemass*' bass player Leif Edling in the line-up for six months, but as a lead singer. *Trilogy* also made a five-track demo with Ian on vocals. He also made a short session with the band *Stitch*, but nothing was recorded. They split in September 1984 when Ian joined *Europe*, Christoffer joined and recorded an outstanding single with the band *Vision* the same year. In 1992 Ian reformed *Trilogy* and they did some odd cover gigs, but after *Europe* split they started working harder on original material. The debut contains some serious riffing hard rock with strong 70s influences. One could say *Trilogy* takes over in the heavier regions where *Europe* left off. The musical qualities are top notch, while the vocals are a weaker link. The Japanese, European and Swedish versions have different artwork but contain the same tracks. The band was working on the second album, that was said to be stronger, however nothing ever came out. Hofgaard is now found in the band *Mud & Blood*.

1994 CD - XRCN-1171

1995 CD - REALCD 3

1994 ■	LUST PROVIDER	CD	Zero (Japan)	XRCN-1171
1995 ■	LUST PROVIDER	CD	MNW ILR	REALCD 3
	Swedish release. Different artwork.			
1995 □	LUST PROVIDER	CD	Long Island	LIR 00074
	European release.			

TRISTITIA

Stefan Persson: v, Luis B. Galvez: g/b/k

Halmstad - The band was formed in 1992 by Luis B. Galvez. He drafted singer Thomas "Devil Lee Rot" Karlsson and Harri Juvonen on bass (*Pagan Rites, Devil Lee Rot*). They recorded their debut demo *Winds Of Sacrifice* in 1993. The second demo effort was entitled *Reminiscences Of The Mourner*. The line-up was now completed with drummer Bruno Nilsson. Atmospheric symphonic black metal in a very doomy direction. Very deep male vocals with a hopelessly Swedish accent. Occasional angelic female vocals and choir parts. Quite a lot of variations. Luis was in *Pagan Rites* for a short period. Thomas is ex-*Autopsy Torment/Pagan Rites* and also goes under the name Devil Lee Rot. Bruno was now out of the band and bass player Adrian Letelier (ex-*Pagan Rites*) was in the ranks only on *Crucidiction*. The track *Prelude Of Solitude* can be found on the compilation *The Holy Bible* (Holy), *Final Lament* on *Holy Bible Vol 2* (1999 Holy Records) and *The Other Side* on *Holy Bible Vol 3* (1999 Holy Records). *The Last Grief* saw a style change, from death metal to dark doom-oriented heavy metal with quite atmospheric and soft passages. The sound also changed drastically because of singer Rickard Bengtsson (*Last Tribe*). On the last album, *Garden Of Darkness*, the band featured Luis and, again death-style singer Stefan Persson. However, the style was still very dark and doom-oriented metal. The latest news on the band's website was dated 2008 and says the band has problems finding a steady line-up. Luis also has the side project *Gardeniathan*, which is more gothic/acoustic.

Three with darkness

1996 CD - HOLY 21 CD

2000 CDd - HOLY 21 CD

2002 CDd - HOLY 80 CD

1995 □	ONE WITH DARKNESS	CDd	Holy	HOLY 11 CD
1996 ■	CRUCIDICTION	CD	Holy	HOLY 21 CD
2000 ■	CRUCIDICTION	CDd	Holy	HOLY 21 CD
	New artwork. Bonus: One With Darkness/Winds Of Sacrifice/Dance Of The Selenities/			
	Dancing Souls/Kiss The Cross			
2000 □	THE LAST GRIEF	CDd	Holy	HOLY 58 CD
2002 ■	GARDEN OF DARKNESS	CDd	Holy	HOLY 80 CD
2005 □	ONE WITH DARKNESS	CDd	Holy	HOLY 11 CDX
	Bonus: Prelude Of Solitude/The Other Side/Envy The Dead/Mark My Words			

TRITON ENIGMA

Kitty Saric: v, Thomas Nilsson: g/b/k, Ronnie Bergerståhl: d/b/g/k

Stockholm/Katrineholm - *Triton Enigma* play high-class melodic death metal, quite similar to *Arch Enemy*, not only because of female ultra-growler Kitty, but also the style of music. Great and powerful melodic and technical death metal indeed. Kitty is also in thrashers *Decadence*, Bergerståhl has been in bands like *World Below, Julie Laughs Nomore, Centinex, Grave, Amaran* and *Demonical*, while Nilsson is ex-*Julie Laughs Nomore*.

2008 CD - OGR 31

2008 ■	BLACK LIES	CD	Open Grave Records	OGR 31

TRIUMPHATOR

Daniel "Arioch" Rosten: v/g, Marcus Tena: g/b

Linköping - Tena (head of Shadow Records) and the members of the band *Blasphemous* formed *Triumphator* in 1995. Their debut demo *The Triumph Of Satan* was released in 1996. In 1997 guitarist Linus "Hellreaper" Köhl and drummer Martin "Skeleton" Axenrot (*Morgue, Nephenzy Chaos Order, Opeth, Nifelheim, Bloodbath, Funeral Frost* etc.) were sacked. After this, the band was put on ice for a few years, then Arioch (*Funeral Mist*) was drafted. Mogge Håkansson (*Marduk*) has written the lyrics to *Heralds Of Pestilence*. Violent and chaotic black metal. The album was recorded at Studio Abyss. Fredrik Andersson (ex-*Marduk*) played drums on the album. Joel "Draugen" Andersson (ex-*Dark Funeral, Svartsyn*) played on one song and did some live shows with the band. In 2002 Regain Records picked them up, but they were put on hold.

1998	☐	The Ultimate Sacrifice	7"	Mark Of The Devil	DEVIL 001	
		Tracks: Redeemer Of Chaos/Heralds Of Pestilence. 300 copies.				
1999	☐	The Ultimate Sacrifice	CDSd 2tr	Holycaust	S810-06	
2000	■	WINGS OF ANTICHRIST	CD	Necropolis	NR 48	
2000	☐	WINGS OF ANTICHRIST	LPg	Merciless	MRSLP 017	
2002	☐	The Ultimate Sacrifice	12" 3tr PD	Grim Rune	GRP 003	
		Tracks: Redeemer Of Chaos/Heralds Of Pestilence/From Under Below. 300 copies.				
2006	☐	WINGS OF ANTICHRIST	CD	Listenable Records	POSH 079	
		New artwork. Bonus: From Under To Below/Burn The Heart Of The Earth (live)/Redeemer Of Chaos/Heralds Of Pestilence/Burn The Heart Of The Earth (live video)				

2000 CD - NR 48

TRIX

Jari "Lefvendahl" Levedahl: v, Anders Halling: g,
Jan Sahlberg: g, Mats "Matte" Sundberg: b, Max Ullrich: d

Visby - The A-side is a bit reminiscent of the first *Ocean* (Karlshamn) single, while the B-side owes more to UK rockers *UFO*. Good, solid rocking hard rock.

1979	■	Nya vindar/Angelika	7"	Wessman & Pettersson Skivor	WSP 01

1979 7" - WSP 01

TROUBLE

Gunnar Jönsson: v/b, Gunnar Palmquist: d/v, Sture Öberg: g, Tobbe Johansson: g

Skara/Skövde - Good, solid hard rock in the 80s format. Not as heavy as their American namesake, but still well worth checking out. These Swedes owe more to bands like *Saxon*, *Gotham City* and *220 Volt*, with a touch of *Thin Lizzy*. The album is a sought after item, released in a small edition. The band also recorded a great eight track demo with unreleased material, entitled *Stand Up For Rock* (1982 Musikstudion).

1985	■	WARRIOR	LP	Artist	ARLP-85031	$$

Unofficial release:

1996	☐	WARRIOR	CD	Scandinavian Metal Attack	001

1985 LP - ARLP-85031

TROUBLED HORSE

Martin Heppich: v/g, John Hoyles: g, Ola Henriksson: b, Jens Henriksson: d

Örebro - *Troubled Horse* were formed by Heppish. Hoyles is also in *Spiders* and was previously in *Witchcraft*. *Troubled Horse* treads the same type of great, retro-style, seventies, riff-oriented hard rock path as the latter. Heppish sounds quite similar to *Pentagram* front man Bobby Liebling.

2010	☐	Bring My Horse Home/Shirleen	7"	Crusher Records	CR 011
2012	■	STEP INSIDE	CD	Rise Above Records	RISECD 148
		First edition in slipcase.			
2012	☐	STEP INSIDE	LPg	Rise Above Records	RISELP 148
		300 red, 300 blue, 300 black vinyl.			

2012 CD - RISECD 148

TRUCK

Roger Holegård: v/g, Roffe "Zip" Carsbring: g,
Sten "Plutten" Larsson: b, Thomas Wiklund: d

Stockholm - Roger is ex-*Neon Rose* and *Wasa Express*. This band's first single is quite poppy. *Impala* is however very good straightforward hard rock and the band later recorded a live-demo that was unfortunately never released. It is said to be a classic. Thomas was ex-*Neon Rose/ Uppåt Väggarna* and Plutten was ex-*Outsiders*, *Rocket*, Magnus Uggla and also backed UK popsters *New World* (who recorded *Sister Jane* and *Tom Tom Turnaround*). Plutten is the brother of Stanley Larsson (*Neon Rose*).

1980	☐	Lägg Inte På Din Lur/Jag Vill Ha	7"	Fontana	6016 028
1981	■	Impala/Taktfast Takt	7"	Fontana	6016 037

1981 7" - 6016 037

TRUCKFIGHTERS

Oskar "Ozo" Cedermalm: v/b, Niklas "Dango" Kjellgren: g, Oscar "Pezo" Johansson: d

Örebro - Stoner rockers *Truckfighters* were formed in 2001 by Dango and Ozo, who also run Fuzzorama Records, originally influenced by the grunge wave. They found drummer Andreas "Paco" von Ahn, who left immediately and was replaced by Oscar "Pezo" Johansson. Late 2001 they recorded their first demo and second demos, before they did the split with *Firestone*. In 2002 guitarist Winfred "Fredo" Kennerknecht was added to the line-up. In 2004 Pezo left the band and Paco was back, replaced by Pezo in 2007. In 2008 Fredo had to leave because of a sleeping disorder. After the album *Mania*, Pezo was out, replaced by Pedro, who was replaced by Fredrik "Frongo" Larsson, replaced by Pezo, replaced by Danne "McKenzo" McKenzie (*Mustasch*) in 2012. The track *Analougus* is found on *Fuzzcollection Volume 1* (2004 Fuzzorama) and *Freewheelin* on *Road To Nowhere* (2007 Poison Tree). *Hidden Treasures Of Fuzz - The Anniversary Of The Century*, is a collection of old demos. By the way, their original grunge influences were totally thrown out the window on the first release. *Truckfighters*, which is actually Josh Homme's favourite band, plays outstanding seventies retro-style heavy fuzzy stoner. In 2012 the *Fuzzomentary* movie about the band was released on DVD. The album *Universe* is set for release 2014, now featuring new drummer Andre "Poncho" Kvarnström.

2005 CD - FUZZCD 004

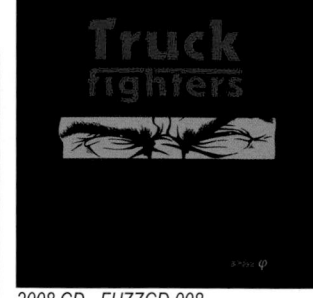

2008 CD - FUZZCD 008

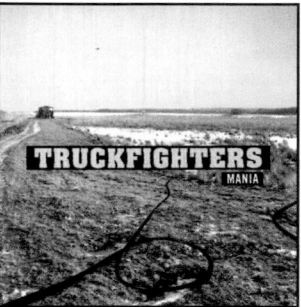

2009 CD - FUZZCD 010

2013 3LP - FUZZLP 006

2003	☐	FUZZSPLIT OF THE CENTURY (split)	CD	Fuzzorama Records	FUZZCD 001

Split with Firestone. Tracks: The Special Theory Of Relativity/Nitro/Helium 28/New Woman/Valium

2003	☐	FUZZSPLIT OF THE CENTURY (split)	LP	Fuzzorama Records	FUZZLP 001 $

Yellow vinyl.

2004	☐	Truckfighters Do Square – Square Do Truckfighters (split)	7"	Fuzzorama Records	FUZZLP 002

Split with Square. Tracks: Frizzy Man Part 1/Frizzy Man Part 2

2005	■	GRAVITY X	CD	Fuzzorama Records	FUZZCD 004
2005	☐	GRAVITY X	CD	Meteor City (USA)	996
2008	■	PHI	CD	Fuzzorama Records	FUZZCD 008
2008	☐	PHI	CD	Poison Tree (USA)	PTR 005
2009	■	MANIA	CD	Fuzzorama Records	FUZZCD 010
2009	☐	MANIA	LPg	Fuzzorama Records	FUZZLP 003

500 copies.

2011	☐	HIDDEN TREASURES OF FUZZ	LP	Fuzzorama Records	FUZZLP 005

500 copies, orange vinyl.

2012	☐	MANIA	CDd	Tee Pee (USA)	TPEE 90144-2
2013	■	GRAVITY X AND PHI - TRIPLE VINYL	3LP	Fuzzorama Records	FUZZLP 006

All three discs in different colours. Gravity X, Phi and demos.

TRUTH

David Fremberg: v, Sven Cirnski: g, Jens Lundahl: b, Jaime Salazar: d

Malmö - It all started back in 2001 when Sven, guitarist in *Bad Habit* wrote some heavier songs, inspired by bands like *Eric Gales Band* and Stevie Salas' band *Nicklebag*. He recorded the songs using Jens and Jaime, plus singer Pete Sandberg (*Alien, Madison, Von Rosen* etc). However, what was supposed to be Sven's solo album, suddenly became Pete Sandberg's album *Push*, because his name was more sellable. Several years later, American label Grooveyard Records loved the songs but not the singer and convinced Sven to pick up the pieces and get his redemption. With *Andromeda/Constancia* singer David Fremberg doing the aforementioned style way better justice, Sven re-recorded a couple of the old songs and wrote another bunch of high-octane riff rock anthems. A killer album for fans of heavy bluesy riffs and grooves.

2008 CD - GYR 039

2008	■	MACHINE	CD	Grooveyard Records	GYR 039

TRYCKVÅG

Mats "Attaque" Håkansson: v/g, Mikael Höglund: b, Thomas "Tom P" Broman: d

Mora - Great melodic hard rock in the same vein as the Canadian band *Santers*. The band was formed in 1978, when bassist Höglund was invited to jam with the boys from the band *Wild Zephyr*, featuring Mats Attaque, Bosse Berglund and Ingemar Sallman. They took the new name *Trash* and started playing covers by *Thin Lizzy, Black Sabbath, Rush* etc. In 1979 they were given the opportunity to play on Swedish television and decided to change the name to *Tryckvåg* ("shock wave" in English). A producer for the show liked the band and one of the songs, *White Wizard*, was entered in the *Europatoppen* radio show, where it ended up last place. The band now started dividing into two camps, where two wanted to do more metal and the other two blues. Ingemar and Bosse were out and now drummer Thomas Broman entered and Mats also took over the vocals. They now drafted guitarists Lars-Erik Wilkensson and Scotsman Donald Burnette. A couple of years later Donald moved back to Scotland. They now drafted singer Conny Lind. The band won a bandstand gaining them a contract with CBS. However, the band failed to impress in the studio and the deal fell through. In 1983 Conny got the boot and a year later so did Lars-Erik. The band, now as a trio, recorded their first and only single, using session keyboardist Robert Widell in the studio. In 1987 the trio relocated to Stockholm, where Conny had already moved. They tried to make it work for a while, but finally ended up in different bands. Conny and Tomas played in *Odessa* while Mikael was in *Bang Bang*. They joined forces

Tryckvåg, gigging and giggling in Dalarna.

and formed **Sin City**. When Conny moved to the US to join Alex Masi, the others found singer Leif Sundin and they became **Great King Rat**. Mikael later recorded with UK band **Thunder**, Conny has made it on record with **State Of Mind**, **Amaze Me** and **Raceway**, Mats moved to the US to join **Mogg** and Tomas later joined **Electric Boys**. On John Norum's album *Face The Truth* the song *Good Man Shining* was written by Mats Attaque/Mikael Höglund/Tomas Broman/John Norum/Glenn Hughes. Mats later returned to Sweden and Broman returned to playing with John Norum. In 1999 the band released a pro-printed CD-R compilation *Demolition*, featuring all the band's unreleased demos. In 2012 Broman and Höglund formed the new band **Bridge To Mars** together with Jocke "JJ" Marsh (ex-**Spellbound**, Glenn Hughes).

1985 ■ Stay The Night/It's A Party Tonight..7" BMO...CTR-286 $

1985 7" - CTR-286

TUBE SCREAMER
Jerry Magnusson: v, Martin Friberg: g, Stefan Magnusson: b, Pelle Skoglund: d
Göteborg - The band was formed in 1992. Jerry and Stefan had previously recorded some demos with the band **Hangman Jury**. Heavy doom-grunge metal with whiskey-stained vocals. A touch of **Alice In Chains** and a hint of **Soundgarden** mixed with a shot of **Black Label Society**. Great stuff! Recorded at Studio Fredman. After the MCD (self-financed but released on the Strontium label) guitarist Christian Smedström (ex-**Full Metal Jacketz**) was added to the line-up. When the band split in 1997 Christian and Stefan formed **The Awesome Machine**.

1995 ■ No More Lies...MCD 6tr Strontium ....ASP 005
   Tracks: Intro/Child/Shine/Don't Lie/Kishore/Bye Bye Sucker

1995 MCD - ASP 005

TUMBLEWEED
Stefan Borg: v, Torbjörn Andrén: g, Jim Olsson: b, Mats Almstedt: d
Eksjö - *In The Raw* is a pretty good **AC/DC**-style hard rocker with quite squeaky vocals. The band also recorded the live tape *Live At Opus 1* in 1992. **Tumbleweed** are still active as a cover band, still featuring Borg, Andrén and Olsson, now flanked by second guitarist Michael Carlsson and drummer Tor Amrén. Stefan Borg previously recorded a single with the band **Fair Child**.

1991 ■ In The Raw..MCD 4tr Opus ....OPUS 004
   Tracks: Welcome To The Wrecking Ball/Too Hot To Handle/Who Do You Think You Are/
   One Night Stand

1991 MCD - OPUS 004

TUMULT
Bruno Lundgren: g/v, Hasse Andersson: g, Tomas Johansson: b, Anders Prag: d
Vetlanda - A-side is hard rock in the vein of heavier **Motvind**, while the B-side is more rock.

1983 ■ Så svårt/Vinterns första snö..7" private ....TMC 001

TURBO
Ola Persson (now Calle Engelmarc): v/g, Håkan Jacobsson: g,
Christian Karlsson: b, Paul Gustavsson (now Bergholtz): v/d
Mörrum/Asarum - Ola was previously playing in the band **TNT**, together with Janne Stark and Pelle Thuresson, where the song *Asfaltsrock* was actually written and demoed in 1977. The band evolved into **Paradize** and Ola was replaced by Kenth Eriksson in 1978. Ola now formed **Turbo** and recorded one single, released on the same "label" (not really a lable, but actually a studio) as **Paradize**. Håkan, brother of **Overdrive** guitarist Kjell Jacobsson, was replaced by Andrija Veljaca (ex-**Horoscope**) in 1981 and they recorded a demo was with Ola on vocals. The band soon changed its name to **Mercy**. More demos and rehearsal recordings were made, but later in 1981, Ola quit and **Mercy** continued as a trio for a while, before drafting singer Messiah Marcolin, and the rest is history. Straightforward 80s heavy metal, sung in Swedish. Håkan later joined **Hatchet** and sadly committed suicide in 2007. Christian played with **Ocean** and Paul was later in **High Voltage**, **Overheat** and today plays in a cover band. Ola later changed his name to Carl Ola "Calle" Engelmarc and is currently in the bands **Feral Ghost** and **Beta Male Hearts** (under the name Carlos Fandango). He's also backing English singer Nicolette Street.

Så svårt / Vinterns första snö

1983 7" - TMC 001

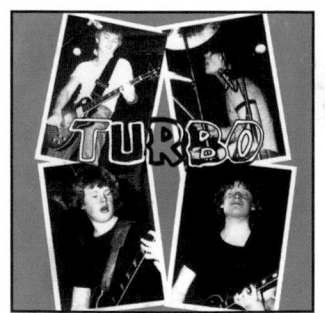

1980 7" - ORI 0706 S

1980 ■ Nattens barn/Asfaltsrock..7" ORI ....ORI 0706 S $$
   250 copies

TURBOCHARGED
Ronnie "Ripper" Olsson: b/v, Nicklas "Old Nick" Johnsson (now de Melo): g,
Fredrik "Freddie Fister" Hultman: d
Forshaga - **Turbocharged** play high-octane punk-fuelled thrash metal, quite crude and brutal. A bit reminiscent of **Kreator** and even **Venom** at times. The band was formed already back in 2000, but didn't record their first demo, *Branded Forever*, until 2008, followed by *Arrogantus Metallus* in 2009. Ronnie was also in **Gehennah** and **Vomitory**. Nick also has his solo project **Dragnagl**.

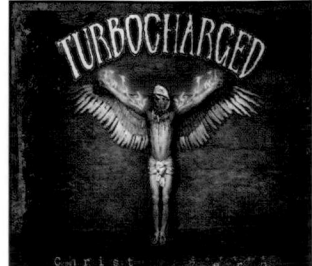

2012 CD - CR 018

2010 □	ANTIXIAN	...LP	Hellrocker Records	...002
	300 copies.			
2011 □	ANTIXIAN	...CD	Chaos Records	...CR 004
	Different artwork.			
2012 ■	CHRIST ZERO	...CDd	Chaos Records	...CR 018
2013 □	AREA 666	...CD	Chaos Records	...CR 024

TURNING POINT

Tord Persson: v, Leif Tarvainen: g, Johan Brodin: g, Ulrik "Urrke" Thunman: b, Jonas Calsson: d

Gävle - A good, quite mellow melodic hard rock band with a singer that reminds a lot of **White Lion**/**Freak Of Nature**'s Mike Tramp. After the album was recorded there were several changes in the crew and only the singer remained a year after the release of the album. The above line-up also recorded a cover of **Thin Lizzy**'s *Emerald*, which is featured on the *Lizzy Songs* (95 SMC) compilation. The album was recorded with drummer Robin Jönsson and bass player Michael Blomberg. Jonas is ex-**Nasty Groove** and Ulrik was previously found in **King Size**, later in **Maryslim**. Late 1995 the line-up had once again changed and the last known constellation features Tord, guitarists Fredric Arvidsson and Mikael Olofsson, Ulrik and Jonas.

1994 ■	RIVER DANCE	...CD	SMC	...SMC 10141
1994 □	Streets Of Roses/I Will Return	...CDS 2tr	SMC	...SMC CDS 11141

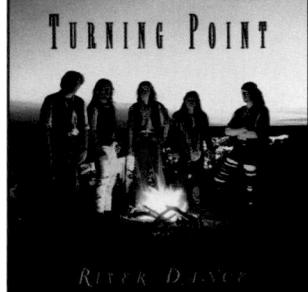

1994 CD - SMC 10141

TUSEN & EN NATT

Eva Olin: v, Patrik Rosman: g, Annika Ohlsson: k, Mattias Kanje: b, Patrik Olofsson: d

Lund - Formed in 1986, influenced by Marie Fredriksson, TomPetty and Mats Ronander. The A-side offers some really good up-tempo AOR, while the B-side is a ballad. The band didn't consider themselves AOR, but more of a pop/rock band, however the A-side clearly qualifies.

1987 ■	Ensam vid havet/I vår lilla värld	...7"	private	...PR 10

1987 7" - PR 10

TWELVESTEP

Lennart Nilsson: v, Marco Kuru: g, Jonas Prahl: g, Jimmy Paulsson: b, Kristoffer Andersson: d

Halmstad - **Twelvestep** were formed in 2004 as a side project of some of the members of the band **Spine**. In 2005 they recorded their first self-financed demo EP, which caught the attention of NLP Records, who featured the band on the compilation *Revolver: Hard Rock And Metal Edition Vol 2* (2004 NLP). After this yet another demo EP followed, *No Tomorrow*. They were soon picked up by Pure Rock Entertainment who put them in the studio with producer Rickard Bengtsson (**Spiritual Beggars, Opeth, Arch Enemy**) and the debut was recorded. **Twelvestep** play really tight, great-sounding modern metal-core oriented melodic death metal with touches of **In Flames** and **Soilwork** as well as **Avatar**.

2008 ■	WORST CASE SCENARIO	...CD	Pure Rock Entertainment	...859700468845

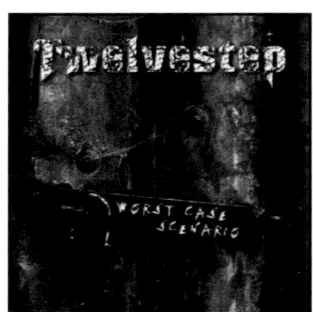

2008 CD - 859700468845

TWILIGHT

Katja Hildén: v, Bitte Johansson: g, Ann-Marie Landtblom: k, Lena Melin: b, Anette Jönsson: d

Stockholm - Good melodic hard rock with good femme vocals. One track in Swedish and one in English. Produced by Hempo Hildén (**Trash, Norum** etc.), who is the brother of Katja.

1983 ■	Rosen/Street Song	...7"	Apollo	...APS 021

1983 7" - APS 021

TWILIGHT PROJECT

Clas Hernegård: v

Jönköping - This is actually the brainchild of singer Clas, who invites different musicians to play on his recordings. It all actually started under the name **Zaragone**, who recorded a demo in 1983. On the MLP the musicians are guitarists Roger Ljunggren and Mats Andersson, keyboardist Jocke Öberg, bassist Staffan Schön and drummer Mikael Hilmer. Two members from **Renegade** are also helping out on backing vocals. **Twilight Project** produce good, slightly progressive hard rock in the vein of early **Rainbow**. Guitarist Roger Ljunggren wrote the song *Don't Close Your Eyes* that was recorded as a single by **Madison**. However, it was recorded without Roger's permission and he stopped the release. The recordings of an album by **Twilight Project** were started in 1995 and it is planned to be released some time in 1996, but still hasn't surfaced. Clas runs the record shop *Zaragon* in Jönköping. There's still basic tracks for an album laid down, and an album could actually be happening. Sometime...

1989 ■	Twilight Project	...MLP 4tr	private	...MTR-005 $
	Tracks: Starchild/Lord Of The Rings/Into The Fire/Fallen Rainbow.			

1989 MLP - MTR-005

TWILIGHT ZONE

Ulf Andersson: v, Hante Andersson: g, Thomas Hunstrand: g,
Jimmy Högfeldt: k, Magnus Sjöquist: b, Stefan Eriksson: d

Trollhättan - Formed in 1985. When the single was recorded the band was a sextet, but they later dropped guitarist Thomas and on their later demos they were five. They later changed their name to **Miss Willis Flower Child** and recorded some high-class, 70s-influenced demos. The single however is traditional AOR. The band still exists under the name **Miss Willis** and has released an outstanding MCD.

1989 7" - HS 1225

1989 ■ Feel The Heat/Dangerous	7"	Hövik	HS 1225

TWIN AGE

Johan Hansson: v, John Löwenadler: g, Carl Johan Kilborn: k,
Petter Pettersson: b, Jörgen Hanson: d/k

Göteborg - Formed in 1993 as a **Dream Theater** cover band, but as the members began writing originals the style changed to progressive/symphonic rock similar to the likes of **Marillion** and **IQ**.

1996 ■ MONTH OF THE YEAR	CD	Altair	TA 9601
1997 ☐ LIALIM HIGH	CD	Altair	TA 9702
2000 ☐ MOVING THE DECKCHAIRS	CD	Record Heaven	RHCD 31

1996 CD - TA 9601

TWIN EARTH

Oscar Björklund: v/g, John Sjölin: g, Kristoffer Gottberg: b, Daniel Halén: d

Mora - Outstanding riff-oriented stoner-type hard rock in the vein of **Spirit Caravan**, **Spiritual Beggars** and with a strong touch of **Black Sabbath**. Singer Oscar is quite unusual for the genre and sings with a bluesy and higher pitch than several of his colleagues. Right after Christmas 2000 bassist Joakim Nauclér was replaced by Kristoffer. The band can also be found on the compilations *Molten Universe Volume One* (Molten Universe 99 - track: *Obelix*), *The Mob's New Plan* (Waterdragon 00), *Judge Not* (Underdogma 00) and *Sacred Groove* (Monstruo de Gila 01). Sjölin and Halén are also found in death metal band **Craft**.

2001 ■ BLACK STARS IN A SILVER SKY	CD	Beard Of Stars	CD BOS 15
2004 ☐ SOUTH OF THE BOARDER	CD	Beard Of Stars	CD BOS 24

2001 CD - CD BOS 15

TWINBALL

Daniel Samuelsson: v/b, Tee Park: g, Lollo Sköllermark: g, L.E Pettersson: d

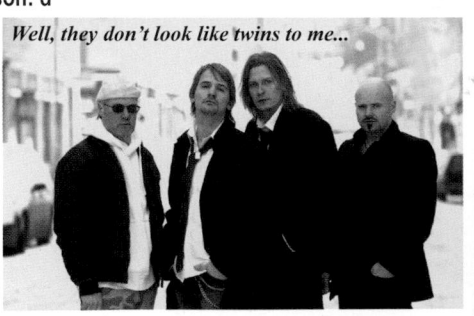

Well, they don't look like twins to me...

Västerås - **Twinball** were formed in 1997 and started out as a **Thin Lizzy** cover band, at the time called **Bad Reputation**. The line-up then featured Adde Psilander on vocals and Olle Frodin on drums, while L.E was handling the bass. In April 2000 the band was revamped, where Frodin left, L.E. went back to drumming and singer Samuelsson was drafted. In 2001 they started writing original material, recorded two songs and were offered a deal with Sweden Rock Records. The name was now changed to **Twinball** and the line-up on the debut album featured Daniel on vocals, Tee and Lollo on guitars, Adde on bass and L.E. on drums. In June 2003 Adde decided to leave the band and Daniel took over the bass as well. The band now recorded the second album, *Slave*. **Twinball** play excellent groovy melodic hard rock with nice riffing a bit like a mix of Swedish colleagues like **Mister Kite** and **Dogpound**. *Website: www.twinball.com*

2002 CD - SRR 003

2002 ■ REMNANTS OF A BROKEN SOUL	CD	Sweden Rock Records	SRR 003
2006 ☐ SLAVE	CD	Fishing Dog Records	BRC 001
2006 ☐ SLAVE	CD	Spiritual Beast (Japan)	POCE-16001
Bonus: Promises			

TWINS CREW

Andreas Larsson: v, Dennis Janglöv: g, David Janglöv: g,
Fredrik Hammar: b, Nicko Dimarino: k, Uno Eriksson: d

Stockholm - **Twins Crew** were formed by the Janglöv twins in 2007 influenced by bands like **Helloween**, **Iron Maiden** and **Stratovarius**. The band recorded two MCDs in 2008-2009, before releasing their own full-length album. This quite honestly sounds way better than many other big label releases. Nice package, great songs, killer vocals and killer guitarists. Melodic power metal, but with a heavier touch at times, a bit like mixing **Helloween** and **Nevermore** with a proggy touch. Before the 2013 album, the band was reinforced by former **Arconova** keyboardist Nicko. *Website: www.twinscrewband.com*

2008 MCDp - TC0801563

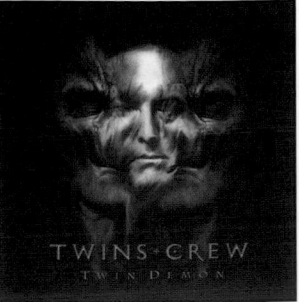

2009 MCDp - TC0801986

2008 ■	Twins Crew	.MCDp 5tr	private	.TC0801563

Tracks: Davy Jones/Breaking The Line/Beauty And The Beast/Raven Souls/Different Kind Of Love

2009 ■	Twins Demon	.MCDp 6tr	private	.TC0801986

Tracks: 777/Twin Demon/Legions Of The Dead/Heavy Metal Nation/Fire Of Anger/The End Of Forever

2011 ■	JUDGEMENT NIGHT	.CDd	private	TC03
2011 ☐	THE NORTHERN CRUSADE	.CDd	Scarlet Records	SC 243-0
2011 ☐	THE NORTHERN CRUSADE	.LP	private	TC 004 LP

250 copies. Numbered. Different artwork.

2011 CDd - TC03

TWO EAGLES REQUEST (aka T.E.R)

Linus Holgersson: v, Mats Pettersson: g, Patrik Johansson: g, Per Sandberg: b, Michael Rothsten: k, Peter Johansson: d

Söderhamn - Initially formed by Per as an anti-teacher band, ***Torsten Elms Rivaler*** (Torsten Elm was their headmaster). In 1985 he teamed up with Patrik. The initials and logo stuck, but the name was changed. The first MLP features Per, Patrik and drummer Marcus Fornander. The above line-up was finalised in 1992. Mid-heavy hard rock with the roots in the 80s metal scene this band shows fine potential. The track *Memories I*, from the MCD, was used as soundtrack for the movie *Hatman*. It seems this band releases a record every fifth year (the ***Def Leppard*** syndrome, eh?). Well, to be honest they did release the demo *Sick World* in 1996. In 1997 the song *Doped* appeared on the compilation *Rape-Cake-Records Nr: 4* and in 1998 the song *So What!* was featured on the compilation *Bay Of Tunes*. On *Stained* the band had adopted a much heavier edge and the line-up had also changed. Keyboard player Michael Rothsten was out while guitarist Mats and singer Linus was in (Per had previously handled the lead vocals, too). It was produced by Mick Nordström (***Modest Attraction, Cornerstone, Spearfish***).

1990 MLP - PLC911-04

1990 ■	Out Of The Dark	MLP 4tr	private	PLC911-04

Tracks:Go Away/Memories I/Memories II/Lighnin'

1995 ☐	Two Eagles Request	.MCD 5tr	Fnörp Rec.	PLC2005/01

Tracks: All That She Wants/10.000 Reasons/Man In The Moon/I Wish/War

2000 ■	STAINED	.CD	Fnörp	TERCD 001

2000 CD - TERCD 001

TWO FRANKLIN GROVE

Patric Franklin: v/g, Niclas Franklin: b

Jönköping - Groove-oriented 70s hard rock with touches of ***Cream***, Hendrix etc. Niclas was a member of Christian hard rockers ***Leviticus*** between 1988 and 1990. Drummer Mick Nordström (***Modest Attraction, Cornerstone, Spearfish***) and Peo Pettersson (solo, ***Axia, Leviticus***) are making guest appearances on the recording.

1996 ■	Tango	.MCDp 4tr	private	TFG 001

Tracks: Tango/People/Hunting For Love/See His Face

1996 MCDp - TFG 001

TWO ROCKS (aka 2 ROCKS)

Thomas Brandt: v, Benny Jansson: g/b

Stockholm - Great, high-quality AOR with catchy but guitar-dominated songs. Thomas later worked with weirdo-comic Svullo and Benny later appeared in ***Racketeer, Johansson Brothers, Snake Charmer, Trail Of Tears*** and has made several solo albums. Busy Guy! The band recorded more material meant for a follow-up album that wasn't released due to lack of funds. ***Two Rocks*** later changed their name to ***Power United*** and recorded some interesting demos. Thomas also did some vocals on the CD by ***Flintstens Med Stanley***.

1992 ☐	WHEN SANITY IS ACTING KIND OF WILD	.CD	Lionheart	LHCD 102
1992 ■	WHEN SANITY IS ACTING KIND OF WILD	.LP	Lionheart	LHLP 102
1992 ☐	WHEN SANITY IS ACTING KIND OF WILD	.LP	FM Revolver (UK)	WGFMLP 174

Different artwork

1992 ☐	WHEN SANITY IS ACTING KIND OF WILD	.CD	FM Revolver (UK)	WGFMCD 174

1992 LP - LHLP 102

TYBURN

Anders Jakobsson: v, Joacim Persson: g, Fredrik Reinedahl: g, Jonas Andersson: b, Henrik Bergström: d

Kristinehamn - Formed in 1990. Made their first demo *In My Mind* in 1992. This band's initial appearance on record was on the compilation-CD *Zalt* (1993 Zalt). The 5-track contains some concrete heavy thrash songs in the vein of ***Metallica*** with elements of ***Pantera***. The band later changed its name to ***Soulquake System*** and made more releases.

1994 ■	Fragments	.MCD 5tr	private	TYBCD 94

Tracks: Fragments/As Time Ceased/Through A Veil Of Black/In Life As In Death/Jenny Cries No More

1994 MCD - TYBCD 94

TYFUZ

Mats Johansson: v/k/g, Tomas Engberg: g, Kjell Arne Engberg: k/g,
Görgen Olsson (now Loviken): b, Pontus Andersson: d

Sundsvall - Tyfus were formed in 1976 and split in 1980 when 3/5 had to do their military service. They recorded some demos before the single, but nothing besides the 7" was ever released. Görgen, who changed his last name to Loviken, was later in **Brända Barn** and some of the others played in cover bands. Side A is melodic pop/rock while side 2 is a straightforward hard rocker.

1980 ■ Häng På/Arbetslös ....7" Tyf.....................................KAS 801

1980 7" - KAS 801

TYRANT

Daniel "Forn" Bragman: v, Peter Bjärgö: g, Daniel Ekeroth: b, Andreas Jonsson: d

Eskilstuna/Stockholm - Formed in Eskilstuna around 2006-2007. They recorded some demos but never managed to get a deal. The debut was initially only supposed to be released as a vinyl in 666 copies, but Listenable managed to convince the band to let them release it on CD. The band was then offered to open for **Gorgoroth**, which they happily accepted, until they found it was actually a tour of 25 gigs! However, they did it and it went great. Peter Bjärgö (aka Pettersson) is also in **Meanwhile, Arcana, Crypt Of Kerberos, Ileus** and **Macrodex**, Bragman and Jonsson are found in **Vinterland** and **The Black**, while Ekekroth, who also wrote the *Swedish Death Metal* bible, is found in **Insision** and **Dellamorte**. *Tyrant* play really old and cold-sounding black metal, similar to **Bathory** and **Hellhammer**. The vocals sounds as if Lemmy and Cronos had a bastard son.

2007 LP - HELL 001

2007 ■ RECLAIM THE FLAME...LP Hell's Cargo ....HELL 001
   666 copies + poster. Bonus: Die In Fire (Bathory cover)
2008 ☐ RECLAIM THE FLAME...CD Listenable.........................POSH 096
2009 ■ GO AHEAD, RAISE THE DEAD (split)................. LPg Agipunk.................................AG 62
   Split with Alehammer. Tracks: Go Ahead, Raise The Dead/Hell To Pay/I'll Burn That Bridge (Before You Can Cross It)/Hungry Flame. 150 black/clear splatter + 850 black vinyl.

2009 LPg - AG 62

TYRON

Niklas Johansson: v, Tommy Nilsson: g, Hans Johansson: g,
Kent Klaveness: k, Magnus Sedenberg: b, Leif Dristig: d

Karlskrona - This band had been around since the early 80s, but their only release was the single. They did record a full-length album, but it was never released. *Tyron* is a good, quite slick AOR band. Sedenberg later ended up as guitarist in **Baltimoore**.

1988 ■ Into The Night/Caught In.......................................7" private ....TYR 001

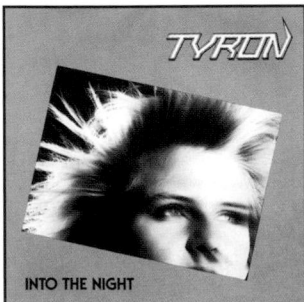

1988 7" - TYR 001

TYROX

Patrik Lindblom: v, Johan Bokström: g/k, Hans Grübeck: k,
Thomas Mann: b, Janne Berg: d

Eskilstuna - Melodic hard rock. Patrik was later replaced by Lena Dahlström (*Avalon*). The band no longer exists. Johan has also recorded a solo CDS in a far more commercial vein.

1986 ■ I Believe In You/The Last Farewell............................7" private ....BSM 006

1986 7" - BSM 006

TÖRSTEN DRICKER

Anna-Lena Nilsson: v, Anna Mattiasson: v, Pär Olsson: g, Jan-Anders Larsson: g,
Ulf Grenholm: b/v, Jan Gustafsson: d

Krokom/Hissmofors - Törsten Dricker (something like "the thirst is drinking"… well, don't ask me) were formed in 1977, featuring Rutger Tåqvist (g), Kjell Ali Bergman (g), Rolf Sandås (b) and Ulf Grenholm on drums. Anna joined in 1986, and not long after, Ulf Olsson replaced Grenholm on the drums (he switched to bass). Ulf Olsson's brother Pär joined on guitar, replacing Kjell. Anna was replaced by her sister Mona in 1990 and Rutger was replaced by Jan-Anders. They entered the Rock SM and ended up third in the finale. The band actually plays quite decent classic hard rock and throws in some covers of **Black Sabbath** and **Status Quo**, for good measure. Not the heaviest production, but good enough. After the first album singer Mona Mattisson was replaced by Anna-Lena and the returning Anna, and drummer Ulf Olsson by Jan Gustafsson. Grenholm sadly passed away in 2006.

1990 7" - JRS 9011

1992 CD - TDCD92

1990 ■ We're Gonna Blow Your House Down/The Rainbow ....7" John's Records ....JRS 9011
1992 ■ REALLY MIRACLES ....CD private TDCD92
1997 ☐ SOMEWHERE BETWEEN HEAVEN AND HELL ....CD private ....HOME 003

U.N.IT

Mathias Johansson: v/g, Peter Jonasson: g,
Mattias Kindefors: b, Christian Ljungberg: d/k

Linköping - **U.N.IT** (quite a witty name!) are a grade A progressive/symphonic hard rock band very reminiscent of late **Rush** with a touch of **Magnum**. Outstanding musicians and long multi-coloured songs. Highly recommended, sadly missed.

1995 ☐ U.N.IT..MCD 3tr   private..SBR-S004
     Tracks: Salvation/Castle In The Clouds/Time Traveller
1998 ■ DREAMDANCE ....CD   Loud 'N Proud....................................LNP 002

1998 CD - LNP 002

UGLY, THE

Ingemar "Inky" Gustafson: v, Johan Eriksson: g,
Per Reinaldo: g, Peter Jonsson: b, Henrik Östensson: d

Stockholm - Brutal black metal in the vein of **Marduk** and **Lord Belial**. *The Ugly* were formed in 2004. The band recorded two demos before the album, *The Birth* (2005) and *Diggin' Graves* (2006), the first one even recorded without a drummer in the band. They were initially more thrash-oriented, but gradually went all black metal. Östensson has also been in **Genocrush Ferox**, **Cromb** and **Hate Patrol**. Reinaldo (**Skitarg**), who replaced former guitarist Lars Sundström in 2006, is also a solo artist where he mixes soft melancholic pop and indie rock, quite far from **The Ugly**. After the album the line-up changed, now featuring Gustafsson and Rinaldo, alongside drummer Fredrik Widigs (**Demonical, Soils Of Fate, Witchery, Vomitous, Angrepp, Carnalized, Desaiha, Bodysbatch**) and bassist Bobbe Nordin (**Lethal**).

2008 ■ SLAVES TO THE DECAY ....CDd   Dental Records..............................DR 190710

2008 CDd - DR 190710

UMEÅ SMALL BAND

See Small Band

UNAMEUS

Michael Dean Hughes: v, Peter "Daniels" Nilsson: g, Ulf "Chris Laney" Larsson: k,
Jonas "Jonni Hex" Andersson: b, Kenny Krueger: d

Helsingborg - According to the band themselves, they sound like a mix of **Cinderella** and **Simple Minds**, well... they actually sound like a heavier and more psychedelic version of early **Simple Minds**. Well performed. Ulf was ex-**Scratch** and **17**. The band featured the song *Paper Tigers* on the Ebony collection *Full Force 3*. As they couldn't find a name, they actually leave it up to the listener - U-name-us. Ulf later found great success as a producer and also played with **Zan Clan** and **Randy Piper's Animal**, and is now doing his solo stuff as Chris Laney, plus he's in **Shotgun**.

1989 MLP - SRT 9KLS 2349

1989 ■ Unameus...MLP 4tr   Risque..................................SRT 9KLS 2349
     Tracks: The Assassins Eyes/Don't Leave Me Alone/Shoot It Up/Gimme All You Got (live)

UNANIMATED

Micke Jansson (now Broberg): v, Jonas "Jojje" Bohlin: g,
Richard "Daemon" Cabeza: b, Peter Stjärnvind: d

Årsta (Stockholm) - The band was formed in 1989 with Jojje, Peter, Richard (on bass and vocals) and guitarist Chris Alvarez. Jonas replaced Chris the subsequent year, and in 1991 they recorded their debut demo *Firestorm*. Richard left to join **Dismember** and Micke came in on vocals, while the bass work was taken over by Daniel Lofthagen. Peter has also been in the band **Merciless** and plays on their album *Unbound*. Jonas also had a band on the side, pop/rock band **Mavrodaphne**, that released a CDS in 1994. After the debut, **Unanimated** recorded the EP *TBA Alnum 2*, but it was never released. On the second album Richard had again replaced Daniel, but he was still a member of **Dismember**. Keyboard player Jocke was then added to the line-up. The music was inspired by bands like **Bathory**, **Venom**, **Celtic Frost** and **Slayer**, of whom I find the latter to be the closest in comparison. The band broke up in 1996 and Peter joined **Face Down**. **Unanimated** finally reformed in 2007, however second guitarist Jonas Mellberg was out and so was keyboardist Jocke Westman. *In The Light Of Darkness* was produced by Tore "Necromorbus" Stjerna. After the album Sethlans Davide "Set Teitan" Totaro (**Dissection, Bloodline, Watain**) was added to the line-up and in 2012 Stjärnvind was replaced by Andreas Schultz. Cabeza has also been in **General Surgery** and **Murder Squad**, Bohlin in **Zebulon**, Jansson in **Celestial Pain** and Stjärnvind in **Krux, Nifelheim, Entombed, Face Down** etc.

1994 CD - 76962-32209-2

1993 LP - NFR 004

1994 CD - NFR 009

1993 ■ IN THE FOREST OF THE DREAMING DEAD ....LP   No Fashion....................................NFR 004

1993	☐	IN THE FOREST OF THE DREAMING DEAD	CD	No Fashion	NFR 004
1994	■	IN THE FOREST OF THE DREAMING DEAD	CD	Pavement (USA)	76962-32209-2
		New artwork.			
1994	■	ANCIENT GOD OF EVIL	CD	No Fashion	NFR 009
1994	☐	ANCIENT GOD OF EVIL	CD	Toy's Factory (Japan)	TFCK-88749
		Bonus: Storms From The Skies Of Grief/Outro			
2008	☐	ANCIENT GOD OF EVIL	CD	Regain Records (USA)	REG-CD-1054
		Bonus: Die Alone			
2008	☐	IN THE LIGHT OF DARKNESS	CD	Regain Records (USA)	REG-CD-1055
		Bonus: Buried Alive (Venom cover)			
2009	☐	IN THE LIGHT OF DARKNESS	CD	Regain Records	RR 161
2009	☐	IN THE LIGHT OF DARKNESS	LP	Regain Records	RR 161
		Bonus: Blackness Of The Fallen Star (re-recording)			
2009	☐	IN THE LIGHT OF DARKNESS	CD	Paranoid Records (Brazil)	n/a
2009	☐	ANCIENT GOD OF EVIL	CD	Regain Records	RR 148
		Bonus: Die Alone			
2009	☐	IN THE FOREST OF THE DREAMING DEAD	CD	Regain Records	RR 149
		Bonus: The Call (demo 1991)/Through The Gates/The Blackness Of The Fallen Star/ Storms From The Skies Of Grief/In The Forest Of The Dreaming Dead. New artwork.			
2009	■	IN THE LIGHT OF DARKNESS	LPg	War Anthem Records	WAR 129 LP
		400 copies.			

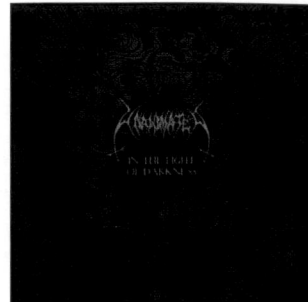

2011 LPg - WAR 129 LP

UNCANNY

Jens Törnroos: v, Fredrik Norrman: g, Johan Jansson: g,
Mattias "Kryptan" Norrman: b, Kenneth Englund: d

Avesta - Death metal that varies from ultra-speed to really doomy parts. Well-arranged guitar work and traditional death vocals. The band was formed in 1990 and released two demos before again using Dan Swanö to record the debut split. The band split in the mid-nineties and Fredrik joined ***Katatonia***, drummer Kenneth Englund went to ***Dellamorte*** and ***Moondark***, guitarist Mats Forsell had his band ***Fulmination*** and Jens was also found in the band ***Uncurbed***. In 2008 the band reunited. Now bassist Mattias "Kryptan" Norrman (***Katatonia, Dellamorte***) had replaced Christoffer Harborg and guitarist Johan Jansson (***Interment, Demonical***) had replaced Mats Forsell. The 2011 release is a compilation of the split plus demos *Transportation Of The Uncanny* (1991) and *Nyklagia* (1992). In 2012 the band recorded the new single *The Path Of Flesh*.

1994 CD USR 008

1994 CD - USR 008 (reissue)

1993	☐	UNCANNY/ANCIENT RITES (split)	LP	Warmaster	WAR 001
		Split with Belgian band Ancient Rites. Tracks: Cease From Reality/Determination To Win/ Profligacy Of Power/Soul Incest/Why My Intestines?/Brain Access. Poster.			
1994	■	SPLENIUM FOR NYKTOPHOBIA	CD	Unisound	USR 008
1994	☐	SPLENIUM FOR NYKTOPHOBIA	LP	Unisound	USR 008
1994	☐	SPLENIUM FOR NYKTOPHOBIA	LP PD	Unisound	USR 008
1994	■	SPLENIUM FOR NYKTOPHOBIA	CD	Unisound	USR 008
		Reissue with new artwork.			
2010	☐	SPLENIUM FOR NYKTOPHOBIA - MCMXCI-MCMXCIV	3LPg box	The Crypt	CRYPT 11
		500 copies in black or Purple/black vinyl. Two posters. In box.			
2011	■	SPLENIUM FOR NYKTOPHOBIA - MCMXCI-MCMXCIV	2CD	Dark Descent	DDR 021 CD
2012	☐	The Path Of Flesh/Creation's Tomb	7"	Dark Descent	DDR 051 EP
		Printed on black, white and green vinyl.			

2011 2CD - DDR 021 CD

UNCHAINED

Pelle "Lenny De Rose" Seather: v, Anders "Andy McLine" Ellin: g,
Anders "Nils Altzar" Altzarfeldt: k, Jan "Ian Dee Jr" Dahlquist: b,
Jan "John South" Söderström: d

Västerås - High-class melodic hard rock with hints of late ***Deep Purple***. Pelle was ex-***Glory North***, later in ***Macbeth*** and in 1994 he released an album with the band ***Schizophrenic Circus***. He was later in bands like ***Zello*** (also featuring Altzarfeldt), ***Zeelion*** and he is today in ***Grand Design***. Pelle is also a renowned producer, running Studio Underground. The 7" was produced by Christer Åkerberg (ex-***Trettioåriga Kriget***).

1987	■	Queen Of The Night/Fighting Fire	7"	Nutida Musik	UNC-188 $

1987 7" - UNC-188

UNCHAINED

Per Karlsson (now Lengstedt): v, David Blomé: g, Peter Ericsson: g,
Mattias Osbäck: b, Martin Michaelsson: d

Karlskrona - ***Unchained*** were formed in 1999, out of the ashes of the band ***Psyche Force***. They recorded a number of demos before the album and several members came and went, such as bass player Mathias Ericsson (***Nepharitus***), bass player Oskar Nilsson (***Paganizer, Carve, Thundereyes***) and singer Sebastian Viitanen (***Buszer***). After the 2002 demo *Like The Candle*, ***Locomotive Breath*** singer Mattias Osbäck took over the bass work from Mathias Ericsson, and this line-up was kept until the band folded in 2006. Blomé was also a live guitarist for

2004 MCD - SRP 031

Locomotive Breath and today plays in *Stacy's Inn*, together with Osbäck and Michaelsson (also in *Istapp*). Per Lengstedt (formerly Karlsson) joined the reunited *Overdrive* in 2004 and also sings in *Portrait*. Peter Ericsson was also in *Disruption*. *Unchained* play excellent melodic power metal with a nice touch of *Iron Maiden*. The band folded in 2006.

2004 ■	My Guide	MCD 4tr	Sound Riot	SRP 031
	Tracks: My Guide/Open Your Eyes/Like The Candle/My Guide (pre-production)			
2005 ■	UNCHAINED	CD	Sound Riot	SRP 029

2005 CD - SRP 029

UNDECIMBER

Patrik "Snakes" Ransäter: v/g, Emma "Lash" Kronborg: g, Mikael "Mizzy" Carling: b, Peter "Zkipper" Jansson: d

Stockholm - *Undecimber* were formed in 2007 from the ashes of the band *Reactor*, who had a strong industrial sound. They recorded the demo *Negotiate This*, which they later tried to withdraw. Some of the songs were reworked to fit *Undecimber*'s sound. The band plays industrial-sounding goth metal with plenty of synths. Dark and gothy vocals. A bit similar to *HIM* or Swedish colleagues *Maialse*, or *Tiamat* for that matter. They also have a close working relationship with author Åsa Schwarz and their song *Demon My Love* was used to market her novel *Och fjättra Lilith i kedjor*. Carling is also found in *Deed*.

2008 ☐	Silence Divine	MCD 3tr	Real Wicked	- -
	Tracks: Death By Design/Silence Divine/Take This Life			
2011 ■	SEVEN NIGHTS OF SIN	CD	Downfall Records	FALLCD 025

2011 CD - FALLCD 025

UNDERGÅNG

Afsihn "Affe/Afrika Bambaataa" Piran: v, Crippe "Crip Cristoferson" von Fraucht: v, Einar "Edgar Allan Coe" Petersson: g, Johannes "Johnny Weissmüller" Wanngren: g, Frank "Fritz Müllweisser" Guldstrand: b, Uno "Uno Svenningsson" Bruniusson: d

Uppsala - Not to be confused with Danish band *Undergang*. *Undergång* play crossover hardcore/thrash/metal. Some of the early stuff is very close to punk. The band was formed by classmates Affe and Crippe, who at first was going to form a *Mob-47*-style punk band and call it *Pappskalle* (dimwit), but scrapped the idea and drew influences from bands like *DS-13*, *What Happens Next?* and *Gordon Solie Motherfuckers*. The band released its first demo, *Pönk*, in 2002, followed by *Klipp dig och skaffa dig ett job* (2004), *Putting The Arm In Armageddon* (2004), *Live At The Fritidsgård* (2004), *Armegeddon Sessions* (2004) and the compilation *Chung Mackan Can Suck It* (2005). Wanngren is also in *Dr Living Dead* and *Leprosy*. On *Apocalypse... Now* all lead guitars were recorded by Jonas Ahlström and drums by Victor Ahlström. It's actually a 7" EP with 15 tracks! *The Mother Of Armageddon* is an LP played on 45 and with 23 tracks. Bruniusson is also in *In Solitude* and Piran is in *Obnoxious Youth*.

2007 7" - SOR #002

2010 7" - HHR 093

2007 ■	Apocalypse... Now!	7" 15tr	Shelf Ornament Records	SOR #002
	Tracks: March To The Youthcenter/Annihilation/Work Can Suck It!/I'd Rather Stay At Home/The Loser Crew/Flip That Can Up/Invasion/Knife Assault/For What Cause?/Alternayouth/Fuck Your Approach/Pump 'Em Full Of Lead/Consumer Of Children/Lobotomixed Youth/Undergång.			
2010 ■	...And You Will Live In Terror	7" 9tr	High Roller Records	HHR 093
	Tracks: Beyond/(We Are) Armageddon/Vision Of Genocide – Put To Death/Trailer Trash/Re-Animated Corpses/Toxic Addiction/Special Treatment/The Executioner/Slave/You're Fucked. 150 orange + 350 black vinyl.			
2011 ■	THE MOTHER OF ARMAGEDDON	LP	Monument Records	MON 029
	Black or black/blue splatter vinyl. Plays on 45 rpm.			

2011 LP - MON 029

UNDIVINE

Tommy Holmer: v, Erik Kumpulainen: g, Sami Mäki: g, Kristofer Nilsson: b, Jonas Lindström: d

Gävle - *Undivine* were formed in 2005 by Kumpulainen (*In Aeternum*, *Mortellez*), Nilsson (*Sectu*, *Ereb Altor*, *Machine*, *Isole*, *Withered Beaury*, *Mortellez*) and Robert Fältström (*In Aeternum*, *Mortellez*), intitially as *Svartalv*. Nilsson drafted *Withered Beauty* colleague Lindström (*Isole*, *Ereb Altor*, *Demonical*). A while later they also found singer Holmer (*Necrocide*, *Rimthurs*, *Zweihander*, *Planet Rain*). Sami Mäki (*Altered Aeon*, *Planet Rain*, *Theory In Practice*) completed the band. In February 2006 they recorded the demo *Behind Thy Eyes*, and in the studio they changed their name to *Undivine*. The demo was released by Demonical Records in 150 hand-numbered copies. *Undivine* play melodic black/death metal a bit similar to *Sacramentum* meets *Lord Belial*. *Deceitful Calm* was actually recorded already in 2006. Website: www.undivine.se

2008 CD - OFFERING 007

2008 ■	A DECEITFUL CALM	CD	Aural Offerings	OFFERING 007
2009 ■	INTO DUST	CD	Northern Silence Productions	NSP 083

2009 CD - NSP 083

UNGRATEFUL, THE

Magnus "Lillis" Lundbäck: v, Dick "Dikk" Börtner: g,
Michael Alltoft: b, Peter "Ke" Lundberg: d

Göteborg - A great band with a varied and quite indefinable style, *Beauty Of Disgrace* could fit in somewhere between **Metallica** and **Skid Row**, while the follow-up has a far more experimental touch and a heavier approach. The boys (minus Lillis) were previously known as **Time Bomb Boys** and the style then was sleaze. After the first CD, guitarist Lennart Widegren left to study at G.I.T. (Guitar Institute Of Technology) in the US. Before **The Ungrateful** he recorded a single with melodic rockers **Midnight Blue**, and before that, he and Dikk recorded an album and some singles with **Boulevard**. Dikk is also part of industrial band **Mike Tajson** and in 1982 he had two tracks on the Pang-compilation *Heavy Metal* with the band **Steelmade**. The second album was released through Megarock Records. Lillis later founded Gain Records

1993 CD - UFCD 001

1994 CD - UFCD 002

1993 ■	BEAUTY OF DISGRACE	CD	private	UFCD 001
	500 copies.			
1994 ■	NEW BLOOD	CD	private/Megarock	UFCD 002

UNGUIDED, THE

Roland Johansson: v/g, Richard Sjunnesson: v, Roger Sjunnesson: g,
Henric Carlsson: b, John Bengtsson: d

Falkenberg - Formed in 2010 by former **Sonic Syndicate** members Richard (growl) and Roland (clean vocals) as they wanted to go back to the original sound and style of **Sonic Syndicate**. They drafted former colleagues Roger and John, plus **Cipher System**'s Henric (ex-**Eternal Grief**, **Nightrage**). *Hell Frost* would be the perfect follow up for **Sonic Syndicate**'s *Only Inhuman* as this one picks up where it left off.

Maybe in need of some photo guidance?

2011 CDS - DZCD015

2011 □	Nightmareland	CDS 2tr	Despotz	DZCD016
	Tracks: Green Eyed Demon/Pathfinder. 616 numbered copies in Jakebox.			
2011 ■	Nightmareland	CDS 2tr	Despotz	DZCD015
	Tracks: Green Eyed Demon/Pathfinder.			
2011 □	HELL FROST	CD	Despotz	DZCD 017
2011 □	HELL FROST	CD	Despotz	DZCD 018
	Bonus: The Miracle Of Mind. In Jakebox.			
2011 □	HELL FROST	CD	Avalon Marquee (Japan)	MICP-11034
	The Miracle Of Mind (SPARK! cover)			
2012 ■	Phoenix Down	MCD 4tr	Despotz	LC 27829
	Phoenix Down in four different versions. 500 copies.			
2012 □	HELL FROST	LP PD	Despotz	DZLP 004
	500 copies.			

2012 MCD - LC 27829

UNHOLY

Mattis Hagman: v, Janne Wiklund: g, Henke Svensson: g, Johan Hamrin: b, Mårten Magnefors: d

Nacksta (Sundsvall) - They have been described as "*Pantera*-goes-death", well I partly agree as the band has components from thrash and hardcore as well as death metal. *Unholy* is also featured on the *Metal North* compilation (1993, Massproduktion, MASS CD-57), with the songs *Eaten By Time* and *Love – A Losers Game*. Henke was later in **Relevant Few** and Wiklund in **Left Hand Solution.**

1994 ■ Abused ....MCD 4tr Massproduktion .... MASS CDS 62
   Tracks: Just A Thought/Abused/1,2,3,4/Ensam Själ

1994 MCD - MASS CDS 62

UNICORN

Dan Swanö: v/d, Anders Måreby: g/cello, Peter Edwinzon: k

Finspång/Örebro - A very good progressive band in the vein of **Marillion** and at times **Saga**. The drummer and lead singer Dan Swanö, is usually found in death metal bands like **Edge Of Sanity, Pan-Thy-Monium, Karaboudjan** etc. Peter was ex-**Attention** and was together with Dan also found in US-indie-style band **Subway Mirror**. The **Genesis** cover *Afterglow* is found on the compilation *The River Of Constant Change* (95 Mellow). The bands second album is a symphonic masterpiece with beautiful melodies, progressive parts, and great variations performed with musical perfection. Dan's brother Dag "Tom Nouga" Swanö plays bass on the second album and Dan, on the other hand, plays on Tom's recordings. The line-up on the early demos reissued in 2001 consisted of: Dan (v/d), Peter (k), Anders (g/v) and Per Runesson (b). The demo *A Collection Of Worlds* was originally recorded back in 1989. Recommended. Dan has later on played with bands like **Bloodbath, Darkcide, Nightingale, Demiurg, Frameshift** etc etc. and in 2013 he picked up his progressive/symphonic side in **Witherscape**.

1993 CD - MMP 155

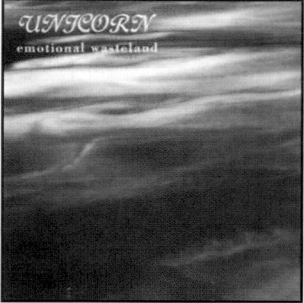

1993 ■ EVER SINCE ....CD Mellow.............................. MMP 155
1995 ■ EMOTIONAL WASTELAND.................................CD Mellow.............................. MMP 278
2001 □ A RECOLLECTION OF WORLDS ....4CD ERUF .... MORK 001
   All four Unicorn-demos on four CDs in a limited edition box-set.
2001 □ A COLLECTION OF WORLDS II/THE WEIRDEST TALES ....2CD Spam .... SPAM 005

1995 CD - MMP 278

UNION MAC

Kristoffer Lagerström: v/k, Mikael Klevengård: g/k, Imre Daun: d

Stockholm/Göteborg - **Union Mac** were formed by former **Spin Gallery** singer Lagerström and guitarist/keyboardist Klevengård. They drafted Daun, who has previously played with bands like **Don Patrol, Kharma, Salute, Hope, Gypsy Rose, White Wolf**, as well as pop artists like Magnus Carlsson, Carola, and **Herreys**. **Union Mac** play quite slick eighties-sounding AOR similar to **Magnum, Saga, Asia** and **Toto**. Good-quality stuff, but not the most exciting effort in the genre.

2007 ■ LOST IN ATTRACTION..CD Escape Music .... ESM 146
2007 □ LOST IN ATTRACTION..CD Spiritual Beast (Japan) SBCD-1050

2007 CD - ESM 146

UNITED

Patrick Aalhuizen: v, Stefan Morén: g, Pea Eliasson: k, Peter Forsell: b, M-E Björklund: d

Vansbro - Good melodic hard rock. The song *Hooked On A Feeling* is written by UK pop-composer Jonathan King. The Swedish group **Blue Swede´s** version, reached no 1 in the US-charts. Their lead singer Björn Skifs (also from Vansbro), makes a guest appearance on this recording. Stefan was also in **Keen Hue**, a band he rejoined and is still in. He also released two hard rocking solo albums.

1988 ■ Hooked On A Feeling/Hearts On Fire ....7" Startklart SKRS-007

1988 7" - SKRS-007

UNITED ENEMIES

Anders "Andy Pierce" Persson: v, Mats Jeppsson: g, Christian Fridlund: b, Richard "Ricci" Dahl: d

Malmö - **United Enemies** were formed in 2002 when **Nasty Idols/Machinegun Kelly** singer Pierce wanted to get some of his songs out. He drafted the members from the punkabilly band **69-Hard** and recorded a raw, punkish sleaze rock record. Dahl is also currently in **Nasty Idols** and Jeppsson was ex-**Raise Cain**.

2004 □ United Enemies..MCD 4tr Power Music 264-766
   Tracks: Love Kills/The Misfits/Dead Boy/Down
2007 ■ ALL THE SICK THINGS WE DO................................CD Swedmetal SM-13-CD

2007 CD - SM-13-CD

UNITED FOOLS

Alan Dzafo: v/g, Mattias Strelvik: g, Johnny Johansson: b, Zlaja Prozorac: d

Göteborg - Basic hard rock with a modern touch, at times similar to *The Cult*-meet-*The Almighty*. The band was formed in 1998, initially only featuring musicians with a Bosnian origin. Strelvik and Johansson however changed the concept. Johnny later played guitar in *Disdain* and *Ruined Soul*.

2002 ■ UNITED FOOLS ....CD   Mad Dog Records.............................MDR 001

2002 CD - MDR 001

UNIVERSAL FLYTRAP

Magnus Bengtsson: v, Magnus Cassersjö: g,
Peter Bondesson: g, David Bodén: b, Jan Fredlund: d

Älmhult - This oddly named band was formed in 1990, under the even more odd moniker *Chyzpa Fudge*. There are some influences from *Zeppelin*, some from *Black Crowes*, some from *Stone Temple Pilots* and even some from *Bad Religion*... Pretty good stuff though. The band split in 1994 and Cassersjö is now found in online project *Hellvalla Burn*. The track *Prepared Geezer* can be found on the *0476* compilation.

1994 ■ Drughog ....MCD 4tr   private .... UNIFLY 001
          Tracks: Drughog/Pale Acid Stains/A Gun Is A Strange Obsession/Hollow.

1994 MCD - UNIFLY 001

UNIVERSE

Kjell Wallén: v, Michael Kling: g, Per Nilsson: g,
Freddie Kriström: k, Hasse Hagman: b, Anders Wetterström: d

Upplands Väsby - A very good and underrated band with power, melody and class. They supported *Nazareth* on their 1984 Swedish tour. The band recorded a demo in 1988, which showed a more AOR-ish side. After this they unfortunately split. They were one of the four bands on Sonet Records compilation *Swedish Metal* (84 Sonet). The album is an underrated classic, especially tracks like *Looking For An Answer* and *Question Of Time*. Before the album was recorded the band featured Mic Michaeli on keyboards, but he left and later joined *Europe*. The band reformed and recorded a new and highly interesting album in 2002, now featuring Janne Åström (*Hot Soup*) on vocals. The album was set to be released during 2002, but unfortunately things were again put on hold. However in 2011 the band picked up the loose ends and the album is now being finished for a release in 2013. Here's hoping! The current line-up features Kling (who was once in *WC* with John Norum), Nilsson, Wetterström and Erik Mårtensson (*Eclipse, W.E.T*).

1985 7" - SMS-2

1985 ● Rollin' On/Woman ....7"   Sonet SMS-2
          No artwork.
1985 ■ UNIVERSE...LP   Sonet SMLP-3
1995 □ UNIVERSE...CD   Sonet ....SMCD 3/527 525-2
1995 □ UNIVERSE...CD   Soundholic (Japan)...................SHCD 1-0005
          The Sonet-release re-packed with extra booklet and sticker

1985 LP - SMLP-3

UNLEASHED

Johnny Hedlund: v/b, Fredrik Lindegren: g,
Tomas Olsson (now Måsgård): g, Anders Schultz: d

Stockholm - When *Nihilist* split in 1989, Johnny formed *Unleashed* and the others went on to form *Entombed*. On *...Revenge* the members were Johnny, guitarist Fredrik Lindegren, drummer Anders and singer/guitarist Robert Sennebäck (*Carnage, Dismember*). Sennebäck was replaced by Olsson (Måsgård) in 1990. They started out playing fast and brutal death metal, but on the third album *Across The Open Sea* they adopted some heavy influences in the vein of *Saint Vitus* and *Cathedral*. They even do a cover of *Judas Priest*'s *Breaking The Law*. The *Live In Vienna '93* was originally out as a bootleg, but Century Media released it as an "official bootleg" at a lower price rate than the original bootleg. On *Victory* the style had turned even more towards heavy rock with almost clean vocals. After *Warrior*, Fredrik Lindegren (*Loud Pipes*) was replaced by Fredrik Folkare (*Scudiero, Skarr, Necrophobic, Hellinor*). *Hell's Unleashed* is an outstanding slab of heavy, crushing doom/death-oriented metal. It actually ranges from high-speed stuff, through *Motörhead*-style crushers to pure doom. Great stuff! Unfortunately, due to their Viking-style lyrics and approach, they were falsely accused of being national socialists which they suffered from for quite some time. The *Immortal Glory* box set features a disc entitled *The Halls Of Asgard*, which features previously unreleased bonus tracks, also including a cover of *Venom*'s *Countess Bathory*.
Website: www.unleashed.nu

1991 7" - CM7 010

1991 7" - CBR-S 124

1991 ■ ... Revenge..7" 3tr   CBR ....CBR-S 124 $($)
          Tracks: The Utterdark Revenge/Unleashed/Where Life Ends
1991 ■ And The Laughter Has Died...7"   Century Media CM7 020
          Tracks: The Dark One/Where Life Ends
1991 □ AND THE LAUGHTER HAS DIED/REVENGE ....CD   private .... UL 002

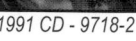

1991 CD - 9718-2

Year		Title	Format	Label	Catalog
1991	■	WHERE NO LIFE DWELLS	CD	Century Media	9718-2
1991	□	WHERE NO LIFE DWELLS	LP	Century Media	9718-1
1991	□	WHERE NO LIFE DWELLS	CD	Century Media (USA)	7718-2
1992	□	SHADOWS IN THE DEEP	CD	Century Media	849732 2
1992	■	SHADOWS IN THE DEEP	LP	Century Media	089732 1
1992	□	SHADOWS IN THE DEEP	CD	Century Media (USA)	7732-2
1993	□	ACROSS THE OPEN SEA	CD	Century Media	770552 2
1993	□	ACROSS THE OPEN SEA	LP	Century Media	770552 1
1994	□	LIVE IN VIENNA '93	CD	Century Media	770562 2
1994	□	LIVE IN VIENNA '93	CD	Century Media (USA)	7756 2
1995	□	VICTORY	CD	Century Media	770902 2
1995	□	VICTORY	LP	Century Media	770902 1
1995	□	VICTORY	LP PD	Century Media	770902 1P
1995	□	VICTORY	CD	Century Media (USA)	7790 2
1996	□	EASTERN BLOOD – HAIL TO POLAND	CD	Century Media	77118-2
1997	□	WARRIOR	LP	Century Media	77124-1
1997	□	WARRIOR	CDd	Century Media	77124-2

1992 LP - 089732 1

2001 □ WHERE NO LIFE DWELLS/…AND THE LAUGHTER HAS DIED ....CD Century Media 77386-2
Bonus: The Dark One/If They Had Eyes (The Watchers Of The Earth)/Dead Forever/Un-
leashed/Where Life Ends/The Utter Dark Revenge/Violent Ecstasy/Before The Creation
Of Time (video)/The One Insane (video)

2001	□	WHERE NO LIFE DWELLS/…AND THE LAUGHTER HAS DIED	CD	Century Media (USA)	7718-2
2001	■	SHADOWS IN THE DEEP/ACROSS THE OPEN SEA	CD	Century Media (USA)	7732-2
2002	■	HELL'S UNLEASHED	CD	Century Media	77424 2
2002	□	HELL'S UNLEASHED	LP	Century Media	77424 1
2002	□	HELL'S UNLEASHED	CD	Century Media (USA)	8124-2
2002	□	VICTORY/WARRIOR	CD	Century Media (USA)	8057-2
2003	□	…AND WE SHALL TRIUMPH IN VICTORY	6LP PD box	Century Media	77544-0/6

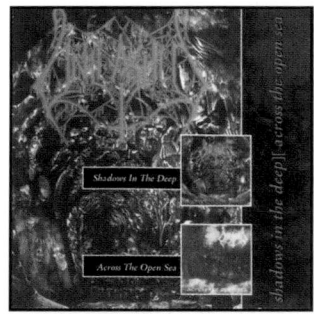

2001 CD - 7732-2

Box set with specially numbered picture discs. Where No Life Dwells, Shadows In The
Deep, Across The Open Sea, Victory, Warrior and Hell's Unleashed. Bonus: The Dark One/
Where Life Ends/The Utter Dark Revenge/Violent Ecstacy/Breaking The Law (Judas
Priest cover)/If They Had Eyes/Dead Forever/Unleashed/Ace Of Spades (Motörhead
cover). 2000 numbered copies.

2004	□	SWORN ALLEGIENCE	CD	Century Media	77524-2
2004	□	SWORN ALLEGIENCE	CD	Fono (Russia)	FO 398 CD
2004	□	SWORN ALLEGIENCE	CD	Icarus Music (Argentina)	ICARUS 077
2004	□	SWORN ALLEGIENCE	CD	Century Media (USA)	8224-2

Bonus: To Miklagård/Long Live The Beast

2004	□	WARRIOR	CD	Fono (Russia)	FO 443 CD
2005	□	WHERE NO LIFE DWELLS	CD	Fono (Russia)	FO 442 CD

Bonus: The Dark One/If They Had Eyes (The Watchers Of The Earth)/Dead Forever/Un-
leashed/Where Life Ends/The Utter Dark Revenge/Violent Ecstasy/Before The Creation
Of Time (video)/The One Insane (video)

2002 CD - 77424 2

2005	□	HELL'S UNLEASHED	CD	Fono (Russia)	FO 557 CD
2006	■	MIDVINTERBLOT	CD	Steamhammer	SPV 97952
2006	□	MIDVINTERBLOT	CD	Steamhammer/Soyus (Russia)	SPV 97952
2006	□	MIDVINTERBLOT	LP	Animate Records	AR 017

777 black, 111 gold, 222 yellow/blue vinyl.

2006	□	MIDVINTERBLOT	CD	Icarus Music (Argentina)	ICARUS 394
2006	□	SHADOWS IN THE DEEP	LP	Century Media	9732-1

Light grey vinyl

2006	□	SHADOWS IN THE DEEP	CD	Century Media	997604-2

Bonus: The Final Silence/Bloodbath/Shadows In The Deep/Never Ending Hate/Onward
Into Countless Battles/The Immortals

2006	□	SHADOWS IN THE DEEP	CD	Century Media	77604-2
2006	□	SHADOWS IN THE DEEP	CD	Icarus Music (Argentina)	ICARUS 863
2006	□	ACROSS THE OPEN SEA	CD	Century Media	997605-2

Bonus: The One Insane (video)

2006 CD - SPV 97952

2007	□	ACROSS THE OPEN SEA	CD	Century Media	77605-2
2007	□	SHADOWS IN THE DEEP	CD	Soyus (Russia)	77604-2
2006	□	VICTORY	CD	Century Media	997608-2

Bonus: Revenge/The Defender/In The Name Of God/Against The World/Victims Of War/
Beserk

2006	□	VICTORY	CD	Century Media	77608-2
2006	□	WARRIOR	CD	Century Media	997609-2
2006	□	WARRIOR	CD	Century Media	77609-2
2008	□	VIKING RAIDS (1991-2004 BEST OF UNLEASHED)	CD	Century Media	997826-2
2008	□	VIKING RAIDS (1991-2004 BEST OF UNLEASHED)	CD	Century Media (USA)	18526-2
2008	□	LIVE IN VIENNA '93	LP+7"	Kneel Before The Master's Throne	Kneel 017

Clear vinyl. Poster.

2008	□	IMMORTAL GLORY	10CD box	Century Media	- -

Wooden box. 2000 copies. Albums: Where No Life Dwells/Shadows In The Deep/Live In
Vienna 1993/Across The Open Sea/Victory/Eastern Blood – Hail To Poland/Warrior/Hell's
Unleashed/Sworn Allegiance/The Halls Of Asgard

2008	□	HAMMER BATTALION	CD	Steamhammer	SPV 92292

2010 LP (white) - 2481-1

2008 ☐ HAMMER BATTALION	...LP	Steamhammer	SPV 92291 LP
2008 ☐ HAMMER BATTALION	...CD	Steamhammer/Soyus (Russia)	SPV 92292
2008 ☐ HAMMER BATTALION	...CD	Icarus Music (Argentina)	ICARUS 515
2010 ☐ VIKING RAIDS (1991-2004 BEST OF UNLEASHED)	...2LP	Animate Records	AR 031

100 blue/yellow + 566 black vinyl.

2010 ☐ WHERE NO LIFE DWELLS	...LP	Century Media	997999-1

100 blue + 100 grey + 100 white + 100 red + 100 clear vinyl.

2010 ☐ WHERE NO LIFE DWELLS	...LPg+CD	Century Media	9979991-2

700 copies. T-shirt. CD bonus: The Dark One/If They Had Eyes (The Watchers Of The Earth)/Dead Forever/Unleashed/Where Life Ends/The Utter Dark Revenge/Violent Ecstasy/Before The Creation Of Time (video)/The One Insane (video)

2010 ☐ AS YGGDRASIL TREMBLES	...CD	Nuclear Blast	2481-2
2010 ☐ AS YGGDRASIL TREMBLES	...CDd box	Nuclear Blast	2481-5

2011 LP - 998110-1

Bonus: Evil Dead (Death cover). Leather bracelet + numbered certificate. 500 copies.

2010 ☐ AS YGGDRASIL TREMBLES	...CDd	Nuclear Blast	2481-0

Bonus: Evil Dead (Death cover).

2010 ■ AS YGGDRASIL TREMBLES	...LP	Nuclear Blast	2481-1

Black vinyl + 250 copies in white vinyl.

2010 ☐ AS YGGDRASIL TREMBLES	...CD	Icarus Music (Argentina)	ICARUS 602
2011 ☐ EASTERN BLOOD – HAIL TO POLAND	...2LP	Animate Records	AR 035

566 copies.

2011 ■ SHADOWS IN THE DEEP	...LP	Century Media	998110-1

New artwork.

2012 ☐ WHERE NO LIFE DWELLS	...CD	Century Media	998311-2
2012 ☐ WHERE NO LIFE DWELLS	...CD	Icarus Muaic (Argentina)	ICARUS 862
2012 ■ ODALHEIM	...LPg	Nuclear Blast	NB 2809-1

Pressed in black, red and 250 copies white vinyl. Poster.

2012 LPg - NB 2809-1

2012 ☐ ODALHEIM	...CD	Nuclear Blast	NB 2809-2

First press with slipcase.

2012 ☐ ODALHEIM	...CD	Icarus Music (Argentina)	ICARUS 936

UNLIGHT ORDER

Alexander "Soahc" Holmberg: v/b, Fredrik Eklöf: b, Simon "Moloch" Holmberg: g/d

Linköping/Kalmar - Formed in 2004 and recorded the demo *Blooddawn* in 2005, followed by *Blooddawn Awaits* later the same year. Old-school-influenced black metal, but more doom-oriented and with a quite melodic touch. Quite poorly produced and not very well-played. Growl that sounds a bit out of breath at times. The band changed their name to *Zworn* and recorded a couple more demos before they broke up in June 2010. Miloch is also in *Saved By Insanity*.

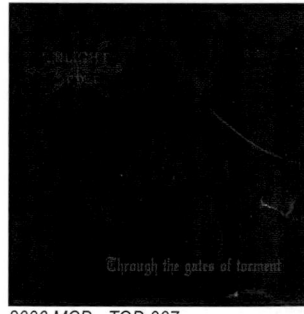

2006 ■ Through The Gates Of Torment	...MCD 5tr	Temple Of Darkness	TOD 007

Tracks: Vault Of The Mind/Through The Gates Of Torment/Key To The Night/Sacrificed/Shine. 1000 copies.

2006 MCD - TOD 007

UNMOORED

Christian Älvestam: v/g/k/b,
Thomas "Plec" Johansson: g,
Henrik Schönström: d

Ship ahoy!

Skövde - Formed in 1994 by Christian, guitarist Rickard Larsson and bassist Torbjörn Öhrling. They recorded the first demo *Wood Chuck Tune* in 1994 with the aid of a drum machine. A drummer was recruited and they recorded the second demo *In The Shadow Of The Obscure* in 1995. It was not until the third demo *More To The Story Than Meets The Eye* (1997), they received interest from Pulverised and were finally signed. The debut album was recorded already in 1997, but not released until two years after. It was recorded at Studio Sunlight and produced by Tomas Skogsberg. Before the recording of the second album drummer Niclas Wahlén left the band, but was replaced by *Thy Primordial/Dawn* drummer Jocke Pettersson. Straightforward death with an almost punk-/garage-attitude, sometimes flirting with doom metal. The second album was recorded at Studio Abyss and produced by Tommy Tägtgren. On *Indefinite Soul Extinction* the line-up had totally changed, seeing Älvestam as the only remaining member. Guitarist Rickard Larsson was replaced by Thomas "Plec" Johansson, bassist Torbjörn Öhrling was out and drummer Jocke Pettersson was replaced by Henrik Schönström. In 2004 the trio recorded a new album, now under the name *Torchbearer*.

1999 CD - ASH 008 CD

1999 ■ CIMMERIAN	...CD	Pulverised	ASH 008 CD
2000 ■ KINGDOM OF GREED	...CD	Pulverised	ASH 012 CD
2003 ☐ INDEFINITE SOUL EXTINCTION	...CDd	Code 666	SPV 085-148462

2000 CD - ASH 012 CD

UNPURE

Kolgrim: b/v, Hräsvelg: v/g, Jonathon: d

Stockholm - The band was formed in 1991 by Kolgrim and Hräsvelg. They were accompanied by Åberg and Victor "Vic" Andersson, both on guitar and recorded their first demo, *Demo 1 – XCII*, in 1993. The guitarist Surth (*Svartsyn, Satans Vind*), Poock and Åberg went in and out of the band and on the first album they were handled by Hräsvelg himself. On *Coldland* Vic (ex-*Bonegrinder, Celestial Pain*) returned and John Blackwar (*Celestial Pain*) joined. On the third album the line-up had once again changed, with Hräsvelg now handling the guitars and drummer Jonathon was in the ranks. Death/Black metal with occasional thrash/power metal influences and vocals quite similar to Cronos of *Venom*. Kolgrim is also in *Incursion, Svartsyn* and *Illska*. Hrägsveld is also in the latter. The band is also found on a number of compilations, such as: *Nynäs Rocks* (93 Nynäs, track: *Lust Of Darkness*), *With Us Or Against Us* (95 Napalm, track: *Lust Of Darkness*), *Headbangers Against Disco 2* (97 track: *Metal Night*), *From The Underground* (97, track: *Sabbath*), *Voices Of Death Pt II* (00, track: *Forever Lost*), *Return Of Darkness And Hate* (01, track: *Incubus*) and the *Alice Cooper* tribute *Thinking About Alice* (01, track: *The Black Widow*). In 2011 Hampus "H. Death" Eriksson was added on guitar/vocals.

1996 CD - NPR 022

2001 CD - DKCD 016

2004 CD - ARcd018

1995 ☐	UNPURE	CD	Napalm	NPR 011	
1996 ■	COLDLAND	CD	Napalm	NPR 022	
2001 ☐	Sabbatical Splittombstone (split)	7"	Iron Pegasus	I.P.S. 03	

Split with Sabbat. Tracks: Warfare/War Of Vengeance.

2001 ■	TRINITY IN BLACK	CD	Drakkar	DKCD 016	
2004 ■	WORLD COLLAPSE	CD	Agonia Records	ARcd018	
2004 ☐	WORLD COLLAPSE	LPg	Agonia Records	ARlp011	

500 copies. Poster. Bonus: A Chalice Full Of Blood/Hungry Slave

UNREAL

Peter Birgersson: v/g, Dennis Stenberg: g, Jimmy Taskinen: b, Gunnar Dahlgren: d

Landskrona - Average quality metal with influences from *Metallica, Judas Priest* etc. Vocals of a less interesting kind. In 2000 the band recorded a new 2 track demo.

1998 ■ Unreal ....MCD 5tr private .... AGAKRAX 999
Tracks: Haunted/Falling/Magic Man/Man's Best Friend/Heartland

1998 MCD - AGAKRAX 999

UNSOLVED

Martin Persson: v, Tony Lang: g, Gabriel Bjäreborg: g, Cliff Nilsson: b, Niclas Persson: d

Kristianstad - When the band *Morpheena* called it a day in 2008 guitarist Tony and drummer Niclas formed the band *Unsolved*. Produced by Adde Larsson and Jens Bogren (*Opeth, Soilwork, Paradise Lost, Urbandux*). Great post-grunge in the vein of *Creed* and *Alter Bridge*. On the second album, *Tabula Rasa*, bassist Bjäreborn had switched to guitar and second guitarist Cliff Nilsson were been added to the line-up.
Website: www.unsolved.se

2011 CDd - ilumnicd 007

2011 ■	LOST	CDd	Ilumnirec	ilumnicd 007	
2012 ☐	TABULA RASA	CD	Sliptrick Records	Slp012.033	

UPPGÅNG 34

Nils Thomasson: g/v, Lars-Eric Sundström: g, Ulric Johansson: b, Michael Hurtig: d

Östersund - Despite the odd name (Entrance 34), this is a brilliant, fusion-oriented instrumental hard rock band, a bit like a mix of *Wishbone Ash* meets Zappa. Great musicians and great music. Hurtig and Johansson was later in pop band *Café M*.

1981 ■ Ladgårdsdrömmar .... 7" 4tr Heavy Metal Records .... HMREP 1001
Tracks: Härlig jakt/7000 människor/Hallelulep/Spricker

1981 7" - HMREP 1001

UPPÅT VÄGGARNA

Johan Vallin: v/g, Dante Holmberg: g, Dan "Svarten" Svensson: b, Hans Karlander: b, Thomas Wiklund: d

Stockholm - This is a rare and highly interesting piece of vinyl for fans of the early 70s-hard rock. They are very reminiscent of *November*, especially the track *Jag Färdas*. Thomas later joined *Neon Rose*, Dante went to *Strix-Q*, while "Svarten" became an appreciated sound engineer and handled the live sound for *Wasa Express* several years.

1971 ■ Jag Hatar Politik/Jag Färdas .... 7" Efel .... SEF 45 $$

UPPÅT VÄGGARNA
SEF 45 / Efel
JAG HATAR POLITIK
JAG FÄRDAS
1971 7" - SEF 45

URBANDUX

Oscar "DemonZ" Zubelzu: v, Jose Pascual: g, Richard Martos: b, Adde Larsson: d

Göteborg - I'm not really sure as to if this is to be considered a Spanish or Swedish band. The two main members, Zubelzu and Pascual recorded the first album, *Songs From The Flesh*, while living in Spain. They then moved to Göteborg in 2005, added some Swedish blood to the line-up and released the follow-up, *The Aftermath*. The album featured Zoltan Csörsz (*The Flower Kings, Art Metal*) on drums and a guest solo from Mattias Ia Eklundh (*Freak Kitchen*). *Urbandux* play quite interesting modern melodic poppy metal a bit similar to *Incubus* and *Shinedown*. *Eleven Eleven* was produced by Jens Bogren (*Opeth, Paradise Lost, Soilwork*). The band broke up in 2011 and in 2012 guitarist Jose was seeking members for his new heavier band *Words For The Lost*. *Another Brick In The Wall* is a cover of *Pink Floyd*.

2004 CD - n/a

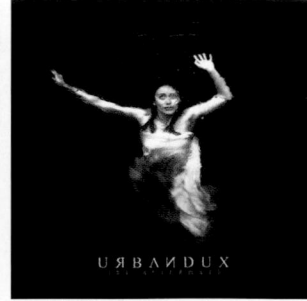

2008 CDd - 63447983993

2008 MCDp - 63447978717

2009 CD - ILUMNICD 003

2004	■	SONGS FROM THE FLESH	CD	Geisha Records	n/a
2008	■	THE AFTERMATH	CDd	P.R.O Records	63447983993
2008	■	Another Brick In The Wall/Bozo/Seltzer Water	MCDp 3tr	P.R.O Records	63447978717
2009	■	ELEVEN ELEVEN	CD	Ilumnirec	ILUMNICD 003

UTUMNO

Jonas Stålhammar: v, Dennis Lindahl: g,
Staffan Johansson: g, Dan Öberg: b, Johan Hallberg: d

Västerås - Formed in 1990, initially as *Carnal Redemption*. *Utumno* comes from *The Lords Of The Ring*, and was a fortress (also named Udûn). The band recorded their first demo, *Desolation Doman*, the year they were formed, followed by *Twisted Emptiness* later the same year. Technical death metal with some awesome drum work, quite similar to early *Entombed*. The vocals are closer to thrash in style. Jonas is also found in *God Macabre*, where he handles the guitar. Recorded at Sunlight Studios. Hallberg, who was also in *Cranium*, passed away in 2001. Johansson is also in *Abhoth*, while Stålhammar has played with *Bombs Of Hades, Darkcreed, God Macabre, Macabre End, The Crown* and *Abhoth*.

1991 7" - CTR 001 EP

2009 LP - CRYPT 04

1991	■	The Light Of Day	7"	Cenotaph Records	CTR 001 EP
		Tracks: Saviour Reborn/In Misery I Dwell			
1993	☐	Across The Horizon	MCD 6tr	Cenotaph Records	CTR 007 CD
		Tracks: The Light Of Day/I Cross The Horizons/In Misery I Dwell/Saviour Reborn/Sunrise/ Emotions Run Cold (Saints And Sinners)			
2009	■	ACROSS THE HORIZON	LP	The Crypt	CRYPT 04
		250 black + 250 purple vinyl. Bonus: Saviour/Reborn/In Misery I Dwell			
2010	☐	ACROSS THE HORIZON	CD	Cyanide Syndicate Records	CSR 002 CD

VA-DÅ

David Kronlid: v/p, Christer Sunesson: v/g, Gotte Ringkvist: flutes/lute-guitar,
Stefan Brisland: violin/sampling, Björn Eriksson: b, Lars Forslund: d

Sundsvall - This is a great and very original band. They mix the heaviness of bands like **Mental Hippe Blood** and **Skintrade** with traditional Swedish folkmusic, like a 90s version of **Kebnekajse**. The instrumentation is quite original. *Red, White, Grey* is the same album as *Va-då*, but with English lyrics. David and Christer have previously recorded two singles with **Jezebel**. Va-då means, approximately "so what?"

1995 □	Trams	CDS	Massproduktion	MASSCDS 66
1995 □	VA-DÅ	CD	Massproduktion	MASSCD 64
1997 ■	RED, WHITE, GREY	CD	Pyrrhic (Cananda)	PYR CD-M641

Same as the above, but with English lyrics.

1997 CD - PYR CD-M641

VAGH

Jonas Blum: v, Tommy "Robin Vagh" Silfvenius: g/k,
Jan-Åke Jönsson: b, Anders Rosell: k/d

Norrköping - **Vagh** were initiated by Robin in 2000. *Sands Of Time* was lacking a bit of thin production. The second album features guest spots from singer John Marshall Gibbs and guitarists David Persson and Henrik Hansson. Unfortunately also this one lacks from quite bad production. The music is really good melodic hard rock. After the second album the line-up was reinforced by keyboardist Tom Rask. Robin immediately started working on the third album, but lack of funds and a feeling it wasn't up to par put the project to a halt. Instead he decided to change it into the **Optimysical** project in 2006, using a variety of musicians and singers to reach his musical goals. It also sounds way better.

2002 CD - SCSP 001

2004 CD - SCSP 002

2002 ■	SANDS OF TIME	CD	Slick City Slackers	SCSP 001
2004 ■	INTO THE FUTURE ZONE	CD	Slick City Slackers	SCSP 002

VAINS OF JENNA

Jesse Forte: v, Niklas "Nicki Kin" Lundahl: g,
Joakim "JP White" Petersson: b, Emil "Jacki Stone" Petersson: d

Falkenberg - Sleaze rockers **Vains Of Jenna** were formed in January 2005. The band moved to the US and recorded a couple of demos under the supervision of former **Guns 'N Roses** guitarist Gilby Clarke. In 2006 they were discovered by *Jackass* star Bam Margera, who signed the band to his Filthy Note Records. In 2008 the band returned back to Sweden. In 2010 they parted ways with singer Jimmy "Lizzy DeVine" Johansson, who was replaced by American singer Jesse Forte. In January 2012 they made it official they were quitting because they felt they needed to move on with their lives. **Vains Of Jenna** were a pretty good sleaze band in the vein of **Buckcherry**-meet-**Guns 'N Roses** with great vocals. After the band's break-up Forte was announced as the new singer of **Lynch Mob**. *Reversed Tripped* is an all covers album where the band sleazifies songs by **The Beatles, Eddy Grant, Bob Dylan, Mountain, Ten Years After, Deep Purple** etc. In 2011 the extended *We Can Never Die Vol 2* was released digitally through RSL.

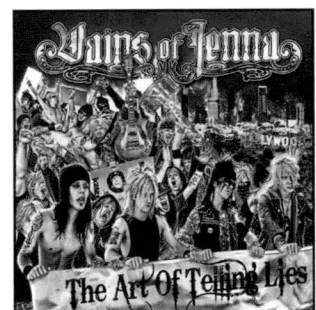
2009 CDd - 648060090922

2010 MCDp - 64806091028

2005 □	Baby's Got A Secret	MCD 4tr	private	- -

Tracks: Get On The Ride/Baby's Got A Secret/One Last Pleasure/Jumping Jack Flash (Rolling Stones cover)

2006 □	LIT UP/LET DOWN	CD	RSL/Raw Noize Records	CD 06062
2006 □	LIT UP/LET DOWN	CD	Outlook Music	OTLK 1008
2006 □	THE DEMOS	CD	RSL/Raw Noize Records	CD 09062
2009 ■	THE ART OF TELLING LIES	CDd	RSL/Raw Noize Records	648060090922
2010 ■	We Can Never Die	MCDp 6tr	RSL/Raw Noize Records	648060091028

Tracks: We Can Never Die/Everybody Loves You When You're Dead (2010 mix)/The Art Of Telling Lies (2010 mix)/Better Off Alone (2010 mix)/We Can Never Die (long play)/Better Off Alone (radio edit)

2011 □	REVERSED TRIPPED	CD	Cleopatra Records	CLP 4797
2011 ■	REVERSED TRIPPED	LP	Cleopatra Records	CLP 4798

2011 LP - CLP 4798

VALENZE

Magnus Severin: v/g, Ulf Johansson: g, Jan Hultin: k,
Mats Larsson: b, Richard Grönlund: d

Gimo - **Valenze** were formed in 1980, initially named **Zendragh** influenced by **Hansa Band** and **Thin Lizzy**. They briefly changed name to **Skyfall**, before going for **Valenze**. The 1984 single is really good melodic hard rock sung in Swedish. In 1990 Hultin moved to Stockholm and Per Selander (ex-**Convention**) replaced him. In 1991 the band switched to playing covers and in 1992 they recorded an original album. In 1993 Selander quit and the band again plays mostly covers.

1984 ■	Sakta faller regnet/Vill du	7"	Pärla Records	PNLS 022
1992 □	20 ÅR I GARAGET	CD	private	n/a

1984 7" - PNLS 022

VALINORS TREE

Ola Sivefäldt: v/g, John Lönnmyr: k, Anders Lindgren: b, Mattias Jarthed: d

Falköping - Highly interesting progressive/symphonic hard rock similar to **Anekdoten** or **Tristan Park**. *Kingdom Of Sadness* contains only four songs, but they are over 40 minutes. The band recorded a new four-track demo in 2002.

1998 CD - RHCD 13

1998 ■	KINGDOM OF SADNESS	CD	Record Heaven	RHCD 13
2000 □	...AND THEN THERE WERE SILENCE	CD	Record Heaven	RHCD 29

VALKYRJA

Andreas "A.L" Lind: v, Simon "S.W" Wizén: g, A. Hed: g, Jocke Wallgren: d

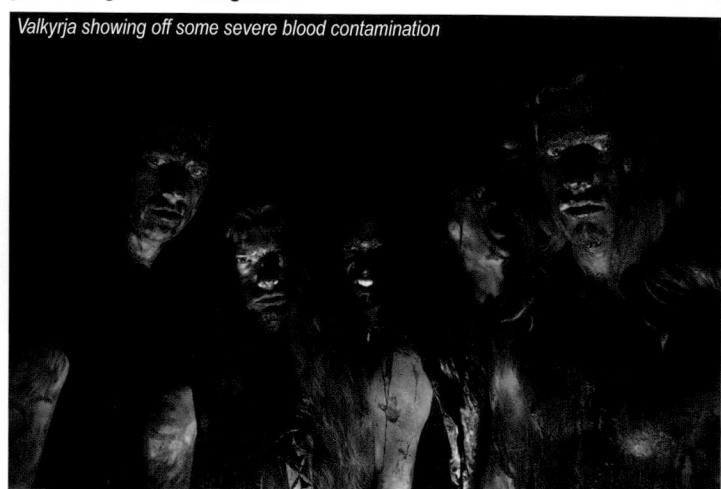

Valkyrja showing off some severe blood contamination

Stockholm - Formed in 2004. Despite the name the band has nothing to do with pagan, heathen or Viking metal. In 2005 the band released the first demo *Funeral Voices*, at the time featuring Lind, Wizén, bassist J Lindgren, drummer Skall and guitarist Joakim "Xephroth", followed by *Far Beyond* later the same year. It was released in 200 copies by Deathkrush, and also features the first demo. On the debut album the line-up had changed, now featuring Wizén, Lind, Wallgren, Hed and Lindgren. High-speed, old-school-oriented death metal. Well-played, but not very sophisticated in its compositions. *The Invocation Of Demise* and *Contamination* were recorded by Tore Stjerna at Necromorbus Studio. The Metal Blade reissue of *The Invocation Of Demise* has new artwork. After the album, bassist M.A was out of the band and after *Contamination* he was replaced by Vlad "VP" Lefay (ex-**Diabolical**). Simon (**Die Hard**), Vlad and Jocke (**Vituperation**) are also found in **Ondskapt**.

2007 CD - NSP 053

2007 ■	THE INVOCATION OF DEMISE	CD	Nothern Silence Productions	NSP 053
	Also 100 copies in metal box, numbered + patch.			
2007 □	THE INVOCATION OF DEMISE	LP	Nothern Silence Productions	NSP 053
	100 copis grey/white splatter + patch, 160 grey/white splatter + 260 black vinyl..			
2009 □	THE INVOCATION OF DEMISE	CD	Metal Blade	3984-14740-2
	New artwork.			
2009 □	THE INVOCATION OF DEMISE	CD	Fono (Russia)	FO 812 CD
2010 □	CONTAMINATION	CD	Metal Blade	3984-14790-2
2010 □	CONTAMINATION	2LPg	W.T.C Productions	- -
	100 coloured vinyl with poster and patch + 400 black vinyl. Different artwork.			

VALLEY

Miko Walldén: g/v, Lars Fransson: g/v, Christer Windahl: b/v, Göran Lundgren: d

Stockholm - Quite good melodic hard rock/metal. Mid-quality vocals and a bit amateurish, but collectors should check it out. The cover says *Valley* and the label says *Walley*.

1981 7" - VD 1

1981 ■	Take Me Through The Night/The Neon Kings Of The Night	7"	private	VD 1

VAMPA

Ola Ahlsén: g/v, Robert Fossengen: g/v, Robert Scholtyssek: b, Per Ljungqvist: d

Stockholm - Puberty metal. The name means vamp. Very young and amateurish metal with slightly punkish vocals sung in Swedish. For collectors only. Scholtyssek later took the stage name Schotz and Fossengren changed his to Foss. They formed **9T9**, later known as **Russell**. Fossengren is now in pop duo **Lucid Dreams Ave**.

1982 7" - BMB 107

1982 ■	Plugget/Blå Tåget/Blackout	7" 3tr	BMB	BMB 107

VAMPIRE

Hand Of Doom: v/d, Black String: g, Command: b

Göteborg - Raw death metal in the vein of early **Entombed** meets **Repugnant**. Formed in 2011.

2013 7" - TTD 020

2012 ■	Vampire	7" 4tr	To The Death	TTD 020
	Tracks: At Midnight I'll Possess Your Corpse/Jaws Of The Unknown/The Night It Came Out Of The Grave/Under The Grudge. 200 red, 500 goat yellow (45 rpm), 200 puke yellow (33 rpm), 100 black vinyl copies. Patch.			

VANADIS

Jan Göransson: v, Carl Månsson: g, Gry Anders Nilsson: g,
Per-Olof Buhre: b, Mats Henriksson: d

Helsingborg - Carl Månsson started out in the band *Aniara* in 1975, a band that later evolved into *Vanadis*. Pretty good 70s-sounding hard rock, sounds a bit influenced by bands like *Neon Rose* or *Solid Ground*. Not to be confused with Ulricehamn band *Vanadis*, who were featured on the compilation *Rock On, Roll On* (1980 Pang). The band split in 1979 when military service made it difficult to get it together. Månsson later played with *Boogie Liquor Band*, which became *Bai Bang* and today has his solo project *Manssrock*. He also made a stint with *Huw Lloyd Langton Group* and played on the album *On The Move*. Nilsson was later in blues rockers *Cold Shot*.

1979 ■ Heaven Can Wait/Do Me A Favor ....7" CF Records..................................CFR-S-7001

1979 7" - CFR-S-7001

VANDÖD

Niclas Ankarbranth: v, Henrik Wendel: g, Ville Kemi: b, Daniel Wikforss: d

Malmö - Formed in 2004 by Wendel and Wikforss. They drafted singer Ankarbrandt and started recording demos. They now drafted Kemi. In 2007 Ville Kemi was replaced by Martin "Zarathustra" Linde, but when Martin left, Ville returned. Wendel is also found in *Pyramido* and *Deathboot*, Wikforss in *Vanity Dies Hard* and *Subfret* while Kemi has been in various bands like *Fall Ov Seraphim, Obscure Divinity, Misteltein* and *Shadow Cult*. As is quite a mix of styles and sounds ranging from classic high-speed black metal to industrial to bombastic choirs and vocals ranging from clean deep goth-style to guttural growls, at times with the addition of horns and stuff. Quite schizophrenic. Niclas is also in the band *The Gardnerz*.

2007 ☐ AS ....CD Ex Mortem ....XMR 001
2008 ■ AS ....LP Possession Productions PS48

2008 LP - PS48

VANESSA

Richard Holmgren: v/b, Peter Ledin: g, Peppe Vikman: d

Västerås - *Vanessa* recorded their first demo in 1992, and a second in 1993, before they were signed by Long Island. A great band influenced by *Black Sabbath* during the *Heaven And Hell* era. High-quality musicians, vocals and song material. Highly recommended. Ledin was ex-*Acis* and is now in *Blackworld*, while Holmgren has been in *Apostasy, Scaar, Wolf, Soulskinner, Haterush, Grand Design* and is also in *Blackworld*. The album features guest spots from Bobby Vargkvist (*Bewarp, Espinoza, Emerald*), Richard Fasth, Mikael Johansson and Jonas Sandquist.

1995 ■ VANESSA ....CD Long Island Records........................ LIR 00126

1995 CD - LIR 00126

VANGUARD

Ralf "Brasse" Wernborg: v, Sven-Erik "Sverka" Wernborg: g, Stefan Rosell: g,
Mikael "Mikke" Andersson: b, Eric "Erca" Lindesvärd: d

Ödeshög/Mjölby - Formed in 1982 under the name *Poleaxe* by Andersson and guitarist Peo Axelsson. Both had played in punk band *Blackmail* (released the single *Statusjakt* on Pang Records in 1982). The Wernborg brothers joined later in 1982 and Lindesvärd completed the line up. In 1983 Peo left to form the band *King's Club*. He was soon replaced by Rosell. They now changed the name to *Vanguard*. Classic 80s heavy metal in the vein of early *Tygers Of Pan Tang*, but with better vocals. Not bad at all. In 1987 they entered Rock SM. The song *All Night Long* was featured on the *Double Up* compilation. They added keyboard player Per-Anders Forsén. Eric left and was replaced by Lubbe Johansson, just shortly before the band broke up in 1988. The band split into the two bands *Avenue* (later *Lone Ranger*) and *Déjà Vu*. The band reunited for some shows in 2004, 2006 and 2007. Members have later appeared in bands like *Pseudo Sun, Guranisten, Limetreesword, Skrot* and *Cha*. Peo is now in *The Reehab*.

1984 ■ V... MLP 4tr private .... VAN-8404 MX $
    Tracks: Scarce For The Future/H.M. Paradise/Beast On The Run/Lady Of Madness.

1984 MLP - VAN-8404 MX

VANGUARD

Björn Jonasson: v, Stefan "Sulan" Hemgren: g, Thomas Ronnhammar: g,
Johan Dahlgren: k, Fredrik Mielke: b, Göran Hemgren: d

Stockholm - The four track MCD by *Vanguard* looks quite cheap and simple, but don't let the artwork fool you. The band delivers good solid melodic hard rock in the same vein as *220 Volt* and *Europe*'s debut album. The band was formed in the late 80s. The MCD was actually never properly mixed, since the tapes were stolen and the rough mix was used. Göran was later in thrash band *Scape Goat*, while Fredrik and Thomas were in the band *Tribe*. The band split in 1995.

1992 ■ Vanguard..MCD 4tr private ....(VGCD 001)
    Tracks: Crusader/Love IS An Angel/Dead Night/Evil Power.

?? MCD - (VGCD 001)

VANHELGD

Jimmy Johansson: g/v, Mattias Frisk: g/v, Viktor Gustafsson: b, Björn Andersson: d

Mjölby/Stockholm - Vanhelgd, which means desecration or profanation, were formed in 2007. Gustafsson and Andersson are also in *Ocean Chief*, while Johansson and Frisk are in *Ceremonial Execution* and *Blump*. *Vanhelgd* play old-school, blackish death metal. Bass player Gustafsson was out of the band in January 2013.

2008 ☐	CULT OF LAZARUS	CD	Crematorium Records	CR 006
2009 ☐	CULT OF LAZARUS	LP	Nuclear War Now!	ANTI-GOTH 131
	New artwork. Poster. Also die hard version on bronze vinyl + patch and sticker.			
2010 ■	Praise The Serpent/The Triumph Of Death	12"	Nuclear War Now!	ANTI-GOTH 170
	250 copies + woven patch			
2011 ☐	CHURCH OF DEATH	LP	Nuclear War Now!	ANTI-GOTH 175
	Poster. 100 dark greed vinyl + 400 black vinyl.			
2011 ☐	CHURCH OF DEATH	LP PD	Nuclear War Now!	ANTI-GOTH 175
	Die hard edition. Poster, patch, sticker.			
2011 ■	CHURCH OF DEATH	CD	Nuclear War Now!	ANTI-GOTH 175

2010 7" - ANTI-GOTH 170

2011 CD - ANTI-GOTH 175

VANITY BLVD

Anna "Cindi Savage" Alfredsson: v, Martin "Marty" Falkeström: g, Emil "Traci Trexx" Skoglund: g, Ted: b, Fredrik "Frecko" Källström: d

Avesta/Flen - Vanity Blvd were formed in 2005 by singer Cindi and bass player Roxy. After a couple of months they entered Black Lounge Studios with producer Jonas Kjellgren (*Scar Symmetry*) to record their first demo. In 2006 they recorded the second demo, *Playin' It Ruff*. They were spotted by Ryan Roxie (*Alice Cooper*) and producer Chris Laney who recorded the band's debut. Shortly after Roxy wanted out and she was replaced by Ted. In 2007 the band was picked up by Gain Music (*Hardcore Superstar, Mustasch* etc) who released the digital single *Share My Pain*. Late 2007 Marty entered as rhythm guitarist and the debut album was recorded. In the summer of 2008 Ted left and Marty took over the bass. Right after the release of the album Marty left and was replaced by Peder "Pete Ash" Rongvall. Drummer Frecko has also been replaced by Gebba (*Wounded*). *Vanity Blvd* play really good ass-kicking sleazy melodic hard rock in the vein of *Vain* meets *Saraya*. Anna is not your average sleazy screamer, but has a slightly mellower and more balanced lower voice, which made me think of Lita Ford. Most of the songs on the first album were co-written by Emil's sister Anna Skoglund.

2008 ■	ROCK 'N ROLL OVERDOSE	CD	Gain	GPCD 057

2008 CD - GPCD 057

VANITY DIES HARD

Kalle Kronhamn: v, Christoffer Sjöstrand: g, Robin Sjöstrand: b, Daniel Wikforss: d

Malmö - Vanity Dies Hard were formed in 1999 (although one of the members used the name already back in 1993-95), but the name and musical direction wasn't set in stone until around 2001, when the demo *Spring Never Came* was recorded. Before the album the band recorded three more demos, *Bone Cabaret* (2002), *Make Me Stay* (2003) and *Printed To Soothe* (2005). The band calls their style "unpretentious progressive metal". They have a really interesting sound and style mixing modern metal and progressive elements and even adding some growls here and there, but as a spice. Powerful, tight, melodic and unique. In 2007 the band also released the pro-printed CD-R EP *What Had To Be Done*. Wikforss is also in *Vandöd*, *Sunhole* and *Subfret*, Kronhamn in *Subfret* (as drummer), *Sunhole* and *Disaster*, Christoffer Sjöstrand in *Subfret* and *Sunhole*, while Robin is in *Origin Blood*.
Website: www.vanitydieshard.com/

Die hard!

2006 ■	WHEN TORCHING THE DAY	CDd	RAHW Productions	RAHW 003

2006 CDd - RAHW 003

VANMAKT

Mattias "Gorgoth/Morg" Svensson: v, Victor "Vladr" Dahlgren: b, Magnus Wohlfart: g

Karlskrona - Vanmakt (powerlessness) recorded the demo *Diaboli Iubeo, Para Vindicta* in 2006. On *Vredskapta mörkersagor* the line-up featured Gorgoth, Vladr alongside guitarists Kristoffer "Satygh" and Christian "Aámoth" Sonesson (*Nidrike, The Autumn Transition*) and drummer Joakim "Graál" Petersson. The album also features guest vocals from Jonas Renvaktar (*Istapp, Spawn Of Possession*). On *Ad Luciferi*, mixed by Tore Stjerna, the drums were played by session drummer Liedheim (*Nidrike*). Black metal in the vein of *Dark Funeral* and *Mayhem* with a touch of *Dissection*. The band now also featured Liedheim on drums. Former guitarist Sonesson died in a tragic work accident at Cascades Djupafors, Kallinge, on June 9, 2009.

2007 CDd - ASH 032 CD

2007 ■	VREDSKAPTA MÖRKERSAGOR	CDd	Pulverised	ASH 032 CD
2009 ■	AD LUCIFERI REGNUM	CD	Pulverised	ASH 055 CD

2009 CD - ASH 055 CD

VANTAGE

Göran Hellsén: v, Per Eriksson: g, Mats Lööf: g,
Håkan Bengtsson: k, Mats Östensson: b, Jonas Lööf: d

Borlänge - *Vantage* are a mid-class AOR band with quite a commercial touch, soft keyboards and toned down guitar. The B-side is a typical 80's ballad. Jonas later joined the remains of *Six Feet Under*, then called *Six Feet*. They were signed to EMI but split due to internal problems. Jonas was later in all-star band *King Siguurd*, also featuring Tomas Larsson (*Six Feet Under, Yeah Bop Station* etc), Hempo Hildén, Anders Bojfeldt (*United*) and Christer Cedergren.

1985	■	Smiling At You/Time To Live	7"	CUF Skivklubb	CUF 001

1985 7" - CUF 001

VARG, EMMA

Emma Varg: v

Göteborg - Emma was discovered through the Swedish TV show *Fame Factory*. *Cannonball*, written by Matti Alfonzetti and Johan Lyander, is straightforward melodic hard rock, while *Why* is more like a heavier version of Alanis Morisette. She also released the digital single *This Time* in 2006. Emma later joined metal band *Those We Don't Speak* of and is now in modern metal band *Maniquin*, featuring former members of *Lambretta*.
Website: www.emmavarg.com

2005	■	Cannonball/Why (So Easily)	CDS	Mariann Grammofon AB	MLPCDS 423

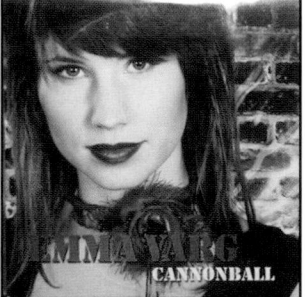
2005 CDS - MLPCDS 423

VARGAVINTER

Hughin: v/b, Gavhin: g, Munhin: d

Medelpad - *Vargavinter*, which means bitter winter or "wolf winter" in Swedish, recorded the demo *Adonai Dead* in 1993. Fast melodic death with the occasional flute. Not to be confused with the jazz group that released *Röster från alla land* (1980) or the Swedish folk/proggband from 1976-1980. A second album entitled *Minnen från fornstora dagar* was supposed to be released in 1998, but never happened. *Vargavinter* played fast old-school style black metal, quite melodic at that. The band was rumoured to be a side project of members of *Defleshed*.

1997	■	FROSTFÖDD	CD	Invasion	IR 046
1996	☐	FROSTFÖDD	LP PD	Invasion	IR 046
		500 copies.			

1997 CD - IR 046

VARGR

Henrik Nordvargr Björkk: v/g/k/b/d

Karlstad - *Vargr*, which means "wolf" in old Swedish, play very primeval, old-school, primitively recorded industrial black metal, sounding a bit like an even more primitive *Bathory* mixed with *Kraftwerk* and a steel mill. Henrik has also recorded various style industrial/ambient/electronic/drone/noise under names like *Muskel, Hydra Head 9, Vampiir Kremator, Toroidh, MZ. 412*. In *Vargr* he is showing more of his industrial, primitive old-school black metal side, like raw *Burzum* or *Bathory* with an industrial side. *Vargr* has also released a number of CD-R albums/EPs on his own 205 Recordings label.

2007	☐	NORTHERN BLACK SUPREMACY	CD	20 Buck Spin	spin:017
2007	☐	WEHRMACHT SATANAS	CD	Eternal Pride Productions	EPP 007
2008	■	STORM OF NORTHERN EVIL	CD	Total Holocaust Records	THR-110
2010	☐	Vargr/Armatus (split)	7"	Werewolf Records	EVII-023
		Split with Armatus. Track: Untitled. 300 hand numbered copies.			

2008 CD - THR-110

VASSAGO

Niclas "Pepa/Vassago" Andersson: v/g, Mikael "Sin/Bloodlord" Backelin: d

Göteborg/Trollhättan - The band was formed in 1987 by Mikael and Niclas from *Lord Belial*, but this is even heavier and more brutal than their original band. They were initially called *Sadist* and did some recordings during 1987-88, but nothing happened. The band was put on hold for some years and in 1994 they recorded the demo *Nattflykt* as *Vassago*. It's more or less Mikael's solo project and Niclas is just a session member. Anders Backelin (also *Lord Belial*) is also found on bass.

1996	☐	HAIL WAR (split)	LP	Total War productions	- -
		Split with Antichrist. 500 copies, hand numbered.. Tracks: Kill In Satan's Name/Abysmaic Downfall To The Kingdom Where I Will Rule Eternally/Stoned By Mortals/Suicide For Satan/Anal Fistfuck/Blood Of Christ			
1999	■	KNIGHTS FROM HELL	CD	No Fashion	NFR 038
2002	☐	KNIGHTS FROM HELL	CD	Mercenary Music (USA)	CD 71301

1999 CD - NFR 038

VATTEN

Tomas Ernvik: v/g/k, Sven Lindvall: b, Bengt "Bengan" Andersson: d

Göteborg - This band's releases are quite varied, the first one being the heaviest and best. At times it's quite reminiscent of early 70s **Mahogany Rush** with some biting guitar work. The other records tend to be softer and more bluesy. They actually recorded another album before *Tungt Vatten*, but under the name **Rockoratoriet Brinnande** and in a totally different musical direction. On *Tungt Vatten* the bass is handled by Thomas Lidbjer and the drums by Anders Kjellberg. They were replaced by Björn Millton and Dan Gansmoe (**Jerusalem**) respectively. However the first 7" was recorded with Anders Mossberg on bass and the versions are different from the versions on the second album. *Vattendrag* was recorded with Tomas, Sven and drummer Matte Marklund. Sven Lindvall has also recorded with **Nord** and is more or less a session player. Tomas and Matte also released a single with the band **Emma's Boogie Band**. All the albums are quite scarce, but the debut is a really expensive gem. The band later featured a fourth member, more or less official, Mats Eriksson on keyboards. A later incarnation of the band featured Ernvik, bassist/singer Alf Rikner and drummer Peter Widehammar. **Vatten** that released the single *Kaffepannan* on CBS is not the same band. The song *The Dreamer* was featured on the compilation *Greenbelt Live*. **Vatten** means water.

1975 LPg - PROP 7756

1980 LP - GUTS-003

1992 7" - GUTS-1009

1975 ■	TUNGT VATTEN	LPg	Prophone	PROP 7756	$$
1979 ☐	The Dreamer/Rely Back	7"	Gutta	GUTS-001	
	Not the same versions as on the album.				
1980 ■	PLAIN WATER	LP	Gutta	GUTS-003	
1981 ☐	SMÄLTVATTEN	LP	Gutta	GUTS-004	
1984 ☐	VATTENDRAG	LP	Gutta	GUTS-007	
1992 ☐	DIGGIN' THE ROOTS	LP	Gutta	GUTS-008	
1992 ☐	DIGGIN' THE ROOTS	CD	Gutta	GUTS-008	
1992 ■	You´ll Never Know/Ernvik Boogie	7"	Gutta (promo)	GUTS-1009	

VELVET CRASH

Henrik Olsson: v/g, Magnus Johansson: g, Mikael Svantesson: b, Patrick Fransson: d

Partille - The band was formed in 1996 under the name **Gooseberry**, but changed their name to **Velvet Crash** the year after. The record was produced by CT Rohdell of **M.ill.ion**. Great, powerful and heavy, yet melodic hard rock with a 90s indie touch, in the vein of **Human Rage**. Fat and riffy guitars, good vocals and driving songs.

1999 CD - VC-DC 111

| 1999 ■ | SLIP INTO CHAOS | CD | private | VC-DC 111 |

VEMOTH

Olof "Behemiron" Luhr: v, Ola "Draugald" Högblom: g,
Markus "Adimirion" Kvarnlöf: b, Kalle "Toxal" Jansson: d

Lindesberg - Formed in the end of 2004. **Vemoth** (or vemod) means melancholy in Swedish. The band entered Studio Seven with Ronny Milianovicz and Thomas Ohlsson in January 2005 to record the demo *Blodregn*. Nothing happened so they returned to record the debut album *Köttkroksvals* again with Ronny and Thomas. Black metal similar to **Watain**, **Marduk** and **Dissection**. Toxal and Draugald are ex-**Maramon**.

2009 CD - DR 190810

2006 ☐	KÖTTKROKSVALS	CD	Temple Of Darkness	TOD 006
2006 ☐	KÖTTKROKSVALS	LP PD	Temple Of Darkness	TOD 006
	500 copies.			
2009 ■	THE UPCOMING END	CD	Dental Records	DR 190810

VENI DOMINE

Fredrik Ohlsson (now Sjöholm): v/g, Torbjörn Weinesjö: g, Thomas Weinesjö: d

Stockholm - A highly interesting Christian band. **Veni Domine** was formed in 1987, as **Seventh Seal**, by the Weinesjö brothers and Anders Olofsson. Fredrik joined later the same year. The band recorded three demos, *Glorify* (1987), *Seventh Seal* (1988) and *Seventh Seal* (1989, different demo) before the debut, where bass player Magnus Thorman had joined. **Veni Domine** produces well played progressive metal with a strong touch of **Queensrÿche**. High-pitched vocals, long multi-tempo songs and interesting arrangements. The debut unfortunately suffered from lack of support. Keyboards on the debut were played by Per Anders Danielsson, who sadly passed away in 2005. The follow-up saw Mats Lidbrandt handling the keyboards. The first three albums were produced by the Wahlquist bros (**Heavy Load**). Singer Fredrik also recorded an album with the band **Zoic**, lead by **Candlemass** guitarist Lasse Johansson. On *Spiritual Wasteland* ex-**Bishop Garden** man Mathias Wilhelmsson was added to the line-up and Gabriel replaced bass player Magnus Thorman. The keyboards on this release were handled by Mattias Cederlund. Things went all quiet for several years, until the album *IIII – The Album Of Labour*, suddenly

Rocking until Babylon falls!

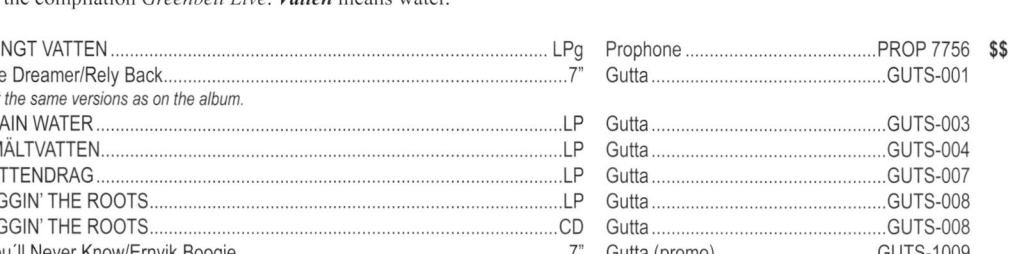

appeared. The reason was, among other things, that Fredrik went through some problems with his throat. It also took two and a half years for the album to be released after completion. Keyboardist Lidbrandt was used again. The album was a bit darker than the previous releases. Both Weinesjö brothers have played in *Audiovision* and *Hero*, while Thomas has also been in *Saviour Machine* and Torbjörn in *DivineFire*. *Tongues* saw the band stripped down to a trio, with guest appearances by bassists Peter Carlsohn, Andreas Olsson (*Narnia*), Gary Kuhstoss and Sven "Ez" Gomér (*Jet Circus*). The style had changed even more on this album, showing an even broader musical spectrum, doomy, yet still progressive, but not as metal as before and quite dark with quite a lot of quirky things happening in the arrangements. A really interesting album. In 2011 Olov Andersson (*Audiovision, Golden Resurrection, Grand Trick*) was added on keyboards. In 2012 the band started recording a new album to be released in 2013.
Website: www.venidomine.com

1992 CD - ECD 7028

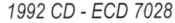

1998 CD - MASCD0133

1992	■	FALL BABYLON FALL	CD	Edge (UK)	ECD 7028
1994	□	MATERIAL SANCTUARY	CD	Thunderload	TLCD 9401
1994	□	MATERIAL SANCTUARY	CD	Alliance Music	ALD 047
1995	□	MATERIAL SANCTUARY	CD	Massacre	MASS 074
1997	□	MATERIAL SANCUARY	CD	Thunderload	TLCD9701
1997	□	FALL BABYLON FALL	CD	Thunderload	TLCD9702
1997	□	FALL BABYLON FALL	CD	Massacre	MASCD0127
		Bonus: Visions.			
1998	■	SPIRITUAL WASTELAND	CD	Massacre	MASCD0133
1998	□	SPIRITUAL WASTELAND	CD	Thunderload	TLCD9803
2004	■	IIII – THE ALBUM OF LABOUR	CD	Rivel Records	RRCD 017
2006	□	23:59	CD	MCM	MCM-2005-29
2007	□	TONGUES	CD	MCM	MCM 2007-35

2004 CD - RRCD 017

VERGELMER

Tobbe "Ebboth" Leffler: v/b, Mathias "Nazgul" Kamijo: g,
Yngve Liljebäck: g, Martin "Grimulv" Gärdeman: d

Åtvidaberg - Formed in 1993 out of the remains of *Abemal*. Recorded two demos, *In Darkness Forever* (1993) and *In The Dead Of Winter* (1994), and started spreading the word. Drummer Maunghrim left in 1994 and bass player Grimulv switched his bass for the drums, guitarist Yngve quit but later rejoined and singer Ebboth took over the bass. In 1995 the band recorded the demo *The Third Winter*. Mathias is also found in *Algaion*, with whom Tobbe is a session guitarist. Evil black metal. The band has also recorded a MCD, as yet unreleased, entitled Origo Malitiae. Leffler is also found in *When Nothing Remains, Algaion* and *Nephenzy Chaos Order*, Kamijo in *Morifade, Algaion, The Abyss* and *Nephenzy Chaos Order*, while Liljebäck and Gärdeman are ex-*Abemal*. Old-school, lo-fi black metal with screeching vocals, a bit similar to early *Dissection*.

1997	■	LIGHT THE BLACK FLAME	CD	Cacaphonous	NIHIL20CD

1997 CD - NIHIL20CD

VERITATE

Niklas Olausson: v, Ritchie "LaRoux" Riekwel: g, Christofer Norrman: g,
Annika Argerich: k, Björn Ahlström: b, Conny Johansson: d

Lund - *Veritate* were formed in 2003 by former *Cult Disciples* members Ritchie and Annika. The band also recorded two demos, *Exploitation Of Human Disturbance* (2004) and *Medical Miracles* (2006) before the first album. *The Rise Of Hatröss* is an official release of the band's two demos. *Veritate* play theatrical and quite dramatic doom metal with a hint of operatic vocals, a bit like mixing *Candlemass, Mercyful Fate* and *Manowar*, unfortunately not even close in quality though. The band initially featured singer Johan "C.L.A.W" Knuutinen, but he was replaced by Olausson before *The Chosen One*. This release shows a big improvement.
Website: www.veritate.se/

2008 CD - VER 001

2011 CDS - KMR-MCD001

2008	■	STRAIGHT INTO HELL	CD	private	VER 001
2009	□	THE RISE OF HATRÖSS	LP	Killer Metal Records	KMRLP 007
		100 grey + 400 black vinyl.			
2011	■	The Chosen One/Den utvalde	CDS	Killer Metal Records	KMR-MCD001
		1000 copies.			

VERMIN

Jimmy Sjöqvist: v/g, "Handy" David Melin: g/v,
Timmy Persson: b, Mathias Adamsson: d

Nässjö - *Vermin* were formed in 1991 and recorded their first demo a year after. The initial line-up consisted of Jimmy and Mathias accompanied by guitarist Moses Shtieh and bassist Johan Svensson. The second demo, released the same year, was entitled *Life Is Pain* and resulted in the band being offered to participate on compilations such as *Extreme Close Up*. The next

1994 CD - CHAOSCD 01

demo, *Scum Of The Earth* lead to a deal with Chaos Records. The first album is a compilation of the first three demos. After the first album David Melin replaced Johan on bass and in 1997 he took over the guitar as Moses quit and Timmy joined on bass. The band started out playing traditional death metal, but gradually evolved in to heavy and brutal death rock/metal in the vein of **Entombed**. The second and third releases were produced by Tomas Skogsberg. Persson and Sjöqvist are also found in **El Camino** and **Karneywar**, while Melin has been found in **The Obscene**.

1994 ■	OBEDIENCE TO INSANITY	CD	Chaos	CHAOSCD 01
1995 ☐	PLUNGE INTO OBLIVEON	CD	Chaos	CHAOSCD 03
1998 ☐	MILLENIUM RIDE	CD	No Fashion	NFR 030
1998 ☐	MILLENIUM RIDE	CD	Metal Blade	3984-14293-2
2000 ☐	FILTHY F***ING VERMIN	CD	No Fashion	NFR 046
2013 ■	PLUNGE INTO OBLIVEON	CD	Punishment 18 Records	P18R 055
2013 ☐	IN DARKNESS DWELLS	LP	To The Death	TTD 026

2013 CD - P18R 055

VERMINOUS
Linus "Germaniac" Björklund: v/g, Pelle "Piss" Melander: g,
Simon Frödeberg: b, Andreas "Agge Bones" Johansson: d
Kristianstad/Åhus - *Verminious* rose out of the ashes of the band **Delve**, who recorded a demo in 2001 and an EP in 2002, before changing their name in 2002, initially featuring Germaniac, Pelle Piss and Agge Bones. They were picked up by Nuclear War Records who released the debut EP. In August 2011 the band booked the studio to record their second album, *The Unholy Communion*, still waiting to be unleashed. Johansson has also recorded with **Evildoer**, Melander with **Sgt. Carnage** and Frödeberg with **Evildoer**, **Sgt. Carnage**, **Infernal Hellfire** and **Logic Severed**. **Verminious** play old-school death metal in the vein of **Repugnant** and **Kaamos**.
Website: www.verminous.com

2003 CD - XM 008 CD

2003 ☐	Smell The Birth Of Death	7" 5tr	Nuclear War Now	NWR 006
	Tracks: Intro/Verminious Fluids/Salvation By Extermination/Resuscitation Of The Dead/ Chaos In The Flesh. 518 copies.			
2003 ■	IMPIOUS SACRILEGE	CD	Xtreem Music	XM 008 CD
2009 ☐	Smell The Birth Of Death	MCD 4tr	Nuclear War Now	NWR 006
	Tracks: Intro-Verminious Fluids/Salvation By Extermination/Resuscitation Of The Dead/ Chaos In The Flesh. 500 copies.			

VETERNUS
David "Dave Grave" Indelöf: v/g, Anonymous: b, Patrik "Possessor": d
Uppsala - Formed in 2009 and recorded the first demo, *Perpetual Insanity*, the same year. Old-school lo-fi black metal recorded in the Nacka Fritidsgård Studio, which it also sounds like.

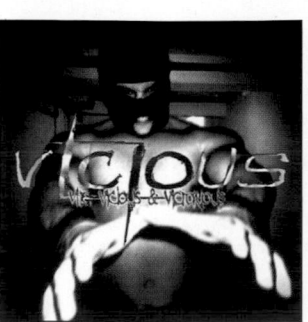
2010 7" - DR013/MSUO-09

2010 ■	Awaken The Grave/Morbid Destruction	7"	Detest/Me Saco Un Ojo	DR013/MSUO-09
	100 red and 400 black vinyl.			

VIA TOKYO
Mats Johansson: v, Peter Danielsson: v/g, Staffan Grenklo: k,
Anders Laursen: b, Eric Forsmark: d
Stockholm - AOR with poppy overtones, but hints of **Saga**. Like a more rough-edged version of Swedish symph/pop-band **Factory**. The B-side is actually quite good. This band came second in the Rock SM competition that gave **Europe** their breaktrough in Sweden. The first price was an LP recording and the second was the recording of a 7", both on Hot Records. Danielsson was also in **Prins Valiant, Zeppelin** cover band **Moby Dick** (also featuring Björn Lodin), **Aurora** and is now found in cover band **Lime House**. Grenklo was also in **Aurora** and **Spray**. The band changed their name to **Go/No Go** and was also in Rock-SM.

1982 7" - HOTS 8201

1982 ■	Man I Uniform/Zansibar	7"	Hot Records	HOTS 8201

VICIOUS
Daniel Wahlström: v, Simon Jarrolf: g, Pontus Pettersson: g,
Håkan Stuvemark: b, Fredrik Eriksson: d
Västerås - The band was formed in 1999 as **Rage Anthem**, changed it to **Wargasm** in 2001 and the year after they became **Vicious**. The first demo, *Pure Evil (Straight From Hell)* was unearthed in 2001, followed by *Chains Won't Hold It Back* in 2002. The debut album features singer Henrik Wenngren (**Autumn Dweller, Skyfire, Zavorash, Mornaland, Favilla**). High-quality melodic death metal in the vein of **Dimenzion Zero** and **The Haunted**. The second album, *Emotionally Disqualified* followed in the same vein. Eriksson is also in **Vilefuck**. The band has also recorded a third album, *Burn With Grace*, produced by Jonas Kjellgren, which has yet to be released. Judging from the samples on MySpace, it's the band's best effort. Killer

2004 CD - SRP 027

melodic alternative thrashy death-oriented metal, mixing clean and harsh vocals. In 2010 the band, now featuring Wahlström, Pettersson, Jarrolf and drummer Pablo Munoz, changed their name to **Grand Exit** and released the digital album *Burn With Grace*. The bass duties are now handled by Magnus Wall (**Thronaeon, Soulbreach, Abhoth** etc). In 2012 they recorded the new, as yet unreleased, album *The Dead Justifies The Means*.

| 2004 ■ | VILE, VICIOUS AND VICTORIOUS | CD | Sound Riot | SRP 027 |
| 2008 ■ | EMOTIONALLY DISQUALIFIED | CD | Scarlet Records | SC 159-2 |

2008 CD - SC 159-2

VICIOUS ART
Jocke Widfeldt: v, Tobbe Silman: g, Matti Mäkelä: g,
Jörgen Sandström: b/v, Robert Lundin: d

Stockholm - *Vicious Art* were formed in 2002 by Mäkelä and Lundin, both ex-**Dark Funeral**, who were joined by Widfeldt (**Dominion Caligula, Obscurity**), who also handled the bass initially and Sillman (**Guidance Of Sin, The Dead**). The foursome recorded a demo in 2003. Early 2004 Sandström (**Entombed, Grave, Krux, Torture Division** etc.) joined forces and Widfeldt could concentrate on vocals. They were soon signed by Threeman Records. The band recorded an EP on their own, but it was soon picked up by Mighty Music and released on their sub label Prutten Records. In the summer of 2007 the second album was recorded, but in 2009 they decided to put the band on hold due to personal issues and lack of motivation. However in 2011 they picked up the pieces and recorded three new tracks, just to split again in November the same year. *Vicious Art* play solid, riff-oriented and aggressive old-school-style death metal with a thrashy touch, a bit like **Dismember** meets **Morbid Angel**. High-quality stuff!

2008 CD - PMZ 37

2004 □	FIRE FALLS AND THE WAITING WATERS	CD	Threeman Records	TRECD 017
2005 □	Weed The Wild/Tanja Joins The Beating/Exit Wounds	7" 3tr	Prutten Records	PRUT 013
	200 copies.			
2008 ■	PICK UP THIS SICK CHILD	CD	Mighty Music	PMZ 37

VICTIM
Karl-Johan Karlsson: v/g, Ulf Sandberg: g, Hans Sandberg: b, Jonas Nilsson: d

Vimmerby - Quite amateurish Christian hard rock/metal in the vein of **Lezlie Paice** or **Turbo**. Horrible vocals, while the riffs are promising.

| 1982 ■ | Det Var Då Han Vann/Framtid Med Hopp | 7" | Pang | PSI 054 |
| | *The single was issued both with and without picture sleeve.* | | | |

1982 7" - PSI 054

VICTORY
Erik Rosenberg: v/g, Henrik Selin: g, Göran Åhlfeldt: k,
Mikael Carlsson: b, Kenneth Gradin: d

Laxå - Formed in 1981. The first single is pretty decent traditional melodic hard rock with Swedish vocals and a Christian message. Like a more hard rock-oriented **Magnum Bonum**. On the album the band had become much more pop-oriented. The second single is really good melodic hard rock, but with quite poppy choruses. Later on they changed their name to **Reel X**, became even more pop-oriented and changed some members. In 1991 the band split.

1983 ■	Ska hon aldrig ge upp?/Vänd om	7"	Stanley & Andrew Music	SAM 5200004
1985 □	VICTORY	LP	Twilight Records	TRLP 852
1986 □	Älskar älskar älskar dig/För mig bort i Eden	7"	Twilight Records	TRS 864

1983 7" - SAM 5200004

VICTORY
Simon Asikainen: v/k, Thomas Forslund: g, Peter Ulving: b, Sverker Hemring: d

Stockholm - Great melodic metal with nice guitar work and good solid vocals. In 1989 Asikainen recorded a single with the band **Knockout** and later sang in Danish band **Naked Rain**.

| 1986 ■ | Don't Go Away/Hot Ice | 7" | Kristall Salongen AB | KR 0100 |

1986 7" - KR 0100

VIDUNDER
Martin Prim: g/v, Linus Larsson: b, Jens Rasmussen: d

Växjö - *Vindunder* were formed in 2011. Seventies-style hard rock quite sparse on the guitar distortion. Similar to **After Life** and **Norrsken**. Decent, but quite simple and harmless. Ok, but a bit limited vocals. Before the album drummer Jonas Sjöqvist was replaced by Jens.

| 2011 ■ | Asmodeus/Witches Shuffle | 7" | Crusher Records | CR 015 |
| 2013 □ | VIDUNDER | CD | Crusher Records | CRCD 021 |

2011 7" - CR 015

VII GATES

Christer Elmgren: v, Robert Makek: g, Jonas "JJ Rockford" Arvidsson: g, Nicola Posa: b, Ingemar Erlandsson: d

Halmstad - Formed in 1999 and released the fourteen-track CD-R album *The Madman Inside* in 2002, at the time featuring Arvidsson, Erlandsson, Elmgren, Makek, keyboardist Mats Andreasson and bassist Magnus Jacobsson. The debut album, *Fire Walk With Me*, features guest solos from Kee Marcello, Chris Amott, Janne Stark, Tommy Denander plus guest vocals from Apollo Papathanasio (*Time Requiem, Spiritual Beggars, Firewind* etc). *In Hoc Signo Vinces* features guest spots from Rick Altzi (*Thunderstone, Sanity*). Guitarist Jonas "JJ Rockford" Arvidsson was fired after the release of the last album. He now plays with the band *The Rockford Heroes*. He was replaced by Robin Pålsson. *VII Gates* play classic melodic power metal/heavy metal with high-pitched vocals.

2003 CD - SRP 025

2008 CD - LMC 249

2003 ■	FIRE WALK WITH ME	CD	Sound Riot	SRP 025
2003 ☐	FIRE WALK WITH ME	CD	CD-Maximum (Russia)	CDM 0704-1887
2008 ■	IN HOC SIGNO VINCES	CD	Lion Music	LMC 249

VIKSTRÖM, THOMAS

Thomas Vikström: v

Stockholm - Thomas started his career in the glam band *Octagon* under the name Tommy Senseless. He then worked at the Swedish Folkopera for two seasons having the leading role in two operas *Barefoot Life* and *The Adventures of Hoffman* (Thomas' father is the very famous opera singer Sven-Erik Vikström) and the musical *Miss Saigon*. In 1987 the band *Scandinavian Dynamite* was formed and when Thomas joined in 1988 they changed their name to *Talk Of The Town*. They had a massive hit with the single *Free Like An Eagle*. He then toured with *Talisman*... as keyboard player... and did the vocals on some of their demos. *Talk Of The Town* reformed, but split in 1992 when he joined the heavy rockers *Candlemass*, with whom he recorded *Chapter VI*. When *Candlemass* decided to take a break Thomas was offered to do a solo album and this album shows yet another side of him. *If I Could Fly* contains very laid back and poppy AOR but he's backed up by guests like Jeff Scott Soto, Pontus Norgren (*Great King Ratt, The Poodles, HammerFall*), Johan Kullberg (*Talk Of The Town, Lion's Share*), Marcel Jacob etc. The album didn't do too well and he was dropped from Virgin in 1994. Thomas was also working a lot with his successful *Queen* cover band named *Silvia* (The queen of Sweden) and was also in the successful cover band *Horny Strings* together with Marcel Jacob, Jake Samuel and Tommy Denander (*ATC, Radioactive*, solo, etc.). In late 1994/beginning of 1995 Thomas was part of Nikolo Kotzevs project *Brazen Abbot* together with Glenn Hughes, Göran Edman, Mic Michaeli, Ian Haugland and Svante Henrysson. A great platter in the early-*Purple* vein with a bluesy touch. He has also made some impressive demos with prog metal band *Afterglow*, which later became *Mind's Eye*. Thomas has later recorded albums with bands like *Stormwind, Covered Call, 7Days, Silent Memorial, Dark Illusion, Therion*, etc.

Young man, no blues

1993 CD - 8921202

1993 ☐	Images Dancing/I Wanna Be With You	CDSp 2tr	Virgin	IMCD 1
1993 ■	IF I COULD FLY	CD	Virgin	8921202
1994 ☐	If I Could Fly/Love Touch	CDSp 2tr	Virgin	IFCD 2

VILDHJARTA

Daniel Ädel: v, Robert Luciani: v, Daniel Bergström: g, Calle Thomér: g, Jimmie Åkerström: g, Johan Nyberg: b, David Lindkvist: d

Hudiksvall - The name (actually vildhjärta) means "wild heart" and was taken from the Swedish version of the game *Dungeons And Dragons*. Formed in 2005 by Bergström, Åkerström and Nyberg. Very mixed, energetic, experimental and musically advanced modern metal. A bit like *CB Murdoc*-meet-*Meshuggah*-meet a grinder. Mixing screamo, growl, clean vocals, you name it. Oustanding stuff! The band recorded the EP *Omnislash* in 2009. They also recorded some demo tracks which were spread on the web and caught the interest of Century Media. Great musicians, interesting music. The band calls their musical style "Djent". Singer Luciani was replaced by Vilhelm Bladin in 2011. In August 2012 Åkerström was sacked.

2011 CDd - 18844-2

2011 ■	MÅSSTANDEN	CDd	Century Media	18844-2

VILEFUCK

Allex: v, Tom: g, Henke: b, Fredrik "Fredde" Eriksson: d

Västerås - Vilefuck were formed in 2004 and recorded their first demo *Livet är värdelöst* in 2005, followed by *Scumfucks* (2005), *The Beast Within* (2006), *Thrashing Fucking Metal* (2007) and *Intoxicated By Madness* (2008). Quite good, fast and furious thrash metal a bit similar to *Kreator* meets *F.K.Ü.*. Fredde is also in *Vicious*. The track *Fuck The System* is featured on the compilation *Obscene Extreme 2010* (2010 Obscene Productions, OBP 091).

2009 ■	WHAT LIES AHEAD IS ALREADY DEAD	CD	F.D.A Rekotz	FDA 20

2009 CD - FDA 20

VILDSVIN

Fredrik Thomander: v/b, Roger Öjersson: g, Peter Månsson: d

Varberg/Stockholm - It's not easy to describe this band. The name means wild boar. Their style varies from powerful almost hardcore riffs with rap vocals to almost ridiculously simple poppy choruses. They sing in Swedish and the lyrics are very sarcastic and funny. Fredrik was previously with the band **Grand Slam** together with Zinny Zan and Fredrik's brother Martin (**Electric Boys**). On the second album the vocals were changed from rap to melodic vocals. The band had also left the heavier side for more Brit-pop influences. Fredrik Thomander is now working together with Anders Wikström (**Treat**, ex-**Mental Hippie Blood**) as the songwriting duo **Epicentre**. They have written songs for artists such as **N'Sync, A-Teens, Backyard Babies** and Jessica Folker. One of the most misplaced live situations I have witnessed was when **Vildsvin** supported **Status Quo** on a Sweden tour..., a strange combination. Öjersson surprisingly turned up as bass player in heavy riff rockers **Kamchatka**.

1994 CDS - TATI 119

1995 CDS - TATI 122

Year		Title	Format	Label	Cat. No.
1994	■	Cykla Till Månen/Öga För Öga	CDS 2tr	The Record Station	TATI 119
1995	□	Fel Stajl/(disco version)/(DJ remix)	MCDp 3tr	The Record Station	TATI 120
1995	□	GRISFESTEN	CD	The Record Station	STAT 49
1995	■	Borta/Herr Viklund	CDS 2tr	The Record Station	TATI 122
1995	□	Schnügg/Du Suger Stort	CDS 2tr	The Record Station	TATI 128
1995	□	Kycklingnudlar Blues/Blind	CDS 2tr	The Record Station	TATI 133
1996	■	TILL EDER TJÄNST	CD	The Record Station	STAT 53
1996	□	Saga Utan Lyckligt Slut/Somna Om	CDS 2tr	The Record Station	TATI 136
1996	□	Den Riktiga Världen	MCD 3tr	Record Station	TATI 140
		Tracks: Den Riktiga Världen/Cykla Till Månen/Fröken Theresa På Charterresa			
1997	□	Vi Ses Igen/Med Stil	CDS 2tr	Record Station	TATI 149
1997	□	ISKALLT BEGÄR	CD	Record Station	STAT 57

1996 CD - STAT 53

VINDICTIV

Göran Edman: v, Stefan Lindholm: g, Pontus Larsson: k,
Björn "Nalle" Påhlsson: b, Zoltan Csörsz: d

Stockholm - **Vindictiv** is the brainchild of excellent guitarist Stefan Lindholm initiated in 2004. He drafted keyboardist Larsson and started working on songs. They found **Seventh Wonder** singer Tommy Karevik and recorded the first demo. *The Beginning* (2004). Tommy however left and by pure luck Stefan hooked up with renowned singer Edman (**Malmsteen, Norum, Madison, Kharma, Glory** etc). Stefan also drafted bassist Nalle Påhlsson (**Zan Clan, Treat, Therion**) to lay down the bass lines and finally he got hold of drummer Mikael Wikman (**Thåström, Alien, Dr Alban** etc). In 2010 Stefan also realeased an album with the band **Firecracker**, also featuring Pontus Larsson and former **Vindictiv** vocalist Tommy Karevik. On the second album the drums were handled by Zoltan Csörsz (**The Flower Kings, Art Metal**). Stefan also plans to release a solo album under the name **Stefan Lindholm's Supernova**. **Vindictiv** play outstanding progressive melodic metal with quite catchy hooks, a bit like the missing link between **Dream Theater** and **Royal Hunt**, at times a bit similar to **Saint Deamon**. A great band!

If I only had one more finger...

2008 CD - ESM 164

Year		Title	Format	Label	Cat. No.
2007	□	VINDICTIV	CD	Soundholic (Japan)	TKCS-85185
		Bonus: David's House			
2008	■	VINDICTIV	CD	Escape Music	ESM 164
2009	□	GROUND ZERO	CD	Bickee Music (Japan)	HMCX-1030
		Bonus: The Sacrifice			
2009	■	GROUND ZERO	CD	Escape Music	ESM 190
2013	□	CAGE OF INFINITY	CD	Escape Music	ESM 252

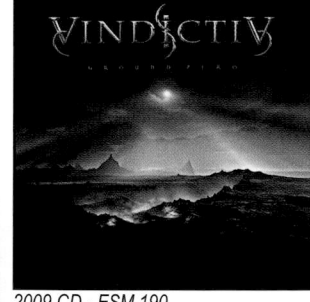

2009 CD - ESM 190

VINTERLAND

Daniel Forn Bragman: v/g/b, Pehr Larsson: g, Andreas Jonsson: d

Strängnäs - Formed in 1992 under the name **Grimoires**. Pehr was also in the band **Maze Of Torment** for a period. Black metal in the vein of **Dark Funeral** and **Dissection**. Produced by Dan Swanö, who also played keyboards on the album. When reading the poems in the booklet one might suspect the boys were more into studying occultism than English - "Now have the twilight already falled". Yep! The album title was *Wings Of Sorrow*, but since it says *Welcome To My Last Chapter* on the front cover, they re-printed the CD and changed the title. The 2007 release is a fifteenth anniversary deluxe box. Bragman is also found in **The Black, Tyrant** and **Porphyria**, Larsson is also in **Harmony** and **Torment**, while Jonsson has been in **The Black, NunFuckRitual, Tyrant** and **Porphyria**.

1996 CD - NFR 017

Year		Title	Label	Cat. No.
1996	■	WINGS OF SORROW (WELCOME TO MY LAST CHAPTER)	No Fashion	NFR 017
		First pressing had Wings Of Sorrow on the tray card.		
1996	□	WINGS OF SORROW (WELCOME TO MY LAST CHAPTER)	No Fashion	NFR 017
2007	■	WELCOME TO MY LAST CHAPTER	Temple Of Darkness	TOD 020
		Bonus: Freezing Moon (Mayhem cover). Deluxe clamshell box with poster, sticker, certificate and new artwork. 2000 copies.		

2007 CD box - TOD 020

VINTERSORG

Andreas "Vintersorg" Hedlund: v, Mattias Marklund: g

Skellefteå - Formed in 1994 under the name *Vargatron* (Wolves throne), but as things didn't evolve as planned Andreas split the band in the summer of 1996 and resurrected it as his solo project under the name *Vintersorg*, meaning "winter sorrow" In 2001 he also became lead singer of Norwegian deathsters *Borknagar*. Session keyboardist Mikael Israelsson was also found in progressive hard rockers *Kharma Cosmic*, later *Black Bonzo*. Other guest-musicians found on the albums are keyboardists Marcus "Vargher" Norman (drum programming) and Nils Johansson, singer Cia Hedmark and guitarist Andreas Frank. All the album layouts have been done by Jens Rydén. On *Cosmic Genesis* Mattias Marklund (*Casket Casey, TME*) joined the band as a full time member. The next album was entitled *Visions From The Spiral Generator* and featured Asgeir Mickelsson (*Spiral Architect, Borknagar*) on drums. *Fragments & Alternatives* contains remixes, alternative takes and three new songs. *Solens rötter* also featured Johan Lindgren on bass and Nils Johansson on keyboards. Andreas also works as a math teacher and can be found in bands like *Fission, Havayoth, Cosmic Death, Waterclime* and *Cronian*. Both Andreas and Mattias were also part of the band *Otyg*, in a similar genre.

The sons of the desert

1998 MCD - NPR 049

1998 ■	Hedniskhjärtad	MCD 5tr	Napalm Records	NPR 049
	Tracks: Norrland/Stilla/Norrskensdrömmar/Hednaorden/Tussmörkret			
1998 □	TILL FJÄLLS	CDd	Napalm Records	NPR 056
1998 □	TILL FJÄLLS	CD	Napalm Records	NPR 056
1999 □	ÖDEMARKENS SON	CD	Napalm Records	NPR 072
2001 □	COSMIC GENESIS	CD	Napalm Records	NPR 085
	First 5000 were a special edition with slipcase.			
2001 □	COSMIC GENESIS	CD	Irond (Russia)	CD 01-42
2002 ■	VISIONS FROM THE SPIRAL GENERATOR	CD	Napalm Records	NPR 107
2002 □	VISIONS FROM THE SPIRAL GENERATOR	CD	Irond (Russia)	CD 02-291
2002 □	FRAGMENTS & ALTERNATIVES	CD	Napalm Records	n/a
2002 □	ÖDEMARKENS SON	CD	Irond (Russia)	CD 02-291
2003 □	TILL FJÄLLS & HEDNISKHJÄRTAD	CD	Irond (Russia)	CD 03-477
2004 □	THE FOCUSING BLUR	CD	Napalm Records	NPR 137
2004 □	THE FOCUSING BLUR	CD	Irond (Russia)	CD 04-776
2004 □	THE FOCUSING BLUR	CD	Icarus Music (Argentina)	ICARUS 060
2005 □	TILL FJÄLLS	CD	Icarus (Argentina)	ICARUS 152
2005 □	ÖDEMARKENS SON	CD	Icarus (Argentina)	ICARUS 154
2005 □	COSMIC GENESIS	CD	Icarus (Argentina)	ICARUS 155
2005 □	VISIONS FROM THE SPIRAL GENERATOR	CD	Icarus Music (Argentina)	ICARUS 156
2006 □	COSMIC GENESIS + VISIONS FROM THE SPIRAL GENERATOR	CDd	Scarcrow (Mexico)	SC 06002
2007 □	SOLENS RÖTTER	CD	Napalm Records	NPR 211
2007 □	SOLENS RÖTTER	CD	Irond (Russia)	CD 07-1306
2007 □	SOLENS RÖTTER	CDd	Scarecrow Records (Mexico)	SC07333
2008 □	Hedniskhjärtad	MCD 5tr	Mazzar Records (Russia)	MYST CD 386
2011 □	JORDPULS	CD	Napalm Records	NPR 367
2011 □	JORDPULS	CD	Icarus Music (Argentina)	ICARUS 721
2012 ■	ORKAN	CD	Napalm Records	NPR 429

2012 CD - NPR 429

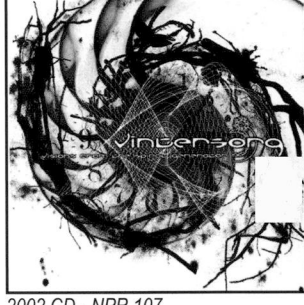

VIOLENT DIVINE

Michael "Mike Divine" Ahlström: v, Mikael "Q" Qvist: g,
Klaus Gauffin: b, Gustaf "Gus" Liljenström: d

Norrköping - *Violent Divine* were formed in late 2005. *In Harm's Way* was produced by Pontus Norgren (*HammerFall, The Poodles* etc). In 2012 the band made some drastic changes in the line up with Mike being the only remaining member, now flanked by guitarist S.J, bassist Oscar and drummer Magnus. *Violent Divine* started out as a sleaze/glam oriented metal band, but it gradually changed to quite classic melodic metal, similar to later days Ozzy Osbourne mixed with modern *Mötley Crüe* and with a touch of *Hardcore Superstar*. Good band. Ahlström was formerly in *Avenue, Marshal Kane* and *Blueplastic*, Qvist in *Avenue, Marshal Kane, Sleazy* and *Starsky*, Gauffin in *Abandoned Sphinx, Millhouse* and *Starsky* and Liljenström in *Millhouse, Battle Station, Marshal Kane* and *Big Hoss & The Animal*. A new album is in the making.

2010 CD - SM-024-CD

2006 CD - CR 0010

2006 ■	VIOLENT DIVINE	CD	Chavis Records	CR 0010
2009 □	IN HARM'S WAY	CD	Misty Recordings	MISTYVD1
2010 ■	RELEASE THE HOUNDS	CD	Swedmetal	SM-024-CD

VIOLENT WORK OF ART

Tobias Eng: v, Anders Gyllensten: g, Wincent Persson: g,
Victor "Otto V. Mad" Eng: b, Magnus "MP" Pettersson: d, Tobias Turesson: sampling

Växjö - The band was previously known as *Trashhole* and recorded a more speed metal-oriented album for Blackbird Records, which was never released. *Violent Work Of Art* play hardcore/power metal in the vein of *Biohazard* and *Pantera*, but at times with an industrial touch. Great quality stuff. Anders was previously in *Corrosive*. Wincent is now in *Killbilly 5'ers*.

2005 CD - SM-05-CD

1995 ☐	Violent Work Of Art	MCD 5tr	private	VWOA 001

Tracks: Unemotional/Melt/Failure/Worm/Strange Play

1996 ☐	BREEDINGDANCE	CD	Download Records	DLR 001
2005 ■	THE WORST IS YET TO COME	CD	Swedmetal	SM-05-CD
2006 ☐	Violent Work Of Art	MCD 5tr	Swedmetal	VWOA 001
2006 ☐	Hard	MCD 5tr	Swedmetal	VWOA 002

Tracks: Another Dream/Poisoned/Grindstone/Written In Blood/Within

2007 ■	[AUTOMATED SPECIES]	CD	Swedmetal	SM-12-CD

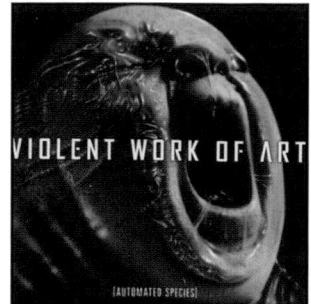
2007 CD - SM-12-CD

VIPERINE

Hussni Mörsare: v/g, Payre Kankanranta: g, Erik Tornberg: b, Mark Buffalo: d

Kalix - In the spring of 2002 *Winterlong* members Mörsare, Tornberg (ex-*Star Queen*) and drummer Tony Erkkilä were suddenly bandless. They teamed up with guitarist Kankanranta (ex-*Karyan, Bourbon Boys*) and formed *Viperine*. A first three-track demo was recorded in 2002. After this they ran into some drummer problems and Mark Buffalo replaced Tony in December 2003. After the album Kankanranta left and after this the band split. *Viperine* play classic high-speed, German-sounding power metal similar to *Primal Fear* meets UKs *Dragonforce*. Kankanranta (now named Pär Hulkoff) and Mörsare were later in *Raubtier*.

2004 ■	THE PREDATOR AWAKENS	CD	Metal Rules	- -

2004 CD -

VIRGIN SIN

Stefan "Dagon" Johansson: v, Andy "SS-66" Rydell: g,
Stefan "Zoak" Nordeng: b, Martin "Schreck" Schönherr: d

Malmö - The band was formed by Dagon (ex-*Dark Ages*) in 1982. On the first single, side A was recorded in 1988 featuring Dagon on vocals and bass, Andy Rydell (*Driller Killer*) on guitar and Clifford "Cliff" Lundberg (*Machinegun Kelly, Driller Killer*) on drums (the above line-up), while side B is a rehearsal recording from 1985 with Rickard "Mr Maniac" Göransson on drums instead of Cliff. Slightly reminiscent of *Sodom*. The band reformed in 1998, now featuring Dagon, Zoak and Schreck (*Splattered Mermaids, RazorRape, Deranged*). *Seduction Of The Innocent* was just as brutal, but with a more thrashy approach, and *Brotherhood Of Freaks* was in the same style, but slightly refined and with better production, sounding a bit like a mix of *Kreator*, *Raven* and *Exodus*. Bass player SS-66 was Andy Rydell under a new moniker. In 2006 Dagon moved to Florida. He has now created a new overseas *Virgin Sin*.

1999 7" - TTD 004

1999 ■	Make 'Em Die Slowly	7" 4tr	To The Death	TTD 004

Tracks: Exterminator/Sadistic Rape/Night Of Hell/Killing Is My Only Joy. 500 copies.

2005 ☐	Seduction Of The Innocent	10" 5tr	To The Death	TTD 010

Tracks: Sane InSide Sanity/Skinned Alive/Mark Of The Beast/War Cry/Awaiting The Wicked

2007 ■	BROTHERHOOD OF FREAKS	CD	Mondongo Canibale Records	MCR 008

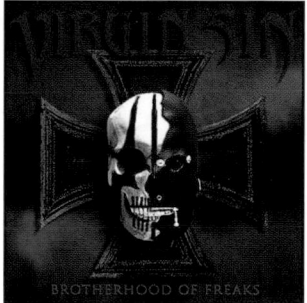
2007 CD - MCR 008

VISCERAL BLEEDING

Martin Pedersen: v, Peter Persson: g, Martin Eklöv: b, Tobias Persson: d

Kalmar - *Visceral Bleeding* were formed in 1999 by guitarist Peter Persson and drummer Niklas Dewerud, influenced by bands like *Suffocation*, *Cannibal Corpse* and *Monstrosity*. They were joined by singer Dennis Röndum, bassist Calle Löfgren and guitarist Marcus Nilsson. They recorded their first demo, *Internal Decomposition* in 2000, followed by *State Of Putrefaction* in 2001. After the release of *Remnants Of Depravation*, Dewerud had to leave because of time issues and wanted to continue playing bass in *Spawn Of Possession*. He was replaced by Tobias Persson. After *Transcend Into Ferocity* Röndum quit to devote his time to *Spawn Of Possession*. He was replaced by Martin Pedersen. Before the release of *Absorbing The Disarray*, Marcus Nilsson left and was replaced by Martin Bernheden. After the release bassist Calle Löfgren left and was replaced by Martin Eklöv. In 2009 the last remaining original member, Peter Persson quit and was replaced by Benny Bats.

Still bleeding

2007 CD - WT 055

2002 ☐	REMNANTS OF DEPRAVATION	CD	Retribute Records	RET 008
2004 ☐	TRANSCEND INTO FEROCITY	CD	Neurotic Records	NRT 040002
2005 ☐	REMNANTS REVIVED	CD	Neurotic Records	NRT 050004

Bonus: Dreaming In Red (Dismember cover)/Carved Down To The Bone (Remake)/ Stripped Raped And Strangled (Cannibal Corpse cover)

2007 ☐	ABSORBING THE DISARRAY	CD	Neurotic Records	NRT 060012
2007 ■	ABSORBING THE DISARRAY	CD	Willlowtip (USA)	WT 055
2009 ☐	TRANSCEND INTO FEROCITY	CD	Willlowtip (USA)	WT 076
2009 ■	REMNANTS REVIVED	CD	Willlowtip (USA)	WT 077

2009 CDd - WT 077

VISION

Donald Burnett: v, Christoffer Hoofgard: g, Pauli Väsäinen: g,
Tapio Karinanta: k, Per Öhman: b, Thorbjörn Sommer: d

Stockholm - Not the same band that recorded the single *Nattens lekar/Fredagshjälte*. This is very high-class melodic hard rock/AOR with a touch of early *Saga* (*Silent Knight* era), especially the guitars. Really impressive guitar/keyboard work and outstanding song material. The vocals are average. Well worth checking out. Christoffer was previously in the band *Hang 'Em High* that recorded two songs for the compilation album *Promotion Music 92* and is was later found in the band *Trilogy*.

1984 ■ Changes/Dreamland ....7"   private ....VISION 1

1984 7" - VISION 1

VITAL SIGN

Jens Lundvik: v, Svenne Mårtensson: g, Rune Bertilsson: k,
PO Larsson: b, Ralf Bjurbo: d

Söderhamn - *Vital Sign* are a Christian melodic hard rock band in the vein of *Guardian*, *Leviticus* and *XT*. Lundvik, ex-*Disciple* and *Messenger*, later appeared in pop band *B.I.G* together with Peo Thyrén (*Easy Action, Sha-Boom*), PO in *XT* and Bertilsson in *Air Condition* and *Solution*. Unfortunately the band only made this one album.

2001 ■ VITAL SIGN...CD   private ....VSCD 001

2001 CD - VSCD 001

VITALITY

Jonas Söderholm: v, Bob Colliander-Nelson: g, Dennis Andersson: b, Martin Olsson: d

Karlshamn - Formed in 1993 out of the band *Doctor Dolittle*. Started doing covers of *Living Colour, Mr Big, Dream Theater* etc. Great slightly progressive hard rock. A young band that unfortunately disappeared. *Love Rears Its Ugly Head* is found on the local compilation *Nu* (1994).

1997 ■ Deep/Cage/Four As One/Illusion ....MCD 4tr   private VITCD01

1997 MCD - VITCD01

VIVALDI (GROUP)

Ralph Peeker: v, Niklas Lindbäck: g, Ola Malmkvist: k,
Niclas Johansson: b, Klaus Kernchen: d

Göteborg - Melodic hard rock. The A-side is pretty close to early *Treat*, with powerful guitars and catchy choruses. Singer Ralph, makes a pretty good performance. The B-side is a traditional power ballad in the true Treat/Europe-vein. Peeker later recorded some solo stuff, fronted *Snowstorm*, then changed career and became a professor of urology. He's still in cover band *Payback Time*.

1986 ■ Run Away/Waiting For You..7"   Platina ....PL 18 $$

VIVID

Jon-Henric Andersson: v/k, Göran Landgren: v/g, Greger Rönnqvist: v/g,
Tryggve Knutsson: g, Leif Thorpemo: b, Jörgen Rönnqvist: d

Strömsund - Formed under the name *Fire* already back in 1982, became *Black Fire* and in 1984 they changed it to *Vivid*. In 1989 the band folded, but ten years later they decided to give it a new shot. They picked the best songs from the old era and recorded the CD. Eighties-style melodic heavy metal, similar to the first two *Europe* albums. Musically it's decent, but the production is quite horrible.

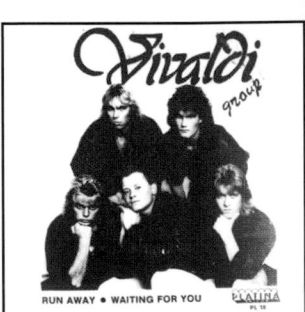
1986 7" - PL 18

2000 □ TIME OF REVELATIONS...CD   private ....TLSCD 6800

VOID MOON

Jonas Gustavsson: v/g, Erika Wallberg: g, Peter Svensson: b, Thomas Hedlund: d

Malmö - *Void Moon* were formed in 2009 by the members of *Cult Ov The Fox*. Drummer Hedlund has previously played with bands like *Autopsy Torment, The Ancient's Rebirth, Pagan Rites, Tristitia, Entity* and *Fall From Grace*. In the winter of 2009 the band recorded a five-track demo, from which four were released as the debut EP. On *On The Blackest Of Nights*, the line-up was completed by guitarist Erika Wallberg. Classic-sounding, doom-oriented metal.

2010 ■ Through The Gateway ....7" 4tr   Metalbound Records.........................MBR 001
    Tracks: The World And The Abyss/The Burning Court/Through The Gateway/Kallocain
    (Pt. 1). 500 copies + 100 copies in blue vinyl + patch.
2012 □ ON THE BLACKEST OF NIGHTS ....CDd   Cruz Del Sur Music............................CRUZ58

2010 7" - MBR 001

VOLTURYON

Olle Ekman: v, Johan Gustafsson: g, Andreas Olander: g, Stefan Eriksson: b, Christian Netzell: d

Falun/Borlänge - It all began in 2005 when Johan (*Evangeli*) and Christian (*In Mourning*) started jamming. Realizing this was too good to waste, they formed *Volturyon*. The first demo, *Forever Suffer*, was released in 2006 and the band was soon picked up by German label Obscure Domain. Before the recording Olle Ekman (*Deals Death, Lethal Attack, Pergolos, Död*) replaced singer Tobias Netzell (*In Mourning, October Tide*). The debut album, *Blood Cure*, was recorded in Black Lounge Studio by Jonas Kjellgren (*Scar Symmetry, Centinex*). Technical death metal with an American touch, a bit similar to *Cannibal Corpse*. In December 2009 the band again hit the Black Lounge studio to record the follow-up, *Coordinated Mutilation*, which was a bit more brutal than the debut. After the release Olle left the band, but Alexander Högbom (*Spasmodic*) soon filled the spot. Eriksson is ex-*Cryonic Temple*. In April 2012 the band and Netzell parted ways.

2008 CD - OD-005-2008

2011 CD - UG 032

| 2008 ■ BLOOD CURE | CD | Obscure Domain | OD-005-2008 |
| 2011 ■ COORDINATED MUTILATION | CD | United Guttural | UG 032 |

VOMITORY

Erik Rundqvist: v/b, Urban Gustafsson: g, Peter Östlund: g, Tobias Gustafsson: d

Forshaga - *Vomitory* were formed in 1989 by Urban Gustafsson and guitarist Ronnie "Ripper" Olsson. They drafted drummer (and Urban's brother) Tobias (ex-*Eureka, Syrus, Bay Laurel*), bassist Bengt Sund and guitarist Ulf Dalegren and recorded their first demo in 1992. Next up they recorded the 7" featuring the same line-up. The first 1 000 copies were released with a misprinted negative cover, while the correctly printed version was only released in 500 copies and could be considered more of a rarity. The band recorded a demo in 1993, now featuring Thomas Bergqvist on bass. In 1995 the band was featured on the compilation *Repulsive Assault* (95 Repulse) with the demo track *Through Sepulchral Shadows*, taken from the demo of the same title. After the album Bergqvist and Olsson left the band and were replaced by singer Jussi Linna and bassist Erik Rundqvist. On *Revelation,* Erik also took over the vocal duties. The style is fast and furious but well-played, old-school death metal with the common growling vocals. Great, powerful and fat production. Revelation… was produced by Berno Paulsson and Clifford "Cliff" Lundberg from *Driller Killer* is guesting. Their version of Pugh Rogefeldt's old 70s hit *Dinga Linga Lena* is quite the ultimate kind of slaughter. The band has also been featured on compilations, such as a CD released with the Israeli version of Metal Hammer magazine, *Death Campaign* (Metal Blade), *Born In Fire Vol 4* and *The Plague*. In 2005 second guitarist Peter Östlund (*The Law, Dispirited*) was added to the line-up. Tobias has also played with bands like *Torture Division*, *God Among Insects* and *The Project Hate MCMXCIX*. In 2011 the band released the live DVD *Dead & Drunk*, recorded in Karlstad at the band's 20th anniversary gig. The band has decided to call it quitz in the end of 2013.
Website: www.vomitory.net

Sick, sicker, Vomitory!

1993 □ Moribund/Dark Grey Epoch	7"	Witchhunt	9309
1000 misprinted negative artwork + 500 correct.			
1996 ■ RAPED IN THEIR OWN BLOOD	CD	Fadeless	FAD 002 CD
1997 □ RAPED IN THEIR OWN BLOOD	CD	Pavement (USA)	76062-32338-2
1999 □ REDEMPTION	CD/d	Fadeless	FAD 005 CD
First 1000 copies released in digi-pack.			
1999 □ Vomitory 1989-1999	10" 5tr PD	Fadeless	FAD 007
10 year anniversary picture disc. Tracks: The Act Of War/Dead Cold/Undivulged/Extremity Retained/Christ Passion (Sodom cover). 667 copies (the number corresponding with the postal code of the member's home town)			
1999 □ Vomitory Goes Pugh/Procreate Insanity	7" 4tr	Hangnail	HANGNAIL 001
Split with Murder Corporation. Tracks The Voyage/Dinga Linga Lena (Pugh Rogefeldt cover)			
1999 □ REDEMPTION	CD	The Plague	Plague 006
2000 □ REVELATION NAUSEA	CD	Metal Blade	3984-14350-2
2000 □ REVELATION NAUSEA	CD	Fono (Russia)	FO 24 CD
2000 □ RAPED IN THEIR OWN BLOOD	CD	The Plague	Plague 003
2002 □ BLOOD RAPTURE	CD	Metal Blade	3984-14391-2
2002 □ BLOOD RAPTURE	CD	Fono (Russia)	FO 136 CD
2002 □ REDEMPTION	CD	CD-Maximum (Russia)	CDM 1002-996
2003 □ REDEMPTION	CD	Fadeless	FAD 010
The tracks from the 1999 10" featured as bonus.			
2004 □ PRIMAL MASSACRE	CD	Metal Blade	3984-14486-2
2004 □ PRIMAL MASSACRE	CD	Fono (Russia)	FO 364 CD
2007 □ RAPED IN THEIR OWN BLOOD	LP	Animate Records	AR 013
100 coloured vinyl + 566 black.			
2007 □ REDEMPTION	LP	Animate Records	AR 014
100 coloured vinyl + 566 black.			
2007 ■ TERRORIZE BRUTALIZE SODOMIZE	CD	Metal Blade	3984-14618-2

1996 CD - FAD 002 CD

2007 CD - 3984-14618-2

2007 ☐ TERRORIZE BRUTALIZE SODOMIZE	CD+DVD	Metal Blade	3984-14618-2
2007 ☐ TERRORIZE BRUTALIZE SODOMIZE	CD	Fono (Russia)	FO 689 CD
2009 ☐ CARNAGE EUPHORIA	CD	Metal Blade	3984-14736-2
2009 ☐ CARNAGE EUPHORIA	CD+DVD	Metal Blade	3984-14736-0
2009 ☐ CARNAGE EUPHORIA	CD	Fono (Russia)	FO 782 CD
2009 ☐ CARNAGE EUPHORIA	LP	Cyclone Empire	CYC-080-1

500 copies on transparent red vinyl.

| 2011 ■ OPUS MORTIS VIII | CD | Metal Blade | 3984-14995-2 |
| 2011 ☐ OPUS MORTIS VIII | CDd | Metal Blade | 3984-14995-0 |

Bonus: Nervegasclouds 2011/Raped In Their Own Blood 2011/Redemption 2011/The Voyage 2011

| 2011 ☐ OPUS MORTIS VIII | LPg | Cyclone Empire | CYC-081-1 |

500 copies on white vinyl.

| 2011 ☐ RAPED IN THEIR OWN BLOOD/REDEMPTION | CD | Vomitory productions | VOM 11666 |

Both albums without the track Ashes Of Mourning Life (God Macabre cover).

2011 CD - 3984-14995-2

VOMITOUS

Andreas Tseung: v, Anders Johansson: v, Christian Lundgren: g, Michael Bergström: g, Gustav Trodin: b, Herbert Alarcon Cerna: d

Stockholm/Skövde/Uppsala - Yet another grindcore-infused death metal band using the gory chapters of the medical encyclopaedia for lyrical inspiration, similar to **Regurgitate**. Heavily distorted, guttural and indecipherable vocals. Well-played and quite heavy at times. Trodin is also in **Flesh Throne**, **Carnalized** and **MP5K**, Lundgren is in **Carnalized**, **Miseration** and **Quest Of Aidance**, Tseung in **Extirpated** and Anders Johansson in **Carnalized**, **Deranged** and ex-**Quest Of Aidance**.

| 2007 ☐ SUPREME ENGORGEMENT OF EXQUISITE DISEMBOWELMENT (sp) | CD | Severed Records | SR-042 |

Split with Inhuman Dissiliency. Tracks: Infectious Urethal Leakage/Engorgement Of Stillborn Corpses/Asphyxiation By Ejaculation/Infectious Necrophilia (demo 2004)

| 2010 ■ Surgical Abominations Of Disfigurement | MCD 4tr | Severed Records | SR-130 |

Tracks: Deranged Entanglement Of Severed Heads/Intrauterine Decimations/Maggot Infestation Amongst Defiled Amputees/Atrocious Defecation Upon The Dead

2010 MCD - SR-130

VON BENZO

Jay Smith: v, Niklas Svärd: g, Richard Larsson: k, Attila Terek: b, Magnus Hoff: d

Helsingborg - **Von Benzo** were formed in 2005, released a single and the debut album (without keyboardist Richard) by themselves and without any big interest. However, when singer Jay won the 2010 Swedish *Idol* it all changed. Jay released a solo album and **Von Benzo** was picked up by Sony Music. The band plays decent post-grunge, with Jay's raspy vocals as the icing on the cake. The second album stepped the game up a bit and fans of bands like **Nickelback**, **Daughtry** and **Shinedown** should check it out.
Website: www.vonbenzo.com

2009 CDd - VB 902

2011 CD - 88697994892

2009 ☐ Die Beautiful/Bad Father, Bad Son	CDS	Orange Haze	VB 901
2009 ■ VON BENZO	CDd	Orange Haze	VB 902
2011 ■ YES KIDS IT'S TRUE	CD	Epic	88697994892

VON PANZER

Andreas "KP" Johansson: v, Jimmy "Jimbo" Petersson: g, Fredrik Ahlo: g, Dag Swanö: b, Niclas "Klajja" Kleist: d

The panzer boys prepared for war

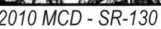

2008 CD - VonP 002

2010 CD - VonP 003

Norrköping - **Von Panzer** was formed in 2005 by drummer Kleist, initially featuring himself, guitarist Olof Sundfeldt and bassist Marko Lehto. In 2006 they were reinforced by singer Andreas "KP" Johansson. In 2007 the band made its first live gig, now featuring Klajja, KP, Olof, bassist Roger Svensson and guitarist Jimmy "Jimbo" Petersson. On the second album Roger had been replaced by Gabriel "Gabbe" Österlund. In 2011 the band released a CD single featuring new guitarist Martin Lindström, who had replaced Olof. The single also contains a cover of **Hawkwind**'s *Silver Machine*, featuring Klajja on vocals. **Von Panzer** play heavy, quite rough edged basic doomy hard rock. The vocals are the band's weak link, not bad, but not as raw as the music demands. On the third album, *Marching*, Dag Swanö (**Nightingale** etc) had replaced Gabbe and Fredrik Ahlo had replaced Lindström. Kleist is also found in rockers **Brewmaster**.

2006 ☐	Bullet/Working Man	CDSp 2tr	private	VonP 001
2008 ■	VON PANZER	CD	private	VonP 002
2010 ■	VON PANZER II	CD	private	VonP 003
2011 ☐	War Of The Worlds	MCDp 3tr	private	VonP 004
	Tracks: War Of The Worlds/Silver Machine (Hawkwind cover)/Working Man (live)			
2013 ■	MARCHING	CD	private	VonP 005

2013 CD - VonP 005

VON ROSEN
Pete Sandberg: v, Magnus Rosén: b

Göteborg - It all started when Magnus, who had previously played with for instance **Kung Sune**, started writing hard rock songs and recorded some demos using singers Jim Jidhed (**Alien**) and Mads Clausen (**Biscaya**). He then teamed up with singer Pete Sandberg (ex-**Sir Maxwell**) and they formed a duo named after Magnus. Other musicians found on the singles were keyboardist Mats Olausson (**Malmsteen, Glory, Motvind**), guitarist Per Alm, and drummer Bengt-Åke Andersson. The singles contain high-quality AOR, well worth checking out. Some more demos were recorded and an album was planned, but when Pete joined **Madison** and later on **Alien**, things fizzled out. Pete has later on been in **Snake Charmer**, **Bewarp**, **Silver Seraph** and has recorded some solo albums. Magnus later joined **Billionaires Boys Club**, **Arose**, **Keegan** and of course **HammerFall**. He now does his jazz-oriented solo bass thing and plays in rock band **Glam**.

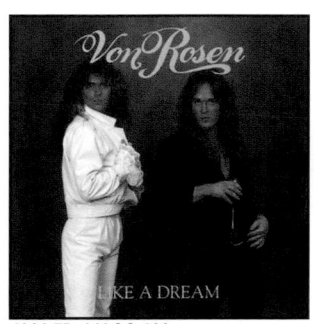

1986 7" - MAGS 100   *1987 7" - MAGS 101*

1986 ■	Like A Dream/You Are The Queen	7"	Magic	MAGS 100
1987 ■	Someone Like You/Time	7"	Magic	MAGS 101

VONDUR
Tony "It" Särkää: v, Jim "All" Berger: g

Stockholm - The solo project of **Abruptum**/**Ophthalamia** singer Tony. In 1993 he initiated his solo project **Vondur**, which means "evil" in Icelandic. He was also joined by Jim "All" Berger. Some of the songs however date as far back as 1985. Musically this is high-speed, ultra-distorted death metal with spoken warped and evil Icelandic vocals and programmed drums. Some tracks are just spoken words to a synth background. On *Beitir Hnitar Skera Djupur* he tries to "sing" with a clean voice and it all sounds like a bad punk-song. The production is among the worst I've ever heard. There is however one small light in the darkness, the ending track *Höfding Satan*, where at least the music (a soft piano ballad) is really good. I could however do without the spoken words. Tony was the founder of the Swedish satanic association *The Black Circle*. The *Galactic Rock 'N Roll Empire* contains covers of bands such as **Judas Priest**, **Mötley Crüe** and Elvis Presley. *No Compromise* is a collection of the band's complete recordings.

Uncompromisingly evil men

1998 MCD - NR 025

1996 ☐	STRIDSYFIRLYSNING	CD	Necropolis	NR 010
1998 ■	The Galactic Rock 'N Roll Empire	MCD 7tr	Necropolis	NR 025
	Tracks: Kill Everyone/Rocka Rolla (Judas Priest cover)/Red Hot (Mötley Crüe cover)/ Love Me Tender (Elvis cover)/You Don't Move Me I Don't Give A Fuck/Panzur Legions Of Vondur/The Raven's Eyes Are As Mirrors Of The Bottom Of Satan's Black Halls			
2011 ■	NO COMPROMISE!	2CDd	Osmose	OPCD249
2011 ☐	NO COMPROMISE!	2LPg	Osmose	OPLP249
	250 black, 260 green, 250 orange copies.			

2011 2CDd - OPCD249

VORNTH
Erik Hartmann: v/g, Erik Kjönsberg: g, Tobias Pettersson: b, Marcus Fors: d

Uddevalla - The band was formed in 2002 and recorded the demo *Die Hard* in 2006. Speed metal. Pettersson is also in **RAM**, **Jormundgand** and ex-**Incendium**, Fors is in **XUL** and ex-**Incendium**, **Jormundgand**, **Grond** while Kjönsberg is in **Sadistic Grimness**, **XUL** and also ex-**Jormundgarn** and **Grond**. The debut album is also due out on Iron Tyrant late 2013.

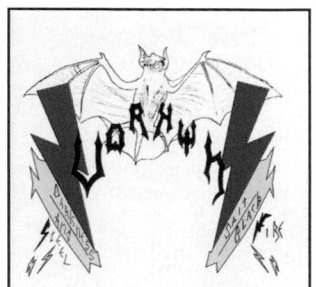

2009 ■	Darkness And Steel/Spit Black Fire	7"	private	7987202
2013 ☐	Evil Blood/Grave Of The Living	7"	Iron Tyrant	ITR 31 EP

2009 7" - 7987202

VOYAGER

Stefan Fröyen: v, Marcus Johansson: v/g, Danjel Garpenbring: b, Andreas Ohlsson: d

Leksand - The band was formed in 1996 under the moniker *Swinefuck*, then changed to *Snake Of Christ* after a *Danzig* tune, and finally stuck with *Voyager*. The band recorded its first demo in 1997, followed by *Demo II* in 1998. *Voyager* also appears on *Molten Universe Volume 1*. In 2004, after recording loads of demos not finding a suitable label, the band sadly folded. *Voyager* play really good melodic stoner, well worth checking out. Marcus, Danjel and Andreas are now found in retro rockers *The Saigon Sickness*.

1999 ☐ Four Bastards Trying To Sort Things Out.............................MCD 4tr Planet 666..................................... PL 666-001
    Tracks: Northumbria/Unstoned/Curse Not Prize/Fragments?
2001 ■ DEAD TUNES FOR THE UNWANTED.......................................CD Powerhead....................................... PHR 001

2001 CD - PHR 001

VREDGAD

Christer "Pnax" Sverla: v/g

Stockholm - *Vredgad* (means angered) recorded the demo *Vredens natt* in 2005. Even though it's Pnax solo thing, Fredrik "Niltor" Romlin (*Psykotisk, Tyranex, Monoscream, Ornias*) was a session member on bass and drums. Raw, fast, old school black metal.

2006 ■ PSYKOTISK/VREDGAD (split) ....CD Regimental....................................... REG 050
    Tracks: Början på slutet/Vedergällningens tid/Hatets natt/Skymning i skogen/Mord. 1000 copies.

2006 CD - REG 050

VULCANO

Anette Karlsson: v, Karin Gustavsson: v, Daniel Nilsson: g, Gert Svensson: g, Johan Sjöqvist: k, Marko Salmi: b, Joakim Kronlid: d

Nödinge - The A-side is very amateurish AOR with female vocals. The B-side is a horrible ballad together with a choir. For collectors only.

1986 ■ Nu vet jag var jag står/När mörkret faller ....7" Fritid Musik ....FM 01

1986 7" - FM 01

VULTURE CAVALRY

Jens Kemgren: v/g, Paul Flensby: b, Jimmy Lexe: d

Karlshamn - *Vulture Cavalry* released their first demo, *Gone In The Morning*, in 2000, at the time featuring drummer Christian Stenbäck. On the second effort, *Looks Like Invisible* (2001) Lexe had replaced Stenbäck. The band signed a deal with Soundport (owned by Jimmy's father, Kjell Jacobsson, also guitarist in *Overdrive*) and the album *Blackwing* was released. Unfortunately Kemgren relocated and the band folded. The style is great retro-style hard rock with a touch of *Badlands*. Kemgren later joined sleaze rockers *Danger*, while Lexe recorded an album with *Locomotive Breath* and today is in heavy rockers *Unfaithful*. Flensby recorded an album with thrash/death metal band *Hydrogen*.

2002 CDS - SP 100101

2002 ☐ Gravity Greetings/Living Loud...............................CDSp 2tr Soundport .... SP 100101
2003 ■ BLACKWING ....CD Soundport .... SP 100103

2003 CD - SP 100103

VÖRGUS

Kenneth "Nenne Vörgus" Nyholm: v/b, Harry "Straight-G" Virtanen: g, Micke "Killalot" Nyholm: d

Stockholm - Well, the name says it all. *Vörgus* is sug röv (suck ass) spelled backwards. Kenneth is also in *Serpentine, Deformity* and *Internal Decay*, while Virtanen has played with *Pandemonic, Internal Decay, Chainsaw, Deformity, Serpentine* and is also in *Morito Ergo Sum*. Mikke has also been in *Deformity*, plus *Sorg, Ad Indinitum* and is also in *Shadowsoul*. *Vörgus* was formed back in 1994, at the time featuring singer Oppegaard. The band recorded the demos *Vörgus Is The Law* (2001) and *The Evil Dominator* (2002) before parting ways with the singer and then entering Necromorbus Studio to record the *Pure Perkele* (2003) demo. The vocals were now handled by Nenne. Another demo, *Vörgusized*, was recorded by Mike Wead in 2004. The demo also contains some covers of *Impaled Nazarene* and *Motörhead*, which would give you an indication of the band's style and sound, which is like a mix of the two with a strong hint of *Venom*. The demo was re-released in 2007 by Mexican labels Executor666/ Iron Blood Death Corporation with some additional tracks. In December 2008 the band started recording their first full length album, *Hellfueled Satanic Action*, which was released by French Inferno Records in 2009.

2007 CD - IBDC.666004

2007 ■ VÖRGUSIZED ....CD Iron Blood & Death/Executor 666 IBDC.666004
    999 copies.
2009 ■ HELLFUELED SATANIC ACTION ....CD Infernö Records .... IR 005 CD
    1000 copies.

2009 CD - IR 005 CD

W.E.T

Lollo Öberg: v/g, Sonny Dahl: g, Jerry Prütz: b, Jörgen Borman: d

Linköping - Formed in 1987. On the first 7" Lollo plays bass and singer/guitarist Morgan Svensson was in the band. In 1987 Lollo also recorded a MLP with *Hazy*, but was never a member of the band. Jerry replaced Morgan before *Sex On The Line*. A great band whose first album was at times quite reminiscent of early *Van Halen*. The single *Sex On The Line* entered some non-Swedish charts and the video was shown on Swedish TV. *W.E.T* (Weird Electric Temple or Weird Electric Treatment or Wild Energetic Tempo or...) was a very energetic live band that supported several big Swedish acts. The band is also found on the compilation *Swedish Metal* (95 XTC), and they recorded a track for the '96 Backstage compilation, this time a cover of the band *Sator*. *W.E.T*'s second album is actually a big step forward with its untrendy, straightforward, hooligan hard rock 'n roll. Highly recommended. Jerry was a host for the heavy metal TV-show *Diezel* and he's a frequent writer for *Close-Up* magazine. The third album was a very strange experiment where the band explored the territory of straightforward country-tinged rock, a far cry from the early heavies. The band has however returned to their former heaviness, maybe with a more *AC/DC*-influenced touch, which is proved by a 3-track demo recorded after the last album. The band actually released the CD-R album *Fifteen Years With Constant Eartrouble* as an anniversary release. Jerry today has his blues rock band *Circus Prütz*.

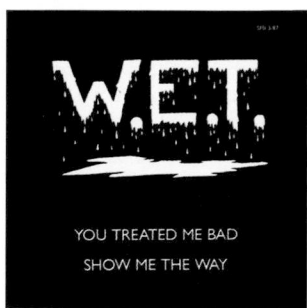

1987 7" - SFSI 3/87

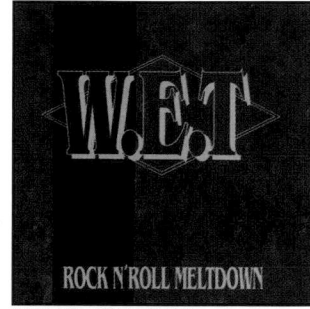

1989 7" - DELTA S-002

1987	■	You Treated Me Bad/Show Me The Way	7"	Rockarusellen	SFSI 3/87
1989	■	Sex On The Line/Beat The Meat (live)	7"	Delta	DELTA S-002
1991	☐	Under The Blue/Massive Attack/Thin Ice	CDS 3tr	HSM	HSMCD 008
1991	☐	ROCK & ROLL MELTDOWN	CD	HSM	HSM CD 009
1991	■	ROCK & ROLL MELTDOWN	LP	HSM	HSM LP 009
1995	☐	WIERD ELECTRIC TENSION	CD	HSM	HSM CD 015
1995	☐	WIERD ELECTRIC TENSION	LP	HSM	HSM LP 015
1998	☐	WALKING STRAIGHT	CD	Sonus	SONCD 012

1991 LP - HSM LP 009

W.E.T

Jeff Scott Soto: v, Robert Säll: g, Erik Mårtensson: b/g/k

Stockholm/Los Angeles - *W.E.T* are something of an all-star melodic rock band and the name comes from the members' original bands *Work Of Art* (Säll), *Eclipse* (Mårtensson) and *Talisman* (Soto). Many all-star projects tend to not deliver what the names promise. This is however not the case when it comes to *W.E.T*. Great, catchy melodic hard rock with influences drawn from the members' original bands melting into a nice musical blend. Drums on the album were played by Robban Bäck (*BALLS, Eclipse, Billion Dollar Babies, Sabaton*). On *Rise Up* they continued in the same style, but now the band felt more like a tight band unit.

2009	☐	W.E.T	CD	Frontiers Records	FRCD 434
2009	☐	W.E.T	CD+DVD	Frontiers Records	FRCD 434
		DVD with videos, interview and "making of".			
2009	☐	W.E.T	CD	King Records (Japan)	KICP-1451
		Bonus: Comes Down Like Rain (acoustic)			
2011	☐	W.E.T	LP PD	Inner Wound	IW 83006
		300 copies.			
2012	■	RISE UP	CD	Frontiers Records	FRCD 594
2013	☐	RISE UP	LP	Inner Wound	IW83024
2013	☐	RISE UP	CD	Icarus Music (Argentina)	ICARUS 1090

2012 CD - FRCD 594

W.O. BAND

Peter Forkelid: g/v, Stephan Brisfjord: g/v, Peder Andersson: b, Kjell Claeson: d

Tranås - Punkish hard rock sung in Swedish, featuring former *Rövsvett* guitarist/singer Forkelid.

1982	■	Rostig kärlek/Fredagsflickan	7"	Pang	PSI 057

1982 7" - PSI 057

WAGABOND, THE

Peter "Walle" Wahlberg: v, Johan "J" Roos: g, Fredrik "Fredrock" Wahledow: g, Thomas "Fikarn" Johansson: b, Magnus "Manne" Kristiansson: d

Kalmar - Formed in 1978. Magnus and Fredrik played in the band *Illusion*, while Peter and Johan had played in bands together. The four got together and also drafted singer Peter. They wrote two songs and immediately booked Studio Decibel in Stockholm. Only Peter had a drivers licence, but because he had his arm in plaster, Magnus had to shift gear while they were driving. Good, solid hard rock, at times similar to *Solid Ground* in their better moments. For some reason some have labelled this as punk, but this is definitely really good, well-played hard rock with great, biting guitar solos. Despite the titles, the vocals are in Swedish. The cover is just an insert printed on both sides. On the same label as *Kung Tung*. The band finally split, but have reunited now and then. Magnus later played with *Fuzzters, Apollo Drive* and in various cover bands.

1979	■	This Is Life/Wagabond	7"	Grisbäck	GRIS 7906
		Red vinyl. 1000 copies.			

1979 7" - GRIS 7906

WAITING RAIN, THE

Mattias "Mylon Hymat" Davidsson: v/g, Anders "Andrew North" Norberg: b,
Ole "Olly Chaos" Knudsen: d

Göteborg - *The Waiting Rain* started out as *Caragorgya* and moved from Skellefteå to Göteborg in 1991. A melodic straightforward hard rock band, influenced by *The Cult*. On the album they had some guest musicians from bands like *Tornado Babies*, *Mary Beats Jane*, *The Leather Nun* etc. The band split in 1994. Davidsson has since recorded lots of material under his own name, but in a synth-pop-oriented vein.

1990	■	Sail/Mad World	7"	A Westside Fabrication	We 018
1992	☐	ANOTHER MENTAL EARTHQUAKE	CD	A Westside Fabrication	WeCD 036

1990 7" - We 018

WALK AWAY

Roger "Roy Bartello" Bertilsson: v, Micke "Mike Alley" Hörnlund: g,
John "GB Junior": k, Tony "Cool" Andersson: b, Tony "Shield" Skiöld: d

Arboga - Great, high-quality, southern-influenced AOR with a touch of *Tangier* or *Bon Jovi*. Highly recommended. Recorded in 1989, but not made public until 1990. Tony later recorded a CD with the band *Rampant* in 2005. The band existed between 1989-1992.

1989	■	We'll Meet Again/I Believe In Love	7"	SGV	SGV-89117

1989 7" - SGV-89117

WANTON

Roger Westberg: v/g, Jari Laakonen: g, Claes Johnson: b, Stefan Book: d

Olofström - Traditional straight ahead 80s metal with strong influences from the British metal scene. Initially called *Charizma*. Definitely worth checking out if you're into bands like *Vardis*, *Red Alert*, *Oxym*, *Buffalo* etc. The single was produced by Christer Åkerberg (*Trettioåriga Kriget*).

1984	■	Motorcycle Man/I Want You	7"	CTR	CTR-1283 $

1984 7" - CTR-1283

WAR/TOTAL WAR

Jim "All" Berger: v, David "Blackmoon" Parland: g,
David "Impious" Larsson: b, Lars Szöke: d

Stockholm - The band started as a project that was meant to change members between each record, but became more of a set band. Drums on the debut were played by Peter Tägtgren (*Pain, Hypocrisy, The Abyss, Bloodbath, Marduk* etc) and bass by Michael Hedlund (*Hypocrisy, Repugnant, The Abyss*). Parland has previously played with *Necrophobic* and *Dark Funeral* and was later in *Infernal*. Lars and Michael are also found in *Hypocrisy*, while Jim is found in *Ophthalamia* and *Vondur*. The band's philosophy is they are against life, against humanity, against goodness and of course against Christianity. Brutal black metal. On *We Are War* the line-up consisted of Berger, Parland and Larsson (*In Aeternum, Adversary, Behemoth, Infernal*), while Szöke (*Epitaph, The Abyss, Hypocrisy*) was just a session-drummer. This, as Tony "It" Särkää (*Ophthalamia, Insicion, Vondur, Abruptum*), who played guitar on the debut, had decided to leave the black metal genre all in all (?!). The album was recorded already in 1997 and mastered by James Murphy (*Testament*, solo). In 2001 the band changed its name to *Total War*, because of another band called *War*. *We Are... Total War* is a re-mastered compilation of both earlier releases. A cover of *Bathory*'s War is found on the tribute *In Conspiracy With Satan* (1998 No Fashion/Hellspawn). David Parland sadly took his own life March 19, 2013.

1998 MCD - NR 019

1998	■	Total War	MCD 7tr	Necropolis	NR 019
		Tracks: Satan/I Am Elite/Total War/The Sons Of War/Revenge/Rapers Of Satan/Satan's Millennium			
1999	■	WE ARE WAR	CD	Necropolis	NR 036 CD
1999	☐	WE ARE WAR	LP	Necropolis	NR 036 LP
1999	☐	WE ARE WAR	CDd	Necropolis	NR 036 DIGI
		Pop-sticker.			
1999	☐	WE ARE WAR	LP	Merciless Records	MRSRLP 009
		1000 copies.			
2001	☐	WE ARE... TOTAL WAR	CD	Hellspawn	HELL 7
		Released under the name Total War.			
2001	■	WE ARE... TOTAL WAR	CD	Necropolis (USA)	NR 077
2001	☐	WE ARE... TOTAL WAR	CD	Orion Music (Argentina)	OME 003

1999 CD - NR 036 CD

WARCOLLAPSE

Jalle Karlsson: v, Emil Sandebäck: g, Janne Karlsson: b, Kalle Andersson: d

Färjestaden - The first 7" showed traces of punk, while the MCD is dark and slow doom with traces of melting lava. Death inspired vocals. Janne was previously in *Dom Där* and Jalle has played with punksters *Disaccord* and *Crude S.S.*. The band has now split. Kalle and Emil have a new band called *Smol*. Kalle is also found in *3-Way Cum* and *Senseless*. Doom-crust-metal?

2001 CD - NR 077

1994	■	Massgenocide (split)	7"	Elderberry	E.B 007

Split with Extinction Of Mankind. Tracks: Massgenocide/Scorned By Bombfighters

1994 ☐ Indoctri-nation ...... 7" 4tr Elderberry ...... E.B 008
Tracks: Rewinding History/Bleakness Over Battlefields/Indoctri-nation/Encaged

1994 ☐ Indoctri-nation ...... 7" 4tr Tribal War Asia (Japan) ...... - -

1994 ☐ Drunk Collapsed Destroyed (split) ...... 7" 4tr Crust Records CRUST-07-008
Split with Disrupt. Tracks: Destroy To Create/Skin Colour Terror

1995 ☐ Crust As A Fuck Existence ...... MCD 4tr Distortion (Germany) ...... DISTCD 18
Tracks: It's Time To.../Massgenocide/Crust As Fuck Existence/Encaged-Death-Dist-Mix

1996 ☐ Wandering In darkness ...... 7" 5tr Scream Records ...... SR 007
*Tracks: Wandering In Darkness 1 and 2/Bloodtrade/Warcollapse/Rewinding History/
Indoctri-Nation*

1998 ☐ DIVINE INTOXICATION ...... CD Mind Control ...... No. 7

1998 ☐ DIVINE INTOXICATION ...... LP Mind Control ...... MCLP 9

1999 ☐ DIVINE INTOXICATION ...... CD Malarie Records ......

2003 ☐ Crap, Scrap And Unforgivable Slaughter ...... 7" 3tr First Blood Family ...... FBF 005
Tracks: Beginning Of The End/In Darkness.../The Blood Runs Red

2004 ☐ Live Intoxication ...... 10" MLP 11tr Malarie Records ...... - -
*Tracks: Warcollapse/Booze, Violence And Misery/Tranquilized/Skin-Colour Terror/
Indoctri-Nation/Phetamine Rush/Marrowness/As The Bombing Ends/No Hope/Nauseating
Nightmare/Encaged*

2007 ■ DEFY! ...... CD Profane Existance ...... EXIST 104

2007 ☐ DEFY! ...... LP Profane Existance ...... EXIST 104

2007 ☐ DEFY! ...... LP Profane Existance ...... EXIST 104
200 copies hand-numbered. Exclusive artwork. Button or poster in some copies.

2007 ☐ THE FINAL END: 15 YEARS OF MISERY AND DESPAIR ...... CD Helvet Records ...... HEL 010

2009 ☐ Crust As A Fuck Existence ...... MLP 4tr Insane Society Records ...... IS 092

2011 ☐ Crap, Scrap And Unforgivable Slaughter Vol. 2 ...... MLP 5tr Blindead Productions ...... DEAD 012
*Tracks: Óvænt(Purrkur Pillnikk cover)/Vi blev rädda (Missbrukarna cover)/Krav (Bannlyst
cover)/Reklamfremstöd (War Of Destruction cover)/Maailma Ilman Vihaa (Rattus cover)*

1994 7" - E.B 007

2007 CD - EXIST 104

WARHAMMER

**Wiktor Söderström: v, Gabriel Österlund: g, Bo Åkesson: g,
Rickard Cidh: b, Magnus Lindh: d**

Norrköping - Run of the mill metal with incredibly patchy lyrics, such as "*Blood, blood and
honour/Walk through fire and death/Back, back for glory/Until victory or death*" or "*You can't
run, cannot hide the hammer of war/Feel the power, there's metal in the air*". Sheer poetry... After
Warhammer split Wiktor, Gabriel and Magnus formed the band ***Seven***, a far better instalment
which no longer exists. Magnus is now found in the band ***Last Temptation***.

1995 ■ Riders ...... MCD 4tr private ...... CDWAR 01
Tracks: Riders/Blood And Honour/Alone/Warhammer. 500 copies.

1995 MCD - CDWAR 01

WARNING

**Eric Wikström: v, Krister Lindman: g, Joachim Lindbäck: g,
Stefan Åberg: b, Johan Henriksson: d**

Älvsbyn - The original line-up featured guitarist Mikael "Mike Wead" Wikström and drummer
Janne Lindh, but they moved to Stockholm where Lindh joined ***Candlemass*** and Wikström
ended up in bands like ***Maninnya Blade*** and ***Hexenhaus***. ***Warning*** split in 1987 when Johan
also made his way to the capitol and joined ***Maninnya Blade***. Excellent dark metal in the vein
of ***Hexenhaus*** and ***Destiny***.

1987 ■ Armageddon/Sword And Sorcery ...... 7" Active Music ...... HEJ S-024 $

1987 7" - HEJ S-024

WATAIN

Erik Danielsson: v/b, Per Forsberg: g, Håkan Jonsson: d

Uppsala - Formed in 1998 by Christian Blom and Erik, formerly of black/thrash-band ***Blood-
soil***. The name ***Watain*** was taken from a ***VON***-song. They are one of the small circle of bands
considered true black metal. Aggressive black metal with lots of riffing and intense musical
patterns, a bit reminiscent of ***Marduk*** and ***Dissection***. They recorded the demos *Go Fuck Your
Jewish God* (1998) and *Black Metal Sacrifice* (1999). In 2001 the live-tape *Ritual Macabre*
was released through Brazilian label Sacriligious Warfare, only on cassette and in 666 copies.
Christian was sacked after the recording of the album. The first single was recorded in guitarist/
bassist Tore "Necromorbus" Stjerna's studio. The band says their music is "meant for die-hard
Black/Death maniacs only" and that they "are not to be looked upon as a part of today's loath-
some false metal scene". Tore is also found in ***Funeral Mist***. As all the early records are in
limited small editions, they are all sold out, so the chances of finding the band's early originals
are pretty slim. The track *My Fists Are Him* can also be found on the compilation *Sounds Of
Pandemonium*. On *Casus Luciferi* Tore Stjerna was out of the band and Erik handled bass and
vocals himself. Live the band is reinforced by guitarist Sethlans Davide "Set Teitan" Totaro and
bassist Alvaro Lillo, who replaced Jonas "Whorth/Mörk" Lindskog (***Malign***). Stjerna however

1999 7" - GRI 002

continued producing the band. When the band released *Lawless Darkness* they were suddenly the hype of the year and even won a Grammy in 2011 for best hard rock. Their dramatic live act featuring fire, rotten blood and all kinds of paraphernalia is something in-between a Satanic sermon and a concert. Nothing for the fainthearted. Jonsson is also in **Die Hard**. *Lawless Darkness* contains a cover of **Death SS** track *Chains Of Death*. *Opus Diaboli* was released in the commemoration of **Watain**'s 13 yeat anniversary and the DVD is live and documentary. Watain play tight, well-produced and well-arranged riffy black metal in the vein of **Dissection** or a better produced and updated **Bathory**. *The Wild Hunt* was more progressive and orchestrated.
Website: www.templeofwatain.com

2000 CD - DKCD 012

2001 7" - SPK EP 012

2003 CD - DK CD 032

2007 2LPg - NED 013

1999 ■	The Essence Of Black Purity/On Horns Impaled	7"	Grim Rune	GRI 002	
	300 numbered copies.				
2000 ■	RABID DEATH'S CURSE	CD	Drakkar Productions	DKCD 012	
	1000 copies.				
2000 □	RABID DEATH'S CURSE	LPg	End All Life	EAL015	
	Bonus: Curdle The Blood (Sabbat cover). 350 hand-numbered copies.				
2001 ■	The Misantropis Ceremonies	7"	Spikekult	SPK EP 012	
	Split with Diabolicum. Track: My Fists Are Him. 300 copies.				
2003 ■	CASUS LUCIFERI	CD	Drakkar Productions	DK CD 032	
2003 □	CASUS LUCIFERI	LP	Norma Evangelium Diaboli	NED 003	
2004 □	RABID DEATH'S CURSE	CD	Drakkar Productions	DKCD 012/2	
	Second press. Bonus: When Heavens End (Dödheimsgard cover). New artwork..				
2004 □	RABID DEATH'S CURSE	LP PD	Apocalyptor (Australia)	AR 08	
	300 copies. First 100 with poster, sticker and extra insert.				
2007 □	SWORN TO THE DARK	CDd	Seasons Of Mist	SOM 148	
2007 □	SWORN TO THE DARK	CDd	Ajna Offensive (USA)	FLAME 42	
2007 □	SWORN TO THE DARK	CDd	Pulverised	ASH 029 CD	
2007 □	SWORN TO THE DARK	CD	CD-Maximum (Russia)	CDM 2812	
2007 ■	SWORN TO THE DARK	2LPg	Norma Evangelium Diaboli	NED 013	
2008 □	SWORN TO THE DARK	2LP PD	Norma Evangelium Diaboli	NED 019	
	999 copies, but 3 different B-sides on disc 1, 333 copies of each.				
2008 □	CASUS LUCIFERI	CDd	Seasons Of Mist	SOM 185	
	Bonus: Watain (Von cover)				
2008 □	CASUS LUCIFERI	2LP PD	Norma Evangelium Diaboli	NED 018	
	999 copies. 333 copies of each with different B-side pics on disc 1.				
2008 □	RABID DEATH'S CURSE	CD	Seasons Of Mist	SOM 187	
	Bonus: The Essence Of Black Purity				
2008 □	RABID DEATH'S CURSE	LP PD	Norma Evangelium Diaboli	NED 017	
	999 copies.				

2010	☐	Reaping Death/The Return Of Darkness And Evil (Bathory cover) .... CDSpg	Seasons Of Mist SOM203SRM
		Special CDS featured in Sweden Rock Magazine #70..	
2010	■	Reaping Death/Chains Of Death (Death SS cover) ....7" PD	Seasons Of Mist .... SOM 203 E
		1300 copies.	
2010	■	LAWLESS DARKNESS ....CD	Seasons Of Mist ....SOM 203
2010	☐	LAWLESS DARKNESS ....CDd	Seasons Of Mist ....SOM 203D
		Bonus: Chains Of Darkness (Death SS cover)	
2010	☐	LAWLESS DARKNESS ....CD	Nippon Colombia (Japan) COCB-60027
2010	☐	LAWLESS DARKNESS ....CDd box	Seasons Of Mist .... - -
		1000 copies. Leather wrapped book, necklace, black candle, poster flag, 10 Tarot cards.	
2010	☐	LAWLESS DARKNESS 2LPg	Norma Evangelium Diaboli .... NED 025
		2500 copies. Poster.	
2010	☐	LAWLESS DARKNESS ....CD	Soyus Music (Russia) ....SOM 203
2010	☐	LAWLESS DARKNESS ....CD	Icarus Music (Argentina).............. ICARUS 794
2012	☐	OPUS DIABOLI..2CD+DVD	His Master's Noise ....FTW 001
2012	☐	OPUS DIABOLI.......................................2LP+2CD+DVD box	His Master's Noise ....FTW 001 LTD $
		1000 copies. Live CD/LP/DVD box. Postcards, photo book. Signed and numbered insert.	
2012	☐	THE VINYL REISSUES ....4LPg box	Seasons Of Mist ....SOM 267 $$
		All four albums in a leather covered wooden box, in four different colours: grey/white splatter, grey, transparent red and clear. 1000 copies.	
2012	☐	RABID DEATH'S CURSE 2LPg	Seasons Of Mist .... SOM 187LP
		Bonus. The Essence Of Black Purity. New artwork.	
2012	☐	CASUS LUCIFERI 2LPg	Seasons Of Mist .... SOM 185LP
		Bonus: Watain (VON cover)	
2012	☐	LAWLESS DARKNESS 2LPg	Seasons Of Mist .... SOM 203LP
2013	☐	All That May Bleed/Play With The Devil...7"	Century Media FTW002/9983481
		2000 black + 500 red with sticker.	
2013	☐	All That May Bleed/Play With The Devil.........................7" PD	Century Media FTW002/9983481
		500 copies.	
2013	☐	THE WILD HUNT ....CD	Century Media FTW003/9983062
2013	☐	THE WILD HUNT ....CDd book	Century Media 9983060
2013	☐	THE WILD HUNT 2LP	Century Media 9983061
2013	☐	THE WILD HUNT ....2LP+CD+7" box	Century Media ....9983069 $$
2013	☐	THE WILD HUNT ....CD	Century Media (USA)............................9006-2
2013	☐	THE WILD HUNT 2LP	Century Media (USA)............................90063
		White label, special artwork, bootleg style press. 500 hand-numbered copies.	

2010 7" PD - SOM 203 E

2010 CD - SOM 203

WATERCLIME
Andreas Hedlund: v/g/b/k/d

Skellefteå - A one-man project created in 2005 by the mastermind of *Vintersorg*, Andreas Hedlund, also in *Otyg*, *Fission*, *Havayoth*, *Borknagar* and *Cronian*. The music of *Waterclime* is quite different from the folky rock of *Vintersorg*. Here we are talking symphonic/progressive hard rock more in the vein of *Marillion* meets late *Opeth*, at times with a touch of *Uriah Heep*. Actually really good stuff for prog fans. The debut also features guest spots from guitarists Mathias Marklund and Magnus Lindgren, as well as singer Cia Hedmark.

2006	☐	THE ASTRAL FACTOR...CD	Lion Music......................................LMC 164
2007	■	IMAGINATIVE ....CD	Lion Music......................................LMC 218

2007 CD - LMC 218

WATERLINE
**Gunnar Janupe: v, Kricke Petersson: g, Esbjörn Larsson: g, Jörgen Munk: k,
Per Andersson: k, Lars Ottosson: b, Peder Jonsson: d**

Göteborg - Great melodic hard rock in the vein of *Bad Habit*. Janupe was also in *Snowstorm*.

1990	■	Tid/Cold Eyes...7"	Hövik Records ....HS 1232

1990 7" - HS 1232

WAVING CORN
**Anton Renborg: v, Henrik "Henke" Johansson: g, Joacim "Jocke" Persson: g,
Mattias Hedenborg: b, Johan "Joje" Lindskoog: d**

1995 CD - APCY-8233

Örebro - The band started out as a side project doing covers of *Rage Against The Machine*, *Red Hot Chili Peppers* etc. They wrote some original songs, recorded a demo and suddenly they were offered a deal with Roadrunner. Not surprisingly, in the vein of *Red Hot Chili Peppers* meets *Rage Against The Machine*. Joje was also a member of hard rockers *Crossroad Jam*, Anton played guitar in thrashers *Cripple*, while Matte, Jocke and Henke were members of *Under The Sun*. The non-CD track *Fish In Gold* can also be found on the compilation *Backstage: Högtalarterror '94*. The band split in mid-'95.

1995	☐	TEARSURF...CD	Roadrunner Records ....RR 8960 2
1995	■	TEARSURF...CD	Apollon/FEMS (Japan)..................APCY-8233
1995	■	Doin' It ....MCD 4tr	Roadrunner Records ....RR 2336 3
		Tracks: Doin' it/Sunshade/Rhymin' & Stealin' (non-CD Beastie Boys song)/Stranded	

1995 MCD - RR 2336 3

WEED, THE

Peter Lidebrandt: v, Bengt Ljungberger: g, Sture Kaveus: g,
Mats Johansson: b, Joakim Sandgren: d

Stockholm - The first single is not hard rock, but closer to new wave, however things changed on the album. *Metallfågel* (metal bird) contains good melodic 80s hard rock, with highlights like *Gått T, Fågeln, Människor* and *Roddbåt*. Vocals in Swedish. The album artwork was made by Flavia Canel (***Living Sacrifice, Aphrodite, Drain***). Bengt was later found in ***AB/CD***, while Sture played in a disco band. At one time they had a bass player called Johan "Chatte" Bergquist.

1982 ☐	Media/Cancer	7"	Weed Records	WEED ETT
1984 ■	METALLFÅGEL	LP	Rosa Honung	ROSA LP 16

1984 LP - ROSA LP 16

WHAM GLAM BOYS

Anders Strengberg: v/b, Torgny Berlin: g, Magnus Rosling: g, Jörgen Lindau: d

Hässleholm - Not really sure if this one qualifies in here, but see this more as a warning. Even though Strengberg has been in several metal bands such as ***Mercy*** and ***Sacrifice***, this is a pure cover band. The CD contains covers only, a strange mix of pop, synth and hard rock. The hard rock/metal covers are of ***Whitesnake, AC/DC, Van Halen, Yes*** and ***Toto***, plus there are decently heavy versions of songs by ***Factory*** and ***Pink Floyd*** (with exaggerated English pronunciation). This is probably only to be seen as a marketing CD for a medium-quality cover band.

1995 ■	CENTERFOLD	CD	Starrec	SRCD 9514

1995 CD - SRCD 9514

WHIMZY

Lasse Gudmunsson: v, Stefan Fagerlund: g, Per "Dohlken" Dohlk: b, Perra Ahlberg: d

Uppsala - Previously known as ***Screw***, but changed it to ***Whimsy*** in 1993. Straigh, simple heavy metal, quite amateurish. If there was a competition in out-of-pitch chorus vocals, ***Whimsy*** would surely win. ***Meshuggah*** did a live-cover of the song *Attacked By A Shark* on the *Power From The North* compilation. On *Heaven Or Hell*, which was more classic hard rock, Lasse replaced Stefan Flodström, and it's also the band's best effort, even though it doesn't say much. Gudmunsson is now in ***Lizard Eye*** and ***Angel King***.

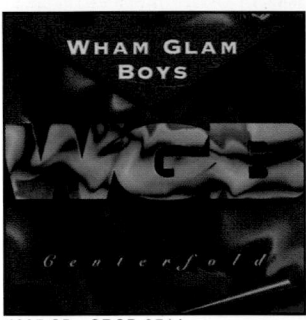

1994 ☐	GAMBLING WITH THE FUTURE	CD	Büms	48123
1996 ☐	Reason To	MCD 4tr	private	WEPCD 09604-11
	Tracks: Spit Like This/Jack The Ripper/The Gambler/Got A Reason			
1997 ■	HEAVEN OR HELL	CD	private	WLPCD 09710-21

1997 CD - WLPCD 09710-21

WHIPPED CREAM

Elisabeth Punzi: v/g, Jörgen Cremonese: g/v, Jonas Sonesson: b, Fredrik Sandsten: d

Göteborg - ***Whipped Cream*** started out in a softer, ***Pink Floyd***-meet-***The Beatles***-style, but on *Horse Mountain* they made a 90 degree turn and produced a really heavy album with hints of old 70s acts like ***Pink Fairies, Lucifer's Friend*** and Hendrix. An album well worth investing in, while the earlier stuff are for collectors only. ***Whipped Cream*** was actually the first Swedish band to do a session recording for John Peel at BBC One. Drummer Lars-Erik Grimelund was replaced by Fredrik after *Observatory Crest* (***Captain Beefheart*** cover). After *Horse Mountain* Jonas and Fredrik were sacked. A cover of ***Pink Floyd***'s *Shine On You Crazy Diamond* can be found on the *King Kong* compilation 7" (KK 005 - 1994), *Wishing* on *Swedish Exotica Vol 2* (90 Topyscan), *This Time, Next Time* on *Swedish Exotica Vol 3* (91 Psyche), *$1.000.000 Project* on *Snapology* (93 MNW Snap!). Jörgen has also produced other bands, like ***H*E*A*L*** and ***Destiny***. ***Whipped Cream***'s fourth album entitled *Possessed* was supposed to be released in 1996, but never happened. The new line-up that would appear on this release consisted of of Elisabeth, Jörgen, Snowy Shaw (g) (***King Diamond, Dream Evil, Therion***), Sharlee D'Angelo (b) (***Mercyful Fate, Arch Enemy***) and Charlie Storm (k) (***Mike Tajson***). And after having heard some advance tracks I assure you it would have been a killer in the heavy rock genre.

1991 LP - RA 73

1994 CD - SNAP 14

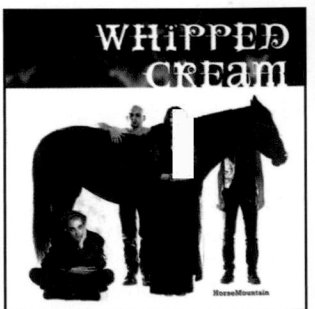

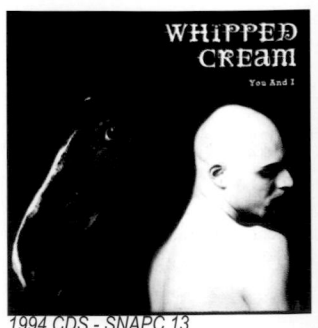

1991 ■	& OTHER DELIGHTS	LP	MNW Radium	RA 73
1991 ☐	& OTHER DELIGHTS	CD	MNW Radium	RA 73
1991 ☐	Come Together/Silver III/Wishing	MCD 3tr	MNW Radium	RACD 87
1992 ☐	Wait For A Minute/Silver part 3/Come	MCD 3tr	MNW Snap	SNAPC 3
1992 ☐	Wait For A Minute	MLP 4tr	MNW Snap	SNAPT 3
	Tracks: Wait For A Minute/Come Now Gently/Silver Part 3/Wait For A Minute			
1992 ☐	TUNE IN THE CENTURY	CD	MNW Snap	SNAP 3
1992 ☐	Observatory Crest/Something New/Silver Part 2	MCD 3tr	MNW Snap	SNAPC 8
1992 ☐	Observatory Crest/Something New/Silver Part 2	MLP 3tr	MNW Snap	SNAPT 8
1994 ■	HORSE MOUNTAIN	CD	MNW Snap	SNAP 14
1994 ☐	& OTHER DELIGHTS	CD	MNW Snap	RESNAP 1
1994 ■	You And I/...And I Have This Dream	CDS	Snap	SNAPC 13
1996 ☐	HORSE MOUNTAIN	CD	Columbia (Japan)	COCY-78880
1996 ☐	& OTHER DELIGHTS	CD	Columbia (Japan)	COCY-80253

1994 CDS - SNAPC 13

WHIPPING PRINCESS

Jenny Jonasson: v, Simon Söderberg: g, Karl Hinterleithner: b, Linus Henriksson: d

Malmö - Formed by Karl who teamed up with singer Jenny. In September 2010 Henriksson was drafted, and at Christmas came, not only Santa Claus, but also guitarist Söderberg. The track *State Of Hate* is featured on the *Punk Kills Seventeen* compilation. Quite raw and untamed power metal with great rough-edged yet melodic vocals from Jenny.
Website: www.whippingprincess.com

2011 ■ Let You And Me Be One ....MCDp 5tr   private ....WHP 2011
        Tracks: State Of Hate/Evil Mind/Let You And Me Be One/Theatre Of Pain/Endless Pain

2011 MCDp - WHP 2011

WHIRLING

A "AE" Pettersson: v/g/b, Johdet: g/b, J Marklund: d

Skellefteå - *Whirling* may feature members from some well-known death metal bands, but here they explore quite different musical aeons. This band play avantgard-ish, quite progressive and experimental and even psychedelic dark metal, a bit like mixing **LIK** and **Joy Division** with mixed clean (quite avant-garde style) vocals and some growl/screech. Not sure how this will go down in BM circuits. Pär Gustafsson (**Bergraven, Nex**) is also session singer (growl) on the album. Marklund is also in **LIK, Sorgeldom** and **Kaos Sacramentum**, while Johdet (aka Jodöden) is also in **Sorgeldom** and Pettersson in **Lönndom, LIK, Armagedda, Leviathan** and **De Arma**.

2010 ■ FACELESS PHENOMENA ....CDd   Eisenwald Tonschmeide ....EISEN 046

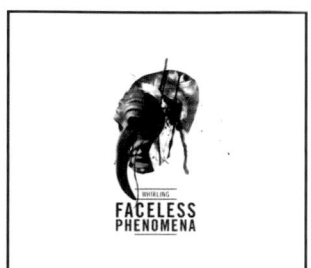

2010 CDd - EISEN 046

WHITE

Bo Anders Holm: v/g, Göran Prahl: b, Göran Olsson: d

Malmö - Formed in the late sixties by Bo Anders. Prahl replaced Ralf Jibert in 1978. This is actually a true late seventies gem. At times it reminds me of *Wishbone Ash*, complex and varied hard rock with the emphasis on great riffs. You can still find it at a fair price, so don't hesitate. Get it while you can. The album was actually recorded in three languages, Swedish, Danish and English. However only the Swedish emerged on record. A live show was also recorded for the Swedish national radio. In 1979, after the album was recorded, Göran Olsson was replaced by 15 year old Tomas Grün. The band split in 1981. Prahl and Olsson later played together in several bands in a more progressive and jazzy vein. Olsson also recorded with the band *Mobile* and rock 'n roller *Kal P. Dal*. Olsson later resurfaced in psychedelic band *Drahk von Trip*.

1979 LP - 2379 155

1979 ■ I DENNA SAMLING ....LP   Polydor...2379 155 $

WHITE CAT

Magnus Hay: v, Mikael Jansson (now Åsberg): g,
Tony Topp: b/k, Martin Larsson: d

Vänersborg - Formed in 1986, split in 1989. Great melodic metal with quite funky bass playing and decent vocals. The band entered a bandstand and ended up on second place. *White Cat* used to play in long white coats with the logo on their backs, and one witty presenter announced the band as aids doctors…

1989 ■ With You/Bet Your Life ....7"   CUF ....CUF 011
        500 copies.

1989 7" - CUF 011

WHITE LINE

Anders "Randy Wiz" Hedberg: v, Stephen Z Svensson: g,
Peter "Pee" Carlhed: b, Magnus "C.M." Odéen: d

Västerås - The band existed between 1984 and 1987. Quite OK melodic metal with prominent guitars, mid-league vocals and the occasional keyboard. In the same musical territory as UK-band *Stampede*. Judging from cover, the guitarist seems kinda feminine. Singer Anders later joined Christian hard rockers *Revelation*.

1984 ■ Wiped Out/Running/Too Fast (For Love) ....7"   Studio 84..S-8402
        1000 copies.

1984 7" - S-8402

WHITE NIGHT

Magnus Nordlund: v, Micke Larsson: g, Håkan Eriksson: b, Stefan Larsson: d

Luleå - Formed in 1985, by Magnus and Micke, as *Gin Fizz*. When, at a bandstand, someone presented them as "Gin Fis" (gin fart), they changed their name. A very good band, not in the heavy AOR-category but still not too slick or soft. Great vocals and some really good songs.

1993 ■ I CAN SEE YOU ....CD   Rebel ....RRCD 9301

1993 CD - RRCD 9301

WHITE SILVER

Henrik Hagedorn: v, Jocke Ludvigsson: g, Issel: b, Patrik Douglas: d

Göteborg - Modern melodic mall metal in the vein of *Nickleback*, *Hoobastank* etc. High-class, but quite run-of-the-mill stuff without any personality.

2005 ■	At Last We Burn	MCDd 4tr	Atenzia	ATZ 02041
	Tracks: In Brief/GET UP!/Guitar Face/Siren Song			

2005 MCDd - ATZ 02041

WHITENESS

Henrik Gustavsson: v, Erik Johansson: g, Patrik Karlsson: k,
Magnus Östlund: b, Peter Gustafsson: d

Hjo - Good melodic hard rock with nice keyboards. In the same vein as early *Treat*. Really good production. The B-side is a typical metal-ballad with strong *Europe* influences. Slightly "Swedish" vocals.

1988 ■	Once Upon A Time/Island In A Forgotten Sea	7"	BABA	BABA 001

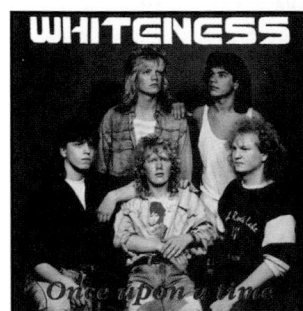

1988 7" - BABA 001

WHO'S NEXT

Conny Lönn: v, Jörgen Nilsson: g, Mats Gustavsson: k,
Thomas Karlsson: b, Jan Pettersson: d

Halmstad - AOR in the vein of early *Yale Bate* or *Treat* with prominent keyboards. Good vocal capacity also quite close to *Yale Bate*'s Alis Magnum. High quality on the instrumental side as well, but unfortunately the sound is a bit too thin. Probably the only Swedish hard rock 7" ever released on the dubious Büms label. Conny sings on the *Side By Side* project recording, where Jörgen also adds a guitar solo.

1989 ■	Crazy Nights/Fool	7"	Büms	S 90116
1990 □	WHAT'S BEYOND	LP	Büms	141 23

1989 7" - S 90116

WHYTE ASH

Mikael Monks: v, Henry Pyykkö: g, Andreas Eriksson: g,
Jimmy Thell: b, Mattias Borg: d

Örebro - *Whyte Ash* were formed in January 2008 by former *Burning Saviours* members Monks and Pyykkö and former *Grand Frontiers* members Thell, Eriksson and Isak Ahlman. Leaving their former retro rock and moving into a classic heavy metal territory, they formed *Whyte Ash*. In February 2008 they recorded their first three-track demo and was soon picked up by Transubstans sub-label Denomination Records. In 2009, before the album, Ahlman was replaced by Borg (ex-*2 Ton Predator* and *Manifest*). *Whyte Ash* plays high-class classic heavy metal in the vein of bands like *Wolf*, *Accept* and *Primal Fear*. Good stuff.

2010 ■	I WILL REMAIN	CD	Denomination Records	DEN 001

2010 CD - DEN 001

WIGELIUS

Anders Wigelius: v, Jake Svensson: g, Chris Pettersson: b, Erik Wigelius: d

Karlstad - In 2011 singer Anders was in the Swedish True Talent show, where he qualified doing a *Journye*'s *Don't Stop Believing*. If that's your bag, Reinventions is a safe buy. High quality commercial AOR in the same style as *Bad Habit*, *H.E.A.T*, *Houston* etc. Erik is ex-*Platitude*.

2012 ■	R3INV3NT1ONS	CD	Frontiers	FR CD 561
2012 □	R3INV3NT1ONS	CD	Icarus Music (Argentina)	ICARUS 993

WILD BUNCH, (THE)

Jorma "Joe" Linna: g, Inge "Uncle Handsome" Norlin: b/v, Mikael "Mike Tall" Talvitie: d

Hallstahammar - Formed by former punksters Elofsson, guitarist Jorma and Mikael Talvitie. Linna, previously with the band *FKM* (aka *Få Kända Män*), while Talvitie recorded a single with pop/rockers *Skymning*. The A-side of the debut single is traditional *Status Quo* boogie, while the B-side is more towards the *Georgia Satellites* straightforward hard rock & roll. Nothing spectacular. The first album follows in the same tradition, like a mix of the two aforementioned bands. On the first LP guitarist Linna by Hans "Haze Gladys" Elofsson was out, Norlin had switched from bass to guitar and bassist Mats "Mädz" Norlin had been added to the line-up. The final line-up, before they split, featured Inge, Hasse, Mats and drummer Johan Karlsson.

1990 LP - 2453

2012 CD - FR CD 561

1986 □	Runaway/Bad Boys	7"	Alpha	ONESIN 025
1988 □	DON'T STOP THE PARTY	LP	private	WBLP 01
1990 ■	CITY DUMP ROCK 'N ROLL	LP	UNI	2453
1993 □	ELVIS HAS LEFT THE BUILDING	CD	private	WBCD 003

WILD CAT SLEEZY
Fredrik Hansson: v/g, Jonas Holst: g, Niklas Lindberg: b, Richard Evén: d

Täby/Stockholm - Young, straighforward, sleaze-tainted metal-band of average quality. The recording of the single the band won in the Week Of Rock '97 competition. The drums on the single were handled by Oscar Razl Hagberg. The singles and album were produced by Micke Moberg.

1998	■	Unborn Son/Warrior/On Clouds	MCD 3tr	Mimo Sound	MI-MO CDS003
2001	□	Happy When I'm Drinking	CDS 1tr	private	-
		One track promo-single.			
2001	□	HAPPY WHEN I'M DRINKING	CD	Mimo Sound	MIMO-CDR-002

1998 MCD - MI-MO CDS003

WILD ONE
Per Sahlberg: v/g, Patrik Belgrave: g, Christo Svahn: b, Marko Nuutinen: d

Borås - A young band with great potential. The album at times suffers from bad production, it's however quite good for being a product of Büms (in the vein of *Dokken*). Patrik, who was in the finale of the 1992 Guitar Heros competition, also has a solo killer-track on the compilation-CD *Guitar Heroes Of Sweden Part 2*.

1991	□	WILD ONE	CD	Büms	CD 30123

WILDBORN
Bo Thörnhult: v/k, Janne Sjödin: g, Peter Carlberg: g/k,
Björn Persson: b, Magnus Dahlquist: d

Gävle - The band was formed in the late seventies as *Marcus Brutus Band*, where Thörnhult handled the drums. *Wildborn* plays very commercial AOR. The band later changed their name to *Bigfoot*, but with new singer Robert Steen and unfortunately only as a cover band. The first release was a good solid melodic metal effort, while the second is very commercial poppy hard rock in the vein of *Snowstorm*.

1985	■	I Wonder/You Ain't Foolin' Me	7"	private	WAP 851
1986	□	Sommarflickor/You Don't Want Me	7"	Platina	PL 16

1985 7" - WAP 851

WILDMARKEN
Janne Åhman: v, Tomas Jansson: g, Hans Forslund: g,
Lars Byström: b, Sven-Åke Westman: d

Sollefteå - *Wildmarken* (the wilderness) are a good solid mid-heavy hard rock band, somewhere in between *Motvind* and *Neon Rose*. The sound was quite undramatic, but still heavy. Both albums are great. Check out the track *Vad Vill Dom* from the second album, a killer. The vocals are in Swedish. Janne, Tomas and Lars recorded a single with the band *Circus* in 1980, in a more commercial vein. Lars also appeared in *Neon Rose* and *Dave And The Mistakes*, and Janne in *Stolt*. *Wildmarken* reunited in 2005. The albums are slated to be reissued by EMI.

1976	□	WILDMARKEN	LP	EMI	4E 062-35312
1977	■	OCH NU PÅ SJUTTIOTALET	LP	EMI	7C 062-35485

1977 LP - 7C 062-35485

WILDNESS
Johan Hagström: g/v, Johan Karlsson: g, Jonas Nordblom: k/g,
Mikael Olsson: g, Ulf Hammarlund: d

Färgelanda - A young classic NWoBHM style band (14-15 year olds) with high ambitions. The track *Quasimodo*, which showed a great improvement, is found on the *Färgelanda spelar och sjunger* (1988 OMIC) compilation. Hammarlund was later found in *Fuelhead*.

1987	■	Dreams/Dollburner	7"	private	SO-1

1987 7" - SO-1

WILHELMSSON, DAVID
See Rock, Dave

WINDWALKER
Per Sandgren: g/b/v, Daniel Bryntse: v/d/g/b/k

Gävle - Formed in 1994. Death-ish metal with elements of traditional hard rock and even grunge. Per and Daniel are also found in doom bands *Forlorn* and *Isole*. Bryntse has also played with *Ereb Altor, Withered Beauty, Sorcery, Theory In Practice, Nightchant, Morannon* and *Februari 93*. The band also recorded the demo *Seeker* in 1995.

1997	■	DANCE OF THE ELVES	CD	Voices Of Death	VODCD 002

1997 CD - VODCD 002

WINTERLONG

Thorbjörn Englund: g/b

Kalix - Winterlong were formed in 1998 by guitarist Thorbjörn Englund. Shredding guitarist, tight outfit, good vocals. Lars Eric Mattsson (who runs Lion Music) guests on a few tracks on the debut. The band featured Englund on guitar, plus singer/guitarist Hussni Mörsare (*Viperine, Raubtier*), bassist Erik Tomberg and drummer Toni Erkkilä (ex-*Star Queen*). After the album Thorbjörn fired the entire band, who all went on to form the band *Viperine*. Englund now used singer Mikael Holm, keyboardist Mistheria, drummers Anders Johansson (*HammerFall* etc) and Andreas Lill. On the third, self-titled release Holm handled the vocals, Peter Uvén played bass and Leif Eriksson sat behind the drums. Payre Kankanranta/Hulkoff (*Raubtier*) guests on guitar and Misteriah on keyboards. *Longing For Winter* is a best of featuring four new tracks. *Winterlong* play melodic power metal with a neoclassical touch and great guitar work from Englund. However the production is at times a bit thin and lacks power.

2001 CD - LMC 2104 2

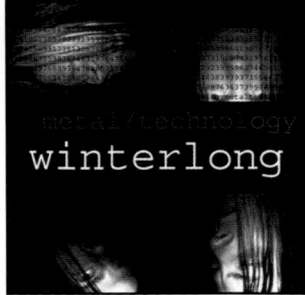

2005 CD - LMC 161

2001 ■	VALLEY OF THE LOST	CD	Lion Music	LMC 2104 2
2001 □	VALLEY OF THE LOST	CD	Fono (Russia)	FO112CD
2002 □	VALLEY OF THE LOST	CD	King Records (Japan)	KICP 858
	Different artwork.			
2003 □	THE SECOND COMING	CD	Lion Music	LMC 075
2004 □	WINTERLONG	CD	Lion Music	LMC 126
2005 ■	METAL/TECHNOLOGY	CD	Lion Music	LMC 161
2008 □	LONGING FOR WINTER	CD	Lion Music	LMC 236

WISDOM CALL

Christian Liljegren: v, Stefan Olsson: g, Fredrik Åberg: g,
Per Hallman: k, Andreas Olsson (now Passmark): b, Andreas Johansson: d

Stockholm - This is more of a side project launched by *Narnia* singer Christian (ex-*Modest Attraction*, also in *Golden Resurrection, Divine Fire, Audiovison, Flagship*). Melodic heavy metal with a strong Christian message. The album also contains two old *Modest Attraction*-tracks. Andreas Olsson (now Passmark) is/was also found in *Stormwind, Narnia, Royal Hunt, Work Of Art* etc. Johansson is also a member of the latter. In 2002 Christian recorded a solo album with hymns and ballads in Swedish.

2001 CD - CLC 003

2001 ■	WISDOM CALL	CD	C.L. Music&Publishing	CLC 003
2001 □	WISDOM CALL	CD	Massacre	MASCD 0287
2001 □	WISDOM CALL	CD	Art Music Group (Russia)	AMG 020

WIT

Pece Masalkovski: v/g, Peter Broch: b, Johan Helgesson: d

Malmö - Wit was founded in 2004 by Pece together with childhood frined Broch. They drafted drummer Helgesson (*The Drugs, Original Sin, Pete Sandberg's Jade*). *Wit* is an excellent retro-oriented power trio mixing the seventies hard rock with the sixties psychedelica, in the vein of *Graveyard, Witchcraft* or US band *Rival Sons*. A great band!

2006 MCD - DANGCD 002

2006 ■	Wit	MCD 6tr	Dang-A-Lang Music	DANGCD 002
	Tracks: Rebel Girl/Tippy Toe Dance/Shake It/Demonic/A Little Love/Breakout			

WITCHCRAFT

Magnus Pelander: v/g, Mats Arnesen: b, Fredrik Jansson: d

Örebro - When the band *Norrsken* fell apart, Magnus decided to do a tribute-single to his idols Bobby Liebling (*Pentagram*) and Roky Erickson. He gathered some friends just for the recording, but it all evolved into a band. The line-up on the first recording were, besides Magnus, guitarist John Hoyles, bassist Ola Henriksson and his brother, drummer Jens Henriksson. The two latter are also found in *Great Mammoth*. Musically the band is very close to early seventies *Pentagram, Blue Cheer* etc. When listening to the recording, both sound and musically it's very hard to imagine it was recorded in 2001. It sound exactly like an old seventies four-track recording, in a positive way. A must for fans of the aforementioned. In 2004 The band was picked up by UK label Rise Above and the debut was released. The line-up now featured Pelander, Hoyles, Henriksson and drummer Jonas Arnesén. On the follow-up, *Firewood*, there is a hidden track after the last track, a cover of *Pentagram*'s *When The Screams Come*. On *The Alchemist* drummer Arnesén had been replaced by Fredrik Jansson (*Abramis Brama, Count Raven*). In 2010 Pelander released a solo EP through Svart Records, while the Henriksson brothers and Hoyles have released an EP and aln album with the band *Troubled Horse*. Hoyles is also in the band *Spiders*, while Jens is also in *The Wait*.

Website: www.witchcrafthome.com

Retro rock sorcerers summoning the force

2002	■	No Angel Or Demon/You Bury Your Head	7"	Primitive Art	PAR 026	$
		First 500 copies pressed in blue vinyl and comes with free post card.				
2004	□	WITCHCRAFT	CD	Rise Above	RISECD 047	
2004	□	WITCHCRAFT	LP	Rise Above	RISELP 047	
2004	□	WITCHCRAFT	CD	The Music Cartel (USA)	TMC 80	
2005	□	WITCHCRAFT	LP PD	Rise Above	RISEPLP 047	
		500 copies.				
2005	○	Chylde Of Fire (split)	7"	Rise Above	RISE7 64	
		500 copies. No picture sleeve. Split with Circulus.				
2005	□	FIREWOOD	CD	Rise Above	RISECD 062	
2005	□	WITCHCRAFT	CD	Leafhound Records (Japan)	LHR 035	
		Bonus: Yes I Do				
2005	□	FIREWOOD	CD	Leafhound Records (Japan)	LHR-036	
		Bonus: The Invincible				
2005	□	FIREWOOD	LPg	Rise Above	RISELP 062	
		Bonus: The Invincible. 500 gold + 500 black vinyl.				
2006	□	FIREWOOD	CD	Candlelight (USA)	CDL0317CD	
2007	□	THE ALCHEMIST	CDd	Rise Above	RISECD 103	
2007	□	THE ALCHEMIST	LP	Rise Above	RISELP 103	$$
		1st press: 25 blue, 100 clear, 500 magnolia, 400 magnolia sparkle, 500 black. 2nd press: 500 red. 3rd press: 300 black sparkle, 300 green, 300 purple. 4th press: 400 neon orange, 400 yellow.				
2007	□	THE ALCHEMIST	CD	Candlelight (USA)	CDL0387CD	
2007	□	THE ALCHEMIST	CD	Leafhound Records (Japan)	LHR-028	
		Bonus: Sweet Honey Pie (Roky Ericson cover)				
2008	■	If Crimson Was A Colour/I Know You Killed Someone	7"	Rise Above	RISE7 87	
		First press: 225 black, 525 clear, 336 red. Second press: 100 blue, 200 green, 200 brown.				
2007	□	The Sword/Witchcraft (split)	MLP 5tr	Kemado Records	KEM 058	
		Split with The Swods. Tracks: You Bury Your Head/Queen Of Bees/Sorrow Evoker. 500 black, 1000 purple marble, 1000 green marble vinyl.				
2012	□	WITCHCRAFT	2LPg + 7"	Rise Above	RISELP 154	
		Bonus: Yes I Do (Pentagram cover). 400 copies with 7" in white and 400 in black, 100 in clear and 400 in silver vinyl.				
2012	□	FIREWOOD	LPg +7"	Rise Above	RISELP 155	
		Bonus: The Invisible/When The Screams Come (Pentagram cover). 400 copies with 7" in white and 400 in black, 100 in clear and 400 in bronze vinyl.				
2012	□	THE ALCHEMIST	LP	Rise Above	RISELP 156	
		100 clear, 400 red marble, 400 purple and 400 black vinyl.				
2012	□	WITCHCRAFT	CD	Metal Blade (USA)	3984-15105-2	
2012	□	FIREWOOD	CD	Metal Blade (USA)	3984-15106-2	
		Hidden bonys track: When The Screams Come				
2012	■	LEGEND	2LPg	Nuclear Blast	NB 2956-1	
		Poster. Black vinyl, 250 clear and 150 blue vinyl. Bonus: By Your Definition				
2012	□	LEGEND	CDd	Nuclear Blast	NB 2956-2	
		Bonus: By Your Definition				
2012	□	LEGEND	CD	Icarus (Argentina)	ICARUS 1016	
2012	□	LEGEND	CDd	Scarecrow (Mexico)	SR 07808	

2002 7" - PAR 026

2008 7" - RISE7 87

2012 2LPg - NB 2956-1

WITCHERY

Erik "Legion" Hagstedt: v, Richard "Rille Corpse" Rimfält: g, Patrik Jensen: g, Charles Petter "Sharlee D'Angelo" Andreasson: b, Martin Axenrot: d

Göteborg - It all began in April 1997, when **Satanic Slaughter** was about to record in Göteborg and singer Ztephan Dark fired the rest of the band. The band, featuring Tony "Toxine" Kampner (on guitar), Micke, Patrik and Richard, continued without Mr Dark and formed **Witchery**. They found Sharlee and the band was complete. The boys have previously been spotted in **Seance** (Micke, Patrik, Richard, Tony), **Dismember/Infernal** (Richard, Tony), **The Haunted** (Patrik) and **Mercyful Fate/Illwill/Dismember** (Sharlee). The debut saw influences from metal, thrash and a slight touch of death. On the third album drummer Micke "Mique" Pettersson was replaced by Martin Axenrot (**Nifelheim, Opeth, Bloodbath**). *Witchburner* contains covers of bands like **W.A.S.P, Accept, Judas Priest** and **Black Sabbath**. Hank Shermann (**Mercyful Fate, Zoser Mez, Gutrix**) guests on *Symphony For The Devil*. Hank, as well as Marcus Sunesson also adds guitars on *Don't Fear The Reaper*. On *Witchkrieg* singer Tony "Toxine" Kampner had been replaced by Erik "Legion" Hagstedt (**Marduk, Ophthalamia, Devian**). The album also features guest spots from prominent musicians such as **Slayer**'s Kerry King, Gary Holt and Lee Altus from **Exodus/Heathen**, Jim Durkin from **Dark Angel** and Hank Sherman. **Witchery** play top-notch thrashy death metal a bit similar to **Arch Enemy** meets **The Haunted** in their prime.

1998 CD - NR 029

1999 MCD - NR 034

1999 CDd - NR 041-2

1998	■	RESTLESS & DEAD	CD	Necropolis	NR 029
1998	□	RESTLESS & DEAD	LP	Necropolis	NR 029 LP
1998	□	RESTLESS & DEAD	CD	Toy's Factory (Japan)	TFCK-87167
		Bonus: The Howling/Into The Catacombs/Breath Of Serpent That Rules The Cold World				
1999	■	Witchburner	MCDd 7tr	Necropolis	NR 034
		Tracks: Fast As A Shark (Accept)/I Wanna Be Somebody (W.A.S.P)/Riding On The Wind (Judas Priest)/Neon Knights (Black Sabbath)/The Howling/The Executioner/Witchburner				

1999	☐	Witchburner	MLP 7tr PD	Merciless Records	MRSRLP 012
1999	■	DEAD, HOT AND READY	CDd	Necropolis	NR 041-2
1999	☐	DEAD, HOT AND READY	LP	Merciless Records	MRSRLP 014
		300 blue + 700 black vinyl.			
1999	☐	DEAD, HOT AND READY	CD	Toy's Factory (Japan)	TFCK-87202
		The Witchburner MCD tracks as bonus.			
2001	☐	SYMPHONY FOR THE DEVIL	CD	Necropolis (USA)	NR 066-2
2001	☐	SYMPHONY FOR THE DEVIL	CD	Music For Nations	CDMFN 273
2001	☐	SYMPHONY FOR THE DEVIL	LP	Music For Nations	MFN 273
2001	☐	SYMPHONY FOR THE DEVIL	CD	Toy's Factory (Jap)	TFCK 87249
		Bonus: Enshrined/The One Within			
2006	☐	DON'T FEAR THE REAPER	CD	Century Media	77505-2
2006	☐	DON'T FEAR THE REAPER	CD	Century Media (USA)	8205-2
		Bonus: Legion Of Hades			
2006	☐	DON'T FEAR THE REAPER	CD	Encore Records (Brazil)	MM 001
2006	☐	DON'T FEAR THE REAPER	CD	Icarus Music (Argentina)	ICARUS 213
2010	■	WITCHKRIEG	LP	Century Media	998015-1
		150 brown marbled + 1400 black vinyl.			
2010	☐	WITCHKRIEG	CD	Trooper (Japan)	XNTE-00016
		Bonus: Cloak & Dagger/Hung Drawn And Quatered			
2010	☐	WITCHKRIEG	CDd	Century Media	998015-8
		Bonus: Hung Drawn And Quatered			
2011	☐	WITCHKRIEG	CD	Mazzar (Russia)	MZR CD 458
2011	■	DON'T FEAR THE REAPER	LP	Night Of The Vinyl Dead	Night 108
		350 hand numbered copies. Orange vinyl in clear plastic sleeve.			

2010 LP - 998015-1

2011 LP - Night 108

WITCHGRAVE

Jocke Norberg: v/g/b, Gabriel "Gabbe" Forslund: g, Tobbe Ander: g, Sven Nilsson: d

Växjö - It all started in 2008, when Jocke wrote some songs. He invited Sven to join and they recorded four tracks, where Gabbe laid down a guest solo. He was later offered to join the band. All three had previously played together in the band Eviscerated, and Gabbe and Sven are also members of thrash band *Antichrist*. The band has been described as sounding like *Mercyful Fate* with Cronos on vocals, which I feel is not too far from the truth. After the first single Ander (*Leukemia, Slingblade, Jigsore Terror*) was added to the line-up.

2009	■	The Devil's Night	MLP 4tr	High Roller Records	HRR 087
		Tracks: The Devil's Night/Eyes Of The Undead/Satanic Slut/Beg For Mercy. 500 copies.			
2013	☐	WITCHGRAVE	LP	High Roller Records	HRR 284
		500 copies. Poster.			
2013	☐	WITCHGRAVE	CD	High Roller Records	HRR 284 CD

2009 MLP - HRR 087

WITHERED BEAUTY

Daniel Bryntse: v/g/d, Magnus Björk: g/v, Tobias Björklund: b/v

Gävle - Formed in 1993 by Magnus and Daniel. Recorded their first demo *Screams From The Forest* in 1994 and *Through The Silent Skies* the year after. Daniel was also part of *Theory In Practice* for a short period in 1998. He recorded one album with *Windwalker* in 1997, One with folk-rockers *February 93* and is still found in doomsters *Forlorn*, who had one track on the compilation *Absolute Helges 1*. Magnus is now in pop-band *Holiday The Maggie*. The band has its base in Gävle, but the members are spread over a 400 kilometre area. The band is also featured on the compilations *Death Is Just The Beginning Vol IV* (Track: *Immortality Is Mine*). After the album the band was dropped from Nuclear Blast and Magnus left. He was soon replaced by William Blackmon (*Gadget*). The band was also completed with drummer Jonas Lindström. The new line-up recorded the song *The Fairest One* for the compilation *The Voices Of Death 4*.

1998	■	WITHERED BEAUTY	CD	Nuclear Blast	NB 316-2
1998	☐	WITHERED BEAUTY	CD	Nuclear Blast America	NBA 6316-2
2008	☐	WITHERED BEAUTY	CDd	Metal Mind	MASS CD 1234 DG
		2000 copies.			

1998 CD - NB 316-2

WITHERSHIN

Georg "Nine": v, Gustav "Hizon" Totenlieb: g, Andreas "Natt" Fröberg: g,
Oskar "Hex" Tornborg: b, Oskar "Zek" Jakobsson: d

Stockholm - *Withershin* (and old Celtic word meaning to go counter clockwise against time) were formed in 2006. After a year they recorded the CD-R demo *Chaos Discipline* after which singer Joakim Trana (*Rozenhill*) was replaced by Nine. *Withershin* plays old school influenced, yet technical and well-produced black metal, at times similar to early *Dissection* meets *Watain* and with a touch of bands like *Belphegor*, but also old *Bathory* in terms of energy.

2008	■	ASHEN BANNERS	CD	Canonical Hours	CH 002
2011	☐	The Hungering Void	10" 3tr	Canonical Hours	CHLP 002
		Tracks: Wherein I Exalt/The Hungering Void/Crossing The Threshold			

2008 CD - CH 002

WITHIN REACH

Denny Axelsson: v, Björn Hahne: g, Robin Sundkvist: g,
Magnus Brolin: b, Jocke Eriksson: d

Arboga - Formed in 95/96 by the remains of hardcore band *Lifeless Image* and *Passage 4*. *Within Reach* started out as a pure, old-school hardcore band, influenced by bands like *Gorilla Bisquits*, *7 Seconds*, *Judge* etc. Some of the albums are recorded by Pelle Saether at Underground. Robin was added to the line-up in 1998. On *Fall From Grace*, produced by Mathias (*Millencollin*) and Mieszko Talarczyk (*Nasum*) the band adopted a heavier sound, more akin to *Entombed*. The band can also be found on compilations such as *This Is Bad Taste Vol 3, Stronger Than Ever, "Cheap Shots Vol 3, Still Screaming* (all on Burning Heart), *Cheap Shots America* (Epitaph), *Area 51* (I Scream/Victory), *Close Up* (2000 Close Up). Before *Complaints Ignored*, guitarist Jonas Lewén joined the band and Denny replaced Magnus Thörnkvist. Denny has also been in *Blinded Colony*, *The Bereaved* and *Maramon*.

1997 CD - JABSCO 004

1999 MCD - JABSCO 020

Year		Title	Format	Label	Cat. No.
1996	☐	The Light Will Return	MCD 5tr	1:st Unit	First: 1
		Tracks: Within Reach/Not Just Words/Arise/Break Up(Break Free)/The Fire			
1996	☐	Something's Not Right	MCD 8tr	Sidekicks/Burning Heart	JABSCO 002
		Tracks: Friend?/Time's Up/Sick Scene/Time To Unite/Promises/Hear My Words/What Will It Take/Alternatives			
1997	■	STRENGTH THROUGH DIVERSITY	CD	Sidekicks/Burning Heart	JABSCO 004
1999	■	Reconsider/Reconstruct	MCD 7tr	Sidekicks/Burning Heart	JABSCO 020
		Tracks: Reconsider-Reconstruct/My Intentions/For Me/Aim/Enemy/What's Left Now?/Vultures			
2000	☐	1125/WITHIN REACH (split)	7"	Shing Records (Poland)	- -
		Split with 1125. Tracks: Feel The Beat/Bullyparade/Lexicon Devil			
2000	☐	FALL FROM GRACE	CD	Bad Taste	BTR 37 CD
2001	■	COMPLAINTS IGNORED	CD	Bad Taste	BTR 52 CD

2001 CD - BTR 52 CD

WITHIN Y

Andreas Solveström: v, Mikael Nordin: g, Niknam Moslehi: g,
Jonas Larsson: b, Erik Hagström: d

Göteborg - *Within Y* were formed in 2002 by singer Solveström (*Amaranthe, Evildoer*) and guitarists Niklas Almén and Mikael Nordin. They drafted drummer Thim Blom (*Gardenian*) and bassist Mattias Wänerstam and recorded their first demo *Feeble And Weak* the same year. The debut album saw the light in 2004. Another demo was recorded in 2005 and the band was soon picked up by Gain (*Hardcore Superstar, Mustasch* etc), who released their second album *Portraying Dead Dreams*. On this album Almén had been replaced by Niknam Moslehi. *Within Y* play tight, powerful and heavy, yet quite melodic death metal similar to *Soilwork*, *The Haunted* and early *Machine Head*. On *The Cult* bassist Wänerstam had been replaced by Jonas Larsson and drummer Blom by Erik Hagström.

2003 CD - KARMA 020

2011 CD - GPCD 85

Year		Title	Format	Label	Cat. No.
2003	■	EXTENDED MENTAL DIMENSIONS	CD	Karmageddon	KARMA 020
2006	☐	PORTRAYING DEAD DREAMS	CD	Gain Productions	GPCD 30
2009	☐	THE CULT	CD	Gain Productions	GPCD 49
2011	■	SILENCE CONQUERS	CD	Gain Productions	GPCD 85

WITHOUT GRIEF

Jonas Granvik: v, Daniel Thide: g, Tobias Ols: g, Björn Tauman: b, Patrik Johansson: d

Stockholm - Melodic death with the Göteborg-touch, similar to early *Dark Tranquillity*. After the first album guitarist Daniel replaced Nicklas Lindh and Björn replaced bass player Ola Berg. Drummer Patrik was later found in *Stormwind* and now plays with *Yngwie Malmsteen*.

Year		Title	Format	Label	Cat. No.
1998	■	DEFLOWER	CD	Serious Entertainment	SE 008 CD
1999	■	ABSORBING THE ASHES	CD	Serious Entertainment	SE 018 CD
1999	☐	ABSORBING THE ASHES	CD	Soundholic (Japan)	SHCD1 0027
		Bonus: Iron Fist (Motörhead cover)			

1998 CD - SE 008 CD

WIZ

Freddy Persson: v, Martin Karlsson: g, Jake Fredén: g,
Johan Weicht: b, Stefan Lindquist: d

Göteborg - It all started back in 1996 when Weicht and Lindquist entered a bandstand with their band *Children Of The Grave*. Guitarist Magnus Hansson was in a rival band, but Weicht and Hansson decided to leave their respective bands to form a new unit. Lindquist was drafted and they also asked *Vapid* guitarist Fredén to join. *Wiz* was formed. They finally found singer Persson (*Sten & Stalin*). Hansson however left the band. In 1998 Persson and Fredén formed the band *Nostradameus*, just to enter a competition and were suddenly signed by AFM Records. In 1999 *Wiz* recorded a new demo after which Lindquist left, to be replaced by Fredrik "Figge" Johansson, who left after two rehearsals and Lindquist was convinced to return. They recorded

1999 CD - SE 018 CD

another demo in the fall of 1999, after which guitarist Karlsson joined. As *Nostradameus* took off the band was temporarily put on hold. About a year later a new demo was recorded, followed by two more during 2002-2003 before the band was picked up by Spanish label Arise. *Wiz* style is quite different from *Nostradameus*, heavier and with a less commercial sound and style, more akin to bands like *Tad Morose*.

2004 ■	SHATTERED-MIND-THERAPY	CD	Arise	ARISE 052	
2004 □	SHATTERED-MIND-THERAPY	CD	Victor (Japan)	VICP-62628	

Bonus: Labyrinth/The Call

2004 CD - ARISE 052

WIZZ
**Göran "George King" Kunstberg: b/v, Mikael Gillstedt: g,
Robert "Kee" Klavinger: k, Janne Pihl: b, Tomas "Collins" Gustavsson: d**

Eskilstuna - A good solid hard rock band in the vein of *Deep Purple*. Well worth looking for. After the album Bernt Ek (*Bedlam, Station, Grace, Wildliw*) joined the band on vocals, but after a year it fell apart. Göran was ex-*Treasure* and later joined *King & Rozz*, later found in the folkish *Urban Turban*, *Dromba* and *Icon X*. He is now also working as a bagpipe tutor (!).

1984 ■	CRAZY GAMES	LP	Fingerprint	FINGLP 004	
1993 □	CRAZY GAMES (split)	CD	Hot Metal	SPLIT 012	

Split with Saigon, both albums on one disc.

1984 LP - FINGLP 004

WIZZARD
**Matti Norlin: v/g, Hans-Erik Jansson: g, Mikael Rönnberg: k,
Eskil Rönnberg: b, Michael Hallberg: d**

Hoting - Fast 80s heavy metal with double-bass-drum work, but still with a touch of melody. The B-side is an attempt to make a radio-oriented song. OK stuff. Good vocals and good musicians. They won several local band battles. Matti was only 13 years old at the time. He is today found in the excellent band *Badge* and has recorded with wacky duo *Matti & Haake* and also released a blues-CD entitled *Pre-War Blues*, under his own name. The band changed their name to *Charity* and released another 7" the year after.

1986 ■	Ninya Warriors/Suzie	7"	Wizzard Music	WIZ S 01	$$

1986 7" - WIZ S 01

WIZZY BLAZE
**Anders "John Royce" Jönsson: v, Rickard "Rick Martins" Mårtensson: g,
Erik "Volin" Briselius: b, Jörgen "Stanley" Olsson: d**

Malmö - Great melodic metal/hard rock in the vein of *Praying Mantis*. Nice guitar harmonies. Check it out! They started out in 1983 under the name *Syrinx* and changed their name to *Wizzy Blaze* in 1985. Anders was later bass player in *Aces High*, Erik later joined *Syron Vanes* and Stanley was found in *Nasty Idols*/*Machinegun Kelly*. At one time *Nasty Idols* bass player Dick Qwarforth was in the band.

1987 ●	So Many Days/Too Far To Reach	7"	private (promo)	WIB 0001

1987 7" - WIB 0001

WOLF
**Niklas Stålvind (aka Olsson): v/g, Johannes "Axeman" Losbäck: g,
Anders Modd: b, Richard Holmgren: d**

Örebro - Formed in 1995, initially called *Wolverine* (not to be confused with the Swedish namesakes). The band recorded two demos in 1995 and 1996. On the first album the line-up featured singer/guitarist Niklas Olsson (later Stålvind), bassist Mikael Goding and drummer Daniel Bergkvist. Great powerful 80s-influenced heavy metal with a 90s touch. The cover on the debut album was made by the famous Swedish artist Hans Arnold, who also made covers for *Spiritual Beggars*, *Plankton* and *ABBA*. It was recorded at Studio Abyss and co-produced by Peter Tägtgren. Guitarist Henrik Johansson is featured on the cover, but he was actually added to the line-up after the recording. In 2001 he was replaced by Johan Bülow (*Fallen Angel*). *Black Wings* has a strong touch of vintage *Iron Maiden*. Great vocals and highly interesting dual guitar work. *Evil Star* features a cover of *Blue Öyster Cult*'s classic *Don't Fear (The Reaper)*. The *Black Flame* saw another change of line-up, now featuring Niklas Olsson (who had changed his name to Stålvind), guitarist Johannes Losbäck (*Power Unit, Decameron, Seventh One*), bassist Goding and new drummer Tobias Kellgren (*Seventh One, Dissection, Decameron, Soulreaper, Satanized, Swordmaster*). On *Ravenous* the line-up had totally changed again seeing Stålvind and Losbäck as the only remaining members, now flanked by drummer Richard Holmgren (*Vanessa, Soulskinner, Haterush, Grand Design*) and bassist Anders Modd (*Tad Morose, Grand Design, Scaar, Apostacy*). The album also features guest spots from Mark Boals and Roy Z. Losbäck has now been replaced by Simon Johansson. The two debut singles on Beast Records in 1999 were just made up stories by the band, and don't even exist.
Website: www.wolf.nu

2000 CD - NFR 43

2001 MCD - NFRCD 52

And they say you shouldn't cry Wolf...

Year		Title	Format	Label	Catalog
2000	■	WOLF	CD	No Fashion	NFR 43
2000	□	WOLF	LP	No Fashion	NFRLP 43
2000	□	WOLF	CD	Prosthetic Records (USA)	10014-2
2001	■	Moonlight	MCD 4tr	No Fashion	NFRCD 52

Tracks: Moonlight (radio edit)/The Parasite/Moonlight (album version)/Electric Raga (previously unreleased)/Moonlight (video)

Year		Title	Format	Label	Catalog
2002	■	A World Bewitched	CDS	No Fashion	NFRCD 55 CDS PROMO
2002	□	Night Stalker/Die By The Sword (Slayer cover)	7"	Rage Of Achilles	ILIAD 030
2002	□	BLACK WINGS	CD	No Fashion	NFR 055
2002	□	BLACK WINGS	LP	No Fashion	NFRLP 055
2002	□	BLACK WINGS	CD	Irond (Russia)	CD 02-242
2004	□	EVIL STAR	CD	No Fashion	NFR 63
2004	□	EVIL STAR	CD	Prosthetic Records (USA)	6561910013-2

Bonus: Die By The Swords (Slayer cover)/I'm Not Afraid Of Life (Ramones cover)

Year		Title	Format	Label	Catalog
2004	□	Wolf's Blood	CDS	No Fashion	NFR 67
2005	□	EVIL STAR	2LPg	Immortal Vinyl Records	IVR 003

Bonus: Déjá Vu/I'm Not Afraid Of Life (Ramones cover). Black/white splatter vinyl. 500 copies.

Year		Title	Format	Label	Catalog
2005	□	EVIL STAR	CD	Massacre Records	MAS CD 424

Bonus: Die By The Swords (Slayer cover)/I'm Not Afraid Of Life (Ramones cover)

Year		Title	Format	Label	Catalog
2005	□	WOLF	CD	Massacre Records	MAS CD 446

Bonus: Electric Raga/Moonlight (radio edit). New artwork.

Year		Title	Format	Label	Catalog
2005	□	BLACK WINGS	CD	Massacre Records	MAS CD 447

Bonus: Moonlight (video). New artwork.

Year		Title	Format	Label	Catalog
2006	■	THE BLACK FLAME	CD	Century Media	77620-2
2006	□	THE BLACK FLAME	CD	Prosthetic Records (USA)	6561910038-2
2007	□	THE BLACK FLAME	LP	Blackcave Records	7290 SE1

500 copies hand-numbered and signed.

Year		Title	Format	Label	Catalog
2009	□	RAVENOUS	CD	Century Media	997844-2
2009	□	RAVENOUS	CD	Century Media (USA)	8544-2
2009	□	RAVENOUS	CD	Soundholic (Japan)	YZSH-1011

Bonus: 6 Steps

Year		Title	Format	Label	Catalog
2009	□	RAVENOUS	CD	Magnum Music (Taiwan)	CM 997844-2
2011	□	LEGIONS OF BASTARDS	CDd	Century Media	998086-8

Bonus: 6 Steps/Method To Your Madness (Metal Church cover)

Year		Title	Format	Label	Catalog
2011	■	LEGIONS OF BASTARDS	CD	Century Media	998086-2
2011	□	LEGIONS OF BASTARDS	LP+CD	Century Media	998086-1

Bonus: 6 Steps/Method To Your Madness (Metal Church cover). Red vinyl.

2002 CDS - NFRCD 55 CDS PROMO

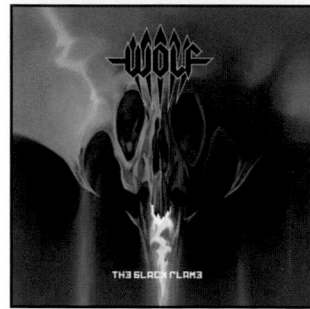

2006 CD - 77620-2

2011 CD - 998086-2

WOLVERINE

**Stefan Zell: v, Mikael Zell: g, Thomas Jansson: b,
Per Henriksson: k, Marcus Losbjer: d/v**

Söderhamn - The band was formed in 1992 under the name *Arachnofobia*. After various line-up changes Stefan and drummer Henrik Johansson formed *Pornographical Harmony*. The band evolved into *Book Of Hours* and later, in 1999, released an album on Record Heaven. In 1995 Stefan and Marcus teamed up with former friend and former *Arachnofobia* colleague Björn Renström and his brother Mikael and *Wolverine* was a fact. They recorded the first demo *Land Of The Midnight Sun*. Björn left and in 1997 he was sadly killed in a car crash. Sami Mäki replaced Björn and they recorded the *North*-demo in 1997. In 1998 they took a break, with Sami leaving and Mikael joining *Book Of Hours*. They however reformed and recorded the song *A Fairytale* for the local compilation *Heden Ceden -98*. Now Mikael left *Book Of Hours* and in 1998 they recorded *A Pleasant Shade Of Grey Part 12* for the *Fates Warning* tribute *Through Different Eyes*. The debut MCD is progressive metal with additional death-ish vocals and the line-up now also featured guitarist Carl-Henrik Landegren. In December 1999 former *Book Of Hours* man Per Broddesson also joined the *Wolverine*-ranks to replace guitarist Carl-Henrik Landegren who decided to leave. The album is killer-prog in the vein of *Evergrey* with clean and very good vocals. On the album Andreas Baglien was added to the line-up and after the recording Stefan decided to concentrate on the vocals and Thomas Jansson came into the ranks. The line-up on *The Window Purpse* featured Stefan Zell on bass and vocals, Mikael Zell and Per Broddesson on guitars, Andreas Baglien on keyboards and Marcus Losbjer on drums. On this album they actually draw quite close to early *Pain Of Salvation*, heavy melancholic prog metal. On the follow-up, *Cold Light Of Monday* new bassist Thomas Jansson let Stefan concentrate on singing. The album features guest spots from people like Urban Breed (*Tad Morose, Bloodbound*), Fredrik Sjöholm, Jamina Jansson and P-O Larsson. This album also showed a new side of the band, much more laid back and almost ambient at times. Not really the band's strongest effort. On *Still* the line-up had again changed, now seeing keyboardist Per Henriksson replacing Andreas Baglien and guitarist Per Broddesson out of the band. The band also picked up speed again on the last two releases. In March 2012 the band announced Mikael Zell was taking a break from the band. He was temporarily replaced by Jonas Jonsson, who played a guest solo on the band's second demo. However in December 2012, the band announced Jonas was a permanent member of the band.

Website: www.wolverine-overdose.com/

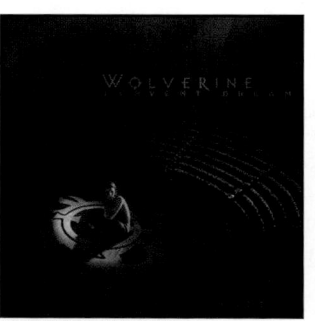

1999 MCD - ZEG 0799

2003 CD - MOSH 908 CD

2001 CD - DVS 005

2006 CD - CANDLE 146 CD

1999 ■	Fervent Deam	MCD 5tr	Zizania Entertainment Group	ZEG 0799

Tracks: Whispers On The Wind/Echoes/More Than Grief/Again?/Last Words

2001 ☐	Fervent Deam	MCD 7tr	Emerald Factory	-

Bonus: Time/Resistance

2001 ■	THE WINDOW PURPOSE	CD	DVS	DVS 005
2003 ■	COLD LIGHT OF MONDAY	CD	Earache	MOSH 908 CD
2005 ☐	THE WINDOW PURPOSE	CD	Earache	MOSH 912 CD

Bonus: Again! New artwork.

2006 ■	STILL	CD	Candlelight	CANDLE 146 CD
2006 ☐	STILL	CD	Candlelight (USA)	CDL 307
2011 ■	COMMUNICATION LOST	CD	Candlelight	CANDLE 328 CD
2011 ☐	COMMUNICATION LOST	CD	Candlelight (USA)	CDL 502

2011 CD - CANDLE 328 CD

WOMBBATH

Tomas Lindfors: v, Håkan Stuvemark: g, Tobbe Holmgren: g,
Richard Lagberg: b, Roger Enstedt: d

Sala - Formed in 1990 under the name *Seizure*, but soon changed it to *Wombbath*. The demo *Brutal Mights* was released in 1991. Thrash with touches of death metal and some more technical passages. Tomas voice could be placed somewhere between traditional hardcore and death metal. Roger Enstedt is a killer drummer, incredibly tight and fast, and was later in *Steel Attack*. After the album singer Tomas Lindfors (*In Thy Dreams*) was replaced by Daniel Samuelsson (*Disgrace, Turning Crosses*). Stuvemark was also in *In Thy Dreams*. The band split in 1995.

1992 ■	Several Shapes /Intro/Corporal Punishment	7" 3tr	Thrash Records/Infest	Thin 001
1993 ☐	INTERNAL CAUSTIC TORMENTS	CD	Thrash Records/Infest	Thin 002
1993 ☐	INTERNAL CAUSTIC TORMENTS	CD	Infest Records/Thrash	CD 852102
1994 ☐	Lavatory	MCD 4tr	Napalm Records	NPR 003

Tracks: Descent Into A Maelstrom/Laughter Through Thousand Winds/Lies After Cries Of Hope/Lavatory Suicide Remains

2009 ☐	INTERNAL CAUSTIC TORMENTS	LP	Letargo Records (Mexico)	LR 001

300 hand-numbered copies on clear vinyl.

2010 ☐	INTERNAL CAUSTIC TORMENTS	CD	Necroharmonic Productions	Sleazy 029

Bonus: Beyond The Gloomy/Brutal Mights/Tales From The Darkside/Unholy Madness/ Intro/Several Shapes/Corporal Punishment/Beyond The Gloomy (unrel version)

1992 7" - Thin 001

WONDERFLOW

Per Ljungberg: v, Nicklas Stenmo: g, Dick Magnusson: b, Max Thornell: g

Växjö - The band was previously known as *Furbowl*, but when singer bass-player Johan Axelsson was replaced by Per and Dick, they changed their name and label. Their MCD shows a band that has come a long way since the *Furbowl* days. High-quality power metal with interesting musical twists, melodic touches and an incredible energy. Great personal vocals by Per, who is part-Egyptian. Should attract fans of anything between *Jethro Tull* to *Black Sabbath*. Check out the awesome title-track, a true killer! A full-length album was supposed to follow, but unfortunately never happened. Thornell later joined *Hearse* and *Satanarchy*.

1996 ■	20th Century Egyptian	MCD 5tr	MNW Zone	MNWCDS 220

Tracks: 20th Century Egyptian/Sleepin´ In The House Of Love/Swervedriver/In God´s Grace/She Calls Me Silence.

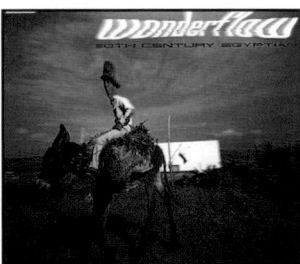

1996 MCD - MNWCDS 220

WONDERLAND

Jens Lundström: v, Roger Björk: g, Pelle Larsson: g,
Jocke Öberg: k, Anders Jansson: b, Mikael Hilmersson: d

Jönköping - *Wonderland* produce high-quality melodic hard rock in the vein of late eighties *Dokken*. Heavy guitars and first-rate vocals. Hilmersson also released an album with the band *Colorblind* in 1995 and Pelle had recorded a solo single under his first name. Unfortunately only one album came out of the band.

1996 ■	IS THIS...	CD	Alfa Records (Japan)	ALCB-3164
1997 ☐	IS THIS...	CD	High Rock	HRR970208

1996 CD - ALCB-3164

WONDERLAND

Klas Ling: v, Per Andersson: g, Bo Karlsson: k,
Joakim Lundberg: b, Joakim Jansson: d

Göteborg - Formed already in the early 80s out of Per's previous band *Stage*, and recorded their first demo in 1984. After a long break they reunited in 1994, but not much happened. Finally in 2008 the band got their shit together and recorded and excellent powerful melodic rocker with a proggy touch.

2008 ■	SEVEN WONDERS	CDd	private	WLD 001

2008 CDd - WLD 001

WONDERLAND DEMENTATION DEPT.

Daniel Palm: v, Fredrik Andersson: g, Christian Lundqvist: b, Niklas Sandell: d

Göteborg - Wonderland Demantation Department were spawned in Göteborg around 2004 aiming to mix hardcore, metal, emocore and sludge. They have actually succeeded blending all these styles into an original brew, at times sounding like a mix of *The Offspring*, *Terrorvision* and *System Of A Down*. Christian was ex-*Belltown*. Early 2005 the debut album was finished. The album features guest vocals from Tony Jelencovich (*Massive Audio Nerve, B-Thong, Transport League* etc). The band followed it up with the seven-track CD-R album *Conquest Of The Last Frontier* in 2007. Drummer Niklas (*Benevolent*) had now been replaced by Anton Broberg.

2005 ■	THE AWKWARD SILENCE	CD	Mind Riot Records	MRR 02

2005 CD - MRR 02

WOOD

Åke Noréen: v, Niklas Kahl: g, Anders Lindén: k, Krister Jonsson: b, Eric Lindstedt: d

Karlskoga - This band really gives you a 70s flashback. *Led Zeppelin* and *Deep Purple* are two bands that really come to mind. Singer Åke (ex-*Jet Airliner*) has his similarities with the almighty Robert Plant. Good stuff. Unfortunately all that came out of this band was one album. Not surprising though, when considering what label they were on... in Sweden that is.

1997 ☐	La La Love You/Sparrow	CDS	Woodworks	WWCDS 101
1997 ■	GRAND ROCK	CD	Epic	EPC 485090 2

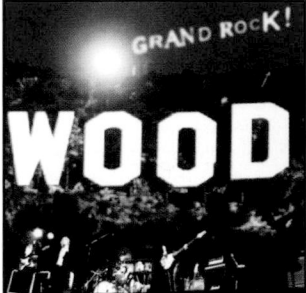

1997 CD - EPC 485090 2

WOODS OF INFINITY

Daniel "Ravenlord" Engberg: v, Andréas "Melkor" Sellstedt: g/b

Umeå - Woods of Infinity were formed in 1999, initially as a duo featuring Ravenlord and Melkor. The first demo, *Skog*, was recorded the same year. It included the song *Worship Up*, later released on the *I-20* EP. The band also featured drummer Bruthor. They recorded two more demos, *Trollhämnd* and *Gaggenau*, before the *I-20* EP was released. In 2001 they released the cassette *Förintelse & Libido* in 1000 copies. In 2003 they were also featured on a three-way split with *Armagedda* and *Total Holocaust*, released by Sombre Records. Ravenlord also has the odd, and totally useless, acoustic pop side project *Kuk med ollon* (Dick with head), which takes away (if they had any) credibility. Not sure how to categorise *Woods Of Infinity*. At times they sound a bit like *Shining*, with very badly recorded music and desperate screeching vocals. Sorry, but I just don't get it at all. The 7" *Frozen Nostalgia* has one "Adolf" side and one "Bormann", which together with the lyrics dealing with for instance paedophilia makes me wonder a bit..., plus the fact that *Hejdå* contains a cover of Barry Manilow.

2002 7" - - -

2001 ☐	I-20	7" 4tr	Djävulskap Produktion	Fanskapt 001
	Bootleg version in 333 copies. Tracks: Summon The Lord Of Blasphemy/ Render God/ Silence After War/Worship Us			
2002 ■	Missfostret Tellus (split)	7"	Sombre Records	- -
	Split with Armagedda. Track: Missfostret Tellus			
2003 ☐	I-20	7" 4tr	Total Holocaust Records	THR 08
	666 copies. Tracks: Worship Us/Silence After War/Render God/Oförmögen att bringa reda i kaotiska tankar			
2003 ■	Lidande upphöjt till två (split)	7"g	Klaxon	KLX 003
	666 copies. Split with Horna. Track: Lidande upphöjt till två			
2004 ☐	F & L	CD	Total Holocaust Records	THR 70
2005 ☐	HEJDÅ	CD	Total Holocaust Records	THR 88
2005 ☐	Woods Of Infinity/Joyless (split)	7"g EP	Iron Flames	- -
	Split with Joyless. Tracks: Uppgivet hjärta/Edyllion			
2005 ☐	LJUSET	CD	Total Holocaust Records	THR 91
2006 ☐	LJUSET	2LPg	Niessedrion Records	N.D 008
2007 ☐	HAMPTJÄRN	CD	Supernal Music	FERLY 040CD
2008 ■	HEJDÅ	LP+7"	Obscure Abhorrence Productions	- -
	Bonus: 7" with Det som hände/Köld. 100 hand-numbered on green vinyl + 400 black vinyl. Different artwork.			
2008 ☐	Hopplös väntan	MCD 7tr	Supernal Music	FERLY 059MCD
	Tracks: Labrador/Backenvägen/Karnevals/Törnrosasömnen/Snår & skare/Taken/Darkness And Death I + II			
2008 ☐	HOPPLÖS VÄNTAN	LP	Obscure Abhorrence Productions	OAP 084
	Bonus: Taken/Rent hat. (Darkness And Death is removed) 150 purple splatter vinyl + 350 black.			
2008 ☐	Frozen Nostalgia	7"	Obscure Abhorrence Productions	- -
	Tracks: Summer IS Not My Friend/Excursions Into The Uncanny Valley. 100 on brown vinyl + 400 black.			
2009 ☐	Old Ugly Trees (split)	7"g 4tr	Devoted Art Propaganda	NMS 003
	Split with Arkha Sva. Tracks: Pappa Satan/Hjässa. 166 on red vinyl + poster, 500 black.			
2010 ■	FÖRINTELSE & LIBIDO	CDd	Those Opposed Records	TOR 026
	New artwork.			

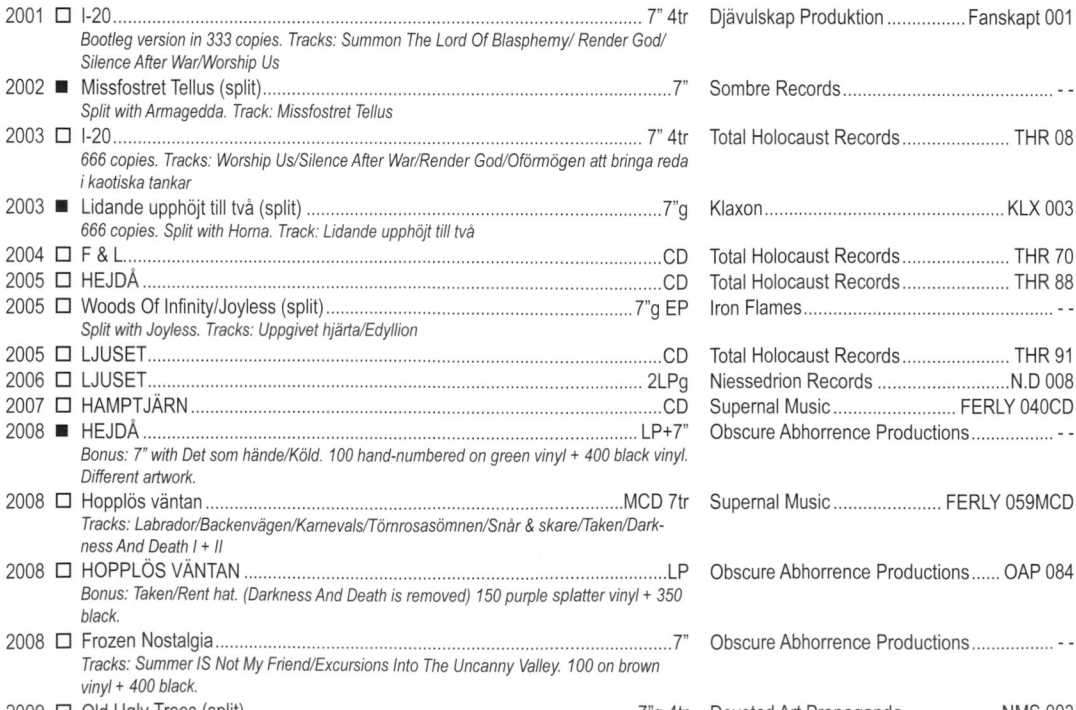

2003 7"g - KLX 003

2008 LP - - -

2010 CDd - TOR 026

2010 □	Anti Zionist (split) ....7"	InnerWar	- -

Split with Armageddon. Track: Avklädd, klädd och oförstädd. 300 hand-numbered copies.
Yellow or black vinyl.

2011 ■	FÖRLÅT ....CDd	Obscure Abhorrence Productions	- -

500 copies.

2011 □	FÖRLÅT ....CD	Obscure Abhorrence Productions	- -

2011 CDd - - -

WORK OF ART

Lars Säfsund: v, Robert Säll: g/k, Herman Furin: d

Stockholm - The band originates back to 1992 when Furin and Säll went to music school together. Fifteen years later they managed to convince singer Säfsund to join. In January 2007 they released their first demo, which lead to a deal with Frontiers Records. **Work Of Art** play outstanding AOR with a touch of westcoast, a bit similar to bands like **Giant** and **Journey**, with Säfsund hitting all notes with perfection. The band also uses live musicians, bassist Andreas Passmark (**Stormwind, Narnia, Harmony, DivineFire, Wisdom Call**) and keyboardist Jonas Gröning, who also play on *In Progress*. In 2012 the band supported **Toto** on tour. Säfsund is also in **W.E.T** and Säfsund sings with Italians **Lionville**.
Website: www.woa.se

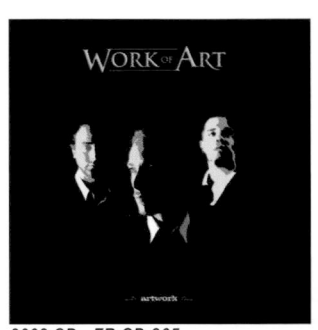

2008 CD - FR CD 365

2008 ■	ARTWORK....................................CD	Frontiers Records ....FR CD 365
2008 □	ARTWORK....................................CD	King Records (Japan)....................KICP-1295
	Bonus: Camelia (acoustic)	
2011 □	The Great Fall ....MCDgp 3tr	Frontiers Records ....FR PR CD 025
	Promo MCD. Tracks: The Great Fall (edit)/Once Again (acoustic)/Until You Believe (acoustic).	
2011 □	IN PROGRESS ....CD	Frontiers Records ....FR CD 524
2011 ■	IN PROGRESS ....CD	King Records (Japan)....................KICP-1587
	Bonus: Fall Down (acoustic)	

2011 CD - KICP-1587

WORLD BELOW

Mikael Danielsson: v/b, Jonas Kjellgren: g/v, Ronnie Bergerstähl: d

Avesta - **World Below** were formed by Jonas Kjellgren (**Scar Symmetry, Centinex, Dellamorte, Carnal Forge** etc) in 1999, but as **Beyond The Sun**. They recorded a two-track demo, but the project was put to rest, until 2002. Singer Danielsson (**Sideburners, Mystery Machine, Turabus**) joined and soon drummer Stefan Westerberg (**Steel Attack, Leech, Carnal Forge**) was drafted to complete the trio. They recorded the first album *Sacrifices To The Moon*, released in 2004. After this the line-up changed quite drastically seeing Ronnie Bergerstähl (**Demonical, Centinex, Grave, Julie Laughs No More**) replacing Westerberg while Per Nilsson (**Scar Symmetry**) was added on second guitar. This line-up recorded the album *Maelstrom*. After this, Nilsson left to devote his time to **Scar Symmetry** and soon also Mikael Danielsson took a time-out. In the spring of 2006 Kjellgren wanted to pick up the pieces, summoned Bergerstähl and Danielsson and recorded the band's third album, *Repulsion*. **World Below** play excellent heavy doom metal in the same vein as **Solitude Aeternus** meets early **Trouble** with a touch of **Sorcerer**.

2005 CD - PSY 019

2006 CD - PSY 028

2004 □	SACRIFICES TO THE MOON ....CDd	Doom Symphony ....DS CD-003
2005 ■	MAELSTROM ....CD	PsycheDOOMelic Records ....PSY 019
2005 □	MAELSTROM ....LP	Hellion Records ....HE 400605
	Brown vinyl. Different artwork. 500 copies.	
2006 ■	REPULSION ....CD	PsycheDOOMelic Records ....PSY 028

WORLD OF SILENCE

Mathias Sandquist: v, Mikael Dahlquist: g,
Thomas Heder: k, Fredric Danielsson: b, Bruno Andersen: d

Karlstad - Killer progressive hard rock. Guitarist Micke was also found in dance-band **Candela**. The band did a cover of **The Beatles**' *Strawberry Fields Forever* on *A Black Mark Tribute* (97 Black Mark) and **Depeche Mode**'s *Black Celebration* on *Vol II* (98 Black Mark). Dahlquist, plus *The Beginning Of The End* on *Jukebox Collection* (95 RFM). Heder and Danielsson recorded two albums with **Godgory** in 1995-1996. Dahlquist and Danielsson are found in **Dogpound**.

1997 CD - BMCD 127

1996 □	WINDOW OF HEAVEN.....................CD	Black Mark ....BMCD 100
1997 ■	MINDSCAPES ....CD	Black Mark ....BMCD 127

WORSHIP

Daniel: v/g, Walker: g/v, Peter: d, Maaw: b.

Älmhult - Totally horrible amateurish hard rock/metal with a singer who sings rather than well and a band that hasn't fully discovered the art of timing and playing tight.

1987 ■	Queen Of Hearts/Strangers In The Night/Take Me High.............7" 3tr	WIP 001

1987 7" - 001

WRAPTORS

Niklas Fridh: v/g, Pål Callmer: g, Fredrik Persson: b, Kristofer Rönstrom: v/d

Malmö - Wraptors mix all kinds of musical elements, from seventies hard rock, sixties rock to quirky pop to total musical insanity. It's a bit like mixing *System Of A Down*, Zappa, *Foo Fighters*, *Them Crooked Vultures* and *Devo*. Callmer is also in *Deathening* and previously in *Supraload* and *Murderplan*, while Fridh is also in *Deathening*. The band sadly split in 2012. *Website: www.wraptors.se*

2011 ■ WRAPTORS ....CD Rakamarow Records ....RAKREC 002

2011 CD - RAKREC 002

WULCAN

Peter Sundell: g/v, Tommy Palm: g, Jan Borg: g, Kent Fagerberg: b, Christian Sundell: d

Nässjö - Wulcan were formed under the name *Paradox*, and at the time drummer Christian was only eight (8!!) years old. Sundell also joined the funk-rock band *Mark V* in 1983, where he met Anders Rydholm, together with whom he formed the band *In & Out*, and they later formed the band *Promotion*. Peter also recorded a solo single in a more AOR-oriented vein. The band *Promotion* later evolved into *Grand Illusion* and Peter was also found in *Decoy* and *Northern Light*. The first single is killer heavy metal, the A-side with a touch of early *Dio* and *Black Sabbath*, while the B-side is more melodic straightforward hard rock/metal. After the first single bass player Kent Fagerberg replaced Lennart Ljungdahl. The second single is more in the vein of *Treat*, *Madison* etc. with the A-side being a ballad and the B-side a great melodic up-tempo AOR rocker. Both recordings are well worth investing in.

1982 7" - 820116-1

1982 ■ Mysterier/Travellin'...7" private ....820116-1 **$$**
1986 ■ No More/Out In The World...............................7" Team Lucas ....LUC 101

1986 7" - LUC 101

WULFGAR

Emil Augustsson: v, Jimmie Mattisson: g, Reine Karlsson: g, Morgan Löfstedt: b, Thommy Lindskog: d

Bromölla - Wulfgar (the name taken from the poem *Beowulf*) were formed in 2005. The band recorded their first demo *Hate For Mankind* in 2006, followed by *Wendigo* later the same year, after which they were picked up by Kampas Records. The debut was recorded by Johan Blomström (*Blinded Colony, Overdrive, Band Of Spice*) at Studio Sound Palace. After the first album Reine Karlsson replaced guitarist Max Lindqvist. In 2012 bassist Morgan took over singer Emil's task and they drafted new bass player Adam Nilsson (*Nattsmyg*). A Viking-influenced death metal band, in the vein of *Amon Amarth*. Lindskog is also in *Nymf*.

2007 ■ WITH GODS AND LEGENDS UNITE.........................CD Kampas Records ....KMPS 002
2010 ☐ MIDGARDIAN METAL ....CD Trollzon Records...................................TZ 024

2007 CD - KMPS 002

WYNJA

Åse Mauritzdotter Westin: v, flute, Robert Lindberg: g, Daniel Norlin: b, Jörgen Svedberg: fiddle, Dag Holmgren: d

Burträsk - Wynja is an ancient stone representing love, happiness and peace in the Nordic mythology. Really interesting folk-rock mixing fiddle, flute and heavy guitars. In the same vein as *Kebnekajse*, *Sten*, *Hoven Droven* and Kenny Håkansson. Svedberg, Lindberg and Holmgren later formed the band *0914*.

1997 ■ 20 GRADER KALLT...CD Siljum...BGS CD 9709

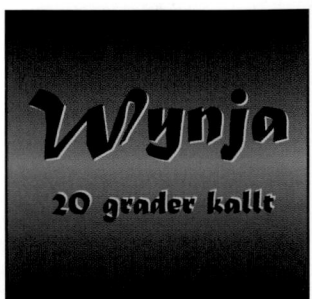

1997 CD - BGS CD 9709

WYVERN

Toni Kocmut: v, Jonas Bendt: g, Andreas Sjöström: g, Petter Broman: b, Peter Nagy: d

Södertälje/Stockholm - High-quality melodic power metal with a touch of *Blind Guardian* and Swedish colleagues *Nocturnal Rites*. At times similar to *Falconer* when the folky influences set in. The band was formed in 1993 by Berndt and Sjöström, and recorded the first demo, *March Of Metal* in 1996. The vocals were here handled by Albrecht Märchenstoltz. It was followed by *The Ancient Sword* in 1994, where David Sterling handled the vocals. Micke Henriksson played drums on the demos, while the first album featured Thomas Väänänen (*Thyrfing*). On the second album Sterling was replaced by Toni Kocmut (ex-*Sins Of Omission* and *Mournful*), and Väänänen by Peter Nagy (*Eternal Oath, Mörk Gryning, Faceshift, Hypocrite*). Broman and Sjöström were also in *Diverge*, while Jonas was ex-*Mörk Gryning*, *Mortifier* and *Diabolical*. After the second album Henrik Hedberg (*Amaranth, Hypocrite, Mörk Gryning*) replaced Jonas Berndt.

1998 CD - 007396-2 B.O

1998 ■ THE WILDFIRE...CD B.O Records ....007396-2 B.O
2001 ■ NO DEFIANCE OF FATE..CDd No Fashion ....NFR 051

2001 CDd - NFR 051

X-ERYUS
Sören Lindmark: v/g, Anders Fransson: g, Joakim Patsonen: k,
Stefan Hozjan: b, Patrick Fransson: d

Torup - It all started already back in 1980 under the name *Killers*. In 1983 the band, now featuring Lindmark, Hozjan and Anders Fransson, changed their name to *Savagers* and released the mega rare MLP *Preachers Of Steel*. In 1985 they recorded a new demo, did some gigs and bandstands, but nothing happened. In 1990 they resurrected, drafted Pasonen and Patrick Fransson and took the name *X-Eryus*. They recorded the album *Expose*, but things faded out in 1991. *Expose* is a pretty good melodic hard rocker following in the footsteps of *Treat* and *Europe*.

1990 ■ EXPOSE ....LP Büms Records ....25123 $

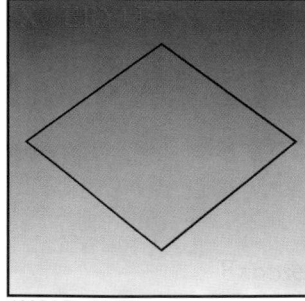
1990 LP - 25123

X-HALE
Tony "Karl" Krusing: v, Anders "Brill" Landin: g, Magnus "Pantho" Olsson: g,
Magnus "Manne" Pettersson: b, Pelle Hörndal: d

Jönköping - Very *Thin Lizzy* influenced hard rock with great guitar harmonies, vocals more in the vein of *Snowstorm*. Formed in 1977, and split in 1981, when Magnus, Magnus and Pelle formed the excellent AOR band *Fortune*. Olsson is today found in melodic rockers *Blind Alley*.

1981 ■ UFOt och jag/Hjälten...7" Sjöbo Påpp SPR-010

1981 7" - SPR-010

X-IT
Claes Alin: v/d, Ulf Högberg: g, Michael Ojala: g, Johan Axelsson: k, Thomas Nilsson: b

Trollhättan - The A-side is a bit too close to pop/rockers *Noise* for comfort. The B-side is musically a pretty good up-tempo melodic hard rocker, but the vocals (in Swedish) are horrible.

1983 ■ Svaga pojkar/Ocean ....7" Pang ....PSI 060

1983 7" - PSI 060

X-PERIENCE
Kent Rune Johansson: g, Tomas Hartman: k, Morgens Widmark: b, Ismo Immonen: d

Laxå - The band was formed in 1975 under the name *Cruel*, initially mostly playing covers. After guitarist Per-Arne Fallén quit, they became a trio featuring Johansson, Widmark and Immonen and went under the name *Trans AM*, playing hard rock. In 1979 they drafted Hartman and became *Arrow*, which changed to *X-Perience* in 1980. The single was recorded in the Ljudspåret Studio in Göteborg. The A-side is quite a poppy thing in the vein of *Factory*, while the B-side is great melodic hard rock, like a heavier *Saga*. The title on the record actually says *Give Me Some Love*. In 1982 the band entered a bandstand with the song *Summer In July* and won. The band however split in 1983. A reunion featuring new drummer Stefan Jacobsson replacing Immonen, plus second guitarist Morgan Bohman added, took place in 1985. They recorded a demo, but the band split. They also did a one-off reunion in the early nineties.

1981 7" - X-PES 101

1981 ■ Casanova/Gimme Some Love ....7" private............................X-PES 101 $
    Several of the copies look damaged, but plays fine.

X-RAY
Peo Pettersson: v/g, Henrik "Henkan" Norrström: g/v, Lasse Eriksson: k,
Tommie Pettersson: k, Otto Lövgren: b, Clas Johansson: d

Skara - Formed in 1980, split 1987. This is hard rock with a strong glam rock 'n' roll feel. Peo later joined Christian hard rockers *Leviticus* and *Axia*. He has also made several solo releases. The band supported Joan Jett on a Sweden-tour in the mid-80s. Tommie was later in *Trace*.

1984 ☐ Mr. Razzle Dazzle/That Will Be All Tonight ....7" private S-1702
1986 ■ Time For Promotion/Just A Question Of Time..................7" Pop Produktion S-1704

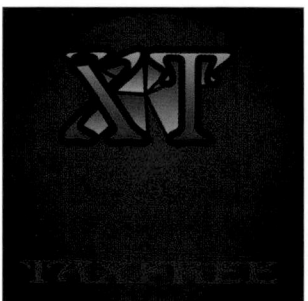
1986 7" - S-1704

XT
Sonny Larsson: v, Björn Stigsson: g, Niklas Johnson: k,
Johan Stark: b, Kjell Andersson: d

Örebro/Hjo - The band was formed in 1991. Sonny was ex-*Motherlode*, while Björn had recorded four albums with his former band *Leviticus* and a solo-album entitled *Together With Friends*, where Sonny participated. The first album was a slick AOR platter with programmed drums and weak songs. *Taxfree* showed a lot more promise and the boys were helped out by *Modest Attraction* drummer Mick Nordström, Niklas Johnsson and bassist P-O Larsson, the latter was also on the first album. On the band's third album the sound had again turned heavier and is actually a great powerful heavy rocker. It was recorded with the above line-up. Sonny was later working with rockers *Kings Of Modern Swing*, who released a MCD in January 1996, and is now in the reunited *Motherload*.

1993 CD - VIVAD 113   *1993 CD - XRCN-1076*

1992 ☐	XT	CD	Viva	VAVAD 104
1993 ☐	XT	CD	Zero (Japan)	XRCN-1075
1993 ☐	All Your Love/I Call Your Name	CDS 2tr	Viva	VIVAS 02
1993 ■	TAXFREE	CD	Viva	VIVAD 113
1993 ■	TAXFREE	CD	Zero (Japan)	XRCN-1076
1995 ■	EXTENDED EMPIRE	CD	Viva	VIVAD 135

1995 CD - VIVAD 135

X-UNION

Börje Reinholdsson: v, Ulf Larsson: g, Micke Reinholdsson: b, Lars Öhman: d

Umeå - The band was formed in 1989 under the name *Mr Tiger*. They recorded the CD *Identitet... Rock 'n Roll* (92 Büms) under this name before becoming *X-Union*. They added more edge to their sound and started singing in English. The single showed great promise and the album was a really good piece of *Kiss*-style basic hard rock. The track *The Morning Will Come* is also found on the American compilation *Best Unsigned European Bands* ('94 Showcase). *X-Union* contributed with their version their version of *White Christmas* on the *Released By X-mas* compilation. Börje has also released two albums with the band *Balthazars Machine*.

1995 MCD - ZRCD 003

| 1995 ■ | The Morning Will Come/I'm A Rock 'N Roller | CDS 2tr | Zakana | ZRCD 003 |
| 1997 ☐ | DASH | CD | MM Records | MMCD 002 |

XXX

Robert "Rob Nasty" Jonasson: b/v, Kristoffer "Chris Loud"/"X": g.
Tommy "Snowy Shaw" Helgesson: d/v

Göteborg - Snowy Shaw, the man the myth the legend, produced an album with glam rockers *Loud 'N Nasty* and ended up forming a band with two of the members. We are talking true seventies glitter hard rock influenced by the school of Chin & Chapman, such as *The Sweet*, *Suzi Quatro* and *Mud*, but with a heavier edge. A great album. They also do a really good cover of *Cheap Trick*'s *I Want You To Want Me*. Unfortunately Chris was conned out of the band's money etc and disappeared from the face of the earth. Rob is also in slease/glamsters *Danger* and Snowy has a zillion projects going, besides being in *Therion*, *Notre Dame* and his solo stuff.

Snowy, loud and nasty Swedes

2009 CD - PER 2142

2009 ☐	HEAVEN, HELL OR HOLLYWOOD	CD	Snowy Shaw Production	WOW 046
2009 ■	HEAVEN, HELL OR HOLLYWOOD	CD	Perris Records (USA)	PER 2142
2009 ☐	HEAVEN, HELL OR HOLLYWOOD	CD	King Records (Japan)	KICP-1330
	Bonus: What's Wrong With The Children Today?/Little Miss Pretty			

XINEMA

Mikael Askemur: v/k/b/g, Sven Larsson: g, Jonas Thurén: d/v

(Dalarna) - Prog trio *Xinema* were formed in 1999, intially named *Madrigal*. Excellent symphonically influenced prog, sounding a bit like a mix of *Asia* and *Saga*. Sven later went solo.

| 2002 ☐ | DIFFERENT WAYS | CD | Unicorn Records | UNCR-5004 |
| 2006 ■ | BASIC COMMUNICATION | CD | Unicorn Records | UNCR-5035 |

2006 CD - UNCR-5035

XORIGIN

Johannes Stole: v/k, Daniel Palmqvist: g

Stockholm/Norway - The band was originally formed in Los Angeles under the name *Orange Crush* in 1999, while the members where studying music at the Musicians Institute. The founding members Johannes Stole and Daniel Palmqvist later went back to their home countries, Norway and Sweden, and continued collaborating on various projects in between their other engagements. Johannes has released a critically acclaimed album with progressive rock band *P:O:B*. Daniel has released an instrumental solo album and is also in *The Murder Of My Sweet*. Daniel Flores (*The Murder Of My Sweet, Mind's Eye, Codex* etc) plays drums on the album. *Xorigin* play classic eighties-sounding AOR with great vocals and high-class guitar playing.

| 2011 ■ | STATE OF THE ART | CD | Frontiers Records | FR CD 526 |

2011 CD - FR CD 526

XSAVIOR

Göran Edman: v, Benny Jansson: g, Matt Norberg: k,
Mathias Garnås: b, Daniel Flores: d

Stockholm - High-class melodic progressive hard rock with a nice theatrical touch. At times it sounds like the missing link between *Asia* and *Queen* with a bit of *Dream Theater* thrown in for good measure. Highly intricate, well-written and well-produced songs with a bunch of outstanding name musicians from the Swedish scene, from bands like *Mind's Eye, Tears Of Anger, Snake Charmer, Two Rocks, Tears Of Anger, Norum, Malmsteen, Madison and Kharma*.

2005 ■	CALEIDOSCOPE	CD	Atenzia	ATZ 02039
2005 ☐	CALEIDOSCOPE	CD	Gencross (Japan)	GCCY-1001
	Bonus: Day Of Deliverance			

2005 CD - ATZ 02039

YALE BATE

Magnus "Alis Magnum" Ahlström: v, Johan "Jonah Dee" Norberg: g,
Christian "Chris Di Neen" Sandquist: k, Andreas "Andy Clarke" Claesson: b,
Jakob "Jake Samuels" Samuelsson: d

Lidingö (Stockholm) - It all started back in January 1985 when Ahlström and Norberg, with the only common musical denominator being a liking of *Alice Cooper*, decided to start a band. The band recorded their first four-track demo at producer Magnus Frykberg's home studio. In April 1985 Claesson joined and two months later drummer Samuelsson came on board. In February 1986 Claesson was fired and replaced by Pontus Egberg (later in *Lion's Share* and *The Poodles*). The band split in April 1986, but reformed in September the same year. In May the following year keyboardist Sandquist was drafted. The band entered and won the Lidingörock bandstand, and the first prize was to record a single. The band then entered the Rock SM in 1988 and won their youth class. They now unearthed the MLP *On The Prowl*. *Yale Bate* was at the time as a pure AOR band. They were picked up by City Records and changed into a honky tonk rockin' act. Jakob quit in 1990 to join *Talisman* and was replaced by Tony Madsen, who made his live debut only six days later. The new line-up recorded a new album, signed a deal with BMG Publishing and broke up in the end of January 1991. Jake was also in *Totem*, later switched to lead vocals and became lead singer of *Jekyll 'N Hyde*, *The Ring*, *Treasure Land* and is now fronting *The Poodles*. *On The Prowl* was produced by Tommy Denander. Johan later joined glam-popsters *Sha-Boom*. Mia Kempff (*Yeah Bop Station*, *Good Clean Fun* etc.) sings on one track on the album.

1987 7" - TM-5

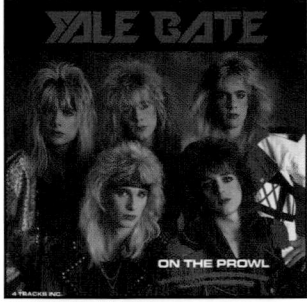
1988 MLP - YB 002

1987	■	Winds Of Change/Comin' Home ....7"	Twin Music TM-5	
1988	■	On The Prowl .... MLP 4tr	private .... YB 002	
		Tracks: Dancin' Outta Control/Take It/Closer To Your Heart/(Why Don't You) Come Along.		
1990	■	Get Movin' (Use Your Body)/This Time It's For Real....................7"	City Records CITY-11	
1990	□	Down To The River/Coolest Cat In Town ....7"	City Records CITY-9	
1990	□	BUSINESS OR PLEASURE ....CD	City Records CD-4	$$

Unofficial releases:
2003	□	ON THE PROWL ....CD	Time Warp .... - -	
		Italian bootleg		

1990 7" - CITY-11

YANKEE HEAVEN

Anette Johansson: v, Mats Edström: g, Kenny Wendel: k,
Pierre Ekström: b, Jan Snarberg: d

Jönköping - A good AOR band in the traditional vein. The band was formed in the early nineties when Wendel and Snarberg had left *Angelez*. Anette's strong clean voice is one of the main strengths in the band's music. Anette (later known as Nettie Q, married to Snarberg) and Mats later formed melodic hard rockers *Shiva*.

1994	■	UNCLASSIFIED........................CD	private YHCD-9404	

1994 CD - YHCD-9404

YEAH BOP STATION

Mia Kempff: b/v, Thomas Larsson: g/v,
Klara Kempff: d

Stockholm/Borlänge - *Yeah Bop Station* are, despite the name, a great melodic hard rock band, even though Mia and Klara were foremost known for their pop hit *Hallå hela pressen* with the band *Chattanooga*. Thomas was ex-*Six Feet Under/Jammer* and has later recorded with *Baltimoore*, Glenn Hughes and solo. The non-CD track *Crying Out For Love* can be found on the compilation *Backstage: En Himla Massa Oväsen*. The band started working on a second album, but it was unfortunately never finished. Mia was also found in *Good Clean Fun*.

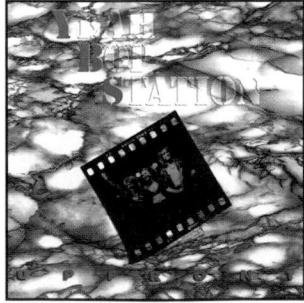
1992 LP - BMLP 001

1992 LP - - -

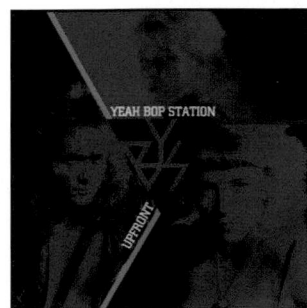
1992 CD - XRCN-1027

1992	□	UPFRONT ....CD	Blue Metal...................... BMCD 001	
1992	■	UPFRONT ....LP	Blue Metal...................... BMLP 001	
1992	■	UPFRONT ....LP	Little Rock/Pyramid Enterprise (Russia)....... - -	
		Says "For promotion only". Different artwork.		
1992	■	UPFRONT........................CD	Zero (Japan) XRCN-1027	
		Different artwork.		
1992	■	My Blue Moon ....MCD 3tr	Blue Metal...................... BMCDS 001	
		Tracks: My Blue Moon/Don't Turn Your Back On Me Now/Easy Livin'.		
1992	□	Don't Turn Your Back On Me Now/Flashback Rabbits........................CDS 2tr	Blue Metal...................... BMCDS 002	
1992	□	Over And Done ....MCD 3tr	Blue Metal...................... BMCDS 003	
		Tracks: Over And Done/Don't Like To Work/Still Want You Back.		

1992 MCD - BMCDS 001

YEAR OF THE GOAT

Thomas Eriksson (now Sabbathi): v/g
Don Palmroos: g
Jonas Mattsson: g
Mikael Popovic: k
Tobias Resch: b
Fredrik Hellerström: d

Year of the goat - 1970?

Norrköping - *Year Of The Goat* were formed by drummer Fredrik in 2006. Quite dynamic and mellow 70s influenced hard rock, a bit in the same vein as *Ghost* or *The Devil's Blood* in the sense that you expect something much heavier from the name and approach. A bit reminiscent of *Epitaph*, *Coven*, *Black Widow* or Swedish colleagues *Graveyard*. Outstanding stuff indeed! Eriksson (now Sabbathi) is also found in doom band *Griftegård*. The track *Missa Niger* is non-album, and also features chanting from *Saturnalia Temple* singer Tommie Eriksson. Popovic was added after the first release, and Per Broddesson replaced by Palmroos. Highly recommended.

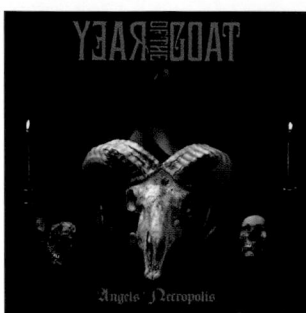

2011 MLP - VAN 057v

2011	☐	Lucem Ferrem	MCD 4tr	Ván Records	VAN 057
		Tracks: Of Darkness/Vermillion Clouds/Dark Lord (Sam Gopal cover)/Lucem Ferre.			
2011	☐	Lucem Ferrem	MCDd 4tr	Ván Records	VAN 057
2011	■	Lucem Ferrem	MLP 4tr	Ván Records	VAN 057v
		Same tracks on both sides. White vinyl. Different artwork.			
2011	☐	Lucem Ferrem	MLP 4tr	Ván Records	VAN 057v
		Same tracks on both sides. 275 copies in purple vinyl. Different artwork with purple print.			
2012	☐	This Will Be Mine/Missa Niger	7"	Ván Records	VAN 70
		Red vinyl			
2012	☐	ANGELS NECROPOLIS	CDd	Ván Records	VAN 073
2012	■	ANGELS NECROPOLIS	LP	Ván Records	VAN 073v
		Different artwork.			

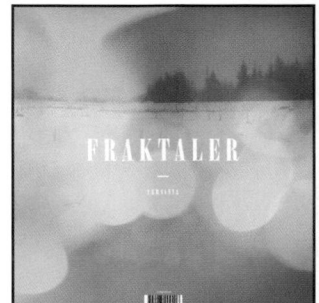

2012 CD - VAN 073v

YERSINIA

Mattis Engman: v, Sebastian Sjögren: g, Hannes Almén: b, Per Svensson: d

Uppsala - Metalcore, mostly sung in Swedish. The band was formed in 2008 initially in a more scream-oriented vein, but became heavier before they made their first demo EP, *Yesinia*, together with Daniel Bergstrand. In 2009 a second demo EP was recorded, entitled *Lejonhjärta*. In 2011 the digital EP *Aldrig mera vinter*, was released. Not to be confused with the German death metal band. *Fraktaler* contains *Aldrig mera vinter* as bonus.
Website: www.yersinia.se

2010	☐	EFTER OSS SYNDAFLODEN	CDd	Black Star Foundation	BSF 042
2012	■	FRAKTALER/ALDRIG MERA VINTER	LP	Snapping Fingers Snapping Necks	SFSN004EP
		250 copies.			

2012 LP - SFSN004EP

YGGDRASIL

Magnus Wohlfart: v/g, Benny Olsson: g, Gustaf Hagel: b, Jacob Blecher: d

Höör - New year 2000-2001 Wohlfart and Hagel (ex-*Broken Dagger*) joined forces to form a new project forging metal and Scandinavian folk music. *Yggdrasil* (the immense world tree in Norse mythology) was born. They recorded first demo, *Kvällning*, in 2002, followed by *I nordens rike* in 2003. The duo initially used drummer Jeremy Child (*Broken Dagger, Lömska Planer, Folkearth*). The first two albums were initially released by the label Det Germanske Folket, and later reissued by Grand Master Music. Before *Irrbloss* (will-o-wisp) guitarist Benny Olsson and drummer Jacob Blecher (*Dibbukim, Pandemonium*) completed the band. *Yggdrasil* play folk-influenced death metal, at times similar to *Otyg*, and at times mixing in instruments like keyharp and fiddle. On *Irrbloss* the addition of clean vocals were a bit more prominent. Wohlfart is also found in *Dibbukim, Pandemonium, Nae'blis, Vanmakt, Broken Dagger, Anti-Christian Assault, Folkearth* and *Trymheim*.
Website: www.yggdrasil-sweden.com

2009 CD - Ger 028   *2011 CD - GMM 010*

2007	☐	KVÄLLSVINDAR ÖVER NORDRÖNT LAND	CD	Det Germanske Folket	GER 017
2009	■	VEDERGÄLLNING	CD	Det Germanske Folket	Ger 028
2011	☐	KVÄLLSVINDAR ÖVER NORDRÖNT LAND	CD	Grand Master Music	GMM 009
		Bonus: Gryningstid (edit)			
2011	■	VEDERGÄLLNING	CD	Grand Master Music	GMM 010
		Bonus: Tusenårslunden			
2011	■	IRRBLOSS	CD	Grand Master Music	GMM 011

YNGSTRÖM TRIO, CLAS

See Sky High

2011 CD - GMM 011

ZAN, ZINNY J

Bo "Zinny Zan" Stagman: v

Stockholm - Zinny actually started out behind the drums, initially as punk rocker Bosse Belsen (**Belsen Boys, Alarm X**), but after seven years he picked up the microphone in the punk band **Brilliant Boys**. Zinny and Dan "Danny Wild" Lagerstedt also had a band called **Zinny & Danny**, who had recorded a demo that caught the attraction of Tandan owner Sanji Tandan. In 1982 he joined glam-rockers **Easy Action** and recorded one album and some EPs before he quit. He then teamed up with sleaze rockers **King Pin**, previously known as **Shylock**. They recorded some highly acclaimed demos, from which some of the songs would appear on the bands debut *Welcome To Bop City*. The style was guitar-dominated hard rock with glammish overtones. The album was first released under the **King Pin** banner, but in 1988 re-issued under the band's new name **Shotgun Messiah**. When Zinny was sacked from/left **Shotgun Messiah** in April 1990, he formed **Grand Slam** together with brothers Fredrik (**Vildsvin**) and Martin Thomander (**Electric Boys**) on bass and guitar respectively. Drummer Anders Johansson (**HammerFall** etc) was soon replaced by Jacob "Jake Samuel" Samuelsson (**Yale Bate, Talisman, Jekyll & Hyde, The Ring, The Poodles** etc). The band was dropped and Zinny took a long vacation before he started doing cover gigs with the boys that later became **Zan Clan** in 1994. When the second **Zan Clan** album didn't happen Zinny took it overseas and found a deal with Fastlane Records who released his solo album *City Boy Blues*, which was actually what was supposed to be the second **Zan Clan** album. The musicians on *City Boy Blues* are more or less the same as on the first **Zan Clan**; guitarists Christian Baraldi and Sören Swanson, drummer Matthew Baraldi, plus bassist Vince Frances, and guest guitarist Johan Glössler and Kee Marcello.

2002 CD - FLR 004

2002 ■ CITY BOY BLUES...CD Fastlane Records.............................FLR 004

ZAN CLAN

Bo "Zinny Zan" Stagman: v, Pontus Norgren: g, Ulf "Chris Laney" Larsson: g, Pontus Egberg: b, Johan "Koleberg" Kullberg: d

2005 CD - BECD 003

Stockholm - See Zan, Zinny J, for the beginning, and continuation of the history. The line-up now featured Zinny on vocals, guitarists Christian Baraldi and Sören Swanson, bassist Perra Tedblad and drummer Matthew Baraldi. The debut is a mid-class rocker with influences from rock, sleaze, traditional hard rock and all kind of directions. Zinny and his clan-members were finishing up the recordings of a new album in March 1996, due to be released later that year. However the album never happened. In 2002 Zinny got a solo deal with Fastlane Records and released the album *City Boy Blues*, which were actually the tracks supposed to be the second **Zan Clan** CD. In 2005 he resurrected **Zan Clan** with a completely new line-up featuring Pontus Norgren (**Great King Rat, The Ring, The Poodles, HammerFall**) and former **Seventeen**-singer/guitarist Ulf "Chris Laney" Larsson on guitars, Pontus Egberg (**The Poodles, Lion's Share** etc) on bass and Johan Koleberg (**Lion's Share, Talk Of The Town**) on drums. The new stuff sounds way more powerful than the debut. Since **Easy Action** was reformed, **Zan Clan** has been put on the backburner. *Kickz The Livin' Shit* is a live album.

1994 CD - SMC 10131

2006 CD - PER 1752

1994 ■	CITIZEN OF WASTELAND	CD	SMC	SMC 10131	
2005 ■	WE ARE ZAN CLAN, WHO THE F**K ARE YOU?	CD	GMR	BECD 003	
2005 □	WE ARE ZAN CLAN, WHO THE F**K ARE YOU?	CD	Perris Records (USA)	PERR 012	
	Bonus: Surrender (Cheap Trick cover)				
2006 ■	KICKZ THE LIVIN' SHIT... OUTTA STOCKHOLM	CD	Perris Records (USA)	PER 1752	

ZANE

Tommy Strömstedt: v, Björn Persson: g, Moreno Tondo: g/v, Per "Zeb" Strömstedt: b, Mario Somenzi: d

Malmö - The single is really good and heavy seventies hard rock with a touch of **Black Sabbath**. **Zane** also contributes with the tracks *Malmö City* on the *Vykort från Malmö* (1980 Amalthea) compilation.

Step aside · Damage

1976 7" - MMS 103

1976 ■ Step Aside/Damage ....7" MM.........................MMS 103 $

ZAP YANKEEFY

Fredrik Karlsson: v, Anders Jönsson: g, Joakim Karlsson: b, Adam Pavlovic: d

Bromölla - As the four songs (actually only three stated on the cover) are so very different from each other a simple categorisation is out of the question. The style is based on good solid seventies-influenced hard rock. However the fourth track on the CD, strangely untitled, is wimped-out synth-pop á la **Ace Of Base**. It probably shouldn't even have been there. Pavlovic also played drums on the final **Mercy** album *Underground* and recorded a MCD with the band **Peak** in 1996.

1994 MCDp - Zy-CDS-190894

1994 ■ Afro American Girl.......................................MCDp 4tr private.....................Zy-CDS-190894
Tracks: Afro American Girl/Coming To Get Ya'/Troops Drawing Nearer.

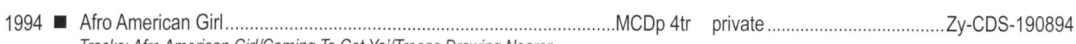

ZAVORASH

Totalscorn/Zablogma: v, Zagzakel/Nil: g,
Joachim "Gideon" Forsberg: b, Tore "I. Hate" Stjerna: d

Stockholm - Nihilistic black metal band *Zavorash*, which stands for Za Vorbashtar Raz Shapog, meaning The Legion Of Revenge in Black Speech (see *Lords Of The Ring* by J.R.R Tolkien), were formed in Stockholm suburb Sigtuna in 1996. The initial members were singer Zablogma and guitarists Zagzakel and Zagrash. The first demo, *Za Vorbashtar Raz Shapog*, was recorded in 1997, on which the band didn't have a drummer but programmed the drums. It was followed by *In Odium Veritas* in 1998, where drummer Tore Stjerna had been drafted. The track *Truth And Sorrow* was featured on the compilation *Voices Of Death Part II* (1998 VOD Records). *In Odium Veritas* was released on cassette by Elven Witchcraft in 1999. In 1999 Zagzakel left and the band drafted *Mornaland* guitarist Henrik Wenngren, while the band used a session bassist. Now Zagrash left the band and Zablogma left Sweden for studies. In 2002 the band resurfaced when Zablogma returned and hooked up with Zagzakel. Interest from Kvarforth's label Selbstmord brought a reunion to reality. The band returned, with new stage names where Zagzakel became Nil, Zablogma became Totalscorn (also in *IXXI*) and Necromorbus became I. Hate. Early 2003 the band drafted bass player Joachim "Gideon" Forsberg (*Overlord, Prometheus*). The first album is basically the second demo with three new tracks added. The style is fast and straightforward old-school black metal similar to *Ofermod* and *Immortal*, with a bit different, but still guttural vocals. Since drummer Tore "Necromorbus/I. Hate" Stjerna (*Funeral Mist, Watain, Ofermod, In Aeternum, Blackwitch, Nex, Chaos Omen* etc) is in the band it vouches for high quality.

2003 LP - PT 083

2004 CD - FPG 27

2006 CD - THR 94

2003 ☐	IN ODIUM VERITAS 1996-2002	CD	Selbstmord Services	CELLAR 012
2003 ■	IN ODIUM VERITAS	LP	Perverted Taste	PT 083
	White vinyl.			
2004 ■	ZAVORASH	CD	Oaken Shield	FPG 27
	Same as In Odium Veritas.			
2006 ■	NIHILISTIC ASCENSION & SPIRITUAL DEATH	CD	Total Holocaust Records	THR 94

ZEBULON

Klas Morberg: v/g, Håkan Morberg: v/g,
Johan "Jojje" Bohlin: b, Thomas "Snake" Johnsson: d

Södertälje - *Zebulon* were formed in 1997, out of the ashes of death metal band *Desultory*, and they recorded their first demo as *Zebulon* in 1998. The band had now changed direction towards the sludge/doom-style of *Queens Of The Stone Age*, *Monster Magnet* and *Nebula*. The name comes from the old western-hero Zebulon Macahan. Jojje is ex-*Unanimated*. In 2009 the entire line-up reformed *Desultory*.

The Macahans?

2000 10" - PRISON 001-1

2004 CD - PRISON 046-2

2000 ■	Cape Canaria	10" 4tr	People Like You	PRISON 001-1
	Tracks: Overflow/The Day/Burning Fuel/Goddamned. Red vinyl.			
2000 ☐	Cape Canaria	MCDd 4tr	People Like You	PRISON 001-2
2001 ☐	VOLUME ONE	CDd	People Like You	PRISON 024-2
2001 ☐	VOLUME ONE	LP	People Like You	PRISON 024-1
2004 ■	TROUBLED GROUND	CD	People Like You	PRISON 046-2

ZEELION

Pelle "Lenny De Rose" Saether: v, Magnus "Sudden" Söderman: g, Mats Olsson: k,
Lasse "Jonathan Oke" Lindén: b, Fredrik "Fredo" Österlund: d

Västerås - An all-star band indeed. Pelle has been a member of bands like *Schizophrenic Circus*, *Glory*, *Unchained*, *Macbeth* and is still a driving force behind *Zello*, where Mats is also found. He is also the owner of Studio Underground. Magnus and Lasse have previously played with *Rosicrucian* and *Slapdash*. Fredo is also ex-*Schizophrenic Circus*. Magnus is also found in *Lost Souls* and Lasse in *Carnal Forge*. The band started recording their second album already in 2002. Söderman has also been a member of *Powerage*, *Atrocity* and *Axenstar*. *Zeelion* play high-class melodic hard rock/metal, a bit reminiscent of *Talisman* meets Yngwie Malmsteen meets *Nocturnal Rites*. Today, Pelle is fronting melodic eighties-style hard rockers *Grand Design*, also featuring guitarist Janne Stark, who also came up with the *Zeelion* name, logo and artwork for *Steel Attack*.

1999 CD - 4 018996100839

2006 CD - LMC 170

1998 ☐	ZEELION	CD	Avex (Japan)	AVCB-66034
	Bonus: Take It To The Limit			
1999 ■	ZEELION	CD	AOR Heaven	4 018996100839
	Different artwork.			
2006 ■	STEEL ATTACK	CD	Lion Music	LMC 170

ZEIT

Michael Ohlsson: v, Håkan Gustavsson: g, Mats Rajaniemi: g, Christer Rössler: k, Lars-Gunnar Ström: b, Magnus Gustafsson: d

Hofors - Good melodic hard rock, like a heavier *Magnum Bonum* with the addition of keyboards. Vocals in Swedish. Michael later joined *Zircus* and is now found in symphonic rockers *New Clear Days*.

1980 ■ För Ung/Dra Iväg ....7" Click S-8280

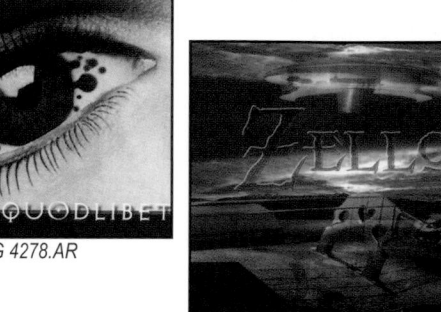

1980 7" - S-8280

ZELLO

Pelle Saether: v, Janne Stark: g, Anders Altzarfeldt: k, Lennart Glenberg-Eriksson: violin, Danne Lindell: b, Svetlan Råket: d

Västerås - *Zello* are a high-quality symphonic band pretty close to *Kansas* in their early prime. Even though the band had no guitarist on the first two albums, it's nothing that you immediately hear. On the first album the drums were handled by Jamil Batal (ex-*Schizophrenic Circus*). Pelle is ex-*Schizophrenic Circus, Unchained, Macbeth* etc and later found in *Zeelion*. Anders is also ex-*Unchained* and later in *EAR*, where Svetlan was also found. Lennart is also playing with comedian band *Bröderna Slut*. The band also did outstanding and original versions of *As The Moon Speaks, Astral Lady* and *As The Moon Speaks (Return)* on the *Captain Beyond* tribute *Thousand Days Of Yesterdays* (99 - Record Heaven). After public demand for guitar on the album, it was partly rerecorded with Janne Stark (*Overdrive, Locomotive Breath, Paradize, Constancia* etc) adding guitars, as *First Chapter, Second Verse*, also featuring some new tracks. Pelle later formed the band *Grand Design*, where Janne is now also found.

1999 CD - FGBG 4278.AR

1996 □ ZELLO..CD APM ....APM 9614 AT/SYMPHILIS 6
1999 ■ QUODLIBET..CD Musea.....................................FGBG 4278.AR
2004 ■ FIRST CHAPTER, SECOND VERSE.................CD Lion Music...LMC 117

2004 CD - LMC 117

ZEN

Martin Jämtlid: g/v, Mikael Lindgren: b, Janne "Jie" Zelf: d

Stockholm - *Zen* started out in a punkier vein with a track on the compilation *Swedish Sins*, but later changed to 70's influenced heavy, fuzz-tainted hard rock. Before the album the band recorded a four-track demo with the same title, where two of the tracks; *Sweettalk* and *Stillborn*, didn't make the album. Jie is ex-*Dirty Old Men*.

1999 □ So Very Zen .... 10" 4tr Froghouse...................................... FROG 006
Tracks: Ugly Truth/Star/Losin/God Of Guilt N' Greed. Pressed in orange vinyl.
2003 ■ THE SOUND OF SHIT HAPPENING............................CD Muse Entity Records/GMR ....MERCD 004

2003 CD - MERCD 004

ZERO ILLUSIONS

Björn Asking: v, Janne Lüthje: g, Tomas Reinersson: b, André Holmqvist: d

Göteborg - *Zero Illusions* were formed in 2004 out of the ashes of the band *Pain And Passion* (recorded one album in 2003), featuring all members except Tomas. The band plays excellent heavy grinding metal sounding a bit like a mix of *Saxon* and *Black Label Society*.

2008 □ ENTER ETERNITY ....CD private ....ZI 0805
2010 ■ OBLIVION..CD private ....ZI 1012

ZETA

Mikael "Micke" Moberg: v/g, Hasse "Bie" Carlsson: g, Mats Gran: b, Anders Carlsson: d

Fisksätra (Stockholm) - Formed as *Z* in 1975, initially featuring Moberg, guitarist Conny Undin, bassist Leif Zetterström and drummer Per Ingels. In 1977 the line-up changed drastically seeing Moberg flanked by Mats Gran on bass and Björn Malmros on drums, and the band now put a lot more effort into it, which resulted in a TV performance. Hasse Carlsson was added to the line-up. The first single is melodic hard rock with an early 70s/late 60s touch. The track *Walking Down The Starway* was featured on the compilation *Swedish Tracks* (1979 Sonet). The line-up on the second single featured Moberg on vocals, Anders Carlsson, Mats Gran, Bie Carlsson and choir girls Lena and Mia Janes. The style was now a bit more in the vein of *Magnum Bonum*. The final line-up of the band saw Carlsson replaced by Pelle Siren. Moberg later formed the band 2001 and after this he recorded an excellent AOR platter with the duo *Moberg-Talton*. He has later recorded solo albums under the moniker *The Moon Man/The Man From The Moon* and also appeared in the band *Bedlam*.

2010 CD - ZI 1012

1978 ○ Speleman/Walking Down The Starway...7" Sonet/Swedish Tracks ....DÄFT 6
Red vinyl. No artwork.
1979 ■ Vicken Tjej/Blinka Lilla Rock 'n Roll ....7" Sonet T-7967

1979 7" - T-7967

ZEUDO

Anna Jedler: v, Johan Bäckström: g, Johan Gottberg: k,
Christer Norrsell: b, Tomas Hurtig: d

Stockholm - Formed in 1984, inspired by *Genesis* and *Marillion*. Musically, this is quite good slightly symphonic melodic hard rock in the vein of *Story*, *Saga* or *Asia* with nice rough-edged guitars and pompy keyboards. Well worth looking for. The band split after the MLP was released.

1986 ■ A Wish From A Dream.. MLP 5tr   Utopia Records.................................UTP 186

Tracks: Don't Reach For My Shadow/Afterwish/He's A Leo/Underneath The Arches/
Dreams.

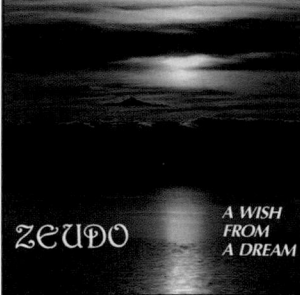
1986 MLP - UTP 186

ZILCH

Petter Englund: v, Mattias: g, Andreas Nilsson: b, Marcus Nilsson: d

Trottatorp - Formed in 1994. In 1999 Mattias left and was replaced by Martin Olsson. Musically *Zilch* produces quite basic hard rock with a garagy slightly stoner:ish attitude and sound topped with non-aggressive and quite cool vocals. Not bad at all.

1999 ■ Fire Down Below/Super System ....7"   private ....Z 001
Clear vinyl.

1999 7" - Z 001

ZIRCUS

Michael Ohlsson: v, Joakim Åberg: g, Tobbe Damberg: g,
Hasse Rosén: b, Niklas Tillman: d

Gävle - Formed in 1983 and split in the end of 1989. Michael and Hasse formed the symphonic melodic band *New Clear Daze*, who released a CD in 1993. The 7" contains two quite predictable tracks in the 80's melodic hard rock mould. The band recorded some great demos after the single, but they were unfortunately never vinylized. Michael has previously recorded with the band *Zeit*. Tobbe was earlier found in the band *Skydiverse*.

1989 ■ Jenny/Crazy 'Bout Girls ....7"   Bozz/Elektra....................................BOS 1034

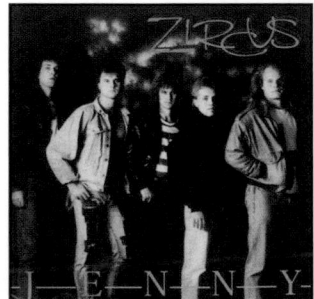
1989 7" - BOS 1034

ZOIC

Fredric Olson: v, Lasse Johansson: g, Mats "Mappe" Björkman: g,
Peter Edwards: b, Janne Lindh: d

Stockholm - When *Candlemass* took a break, and Leif Edling formed *Abstrakt Algebra*, *Candlemass* members Lasse, Mats and Janne formed the band *Zoic*. They drafted *Veni Domine* singer Fredric Olson and bassist Peter Edwards. *Zoic* is quite different from *Candlemass*, more in the vein of *Crimson Glory*, especially with Olson's high pitch vocals, but with a less proggy and more doomy approach. *Crimson Glory* singer Midnight was actually supposed to guest on the album, but it never happened. Not bad, but lacks a bit in the song department. In 2004, when *Candlemass* was having another break, Johansson and Lindh formed the band *Creozoth*.

1996 ■ TOTAL LEVEL OF DESTRUCTION...CD   Powerline Records.........................PLRCD 01
1996 ☐ TOTAL LEVEL OF DESTRUCTION...CD   Soundholic (Japan)....................SHCD1-0011

1996 CD - PLTCD 01

ZOMBIEKRIEG

Axel Widén: v, el Guapo: g, Martin Meyerman: g, Martin Petersson: b, Manne: d

Göteborg - *Zombiekrieg* play tight and well-played high-speed thrash with Swedish harsh/ screeching vocals. Great-sounding band, tight and powerful, similar to early *Megadeth* and *Metallica* meets *Kreator*. Widén was also in *Marionette*, *Mindfall* and *Poem*, Petersson has been in *Nominon* and Meyerman in *Massive Audio Nerve*. The line-up on the debut featured singer Axel, guitarist el Guapo, bassist Petersson and drummer Peter.

2010 ■ UNDANTAGSTILLSTÅND ....CD   GMR ....GMRCD 9022
2013 ☐ DEN VÄNSTRA STIGENS LJUS ....CD   GMR ....GMRCD 9035

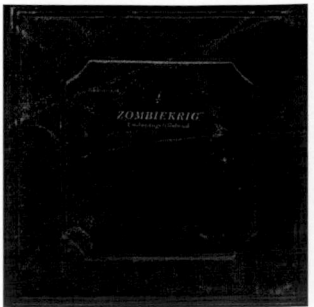
2010 CD - GMRCD 9022

ZONARIA

Simon Berglund: v/g, Emil Nyström: g, Markus Åkebo: b, Emanuel Isaksson: d

Umeå - *Zonaria* were formed in 2002 by fifteen year old Berglund and Nyström. In 2004 they recorded the demo *Evolution Overdose*. In 2005, seventeen-year-old drummer Isaksson and bassist Jerry Ekman were drafted. In 2006 the band entered the studio with Jonas Kjellgren (*Scar Symmetry*, *Carnal Forge*) to record the demo *Rendered In Vain*, which also featured some guest vocals from Christian Älvestam (*Unmoored, Scar Symmetry* etc.). Now Pivotal signed the band and the band again entered the studio with Kjellgren to record the debut album. After the album bass player Jerry Ekman was replaced by Markus Åkebo. The band now moved on to Century Media for the release of the follow-up, produced by Fredrik Nordström (*Dream Evil, Dimmu Borgir* etc). After the second album guitarist Caleb Bingham (*Ascension*) reinforced the band

and let Simon concentrate on singing. In Janury 2011bassist Max Malmer (*Folkmord, Death Maze, Apocalyst*) replaced Åkebo. *Zonaria* play well-produced melodic death metal with nice guitar harmonies, similar to *Dimmu Borgir* with a touch of *Scar Symmetry* (minus the clean vocals). In January 2013 Rickard Lundmark (*Feral*) replaced Isaksson.

2007	☐	INFAMY AND THE BREED	CD	Pivotal Recordings	PR 003
2008	☐	THE CANCER EMPIRE	CD	Century Media	997820-2
2012	■	ARRIVAL OF THE RED SUN	CD	Listenable Records	POSH 186

2012 CD - POSH 186

ZONATA

Johannes Nyberg: v/k, John Nyberg: g, Niclas Karlsson: g,
Mattias Asplund: b, Mikael "Cameron Force" Hörnqvist: d

Borås - Formed in 1998 and the track *Gate Of Fear* was featured on the *Rock Hard* compilation in 1999. The line-up featured Johannes, John, Mikael, guitarist Henrik Karlsson and bassist Johan Elving. After *Tunes Of Steel* second guitarist Henke Karlsson left the band and Elving was replaced by Mattias Asplund. The artwork for *Reality* was made by *Iron Maiden*'s former cover artist Derek Riggs. Great power metal, similar to *Insania*, *Steel Attack* etc. On *Buried Alive* second guitarist Niclas Karlsson (*Fraternia, Conviction, Fierce Conviction, Crystal Eyes*) had been added to the line-up. *Exceptions* is a compilation. Hörnqvist is now in *Enbound* and was formerly in *Ablaze*, *IronWare* and *Poem*. *Zonata* disbanded in 2003.

1998 MCD - MOLLA 101

1998	■	Copenhagen Tapes	MCD 5tr	private	MOLLA 101
		Tracks: Sonat A/Gate Of Fear/Glory And Fame/Magic Sword/Sonat B			
1999	☐	TUNES OF STEEL	CD	Century Media	77253 2
1999	☐	TUNES OF STEEL	CD	Victor (Japan)	VICP 60952
2001	■	REALITY	CD	Century Media	77324 2
2001	☐	REALITY	CD	Victor (Japan)	VICP 61345
2002	☐	BURIED ALIVE	CD	Soundholic (Japan)	TKCS-85051
		Bonus: The Search For The Light			
2002	☐	BURIED ALIVE	CD	Century Media	77393-2
2002	☐	BURIED ALIVE	CD	Fono (Russia)	FO 178 CD
2007	☐	EXCEPTIONS	CD	Century Media	77393-2

2001 CD - 77324 2

ZONE ZERO

Anders "Lissa" Listaniels: v, Torben "Tobben" Stenberg: g, Håkan Göras: g,
Lars Thörnblom: b, Lars "Leo/Lasse Lee" Lindberg: d

Gagnef/Leksand - *Zone Zero* were formed in 1980. They recorded their first two-track demo in 1981, followed by a five-track demo later the same year. The single, recorded in 1982, is often entitled *Heavy Metal*, as it's printed on the front cover. Heavy metal in the true Viking manner. Quite close to early *Heavy Load* or *Gotham City*. Mid-league stuff. The band reunited with the original line-up in 2004 and recorded some new songs.

1982	■	Win Or Die/Evil Dream	7"	Pang	PSI 021	$$

1982 7" - PSI 021

ZOOL

Martin Häggström: v, Henrik Flyman: g, Kasper Gram: b,
Andreas Lindahl: k, Kenneth Olsen: d

Stockholm - Henrik was once the main-man behind the band *Moahni Moahna*, where Martin was the singer. When things took a halt in the late nineties the two decided to form *ZooL*. They engaged former *Moahni Moahna* colleague Stefan Edström (b), *Afterglow/Mind's Eye* drummer Daniel Flores and keyboard player Andreas Lindahl for the album. The above line-up was not established until after the album was recorded and ready. Kasper is ex-*Wuthering Heights* and also found in *Manticora*, while Kenneth was found in *Royal Hunt*, meaning both are Danes. Keyboardist Richard Andersson guests. If you were into *Moahni Moahna*'s first album *Temple Of Life* or early *Rainbow*, you will love *ZooL*! Highly recommended. Flyman later appeared in *Evil Masquerade* and Lindahl in *Platitude*.

2002 CD - LU 20014 2

2002	■	ZOOL	CD	Lucretia Records	LU 20014 2
2002	☐	ZOOL	CD	CD-Amximum (Russia)	CDM 0702-938

ZPEEDFREAK

Jonny Granberg: v, Fredrik Håkansson: g, Micke Lidén: b, Ulf "Knirk" Johansson: d

Sundsvall - *Zpeedfreak* were formed by former *Moonshine* members Håkansson and Johansson in 2002. The debut is unfortunately not very exciting, with below par vocals and slightly sloppy playing. The second release is slightly better.

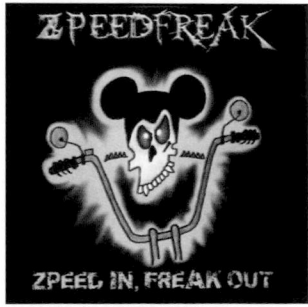

2010	☐	PAYBACK TIME	CD	private	ZPEED2010
2012	■	ZPEED IN, FREAK OUT	CDp	private	ZPEED2012

2012 CDd - ZPEED2012

ÅHLIN, MAGNUS

Magnus Åhlin: v/g/b, Ulric Åhlin: b, Gino Renebrandt: d

Eksjö - The first single is quite poppy AOR/melodic rock, while *Love Is A Day Away* is pretty decent melodic hard rock, and *No Time To Rest* has a reggae touch, but still rock. Peter Ekdahl plays tambourine and Hårdrockande Snaggle adds hand claps.

1982 □	Heart Burning Bright/Bomba molnen med centrifugerade guldfiskar	7"	private	SS-OM-999	
	500 copies.				
1983 ■	Love Is A Day Away/No Time To Rest	7"	private	SS-OM-997	
	500 copies.				

1983 7" - SS-OM-997

ÄNGLAGÅRD

Jonas Engdegård: g, Thomas Johnson: k, Anna Holmgren: flute, Johan Brand (aka Högberg): b, Mattias Olsson: d

Stockholm - The band was formed in 1991 by Tord and Johan, but the line-up wasn't complete until Anna joined in the spring of 1992. This has to be Sweden's #1 band in the symphonic/progressive rock category accompanied by the likes of **Anekdoten** and **The Flower Kings**. The first album consists of four very long, very good and very well-played songs with lots of mellotron, Hammond organ, flute and distorted guitar. *Änglagård* were invited to play at the Progfest in USA in 1993 and 1994, where they made an enormous impact. The single, already very rare, was released through the English magazine Ptolematic Terrascope. They are featured with one track on the compilation-CD *Progfest 94* (95 Musea) and *Gånglåt från Knapptibble* was also featured on the Hurricane Katrina benefit album *After The Storm* (2006 Near Fest). The band sadly split, but reunited in 2002, but without singer/guitarist Tord Lindman. They did a few gigs, took a long break and returned again in 2011, and released the excellent *Viljans öga*. Late 2012 Tord returned, Linus Kåse replaced Thomas and Erik Hammarström replaced Mattias (**Pineforest Crunch, White Willow**). Both are ex-**Brighteye Brison**.

1993 CD - MELLO 004

1995 CD - HYB CD 010

1993 ■	HYBRIS	CD	Mellotronen	MELLO 004	$
1993 □	HYBRIS	LP	Colours	COSLP 013	$
1994 ○	Gånglåt Från Knapptibble (split)	7"	Ptolematic Terrascope	-	$
	Released together with Ptolematic Terrascope Vol. 4 1994 (#16). No artwork.				
1995 ■	EPILOG	CD	private	HYB CD 010	
1995 □	EPILOG	CD	Exergy Music	EX 10	
1995 □	EPILOG	LPg	Gates Of Dawn (USA)	GOD 002	
	Second pressing is without booklet, but with lyric sheet.				
1997 □	BURIED ALIVE!	CD	Musea	FGB 4116.AR CD4	
	Recorded at the LA Progfest in 1994.				
1997 □	BURIED ALIVE!	CD	Si-Wan (Korea)	n/a	
2000 □	HYBRIS	CD	Mellotronen	MELLOCD 4004	
	Bonus: Gånglåt från Knapptibble				
2003 □	HYBRIS	CDd	Exergy Music	EX 9	
2009 □	HYBRIS	CDd	Änglagård Records	ANG 01	
	Bonus: Gånglåt från Knapptibble. Re-mastered.				
2010 □	EPILOG	2CD	Änglagård Records	ANG 02	
	Bonus: Rösten				
2012 ■	VILJANS ÖGA	CD	Änglagård Records	ANG 03CD	
2012 □	VILJANS ÖGA	2LP	Änglagård Records	ANG 03LP	
	1500 black vinyl, 500 copies clear vinyl with postcards.				
2013 □	HYBRIS	CDvg	Arcangelo (Japan)	ARC-3035	
2013 □	EPILOG	2CDvg	Arcangelo (Japan)	ARC-3036/37	
2013 □	VILJANS ÖGA	CDv	Arcangelo (Japan)	ARC-3038	

2012 CD - ANG 03CD

Unofficial releases:

1993 □	1993-12-18 MARX INN, MILWAUKEE, WI	CD	- -	- -

ÖRBY MIX

Bo Lönnberg, Rolf Johansson, Lars Berg, Hans Lönnberg

Stockholm - **Örby Mix** play really good pomp-oriented melodic hard rock with an American touch. Good vocals and nice guitars. Not bad at all.

1982 ■	Tomma glas/Ge mig tid	7"	Pang	PSI 064

1982 7" - PSI 064

ÖVERSLAG

Torbjörn Andersson: v/b, Mats Andersson: g, Peter Hoffman: g, Christer Örnberg: d

Stockholm - Formed in 1976, influened by the classic hard rock bands, but also drawing some influences from punk, which shows in the vocal delivery. *Överslag* play very straightforward, seventies-sounding hard rock 'n' roll similar to **Ocean** or **Spin Air**. For collectors only.

1980 ■	Varför får man inte va' annorlunda/Farbror polisen	7"	Noon Records	SNS 802	$

1980 7" - SNS 802

ANGEL KING

Lasse Gudmundsson: s, Thomas Jacobsson: g, Robin Ericsson: b, Mats Ericsson: d

Stockholm - *Angel King* are a new band with a bunch of old foxes. Thomas is ex-*Snakes In Paradise*, *Bedlam* etc., Lasse is also in *Lizard Eye*, Robin is in *Degreed*. *Angel King* plays solid, standard-formula sleazy hard rock with a touch of 70s *Kiss*.

2012 ☐ WORLD OF PAIN...CD Yesterrock...Y201227

2012 LP - AMAXA01

AMAXA

Erik Broström: v, Peter Pedersén: g, Anders Broström: b, Jimmy Halvarsson: d

Stockholm - A good band with nice riffs, but lacking a bit in originality. *Amaxa* draw their influences from bands like *Atomic Rooster, Led Zeppelin, Grand Funk* etc.

2012 ■ AMAXA..LP Mandarin.................................... AMAXA 01

ANGUISH

Johan Dee: v, David Eriksson: g, Christoffer "Kribbe" Frylmark: g,
Anton Eriksson: b, Rasmus Jansson: d

Uppsala - Formed in 2007 and released their first demo *Dawn Of Doom* in 2010. Crushing doom metal, quite similar to early *Candlemass*, but lacking in the vocal department. Anton Johansson played bass on the split.

2011 ☐ Anguish/Black Oath (split)...............................7" Unholy Domain Records............................n/a
    Split with Black Oath. 300 copies. Track: The Veil
2012 ☐ THROUGH THE ARCHDEMON'S HEAD ....CD Dark Descent...............................DDR054CD
2012 ☐ THROUGH THE ARCHDEMON'S HEAD ....2LP Dark Descent...............................DDR054LP
    Black or grey vinyl.

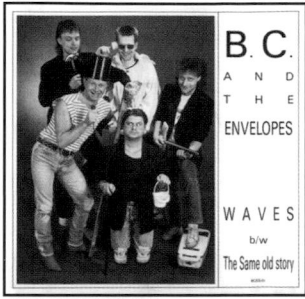

1988 7" - BCES-01

B.C AND THE ENVELOPES

Åke Swahn: v, Pelle Robertsson: g, Olle Hellström: k,
Mats Engberg: b, Thorbjörn Harr: d

Umeå - Strange name, but a great band, playing powerful and high-quality AOR. Olle has since made a solo career in pop.

1988 ■ Waves/The Same Old Story.................................7" private BCES-01

BEAST

Maria Eriksson: v, Elias Jubran: g, Kalle Lagergren: b, Mattias Karlsson: d

Stockholm - The band was formed in 2009 with the members coming from the hardcore and punk scene and bands like *Imperial Leather*, *The Kind That Kills* and *Social Pressure*. Quite garagey, energetic, great hard rock, similar to *Danko Jones*, with great vocals from Maria!

2012 7" - GAP 022

2011 ☐ Beast.. 7" 4tr private ....(BEAST001)
    Tracks: Rage/Nightrider/Do It/ Creatures.100 red and 300 black vinyl copies.
2012 ■ Devil's Throat/Buckle Up......................................7" Gaphals .... GAP 022
    277 black vinyl copies.
2012 ☐ Disguice / Disaster .... 7" 4tr Green Menace Records..................... GMR 16
    Tracks: Disguice / Disaster/Unholy One/Time To Escape/Dark Road. 300 black vinyl copies.

BENEVOLENT

Johan Samuelsson: v, Joel Nilsson: g, Christoffer Norén: g,
Robin Halldin: b, Niklas Sandell: d

Göteborg - Very interesting progressive and technival melodic metal core, like a mix of *Meshuggah*, *Mastodon* and *Khoma*. The band was formed in 2006. Nilsson has also played with *Dead By April* as a live musician and Sandell is ex-*Wonderland Dementation Dpt.*.

2010 MCDd - DTM 020

2010 ■ Evolve ....MCDd 3tr Dead Tree Music...............................DTM 020
    Tracks: Evolve/Shreds/Personae
2013 ☐ THE WAVE...CD Rambo Music...............................BENCD 001

BEYOND ALL RECOGNITION

David Söhr: v, David Eriksen: g, Paul Gidlöf: g,
Pontus Bergström Warren: b, Edwin Jansson: d

Västerås - Formed in 2011. The band play a mix of melodic death metal, hardcore and dubstep, or dubcore as the band calls it. Söhr and Gidlöf were ex-*Affecti Veternus*.

2012 CD - NPR 440

LATE ADDITIONS

2011 ☐	This Is Dubcore	MCD 5tr	Napalm			- -

Tracks: Remains Of A Memory/Mark This Earth/Tale Of A Traitor/True Story/From Another Point Of View

2012 ■	DROP=DEAD	CD	Napalm	NPR 440

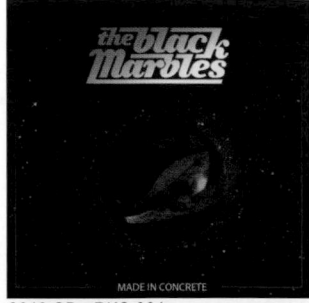

2013 CD - RKC 001

BLACK MARBLES, THE

Kaj Paxéus: v, Philip Karlsson: g, Krister Selander: b, Tobbe Bövik: d

Göteborg - Bövik has also been found in *The Awesome Machine* and *On Parole*. The Black *Marbles* play really great rock-oriented hard rock, drawing influences from various styles, but making it sound really tight and consistent.

2013 ■	MADE IN CONCRETE	CD	TBM Productions	RKC 001
2013 ☐	MADE IN CONCRETE	LP	TBM Productions	RKC 001 LP

BLACKWOOD

Mårten Larsson: v, Andreas Magnusson: g, Magnus Sandberg: g, Mikael Elofsson: b, Tomas Andersson: d

Östersund - Quite grunge-oriented heavy rock. Musically it's heavy rock, while the vocals are more Eddie Vedder-ish. Decent. In 1998 the band made two releases under the name *Saltmine*, then featuring drummer Peter Wikström, and still in the same musical vein.

2011 MCDp - 340065 006467

1995 ☐	Otherwise	MCD 5tr	private	PEAK 19951

Tracks: Lost/Green Sweat/When I Lie/Pretend/Otherwise

BLOODLIT

Mladen Milojkovic: v, Dennis Carlsson: g, Tord Ottergren: g, Andrëas Larsson: b, Marcus Rudenvall: d

Borås - Hard-edged metal with strong influences from *Mustasch* and *Motörhead*, mixed with *Metallica*. The band was formed in 2006 by Carlsson and Ottergren. The band initially featured drummer Markus Johansson, who was replaced by Rudenvall in 2009.

2011 ■	Take What's Mine	MCDp 6tr	private	340065 006467

Tracks: Take What's Mine/Surf In USA/Still I Feel/Atrocity/Vulture/Misleading Attention

2013 ☐	DEAD ON	CD	private	BEF 1301

2010 CD - SR-0090

BRING YOUR OWN KNIFE

Anton Sööder: v, Jacob Ottosson: g, Tomas Nyiri: g, Jesper Thorin: b, Robin Österberg: d

Motala - The band recorded their first demo in 2008 and the digital live album *Live From Gothenburn* in 2010 and in September the same year bass player Joel Ek was replaced by Thorin. In 2011 the band also recorded a digital EP. Good, standard melodic death metal/metalcore.

2010 ■	END	CD	Sleazy Rider	SR-0090

CORROSIVE CARCASS

Jonathan Sjöblom: v, Christian Kanto: g, Mikael Lindorf: g, Peter Koistinaho: b, Markus Janis: d

Hofors - Formed by Fredrik Lindorf and Markus in 2004, followed by Peter and Mikael. In 2007 Jonathan joined. Fredrik left, guitarist Markus took over his drums and Christian finally joined in 2009. Old-school style death metal similar to *Marduk* and *Dark Funeral*.

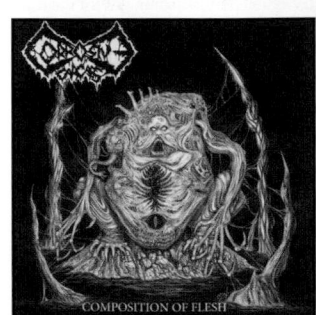

2012 CD - ABYSS 033 CD

2012 ■	COMPOSITION OF FLESH	CD	Abyss Records	ABYSS 033 CD

DEALS DEATH

Olle Ekman: v, Sebastian Myrén: g, Erik Jacobsson: g, Fredrik Ljung: b, Janne Jaloma: d

Falun/Göteborg - Formed in 2008 in Borlänge and later relocated to Göteborg. Jaloma has also been found in *Chronic Torment*, *Anubis* and *Ruined Soul*, Ljung in *Disdain*, Ekman has growled in *Död*, *Volturyon*, *Lethal Attack* and *Pergolos* and Jalorma is also in *Confidence*.

2012 CD - SPI421 CD

2012 ■	ELITE	CD	Spinefarm	SPI421 CD
2013 ☐	POINT ZERO SOLUTION	CD	Spinefarm	SPI444 CD

870

DEATH WOLF

Valentin Maelstrom: v, Marcus "Markko" Bäckbrant: g,
Morgan "Mogge/Steinmeyer" Håkansson: b, Mikael "Hrafn" Karlsson: d

Norrköping - In 2011 *The Devil's Whorehouse* simply changed their name to *Death Wolf*, as they figured they had outgrown the old name. Same members, same style. *Danzig/Samhain*-influenced dark metal/hard rock with punkish influences. See *Devil's Whorehouse, The*.

2011	☐	DEATH WOLF	CD	Blooddawn	BLOOD 051
		Sticker in the first 1000 copies.			
2012	■	Bloodscent	7"	Blooddawn	BLOOD 056
		Tracks: Snake Mountain/Sudden Bloodletter. White vinyl. 500 copies			
2013	☐	II: BLACK ARMOURED DEATH	CD	Century Media	88612
2013	☐	II: BLACK ARMOURED DEATH	CD	Century Media	9981618
2013	☐	II: BLACK ARMOURED DEATH	LP	Century Media	9981618

2012 7" - BLOOD 056

DEATH TYRANT

Daniel "Nárgraðr Agartha" Bornstrand: v, Thomas Backelin: g,
Dennis Antonsson: g, Anders Backelin: b, Joakim Antonsson: d

Vänersborg - When *Lord Belial* were put to rest the Backelin brothers formed *Death Tyrant* to continue their melodic death/black metal journey in a similar style. They recorded the demo *The Dark Abyss* in 2010. Antonsson is ex-*Trident, Nox Aurea, The Cold Existence*.

2013	■	OPUS DE TYRANIS	CD	Non-Serviam Records	NSR 666

2013 CD - NSR 666

DESULTOR

Markus Joha: v/g, Ibrahim Stråhlman: d

Stockholm - Great-sounding, well-played technical death metal with mixed growling and clean vocals. Stråhlman is also in *Auberon*, while Joha is ex-*Machinery*. The album also features Pablo Magallanes (*Demonical*), Fredrik Klingwall (*Loch Vostock*) and Ragnar Rage.

2012	■	MASTERS OF HATE	CD	Abyss Records	ABYSS 026 CD
2012	☐	MASTERS OF HATE	LP	Abyss Records	ABYSS 001 LP
		400 transparent red + Sticker. 100 die hard - sticker, patch, button.			

2012 CD - ABYSS 026 CD

DIAMOND DAWN

Alexander Strandell: v, Jhonny Göransson: g, Olle Lindahl: g,
Mikael Planefeldt: b, Niklas Arkbro: k, Efraim Larsson: d

Göteborg - This new, up-and-coming AOR band was formed in 2011 and gained much attention with their first demo track *Standing As One*, resulting in a deal with Frontiers Records. Excellent AOR in the same league and vein as *H.E.A.T, Houston* etc.

2013	■	OVERDRIVE	CD	Frontiers Records	FR CD 588
2013	☐	OVERDRIVE	CD	Icarus Music (Argentina)	ICARUS 1092

EDGE

Johan Forss: v/g/k, Tobias Andersson: g/k, Torbjörn Brogren: b, Olle Rodéhn: d

Karlskoga - Formed in 2011 by former *Shadowland/Seven Wishes* member Andersson and Forss. They drafted *Shadowland* colleague Rodéhn and *Heads Or Tales* bassist Brogren and there was *Edge*. The band plays high-quality melodic hard rock similar to *H.E.A.T, Talisman* etc.

2013	■	HEAVEN KNOWS	CD	Escape Music	ESM 247

2013 CD - FR CD 588

ERUPTED

Daniel Ocic Sundberg: v, Tobias Pettersson: g,
Jonas Davidsson: g, Cedrik Petersson: b, Jonte Holm: d

Växjö - Formed in 2010 as *Carnivore*, but changed name to *Erupted* in 2011, when they also recorded their first demo. Old-school death metal.

2012	☐	IN THE GRIP OF CHAOS	CD	Abyss Records	ABYSS 042 CD

FETUS STENCH

Andreas Björnson: v/g, Kristian Karlsson: b, Emil Wiksten: d

Karlstad - Wiksten is also in *Aeon* and *Blood Red Throne*, while Karlsson is also in *The Law* and *Inferior*. Death metal in the vein of *Morbid Angel*.

2012	☐	STILLBIRTH	CD	Abyss Records	ABYSS 037 CD

2013 CD - ESM 247

LATE ADDITIONS

GARDNERZ, THE
Niclas Ankarbranth: v, Wilhelm Lindh: g, Francisco Martin: b, Vedran Bencic: d

Landskrona - Formed in 2008. Well-played and well-produced doom-oriented death metal. Ankarbranth is also found in *Vandöd*.

2011 ■	THE SYSTEM OF NATURE	CDd	Abyss Records	ABYSS 030 CD
	Bonus: Bloody Vengeance (Vulcano cover)/Servants Of Warsmen (Winter cover)			
2011 ☐	THE SYSTEM OF NATURE	LP	Mechanix Records	MCHX 1001-1
	500 copies.			
2012 ☐	It All Fades	MCD	Abyss Records	ABYSS 046 CD
	Tracks: Don't Look Back/A Horrible Disease/Transylvanian Hunger (Darkthrone cover)/It All Fades/Melatoni/Erasing Bad Specimen			

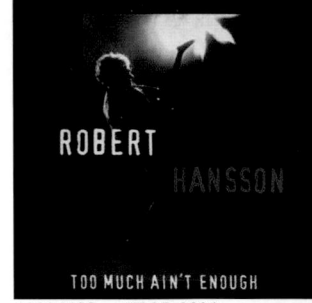

2011 CDd - ABYSS 030 CD

HANSSON, ROBERT
Robert Hansson: g/b/d

Göteborg - Robert Hansson started his career doing his own MCD, playing and programming all of it himself. Style-wise, this is really great melodic shredding with fusion-overtones. Robert has later recorded with bands and projects like *Human Race, Rawburt, Treborian* and *Bonkyman*. For fans of guys like Steve Lukather, Joe Satriani and Neal Schon.

1996 ■	Too Much Ain't Enough	MCDp 3tr	private	TRCD 9601
	Tracks: Too Much Ain't Enough/Starfall/Hurdy Gurdy			

1996 MCDp - TRCD 9601

HYPERBOREAN
Magnus Persson: v, Andreas Blomqvist: g, Max Lindberg: b

Örebro/Stockholm - Formed in 2000 and recorded their first demo, *Of Malice*, in 2002. The recording featured guest drummer Fredrik Widigs (*Angrepp, Demonical, The Ugly*).Quite technical and melodic black metal, a bit like *Dissection* mixed with *Amon Amarth*.

2011 ☐	THE SPIRIT OF WARFARE	CD	Abyss Records	ABYSS 022 CD

I AM HUNGER
Fredrik Forsberg: v, Andreas Ehrnberg: g,
Lars Nordén: g, Love Forsberg: b, Ulf Bogren: d

Trollhättan - *I Am Hunger* plays high-quality technical metalcore with a touch of *Bring Me The Horizon* and *Neurosis*. The band split in 2012. Some of the members continued in *GUST*.

2011 ■	ODIUM	CDd	Snapping Fingers Snapping Necks	SFSN002CD

2011 CDd - SFSN002CD

LAVETT
Daniel Heiman: v, Manne Engström: g, Andreas Olavi: g,
Henric Liljestrand: b, Chistian Silver: d

Varberg - *Lavett* feature quite an impressive line-up. Manne (*Fatal Embrace*), Olavi (*Serenade For June, Inhale*), Silver (*Sundown, Beseech, Painfield, As You Drown*) and top notch singer Heiman (*Lost Horizon, Heed, Sarea,* etc). It's quite surprising what made this line-up record such a pop-oriented album. Pop-metal in the vein of *Dead By April*.

2012 ☐	FIND YOUR PURPOSE	CD	RoastingHouse	RHRCD688-2

LEGIONS OF WAR
Zyklon: v/g, Widowreaper: g, Hellwind: v/b, Martin "C. Stalinorgel" Hogebrandt: d

Tanum - These death-oriented, old-school thrashers recorded their first demo, *Proclamation Of War* in 2005, followed by *In The Sniper's Eye* (2007) and *Mission To Kill* (2009), before they were featured on the *Extreme Aggression* compilation in 2008, and then picked up by Inferno Records. Hogebrandt is also found in *Suicidal Winds, Mindblaster* and *Conspiracy*.

2009 ☐	TOWARDS DEATH	CD	Infernö Records	IR 003 CD
	1000 copies.			
2011 ■	Riding With Blitz/Shellshocks	CDS	Infernö Records	n/a

2011 CDS - ??

MAGNUS KARLSSON'S FREEFALL
Magnus Karlsson: v/g/b/k

Höör - Magnus Karlsson is one of Sweden's prime string benders and melodic metal composers who has worked with bands like *Last Tribe, Planet Alliance, Midnight Sun*, as well as *Starbreaker, Allen Lande* and *Primal Fear*. When Magnus goes solo, it's no different. High-class melodic metal with classy guitar playing. Guests: Herman Saming (*A.C.T*), Mike Andersson (*FullForce*), Rickard Bengtsson (*Last Tribe*), Rick Altzi (*Sanity*), Daniel Flores etc.

2013 CD - FRCD 607

| 2013 ■ | MAGNUS KARLSSON'S FREEFALL | CD | Frontiers Records | FRCD 607 |
| 2013 □ | MAGNUS KARLSSON'S FREEFALL | CD | Avalon Marquee (Japan) | MICP-11094 |

MAMONT

Karl Adolphsson: v/g, Jonathan Wårdsäter: g, Victor Wårdsäter: b, Jimmy Karlsson: d

Stockholm/Nyköping - *Lugnoro* and *Alonzo* have a great label mate in *Mamont*, who bring on their best-sounding seventies-sound with an additional stoner touch. Quite jam-oriented.

| 2012 ■ | PASSING THROUGH THE MASTERY DOOR | CDd | Ozium Records | OZIUM002 |
| 2013 □ | PASSING THROUGH THE MASTERY DOOR | LP | Bilocation | 12 |

100 blue, 200 orange and 200 black vinyl copies.

2012 CDd - OZIUM002

MANDYLION

Magnus Blomkvist: v, Andreas Spåls: g/b, Leif Olsson: g

Storvik - The band was formed in 1997 from the remains of death metal bands *Soliloquy* and *Encined*. Quite atmospheric doom metal with a slightly gothic touch. Not over-exciting vocals though and a slightly underwhelming sound. Micke Ahlin played drums on the recording.

| 1999 □ | Haunted Heart | MCD 4tr | private | - - |

Tracks: Disintegration/Only When You Fall/Fountain/Night Under Command By The Grave

MARGOTH AND THE JABS

Margot: v, Åke Bylund: v/d, Roger Jonsson: b, Per Alpne: g, Tomas Json Stendius: d

Stockholm - *Thor* is good solid melodic hard rock with low key, high vibrato female vocals. *JABS* stands for Jonsson, Alpne, Bylund, Stendius, all members of popsters *Mörbyligan*. *Thor* was also released in Swedish on *Mörbyligan*'s album *Vikingarock* (1984). *Margoth & The Jabs*' version is also found on the *Mörbyligan* compilation *Tors återkomst* (1995). Bylund died in 2005. Margot was just a singer hired for this recording.

| 1988 ■ | Child Of The Northern Lights/Thor | 7" | Audiovision | - - $ |

1988 7" - - -

MASSDISTRACTION

Mikkjal G. Hansen: v, Jon Hjalmarsson: g, Ali Nassadjpoor: g,
Kalle Möllerström: b, David Larsson: d

Malmö - The band was formed in 2007. *Massdistraction* play outstanding, tight, energetic and well-played thrash with brutal vocals.

| 2012 ■ | FOLLOW THE RATS | CD | Target/Misty Music | PMZ 75 |

2012 CD - PMZ 75

MINDSHIFT

Marcus "Mao" Uggla: v, Jay Matharu: g, Johan Lund: g,
Eddie Siojo: b, Joakim Olausson: d

Stockholm - *Mindshift* were founded in 2004. On *No Regrets* Jay had replaced Rickard Gustavsson, Eddie replaced Dennis Langkjaer and Joakim replaced Marty Martszchanty. The album contains a bonus DVD with "the making of". In 2013 Johan Björn was replaced by Marcus Mao Uggla (*Blowsight, Slavegrind*). Great melodic metal. On *Evilution* Marcus (also bassist in *Blowsight*) replaced Johan Björn and the syle went modern aggro metal.

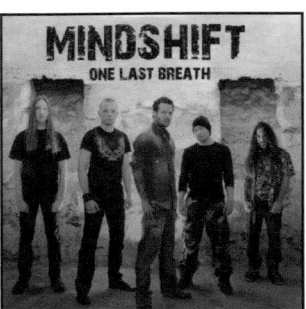

2011 ■	One Last Breath	MCDp 3tr	private	- -
	Tracks: My Infamy/This Pain In Me/Havoc In Mind			
2012 □	NO REGRETS	CD+DVDd	private	- -
2013 □	Evilution	MCD 4tr	private	- -

Tracks: Farewell/My Dark Passenger/Into Your Hands/The Burning Hate

2011 MCDp - - -

NECROCURSE

Per "Hellbutcher" Gustavsson: v, Martin "Mörda" Andersson: g,
Stefan Rodin: g, Johan Bäckman: b, Nicklas Rudolfsson: d

Uddevalla - This all-star band, with members from band such as *Nifelheim*, *Runemagick*, *Masticator* and *Sabotage* was initiated in 2004, but didn't make any serious recordings until 2010. In 2011 it all exploded. No frills, straight death metal in the vein of *Dismember* and *Runemagick*.

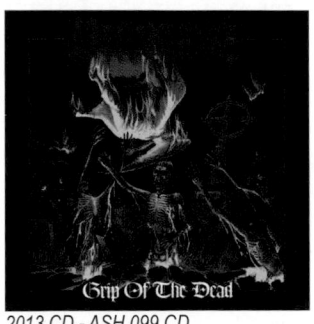

2011 □	Chaos Carnage Cataclysm/Shape of Putrid Abomination	7"	Aftermath Music	Chapter 63
	500 copies.			
2011 □	Insane Curse Of Morbidity/Dust To Flesh (The Evocation)	7"	Aftermath Music	Chapter 65
	500 copies.			
2012 □	Shape Of Death	shape MCD 5tr	Aftermath Music	Chapter 66

Tracks: Both singles + Souls Of A Thousand Funerals. 500 copies.

2013 CD - ASH 099 CD

LATE ADDITIONS

2013 ■	GRIP OF THE DEAD	CD	Pulverised	ASH 099 CD
2013 □	GRIP OF THE DEAD	CDd	Pulverised	ASH 099 DG
2013 □	GRIP OF THE DEAD	LP	To The Death	TTD 028

Bonus: Souls Of A Thousand Funerals. 400 orange and 100 black vinyl.

NIGHT

Oskar Andersson: v, Calle Englund: g, Sammy Ouirra: b, Linus Lundgren: d

Linköping - Another great addition to the NWoSHM, sounding like true NWoBHM from the 80s.
If you're into bands like **Jameson Raid** and early **Tygers Of Pan Tang** (but with better vocals).

2012 □	Stand Your Ground/Hard Working Man	7"	Gaphals	GAP 026

200 white and 300 black vinyl copies.

2013 ■	Gunpowder Treason/Into The Night	7"	Gaphals	GAP 043

200 white and 300 black vinyl copies.

2013 7" - GAP 043

NOCTURNAL

Linus Ekermo: v, Kalle Svensson: g, Max Monryd: b, Dennis Skoglund: d

Linköping - **Nocturnal**, formed early 2011, plays solid seventies sounding hard rock with a good
amount of riffs, in the vein of **Witchcraft**.

2012 ■	Until The Morning Light/Black Magic	7"	Gaphals	GAP 023

1st press: 300 black, 2nd press (2013) 250 purple + 250 white vinyl.

2013 □	One Of A Kind/Night Rainbow	12"	Gaphals	GAP 034

500 copies.

2013 □	NOCTURNAL	CDd	Gaphals	GAP040

1000 copies.

2013 □	NOCTURNAL	LP	Gaphals	GAP040

500 black, 250 dark red and 250 dark yellow.

2012 7" - GAP 023

NUBIAN ROSE

**Sofia Lilja: v, Christer Åkerlund: g, Thomas Lindgren: g,
Fredrik Åkerlund: k, Henrik Uhrbom: b, David Algesten: d**

Stockholm - High-class, melodic, 80s-style hard rock/AOR with a touch of **Heart**, fronted by
vocal coach Lilja. Features guest vocals from Mats Levén.

2013 ■	MOUNTAIN	CD	Funkylord Dynasty	NR12001

2013 CD - NR12001

OBNOXIOUS YOUTH

Afsihn "Affe" Piran: v, John Zeke: g, Oliver Ahlström: b, Frans Utterström: d

Stockholm - This is definitely a borderline band. Mix hardcore, punk and high speed death metal
and this is what you'll get. Not too far från Piran's band **Undergång**.

2011 □	THE ETERNAL VOID	LP	n/a	n/a
2013 ■	Suck On The Cross	7" 4tr	Primitive Art	PAR 033

*Tracks: Hell On Earth/Suck On The Cross/Cut The Throat/Conquest For Death (Necros
cover).166 red and 500 black vinyl copies.*

PETER MARTINSSON GROUP

Peter Martinsson: g

Uppsala - Peter started his career in the sevenies playing in hard rockers **Plebb** and **Purple
Haze**. After some years in various constellations he finally struck a deal with US guitar label
Grooveyard. Instrumental melodic hard rock/rock/blues, Satriani meets Bonamassa. Great!

2012 ■	GUITAR STATE OF MIND	CDd	Grooveyard Records	GYR 097

2013 7" - PAR 033

PRAY FOR LOCUST

Tintin Andersen: v, Jerry Engström: g, Stefan Schyberg: g, Kvasi: b, Simon Corner: d

Stockholm - **Pray For Locust** was formed in 2009, influenced by bands like **The Haunted**,
Pantera and **Slayer**, but also **The Refused** and **Machine Head** which made the band move into
a heavier territory, sounding a bit more in the vein of **Children Of Bodom**.

2012 □	SWARM	CD	Supernova	SUPERCD 012

REAKTOR 4

"P G": v/g, "Lex A": g/k, Johan "J" Goksöyr: g/programming

Strömstad - **Reaktor 4** are an industrial, quite synth-based, melancholic death metal band
formed in 2007. They recorded their first demo the same year and released the debut in 2009.

2012 CDd - GYR 097

Jonas "Nattdal/B" Bergqvist (*Lifelover*) guests on vocals on the album.

2009 ■ REAKTOR 4 ....CD   Total Holocaust Records ....THR 118

REEHAB, THE
Sven Östlind: v/g, Peo Axelsson: b, Johan Månsson: g, Jesper Waltersson: d

Lindome - **The Reehab** play straight ahead, good, solid melodic, bluesy hard rock with some classic rock thrown in. A new release is planned for 2013. Peo is ex-*Vanguard* and *Poleaxe*.

2012 □ Revolution ....MCDp 5tr   StoneFree REEHAB002

2009 CD - THR 118

RESISTANCE, THE
Marco Aro: v, Jesper Strömblad: g, Glenn Ljungström: b, Christofer Barkensjö: d

Göteborg - Göteborg all stars indeed! These former members of bands like **In Flames, The Haunted, Grav, Facedown** etc. joined forces in 2012 and formed **The Resistance**. True to their former bands they stick to death metal

2013 □ Rise From Treason/My Fire/Slugger/Face To Face .... 7" 4tr   Edel.................................0208481EREP
2013 ■ SCARS...CDd   Edel.................................0208478ERE
2013 □ SCARS...LP   Edel.................................0208709ERE

2013 CD - 0208704EREP

REVELATIONS
Thomas Berggren: v, Anders Stafrén: g, Daniel Ramirez: b, Janne Backlund: d

Stockholm - Formed in 2012. Seventies-influenced hard rock sounding like a mix of **Iron Maiden** and **Black Sabbath**. In 2013 Lasse Gudmunsson (**Angel King, Lizard Eye**) replaced Thomas.

2012 □ Warning..MCD 4tr   private ....REVCD 001
    Tracks: Strange Dreams/Under The Gun/Another Lie/Jealousy

ROCKA ROLLAS
Joe Liszt: v, Cederick Forsberg: g/b/d

Sandviken - Killer retro heavy metal with killer vocals and shredding guitars from the multi talented Cederick. Highly recommended for fans of **Raven, Air Raid, Enforcer** etc. Josef Mineur sings on the debut. Cederick also has two metal side projects called **Blazon Stone** and **Mortyr**.

2011 ■ THE WAR OF STEEL HAS BEGUN ....CD   Stormspell Records SSR-DL75
    1000 copies.
2012 □ Conquer ....MLP 4tr   Underground Power.............................UP003
    300 copies. Tracks: Bloodbath/Conquer/Living The Metal Storm/Steelwheeler
2012 □ Conquer ....MCD 4tr   Stormspell Records SSR-DL-98
2013 □ METAL STRIKES BACK ....CD   Stormspell Records ....SSR-DL-105 CD

2011 CD - SSR-DL75

ROUGH ROCKERS
Peter Ljungberg: v, Magnus Hällström: g/b/d

Stockholm - **Rough Rockers** play, despite the slightly silly name, hard rock with influences from the 70s **Sweet**, **Uriah Heep** and even some **Sabbath**y moments. Average quality stuff. Peter is also found in **Movin' Globe** and **Eterno**.

2013 ■ Pimped & Poisoned ....MCDp 5tr   private ....(C13-1044)
    Tracks: No More Heroes/The Vicious Circle/Rough Rocker/Speedrocker/Rebel At Heart

2013 CD - IW83026

SAFFIRE
Tobias Jansson: v, Victor Olsson: g, Dino Zuzic: k, Magnus Carlsson: b, Anton Roos: d

Göteborg - **Saffire** were formed in 2006 by Victor and Dino and recorded three demos, before recording the debut with producers Fredrik Nordström and Henrik Udd. The band plays excellent melodic heavy rock in the vein of **ColdSpell** with a touch of **Mustasch**. Roos is also in **Elevener**.

2013 ■ FROM ASHES TO FIRE ....CD   Inner Wound IW83026

SCANDAL CIRCUS
Johan Jonvén: v, Pelle "Eliaz" Eliasson: g, Carl Malmqvist: b, Andreas Båge: d

Helsingborg - Formed in 2011, when Pelle (**Bai Bang**), Andreas (**Dawn Of Oblivion**) and Carl left the band **Mindfuel**. They found singer Johan and Scandal Circus was a fact. Great, riff-oriented heavy melodic metal in the vein of **Ammotrack** or **Fuelhead**.

2012 ■ IN THE NAME OF ROCK 'N' ROLL ....CD   private ....MECD 1009

2012 CD - MECD 1009

LATE ADDITIONS

SPASMODIC

Alexander Högbom: v, **Johan Haglund:** g, **Johan Kvategård:** g,
Tommy Haglund: b, **Jimmy Holmgren:** d

Ludvika - The band *Metaphor* were formed in 2002, changed some members and their name in 2004 and recorded the demo *Soon To Be Lacerated* the year after. Johan Haglund has also been found in *Ikhon*, Kvastgård in *Mother Of God* and Högbom in *Volturyon* and is now fronting *October Tide*. *Cannibal Corpse*-style brutal death metal. Masse "Caligula" Broberg guests.

2010 ■ Carve Perfection EP ....MCD 4tr Emric... E1003
  Tracks: Carve Perfection/Cutting Room/Snip Snip Sweetheart/Self Starvation

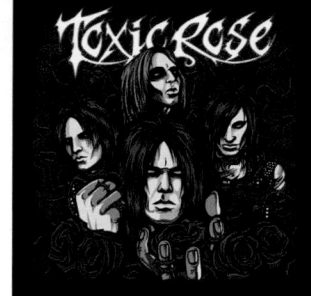

2010 MCD - E1003

TOXIC ROSE

Anders "Andy Txr" Arvidsson: v, **Tom Wouda:** g,
Göran Berggren: b, **Michael "Sweet" Hosselton:** d

Stockholm - Formed in 2010. Tom (*Gemini Five*), Andy and Michael, both *Lipstixx 'N Bulletz* and Göran ex-*Sexydeath*. Michael is the brother of *Crashdïet* drummer Martin Sweet. *Toxic Rose* plays glammy metal, but with a raw edge and a modern touch. Great band!

2012 ■ Toxic Rose ....MCD 5tr City Of Light ....COL 01
  Tracks: A Song For The Weak/Set Me Free/Follow Me/Black Bile/Fear Lingers On
2013 ☐ Don't Hide In The Dark/I Drown In Red..........................7" Burning Skull Records .... BRS 001
  350 copies.

2012 MCD - COL 01

TUNGSTEN AXE

Dick Mattsson: v/g, **Johan Sjögren:** g, **Robbin Wännström:** b, **Andreas Mattsson:** d

Falun - Formed in 2009. Released their first demo in 2011, in 100 copies with a patch. *Tungsten Axe* play great, classic NWoBHM, sounding very 80s-authentic, similar to *Wolf*, *Trespass* etc.

2013 ■ SWEDISH IRON ....CD Iron Shield Records .... ISR 017-13/C
  1000 copies.

2013 CD - ISR 017-13/C

TYRANEX

Linnea Landstedt: v/g, **Martin Zettmar:** g, **Stefan Thylander:** b, **Johannes Lindström:** d

Stockholm - The band was formed in 2005 by Linnea and singer Paloma Estrada, later joined by Stefan and drummer Fredrik Romlin (*Vredgad, Ornias*), replaced by Tuukka Frank, replaced by Johannes. Paloma left and Linnea took over the vocals. Good, energetic old-school thrash.

2011 ■ EXTERMINATION HAS BEGUN...............................CD Infernö Records IR011CD
  1000 copies.
2011 ☐ EXTERMINATION HAS BEGUN...............................LP Journey's End Records....................JERLP003
  100 white and 400 black vinyl copies.

2011 CD - IR011CD

VARGTON PROJECT

Björn Jansson: v, **Mats Hedberg:** g, **Morgan Ågren:** d

Stockholm - Formed in 2006. *Vargton Project* are like a metal version of *Mahavishnu Orchestra* or the proggy side of *King Crimson* with a touch of heavy Zappa. Vargton means wolf tone.

2011 ☐ PROGXPERIMENTAL ....CD Lion Music................................... LMC 307

WITHERSCAPE

Dan Swanö: v/k/d, **Ragnar Widerberg:** g/b

Örebro - Dan Swanö started exploring progressive/symphonic rock already in the band *Unicorn.*, later in *Nightingale*. However, he became more or less synonymous with classic Swedish death metal. In *Witherscape* he produces highly intricate progressive/symphonic heavy rock mixing clean and growling vocals. The musical brew also features Ragnar's outstanding guitar playing. Great prog!

2013 ■ THE INHERITANCE..CD Century Media 5051099-83462
2013 ☐ THE INHERITANCE..CDd Century Media 5051099-83460
2013 ☐ THE INHERITANCE..LP Century Media 5051099-83461

2013 CD - 5051099-83462

The names are presented as First name+Last name and the bands in which the person has in some way been involved (member, guest, production etc). Bands in paretheses means they are only stated in the Peripheral bands section.

A Hallgren .... Nightfall
A Lindén .... Nightfall
A Skare .... Bolt
A. Hed .... Valkyrja
Aamon (aka Siddtraaharta) .... Ornias
Aaron Coombs .... King Chrome
Abbe Enhörning "Abbey" .... Axewitch
Adam Aronsson "Verrot" .... Elimi
Adam Butler .... Dynamite
Adam Gelotte .... Coldtears
Adam Gilderstam .... Morpheena
Adam Grahn .... Pax
Adam Grembowski .... Exanthema
Adam Hector .... Bullet
Adam Johansson .... 8-Point Rosie
Adam Johansson (aka Dahlberg) .... Barrelhouse
Adam Kårsnäs .... R.A.W
Adam Lindberg .... Axenstar
Adam Lindmark .... Morbus Chron
Adam Magnusson .... Transport League Denial
Adam Nilsson .... Nattsmyg, Wulfgar
Adam Pavlovic .... Peak, Mercy, Zap Yankeefy
Adam Skogvard .... Book Of Hours, Imperious
Adam Zaars "D.D. Sars" .... Tribulation (2), Enforcer,
.... Repugnant
Adde Mitroulis .... (see Andreas Mitroulis)
Adde Psilander .... Twinball, Slip Into Silk
Adimirion .... Vemoth, Angst
Adreas Edin .... Apostasy
Adrian Erlandsson .... The Haunted, Decameron
.... Hyperhug, Netherbird, Nifelheim,
.... H.E.A.L, At The Gates
Adrian Hörnquist .... Thornclad
Adrian Kanebäck .... Morifade, Nephenzy (Chaos Order)
Adrian Lawson "Outlaw" .... IXXI, Angrepp
Adrian Letelier "Black Agony" .... Pagan Rites, Tristitia
Adrian Westin .... By Night, Trendkill
Af Dictator .... Mordichrist
Afsihn Piran "Affe/Afrika Bambaataa" .... Undergång
.... Obnoxious Youth
Agneta Ölund (now Eriksson) "Nulle" .. Revanch, Shalalee
Agust Ahlberg .... The Embodied
Ah Fhinsta .... Abyssos
Ajax Stargazer .... Flintstens Med Stanley
Aki Järvinen .... Develop
Aki Ollila .... Panama
Alan Dzafo .... United Fools
Alban Herlitz .... Road Ratt
Albert "Killerpenguin" .... Satan's Penguins
Albert Cervin .... Cavalince
Albert Gustavsson .... Dimma
Albin Andersson .... Blackshine
Albin Bennich .... Man.Machine.Industry
Albin Gillgren .... De Tveksamma
Albin Johansson .... Amsvartner
Albin Rönnblad Ericsson ....
.... New Keepers Of The Water Towers
Albrecht Märchenstoltz .... Wyvern
Alec Björedal .... Blind Alley
Aleena Gibson .... Kaipa
Alex "Aids" .... Morbid Insulter
Alex "Nordsjäl" .... Dimhymn
Alex Bengtsson .... Ablaze My Sorrow
Alex Dahlqvist .... Cavalince
Alex Dzaic .... Illfigure
Alex Friberg .... Trident
Alex Frigren .... Dechas
Alex Hellid .... Nihilist, Entombed
Alex Kallonas .... Panama Red
Alex Lycke .... Smokey Bandits
Alex Räfling .... Mega Slaughter
Alex Stjärnfeldt .... Mr. Death
Alex Swerdh "Alec Farrara" 17
Alex Tollin .... Sanctrum
Alex Vega .... Steelwing
Alex Wehlin .... Molly's Gusher
Alex Zaino .... Obrero
Alexander Andersson .... Obscene, Svartnar,
.... Eldrimner, Marionette
Alexander Ånfalk "Alex" .... Defueld
Alexander Berg "Alex" .... Beyond Visions
Alexander Brorsson "Alex" .... Dust Bowl Jokies
Alexander Danielsson .... Strike
Alexander Frisborg .... Divine Baze Orchestra
Alexander Gabay .... Plain Zero
Alexander Gustavsson .... Heel
Alexander Hedlund .... Big Wave
Alexander Holmberg "Soahc" .... Unlight Order
Alexander Högbom "Alex" .... Spasmodic
.... Volturyon, October Tide
Alexander Jonsson "Alex/Alx" .... Tough Trade
.... Rejected, Torch, Days Of Anger, Scaar, Fatal Smile
Alexander Kirst .... Hearts Alive
Alexander Kronlund .... Superstition
Alexander Larsson .... Svartnad
Alexander Lindgren .... Sarea
Alexander Losbäck (Holstad) "Alex" .... Decameron
.... Despite, Bishop Garden, Cardinal Sin
Alexander Lyrbo .... Nominon
Alexander Malmström .... Galaxy Safari
Alexander Milsten .... Buszer
Alexander Nilsson "Alex" .... Flood
Alexander Nord .... Scarpoint
Alexander Nordqvist .... Sherlock Brothers
Alexander Orest .... Sanctifica, Crimson Moonlight
Alexander Oriz .... Sanchez, Oriz
Alexander Persson .... As You Drown
Alexander Sekulovski "Saso" ... The Mushroom River Band
Alexander Strandell .... Diamond Dawn
Alexander Svenningsson .... Dead By April
Alexander Timander .... 8 Point Rosie
Alexander Wegebro .... Torn Apart
Alexander Wik Fridén "Frid" .... Irrbloss
Alexandra Isberg .... New Bulsara
Alexandra Jardwall .... Shineth
Alexis Xanthopolous "Titan" .... Hydra (2)
Alexx Hedlund .... Dreamland
Alf Bengtsson "Daffy" .... Asoka
Alf Hagström .... Teamwork
Alf Johansson .... Scaar, Tough Trade, Days Of Anger
Alf Rikner .... Vatten
Alf Roger Arvidsson .... Sonic Walthers
Alf Strandberg .... Spellbound
Alf Svensson .... At The Gates, Diabolique
.... Midvinter, Grotesque, Oxiplegatz
Alf Thorell .... Riksväg 77
Alf Wemmenlind .... Mister Kite
Alfred Fridhagen .... Golden Resurrection
Alfred Johansson .... Amsvartner
Ali Nassadjpoor .... Massdistraction
Alice Persell .... Nox Aurea
Allan Fredriksson .... Remo
Allan Lundholm .... Circle Of Chaos
Allan Sundberg .... Dry Dive
Alvaro Lillo .... Watain
Alvaro Romero .... Imperial Domain
Alvaro Svanerö .... Loch Vostock
Alx Reuterskiöld .... Closer (1)
Amadou Jobe .... Side By Side
Ambjörn Furenhed .... Soniq Circus
Amducious .... Nidsang
Amir Tehrani .... Convinced
Amit Mohla .... Degradead
Anden Andersson .... Steel Attack
Anderas Hermansson .... Skinfected, The Mist Of Avalon
Anders Almgren .... Guns 'N' Horses
Anders "Eparygon" .... Sorhin
Anders "Nanne" .... Doom Dogs
Anders Ahlbäck .... Obitus
Anders Aldrin .... Stand By
Anders Allhage "Andy La Rocque" .... Astroqueen, Illwill,
.... The Awesome Machine, Prophanity, EF Band,
.... Swedish Erotica, Arise, Midvinter, King Of Asgard
.... Mortum, Puteraeon, Time Code Alpha, The Embodied,
... Falconer, Swordmaster, Sacramentum, Taetre, Katana,
.... The Cold Existance, Eventide, Lord Belial, Runemagic
Anders Altzarfeldt "Nils Altzar" .... Unchained (1), Zello
.... Locomotive Breath
Anders Andersson .... Supreme Majesty
Anders Andersson .... Damned Nation, Pantheon
Anders Arstrand "Andy Kentacky" .... Explode
Anders Arvidsson "Andy Lipstixx/Txr" .... Lipstixx 'N' Bullets
.... Toxic Rose
Anders Axelsson "Drette" .... Total Terror
Anders Backelin "Bloodlord" .... Lord Belial, Death Tyrant,
.... Skin Infection, Shattered, Vassago
Anders Bartonek .... Fingerspitzengefüh,
.... Forkeyed, Switch Opens
Anders Bengtsson .... Gallery (1)
Anders Bentell "Ben Tell/Mjölner" .... Rolene, Roadrats
.... Bajen Death Cult, Order Of Isaz
Anders Bergé .... Solid Ground (1)
Anders Bergman .... Jonah Quizz
Anders Berlin .... Miss Beahaviour, Timescape,
.... Shineth, Eclipse
Anders Bertilsson .... Coldworker
Anders Biederbeck .... Axia
Anders Billing .... Bussiga Klubben
Anders Björk .... Searing I
Anders Björler .... At The Gates, The Haunted
Anders Blomstrand .... Ton Of Bricks
Anders Bohlin .... Brigada Illuminada
Anders Borgström .... Rough Diamonds
Anders Brolycke .... Sacramentum
Anders Brorsson .... Ablaze My Sorrow
Anders Broström .... Amaxa
Anders Carlberg .... Outshine
Anders Carlsson .... Zeta
Anders Carlsson .... Gordon Fights
Anders Carlsson .... Retrace
Anders Carlström .... A Swarm Of The Sun,
.... Come Sleep, Lingua
Anders Carolusson .... Gypsy
Anders Christell "Andy Cristell" .... Electric Boys
.... Roadrats, Rolene, Livin' Sacrifice
Anders Dahm .... Core Of Nation
Anders E Rudström 454
Anders Edlund .... Solution .45, Angel Blake,
.... Incapacity, Solar Dawn
Anders Einarsson .... Meadow
Anders Ekman .... Abhoth
Anders Ekman "Butch" .... Bombs Of Hades, Abhoth
Anders Ellin "Andy McLine" .... Unchained (1)
Anders Eltebo "Al De'Elt" .... Rough Diamonds
Anders Engberg "Andy" .... Cut 4, Sorcerer, Lion's Share
Anders Ericson .... Capricorn
Anders Eriksson "Flame" .... Satan's Penguins
.... Bloodbanner, Hydra (2)
Anders Exo Ericson Kragh .... Sectu
Anders Fagerstrand .... Pagan
Anders Falestål .... Comandatory
Anders Fernlund .... To Africa With Love
Anders Flusch "Rudy" .... Trash
Anders Folbert "Andy T" .... Scratch (1)
Anders Forsberg .... Angel Heart
Anders Forsse .... Rockvaktmästarna
Anders Franssohn .... Ammotrack
Anders Fransson "Andy Double-Hammer" .... Savagers,
.... X-Eryus
Anders Freimanis "Freiman" .... Hetsheads, Blackshine
Anders Fridén .... Cipher System, Dark Tranquillity,
.... Dimension Zero, In Flames, Ceremonial Oath,
.... In Flames, Passenger
Anders Frykebrant .... Silent Scythe
Anders Fäldt .... The Legion
Anders Fältsjö .... Fatal Attraction
Anders Fästader (aka Nilsson) "Nippe" .... Advice
.... Titanic Truth, John Norum, Great King Rat,
.... Southfork, Conny Bloom
Anders Glambeck "Bambi" .... Pussy Galore
Anders Granlund .... Railroad
Anders Green .... Comecon
Anders Grönlund .... Ocean (2)
Anders Gustafsson .... Peak
Anders Gustafsson .... ATC
Anders Gustafsson "Gus" .... It's Alive
Anders Gyllensten .... Devourment, Violent Work Of Art
Anders Gärdelind "Jeff Lynn" .... Cheri
Anders Göth .... Meadow In Silence
Anders Haga .... Black Rose
Anders Hagerborn .. Infernal Gates, Kisses From The Past
Anders Hahne "Andy Seymore" .... Syron Vanes
Anders Hallin .... Maniac
Anders Halling .... Trix
Anders Hammarström .... Double Deuce
Anders Hammer .... Disdain, Dragonland
Anders Hanser .... Excretion
Anders Hansson .... Amon Amarth
Anders Harning .... Bozeman's Simplex
Anders Hedberg "Randy Wiz" .... White Line
Anders Hedlund .... Altered Aeon
Anders Hedström .... Magnolia
Anders Henriksson .... Kingsize
Anders Henriksson (now Pellving) .... Pride
Anders Hjärtström .... Stormcrow, Miss Behaviour
Anders Holmberg .... Expulsion
Anders Holmqvist .... Proud
Anders Holmström .... Parasite, Rebelene
Anders Håkansson "Andy" .... Kaptain Sun
Anders Häggkvist .... Destynation, Eternia
Anders Härén .... My Own Grave
Anders Iwers .... Rickshaw, Tiamat,
.... Cemetary, Ceremonial Oath
Anders J:son .... Aces High
Anders Jacobsson .... Coldworker, Route Nine,
.... Necrony, (Nasum)
Anders Jacobsson .... Amkeni
Anders Jacobsson .... Draconian
Anders Jacobsson .... Gregor Samsa
Anders Jakobsson .... Soulquake System, Tyburn
Anders Janfalk .... All Ends, Celestial Decay
Anders Janocha .... Horoscope (2)
Anders Jansson .... Wonderland (1)
Anders Jansson .... Etos
Anders Jansson .... Ramm, Heel
Anders Jansson .... Karma
Anders Jansson .... It's Alive, Mother Groove
Anders Jivarp .... Dark Tranquillity
Anders Johansson .... Silver Mountain, Keegan,
.... Yngwie Malmsteen, Mountain Of Power, Winterlong,
.... Bakteria, FullForce, Hammerfall, Aces High, Art Metal,
.... Geff, Billionaires Boys Club, Dave Nerge's Bulldog,
.... Hammerfall, Johansson (Brothers), Mansson,
.... Planet Alliance, Shining Path, Snake Charmer,
Anders Johansson .... Cavus
Anders Johansson .... Doctor Weird
Anders Johansson .... Sadatron
Anders Johansson .... Gosh!
Anders Johansson .... Sabotage
Anders Johansson "Andy" .... Diablo Swing Orchestra
Anders Johansson "Trazan" .... Vomitous, Carnalized,
.... Deranged, Quest Of Aidance
Anders Johansson .... Green Sleeves, Heartcry, Johannes
Anders Jonasson .... Lemon Bird
Anders Jonsson .... Danger (1)
Anders Jonsson .... Stormcrow
Anders Josefsson .... Time Code Alpha
Anders Jönsson .... Zap Yankeefy
Anders Jönsson "John Royce" .... Wizzy Blaze, Aces High
Anders Kampe .... Carizma Rain
Anders Karlsson .... Mindless (Sinner)
Anders Karlsson .... Pax Romana
.... Stefan Herde And His Broomdusters
Anders Karlsson .... Foobar The Band
Anders Karlsson .... Big Train
Anders Karlsson .... Gypsy
Anders Karlsson .... Regent, Madison
Anders Karlsson "Kalkan" .... Side By Side
Anders Kiel .... Loréne
Anders Kjellberg .... Vatten
Anders Kjellman .... Disdain
Anders Kritz .... Roterock
Anders Köllerfors .... Heartcry
Anders Körmark .... Anyway
Anders Lago .... 7:e Himlen
Anders Landin "Brill" .... X-Hale, Tanaque
Anders Larsson .... Status Two
Anders Larsson .... Impale
Anders Laursen .... Via Tokyo
Anders Levander .... Gondoline
Anders Lilja .... Johan Randén
Anders Lind .... Syron Vanes
Anders Lindberg .... Edge Of Sanity
Anders Lindberg .... Cane
Anders Lindberg .... The Porridgeface
Anders Lindén .... Johnny Engström Band
.... Damned Nation, Wood
Anders Lindgren .... Valinors Tree
Anders Lindgren .... Jonah Quizz
Anders Lindmark .... Coldspell, R.A.W, Dalton
Anders Lindström "Boba Fett" .... The Gloria Story
.... (Hellacopters)
Anders Linusson .... Band Of Spice,
.... The Mushroom Band, Spice And The RJ Band
Anders Listaniels "Lissa" .... Zone Zero
Anders Ljung .... Casablanca, (Space Age Baby Jane)
Anders Ljunggren .... Simson
Anders Loos "Andy" .... Glory, Lion's Share, Covered Call
Anders Looström .... Memory Garden
Anders Lundin .... Cromlech, Ablaze My Sorrow
Anders Lundquist .... Diva
Anders Lundqvist .... Taurus
Anders Lundström .... House Of Shakira
Anders Lundvall "Eligor" .... Thornium, Descending
Anders Löfgren .... Rubbet
Anders Löfgren .... Razorblade
Anders Löfgren "Zathanel" .... Sorhin, Midvinter
.... Blot Mine, Setherial, Blackwinds
Anders Magnell .... Proud
Anders Malmer .... Hyperhug
Anders Malmström "Wouthan" .... Immemoreal,
.... Prophanity, Puteraeon, Nominon
Anders Mantler .... Burning Engines
Anders Martinsgård .... Ponamero Sundown
Anders Moberg .... Blind Alley, Hellspray
Anders Moberg .... Tippen Ruda
Anders Modd "Modden" .... Tad Morose, Wolf,
.... Grand Design
Anders Mossberg .... Tonvikt, Jerusalem
.... Vatten, Elsy Band
Anders Måreby .... Unicorn
Anders Möller "Karl-Ingvar" .... Black Ingvars
.... Big Easy, Swedish Erotica
Anders Nauclér "Karagat" .... Misteltein, Enshrined
Anders Nilsson .... Croc
Anders Nilsson .... Headline (1)
Anders Norberg "Andrew North" .... The Waiting Rain
Anders Nordh .... Life
Anders Nordin .... Opeth, Steel
Anders Nordström .... Big Price
Anders Nyander .... Sgt. Carnage, Vermonious
.... Non Serviam, In Black
Anders Nyberg .... Bussiga Klubben
Anders Nyberg .... Spinning Black Circle
Anders Nyberg .... Posh Filth
Anders Nyberg .... Naked
Anders Nyström .... Degradead
Anders Nyström "Sombreius Blackheim" .... Katatonia,
.... Bewitched, Diabolical, Bloodbath
Anders Odenstrand "Oden" .... Glorious Bankrobbers,
.... Mental Hippie Blood
Anders Olinder .... Crier
Anders Olofsson .... Veni Domine
Anders Olofsson .... Gudars Skymning
Anders Olofsson .... Young Force
Anders Olsson .... Horoscope (1)

NAME INDEX

Anders Olsson ... Jar
Anders Olsson ... De Tveksamma
Anders Olsson ... Eternal Desire
Anders Oredsson ... Dorian Gray
Anders Palme ... Physical Attraction
Anders Pers "AE" ... Avsky, Omnizide
Anders Persson ... Katana, Last Kingdom
Anders Persson ... Portrait
Anders Persson ... Revenge
Anders Persson ... TRP
Anders Persson "Andy Pierce" ... Machinegun Kelly
... United Enemies, Nasty Idols
Anders Pettersson "P" ... Succé
Anders Plassgård ... Cartago
Anders Prag ... Tumult
Anders Pålsson ... Bulldogs
Anders Ringman ... Chris Laney
Anders Romppanen ... Tomterockers
Anders Rosander ... Section 8
Anders Rosdahl ... Siebenbürgen
Anders Rosell ... Vagh
Anders Rosén ... Hagen
Anders Rothman ... Jonny Cartong
Anders Rundblad ... Motvind
Anders Rybank ... Coastline Ride
Anders Rydholm ... Code, Peter Sundell,
... Grand Illusion, Promotion
Anders Rödin ... Meadows End
Anders Rönnblom "LA" ... Romance, Desert Rain,
... Killer Bee
Anders Rösarne ... Abandoned Splhinx
Anders Sandlund ... Laudamus
Anders Sandström ... Eternal
Anders Sandström "Sledge" ... Absorbing The Pain
Anders Schultz ... Unleashed
Anders Sellin ... Boogietryck
Anders Sevebo ... Backdraft, Blue Matter, Cellout
Anders Sjöholm ... The Forsaken, Omnious
Anders Skoog ... Capricorn, Dogface
Anders Stafrén ... Revelations
Anders Steen ... Switchblade
Anders Stigert ... The Darksend
Anders Strengberg ... Espinoza, Mercy, Neofight
... Sacrifice, Wham Glam Boys
Anders Strokirk "Atte" ... Hetsheads, Blackshine,
... Mykorrhizza, Necrophobic
Anders Ström ... Ton Of Bricks, NME Within,
... Ice Age, Ton Of Bricks
Anders Stub ... Mother Superior, 454, Six Pack Sonic
... Big Fish, (Anders)
Anders Sundelin ... Silverwings
Anders Swanholm ... Quadruple
Anders Svedberg ... Limit
Anders Söderberg ... Motvind
Anders Söderström ... Rockvattnä
Anders Tallfors ... Captain Crimson
Anders Teglund ... Cult Of Luna
Anders Theander "Theo" ... Spin Gallery, Pathos,
... Bewarp, Eurock, Sapphire Eyes
Anders Thorstensson ... Backwater
Anders Tibbling ... Steamboat Willies
Anders Tillaeus ... Drabness
Anders Tingsvik ... Heartcry
Anders Tång ... Grief Of Emerald
Anders Tönnäng ... Cornel Band
Anders Uddberg ... Deep Diver
Anders Unoson "Andy McQueen" ... Gasoline Queen
Anders Wallberg ... Nation
Anders Wallentoft ... Axewitch, Hexagon
Anders Wallin ... Helium Head, Nemesis
Anders Waltersson ... Nemesis
Anders Wenander ... The Awesome Machine
Anders Westling ... Averon
Anders Westling ... Panic
Anders Westman ... Third Stone
Anders Westring ... Guns 'N' Horses
Anders Wetterström ... Talk Of The Town, Universe
Anders Viberg ... Cartago
Anders Wickström ... Cowboy Prostitutes
Anders Wigelius ... Wigelius
Anders Wigestam ... Laudamus
Anders Wikström ... Borderline (2)
Anders Wikström "Gary" ... Mental Hippie Blood, Treat
Anders Zackrisson ... Eternia, Heel,
... Nocturnal Rites, Gotham City
Anders Zerath ... On The Rocks
Anders Åberg ... Sparzanza
Anders Åhlund ... Lotus (1), Nasty Groove, Saigon
Anders Åhslund ... De Tveksamma
Anders Åkerfeldt "John Akefeldt" ... Cheri
Anders Åström ... Iodine Jupiter
Anders Öhman ... Inzight
Anders Östberg "Johnny Fuzz" ... Remuda Dust
Anders Östman ... Leash
Andi Kravljaca ... Silent Call, Elsesphere
... Celestial Decay, Seventh Wonder
André Alvinzi ... Coldworker, Carnal Grief
André Andersson ... Backyard Bullets
André Andersson ... Sherlock Brothers
Andre Daniel ... Supergroupies
André Drexler ... Nonworkinggeneration
Andre Gonzales ... By Night, Trendkill, Despite
Andre Holmqvist ... Pain And Passion, Zero Illusions
Andre Kvarnström "Poncho" ... Truckfighters
André Nilsson ... Fleshcut
André Nylund ... Azure, Embracing
André Nyvoll ... Mystery, Lovebone
André Robsahm ... Miosis
André Samuelsson ... Her Whisper
André Skaug ... Black Dog, Clawfinger, Liquidust
André Swahn ... The Rifles
Andrea Green ... Faithful Darkness
Andrea Martinsson ... Sunset Blade
Andreas "Stigmata/S/Non" ... Lifelover, IXXI
Andreas Albihn ... Tenebre, Embraced
Andreas Allenmark ... Anata, Cipher System, Exhale Swe
Andreas Alriksson "Ankan" ... Entropy
Andreas Andersson ... Majectic Vanguard
Andreas Andersson ... Prisca
Andreas Andersson ... Buszer
Andreas Antonsson ... Hollow Breed
Andreas Aspell ... Jet Airliner
Andreas Augustsson ... Tore And The No Smokers
Andreas Axelsson "Dread/Drette/" ... Mourning, Incapacity,
... Tormented, Necronaut, Infestded, Paganizer,
... Ribspreader, Marduk, Edge Of Sanity
Andreas Axelsson "Ascaroth" ... Mörker
Andreas Baglien ... Wolverine
Andreas Barringer ... Blind Dog
Andreas Bengtsson ... Deville
Andreas Bergh "Vinnie Whiplasher" ... Swordmaster,
... Deathstars, The Crown (Crown Of Throns)
Andreas Bergström ... Ridge
Andreas Björler ... Evocation
Andreas Björnsson ... Fetus Stench
Andreas Blomberg ... Comandatory
Andreas Blomqvist ... Seventh Wonder
Andreas Blomqvist ... Hyperborean
Andreas Bolldén "Skullthrasher" ... Immaculate
Andreas Bonnevier ... Gondoline
Andreas Brattlund-Klein ... Frenzy
Andreas Brisheim ... Paganizer
Andreas Brobjer ... Richard Andersson, Platitude
Andreas Brodén ... Elevener
Andreas Byhlin ... Singer
Andreas Bünger ... Necrovation
Andreas Båge ... Dawn Of Oblivion,
... Mindfuel, Scandal Circus
Andreas Båtsman ... Ghamorean
Andreas Carlsson "Andy" ... Denied
Andreas Carlsson "Dea" ... Ribspreader, Sinners Burn,
... Another Life, Paganizer, Carve
Andreas Claesson "Andy Clarke" Freddie Field, Yale Bate
Andreas Classen ... Shining
Andreas Dahlgström ... Thronaeon, Godhate
Andreas Dahlqvist ... Cavalince
Andreas de Vera (now Vollmer) ... Steel Attack
Andreas Deblén ... Satanic Slaughter
Andreas Dimeo ... Opeth
Andreas Edlund ... Backhander, Skyfire, Chaos Feeds Life
Andreas Edmark ... Skinfected
Andreas Ehrnberg ... I Am Hunger
Andreas Eklund ... Prisoner, Sabbtail, House Of Shakira
... Radioactive, Sayit
Andreas Ekström ... Switchblade
Andreas Engberg ... Painfield, Massive Audio Nerve
Andreas Engman ... Searing I
Andreas Eriksson ... Lowrider
Andreas Eriksson ... Dimmz
Andreas Eriksson ... Whyte Ash
Andreas Eriksson ... Captain Crimson
Andreas Evaldsson ... Centinex
Andreas Fors ... Punishment, Infanticide
Andreas Frank ... Vintersorg
Andreas Frisk ... Cauterizer
Andreas Fritz ... Heavy Load
Andreas Fröberg "Natt" ... Angrepp, Withersin
Andreas Fullmestad ... Dawn
Andreas Fäldt ... Skin Infection
Andreas Gerdén ... Inevitable End
Andreas Gerdin "Gordon" ... Machinae Supremacy
Andreas Grufstedt ... From Behind
Andreas Grövle ... Million
Andreas Gustafsson ... Demental
Andreas Gärtner ... The Carpet Knights
Andreas Hahne ... Souldivider
Andreas Hall ... Carnival Sun
Andreas Halvardsson ... Diablo Swing Orchestra
Andreas Hanberger ... Soniq Circus
Andreas Hansson ... Cherokee
Andreas Hansson "Hasse" ... Die Hard
Andreas Hedlund "Vintersorg" ... Vintersorg, Otyg
... Hanvayoth, Fission, Waterclime
Andreas Hedman ... Core Of Nation
Andreas Hedström ... Excessum, Grief Of Emerald,
... Descending, Sadistic Grimness
Andreas Helander ... Freternia
Andreas Heleander "Andy" ... Debbie Ray, Plan 9
Andreas Hellgren ... Cervello
Andréas Henemyr ... Fuelhead
Andreas Henriksson ... Plan Three
Andreas Henriksson ... Somber
Andreas Hermansson ... The Mist Of Avalon, Skinfected
Andreas Hindenäs "Andy" ... Shadowgarden, Draconian
Andreas Holma ... Hypocrisy
Andreas Holmberg ... M.A.C
Andreas Holmberg ... Tiamat
Andreas Häggström ... Mortalicum
Andreas Iverhed ... 454, Big Fish
Andreas J ... Idiot
Andreas Jennische "Lenny" ... Ninnuam
Andreas Joelsson ... Igneous Human
Andreas Johansson ... Cult Of Luna
Andreas Johansson ... Deranged, Havok
Andreas Johansson ... Fatal Embrace, Gates Of Ishtar,
... Skinfected, Dead Silent Slumber
Andreas Johansson ... Divinefire, Narnia,
... System Breakdown, Wisdom Call
Andreas Johansson "KP" ... Von Panzer
Andreas Johansson "Toya" ... Saint Deamon,
Ride The Sky
Andreas Johansson "Agge Bones" ... Verminious,
... Evildoer, Delve
Andreas Johansson "Andy Stormchild" ... Air Raid
Andreas Jonasson ... Sharp Nine
Andreas Jonasson ... Extaz
Andreas Jonsson ... Tyrant, The Black, Vinterland, Flesh
Andreas Karlsson ... Sundown
Andreas Karlsson ... Dimmz
Andreas Karlsson ... Draconian
Andreas Karlsson "Isidor" ... Thy Primordial
Andreas Kloss ... Sparzanza
Andreas Klügel ... Sacrifice, Crier
Andreas Krenz ... M-Train
Andreas Kronqvist ... Elsesphere
Andreas Lagerin ... Nocturnal Alliance, Enemies Swe
Andreas Larsen ... Shining, Livsnekad
Andreas Larsson ... Twins Crew
Andréas Larsson ... Bloodlit
Andreas Larsson "Adde" ... Merrygold,
... Massive Audio Nerve, Man.Machine.Industry,
... Unsolved, Urbandux
Andreas Lidberg "Janos" ... Street Talk, Sacrifice, Solitude
Andreas Lill ... Winterlong
Andreas Lind "A.L" ... Valkyrja
Andreas Lindahl ... Platitude, Audivision, ZooL,
... Crash The System, The Murder Of MySweet,
... Loch Vostock, Wuthering Heights
Andreas Lindmark ... Maninnya Blade
Andreas Lindmark ... Lineout
Andreas Lindqvist ... Sherlock Brothers
Andreas Lindqvist ... Tie 28
Andreas Lundin ... Misanthropian
Andreas Magnusson ... Saltmine, Blackwood
Andreas Mallander "Andy" ... Keehole
Andreas Malm ... Plan Three
Andreas Mattsson ... Tungsten Axe
Andreas Melander ... Comandatory, Seventribe
Andreas Melander ... Black Web
Andreas Melberg ... Closer (2)
Andreas Mellkvist ... Sanctification
Andreas Michols ... Dreamline
Andreas Mitroulis "Uther Pendragon" ... Overdeth
... Dethronement, Entrails, Jigsore Terror
Andreas Morling "Antz" ... Subtopia, Subztain
Andreas Månsson ... Solar Dawn
Andreas Mårtensson ... Sonic Syndicate
Andreas Mäkelä ... Memory Garden
Andreas Niemi "Adrian de Crow" ... Opera Diabolicus,
... Akilles, Deletion
Andreas Nilsson ... Source (2)
Andreas Nilsson ... Hellbelly
Andreas Nilsson ... Zilch
Andreas Nilsson ... Ancient Wisdom, Naglfar, Midvinter
Andreas Nilsson "Nizze" ... Calm Chaos
Andreas Nilsson "Velvet" ... Azure
Andreas Nilzon "Astaroth" ... Satariel, The Moaning,
... Satarie, Incinerator
Andreas Nordkvist ... Sticky Sweet
Andreas Novak ... Deacon Street Project, Afterglow,
... House Of Shal´kira, Mind's Eye, Novak
Andreas Ohlsson ... Voyager
Andreas Olander ... Volturyon
Andreas Olavi ... Serenade For June, Inhale, Lavett
Andreas Olsson ... (see Andreas Passmark)
Andreas Olsson ... Self Deception
Andreas Ottosson ... Blue Skies Bring Tears
Andreas Palm "Rick Meister" ... Damien, Hexenhaus,
... Maninnya Blade
Andreas Passmark (aka Olsson) ... Divinefire, Narnia,
... Stormwind, WisdomCall, 7Days, Harmony, Novak,
... Veni Domine, Daniel Palmqvist, Work Of Art
Andreas Pelli ... Chaossworn
Andreas Persson "Diablo" ... Bulletsize
Andreas Pettersson "AE/A/Sir A" ... Whirling, LIK,
... Armagedda, Leviathan, Lönndom
Andreas Ragnarsson ... Frame
Andreas Risberg ... Macrocosmic Emotions
Andreas Salomonsson ... Aphasia
Andreas Sandberg ... Mozkovitch
Andreas Sandberg "Dr. Ape Grüber" ... Dr. Living Dead,
... Ouijabeard
Andreas Schultz ... Unanimated
Andréas Sellstedt "Melkor" ... Woods Of Infinity
Andreas Siegrist ... Source Of Ignition
Andreas Silén ... Lack Of Faith
Andreas Sjöberg ... Plague Warhead, Allegience, Ashes
Andreas Sjösted "Re'carrdo" ... Seventribe
Andreas Sjöström ... Wyvern
Andreas Skoglund ... Brigada Illuminada
Andreas Sonderlid ... Firestone
Andreas Spåls ... Mandylion
Andreas Stahre "Mort" ... Mort
Andreas Stenfeldt "Andy Stone" ... Stingray
Andreas Stenlund ... TME
Andreas Stoltz ... Hollow, Auberon
Andreas Strandh ... Sister Sin
Andreas Ström ... Suicidal Winds, Conspiracy
Andreas Strömbäck ... Cowboy Prostitutes
Andreas Sundh ... Hell N' Diesel
Andreas Svensson ... Rising, Remo
Andreas Svensson "Andrey" ... Kaptain Sun
Andreas Svensson "Dregen" ... Backyard Babys,
... Conny Bloom, (Hellacopters)
Andreas Sydow ... Darkane
Andreas Söderberg "Andy" ... Belladonna
Andreas Söderin ... Seventh Wonder
Andreas Söderlund "Metalwarrior" ... Abyssos, Ishtar
Andreas Söderlund "Söder" ... Holocaust, Degrade
Andreas Sölveström "Andy" ... Within Y, Cipher System,
... Dragonland, Evildoer, Amaranthe, Galaxy Safari
Andreas Tomasson ... Revengia
Andreas Tseung ... Vomitous
Andreas Tönnerheim ... New Breed
Andreas Wahl ... Therion, Hexenhaus
Andreas Wahlberg ... Cherokee, Kansas City Roller
Andreas Wallström ... Rosicrucian
Andreas Vaple ... Azotic Reign, King Chrome
Andreas Westerling ... Downstroke
Andreas Westerlund ... Cheerleader
Andreas Wiberg ... Empty Guns
Andreas Widén ... Prime
Andreas Wiik ... Beseech
Andreas Wiil ... Freedom Bleeder, Firestone
Andreas Wikström ... Nasheim, Stoneload
Andreas Vingbäck "Heljamadr" ... Domgård
Andreas Winkler ... The Mist Of Avalon
Andreas von Ahn "Paco" ... Truckfighters
Andreas Åkerberg ... All Hell
Andreas Åkerlind ... Anachronaeon
Andreas Åkerlund ... Forkeyed
Andreas Öman ... Searing I
Andreas Östberg "Andy Be Bop" ... Rickshaw
Andreas Österlund ... Ozium
Andrée Theander ... Cap Outrun
Andrei Amartinesei ... Burning Saviours
Andrew Axelsson ... Slyside, Bedroom Love
Andrija Veljaca "Weechking" ... Mercy, Horoscope, Turbo
Andy "Oh My God" ... Lillasyster
Andy Alkman ... Hellfueled
Andy Andersson ... Slow Train
Andy Blakk ... Sanchez
Andy Christell ... (see Andreas Christell)
Andy Dawson ... Crazy Lixx
Andy Goodwyn ... EF Band
Andy Haller ... Original Sin
Andy K ... Skellington
Andy La Guerin ... Mean Streak
Andy La Rocque ... (see Anders Alhage)
Andy Malaecek ... Last Autumn's Dream
Andy Rose. Rampant, Richard Andersson, Time Requiem
Andy Rydell "SS-66" ... Virgin Sin, (Drille Killer)
Andy Shore ... Arconova
Andy Skinner ... Notorious
Anette Ax (aka Richardsdotter) ... Anette Ax
Anette Blyckert (now Olzon) ... Alyson Avenue, Disdain,
... Pain, Scarpoint, Sapphire Eyes
Anette Johansson ... Yankee Heaven, Shiva
Anette Jönsson ... Twilight
Anette Karlsson ... Vulcano
Anette Wigenius ... Million
Anfinn Skulevold ... Abhoth
Angel M ... System Shock
Angela Ahola ... A Canorous Quintet
Angela Esposito ... Lights Out
Angela Gossow ... Arch Enemy
Angelica Häggström ... Stormwind
Angelica Rylin ... The Murder Of My Sweet,
... Crash The System
Angelo Mayer ... Celestial Decay
Angelo Mikai ... Captor
Angelo Modafferi ... Million

NAME INDEX

Ann Ekberg ... Deathstars
Ann Åkerman ... Dead Silent Slumber
Anna Alfredsson "Cindi Savage" ... Vanity Blvd
Anna Carlsdotter ... Mortum
Anna Ekblad ... Ningizzia
Anna Hanser ... Nerved
Anna Hellgren ... Happy Hour
Anna Holmgren ... Änglagård
Anna Jedler ... Zeudo
Anna Kjellberg ... Drain (S.T.H)
Anna Mattiasson ... Törsten Dricker
Anna Nyhlin ... Therion
Anna Sandberg ... Siena Root
Anna Sofi Dahlberg ... Anekdoten
Anna Svensson ... Svartsyn
Anna Wallenborg "Pandora" ... Joke
Anna-Kaisa Avehall ... Dark Tranquillity
Anna-Karin Nylén ... Cut Out
Anna-Lena Elfving ... Panic
Anna-Lena Nilsson ... Törsten Dricker
Anne Ekman ... Broken Glass
Anneli Storå ... Laudamus
Anneli Zachrisson ... Adams Eve
Anni Lovisa Sundqvist "Anni De Vil" ... Hysterica
Anni Thulin ... Book Of Hours
Annica Jensen ... Gilt
Annie Kratz-Gutå ... Annie For President
Annika Argerich ... Cult Disciples, Stonelake, Veritate
Annika Burman ... Sayit
Annika Jansson ... Shee
Annika Ohlsson (now Helander Isby) ... Tusen & En Natt
Annlouice Lögdlund ... Diablo Swing Orchestra
Ann-Marie Landtblom ... Twilight
Ann-Sofi Elert ... Necromicon
Ann-Sofie Hoyles ... Spiders
Anonymous ... Veternus
Anssi Alatalo ... CC Rock
Anthon Johansson ... Black Bonzo, Gin Lady
Anthony Cedergren ... Love Child, Trazy, Seven Wishes
Anthony Rascal ... Chains
Anton Broberg ... Wonderland Dementation Dpt.
Anton Eriksson ... Meadows End
Anton Eriksson ... Anguish
Anton Fingal ... Screamer
Anton Grönholm ... Sanctuary In Blasphemy
Anton Hedberg ... Cemetary (1213)
Anton Hinterlach ... Nattsmyg
Anton Johansson ... Chaossworn
Anton Johansson ... Mister Kite
Anton Johansson ... Anguish
Anton Klaesen ... Naked
Anton Körberg ... The Poodles
Anton Lindsjö ... Hasse Fröberg & Musical Companion
Anton Modig ... Marionette
Anton Renborg ... Waving Corn, Cripple
Anton Roos ... Elevener, Saffire
Anton Ryvang "Anthony Fox" ... Billion Dollar Babies
Anton Solli ... Snakepit Rebels, Guardian Angels
Anton Strömberg ... Legia
Anton Sunesson ... Antichrist
Anton Svedin ... Soreption
Anton Svensson ... Affecti Veternus
Anton Wanstadius ... Stench, Necrovation
Anton Östergren ... Last Laugh (2)
Antonio Juhlin "Julle" ... Fistfunk
Antonio Ravina da Silva ... Subcyde, Circle Of Chaos
Antonio Saluena ... Talk Of The Town
Antti Lindholm ... The Duskfall
Antti Mäkinen ... Lucy
Antti Remes ... Lugnoro
Apollo Papathanasio ... Gardenian, Evil Masquerade, ... Time Requiem, VII Gates, Craze, Faith Taboo, ... Majestic, Meduza, Spiritual Beggars
Arabella Vitanic ... Alyson Avenue, Sapphire Eyes
Aram Yildiz ... The Mist Of Avalon
Archaic ... Durthang
Arganas ... Nåstrond
Ariel Sanga ... Darklands
Aris Restaino ... Cane
Arne Arvidsson ... Tom Trick
Arne Blomqvist ... Sky High
Arne Larsson ... Scatcats
Arne Sandved "Ace Greenwood" ... Syron Vanes
Arne Öhrström ... Fire
Arnold Compier ... Cool For Cats
Arnold Lindberg ... Deathening, Murderplan
Aron Engberg ... Sanctifica
Aron Parmerud ... Marionette
Arthur Börjesson ... Assault
Arto Jetsonen ... Deep Zilents
Arto Karttunen ... Fantasy
Arto Pyykkö ... Cicero
Arttu Malkki "Amath" ... Diabolicum, Equinox Ov The Gods, ... Aeon (2), Sanctification, Defaced Creation, Souldrainer
Artur Meinild ... Evil Masquerade
Arvid Eriksson ... Big Fish
Arvid Hammar ... Excessum
Arvid Jonsson ... Mozkovitch
Arvid Sjögedahl ... Los Sin Nombre
Arvin Yarollahi ... Carizma Rain
Asgeir Mickelsson ... Vintersorg
Asko Nisula ... Dear Mutant
Assar Andersen ... Backtalk
Aster ... Shotgun Bluez
Atahan Tolunay ... Taketh
Atilla Szabo ... Kharma
Attila Publik ... Lost Horizon
Attila Terek ... Von Benzo
August Holmgren ... Eternity Remains
August Lengquist ... Blue Skies Bring Tears
Aulis Hultin ... Frozen Eyes
Avernus ... Sanctum Sanguis Apati
Avondo ... Obscuro
Avsky ... IXXI, Ondskapt
Axel Axelsson Johnsson "Acerbus" ... IXXI, Ondskapt
Axel Hjelm ... Born Of Sin
Axel Janossy ... The Embodied
Axel Jonsson ... Calm
Axel Jonsson ... Maze Of Time
Axel Karlsson ... Distorted Wonderland
Axel Sjöberg ... Spiders, Graveyard
Axel Söderberg ... Horisont
Axel Widén .Marionette, Zombiekrieg, The Cold Existance
Axl Ludwig ... Pretty Wild
B. Lindgren ... Blue Orange
B-O Kjellsson ... Killbilly 5'ers
Babbaen ... Julie Laughs Nomore
Babis Tasiopoulos "Argati" ... Damnatory, Brainwave
Badde Abrahamsson ... Tom Trick
Bajen Månsson ... Curse
Barbro Olsson ... Sahara (1)
Bard ... Misericordia
Bartek/Bartosz Nalezinski ... Supreme Majesty Mortum
Basse Blyberg (aka Sebastian) ... House Of Shakira ... Jupiter Society
Basse Norberg ... Metal Mercy
Bassel Elharbiti ... Mayadome, Imperial Domain, ... Fatal Smile (1)
Behemiron ... Vemoth
Benga Ragnewall ... BB Rock
Bengt Ahlström ... Bengalen
Bengt Alexandersson ... Spectra
Bengt Almquist ... Flame
Bengt Andersson "Bengan" ... Vatten, Niva, Peo
Bengt Bäcke ... Greenleaf
Bengt Danielsson ... Genesaret
Bengt Fisher ... EF Band, (Epizootic)
Bengt Igefors "Boogie" ... Colorblind, Metal Mercy
Bengt Johansson ... Too Late
Bengt Johansson "Kärnkraft" ... Ocean (1)
Bengt Johnsson ... Espinoza
Bengt Ljungberger "Bengus" ... AB/CD, The Weed
Bengt Lundberg ... Overture
Bengt Mikaelsson ... Rockvattnä
Bengt Nilsson ... After Life
Bengt Randén ... Johan Randén
Bengt Rönning ... Paradise (3)
Bengt Sandblom ... Flash
Bengt Skarin ... Nebulosa
Bengt Sund ... Vomitory
Bengt Svensson ... Blåeld
Bengt Thand ... Carrie
Bengt Walter ... Tears
Bengt Weber ... Mentor's Wish
Bengt-Åke Andersson ... Von Rosen
Benjamin Boräng ... Innocent Rosie
Benjamin Jennebo ... Smash Into Pieces
Benjamin Koverman ... Enshrined
Benjamin Vallé ... Nine
Benke Brogwall "Benkr" ... Celestial Pain
Benke Sandberg ... Overload
Benna Sörman ... Alexander Lucas
Bennie Fors "B-Force" ... Dark Funeral, Omnizide, Epitaph
Benno Megarelli ... Neon Rose
Benny Ahlquist ... Gallery (2), Rhapsody (Sweden)
Benny Andersson ... Stand By
Benny Bats ... Viceral Bleeding
Benny Björkh ... Bang & Out
Benny Carlsson ... Rat Salad
Benny Eriksson ... Smokey Bandits
Benny Eriksson ... Ironware
Benny Hadders ... Blåeld, Cross
Benny Hagstedt ... Syconaut
Benny Halvarsson "Blomman" ... Julie Laughs Nomore
Benny Hägglund ... Fission, TME
Benny Jansson ... Johansson Brothers, (Erika), ... Avenue, Dave Nerge's Bulldog, Benny Jansonn, ... Ride The Sky, Snake Charmer, Tears Of Anger, ... Xsavior, Two Rocks, Ruined Soul
Benny Johansson ... Kliché
Benny Larsson "Bempa/Winter" ... Plague Warhead, ... Edge Of Sanity, Ophthalamia, ... Total Terror, Pan-Thy-Monium
Benny Lundgren ... Crier
Benny Olsson ... Yggdrasil
Benny Persson ... Denied
Benny Söderberg ... Clockwise, Fortune (2)
Benny Åkermark ... Impiety
Benton Wiberg ... Sister Sin
Berndt Baumgartner ... Rydell & Quick
Berne Svanberg: v/d ... Fagin
Berno Paulsson ... Deranged, Insision, Killaman, ... Blind Dog, Defleshed, Diabolique, The End, ... Excretion, Kaamos, Serpent, Vomitory
Bernst-Gunnar ... Leukemia
Bernt Ek ... Alien, Prisoner, House Of Shakira, ... Wizz, Bedlam, Grace
Bernt Olofsson ... Phoenix, Nagazakii
Berra Holmberg ... Heartbreak Radio
Bert Andersson ... Alien
Bert Bratén ... Succé, Frozen Fire
Bert Forslund ... Succé
Bert Lundgren ... Raise Cain
Bert Ringblom ... Pejling
Bert Östlund ... 7:e Himlen
Bertil Harding ... Rockvaktmästarna
Bertil Karlsson ... Succé
Bertil Nieminen "Beppe" ... Tornado Babies
Bertil Stenström ... Airlines
Bertil Sörensson ... Jerusalem
Berto Hjert "Drumtormentor" ... Holocaust, Degrade
Billy Eriksson ... Molly's Gusher
Billy Nordström ... The Case
Bino Rindestig ... Nasty Groove, Steven Anderson
Birger Löfman .. Biscaya, Motvind, Hawk, Destiny, Fretless
Birger Wallsten ... Oxan
Birger Wikström ... Motherpearl
Bitte Johansson ... Twilight, Revanch
Bizmark ... Netherbird
BJ Laneby "Berra" ... Million
BJ Lindström ... Keen Hue
Bjarne Gudmundsson ... DeVan, (The New Wind)
Bjarne Elvsgård ... Moonshine, Corroded
Bjarne Johansson "BC Strike" ... Shotgun Messiah, ... Swedish Erotica
Bjarne Olson ... Sonic Walthers, Mary Beats Jane
Björn (Erik) Melander ... Gotham City, Mogg, ... Glory Bells (Band), IMarc Quee
Björn Aggemyr ... Råg I Ryggen
Björn Ahlqvist ... Ceremonial Executi, Closer (2)
Björn Ahlström ... Veritate
Björn Algers ... Plector
Björn Andersson ... Ocean Chief, Vanhelgd
Björn Arvidsson ... Tomterockers
Björn Asking ... Zero Illusions, Pain And Passion
Björn Billgren ... Dexter Jones' Circus Orchestra
Björn Dahlberg ... Mister Kite
Björn Danielsson ... Cosmic Junk
Björn Demelin ... Scar
Björn Drott ... Angelez
Björn Ebbsjö ... Advice
Björn Edlund ... Reinxeed
Björn Eliasson ... Cloudscape, Doctor Weird
Björn Englén ... Yngwie Malmsteen, Mountain Of Power
Björn Eriksson ... The Cold Existence, Leif Edlin, ... Jupiter Society
Björn Eriksson ... Godhate
Björn Eriksson ... Va-Då?
Björn Eriksson ... Attention (1)
Björn Flodkvist ... Enter The Hunt, Gone, Candlemass
Björn Follin ... Spaps
Björn Fors ... Stallion Four
Björn Fryklund ... Eaglestrike, Full Strike, Freak Kitchen
Björn Gelotte ... In Flames, All Ends
Björn Gottfridsson ... Hollowe Breed
Björn Gramell "Churchburner" ... Damnation
Björn Gustafsson ... Sahara (1)
Björn Gustavsson ... Spearfish
Björn Göransson ... Layout
Björn Hahne ... Within Reach
Björn Hansén ... Loudhell
Björn Hansson ... Stormwind
Björn Hansson ... Crut
Björn Hansson ... Lugnoro
Björn Hellmark ... Hellmark, GRK
Björn Holm ... Onyx
Björn Holmberg "Sasrof" ... Setherial, Bloodline ... Diabolicum, Hyena
Björn Holmdén ... Svarte Pan
Björn Holmquist "Bobo" ... Mellow Poetry
Björn Holstensson ... Jackwave
Björn Homquist ... Mayadome
Björn Höglund "Grizzly" ... Easy Action, 220 Volt
Björn Inge "Binge" ... November, Mårran
Björn Jansson ... Avenue, Power, Crash The Syatem, ... Ride The Sky, Tears Of Anger, Vargton Project
Björn Johansson ... Meadows End
Björn Johansson ... Eternal Lies
Björn Johansson "Chris" ... Godhate
Björn Johansson ... The Björn
Björn Jonasson ... Vanguard (2)
Björn Jonsson ... Primitive Symphony, Paganizer
Björn Jonsson ... Stormrider, Blodsrit
Björn Jönsson ... Jeanne D'Arc
Björn Klingvall ... Heartcry
Björn Kristensen "The Animal" ... Bathory
Björn Kromm "Ace Chrome" ... Keehole, Hydrogen, Cellout
Björn Kvalvik ... Crowpath
Björn Larsson ... Mordbrand, The Law
Björn Lindbom "Ricky Delin" ... Prisoner, ... Sencelled, Houston
Björn Lindborg ... Brazen Riot
Björn Lindqvist ... Muddy Road
Björn Lodin ... Baltimoore, Bedlam, Mountain Of Power, ... BALLS, Six Feet Under, Rainfall, Swedish Metal Aid
Björn Lodmark ... Street Talk
Björn Lundberg ... Nerved
Björn Lundkvist ... Baltimoore, Balls
Björn Malmros ... Zeta
Björn Melin ... Raceway
Björn Midborg ... Kaross
Björn Millton ... Vatten
Björn Mohlin ... Boogie Liquor Band
Björn Nielsen ... Roswell
Björn Nilsson ... Roswell
Björn Nilsson ... Barrelhouse
Björn Nilsson ... Horizon (2)
Björn Nygren ... Empire
Björn Nyström "Nysse" ... Råg I Ryggen
Björn Olsson ... Sonic Walthers
Björn Oscarsson "Nalle" ... Blue Balls
Björn Pehrson ... Human Cometh
Björn Persson ... Zane
Björn Persson ... Doctor Weird
Björn Persson "Rolle" ... Wildborn, Marcus Brutus Band
Björn Petersson ... Renegade (2)
Björn Pettersson ... In Mourning
Björn Påhlsson "Nalle/Nalcolm" ... AB/CD, Vindictiv, ... Easy Action, Treat, Alfonzetti, Hardcore Circus, ... Mountain Of Power, Last Autumns Dream, ... Chris Laney, Therion, Glen Spove, (Do*In*It)
Björn Rehnqvist "Bear" ... Somber
Björn Renström ... Wolverine
Björn Roos ... Anyway
Björn Rydé ... Orphan Gypsy
Björn Rydman ... Meadows End
Björn Schagerström ... Liquid Phase
Björn Sjöblom ... Mothers Pride
Björn Stenmark ... Loudhell
Björn Stigsson ... Björn Stigsson, Leviticus, XT
Björn Strandh ... Sobre Nocturn
Björn Strid "Speed" ... Darkane, Soilwork, ... The Night Flight Orchestra, Terror 2000, Scarpoint
Björn Sundström ... Hero
Björn Svensson ... Cryonic Temple
Björn Svensson ... Crier, Sacrifice
Björn Svensson "Varulf" ... Skitarg
Björn Tauman ... Renaissance Of Fools, ... Chainwreck, Without Grief
Björn Thelberg ... Spazmosity
Björn Thorup "Azazel/Folkilsk/Aggressor ... Styggelse ... Fear The Future, Pagan Rites
Björn Uhr ... Solid Ground (1) Attack, Clown, Tempelrock
Björn Vasseur ... Spazmosity
Björn Wahlström ... Forkeyed
Björn Wennerborg ... Backwater
Björn Wennås ... Spacebone
Björn Wijk ... Scratch (2)
Björn Wikholm ... Parafine
Björn Wilander ... Dirty Passion
Björn Åsander ... Line Up, Reckless, Chiron
Björn Öhrfeldt ... Pagan
Blash Borden ... Immemoreal
Blotgast ... Dråpsnatt
Bo Anders Holm ... White
Bo Andersson ... Silicon Valley
Bo Andersson "Bobo" ... Highbrow, Glory Bells (Band)
Bo Berggren ... Street Level
Bo Eriksson ... Stefan Rosqvist Band
Bo Falk ... Sarcazm
Bo Falk "Bosse" ... Scatcats
Bo Florin ... Raise Cain
Bo Georgsson ... Conquest
Bo Johan Renck ... New Brand
Bo Johander "Ramone" ... Ten 67
Bo Karlsson ... Wonderland (2)
Bo Karlsson "Chaq Mol" ... Dark Funeral, Skellington, ... Mordichrist
Bo Lindmark "Bosse" ... Dalton, R.A.W, Team Custard
Bo Lönnberg ... Örby Mix
Bo Magnusson ... Tatch
Bo Malmqvist "Falsterbosse" ... Asoka
Bo Nilsson ... Neofight
Bo Persson (now Hoflin) ... Fire
Bo Petersson ... Parasite
Bo Stagman "Zinny Zan" ... Easy Action, Tribal Ink, ... Shotgun Messiah, Zinny J Zan, King Pin ... Zan Clan, Chris Laney
Bo Stenlund ... Dream
Bo Werner ... (See Ulf Sundberg)
Bo Svärd ... Spinnrock

NAME INDEX

Bo Thörnhult .... Marcus Brutus Band, Wildborn
Bo Åberg .... Pejling
Bo Åkesson .... Warhammer
Bo Åström "Bosse" .... Sergeant, Boogietryck, ... Black Cat Moan
Bob Colliander-Nelson .... Vitality
Bob May .... Stitch
Bob Rowlands .... Oberon
Bob Ruben .... Kayser
Bobban Michaljlovic .... Side By Side
Bobbe Nordin .... Lethal
Bobbe Wallentin .... Scamps
Bobby Dawn .... Rickshaw
Bobby Horvath .... Proud
Bobby Lycon .... Shotgun Messiah
Boel Lidgren .... Six Feet Under
Bonde Svedberg .... Hallonbomb
Bosse Andersson .... After Life
Bosse Berglund .... Tryckvåg
Bosse Bäckström .... Amkeni
Bosse Eriksson .... Dedication
Bosse Ferm .... Blåkulla
Bosse Gärds .... Eternal
Bosse Karlsson .... After Twelve
Bosse Källström .... Rampant
Bosse Lantz .... Råg I Ryggen
Bosse Lindblom .... Pink Panther
Bosse Lundström .... Misert Loves Co., Midas Touch
Bosse Nikolausson .... Charizma
Bosse Norman .... Bullseye
Bosse Westerlund .... Nattfrost, Göran Nordh
Brian Frank "Bee" .... Desert Rain, Killer Bee
Brian Petersen .... Origin Blood
Brian Young .... Human Clay, Talisman
Brice Leqlerc .... Netherbird, Dissection
Britt-Marie Ebbersten "Marydeath" .... Hysterica
Bruno Andersen .... World Of Silence
Bruno Edling .... Cross
Bruno Lundgren .... Tumult
Bruno Nilsson .... Tristitia
Brynjar Helgetun .... Ribspreader, ... Those Who Bring TheTorture, Saved By Insanity
Bubby Goude .... Divine Sin
Bård Torstensen .... Clawfinger
Börje Forsberg "Boss" ...... Bathory, Jennie Tebler, Motvind
Börje Gyllsén .... Transit
Börje Olevald .... Sky High
Börje Reinholdsson .... Mr. Tiger, X-Union, ... Balthazar's Machine
Börje Westberg .... Cut Out
CM Häger .... One Minute Left
C.S Johansson "Perversion Trauma/CJ Sodomizer" .... Karnarium, Pagan Rites, Funeral
Cab Castervall .... See Mikael Castervall
Cain Gordon .... Painfield
Calle Boman "Tuka" .... Dogpound, Space Probe Taurus
Calle Bäckström .... Sectu
Calle Engelmarc (aka Ola Persson) .... Paradize, Madison, ... Turbo, Mercy, Big Easy
Calle Englund .... Night
Calle Fransson "Najse" .... Treblinka, Expulsion
Calle Fredriksson .... One Minute Left
Calle Fäldt "Krizzy Field" .... Crazy Lixx, Pretty Wild
Calle Grimmark .... (See Carl Johan Grimmark)
Calle Johannesson .... Sparzanza
Calle Larsson "Charlie D" .... Sarea
Calle Lennartsson .... Soniq Circus
Calle Löfgren .... Viceral Bleeding
Calle Sjöström .... Obrero, Unchaste
Calle Sundberg .... Reinxeed
Calle Thomér .... Vildhjarta
Camilla Cruse .... Simson
Captain Cannibal .... Gehennah
Carina Englund .... Overload
Carino Malmros .... Solid
Carl Ahlander .... The Gloria Story
Carl Baumann .... Lugnoro
Carl Bergendahl .... Scenteria
Carl Berglund .... Haterush
Carl Birath .... Insision
Carl Colt .... Time Gallery, Pete Sandberg
Carl Dahlberg .... Osukaru
Carl Engström .... Infernal (666)
Carl Fritzell .... Somber
Carl Janfalk .... A*Teem
Carl Johan "CJ" .... Osukaru
Carl Johan Grimmark "CJ/Calle" .... System Breakdown, ... Locomotive Breath, Sanctifica, Audiovision, ... Flagship, Fullforce, Hardcore Circus, Grimmark, ... Divinefire, Planet Alliance, Narnia
Carl Johan Kilborn .... Twin Age
Carl Karlsson .... Grief Of Emerald
Carl Lagerholm .... (See Mikael Swärd)
Carl Larsson .... Lithium
Carl Leijon .... Noctes
Carl Lindblad .... Mother Of God
Carl Linnaeus "Carlos Satanos" .... Rickshaw,Chillihounds, ... Abandon
Carl Malmqvist .... Scandal Circus
Carl Manstrand .... Jayce Landberg
Carl Moser .... Lynx, Dunder
Carl Månsson .... Vanadis
Carl Nordblom "Conjurer/Tiburtius" .... Morbid Insulter, ... Matricide
Carl Olsson .... Eternal Desire
Carl Ottosson .... Mascot Parade
Carl Paulsen .... Devilicious
Carl Stjärnlöv .... Devian, Diabolical
Carl Westholm "Calle" ...... Candlemass, Abstrakt Algebra, ... (Carptree), Leif Edling, Jupiter Society
Carl Williams .... Solitude (2)
Carl Wochatz "Warslaughter" .... Kill, Bestial Mockery
Carl Åbjörnsson .... Deed
Carl-Filip Björck .... Ravaged
Carl-Gustav Bäckström "C-G" .... Mörk Gryning, Sectu, ... Wyvern, C.B Murdoc
Carl-Henrik Landegren .... Wolverine
Carl-Johan Kvaldén .... Genesaret
Carl-Johan Lindblad .... Moonville, Memfis
Carl-Johan Lindström "Calle" .... Too Late
Carl-Johan Sillén .... Slowlife
Carl-Johan Sörman .... Prophanity
Carl-Johan Wictor .... Epedemic
Carl-Magnus Palm "Calle" .... Mammuth
Carl-Magnus Petersson .... Solid ground (2)
Carl-Mikael Hildesjö "Mephistopheles" .... Cult Disciples, ... From Behind, Burning Engines
Carl Tore Rohdell "C. Tee" .... Panama, Million
Carlos Del Olmo Holmberg .... Soilwork, The Defaced
Carlos Ibarra .... No Hawaii
Carlos Sepulveda .... Swedens Finest, No Hawaii
Carola Häggkvist (Söögard) .... Stand By, Neon Rose
Carolina Lindwall .... Jet Trail
Caroline Darkness .... Diabolicum
Carsten Rickerman .... Spit It Out
Cary Sharaf .... Crossroad Jam, (Wasa Express)
Cary Wihma .... Panta Rei
Catrin Feymark .... One Without
Cederick Forsberg "Ced" .... Rocka Rollas
Cedrik Petersson .... Erupted
Charles Lundin .... Panama
Charles Petter Andreasson "Sharlee d'Angelo" .... Illwill, ... Arch Enemy, Spiritual Beggars, ... The Night Flight Orchestra
Charles Rytkönen .... Tad Morose, Inmoria, Lefay, ... Morgana Lefay
Charles van Loo .... Horisont
Charlie Arvstrand .... Jayce Landberg
Charlie Härenvall .... Spitfire
Charlie Johansson .... Damn Delicious
Charlie Persson .... Omnispawn
Charlie Storm .... Whipped Cream
Chino Mariano .... Darque
Chips Kisbye .... Badmouth, Dozer, (Hellacopters), ... Mascot Parade, Misdemeanor, Plan 9
Chitral Somapala "Shitty" .... Moonlight Agony
Chrille Andersson .... Non Serviam, Hellspell Mortum
Chrille Eriksson .... Chiron
Chrille Lundin .... Flesh
Chris Adam Hedman Sörbye .... Smash Into Pieces
Chris Alvarez .... Unanimated
Chris Antblad .... Spin Gallery, Deacon Street Project
Chris Catena .... Mountain Of Power, Mind's Eye
Chris Demming .... Deacon Street Project
Chris Eldblom .... Notorious
Chris Goldsmith (Christer Goldschmidt) ...... Gemini Souls, ... Crawley, Scarpoint, Full Strike, ... Pontus Norgren, Coldspell
Chris Laney .... (see Ulf Larsson)
Chris Lee Smith .... The Chair
Chris LeMon .... Badmouth
Chris Loud .... Dracena
Chris Melin .... The Embodied
Chris Palm .... Reingold, Midnight Sun
Chris Pettersson .... Wigelius
Chris Vowden .... Expulsion, Hydrogen, Denied
Chrisse Fricano .... Jonas Hansson
Christer Abrahamsson .... Shore
Christer Andersson .... Hydra (1)
Christer Andersson "Krunt" .... Tad Morose, Inmoria
Christer Andersson "Chris" .... Airborne
Christer Ankarlid .... Fire
Christer Axelsson .... Ellen B
Christer Batholdsson .... Overlord
Christer Bergman .... Jonny Cartong
Christer Bergqvist "C. Carnivore" .... Sadistic Grimness, ... Grief Of Emerald, Dead Silent Slumber, Auberon
Christer Björklund .... Sky High
Christer Boquist .... Maninnya Blade, Diva/Deeva
Christer Carlsson .... Mindless (Sinner), Skinny Horse
Christer Cunat .... Doom Dogs
Christer Elmgren .... VII Gates
Christer Elofsson .... Point Of Existence
Christer Ericsson .... Lonely Hearts
Christer Eriksson .... The Riff
Christer First "Chris J" .... Torch, Crystal Pride
Christer Frost .... Rainfall
Christer Green .... Orient
Christer Gärds .... Eternal
Christer Göransson "Chris G-son" .... Mindless (Sinner), ... Demental, Powerdise, Skinny Horse
Christer Hjort "Chris Crash" .... Bad Business, Nectaris
Christer Holm .... Splash
Christer Häger .... Poor Boys
Christer Jansson .... Splash
Christer Jarefäll .... Elsy Band
Christer Johansson .... Horizon (1)
Christer Johansson .... Big Talk (1)
Christer Johnsson .... Baddies
Christer Johnsson .... Marcus Brutus Band
Christer Jönsson .... EF Band
Christer Karlsson .... Ion Olteanu Band
Christer Karlsson .... Maramon
Christer Kilander .... Solen Skiner
Christer Lindahl .... Rävjunk
Christer Linder .... Rio
Christer Lindgren .... Chai Gang
Christer Lindgren .... Narduz
Christer Lindström .... Maze Of Time
Christer Lindström .... Quiz
Christer Lovichs .... Kliché
Christer Lundgren .... Borderline (2), Mr Quinn
Christer Lundh .... Inferno
Christer Lövgren .... Nasty Groove
Christer Magnusson .... Shee
Christer Malmesjö .... Buckshot O.D.
Christer Mentzer "Chris" ..... Norden Light, Silver Mountain
Christer Nahrendorf .... Solen Skiner
Christer Nilsson .... Faith
Christer Nilsson .... Hallonbomb
Christer Nilsson .... Crut
Christer Nordlander .... Sunflower, Firework
Christer Nordström .... Swedes
Christer Norrsell .... Zeudo
Christer Olsson .... Angel Heart
Christer Olsson .... Forest
Christer Olsson "Chris Light" .... Rough Diamonds
Christer Olsson "Grendel" .... Immemoreal, Prophanity
Christer Paulstrup .... Cosmic Junk
Christer Pedersen .... Nightshade, Apostasy, Dragonland
Christer Pedersen "Zigge" .... Moonlight Agony
Christer Persson .... Elsy Band
Christer Persson .... Keen Hue
Christer Pettersson (now Levell) .... Da President
Christer Rockström .... The Mushroom River Band
Christer Rydell .... Rydell & Quick
Christer Rössler .... Zeit
Christer Salling .... Lost Souls, Inrage
Christer Schill .... Promille, Side By Side, Big Talk (2)
Christer Sjöborg .... Råg I Ryggen
Christer Stålbrandt .... November, (Saga)
Christer Sundell .... Stallion, Misery
Christer Sunesson .... Va-Då?
Christer Sverla "Pnax" .... Ornias, Vredgad
Christer Teglund .... Mascot Parade
Christer Ugglin .... Soniq Circus
Christer Ulander .... Corrosive Sweden
Christer Wiik .... Mentor's Wish
Christer Viklund .... Reinxeed, Caliber 73
Christer Wikström .... Hexagon
Christer Windahl .... Valley
Christer Wolfbrandt .... Tension
Christer Åkerberg .... Trettioåriga Kriget, Source (1), ... Wanton, Movin' Globe, Unchained (1)
Christer Åkerlund .... Nubian Rose
Christer Åsell (now Nääs) .... 220 Volt, Inzight, Magic
Christer Örnberg .... Överslag
Christer Örtefors .... Freak Kitchen, Road Ratt, Eaglestrike
Christfucker .... Anti-Christian Assault
Christian Ahlsén .... Blue Skies Bring Tears
Christian Aho .... Immemoreal, Prophanity, Karnarium
Christian Alsing .... Christian Alsing, Suicide Nation, ... Johan Randén, CB Murdoc
Christian Andersen .... Abramis Brama
Christian Andersson "Chrille" .... Supreme Majesty, ... Mortum
Christian Andolf .... Slowlife
Christian André .... Russell, Cross
Christian Andreasson "Tyrann/S.S. Sexual Death" .... Eidomantum
Christian Baraldi .... Zan Clan, Zinny J Zan
Christian Bednarz .... Sister Sin
Christian Bengtsson .... Moria
Christian Björk .... Sobre Nocturn
Christian Blom .... Watain
Christian Börjesson .... Disdain, Katana
Christian Carlsson .... The Quill
Christian Carlsson "Crippa" .... Excruciate
Christian Doyle .... Fraise
Christian Edström .... In Grey
Christian Eidevald .... Heartcry
Christian Eklöf .... Divine Baze Orchestra
Christian Ericson .... Construcdead
Christian Eriksson .... Three Seasons
Christian Eriksson .... Crypt Of Kerberos
Christian Eriksson "Cribbe" .... Roswell
Christian Eskilsson "Equimanthorn" .... Pest
Christian Fecht .... Captain Freak's Freaky Funksters, ... Battle Station
Christian Fridh .... Pax, (The Bones)
Christian Fridlund .... United Enemies
Christian Gabel .... Mindjive
Christian Grönlund .... Freak Kitchen
Christian Gunnarsson .... Crystal Eyes
Christian Iwung .... Happy Hour
Christian Jansson .... Eleven Pictures, ... Pagandom, Transport League
Christian Jernbro .... Dave Rock
Christian Johansson .... Street Talk
Christian Joselfsson .... Calilio
Christian Kanto .... Corrosive Carcass
Christian Karlsson .... Lava Engine
Christian Karlsson .... Backyard Bullets
Christian Karlsson .... Mercy, Turbo
Christian Karlsson "Bino" .... Seance, Diabolique
Christian Karlzon .... Moonlight Agony
Christian Kimber .... Blowback
Christian Knudsen "Norsken" .... Entropy, Satureye
Christian Larsson .... Pound
Christian Larsson "Draug/Patient C" .... Svart, ... Sanctum Sanguis, Apati, Shining, Livsnekad
Christian Lauritson .... The End
Christian Lecaros .... Craze
Christian Liljegren (aka Rivel) .... Audiovision, Divinefirre, ... Narnia, Flagship, Modest Attraction, Borderline, .. Golden Resurrection, Wisdom Call, Mountain Of Power,
Christian Lindell .... Helvetets Port, Cross Bow, Portrait
Christian Lindersson "Chritus" .. Count Raven, Terra Firma
Christian Lindholm .... Decadence
Christian Lindskog .... Blindside
Christian Ljungberg .... U.N.IT
Christian Lundberg "Kricke" .... Sgt. Sunshine
Christian Lundgren .... Quest Of Aidance, Vomitous, ... Miseration
Christian Lundh .... Crow, Indomitus
Christian Lundqvist .... Wonderland Dementation Dpt, ... (Belltown)
Christian Lundqvist "Kicken" .... The Poodles
Christian Magnusson .... Psyckadeli
Christian Martinsson .... It Will Come
Christian Müenzner .... Spwan Of Possession
Christian Neppenström .... Plankton, Mountain Of Power
Christian Netzell .... Volturyon, In Mourning
Christian Nielsen .... Diva/Deeva
Christian No "de Luxe" .... Svarte Pan
Christian Nordh .... Primitive Symphony
Christian Nyquist .... Lost Horizon
Christian Nyström .... Imperious
Christian Odin "Crippa" .... Full Metal Jacketz
Christian Paulin .... Bluesbreath
Christian Pettersson .... Jayce Landberg
Christian Rehn "Chris/Lord" .... Abyssos, Angtoria, ... Sargoth, Evergrey
Christian Rimmi .... Avatar
Christian Rivel .... (see Christian Liljegren)
Christian Rosen .... Happy Hour
Christian Rosenberg .... Horizont
Christian Saarinen .... Evocation, Cemetary (1213), ... Lake Of Tears
Christian Sandberg .... Maim, Ocean Chief
Christian Sandquist "Chris Di Neen" .... Yale Bate
Christian Selan .... For You (4U)
Christian Silver "Chris" .... Painfield, As You Drown, ... Beseech, Sundown, Lavett
Christian Sjöstrand "Kryddan/Spice" .... Kayser, ... The Mushroom River Band, Spiritual Beggars, ... Band Of Spice, Spice And The RJ Band, Aeon (1)
Christian Skärby .... Chainsaw
Christian Smedlund .... Dieselkopf
Christian Smedström .... Tube Screamer, Mrs. Hippie, ... The Awesome Machine, Full Metal Jacketz, On Parole
Christian Sonesson "Aåmoth" .... Vanmakt, Nidrike
Christian Stenbäck .... Vulture Cavalry
Christian Stinga-Borg .... Morifade
Christian Strömblad .... Nominon, Immersed In Blood
Christian Sture .... H.E.A.L
Christian Sundell .... Grand Illusion, Jet Trail, ... Promotion, Peter Sundell, Wulcan
Christian Svensson .... Frame
Christian Thörnlund "Chris-Tiann" ..... Osukaru, Dirty Dixxx
Christian Vasselbring .... Body Core
Christian Weberyd .... Nemesis
Christian Vidal .... Therion
Christian Widen .... Her Whisper
Christian Wirtl .... Celestial Decay
Christian Åkerberg .... Skymning, Scar Symmetry, ... Miseration,The Project HateMCMXCIX, Syconaut, ... Zonaria, Incapacity, Torch Bearer, Solar Dawn, ... Solution .45, Quest Of Aidance, Unmoored
Christian Öberg .... Memfis
Christo Svahn .... Wild One
Christof Jeppsson .... Craze

Christofer Barkensjö "Chris/Chriss Piss" ... Grave (2), Face Down, Kaamos, Serpent Obscene, Carnal Forge, Blackshine, Construcdeda, Mass Murder Agenda, The Resistance
Christofer Bergqvist ... Fimbultyr
Christofer Björck ... Titan
Christofer Johnsson ... Therion, Demonoid, Carbonized, Liers In Wait, Excruciate
Christofer Malmström ... Agregator, Darkane, Non-Human Level
Christofer Norrman ... Veritate
Christofer Olofsson ... Croc
Christofer Starnefalk ... Moonlight Agony
Christofer Swahn "Swanne" ... Bulletsize
Christoffer Ahl ... Sencelled
Christoffer Andersson ... Captor
Christoffer Antonsson ... Shotgun Bluez
Christoffer Apell ... Solitude (2)
Christoffer Carlsson ... Tore And The No Smokers
Christoffer Forsberg ... Sarea, Sabotage
Christoffer Frylmark ... Anguish
Christoffer Harborg ... Society Gang Rape, Uncanny
Christoffer Hermansson ... Seventh One, Soulreaper
Christoffer Hjertén ... Soulreaper
Christoffer Holm ... Excretion
Christoffer Hofgaard ... Mud & Blood, Trilogy, Vision
Christoffer Johansson ... Damn Delicious
Christoffer Johansson ... Inevitable End
Christoffer Jonsson ... Sonic Ritual
Christoffer Jonsson ... Furor
Christoffer Knutsson ... Implode
Christoffer Larsson ... Slowgate
Christoffer Larsson "Mister" ... Axis Powers
Christoffer Lind "Chris" ... Rat Bat Blue
Christoffer Ling ... Downhearted
Christoffer Lohikoski Svensson "Chris Sleazy Joe ... Dirty Passion
Christoffer Långström ... Torn Apart
Christoffer Melin ... Somber
Christoffer Norén ... Benevolent
Christoffer Rudbeck ... Moria
Christoffer Rörland ... TME, Sabaton, Nocturnal Rites
Christoffer Sandgren ... Scumkill
Christoffer Seidbo ... Croc
Christoffer Silverberg ... Mothers Pride
Christoffer Sjöstrand ... Vanity Dies Hard
Christoffer Svedbo "Zwedda" ... Nifters
Christoffer Svensson ... Screamer
Christoffer Svensson "Sikk Roxx" ... Bai Bang
Christoffer Tideström ... Greasy Saddles
Christoffer Wetterström "Chris" ... Defueld
Christoffer von Renvaktar "Ashuck" ... Istapp
Christopher Amott "Chris" ... Arch Enemy, Shining, VII Gates, Armageddon
Christopher Anderzon ... Prisca
Christopher Dahlmann ... Sapphire Eyes
Christopher Davidsson ... Oriz
Christopher Landstedt "Snetan" ... Cirkus
Christopher Lind ... Red Fun
Christopher Ranåsen ... As You Drown
Christopher Shoori ... Mojobone
Christopher Ståhl ... Highbrow, Talisman, Power
Christopher Vetter ... The Murder Of My Sweet
Christopher Vowden ... Absurd
Cia Backman ... Jupiter Society
Cia Hedmark. Waterclime, Vintersorg, Casket Casey, Otyg
Cia Lindberg ... (see Zia Lindberg)
Claas Wallin ... Pleasure Avenue
Claes Alexander Von Post ... Alexander Lucas
Claes Alin ... X-It
Claes Andersson ... Great Ad
Claes Andreasson "Chris Cain" .. Talent, Heart BreaRadio, Last Autumn's Dream
Claes Annersjö ... Six Feet Under
Claes Aschan ... Cicero
Claes Axelsson ... Ocean (2)
Claes Bergqvist ... BB Rock
Claes Björnberg ... (Umeå) Small Band
Claes Colbin ... Taurus
Claes Edvardsson ... Rain
Claes Engberg ... Abacorn, Shee
Claes Ericsson ... Asoka
Claes Fredriksson "Cari" ... Sister
Claes Hedlund ... Dream
Claes Holmberg ... Tormented
Claes Johansson ... Haze
Claes Johnson ... Wanton
Claes Kollstedt ... Hoarse
Claes Kylemo "Anger" ... Infernal Vengeance
Claes Kåge ... Indian Red
Claes Lindström "Fille" ... Talk Of The Town, Attack, Blacksmith, Benny Jansson
Claes Lundquist ... Solid
Claes Lysén ... Souldivider
Claes Magnusson ... Fortune (1), Blind Alley
Claes Ramberg "Clabbe" ... In Aeternum, Abhoth, Godhate
Claes Wikander ... Crystal Eyes
Claes Wållberg ... Empty Guns, Marshal Kane
Clarence Öfwerman ... Overture
Clas Hernegård ... Twilight Project, Trazer
Clas Hägglund ... Thomas Larsson
Clas Idéhn ... Headline (2)
Clas Johansson ... X-Ray
Clas Magnusson ... Blind Alley
Clas Sjöstrand ... Confidence
Clas Yngström ... Sky High, Mountain Of Power, Thomas Larsson
Classe Byström ... Fatal Smile
Classe Johnson ... Last Temptation
Claudio Lepori ... Rough Diamonds
Claudio Marino ... Roswell
Claus Wildt ... Torch
Cliff Nilsson ... Unsolved
Cliff Stiff ... Rat Pack
Clifford Lundberg "Cliff" ... Machinegun Kelly, Vomitory, Virgin Sin, (Driller Killer)
Cloffe Caspersson ... Maze Of Torment
Conel Winblad ... Göran Nordh
Conleth Hanlon ... Thee Expression
Conny Andersson ... The Itch, Svarte Pan
Conny Andersson "Steven Sleaze" ... Sleazy Joe
Conny Bevelius "C.B. Carella/Demonizer" ... Explode, Nattas
Conny Blomquist "Bloom" ... Conny Bloom, Neon Rose, Electric Boys, Roadrats, Livin' Sacrifice, Rolene, Titanic Truth, Pontus Snibb 3, Crucified Barbara, Chris Laney, Mountain Of Power
Conny Carlsson ... Tore And The No Smokers
Conny Goldschmidt ... Candy Roxx, Ban-Zai, M.O.B
Conny Granqvist ... Suffer
Conny Hall ... Madigan
Conny Höök ... Double Diamond
Conny Jogander ... Stonehenge
Conny Johansson ... Veritate
Conny Johansson ... Rock Squad
Conny Jonsson ... Dog Faced Gods, Ebony Tears
Conny Kokkonen ... Lovebone, Mystery
Conny Lind "Laz Basswood" ... Mud & Blood, Amaze Me, State Of Mind, Raceway, Talk Of The Town, Shock Tilt, Lion's Share, Great King Rat, Tryckvåg
Conny Lindblom ... Hazy
Conny Lönn ... Side By Side, Who's Next
Conny Mattsson ... Morgan Mastling Band
Conny Payne (aka Sundqvist) ... Madison, Alien, Big Easy, Tony Borg, Mindsplit, Regent
Conny Pettersson ... Lion's Share, Anata Starterhead, Trendkilll, Eternal Lies, Revengia
Conny Sparrman ... Central
Conny Thörnqvist ... Akilles
Conny Undin ... Zeta
Conny Vandling ... Taetre
Conny Welén ... Hexenhaus, Mezzrow
Conny Wendel ... M-Train
Conny Wigström ... Agony
Corpse ... Funeral Frost
Coste Apetrea ... Coste Apetrea, Kingsize
Crax ... Dyngrak
Crille Lundin ... Deceiver, Thrown
Crille Pettersson ... King Size
Crippe von Fraucht "Crip Cristoferson" ... Undergång
Crister Olsson "Mats" ... Ereb Altor, Isole, Februari 93
Cristian Sigurdsson ... Bult
Croneström ... In Grey
CT Rohdell ... Million, Velvet Crash
D Arvidsson ... Doom:Vs
Daemon Deggial ... Nefandus
Dag Carlsson ... Arena
Dag Carlsson ... Crush On You
Dag Eliason ... EF Band
Dag Hofer "Hell" ... Bullet
Dag Holmgren ... Wynja, Mr Quinn
Dag Ingebrektsen ... Swedish Erotica
Dag Kristoffersson ... Fimbultyr
Dag Landin "Dagge" ... Morbus Chron
Dag Lundquist ... Trettioåriga Kriget
Dag Nesbö ... Abhoth
Dag Swanö "Tom Nouga/Aag" ... Unicorn, Nightingalle, Pan-Thy-Monium, Karaboudian, Von Panzer
Dag Thornblad ... Shame (2)
Dag-Erik Magneli "Kongo/ K.Lightning" ... Helvetes Port
Damien Hess ... Bloodstone
Dan Andersson ... Boom Club
Dan Andersson "Necrophiliac" ... Mordant
Dan Barrling ... Kiss Of Thunder
Dan Bengtsson ... Deranged, Murder Corporation, Inverted, Pyramido, Crowpath
Dan Boström ... Peo
Dan Bronell ... Evergrey
Dan Bäck ... Disdain, Katana
Dan Cardesjö ... Shenerah
Dan Darforth ... Diabolical
Dan Ellström "Harry" ... Tornado Babies
Dan Eriksson ... Lucky Stiff
Dan Eriksson ... Inmoria
Dan Fondelius ... Count Raven
Dan Fors ... Galleon
Dan Gansmoe ... Jerusalem,, Vatten
Dan Götestam ... Niva
Dan Hansson ... Sharp Nine
Dan Hedlund ... Pyramido
Dan Heikenberg ... Nattsmyg
Dan Hejman ... Body Core
Dan Helgesen ... Don Patrol, Salute, The Jet Circus, Blue Balls
Dan Hellström ... Magic
Dan Högberg "TT Tonic" ... Bad Business
Dan J Ekfeldt ... Bewarp
Dan Johansson ... Omnious
Dan Johansson "Dan J" ... Generous Maria, Transport League, (Mary Beats Jane)
Dan Klasson ... Gallery (2), (Mary Beats Jane)
Dan Kristiansson ... Pride, Transit
Dan Lagerstedt ... Roadrats, Pride
Dan Larsson ... Interment
Dan Larsson ... Advice
Dan Larsson "Funky Dan" ... Tribal Ink
Dan Lindberg ... Leash
Dan Ljungdahl ... Ironware
Dan Lundberg ... Shubend, (Emeth)
Dan Lundgren ... Quadruple
Dan Molén ... Heavy Load
Dan Nordell ... Frozen Fire, Succé
Dan Olandersson ... Morgan Mastling Band, Frozen Fire
Dan Pelleborn ... Airlines
Dan Rigtorp ... Tornado Babies
Dan Ryteniemi ... Gosh!
Dan Segerstedt "Danny Wilde" ... Easy Action
Dan Skavhellen ... Robb and Friends
Dan Stomberg ... Madison, Swedish Erotica, Regent
Dan Swanö "Day DiSyraah" ... Darkcide, Bloodbath, Blowback, Coldworker, Dark Funeral, Dawn, Diabolical Masquerade, Dissection, Evocatio, Altar, Canopy, Pan-Thy-Monium
Dan Swanö "Day DiSyraah" ... Steel, Gates Of Ishtar, Katatonia, Leukemia, My Own Grave, Mörk Gryning, Ophthalamia, Satanic Slaughter, This Haven, Vinterland, A Canorous Quintet, The Bereaved, Darkcide, Darkified, Deadmarch, Defleshed, Demiurg, Edge Of Sanity, Goremention, Mountain Of Power, Necrony, Opeth, Overflas, The Project Hate, Ribspreader, Sacramentum, Therion, Another Life, Infestdead, Unicorn, Odyssey, Nightingale, Total Terror, Witherscape, Karaboudjan, Route Nine, Dan Swanö
Dan Svensson ... Terror 2000
Dan Svensson ... Hearts Alive
Dan Svensson "Svarten" ... Uppåt Väggarna
Dan Tibell ... Heartcry, Jerusalem, Agape, Björn Stigsson
Dan Wande ... Grave (1)
Dan Wernersson ... Orient
Dan Öberg ... Utumno
Dani Cosimi ... Abandon
Daniel Abrahamsson "Contagion" ... Matricide
Daniel Ahlm ... Canopy
Daniel Alfredsson ... Colordream
Daniel Andersson ... Hellspell, Non Serviam, Supreme Majesty
Daniel Andersson ... Memorium
Daniel Andersson ... Soulbreach
Daniel Andersson ... Candy Kicks Ass
Daniel Andersson "Trashcan" ... Rat Pack
Daniel Antonsson ... Dark Tranquillity, Soilwork, Pathos, Dimension Zero
Daniel Arvidsson ... Draconian, Scorched
Daniel Axelsson ... Muddy Road, Lemon Bird
Daniel Backman ... Mammuth
Daniel Barkman ... Macrocosmic Emotion, Buszer
Daniel Beckman ... Slumber
Daniel Bentzer ... Lava Engine
Daniel Berg ... Cripple
Daniel Bergenbrandt ... For You (4U)
Daniel Bergkvist ... Wolf, Black Trip
Daniel Bergstrand ... Darkane, Engel, Eternal Autumn, Forcefeed, Loch Vostock, The Mistf Avalon, Sargoth, Scaar, Scarpoint, Thyrfing, Yersinia, Andromeda, Astral Doors, Dark Funeral, Degradead, The Duskfall, Enemy Is Us, Face Down, Helltrain, Infernal (666), Lost Souls, Meshuggah, Nine, Satariel, Seething, Sportlov
Daniel Bergström ... Iscaroth, Vildhjarta
Daniel Bergwall ... Calm
Daniel Bertilsson ... Empty Guns
Daniel Bignert ... Annie For President
Daniel Birath ... Thyreos
Daniel Bivensjö "Bevis" ... Enemies Swe
Daniel Bjerkes ... Saigon
Daniel Björklund ... Slodust
Daniel Björklund ... Oxid
Daniel Björkman ... Necromicon
Daniel Björnarås ... Pagan, Solid
Daniel Bornstrand "Nárgraðr Agartha" ... Death Tyrant
Daniel Boström ... Nightshade
Daniel Bragman "Forn" ... Tyrant
Daniel Bredefelt ... Sacred Night
Daniel Brennare ... Lake Of Tears
Daniel Bryntse "Ragnar" ... Ereb Altor, Withered Beauty, Isole, Windwalker, Theory In Practice, Februari 93
Daniel Bugno ... Arise
Daniel Börefelt ... Oblivious
Daniel Cannerfelt ... In Grey, Anima Morte, Flaggelaton
Daniel Carlsson ... The Curtain
Daniel Carlsson ... Julie Laughs Nomore
Daniel Castman ... Daisy Chain
Daniel Contagion ... Excessum
Daniel Cordero ... Lillasyster, LOK, Rallypack
Daniel Dinsdale ... Sacrilege
Daniel Dlimi ... Equinox Ov The Gods, Sanctifica, Souldrainer, Aeon (2)
Daniel Edström "Thorn" ... Setherial, Blot Mine, Diabolicum
Daniel Ekeroth "Death" ... Dellamorte, Insision, Iron Lamb, Tyrant
Daniel Ekholm "Danne" ... Silent Call
Daniel Elofsson ... Beseech, The Mary Major
Daniel Engberg "Ravenlord" ... Woods Of Infinity
Daniel Engman ... Septic Grave, Soulquake System
Daniel Engström ... Mascot Parade
Daniel Engström ... Syrus
Daniel Eriksson ... Sound Explosion
Daniel Eriksson ... Piper's Dawn, Gorement
Daniel Eriksson ... Ghamorean
Daniel Erlandson ... Eucharist, Diabolique, In Flames, Liers In Wait, Arch Enemy, Armageddon, The*End, Revengia
Daniel Eskilsson ... Majectic Vanguard
Daniel Fjärve ... Source (2)
Daniel Flores ... Alfonzetti, Deacon Street, Benny Jansson ,Daniel Palmqvist, Silent Call, Xorigin, ZooL, 7Days, Afterglow, The Code, Evil Masquerade, Mind's Eye, The Murder Of My Sweet, Novak, Speedy Gonzales, Tears Of Anger, Xsavior, Magnus Karlsson's Freefall, Crash The System
Daniel Forn Bragman ... The Black (2), Vinterland
Daniel Forsén ... My Dead Addiction
Daniel Forslund ... Lack Of Faith
Daniel Fredriksson ... Otyg
Daniel Fredriksson ... East End
Daniel Fritze ... Cult Of The Fox
Daniel Frödén ... Gone
Daniel Gadd ... Skald, Omnispawn
Daniel Garpentoft ... Nominon
Daniel Gese ... Pole Position, Dizziness, Grand Vision, Captain Freak's Freaky Funksters, Miss Beahaviour,
Daniel Gildenlöw ... Crypt Of Kerberos, The Flower Kings, Harmony, Pain Of Salvation
Daniel Grahn ... Brimstone
Daniel Granlund ... Syconaut
Daniel Granstedt ... Headplate
Daniel Green ... Decadence
Daniel Groth ... Grand Stand
Daniel Grüter ... Knockout
Daniel Gustafsson ... Cryonic
Daniel Gustafsson ... Time Code Alpha
Daniel Gustafsson ... Polluted Influence
Daniel Gustafsson ... Mammoth Volume
Daniel Gustavsson ... Sworn
Daniel Göstedt ... Memfis
Daniel Halén ... Craft, Twin Earth
Daniel Hall ... Platitude
Daniel Hammare ... Porklift
Daniel Hannedahl ... Frequency, Lothlorien
Daniel Hedin ... Corrosive Sweden
Daniel Heiman ... Fatal Embrace, Conviction, Crystal Eyes, Disdain, Harmony, Sarea, Heed, Lost Horizon, Lavett
Daniel Henriksson ... Eternal Fear
Daniel Hermansson ... Calm
Daniel Hessel ... Chillihounds
Daniel Hjelm ... Nightshade
Daniel Hojas ... Tribulation (1)
Daniel Holmgren ... Loudhell
Daniel Håkansson ... Diablo Swing Orchestra
Daniel Israelsson ... Dexter Jones' Circus Orchestra
Daniel Jakobsson ... Mammuth
Daniel Jansson "Jansson" ... Greenleaf, Stonewall, Demon Cleener
Daniel Jansson "Nekro/Morn/Deadwood" ... Bloduly, Deadwood
Daniel Johannesson ... Maleficio
Daniel Johansson ... Noctum
Daniel Johansson ... Skinfected
Daniel Johansson ... Cavus
Daniel Johansson ... Degreed
Daniel Johansson ... Ram
Daniel Johansson ... Chive
Daniel Johansson ... Lucid Legend
Daniel Johansson "D.D. Executioner" ... Diabolicum, Kill, Lord Beliial, Sadistic Grimness, Angst
Daniel Jonsson ... Street Talk
Daniel Josefsson ... Rise And Shine
Daniel Kangas ... Absurd
Daniel Karlsson ... Pain Of Salvation
Daniel Karlsson ... Divine Baze Orchestra
Daniel Karlsson "Östnytt" ... Last Laugh (1)

NAME INDEX

Daniel Kvist .... Scams
Daniel Kvist "DK" .... Nightshade, Taetre, Likblek, ... Sacrilege, Dragonland, Snakeskin Angels
Daniel Kåse .... Brighteye Brison
Daniel Landin .... Scenteria
Daniel Larson .... Nightshade
Daniel Larsson .... Body Core
Daniel Larsson .... The Grand Trick
Daniel Lehtihet .... Superstition
Daniel Lidén "Danny" .... Greenleaf, Demon Cleener, Vaka .... Dozer, A Swarm Of The Sun
Daniel Liljekvist .... Katatonia
Daniel Lillman .... Soulgrinder
Daniel Lind .... Skua
Daniel Lindberg .... Bulldoggs, Embraced
Daniel Lindgren "Funestus Inferis" .... Setherial, ... Apostasy, Divine Souls
Daniel Lindström .... De Tveksamma
Daniel Ljung .... Conquest, Valkyrja
Daniel Lofthagen .... Unanimated
Daniel Lundberg "Danne/Necrophilip" .... Sterbhaus, ... Skitarg
Daniel Lundberg "Garion Blackwater" .... Dispatched
Daniel Lundh .... Misanthropian
Daniel Lundstedt .... Art Rebellion
Daniel Löfgren .... Suicide Nation
Daniel Magdic .... Renaissance Of Foo, Pain Of Salvation
Daniel Magnusson .... Major N.A
Daniel Meidal "Mad" .... Abyssos
Daniel Melkersson .... Sub Second Rocket
Daniel Melo .... Stormcrow, Bokor
Daniel Mikaelsson .... Syn:Drom
Daniel Minton .... Gregor Samsa
Daniel Moilanen "Dan Slaughter/Mojjo" .... Deathwitch, ... Lord Belia, Netherbird, The Project Hate, Dracena .... Notre Dame, Relevant Few, Engel, Runemagick
Daniel Mossberg .... Angel Heart
Daniel Mouton "Dannie Boy" .... Hero, Sons Of Thunder
Daniel Mullbäck .... Civil War, Sabaton
Daniel Munoz "Thyphenz/Thyph" .... Thornium
Daniel Mÿhr .... Civil War, Sabaton
Daniel N Sahlin .... In Aeternum
Daniel Nellänge .... Naked
Daniel Niemann .... Destynation, Eternia
Daniel Nilssen "Goretrash" .... Autopsy Torment, ... Devil Lee Rot, Pagan Rites
Daniel Nilsson .... Vulcano
Daniel Nilsson "Dee" .... Infernal Vengeance
Daniel Nilsson "Dadde" .... Taetre
Daniel Nilsson-Sahlin .... Setherial
Daniel Nitsche .... Amethyst
Daniel Nordlund .... Meadows End
Daniel Norlin .... Wynja
Daniel Nyberg .... Rat Pack
Daniel Nygaard .... Amsvartner
Daniel Nygren .... Mother Of God
Daniel Nöjd .... Evergrey
Daniel Ocic Sundberg .... Erupted
Daniel Olsson .... Tad Morose, Trail Of Murder
Daniel Ortega .... Bokor
Daniel Ovyar-Hosseini .... Sludge
Daniel Palm .... Wonderland Dementation Dpt.
Daniel Palmquist .... Scudiero, Daniel Palmquist, ... Crash The System, The Murder Of My Sweet, Xorigin
Daniel Paulsson .... Payback
Daniel Pecovnik "Io" .... Joke
Daniel Pennbrant .... Slow Train
Daniel Persson .... Section 8
Daniel Persson .... Chained
Daniel Persson .... Igneous Human
Daniel Persson .... Morgana Lefay
Daniel Persson "Dani" .... Babylon Bombs
Daniel Plaza .... Downhearted
Daniel Pålsson .... Cloudscape
Daniel Ramirez .... Revelations
Daniel Riddersjö .... Ape
Daniel Ridell .... El Camino
Daniel Rostén "Arioch/Mortuus" .... Funeral Mist .... Triumphator, Marduk
Daniel Ruud .... Cripple
Daniel Sahlin-Nilsson .... Conquest, In Aeternum, ... Setherial
Daniel Saidi .... Midfortune
Daniel Samuelsson .... Slip Into Silk, Twinball
Daniel Schröder .... Coldworker
Daniel Silfver .... Asphyxiation
Daniel Sjölund .... Divine Souls
Daniel Sjöstrand .... Motherpearl
Daniel Sköld .... Disruption, Nymf
Daniel Stenberg .... Incinia
Daniel Stenå "Danny Hitman" .... Stingray
Daniel Strachal "Dudde" .... Lobotomy
Daniel Strid .... Eternal Desire
Daniel Sundberg .... Confess
Daniel Sundbom .... Persuader, Guillotine
Daniel Svensson .... Hebron
Daniel Svensson .... Galaxy
Daniel Svensson .... In Flames, Sacrilege
Daniel Svensson "Daco" .... Eye
Daniel Söderberg .... Blackrain, Justaquickstop
Daniel Söderfeldt .... Demon Cleener
Daniel Sörén .... Harvey Wallbanger
Daniel Taylan .... New Brand
Daniel Tegnvallius .... Killbillyb 5'ers
Daniel Thelin .... Sanctifica
Daniel Thide .... Without Grief
Daniel Tiger .... Amethyst, Meadows End
Daniel Tolegård .... Astroqueen
Daniel Wahlström .... Vicious
Daniel Vala .... Obscurity
Daniel Wallenborg .... Hearts Alive
Daniel Valström (aka Nilsson) "Daaz" .... Syconaut, ... Quest Of Aidance
Daniel Vandija .... Puteraeon
Daniel Varghamne "Dannee Demon" .... Dream Evil
Daniel Westerberg .... Infanticide, Punishment
Daniel Wickström .... Layout
Daniel Wikforss .... Vandöd, Vanity Dies Hard
Daniel Wikstén .... Incinerator
Daniel Wilén "Dannie" .... Calm Chaos
Daniel Zangger Borch .... Alien, Shere Khan
Daniel Åsén .... Syn:Drom
Daniel Ädel .... Vildhjarta
Daniel Änghede .... Astroqueen
Daniel Öman .... 2 Years After
Daniel Önnerlöv "Jack el Cozmo" .... Remuda Dust
Daniele Soravia .... Cans
Danile Kallin .... Immaculate
Danjel Garpenbring .... Voyager
Danjel Södervall .... Human Rage
Danne Andersson .... Greed
Danne Eriksson .... Tad Morose
Danne Irmalm .... Blåeld
Danne Johansson .... Quadruple
Danne Lindell .... Zello
Danne Lundsbye .... Blackmail
Danne McKenzie "McKenzo" .... Mustasch, Truckfighters
Danne Neldell .... Shotgun Bluez
Danne Palm .... Marulk
Danne Pettersson .... Lafayette
Danne Roos .... Crush On You
Danny Cräsh .... Danger (2)
Danny Driver .... Rat Pack
Danny Gill .... Cans, Gypsy Rose
Danny Jacob .... Grand Illusion
Danny Karlsson .... Bedroom Love
Danny Rexon .... Crazy Lixx
Dan-Ola "Danne" Persson .... Entity, The Ancient's Rebirth
Dante Holmberg .... Uppåt Väggarna
Dave Dufort (now Gerian Germaine) .... EF Band
Dave Janney .... Sarcasm
Dave Nerge .... Highbrow, Dave Nerge's Bulldog .... Moosters, Aphrodite
Dave O'Neil .... Hellennium
Dave Persson .... Crystal Blue
David Algesten .... Nubian Rose
David Andersson .... Borderline (1)
David Andersson .... Downstroke
David Andersson .... Headache
David Andersson .... Lisa Gives Head
David Andersson .... The Night Flight Orchestra, ... Mean Streak, Soilwork
David Andersson .... Skin Infection
David Asp "Grimoire" .... Opera Diabolicus, Akilles
David Augustsson .... Denial
David Axelsson "Dave Dalone" .... H.E.A.T
David Berlin .... Mother Superior
David Blomé .... Locomotive Breath, Unchained (2)
David Blomqvist .... Necronaut, Dismember, ... Dagger, Entombed, Carnage
David Bodén .... Universal Flytrap
David Borg-Hansen .... Hellennium
David Braic .... Mandrake Root
David Brandt .... Aces High, Project L.E.E
David Brink .... Morpheus
David Carlsson .... Overture
David Castillo .... Draconian
David Clewett .... Plan Three
David Dahl .... Taketh
David Delring .... Original Sin, Espinoza
David Ekevärn .... Ghamorean, Apostasy, ... Those Who Bring The Torture
David Eliasson .... Torn Apart
David Eriksson .... Anguish
David Fange .... Sten
David Flood .... Johan Randén
David Forsberg .... Skogen Brinner
David Fredriksson .... Abandon
David Fremberg .... Andromeda, Constancia, Truth, Richard Andersson's Space Odyssey, Mountain Of Power
David Fridefors .... Remo
David Funck .... Diploma
David Gabrielsson .... By My Fear, Erottica
David Giese .... Big Fish
David Hellman "Dave Lepard" .... Crash Diet
David Henriksson .... Demental
David Henriksson .... Insania (StockholmHeel
David Hermansson "Dave Destructor" .... Air Raid
David Holgersson .... Syconaut
David Hult "Criss David" .... Danger Avenue
David Indelöf "Dave Grave" .... Veternus, Noctum
David Isberg .... Opeth
David Israelsson .... Dexter Jones' Circus Orchestra
David Janglöv .... Twins Crew
David Johannesson .... Mustasch, Sparzanza, Dave Rock
David Johansson .... Coldtears
David Johansson .... Kongh
David Johansson .... Renegade Five
David Jonasson .... Heel
David Kalitziki "James Deerider" .... Remuda Dust
David Karlsson .... Syn:Drom
David Kronlid .... Va-Då?
David L. .... Meadow In Silence
David Larsson .... Narduz
David Larsson "Impious" .... WAR, Total War, ... Infernal, In Aeternum
David Larsson .... Massdistraction
David Larsson "Natt" .... Mörker
David Lecander .... Confidence
David Lindegren .... Amethyst
David Lindell .... Stonelake
David Lindkvist .... Vildhjarta
David Lindqvist .... Dieselkopf
David Lundsten .... Scumkill
David Malm .... Outshine
David Mauritzon .... Oriz
David Melin "Handy" .... Vermin
David Nilsson "Hook" .... Feral
David Nowén .... Damnatory
David Nuctemeron .... Grotesque
David Nyström .... Far North
David Ohlsson .... Incrave, Evergrace
David Parland "Blackmoon" .... WAR, Total War, ... Dark Funeral, Necrophobic, Infernal
David Persson .... The Painted Man
David Persson .... Vagh
David Reece .... Reece/Kronlund, Gypsy Rose, Salute
David Rosén .... Holocaustia, Sworn
David Sandström .... 2 Years After
David Sandström .... Chained
David Schelin-Andersen .... Astrophobos
David Seiving .... Crimson Moonlight
David Sivelind .... Cap Outrun
David Sterling .... Wyvern
David Stranderud "Slaughter" .... Autopsy Torment, ... Cross Bow, Portrait
David Sundberg "Dave" .... Sister Sin
David Sundbom "Dave" .... Skiller
David Swan Montgomery .... Jonas Hansson Band
David Svartz .... The Legion
David Svensson .... Close Quarters
David Szücs .... Degradead
David Söhr .... Affecti Veternus
David Sörén .... Tribulation (1), Harvey Wallbanger
David Taylor .... Dakks
David Wallin .... Stormwind, Meduza, Blacksmit, ... Pain, Shineth
David Wikberg .... Idiot
David Wiktorsson .... Skald
David Wilhelmson "Dave Rock" .... Dave Rock, ... Renegade Five
David Wiltz .... Man.Machine.Industry
David Zackrisson .... Liquid Phase
David Zackrisson .... Beardfish
David Åkesson .... Moonlight Agony
Davide Tataro "Set/Sethlans Teitan" .... Dissection, ... Unanimated, Watain, Arckanum
Davor Tepic .... Embraced
Dawid Dahl .... Angrepp
Dejan Milenkovits .... Enshrined
Dejan Rosic .... Screamer
Demis Skoupras .... Payback
Denis Boardman .... Gloomy Sunday
Dennie Linden .... Ablaze My Sorrow
Dennis "DNA" .... Man.Machine.Industry
Dennis Andersson .... Vitality
Dennis Antonsson .... Death Tyrant
Dennis B. Nagy .... Crow, Indomitus
Dennis Berg .... Abramis Brama
Dennis Berntsson .... Sektor Skandal
Dennis Blomberg .... Paganizer
Dennis Bobzien .... Cryonic, Apostasy
Dennis Brandeby .... Foobar The Band
Dennis Buhl .... Evil Masquerade
Dennis Buhr .... Spinning Black Circle
Dennis Camenborn .... Guardian Angels
Dennis Carlin "Erebus" .... Hydra (2)
Dennis Carlsson .... Bloodlit
Dennis Carlsson .... The Painted Man
Dennis Ehdahl .... Sins Of Omission
Dennis Ehrnstén .... Korea
Dennis Ekdahl .... Raise Hell, Rutthna, Siebenbürgen
Dennis Enarsson .... Raving Mad
Dennis Forsberg .... Fretless
Dennis Hoffman "Dee Fearless" .... Gasoline Queen
Dennis Janglöv .... Twins Crew
Dennis Johansson "Dempa" .... Crystal Ocean
Dennis Jonbarn .... Spit It Out
Dennis Langkjaer .... Mindshift
Dennis Larsson .... Dawn
Dennis Larsson "L Svartvén" .... Styggelse, Likblek
Dennis Liljedahl .... In Grey
Dennis Lindahl .... Utumno
Dennis Lindegren .... Blåkulla
Dennis Nilsson .... Demon Seed, Dispatched
Dennis Nybratt .... Swedish Erotica, Steelwings
Dennis Olsson .... Griftegård
Dennis Olsson .... Seething, Forcefeed
Dennis Printz .... Axewitch, Sleazy Roze
Dennis Pålsson .... Rise And Shine
Dennis Röndum .... Viceral Bleeding, Spwan Of Possession
Dennis Sand .... Enjoy The View
Dennis Sjödin .... Gudars Skymning
Dennis Starkenberg .... In Grey
Dennis Stenberg .... Unreal
Dennis Strömberg "Damp" .... Last Laugh (1)
Dennis Vestman .... Carnal Forge, Steel Attack, ... Grand Design
Dennis Warelius .... Solitude (2)
Dennis Westerberg .... Seventribe
Dennis Widén "Angerbodor" .... The Goddamned, ... Moria, The Ancient's Rebirth, Pagan Rites
Dennis Zielinski .... Egonaut
Dennis Österdahl .... Eaglestrike, Elsy Band, Big Easy, ... Big Wave, Human Race, Lommi
Denny Axelsson .... The Bereaved, Blinded Colony, ... Maramon, Within Reach
Denny Edström .... Conquest
Deobrugia .... Spetälsk
Devo Andersson .... (See Magnus Andersson)
Dick Bengtsson .... After Life
Dick Bewarp .... Bewarp, (AHA)
Dick Börtner "Dikk" .... The Ungrateful, Innocent Rosie, ... Boulevard
Dick Greuz .... Grace
Dick Johnsson .... Steel Attack
Dick Karlsson .... Dunder
Dick Lundberg .... Dellamorte
Dick Löwgren .... Armageddon, In Flames, Cromlech, ... Last Tribe, Meshuggah, Time Requiem, Arch Enemy
Dick Magnusson .... Wonderflow
Dick Mattsson .... Tungsten Axe
Dick Qwarfort .... Syron Vanes, Nasty Idols, ... Quadruple, Wizzy Blaze
Diddi Kastenholt .... Bai Bang, Boogie Liqore Band, ... Double Trouble
Dille Diedricson .... Don Patrol
Dimitri Jungi .... Spazmosity
Dimitri Keiski .... Insania (Stockholm)
Dimitris Loakimoglou .... System Shock
Dino Medanhodzic .... Carnal Forge, Soulbreach
Dino Nicolaides "Dynamit" .... Oxan
Dino Zuzic .... Saffire
Dirk Verbeuren .... Soilwork, Jupiter Society
Divina Korhonen .... Mort
DJ King D .... Mothers Pride
Doc Patric Schannong "Pat Shannon" .... Bad Habit
Dogantimur .... Svartrit
Don Krim .... Scams
Donald Burnett .... Vision, Tryckvåg
Don-Allan "Deobrigula" Palmroos .... Misericordia
Dougie Lawton .... Kingsize
Douglas .... Slodust
Dr. Sundén .... (see Erik Sundén)
Dragan Tanacovic .... Dark Tranquillity Kharma
Duncan Burbury "Burberry" .... Notorious
Dödskommendanten .... Bloodline
E Skare .... Bolt
E. Strömqvist .... Blue Orange
Ed Warby .... Demiurg
Edd Liam .... Crazy Lixx
Edde Weile .... Mansson
Eddi Eriksson .... Tears
Eddie Marcolin "Messiah" .... Candlemass, Stillborn, ... Memento Mori, Mercy
Eddie Bloodbath .... Odenwrath
Eddie Erixon .... Thunder
Eddie Nilsson .... Gods Incorporated
Eddie Partos .... Mindcollapse
Eddie Persson .... TRP, Little Yankees
Eddie Siojo .... Mindshift
Eddy Malm .... Heavy Load, Torsten, Highbrow
Edgar Allen"Paul" .... Original Sin
Edo Seleskovic .... Speedfreaks
Eduardo Fernandez-Rodrigues .... Sgt. Sunshine, ... The Carpet Knights
Edvard Hansson .... New Keepers Of The Water Towers
Edward Nyström .... Great Ad
Edvin Aftonfalk "Edde" .... Morbus Chron
Edvin Holm .... Stereo Generator
Edvin Norrman .... Mama Kin
Eero Koivisto .... Highbrow, Red Baron, Yngwie Malmsteen

NAME INDEX

Efraim Juntunen .... Guillotine, Persuader
Efraim Larsson .... Diamond Dawn
Egon Danielsson .... Headache
Ehsan Kalantarpour .... Slumber
Einar Petersson "Edgar Allan Coe" .... Undergång
Einar Magnusson .... All Hell
Eirikur Haukson "Eric Hawk" .... Gardenian
Eiron Johansson .... Thomas Larsson, Baltimoore,
.... Mojobone, Thomas Larsson
Ekko Karttunen .... Fantasy
El Barkus .... Mother's Hope
el Guapo .... Zombiekrieg
Elena Schirenc .... Diabolicum
Elias Dellow .... The Brimstone Days
Elias Holmlid .... Opera Diabolicus, Dragonland, Disdain
Elias Håkansson .... Mama Kin
Elias Jubran .... Beast
Elias Jäderberg Nilsson .... Slodust
Elias Modig .... Nerved
Elias Niemi "Core" IXXI
Elin Eriksson "Hell'n" .... Hysterica
Elin Hedlund .... Armauk
Elin Johansson .... Seven Tears
Elin Melgareijo .... For You (4U)
Elinor Hasson .... Jet
Elinor Mårtensson .... Pride
Elinor Stenlund .... Laudamus
Elisabeth Magnusson .... Algaion
Elisabeth Punzi .... Whipped Cream
Elize Ryd .... Amaranthe, Dragonland
Ellen Hjalmarsson .... Carizma Rain
Elliot Hofvander .... Confess
Elvis Campbell "47" .... Asteroid
Emanuel Hedberg .... Baltimoore
Emanuel Isaksson .... Zonaria
Emanuel Johansson .... Ruined Soul
Emanuel Odh .... Degrade
Emanuel Wärja .... Admonish
Emanuel Åström .... Dispatched
Emil Abrahamsson .... Sworn
Emil Anter .... Sanctrum
Emil Asbjörnsen .... Blofly
Emil Augustsson .... Wulfgar
Emil Bygde .... Defueld
Emil Dragutinovic.. Marduk, Devian, The Legion, Nominon
Emil Ekbladh .... Dirty Passion
Emil Eriksson .... Sanchez, Oriz
Emil Fredenmark .... Imperious
Emil Fredholm .... Fortune (2), Plankton,
.... Alfonzetti, Mountain Of Power
Emil Frisk .... Cipher System
Emil G. Koverot "Brisheim" ... Skald, Carve, Portal, Blodsrit
Emil Gammeltoft .... Nerved
Emil Gustavsson .... Aggregate
Emil Holmgren "P.W.S" .... Chainsaw, Odenwrath
Emil Ilic .... Mega Slaughter
Emil Johansson .. Suicidal Winds, Ill-Natured, Axis Powers
Emil Karlsson .... Taketh, Admonish
Emil Kyrk .... Confidence, Hell 'N Diesel
Emil Lantz .... Chainwreck, Brazen Riot
Emil Larsson .... Dispatched
Emil Lundin "Atum/Abtriakon" .... Ofermod, Dödfödd
Emil Malm .... Plain Zero
Emil Norberg .... Persuader
Emil Norman .... Toxaemia
Emil Nyström .... Zonaria
Emil Nässtrom .... Saved By Insanity
Emil Nödtveidt "Naughty Nightmare Indutries"
.... Swordmaster, Deathstars, Sacramentum,
.... Ophthalamia, Nifelheim
Emil Oscarsson .... Cervello
Emil Petersson "Jacki Stone" .... Vains Of Jenna
Emil Rolof .... Lugnoro
Emil Sandebäck .... Warcollapse
Emil Sandin .... Kayser
Emil Sjöstrand .... Reenact
Emil Skoglund "Traci Trexx" .... Vanity Blvd
Emil Svensson "E Forcas" .... Die Hard, Degial
Emil Tillman .... Oferd, Svarti Loghin
Emil Westerdahl .... Inevitable End
Emil Wigelius .... Diploma
Emil Wiksten .... Aeon, Fetus Stench
Emil Wållberg .... The Gypsies
Emil Wärmedal .... Cavalince
Emil Åström .... Terrorama
Emil Öberg .... Lancer
Emma Dahlqvist .... Aphasia
Emma Fredriksson .... Deed
Emma Gelotte .... All Ends
Emma Hellström .... The Provenance
Emma Karlsson (now Rudolfsson) "Lady Death"
.... Deathwitch, Dracena, Runemagick
Emma Kronborg "Lash" .... Undecimber
Emma Lee Gunnari .... Osukaru
Emma Varg .... Emma Varg
Enberg .... Space Probe Taurus
Enes Sabanovic .... Maitreya
Enzo Galione .... Shame (1)
Eric Asplund .... Rain
Eric Björkman (aka Likagod) .... Screamin' Mother
Eric Björner .... Kamasutra
Eric Bäckman "Cat Casino" .... Deathstars
Eric Diurlin .... Powerbreeze
Eric Forsmark .... Via Tokyo
Eric Gjerdrum "Young" .... Crash Dïet, Pandemonic
Eric Holberg .... Scarpoint
Eric Holmberg .... One Hour Hell
Eric Jacobsson .... Deals Death
Eric Jexén .... Galaxy
Eric Johansson .... Dumper
Eric Jonasson .... For You (4U)
Eric Krona .... Algaion
Eric Liljeros .... Mentor's Wish
Eric Lindesvärd "Erca" .... Vanguard
Eric Lindstedt .... Wood
Eric Ljung .... Nifelheim
Eric Losman .... Strike
Eric Massicotte "Syre" .... Hyena
Eric Månsson .... Boogie Liquor Band, Bai Bang
Eric Nilsson .... Mozkovitch
Eric Nordin .... Rise And Shine
Eric Nytomt "De Van" .... DeVan, Eric De Van
Eric Olausson .... Hostile Cell
Eric Rauti .... NME Within, Torch, Dreamland
.... Infinity, Ruined Soul, Opera Diabolicus
Eric Wikström .... Warning
Erik "Tyrant" Gustavsson .... Necronaut, Black Trip, Ram,
.... Nifelheim, Therion, Dismember, Maleficio
Erik Almström .... Bullet
Erik Amkoff .... Jimmy Nielsen & Band
Erik Andersson .... Skin Infection, Shattered
Erik Andersson .... Godgory, Grave Flowers
Erik Andersson .... Shattered
Erik Anell .... Skull Parade, Art Rebellion
Erik Arvidsson .... Flame
Erik Barthold .... Left Hand Solution, Darklands
Erik Bergkvist .... Setherial
Erik Bernholm .... Slick Stuff
Erik Billing .... Deathboot
Erik Birgersson .... Daisy Chain
Erik Björkman (aka Likagod) .... Iodine Jupiter, Canopy
Erik Björkegren "EB" .... Deviant, St. Erik
Erik Björn Nielsen .... Silver Mountain
Erik Blodyx .... Dark Legions, Lethal
Erik Blomkvist "EZ" .... Platitude
Erik Briselius "Rix Volin" .... Syron Vanes, Wizzy Blaze
Erik Broström .... Amaxa
Erik Bäckwall .... Dozer, Greenleaf
Erik Carling .... Kamasutra
Erik Dahlquist .... Suicidal Seduction
Erik Dahlström .... Excessum
Erik Danielsson "E" .... Damnation, Armagedda,
.... Black Trip, Degial, Dissection, Necronaut,
.... Atlantic Tide, Shining, Switchblade, Watain
Erik Ekestubbe .... My Endless Wishes
Erik Eklund .... Self Deception
Erik Engbo .... Plector
Erik Engström .... Mindjive
Erik Fastén .... Plain Zero
Erik Fernold "Svajjen" .... Crystal Ocean
Erik Forsgren .... Slowgate, Reinxeed
Erik Gornostajev .... The Storyteller
Erik Grahn .... Nasheim, Lethal
Erik Grandin...... Loch Vostock, Mayadome, Mellow Poetry
Erik Grawsjö .... Månegarm
Erik Grönwall .... H.E.A.T
Erik Gustavsson "Tyrant" .... Black Trip, Dagger,
.... Pagan Rites, Nifelheim
Erik Gärdefors .... Insult
Erik Hagstedt "Legion" .... Devian, Ophthalamia,
.... Marduk, Witchery
Erik Hagström .... Within Y
Erik Hall .... Crowpath
Erik Halläsen .... Anaemia
Erik Halvorsen "Beast X Electric" .... Swordmaster,
.... Deathstars
Erik Hammarbäck "Eric Rivers" .... H.E.A.T
Erik Hammarström .... Brighteye Brison, Änglagård
Erik Hartmann .... Vornth
Erik Heikne .... Miss Beahaviour
Erik Hjalmarsson .... Six Feet Under, Thomas Larsson,
.... Jammer
Erik Holmberg .... Sencelled
Erik Häggström .... Reflex
Erik Jansson .... Portrait, Impale
Erik Jayce Landberg .... Jayce Landberg
Erik Johansson .... Aspected, 2 Years After
Erik Johansson .... Whiteness
Erik Kjönsberg .... Vornth, Sadistic Grimness
Erik Kumpulainen .... Undivide
Erik Kurtsson .... The Grand Trick
Erik Larsson .... Poor Boys
Erik Likagod (aka Björkman) .... Iodine Jupiter, Canopy
Erik Lindekrans .... Panic
Erik Lindkvist .... Cavokey
Erik Lindstedt .... Johnny Engström Band
Erik Ljungkvist .... Skymning, Arise
Erik Lundberg .... Reflex
Erik Lööv .... De Tveksamma
Erik Mjörnell .... Mirador
Erik Molarin .... The Mary Major, Beseech
Erik Månsson .... Trendkill, Eternal Lies
Erik Mårtensson .... Eclipse, W.E.T (2), Universe,
.... Audiovision, Shineth
Erik Nilsson .... A Swarm Of The Sun
Erik Nilsson .... Faithful Darkness
Erik Norbeck .... Iscaroth
Erik Nordström .... S:t Erik
Erik Nyberg "Hat" .... Nidsang
Erik Odsell .... Pandemonium
Erik Olofsson .... Cult Of Luna
Erik Olsson .... Manticore
Erik Oskarsson .... Nightingale, Blackbird
Erik Palmqvist .... Thyreos
Erik Palmqvist .... Powertrip
Erik Persson .... Memoria
Erik Persson .... Suma
Erik Peterson .... Impious
Erik Petschler .... Human Rage
Erik Pettersson .... Higher Ground
Erik Qvick .... Nirvana 2002
Erik Rosenberg .... Victory (1)
Erik Rundqvist .... Vomitory
Erik Rutan .... In Battle
Erik Röjås .... Sterbhaus, Decadence, Netherbird
Erik Sahlström "Tormentor/Destormo" ... Serpent Obscene,
.... Maze Of Torment, Death Breath, Nominon,
.... Crucifyre, Deceiver, (General Surgery)
Erik Sandquist .... Stillborn
Erik Sayenga .... Mordichrist
Erik Sjödin .... Helvetets Port
Erik Sjögren .... The Citadel
Erik Sjökvist .... The Durango Riot
Erik Sjölander .... The Mist Of Avalon
Erik Skogberg "Expulser" .... Morbid Insulter
Erik Skoglund .... 21 Lucifers, Miosis
Erik Soukkan .... Fistfunk
Erik Stenemo .... Casablanca
Erik Stenström .... Soulbreach
Erik Strömblad .... Fake
Erik Sundén "E/Dr." .... Blodskald, Sorgeldom,
.... Kaos Sacramentum
Erik Sundler .... Space Probe Taurus
Erik Sundquist .... Last View
Erik Svensson .... Neon Rose
Erik Söderlund .... Iscaroth
Erik Söderman .... Nostradameus
Erik Thyselius .... Construcdead, Face Down,
.... Scarpoint, Terror 2000
Erik Tomberg .... Winterlong
Erik Tordsson .... Crimson Moonlight
Erik Tornberg .... Viperine
Erik Trazom Olsson .... Pandemonium
Erik Wall .... Bloodshed
Erik Wallberg .... Mozkovitch
Erik Wallin .... Shaker
Erik Wallin "Pedro el Guero" ... Trash Amigos, Harm's Way,
.... Merciless, Death Breath
Erik Ward .... No Hawaii
Erik Wennerholm .... Bokor
Erik Werholt .... Prisca
Erik Wigelius .... Platitude, Wigelius
Erik Wilhelmsson .... Orphan Gypsy
Erik Wiss .... Cap Outrun
Erik Wulff "Erkblerk den Förskräcklige" .... Istapp
Erik Wåke .... Anxious
Erik Vårdstedt .... Annie For President
Erik Öster "Eric Richards" .... Hungry Head Hunters
Erik_Danielsson "Sigge" .... Hades
Erika Roos .... Siebenbürgen
Erika Wallberg .... Void Moon, Cult Of The Fox
Erland Wicklund .... Project UPA
Erlend Caspersen .... Spwan Of Possession
Erlend Jegstad .... Outshine
Erlend Ottem .... Clawfinger, Fuck Bitch
Ermin Mujnovic .... Detest
Ernesto Grande .... Mainline
Errol Norstedt .... Europe
Esa Englund .... Silverdollar
Esa T Ahonen "Freewheeler" .... Cryonic Temple
Esben Willems .... Marulk
Esbjörn Johansson .... Galleon, Helium Head
Esbjörn Larsson .... Waterline
Eskil Rönnberg .... Wizzard, Charity
Esko Heino .... Ypzilon
Esko Salow .... Pathos
Esse Nilsson .... Allan Beddo Band
Esse Swerin .... Suspekt
Etienne Belmar .... Lobotomy
Eva Aggesjö-Abrahamsson .... Broke N Blue
Eva Beckman .... Street Level
Eva Kemppainen .... Robb and Friends
Eva Myrdal .... Revanch
Eva Olin .... Tusen & En Natt
Eva-Marie Larsson .... Dark Tranquillity
Evert Gyllsén .... Transit
Ewo Solvenius .... Igneous Human
Ez Gomer .... (see Sven Gomér)
F. Fuze .... Paradize (2)
F. Kallvik .... Blue Orange
F. Sunny .... Paradize (2)
F.M (aka Shattenführer/Fullmåne) .... Jotunheim
Fabian Ericson .... Miosis
Fabian Gustavsson .... Andromeda
Fabian Helge .... Brutaliator
Fabian Stanojevic .... Allan Beddo Band
Fabian Völker "Winterheart" .... Armagedda
Fabien Perreau "Fabz" .... Blowsight
Fadi Ghanime .... Immaculate
Federico de Costa .... Qoph, Black Dog, Stonesilk
Felipe Plaza Kutzbach .... Nifelheim
Felipe Queiroz .... Goddefied
Felix Lehrmann .... The Flower Kings
Felix Reinhard .... Forkeyed
Felix Öhlén "Fix" .... Lifelover
Fiama Fricano .... Jonas Hansson
Filip Brandelius .... Adept
Filip Fransson .... El Gordo
Filip Karlsson .... Lucid Legend
Filip Lange .... Lugnoro
Filip Leo (aka Carlsson) "Fille" .... Thornclad,
.... Satanic Sllaughter, Corporation 187
Filip Norman .... Qoph
Filip Radovic .... Silicon Valley
Filip Rapp .... The Gloria Story
Filip Runesson .... Antichrist
Fille Lindström .... (see Claes Lindström)
Finn Zieler .... Nocturnal Alliance, Detest
Flavia Canel .... Blowsight, The Weed, Aphrodite,
.... Drain (S.T.H), (Livin' Sacrifice)
Floyd Konstantin .... Destiny
Forn Paananen .... Funeral Frost
Francisco Martin .... The Gardnerz
Franco Bollo .... Tenebre, Funhouse
Franco Mavica .... Dunder
Franco Santuione .... Reptile Smile, Glory Bells (Band),
.... Electric Boys
Frank Andersson .... Burning Saviours
Frank Bakken .... Sons Of Thunder
Frank Granström .... Steve Roper Band
Frank Guldstrand "Fritz Müllweisser" .... Undergång
Frank Holm .... Romance
Frank Inered .... Dedication
Frank Kooistra "Frankie Rich" .... Billion Dollar Babies,
.... Mustain
Frank Roleau .... Limiless
Frank Rönningen .... Erika Evenlind
Frank Stenbom .... Gotham City, (Oz)
Frank Stenbro .... Headache
Frank Sundström .... Abacorn
Frank Thomsen .... Frank Thomsen
Frank Thunström .... Diploma, Mozkovitch
Frank_Roxenby .... New Brand
Frans Karlsson .... Lucid Legend
Frans Mittermayer .... Pinch
Frans Perris .... Infra
Frans Utterström .... Obnoxious Youth
Fransisco Lundberg .... Phoenix
Fransisco Rencoret .... Roachpowder
Frasse Franzén .... Dogman
Frasse Welin-Berger .... Six Pack Sonic
Fred Donelly .... Avalon/Avalone
Fred Estby .... A Mind Confused, Cryonic Temple,
..... Dagger, Death Breath, Degial, Dismember, Hypocrite,
.... Misdemeanor, Centinex, In Battle, In Solitude,
.... Legia, Meshuggah, Nine, Carnage, Necronaut
Fred Hellbelly .... Revokation
Fred Norrman .... Katatonia
Fredde Grahn .... Renegade (1)
Fredde Hänninen "Throllv" .... Rimfrost
Fredde Lundberg .... Divine Sin
Fredde Olsson .... Slitage
Freddie Allen .... Houston
Freddie Eugene .... (See Fredrik Lindgren)
Freddie Kriström .... Universe
Freddie Kvarnebrink "Cocker" .... Hate Gallery
Freddie Rein .... Middleage
Freddy Andersson .... Sacramentum
Freddy Hedefalk .... Big Price
Freddy Olofsson .... Celestial Decay
Freddy Persson .... Nostradameus, Wiz
Freddy Sövik "Johnny Schlong" .... Evil's Eye
Freddy Zielinsky .... Ablaze, Ironware
Frederic Hugues .... Sabbtail
Frederik Björling .... Little Yankees
Frederik Groove .... Thee Expression
Fredric Arvidsson .... Turning Point
Fredric Danielsson "Figge" ... Dogpound, World Of Silence
Fredric Edin .... Apostasy
Fredric Gråby "Wredhe" .... Shining, Ondskapt, Bloodline
Fredric Josefsson/Käld .... Cornerstone, Stonefuze
Fredric Norburg .... Crossroad Jam

NAME INDEX

Fredric Olson .... Zoic, Veni Domine
Fredric Ryttergård .... Human Rage
Fredrick Lindquist .... Crystal Pride
Fredrick Sandberg .... Deranged
Fredrik "Gädda" .... Hels
Fredrik Adler .... Darque
Fredrik Ahlo .... Von Panzer
Fredrik Andersson "Thorn" .... Incinerator, Satariel
Fredrik Andersson "Joe Bourbon" .... Remuda Dust
Fredrik Andersson "Fred" .... The Durango Riot
Fredrik Andersson "Freddie Panzer" .... Suicidal Winds,
.... Axis powers
Fredrik Andersson "Fred The Dead" .... This Ending,
.... Amon Amarth, Allegiance, Guidance Of Sin,
.... A Canorous Quintet, Triumphator, Marduk, Freevil,
.... Moment Manics, The Dead
Fredrik Andersson .... Thunder
Fredrik Andersson .... Chive
Fredrik Andersson .... Wonderland Dementation Dpt.
Fredrik Arnesson .... Ablaze My Sorrow, Cromlech
Fredrik Askenström .... Sencelled
Fredrik Aspelin .... S:t Erik
Fredrik Beckmann .... Motherlode
Fredrik Bergener .... Karma
Fredrik Bergengren .... Colorstone, Pete Sandberg,
.... Time Gallery
Fredrik Bergenstråhle .... Kerberos, Chris Laney, Loud
Fredrik Bergh ...... Alyson Avenue, Bloodbound, Street Talk
Fredrik Blomberg "Ztikkan" .... Crystal Ocean
Fredrik Blomkvist "Stitch" .... Transport League,
.... Massive Audio Nerve
Fredrik Bodin .... Pearly White
Fredrik Boëthius .... C.B Murdoc, Mörk Gryning
Fredrik Borg .... From Behind
Fredrik Brockert .... Siebenbürgen
Fredrik Broqvist .... Sideburn, Mangrove
Fredrik Bultmark .... Spacebone
Fredrik Burstedt .... Moahni Moahna
Fredrik Burström .... Laudamus
Fredrik Cardona "Fred/Fredda" (aka Holmberg) ....
.... Blackshine, Deviant, The Satellite Circle, Hetsheads
Fredrik Carlsson .... Exanthema
Fredrik Carlsson .... Outshine
Fredrik Cronsten .... Mother Superior
Fredrik Dahllöf .... Indian Red
Fredrik Danielsson .... Godgory, World Of Silence
Fredrik Degerström "Spider" .... Bewitched, Auberon,
.... Guillotine
Fredrik Edholm .... Last Laugh (2)
Fredrik Ekberg "Fredric Alicia" .... Alicate
Fredrik Eklöf .... Unlight Order
Fredrik Elander .... God B.C.
Fredrik Elemalm "Freddy" .... Cryonic
Fredrik Emneus .... Fatal Smile (1)
Fredrik Enqvist .... Carpe Wade
Fredrik Ericsson .... In Thy Dreams
Fredrik Eriksson .... Quarterback Beat
Fredrik Eriksson .... Silent Scythe, (Crimson Tide)
Fredrik Eriksson "Athel W" .... Blot Mine
Fredrik Eriksson "Fredde" .... Vilefuck, Vicious
Fredrik Eriksson .... Eternal Desire
Fredrik Eriksson .... Alyson Avenue
Fredrik Eriksson "Frippe" .... Morifade,
.... Tad Morose, Solitude (1)
Fredrik Erneroth "Fredde" .... Temperance
Fredrik Evertsson .... Burning Saviours
Fredrik Fagerlund .... Jonny's Bomb
Fredrik Feldt "Freddie Field" .... Freddie Field
Fredrik Fencke .... Optimystical
Fredrik Finnander .... The Mushroom River Band,
.... Rise And Shine, Kayser, Aeon (1)
Fredrik Flink .... Middleage
Fredrik Folkare .... Siebenbürgen, Eclipse, Firecracker,
.... Scudiero, Constancia, Unleashed
Fredrik Forsberg .... I Am Hunger
Fredrik Forsén "Hilding" .... R&R
Fredrik Forsfjäll "FoaF" .... Calm Chaos
Fredrik Forssblad .... Mac & Ploids
Fredrik Frykman .... Lucy, Sabbtail
Fredrik Furberg .... Borderline (2)
Fredrik Gahm .... Nugatory
Fredrik Gleisner .... Rise And Shine
Fredrik Glimbrand .... Atlantis, Mercury Fang, Misth
Fredrik Gomersson .... Inhale
Fredrik Groth .... The Storyteller
Fredrik Grünberger .... Afterglow, Mind's Eye
Fredrik Grähs .... Quarterback Beat
Fredrik Gröndahl .... Crystal Eyes
Fredrik Gunnarsson .... Razorblade
Fredrik Haake .... Meldrum
Fredrik Hall .... Silverdollar
Fredrik Hamberg .... Facequake
Fredrik Hammar .... Sterbhaus, Twins Crew
Fredrik Hansson "Hellvis" ...... Boogieman, One Minute Left
Fredrik Hansson .... Wild Cat Sleezy
Fredrik Hedberg "Fredde" .... Defueled
Fredrik Hedström .... Persuader
Fredrik Heghammar .... Fred's Fuel

Fredrik Helgesson .... Grief Of Emerald, Obligatorisk Tortyr
Fredrik Hellerström .... Year Of The Goat
Fredrik Helmersson "Nellie" .... Sonic Temple
Fredrik Hermansson .... Pain Of Salvation
Fredrik Hjärtström .... Septic Grave
Fredrik Holm .... Takida
Fredrik Holmberg "Fredda" .... (See Fredrik Cardona)
Fredrik Hugosson .... Ginger Trees
Fredrik Huldtgren .... Canopy
Fredrik Hultman "Freddie Fister" .... Turbocharged
Fredrik Håkansson .... Zpeedfreak, Moonshine
Fredrik Hänhel .... Fallen Angel
Fredrik Isaksson "Fredda" .... Grave (2), Therion,
.... Bajen Deathe Cult, Excruciate, Denied
Fredrik Jacobsen .... Rosicrucian, Slapdash, Atrocity
Fredrik Jacobsson "Beretorn" .... Throne Of Ahaz,
.... Ancient Wisdom
Fredrik Jansson .... Orient
Fredrik Jansson .... Atlantic Tide, Witchcraft,
.... Abramis Brama, Count Raven
Fredrik Jansson .... Sticky Sweet
Fredrik Jansson .... Steamroller, Maniac
Fredrik Jernberg ... Red Fun, Guardian Ange, Rat Bat Blue
Fredrik Joakimsson .... Cloudscape
Fredrik Joelsson .... Fimbultyr
Fredrik Johannesen .... Iniuria
Fredrik Johansson .... Morifade
Fredrik Johansson .... Dimension Zero, All Ends
Fredrik Johansson .... The Goddamned, Draconian
Fredrik Johansson "Fidde" .... Hardcore Superstar
Fredrik Johansson .... Suicide Nation, Dark Tranquillity
Fredrik Johansson "Figge" .... Wiz
Fredrik Johansson "Lillis" .... Dear Mutant, Bokor
Fredrik Johansson .... Fairness
Fredrik Johansson .... Blackburns
Fredrik Johansson .... Disdain
Fredrik Johansson .... Bishop Garden
Fredrik Johansson (now Järnberg) .... Altar
Fredrik Johnsson "Af Necrohell" .... Deathwitch,
.... Immersed In Blood, Runemagick
Fredrik Jonsson .... Dexter Jones' Circus Orchestra
Fredrik Jordanius .... Ablaze, Conviction,
.... Rising Fate, Egonaut
Fredrik Josefsson .... Dreamland, Infinity
Fredrik Josefsson .... Close Quarters
Fredrik Junhammar .... Narnia
Fredrik Karlén .... Merciless
Fredrik Karlsson "Mussla" .... Dispatched
Fredrik Karlsson "Balle" .... Paganus
Fredrik Karlsson "Missfall" .... Funeral Dirge
Fredrik Karlsson .... Hexagon
Fredrik Karlsson .... Sinkadus
Fredrik Karlsson .... Demon Seed, Dispatched
Fredrik Karlsson .... Zap Yankeefy
Fredrik Kelemen .... Lancer
Fredrik Kihlberg .... Cult Of Luna
Fredrik Kjörling .... Mellow Poetry, Mayadome
Fredrik Klingwall .... In Grey, Flaggelation,
.... Desultor, Loch Vostock, Machinery, Anima Morte
Fredrik Kretz .... Outshine
Fredrik Källberg .... Sherlock Brothers
Fredrik Källström "Frecko" .... Vanity Blvd
Fredrik Lager .... Seven Tears
Fredrik Larsson .... Mentor's Wish
Fredrik Larsson .... Dispatched
Fredrik Larsson .... Hammerfall,
.... Deathdestruction, Crystal Age
Fredrik Larsson .... Taste
Fredrik Leijström .... Malaise
Fredrik Liefvendahl "Trizze Trash" .... Grand Magus,
.... Abramis Brama, Backdraft
Fredrik Lind .... Loudhell
Fredrik Lindegren .... Unleashed
Fredrik Lindehall .... Sharp Nine
Fredrik Lindén .... Fallen Angel
Fredrik Lindgren "Freddie Eugene" .... Born Of Fire,
... Harm's Way, Atlantic Tide, Terra Firma, Rise And Shine
Fredrik Lindgren .... Cut Out
Fredrik Lindgren .... Headache
Fredrik Lindholm .... For You (4U)
Fredrik Lindorf .... Corrosive Carcass
Fredrik Lindqvist .... Ritual
Fredrik Lindqvist .... Lineout, (Totalt Jävla Mörker)
Fredrik Lindvall .... Mr. Tiger
Fredrik Linfjärd .... Stabwound, Shubend
Fredrik Ljung .... Disdain, Deals Death
Fredrik Ljunge .... Colorblind, Thore Goes Metal
Fredrik Lundberg .... Attention (2)
Fredrik Lundberg ... Morgana Lefay, Lefay, Fantasmagoria
Fredrik Lundstedt ...... Distorted Wonderland, Art Rebellion
Fredrik Löfdahl .... Railroad
Fredrik Lösnitz .... Kaross
Fredrik Magnusson .... Chasticement
Fredrik Mannberg "Spider" .... Guillotine, Nocturnal Rites
Fredrik Meister .... Despite
Fredrik Melander "Fredrick Hanoi" .... Bathory
Fredrik Mielke .... Vanguard (2)
Fredrik Molin "Molle" .... Paganus

Fredrik Muskos .... Slitage
Fredrik Nilsson "Endymion" .... Spetälsk,
.... Misericordia, Satanic Slaughter
Fredrik Nilsson .... Sinners Burn
Fredrik Nilsson .... Dreamline
Fredrik Nilsson .... Otyg
Fredrik Nilsson .... Timeless Miracle
Fredrik Nilsson .... Jezider
Fredrik Nordin .... Greenleaf, Dozer
Fredrik Nordin .... Thyreos
Fredrik Nordstrandh .... Lechery
Fredrik Nordström .... Burst, In Aeternum, Mean Streak,
.... Covered Call, Dark Tranquillity, Denial, Devian,
.... Marionette, Pain And Passion, The Storyteller,
.... Zonaria, Dream Evil
Fredrik Norlander "Phobos" .... Joke
Fredrik Norman .... Three Minute Madness
Fredrik Normark .... Gin Lady
Fredrik Norrman .... Subdive, Dellamorte,
.... Uncanny, October Tide
Fredrik Notling .... M.O.B
Fredrik Nygren .... Sorcery
Fredrik Ohlsson (now Sjöholm) .... Veni Domine
Fredrik Olofsson .... Captor
Fredrik Olsson "Equilibrian Epicurius" . Lost Horizon, Heed
Fredrik Pellbrink .... Entrench
Fredrik Pernros .... Azure, My Endless Wishes
Fredrik Persson .... Kamasutra, Wraptors
Fredrik Persson .... Broken Glass
Fredrik Persson .... Syrus
Fredrik Petersson .... Oppression
Fredrik Petersson .... Skinfected
Fredrik Pettersson .... The Goddamned
Fredrik Pettersson .... Another Life
Fredrik Pettersson .... Section Eight
Fredrik Pihl .... Fredrik Pihl
Fredrik Pihlström (aka Lundquist) .... Obrero
Fredrik Plahn .... Prey, Sound Explosion
Fredrik P-zon .... Quarterback Beat
Fredrik Pålsson .... Takida
Fredrik Pålsson .... Comecon
Fredrik Rehnqvist .... Blackburns
Fredrik Rehnström .... Cult Of Luna
Fredrik Reinedahl .... Burst, Soulquake, Tyburn
Fredrik Rhodin .... Jennie Tebler's Out Of Oblivion,
.... Screwball.Sthlm
Fredrik Romlin "Niltor" .... Vredgad, Psykotisk,
.... Ornias, Tyranex
Fredrik Samuelsson "Feje" .... Pussy Galore
Fredrik Sandberg .... Moonstruck
Fredrik Sandsten .... H.E.A.L, Whipped Cream
Fredrik Scherman .... Mentor's Wish
Fredrik Schälin .... Anata
Fredrik Schönbeck .... Stonesilk
Fredrik Sjöholm .... Wolverine, Divinefire
Fredrik Skoog .... Frank Thomsen
Fredrik Stenberg .... Road Ratt
Fredrik Strömkvist .... Memorium
Fredrik Ståhl .... Bussiga Klubben
Fredrik Sundin .... Sargoth
Fredrik Sunnefeldt "F Sunny" .... Paradize
Fredrik Svensson .... Gabria,
.... Headline, The Kaars
Fredrik Swedberg .... Request
Fredrik Söderberg "Chainsaw Demon" ...... Cranium, Dawn
Fredrik Söderberg .... Soreption
Fredrik Söderlund .... Parnassus, Murderplan,
.... Octinomos, Algaion
Fredrik Söderström .... Greed
Fredrik Söderström .... Posh Filth, Cavus
Fredrik Thomander .... Vildsvin
Fredrik Thordendahl .... Meshuggah, Blacksmith,
...... C.B Murdock, Fredrik Thordendahl's Special Defects
Fredrik Thörnblom .... Lizard Eye
Fredrik Thörnqvist .... Expulsion
Fredrik Trossö .... Anxious
Fredrik Täck .... Tenebre
Fredrik Wahledow "Fredrock" .... Wagabond
Fredrik Wallenberg .... Sarcasm, Skitsystem
Fredrik Wallin .... Equinox Ov The Gods
Fredrik Wattwil .... Disciple
Fredrik Weileby .... Sparzanza
Fredrik Welin-Berger "Frasse" .. Six Pack Sonic, Fuzzdevil
Fredrik Wester "Plague" .... Lord Belial
Fredrik Westin .... Corroded
Fredrik Widigs .... Angrepp, The Ugly, Hyperborean,
.... Demonical, Witchery
Fredrik Winero .... Sahara (2)
Fredrik Wolff (aka Torstenfelt) "Obehag" .... Apati
Fredrik Von Gerber "Freddie" ...... Red Fun, Easy Action,
.... Rat Bat Blue, Bam Bam Boys, Glen Spove
Fredrik Zackrisson .... Black Dog
Fredrik Åberg .... Loud, Wisdom Call
Fredrik Åkerlund .... Nubian Rose
Fredrik Åkesson ...... Arch Enemy, Clockwise, Human Clay,
.... Shock Tilt, One Cent, Opeth Sabbtail,
.... Southpaw, Talisman, Jupiter Society
Fredrik Åstrand .... Belsebub

Fredrik Ärletun .... Plastic Pride
Fredrik Öberg .... Snakes In Paradise
Fredrik Österlund "Fredo" .... Zeelion
Fredrika Berggren .... Sound Explosion
Frida Lundström .... Liquid Scarlet
Frida Ståhl .... Meldrum
Frida Viberg .... My Endless Wishes
Fritz Quathoff .... Harvey Wallbanger
Fritz .... (See Gunnar Fritzell)
Frozthirw .... Rimfrost
Fullmåne .... Funeral Frost, Jotunheim
Funeral Whore .... Karnarium
Gabby Force .... Chains
Gabriel Aadland .... Chillihounds
Gabriel Axelsson .... Mason
Gabriel Bjäreborg .... Unsolved
Gabriel Engberg .... Painfield
Gabriel Eskilsson .... The Rifles
Gabriel Forslund "Gabbe" .... Witchgrave, Antichrist
Gabriel Hellmark .... Adept
Gabriel Rauhofer .... Self Deception
Gabriel Österlund "Gabe Colt/Gabbe" ...... Blazing Guns,
.... Von Panzer, Seven, Warhammer
Galle .... (See Jan-Ove Johansson)
Gareth Brandt .... Damien
Gari Krajacic .... Brainwave
Gary Cooper "Mudbone" .... Shining Path
Gavhin .... Vargavinter
Geir Rönning .... Deacon Street Project, Prisoner,
.... Talk Of Town, Radioactive, Rainmaker
Gene Zider "Zeth" .... Asphyxiation
Georg "Nine" .... Withersin
Georg Härnsten "Egg" .... Dynazty, Chris Laney
Georg Rozello .... Avalon/Avalone
Georg Trolin .... Panta Rei
George Atlagic "Jolle" .... The Quill, N.J.B
George Bravo .... Fuck Bitch, Roachpowder, Skintrade
George Ellgren .... Anxious
George Gustavsson "Little" .... (See Jörgen Tjusling)
George Kollias .... System Shock
George Svensson "Swanson" .... Nasty Idols
George Wallen "Georg Allen" .... Gemini Souls
Georgios Karvelas .... Dechas
Gerard Stenlund .... Three Minute Madness
Gerian Germaine (Dave) Dufort .... EF Band
German Pascual . Divinefire, Mind's Eye, Narnia, Afterglow
Gernot Iversen .... Overdrive, High Voltage
Geron Fritiofsson .... Parazite
Gert Daun (aka Erikson) .... Horizon (2), Andromeda
Gert Karlsson .... Adventure
Gert Svensson .... Vulcano
Gert-Inge Gustafsson .... Steelwings
Gert-Åke Nilsson .... Pax Romana
Gino Renebrandt .... Pax Romana
Girilal Barrs .... Kapoor
Giulio Capone .... Treasure Land
Glen Gilbert .... Hide The Knives
Glenn Borgquist .... Heavy Cargo
Glenn Eriksson .... Crow, Incolmitus
Glenn Fransson .... HÄF Band
Glenn Grylin .... Revenge
Glenn Hughes .... Snakes In Paradise
Glenn Jonsson .... One Cent
Glenn Larsson .... Meadow
Glenn Laurén .... Frequency
Glenn Ljungkvist "Glen McKee" .... Alicate
Glenn Ljungström .... In Flames, Dimension Zero,
.... The Resistance
Glenn Spove .... Glen Spove
Glenn Stenlöf .... Fair Child
Glenn Svensson .... The Duskfall
Glenn Sykes .... Regurgitate
Glenn Verho .... Bloodshed
Glyn Grimwade .... Rosicrucian
Gobbe Henningsson .... Antichrist
Gonzalo Lopez .... Request
Gordon Danielsson .... Paradise (3)
Gordon Johnston .... Coercion
Gorethrash .... Autopsy Torment
Gorgorium .... (see Kalle Antonsson)
Gorgoth .... Nidrike
Gothard Stenlund .... Heel
Gotte Ringkvist .... Va-Då?
Gottfrid Åhman .... In Solitude
Graav .... (See Stefan Sandström)
Greger Andersson "Greg" .... Eric De Van, DeVan
Greger Gerlehagen "Ian Greg" .... Torch
Greger Rönnqvist .... Vivid
Grendel .... Blodulv
Greta Zachoszcz "Gosia" .... Merrygold
Greta Zackrisson .... Eggs On Legs
Grigoriou Cornel .... Cornel Band
Grim .... Fear The Future
Grim Vindkall .... (see Jonas Almen)
Grimner .... Mörker
Gry Anders Nilsson .... Vanadis
Guillaume Le Huche "Isphael Wing" .... Katatonia
Gunilla Ericsson .... Tears

Gunnar Berglindh ... Cauterizer
Gunnar Dahlgren ... Unreal
Gunnar Forselius ... Tom Trick
Gunnar Fritzell "Fritz" ... Behemoth
Gunnar Green ... Hexagon
Gunnar Hagman ... Bedrock Zity
Gunnar Hallin ... Neon Rose, Bam Bam Boys, Easy Action
Gunnar Hammar ... Amaran
Gunnar Hård Af Segerstad ... Disdain, Fraise
Gunnar Janupe ... Nadir, Waterline, (Snowstorm)
Gunnar Johansson ... Kings N' Fools
Gunnar Jonsen ... TBC
Gunnar Jönsson ... Trouble
Gunnar Kastman (aka Andersson) ... Half Man
Gunnar Kindberg ... Destiny
Gunnar Lööf ... Southfork
Gunnar Maxén ... Brother Ape
Gunnar Michaeli "Mic" ... Europe, Universe, ... Last Autumn's Dream, Audiovision, Thore Skogman
Gunnar Nilsson ... Beneath The Frozen Soil
Gunnar Norgren ... Chronic Decay
Gunnar Palmquist ... Trouble
Gunnar Söderström ... Through Time Tomorrow
Gunnar Westberg ... Kaipa
Gunnar Wiklund ... Morgan Mastling Band
Gurkha ... Eleven Pictures
Gus G (Kostas Karamitroudis) ... Arch Enemy, Cans, ... Dream Evil
Gustaf "Kallbrand "Sundin ... Styggelse
Gustaf Albinsson ... No Hawaii
Gustaf Hagel ... Yggdrasil, Broken Dagger
Gustaf Hedtström ... Motherpearl
Gustaf Heinemann Ljungström ... Noctum
Gustaf Hielm ... Dark Funeral, Meshuggah, ... Pain Of Salvation, Non-Human Level
Gustaf Hjortsjö ... Bullet
Gustaf Jorde ... Man.Machine.Indust, Raubtier, ... Defleshed, Enemy Is Us, Deviant, Searing I
Gustaf Liljenström "Gus" ... Violent Divine, Battle Station, ... Marshal Kane, Captain Freak's Freaky Funksters
Gustaf Lindström "Grga/Carlos Satano" ... Iron Lamb, ... Ghost, Repugnant
Gustaf Ljungström ... Fallen Angel
Gustaf Malmberg ... Orphan Gypsy
Gustaf Skürk ... Steelwing
Gustaf von Segebaden ... Cranium
Gustav Alander ... Coldtears
Gustav Bergqkvist "Tank Hooker" ... Panzer Princess
Gustav Bergström ... Titan
Gustav Elowsson "Gurra" Crimson Moonlight, Exhale Swe
Gustav Grenstam "Golgara" ... Life Illusion
Gustav Grusell ... Freedom Bleeder
Gustav Hedlund "Lestat" ... Sister
Gustav Johansson ... Implode
Gustav Jonsson ... The Session
Gustav Karlsson ... Sordid Death
Gustav Köllerström ... Platitude
Gustav Larsson ... Titan
Gustav Lithammer ... Adept
Gustav Ljung "Gurra" ... Stallion Four
Gustav Ljungberg ... Shenerah
Gustav Nahlin ... Nostradameus
Gustav Totenlieb "Hizon" ... Withersin
Gustav Trodin ... Vomitous
Göran Alnestrand ... Cornel Band
Göran Andersson ... 1 Way Street
Göran Andersson ... Spinnrock
Göran Bartol ... Roswell
Göran Bengtsson ... Jeremiah
Göran Berg ... Neofight
Göran Berggren ... Toxic Rose
Göran Böwing ... Fred's Fuel
Göran Edman ... Crash The System, Benny Jansson, ... Flintstens med Stanley, Johansson (Brothers), ... Thomas Larsson, Madison, Yngwie Malmsteen, ... Geff, Glory, Snake Charmer, Time Requiem, Xsavior, ... Covered Call, John Norum, Regent, Silent Call, ... Swedish Erotica, Talisman, Richard Andersson, ... Kharma, Karmakanic, Mårran, Reingold, Street Talk, ... Vindictive, Jayce Landberg
Göran Edquist ... Paradise (3), Simson
Göran Ekstrand ... Motvind
Göran Eliasson ... Notorious
Göran Elmquist ... 17, Alfonzetti, Rising, Stand By, ... Bam Bam Boys, Dream Bank
Göran Eriksson ... Reazon
Göran Eriksson ... Rubbet
Göran Eriksson ... Godhate, Thronaeon
Göran Fagerli ... Fire & Ice
Göran Finnberg ... Nattas
Göran Florén "G G Florence" ... Avalon/Avalone
Göran Florström ... Generous Maria
Göran Fors ... Galleon, Spektrum
Göran Forssén ... Quix, Sapphire Eyes
Göran Greus ... Fantasy
Göran Hansson ... Lotus (1)
Göran Hellsén ... Vantage
Göran Hemgren ... Vanguard (2)
Göran Holmberg ... Manticore
Göran Jacobson ... Quicksand Dream
Göran Johansson "Chorozon" ... Setherial, Torchbearer, ... Chaosdemon
Göran Johnsson . Cross, Grand Stand, Galleon, Spektrum
Göran Kunstberg "George King" ... Wizz, King & Rozz, ... Treasure
Göran Landgren ... Vivid
Göran Larnö ... Electra Top Raiders
Göran Levén ... Ambush
Göran Lundgren "Guru" ... Skellington
Göran Lundgren ... Valley
Göran Nikolausson ... Charizma
Göran Nordh "Glory North"Glory Bells (Band), Göran Nord
Göran Norman ... Scheitan
Göran Nylén ... Quinzy
Göran Nyström ... Majestic Dimension
Göran Olsson ... White
Göran Palm ... Young Force
Göran Persson ... Frozen Fire
Göran Prahl ... White
Göran Pripp ... The Riff
Göran Pärnils ... Panic
Göran Sjöberg ... King Koole
Göran Sjöberg ... Rockvaktmästarna
Göran Sonesson ... GRK
Göran Sten ... Misery
Göran Svensson ... Young Force
Göran Werner ... Lonely Hearts
Göran Åhlfeldt ... Victory (1)
Görgen Olsson (aka Loviken) ... Tyfuz
Gösta Eliasson ... Headache
Gösta Hjelmquist ... Solid Ground (1)
H Fossmo ... Plutonium
H. Sebastian ... Gemini Souls
H.B. Jewel ... Belladonna
Haakon Sjöquist ... Oblivion
Hakim Hietikko ... Dechas
Hal Marabel "Jonsson" (aka Hal/Hjalmar) ... Bad Habitt ... Midnight Sun, Bai Bang, Project L.E.E
Halvar ... Blodskald
Hampus Eriksson "Hampe Death" ... Degial
Hampus Erix "Hank" ... Houston
Hampus Grönberg ... Kamasutra
Hampus Hallgard "Hampe" ... The Brimstone Days
Hampus Klang ... Jigsore Terror, Bullet, ... Hypnosia, Lenny Blade
Hampus Landin ... Miss Beahaviour, Neondaze
Hampus Olsson ... Carnalist
Hampus Södergren "Action" ... Dust Bowl Jokies
Hank A*Teem ... A*Teem
Hanna Rejdvik ... Aphasia
Hannah Holgersson ... Therion
Hannes Almén ... Yersinia
Hannes Hansson ... Mustasch
Hannes Rognås ... Assault
Hannes Råstam ... Blåkulla
Hannes Van Dahl ... (see Karl-Hannes Van Dahl)
Hannu Kiviaho ... Ingo & Floyd
Hannu Rajala ... Shock Tilt
Hans Alsing ... Overture
Hans Andersson ... Genie
Hans Andersson "HB/Hasse" ... Token, Fatal Smile, ... Fire & Ice, Scudiero, Mindsplit
Hans Arleklint ... Steamboat Willies
Hans Asp ... Frontiers
Hans Bell ... Burn
Hans Bergqvist ... Forest
Hans Bruhn "B Broccoli" ... Fruitcake
Hans Carlsson ... Horde Of Hel, In Battle, ... Diabolical, Odhinn
Hans Carlsten ... Comatose
Hans Derestam "Hasse" ... Blues Bag, Moosters
Hans Diechle ... Lucky Stiff
Hans Dimberg ... Blind Alley, Fortune (1)
Hans Ekman ... Chai Gang
Hans Elofsson "Haze Gladys" ... The Wild Bunch
Hans Engström ... Alex's Pro
Hans Eriksson "H Asparagus" ... Fruitcake, Lotus (2)
Hans Fogelberg ... Tears
Hans Forslund ... Wildmarken
Hans Forslund ... Calm
Hans Forsman ... Double Deuce
Hans Fröberg "Hasse" ... Barrelhouse, Spellbound, ... Hasse Fröber & Listening Companion, ... The Flower Kings, (Solid Blue)
Hans Grübeck ... Tyrox
Hans Gustavsson ... Belsebub
Hans Hernberg "Alex Hill" ... Burn
Hans Hogedal ... Tonvikt
Hans Johansson (now Dalzon) ... Million
Hans Johansson ... Pain And Passion, Biscaya, ... Moahni Moahna
Hans Johansson ... Tyron
Hans Karlander ... Uppåt Väggarna
Hans Karlin ... Cryonic Temple
Hans Lagerström ... Gallery (2)
Hans Larsson ... Airlines
Hans Larsson ... Tatch
Hans Liljegren ... Paralyce
Hans Lindström ... Cane
Hans Ludwig ... Black Cat Moan
Hans Lundin ... Vargton, Kaipa, Hagen
Hans Lönnberg ... Örby Mix
Hans Montin ... Shock Tilt
Hans Månsson ... Svarte Pan
Hans Nilsson ... Liers In Wait, Dimension Zero, ... The Great Deceiver, Luciferion, Diabolique, Crystal Age
Hans Nilsson ... M-Train
Hans Olsson ... Naughty Boys
Hans Persson "Haynes Phersson" ... Cloudscape, ... Doctor Weird
Hans Persson ... Pole Position
Hans Persson ... Aquila
Hans Rasmusson ... Art Rebellion
Hans Rosander ... Greasy Saddles
Hans Sandberg ... Victim
Hans Schakonat ... Kalajs
Hans Söder "Spider" ... ATC
Hans Tanska ... Diary
Hans-Erik Hall ... Teamwork
Hans-Erik Jansson ... Charity, Wizzard
Hansi Borgström ... Status Two
Hansi Cross ... Cross, Spektrum, Blåeld
Hansi Fellbrink ... Cherry Red, Roulette
Hans-Olof Childs ... Make Up
Hante Andersson ... Miss Willis, Twilight Zone
Harald Hansen ... S.L.R
Harald Lund ... Sabbtail
Harald Nygren ... Blåeld
Haraldur Briem "Joe Nebel" ... Sludge
Harri Juvonen "Sado/Fiend/von Hell" ... Devil Lee Rot, ... Tristitia, Pagan Rites
Harri Kolari ... Blastrock
Harri Sillsten ... Deep Zilents
Harri Tuovila ... Griffen, Pink Panther
Harry Granroth ... Ram
Harry Kemppainen "Kody" ... King Pin, Shotgun Messiah
Harry Kjövik ... Renegade Five
Harry Virtanen ... Chainsaw, Pandemonic
Hasse Andersson ... Tumult
Hasse BruniussonThe Flower Kings, Karmakanic, Rävjunk
Hasse Carlsson "Bie" ... Zeta
Hasse Chapskate ... Blue Balls
Hasse Frendin ... Allan Beddo Band
Hasse Gustafson ... Nattfrost
Hasse Gustavsson (now Gatu) ... Arrowz
Hasse Hagman ... Universe
Hasse Hermanssen (aka Hermansen) ... Staiger, Greyhate
Hasse Hurnasti ... Poor Boys
Hasse Johansson ... Meadow
Hasse Jönsson ... Shame (2)
Hasse Karlberg ... Hasse Karlberg
Hasse Karlsson ... In Battle, Diabolical
Hasse Olausson ... Sky High
Hasse Ottosson ... Overload
Hasse Rosén ... Hagen, Zircus
Hasse Sörensen ... Puteraeon
Hasse Torensjö ... Prospect
Hasse Worzel ... Firecracker
Hazze Wazzéen ... Sahara (2)
Heidi Lehmus ... Lights Out
Heikki Kiviaho ... Ingo & Floyd
Heino Särkioja ... Ma Connection
Helen Froh (now Årjes) ... Robb and Friends
Helen Jennerwall ... Livin' Sacrifice
Helen Polstam ... Love Injection
Helena Kihlstrand ... Ice Age
Helena Pettersson ... Drama
Helena Rosendahl ... Coastline
Helena Wahlgren ... II Shy
Heljamadr ... (see Andreas Vingbäck)
Hell Mike Motorbike ... Dark Legions
Hempo Hildén ... (see Henrik Hildén)
Henka Ahlberg "Gator" ... Kazjurol
Henka Johansson ... The Citadel, Clawfinger
Henkan Thomsen ... Don Patrol
Henke Borg ... SnakeStorm
Henke Forss ... Dawn, Niden Div. 187, In Flames
Henke Karlsson ... Stillborn, Gosh!
Henke Kolbjer ... Soils Of Fate
Henke Lönn ... Hellfueled
Henke Skoog ... Nominon, Eviscerated
Henke Svensson ... Unholy, Relevant Few
Henning Eckerborn ... Oxan
Henning Nielsen ... Born Of Sin
Henri Gylander ... Ginger Trees
Henric Carlsson ... The Unguided, Eternal Grief, ... Nightrage, Cipher System
Henric Heed ... Inverted
Henric Johansson ... Peo
Henric Liljestrand ... Lavett
Henric Merkel ... Illfigure
Henric Ohlsson ... Diabolical
Henric Ottosson "Otto" ... Maim
Henric Von Boisman ... Dry Dive
Henrik Allbjer ... The Goddamned, Moria
Henrik Andersson "Hea" ... Dogpound
Henrik Andersson ... Power Unit
Henrik Andersson ... Skywalkers
Henrik Andersson ... Three Minute Madness
Henrik Andreasson ... House Of Shakira
Henrik Antonsson ... Rickshaw
Henrik Axelsson ... Implode
Henrik Bengtsson ... The Ancient's Rebirth
Henrik Bergman ... The Graviators
Henrik Bergquist ... The Poodles, Fortune (2), ... Four Sticks, Southfork
Henrik Bergström ... Soulquake System, Tyburn
Henrik Bladh ... Academy
Henrik Block "Hank Black" ... Gabria
Henrik Blomquist ... Face Down, Mass Murder Agenda
Henrik Blomqvist ... As You Drown
Henrik Boman ... Switchblade
Henrik Borg "Henke" ... Entropy, Satureye
Henrik Brander ... Carnal Grief
Henrik Brannerydh ... The Storyteller
Henrik Bringås ... Sacred Night
Henrik Bringås ... Mascot Parade
Henrik Brockmann ... Evil Masquerade
Henrik Brun "Mange" ... Entropy
Henrik Brynolfsson "Hempa" ... Mykorrhiza, ... Excruciate, Internal Decay
Henrik Båth ... Harmony (2), Darkwater, ... Heartbreak Radio
Henrik Börjesson ... Humble Bee
Henrik Christensson ... Miscellany
Henrik Claesson ... Frekvens
Henrik Crantz ... Soils Of Fate
Henrik Dahlberg ... Iniuria
Henrik Danhage ... Evergrey, Deathdestruction, ... In Flames, Lillasyster
Henrik Deleskog ... Hero
Henrik Doltz Nilsson ... Crucifyre
Henrik Drake ... Anata
Henrik EdenhedDead By April, Straight Frank, Downstroke
Henrik Ekeroth "Typhos" ... Dark Funeral, Infernal (666)
Henrik Englund ... Scarpoint
Henrik Eriksson "YX" ... Stormrider
Henrik Evertsson "Henke" ... Blowback
Henrik Fellermark ... Reinxeed
Henrik Flyman ... Evil Masquerade, ZooL, Moahni Moahna
Henrik Forslund ... Sarcasm
Henrik Georgsson ... Sanctifica
Henrik Grüttner ... Skraeckoedlan
Henrik Gustafson ... Core Of Nation
Henrik Gustavsson ... Whiteness
Henrik Hagedorn ... White Silver, Serenade For June
Henrik Hansson ... Vagh
Henrik Hedberg ... Wyvern, Amaranth, Hypocrite ... C.B Murdoc, Mörk Gryning
Henrik Hedelund ... Memfis
Henrik Hedman ... Celestial Decay
Henrik Helenius ... In Solitude
Henrik Hildén "Hempo/Hobo" ... Baltimoore, John Norum, ... Midnight Sun, Shock Tilt, Twilight, MandrakeRoot, ... Flintstens med Stanley, Trash, Ball, Splash
Henrik Huldtgren "H." ... Lifelover
Henrik Högl ... Mortalicum
Henrik Ivarsson ... Crowpath
Henrik Jansson "Nagge" ... Beyond Visions
Henrik Johansson ... Apostasy, Wolf
Henrik Johansson ... Excessum, Bloodlust
Henrik Johansson "Henke" ... Waving Corn
Henrik Johansson ... Thunder
Henrik Johansson ... Book Of Hours, Wolverine
Henrik Johansson ... Nocturnal Alliance, Detest
Henrik Juhano ... Disdained, Insania (Stockholm)
Henrik Karlsson ... Zonata
Henrik Karlsson "Henke" ... Cryonic
Henrik Karlsson ... Epedemic
Henrik Kentsson ... Solitude (2)
Henrik Kihlberg ... Porklift
Henrik Kindvall "Gjallar" ... Nidrike, Skald
Henrik Kjellberg ... Nocturnal Rites, Jonny's Bomb
Henrik Klefbäck ... Empty Guns
Henrik Larsen ... Stormrider
Henrik Larsson ... Red Baron
Henrik Larsson ... Diabolique, Tenebre
Henrik Lind ... Rävjunk
Henrik Lindahl ... Fuzzdevil, Six Pack Sonic
Henrik Lindberg ... Fat Nelly
Henrik Lindemo ... Sorcery, Outrider
Henrik Lindén "Stanley Hawk" ... On The Rocks, Crier, ... Sacrifice, Pete Sandberg
Henrik Lindenmo ... Isole, Outremer
Henrik Lindqvist ... Nine, Outlast
Henrik Lingman ... Jezider
Henrik Lovén ... Guns 'N' Horses
Henrik Lundberg ... Masquerade, House Of Heavy
Henrik Lundgren ... Abandoned Splhinx
Henrik Lundqvist ... Bozeman's Simplex
Henrik Mawe ... Firecracker
Henrik Meijner ... Cromlech

NAME INDEX

Henrik Mikaelsson ... Hate Ammo, Live Elephant
Henrik Nilsson ... Gondoline
Henrik Norén ... Switchblade
Henrik Norrström "Henkan" ... X-Ray
Henrik Nygren ... Embracing
Henrik Nygren ... Miscellany
Henrik Näslund ... Meadows End
Henrik Ohlin "Pär-Ingvar" ... Black Ingvars
Henrik Ohlsson ... Theory In Practice, Mutant, Scar Symmetry, Altered Aeon, Legia
Henrik Olin ... Obscene
Henrik Olofsson ... Mammuth
Henrik Olsson "Baffe" ... Black Dog, It's Alive
Henrik Olsson ... Bloodbound
Henrik Olsson ... Velvet Crash
Henrik Orgna ... Cleopatra
Henrik Paahle ... Autopsy Torment
Henrik Palm ... Sonic Ritual, In Solitude, Chainwreck
Henrik Paulsson ... Mothercake
Henrik Persson ... Mourning Sign
Henrik Persson ... By Night
Henrik Petersson ... Screamer, Erottica
Henrik Pommer ... The Defaced
Henrik Randén ... Johnny Engström Band
Henrik Renström ... Freedom Bleeder
Henrik S Johansson ... Thyreos
Henrik Samuelsson ... Another Hell
Henrik Sandelin ... Avatar
Henrik Schönström ... Enshrined, Torch Bearer, Incapacity, Quest Of Aidance, Solar Dawn, Spawn Of Possession, Unmoored
Henrik Sedell ... Axenstar
Henrik Seeman ... Stormwind
Henrik Selin ... Victory (1)
Henrik Serholt ... Fatal Embrace, Lothlorien
Henrik Siberg ... The Gloria Story
Henrik Sjöwall ... The Defaced
Henrik Sproge ... Sarea, Miss Behaviour
Henrik Stenroos ... Manimal
Henrik Sunding "Nachtzeit/Norden"Durthang, Hypothermia
Henrik Sundström ... Ghamorean
Henrik Svegsjö ... Thyrfing
Henrik Swerkersson ... Arena
Henrik Söderqvist "Honken" ... Blackrain, Justaquickstop
Henrik Thall ... Grave (1)
Henrik Thomsen ... Jim Jidhed, Salute, The Black, Hope
Henrik Tranemyr ... The Bereaved, Maramon
Henrik Trysberg ... Another Hell
Henrik Uhrbom ... Nubian Rose
Henrik von Harten ... Miosis
Henrik Weimedal ... Morifade
Henrik Wendel ... Pyramido, Vandöd, Deathboot
Henrik Wenngren ... Vicious, Autumn Dweller, Skyfire, Dust, Mornaland, Zavorash
Henrik Westerlund ... Denied
Henrik Wetterholm ... Legbone
Henrik Wiklund ... Lineout, Misfortune
Henrik Åberg "Baron De Samedi" ... Battlelust, Gates Of Ishtar, Incinerator, Necromicon
Henrik Öhlund ... Incinia
Henrik Östensson "Henke" ... Genocrush Ferox, The Ugly
Henry Forsén ... Rockvattnä
Henry Lampeinen ... Firework
Henry Pyykkö ... Burning Saviours, Whyte Ash
Henry Ranta ... The Defaced, Soilwork, Terror 2000
Herbert Alarcon Cerna ... Vomitous
Herman Danielsson ... Downhearted
Herman Engström ... Sundown
Herman Furin ... Work Of Art
Herman Saming ... Locomotive Breath, A.C.T, Magnus Karlsson's Freefall
Heval Bozarslan ... Sarcasm
HG Hogström ... Circle Of Chaos
Hibernal ... Terra Tenebrosa
Hilding Marshmallow ... Flintstens Med Stanley
Hillel Tokazier ... Ball
Hjalle Klitse Kyrö ... Mort
Hjalmar Nielsen ... Lord Belial, Born Of Sin
Hobbe Housmand ... Celestial Decay
Holger Thorsin ... Noctes
Homping ... Gas
Hornaeus Nebelhammer ... Fenria
Howie Simon ... Talisman
Hravn Decmiester ... Rimfrost
Hrimner ... Domgård
Hräsvelg ... Unpure
Hubertus Liljegren ... Audiovision, Crimson Moonlight, Sanctifica
Hughin ... Vargavinter
Hugo Bryngfors ... Loss, Mental Crypt
Hugo Thorsin ... Noctes
Hugo Tigenius ... Slodust
Hussni Mörsare ... Winterlong, Raubtier, Viperine
Håcan Åström ... Ma Connection
Håkan Agnsäter ... Solen Skiner
Håkan Almbladh ... Enjoy The View
Håkan Almquist ... Erika Evenlind
Håkan Andersson ... Leviticus, Björn Stigsson
Håkan Andersson ... Haze
Håkan Arnell ... Blåeld
Håkan Bengtsson ... Vantage, Junction
Håkan Bjurquist ... Oxiplegatz
Håkan Björklund ... Apostasy
Håkan Brunnkvist "Bronco" ... Mother's Hope
Håkan Calmroth ... Roachpowder, Skintrade
Håkan Dalsfelt ... Dexter Jones' Circus Orchestra
Håkan Danielsson ... Thalamus
Håkan Ekblad ... Alcatraz
Håkan Englund "Hawkan" ... Mother's Hope
Håkan Eriksson ... Inzight, Blackshine, Face Down
Håkan Eriksson ... White Night
Håkan Ficks ... The Durango Riot
Håkan Fransson ... Elsy Band
Håkan Fredriksson ... Renegade Five
Håkan Fridell ... Aphasia
Håkan Fridhagen ... Trazer
Håkan Fried ... Kansas City Rollers, Cherokee
Håkan Frisk ... 1 Way Street, Kiss Of Thunder
Håkan Goldbeck ... David Harleyson Powertrio
Håkan Granat ... Mercury Fang, Misth
Håkan Gustafsson ... Gypsy Rose
Håkan Gustavsson ... Solid ground (2)
Håkan Gustavsson ... Zeit
Håkan Göras ... Zone Zero
Håkan Hallmén ... Rio
Håkan Hammarström ... Etos
Håkan Haugland "Ian" ... Europe, Ten 67, Stitch, Yngwie Malmsteen, Trilogy, Axia, Baltimoore, Last Autumn's Dream, Candlemass, Clockwise, Coldspell, Chris Laney, Niva, R.A.W, Thore Skogman
Håkan Hedlund "Steve Streaker" ... Torch, Crystal Pride
Håkan Hellgren ... Armatur
Håkan Hemlin ... Steven Anderson, NME Within, Shining, Through Time Tomorrow
Håkan Henriksen ... Galaxy
Håkan Holmström "Philip Junior" ... Trazy Goes Crazy
Håkan Holmström ... Demon Seed
Håkan Höglund ... Jaguar
Håkan Ivarsson ... Fraise
Håkan Jacobsson ... Mercy, Turbo
Håkan Jardmo ... Arrow, Renegade (1)
Håkan Johansson ... Axia
Håkan Johansson ... Poor Boys
Håkan Johansson ... Body Core
Håkan Johnson "Gurra" ... Roach
Håkan Jonsson ... Watain, Die Hard
Håkan Karlsson ... Crush On You
Håkan Karlström ... Black Rose
Håkan Kjellberg ... Onyx
Håkan Lanz ... The Brimstone Days
Håkan Lindkvist "Sueppe" ... Rozz The Bozz
Håkan Linn "E.Zee Lynn" ... Hungry Head Hunters
Håkan Ljunggren ... Lezlie Paice
Håkan Ljungtegen ... Spit It Out
Håkan Malmberg ... Promotion
Håkan Mellquist ... Source (1)
Håkan Mjörnheim ... Alex's Pro
Håkan Morberg ... Desultory, Zebulon
Håkan Mårtensson ... After Twelve
Håkan Nilsson ... Hallonbomb
Håkan Nilsson ... Beyond Visions
Håkan Norgren ... Diavox
Håkan Nyander ... Supreme Majesty, Sanzia, Cloudscape, In Black
Håkan Oksanen ... Drama
Håkan Ollars "Insis" ... Shining
Håkan Olofsson ... Nadir
Håkan Olsson ... Gondoline
Håkan Olsson ... Celestial Decay
Håkan Persson "Måsen" ... Skintrade, Bang & Out, Roachpowder
Håkan Rangemo ... Sabbtail, David Harleyson Powertrio
Håkan Ring ... Destiny
Håkan Sjödin "Alastor Mysteriis" ... Setherial, In Battle, Diabolicum, Blackwinds
Håkan Skoger ... Gardenian, Headplate, Passenger
Håkan Skoog "Fucko" ... Prowoke
Håkan Sten ... Marc Quee
Håkan Stiernström ... Gilt
Håkan Stolt ... Fortuna
Håkan Strind "H-Can" ... Debbie Ray, Ironware
Håkan Stuvemark ... Vicious, In Thy Dreams, Wombbath
Håkan Ståhl ... Fullmakt
Håkan Svantesson "Kane Insane" ... Evil's Eye, Destiny
Håkan Tingshagen ... Chiron
Håkan Tyresten ... Motorcity Madhouse
Håkan Wedin ... Ivory
Håkan Windahl ... Interaction, Mörrum's Own, To Africa With Love
Håkan Zetterkvist ... The Case
Ian-Paolo Lira ... Lillasyster, Rallypack
Ib Odd Vegger ... Dechas
Ibrahim Stråhlman ... Auberon, Desultor
Ids Olniansky ... Dibbukim
Ida Stenbacka "Evileye" ... Crucified Barbara
Ignatius of Loyola ... Saturnalia Temple
Igor Jevtic ... In Grey
Illbrand ... Domgård
Ilmo Venja ... Embracing
Ilpo Ylitalo "Paul Curry" ... Burn
Iman Solgarian ... Stormwind
Iman Zolgharnian ... Cauterizer, Ebony Tears, Dog Faced Gods
Imre Daun "Steve Speed" ... The Black (1), Don Patrol, Gypsy Rose, Hope, Kharma, Salute, Union Mac
Ina Jönsson ... Ten 67
Inge Norlin "Uncle Handsome" ... The Wild Bunch
Inge Tillberg ... Tejp
Ingemar Bergman ... Kaipa
Ingemar Erlandsson ... VII Gates
Ingemar Gustafson "Inky" ... The Ugly
Ingemar Henning ... Stillborn
Ingemar Lundberg ... Maninnya Blade
Ingemar Mårtensson ... Emotion
Ingemar Sallman ... Tryckvåg
Ingemar Sollgard ... In The Colonnades
Ingemar Stenqvist ... Silver Mountain
Ingemar Woody ... Annie For President
Ingmar Eriksson ... Big Times
Ingo Andersson ... Suspekt
Ingo Blomqvist ... Mac Bladgick
Ingvar Bengtsson ... Headline (1)
Ingvar Sandgren ... Abandon
Ingvar Sylegård ... Arrowz
Ioan Nuca ... Morpheena
Iodine Jupiter ... (See Viktor Wennerkvist)
Ion Olteanu "Nutu" ... Ion Olteanu Band
Irene Tuomainen ... Chai Gang
Irfan Cancar ... Sanctrum
Irrbloss ... Irrbloss
Isaac Ingelsbo ... Kaross
Isaac Isaacson ... Nation
Isak Ahlman ... Whyte Ash
Isak Nordblom ... Oblivious
Isak Snow ... Smash Into Pieces
Isak Stenvall ... Lancer
Ismo Immonen ... X-Perience
Ismo Varonen "Hero O'Hara" ... Hiroshima
Ismo Ylitalo "Pete Curry" ... Burn
Isojärvi ... Irrbloss
Isse Isaksson ... Dionda
Issel ... White Silver
Isti ... Atrox
Ivan Höglund "Ivve" ... Pretty Wild, Eye
Ivan Persic ... Peo
Ivana Baukart "Hel" ... Misteltein, Tenebre
Ivar Anås ... Coldtears
Ivar Edding ... Netherbird
Ivar Helenius ... Teamwork
Ivar Katranka ... Hades
Izmo Hedlund "Ledderfejs" ... Terra Firma, Atlantic Tide
Izzy Stormrider ... Odenwrath
J Hallbäck ... Orcivus
J Hietala ... Paletoe
J Kvarnbrink "Tehôm" ... (See Johannes Kvarnbring)
J Lindgren ... Valkyrja
J Marklund "JM" ... Kaos Sacramentum, LIK Armagedda, Lönndom, Sorgeldom, Whirling
J Meddigo ... See Joel Lindholm
J. Demiser ... Sadistic Grimness
J.C. Petersson ... Full Metal Jacketz
Jaanus Kalli ... Misanthropian
Jacek Kedzierski ... Exanthema
Jack Daniel Andersson "J.D" ... 17
Jack Karlsson ... Los Sin Nombre
Jack Kelly ... Heartcry
Jack Pot ... Rat Pack
Jac Rytterholm ... Skellington
Jack White ... Alicate
Jacob Alm ... Mornaland
Jacob Andersson ... Flaggelation
Jacob Berglund ... A Swarm Of The Sun
Jacob Blecher ... Pandemonium, Yggdrasil, Dibbukim
Jacob Bramsell ... Nattsmyg
Jacob Fredén "Jake" ... Nostradameus, Wiz, Arise
Jacob Hallegren ... Angrepp, Månegarm
Jacob Hellner ... Enter The Hunt
Jacob Jennische ... Spacebone
Jacob Lovén ... Plan Three
Jacob Magnusson ... Eventide
Jacob Nordangård ... Captor
Jacob Sickenga "Jake S:t Snake" ... Reptile Smile
Jacob Wennerqvist ... The Storyteller
Jacqueline Anagrius ... Chai Gang
Jaime Salazar ... Diabolique, The Flower Kings, Karmakanic, Pete Sandberg's Jade, Stonelake, Smiling Dog, Bad Habit, Timeless Miracle, Blakk Totem, Last Tribe, Midnight Sun, Reingold, Opus Atlantica, Pax, Planet Alliance, Project L.E.E, Truth, Moahni Moahna
Jake Svensson ... Wigelius
Jakob Andersson "Steril Vwrede" ... Blot Mine
Jakob Asp ... Dechas
Jakob Burstedt ... Lithany, Moloken
Jakob Forsberg ... Mirador
Jakob Herrmann ... The Fuzes
Jakob Jennische ... Dimma, Fuzzdevil, 454, Six Pack Sonic
Jakob Johansson "Bob Gentle" ... Tribulation (2), Stench
Jakob Lagergren ... Syron Vanes
Jakob Lecinzky ... Lobotomy
Jakob Löfdahl ... Body Core
Jakob Martinsson "Jake" ... The Durango Riot
Jakob Papinniemi ... Adept
Jakob Persson ... Narnia
Jakob Reinhard ... Last View
Jakob Samuelsson "Jake Samuel" ... The Poodles, The Ring, Talisman, Yale Bate, Midnight Sun, Freddie Field, Jekyll & Hyde, Blakk Totem, Treasure Land
Jakob Strand ... Oppression
Jakub Orzechowski ... Dimma
Jalle Ahlström ... Agape
Jalle Karlsson ... Warcollapse
James Bradley Jr. ... Sky High
Jamie Borger ... Alfonzetti, Human Clay, Six Feet Under, Swedish Erotica, Capricorn, Last Autumn's Dream, Treat
Jamil Batal ... Zello, Schizophrenic Circus
Jamil Pannee ... No Hawaii
Jamina Jansson ... Wolverine
Jan Aggemyr ... Råg I Ryggen
Jan Altsjö "Auwa" ... Mother Ice Dog
Jan Andersson ... Bedrock Zity
Jan Andersson ... Päst
Jan Andersson ... Jar
Jan Andersson ... Far North
Jan Arvidsson ... Side By Side
Jan Axel Blomberg "M Hellhammer" ... Shining
Jan Bengtsson ... Lohengrin
Jan Bengtsson ... Skånska Mord
Jan Bergman ... Boom Club
Jan Bergström ... Grand Slam
Jan Bingegård ... Sabbtail
Jan Björk ... Boogie Liquor Band
Jan Blomquist "Blomman" ... Hexenhaus, Maninnya Blade, Slowgate
Jan Borg ... Wulcan
Jan Brynsten ... Motvind
Jan Carlsson ... H2O
Jan Cederlund ... Thalamus, Sky Of Rage
Jan Dahlberg ... Meadows End
Jan Dahlquist "Ian Dee Jr" ... Unchained (1)
Jan Dalquist ... Tale, Unleashed
Jan Eliasson ... Born Electric, Crash
Jan Erik Liljeström ... Anekdoten
Jan Fagerberg ... Fake
Jan Fredlund ... Universal Flytrap
Jan Granvik "Granwick" ... Jan Granwick, Grave (1), Glory, Clockwise, Gemini Souls, Glory Bells (Band)
Jan Gripstedt "Jamie S:t Jan" ... 17
Jan Gustafsson ... Törsten Dricker
Jan Göransson ... Vanadis
Jan Hedlund ... Coastline
Jan Hellenberg ... The Cold Existence
Jan Hermansson ... Spectra
Jan Hotverber ... Jimmy Nielsen & Band
Jan Hultin ... Valenze
Jan Iso-Aho ... Blacklight
Jan J Cederlund "Janne" ... Sky Of Rage, Thalamus, Cryonic Temple
Jan Jansson "Jason" .. Mental Crypt, Loss, Grave Flowers
Jan Johannesson ... Fortune (1)
Jan Johansen ... Thore Skogman, Deacon Street Project
Jan Johansson ... Obscurity
Jan Johansson ... Allan Beddo Band
Jan Jämte ... Plastic Pride
Jan Karlsson ... Trazer
Jan Kvillsäter "Nane" ... Kaipa, (Good Clean Fun)
Jan Larsson ... Meduza
Jan Lindberg ... Maninnya Blade, Slowgate
Jan Lindblom ... Armauk
Jan Lindekrantz ... Stonehenge
Jan Lindh "Janne" ... Candlemass, Creozoth, Narduz, Warning, Candlemass, Zoic
Jan Lindström ... Soulquake System
Jan Lissnils ... Reptile Smile
Jan Lundberg ... Alien
Jan Melander ... Transit
Jan Minolf ... Fortuna
Jan Morge ... Eurock
Jan Morin ... Grace
Jan Mårtensson ... The Curtain
Jan Mörk ... Steamboat Willies
Jan Nilsson ... Simson
Jan Nilsson ... Neofight
Jan Nordbring ... Peo
Jan Norell ... Sadatron
Jan Ogrodowczyk ... Downhearted
Jan Petersson ... Red Baron
Jan Pettersson ... Who's Next
Jan Rognås "Fidde" ... Shaggy
Jan S Eckert ... Grimmark
Jan Sahlberg ... Trix

Jan Sallander....Nox Aurea, The Cold Existence
Jan Samefors....Disciple, Emotion
Jan Sandberg....Bullhorn, Haterush, Ten Foot Pole
Jan Schankman....Human Cometh
Jan Snarberg....Yankee Heaven, Angelez
Jan Strandh....Morifade, Niva, Flintstens med Stanley, Sobre Nocturn
Jan Svedberg....Bootleg
Jan Söderholm....Dorian Gray
Jan Söderström "John South"....Unchained (1)
Jan Thore Grefstad....Saint Deamon
Jan Walles "Rio Sunwill"....Explode
Jan Åkesson....Stonelake
Jan Åström....Pontus Norgren
Jan-Anders Larsson....Törsten Dricker
Jana Persson....Fullmakt
Jane Björck....Fat Nelly
Jan-Egil Bogvald....Deep Diver, Tears
Janek Hellqvist....Misanthropian
Jan-Erik Andersson....Electra Top Raiders
Jan-Erik Bäckström....Europe, John Norum
Jan-Erik Falk....Pax Romana
Jan-Erik Liljeström....Junction
Jan-Erik Persson....Brimstone
Janet Jones Simmonds....Siena Root, Meldrum
Jani Erickson....Darklands
Jani Karvola....Evocation
Jani Kataja....Sideburn, Mangrove, Dagger
Jani Myllärinen....House Of Usher
Jani Ruhala....House Of Usher
Jani Salonen....Seventribe
Jani Stefanovic....Crimson Moonlight, Incapacity, Quest Of Aidance, Solution .45, Miseration, Divinefire
Janne Andersson....Bad Habit
Janne Andreasson....Tatch
Janne Apelholm....Roterock
Janne Arkegren....Angeline
Janne Arvidsson....Goddefied
Janne Backlund....Revelations
Janne Bark....Tears
Janne Bengtsson....Half Man
Janne Berg....Tyrox
Janne Berggren....Ivory
Janne Blom....Tears, Deep Diver
Janne Blondell....Eurock
Janne Borg....Highway
Janne Buchar....Crut
Janne Buckley....Parafine
Janne Buhr....Ma Connection
Janne Christoffersson "JB"....Necronaut, Spiritual Beggars, Grand Magus
Janne Ekberg....Destiny
Janne Eklund....Mogg
Janne Fernström....Kings N' Fools
Janne Grunditz....Jackwave
Janne Gummesson....Paradize (1)
Janne Gustavsson....Shaggy
Janne Hansen....The End
Janne Hedström....Lifeline
Janne Heikkinen....Eternal Darkness
Janne Henriksson....Deep Zilents
Janne Hyytiä....Insision
Janne Ivarsson....Facebreaker
Janne Jaloma....Confidence, Deals Death
Janne Jarvis....Hate Gallery
Janne Jernestrand....Fullmakt
Janne Johansson (now Ström)....Detest, Slug, Trace
Janne Junttila "JJ Taneli"....Tough Trade
Janne Karlsson "Loffe"....Mörrum's Own
Janne Karlsson....Warcollapse, (Dom Där)
Janne Karlsson....Siebensünden
Janne Kenttäkumpu Bodén....Evocation
Janne Korpela....Pound
Janne Lenell....Mystery, Lovebone
Janne Liljeqvist....Månegarm
Janne Lindgren....The Chair
Janne Lund....Slodust
Janne Lund....Fortune (2), Sabbtail
Janne Lundberg....Grace
Janne Lüthje....Zero Illusions, Pain And Passion
Janne Löwstrand....Sergej The Freak
Janne Murén....Reazon
Janne Nikolausson....Charizma
Janne Nilsson....Kliché
Janne Näsström....The Citadel
Janne Olander....Barrelhouse, (Solid Blue)
Janne Olsson....Head Force
Janne Persson....Notorious, Maze Of Time
Janne Persson....Jackwave
Janne Pihl....Wizz
Janne Posti....Chaossworn
Janne Rehnquist....Hellspray
Janne Risberg....Danger (1)
Janne Rosenholm....Movin' Globe
Janne Rudberg (now Björkenfjäll)....Morpheus
Janne Rydqvist....Repulz
Janne Röök....Exanthema
Janne Saarenpää....Netherbird, The Crown/Crown Of Thorns
Janne Sjödin....Marcus Brutus BandWildborn
Janne Skåhlberg....Slick Stuff
Janne Skärming....GSO
Janne Spanedal....Feed
Janne Stark....Overdrive, Locomotive Breath, Grand Design, Paradize, Planet Alliance, Constancia, BALLS, Zello, Mountain Of Power, Mörrum's Own, The Kaars, Thalamus, Spearfish, Narnia, M.O.B, From Behind, Faith, Blinded Colony, Alyson Aenue, VII Gates, Ruined Soul, Tomas Bergström's Fantasy
Janne Ström....Nocturnal Alliance
Janne Svensson....Facequake
Janne Söderlund "Evil J"....Cryonic Temple
Janne Tillman "Goat"....Isengard, Powerdise
Janne Wiklund....Left Hand SolutionUnholy
Janne Wännström....Jet
Janne Zelf "Jie"....Zen, Dirty Old Men
Janne Åhman....Wildmarken
Janne Åström....Universe
Janne Ördén "Bror Duktig"....Publikförakt AB
Janneck Larsson....Foobar The Band, Sergej The Freak
Jannicka Segemark....II Shy
Jannike Lindström "Nicki Wicked"....Crucified Barbara
Jan-Olof Jansson....Kalajs
Jan-Olof Karlsson....Jesusexercise
Jan-Olof Sjögren....Notredame
Jan-Olov Persson....Pearly White, Thrashon
Jan-Ove Johansson "Galle"....Dead End Street, Dead End Space, Johnny Engström Band
Janusz Fursa....Hellspray
Jan-Åke Jönsson....Vagh
Jan-Åke Österberg....Infernal Gates
Jari Forsman....Lazy
Jari Katila....Mud & Blood, Power
Jari Kuittinen....Gloomy Sunday
Jari Kujansuu....New Bulsara, Laroche, Cheers
Jari Kuusisto....In Thy Dreams, Carnal Forge
Jari Laakonen....Wanton
Jari Laakso....Loréne
Jari Lefvendahl....Trix
Jari Lindholm....Slumber
Jari Salonen....Human Rage, Denied
Jari Tissari....Lisa Gives Head
Jari Ylitalo....Bacon
Jarlau Wiahl....Fleshcut
Jarle Strand....Motorcity Madhouse
Jarmo Heikkinen....Spitfire
Jarmo K....Syron Vanes
Jarmo Kuurola....Eternal Darkness
Jarmo Lindell....Annie For President
Jarmo Miettinen....Quiz
Jarmo Mäkkeli....Dynamiet Wasteland
Jarmo Piiroinen....Alyson Avenue
Jarmo Sääskilahti....Pantheon
Jarmo Vehmanen....Lisa Gives Head
Jason Bieler....Talisman
Jason Stitch....Chains
Jauni Niemi....Lion's Share
Jay Lee Keen....To Africa With Love
Jay Matharu....Mindsplit
Jay Smith....Von Benzo
Jean Paul Gaster....King Hobo
Jeanette Müller....Revanch
Jean-Paul Asenov....Deranged
Jeff Scott Soto "Umberto Torres"....Talisman, Humanimal, Bakteria, Human Clay, Yngwie Malmsteen, Crossroad Jam, Thomas Vikström, Audiovision, Laudamus, W.E.T (2)
Jeffrey Branscher....Crier
Jejo Perković....Candlemass, Mustasch, Abstrakt Algebra, (Brick)
Jennie Tebler....Jennie Tebler's Out Of Oblivion, Jennie Tebler, Bathory,
Jennifer Sikström....Sommoned Tide
Jenny Back....Lights Out
Jenny Bogne....Soulless
Jenny Frohagen....Ningizzia
Jenny Jonasson....Whipping Princess
Jenny Landt....Tenebre
Jenny Lindahl....Misdemeanor
Jenny Möllberg....Misdemeanor
Jenny Persson....Miscellany
Jens Almgren....Desultory
Jens Andersson....Horizon (2)
Jens Axén....Treasure
Jens Berglund....Acis
Jens Björk....El Gordo
Jens Blomdal "Agilma"....Diabolical
Jens Blylod....Sound Explosion
Jens Bock....Count Raven, Jayce Landberg
Jens Bogren....Draconian, Lion's Share, Saint Deamon, Starterhead, Unsolved, Urbandux
Jens Boman....Construcdead, Darkane, The Defaced, Darkane
Jens Bäckelin....Sanctuary In Blasphemy, Iron Lamb
Jens C Mortensen....One Hour Hell, Carnal Forge, Slapdash
Jens Carlsson....Persuader
Jens Cedergren....Panama Red
Jens Englund....Memoria
Jens Ericson....Skull Parade
Jens Florén....Lommi
Jens Frank....Lovehandles
Jens Gillback....Paperback Freud
Jens Grundelius "Dubben/Gene Ball"....Stonehenge, Trash
Jens Gustafsson....Griftegård, Dear Mutant
Jens Heath....Gosh!
Jens Henriksson....Witchcraft, Troubled Horse
Jens Johansson....Murder Corporation, Mega Slaughter
Jens Johansson "Pedro Herrera"....Bakteria, Hammerfall, Benny Jansson, Yngwie Mlmsteen, Art Metal, Dave Nerge's Bulldog, Johansson (Brothers), Shining Path, Silver Mountain, Nocturnal Rites
Jens Johansson....Extaz
Jens Johansson. Society Gang Rape, Uncanny, Interment
Jens Jokinen....Redstorm
Jens Kemgren "Jesse Kid"....Danger (2), Vulture Cavalry
Jens Kidman....Embracing, Scarpoint, Meshuggah
Jens Kjerrström....Brutaliator, Obligatorisk Tortyr
Jens Klovegård....Abhoth, Axenstar, Godhate, Thronaeon
Jens Lundahl....Blakk Totem, Silver Seraph, Truth
Jens Lundgren....Bai Bang
Jens Lundsbye....Blackmail
Jens Lundström....Wonderland (1)
Jens Lundvik....Vital Sign, Disciple
Jens Malmborg....No Rules
Jens Mårtensson....Rosicrucian
Jens Näsström "Dr. Schitz"....Morbid
Jens Pedersen "Killheiler"....Kill
Jens Persson....Love Child, Trazy, Seven Wishes
Jens Rasmussen....Vidunder
Jens Rosander....Greasy Saddles
Jens Rydén....Vintersorg, Ancient Wisdom, Persuader, Setherial, Thyrfing, Profundi, Dead Silent Slumber
Jens Rydman....Naglfar
Jens Storm....Paperback Freud
Jens Tillqvist "J-son"....Göran Nordh
Jens Törnroos....Interment, Uncanny
Jens Westberg....Stonelake
Jens Vestergren "Doc"....Malison Rogue
Jens Westin....Man.Machine.Indust, Corroded, Dr Booster
Jens Wide....Mother Misery, Clench
Jens Åkesson....Dimmz
Jensa Carlsson....Dead Silent Slumber
Jensa Paulsson....Grave (2)
Jensen....Eternity Remains
Jenziih....Semremedy
Jeppe Wihlborg....Epedemic
Jeremy Child....Stonelake, Yggdrasil, Broken Dagger
Jerker Avander....Lineout, (Totalt Jävla Mörker)
Jerker Dahlén....Taurus
Jerker Edman "Jee Eden"....Skinny Horse, Demental, Mindless, Mindless Sinner
Jerker Johansson....Skin Infection, Sacrifice
Jerry Backelin....Born Of Sin
Jerry Ekman....Zonaria
Jerry Engström....Pray For Locust
Jerry Ericsson....Fredrik Thordendah's Special Defects
Jerry Grimaldi....Heartcry
Jerry Karlsson....Axia
Jerry Kronqvist "Läppen/Krown"....Hyste'riah G.B.C
Jerry Magnusson....Tube Screamer
Jerry Nilsson....Electra Top Raiders
Jerry Prütz....W.E.T (1)
Jerry Repo....Adept
Jerry Rutström....Maninnya Blade, Slowgate
Jerry Sahlin....A.C.T
Jerry Torstensson....Paganus, Draconian, Shadowgarden
Jerry Östman....Defueld
Jesper Adefelt....Degreed
Jesper Andersson....Headline (1)
Jesper Arkerud (now Oldberg) "Glasse"....Publikförakt AB
Jesper Arnö....Carizma Rain
Jesper Aronsson....Skogen Brinner
Jesper Bagge....Evercry, Marble Arch
Jesper Bood....Cauterizer
Jesper Enander....Spazmosity
Jesper Granath "Ratt B"....God B.C.
Jesper Heijkenskjöld....SnakStorm
Jesper Johansson....Morifade
Jesper Karlsson....Odyssey (2)
Jesper Klarqvist "Jeppe"....Generous Maria
Jesper Kviberg....Knockout
Jesper Landén....Maze Of Time
Jesper Larsson....Carnage, Medicine Rain
Jesper Lindbergh "Jeppe"....Bedroom Love, The Painted Man
Jesper Lindstedt....Blue Matter
Jesper Liveröd....Burst
Jesper Löfgren....A Canorous Quintet, This Ending, Guidance Of Sin
Jesper Magnusson....Bullseye, Caligula
Jesper Malm....Neondaze
Jesper Malmgren....Illfigure
Jesper Miller....Carizma Rain
Jesper Nyberg....Galaxy Safari
Jesper Persson....Alicate, Carnival Sun
Jesper Persson....Hearts Alive
Jesper Pihl....Långfinger
Jesper Rydberg....Dawn Of Oblivion
Jesper Skarin....Fingerspitzengefühl, Switch Opens
Jesper Sporre "Gyp Casino"....Roadrats, Rolene
Jesper Starander....Blofly, Sharp Nine
Jesper Stolpe....Draconian
Jesper Strömblad....In Flames, All Ends, Ceremonial Oath, Hammerfall, Dimension Zero, The Resistance
Jesper Thorsson....Afflicted
Jesper Wallgren....Nonworkinggeneration
Jesper Waltersson....Reehab
Jesper Örtegren....Closer (1)
Jesse Andersson....Cartago
Jesse Forte....Vains Of Jenna
Jesse Lindskog....Nostradameus, Dreamland
Jessica Johansson....Convinced
Jessica Strandell....Crypt Of Kerberos
Jhonny Bergman "Berget"....Man.Machine.Industry, Rosicrucian, Slapdash
Jhonny Göransson....Diamond Dawn
Jim Berger "All"....Ophthalamia, Vondur, WAR, Total War
Jim Edström....Another Hell
Jim Edwards....Malaise, Misert Loves Co.
Jim Gustavsson "Clim"....AB/CD
Jim Hellström....Spinnrock
Jim Jidhed....Alien, Von Rosen, Heartbreak Radio, Radioactive, Sayit, Jim Jidhed
Jim Johnsson....Interaction
Jim Kjell....Gardenian
Jim Olsson....Tumbleweed
Jim Riggo....Prosperity
Jim Sundström....Idiot
Jimi Andersson....Shattered
Jimi Fagerstig "The Demon"....Autopsy Torment, Devil Lee Rot
Jimi Toivanen....Sommoned Tide
Jimmie Bergkvist....Rising Faith
Jimmie Fornel....Los Sin Nombre
Jimmie Isacsson....Oblivion
Jimmie Mattisson....Wulfgar
Jimmy Nielsen....Jimmy Nielsen & Band
Jimmie Nyhlén "Naahz/Nazgûl"....Blodsrit, Primitive Symphony
Jimmie Ogefalk "Knudan"....Fleshcut
Jimmie Olausson....The Cold Existence
Jimmie Olsson....Sticky Sweet
Jimmie Rudolfsson "Lee Cooper"....Danger Avenue
Jimmie Strimell....Despite, Dead By April, Dragonland, Deathdestruction, Scarpoint, Cipher System
Jimmie Svensson....Fuelhead, Wildness
Jimmie Åkerström....Vildhjarta
Jimmy Ahovalli "Mattanten"....Skitarg, Sterbhaus
Jimmy Andersson "Jamie"....Sister
Jimmy Bergman "Car Crash Jim"....Man.Machine.Industry
Jimmy Bergström....Ghamorean
Jimmy Borgström....Caliber 74
Jimmy Carlsson (now Svärdhagen)....Prisca
Jimmy Drexler....Nonworkinggeneration
Jimmy Edström "Hora/Jim Voltage/Gorethrash"....Kill, Lenny Blade, Pagan Rites, Devil Lee Rot, Karnarium, Autopsy Torment
Jimmy Ek....Sacrifice, Crier
Jimmy Fjällendahl....Raise Hell
Jimmy Gunnarsson....Moonville
Jimmy Halvarsson....Amaxa
Jimmy Hedlund....Supreme Majesty, Falconer
Jimmy Hiltula "J Basher"....Sister Sin, Maleficio
Jimmy Holmgren....Spasmodic
Jimmy Holmström....Stitch
Jimmy Hurtig....Mother Of God
Jimmy Högfeldt....Miss Willis, Twilight Zone
Jimmy Johansson....The Fuzes
Jimmy Johansson "Dolla"....Ceremonial Executioner, Vanhelgd, Bloodshed Nihil
Jimmy Johansson "Jay"....H.E.A.T
Jimmy Johansson....H2O
Jimmy Johansson....The Fuzes
Jimmy Johansson "Lizzy DeVine"....Vains Of Jenna
Jimmy Karlsson....Gorement
Jimmy Larsen....Bokor
Jimmy Larsson....Shattered
Jimmy Lee Lou....Dawn Of Oblivion
Jimmy Lexe....Locomotive Breath, Vulture Cavalry
Jimmy Lindbergh....Mother Misery
Jimmy Lundin....Renegade Five
Jimmy Lundmark....Altar
Jimmy Lundqvist....Entrails
Jimmy Mattson....Loch Vostock
Jimmy Nilsson "Death"....Devil Lee Rot
Jimmy Nilsson "Soulmolester"....Mordant
Jimmy Norberg....Outshine
Jimmy Olausson....Engel, Marionette
Jimmy Paulsson....Twelvestep
Jimmy Persson....Soilwork
Jimmy Persson "LJ Roger"....Paradize (2)
Jimmy Persson....Faithful Darkness

NAME INDEX

Jimmy Petersson "Jimbo" ... Von Panzer
Jimmy Pinaitis ... Driver
Jimmy Sjöqvist ... El Camino
Jimmy Sjöqvist ... Vermin
Jimmy Stridh ... Smokey Bandits
Jimmy Svensson ... Deception
Jimmy Svensson ... Entity
Jimmy Taskinen ... Unreal
Jimmy Thell ... Whyte Ash
Jimmy Thunlind ... Karaboudjan
Jimmy Thörnfeldt ... Cherokee
Jimmy Wahlsteen ... Blue Matter, Qoph
Jimmy Wandroph ... Alien
Jimmy Wave ... Arconova
Jimmy Widegren ... Malaise
Jimmy Värn ... Malaise
Jimmy Årjes ... Big Times
Jimmy Öster ... Drabness
Joachim Dahlberg ... Closer (1)
Joachim Eversholt "Gwahlar" ... Mordgrim
Joachim Floke ... Cross
Joachim Forsberg "Gideon" ... Zavorash
Joachim Hansson ... Spin Air
Joachim Hellström ... Horizon (1)
Joachim Lindbock ... The Duskfall
Joachim Lindbäck ... Warning
Joachim Nordlund ... Sky Of Rage, Astral Doors
Joachim Sjöström ... Buckshot O.D.
Joachim Sveder ... Singer
Joachim Uddling ... Talk Of The Town
Joachim Walter ... Colordream
Joachim Åslund ... Thalamus
Joacim Brunnberg ... Nerved
Joacim Cans ... Hammerfall, Cans, Nostradameus, Lost Horizon, Mrs. Hippie
Joacim Carlsson ... Afflicted, Dismember, Face Down, (Proboscis), (General Surgery)
Joacim Kjellgren ... Adams Eve
Joacim Lundberg ... Infinity
Joacim Nordlund ... Astral Doors
Joacim Olofsson ... Outremer, In Solitudude, In Aeternum
Joacim Persson ... Fallen Angel, Tyburn
Joacim Persson "Jocke" ... Waving Corn
Joacim Sandin ... Bai Bang
Joacim Starander ... Blofly, Sharp Nine
Joakim Lindquist "Michael Ross" ... Cheri
Joakim Andersson ... Scar
Joakim Antman ... Decadence
Joakim Antonsson ... Death Tyrant, Nox Aurea, The Cold Existence
Joakim Attoff ... Stefan Rosqvist Band
Joakim Bengtsson "Devlin" ... Pompei Nights
Joakim Bergman ... Reenact
Joakim Björkegren "Kim" ... It's Alive, Lazy
Joakim Björkelid ... Immaculate
Joakim Blomdahl ... Scratch (2)
Joakim Bloohm ... Hardcore Circus
Joakim Brodén ... Sabaton
Joakim Bröms ... Into The Void, Blastrock
Joakim Bylander ... Equinox Ov The Gods
Joakim Diener ... Another Life
Joakim E Ramsell "Jocke" ... RFP, Surrender
Joakim Eriksson ... Diesel Down
Joakim Fasth ... Soulless
Joakim Floke ... Dionysus, Elsesphere, Meduza
Joakim Granlund "Jens-Ove/Jojje" ... Leukemia
Joakim Granvold ... Myrah
Joakim Gustafsson ... Ninnuam
Joakim Gustavsson ... Centinex
Joakim Göthberg "Jocke/af Gravf" ... Marduk, Miscreant, Sarea, Darkified, Nifters, Moment Maniacs, Dimension Zero, Cardinal Sin
Joakim Hammare "Jocke" ... Satureye
Joakim Hansson ... Sorcery
Joakim Heder ... Morgana Lefay
Joakim Hedestedt (aka Harju) ... Face Down, Nation Beyond, Construcdead, Mass Murder Agenda
Joakim Holgersson ... The Jet Circus
Joakim Jarlsén "Jake The Snake" ... Paperback Freud
Joakim Jacobsson ... Idiot
Joakim Jansson ... Wonderland (2)
Joakim Janthe ... Eric De Van
Joakim Johansson ... Convinced
Joakim Jonsson ... Mornaland, Dust, Skinfected, The Mist Of Avalon, Skyfire, Axenstar, Assailant, Autumn Dweller
Joakim Jönsson ... The Carpet Knights
Joakim Karlsson ... Skyfire
Joakim Karlsson ... Zap Yankeefy
Joakim Karlsson ... Backyard Bullets
Joakim Karlsson ... Craft
Joakim Karlsson ... Gin Lady, Black Bonzo
Joakim Knutsson "Beered" ... Satanarchy, Rise And Shine
Joakim Kristensson ... Thyrfing, Rutthna
Joakim Kronlid ... Vulcano
Joakim Kulo ... Raise Hell
Joakim Lahgerkranser "Lahger" ... Diesel Down
Joakim Larsson "Joe/Jocke" ... Treat, Power, Thomas Larsson, Jammer, John Norum, Six Feet Under, Swedish Erotica, Baltimoore
Joakim Larsson "Joey Tempest" ... Europe, Swedish Metal Aid
Joakim Loften "Isti" ... Atrox
Joakim Lundberg ... Morgana Lefay
Joakim Lundberg "Jake E/Jake Steel" ... Amaranthe, Dragonland, Dream Evil, Opera Diabolicus, Dreamland
Joakim Lundberg ... Wonderland (2)
Joakim Lundholm ... 220 Volt, Swedish Metal Aid
Joakim Malmborg ... Inevitable End
Joakim Marsch "JJ/Jocke" ... JJ Marsch, Spellbound
Joakim Mikiver ... Prosperity
Joakim Nauclér ... Twin Earth
Joakim Nilsson ... Graveyard, Norrsken
Joakim Norlander ... Skellington
Joakim Ohlsson ... Siebenbürgen
Joakim Olausson ... Mindshift
Joakim Olofsson ... Milky
Joakim Olsson ... Supreme Majesty, Deep Quest
Joakim Olsson ... Nugatory
Joakim Patsonen ... X-Eryus
Joakim Petersson "JP White" ... Vains Of Jenna
Joakim Petersson "Graál" ... Vanmakt
Joakim Pettersson ... Cranium, Niden Div. 187
Joakim Rhodin ... Screwball.Sthlm
Joakim Rosén ... The Provenance, Laethora, Damnatory
Joakim Rönström ... Meadows End
Joakim Samuelsson ... Nifters
Joakim Sandberg "Jake/Jocke" ... Aces High, Mountain Of Power, Mansson
Joakim Sandgren ... The Weed
Joakim Sandin ... Pete Sandberg's Jade
Joakim Sjöberg ... Freak Kitchen
Joakim Staaf-Sylsjö ... Skywalkers
Joakim Stabel ... Atlantic Tide, Hetsheads, Blackshine
Joakim Sterner ... Necrophobic
Joakim Strandberg ... Pain Of Salvation
Joakim Strandberg-Nilsson ... Faithful Darkness, Nonexist
Joakim Ståhl ... The Gloria Story
Joakim Svalberg ... Yngwie Malmsteen, Opeth
Joakim Svedlund ... Lipkin
Joakim Svensson "Jocke" ... Oblivious
Joakim Svensson ... Entrails, Skogen, (Birdflesh)
Joakim Söderlind ... II Shy
Joakim Thell ... Blind Dog
Joakim Trana ... Withershin
Joakim Törnqvist ... Oppression
Joakim Wassberg "Jocke" ... Equinox Ov The Gods, Souldrained, Defaced Creation
Joakim Westman ... Story
Joakim Wickgren ... Aggregate
Joakim Widén ... The Goddamned, Moria
Joakim Wiklund ... Nightscape
Joakim Wikström ... Promotion
Joakim Åberg ... Pole Position, Grand Vision
Joakim Åberg ... Zircus
Joakim Åström ... Calm Chaos
Joakim Åström ... Spinning Black Circle, April Divine
Joakim Öhman ... Suffer
Joan Ericsson ... DeVan
Joan Sallrot "Kid" ... The Gloria Story
Joan Vieru ... Cheerleader
Joaquin Calafell ... Neon Rose
Jock Millgård "Tai/Russel" ... Cross, Russell, 9T9, Cross
Jocke Andersson ... Loréne
Jocke Berg ... Hardcore Superstar
Jocke Carlsson ... Too Late
Jocke de Vil ... Inhale
Jocke Diener ... Paganizer
Jocke Därth ... Nocturnal Alliance
Jocke Eriksson ... Lifeless Image, Within Reach
Jocke Fleetwood ... Steel Arrows
Jocke Hammar ... Chronic Decay
Jocke Johansson ... Straight Up
Jocke L ... Opéra
Jocke Lindström ... Mr. Death
Jocke Ludwigson ... Eternal Lies
Jocke Ludvigsson ... White Silver
Jocke Lundgren ... Hellfueled
Jocke Lundström ... The Storyteller
Jocke Mårdstam ... Slitage, Left Hand Solution
Jocke Nilsson ... The Point
Jocke Nilsson ... Angeline
Jocke Norberg ... Witchgrave
Jocke Olofsson ... Sorcery, Outrider, Dominion, In Aeternum
Jocke Olsson ... Feed
Jocke Olsson ... Fat Nelly
Jocke Olsson ... Rickshaw
Jocke Persson ... Section 8
Jocke Persson ... Soulquake System
Jocke Pettersson "Morth" ... Lobotomy, Dawn, Regurgitate, Niden Div. 187, Solar Dawn, Thy Primordial, Unmoored, Ocean Chief, Regurgitated
Jocke Puuraid ... Fierce Conviction
Jocke Rehnholm ... Sanctification
Jocke Reiskog ... Reizon band
Jocke Ringdahl ... Paganizer, Sinners Burn
Jocke Roberg ... Astral Doors
Jocke Schön ... Airborne
Jocke Sjöberg ... Frozen Eyes, Freak Kitchen
Jocke Sjöström "Jox" ... Death Organ
Jocke Skoog ... Clawfinger, Scarpoint
Jocke Stoor ... Team Custard
Jocke Ståhl ... Bullseye
Jocke Svanberg ... Alfonzetti
Jocke Th ... Reizon band
Jocke Uddling ... Glen Spove
Jocke Unger ... Immersed In Blood, Sgt. Carnage, Supreme Majesty
Jocke Wallgren "J." ... Ondskapt, Valkyrja
Jocke Warneryd ... God B.C.
Jocke Westman ... Unanimated
Jocke Widfeldt ... The Project Hate MCMXCIC, Dominion Caligula, Vicious Art
Jocke Åberg ... Skydiverse
Jocke Åhslund ... Greenleaf, Payback
Jocke Öberg ... Twilight Project, Wonderland (1)
Jocke Ölund ... Tormented
Jocke Östlund ... Section Eight
Jodöden (aka Johdet) ... Sorgeldom, Whirling
Joe Comeau ... Tad Morose
Joe Liszt ... Rocka Rollas
Joe Nebel ... Sludge
Joel Andersson ... Blinded Colony
Joel Andersson ... Insision, Nominon, Immersed In Blood, Inverted
Joel Andersson "Draugen" ... Triumphator, Svartsyn, Dark Funeral
Joel Andersson ... Crawley
Joel Apelgren "Joey Fox" ... Dynazty
Joel Berntson ... Divine Baze Orchestra
Joel Carlsson ... Covered Call
Joel Carnstam ... Skogen Brinner
Joél Cirera "Joey" ... Crazy Lixx, Omnious, Enshrined
Joel Edegran ... Dechas
Joel E. Sundin ... Entrench
Joel Ek ... Cheerleader
Joel Eiasson ... Innocent Rosie
Joel Fornbrandt ... Coldworker
Joel Geffen "Nefaustus" ... Bloodshed, Rev. 16:8
Joel Görsch ... Memorium
Joel Holmström "Johell" ... Feral
Joel Kuronen ... System Shock
Joel Lindberg ... Liquid Scarlet
Joel Lindell ... Laethoria, The Provenance
Joel Linder ... Tenebre, Pole Posittion, Majestic, Rebels, Reptilian
Joel Lindholm "J Megiddo" ... Patronymicon, Shining, Degial, Patronymicon
Joel Lööf ... Divine Baze Orchestra
Joel Nevrup ... 2 Years After, Aspected
Joel Nilsson ... Benevolent, Dead By April
Joel Pettersson ... El Gordo
Joel Pälvärinne "Ace Tormenta" ... Eidomantum
Joel Starander ... Heartbreak Radio, Geisha, Kharma
Joel Uhr ... Fistfunk
Joel Viklund "Terrorgoat" ... Nidsang, Fenria
Joel Widegren Lundström ... Furor
Joel Öhlund ... Shaker
Joey Nine ... Crucified Barbara
Joey Tempest ... (see Joakim Larsson)
Johan "Nephente" ... Netherbird, Fear The Future
Johan Abbing ... Bozeman's Simplex
Johan Abelsson ... Majectic Vanguard
Johan Adamsson ... Misanthropian
Johan Adler ... Eric De Van, Devan, Eternal Oath
Johan Agerberg ... Pride
Johan Ahlberg ... Centinex, Subdive
Johan Ahlgren ... Subdive
Johan Aldgård ... Faithful Darkness
Johan Anderberg ... Deranged, Murder Corporation
Johan Andersson ... Sektor Skandal
Johan Andersson ... Middleage
Johan Andersson ... Sherlock Brothers
Johan Andersson ... Slyside
Johan Andersson ... Fair Child
Johan Andersson ... Sonic Walthers
Johan Andersson ... Acis
Johan Andersson ... Blackburns
Johan Andreassen ... Hostile Cell, Headplate, All Ends, Amaranthe
Johan Andreasson ... Scenteria
Johan Asplund ... Auberon
Johan Augustsson ... Buszer, No Rules
Johan Axelsson (now Liiva) ... Carnage, Devourment, Furbowl, Killaman, Murder Corporation, Sarea, Shineth, Hearse, Nonexist, Wonderflow, Misteltein, Deranged,
Johan Axelsson ... X-It, Heartbreak Radio
Johan Backman ... Astroqueen
Johan Bengs "Sir Alex" ... Panzer Princess
Johan Bengtsson "Johnny Benson" ... Pretty Wild, Bai Bang
Johan Bengtsson ... Corrosive Sweden
Johan Berg ... Slingblade, Posh Filth
Johan Bergebäck (now De Faux) ... Morpheus, Nifelheim, Dismember, Necrophobic
Johan Bergkvist ... Bishop Garden
Johan Berglund ... Ribspreader, Demiurg, This Haven
Johan Bergquist "Chatte" ... The Weed
Johan Bergquist ... Elevener
Johan Bergström ... Havok, Splattered Mermaids
Johan Berlin ... Timescape, Eclipse
Johan Bernspång ... Osukaru, Katana
Johan Billerhag "Billy St John" ... Memento Mori, Hexenhaus, Parasite
Johan Björn ... Mindshift
Johan Blidell ... Ocean (2)
Johan Blom ... Confess
Johan Blomdahl ... Diesel Down
Johan Blomquist ... Backyard Babies, Haystack
Johan Blomström ... Blinded Colony, Wulfgar, The Graviators, Fourever, Calm, Overdrive
Johan Bobäck ... Moahni Moahna
Johan Boding "Joan Strauss" ... Candy Roxx, Ban-Zai
Johan Bohlin "Jojje" ... Zebulon
Johan Bokström ... Tyrox
Johan Bolin ... Desultory
Johan Bonnier ... Rydell & Quick
Johan Boqvist ... Memfis
Johan Borelius ... Great Ad
Johan Brandberg ... Meadows End
Johan Brodin ... Turning Point
Johan Broman ... Prisca
Johan Brusell ... Sheik Ahmeed
Johan Brändström ... Conquest
Johan Burman ... Miscreant
Johan Bülow ... Altar, Wolf, Fallen Angel
Johan Bäckman ... Section Eight
Johan Bäckman ... Necrocurse
Johan Bäckström ... Gondoline
Johan Bäckström ... Zeudo
Johan Carlsson ... Dawn Of Decay, Sparzanza, Moaning Wind
Johan Carlsson ... The Curtain
Johan Carlzon (aka Karlsson) ... Abandon, Relevant Few
Johan Clasén ... Solid ground (2)
Johan Coma Svensson ... Straight Frank
Johan Cronqvist ... Havok
Johan Dahl ... Taketh
Johan Dahlén ... Stereo Generator
Johan Dahlgren ... Vanguard (2)
Johan Dahlström ... Atrox
Johan Dahlström ... Silver Mountain, Colorstone
Johan Dahnberg ... The Grand Trick
Johan Danielsson "Joe" ... Andra Band, Rockbox
Johan Danielsson ... Mustain
Johan De Daux (aka Bergebäck) ... Morpheus, Nifelheim, Dismember, Necrophobic
Johan De Farfalla ... Opeth
Johan Dee ... Anguish
Johan Dirfors ... Disdain
Johan Dyyk ... Stormcrow
Johan Eckerblad ... Broken Glass
Johan Edberg ... Reenact
Johan Edlund ... Nihilist, Apostasy
Johan Edlund "Joey Eden" ... Pompei Nights
Johan Edlund "Hellslaughter" ... Treblinka, Tiamat, Lucyfire, Expulsion
Johan Ejerblom ... Implode
Johan Ekelund ... Nerved
Johan Ekman ... Theory In Practice, Incantation
Johan Ekström ... Corporation 187
Johan Elving ... Zonata
Johan Englund ... Movin' Globe
Johan Engström ... Mentor's Wish
Johan Enocksson ... Epitaph (1)
Johan Ericson ... Shadowgarden, Doom: Vs, Draconian
Johan Ericsson "Jojje" ... Sargatanas Reign
Johan Ericsson ... Bulldogs
Johan Eriksson ... Dreamland
Johan Eriksson ... Timescape
Johan Eriksson ... The Ugly
Johan Eriksson ... Tie 28
Johan Eriksson ... Revolution Riot, Sister Sin
Johan Erneroth "B-Häng" ... Temperance
Johan Eskilsson ... Dead By April, Cipher System
Johan Evertsson ... Motherlode, Giant
Johan Fahlberg ... Deacon Street Project, Denied, Insania (Stockholm)
Johan Falk ... Evergrace, Incrave
Johan Feldtmann ... Harvey Wallbanger
Johan Flodell ... Slowlife
Johan Fogelberg ... Syconaut, Exhale Swe
Johan Folke ... Fatal Smile (1)
Johan Folker ... The Downtown Clowns
Johan Folkesson ... Switchblade
Johan Forsberg ... Deletion
Johan Forsell ... One Minute Left
Johan Forss ... Edge
Johan Forssén "John Allan" ... Steel Attack
Johan Fransson ... Ellen B
Johan Fredriksson ... Memory Garden
Johan Fredriksson ... Silverwings

Johan Freij ..... Anyway
Johan Frisk ..... Blackburns
Johan Gabrielsson "1853" ..... Lifelover
Johan Gardestedt ..... Atrox
Johan Glössler ..... Karmakanic, Zinny J Zan
Johan Gottberg ..... Zeudo
Johan Granström ..... Glory
Johan Gummesson ..... Setback
Johan Gustafsson ..... Bubonic Plague
Johan Gustafsson ..... Volturyon
Johan Gärdt ..... Convinced
Johan Haag ..... Freedom Bleeder, Dimma
Johan Haglund ..... Skywalkers, Spasmodic
Johan Hagström ..... Wildness
Johan Hallander ..... Shining
Johan Hallberg "Necro Nudist" ..... Cranium, Utumno
Johan Hallberg ..... Splattered Mermaids
Johan Hallbäck ..... Daemonicus
Johan Haller ..... Hypocrite
Johan Hallgren ..... Pain Of Salvation
Johan Hallström ..... Bullseye
Johan Hammarlund ..... Porklift
Johan Hamrin ..... Unholy
Johan Hansen ..... C.B Murdoc
Johan Hansson ..... Sahara (1)
Johan Hansson ..... Crematory
Johan Hansson ..... Emerald
Johan Hansson ..... Limiless, Mandala, Tippen Ruda
Johan Hansson ..... Twin Age
Johan Hartman ..... Disdained
Johan Havås ..... Grief Of Emerald
Johan Hedin ..... Stingray
Johan Hedlund "Dezo" ..... Machinae Supremacy
Johan Hedlund ..... Slowgate, Corrupt
Johan Hedman ..... Defleshed, Sarcasm
Johan Hedman ..... Freedom Bleeder
Johan Hedman ..... Infernal Gates
Johan Hegg ... Amon Amarth, The Project Hate MCMXCIX
Johan Helander ..... Marshal Kane
Johan Helgesson ..... Debase, The Drugs, The Itch,
.. Nation Beyond, Original Sin, Pete Sandberg's Jade, Wit
Johan Henriksson ..... Maninnya Blade, Slowgate, Warning
Johan Herlogsson ..... Norden Light
Johan Hidén ..... Abacorn
Johan Hjelm ..... Aeon (2), Defaced Creation
Johan Holm ..... The Graviators
Johan Holmberg ..... G.O.L.D
Johan Holmström ..... Keystone
Johan Holst ..... Jet Trail
Johan Huldtgren ..... Obitus
Johan Husgafvel ..... Pain, 8th Sin
Johan Häggman ..... Anyway
Johan Häll ..... Layout, Hellspray, M.ill.ion
Johan Högberg ..... Änglagård
Johan Hörnquist ..... Shredhead
Johan Igard ..... Nonexist
Johan Isacsson ..... Oblivion
Johan Jahlonen ..... Asperity
Johan Jalonen Penn ..... Steel Attack, Blackworld
Johan Jansson ..... Iniuria
Johan Jansson "Chainsaw/Jonken" ..... Dellamorte,
..... Regurgitate, Interment, Centinex,
..... Demonical, Uncanny, Moondark
Johan Jansson ..... Lucy, Frenzy
Johan Johannesson ..... Brutaliator
Johan Johansson "Glen Metal" ..... Cryonic Temple
Johan Johansson "J.J. Scat" ..... Boogieman
Johan Johnsson ..... Assault
Johan Jonasson "J.J. Glitter" .... Danger (2), Dethronement
Johan Jonvén ..... Scandal Circus
Johan Jämtberg ..... Broken Glass, Il Shy
Johan Kaiser ..... Mindcollapse
Johan Kalin ..... Spaps
Johan Karlsson "Johnny Nightshredder" ..... Air Raid
Johan Karlsson ..... The Wild Bunch
Johan Karlsson (Carlzon) ..... Relevant Few, Abandon
Johan Karlsson ..... Shattered
Johan Karlsson ..... Wildness
Johan Kempe ..... Sargoth
Johan Kihlberg ..... Impera
Johan Klevenskog ..... Mort
Johan Klitkou ..... Souldrainer, Chasticement
Johan Knuutinen "C.L.A.W" ..... Veritate
Johan Kronlund ..... Houston
Johan Kullander ..... Infernal Vengeance
Johan Kullberg "Koleberg/J.K Impera" ..... Chris Laney,
..... Frontiers, Lion's Share, Therion, Zan Clan, Prisoner,
..... Talk Of The Town, Thomas Vikström, Dark Illusion
Johan Kuurne ..... Moria
Johan Kvastgård ..... Mother Of God, Spasmodic
Johan Lagander ..... Sarea
Johan Lagher "Shamaatae" ..... Arckanum, Dawn, Sorhin
Johan Landhäll ..... Iniuria
Johan Langell ..... Pain Of Salvation
Johan Lannering ..... Hyperhug
Johan Larsson ..... Hammerfall, In Flames
Johan Larsson "Aeon" ..... Mörk Gryning, C.B Murdoc
Johan Larsson ..... Sarea
Johan Larsson ..... State Of Mind
Johan Larsson ..... Atrox
Johan Larsson ..... Seance
Johan Laux ..... Overlord, Spit It Out
Johan Liefvendahl ..... Seventh Wonder
Johan Liiva (aka Axelsson) ..... Carnage, Devourment,
..... Killaman, Murder Corporation, Sarea, Shineth,
..... Wonderflow, Misteltein, Deranged, Furbowl,
..... Hearse, Nonexist
Johan Lindberg ..... 9th Plague
Johan Lindblom ..... Surrender
Johan Lindén ..... Omnious
Johan Linder ..... Malaise
Johan Lindgren ..... Vintersorg, TME
Johan Lindh ..... Saved By Insanity
Johan Lindqvist ..... Nine
Johan Lindskoog "Joje" ..... Waving Corn,
..... Crossroad Jam, Buckshot O.D.
Johan Lindstedt ..... Astral Doors
Johan Lindstrand ..... The Crown/Crown Of Thorns,
..... One Man Army And The Undead Quartet, Impious
Johan Lindström ..... Rio, Avenue, Lifeline, Tornado Soup
Johan Lindström ..... Mustain, Svarti Loghin
Johan Ling "Joe" ..... Crossing Oceans, NME Within
Johan Ljung "Hellterror" ..... Mörk Gryning,
..... Blackmoon, C.B Murdoc
Johan Lund ..... Mindshift
Johan Lundell ..... Serpent
Johan Lundgren ..... Sunflower
Johan Lundström ..... Liquid Scarlet
Johan Lyander ..... Ellen B, Emma Varg
Johan Längquist ..... Candlemass, Jonah Quizz,
..... Impulsia, Notorious
Johan Löfgren ..... Lack Of Faith, Steel Attack
Johan Lönn ..... Noctes
Johan Lönnroth ..... Crypt Of Kerberos
Johan Magnberg ..... Ginger Trees
Johan Magnusson ..... Construcdead, Carnal Forge
Johan Magnusson ..... Calm
Johan Malmgren "Kid Tiffany" ..... Candy Roxx
Johan Martinsson ..... Enjoy The View
Johan Meiton ..... SnakeStorm, (Dia Psalma)
Johan Melander ..... Excruciate
Johan Melin "John Mell" ..... Scratch (1)
Johan Mellryd ..... Skin Infection
Johan Mortiz ..... Throne Of Ahaz
Johan Mossberg ..... Lucky Stiff
Johan Murmester "Meanos" ..... Nattas
Johan Månsson ..... Reehab
Johan Niemann ..... 220 Volt, Lithium, Crash The System,
..... Therion, Afterglow, Demonoid, Evergrey,
..... Evil Masquerade, The Murder Of My Sweet, Sectu,
..... Tears Of Anger, Novak, Mind's Eye, Marcus Jidell
Johan Nilsson ..... Abandon, Relevant Few
Johan Nilsson ..... Ghamorean
Johan Nilsson "Goomba" ..... Maitreya
Johan Nilsson "Joleni" ..... Semlah, Stronghold
Johan Nilsson ..... Mac & Ploids
Johan Norberg "Jonah Dee" ..... Yale Bate
Johan Nord ..... Netherbird
Johan Nordenfeldt ..... Cross
Johan Nordgren ..... Ritual
Johan Nordlund ..... This Gift Is A Curse
Johan Norell ..... Mercy
Johan Norgren ..... Stand By
Johan Norman ..... Dissection, Runemagick, Deletion,
..... Soulreaper, Trident, Sacramenum, Decameron
Johan Norström ..... Terrortory
Johan Nyberg ..... Vildhjarta
Johan Nylund ..... Aggregate
Johan Nyman ..... New Breed
Johan Nyqvist ..... Big Train
Johan Nyström ..... Blacksmith, Meadow
Johan Nääs ..... Soulquake System, Motorcity Madhouse
Johan Ohlsson ..... Ridge
Johan Ohlsson ..... Immersed In Blood, Inverted
Johan Olsen ..... Carnal Grief
Johan Olsson "Savage" ..... Inevitable End
Johan Olsson ..... To Africa With Love
Johan Olsson ..... Aquila
Johan Olsson ..... Evildoer, Blinded Colony, Dead By April
Johan Orre ..... Hypnosia, Dethronement
Johan Oudhuis ..... Lake Of Tears
Johan Paavola ..... Borderline (2), Mr Quinn
Johan Palmberg ..... Covered Call
Johan Palovaara ..... Machinae Supremacy
Johan Paulsson ..... Sins Of Omission
Johan Persson ..... Mind's Eye, Scudiero
Johan Persson ..... Disdained
Johan Petersson ..... Jackwave
Johan Pettersson ..... Ocean Chief
Johan Pettersson ..... Nightvision
Johan Pettersson ..... Grand Slam
Johan Pettersson ..... Liquid Phase
Johan Pettersson ..... In The Colonnades
Johan Randén ..... Johan Randén, Time Code Alpha,
..... Platitude, Quest Of Aidance
Johan Rask ..... Majestic Dimension
Johan Reinholdz ..... Andromeda, Skyfire,
..... Opus Atlantica, Nonexist
Johan Reiven ..... Transport League, Ram, Hyperhug, LOK
Johan Rockner ..... Dozer, Greenleaf
Johan Romert ..... Reckless
Johan Roos "J" ..... Wagabond
Johan Rosenberg ..... Kisses From The Past
Johan Rudberg "Skuggan" ..... Mordbrand, The Law
Johan Rudberg ..... Excruciate
Johan Runesson ..... Lemon Bird
Johan Rydberg ..... Sanzia, Supreme Majesty, In Black
Johan Rydin ..... Memoria
Johan Rylander ..... Guns 'N' Horses
Johan Rönn ..... Shame (2)
Johan Sahlén "Dr. A Force" ..... The Black (1)
Johan Sahlin "Master Motorsåg" ..... Bestial Mockery
Johan Samuelsson ..... Benevolent
Johan Sandberg "John Blackwar" .. Celestial Pain, Unpure
Johan Sandquist ..... Colorstone
Johan Saxin ..... Omnious
Johan Schüster ..... Blinded Colony
Johan Segui ..... Rebelene
Johan Sellman ..... Shredhead
Johan Sigfridsson ..... Panic
Johan Sigurdsson "G" ..... Aspected
Johan Sikberg ..... Brigada Illuminada
Johan Sjöberg ..... Optimystical
Johan Sjöberg ..... Tough Trade, Rejected
Johan Sjöberg ..... Stonesilk, Token
Johan Sjögren ..... Meshuggah, Bubonic Plague
Johan Sjögren ..... Tungsten Axe
Johan Sjölin ..... Slick Stuff
Johan Sjöqvist ..... Vulcano
Johan Sjöström ..... The Morning After
Johan Skough ..... Delve
Johan Skugge ..... Singer
Johan Sohlberg ..... Bloodbound, The Storyteller
Johan Spinord ..... Black Rose
Johan Sporre ..... Despite, Marionette
Johan Stark ..... XT
Johan Stentorp ..... Pete Sandberg, Time Gallery
Johan Sterner ..... Spearfish, Armatur
Johan Strende ..... Impale, Silent Scythe
Johan Strömberg ..... Hawk, Motvind
Johan Sundborger ..... Defueld
Johan Svensson ..... Vermin
Johan Svensson ..... Hostile Cell
Johan Svensson ..... Insult
Johan Sånesson ..... Pandemonium
Johan Söderberg ..... Dechas
Johan Söderberg ..... Amon Amarth
Johan Söderhielm ..... Nifters
Johan Söderman ..... Long John
Johan Thoren ..... Imperious
Johan Thornberg "Barsk" ..... Nominon, Insision
Johan Thorstensson ..... Insult
Johan Thosell ..... Human Rage
Johan Thörgren ..... A Mind Confused
Johan Thörn ..... Nattsvart
Johan Thörngren ..... Kaamos, Serpent Obscene
Johan Törnqvist ..... A*Teem
Johan Vallin ..... Uppåt Väggarna
Johan Voxberg "Johnny Wizzer" ..... Lipstixx 'N' Bullets
Johan Wadelius ..... Marble Arch, Evercry
Johan Wahlström ..... Fullmakt
Johan Wallin "Sid E Burns" ..... Repugnant, Iron Lamb
Johan Wallqvist "Ewan" ..... Eleven Pictures
Johan Vegna "Joe Sleaze" ..... Sleazy Joe
Johan Weicht ..... Wiz
Johan Westerberg ..... Suma
Johan Westerlund ..... Auberon, Embracing
Johan Westman "Vebba" ..... Machinery
Johan Wiberg ..... Dawn Of Time, Reclusion
Johan Wickenberg ..... Hellbelly
Johan Widerberg ..... Lovehandles
Johan Wikforss ..... Subcyde, Centinex
Johan Wikmark ..... Deviant
Johan Wikström ..... Mentor's Wish
Johan Ylenstrand (Wold) ..... Crimson Moonlight,
.... Sordid Death, Exhale Swe, Inevitable End, Miseration,
Johan Zackrisson ..... Pagandom
Johan Åberg "Johnny Sleaze" ..... Sleazy Joe
Johan Åkerman ..... Sheik Ahmeed
Johan Öberg ..... Loaded
Johan Öhrnell ..... Quiz
Johan Öijen ..... Brighteye Brison
Johan Öman ..... Moloken
Johan Österberg "John Lesley" ..... Decollation,
..... Diabolique, The Great Deceiver
Johann Laux ..... Spit It Out
Johann Nyström ..... Notorious
Johann ..... Band Of Spice, Spice And The RJ Band
Johanna Andersson ..... Dark Tranquillity
Johanna DePierre ..... Amaran
Johannes Abrahamsson ..... Hypothermia
Johannes Andersson "Jonka" ..... Tribulation (2),
..... Non Serviam, Stench
Johannes Berg ..... Semlah, Castillon Dionysus
Johannes Bergion ..... Diablo Swing Orchestra
Johannes Eckerström ..... Avatar
Johannes Forsberg ..... Amethyst
Johannes Hultin ..... Darkness
Johannes Karlsson ..... Safemode
Johannes Kvarnbring "J/Tehôm" ..... Ofermod,
..... Mortuus, Dödfödd
Johannes Lindström ..... Tyranex
Johannes Losbäck "Axeman" ..... Wolf, Power Unit
..... Seventh One, Decameron
Johannes Malmqvist ..... The Brimstone Days
Johannes Nilsson ..... Asteroid
Johannes Nordström ..... Jonny's Bomb
Johannes Nyberg ..... Zonata
Johannes Olsson ..... Sleazy Joe
Johannes Pedro ..... Bloodshed
Johannes Persson ..... Plastic Pride, Cult Of Luna
Johannes Sande ..... Humble Bee
Johannes Stole ..... Xorigin
Johannes Sundblad ..... Kamasutra
Johannes Svensson ..... Ridge
Johannes Söderqvist "Hampe" ..... Paganus
Johannes Thyr ..... Armauk
Johannes Timander ..... 8 Point Rosie
Johannes Wanngren "Dr. Toxic/Johnny Weissmüller"
..... Dr. Living Dead, Undergång, Ouijabeard
Johannes Åberg "Architect" ..... Skymning
Johdet (aka Jodöden) ..... Whirling, Sorgeldom
Johhny Rydh ..... Crystal Ocean
John "Johnie Wilde" ..... Gabria
John "GB Junior" ..... Walkaway
John Aho ..... Prosperity
John Alfredsson ..... Avatar
John Andersson ..... Omnispawn
John Bengtsson ..... Sonic Syndicate, The Unguided
John Berg ..... Dynazty
John Berger "Gehenna" ..... Morbid
John Bresäter ..... Somber
John Carlsson ..... Strangulation
John Carlsson ..... Eternal Autumn
John Carlsson ..... Plutonium
John Donelly ..... Clown
John Egnell ..... Nightvision
John Falk ..... Sorcery, In Aeternum
John Forsberg ..... Interment
John Frölen "Fröléti" ..... In Battle, Odhinn
John Gelotte ..... Source (2)
John Henriksson ..... My Own Grave, Angtoria
John Hermansen (aka Hermansson) ..... Greenleaf,
..... Stonewall Noise Orchestra, The Awesome Machine,
..... Mother Misery, Sixcoverkisssongs, Staiger, Greyhate
John Hoyles ..... Witchcraft, Spiders,
..... Greenleaf, Troubled Horse
John Huldt "K" ..... Fall Ov Serafim, Crazy Lixx, John Huldt
John Jacobsson ..... Tomterockers
John L. Swedenmark ..... Mirage
John Levén ..... Clockwise, Europe, Pontus Norgren,
..... Yngwie Malmsteen, Last Autum's Dream,
..... Jayce Landberg, Thore Goes Metal, Southpaw
John Lillestrand ..... Lisa Gives Head
John Lindén ..... Eleven Pictures
John Linden ..... Supergroupies
John Lindholm ..... Mother's Hope
John Lönnmyr ..... Valinors Tree
John Löwenadler ..... Twin Age
John Marshall Gibbs ..... Vagh
John McRis ..... System Shock
John Melander ..... Born Electric, Crash
John Miller ..... Source (1)
John Newman ..... Temptation
John Norum ..... John Norum, Europe,
..... Mountain Of Power, Midnight Sun
John Nyberg ..... Zonata
John Odhinn Sandin ..... Diabolicum
John Prodén ..... Destiny
John Påäg ..... Dedication
John Ridge (aka John Boutkam) ..... EF Band
John Rosth ..... It's Alive
John Råd Juvas ..... Canopy
John Sandin (aka Östlund) "Odhinn" ..... Horde Of Hel
John Sjöberg ..... Affecti Veternus
John Sjölin "Doe" ..... Craft, Twin Earth
John Svensson Rehnström ..... Faithful Darkness
John Thorner ..... Igneous Human
John Vesanen ..... Avalon
John Vigebo ..... Blackrain, Justaquickstop
John Viksten ..... Boom Shanker Group
John Wreibo (now Lindqwister) ..... Lisa Gives Head
John Zeke ..... Obnoxious Youth
John Zwetzloot ..... Dissection, The Haunted,
..... Nifelheim, Cardinal Sin
John Östlund ..... Odhinn
Johnnie Gunter ..... Siebenbürgen
Johnnie Nilsson "Colour" ..... Panndeads
Johnnie Tiborn ..... Polluted Influence
Johnny Berntsson ..... Elsesphere
Johnny Blackout ..... Blinded Colony
Johnny Darabandt ..... Shakespeare

NAME INDEX

Johnny Dee ... Phoenix
Johnny Dordevic ... Entombed, Carnage
Johnny Eliasson ... Rebels
Johnny Engström ... Dead End Street, Dead End Space, Johnny Engström Band
Johnny Fagerström ... Lucifer
Johnny Georgsson ... Conquest
Johnny Granström ... Ocean (1), Interaction
Johnny Hagel ... Blackshine, Cemetary (1213), Sundown, Tiamat, Lithium, Order Of Isaz, Sorcerer
Johnny Hedlund ... Unleashed, Nihilist, Bajen Death Cult
Johnny Johansson ... Akilles
Johnny Johansson ... Calm Chaos
Johnny Johansson ... Disdain, Ruined Soul, United Fools
Johnny Jonsson ... Prosperity
Johnny Leadfinger ... Blazing Guns
Johnny Lehto ... Grief Of Emerald
Johnny Liiva ... Arch Enemy
Johnny Lindquist ... Jonny's Bomb
Johnny Lundgren ... Quadruple
Johnny Mattsson ... Crystal Pride
Johnny Pettersson ... Lucy
Johnny Pettersson ... Texas Ego
Johnny Reinholm ... Nemesis
Johnny Sandin ... Seventh Wonder
Johnny Söderkvist ... Tension
Johnny Wranning ... Månegarm, Ebony Tears, Dog Faced Gods, Miscreant
Johnny Öhlin ... Dionysus, Nation
Johny Fagerström ... Belsebub
Johny Tango ... A*Teem
Jokke Pettersson ... Kayser
Jokke Rosén ... Gallery (1)
Jolene Fredricson ... Paganus
Jompa Gustafsson ... Razorblade
Jompa Nymark ... One Hour Hell
Jon Agrell ... Hellbelly
Jon Bålefalk ... Evergrace, Incrave
Jon Bäcklund "Necrofucker" ... Srodek
Jon Dehlén ... Implode
Jon Ericsson ... Stardog
Jon Gamble ... Ritual
Jon Grinde ... Mothers Pride
Jon Hjalmarsen ... Massdistraction
Jon Jeremiah ... Decollation
Jon Mortensen ... The Embodied
Jon Nilsson "Silver" ... Billion Dollar Babies
Jon Nödtveidt "Shadow" ... Ophthalamia, Midvinter, Dissection, The Black, Diabolicum
Jon Persson ... Street Talk
Jon Peterson ... Attention (2)
Jon Rekdahl ... Blidside, Fuck Bitch
Jon Robbins ... Human Cometh
Jon Skäre ... Mindsplit
Jon Solander ... In Mourning
Jon Stavert ... Jet Trail, Promotion
Jon Stinnerbom ... Mama Kin
Jon Sundberg ... Babylon Bombs, Backdraft
Jon Söder ... Sten
Jon Wallner ... Hoarse
Jonas A. Holmberg ... This Gift Is A Curse
Jonas Ahlberg ... Centinex
Jonas Ahlmark ... Ghamorean
Jonas Ahlström ... Undergång
Jonas Albrektsson ... Indungeon, King Of Asgard, Niden Div 187, Thy Primordial, Ceremonial Oath, Infernal Vengeance
Jonas Almen "Grim Vindkall" ... Domgård, Svartrit, Nox Aurea, Snakeskin Angels
Jonas Almquist ... Månegarm
Jonas Andersson ... Scratch (2), Unameus, 17
Jonas Andersson (now Beijer) ... NME Within
Jonas Andersson "Jonkan" ... Hemligt Uppdrag
Jonas Andersson "Jonni Hex" ... Unameus, 17, Gallery, Scratch (2)
Jonas Andersson ... Tyburn
Jonas Andersson ... Tale
Jonas Aneheim ... Goddefied
Jonas Arnberg ... Fimbultyr
Jonas Arnesén ... Witchcraft
Jonas Arvidsson "JJ Rockford" ... VII Gates
Jonas Asplind ... Orphan Gypsy
Jonas Axelsson ... Agape
Jonas Bendt ... Wyvern
Jonas Bergqvist "Nattdal/B" ... Lifelover, IXXI, Dimhymn
Jonas Berndt "Goth Gorgon" ... Mörk Gryning, Diabolical
Jonas Björle ... At The Gates, The Haunted
Jonas Blom ... One Man Army, Grief Of Emerald, Trident, Runemagick
Jonas Blum ... Majestic, Optimystical, Pole Positio, Rebels, Reptilian, Vagh
Jonas Bohlin "Jojje" ... Unanimated
Jonas Bryssling ... Spwan Of Possession
Jonas Bülund "Evil Ed Engine" ... Nattas
Jonas Calsson ... Turning Point, Nasty Groove
Jonas Carlsson ... Carnal Grief
Jonas Cederteg ... Laudamus
Jonas Christophs ... Big Talk (2)
Jonas Dahlström "Yonas Af" ... Ton Of Bricks, Illwill, Lord Belial
Jonas Davidsson ... Erupted
Jonas Derouche ... Carbonized
Jonas Eckerström ... Serenade For June, Cromlech
Jonas Edahl ... Pleasure Avenue
Jonas Edström ... Meduza, Savage Skülls
Jonas Ehlin ... Astrophobos
Jonas Ekdahl ... Deathdestruction
Jonas Eliasson ... Hydra (1)
Jonas Engdegård ... Änglagård
Jonas Ericson ... The Satellite Circle
Jonas Eriksson ... Lake Of Tears
Jonas Eriksson ... Skydiverse
Jonas Eriksson ... Serpent Obscene
Jonas Erixon "Kim Miguel" ... Alicate
Jonas Erkers ... Degreed
Jonas Falk ... Neon
Jonas Forsen ... Moonstruck
Jonas Franke-Blom ... Abuzimbel
Jonas Fritzon ... Bronto
Jonas Gembäck ... Carizma Rain
Jonas Granvik ... Without Grief, Azure
Jonas Gröning ... Work Of Art
Jonas Gustafson ... Souldivider
Jonas Gustafsson ... Infernal Gates
Jonas Gustavsson ... Void Moon
Jonas Hagström ... Dynamite
Jonas Hallberg ... Danger (2), Mindcollapse
Jonas Hallberg ... Maryscreek
Jonas Hallgren ... Crypt Of Kerberos
Jonas Hallström ... Pax Romana
Jonas Hansson ... Stingray
Jonas Hansson ... Book Of Hours
Jonas Hansson ... Silver Mountain, Jonas Hansson Band, Jonas Hansson, Mountain Of Power
Jonas Hartikainen ... Burning Saviours
Jonas Hedgren ... Råg I Ryggen
Jonas Hedlund ... TNT
Jonas Heghammar ... Fred's Fuel
Jonas Heidgert ... Dragonland
Jonas Hellborg "Jesus Ruiz" ... Bakteria, Art Metal, Shining Path
Jonas Hellgren ... Evolution
Jonas Hellgren ... Darkness
Jonas Hellström ... Crier
Jonas Hermansson ... Million
Jonas Hollsén ... Bullhorn, Ten Foot Pole
Jonas Holst ... Wild Cat Sleezy
Jonas Hygren ... Skin Infection, Sacrifice
Jonas Hägg ... Mayadome, Mellow Poetry
Jonas Högberg ... The Björn
Jonas Höglund ... The Gypsies
Jonas Hörnqvist ... Treasure Land, Ruined Soul, Calilio
Jonas Isacsson ... Horizont, Dark Legions
Jonas Jarlsby ... Avatar
Jonas Jeppsson ... Ammotrack
Jonas Johansson ... Stonechurch
Jonas Johansson ... Psyckadeli
Jonas Jönsson ... Ridge
Jonas Jörgensen ... It Will Come
Jonas Kangur "Skinny Disco" ... Deathstars, Revolution Riot, Netherbird
Jonas Karlberg ... Roach
Jonas Karlgren ... Nation Beyond, Debase
Jonas Karlsson ... Spawn Of Possession
Jonas Karlsson ... Stereo Generator
Jonas Karlsson ... Taketh, Admonish
Jonas Kimbrell ... Dispatched
Jonas Kjell ... Stefan Herde And His Broomdusters, Fair Child
Jonas Kjellgren "The Box" ... In Mourning, Dellamorte, Nightscape, Ruined Soul, Steel Attack, Vicious, Altered Aeon, Arise, Rimfrost, Skyfire, Carnal Forge, Centinex, Chainwreck, Dawn Of Silence Dedication, Degradead, Dellamorte, Flaggelation, Raubtier, TorchbBearer, Vanity Blvd, Volturyon, Zonaria, October Tide, Quest Of Aidance, Scar Symmetry, World Below
Jonas Kronberg ... Aggressive Chill, Suicide Nation
Jonas Kulhammar ... Abramis Brama
Jonas Källsbäck ... Cap Outrun, Axia, Mean Streak, Peo, Jupiter Society, The Night Flight Orchestra,
Jonas Langebro ... Bai Bang
Jonas Larsson ... Within Y
Jonas Larsson ... Colordream
Jonas Larsson ... Traumatic
Jonas Lembke ... Fred's Fuel
Jonas Lewén ... Within Reach, Molly's Gusher, Cowboy Prostitutes, All Hell
Jonas Liberg ... Orient
Jonas Lidström ... Mindsplit
Jonas Lindblad "Lindblood" ... Deletion, Puteraeon, Taetre
Jonas Lindgren ... Sacred Night
Jonas Lindgren ... Carnal Grief
Jonas Lindskog "Whorth/Mörk" ... Watain, Malign
Jonas Lindström ... Withered Beauty, Ereb Altor, Isole, Undivide
Jonas Ludvigsson ... Naughty Boys
Jonas Lugner ... Nectaris
Jonas Lundberg ... Hawk, Candy Kicks Ass, Haystack
Jonas Lööf ... Six Feet Under, Vantage
Jonas Magnusson ... Facebreaker, Ashes
Jonas Malmqvist ... The Grand Trick
Jonas Mattsson "Joinus" ... Devian, Sargatanas Reign, Nominon, Silencer, Incinerator, Year Of The Goat
Jonas Mejfeldt ... Necromicon
Jonas Mellberg ... Unanimated, Therion
Jonas Moström ... Absorbing The Pain
Jonas Myrenberg ... Siena Root
Jonas Mähl "Shugatraa" ... Psykotisk
Jonas Nilsson ... Dawn Of Oblivion
Jonas Nilsson ... Sins Of Omission, Raise Hell, Mortifier
Jonas Nilsson ... Shame (2)
Jonas Nilsson ... Victim
Jonas Nilsson ... Carnalist
Jonas Nordblom ... Wildness
Jonas Nordin ... The Satellite Circle
Jonas Nordqvist ... GSO
Jonas Nyrén ... Armageddon, In Thy Dreams
Jonas Nyström ... Buckshot O.D.
Jonas Ohlsson ... Mr. Death, Sceptic Grave, Maitreya, Point Of Existence
Jonas Olsson ... Cross, Talk Of The Town, ATC, Cheerse
Jonas Olsson ... Red Surface
Jonas Ottander ... Bussiga Klubben
Jonas Pannee ... No Hawaii
Jonas Paulsson ... My Dead Addiction, Sanzia
Jonas Pedersen ... Odyssey (2)
Jonas Persson ... M-Train
Jonas Persson ... Psychotic Supper
Jonas Petersson ... Glorious Bankrobbers, Greed, Mental Hippie Blood
Jonas Polling ... Blastrock
Jonas Prahl ... Twelvestep
Jonas Pålsson ... Mothers Pride
Jonas Radehorn ... The Citadel
Jonas Ragnarsson ... Crawley
Jonas Reingold ... Kaipa, Mansson, Pete Sandberg's Jade, Time Requiem, The Downtown Clowns, The Flower Kings, Karmakanic, Midnight Sun, Opus Atlantica, Reptilian, Reingold
Jonas Remne ... Thornclad
Jonas Renkse "Lord Seth" ... Bloodbath, Katatonia, October Tide
Jonas Renvaktar ... Spawn Of Possessio, Vanmakt, Disruption
Jonas Renöfeldt ... Evercry
Jonas Rydberg ... Burst
Jonas Rörling "GIBLI" ... Machinae Supremacy
Jonas Sandberg ... Construcdead
Jonas Sandkvist ... Glory
Jonas Sandquist ... Vanessa
Jonas Sandquist ... Sven Hahne & Prästrock
Jonas Sjödin ... Broken Glass
Jonas Sjögren ... Skyfire, Backhander
Jonas Sjöholm ... Heads Or Tales
Jonas Sjöqvist ... Vidunder
Jonas Skoog ... Closer (2)
Jonas Sköld ... Galaxy
Jonas Sonesson ... Whipped Cream
Jonas Stadling ... Russell
Jonas Stenlund ... Chained, Laudamus
Jonas Stoor ... Team Custard
Jonas Strandberg "Jam" ... The Chair
Jonas Strandell ... Eternal Darkness, Crypt Of Kerberos
Jonas Ström ... Faith Taboo
Jonas Strömberg ... Beseech, The Mary Major
Jonas Stålhammar ... The Crown/Crown Of Thorns, Space Probe Taurus, God Macabre, Macabre End, Utumno, Bombs Of Hades
Jonas Stålne Stensvik ... Slowlife
Jonas Svensson "Johnny Walker" ... Stingray
Jonas Söderholm ... Vitality
Jonas Söderlind ... Morgana Lefay
Jonas Tengner "Leviathan/Nebiros/Nord" ... Ofermod, Malign
Jonas Thegel "Jona Tee" ... H.E.A.T
Jonas Thurén ... Xinema, Madrigal
Jonas Tillheden ... Bulletrain
Jonas Torndal ... Grave (2)
Jonas Tornemalm ... Epitaph (2), Sound Explosion
Jonas Torrestad ... Remo
Jonas Tropp ... Golden Dawn
Jonas Tångström "Johnny D'Fox" ... Swedish Erotica
Jonas Udd ... Bult
Jonas Wahlberg ... Stonewall Noise Orchestra
Jonas Wallinder ... Pantokrator
Jonas Warnerbring ... Råg I Ryggen, Shame (2)
Jonas Westerlund "Johnny Wee" ... Nasty Idols
Jonas Wickström ... Angel Heart
Jonas Wigstad ... Mosez, Ground Mower
Jonas Wiik ... Mr Quinn
Jonas Wikstrand ... Enforcer
Jonas Wimar ... Payback
Jonas Wincent ... Harvey Wallbanger
Jonas Wirsén ... Darklands
Jonas von Renvaktar "Mordechai" ... Istapp
Jonas Ydlinge ... Moonville, Impale
Jonas Ygnell ... H.E.A.L
Jonas Åhlen ... Siena Root, Backdraft, Chainsaw
Jonas Åkerlund "Vans McBurger" ... Bathory
Jonas Öhgren ... Railroad
Jonas Öhlund ... Pride, Linehouse
Jonas Österberg ... Epitaph (2)
Jonas Östman "J.R" ... Gotham City, Mogg, Alfonzetti, Dark Illusion, Yngwie Malmsteen, Skintrade, Glory, Gemini Souls, Mental Hippie Blood
Jonatan Berg ... Shadows Past
Jonatan Björkborg "Bjoerkborg" ... Malison Rogue
Jonatan Forssander ... Disruption
Jonatan Hedlin ... Canopy
Jonatan Larsson ... Despite
Jonatan Näslund ... Colossus
Jonatan Östling ... Hearts Alive
Jonathan Blomberg ... The Björn
Jonathan Blomberg ... Source (2)
Jonathan Carlemar ... Seven Tears
Jonathan Enmark ... Carpe Wade
Jonathan Eriksson ... Skogen Brinner
Jonathan Granlund Pennheim ... Ground Mower
Jonathan Hjalmarsson ... Iscaroth
Jonathan Holmgren ... Auberon, Amsvartner
Jonathan Hultén "Evil Kid Joe" ... Tribulation (2), Stench
Jonathan Jansson "Steele" ... Pantokrator, Crimson Moonlight, Sanctifica
Jonathan Johnsson ... Crystal Eyes
Jonathan Jonsson "Jonte" ... Lethal
Jonathan Larocca Ramm ... Graveyard
Jonathan Nordenstam ... Laethoria
Jonathan Nyberg ... Crystal Eyes, Enbound
Jonathan O. Gonzales ... Strangulation
Jonathan Stenberg ... Evergrace, Incrave
Jonathan Sjöblom ... Corrosive Carcass
Jonathan Thorpenberg ... Eternity Remains
Jonathon ... Unpure
Jonaz Bylund ... Bibleblack
Jonaz Lindgren ... Swedens Finest, Gosh!
Jon-Henric Andersson ... Vivid
Joni Laine ... Skiller
Joni Mäensivu "Gösta" ... Eternal Oath
Joni Salo ... Chaossworn
Jonna Enckell ... The Project Hate MCMXCIX
Jonna Sailon ... All Ends
Jonne Brolin ... Subtopia
Jonnie Carlsson ... Captor
Jonnie Täll ... The Provenance, Laethoria
Jonny Andersson ... Rockvaktmästarna
Jonny Birtner ... Silverwings
Jonny Bogren ... Immersed In Blood
Jonny Edvardsson ... Seventh One, Power Unit
Jonny Granberg ... Zpeedfreak
Jonny Gustavsson "Superstar" ... Plan 9
Jonny Gustavsson ... Hemligt Uppdrag
Jonny Lehto ... Decameron
Jonny Lindberg ... Chiron
Jonny Lindqvist ... Arrows, Mogg, Nocturnal Rites, Tippen Ruda
Jonny Nielsen "Carnage" ... Mordant
Jonny Pettersson ... Syn:Drom
Jonny Putrid ... Serpent Obscene, Revokation
Jonny Rantala ... Redsun
Jonny Reinholm ... Shock Tilt, Thore Skogman
Jonny Scaramanga ... Kee Marcello
Jonny Wemmenstedt ... Straight Frank, Nestor
Jonny Wester ... Solution
Jonny Westerbäck ... The Bereaved
Jonny Zasella ... Foobar The Band
Jonte Eliasson ... Lohengrin
Jonte Holm ... Erupted
Jonte Johansson ... Ginger Trees
Joonas Ahonen ... Insision
Joonas Niskanen ... One Without
Jori Helminen ... Scudiero
Jorma Kujansuu ... Cheers
Jorma Kytölä ... Raceway
Jorma Linna "Joe" ... The Wild Bunch
Josabeth Leidi ... Satanarchy, Rise And Shine,
José Gomez-Sanchez "Joe Canner" ... Dr Dream, Empire Saint, Fierce Conviction, Sanchez, Conviction
Jose Pascual ... Urbandux
Josef Davidsson ... Evergrace, Incrave
Josef Mineur ... Rocka Rollas
Josef Torvaldsson ... Memoria
Josefin Berg ... Myrah
Josefin Qvarnström ... February 93
Joseph Astorga ... Despite
Joseph Skansås ... All Ends
Joseph Tholl ... Enforcer, Black Trip, Corrupt
Josephine Forsman ... Casablanca
Josephine Kersten ... Blue Skies Bring Tears
Jouko Kinnonen "Jake" ... Pussy Galore
Jouni Heikkinen ... Spitfire

Jouni Parkkonen "Joppe Jouppo" ... Chronic Torment
Jovan Bojcevski ... Suma
Juan Gauthier ... Point Of Existence, T.A.R
Judas Isaksson "Priestor Af Hellgoat" ... Necroplasma
Juha Nurmenniemi "Juba" ... Ambush, Rampant, (Darxtar)
Juha Helttunen ... Strangulation
Juha Koikeroinen ... H2O
Juha Ojajärvi ... Syconaut
Juha Sulasalmi ... Nominon
Juho Korhonen ... Malaise, The Mist Of Avalon
Jukka Kaupaamaa ... Crystal Eyes
Jukka Kemppainen "JK Knoxx" ... Enemies Swe, ... King Pin, Shotgun Messiah
Jukka Vouti ... Pussy Galore
Julian Loaiza ... Circle Of Chaos
Julie Greaux ... Talisman
Julius "Farnargh" Chmielewski ... Misteltein, ... Fall Ov Seraphim, Supreme Majesty, Embraced
Junita Stomberg ... Amity
Juoko Kinnunen "Jake Killer" ... Hiroshima
Juris Salmins ... Motvind
Jussi Linna ... Vomitory
Jussi Pöysälä ... Grave (1)
Juuso Savolainen ... Safemode
Jylle Sandberg ... Ban-Zai
Jögge Sundqvist ... Rockvattnä
Jörgen Carlsson ... Morgan Mastling Band
Jörgen Olsson "Stanley" ... Wizzy Blaze, Nasty Idols, ... Machinegun Kelly
Jörgen Ahr ... Reazon
Jörgen Alriksson ... Buckshot O.D.
Jörgen Anderson "Jamie" ... Maeday
Jörgen Andersson ... Bloodbound, Baltimoore
Jörgen Andersson ... Sanchez
Jörgen Andersson ... Torch, The Citadel, Bloodbound
Jörgen Andersson ... Avenue
Jörgen Andersson ... Extasy
Jörgen Andersson ... Mammoth Volume
Jörgen Arvidsson "Jamie Tease" ... Lipstixx 'N' Bullets
Jörgen Aspring (now Miller) ... Overdrive
Jörgen Berglund ... Rio
Jörgen Bihagen "Holger" ... R&R
Jörgen Birch Jensen ... Pete Sandberg's Jade, ... Silver Seraph, Bai Bang
Jörgen Björk ... Driver, Dumper
Jörgen Björnström ... Septic Grave, The Embraced
Jörgen Bolmstad "Jojje" ... Hardcore Circus, Big Thing
Jörgen Borman ... W.E.T (1)
Jörgen Bröms ... Afflicted, Abhoth, Dissober
Jörgen Bylander ... Sanctification, Defaced Creation
Jörgen Carlsson ... M.A.C
Jörgen Cremonese ... Destiny, Whipped Cream
Jörgen Ek "Pastor" ... Crystal Ocean
Jörgen Ekener ... Kisses From The PaShee
Jörgen Engström ... Sticky Sweet
Jörgen Eriksson ... Squetters
Jörgen Fahlberg ... Left Hand Solution
Jörgen Fardvik ... Suicide Nation, Adams Eve
Jörgen Gustavsson "George" ... Rebelene
Jörgen Hallberg ... Daydream
Jörgen Hanson ... Twin Age
Jörgen Hansson ... Balthazar
Jörgen Holmberg ... Gilt
Jörgen Jern ... Plague Angel
Jörgen Kristensen ... Abhoth, Suffer, Dead Awaken
Jörgen Lantto ... Black Cat Moan
Jörgen Larsson ... Gosh!
Jörgen Lejon ... Kings Of Modern Swing
Jörgen Lindau ... Wham Glam Boys
Jörgen Lindgren ... Live Elephant
Jörgen Lindhe ... Flegma, Obscurity, S.K.U.R.K
Jörgen Lindhult "Jukken" ... Mother's Hope
Jörgen Lindmark ... Meshuggah
Jörgen Löfberg ... Agregator, Darkane, The Defaced
Jörgen Munk ... Waterline
Jörgen Månsson ... Torsten
Jörgen Nilsson ... Who's Next, Side By Side
Jörgen Olausson ... Heartcry
Jörgen Olsson ... Heed
Jörgen Olsson ... Air Condition
Jörgen Olsson ... Seventh One, Heed
Jörgen Paulsson ... Authorize
Jörgen Persson ... Side By Side
Jörgen Persson "Jögge" ... Exanthema
Jörgen Persson ... Daemonicus
Jörgen Rönnqvist ... Vivid
Jörgen Sandström ... Entombed, Deadmarch, ... Death Breath, Grave (2), Vicious, ... The Project Hate, Torture Division
Jörgen Schelander ... Mercury Fang, Novak, ... Audiovision, Tomas Bergsten's Fantasy, Misth
Jörgen Sigvardsson "Sigge" ... Angeline
Jörgen Sjöberg ... Beseech
Jörgen Sjöström ... Satanic Slaughter
Jörgen Ström ... Beseech, The Mary Major
Jörgen Svahn ... Detest
Jörgen Svedberg ... Wynja
Jörgen Svensson ... State Of Mind
Jörgen Sverin ... Stitch
Jörgen Söderberg ... Griffen
Jörgen Thullberg ... Mr. Death, Treblinka, Tiamat
Jörgen Thuresson ... Faith
Jörgen Tjusling (aka Little George Gustafsson) ... Lommi, ... Eaglestrike, Elsy Band, Human Race, The Jet Circus
Jörgen Wall ... Screamin' Mother, Ingo & Floyd
Jörgen Westerberg ... Fortuna
Jörgen Winblad "Conel" ... Stitch
Jörgen Zetterberg ... Caligula
Jörgen Örnhem ... Dethronement
JörgenThorsson ... Shenerah
K. Ailo ... Chronic Torment
K. Fjällbrandt "Hraegelmir" ... Domgård
Kacper Rosanski "Mickey Mouth" ... Nattas, Bibleblack
Kahl Hellmer ... Machinae Supremacy
Kai Jaakkola ... The Duskfall, Necromicon
Kai Lethola ... Shere Khan
Kai Molin ... The Duskfall
Kai Nurmi ... Onyx
Kai Partanen "Ishtar" ... Curse
Kaj Högberg ... Proud
Kaj Leissner "Kai" ... Arise
Kaj Löfven "Dubbdäck Doom Culta" ... Sportlov
Kaj Mattsoff ... Dakks
Kaj Nordstrand ... 7th Planet
Kaj Palm "Gimbrynjer" ... Matricide, Excessum
Kaj Paxéus ... The Black Marbles
Kaj Podgorski ... 1 Way Street
Kaj Roth ... Human Cometh
Kaj Söderström "Coda" ... Trash, Splash
Kaj Ukura ... Blacklight
Kajsa Eldh ... Brickhouse
Kali Ma ... Thornium
Kalle Antonsson "Gorgorium" Diabolicum, Kill, Warcollapse
Kalle Berlin ... Mammoth Volume
Kalle Bondesson "Taurtheim" ... Throne Of Ahaz
Kalle Carlsson ... Nation
Kalle Dettner ... Superstition
Kalle Granström ... A Swarm Of The Sun
Kalle Gustafsson ... Bubonic Plague
Kalle Jansson "Toxal" ... Vemoth
Kalle Johansson ... (see Kalle Nimhagen)
Kalle Kjellberg ... Furor
Kalle Kronhamn ... Vanity Dies Hard
Kalle Lagergren ... Beast
Kalle Lilja ... Långfinger
Kalle Lindström ... Sheik Ahmeed
Kalle Lundin ... Amsvartner
Kalle Magnusson ... Hellmark
Kalle Metz ... Flegma, Tenebre
Kalle Möllerström ... Massdistraction
Kalle Nimhagen (aka Johansson) ... Deathening, ... Embraced, Burning Engines
Kalle Pettersson "Graveyard" ... Taetre, Snakeskin Angels
Kalle Sandström ... Pound
Kalle Sellbrink ... The Grand Trick
Kalle Sjödin ... Maze Of Torment
Kalle Sjöstrand ... Kaross
Kalle Stridh ... Diesel
Kalle Svedåker ... Gormathon
Kalle Ullbrandt ... Anachronaeon
Kalle Wallin ... Pandemonium
Kalle Wanngård "Yeti" ... Paperback Freud
Kalle Åslund ... Shaker
Kam Lee ... Bone Gnawer
Karel Brydniak ... Request
Kari Hokkanen ... Stillborn
Kari Kainulainen ... Amaran, Mourning Sign
Kari Korkala ... Grave (1)
Kari Stehag ... Black Dog
Kari Säveläa ... Diavox
Kari Tapio ... Blizzard
Kari Varonen "Luke Powerhand" ... Hiroshima
Karim Elomary ... Internal Decay
Karin Axelsson ... Sonic Syndicate
Karin Blomqvist ... Dracena, Deathwitch
Karin Gustavsson ... Vulcano
Karin Sjögren ... Loud
Karl Alling ... Elimi
Karl Baker ... Thee Expression
Karl Beckman "Bastard" ... Infernal Vengeance
Karl Bäckman ... Mithotyn, Indungeon, King Of Asgard
Karl Envall "Drunkschwein" ... Revokation, Kaamos
Karl Granehed "Charlie" ... Electric Eastwood
Karl Gustaf Westman "KG West" ... Siena Root
Karl Hannus ... Sordid Death
Karl Hinterleithner ... Whipping Princess
Karl Landin ... Moonlight Agony
Karl Lindén "Mori" ... Infernal Vengeance
Karl Magnus NE ... Nåstrond
Karl Nilsson "Karl Kidd" ... Axis Powers
Karl Nylin ... Sobre Nocturn
Karl Obbel ... Cipher System
Karl Olsson ... Angrepp
Karl Persson ... System Breakdown
Karl Sjöblad "Clarious Thump" ... Mac Bladgick
Karl Stork ... Aeon (1)
Karl Torstensson ... Nine
Karl Tunander "Thunder" ... Hydra (2)
Karl Wahllöf "Kalle" ... Insult
Karl Walfridsson ... Pantokrator
Karl Wassholm ... Darkwater
Karl-Jan Kristiansson "Vincent/Sexual Goatlicker" ... Autopsy Torment, Pagan Rites, Devil Lee Rot
Karl Åke Wallin ... Giant
Karl-Hannes Van Dahl ... Evergrey, Marcus Jidell
Karl-Johan Karlsson ... Victim
Karl-Johan Samuelsson ... Indian Red
Karl-Oskar Wiman "Kalle" ... Stonechurch
Karl-Otto Ahlberg ... King Koole
Karl-Peter "Per" Resac ... Baddies
Karl-Wilhelm Arvidsson ... Chicks With Guns
Karsten Larsson ... Dawn, Choir Of Vengeance, ... Falconer, King Of Mithotyn
Kaspar Dahlberg ... Dionysus, Treasure Land, ... Sahara (2), Ride TheStormwind
Kaspar Larsson ... Killaman, Withering Surface
Kasper Gram ... Evil Masquerade, ZooL
Kasper Lindgren ... Straight Frank, Prime Sth
Katarina Lammi "Kattis" ... Society Gang Rape
Katarina Lilja ... Therion
Katja Andersson ... A Virgin's Delight
Katja Hilldén ... Twilight
Kauno Vaattovaara ... Lynx
Kay Backlund ... Lion's Share
Kay Söderström ... Ball
Kecke Ljungberg ... Satanic Slaughter
Kee Bergman ... Keehole
Kee Marcello ... (see Kjell Löfbom)
Keijo Ruprecht ... Dakks
Keith Almgren ... Inferno
Kemper Lieath ... Sadistic Grimness
Ken Johansson ... Memory Garden
Ken Olsson ... Pagan, Solid
Ken Sandin ... (See Ulf Sandin)
Ken Savefjord ... Mercury Fang
Ken Sundberg ... Ion Olteanu Band Stitch
Kennet Berggren ... Lifeless Image
Kennet Englund ... Interment, Moondark, ... Dellamorte, Subdive, Uncanny, Centinex
Kennet Jansson ... Seven, Last Temptation
Kenneth Andersson ... Side By Side
Kenneth Arnestedt ... Mega Slaughter
Kenneth Asplund ... Neon
Kenneth Augustsson ... Stallion
Kenneth Berg ... TBC
Kenneth Braman ... The Chair
Kenneth Eriksson ... Ellen B
Kenneth Fahlman ... Mac & Ploids
Kenneth Forsell ... Hallonbomb
Kenneth Gagner "Thunderbolt" ... Likblek, ... Swordmaster, Snakeskin Angels
Kenneth Gradin ... Victory (1)
Kenneth Hansson ... Prowoke
Kenneth Helgesson ... Degradead
Kenneth Holmström ... Spectra, Sten Sandberg
Kenneth Jern ... Plague Angel
Kenneth Johnsson ... Baddies
Kenneth Johnsson ... The Citadel, Torch, Tad Morose
Kenneth Jonsson ... Sektor Skandal
Kenneth Jonsson ... Sanchez
Kenneth K Gilbert ... Her Whisper
Kenneth Lamberg ... Bullhorn
Kenneth Lantz ... Decadence
Kenneth Lillqvist ... Golden Resurrection
Kenneth Lindberg ... Etos
Kenneth Nordqvist "Zone" ... Slam
Kenneth Nyholm "Nenne Vörgus" ... Vörgus
Kenneth Nyman ... Coercion
Kenneth Olofsson ... Slowgate
Kenneth Olofsson ... Romance
Kenneth Olsen ... ZooL
Kenneth Olsson ... Ten Foot Pole
Kenneth Pettersson ... Tears, Deep Diver
Kenneth Roos ... Tiamat
Kenneth Seil ... Scar Symmetry
Kenneth Siewertsson ... Treat
Kenneth Skoog ... Kenneth Skoog
Kenneth Sundqvist ... Dreamline
Kenneth Sylwan ... Rävjunk
Kenneth Vikland ... Phoenix
Kenneth Wiklund ... Centinex
Kennth Holmberg ... Dream
Kenny Boufadene ... One Without
Kenny Bryngelsson ... Shenerah
Kenny Elfström ... Slyside
Kenny Gustavsson ... Tornado Babies
Kenny Krueger ... Unameus
Kenny Leckremo ... H.E.A.T
Kenny Lindal ... Dream
Kenny Lundstedt ... Internal Decay
Kenny Wendel ... Yankee Heaven, Angelez
Kenny-Oswald Sjödin ... Gudars Skymning
Kent Abrahamsson ... Steve Eastside Band
Kent Bengtsson "Tjobbe" ... Asoka
Kent Bill ... Brat Pack
Kent Brandin ... Queen Obscene
Kent Engberg ... Fallen Angel
Kent Fagerberg ... Wulcan
Kent Franklin ... Stonefuze, Cornerstone
Kent G Svensson ... Hellfueled
Kent Gustafsson ... Queensland, Adventure
Kent Hedlund ... Firework
Kent Helgesson ... HÅF Band
Kent Hofling ... Sargoth
Kent Jansson ... Six Feet Under, Keen Hue
Kent Johansson ... Ivory
Kent Jonsson ... Dexter Jones' Circus Orchestra
Kent Jädestam ... Jennie Tebler, ... Jennie Tebler's Out Of Oblivion
Kent Karlsson ... Göran Nordh
Kent Klaveness ... Tyron
Kent Kroon ... Cool For Cats, Notorious, Cross
Kent Nei ... Hels
Kent Nordström ... Diva
Kent Paul Svensson ... Crossroad Jam
Kent Persson ... Balthazar
Kent Pettersson ... Allan Beddo Band
Kent Ploog ... Sabbtail
Kent Rune Johansson ... X-Perience
Kent Spjuth ... Dunder
Kent Österlöv ... Madigan
Kenta Krull ... Neon Rose
Kenta Svensson ... Ocean (1), Overdrive, Carnival Sun
Kenth Edvardsson ... Jonah Quizz
Kenth Ericsson ... Overdrive, Paradize (1), Interaction
Kenth Lindh ... Dreamline
Kenth Lindstrand ... Shame (2)
Kenth Sandell ... Neon
Kent-Åke Philipsson "Lord K/Kenta" .. God Among Insects, ... Torture Division, The Project Hate MCMXCIX, ... Odyssey, Deadmarch, Leukemia
Kerim Kalkan ... Timescape
Kerry Lundberg ... Reinxeed
Kevin Rehn Eires "Yohio" ... YOHIO, Seremedy
Kevin Talley ... Soils Of Fate
Kevin Vahlberg ... Caliber 71
KG West ... (See Karl Gustaf Westman)
Khaled El Tayara ... Hellennium
Kiana Svalold ... Liquidist
Kicke Grape ... Revanch
Kicki Höijertz ... Left Hand Solution, Siebenbürgen
Kieven Klevmyr ... Sanchez
Kim Andreasson ... Skymning
Kim Arnell ... Nephenzy /Chaos Order, ... Sobre Nocturne, Morifade
Kim Blomqvist ... Internal Decay
Kim Boman ... Malaise
Kim Bäckström "Slim" ... Silverfish
Kim Carlsson "( )" ... Lifelover, Dimhymn, Hypothermia
Kim Chevélle ... Pretty Wild
Kim Eriksson "Maturz" ... Elimi
Kim Gabrielsson ... Sky High, Crossing Oceans
Kim Gustafsson ... The Goddamned
Kim Gustavsson ... Taketh, System Shock
Kim Gustavsson ... Excessum
Kim Kajjuuti "Caine" ... Empire Saint
Kim Laakso ... Ninnuam
Kim Lantto ... Comatose
Kim Lindstén ... My Dead Addiction
Kim Norberg ... Freedom Bleeder
Kim Pettersson ... Opeth
Kim Salmi ... Damnatory
Kim Sandström ... Stillborn
Kim Simon ... Supergroupies
Kim Stockkfelt ... Lugnoro
Kim Stranne ... Anaemia
Kim Thalén "Keuron" ... Diabolical
Kim Turesson "Kim Sleaze" ... Sleazy Joe
Kim Widfors ... Timeless Miracle, Trapped
Kimmo Värynen "Kim Wyn" ... Madigan
Kimmo Holappa ... Chainwreck, Demon Cleener
Kimmo Morja ... Spitfire, Rozz The Bozz
Kimmo Ylitalo ... Bacon
Kimmy Sjölund ... Thyrfing
Kitty Saric "Metallic Kitty" ... Decadence, Netherbird, ... Triton Enigma
Kjell Adolfsson ... Hebron
Kjell Allinger ... Ion Olteanu Band
Kjell Andersson ... Teamwork, Björn Stigsson, ... XT, Leviticus
Kjell Andersson ... Azotic Reign, Altered Aeon
Kjell Arne Engberg ... Tyfuz
Kjell Berg ... Bulletsize
Kjell Bergendahl ... Renaissance Of Fools, Thalamus, ... Mountain Of Power
Kjell Claeson ... W.O. Band
Kjell Danielsson ... Lotus (1)
Kjell Elmlund ... Mental Crypt, Loss
Kjell Enblom ... Maze Of Torment, Harmony (1)
Kjell Eriksson (now Nietzche) "Shelly" ... Paradise (2), ... Yngwie Malmsteen, Red Baron
Kjell Gustafsson ... Silver Mountain

NAME INDEX

Kjell Gustavsson ... Air Condition
Kjell Haraldsson ... Hasse Fröberg & Music Companion, ... Dreamline, JJ Marsch
Kjell Holboe ... Core Of Nation
Kjell Jacobsson. Ocean (1), Overdrive, Locomotive Breath
Kjell Jansson ... Manticore
Kjell Jennstig ... Colt 46
Kjell Johansson ... Rampant
Kjell Johansson ... Hemligt Uppdrag
Kjell Klaesson ... Grand Illusion
Kjell Löfbom "Kee Marcello" ... Europe, Easy Action, ... Killer Bee, Loud 'N' N Proud, Sayit, Supergroupies, ... VII Gates, Zinny J Zan, Candy Roxx, Eclipse, Red Fun, ... Rat Bat Blue, Swedish Metal Aid, Kee Marcello
Kjell Nilsson ... Jeremiah
Kjell Segebrant ... Moosters
Kjell Svensson ... Nattsvart
Kjell Wallén ... Universe, Airlines
Kjell-Arne Lindvall ... Genesaret
Kjell-Åke Norén ... Rhapsody (Sweden)
Kjell-Åke Svensson ... On The Rocks
Kjetil Hektoen ... The Legion
Kjukken ... Mother's Hope
Klara Gripe ... Netherbird
Klara Kempff ... Yeah Bop Station
Klara Rönnqvist Fors "Force" ... Crucified Barbara
Klas Andelhell ... Jerusalem
Klas Berg ... Chiron
Klas Bergwall ... Nemesis, Candlemass
Klas Bohlin ... Beseech
Klas Holmgren ... Gin Lady, Black Bonzo
Klas Hägglund ... Stonecake, Sky High, Death Organ
Klas Ideberg "Cliff T" ... Hyste'riah G.B.C, Darkane, ... The Defacaced, Terror 2000
Klas Ling ... Wonderland (2)
Klas Lövgren ... Third Stone
Klas Morberg ... Desultory, Zebulon
Klas Pettersson ... Sons Of Thunder
Klas Rydberg ... Spinning Black Circle, Cult Of Luna
Klas Wistedt "Juck" ... Tiamat, Treblinka
Klas Wollberg ... Axewitch
Klasse Sundberg ... Grand Stand
Klatuu (aka Kee Marcello) ... (See Kjell Löfbom)
Klaus Gauffin ... Abandoned Splhinx Violent Divine
Klaus Kernchen ... Vivaldi (group)
Knoven ... Solid Rox
Knut Akselsen ... Silver Mountain
Knut Hassel ... Destiny, 7th Planet, Gudars Skymning
Knut Owe Wallin ... Giant
Kolgrim ... Svartsyn, Unpure
Konstantin Papavassiliou ... Saturnalia Temple, ... A Mind Confused, Kaamos
Koothat ... Bathory
Korpr ... Nidsang
Kprl. Sigge Hall ... Skitarg
Kricke Petersson ... Waterline
Kricke Zetterquist ... Snakepit Rebels
Kriegwulff ... Blodulv
Krille Eriksson ... Houston
Krille Johansson ... M.A.C
Krille Kellerman ... Aggressive Chill
Kriss Biggs ... Scams
Kriss Lenmark ... Legia
Kristeian ... Midvinter, Melek Taus
Krister Albertsson ... Gardenian, Sarcazm
Krister Andersen "Spud" ... One Hour Hell
Krister Andersen ... Steelwings
Krister Andersson "Chris Reeve" ... Dispatched
Krister Andersson ... Tomterockers
Krister Angelovski ... Mistie, Seventribe
Krister Bengtsson ... Onyx
Krister Björkholm ... Grand Vision
Krister Boquist ... Diva
Krister Hermansson ... The Poodles
Krister Jacobsson ... Motvind
Krister Johnsson ... Story
Krister Jonsson ... Wood
Krister Jonsson ... Karmakanic, Rebels
Krister Karlsson ... King Koole
Krister Linder ... Enter The Hunt
Krister Lindman ... Warning
Krister Pirkkanen ... Genie
Krister Rispling ... King Pin
Krister Saarinen ... Brainwave
Krister Selander ... The Black Marbles
Krister Sundqvist ... Anaemia
Krister Taimi ... Crystal Pride
Kristian Andrén ... Tad Morose, Street Talk, ... Fi5th Reason, Memento Mori, Meduza, Bibleblack, ... Bloodbound, Cemetary,The Great Deceiver, ... Grotesque, Diabolique
Kristian Bäckbrant "Bäckis" ... Brewmaster
Kristian Carlin "Gutsfucker" ... Holocaust
Kristian Carlin ... Degrade
Kristian Enkvist ... Rising Faith
Kristian Halvarsson "Kribbe" ... Blodsrit
Kristian Hasselhuhn ... Inverted
Kristian Hermansson ... Cleopatra
Kristian Houtari ... Torch, Griffen, Scaar, Days Of Anger
Kristian Järvenpää ... Decadence
Kristian Kallio ... Frame
Kristian Karlsson ... The Law, Fetus Stench
Kristian Kaunissaar ... Portal
Kristian Lampila Ton Of Bricks, Relevant Few, Gooseflesh
Kristian Larsen ... Osukaru, Titan
Kristian Lindström ... Amethyst
Kristian Lönnsjö ... Ablaze My Sorrow
Kristian Metsälä "Bobby Hott" ... Belladonna
Kristian Möllerström ... Macrocosmic Emotions
Kristian Niemann ... Lithium, Sorcerer, Therion, Canopy, ... Notre Dame, Moonlight Agony, Demonoid
Kristian Svensson ... Lechery
Kristian Wallin ... Morifade, Danger (2), Rising Faith
Kristian Ward ... Mama Kin
Kristian Wåhlin "Bullen/Necrolord/Chris Steele" ... Liers In Wait, Decollation, Netherbird, ... Diabolique, Grotesque
Kristian Zackrisson ... Liquid Phase
Kristian Åkesson ... Fistfunk
Kristian Östergren ... Nadir
Kristina Johansson ... Firestone
Kristina Karlsson ... Slingblade
Kristofer Bergman ... One Without
Kristofer Elemyr (aka Nilsson) . Sectu, Undivine, Ereb Altor
Kristofer Eng ... Stormwind, Brighteye Brison, Flagship
Kristofer Greczula ... Damn Delicious
Kristofer Möller ... Horisont
Kristofer Nilsson ... (See Kristofer Elemyr)
Kristofer Rönstrom ... Wraptors
Kristofer Samuelsson ... Sanity
Kristofer Stjernqvist ... Nymf
Kristofer von Wachenfeldt ... Seven Tears, Platitude
Kristofer Örstadius§9th Plague
Kristoffer "Chris Loud"/X" ... XXX, Loud 'N' Nasty
Kristoffer "Satygh" ... Vanmakt
Kristoffer af Dolphins Andersson "Ushatar" ... Nefandus, ... Sargatanas Reign, Nefandus, The Legion
Kristoffer Ahlberg ... Stormrider
Kristoffer Andersson ... Last Tribe, Twelvestep
Kristoffer Bäcklund ... Sonic Syndicate, Avatar
Kristoffer Bäckström ... Moloken
Kristoffer Englund ... Another Hell
Kristoffer Folin ... Plan Three
Kristoffer Gildenlöw ... Pain Of Salvation
Kristoffer Gottberg ... Twin Earth
Kristoffer Griedl ... Defleshed
Kristoffer Göbel ... Destiny
Kristoffer Hell ... Sanctification
Kristoffer Hessö ... Denial
Kristoffer Hjelm ... Born Of Sin
Kristoffer Johnsson ... Chicks With Guns
Kristoffer Lagerström ... Spin Gallery, ... Union Mac, Radioactive
Kristoffer Olivius "Wrath/Wrathyr" ... Setherial, Bewitched, ... Bloodline, Naglfar, Ancient Wisdom, Nocturnal Rites
Kristoffer Palm "Kristo Napalm" ... Nightshade
Kristoffer Pettersson ... Scumkill
Kristoffer Sjödal ... Norrsken
Kristoffer Sundberg ... Madrigal
Kristoffer Svensson ... Dethronement, Exanthema
Kristoffer Söderström ... Takida
Kristoffer Widman "Snipe/Viking Slammer" .. Mac Bladgick
Kristoffer von Wachtenfeldt ... Osukaru
Kristoffer Österman ... Slowlife
Kristopher Lind "Chris Lynn/Linn" ... Easy Action
Krizzy Field ... Pretty Wild
Krook ... Flash
Kujtim Gashi ... Crystal Eyes, Damnatory
Kurre Persson ... Råg I Ryggen
Kurt Gustafsson ... Street Level, Checkpoint Charlie
Kurt Kästner ... Shaggy
Kurt-Anders Svensson ... Tonvikt
Kurt-Ove Åhs ... Hangover
Kutchek Gorealis ... Dark Legions
Kvist ... Patronymicon
Kyrkbrand ... Svartnatt
L.E Pettersson ... Twinball
Lacki Miliadis ... Liquidist
Lage Malmsten ... Blåeld
Lage ... Blodskald
Lake Skoglund ... Glorious Bankrobbers, ... Mental Hippie Blood
Lalle Larsson ... Karmakanic, Fredrik Pihl
LAO ... Cowboy Prostitutes
Lars Abrahamsson ... Broke N Blue
Lars Adolfsson "Orm" ... Domgård
Lars Andersson ... Gone
Lars Andersson "Kula" ... Co Stone
Lars Andersson "Messias" ... Panndeads
Lars Andersson ... Lezlie Paice
Lars Axelsson ... Black Cat Moan, Red Baron
Lars Berg ... Örby Mix
Lars Bergbom ... Plain Zero
Lars Berger ... Electric Earth, Rising, Gooseflesh
Lars Boquist "Lasse" ... Dizziness, Neondaze, ... Pole Position, Reptilian
Lars Borgström ... Cross
Lars Broddesson ... Excessum, Marduk
Lars Byström ... Wildmarken, Neon Rose
Lars Carlberg ... Bokor
Lars Carlsohn ... Agape
Lars Christmansson "Chriss" ... Lion's Share, Audiovision, Road II Ruin, Ten 67, Deacon Street Project
Lars Crantz ... Suspekt
Lars Dahlqvist "Quast" ... Eurock
Lars Danielsson ... S.L.R
Lars Dannesäter ... N.J.B
Lars Eklund ... (Umeå) Small Band
Lars Elf ... Generous Maria
Lars Eliasson ... Born Electric, Crash, Tatch
Lars Eric Mattsson ... Winterlong
Lars Eriksson ... Notredame
Lars Forslund ... Va-Då?
Lars Fransson ... Valley
Lars Furberg "Fubbe" ... Tears, Deep Diver
Lars Gabrielsson ... Negro
Lars Gillén ... Steve Roper Band, TBC
Lars Grahn ... Corrosive Sweden
Lars Gunnar Selinder ... Empire
Lars Gunnarsson ... This Gift Is A Curse
Lars Gustavsson "Skunken" ... Rebelene
Lars Göransson ... Quix
Lars Hagman "Hagis" ... Backtalk
Lars Hallbäck ... Extasy
Lars Hasselfeldt ... Cleopatra
Lars Hemlin ... Spaps
Lars Henriksson ... Nirvana 2002
Lars Hillgren ... Pejling
Lars Hjelm ... Nagazaki
Lars Hoflund ... Alex's Pro
Lars Holmlund ... Firework
Lars Hultman ... Dizziness, Grand Vision
Lars Häglund . Transport League, B-Thong, Concrete Stuff
Lars Hägglund ... Sergeant, Boogietryck
Lars Isaksson ... Meadow
Lars Jelleryd ... Lobotomy
Lars Jerkell "Crash" ... H.E.A.T
Lars Johansson "Lasse" ... Creozoth, Candlemass, Zoic
Lars Johansson ... Cut Out
Lars Johansson ... Dominion Caligula
Lars Johansson ... Panic
Lars Johansson ... Blacksmith
Lars Jönsson ... Mothercake
Lars Karlsson "Angelreaper" ... Mordant, Shattered
Lars Karlsson ... Notredame
Lars Lagergren ... Rock Squad
Lars Landegren "Slarre" ... Grand Slam
Lars Levin ... Excruciate, Mykorrhiza
Lars Lindberg "Leo/Lasse Lee" ... Zone Zero
Lars Lindén "Lasse/Jonathan Oke" ... Carnal Forge, ... Slapdash, Rosicrucian, Zeelion, Apostasy
Lars Lindgren ... Drama
Lars Lundin ... Big Easy
Lars Löfven "Hell Y Hansen" ... Sportlov, Defleshed
Lars Martinsson "Lazr" ... The Legion, Pinch
Lars Martinsson ... Bosse
Lars Melin ... Coastline
Lars Monat ... Forest
Lars Mossberg ... Remo
Lars Nilsson ... Black Web
Lars Nilsson ... Firework
Lars Nordén ... I Am Hunger
Lars Noren ... Hangover
Lars Normalm ... Plankton
Lars Ottosson ... Waterline
Lars Palmqvist "Lerta" ... Last Temptation, ... Scar Symmetry, Mirador
Lars Pollack ... Baltimoore
Lars Rapp ... Conviction
Lars Risberg ... Gregor Samsa
Lars Rosenberg ... Entombed, Serpent, ... Therion, Carbonized, Roachpowder
Lars Rulander ... Air Condition
Lars Sköld ... Leif Edling, Jupiter Society, Tiamat
Lars Ståhl ... Develop
Lars Sundström ... The Ugly
Lars Svensson "Lasse Pop" ... Pussy Galore
Lars Szöke ... Hypocrisy, Epitaph (2), WAR, ... Total War, The Abyss
Lars Säfsund "Lee Hunter" ... Enbound, Work Of Art
Lars Söderberg ... Diabolical, Maitreya
Lars Söderberg ... Seething
Lars T.C. Anderson ... Spit It Out, Lezlie Paice
Lars Thorsén ... Lucifer
Lars Thörnblom ... Zone Zero
Lars Tängmark ... Dawn, Choir Of Vengeance, ... King Of Asgard
Lars Uddberg ... Steamboat Willies
Lars Underdal ... Co Stone
Lars Walfridsson ... Majectic Vanguard, Taketh
Lars Wallgren ... Thunderhog
Lars Wallin "Walle" ... Co Stone
Lars Westerlund ... Mercenary Mustangs
Lars Wiklund ... Torsten
Lars Öhman ... Mr. Tiger, X-Union
Larsa Bengtsson ... Parazite, Livin' Parazite
Larsa Johansson ... Authorize
Larsa Åström ... Raceway
Lars-Eric Sundström ... Uppgång 34
Lars-Erik Grimelund ... Whipped Cream
Lars-Erik Wilkensson ... Tryckvåg
Lars-Gunnar Ström ... Zeit
Lars-Göran Persson ... Dream
Lars-Göran Petrov "L-G/Drutten" ... Morbid, Entombed, ... Comecon, Nihilist, Hypocrite, Nine, ... The Project Hate MCMXCIX
Lars-Göran Siljeholm ... Junction
Lars-Henry " Lasse" Karlsson ... Export
Lars-Håkan "Larsken" Svensson ... Inverted
Lars-Inge Strömberg "Singe" ... Stonewall Noise Orchestra
Lars-Ola Fritzon ... On The Rocks
Lars-Roland Svensson ... Promille
Larsy Sundberg ... King Size
Lars-Åke Eriksson ... Double Diamond
Lars-Åke Löwin ... Mason
Lars-Åke Nilsson ... Keen Hue
Lars-Åke Nilsson ... Air Condition
Larz Hjelm ... Phoenix, Nagazaki
Lasse Alehag ... Oxan, Unchained
Lasse Andersson ... Ambush
Lasse Andersson ... Status Two
Lasse Bjarnetoft ... Shame (2)
Lasse Byström ... Neon Rose
Lasse Bäcke ... Cryonic Temple
Lasse E. Engström ... Project L.E.E
Lasse Eliasson ... Lohengrin
Lasse Eriksson ... Centinex
Lasse Eriksson ... X-Ray
Lasse Falck ... Houston
Lasse Fallman ... Straight Up
Lasse Gidbo ... David Harleyson Powertrio
Lasse Grönnå ... Publikförakt AB
Lasse Gudmundsson ... Angel King, Lizard Eye, ... Revelations, Whimzy
Lasse Gustavsson ... Midas Touch
Lasse Hajagos "Dilldoo" ... Bedlam Erixon
Lasse Hallberg ... Clown
Lasse Hallin ... Maniac
Lasse Hedlund ... Raceway
Lasse Hedlund ... Cheyenne
Lasse Hermansson ... Headline (2)
Lasse Holmgren ... Ten Foot Pole, G.S.O, Bullhorn
Lasse Hägg ... Helium Head
Lasse Johansson ... Prospect
Lasse Johansson ... Stonelake
Lasse Johansson ... Movin' Globe
Lasse Johansson ... Stallion
Lasse Lekberg ... Guardian Angels, Snakepit Rebels
Lasse Levander ... Steve Eastside Band
Lasse Lundgren ... Scamps
Lasse Malmberg "Lace" ... Maeday
Lasse Martinsson ... The Storyteller
Lasse Mårtén ... Fistfunk
Lasse Nilsson Wihk ... Ellen B
Lasse Nordström ... Kalajs
Lasse Nyström ... Stitch
Lasse Olausson ... The Awesome Machine,Stoneflow
Lasse Olsson ... Spectra, Ellen B
Lasse Ortega ... Coercion
Lasse Pajula ... Spitfire
Lasse Starö ... Pax Romana
Lasse Wahlman ... Highbrow
Lasse Wester ... Pearly White, Thrashon
Lasse Vänngård ... Lotus (1)
Lawen Palmgren "Getaz" ... Kill, Likblek
Lawrence Dinamarca ... Loch Vostock, Carnal Forge
Lawrence Mackrory "Larry/Thermoss" ... F.K.Ü, Sportlov, ... Andromeda, Darkane, The Duskfall, Enemy Is Us, ... Forcefeed, Seething
Lawrence West ... Crawley, Damien
LE Ericsson ... Jar
L-E Limnell ... Guidance Of Sin
Leere (aka Casado) ... Silencer
Leffe Lindström ... Stitch
Leffe Persson ... Suspekt
Leffe Unnemark ... Redsun
Legion ... Dark Legions
Leif Alderskanz ... Swedes
Leif Andersson ... Allan Beddo Band, Metal Mercy
Leif Bergquist ... Purple Haze, Plebb
Leif Bertilsson ... Solution
Leif Carlsson ... Magic
Leif Collin "Gülf Tysk" ... Cryonic Temple
Leif Cuzner ... Nihilist
Leif Dristig ... Tyron
Leif Edling ... Candlemass, Abstrakt Algebra, ... The Project Hate MCMXCIX, Jupiter Society, ... Nemesis, Leif Edling, Krux
Leif Ehlin: ... Romance, Desert Rain
Leif Eriksson ... Winterlong
Leif Eriksson ... Maninnya Blade, Slowgate
Leif Erixon ... Damned Nation, Easy Street

Leif Fors ... Hazy
Leif Goldkuhl ... Colt 45
Leif Grabbe ... Angeline, Heel, M.A.D, Ramm
Leif Halldén ... Splash
Leif Hedberg ... Retrace
Leif Högberg ... Apostasy
Leif Isberg ... Grand Stand
Leif Jarl ... Promille
Leif Jergefeldt ... Fire
Leif Johansson ... Armatur
Leif Laestander ... Genie
Leif Larsson ... Maninnya Blade
Leif Larsson ... Clown
Leif Larsson ... Ram, Frozen Eyes, NME Within, Black Ingvars
Leif Liljegren "Lillen" ... Treat
Leif Ljungkvist ... Pax Romana
Leif Mases ... Kaipa
Leif Mårtensson ... Motvind
Leif Olsson ... Mandylion
Leif Persson ... Make Up
Leif Petersson ... Backyard Bullets
Leif Starck ... Crazy Visions, Tencider
Leif Strandqvist ... Adams Eve
Leif Sundin ... Treat
Leif Sundin ... Great King Rat, John Norum, Johansson Brothers
Leif Tarvainen ... Turning Point
Leif Thorpemo ... Vivid
Leif Training ... Baddies
Leif Westergren ... Flame
Leif Westfahl ... Dalton
Leif Zetterström ... Zeta
Leif Åhman ... Smiling Dog, HÅF Band
Leif Östman ... Panta Rei
Leini ... Guidance Of Sin
Lelle Gustavsson ... Psychotic Supper
Lempe Rodin ... Rainfall
Lena Dahlström "Lana Dale" ... Avalon, Tyrox
Lena Johansson ... Lifeline
Lena Karlsson ... Shore
Lena Melin ... Twilight
Lena Persson ... Cross Bow
Lena Pettersson ... Sinkadus
Lena Vikström ... Gallery (1)
Lennart "Stonte Kramer" ... Horoscope (2)
Lennart Andersson ... Spectra
Lennart Andersson ... Source (1)
Lennart Blomqvist ... Nattfrost
Lennart Esbjörnsson ... Tornado Babies
Lennart Glenberg-Eriksson ... Zello, Ebony Tears, Dog Faced Gods
Lennart Gustafsson "Lello" ... Queensland
Lennart Holmgren ... Solen Skiner
Lennart Johansson ... Print
Lennart Karlsson "Leonid" ... Seven Wishes
Lennart Kåge ... Blues Bag
Lennart Ljungdahl ... Wulcan
Lennart Löfgren ... Splash
Lennart Nilsson "Ledde" ... Side By Side
Lennart Nilsson ... Twelvestep
Lennart Nyberg ... Roterock
Lennart Salthammer ... Dr Booster
Lennart Specht ... Nostradameus, Pathos, Fejd
Lennart Staaf ... Scamps
Lennart Thand ... Carrie
Lennart Usterud ... Nebulosa
Lennart Widegren ... Boulevard, Midnight Blue, The Ungrateful
Lennart Östlund ... Chris Laney, Loud
Lenny Bladh "Venom/Blade" ... Pagan Rites, Incinerator, Lenny Blade, Funera,l Bullet, Devil Lee Rot, Hypnosia, Nominon
Leo Dahlin ... Black Dog
Leo Hansson ... Supergroupies
Leo Hed ... Lazy
Leo Margarit ... Pain Of Salvation
Leo Pignon ... A Canorous Quintet, Niden Div.187, This Ending
Lesli Liljegren ... Kerberos
Lestat ... Sister
Lexi ... Devlin
L-G Forsman ... TBC
L-G Jonasson ... Arise
L-G Persson ... The Storyteller
L-G Petrov ... (see Lars-Göran Petrov)
Liedheim ... Vanmakt, Nidrike
Liikböhr ... Svartnatt
Lik ... Helgedom, Svartrit
Liljan Liljekvist ... Left Hand Solution
Linda Emanuelsson ... Madrigal
Linda Gustafsson ... Seven Wishes
Linda Johansson ... Sinkadus
Linda Rudin ... Scumkill
Linda Setterborn ... Psyckadeli
Linder ... Semremedy
Linkan Andersson ... Livin' Parazite, Parazite
Linn Carlshaf ... Nattsmyg
Linn De Wilde ... Skald
Linnea Helgé (aka Liny Wood) ... Loud
Linnea Landstedt ... Tyranex
Linnéa Olsson ... Slingblade, Sonic Ritual
Linus ... Circuit
Linus Abrahamsson ... Mister Kite, Viceral Bleeding, Nocturnal Alliance, The Codex, Nonexist
Linus Bergström ... Amkeni
Linus Björklund "Germaniac" ... Delve, Verminious
Linus Brahamsson ... Peo
Linus Carlsson ... Kamchatka
Linus Ekström "Lord Khazad" ... Hydra (2), Siebenbürgen
Linus Fransson ... Skua
Linus Fritzson ... Chicks With Guns
Linus Henriksson ... Whipping Princess
Linus Holgersson ... Thunder, Two Eagles Request
Linus Johansson ... Marionette
Linus Jägerskog ... Burst
Linus Kåse ... Audiovision, Narnia, Flagship, Brightey Brison, Änglagård
Linus Köhl "Hellreaper" ... Triumphator
Linus Larsson ... Vidunder
Linus Lundgren ... Night
Linus Melchiorsen ... Los Sin Nombre, Maitreya, Powerdise, Demental, Isengard
Linus Nirbrant "Mr. Jones" ... The Dead, A Canorous Quintet, Guidance Of Sin, This Ending
Linus Nylen ... Godphobia
Linus Olsson ... Toxaemia
Linus Olsson ... The Scams
Linus Palmkvist ... Sludge
Linus Palmqvist ... Hellennium
Linus Pettersson ... Supreme Majesty
Linus Pilebo ... Humble Bee
Linus Pilebrand ... It Will Come, Beneath The Frozen Soil
Linus Sydstrand "Limpan" ... Alonzo
Linus Wiklund ... Roachpowder
Linus Wikström ... Frequency, Lothlorien
Liny Wood ... (See Linnéa Helgé)
Lisa Bohwalli Simonsson ... Siebenbürgen
Lisa Bouvin ... Fourever
Lisa Johansson ... Shadowgarden, Draconian
Lisa Svanström ... Frenzy
Liv Jagrell ... Sister Sin, Hysterica, Fuelhead
Lix Tetrax ... Mordichrist
Lizette von Panjott ... Spektrum, Cross
LO Johansson ... Thomas Larsson
Loke Rivano "Luke" ... Crazy Lixx
Loke Svarteld ... Arckanum
Lollo Andersson ... Cross
Lollo Sköllermark ... Twinball
Lollo Öberg ... Hazy, W.E.T (1)
Lonne Bergman ... Tribal Ink
Lord Therramon ... Dom Dracul
Lori Linstruth ... Ice Age, Mountain Of Power
Lotta Brolin ... Burning Engines
Lotta Högberg ... Scheitan
Lotta Höglin ... Beseech, The Mary Major
Lotta Pettersson ... Sunset Blade
Louise Eriksson ... Happy Hour
Louise Halldin ... It Will Come
Louse Hoffsten ... Sky High
Love Florgård ... Forkeyed
Love Forsberg ... I Am Hunger
Love Forsberg "Billy" ... Siena Root
Love Magnusson "Rob" ... Dynazty
Love Utterström "Dr. Mania" ... Dr. Living Dead
Lovisa Hallstedt ... Siebenbürgen
Lubbe Johansson ... Vanguard
Luca D'Andria "Isabelle" ... Cowboy Prostitutes
Lucas Ekström ... Alexander Lucas
Lukas Landerö (aka Sunesson) ... The Itch, Tenebre
Luciano Peirone ... Milky
Lucichrist ... Battlelust
Ludvig Eklund ... Abandoned Splhinx
Ludvig Engellau ... Demonical
Ludvig Friberg ... Memoria
Ludvig Johansson ... Apostasy
Ludvig Johansson ... Ghamorean Apostacy
Ludwig Larsson ... Mårran
Ludvig Svartz ... Soilwork
Ludwig Witt ... Shining, Grand Magus, Spiritual Beggars
Ludvig von Sersam "Ludde" ... Deathboot
Luis B. Galvez ... Tristitia
Lukas Bergis ... System Shock
Lukas Gren ... Madrigal
Lukas Häger "Spine" ... Reveal
Lukas Sunesson ... (See Lukas Landerö)
Lukasz Strach ... Ablaze
Lukasz ... Zombiekrieg
Luna ... Fear The Future
Lyris M. Karlsson ... Electric Earth
M Hellhammer ... (See Jan Axel Blomberg)
M. Lamming ... Spazmosity
M. Ljungberg ... Blue Orange
Maaw ... Worship
Mac ... Export
Mackan Andersson ... Kiss Of Thunder
Mackan ... Flash
Macke "Machabuzz" ... Rickshaw
Macke Strandberg ... Galaxy Safari
Madeleine Svensson ... Seven Tears
Mads Clausen ... Biscaya, Time Code Alpha
Magnus 155 ... Transport League, Massive Audio Nerve
Magnus Af Nestergaard ... Her Whisper
Magnus Ahlström "Alis Magnum" ... Yale Bate
Magnus Alakangas "Azazel" ... Satariel
Magnus Alkangas ... Morthirim
Magnus Alkarp ... Team Custard
Magnus Anderson ... Silicon Valley
Magnus Andersson ... The End
Magnus Andersson "Devo" ... Allegiance, IXXI, Nephenzy (Chaos Order), Misericordia, Horde Of Hel, Nefandus, Sargatanas Reign, Marduk, Dear Mutant, Devil's Whorehouse, Cardinal Sin, Overflash, Flagellated Seraph, Illfigure
Magnus Andersson ... Tale
Magnus Andersson (now Härsjö) ... Big Easy, Big Wave
Magnus Andersson ... Brickhouse
Magnus Andreasson "Adde" ... Hardcore Superstar, Dorian Grey
Magnus Arndtzen ... Stonesilk
Magnus Arens "Nasty" ... Gin N' It
Magnus Arnar ... Ground Mower, The Quill, King Chrome
Magnus Axx ... Swedish Erotica
Magnus Barthelsson ... Therion, Order Of Isaz
Magnus Bengtsson ... Universal Flytrap
Magnus Bergqvist ... Dexter Jones' Circus Orchestra
Magnus Bergström ... Draconian
Magnus Bierfeldt ... Pussy Galore
Magnus Birgersson ... Electra Top Raiders
Magnus Björk ... The Storyteller, Februari 91, Withered Beauty
Magnus Blom ... Solitude (1)
Magnus Blomkvist ... Mandylion
Magnus Boström ... Daemonicus
Magnus Brink ... Revenge
Magnus Broberg "Masse/Emperor Magus Caligula ... God Among Insects, Dark Funeral, Hypocrisy
Magnus Brolin ... Lifeless Image, Within Reach
Magnus Brunzell "Max Newman" ... Candy Roxx, Ban-Zai
Magnus Bureteg ... Taste
Magnus Bång ... Abuzimbel
Magnus Carlberg ... Ingo & Floyd
Magnus Carlsson ... Oberon
Magnus Carlsson "Mackan" ... Shaggy
Magnus Carlsson ... Ablaze My Sorrow
Magnus Carlsson ... Saffire
Magnus Cassersjö ... Universal Flytrap
Magnus Dahlquist ... Wildborn
Magnus Danielsson ... Muddy Road
Magnus Danneblad "Dan Blade" ... Mindless Sinner, Skinny Horse, Mindless, Demental
Magnus Delborg ... Horisont
Magnus Edberg ... Reenact
Magnus Egerbladh Öberg ... Shredhead
Magnus Ek ... Axenstar, Miscreant
Magnus Ekberg ... King Koole
Magnus Ekwall ... The Quill, Quil
Magnus Eliasson ... Sahara (2)
Magnus Emilsson ... Non Serviam
Magnus Engdahl ... Schizophrenic Circus, Dynamite Wasteland
Magnus Eriksson ... Tension
Magnus Eronen ... Moaning Wind, Sparzanza, Space Probe Taurus
Magnus Ewald ... The Mist Of Avalon
Magnus Fasth ... Captor
Magnus Flink "Flingan" ... Deceiver
Magnus Florin ... Lava Engine
Magnus Forsberg ... Bombs Of Hades, Tribulation (1)
Magnus Frid ... Optimystical
Magnus Fritz ... Abuzimbel
Magnus Gehlin ... In The Colonnades
Magnus Gillberg "Nagrinn" ... Misteltein
Magnus Grundström ... Absorbing The Pain, Killer Bee
Magnus Gustavsson ... Angelize
Magnus Gustavsson ... Happy Cakes, Zeit
Magnus Gustavsson ... Fatal Smile
Magnus Göransson ... Mindfuel
Magnus Göransson ... Silverfish
Magnus Hall ... Angelize
Magnus Hansson ... Wiz
Magnus Hansson ... Power Unit, Miscellany
Magnus Hansson ... Harvey Wallbanger
Magnus Hansson ... Psyckadeli
Magnus Hasselstam ... Gudars Skymning
Magnus Hay ... White Cat
Magnus Hedin "Bonum" ... Mother Ice Dog, Overflash, Axewitch, Downbound Train
Magnus Hedlund ... Big Business
Magnus Hedquist ... Death Breath
Magnus Hellman "Dirk" ... Goddefied
Magnus Henriksson ... Eclipse
Magnus Hoff ... The Darksend, Von Benzo
Magnus Holmberg ... Harmony (2), Darkwater
Magnus Hultgren ... Demental
Magnus Hultman ... Cross Bow, Cult Of The Fox
Magnus Häggman ... Abandon
Magnus Hälleblad ... Danger (1)
Magnus Hällström ... Rough Rockers
Magnus Högdahl ... Skull Parade, Black Dog
Magnus Hörberg ... Sad Wings
Magnus Hörnqvist ... Calilio, Treasure Land
Magnus Ingels ... Enemy Is Us
Magnus Jacobsson ... VII Gates
Magnus Jacobsson ... Miss Beahaviour
Magnus Jakobsson ... Armatur
Magnus Jarl ... Straight Up, Sleazy Roze, Axewitch
Magnus Jernström ... Mangrove
Magnus Johansson ... Pain Of Salvation, Project Hate
Magnus Johansson ... Velvet Crash
Magnus Jonsson ... Jimmy Nielsen & Band
Magnus Jonsson ... Oberon
Magnus Jönsson ... Damned Nation, Easy Street, Shadowland
Magnus Karkea ... Obrero
Magnus Karlsson ... Chainwreck
Magnus Karlsson ... King Koole
Magnus Karlsson ... Renaissance Of Fools, Thalamus, Leech, Machina
Magnus Karlsson ... Last Tribe, Midnight Sun, Magnus Karlsson's Freefall, Planet Alliance, The Codex
Magnus Karlsson ... Altar
Magnus Karlsson-Mård ... Outremer, Sorcery
Magnus Klavborn ... Engel, Headplate
Magnus Klintö ... Mercy
Magnus Knutas ... Kaross
Magnus Kristensson ... Mister Kite
Magnus Kristiansson "Manne" ... Wagabond
Magnus Källström ... My Endless Wishes
Magnus Kärnebro (aka Lindgren) ... Gin Lady, Black Bonzo
Magnus Könberg ... Psycho Circus
Magnus Lange ... Cheerse
Magnus Larsson ... Dozer
Magnus Larsson My Dead Addiction, Sanzia, Zap Yankefy
Magnus Larsson ... Destynation, Eternia
Magnus Leijon ... Solsting
Magnus Leo ... Third Stone
Magnus Lind ... Skull Parade, Calilio, Treasure Land, Blue Balls
Magnus Lind ... Last Temptation
Magnus Lindberg ... Cult Of Luna, Lineout
Magnus Lindblom ... Persuader
Magnus Lindbloom ... Cervello
Magnus Lindgren ... Waterclime
Magnus Lindgren (now Kärnebro) ... Black Bonzo
Magnus Lindh ... Keystone
Magnus Lindh ... Warhammer, Seven
Magnus Lindh ... Tanaque
Magnus Lindqvist ... Elevener
Magnus Lindqvist ... Reazon
Magnus Lindvall ... Maze Of Torment, Soils Of Fate
Magnus Linhardt ... Falconer, Choir Of Vengeance
Magnus Ljungkvist ... Trazer
Magnus Ludvigsson ... Neocori
Magnus Lund ... Mac & Ploids
Magnus Lundbäck "Lillis" ... Tai Rose, The Ungrateful
Magnus Lundin ... M-Train
Magnus Lundström "Magnum" ... Blazing Guns
Magnus Löfgren ... Mort
Magnus Lövgren ... Enigmatic
Magnus M. Jonsson ... Steve Roper Band
Magnus Malte Olsson ... God Kills
Magnus Mets ... Mistie
Magnus Mild ... Majestic Dimension
Magnus Mörth ... Scudiero
Magnus Nelin ... Cherry Red, Roulette
Magnus Nilsson ... The Grand Trick
Magnus Nilsson "Manuck" ... Time Requiem, God B.C, Richard Andersson, Richard Andersson's Space Odyssey
Magnus Nilsson ... The Carpet Knights
Magnus Noberg "Nobby" Nation, Dionysus, Saint Deamon
Magnus Nordh ... Time Requiem, Majestic
Magnus Nordlund ... Headline (1)
Magnus Nordlund ... White Night
Magnus Nyström ... TRP
Magnus Nörrenberg ... Brickhouse
Magnus Odéen "C.M." ... White Line
Magnus Olsfelt ... The Crown (Crown Of Throns)
Magnus Olsson ... Meadows End
Magnus Olsson ... Sacrifice
Magnus Olsson "Pantho" .. X-Hale, Fortune (1), Blind Alley
Magnus Olsson "Balou" ... Panic
Magnus Olsson "Draken" ... Electric Earth, Rat Salad
Magnus Olsson ... Sten
Magnus Olsson ... Demons Of Dirt
Magnus Olsson ... Septic Grave
Magnus Olsson ... Proud
Magnus Paulsson ... G.O.L.D
Magnus Pelander ... Norrsken, Witchcraft
Magnus Persson ... Hellspray
Magnus Persson ... Kingsize

NAME INDEX

Magnus Persson ... Hide The Knives
Magnus Persson ... Moonstruck
Magnus Persson ... Hyperborean
Magnus Persson ... Stoneflow
Magnus Petersson ... Paradize (1)
Magnus Pettersson "Manne" ... X-Hale, Fortune (1)
Magnus Pettersson "MP" ... Violent Work Of Art
Magnus Pettersson ... Fatal Attraction
Magnus Pettersson ... Corporation 187
Magnus Qvist ... Gregor Samsa
Magnus Rosén ... Billionaires Boys Club, Fullforce, Heartbreak Radio, Keegan, Planet Alliance, Shame (1), Von Rosen, Hammerfall, (Arose)
Magnus Rosén ... Fagin
Magnus Rosling ... Wham Glam Boys
Magnus Rydman ... Rise And Shine
Magnus Sahlgren ... Tiamat, Dismember, Lake Of Tears
Magnus Sandberg ... Saltmine, Blackwood
Magnus Sedenberg "Mankan" ... Baltimoore, Disruption, Crucified Barbara, Silver Seraph, Spawn Of Possession, Tyron
Magnus Severin ... Valenze
Magnus Sivertsson ... Skywalkers
Magnus Sjölin ... Agony
Magnus Sjöquist ... Twilight Zone
Magnus Skoglind "Baus" ... Red Surface
Magnus Stenberg ... Castillon
Magnus Stenvinkel ... Nerved, Powerbreeze
Magnus Strandberg ... Sonic Temple
Magnus Strömberg ... Biscaya
Magnus Styrén ... Akilles
Magnus Svensson ... Sonic Syndicate
Magnus Svensson ... Jesusexercise
Magnus Söderman "Sudden" ... Zeelion, Slapdash, The Project Hate MCMXCIX, Inrage, Rosicrucian
Magnus Tallåker ... Hellspray, Arrow, Renegade (1)
Magnus Tengby "Lars-Ingvar" ... Black Ingvars
Magnus Thorman ... Veni Domine
Magnus Thorn ... CC Rock
Magnus Thurin ... Cryonic Temple
Magnus Thörnkvist ... Within Reach
Magnus Timmerås ... Rickshaw
Magnus Trulsson ... Emerald
Magnus Törnkvist ... Lifeless Image
Magnus Ulfstedt ... Eclipse, Torch, Grand Design
Magnus Van Wassenaar ... Mindless (Sinner)
Magnus Vesterlund ... Black Rose
Magnus Vinblad ... Plastic Pride
Magnus Wahlberg ... The Itch
Magnus Wall ... Thronaeon, Soulbreach, Abhoth, Godhate, Haterush, Vicious, (Grand Exit)
Magnus Weidenmo ... Spin Gallery, Deacon Street Project
Magnus Wennerholm ... Cavokey
Magnus Westman ... Mindfuel
Magnus Wikholm ... Gallantry, God Kills
Magnus Wikmark ... Deviant, St.Erik
Magnus Windo ... Plain Zero
Magnus Winterwild (aka Eriksson) ... Axenstar
Magnus Wohlfart ... Broken Dagger, Dibbukim, Vanmakt, Yggdrasil, Anti-Christian Assault, Nae'blis
Magnus Zotterman ... Mindjive
Magnus Åsard ... Closer (1)
Magnus Åhlström ... Tomterockers
Magnus Öberg ... Heel, Ramm
Magnus Ödling "Infaustus/Necroghoul" ... Blackwinds, Fenria, Setherial
Magnus Öhlander ... Cipher System
Magnus Östborg ... Liquidust, Reckless
Magnus Österman ... Destiny
Magnus Östgren ... Beardfish
Magnus Östlund ... Whiteness
Magnus Caligula ... (See Masse Broberg)
Mahan Ahmadi ... Havok
Maja Olsson Sax ... Carizma Rain
Majja Persson ... Fourever
Make Pesonen ... Eternal Darkness
Malena Bengtsson ... Temperance
Malin Almén ... Hin Haley
Malin Andersson ... Lights Out
Malin Ekholm Drain (S.T.H), Aphrodite, Swedish Metal Aid
Malin Ekstrand ... Brickhouse
Malin Karlsson ... Fourever
Malin Quick ... Rydell & Quick
Malin Yildiz ... The Mist Of Avalon
Mally Hoxell ... (See Mats Håxell)
Malte Nordström ... Cross Bow, Cult Of The Fox
Mange Ericsson ... Steel Arrows
Mange Roos ... Hypnosia
Manne Engström ... Fatal Embrace, Lavett
Manne Ikonen ... Book Of Hours
Manne Svensson ... Epitaph (1)
Manuel Gonzales ... (see Anders Johansson)
Manuel Korsoski ... Major N.A
Manuel Lewys ... Crash The System, Machinery
Manx Gustafsson (Tummalid) ... Debbie Ray, Plan 9
Marc Gransten ... Trilogy
Marc Grewe ... Comecon
Marcel Jacob ... Radioactive, Billionaires Boys Club, Deacon Street, Europe, Impulsia, Jim Jidhed, Power, Johansson Brothers, Last Autumn's Dream, Lion's Share, Yngwie Mlmsteen, John Norum, The Poodles, Richard Andersson's Space Odyssey, Thomas Vikström, Humanimal, Locomotive Breath, Speedy Gonzales, Human Clay, Highbrow,Talisman
Marcelo Quiroga "Marc Quee" ... Marc Quee, Talisman
Marco Viita "Marc White" ... Sanchez
Marco A. Nicosia ... Silverdollar, Fi5th Reason, Hexenhaus
Marco Aro ... Face Down, The Haunted, The Resistance
Marco Ayala ... Seventribe
Marco Bjurling ... Redsun
Marco Eronen ... The Duskfall
Marco Hildén ... Cult Of Luna
Marco Kuru ... Twelvestep
Marco Ledri ... Soniq Circus
Marco Malasagna ... Acis
Marco Nicolaidis ... Crystal Eyes
Marco Oxala ... Psychotic Supper
Marco Pennbrant ... Slow Train
Marco Tapani ... Masquerade, Flintstens Med Stanley
Marcu Lehto ... Kansas City Rollers
Marcus "Machabuzz" ... Rickshaw
Marcus Aldén ... Mojobone
Marcus Andersson ... Chive
Marcus Andersson ... New Breed
Marcus Ankarberg ... Sinners Burn
Marcus Backlund ... The Storyteller
Marcus Bergman ... Madrigal
Marcus Berndtsson ... Elsy Band
Marcus Bertilsson ... Inevitable End, Miseration
Marcus Bigren ... Hollow
Marcus Boholm ... Smokey Bandits
Marcus Brandel ... Seventribe
Marcus Bressler ... Denial
Marcus Bäckbrant "Markko" ... Brewmaster, Devil's Whorehouse, Hanvayoth, Naglfar
Marcus Calmborg ... Lucy
Marcus Christensen ... Her Whisper
Marcus Dahlström ... Safemode, Blidside
Marcus Dahlström ... Coldtears
Marcus E. Norman "Vargher" ... Bewitched, Vintersorg, Throne Of Ahaz, Ancient Wisdom
Marcus Edvardsson ... Souldrainer, Chasticement, Aeon, In Battle, Sanctification
Marcus Ehlin ... Siebenbürgen, Devlin
Marcus Eliasson ... Heel, Ramm
Marcus Enochsson ... Soniq Circus
Marcus Eriksson ... Anxious
Marcus Fors ... Vornth
Marcus Fren ... Sanzia
Marcus Fritiofsson ... Loaded
Marcus Hammarström ... Sterbhaus, Elvira Madigan
Marcus Hamrin "Mackie" ... Kaptain Sun
Marcus Hanser ... Nerved
Marcus Hellgren ... Sherlock Brothers
Marcus Hinze ... Mortuus
Marcus Häll "Hell" ... Mordant
Marcus Högberg "Mack Daniels" ... Stingray
Marcus Höher ... Platitude
Marcus Jidell ... Evergrey, Hysterica, Alfonzetti, Pain, Jekyll & Hyde, The Ring, Impulsia, Jupiter Society, Marcus Jidell
Marcus Joha ... Desultor
Marcus Johansson ... Amsvartner
Marcus Johansson ... Voyager
Marcus Jonsson "Mackan" ... Genocrush Ferox, Insision, Pandemonium, Flaggelation, Bloodshed, Spazmosity, Decadence
Marcus Jäderholm Mother Misery, Staiger, Greyhate, RFP
Marcus Klack ... Fistfunk
Marcus Käck ... Shenerah
Marcus Källström ... Sky High, Death Organ, Jammer, Six Feet Under, Stonecake, Bacon
Marcus Liliequist ... Radioactive, Spin Gallery, Karmakanic, Jim Jidhed, The Flower Kings, Deacon Street
Marcus Lindelöf "Demigorgon Bile" ... Cult Disciples
Marcus Losbjer ... Midfortune, Wolverine
Marcus Lundberg ... Devian
Marcus Lundgren ... Neondaze
Marcus Melander ... Cervello
Marcus Mustafa ... Gosh!
Marcus Nilsson ... Viceral Bleeding
Marcus Nilsson ... Zilch
Marcus Nordenberg ... Lion's Share
Marcus Nowak ... CC Rock, Heads Or Tales
Marcus Nygaard ... Amsvartner
Marcus Nygren ... 8 Point Rosie, Enbound
Marcus Olofsson ... Terrortory, Searing I
Marcus Olsson ... Mozkovitch
Marcus Palm ... Loaded
Marcus Pedersen "Leviathan" ... The Black (2), Crypt Of Kerberos
Marcus Pehrsson "Stene" ... Last Laugh (1)
Marcus Persson ... Niva
Marcus Pousette "Kelly Morgue" ... Panzer Princess
Marcus Rosell ... Assault
Marcus Rudenvall ... Bloodlit
Marcus Sjöblom ... Cleopatra
Marcus Sjösund ... 8 Point Rosie
Marcus Sjöwall ... Shineth
Marcus Sköld ... Dreamland
Marcus Stark ... Mustain
Marcus Strandberg ... Chive
Marcus Sundquist ... Heave
Marcus Sunesson ... The Haunted, Witchery, The Crown (Crown Of Thorns), Engel
Marcus Tena ... Triumphator
Marcus Thorell ... The Embodied
Marcus Törnquist ... Prime
Marcus Uggla "Mao" ... Mindshift, Blowsight
Marcus Wahlström ... Subztain
Marcus Weimer ... Sten
Marcus Wesslén ... Eternal Lies, By Night, Dead By April, Trendkill
Marcus Von Boisman ... Dry Dive
Marcus Åblad ... Nestor
Marek Dobrowolski ... Dawn Of Time, One Man Army & The Undead Quartet, Reclusion
Margaretha Folkesson ... Sky High
Maria Eriksson ... Beast
Maria Eriksson "Bitchie" ... Hysterica
Maria Isaacs ... Big Business
Maria Landberg "Mia" ... Livin' Sacrifice
Maria Larsson ... Paganus
Maria Rådsten ... The Murder Of My Sweet, Mountain Of Power, Divinefire, Mercury Fang, Divinefire, Misth
Maria Sjöholm ... Drain (S.T.H)
Maria Tern (aka Landberg) "RockZilla" ... Hysterica, Aphrodite, Shalalee
Maria Weimer ... Sten
Mariana Holmberg ... Left Hand Solution
Marianne Flynner ... Clown
Marianne Hall ... Aphrodite, Livin' SacShalalee
Marie Andersson ... Publikförakt AB
Marie Dagerborn (now Skoglund) ... Livin' Sacrifice
Marie Melin ... Side By Side
Marie-Louise Ehrs (now Gunnarsson) "Mackan" ... Society Gang Rape
Marika Andersson ... Layout
Marika Willstedt ... Spin Gallery, Impulsia
Mario Santos Ramos ... Hate Ammo, Chainsaw
Mario Somenzi ... Zane
Marios Iliopoulos ... Ruined Soul
Marita Vikström ... Negro
Marius Tömte ... Space Probe Taurus
Mark Boals ... Yngwie Malmsteen, The Codex
Mark Buffalo ... Viperine
Mark E Gunnardo ... CC Rock, Nocturnal Alliance
Mark Tholin ... Magnolia
Mark Tysper ... Tommy Tysper & The Kids
Mark Zonder ... Cans
Mark Åkerblom ... Side By Side
Marko Grönholm ... Peo
Marko Lehto ... Von Panzer
Marko Nuutinen ... Wild One
Marko Palmén ... Evocation
Marko Salmi ... Vulcano
Marko Siila ... Enemies Swe
Marko Tervonen ... The Crown (Crown Of Throns)
Marku Larsson (Väkevä) ... Cartago
Markus Albertsson ... Tad Morose, Bloodbound
Markus Aldén ... Sky High, Bacon
Markus Andé ... Månegarm
Markus Berg ... Stallion Four
Markus Berglund "El Barkus" ... Mother's Hope
Markus Edvardsson ... Sanctification, Aeon
Markus Ekborg ... Enjoy The View
Markus Elfström ... Prospect
Markus Fagervall ... Liquid Scarlet
Markus Fristedt "Mark Black" ... Dream Evil, Notre Dame, Massive Audio Nerve, Ton Of Bricks
Markus Gunnarsson ... M.A.C
Markus Görsch ... Memorium
Markus Harju ... Omnispawn
Markus Hill ... Slumber
Markus Hinze ... Ondskapt
Markus Isberg ... Machinery
Markus Jaan ... Swedens Finest
Markus Janis ... Corrosive Carcass
Markus Johansson ... Bloodlit
Markus Johansson ... Fatal Smile (2)
Markus Johansson ... Egonaut
Markus Johnsson ... Eucharist
Markus Karlsson ... Johan Randén
Markus Kinell ... Mindfuel
Markus Kvarnlöf "Adimirion" ... Vemoth
Markus Källström ... Mojobone
Markus Lidström ... Embracing
Markus Lindahl "Big Mac" ... Feral
Markus Lindström ... Lithany
Markus Linfeldt ... Fuck Bitch
Markus Lundberg ... Sarea, Sargatana's Reign
Markus Neuendorf ... Kaross
Markus Nilsson ... Body Core
Markus Nilsson ... Soniq Circus
Markus Nilsson ... Deville
Markus Nordberg ... Cemetary (1213), Ceremonial Oath
Markus Nordenberg ... Big Price, Coastline Ride
Markus Nowak ... Renegade Five, Heads Or Tales, CC Rock
Markus Persson "Mackan" ... Merrygold
Markus Pesonen "Make/The Black" ... The Black (2)
Markus Ramström ... Black Web
Markus Rüden ... Carbonized, Morpheus
Markus Rytilahti ... Syconaut
Markus Sigfridsson ... 7Days, Darkwater, Harmony (2)
Markus Sjökvist "Fjelltrone" ... Fjelltrone, Setback
Markus Sukuvaara ... Silverfish
Markus Sundbom ... Assailant
Markus Sundquist ... Nightscape
Markus Wallén ... Body Core
Markus Wiberg ... Dirty Passion
Markus Ydkvist ... Million
Markus Åkebo ... Zonaria
Markus Åkesson ... Deville
Markus Östman ... Da President
Marre Eriksson ... Misert Loves Co., Lost Souls, Damien
Marry Virtanen "Straight-G" ... Vörgus, Pandemonic, Internal Decay
Marten Cederberg ... Absurd
Martin Svensson "Metal" ... The Generals
Martin Nilsson "Stray" ... Sonic Temple
Martin Ahx ... Darkified
Martin Albinsson ... Nattsmyg
Martin Alowerson ... Reenact
Martin Anderson ... Subcyde
Martin Andersson ... Astrophobos
Martin Andersson ... Necrocurse, Ton Of Bricks, Elixir, Sabotage
Martin Andreasson ... Bult
Martin Axenrot "Axe/Devastator/Skeleton" ... Bloodbath, Nifelheim, Opeth, Triumphator, Funeral Frost, Satanic Slaughter, Nephenzy (Chaos Order), Witchery
Martin Bengtsson ... Armageddon, Arch Enemy, Lechery
Martin Berg ... Sign
Martin Bergman ... Blinded Colony
Martin Bergman ... Evildoer
Martin Bermheden ... Mort
Martin Bohgard ... Cervello
Martin Boman ... Marble Arch, Evercry
Martin Brandström ... Dark Tranquillity
Martin Brisshäll ... Motherpearl
Martin Brorsson ... S.K.U.R.K, Flegma
Martin Bullit ... Latex
Martin Carlsson ... Hell N' Diesel
Martin Carlsson ... Pagandom
Martin Claësson (now Härenstam) ... Narnia
Martin Danielsson ... Limiless
Martin Danielsson ... Malaise
Martin Davidsson ... Increave, Evergrace
Martin Eklöv ... Splattered Mermaids, Viceral Bleeding
Martin Emil ... Eleven Pictures
Martin Ericsson ... Shaker
Martin Eriksson "E-Type" ... The Poodles, Maninnya Blade
Martin Eriksson ... Shubend
Martin Erlandsson "Rhyder" ... Chains
Martin Eversholt "Grimner" ... Mordgrim
Martin Fairbanks ... The Graviators, Nymf
Martin Falkeström "Marty" ... Vanity Blvd
Martin Floberg "Marvin Flowberg/The Butcher" ... Enbound
Martin Fogander ... Los Sin Nombre, Powerdise, Maitreya
Martin Franzén ... Dechas
Martin Friberg ... Tube Screamer
Martin Furst ... Pax
Martin Furängen ... Lost Horizon, Luciferion
Martin Fürst ... Sten Sandberg
Martin Färdigh ... Coldtears
Martin Germ Bermheden ... Enshrined
Martin Ghaoui ... Screwball.Sthlm
Martin Glaever ... Arsenite
Martin Grahage ... The Fuzes
Martin Gustafsson "Draupin" ... Darkified, Plague Warhead, Allegience
Martin Gärdeman "Grimulv" ... Vergelmer
Martin Haglund ... Pound, Astral Doors
Martin Halfdan ... Infernal (666), Necrophobic
Martin Hallberg ... Screamer
Martin Hallin "Khaos" ... Nephenzy (Chaos Order)
Martin Hambitzer ... Deville
Martin Hamrén ... Evolution
Martin Hanner ... Skyfire, Chaos Feeds Life
Martin Hansén "Demon" ... Nifelheim
Martin Hedberg ... Motherlode, Tornado Soup
Martin Hederberg ... Close Quarters
Martin Hedin ... Andromeda
Martin Hedström ... Biscaya, Pagan, Hawk
Martin Hellström ... Assault
Martin Henricsson ... Souldivider
Martin Henriksson ... Dark Tranquillity
Martin Heppich ... Troubled Horse
Martin Hjerpe ... The Storyteller

Martin Hogebrandt .... Suicidal Winds, Conspiracy, Mindblaster, Legions Of War
Martin Hosselton "Sweet" .... Crash Diet
Martin Hoväng .... Psycho Circus
Martin H-Son .... Full Metal Jacketz
Martin Hållqvist .... Facequake
Martin Häggström .... Moahni Moahna, ZooL, Angtoria
Martin Högvall .... Barrelhouse
Martin Jensen .... Attention (1)
Martin Joelsson .... Hell N' Diesel
Martin Johansen .... Hide The Knives
Martin Johansson .... Nestor
Martin Johansson .... Haze
Martin Jämtlid .... Zen
Martin Karlegård .... Reptile Smile
Martin Karlsson .... Cellout
Martin Karlsson .... Hydrogen
Martin Karlsson "KK" .... Close Quarters
Martin Karlsson .... Lechery, By Night
Martin Karlsson .... Livin' Parazite, Parazite, Revengia, Eternal Lies
Martin Karlsson .... Sideburn
Martin Karlsson .... Bloodshed, Mykorrhiza, Die Hard
Martin Karlsson .... Hydrogen
Martin Karlsson .... Wiz
Martin Karlsson .... Madrigal
Martin Knutar .... Divine Sin
Martin Kronlund .... Elevener, Jet Trail, Lotus (2), Salute, Silent Call, Dogface, Gypsy Rose, Reece/Kronlund, Develop, Lover Under Cover
Martin Källström .... Corroded
Martin Langen .... Faithful Darkness
Martin Larsson .... Fi5th Reason
Martin Larsson .... House Of Shakira, Mercury Fang, Misth
Martin Larsson .... Skraeckoedlan
Martin Larsson .... White Cat
Martin Larsson .... At The Gates, House Of Usher
Martin Latvala .... As You Drown
Martin Lind .... Skua
Martin Lindberg .... New Bulsara
Martin Lindberg .... Hellennium
Martin Linde "Zarathustra" .... Vandöd
Martin Lindström .... Von Panzer
Martin Lindkvist .... Nine
Martin Lopez .... Amon Amarth, Opeth
Martin Lous-Christensen .... Queen Obscene
Martin Lundgren .... Drabness
Martin Löwe Sörensen .... Dragonland
Martin Magnusson .... Convinced
Martin Mellström .... Moonlight Agony
Martin Mendez .... Opeth
Martin Meyerman .... Massive Audio Nerve, Zombiekrieg
Martin Michaelsson "Fjalar" .... Unchained (2), Istapp
Martin Missy .... Obrero
Martin Nadersson .... Heed
Martin Nilsson .... Souldivider
Martin Nilsson .... No Rules
Martin Nilsson .... Lucid Legend
Martin Norén .... Admonish
Martin Ohlsson .... Mothercake
Martin Olsson .... Cap Outrun
Martin Olsson .... Zilch
Martin Olsson .... Vitality
Martin Olsson .... Flegma, Devilicious
Martin Olsson .... Sabotage
Martin Palme .... Physical Attraction
Martin Pedersen .... Viceral Bleeding
Martin Persner .... Roswell
Martin Persson .... Sins Of Omission, Mörk Gryning, Dismember
Martin Persson .... Sarea
Martin Persson .... Unsolved
Martin Petersson .... Zombiekrieg, Nominon
Martin Pettersson .... Shubend
Martin Prim .... Vidunder
Martin Pudas .... Daemonicus, Hate Ammo
Martin Qvist "Goatnecro" .... The Ancient's Rebirth, Ablaze My Sorrow, Immemoreal
Martin Ramberg .... Rising
Martin Restin .... Solar Dawn, Enthralled
Martin Rydin .... Memoria
Martin Rydlund .... Seven Tears
Martin Sandberg "Max Martin/White" .... It's Alive
Martin Sandvik .... Hardcore Superstar
Martin Schabbauer .... Print
Martin Scherman .... Leash
Martin Schirenc .... Diabolicum
Martin Schulman .... Centinex, Demonical, Interment
Martin Schönherr "Schreck" .... Virgin Sin, Fleshcut, Splattered Mermaids, Deranged
Martin Solymar "Black Curse" .... Kill
Martin Stangefeldt .... Demon Cleener
Martin Stenquist .... Dyngrak
Martin Stridh .... Armauk
Martin Ström .... Asteroid
Martin Sundberg .... Mass Murder Agenda
Martin Svensson .... Siena Root
Martin Svensson .... Anaemia
Martin Svensson .... Slip Into Silk
Martin Sventorp .... Frank Thomsen
Martin Sällström "Necro" .... Pest
Martin Söderqvist .... Debbie Ray, Hostile Cell
Martin Sörbom .... Hoarse
Martin Thornell .... Nifters
Martin Thorsén "Vires" .... The Darksend
Martin Tilander .... Conviction, Fierce Conviction, Freternia, Crystal Eyes, Sanchez
Martin Tjusling .... Eldrimner
Martin Tomander "Slim" .... Electric Boys
Martin Torsson .... Evocation
Martin Tronson "Marty" .... Babylon Bombs
Martin Ulvgård .... Svarte Pan
Martin Unosson "Mart Wildheart" .... Misfortune, Gasoline Queen
Martin van Drunen .... The Project Hate MCMXCIX
Martin Vangbo .... Slip Into Silk
Martin Viberg .... My Endless Wishes
Martin Viklander .... Eternal Oath
Martin Von Druinen .... Comecon
Martin Von Schmalensee .... Power
Martin Westerstrand Skans .... Lillasyster, LOK, Rallypack, Scarpoint
Martin Wezowski "Bollack" ... Merrygold, Burning Engines, Original Sin, The Drugs, Majestic, From Behind
Martin Wiberg "Marino Funketti" .... Mac Bladgick
Martin Wijkström .... Burning Saviours
Martin Wiklund .... Stardog
Martin Zettmar .... Tyranex
Martin Åkesson .... Impious
Martin Öhman .... Fuzzdevil, Six Pack Sonic
Martin Östman .... Da President
Martina Axén .... Drain (S.T.H), Aphrodite
Martina Edoff .... The Poodles, Novak
Martina Hornbacher .... Therion
Marty Martszchanty .... Mindshift
Martyn Karlsson .... Bai Bang
Masse Broberg "Emperor Magus Caligula" .... Demonoid, Sanctifica, Sportlov, Dominion Caligola, Spasmodid, The Project Hate MCMXCIX
Mathew Bethancourt .... Dexter Jones' Circus Orchestra
Mathias Adamsson .... Vermin
Mathias Adolfson "Mr. Pillow" .. Stonewall Noise Orchestra
Mathias Beckius .... Soniq Circus
Mathias Bladh .... Falconer
Mathias Bäck .... Sartinas
Mathias Edin .... Apostasy
Mathias Elovsson .... Kapoor
Mathias Ericsson .... Unchained (2), Nefaritus
Mathias Fiebig .... Carve
Mathias Färm .... The Bereaved, Nine
Mathias GarGarnas .... Benny Jansson
Mathias Garneij .... Plan Three
Mathias Garnås .... Ride The Sky, Xsavior
Mathias Gattefors "Matte" .... Blue Matter
Mathias Gustaffsson .... Firestone
Mathias Hedestig .... Caliber 69
Mathias Hellström .... Feed
Mathias Henrysson .... Chainwreck
Mathias Holm .... Mindsplit, Mathias Holm
Mathias Johansson "Matt The Desert Fox" .... Axis Powers, Suicidal Winds
Mathias Johansson .... U.N.IT
Mathias Järrebring "Farbaute" .... Prophanity
Mathias Kamijo "Nazgul/M Flatline" .... Algaion, Vergelmer, Nephenzy (Chaos Order), The Abyss, Morifade
Mathias Karlsson .... Macrocosmic Emotions
Mathias Lodmalm .... Sundown, Cemetary (1213), Lake Of Tears, Fatal Embrace
Mathias Lönngren .... Through Time Tomorrow
Mathias Marklund .... Waterclime
Mathias Mohlin .... Sanctification
Mathias Nilsson .... Danger (2), Mindcollapse, Skogen, Entrails
Mathias Nylén .... Live Elephant
Mathias Persson .... Metal Mercy
Mathias Pettersson "Matt Cosby" .... Pompei Nights
Mathias Pettersson .... Calm
Mathias Roitto .... Deed
Mathias Rosén .... Deletion, Eye
Mathias Samuelsson .... Double Deuce
Mathias Sandquist .... World Of Silence
Mathias Svensson "Skadeglade" .... Styggelse
Mathias Söderström .... Demon Seed
Mathias Ulfheim .... TNT
Mathias Wendt .... Negro
Mathias Wilhelmsson .... Veni Domine, Bishop Garden
Mathias Öjermark .... Obrero
Mathilda Lückner .... Peo
Maths Sundwall .... Lohengrin
Matias Klint .... De Tveksamma
Matias Kupiainen .... Ruined Soul
Matilda Karlsson .... Mykorrhiza
Matilda Persson .... Fourever
Mats Almstedt .... Tumbleweed
Mats Andersson .... Blacksmith
Mats Andersson .... Twilight Project
Mats Andersson "Sammy" .... Cheri
Mats Andersson .... Överslag
Mats Andersson .... Sleeping Ape
Mats Andersson .... Bullhorn, Mainline
Mats Andersson .... Glory Bells (Band)
Mats Andersson .... Evolution
Mats Andreasson .... VII Gates
Mats Annemalm .... Abuzimbel
Mats Arnesen .... Witchcraft
Mats Bengtsson .... King Koole
Mats Bergentz .... Silver Mountain, Mister Kite
Mats Berggren "Mabbe" .... Moondark
Mats Berggren .... Miss Willis
Mats Berglén .... Revenge
Mats Berglund .... Speednauts
Mats Bergman .... Bootleg
Mats Bjuhr .... Red Surface
Mats Björklund .... Quadruple
Mats Björkman .... Aces High
Mats Björkman "Mappe" .... Candlemass, Zoic, Nemesis, ATC
Mats Blomberg "Nauthis" .... Prophanity, Inverted
Mats Blomstrand .... Steve Eastside Band
Mats Blyckert .... Abhoth, Suffer, Dead Awaken
Mats Bostedt .... Develop, Gypsy Rose, Tai Rose
Mats Brandström .... Locomotive Breath
Mats Brandt .... Brigada Illuminada
Mats Byström "Matt" .... Paradise (2), Sergeant, Boogietryck, Desert Rain, Killer Bee
Mats Dacke .... It Will Come
Mats Dahlberg "Dalton" .... Speedy Gonzales, Treat, Dalton, Highbrow, Yngwie Malmsteen
Mats Dahlberg .... Galaxy
Mats Dahlberg .... Eternia
Mats Danielsson .... Crut, Genesaret
Mats Demelin .... Scar
Mats Drehmer .... Boom Shanker Group
Mats Edström .... Yankee Heaven, Shiva, Arrow, Second Heat
Mats Ekstrand .... Adventure
Mats Eldblom .... In Aeternum
Mats Elf .... Sektor Skandal
Mats Engberg .... B.C And The Envelopes
Mats Ericsson .... Angel King, Degreed
Mats Eriksson .... Vatten
Mats Eriksson "Marre Martini" .... Lost Souls, Damiel
Mats Eriksson .... Lynx
Mats Eriksson-Wigg .... Mathias Holm
Mats Flodin .... Firework
Mats Flygelholm .... Headline (1)
Mats Forsell .... Uncanny
Mats Fransson .... Disciple
Mats Frimodigs .... 1 Way Street, Keen Hue
Mats Förare "Matt Driver" .... Glory Bells (Band), Glory
Mats Gesar .... Thalamus
Mats Gihl .... Torsten
Mats Glenngård .... Coste Apetrea
Mats Gran .... Zeta
Mats Grundström "Oloph Skam" .... Shame (1)
Mats Gunhamre .... Inferno
Mats Gustavsson .... Who's Next
Mats Hagman .... Morgan Mastling Band
Mats Halldin .... Frequency
Mats Hallstensson .... House Of Shakira, Novak
Mats Hammarström .... Carpe Wade
Mats Hansson .... Sonic Walthers, Mustasch, Tornado Babies
Mats Hedberg .... Vargton, Glen Spove
Mats Hedén "Fox Skinner/Lodbror" .... Grand Magus, Bajen Death Cult
Mats Hedström .... Rat Bat Blue
Mats Hellberg .... Robb and Friends
Mats Helli .... Meadows End
Mats Henriksson .... Vanadis
Mats Hermansson .... Lynx
Mats Hillström .... Lipkin
Mats Hjerp .... Silverdollar
Mats Holm .... Gods Incorporated
Mats Håkansson "Matt/s Attaque" .... Tryckvåg, Mogg
Mats Håxell "Malli/Mally Hoxell" .... Raceway, Pike, Steven Anderson
Mats Ingwall "Rio" .... Candy Roxx
Mats Jacobsson .... Talk Of The Town
Mats Jeppsson .... Project L.E.E, Raise Cain, United Enemies
Mats Johansson .... Malison Rogue
Mats Johansson .... The Quill, Quil
Mats Johansson "Sir Richard Fireburn" .... The Black (1), Heartbreak Radio, Hope
Mats Johansson "Stam" .... Mustasch
Mats Johansson "M.J. Masen" .... Scratch (1), To Africa With Love
Mats Johansson "Randy Johansen" .... Candy Roxx
Mats Johansson .... The Weed
Mats Johansson .... Mason, Rough Diamonds
Mats Johansson .... A Virgin's Delight
Mats Johansson .... Skinny Horse, Axewitch, Mindless (Sinner)
Mats Johansson .... Dawn Of Silence
Mats Johansson .... New Bulsara
Mats Johansson .... Via Tokyo
Mats Johansson .... Tyfuz
Mats Jonasson "Matte" .... Red Baron
Mats Josephson "J.R" .... Roach
Mats Järnil "Matte" .... The Duskfall, Crawley, Helltrain, Inrage, Lost Souls
Mats Karlsson .... Heed, Seventh One
Mats Karlsson .... 220 Volt
Mats Karlsson .... Karma
Mats Karpestam .... Korea
Mats Klang .... Stefan Herde And His Broomdusters, Pax Romana
Mats Larsson (now Seiterö) .... Nifters
Mats Larsson .... Valenze
Mats Levén "Brajan" .... AB/CD, Abstrakt Algebra, Audiovision, Alfonzetti, Candlemass, Chris Laney, Capricorn, Crash The System, Spearfish, Dogface, Nubian Rose, Yngwie Malmsteen, Gypsy Rose, Hardcore Circus, Jupiter Society, Malison Rouge, Opera Diabolicus, Swedish Erotica, Therion, Pontus Norgren, Sabbtail, Southpaw, Treat
Mats Lidbrandt .... Veni Domine
Mats Liedholm .... Sorcerer
Mats Lilienberg "Johnny Cherobiano" .... Bonkyman, Human Race
Mats Lindberg (1) .... Kaipa, Trettioåriga Kriget
Mats Lindberg (2) .... Kaipa
Mats Lindbergh .... Shere Khan
Mats Lindfors .... Angeline, Bai Bang, John Norum, Talisman, Grand Slam
Mats Lindström .... Lifeline
Mats Lingman .... King Chrome
Mats Lundberg .... Erika Evenlind
Mats Lyborg .... Sgt. Carnage
Mats Löfgren .... Kaipa
Mats Lööf .... Vantage
Mats Mattsson .... Alcatraz
Mats Melin (now Hedfors) .... Red Baron
Mats Nehl .... Bloodshed
Mats Nelin .... Roulette, Cherry Red, Rain
Mats Nilsson .... Half Man
Mats Nilsson .... Thunderhog
Mats Nilsson .... Pleasure Avenue
Mats Nilsson .... Maryscreek
Mats Norberg .... Magic
Mats Nordrup .... Crematory
Mats Norlin "Mädz" .... The Wild Bunch
Mats Norman .... S:t Erik
Mats Norman .... Smokey Bandits
Mats Norström "Finlay" .... Ambush
Mats Ohlsson .... Generous Maria
Mats Olausson .... Glory, Geff, Von Rosen, Motvind, Yngwie Malmsteen, Nadir, Sayit, Talisman, Lion's Share, Houston, Gypsy Rose, Eclipse, Bam Bam Boys, Baltimoore, Radioactive
Mats Olsson .... Dog Faced Gods
Mats Olsson .... The End
Mats Olsson .... Ivory
Mats Olsson .... Zeelion
Mats Ottosson .... Shiva, Arrow, Renegade (1)
Mats Petersson "Staa" .... Locomotive Breath, Deception
Mats Pettersson .... Carrie
Mats Pettersson .... Two Eagles Request, Thunder
Mats Pettersson .... Powerdise
Mats Rajaniemi .... Zeit
Mats Rambin .... Exciters
Mats Reiniusson .... Overture
Mats Rendlert .... Dreamland, Infinity, Hammerfall, Cans
Mats Ringström .... Fagin
Mats Ronander .... Pontus Snibb 3
Mats Rubarth .... Casablanca
Mats Rundlou .... Darque
Mats Rydström .... Pontus Snibb 3, Backdraft, Abramis Brama
Mats Sandborg .... Alien
Mats Sannetorp .... Inzight
Mats Segerdahl .... Sinkadus
Mats Stattin .... Naked
Mats Ström .... Screwball.Sthlm
Mats Ström .... Overture
Mats Ståhl .... Candlemass, Gone, Enter The Hunt
Mats Ståhl .... Sapphire Eyes
Mats Sundholm .... TRP
Mats Svensson .... Art Rebellion
Mats Svensson .... Crier, Sacrifice
Mats Svensson .... Sinkadus
Mats Svensson .... Double Diamond
Mats Söderbom .... Keystone
Mats Tropp .... Golden Dawn
Mats Uhrlander .... 1 Way Street
Mats Vassfjord .... Chris Laney, Grand Design, Pink Panther, Scaar, Impera
Mats Wennhag .... Chai Gang
Mats Wernvall .... Pejling
Mats Wikberg .... Bloodstone
Mats Ymell .... Knockout

NAME INDEX

Mats Yngvesson ... Pantheon
Mats Ångman ... Notredame
Mats Öberg ... Fredrik Thordendah's Special Defects
Mats Öbergh ... Blåkulla
Mats Ögren ... Paradise (3)
Mats Öhlen ... Emmas Boogie Band
Mats Öhr ... Hin Haley
Mats Ördén "Maniac" ... Publikförakt AB
Mats Östensson ... Sky High, Vantage
Matt Drumhead ... Stingray
Matt Norberg ... Xsavior
Matt Schelin ... Eye
Matt Vereez ... Crossroad Jam
Matte Andersson ... Loss, Godgory
Matte Andersson ... Grave Flowers, (Mantaray K-D)
Matte Andersson ... Relentless
Matte D ... Despite
Matte Johansson ... Posh Filth
Matte Lindblom ... Overload
Matte Lindgren ... Tom Trick
Matte Lundberg ... Trix
Matte Marklund ... Vatten, Emmas Boogie Band
Matte Modin "Dominator/Fjällhammer" ... Dark Funeral, Sportlov, Thronaeon, Defleshed, Infernal (666), Nonexist, Stallion Four
Matte Norberg ... Greasy Saddles
Matte Nordrup ... Regurgitate
Matte Rydstrand ... Snakepit Rebels
Matte Ågren ... One Hour Hell
Matteo Gambacorta ... Spiders
Matthew Baraldi ... Zan Clan
Matthias "Matt Haze" ... Chains
Matthias Segerström ... Epitaph (2)
Matti Alfonzetti (aka Hohilla) ... Skintrade, Alfonzetti, The Poodles, Impera, Bai Bang, Damn Delicious, Glen Spove, Talisman, Emma Varg, Bam Bam Boys, Damned Nation, Road II Ruin
Matti Almsenius ... Revengia, The*End, Eucharist
Matti Eklund ... Coldspell
Matti Joutsen ... Queensland, Adventure
Matti Kärki ... Carnage, Dismember, Therion, Carbonized
Matti Larsson ... M.A.D
Matti Lovell ... Suicide Nation
Matti Lundell ... The Great Deceiver
Matti Mäkelä "Dominion" ... Dark Funeral, Dominion Caligula, Vicious Art
Matti Norlin ... Charity, Wizzard
Matti Vourinen ... Tears
Mattias Andersen ... The Defaced
Mattias Andersson ... Hin Haley
Mattias Ankarbranth ... The Carpet Knights
Mattias Arreflod ... Exanthema
Mattias Asplund ... Zonata
Mattias Athlei ... The Fuzes
Mattias Aurelius ... Sadatron
Mattias Axelsson ... Miosis
Mattias Bergkvist ... Flood
Mattias Berglund ... Gorement
Mattias Bernhardsson ... Nocturnal Rites
Mattias Björklund "Lord Aganaroth" .. Sapfhier, Exanthema
Mattias Bolander ... One Man Army
Mattias Borg ... 2 Ton Predator, Whyte Ash
Mattias Borgh ... Crypt Of Kerberos
Mattias Boström "Buffa" ... Nihilist
Mattias Bylund ... Killer Bee
Mattias Bäck ... Cromlech
Mattias Carlsson "Lalle" ... Too Late
Mattias Carlsson ... Nestor
Mattias Cederlund ... Bishop Garden, Veni Domine
Mattias Danielsson ... Latex
Mattias Davidsson "Mylon Hymat" ... The Waiting Rain
Mattias Ekblad ... Sins Of Omission
Mattias Eklundh "Ia" ... Freak Kitchen, Art Metal, Frozen Eyes, Evergrey, Mister Kite, Pagan, Urbandux, Pagan, Audiovision, Fredrik Pihl, Blackmail, Disdain, Locomotive Breath, Planet Alliance, Johan Randén, Soilwork, Mattias Eklundh, Laudamus
Mattias Eliasson ... Fatal Smile
Mattias Eliasson ... Soulreaper
Mattias Engstrand ... Theory In Practice
Mattias Engström ... Memfis
Mattias Eriksson ... Oriz
Mattias Eronn ... Plague Warhead
Mattias Fasth ... Soulless
Mattias Fiebig ... Paganizer, Ribspreader, Blodsrit, Portal
Mattias Fransson "Lurgo" ... Cripple
Mattias Fredriksson ... Nephenzy (Chaos Order)
Mattias Fredriksson ... On Parole
Mattias Friberg ... Switchblade
Mattias Frisk "Flesh" ... Ceremonial Execution, Vanhelgd
Mattias Grahn ... Naglfar
Mattias Gustafsson ... In Solitude
Mattias Gustavsson ... Liers In Wait
Mattias Göransson ... In Black
Mattias Hansson ... Searing I
Mattias Hedberg ... Sound Explosion
Mattias Hedenborg ... Fallen Angel, Waving Corn
Mattias Heldevik ... Itchy Daze
Mattias Hellberg ... Hellacopters
Mattias Helmer ... Silverwings, Paralyce
Mattias Henriksson ... Metal Mercy, Colorblind
Mattias Holm ... Stonefuze, Cornerstone
Mattias Holmgren ... Skyfire, Embracing, Naglfar, Azure, Dead Silent Slumber
Mattias Håkansson ... Taste
Mattias Höijer ... Shiva, Arrow
Mattias Jakobsen ... Oppression
Mattias Jarthed ... Valinors Tree
Mattias Johansson ... Divine Baze Orchestra
Mattias Johansson "Matte Hellcore" ... Ninnuam
Mattias Johansson "Dogge" ... Itchy Daze
Mattias Johansson "Matt Machine". Reinxeed, Pantokrator
Mattias Johansson "Mäbe" ... Dissection
Mattias Johansson "Panzer" .. Fear The Future, El Camino
Mattias Jonsson ... The Social ScumbagPäst
Mattias Jonsson ... Empty Guns
Mattias Kanje ... Tusen & En Natt
Mattias Karlsson ... Taste
Mattias Karlsson ... Dynamite
Mattias Karlsson ... Beast
Mattias Kennhed ... House Of Usher
Mattias Kindberg ... Frenzy
Mattias Kindefors ... Powerdise, U.N.IT
Mattias Klein ... Itchy Daze
Mattias Kun ... Mistie
Mattias Lamppu ... Centinex
Mattias Larsson ... Subdive
Mattias Larsson ... Takida
Mattias Lilja ... Thyreos
Mattias Lilja ... Divine Souls
Mattias Lind "Buffeln" ... Raubtier
Mattias Lindberg ... Reinxeed
Mattias Ljung ... Hearse
Mattias Lundberg ... Flood
Mattias Lövdahl ... Eternal Fear
Mattias Marklund ... Vintersorg, TME, Casket Casey, Otyg
Mattias Mattsson ... Anxious
Mattias Merking ... Blofly
Mattias Nielsen ... Subtopia, Subztain
Mattias Nilsson ... Payback
Mattias Norrman "The Crypt/Cryptan" ... Dellamorte, Moondark, Katatonia, October Tide
Mattias Ohlsén ... Sencelled
Mattias Olsson ... Änglagård
Mattias Orre ... Side By Side
Mattias Osbäck ... Locomotive Breath, Unchained, Mörrum's Own, From Behind
Mattias Pedersén ... Traction
Mattias Persson ... Another Hell
Mattias Persson "Matte" ... Bulletrain
Mattias Pettersson ... Goddefied
Mattias Rasmussen ... Spacebone
Mattias Reinholdsson ... Book Of Hours
Mattias Rydell ... Big Thing, Hellspray
Mattias Ryderman ... Celestial Decay
Mattias Schlyter ... Cult Disciples
Mattias Schyberg ... Cut 4
Mattias Skoog ... Sorhin, Enslavement
Mattias Starander ... Transport League, Major N.A
Mattias Strelvik ... United Fools
Mattias Sundberg ... Midfortune
Mattias Svanborg "Sternberg" ... Arise
Mattias Svensson ... Nifters
Mattias Svensson ... Redsun
Mattias Svensson "Gorgoth/Morg" ... Vanmakt, Nidrike
Mattias Svensson "Perish" ... Elimi
Mattias Svensson "Moon" ... Sludge
Mattias Svensson "Swaney" ... The Defaced, Kayser
Mattias Thomasén ... Eternal Fear
Mattias Tranberg "Krs Krstal" ... Evil's Eye
Mattias Warnelio ... Skull Parade
Mattias Wellhag ... House Of Heavy
Mattias Wester ... Astroqueen
Mattias Westlund ... Brazen Riot
Mattias Wetterhall ... Miss Beahaviour, Sarea
Mattias Willis ... Plan Three
Mattias Wänerstam ... One Without, Within Y
Mattias Värmby ... Rise And Shine
Mattias Åhlén ... Token
Mattias Åhrman "Harry" ... Die Hard
Mattias Åström ... Staiger, Greyhate
Mattis Engman ... Yersinia
Mattis Hagman ... Unholy
Mattis Hällström ... Solsting
Matts Tohver ... Motvind
Maturz ... Snötårar
Matz Ekström ... Nemesis, Candlemass
Matz Matsson ... Kiss Of Thunder
Matz Winroth ... Alcatraz
Maunghrim ... Vergelmer
Mauritz Petersson ... Cap Outrun, Backwater
Mauritz Vetterud ... Hero
Max Bergman ... My Own Grave
Max Bergman ... Brother Ape
Max Carlberg ... Aeon (2)
Max Collin ... Lobotomy
Max Flamer ... Crazy Lixx
Max Flövik ... Rallypack, Lillasyster
Max Hansen ... Peak
Max Lindberg ... Hyperborean
Max Lindqvist ... Wulfgar
Max Lorentz ... Mårran, Bai Bang
Max Malmer ... Zonaria
Max Malmgren ... Illfigure, Abuzimbel
Max Martin (see Martin Sandberg) ... Pain
Max Olsson ... Enjoy The View
Max Seppälä ... Eventide
Max Thornell ... Devourment, Hearse, Satanarchy, Furbowl, Jesusexercise, Wonderflow
Max Ullrich ... Trix
Max Åhman ... Coste Apetrea
Max Åhman ... Kaipa
Maxi Dread ... Siena Root
M-E Björklund ... United
Mehdi Vafaei ... Abandon
Melek Taus ... Melek Taus
Melissa Swan "Vampirella" ... Notre Dame
Melker Ryymin ... Equinox Ov The Gods
Messiah Marcolin ... Satariel
Metal Mike Chlasciak ... Cans
Mia Hansson ... Revanch
Mia Karlsson "Coldheart" ... Crucified Barbara, Babylon Bombs, Bonafide, Mind's Eye
Mia Kempff ... Yale Bate, Yeah Bop Station
Mia Larsson "Necrohell" ... Pagan Rites, Dracena
Mia Lorentzon ... Akilles
Mia Moilanen ... Fourever
Mia Möllberg ... Misdemeanor
Mia Ståhl ... Deadmarch
Mia Tern ... Revanch
Mia Von Barde ... Hazy
Micael Delaoglou "Mikkey Dee" .. Nadir, Heartbreak Radio, Geisha, The Jet Circus, John Norum
Micael Hellström ... Boom Shanker Group
Micael Larsson ... Rat Salad
Micael Lundberg ... Loréne
Micael Magnusson "Vån/Michael Grimm" ... Glanzig, Supergroupies, Easy Action
Micael Stålbom ... Kalajs
Micael Svan ... Myrah
Micael Wennbom ... Corrupt
Micael Wikström ... Averon
Micael Zetterberg ... Spetälsk
Micce Andersson ... Ningizzia, Forest Of Shadows
Michael (Maciek) Van De Graaf ... Afflicted
Michael Ahlander ... Mirage
Michael Ahlström "Mike Divine" ... Violent Divine, Avenue, Marshal Kane
Michael Alexandersen ... Axia
Michael Alforth ... Trazy Goes Crazy
Michael Alltoft ... The Ungrateful
Michael Amberg ... Treasure
Michael Amott "Mike" ... Arch Enemy, Spiritual Beggars, Candlemass, Deranged, Furbowl, Mojobone, Carnage
Michael Andersson ... Miosis
Michael Andersson ... Bonedog
Michael Ardenheim ... Tonvikt
Michael Backlund ... Heavy Load
Michael Beck ... Silicon Valley
Michael Bergström ... Vomitous
Michael Bergvall ... Terrortory
Michael Blair ... Shredhead
Michael Blomberg ... Turning Point
Michael Bohlin ... Attention (1), 8th Sin, Pain
Michael Borgh ... Livin' Sacrifice
Michael Borup ... Mansson
Michael Broberg ... Panic
Michael Carlsson ... Quolio
Michael Carlsson ... Tumbleweed
Michael Carlsson "Nocturnal Skullsdomiser" ... Sadistic Grimness
Michael Carlström ... Pike
Michael Christmansson ... Neocori
Michael Dahlquist ... Scudiero
Michael Daxberg ... Demon Seed
Michael Dean Hughes ... Unameus
Michael Ehrnstén ... Korea
Michael Elverson ... Temptation
Michael Fantel ... Tanaque
Michael Fridh ... Pax
Michael Fuhrman ... Akilles
Michael Garesjö ... Pink Panther
Michael Gunnarson ... Interment
Michael Gustafsson ... Quiz
Michael Hahne ... Misert Loves Co., Lost Souls
Michael Hallberg ... Charity, Wizzard
Michael Hedlund ... Happy Hour
Michael Hedlund ... WAR, Total War
Michael Hjelte "Hero" ... Hero, Sons Of Thunder
Michael Hosselton "Sweet" ... Toxic Rose
Michael Hurtig ... Uppgång 34
Michael Håkansson ... Engel, All Ends, Dark Tranquillity, The Project Hate MCMXCIX, Embraced, Mortum, Evergrey, The Forsaken
Michael Johansson ... Stallion
Michael Johansson ... Side By Side
Michael Johnson "Miche" ... Abacorn
Michael Jönsson ... Eurock
Michael Karlsson ... The Grand Trick
Michael Karlsson ... Loaded
Michael Kling ... Universe
Michael Körner ... Tenebre
Michael Lagesson ... Colt 48
Michael Larsson ... Coldspell, R.A.W, Lover Under Cover
Michael Levenstad ... Horizon (2)
Michael Lindman ... Steelwings
Michael Ludvigsson ... Infra
Michael Lundberg ... Crystal Pride
Michael Lundholm ... Mud & Blood
Michael Mehler ... Panndeads
Michael Mino ... Sgt. Sunshine
Michael Mueller ... Constancia
Michael Månsson "Manson" ... Mansson
Michael Nicklasson ... Sarcazm, Luciferion
Michael Nilsson ... Transit
Michael Nilsson ... Buckshot O.D.
Michael Nilsson ... Quiz
Michael Nordmark ... Steven Anderson
Michael Norrby ... Saturnalia Temple
Michael Norrman ... Interment
Michael Nyström ... Sargoth
Michael Ohlsson ... Hagen, Zircus, Zeit
Michael Ojala ... X-It
Michael Oran ... Mental Hippie Blood
Michael Persson ... Spit It Out
Michael Pethrus ... Axia
Michael Pettersson "Doomfanger" ... Bestial Mockery
Michael Pihl "Micki" ... Last Temptation
Michael Pyykkö ... Academy
Michael Qvarsell ... Traction
Michael Rank Jensen ... Grand Stand
Michael Rodin ... Jammer
Michael Rothsten ... Two Eagles Request
Michael Sahlström ... Silver Seraph, Dorian Grey
Michael Samuelsson ... Bloodstone, Cauterizer
Michael Siegrist ... Source Of Ignition
Michael Sjöö ... Seven Tears
Michael Stark ... Gallantry
Michael Stattin ... TBC
Michael Stein ... Prospect
Michael Stenbom ... Headache
Michael Stolt ... The Flower Kings
Michael Storm ... Jayce Landberg
Michael Svanberg ... Screamin' Mother
Michael Svensson ... Depzon
Michael Szemler ... Nightvision
Michael Ulvsgärd ... The Jet Circus, Jerusalem
Michael Uppman (now Storck) "Mike Lestat" ... Explode, Yngwie Malmsteen, Creozoth, Highbrow, Paradise (2)
Michael Wallin ... Big Easy
Michael Van de Graaf ... Defender
Michael Wedberg ... The Riff
Michael Westerlund ... Screamin' Mother
Michael Winkler ... Fagin
Michael Von Knorring ... Norden Light, Yngwie Malmsteen
Michael Åberg ... Nostradameus, Destiny
Michael Åhden ... Steve Roper Band
Michaela Löfving ... Svartsyn
Miachail Rinakakis ... Air Raid
Miche Johansson ... Parafine
Michel Baioni ... Cervello
Michel Bärzén ... Degradead
Michel Isberg ... Machinery
Michel Strand ... Syron Vanes
Michelle Maiden ... Reptile Smile
Michelle Meldrum (Norum) ... Meldrum, John Norum
Michelle Ristik "Michel Rice" ... Avalon
Micke Ahlin ... Mandylion
Micke Ahlquist ... S.L.R
Micke Andersson ... Divine Sin, Moribund
Micke Blomberg ... Galaxy Safari
Micke Brandtler ... Backtalk
Micke Broberg (aka Jansson). Unanimated, Celestial Pain
Micke Dahlén ... Clawfinger
Micke Danielsson ... Neofight
Micke Därth ... Peo, Nocturnal Detest
Micke Friman ... Fantasy, Tomas Bergsten's Fantasy
Micke Fröling "Mike" ... Abacorn
Micke Green ... Sacred Night
Micke Hansen ... One Hour Hell
Micke Hansson ... Debase
Micke Henriksson ... Wyvern
Micke Hujanen ... AB/CD, 220 Volt
Micke Hörnlund "Mike Alley" ... Walkaway
Micke Jakobsson ... Pandemonic, Soils Of Fate, Internal Decay, Denied
Micke Jansson ... Outremer
Micke Jansson ... Degreed
Micke Jansson (now Broberg) Unanimated, Celestial Pain
Micke Jansson ... Happy Cakes
Micke Johansen ... Nattfrost
Micke Johansen ... Göran Nordh

Micke Jonsson ..... Body Core
Micke Jönsson ..... Mercenary Mustangs
Micke Karlsson ..... Chronic Decay
Micke Karlsson ..... Meadow In Silence
Micke Kjellman ..... Sanctuary In Blasphemy
Micke Kvist ..... Silent Call, Elsesphere
Micke Ladréhn ..... Bonedog
Micke Larsson ..... White Night
Micke Lidén ..... Zpeedfreak
Micke Lindvall ..... Crematory
Micke Lövquist ..... Punishment
Micke Moberg ..... Bedlam
Micke Mujanne "Mike Mocadem" ..... Stonehenge
Micke Myhr ..... Posh Filth
Micke Nicklasson ..... Liers In Wait
Micke Nilsson ..... Raceway
Micke Nilsson ..... Bonafide, Brickhouse
Micke Nyholm "Killalot" ..... Vörgus
Micke Olsson ..... Cheryenne
Micke Oretoft ..... Katatonia
Micke Palmström ..... Crystal Blue
Micke Pettersson "Mique Flesh" ..... Seance, Witchery
Micke Riesbeck ..... Debase
Micke Sjöstrand ..... Chronic Decay, Hypnosia
Micke Strömberg ..... Headache
Micke Ståhl ..... Cheryenne
Micke Svanberg "Lord Ahriman" ..... Dominion Caligula, Dark Funeral
Micke Swed ..... Authorize
Micke Svennerbrandt ..... The Point
Micke Söderlund ..... Red Rocket
Micke Ullenius ..... Pandemonic
Micke Wickström ..... Steve Eastside Band
Micke Värn ..... Galleon
Micke Åsentorp ..... Fantasmagoria, Lefay
Micke Öberg ..... Cryonic
Micke Öster ..... Skydiverse
Micke Österberg "Nattfursth" ..... Sorhin
Mickey Sweet ..... Lipstixx 'N' Bullets
Micko Twedberg ..... Nation Beyond, Debase, Pretty Wild, Cloudscape
Mieszko Talarczyk ..... Ribspreader, Altar, The Bereaved, Blodsrit, Nine, Regurgitate, (Nasum)
Miguel Cabrera ..... Havok
Miguel Robaina ..... Memento Mori
Miguel Santana ..... Glory Bells (Band)
Mihalj Stefko ..... The Darksend
Miika Rudin ..... Scumkill
Miika Vains "Von Silli" ..... Chronic Torment
Mija Folkesson ..... Sky High
Mika Eronen ..... Immaculate
Mika Hakola "Michayah/Belfagor" ..... Nefandus, Ofermod
Mika Itäranta ..... Pound, Astral Doors, Sky Of Rage
Mika Kahilainen ..... Dionda
Mika Kajanen ..... Faceshift, Godphobia
Mika Korpi ..... Flintstens Med Stanley
Mika Lagreen ..... Facebreaker
Mika Luttinen ..... The Crown (Crown Of Throns)
Mika Savimäki ..... Belsebub, Lucifer
Mika Tikkanen "Robin Nelson" ..... Oberon
Mika Vai ..... Mrs. Hippie
Mika Vainio "Dyna Mike" ..... Hardcore Superstar
Mikael "Damien" ..... Midvinter
Mikael Ahlqvist ..... Renegades
Mikael Almgren ..... Allegiance, Maitreya
Mikael Andersson "Mike" ..... Planet Alliance, Cloudscape, Fullforce, Mountain Of Power, Alyson Avenue, Magnus Karlsson's Freefall, Doctor Weird
Mikael Andersson "Mikke" ..... Vanguard
Mikael Andersson "Micke Nord" ..... Nord, BALS, Mountain Of Power, Locomotive Breath, Red Baron, Angeline
Mikael Andersson ..... Amaran
Mikael Andersson ..... Extasy
Mikael Andersson ..... Il Shy
Mikael Andersson ..... Allan Beddo Band
Mikael Andersson ..... Story
Mikael Andersson ..... The Björn
Mikael Andersson ..... Ceremonial Oath
Mikael Andersson ..... Indungeon, Lucifer, Thy Primordial
Mikael Andersson ..... Horoscope (2)
Mikael Aronsson ..... My Own Grave
Mikael Askemur ..... Xinema
Mikael Back ..... Beseech
Mikael Backelin "Sin/Bloodlord/Micke" ..... Vassago, Lord Belial, Latex, Skin Infection
Mikael Baden ..... CC Rock
Mikael Bakajek ..... Freternia
Mikael Bauer ..... Embracing
Mikael Berg ..... Request
Mikael Berggren ..... Kaross
Mikael Bergman ..... Deranged, The Darksend
Mikael Bergström ..... Absurd
Mikael Berner ..... Street Talk, Saigon
Mikael Bielinski ..... Egonaut
Mikael Birgersson "Hellcop" ..... Gehennah, Dawn Of Decay
Mikael Blixt ..... Subdive
Mikael Blohm ..... Crystal Eyes
Mikael Bohlin ..... Coastline Ride
Mikael Bojko ..... Backstreet
Mikael Broman ..... Astrophobos
Mikael Brunkvist ..... Slumber
Mikael Brunzell ..... Lucy
Mikael Bäcklin "Mike Spider" ..... Gasoline Queen
Mikael Böhlin ..... Steel Attack
Mikael Böhnke ..... Million
Mikael Börjesson ..... Gypsy
Mikael Carling "Mizzy" ..... Undecimber, Deed
Mikael Carlsson ..... Victory (1)
Mikael Carlsson ..... Lover Under Cover
Mikael Carlsson ..... Tom Trick
Mikael Carlsson ..... Rubbet
Mikael Carlsson ..... Easy Street
Mikael Castervall "Cab" ..... Hypnosia, Funeral, Portrait
Mikael Dahl ..... Crystal Eyes
Mikael Dahlbom ..... Remo
Mikael Dahlquist ..... Godgory, World Of Silence, Dogpound
Mikael Danielsson ..... World Below
Mikael Davidsson "Divine" ..... Pussy Galore
Mikael de Bruin ..... Ammotrack
Mikael Delén ..... Lovehandles
Mikael Dimle "Mike Randle" ..... Empire Saint
Mikael Edebro ..... Lugnoro
Mikael Edvinsson ..... Shore
Mikael Eklöv ..... Headline (2)
Mikael Ellgren-Svensson ..... Gallery (2)
Mikael Elofsson ..... Saltmine, Blackwood
Mikael Englund ..... Backstreet
Mikael Engström ..... Mortalicum
Mikael Ericsson ..... Double Deuce
Mikael Eriksson ..... Prisoner, House Of Shakira
Mikael Eriksson ..... Brazen Riot
Mikael Eriksson ..... Demons Of Dirt
Mikael Eriksson ..... Third Stone
Mikael Eriksson ..... Cheers
Mikael Erlandsson "Eden" ..... The Black (1), Radioactive, Last Autumns Dream, Salute, Heartbreak Radio, Lover Under Cover, Sapphire, Talent, Don Patrol, Crash
Mikael Falk ..... Headline (2)
Mikael Fasth ..... Lucifer
Mikael Folkesson ..... Love Child, Trazy
Mikael Forsberg ..... Los Bohemos
Mikael Forsberg ..... Syrus
Mikael Fredriksson ..... Maleficio
Mikael Fredriksson ..... Grand Vision, Sleazy Roze
Mikael Freij ..... Rockvaktmästarna
Mikael Fässberg ..... Bonafide, Burning Engines, From Behind
Mikael Garcia ..... Overdeth
Mikael Gillstedt ..... Wizz
Mikael Goding ..... Wolf
Mikael Granbacke (aka Degerman) "Asael" ..... Satariel, Torch Bearer
Mikael Grankvist ..... The Moaning, Satariel, Incinerator
Mikael Green ..... Red Baron
Mikael Gustafsson ..... Crut
Mikael Gustafsson ..... Dream
Mikael Gustavsson ..... Igneous Human
Mikael Gustavsson ..... Crier, Sacrifice
Mikael Gyllenstig ..... Motvind
Mikael Hagberg ..... Project UPA
Mikael Hallberg ..... Lack Of Faith
Mikael Hallsten ..... Silverwings
Mikael Hansson ..... Lion's Share
Mikael Hed ..... Heartcry, Johannes
Mikael Hedlund ..... Hypocrisy, Dark Funeral, The Abyss
Mikael Hedström ..... Big Price, Paradise (1)
Mikael Hermansson ..... Headline (2)
Mikael Hilmer ..... Twilight Project
Mikael Hilmersson ..... Metal Mercy, Wonderland, Colorblind
Mikael Holm ..... Winterlong
Mikael Holmberg ..... Head Force
Mikael Holmquist ..... Arrows
Mikael Holst ..... Timeless Miracle
Mikael Hurtig ..... Croc
Mikael Höglund ..... Audiovision, Alfonzetti, Great King Rat, Jekyll & Hyde, Neocori, Tryckvåg
Mikael Hörnqvist "Mike Cameron Force" ..... Zonata, Enbound, Ablaze
Mikael Israelsson ..... Vintersorg, Black Bonzo
Mikael Jacobsson ..... Devilicious
Mikael Jansson ..... Glorious Bankrobbers
Mikael Jansson ..... Outremer, Sorcery
Mikael Jansson ..... Sorcery
Mikael Jansson (now Åsberg) ..... White Cat
Mikael Jansson "Mike Metalhead" ..... Celestial Pain, Unanimated
Mikael Jansson ..... Mental Hippie Blood
Mikael Johannesson ..... Limitless, Lovehandles, Tippen Ruda, Mandala
Mikael Johansson ..... Vanessa
Mikael Johansson ..... Balthazar
Mikael Johansson ..... Cut Out
Mikael Johansson ..... Misery
Mikael Jonasson "Snobben/Snoopy" ..... Gemini Five
Mikael Jonsson ..... Extaz
Mikael Junell ..... Grace
Mikael Jönsson ..... TRP
Mikael Kallin ..... Amethyst
Mikael Karlsson "Hravn/Hrafn" ..... IXXI, Devil's Whorehouse
Mikael Karlsson "Lyris" ..... Rat Salad
Mikael Karlsson ..... Gallows End
Mikael Karlsson "N. Sadist" ..... Patrynomicon
Mikael Klevengård ..... Union Mac
Mikael Kling ..... Universe, Europe, John Norum
Mikael Kvist ..... Elsesphere
Mikael Kähäri ..... Sahara (1)
Mikael Källgren ..... Source Of Ignition
Mikael Lagerblad ..... One Man Army
Mikael Lans ..... Quinzy
Mikael Larson ..... R.A.W
Mikael Larsson (now Krusenberg) "Mike" ..... 220 Volt
Mikael Larsson ..... Brazen Riot
Mikael Larsson ..... Lake Of Tears
Mikael Larsson ..... Mammuth
Mikael Lavér "Mike" ..... DeVan, Optimystical, Dynazty
Mikael Lejon ..... Madigan
Mikael Lindahl ..... Elsesphere
Mikael Lindbom ..... Sabotage
Mikael Lindevall ..... Afflicted, Proboscis
Mikael Lindgren ..... Zen
Mikael Lindgren ..... Divine Souls
Mikael Lindholm ..... Shineth
Mikael Lindkvist ..... Heads Or Tales
Mikael Lindorf ..... Corrosive Carcass
Mikael Lindqvist ..... Taketh
Mikael Lindström ..... Quinzy
Mikael Long "Herman" ..... R&R
Mikael Loorenz ..... Mörrum's Own
Mikael Ludvigsson ..... Live Elephant
Mikael Lundén ..... Cheers
Mikael Lundgren ..... Gilt
Mikael Lundholm "Mike Thorn" ..... Damien
Mikael Lundqvist ..... Disruption
Mikael Lång ..... Casket Casey, Soulreaper
Mikael Lägermo ..... Emotion
Mikael Läth ..... Captain Crimson
Mikael Löfgren ..... Kings N' Fools
Mikael Löfqvist "Bigswede" ..... Cryonic
Mikael Lövdal ..... Grand Vision
Mikael Magnusson ..... Boulevard, Easy Action
Mikael Malmborg ..... Shiva
Mikael Mangs Edwardsson ..... Miosis
Mikael Marjanen (now Monks) ..... Burning Saviours, Whyte Ash
Mikael Markström ..... Nasheim, Lethal
Mikael Martinsson ..... Sunset Blade
Mikael Medin ..... Marionette
Mikael Moberg "Micke" ..... Zeta, Moberg-Talton
Mikael Moberg ..... Timescape
Mikael Mujanne "Mike Mocadem" ..... Trash
Mikael Myllynen ..... Madison
Mikael Mörk ..... Lezlie Paice
Mikael Nicklasson "Micke" ..... Luciferion
Mikael Nilsson ..... The Bereaved, Behemoth
Mikael Nilsson "Nattramn" ..... Silencer
Mikael Nilsson ..... The End, Oxid
Mikael Nilsson "Mikey/Mikkey Nielsen" ..... Heavy Cargo, Nasty Idols, Bai Bang, Sapphire Eyes, Alyson Avenue
Mikael Nordh ..... Cicero
Mikael Nordin ..... Within Y
Mikael Nordlander ..... Powerbreeze
Mikael Nordström "Mick" ..... Bengalen, Charizma, Cornerstone, Lava Engine, Modest Attraction, Flagship, Stonefuze, Two Eagles Request, Spearfish, Two Franklin Groove, XT
Mikael Nordström ..... Spazmosity
Mikael Norén ..... Impious, Enthralled
Mikael Nox Pettersson ..... Avsky, Craft, Omnizide
Mikael Ohlsson ..... Fake
Mikael Olander ..... The Rifles
Mikael Olervo ..... Shredhead
Mikael Olofsson ..... Turning Point
Mikael Olsson ..... Bozeman's Simplex
Mikael Olsson ..... Wildness
Mikael Palm "Mike Mayson" ..... Stingray
Mikael Pergel (aka Bennich) ..... Fortuna
Mikael Persson ..... Naughty Boys
Mikael Persson ..... Bai Bang
Mikael Persson ..... On The Rocks
Mikael Pettersson "Mique Flesh/Mickie" ..... Freevil, Satanic Slaughter
Mikael Pettersson ..... Stench
Mikael Pireng "Edgy Led" ..... Keehole
Mikael Planefeldt ..... Diamond Dawn
Mikael Popovic ..... Year Of The Goat
Mikael Qvist "Q" ..... Marshal Kane, Violent Divine, Sleazy Roze
Mikael Reinholdsson ..... Mr. Tiger, X-Union
Mikael Renström ..... Wolverine
Mikael Rosengren ..... Damned Nation, Constancia, Scudiero, Token
Mikael Ross ..... Frozen Fire
Mikael Rydén ..... Sacramentum
Mikael Rönnberg ..... Charity, Wizzard
Mikael Saario ..... Backstreet
Mikael Sahlström ..... Dorian Gray
Mikael Sandorf ..... Helltrain, The Duskfall, Gates Of Ishtar
Mikael Sandström ..... Torn Apart
Mikael Sandvik ..... Naughty Boys
Mikael Schelin "Mist" ..... Ophthalamia, Ofermod, Malign
Mikael Sehlin ..... Degradead, Engel
Mikael Sjöberg ..... Crypt Of Kerberos
Mikael Sjöbom ..... Ivory
Mikael Sjölund ..... Decadence
Mikael Sjöstrand ..... Hypnosia
Mikael Sjöstrand ..... Request
Mikael Sjöström "Abbe" ..... Airborne
Mikael Skager ..... Polluted Influence
Mikael Stanne ..... Dark Tranquillity, In Flames, Hammerfall, Arise
Mikael Stark "Mike" ..... Steel Attack
Mikael Strandberg "Strampan" ..... Stormrider
Mikael Stålberg ..... Inzight
Mikael Sundh ..... Etos
Mikael Sundkvist ..... Conquest
Mikael Sundvisson ..... The Gypsies
Mikael Svantesson ..... Velvet Crash
Mikael Svennberg "Ludde" ..... Nattsvart
Mikael Svensson "Mike C" ..... Backhander
Mikael Swärd (now Carl Lagerholm) ..... Renegade (2)
Mikael Söderström ..... Nocturnal Rites
Mikael Talvitie "Mike Tall" ..... The Wild Bunch
Mikael Tanneståhl "Mike T Thundersteel" ..... Paperback Freud
Mikael Thelin ..... Sommoned Tide
Mikael Thomsen ..... Downbound Train
Mikael Thorne ..... Humble Bee
Mikael Tossavainen "Mike Toza" ..... Tribulation (1)
Mikael Touminen ..... Fingerspitzengefühl, Switch Opens
Mikael Underdahl ..... Peak
Mikael Vaarala ..... Dr Dream
Mikael Vanhanen "Mika 3,5" ..... Chronic Torment
Mikael Vannequé ..... Bloodshed
Mikael Wassholm ..... Ashes, Facebreaker
Mikael Wedin ..... Obscene
Mikael Wennergrund ..... Limiless
Mikael Wester ..... Boom Shanker Group
Mikael Widlöf ..... Embracing
Mikael Widmark ..... Demons Of Dirt
Mikael Wiking ..... Bedrock Zity
Mikael Wikman ..... Vindictiv, Alien, Tony Borg
Mikael Wikström "Mike Wead" ..... Hexenhaus, Abstrakt Algebra, Bibleblack, Candlemass, Hexenhaus, Memento Mori, Warning, Maninnya, Fi5th Reason, Heave, The Project Hate MXMXCIX, Chainsaw, The Haunted, Her Whisper, Memory Grden, Nattas, Kee Marcello
Mikael Wilhelmsson ..... Aggressive Chill
Mikael Von Knorring ..... Norden Light
Mikael Wretfors ..... Orphan Gypsy
Mikael Wängkvist ..... Frekvens
Mikael Zakrisson ..... Central
Mikael Zell ..... Wolverine
Mikael Zetterberg ..... Terrorama, Spetälsk
Mikael Åhlin "Mike Thaison" ..... Seventribe
Mikael Åkerblom ..... As You Drown
Mikael Åkerfelt ..... Opeth, Katatonia, Bloodbath, Steel
Mikael Åkerman "Micke" ..... Ypzilon
Mikael Åkerström ..... As You Drown
Mikael Öberg ..... The Project Hate MCMXCIX, Infanticide, Punishment, Deadmarch
Mikael Östberg ..... Torsten
Mikael Österberg "Nattfurst" ..... Algaion
Mikael Östermalm ..... Slowlife
Mike Amott ..... (See Michael Amott)
Mike Down ..... The Point
Mike Hill ..... Badmouth
Mike Larsson ..... John Norum
Mike Roos ..... Naked
Mike Svensson ..... S.K.U.R.K
Mike Szymanski ..... Middleage
Mike T Thundersteel ..... Paperback Freud
Mike Thorn ..... (see Mikael Lundholm)
Mike Wead ..... (see Mikael Vikström)
Mike Åberg ..... April Sky
Mikka "Sadist" ..... Nifelheim
Mikkey Dee ..... (see Micael Delaoglou)
Mikkie Nielsen ..... (see Mikael Nilsson)
Mikkjal G. Hansen ..... Massdistraction
Mikko Härkin ..... Solution .45
Mikko I. Petersen ..... Epedemic
Mikko Karvonen ..... D.I.Y
Mikko Korsbäck ..... Insania (Stockholm)
Mikko Savela ..... Amsvartner
Mikko Walldén ..... Valley
Mille Wendel ..... Bai Bang, Boogie Liquor Band
Mini ..... Blowsight
Miqael Persson ..... Heavy Cargo, Seven
Mirjam Andersson ..... Anxious
Mirko Varis "Hangover" ..... Chronic Torment
Misha Sedini ..... Man.Machine.Industry, Lingua, Come Sleep
Mistheria ..... Winterlong

NAME INDEX

Mjorga ... Incinia
Mladen Milojkovic ... Bloodlit
Moa Holmsten ... Meldrum, Abramis Brama
Mogge Lundin ... 2 Ton Predator
Mojje Andersson ... Hell N' Diesel
Mona Mattisson ... Törsten Dricker
Monica Blom ... Frozen Fire
Monica Falk ... Frozen Fire
Monica Larsson ... Bang & Out
Morbid Juttu ... Deathwitch
Moreno Tondo ... Zane
Morgan Alm ... Silver Mountain
Morgan Andersson "Mogge" ... Beyond Visions
Morgan Blomquist ... Axia
Morgan Bohman ... X-Perience
Morgan Eklöv ... Magic
Morgan Eriksson ... Live Elephant
Morgan Evans ... Killer Bee
Morgan Gottfridsson ... Drabness
Morgan Gredåker ... Beseech
Morgan Hansson ... Havayoth, Naglfar
Morgan Hansson ... By My Fear
Morgan Hellman "MC Hellbound" ... Downbound Train
Morgan Håkansson ... Nefandus
Morgan Håkansson "Mogge/Steinmeyer/Evil" ... Marduk,
... Sargatanas Reign, Triumphator,
... Abruptum, Devil's Whorehouse
Morgan Höglund ... Romance
Morgan Jacobsson ... Tai Rose
Morgan Jensen "Lefay" ... Swedish Erotica
Morgan Johansson ... Crystal Blue
Morgan Johansson ... Panama
Morgan Johansson ... Nugatory
Morgan Kane ... Marshal Kane
Morgan Korsmoe ... Mårran
Morgan Lie (Peter) ... Auberon, Bone Gnawer,
... Saved By Insanity, Hate Ammo
Morgan Lundin ... The Project Hate MCMXCIX
Morgan Löfstedt ... Wulfgar
Morgan Mastling ... Morgan Mastling Band
Morgan Mathiasson ... Tencider, Crazy Visions
Morgan Nordbekk ... Aeon (2)
Morgan Pettersson "Cake" ... Glanzig, Boulevard,
... Midnight Blue, B-Thong, Ram
Morgan Pettersson ... Human Cometh
Morgan Ramstedt ... Stormrider
Morgan Rosenquist ... Covered Call, Priority
Morgan Rosörn "Mogge" ... Aggregate
Morgan Sjöberg ... Naughty Boys
Morgan Svedlund ... Equinox Ov The Gods, Hin Haley
Morgan Svensson "Svisse" ... Prime, W.E.T (1)
Morgan Valentin ... Naughty Boys
Morgan Zocek ... Black Dog, Sideburn
Morgan Ågren ... Glory, Kaipa, Tippen Ruda,
... Fredrik Thordendahl's Special defects, Vargton
Morgens Widmark ... X-Perience
Morten Skaug ... Black Dog
Mortifier ... Orcivus
Moses Jonathan Elfström ... Crystal Age
Moses Shtieh ... Vermin
Mr. South ... Dirty Old Men
Munhin ... Vargavinter
Murre ... Solid Rox
Mutated Martin ... Revolting
Måns Jaktlund ... Ninnuam
Måns P. Månsson ... Gone
Måns Welander "Manster" ... Delve
Mårten Andersson ... Mountain Of Power,
... Jonas Hansson Band
Mårten Bergkvist ... Miosis
Mårten Björkman ... Octinomos, Algaion
Mårten Edlund ... Gotham City
Mårten Eriksson ... G.O.L.D
Mårten Eriksson ... Limit
Mårten Eriksson ... Reflex
Mårten Hagström ... Meshuggah
Mårten Hansen ... October Tide, This Ending,
... A Canorous Quintet, Sins Of Omission
Mårten Hedener ... Debase
Mårten Jansson ... Immaculate
Mårten Larsson ... Saltmine, Blackwood
Mårten Löwe Sörensen ... Amaranthe
Mårten Magnefors ... Darklands, Unholy
Mårten Matsson ... Månegarm
Mårten Ronsten ... Bacon
Mårten Sandberg "Marty Marteen" ... Hexenhaus,
... Fi5th Reason, Memento Mori, Nagazaki
Mårten Sandén ... Nightvision
Mårten Tromm ... Iodine Jupiter, (Baby Jesus)
Mårten Wanning "Rigor Martini" ... Hungry Head Hunters
Måsen Persson ... (see Håkan Persson)
Möller ... Blodskald
Mörkestöl ... Domgård
N. Sadist ... Patronymicon
Nabemih ... Ondskapt
Nad Sylvan ... Time Code Alpha
Nader Moini ... Drabness
Nakko H ... Sabbtail
Nalle Oskarsson ... Norden Light
Nalle Påhlsson ... (see Björn Påhlsson)
Nappe Benchemsi ... Agony
Narstrand ... Dråpsnatt
Natalie Duarte ... Myrah
Nathan James Biggs ... Sonic Syndicate
Neanderthal ... Northern Darkness
Neil Detlofson ... Sun Island
Neil Taylor ... Skold
Nenia ... Mordichrist
Nephente (Johan) ... Fear The Future, Netherbird
Nic Savage ... Steelwing
Nic Svensson ... Reinxeed
Nicci Wallin "Flint" ... AB/CD, Nord
Nick d'Virgillo ... Karmakanic
Nick Döring ... Opeth
Nick Marino ... Yngwie Malmsteen
Nicke Andersson "Royale" ... Hellacopters, Dismember,
... Entombed, Necronaut, Nihilist, Death Breath
Nicke Borg ... Backyard Babies
Nicke Engwall ... Ponamero Sundown
Nicke Ericsson ... Raving Mad
Nicke Erikson ... Atrox
Nicke Grabowski ... The Forsaken
Nicke Hagen ... Epitaph (1)
Nicke Holstenson ... Nominon
Nicke Johansson ... Dark Legions, Hexenhaus
Nicke Karlsson ... Soils Of Fate
Nicke Källström ... Corroded
Nicke Landin ... Detest
Nicke Olsson ... Mort
Nicke Stenemo ... Furbowl
Nicke Wadström ... Dionda
Nickey Argento ... Memento Mori
Nicklas Andersson ... Blacksmith
Nicklas Andersson ... Adams Eve
Nicklas Andersson ... Mammoth Volume
Nicklas Arvidsson ... Metal Mercy
Nicklas Berg ... Anekdoten
Nicklas Bergström ... Malaise
Nicklas Brommare ... Solsting
Nicklas Bäckström ... Lithany, Moloken
Niklas Ekelund ... Daydream
Nicklas Eriksson ... A Mind Confused,
... Kaamos, Serpent Obscene
Nicklas Franzén ... Brazen Riot
Nicklas Hansson ... Ravaged
Nicklas Holmgren ... Nasheim, Embracing
Nicklas Johansson "Nick/The Ripper" ... Slowgate
... Maninnya Blade, Hexenhaus
Nicklas Johansson "Old Nick" ... Turbocharged
Nicklas Johnsson ... Mentor's Wish, Full Strike
Nicklas Jonsson ... Fatal Smile (2)
Nicklas Keijser ... This Haven
Nicklas Lilja ... Piper's Dawn, Gorement
Nicklas Lindgren ... Sonic Temple
Nicklas Lindh ... 21 Lucifers, Without Grief
Nicklas Lindquist ... Arrows
Nicklas Linnes ... Chasticement
Nicklas Magnusson .. Nightshade, Dragonland, Prophanity
Nicklas Michaelsson "Gaddur" ... Omnizide
Nicklas Rudolfsson "Terror/Priest 4" ... Dracena,
... The Funeral Orchestra, Swordmaster,
... Necrocurse, Runemagic, Deathwitch
Nicklas Silfverin ... Colordream
Nicklas Stenemo ... Wonderflow
Nicklas Sundqvist ... Necromicon, Morthirim
Nicklas Svensson "Wortael" ... Throne Of Ahaz
Nicklas Svärd "Nick Sword" ... Terror 2000
Nicklas Tärnhamn ... Tanaque
Nicklas Wallén ... Body Core
Nicklas Wintersteller ... Spaps
Nicklas Åhlund ... Black Bonzo
Nicklas Åström ... Sommoned Tide
Nicko DiMarino ... Demon Seed, Arconova, Twins Crew
Niclas Andersson "Pepa" (now Green) ... Sacramentum,
... Latex, Dracena, Lord Belial, Vassago
Niclas Ankarbranth ... Vandöd, The Gardnerz
Niclas Blomquist ... Queen Obscene
Niclas Boman ... Fimbultyr
Niclas Brönner ... Abuzimbel
Niclas Cruse ... Simson
Niclas Engelin ... Engel, Gardenian, In Flames,
... Passenger, Sarcazm, Ice Age
Niclas Erickson "Nicke" ... Ypzilon
Niclas Ericson ... Axia
Niclas Flodberg ... King Size
Niclas Franklin ... Two Franklin Grove
Niclas Frohagen ... Shubend, Forest Of Ningizzia
Niclas Granath ... Abacorn, Destiny, Sabbtail
Niclas Gröndahl ... Shakespeare
Niclas Gustafsson "Nickrock" ... Skiller
Niclas Gustavsson ... Print
Niclas Hedenström ... Grand Vision
Niclas Johansson ... Vivaldi (group)
Niclas Johnsson ... Full Strike
Niclas Karlsson ... Freternia, Zonata, Fierce Conviction,
... Conviction, Crystal Eyes
Niclas Kleist ... Brewmaster, Von Panzer
Niclas Lillman ... Soulgrinder
Niclas Lindblom ... Miss Beahaviour
Niclas Linde ... Eventide
Niclas Lundgren ... Meshuggah
Niclas Lundgren "Ankan" ... Carnival Sun
Niclas Mellander ... NME Within
Niclas Nilsson ... God Macabre
Niclas Nordlander ... Big Business
Niclas Nordqvist ... Project UPA, Rio
Niclas Olsson ... Shiva, Alyson Avenue, Second Heat,
... Sapphire Eyes
Niclas Olsson "Nicke" ... Hydrogen
Niclas Persson ... Unsolved, Morpheena
Niclas Rundkvist ... Negro
Niclas Rådberg ... Decadence
Niclas Sigevall ... Reptile Smile, John Norum,
... Annie For President, Dream Bank, Electric Boys
Niclas Sjölin ... Slick Stuff
Niclas Sjöquist ... Setback
Niclas Staberg ... Solitude (2)
Niclas Stålfors ... Lowrider
Niclas Swedentorp ... Coldspell
Niclas Svensson ... Slingblade
Niclas Wahlén ... Unmoored
Niclas Wilhelmsson ... Bishop Garden
Niclas Åberg ... Hypocrite
Nico Elgstrand "Moosebach" ... Terra Firma
... Satanarchy, Entombed
Nico Pedersen ... Lithium
Nicola Posa ... VII Gates
Nidas Hammargren ... Aggressive Chill
Nidhägg ... (see Sebastian Ramstedt)
Nielz Lindström ... Nation Beyond
Nigris ... Bloodline
Nikkey Argento ... Slowgate
Nikki Andersen ... Aces High
Niklas Ahlin ... Galaxy
Niklas Almén ... Within Y
Niklas Andersson "Nicke" ... Export
Niklas Andreasson ... By My Fear
Niklas Arkbro ... Diamond Dawn
Niklas Axelsson ... In Grey
Niklas Bentholm ... Candy Kicks Ass
Niklas Björnör ... Alonzo
Niklas Boström ... Mac & Ploids
Nicklas Brant ... Espinoza
Niklas Brevestedt ... Guns 'N' Horses
Niklas Brodd ... Evercy, Marble Arch
Niklas Bruzell "Nicki" ... Pussy Galore
Niklas Böhme ... Greasy Saddles
Niklas Börjesson "N. Carrot" ... Fruitcake, Lotus (2)
Niklas Dahlin ... Insania (Stockholm), Disdained
Niklas Dernebo ... Linehouse
Niklas Dewerud .... Viceral Bleeding, Spawn Of Posession
Niklas Edberger ... Leviticus
Niklas Ek ... Cheerleader
Niklas Ekander ... Guns 'N' Horses
Niklas Ekstrand ... Tiamat, Face Down
Niklas Eriksson ... Colossus
Niklas Fagerström "Nic Red" ... Blowsight
Niklas Falk ... Sergej The Freak
Niklas Fjärve ... Source (2)
Niklas Franklin ... Leviticus, Two Frankling Grove
Niklas Fridh ... Wraptors, Deathening
Niklas' Gidlund "Nibbe" ... Bulletsize
Niklas Hammarberg ... Higher Ground
Niklas Hanell ... El Camino
Niklas Hasselberg ... Inferno
Niklas Holmkvist ... Token
Niklas Holstensson ... Nominon, Thy Primordial
Niklas Hoven "Nic Lester" ... Billion Dollar Babies
Niklas Hultman ... Earthquake
Niklas Högberg . Johnny Engström Band, Dead End Street
Niklas Isfeldt ... Dream Evil
Niklas Jansson "Nikki Oi" ... Boogieman
Niklas Jerberg ... Lezlie Paice, Livin' Parazite
Niklas Johansson ... Suicide Nation
Niklas Johansson ... Tyron
Niklas Johnsson ... XT
Niklas Jonsson "Nikki" ... Battle Station,
... Captain Freak's Freaky Funksters
Niklas Jonsson ... Singer
Niklas Kahl ... Wood
Niklas KarlssonPandemonic, Soils Of Fate, Construcdead
Niklas Karlsson ... Section 8
Niklas Kilenstam ... Thee Expression
Niklas Kjellgren "Dango" ... Truckfighters
Niklas Kullström ... Captor
Niklas Kupper ... Loch Vostock, Searing I
Niklas Kvarforth ... (see Niklas Olsson)
Niklas Källström ... Takida
Niklas Laihanen ... Haze
Niklas Liliengren ... Godphobia
Niklas Lindberg ... Wild Cat Sleezy
Niklas Lindbäck ... Vivaldi (group)
Niklas Lindeke ... Carnalist
Niklas Lindström ... In Solitude
Niklas Lundahl "Nicki Kin" ... Vains Of Jenna
Niklas Lundgren ... Comandatory
Niklas Lövgren ... Gods Incorporated
Niklas Matsson ... Backdraft, Bonafide, Pontus Snibb 3
Niklas Munter ... (Umeå) Small Band
Niklas Murbäck ... Slodust
Niklas Möller ... Ironware
Niklas Nilsson "Nicke" ... Dust Bowl Jokies
Niklas Nilsson ... Macabre End
Niklas Nord ... Gallows End
Niklas Olausson "Nico Noon" ... Scratch (1),
... To Africa With Love
Niklas Olausson ... Broken Dagger, Veritate
Niklas Olniansky ... Dibbukim
Niklas Olsson "Kvarforth" ... Shining, Diabolicum,
... Funeral Dirge, Livsnekad
Niklas Olsson ... Asphyxiation
Niklas Ottosson ... Blue Skies Bring Tears
Niklas Pelli "Nicke" ... Mörker, Chaossworn
Niklas Pettersson ... Scenteria
Niklas Rehn ... Altered Aeon
Niklas Rollgard "Nick" ... Gallery (1), 17
Niklas Rudolfsson ... Sacramentum
Niklas Rundquist ... Iodine Jupiter
Niklas Samuelsson ... Sargatanas Reign
Niklas Sandell ... Wonderland DementaBenevoent
Niklas Sandell ... Paralyce
Niklas Sandin ... Siebenbürgen, Amaran
Niklas Sjöberg ... The Graviators, Nymf
Niklas Sjöström ... Raise Hell
Niklas Skogqvist "Don Foster" ... Sterbhaus,
... Skitarg, Decadence
Niklas Sköld "Nick Shields" ... Decollation
Niklas Sposato ... Swedens Finest
Niklas Stålvind (aka Olsson) ... Wolf, Ruined Soul
Niklas Sundin ... Laethoria, Dark Tranquillity,
... Hammerfall, In Flames
Niklas Svensson ... Blinded Colony, Carnival Sun
Niklas Svensson ... The Moaning, Gates Of Ishtar,
... Throne Of Ahaz, The Everdawn
Niklas Svärd ... Von Benzo
Niklas Thorn ... Fatal Tabasco
Niklas Tillman ... Zircus
Niklas Tärnhamn ... Tommy Tysper & The Kids
Niklas Welin "Douglas" ... Slodust
Niklas Westberg ... April Divine
Niklas Wester ... Self Deception
Niklas Wiik ... Prowoke
Niklas Wiklund ... Stardog
Niklas Öberg ... Skellington
Niklas Österlund ... Headplate
Niknam Moslehi ... Within Y
Nilo Kovacic ... Hellspray, Layout
Nils Andersson ... The Carpet Knights
Nils Angnarsson ... Carpe Wade
Nils Berggren ... Sergeant
Nils Bielfeld "Nisse" ... RFP, Surrender,
... Sixcoveredkisssongs, Clench
Nils Ekblad "Sledge Nelson" ... Mac Bladgick
Nils Ekholm ... Robb and Friends
Nils Erikson ... Karmakanic
Nils Eriksson "Snake" ... Nocturnal Rites, Guillotine
Nils Fjellström "Fastfills/Dominator" ... A*Teem,
... Dark Funeral, In Battle, Souldrainer,
... Aeon (2), Chasticement, Sanctification
Nils Ingvar Ekholm ... The End
Nils Johansson ... Vintersorg, Melek Taus
Nils Lindroth "Chaos" ... Mordant
Nils Lindström ... The Drugs
Nils Molin ... Dynazty
Nils Norberg ... Nocturnal Rites, Azure
Nils Olsson ... Dreamland
Nils Olsson ... Massive Audio Nerve
Nils Patrik Johansson ... Lion's Share, Astral Doors,
... Richard Andersson's Space Odyssey,
... Ruined Soul, Civil War
Nils Reuterswärd ... Tom Trick
Nils Thomasson ... Uppgång 34
Nils-Åke Andersson ... Etos
Nina Fernandez ... Red Rocket
Nina Moilanen ... Fourever
Nina Persson ... Backyard Babies
Nina Ramsby ... Shredhead
Nina Söderqvist ... Panic
Nino Vukovic ... Immaculate
Nippe Ungerh ... Alonzo
Nisse Carlsson ... Tom Trick
Nisse Drechsel ... Ravaged
Nisse Karlén ... Sacramentum
Nisse Nilsson ... Thy Primordial
Nisse Nordin "Niels-Ingvar" ... Black Ingvars
Nitesh Mistry ... Stoneload
Nono Söderberg ... Ball
Nysse Nyström ... (See Björn Nyström)
Odd Larsson ... Harmony (1)
Oggie Jacobi ... Sun Island
Ola af Trampe ... Code, Killbilly 5'Ers, Grand Illusion
Ola Ahlsén ... Vampa

Ola Andersson ... A.C.T
Ola Andersson ... Embracing
Ola Berg ... Without Grief, 21 Lucifers
Ola Berg ... Silverdollar
Ola Blomqvist ... Spetälsk, Griftegård
Ola Carlsson ... Black Rose
Ola Colbin ... Taurus
Ola Englund ... Scarpoint, Subcyde, Sorcerer
Ola Eriksson ... Ambush
Ola Flink ... Soilwork
Ola Frenning ... Soilwork
Ola Fröjd ... Cross Bow
Ola Grönlund ... Meduza, Savage Skülls
Ola Halén ... Insania (Stockholm), Shadows Past
Ola Hedman ... Fraise
Ola Hellquist ... Lowrider
Ola Hellström ... Fire & Ice
Ola Henriksson ... Witchcraft, Troubled Horse
Ola Håkansson ... Denial
Ola Höögblom "Draugald" ... Vemoth
Ola Jansson ... Dark Illusion
Ola Johansson ... A Virgin's Delight
Ola Johansson ... Spearfish, Covered Call
Ola Johansson ... Road Ratt
Ola Johansson ... T'Bell
Ola Johansson ... Agape
Ola Karlsson ... Balthazar's Machine
Ola Karlsson ... Grand Illusion, Killbilly 5'ers
Ola Larsson ... Brimstone
Ola Lindgren ... Grave (2), Spazmosity, Putrefaction
Ola Lindström ... Hide The Knives
Ola Lindström ... Dalton
Ola Lindström ... Dieselkopf
Ola Lugner "Rich 'N Famous" ... Bad Business, Nectaris
Ola Lundberg "Machine" ... Skymning
Ola Malmkvist ... Vivaldi (group)
Ola Malmström ... Outremer, Sorcery
Ola Mohlin ... Cosmic Junk
Ola Nilsson ... Core Of Nation
Ola Ohlsson ... Gotham City
Ola Paulsson ... Caligula
Ola Persson ... (see Calle Engelmarc)
Ola Persson ... Averon
Ola Pettersson ... Syron Vanes
Ola Püschel ... Flegma
Ola Renkse ... Livin' Parazite, Parazite
Ola Ruud ... Simson
Ola Salo ... M.O.B
Ola Sivefäldt ... Valinors Tree
Ola Sjöberg ... God Macabre, Macabre End, ... Space Probe Taurus
Ola Sjödin ... Psycho Circus
Ola Sjöstedt ... Sanzia
Ola Strandberg ... Spellbound, ... Hasse Fröberg & Musical Companion
Ola Sundqvist ... Ma Connection
Ola Sundström ... Sub Second Rocket
Ola Svedin ... Syron Vanes
Ola Svensson ... Into The Void
Ola Svensson ... Faith Taboo
Ola Wentrup ... Blastrock, Into The Void
Ola Wikström ... Sanity, Sign, M.A.C
Olaf Hayer ... Dionysus
Olaf Landen ... Obscene, Svartnar
Olavi Mikkonen ... Amon Amarth
Ole Knudsen "Olly Chaos" ... The Waiting Rain
Ole Öhman "Bone W Machine/Inferno" ... Deathstars, ... Ophthalamia, Swordmaster, Dissection
Oliver Ahlström ... Obnoxious Youth
Oliver Eek ... Divine Baze Orchestra
Oliver Gille Vowden ... Ponamero Sundown
Oliver Mets ... Exanthema
Oliver Vowden ... Hydrogen
Olle Bergqvist ... D.I.Y
Olle Bodén ... Mercury Fang, Misth
Olle Borg ... In The Colonnades
Olle Boson ... Dirty Old Men
Olle Carlsson ... Daydream
Olle Cederborg ... Closer (1)
Olle Dahlstedt ... Blue Matter, Entombed, Misert Loves Co.
Olle Dickson ... Los Sin Nombre
Olle Ekman ... Volturyon, Deals Death
Olle Ekstubbe ... Cartago
Olle Ferner ... 21 Lucifers, Enemy Is Us
Olle Frodin ... Twinball
Olle Hellström ... B.C And The Envelopes
Olle Hillborg ... Glorious Bankrobbers
Olle Häggberg ... Cavalince
Olle Jansson ... Sargoth, Impious
Olle Karvonen ... Diploma
Olle Lindroth Shadows Past
Olle Lingwall ... Jonny's Bomb
Olle Mårthans ... Chainwreck, Dozer, Greenleaf
Olle Nilsson ... Colorstone, Dimma
Olle Nyberg ... Sky High
Olle Nyberg ... Motvind
Olle Olausson ... Horoscope (1)
Olle Pettersson ... In The Colonnades
Olle Risberg ... Three Seasons
Olle Rodéhn ... Shadowland, Edge
Olle Rönnbäck ... Åke Eriksson & Bedlam
Olle Siljeholm ... Cross
Olle Sjögren ... Liquid Scarlet
Olle Sjölund ... Spinning Black Circle
Olle Södergren "Olli Cox" ... Pompei Nights
Olle Töpel ... One Without
Olle Zimmerman ... Dreamhunter, Lifeline
Olle Öjebo ... Silverfish
Olli Herman Kosunen "H. Olliver Twisted" ... Crash Diet
Olof Bergeus "Hoss" ... Bosse
Olof Gardestrand ... Mirador
Olof Gardeström ... Another Hell
Olof Gustafsson ... Deed
Olof Gustafsson ... No Rules
Olof Holgersson ... Beneath The Frozen Soil
Olof Jernryd ... Brickhouse
Olof Karlsson ... Crush On You
Olof Landén ... Svartnar
Olof Larsson ... Horoscope (2)
Olof Lindgren ... Pagan, Distorted Wonderland
Olof Luhr "Behemiron" ... Vemoth
Olof Lönnroth "Puss Packard" ... Evil's Eye
Olof Martinsson ... Mindblaster
Olof Mörck ... Ruined Soul, Amaranthe, Dragonland
Olof Oljelund ... Innocent Rosie
Olof Stolt "Viusiudad" ... Reveal
Olof Sundfeldt ... Von Panzer
Olof Wikstrand "Enforcer" ... Enforcer, Corrupt, Oppression
Olov Andersson ... Veni Domine, Audiovisnion, Cross, ... Golden Ressurrection, Grand Stand, Spektrum, Hero
Olov Andersson ... Liquid Scarlet
Olov Ericsson ... Cut Out
Olov Groth ... The Citadel
Olov Häggmark ... Terrortory
Olov Knutsson ... Corporation 187
Olov Nilsson ... Live Elephant
Olov Norberg ... Hate Ammo, Live Elephant
Olov Öhman ... Tie 28
Olton ... Earthquake
Omar Ahmed ... Mefisto
Onkel ... Kill, Nifelheim
Orcus ... Blodulv
"Ornias" Sundelin ... Svartsyn
Orvar Säfström ... Entombed, Nirvana 2002
Orvar Wennström ... The Drugs, Reptilian, Original Sin
Oscar Björklund ... Twin Earth
Oscar Borgenstam "Dr. Dawn" ... Dr. Living Dead
Oscar Carlquist ... Ram
Oscar Dronjac ... Hammerfall, Cans, ... Crystal Age, Ceremonial Oath
Oscar Ekelund ... A Virgin's Delight
Oscar Kaleva ... Innocent Rosie
Oscar Leander "Vice" ... Deathstars
Oscar Lindström ... Sven Hahne & Prästrock
Oscar Moritz ... Immaculate
Oscar Nilsson ... Miseration, Despite, Saint Deamon, ... One Without, Quest Of Aidance
Oscar Olandersson ... Motherpearl
Oscar Olsson ... The Curtain
Oscar Petersson "Oz Osukaru" ... Katana, Osukaru, Eye
Oscar Petterson ... Eldrimner
Oscar Razl Hagberg ... Wild Cat Sleezy
Oscar Rolfsson "O. Thunder" ... Helvetets Port
Oscar Ryden ... Kongh
Oscar Simonson ... Ape
Oscar Zubelzu "DemonZ" ... Urbandux
Oscar Tillman ... Fi5th Reason
Oskar Andersson ... Night
Oskar Belin ... Bloodbound
Oskar Cedermalm "Ozo" ... Truckfighters, ... Firestone, Greenleaf
Oskar Eriksson ... Nine
Oskar Fjäll ... Kansas City Rollers
Oskar Forsberg ... Hellbelly
Oskar Forss ... Therion
Oskar Fredén ... Holocaustia
Oskar Höglund ... Hollowe Breed
Oskar Jakobsson "Zek" ... Withersin
Oskar Johansson "Pezo" ... Truckfighters
Oskar Karlsson ... Sarcasm, Everdawn, Helltrain, ... Gates Of Ishtar, The Duskfall, Defleshed, Scheitan
Oskar Kvant ... Kerberos
Oskar Lindholm ... Amethyst
Oskar Ling ... Pax
Oskar Lumbojev ... Ablaze
Oskar Lundström ... Siena Root
Oskar Montelius ... Civil War, Sabaton
Oskar Nilsson ... Carve, Paganizer, Unchained (2)
Oskar Norberg ... Assailant
Oskar Odelbo ... Sanctrum
Oskar Pålsson ... Coldworker, Relentless
Oskar Tornborg "Hex" ... Withersin
Oskar Westesson ... Pandemonium
Oskar Wiklund ... Savage Skülls
Oskar Åstedt ... Steelwing
Oskari Katainen ... Fimbultyr
Ottar Vigurst ... Clawfinger
Otto Almqvist ... Legbone
Otto Lövgren ... X-Ray
Otto Wiklund "Moloch" ... In Battle, Odhinn, Setherial
Ove Eriksson ... Team Custard
Ove Jansson ... The Morning After
Ove Jonsson ... Easy Street
Ove Jonsson ... Eternal Fear
Ove Kilström ... Ban-Zai
Ove Lundquist ... Crystal Blue
Ove Nordin ... Renegade (2)
Ove Thorell ... Riksväg 77
Ove Wulff ... Mercenary Mustangs
Owe Lingvall ... Nocturnal Rites
P A Danielsson ... Lion's Share
P Warenmark ... Rio
P.O Häll ... Big Thing
Pablo Munoz ... Vicious
Padde Holmgren ... Fleshcut
Pajen Karlsson ... Renegades
Paloma Estrada ... Tyranex
Paolo Mendonca ... Develop
Parik Wallin ... Roterock, Tomterockers
Partic Axelsson ... Panama Red
Pasi Humppi ... Ablaze, Freternia, Ironware
Pasi J Lappi ... Heave
Pasi Jaskara "Batong" ... Chronic Torment, ... Dawn Of Time, Reclusion
Pasi Lundegård ... Noctes
Pasi Oksa ... Pike
Pasi Salo ... By My Fear
Pasi Viitasalo "Izaph" ... Funeral Frost
Pate Lundberg ... Fleshcut
Patric Brundin ... Faith Taboo
Patric Carlsson ... Driver
Patric Carlsson ... Half Man, Skånska Mord
Patric Carlsson ... Anachronaeon
Patric Carsana ... Lobotomy
Patric Erixcon ... Asoka
Patric Fagerberg ... Psychotic Supper
Patric Franklin ... Two Franklin Grove
Patric Fransson "Valentino" ... Avalon/Avalone
Patric Hedberg ... Blacklight
Patric Ifverson ... Sub Second Rocket
Patric Köpman ... Bang & Out
Patric Wahlquist ... Candy Kicks Ass
Patric Wilén ... Calm Chaos
Patricio Carasco ... Bronto
Patrick Aalhuizen ... United
Patrick Arnehall ... Shotgun Bluez
Patrick Axelsson ... Line Up
Patrick Backlund ... Mortalicum, Quicksand Dream
Patrick Berg ... Sad Wings
Patrick Bruss ... Ribspreader
Patrick Carlsson ... Evergrey
Patrick Fransson ... Velvet Crash
Patrick Fransson ... X-Eryus
Patrick Halvarsson ... Paganizer
Patrick Hedqvist ... Raceway
Patrick Jensen ... The Haunted
Patrick Johansson "Patsy" . Prophanity, The Rapture, Arise
Patrick Johansson ... Burn
Patrick Jonsson ... Far North
Patrick Kullberg "Hrimner" ... Domgård, Nox Aurea
Patrick Leandersson ... Black Bonzo
Patrick Nygren ... Blacklight
Patrick Odepark ... Phoenix
Patrick Olsson ... Slick Stuff
Patrick Salin ... Junction
Patrick Wallin ... Tomterockers
Patrik "Possessor" ... Veternus
Patrik Albin ... Benny Jansson
Patrik Alfredsson ... Ocean (2)
Patrik Alm ... Pete Sandberg
Patrik Andersson ... Sartinas
Patrik Andersson ... Long John
Patrik Andersson ... Mogg
Patrik Andersson ... Suffer
Patrik Andersson ... Arrows
Patrik Andersson ... Railroad
Patrik Andersson ... Apostle
Patrik Andersson ... Hydra (1)
Patrik Andersson ... This Gift Is A Curse
Patrik Andersson "Onkel" ... Autopsy Torment
Patrik Andersson Winberg ... Doom Dogs
Patrik Appelgren ... Power, State Of Mind, Treat, Highbrow
Patrik Axelsson ... Chiron, Reckless
Patrik Backlund ... Quicksand Dream
Patrik Belgrave ... Wild One
Patrik Bengtsson ... Quadruple
Patrik Berg ... Shadows Past
Patrik Bergholm ... TNT
Patrik Berglin ... Mothercake, Skånska Mord
Patrik Berglund ... Renegade (2)
Patrik Björklund ... D.I.Y
Patrik Bolwede ... Eternity Remains
Patrik Borgkvist "Pat" ... 17, Gallery (1)
Patrik Byström "Sico" ... Cryonic
Patrik Carlsson ... Patrik Carlsson
Patrik Carlsson ... Aquila, Fretless
Patrik De Vee ... Time Gallery
Patrik Douglas ... Serenade For June, White Silver
Patrik Eklund ... Balthazar's Machine
Patrik Eklöf ... Blacksmith
Patrik Engelbrektsson ... Earthquake, Dogface, Tai Rose
Patrik Englund "Petter" ... Mothercake
Patrik Engström ... Gordon Fights
Patrik Eriksson ... Fatal Attraction
Patrik Essén ... Katana
Patrik Essman ... Myrah
Patrik Fernlund ... Piper's Dawn, Gorement
Patrik Fliesberg ... Bozeman's Simplex
Patrik Forsberg "Pat Kramer" ... Billion Dollar Babies
Patrik Fransson ... Fraise
Patrik Frisk ... Smash Into Pieces
Patrik Fryklund ... Hangover
Patrik Frögéli "Pata" ... Bloodshed, Rev. 16:8, Decadence
Patrik Gardberg ... Solution .45, Divinefire, Ammotrack, ... Mean Streak, Torch Bearer, Quest Of Aidance
Patrik Grip ... Superstition
Patrik Gustavsson ... Azotic Reign
Patrik Hallgren ... Self Deception
Patrik Halvarsson-Myrén "Saphanoz" ... Sinners Burn, ... Blodsrit, Ribspreader, Primitive Symphony
Patrik Hansson ... Time Code Alpha
Patrik Heath ... Gosh!
Patrik Herrstedt "PsychoPatrik" ... Road Ratt
Patrik Herrström ... Eleven Pictures
Patrik Hjalmarsson ... Lucy
Patrik Holmgren ... Craze
Patrik Holmström ... Flood
Patrik Holtentjärn ... Regent
Patrik Hultin ... Burst
Patrik Hurtig ... The Rest
Patrik Högberg "Mord" ... Armagedda
Patrik Instedt ... Candlemass
Patrik Isaksson ... Pontus Norgren
Patrik Israelsson ... Sten
Patrik J. Sten ... (See Patrik Jerksten)
Patrik Janson ... Platitude
Patrik Jansson ... Defueld, Hagen
Patrik Jemteborn ... Extaz
Patrik Jensen Dawn, Satanic Slaughter, Seance, Witchery
Patrik Jerksten "J Sten/Pat Power" ... Transport League, ... Dream Evil, Passenger
Patrik Johansson ... Prey, Stormwind Chainwreck, ... Scudiero, Yngwie Malmsteen, Without Grief, Token
Patrik Johansson "Pata" ... Bloodbound, Dawn Of Silence
Patrik Johansson ... Angel Heart
Patrik Johansson ... Dynamite Wasteland
Patrik Johansson ... Sargoth
Patrik Johansson ... Two Eagles Request
Patrik Johnsson ... Memoria
Patrik Jonsson ... Traumatic
Patrik Jonsson ... Bullhorn, GSO
Patrik Juutilainen ... Come Sleep, Lingua
Patrik Järlefalk "Mojen" ... Paralyce, Taste
Patrik Karlsson ... Heavy Load
Patrik Karlsson ... Aphasia
Patrik Karlsson ... Whiteness
Patrik Karlsson ... This Haven
Patrik L. Johansson ... Sorcery
Patrik Larsson ... Sven Hahne & Prästrock
Patrik Larsson ... Assailant
Patrik Larsson ... The Downtown Clowns
Patrik Larsson ... Solitude (2)
Patrik Lindblom "Lind" ... Tough Trade, Tyrox
Patrik Lindgren ... Thyrfing
Patrik Lindqvist ... Greasy Saddles
Patrik Lindqvist ... Section Eight
Patrik Ljungblad ... Iron Shit Snakes
Patrik Lund (now von Porat) ... Freternia
Patrik Lundh ... Crowpath
Patrik Lundström ... Sven Hahne & Prästrock
Patrik Lundström ... Kaipa, Ritual
Patrik Lägermo ... Emotion
Patrik Magnusson ... Pandemonium
Patrik Magnusson ... Spaps
Patrik Marchente ... Rosicrucian
Patrik Mattsson "Ulverheim" ... Thornium, ... Forsaken, Cryptic
Patrik Mattsson ... Deletion
Patrik Muhr ... Incinia
Patrik Myrén ... Paganizer
Patrik Mårtensson "Baalzephon" ... Misteltein
Patrik Nikolic ... Heave
Patrik Nilsson ... Crucifyre, Concrete Sleep
Patrik Nilsson ... Rebels
Patrik Nordendahl ... Destynation, Eternia
Patrik Nordlander ... Motherlode
Patrik Nyman ... Itchy Daze
Patrik Nyström ... Dedication
Patrik Olofsson (now Virdhall) ... Tusen & En Natt
Patrik Olsson ... Miscellany
Patrik Pelander ... Iniuria
Patrik Persson ... Qoph

NAME INDEX

Patrik Persson ... Frank Thomsen
Patrik Persson ... The Forsaken
Patrik Pettersson ... TME, Casket Casey
Patrik Ransäter "Snakes" ... Undecimber
Patrik Reimers ... M.O.B
Patrik Rosman ... Tusen & En Natt
Patrik Räfling "Putte" ... Mega Slaughter, Full Strike, Hammerfall
Patrik Sahlgren ... Academy
Patrik Schultz ... Death Organ
Patrik Schulz ... Scratch (2)
Patrik Selén ... Lafayette
Patrik Silén ... Keen Hue
Patrik Sjöberg ... Azotic Reign
Patrik Sjölund ... Texas Ego
Patrik Skoglöw ... Arise
Patrik Sporrong "Pat" ... F.K.Ü, Lost Souls, Kapoor, Midas Touch
Patrik Stenman ... Tie 28
Patrik Stoor ... Heave
Patrik Strömberg ... Marshal Kane
Patrik Sundkvist ... Necromicon
Patrik Sundqvist ... Stardog
Patrik Svensson ... Inverted
Patrik Sviberg ... Atlantis, Raceway
Patrik Svärd ... Cloudscape, Doctor Weird, Second Heat
Patrik Syk ... The Cold Existence
Patrik Södergren "Stevie Rose" ... Bad Habit
Patrik Söderkvist "Patrick Fox" ... Burn
Patrik Söderström ... Frontiers
Patrik Thorngren ... Spacebone
Patrik Tibell ... Amity, CC Rock, Flintstens Med Stanley, Railroad, Trazy Goes Crazy, T'Bell
Patrik Törnblom (aka Ulfström) ... Silent Call
Patrik Törnkvist ... The Moaning, Helltrain, The Everdawn
Patrik Wall ... Plector, Apostasy
Patrik Wirén ... Man.Machine.Industry, Midas Touch, Misery Loves Co.
Patrik Västilä ... Insania (Stockholm)
Patrik Ylmefors ... Moloken
Patrik Zakrisson ... Lipkin
Patrik Öberg ... Ghamorean
Paul Allen ... Espinoza
Paul Börjesson ... Cornel Band
Paul DeCarli ... Skold
Paul Dexter ... Little Yankees
Paul Eriksson ... East End
Paul Fernandez ... Knockout
Paul Flensby ... Hydrogen, Vulture Cavalry
Paul Gidlöf ... Affecti Veternus
Paul Grey ... Heavy Load
Paul Gustafsson (now Bergholtz) ... Mercy, Turbo, Overdrive
Paul Humble ... Seamroller
Paul Johansson ... Outremer, In Solitude, In Aeternum, Sorcery
Paul Mäkitalo "Themgoroth" ... Dark Funeral, Bloodshed, Infernal, Setherial, In Aeternum
Paul Pettersson ... Crystal Eyes
Paul Schöning ... Pathos
Paul Sundlin "Palle" ... Life
Paul Sörensson ... Sonic Walthers
Paul Utter ... Rising
Paul Vahala ... Tornado Babies
Paul Zanichelli ... Parasite, Rebelene, To Africa With Love
Pauli Väsäinen ... Vision
Payre Kankanranta (now Pär Hulkoff) ... Viperine, Winterlong, Raubtier, The Storyteller
Pea Eliasson ... United
Pece Masalkovski ... Wit
Peder Andersson ... W.O. Band
Peder Berglund ... Acis
Peder Bergstrand ... Greenleaf, Lowrider
Peder Borgemo ... Hebron
Peder Carlsson ... Backyard Babies
Peder Clevberger ... Fuzzdevil, Six Pack Sonic
Peder Johansson ... S.L.R, Falconer
Peder Jonsson ... Waterline
Peder Karlsson ... Last Laugh (2), Miseration
Peder Lindblom ... New Bulsara
Peder Lundgren ... Orient
Peder Rongvall "Pete Ash" ... Vanity Blvd
Peder Sandström ... Assailant
Peder Skoglund ... Lovebone, Mystery
Peder Sundqvist ... Assailant, Hate Ammo
Pedro Pico "Mr Dim" ... Trash, Harm's Way
Peer Stappe "Zack Booner" ... Rydell & Quick, Loud, Lonely Hearts
Pehr Larsson .. Vinterland, Maze Of Torment, Harmony (1)
Pehr Severin ... Corporation 187, Daisy Chain
Pekka Adolfsson ... Göran Nordh
Pekka Kiviaho "Power" ... One Man Army, Persuader, Auberon
Pekka Lindqvist ... Traumatic
Pekka Ollinen "Stixx" ... House Of Heavy, Shotgun Messiah, King Pin
Pekka Similä ... Deep Zilents
Pelle Alsing ... Moosters
Pelle Andersson ... Status Two
Pelle Andersson ... Seven Wishes
Pelle Andreasson ... Eternity Remains
Pelle Berglund ... Powerbreeze
Pelle Ekegren ... Cauterizer, Grave (2), Coercion
Pelle Ekman ... Dyngrak
Pelle Eliasson "Eliaz". Bai Bang, Scandal Circus, Mindfuel
Pelle Engvall ... Svarte Pan, The Carpet Knights
Pelle Ferner ... Rat Pack
Pelle Henricsson ... Shredhead
Pelle Hindén ... Aquila, Fretless, Eternal
Pelle Höglund ... Mason
Pelle Hökengren ... Solsting
Pelle Hörndal ... X-Hale, Fortune
Pelle Jernryd ... Brickhouse
Pelle Johansson ... Laudamus
Pelle Johansson ... Dawn Of Silence
Pelle Karlsson "DeLuxe" ... Inhale
Pelle Karlsson ... Repulz
Pelle Larsson ... Wonderland (1)
Pelle Liljenberg ... Coercion
Pelle Melander "Piss" ... Verminious, Sgt. Carnage
Pelle Nilsson ... Atrox
Pelle Persson ... Heavy Cargo
Pelle Petersson ... Green Sleeves, Heartcry, Johannes, Emotion
Pelle Robertsson ... B.C And The Envelopes
Pelle Rönningås ... Dr Booster
Pelle Saether "Lenny De Rose" ... Zeelion, Unchained, Grand Design, Schizophrenic Circus, Zello ... The Bereaved, The Cold Existance, Corporation 187, Crimson Moonlight, Diabolical, Draconian, Ironware, Lick The Dog, Maleficio, Mindjive, Nightshade, Nox Aurea, Shattered, Sherlock Brothers, Subdive, Thalamus, Apostasy, Bullhorn, Cryonic Temple, Darkwater, Diablo Swing Orchestra, Ebony Tears, Facequake, Griffen, Harmony, Middleage, Mithotyn, Mother Misery, Psychotic Supper, Rising Faith, Renaissance Of Fools, Steel Attack, Terror 2000, Within Reach, Dog Faced Gods,
Pelle Siren ... Zeta
Pelle Skoglund ... Tube Screamer
Pelle Smuts ... Oberon
Pelle Ström ... Agony, Comecon, Omnitron
Pelle Thambert ... Onyx
Pelle Thuresson ... Overdrive, Paradize (1)
Pelle Thörnqvist ... Sunflower
Pelle Wilhelmsson ... Kisses From The Past
Pelle Åhman "Hornper" ... In Solitude
Pelle Åkerlind ... Morgana Lefay, Bloodbound, Trail Of Murder
Pelle Öberg ... Infanticide, Punishment
Pentti Von Fürstenrecht ... Big Times
Peo Axelsson ... Vanguard, Reehab
Peo Gaasvik ... Frontiers
Peo Hedin ... Absorbing The Pain, Killer Bee
Peo Moogvall ... Blastrock
Peo Olofsson ... M.A.D
Peo Petersson ... Ypzilon
Peo Pettersson ... Axia, Amity, Leviticus, Galaxy, Flintstens Med Stanley, Nocturnal Alliance, Two Franklin Groove, X-Ray, Peo
Peo Thyrén "Alex Tyrone" ... Easy Action, Candy Roxx
Peppe Vikman ... Vanessa
Per Ahlström ... Lazy, Shed
Per Ahre ... Stabwound
Per Aldeheim ... It's Alive, Pain
Per Alm ... Von Rosen
Per Almgren ... Head Force
Per Almquist ... Eternal Oath
Per Anders Danielsson ... Veni Domine
Per Anders Sahlström ... Dorian Gray, Priority
Per Andersson ... Electric Eastwood
Per Andersson ... Colt 49
Per Andersson ... Wonderland (2)
Per Andersson ... Keen Hue
Per Andersson ... Waterline
Per Ax ... Excruciate
Per Axelsson ... Eggs On Legs
Per Berglund ... Merrygold
Per Bergquist ... The Bereaved, Closer (2)
Per Billengren ... Renegade (1)
Per Björklund ... Oblivious
Per Blom ... John Norum
Per Blomgren ... Hangover
Per Blückert ... Traction
Per Boder ... Space Probe Taurus, God Macabre, Macabre End, Mordbrand
Per Broberg ... Dawn Of Oblivion
Per Broddesson ... Book Of Hours, Wolverine, Griftegård, Year Of The Goat, Optimystical
Per Bruun ... Jaguar, (Fläsket Brinner)
Per Cederberg "Glitz" ... Revolution Riot
Per Dohlk "Dohlken" ... Whimzy
Per Elberg ... Jonny Cartong
Per Ellwerson ... Mother Superior
Per Elmquist ... Exciters
Per Elofsson ... Nocturnal Rites
Per Englund ... Blacksmith, 220 Volt, Dedication, Mandrake Root, Motherlode
Per Engström ... Blizzard
Per Eriksson ... Carrie
Per Eriksson "Sodomizer" ... 21 Lucifers, Bloodbath
Per Eriksson ... Paradise (1)
Per Eriksson ... Vantage
Per Eriksson ... Genocrush Ferox
Per Eriksson ... Powertrip
Per Forsberg ... Watain
Per Forsell ... Nattsvart
Per Fransson ... Soulbreach
Per Fällström ... Downstroke
Per Giöbel ... Motvind
Per Gustavsson "Hellbutcher" ... Necronaut, Nifelheim, Necrocurse, Pagan Rites
Per Gustavsson ... Gods Incorporated
Per Gustavsson ... Bussiga Klubben
Per Gyllenbäck ... Deranged
Per Hallman ... Stormwind, Wisdom Call, Brighteye Brison
Per Hansson ... Russell
Per Hedtjärn ... Ellen B
Per Hellqvist "Kraath" ... Blackwinds, Setherial
Per Henriksson ... Wolverine
Per Hesselrud ... D.I.Y, Bosse
Per Holma ... Sunset Blade
Per Holmstedt ... The Morning After
Per Husebö "Dirge Rep" ... Craft
Per Häggblom ... Shock Tilt
Per Ingels ... Zeta
Per Ivarsson ... Side By Side
Per Johansson ... Borderline (1)
Per Johansson ... Rubbet
Per Johansson ... Buszer
Per Jungberger ... Furbowl
Per Karlsson "Perry" ... Dreamhunter, Lifeline
Per Karlsson "Perra" ... Bergraven, Nominon, In Aeternum, Nex, Interment, Suffer, Altar, Wortox, Serpent, Die Hard, T.A.R
Per Karlsson ... April Divine
Per Karlsson ... Conquest, Blot Mine, Setherial
Per Korpås ... Source (2)
Per Larsson ... Lynx
Per Lefvert ... Greasy Saddles
Per Lengsted (aka Karlsson) "Periloz" ... Overdrive, Portrait, Unchained (2)
Per Lidén ... Renegade Five
Per Liljefors ... Cross, ATC, Cheese
Per Lindstedt (aka Andersson) "Jeff Keegan" ... Arrowz, Keegan
Per Lindström ... Machinery, In Grey, Flaggelation
Per Ljungberg ... Wonderflow
Per Ljungqvist ... Vampa
Per Lundgren ... Empire
Per Lundh ... Empire
Per Lundqvist ... Taurus
Per Magnusson ... Razorblade
Per Melander ... Delve
Per Mikaelsson ... Heel
Per Mårtensson . Mojobone, Stonecake The Morning After
Per Möller Jensen ... The Haunted
Per Nilsson ... Kaipa
Per Nilsson ... World Below, Scar Symmetry, Altered Aeon
Per Nilsson ... Hagen, Legia
Per Nilsson ... Universe
Per Nordbring ... Peo
Per Nylin ... Dave Rock, Renegade Five
Per-Ola Vikström "Peo" ... Sunset Blade
Per Olofsson ... Blastrock
Per Olofsson ... Into The Void
Per Olsson "Rikki Bullet" ... Lipstixx 'N' Bullets
Per Ousbäck ... Jaguar
Per Persson (now Pilhjerta) ... Cult Of The Fox
Per Qvarnström ... By Night
Per Reinaldo "Barnet" ... Skitarg, The Ugly
Per Richard ... Heave
Per Romwall ... Hostile Cell
Per Runesson ... Unicorn
Per Ryberg ... Enigmatic
Per Rydberg ... Averon
Per Rylander ... Diary
Per Sahlberg ... Wild One
Per Sandberg ... Two Eagles Request
Per Sandgren ... Windwalker
Per Sandlund ... Fatal Attraction
Per Schelander ... House Of Shakira, Pain Of Salvation, Tomas Bergsten's Fantasy
Per Selander ... Valenze
Per Sjögren ... Meshuggah
Per Soläng ... Corroded
Per Sparring "Billie/St Caramel Jr III" ... Evil's Eye
Per Stadin ... Billionaires Boys Club, Yngwie Malmsteen, Dave Nerge's Bulldog, Geff, Silver Mountain, Snake Charmer
Per Stenbeck ... Outshine
Per Strömstedt "Zeb" ... Zane
Per Sundberg ... Crimson Moonlight
Per Sundström ... Panzer Princess
Per Svensson ... Promotion, Grand Illusion, Code
Per Svensson ... Yersinia
Per Svensson ... G.O.L.D
Per Söderberg ... Blizzard
Per Telg ... Moonstruck
Per Wallgren ... Syrus
Per Wallmark ... Side By Side
Per Warger ... Quinzy
Per Westergren ... Million
Per Wiberg "Wibärj" ... Bacon, Baltimoore, Sky High, Spiritual Beggars, Mojobone, Boom Club, Opeth, King Hobo, Death Organ
Per Widell "Pistolper" ... Cowboy Prostitutes
Per Wikström ... Noctum
Per Wilhelmsson ... Orphan Gypsy
Per Yngve Ohlin "Dead" ... Morbid
Per Åhlund ... Calm
Per Öhman ... Vision
Per Öhman ... Reflex
Per-Anders Enebro ... A*Teem
Per-Arme: b ... Armauk
Per-Arne Fallén ... X-Perience
Percy Mejhagen ... Cellout
Per-Erik Karlsson "Thunaraz/Devothan" ... Blot Mine, Treasure, Setherial
Per-Erik Tageson "Lillen" ... The Session
Per-Erik Thorp ... Liquid Phase
Per-Håkan Skånberg ... Hawk
Per-Martin Pettersson ... Plebb
Per-Ola Embretsén "MadDog" ... Gasoline Queen
Per-Ola Olsson ... Tad Morose
Per-Ola Pettersson ... Paradize (2)
Per-Olof Andersson ... Borderline (2)
Per-Olof Andersson ... Abramis Brama
Per-Olof Buhre ... Vanadis
Per-Olof Hogebrandt ... Mindblaster
Per-Olof Johansson ... Sleazy Roze
Per-Olof Wester ... Daemonicus
Per-Olov Engman ... Promille
Per-Ove Johansson ... Axewitch
Per-Owe Johansson "P-O" ... Depzon
Per-Ove Nilsson ... Oxid, The End
Per-Owe Solvenius "Ewo" . Confidence, Trident, Darkness
Perra Ahlberg ... Whimzy
Perra Eriksson ... Razorblade
Perra Johansson ... Coldspell, Lover Under Cover
Perra Johansson ... Inrage, Lost Souls, Lafayette, Crawley
Perra Tedblad ... Zan Clan
Perre Lindberg ... Los Bohemos
Perry Geson ... Cavokey
Perti Hellala ... Kings N' Fools
Pertti Tikkanen ... Shock Tilt
Per-Åke Holmberg "Sticky Bomb" ... Bonafide
Per-Åke Persson ... Colt 47
Pete Ash ... Vanity Blvd
Pete Blakk ... Notre Dame
Pete Cockcroft ... Paradise (2)
Pete Dolls ... Denied
Pete Meete ... To Africa With Love
Pete Peeters ... Fat Nelly
Pete Sandberg ... Alien, Billionaires Boys Club, Keegan, Mansson, Midnight Sun, Snake Charmer, Bewarp, Madison, Opus Atlantica, Pete Sandberg, Pete Sandberg's Jade, Silver Seraph, Von Rosen
Peter "Stonebreaker" ... The Chair
Peter Alstermark ... Cartago
Peter Andersson ... Odyssey (1)
Peter Andersson ... Enigmatic
Peter Andersson (Weiner) ... Luciferion, Sarcazm
Peter Andersson "Lato" ... Rising
Peter Andersson "P-Son" ... N.J.B, Meadow
Peter Andersson ... GRK
Peter Andersson ... New Breed
Peter Andersson ... Niva, Axia, Mean Streak
Peter Andersson ... Stallion, Misery
Peter Andersson ... Tornado Soup
Peter Andersson ... Raving Mad
Peter Arnildstam ... Earthquake
Peter Arvidsson ... Driver, Dumper
Peter Asp ... A.C.T
Peter Asp ... Stillborn
Peter Axelsson ... Rio
Peter Axelsson ... Dedication
Peter Beckman ... Greasy Saddles
Peter Bengtsson ... Big Talk (2)
Peter Berg ... Machinery, Colossus
Peter Bergkvist ... Maryscreek
Peter Birgersson ... Unreal
Peter Bjärgö (aka Pettersson) ... Tyrant, Crypt Of Kerberos, Flesh (The Pete Flesh Deathtrip)
Peter Björklund ... Double Diamond
Peter Björklund ... Print
Peter Blomberg "Blomman" ... Belsebub
Peter Blomqvist ... Subtopia
Peter Bodefjord ... Norden Light
Peter Bondesson ... Universal Flytrap
Peter Borg ... Panama Red
Peter Broch ... Wit

Peter Broman … Amaze Me
Peter Bäcke … Prey
Peter Callander … Apostle
Peter Carlberg … Marcus Brutus Band, Wildborn
Peter Carlfors … Dieselkopf
Peter Carlhed "Pee" … White Line
Peter Carlsohn … Veni Domine, Jerusalem
Peter Carlsson … Bedlam
Peter Dahl … Story
Peter Dahlgren … Ozium
Peter Dahlstrand … Allan Beddo Band
Peter Dahlström … Brother Ape
Peter Damin … Another Life, Renegade Five
Peter Danielsson … Frekvens
Peter Danielsson … Via Tokyo, Aurora
Peter Degerfelt … Dr Booster
Peter Derenius … Maleficio
Peter Diephuis … Jonny Cartong
Peter Dolving … The Haunted, Sparzanza, Coldtears
Peter Edwards … Zoic
Peter Edwinzon … Attention (1), Unicorn
Peter Ehlebrink … Haze
Peter Eklund "Equimanthorn" … Dark Funeral,
… Ponamero Sundown
Peter Eklund … Solid Ground (1)
Peter Ekman … Prospect
Peter Ekström … Great Ad
Peter Eliasson "Griffin" … Belladonna
Peter Ellström … Lancer
Peter Emanuelsson … Spazmosity
Peter Emilsson … Crossroad Jam
Peter Engström … Cipher System
Peter Ericson … Glory
Peter Ericsson … Unchained (2), Disruption
Peter Eriksson … Sparzanza
Peter Eriksson … Inzight
Peter Eriksson … Keen Hue
Peter Eriksson … Rävjunk
Peter Eriksson … Spacebone
Peter Espinoza … Original Sin, Bai Bang, Gin N' It,
… Majestic, Mansson, Steelwings, Espinoza,
… Nasty Idols, Reingold, Sad Wings
Peter Eyre … Coste Apetrea
Peter Fjällström … Last Laugh (2)
Peter Forkelid "Pim" … Sons Of Neverland, W.O. Band
Peter Forsberg … Stockholm Showdown
Peter Forsell … United
Peter Forss … Bonedog
Peter Franzén … Drama
Peter Fredricksson … Regent, Madison
Peter Frögéli … Decadence, Rev 16:8, Bloodshed
Peter Furulid … Sorcerer
Peter Füle … Milky
Peter Gidlund … Inzight
Peter Gottlieb … Electric Earth
Peter Grehn … Morgana Lefay, Lefay, Fantasmagoria
Peter Grimhall … Chai Gang
Peter Grundström … Stonelake
Peter Gustafsson … Queen Obscene
Peter Gustafsson … Whiteness
Peter Gustafsson … M.O.B
Peter Gustavsson … Angelize, Broke(N)Blue
Peter Haga … Black Rose
Peter Haglund "Pete Destroyer" … Axis Powers,
… Suicidal Winds
Peter Halvarsson … Divine Sin
Peter Hansson … Therion
Peter Hedberg … Fatal Smile (1), Freedom Bleeder
Peter Hedman … Sorcery
Peter Hellström … Gone
Peter Henningsson … Impale, Silent Skythe
Peter Henriksson "Henrix/Slim Pete" … Jekyll & Hyde,
… Ponamero Sundown, Gemini Five, Slingblade
Peter Hermansson … 220 Volt, Talisman, John Norum,
… Annie For President, Grand Design
Peter Hoffman … Överslag
Peter Horvath … Proud
Peter Huss … Ruined Soul, Apostasy Shining
Peter Hynyadi "Krist" … Glanzig
Peter Hägglund … Terrortory
Peter Hägglund (now Lans) "Pete" … (See Peter Lans)
Peter Högberg … Nightvision
Peter Ingman "Perry" … Pussy Galore
Peter Iwers … In Flames
Peter Jacobson … Fagin
Peter Jacobsson "Pete Black/Blakk" … Geisha, Trazer,
… Blakk Totem
Peter Jakobsson … Genie
Peter Jakobsson … Suicide Nation
Peter Jansson … Crypt Of Kerberos, Maze Of Torment
Peter Jansson "Zkipper" … Undecimber
Peter Jeansson … Norden Light
Peter Johansson … Axenstar, Miscreant
Peter Johansson "Bobby" … Ape
Peter Johansson "Pjorra" … Ape
Peter Johansson … Meadow
Peter Johansson … Silverwings
Peter Johansson … Thalamus
Peter Johansson … Two Eagles Request
Peter Johansson … Empire Saint
Peter Johansson … The Session
Peter Jonasson … U.N.IT
Peter Jones … Line Up
Peter Jonsson … The Ugly
Peter Jonsson … Enigmatic
Peter Josefsson … Overdeth
Peter Jägerhult "PJ" … Attack, Tempelrock, Biscaya, Trash
Peter Jönsson … Sanctification
Peter Kadar … Amkeni
Peter Kahm … It's Alive, Ebony Tears
Peter Kantonmaa "Waylon" … Raubtier
Peter Karlsson "Bitchfire" … Mordant
Peter Karlsson "Pete Flesh" … Maze Of Torment,
… Deceiver, Thrown, Flesh
Peter Karlsson/Holm … The Quill, Quil
Peter Karlsson … Saturnalia Temple
Peter Karlsson … King Koole
Peter Karlsson … My Dead Addiction
Peter Karlsson … Far North
Peter Karlsson … Harmony (1)
Peter Kihlberg … Fairness
Peter Kim … Miscreant
Peter Kjellin … Plan Three
Peter Klintberg … Cartago
Peter Koistinaho … Corrosive Carcass
Peter Korsgard … Foobar The Band
Peter Kronberg … Section Eight, Asperity
Peter Kvick … Crystal Pride
Peter Kvist … Los Bohemos
Peter Laestadius … Comatose
Peter Lagestam … Rainfall
Peter Laitinen … Imperial Domain
Peter Lake … Mutant, Theory In Practice
Peter Lans (aka Hägglund) "Pete" … Inrage,
… Lost Souls, F.K.Ü
Peter Larsson … Anxious
Peter Larsson … Cavus
Peter Laustsen . Rimfrost, Nox Aurea, The Cold Existence
Peter Lazar … Time Code Alpha
Peter Ledin … Vanessa, Acis, Blackworld, Grand Design
Peter Lidebrandt … The Weed
Peter Lidén … Terrorama
Peter Lidström … Sahara (2)
Peter Lilja … Half Man
Peter Limber … Saltmine
Peter Lindberg … Armatur
Peter Lindell … Physical Attraction
Peter Lindgren … Steel, Opeth
Peter Lindh … Lafayette
Peter Lindholm … Enemy Is Us
Peter Lindqvist … Chainsaw, Decadence, Canopy
Peter Lindskog … Interaction
Peter Lindström … Neon
Peter Ljungberg … Rough Rockers, Movin' Globe
Peter Lundberg … Embracing
Peter Lundberg "Ke" … The Ungrateful
Peter Lundberg … Higher Ground
Peter Lundell … Darkness
Peter Lundell … Helium Head
Peter Lundén "London" … Crash Diet
Peter Lundgren … Destiny, 7th Planet
Peter Lundgren … Marc Quee
Peter Lundin … Cicero
Peter Lundin … CC Rock
Peter Lundin … Spearfish
Peter Lundström … Los Bohemos
Peter Lundström … Agony
Peter Löf … Thyrfing
Peter Magnusson … Cherokee
Peter Magnusson … Sub Second Rocket
Peter Malmersjö … Solid ground (2)
Peter Martinsson … Plebb, Purple Haze,
… Peter Martinsson Group
Peter Melin … Black Cat Moan
Peter Mellgren "Bad-Ass Bobby" … A*Teem
Peter Mikaelsson … One Cent
Peter Milefors … Darque
Peter Morén … Inmoria, Steel Attack, Tad Morose
Peter Morgan Lie … (See Morgan Lie)
Peter Mosebach "Mose" … Too Late
Peter Månsson … Depzon
Peter Månsson … Vildsvin
Peter Mårdklint … Tenebre, All Ends, Embraced
Peter Nagy (-Eklöf) "Draakh Kimera" … Hypocrite,
… Wyvern, Defender, Sectu, Eternal Oath,
… Faceshift, Mörk Gryning
Peter Nilsson … Nominon, Fafner
Peter Nilsson … Stormwind, Glory
Peter Nilsson "Daniels" … Unameus
Peter Nilsson … Tension
Peter Nilsson … Young Force
Peter Nordholm … Don Patrol
Peter Nordin … Meshuggah
Peter Nordin … Anekdoten
Peter Nordin … Regent
Peter Nordstedt … Reptile Smile
Peter Norstedt … Spinning Black Circle
Peter Nylén … Gondoline
Peter Ogestad … Silent Scythe
Peter Olander … 220 Volt
Peter Olsen … Kings Of Modern Swing
Peter Olsén … Mac & Ploids
Peter Olsson … Power, Europe
Peter Olsson … Head Force
Peter Olsson … Adventure
Peter Olsson … Deep Zilents
Peter Olsson … Limit
Peter Otterborg … Dreamhunter, Lifeline
Peter Ottosson … Green Sleeves
Peter Palmdahl "Carnivore" … Deathwitch,
… Runemagick, Dissection
Peter Pedersén … Amaxa
Peter Persson … The Case
Peter Persson … Soulless
Peter Persson … The Painted Man
Peter Persson … Viceral Bleeding
Peter Petersson … Snakes In Paradise
Peter Pettersson … (see Peter Bjärgö)
Peter Pohlin … Stoneflow
Peter Rhode … Pussy Galore, Side By Side
Peter Ristiharju … Maramon
Peter Robsahm … Robb and Friends
Peter Rosenbach "Rozz" … Rozz The Bozz, King & Rozz
Peter Rudström … 454
Peter Ruhdberg … Midfortune
Peter Rundström … Motherlode
Peter Samuelsson … Nifters
Peter Samuelsson … Gallows End
Peter Sandberg … Naughty Boys
Peter Sandberg "Udd" … Yngwie Malmsteen,
… Glory Bells (Band), Råg i Ryggen
Peter Sandqvist … Make Up
Peter Sehlin … Steel Arrows
Peter Sehlstedt … The Case
Peter Selin … Left Hand Solution
Peter Shapiro … Reptile Smile
Peter Sigfridsson … Majectic Vanguard
Peter Sjöberg … (see Peter Lake)
Peter Sjödin … Corroded
Peter Sonefors … Overload, Gormathon
Peter Späth … Steel Attack
Peter Stange … Brainwave
Peter Stenlund … Laudamus
Peter Stjärnvind "Insulter" … Damnation, Entombed,
… Regurgitate, Born Of Fire, Face Down,
… Merciless, Murder Squad, Nifelheim,
… Dismember, Unanimated, Black Trip
Peter Strandberg … Heartbreak Radio
Peter Stålfors … Dream Evil
Peter Stålhammar … Young Force
Peter Sundell … Deacon Street, Wulcan,
… Grand Ilusion, Promotion, Peter Sundell
Peter Sundell … Bluesbreath
Peter Svensson … Gypsy Rose
Peter Svensson … Cross Bow, Devil Lee Rot,
… Void Moon, Cult Of The Fox
Peter Svensson "TrumPeter" … Locomotive Breath,
… Mercy, Mountain Of Power, Mörrum's Own,
… Constancia, Faith, The Kaar's
Peter Särnegårdh … Suma
Peter Söderlind … Ape
Peter Söderström … Bosse, Frontiers, Jupiter Society
Peter Thederan … Black Rose
Peter Thorne … Iron Shit Snakes
Peter Tillgren … East End
Peter Tuthill … Despite, Carnal Forge, Dog Faced Gods
Peter Türsch … Balthazar
Peter Tägtgren … Amon Amarth, Arckanum, Astral Doors,
… Bloodbath, Gardenian, Marduk, Naglfar, Ophthalamia,
… Scarpoint, Sorhin, 8th Sin, Thyrfing, Wolf, Algaion,
… Allegiance, Corporation 187, Dark Funeral, Dawn,
… Hysterica, Sanctification, WAR, Total War, The Abyss,
… Pain, Hypocrisy
Peter Udd … (see Peter Sandberg)
Peter Ulvén … Embracing, April Divine, Azure
Peter Ulving … Victory (2)
Peter Uvén … Winterlong, Slowgate, Powertrip
Peter Valefors … Hearts Alive
Peter Vilhelmsson "Pete Meat" … Scratch (1)
Peter Wahlberg "Walle" … Wagabond
Peter Waites … Forcefeed, Malaise, Seething
Peter Wendin … Eternal Oath
Peter Westby … Il Shy
Peter Westerberg … Bishop Garden
Peter Westin … Solution
Peter Westin … Airlines
Peter Westman "Pedda" … Lick The Dog
Peter Wiberg … Ironware, Freternia
Peter Wichers … The Defaced, Soilwork
Peter Widding … Ghamorean
Peter Widehammar … Vatten
Peter Wigeborn … Sworn
Peter Wikberg "PeeWee" … Squetters
Peter Wikström … Saltmine
Peter Wildoer … Armageddon, Agregator, Darkane,
… Dawn Of Oblivion, Arch Enemy, Time Reqiem,
… Grimmark, Majestic, Silver Seraph,
… Stefan Rosquist Band, Non-Human Level
Peter Wingård … Depzon
Peter Wold … Akilles
Peter Ytterman … Double Diamond
Peter Zyreén … Story
Peter Åhs … Rhapsody (Sweden), Extasy, Shaggy
Peter Åström … Three Minute Madness
Peter Öberg … Ramm
Peter Östling … Six Feet Under
Peter Östlund … The Law, Vomitory
Peter Östman … Sergeant, Boogietryck
Peter Östros … Insania (Stockholm)
Pether Mentzer … Manimal
Pether Svedjewik … Razorblade
Petja Lepola … Hate Gallery
Petra Albrecht … Piper's Dawn
Petra Kvännå … Mojobone, Nerved, Sky High
Petra Vadsten … Quarterback Beat
Petri Aho … Mourning Sign
Petri Kinnunen … Da President
Petri Kuusisto … Steel Attack, In Thy Dreams,
… Asperity, Carnal Forge
Petri Pöllänen … Terrorama
Petri Ranki "T-Bird" … Plan 9
Petri Riipi … Angelize
Petri Tarvainen … Eternal Oath, Faceshift
Petri Vehviläinen … Naked
Petrus Engelhart … Steamboat Willies
Petrus Kukulski … Ion Olteanu Band
Petrus Lindström … Hollowe Breed
Petter Adsten … Furor
Petter Boström … Cap Outrun
Petter Broman … Wyvern
Petter Dennevi … Starterhead
Petter Englund … Skånska Mord, Zilch
Petter Eriksson … Higher Ground
Petter Flemberg … Skin Infection
Petter Furå "Pete Fury" … Malison Rogue
Petter Heinemann "Temple" … Reveal
Petter Johansson … Torn Apart
Petter Karlsson … Therion, Diablo Swing Orchestra,
… Notre Dame, Sobre Nocturn
Petter Karlsson … Distorted Wonderland
Petter Nilson … Terrorama
Petter Nilsson "Svarte Petter" … Feral
Petter Pettersson … Twin Age
Petter Samuel Freed … 2 Ton Predator,
… The Project Hate MCMXCIX
Petter Stenmarker … Crimson Moonlight, Oblivion
Petter Swartz … Illfigure
Petter Tavér … Comatose
Petter Ter-Borch … Marble Arch, Evercry
PH Holgersson … Paletoe
Phamarus … Diabolical
Phanatos … Screams Over Northland
Phil Alex Cirone … Craft, Shining
Phil Levy … God Kills
Philip Borg … Imperial Domain
Philip Karlsson … The Black Marbles
Philip Monell … Attention (1)
Philip Svennefeldt "Inquisitor" … Helvetets Port, Portrait
Philip Von Segebaden "Grave Raper" … Cranium, Dawn,
… Afflicted, Defender
Pia Kjellborn … Revanch
Pia Nyström … Ice Age
Piatos Dimitrios "Mr Dim" … Born Of Fire
Pierre Andersson … Calm
Pierre Andersson … Source (2)
Pierre Breidensjö … Avenue
Pierre Carnbrand-Lindsjöö "P-Air" … Fistfunk
Pierre Ekström … Yankee Heaven
Pierre Erixon … Gregor Samsa
Pierre Glans … Blind Alley
Pierre Knutsson … Dieselkopf
Pierre Lopez … Nymf
Pierre Nilsson … Allan Beddo Band
Pierre Oxenryd … Moonville
Pierre Petterson … Taste
Pierre Richter … God B.C., Agregator
Pierre Stam … In Mourning
Pierre Swärd … Thomas Larsson
Pierre Törnkvist … The Moaning, Helltrain,
… The Everdawn, Scheitan
Pierre Wensberg … Roach, Radioactive, Elevener,
… Prisoner, Heartbreak Radio
Pierre Wilhelmsson … Månegarm
Pierre Östh … Diary
Pierro Mengarelli … Neon Rose
Piotr Jastrzebski … Shakespeare
Piotr Wawrzeniuk … Therion, Carbonized, Serpent
Patrik Saari "PM" … Lizard Eye
P-O Larsson … Wolverine, Vital Sign, XT
P-O Sedin … Killer Bee
P-O Söderbäck "Wolfie" … Bombs Of Hades
Poa Åhlslund … Project UPA

NAME INDEX

Pontus "Penetrator" ... Morbid Insulter
Pontus Andersson ... Cipher System, Satureye, Eternal Grief, Entropy
Pontus Andersson ... Tyfuz
Pontus Andersson ... SnakeStorm, (Dia Psalma)
Pontus Arkerud (now Oldberg) ... Publikförakt AB
Pontus Arvidson ... Chainsaw
Pontus Borg ... Roach
Pontus Carmbrandt ... Enemies Swe
Pontus Cervin ... Toxaemia
Pontus Dahlström ... Somber
Pontus Egberg ... Lion's Share, Yale Bate, Dark Illusion, The Poodles, Steamroller, Zan Clan
Pontus Ekwall "Chris" ... Kazjurol
Pontus Hjelm ... Marionette, Dead By April
Pontus Holmgren ... Stand By
Pontus Hultgren ... Amkeni
Pontus Jansson ... Miscreant, Utumno
Pontus Jansson ... Axenstar
Pontus Jonsson ... Demons Of Dirt
Pontus Jordan ... Horisont
Pontus Landgren ... Svartnad
Pontus Larsson ... Firecracker, Vindictiv
Pontus Lekaregård (aka Larsson) ... Eternal, Aquila
Pontus Lindmark ... Cloudscape
Pontus Lindmark ... Faithful Darkness
Pontus Lindmark ... Miscellany
Pontus Lindqvist ... Enter The Hunt, Omnitron
Pontus Lundin ... Skald
Pontus Lundström ... Earthquake
Pontus Mantefors ... Diablo Swing Orchestra
Pontus Nelderup ... Anyway
Pontus Norgren ... 17, Divinefire, Four Sticks, Gallery, Great King Rat, Hammerfall, House Of Shakira, Humanimal, Hysterica, Impulsia, Jekyll & Hyde, Locomotive Breath, Mercury Fang, Pontus Norgren, The Poodles, The Ring, Seven Wishes, Talisman, Token, Thomas Vikström, Violent Divine, Zan Clan
Pontus Norman ... Excessum
Pontus Pedersén ... Traction
Pontus Pettersson (now Lennander) ... Stonechurch
Pontus Pettersson ... Vicious
Pontus Pfeiffer ... Arconova
Pontus Redig ... Miasmal
Pontus Sjösten ... Satanic Slaughter, Denata
Pontus Sköldhammar ... Psyckadeli
Pontus Snibb ... Bonafide, Brickhouse, Pontus Snibb 3, Mountain Of Power
Pontus Swanberg ... Sanchez
Pontus Svensson ... Nymf
Pontus Svensson ... Red Rocket
Pontus Wallin ... Last Laugh (1)
Pontus Åkesson ... Nightscape
Preem Sandell ... Johan Randén
Professor X (aka Avernus) ... Apati
Putte Eriksson ... Manticore
Putte Leander ... Authorize
Pyngas ... Temptation
Pål Callmer ... Wraptors, Deathening, Murderplan
Pähr Nilsson ... Cavalince
Pär Anders Frånberg "Bajen" ... Scamps
Pär Alfredsson ... Orient
Pär Berndtsson ... Elsy Band
Pär Boberg ... Gloomy Sunday
Pär Edwardsson (aka Per) ... Eaglestrike, Biscaya, Million, Damned Nation, Hawk, Human Race
Pär Ericsson ... EF Band
Pär Forsgren ... Steve Roper Band
Pär Fransson ... Another Life, The Project Hate MCMXCIX
Pär Gunnarsson "Pärsan" ... Sadatron
Pär Gustafsson "Bergraven" (now Stille) ... Bergraven, Nex, Whirling
Pär Hagström ... System Breakdown
Pär Hallgren ... Sgt. Sunshine, The Carpet Knights, Deathening
Pär Hjulström ... Maramon, Motherlode
Pär Ivy ... Diabolical
Pär Johansson "Aemelgoth" ... Azure, Satariel, Demiurg, Miseration, Torch Bearer
Pär Lindh ... Manticore
Pär Lindholm ... Negro
Pär Lundgren ... Extaz
Pär Nilsson ... This Haven
Pär Norén ... Mercenary Mustangs
Pär Olsson ... Törsten Dricker
Pär Sundström ... Sabaton
Pär Svensson ... Relentless, Valkyrja
Pär Thornell ... Allegiance
Pär Wahlquist ... Slam
Pär Wallmark ... Last Tribe
Pär Wennerström ... Horizon (2)
Pär Villsé ... Cross
Pär Åström ... Angeline
Quint Starkie ... Marc Quee, Tommy Tysper & The Kids
Radis Davis ... Tension
Rafael Andersson ... 9th Plague
Rafael Martinez ... Stallion, Misery
Ragnar Larsson ... Skywalkers
Ragnar Rage ... Desultor
Ragnar Widerberg ... Witherscape
Ragnar Zolberg ... Pain Of Salvation
Ragne Wahlquist ... Heavy Load, Maeday, Morbid, Long John, Isengard, Da President, Blizzard
Raimo Bikanen "Quick" ... Hiroshima
Raimo Flink ... Frekvens
Rainer Fetcher ... Tatch
Ralf Bjurbo ... Vital Sign
Ralf Gyllenhammar "Lennart" ... B-Thong, Mustasch, Sparzanza, Pontus Snibb 3
Ralf Jedestedt "Geff" ... Geff
Ralf Jibert ... White
Ralf Petersson ... Axewitch
Ralf Söderström ... Curse
Ralf Wernborg "Brasse" ... Vanguard
Ralph Peeker ... Vivaldi (group)
Ralph Pettersson ... Straight Up
Ralph Rydén "Raideen" (aka Lindgren) ... Hexenhaus, Hydrogen, Lizard Eye, Mercy, Spin Air, Keehole, Keegan
Rami Tainomo ... The Social Scumbags
Raimo Pikanen "Quick" ... Hiroshima
Ramon Novak ... Devourment
Randy Joy ... Badmouth
Rasmus Andersson ... Major N.A
Rasmus Blomqvist ... Ginger Trees
Rasmus Bogegård ... Stereo Generator
Rasmus Booberg ... New Keepers Of The Water Towers
Rasmus Ejneberg ... Close Quarters
Rasmus Ekman ... Comecon, Omnitron
Rasmus Grahm ... Blofly
Rasmus Göransson "Raz Cadillac" ... Belladonna
Rasmus Jansson ... Anguish
Rasmus Ström ... Primitive Symphony
Rasmus Söderling ... Gordon Fights
Rasmus Uhlin ... Big Talk (1)
Rasmus Weinheim ... Middleage
Rauno Luoto ... Lipkin
Rauno Morja ... Spitfire
Ravenlord ... Hypothermia
Ray Grönlund ... Hyste'riah G.B.C
Raymond Liljegren ... Tomterockers
Raymond Henning Lindbladh ... Golden Dawn
Raymond Nykvist ... Oferd, Svarti Loghin
Rebecka Heijel ... Beyond Visions
Reidar Horghagen "Horgh" ... Hypocrisy, Pain
Reidar Paulsen ... Jerusalem
Reijo Suonuieri ... Cane
Reijo Väliaho ... Spitfire
Reine Alexandersson "Ray Alex" ... Glory, Jar
Reine Dahlström ... Panama, Fretless
Reine Heyer ... Debbie Ray
Reine Johansson ... Karma
Reine Johansson ... Plan 9
Reine Karlsson ... Wulfgar
Reine Svensson ... Outshine
Reino Naatikka ... Happy Cakes
Rene Lintunen ... Shock Tilt
René Sebastian ... Denied
Rex Gisslén "Luger" ... Candy Roxx, T.A.R
Ricard Andersson ... Freeway
Ricard Harrysson ... Spiders
Richard Abrams ... Hypothermia
Richard Allercrantz ... Panama Red
Richard Andersson ... Richard Andersson, Majestic, Mansson, Richard Andersson's Space Osyssey, Silver Seraph, Time Requiem, Karmakanic, Moahni Moahna
Richard Averdahl ... M.O.B
Richard Bergholtz ... Sacrilege
Richard Bryngelsson ... Siebenbürgen
Richard Bång ... Ground Mower
Richard Cabeza "Daemon" ... Unanimated, Damnation, Dismember, Dark Funeral, Murder Squad, Born Of Fire
Richard Caesar ... Kayser
Richard Dahl "Rikki" ... Nasty Idols, United Enemies, Bewarp, (69-Hard)
Richard Davidsson ... East End
Richard Eriksson ... Attention (2)
Richard Evén ... Wild Cat Sleezy
Richard Evensand (aka Rickard) ... Lion's Share, Demonoid, Ebony Tears, Dog Faced Gods, It's Alive, Jekyll & Hyde, Southpaw, Paralyce, Therion, Sorcerer
Richard Fasth ... Vanessa
Richard Fehling "Bax" ... Bad Habit
Richard Fredriksson ... Arsenite
Richard Grönlund ... Valenze
Richard Hallifax ... Crazy Visions
Richard Holmgren (aka Rickard) ... Wolf, Grand Design, Haterush, Blackworld, Scaar, Vanessa
Richard Jennische ... Dimma
Richard Karlsson ... Blacklight
Richard Karlsson "Pinnen" ... Sinners Burn
Richard Lagberg ... Wombbath
Richard Lagergren "St. Erben" ... Eidomantum, Portrait
Richard Larsson ... The Defaced
Richard Larsson ... Sabaton, Skyride
Richard Larsson ... Deception
Richard Larsson ... The Night Flight Orchestra, Von Benzo
Richard Lion ... Tenebre, Flegma
Richard Lundgren ... Hellmark, GRK
Richard Martinsson ... Choir Of Vengeance, Mithotyn
Richard Martos ... Outshine, Urbandux
Richard Nilsson ... Auberon
Richard Nyman ... Calm
Richard Ohlsson ... Stefan Herde And His Broomdusters
Richard Persson ... Headline (1)
Richard Riekwel "Ritchie La Roux" ... Cult Disciples
Richard Rimfält "Rille/Corpse" ... Seance, Witchery
Richard Ryden ... The Point
Richard Schill ... Livsnekad
Richard Sjunnesson ... The Unguided, Sonic Syndicate, Faithful Darkness
Richard Sjöberg ... God Kills
Richard Svensson ... Renegades
Richard Söderstedt ... Slyside
Richard Warldén ... Downbound Train
Richard Öberg ... Ramm
Rick Altzi ... (see Rickard Thornberg)
Rick Gustafson ... Odyssey, Memeory Garden
Rickard "Lord Of The Deeps" ... Pagan Rites
Rickard Alriksson ... Necrony
Rickard Andersson ... Enemies Swe
Rickard André ... Tony Borg, Brat Pack, Alien, (Rossall & The Gang)
Rickard Armén ... Double Deuce
Rickard Bengtsson ... Pantokrator, Spiritual Beggars, Armageddon, Tristitia, Last Tribe, Twelvestep, Magnus Karlsson's Freefall
Rickard Bengtsson ... The Generals
Rickard Bergman ... Bathory
Rickard Biström ... Sinkadus
Rickard Cidh ... Warhammer
Rickard Dahlberg ... Face Down, Construcdead
Rickard Dahlin ... Maze Of Torment
Rickard Donatello ... Screamin' Mother, Iodine Jupiter
Rickard Ekvall ... Bulldogs
Rickard Eriksson ... Goddefied
Rickard Eriksson ... Borderline (1)
Rickard Evensand ... (see Richard Evensand)
Rickard Forslund ... Tribal Ink
Rickard Gustafsson "Richie" ... Kaptain Sun
Rickard Gustavsson ... Mindshift
Rickard Gustafsson ... Golden Resurrection, Pantokrator
Rickard Göransson "Mr Maniac" ... Virgin Sin
Rickard Harrysson "Ricky" ... Sister Sin, Babylon Bombs
Rickard Harrysson ... Fantasmagoria
Rickard Hednar ... The Generals
Rickard Holmgren ... (see Richard Holmgren)
Rickard Hux Flux Netterman ... Impulsia, Fuck Bitch, Fistfunk
Rickard Höggren ... Degial
Rickard Jakobson ... Apostle
Rickard Johansson ... Fatal Smile (2)
Rickard Johansson ... Coldtears
Rickard Johansson ... Keehole
Rickard Johansson "Dick" ... The Generals
Rickard Jonsson ... Feed
Rickard Kalm ... Marduk
Rickard Larsson ... Unmoored
Rickard Larsson ... Bokor
Rickard Larsson ... Orphan Gypsy, Sabaton, Skyride
Rickard Ligander ... Pagandom
Rickard Lundmark "Damien" ... Feral, Zonaria
Rickard Löfgren ... Dawn Of Decay
Rickard Magnusson ... Embracing
Rickard Mattsson "Maston" ... Cirkus
Rickard Mentzer ... Manimal
Rickard Mårtensson "Rick Martins" ... Wizzy Blaze
Rickard Ny "Snicken" ... Demon Cleener, Stonewall Noise Orchestra
Rickard Ozols ... Spinnrock
Rickard Persson ... The Citadel
Rickard Persson ... Diabolical
Rickard Rimfält "Corpse" ... Satanic Slaughter, Seance
Rickard Rolf ... November, Mårran
Rickard Roskvist ... Horizon (2)
Rickard Sahlén ... Caliber 70
Rickard Schill ... Shining, Livsnekad
Rickard Sievert ... Project UPA
Rickard Sporrong ... Eternal Autumn, Midas Touch
Rickard Stenmark ... Cross
Rickard Thelin ... Sommoned Tide
Rickard Thornberg "Rick Altzi" ... Sanity, Treasure Land, Magnus Karlsson's Freefall, Frequency, VII Gates
Rickard Thulin ... Imperious, Coercion
Rickard Vickhoff "Rikki" ... Sister
Rickard Wahlberg ... Omnispawn
Rickard Westerberg ... Core Of Nation
Rickard Wyöni ... A Mind Confused
Rickard Zander ... Barrelhouse, Evergrey, (Solid Blue)
Rickard Öström "LH" ... Lifelover
Ricki Aresu ... Craze
Ricky B Delin ... (see Björn Lindbom)
Ricky Stahre ... Sticky Sweet
Rigmor Gustafsson ... Shalalee
Rikard Andersson ... Angtoria
Rikard Borginger ... Lemon Bird
Rikard Edlund ... Norrsken, Graveyard
Rikard Eriksson ... Jezider
Rikard Jansson ... Regurgitate
Rikard Järlefalk ... Silverwings
Rikard Kottelin "Tiwaz" ... The Legion
Rikard Larsson "Rich Wine" ... Supreme Majesty, Sanzia, Mercy, In Black, Sacrifice, Crier
Rikard Löfgren ... Hellfueled
Rikard Löfgren ... Sparzanza, Bay Paurel
Rikard Magnusson "R. Fleshripper" ... Sadistic Grimness, Ill-Natured
Rikard Mårtensson ... Päst, Social Scumbags
Rikard Nilsson ... Motherlode
Rikard Nilsson ... Non Serviam
Rikard Olsson ... Priority
Rikard Ottosson ... Maim
Rikard Persson ... Soreption
Rikard Petersson ... Moonlight Agony
Rikard Quist ... Reece/Kronlund, Gypsy Rose
Rikard Sjöblom ... Beardfish, Gungfly
Rikard Sundén ... Civil War, Sabaton
Rikard Swahn "Ritchi" ... Skiller
Rikard Wermén .. Deranged, Murder Corporation, Killaman
Rikard Öberg ... Heel, Ramm
Rikki Force ... Blazing Guns
Riley Ericson ... Steelwing
Rille Eriksson ... Impiety
Rille Lundell ... Hate Gallery
Rille Svensson ... Mortum, Supreme Majesty
Rimbert Vahlström "Rimmy Hunter" ... Syron Vanes
Rino Fredh ... Seventh One
Risperdal ... Terra Tenebrosa
Ritchie Riekwel "LaRoux" ... Veritate
Rius ... Misericordia
Roald Olsen ... Tears
Rob Guz ... Massive Audio Nerve
Rob Hammarström "Cold" ... Pompei Nights
Rob Rocker ... Serpent Obscene
Rob Wikman ... Phoenix
Robban Blennerhed ... BB Rock
Robban Eriksson ... The Project Hate MCMXCIX
Robban Eriksson ... Slyside
Robban Jacobsson ... Axia
Robban Larsson ... Asoka
Robban Persson ... Axewitch, Straight Up
Robban Wettersten "Pisk" ... Aska
Robbin Wännström ... Tungsten Axe
Robby Rockbag ... Steelwing
Roberg Persson ... Nox Aurea, The Cold Existence
Robert Ahrling ... Mister Kite, Origin Blood, Incapacity
Robert Alsterlind ... Blackmail
Robert Andersson "Robba" ... Morbus Chron
Robert Andersson ... Backwater
Robert Axelsson ... One Man Army
Robert Bengtsson ... Grief Of Emerald
Robert Bergius ... Darklands
Robert Bjärmyr ... Celestial Decay
Robert Björk ... Beneath The Frozen Soil
Robert Breiner ... Nifters
Robert Bunke ... Korea
Robert Bäck "Robban XIII/Robby Rock" ... Eclipse, Prey, BALLS, W.E.T (2), Sabaton, Billion Dollar Babies, Baltimoore
Robert Carlsson ... Disciple
Robert Dunberg "Robban" ... Sterbhaus
Robert Eklundh ... Electric Eastwood
Robert Eng ... Satanic Slaughter, Algaion, Corporation 187, Satanic Slaughter
Robert Engstrand ... Karmakanic
Robert Eriksson ... Raceway
Robert Eriksson (Valerie) "Bobby" ... Mogg
Robert Eriksson "Robban" ... God Kills
Robert Eriksson ... Scar
Robert Ernlund "Robban" ... Treat, Swedish Metal Aid
Robert Fjällsby "Garm Stringburner" ... Gehennah
Robert Forse ... Afterglow, Mind's Eye, Heads Or Tales, Shadowland
Robert Fossengren "Foss" ... Vampa, Russell, (9T9)
Robert Franck ... Maniac
Robert Fransson ... Reckless
Robert Garnold ... Heartbreak Radio, Elevener, Roach
Robert Green ... Born Of Sin
Robert Gustafsson "Geezon" ... Tough Trade
Robert Gustafsson ... Ninnuam
Robert Gustavsson ... Big Talk (1)
Robert Haglund ... Timescape
Robert Hakemo "Rob" ... Gardenian, Gooseflesh, Relevant Few, Ton Of Bricks, Massive Audio Nerve
Robert Hansen ... Beardfish
Robert Hansson "Bobbo" ... Latex
Robert Hansson "Rob" ... Human Race, Treborian, Bonkyman
Robert Hansson "Rob Devilpig" ... Bestial Mockery

Robert Hansson "Bob Ruben" ... Band Of Spice, The Mushroom River Band, Spice And The RJ Band
Robert Hoffman ... Gondoline
Robert Holmberg "Bobby" ... Blacksmith
Robert Hrusovar ... Blood feud
Robert Hylén ... Sargatanas Reign, Griftegård
Robert I Edman ... Maze Of Time
Robert Ivarsson "Mourning" ... Pan-Thy-Monium, Ashes, Ophthalamia
Robert Ivarsson ... Incapacity
Robert Iversen ... Cross, Sorcerer
Robert Jacobsson ... Niva
Robert Johansson "The Slob" ... Backdraft
Robert Johansson ... Eldrimner
Robert Johansson ... Silverfish
Robert Johansson ... Ninnuam
Robert Johansson ... Attention (2)
Robert Jonasson "Robban/Rob Nasty" ... XXX, Danger, Loud 'N' Nasty
Robert Jörgensen "Lefty" ... Machinegun Kelly
Robert Kanto "Amorth Bredlave" ... Azure
Robert Kardell "Gorebert" ... Ceremonial Execution
Robert Karlson ... Nine
Robert Karlsson "Kail" ... Misericordia
Robert Karlsson "Derelict" ... Pan-Thy-Monium
Robert Karlsson ... Prowoke
Robert Karlsson ... As You Drown
Robert Kenndal ... Captain Freak's Freaky Funksters, Battle Station
Robert Klavinger "Kee" ... Wizz
Robert Knutsson ... April Sky
Robert Kratz ... Taste
Robert Krook ... Fatal Smile (1)
Robert Kulka ... Foobar The Band, Chillihounds
Robert Kusen ... Pike
Robert Lamu ... Skraeckoedlan
Robert Larsson ... Borderline (2)
Robert Larsson ... Fierce Conviction
Robert Lendahl ... Forest
Robert Lilja "Rob Paris" ... Danger (2), Dethronement
Robert Lindberg ... Wynja
Robert Lindell "Rob" ... Rozz The Bozz
Robert Lindell "Robban" ... Bulletrain
Robert Lindmark ... Prophanity, Septic Grave
Robert Ljung ... Adept
Robert Lowe ... Candlemass
Robert Luciani ... Vildhjarta
Robert Lundgren ... Plague Angel
Robert Lundin "Gaahnfaust" ... Dominion Caligula, Vicious Art, Dark Funeral
Robert Makek ... VII Gates
Robert Mis ... Attention (1)
Robert Molldius ... Angelez
Robert Monegrim ... Cellout, Reckless
Robert Möller ... Maryscreek
Robert Nilsson ... Badmouth
Robert Nilsson "Bobby Dawn" ... Rickshaw
Robert Nilsson ... Fatal Tabasco
Robert Norberg ... Naughty Boys
Robert Ottosson ... Aggressive Chill
Robert Pecnovnik "Triton" ... Joke
Robert Pehrsson "Reaper" ... Runemagick, Deathwitch, Necronaut, Death Breath
Robert Persson ... The Cold Existence, Nox Aurea
Robert Petersson ... Anata
Robert Peterzon ... Mistie
Robert Pettersson ... Takida
Robert Pörschke ... Mourning Sign
Robert Reinholdz ... Burst
Robert Samuelsson ... Traction
Robert Scholtyssek "Scholtz" ... Russell, Vampa, (9T9)
Robert Sennebäck ... Dismember, Unleashed
Robert Sjöbäck ... Sinkadus
Robert Smedberg ... Section Eight
Robert Spånglund ... Beseech
Robert Stellmar ... Denied, Human Rage, One Cent
Robert Stjärnström "GAZ" ... Machinae Supremacy
Robert Sundelin "Zoid" ... Satariel, Morthirim, Necromicon
Robert Svensson ... Seventribe
Robert Svärdh ... Malaise
Robert Säll ... Work Of Art, W.E.T (2)
Robert Triches ... The Quill, Boom Shanker Group
Robert Tyborn Axt "An-ti-christ" ... Skymning, Immersed In Blood
Robert Vargkvist "Bobby" ... Vanessa, Bewarp, Espinoza, Emerald
Robert Warnqvist ... Damned Nation, Easy Street
Robert Wendelstam "Rob Marcello" ... Alyson Avenue, Chris Laney, Infestdead, Shotgun Messiah
Robert Werngren ... Quiz
Robert Westin ... Frame
Robert Willstedt ... Dragonland, Moonlight Agony
Robert Wirensjö ... Ellen B, Agape
Robert Zima ... Trettioåriga Kriget, Blues Bag
Robert Örnsved ... Castillon
Robert Österberg ... The Crown (Crown Of Throns)
Roberth Ekholm ... Bacon
Roberth Karlsson ... Facebreaker, Pan-Thy-Monium, Edge Of Sanity, Scar Symmetry, Devian, Tormented,
Roberth Steiner ... Polluted Influence
Roberto Granath "Thord" ... Mefisto
Roberto Laghi ... Transport League, Close Quarters, LOK, The Awesome Machine, Deathdestruction, Diablo Swing Orchestra, Electric Earth, Headplate, Hardcore Superstar, Pain And Passion, Stoneflow
Roberto Vacchi Segerlund ... Decadence
Robin Ahnlund ... Safemode
Robin Arnell ... Morifade
Robin Bengtsson ... Bulletrain
Robin Bergh ... Piper's Dawn, Amaran, October Tide, Gorement
Robin Dohlk ... Defleshed
Robin Duvfors ... Last View
Robin Engström ... Lefay, Fantasmagoria
Robin Ericsson ... Angel King, Degreed
Robin Fors ... Nattsmyg
Robin Gillard ... Ravaged
Robin Halldin ... Benevolent
Robin Hirse ... Asteroid
Robin Holgersson ... Eldrimner
Robin Holmberg ... New Keepers Of The Water Towers
Robin Högdahl ... Majestic Dimension
Robin Jensen ... Marionette
Robin Jönsson ... Turning Point
Robin Kvist ... Qoph
Robin Lagerqvist ... Fatal Smile (2)
Robin Larsson ... Tore And The No Smokers
Robin Lindström ... The Cold Existence
Robin Lundgren ... Robeeo
Robin Mattsson ... Meadows End
Robin Pettersson ... Oppression
Robin Pålsson ... VII Gates
Robin Roux "Roux'd" ... Cirkus
Robin Rubio ... Sgt. Sunshine
Robin Sandvik ... Subztain
Robin Sjunnesson ... Sonic Syndicate
Robin Sjöstrand ... Vanity Dies Hard, Origin Blood
Robin Sundkvist ... Within Reach
Robin Svedman ... Admonish
Robin Sörqvist ... Impious
Robin Tesch ... Chiron
Robin Thuresson ... Akilles
Robin Utbult "Rob Thunderbolt" ... Air Raid
Robin Vagh ... (see Tommy Silfvenius)
Robin Verho ... Bloodshed
Robin Westlund ... Godphobia
Roffe Carsbring "Zip" ... Truck
Roger Albinsson "Spy-T" ... Gemini Souls
Roger Averdah ... Atlantis
Roger Bengtsson ... Half Man
Roger Bergsten ... Diabolical, Hectorite, Syn:Drom
Roger Berntsson ... Faith
Roger Berntsson ... Revengia
Roger Bertilsson "Roy Bartello" ... Walkaway
Roger Björk ... Wonderland (1)
Roger Blomberg ... Freevil, Denata
Roger Christiansson ... Solid, Destiny
Roger Claussen ... Head Force
Roger Crossler ... Speedfreaks
Roger Ekelund ... Neofight
Roger Emlid "Mane" ... Sonic Temple
Roger Englund ... Movin' Globe
Roger Engvik ... Meadows End
Roger Enstedt "Raw" ... Steel Attack, Wombbath
Roger Ericson ... Pain And Passion
Roger Ersson ... Slodust
Roger Frejd ... Big Train, Profile
Roger Grönberg "White" ... Nasty Idols
Roger Gustafsson ... The Poodles
Roger Gustafsson ... N.J.B
Roger Hedin ... Bedrock Zity
Roger Helj ... Freeway
Roger Holegård ... Neon Rose, Truck, Mountain Of Power, (Wasa Express)
Roger Jern ... Damned Nation, Dead End Street, Johnny Engström Band
Roger Johansen ... Lazy
Roger Johansson ... Morthirim, Necromicon
Roger Johansson ... Rock Squad
Roger Johansson ... Insision, Killaman
Roger Johansson ... Mercy, Faith
Roger Johansson ... Ablaze My Sorrow
Roger Johansson (now Pontare) ... Nebulosa
Roger Johansson "Rogga" ... Ribspreader, Deranged, Those Who Bring The Torture, Bone Gnawer, Demiurg, Paganizer, Sinners Burn, Carve, Revolting, Puteraeon, Another Life
Roger Karlsson ... Interaction
Roger Karlsson ... Keystone
Roger Kindstrand ... Avenue, State Of Mind
Roger Kääpää ... Nadir
Roger Lagerlund ... Sargoth
Roger Landin ... Doctor Weird, Second Heat, Alyson Avenue, Cloudscape
Roger Lind ... Rock Squad
Roger Lindbladh ... Golden Dawn
Roger Lindroth ... Lovebone, Mystery
Roger Ljunggren ... Niva, CC Rock, Twilight Project, Grand Ilusion, T'Bell
Roger Markström "Phycon" ... Armagedda, Leviathan
Roger Marsden ... EF Band
Roger Mattsson ... The Kaars
Roger Munch ... Espinoza
Roger Nikander ... Robb and Friends
Roger Nilsson ... Arch Enemy, The Quill, Spiritual Beggars
Roger Nordström ... Swedes
Roger Olsson ... Takida
Roger Olsson ... Psychotic Supper
Roger Olsson ... Redsun
Roger Pettersson "Rogga" ... Merciless, Satureye, Entropy
Roger Pettersson ... Chronic Decay
Roger Samuelsson "Lolle" ... Head Force
Roger Sjunnesson ... Sonic Syndicate, The Unguided
Roger Sundquist ... Thronaeon, Godhate
Roger Svensson ... Von Panzer
Roger Svensson "Bogge/B. War" ... Allegiance, Moment Maniacs, Marduk, Devil's Whorehouse
Roger Svensson ... Last Temptation
Roger Teilmann "Hot Rod" ... Gemini Five
Roger Wahlsten ... Bedroom Love
Roger Wasell ... Behemoth
Roger Westberg ... Wanton
Roger Öjersson ... Vildsvin, Kamchatka
Roine Stolt ... The Flower Kings, Kaipa, Karmakanic, Lafayette
Roine Thörnell ... Saigon
Rokki Toni Pietilä ... Eternal Darkness
Rolan Wiberg ... Stonehenge
Roland Chantre ... Crossroad Jam
Roland Christoffersson ... Million
Roland Eriksson ... Carrie
Roland Grapow ... Miss Beahaviour
Roland Johansson ... Sonic Syndicate, The Unguided
Roland Johansson ... Inhale
Roland Josefsson ... Evolution
Roland Rosenqvist "Rolle" ... Giant
Rolf Alex ... Baltimoore, Alex's Pro
Rolf Berg ... Core Of Nation
Rolf Gustafsson "Roffe" ... Andra Band, Rockbox
Rolf Heische ... Frozen Fire
Rolf Hellmark ... Hellmark, GRK
Rolf Holmström ... Axewitch
Rolf Häggblom ... Shock Tilt
Rolf Johansson ... Örby Mix
Rolf Leidestad ... Abramis Brama
Rolf Moberg ... Airlines
Rolf Nordström "Trazan" ... Killer Bee, Limit, Reflex
Rolf Pesonen ... Pagan
Rolf Pilve "Stuka" ... Torch Bearer, Miseration, Solution .45
Rolf Scherrer ... Jaguar
Rolle Hermin ... Tears
Rolle Larsson ... Kings Of Modern Swing
Rolle Persson ... (see Björn Persson)
Rolle Nilsson "Rock" ... Panndeads
Rolph Van Royce ... Maeday
Roman Karpovich ... Seventh Wonder
Ronney Hedlund ... Adams Eve, Elevener
Ronnie Andréson ... Isengard
Ronnie Backlund ... Amaran
Ronnie Bergerståhl ... Amaran, Demonical, Grave (2), Centinex, Julie Laughs Nomore, World Below, Triton Enigma
Ronnie Biveland ... Kliché
Ronnie Björnström "Worm" ... Scumkill, Hate Ammo, Bone Gnawer, Plector, Embracing, Azure, Those Who Bring The Torture
Ronnie Börjesson ... Satanic Slaughter
Ronnie Eriksson ... Frenzy
Ronnie Hagstedt ... Optimystical
Ronnie Hassleqvist ... Electric Eastwood
Ronnie Jaldemark ... Lava Engine, System Breakdown
Ronnie Johansson "Rozen" ... Stockholm Showdown
Ronnie Källback ... Pyramido
Ronnie Lundqvist ... Lack Of Faith
Ronnie Nielsen ... Aeon (1)
Ronnie Nilsson ... Plebb
Ronnie Nyman ... Forcefeed
Ronnie Nyman ... Enemy Is Us
Ronnie Olsson "Ripper" ... Gehennah, Turbocharged, Vomitory, Die Hard
Ronnie Peeters ... Thrashon, Pearly White
Ronnie Pettersson "Ronta" ... Shotgun Bluez
Ronnie Wicklander ... Angelize
Ronny Andersson ... Infinity
Ronny Blylod ... Blackrain, Eternia, Justaquickstop, Destynation
Ronny Eide ... Suffer
Ronny Eriksson ... Magnolia
Ronny Hemlin ... Bibleblack, The Storyteller, Tad Morose, Lack Of Faith, Steel Attack
Ronny Karlsson ... Rock Squad
Ronny Lahti ... Damn Delicious, Stallion
Ronny Lindqvist ... Muddy Road
Ronny Milianowicz ... Saint Deamon, Vemoth, Thyreos, Dionysus
Ronny Normi ... Candy Kicks Ass
Ronny Olsson ... Bluesbreath
Ronny Persson ... Balthazar
Ronny Rasmusson ... Dieselkopf
Ronny Starborg ... Ambush, Rampant
Ronny Svanströmer ... Covered Call
Ronny Westergren ... Stonechurch
Ronny Wikberg ... Squetters
Ronny Zander ... Naked
Rosa Dahl ... Aphasia
Rosa Körberg ... Attack
Rosmarie Gröning "Rosa" ... 7:e Himlen
Rother ... Flegma
Roy El Hoshy ... Boulevard, Midnight Blue
Roy Erlandsson ... Blinded Colony
Roy Östh ... Tonvikt
Ruby Roque ... The Project Hate MCMXCIX
Rudolf Janszky ... Rhapsody (Sweden)
Rudra Fjäll "TRF" ... Angst, Octinomos
Rune Bertilsson ... Vital Sign, Air Condition, Solution
Rune Foss ... Dawn Of Time, Puteraeon, Reclusion, Killaman
Rune Hellgren ... TBC
Rustan Geschwind ... Quoph
Ryan Coyle ... Osukaru
Ryan Roxie ... Casablanca
Ryan Van Poederooyen ... Non-Human Level
Räven Alisic ... Physical Attraction
S.O. Anda ... Major N.A
Sabrina Kihlstrand ... Gardenian, Ice Age
Salvaganesh ... Art Metal
Sam Nilsson ... Danger (1)
Sam Riffer ... (see Samir Eriksson)
Sam Rönnberg ... Bult
Sami Karppinen ... Curse, Therion, Lithium
Sami Miari ... Stillborn
Sami Mäki ... Altered Aeon, Wolverine, Undivide
Sami Nerberg ... Edge Of Sanity
Sami Nieminen ... Eternal Autumn
Sami Tiainen ... Pantheon
Samir Eriksson "Sam Riffer" ... Siena Root
Sammy Carpenter ... Cut 4
Sammy Ouirra ... Night
Sampo Axelsson ... Audiovision, Crawley, Smiling Dog, Lion's Share, Road II Ruin
Sampo Laakkonen ... Scatcats
Samuel Berg ... Damn Delicious
Samuel Emtlind ... Oblivion
Samuel Fredén (Andersson) ... Majectic Vanguard
Samuel Granath ... Pound
Samuel Gustafsson ... Cornerstone, Stonefuze
Samuel Johansson ... Sordid Death
Samuel Larsson ... Mammuth
Samuel Nyman ... Manimal
Samuel Olofsson Jonsson ... Confess
Samuel Persson ... Ghamorean
Samuel Smitz ... Saved By Insanity
Samuel Waermö ... Retrace
Samuel Wistemar ... Ghamorean
Samuel Åhden ... Steve Roper Band
Samuel Öjring ... Suicidal Seduction
Sandra Bergman ... Nattsmyg
Sandro Cajander ... Mefisto
Sandy B Hansen ... Göran Nordh
Sanya ... Siena Root
Sara Fredriksson ... Misdemeanor
Sara Heurlin ... Nation Beyond
Sara L ... Hypothermia
Sara Leni Englund "SatAnica" ... Hysterica
Sara Näslund ... Necromicon
Sara Svensson ... Oxiplegatz
Sarah Jezebel Deva ... Angtoria
Sarah Kreft ... Facequake
Sartez Abdulrahman "Faraj" ... Three Seasons, Siena Root
Sataros ... Arckanum, Sataros Grief
Saul Camara ... Los Sin Nombre
Sauli Ranta ... Beyond Visions
Sayit Dölen ... Sayit, The Jet Circus, Jim Jidhed, Deacon Street
Scott Andersson ... Maim, Morbus Chron
Scott Carlson ... Death Breath
Sean C. Bates ... Diabolical Masquerade
Sebastian Aronsson ... Skymning
Sebastian Eriksson ... A*Teem
Sebastian Gadd ... Stench, Necrovation
Sebastian Gustafsson ... Miss Beahaviour
Sebastian Hed-Pikas ... Dynamite
Sebastian Jansson "Zeb" ... Malison Rogue
Sebastian Kellgren ... Last View
Sebastian Kimber ... Blowback
Sebastian Lilja ... Quarterback Beat
Sebastian Lind ... Il Shy, Jezider
Sebastian Myrén ... Deals Death
Sebastian Nilsson ... A*Teem
Sebastian Nilsson "Zeb" ... Aeon (2)

NAME INDEX

Sebastian Okupsi ... Imperial Domain, Loch Vostock, Mayadome
Sebastian Olsson "Gert Steelheart" ... Thalamus, Cryonic Temple, Eventide
Sebastian Olsson ... Incinia
Sebastian Pedernera ... Lancer
Sebastian Ramstedt "Nidhägg/Vengeance Of Beyond" ... Morpheus, Necrophobic, Nifelheim, Bloduly, Bajen Death Cult
Sebastian Roos ... Miss Beahaviour, Shineth
Sebastian Sander ... Safemode
Sebastian Sippola ... Fortune (2), Four Sticks, Plankton, Southfork, Grand Magus
Sebastian Sjögren ... Yersinia
Sebastian Sjöström ... Confess
Sebastian Sundqvist "Kprl Sigge Hall" ... Skitarg
Sebastian Swahn "Dihm Rust" ... Skiller
Sebastian Westermark ... Feral
Sebastian Viitanen ... Unchained (2), Buszer
Sebiastian Olsson "Gert Steelheart" ... Cryonic Temple
Seike ... Semremedy
Seiya Ogino ... Livsnekad
Selin ... IXXI
Selma Liljenberg ... Merrygold
Seppo (Räftegård) Toivanen ... Love Injection
Serban Carapancea "Seb" ... Blowsight
Seron (aka Morgh) ... Misteltein
Set/Sethlans Teitan ... (see David Tataro)
SG Petersson ... Pax
Shara Peterson ... Eaglestrike
Sharlee d'Angelo ... (see Charles Petter Andreasson)
Sheik Ahmeed ... Sheik Ahmeed
Siavosh Bigonah ... Ghamorean, Ondskapt, Slumber
Sigge Frenzel ... Clown, Grand Slam
Sigge Kron ... Magic, Central
Sigrid Lagander ... Sarea
Simeon Liljegren ... Audiovision, Borderline, Modest Attraction, Disciple
Simi "R Corps" ... Chronic Torment
Simon Algesten "Cee" ... DeVan
Simon Andersson ... Pain Of Salvation, Urbandux, Outshine, Avatar, Christian Alsing, Johan Randén, Darkwater
Simon Asikainen "Tapani" ... Victory (2), Knockout
Simon Axenrot "S Demon" ... Nephenzy (Chaos Order), Satanic Slaughter
Simon Berglund ... Zonaria
Simon Cop ... Titan
Simon Corner ... Pray For Locust
Simon Dahlberg ... Havok
Simon Dahlström ... Lava Engine
Simon Exner ... As You Drown
Simon Follman ... All Hell
Simon Frödeberg ... Evildoer, Verminious, Sgt. Carnage
Simon Galle ... Decadence
Simon Granath ... Affecti Veternus
Simon Grenehed ... Blidside, Fuck Bitch
Simon Hagberg ... Arsenite
Simon Hallén ... Mothers Pride
Simon Hardell ... Cryonic
Simon Hermansson ... Moonlight Agony
Simon Holmberg "Moloch" ... Unlight Order, Saved By Insanity
Simon Jansson ... Armauk
Simon Jarrolf ... Vicious
Simon Johansson ... Abstrakt Algebra, Bibleblack, Fi5th Reason, Memory Garden, Steel Attack, Nattas, Slowgate, Wolf, Chainsaw
Simon Karlsson "Roxx" ... Easy Action, Enemies Swe
Simon Karlsson ... Holocaustia
Simon Lindh ... Crimson Moonlight
Simon Lindholm ... Fraise, Fatal Tabasco
Simon Lundin ... Paganizer
Simon Myrberg "Simon LaRue" ... Panzer Princess
Simon Niklasson ... Origin Blood
Simon Nilsson ... Oppression
Simon Olovsson ... Sterbhaus
Simon Olsson ... Screwball.Sthlm
Simon Rosén "Pilgrim" ... Crimson Moonlight
Simon Roxx ... Ammotrack
Simon Solomon ... Starterhead, Bloodbath, Cowboy Prostitutes
Simon Steensland ... Sheik Ahmeed, (Landberk)
Simon Söderberg ... Roswell, Ghost
Simon Söderberg ... Whipping Princess
Simon Söderström "Cruz" ... Crash Diet
Simon Vegas ... Molly's Gusher
Simon Wettervik ... Forcefeed, Seething
Simon Wizén "S.W" ... Valkyrja, Die Hard, Ondskapt
Simon Åkesson ... Nightscape
Simpen Claezon "Descecrator" ... Pagan Rites
Sinisa Krnjaic ... Drabness
Sir J Marklund ... Grifteskymfning, LIK, Kaos Sacramentum
Sir. N (aka Vanskapt) ... Svartrit, Grifteskymfning, Kaos Sacrmentum, Hädanfärd, Dödfödd
Siri Hagfors ... Mykorrhiza
Sixten Jaskari ... Cut 4, Mandala, Tippen Ruda
Skall ... Valkyrja
Skamfer ... Heresi, Ondskapt
Skid La'Russo "Sadde" ... Innocent Rosie
Slade Doom ... Deathwitch
Slim Tannberg ... Stockholm Showdown
Slurge ... Fleshcut
Smoker ... IXXI
Snowy Shaw ... (see Tommy Helgesson)
Sofia Lilja ... Nubian Rose
Sofia Pettersson ... Paradise (3)
Sonny Andersson ... Dimmz
Sonny Dahl ... W.E.T (1)
Sonny Gröndahl ... After Life
Sonny Jonasson ... Chainwreck
Sonny Larsson ... Motherlode, Kings Of Modern Swing, Björn Stigsson, XT, Silver Mountain, Leviticus
Sonny Mery ... Carnalist
Sonny Svedlund "Sick" ... Dellamorte, Interment
Sorghim ... Rimfrost
Sotiris Geveniotis ... Milky
Spawn ... Fear The Future
Spinegrinder de Sate ... Necroplasma
Stabben Wahlman ... Tejp
Staffan Andersson (now Lindstedt) "Stephen Mavrock" ... Syron Vanes
Staffan Andersson ... Mascot Parade
Staffan Astner ... Clown, Johan Rand, (Bronk)
Staffan Björkman ... Glorious Bankrobbers
Staffan Carlsson ... Sky Of Rage
Staffan Forsell ... Reazon
Staffan Franzén ... Blinded Colony
Staffan Grenklo ... Via Tokyo, Aurora
Staffan Hagberg ... Crut
Staffan Johansson ... B-Thong, Concrete Stuff
Staffan Johansson ... Utumno, Abhoth
Staffan Karlsson ... Snakepit Rebels
Staffan Linder ... Talk Of The Town
Staffan Lindroth ... Shadows Past
Staffan Lundholm ... Bibleblack, Circle Of Chaos
Staffan Persson ... Highbrow
Staffan Scharin ... Talk Of The Town, Alien, Brat Pack
Staffan Schön "Abbe" ... Crut, Twilight Project
Staffan Stavers ... Mandrake Root
Staffan Ström ... Nagazaki
Staffan Winroth ... The Mist Of Avalon, Enemy Is Us
Staffan Österlind ... Burning Engines, Merrygold
Staffe Karlsson ... Mezzrow
Stakka Bo (Bo Johan Renck) ... New Bread
Stanley Larsson ... Neon Rose
Stathis Cassios ... System Shock
Stefan Almqvist ... Eternal Fear
Stefan Andersson ... Ironware
Stefan Andersson ... Rebels
Stefan Andersson ... Spinnrock
Stefan Aronsson ... Beardfish
Stefan Asplund ... Cheryenne
Stefan Axelsson ... Jackwave, Airborne
Stefan Bellnäs ... Crossing Oceans
Stefan Berg ... Meduza, Laudamus
Stefan Berggren "John Stefan" ... Snakes In Paradise, One Cent, Four Sticks
Stefan Bergh ... Great Ad
Stefan Berglund ... Memory Garden
Stefan Bergström ... Alfonzetti, Skintrade, Baltimoore
Stefan Björnshög ... Destiny
Stefan Bogstedt ... Fake
Stefan Book ... Wanton
Stefan Borg ... Fair Child, Tumbleweed
Stefan Brekh ... Sabotage
Stefan Brisland ... Va-Då?
Stefan Byrstedt "Sterta" ... Stockholm Showdown
Stefan Carlsson "Stipen/Pedro Serdito" ... Merciless, Transport League, Trash Amigos, Blackshine, Crystal Ocean, Harm's Way, (Dia Psalma)
Stefan Cronebäck ... Big Business
Stefan Dahlberg ... Defaced Creation
Stefan Damicolas ... Brother Ape
Stefan Edström ... ZooL
Stefan Egeman ... Dogface
Stefan Eklund ... Bubonic Plague
Stefan Ekström ... Carbonized, Morpheus
Stefan Ekström ... Horizon (2)
Stefan Eldevall ... Pax
Stefan Eliasson "Steff" ... Sworn
Stefan Elmgren ... Hammerfall, The Jet Circus, Lost Horizon, Nocturnal Rites, Spearfish, Thyreos, Cans, Fullforce, Full Strike
Stefan Embretsson ... Haterush
Stefan Englund ... Rising Faith
Stefan Englund ... Steve Eastside Band
Stefan Eriksson ... Civil War, Volturyon, Cryonic Temple
Stefan Eriksson ... Notredame
Stefan Eriksson ... Twilight Zone
Stefan Fagerlund ... Whimzy
Stefan Fandén ... Jupiter Society
Stefan Fjellner ... Nightvision
Stefan Flodström ... Whimzy
Stefan Fors ... Crystal Eyes
Stefan Fredin ... Trettioåriga Kriget
Stefan Fröyen ... Voyager
Stefan Granberg ... Anima Morte
Stefan Grundel (aka Olsson) ... Godgory
Stefan Gustafsson ... Hydra (1)
Stefan Gustavsson (now Altzar) ... Pound
Stefan Guteklint ... Opeth
Stefan Göransson ... Diavox
Stefan Hagström ... Daemonicus
Stefan Halldin ... Maryscreek, The SocialPäst
Stefan Hammarström ... Academy
Stefan Harrvik ... Necrophobic, Crematory
Stefan Haugsnes ... Big Easy
Stefan Hellspong ... Hangover
Stefan Hellström "Stiff Hell" ... Mother Misery
Stefan Hemgren ... Vanguard (2)
Stefan Herde ... Stefan Herde And His Broomdusters, Pax Romana
Stefan Holm ... The Forsaken
Stefan Hozjan "Steve Thunderhawk" ... Savagers, X-Eryus
Stefan Högberg ... Divine Souls
Stefan Isebring ... Maitreya
Stefan Jacobsson ... X-Perience
Stefan Jansson ... Devilicious
Stefan Joansson ... Gloomy Sunday
Stefan Johansson ... Promotion
Stefan Johansson ... Satanic Slaughter, Morgue
Stefan Johansson "Dagon" ... Virgin Sin
Stefan Johansson "Yxmarder" ... Blodsrit
Stefan Johansson ... Chillihounds
Stefan Johansson "Mulle" ... N.J.B
Stefan Johansson ... Portal
Stefan Johansson ... Raving Mad
Stefan Johansson ... Shee
Stefan Johansson ... The Grand Trick
Stefan Johansson ... Gypsy
Stefan Johansson ... Keystone
Stefan Jonsson ... Overload, Gormathorn, Morgana Lefay
Stefan Jonsson ... Scatcats
Stefan Jonsson ... Snakes In Paradise, Renegade (2)
Stefan Juhlin ... The Curtain
Stefan Karlsson "Gubben" ... Head Force
Stefan Karlsson "Ztephan Dark" ... Satanic Slaughter
Stefan Karlsson ... Crypt Of Kerberos
Stefan Karlsson ... Iniuria
Stefan Karlsson ... Thore Goes Metal
Stefan Karlsson ... Brutaliator, Obligatorisk Tortyr, Soulreaper
Stefan Karlsson (aka Carlsson) ... Neocori, Memento Mori, Pathos
Stefan Karlsson ... Enigmatic
Stefan Karlström ... Pride
Stefan Kéry ... Europe, John Norum
Stefan Kihlgren ... Horde Of Hel, My Own Grave
Stefan Kjällgren ... Peo
Stefan Klingborg ... Erika Evenlind
Stefan Kronquist "Vrashtar" ... Sargatanas Reign, Angst
Stefan Kuczerski ... Overlord
Stefan Käck ... Golden Resurrection
Stefan Kälfors ... Enter The Hunt, Gone, Omnitron
Stefan Källarsson ... House Of Usher
Stefan Källarström ... Crypt Of Kerberos
Stefan Lagergren "Emetic" ... Expulsion, Treblinka, Mr. Death, Tiamat
Stefan Larsson ... Bathory
Stefan Larsson "The Flea" ... Bad Business, Nectaris
Stefan Larsson ... White Night
Stefan Larsson-Almén ... Treat, Advice
Stefan Lekström ... Fair Child
Stefan Lindahl ... Hels
Stefan Lindgren ... Dark Tranquillity
Stefan Lindholm ... Firecracker, Vindictiv
Stefan Lindquist ... Wiz
Stefan Lindström ... Svarti Loghin
Stefan Lundberg "The Mechanic" ... Skymning, Immersen In Blood
Stefan Lundgren ... Sobre Nocturn, Dawn, Necronomicon, Sectu
Stefan Lönnhagen ... Lafayette
Stefan Löwenborg ... Sven Hahne & Prästrock
Stefan Magnusson ... The Awesome Machine, Tube Screamer
Stefan Malmberg ... Alcatraz
Stefan Mithander "Mr Violece" ... Satanarchy, Gehennah
Stefan Molander "Stephen/Tin Star" ... Gemini Five, Jekyll & Hyde
Stefan Morén ... Keen Hue, United, Stefan Morén
Stefan Nielsen ... Chained
Stefan Nilsson ... Mandrake Root
Stefan Nilsson ... Gates Of Ishtar
Stefan Nilsson ... Depzon
Stefan Nilsson ... Calilio
Stefan Nordeng "Zoak" ... Virgin Sin
Stefan Nordström ... Jezider
Stefan Norén ... Captain Crimson
Stefan Noren ... Blowback
Stefan Norgren ... Eternal Oath, Lion's Share, Seventh Wonder, Faceshift
Stefan Olofsson ... Crazy Visions
Stefan Olsson ... Nord, House Of Shakira, Tippen Ruda
Stefan Olsson ... Human Rage
Stefan Olsson ... Sabotage
Stefan Olsson ... Wisdom Call, Bishop Garden
Stefan Orhamn ... Reckless
Stefan Paparo ... Slow Train
Stefan Persson ... Tristitia
Stefan Persson ... Coercion
Stefan Persson "Steve" ... Tanaque
Stefan Persson ... Scenteria
Stefan Pettersson ... Captain Freak's Freaky Funksters, Savage Skülls, Morifade
Stefan Pettersson "Count Wassberg" ... Sportlov
Stefan Pettersson ... Sleazy Roze
Stefan Pöge ... Desultory
Stefan Rasmusson "Snake Stevens" ... Nightshade
Stefan Ridderstråle ... Alien, Roach
Stefan Rodin ... John Norum, Necrocurse
Stefan Rosell ... Vanguard
Stefan Rosqvist ... Cloudscape, Dawn Of Oblivion, Fullforce, Stefan Rosqvist Band, Scratch (2)
Stefan Roxenby ... New Brand
Stefan Rydberg ... Balthazar
Stefan Rådlund "Stuk" ... M.A.D, Azure
Stefan Sandberg ... Jonny's Bomb
Stefan Sandström "Graav/Stoif" ... LIK, Lönndom, Armagedda
Stefan Schyberg ... Pray For Locust
Stefan Sedvalsson ... Inzight
Stefan Selvander ... Borderline (1)
Stefan Sjöberg ... Point Of Existence, T.A.R
Stefan Sjölander ... Meadows End
Stefan Sköld ... Saigon
Stefan Stigert ... The Darksend
Stefan Storrank ... Bengalen
Stefan Strömberg ... Casket Casey
Stefan Sundholm "Allweather" ... Treasure
Stefan Sundholm ... Infernal Gates
Stefan Suomalainen ... Neocori
Stefan Svanström ... Red Surface
Stefan Svantesson ... Crystal Eyes
Stefan Svensson ... Freternia
Stefan Svensson ... Mystery
Stefan Sverin ... Fake
Stefan Söderberg ... Coercion
Stefan Thuresson ... B-Thong, Concrete Stuff
Stefan Thylander ... Tyranex
Stefan Thörnblom ... Madigan, Griffen
Stefan Tyresten ... Love Injection, Motorcity Madhouse
Stefan Törnblom ... Griffen
Stefan Törnby ... Bronto
Stefan Vesterberg ... Three Minute Madness
Stefan Wallman ... Dizziness
Stefan Wedlund ... Torch
Stefan Weinerhall ... Falconer, Indungeon, Mithotyn
Stefan Westerberg "Steve Steel" ... Steel Attack, Asperity, Carnal Forge, In Thy Dreams, World Below
Stefan Wetterlind ... Million
Stefan Vidmark ... Nightscape, Terrortory
Stefan Väisinen ... Malaise
Stefan Zell ... Book Of Hours, Wolverine
Stefan Zeylon ... Hemligt Uppdrag
Stefan Åberg ... Warning
Stefan Ögren ... Paradise (3)
Stefan Öhman ... Squetters
Stefano Marcesini ... Human Race
Stefano Moggia ... Electra Top Raiders
Steffe Karlsson ... Mezzrow
Steinar Andersson ... Blåkulla
Sten Gustavsson ... Diesel
Sten Kåge ... Blues Bag
Sten Larsson "Plutten" ... Truck
Sten Möller ... Timeless Miracle
Sten Nordell ... Frozen Fire
Sten Sandberg ... Sten Sandberg
Sten Tempelman ... Tempelrock
Sten Widhman ... Hexagon
Sten-Olof Björk "S-O" ... Frozen Fire
Stephan Anderzon ... Dunder
Stephan Brisfjord ... W.O. Band
Stephan Engström ... Straight Up
Stephan Haugsnes ... Big Wave
Stephan Hermansson ... Atrox
Stephan Knutsson ... Shere Khan
Stephan Mohlin ... Modest Attraction
Stéphane Peudupin ... Ningizzia
Stephanie Rudert ... Ninnuam
Stephen Axelsson ... Airborne
Stephen Nykvist ... Crystal Blue, Bedroom Love
Stephen Wikström ... Strike
Stephen Z Svensson ... White Line
Steve Drennan ... Engel
Steve Gardner ... Human Cometh
Steve Marlyn ... Temptation
Steve Mills ... Los Sin Nombre
Steve Ranzow "A.J" ... Espinoza, Desert Rain, Original Sin
Steve Ruprecht ... Dakks
Steve Siros Redstorm ... Redstorm

NAME INDEX

Steve Woltz ... Silencer
Steven Kautzky Andersson ... Nasty Groove,
... Steven Andersson, Pike, The Storyteller, II Shy
Steven Williams ... Motorcity Madhouse
Stevo Bolgakov (aka Bolgakoff) ... Toxaemia, Belsebub
Stevo Neuman ... Tribulation (1)
Stezzo ... Melissa
Stian Grimstad ... Siena Root
Stig Gunnarsson ... Dreamhunter, Lifeline
Stig Hailovic ... Blodulv
Stig Johansson "Sirre" ... Behemoth
Stig Leyonberg ... Teamwork
Stig-Olov Svensson ... Ocean (1)
Stitch ... (see Fredrik Blomkvist)
Stojan Bdarski ... Tribal Ink
Strijd ... Black Circle, Svartr Strijd
Sture Kaveus ... The Weed
Sture Öberg ... Trouble
Styrbjörn Wahlquist ... Heavy Load, Da President
Sulan Von Zoomlander "13" ... Man.Machine.Industry
Sune Hammerström ... The Legion
Sune Olsson ... Paradise (1)
Susanna Salminen ... Katana
Susanne Berger "Sussie" ... Society Gang Rape
Susanne Carlsson ... Pleasure Avenue
Susanne Christensen ... Crystal Pride
Susanne Gillberg ... M.A.D
Susanne Pecovnik "DesDemona" ... Joke
Susie Päivärinta ... The Citadel, Grand Design
Sussi Ax ... Revanch, Stitch
Svante Enefalk ... Beneath The Frozen Soil
Svante Friberg ... Bloodstone
Svante Hedström "Swaint" ... Babylon Bombs
Svante Henrysson ... Yngwie Malmsteen,
... Glory, Marcus Jidell
Svante Lundin ... Gilt
Svante Nordström ... Bronto
Svante Stenberg ... Lohengrin
Svante Wickström ... Fatal Tabasco
Svante Widerström ... Fraise, Fatal Tabasco
Svartedöden (akaSwartadauduz) ... Helgedom, Svartrit
Sven Bjärhall ... Solen Skiner
Sven Cirnski ... Bad Habit, Truth, Raise Cain,
... Snake Charmer, Mountain Of Power,
... Project L.E.E, Blakk Totem, Pete Sandberg
Sven Gomér "Ez" ... The Jet Circus, Leviticus,
... Veni Domine
Sven Hahne ... Sven Hahne & Prästrock
Sven Jensen ... Schizophrenic Circus
Sven Johansson ... King Koole
Sven Karlsson "Mishrak" ... Soilwork, Evergrey,
... Embraced, Misteltein
Sven Kihlström ... Electra Top Raiders
Sven Lanz ... Frozen Fire
Sven Larsson ... Coastline Ride, Street Talk,
... Galleon, Xinema
Sven Lindvall ... Nord, Vatten,
... Jupiter Society, Johan Randén
Sven Nilsson ... Witchgrave, Antichrist
Sven Odén "Swede" ... Enbound
Sven Olov Wallenstein ... Sahara (1)
Sven Regner ... Parafine
Sven Wolf ... My Dead Addiction
Sven Östlind ... Reehab
Sven-Erik Fritiofsson "Fritte" ... Loss, Mental Crypt
Sven-Erik Wernborg "Sverka" ... Vanguard
Sven-Inge Nilsson ... Air Condition, Exciters
Svenne Jansson ... Golden Resurrection
Svenne Mårtensson ... Vital Sign
Svenne Rosendahl ... Månegarm
Svenne Schönfeldt ... Far North
Svenne Svensson ... Suspekt
Sven-Olof Andersson "Lollo" ... Elsesphere
Sven-Olof Nilsson ... Pride
Sven-Åke Westman ... Wildmarken
Sverker Hemring ... Livin' Sacrifice, Victory (2)
Sverker Widgren "Widda/Vidar" ... Demonical, Diabolical
Sverrir Marinosson ... Full Metal Jacketz
Svetlan Råket ... Zello, Time Code Alpha
Sylvain Coudret ... Soilwork
Sylvia Ristik "Sylvia Rice" ... Avalon
Sölvi Blöndal "Silver" ... Mother Superior
Sören Fardvik ... Adams Eve
Sören G Andersson ... Rävjunk
Sören Karlsson ... Etos
Sören Kronkvist ... Crash The System
Sören Lindmark "Whitey X'Ero" ... Savagers, X-Eryus
Søren Nico Adamsen ... Crystal Eyes, Inmoria
Sören Sandved ... Omnious, S.K.U.R.K
Sören Swanson ... Zinny J Zan, Zan Clan
T Malm ... Paletoe
T. Ahlgren ... Plutonium
T.C Rundquist ... Strike
T.J. Johnson ... Sun Island
Tamás Buday ... Nifelheim
Tamra Hope Rosanes ... Alex's Pro
Tapio Flink ... Frekvens
Tapio Karinanta ... Mud & Blood, Vision
Tapio Mäntyranta ... Skitarg
Ted Axelsson "Bundy" ... Bestial Mockery
Ted Jonsson ... Eternal Oath, Slumber
Ted Larsson ... Meadow
Ted Lindström ... Sartinas
Ted Lundström ... Amon Amarth
Ted Mattson ... Forcefeed
Ted Stenlöv ... Dorian Gray, Long John
Ted Wedebrand "Impaler" ... Shining
Ted Wernersson ... Locomotive Breath,
... From Behind, Mandrake Root
Teddy Möller "Ted" ... Searing I, Anima Morte,
... Mayadome, Mellow Poetry, Flaggelation,
... Loch Vostock, Imperial, F.K.Ü
Teddy Skoglund ... Chicks With Guns
Teddy Westlund ... The Murder Of My Sweet
Tee Park ... Twinball
Teijo Järvinen ... Dyngrak
Teo Dahnberg ... The Goddamned, Moria
Terje Hjortander "Terry Haw/H" ... The Jet Circus,
... Leviticus, Forest, Quinzy
Tero Viljanen ... Eternal Darkness, Exanthema
Theo Salsberg ... November
Theo Savidis ... F.K.Ü, Lost Souls
Therese Hanseroth ... Destiny
Therese Runsö ... Lights Out
Therése Thomsson ... Disdained
Thim Blom ... Within Y, Gardenian
Thobias Wall ... Miscellany
Thomas "Tompa" Lindberg ... Ceremonial Oath
Thomas Ahlgren "Hellord" ... Pandemonium, Deranged
Thomas Ahlgren ... Deranged, Eternal Autumn,
... Pandemonium
Thomas Anderberg ... Guardian Angels
Thomas Andersson ... Kings N' Fools
Thomas Andersson ... Black Dog
Thomas Andersson ... Aphasia
Thomas Andersson ... Ypzilon
Thomas Antonsson ... Nostradameus, Pathos, Fejd
Thomas Augustsson ... H2O
Thomas Axelsson ... Crier, Sacrifice
Thomas Backelin "Dark" ... Latex, Decameron, Lord Belial,
... Death Tyrant, Skin Infection, The Cold Existence
Thomas Berg ... Black Rose
Thomas Bergsten ... Revelations
Thomas Bergqvist ... Vomitory
Thomas Berndts ... Red Rocket
Thomas Björk ... Slam
Thomas Blum ... Reptilian
Thomas Bokgren "Van Shaw" ... Danger Avenue
Thomas Brandt ... LOK
Thomas Brandt ... Two Rocks
Thomas Broman ... John Norum, Pontus Norgren,
... Humanimal, Talisman, Road II Ruin, JJ Marsch,
... Electric Boys, Baltimoore, Impulsia,
... Great King Rat, Tryckvåg
Thomas Bursell ... Second Heat, Sapphire Eyes
Thomas Bäckman ... Mathias Holm
Thomas Carfors ... Mogg
Thomas Carlsson "Helge" ... R&R
Thomas Coox ... Big Price
Thomas Daun "Tom Bones" ... Iron Lamb, Ghost,
... Dismember, Crashdïet, Insision,
... Dr. Living Dead, Repugnant
Thomas Drevin ... 220 Volt, Inzight
Thomas Einarsson ... Eucharist
Thomas Ek "Bizzon" ... Authorize
Thomas Eklund "Tom Oakland" ... Burn
Thomas Elmberg ... Da President
Thomas Elnevik ... Blind Dog
Thomas Emblad "Blade" ... Fatal Smile (2)
Thomas Englund ... Freeway
Thomas Engström ... Shaggy, Highway
Thomas Eriksson ... Axenstar
Thomas Eriksson "GG" ... Doom Dogs, Grotesque,
... Runemagic, Fretless
Thomas Eriksson ... April Sky
Thomas Eriksson "Sluggo" ... (see Thomas Sabbathi)
Thomas Eriksson "Tommie Agrippa" .. Damien, Hexenhaus
Thomas Esteman ... Parafine
Thomas Fager ... Quix
Thomas (Ace) Forsberg "Quorthon" ... Quorthon, Bathory
Thomas Forslund ... Victory (2)
Thomas Fransén ... Nebulosa
Thomas Fredriksson ... Sartinas
Thomas Fällgren ... Construcdead, Sins Of Omission
Thomas Gardh ... Mourning Sign
Thomas Gustafsson "G:son" ... Masquerade,
... Dynazty, Detest
Thomas Gustavsson ... Double Diamond
Thomas Hackberg ... Side By Side
Thomas Hageros ... The Rest
Thomas Hallbäck "Tom" ... God B.C.
Thomas Hansson ... Thunderhog
Thomas Hansson ... Coastline
Thomas Hauk ... Fortune (2)
Thomas Heder ... World Of Silence
Thomas Hedgren ... Suicidal Winds
Thomas Hedin ... Corrosive Sweden
Thomas Hedlund ... Overload, Gormathon
Thomas Hedlund "Rex-Inferi" ... Pagan Rites, Void Moon,
... Autopsy Torment, The Ancient's Rebirth,
... Cult Of The Fox
Thomas Hedlund ... Cult Of Luna, Plastic Pride
Thomas Hedner ... Godgory, World Of Silence
Thomas Helgesson ... Backhander, The Itch
Thomas Hellquist ... Clench
Thomas Henriksson ... Come Sleep, Lingua
Thomas Hermansson ... Plan 9
Thomas Hultmark ... Shock Tilt
Thomas Hunstrand ... Twilight Zone
Thomas Huttenlocher ... Big Business
Thomas Hård ... Porklift
Thomas Irgard ... Diesel, Rotinjected
Thomas Isaksson ... Stoneload
Thomas Jacobsson ... Jeremiah
Thomas Jakobsson ... Snakes In Paradise,
... Angel King, Bedlam, (Wildliw)
Thomas Jansson ... Griftegård, Wolverine, Crowpath
Thomas Jansson ... Snakes In Paradise
Thomas Johansson "Plec" ... Dynazty, Implode,
... Mean Streak, Torch Bearer, Unmoored
Thomas Johansson "Fikarn" ... Wagabond
Thomas Johansson "Charles Von Weissenberg"
... Ceremonial Oath, God Macabre,
... Macabre End, Decollation
Thomas Johansson ... Dr Dream
Thomas Johansson ... Love Injection
Thomas Johansson ... Ozium
Thomas Johansson ... Overlord
Thomas Johnson ... Semlah
Thomas Johnson ... Änglagård
Thomas Johnsson "Snake" ... Desultory, Zebulon
Thomas Johnsson ... Impiety
Thomas Jonsson ... Circle Of Chaos
Thomas Josefsson ... Sanchez
Thomas Josefsson ... Outshine, Evocation
Thomas Jutterström ... Splash
Thomas Jäger "B/V" ... Draconian, Marulk
Thomas Jönsson ... Mothercake, Skånska Mord
Thomas Jörlöv ... New Brand
Thomas Kacso ... Nebulosa
Thomas Karlsson "Daemon Deggial" ... Shadowseeds,
... Nefandus, Therion
Thomas Karlsson "Unholy Pope/Devil Lee Rot" ... Tristitia.
... Pagan Rites, Devil Lee Rot,
... Autopsy Torment, Lenny Blade,
Thomas Karlsson ... Who's Next
Thomas Karlsson ... Head Force
Thomas Kihlberg ... Cap Outrun, Backwater
Thomas Kilberg "Paulus" ... Trazy Goes Crazy
Thomas Kjellsson ... Spin Air
Thomas Kraus ... Slowgate
Thomas Kullman ... Renegade (1)
Thomas Larsson ... Thomas Larsson, Jammer, Sky High,
... Mountain Of Power, Baltimoore
Thomas Larsson ... Psycho Circus
Thomas Lassar ... Lifeline, Damned Nation,
... Last Autumn's Dream, Dreamhunter, Crystal Blue
Thomas Lejon "Nirag" ... Omnious, A.C.T, Andromeda,
... Embraced, Fall Ov Serafim
Thomas Lidbjer ... Vatten
Thomas Lindberg ... Leash
Thomas Linde ... Backstreet
Thomas Lindfors ... In Thy Dreams
Thomas Lindgren "TG" ... 8th Sin
Thomas Lindgren ... Repulz
Thomas Lindgren ... Nubian Rose
Thomas Livenborg "Silver Silver" ... Hardcore Superstar
Thomas Lundell ... Eternity Remains
Thomas Lundeskog ... Fortuna
Thomas Lundgren ... Crier, Sacrifice
Thomas Lundgren ... Cherry Red, Roulette
Thomas Lundgren "Jaeger/Lyon" ... Hexenhaus,
... Keegan, Destiny
Thomas Löfgren ... Horizont
Thomas Löfholm ... Maryscreek
Thomas Löyskä ... Second Heat, Alyson Avenue,
... Sapphire Eyes
Thomas Magnusson ... Eventide
Thomas Magnusson ... H2O
Thomas Manell ... Man.Machine.Industry
Thomas Mann ... Tyrox
Thomas Nesslin ... Cherry Red, Roulette
Thomas Netzler ... Dyngrak
Thomas Nilsson "Nibbe" ... M.A.D
Thomas Nilsson ... Hollow
Thomas Nilsson ... X-It
Thomas Nilsson ... Fatal Attraction
Thomas Nilsson ... Triton Enigma, Julie Laughs No More
Thomas Nordh ... Maze Of Time
Thomas Nordmark ... Empire
Thomas Norstedt ... Colossus
Thomas Nyberg ... Time Gallery
Thomas Nyholm ... Damnation Army
Thomas Nyström ... Prey
Thomas Ohlsson ... Axenstar, Apostasy,
... The Project Hate MCMXCIX
Thomas Ohlsson ... Cellout
Thomas Olofsson ... Retrace
Thomas Olofsson ... Crazy Visions, Tencider
Thomas Olsson "TH" ... Julie Laughs Nomore
Thomas Osmark ... Steamboat Willies
Thomas Persson ... Lucy
Thomas Persson ... Mogg, Red Fun
Thomas Persson ... Morgana Lefay
Thomas Petersson ... Tiamat
Thomas Pettersson ... Angelize
Thomas Piehl ... Mother Misery, Clench
Thomas Pålsson ... Head Force
Thomas Rehn ... Dry Dive
Thomas Ronnhammar ... Vanguard (2)
Thomas Ryan ... Shaggy
Thomas Rydberg ... Life
Thomas Sabbathi "Sluggo" (aka Eriksson) ... Griftegård
... Year Of The Goat, Dear Mutant, Bokor
Thomas Selander ... Diesel Down
Thomas Sjöblom ... Internal Decay
Thomas Skogsberg "Mowgli" ... Shere Khan
Thomas Skult ... Bengalen
Thomas Svensson ... Sten
Thomas Thompson ... Spellbound,
... Hasse Fröberg & Musical Companion
Thomas Thorsén ... Damned Nation
Thomas Thulin ... Covered Call, Priority Spearfish
Thomas Thun ... Ebony Tears
Thomas Thörnblom ... Tale
Thomas Wahlberg ... Ninnuam, Julie Laughs No More
Thomas Wahlström ... Excretion
Thomas Wallén ... The Downtown Clowns
Thomas Weinesjö ... Veni Domine, AudiovisioHero
Thomas Widmark ... Romance
Thomas Wikblad ... Mainline
Thomas Wiklund ... Neon Rose, Truck, Uppåt Väggarna
Thomas Vikström ... Afterglow, Mind's Eye, Candlemass,
... Brat Pack, The Poodles, Talisman, Therion, 7Days,
... Covered Call, Dark Illusion, Speedy Gonzales,
... Stormwing, Talk Of The Town, Thomas Vikström,
... 17, Audiovision, Crash The System, Prisoner, Sayit,
... Deacon Street, Divinefire, Flintstens med Stanley,
... Gallery (1), Houston, Hypocrite, Lion's Share,
Thomas Witt ... Europe, John Norum
Thomas Wolf ... Stormwind
Thomas von Wachenfeldt ... De Tveksamma
Thomas Wretman ... Tejp
Thomas Wunger ... Tomterockers
Thomas Väänänen ... Thyrfing, Wyvern
Thomas Åberg ... Kaamos, A Mind Confused
Thomas Åhman ... Firework
Thommy Larsson ... Shore
Thommy Lindskog ... Nymf, Wulfgar
Thor Jeppesen ... Evil Masquerade
Thorbjörn "Turken" ... Shame (1)
Thorbjörn Andersson ... Earthquake, Rising
Thorbjörn Andersson ... Source (1)
Thorbjörn Andersson ... Rising
Thorbjörn Brynedal "Toob" ... Genocrush Ferox
Thorbjörn Englund ... Thorbjörn Englund, Winterlong,
... Raubtier, Sabaton
Thorbjörn Frejd ... Big Train, Profile
Thorbjörn Gräslund "TG" ... Crucifyre
Thorbjörn Harr ... B.C And The Envelopes
Thorbjörn Holm ... Nectaris
Thorbjörn Löfgren ... Lazy
Thorbjörn Persson "Tobbe" ... Rhapsody (Sweden), Extasy
Thorbjörn Ragnesjö ... Heavy Load
Thorbjörn Rapp ... Cartago
Thorbjörn Sommer ... Vision
Thord Brännkärr ... Ninnuam
Thord Jonsson ... Carrie
Thord Klarström ... Gallows End
Thord L. Steen ... Fairness
Thore Skogman ... Thore Goes Metal
Tia Marklund ... Dexter Jones' Circus Orchestra
Tim Bertilsson ... Switchblade, Pinch
Tim Ferm ... Foobar The Band
Tim Hallerhed ... Damn Delicious
Tim Nedergård ... In Mourning
Tim Norell ... Inferno
Tim Sköld "Tim Tim/Sköld" ... Shotgun Messiah,
... Sköld, King Pin
Tim Ängström ... Skraeckoedlan
Tim Öhrström ... Eternity Remains, Avatar
Timmy Leng ... Despite
Timmy Persson ... El Camino, Vermin
Timo Hovinen ... Faceshift
Timo Nilsson ... Emerald, Lovehandles
Tina Leijonberg ... Stormwind
Tina Spångberg ... Björn Stigsson
Tina Strömberg ... Ice Age
Tinna Karlsdotter ... All Ends
Tintin Andersen ... Pray For Locust
Tirre Bendroth "Dione" ... Joke
Tjaback Holmér ... Tears

NAME INDEX

Tjet Gustafson (Pipare) ... Safemode
Tjompen ... Sten
Tobbe "Nachash" ... Funeral Mist
Tobbe Anger ... 2 Ton Predator
Tobbe Broström ... Coldspell, Maniac
Tobbe Bövik ... The Awesome Machine, On Parole, The Black Marbles
Tobbe Damberg ... Zircus, Skydiverse
Tobbe Eliasson ... Shame (1)
Tobbe Geson ... Hydrogen
Tobbe Gustafsson "Ash" ... Fear The Future
Tobbe Holmgren ... Wombbath
Tobbe Höckert "Toby" ... Liquidist
Tobbe Jansson ... Silent Scythe
Tobbe Johansson ... Cowboy Prostitutes
Tobbe Johansson ... Trouble
Tobbe Johansson ... Atrox
Tobbe Jonsson ... Angeline
Tobbe Larsson ... Electric Eastwood
Tobbe Nyberg ... Physical Attraction
Tobbe R "Schizo" ... Melissa
Tobbe Sandström ... Jet
Tobbe Skogh ... Carnival Sun, The Itch
Tobhias Ljung ... The Bereaved, Bibleblack
Tobias Alpadie ... Miseration, Gordon Fights
Tobias Ander "Tobbe" ... Slingblade, Jigsore Terror, Witchgrave, Scams, Leukemia
Tobias Andersson "Toby" ... Seven Wishes, Shadowland, Edge
Tobias Anger ... All Hell, 2 Ton Predator
Tobias Backlin "Toby" ... Calm Chaos
Tobias Backlund ... Chainsaw
Tobias Bernström ... Revengia
Tobias Bertilsson ... Empty Guns
Tobias Birgersson ... Frequency, Lothlorien
Tobias Björk ... Chaos Feeds Life, Skyfire
Tobias Björklund ... Withered Beauty
Tobias Björkman ... Slitage
Tobias Brynedal "Toob" ... Interment, Insision
Tobias Christiansson ... Necronaut, Dismember, Dagger, Grave (2)
Tobias Danielsson "Eazy" ... Revolution Riot
Tobias Danielsson ... Mindjive
Tobias Enbert ... Darkwater, Harmony (2)
Tobias Eng "King Pellinore" Overdeth, Violent Work Of Art
Tobias Ericson ... Last View
Tobias Eriksson "Rogirrek Garm" ... Elimi
Tobias Fischer ... Backyard Babies
Tobias Fjällström "Kheeroth" ... Setherial, Midvinter
Tobias Forge "Mary Goore" . Repugnant, Ghost, Crashdïet
Tobias Fransson ... Attention (2)
Tobias "Grotesque" ... Revolting
Tobias Gustafsson ... Hydrogen, Infernal
Tobias Gustafsson ... Netherbird, Eucharist, Revengia, Armageddon, The*End
Tobias Gustafsson "Tobbe" ... God Among Insects, The Project Hate MCMXCIX, Vomitory, Syrus, Torture Division
Tobias Gustafsson ... Nestor
Tobias Gustavsson ... Straight Frank
Tobias Heideman ... Imperial Domain
Tobias Holst ... Quarterback Beat
Tobias Israelsson ... Plague Angel, Strangulation
Tobias Jacobsson ... This Haven
Tobias Jansson ... Diabolical, Ruined Soul
Tobias Jansson ... Saffire
Tobias Jansson "Toby Jay" ... The Law
Tobias Johansson ... All Hell
Tobias Johansson ... Lothlorien
Tobias Karlsson "Ghost" ... Reveal
Tobias Karlsson ... Osukaru, Katana
Tobias Karlsson ... Ultimate Concern
Tobias R Kellgren "Tobbe" ... Decameron, Seventh One, Soulreaper, Wolf, Sacramentum, Dissection
Tobias Larsson ... Ocean Chief
Tobias Leffler "Tobbe/T Nails/Ebboth" ... Algaion, Nephenzy (Chaos Ordetr), The Cold Exicisence, Vergelmer
Tobias Lepistö ... Myrah
Tobias Lindberg ... Svartnad
Tobias Lindell ... Europe, Aggressive Chill, Ammotrack, H.E.A.T, Heed, Sister
Tobias Lindquist ... Corrupt, Enforcer
Tobias Lund ... Calm
Tobias Martinsson ... The Provenance
Tobias Moen "Tobbe" ... Rat Bat Blue, Red Fun, Silent Call
Tobias Molin ... The Poodles
Tobias Netzell ... Volturyon, In Mourning, October Tide
Tobias Nilsson "Tobbe" ... Superstition
Tobias Nilsson ... Blind Dog, Mindcollapse
Tobias Nyström ... Daisy Chain
Tobias Ogenblad ... Anaemia
Tobias Oja ... Stoneload
Tobias Ols ... 21 Lucifers, Without Grief
Tobias Olsson "Shuffle" ... Boogieman
Tobias Olsson ... Blinded Colony
Tobias Persson ... Closer (2), Viceral Bleeding, Deathboot
Tobias Pettersson ... Divine Baze Orchestra
Tobias Pettersson ... Vornth, RAM
Tobias Pettersson ... Erupted
Tobias Quick "Tobbe" ... Sergej The Freak
Tobias Resch ... Year Of The Goat
Tobias Rosén ... Noctum
Tobias Sidegård "Draugadrottir" ... Necrophobic, Trident, Order Of Isaz, Therion, Bajen Death Cult
Tobias Sillman "Tobbe/Necrobarber" ... The Dead, Crucifyre, Guidance Of Sin, Vicious Art
Tobias Strandvik ... Kamchatka
Tobias Söderström "Deathslaughter" ... Necroplasma
Tobias Tarrach "Toby" ... Alien
Tobias Turesson ... Violent Work Of Art
Tobias Tybåhl ... Prime
Tobias Wernersson ... Supreme Majesty, Little Yankees
Tobias Wiik ... New Breed
Tobias Wulff ... The Carpet Knights
Tobias Öhman ... Far North
Toft Stade ... Shredhead
Togge Rock ... Danger (2)
Tom Berglund ... Subtopia, Subztain
Tom Björn (aka Johansson) ... Memento Mori, Nightingale, Memory Garden
Tom Burton ... Blåeld
Tom S Englund ... Evergrey, Moonlight Agony, Scarpoint
Tom Gardiner ... Solution .45
Tom Gustavsson ... Genesaret
Tom Hallbäck ... Hyste'riah G.B.C
Tom Lind ... Maeday
Tom Mitchell ... Mercy
Tom Nilsson ... Motherlode
Tom Pearson ... Badmouth
Tom Persson ... Disruption
Tom Rask ... Optimystical, Vagh
Tom B Walther ... Avalon/Avalone
Tom Wouda ... Gemini Five, Toxic Rose
Tom Yttergren ... Stereo Generator
Tom Åberg ... April Sky
Tom Åsberg ... Diploma
Tomas Ace Forsberg "Quorthon" ... Bathory, Jennie Tebler
Tomas Adolfsson ... The Session
Tomas Ahlberg ... Pleasure Avenue, Wolf
Tomas Andersson "Juneor" ... Kamchatka, King Hobo, Mountain Of Power
Tomas Andersson ... Freevil, Denata
Tomas Andersson ... Itchy Daze
Tomas Andersson ... Screams Over Northland
Tomas Andersson ... Blackwood
Tomas Antonsson ... Kamasutra
Tomas Asklund "Alzazmon" ... Infernal (666), Dissection, Necromicon, Dark Funeral, Dawn
Tomas Bengtsson "Bäsan" ... Kazjurol
Tomas Bergsten ... Fantasy, Tomas Bergsten's Fantasy
Tomas Bergstrand .. Dawn Of Decay, Fingerspitzengefühl, Switch Opens, Moaning Wind, Rise And Shine
Tomas Björkbacka ... After Twelve
Tomas Bodin ... Karmakanic, Cross, JJ Marsch, The Flower Kings
Tomas Carlsson ... April Sky
Tomas Carlström ... Lava Engine
Tomas Christensen ... Cross
Tomas Claesson ... Disciple
Tomas Djurfeldt ... Mister Kite
Tomas Ederer ... Brimstone
Tomas Edström ... Pantheon
Tomas Elofsson ... Sanctification, In Battle, God Among Insects
Tomas Engberg ... Make Up
Tomas Engberg ... Tyfuz
Tomas Ericson "Witchfinder" ... Helvetets Port
Tomas Eriksson ... Kaipa
Tomas Eriksson ... Magnolia
Tomas Eriksson ... S:t Erik, Devian
Tomas Erlandsson ... A.C.T
Tomas Ernvik ... Vatten, Emmas Boogie Band
Tomas Ferm "John Raymore" ... Empire Saint
Tomas Fredblad ... Ocean (2)
Tomas Fredriksson ... Tai Rose
Tomas Friberg ... Sky Of Rage, Astral Doors
Tomas Gerdoff ... Paradise (1)
Tomas Grün ... White
Tomas Gustafsson "Tompa" ... Entity
Tomas Gustafsson "Tosse" ... Lick The Dog
Tomas Gustafsson ... Reizon Band
Tomas Gustavsson (now Rudström) ... 454, Big Fish
Tomas Gustavsson "Collins" ... Wizz
Tomas Haake ... Meshuggah, Fredrik Thordendah's Special Defects
Tomas Hartman ... X-Perience
Tomas Hedlund "Jim Voltage/Sagittarius" ... Kill, Entity, Cross Bow
Tomas Hermansson ... Love Child, Seven Wishes
Tomas Hjort ... Cross
Tomas Holtinkoski ... Denied
Tomas Hultqvist ... Dark Illusion
Tomas Hurtig ... Grand Stand, Zeudo
Tomas Irgard ... Thunderhog
Tomas Jansson ... Wildmarken
Tomas Jansson ... Power
Tomas Johansson ... Incapacity, Unmoored
Tomas Johansson ... Tumult
Tomas Jonasson ... Croc
Tomas Jonsson ... Loch Vostock, Mellow Poetry
Tomas Jonsson ... Narduz
Tomas Jonsson ... Moment Maniacs
Tomas Josefsson ... Cemetary (1213)
Tomas Jutenfaldt ... Gates Of Ishtar
Tomas Karström ... Source Of Ignition
Tomas Kålen ... Central
Tomas Lagrén ... Suicidal Seduction, BackWardness
Tomas Lewin ... Notorious
Tomas Lindberg "Tompa" ... Sarea, At The Gates, Grotesque, Necronaut, The Crown (Crown Of Throns)
Tomas Lindfors ... Wombbath, In Thy Dreams
Tomas Lindgren ... Plague Warhead
Tomas Lindh "Chappe" ... Team Custard
Tomas Lundin ... M.A.C
Tomas Löfgren ... 7:e Himlen
Tomas Marklund ... Mosez, Ground Mower
Tomas Melin ... Cheryenne
Tomas Modig "T. Cucumber" ... Fruitcake, Lotus (2), On Parole
Tomas Munters ... Coastline
Tomas Musial ... King Size
Tomas Nadersson ... Spitfire
Tomas Naeslund ... Dizziness
Tomas Nielsen ... East End
Tomas Nilsén "TOM" ... Machinae Supremacy
Tomas Nilsson "Zornheym" ... Dark Funeral
Tomas Nilsson ... The Rifles
Tomas Nilsson ... Through Time Tomorrow
Tomas Nilsson .. Suicidal Seduction, Devian, Dark Funeral
Tomas Nordin ... Greed
Tomas Näslund ... Blidside
Tomas Oksanen ... Drama
Tomas Olsson ... Street Talk, Bloodbound
Tomas Olsson (now Måsgård) ... Unleashed
Tomas Olsson ... Blåkulla
Tomas Opava ... Alex's Pro
Tomas Persson ... Rat Bat Blue, Alien
Tomas Persson "Rotten Boy" ... Deathboot
Tomas Persson ... Faith Taboo
Tomas Pettersson ... Prime
Tomas Reinersson "Kiwi" ... Seventh Planet, Zero Illusions
Tomas Salonen ... Kongh
Tomas Sjölander ... Legbone
Tomas Skogsberg ... Afflicted, Axia, Candy Kicks Ass, Damned Nation, Dissection, Close Quarters, God Macabre, In Battle, In The Collonnades, Entombed, Katatonia, Suffer, This Gift Is A Curse, Unmoored, Dismember, The Generals, Legia, Leukemia, Lisa Gives Head, Macabre End, Nihilist, Skintrade, Theory In Practice, Niva, Ebony Tears, Singer, Vermin, Lake Of Tears, Lobotomy
Tomas Snellman ... Itchy Daze
Tomas Stolt ... Disdained, Insania (Stockholm)
Tomas Strand ... Sleeping Ape
Tomas Strömberg ... Setback
Tomas Sunnmo ... Axewitch
Tomas Sörlen ... Scar
Tomas Thorberg "Pomma" ... John Norum, One Cent, Southfork, Four Sticks, Plankton, Snakes In Paradise
Tomas Tornefjell ... Grave (1)
Tomas Wallin ... Solsting
Tomas Wallin ... Takida
Tomas Walther "Tom B" ... Avalon, Avalone
Tomas Varadi ... Peo
Tomas Vasseur ... Crow, Indomitus
Tomas Westerlund ... Freeway
Tomas Wäppling ... Freternia
Tomas Ylivaimo ... Nagazaki, Burn
Tomas Åberg ... To Africa With Love, Deception
Tomas Ängshammar ... Prime
Tomas Ängstgård ... Interment
Tomas Öndemar ... Råg i ryggen
Tomi Peltonen "Tommy Martell" ... Madigan, Griffen, Torch
Tommi Djukin ... Silent Scythe
Tommi Holappa ... Greenleaf, Dozer
Tommi Karppanen ... Tad Morose, Morgana, Lelnmoria
Tommi Konu ... Daemonicus, The Duskfall
Tommi Korkeamäki "Tommy Trigger" ... Blazing Guns
Tommi Larsson "Larssa" ... Mörker
Tommi Partanen ... Coldspell
Tommie Andersson ... Seven Tears
Tommie Eriksson (aka Tommy) "Daemon Kajgal" ... Year Of The Goat, Saturnalia Temple, Enigmatic, Shadowseeds
Tommie Hammar ... Plan Three
Tommie Johansson ... Kliché
Tommie Johansson ... Freternia
Tommie Karlsson ... Sanity
Tommie Lundgren ... Platitude
Tommie Nissilä "Tom-E" ... Revolution Riot
Tommie Petersson "Tban/Rayban" ... Kazjurol
Tommie Pettersson ... X-Ray
Tommie Svanbo ... Aggressive Chill
Tommy "Zombie" ... Ceremonial Execution
Tommy Adolfsson ... Head Force
Tommy Andersson (now Liljegren) "Stommen" ... Stonecake, Anekdoten
Tommy Andersson ... Savage Skülls, Tornado Soup
Tommy Asmola ... Sahara (1)
Tommy Brage ... Hazy, Axewitch
Tommy Braic ... Jet Trail, Mandrake Root
Tommy Carlsson ... Istapp, Devoured, Abomination
Tommy Carlsson ... The Quill, Quil
Tommy Dahlström "Blackblood" ... Diabolicum, Aeon (2), Defaced Creation
Tommy Denander ... 17, ATC, Audiovision, Houston, Impulsia, The Jet Circus, Locomotive Breath, The Poodles, Mountain Of Power, Reece/Kronlund, Ten 67, Yale Bate, Grand Design, Jim Jidhed, Mind's Eye, VII Gates, Cheers, Deacon Street, Rainmaker, Heartbreak Radio, Speedy Gonzales, Talk Of The Town, Spin Gallery, Cool For Cats ... Radioactive, Tommy Denander, Prisoner, Sayit, Impera
Tommy Eklund ... Grand Vision
Tommy Ericsson ... Therion
Tommy Eriksson "Wilbur" ... Semlah, Count Raven
Tommy Falk ... Pete Sandberg
Tommy Folkesson ... Extasy
Tommy Fäldt ... Supreme Majesty
Tommy Grönberg ... Eternal Lies, Fatal Embrace
Tommy Gustavsson ... Plebb, Purple Haze
Tommy Gällhagen ... 7:e Himlen, Horizont
Tommy Haglund ... Spasmodic
Tommy Hammarsten ... Blåeld
Tommy Helgesson "Snowy Shaw" ... Memento Mori, Dream Evil, Therion, XXX, Notre Dame, Illwill, Falconer, Loud 'N' Proud, Kee Marcello, Opera Diabolicus, Whipped Cream, Sabaton
Tommy Hjälmberg ... Allan Beddo Band
Tommy Holmer ... Undivide
Tommy Holmers "Ymer" ... Rimthurs
Tommy Jansson "Jee" ... Skellington
Tommy Johannesson ... Motvind
Tommy Johansson ... Majectic Vanguard, ReinXeed, Golden Resurrection
Tommy Johansson "McJo" ... Mindless (Sinner)
Tommy Johnsson ... Airborne
Tommy Karevik ... Vindictiv, Firecracker, Seventh Wonder
Tommy Karlsson ... Sorcerer
Tommy Karlsson ... Sign
Tommy Larsson ... Fullforce, Heed
Tommy Larsson ... Chasticement
Tommy Magnusson ... No Rules
Tommy Mattsson ... Inzight
Tommy Moberg ... Agony
Tommy Nilsson ... Easy Action, Swedish Metal Aid, R.A.W, Horizont
Tommy Nilsson ... Lifeline
Tommy Nilsson ... Oxid
Tommy Nilsson ... Terrortory
Tommy Nilsson ... Tyron
Tommy Nordell ... Frozen Fire
Tommy Ottemark ... Excretion
Tommy Palevik ... Slyside
Tommy Palm ... Wulcan
Tommy Parkkonen "Tom Alcohol" ... Chronic Torment
Tommy Persson ... Sad Wings
Tommy Pettersson ... Madigan
Tommy Rehn ... Corroded, Moahni Moahna, Angtoria, Lillasyster, YOHIO
Tommy Rudak ... Sanity
Tommy Scalisi Svensson ... Gooseflesh, Rat Salad, Electric Earth
Tommy Silfvenius "Robin Vagh" ... Optimystical, Vagh
Tommy Storback ... Nifters
Tommy Strömstedt ... Zane
Tommy Svanbo "Tommie Rocker/T-Bone" .. Loud 'N' Nasty
Tommy Södergren ... Illfigure
Tommy Söderström ... Steelwings
Tommy Tysper (Pawlicki) ... Tommy Tysper & The Kids
Tommy Tägtgren ... Dispatched, The Forsaken, Omnious, Sterbhaus, Unmoored, Nephenzy (Chaos Order), Flesh, Skyfire, Theory In Practice
Tommy Wirén ... Horoscope (1), Ocean (1)
Tommy Zachariasen "Lone Wolf" ... Rozz The Bozz
Tommy Åberg "Talon" ... Bloodshed, Rev. 16:8, IXXI
Tommy Öberg ... Mornaland, Slumber
Tomo Wihma ... Panta Rei
Tompa Ericsson ... Tears
Tompa Lindberg ... The Great Deceiver
Toni Baioni ... Cervello, Jennie Tebler's Out Of Oblivion
Toni Donello ... The Fuzes
Toni Erkkilä ... Winterlong
Toni Kocmut ... Sins Of Omission, Wyvern
Toni Korhonen ... Dawn Of Time, Reclusion
Toni Lindgren ... Jackwave
Toni Paananen ... System Shock
Tony "Blackwinged/Demogorgon" ... Nefandus
Tony Ajayi ... Åke Eriksson & Bedlam
Tony Andersson ... House Of Shakira

Tony Andersson "Cool" ... Walkaway
Tony Arnesson: v/g ... Spin Air
Tony Bohman ... Jonah Quizz
Tony Borg ... Alien, Tony Borg, Highway, Naked
Tony Brorsson ... Frontiers
Tony Carlsson ... Dirty Old Men
Tony Classon ... Arsenite
Tony Dicander ... Buckshot O.D.
Tony Ekfeldt ... Sad Wings
Tony Elfving ... Steel Attack, Facequake, Lack Of Faith
Tony Engström ... Advice
Tony Eriksson ... Diavox, Morgana LeLefay
Tony Eriksson ... Fat Nelly
Tony Erkkilä ... Viperine
Tony Freed ... Godhate, Thronaeon
Tony Frisk ... (see Tony Sunnhag)
Tony Fryklund ... Sleeping Ape
Tony Gelander ... Rising Faith
Tony Hadarsson ... Fair Child
Tony Hedin "Hanover" ... Hiroshima
Tony Heine ... Aspected
Tony Hellander "Roy Taylor" ... Dream Bank, Titanic Truth, Trash, Stonehenge
Tony Hermansen ... Cavus
Tony Isaksson ... Lucy
Tony Jaensson ... Arena
Tony Jansson ... Mason, Slam
Tony Jelencovich "JJ" ... B-Thong, Lord Belial, NME Within, Taetre Wonderland, Dementation Dpt., Concrete Stuff, Glanzig,Transport League, Ton Of Bricks, Massive Audio Nerve, Iron Shit Snakes, Hostile Cell, DeathDestruction
Tony Johansson "Yoanson" ... Masquerade
Tony Johansson ... Tencider, Crazy Visions
Tony Josefsson ... Sky Of Rage
Tony K Sköld "Shield" ... Rampant, Walkaway
Tony Kampner "Toxine" ... Satanic Slaughter, Witchery, Seance
Tony Kristiansson ... Frank Thomsen
Tony Krusing "Karl" ... X-Hale
Tony Lang ... Unsolved, Morpheena
Tony Lind ... The Mist Of Avalon
Tony Lindberg ... Evolution, Frekvens
Tony Niemistö "Reno" ... John Norum, Geisha, Europe
Tony Niva ... Lion's Share, Peo, Swedish Erotica, Niva, Trazy Goes Crazy
Tony Nyberg ... Line Up, Paradise (2)
Tony Pietilä ... Eternal Darkness
Tony Qwarnström ... Alex's Pro
Tony Richter ... The Darksend, 9th Plague
Tony Rohtla ... Alyson Avenue
Tony Sandberg ... Overload, Gormathon
Tony Sundstrand "Satanic Tony" ... Demorian
Tony Sunnhag (aka Frisk) ... Overload, Gormathon
Tony Svensson ... Hydra (1)
Tony Särkää "It" ... Ophthalamia, 8th Sin, Abruptum, Vondur, WAR, Total War
Tony Thorén ... The Bereaved
Tony Tillerås ... Lezlie Paice
Tony Tomasson ... Caligula
Tony Topp ... White Cat
Tony Ulvan "Odin" ... Isengard, Hazy
Tony Westermark ... Soreption
Tony Westgård ... Love Child, Trazy, Seven Wishes
Tony Westin ... Rain
Tony Wilhelmsson ... Fake
Tony Östman ... Aeon
Tor Adolfsson ... Mykorrhiza
Tor Amrén ... Tumbleweed
Tor Castensson ... Nine
Tor Frykhold ... Coercion
Tor Nygård ... Tonvikt
Tor Nyman ... Oppression
Tor Pentén ... Sideburn, Stonesilk
Tor Sjödén ... New Keepers Of The Water Towers
Torben Ferm ... Norden Light
Torben Stenberg "Tobben" ... Zone Zero
Torbjörn Andersson ... Överslag
Torbjörn Andrén ... Tumbleweed
Torbjörn Brogren ... Heads Or Tales, Edge
Torbjörn Carlsson ... Splash
Torbjörn Edqvist ... Dawn Of Silence
Torbjörn Enberg ... Lucy, Texas Ego
Torbjörn Eriksson ... Cicero
Torbjörn Haraldsson ... Fatal Tabasco
Torbjörn Larsson ... John Norum, Trash, (Macbeth)
Torbjörn Lindberg "T.L" ... Lonely Hearts
Torbjörn Marcusson ... After Twelve
Torbjörn Moen "Tobbe" ... Creozoth, Gotham City
Torbjörn Olsson ... Airlines
Torbjörn Pettersson ... Cheers
Torbjörn Sandberg ... Point Of Existence, T.A.R
Torbjörn Skogh ... Erottica
Torbjörn Stråhle ... Revenge
Torbjörn Tarrach "Toby" ... Highway
Torbjörn Wahrotén ... Epedemic
Torbjörn Wassenius "John Tatum" ... Talent, Heartbreak Radio, Last Autumn's Dream
Torbjörn Weinesjö ... Audiovision, Divinefire, Grand Stand, Hero,Veni Domine
Torbjörn Westerhäll ... Brat Pack
Torbjörn Öhrling ... Unmoored
Tord Carlsson ... Print
Tord Eriksson ... Azotic Reign
Tord Lindman ... Änglagård
Tord Ottergren ... Bloodlit
Tord Persson ... Turning Point
Tord-Martin Pettersson "Pat Raven" ... Candy Roxx
Tore Kjell ... Asoka
Tore Nylund ... Fullmakt
Tore Paulsen ... Thrashon
Tore Stjerna "Necromorbus/Shiva/I. Hate" ... Ondskapt, Unanimated, Watain, Funeral Stench, Armagedda, Ofermod, Vanmakt, Damnation, Orcivus, Nominon, Valkyrja, Nex, Chaos Omen, Zavorash
Torgil Sturesson ... Daydream
Torgny Berlin ... Wham Glam Boys
Torgny Johansson ... Erottica, By My Fear
Torgny Pettersson ... Exciters
Torgny Östlund ... Magic
Torstein Wickberg ... Raise Hell
Torsten Jacobsson "Tott" ... Lucky Stiff
Tosse Wennerholm ... Backtalk
Totalscorn/Zablogma ... Zavorash, IXXI
Totte Martini ... Traumatic
Tove Thörn Lundin ... Kaipa
Toyyi Sjöqvist ... Nattfrost
Travis Neal ... The Bereaved
Trevor Searle ... Steve Roper Band
Tristan Agdler ... Mass Murder Agenda
Trond Vinje ... Dynamiet Wasteland
Truls Mörck ... Graveyard
Tryggve Knutsson ... Vivid
Turid Walderhaug ... Siebenbürgen
Tuukka Frank ... Tyranex
Tyler Voelz ... Nightscape
Tyrone Nilsson ... Big Thing
Tängman ... Siena Root
U. Jensen ... Paradize (2)
Ubbe Rydeslätt ... Snakepit Rebels, The Case, Steel Arrows
Uffe Cederlund "Napolean Pukes" ... Morbid, Entombed
Uffe Johansson ... Repulz
Uffe Nilsson ... Angeline
Uffe Speedfreak "6-10" ... Speedfreaks
Uffe Westberg ... Slam
Ufuk Demir ... Abandon, Relevant Few, Heed
Ulf Ahlberg ... Kalajs
Ulf Andersson ... Jeanne D'Arc
Ulf Andersson ... The Social Scumbags, Päst
Ulf Andersson "Stormlord" ... Bewitched, Naglfar, Nocturnal Rites
Ulf Andersson "Wolf" ... Masquerade, Peo
Ulf Andersson ... Backstreet, Mother's Hope
Ulf Andersson ... Boogietryck
Ulf Andersson (aka Uffe) ... Twilight Zone, Miss Willis
Ulf Bogren ... I Am Hunger
Ulf Carlsson ... Rain
Ulf Cederlund "Uffe" ... Nihilist, Haystack, Murder Squad
Ulf Christiansson ... Jerusalem
Ulf Dalegren ... Allegiance, Vomitory
Ulf Eriksson ... Shenerah
Ulf Forslund ... Genie
Ulf Grenholm ... Törsten Dricker
Ulf Gustafsson ... Riksväg 77
Ulf Gustavsson ... TNT
Ulf Hammarlund "Palle" ... Fuelhead, Wildness
Ulf Hansson ... Psyckadeli
Ulf Helander ... Stormcrow
Ulf Holmberg ... Manticore
Ulf Högberg ... X-It
Ulf Ihrsén ... Surrender
Ulf Ivarsson "Rockis" ... King Hobo, Sky High, Enter The Hunt, Conny Bloom
Ulf Jansson "Blappan" ... Loss, Mental Crypt
Ulf Jansson ... Capricorn
Ulf Johansson "Wolf" ... Impious, Power Supreme, Tribal Ink
Ulf Johansson "Knirk" ... Zpeedfreak, Moonshine
Ulf Johansson ... Evolution
Ulf Johansson ... Mandala, Tippen Ruda
Ulf Johansson ... Valenze
Ulf Kjell ... Tom Trick
Ulf Kronsell ... Locomotive Breath
Ulf Lagerström ... Astral Doors
Ulf Lagestam ... Scamps
Ulf Lagesten ... Carrie
Ulf Larsson "Chris Laney" ... Zan Clan, Casablanca, Alyson Avenue, Dynazty, Vanity Blvd., Unameus, 17, Chris Laney, Scratch (2), Leif Edling, Dark Illusion, Crash Diet, Kyss, Shotgun Messiah
Ulf Larsson "Udo" ... Kazjurol
Ulf Larsson ... X-Union, Mr. Tiger
Ulf Lenneman ... In The Colonnades
Ulf Lundström ... Blizzard
Ulf Magnusson ... Green Sleeves
Ulf Malm ... Boom Shanker Group
Ulf Mellander ... Make Up
Ulf Merkell ... Higher Ground
Ulf Nygårds ... Book Of Hours
Ulf Nylin ... Stabwound, Livsnekad
Ulf Olsson ... Törsten Dricker
Ulf Olsson ... Setback
Ulf Pettersson ... Lotus (1), Galleon, Lake Of Tears
Ulf Pettersson ... Rosicrucian, Mezzrow
Ulf Samuelsson ... Serpent, Suffer
Ulf Sandberg ... Victim
Ulf Sandin "Ken" ... Transport League, Alien, Swedish Erotica, Kee Marcello, Time Code Alpha
Ulf Stöckel ... Comatose
Ulf Sundberg "Bo Werner" ... Mogg, Yngwie Malmsteen, Steamroller, Europe
Ulf Svensson ... Purple Haze
Ulf Sörman ... Castillon
Ulf Thunberg ... Lohengrin
Ulf Tillman ... Isengard
Ulf Torkelsson ... Atlantic Tide, Abramis Brama, Sunflower
Ulf Wahlberg ... Gemini Souls
Ulf Wahlquist ... Baltimoore
Ulf Waldekrantz "Sebastian Gant" ... Candy Roxx
Ulf Wallander ... The Flower Kings
Ulf Wedenbrand ... Polluted Influence
Ulf Wessman ... Hemligt Uppdrag
Ulf Vestlund ... Broke N Blue
Ulf Wiglund ... Quix
Ulf Vinyl Stenberg ... The Jet Circus
Ulf Åhman ... Sky High
Ulf Örtensjö ... Quolio
Ulla Nordin ... Paradise (1)
Ulph Johansson.. Dead Silent Slumber, Azure, Embracing
Ulric Johansson ... Uppgång 36
Ulrica Carnell ... Lifeline
Ulrich Carlsson ... Million
Ulrick Lönnquist ... Sahara (2)
Ulrik Arturén ... Diary
Ulrik Bjuhr ... Ghamorean
Ulrik Fröberg ... Renegade (2)
Ulrik Larsson ... Regent
Ulrik Lindblom ... Lake Of Tears
Ulrik Nilsson ... Generous Maria
Ulrik Seppänen ... Thore Goes Metal
Ulrik Thunman "Urrke" ... Turning Point, King Size, (Maryslim)
Ulrik Zander ... Metal Mercy, Colorblind, Majestic Dimension
Ulrika Beijer ... Broken Glass
Ulrika Bornemark ... The Defaced
Ulrika Karlsson ... Jesusexercise
Ulrika Örn ... Fake
Ulv ... Blodulv, Svartnatt
Uno Bjurling ... Oxiplegatz
Uno Bruniusson "Svenningsson" ... Undergång, In Solitude
Uno Eriksson ... Twins Crew
Uno Helmersson ... Darklands
Uno Sjöström ... Impulsia
Urban Bergman ... Street Level, (Checkpoint Charlie)
Urban Breed ... Bloodbound, Wolverine, Tad Morose, Trail Of Murder
Urban Carli "Ubbe" ... Andra Band, Rockbox
Urban Carlsson ... The Duskfall
Urban Engström ... H2O
Urban Fagerholm ... Kisses From The Past
Urban Fermdal "Bam'C Slammer" ... Adams Eve
Urban Greijer ... Paradise (3)
Urban Gustafsson "Ubbe" ... Andra Band, Rockbox
Urban Gustafsson ... Vomitory
Urban Henriksson ... N.J.B
Urban Larsson ... Fairness
Urban Lundgren ... Borderline (2), Mr Quinn
Urban Lundin "Ubbe" ... Aeon (1)
Urban Mattsson ... Jonny Cartong
Urban Månsby ... Broken Dagger
Urban Nilsson ... Rampant
Urban Robertsson ... Mosez
Urban Skytt ... Crematory, Crucifyre, Regurgitate
Urban Svensson ... Rising
Urban Thorell ... Riksväg 77
Urban Wikström ... Hollow
Urban Åhden ... Hexagon
Urban Österberg ... Black Web, Impiety
Vagelis Baliousis ... System Shock
Valbon Gurmani "Bonnie" ... Cult Disciples
Valentin Maelstrom ... Devil's Whorehouse
Valentin Nilsson ... Obscurity
Valentin Nilsson ... Superstition
Valentine "Charon" Pecovnik ... Joke, Renegades
Valle Daniel Adzic ... Impious, One Man Army
Valle Magnusson ... Jezider
Valter Koivunen ... Spinning Black Circle
Vanja Hadzic ... Lava Engine, Maitreya
Vanskapt (Sir N) ... Helgedom
Varg Strand "Ahldrathan" ... Misteltein, Ishtar, Fall Ov Serafim, My Dead Addiction
Vedran Bencic ... The Gardnerz
Veikko Heikkinen ... Nugatory
Vera Olofsson ... Misdemeanor
Vesa Kenttäkumpu ... Stoneflow, Evocation
Vettfall ... Irrbloss
Vic Zino ... Hardcore Superstar, Crazy Lixx, Chris Laney
Victor Ahlström ... Undergång
Victor Alneng ... Infra
Victor Andersson "Vic Anders" ... Celestial Pain, Unpure
Victor Berg ... New Keepers Of The Water Towers
Victor Brandt ... Entombed, Dominion
Victor Crusner: v/b/k ... Långfinger
Victor Dahlgren "Vladr" ... Vanmakt
Victor Danling ... Implode
Victor Eng "Otto V. Mad" ... Violent Work Of Art
Victor Erdesjö ... Broken Glass, II Shy
Victor Fradera ... Tenebre, Dawn Of Oblivion
Victor Holmström ... Entrench
Victor Karlsson ... Dust Bowl Jokies
Victor Kinnhammar "DiCola" ... Danger Avenue
Wictor Lindström ... The Cold Existence
Victor Nordström ... Degrade
Victor Olofsson ... Reinxeed
Victor Olsson ... Saffire
Victoria Larsson ... Doom Dogs
Vikki Roxx ... Rat Pack
Viktor Ahnfelt ... Spacebone
Viktor Alasalmi ... Last View
Viktor Arfwedson ... Sanctrum
Viktor Ax ... Backwater
Viktor Balkewitsch Persson ... Gordon Fights
Viktor Bergman ... Sonic Ritual
Viktor Bingzelius ... Sterbhaus
Viktor Brunö ... Implode
Viktor Eklund ... Defueld
Viktor Eriksson "Valmer" ... Feral
Viktor Eriksson ... Idiot
Viktor Forss "El Gordo" ... Deathboot, Pyramido
Viktor Friberg ... Downhearted
Viktor Grahnström ... Stonewall Noise Orchestra
Viktor Granlund ... Close Quarters
Viktor Gustafsson ... Vanhelgd
Viktor Gustafsson ... Section 8
Viktor Halldin ... Affecti Veternus
Viktor Helge ... Obligatorisk Tortyr
Viktor Hemgren ... Construcdead, Månegarm
Viktor Klint ... Thornclad, Algaion, Corporation 187
Viktor Kröger ... Furor
Viktor Linder ... Stabwound
Viktor Lindqvist ... Implode
Viktor Olofsson ... Reinxeed
Viktor Skatt "O'Malley" ... Danger Avenue
Viktor Vidlund ... Smash Into Pieces
Viktor Wennerkvist "Iodine Jupiter" ... Iodine Jupiter
Viktoria Johansson ... Powertrip
Viktoria Larsson "Vicky" ... Ice Age, Notre Dame
Vilhelm Bladin ... Vildhjarta, Iscaroth
Vilhelm Norberg ... Plector
Ville Kemi "Shorrgh" ... Misteltein, Mort, Life Illusion, Fall Ov Serafim, Vandöd, Pyramido
Vince Frances ... Zinny J Zan
Vinterfader ... Dråpsnatt
Viusiudad ... Reveal
Viveca Bjerselius ... Lights Out
Vlad Lefay "VP" ... Valkyrja, Diabolical
Vladde Labat ... Sanity
Volkan Akol ... Sanctrum
Waldemar Braathen "Walle" ... Slowlife
Waldemar Sorychta ... Therion
Walker ... Worship
Walter Dego ... Rainmaker
Weine Johansson ... Baltimoore, Thomas Larsson
Werner Lindström ... Tempelrock
Wiktor Söderström ... Warhammer, Seven
Wilgot Hansson ... Coste Apetrea
Wilhelm Fischerström "Fisch" ... Revolution Riot
Wilhelm Lindh ... The Gardnerz
Wilhelm Wallin ... Rävjunk
Will Chandra ... Evergrey
William Blackmon ... Withered Beauty
William Ekeberg "Obizurt" ... Body Core, Broken Dagger, Pandemonium
William Turner ... Solitude (2)
Wincent Persson ... Violent Work Of Art, Killbilly 5'ers
Winfred Kennerknecht "Fredo" ... Truckfighters, Firestone
Witold Östensson ... Odyssey (2)
Wojtek Lisicki ... Luciferion, Lost Horizon
Wolfgang Kempfel ... H.E.A.L
Yari Säisä ... Dr Dream
Yasin Hillborg ... Afflicted, Crucifyre
Yenz Arnsted "Cheyenne/Leonhardt" ... Geisha
Yngve Edvardsson ... Power Unit
Yngve Frank ... Mean Streak, Detest
Yngve Hammervald ... Fire
Yngve Liljebäck ... Vergelmer
Yngve Strömberg "Vinnie Sharpe" ... Badmouth
Yngwie Malmsteen ... Yngwie Malmsteen, Human Clay, Highbrow, (Erika)
Yoga Andersson ... Hin Haley

NAME INDEX

Yohann Bohlinder (now Bonér)............................ Notorious
YOHIO ....(see Kevin Yohio Rehn Eires)
Yonas Lindskog "Mörk" ....Damnation, Malign, Svartsyn
Yvonne Andersson ....Alcatraz
Yüksel Unutmaz "Y/Yxel"...............Fatal Smile (2), 8th Sin
Zach Zuchowski "Odenwrath".........................Odenwrath
Zacharias Ahlvik "Zack" ....8th Sin
Zachary Stephens ....Evergrey
Zache Enochsson...Soniq Circus
Zagzakel/Nil...Zavorash
Zak Tell ....Clawfinger, Scarpoint
Zalle Salbert ....Impulsia
Zandro Santiago ....Dead By April
Zeb Nilsson "Nathzion" ....Diabolicum, Defaced Creation
Zebba Karlsson ....Mezzrow
Zenny Hansson (now Gram, aka Gramm)... Arrowz, Faith,
.......................Treasure, Sacrifice, Crier, Destiny, Spin Air
Zepp Urgard (aka Sepp)....................Yngwie Malmsteen,
....Power, Tippen Ruda
Zia Lindberg (aka Cia) .... Zia Lindberg, Thore Skogman
Zinny Zan...(see Bo Stagman)
Zito Ponz ....Rat Pack
Zlaja Prozorac ....United Fools
Zoltan Csörcz .... Art Metal, Karmakanic, Kee Marcello,
.................Time Requiem, Urbandux, The Flower Kings,
.... Vindictive, Richard Andersson's Space Odyssey
Zoltan Djember ....Overdrive
Zoran Djorem...Seven Tears
Zoran Kukulj ....Scarpoint
Zrinko Culjak..Cemetary (1213)
Zwedda Svedbo..............................Devil's Whorehouse
Zvonko Hvizdak ....Speedfreaks, On Parole
Åke Andersson ....The Case
Åke Borgström....................................Ma Connection
Åke Cromnow...............................Rampant, Ambush
Åke Danielsson..Denata
Åke Eriksson "Bedlam" ....Bedlam, Åke Eriksson, Attack,
.................Bedlam Eriksson, Coste Apetrea, Bluesbreath
Åke Johansson ....Shakespeare
Åke Karlsson "Age".................................Paradize (1)
Åke Möller ....Raving Mad
Åke Noréen..................................Wood, Jet Airliner
Åke Nyström..Keen Hue
Åke Parmerud..Marionette
Åke Reinholtz ....Electra Top Raiders
Åke Sold ....Flame
Åke Svensk ....Riksväg 77
Åke Swahn ....B.C And The Envelopes
Åke Thoresson ....Arena
Åke Walleborn ....Eventide
Åke Wallin..Gallery (2)
Åsa Andersson ....Anxious
Åsa Person ....Meldrum
Åsa Pettersson ....Dracena
Åsa Rosenberg ....Noctes
Åse Mauritzdotter Westin ....Wynja
Örjan Andersson.............................Candy Kicks Ass
Örjan Armgren ....Mason
Örjan Baudin.......................Mother Misery, Clench
Örjan Englin "Dr Rock" ....Ten 67
Örjan Fernström ....Baltimoore
Örjan Gill...Fire & Ice
Örjan Jonsson ....Blizzard
Örjan Mårtensson ....After Twelve
Örjan Wahlström...Cleopatra
Örjan Wiberg ....Queensland
Örjan Örnkloo .... Darkane, Dark Funeral, The Duskfall,
.....................................Nine, Misert Loves Co.
Östen Bidebo "Dan Dark" ....Torch
Östen Johansson...T.A.R

PHOTO CREDITS

The photos in this book have been obtained from various sources such as from the bands, record labels, photographers or managements. Unfortunately in some cases we have not been able to identify the name of the photographer. If your photo has been published without correct credit, please submit correct information and we will be happy to update any future editions of this book and on the book´s website.

Inide cover (OVERDRIVE): Ben GT Nyberg
Inside page 2 (OVERDRIVE): Ozzie Adenborg
JANNE STARK: Ozzie Adenborg
AEON: Jennie Grinde
ALIEN: Ola Bergman
AMON AMARTH: Steve Brown
ANEKDOTEN: Tord Lindman
ANGELINE: Göran Simonsson
ARCH ENEMY: Adde
ARCKANUM: Fredrik Becker
AS YOU DROWN: Anton Hedberg
AT THE GATES: Niklas Sundin
AUDIOVISION: Janne Stark
AXEWITCH: Arne Gustafsson @ Studio Östgötabild
BALLS: FotoHelen

BAI BANG: FROHMs
BEWITCHED: nikdesign.net
BONAFIDE: Jesper Lindgren
CANS: Michael Johansson
CHAINWRECK: Heléne
CONSTANCIA: Daniel Andersson+Magnus Norlén+Elke Mühlhoff@Photopolish
CRYSTAL PRIDE (right); Alice Molander
DARK TRANQUILLITY (b/w): Kenneth Johansson
DEATHSTARS: Martin Wickler
DECADENCE: Michael Johansson
DENANDER, TOMMY: Janne Stark
DISMEMBER: Soile Siirtola
DRAIN: Peter Gehrke
EF BAND: Michael Calvert
EASY ACTION (top): Hans Hatwig
EASY ACTION (bottom): Snowy Shaw
MATTIAS IA EKLUNDH: Lennart Sjöberg
ELECTRIC BOYS: Janne Stark
ENTOMBED: Daniel Falk/framednoise.com
EUROPE (1: top): Göran Lindsjöö © Premium Rockshot
EUROPE (1: mid): Hans Hatwig © Premium Rockshot
EUROPE (1: bott): Torbjörn Calvero © Premium Rockshot
EUROPE (2: top): Torbjörn Calvero © Premium Rockshot
EUROPE (2: bottom): Patric Ullaeus
EUROPE (3: top+mid): Mattias Eliasson
EUROPE (3: bottom) PM Ström
EVIL MASQUERADE: Thomas Trane
EVOCATION: A. Hedberg
FREAK KITCHEN: Patrik Hellström
FULLFORCE: Gabriel Henningsson
GRAND DESIGN: Mats Vassfjord
H.E.A.T: Janne Stark
HAMMERFALL (band): Michael Johansson
HARDCORE SUPERSTAR: Tim Troncke
THE HANUTED: Olle Carlsson
HEAVY LOAD: Göran Lindsjöö © Premium Rockshot
HELLFUELD: Michael Johansson
IMPERA: Talee Savage
IN FLAMES (colour): Patrik Ullaeus
KATANA: Susanne Johansson
KATATONIA: Harry Välimäki
IMPERA: Talee Savage
IODINE JUPITER: Bisse
KRUX: PM Ström
LION's SHARE: Hanna Axelsson
MAN MACHINE INDUSTRY: Soile Siirtola
MACHINAE SUPREMACY: Joakim Åbro
YNGWIE MALMSTEEN (1: top): Mats Påhlsson
YNGWIE MALMSTEEN (1: mid/bottom): Jens Johansson
YNGWIE MALMSTEEN (2: top): Göran Lindsjöö © Premium Rockshot
YNGWIE MALMSTEEN (2: bottom): Christer Wedin
YNGWIE MALMSTEEN (3): Janne Stark
MARDUK: Vallentin Melström
MARYSCREEK: Evil Eye Photos / EvaLinda Grensman
MELDUM: Ozzie Adenborg
MESHUGGAH (bottom): Micke Sandström
MOUNTAIN OF POWER: PM Ström
MUSTASCH: Fredrik Etoall
MÅRRAN: Ludde Loorentz
NEON ROSE: Lars Falck © Premium Rockshot
NEON ROSE (girls): Hans Hatwig © Premium Rockshot
NINE: Jakob Fridholm
NORD: Torbjörn Calvero © Premium Rockshot
JOHN NORUM (Michelle/Scott): Ozzie Adenborg
JOHN NORUM (backstage): Ozzie Adenborg
JOHN NORUM (band): Göran Lindsjöö © Premium Rockshot
JOHN NORUM (w Tone): Göran Lindsjöö © Premium Rockshot
OSUKARU: Johan Fransson
OVERDRIVE (top): Ben GT Nyberg
OVERDRIVE (bottom): Thomas Tjäder
PAIN: Denis Goria
PARADIZE: Ronnie Jönsson
PLANKTON: Annika Leinonen
PORTRAIT: Magdalena Divenska
RAM: Magnus Lindgren
SHAGGY: Bengt H. Malmqvist © Premium Rockshot
SHOTGUN MESSIAH: Sarah Martinsson
SONIC SYNDICATE. Michael Johansson
STANDBY: Jonas Odland
TAD MOROSE: Benny Backeby
TAKIDA: Daniel Wadenius
TALISMAN (b/w): Michael Johansson
TALISMAN (top): Rickard Nilsson
TEARS: Bengt H. Malmqvist © Premium Rockshot
THERION (1: bottom): Axel Jusseit
TWINBALL: Kate Gabor
VANADIS: Ronnie Hellström
VENI DOMINE: MagiComDesign
WATAIN: PM Ström
WOLF: Nikdesign
ZINNY ZAN: Michael Johansson
Inside back cover (Janne Stark): Ben GT Nyberg
Inside back under CD text (John Sykes): Ozzie Adenborg

ROADHOUZE RECORDS

LISTS

As I have stated before, this is not a fully factual-only encyclopedia. I have added some personal views and comments. In line of this, here are some of my favourite bands, albums and songs in the form of my personal top lists. I have also, of course, excluded all bands I play in myself: Grand Design, Mountain Of Power, Overdrive, Paradize, Zello, Planet Alliance, BALLS and Locomotive Breath.

Top 5 Heavy Rock songs of the 1970s
NEON ROSE - Love Rock
NOVEMBER - Rödluvan
RHAPSODY - Strange Vibrations
WHITE - Hit The Sky
WILDMARKEN - Vad vill dom

Top 5 Seventies Hard Rock albums
NEON ROSE - Reload
NOVEMBER - 6:e november
RHAPSODY - Rhapsody
WILDMARKEN - Och nu på sjuttiotalet
SHAGGY - Lesson For Beginners

Top 6 melodic Death/Black Metal albums
ENTOMBED - To Rise, Shoot Straight And Tell The Truth
SOILWORK - The Living Infinite
STERBHAUS - Angels For Breakfast... And God For Lunch
UNLEASHED - Sworn Allegiance
THE HAUNTED - Revolver
SOLUTION .45 - The Black Machine
WATAIN - The Wild Hunt

Top 5 Melodic Hard Rock albums 80s-90s
TALISMAN - Genesis
EUROPE - Europe
JOHN NORUM - Face The Truth
GREAT KING RAT - Great King Rat
YNGWIE MALMSTEEN - Marching Out

Top 6 Stoner bands
SPIRITUAL BEGGARS
KAROSS
SIDEBURN
TRUCKFIGHTERS
ASTEROID
OBLIVIOUS

Top 10 Heavy Metal songs of the 1980s
220 VOLT - Sauron
EF BAND - Devil's Eye
SILVER MOUNTAIN - Man Of No Present Existance
TORCH - Battleaxe
SCRATCH - Metal Breaker
SACRIFICE - Street Fighter
UNIVERSE - Weekend Warriors
DEPZON - Flying On The Sundown
DETEST - Chains Of Hell
SYRON VANES - Born To Rock

Top 4 Technical Metal bands
VILDHJARTA
CB MURDOC
MESHUGGAH
CALM

Top 9 AOR albums
WORK OF ART - In Progress
ECLIPSE - Bleed And Scream
GRAND ILLUSION - Prince Of Paupers
HOUSE OF SHAKIRA - Lint
H.E.A.T - H.E.A.T
ANGELINE - Confessions
MASQUERADE - Masquerade
SNAKES IN PARADISE - Snakes In Paradise
TREAT - Organized Crime
BAM BAM BOYS - Bam Bam Boys

Top 6 Doom albums
SORCERER - Sorcerer
CANDLEMASS - Chapter VI
MORTALICUM - The Endtime Prophecy
KRUX - III - He Who Sleeps Among The Stars
WORLD BELOW - Maelstrom
MEMENTO MORI - Rhymes Of Lunacy

Top 5 Heavy Metal albums
DREAM EVIL - The Book Of Heavy Metal
GRAND MAGUS - Iron Will
NOCTURNAL RITES - The 8th Sin
WOLF - The Black Flame
RAM - Sudden Impact

Top 5 Thrash albums
F.K.Ü - 4: Rise Of The Mosh Mongers
DARKANE - Demonic Art
ARCH ENEMY - Anthems Of Rebellion
IMMACULATE - Atheist Crusade
GUILLOTINE - Blood Money

LISTS

Top 5 Blues Rock albums
SKY HIGH - Freedom
BLUES BAG - Blå påse
BACON - Like It Black
BB ROCK - BB Rock
MOOSTERS - Executioner

Top 5 Progressive Rock/Metal albums
A.C.T - Today's Report
OPETH - Watershed
WITHERSCAPE - The Inheritance
ANDROMEDA - Chimera
NIGHTINGALE - White Darkness

Top 5 Symphonic Rock bands
ÄNGLAGÅRD
BLÅKULLA
BEARDFISH
THE FLOWER KINGS
GALLEON

Top 5 most sought after records

SAVAGERS - Preacher Of Steel (MLP)
DETEST - Thundersteel (MLP)
SCRATCH - Metal Breaker (7")
BATHORY - Bathory (LP - yellow goat)
GOTHAM CITY - Gotham City (7")

Top 5 best cover versions
GHOST - Here Comes The Sun
(The Beatles)
JOHN NORUM - Ditch Queen
(Frank Marino)
OPETH - Bridge Of Sighs
(Robin Trower)
IN FLAMES - World Of Promises (Treat)
SLAPDASH - Free Your Mind
(En Vogue)

Top 5 new heavy metal bands (NWOSHM)
ENFORCER
STEELWING
ROCKA ROLLAS
SCREAMER
SLINGBLADE

Top 5 modern metal bands
CORRODED
THREE MINUTE MADNESS
MORPHEENA
SHERLOCK BROTHERS
CELLOUT

Top 4 controversial bands
BAKTERIA - Lyrics, concept, manifesto
SHINING - Live show
LATEX - Artwork
WATAIN - Pig's blood, anyone?

Top 5 rockers
PONTUS SNIBB 3
BONAFIDE
DYNAMITE
BACKYARD BABIES
BULLET

Top 5 rarest records (test pressings)
NEON ROSE - Whatever Happened To Rock
And Roll (7", 2 copies)
BAKTERIA - Bakteria (CD, 4 promo copies)
JACKWAVE - Rising Star (7", 5 copies)
MADISON - Don't Close Your Eyes (7", 5 copies)
INTERACTION - Silver Lady (7", 6 copies)

Top 10 modern retro Hard Rock bands
MOJOBONE
ABRAMIS BRAMA
MÅRRAN
KAMCHATKA
THE QUILL
GRAVEYARD
GHOST
YEAR OF THE GOAT
GIN LADY
DEVILLE

Top 3 worst covers versions
BLUE BALLS - Motorbreath (Metallica)
VONDUR - Love Me Tender
(Elvis Presley)
VOMITORY - Dinga Linga Lena
(Pugh Rogefeldt)

Top 6 instrumental albums
PLANKTON - Humble Colossus
ÄNGLAGÅRD - Hybris
THOMAS LARSSON - Freeride
JOHAN RANDÉN - Summary
PETER MARTINSSON GROUP - Guitar State
Of Mind
CHRISTIAN ALSING - The Last Robot

Top 5 expensive, price-worthy rarities
SACRIFICE - Street Fighter (7")
TROUBLE - Warrior (LP)
DIZZINESS - Playing With Fire (MLP)
FOUR STICKS - Electric Celebration (CD)
DETEST - Thundersteel (MLP)

Top 5 weirdest (but still great) bands
DIABLO SWING ORCHESTRA
MATTIAS IA EKLUNDH
DEATH ORGAN
BOSSE
SKITARG

Best reunion/return albums
ELECTRIC BOYS - And Them Boys Done Swang
SYRON VANES - Evil Redux
EUROPE - Start From The Dark
THE CROWN - Doomsday King
MOTHERLODE - Tomorrow Never Comes

Top 5 bands singing in Swedish
ABRAMIS BRAMA
MÅRRAN
LOK
ONYX
NATTSVART

Top 5 busiest musicians
Dan Swanö
Tommy Denander
Jaime Salazar
Mats Leven
Göran Edman

19 albums I often listen to (at the moment...)
MOJOBONE - Crossroad Message
GRAND MAGUS - Iron Will
NEON ROSE - Reload
SPIRITUAL BEGGARS - Return To Zero
A.C.T - Today's Report
THALAMUS - Beneath A Dying Sun
FREAK KITCHEN - Spanking Hour
F.K.Ü - 4: Rise Of The Mosh Mongers
NOVEMBER - En ny tid är här
LOK - Naken, blästrad och skitsur
TRUTH - Machine
KAMCHATKA - Bury Your Roots
OPETH - Watershed
DREAM EVIL - The Book Of Heavy Metal
ABRAMIS BRAMA - Smakar söndag
COLDSPELL - Out From The Cold
BLÅKULLA - Blåkulla
NOCTURNAL RITES - The 8th Sin
THE KILLBILLY 5'ERS - Welcome To Town...

5 songs I often listen to (excluding above bands)
B-THONG - Lucified
DREAM EVIL - The Book Of Heavy Metal
SOUTHFORK - Space Revolution
GHOST - Con Clavi Con Dio
DESTINY - Bermuda

My current top 5 favourite songs
FREAK KITCHEN - Taste My Fist
NEON ROSE - Love Rock
NOVEMBER - Rödluvan
ZANITY - Time Out Of Mind
MOJOBONE - Dig Your Own Groove

Songs that fit with bands that don't (or - I wish they would've written more stuff like this!)
WASA EXPRESS - Jag är bäst
MAGNUM BONUM - What You Gonna Do
SNOWSTORM - Going Back (To Hising Island)
CONTACT - Convulsions
PUGH ROGEFELDT - Hog Farm
NATIONALTEATERN - Lägg av!

My top 5 cover art works

OPHTHALAMIA - Via Dolorosa
SPIRITUAL BEGGARS - Another Way To Shine
STERBHAUS - Angels For Breakfast... And God For
Lunch
VENI DOMINE - Fall Babylon Fall
GRAVEYARD - Hisingen Blues

A PREMIUM SELECTION ...

Stora Popboken
– Svensk Rock & Pop 1954–1969
Hans Olofsson
Discographies Sture Hallberg
SOLD OUT

**The Encyclopedia Of Swedish
Hardrock and Heavy Metal
Volume I**
Janne Stark
Bonus CD included
SOLD OUT

**The Rolling Stones i Sverige
– från Baltiska Hallen
till Bredäng**
Börje Lundberg & Ove Tingvall
Bonus CD included

**The Encyclopedia Of Swedish
Hardrock and Heavy Metal
Volume II**
Janne Stark
Bonus CD included
SOLD OUT

YEAH! YEAH! YEAH!
– The Beatles erövrar Sverige
Börje Lundberg & Ammi Bohm
Bonus CD included

**Cadillac Madness – den otroliga
berättelsen om The Hep Stars**
Dan-Eric Landén
Bonus CD included

**The Encyclopedia of Swedish
Progressive Music 1967-1979**
Tobias Pettersson &
Ulf Henningsson (Editor)
Bonus CD included
SOLD OUT

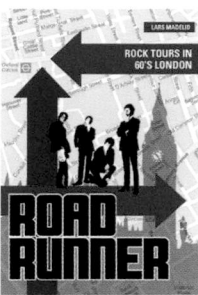

**Roadrunner
- Rock Tours in 60´s London**
Lars-Åke Madelid
English edition
Also available in a Swedish version

**Poster
– Nordens största Poptidning 1974–1980**
Fabian H. Bernstone
& Mathias Brink
Bonus poster included

**The Encyclopedia Of Swedish
Punk 1977-1987**
Peter Jandreus

**Labelography Volume 1
– Progressive U.K. Record Labels**
Jan Pettersson

**The EP Book – Swedish Rock
& Pop Pressings 1954–1969
Second Edition: Expanded
and Revised in Colour**
Roger Holegård

**Boken om OKEJ
– 80-tales största poptidning**
Jörgen Holmstedt
Bonus poster included

**Labelography Volume 2
– Progressive U.K. Record Labels
A First Pressing Identification Guide for
Deram, Harvest, Regal Zonophone
– Singles, EPs and LPs 1966-1980**
Jan Pettersson

**Ny Våg
– Svensk Punk / New Wave / Synth
1977-1982**
Peter Kagerland
New revised edition

**Grönalundsaffischerna!
– 200 klassiker från 70 & 80-talet
illustrerade av Nils Sture Jansson**
Jonas Jansson & Andreas Theve

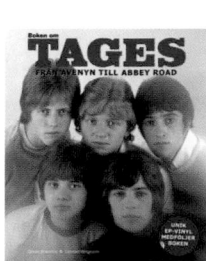

**Boken om Tages
– Från Avenyn till Abbey Road**
Göran Brandels & Lennart Wrigholm
Bonus Vinyl EP included

**Tio i Topp
– med de legendariska
"På försök" 1961-74**
Eric Hallberg & Ulf Henningsson

**The UK 45 rpm sleeves-
A Collector´s Guide to 7"
Record Company Sleeves**
John Delaney

SCEN
Peder Andersson

Find more interesting books on **www.premiumpublishing.com**

THE BONUS CD

This time I have opted for a different type of bonus-CD. Since most "previously unreleased" tracks are now available all over the Internet, I'd instead like to open your ears to some bands that were never actually released (or haven't been yet). These were bands that have made recordings I feel should have been/should be given a proper release. Some of the members are/have been found in other name bands. Prepare yourself to find some new hidden gems!

If you think I forgot to add the year of recording, I did it deliberately. It may be 1994, and it may be 2013. Some stuff is just timeless...

1. AMBUSH
Don't Stop (Let Them Burn) (4.50)
(Music: Sjöholm/Lyrics: Engkvist)
Oscar Jacobsson: v, Adam Hagelin: g, Olof Engkvist: g, Ludwig Sjöholm: b, Linus Fritzson: d
Växjö - The new millennium saw a new wave of classic Swedish metal come alive. Guys that were not even born when heroes like *Heavy Load* walked the earth. *Ambush* was formed November 27, 2012, on a night of beer-splendour, listening to classic 80s heavy metal, feeling nostalgic and frustrated that new productions didn't measure up to the old masterpieces. So they decided to do something about it. Recorded by Jonathan Bark in Studio Vind, Växjö.

2. EDDY MALM BAND
Turn In Down (3.50)
(Music: Malm-Hesselrud/Lyrics: Malm)
Eddy Malm: v, Per Hesselrud: g, Peter Söderström: b, Olof Bergius: d
Stockholm - If you have heard the stuff Eddy did with *Highbrow*, prior to joining Swedish Viking metal originators *Heavy Load*, you will feel at home. The members of the band *Bosse* are fans of classic heavy metal, so naturally they became Eddy's backing band. The track was taken from the band's four-track demo.

3. HELLACOASTER
Mani Jack (3.47)
(Music+Lyrics: Karlsson)
Petter Karlsson: v/g/b/d
Skövde - After leaving *Therion*, Petter wanted to do his own thing. He also wanted to go back to his musical roots of *Judas Priest*, *Slayer*, early *Metallica* and *Manowar*. He recorded a bunch of songs in 2009, a thread he has again picked up. Petter is also the man behind the drums in *Master Massive*.

4. ICE AGE
General Alert (4.03)
(Music: Nyström-Kihlstrand/Lyrics: Kihlstrand)
Sabrina Kihlstrand: v/g, Pia Nyström: g, Viktoria Larsson: b, Tina Strömberg: d
Göteborg - OK, *Ice Age* are actually featured in the book, but since they have not had any legitimate release, I've decided to include them. They deserve it.

5. MASTER MASSIVE
Time Out Of Mind (4.44)
(Music+Lyrics: Strandh)
Tony Niva: v, Jan Stradh: g, Yngve Frank: g, Karl Nyhlin: b, Petter Karlsson: d
Skövde - It all started in *Akt*, followed by *Act*, followed by the band that made me discover guitarist Jan Strandh - *Zanity*. I featured the track *Time Out Of Mind* on one of my previous compilations. *Zanity* later became *Master Massive*. The band recorded numerous outstanding demos and an album that was going to be released by Loud 'N Proud Records, just before they folded. The song is still alive!

6. MACBETH
Sound Of A Hurricane (4.18)
(Music: Larsson-Johansson/Lyrics: Saether)
Pelle Saether: v, Lars Johansson: g, Torbjörn Larsson: b, Mats Hallstensson: k, Håkan Andersson: b
Stockholm - It started around 1983/84 in Boden, in the band *Hexagon*, which featured Lars, Torbjörn and Håkan. The lads relocated to Stockholm. *Macbeth* was formed in 1987, when Torbjörn drafted his former *Glory North* colleague Saether. They split in 1988, when Thorbjörn joined John Norum and Lars was busy with *Candlemass*. Norum liked *Sound Of A Hurricane*, which actually is a bit similar to his song *Face The Truth*. Thorbjörn is now a chief physician and plays covers, Lars is still in *Candlemass,* Pelle is fronting *Grand Design* and Mats is in *House Of Shakira*. A guy presumably named Christer Andersson played drums on this recording.

7. THE HIDDEN
For Gods Ache (2.48)
(Music+Lyrics: Möller)
Teddy Möller: v/g, Peter Leitinen: g, Patrik Sporrong: b, Matte Modin: d
Uppsala - It all started when Teddy (*Mayadome*, now *Loch Vostock, F.K.Ü*) wanted to do a thrash album. He gathered some well reputed friends and recorded the album *Fearful Symmetry*. Unfortunately, it was never released.
Recorded in Blueflame Productions 1999, by Teddy and Fredrik Kjörling.

8. VOLTERGEIST
Desperate Highway (3.53)
(Music: Karlsson/Lyrics: Englund)
Per Englund: v, Mats Karlsson: g, Peter Olander: g, Mike Larsson: b, Peter Hermansson: d
Stockholm - When *220 Volt* took a halt in 1992, Karlsson, Olander, Larsson and Hermansson decided to form a new band . They drafted former *Blacksmith/Motherlode* singer Per and *Voltergeist* was a fact. They recorded a bunch of great demos, did lots of live shows, and sadly split only a year later. Here is a taste of what could have been.

9. PAINKILLAZ
Lost My Religion (4.53)
(Music+Lyrics: Sedenberg/Osbäck/Valdemarson/Hilden)
Mattias Osbäck: v, Manka Sedenberg: g, Anders Waldemarsson: b, Hempo Hildén: d
Karlskrona - A shortlived project which only resulted in some killer demos! The members have also appeared in bands like *Trash, Baltimoore, Locomotive Breath, The Bones, John Norum Band, Silver Seraph* etc.
Drums recorded at PAMA, Karlskrona.

10. ZOOM CLUB
Walking On Stilts (5.05)
(Music: Hermansson-Stark-Hujanen/Lyrics: Hermansson)
Peter Hermansson: v/d, Janne Stark: g, Micke Hujanen: b
Stockholm/Nyhamnsläge - Peter (*220 Volt, Talisman, John Norum*) and Janne (*Overdrive, Locomotive Breath, Grand Design, Constancia*) met in 2010, through their common love of seventies hard rock and especially bands like *Sir Lord Baltimore, Mountain* and *Budgie*. Hujanen (*AB/CD*) joined the subsequent year. Around forty songs are written and ready, but nothing has been released, yet.
Recorded live at rehearsal in 2012.

11. RAWBURT
Psycho Man (3.28)
(Music: Hansson/Lyrics: Jansson-Hansson)
Stefano Marchesini: v, Robert Hansson: g, Jörgen Raneström: b, Jörgen Tjusling: d
Göteborg - After having released two great albums with *Human Race*, Robert made some (more or less strange) solo recordings. Then came silence. Until *Rawburt* was born. The band has recorded several outstanding demos so far.

12. MONICA MAZE BAND
Eyes Of The Living (4.34)
(Music+Lyrics: Larsson/Egberg/af Klintberg/Svärd)
Monica Larsson: v, Pontus Norgren: g, Pontus Egberg: b, Petter Svärd: d
Stockholm - After *Great King Rat* disbanded and before he went solo, guitarist Pontus Norgren replaced Pontus af Klintberg in this highly interesting band, also featuring bassist Egberg (ex-*Lion's Share*), now in *The Poodles* and outstanding singer Monica Larsson. The band recorded two excellent demos, but unfortunately nothing more came out of this.

13. STRAITJACKETS
Stripped To The Bone (4.27)
(Music+Lyrics: Seppenen)
Mattias Wellhag: v, Ulrich Seppenen: g, Stefan Karlsson: g, Henrik Lundberg: b, Joakim Sandberg: d
Skövde/Trollhättan - The band started out as *Glam Slam*, who were featured on the *Rockbox* compilation. They later became *Straitjackets* and recorded an outstanding, still unreleased, album. After this they became *Booster* and recorded yet an unreleased album. Lundberg (ex-*Masquerade*) and Wellhag have also released an album as *House Of Heavy*, while Seppänen and Karlsson are now souther heavy rockers *Rebel Road*.